June 26–July 1, 2016
San Francisco, California, USA

Association for
Computing Machinery

Advancing Computing as a Science & Profession

SIGMOD'16

Proceedings of the 2016 International Conference on

Management of Data

Sponsored by:

ACM SIGMOD

Supported by:

Microsoft, Oracle, Tableau, Alibaba, AT&T, Facebook, Google, IBM, Infosys, Platfora, Recruit, Salesforce, SAP, Snowflake, Amazon Web Services, Cloudera, Esgyn, Hewlett Packard, Intel, Linked In, LogicBlox, MemSQL, Splice Machine, VISA Research, Hewlett-Packard Enterprise, Morgan & Claypool, Elsevier, Springer, and National Science Foundation

Association for
Computing Machinery

Advancing Computing as a Science & Profession

The Association for Computing Machinery
2 Penn Plaza, Suite 701
New York, New York 10121-0701

ISBN: 978-1-4503-3531-7 (Digital)

ISBN: 978-1-4503-4605-4 (Print)

Additional copies may be ordered prepaid from:

ACM Order Department
PO Box 30777
New York, NY 10087-0777, USA

Phone: 1-800-342-6626 (USA and Canada)
+1-212-626-0500 (Global)
Fax: +1-212-944-1318
E-mail: acmhelp@acm.org
Hours of Operation: 8:30 am – 4:30 pm ET

Printed in the USA

Welcome Message from the SIGMOD Chairs

It is our great pleasure to welcome you to SIGMOD 2016, the 2016 edition of the ACM SIGMOD International Conference on Management of Data, at San Francisco, the heart of Silicon Valley. A unique bridge, cable cars, a sparkling bay, a famous prison, and steep streets with beautiful Victorian houses are just a few of the things that make San Francisco one of the world's greatest cities to visit. Located in the Bay Area along the Northern California coast, many attractions beyond those in the city can be easily reached: the world-famous wine country, including Napa and Sonoma Valley, beautiful beaches, the world's largest trees and wonderful hikes in nearby National Parks.

The conference itself is held in the Hyatt Regency Hotel, located in the financial district in downtown San Francisco. The hotel is very conveniently located nearby to many activities and landmarks, making this the ideal spot not only for an exciting conference but also for exploring the area. The banquet will be held in the California Academy of Sciences. The California Academy of Sciences is a Planetarium, Aquarium and Natural History Museum under a Living Roof in San Francisco, and it is among the largest museums of natural history in the world, housing over 26 million specimens.

This year's technical program features 137 papers in 22 sessions; 116 research papers, 17 industrial papers, and 4 invited papers. Research and industrial papers will be mixed together instead of separated into separate tracks as in past years. All papers will be presented at conference sessions, as well as at one of two plenary poster events. There are also 31 demos and 10 tutorials. Instead of running these concurrently with technical presentations, demos are now a separate plenary event in the conference and tutorials have been moved before and after the conference. There is just one panel, the Careers in Industry panel. Finally, this year's conference will feature one keynote, from the inimitable Jeff Dean (Google, USA), who will talk about how deep learning and software systems can support each other, with particular thoughts on the implications for data management. The net effect of these changes is that there are more plenary events, and at most three concurrent events ongoing (from 6 or more concurrent tracks in previous conferences). We hope this will make the SIGMOD experience more communal.

Other technical events of interest include the SIGMOD programming contest, featuring a $7,000 prize for the winning team plus a $3,000 dollar prize for the runner-up donated by Microsoft, with contest participants presenting their work during the poster session; the undergraduate poster competition, featuring 12 undergraduate posters from an outstanding group of young database researchers; the new research symposium on Tuesday night; and the business meeting, also on Tuesday evening.

We made a number of changes in the way we assembled this year's technical program with an eye towards improving review and paper quality. As in past years we had two submission deadlines, but we spread them out more (one in July and one in November). Each submission included one round of revisions, during which reviewers could request specific changes to papers. The vast majority of accepted papers underwent revision, which we believe significantly improved the quality of papers. All submissions were also discussed in a series of conference calls organized by our group leaders; this forced reviewers to defend their positions and helped achieve consensus. A post-review survey revealed 70% of reviewers felt this improved the review process, and 80% reported they worked harder in preparing and defending their reviews. We also asked reviewers and group leaders to request additional reviews when an additional opinion was needed; many papers received four reviews, and some papers received as many as six. Finally, we introduced an online conference organization tool, Confer, which we used to get the community's input about how papers should be grouped together, and which attendees can use throughout the conference to navigate the program.

SIGMOD 2016 is preceded and followed by 10 workshops, including the PhD symposium on Sunday, June 26. These workshops provide an opportunity for small groups of like-minded researchers to discuss areas of interest and new ideas, and we are pleased to see a diverse ecosystem of workshops with competitive submissions evolving at SIGMOD.

We are grateful to the many members of our community who made this technical program possible, especially the 247 reviewers whose hard work resulted in writing more than 2700 reviews for our research, industrial, and demo tracks. This work was coordinated by our fabulous program committee team, including our program track chairs, Alexandra Meliou (UMass Amherst, USA), and Tim Kraska (Brown University, USA), and our 14 group leaders, who coordinated conference calls and guided papers through the review process. The industrial program was created by Tyson Condie (UCLA, USA), and Carlo Curino (Microsoft, USA), and the demo program was organized by Jennie Duggan (Northwestern University, USA), and Aaron Elmore (University of Chicago, USA). Alexandros Labrinidis (University of Pittsburgh, USA), efficiently organized the tutorials program. The undergraduate poster competition was organized by Aditya Parameswaran (University of Illinois, Champaign Urbana, USA), and Anisoara Nice (SAP SE, Canada). Ken Salem organized this year's programming contest (finding shortest paths in a changing graph), and Peter Bailis (Stanford University, USA), and Andy Pavlo (Carnegie Mellon University, USA) organized the poster session. Anant Bhardwaj (MIT, USA), built the Confer online conference software. Finally, last but certainly not least Alekh Jindal helped organize the proceedings, tirelessly hounding authors to get their camera ready submissions uploaded!

SIGMOD is a volunteer effort and involved thousands of hours of work, thousands of emails, and thousands of hours in meetings during the last two years to put together. Please thank all these individuals involved if you see them around the conference. Also congratulate Alex Labrinidis, Alex Meliou, Melanie, Martin, Yunyao, and Stratos who became parents in the meantime.

We also acknowledge all members of the SIGMOD 2016 organizing committee, as well as the SIGMOD Executive Committee, for their invaluable help and guidance throughout the many months leading to the conference. The strong organizing team for SIGMOD 2016 includes finance chair Martin Theobald (University of Ulm, Germany), publicity chair Melanie Herschel (University of Stuttgart, Germany), social media chair Hakan Ferhatosmanoglu (Bilkent University, Turkey), sponsorship chairs Mohamed Mokbel (University of Minnesota, USA) and Stratos Idreos (Harvard University, USA), exhibit chair Huiping Cao (New Mexico State University, USA), local arrangements chairs Enela Pema (Facebook, USA) and Yunyao Li (IBM Research-Almaden, USA), registration chair Mohamed Sarwat (Arizona State University, USA) , workshop local arrangement chair Fei Chen (LinkedIn, USA), web chair Kostas Stefanidis (ICS-FORTH, Hellas), volunteer chair Maria Daltayanni (University of San Francisco, USA), and travel award committee chairs Eugene Wu (Columbia University, USA) and Peter Alvaro (University of California, Santa Cruz, USA. The success of this conference would be impossible without their hard work, persistent dedication, and hours of effort they committed to the conference. We also would like to thank K. Selçuk Candan for providing us with his advice and SIGMOD institutional memory, as well as for his help with logistics throughout the conference planning. We are also grateful to the Microsoft Research Conference Management Toolkit (CMT) team for their extremely prompt and helpful support throughout the complex conference reviewing process. We would also like to extend our appreciation to the student volunteers.

Finally, we would like to thank ACM, and particularly Fran Spinola and April Mosqus for helping with the conference logistics, Diana Brantuas for guidance and help with the budget, Stephanie Sabal for hotel site selection, Ann Lane for conference promotion, and Carolina Erazo for preparing the visa letters. Adrienne Griscti (ACM) and Lisa Tolles (Sheridan) have made the proceedings and the program booklet possible.

This year we are extremely grateful for all our corporate sponsors, whose contributions helped to keep the conference registration fees low, most significantly for student attendees. These include at the Platinum Level: Microsoft, Oracle, and Tableau; at the Gold Level: Alibaba.com, AT&T, Facebook, Google, IBM Research, Infosys, Platfora, Recruit, Salesforce, SAP, and Snowflake; and at the Silver Level: Amazon Web Services, Cloudera, esgyn, HP, Intel, LinkedIn, LogicBlox, memsql, Splice Machine, and Visa Research. Microsoft also supported the programming contest by providing the generous award to the winners. In addition, Microsoft, Google, the National Science Foundation and the SIGMOD Executive Committee have generously funded the SIGMOD 2016 student travel award program, Microsoft's donation provided 16 travel awards, Facebook's donation supported 4 travel awards, Snowflake's donation supported 1 travel award, and the NSF grant covered another 15 travel awards. Finally, the SIGMOD EC provided 27 awards, and covered all 63 free registrations for the student travel program awardees. Last but not least, we would like to thank Salesforce for organizing the reception at Exploratorium on Tuesday night for all SIGMOD attendees.

Welcome to San Francisco, and we hope you enjoy the conference!

Fatma Özcan	**Georgia Koutrika**	**Samuel Madden**	**Alekh Jindal**
General Chair	*General Chair*	*Program Chair*	*Proceedings Chair*

Table of Contents

Session 3 - Logical and Physical Database Design

Session 4 - New Storage and Network Architectures

Session 5 - Graphs 1: Infrastructure and Processing on Modern Hardware

Session 6 - Streaming 1: Systems and Outlier Detection

Session 7 - Approximate Query Processing

Session 8 - Networks and the Web

Session 9 - Data Discovery and Extraction

Session 10 - Data Integration / Cleaning

Session 11 - Spatio / Temporal Databases

Session 12 - Distributed Data Processing

Session 13 - Graphs 2: Subgraph-based Optimization Techniques

Session 14 - Main Memory Analytics

Session 15 - Interactive Analytics ....

Session 16 - Streaming 2: Sketches

Session 17 - Transaction Processing

Session 18 - Transactions and Consistency

Session 19 - Query Optimization

Session 20 - Graphs 3: Potpourri

Session 21: Hardware Acceleration and Query Compilation

Session 22 - Nearest Neighbors and Similarity Search

Demonstrations

Tutorials

Undergraduate Student Abstracts

2016 SIGMOD Conference Organization

General Chairs: Fatma Özcan (IBM Research, USA)
Georgia Koutrika (HP Labs, USA)

Program Chair: Sam Madden (Massachusetts Institute of Technology, USA)

PC Track Chairs: Tim Kraska (Brown University, USA)
Alexandra Meliou (University of Massachusetts, Amherst, USA)

Proceedings Chair: Alekh Jindal (Microsoft, USA)

Tutorials Chair: Alex Labrinidis (University of Pittsburgh, USA)

Industrial Program Chairs: Carlo Curino (Microsoft, USA)
Tyson Condie (University of California, Los Angeles, USA)

Demonstration Chairs: Aaron Elmore (University of Chicago, USA)
Jennie Duggan (Northwestern University, USA)

Workshops Chairs: Anastasia Ailamaki (EPFL, Switzerland)
Barzan Mozafari (University of Michigan, USA)

Poster Chairs: Andy Pavlo (Carnegie Mellon University, USA)
Peter Bailis (Stanford University, USA)

Undergraduate Poster Competition Chairs: Anisoara Nica (SAP SE, Canada)
Aditya Parameswaran (University of Illinois at Urbana Champaign, USA)

Local Organization Chairs: Yunyao Li (IBM Research, USA)
Enela Pema (Facebook, USA)

Finance Chair: Martin Theobald (University of Ulm, Germany)

Sponsorship Chairs: Mohamed Mokbel (University of Minnesota, USA)
Stratos Idreos (Harvard University, USA)

Publicity Chair: Melanie Herschel (University of Stuttgart, Germany)

Social Media Chair: Hakan Ferhatosmanoglu (Bilkent University, Turkey)

Exhibits Chair: Huiping Cao (New Mexico State University, USA)

Registration Chair: Mohamed Sarwat (Arizona State University, USA)

Web/Information Chair: Kostas Stefanidis (ICS-FORTH, Greece)

Travel Award Selection Committee Chairs:	Eugene Wu (Columbia University, USA) Peter Alvaro (University of California, Santa Cruz, USA)
Programming Contest Chair:	Ken Salem (University of Waterloo, Canada)
New Researcher Symposium Chairs:	Julia Stoyanovich (Drexel University, USA) Fabian M. Suchanek (Telecom ParisTech University, France)
Volunteer Chair:	Maria Daltayanni (University of San Francisco, USA)
Local Workshops Chair:	Fei Chen (LinkedIn, Mountain View, USA)
Group Leaders:	Sihem Amer-Yahia (CNRS, France) Magdalena Balazinska (University of Washington, USA) Carsten Binnig (DHBW Mannheim, Germany) Mike Cafarella (University of Michigan, USA) Philippe Cudre-Mauroux (University of Fribourg, Switzerland) Amol Deshpande (University of Maryland, USA) Ihab Ilyas (University of Waterloo, Canada) Justin Levandoski (Microsoft Research, USA) Amelie Marian (Rutgers University, USA) Kyriakos Mouratidis(Singapore Management University, Singapore) Paolo Papotti (QCRI, Qatar) Daisy Zhe Wang (University of Florida, USA)
Program Committee:	Daniel Abadi (Yale, USA) Ashraf Aboulnaga (Qatar Computing Research Institute, Qatar) Foto Afrati (NTU Athens, Greece) Sameer Agarwal (Databricks, Inc, USA) Yanif Ahmad (Johns Hopkins University, USA) Reza Akbarinia (INRIA Sophia Antipolis, France) Gustavo Alonso (ETH Zurich, Switzerland) Peter Alvaro (UC Berkeley, USA) Sihem Amer-Yahia (CNRS/LIG, France) Aijun An (York University, Canada) Arvind Arasu (Microsoft Research, USA) Peter Bailis (UC Berkeley, USA) Magda Balazinska (University of Washington, USA) Zhuowei Bao (Facebook Inc., USA) Denilson Barbosa (University of Alberta, Canada) Srikanta Bedathur (IBM Research, India) Philip Bernstein (Microsoft Research, USA) Carsten Binnig (Brown University, USA) Spyros Blanas (Ohio State, USA) Michael Bohlen (University of Zurich, Switzerland) Francesco Bonchi (Yahoo Labs, Barcelona, Spain) Peter Boncz (CWI, Netherlands)

Program Committee (continued):

Angela Bonifati (Lille 1 University and INRIA, France)
Philippe Bonnet (IT University of Copenhagen, Denmark)
Stephane Bressan (NUS, Singapore)
Nico Bruno (Google, USA)
Michael Cafarella (University of Michigan, USA)
Mark Callaghan (Facebook, USA)
K. Selcuk Candan (Arizona State University, USA)
Kaushik Chakrabarti (Microsoft Research, USA)
Badrish Chandramouli (Microsoft Research, USA)
Kevin Chang (University of Illinois at Urbana-Champaign, USA)
Shimin Chen (ICT, Chinese Academy of Science, China)
Lei Chen (Hong Kong University of Science and Technology, Hong Kong)
James Cheng (CUHK, Hong Kong)
Alvin Cheung (University of Washington, USA)
Fei Chiang (McMaster University, Canada)
Sarah Cohen-Boulakia (LRI Universite Paris Sud, France)
Dario Colazzo (Universite Paris-Dauphine, France)
Tyson Condie (UCLA, USA)
Neil Conway (Typical Set LLC, USA)
Brian Cooper (Google, USA)
Philippe Cudre-Mauroux (University of Fribourg, Switzerland)
Bin Cui (Peking U., China)
Mahashweta Das (HP Labs, USA)
Sudipto Das (Microsoft Research, USA)
Antonios Deligiannakis (Technical University of Crete, Greece)
Amol Deshpande (University of Maryland, USA)
Stefan Dessloch (TU Kaiserslautern, Germany)
Jens Dittrich (Saarland University, Germany)
Luna Dong (Google, USA)
Chris Douglas (Microsoft, USA)
Eduard Dragut (Temple Univ., USA)
Jennie Duggan (Northwestern University, USA)
Curtis Dyreson (Utah State, USA)
Aaron Elmore (University of Chicago, USA)
Alan Fekete (U. Sydney, Australia)
Shel Finkelstein (UCSC, USA)
Peter Fischer (Universitat Freiburg, Germany)
Avrilia Floratou (IBM Almaden, USA)
Tim Furche (Oxford, United Kingdom)
Avigdor Gal (Technion, Israel)
Wolfgang Gatterbauer (CMU Tepper School of Business, USA)
Tingjian Ge (UMass Lowell, USA)
Floris Geerts (University of Antwerp, Belgium)
Rainer Gemulla (Max-Planck-Institut fur Informatik, Germany)
Boris Glavic (IIT Chicago, USA)
Lukasz Golab (University of Waterloo, Canada)

Program Committee (continued):

Todd Green (LogicBlox, USA)
Torsten Grust (U Tubingen, Germany)
Dimitrios Gunopulos (University of Athens, Greece)
Jiawei Han (UIUC, USA)
Wook-Shin Han (POSTECH, South Korea)
Carmem Hara (Universidade Federal do Parana, Brazil)
Oktie Hassanzadeh (IBM Research, USA)
Michael Hay (Colgate, USA)
Bingsheng He (Nanyang Technological University, Singapore)
Katja Hose (Aalborg University, Denmark)
Vagelis Hristidis (UC Riverside, USA)
Stratos Idreos (Harvard University, USA)
Ihab Ilyas (University of Waterloo, Canada)
Zachary Ives (University of Pennsylvania, USA)
Ruoming Jin (Kent State University, USA)
Alekh Jindal (MIT, USA)
Eser Kandogan (IBM Research, USA)
Panagiotis Karras (Skoltech, Russia)
Asterios Katsifodimos (TU Berlin, Germany)
Yannis Katsis (UC San Diego, USA)
Georgios Kellaris (Harvard, USA)
Anastasios Kementsietsidis (Google Inc., USA)
Alfons Kemper (University of Munich, Germany)
Oliver Kennedy (University at Buffalo, USA)
Eamonn Keogh (UC Riverside, USA)
Martin Kersten (CWI, Netherlands)
Daniel Kifer (Penn State, USA)
Christoph Koch (EPFL, Switzerland)
George Kollios (Boston University, USA)
Nick Koudas (University of Toronto, Canada)
Tim Kraska (Brown University, USA)
Hongrae Lee (Google, USA)
Wolfgang Lehner (TU Dresden, Germany)
Alberto Lerner (New York University, USA)
Justin Levandoski (Microsoft, USA)
Chengkai Li (UT Arlington, USA)
Feifei Li (University of Utah, USA)
Guoliang Li (Tsinghua University, China)
Yunyao Li (IBM Research, USA)
Erietta Liarou (EPFL, Switzerland)
Xuemin Lin (University of New South Wales, Australia)
Chengfei Liu (Swinburne University of Technology, Australia)
Eric Lo (Polytecnic University of Hong Kong, Hong Kong)
Guy Lohman (IBM Research, USA)
Jiaheng Lu (University of Helsinki, Finland)
Qiong Luo (Hong Kong University of Science & Technology, Hong Kong)

Program Committee (continued):

Shuai Ma (Beihang University, Beijing, China)
Ashwin Machanavajjhala (Duke U., USA)
Samuel Madden (MIT, USA)
Jayant Madhavan (Google, USA)
David Maier (Portland State University, USA)
Nikos Mamoulis (U. Hong Kong, Hong Kong)
Silviu Maniu (Universite Paris-Sud, France)
Essam Mansour (Qatar Computing Research Institute, Qatar)
Amelie Marian (Rutgers University, USA)
Davide Martinenghi (Politecnico di Milano, Italy)
Gianni Mecca (Universita della Basilicata, Italy)
Alexandra Meliou (UMass Amherst, USA)
Sergey Melnik (Google, USA)
Xiaofeng Meng (Renmin University of China, China)
Sebastian Michel (TU Kaiserslautern, Germany)
Umar Minhas (IBM Research, USA)
Zhou Minqi (East China Normal University, China)
Mohamed Mokbel (Northeastern University, USA)
Kyriakos Mouratidis (Singapore Management University, Singapore)
Barzan Mozafari (University of Michigan, USA)
Hannes Muhleisen (CWI, Netherlands)
Arnab Nandi (Ohio State University, USA)
Vivek Narasayya (Microsoft Research, USA)
Neha Narula (MIT, USA)
Felix Naumann (Hasso Plattner Institute, Germany)
Muhammad Naveed (University of Illinois at Urbana-Champaign, USA)
Rimma Nehme (Microsoft, USA)
Thomas Neumann (TU Munich, Germany)
Christopher Olston (Google, USA)
Dan Olteanu (Oxford University & LogicBlox, United Kingdom)
Beng Chin Ooi (National University of Singapore, Singapore)
Carlos Ordonez (University of Houston, USA)
M. Tamer Ozsu (University of Waterloo, Canada)
Ippokratis Pandis (Cloudera, USA)
Dimitris Papadopoulos (Boston University, USA)
Stavros Papadopoulos (Intel Labs and MIT, USA)
Olga Papaemmanouil (Brandeis University, USA)
Charalampos Papamanthou (UMD, USA)
Stelios Paparizos (Microsoft Research, USA)
Paolo Papotti (QCRI, Qatar)
Srinivasan Parthasarathy (Ohio State, USA)
Alex Passos (Google, USA)
Andy Pavlo (Carnegie Mellon University, USA)
Torben Bach Pedersen (Aalborg University, Denmark)
Jian Pei (Simon Fraser University, Canada)
Peter Pietzuch (Imperial College London, United Kingdom)

Program Committee (continued):

Holger Pirk (MIT, USA)
Evaggelia Pitoura (University of Ioannina, Greece)
Li Qian (Facebook, USA)
Jorge Quiane-Ruiz (Qatar Computing Research Institute, Qatar)
Karthik Ramachandra (Microsoft, USA)
Ravi Ramamurthy (Microsoft Research, USA)
Vijayshankar Raman (IBM Research, USA)
Christopher Re (Stanford University, USA)
Tore Risch (Uppsala Universitet, Sweden)
Florin Rusu (UC Merced, USA)
Russell Sears (PureStorage, USA)
Elaine Shi (Cornell University, USA)
Suvrit Sra (MIT, USA)
Ion Stoica (UC Berkeley, USA)
Kian-Lee Tan (National University of Singapore, Singapore)
Nesime Tatbul (Intel Labs and MIT, USA)
Anthony Tung (National University of Singapore, Singapore)
Daisy Zhe Wang (University of Florida, USA)
Jiannan Wang (UC Berkeley, USA)
Gerhard Weikum (Max-Planck-Institut fur Informatik, Germany)
Till Westmann (Oracle, USA)
Janet Wiener (Facebook, USA)
Xiaokui Xiao (Nanyang Technological University, Singapore)
Xiaochun Yang (Northeastern University, China)
Ken Yocum (Human Longevity, USA)
Cong Yu (Google Research, USA)
Matei Zaharia (MIT, USA)
Kai Zeng (UC Berkeley, USA)
Kevin Zheng (University of Queensland, Australia)
Jingren Zhou (Alibaba, USA)

Demo Program Committee:

Adam Silberstein (Trifacta, USA)
Alekh Jindal (MIT, USA)
Alexandros Labrinidis (University of Pittsburgh, USA)
Alvin Cheung (U. Washington, USA)
Arijit Khan (ETH Zurich, Switzerland)
Beng Chin Ooi (National University of Singapore, Singapore)
Danica Porobic (EPFL, Switzerland)
Darius Sidlauskas (EPFL, Switzerland)
Emad Soroush (Dato, USA)
Eugene Wu (Columbia University, USA)
Guy Lohman (IBM Almaden, USA)
Hannes Muhleisen (CWI, Netherlands)
Herodotos Herodotou (Cyprus University of Technology, Cyprus)
Holger Pirk (MIT, USA)
Isabel Cruz (Univ. of Illinois at Chicago, USA)

Demo Program Committee (continued):

Jagan Sankaranarayanan (NEC Labs, USA)
James Cheng (CUHK, Hong Kong)
Jens Teuber (TU Dortmund, Germany)
Jens Dittrich (Saarland, Germany)
Jeong-Hyon Hwang (SUNY Albany, USA)
Jiannan Wang (University of California, Berkeley, USA)
Jianyong Wang (Tsinghua, P.R. China)
Julia Stoyanovich (Drexel University, USA)
Junho Shim (Sookmyung Women's University, Rep. of Korea)
K. Selcuk Candan (Arizona State University, USA)
Kostis Kyzirakos (CWI, Netherlands)
Lei Chen (HKUST, Hong Kong)
Marco Serafini (QCRI, Qatar)
Martin Kersten (CWI, Netherlands)
Mike Carey (University of California - Irvine, USA)
Mohamed Mokbel (Univ of Minnesota, USA)
Mohamed Sarwat (Arizona State University, USA)
Paolo Papotti (QCRI, Qatar)
Pat Helland (Salesforce, USA)
Paul Brown (Paradigm4, USA)
Peter Bailis (University of California, Berkeley, USA)
Philippe Cudre-Mauroux (Univ. of Freiburg, Germany)
Pinar Tozun (IBM, USA)
Rachel Pottinger (University of British Columbia, Canada)
Ravi Ramamurthy (Microsoft Research, USA)
Reynold Cheng (Univ of Hong Kong, Hong Kong)
Ryan Stutsman (Microsoft Research, USA)
Shel Finkelstein (University of California, Santa Cruz, USA)
Spyros Blanas (Ohio State University, USA)
Sudeepa Roy (University of Washington, USA)
Sudipto Das (Microsoft Research, USA)
Christian Thomsen (Aalborg University, Denmark)
Tingjian Ge (U. Mass Lowell, USA)
Victor Alvarez (Saarland University, Germany)
Willis Lang (Microsoft Jim Gray Systems Lab, USA)
Yinghui Wu (Washington State University, USA)
Ziawasch Abedjan (MIT, USA)

Industrial Program Committee:	Philip Bernstein (Microsoft Research, USA) Nico Bruno (Google, USA) Michael Cafarella (University of Michigan, USA) Mark Callaghan (Facebook, USA) Neil Conway (Mesosphere, USA) Brian Cooper (Google, USA) Chris Douglas (Microsoft, USA) Shel Finkelstein (UCSC, USA) Konstantinos Karanasos (Microsoft, USA) Guy Lohman (IBM Research, USA) Ippokratis Pandis (Amazon Web Services, USA) Karthik Ramachandra (Microsoft, USA) Karthik Ramasamy (Twitter, USA) Russell Sears (PureStorage, USA) Till Westmann (Couchbase, USA) Ken Yocum (Human Longevity, USA) Jingren Zhou (Alibaba, USA)
Tutorials Program Committee:	Selçuk Candan (Arizona State University, USA) Junghoo Cho (University of California, Los Angeles, USA) Alex Delis (University of Athens, Greece) AnHai Doan (University of Wisconsin, USA) Luis Gravano (Columbia University, USA) Guy Lohman (IBM Almaden, USA) Qiong Luo (Hong Kong University of Science & Technology, Hong Kong) Meral Ozsoyoglu (Case Western Reserve University, USA) Alkis Polyzotis (Google, USA) Mohamed Sharaf (University of Queensland, Australia) Peter Triantafillou (University of Glasgow, UK) Stratis Viglas (University of Edinburgh, UK) Jun Yang (Duke University, USA)

Sponsors, Supporters, and Exhibitors

Sponsor:

Platinum Supporters:

Gold Supporters:

Silver Supporters:

Other Supporters:

Platinum Publisher:

MORGAN & CLAYPOOL PUBLISHERS

Silver Publishers:

ELSEVIER

Springer

Student Travel Awards:

NSF

Goods: Organizing Google's Datasets

Alon Halevy[2*], Flip Korn[1], Natalya F. Noy[1], Christopher Olston[1], Neoklis Polyzotis[1], Sudip Roy[1], Steven Euijong Whang[1]

[1]Google Research [2]Recruit Institute of Technology

alon@recruit.ai, {flip, noy, olston, npolyzotis, sudipr, swhang}@google.com

ABSTRACT

Enterprises increasingly rely on structured datasets to run their businesses. These datasets take a variety of forms, such as structured files, databases, spreadsheets, or even services that provide access to the data. The datasets often reside in different storage systems, may vary in their formats, may change every day. In this paper, we present Goods, a project to rethink how we organize structured datasets at scale, in a setting where teams use diverse and often idiosyncratic ways to produce the datasets and where there is no centralized system for storing and querying them. Goods extracts metadata ranging from salient information about each dataset (owners, timestamps, schema) to relationships among datasets, such as similarity and provenance. It then exposes this metadata through services that allow engineers to find datasets within the company, to monitor datasets, to annotate them in order to enable others to use their datasets, and to analyze relationships between them. We discuss the technical challenges that we had to overcome in order to crawl and infer the metadata for billions of datasets, to maintain the consistency of our metadata catalog at scale, and to expose the metadata to users. We believe that many of the lessons that we learned are applicable to building large-scale enterprise-level data-management systems in general.

1. INTRODUCTION

Most large enterprises today witness an explosion in the number of datasets that they generate internally for use in ongoing research and development. The reason behind this explosion is simple: by allowing engineers and data scientists to consume and generate datasets in an unfettered manner, enterprises promote fast development cycles, experimentation, and ultimately innovation that drives their competitive edge. As a result, these internally generated datasets often become a prime asset of the company, on par with source code and internal infrastructure. However, while enterprises have developed a strong culture on how to manage the latter, with source-code development tools and methodologies that we now consider "standard" in the industry (e.g., code versioning and indexing, reviews, or testing), similar approaches do not generally exist for managing datasets. We argue that developing principled and flexible approaches to dataset management has become imperative, lest companies run the risk of internal siloing of datasets, which, in turn, results in significant losses in productivity and opportunities, duplication of work, and mishandling of data.

*Work done while at Google Research.

SIGMOD/PODS'16 June 26 - July 01, 2016, San Francisco, CA, USA

ACM ISBN 978-1-4503-3531-7/16/06.

DOI: http://dx.doi.org/10.1145/2882903.2903730

Enterprise Data Management (EDM) is one common way to organize datasets in an enterprise setting. However, in the case of EDM, stakeholders in the company must embrace this approach, using an EDM system to publish, retrieve, and integrate their datasets. An alternative approach is to enable complete freedom within the enterprise to access and generate datasets and to solve the problem of finding the right data in a post-hoc manner. This approach is similar in spirit to the concept of *data lakes* [4, 22], where the lake comprises and continuously accumulates all the datasets generated within the enterprise. The goal is then to provide methods to "fish" the right datasets out of the lake on the as-needed basis.

In this paper, we describe Google Dataset Search (Goods), such a post-hoc system that we built in order to organize the datasets that are generated and used within Google. Specifically, Goods collects and aggregates metadata about datasets after the datasets were created, accessed, or updated by various pipelines, without interfering with dataset owners or users. Put differently, teams and engineers continue to generate and access datasets using the tools of their choice, and Goods works in the background, in a non-intrusive manner, to gather the metadata about datasets and their usage. Goods then uses this metadata to power services that enable Google engineers to organize and find their datasets in a more principled manner.

Figure 1 shows a schematic overview of our system. Goods continuously crawls different storage systems and the production infrastructure (e.g., logs from running pipelines) to discover which datasets exist and to gather metadata about each one (e.g., owners, time of access, content features, accesses by production pipelines). Goods aggregates this metadata in a central catalog and correlates the metadata about a specific dataset with information about other datasets.

Goods uses this catalog to provide Google engineers with services for dataset management. To illustrate the types of services powered by Goods, imagine a team that is responsible for developing natural language understanding (NLU) of text corpora (say, news articles). The engineers on the team may be distributed across the globe and they maintain several pipelines that add annotations to different text corpora. Each pipeline can have multiple stages that add annotations based on various techniques including phrase chunking, part-of-speech tagging, and co-reference resolution. Other teams can consume the datasets that the NLU team generates, and the NLU team's pipelines may consume datasets from other teams.

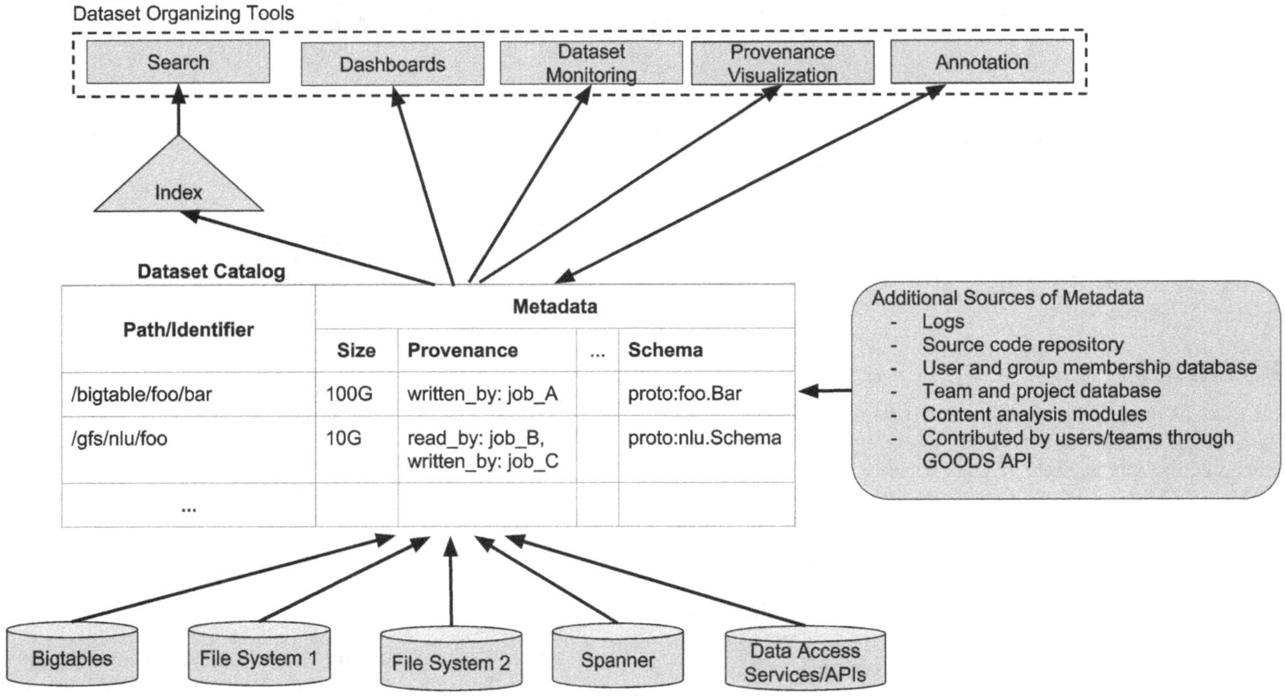

Figure 1: Overview of Google Dataset Search (Goods). The figure shows the Goods dataset catalog that collects metadata about datasets from various storage systems as well as other sources. We also infer metadata by processing additional sources such as logs and information about dataset owners and their projects, by analyzing content of the datasets, and by collecting input from the Goods users. We use the information in the catalog to build tools for search, monitoring, and visualizing flow of data.

Based on the information in its catalog, Goods provides a *dashboard* for the NLU team (in this case, dataset *producers*), which displays all their datasets and enables browsing them by facets (e.g., owner, data center, schema). Even if the team's datasets are in diverse storage systems, the engineers get a unified view of all their datasets and dependencies among them. Goods can *monitor* features of the dataset, such as its size, distribution of values in its contents, or its availability, and then alert the owners if the features change unexpectedly.

Another important piece of information that Goods provides is the dataset *provenance*: namely, the information about which datasets were used to create a given dataset (upstream datasets), and those that rely on it (downstream datasets). Note that both the upstream and downstream datasets may be created by other teams. When an engineer in the NLU team observes a problem with a dataset, she can examine the provenance visualization to determine whether a change in some upstream dataset had caused the problem. Similarly, if the team is about to make a significant change to its pipeline or has discovered a bug in an existing dataset that other teams have consumed already, they can quickly notify those affected by the problem.

From the perspective of dataset *consumers*, such as those not part of the NLU team in our example, Goods provides a *search engine* over all the datasets in the company, plus facets for narrowing search results, to find the most up-to-date or potentially important datasets. Goods presents a profile page for every dataset, which helps users unfamiliar with the data to understand its schema and to create boilerplate code to access and query the data. The profile page also contains the information on datasets with content similar to the content of the current dataset. The similarity information may enable novel combinations of datasets: for example, if two datasets share a primary key column, then they may provide complementary information and are therefore a good candidate for joining.

Goods allows users to expand the catalog with crowd-sourced metadata. For instance, dataset owners can *annotate* datasets with descriptions, in order to help users figure out which datasets are appropriate for their use (e.g., which analysis techniques are used in certain datasets and which pitfalls to watch out for). Dataset auditors can tag datasets that contain sensitive information and alert dataset owners or prompt a review to ensure that the data is handled appropriately. In this manner, Goods and its catalog become a hub through which users can share and exchange information about the generated datasets. Goods also exposes an API through which teams can contribute metadata to the catalog both for the teams own restricted use as well as to help other teams and users understand their datasets easily.

As we discuss in the rest of the paper, we addressed many challenges in designing and building Goods, arising from the sheer number of datasets (tens of billions in our case), the high churn in terms of updates, the sizes of individual datasets (gigabytes or terabytes in many cases), the many different data formats and stores they reside in, and the varying quality and importance of information collected about each dataset. Many of the challenges that we addressed in Goods were precipitated by the scale and characteristics of the data lake at Google. However, we believe that our experience and the lessons that we learned will apply to similar systems in other enterprises.

2. CHALLENGES

In this section, we describe in more detail the challenges that we addressed in building Goods. While some of these challenges are specific to Google's setup, we believe that most of the following points carry over to other large enterprises.

2.1 Scale of the number and size of datasets

While we anticipated the existence of a large number of datasets in the company, the actual count far exceeded our initial calculations. The current catalog indexes over 26 billion datasets even though it includes only those datasets whose access permissions make them readable by *all* Google engineers. We expect that the catalog will more than double in the number of datasets when we index the datasets with restricted access permissions and when we start supporting other storage systems. It is important to note that the catalog already excludes many types of uninteresting datasets (e.g., we discard known "marker" files that are content free) and normalizes paths to avoid obvious redundancies (e.g., we normalize paths corresponding to different shards of the same dataset to a common path and do not store them separately in the catalog).

At this scale, gathering metadata for all datasets becomes infeasible. Indeed, even if we spend one second per dataset (and many of the datasets are too large to process in one second), going through a catalog with 26 billion datasets using a thousand parallel machines still requires around 300 days. Thus, we must develop strategies that prioritize and optimize processing of the datasets.

The scale issue is aggravated by "n-square" problems that arise in metadata inference. For instance, Goods identifies datasets that contain similar or identical content, both overall as well as for individual columns. Comparing any two datasets to each other can already be expensive due to large dataset sizes, but a naïve pairwise comparison of contents of billions of datasets is infeasible.

2.2 Variety

Datasets are stored in many formats (text files, csv files, Bigtables [13], etc.) and storage systems (GoogleFS, database servers, etc.), each with its own type of metadata and access characteristics. This diversity makes it difficult to define a single "dataset" concept that covers all actual dataset types. Hiding this variety and complexity from the users and presenting a uniform way to access and query information about all types of datasets is both a goal and a challenge for Goods.

Even more important is the variety in the cost of metadata extraction, which can change vastly depending on the type and size of the dataset and the type of metadata. Therefore, our metadata-extraction process needs to be differential: we must identify which datasets are important to cover, and then to perform metadata inference based on the cost and benefit for having the particular type of metadata.

Variety also manifests in the relationships among datasets, which in turn affect how we model and store metadata in the catalog. Take for instance a Bigtable dataset [13]. It comprises several column families, with each family inheriting metadata from the containing Bigtable but also having its own metadata and access properties. As a result, we can view column families both as individual datasets and as part of the overall Bigtable dataset. Furthermore, the underlying storage infrastructure for a Bigtable is provided by a distributed file system, and so we can also view the corresponding files as datasets. In the case of Bigtable, the decision to hide these underlying files in favor of the Bigtable dataset seems reasonable. However, a similar decision is less clear in other cases. For instance, we include database tables (specifically, Dremel tables [19]) in our catalog. These tables were created from other files (also in our catalog), and in this case it is meaningful to have both the files and the database tables as separate (but connected) datasets in the catalog given that their access patterns are sufficiently different. Note that this last example illustrates a type of dataset aliasing. Aliases can arise in several ways in our catalog, and we have dealt with each alias type separately depending on the corresponding usage patterns.

Number of datasets	26 billion
Number of paths added per day	1.6 billion
Number of paths deleted per day	1.6 billion
Number of storage systems	6
Number of dataset formats	> 20

Table 1: The scale, variety, and churn of the entries in the Goods catalog.

2.3 Churn of the catalog entries

Every day, production jobs generate new datasets, and old datasets get deleted—either explicitly or because their designated time-to-live (TTL) has expired. In fact, we found that more than 5% (i.e., about 1 billion) of the datasets in the catalog are deleted every day. Almost an equal number of new entries are added back as well. This level of churn adds more considerations to how we prioritize for which datasets we compute the metadata and which datasets we include in the catalog. For example, many of the datasets that have a limited Time-To-Live (TTL) from their creation are intermediate results of a large production pipeline that are garbage collected after a few days. One possibility is to ignore these transient datasets for metadata extraction, or even to exclude them from the catalog. However, there are two considerations. First, some of these datasets have long TTLs (e.g., measured in weeks) and hence their value to users can be high when the datasets are just created. Second, as we discuss later, some of these transient datasets link non-transient datasets to each other and are thus critical in the computation of dataset provenance. Hence, entirely blacklisting transient datasets was not an option for Goods.

2.4 Uncertainty of metadata discovery

Because Goods explicitly identifies and analyzes datasets in a post-hoc and non-invasive manner, it is often impossible to determine all types of metadata with complete certainty. For instance, many datasets consist of records whose schema conforms to a specific protocol buffer [23] (i.e., a nested-relational schema). However, the dataset itself does not reference the specific protocol buffer that describes its content—the association between a protocol buffer and a dataset is implicit in the source code that accesses the dataset. Goods tries to uncover this implicit association through several signals: For instance, we "match" the dataset contents against all registered types of protocol buffers within Google, or we consult usage logs that may have recorded the actual protocol buffer. This inference is inherently ambiguous and can result in several possible matches between a dataset and protocol buffers.

Similarly, Goods analyzes the datasets to determine which fields could serve as primary keys, but relies on an approximate process in order to deal with the scale of the problem—another uncertain inference.

Most of this uncertainty arises because we process the datasets in a post-hoc fashion: we do not require dataset owners to change their workflows in order to associate this type of metadata with the datasets when the owners create the datasets. Instead, we opt to collect dataset metadata that is already logged in different corners

Metadata Groups	Metadata
Basic	size, format, aliases, last modified time, access control lists
Content-based	schema, number of records, data fingerprint, key field, frequent tokens, similar datasets
Provenance	reading jobs, writing jobs, downstream datasets, upstream datasets
User-supplied	description, annotations
Team and Project	project description, owner team name
Temporal	change history

Table 2: Metadata in the Goods catalog.

of the existing infrastructure and then we aggregate and clean the metadata for further usage.

2.5 Computing dataset importance

After we discover and catalog the datasets, reasoning about their relative importance to the users presents additional challenges. To start with, the basic question of what makes a dataset important is hard to answer. Looking at a dataset in isolation can provide some hints, but it is often necessary to examine the dataset in a more global context (e.g., consider how often production pipelines access the dataset) in order to understand its importance.

Note that the notion of importance—and relative importance—comes up prominently in the context of Web search. However, ranking and importance among structured datasets in an enterprise setting is significantly different from the Web search setting: the only explicit links that we have are the provenance links, which do not necessarily signify importance. Furthermore, many of the signals that we can use for Web search (e.g., anchor text) do not exist for datasets, whereas datasets can provide structured context that the Web pages do not have.

In addition to the importance of datasets to the users, a different notion of importance comes up when we prioritize the datasets for which we derive metadata. For example, we would often consider transient datasets to be unimportant. However, if a transient dataset provides a provenance link between non-transient, important datasets, then it is natural to boost its importance accordingly.

2.6 Recovering dataset semantics

Understanding the semantics of dataset contents is extremely useful in searching, ranking, and describing the datasets. Suppose that we know the schema of a dataset and that some field in the schema takes integer values. Now, suppose that through some inference on the dataset contents we are able to identify that these integer values are IDs of known geographic landmarks. We can use this type of content semantics to improve search when a user searches Goods for geographic data. In general, by lifting the level of abstraction from raw bytes to concepts we can make inferences that lead to deeper and cleaner dataset metadata. However, identifying the semantics from raw data is a hard problem even for small datasets [12] because there is rarely enough information in the data to make this inference. Performing such inference for datasets with billions of records becomes even harder.

3. THE GOODS CATALOG

Having described the challenges that we addressed in building Goods, we now turn our attention to the details of the system. We begin by taking a closer look at the Goods catalog, which lies in the core of our system. At a high level, the catalog contains an entry for each dataset that Goods discovers by crawling different storage systems within Google. While each independent storage system within the company may maintain a catalog over datasets that it serves, each such catalog has different types of metadata and data often flows from one system to another in an unfettered fashion. This freedom makes it difficult to obtain a global and unified view of the datasets available throughout the company. The Goods catalog fills this gap and is thus an important contribution in itself, even if we do not consider the services at the top of Figure 1.

The Goods catalog not only contains the individual datasets that we collect by crawling the different storage systems, but also groups related datasets into clusters, which become first-class entries in the catalog. Consider for example a dataset where a new version is produced daily, or even hourly. Our catalog will contain an entry for each version of such a dataset. However, users would often want to think of these versions as a single logical dataset. Furthermore, all these versions are likely to have some common metadata (e.g., owners or schema) and thus collecting metadata separately for each version is wasteful—and often prohibitive—in terms of resources. For these two reasons, we organize these related datasets in a cluster, which becomes a separate entry in the catalog. Goods surfaces this cluster to users as a logical dataset that represents all the generated versions. Goods also uses the cluster to optimize the computation of metadata under the assumption that all datasets in the cluster have similar properties.

In this section, we first describe the types of metadata that we associate with each dataset (Section 3.1) and then describe our mechanism for metadata extraction based on dataset clusters (Section 3.2).

3.1 Metadata

Goods bootstraps its catalog by crawling Google's storage systems (e.g., GoogleFS, Bigtable, database servers) in order to discover what datasets exist and to obtain some basic metadata such as size, owners, readers, and access permissions of datasets. However, most storage systems do not keep track of other important metadata, such as jobs that produced a dataset, teams and users that access it, its schema, and others (Table 2). This information is spread across logs written by processes that access these datasets, is encoded within the datasets themselves, or can be deduced by analyzing the content of the datasets. Thus, in addition to crawling, we perform metadata inference. In what follows, we describe in more detail the different types of metadata (collected and inferred) in the Goods catalog.

Basic metadata - The basic metadata for each dataset includes its timestamp, file format, owners, and access permissions. We obtain this basic metadata by crawling the storage systems and this process usually does not necessitate any inference. Other Goods modules often depend on this basic information to determine their behavior. For example, some of the modules bypass catalog entries that have restricted access or the entries that have not been modified recently.

Provenance - Datasets are produced and consumed by code. This code may include analysis tools that are used to query datasets, serving infrastructures that provide access to datasets through APIs, or ETL pipelines that transform it into other datasets. Often, we can understand a dataset better through these surrounding pieces of software that produce and use it. Moreover, this information helps in tracking how data flows through the enterprise as well as across

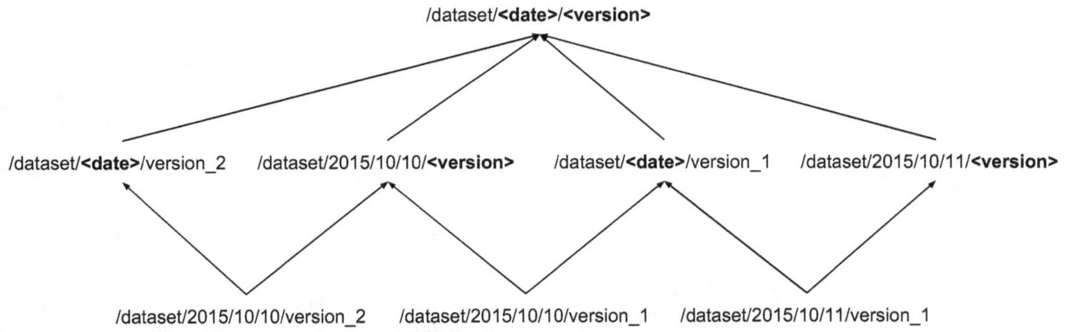

Figure 2: An example of abstraction semi-lattice

boundaries of teams and organizations within the company. Therefore, for each dataset, the GOODS catalog maintains the provenance of how the dataset is produced, how it is consumed, what datasets this dataset depends on, and what other datasets depend on this dataset. We identify and populate the provenance metadata through an analysis of production logs, which provide information on which jobs read and write each dataset. We then create a transitive closure of this graph connecting datasets and jobs, in order to determine how the datasets themselves are linked to one another. For instance if a job J reads dataset D_1 and produces dataset D_2, then the metadata for D_1 contains D_2 as one of its downstream datasets and vice versa. We also take into account timing information in order to determine the earliest and latest points in time when these dependencies existed. However, the number of data-access events in the logs can be extremely high and so can be the size of the transitive closure. Therefore, we trade off the completeness of the provenance associations for efficiency by processing only a sample of data-access events from the logs and also by materializing only the downstream and upstream relations within a few hops as opposed to computing the true transitive closure.

Schema - Schema is another core type of metadata that helps us understand a dataset. The most commonly used dataset formats in Google are not self-describing, and we must infer the schema. Nearly all records within structured datasets at Google are encoded as serialized protocol buffers [23]. The difficulty lies in determining which protocol buffer was used to encode records in a given dataset. Protocol buffers that the majority of Google's datasets use are nearly always checked into Google's central code repository. Thus, we have a full list of them available to match against datasets that we have crawled. We perform this matching by scanning a few records from the file, and going through each protocol message definition to determine whether it could conceivably have generated the bytes we see in those records. Protocol buffers encode multiple logical types as the same physical type, notably string and nested messages are both encoded as variable-length byte strings. Consequently, the matching procedure is speculative and can produce multiple candidate protocol buffers. All the candidate protocol buffers, along with heuristic scores for each candidate, become part of the metadata.

Content summary - For each dataset that we are able to open and scan, we also collect metadata that summarizes the content of the dataset. We record frequent tokens that we find by sampling the content. We analyze some of the fields to determine if they contain keys for the data, individually or in combination. To find potential keys, we use the HyperLogLog algorithm [15] to estimate cardinality of values in individual fields and combinations of fields and we compare this cardinality with the number of records to find potential keys. We also collect fingerprints that have checksums for the individual fields and locality-sensitive hash (LSH) values for the content. We use these fingerprints to find datasets with content that is similar or identical to the given dataset, or columns from other datasets that are similar or identical to columns in the current dataset. We also use the checksums to identify which fields are populated in the records of the dataset.

User-provided annotations - We enable dataset owners to provide text descriptions of their datasets. These descriptions are critical to our ranking, and also help us filter out datasets that are experimental or that we should not show to the users.

Semantics - GOODS combines several noisy signals in order to derive metadata about dataset semantics. For datasets whose schema conforms to a protocol buffer, GOODS can examine the source code that defines the protocol buffer and extract any of the attached comments. These comments are often of high quality and their lexical analysis can provide short phrases that capture the semantics of the schema. As an actual example, some of the datasets in the GOODS catalog conform to a protocol buffer with a field cryptically named `mpn`. However, the source code contains the comment "`//Model Product Number`" above the field, which disambiguates its semantics. GOODS can also examine the dataset content and match it against Google's Knowledge Graph [11], to identify entities (e.g., locations, businesses) that appear in different fields.

In addition to the metadata listed above, we collect identifiers for teams that own the dataset, a description of the project to which a dataset belongs, and the history of the changes to the metadata of the dataset.

Finally, our infrastructure (Section 4) allows other teams to add their own types of metadata. For instance, a team may rely on different types of content summaries, or provide additional provenance information. The GOODS catalog is becoming the unifying place for teams to collect their metadata and to access it.

3.2 Organizing datasets into clusters

The 26B datasets in the GOODS catalog are not completely independent from one another. We often see different versions of a dataset that are being generated on a regular basis, datasets that are replicated across different data centers, datasets that are sharded into smaller datasets for faster loading, and so on. If we can identify natural clusters to which datasets belong, then not only we can provide the users with a useful logical-level abstraction that groups together these different versions but we can also save on metadata extraction, albeit potentially at the cost of precision. That is, instead of collecting expensive metadata for each individual dataset, we can collect metadata only for a few datasets in a cluster. We can then propagate the metadata across the other datasets in the cluster. For instance, if the same job generates versions of a dataset daily, these datasets are likely to have the same schema. Thus, we do not

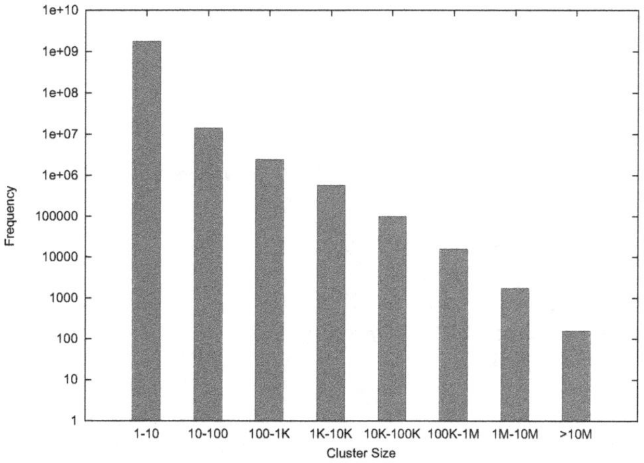

Figure 3: Distribution of cluster sizes. The X axis is the number of datasets in a cluster (cluster size). The Y axis is the number of clusters of the corresponding cluster size.

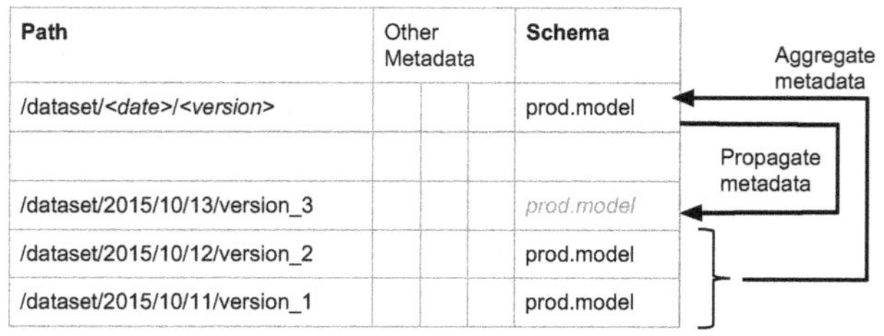

Figure 4: An example of propagating the *owners* metadata to an unanalyzed dataset through the cluster's representative element.

need to infer the schema for each version. Similarly, if a user provides a description for a dataset, it usually applies to all members of the cluster and not just the one version. When the clusters are large, the computational savings that we obtain by avoiding analysis of each member of the cluster can be significant.

For clustering to reduce the computational overhead, the clustering itself should be cheap. Clustering techniques that require investigating the contents of a dataset can overshadow the computational savings that we obtain by avoiding repetitive metadata extraction. Fortunately, the paths of the datasets often give hints on how to cluster them via embedded identifiers for timestamps, versions, and so on. For example, consider a dataset that is produced daily and let `/dataset/2015-10-10/daily_scan` be the path for one of its instances. We can *abstract* out the day portion of the date to get a generic representation of all datasets produced in a month: `/dataset /2015-10-<day>/daily_scan`, representing all instances from October 2015. By abstracting out the month as well, we can go up the hierarchy to create abstract paths that represent all datasets produced in the same year: `/dataset/2015-<month>-<day>/daily_scan`.

By composing hierarchies along different dimensions, we can construct a *granularity semi-lattice* structure where each node corresponds to a different *granularity* of viewing the datasets. Figure 2 shows an example of such a semi-lattice obtained by composing two hierarchies—one along date and the other along version number.

Table 3 lists the abstraction dimensions that we currently use to construct the granularity semi-lattice for each dataset. By abstracting out the various dimensions from all dataset paths, we eventually obtain a set of semi-lattices whose non-leaf nodes represent different choices for grouping datasets into clusters. We can optimize the selection of clusters with a suitable objective function over the current state of the catalog, but the daily catalog churn can cause a frequent recomputation of clusters. Therefore, users may see different clusters (representing logical datasets) from day to day, which can be confusing. We adopted a simple solution that works well in practice: we create an entry only for the top-most element of each semi-lattice. Going back to the example of Figure 2, the catalog would have an entry for the cluster `/dataset/<date>/<version>`, representing the three datasets at the bottom of the lattice. This approach keeps the number of cluster entries low, guarantees that each dataset maps to exactly one cluster, and maintains a stable set of clusters over time.

After we compute the clusters, we obtain the metadata for each cluster by aggregating the metadata for individual members. For instance, if we know the schema for several members of the cluster, and it is the same for all of them, we can propagate this schema for the cluster as a whole (Figure 4). Whether to materialize this propagated information or simply to compute it on-demand is an application-specific design decision. In our case, we compute it on demand to differentiate explicitly between propagated metadata and metadata that we obtained through real analysis.

Figure 3 shows a distribution of the number of datasets within each cluster in our catalog. The figure shows that clustering can compress dramatically the set of "physical" datasets into a much smaller set of "logical" datasets, thus making it easier for users to inspect the catalog. Moreover, the computational savings from metadata smearing are significant, particularly for the extremely large clusters.

4. BACKEND IMPLEMENTATION

In this section, we focus on the implementation details of building and maintaining the catalog that we described in Section 3. We discuss the physical structure of the catalog, our approach to scaling up the modules that populate the catalog, consistency and garbage collection, and finally, fault tolerance.

4.1 Catalog storage

We use Bigtable [13], a scalable, temporal key–value store, as the storage medium for our catalog. Each row represents one dataset or a dataset cluster (Section 3.2), with the dataset path or cluster path as the key. Bigtable offers per-row transactional consistency, which is a good fit as most (although, not all) of the processing in our system is per dataset. For instance, we can infer a schema for a dataset without looking at entries for other datasets; we can analyze the content of a dataset by examining a single row.

There are some aspects of our system that deviate from this per-dataset processing. For example, we aggregate information from multiple rows into logical datasets in our abstraction lattice (Section 3.2). Propagating metadata across datasets in the same cluster also does not conform to the model of processing each dataset independently. However, this metadata propagation is best effort and does not require strong consistency.

At the physical level, a Bigtable comprises several independent column families. We keep data that is accessed only by batch jobs (vs. served to a frontend tool) in separate column families that we tuned for batch processing (highly compressed, and not memory-resident). For instance, our largest column family contains raw provenance data that we use to compute the provenance graph but that we do not directly serve at the front end (Section 5): There, we serve the provenance information only at the level of abstracted

Abstraction Dimension	Description	Examples of paths with instances
Timestamps	All specifications of dates and times	/gfs/generated_at_**20150505T20:21:56**
Data-center Names	Specification of data center names	/gfs/**oregon**/dataset
Machine Names	Hostnames of machines (either user's or one in the data center)	/gfs/dataset/**foo.corp.google.com**
Version	Numeric and hexa-numeric version specifications	/gfs/dataset/**0x12ab12c**/bar
Universally Unique Identifier	UUIDs as specified in RFC4122[6]	/gfs/dataset/**30201010-5041-7061-9081-F0E0D0C0B0AA**/foo

Table 3: The dimensions that Goods uses to abstract dataset paths. The examples illustrate portions of the paths that correspond to the abstraction dimensions.

dataset clusters. Thus, we can aggressively compress this large column family.

We store two kinds of metadata for each row in our Bigtable-backed catalog: (a) metadata for the datasets (Section 3); (b) metadata about the outcome of the modules that processed a given dataset, *status metadata*. The status metadata lists each module that processed a particular entry, with timestamp, success status, and error message, if any. We use the status metadata to coordinate execution of modules (Section 4.2), and for our own inspection of the system (What fraction of datasets has module X processed successfully? What is the most common error code?). In conjunction with Bigtable's temporal data model, the status metadata was also extremely useful for debugging. We configure the Bigtable to retain multiple generations of the status metadata, allowing us to see what our modules have been doing over time (e.g., on a given problematic dataset, when did the module start emitting an error? is the error deterministic?).

4.2 Batch job performance and scheduling

Our system is comprised of two types of jobs: (1) a large number of diverse batch-processing jobs; and (2) a small number of jobs that serve our front end and the API. In addition, we designed the system to be extensible and to accommodate crawlers for new sources of datasets and provenance and other metadata, and new analysis modules. Some of our batch jobs are fairly quick and typically finish a full pass over our catalog in a few hours; others, such as the ones that analyze the content of the datasets, take many days to catch up with a fresh crawl that added new datasets to the catalog. We schedule such jobs to run in geographical proximity to the datasets that they analyze, which are distributed worldwide.

We allow all the jobs to run independently from one another: we do not restrict the order in which jobs run, or constrain whether or not they run concurrently. Some of the jobs may be broken at any given time and we can take them offline temporarily. Each job includes one or more modules, such as crawlers or analyzers.

Individual modules often depend on other modules and cannot process a given dataset until some other modules processed it. For example, the module that computes fingerprints for columns needs to know a dataset's schema, and hence has a dependency on the module that determines the schema of a dataset—a so-called *Schema Analyzer* module. The modules coordinate their execution with one another at the granularity of individual Bigtable rows, using the status metadata that we mentioned earlier. If a module A must (successfully) process a row before module B, then when module B examines a row, it checks for a status metadata entry indicating a successful visit by module A. If no such status entry is present, then module B bypasses that row; it will try again next time it runs. If module A re-processes a row, then upon its next visit to the row, module B will also re-process it, to propagate the freshest metadata (e.g. re-fingerprint based on the updated schema). Modules also use their own status metadata to avoid re-processing rows they have already processed within a configurable freshness window.

Most jobs are configured to run daily, and finish comfortably in 24 hours. When jobs overrun their daily cycle, we optimize and/or add parallelism. These jobs use each 24-hour cycle to process new catalog rows and/or refresh already-processed ones that have fallen outside the freshness window.

After a large influx of new datasets (e.g. incorporating a new source of dataset paths), our most heavyweight job, the Schema Analyzer, takes days, or sometimes weeks, to catch up. We use a simple prioritization mechanism to ensure that our most important datasets do not get neglected by the Schema Analyzer during this "catch-up" scenario: We heuristically designate datasets having user-supplied annotations or high provenance centrality as "important," and schedule two instances of the job: one instance processes only the important datasets and can get through them quickly, and another instance aims to process all datasets but may get only to a fraction of them by day's end. In practice, as with Web crawling, ensuring good coverage and freshness for the "head" of the importance distribution is enough for most user scenarios.

Our large crawler jobs perform "blind writes" to the catalog: They read data from a source and write all of the data to our Bigtable. Bigtable does not distinguish between insertions and updates, so this approach yields a combination of no-op updates and insertions. This approach is more efficient than doing a read of our catalog to anti-join it with the new source crawl. However, we must take care to avoid no-op writes in certain cases, because it can cause dependent modules to re-run needlessly, or block garbage collection (see Section 4.4).

4.3 Fault tolerance

With such a large number and variety of datasets being analyzed, we encounter many different kinds of problems. For modules that process individual datasets, we record per-dataset errors in the status metadata of the dataset's entry in the catalog. Status metadata that indicates that a module finished with an error, triggers (a bounded number of) retries. The modules that do not process each dataset in isolation (e.g. provenance linking), rely on a job-wide status metadata entry that indicates the start time of a job and whether the job succeeded. For example, the provenance-linking module incorporates a dataset–job link into the transitive provenance graph only if the link's timestamp is more recent than the last successful execution of the module (as recorded in the module-wide status metadata). This approach is conservative: we may redo some Bigtable writes if the previous execution of the module failed part-way. However, this approach ensures that the resulting provenance graph is correct because Bigtable writes are idempotent. Furthermore, it enables us to mark the recorded job-provenance information as "consumed," a feature that becomes critical for garbage collection, as we discuss later.

Several of our modules that examine content of datasets use a variety of libraries specific to different file formats. At times, these libraries crash or go into infinite loops. (While we work to track down and eliminate these cases, it is not feasible to eradicate them entirely, especially given the evolving nature of files and file formats in our environments.) Because we cannot have long-running analysis jobs crashing or hanging, we sandbox such potentially dangerous jobs in a separate process. We then use a watchdog thread to convert long stalls into crashes while allowing the rest of the pipeline to proceed.

We replicate our catalog at multiple geographical locations. Writes go to a master and get replicated asynchronously in the background elsewhere.

4.4 Garbage collection of metadata

We ingest and create a huge volume of data daily. A nontrivial fraction of this data is transient. After we consume such transient data to build the provenance graph, we can remove the entries that correspond to the deleted datasets, as long as our modules have consumed the associated metadata to update the catalog. We initially favored a simple, conservative approach to garbage collection. For instance, we would delete a row if it had not been updated for one week. However, a few incidents in which our catalog became badly bloated taught us that aggressive garbage collection is necessary. Early in our project, on two occasions we had to disable all crawlers and non-garbage-collection-related analysis modules for several days to recover from this situation.

The garbage-collection mechanism that we have implemented currently addresses several constraints that we discovered along the way:

1. Conditions for removing rows are best expressed as declarative predicates that use both metadata and statuses of other modules that may have accessed or updated the row. For example, we have the following condition on when we can remove a dataset from the Goods catalog: "the dataset has been deleted from the storage system, and its most recently updated provenance information has been processed by a transitive provenance linker module that finished successfully."

2. When we delete an entry from a catalog, we must ensure that we do not create so-called "dangling rows": Recall that Bigtable does not differentiate between insertions and updates. Thus, when we remove a row, we must ensure that no other concurrently running module will add that row back with only partial information (specifically, only the information that the specific module is responsible for). For example, assume that there is a race condition between the garbage collector and a metadata-inference module that is examining the same row. The garbage collector removes the row and then the metadata-inference module inserts the row back; this row will contain only the information that this module infers. This sequence results in loss of information about where the corresponding dataset was crawled, possibly compromising the integrity of other modules.

3. All other module must be able to run independently of and simultaneously with the garbage collection.

Bigtable supports *conditional mutations*, which are stylized transactions that update or delete a Bigtable row if a given predicate yields true, in a transactional fashion. Having Bigtable updates from all modules to be conditioned on the row not having been deleted, proved to be too expensive: Conditional mutations incur substantial log-structured read overhead.

Our ultimate design permits all modules other than the garbage collector to perform non-transactional updates. To enable this flexibility, the garbage collection occurs in two phases: (a) In the first phase, we use declarative predicates that approve removing a catalog row (see the first condition above). However, in this first phase our garbage collector does not actually delete the Bigtable entry, but puts a special *tombstone* marker on it. (b) 24 hours later (see below for more on this threshold), if the row still meets the deletion criteria, we delete it; otherwise, we remove the tombstone.

At the same time, all other modules conform to the following constraints: (a) they can perform non-transactional updates; (b) they ignore the rows with the *tombstone* marker to avoid updating the rows that are slated for deletion; (c) a single iteration of a module cannot remain live for more than 24 hours (our module scheduling mechanism enforces this).

This design satisfies the three conditions above while preserving the efficiency of the entire system.

5. FRONT END: SERVING THE CATALOG

We have so far focused on the process for building and maintaining the Goods catalog. In this section, we describe the main services enabled by the metadata that we collect in Goods (cf. the top part of Figure 1).

5.1 Dataset profile pages

The first service is to export the metadata for a specific dataset in an easy-to-view *profile page* for the dataset. Specifically, the profile-page service accepts as input the path of a dataset or a dataset cluster and generates an HTML page from the metadata stored in the catalog. The service also provides methods to edit specific parts of the metadata, to allow users either to augment or to correct the information stored in the catalog.

The profile page renders most of the dataset metadata that we described in Section 3. When presenting the profile page to the users, we must balance the need to present the metadata in a comprehensive way with the desire to keep the amount of information on the page manageable. The manageable size is important both not to overwhelm the users with too much information and to avoid transferring large amounts of information. Consider provenance information, for example: Popular datasets may be read by tens of thousands of jobs and have tens of thousands of datasets downstream from them. Incidentally, jobs such as Goods modules, which need to access every dataset in the company, have potentially billions of datasets upstream from them. To avoid transferring and trying to present such overwhelming amounts of information to the users (which would be futile to do anyway), we compress provenance metadata offline, whenever it becomes too large, using the same abstraction mechanism that we introduced in Section 3.2. We then use this compressed provenance to render the profile page. If the compressed version is still too large, then our last resort is to retain only a number of most recent entries.

The profile page of a dataset cross-links some of the metadata with other, more specialized, tools. For example, the profile page links the provenance metadata, such as jobs that generated the dataset, to the pages with details for those jobs in job-centric tools. Similarly, we link schema metadata to code-management tools, which provide the definition of this schema. Correspondingly, these tools link back to Goods to help users get more information about datasets.

The profile page also provides *access snippets* in different languages (e.g., C++, Java, SQL) to access the contents of the dataset. We custom-tailor the generated snippets for the specific dataset: For example, the snippets use the path and schema of the dataset (when known), and users can copy-paste the snippets in their respective programming environment. The goal behind these snippets is to complement the content metadata in the profile page: the latter provide schema-level information about the contents of the dataset, whereas the snippets provide a handy way to inspect quickly the actual contents or to analyze the contents through code.

Overall the intent of a profile page is to provide a one-stop shop where a user can inspect the information about a dataset and understand the context in which the dataset can be used in production. This feature makes the profile page a natural handle for sharing a dataset among users or linking to dataset information from other tools. As an example of the latter, Google's filesystem browser provides direct links to GOODS dataset-profile pages when users examine the contents of a directory.

5.2 Dataset search

Profile pages allow users to view information about specific datasets, but how can a user find datasets of interest? This task is where our dataset-search service comes in.

Dataset search allows Googlers to find datasets using simple keyword queries. The service is backed by a conventional inverted index for document retrieval, where each dataset becomes a "document" and we derive the indexing tokens for each document from a subset of the dataset's metadata. As is common in this context, each token can be associated with a specific section of the index. For example, a token derived from the path of the dataset is associated with the "path" section of the index. Accordingly, the search atom "path:x" will match keyword "x" on dataset paths only, whereas the unqualified atom "x" will match the keyword in any part of a dataset's metadata. Table 4 summarizes the main sections in the dataset-search index and their meaning in queries.

Qualified token	Where token matches
path:*a*	Path of the dataset
proto:*a*	Name of protocol buffer
read_by:*a* written_by:*a*	Names of jobs reading/writing the dataset
downstream_of:*a* upstream_of:*a*	Paths of datasets downstream/upstream of the dataset
kind:*a*	Type of the dataset
owner:*a*	Owners of the dataset

Table 4: Examples of qualifying a search token *a* so that it matches different sections of the index. A search query may comprise several qualified and unqualified tokens.

The extraction of indexing tokens follows from the type of queries that the index must cover. As an example, we want to support partial matches on the dataset path, where a user may search for "x/y" to match a dataset with path "a/x/y/b" (but not one with "a/y/x/b"). One approach is to index every sub-sequence of the path along common separators (e.g., for path "a/x/y/b" extract the indexing tokens "a/x","x/y", ..., "a/x/y", "x/y/b", and so on). However, this approach results in a blow-up in index size. Instead, we break up the dataset's path along common separators and then associate each resulting token with its position in the path. Going back to our example, the path "a/x/y/b" gets mapped to the indexing tokens "a", "x", "y", and "b", in that sequence. When the user issues a search query with a partial path, our service parses the partial path the same way and matches the query's tokens against consecutive tokens in the index. We followed a similar scheme when indexing the names of protocol buffers, which can be qualified with a namespace (e.g., "foo.bar.X"). In this fashion, a user can search for all datasets whose schema matches any protocol buffer under a specific namespace.

Matching search keywords to datasets is only the first part of the search task. The second part is deriving a scoring function to rank the matching datasets, so that the top results are relevant for the user's search. Scoring is generally a hard problem and part of our ongoing work involves tuning the scoring function based on our users' experience. In what follows, we describe some heuristics that informed the design of the scoring function thus far.

- *The importance of a dataset depends on its type.* For instance, our scoring function favors a Dremel table [19] over a file dataset, all else being equal. The intuition is that a dataset owner has to register a dataset as a Dremel table explicitly, which in turn makes the dataset visible to more users. We interpret this action as a signal that the dataset is important and reflect it in our final scoring.
- *The importance of a keyword match depends on the index section.* For instance, a keyword match on the path of the dataset is more important than a match on jobs that read or write the dataset, all else being equal. This heuristic reflects the types of searches that we observe in practice.
- *Lineage fan-out is a good indicator of dataset importance.* Specifically, this heuristic favors datasets with many reading jobs and many downstream datasets. The intuition is that if many production pipelines access the dataset, then most likely the dataset is important. One can view this heuristic as an approximation of PageRank in a graph where datasets and production jobs are vertices and edges denote dataset accesses from jobs. An interesting artifact of this heuristic and the nature of Google's production pipelines (and potentially pipelines in other enterprises as well) is assignment of inordinately high scores to certain datasets simply because they are consumed indirectly by many internal pipelines—even if they may not be useful to most users. One such example is Google's Web crawl, which numerous pipelines consume (often indirectly) in order to extract different types of information. Hence, it becomes important to tune and control the contribution of this heuristic to the overall ranking function, otherwise these datasets tend to get ranked high even for vaguely related searches.
- *A dataset that carries an owner-sourced description is likely to be important.* Our user interface enables dataset owners to provide descriptions for datasets that they want other teams to consume. We treat the presence of such a description as a signal of dataset importance. If a keyword match occurs in the description of a dataset then this dataset should be weighted higher as well.

Our scoring function incorporates these heuristics as well as other signals, and as with any similar setting, tuning the contribution of different signals has been an ongoing effort in our team. Note that we do not claim that the heuristics that we mentioned are complete. In fact, an interesting research problem is understanding the factors that influence dataset importance at search time (when the search keywords provide some indication of the user's intent) but also in a static, more global context that considers the usage of a dataset in relation to other datasets, jobs, and teams in the enterprise. This static context is relevant for our backend, as an additional signal on what datasets we should prioritize for metadata extraction.

In addition to the keyword search, GOODS presents metadata facets for some of the categorical metadata in the catalog, such as dataset owners and dataset file formats. These facets give users an overview of the matching datasets, and help them formulate subsequent drill down queries significantly easier.

5.3 Team dashboards

The Goods dashboard is a configurable one-stop shop for displaying all the datasets generated by a team along with interesting metadata per dataset, such as various health metrics, other dashboards, and whether or not the storage system in which the dataset resides is online. Goods updates the content of a dashboard automatically as it updates the metadata of the datasets in the dashboard. Users can easily embed the dashboard page within other documents and share the dashboard with others.

The Goods dashboard also provides the means to monitor datasets and fire alerts if certain expected properties fail to hold (e.g., a dataset should have a certain number of shards or should have a certain distribution of values). Users can set up this type of monitoring with a few clicks and Goods is then responsible for checking the monitored properties for the corresponding datasets and to propagate any alerts to an in-house monitoring UI. In addition to performing fixed validation checks, Goods can generate checks by learning trends for a few common properties of interest. For example, if the size of a dataset historically increases by 10% for each version, then Goods can recommend a corresponding check that the next dataset size should be within some range around the projected size.

6. LESSONS LEARNED

In our efforts to build Goods we encountered many pitfalls—some that were avoidable and some that were hard to anticipate. In this section, we summarize some of the lessons that we have learned along the way.

Evolve as you go — We started building the catalog with dataset discovery as the target use case. Soon we realized that engineers were using Goods in a variety of ways, some of which deviated from or refined the initial use case. Here are the main trends that we observed in our usage logs or learned from our users:

- *Audit protocol buffers* Certain protocol buffers may contain personally identifiable information and so any datasets using these protocol buffers must adhere to strict usage and access policies. Using Goods, engineers can easily find all datasets conforming to a sensitive protocol buffer and alert the dataset owners in case of policy violations.

- *Re-find datasets* Engineers generate many "experimental" datasets as part of their work, but often forget the paths when they want to share these datasets or continue working on them. Usually these datasets can be easily re-found with a simple keyword search.

- *Understand legacy code* Up-to-date documentation for legacy code can be hard to find. Goods exposes a provenance graph that engineers can use to track previous executions of legacy code along with input and output datasets, which in turn can provide useful clues for the underlying logic.

- *Bookmark datasets* A dataset's profile page is a natural one-stop-shop for information about the dataset. Users bookmark these pages for easy access and also to share datasets with other users.

- *Annotate datasets* The Goods catalog serves as a hub for dataset annotations that can be shared across teams. For example, teams can tag their datasets with different levels of privacy in order to warn engineers about the intended usage of the datasets and also to facilitate policy checks.

It is noteworthy that the last feature was built by a different team within Google, one who piggybacked on the infrastructure that we developed. This outside contribution validated our goal to help create a company-wide ecosystem of tools around dataset management.

As we were developing Goods, we had several meetings with teams inside Google to discuss their pain points in dataset management. We realized very quickly the need for a holistic suite of data-management tools beyond search, including dashboards to monitor dataset health, automated dataset testing, and tools to understand differences among datasets. Our extensible design enabled us to support some of these use cases with a relatively small incremental effort. Moreover, some of these tools can enhance the catalog with additional metadata that apply in other use cases. For example, datasets that users explicitly included in data dashboards for monitoring were clearly important datasets and therefore we could boost their ranking.

Use domain-specific signals for ranking — As mentioned in Section 2, the problem of ranking datasets has unique characteristics when compared to ranking problems in other domains (e.g., Web ranking). Our experience with Goods confirmed this observation. For example, we have found that provenance relationships among datasets provide a strong domain-specific ranking signal. Specifically, it is common for teams to generate denormalized versions of some "master" dataset in order to facilitate different types of analysis of the master data. These denormalized datasets can match the same search keywords as the master dataset, yet it is clear that the master dataset should be ranked higher for general-purpose queries or for metadata-extraction. Another example comes from provenance relationships that cross team boundaries, when the dataset from one team is processed to create a dataset in the scope of another team or project. In this case, we can boost the importance of the input dataset as evidenced by its usage by an external team. The output dataset is also important, since we can view it as an origin of other datasets within the external project.

Identifying the type of provenance relationships is an interesting research problem, especially in the context of post-hoc metadata inference. There are several signals that we can leverage in this direction, including content similarity among datasets, known provenance relationships, and crowdsourced information such as the owner-provided descriptions. Once we categorize these relationships we then have to reason about them in the context of ranking, a problem that itself involves a different set of challenges.

Expect and handle unusual datasets — Given the large number of datasets in the catalog, we ran into many unexpected scenarios in our early days. We solved some of them as one-off cases with dedicated code while others required a system-level redesign. For example, the abstraction mechanism described in Section 3.2 employs special logic to extract out unconventionally specified dates (for example, "05Jan2015") and versions. Handling of certain datasets that caused our analyzers to crash due to issues in third party libraries outside our codebase required the sandboxing mechanism described in Section 4.3. We adopted the strategy of going with the simplest albeit adhoc solution first and generalized it as and when required.

Export data as required — The storage medium for the Goods catalog is a key-value store and the search service is backed by a conventional inverted index. However, neither of these structures are suitable for visualizing or performing complex path queries over the provenance graph. To support such use cases, we set up a daily export of the catalog data as subject–predicate–object triples. We then import these triples into a graph-based system that supports path queries and exposes an API that is more amenable for visualization. For use cases that require more powerful query processing capabilities that our storage medium does not support natively, the easiest strategy is to export the catalog data to a suitably specialized engine.

Ensure recoverability — Extracting the metadata of billions of datasets is expensive. In stable state, we process one day's worth of new datasets in a single day. Losing or corrupting a significant chunk of the catalog can take weeks to recover unless we dedicate significant additional computational resources to recovery. Moreover, we may not even be able to recompute some of the metadata after significant data loss. For example, some transient files link input and output datasets in the provenance graph. If we loose the provenance data that we inferred from these transient files, we will not be able to recover it.

To ensure recoverability we have configured Bigtable to retain a rolling window of snapshots over several days, but we have also built custom-tailored recovery schemes specifically for GOODS. Specifically, we have added a dedicated process to snapshot high-value datasets (those in which users have explicitly expressed interest through annotations) in a separate catalog in order to guard against data loss. Another process replicates the subset of the catalog that powers the profile pages so that the service remains available even if the main catalog goes offline. Furthermore, we use the GOODS dataset-monitoring service for the catalog itself (which is another structured dataset!) to ensure early detection of data corruption and deletion. We arrived at this combined approach based on our experience of repairing the catalog on several occasions, some of which caused major outages to the user-facing services.

7. RELATED WORK

We can characterize GOODS as a data lake, an approach to store massive amounts of data in easy-to-access repositories, without having to pre-categorize them when they are created. Specifically, GOODS is a system to organize and index the data lake of all Google datasets. Similar efforts are underway in other companies, such as the data-lake management system developed in IBM Research [22] or data-lake offerings in cloud services [1]. We do not have the complete details for these systems, but the distinguishing features of GOODS seem to be the scale of the lake and the post-hoc approach to metadata inference. GOODS also shares the goals and ideas of Dataspaces [16], and we can view it as a concrete implementation of that idea.

DataHub [8, 9, 10] is a collaborative version-management system for datasets that is similar in spirit to software version control systems like Git and SVN. DataHub enables many users to analyze, collaborate, modify, and share datasets in a centralized repository. Data-management systems such as CKAN [3], Quandl [5], and Microsoft Azure Marketplace [2] are repositories of data from multiple sources, organized for distribution and sharing. In all these systems, dataset owners actively choose to contribute their datasets to the system or to annotate the datasets with metadata. The main focus of GOODS is to create a catalog in a post-hoc manner, while the engineers continue to create and maintain the datasets in their current environment. The engineers do not need to change any of their practices in order for GOODS to provide access to their datasets.

Researchers have proposed several systems [12, 26, 7] to extract HTML tables from the Web, to annotate their schema, and to implement a search service for this type of Webtables. However, much of the machinery in Webtable systems is devoted to the identification of HTML tables that hold data (and are not merely used for layouts), something that is not necessary for the kind of structured datasets that GOODS handles. Furthermore, metadata such as provenance, owners, or project affiliation are absent for Webtables but are very important for datasets.

Fast and efficient file search has become necessary for storage systems. Spyglass [18] is a metadata-search system that improves file management by allowing complex, ad hoc queries over file metadata. Propeller [25] also provides fast file-search services and updates its file indices in a real-time and scalable fashion. In comparison, the datasets in GOODS are not in a single storage system and therefore do not have as much readily available metadata, making search a significantly more challenging problem. In addition, GOODS aims to provide a suite of tools for dataset management that go beyond search.

Previous studies have looked into the problem of indexing and searching a large corpus of structured datasets [21, 17]. The developed techniques could be used to power the search service of GOODS, but they would not solve the main challenges that we outlined in Section 2. However, these techniques may become more relevant if GOODS needs to index the actual content of datasets, in which case the catalog will increase significantly in size.

Provenance management has been studied extensively in the literature [14]. Some examples are the PASS [20] and Trio [24] systems to maintain the provenance of files and database records, respectively, and Datahub [10] as a system to maintain versions of datasets. These systems assume that provenance information is either given or can be retrieved reliably through special instrumentation of the processes that access the data. By contrast, GOODS has to rely on much weaker signals for provenance inference while also relying on provenance as a strong signal for dataset ranking.

8. CONCLUSIONS AND FUTURE WORK

In this paper, we have described a system that provides access to metadata about billions of datasets within an enterprise. As might be expected with a system of this scale, we had to solve many challenges—some that we expected and some that we had not. The resulting system provides real value for engineers at Google and already supports many data-management use cases—again, some that we had anticipated and some that grew out of feedback from users who were using the system.

Many significant challenges remain, however. First, we are still far from fully understanding how to rank datasets, how to identify important datasets, and whether or not approaches are similar to ranking of web pages. We discussed some of the signals that we use for ranking in Section 5.2, but we know from the users' feedback that we must improve ranking significantly. We need to be able to distinguish between production and test or development datasets, between datasets that provide input for many other datasets, datasets that users care about, and so on.

Second, because the teams generate their datasets independently and some provide a lot more metadata about the data than others, we need to rely on other, weaker, signals in order to fill the missing metadata about a dataset. We plan to integrate the data with a larger knowledge graph that links together many of the Google's resources, such as datasets, code, and teams. For instance, knowing which code generated a dataset can provide clues to its content. Knowing what are the projects that the team that is responsible for a dataset works on can fill out some of the missing metadata. We believe that there are multiple connections like these ones that would allow us to propagate some of the missing metadata between related entities.

Third, understanding the semantics of the data inside the datasets is another source of information that would make our services—search, in particular—more useful to the users. Again, we can rely on other knowledge structures at Google, such as the Knowledge

Graph (which other companies also have) to gain some understanding of these semantics.

Fourth, modifying existing storage systems to register their datasets with GOODS at the time when the datasets are created can improve the freshness of the catalog. This approach, however, is contrary to the non-invasive post-hoc approach that we have described in this paper. Exploring a combination of the two approaches is future work.

Finally, we hope that systems such as GOODS will provide an impetus to instilling a "data culture" at data-driven companies today in general, and at Google in particular. As we develop systems that enable enterprises to treat datasets as core assets that they are, through dashboards, monitoring, and so on, it will hopefully become as natural to have as much "data discipline" as we have "code discipline."

9. ACKNOWLEDGMENTS

We would like to thank John Wilkes for his insightful comments which helped us improve the paper. We would also like to thank Lorenzo Martignoni and Andi Vajda who helped us in collecting and visualizing provenance metadata, respectively. Finally, we would like to thank our interns, Dominik Moritz, Arun Iyer, Xiao Cheng, Hui Miao, Subhabrata Mukherjee and Jaeho Shin, who have contributed to the features of our system.

10. REFERENCES

[1] Azure data lake. https://azure.microsoft.com/en-us/solutions/data-lake/.

[2] Azure marketplace. http://datamarket.azure.com/browse/data.

[3] CKAN. http://ckan.org.

[4] Data lakes and the promise of unsiloed data. http://www.pwc.com/us/en/technology-forecast/2014/cloud-computing/features/data-lakes.html.

[5] Quandl. https://www.quandl.com.

[6] A universally unique identifier (uuid) urn namespace. https://www.ietf.org/rfc/rfc4122.txt.

[7] S. Balakrishnan, A. Y. Halevy, B. Harb, H. Lee, J. Madhavan, A. Rostamizadeh, W. Shen, K. Wilder, F. Wu, and C. Yu. Applying webtables in practice. In *CIDR 2015, Seventh Biennial Conference on Innovative Data Systems Research, Asilomar, CA, USA*, 2015.

[8] A. P. Bhardwaj, S. Bhattacherjee, A. Chavan, A. Deshpande, A. J. Elmore, S. Madden, and A. G. Parameswaran. DataHub: Collaborative data science & dataset version management at scale. In *CIDR 2015, Seventh Biennial Conference on Innovative Data Systems Research, Asilomar, CA, USA*, 2015.

[9] A. P. Bhardwaj, A. Deshpande, A. J. Elmore, D. R. Karger, S. Madden, A. G. Parameswaran, H. Subramanyam, E. Wu, and R. Zhang. Collaborative data analytics with DataHub. *PVLDB*, 8(12):1916–1927, 2015.

[10] S. Bhattacherjee, A. Chavan, S. Huang, A. Deshpande, and A. G. Parameswaran. Principles of dataset versioning: Exploring the recreation/storage tradeoff. *PVLDB*, 8(12):1346–1357, 2015.

[11] A. Brown. Get smarter answers from the knowledge graph. http://insidesearch.blogspot.com/2012/12/get-smarter-answers-from-knowledge_4.html, 2012.

[12] M. J. Cafarella, A. Y. Halevy, D. Z. Wang, E. Wu, and Y. Zhang. Webtables: exploring the power of tables on the web. *PVLDB*, 1(1):538–549, 2008.

[13] F. Chang, J. Dean, S. Ghemawat, W. C. Hsieh, D. A. Wallach, M. Burrows, T. Chandra, A. Fikes, and R. E. Gruber. Bigtable: A distributed storage system for structured data. *ACM Trans. Comput. Syst.*, 26(2):4:1–4:26, June 2008.

[14] J. Cheney, L. Chiticariu, and W.-C. Tan. Provenance in databases: Why, how, and where. *Found. Trends databases*, 1(4):379–474, Apr. 2009.

[15] P. Flajolet, E. Fusy, G. O., and F. Meunier. Hyperloglog: The analysis of a near-optimal cardinality estimation algorithm. *Analysis of Algorithms (AOFA)*, 2007.

[16] M. Franklin, A. Halevy, and D. Maier. From databases to dataspaces: A new abstraction for information management. *SIGMOD Rec.*, 34(4):27–33, Dec. 2005.

[17] I. Konstantinou, E. Angelou, D. Tsoumakos, and N. Koziris. Distributed indexing of web scale datasets for the cloud. In *Proceedings of the 2010 Workshop on Massive Data Analytics on the Cloud*, MDAC '10, pages 1:1–1:6, 2010.

[18] A. W. Leung, M. Shao, T. Bisson, S. Pasupathy, and E. L. Miller. Spyglass: Fast, scalable metadata search for large-scale storage systems. In M. I. Seltzer and R. Wheeler, editors, *FAST*, pages 153–166. USENIX, 2009.

[19] S. Melnik, A. Gubarev, J. J. Long, G. Romer, S. Shivakumar, M. Tolton, and T. Vassilakis. Dremel: interactive analysis of web-scale datasets. *Commun. ACM*, 54(6):114–123, 2011.

[20] K.-K. Muniswamy-Reddy, D. A. Holland, U. Braun, and M. Seltzer. Provenance-aware storage systems. In *Proceedings of the Annual Conference on USENIX '06 Annual Technical Conference*, pages 43–56, 2006.

[21] P. Rao and B. Moon. An internet-scale service for publishing and locating xml documents. In *Proceedings of the 2009 Int'l Conference on Data Engineering (ICDE)*, pages 1459–1462, 2009.

[22] I. Terrizzano, P. M. Schwarz, M. Roth, and J. E. Colino. Data wrangling: The challenging journey from the wild to the lake. In *CIDR 2015, Seventh Biennial Conference on Innovative Data Systems Research, Asilomar, CA, USA*, 2015.

[23] K. Varda. Protocol buffers: Google's data interchange format. *Google Open Source Blog, Accessed July*, 2008.

[24] J. Widom. Trio: A system for integrated management of data, accuracy, and lineage. In *CIDR*, pages 262–276, 2005.

[25] L. Xu, H. Jiang, X. Liu, L. Tian, Y. Hua, and J. Hu. Propeller: A scalable metadata organization for a versatile searchable file system. Technical Report 119, Department of Computer Science and Engineering, University of Nebraska-Lincoln, 2011.

[26] M. Yakout, K. Ganjam, K. Chakrabarti, and S. Chaudhuri. InfoGather: entity augmentation and attribute discovery by holistic matching with web tables. In K. S. Candan, Y. Chen, R. T. Snodgrass, L. Gravano, and A. Fuxman, editors, *SIGMOD Conference*, pages 97–108. ACM, 2012.

Multi-Source Uncertain Entity Resolution at Yad Vashem

Transforming Holocaust Victim Reports into People

Tomer Sagi
Hewlett Packard Labs
Guttwirt Industrial Park
Technion City, Haifa, Israel
tomer.sagi@hpe.com

Avigdor Gal
Technion - Israel Institue of Technology
Technion City, Haifa, Israel
avigal@ie.technion.ac.il

Omer Barkol
Hewlett Packard Labs
Guttwirt Industrial Park
Technion City, Haifa, Israel
omer.barkol@hpe.com

Ruth Bergman
Hewlett Packard Labs
Guttwirt Industrial Park
Technion City, Haifa, Israel
ruth.bergman@hpe.com

Alexander Avram
Yad Vashem
Jerusalem, Israel
alexander.avram@yadvashem.org.il

ABSTRACT

In this work we describe an entity resolution project performed at Yad Vashem, the central repository of Holocaust-era information. The Yad Vashem dataset is unique with respect to classic entity resolution, by virtue of being both massively multi-source and by requiring multi-level entity resolution. With today's abundance of information sources, this project sets an example for multi-source resolution on a big-data scale. We discuss a set of requirements that led us to choose the MFIBlocks entity resolution algorithm in achieving the goals of the application. We also provide a machine learning approach, based upon decision trees to transform soft clusters into ranked clustering of records, representing possible entities. An extensive empirical evaluation demonstrates the unique properties of this dataset, highlighting the shortcomings of current methods and proposing avenues for future research in this realm.

1. INTRODUCTION

Cultural heritage institutes are tasked with recording, researching, and preserving a culture, often after a severe catastrophe causing a heightened sense of urgency in preserving the records of this culture. These organizations have collected, over the years, troves of analog artifacts, including films, audio recordings, documents, and pictures. Digitization of these artifacts and extraction of metadata and texts, either manually or via OCR techniques, has created a deluge of raw data through which researchers can sift, attempting to create coherent narratives of the culture now extinct. Recent attempts such as the EHRI project [4] are creating infrastructure enabling researchers around the globe to access disparate sources of information using a unified interface with underlying common semantics. However, with the growing amounts of data, data integration problems arise. A first step towards recreating the story of a specific person, community, or place is the unification of all information pertaining to these entities, overcoming different source schemas, languages, political, and historical idiosyncrasies.

SIGMOD'16, June 26-July 01, 2016, San Francisco, CA, USA

DOI: http://dx.doi.org/10.1145/2882903.2903737

Figure 1: Guido and Massimo Foa, 1944

As an example, we bring the story of Guido and Massimo Foa. Figure 1 shows a picture titled "Guido and Massimo Foa, Cuorgnè, 1944". From the picture we can deduce that there were once a father and son named Guido and Massimo (who is who?) and in 1944 they resided in Cuorgnè, Italy. The Yad Vashem Names Project,[1] has been collecting Holocaust victim reports since 1953. Among these are three reports, whose extracted data is presented in Table 1.

Yad Vashem also commemorates non-Jewish individuals who risked their lives to save Jewish people during the Holocaust. One of those commemorated is Clotilde Boggio, who hid a child named Massimo from the Nazis in a village called Cuorgnè from 1944 to 1945. Taking into account the information in these four sources, a graph such as in Figure 2 can be established. During the construction process, data integration decisions need to be taken, *e.g., do all of the rows in Table 1 refer to the same person?*.

[1]http://www.yadvashem.org/yv/en/remembrance/names/ retrieved June, 2015

BookID	First	Last	Gender	DOB	Birth	Permanent	War	Death	Spouse	Mother	Father
1016196	Guido	Foa	Male	1936-08-02	Torino, Italy	Torino, Italy				Estela	Italo
1059654	Guido	Foa	Male	1920-11-18	Torino, Italy	Torino, Italy		Auschwitz	Helena	Olga	Donato
1028769	Guido	Foy	Male	1920-11-18	Turin, Italy	Canischio, Italy	Turin, Italy			Olga	Donato

Table 1: Three victim reports from the Yad Vashem Names Project DB

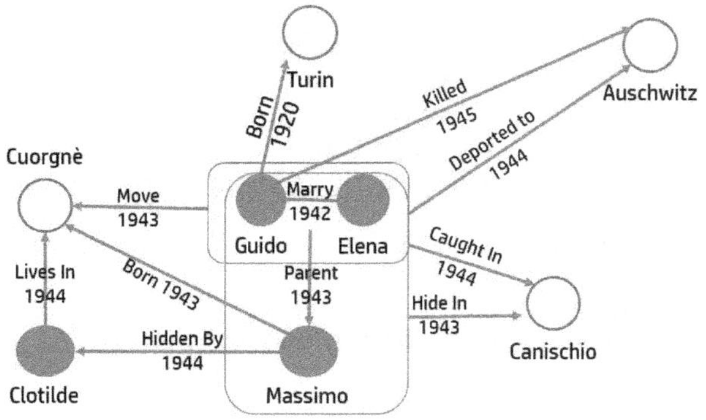

Figure 2: Knowledge graph of Guido Foa

Furthermore, extraction of the three records presented in Table 1 is not trivial. A simple query selecting those records whose first name is Guido and last name is Foa would have missed the third record, which nevertheless contains valuable information.

Narratives are stories told as a sequence of events. Weaving information to form narratives has traditionally been a manual process, performed by expert historians. For example, Massimo Foa, Guido's son, grew up to be a historian and wrote a book describing his parents' story, which enables the validation of the knowledge graph (Figure 2). The challenge we tackle in this work is to create a robust automatic procedure to identify and collect all information pertaining to a single entity from over 500,000 sources in the Yad Vashem database, as a stepping stone towards automatically creating narratives for each entity in the database.

This data integration challenge can be positioned within the scope of the research area of entity resolution (also known as entity matching, record linkage, and deduplication) [22, 10, 17, 18, 8]. Entity resolution (ER) is at the heart of the data integration problem. The task entails creating a single entity from a collection of data records, each revealing some aspects of the entity, with no common identifier to rely upon. Examples include identifying accounts belonging to the same customer in different operational systems, merging customer accounts following a bank merger, *etc.*

Creating narratives from a set of facts poses a new challenge, which is non-characteristic of ER applications. Many ER applications require a single crisp answer as the outcome of the process, while here the outcome is a ranked list of possible narratives, which depends on the created ER clusters. Only in rare cases (such as the example given above) one would be lucky enough to find a single narrative that dominates the others. In most cases, we are faced with subjective details of events and based on the context may choose one narrative over another. To support such flexibility we use an entity blocking algorithm, MFIBlocks, to create soft blocks (clusters) and apply a machine learning method using decision trees to transform blocks into ranked associations of records to form entities.

This paper tells the story of cultural heritage institutions, such as Yad Vashem, and their effort to collect large amounts of information about the past. However, the multi-source entity resolution task may be relevant to any application that uses multiple disparate sources of information pertaining to the same people and events. While the described project was motivated by a desire to piece together stories from a lost culture, we believe its implications may benefit modern applications looking to automatically construct coherent narratives from a multitude of sources.

The rest of the paper is structured as follows. Background on the Yad Vashem Names Project is given in Section 2. We then cast the challenge as an entity resolution problem (Section 3). The multi-source entity resolution problem of Yad Vashem and the techniques we used to resolve it are given in Section 4. We report on an extensive empirical evaluation of the techniques (Section 5) and discuss the implications of this work and avenues for future research in Section 6.

2. THE YAD VASHEM NAMES PROJECT

In 1953 Yad Vashem was established as both a research institute and a memorial. One of its major tasks, beginning in 1954, was the registration of Holocaust victims' names on "Pages of Testimony" containing the names and biographic details of individual victims.

A national campaign of collecting Pages of Testimony in Israel between 1955-1957 resulted in 800,000 names registered by family members and friends. Collection efforts continued: during the 1980's the average number of incoming Pages of Testimony was 14,000-15,000 a year. Following the fall of the Iron Curtain and through the 1990's, the yearly average has risen to 30,000, largely in Russian. Pages of Testimony are preserved in the Hall of Names.

In September 1991 began the extraction of names and biographic data from the Pages of Testimony. This digitization project would later extend to all name resources in Yad Vashem, including the Archives and the Library. By the end of 1998, the Hall of Names digitized 470,000 Pages of Testimony. In addition, 500,000 names from major deportation lists were extracted through OCR.

In spring 1999, in agreement with the International Commission of Eminent Persons dealing with Swiss dormant bank accounts, Yad Vashem, Tadiran Systems Ltd., and Manpower Israel processed the remaining 1.1 million Pages of Testimony and scanned the entire collection. In parallel, in April 1999 Yad Vashem led a renewed campaign of collecting Pages of Testimony resulting in 400,000 Pages of Testimony and 50,000 photographs by the end of 2000.

The data was gathered into a database supported by a cataloging and retrieval system. Efforts have been made to streamline and standardize the data and to create advanced retrieval tools. The Central Database of Holocaust Victims' Names was launched on the Internet in November 2004 and is available in Hebrew, English, Russian, Spanish, and German. It registered 14 million visits in 2014. The database is comprised of name records based on Pages of Testimony

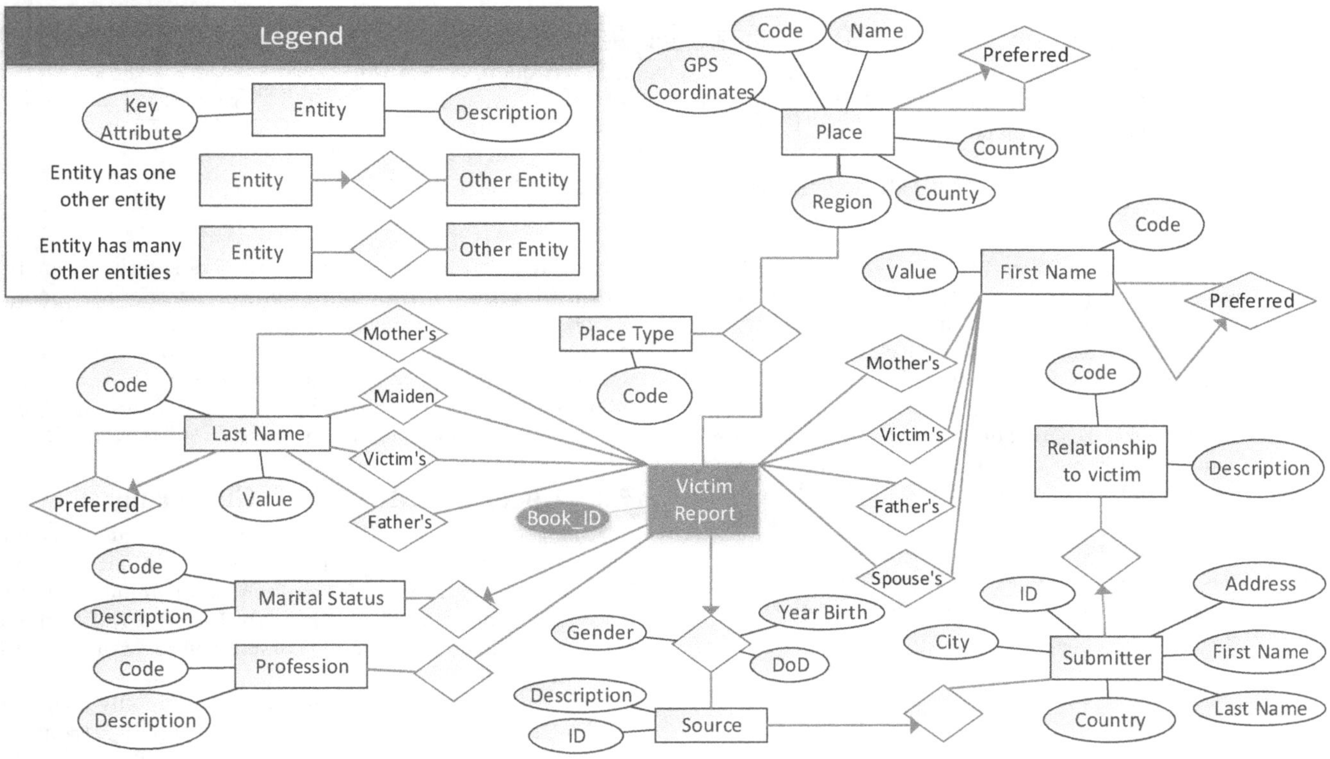

Figure 3: Entity Relationship Diagram of the Names Project Database

and archive material such as lists of transports and deportation, inmates in camps and ghettos, police registration and property confiscation, as well as memorial books and commemoration projects. Among them, for example, deportation lists from Drancy to Auschwitz and Sobibor, card files of inmates in Mauthausen, and lists of inmates in ghettos in Transnistria.

The sources are written in Hebrew, Latin, Cyrillic and Greek alphabets, in over 30 languages; the greatest part are handwritten, making the process of deciphering more complicated. During the registration process, speakers of one language wrote unfamiliar names and places in foreign languages, resulting in a vast array of different spellings and semantic variants.

In the extraction process, names and places are registered, barring typing mistakes, exactly as they appear in the source to preserve accuracy. Equivalence classes of first names, last names and places, as well as professions, personal titles and family relations, were created to help deal with multiple spellings and variants. The preprocessing of all misspelling and name synonyms led to a large yet relatively clean Names project database.

Figure 3 provides an entity-relationship diagram of the Names Project database. The central entity is the victim report, assigned a sequential BookID when entered to the database. The database contains 6.5 million victim report records and their auxiliary information such as names and places. Of these, a third was obtained from Pages of Testimony and the others extracted from various lists. For testimonies, information regarding the submitter is recorded as well. However, no unique id exists for a submitter. Thus, the same person may have submitted multiple testimonies, about different people (or the same), but there is no definite method of verifying this automatically without retrieving the original documents and matching handwriting style. Taking a straightforward approach and grouping the submitters by first name, last name, and city, results in 514,251 different submitters. Some are obvious duplicates, misspellings of names and city names, usage of a nickname, or a different transliteration of the foreign name, but short of performing entity resolution on the submitter data, we must remain with this figure. In addition to the testimony submitters, 16,656 victim lists, gathered from various sources such as transportation manifests and concentration camp records, comprise the rest of the sources.

3. UNCERTAIN ENTITY RESOLUTION

In this section we introduce the uncertain entity resolution model that was used to analyze the Yad Vashem's Names Project database. We start with an overview of the entity resolution process (Section 3.1), followed by the introduction of its two major components. We use the MFIBlocks algorithm to generate possibly overlapping (soft) record collections (clusters) (Section 3.2). Then, we propose the use of the alternating decision tree (ADT) algorithm to transform soft clusters into ranked associations that can later serve in performing flexible certainty querying in Section 3.3.

3.1 Entity Resolution Model

Entity resolution is a long standing problem in data integration. Straightforward algorithms, comparing all entity pairs in a database, quickly become unfeasible as the number of pairs grows quadratically with the size of the dataset.

Therefore, the prevalent work-flow model used by entity

rid	items
1000069	YB_1927,P1_Lubaczow, P2_Lubaczo, P3_Lwow, P4_Poland, F_Avraham, L_Kesler
1000069	P1_Lwow, P2_Lwow, P3_Lwow, P4_Poland, F_Avraham, L_Apoteker,G_0
1000069	P1_Antopol, P2_Kobryn, P3_Polesie, P4_Poland, F_Yitzhak, F_Avraham, L_Postel, G_0
1000069	P4_Poland, F_Yitzhak, L_Postel, G_0

Table 2: Sample records in item-bag form

resolution processes (See Figure 4) contains a *blocking* phase. In this phase *clusters*, groups of records, are created, effectively reducing the general Cartesian product of all records to a run over the Cartesian records in each group. In practice, blocking techniques manage to reduce the number of pair-wise comparisons by 87-97% at the cost of a generally acceptable loss in recall. Following the blocking phase, pairwise comparison is performed using similarity measures (*e.g.*, [11, 9, 23]), machine learning techniques such as SVM and decision trees (*e.g.*, [20, 21, 3, 7, 19]), or probabilistic logic.[2] These comparisons are then used to classify tuple pairs as matched using some predefined threshold. Finally, the pairwise classification serves as a basis for clustering tuples into entities.

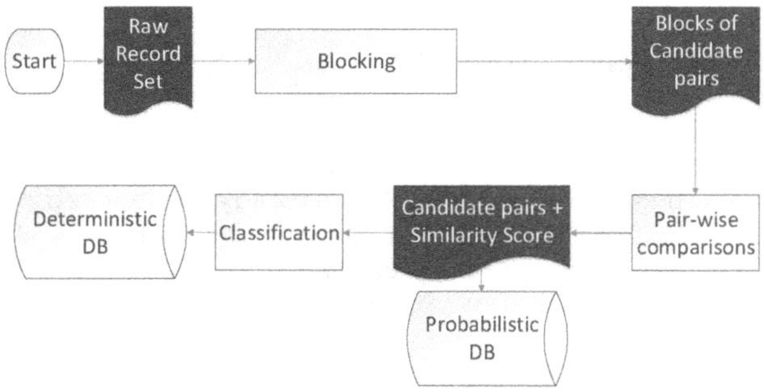

Figure 4: Generic ER Process

The ER process, as described above and as being practically used for many years, lacks the ability to accommodate multiple, possible views of a dataset. Entity resolution is inherently an uncertain process because the decision to map a set of tuples to the same entity cannot be made with certainty unless these are identical in all of their attributes or have a common key. Making deterministic decisions at various stages of the process may lead to inaccurate results and loss of information [13].

Several recent works have advocated for the use of probabilistic databases to represent the multiple views of the outcome of entity resolution (*e.g.*, [1, 2, 15]). The essence of this extension to standard ER processing is that pairwise comparisons can be reasoned about and stored in a probabilistic database, thus effectively retaining all matching information, and adding a same-as uncertain semantic relation between entities. With such models, entities can be resolved at query time or alternative solutions can be presented, ranked according to some measure of likelihood.

Uncertain ER is therefore an ER process whose outcome is probabilistic rather than deterministic [13]. The shift towards uncertain ER requires foregoing crisp clustering and predefined similarity thresholding. We next focus on adapting the blocking and clustering phases to uncertain ER.

3.2 Uncertain ER via Soft Clustering

Among the available blocking algorithms that offer soft clusters, clusters that may share records as an outcome, we have selected MFIBlocks, due to four major unique features that make it best suited for the analysis of the Yad Vashem data. For s detailed literature comparison, we refer the interested reader to [16].

Firstly, MFIBlocks waives the need to manually design a blocking key, the value of one or more of a tuple's attributes. Blocking keys in contemporary blocking algorithms have to be carefully designed to avoid false negatives by assigning matching tuples to different blocks. Therefore, attributes in the blocking key should contain few errors and missing values and the design of a blocking key should take into account the frequency distribution of values in the attributes of the blocking key to balance block sizes. Such careful key design comes with the risk of over fitting the keys to the designer perspective, thus preventing a fair evaluation of alternative matching methods. MFIBlocks "lets the data talk" by allowing any combination of attributes to serve as a key, as long as the decision can be supported by the data at hand.

Second, MFIBlocks localizes the search for similar tuples and is able to uncover blocks of tuples that are similar in multiple, possibly overlapping sets of attributes. MFIBlocks allows a dynamic, automatic, and flexible selection of a blocking key, so that different blocks can be created based on different keys. This approach is in line with the required analysis of the Yad Vashem dataset, where the current perception of a single-key-fits-all no longer holds. In particular, this task should allow multiple levels of granularity, based upon the narrative a researcher wishes to follow. For example, in the story of Guido and Massimo Foa, the finest granularity deals with the life of Guido Foa. A different narrative involves the whole Foa Family (coarser granularity), while another may be interested in all the Jews of Turin.

Blocks created by the algorithm are constrained to satisfy the *compact set* (CS) and *sparse neighborhood* (SN) [6] properties. As such, local structural properties of the dataset are used during the discovery and evaluation of tuple clusters and the number of comparisons for each tuple is kept low, even though the same tuple can appear in several clusters (using multiple keys) simultaneously. For the Yad Vashem dataset, the ability to tune the compact set and sparse neighborhoods properties provides flexibility in determining the granularity of the entity resolution process (*e.g.*, by family versus by person). By allowing a looser compact set setting

[2]see http://www.umiacs.umd.edu/~getoor/Tutorials/ER_KDD2013.pdf for a tutorial on these methods.

and denser neighborhoods, entities can be broadened from a single individual to a nuclear family, or broader social units.

Finally, MFIBlocks is designed to discover entity sets of matching tuples with largely varying sizes. MFIBlocks effectively utilizes a-priori knowledge of the size of matching entity sets, by discovering clusters of the appropriate size having the largest possible commonality. For the Yad Vashem dataset, archival experts estimate that the maximal number of duplicates can be eight records or less. This estimate is based upon the source structure of the Names project database being mostly first-person testimonials. It was anecdotally supported by pilot runs with parameter settings that induced much larger blocks but never produced valid sets with more than seven records.

For completeness, we next present the MFIBlocks algorithm, starting with MFIs, maximum frequent itemsets. We omit some of the configuration options and implementation details for brevity. For a detailed description see [16].

3.2.1 Maximally Frequent Itemsets

Let $M = \{i_1, i_2 \ldots, i_k\}$ be a set of distinct items from which records in a database D are built. A record $r_i \in D$ is composed of a record id (rid) and a set of items $I_i \subseteq M$. Given an item set $I \subseteq M$, the *support* of I in D is defined as the set of records whose item set contains I. I is *frequent* if the size of its support is larger than some threshold *minsup*. I is maximal (*MFI*, Maximal Frequent Itemset) if no frequent item-set I' exists such that $I \subset I'$.

Table 2 presents some records from the Yad Vashem dataset after preprocessing. Each record is presented as a record id (rid) and a bag of items that is created by prefixing a field reference to the value of this field for this record (nulls are omitted). Thus, the item representing the first name Avraham appears as F_Avraham. Given the item set $I = \{\text{F\_Yitzhak}, \text{L\_Postel}, \text{G\_0}\}$, the last two rows in Table 2 serve as the support of I. $minsup = 2$ is the highest value for which I is a frequent item set. There is no other frequent item set in this example that strictly subsumes I, and therefore I is maximally frequent.

3.2.2 The MFIBlocks *Algorithm*

Let D be a database of n records $\{r_i \in D : i \in [1, n]\}$, then the result of MFIBlocks is a set $\mathcal{B}$ of m (possibly overlapping) record blocks $\{B_j \in \mathcal{B} : j \in [1, m] | B_j \subseteq D\}$.

Algorithm 1 is supplied with two parameters. $MaxMinSup$ is the maximal value of the $minsup$ parameter for record blocks. Thus, if $MaxMinSup$ is set to some arbitrary k, then blocks with a support larger than k are discarded. The second parameter effectively limits the overlap between blocks. The sparse neighborhood condition limits this overlap by capping the number of blocks in which a single record may participate.

Generating the record blocks is done in two phases. The first mines MFIs from the database using, *e.g.*, Borgelt's FPGrowth algorithm [5] (line 6) and finds their supporting blocks (line 7). The second phase entails scoring and pruning low-scoring blocks. In line 8, blocks whose size is larger than $minsup \times p$ are pruned. Lines 9-14 update $minTh$ by finding the minimal block score that will prune those blocks violating the sparse-neighborhood condition. These blocks are then filtered in line 15 and the pairs they contain are filtered from the result set in line 16. This process is done repeatedly, requiring a decreasing $minsup$ for candidate blocks at

```
   Input: Database D; MaxMinSup; p
   Result: Set of candidate pairs M
   // Set of Covered Records
1  P = ∅ ;
   // Set of Candidate Pairs
2  M ← ∅;
3  minsup ← MaxMinSup;
4  minTh ← 0 ;
5  while minsup ≥ 2 ∧P ≠ D do
       // mine MFI from uncovered records
6      MFIs ← MFI(D \ P,minsup);
7      Blocks ← FindSupport(MFIs);
       // Filter blocks
8      Blocks ← Blocks.filter(B -> B.size ≤ minsup · p ) ;
       // Set minTh by NG limitation
9      foreach B ∈ Blocks do
10         foreach (r_i, r_j) ∈ B do
11             CandidatePairs ← (r_i, r_j);
12             minTh ← UpdateByNG((r_i, r_j));
13         end
14     end
       // filter blocks violating minTh
15     Blocks ← Blocks.filter(B -> Score(B) > minTh ) ;
16     CandidatePairs ← CandidatePairs.filter(pair ->
        pair.B ∈ Blocks) ;
17     P ← P ∪ {r_i|∃(r_i, r_j) ∈ CandidatePairs};
18     P ← P ∪ {r_j|∃(r_i, r_j) ∈ CandidatePairs};
19     M ← M∪CandidatePairs;
20     minsup − − ;
21 end
```

Algorithm 1: Simplified MFIBlocks Algorithm

each iteration and maintaining a set of covered records (P) and candidate pairs (M). The algorithm terminates when all records are covered or after *minsup* is down to one.

3.3 From Soft Clustering to Ranked Resolution

Following the blocking phase, record pairs in the same block are candidates for duplication resolution. The nature of the Yad Vashem application requires flexibility in deciding **the extent** to which record pairs are resolved to be duplicates. Such flexibility allows Yad Vashem to tune their usage of the entity clusters to the accuracy required for different applications. For example, a user app relaying historical information, such as the number of people perished in the Holocaust in various parts of Europe, requires a single deterministic answer. On the other hand, a person searching for perished relatives can control the size of the response by tuning a **certainty** parameter in a Web-query interface. Therefore, the output of the entity resolution is a ranked list of results, associating a similarity value for each match, rather than a binary match/ non-match decision.

To create a ranked resolution we use a classifier that learns the appropriate similarity value. The extremely multi-source nature of this dataset causes concern when choosing a classifier as data items available for classification vary. For example, one record may contain only a first name, a last name and a birth year while another record may additionally contain a father's names but not a birth year. Thus, we are required to use techniques that are robust to disparity between record attributes.

We chose the alternating decision trees (ADTrees) classifier [12], which supplies a single decision tree, easily interpretable, yet robust to variability in both training and testing data. Furthermore, the technique provides each match with a prediction score, allowing ranking of the results and tuning accuracy versus number of returned results.

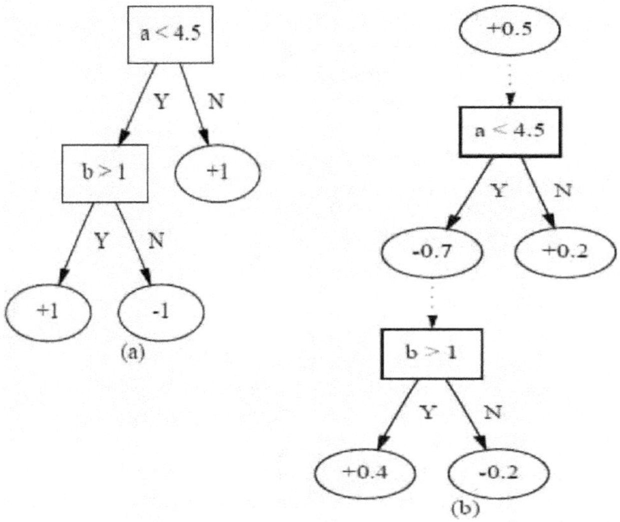

Figure 5: Decision tree standard representation (a) and as an ADTree (b) [12]

For exposition completeness we briefly describe ADTrees. Consider the examples in figures 5 and 6. Figure 5(a) contains a standard decision tree. The tree includes two decision nodes and three prediction leaves. The tree performs a binary classification of $(a, b) \in R^2$ into $\{-1, +1\}$. The example in Figure 5(b) implements the same binary classification using an alternating decision tree (ADTree). It consists of two types of nodes: *Splitter* nodes, marked with rectangles, which act as decision nodes, and *prediction* nodes (in elipses), each of which holds a real valued number that can be semantically understood as the confidence gain that a state adds to the classification. The value in a leaf node is computed as the sign of the sum of all prediction nodes on the path from the root to the leaf. This way, in the example, for $(a, b) = (3.9, 0.9)$ the value would be $\mathtt{sign}(+0.5 - 0.7 - 0.2) = -1$.

General alternating decision trees allow each splitter node to split more than once. Semantically, this allows to create a `Union` phrase for different decision criteria. The resulting score would be the sum of the prediction nodes in the traversed sub-tree that is spanned from the root to all the accepted leaves. In Figure 6, an additional splitter child node was added to the two internal prediction nodes. In this case, the input $(a, b) = (3.9, 0.9)$ would result in three leafs, and its value would be $\mathtt{sign}(+0.5 + 0.3 - 0.7 - 0.1 - 0.2) = -1$.

The constructed ADTree is much denser comparing to standard decision trees, which contributes immensely to the ease with which it can be understood. An additional feature, which we exploit, is the ability to disregard the `sign` operation and use the resulting score as a confidence score with respect to the classification at hand. This score serves

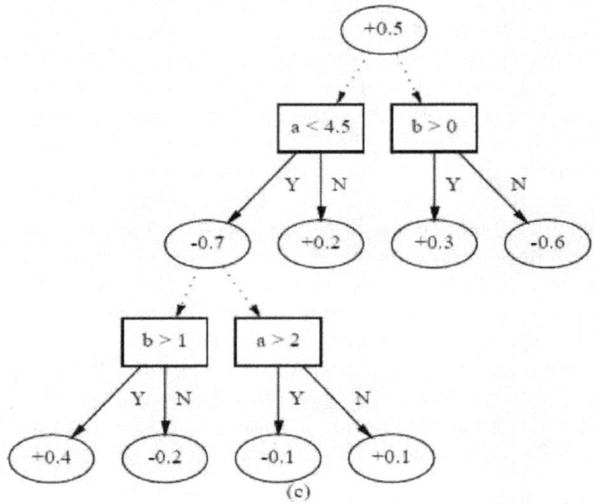

Figure 6: A general alternating tree [12]

as the basis of a ranked decision instead of a deterministic classification. Finally, this method allows graceful handling of missing values, as in such cases the computation considers only reachable decision nodes [12]. In many cases, accuracy will not be degraded significantly, which is a crucial property when regarding our multi-source schema-diverse dataset.

4. MULTI-SOURCE ENTITY RESOLUTION IN THE NAMES PROJECT

We now present the details of the instantiation of uncertain entity resolution in the Names Project, allowing for multiple levels of resolution and incorporating information about multiple sources.

4.1 Data Preparation

From the data described above, two subsets were extracted, of which one was tagged.

ItalySet A homogeneous dataset comprised of all records having *Italy* as the victim's place of residence. This Dataset contains 9499 tagged records and is available for public use.[3]

RandomSet A stratified random sample of the full dataset. Six geographical regions were selected from the dataset, each representing a different pre-Holocaust Jewish community. Differences were either cultural-linguistic or in the progression of persecution during WWII itself. This dataset contains 100,000 records.

Each field in the original data was given a unique prefix, which was added to the items. Thus, when the literal 'Moshe' appears in the first name field of a record, it is entered in that record's item bag as 'FN_Moshe'. A person may have multiple occurrences in some attributes, such as first name, and war-time place. This is supported by the bag-of-items model used by the MFIBlocks algorithm and the items are added independently.

[3] https://github.com/tomersagi/yv-er

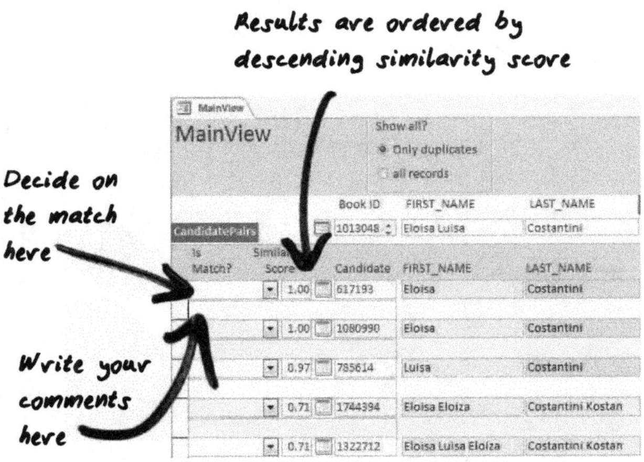

Figure 7: Screen-shot from Tagging Application User Guide

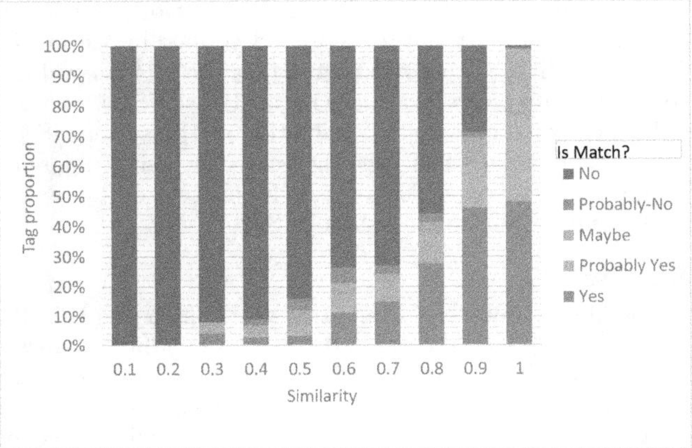

Figure 8: Tag-Similarity Comparison

To obtain expert tags, MFIBlocks was run several times and with several configurations on the Italy set. The candidate pairs from this process were bundled into a tagging application (see screen-shot from user manual in Figure 7). The application presents users with the candidate matches sorted by similarity while highlighting the differences between the records. Yad Vashem archival experts tagged each pair with one of the following {*Yes, Probably Yes, Maybe, Probably No, No*}. A *Maybe* tag indicates that the information contained in the pair is insufficient to decide whether they constitute a matched pair. Figure 8 presents an analysis of the expert tags assigned to candidate pairs. We examined the proportion of pairs assigned to each tag for similarity bins from 0.1 to 1.0. The analysis focused on aberrations such as low scoring pairs assigned a *Yes* tag or high scoring pairs assigned a *No* tag. These were used to validate tagging and tweak our similarity function.

Following the qualitative analysis, the tagged set was simplified by combining *Yes* with *Probably Yes* and *No* with *Probably No*. The revised tagged set was used to both train the classifier and experiment with different configurations of the system (See Section 5). Since the exhaustive set of pairs (45×10^6 for the Italian set) is too large for humans to review, we concede that there may well be additional matched pairs not found by any configuration and therefore remain untagged (false negatives). In addition, we invite future researchers to carefully examine any false positives reported by the algorithms, as these may contain pairs that were untagged by omission. We welcome submissions of such suspect pairs to the correspondent author from Yad Vashem for validation.

Finally, to facilitate the ADT algorithm, 48 similarity features over matched record pairs were defined. We constructed every conceivable similarity feature given the record attributes, assuming these will be pruned by the ADT algorithm. The algorithm constructs the most efficient decision tree given the training data, and omits any similarity features that do not contribute to accuracy. For each feature, one of three types of comparisons was applied. First, categorical attributes, such as name, gender and profession, are compared using a binary similarity feature. Second, the trinary option was applied to attribute values with a small number of words, those for which less than 5% of the records have more than two words. Finally, for the non-discrete attributes, a normalized distance was used, using Yad Vashem expert opinion to tune the normalization factor. The final list of features is as follows. Due to the unique properties of ADT, if a record does not have a value for some attribute, then that feature is not used for the matched pair.

sameXName For each of the seven attributes (First, Last, Spouse, Father, Mother, Mother's Maiden, Maiden) the corresponding feature is valued *yes* when all of the matched pairs' names of this type were the same, *partial* when only some were the same and *no* if none matched. For example, comparing a record with first names {John, Harris} with another record whose first name is John would result in *partial*.

XnameDist For each of the seven names, a corresponding feature calculates the Jaccard similarity (a value of 1.0 is perfectly similar) between the corresponding names and taking the maximum over multiple names. This feature is included since we encountered some cases of clerical errors (Bella->Della) even though extensive preprocessing by Yad Vashem experts should preclude most typos, spelling mistakes, and multiple spelling and pronunciation induced versions of a name.

BXDist For each of the birth date components (day, month, and year) this feature measures the distance between the values, normalized by a maximal distance (31 for days, 12 for months, 100 for years).

samePlaceXPartY For each of the four place types (Birth, Permanent, War-time, Death), and for each of the four place components (City, County, Region, Country) a feature is valued *yes* if the place part is the same.

PlaceXGeoDistance For each of the four place types, this feature represents the distance in KM between the same place type in the two compared records. For example, for two records with birth places of Turin and Moncalieri, the value would be 9 (KM).

sameSource This feature is valued *true* if the records are from the same list or are pages of testimony submitted by the same person.

sameGender This features is valued *true* if the records are of the same gender.

sameProfession This features is valued *true* if the records have the same profession code.

Schema reconciliation of the various sources was performed continuously over the 60 years in which the data was col-

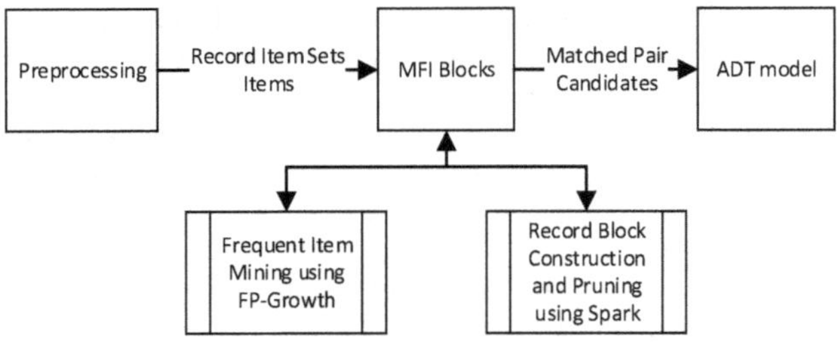

Figure 9: System Architecture

lected. We have reasonable confidence in the semantics of the different place attributes (Birth, Death, Permanent, War-time). Therefore, we do not compare place values across attributes (e.g., Birth to Permanent). The high accuracy result ($\sim 95\%$, see Section 5.4) obtained by the ADT algorithm, choosing only 8-10 features of the 48 defined, allowed us to conclude the feature evaluation process at a relatively early stage of the project.

4.2 System Architecture

The system architecture is presented in Figure 9. A preprocessing step converts the records to a collection of pairs (record id, item-set) and creates an index that maps each item to the list of records in which it appears. The dataset is then fed to the MFIBlocks algorithm using Borgelt's FP Growth [5] algorithm to mine frequent items and an Apache Spark-based distributed algorithm to process the MFIs and create blocks. Finally, a trained ADT model is used for classification and similarity calculation.

The MFIBlocks algorithm was modified for the purpose of this project as follows. The original MFI algorithm assumed a collection of q-grams in the records' item-sets. However, in this dataset, dates and geo locations supplant textual data such as names and places. Therefore, we experimented with replacing the union of Jaccard Similarity between item q-grams used to score blocks in the original work with a custom item similarity score defined as follows (Eq. 1).

$$f_{sim}(i_1, i_2) = \begin{cases} 0 & type(i_1) \neq type(i_2) \\ jw(i_1, i_2) & type(i_1) = Name \\ 1 - \frac{|i_1 - i_2|}{50} & type(i_1) = Year \\ 1 - \frac{monthDiff(i_1, i_2)}{12} & type(i_1) = Month \\ 1 - \frac{dayDiff(i_1, i_2)}{31} & type(i_1) = Day \\ Max(0, 1 - \frac{geoDist(i_1, i_2)}{100}) & type(i_1) = Geo \end{cases} \tag{1}$$

Using the similarity features described above, the ADT tree was trained and accessed at run-time using Weka 3.6 [14]. A fragment of the final model is described in Figure 10. For each candidate record pair, all branches whose conditions match the features of this pair are traversed and their value accumulated to the overall similarity score. For example, a pair that has different father names, whose distance between father names is 0.2, and no mother first name in one of the records would score $-1.3 + -0.25 = -1.55$. To calculate accuracy, we use the default classification of values lower than or equal to zero to *non-match* and above zero to *match*. However, as previously discussed, there is merit in retaining the similarity score as well. The full tree under different experimental conditions is described in Section 5.5, and presented in tables 7 and 8.

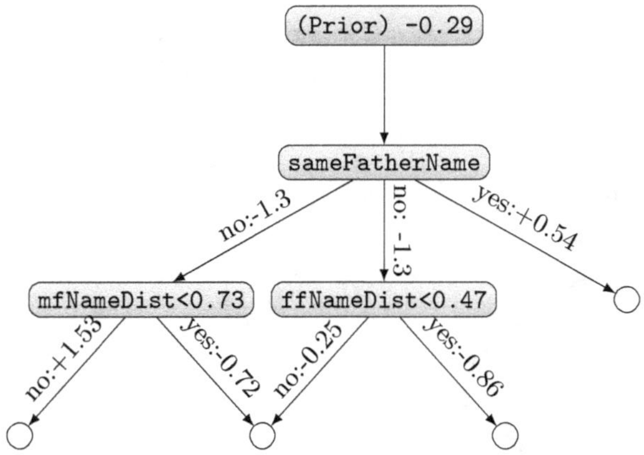

Figure 10: Fragment of Final ADT tree

5. EMPIRICAL EVALUATION

In this section we present evaluations performed on the Yad Vashem dataset and its subsets described in Section 2. We begin with the experiment setup (Section 5.1), an evaluation of the data pattern variance in the dataset (Section 5.2), and a performance oriented evaluation of the system (Section 5.3). Evaluation of the ADT classifier using different feature sets is given in Section 5.4. Finally, we evaluate the full system on the Italian subset in Section 5.5.

5.1 Set-up

Classifier training and evaluation was done on an HP Ultrabook laptop with 4 cores and 8GB RAM. MFIBlocks was run on an HP DL380 server with 24 cores and 64GB RAM of which 30GB were allocated to the JVM heap and 30GB to an Apache Spark 1.2.1 pseudo cluster. The single-threaded implementation of FPGrowth [5] was used by MFIBlocks to mine frequent item sets and was the most efficient known sequential version of this algorithm at the time of publication. However, as the following evaluation shows, the sequential nature of the algorithm caused it to be the bottleneck of the system as it could only utilize one of the 24 cores available on the server and accounted for 90% of the runtime.

5.2 Data Patterns

An important ramification of the multi-source nature of this dataset is the expected schema variability between sources. In order to examine this variability, we performed a pattern count over the entire dataset. Records share a pattern if the same item types appear. As Figure 11 shows, over four million records share less then one hundred patterns (*more* column) while about 19,000 different patterns have less than ten records each. The most prevalent pattern is shared by half a million records and contains only FirstName, LastName, Gender, and Permanent Place. The full information pattern containing all possible item types is shared by only 40,191 records.

In Table 3 we report on the prevalence of item types in the full dataset and in the public subsets provided. As expected, prevalence of the stratified random sample of 100,000 records is very similar to that of the full dataset. Notable differences relate to higher prevalence of Place information since it was specifically used to create the stratified sample. The homogeneity of the Italy sample is a probable antecedent to its different data pattern. Notably, a Person's father name was

Item Type	Full Set		10K Italy Set		100K Set	
	Records	% of Total	Records	% of Total	Records	% of Total
Last Name	6,478,181	98%	9,402	99%	96,656	97%
First Name	6,352,481	97%	9,402	99%	97,527	98%
Gender	5,778,172	88%	9,223	97%	86,474	86%
DOB	4,185,298	64%	6,345	67%	65,005	65%
Father's Name	3,452,056	52%	7,392	78%	49,019	49%
Mother's First Name	2,639,497	40%	5,583	59%	39,816	40%
Spouse Name	1,759,845	27%	2,022	21%	25,964	26%
Maiden Name	819,618	12%	1,201	13%	12,399	12%
Mother's Maiden Name	758,303	12%	1,954	13%	11,950	12%
Permanent Place	4,634,209	70%	8,348	88%	83,308	83%
Wartime Place	3,841,196	58%	6,806	72%	70,009	70%
Birth Place	2,344,618	36%	8,563	90%	58,399	58%
Death Place	2,253,248	34%	5,675	60%	42,541	43%
Profession	2,332,427	35%	2,559	27%	27,209	27%

Table 3: Item Type Prevalence

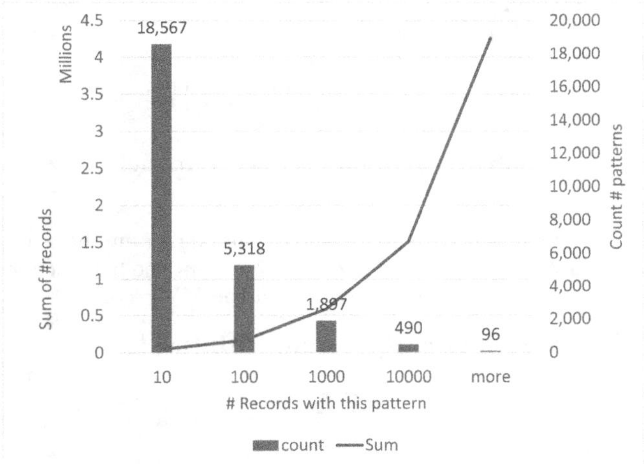

Figure 11: Data Pattern Counts

a major part of their identity in this community and, thus, appears in most records.

In addition to prevalence, we examined the cardinality of each item type. Low cardinality items have the potential to be good markers for matched record pairs and be used as the basis for entity clusters, while high cardinality items are often discarded by the blocking algorithm, although may still be used by the classifier. For example, using Gender as the basis for a block will contribute little to the block's quality. By using the MFIBlocks algorithm we ensure high cardinality items are not used as block keys. However, these items are available for the classifier. In this case, Gender may disqualify candidate pairs of different genders. Table 4 presents the cardinality and average number of records per item for the dataset items on the two sample subsets. One should note that even if a field has high cardinality, the extremely diverse data patterns in this dataset significantly lower the probability of records sharing many high-cardinality items.

5.3 Performance

In our second evaluation we examine how the system's runtime scales with dataset size and the *minsup* parameter. We employ the method reported in [16] to prune the .03% most frequent items and compare the runtime with and without pruning. Figure 12 shows the runtime in seconds, plotted at log scale against the *minsup* parameter value for four test conditions. Series 6.5M indicates the full dataset of 6.5 million records, 600K is a random sample of 600,000 records.

Results indicate that runtime increases exponentially as *minsup* decreases, and linearly with dataset size. Detailed analysis of runtime revealed that the FPGrowth implementation, being sequential, was the performance bottle neck of this set-up as it used only a single core and could not be trivially parallelized using the Spark cluster.

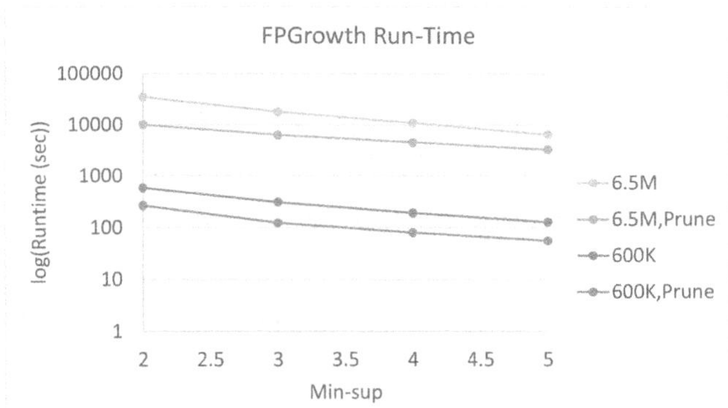

Figure 12: Run-time comparison

5.4 ADT Classifier

Next, we examine the accuracy of the ADT classifier over the candidate pairs returned by the MFIBlocks algorithm under various conditions. Recall that the golden standard is tagged by three tag types: *Yes, No, and Maybe.*

The semantics of the *Maybe* tagged pairs is that they do not carry enough information to be correctly classified. When training the classifier, should we keep such pairs as a distinct group to be identified at run-time as well? Do we classify these as non-matches? Or do we omit these examples? It should be noted that of the 10,017 tagged pairs, 611 were tagged as *Maybe* limiting the effect on accuracy to a 6% difference. As demonstrated in Table 5, accuracy levels

Item Type	10K Italy Set		100K Set	
	Items	Rec/Item	Items	Rec/Item
Last Name	1,495	6	20,541	5
First Name	775	12	1,544	63
Gender	2	4,612	2	43,237
Maiden Name	505	2	5,019	2
MMN	496	4	4,731	3
MFN	382	15	825	48
Profession	355	7	2,115	13
Spouse Name	430	5	955	27
Father's Name	372	20	777	63
Birth Day	31	127	31	738
Birth Month	12	332	12	2,068
Birth Year	98	64	119	541
Birth City	670	12	9,519	6
Birth County	278	19	1,112	44
Birth Region	91	86	151	223
Birth Country	33	259	52	1,116
War City	290	23	6,976	8
War County	114	30	1,715	25
War Region	54	116	195	218
War Country	20	338	45	1,556
Perm. City	226	36	8,328	10
Perm. County	73	70	1,051	73
Perm. Region	19	425	81	800
Perm. Country	1	8,348	23	3,622
Death City	209	26	3,802	11
Death County	87	7	924	13
Death Region	53	19	238	80
Death Country	18	310	45	945

Table 4: Item Type Cardinality

Condition	N	Accuracy
Maybe:=No	10,016	94.2%
Maybe values omitted	9,406	96.4%
Identify Maybe values	10,016	95.1%

Table 5: Classifier Quality - *Maybe* values

are stable around 95% in all configurations, with a slight advantage to the model trained on a set without *Maybe* values.

We attempt to avoid over-fitting of the ADT model by removing a unique source to the Italian dataset. This person, which we will refer to by his initials MV, supplied 1,400 of the 9,499 records in the Italy subset, which is unusual by any standard, and uncommon in the general Yad Vashem dataset, where most submitters submit 1-5 testimony pages. Furthermore, MV submitted a unique data pattern for all his submissions, namely {FirstName, LastName, FatherName, BirthPlace, Death Place}. While this submitter provides valuable information, including these reports in the classification model runs the risk of over fitting the model to the Italian sub-set, since the phenomenon of a single person submitting over a 1,000 pages of testimony is extremely rare and occurs only twice more in 6.5 million records. Of the 10,016 tagged pairs, 3,183 are pairs involving an MV record and so the reduced dataset is comprised of 6,833 tagged pairs.

As Table 6 shows, model accuracy drops by 2.3% when MV reports are removed. However, comparing the two models (tables 7 and 8), we observe that the MV-less model puts

Condition	N	Accuracy
With MV	9,406	96.5%
Without MV	6,833	94.2%

Table 6: Classifier Quality - *Maybe* values

: -0.289			
(1)sameFFN = no:	-1.314		
		(6)MFNdist < 0.728:	-0.718
		(6)MFNdist ≥ 0.728:	1.528
		(8)FFNdist < 0.471:	-0.863
		(8)FFNdist ≥ 0.471:	-0.247
(1)sameFFN ≠ no:	0.539		
(2)sameFN = no:	-1.475		
		(7)FNdist < 0.728:	-0.371
		(7)FNdist ≥ 0.728:	1.241
(2)sameFN ≠ no:	0.791		
		(5)FFNdist < 0.609:	-0.734
		(5)FFNdist ≥ 0.609:	0.757
		(10)SNdist < 0.738:	-0.982
		(10)SNdist ≥ 0.738:	0.786
(3)B3dist < 1.5:	1.142		
(3)B3dist ≥ 1.5:	-0.29		
(4)LNdist < 0.671:	-1.454		
(4)LNdist ≥ 0.671:	-0.078		
		(9)MNdist < 0.606:	-0.978
		(9)MNdist ≥ 0.606:	1.58

Table 7: Full dataset ADT model

less emphasis on father name (FFN) and higher emphasis on same first name, which may better represent the behavior of a general subset of this dataset than the MV records.

5.5 System Quality - Italian Dataset

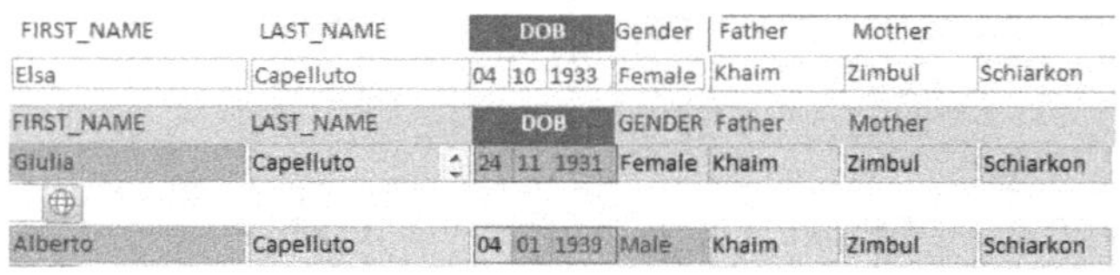

Figure 13: Meaningful False Positives - The Capelluto Children

In this section we examine the quality of results using the Italian dataset with different configuration parameters. The configurable options were as follows.

- **Neighborhood Growth** (*NG*): A parameter of the MFIBlocks algorithm controlling the amount of overlap allowed between clusters. The higher *NG* is, the more overlap may be present.
- **MaxMinSup**: As explained in Section 3.2, the *MaxMinSup* parameter determines the starting support level required by the MFI mining phase. MFIBlocks runs iteratively with decreasing *minsup* levels. For example, given $MaxMinSup = 5$, MFIBlocks would iteratively run with *minsup* values of {5,4,3,2}.
- **Expert Weighting**: Block score function can be weighted by item type. When this parameter is set to *true*, we use an expert derived weighting scheme rather than uniform item weights.
- **Expert Item Similarity** (***ExpertSim***): In [16], block scores are calculated based upon the Jaro-Winkler similarity function between items. While this

Rule	Score	Sub-rule	Score
:	-0.132		
(1)sameFN = no:	-1.461		
		(9)FFNdist < 0.539:	-0.486
		(9)FFNdist ≥ 0.539:	0.433
(1)sameFN ≠ no:	0.61		
		(2)sameFFN = no:	-1.296
		(2)sameFFN ≠ no:	1.171
		(5)MFNDist < 0.708:	-0.962
		(5)MFNDist ≥ 0.708:	0.557
		(7)DPGeoDist < 223:	-0.532
		(7)DPGeoDist ≥ 223:	1.088
(3)B3dist < 4.5:	0.674		
		(10)B3dist < 1.5:	0.431
		(10)B3dist ≥ 1.5:	-0.379
(3)B3dist ≥ 4.5:	-0.906		
(4)LNdist < 0.671:	-1.292		
(4)LNdist ≥ 0.671:	-0.1		
		(6)MNdist < 0.606:	-0.938
		(6)MNdist ≥ 0.606:	1.516
(8)SNdist < 0.663:	-0.765		
(8)SNdist ≥ 0.663:	0.978		

Table 8: ADT model without MV records

method makes sense for q-grams derived from textual fields, we experiment with an expert knowledge-based function (Eq. 1), taking into account date part distance and geographical distance.

- **Same Source Discard (*SameSrc*)**: following the blocking stage, candidate pairs can be discarded if emanating from the same source. It is deemed unlikely that the same person would appear twice in the same source, since this implies that a person was named twice in the same victim list or that a single witness filed two pages of testimony about the same person.
- **Classification (*Cls*)**: Binary parameter. When set to true the ADT classifier filters low scoring matches, rather than just output a similarity score.

A Cartesian product of all parameter values is prohibitively large. We therefore report on the effect of running the full range of NG and $MaxMinSup$ and then fix NG and $MaxMinSup$ to the values returning the best results and vary each of the other conditions one at a time.

Before delving into the results, we return to the motivation of this dataset, which is to enable automated construction of narratives from multiple disparate sources. Figure 13 captures two candidate pairs from the tagging application given to Yad Vashem researchers with candidate pairs from the MFIBlocks algorithm's results. Elsa Capelluto, age 11 at death, is suggested to be matched with Giulia Capelluto (age 13), and Alberto Capelluto (age 5). The records share a last name, father name, and mother name. Also (not shown in the image) all records are associated with the island of Rhodes (Controlled by Italy at the time, now part of Greece). While these two candidate pairs are obvious false positives with respect to a single person entity matching task, they may be significant to users of Yad Vashem data seeking to create narratives for families. Families often share many common properties, as the Capelluto family (Mother Zimbul and Sisters Elsa and Guilia pictured in Figure 14) demonstrates. Thus, we may wish to retain these pairs in a familial entity resolution task. These three pages of testimonies share a source, the aunt of these children, and thus they are discarded if the sameSrc feature is used.

Figure 15 presents the F-1 score of the different NG and

Figure 14: Capelluto Family Picture

$MaxMinSup$ configurations. The horizontal axis designates the NG value used while each line corresponds to a different $MaxMinSup$ value as specified by the legend. Results indicates peak F-1 score is obtained at a NG value of 3.5 for $MaxMinSup = 4$ and a value of three for $MaxMinSup = 5$ and $MaxMinSup = 6$. However, when taking into account that these results are to be filtered using a classifier and sameSrc, one would prefer higher Recall over Precision, and thus, an in-depth analysis (see Figure 16) reveals that in order to maximize Recall and with a relatively low price to pay in Precision, $MaxMinSup = 5$, and NG between three and four are the preferred parameter settings. These values are in line with previous findings [16].

Condition	Recall	Precision	F-1
Base	0.770	0.172	0.279
Expert Weighting	0.886	0.151	0.256
ExpertSim	0.872	0.118	0.205
SameSrc	0.691	0.241	0.350
Cls	0.850	0.204	0.328
SameSrc + *Cls*	0.660	0.325	0.427

Table 9: Quality under Varying Conditions

We now report results for the average over three runs

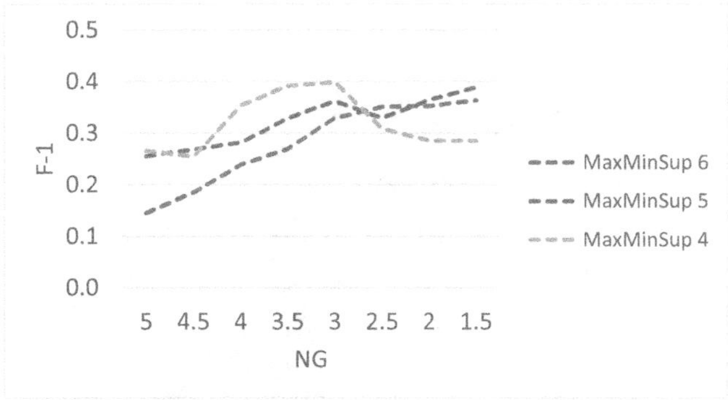

Figure 15: F-1 score By NG and MaxMinSup

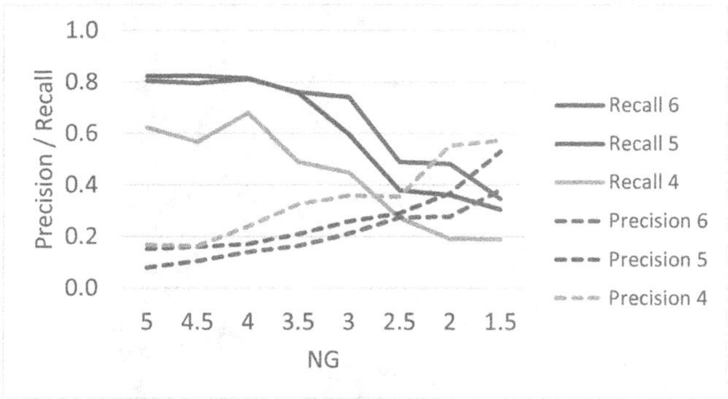

Figure 16: Precision and Recall By NG and MaxMinSup

where $minsup \in \{5, 4, 3, 2\}$ ($MaxMinSup = 5$) and NG varies between three and four (3, 3.5, 4). Table 9 summarizes the experiments on the binary conditions defined above. For all rows, the number reported indicate the average between three runs with varying NG. We provide the results for the null condition in the first row (Base) for reference. Applying expert weighting to item types provided a significant boost in Recall with only a minor drop in Precision and since other conditions were expected to impact Recall negatively, we opted to continue the rest of the experiments with this condition set to *true*. Using the hand crafted expert similarity function was detrimental to both Precision and Recall. Using the two filter conditions (*SameSrc* and Cls) improved Precision at the expense of Recall, increasing the overall F-1 score up to 0.43 when both were used.

Of the results reported above, only the negative effect of using a hand crafted similarity function is surprising at first. However, one should keep in mind that the suitability of the MFIBlocks algorithm to the entity resolution task hangs upon the special properties of the block scoring function used, and specifically set-monotonicity [16]. This property is lost once a non-monotonic custom similarity function is used.

Finally, to better understand the algorithm's misclassification, we manually evaluated 100 pairs from the set of about 1700 false positives. Of the pairs evaluated, we found 94 to be in fact true positives that were missing from the golden standard. We therefore returned the all untagged pairs from the false positive set for tagging by Yad Vashem experts. We expect most of these pairs to be tagged as true. Therefore, we expect the performance figures to be higher than reported here in absolute terms while retaining the relative performance of the different conditions.

6. CONCLUSIONS AND OPEN QUESTIONS

We presented the entity resolution project at Yad Vashem, which represents a unique opportunity to apply state-of-the-art research prototypes to a real-life dataset. We have shown that MFIBlocks scales well with the size and complexity of this dataset. Quality of results for the Italy subset is encouraging and we hope foretells good results on the general dataset as well. We have investigated alternatives in handling a Maybe tag and investigated a few methods for incorporating domain knowledge to improve upon the performance of the employed tools.

The model of uncertain entity resolution can generalize to many more domains beyond multi-sourced historical data. Nevertheless, by providing a deep analysis of this model in a specific domain carries the benefits of highlighting unique characteristics in a way that is more accessible to researchers and industrial partners alike. We believe that the uncertain entity resolution concept carries much potential in the new realms of big data, where volume, variety, and veracity of data pose new challenges to the database community.

We feel the question of the potential benefits and appropriate methods of incorporating domain knowledge in entity resolution is far from resolved. Furthermore, the unique properties of this project prompted us to pose some additional questions which were only partially addressed within the limited scope of this paper. How can we exploit implicit and explicit knowledge about record sources in the multi-source setting? Can we effectively perform entity resolution on different levels of resolution, *e.g.,* families in this dataset. The inter-record relationships in this dataset open the door to questions such as how to perform entity resolution at the edge and sub-graph level and not just at the node level? We leave these questions for future research.

For Yad Vashem, this project is a corner-stone for future applications that will enable researchers and the general public to gain insight into the lives and tragedies of Holocaust-era individuals and communities. For example, Yad Vashem has sponsored a Hackathon[4] in which many of the submitted applications were based upon the ability to resolve entities and suggested methods to automatically extract narratives from Yad Vashem data. At the time of publication, Yad Vashem is actively engaged in integrating the results of the project into its databases and applications.

7. ACKNOWLEDGMENTS

We wish to extend our thanks to Sapir Golan for his invaluable technical assistance.

8. REFERENCES

[1] P. Andritsos, A. Fuxman, and R. Miller. Clean answers over dirty databases: A probabilistic approach. In *ICDE*, page 30, 2006.

[2] G. Beskales, M. A. Soliman, I. F. Ilyas, and S. Ben-David. Modeling and querying possible repairs in duplicate detection. *Proc. VLDB Endow.*, 2(1):598–609, 2009.

[4]https://youtu.be/sgoVF5qKuPQ Innovation in the Service of Memory, retrieved February 17th, 2016

[3] M. Bilenko and R. J. Mooney. Adaptive duplicate detection using learnable string similarity measures. In *Workshop on Data Cleaning, Record Linkage, and Object Consolidation.* ACM SIGKDD, 2003.

[4] T. Blanke and C. Kristel. Integrating Holocaust Research. *International Journal of Humanities and Arts Computing*, 7(1-2):41–57, 2013.

[5] C. Borgelt. An implementation of the fp-growth algorithm. In *Proceedings of the 1st international workshop on open source data mining: frequent pattern mining implementations*, pages 1–5. ACM, 2005.

[6] S. Chaudhuri, V. Ganti, and R. Motwani. Robust identification of fuzzy duplicates. In *ICDE05*, pages 865–876, 2005.

[7] P. Christen. FEBRL: a freely available record linkage system with a graphical user interface. In *HDKM*, 2008.

[8] P. Christen. A Survey of Indexing Techniques for Scalable Record Linkage and Deduplication. *IEEE Transactions on Knowledge and Data Engineering*, 24(9):1537–1555, 2012.

[9] W. W. Cohen. Data integration using similarity joins and a word-based information representation language. *ACM Trans. Inf. Syst.*, 18:288–321, July 2000.

[10] A. K. Elmagarmid, P. G. Ipeirotis, and V. S. Verykios. Duplicate record detection: A survey. *IEEE Transactions on Knowledge and Data Engineering*, 19(1):1–16, 2007.

[11] I. P. Fellegi and A. B. Sunter. A theory for record linkage. *Journal of the American Statistical Association*, 64(328), 1969.

[12] Freund, Yoav and L. Mason. The alternating decision tree learning algorithm. *International Conference on Machine Learning*, 99:124–133, 1999.

[13] A. Gal. Tutorial: Uncertain entity resolution. *PVLDB*, 7(13):1711–1712, 2014.

[14] M. Hall, H. National, E. Frank, G. Holmes, B. Pfahringer, P. Reutemann, and I. H. Witten. The WEKA Data Mining Software : An Update. *SIGKDD Explorations*, 11(1):10–18, 2009.

[15] E. Ioannou, W. Nejdl, C. Niederée, and Y. Velegrakis. On-the-fly entity-aware query processing in the presence of linkage. *PVLDB*, 3(1):429–438, 2010.

[16] B. Kenig and A. Gal. MFIBlocks: An effective blocking algorithm for entity resolution. *Information Systems*, 38(6):908–926, Sept. 2013.

[17] H. Köpcke, A. Thor, and E. Rahm. Evaluation of entity resolution approaches on real-world match problems. *Proceedings of the VLDB Endowment*, 3(1):484–493, 2010.

[18] F. Naumann and M. Herschel. An introduction to duplicate detection. *Synthesis Lectures on Data Management*, 2(1):1–87, 2010.

[19] S. Rong, X. Niu, E. W. Xiang, H. Wang, Q. Yang, and Y. Yu. A machine learning approach for instance matching based on similarity metrics. In *The Semantic Web - ISWC 2012 - 11th International Semantic Web Conference, Boston, MA, USA, November 11-15, 2012, Proceedings, Part I*, pages 460–475, 2012.

[20] S. Sarawagi and A. Bhamidipaty. Interactive deduplication using active learning. In *KDD*, pages 269–278, 2002.

[21] W. Winkler. Methods for record linkage and bayesian networks. Technical Report RRS2002/05, US Bureau of the Census, Washington, D.C., 2002. Statistical Research Report Series.

[22] W. E. Winkler. Overview of record linkage and current research directions. *Current*, (2006-2):1–28, 2006.

[23] C. Xiao, W. Wang, X. Lin, and J. Yu. Similarity joins for near duplicate detection. In *WWW*, 2008.

A Hybrid Approach to Functional Dependency Discovery

Thorsten Papenbrock
Hasso Plattner Institute (HPI)
14482 Potsdam, Germany
thorsten.papenbrock@hpi.de

Felix Naumann
Hasso Plattner Institute (HPI)
14482 Potsdam, Germany
felix.naumann@hpi.de

ABSTRACT

Functional dependencies are structural metadata that can be used for schema normalization, data integration, data cleansing, and many other data management tasks. Despite their importance, the functional dependencies of a specific dataset are usually unknown and almost impossible to discover manually. For this reason, database research has proposed various algorithms for functional dependency discovery. None, however, are able to process datasets of typical real-world size, e.g., datasets with more than 50 attributes and a million records.

We present a hybrid discovery algorithm called HyFD, which combines fast approximation techniques with efficient validation techniques in order to find *all minimal functional dependencies* in a given dataset. While operating on compact data structures, HyFD not only outperforms all existing approaches, it also scales to much larger datasets.

1. FUNCTIONAL DEPENDENCIES

A functional dependency (FD) written as $X \rightarrow A$ expresses that all pairs of records with same values in attribute combination X must also have same values in attribute A [6]. The values in A *functionally depend* on the values in X. Consequently, keys in relational datasets express functional dependencies, because they uniquely determine all other attributes. Functional dependencies also arise naturally from real-world facts that a dataset describes. In address datasets, for instance, a person's *firstname* might determine the *gender* attribute, the *zipcode* might determine *city*, and *birthdate* should determine *age*.

The most important use for functional dependencies is schema normalization [5]. Normalization processes systematically decompose relations with their functional dependencies to reduce data redundancy. But functional dependencies also support further data management tasks, such as query optimization [22], data integration [17], data cleansing [3], and data translation [4]. Although we find many such use cases, functional dependencies are almost never specified as concrete metadata. One reason is that they depend not only on a schema but also on a concrete relational instance. For example, *child* $\rightarrow$ *teacher* might hold for kindergarten children, but it does not hold for high-school children. Consequently, functional dependencies also change over time when data is extended, altered, or merged with other datasets. Therefore, discovery algorithms are needed that reveal all functional dependencies of a given dataset.

Due to the importance of functional dependencies, many discovery algorithms have already been proposed. Unfortunately, none of them is able to process datasets of real-world size, i.e., datasets with more than 50 columns and a million rows, as a recent study showed [20]. Because the need for normalization, cleansing, and query optimization increases with growing dataset sizes, larger datasets are those for which functional dependencies are most urgently needed. The reason why current algorithms fail on larger datasets is that they optimize for either many records *or* many attributes. This is a problem, because the discovery of functional dependencies is by nature quadratic in the number of records n and exponential in the number attributes m. More specifically, it is in $\mathcal{O}(n^2(\frac{m}{2})^2 2^m)$ as shown by Liu et al. [15]. Therefore, any truly scalable algorithm must be able to cope with both large schemata *and* many rows.

To approach such datasets, we propose a novel hybrid algorithm called HyFD, which combines row- and column-efficient discovery techniques: In a first phase, HyFD extracts a small subset of records from the input data and calculates the FDs of this non-random sample. Because only a subset of records is used in this phase, it performs particularly column-efficient. The result is a set of FDs that are either valid or almost valid with respect to the complete input dataset. In a second phase, HyFD validates the discovered FDs on the entire dataset and refines such FDs that do not yet hold. This phase is row-efficient, because it uses the previously discovered FDs to effectively prune the search space. If the validation becomes inefficient, HyFD is able to switch back into the first phase and continue there with all results discovered so far. This alternating, two-phased discovery strategy clearly outperforms all existing algorithms in terms of runtime and scalability, while still discovering *all minimal FDs*. In detail, our contributions are the following:

(1) *FD discovery.* We introduce HyFD, a hybrid FD discovery algorithm that is faster and able to handle much larger datasets than state-of-the-art algorithms.

(2) *Focused sampling.* We present sampling techniques that leverage the advantages of dependency induction algorithms while, at the same time, requiring far fewer comparisons.

SIGMOD'16, June 26-July 01, 2016, San Francisco, CA, USA

DOI: http://dx.doi.org/10.1145/2882903.2915203

(3) *Direct validation.* We contribute an efficient validation technique that leverages the advantages of lattice traversal algorithms with minimal memory consumption.

(4) *Robust scaling.* We propose a best-effort strategy that dynamically limits the size of resulting FDs if these would otherwise exhaust the available memory capacities.

(5) *Exhaustive evaluation.* We evaluate our algorithm on more than 20 real-world datasets and compare it to seven state-of-the-art FD discovery algorithms.

In the following, Section 2 discusses related work. Then, Section 3 provides the theoretical foundations for our discovery strategy and Section 4 an overview on our algorithm HyFD. Sections 5, 6, 7, and 8 describe the different components of HyFD in more detail. Section 10 evaluates our algorithm and compares it against seven algorithms from related work. We then conclude in Section 11.

2. RELATED WORK

The evaluating work of [20] compared the seven most popular algorithms for functional dependency discovery and demonstrated their individual strengths and weaknesses. Some effort has also been spent on the discovery of *approximate* [12] and *conditional* [3,7] functional dependencies, but those approaches are orthogonal to our research: We aim to discover *all minimal* functional dependencies without any restrictions or relaxations. Parallel and distributed dependency discovery systems, such as [10] and [14], form another orthogonal branch of research. They rely on massive parallelization rather than efficient pruning to cope with the discovery problem. We focus on more sophisticated search techniques and show that these can still be parallelized accordingly. In the following, we briefly summarize current state-of-the-art in non-distributed FD discovery.

Lattice traversal algorithms: The algorithms Tane [12], Fun [18], Fd_Mine [25], and Dfd [1] conceptually arrange all possible FD candidates in a powerset lattice of attribute combinations and then traverse this lattice. The first three algorithms search through the candidate lattice level-wise bottom-up using the *apriori-gen* candidate generation [2], whereas Dfd applies a depth-first random walk. Lattice traversal algorithms in general make intensive use of pruning rules and their candidate validation is based on stripped partitions (also called position list indices). They have been shown to perform well on long datasets, i.e., datasets with many records, but due to their candidate-driven search strategy, they scale poorly with the number of columns in the input dataset. In this paper, we adopt the pruning rules and the position list index data structure from these algorithms for the validation of functional dependencies.

Difference- and agree-set algorithms: The algorithms Dep-Miner [16] and FastFDs [24] analyze a dataset for sets of attributes that agree on the values in certain tuple pairs. These so-called agree-sets are transformed into difference-sets from which all valid FDs can be derived. This discovery strategy scales better with the number of attributes than lattice traversal strategies, because FD candidates are generated only from concrete observations rather than being generated systematically. The required maximization and minimization of agree- and difference-sets respectively, however, reduces this advantage significantly. With regard to the number of records, Dep-Miner and FastFDs scale much worse than the previous algorithms, because they need to compare all pairs of records. Our approach also compares records pair-wise, but we choose these comparisons carefully.

Dependency induction algorithms: The Fdep [9] algorithm also compares all records pair-wise to find all *invalid* functional dependencies. This set is called *negative cover* and is stored in a prefix tree. In contrast to Dep-Miner and FastFDs, Fdep translates this negative cover into the set of valid functional dependencies, i.e., the *positive cover*, not by forming complements but by successive specialization: The positive cover initially assumes that each attribute functionally determines all other attributes; these functional dependencies are then refined with every single non-FD in the negative cover. Apart from the fact that the pair-wise comparisons do not scale with the number of records in the input dataset, this discovery strategy has proven to scale well with the number of attributes. For this reason, we follow a similar approach during the induction of functional dependency candidates. However, we compress records before comparison, store the negative cover in a more efficient data structure, and optimize the specialization process.

The evaluation section of this paper provides a comparison of our approach with *all* mentioned related work.

3. HYBRID FD DISCOVERY

We begin this section by formally defining *functional dependencies* (FDs). We then discuss sampling-based FD discovery and our hybrid discovery approach.

Preliminaries. Our definition of a functional dependency follows [23]: A functional dependency (FD) written as $X \rightarrow A$ is a statement over a relational schema R, where $X \subseteq R$ and $A \in R$. The FD is valid for an instance r of R, iff for all pairs of tuples $t_1, t_2 \in r$ the following is true: if $t_1[B] = t_2[B]$ for all $B \in X$, then $t_1[A] = t_2[A]$. In other words, the values in X functionally determine the values in A. We call the determinant X the FD's *left hand side* (Lhs), and the dependent A the FD's *right hand side* (Rhs). Moreover, an FD $X \rightarrow A$ is a *generalization* of another FD $Y \rightarrow A$ if $X \subset Y$ and it is a *specialization* if $X \supset Y$. The FD $X \rightarrow A$ is *non-trivial* if $A \notin X$ and it is *minimal* if no B exists such that $X \backslash B \rightarrow A$ is a valid FD, i.e., if no valid generalization exists. To discover all FDs in a given relational instance r, it suffices to discover all minimal, non-trivial FDs, because all Lhs-subsets are non-dependencies and all Lhs-supersets are dependencies by logical inference.

The discovery of all minimal, non-trivial FDs can best be modeled as a graph search problem: The graph is a powerset lattice of attribute combinations and an edge between the nodes X and XA represents the FD candidate $X \rightarrow A$. Figure 1 depicts an example lattice and its FDs and non-FDs. In all such lattices, FDs are located in the upper part of the lattice; non-FDs are located at the bottom. A virtual border separates the FDs and non-FDs. All minimal FDs, which we aim to discover, reside on this virtual border line.

Sampling-based FD discovery. For a relational instance r, a sample r' of r contains only a subset of records $r' \subset r$. Because r' is smaller than r, discovering all minimal FDs on r' is expected to be cheaper than discovering all minimal FDs on r (with any FD discovery algorithm). The resulting r'-FDs can, then, be valid or invalid in r, but they exhibit three properties that are important for our hybrid algorithm:

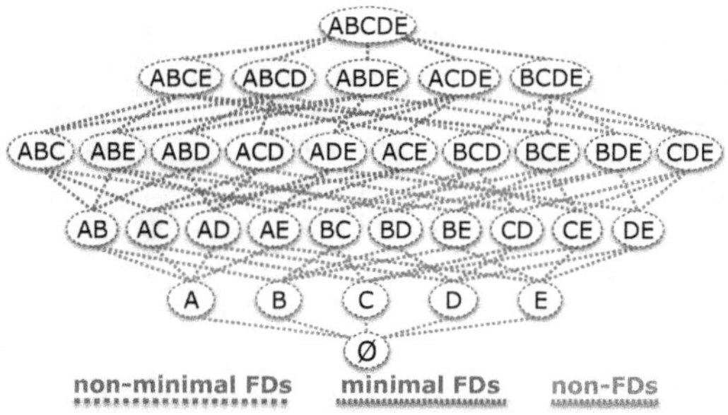

Figure 1: FD discovery in a power set lattice.

(1) *Completeness:* The set of r'-FDs implies the set of r-FDs, i.e., we find an $X' \to A$ in r' for each valid $X \to A$ in r with $X' \subseteq X$. Hence, all $X \to A$ are also valid in r' and the sampling result is complete. To prove this, assume $X \to A$ is valid in r but invalid in r'. Then r' must invalidate $X \to A$ with two records that do not exist in r. So it is $r' \not\subset r$, which contradicts $r' \subset r$.

(2) *Minimality:* If a minimal r'-FD is *valid* on the entire instance r, then the FD must also be minimal in r. This means that the sampling cannot produce non-minimal or incomplete results. In other words, a functional dependency cannot be valid in r but invalid in r'. This property is easily proven: If $X \to A$ is invalid in r', then r' contains two records with same X values but different A values. Because $r' \subset r$, the same records must also exist in r. Therefore, $X \to A$ must be invalid in r as well.

(3) *Proximity:* If a minimal r'-FD is *invalid* on the entire instance r, then the r'-FD is still *close* to specializations that are valid in r. In other words, r'-FDs are always located closer to the virtual border, which holds the true r-FDs, than the FDs at the bottom of the lattice. Therefore, any sampling-based FD discovery algorithm approximates the real FDs. The distance between r'-FDs and r-FDs still depends on the sampling algorithm and the entire data.

In summary, a sampling-based FD discovery algorithm calculates a set of r'-FDs that are either r-FDs or possibly close generalizations of r-FDs. In terms of Figure 1, the result of the sampling is a subset of solid lines.

The hybrid approach. Recently, the authors of [20] made the observation that current FD discovery algorithms either scale well with the number of records (e.g., DFD) or they scale well with the number of attributes (e.g., FDEP). None of the algorithms, however, addresses both dimensions equally well. Therefore, we propose a hybrid algorithm that combines column-efficient FD induction techniques with row-efficient FD search techniques in two phases.

In Phase 1, the algorithm uses column-efficient FD induction techniques. Because these are sensitive to the number of rows, we process only a small sample of the input. The idea is to produce with low effort a set of FD candidates that are according to property (3) *proximity* close to the real FDs. To achieve this, we propose focused sampling techniques that let the algorithm select samples with a possibly large impact on the result's precision. Due to sampling properties (1) *completeness* and (2) *minimality*, these techniques cannot produce non-minimal or incomplete results.

In Phase 2, the algorithm uses row-efficient FD search techniques to validate the FD candidates given by Phase 1. Because the FD candidates and their specializations represent only a small subset of the search space, the number of columns in the input dataset has a much smaller impact on the row-efficient FD search techniques. Furthermore, the FD candidates should be valid FDs or close to valid specializations due to sampling property (3) *proximity*. The task of the second phase is, hence, to check all FD candidates and to find valid specializations if a candidate is invalid.

Although the two phases match perfectly, finding an appropriate, dataset-independent criterion for when to switch from Phase 1 into Phase 2 is difficult. If we switch too early into Phase 2, the FD candidates approximate the real FDs only poorly and the search space becomes large; if we remain too long in Phase 1, we might end up analyzing the entire dataset with only column-efficient FD induction techniques, which is very expensive on many rows. For this reason, we propose to switch between the two phases back and forth whenever the currently running strategy becomes inefficient.

For Phase 1, we track the *sampling efficiency*, which is defined as the number of new observations per comparison. If this efficiency falls below an optimistic threshold, the algorithm switches into Phase 2. In Phase 2, we then track the *validation efficiency*, which is the number of discovered valid FDs per validation. Again, if this efficiency drops below a given threshold, the validation process can be considered inefficient and we switch back into Phase 1. In this case, the previous sampling threshold was too optimistic, so the algorithm dynamically increases it.

When switching back and forth between the two phases, the algorithm can share insights between the different strategies: The validation phase obviously profits from the FD candidates produced by the sampling phase; the sampling phase, in turn, profits from the validation phase, because the validation hints on interesting tuples that already invalidated some FD candidates. The hybrid FD discovery terminates when Phase 2 finally validated all FD candidates. We typically observe three to eight switches from Phase 2 back into Phase 1 until the algorithm finds the complete set of minimal functional dependencies. This result is correct, complete, and minimal, because Phase 1 is complete and minimal, as we have shown, and Phase 2 finally releases a correct, complete, and minimal result as shown by [12].

4. THE HYFD ALGORITHM

We implemented the hybrid FD discovery approach as the HYFD algorithm. Figure 2 gives an overview of HYFD showing its components and the control flow between them. In the following, we briefly introduce each component and their tasks in the FD discovery process. Each component is later explained in detail in their respective sections. Note that the `Sampler` and the `Inductor` component together implement Phase 1 and the `Validator` component implements Phase 2.

(1) `Preprocessor`. To discover functional dependencies, we must know the positions of same values for each attribute, because same values in an FD's LHS can make it invalid if the according RHS values differ. The values itself, however, must not be known. Therefore, HYFD's `Preprocessor` component first transforms the records of a given dataset into compact *position list indexes* (PLI). For performance reasons, the component also pre-calculates the inverse of this index, which is later used in the validation step. Be-

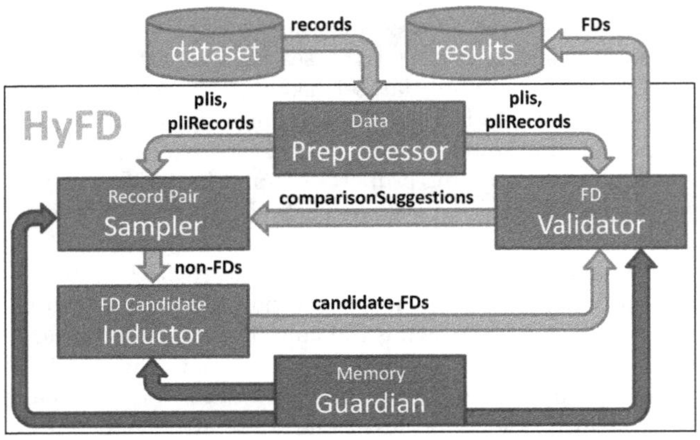

Figure 2: Overview of HyFD and its components.

cause HyFD uses sampling to combine row- with column-efficient discovery techniques, it still needs to access the input dataset's records. For this purpose, the `Preprocessor` compresses the records using the PLIs as dictionaries.

(2) `Sampler`. The `Sampler` component implements the first part of a column-efficient FD induction technique: It starts the FD discovery by checking the compressed records for FD-violations. An FD-violation is a pair of two records that match in one or more attribute values. From such record pairs, the algorithm infers that the matching attributes cannot functionally determine any of the non-matching attributes. Hence, they indicate non-valid FDs or short *non-FDs*. The schema $R(A, B, C)$, for instance, could hold the two records $r_1(1, 2, 3)$ and $r_2(1, 4, 5)$. Because the A-values match and the B- and C-values differ, $A \not\rightarrow B$ and $A \not\rightarrow C$ are two non-FDs in R. Finding all these non-FDs requires to systematically match all records pair-wise. Because this quadratic complexity does not scale in practice, the `Sampler` carefully selects only a subset of record pairs, namely those that indicate possibly many FD-violations. For the selection of record pairs, the component uses a deterministic, focused sampling technique that we call *cluster windowing*.

(3) `Inductor`. The `Inductor` component implements the second part of the column-efficient FD induction technique: From the `Sampler` component, it receives a rich set of non-FDs that must be converted into *FD-candidates*. An FD-candidate is an FD that is minimal and valid with respect to the chosen sample – whether a candidate is actually valid on the entire dataset is determined in Phase 2. The conversion algorithm is similar to the FDEP algorithm [9]: We first assume that the empty set functionally determines all attributes; then, we successively specialize this assumption with every known non-FD. Recall the example schema $R(A, B, C)$ and its known non-FD $A \not\rightarrow B$. Initially, we define our result to be $\emptyset \rightarrow ABC$, which is a short notation for the FDs $\emptyset \rightarrow A$, $\emptyset \rightarrow B$, and $\emptyset \rightarrow C$. Because $A \not\rightarrow B$, the FD $\emptyset \rightarrow B$, which is a generalization of our known non-FD, must be invalid as well. Therefore, we remove it and add all valid, minimal, non-trivial specializations. Because this is only $C \rightarrow B$, our new result set is $\emptyset \rightarrow AC$ and $C \rightarrow B$. To execute the specialization process efficiently, the `Inductor` component maintains the valid FDs in a prefix tree that allows for fast generalization look-ups. If the `Inductor` is called again, it can continue specializing the FDs that it already knows, so it does not start with an empty prefix tree.

(4) `Validator`. The `Validator` component implements a row-efficient FD search technique: It takes the candidate-FDs from the `Inductor` and validates them against the entire dataset, which is given as a set of PLIs from the `Preprocessor`. When modeling the FD search space as a powerset lattice, the given candidate-FDs approximate the final FDs from below, i.e., a candidate-FD is either a valid FD or a generalization of a valid FD. Therefore, the `Validator` checks the candidate-FDs level-wise bottom-up: Whenever the algorithm finds an invalid FD, it exchanges this FD with all its minimal, non-trivial specializations using common pruning rules for lattice traversal algorithms [12]. If previous calculations yielded a good approximation of the valid FDs, only few FD candidates need to be specialized; otherwise, the number of invalid FDs increases rapidly from level to level and the `Validator` switches back to `Sampler`. The FD validations themselves build upon direct refinement checks and avoid the costly hierarchical PLI intersections that are typical in all current lattice traversal algorithms. In the end, the `Validator` outputs all minimal, non-trivial FDs for the given input dataset.

(5) `Guardian`. FD result sets can grow exponentially with the number of attributes in the input relation. For this reason, discovering complete result sets can sooner or later exhaust any memory-limit, regardless of how compact intermediate data structures, such as PLIs or results, are stored. Therefore, a robust algorithm must prune the results in some reasonable way, if memory threatens to be exhausted. This is the task of HyFD's `Guardian` component: Whenever the prefix tree, which contains the valid FDs, grows, the `Guardian` checks the current memory consumption and prunes the FD tree, if necessary. The idea is to give up FDs with largest left-hand-sides, because these FDs mostly hold accidentally in a given instance but not semantically in the according schema. Overall, however, the `Guardian` is an optional component in the HyFD algorithm and does not contribute in the discovery process itself. Our overarching goal remains to find the *complete* set of minimal FDs.

5. PREPROCESSING

The `Preprocessor` is responsible for transforming the input data into two compact data structures: *plis* and *pliRecords*. The first data structure *plis* is an array of *position list indexes* (PLI). In the literature, these PLIs are also known as *stripped partitions* [8, 12]. A PLI, denoted by π_X, groups tuples into equivalence classes by their values of attribute set X. Thereby, two tuples t_1 and t_2 of an attribute set X belong to the same equivalence class if $\forall A \in X : t_1[A] = t_2[A]$. These equivalence classes are also called *clusters*, because they cluster records by same values. For compression, a PLI does not store clusters with only a single entry, because tuples that do not occur in any cluster of π_X can be inferred to be unique in X. Consider, for example, the relation Class(Teacher, Subject) and its tuples (Brown, Math), (Walker, Math), (Brown, English), (Miller, English), and (Brown, Math). Then, $\pi_{\{Teacher\}} = \{\{1, 3, 5\}\}$, $\pi_{\{Subject\}} = \{\{1, 2, 5\}, \{3, 4\}\}$, and $\pi_{\{Teacher,Subject\}} = \{\{1, 5\}\}$. Such PLIs can efficiently be implemented as sets of record ID sets, which we wrap in PLI objects.

To check a functional dependency $X \rightarrow A$ using only PLIs, we can test if every cluster in π_X is a subset of some cluster of π_A. If this holds true, then all tuples with same values in

X have also same values in A, which is the definition of an FD. This check is called *refinement* (see Section 8) and was first introduced in [12].

Algorithm 1 shows the `Preprocessor` component and the two data structures it produces: The already discussed *plis* and a PLI-compressed representation of all records, which we call *pliRecords*. For their creation, the algorithm first determines the number of input records *numRecs* and the number of attributes *numAttrs* (Lines 1 and 2). Then, it builds the *plis* array – one π for each attribute. This is done by hashing each value to a list of record IDs and then simply collecting these lists in a PLI object (Line 4). When created, the `Preprocessor` sorts the array of PLIs in descending order by the number of clusters (including clusters of size one, whose number is implicitly known). This sorting improves the FD-candidate validations of the `Validator` component, which we discuss in Section 8.

Algorithm 1: Data Preprocessing

```
Data: records
Result: plis, invertedPlis, pliRecords
1 numRecs ← |records|;
2 numAttrs ← |records[0]|;
3 array plis size numAttrs as PLI;
4 plis ← buildPlis(records);
5 plis ← sort(plis, DESCENDING);
6 array pliRecords size numRecs × numAttrs as Integer;
7 pliRecords ← createRecords(invertedPlis);
8 return plis, invertedPlis, pliRecords;
```

With the *plis*, the `Preprocessor` finally creates dictionary compressed representations of all records, the *pliRecords* (Lines 6 and 7). A compressed record is an array of cluster IDs where each field denotes the record's cluster in attribute $A \in [0, numAttrs[$. We extract these representations from the *plis* that already map cluster IDs to record IDs for each attribute. The PLI-compressed records are needed in the sampling phase to find FD-violations and in the validation phase to find LHS- and RHS-cluster IDs for certain records.

6. SAMPLING

The idea of the `Sampler` component is to analyze a dataset, which is represented by the *pliRecords*, for FD-violations, i.e., non-FDs that can later be converted into FDs. To derive FD-violations, the component compares records pair-wise. These pair-wise record comparisons are robust against the number of columns, but comparing all pairs of records scales quadratically with their number. Therefore, the `Sampler` uses only a subset, i.e., a sample of record pairs for the non-FD calculations. The record pairs in this subset should be chosen carefully, because some pairs are more likely to reveal FD-violations than others. In the following, we first discuss how non-FDs are identified; then, we present a deterministic focused sampling technique, which extracts a non-random subset of promising record pairs for the non-FD discovery; lastly, we propose an implementation of our sampling technique.

Retrieving non-FDs. A functional dependency $X \to A$ can be invalidated with two records that have matching X and differing A values. Therefore, the non-FD search is based on pair-wise record comparisons: If two records match in their values for attribute set Y and differ in their values for attribute set Z, then they invalidate all $X \to A$ with $X \subseteq Y$ and $A \in Z$. The corresponding FD-violation $Y \not\to Z$ can be efficiently stored in bitsets that hold a 1 for each matching attribute of Y and a 0 for each differing attribute Z. To calculate these bitsets, we use the `match()`-function, which compares two PLI-compressed records element-wise. Because the records are given as Integer arrays (and not as, for instance, String arrays), this function is cheap in contrast to the validation and specialization functions used by other components of HyFD.

Sometimes, the sampling discovers the same FD-violations with different record pairs. For this reason, the bitsets are stored in a set called *nonFds*, which automatically eliminates duplicate observations. For the same task, related algorithms, such as FDEP [9], proposed prefix-trees, but these data structures consume much more memory and do not yield a better performance. Reconsidering Figure 1, we can easily see that the number of non-FDs is much larger than the number of minimal FDs, so storing the non-FDs in a memory efficient data structure is crucial.

Focused sampling. FD-violations are retrieved from record pairs, and while certain record pairs indicate important FD-violations, the same two records may not offer any new insights when compared with other records. So an important aspect of focused sampling is that we sample *record pairs* and not *records*. Thereby, only record pairs that match in at least one attribute can reveal FD-violations; comparing records with no overlap should be avoided. A focused sampling algorithm can easily assure this by comparing only those records that co-occur in at least one PLI-cluster. But due to columns that contain only few distinct values, most record pairs co-occur in some cluster. Therefore, more sophisticated pair selection techniques are needed.

The problem of finding promising comparison candidates is a well known problem in duplicate detection research. A popular solution for this problem is the *sorted neighborhood* pair selection algorithm [11]. The idea is to first sort the data by some domain-dependent key that sorts similar records close to one another; then, the algorithm compares all records to their w closest neighbors, where w is called *window*. Because our problem of finding violating record pairs is similar to finding matching record pairs, we use the same idea for our focused sampling algorithm.

At first, we sort similar records, i.e., records that co-occur in certain PLI-clusters, close to one-another. We do this for all clusters in all PLIs with different sorting keys each. Then, we slide a window over the clusters and compare all record pairs within this window. Because some PLIs produce better sortations than others in the sense that they reveal more FD-violations than others, the algorithm shall automatically prefer more efficient sortations over less efficient ones. This can be done with a progressive selection technique, which is also known from duplicate detection [21]: The algorithm first compares all records to their direct neighbors and counts the results; afterwards, the result counts are ranked and the sortation with the most results is chosen to run a slightly larger window ($w + 1$). The algorithm stops continuing best sortations, when all sortations have become inefficient. In this way, the algorithm automatically chooses most profitable comparisons. When adapting the same strategy for our FD-violation search, we can save many comparisons: Because efficient sortations anticipate most informative comparisons, less efficient sortations become quickly inefficient.

```
Algorithm 2: Record Pair Sampling
   Data: plis, pliRecords, comparisonSuggestions
   Result: nonFds
1  if efficiencyQueue = ∅ then
2      for pli ∈ plis do
3          for cluster ∈ pli do
4              cluster ← sort(cluster, ATTR_LEFT_RIGHT);
5      nonFds ← ∅;
6      efficiencyThreshold ← 0.01;
7      efficiencyQueue ← new PriorityQueue;
8      for attr ∈ [0, numAttributes[ do
9          efficiency ← new Efficiency;
10         efficiency.attribute ← attr;
11         efficiency.window ← 2;
12         efficiency.comps ← 0;
13         efficiency.results ← 0;
14         runWindow(efficiency, plis[attr], nonFds);
15         efficiencyQueue.append(efficiency);
16 else
17     efficiencyThreshold ← efficiencyThreshold / 2;
18     for sug ∈ comparisonSuggestions do
19         nonFds ← nonFds ∪ match(sug[0], sug[1]);
20 while true do
21     bestEff ← efficiencyQueue.peek();
22     if bestEff.eval() < efficiencyThreshold then
23         break;
24     bestEff.window ← bestEff.window + 1;
25     runWindow(bestEff, plis[bestEff.attribute], nonFds);
26 return newFDsIn(nonFds);
   function runWindow(efficiency, pli, nonFds)
27 prevNumNonFds ← |nonFds|;
28 for cluster ∈ pli do
29     for i ∈ [0, |cluster| − efficiency.window [ do
30         pivot ← pliRecords[cluster[i]];
31         partner ← pliRecords[cluster[i + window − 1]];
32         nonFds ← nonFds ∪ match(pivot, partner);
33         efficiency.comps ← efficiency.comps + 1;
34 newResults ← |nonFds| − prevNumNonFds;
35 efficiency.results ← efficiency.results + newResults;
```

Finally, the focused sampling must decide on when the comparisons of records in a certain sortation, i.e., for a certain PLI, become inefficient. We propose to start with a rather strict definition of efficiency, because HYFD will return into the sampling phase anyway, if the number of identified FD-violations was too low. So an efficiency threshold could be 0.01, which is one new FD-violation within 100 comparisons – in fact, Section 10 shows that this threshold performs well on *all* dataset sizes. To relax this threshold in subsequent iterations, we double the number of comparisons whenever the algorithm returns to the sampling phase.

The sampling algorithm. Algorithm 2 implements the focused sampling strategy introduced above. It requires the *plis* and *pliRecords* from the `Preprocessor` and the *comparisonSuggestions* from the `Validator`. Figure 3 illustrates the algorithm.

The priority queue *efficiencyQueue* is a local data structure that ranks the PLIs by their sampling efficiency. If the *efficiencyQueue* is empty (Line 1), this is the first time the `Sampler` is called. In this case, we need to sort all clusters by some cluster-dependent sorting key (Lines 2 to 4). As shown in Figure 3.1, we sort the records in each cluster of attribute A_i's PLI by their cluster number in attribute A_{i-1} and, if

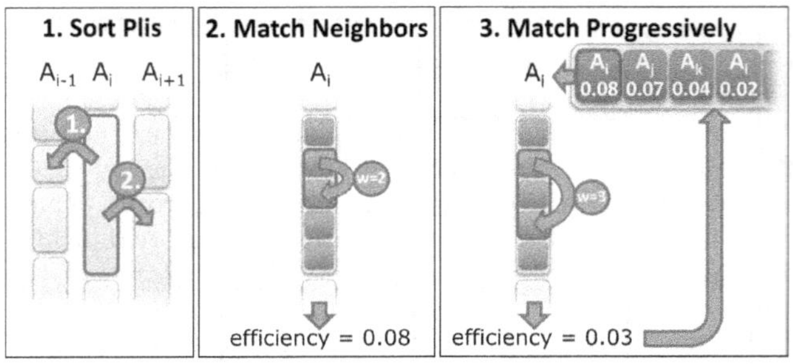

Figure 3: Focused sampling: Sorting of Pli clusters (1); record matching to direct neighbors (2); progressive record matching (3).

numbers are equal or unknown, by the cluster number in A_{i+1}. The intuition here is that attribute A_{i-1} has more clusters than A_i, due to the sorting of *plis* in the `Preprocessor`, which makes it a promising key; some unique values in A_{i-1}, on the other hand, do not have a cluster number, so the sorting also checks the PLI of attribute A_{i+1} that has larger clusters than A_i. However, the important point in choosing sorting keys is not which $A_{i+/-x}$ to take but to take different sorting keys for each PLI. In this way, the neighborhood of one record differs in each of its PLI clusters.

When the sorting is done, the algorithm initializes the *efficiencyQueue* with first *efficiency* measurements. The efficiency of an attribute's PLI is an object that stores the PLI's sampling performance: It holds the attribute identifier, the last window size, the number of comparisons within this window, and the number of results, i.e., FD-violations first revealed with these comparisons. An efficiency object can calculate its efficiency by dividing the number of results by the number of comparisons. For instance, 8 new FD-violations in 100 comparisons yield an efficiency of 0.08. To initialize the efficiency object of each attribute, the `Sampler` runs a window of size two over the attribute's PLI clusters (Line 14) using the *runWindow*()-function shown in Lines 27 to 35. Figure 3.2 illustrates how this function compares all direct neighbors in the clusters with window size two.

If the `Sampler` is not called for the first time, the PLI clusters are already sorted and the last efficiency measurements are also present. We must, however, relax the efficiency threshold (Line 17) and execute the suggested comparisons (Lines 18 and 19). The suggested comparisons are records pairs that violated at least one FD candidate in Phase 2 of the HYFD algorithm so that they probably also violate some more FDs. With the suggested comparisons, Phase 1 incorporates knowledge from Phase 2 to focus the sampling.

No matter whether this is the first or a subsequent call of the `Sampler`, the algorithm finally starts a progressive search for more FD-violations (Lines 20 to 25): It selects the efficiency object *bestEff* with the highest efficiency in the *efficiencyQueue* (Line 21) and executes the next window size on its PLI (Line 25). This updates the efficiency of *bestEff* so that it might get re-ranked in the priority queue. Figure 3.3 illustrates one such progressive selection step for a best attribute A_i with efficiency 0.08 and next window size three: After matching all records within this window, the efficiency drops to 0.03, which makes A_j the new best attribute.

The `Sampler` algorithm continues running ever larger windows over the PLIs until all efficiencies have fallen below the current *efficiencyThreshold* (Line 22). At this point, the row-efficient discovery technique has apparently become inefficient and the algorithm decides to proceed with a column-efficient discovery technique.

7. INDUCTION

The `Inductor` component concludes the column-efficient discovery phase and leads over into the row-efficient discovery phase. Its task is to convert the *nonFds* given by the `Sampler` component into corresponding minimal FD-candidates *fds*. These FD-candidates are stored in a data structure called *FDTree*, which is a prefix-tree optimized for functional dependencies. Figure 4 shows three such FDTrees with example FDs. First introduced by Flach and Savnik in [9], an FDTree maps the LHS of FDs to nodes in the tree and the RHS of these FDs to bitsets, which are attached to the nodes. A RHS attribute in the bitsets is marked if it is at the end of an FD's LHS path, i.e., if the current path of nodes describes the entire LHS to which the RHS belongs to.

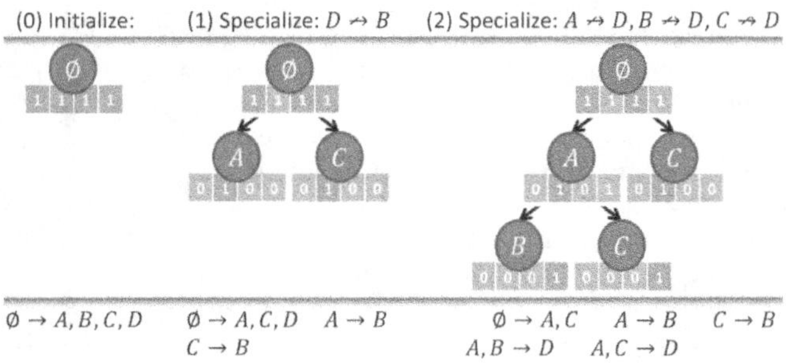

Figure 4: Specializing the FDTree with non-FDs.

Algorithm 3 shows the conversion process in detail. The `Inductor` first sorts the *nonFds* in descending order by their cardinality, i.e., the number of set bits (Line 1). The sorting of FD-violations is important, because it lets HYFD convert non-FDs with long LHSs into FD-candidates first and non-FDs with ever shorter LHSs gradually later achieving much stronger pruning in the beginning. In this way, the prefix-tree of candidate-FDs *fds* grows much slower, significantly reducing the costs for early generalization look-ups.

When the `Inductor` is called for the first time, the FDTree *fds* has not been created yet and is initialized with a schema R's most general FDs $\emptyset \rightarrow R$, where the attributes in R are represented as integers (Line 4); otherwise, the algorithm continues with the previously calculated *fds*. The task is to specialize the *fds* with every bitset in *nonFds*: Each bitset describes the LHS of several non-FDs (Line 5) and each zero-bit in these bitsets describes a RHS of a non-FD (Lines 6 and 7). Once retrieved from the bitsets, each non-FD is used to specialize the FDTree *fds* (Line 8).

Figure 4 exemplarily shows the specialization of the initial FDTree for the non-FD $D \not\rightarrow B$ in (1): First, the `specialize`-function recursively collects the invalid FD and all its generalizations from the *fds* (Line 10), because these must be invalid as well. In our example, the only invalid FD in the tree is $\emptyset \rightarrow B$. HYFD then successively removes these non-FDs from the FDTree *fds* (Line 12). Once removed, the non-FDs are specialized, which means that the algorithm *extends* the LHS of each non-FD to generate still valid specializations (Line 17). In our example, these are $A \rightarrow B$ and $C \rightarrow B$. Before adding these specializations, the `Inductor` assures that the new candidate-FD are minimal by searching the *fds* for generalizations of the candidate-FDs (Line 18). Figure 4 also shows the result when inducing three more non-FDs into the FDTree. After specializing the *fds* with all *nonFds*, the prefix-tree holds the entire set of valid, minimal FDs with respect to these given non-FDs [9].

Algorithm 3: Functional Dependency Induction

```
Data: nonFds
Result: fds
1  nonFds ← sort(nonFds, CARDINALITY_DESCENDING);
2  if fds = null then
3      fds ← new FDTree;
4      fds.add(∅ → {0, 1, ..., numAttributes});
5  for lhs ∈ nonFds do
6      rhss ← lhs.clone().flip();
7      for rhs ∈ rhss do
8          specialize(fds, lhs, rhs);
9  return fds;
   function specialize(fds, lhs, rhs)
10 invalidLhss ← fds.getFdAndGenerals(lhs, rhs);
11 for invalidLhs ∈ invalidLhss do
12     fds.remove(invalidLhs, rhs);
13     for attr ∈ [0, numAttributes[ do
14         if invalidLhs.get(attr) ∨
15             rhs = attr then
16             continue;
17         newLhs ← invalidLhs ∪ attr;
18         if fds.findFdOrGeneral(newLhs, rhs) then
19             continue;
20         fds.add(newLhs, rhs);
```

8. VALIDATION

The `Validator` component takes the previously calculated FDTree *fds* and validates the contained FD-candidates against the entire input dataset, which is represented by the *plis* and the *invertedPlis*. For this validation process, the component uses a row-efficient lattice traversal strategy. We first discuss the lattice traversal; then, we introduce our direct candidate validation technique; and finally, we present the specialization method of invalid FD-candidates. The `Validator` component is shown in detail in Algorithm 4.

Traversal. Usually, lattice traversal algorithms need to traverse a huge candidate lattice, because FDs can be everywhere (see Figure 1 in Section 3). Due to the previous, sampling-based discovery, HYFD already starts the lattice traversal with a set of promising FD-candidates *fds* that are organized in an FDTree. Because this FDTree maps directly to the FD search space, i.e., the candidate lattice, HYFD can use it to systematically check all necessary FD candidates: Beginning from the root of the tree, the `Validator` component traverses the candidate set breath-first level by level.

When the `Validator` component is called for the first time (Line 1), it initializes the *currentLevelNumber* to zero (Line 2); otherwise, it continues the traversal from where it stopped before. During the traversal, the set *currentLevel* holds all FDTree nodes of the current level. So before entering the level-wise traversal in Line 5, the `Validator` initializes the *currentLevel* using the `getLevel()`-function (Line 3). This function recursively collects all nodes with depth *currentLevelNumber* from the prefix-tree *fds*.

Algorithm 4: Functional Dependency Validation

```
   Data: fds, plis, pliRecords
   Result: fds, comparisonSuggestions
 1 if currentLevel = null then
 2    currentLevelNumber ← 0;
 3 currentLevel ← fds.getLevel(currentLevelNumber);
 4 comparisonSuggestions ← ∅;
 5 while currentLevel ≠ ∅ do
      /* Validate all FDs on the current level */
 6    invalidFds ← ∅;
 7    numValidFds ← 0;
 8    for node ∈ currentLevel do
 9       lhs ← node.getLhs();
10       rhss ← node.getRhss();
11       validRhss ← refines(lhs, rhss, plis, pliRecords,
                              comparisonSuggestions);
12       numValidFds ← numValidFds + |validRhss|;
13       invalidRhss ← rhss.andNot(validRhss);
14       node.setFds(validRhss);
15       for invalidRhs ∈ invalidRhss do
16          invalidFds ← invalidFds ∪ (lhs, invalidRhs);
      /* Add all children to the next level */
17    nextLevel ← ∅;
18    for node ∈ currentLevel do
19       for child ∈ node.getChildren() do
20          nextLevel ← nextLevel ∪ child;
      /* Specialize all invalid FDs */
21    for invalidFd ∈ invalidFds do
22       lhs, rhs ← invalidFd;
23       for attr ∈ [0, numAttributes[ do
24          if lhs.get(attr) ∨ rhs = attr ∨
25             fds.findFdOrGeneral(lhs, attr) ∨
26             fds.findFd(attr, rhs) then
27             continue;
28          newLhs ← lhs ∪ attr;
29          if fds.findFdOrGeneral(newLhs, rhs) then
30             continue;
31          child ← fds.addAndGetIfNew(newLhs, rhs);
32          if child ≠ null then
33             nextLevel ← nextLevel ∪ child;
34    currentLevel ← nextLevel;
35    currentLevelNumber ← currentLevelNumber + 1;
      /* Judge efficiency of validation process */
36    if |invalidFds| > 0.01 * numValidFds then
37       return fds, comparisonSuggestions;
38 return fds, ∅;
```

On each level (Line 5), the algorithm first validates all FD-candidates removing those from the FDTree that are invalid (Lines 6 to 16); then, the algorithm collects all child-nodes of the current level to form the next level (Lines 17 to 20); finally, it specializes the invalid FDs of the current level which generates new, minimal FD-candidates for the next level (Lines 21 to 33). The level-wise traversal stops, if the validation process becomes inefficient (Lines 36 and 37). Here, this means that more than 1% of the FD-candidates of the current level were invalid and the search space started growing rapidly. HyFD then returns into the sampling phase. We use 1% as a static threshold for efficiency of this phase, but our experiments in Section 10.5 show that any small percentage performs well here due to the observed high growth rate of invalid FD-candidates. The validation terminates when the next level is empty (Line 5) and all FDs in the FDTree *fds* are valid. This also ends the entire HyFD algorithm.

Validation. Each node in an FDTree can harbor multiple FDs with the same LHS and different RHSs (see Figure 4 in Section 7): The LHS attributes are described by a node's path in the tree and the RHS attributes that form FDs with the current LHS are marked. The `Validator` component validates all FD-candidates of a node simultaneously using the ***refines***()-function (Line 11). This function checks which RHS attributes are *refined* by the current LHS using the *plis* and *pliRecords*. The refined RHS attributes indicate valid FDs, while all other RHS attributes indicate invalid FDs.

Figure 5 illustrates how the ***refines***()-function works: Let $X \rightarrow Y$ be the set of FD-candidates that is to be validated. At first, the function selects the *pli* of the first LHS attribute X_0. Due to the sorting of *plis* in the `Preprocessor` component, this is the PLI with the most and, hence, the smallest clusters of all LHS attributes. For each cluster in X_0's PLI, the algorithm iterates all record IDs r_i in this cluster and retrieves the according compressed records from the *pliRecords*. A compressed record contains all cluster IDs in which a record is contained. Hence, the algorithm can create one array containing the LHS cluster IDs of X and one array containing the RHS cluster IDs of Y. The LHS array, then, describes the cluster of r_i regarding attribute combination X. To check which RHS PLI these LHS clusters refine, we map the LHS clusters to the corresponding array of RHS clusters. We fill this map while iterating the record IDs of a cluster. If an array of LHS clusters already exists in this map, the array of RHS clusters must match the existing one. All non-matching RHS clusters indicate refinement-violations and, hence, invalid RHS attributes. The algorithm immediately stops checking such RHS attributes so that only valid RHS attributes survive until the end.

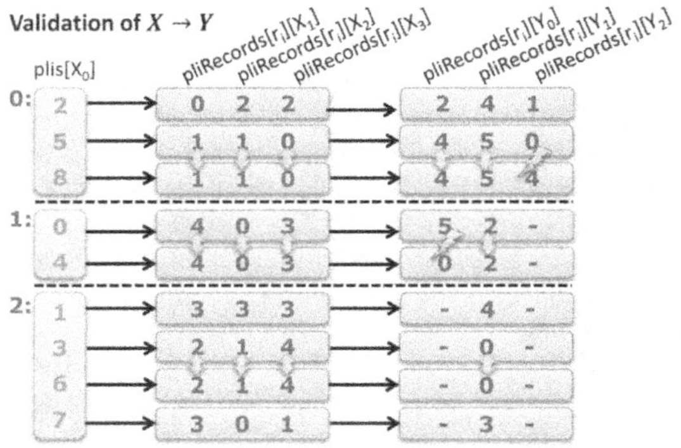

Figure 5: Directly validating FD-candidates $X \rightarrow Y$.

In comparison to other PLI-based algorithms, such as TANE, HyFD's validation technique avoids the costly hierarchical PLI intersections. By mapping the LHS clusters to RHS clusters, the checks are independent of other checks and do not require intermediate PLIs. The direct validation is important, because the `Validator`'s starting FD candidates are – due to the sampling-based induction part – on much higher lattice levels and successively intersecting lower level PLIs would undo this advantage. Furthermore, HyFD can terminate refinement checks very early if all RHS attributes are invalid, because the results of the intersections, i.e., the intersected PLIs are not needed for later intersections. Not storing intermediate PLIs also has the advantage of demanding much less memory – most PLI-based algorithms fail at processing larger datasets, for exactly this reason [20].

Specialization. The validation of FD candidates identifies all invalid FDs and collects them in the set *invalidFds*. The specialization part of Algorithm 4, then, extends these invalid FDs in order to generate new FD candidates for the next higher level: For each invalid FD represented by *lhs* and *rhs* (Line 21), the algorithm checks for all attributes *attr* (Line 23) if they specialize the invalid FD into a new minimal, non-trivial FD candidate $lhs \cup attr \rightarrow rhs$. To assure minimality and non-triviality of the new candidate, the algorithm tests the following:

(1) *Non-triviality*: $attr \notin lhs$ and $attr \neq rhs$ (Line 24)

(2) *Minimality 1*: $lhs \not\rightarrow attr$ (Line 25)

(3) *Minimality 2*: $lhs \cup attr \not\rightarrow rhs$ (Lines 24 and 29)

For the minimality checks, the `Validator` algorithm recursively searches for generalizations in the FDTree *fds*. This is possible, because all generalizations in the FDTree have already been validated and must, therefore, be correct. The generalization look-ups also include the new FD candidate itself, because if this is already present in the tree, it does not need to be added again. The minimality checks logically correspond to candidate pruning rules, as used by lattice traversal algorithms, such as TANE, FUN, and DFD.

If a minimal, non-trivial specialization has been found, the algorithm adds it to the FDTree *fds* (Line 31). The adding of a new FD into the FDTree might create a new node in the graph. To handle these new nodes on the next level, the algorithm must add them to *nextLevel*. When the specialization has finished with all invalid FDs, the `Validator` moves to the next level. If the next level is empty, all FD-candidates have been validated and *fds* contains all minimal, non-trivial functional dependencies of the input dataset.

9. MEMORY GUARDIAN

The memory `Guardian` is an optional component in HYFD and enables a best-effort strategy for FD discovery for very large inputs. Its task is to observe the memory consumption and to free resources if HYFD is about to reach the memory limit. Observing memory consumption is a standard task in any programming language. So the question is, what resources the `Guardian` can free if the memory is exhausted.

The PLI data structures grow linearly with the input dataset's size and are relatively small. The number of FD-violations found in the sampling step grows exponentially with the number of attributes, but it takes quite some attributes to exhaust the memory with these compact bitsets. The data structure that grows by far the fastest is the FDTree *fds*, which is constantly specialized by the `Inductor` and `Validator` components. Hence, this is the data structure the `Guardian` must prune.

Obviously, shrinking the *fds* is only possible by giving up some results, i.e., giving up completeness of the algorithm. In our implementation of the `Guardian`, we decided to successively reduce the maximum LHS size of our results; we provide three reasons: First, FDs with a long LHS usually occur accidentally, meaning that they hold for a particular instance but not for the relation in general. Second, FDs with long LHSs are less useful in most use cases, e.g., they become worse key/foreign-key candidates when used for normalization and they are less likely to match a query when used for query optimization. Third, FDs with long LHSs consume more memory, because they are physically larger, and preferentially removing them retains more FDs in total.

To restrict the maximum size of the FDs' LHSs, we need to add some additional logic into the FDTree: It must hold the maximum LHS size as a variable, which the `Guardian` component can control; whenever this variable is decremented, the FDTree recursively removes all FDs with larger LHSs and sets their memory resources free. The FDTree also refuses to add any new FD with a larger LHS. In this way, the result pruning works without changing any of the other four components. However, note that the `Guardian` component prunes only such results whose size would otherwise exceed the memory capacity, which means that the component in general does not take action.

10. EVALUATION

FD discovery has shown to be quadratic in the number of records n and exponential in the number of attributes m [15]. This also holds for HYFD: Phase 1 is in $\mathcal{O}(mn^2 + m^2 2^m)$, because in the worst case n^2 records are compared with comparison costs m and for each of the m possible RHS attributes, 2^{m-1} LHS attribute combinations must be refined $m - 1$ times in the negative cover. Phase 2 is also in $\mathcal{O}(mn^2 + m^2 2^m)$ as shown in [15], because our complexity is the same as for TANE. Note that each phase can (potentially) discover all minimal FDs without the other. The following experiments, however, show that HYFD is able to process significantly larger datasets than state-of-the-art FD discovery algorithms in less runtime. At first, we introduce our experimental setup. Then, we evaluate the scalability of HYFD with both a dataset's number of rows and columns. Afterwards, we show that HYFD performs well on different datasets. In all these experiments, we compare HYFD to seven state-of-the-art FD discovery algorithms. We, finally, analyze some characteristics of HYFD in more detail and discuss the results of the discovery process.

10.1 Experimental setup

Metanome. HYFD and all algorithms from related work have been implemented for the *Metanome* data profiling framework (www.metanome.de), which defines standard interfaces for different kinds of profiling algorithms. Metanome also provided the various implementations of the state of the art. Common tasks, such as input parsing, result formatting, and performance measurement are standardized by the framework and decoupled from the algorithms [19].

Hardware. We run all our experiments on a Dell PowerEdge R620 with two Intel Xeon E5-2650 2.00 GHz CPUs and 128 GB RAM. The server runs on CentOS 6.4 and uses OpenJDK 64-Bit Server VM 1.7.0_25 as Java environment.

Null Semantics. Real-world data often contains `null` values. So a schema $R(A, B)$ could hold the two records $r_1 = (\perp, 1)$ and $r_2 = (\perp, 2)$. Depending on whether we choose the semantics `null` = `null` or the semantics `null` $\neq$ `null`, the functional dependency $A \rightarrow B$ is `false` or `true` respectively. Hence, the `null` semantics changes the results of the FD discovery. Our algorithm HYFD supports both settings, which means that the semantics can be switched in the `Preprocessor` (PLI-construction) and in the `Sampler` (*match*()-function) with a parameter. For the experiments, however, we use `null` = `null`, because this is how related work treats `null` values [20].

Datasets. We evaluate HYFD on various synthetic and real-world datasets. Table 1 in Section 10.4 and Table 2 in

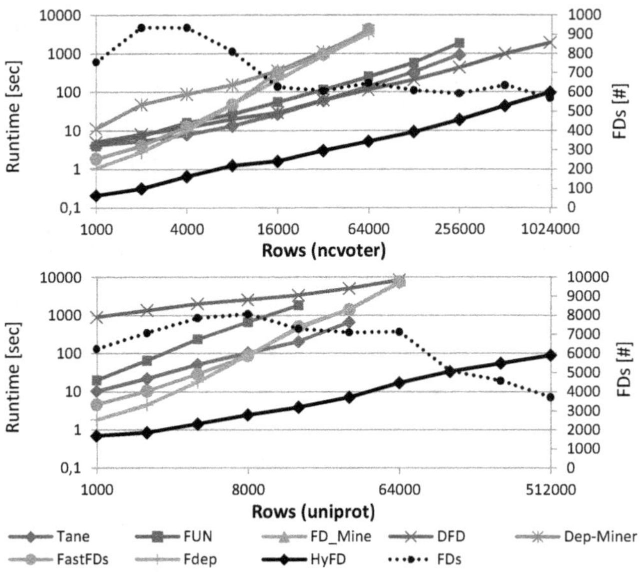

Figure 6: Row scalability on *ncvoter* and *uniprot*.

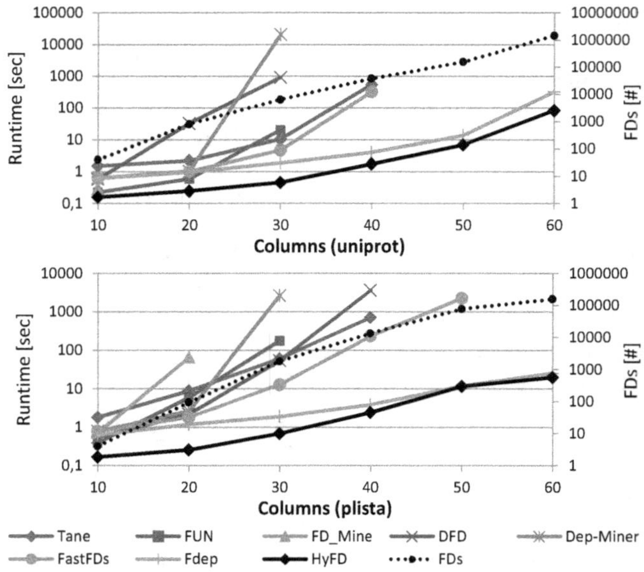

Figure 7: Column scalability on *uniprot* and *plista*.

Section 10.5 give an overview of these datasets. The data shown in Table 1 was already used in [20]. We also use the *plista* [13] dataset containing web log data, the *uniprot*[1] dataset storing protein sequences, and the *ncvoter*[2] dataset listing public voter statistics. The datasets listed in Table 2 have never been analyzed for FDs before, because they are much larger than the datasets of Table 1 and most of them cannot be processed with any of the related seven FD discovery algorithms within reasonable time (<1 month) and memory (<100 GB): The *CD* dataset contains CD-product data, the synthetic *TPC-H* dataset models business data, the *PDB* dataset stores protein sequence data, and the *SAP_R3* dataset holds data of a real SAP R3 ERP system.

10.2 Varying the number of rows

Our first experiment measures the runtime of HyFD on different row numbers. The experiment uses the *ncvoter* dataset with 19 columns and the *uniprot* dataset with 30 columns. The results, which also include the runtimes of the other seven FD discovery algorithms, are shown in Figure 6. A series of measurements stops if either the memory consumption exceeded 128 GB or the runtime exceeded 10,000 seconds. The dotted line shows the number of FDs in the input using the second y-axis: This number first increases, because more tuples invalidate more FDs so that more larger FDs arise; then it decreases, because even the larger FDs get invalidated and no further minimal specializations exist.

With our HyFD algorithm, we could process the 19 column version of the *ncvoter* dataset in 97 seconds and the 30 column version of the *uniprot* dataset in 89 seconds for the largest row size. This makes HyFD more than 20 times faster on *ncvoter* and more than 416 times faster on *uniprot* than the best state-of-the-art algorithm respectively. The reason why HyFD performs so much better than current lattice traversal algorithms is the fact that the number of FD-candidates that need to be validated against the many rows is greatly reduced by the `Sampler` component.

[1] www.uniprot.org

[2] www.ncsbe.gov/ncsbe/data-statistics

10.3 Varying the number of columns

In our second experiment, we measure HyFD's runtime on different column numbers using the *uniprot* dataset and the *plista* dataset with 1,000 records each. Again, we plot the measurements of HyFD with the measurements of the other FD discovery algorithms and cut the runtimes at 10,000 seconds. Figure 7 shows the result of this experiment.

We first notice that HyFD's runtime rather scales with the number of FDs, i.e., with the result size than with the number of columns. This is a desirable behavior, because the increasing effort is compensated by an also increasing gain. We further see that HyFD again outperforms all existing algorithms. The improvement factor is, however, smaller in this experiment, because the two datasets are with 1,000 rows so small that comparing all pairs of records, as FDEP does, is feasible and probably the best way to proceed. HyFD is still slightly faster than FDEP, because it does not compare all record pairs; the overhead of creating PLIs is compensated by then being able to compare PLI compressed records rather than String-represented records.

10.4 Varying the datasets

To show that HyFD is not sensitive to any dataset peculiarity, the next experiment evaluates the algorithm on many different datasets. For this experiment, we set a time limit (TL) of 4 hours and a memory limit (ML) of 100 GB. Table 1 summarizes the runtimes of the different algorithms.

The measurements show that HyFD was able to process all datasets and that it usually performed best. There are only two runtimes, namely those for the *fd-reduced-30* and for the *uniprot* dataset, that are in need of explanation: First, the *fd-reduced-30* dataset is a generated dataset that exclusively contains random values. Due to these random values, all FDs are accidental and do not have any semantic meaning. Also, all FDs are of same size, i.e., 99% of the 89,571 minimal FDs reside on lattice level three and none of them above this level. Thus, bottom-up lattice traversal algorithms, such as TANE and FUN, and algorithms that have bottom-up characteristics, such as DEP-MINER and FAST-

Dataset	Cols [#]	Rows [#]	Size [KB]	FDs [#]	TANE [12]	FUN [18]	FD_MINE [25]	DFD [1]	DEP-MINER [16]	FASTFDs [24]	FDEP [9]	HYFD
iris	5	150	5	4	1.1	**0.1**	0.2	0.2	0.2	0.2	**0.1**	**0.1**
balance-scale	5	625	7	1	1.2	**0.1**	0.2	0.3	0.3	0.3	0.2	**0.1**
chess	7	28,056	519	1	2.9	1.1	3.8	1.0	174.6	164.2	125.5	**0.2**
abalone	9	4,177	187	137	2.1	0.6	1.8	1.1	3.0	2.9	3.8	**0.2**
nursery	9	12,960	1,024	1	4.1	1.8	7.1	0.9	121.2	118.9	46.8	**0.5**
breast-cancer	11	699	20	46	2.3	0.6	2.2	0.8	1.1	1.1	0.5	**0.2**
bridges	13	108	6	142	2.2	0.6	4.2	0.9	0.5	0.6	0.2	**0.1**
echocardiogram	13	132	6	527	1.6	0.4	69.9	1.2	0.5	0.5	0.2	**0.1**
adult	14	48,842	3,528	78	67.4	111.6	531.5	5.9	6039.2	6033.8	860.2	**1.1**
letter	17	20,000	695	61	260.0	529.0	7204.8	6.0	1090.0	1015.5	291.3	**3.4**
ncvoter	19	1,000	151	758	4.3	4.0	ML	5.1	11.4	1.9	1.1	**0.4**
hepatitis	20	155	8	8,250	12.2	175.9	ML	326.7	5576.5	9.5	0.8	**0.6**
horse	27	368	25	128,727	457.0	TL	ML	TL	TL	385.8	7.2	**7.1**
fd-reduced-30	30	250,000	69,581	89,571	**41.1**	77.7	ML	TL	377.2	382.4	TL	513.0
plista	63	1,000	568	178,152	ML	ML	ML	TL	TL	TL	26.9	**21.8**
flight	109	1,000	575	982,631	ML	ML	ML	TL	TL	TL	216.5	**53.4**
uniprot	223	1,000	2,439	>2,437,556	ML	ML	ML	TL	TL	TL	ML	>**5254.7**

Results larger than 1,000 FDs are only counted **TL**: time limit of 4 hours exceeded **ML**: memory limit of 100 GB exceeded

Table 1: Runtimes in seconds for several real-world datasets (extended from [20])

FDs, perform very well on such an unusual dataset. The runtime of HYFD, which is about 9 minutes, is an adequate runtime for any dataset with 30 columns and 250,000 rows.

The *uniprot* dataset is another extreme, but real-world dataset: Because it comprises 223 columns, the total number of minimal FDs in this dataset is much larger than 100 million. This is, as Figure 7 shows, due to the fact that the number of FDs in this dataset grows exponentially with the number of columns. For this reason, we limited HYFD's result size to 4 GB and let the algorithm's `Guardian` component assure that the result does not become larger. In this way, HYFD discovered all minimal FDs with a LHS of up to four attributes; all FDs on lattice level five and above have been successively pruned, because they would exceed the 4 GB memory limit. So HYFD discovered the first 2.5 million FDs in about 1.5 hours. One can compute more FDs on *uniprot* with HYFD using more memory, but the entire result set is – at the time – impossible to store.

The datasets in Table 1 brought all state-of-the-art algorithms to their limits, but they are still quite small in comparison to most real-world datasets. Therefore, we also evaluated HYFD on much larger datasets. This experiment reports only HYFD's runtimes, because no other algorithm can process the datasets within reasonable time and memory limits. Table 2 lists the results for the single-threaded implementation of HYFD (left column) that we also used in the previous experiments and a multi-threaded implementation (right column), which we explain below.

The measurements show that HYFD's runtime depends on the number of FDs, which is fine, because the increased effort pays off in more results. Intuitively, the more FDs are to be validated, the longer the discovery takes. But

Dataset	Cols [#]	Rows [#]	Size [MB]	FDs [#]	HYFD [s/m/h/d]	
TPC-H.lineitem	16	6 m	1,051	4 k	**39 m**	4 m
PDB.POLY_SEQ	13	17 m	1,256	68	**4 m**	3 m
PDB.ATOM_SITE	31	27 m	5,042	10 k	**12 h**	64 m
SAP_R3.ZBC00DT	35	3 m	783	211	**4 m**	2 m
SAP_R3.ILOA	48	45 m	8,731	16 k	**35 h**	8 h
SAP_R3.CE4HI01	65	2 m	649	2 k	**17 m**	10 m
NCVoter.statewide	71	1 m	561	5 m	**10 d**	31 h
CD.cd	107	10 k	5	36 k	**5 s**	3 s

Table 2: Single- and multi-threaded runtimes on larger real-world datasets.

the *CD* dataset shows that the runtime also depends on the number of rows, i.e., the FD-candidate validations are much less expensive if only a few values need to be checked. If both the number of rows and columns becomes large, which is when they exceed 50 columns and 10 million rows, HYFD might run multiple days. This is due to the exponential complexity of the FD-discovery problem. However, HYFD was able to process all such datasets and because no other algorithm is able to achieve this, obtaining a complete result within some days is the first actual solution to the problem.

Multiple threads. We introduced and tested a single-threaded implementation of HYFD to compare its runtime with the single-threaded state-of-the-art algorithms. HYFD can, however, easily be parallelized, because the comparisons in the `Sampler` component are like the validations in the `Validator` component independent of one another. We implemented these simple parallelizations and the runtimes reduced to the measurements shown in the right column of Table 2 running 32 parallel threads. Compared to the parallel FD discovery algorithm PARADE [10], HYFD is 8x (*POLY_SEQ*), 38x (*lineitem*), 89x (*CE4HI01*), and 1178x (*cd*) faster due to its novel, hybrid search strategy – for the other datasets, we stopped PARADE after two weeks.

10.5 In-depth experiments

Memory consumption. Many FD discovery algorithms demand a lot of main memory to store intermediate data structures. The following experiment contrasts the memory consumption of HYFD with its three most efficient competitors TANE, DFD, and FDEP on different datasets (the memory consumption of FUN and FD_MINE is worse than TANE's; DEP-MINER and FASTFDs are similar to FDEP [20]). To measure the memory consumption, we limited the available memory successively to 1 MB, 2 MB, ..., 10 MB, 15 MB, ..., 100 MB, 110 MB, ..., 300 MB, 350 MB, ..., 1 GB, 2 GB, ..., 10 GB, 15 GB, ..., 100 GB and stopped increasing the memory when an algorithm finished without memory issues. Table 3 lists the results. Note that the memory consumption is given for complete results and HYFD can produce smaller results on less memory using the `Guardian` component. Because DFD takes more than 4 hours, which is our time limit, to process *horse*, *plista*, and *flight*, we could not measure the algorithm's memory consumption on these datasets.

Dataset	TANE	DFD	FDEP	HYFD
hepatitis	400 MB	300 MB	9 MB	**5 MB**
adult	5 GB	300 MB	100 MB	**10 MB**
letter	30 GB	400 MB	90 MB	**25 MB**
horse	25 GB	-	100 MB	**65 MB**
plista	> 100 GB	-	800 MB	**110 MB**
flight	> 100 GB	-	900 MB	**200 MB**

Table 3: Memory consumption

Due to the excessive construction of PLIs, TANE of course consumes the most memory. DFD manages the PLIs in a PLI-store using a least-recently-used strategy to discard PLIs when memory is exhausted, but the minimum number of required PLIs is still very large. Also, DFD becomes very slow on low memory. FDEP has a relatively small memory footprint, because it does not use PLIs at all. HYFD uses the same data structures as TANE and FDEP and some additional data structures, such as the comparison suggestions, but it still has the overall smallest memory consumption: In contrast to TANE, HYFD generates much fewer candidates and requires only the single-column PLIs for its direct validation technique; in contrast to FDEP, it stores the non-FDs in bitsets rather than index lists and uses the PLIs instead of the original data for the record comparisons.

Efficiency threshold. HYFD requires a parameter that determines when Phase 1 or Phase 2 become inefficient: It stops the record matching in the `Sampler` component if less than x percent matches delivered new FD-violations and it stops the FD-candidate validations in the `Validator` component if more than x percent candidates have shown to be invalid. In the explanation of the algorithm and in all previous experiments, we set this parameter to 1% regardless of the datasets being analyzed. The following experiment evaluates different parameter settings on the *ncvoter_statewide* dataset with ten thousand records.

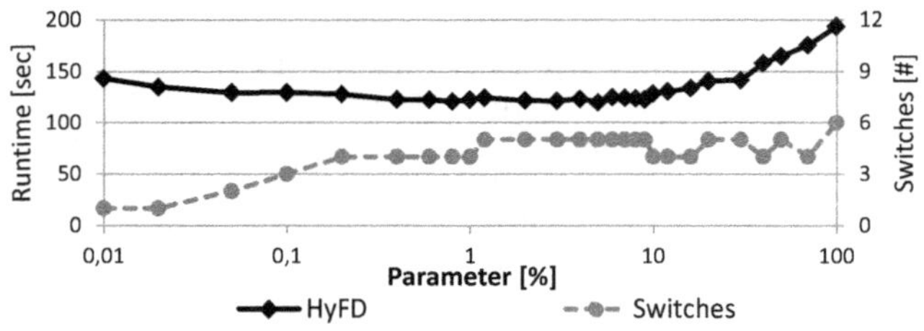

Figure 8: Effect of HyFD's only parameter on 10 thousand records of the *ncvoter_statewide* dataset.

The first line in Figure 8 plots HYFD's runtime for parameter values between 0.01% and 100%. It shows that HYFD's performance is not very sensitive to the efficiency threshold parameter. In fact, the performance is almost the same for any value between 0.1% and 10%. This is because the efficiency of either phase falls suddenly and fast so that all low efficiency values are met quickly: The progressive sampling identifies most matches very early and the validation generates many new, largely also invalid FD-candidates for every candidate tested as invalid.

However, if we set the parameter higher than 10%, then HYFD starts validating some lattice levels with too many invalid FD-candidates, which affects the performance negatively; if we, on the other hand, set the value lower than 0.1%, HYFD invests too much time on sampling than actually needed, which means that it keeps matching records although all results have already been found. We observed the same effects an different dataset, so we propose 1% as the default efficiency threshold for HYFD.

The second line in Table 8 depicts the number of switches from Phase 2 back into Phase 1 that HYFD made with the different parameter settings. We observe that four to five phase-switches are necessary on *ncvoter_statewide* and doing fewer or more switches is disadvantageous for the performance. Note that HYFD did these switches on different lattice-levels depending on the parameter setting, i.e., with low thresholds it switches earlier; with high thresholds later.

10.6 Result analysis

The number of FDs that HYFD can discover is very large. In fact, the size of the discovered metadata can easily exceed the size of the original dataset (see the *uniprot* dataset in Section 10.4). A reasonable question is, hence, whether complete results, i.e., *all* minimal FDs, are actually needed. Schema normalization, for instance, requires only a small subset of FDs to transform a current schema into a new schema with smaller memory footprint. Data integration also requires only a subset of all FDs, namely those that overlap with a second schema. In short, most use-cases for FDs indeed require only a subset of all results.

However, one must inspect all functional dependencies to identify these subsets: Schema normalization, for instance, is based on closure calculation and data integration is based on dependency mapping, both requiring complete FD result sets to find the optimal solutions. Furthermore, in query optimization, a subset of FDs that optimizes a given query workload by 10% is very good at first sight, but if a different subset of FDs could have saved 20% of the query load, one would have missed some high optimization potential. For these reasons and because we cannot know which other use cases HYFD will have to serve, we discover all functional dependencies – or at least as many as possible.

11. CONCLUSION & FUTURE WORK

In this paper, we proposed HYFD, a hybrid FD discovery algorithm that discovers all minimal, non-trivial functional dependencies in relational datasets. Because HYFD combines row- and column-efficient discovery techniques, it is able to process datasets that are both long and wide. This makes HYFD the first algorithm that can process datasets of relevant real-world size, i.e., datasets with more than 50 attributes and a million records. On smaller datasets, which some other FD discovery algorithms can already process, HYFD offers the smallest memory footprints and the fastest runtimes; in many cases, our algorithm is orders of magnitude faster than the best state-of-the-art algorithm. Because the number of FDs grows exponentially with the number of attributes, we also proposed a component that dynamically prunes the result set, if the available memory is exhausted.

A task for future work is the development of use-case-specific algorithms that leverage FD result sets for schema normalization, query optimization, data integration, data cleansing, and many other tasks. In addition, knowledge of the use-case might help develop specific semantic pruning rules to further speed-up detection. The only reasonable semantic pruning we found was removing FDs with largest left-hand-sides, because these are most prone to being accidental, and we only apply it when absolutely necessary.

Acknowledgements. We thank Tobias Bleifuß for the idea of compressing non-FDs as bitsets and the authors of [20] and [10] for providing code and data for our comparative evaluation.

12. REFERENCES

[1] Z. Abedjan, P. Schulze, and F. Naumann. DFD: Efficient functional dependency discovery. In *Proceedings of the International Conference on Information and Knowledge Management (CIKM)*, pages 949–958, 2014.

[2] R. Agrawal and R. Srikant. Fast algorithms for mining association rules in large databases. In *Proceedings of the International Conference on Very Large Databases (VLDB)*, pages 487–499, 1994.

[3] P. Bohannon, W. Fan, and F. Geerts. Conditional functional dependencies for data cleaning. In *Proceedings of the International Conference on Data Engineering (ICDE)*, pages 746–755, 2007.

[4] C. R. Carlson, A. K. Arora, and M. M. Carlson. The application of functional dependency theory to relational databases. *Computer Journal*, 25(1):68–73, 1982.

[5] E. F. Codd. A relational model of data for large shared data banks. *Communications of the ACM*, 13(6):377–387, 1970.

[6] E. F. Codd. Further normalization of the data base relational model. *IBM Research Report, San Jose, California*, RJ909, 1971.

[7] G. Cormode, L. Golab, K. Flip, A. McGregor, D. Srivastava, and X. Zhang. Estimating the confidence of conditional functional dependencies. In *Proceedings of the International Conference on Management of Data (SIGMOD)*, pages 469–482, 2009.

[8] S. S. Cosmadakis, P. C. Kanellakis, and N. Spyratos. Partition semantics for relations. *Journal of Computer and System Sciences*, 33(2):203–233, 1986.

[9] P. A. Flach and I. Savnik. Database dependency discovery: a machine learning approach. *AI Communications*, 12(3):139–160, 1999.

[10] E. Garnaud, N. Hanusse, S. Maabout, and N. Novelli. Parallel mining of dependencies. In *Proceedings of the International Conference on High Performance Computing & Simulation (HPCS)*, pages 491–498, 2014.

[11] M. A. Hernández and S. J. Stolfo. Real-world data is dirty: Data cleansing and the merge/purge problem. *Data Mining and Knowledge Discovery*, 2(1):9–37, 1998.

[12] Y. Huhtala, J. Kärkkäinen, P. Porkka, and H. Toivonen. TANE: An efficient algorithm for discovering functional and approximate dependencies. *The Computer Journal*, 42(2):100–111, 1999.

[13] B. Kille, F. Hopfgartner, T. Brodt, and T. Heintz. The plista dataset. In *Proceedings of the International Workshop and Challenge on News Recommender Systems*, 2013.

[14] W. Li, Z. Li, Q. Chen, T. Jiang, and H. Liu. Discovering functional dependencies in vertically distributed big data. *Proceedings of the International Conference on Web Information Systems Engineering (WISE)*, pages 199–207, 2015.

[15] J. Liu, J. Li, C. Liu, and Y. Chen. Discover dependencies from data – a review. *IEEE Transactions on Knowledge and Data Engineering (TKDE)*, 24(2):251–264, 2012.

[16] S. Lopes, J.-M. Petit, and L. Lakhal. Efficient discovery of functional dependencies and Armstrong relations. In *Proceedings of the International Conference on Extending Database Technology (EDBT)*, pages 350–364, 2000.

[17] R. J. Miller, M. A. Hernandez, L. M. Haas, L.-L. Yan, H. Ho, R. Fagin, and L. Popa. The Clio project: Managing heterogeneity. *SIGMOD Record*, 30(1):78–83, 2001.

[18] N. Novelli and R. Cicchetti. FUN: An efficient algorithm for mining functional and embedded dependencies. In *Proceedings of the International Conference on Database Theory (ICDT)*, pages 189–203, 2001.

[19] T. Papenbrock, T. Bergmann, M. Finke, J. Zwiener, and F. Naumann. Data profiling with metanome. *Proceedings of the VLDB Endowment*, 8(12):1860–1871, 2015.

[20] T. Papenbrock, J. Ehrlich, J. Marten, T. Neubert, J.-P. Rudolph, M. Schönberg, J. Zwiener, and F. Naumann. Functional dependency discovery: An experimental evaluation of seven algorithms. *Proceedings of the VLDB Endowment*, 8(10):1082–1093, 2015.

[21] T. Papenbrock, A. Heise, and F. Naumann. Progressive duplicate detection. *IEEE Transactions on Knowledge and Data Engineering (TKDE)*, 27(5):1316–1329, 2015.

[22] G. N. Paulley. Exploiting functional dependence in query optimization. Technical report, University of Waterloo, 2000.

[23] J. D. Ullman. *Principles of Database and Knowledge-Base Systems: Volume II: The New Technologies*. W. H. Freeman & Co., New York, NY, USA, 1990.

[24] C. Wyss, C. Giannella, and E. Robertson. FastFDs: A heuristic-driven, depth-first algorithm for mining functional dependencies from relation instances extended abstract. In *Proceedings of the International Conference of Data Warehousing and Knowledge Discovery (DaWaK)*, pages 101–110, 2001.

[25] H. Yao, H. J. Hamilton, and C. J. Butz. FD_Mine: discovering functional dependencies in a database using equivalences. In *Proceedings of the International Conference on Data Mining (ICDM)*, pages 729–732, 2002.

Ontological Pathfinding: Mining First-Order Knowledge from Large Knowledge Bases

Yang Chen† Sean Goldberg† Daisy Zhe Wang† Soumitra Siddharth Johri‡
Department of Computer and Information Science and Engineering
University of Florida
†{yang,sean,daisyw}@cise.ufl.edu ‡soumitra.johri@ufl.edu

ABSTRACT

Recent years have seen a drastic rise in the construction of web-scale knowledge bases (e.g., Freebase, YAGO, DBPedia). These knowledge bases store structured information about real-world people, places, organizations, etc. However, due to limitations of human knowledge and information extraction algorithms, these knowledge bases are still far from complete. In this paper, we study the problem of mining first-order inference rules to facilitate knowledge expansion. We propose the Ontological Pathfinding algorithm (OP) that scales to web-scale knowledge bases via a series of parallelization and optimization techniques: a relational knowledge base model to apply inference rules in batches, a new rule mining algorithm that parallelizes the join queries, a novel partitioning algorithm to break the mining tasks into smaller independent sub-tasks, and a pruning strategy to eliminate unsound and resource-consuming rules before applying them. Combining these techniques, we develop the first rule mining system that scales to Freebase, the largest public knowledge base with 112 million entities and 388 million facts. We mine 36,625 inference rules in 34 hours; no existing approach achieves this scale.

Keywords

Knowledge bases; data mining; first-order logic; scalability

1. INTRODUCTION

Recent years have seen tremendous research and engineering efforts in constructing large knowledge bases (KBs). Examples of these knowledge bases include DBPedia [4], DeepDive [39], Freebase [8], Google Knowledge Graph [7], NELL [9], OpenIE [5, 18], ProBase [53], and YAGO [6, 24, 35]. These knowledge bases store structured information about real-world people, places, organizations, etc. They are constructed by human crafting (DBPedia, Freebase), information extraction (DeepDive, OpenIE, ProBase), reasoning and inference [12, 46], knowledge fusion [52, 16], or combinations of them (NELL).

In this paper, we focus on the problem of mining first-order inference rules to support knowledge expansion. An inference rule is a first-order Horn clause to discover implicit facts. As an example, the following rule expands knowledge of people's birth places:

$$\text{wasBornIn}(x, y), \text{isLocatedIn}(y, z) \rightarrow \text{wasBornIn}(x, z).$$

Rules are useful in a wide range of applications: knowledge reasoning and expansion [12, 46], knowledge base construction [9], question answering [14], knowledge cleaning [19, 44], knowledge base maintenance [48], Markov logic learning [27], etc.

Mining Horn clauses has been studied extensively in inductive logic programming. However, today's knowledge bases pose several new challenges. First, knowledge bases are often prohibitively large. For example, as of this writing, Freebase has 112 million entities and 388 million facts. None of the existing rule mining algorithms efficiently support KBs of this size. Second, knowledge bases implement the open world assumption, implying that we have only positive examples for rule mining. To address these challenges, a number of new approaches are proposed: SHERLOCK [47], AMIE [20], Markov logic structure learning [26, 27], etc. Still, new techniques need to be invented to scale up state-of-the-art approaches to knowledge bases of billions of facts.

In this paper, we propose the Ontological Pathfinding algorithm (OP) to tackle the large-scale rule mining problem. We focus on scalability and design a series of parallelization and optimization techniques to achieve web scale. Following the relational knowledge base model [12], we store inference rules in relational tables and use join queries to apply them in batches. The relational approach outperforms state-of-the-art algorithms by orders of magnitude on medium-sized knowledge bases [12]. To scale to larger knowledge bases, we parallelize the mining algorithm by dividing the input knowledge base into smaller groups running parallel in-memory joins. The parallel mining algorithm can be implemented on state-of-the-art cluster computing frameworks to achieve maximum utilization of available computation resource.

Furthermore, even if we parallelize the mining algorithm, the parallel tasks are dependent on each other. In particular, the tasks need to shuffle data between stages. As the knowledge bases expand in scale, shuffling becomes the bottleneck of the computation. This shuffling bottleneck motivates us to introduce another layer of partitioning on top of the parallel computation, a partitioning scheme that divides the mining task into smaller *independent* sub-tasks. Each partition still runs the same parallel mining algorithm as before, but on a smaller input. Since each partition is independent from each other, the results are unioned in the end; no data exchange occurs during computation. Our experiments show that we accomplish the Freebase mining task within 34 hours that does not finish in 5 days without partitioning.

One major performance bottleneck is caused by large degrees of join variables in the inference rules. Applying these rules in the mining process generates large intermediate results, enumerating

SIGMOD'16, June 26-July 01, 2016, San Francisco, CA, USA

DOI: http://dx.doi.org/10.1145/2882903.2882954

all possible pair-wise relationships of the joined instances. As a result, these rules are often of low quality. Based on this observation, we use non-functionality as an empirical indication of inefficiency and inaccuracy. In our experiments, we determine a reasonable functional constraint and show that 99% of the rules violating this constraint turn out to be false. Removing those rules reduces runtime by more than 5 hours for a single mining task. Combining our approaches, we develop the first rule mining system that scales to Freebase, the largest public knowledge base with 112 million entities and 388 million facts. We mine 36,625 inference rules in 34 hours; no existing approach achieves this scale.

In summary, we make the following contributions to achieve scalability in mining first-order rules from large knowledge bases:

- We design an efficient rule mining algorithm that evaluates inference rules in batches using join queries. The algorithm runs in parallel by dividing the knowledge base into smaller groups running parallel in-memory joins;
- We design a novel partitioning algorithm to divide the mining task into small independent sub-tasks. Each sub-task is parallelized, running the same mining algorithm, but operates on small inputs. Data shuffling is unnecessary among sub-tasks;
- We define the non-functionality score to prune dubious and inefficient rules. We experimentally determine a reasonable functional constraint and show the constraint improves efficiency and accuracy of the mining algorithm;
- We conduct a comprehensive experiment study to evaluate our approaches over public knowledge bases, including YAGO and Freebase. Our research leads to a first rule set for Freebase, the largest knowledge base with hundreds of millions of facts. We publish the code and data repository online[1].

The remainder of this paper is organized as follows. Section 2 discusses related works. Section 3 defines the first-order mining problem. Section 4 introduces the underlying background knowledge. Section 5 introduces the Ontological Pathfinding algorithm in detail. Section 6 describes the partitioning algorithm. Section 7 presents the experiment study, and Section 8 concludes the paper.

2. RELATED WORK

Mining Horn clauses. Mining Horn clauses [25] has first been studied in Inductive Logic Programming (ILP) literature [41, 37, 42]. Recently, SHERLOCK [47] and AMIE [20] have extended it to mining first-order inference rules from knowledge bases by defining new metrics to address the open world assumption made by the knowledge bases. AMIE achieves the state-of-the-art efficiency using an in-memory database to support the projection queries for counting. Sherlock and AMIE have mined 30,912 and 1090 inference rules from 250K (OPENIE [5, 18]) and 948K (YAGO2 [24]) distinct facts, respectively. Still, none of these approaches scales to the Freebase size. To solve this scalability problem, we adopt the mining model of AMIE, described in Section 3, and scale it up using a series of parallelization and optimization techniques.

Parallel computing. In recent years, various data processing frameworks have been proposed and developed to facilitate large-scale data analytics, including in-databases analytics [23, 51, 31, 38, 50], MapReduce [15], FlumeJava [11], Spark [55, 54], GraphLab [34, 33], Datapath [13, 3], etc. These systems are effective in a variety of data mining and machine learning problems. Given no previous work that scales up the rule mining algorithms to the web, we are motivated to leverage state-of-the-art parallel computing techniques. The parallel mining algorithm we propose combines the relational model [12] and the MapReduce programming paradigm [15], consisting of a sequence of parallel operations on the KB tables. We implement and evaluate it on Spark in favor of its efficient pipelining of parallel operations using distributed caches.

Functional Constraints. Constraints have proven helpful in a wide range of knowledge base construction and expansion problems. NELL employs a set of coupling constraints to prevent "semantic drifts" in constructing the knowledge base [10]. A particularly useful class of constraints is functional constraints. The N-FOIL algorithm [30] for NELL uses functional constraints to provide negative examples for ILP learners. [32, 44] mines functional constraints from automatically constructed knowledge bases. [12] applies functional constraints to detect contradictions and ambiguous entities for the knowledge expansion problem. [46] leverages functionality properties of predicates to scale up textual inference to the web. These works of speeding up knowledge and textual inference tasks by leveraging functionality properties of predicates inspire us to apply them to the mining problem by extending the notion of functionality to Horn clauses to prune erroneous rules.

Mining association rules. Since the first introduction of association rule mining in [1], researchers have developed a number of improvements [2, 40, 45, 22]. In particular, the Direct Hashing and Pruning algorithm [40] partitions itemsets into buckets and prunes buckets that violate the minimum support constraint. The Partition Algorithm [45] partitions the transactions database and processes one partition at a time. These partitioning approaches depend on the assumption that transactions independently contribute to the itemset counts in a transactions database. In a first-order knowledge base, the facts are interconnected by the rules and arguments. This dependency will be lost if we directly partition the knowledge base in the state-of-the-art ways. In our approach, we preserve data dependency by relaxing the non-overlapping requirement and designing a new algorithm that partitions the knowledge base into independent but possibly overlapping partitions.

Mining frequent subgraphs. The rule mining problem is closely related to mining frequent subgraphs [17, 56, 29, 28], where the knowledge base is represented as a single directed graph. The major difference is the notion of a subgraph: In the first-order rule mining problem, a subgraph is a graph pattern where the edges are labeled but vertices are variables. This leads to an important consequence we address in this paper: A more sophisticated counting algorithm is needed to count the frequencies of *grounded* subgraphs [43], namely, subgraphs with variables substituted by constants. The grounding problem of parameterized subgraphs is not addressed in the frequent subgraph mining literature.

3. FIRST-ORDER MINING PROBLEM

We study the problem of mining first-order inference rules from web-scale knowledge bases: Given a knowledge base of (subject, predicate, object) (or (s, p, o)) triples, we mine first-order Horn clauses of form

$$(\mathbf{w},\ \mathbf{B} \to H(x, y)), \tag{1}$$

where the body $\mathbf{B} = \bigwedge_i B_i(\cdot, \cdot)$ is a conjunction of predicates, H is the head predicate, and $\mathbf{w}$ is a scoring metric reflecting the likelihood of the rule being true.

As in AMIE [20] and other ILP systems [36, 49], we use a language bias and assume the Horn clauses to be connected and closed. Two atoms are connected if they share a variable. A rule is *connected* if every atom is connected transitively to every other atom in the rule. A rule is *closed* if every variable appears at least twice in different predicates. This assumption ensures that the rules do not contain unrelated atoms or variables.

[1] http://dsr.cise.ufl.edu/projects/probkb-web-scale-probabilistic-knowledge-base.

Our primary focus of this paper is *scalable mining*. Previous approaches [20, 47] scale to knowledge bases of 1 million facts, but no existing work mines inference rules from the 112 million entities and 388 million facts of Freebase. We investigate a series of parallelization and optimization techniques to achieve this scale, and we study how to use state-of-the-art data processing systems, e.g., Spark, to efficiently implement the parallel algorithms.

The first-order mining problem has similarities with association rule mining in transactions databases [20], but they are essentially different. In first-order rules, the atoms are *parameterized* predicates. Each parameterized predicate can be *grounded* to a set of ground atoms. Depending on the size of the knowledge base, each rule can have a large number of possible ground instances. This makes mining first-order knowledge more challenging than mining traditional association rules in transactions databases.

3.1 Scoring Metrics

We review the support and confidence metrics for first-order Horn clauses. They have counterparts in association rule mining in transactions databases, but are different from them as discussed above.

Support. The *support* of a rule is defined to be the number of distinct pairs of subject and object in the head of all instantiations that appear in the knowledge base:

$$\text{supp}(\mathbf{B} \to H(x, y)) := \#(x, y) : \exists z_1, \ldots, z_m : \mathbf{B} \wedge H(x, y). \tag{2}$$

In Equation (2), $\mathbf{B}$ and H denote the body and head, respectively. $z_1, \ldots, z_m$ are the variables of the rule in addition to x and y.

Confidence. The *confidence* of a rule is defined to be the ratio of its predictions that are in the knowledge base:

$$\text{conf}(\mathbf{B} \to H(x, y)) := \frac{\text{supp}(\mathbf{B} \to H(x, y))}{\#(x, y) : \exists z_1, \ldots, z_m : \mathbf{B}}. \tag{3}$$

For each rule, we compute its support and confidence, and set $\mathbf{w} = (\text{supp}, \text{conf})$ in (1). The support and confidence metrics together determine the quality of a rule. [20, 47] introduces other scoring functions, e.g., head coverage, PCA confidence, statistical relevance. These metrics can be implemented using the same principle as we propose in this paper.

4. PRELIMINARIES

Before describing the OP algorithm in detail, we introduce the notion of knowledge bases, their relational model, and Spark.

4.1 Knowledge Bases

In this paper, we model a *knowledge base* as a collection of (subject, predicate, object) facts $\Gamma = \{(s, p, o)\}$ with the following semantics:

- Each subject or object refers to a real-world *entity*. For example, Barack Obama, USA are well-known entities.
- Each predicate specifies relationships among its subjects and objects. We call each relationship a *fact*. For example, the fact (Barack Obama, wasBornIn, USA) specifies that Barack Obama was born in the USA.
- Each entity belongs to one or more types. Correspondingly, each predicate specifies a binary relation between one or more pairs of types. For example, the wasBornIn predicate specifies a binary relation between Person and Place. We call these types *domain* and *range* of the predicate, respectively.
- We call the predicates, along with their domains and ranges, the *schema* of the knowledge base.

Example 1. As a concrete example, in Freebase, the predicates are called *properties*. Each property belongs to a specific type, written as domain/type/property, where a domain denotes a manual division of Freebase consisting of related types[2]. Thus, a predicate "film/film/country(x, y)" means film x is produced in country y. The inference rules are interpreted accordingly, illustrated below:

film/film/sequel(x, z), film/film/country$(z, y) \to$ film/film/country(x, y).

The rule states that if a film x has a sequel z, and the sequel z is produced in country y, then film x is produced in country y. □

4.2 Relational Knowledge Base Model

[12] introduces a relational model for probabilistic knowledge bases. In this section, we review the model for inference rules. This relational representation allows us to compactly store inference rules and apply them in batches using join queries. The main challenge with inference rules is that they have flexible structures, conflicting with the relational tables with fixed columns. To adapt for their structures, we use the concept of structural equivalence so that each equivalent class has a fixed table format.

Definition 1. Two first-order clauses are defined to be *structurally equivalent* if they differ only in entities, types, and predicates.

It is verifiable that the structural equivalence relation in Definition 1 is an equivalence relation. Thus, first-order clauses can be divided into equivalent classes accordingly. Since the first-order clauses in each equivalent class differ only in entities, types, and predicates, it suffices to use these elements to identify inference rules in an equivalence class. In other words, each equivalent class can be stored in a fixed-column table, with the columns being entities, types, and predicates.

Example 2. Consider the following inference rules:

1. $\forall x \in$ Person, $\forall y \in$ Person:
   isMarriedTo$(x, y) \to$ isMarriedTo(y, x);
2. $\forall x \in$ Book, $\forall y \in$ Person:
   influences$(x, y) \to$ isInterestedIn(y, x);
3. $\forall x \in$ Person, $\forall y \in$ Actor, $\forall z \in$ Movie:
   directed(x, z), actedIn$(y, z) \to$ influences(x, y);
4. $\forall x \in$ Person, $\forall y \in$ Actor, $\forall z \in$ Org:
   worksAt(x, z), worksAt$(y, z) \to$ influences(x, y).

Rules 1 and 2 are structurally equivalent since their only differences are the predicates (isMarriedTo, influences, isInterestedIn) and types (Person, Book). Similarly, Rules 3 and 4 are structurally equivalent. Therefore, we store Rules 1 and 2 in one table with the columns specifying the predicates of the head and body, as shown in Table 1 (left). We store Rules 3 and 4 in Table 1 (right), its columns storing the head and first, second predicates of the rule body. We have omitted the types since they are not involved in the join queries to evaluate the rules, as we discuss in Section 5.2.

Head	Body
isMarriedTo	isMarriedTo
isInterestedIn	influences

Head	Body1	Body2
influences	directed	actedIn
influences	worksAt	worksAt

Table 1: (Left) Relational table for rules 1 and 2. (Right) Relational table for rules 3 and 4.

The rules in one table are interpreted in the same way. For example, both rules in Table 1 (left) mean "if Body(x,y) holds, then Head(x,y) holds". By classifying the rules into structurally equivalent classes, we are able to store them into fixed-column tables and perform relational queries to evaluate them in batches. □

[2]In Freebase, domains are used to conceptually organize the types. We do not use this terminology elsewhere in the paper.

R1: $\text{Person}_1 \xrightarrow{\text{isMarriedTo}} \text{Person}_2 \xrightarrow{\text{livesIn}} \text{City} \xleftarrow{\text{livesIn}} \text{Person}_1$	$\text{isMarriedTo}(P_1, P_2), \text{livesIn}(P_2, C) \rightarrow \text{livesIn}(P_1, C)$
R2: $\text{Person} \xrightarrow{\text{directed}} \text{Movie} \xleftarrow{\text{actedIn}} \text{Actor} \xleftarrow{\text{influences}} \text{Person}$	$\text{directed}(P, M), \text{actedIn}(A, M) \rightarrow \text{influences}(P, A)$
R3: $\text{Person} \xrightarrow{\text{worksAt}} \text{Organization} \xleftarrow{\text{worksAt}} \text{Actor} \xleftarrow{\text{influences}} \text{Person}$	$\text{worksAt}(P, O), \text{worksAt}(A, O) \rightarrow \text{influences}(P, A)$

Figure 1: (Left) Cycles from Example 3. The first and last nodes in R1-R3 denote the same start and end node in the cycle. (Right) Corresponding rules.

4.3 Spark Basics

Spark is a cluster computing framework. Based on its core idea of resilient distributed datasets (RDDs)–read-only collections of objects partitioned across a set of machines–it defines a set of parallel operations. Using these operations, Spark allows users to express a rich set of computation tasks. The operations we use in this paper are listed below:

- `map/flatMap` Transforms an RDD to a new RDD by applying a function to each element in the input RDD.
- `groupByKey` Transforms an RDD to a new RDD by grouping by a user-specified key. In the result RDD, each key is mapped to a list of values of the key.
- `reduceByKey` Transforms an RDD to a new RDD by grouping by a user-specified key and performs a reduce function to the values of each key. In the result RDD, each key is mapped to the result value of the reduce function.

In our parallel rule mining algorithm, we represent the set of facts $\{(s, p, o)\}$ and the set of rules $\{(h, b_1, b_2)\}$ as two RDDs and express the algorithm using the above parallel operations.

5. ONTOLOGICAL PATHFINDING

The Ontological Pathfinding (OP) algorithm is similar to relational pathfinding [42], but instead of finding paths over an entity-relationship graph, the OP algorithm searches the domain-range schema graph. The schema graph constrains the search space to syntactically correct rules according to the arguments of each predicate. After constructing candidate rules, OP partitions them into smaller independent parts. It accepts a maximum size argument s, a maximum rules size m, and partitions the candidate rules, making a best effort to satisfy the size requirements. Finally, OP prunes candidate rules with respect to the functional constraint t and evaluates the rule batches using the parallel mining algorithm.

Algorithm 1 summarizes the major steps of Ontological Pathfinding to mine inference rules from a knowledge base Γ. We explain each step in detail in the following sections.

Algorithm 1 Ontological Pathfinding(Γ, t, s, m)

```
M ← construct-rules(Γ.schema)
{(Γ_i, M_i)} ← partition(Γ, ∅, M, s, m)
rules ← ∅
for all (Γ_i, M_i) do
    M_i ← prune(Γ_i, M_i, t)
    rules ← rules ∪ parallel-rule-mining(Γ_i, M_i)
return rules
```

5.1 Rule Construction

As discussed in Section 4.1, all entities and predicates are *typed* in a knowledge base, i.e., each entity belongs to one or more types, and each predicate has a domain and a range. Typing restricts the predicates that can be combined to form candidate rules: they must have corresponding types for the joining variables. In this section, we utilize the schema to construct candidate rules.

Definition 2. The *schema graph* of a knowledge base is defined to be a graph $G_\Gamma = (V, E)$, where $V = \{v_1, \ldots, v_{|V|}\}$ is the set of nodes representing types and $E = \{e_p(v_i, v_j)\}$ is the set of labeled directed edges representing typed predicates p with v_i as the domain and v_j as the range.

In a web-scale knowledge base like YAGO and DBPedia, we often have a *type hierarchy* to divide types into subtypes for finer classification. For instance, the "Person" type has subtypes including "Actor", "Professor". These types are related by the "subClassOf" edges. In Figure 2, we have a "subClassOf" edge from "Actor" to "Person", indicating that "Actor" is a subtype of "Person". To construct candidate rules, the subclasses need to inherit all the edges from their ancestors. The inherited edges are defined in Definition 3 using the following notations: 1. $A(v)$ denotes the ancestor nodes u of v such that there is a path from v to u with all edges labeled as "subClassOf"; and 2. $E(u/v)$ denotes the neighboring non-subClassOf edges of u with at least one u substituted by v.

Definition 3. We define the *schema closure graph* of a schema graph $G = (V, E)$ to be $G' = (V, E \cup E')$ where

$$E' = \bigcup_{v \in V, u \in A(v)} E(u/v).$$

Example 3. In Table 2, we provide an example schema from the YAGO knowledge base. Its schema graph is shown in Figure 2. In this graph, each type in the domain and range columns is represented as a node, and each row in Table 2 is represented as an edge from domain to range. Since Actor is a subclass of Person, we infer additional edges by having Actor inherit Person's non-subClassOf edges, as shown by dashed arrows in Figure 2. □

Predicate	Domain	Range
livesIn	Person	City
isMarriedTo	Person	Person
worksAt	Person	Organization
directed	Person	Movie
influences	Person	Actor
actedIn	Actor	Movie
subClassOf	Actor	Person

Table 2: Example KB schema from YAGO knowledge base.

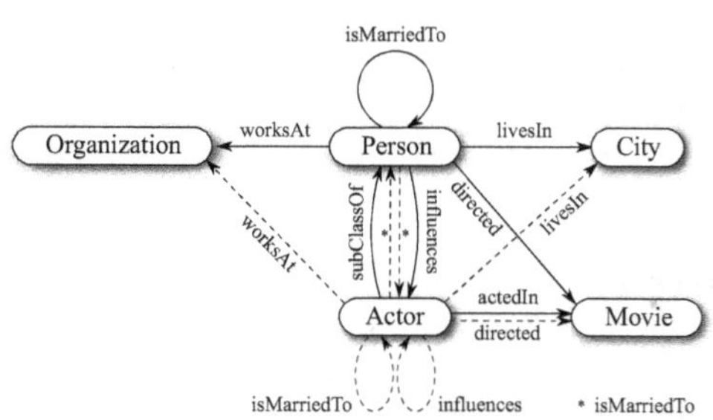

Figure 2: Example schema closure graph. Dashed arrows indicate inherited edges.

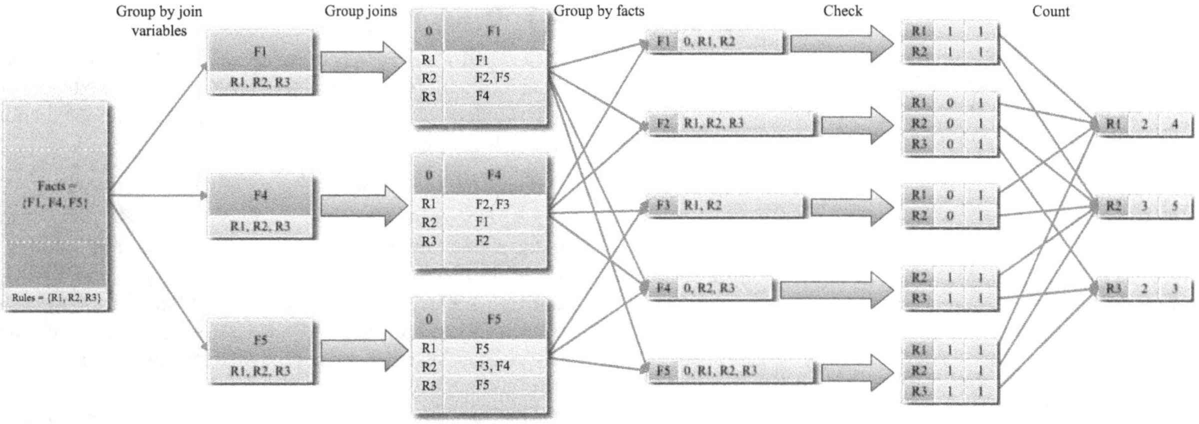

Figure 3: Parallel rule mining: KB divided into groups by join variables, each group running GROUP-JOIN to apply inference rules.

Following Definition 3, Algorithm 2 shows how to compute the closure of a specific node v in a schema graph G by DFS. When visiting a node v, we recursively visit its ancestors (Line 3) and add their neighboring edges to v (Line 4). Visiting each unvisited node in G yields its schema closure graph.

Algorithm 2 Closure($G = (V, E), v$)

```
1: if !v.visited then
2:     for all e_subClassOf(v, u) ∈ E do
3:         Closure(G, u)
4:         E ← E ∪ E(u/v)
5:     v.visited ← True
```

By traversing the closure graph, we identify a syntactically correct rule when we detect a cycle. For instance, Figure 1 (Left) shows three example cycles from Example 3, and Figure 1 (Right) shows the corresponding rules constructed from the cycles. Although we have directed edges in the schema graph, we traverse it in an undirected manner: from any vertex v, we visit its neighbors from both incoming and outgoing edges. R3 shows an example path containing an inherited edge, Actor $\xrightarrow{\text{worksAt}}$ Organization, inherited from Actor's ancestor, Person.

5.2 Parallel Rule Mining

Given the relational knowledge base model in Section 4.2, we store candidate inference rules in tables, allowing us to apply them in batches by joining the rules and facts tables. Furthermore, we design a parallel rule mining algorithm that divides the knowledge base into groups running parallel in-memory group joins. We introduce the algorithm with the following equivalent class of rules:

$$p(x, y) \leftarrow q(x, z), r(y, z).$$

In Section 5.2.1, we generalize it to other rule classes. We present Algorithm 3 using Spark primitives, but we note that it is a general parallel algorithm consisting of basic parallel operations, conforming to the MapReduce paradigm. Figure 3 illustrates how Algorithm 3 transforms datasets using parallel operations.

In Step 1, we map each (s, p, o), i.e., (subject, predicate, object), triple to a pair $(o, (p, s))$, o serving as a key for the GroupByKey operation that follows. In Step 2, the GroupByKey operation groups all $(o, (p, s))$ tuples with the same object o into one group. This ensures the tuples with the same joining variable (o) are in the same group. In addition, we broadcast the rule table to each group to ensure all relevant data are collocated for the joins. Consequently, the groups run disjoint in-memory group-joins, Algorithm 4, and are executed in parallel.

Algorithm 3 Parallel Rule Mining

Require: `facts` = {(`pred`, `sub`, `obj`)}
Require: `rules` = {(`ID`, `head`, `body1`, `body2`)}

1: **`Map`** each fact (`pred`, `sub`, `obj`) ∈ `facts` to (`obj`, (`pred`, `sub`)).
2: **`GroupByKey`** `obj`, yielding a list of {(`pred`, `sub`)} pairs for each `obj`.
3: **`FlatMap`** the (`obj`, {(`pred`, `sub`)}) pairs to GROUP-JOIN(`obj`, {(`pred`, `sub`)}, `rules`), using Algorithm 4, yielding a list of {(`pred`, `sub`, `obj`), `rule.ID`)} pairs.
4: **`ReduceByKey`** (`pred`, `sub`, `obj`), deduplicating the `rule.ID` s for each (`pred`, `sub`, `obj`) triple.
5: **`FlatMap`** the ((`pred`, `sub`, `obj`), {`rule.ID`}) tuples to CHECK({`rule.ID`}), using Algorithm 5, yielding a list of {`rID`, (`correct`, `1`)}pairs.
6: **`ReduceByKey`** `rule.ID`, summing the `correct` and `1` values.
7: **`Map`** each (`rule.ID`, (`sum`, `count`)) to (`rule.ID`, `sum/count`) pairs.

The GROUP-JOIN algorithm is an in-memory hash-join. Since the join variable o is matched by the previous GroupByKey, GROUP-JOIN matches predicates to the rule body. It starts by hashing the input list of (p, s) pairs by predicate p (Line 3), creating a list of subjects for each p. This hash table is used to retrieve joined entities to be output as the subject and object as inferred by the rule. For each rule, its body predicates match two lists of subjects from the hash table. The algorithm infers the rule head with combinations of subjects from the two matched lists (Lines 4-7).

In the GROUP-JOIN algorithm, we output the input facts (Line 2) and the inferred facts (Line 7). Each triple is output as a key, with the value being the positive ID of the rule if it is inferred by that rule, or 0 if it is from the input knowledge base. These IDs are used to verify the inference results: if a fact is associated with an ID of 0, it exists in the input knowledge base; otherwise, it is inferred by inference rules specified by the ID list.

Algorithm 4 GROUP-JOIN(`obj`, `ps` = {`pred`, `sub`}, `rules`)

```
1: for all (pred, sub) ∈ ps do
2:     emit ((pred, sub, obj), 0)
3: preds ← ps.groupBy(pred)
4: for all r ∈ rules do
5:     for all sub1 ∈ preds.get(r.body1) do
6:         for all sub2 ∈ preds.get(r.body2) do
7:             emit ((r.head, sub1, sub2), r.ID)
```

In Step 4, we group by the output facts, each group computing a list of rule IDs that generate the fact. Algorithm 5 processes this list and determines if each rule is generating a correct fact by searching for 0 in the list. It outputs a (ID, (c, 1)) tuple for each rule, where c indicates the correctness of the inferred fact. Thus, the component-wise sum of the (c, 1) tuples for each rule is the number of correct and total facts, respectively, inferred by the rule. Steps 6 and 7 group by the rules, sum the correct and total counts, and compute the confidence of each rule.

Algorithm 5 CHECK(`rs = {rule.ID}`)

```
correct ← rs.contains(0)
for all rule.ID ∈ rs do
    emit(rule.ID, (correct, 1))
```

The correctness of Algorithm 3 follows from the fact that the entire set of rules is broadcast to each group and that the groups are disjoint from each other (recall that they are grouped by key o). Therefore, Step 3 properly applies rules to the facts. In Step 5, Algorithm 5 generates individual correct (0 or 1) and total (1) counts for rules inferring each fact. Since each fact contains the "0" flag to determine its correctness, aggregating the results from all facts generates final correct and total counts for each rule.

5.2.1 General Rule Mining

To generalize Algorithm 3 to other rule classes, we recall from Section 3 that the Horn clauses are assumed to be *connected* and *closed*. Thus, for a general rule with rule ID $\dot{r}$:

$$h(x, y) \leftarrow b_1, b_2, \ldots, b_k,$$

we can arrange the body atoms so that each b_i is connected to b_{i+1}, $i = 1, \ldots, k-1$, and b_k is connected to $h(x, y)$, by a shared variable $\mathbf{z_i}$. The general rule mining algorithm, Algorithm 6, allows $\mathbf{z_i}$ to be vectors and to contain repeated variables.

Algorithm 6 General Rule Mining

```
Require: facts = {(p, x, y)}
Require: rules = {(ṙ, h, b_1, ..., b_k)}
1: j_1 ← facts
2: for all pairs (b_i, b_{i+1}) with shared variable z_i do
3:     j_i ← j_i.GroupByKey(z_i)
4:     f_{i+1} ← facts.GroupByKey(z_i)
5:     if i + 1 < k then
6:         j_{i+1} ← {(z_{i+1}, (ṙ, x_{i+1}))} =
               GROUP-JOIN(j_i, f_{i+1}, rules)
7:     else
8:         j_k ← {((h, x, y), ṙ)} = GROUP-JOIN-LAST(j_i, f_k, rules)
9: Process join result j_k, as in Steps 4-7 of Algorithm 3.
```

Algorithm 6 joins two body atoms at a time. j_i denotes the result of joining $b_1, \ldots, b_i$, and is used as the operand for joining the next rule body, f_{i+1}, in each iteration. The GROUP-JOIN and GROUP-JOIN-LAST methods in Lines 6 and 8 implement the rule semantics. GROUP-JOIN performs the join and outputs the tuples with the next shared variable $\mathbf{z_{i+1}}$ as the key, along with the rule ID, $\dot{r}$, and any variables referred to by the head or subsequent body atoms. GROUP-JOIN-LAST completes the join and infers facts from the rules, generating a list of (fact, rule ID) pairs as in Algorithm 4 to be further processed to evaluate the confidence of each rule, as in Steps 4-7 of Algorithm 3.

As a remark, we note that Algorithm 6 requires the input rules be of the same form. Thus, if there are N equivalent classes (defined in Section 4.2) of rules, we need N rule tables and N calls of Algorithm 6 to complete the mining task. On the other hand, each run of Algorithm 6 is highly efficient and optimized as we apply the rules in batches and in parallel. Thus, our approach trades off between generality and efficiency.

5.3 Rule Pruning

One performance barrier we observe in the candidate rules is that some of them generate prohibitively large intermediate results due to large-degree variables in the joining predicates, as demonstrated by the following example:

$$\text{diedIn}(x, z), \text{wasBornIn}(y, z) \rightarrow \text{hasAcademicAdvisor}(x, y) \quad (4)$$

In the above rule, we have variable z as the joining variable. Meanwhile, in places with large populations, e.g., New York City, the California state, etc, there may be hundreds of thousands of people who were born or dead. Rules like this are untrustworthy, as most of the intermediate results are irrelevant enumerations of the involving arguments (x, y in Rule (4)).

This large join problem is not uncommon among candidate rules as they are constructed from the KB schema with no validation using the facts. Thus, rules can accidentally have irrelevant predicates that coincide with the join variable with a large degree. To detect these rules, we use histograms to determine the functional property of inference rules:

- Predicate Histogram $H^0 = \{(p, |\{p(\cdot, \cdot)\}|)\}$;
- Predicate-Subject Histogram $H^1 = \{(p, x, |\{p(x, \cdot)\}|)\}$;
- Predicate-Object Histogram $H^2 = \{(p, y, |\{p(\cdot, y)\}|)\}$.

In a functional notation, we write $H^0(p) = |\{p(\cdot, \cdot)\}|$, $H^1(p, x) = |\{p(x, \cdot)\}|$, and $H^2(p, y) = |\{p(\cdot, y)\}|$. H^0 is used to compute the size of a KB partition, as explained in Section 6. H^1 and H^2 determine the size of intermediate results. For instance, the size of the join for Rule (4) can be computed by

$$\sum_z H^2(\text{diedIn}, z) \cdot H^2(\text{wasBornIn}, z).$$

In the definition below, we omit the position descriptors (H^1, H^2) and use $H(p, z)$ to denote the histogram entry for predicate p and join variable z in a general rule, the position of z determined by the join under consideration.

Definition 4. For a connected, closed rule r:

$$h \leftarrow b_1, \ldots, b_l,$$

we define the *non-functionality* of r as

$$\text{NF}(r) = \max_{b_i, b_j \text{ connected by } z} \{\min(H(b_i, z), H(b_j, z))\}. \quad (5)$$

A *functional constraint* t accepts rules r with $\text{NF}(r) \leq t$.

According to Definition 4, a functional constraint requires each join, represented by a pair of connected atoms of the rule, have a join variable z with no more than t joined instances as determined by $\min(H(b_i, z), H(b_j, z))$, z ranging over all joined values. We use non-functionality as an empirical indication of rule correctness. Viewing a knowledge graph as a sparse natural graph–e.g., Freebase and YAGO2s has a sparsity of 3.11×10^{-8} and 9.82×10^{-7}, respectively–we justify our approach by the empirical power-law degree distribution of natural graphs that only a few entities in a knowledge graph have a large degree [21], implying that neighbors of large degree entities are unlikely inter-connected with one another as suggested by the non-functional joins.

In our experiment, we observe that violations of functional constraints are strong indications of incorrectness of the rules, and more than 99% of the non-functional rules are wrong. Removing those erroneous rules improves performance and rule quality. By varying the constraint t, we show that a reasonable choice lies between 50 and 250 and set $t = 100$ in the default configuration. We experimentally justify our choice in Section 7.4.

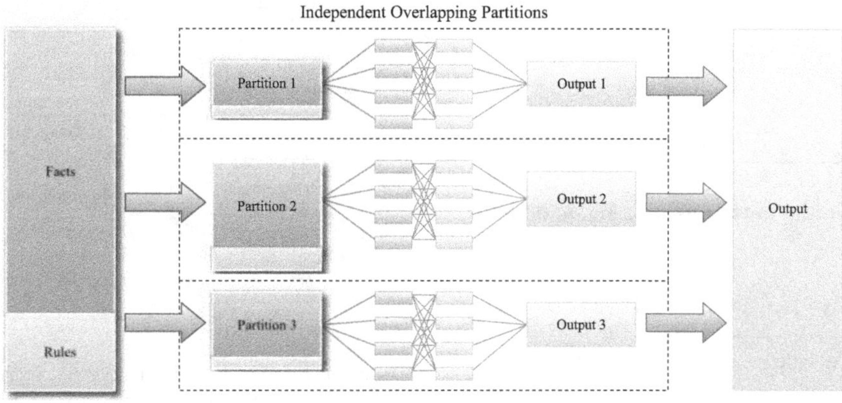

Figure 4: Partitioning algorithm: KB partitioned into smaller overlapping parts running independent mining algorithm instances.

Example 4. As an example, Table 3 shows a histogram from the YAGO2 knowledge base containing the number of people born and died in New York City, London, and Montreal.

wasBornIn	NYC	1287
wasBornIn	London	1584
wasBornIn	Montreal	618
diedIn	NYC	737
diedIn	London	951

Table 3: Histogram for "wasBornIn" and "diedIn".

Using this histogram, we determine the non-functionality of Rule (4) to be 951, the joining variable z being NYC and London. The total number of facts inferred by Rule (4) is $1287 \times 737 + 1584 \times 951 = 2\,454\,903$, 734 times larger than the head predicate hasAcademicAdvisor (H^0(HasAcademicAdvisor) $= 3340$). □

Analysis. To analyze Algorithm 3, we study the size of its intermediate result, which is dominated by joining the rule body. Suppose we have facts tables S, T, rules table M, and a functional constraint t. We denote the histograms by H_S and H_T, the position of the join variable implied by context of the rule. We use $M[\cdot]$, $\hat{M}[\cdot]$ to denote the projection and distinct projection of table M to the specified columns, respectively. The join size is then given by:

$$\begin{aligned}
&\sum_z \sum_{(p,q)\in M[b_1,b_2]} H_S(p,z)\cdot H_T(q,z) \\
\le& t\sum_z \sum_{(p,q)\in M[b_1,b_2]} \max\{H_S(p,z), H_T(q,z)\} \\
\le& t\sum_z \sum_{(p,q)\in M[b_1,b_2]} (H_S(p,z) + H_T(q,z)) \\
=& t\Big(\sum_z \sum_{(p,q)\in M[b_1,b_2]} H_S(p,z) + \sum_z \sum_{(p,q)\in M[b_1,b_2]} H_T(q,z)\Big) \\
\le& t\Big(|M|\sum_z \sum_{p\in \hat{M}[b_1]} H_S(p,z) + |M|\sum_z \sum_{q\in \hat{M}[b_2]} H_T(q,z)\Big) \\
\le& t(|M||S| + |M||T|) \\
=& t|M|(|S|+|T|), \qquad (6)
\end{aligned}$$

where the first inequality follows from Definition 4. Hence, The time complexity of Algorithm 3 is dominated by $O(t|M|(|S| + |T|))$. In case of a self-join, we have $S = T$, and the complexity reduces to $O(t|M||S|)$. More generally, for longer rules, the complexity is $O(t^{l-1}|M||S|)$, where l is the body length of the rule. In practice, as we show in Section 7.4, a reasonable t lies between 50-250. Comparing with a direct join of facts and rules, $O(|M||S|^l)$, we achieve a notable improvement with pruning.

6. PARTITIONING

Even if we parallelize the rule mining algorithm, it still suffers from data shuffling between stages when the knowledge base expands in scale. In this section, we introduce another level of partitioning that divides the KB into a set of independent but possibly overlapping partitions running smaller instances of the rule mining algorithm, as shown in Figure 4.

The partitioning algorithm improves performance by accepting a size constraint and returns partitions that satisfy the constraint. The smaller partitions are more efficiently processed than the entire KB. We begin by introducing the notions of Γ-partition and Γ-size. They allow us to determine the size of a partition. We utilize this information to assign each rule to an appropriate partition.

Definition 5. Denote the predicates in rule $r = p_0 \leftarrow p_1, \ldots, p_l$ by $\Gamma(r) = \{p_0, p_1, \ldots, p_l\}$. We define the *Γ-partition*, with respect to rules $M_i = \{r_1, \ldots, r_m\}$, to be the set of predicates

$$\Gamma(M_i) = \bigcup_{i=1}^{m} \Gamma(r_i).$$

Given an input KB Γ and partitioned rules $M = \{M_1, \ldots, M_k\}$. Let $\Gamma_i = \{p(x,y) \in \Gamma | p \in \Gamma(M_i)\}$ be the partition of facts induced by M_i. Then Γ_i contains all facts we need to evaluate rules $r \in M_i$. Thus, (Γ_i, M_i) defines an *independent* partition of the input KB. Running Algorithm 6 on (Γ_i, M_i) returns the mining results for rules M_i. The size of the partition indicates how long the algorithm runs and can be determined using the predicate histogram H^0 from Section 5.3.

Definition 6. We define the *Γ-size* of a rule set M_i with respect to KB Γ to be

$$\sigma(\Gamma, M_i) = |\Gamma_i| = \sum_{p\in\Gamma(M_i)} H^0(p), \qquad (7)$$

where $H^0 = \{(p, |\{p(\cdot,\cdot)\}|)\}$ is the predicate histogram.

Example 5. Consider the knowledge base Γ and rule table M in Figure 5. M is partitioned into two parts, M_1 and M_2 (initially without the last row, r). According to Definition 5, we have:

$$\Gamma(M_1) = \{P_1, Q_1, R_1, P_2, Q_2, R_2\},$$
$$\Gamma(M_2) = \{P_3, Q_3, R_3, P_4, Q_4, R_4\}.$$

	h	b1	b2
M_1	P_1	Q_1	R_1
	P_2	Q_2	R_2
M_2	P_3	Q_3	R_3
	P_4	Q_4	R_4
r	P_2	Q_3	R_4

M

Figure 5: Rule table M, initial partitions M_1, M_2, and unpartitioned rule r.

Assuming each predicate has 1 fact, namely, $H^0(P_i) = H^0(Q_i) = H^0(R_i) = 1$, we have $\sigma(\Gamma, M_1) = \sigma(\Gamma, M_2) = 6$. Now consider the addition of rule $r = (P_2, Q_3, R_4)$. We have:

$$\Gamma(M_1 \cup \{r\}) = \{P_1, Q_1, R_1, P_2, Q_2, R_2, Q_3, R_4\},$$
$$\Gamma(M_2 \cup \{r\}) = \{P_3, Q_3, R_3, P_4, Q_4, R_4, P_2\}.$$

Consequently, $\sigma(\Gamma, M_1 \cup \{r\}) = 8$, $\sigma(\Gamma, M_2 \cup \{r\}) = 7$. Adding r to M_2 incurs a smaller increase of size than adding it to M_1. □

Given an upper bound of the Γ-size s and the number of rules m for each partition, our goal is to find a partition $\{M_1, \ldots, M_k\}$ of M that satisfies the following constraints:

$$\text{(C1)} \quad \sigma(\Gamma, M_i) \leq s, \quad 1 \leq i \leq k$$
$$\text{(C2)} \quad |M_i| \leq m, \quad 1 \leq i \leq k$$
$$\text{(C3)} \quad \bigcup_{i=1}^{k} M_i = M,$$
$$\text{(C4)} \quad M_i \cap M_j = \varnothing, \quad 1 \leq i < j \leq k$$

We seek to find a partition $\{M_1, \ldots, M_k\}$ with as a small k as possible. Without a priori knowledge of the optimal k, we use a recursive binary partitioning scheme in Algorithm 7. In each recursive step, the input rule set M is partitioned into two smaller parts, M_1 and M_2. The algorithm terminates when all partitions satisfy the size constraints (C1) and (C2). The partitions satisfy the completeness and disjointness constraints (C3) and (C4) at each recursive step as M is partitioned into M_1 and M_2 by Algorithm 8 such that $M_1 \cup M_2 = M$ and $M_1 \cap M_2 = \varnothing$.

Algorithm 7 RecPartition(Γ, Π, M, s, m)

```
1: if σ(Γ, M) ≤ s and |M| ≤ m then
2:    Π ← Π ∪ {M}
3: else
4:    (M1, M2) ← 2-Partition(Γ, M)
5:    if M1 = ∅ then
6:       Π ← Π ∪ {M2}
7:    else if M2 = ∅ then
8:       Π ← Π ∪ {M1}
9:    else
10:      RecPartition(Γ, Π, M1, s, m)
11:      RecPartition(Γ, Π, M2, s, m)
```

Specifically, we first determine whether to partition the input M by checking if it already satisfies the size constraints (C1) and (C2) (Line 1). If it does, we add it to the final set of partitions and return (Line 2); otherwise, we use a binary partitioning algorithm to partition the rules (Line 4) and recursively partition the sub-parts (Lines 10-11). Lines 5-8 handle special cases where the size constraint (C1) cannot be satisfied. This happens when $s < H^0(p)$ for some predicate p. The binary partitioning algorithm is described in Algorithm 8, using a greedy assignment strategy: each rule is assigned to the partition with a smaller increase in size (Lines 4-9). Note that in Lines 4-5, we add a penalty term $p(\Gamma, M)$ to penalize the larger partition, preventing it from absorbing all subsequent

Algorithm 8 2-Partition(Γ, M)

```
1: M1 ← ∅
2: M2 ← ∅
3: for all r ∈ M do
4:    Δ1 ← σ(Γ, M1 ∪ {r}) − σ(Γ, M1) + p(Γ, M1)
5:    Δ2 ← σ(Γ, M2 ∪ {r}) − σ(Γ, M2) + p(Γ, M2)
6:    if Δ1 < Δ2 then
7:       M1 ← M1 ∪ {r}
8:    else
9:       M2 ← M2 ∪ {r}
10: return (M1, M2)
```

rules, as duplicate predicates do not increase the partition size. In our experiments, we set $p(\Gamma, M) = \frac{1}{50}\sigma(\Gamma, M)$.

Analasis. Algorithm 7 makes a best effort to satisfy the size requirement s. If $H^0(p) > s$ for some predicate p, Algorithm 7 returns in Lines 5-8 without partitioning the predicate. Assuming Algorithm 7 results in N partitions $\{M_1, \ldots, M_N\}$, the size of the largest partition being s_m, then the overall time complexity to evaluate the partitioned facts and rules tables, based on (6), is:

$$\sum_{i=1}^{N} O(t^{l-1} s_m |M_i|) = O\left(t^{l-1} s_m \sum_{i=1}^{N} |M_i|\right) = O(t^{l-1} s_m |M|), \tag{8}$$

where t is the functional constraint and l is the length of the rule body as in Section 5.3. The time complexity is bounded with respect to the largest partition instead of the input knowledge base. Thus, partitioning reduces time complexity from $O(t^{l-1}|\Gamma||M|)$ to $O(t^{l-1} s_m |M|)$, allowing us to control the complexity by tuning the size constraints for very large knowledge bases.

Since Γ-partitions are induced from partitions of inference rules (Definition 5) and rules from different partitions may contain duplicate head or body predicates, the Γ-partitions may overlap, as illustrated by the addition of rule r in Example 5. To measure this overlap, we introduce the notion of *degree of overlap*.

Definition 7. The *degree of overlap* (DOV) of a set of rule parts $M = \{M_1, M_2, \ldots, M_k\}$ is defined to be

$$\text{DOV}(M) = \frac{\sum_i \sigma(\Gamma, M_i)}{\sigma\left(\Gamma, \bigcup_i \Gamma(M_i)\right)}. \tag{9}$$

In Equation (9), the numerator $\sum_i \sigma(\Gamma, M_i)$ is the total size of the partitions we make to evaluate the inference rules. The denominator $\sigma\left(\Gamma, \bigcup_i \Gamma(M_i)\right)$ is the size of the KB induced by rules M. A DOV greater than 1 indicates overlapping partitions.

Example 6. Consider the partitioning scheme from Example 5. While the initial partitions M_1 and M_2 are disjoint, adding r to M_1 or M_2 results in overlapping partitions:

$$\text{DOV}(\{M_1, M_2\}) = \frac{6+6}{12} = 1;$$
$$\text{DOV}(\{M_1, M_2 \cup \{r\}\}) = \frac{6+7}{12} = 1.0833;$$
$$\text{DOV}(\{M_1 \cup \{r\}, M_2\}) = \frac{8+6}{12} = 1.1667. \quad □$$

Partition Independence. We conclude this section by remarking the difference between partitioning in Algorithm 7 and parallelization in Algorithm 3. Algorithm 7 breaks the input knowledge base into smaller independent partitions so that each partition runs its own instance of Algorithm 3. Algorithm 3 divides the input knowledge base into correlated groups running sub-procedures of a single mining task. Algorithm 3 is used by Algorithm 7 as the parallel mining algorithm in each partition. The two-level partitioning-parallelization scheme is elucidated in Figure 4. These techniques combined scale the rule mining algorithm to Freebase.

7. EXPERIMENTS

We validate our approaches by mining inference rules from YAGO and Freebase. Our work contributes the first rule set for Freebase–36,625 first-order inference rules. In this section, we present our results, compare with the state-of-the-art KB rule mining algorithm, AMIE [21], and analyze individual techniques from Sections 5 and 6. We begin by describing the datasets and experiment setup.

YAGO. YAGO is a knowledge base derived from Wikipedia, WordNet, and GeoNames. Its newest version, YAGO2s, has more than 10M entities and 120M facts, including the schema, taxonomy, core facts, etc. We use the schema for rule construction and the core 4.48M binary facts for rule evaluation.

Freebase. Freebase is a community-curated knowledge base of well-known people, places, and things, containing 112M entities and 2.68B facts, as of current writing. We preprocess the dataset by removing the multi-language support and use the remaining 388M facts. The datasets statistics are summarized in Table 4 (Left).

KB	Size
YAGO2	# Entities = 834,554 # Facts = 948,047
YAGO2s	# Entities = 2,137,468 # Facts = 4,484,907
Freebase	# Entities = 111,781,246 # Facts = 388,474,630

Max length	3
Max Γ-size	3M (YAGO) 10M (Freebase)
Max # of rules	1000
Functional constraint	100
Min support	0
Min confidence	0.0

Table 4: (Left) Datasets statistics. (Right) Default parameters.

Experiment setup. We conduct all experiments on a 64-core machine running on AMD Opteron processors at 1.4GHz, with 512GB RAM and 3.1TB disk space. The OP and AMIE algorithms are implemented in Spark and Java/SQL, respectively, running on Spark 1.3.0, Java 1.8, and PostgreSQL 9.2.3.

Default parameters. Unless otherwise specified or the current parameter is under evaluation, we use the default parameters in Table 4 (Right) for the experiments. We determine the parameters by trying multiple parameter combinations and comparing the performance and result rules. For Freebase experiments in Sections 7.2 to 7.4, we report the result of one class of length 3 rules.

Rule set precision. We evaluate a rule set by assessing its most confident rules, i.e., with a minimum confidence of 0.6 and supporting at least 2 facts. Under this constraint, we define the *precision* of a rule set as the percentage of rules satisfying the above threshold that we consider correct. Each rule is rated by two independent human judges. In case of a disagreement, the judges conduct a detailed discussion until a final decision is made. We sample at most 300 rules from each rule set for human inspection.

7.1 Overall Result

To evaluate performance of the OP algorithm and compare with the state-of-the-art, we run the OP and AMIE algorithms on Freebase and YAGO. As a result, OP mines 36,625 rules in 33.22 hours from Freebase, contributing the largest first-order rules repository created from public knowledge bases. We compare the detail performance metrics, including the number and precision of mined rules, and the runtime for each knowledge base, in Table 5.

In terms of efficiency and scalability, OP outperforms AMIE in all the experiments we run. For Freebase, AMIE takes more than 5 days to generate a single rule (AMIE outputs an inference rule once it has determined its quality), whereas OP finishes in 33.22 hours. For the smaller YAGO2s KB, AMIE mines 278 rules in 5 days while OP mines 312 rules in 19.40 minutes. For YAGO2, due to its small size, partitioning and parallelization have limited advantage, so OP is only 0.97 minutes faster. The quantity of mined rules is large: 36,625 first-order rules from Freebase, spanning a variety of topics: film, book, music, computer, etc, as shown in Figures 6 and 11(3). OP mines fewer rules from YAGO2 and YAGO2s because their sizes are much smaller, and their schemas are incomplete. Possible domain and range values are missing from overloaded predicates, so the rule construction algorithm generates a subset of all possible rules from the available schema. Using a more accurate schema, e.g., the Freebase schema, improves recall.

Dataset	Algorithm	# Rules	Precision	Runtime
YAGO2	OP AMIE	218 1090	0.35 0.46	3.59 min 4.56 min
YAGO2s	OP AMIE	312 278+	0.35 N/A	19.40 min 5+ d
Freebase	OP AMIE	36,625 0+	0.60 N/A	33.22 h 5+ d

Table 5: Overall mining result.

In terms of precision, Freebase rules achieve 0.60, outperforming YAGO rules by more than 0.1. The precision benefits from Freebase's cleaner data and schema. To illustrate, consider Rule (1) in Figure 6 with predicates "film/film/sequel" and "film/film/-country". These predicates impose precise constraints on the data: "sequel" refers to the sequel of a film, and "country" refers to the producing country of a film. Such constraints ensure that Freebase predicates contain fine-grained and accurate data instances. On the other hand, because 1) YAGO has fewer predicates, and 2) YAGO predicates are less well-defined, YAGO generates fewer rules with lower quality. Consider the "create" predicate from YAGO2s: the domain is possibly writer, musician, filmmaker, author, etc, and the range can be book, music, film, novel, etc. Thus, "create" can be combined with any matching predicates to form candidate rules, leading to spurious results. The rule "created(x, z), created$(y, z) \rightarrow$ isMarriedTo(x, y)" illustrates this situation. Other predicates, like "playsFor", "owns", "influences", are similarly misused.

Figures 7(a)(b) report OP's performance for one class of rules of each length from 2 to 5. We mine 1,006 and 83,163 for YAGO2s (lengths 4 and 5) and Freebase (length 4) in 8.62 and 82.77 hours, respectively. For rule construction, because the schema is much smaller than the knowledge base, it takes 13.64 and 0.94 minutes for YAGO2s and Freebase, accounting for less than 3% of the runtime. The construction process for YAGO2s is slower than for Freebase since its predicates are heavily overloaded, as we discuss above, resulting in expensive joins, especially for long rules.

Analyzing the rules, we observe that 90.3% of them reduce to lengths 2 and 3 rules, as shown in Figure 7(c). We classify these rules as trivial extensions and composite rules. We call a rule *trivial extension* of another rule if it can be reduced to the other rule by applying and removing any valid rules from its body. In Figure 6, Rule (4) is a trivial extension of Rule (3) since the rule book/book/first_edition$(x, u) \rightarrow$ book/book_edition/book(u, x) infers that $v = x$ in (4). By replacing v with x and removing the applied rule, it reduces to (3). We call a rule *composite* if it can be rewritten by chaining shorter rules. For instance, Rule (5) in Figure 6 is a composite rule of (1) and (2). Rule (6) gives an example of correct and irreducible length 4 rule.

	Confidence	Rule
(1)	0.81	film/film/sequel(x, z), film/film/country(z, y) $\rightarrow$ film/film/country(x, y)
(2)	0.44	film/film/country(x, z), location/country/official_language(z, y) $\rightarrow$ film/film/language(x, y)
(3)	1.0	book/book/first_edition(x, y) $\rightarrow$ book/book/editions(x, y)
(4)	1.0	book/book/first_edition(x, u), book/book_edition/book(u, v), book/book/first_edition(v, y) $\rightarrow$ book/book/editions(x, y)
(5)	0.41	film/film/sequel(x, u), film/film/country(u, v), location/country/official_language(v, y) $\rightarrow$ film/film/language(x, y)
(6)	0.89	music/music_video/music_video_song(x, u), music/composition/recorded_as_album(u, v), music/album/artist(v, y) $\rightarrow$ music/music_video/artist(x, y)

Figure 6: Example Freebase rules.

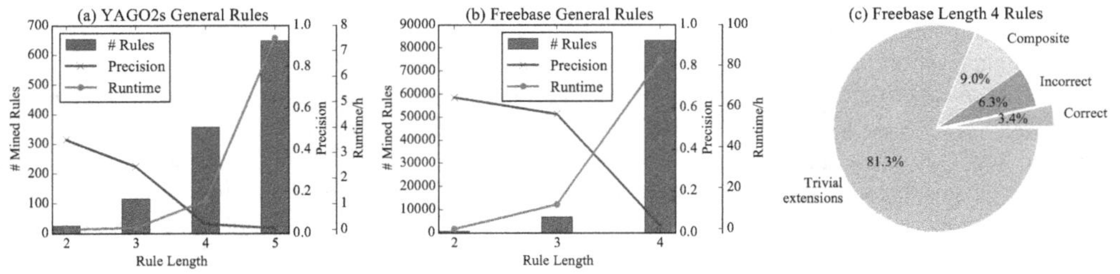

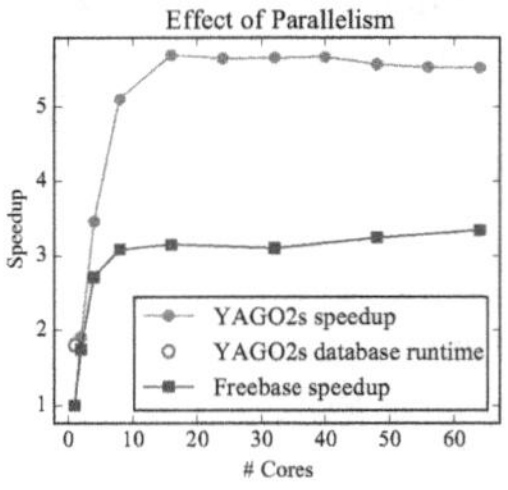

Figure 7: (a)(b) OP performance for mining lengths 4 (YAGO and Freebase) and 5 (YAGO) rules. (c) Quality of Freebase length 4 rules.

Figure 8: Effect of parallelism.

The trivial extensions and composite rules provide little knowledge in addition to lengths 2 and 3 rules. Thus, their distribution in Figure 7(c) implies limited benefits from mining longer rules. We remove those rules and evaluate the remaining rules as we do with length 2 and 3 rules. As a result, the precision is much lower than the lengths 2 and 3 rules: 0.04 for YAGO2s and 0.03 for Freebase, as reported in Figure 7. These results suggest the primary and foundational importance of shorter rules in a knowledge base. We therefore limit the maximum length to 3 in the default setting.

In summary, the overall results justify the benefits of OP algorithm to mine web-scale knowledge bases. In the remainder of this section, we examine individual techniques of parallelism, partitioning, and rule pruning in greater details and show how they improve the performance and quality of the rule mining task.

7.2 Effect of Parallelism

We evaluate the effect of parallelism by comparing the parallel mining algorithm with a SQL implementation on PostgreSQL. We vary the number of cores for parallel mining from 1 to 64 and report in Figure 8 the relative speedup compared to running on 1 core. As a result, the parallel mining algorithm achieves a speedup of 5.70 and 3.34 on YAGO2s and Freebase, respectively. Comparing with the SQL approach, parallel mining achieves a speedup of 3.16 on YAGO2s and a much higher speedup on Freebase–the SQL queries do not scale to Freebase in the experiments on PostgreSQL and on an in-house parallel database system, Datapath [3]. The speedup results from 1) the SQL query performs one large join while Algorithm 3 runs smaller joins in parallel; 2) the shuffling step in Spark is more efficient than the deduplication operation in PostgresSQL given a large output from previous joins.

These results attest to the overall advantage of parallelizing the rule mining algorithm. Nonetheless, we see the parallelization does not make full use of available 64 processors, because the output sizes and performance of GROUP-JOINs vary greatly among groups, depending on the data distribution, and is dominated by the slowest joins among the groups. Moreover, the efficiency of the shuffling step is restricted by data dependency among parallel workers.

7.3 Effect of Partitioning

Partitioning is a key step in scaling up the mining algorithm. By setting a maximum Γ-size s and number of rules m, the partitioning algorithm breaks the input knowledge base into parts with no larger than the specified size. Our experiments show the OP algorithm completes the Freebase mining task in 1.39 days with partitioning, which otherwise takes more than 5 days with no success.

The result of Freebase partitioning is illustrated in Figure 9: in the left figure, we set $s = $ 20M and $m = $ 2K; in the right figure, we set $s = $ 200M and $m = $ 10K. For the former case, we have 65 partitions, all running faster than partitions from the latter case, with the fastest partition finishing in 14.18 seconds and the slowest in 1.17 hours. For the latter case, we have 5 large partitions, the fastest taking 4.58 hours to finish and the slowest taking 1.27 days.

The effect of choosing different partition sizes is shown in Figures 10(a)-(c) for Freebase and Figure 10(d) for YAGO2s. In the Freebase experiments, the effect of partitioning is substantial: as we vary s from 200M to 5M and m from 10K to 1K, the total runtime decreases from 2.55 days to 5.06 hours. The reason for such speedup is because the partitioning algorithm manages to split the input knowledge base into smaller ones that are more efficiently joined, and the overhead of the overlap is less significant as the benefit from joining smaller tables. This benefit can be further verified by the decline of runtime of the largest partitions from 1.27 days to 38.14 minutes as we lower the size constraints, as shown in Figure 10(b), indicating that the partitions are more efficiently joined because of their smaller sizes. Consequently, the overall runtime significantly drops despite partition overlaps.

In Figure 10(c), we show the DOV increases from 1.14 to 1.35 as we create smaller partitions. The increasing DOV means we spend more time partitioning Freebase: from 2.45 minutes to 61.43 minutes. Comparing with Figure 10(a), we see the reduction from joining smaller partitions has greater impact on the total runtime.

On the other hand, if s and m become too small, the overhead of overlapping partitions begins to dominate. The overlapping effect is shown in Figure 10(d) as we partition the 4.48M YAGO2s into smaller parts: while we improve the runtime of the slowest partition from 5.80 minutes to 1.79 minutes, the total runtime rises to 29.60 minutes after hitting the optimum of 19.40 minutes when $s = $ 3M and $m = 500$. The fall of performance is caused by the growing number of overlapping partitions. The extreme case of applying one rule at a time, taken by state-of-the-art approaches, is equivalent to having one rule in each partition. Given a large search space of candidate rules, it implies a large number of queries, hence too much overlapping overhead for it to be efficient.

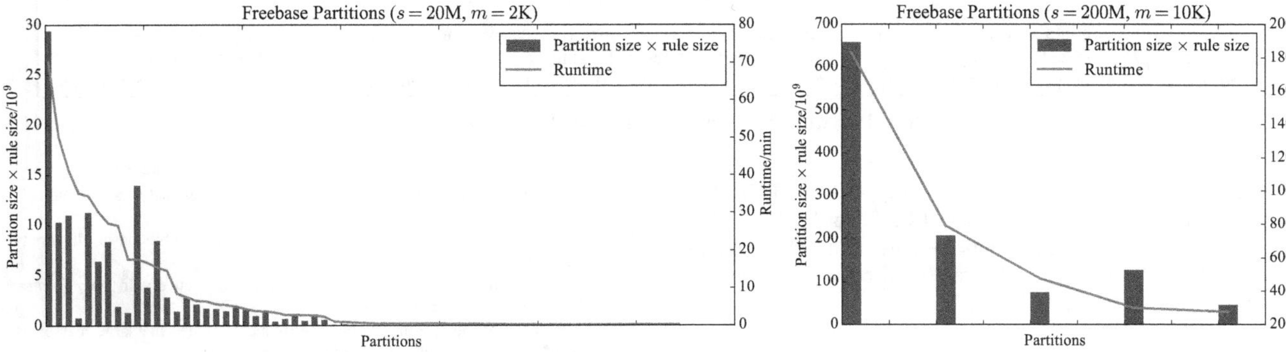

Figure 9: Sizes and runtime of Freebase partitions.

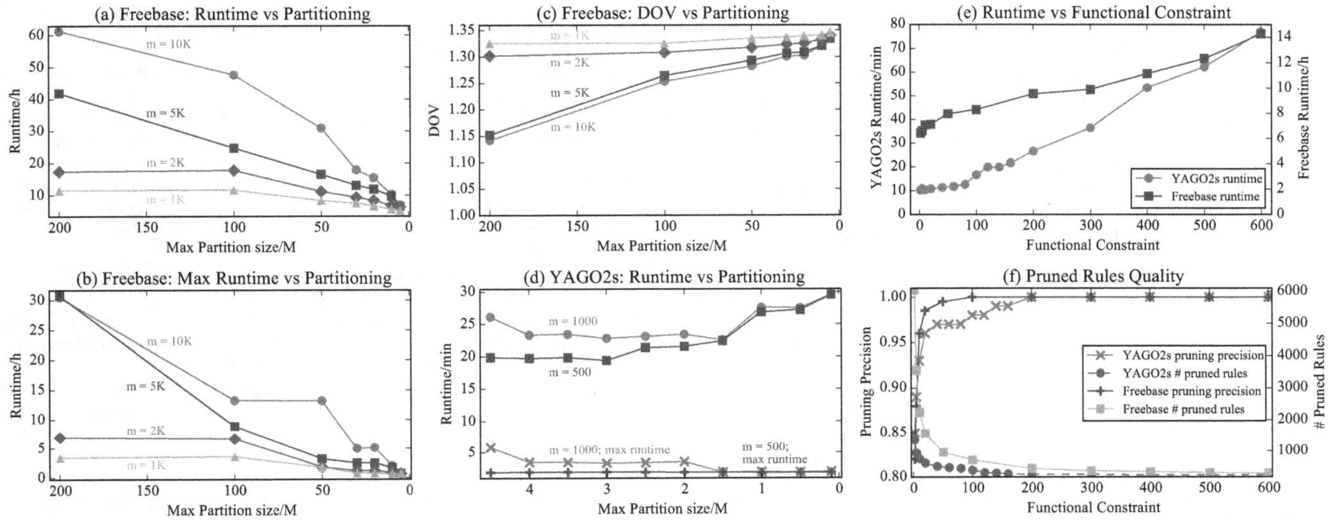

Figure 10: (a)-(d) Runtime by varying partition sizes. (e)-(f) Runtime and accuracy by varying functional constraints.

7.4 Effect of Rule Pruning

The functional constraint t affects the mining algorithm in terms of both performance and quality. To evaluate the accuracy, we define the *pruning precision* of pruned rules as the percentage of those rules that we consider erroneous. Thus, a high pruning precision indicates that erroneous rules are pruned as desired and justifies the proposed approach. As we vary the functional constraint t and prune violating rules, we report the runtime, number and pruning precision of pruned rules in Figures 10(e)(f).

We make two observations from Figures 10(e)(f): (1) When $t \geq 200$, the pruning precision reaches its maximum value of 1.0–all pruned rules are erroneous. However, the runtime grows from 9.55 hours to 14.27 hours, indicating wasted computation in evaluating wrong rules that should otherwise be eliminated by setting a smaller t. (2) On the other hand, decreasing t from 50 to 2 causes the pruning precision to drop sharply from 0.995 to 0.82 while improving runtime only by 1.54 hours from 7.97 to 6.43 hours.

From the above observations, we see the rule pruning process improves both performance and quality provided we choose a proper t constraint. Based on Figure 10(f), a value between 50 and 250 is reasonable. In our default setting, we have $t = 100$ and detect 101 and 2352 non-functional rules from YAGO2s and Freebase, respectively. For Freebase, more than 99% rules are correctly pruned. Rules (1) and (2) from Freebase in Figure 11 illustrate the common reason why functional constraints are violated: in Freebase and other knowledge bases, we have many-one, many-few, and many-many predicates. The "location/location/containedBy" predicate in Rule (1), for example, is a many-few predicate. The rule construction algorithm, based on the KB schema, is unaware of the functionality properties of the predicates. When the *one* or *few* variable happens to be the join variable, the rule violates the functional constraint. Rule (3) is an incorrectly pruned rule due to a low $t = 5$ functional constraint. The "computer/computer_processor/variants" predicate defines an equivalence relation: variants of a computer processor are variants of each other. According to the sparsity of natural graphs [21], we reduce pruning errors by raising the functional constraint t.

8. CONCLUSION

In this paper, we address the scalable first-order rule mining problem. We present the Ontological Pathfinding algorithm to mine first-order inference rules from web-scale knowledge bases. We achieve the Freebase scale via a series of parallelization and optimization techniques: a relational knowledge base model that applies inference rules in batches, a rule mining algorithm that parallelizes the join queries, a novel partitioning algorithm that divides the mining task into smaller independent sub-tasks, and a rule pruning strategy to detect incorrect and resource-consuming rules. Combining these techniques, we mine the first rule set for Freebase, the largest public knowledge base with 388 million facts and 112 million entities, in 34 hours. No existing system achieves this scale. We publish our code and data repositories online.

	Rule
(1)	location/location/containedby(x, z), location/location/contains(z, y) $\rightarrow$ location/location/contains_major_portion_of(x, y)
(2)	engineering/engine_category/engines(z, x), engineering/engine_category/engines(z, y) $\rightarrow$ engineering/engine/variants(x, y)
(3)	computer/computer_processor/variants(x, z), computer/computer_processor/variants(y, z) $\rightarrow$ computer/computer_processor/variants(x, y)

Figure 11: Example rules violating functional constraints.

Acknowledgements. This work is partially supported by NSF IIS Award # 1526753, DARPA under FA8750-12-2-0348-2 (DEFT/CU-BISM), and a generous gift from Google. We also thank Dr. Milenko Petrovic and Dr. Alin Dobra for the helpful discussions on query optimization.

9. REFERENCES

[1] R. Agrawal, T. Imieliński, and A. Swami. Mining association rules between sets of items in large databases. In *ACM SIGMOD Record*, 1993.

[2] R. Agrawal, R. Srikant, et al. Fast algorithms for mining association rules. In *Proceedings of the VLDB Endowment*, 1994.

[3] S. Arumugam, A. Dobra, C. M. Jermaine, N. Pansare, and L. Perez. The datapath system: a data-centric analytic processing engine for large data warehouses. In *SIGMOD*. ACM, 2010.

[4] S. Auer, C. Bizer, G. Kobilarov, J. Lehmann, R. Cyganiak, and Z. Ives. *Dbpedia: A nucleus for a web of open data*. Springer, 2007.

[5] M. Banko, M. J. Cafarella, S. Soderland, M. Broadhead, and O. Etzioni. Open information extraction for the web. In *IJCAI*, 2007.

[6] J. Biega, E. Kuzey, and F. M. Suchanek. Inside yago2s: a transparent information extraction architecture. In *WWW*, 2013.

[7] G. O. Blog. Introducing the knowledge graph: thing, not strings. http://googleblog.blogspot.com/2012/05/introducing-knowledge-graph-things-not.html.

[8] K. Bollacker, C. Evans, P. Paritosh, T. Sturge, and J. Taylor. Freebase: a collaboratively created graph database for structuring human knowledge. In *SIGMOD*. ACM, 2008.

[9] A. Carlson, J. Betteridge, B. Kisiel, B. Settles, E. R. Hruschka Jr, and T. M. Mitchell. Toward an architecture for never-ending language learning. In *AAAI*, volume 5, page 3, 2010.

[10] A. Carlson, J. Betteridge, R. C. Wang, E. R. Hruschka Jr, and T. M. Mitchell. Coupled semi-supervised learning for information extraction. In *Proceedings of WSCM*, 2010.

[11] C. Chambers, A. Raniwala, F. Perry, S. Adams, R. R. Henry, R. Bradshaw, and N. Weizenbaum. Flumejava: easy, efficient data-parallel pipelines. In *ACM Sigplan Notices*, volume 45, pages 363–375. ACM, 2010.

[12] Y. Chen and D. Z. Wang. Knowledge expansion over probabilistic knowledge bases. In *SIGMOD Conference*, pages 649–660, 2014.

[13] Y. Cheng, C. Qin, and F. Rusu. Glade: big data analytics made easy. In *SIGMOD*, 2012.

[14] P. Clark, J. Thompson, and B. Porter. A knowledge-based approach to question-answering. In *In the AAAI Fall Symposium on Question-Answering Systems, AAAI*, 1999.

[15] J. Dean and S. Ghemawat. Mapreduce: simplified data processing on large clusters. *Communications of the ACM*, 51(1):107–113, 2008.

[16] X. Dong, E. Gabrilovich, G. Heitz, W. Horn, N. Lao, K. Murphy, T. Strohmann, S. Sun, and W. Zhang. Knowledge vault: A web-scale approach to probabilistic knowledge fusion. In *SIGKDD*, 2014.

[17] M. Elseidy, E. Abdelhamid, S. Skiadopoulos, and P. Kalnis. Grami: Frequent subgraph and pattern mining in a single large graph. *Proceedings of the VLDB Endowment*, 2014.

[18] O. Etzioni, A. Fader, J. Christensen, S. Soderland, and M. Mausam. Open information extraction: The second generation. In *IJCAI*, 2011.

[19] A. Fader, S. Soderland, and O. Etzioni. Identifying relations for open information extraction. In *EMNLP*, 2011.

[20] L. A. Galárraga, C. Teflioudi, K. Hose, and F. Suchanek. Amie: association rule mining under incomplete evidence in ontological knowledge bases. In *Proceedings of the 22nd international conference on World Wide Web*, 2013.

[21] J. E. Gonzalez, Y. Low, H. Gu, D. Bickson, and C. Guestrin. Powergraph: Distributed graph-parallel computation on natural graphs. In *OSDI*, 2012.

[22] J. Han and J. Pei. Mining frequent patterns by pattern-growth: methodology and implications. *ACM SIGKDD explorations newsletter*, 2000.

[23] J. M. Hellerstein, C. Ré, F. Schoppmann, D. Z. Wang, E. Fratkin, A. Gorajek, K. S. Ng, C. Welton, X. Feng, K. Li, et al. The madlib analytics library: or mad skills, the sql. *VLDB*, 2012.

[24] J. Hoffart, F. M. Suchanek, K. Berberich, and G. Weikum. Yago2: a spatially and temporally enhanced knowledge base from wikipedia. *Artificial Intelligence*, 194:28–61, 2013.

[25] A. Horn. On sentences which are true of direct unions of algebras. *The Journal of Symbolic Logic*, 1951.

[26] T. N. Huynh. Discriminative learning with markov logic networks. Technical report, DTIC Document, 2009.

[27] S. Kok. *Structure Learning in Markov Logic Networks*. PhD thesis, University of Washington, 2010.

[28] M. Kuramochi and G. Karypis. Frequent subgraph discovery. In *Data Mining, 2001. ICDM 2001*. IEEE, 2001.

[29] M. Kuramochi and G. Karypis. Finding frequent patterns in a large sparse graph*. *Data mining and knowledge discovery*, 2005.

[30] N. Lao, T. Mitchell, and W. W. Cohen. Random walk inference and learning in a large scale knowledge base. In *Proceedings of EMNLP*, 2011.

[31] K. Li, D. Z. Wang, A. Dobra, and C. Dudley. Uda-gist: an in-database framework to unify data-parallel and state-parallel analytics. *Proceedings of the VLDB Endowment*, 2015.

[32] T. Lin, O. Etzioni, et al. Identifying functional relations in web text. In *EMNLP*, 2010.

[33] Y. Low, D. Bickson, J. Gonzalez, C. Guestrin, A. Kyrola, and J. M. Hellerstein. Distributed graphlab: a framework for machine learning and data mining in the cloud. *VLDB*, 2012.

[34] Y. Low, J. Gonzalez, A. Kyrola, D. Bickson, C. Guestrin, and J. M. Hellerstein. Graphlab: A new parallel framework for machine learning. In *UAI*, July 2010.

[35] F. Mahdisoltani, J. Biega, and F. Suchanek. Yago3: A knowledge base from multilingual wikipedias. In *CIDR*, 2015.

[36] S. Muggleton. Inductive logic programming: derivations, successes and shortcomings. *ACM SIGART Bulletin*, 1994.

[37] S. Muggleton. Inverse entailment and progol. *New generation computing*, 1995.

[38] F. Niu, C. Ré, A. Doan, and J. Shavlik. Tuffy: Scaling up statistical inference in markov logic networks using an rdbms. *VLDB*, 2011.

[39] F. Niu, C. Zhang, C. Ré, and J. W. Shavlik. Deepdive: Web-scale knowledge-base construction using statistical learning and inference. In *VLDS*, pages 25–28, 2012.

[40] J. S. Park, M.-S. Chen, and P. S. Yu. An effective hash-based algorithm for mining association rules. *SIGMOD Record*, 1995.

[41] J. R. Quinlan. Learning logical definitions from relations. *Machine learning*, 5(3):239–266, 1990.

[42] B. L. Richards and R. J. Mooney. Learning relations by pathfinding. In *Proc. of AAAI-92*, 1992.

[43] M. Richardson and P. Domingos. Markov logic networks. *Machine learning*, 62(1-2):107–136, 2006.

[44] A. Ritter, D. Downey, S. Soderland, and O. Etzioni. It's a contradiction—no, it's not: a case study using functional relations. In *EMNLP*, 2008.

[45] A. Savasere, E. Omiecinski, and S. B. Navathe. An efficient algorithm for mining association rules in large databases. In *Proceedings of the VLDB Endowment*, 1995.

[46] S. Schoenmackers, O. Etzioni, and D. S. Weld. Scaling textual inference to the web. In *Proceedings of the Conference on Empirical Methods in Natural Language Processing*, 2008.

[47] S. Schoenmackers, O. Etzioni, D. S. Weld, and J. Davis. Learning first-order horn clauses from web text. In *Proceedings of the 2010 Conference on Empirical Methods in Natural Language Processing*, 2010.

[48] J. Shin, S. Wu, F. Wang, C. De Sa, C. Zhang, and C. Ré. Incremental knowledge base construction using deepdive. *Proceedings of the VLDB Endowment*, 2015.

[49] B. Tausend. Representing biases for inductive logic programming. In *Machine Learning: ECML-94*. Springer, 1994.

[50] D. Z. Wang, Y. Chen, C. Grant, and K. Li. Efficient in-database analytics with graphical models. *IEEE Data Engineering Bulletin*, 2014.

[51] D. Z. Wang, M. J. Franklin, M. Garofalakis, J. M. Hellerstein, and M. L. Wick. Hybrid in-database inference for declarative information extraction. In *SIGMOD*, 2011.

[52] D. Wijaya, P. P. Talukdar, and T. Mitchell. Pidgin: ontology alignment using web text as interlingua. In *CIKM*, 2013.

[53] W. Wu, H. Li, H. Wang, and K. Q. Zhu. Probase: A probabilistic taxonomy for text understanding. In *SIGMOD*. ACM, 2012.

[54] M. Zaharia, M. Chowdhury, T. Das, A. Dave, J. Ma, M. McCauley, M. J. Franklin, S. Shenker, and I. Stoica. Resilient distributed datasets: A fault-tolerant abstraction for in-memory cluster computing. In *NSDI*. USENIX Association, 2012.

[55] M. Zaharia, M. Chowdhury, M. J. Franklin, S. Shenker, and I. Stoica. Spark: cluster computing with working sets. In *Proceedings of the 2nd USENIX conference on Hot topics in cloud computing*, pages 10–10, 2010.

[56] L. Zou, L. Chen, and M. T. Özsu. Distance-join: Pattern match query in a large graph database. *Proceedings of VLDB*, 2009.

Extracting Databases from Dark Data with DeepDive

Ce Zhang, Jaeho Shin, Christopher Ré
Stanford University
Palo Alto, CA
{czhang,jaeho,chrismre}@cs.stanford.edu

Michael Cafarella
University of Michigan
Ann Arbor, MI
michjc@umich.edu

Feng Niu
Lattice Data, Inc.
Palo Alto, CA
feng.niu@lattice.io

ABSTRACT

DEEPDIVE is a system for extracting relational databases from *dark data*: the mass of text, tables, and images that are widely collected and stored but which cannot be exploited by standard relational tools. If the information in dark data — scientific papers, Web classified ads, customer service notes, and so on — were instead in a relational database, it would give analysts a massive and valuable new set of "big data."

DEEPDIVE is distinctive when compared to previous information extraction systems in its ability to obtain very high precision and recall at reasonable engineering cost; in a number of applications, we have used DEEPDIVE to create databases with accuracy that meets that of human annotators. To date we have successfully deployed DEEPDIVE to create data-centric applications for insurance, materials science, genomics, paleontologists, law enforcement, and others. The data unlocked by DEEPDIVE represents a massive opportunity for industry, government, and scientific researchers.

DEEPDIVE is enabled by an unusual design that combines large-scale probabilistic inference with a novel developer interaction cycle. This design is enabled by several core innovations around probabilistic training and inference.

1. INTRODUCTION

DEEPDIVE is a system for extracting structured data from unstructured *dark data.* Dark data is the mass of text, tables, and images that is collected and stored but which cannot be queried using traditional relational database tools. Consider the set of text notes about insurance claims, or scientific papers, or internet classified ads; these different sources contain valuable information that is not in a relational format, but in principle should be amenable to analysis by relational tools. Currently, organizations pay the cost of collecting and maintaining dark data, but cannot exploit it. DEEPDIVE consumes dark data and populates a relational database that can be used with standard data management tools, such as OLAP query processors, visualization software like Tableau, and analytical tools such as R or Excel.

SIGMOD'16, June 26-July 01, 2016, San Francisco, CA, USA

ISBN 978-1-4503-3531-7/16/06...$15.00

DOI: http://dx.doi.org/10.1145/2882903.2904442

Dark data often holds information that is not available in any other format. For example, an insurance company's claim notes resemble a small blog dedicated to a single claim, with entries authored by many different individuals. They will contain service representatives' notes from customer interactions, bills from doctors who treat claimants, reports from car repair shops, and so on. Simple claims might have a single text note, but more complicated claims might have hundreds. If this information were in a relational database instead of text, it would be possible to use simple SQL queries to answer a range of useful questions, including:

- Which doctors were responsible for the most claims?
- Is the distribution of injury types changing over time?
- Do certain inspectors yield larger claims than others?

Because success in analytical tasks is often limited by the data available [18], the information embedded in dark data can be massively valuable. In some cases, the data is so valuable that institutions have hired human beings to manually read documents and populate a relational database by hand [37]. However, this practice is expensive, incredibly slow, and surprisingly error-prone.

DEEPDIVE can extract structured databases from dark data accurately and vastly more quickly than human beings. Of course, information extraction has been an area of active academic investigation since at least the early 1990s [1]. DEEPDIVE is distinctive because of its ability to produce databases of extremely high accuracy with reasonable amounts of human engineering effort. In a remarkable range of applications, DEEPDIVE has been able to obtain data with precision that meets or beats that of human annotators. DEEPDIVE's high quality is possible because of a unique design based around probabilistic inference and a specialized engineering development cycle; they are underpinned by several technical innovations for efficient statistical training and sampling.

DEEPDIVE is an open source project that has been under development since 2011. We have used it to extract high-quality information in a number of disparate areas, including genomics, insurance, Web classified ads, materials science, paleontology, and others. We believe that creating and exploiting extracted information from dark data (nowadays often sitting around in rapidly-growing data lakes) represents a massive opportunity for academia, industry, and government. We have deployed many of these extracted datasets to domain-specific users and have been gratified to see the information enable novel and remarkable domain-specific results.

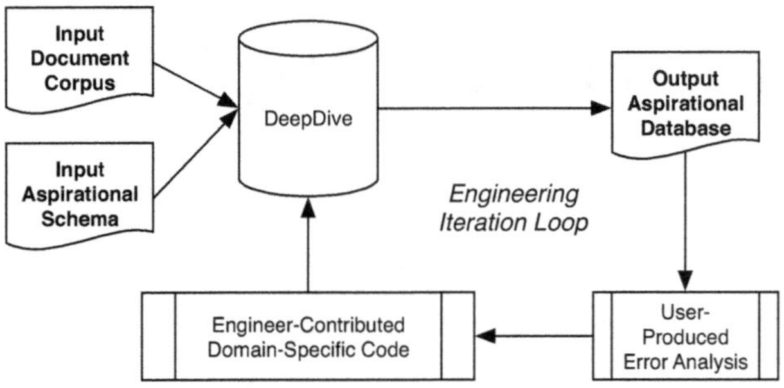

Figure 1: The typical DEEPDIVE user interaction cycle. A knowledge engineer runs DEEPDIVE to obtain an output, evaluates its quality, then adjusts the input rules and runs DEEPDIVE again.

In this paper we will discuss the core elements of the DEEPDIVE software architecture, as well as a number of applications driven by DEEPDIVE, drawn from both academic and industrial settings. Many of the algorithms and technical components behind DEEPDIVE have been documented previously; this paper is the first to offer a comprehensive look at the software that ties the technical elements into a coherent whole. Although DEEPDIVE is designed to handle multiple media types, we will primarily focus on text.

In this paper we discuss:

- Design goals for DEEPDIVE (Section 2)
- DEEPDIVE's software architecture (Section 3)
- A brief overview of the technical components needed to implement the above architecture (Section 4)
- The DEEPDIVE development cycle (Section 5)
- An overview of DEEPDIVE-enabled applications, including insurance, materials science, and human trafficking (Section 6)

Finally, we conclude with a discussion of related and future work.

2. USER INTERACTION AND DESIGN CRITERIA

DEEPDIVE's overriding goal is to extract data with very high quality. Figure 1 shows DEEPDIVE's core inputs and outputs. The user presents DEEPDIVE with an *input document corpus* and an *input aspirational schema* to populate with information from that corpus. For example, if the *document corpus* were a collection of genomics research papers, the *aspirational schema* might be (gene, phenotype). DEEPDIVE then emits an *output aspirational table* that has the given schema and uses information found in the input corpus.

The success of a single DEEPDIVE run is determined by the quality — the precision and recall — of the output aspirational table. DEEPDIVE obtains high quality by asking an engineer to repeatedly examine the output table, diagnose any problems, and repair problems by contributing domain-specific code. By repeatedly going through this iterative improvement cycle, a DEEPDIVE engineer should be able to obtain extremely high accuracy data.

DEEPDIVE's success is entirely dependent on effective and rapid execution of this iterative development cycle. In this section we discuss the motivation behind this developer model, as well as the system design criteria driven by the model.

2.1 Iterative Development Model

We have observed that when working on an information extraction task, it is very easy to spend one's time poorly. Even well-trained computer scientists will work in an *ad hoc* fashion and contribute useless features, laboriously perfect features that have little impact, solve error cases that are obvious rather than common, fiddle with the statistical infrastructure, rarely know when to add more training data, and fall victim to common (though sometimes subtle) statistical errors. In short, even the best of us flail aimlessly in the face of a low precision or recall number.

This process superficially resembles that of *performance debugging*, an area where it is famously easy for a software engineer to spend huge amounts of time flailing, making changes that do not yield concrete results. But in contrast to extractor development, the software engineer who wants to make a slow piece of software run fast can pursue several methods that are very effective, if not always practiced.

An effective engineer knows the wisdom in Amdahl's Law, and will focus only on the slowest component. Identifying the slowest component is often counterintuitive, so she heavily instruments the code before making any changes. Finally, she knows that she should make performance improvements piecemeal, because solving one can change the overall picture of which components are now the bottleneck. By repeatedly applying this deeply-ingrained, reliable, and predictable discipline, the engineer can obtain a fast piece of software.

DEEPDIVE aims to use a similar development cycle to obtain high accuracy. The human engineer identifies the most common error in the output table. She then examines the relevant region of the raw input corpus, plus DEEPDIVE's instrumented extraction decision. This information enables the engineer to solve the error class, rerun the system, and move onto the next error. We describe the developer experience in more detail in Section 5.

2.2 System Design Criteria

In order to support the above developer workflow, DEEPDIVE has three core design criteria:

- **Mechanism independence** — Human developers improve accuracy by contributing domain information, *not* by changing the statistical procedure.
- **Integrated processing** — The interrelated steps of extraction, cleaning, and integration should all be handled simultaneously.
- **Debuggable decisions** — Any extraction error made by the system should be analyzable and tied to a root cause that can be understood and fixed by a human engineer.

2.3 Mechanism Independence

In an effort to obtain either high accuracy or faster runtimes, it is commonplace for machine learning engineers to modify the core statistical procedure for a given task. Machine learning conferences focus heavily on novel methods, often justified with experiments showing improved accuracy numbers for a workload of tasks. This practice is disastrous from an engineering point of view, encouraging the developer to fiddle with the most error-prone and difficult-to-debug portion of the system. It also distracts the developer from contributing what a human is uniquely able to contribute, and what usually solves real extraction problems: additional problem-specific domain knowledge.

Unlike machine learning toolkits such as MLib, MADLib, or SAS, DeepDive does not offer the user an elaborate suite of statistical algorithms. The training and inference procedure is not controllable by the developer. Rather, the developer uses a high-level datalog-like language called **DDlog** to describe the structured extraction problem. DeepDive then figures out how to most efficiently perform the extraction task described by the developer.

This approach should sound very familiar to readers in the database community, which has long favored high-level languages over direct user control of the query processing mechanism. However, this design choice posed a serious technical challenge well into the 1980s, until it eventually became known how to build a query processing system that could obtain acceptable performance. DeepDive faced a similar technical challenge: a system for probabilistic inference that is efficient enough that users can generally rely on it. Addressing this challenge was a key hurdle in building DeepDive (though DeepDive is not the only possible way to use these efficient training and inference techniques). We describe it in more detail in Section 4.

2.4 Integrated Processing

DeepDive handles in a single platform several processing steps that in the past have been treated as distinct: extraction, integration, and cleaning. This approach may seem unwisely ambitious, since each individual step has been the focus of dedicated software products. But in contrast to the past *siloed processing* model, we believe that *integrated processing* is crucial for supporting the developer workflow above. The key is that integrated processing allows the developer to solve extraction problems where they are easiest to solve.

Consider when the DeepDive developer wants to create a book catalog out of book review web pages, using a siloed system of two steps: extraction, followed by integration with a partial catalog. Imagine the target schema is **(bookTitle, author, uniqueId, price)** and the extractor has a very high precision of 98%. The remaining 2% of emitted tuples are not books, but are movies that were incorrectly extracted, due to a mistake made by the extractor's NLP parser. The downstream integration module fails to integrate some of the correct extractions (because they are novel) and all of the incorrect ones (because the existing database does not contain movies).

In a siloed system, the extractor will appear to be providing incorrect data to the integrator, which of course will fail. The team responsible for the integration system will naturally ask the extractor team to fix the problem, with the reasoning that no system can integrate incorrect data[1]. Unfortunately, NLP parsing problems are likely extremely difficult for the extraction team to repair, forcing them to either devote huge technical resources to solving the problem, or devote human resources to manually reviewing the extractor's output.

It would be vastly simpler for the integration team to simply filter out extracted tuples that contain movie titles (for which there are free and high-quality downloadable databases). However, this easy fix will not be apparent in the siloed system; it is only apparent to an engineer responsible for integrated end-to-end data quality.

It may seem artificial to say that the siloed "extractor" cannot use dictionaries; we entirely agree. Using separate software components for each stage — written and maintained by separate teams — will inevitably lead to these artificial distinctions, which will lead to poor engineering decisions. In an integrated system, the developer simply asks whether the final data product is good enough; if the answer is no, the developer picks the most convenient place to fix the most important problem.

There may also be a further statistical advantage in incorporating multiple sources of information during the joint inference task.

2.5 Debuggable Decisions

Our final design goal is that DeepDive should enable *debuggable decisions*. When the developer has identified an extraction error, she must be able to examine what incorrect decision DeepDive made, and diagnose why it happened. Satisfying this goal has three practical impacts on the system:

- DeepDive uses human-understandable features that are implemented in traditional Python code, not the opaque features yielded by deep learning systems. In Section 5 we describe how to use this approach and still obtain some of the feature induction advantages associated with deep learning.
- All weighted decisions are described using calibrated probabilities, not scores. This allows humans to examine individual and intermediate decisions, then decide whether the intermediate decision was correct or not. Doing so is impossible unless the numerical value is human-comprehensible. This places additional requirements on our probabilistic inference mechanism.
- It retains a statistical "execution history" and can present it to the user in an easy-to-consume form. For example, our debugging tool always presents, for each feature, the number of times the feature was observed in the training data. This allows engineers to detect whether the feature has an incorrect weight due to insufficient training data.

In the following section we describe the overall DeepDive architecture, and discuss how it meets these three design criteria.

3. SYSTEM OVERVIEW

Figure 2 shows DeepDive's three execution phases:

1. In *candidate generation*, DeepDive applies a user-defined function (UDF) to each document in the input corpus to yield candidate extractions. For example, the book price extractor might emit every numerical value from each input webpage. The goal of the candidate generator is to eliminate "obviously" wrong outputs (such as non-numeric prices). The candidate generation step is thus intended to be *high-recall, low-precision*.

[1]Could the extractor team respond that 98% is "good enough"? There is no way to answer this question without an integrated end-to-end evaluation. Consider the similar problem of evaluating whether a given function in a piece of software is "fast enough." For a function considered in isolation, the question is impossible to answer. One needs to know the function's role in an overall program — the performance requirements, how often the function is called, etc.

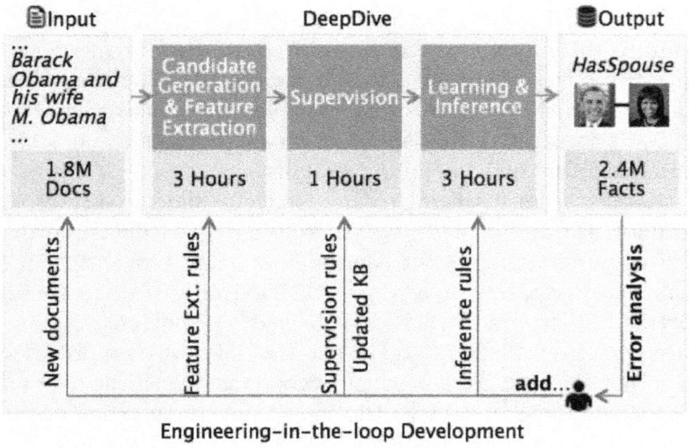

Figure 2: DeepDive takes as input dark data — such as unstructured documents — and outputs a structured database. The runtimes here are for the TAC-KBP competition system. To improve quality, the developer adds new rules and new data with error analysis conducted on the result of the current snapshot of the system. DeepDive provides a declarative language to specify each type of different rules and data, and techniques to incrementally execute this iterative process.

The system also applies user-defined feature functions to each candidate. For example, one feature might indicate whether the candidate has a $ symbol to its left. We believe that improving feature quality is one of the core mechanisms by which a statistical system can improve its quality [2]. Unlike some statistical frameworks in which features are largely or entirely synthetic — say, deep learning — we strongly believe that all features should be comprehensible by humans, so as to permit downstream debugging.

2. In *supervision*, DeepDive applies user-defined *distant supervision rules* to provide labels for some of the candidates. For example, we might know the true price for a subset of downloaded Web pages because of a previous hand-annotated database. Supervision rules do not have to label each candidate: they are intended to be *low-recall, high-precision.* Distant supervision rules in some cases may be more error-prone than direct human label generation, but the former allows us to fix and reexecute rules, and also to generate massively more labeled examples.

3. In *learning and inference*, we construct a graphical model that represents all of the labeled candidate extractions, train weights, then infer a correct probability for each candidate. At the end of this stage, we apply a threshold to each inferred probability and thereby obtain the extractions that will be placed in the output database.

Every time the developer makes a pass through the Figure 1 iteration loop — that is, each time she changes a candidate generation UDF, a feature UDF, or the distant supervision rules — we rerun DeepDive to obtain a new output table. The user can also specify many smaller-bore task-specific details: where to find input data, the schema of the output, how to incorporate information about multiple possible extractions, and so on. The user provides this information using **DDlog**.

3.1 Candidate Generation and Feature Extraction

All data in DeepDive is stored in a relational database. The first phase populates the database using a set of SQL queries and user-defined functions (UDFs). By default, DeepDive stores all documents in the database in one sentence per row with markup produced by standard NLP pre-processing tools, including HTML stripping, part-of-speech tagging, and linguistic parsing. After this loading step, DeepDive executes two types of queries: (1) *candidate mappings*, which are SQL queries that produce possible mentions, entities, and relations, and (2) *feature extractors* that associate features to candidates.

Example 3.1. *Candidate mappings are usually simple. Here, we create a relation mention for every pair of candidate persons in the same sentence (s):*

$$\textit{(R1)}\ \texttt{MarriedCandidate}(m1, m2)\ \text{:-}\ \texttt{PersonCandidate}(s, m1), \texttt{PersonCandidate}(s, m2).$$

Candidate mappings are simply SQL queries with UDFs that look like low-precision but high-recall ETL scripts. Such rules must be high recall: if the union of candidate mappings misses a fact, DeepDive will never extract it.

We also need to extract features. Here we extend classical Markov Logic in two ways: (1) user-defined functions and (2) weight tying, which we illustrate by example.

Example 3.2. *Suppose that UDF* phrase$(m1, m2, sent)$ *returns the phrase between two mentions in the sentence, e.g., "and his wife" in the above example. The phrase between two mentions may indicate whether two people are married. We would write this as:*

$$\begin{aligned}\textit{(FE1)}\ &\texttt{MarriedMentions}(m1, m2)\ \text{:-}\\ &\texttt{MarriedCandidate}(m1, m2), \texttt{Mention}(s, m1),\\ &\texttt{Mention}(s, m2), \texttt{Sentence}(s, sent)\\ &weight = \mathsf{phrase}(m1, m2, sent).\end{aligned}$$

One can think about this like a classifier: This rule says that whether the text indicates that the mentions m1 and m2 are married is influenced *by the phrase between those mention pairs. The system will infer based on training data its confidence (by estimating the weight) that two mentions are indeed indicated to be married.*

Technically, phrase returns an identifier that determines which weights should be used for a given relation mention in a sentence. If phrase returns the same result for two relation mentions, they receive the *same* weight. In general, phrase could be an arbitrary UDF that operates in a per-tuple fashion. This allows DeepDive to support common examples of features such as "bag-of-words" to context-aware NLP features to highly domain-specific dictionaries and ontologies. In addition to specifying sets of classifiers, DeepDive inherits Markov Logic's ability to specify rich correlations between entities via weighted rules. Such rules are particularly helpful for data cleaning and data integration.

3.2 Supervision

Just as in Markov Logic, DeepDive can use training data or evidence about any relation; in particular, each user relation is associated with an evidence relation with the same

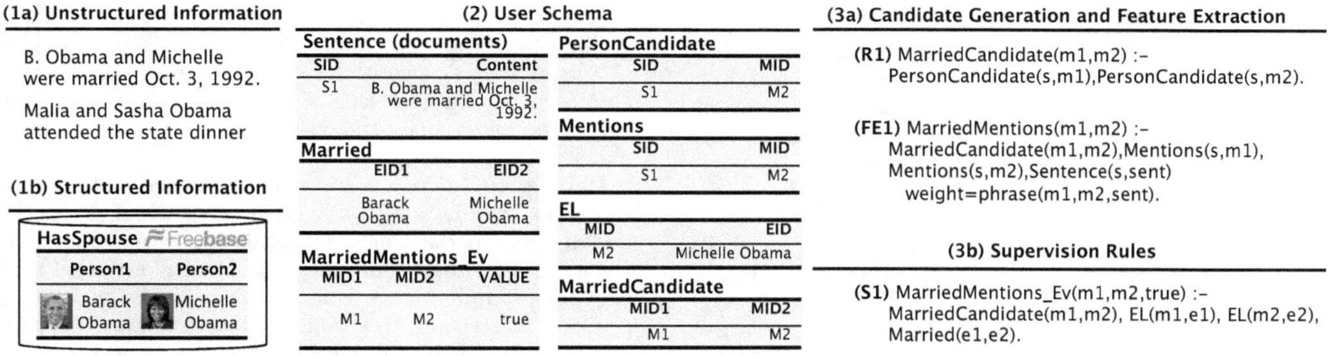

Figure 3: An example DEEPDIVE deployment.

schema and an additional field that indicates whether the entry is true or false. Continuing our example, the evidence relation *MarriedMentions_Ev* could contain mention pairs with positive and negative labels. As a rule, we use distant supervision to obtain labels rather than manual efforts.

EXAMPLE 3.3. *Distant supervision [20, 33] is a popular technique to create evidence in information extraction systems. The idea is to use an incomplete database of married entity pairs to* heuristically *label (as* **True** *evidence) all relation mentions that link to a pair of married entities:*

$$\texttt{(S1) MarriedMentions\_Ev}(m1, m2, true) :\text{-} \; \texttt{MarriedCandidates}(m1, m2), \texttt{EL}(m1, e1), \texttt{EL}(m2, e2), \texttt{Married}(e1, e2).$$

Here, `Married` is an (incomplete) list of married real-world persons that we wish to extend. The relation EL is for "entity linking" that maps mentions to their candidate entities. At first blush, this rule seems incorrect. However, it generates noisy, imperfect examples of sentences that indicate two people are married. Machine learning techniques are able to exploit redundancy to cope with the noise and learn the relevant phrases (e.g., "and his wife"). Negative examples are generated by relations that are largely disjoint (e.g., siblings). Similar to DIPRE [6] and Hearst patterns [19], distant supervision exploits the "duality" [6] between patterns and relation instances; furthermore, it allows us to integrate this idea into DEEPDIVE's unified probabilistic framework.

3.3 Learning and Inference

In the learning and inference phase, DEEPDIVE generates a factor graph, similar to Markov Logic, and uses techniques from Tuffy [36]. The inference and learning are done using standard techniques (Gibbs Sampling) that we describe below after introducing the formal semantics.

As in Figure 4, DEEPDIVE explicitly constructs a factor graph for inference and learning using a set of SQL queries. Recall that a factor graph is a triple $(V, F, \hat{w})$ in which V is a set of nodes that correspond to Boolean random variables, F is a set of hyperedges (for $f \in F$, $f \subseteq V$), and $\hat{w} : F \times \{0,1\}^V \to \mathbb{R}$ is a weight function. In DEEPDIVE, each variable corresponds to one tuple in the database, and each hyperedge f corresponds to the set of groundings for a rule γ. In DEEPDIVE, V and F are explicitly created using a set of SQL queries. These data structures are then passed to the sampler, which runs outside the database, to estimate the marginal probability of each node or tuple in the database. (In principle there could be some data movement advantages to running the sampler inside the core database system, but probably not enough to warrant the additional code complexity.) Each tuple is then reloaded into the database with its marginal probability.

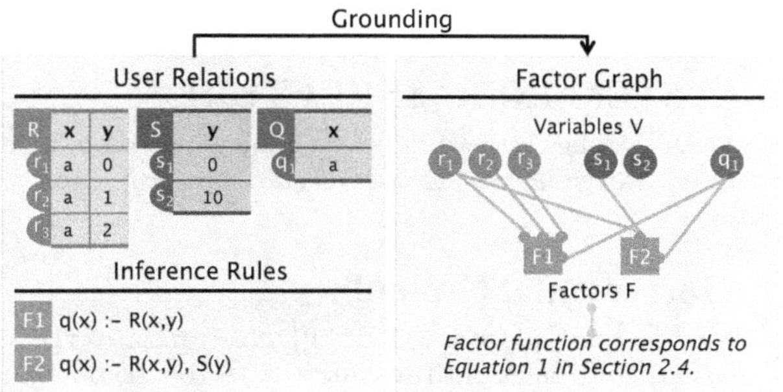

Figure 4: Schematic illustration of grounding. Each tuple corresponds to a Boolean random variable and node in the factor graph. We create one factor for every set of groundings.

EXAMPLE 3.4. *Take the database instances and rules in Figure 4 as an example, each tuple in relation R, S, and Q is a random variable, and V contains all random variables. The inference rules F1 and F2 ground factors with the same name in the factor graph as illustrated in Figure 4. Both F1 and F2 are implemented as SQL in* DEEPDIVE.

To define the semantics, we first define the concept of *possible world*: a possible world is a function that assigns each variable a truth value. Let $\mathcal{I}$ be the set of all possible worlds, for each factor f and a possible world I, we use $\hat{w}(f, I)$ as the value returned by factor f for possible world I. We then define $\hat{W}(F, I) = \sum_{f \in F} \hat{w}(f, I)$, and then the probability of a possible world is the following function:

$$\Pr[I] = Z^{-1} \exp\left\{\hat{W}(F, I)\right\} \text{ where } Z = \sum_{I \in J} \exp\left\{\hat{W}(F, I)\right\}$$

The main task that DEEPDIVE conducts on factor graphs is statistical inference, i.e., for a given node, what is the marginal probability that this node takes the value 1? This marginal probability is defined as follows. Given a variable v, let $\mathcal{I}_+$ be the set of all possible worlds in which v is assigned to true, the marginal probability of v is $\sum_{I \in \mathcal{I}_+} \Pr[I]$.

3.4 Execution

DEEPDIVE runs the above three phases in sequence, and at the end of the learning and inference, it obtains a marginal probability p for each candidate fact. To produce the output database, DEEPDIVE applies a user-chosen threshold, e.g., $p > 0.95$. For some applications that favor extremely high recall at the expense of precision, it may be appropriate to lower this threshold.

Typically, the developer will need to perform an *error analysis* and repeat the development cycle. Error analysis is the process of understanding the most common mistakes (incorrect extractions, too-specific features, candidate mistakes, etc.) and deciding how to correct them [40]. To facilitate error analysis, users write standard SQL queries or use the Mindtagger tool [45]. We will describe these methods in more detail in Section 5.

4. SYSTEM INFRASTRUCTURE

DEEPDIVE relies on two novel technological components for *incremental grounding* as well as *statistical inference and learning.*

4.1 Incremental Grounding

Grounding takes place when DEEPDIVE translates the set of relations and rules into a concrete factor graph upon which probabilistic inference is possible. Because DEEPDIVE is based on SQL, we are able to take advantage of decades of work on incremental view maintenance. The input to this phase is the same as the input to the grounding phase, a set of SQL queries and the user schema. The output of this phase is how the output of grounding changes, i.e., a set of modified variables ΔV and their factors ΔF. Since V and F are simply views over the database, any view maintenance techniques can be applied to incremental grounding. DEEPDIVE uses the DRED algorithm [17] that handles both additions and deletions. Recall that in DRED, for each relation R_i in the user's schema, we create a *delta relation,* R_i^δ, with the same schema as R_i and an additional column *count.* For each tuple t, $t.count$ represents the number of derivations of t in R_i. On an update, DEEPDIVE updates delta relations in two steps. First, for tuples in R_i^δ, DEEPDIVE directly updates the corresponding counts. Second, a SQL query called a *"delta rule"*[2] is executed which processes these counts to generate modified variables ΔV and factors ΔF. We found that the overhead of DRED is modest and the gains may be substantial, so DEEPDIVE always runs DRED–except on initial load.

4.2 Statistical Inference and Learning

The main task that DEEPDIVE conducts on factor graphs is statistical inference, i.e., for a given node, what is the marginal probability that this node takes the value 1? Since a node takes value 1 when a tuple is in the output, this process computes the marginal probability values returned to users. In general, computing these marginal probabilities is ♯P-hard [50]. Like many other systems, DEEPDIVE uses Gibbs sampling [43] to estimate the marginal probability of every tuple in the database.

[2]For example, for the grounding procedure illustrated in Figure 4, the delta rule for $F1$ is $q^\delta(x) : -R^\delta(x,y)$.

Efficiency and Scalability. There are two components to scaling statistical algorithms: *statistical efficiency,* roughly how many steps an algorithm takes to converge, and *hardware efficiency,* how efficient each of those step is. We introduced this terminology and studied this extensively in a recent paper [55].

DimmWitted [55], the statistical inference and learning engine in DEEPDIVE, is built upon our research of how to design a high-performance statistical inference and learning engine on a single machine [29, 41, 54, 55]. DimmWitted models Gibbs sampling as a "column-to-row access" operation: each row corresponds to one factor, each column to one variable, and the non-zero elements in the matrix correspond to edges in the factor graph. To process one variable, DimmWitted fetches one column of the matrix to get the set of factors, and other columns to get the set of variables that connect to the same factor. In standard benchmarks, DimmWitted was 3.7× faster than GraphLab's implementation without any application-specific optimization. Compared with traditional work, the main novelty of DimmWitted is that it considers *both* hardware efficiency and statistical efficiency for executing an inference and learning task.

- **Hardware Efficiency** DEEPDIVE takes into consideration the architecture of modern Non-uniform memory access (NUMA) machines. A NUMA machine usually contains multiple nodes (sockets); each socket contains multiple CPU cores. To obtain high hardware efficiency, one wants to decrease the communication across different NUMA nodes.
- **Statistical Efficiency** Pushing hardware efficiency to the extreme might suffer on statistical efficiency because the lack of communication between nodes might decrease the rate of convergence of a statistical inference and learning algorithm. DEEPDIVE takes advantage of the theoretical results of model averaging [57] and our own results about lock-free execution [29, 41].

When performing extraction from a corpus of 0.3 million papers from the paleobiology literature, the factor graph contains more than 0.2 billion random variables and 0.3 billion factors. On this factor graph, DEEPDIVE is able to run Gibbs sampling on a machine with 4 sockets (10 core per sockets), and we find that we can generate 1,000 samples for all 0.2 billion random variables in 28 minutes. This is more than 4× faster than a non-NUMA-aware implementation.

Incremental Inference. Due to our choice of incremental grounding, the input to DEEPDIVE's inference phase is a factor graph along with a set of changed variables and factors. The goal is to compute the output probabilities computed by the system. Our approach is to frame the incremental maintenance problem as approximate inference. Previous work in the database community has looked at how machine learning data products change in response to both to new labels [25] and to new data [9, 10]. When extracting databases from dark data, both the program and data change on each iteration. Our system can cope with both types of change simultaneously.

There are two popular classes of approximate inference techniques: *sampling-based materialization* (inspired by sampling-based probabilistic databases such as MCDB [22]) and *variational-based materialization* (inspired by techniques for approximating graphical models [49]). We conducted an experimental evaluation of these two approaches on a diverse set of DEEPDIVE programs. We found these two approaches are sensitive to changes in the size of the factor graph, the sparsity of correlations, and the anticipated number of future changes. The performance varies by up to two orders of magnitude in different points of the space. To automatically choose the materialization strategy, we use a simple rule-based optimizer.

5. DEVELOPING AND DEBUGGING

The main claim for DEEPDIVE is that it enables data quality that is much higher than previous or competing systems. But so far we have covered mainly how to match our three design criteria of mechanism independence, integrated processing, and debuggable decisions. DEEPDIVE meets these criteria by framing extraction as a single integrated probabilistic inference task, along with infrastructure that can perform fast and accurate probabilistic inference without any one-off hacking of the inference procedure, plus some code that generates log-like data about DEEPDIVE's decisions.

In this section we describe how these advantages translate into DEEPDIVE's reliably high-quality output.

5.1 Improvement Iteration Loop

DEEPDIVE reaches high accuracy by enabling an efficient *improvement iteration loop.* The basic steps in this loop are described in Figure 1. As mentioned in Section 2, this developer loop is inspired by engineering behavior in traditional performance debugging settings: the engineer repeatedly runs the system, carefully diagnoses problems, and makes minimal modifications to address only the diagnosed problems. Performing this cycle is not easy — new students require lots of training in order to do it — but can be done reliably and repeatedly. Put another way, a good software engineering team can reliably obtain better performance by applying systematic effort to the problem.

In contrast, most machine learning-driven efforts in our experience do not exhibit either reliable accuracy improvement over time or systematic practice by engineers. Instead, the accuracy improvement over time is often fitful and unreliable. The engineering practice is often characterized by tinkering with the core statistical machinery and opaque "rules of thumb" that often lead to wasted or low-productivity effort.

We have devoted substantial time to evolving a systematic engineering practice that yields reliable improvements to extraction quality over time. Below we describe how the engineer identifies and remedies accuracy errors, plus some dead ends and common failure modes we have observed while building DEEPDIVE.

5.2 Fixing Failure

Rapidly identifying and repairing accuracy errors is the core mechanism by which DEEPDIVE obtains high accuracy. The first step in this process is when an engineer produces an *error analysis.* This is a strongly stylized document that helps the engineer determine:

- The true precision and recall of the extractor
- An enumeration of observed extractor failure modes, along with error counts for each failure mode. For example, a flawed extractor for medical doctors might incorrectly yield city names because they appear after the term *Dr.*

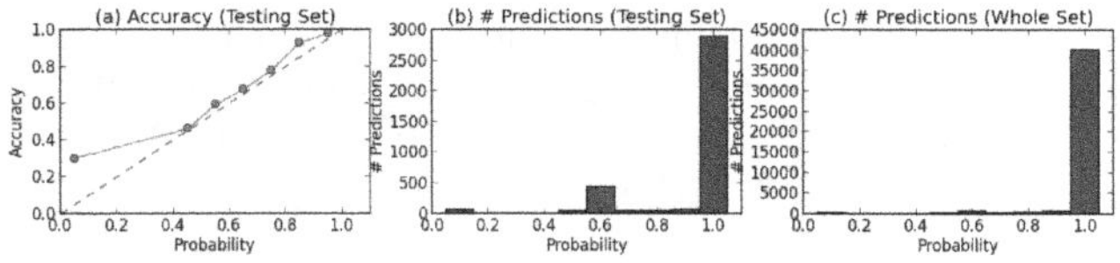

Figure 5: Example plots emitted by DEEPDIVE after training. From left-to-right: a probability calibration plot, a histogram of the different emitted probabilities for the test set, and a histogram of different emitted probabilities for the training set.

- For the top-ranked failure modes, the underlying reason DEEPDIVE made a mistake.

The error analysis document plays a role similar to the software engineer's performance instrumentation tool. Unfortunately, unlike most performance tools, producing the error analysis cannot be wholly automated. It requires a human being to:

1. Manually mark a sample of emitted extractions — usually roughly 100 — as correct or incorrect. This sample will be used to compute DEEPDIVE's *precision.*
2. Manually mark a sample of correct answers from the documents — usually roughly 100 — as correctly or incorrectly-extracted. This sample will be used to compute DEEPDIVE's *recall.*
3. Place each extraction failure into one of several "failure mode buckets." These buckets are not hard-coded in advance, and are not strictly defined; they are more akin to semantic tags applied by the engineer to errors that seem similar. Examples include *bad doctor name from addresses*, or *bad gene name from capitalized title*, or *missed price extraction when preceded by Euro symbol.*

Producing the error analysis requires human annotation and can be time-consuming. (Though note that the person producing the above document can be someone other than the core DEEPDIVE engineer, and in the case of highly-technical input corpora, the primary DEEPDIVE engineer might not be qualified to produce it.)

The error analysis document also includes information the user does not have to generate manually: commodity statistics that describe the inputs and outputs, checksums of all data products and code, and summaries of features, including their learned weights and observed counts. It also has a version checksum and references to GitHub versions that contain the relevant feature functions and distant supervision code.

After producing the error analysis, the engineer sorts the failure mode buckets in descending order of frequency. She always tries to address the largest bucket first. Bugs usually fall into one of three categories:

1. The *candidate generator* failed to identify the extraction, or through a preprocessing error emitted a nonsense candidate (perhaps due to a bad character in the input, or an OCR failure in the case of hand-written forms) . This is easily checked by testing whether the correct answer was contained in the set of candidates evaluated probabilistically.
2. There is not a *feature function* that can successfully distinguish the right answer. The engineer checks for this

failure by examining each incorrect example in the current bucket, and asking whether the observed features would be sufficient for a human being to distinguish a correct from incorrect answer.

For example, if the doctor extractor has just a single feature — *is 'Dr' to the left of the candidate?* — then clearly there is not sufficient feature information for DEEPDIVE to emit the correct result, and the engineer should add a new feature function.

3. If there is sufficient feature information, but DEEPDIVE still yielded an incorrect result, then the learned feature weights are likely incorrect, most often due to insufficient *distant supervision rules*. This can easily happen when the distant supervision rules provide few or no labels for certain feature values.

   For example, if the extractor has two features — *is 'Dr' to the left of the candidate?* and *is the candidate inside an address?* — then the distant supervision rules must provide labels for candidates that exhibit both features. If the distant supervision rules instead just happen to label non-address examples, then DEEPDIVE will not have enough evidence to correctly compute the relative weights of these features. The engineer should add a new distant supervision rule to cover this case.

That is all. The DEEPDIVE engineer repeatedly creates the error analysis, then diagnoses the reason behind the most important errors. Do this enough times, and DEEPDIVE can rapidly obtain extremely high data quality.

In addition, after each training run, DEEPDIVE emits the diagrams shown in Figure 5. This data helps the engineer understand the system's probabilistic output without having to understand the statistical algorithm. The leftmost diagram is a *calibration plot* that shows whether DEEPDIVE's emitted probabilities are accurate; *e.g.*, for all of the items assessed a 20% probability, are 20% of them actually correct extractions? In the case shown here, the actual red line does not reflect the ideal dotted blue line, suggesting DEEPDIVE lacks sufficient feature evidence to compute entirely correct probabilities. The center and right diagrams show a histogram of predictions in various probability buckets for the test and training sets, respectively. Ideal prediction histograms are U-shaped, with the vast majority of items receiving a probability of either 0% or close to 100%. The center (test set) histogram here is worrisome, suggesting that for many test cases, DEEPDIVE does not have enough evidence to push its belief either to zero or 1.

5.3 Design Choices

Making the engineer as productive as possible has been a driving force in the last few years of DEEPDIVE development. We have made a number of nonobvious design choices and pulled back from a few interesting dead ends.

Human-understandable features only — All of the features that DEEPDIVE uses are easily human-understandable. This decision stands in sharp contrast to recent deep learning trends that deemphasize manual feature engineering in favor of manually-designed networks and training procedures that can yield effective but opaque features.

Note that human comprehensibility is core to the debugging loop described above. In our view, the human engineer must be able to determine whether an observed mistake was due to a lack of effective features or due to some other source of failure; that determination is impossible if the feature set is not comprehensible.

In the past year we have introduced a *feature library* system that automatically proposes a massive number of features that plausibly work across many domains, and then uses statistical regularization to throw away all but the most effective features. This method gives a bit of the feel of deep learning, in that some features come "for free" with no explicit engineer involvement. However, the hypothesized features are designed to always be human-understandable; we describe the space of all possible features using code-like "feature templates" instead of the opaque network designs common in deep learning.

Distant supervision — Our standard development loop never calls upon anyone to manually label training data examples. The only explicit human labels come during the error analysis phase, after the system has already been trained. This decision stands in contrast to most previous supervised trained systems, which rely on huge numbers of manually-labeled examples.

We use distant supervision for three reasons. First, it is far less burdensome than manual labeling and thus enables rapid execution of the improvement iteration cycle. Second, we have found in other work that the massive number of labels enabled by distant supervision rules may simply be more effective than the smaller number of labels that come from manual processes, even in the face of possibly-higher error rates [53]. Third, distant supervision rules can be revised, debugged, and cheaply reexecuted; in contrast, a flaw in the human labeling process can only be fixed by expensively redoing all of the work.

Few deterministic rules — This point is best described as an engineering failure mode we now actively strive to avoid. When faced with an extraction task, it is often possible to rapidly obtain middling data quality by writing a simple regular expression. For example, simply extracting capitalized words after *Dr.* would indeed give a healthy number of correct doctor extractions. This approach can be extremely appealing from an engineering perspective, as it is quick to write and relies entirely on well-understood software libraries instead of probabilistic machinery that may seem novel or surprising.

However, this approach is also a dead end for all but the most trivial extraction targets. A conscientious engineer, having met with success after writing the first regular expression, will quickly address the remaining quality bugs by writing a second. In our experience, this second deterministic rule will indeed address some bugs, but will be vastly less productive than the first one. The third regular expression will be even less productive. Very quickly, the engineer will have written a depressing page full of increasingly-obscure regular expressions that are hard to debug, hard to maintain, and still do not obtain human-level quality.

We have seen this pattern in new DEEPDIVE engineers many, many times. It has led to failure every single time but two: when extracting phone numbers and email addresses. There is a real cognitive resistance to adopting the development cycle described above; it appears to run strongly against common engineering habit, perhaps similar to the way habits for effective performance debugging can be very counterintuitive. Training new engineers in the DEEPDIVE debugging methodology can be initially difficult, but once these engineers are trained, they are enormously effective. Indeed, over the last several years, improvements in tools, practices, and training have enabled experienced DEEPDIVE engineers to produce many novel and high-quality databases in 1-2 days, down from several months originally.

6. APPLICATIONS

We now explore several applications in detail, to give a flavor for the kinds of applications DEEPDIVE can enable.

6.1 Medical Genetics

The body of literature in life sciences has been growing rapidly for years, to the extent that it has become unrealistic for scientists to perform research solely based on reading and memorization (even with the help of keyword search). As a result, there have been numerous initiatives to build structured databases from the research literature. For example, OMIM is an authoritative database of human genes and genetic disorders. It dates back to the 1960s, and so far contains about 6,000 hereditary diseases or phenotypes. Because OMIM is curated by humans, it has been growing at a rate of roughly 50 records / month for many years. In collaboration with Prof. Gill Bejerano at Stanford, we are developing DEEPDIVE applications in the field of medical genetics. Specifically, we use DEEPDIVE to extract mentions of genes, diseases, and phenotypes from the literature, and statistically infer their relationships.

Consider a very simple schema of *regulate* relationships that consists of (**gene**, **phenotype**, **research-paper**). This database can be crucial for treating genetic illnesses: consider a patient who arrives at the doctor with a symptom that the doctor believes is likely to be genetically-linked. The doctor takes two steps to find a possible clinical intervention: (1) she runs a test on the patient to determine which genes are atypical, (2) she checks the scientific literature to see if there is any known linkage between the patient's symptom and the atypical genes. This second step — sometimes known informally as "asking Doctor Google" — can be hugely time-consuming: the scientific literature is vast, genes and phenotypes are often known by different names, and identifying a relevant relationship between a gene and phenotype often requires reading and understanding the paper. Doctors can spend large amounts of time researching rare genetic illnesses, and if Googling does not yield immediate results, it can be difficult for the doctor to distinguish between humanity's lack of clinical knowledge on a topic vs. an especially challenging Internet browsing effort. As a result, doctors spend a large amount of time performing research instead of treating patients, and in some cases may fail to identify literature that is crucial for formulating treatment.

If the doctor had access to a high-quality version of the (**gene**, **phenotype**, **research-paper**) database, it would be simple and quick to look up patient information. DEEPDIVE enables the construction of this database.

6.2 Pharmacogenomics

Understanding the interactions of chemicals in the body is key for drug discovery. However, the majority of this data resides in the biomedical literature and cannot be easily accessed. The Pharmacogenomics Knowledgebase is a high quality database that aims to annotate the relationships between drugs, genes, diseases, genetic variation, and pathways in the literature. With the exponential growth of the literature, manual curation requires prioritization of specific drugs or genes in order to stay up to date with current research. In collaboration with Emily Mallory and Prof. Russ Altman [30] at Stanford, we are developing DEEPDIVE applications in the field of pharmacogenomics. Specifically, we use DEEPDIVE to extract relations between genes, diseases, and drugs in order to predict novel pharmacological relationships.

6.3 Materials Science

The world of semiconductors offers a scenario similar to that of medical genetics. There is a large universe of chemical formulas from which it is possible to create semiconductors with different technical physical properties, such as *electron field mobility*. It would be useful for a semiconductor engineer to have a handbook of semiconductor materials and their properties, using which she could simply look up a desirable set of numbers for any specific application. Unfortunately, there is no such handbook — the evolving research literature itself is the best source of information on semiconductors data. As a result, engineers can spend large amounts of time rifling through the scientific literature in the search for just the right material.

In conjunction with researchers at Toshiba Corporation, we have worked since the fall of 2014 to create this database of semiconductors and their properties.

6.4 Fighting Human Trafficking

Human trafficking is an odious crime that uses physical, economic, or other means of coercion to obtain labor from human beings. Trafficked individuals are often used in sex work or factory work. Unfortunately, identifying human trafficking victims in the United States can often be difficult for authorities — the individuals may be kept from regular contact with friends or family, and may be unable, afraid, or too ashamed to contact law enforcement by themselves. (Trafficking patterns differ from country to country.) It would be far better if law enforcement could proactively identify and investigate possible trafficking victims.

Somewhat surprisingly, there is data online that may contain evidence of trafficking activity. Like many other forms of commerce, sex work advertising is now online; there are many websites where providers of sex services post ads containing price, location, contact information, physical characteristics, and other data. Details differ across sites, but in most cases the posts resemble Craigslist-style textual classified ads: they have very little structure, lots of extremely nonstandard English, and tend to contain the same data values. It is easy to imagine a relational schema that would capture most of the relevant data in these ads.

There is additional information available on discussion forum websites where users of sex services post information about their experiences. Again, these posts are primarily textual, but tend to contain similar information: when the encounter took place, what happened, the sex worker's details, etc. For a surprisingly large percentage of forum posts, there is enough contact information for us to identify the relevant sex worker ad. The posts are also remarkably candid, describing both the illegal activity itself as well as details about the sex worker (*e.g.*, evidence of drug abuse or physical abuse) that would never have been found in the original advertisement.

It was initially surprising to us that forum writers are willing to be so forthcoming. There appears to be a strong social element to the forum posts, roughly similar to what can be observed in Amazon and Yelp discussion fora; domain experts in sex commerce have reported to us that this finding is not surprising to them.

We ran DEEPDIVE on approximately 45M advertisements and 0.5M forum posts, creating two distinct structured tables. We can use this data in many different ways:

- Statistics from advertisements can be used by themselves to identify trafficking warning signs. For example, a sex worker who posts from multiple cities in relatively rapid succession may be moved from place to place by traffickers in order to be kept disoriented and easy to manage. A worker who posts an unusually low price or is willing to engage in extremely risky practices may also be doing so as a trafficking victim. We have shipped extracted data for other companies to use in law enforcement products; this data has been deployed to several law enforcement agencies and has been used in at least one arrest.
- Using price data from the advertisements alone, we can compute aggregate statistics and analyses about sex commerce in the United States. We are writing a paper with economists and political scientists about the relationship between pricing in the sex economy in individual cities and the licit economies in those places.
- Using the joined advertisement and forum tables, we can use forum posters' comments about experiences to identify sex workers who may be in danger. For example, signs of drug or physical abuse on their own are worrisome on their own, and may also be evidence of possible trafficking. Engineers at Lattice Data (`http://lattice.io`), a startup company designed to commercialize DEEPDIVE, have used this data to create a user-facing faceted search tool for law enforcement officers.

This work was done as part of the DARPA MEMEX project and has been covered on 60 Minutes and other news sources.

7. RELATED WORK

Knowledge Base Construction (KBC). KBC has been an area of intense study over the last decade, moving from pattern matching [19] and rule-based systems [28] to systems that use machine learning for KBC [5, 8, 13, 14, 34]. Many groups have studied how to improve the quality of specific components of KBC systems [33, 51]. DEEPDIVE's effort to extract structured databases from dark data can be seen as an effort to ease and accelerate the KBC process. DEEPDIVE has many common features to Chen and Wang [11], Google's Knowledge Vault [13], and a forerunner of DEEPDIVE, Tuffy [36]. We focus on the incremental evaluation from feature extraction to inference.

DEEPDIVE's model of KBC is motivated by the recent attempts of using machine learning-based technique for KBC [3, 4, 24, 38, 46, 52, 56] and the line of research that aims to improve the quality of a specific component of KBC system [7, 12, 15, 21, 26, 27, 31–33, 35, 39, 42, 47, 48, 51, 53, 54]. When designing DEEPDIVE, we used these systems as test cases to justify the generality of our framework. In fact, we find that DEEPDIVE is able to model thirteen of these popular KBC systems [15,23,26,27,31–33,35,39,42,51,53,54].

Declarative Information Extraction. The database community has proposed declarative languages for information extraction, a task with similar goals to knowledge base construction, by extending relational operations [16, 28, 44], or rule-based approaches [34]. These approaches can take advantage of classic view maintenance techniques to make the execution incremental, but they do not study how to incrementally maintain the result of statistical inference and learning, which is the focus of our work.

Data Cleaning and Integration. Data cleaning and integration systems have been active research topics in academia, with moderate deployment in industrial settings. Many deployed systems to date have focused on generating precise and correct integrations for traditional transaction-focused systems, such as merged human resources databases.

A newer set of software systems, such as Wrangler and Tamr, have focused on data ingest, cleaning, and integration for analytical purposes. To the best of our knowledge, these systems are focused more on ingesting diverse sources of structured data rather than free-form dark data, but the line between the two can be hazy (*e.g.*, template-driven electronic medical records with a mixture of structured and unstructured components). More importantly, these systems are rule-driven rather than probabilistic, which we believe will lead to the higher maintenance costs and lower data quality we described in Section 5.3. We have found that probabilistic inference and an effective accompanying engineering cycle are core to DEEPDIVE's success in obtaining reliably high quality.

8. CONCLUSIONS AND FUTURE WORK

We have demonstrated DEEPDIVE's ability to obtain high-quality databases in many different domains. We believe there is a vast amount of future work in applying DEEPDIVE to novel problems in the sciences, medicine, finance, and other real-world domains with huge amounts of dark data. We have been repeatedly surprised by the sheer number and variety of problems that can be addressed using DEEPDIVE's results.

Much of the future technical work on DEEPDIVE entails reducing the amount of developer effort needed to obtain high quality. This work can be reduced using novel developer tools, novel data-centric methods, or some combination.

For example, over time we have modified DEEPDIVE to require *less* information from the user, not more. Users have fairly limited direct control over the machine learning elements of our knowledge base construction procedure, especially compared to what is possible given most standard machine learning toolkits. However, it is still possible for users to make inadvertent and hard-to-debug errors. For example, consider a user who has provided the above-listed feature, which we might call $isGene_{f1}$. This is an entirely reasonable piece of feature code, and is likely just one of several features the system uses when classifying an in-document string as **is-gene** or not.

However, now consider what happens when the user has also provided a distant supervision rule. Distant supervision rules are algorithmic methods for generating labeled data; they can be less accurate than traditional hand-labeled data examples, but when applied to a large corpus they can generate far more labeled data than is possible with hand-marking.

Unfortunately, if the distant supervision rule is identical to or extremely similar to a feature function, standard statistical training procedures will fail badly. Even if the user has provided a large number of helpful features, there is one that *perfectly* predicts the labeled answer, and so the training procedure will build a model that places all weight on the single feature that overlaps with the supervision rule. The trained statistical model will — reasonably enough — have little effectiveness in the real world, in which the feature and the truth do not perfectly overlap. This failure mode is extremely hard to detect: to the user, it simply appears that the training procedure has failed. Worse, it has failed after the user has been conscientious enough to provide what should have been a high-quality feature function. Continuing to address such DEEPDIVE engineering failure modes is an ongoing project.

9. ACKNOWLEDGMENTS

We gratefully acknowledge the support of the Defense Advanced Research Projects Agency (DARPA) XDATA Program under No. FA8750-12-2-0335 and DEFT Program under No. FA8750-13-2-0039, DARPA's MEMEX program and SIMPLEX program, the National Science Foundation (NSF) CAREER Awards under No. IIS-1353606 and No. IIS-1054913, the Office of Naval Research (ONR) under awards No. N000141210041 and No. N000141310129, the National Institutes of Health Grant U54EB020405 awarded by the National Institute of Biomedical Imaging and Bioengineering (NIBIB) through funds provided by the trans-NIH Big Data to Knowledge (BD2K, http://www.bd2k.nih.gov) initiative, the Sloan Research Fellowship, the Moore Foundation, American Family Insurance, Dow, Google, Yahoo!, and Toshiba. Any opinions, findings, and conclusions or recommendations expressed in this material are those of the authors and do not necessarily reflect the views of DARPA, AFRL, NSF, ONR, NIH, or the U.S. government.

10. REFERENCES

[1] *MUC6 '95: Proceedings of the 6th Conference on Message Understanding*, Stroudsburg, PA, USA, 1995. Association for Computational Linguistics.

[2] M. R. Anderson, D. Antenucci, V. Bittorf, M. Burgess, M. J. Cafarella, A. Kumar, F. Niu, Y. Park, C. Ré, and C. Zhang. Brainwash: A data system for feature engineering. In *CIDR 2013, Sixth Biennial Conference on Innovative Data Systems Research, Asilomar, CA, USA, January 6-9, 2013, Online Proceedings*, 2013.

[3] M. Banko, M. J. Cafarella, S. Soderland, M. Broadhead, and O. Etzioni. Open information extraction from the web. In *IJCAI 2007, Proceedings of the 20th International Joint Conference on Artificial Intelligence, Hyderabad, India, January 6-12, 2007*, pages 2670–2676, 2007.

[4] D. Barbosa, H. Wang, and C. Yu. Shallow information extraction for the knowledge web. In *29th IEEE International Conference on Data Engineering, ICDE 2013, Brisbane, Australia, April 8-12, 2013*, pages 1264–1267, 2013.

[5] J. Betteridge, A. Carlson, S. A. Hong, E. R. H. Jr., E. L. M. Law, T. M. Mitchell, and S. H. Wang. Toward never ending language learning. In *Learning by Reading and Learning to Read, Papers from the 2009 AAAI Spring Symposium, Technical Report SS-09-07, Stanford, California, USA, March 23-25, 2009*, pages 1–2, 2009.

[6] S. Brin. Extracting patterns and relations from the world wide web. In *The World Wide Web and Databases, International Workshop WebDB'98, Valencia, Spain, March 27-28, 1998, Selected Papers*, pages 172–183, 1998.

[7] R. C. Bunescu and R. J. Mooney. Learning to extract relations from the web using minimal supervision. In *ACL 2007, Proceedings of the 45th Annual Meeting of the Association for Computational Linguistics, June 23-30, 2007, Prague, Czech Republic*, 2007.

[8] A. Carlson, J. Betteridge, B. Kisiel, B. Settles, E. R. H. Jr., and T. M. Mitchell. Toward an architecture for never-ending language learning. In *Proceedings of the Twenty-Fourth AAAI Conference on Artificial Intelligence, AAAI 2010, Atlanta, Georgia, USA, July 11-15, 2010*, 2010.

[9] F. Chen, A. Doan, J. Yang, and R. Ramakrishnan. Efficient information extraction over evolving text data. In *Proceedings of the 24th International Conference on Data Engineering, ICDE 2008, April 7-12, 2008, Cancún, México*, pages 943–952, 2008.

[10] F. Chen, X. Feng, C. Re, and M. Wang. Optimizing statistical information extraction programs over evolving text. In *IEEE 28th International Conference on Data Engineering (ICDE 2012), Washington, DC, USA (Arlington, Virginia), 1-5 April, 2012*, pages 870–881, 2012.

[11] Y. Chen and D. Z. Wang. Knowledge expansion over probabilistic knowledge bases. In *International Conference on Management of Data, SIGMOD 2014, Snowbird, UT, USA, June 22-27, 2014*, pages 649–660, 2014.

[12] M. Craven and J. Kumlien. Constructing biological knowledge bases by extracting information from text sources. In *Proceedings of the Seventh International Conference on Intelligent Systems for Molecular Biology, August 6-10, 1999, Heidelberg, Germany*, pages 77–86, 1999.

[13] X. L. Dong, E. Gabrilovich, G. Heitz, W. Horn, K. Murphy, S. Sun, and W. Zhang. From data fusion to knowledge fusion. *PVLDB*, 7(10):881–892, 2014.

[14] O. Etzioni, M. J. Cafarella, D. Downey, S. Kok, A. Popescu, T. Shaked, S. Soderland, D. S. Weld, and A. Yates. Web-scale information extraction in knowitall: (preliminary results). In *Proceedings of the 13th international conference on World Wide Web, WWW 2004, New York, NY, USA, May 17-20, 2004*, pages 100–110, 2004.

[15] M. Fan, D. Zhao, Q. Zhou, Z. Liu, T. F. Zheng, and E. Y. Chang. Distant supervision for relation extraction with matrix completion. In *EMNLP*, 2014.

[16] G. Gottlob, C. Koch, R. Baumgartner, M. Herzog, and S. Flesca. The lixto data extraction project - back and forth between theory and practice. In *Proceedings of the Twenty-third ACM SIGACT-SIGMOD-SIGART Symposium on Principles of Database Systems, June 14-16, 2004, Paris, France*, pages 1–12, 2004.

[17] A. Gupta, I. S. Mumick, and V. S. Subrahmanian. Maintaining views incrementally. In *Proceedings of the 1993 ACM SIGMOD International Conference on Management of Data, Washington, D.C., May 26-28, 1993.*, pages 157–166, 1993.

[18] A. Y. Halevy, P. Norvig, and F. Pereira. The unreasonable effectiveness of data. *IEEE Intelligent Systems*, 24(2):8–12, 2009.

[19] M. A. Hearst. Automatic acquisition of hyponyms from large text corpora. In *14th International Conference on Computational Linguistics, COLING 1992, Nantes, France, August 23-28, 1992*, pages 539–545, 1992.

[20] R. Hoffmann, C. Zhang, X. Ling, L. S. Zettlemoyer, and D. S. Weld. Knowledge-based weak supervision for information extraction of overlapping relations. In *The 49th Annual Meeting of the Association for Computational Linguistics: Human Language Technologies, Proceedings of the Conference, 19-24 June, 2011, Portland, Oregon, USA*, pages 541–550, 2011.

[21] R. Hoffmann, C. Zhang, and D. S. Weld. Learning 5000 relational extractors. In *ACL 2010, Proceedings of the 48th Annual Meeting of the Association for Computational Linguistics, July 11-16, 2010, Uppsala, Sweden*, pages 286–295, 2010.

[22] R. Jampani, F. Xu, M. Wu, L. L. Perez, C. M. Jermaine, and P. J. Haas. MCDB: a monte carlo approach to managing uncertain data. In *Proceedings of the ACM SIGMOD International Conference on Management of Data, SIGMOD 2008, Vancouver, BC, Canada, June 10-12, 2008*, pages 687–700, 2008.

[23] N. Kalchbrenner, E. Grefenstette, and P. Blunsom. A convolutional neural network for modelling sentences. In *Proceedings of the 52nd Annual Meeting of the Association for Computational Linguistics, ACL 2014, June 22-27, 2014, Baltimore, MD, USA*, pages 655–665, 2014.

[24] G. Kasneci, M. Ramanath, F. M. Suchanek, and G. Weikum. The YAGO-NAGA approach to knowledge discovery. *SIGMOD Record*, 37(4):41–47, 2008.

[25] M. L. Koc and C. Ré. Incrementally maintaining classification using an RDBMS. *PVLDB*, 4(5):302–313, 2011.

[26] S. Krause, H. Li, H. Uszkoreit, and F. Xu. Large-scale learning of relation-extraction rules with distant supervision from the web. In *ISWC*, 2012.

[27] J. Li, A. Ritter, and E. H. Hovy. Weakly supervised user profile extraction from twitter. In *Proceedings of the 52nd Annual Meeting of the Association for Computational Linguistics, ACL 2014, June 22-27, 2014, Baltimore, MD, USA, Volume 1: Long Papers*, pages 165–174, 2014.

[28] Y. Li, F. R. Reiss, and L. Chiticariu. SystemT: A declarative information extraction system. In *The 49th Annual Meeting of the Association for Computational Linguistics: Human Language Technologies, Proceedings of the Conference, 19-24 June, 2011, Portland, Oregon, USA*, pages 109–114, 2011.

[29] J. Liu, S. J. Wright, C. Ré, V. Bittorf, and S. Sridhar. An asynchronous parallel stochastic coordinate descent algorithm. In *Proceedings of the 31th International Conference on Machine Learning, ICML 2014, Beijing, China, 21-26 June 2014*, pages 469–477, 2014.

[30] E. K. Mallory et al. Large-scale extraction of gene interactions from full text literature using deepdive. *Bioinformatics*, 2015.

[31] M. Marchetti-Bowick and N. Chambers. Learning for microblogs with distant supervision: Political forecasting with twitter. In *EACL*, 2012.

[32] B. Min, R. Grishman, L. Wan, C. Wang, and D. Gondek. Distant supervision for relation extraction with an incomplete knowledge base. In *NAACL-HLT*, 2013.

[33] M. Mintz, S. Bills, R. Snow, and D. Jurafsky. Distant supervision for relation extraction without labeled data. In *ACL 2009, Proceedings of the 47th Annual Meeting of the Association for Computational Linguistics and the 4th International Joint Conference on Natural Language Processing of the AFNLP, 2-7 August 2009, Singapore*, pages 1003–1011, 2009.

[34] N. Nakashole, M. Theobald, and G. Weikum. Scalable knowledge harvesting with high precision and high recall. In *Proceedings of the Forth International Conference on Web Search and Web Data Mining, WSDM 2011, Hong Kong, China, February 9-12, 2011*, pages 227–236, 2011.

[35] T.-V. T. Nguyen and A. Moschitti. End-to-end relation extraction using distant supervision from external semantic repositories. In *ACL*, 2011.

[36] F. Niu, C. Ré, A. Doan, and J. W. Shavlik. Tuffy: Scaling up statistical inference in markov logic networks using an RDBMS. *PVLDB*, 4(6):373–384, 2011.

[37] S. E. Peters et al. A machine reading system for assembling synthetic Paleontological databases. *PloS ONE*, 2014.

[38] H. Poon and P. M. Domingos. Joint inference in information extraction. In *Proceedings of the Twenty-Second AAAI Conference on Artificial Intelligence, July 22-26, 2007, Vancouver, British Columbia, Canada*, pages 913–918, 2007.

[39] M. Purver and S. Battersby. Experimenting with distant supervision for emotion classification. In *EACL 2012, 13th Conference of the European Chapter of the Association for Computational Linguistics, Avignon, France, April 23-27, 2012*, pages 482–491, 2012.

[40] C. Ré, A. A. Sadeghian, Z. Shan, J. Shin, F. Wang, S. Wu, and C. Zhang. Feature engineering for knowledge base construction. *IEEE Data Eng. Bull.*, 37(3):26–40, 2014.

[41] B. Recht, C. Re, S. J. Wright, and F. Niu. Hogwild: A lock-free approach to parallelizing stochastic gradient descent. In *Advances in Neural Information Processing Systems 24: 25th Annual Conference on Neural Information Processing Systems 2011. Proceedings of a meeting held 12-14 December 2011, Granada, Spain.*, pages 693–701, 2011.

[42] S. Riedel, L. Yao, and A. McCallum. Modeling relations and their mentions without labeled text. In *Machine Learning and Knowledge Discovery in Databases, European Conference, ECML PKDD 2010, Barcelona, Spain, September 20-24, 2010, Proceedings, Part III*, pages 148–163, 2010.

[43] C. P. Robert and G. Casella. *Monte Carlo Statistical Methods*. Springer-Verlag New York, Inc., Secaucus, NJ, USA, 2005.

[44] W. Shen, A. Doan, J. F. Naughton, and R. Ramakrishnan. Declarative information extraction using datalog with embedded extraction predicates. In *Proceedings of the 33rd International Conference on Very Large Data Bases, University of Vienna, Austria, September 23-27, 2007*, pages 1033–1044, 2007.

[45] J. Shin, C. Ré, and M. J. Cafarella. Mindtagger: A demonstration of data labeling in knowledge base construction. *PVLDB*, 8(12):1920–1931, 2015.

[46] F. M. Suchanek, M. Sozio, and G. Weikum. SOFIE: a self-organizing framework for information extraction. In *Proceedings of the 18th International Conference on World Wide Web, WWW 2009, Madrid, Spain, April 20-24, 2009*, pages 631–640, 2009.

[47] M. Surdeanu, S. Gupta, J. Bauer, D. McClosky, A. X. Chang, V. I. Spitkovsky, and C. D. Manning. Stanford's distantly-supervised slot-filling system. In *Proceedings of the Fourth Text Analysis Conference, TAC 2011, Gaithersburg, Maryland, USA, November 14-15, 2011*, 2011.

[48] M. Surdeanu, D. McClosky, J. Tibshirani, J. Bauer, A. X. Chang, V. I. Spitkovsky, and C. D. Manning. A simple distant supervision approach for the TAC-KBP slot filling task. In *Proceedings of the Third Text Analysis Conference, TAC 2010, Gaithersburg, Maryland, USA, November 15-16, 2010*, 2010.

[49] M. J. Wainwright and M. I. Jordan. Log-determinant relaxation for approximate inference in discrete markov random fields. *IEEE Transactions on Signal Processing*, 54(6-1):2099–2109, 2006.

[50] M. J. Wainwright and M. I. Jordan. Graphical models, exponential families, and variational inference. *Foundations and Trends in Machine Learning*, 1(1-2):1–305, 2008.

[51] L. Yao, S. Riedel, and A. McCallum. Collective cross-document relation extraction without labelled data. In *Proceedings of the 2010 Conference on Empirical Methods in Natural Language Processing, EMNLP 2010, 9-11 October 2010, MIT Stata Center, Massachusetts, USA, A meeting of SIGDAT, a Special Interest Group of the ACL*, pages 1013–1023, 2010.

[52] A. Yates and O. Etzioni. Unsupervised resolution of objects and relations on the web. In *Human Language Technology Conference of the North American Chapter of the Association of Computational Linguistics, Proceedings, April 22-27, 2007, Rochester, New York, USA*, pages 121–130, 2007.

[53] C. Zhang, F. Niu, C. Ré, and J. W. Shavlik. Big data versus the crowd: Looking for relationships in all the right places. In *The 50th Annual Meeting of the Association for Computational Linguistics, Proceedings of the Conference, July 8-14, 2012, Jeju Island, Korea - Volume 1: Long Papers*, pages 825–834, 2012.

[54] C. Zhang and C. Ré. Towards high-throughput gibbs sampling at scale: a study across storage managers. In *Proceedings of the ACM SIGMOD International Conference*

on Management of Data, SIGMOD 2013, New York, NY, USA, June 22-27, 2013, pages 397–408, 2013.

[55] C. Zhang and C. Re. Dimmwitted: A study of main-memory statistical analytics. *PVLDB*, 7(12):1283–1294, 2014.

[56] J. Zhu, Z. Nie, X. Liu, B. Zhang, and J. Wen. StatSnowball: a statistical approach to extracting entity relationships. In *Proceedings of the 18th International Conference on World Wide Web, WWW 2009, Madrid, Spain, April 20-24, 2009*, pages 101–110, 2009.

[57] M. Zinkevich, M. Weimer, A. J. Smola, and L. Li. Parallelized stochastic gradient descent. In *Advances in Neural Information Processing Systems 23: 24th Annual Conference on Neural Information Processing Systems. Vancouver, Canada, December 6-9, 2010.*, pages 2595–2603, 2010.

Estimating the Impact of Unknown Unknowns on Aggregate Query Results

Yeounoh Chung[1] Michael Lind Mortensen[2] Carsten Binnig[1] Tim Kraska[1]

[1]Brown University
{yeounoh_chung, carsten_binnig, tim_kraska}@brown.edu

[2]Aarhus University
illio@cs.au.dk

ABSTRACT

It is common practice for data scientists to acquire and integrate disparate data sources to achieve higher quality results. But even with a perfectly cleaned and merged data set, two fundamental questions remain: (1) is the integrated data set complete and (2) what is the impact of any unknown (i.e., unobserved) data on query results?

In this work, we develop and analyze techniques to estimate the impact of the unknown data (a.k.a., *unknown unknowns*) on simple aggregate queries. The key idea is that the overlap between different data sources enables us to estimate the number and values of the missing data items. Our main techniques are parameter-free and do not assume prior knowledge about the distribution. Through a series of experiments, we show that estimating the impact of *unknown unknowns* is invaluable to better assess the results of aggregate queries over integrated data sources.

1. INTRODUCTION

In the past few years, the number of data sources has increased exponentially because of the ease of publishing data on the web, the proliferation of data-sharing platforms (e.g., Google Fusion Table [19] or Freebase [15]), and the adoption of open data access policies, both in science and government. The success of crowdsourcing [11, 13, 31, 30, 39, 2, 52, 16] provides another virtually unlimited source of information. This deluge of data has enabled data scientists, both in commercial enterprises and in academia, to acquire and integrate data from multiple data sources, achieving higher quality results than ever before. It is therefore not surprising that industry and academia alike have developed highly sophisticated systems and tools to assist data scientists in the process of data integration [29]. However, even with a perfectly cleaned and integrated data set, two fundamental questions remain: (1) do the data sources cover the complete data set of interest and (2) what is the impact of any unknown (i.e., unobserved) data on query results?

SIGMOD'16, June 26-July 01, 2016, San Francisco, CA, USA

ISBN 978-1-4503-3531-7/16/06...$15.00

DOI: http://dx.doi.org/10.1145/2882903.2882909

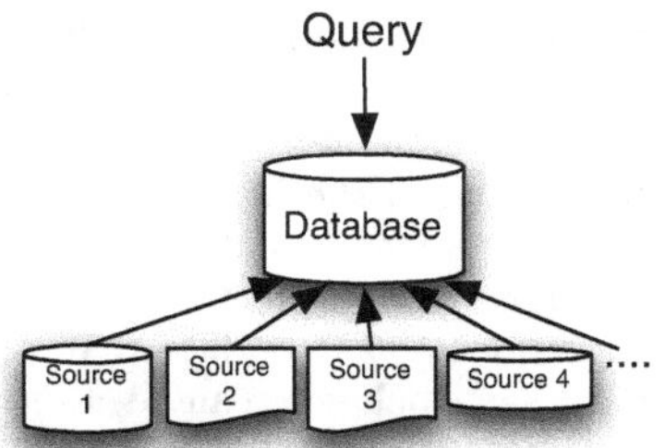

Figure 1: Simple data integration scenario where multiple data sources overlap but are not necessarily complete.

1.1 Unknown Data

In this work, we develop techniques to estimate the impact of the unknown data on aggregate queries of the form `SELECT AGGREGATE(attr) FROM table WHERE predicate`.

We assume a simple data integration scenario, as depicted in Figure 1. Several domain-related data sources are integrated into one database, preserving the lineage information for each data item or record. Naturally, these data sources overlap with each other, but even when put together they might not be complete. For example, all data sources in Figure 1 might list U.S. tech companies but some smaller companies might not be mentioned in any of the sources. This data integration scenario applies to a wide range of use cases ranging from crowdsourcing (where every crowd-worker can be considered a single data source [13]) to data extraction from web pages.

Estimating the impact of the unknown data (data items that are not observed in any data source) is particularly difficult as we know neither how many unique data items are missing nor their values; thus, we deal with **unknown unknowns**. This characteristic distinguishes our work from what is generally known as *missing data*, or *known unknowns*, estimation in Statistics [1, 44, 41], which tries to estimate the value of unknown (missing) attributes for known records. At a first glance, it may seem impossible to estimate the impact of *unknown unknowns*; however, for a large class of data integration scenarios, the analysis of overlap of multiple data sources makes it feasible.

1.2 A Running Example

To demonstrate the impact of *unknown unknowns*, we pose a simple aggregate query to calculate the number of all employees in the U.S. tech industry, `SELECT SUM(employees) FROM us_tech_companies`, over a crowdsourced data set. We used techniques from [13] to design the crowdsourcing tasks on Amazon Mechanical Turk (AMT) to collect employee

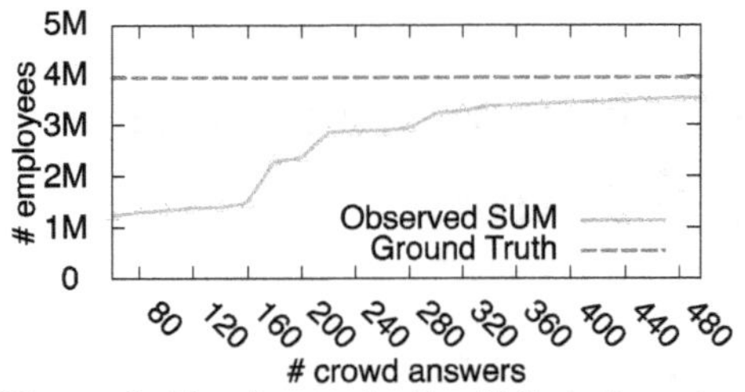

Figure 2: Employees in the U.S. tech sector

numbers from U.S. tech companies.[1] The data was manually cleaned before processing (e.g., entity resolution, removal of partial answers). Figure 2 shows the result.

The red line represents the ground truth (i.e., the total number of employees in the U.S. tech sector) for the query [40], whereas the grey line shows the result of the observed SUM query over time with the increasing number of received crowd-answers. The gap between the observed and the ground truth is due to the impact of the *unknown unknowns*, which gets smaller at a diminishing rate as more crowd-answers arrive.

While the experiment was conducted in the context of crowdsourcing, the same behavior can be observed with other types of data sources, such as web pages. For instance, suppose a user searches the Internet to create a list of all solar energy companies in the U.S. The first few web pages will provide the greatest benefit (i.e., more new solar companies), while after a dozen web pages the benefit of adding another web page diminishes as the likelihood of duplicates increases. The rate of increasing overlap of data sources is indicative of the completeness of the data set.

1.3 A Naïve Solution

The same type of diminishing effect is also known as the *Species Accumulation Curve* in Ecology [48], where the rate of new species discovered decreases with increasing cumulative effort to search. Measuring species richness (i.e., counting species) is critical in many ecological studies. Plotting a *Species Accumulation Curve* provides a way to estimate the number of additional species to be discovered.

These species estimation techniques lay the foundation for estimating the impact of unknown unknowns on aggregate query results. A naïve solution for the SUM query from Section 1.2 would be to first estimate the number of *unknown data* items using species estimation techniques [47] and then use *mean substitution* to estimate their value [38]. This assumes that the missing items have (on average) the same attribute value as the observed (known) data items.

The naïve approach has a couple of drawbacks. First, species estimation has very strict requirements on how data is collected. Almost every data integration scenario violates these requirements, causing the estimator to significantly over/underestimate the number of missing data items.

Second, it ignores the fact that the attribute values of the missing items may be correlated to the likelihood of observing certain data items. For example, large tech companies like Google with many employees are often more well known and thus, appear more often in data sources than smaller start-ups, creating a biased data set. This is problematic since it also biases the mean and with it the estimate.

[1] More precisely, we only asked for companies with a presence in Silicon Valley, as we found it provides more accurate results (see also Section 6).

In the statistics literature, this second problem is referred to as *Missing Not At Random* (MNAR) [38, 44], where the missingness of a data item depends on its value. There are many statistical inference techniques dealing with MNAR [1, 10, 9, 1, 53, 41], but nearly all the techniques require at least partial knowledge of the record. For example, in the case of surveys, people with a high salary might be more reluctant to report their salary but have no problem stating their home address or how many children they have. Existing MNAR techniques use the reported values (e.g., the address) to infer the missing attributes. Unfortunately, this is not possible in the case of *unknown unknowns*, as we miss the entire record.

1.4 Contributions

This work is a first step towards developing techniques to estimate the impact of the *unknown unknowns* on query results. Our focus is on simple aggregate queries, especially *SUM*-aggregates, but we also touch upon other aggregations like *COUNT*, *AVG*, *MIN*, and *MAX*. We design techniques that can deal with the peculiarities of the data integration scenarios discussed before, such as uneven contributions from different sources (bias of data sources).

In this work, we use crowdsourced data sets because they are easier to collect, but the techniques are general and apply to almost all data integration scenarios that combine overlapping data sources. While we do not argue that the proposed techniques can predict black-swan-like data items (i.e., extremely rare data items), we will show that our techniques can provide useful estimates under more "normal" circumstances, which we will define more formally. For instance, in the example of Figure 2, we can get an almost perfect estimate of the impact of the *unknown unknowns* after only 350 crowd-answers. In addition, by building upon recent work on the Good-Turing estimator [32], we are able to provide an upper bound for our estimates under easy to understand conditions. In summary we make the following contributions:

- We formalize the problem of estimating the impact of *unknown unknowns* on query results and describe why existing techniques for species estimation and missing data estimation are not sufficient.
- We develop techniques to estimate the impact of the *unknown unknowns* on aggregate query results.
- We derive a first upper bound for *SUM*-aggregate queries.
- We examine the effectiveness of our techniques via experiments using both real and synthetitc data sets.

In the following, we first formalize our problem statement (Section 2), present techniques to estimate the impact of *unknown unknowns* for sum-queries (Section 3), and propose an upper bound estimate (Section 4). Section 5 extends these techniques to other aggregate functions and in Section 6, we evaluate our techniques, followed by related work and conclusion.

2. THE IMPACT OF UNKNOWN UNKNOWNS

In this Section, we define *unknown unknowns*, explain how data integration over multiple sources can be regarded as a sampling process and formally define our estimation goal. For convenience Appendix A contains a symbol-table.

For the purpose of this work, we treat data cleaning (e.g., entity resolution, data fusion, etc.) as an orthogonal problem. Any data cleaning techniques [1, 12, 23, 35, 36, 34]

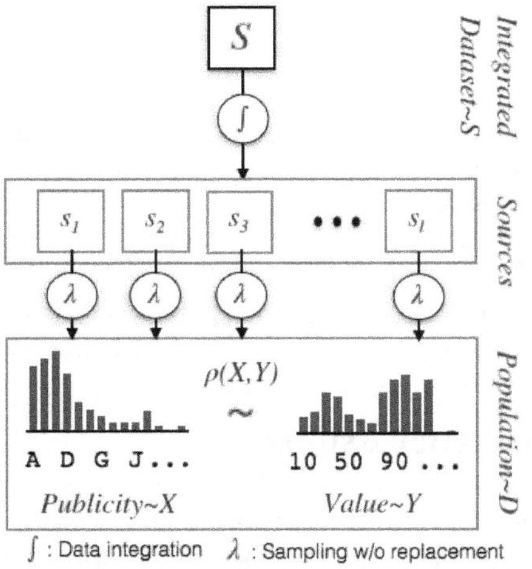

Figure 3: A sampling process for the integrated database.

can be applied to our problem without altering the problem context. While data quality can influence the estimation quality, studying it goes beyond the scope of this paper [47]. We assume that after a proper data cleaning process we have one instance per observed entity and know exactly how many times the entity was observed across multiple data sources.

2.1 Unknown Unknowns

We assume that queries are of the form `SELECT AGGREGATE(attr) FROM table WHERE predicate`, that *table* only contains records about a single entity class (e.g., companies) and that a record in *table* corresponds to exactly one real-world entity (e.g., IBM). Thus, in the remainder of the paper we use record, entity and data item interchangeably.

DEFINITION 1. *(Unknown Unknowns) Let Ω be the universe of unknown size of all valid unique entities r for a given entity class, and let $attr_A(r)$ be the value of attribute A of r. Then the ground truth $D \subseteq \Omega$ is defined as a set of entities that satisfy the predicate, i.e., $D = \{r \in \Omega \mid predicate(r)\}$, where its size $N = |D|$ is not known. Let S be a sample with replacement from D and c be the number of unique entities in S. Unknown unknowns U refers to any unobserved entity r that exists in D but not in S: $U = D - S$ with size $N - c$.*

For our running example, Ω would be the universe of all companies in the world, D all tech companies in the US and $\sum_{r \in D} attr_{empl}(r)$ be the true number of U.S. tech sector employees. S would be a sample with duplicates and *unknown unknowns* would be every company which is not in S.

What we aim to achieve is a good estimate of the ground truth: `SELECT AGGREGATE(attr) FROM D`, when we only have S. Note, that we drop the *predicate* from the query, since every item in D already has to fulfill the *predicate*. In this work, we assume that we neither know all entities in D nor its size (i.e., *open world* assumption). This distinguishes our problem from the problem of *missing data* [38, 44, 45], which refers to incomplete data or missing attribute values.

2.2 Data Integration As Sampling Process

Data integration refers to the process of combining different data sources under a common schema [12]. For the purpose of this work, we assume that data sources are independent samples (e.g., data sources are not copies from each other and instead are independently created), and we model the data integration process as a multi-stage sampling process as shown in Figure 3.

We assume l data sources $s_1 ... s_l$, each sampling $n_j = |s_j|$ data items from the ground truth D (e.g., the complete set of tech companies in the US with their respective number of employees), **without replacement**, since a data source typically only mentions a data item once. We also assume that every data item $d_i \in D$ has a *publicity* likelihood p_i of being sampled, following some distribution X. Likewise, the attribute values (e.g., the number of employees) have a certain likelihood to appear in the ground truth, referred to as *value likelihood*, again following some distribution Y. These two distributions are possibly correlated making the *publicity-value correlation* bigger or smaller than 0: $\rho \neq 0$.

The data sources l are then integrated into a single integrated data set S of size $n_S = \sum_{j=1}^{l} n_j$. Although each source samples without replacement from $N = |D|$ different classes (i.e., unique data item), S contains duplicates because every data source is sampling from the same underlying truth D. If l is sufficiently large, S **approximates a sample with replacement** from D, which is why species estimation techniques work in the first place (we analyze the effects of smaller l in Section 3.4 and 6). The number of unique data items c in S is likely to be smaller than N. In contrast, the end-user only sees a view of S, referred to as the integrated database K (for *Known* data), which contains only one entity per unique entity in S.

This data integration model covers a large class of use cases from web integration to crowdsourcing. In the latter case, each crowd worker can be regarded as a separate data source s_j since it is known that workers also sample without replacement from D [47]. While extremely powerful, there are scenarios where this sampling model does not apply. Most importantly, data sources are not always independent [25]. Furthermore, the number of data sources l has to be large enough to have sufficient overlap between the sources (see Section 6). If any of these assumptions are violated, then only low-quality estimations are possible.

2.3 Problem Statement

We are interested in estimating the impact of *unknown unknowns* (U) to adjust aggregate query results.

DEFINITION 2. *(The Impact of Unknown Unknowns) Given an integrated database K, the impact of unknown unknowns is defined as the difference between the current answer ϕ_K of the aggregate query over the database K and the answer over the ground-truth ϕ_D:*

$$\Delta = \phi_D - \phi_K \tag{1}$$

Our goal is to estimate the answer on the ground-truth by estimating Δ based on S:

$$\hat{\phi}_D = \phi_K + \hat{\Delta}(S) \tag{2}$$

Note that this definition works for all common aggregates including *MIN* and *MAX*, where $\hat{\Delta}$ would be the positive or negative adjustment to the observed *MIN*/*MAX* value.

3. SUM QUERY

In this section, we focus on *SUM*-aggregates to illustrate our estimation techniques. We first formalize the naïve estimator (Section 3.1), which was informally introduced in the introduction. We then develop the *frequency* estimator by making *naïve* estimator more robust to the *publicity-value correlation* (Section 3.2). Afterwards, we describe the more sophisticated *bucket* estimator (Section 3.3). Finally, we develop a *Monte-Carlo* estimator which is better suited for a smaller set of data sources (Section 3.4).

3.1 Naïve Estimator

Estimating the impact of *unknown unknowns* for *SUM* queries is equivalent to solving two sub-problems: (1) estimating how many unique data items are missing (i.e., the *unknown unknowns* count estimate), and (2) estimating the attribute values of the missing data items (i.e., the *unknown unknowns* value estimate). The *naïve* estimator uses the *Chao*92 [7] species estimation technique to estimate the number of the missing data items, and *mean substitution* [38] to estimate the values of them.

Let $\phi_K = \sum_{r \in K} attr(r)$ be the current sum over the integrated database, then we can more formally define our *naïve* estimator for the impact of *unknown unknowns* as:

$$\Delta_{naive} = \underbrace{\frac{\phi_K}{c}}_{\text{Value estimate}} \cdot \underbrace{(\hat{N} - c)}_{\text{Count estimate}} \quad (3)$$

$\hat{N}$ is the estimate of the number of unique data items in the ground truth D, and c is the number of unique entities in our integrated database K (thus, $\hat{N} - c$ is our estimate of the number of the unknown data items). ϕ_K/c is the average attribute value of all unique entities in our database K.

3.1.1 Chao92 estimator

Throughout the paper, we use the popular *Chao*92 estimator. Many species estimation techniques exist [3, 6], but we choose *Chao*92 since it is more robust to a skewed publicity distribution. The *Chao92* estimator uses *sample coverage* to predict $\hat{N}$. The sample coverage C is defined as the sum of the probabilities p_i of the observed classes. Since the true distribution $p_1 ... p_N$ is unknown, we estimate C using the Good-Turing estimator [14]:

$$\hat{C} = 1 - f_1/n \quad (4)$$

The f-statistics, e.g., f_1, represent the frequencies of observed data items in the sample, where f_j is the number of data items with exactly j occurrences in the sample. f_1 is referred as *singletons*, f_2 *doubletons*, and f_0 as the *missing data* [4]. Sample coverage measures the ratio between the number of singletons (f_1) and the sample size (n). This ratio changes with the amount of duplicates in the sample. The high-level idea is that the more duplicates that exist in our sample S compared to the number of singletons f_1, the more complete the sample is (i.e., higher sample coverage).

In addition, the *Chao92* estimator explicitly incorporates the skewness of the underlying distribution using *coefficient of variance* (*CV*) γ, a metric that is used to describe the dispersion in a probability distribution [7]. A higher *CV* indicates a higher variability among the p_i values, while a $CV = 0$ indicates that each item is equally likely (i.e., the items follow a uniform distribution).

Given the publicity ($p_1 \cdots p_N$) that describe the probability of the i-th class being sampled from D, with mean $\bar{p} = \sum_i p_i/N = 1/N$, *CV* can be expressed as follows:

$$\gamma = \left[\sum_i (p_i - \bar{p})^2 / N \right]^{1/2} / \bar{p} \quad (5)$$

However, since p_i is not available for all data items, *CV* has to be estimated using the f-statistic:

$$\hat{\gamma}^2 = \max \left\{ \frac{\frac{c}{\hat{C}} \sum_i i(i-1) f_i}{n(n-1)} - 1, 0 \right\} \quad (6)$$

The final *Chao92* estimator for $\hat{N}_{Chao92}$ can then be formalated as:

$$\hat{N}_{Chao92} = \frac{c}{\hat{C}} + \frac{n(1-\hat{C})}{\hat{C}} \cdot \hat{\gamma}^2 \quad (7)$$

3.1.2 The Estimator

$\hat{N}_{Chao92}$ is our estimate for N, and comparing this to c provides us with a means of evaluating the completeness of S. By substituting $\hat{N}_{Chao92}$ for $\hat{N}$, the final *naïve* estimator can be written as:

$$\Delta_{naive} = \frac{\phi_K}{c} \cdot (\hat{N}_{Chao92} - c) = \frac{\phi_K \cdot f_1 \cdot (c + \hat{\gamma}^2 n)}{c \cdot (n - f_1)} \quad (8)$$

Note, that the *naïve* estimator does not consider any *publicity-value correlation* and thus tends to over-estimate (or under-estimate) the ground truth.

3.2 Frequency Estimator

We developed a simple variation of the *naïve* estimator, which makes direct use of the frequency statistics to improve estimation quality. All coverage-based species estimation methods give special attention to the singletons f_1; the data items observed exactly once. The idea is that those items, in relation to the sample size n, give a clue about how well the complete population is covered. A ratio of f_1/n close to 1 means that almost every sample is unique, indicating that many items might still be missing. Conversely, a ratio close to 0 indicates all unique values have been observed several times, decreasing the likelihood of any unknown data. We use a similar reasoning to improve our value estimation. The key idea is that singletons are the best indicator of missing data items, and that their average value might be a better representation of the values of the missing items. Let ϕ_{f_1} be the sum of all singletons, $\sum_{r \in singletons} attr(r)$ and $\hat{N}_{Chao92}$ again be the *Chao*92 count estimate. Then the estimator can be defined as:

$$\Delta_{freq} = \frac{\phi_{f_1}}{f_1} \cdot (\hat{N}_{Chao92} - c) = \frac{\phi_{f_1} (c + \hat{\gamma}^2 n)}{n - f_1} \quad (9)$$

While this estimator still does not directly consider the *publicity-value correlation*, it is more robust against popular high-impact data items (i.e., data items with extreme *attribute* values). For example, in our running employee example, big companies that are highly visible like Google or IBM can significantly impact the known value estimate ϕ_K/c. However, through using the average value of the singletons, ϕ_{f_1}/f_1, it is reasonable to assume that those companies will not stay as singletons very long in any sample and thus will not impact the average value for the *unknown unknowns*. This estimator is surprisingly simple and becomes even simpler if we assume $\hat{\gamma}^2 = 0$:

$$\Delta_{freq} = \frac{\phi_{f_1} \cdot c}{n - f_1} \quad (10)$$

Note, that $\hat{\gamma}^2 = 0$ makes it a Good-Turing estimate, which also converges to the ground truth even for skewed publicity values; it might just take a bit longer [7]. While Δ_{freq} is not the best estimator (see Section 6) the simplicity makes it still useful to quickly test if an aggregate query result might be impacted by any *unknown unknowns*.

3.3 Bucket Estimator

The problem with the previous two estimators is that they do not directly consider a correlation between publicity and attribute values. We designed the *bucket* as a first estimator designed for *unknown unknowns* with *publicity-value correlation*. The idea of the estimator is to divide the attribute value range into smaller sub-ranges called buckets, and treat each bucket as a separate data set. We can then estimate the *impact of unknown unknowns* per bucket (e.g., large, medium, or small companies) and aggregate them to the overall effect:

$$\Delta_{bucket} = \sum_i \Delta(b_i) \tag{11}$$

Here Δ_{b_i} refers to the estimate per bucket and both the *frequency* or *naïve* estimator could be used. Using buckets has two effects: first, it provides more detailed estimates of what types of companies are missing; second, it decreases the variance of item values per bucket, making the estimate less prune to outliers (e.g., items with extreme low and high values can be "contained" in separate buckets).

The challenge with the *bucket* estimator is to determine the right size for each bucket. If the bucket size is too small, the bucket contains almost no data items. In an extreme case of having a single data item per bucket, no count or proper value estimation is possible. If the bucket size is too big, then the *publicity-value correlation* can still bias the estimate. In fact, the case with a single bucket is equivalent to using just the *naïve* or *frequency* estimator. In the following we describe two bucketing strategies.

3.3.1 Static Bucket

An easy way to define buckets is to divide the observed value range into a fixed n_b number of buckets of size w_i:

$$w_i = \frac{(a_{max} - a_{min})}{n_b} \tag{12}$$

where a_{min} (a_{max}) refers to the min (max) observed attribute value. Afterwards we apply Δ_{naive} per bucket. It is important to note that the estimate goes to infinity with buckets which only contain singletons due to division-by-zero ($n - f_1 = 0$, see equation 8), which can significantly increase the error of the estimate for very small buckets.

The optimal number of buckets varies depending on the underlying publicity distribution (see Appendix B); unfortunately, the true publicity distribution is not known and we cannot predetermine the right number (or size) of static buckets. To this end, we found that static buckets based estimation is of little practical value.

3.3.2 Dynamic Bucket

To overcome the previously mentioned issues, we developed several alternative statistical approaches to determine the optimal bucket boundaries over time. The most notable are our uses of the error estimate/upper bounds from Section 4 and of treating f_1 as a random variable (see also Section 3.5). Surprisingly, we achieve the best performance across all our real-world use cases and simulations using a rather simple conservative approach, referred to as $\Delta_{Dynamic}$.

The core idea behind our dynamic strategy $\Delta_{Dynamic}$ is to sort the *attribute* values of S and then recursively split the range into smaller buckets only if it minimizes the estimated impact of *unknown unknowns*, i.e., the absolute Δ value. Intuitively, this is controversial since either under- or overestimation could be better for different use cases. However, there is a more fundamental reason behind this strategy.

The Foundation: Whenever we split a data set into buckets, each bucket contains less data than before the split, and the chance of an estimation error increases due to the *law of large numbers* (i.e., the less data the higher the potential variance) [32, 28]. To illustrate this, we consider the simplest case of a uniform *publicity* distribution ($\hat{\gamma} = 0$) and an even bucket split. In this case, the $Chao92$ estimate for

Algorithm 1: Dynamic bucket generation

```
Input  : S
Output: List of buckets
b0 = (minValue(S), maxValue(S)) ;  /* init bucket b0 */
todo = [b0];                        /* list with b0 */
δmin = abs(Δ(b0)) ;                 /* Δ estimate over b0 */
bkts = [] ;                         /* final bucket list */
while !todo.empty do
    b = todo.pop ;                  /* remove first element */
    δtmp = δmin − abs(Δ(b));
    tmp = (null, null) ;            /* Empty pair */
    for unique r ∈ b do
        (t1, t2) = split(b, r.value) ;
        if δmin > δtmp + abs(Δ(t1)) + abs(Δ(t2)) then
            δmin = δtmp + abs(Δ(t1)) + abs(Δ(t2));
            tmp = (t1, t2);
        end
    end
    if tmp ≠ (null, null) then
        todo.add(t1, t2);
    else
        bkts.add(b);
    end
end
return bkts;
```

$\hat{N}$ is greater than or equal to the estimate before the split:

$$\hat{N}_{Chao92} = \frac{c}{1 - f_1/n} = \overbrace{\frac{n \cdot c}{n - f_1}}^{\text{Before split}} \le \underbrace{\frac{n_{b1} \cdot c_{b1}}{n_{b1} - f_{1_{b1}}} + \frac{n_{b2} \cdot c_{b2}}{n_{b2} - f_{1_{b2}}}}_{\text{After split}} \tag{13}$$

When we split the data exactly into halves, it follows that $c_{b1} = c_{b2} = c/2$ (i.e., we split in regard to the unique values). With a uniform publicity distribution, every item is equally likely, and therefore we can assume that both buckets contain roughly the same amount of data after the split: $n_{b1} = n_{b2} \approx n/2$. However, in contrast to n and c, the number of singletons (f_1) can vary significantly between the buckets. In fact, we know that the estimators only stabilize if every item was observed several times [7] and as a consequence n has to be significantly larger than c and c significantly larger than f_1 ($n \gg c \gg f_1$); if we split, there is a higher chance that we unevenly distribute the f_1 among the buckets.

To model the uneven distribution of f_1 we introduce another parameter $\alpha \in [0, 1]$ and set $f_{1_{b1}} = \alpha \cdot f_1$ and $f_{1_{b2}} = (1-\alpha) \cdot f_1$. As a result the inequality in equation 13 becomes:

$$\underbrace{\frac{n \cdot c}{n - f_1}}_{\text{Before split}} \le \underbrace{\frac{\frac{n}{2} \cdot \frac{c}{2}}{\frac{n}{2} - \alpha \cdot f_1} + \frac{\frac{n}{2} \cdot \frac{c}{2}}{\frac{n}{2} - (1 - \alpha) \cdot f_1}}_{\text{After split}} \tag{14}$$

Appendix C shows that the right hand side of the above inequality has its global minimum at $\alpha = 0.5$, which evaluates to $nc/(n - f_1)$ ($\hat{N}$ before split), and that the inequality always holds. Thus, it can be seen that splitting a data set into buckets not only potentially increases the error, but it does so in a monotonic way.

Yet, this does not mean that the *sum* estimate Δ always increases as well. Especially with a *publicity-value correlation*, the overall estimate of Δ over all buckets can still decrease as the average *attribute* values per bucket differ. This is in-line with our original motivation to use buckets, as we wanted to get a more detailed *unknown unknowns* estimate (e.g., how many small companies vs. large companies are missing). Bringing these two observations together, we can assume for many real-world use cases that whenever our estimate of the impact of unknown unknowns Δ increases after a split, it has a significant chance of being caused by the increasing error in $\hat{N}$, whereas when it decreases it potentially improves the estimate due to the more detailed unknown estimate. While it does not always have to be the case (e.g., if the publicity-value correlation is negative) it is still an indicator for many real-world use cases (see Section 6). Based on the observations, we have devised the conservative bucket splitting strategy: only split the bucket if the overall estimate for Δ is minimized.

The Algorithm: Algorithm 1 shows the final algorithm. First we add a bucket which covers the complete value range of S to the *todo* list (line 2) and calculate the current Δ over S (line 3). Note that we take the absolute values of all estimates (Δ) to underestimate the impact of *unknown unknowns* even for the case of having negative attribute values (e.g., net losses of companies). Afterwards, we check recursively if we can split the bucket to minimize Δ until no further "underestimation" is possible (line 5-21).

We therefore remove the first bucket from the *todo* list (line 6) and calculate the Δ over S without the impact of this bucket b (line 7). Note, that during the first iteration δ_{tmp} will be 0. Afterwards, for every unique record in b, we split the current bucket b into two temporary buckets t_1 and t_2 based on the record's attribute value (line 10). If the resulting estimate using this split is bigger than any previously observed minimums (line 11), we set the new minimum to this value (line 12) and store the new buckets (line 13). When the for-loop of line 9-15 finishes and if at least one new bucket was found (line 16), *tmp* will contain the new split point, which minimizes δ for the bucket, and δ_{min} the new minimum value of δ. These buckets are then added to the *todo* list (line 17) to check, if splitting them again would further lower the estimate. On the other hand, if *tmp* is empty, the algorithm wasn't able to further split the bucket and the current bucket without any additional splits is added to the final bucket list (line 19). If no buckets are left in the *todo* list, the algorithm terminates and *bkts* contains the final list of buckets.

3.4 Monte-Carlo Estimator

As our experiments show, the previous estimator actually performs very well (see Section 6). However, what it does not consider is the effect of uneven contributions from data sources (i.e., one data source contains much more data than another) and the peculiarities of the sampling process itself. The *Chao*92 species estimation, like almost all other estimators, assumes sampling *with* replacement, whereas our data sources sample *without* replacement from the underlying ground truth. The reason why the *Chao*92 still works is that with a reasonably high number of data sources, the integrated data source S approximates a sample with replacement [47]. However, with either a small number of data sources or uneven contributions from sources (i.e., some sources are significantly bigger than others), S diverges significantly from a sample done with replacement, resulting in significant over- or under-estimation. In the case of crowdsourcing, the workers which provide significantly more data items than other workers are referred to as *streakers* [47].

To address these issues, we present a *Monte Carlo*-based (MC) estimator for $\hat{N}$. The idea is that we simulate the sampling process to find the most likely distribution with population size N, which best explains the observed sample including how many items s_j every data source j contributes. More formally, given $(s_1, ..., s_l)$ what we seek is a set of parameters Θ (e.g., the distribution parameters) for the MC simulation, which minimize some distance function Γ between the observed data S and the simulated data Q_Θ:

$$\underset{\Theta}{\operatorname{argmin}}\, \Gamma(S, Q_\Theta | l, [s_1, ..., s_l]) \qquad (15)$$

In the following we first describe the MC method for generating Q_Θ given a distance function Γ and a search strategy to find the optimal parameter Θ[20].

3.4.1 Monte-Carlo Method

In contrast to the other estimators, the *Monte-Carlo* estimator requires an assumption about the shape of the underlying *publicity* distribution; in this work, we use an exponential distribution for *publicity*, from which data source j samples n_j data items. Accordingly, the parameter Θ has two components: θ_N specifies the assumed number of data items, and θ_λ governs the shape (skew) of *publicity* distribution. Note, that the assumption of the exponential distributions makes the MC method a parametric model. The goal of the MC simulation is to determine how well θ_N and θ_λ help to explain the observed S.

Algorithm 2 outlines our MC algorithm. First, we use an exponential distribution with skew θ_λ to sample *publicity* $(p_1 \cdots p_{\hat{N}})$ for $\theta_{\hat{N}}$ items (line 1), and then we initialize the distance to 0 (line 2). Afterwards, we repeat the following procedure *nbRuns* times. For every data source (line 5) we sample n_j data items according to E, but also without replacement (line 6). The sampled items are added to Q to form a histogram (line 7) for the particular run. After simulating l sources, Q contains the simulated version of S.

To finally compare the simulated sample Q with the observed sample S, we make use of the discrete KL-divergence metric [24]. However, this requires transforming S and Q into a frequency statistic and indexing them to ensure that the right items are compared with each other (line 9).

After the indexing we have two comparable frequency statistics for S and the simulation: F_S and F_Q. However, S might contain less than $\hat{N}$ unique data items, for which the KL-divergence is not defined. We therefore adjust F_S and assign a small non-zero probability to the missing extra unique items (line 10). Finally, the two frequency statistics can be compared using the standard KL-Divergence metric and added to the total distance (line 11). After all the simulation runs the average distance is returned (line 13).

3.4.2 Search Strategy

We can now simulate the observed sampling process leading to S, but we still need a way to find the optimal Θ, which best explains the observed sample S. The difficulty is that even though the KL-divergence cost function is convex, the integer variable $\hat{N}$ prevents us from using tractable optimization algorithms (e.g., gradient descent). Furthermore, the distance function can be quite sensitive to small amounts of noise in D.

We therefore make the estimator more robust by first performing a grid search for Θ (line 5-10). We vary θ_N between $c \leq \hat{N} \leq \hat{N}_{Chao92}$ with a step-size $(\hat{N}_{Chao92} - c)/10$ and θ_λ between $-0.4 \leq \lambda \leq 0.4$ (i.e., almost no to heavy skew) with

Algorithm 2: Monte Carlo method

```
Input  : θ_N̂, θ_λ, S, [n_1, ..., n_l], nbRuns
Output: Average distance
1  E = dist(θ_N̂, θ_λ);                /* publicity of N̂ items */
2  Γ = 0.0;                            /* default value */
3  for i = 1 to nbRuns do
4      Q = [];                         /* simulated model */
5      for j = 1 to l do
6          s_i = sample(n_j, E);       /* w/o repl */
7          Q.add(s_i);
8      end
9      (F_S, F_Q) = indexing(S, Q);
10     F'_S = smooth(F_S, F_Q);
11     Γ += klDiv(F'_S, F_Q);          /* KL-divergence */
12 end
13 return Γ/nbRuns;
```

Algorithm 3: Monte-Carlo based $\hat{N}$ estimation

```
Input  : [s_1, ...s_l], c, N̂_Chao92, nbRuns
Output: Estimated number of unique data items, N̂
1  D_KL = [];                                  /* KL-divergence */
2  n = sizes([s_1, ..., s_l]);                 /* [n_1, ..., n_l] */
3  Θ_N̂ = [c : (N̂_Chao92 − c)/10 : N_Chao92];
4  Θ_λ = [−0.4 : 0.1 : 0.4];
5  for θ_N̂ ∈ Θ_N̂ do
6      for θ_N̂ ∈ Θ_λ do
7          Γ = monteCarlo(θ_N̂, θ_λ, n, n_r);  /* Alg 2 */
8          D_KL.add(Γ);
9      end
10 end
11 p = curveFit(Θ_N̂, Θ_λ, D_KL, 2);          /* 2-D curve fit */
12 [N̂, λ] = argmin_{λ∈[−0.4,0.4], N̂∈[c, N̂_Chao92]} {p(N̂, λ)} ; /* min on the curve */
13 return N̂;
```

a step-size 0.1 (line 2 and 3). The step sizes are chosen to be small enough to efficiently model the convex curve, but large enough to be robust to any noise. Afterwards, we fit a two-dimensional curve using least-squares curve fitting (line 11) and return the $\hat{N}_{MC}$ with the minimum D_{KL} on the fitted curve as the final count estimate (line 11).

Finally, to estimate the total difference, we use our *naïve* estimation technique with $\hat{N}_{MC}$. The estimate is more robust and over-estimates less than the original *naïve* estimator as our MC method always penalizes any unmatched unique items in Q. In other words, the MC estimator favors solutions where $\hat{N}$ is closer to the number of observed unique items c.

3.5 Other Estimators

During the course of developing the above estimators, we explored various alternatives. For example, we experimented with alternative static bucket strategies (see also Appendix B). Furthermore, we noticed that many proposed techniques can be combined. For instance, we can use the *frequency* estimator, instead of the *naïve* estimator, with the *bucket* (i.e., *Dynamic Bucket* approach) estimator or the *Monte-Carlo* estimator; furthermore, we can also combine the *Monte-Carlo* estimator with the *bucket* estimator.

However, since the *Monte-Carlo* estimator requires larger sample size for accurate estimates, applying it to a smaller bucket often degrades the estimation quality. Also, our experiences tell us that the difference between the *naïve* and *frequency* estimators does not help much for the *bucket* approach (see Appendix D). Therefore, we focus on the original techniques for the evaluation of this work.

4. ESTIMATION ERROR UPPER BOUND

In this section, we derive an estimation error upper bound, specifically, the worst case estimation error of the *naïve* estimator (Equation 3): the product of the worst case count and the worst case value estimates. The same upper bound can easily be applied to each bucket in the *bucket* estimator, as well as the *Monte-Carlo* estimator.

The *Chao*92 count estimation is based on *sample coverage* plus a correction for the skew $\hat{\gamma} > 0$. Recent work proposed an error bound of the Good-Turing estimator for the ground truth *unknown unknowns* distribution mass (M_0) [32]:

$$M_0 \leq \frac{f_1}{n} + (2\sqrt{2} + \sqrt{3}) \cdot \sqrt{\frac{\log 3/\epsilon}{n}} \tag{16}$$

which holds with **probability at least** $1 - \epsilon$ over the choice of the sample with $n = |S|$. The confidence parameter ϵ governs the tightness of this bound (we use $\epsilon = 0.01$ for 99% confidence). Based on equation 16, we bound $Chao92$:

$$\begin{aligned}\hat{N}_{Chao92} &= \frac{c}{\hat{C}} + \frac{n(1-\hat{C})}{\hat{C}} \cdot \hat{\gamma}^2 \\ &\approx \frac{c}{\hat{C}} = \frac{c}{1 - M_0} \\ &\leq \frac{c}{1 - (\frac{f_1}{n} + (2\sqrt{2} + \sqrt{3}) \cdot \sqrt{\frac{\log\log 3/\delta}{n}})}\end{aligned} \tag{17}$$

Notice, that we can omit $\hat{\gamma}$ as it only makes the $Chao92$ converge faster, but does not influence the asymptotic estimate, which is based on the sample coverage.

As the distribution of the *mean substitution* ($\frac{\phi_K}{c}$) tend to a normal distribution (*Central Limit Theorem*), we define the worst case estimate of the ground truth *attribute* mean value ($\frac{\phi_D}{N}$) with the help of the sample standard deviation (σ_K):

$$\frac{\phi_D}{N} \leq \frac{\phi_K}{c} + z \cdot \sigma_K \tag{18}$$

Here z controls the confidence of the bound, and we use $z = 3$ based on the three-sigma rule of thumb [50] to have nearly all values with 99.95% confidence lie below the upper bound. The final upper bound is then the simple multiplication of the two worst case estimators (we present the results in Section 6.4):

$$\Delta_{bound} = \frac{(\frac{\phi_K}{c} + z \cdot \sigma_K) \cdot c}{1 - (\frac{f_1}{n} + (2\sqrt{2} + \sqrt{3}) \cdot \sqrt{\frac{\log\log 3/\delta}{n}})} \tag{19}$$

5. OTHER AGGREGATE QUERIES

In the following, we describe how the same techniques for *SUM*-aggregates can be applied to other aggregates for estimating the impact of *unknown unknowns*.

COUNT: Estimating *COUNT* is easier than *SUM* as it only requires estimating the number of unknown data items, but not their values. For instance, one could either directly use the *Chao*92 estimator or the techniques proposed in [47]. In addition, the *bucket* and *Monte-Carlo* approaches can be used simply by skipping the second step, i.e., not multiplying the estimated count with the value estimates.

AVG: The simplest way to estimate the *AVG* with *unknown unknowns* is to use the *AVG* over the observed sample S (i.e., the law of large numbers). This is reasonable because of the law of large numbers. However, S might be biased due to a *publicity-value correlation* and need to be corrected. One way to deal with the bias is to use our *bucket* approach with a simple modification on how the Δ_b per bucket are aggregated (e.g., weighted average of averages by the number of unique data items ($\hat{N}_{Chao92}$) per bucket).

MAX/MIN: At a first glance, it seems impossible to estimate *MIN* or *MAX* in the presence of *unknown unknowns*. However, we can still do better than simply returning the observed extreme values by reporting when we believe that the observed minimum or maximum value is the true extreme values. This is already very helpful in many integration scenarios and easy to do with our *bucket* estimator. The strategy divides the observed value range of S into consecutive sub-ranges (i.e., buckets); the number of *unknown unknowns* as well as their values are estimated per bucket. If the estimated *unknown unknowns* count in the highest (lowest) value range bucket is zero, then we say that we have observed the true maximum (minimum) value and only then report the highest (lowest) value.

6. EXPERIMENTS

We evaluated our algorithms on several crowdsourced and synthetic data sets to test their predictive power. Crowdsourcing allowed us to generate many real data sets and avoided the licensing issues which often comes with other data sources. We designed our experiments to answer the following questions:

- How does the estimation quality between the different estimators compare on real-world data sets?
- What is the sensitivity of our estimators in regard to data skew (*publicity-value correlation*) and streakers/imbalance of data sources?
- How useful is the upper bound?
- How early are accurate *MIN/MAX* estimates possible?

6.1 Real Crowdsourced Data

We evaluated the estimation techniques on a number of real-world data sets, each gathered independently using Amazon Mechanical Turk, following the guidelines in [13]. Here we chose four representative data sets and four aggregate queries, which show different characteristics we encountered during the evaluation.

1. **US tech revenue & employment**: For the query: *how much revenue does the US tech industry produce?*, i.e., `SELECT SUM(revenue) FROM us_tech_companies`, we used the crowd to collect US[2] tech company names and revenues. Similarly, in an independent experiment we asked for US tech company names and number of employees, in order to answer the question: *how many people does the US tech industry employ?*, i.e., `SELECT SUM(employees) FROM us_tech_companies`. We selected the two data sets as they exhibit a steady arrival of unique answers from crowd workers.
2. **US GDP**: As a proof-of-concept experiment, we asked crowd workers to enter a US state with its GDP. This data set suffered from streakers.
3. **Proton beam**: Together with researchers from the field of Evidence Based Medicine (EBM) at Brown university we created a platform for abstract screening and fact extraction and spent over $6,000 on AMT, to screen articles about 4 different topics. Here we utilize the results on one of these, namely Proton beam: a set of articles on the benefits and harms of charged-particle radiation therapy for patients with cancer. Part of the abstract screening asked workers to supply the number of patients being studied. The question we aim to answer is *how many people, in total, participated in these type of studies*: `SELECT SUM(participants) FROM proton_beam_studies`. This data set and research question is grounded in a real world problem and unlike the other queries, this one does not have a known answer.

[2]We asked for companies in Silicon Valley to get a representative sample of US tech companies; without restrictions we received too many tiny computer shops and even non-US based companies.

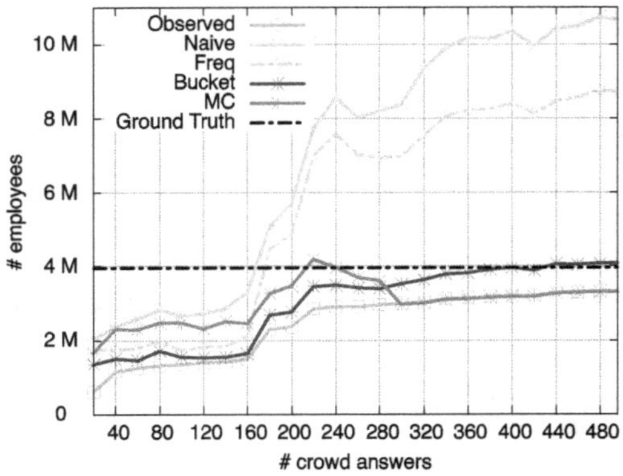

Figure 4: The best US tech-sector employment

We paid between 2 and 35 cents per task. For the Proton beam experiment we designed a qualification test to filter out bad workers, the other experiments were done without qualification tests. Data cleaning was done manually: if workers disagreed on the value (e.g., the number of employees of a company) we used the average.

In the following we describe the results for every data set and the following estimators: *Naïve* (naive) (Section 3.1), *frequency* (Freq) (Section 3.2), *bucket* (Bucket) (Section 3.3), and *Monte-Carlo* (MC) (Section 3.4) estimators (other estimators did not perform that well or had the same performance and are only shown in Appendix B and D).

6.1.1 US Tech-Sector Employment

Figure 4 shows the *SUM* estimates from the different estimators (colored lines) for our running example `SELECT SUM(employees) FROM us_tech_companies` as well as the observed *SUM* (grey line) over time (i.e., with an increasing number of crowd-answers). As the ground-truth (dotted black line) we used the US tech sector employment report from the Pew Research Center [40].

Both the *naïve* and *frequency* estimators heavily overestimate the impact of *unknown unknowns*. The *frequency* estimator does slightly better than the *naïve* estimator, which indicates that some big companies have a high publicity likelihood and were observed early on by several sources.

In contrast, the *MC* estimator does well until it falls back to the observed query result. This can be explained by a peculiarity of this experiment. After roughly 280 crowd-provided data item, all remaining companies have a rather uniform publicity likelihood. In such a case, the *MC* estimator has a tendency to favor count estimates, which are similar to the number of observed items: $\hat{N}_{MC} \sim c$. A major drawback of our *MC* estimation technique.

Finally, the *bucket* estimator provides the best estimate (4053160.57 at 500 crowd answers), which is only $\sim$ 2.5% above the ground truth (3951730). While it is possible that the *bucket* estimator might require more data to converge, it is also possible that the ground truth is inaccurate: the

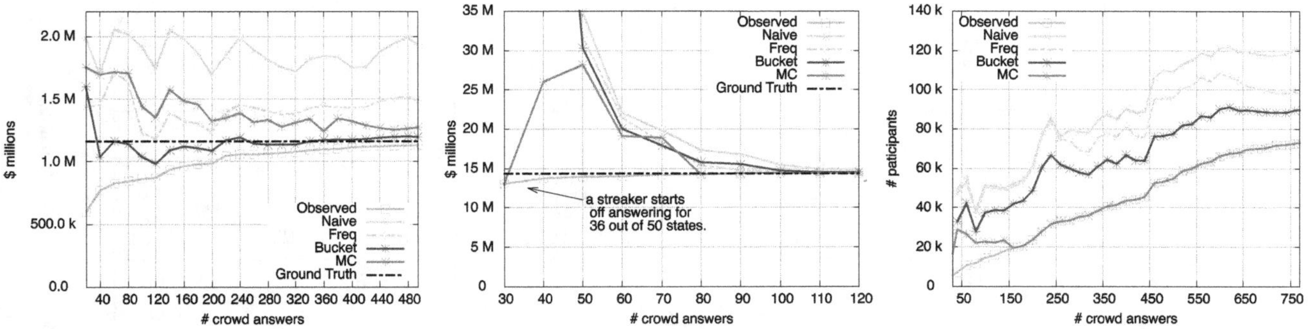

(a) US Tech Revenue (b) US GDP (c) Proton Beam

Figure 5: Real data experiments with aggregate SUM query

employment statistics can vary widely based on many factors (e.g., inclusion or exclusion of part-time employees). We also speculate that there exist many smaller start-ups overlooked by survey agencies, due to the high data collection cost. In contrast, a school of crowd workers can more easily find smaller start-ups and their number of employees on web-pages. Thus, the *bucket* estimate could be closer to the ground truth than the one by the Pew Research Center. This is an astonishing result as the cost of crowdsourcing (e.g., \$50.00 per 500 crowd-answers for US tech revenue & employment experiments) is probably only a small fraction of the cost of survey research by any major agency.

6.1.2 US Tech-Sector Revenue

Figure 5(a) shows the results for the US tech-sector revenue. In this data set, both the *naïve* and the *frequency* techniques overestimate the ground truth significantly because of the *publicity-value correlation*. While both estimators will eventually converge to the ground truth, it requires significantly more crowd-answers than what we collected.

Again, both *Monte-Carlo* and *bucket* estimators provide better estimates than *naïve* and *frequency* estimators .Yet, *Monte-Carlo* still overestimates, whereas *bucket* gives an almost perfect estimate after 240 answers. However, it can also be observed that the bucket estimator slightly overestimates at the end of the experiment. This happens because one crowd worker suddenly reported a few unique companies causing the estimator to believe that there were more. Again, we cannot say with 100% certainty that our assumed ground-truth is actually the real ground truth and the *bucket* estimate might or might not be the real value.

6.1.3 GDP per US State

Figure 5(b) shows the estimate quality for our GDP experiment. To clean the data, we substituted the crowd reported GDP values with the values from [51]. This experiment suffered from streakers, i.e., uneven contributions from crowd workers. A single crowd-worker reported almost all answers in the beginning; this kind of aggressive behavior results in unusually high f_1, which throws off the estimators.

As the figure shows, only the *Monte-Carlo* based technique can actually deal with streakers and provides a reasonable estimate even in the beginning. However, it should also be noted that all estimators converge after 100 samples (for $N = 50$). Furthermore, except for the *Monte-Carlo* estimator, there is no difference between the other estimators.

6.1.4 Proton Beam

Finally, results for Proton beam are shown in Figure 5(c). Again the *Monte-Carlo* estimator follows the observed line, which makes the estimates less interesting. Furthermore, we suspect that the *naïve* and the *frequency* estimators overestimate with constantly increasing number of unique data items (reviewed articles). By manually examining the data set, we confirm that this crowdsourcing experiment did not encounter any streakers, which may cause our estimators (e.g., *bucket*) to fail. Note that the *bucket* estimator converges to roughly $95k$, which we consider to be the best estimate of the number of participants for this particular type of cancer therapy effectiveness study.

6.1.5 Discussion

Overall, our *bucket* estimator has the highest accuracy. The only exception is when streakers are present, making the *Monte Carlo* perform better. However, it should also be noted, that the run-time of the *Monte-Carlo* estimator is significantly higher than the other estimators. While not a serious issue for our experiments (roughly 3.5s for *Monte-Carlo* vs. 0.2s for *bucket*), it could be significant for larger data sets, as the run-time scales linearly with sample size (the inner loop in Algorithm 2 depends on the sample size). In the remainder we analyze the different estimators in more depths using simulations and make final recommendations about which estimator to use at the end of the section.

6.2 Synthetic Data Experiment

To explore the estimation quality more systematically, we used a synthetic data set with $N = 100$ unique items, each having a single attribute-value ranging from 10 to 1000 ($attr = 10, 20, 30, ..., 1000$). We further simulated the sampling process outlined in Section 2 and used an exponential distribution with parameter λ to model various publicity distributions ($\lambda = 0$: uniform; $\lambda = 4$: highly skewed). Finally, our simulation allowed us to vary the *publicity-value correlation* ($\rho = 0$: no correlation; $\rho = 1$: perfect correlation - the most frequent item also has the largest value).

Figure 6 shows the results for various synthetic data experiments, each of which is repeated 50 times and the results averaged (we omit the error bars for better readability). From left to right, we vary the number of simulated crowd-workers (i.e., sources) from $w = 100$, 10 to 5. From top to bottom, we first assume no publicity skew and no *publicity-value correlation* ($\lambda = 0, \rho = 0$), a for species estimation techniques often ideal scenario, we then show the more realistic scenario with skew and publicity-value correlation ($\lambda = 4, \rho = 1$), and finally simulate an environment where some rare items might contain high values ($\lambda = 4, \rho = 0$).

Ideal: Looking at the top-left figure with a uniform publicity distribution and a hundred workers, we can see that all

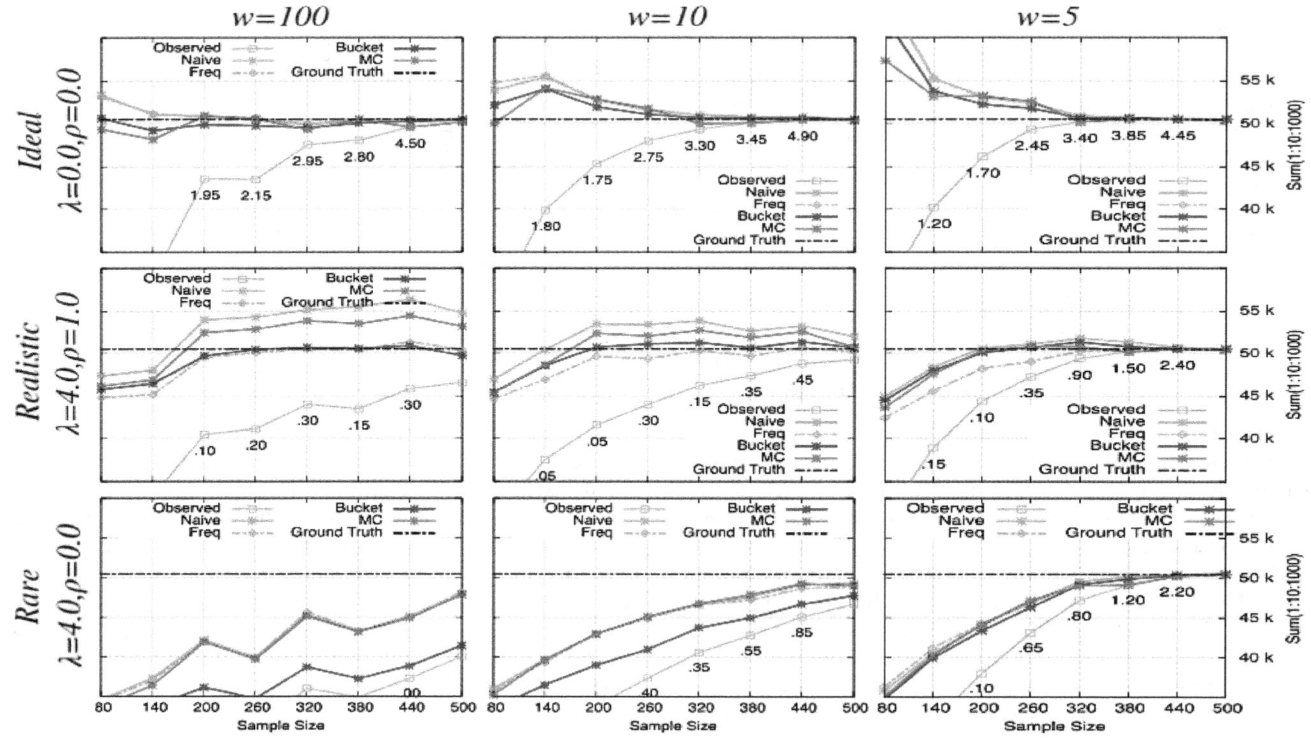

Figure 6: Synthetic data with varying number of sources (w), degrees of publicity skew (λ) & publicity-value correlation (ρ).

estimators perform very well from the beginning. This is not surprising since all estimators work best with sampling with replacement from a uniform publicity distribution; having many workers sampling without replacement from a uniform distribution approximates sampling with replacement. With fewer numbers of workers sampling from the uniform distribution (top row), all estimators start to overestimate slightly. We conclude that *under the ideal conditions (i.e., the original assumptions of species estimation technique) all estimators perform equally well.*

Realistic: The middle row shows the scenarios which best resemble real-world use cases with a skewed *publicity* distribution and positive *publicity-value correlation.* In this case, the *bucket* estimator always provides the best estimates. However, in contrast to the real-world experiments the *frequency* estimator also performs well. This is due to a couple of reasons: Firstly, the *publicity* is highly skewed and perfectly correlated to the values. Secondly, the item values are evenly spaced. This helps the *frequency* estimator to under-estimate as *singletons* consist of only rare low-valued items from the tail – a peculiarity of this simulation. Also, with 5 evenly contributing workers almost all estimators perform about the same. However, the *bucket* estimator has less variance (not shown). We conclude that *under the more realistic conditions the bucket estimator performs the best and does not over-estimate.*

Rare events: Finally, we see in the bottom row that the *bucket* estimator is not the best choice. This is the case where we have skewed *publicity*, but no *publicity-value correlation.* In fact, all estimators perform poorly in this scenario, even with a lot of data sources (d). As the *publicity* distribution tail can take on any values (i.e., no *publicity-value correlation*, the tail (i.e., *singletons*) can contain many high-impact values or "black-swan" events. In this case, because it conservatively favors underestimation, the *bucket* estimator performs worse. In summary, *none of the estimators are able to predict black-swan events or the long tail; all the estimators underestimate the ground truth.*

6.3 Streakers

We have seen in Section 6.1.3 that the estimators can heavily overestimate in the presence of streakers. We now examine the effects of streakers using the synthetic data set with $n = 20$, $\lambda = 1.0$ and $\rho = 1.0$.

First, we consider an extreme case where each source successively provides all $N = 100$ data items; first, one data source contributes $n = 100$ items and then the second source starts to contribute its $n = 100$ items, and so on. Figure 7(a) shows that *Monte-Carlo* simply defaults to the observed sum from one source ($n = 100$), whereas all other estimators fail. This is because of the fact that all *Chao*92-based estimators assume a sample with replacement; an assumption which is strongly violated in this case. Only *Monte-Carlo* is more robust against streakers as it tries to best explain the observed S using simulation.

Next, we consider a more moderate case where we inject a single streaker (i.e., an overly ambitious crowd-worker). In Figure 7(b), a streaker is injected at the sample size $n = 160$, contributing all $N = 100$ unique data items directly afterwards. Similar to the previous case, all estimators, except *Monte-Carlo*, heavily overestimate in the presence of a streaker. Again, the reason is that *Monte-Carlo* uses simulation to explain the observed sample S instead of assuming that S was created using sampling *with* replacement.

6.4 Other Queries & Upper Bound

In this subsection we present results for other aggregate queries than *SUM* using the techniques from Section 5. As before we use synthetic data with 100 unique data items

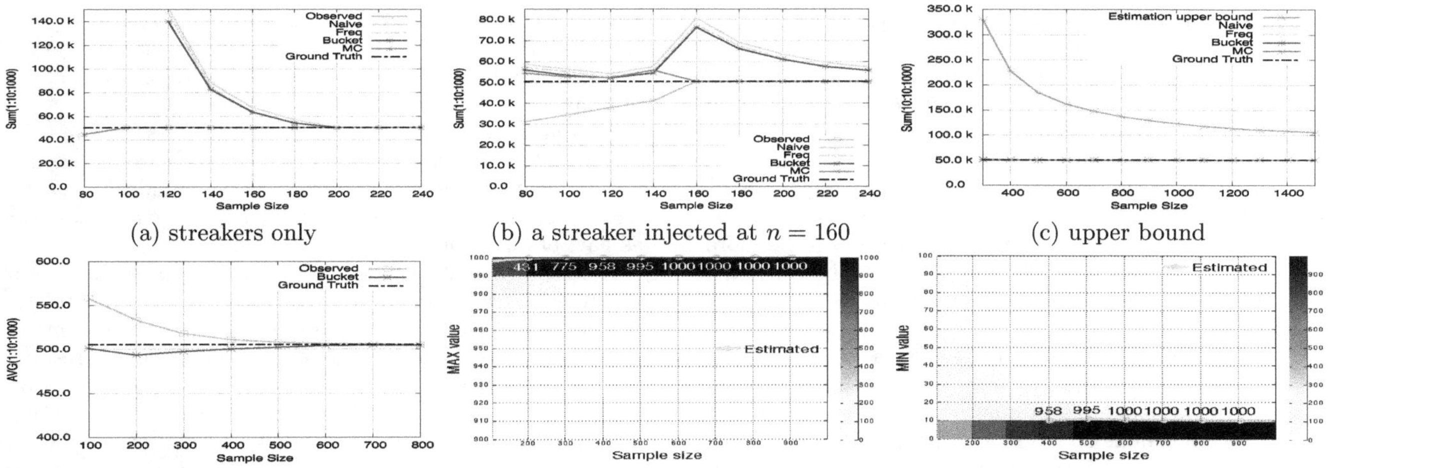

(a) streakers only (b) a streaker injected at $n = 160$ (c) upper bound

(d) AVG (e) MAX (f) MIN

Figure 7: Streaker effect (a-b), estimation upper bound (c), AVG query (d) and aggregate MAX/MIN queries (e)(f) experiments using a synthetic data ($\lambda = 1.0$, $\rho = 1.0$: larger values are more likely)

(e.g., with values $\{10, 20, 30, ..., 1000\}$) integrated over 20 sources with $\lambda = 1.0$ and a publicity-value correlation $\rho = 1.0$. The experiments are repeated 1000 times.

AVG: Figure 7(c) shows the observed (gray line) and estimated (blue line) for a simple average query of the form `SELECT AVG(attr) FROM table`. We only show the *bucket* estimation, as other estimates exactly overlap the observed *AVG* query results (i.e., when all *unknown unknowns* assume the same observed mean value, the *AVG* query result is the same as the observed). As with the sum-aggregates, our dynamic bucket estimator is able to correct the bias of the average because of the publicity-value correlation and provides an almost perfect estimate in this scenario.

MIN/MAX: Figure 7(d-e) compactly visualizes the observed *MIN or* MAX query results. The heat-map shows when the real MIN/MAX value was observed in the data set (the darker the color the more often the result was observed given a number of samples over the 1000 repetitions). The green line shows on average, which value was reported if the *unknown unknowns* count estimate for the highest (*MAX*) / lowest (*MIN*) bucket was zero. The text next to the green line shows how often over the 1000 repetitions the MIN/-MAX value was reported for a given sample size. As it can be seen the average is almost perfect for both *MAX* and *MIN* (note the actual minimum value is 10). That is, whenever our estimation technique for *MAX*/*MIN* reports a value, the user can have more trust in it. It should be noted, tough, that it is impossible to estimate rare extreme values (black swans). Thus, it is only possible to improve upon the confidence but not eliminate any doubts in the results.

Upper Bound: Finally in Figure 7(f) we show the upper-bound from Section 4 using the same synthetic data set. As it can be seen, the bound is very loose (i.e., very large compared to our estimates) and becomes tighter as we observe more data (the real data set results are similar and omitted for space constraints). While the upper bound provides a valuable insight, it may still be too loose for many real-world scenarios and we hope to improve it in the future.

6.5 Summary

Which Estimator To Use: While the *Monte Carlo* or *bucket* estimators always dominate all the others, there is no clear winner between them. The *bucket* estimator performs exceptionally well unless the data sources are imbalanced. It provides the best performance on the real-world use cases (except on the GDP experiment, which suffers from streakers); furthermore, it performs at least as good as other estimators in the simulations from Section 6.2 (except for the *rare event* case, in which all estimators fail to predict black-swan events). However, when the data sources are imbalanced the *Monte Carlo* estimator wins.

Bucket estimator is a *Chao*92 based method, and thus, a *nonparametric model*, which does not require assumptions about the underlying distribution. However, it assumes a single sample without replacement, which is not an issue as long as enough independent data sources exist (in our simulations, 5 sources are often sufficient, see Appendix E) and contribute evenly (i.e., no streakers). Also, the authors of [7] found that *Chao*92 estimator is inaccurate with very low sample coverage C (i.e., observed items are mostly *singletons*) and reported results for cases with $C \geq 0.395$ only. On the other hand, *Monte-Carlo* estimator is a form of a *Data-Analytic Methods*[20] and really good at adjusting to the specifically observed sampling scenario (i.e., streakers), but at a cost of being a *parametric model*. The method assumes an exponential distribution to model the *publicity* distribution, which can be good or bad depending on the true shape of the underlying distribution.

Thus, our recommendation is to use *bucket* estimator, if the predicted sample coverage $\hat{C}$ (Equation 4) is greater than 40%, and when the analyst knows that enough data sources contribute evenly to the sample, and, otherwise, to use the more conservative *Monte Carlo* method.

Trust In The Results: With any types of estimators the main question arises: *How can we trust the estimate?* In 1953, Good, who worked with Turing on the estimators, already pointed out that "I don't believe it is usually possible to estimate the number of species ... but only an appropriate lower bound to that number. This is because there is nearly always a good chance that there are a very large number of extremely rare species"[3]. In estimating the Impact of *unknown unknowns*, this statement is even more critical as the rare items can have extreme values.

Nonetheless, species estimation techniques are extensively used in biology and even helped to decipher the Enigma machine [14]. We actually believe that it comes down to a simple question: *What do you trust more? A potentially wrong answer as no missing data is considered or a potentially wrongly corrected result.* Now, knowing that with enough data sources and no *streakers*, our *bucket* estimator tends to under-estimate the ground truth; in this case, one can generally say that it can only improve the estimates (see the simulations and real-world experiments). Unfortunately, without enough sources or in the presence of *streakers*, the answer is less obvious since the estimators might over-estimate more often. Thus, the answer to the question actually lies somewhere in the middle; to this end, the estimation error upper bound can guide the decision. Overall, we believe, that knowing something is wrong and a best guess about the hidden ground truth is better than staying on the blind-side. In this work, we made a first step in the direction, while a lot remains to be done including developing tighter bounds, better ways to deal with the imbalance of sources, and easier ways to convey the meaning (and assumptions) of the estimates to the user.

7. RELATED WORK

Traditional query processing assumes the database to be complete (i.e., closed world assumption). Furthermore, nearly all sampling-based query processing techniques assume knowledge of the population size [18]; hence, none of these are suitable for our problem with *unknown unknowns.* To the best of our knowledge, this is the first work on estimating the impact of the *unknown unknowns* on query results (i.e., aggregate query processing in the *open world*).

Species estimation: Most related to this work are the various species estimation techniques, like *Chao*92 [7, 5, 3]. Recent work [49] in this area even tries to estimate the shape of the population (e.g., support size, N). We could use these techniques in place of *Chao*92 to estimate the number of *unknown unknowns*, but not to directly estimate the *impact of unknown*, as the shape does not concern the values of *unknown unknowns.*

Species estimation techniques have also been used to estimate the size of search engine indexes and the deep web [26]. The problem is similar to our *unknown unknowns* count estimation [27]. Yet again, this line of work does not consider the *unknown unknowns* value.

Similar species estimation techniques have been used in the context of distinct value estimation for a database table [18, 8]. However those techniques leverage the knowledge of the table size to avoid over-estimation.

Survey Methodology & Missing Data: There is a vast body of literature on sampling-based statistical inferences to estimate population statistics [46, 33, 21] or techniques to deal with missingness of values [44, 1, 10, 9, 53].

However, *unknown unknowns* is different from the missing data; missingness refers to the case when the existence of record is known, but one or more attribute values are missing; most of the techniques assume the knowledge of population size to categorize something as missing (e.g., among this many people asked, only that many people responded, etc.). In addition, the cause of missingness (e.g., missing completely at random, missing at random, missing not at random) needs to be known to select appropriate techniques. The statistical inference techniques (e.g., multiple imputation based EM/maximum likelihood estimation [1, 10], propensity score estimation [9], or *Markov Chain Monte Carlo* simulation [1, 53]) used to fill the missing attributes make their inference based on the known non-missing attributes of the record. In the case of *unknown unknowns*, these assumptions are violated as the entire record (i.e., all attributes) are missing.

Missing data is also studied in the database community [41, 38, 22] with respect to data cleaning; however, since traditional RDBMS query processing function under the *closed world* assumption, they do not consider *unknown unknowns* as part of query processing.

Recent works [22, 42] defined database completeness in a partly *open world* semantic (i.e., database can be incomplete, which causes incorrect query results) and use the completeness information to denote the completeness of query results. Similar in spirit to our work, they investigate the impact on query results of entire database records that may be missing [42]; however, they also assume the knowledge of population size (e.g., there are 7 days in a week) to define the completely missing records and measure the completeness.

Sampling-Based Query Processing: To cope with aggregates over large data sets, sampling based estimation techniques have been proposed as part of query processing [37, 17, 43]. One limiting aspect of any sampling based estimation techniques, though, is that they assume a complete database (i.e., *closed world*).

8. CONCLUSION

Integrating various data sources into a unified data set is one of the most fundamental tools to achieve high quality answers. However, even with the best data integration techniques, some relevant data might be missing from the integrated data set. In this work, we have developed techniques to quantify the impact of any such missing data on simple aggregate query results. The challenge lies in the fact that the existence and the value of the missing data is unknown. To our knowledge, this is the first work on estimating the impact of *unknown unknowns* on query results.

By nature, our techniques cannot predict black swan events (i.e., extremely rare data items). However, based on our evaluation results, we believe that the proposed techniques can provide valuable insights for users; rather than blindly believing a query result over an integrated data source, the user gets an idea of what the true answer might be.

There are several interesting future directions. Currently, none of our estimators works best under all circumstances. The *Monte-Carlo* estimator is robust against streakers, whereas the *bucket* estimator provides the most accurate results without streakers. Developing a robust estimator in any scenario is an important area of future work. Similarly, developing tighter error-bounds for the techniques is important. Finally, extending the results to more complex aggregate queries (e.g., with joins) also remains for future work.

This work is an important step towards providing higher quality query results. After all, we live in a big data world where even an integrated data set over multiple sources is possibly incomplete.

9. ACKNOWLEDGMENTS

This research is funded in part by the Intel Science and Technology Center for Big Data, the NSF CAREER Award IIS-1453171, the Air Force YIP AWARD FA9550-15-1-0144, NSF IIS-1514491, and gifts from SAP, Mellanox, Amazon, and Oracle.

10. REFERENCES

[1] P. D. Allison. Handling missing data by maximum likelihood. In *SAS global forum*, pages 1–21, 2012.

[2] S. Amer-Yahia, A. Doan, J. Kleinberg, N. Koudas, and M. Franklin. Crowds, clouds, and algorithms: Exploring the human side of "big data" applications. In *Proc. of SIGMOD*, pages 1259–1260, 2010.

[3] J. Bunge and M. Fitzpatrick. Estimating the Number of Species: A Review. *Journal of the American Statistical Association*, 88(421), 1993.

[4] K. P. Burnham and W. S. Overton. Estimation of the Size of a Closed Population when Capture Probabilities vary Among Animals. *Biometrika*, 65(3), 1978.

[5] A. Chao. Nonparametric Estimation of the Number of Classes in a Population. *SJS*, 11(4), 1984.

[6] A. Chao. Species estimation and applications. In *Encyclopedia of Statistical Sciences, 2nd Edition*, pages 7907–7916. Wiley, New York, 2005.

[7] A. Chao and S. Lee. Estimating the Number of Classes via Sample Coverage. *Journal of the American Statistical Association*, 87(417):210–217, 1992.

[8] M. Charikar, S. Chaudhuri, R. Motwani, and V. Narasayya. Towards estimation error guarantees for distinct values. In *Proc. of PODS*, pages 268–279. ACM, 2000.

[9] R. B. D'Agostino Jr and D. B. Rubin. Estimating and using propensity scores with partially missing data. *Journal of the American Statistical Association*, 95(451):749–759, 2000.

[10] A. P. Dempster, N. M. Laird, and D. B. Rubin. Maximum likelihood from incomplete data via the em algorithm. *Journal of the royal statistical society. Series B (methodological)*, pages 1–38, 1977.

[11] A. Doan, R. Ramakrishnan, and A. Y. Halevy. Crowdsourcing systems on the world-wide web. *Commun. ACM*, 54(4):86–96, Apr. 2011.

[12] D. Florescu, D. Koller, and A. Y. Levy. Using probabilistic information in data integration. In *Proc. of VLDB*, pages 216–225, 1997.

[13] M. J. Franklin, D. Kossmann, T. Kraska, S. Ramesh, and R. Xin. Crowddb: Answering queries with crowdsourcing. In *Proc. of SIGMOD*, pages 61–72, 2011.

[14] I. J. Good. The Population Frequencies of Species and the Estimation of Population Parameters. *Biometrika*, 40(3/4), 1953.

[15] Google. Freebase. https://www.freebase.com, 2015. Accessed: 2015-07-08.

[16] D. Haas, M. Greenstein, K. Kamalov, A. Marcus, M. Olszewski, and M. Piette. Reducing error in context-sensitive crowdsourced tasks. In *First AAAI Conference on Human Computation and Crowdsourcing*, 2013.

[17] P. J. Haas. *Hoeffding Inequalities for Join Selectivity Estimation and Online Aggregation*. IBM, 1996.

[18] P. J. Haas et al. Sampling-based estimation of the number of distinct values of an attribute. In *Proc. of VLDB*, 1995.

[19] A. Y. Halevy. Data publishing and sharing using fusion tables. In *CIDR*, 2013.

[20] W. K. Hastings. Monte carlo sampling methods using markov chains and their applications. *Biometrika*, 57(1):97–109, 1970.

[21] L. Kish. *Survey sampling*. John Wiley and Sons, 1965.

[22] W. Lang, R. V. Nehme, E. Robinson, and J. F. Naughton. Partial results in database systems. In *Proceedings of the 2014 ACM SIGMOD international conference on Management of data*, pages 1275–1286. ACM, 2014.

[23] U. Leser and F. Naumann. Query planning with information quality bounds. In H. Larsen, T. Andreasen, H. Christiansen, J. Kacprzyk, and S. Zadrożny, editors, *Flexible Query Answering Systems*, volume 7 of *Advances in Soft Computing*, pages 85–94. Physica-Verlag HD, 2001.

[24] M. Lexa. Useful facts about the kullback-leibler discrimination distance. https://scholarship.rice.edu/bitstream/handle/1911/20061/Lex2004Dec8UsefulFact.PDF?sequence=1&isAllowed=y, 2004. Accessed:2015-07-08.

[25] X. Li, X. L. Dong, K. Lyons, W. Meng, and D. Srivastava. Truth finding on the deep web: Is the problem solved? *PVLDB*, 6(2):97–108.

[26] J. Liang. Estimation Methods for the Size of Deep Web Textural Data Source: A Survey. cs.uwindsor.ca/richard/cs510/survey_jie_liang.pdf, 2008. Accessed: 2015-07-08.

[27] J. Lu and D. Li. Estimating deep web data source size by capture—recapture method. *Inf. Retr.*, 13(1):70–95, Feb. 2010.

[28] R. Lynch and B. Kim. Sample size, the margin of error and the coefficient of variation. *InterStat*, 2010.

[29] M. Magnani and D. Montesi. A survey on uncertainty management in data integration. *J. Data and Information Quality*, 2(1):5:1–5:33, July 2010.

[30] A. Marcus, E. Wu, D. R. Karger, S. Madden, and R. C. Miller. Demonstration of qurk: a query processor for humanoperators. In *Proc. of SIGMOD, SIGMOD 2011, Athens, Greece, June 12-16, 2011*, pages 1315–1318, 2011.

[31] A. Marcus, E. Wu, S. Madden, and R. C. Miller. Crowdsourced databases: Query processing with people. In *Proc. CIDR 2011, Asilomar, CA, USA, January 9-12, 2011*, pages 211–214, 2011.

[32] D. A. McAllester and R. E. Schapire. On the convergence rate of good-turing estimators. In *COLT*, pages 1–6. Citeseer, 2000.

[33] J. McClave and T. Sincich. *Statistics*. Pearson, 2013.

[34] W. Meng, K.-L. Liu, C. Yu, W. Wu, and N. Rishe. Estimating the usefulness of search engines. In *Data Engineering, 1999. Proceedings., 15th International Conference on*, pages 146–153, Mar 1999.

[35] F. Naumann, J.-C. Freytag, and U. Leser. Completeness of integrated information sources. *Inf. Syst.*, 29(7):583–615, Sept. 2004.

[36] M. T. Neiling and H.-J. Lenz. Data integration by means of object identification in information systems. In *Proc. of European Conference on Information Systems*, 2000.

[37] F. Olken and D. Rotem. Simple random sampling from relational databases. In *VLDB*, volume 86, pages 25–28, 1986.

[38] J. W. Osborne. *Best practices in data cleaning: A complete guide to everything you need to do before and after collecting your data*. Sage, 2012.

[39] A. Parameswaran and N. Polyzotis. Answering Queries using Humans, Algorithms and Databases. In *Proc. of CIDR*, 2011.

[40] Pew Research Center. How u.s. tech-sector jobs have grown, changed in 15 years. http://pewrsr.ch/PtqZDA, 2014. Accessed: 2015-07-08.

[41] E. Rahm and H. H. Do. Data cleaning: Problems and current approaches. *IEEE Data Eng. Bull.*, 23(4):3–13, 2000.

[42] S. Razniewski, F. Korn, W. Nutt, and D. Srivastava. Identifying the extent of completeness of query answers over partially complete databases. In *Proc. of SIGMOD*, pages 561–576. ACM, 2015.

[43] J. Rice. *Mathematical statistics and data analysis*. Cengage Learning, 2006.

[44] D. B. Rubin. Inference and missing data. *Biometrika*, 63(3):581–592, 1976.

[45] B. Saha and D. Srivastava. Data quality: The other face of big data. In *IEEE 30th International Conference on Data Engineering, Chicago, ICDE 2014, IL, USA, March 31 - April 4, 2014*, pages 1294–1297, 2014.

[46] R. Sapsford. *Survey Research*. SAGE Publications, 1999.

[47] B. Trushkowsky, T. Kraska, M. J. Franklin, and P. Sarkar. Crowdsourced enumeration queries. In *ICDE*, pages 673–684, 2013.

[48] K. I. Ugland, J. S. Gray, and K. E. Ellingsen. The species–accumulation curve and estimation of species richness. *Journal of Animal Ecology*, 72(5):888–897, 2003.

[49] G. Valiant and P. Valiant. Estimating the unseen: an n/log (n)-sample estimator for entropy and support size, shown optimal via new clts. In *Proceedings of the forty-third annual ACM symposium on Theory of computing*, pages 685–694. ACM, 2011.

[50] Wikipedia. 68–95–99.7 rule. https://en.wikipedia.org/wiki/68-95-99.7_rule, 2015. Accessed: 2015-07-08.

[51] Wikipedia. List of u.s. states by gdp. https://en.wikipedia.org/wiki/List_of_U.S._states_by_GDP, 2015. Accessed: 2015-07-08.

[52] T. Yan, V. Kumar, and D. Ganesan. Crowdsearch: Exploiting crowds for accurate real-time image search on mobile phones. In *Proc. of MobiSys*, pages 77–90, New York, NY, USA, 2010. ACM.

[53] Y. C. Yuan. Multiple imputation for missing data: Concepts and new development (version 9.0). *SAS Institute Inc, Rockville, MD*, 2010.

APPENDIX

A. SYMBOL TABLE

Ω	Universe of all valid entities (unknown size)
r	A valid unique entity or data item
D	Ground truth or the underlying population
S	Observed sample of size $n = \|S\|$, with duplicates
K	Integrated database with only unique entities from S
U	*Unknown unknowns* that exist in D, but not in S or K
M_0	*Unknown unknowns* distribution mass in D
c	The number of unique data items in S; $c = \|K\|$
s_j	Source j with $n_j = \|s_j\|$ data items
N	The size of the ground truth; $N = \|D\|$
ϕ	The aggregated query result: e.g., ϕ_D (over D)
Δ	*The impact of unknown unknowns*: $\Delta = \phi_D - \phi_K$
f_j	A frequency statistic, i.e., the number of data items with exactly j occurrences in S.
F	The set of frequency statistics, $\{f_1, f_2, ..., f_n\}$
ρ	The correlation between publicity and value distributions, i.e., *publicity-value correlation*
γ	Coefficient of variance (data skew measure)
C	Sample coverage, also $C = 1 - M_0$

Table 1: Symbols

B. STATIC BUCKET BASED ESTIMATOR

In Section 3.3.1, we state that the optimal number of buckets depends on the underlying *publicity* distribution. Here, we elaborate on this with the two examples.

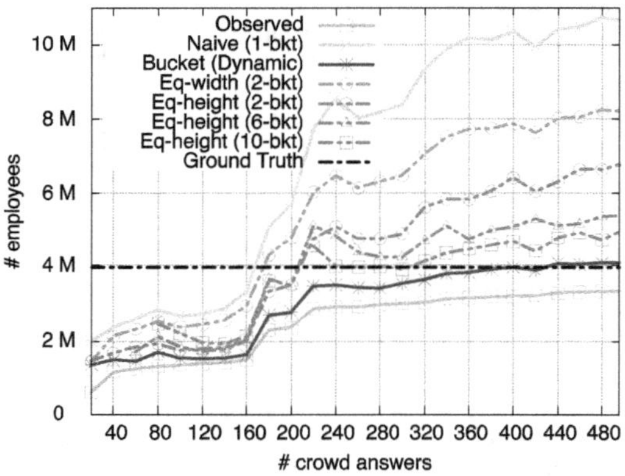

Figure 8: The best US tech-sector employment estimation with static buckets. Splitting into more buckets improves estimation. Eq-width (6-bkt, 10-bkt) are missing due to some of the buckets are empty.

Figure 8 shows the US tech-sector employment estimates by various estimators: *Naive* (1-bucket), *Bucket* (a.k.a., *Dynamic Bucket*), and *Static Bucket* (Eq-width and Eq-height). In this particular example, splitting into more buckets improves estimation, as the underlying *publicity* distribution is skewed and correlated to the values (i.e., larger companies are more well known).

In contrast, in the simulated case in Figure 9, splitting into less (e.g., *Naive*) improves estimation as the underlying *publicity* is uniform. Notice, that in both examples above, the *bucket* estimator yields the best estimates, dynamically resizing buckets on its own.

Also notice, that we consider two variants of static buckets: the one described in the paper, **equi-width**, which divides the observed value range into a fixed number of buckets, and another obvious variant, **equi-height**, which divides the observed sample, sorted by value, evenly into a

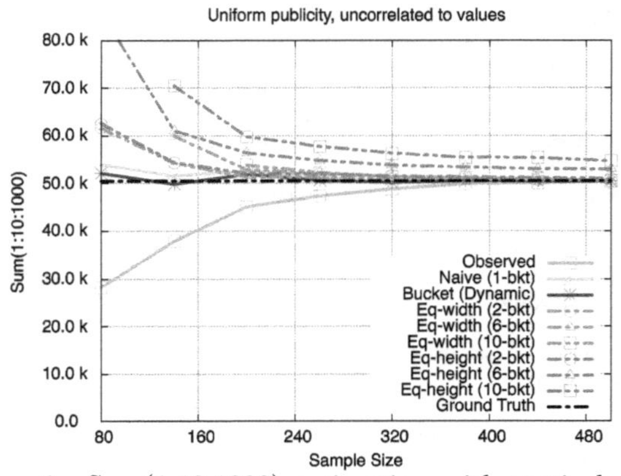

Figure 9: Sum(1:10:1000) estimation with static buckets. Splitting less (e.g., *Naive*) improves estimation. Data points are missing when some buckets contain *singletons* only (i.e., infinite estimation).

fixed number of buckets. Both static bucket types are simple to use, but they require parameter tuning for the optimal number of buckets, which is hard to predict without knowing the true *publicity* distribution.

C. THE INCREASE IN COUNT ESTIMATE AFTER BUCKET SPLIT

In equation 14, we claimed that the count estimation ($\hat{N}_{Chao92} = nc/(n - f_1)$) of a bucket increases after splitting the bucket, if data items are evenly distributed over the *attribute* value range, and there is no *publicity-value correlation*:

$$\hat{N}_{Chao92} = \frac{c}{1 - f_1/n} = \overbrace{\frac{n \cdot c}{n - f_1}}^{\text{Before split}} \leq \underbrace{\frac{\frac{n}{2} \cdot \frac{c}{2}}{\frac{n}{2} - \alpha \cdot f_1} + \frac{\frac{n}{2} \cdot \frac{c}{2}}{\frac{n}{2} - (1 - \alpha) \cdot f_1}}_{\text{After split}}$$

The α parameter governs the split of the original singleton count (f_1) into a pair of smaller buckets. We assume n and c are evenly distributed between the split buckets, as items are evenly distributed over the value range, and all values are equally likely (no *value-publicity correlation*). We now show that the above inequality holds by showing that the right hand side (after split) is minimized at $nc/(n - f_1)$. Note that $nc/(n - f_1)$ is a positive number as $n \geq f_1 \geq 0$ and $c \geq 0$.

To find the minimum, we take the first derivative of the right hand side (denoted by $\mathcal{R}$) with respect to α:

$$\mathcal{R}' = \frac{-c \cdot f_1 \cdot n}{4(-(1-\alpha) \cdot f_1 + \frac{n}{2})^2} + \frac{-c \cdot f_1 \cdot n}{4(-\alpha \cdot f_1 + \frac{n}{2})^2}$$

Solving $\mathcal{R}' = 0$, we get $\alpha = 0.5$; we have $\mathcal{R}(0.5) = nc/(n - f_1)$ as shown below:

$$\mathcal{R}(0.5) = \frac{\frac{n}{2} \cdot \frac{c}{2}}{\frac{n}{2} - 0.5 \cdot f_1} + \frac{\frac{n}{2} \cdot \frac{c}{2}}{\frac{n}{2} - (1 - 0.5) \cdot f_1} = \frac{\frac{n}{2} \cdot \frac{c}{2} + \frac{n}{2} \cdot \frac{c}{2}}{\frac{n}{2} - 0.5 \cdot f_1} = \frac{n \cdot c}{n - f_1}$$

Finally, we show $\mathcal{R}(0.5) = nc/(n - f_1)$ is the minimum by ensuring $\mathcal{R}''(0.5) > 0$:

$$\mathcal{R}'' = \frac{c \cdot f_1^2 \cdot n}{2(-(1-\alpha)\cdot f_1 + \frac{n}{2})^3} + \frac{c \cdot f_1^2 \cdot n}{2(-\alpha \cdot f_1 + \frac{n}{2})^3}$$

$$\mathcal{R}''(0.5) = \frac{c \cdot f_1^2 \cdot n}{2(-(1-0.5)\cdot f_1 + \frac{n}{2})^3} + \frac{c \cdot f_1^2 \cdot n}{2(-0.5 \cdot f_1 + \frac{n}{2})^3}$$

$$= \frac{c \cdot f_1^2 \cdot n}{(-0.5 \cdot f_1 + \frac{n}{2})^3} = \frac{8c \cdot f_1^2 \cdot n}{(-f_1 + n)^3}$$

Note that $n \geq f_1$, and this makes $\mathcal{R}'' > 0$; $\mathcal{R}$ is minimized at $nc/(n - f_1)$ and the inequality holds true:

$$\overbrace{\frac{n \cdot c}{n - f_1}}^{\text{Before split}} \leq \underbrace{\frac{\frac{n}{2} \cdot \frac{c}{2}}{\frac{n}{2} - \alpha \cdot f_1} + \frac{\frac{n}{2} \cdot \frac{c}{2}}{\frac{n}{2} - (1-\alpha) \cdot f_1}}_{\text{After split}}$$

D. OTHER ESTIMATORS

Many proposed techniques can be combined: we can use the *frequency* estimator, instead of the *naïve* estimator, with the *bucket* (i.e., *Dynamic Bucket* approach) estimator or the *Monte-Carlo* estimator. We can also combine the *Monte-Carlo* estimator with the *bucket* estimator.

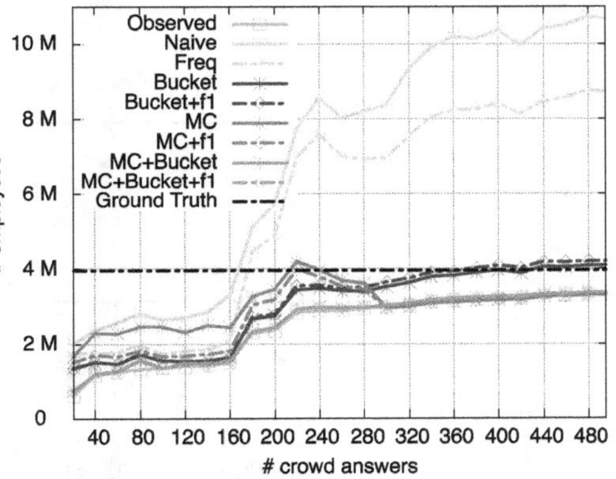

Figure 10: The best US tech-sector employment estimation with other estimators

However, as the *Monte-Carlo* estimator requires large sample sizes to be accurate, combining it with *bucket* estimator often results in lower estimation quality (i.e., each bucket contains a smaller sample). Furthermore, each bucket (a smaller value range) entails a part of the underlying *publicity* distribution; hence, the *publicity* distribution per bucket appears more uniform. As a major drawback, the *Monte-Carlo* estimator exhibits a tendency to favor its count estimate $\hat{N}_{MC} \sim c$ (see Section 6.1.1). Such tendency gets more imminent in *Monte-Carlo* with *Bucket* estimator as seen in Figure 10. Similarly, we found that the difference between the *naïve* and *frequency* estimators is not significant for the *bucket* estimator (i.e., uniform *publicity*).

E. NUMBER OF SOURCES

Bucket estimator is non-parametric and works well with with both uniform and skewed distributions; however, it assumes a sample S sampled with replacement. This assumption is appropriate as long as enough independent data sources contribute evenly to S.

In Figure 11, we illustrate this with a synthetic data (skewed *publicity* correlated to item *attribute* values). In this particular example, more than 5 sources result in enough overlaps for *bucket* to estimate accurately; however, the minimum number of sources would vary with the date set. In addition, *Monte-Carlo* estimator converges faster as it does not assume a sample sampled with replacement.

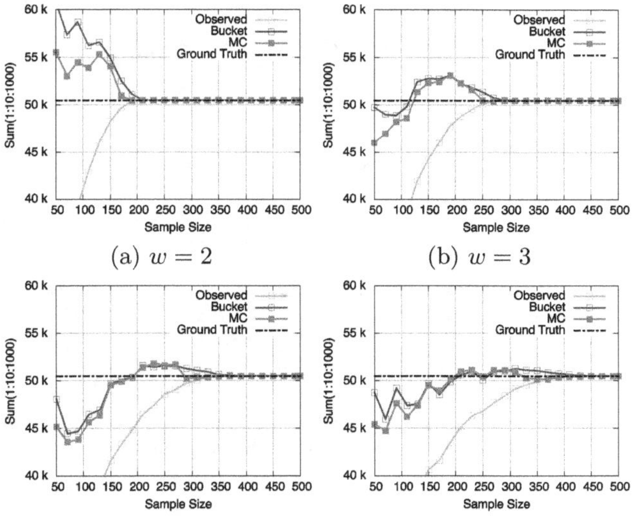

(a) $w = 2$ (b) $w = 3$ (c) $w = 4$ (d) $w = 5$

Figure 11: Synthetic data ($\lambda = 4.0, \rho = 1.0$) with varying number of sources (w). *Bucket* estimator performs better with more independent sources (i.e., more overlaps).

F. A TOY EXAMPLE

In this section, we walk through the different estimators step by step using a simple toy example. Again, we use the same query, `SELECT SUM(employee) FROM K`, from the introduction but over a very simplistic data set, shown in Figure 12. It should be noted, that this toy example can not convey any statistical properties because of its small size, but we can explain the general reasoning behind the techniques using the example.

Figure 12 shows the data integration scenario of our example. We assumes that the ground truth D consists of 5 companies $\{A, B, C, D, E\}$ (the bubble on the top), with different numbers of employees (e.g., company A has 1000, whereas company B has 2000). In the beginning we have four data sources $\{s_1, s_2, s_3, s_4\}$ and they sample without replacement from D. For instance data source s_1 lists companies A, B, and D. In the example we also assume a *publicity-value correlation*; that is, the biggest company D appears in all data sources ($\{s_1, s_2, s_3, s_4\}$), while smaller companies appear in fewer sources. To show how the estimates improve, we assume that the data source s_5 is added later on (visualized through the plus). The tables in Figure 12(b) show the integrated database before (top) and after (bottom) adding the fifth data source. For convenience, the last column shows, how many times each company was observed across the multiple data sources.

Table 2 shows the estimates by different estimators before and after adding the fifth data source. We exclude *Monte-Carlo* estimator due to its simulation based nature. The top row contains the relevant statistics of K. For instance, with 4 data sources, the number of observed items / sample size is $n = 7$, the number of observed unique items is $c = 3$ (i.e., companies A, B, and D from the top table in Figure 12(b)),

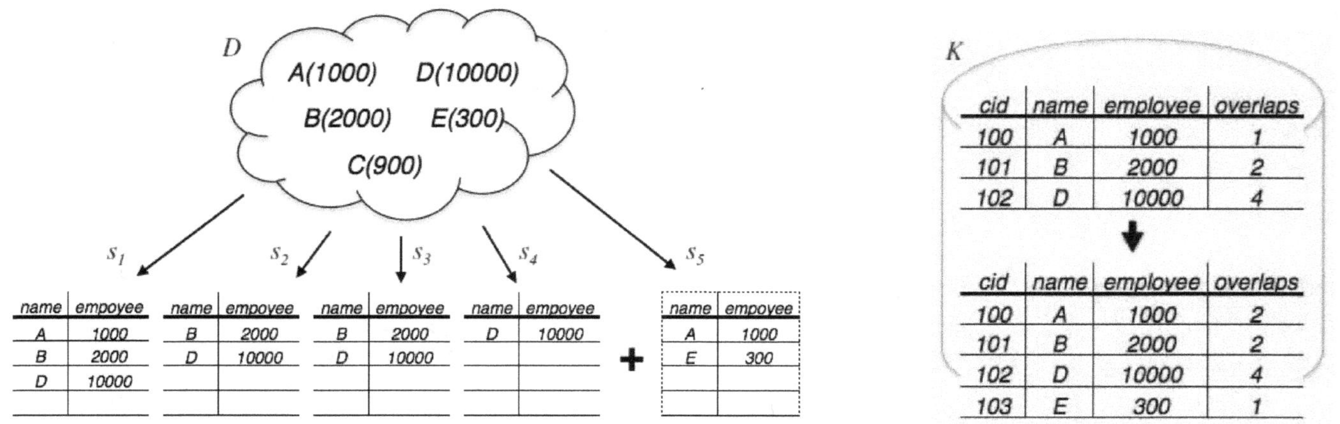

(a) Multiple sources s_i sampled without replacement from the unknown population D. s_5 is added later to the original integrated database.

(b) Integrated Database K, before (top) and after (bottom) adding s_5

Figure 12: A toy example for `SELECT SUM(employee) FROM K`

	before adding s_5 ($n = 7$, $c = 3$, $f_1 = 1$, $\hat{\gamma}^2 = 0.1667$)	after adding s_5 ($n = 10$, $c = 4$, $f_1 = 1$, $\hat{\gamma}^2 = 0$)
Ground Truth	$\phi_D = 1000 + 2000 + 900 + 10000 + 300 = 14200$	
Observed	$\phi_K = 1000 + 2000 + 10000 = 13000$	$1000 + 2000 + 10000 + 300 = 13300$
Naive	$\phi_K + \Delta_{naive} = \phi_K + \frac{\phi_K \cdot f_1 \cdot (c + \hat{\gamma}^2 n)}{c \cdot (n - f_1)}$ $= 13000 + \frac{13000 \cdot 1 \cdot (3 + 0.1667 \cdot 7)}{3 \cdot (7 - 1)}$ ≈ 16009	$= 13300 + \frac{13300 \cdot 1 \cdot (4 + 0 \cdot 9)}{4 \cdot (9 - 1)}$ ≈ 14962
Freq	$\phi_K + \Delta_{freq} = \phi_K + \frac{\phi_{f_1}(c + \hat{\gamma}^2 n)}{n - f_1}$ $= 13000 + \frac{1000\,(3 + 0.1667 \cdot 7)}{7 - 1}$ ≈ 13694	$= 13300 + \frac{300\,(4 + 0 \cdot 9)}{9 - 1}$ $= 13450$
Bucket	$\phi_K + \Delta_{bucket} = \phi_K + \Delta_{b_1:\{A,B\}} + \Delta_{b_2:\{D\}}$ $= \phi_K + \{\Delta_{naive}\}_{b_1} + \{\Delta_{naive}\}_{b_2}$ $= 13000 + \frac{3000 \cdot 1 \cdot (2 + 0 \cdot 3)}{2 \cdot (3 - 1)}$ $+ \frac{10000 \cdot 0 \cdot (1 + 0 \cdot 4)}{1 \cdot (4 - 0)}$ $= 14500$	$= \phi_K + \Delta_{b_1:\{A,E\}} + \Delta_{b_2:\{B\}} + \Delta_{b_3:\{D\}}$ $= \phi_K + \{\Delta_{naive}\}_{b_1} + \{\Delta_{naive}\}_{b_2} + \{\Delta_{naive}\}_{b_3}$ $= 13300 + \frac{1300 \cdot 1 \cdot (2 + 0 \cdot 3)}{2 \cdot (3 - 1)}$ $+ \frac{2000 \cdot 0 \cdot (1 + 0 \cdot 2)}{1 \cdot (2 - 0)} + \frac{10000 \cdot 0 \cdot (1 + 0 \cdot 4)}{1 \cdot (4 - 0)}$ $= 13950$

Table 2: `SELECT SUM(employee) FROM K` results with different *unknown unknowns* estimators: *bucket* estimator gives the most accurate estimation of ϕ_D,

the number of singletons $f_1 = 1$ (i.e., company D as it is the only company, which was observed exactly ones across the data sources). and the calculated *coefficient of variance (CV)* $\gamma = 0.1667$ calculated over the sample.

Before adding the fifth data source, the observed total sum is $\phi_K = 1000 + 2000 + 10000 = 13000$, after adding the fifth data source $\phi_K = 1000 + 2000 + 10000 = 13300$. In this example, the observed total sum does not converge to the ground truth of 14200

Table 2 shows the values with calculations for the different estimators. As it can be seen, the naïve estimator performs the worse; the estimator is quite far off, especially with 4 data sources. The reason is the value estimator (*mean substitution*) used. The average number of employees is $\phi_K/3 \approx 4333$. Thus all missing companies (i.e., *unknown unknowns*) are also assumed to be that big. Now knowing that bigger companies are more likely to be sampled, now the naïve estimator heavily over-estimates.

In contrast, the *frequency* estimator performs much better than the naïve estimator because it assumes that the missing companies have the average value over *singletons*, which includes A, but not the extremely big company D; the missing companies are assume to have a value of $\phi_{f_1}/1 = 1000$. Because less popular companies are more likely to be smaller (i.e., the *publicity-value correlation*), this yields to a much better estimate.

Finally, the *bucket* estimator performs the best. Before adding the fifth source, the algorithm creates two buckets: $b_1 : \{A, B\}$ and $b_2 : \{D\}$. The estimate quality of *bucket* persists even after we add s_5 (i.e., *Bucket* is the best). In this case, the *bucket* estimator generates $b_1 : \{A, E\}$, $b_2 : \{B\}$ and $b_3 : \{D\}$. The *bucket* estimator automatically groups the small companies (A and E) together and uses their average number of employees for the missing companies (all other buckets have unknown count estimation of 0); in this example, the *bucket* estimator has a smoothed value in between 300 and 1000. This is particularly more desirable compared to the case of the *frequency* estimator: E is the new one and only *singleton* and ϕ_{f_1} is now 300.

Constraint-Variance Tolerant Data Repairing

Shaoxu Song Han Zhu Jianmin Wang
Tsinghua National Laboratory for Information Science and Technology
KLiss, MoE; School of Software, Tsinghua University, China
{sxsong, zhuhan10, jimwang}@tsinghua.edu.cn

ABSTRACT

Integrity constraints, guiding the cleaning of dirty data, are often found to be imprecise as well. Existing studies consider the inaccurate constraints that are oversimplified, and thus refine the constraints via inserting more predicates (attributes). We note that imprecise constraints may not only be *oversimplified* so that correct data are erroneously identified as violations, but also could be *overrefined* that the constraints overfit the data and fail to identify true violations. In the latter case, deleting excessive predicates applies.

To address the oversimplified and overrefined constraint inaccuracies, in this paper, we propose to repair data by allowing a small variation (with both predicate insertion and deletion) on the constraints. A novel θ-tolerant repair model is introduced, which returns a (minimum) data repair that satisfies at least one variant of the constraints (with constraint variation no greater than θ compared to the given constraints). To efficiently repair data among various constraint variants, we propose a single round, sharing enabled approach. Results on real data sets demonstrate that our proposal can capture more accurate data repairs compared to the existing methods with/without constraint repairs.

Keywords

Data repairing; denial constraints

1. INTRODUCTION

Automatic repairing techniques are often employed for cleaning dirty data, under the supervision of integrity constraints [9]. Typical repairing approaches (minimally) modify the data towards conformance to the constraints [4]. The repair performance thus heavily relies on trustable constraints. Unfortunately, it has been highlighted that both integrity constraints and data could be variant [18]. Recent studies [5, 2] also indicate the fact of inaccurate integrity constraints and inaccurate data co-existence and work on repairing constraints and data at the same time.

SIGMOD'16, June 26-July 01, 2016, San Francisco, CA, USA

DOI: http://dx.doi.org/10.1145/2882903.2882955

Existing studies on simultaneously repairing constraints and data [5, 2] consider imprecise constraints (mainly *functional dependencies*, FDs) that are oversimplified. With such oversimplified constraints, data repairing may erroneously identify correct data as violations (see examples below). The constraint repairing is thus to *refine* the oversimplified constraints, via inserting more predicates (attributes in FDs).

As one of the most direct motivations of this study, we first note that, besides oversimplified, the imprecise constraints could also be overrefined. That is, too many predicates (attributes) are specified in a constraint so that it overfits the data. Owing to such overfitting, the overrefined constraints fail to identify some truly dirty data (also see examples below). In this case, constraint *simplification*, by deleting excessive predicates (attributes), may apply.

In this study, we propose to address both constraint variances, *oversimplified* and *overrefined*. By *oversimplified*, we mean too few predicates specified in a constraint, such that many (correct) data will be identified as violations to the constraint, e.g., φ_1 in Example 1. On the other hand, by *overrefined*, we mean too many predicates specified in a constraint, such that no (incorrect) data could be identified as violations to the constraint, e.g., φ_3 in Example 1.

Example 1. *Consider an example Income relation in Figure 1(a). To support the order relationships on numeric values such as* Income, Tax, *we use a general notation of* denial constraints *(*DCs*) [7]. (See Example 3 for* DCs *on numerical attributes. As special cases,* FDs *can be represented by* DCs*.)*

Suppose that the following DC *is given.*

$$\varphi_1 : \forall t_\alpha, t_\beta \in R, \neg(t_\alpha.\mathsf{Name} = t_\beta.\mathsf{Name} \land t_\alpha.\mathsf{CP} \neq t_\beta.\mathsf{CP})$$

It states that for any $t_\alpha, t_\beta \in R$, they should not *have the same* Name *but different* CP *(Cellphone number), i.e., an* FD Name$\rightarrow$CP*. This constraint, stating that* Name *can determine* CP*, is obviously imprecise. With this oversimplified φ_1, many data values (in red) need to be modified in Figure 1(b), most of which are indeed correct.*[1]

Referring to [5, 2], a (refinement) repair of constraint is performed by adding attributes to the left-hand-side of FDs*, i.e., inserting predicates in* DCs *as shown in φ_2 below.*

$$\varphi_2 : \forall t_\alpha, t_\beta \in R, \neg(t_\alpha.\mathsf{Name} = t_\beta.\mathsf{Name} \land t_\alpha.\mathsf{Birthday} = t_\beta.\mathsf{Birthday} \land t_\alpha.\mathsf{CP} \neq t_\beta.\mathsf{CP})$$

With the additional Birthday*, φ_2 becomes precise. Consequently, the truly dirty values (only a small proportion with*

[1]Assume that the data repair on CP has the minimum change in this example for simplicity. Repairs on other attributes may be performed in practice.

	Name	Birthday	CP	Year	Income	Tax
t_1	Ayres	8-8-1984	322-573	2007	21k	0
t_2	Ayres	5-1-1960	***-389	2007	22k	0
t_3	Ayres	5-1-1960	564-389	2007	22k	0
t_4	Stanley	13-8-1987	868-701	2007	23k	3k
t_5	Stanley	31-7-1983	***-198	2007	24k	0
t_6	Stanley	31-7-1983	930-198	2008	24k	0
t_7	Dustin	2-12-1985	179-924	2008	25k	0
t_8	Dustin	5-9-1980	***-870	2008	100k	21k
t_9	Dustin	5-9-1980	824-870	2009	100k	21k
t_{10}	Dustin	9-4-1984	387-215	2009	150k	40k

(a)

	··· CP
t_1	··· 564-389
t_2	··· 564-389
t_3	··· 564-389
t_4	··· 930-198
t_5	··· 930-198
t_6	··· 930-198
t_7	··· 824-870
t_8	··· 824-870
t_9	··· 824-870
t_{10}	··· 824-870

(b)

	··· CP
t_1	··· 322-573
t_2	··· 564-389
t_3	··· 564-389
t_4	··· 868-701
t_5	··· 930-198
t_6	··· 930-198
t_7	··· 179-924
t_8	··· 824-870
t_9	··· 824-870
t_{10}	··· 387-215

(c)

	··· CP
t_1	··· 322-573
t_2	··· 564-389
t_3	··· 564-389
t_4	··· 868-701
t_5	··· ***-198
t_6	··· 930-198
t_7	··· 179-924
t_8	··· ***-870
t_9	··· 824-870
t_{10}	··· 387-215

(d)

Figure 1: (a) dirty data, and possible repairs w.r.t. (b) oversimplified φ_1, (c) precise φ_2, (d) overrefined φ_3

*hidden digits ***) are repaired in Figure 1(c). (Note that predicates may not be inserted arbitrarily, see Section 2.2 for a detailed discussion on inserting meaningful predicates.)*

On the other hand, a given DC *could also be overrefined.*

$$\varphi_3 : \forall t_\alpha, t_\beta \in R, \neg(t_\alpha.\mathsf{Name} = t_\beta.\mathsf{Name} \wedge t_\alpha.\mathsf{Year} = t_\beta.\mathsf{Year} \wedge t_\alpha.\mathsf{Birthday} = t_\beta.\mathsf{Birthday} \wedge t_\alpha.\mathsf{CP} \neq t_\beta.\mathsf{CP})$$

The Year *information is not necessary to identify a person's* CP*. As illustrated in Figure 1(d), φ_3 overfits the data and fails to identify the truly dirty data in t_5 and t_8. By eliminating the excessive predicates on* Year *from φ_3, the modified constraint (i.e., φ_2 exactly) addresses all the dirty* CP *values.*

Compared to the existing approach [2] (with the trust parameter τ that controls the portion of trusted data), our proposal differs in the following aspects: (1) We employ both predicate insertion and deletion for repairing constraints, rather than only refining constraints (by insertion) without addressing overfitting ones; (2) We consider the advanced refinement with order relationships on numerical values in addition to the (in)equality relationship, e.g., $>$ refines $\neq$, which is not considered in the existing FD-based methods (see more examples in Example 4); (3) Instead of pre-setting a parameter τ ahead on the portion of trusted data, we can try several constraint variations (with different thresholds θ) and select the repair result having a moderate amount of changed data, with neither oversimplified nor overrefined constraints (see more discussions in Section 5.1).

In this paper, we propose a novel *θ-tolerant* repair model, with tolerance on constraint variances: Given a set Σ of constraints over a data instance I, the *θ-tolerant* repair model finds a minimum data repair I' that satisfies at least one of the constraint variants Σ' whose variation upon the given Σ (via predicate insertion and deletion) is within θ.

Challenges. Owing to the inherent hardness of data repairing problems [14, 16], it is not surprising to understand the challenge of the θ-tolerant repair problem (in Section 2.3).

To tackle the θ-tolerant repair problem, a straightforward approach is to compute the data repair results for each constraint *variant* Σ' with variation no greater than θ. A potentially large number of possible constraint repairs (variants) naturally lead to three questions: (1) how to *prune* the constraint variants, (2) how to enable the *sharing* of data repair results among different constraint variants, and (3) how to choose the constraint-variance tolerance threshold θ and the corresponding repair results.

Existing holistic data repair [8] eliminates only the currently observed violations, which may introduce new violations to others; and thus needs multiple rounds of repairing till no new violations coming up. Directly applying the holistic data repair falls short in the following aspects: (1) the multi-round repairing could be inefficient and with possibly unbounded repair cost (so that pruning is not applicable); (2) the ad-hoc repairing in distinct rounds prevents sharing the repair computation among different constraint variants.

Contributions. Our major contributions in this paper are summarized as:

(1) We propose a novel θ-tolerant repair, the first repair model with tolerance of constraint variances on both predicate insertion and deletion.

(2) We devise efficient pruning of possible constraint variants Σ'. By revealing the refinement relationships between constraints, we show that those non-maximal constraint variants w.r.t. refinement are not necessary to be considered. Upper and lower bounds of data repair cost further advance the pruning of candidate constraint variants.

(3) We present a violation-free algorithm for repairing data given a set of constraints (variants). The proposed method guarantees one round repairing without introducing new violations, by putting not only violations but also the suspect data (that may introduce violations after repairing) into the repair context. This one round data repairing also enables sharing repair results among different constraint variants.

(4) Finally, experimental results on real data sets demonstrate that our constraint-variance tolerant (CVtolerant) repair has significantly higher data repair accuracy than the state-of-the-art Unified [5] and Relative [2] approaches. In addition, our proposal shows about 2 orders of magnitude improvement in time costs compared to Relative. Owing to the effective pruning techniques, the time cost of CVtolerant is even comparable to the pure Holistic data repair [8] (which does not consider constraint variants).

2. PROBLEM STATEMENT

Consider a relation scheme R with attributes $attr(R)$. Let predicate space $\mathbb{P}$ be a set of predicates P in the form of $v_1\phi v_2$ or $v_1\phi c$ with $v_1, v_2 \in t_x.A$, $x \in \{\alpha, \beta\}$, $t_\alpha, t_\beta \in R$, $A \in attr(R)$, c is constant, and $\phi \in \{=, <, >, \leq, \geq, \neq\}$ is a built-in operator[2]. A *denial constraint* (DCs) [7]

$$\varphi : t_\alpha, t_\beta, \dots \in R, \neg(P_1 \wedge \dots \wedge P_m)$$

[2]The determination of meaningful predicates in $\mathbb{P}$ over the same attributes or joinable and comparable attribute pairs has been studied in [7], which is not the focus of this study.

states that for any tuples $t_\alpha, t_\beta, \ldots$ from R, all the predicates $P_i \in \mathit{pred}(\varphi), i = 1, \ldots, m$, should not be true at the same time.

For an instance I of R, we say that a list of tuples $t_i, t_j, \cdots \in I$ *satisfies* φ, denoted by $\langle t_i, t_j, \ldots \rangle \models \varphi$, if there exists at least one $P \in \mathit{pred}(\varphi)$ that is not satisfied, e.g., having $I(t_i.A)\overline{\phi}I(t_j.B)$ for a $P : t_\alpha.A\phi t_\beta.B$. Here $I(t_i.A)$ denotes the value of cell $t_i.A$ in I, and $\overline{\phi}$ is the inverse of ϕ (see Table 1). If $\langle t_i, t_j, \ldots \rangle$ satisfies all the predicates in $\mathit{pred}(\varphi)$, it is a violation of φ.

We say that I satisfies φ, written as $I \models \varphi$, if all the distinct tuple lists in I satisfies φ. For a set Σ of φ, $I \models \Sigma$ if and only if $\forall \varphi \in \Sigma$, $I \models \varphi$.

Example 2. *For φ_1 in Example 1, the tuple pair t_1, t_2 in Figure 1(a) violates φ_1 since t_1.Name $=$ t_2.Name whereas t_1.Income $\neq$ t_2.Income, i.e., all predicates in $\mathit{pred}(\varphi_1)$ are true. Instead, tuple pair t_1, t_4 satisfies φ_1, i.e., $\langle t_1, t_4 \rangle \models \varphi_1$, given t_1.Name $\neq$ t_4.Name. In conclusion, I in Figure 1(a) does not satisfy $\Sigma = \{\varphi_1\}$ in Example 1.*

2.1 Data Repair via Value Modification

Data repairing is to find a modification I' of I such that all the violations w.r.t the constraints Σ are eliminated, having $I' \models \Sigma$. Referring to the minimum change principle [4], the data repair I' is expected to be as close as possible to the original I, i.e., minimizing the data repair cost below.

Definition 1. *Let I' denote a repair of I by modifying the attribute values without adding or deleting tuples. The data repair cost is evaluated by the distance between I and I'*

$$\Delta(I, I') = \sum_{t \in I, A \in \mathit{attr}(R)} w(t.A) \cdot \mathit{dist}(I(t.A), I'(t.A))$$

where $\mathit{dist}(I(t.A), I'(t.A))$ is the distance between two values on cell $t.A$ in I and I', and $w(t.A)$ is the weight of cell $t.A$.

The data repair cost could be simply the *count* of cells $t.A$ such that $I(t.A) \neq I'(t.A)$, i.e., with $\mathit{dist}(I(t.A), I'(t.A)) = 1$, while $\mathit{dist}(I(t.A), I'(t.A)) = 0$ if $I(t.A) = I'(t.A)$. Alternatively, the absolute value of difference on numerical values or the edit distance [17] for string values could be considered. The weight $w(t.A)$ can either be the confidence of the original value in cell $t.A$, or simply an equal 1 if no advanced knowledge is provided [14].

Note that there may not exist a repair I' with values from the currently known values $\mathit{dom}(A)$ of each attribute $A \in \mathit{attr}(R)$ that eliminates all the violations. Following the same line in [14], an assignment of *fresh variable* (fv) out of the currently known domain $\mathit{dom}(A)$ is necessary. As stated in [8], a fresh variable fv is a value not in the currently known domain $\mathit{dom}(A)$ and does not satisfy any of the predicates, i.e., ensures eliminating violations. It is worth noting that a denial constraint requires all the predicates should not be true at the same time. That is, tuples do not satisfy a *denial* constraint, e.g., φ_4 below, if they satisfies all the predicates specified in φ_4. Therefore, in order to make the tuples satisfy φ_4, we need some modification on the tuples such that they do not satisfy at least one predicate in φ_4. By specifying that "an fv does not satisfy any of the predicate", it ensures the repaired tuples satisfy the denial constraints. Usually, a cell is repaired to fv only when there is no other alternative from $\mathit{dom}(A)$, and is thus associated with higher cost, having $\mathit{dist}(a, b) < \mathit{dist}(a, \mathit{fv}), a, b \in \mathit{dom}(A)$.

Example 3. *Consider another φ_4 over the relation Income:*

$$\varphi_4 : \forall t_\alpha, t_\beta \in R, \neg(t_\alpha.\mathsf{Income} > t_\beta.\mathsf{Income} \wedge t_\alpha.\mathsf{Tax} \leq t_\beta.\mathsf{Tax})$$

which states that higher income should pay more tax. Tuples $t_1 - t_7$ violate φ_4 with each other, for instance, having t_2.Income $>$ t_1.Income and t_2.Tax $\leq$ t_1.Tax, i.e., $\langle t_2, t_1 \rangle \not\models \varphi_1$. Suppose that there is a data repair I' with the following modifications, on attribute Tax of t_2, t_3, t_5, t_6, t_7. (As we will see soon in Example 4, this is not a rational repair owing to the imprecise φ_4.)

	t_1	t_2	t_3	t_4	t_5	t_6	t_7	t_8	t_9	t_{10}
Tax	0	fv_1	fv_2	3k	fv_3	fv_4	fv_5	21k	21k	40k

Note that $I(t_1.\mathsf{Tax}) = 0$ requires $I(t_2.\mathsf{Tax}) > 0$ referring to φ_4, while $I(t_4.\mathsf{Tax}) = 3k$ indicates $I(t_2.\mathsf{Tax}) < 3k$. However, there is no value in the current $\mathit{dom}(\mathsf{Tax}) = \{0, 3k, 21k, 40k\}$ which is > 0 and $< 3k$. Therefore, the repair $I'(t_2.\mathsf{Tax}) = \mathit{fv}_1$ is assigned by a fresh variable fv_1 (out of $\mathit{dom}(\mathsf{Tax})$, e.g., denoting unknown or not applicable).

Suppose that the count cost is used, having $\mathit{dist}(a, a) = 0, \mathit{dist}(a, b) = 1, \mathit{dist}(a, \mathit{fv}) = 1.1, a \neq b, a, b \in \mathit{dom}(A)$ and fv is a fresh variable. According to the cost function, the total modification cost by this I' is $\Delta(I, I') = 5.5$.

2.2 Constraint Variation via Insertion/Deletion

We consider two types of reasonable constraint variances, via predicate insertion and deletion, respectively.

2.2.1 Predicate Insertion

First, following the same line of adding attributes for refining FDs [5, 2], by adding additional predicates (from predicate space $\mathbb{P}$) into a constraint, some tuples may no longer violate the modified constraint. However, we should not insert two types of predicates that make the DCs useless, (1) insertion leading to trivial DCs, and (2) insertion of predicates with constants, which is not an issue for FDs.

Specifically, if a $P_j : x\phi_j y$ is inserted, such that there exist $P_i : x\phi_i y \in \mathit{pred}(\varphi)$ having $\overline{\phi_i} \in \mathit{Imp}(\phi_j)$ as defined in Table 1, the repaired φ' becomes a *trivial* DC [7]. Since P_i, P_j always cannot be true at the same time, φ' is trivially satisfied. In other words, no violations can be detected by such a trivial DC. Similarly, inserting a predicate $t_\alpha.K = t_\beta.K$ over a declared key attribute K makes any DC trivially satisfied as well, and thus should be avoided. For the same reason, we do not consider inserting predicates with constants either. For instance, inserting a predicate $t_\alpha < 0$ makes all DCs fail to detect any violation in the Income relation in Figure 1.

2.2.2 Predicate Deletion

On the other hand, besides the oversimplified DCs (need predicate insertion), the constraints may already overfit the data (have to remove unnecessary predicates).

However, if too many predicates are eliminated from a DC, the constraint changes from overrefined to oversimplified. Indeed, the more the predicates are deleted, the higher the data repair cost will be (as stated in the following Lemma 1). Hence, a low cost data repair with moderated predicate deletion is preferred (see details in the problem definition below).

2.2.3 Constraint Variation Cost

It is worth noting that the variation of a constraint may need both predicate insertion (for fixing over-simplification) and predicate deletion (for fixing over-refinement).

For example, consider another φ_7.

$$\varphi_7 : \forall t_\alpha, t_\beta \in R, \neg(t_\alpha.\mathsf{Name} = t_\beta.\mathsf{Name} \wedge t_\alpha.\mathsf{Year} = t_\beta.\mathsf{Year} \wedge t_\alpha.\mathsf{CP} \neq t_\beta.\mathsf{CP})$$

To fix this constraint, we need to remove $t_\alpha.\mathsf{Year} = t_\beta.\mathsf{Year}$, and insert $t_\alpha.\mathsf{Birthday} = t_\beta.\mathsf{Birthday}$ in the variant φ'_7 of φ_7. While predicate insertion reduces unnecessary data repairs and the corresponding data repair cost, predicate deletion identifies new violations and increases the data repair cost. In this sense, the "common effect" between predicate insertion and deletion is that, the changed data will be smaller by inserting more predicates (deleting fewer predicates) than that of inserting fewer predicates (deleting more predicates). The data repair cost function consider the effect of predicate insertion and deletion holistically in φ'_7. Similarly, we need a constraint variation cost function to holistically represent the effect of predicate insertion and deletion in φ'_7 as well: (1) To avoid inserting too many predicates such that the constraints overfit the data (*smaller* data change), the constraint variation cost counts *positively* the predicate insertion and should be bounded. (2) To reward the contribution of identifying new violations (*larger* data change), we count *negatively* the predicate deletion towards the cost of constraint variation.

We call Σ' a variant of Σ if all $\varphi' \in \Sigma'$ are obtained by inserting/deleting predicates of a corresponding $\varphi \in \Sigma$. While $\Delta(I, I')$ denotes the cost on modifying data values, we use $\Theta(\Sigma, \Sigma')$ to represent the modification of constraints, in order to avoid potential confusion between data and constraint modifications.

Definition 2. *For a variant Σ' of Σ, the constraint variation cost is defined as*

$$\Theta(\Sigma, \Sigma') = \sum_{\varphi \in \Sigma} edit(\varphi, \varphi')$$

where φ' is a variant of φ, and $edit(\varphi, \varphi')$ is the corresponding cost.

The cost of changing φ into φ' by inserting/deleting predicates is given by

$$edit(\varphi, \varphi') = \sum_{P \in \varphi \setminus \varphi'} c(P) + \lambda \sum_{P \in \varphi' \setminus \varphi} c(P) \tag{1}$$

where $c(P)$ denotes the weighted cost of predicate P, and λ is a weight of a predicate deletion relative to a predicate insertion, having $-1 \leq \lambda \leq 0$, e.g., $\lambda = -0.5$. It is not suggested to count predicate deletion by $\lambda = -1$ so that predicate substitution may have 0 cost.

Example 4 (Example 3 continued). *Note that φ_4 is imprecise, since low-income people do not have to pay tax (equal 0). To address this scenario, we refine φ_4 by substituting predicate $t_\alpha.\mathsf{Tax} \leq t_\beta.\mathsf{Tax}$ with $t_\alpha.\mathsf{Tax} < t_\beta.\mathsf{Tax}$, having*

$$\varphi'_4 : \forall t_\alpha, t_\beta \in R, \neg(t_\alpha.\mathit{Income} > t_\beta.\mathit{Income} \wedge t_\alpha.\mathit{Tax} < t_\beta.\mathit{Tax}).$$

By deleting and inserting a predicate in φ_4, we have the constraint variation cost $edit(\varphi_4, \varphi'_4) = c(\{t_\alpha.\mathit{Tax} < t_\beta.\mathit{Tax}\}) - \frac{1}{2}c(\{t_\alpha.\mathit{Tax} \leq t_\beta.\mathit{Tax}\}) = \frac{1}{2}$, where each predicate has a unit cost $c(P) = 1$ for simplicity and $\lambda = -\frac{1}{2}$.

Finally, with this repaired φ'_4, the irrational data repair I' in Example 3 can be avoided. Indeed, the minimum data repair w.r.t. φ'_4 only needs to modify one cell, $I'(t_4.\mathit{Tax}) = 0$.

Besides unit cost, it is possible to employ the distribution information to distinguish the contribution of attributes (predicates) when evaluating the constraint variance of adding and removing predicates. Consider a weighted cost $c(P)$ of a predicate P w.r.t. a constraint φ

$$c(P) = |\Pr(P) - \Pr(\varphi)|. \tag{2}$$

Intuitively, $\Pr(\varphi)$ estimates the proportion of tuple pairs satisfying φ, while $1 - \Pr(P)$ denotes the proportion of tuple pairs not satisfying P, or equivalently the proportion of tuple pairs that will satisfy the constraint by adding P into φ (referring to the denial semantics in the constraint). The more similar the distributions of tuple pairs satisfying P and φ (leading to more similar $\Pr(P)$ and $\Pr(\varphi)$ as well), the more likely the constraint will be true after adding P into φ, i.e., higher contribution or lower cost of P.

For instance, consider φ_1 with predicate $t_\alpha.\mathsf{CP} \neq t_\beta.\mathsf{CP}$ in Example 1. A predicate $P : t_\alpha.\mathsf{Birthday} = t_\beta.\mathsf{Birthday}$ on attribute Birthday, which has a distribution coinciding better with CP, will leads to more similar $\Pr(P : t_\alpha.\mathsf{Birthday} = t_\beta.\mathsf{Birthday})$ and $\Pr(\varphi : \neg(\cdots \wedge t_\alpha.\mathsf{CP} \neq t_\beta.\mathsf{CP}))$. That is, the predicate P on attribute Birthday has higher contribution to φ and lower cost when added into φ.

In contrast, $t_5[\mathsf{Year}] \neq t_6[\mathsf{Year}]$ but with similar CP values (or more precisely $t_5[\mathsf{CP}] = t_6[\mathsf{CP}]$ in truth data) would contribute negatively in observing similar $\Pr(t_\alpha.\mathsf{Year} = t_\beta.\mathsf{Year})$ and $\Pr(\varphi : \neg(\cdots \wedge t_\alpha.\mathsf{CP} \neq t_\beta.\mathsf{CP}))$ values. In other words, the predicate on attribute Year has lower contribution to φ and higher cost when added into φ.

We have weighed costs $c(P : t_\alpha.\mathsf{Birthday} = t_\beta.\mathsf{Birthday}) \leq c(t_\alpha.\mathsf{Year} = t_\beta.\mathsf{Year})$. The weighted cost similarly applies to predicate removing, following the intuition that removing a higher contribution predicate should have higher cost. Referring to the cost function, for an overrefined φ_3 in Example 1, removing a predicate $P : t_\alpha.\mathsf{Birthday} = t_\beta.\mathsf{Birthday}$ on attribute Birthday, which has a distribution coinciding better with CP, will leads to higher removing cost, i.e., $\lambda c(t_\alpha.\mathsf{Year} = t_\beta.\mathsf{Year}) \leq \lambda c(P : t_\alpha.\mathsf{Birthday} = t_\beta.\mathsf{Birthday})$.

2.3 θ-tolerant Repair Model

Let Φ_i denote the set of possible variants of a constraint φ_i by inserting/deleting predicates. Consider $\mathbb{D} = \Phi_1 \times \cdots \times \Phi_{|\Sigma|}$, where each $\Sigma' \in \mathbb{D}$ corresponds to a possible variant of Σ. By θ-tolerant, we mean allowing a small variation on the constraints Σ, i.e., having constraint variation cost no greater than θ, $\Theta(\Sigma, \Sigma') \leq \theta$.

We take data repairing cost as objective function (to minimize) and constraint repairing cost as constraint θ, following two intuitions: (1) to avoid over-refinement, the constraint variation (cost on inserting and deleting predicates in Definition 2) should not exceed a threshold θ; (2) to avoid over-simplification, i.e., identifying too many correct data as violations, the repairing follows the minimum change principle[3] over data.

Problem 1. *Given a set Σ of constraints and an instance I, the θ-tolerant repair problem is to find a data repair I' of I such that (1) $\Delta(I, I')$ is minimized, and (2) $I' \models \Sigma'$, for some constraint variant Σ' of Σ with $\Theta(\Sigma, \Sigma') \leq \theta$.*

[3]The minimum change principle is widely considered in data cleaning [4], under the assumption that people and machines always try to make mistakes as few as possible.

Table 1: Operator inverse and implication

ϕ	$=$	$\neq$	$>$	$<$	$\geq$	$\leq$
$\overline{\phi}$	$\neq$	$=$	$\leq$	$\geq$	$<$	$>$
Imp(ϕ)	$=,\geq,\leq$	$\neq$	$>,\geq,\neq$	$<,\leq,\neq$	$\geq$	$\leq$

Similar to data value modification that does not allow adding or deleting tuples, the constraint modification does not consider inserting or removing entire constraints either. The definition of denial constraints requires at least one predicate. Therefore, removing all predicates is not supported. Indeed, we can hardly imagine the meaning of $\neg()$ without any predicate.

While turning everything into a fresh variable definitely forms a feasible repair, it is not necessary. Instead, turning one attribute value into a fresh variable is sufficient to eliminate the violation to a denial constraint (recall that an fv does not satisfy any of the predicate). Referring to the target of minimizing the repair cost in Problem 1, such a repair of turning everything into a fresh variable will never be returned as an optimal repair.

Finding the θ-tolerant minimum repair is highly non-trivial. Indeed, for a fixed set of DCs, the minimum repair problem has already been known to be NP-hard [16]. Owing to this inherent hardness (in the case without constraint modification), it is not surprising to recognize the challenge in the θ-tolerant repair problem. A straightforward approach is to obtain all the possible constraint variants Σ' with $\Theta(\Sigma, \Sigma') \leq \theta$, and find the minimum data repair I' w.r.t. each Σ', respectively.

In the remainder of this paper, we show that not all the constraint variants need to be considered (in Section 3), and sharing of data repairs can be enabled among different constraint variants (in Section 4). For the determination of the constraint variance tolerant threshold θ, we introduce some guideline on the number of repaired cells (in Section 5.1).

3. CONSTRAINT VARIATION

It is worth noting that not all the constraint variants $\Sigma' \in \mathbb{D}$ with cost $\Theta(\Sigma, \Sigma') \leq \theta$ are necessarily to be considered. In the following, we illustrate that some constraint variant may refine another. It enables the pruning of constraint variants that will not generate minimum data repairs for sure.

3.1 Maximal Constraint Variants

To capture the refinement relationship among constraints, we consider the implication between operators [7]. For any two values a and b, if $a\phi_1 b$ always implies $a\phi_2 b$, it is said that $\phi_2 \in Imp(\phi_1)$. The $Imp(\phi)$ of all ϕ are presented in Table 1. For example, we have $\leq \in Imp(<)$ since any $a < b$ always implies $a \leq b$. As restrictions, $<$ is stronger than $\leq$. Given the denial semantics, $<$ refines the constraint with $\leq$, which belongs to $Imp(<)$. The concept of closure of a set of predicates, w.r.t. a denial constraint set, is defined and calculated upon the notation of $Imp(\phi)$ in [7], which is out the scope of this study.

Definition 3. *We call φ_2 a* refinement *of φ_1, denoted by $\varphi_1 \preceq \varphi_2$, if for each $P : x\phi_1 y \in pred(\varphi_1)$, there exists a $Q : x\phi_2 y \in pred(\varphi_2)$ such that $\phi_1 \in Imp(\phi_2)$.*

By inserting additional predicates, each variant φ' of φ is a refinement of φ.

Definition 4. *We call Σ_2 a* refinement *of Σ_1, denoted by $\Sigma_1 \preceq \Sigma_2$, if for each $\varphi_2 \in \Sigma_2$, there exists a $\varphi_1 \in \Sigma_1$ such that $\varphi_1 \preceq \varphi_2$.*

Intuitively, the more the predicates are inserted, the more likely the constraints overfit the data. In other words, the more the constraints are refined (via predicate insertion or substitution), the less the data need to be changed. For instance, two tuples with $t_\alpha.A = t_\beta.A$ violating $\neg(t_\alpha.A \leq t_\beta.A)$ will no longer violate the refinement $\neg(t_\alpha.A < t_\beta.A)$.

Lemma 1. *Given two constraint variants Σ_1, Σ_2 of Σ such that Σ_2 is also a refinement of Σ_1, having $\Sigma \preceq \Sigma_1 \preceq \Sigma_2$, it always has $\Delta(I, I_1) \geq \Delta(I, I_2)$, where I_1 and I_2 are the minimum data repairs w.r.t. Σ_1 and Σ_2, respectively.*

As a result, given possibly higher data repair cost $\Delta(I, I_1)$, the corresponding constraint variant Σ_1 can be ignored.

A variant Σ' of constraint set Σ is said *maximal* w.r.t. the constraint-variance bound θ, if there does not exist any Σ'' such that $\Sigma' \preceq \Sigma''$ and $\Theta(\Sigma, \Sigma'') \leq \theta$. Consequently, any non-maximal Σ' can be directly removed from $\mathbb{D}$.

Pruning Non-maximal Constraint Variants

We say that a variant φ' of constraint φ, $\varphi \preceq \varphi'$, is *maximal*, if there does not exist another variant φ'' such that $\varphi' \preceq \varphi''$ and $edit(\varphi, \varphi'') = edit(\varphi, \varphi')$.

It is obvious to see that any φ' must be maximal in a maximal constraint variant Σ'. (Otherwise, we could build a $\Sigma'', \Sigma' \preceq \Sigma''$, by $\varphi'', \varphi' \preceq \varphi''$, with the same constraint variation cost.) In other words, we only need to consider those maximal φ'_i when obtaining Φ_i for a $\varphi_i \in \Sigma$.

Proposition 2. *For any inserted predicate $P : x\phi y \in pred(\varphi') \setminus pred(\varphi)$, if $\phi \in \{\leq, \geq, \neq\}$, then φ' is not maximal.*

Instead of inserting all the possible predicates (indicated in Section 2.2), we only need to consider the predicates with operators in $\{<, >, =\}$ when obtaining the possible variants Φ_i of a φ_i. The others with $\leq, \geq, \neq$ can be ignored.

Example 5. *Consider φ_1 again in Example 1. Besides φ_2, we may have other variants for φ_1, e.g., by inserting predicates on* Income.

$$\varphi_5 : \forall t_\alpha, t_\beta \in R, \neg(t_\alpha.\mathsf{Name} = t_\beta.\mathsf{Name} \wedge t_\alpha.\mathsf{Income} = t_\beta.\mathsf{Income} \wedge t_\alpha.\mathsf{CP} \neq t_\beta.\mathsf{CP})$$

$$\varphi_6 : \forall t_\alpha, t_\beta \in R, \neg(t_\alpha.\mathsf{Name} = t_\beta.\mathsf{Name} \wedge t_\alpha.\mathsf{Income} \leq t_\beta.\mathsf{Income} \wedge t_\alpha.\mathsf{CP} \neq t_\beta.\mathsf{CP})$$

According to $\leq \in Imp(=)$ in Table 1 for the predicates on Income*, we have $\varphi_6 \preceq \varphi_5$. That is, φ_5 is a refinement of φ_6. According to Proposition 2, the constraint variant φ_6 by inserting a predicate with operator $\leq$ is not maximal.*

The minimum data repair w.r.t. φ_6 is exactly the results in Figure 1(b), with data repair cost 7 (by count). On the other hand, the minimum data repair cost w.r.t. φ_5 is 3 (the same as the results in Figure 1(c)). It verifies the conclusion in Lemma 1 that for $\varphi_6 \preceq \varphi_5$, the minimum data repair cost w.r.t. φ_6 is always no less than that of φ_5 (7>3). Consequently, we can directly ignore the constraint variant φ_6 without computing its data repair (with cost 7).

3.2 Variants with Bounded Data Repair Cost

This section focuses on pruning/removing the unnecessarily considered candidate constraint variants Σ' that would

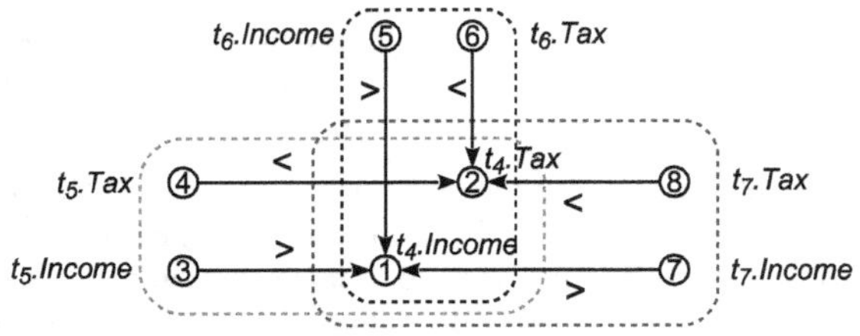

Figure 2: Conflict hypergraph

never generate the minimum data repair. We obtain $\delta_l(\Sigma', I)$ and $\delta_u(\Sigma', I)$, the lower and upper bounds of possible minimum data repairs of I w.r.t. Σ', respectively. Intuitively, for constraint variants Σ' and Σ'', if $\delta_u(\Sigma', I) < \delta_l(\Sigma'', I)$, then Σ'' can be directly discarded.

3.2.1 Conflict Graph for Representing Violations

Given a Σ over I, let us first capture all the violations, upon which the data repair cost bounds can be derived.

Definition 5. *The violation set* $viol(I, \varphi) = \{\langle t_i, t_j, \dots\rangle \mid \langle t_i, t_j, \dots\rangle \not\models \varphi, t_i, t_j, \dots \in I\}$ *is a set of tuple lists that violate* φ.

The violation set of Σ is $viol(I, \Sigma) = \cup_{\varphi \in \Sigma} viol(I, \varphi)$.

We denote $cell(t_\alpha, t_\beta, \dots; \varphi)$ all the cells that are involved in the predicates $pred(\varphi)$ of φ.

$$cell(t_\alpha, t_\beta, \dots; \varphi) = \{v_1 \mid P : v_1 \phi c \in pred(\varphi)\} \cup \{v_1, v_2 \mid P : v_1 \phi v_2 \in pred(\varphi)\}$$

The degree $Deg(\varphi)$ of φ is defined as the number of distinct cells in φ, i.e., $Deg(\varphi) = |cell(t_\alpha, t_\beta, \dots; \varphi)|$.

Following [8], we represent violations in I w.r.t. Σ by a *conflict hypergraph* $\mathcal{G}$, where each vertex is a cell in I. Each violation tuple list $\langle t_i, t_j, \dots\rangle \in viol(I, \varphi)$ forms a hyperedge, consisting of $cell(t_i, t_j, \dots; \varphi)$, in the graph. The data repair problem is thus to find a I' such that all the conflict hyperedge are eliminated.

Example 6. *Consider again* φ_4' *in Example 4.*

$$\varphi_4' : \forall t_\alpha, t_\beta \in R, \neg(t_\alpha.\textsf{Income} > t_\beta.\textsf{Income} \wedge t_\alpha.\textsf{Tax} < t_\beta.\textsf{Tax}).$$

For the relation I in Figure 1(a), the violation set is

$$viol(I, \varphi_4') = \{\langle t_5, t_4\rangle, \langle t_6, t_4\rangle, \langle t_7, t_4\rangle\}.$$

Figure 2 illustrates the conflict hypergraph built upon the violation set, where each node denotes a cell in the relation. Each hyperedge corresponds to a violation tuple list (pair). For instance, the hyperedge for $\langle t_5, t_4\rangle \in viol(I, \varphi_4')$ *consists of* $cell(t_5, t_4; \varphi_4') = \{t_5.\textsf{Income}, t_4.\textsf{Income}, t_5.\textsf{Tax}, t_4.\textsf{Tax}\}$.

3.2.2 Bounds on Minimum Data Repair Cost

To eliminate the violation of a conflict hyperedge, at least one vertex (cell) in the edge should be repaired. We denote

$$\min_{a \in dom(A)} dist(I(t.A), a)$$

the weight of vertex $t.A$, i.e., the minimum cost should be paid to repair $t.A$.

Let $\mathbb{V}^*(\mathcal{G})$ be the *minimum weighted vertex cover* of the hypergraph $\mathcal{G}$ corresponding to Σ, I, with weight

$$\|\mathbb{V}^*(\mathcal{G})\| = \sum_{t.A \in \mathbb{V}^*(\mathcal{G})} \min_{a \in dom(A)} dist(I(t.A), a).$$

Lemma 3. *For any valid repair I' of I, i.e., $I' \models \Sigma$, we have* $\Delta(I, I') \geq \|\mathbb{V}^*(\mathcal{G})\|$.

Since computing $\mathbb{V}^*$ is already known to be NP-hard, we consider an constant factor-f approximation of $\mathbb{V}^*$ [20], i.e., $\frac{\|\mathbb{V}(\mathcal{G})\|}{\|\mathbb{V}^*(\mathcal{G})\|} \leq f$, where f is the maximum degree of hyperedges and $\mathbb{V}(\mathcal{G})$ is an approximation of $\mathbb{V}^*(\mathcal{G})$.

Let $Deg(\Sigma) = \max_{\varphi \in \Sigma} Deg(\varphi)$ be the degree of Σ, i.e., the maximum degree of φ in Σ. It follows $\|\mathbb{V}(\mathcal{G})\| \leq f\|\mathbb{V}^*(\mathcal{G})\| \leq Deg(\Sigma)\Delta(I, I')$. Therefore, we define the lower bound of minimum data repair cost as

$$\delta_l(\Sigma, I) = \frac{\|\mathbb{V}(\mathcal{G})\|}{Deg(\Sigma)}.$$

Recall that the violation can be eliminated by simply assigning any cell in a hyperedge to fresh variable fv. Since $\mathbb{V}(\mathcal{G})$ covers all the hyperedges, assigning all the cells in $\mathbb{V}(\mathcal{G})$ forms a valid data repair. We thus define the upper bound of the minimum data repair cost as

$$\delta_u(\Sigma, I) = \sum_{t.A \in \mathbb{V}(\mathcal{G})} dist(I(t.A), fv).$$

Example 7 (Example 6 continued). *Consider the conflict graph $\mathcal{G}$ in Figure 2. Suppose that the count cost is used, having $dist(a, b) = 1, a \neq b, a, b \in dom(A)$. That is, each vertex has weight 1. Let $AMWVG(\mathcal{G}) = \{t_4.\textsf{Tax}\}$ be an approximate minimum weighted vertex cover, with $\|AMWVG(\mathcal{G})\| = 1$. Referring to the number of 4 cells in φ_4', we have $Deg(\Sigma) = Deg(\varphi_4') = 4$. The lower bound of minimum data repair cost is $\delta_l(\Sigma, I) = 0.25$. Similarly, suppose that $dist(a, fv) = 1.1, a \in dom(A)$. The upper bound of minimum data repair cost can be computed as $\delta_u(\Sigma, I) = 1.1$.*

3.3 θ-tolerant Repair Algorithm

Consider a set $\mathbb{D}$ of constraint variation candidates Σ_i for Σ, whose variations are bounded by θ, $\Theta(\Sigma, \Sigma_i) \leq \theta$. Algorithm 1 returns a data repair $I_{\min} = \arg\min_{I_i} \Delta(I, I_i)$, where I_i is the minimum repair of I w.r.t. $\Sigma_i, i = 1, \dots, |\mathbb{D}|$.

First, it is notable that Σ itself, with $\Theta(\Sigma, \Sigma) = 0 \leq \theta$, should be a valid constraint "variation" candidate. Therefore, the upper bound $\delta_{\min}$ of the θ-tolerant minimum data repair can be initialized as $\delta_u(\Sigma, I)$ in Line 1.

For each variant Σ_i, if the lower bound $\delta_l(\Sigma_i, I)$ is no greater than the previously known upper bound $\delta_{\min}$ (Line 3), the data repair over Σ_i, I should be processed. (See the following section for the DATAREPAIR function.) Lines 5-7 update the bound $\delta_{\min}$, once a better result I_i is found.

Algorithm 1 θ-TOLERANTREPAIR($\mathbb{D}, \Sigma, I$)

Input: An instance I, a constraint set Σ, and a set $\mathbb{D}$ of constraint variants with variation bounded by θ
Output: A minimum data repair $I_{\min}$ w.r.t. $\mathbb{D}$

```
1: δmin := δu(Σ, I)
2: for each constraint variant Σi ∈ D do
3:   if δl(Σi, I) ≤ δmin then
4:     Ii := DATAREPAIR(Σi, I, V(Gi), δmin)
5:     if Δ(I, Ii) < δmin then
6:       δmin := Δ(I, Ii)
7:       Imin := Ii
8: return Imin
```

Example 8. *Consider the relation in Figure 1(a) and $\Sigma = \{\varphi_4\}$ in Example 3. For a $\theta = \frac{1}{2}$, suppose that the (pruned)* *constraint variants are* $\mathbb{D} = \{\Sigma_1, \Sigma_2\}$ *where* $\Sigma_1 = \{\varphi'_4\}$ *in Example 4, and* $\Sigma_2 = \{\varphi''_4\}$ *contains*

$$\varphi''_4 : \forall t_\alpha, t_\beta \in R, \neg(t_\alpha.\mathsf{Income} > t_\beta.\mathsf{Income} \wedge t_\alpha.\mathsf{Tax} = t_\beta.\mathsf{Tax}).$$

Note that both Σ_1 *and* Σ_2 *are maximal w.r.t.* θ.

As shown in Example 6, for Σ_1*, its conflict hypergraph* $\mathcal{G}_1$ *(in Figure 2) can be obtained. We have* $\delta_u(\Sigma_1, I) = 1.1$*, referring to Example 7.*

Similarly, for Σ_2*, we obtain conflict hypergraph* $\mathcal{G}_2$ *with* $\mathbb{V}(\mathcal{G}_2) = \{t_2.\mathsf{Tax}, t_3.\mathsf{Tax}, t_5.\mathsf{Tax}, t_6.\mathsf{Tax}, t_7.\mathsf{Tax}\}$*. Referring to the count cost as introduced in Example 7 and* $Deg(\Sigma_2) = Deg(\varphi'_4) = 4$*, it follows* $\delta_l(\Sigma_2, I) = 5/4 = 1.25$.

With $\delta_u(\Sigma_1, I) < \delta_l(\Sigma_2, I)$*, the constraint variant* Σ_2 *can be further pruned without calling* DATAREPAIR.

Let ℓ be the maximum number of tuples $|\{t_\alpha, t_\beta, \dots\}|$ involved in a φ of Σ. The construction of $\mathcal{G}_i$ for each $\Sigma_i \in \mathbb{D}$ costs $O(|I|^\ell)$. As illustrated in the following section, for a certain set of changing cells $\mathbb{V}(\mathcal{G}_i)$, the DATAREPAIR algorithm runs in $O(|I|^\ell)$ time. Thereby, the θ-TOLERANTREPAIR algorithm runs in $O(|I|^\ell|\mathbb{D}|)$ time. Typical constraints are with $\ell = 1$ or 2, i.e., involving one or two tuples. For instance, linear denial constraints [16, 1] and constant conditional functional dependencies [3] have $\ell = 1$, declaring constraints on single tuples. Functional dependencies and general conditional functional dependencies, with $\ell = 2$, consider constraints involving two tuples. The proposed pruning practically reduces computing time costs but does not improve the complexity.

4. DATA REPAIR

Next, given a set Σ' of constraints (variants), we focus on generating the minimum data repair of I w.r.t. Σ'. In particular, it is expected to share the computation among different constraint variants Σ'.

Existing holistic approach [8] is incapable of the aforesaid sharing, owing to multiple ad-hoc repair rounds. The rationale is that putting only violations into repair context may introduce new violations to others after one round repairing.

In this section, to advance data repair with sharing, we introduce a novel violation-free repair (in Section 4.1) that ensures no new violations introduced after repairing. The idea is to consider in repair context not only the violations but also the suspects that may potentially introduce violations. This one round data repair thus enables sharing among various constraint variants (in Section 4.2).

4.1 Violation Free Data Repair

Since the problem of finding the minimum data repair has already been known to be NP-hard [16], we thereby focus on approximation approaches for repairing. Following the same line of [8], the repairing starts from heuristically selected cells, i.e., the aforesaid $\mathbb{V}(\mathcal{G})$, denoted by $\mathbb{C}$ for simplicity. To perform the one-round violation-free repair, it is essential to guarantee that the modification on cells in $\mathbb{C}$ will not introduce new violations (conflict hyperedges).

4.1.1 Suspects of Potential Violations

Let us first capture the "suspects" that may lead to new violations after modifying the cells in $\mathbb{C}$. Recall that a violation occurs in a tuple list $t_i, t_j, \dots$ w.r.t. φ, when all the predicates in φ are satisfied. Intuitively, if a predicate of φ is

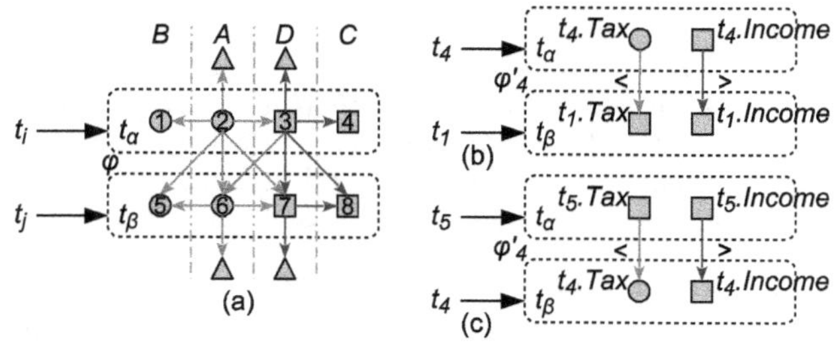

Figure 3: Suspect condition (blue arrow) and repair context (red arrow with operator inverse)

not satisfied, which does not contain cells from $\mathbb{C}$, the repairing on $\mathbb{C}$ will not affect $\langle t_i, t_j, \dots\rangle \models \varphi$. That is, $\langle t_i, t_j, \dots\rangle$ does not need to be suspected.

Definition 6. *The* suspect set $susp(\mathbb{C}, \varphi)$ *of a* φ *is a set of tuple lists* $\langle t_i, t_j, \dots\rangle$ *satisfying all the predicates in* φ *which do not involve cells in* $\mathbb{C}$.

All the tuple lists $\langle t_i, t_j, \dots\rangle$ satisfying the following suspect condition $sc(t_i, t_j, \dots; \varphi)$ w.r.t. $\mathbb{C}$ should be suspected,

$$sc(t_\alpha, t_\beta, \dots; \varphi) = \{I(v_1)\phi c \mid P : v_1\phi c \in pred(\varphi), v_1 \notin \mathbb{C}\} \cup \{I(v_1)\phi I(v_2) \mid P : v_1\phi v_2 \in pred(\varphi), v_1, v_2 \notin \mathbb{C}\}$$

which considers all the predicates on cells in $cell(t_\alpha, t_\beta, \dots; \varphi)$ except those ones from $\mathbb{C}$.

To understand the suspect condition more clearly, let us illustrate an example constraint φ declared on two tuples t_i (as t_α of φ) and t_j (as t_β of φ) in Figure 3(a). Each circle denotes a changing cell from $\mathbb{C}$, while a square is a cell not in $\mathbb{C}$ (that will not be modified). The constant associated in a predicate is represented by a triangle. Each arrow $v_1 \to v_2$ denotes a predicate declared on two cells $v_1\phi v_2$ (or between a cell and a constant $v_1\phi c$). The suspect condition considers predicates with cells not from $\mathbb{C}$, i.e., blue arrows attached on two squares or between squares and triangles. For instance, a suspect condition $I(t_j.D)\phi I(t_j.C)$, i.e., 7→8, corresponds to the satisfaction of predicate $t_\beta.D\phi t_\beta.C \in pred(\varphi)$. Consequently, if all the blue edges specified by predicates in φ are satisfied, i.e., $sc(t_i, t_j; \varphi)$ is satisfied, $\langle t_i, t_j\rangle$ becomes a suspect tuple list (pair).

Lemma 4. *For any* $\mathbb{C}$*, it always has* $viol(I, \varphi) \subseteq susp(\mathbb{C}, \varphi)$.

Lemma 4 states that any tuple list already in violation is naturally suspected. In other words, identifying the suspect set is sufficient to capture all the violations.

Example 9. *Consider again* φ'_4 *in Example 4 over the relation in Figure 1(a). Let* $\mathbb{C} = \{t_4.\mathsf{Tax}\}$ *be the set of changing cells, i.e., an* $\mathbb{V}(\mathcal{G})$ *for the conflict hypergraph* $\mathcal{G}$ *in Figure 2. We have the suspect set* $susp(\mathbb{C}, \varphi'_4) = \{\langle t_4, t_1\rangle, \langle t_4, t_2\rangle, \langle t_4, t_3\rangle, \langle t_5, t_4\rangle, \langle t_6, t_4\rangle, \langle t_7, t_4\rangle, \langle t_8, t_4\rangle, \langle t_9, t_4\rangle, \langle t_{10}, t_4\rangle\}$*. For instance, consider* $\langle t_4, t_1\rangle$ *in Figure 3(b), where* $t_4.\mathsf{Tax} \in \mathbb{C}$ *is denoted by a circle, while other cells not in* $\mathbb{C}$ *are squares. The predicate* $t_4.\mathsf{Tax} < t_1.\mathsf{Tax}$ *on* $t_4.\mathsf{Tax} \in \mathbb{C}$ *is a red arrow, while the blue arrow denotes the other* $t_4.\mathsf{Income} > t_1.\mathsf{Income}$ *whose cells are not in* $\mathbb{C}$.

The suspect condition on $\langle t_4, t_1\rangle$ *is thus* $sc(t_4, t_1, \varphi'_4) = \{I(t_4.\mathsf{Income}) > I(t_1.\mathsf{Income})\}$*. Referring to Figure 1(a), we have* $I(t_4.\mathsf{Income}) = 3k > I(t_1.\mathsf{Income}) = 0$*. That is,* $\langle t_4, t_1\rangle$ *satisfies all the predicates (blue arrow) in* φ'_4 *except* *those (red arrow) with cells from $\mathbb{C}$. Referring to Definition 6, $\langle t_4, t_1\rangle$ is a suspect tuple pair. It is possible that repairs on $t_4.\mathsf{Tax}$ may introduce violations to $t_1.\mathsf{Tax}$, i.e., when $I'(t_4.\mathsf{Tax}) < I(t_1.\mathsf{Tax})$ with all the predicates in φ'_4 satisfied.*

For the violation set $viol(I, \varphi'_4) = \{\langle t_5, t_4\rangle, \langle t_6, t_4\rangle, \langle t_7, t_4\rangle\}$ in Example 6, we have $viol(I, \varphi'_4) \subseteq susp(\mathbb{C}, \varphi'_4)$ by Lemma 4.

4.1.2 Repair Context over Suspects

For each $\langle t_i, t_j, \dots\rangle$ in the suspect set of φ, the following repair context $rc(t_i, t_j, \dots; \varphi)$ ensures that the repaired cells in $\mathbb{C}$ will not satisfy the predicates $P : x\phi y$ declared on $\mathbb{C}$, by specifying the inverse $\overline{\phi}$ of ϕ.

$$\begin{aligned} rc(t_\alpha, t_\beta, \dots; \varphi) = &\{I'(v_1)\overline{\phi}c \mid P : v_1\phi c \in pred(\varphi), v_1 \in \mathbb{C}\} \cup \\ &\{I'(v_1)\overline{\phi}I'(v_2) \mid P : v_1\phi v_2 \in pred(\varphi), v_1, v_2 \in \mathbb{C}\} \cup \\ &\{I'(v_1)\overline{\phi}I(v_2) \mid P : v_1\phi v_2 \in pred(\varphi), v_1 \in \mathbb{C}, v_2 \notin \mathbb{C}\} \cup \\ &\{I(v_1)\overline{\phi}I'(v_2) \mid P : v_1\phi v_2 \in pred(\varphi), v_1 \notin \mathbb{C}, v_2 \in \mathbb{C}\} \end{aligned}$$

Each repair context predicate in $rc(t_\alpha, t_\beta, \dots; \varphi)$ corresponds to the inverse of a predicate in φ with cells from $\mathbb{C}$ (red arrow in Figure 3). For instance, $I(t_\alpha.D)\overline{\phi}I'(t_\beta.A)$, corresponding to 3→6, ensures that the predicate $t_\alpha.D\phi t_\beta.A \in pred(\varphi)$ will not be satisfied after modifying $t_\beta.A \in \mathbb{C}$.

We assemble the repair contexts for each suspect tuple list $\langle t_i, t_j, \dots\rangle$ of all $\varphi \in \Sigma$ to generate a data repair I'.

Proposition 5. *Any assignment that satisfies all the repair contexts forms a valid repair I' without introducing any new violations, i.e., $I' \models \Sigma$.*

Again, the repair cost is expected to be small.

$$\min \sum_{t_i.A \in \mathbb{C}} dist(I(t_i.A), I'(t_i.A)) \quad (3)$$

$$\text{s.t.} \quad rc(t_i, t_j, \dots; \varphi) \qquad \langle t_i, t_j, \dots\rangle \in susp(\mathbb{C}, \varphi), \varphi \in \Sigma$$

Existing solver can be employed to efficiently compute solutions, e.g., liner programming (LP) for numerical values and value frequency map (VFM) for string types [8].

Example 10 (Example 9 continued). *For the suspect tuple list $\langle t_4, t_1\rangle \in susp(\mathbb{C}, \varphi'_4)$, its repair context $rc(t_4, t_1; \varphi'_4) = \{I'(t_4.\mathsf{Tax}) \geq I(t_1.\mathsf{Tax})\}$ is obtained by considering the inverse of each predicate in φ'_4 with cells from $\mathbb{C}$, i.e., red arrow in Figure 3(b). Similarly, $rc(t_5, t_4; \varphi'_4) = \{I'(t_5.\mathsf{Tax}) \geq I(t_4.\mathsf{Tax})\}$ is obtain from the red arrow in Figure 3(c).*

By considering all the tuple pairs in $susp(\mathbb{C}, \varphi'_4)$, we obtain the entire repair contexts in formula (3), as shown in Figure 4(a). Given the repair contexts $I'(t_4.\mathsf{Tax}) \geq I(t_1.\mathsf{Tax}) = 0$ and $I'(t_4.\mathsf{Tax}) \leq I(t_5.\mathsf{Tax}) = 0$, a solution to the problem in formula (3) is $I'(t_4.\mathsf{Tax}) = 0$ (as shown in Example 4).

4.1.3 Problem Solving with Fresh Variable

As mentioned, there may not exist any assignment from the currently known values that can satisfy all the repair contexts. Following the same line of DC-based data repairing [8], we attempt to assign some cells by fresh variable *fv*. Recall that *fv* (denoting values out of the current domain such as unknown or not applicable) does not satisfy any predicate including the repair context predicates. Once a cell is assigned by *fv*, all the repair context predicates involving the cell can be removed. Heuristically, we would select a cell $t.A \in \mathbb{C}$ with the largest number of appearance in the repair contexts, to assign *fv*.

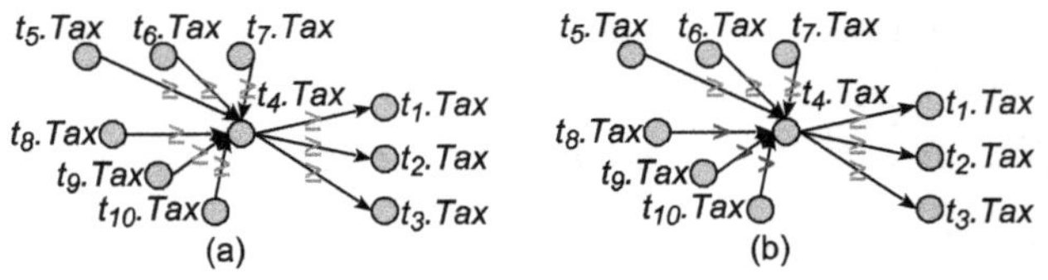

Figure 4: Repair contexts (a) rc_1 and (b) rc_2

The repairing keeps on assigning *fv*, i.e., removing repair context predicates, till the problem with the remaining repair contexts can be solved. The more the repair context predicates are removed, the more likely the problem can be solved. The worst case is the assignment of *fv* for all cells in $\mathbb{C}$ (see more discussions below on performance analysis).

Rather than gradually (slowly) assigning *fv* in each iteration, we are indeed able to identify ahead some cells $t.A$ that must be assigned to *fv*. Let

$$rc(t.A, \Sigma) = \{$$

$$I(v_1)\overline{\phi_1}I'(t.A), I'(t.A)\overline{\phi_2}I(v_2), I'(t.A)\overline{\phi_3}c \in rc(t_i, t_j, \dots; \varphi)$$

$$\mid t \in \{t_i, t_j, \dots\}, v_1, v_2 \notin \mathbb{C}, \langle t_i, t_j, \dots\rangle \in susp(\mathbb{C}, \varphi), \varphi \in \Sigma\}$$

denote all the repair context predicates declared between $t.A$ and a constant c, or between $t.A$ and cell $v_1, v_2 \notin \mathbb{C}$ that cannot be modified. If $rc(t.A, \Sigma)$ is unsatisfiable, we directly assign $I'(t.A) = fv$.

Example 11. *Consider again φ_4 in Example 3, with $\mathbb{C} = \mathbb{V}(\mathcal{G}) = \{t_2.Tax, t_3.Tax, t_5.Tax, t_6.Tax, t_7.Tax\}$ as illustrated in Example 8. Following the same line of Example 10, we compute all the repair contexts for each suspect tuple pair in $susp(\mathbb{C}, \varphi_4)$. Now consider the subset of repair contexts on the cell $t_2.Tax$, i.e., $rc(t_2.Tax, \{\varphi_4\}) = \{I'(t_2.\mathsf{Tax}) > I(t_1.\mathsf{Tax}), I(t_4.\mathsf{Tax}) > I'(t_2.\mathsf{Tax}), I(t_8.\mathsf{Tax}) > I'(t_2.\mathsf{Tax}), I(t_9.\mathsf{Tax}) > I'(t_2.\mathsf{Tax}), I(t_{10}.\mathsf{Tax}) > I'(t_2.\mathsf{Tax})\}$. Given that $I(t_1.\mathsf{Tax}) = 0$ and $I(t_4.\mathsf{Tax}) = 3k$, $rc(t_2.Tax, \{\varphi_4\})$ indeed requires $0 < I'(t_2.\mathsf{Tax}) < 3k$. As presented in Example 3, since there is not value in the current dom(Tax) that meets the requirement, we can directly assign $I'(t_2.\mathsf{Tax}) = fv_1$ by fresh variable, without solving the problem in formula (3) over the entire repair contexts.*

4.2 Enabling Sharing among Problem Solving

To enable sharing, we decompose $\mathbb{C}$ into a set of components $\mathbb{C}_1, \dots, \mathbb{C}_m$, such that for any $v_1 \in \mathbb{C}_i, v_2 \in \mathbb{C}_j$, there does not exist $I'(v_1)\overline{\phi}I'(v_2) \in rc(t_i, t_j, \dots; \varphi)$, for some tuple list $\langle t_i, t_j, \dots\rangle \in susp(\mathbb{C}, \varphi), \varphi \in \Sigma$. That is, the assignment of $v_1 \in \mathbb{C}_i$ will not affect $v_2 \in \mathbb{C}_j$. Let

$$rc(\mathbb{C}, \Sigma) = \bigcup_{\langle t_i, t_j, \dots\rangle \in susp(\mathbb{C}, \varphi), \varphi \in \Sigma} rc(t_i, t_j, \dots; \varphi)$$

denote all the repair contexts in formula (3) for short. Since components are disjoint w.r.t. repair contexts, $rc(\mathbb{C}_k, \Sigma)$ is indeed a projection of $rc(\mathbb{C}, \Sigma)$ on $\mathbb{C}_k$, having $rc(\mathbb{C}, \Sigma) = rc(\mathbb{C}_1, \Sigma) \cup \dots \cup rc(\mathbb{C}_m, \Sigma)$. Consequently, we can solve the problem by resolving the subproblems w.r.t. $rc(\mathbb{C}_k, \Sigma)$ for each component $\mathbb{C}_k$ individually.

Decomposing into components not only accelerates the solution computing but also enhances the possibility of result sharing among (sub)problems. Obviously, the solution can be directly shared, if $rc(\mathbb{C}_k, \Sigma_1) = rc(\mathbb{C}_k, \Sigma_2)$.

To further explore the sharing opportunity, we consider the following refinement relationship among repair contexts.

Definition 7. *We say that* $rc(\mathbb{C}_k, \Sigma_2)$ refines $rc(\mathbb{C}_k, \Sigma_1)$, *denoted by* $rc(\mathbb{C}_k, \Sigma_2) \sqsubseteq rc(\mathbb{C}_k, \Sigma_1)$, *if for each* $x\overline{\phi_1 y} \in rc(\mathbb{C}_k, \Sigma_1)$, *there exists* $x\overline{\phi_2 y} \in rc(\mathbb{C}_k, \Sigma_2)$ *s.t.* $\overline{\phi_1} \in Imp(\overline{\phi_2})$.

That is, the repair contexts in $rc(\mathbb{C}_k, \Sigma_2)$ are more strict (refined). For instance, rc_2 (with $t_8.\mathsf{Tax} > t_4.\mathsf{Tax}$) in Figure 4(b) refines rc_1 (with $t_8.\mathsf{Tax} \geq t_4.\mathsf{Tax}$) in Figure 4(a).

Proposition 6. *For an optimal solution* $I'(\mathbb{C}_k)$ *of* $rc(\mathbb{C}_k, \Sigma_1)$, *if* $I'(\mathbb{C}_k)$ *also satisfies* $rc(\mathbb{C}_k, \Sigma_2)$ *and* $rc(\mathbb{C}_k, \Sigma_2) \sqsubseteq rc(\mathbb{C}_k, \Sigma_1)$, *then* $I'(\mathbb{C}_k)$ *is an optimal solution to* $rc(\mathbb{C}_k, \Sigma_2)$ *w.r.t. the problem in formula (3).*

A natural idea is to materialize the optimal solutions of the previously solved $rc(\mathbb{C}_k, \Sigma_1)$, and reuse them directly when solving $rc(\mathbb{C}_k, \Sigma_2)$. To search the materialized $rc(\mathbb{C}_k, \Sigma_1)$ for $rc(\mathbb{C}_k, \Sigma_2)$, efficient filtering can be applied to fast exclude the repair contexts on distinct $\mathbb{C}_k$.

Example 12. *Let* $rc_1 = rc(\{t_4.\mathsf{Tax}\}, \{\varphi_4'\})$ *denote all the repair contexts in Figure 4(a) in Example 10. Suppose that there is another* rc_2 *of repair contexts on the same* $\mathbb{C} = \{t_4.\mathsf{Tax}\}$ *as shown in Figure 4(b). Note that we have* $I(t_8.\mathsf{Tax}) > I'(t_4.\mathsf{Tax}) \in rc_2$, *whereas* $I(t_8.\mathsf{Tax}) \geq I'(t_4.\mathsf{Tax}) \in rc_1$. *It is similar for* $t_9.\mathsf{Tax}$ *and* $t_{10}.\mathsf{Tax}$. *Referring to* $\geq \in Imp(>)$ *in Table 1, we have* $rc_2 \sqsubseteq rc_1$. *Since the optimal solution* $I'(t_4.\mathsf{Tax}) = 0$ *for* rc_1 *also satisfies all the repair contexts in* rc_2, *according to Proposition 6, we can directly conclude that* $I'(t_4.\mathsf{Tax}) = 0$ *is an optimal solution for* rc_2 *as well.*

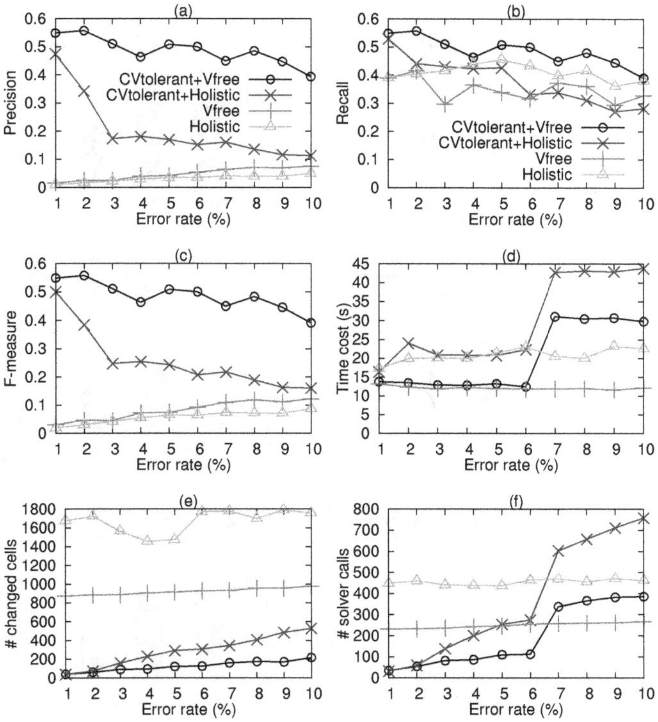

Figure 5: Vfree vs. Holistic data repairing with and without constraint variance tolerance (HOSP)

5. EXPERIMENTAL STUDY

In this section, we compared our proposed θ-tolerant repair with the state-of-the-art approaches (with/without constraint repairs). By default, we consider the unit predicate cost with $c(P) = 1$ and $\lambda = -0.5$ in formula (1). Details on experiment preparation can be found in Appendix D.1.

5.1 Evaluating Proposed Techniques

First, we compare our violation-free (Vfree) data repair algorithm, in Section 4, with the existing Holistic data repair [8]. As DC-based data repair algorithms, both Vfree and Holistic can work together with our proposed constraint-variance tolerant repair CVtolerant, in Section 3.

Figure 5 reports the performance under various error rates (with $\theta = 1$ for CVtolerant, see discussion below on choosing θ). Generally, our proposed Vfree shows higher accuracy in Figure 5(c) than Holistic, especially when working with CVtolerant. The results verify the effectiveness of considering suspects rather than only violations in the repair context.

Time cost of Vfree is significantly lower than that of Holistic, either with or without CVtolerant, as shown in Figure 5(d). The rationale is that our Vfree needs only one round violation-free repair, while Holistic may have multiple rounds for handling newly introduced violations in each round.

The CVtolerant+Vfree approach can always achieve the highest accuracy in Figures 5(a)-(c). The time costs of CVtolerant increase heavily from error rate 0.6 to 0.7. It is because the number of calling DATAREPAIR (in Line 6 of Algorithm 1) increases from 1 to 2. The corresponding number of calling solvers (in Line 9 of Algorithm 2) increases largely as well, as illustrated in Figure 5(f). Nevertheless, owing to our efficient pruning and sharing techniques, most tests can obtain the results by calling DATAREPAIR within 2 times, and the times of calling solver for CVtolerant are comparable to that of without constraint variance.

An interesting result is the slight increase of accuracy with the increase of error rate, by approaches without CVtolerant. The reason is the large number of changed cells by Vfree and Holistic, as shown in Figure 5(e), most of which are indeed not noises and negatively repaired by the inaccurate constraints. With the increase of error rate, some of them become true noises and thus the repair accuracy increases a bit. When more accurate constraints are captured via variance toleration, CVtolerant (either with Vfree or Holistic) shows accuracy decrease with the increase of error rate.

Figure 6 studies the impact of varying the constraint variance tolerance level θ (under an error rate of 7%). With the increase of θ, i.e., with higher tolerance of constraint variances, many negative repairs can be avoided, and the repairing accuracy (precision as well as f-measure) increases. However, when θ increases to 3, no data need to be changed, i.e., the constraints are over-refined and overfit the data.

Observing the number of repaired cells may help in determining θ. A large number of changed cells (under a small θ) indicate that data is overrepaired (with imprecise constraints). In contrast, an extremely small size of repaired cells (under a large θ) means that the constraints are over-refined (overfitting the data without identifying violations).

Similar results are observed over CENSUS, in Figures 7 and 8 analogous to Figures 5 and 6 over HOSP. Specifically, as shown in Figure 7(b), our CVtolerant methods show significantly higher accuracy than those without constraint-variance tolerance. Again, the time cost of Vfree is significantly lower than that of Holistic, either with or without

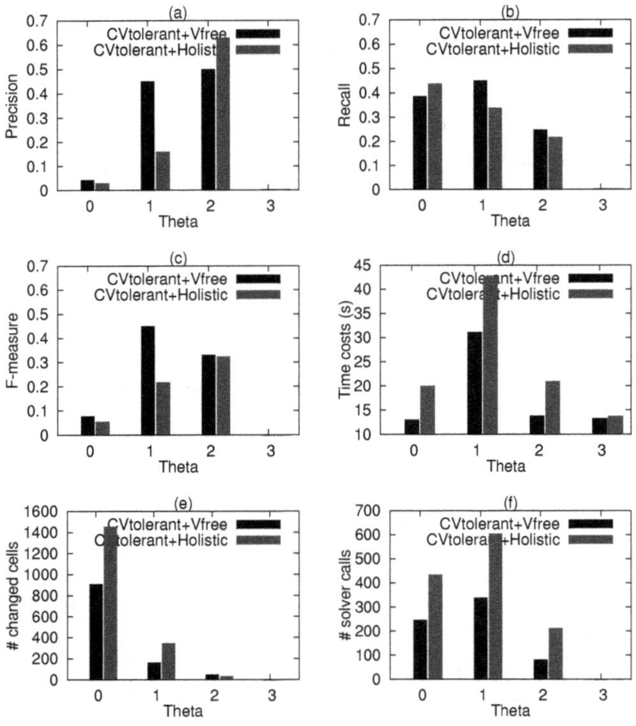

Figure 6: Varying tolerance level θ (HOSP)

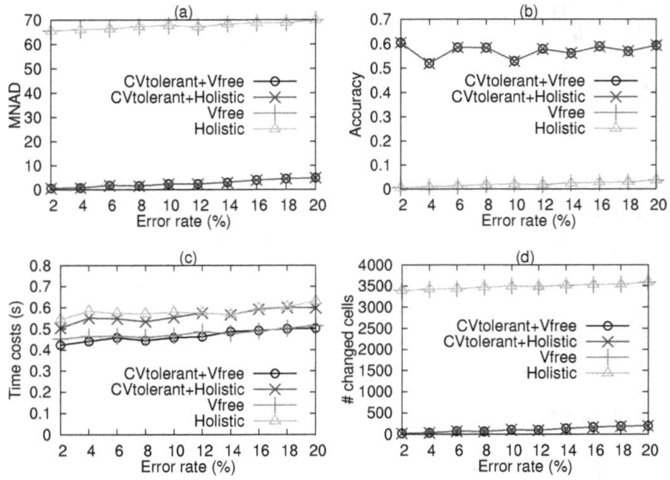

Figure 7: Comparison with and without constraint variance tolerance (CENSUS)

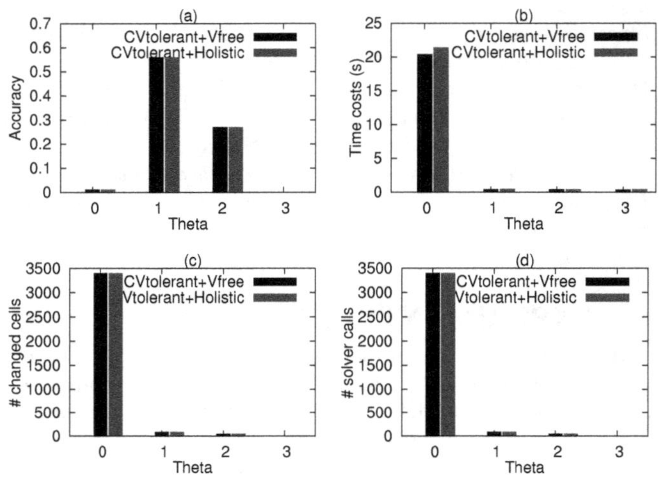

Figure 8: Varying tolerance level θ (CENSUS)

CVtolerant, as shown in Figure 7(d). The accuracy results of Vfree and Holistic are similar, because the constraints employed in this test are liner DCs where the repairing w.r.t. suspect set is similar to that on violation set. Similar to Figure 6(e) over HOSP, Figure 8(c) illustrates that the larger the constraint variance tolerance level θ is, the fewer the number of cells need to be changed. With a moderate $\theta = 1$, i.e., neither oversimplified constraints leading to many changed cells nor overrefined constraints without repairing any data, the accuracy is highest in Figure 8(a), which is also observed in Figure 6(c) over HOSP.

5.2 Comparison to FD-based Repairs

Next, we compared the state-of-the-art approaches using FDs as constraints, over the categorized data HOSP, including (1) Vrepair [14] and Holistic [8] without considering constraint variances, (2) Unified [5] with a unified cost model for both data and constraint repairs, (3) Relative [2] considering the relative trust between data and constraints via a data repair cost threshold, and (4) our proposed CVtolerant.

Figures 9 and 10 report the performance on various error rates and data sizes. In general, our CVtolerant approach shows significantly higher repair accuracy than all the other approaches. The time cost increases almost linearly in the number of tuples, in Figure 10(b). The results verify the complexity analysis (in Sections 3 and 4) of the proposed θ-tolerant repair approach.

The number of changed cells by Unified decreases sharply from 6 to 7 in Figure 11(b). It is because the cost of data repair exceeds that of constraint repair in the unified cost model. Constraint repair is performed rather than data repair, i.e., the number of changed cells drops. Its corresponding accuracy varies significantly as well, from 7 to 8, in Figure 10(a). The results verify again that constraints and data are not equally trustworthy for repairing, as indicated in [2].

The Relative method takes extremely high time costs, as shown in Figure 10(b), which is also reported in [2]. The method uses a fixed threshold τ of data repair cost to filter constraint repairs, rather than the dynamically determined minimum data repair cost bound $\delta_{\min}$ in our proposed algorithms. A large number of constraint and data repairs need to be considered by Relative with very high overhead. Owing to the extremely high time costs, we stop attempting the method with data sizes greater than 1000 in Figure 10 (given the clearly lower accuracy under various error rates, as well as on various # constraints and # attributes below).

In Figures 9(a) and 10(a), CVtolerant with weighted cost shows a bit higher accuracy than CVtolerant with unit cost, and significantly better results compared to the existing Unified and Relative methods. The results verify again that CVtolerant with either weighted or unit cost can improve the state of the art in further selecting the right attribute (predicate) for constraint variation. The improvement of weighted cost compared to unit cost in CVtolerant is not very significant. The reason is that inserting inappropriate predicates,

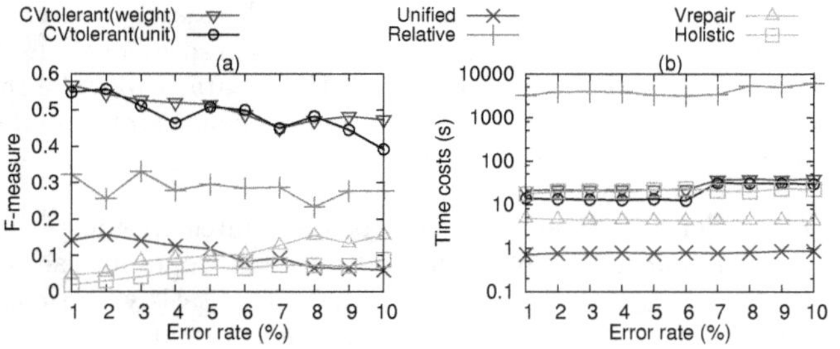

Figure 9: Comparison under FD constraints with various data error rates (HOSP)

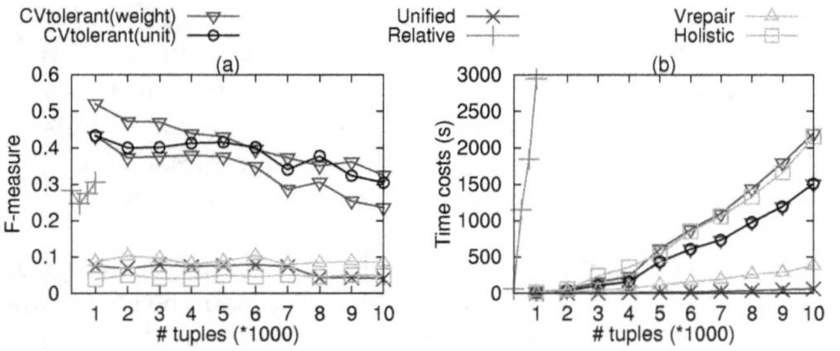

Figure 10: Scalability on number of tuples (HOSP)

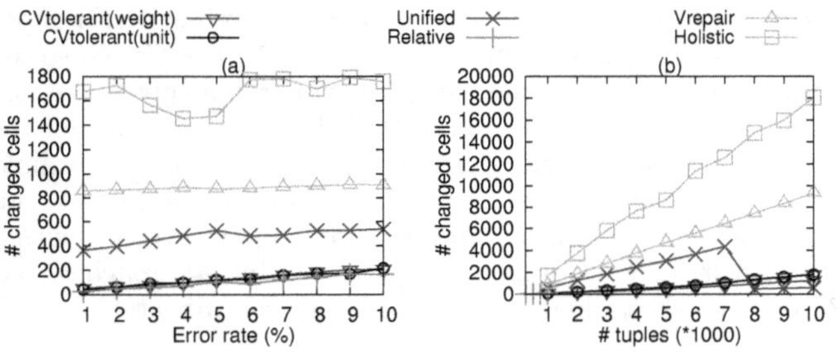

Figure 11: Changed cells (HOSP)

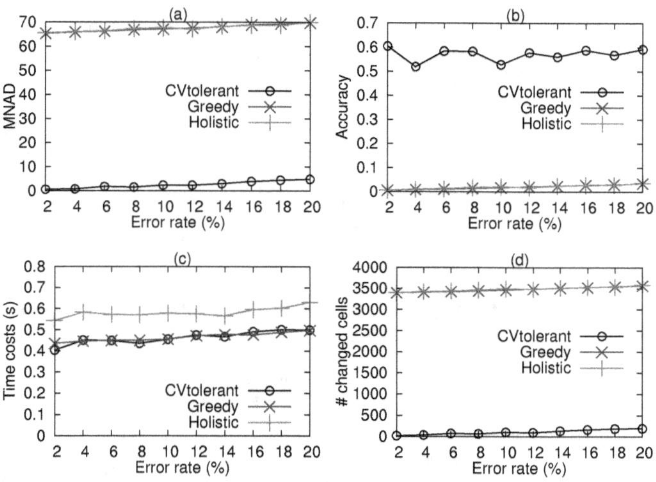

Figure 12: Comparison under DC constraints with various data error rates (CENSUS)

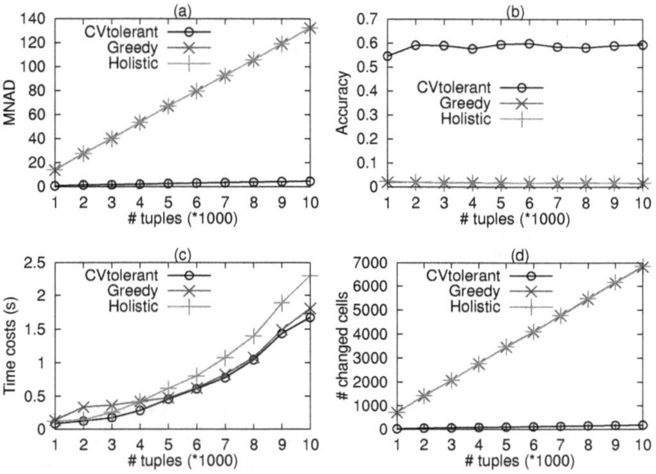

Figure 13: Scalability on num. of tuples (CENSUS)

e.g., on attribute Year with worse coincided distribution, does not help much in refining oversimplified constraints, and thus the data repair cost is high. Instead, inserting the right predicates, e.g., on attribute Birthday with better coincided distribution, does refine the oversimplified constraints, and the corresponding data repair with lower cost will be returned following the minimum change principle. That is, CVtolerant with unit cost on predicates achieves considerably good accuracy as well. Nevertheless, by introducing fine-grain cost of predicates, the right attributes and predicates can be more precisely selected and the repair accuracy improves as reported in Figures 9 and 10.

5.3 Comparison to DC-based Repairs

This experiment over CENSUS considers numerical data repairing by DC-based approaches: (1) Greedy [16] using a modified greedy strategy, (2) Holistic [8] putting violations into repair context, and (3) our proposed CVtolerant.

As shown in Figures 12(a) and 13(a), the MNAD distance (between truth and repair) of our CVtolerant is significantly lower than those of Greedy and Holistic, i.e., more close to the ground truth. Similarly, for the accuracy relative to the introduced noises, in Figures 12(b) and 13(b), CVtolerant shows clear improvement as well. Again, the rationale is that without repairing inaccurate constraints, existing approaches change a large number of cells (that are indeed correct) as illustrated in Figure 13(d). Time costs of CVtolerant are only a slightly higher than existing methods. Indeed, as illustrated in Figure 13(c), all the approaches scale well.

5.4 Evaluation over Various Errors

Real errors could be correlated, that is, errors often appear together in the same tuples on a certain set of attributes, rather than independently appear in random tuple-attribute cells. Such error patterns could be prevalent in real-world. For instance, tuples collected from unreliable sources could involve multiple errors, e.g., not only the Name value contains error but also Birthday.

Figure 14 presents an experiment on various correlation levels of errors, by observing different numbers of errors that appear together in the same tuples with correlations. As shown in Figure 14(a), the accuracy drops a bit with the increase of errors in a tuple (higher error appearance correlation). Nevertheless, the proposed method CVtolerant still clearly outperforms other methods, which is similar to the previous results in Figure 9(a).

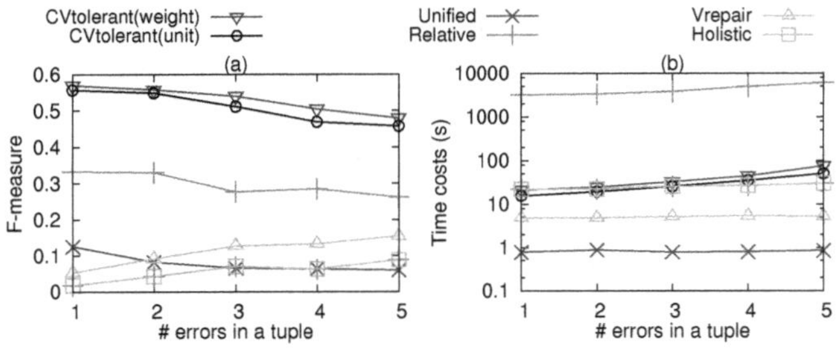

Figure 14: Comparison over correlated errors appearing together (HOSP)

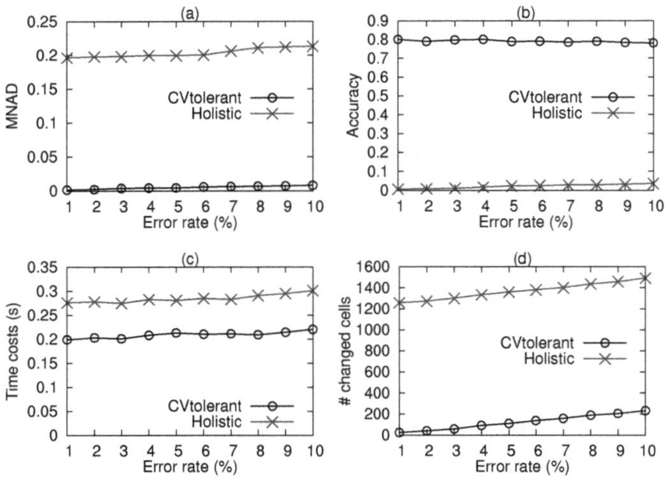

Figure 15: Comparison over real GPS data with errors naturally embedded

The GPS dataset has real errors naturally embedded and the ground truth values (locations) of errors manually labelled. Specifically, we collect GPS readings carrying a smartphone and walking along main roads at campus. The GPS readings are not accurate and may occasionally "jump" away from the trajectory. Since we know exactly the path of walking, a number of 243 dirty points are manually identified (among total 2409 points in the trajectory). The true locations of these dirty points are also manually labeled, as the ground truth. Figure 15 reports the results over the GPS data. As shown, e.g., in Figure 15(b), our proposed method CVtolerant achieves significantly higher accuracy than that of Holistic, which is similar to Figure 12 over CENSUS.

6. RELATED WORK

Integrity Constraints. In this paper, we use a general notation of integrity constraints, denial constraints (DCs) [7]. The reason is that DCs are able to express the semantics of several classes of integrity constraints, e.g., traditional key constraints and functional dependencies (FDs). Since constants can be declared in DCs, the conditional functional dependencies (CFDs) [3] can also be expressed with constants as conditions. The advantage is obvious to employ multiple classes of constraints, which can identify more violations.

Besides manual specification, DCs are often discovered from data [7]. The discovery focuses on finding a minimal cover of DCs that hold in the given training data. Instead, our constraint variance considers a set of maximal DCs with variation to the given DCs bounded by θ. The major difference is that the discovery concerns a concise representation of precise constraints from (usually clean) data, while the repair explores the variants of inaccurate constraints for the minimum repair of dirty data.

Data Repair. To eliminate violations to integrity constraints, the deletion model [6] manages to delete a minimum set of tuples such that the remaining data can satisfy the constraints. Information loss occurs in such deletion.

Rather than deletion, the data modification repair model [21] proposes to modify data values. Most cleaning techniques adopt this modification model, such as Vrepair [14] considering FDs as constraints, Greedy repair [16] under linear DCs, and Holistic repair [8] with general DCs. All these approaches assume that the constraints are accurate, while our study considers the inaccuracies of both constraints and data. We experimentally compare these approaches in Section 5 to demonstrate the superiority of our proposal.

Constraint Repair. When both constraints and data are dirty, existing methods simultaneously repair the constraints and data. Chiang and Miller [5] propose a unified cost model for both data and constraint repairs. With a model of tuple patterns, the description length based cost is the number of tuples not represented by the model (as well as the number of patterns) times the size of FD. A repair of FD increases its size but may reduce the number of tuples not represented by the model (violations to FD). Beskales et al. [2] consider the relative trust between data and constraints via a threshold of data repair cost. The idea is to consider potential constraint repairs whose bounds of data repair cost are within a threshold τ. Compared to the existing approaches, our proposal shows higher repairing accuracy in Section 5.

7. CONCLUSIONS

In this paper, we study the problem of repairing data under imprecise constraints. Besides inserting predicates for oversimplified constraints (as in existing approaches), we argue that the constraints could be overrefined as well, and need predicate deletion. To be tolerant of constraint variances (with both predicate insertion and deletion), a novel θ-tolerant repair model is introduced, which finds a minimum data repair by allowing a small variation on the constraints (with variation no greater than θ). In particular, our method addresses repairing over numerical attributes which are not supported by existing approaches [5, 2].

We devise efficient pruning among different constraint variations. The one-round, violation-free, repair-cost-bounded data repair algorithm further enables sharing the repair computation. Experiments on real datasets demonstrate that our proposal has significantly higher repair accuracy than the state-of-the-art Unified [5] and Relative [2] approaches (with consideration of constraint repair), while the corresponding time cost is comparable to the pure Holistic data repair [8] (which does not consider constraint variant).

Acknowledgement

This work is supported in part by the Tsinghua University Initiative Scientific Research Program; Tsinghua National Laboratory Special Fund for Big Data Science and Technology; China NSFC under Grants 61572272, 61325008, 61370055 and 61202008.

8. REFERENCES

[1] L. E. Bertossi, L. Bravo, E. Franconi, and A. Lopatenko. The complexity and approximation of fixing numerical attributes in databases under integrity constraints. *Inf. Syst.*, 33(4-5):407–434, 2008.

[2] G. Beskales, I. F. Ilyas, L. Golab, and A. Galiullin. On the relative trust between inconsistent data and inaccurate constraints. In *ICDE*, pages 541–552, 2013.

[3] P. Bohannon, W. Fan, F. Geerts, X. Jia, and A. Kementsietsidis. Conditional functional dependencies for data cleaning. In *ICDE*, pages 746–755, 2007.

[4] P. Bohannon, M. Flaster, W. Fan, and R. Rastogi. A cost-based model and effective heuristic for repairing constraints by value modification. In *SIGMOD Conference*, pages 143–154, 2005.

[5] F. Chiang and R. J. Miller. A unified model for data and constraint repair. In *ICDE*, pages 446–457, 2011.

[6] J. Chomicki and J. Marcinkowski. Minimal-change integrity maintenance using tuple deletions. *Inf. Comput.*, 197(1-2):90–121, 2005.

[7] X. Chu, I. F. Ilyas, and P. Papotti. Discovering denial constraints. *PVLDB*, 6(13):1498–1509, 2013.

[8] X. Chu, I. F. Ilyas, and P. Papotti. Holistic data cleaning: Putting violations into context. In *ICDE*, pages 458–469, 2013.

[9] W. Fan. Dependencies revisited for improving data quality. In *PODS*, pages 159–170, 2008.

[10] L. Golab, H. J. Karloff, F. Korn, A. Saha, and D. Srivastava. Sequential dependencies. *PVLDB*, 2(1):574–585, 2009.

[11] L. Golab, H. J. Karloff, F. Korn, D. Srivastava, and B. Yu. On generating near-optimal tableaux for conditional functional dependencies. *PVLDB*, 1(1):376–390, 2008.

[12] N. Karmarkar. A new polynomial-time algorithm for linear programming. In *STOC*, pages 302–311, 1984.

[13] J. Kivinen and H. Mannila. Approximate inference of functional dependencies from relations. *Theor. Comput. Sci.*, 149(1):129–149, 1995.

[14] S. Kolahi and L. V. S. Lakshmanan. On approximating optimum repairs for functional dependency violations. In *ICDT*, pages 53–62, 2009.

[15] Q. Li, Y. Li, J. Gao, B. Zhao, W. Fan, and J. Han. Resolving conflicts in heterogeneous data by truth discovery and source reliability estimation. In *SIGMOD Conference*, pages 1187–1198, 2014.

[16] A. Lopatenko and L. Bravo. Efficient approximation algorithms for repairing inconsistent databases. In *ICDE*, pages 216–225, 2007.

[17] G. Navarro. A guided tour to approximate string matching. *ACM Comput. Surv.*, 33(1):31–88, 2001.

[18] J. E. Olson. *Data Quality: The Accuracy Dimension.* Morgan Kaufmann, 2003.

[19] S. Song, A. Zhang, J. Wang, and P. S. Yu. SCREEN: stream data cleaning under speed constraints. In *SIGMOD*, pages 827–841, 2015.

[20] V. V. Vazirani. *Approximation algorithms.* Springer, 2001.

[21] J. Wijsen. Database repairing using updates. *ACM Trans. Database Syst.*, 30(3):722–768, 2005.

APPENDIX

A. PROOFS

Proof of Lemma 1

Proof. Consider the minimum data repair I_1 w.r.t Σ_1. Given I_2 as the minimum data repair w.r.t Σ_2, the conclusion $\Delta(I, I_1) \geq \Delta(I, I_2)$ is naturally proved by showing that I_1 is also a valid data repair w.r.t Σ_2, i.e., to show $I_1 \models \Sigma_2$.

First, according to the definition of inverse and implication in Table 1, for any $\phi_1 \in \mathit{Imp}(\phi_2)$, it always has $\overline{\phi_2} \in \mathit{Imp}(\overline{\phi_1})$. For instance, $\leq \in \mathit{Imp}(<)$ implies $\geq \in \mathit{Imp}(>)$.

According to Definition 4 of refinement $\Sigma_1 \preceq \Sigma_2$, for each $\varphi_2 \in \Sigma_2$, there exists a $\varphi_1 \in \Sigma_1$ such that $\varphi_1 \preceq \varphi_2$.

Since $I_1 \models \Sigma_1$ (i.e., $I_1 \models \varphi_1$), for any $\langle t_i, t_j \rangle \in I_1$, there must exist some $P : x\phi_1 y \in \mathit{pred}(\varphi_1)$ such that $\langle t_i, t_j \rangle \not\models P : x\phi_1 y$, which can also be written as $\langle t_i, t_j \rangle \models x\overline{\phi_1}y$.

Referring to Definition 3 of refinement $\varphi_1 \preceq \varphi_2$, for each $P : x\phi_1 y \in \mathit{pred}(\varphi_1)$, there exists a $Q : x\phi_2 y \in \mathit{pred}(\varphi_2)$ such that $\phi_1 \in \mathit{Imp}(\phi_2)$. It follows $\overline{\phi_2} \in \mathit{Imp}(\overline{\phi_1})$. In other words, $\langle t_i, t_j \rangle \models x\overline{\phi_1}y$ implies $\langle t_i, t_j \rangle \models x\overline{\phi_2}y$. We have $\langle t_i, t_j \rangle \not\models Q : x\phi_2 y \in \mathit{pred}(\varphi_2)$ as well, i.e., $\langle t_i, t_j \rangle \models \varphi_2$.

To sum up, for each $\varphi_2 \in \Sigma_2$ and $\langle t_i, t_j \rangle \in I_1$, we have $\langle t_i, t_j \rangle \models \varphi_2$, i.e., $I_1 \models \Sigma_2$. As aforesaid, the conclusion $\Delta(I, I_1) \geq \Delta(I, I_2)$ is proved. □

Proof of Proposition 2

Proof. According to the definition of implication in Table 1, for any $\phi \in \{\leq, \geq, \neq\}$, we can always find a ϕ_1 such that $\phi \in \mathit{Imp}(\phi_1), \phi \neq \phi_1$. For instance, for the operator $\geq$, it always has $\geq \in \mathit{Imp}(>)$, and similarly $\leq \in \mathit{Imp}(<), \neq \in \mathit{Imp}(<)$.

For a $P : x\phi y \in \mathit{pred}(\varphi') \setminus \mathit{pred}(\varphi)$, we can always obtain another φ'' via replacing P of φ' by $Q : x\phi_1 y$, such that $\varphi' \preceq \varphi''$ according to Definition 3 of refinement. Their costs are the same $\mathit{inst}(\varphi, \varphi'') = \mathit{inst}(\varphi, \varphi')$. It concludes that φ' is not maximal. □

Proof of Lemma 3

Proof. To eliminate the violation of a tuple list $\langle t_i, t_j, \dots \rangle \not\models \varphi$, at least one cell in $\mathit{cell}(t_i, t_j, \dots; \varphi)$ should be modified. It corresponds to at least one vertex in the hyperedge of $\mathit{cell}(t_i, t_j; \varphi)$.

Considering all the violation tuple lists, any valid data repair should at least modify one vertex for each hyperedge, i.e., a vertex cover of the hypergraph.

The minimum cost of modifying a cell is

$$\min_{a \in dom(A)} \mathit{dist}(I(t.A), a),$$

which is exactly the weight of a vertex. In other words, any valid data repair should have repair cost no less than the weight of the corresponding vertex cover.

Therefore, the weight of the minimum weighted vertex cover $\|\mathbb{V}^*(\mathcal{G})\|$ gives a lower bound of any valid data repair. □

Proof of Lemma 4

Proof. For each $\langle t_i, t_j, \dots \rangle$ in the violation set of φ, we have $\langle t_i, t_j, \dots \rangle$ satisfying all the predicates in φ. Referring to the suspect condition $sc(t_\alpha, t_\beta, \dots; \varphi)$, $\langle t_i, t_j, \dots \rangle$ belongs to suspect set as well. □

Proof of Proposition 5

Proof. The correctness of results $I' \models \Sigma$ includes two aspects.

First, we show that I' eliminates all the violations existing in I. For any $\langle t_i, t_j, \dots \rangle \in I$ that satisfies all the predicates of a $\varphi \in \Sigma$, i.e., a violation, there must have a cell in $cell(t_i, t_j, \dots; \varphi)$ that is selected to $\mathbb{C}$ (a vertex cover). That is, there must have a circle (belonging to $\mathbb{C}$) as illustrated in Figure 3(a).

The repair context $rc(t_i, t_j, \dots; \varphi)$ ensures that all the predicates involving cells from $\mathbb{C}$ (red arrows in Figure 3(a)) are not satisfied. In other words, no violation remains in $\langle t_i, t_j, \dots \rangle$ in the repaired I'.

Next, for the other tuple lists in the suspect sets, which satisfy all the predicates that do not contain cells from $\mathbb{C}$ (blue arrows in Figure 3(a)), the aforesaid assignment of cells in $\mathbb{C}$ (circles) guarantees violation-free for each suspect tuple list as well. □

B. DATA REPAIR ALGORITHM

Algorithm 2 presents the violation-free data repair with the aforesaid sharing enabled. As discussed in Section 4.1.3, by gradually assigning cells to *fv* (in Line 16), the algorithm guarantees to return a solution for each component $\mathbb{C}_k$. Before calling an existing solver (in Line 9), the program first searches the materialized subproblems and solutions. If the conditions in Proposition 6 are satisfied, the materialized solution can be directly reused (Lines 5-7).

Algorithm 2 DATAREPAIR($\Sigma, I, \mathbb{C}, \delta_{\min}$)

Input: An instance I, a constraint set Σ, a set $\mathbb{C}$ of changing cells and a bound of data repair cost $\delta_{\min}$
Output: An assignment of cells in $\mathbb{C}$ for the repair I'

```
1: initialize rc(C, Σ) and project into components
2: for each component C_k of C do
3:   while C_k ≠ ∅ do
4:     search materialized subproblems
5:     if exists some rc(C_k, Σ') whose solution satisfies
         rc(C_k, Σ) and rc(C_k, Σ) ⊑ rc(C_k, Σ') then
6:       I'(C_k) := the solution of rc(C_k, Σ')
7:       C_k := ∅
8:     else
9:       solve rc(C_k, Σ) by existing solver
10:      if rc(C_k, Σ) is solved then
11:        I'(C_k) := the solution returned by the solver
12:        materialize rc(C_k, Σ) with I'(C_k) for reuse
13:        C_k := ∅
14:      else
15:        t.A := the cell with the largest number of appear-
             ance in rc(C_k, Σ)
16:        I'(t.A) := fv
17:        C_k := C_k \ {t.A}
18:   if Δ(I, I') ≥ δ_min then
19:     return null
20: return I'
```

Example 13. *Suppose that we are given a set of (repaired) constraints $\Sigma = \{\varphi_3, \varphi'_4\}$ from Examples 1 and 4, and $\mathbb{C} = \{t_2.\mathsf{CP}, t_5.\mathsf{CP}, t_8.\mathsf{CP}, t_4.\mathsf{Tax}\}$ in Figure 1(a). The repair contexts are $rc(\mathbb{C}, \Sigma) = \{I'(t_2.\mathsf{CP}) = I(t_3.\mathsf{CP}), I'(t_5.\mathsf{CP}) = I(t_6.\mathsf{CP}), I'(t_8.\mathsf{CP}) = I(t_9.\mathsf{CP})\} \cup rc_1$, where rc_1 is the repair contexts in Figure 4(a) computed in Example 10. $\mathbb{C}$ is decomposed into four components $\mathbb{C}_1 = \{t_2.\mathsf{CP}\}, \mathbb{C}_2 = \{t_5.\mathsf{CP}\}, \mathbb{C}_3 = \{t_8.\mathsf{CP}\}, \mathbb{C}_4 = \{t_4.\mathsf{Tax}\}$ w.r.t. the repair context independence. By separately solving $rc(\mathbb{C}_k, \Sigma)$ for each component $\mathbb{C}_k$, the repair results are $I'(t_2.\mathsf{CP}) =$ 564-389, $I'(t_5.\mathsf{CP}) =$ 930-198, $I'(t_8.\mathsf{CP}) =$ 824-870, $I'(t_4.\mathsf{Tax}) = 0$.*

Table 2: Approximation performance

Constraints	Approximation factor
linear DC/constant CFD	$d\|R\|$
binary DC/variable CFD/FD	$2d\|R\|$

To initialize $rc(\mathbb{C}, \Sigma)$, we need to search suspects in I for each tuple with cells from $\mathbb{C}$. The cost is $O(|I|^{\ell})$, where ℓ is the maximum number of tuples $|\{t_\alpha, t_\beta, \dots\}|$ involved in a φ of Σ, as discussed at the end of Section 3. To solve the problem in formula (3), existing LP solvers are employed, e.g., [12] with cost $O(n^{3.5}L)$, where n is the number of variables, i.e., $|\mathbb{C}|$, and L is the number of bits of input. Therefore, for a fixed $\mathbb{C}$, the DATAREPAIR algorithm takes $O(|I|^{\ell})$ time.

Constant Factor Approximation

Theorem 7. *Algorithms 1 and 2 output a repair I' having $\frac{\Delta(I,I')}{\Delta(I,I^*)} \leq d \cdot Deg(\Sigma)$, where $d = \frac{\max_{a \in dom(A), A \in attr(R)} dist(a, fv)}{\min_{a,b \in dom(A), A \in attr(R)} dist(a,b)}$ and I^* is the optimal θ-tolerant repair with the minimum data repair cost.*

Table 2 reports the performance of our approach under several typical integrity constraints. For a set Σ of linear DCs [16, 1], i.e., with all the predicates in the form of $v\theta c$, we have $Deg(\Sigma) \leq |R|$. The approximation bound becomes $d|R|$. Similar situation occurs in constant CFD [3], which also specifies constraints on single tuples. Binary DCs contain only predicates declared on the same attributes of two tuples, in the form of $t_\alpha.A\theta t_\beta.A$. As special cases of binary DCs, the constraints, including FDs and variable CFDs, share the same bounds $2d|R|$. Since all these types of constraints are declared on tuple pairs, the number of involved cells is at most two times the number of attributes, i.e., $Deg(\Sigma) \leq 2|R|$. (See Section 6 for a more detailed introduction of the aforesaid integrity constraint notations.)

In short, for a R with fixed domain, our proposed approach is a constant factor approximation.

C. DISCUSSION ON USAGE

C.1 Relevance to Real World Usage

In practice, it is already difficult for data curators to understand and accept data repairs, which are suggested by tools following the minimum change property. Automatic repairing techniques (towards constraint satisfaction) play largely a role of suggesting repairs rather than determining repairs. In this sense, suggesting multiple possible repairs, instead of only one repair following the minimum change property and constraint satisfaction, could be helpful to data curators in repair selection. Therefore, in order to enhance the real-world usage, our approach (1) obtains multiple repair results w.r.t. various constraint variants (instead of one single minimum repair satisfying one fixed set of constraints), and (2) provides guidelines on evaluating and selecting the returned multiple repair results. The rationale is explained as follows.

(1) To reduce the complexity of considering both data repairs and constraint repairs at the same time, existing studies [5] employ an unified cost function on both data and

constraint repairs, and the repairing still follows the (unified) cost minimality. As also observed in our experimental evaluation, e.g., in Figure 10, the repair result suggested by unified cost minimality could be doubtful and thus with lower repair accuracy. In order to overcome the problem of returning only one minimum repair result, our proposal considers multiple minimum repair results, suggested by various constraint variants (constraint repairs) w.r.t. different constraint variation levels θ.

(2) To practically understand and select data repairs from the multiple results, one may observe the number of repaired cells in a data repair result. A large number of changed cells (under a small θ) indicate that data is over-repaired (with oversimplified constraints). In contrast, an extremely small size of repaired cells (under a large θ) means that the constraints are overrefined (overfitting the data without identifying violations).

C.2 Prevalence of Imprecise Constraints

The book [18] gives an explanation, together with some examples, of why both the data and the metadata (such as integrity constraints) could be inaccurate at the same time. In particular, the metadata, e.g., constraint on $\mathsf{Age} \geq 18$, are often collected from various internal/external sources, and thus could be inaccurate and incomplete. For instance, "the metadata (constraints) could be extracted from the relational database directory or catalog in a relational system, or a COBOL copybook or a PL/1 INCLUDE file that lays out the data in an IMS or VSAM data source". Moreover, "primary key, foreign key, and other referential constraint information, TRIGGER or STORED PROCEDURE logic embedded within the relational system, application source code for programs that insert, delete, and update information in the database" are also sources of metadata collection. Therefore, it is necessary "to verify some of the information to determine the completeness of (meta)data-gathering and to identify areas where one may suspect wrong or missing information".

C.3 Prevalence of Overrefined Constraints

Overrefined constraints could appear in both manually specified constraints and automatically discovered constraints, two common ways of obtaining integrity constraints. (1) For manually specified constraints, for example, a non-minimal super key {Name, Department, Birthday} could be declared, which includes unnecessary attributes to uniquely identify a tuple. This super key is overrefined, given that a candidate key {Name, Department} is sufficient to uniquely identify a tuple. (2) When discovering constraints from data with noises, it is very like that the discovered constraints may overfit the data. For instance, an overrefined constraint φ_3, i.e., Name,Year,Birthday→CP, could be discovered (with high confidence) from the given data set in Figure 1(a). Such discovery of constraints from data with noises, together with some confidence guarantees, is prevalent when there is no clean data available for discovery [13]. Similar scenarios of overrefined constraints that overfit the data occur in sequential dependency discovery [10] and conditional functional dependency discovery [11].

Without addressing these overrefined constraints, as illustrated in Example 1, dirty data might not be identified and repaired. Therefore, special attention on such overrefined constraints is needed.

C.4 When Errors Fit the Constraints

Real-world errors may fall in the specified constraints, that is, tuples with errors indeed satisfy the specified constraints. There are two cases to take care of: (1) For the case of overrefined constraints, which fail to identify the errors, as φ_3 shown in Example 1, our proposed methods can handle this case by removing excessive predicates; (2) For the case of constraints that are indeed accurate, the proposed method of predicate removing or inserting does not help. Indeed, without further knowledge, all the constraint-based repairing methods fail to identify and repair such errors, which satisfy all the (accurate) constraints.

D. ADDITIONAL EXPERIMENTS

D.1 Experiment Preparation

Count cost is employed in evaluating data repair cost, and an equal weight is associated to each cell (in Definition 1). All the experiments are performed on a machine with 2.5GHz CPU and 8GB RAM.

Datasets. The comparison mainly performs over two real datasets, HOSP and CENSUS. The HOSP dataset includes 14 attributes and 20,442 tuples. The CENSUS dataset is with 40 attributes and 299,285 tuples. The HOSP dataset, from US Department of Health & Human Services, mainly contains categorized data, where up to 6 FDs are specified. The CENSUS dataset, part of the UC Irvine Machine Learning Repository, comes up with 3 DCs over numerical values such as Income.

Following the same line of evaluating data repairing [8], errors are introduced in the datasets by producing noises with a certain error rate. An error rate e denotes that $e\%$ of cells in the data are changed.

Criteria. For categorized data, we use *f-measure* to evaluate the accuracy of repairs. Let truth be the set of original cell values that are changed when introducing noises, and repair be the set of repair results. The repair accuracy is given by *f-measure*$= 2 \cdot \frac{precision \cdot recall}{precision + recall}$, where $precision = \frac{|\mathsf{truth} \cap \mathsf{repair}|}{|\mathsf{repair}|}$ and $recall = \frac{|\mathsf{truth} \cap \mathsf{repair}|}{|\mathsf{truth}|}$. Following the same criteria in [8], for the cells repaired by fv, it is counted as a partial 0.5 rather than 1, in $|\mathsf{truth} \cap \mathsf{repair}|$.

For numerical values, we observe mean normalized absolute distance (MNAD) [15], i.e., the distance between I_{truth} (before introducing noises) and I_{repair} (results after repairing). Since the absolute distance measures do not consider the variance of introduced noises I_{noise}, we study the relative accuracy [19] of repairing, $1 - \frac{\Delta(I_{repair}, I_{truth})}{\Delta(I_{repair}, I_{noise}) + \Delta(I_{truth}, I_{noise})}$. According to triangle inequality on distances, in the worst case, $\Delta(I_{repair}, I_{truth}) = \Delta(I_{repair}, I_{noise}) + \Delta(I_{truth}, I_{noise})$, we have the lowest accuracy=0. For the best repair results, $\Delta(I_{repair}, I_{truth}) = 0$, we have accuracy=1.

D.2 Experiments on Predicate Deletion

This experiment evaluates the accuracy and effectiveness of predicate removal. The input constraints are overrefined with excessive predicates and need removal, denoting by negative θ of constraint variance tolerance levels.

First, as illustrated in Figure 16(b), without constraint variance, $\theta = 0$, few data can be correctly repaired (low re-

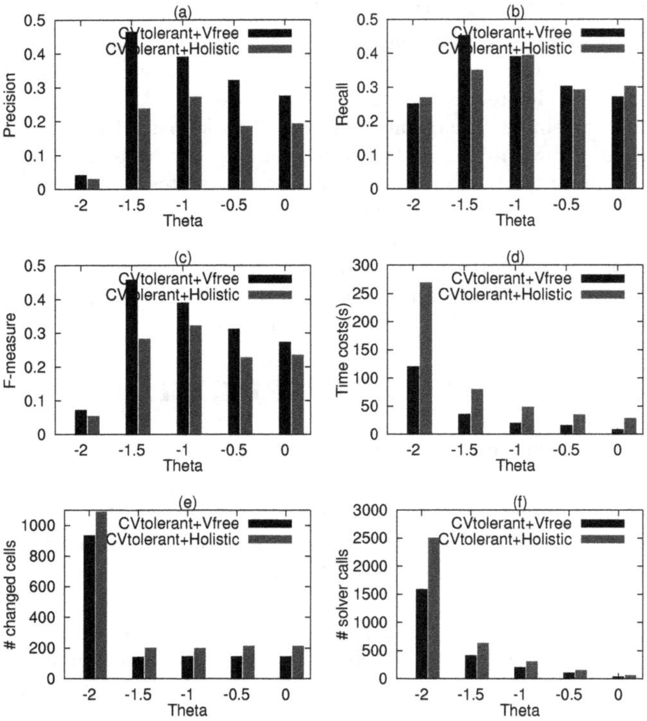

Figure 16: Varying tolerance level θ with predicate removal (HOSP)

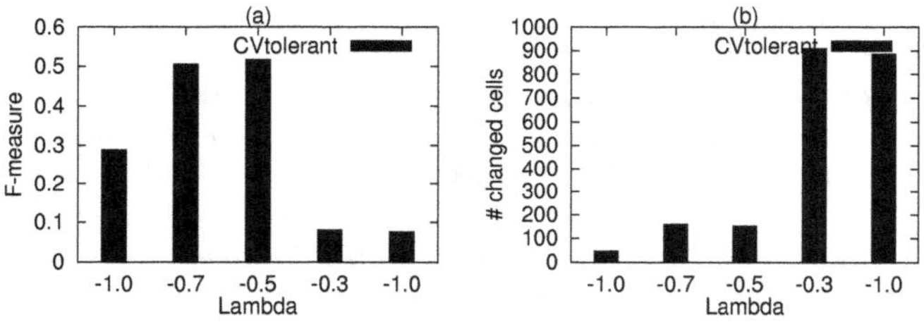

Figure 17: Varying weight λ of predicate deletion (HOSP)

call) under the input overrefined constraints. On the other hand, if too many predicates are removed, e.g., $\theta = -2$, the constraints become oversimplified and a large number of cells will be unnecessarily changed as show in Figure 16(e). Consequently, with a moderate $\theta = -1.5$, i.e., neither oversimplified constraints leading to many changed cells nor overrefined constraints without repairing much data, the accuracy is highest in Figure 16(c). Such phenomenon is also observed in Figure 6(c) of predicate insertion.

D.3 Evaluating the Predicate Deletion Weight

To further distinguish the contributions of predicate insertion and deletion, we conduct another experiment in Figure 17. Instead of a fixed -0.5, we vary the weight λ of predicate deletion, from 0 to -1, relative to predicate insertion. Generally, a smaller λ (closer to -1.0) denotes that more predicate insertions could be afforded, given the same predicate deletion and cost threshold θ. Oversimplified constraints are more likely to be refined and thus fewer cells will be changed in repairing, e.g., weight $\lambda = -0.7$ as shown in Figure 17(b).

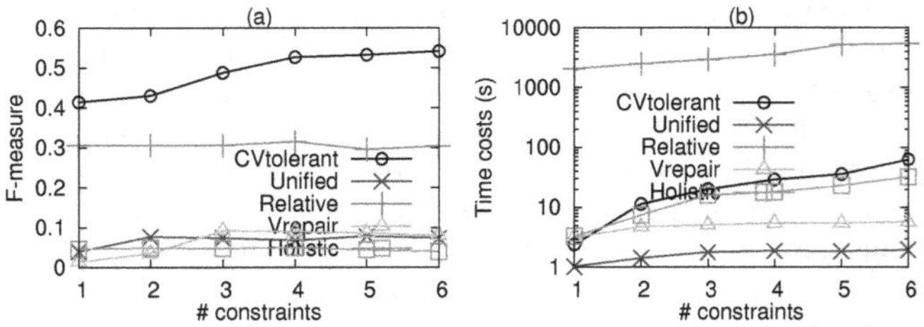

Figure 18: Varying number of FDs (HOSP)

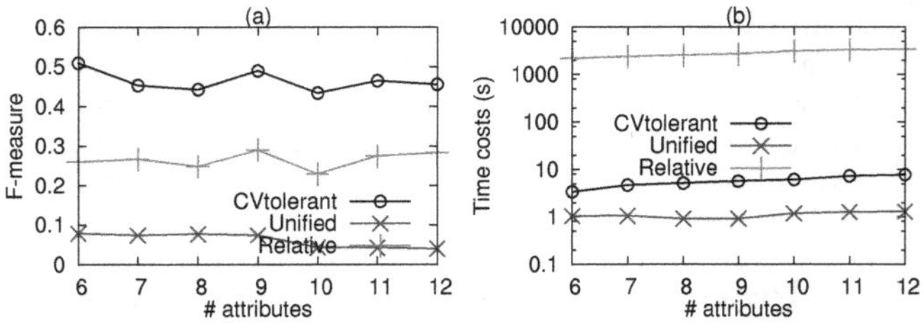

Figure 19: Varying number of attributes (HOSP)

However, for an extremely small $\lambda = -1.0$, the constraints become overrefined and few cells will be repaired. The corresponding accuracy is low as illustrated in Figure 17(a). The results verify our suggestion of avoid setting $\lambda = -1.0$. As shown, a weight $\lambda = -0.5$ (or -0.7), leading to neither oversimplified constraints with many changed cells nor overrefined constraints without repairing much data, achieves the highest repair accuracy.

D.4 Experiments on Various FDs

Figures 18 and 19 report the performance on various numbers of FDs and numbers of attributes. Relative method always tries to repair the data as many as possible (towards the maximum limit τ) in order to minimizing the constraint changes. In this sense, increasing the number of FDs does not help much in reducing unnecessary data repairs and thus has no significant improvement on the repairing accuracy, as shown in Figure 18(a). In contrast, our proposed CVtolerant approach benefits when more constraints are provided.

Figure 19(a) illustrates that with more attributes in a relation, the repairing accuracy is not affected largely. The rationale is that all the constraint repair approaches have mechanism on avoiding inserting many irrelevant predicates into the constraints.

Another interesting result is the slow increase of Relative's time cost (on # constraints and # attributes) in Figures 18(b) and 19(b), in contrast to the result (on # tuples) in Figure 10(b). The reason is that the given constraints are both oversimplified and overrefined, e.g., an FD(State→City) that needs an insertion of Zipcode and a deletion of State. Simply considering more attributes (more FDs) does not help much in reducing the violations to this imprecise FD, and such high (data-repair) cost constraint variants can be efficiently pruned without introducing significantly higher time costs in Figures 18(b) and 19(b). On the other hand, since the high cost data repair is inevitable, the time cost of Relative increases heavily w.r.t. # tuples in Figure 10(b). Nevertheless, our proposed CVtolerant can successfully handle the aforesaid case, with significantly lower time costs in various number of tuples, constraints and attributes.

Interactive and Deterministic Data Cleaning

A Tossed Stone Raises a Thousand Ripples

Jian He[1]* Enzo Veltri[2] Donatello Santoro[2] Guoliang Li[1]
Giansalvatore Mecca[2] Paolo Papotti[3]* Nan Tang[4]

[1]Tsinghua University, China [2]Università della Basilicata, Potenza, Italy [3]Arizona State University, USA
[4]Qatar Computing Research Institute, HBKU, Qatar

{hej13, liguoliang}@tsinghua.edu.cn, ppapotti@asu.edu, ntang@qf.org.qa
{enzo.veltri, donatello.santoro, giansalvatore.mecca}@gmail.com

ABSTRACT

We present FALCON, an *interactive, deterministic, and declarative* data cleaning system, which uses SQL update queries as the language to repair data. FALCON does not rely on the existence of a set of pre-defined data quality rules. On the contrary, it encourages users to explore the data, identify possible problems, and make updates to fix them. Bootstrapped by one user update, FALCON guesses a set of possible SQL update queries that can be used to repair the data. The main technical challenge addressed in this paper consists in finding a set of SQL update queries that is minimal in size and at the same time fixes the largest number of errors in the data. We formalize this problem as a search in a lattice-shaped space. To guarantee that the chosen updates are semantically correct, FALCON navigates the lattice by interacting with users to gradually validate the set of SQL update queries. Besides using traditional one-hop based traverse algorithms (*e.g.*, BFS or DFS), we describe novel multi-hop search algorithms such that FALCON can dive over the lattice and conduct the search efficiently. Our novel search strategy is coupled with a number of optimization techniques to further prune the search space and efficiently maintain the lattice. We have conducted extensive experiments using both real-world and synthetic datasets to show that FALCON can effectively communicate with users in data repairing.

CCS Concepts

•Information systems → Extraction, transformation and loading; Data cleaning;

Keywords

Data Cleaning; Interactive; Deterministic; Declarative

*Work partially done while interning/working at QCRI.

SIGMOD '16, June 26–July 1, 2016, San Francisco, CA, USA.
© 2016 ACM. ISBN 978-1-4503-3531-7/16/06... $15.00
DOI: http://dx.doi.org/10.1145/2882903.2915242

	Date	Molecule	Laboratory	Quantity
t_1	11 Nov	$C_{16}H_{16}Cl$	Austin	200
t_2	12 Nov	statin→$C_{22}H_{28}F$	Austin	200
t_3	12 Nov	$C_{24}H_{75}S_6$	N.Y.→ New York	1000→100
t_4	12 Nov	statin	Boston	200
t_5	13 Nov	statin	Austin	200
t_6	15 Nov	$C_{17}H_{20}N$	Dubai	150

Table 1: Dataset T_{drug} with drug tests.

1. INTRODUCTION

High quality data is important to all businesses, and data cleaning is an important but tedious step. In fact, removing errors in order to get high quality data takes most of data analysts' time [31], and some studies predict a shortage of people with the skills and the know-how for these tasks [33].

Consequently, the number and variety of users who are getting close to the data for data quality tasks are destined to increase, and we cannot assume that only IT staff and data scientists are in charge of the data cleaning process.

The above requirement poses new and interesting research challenges. Indeed, a large body of the research has been conducted on *rule-based data repairing*, which consists of using integrity constraints to identify data errors [11,12,17,25,40], and automated algorithms to enforce these constraints over the data [7,22,23,32,43]. However, in the evolving scenario of data cleaning, these approaches show a serious limitation. Specifically, they assume that data quality rules are declared upfront by domain experts who understand the data and write logical formulas or procedural code. Despite many promising results, these systems have failed short in terms of adoption in industrial tools.

We address the problem of improving the data cleaning process by involving non-expert users as first-class citizens, and present FALCON, a novel system for *interactive* data repairing. FALCON departs from other interactive data cleaning systems [20,27,37,41,46], since it brings together a simple, user-oriented interaction paradigm with the benefits of a declarative, *deterministic*, and expressive data quality language – SQL update (SQLU) queries. In fact, the system is bootstrapped by an update to the data made by the user to rectify an error; based on that, it infers a set of SQLU queries that can be used as data quality rules to correct more errors. We illustrate by example how it works.

Example 1: Table 1 reports a sample real-world dataset T_{drug} for experiments collected from different labs. Each record represents the quantity and date of a test done in a lab over a certain molecule. Errors are highlighted. Consider the following three user updates.

Δ_1: t_3[Laboratory] ← "New York" (from "N.Y.")
Δ_2: t_3[Quantity] ← 100 (from 1000)
Δ_3: t_2[Molecule] ← "$C_{22}H_{28}F$" (from "statin")

There exist multiple interpretations for each update. For instance, two possible semantics behind Δ_1 could be either reformatting all "N.Y." to "New York" as shown in Q_1, or changing all Laboratory values to "New York" as shown in Q'_1, regardless of their original values.

Q_1: UPDATE T_{drug} SET Laboratory = "New York" WHERE Laboratory = "N.Y.";

Q'_1: UPDATE T_{drug} SET Laboratory = "New York";

Similarly, one possible interpretation of Δ_2, as given in Q_2, is that it is specific for Molecule and Date. Hence, it is hard to generalize this update to apply it to other tuples.

Q_2: UPDATE T_{drug} SET Quantity = 100 WHERE Molecule = "$C_{24}H_{75}S_6$" AND Date = "12 Nov";

Update Δ_3 is more interesting. Consider the following three interpretations with different effects. Q_3 repairs errors in both t_2 and t_5. Q'_3 also repairs both t_2 and t_5, but additionally, it modifies t_4[Molecule] to "$C_{22}H_{28}F$", which is an erroneous update, since in Boston they test a different statin molecule. On the other hand, the tuple-specific query Q''_3 only corrects t_2 but misses the chance to repair t_5.

Q_3: UPDATE T_{drug} SET Molecule = "$C_{22}H_{28}F$" WHERE Molecule = "statin" AND Laboratory = "Austin";

Q'_3: UPDATE T_{drug} SET Molecule = "$C_{22}H_{28}F$" WHERE Molecule = "statin";

Q''_3: UPDATE T_{drug} SET Molecule = "$C_{22}H_{28}F$" WHERE Molecule = "statin" AND Laboratory = "Austin" AND Date = "12 Nov" AND Quantity = 200;

From Example 1, one may observe that there might exist a large number of SQLU queries. Indeed, this large number is not surprising, as up to thousands of precise and reliable update queries can be needed in real-world settings, such as Walmart catalog [14]. However, while an update is a perfect starting point for the process of inferring the general scripts, it comes with new challenges in terms of user interactions.

First, the search space for a new update is exponential to the number of the attributes, and domain experts cannot manually validate each of these SQLU queries. We have to assume that a *budget* (*e.g.*, #-user interactions) is given for a specific update. Second, the discovery algorithm must be fast (*e.g.*, able to react in seconds) to enable user interactions. However, each interaction may trigger the update of data, which makes the search space a *dynamic* environment. This *dynamic* behavior, together with the large search space and a budget of user capacity, prevents the use of traditional tools for interactive response, such as precomputing and caching. In order to efficiently manage all potential updates, and effectively interact with users, we propose FALCON, which works as follows.

Workflow. The workflow of FALCON is depicted in Figure 1. ❶ The user examines the data and provides a repair Δ over table T. ❷ Given Δ, FALCON generates a set of SQLU queries as rules. It then selects a query Q whose validity is yet unknown, and asks the user to verify it. ❸ Based on the user verification on Q to be either True (*i.e.*, valid) or False (*i.e.*, invalid), if Q is True, it utilizes Q to repair more data.

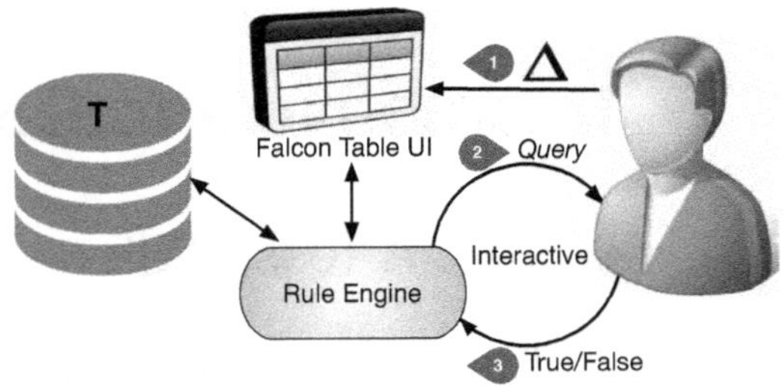

Figure 1: FALCON workflow.

Obviously, FALCON can prune the search space based on the validation on Q. The loop for steps ❷ and ❸ terminates when either all usable queries have been identified, or the user has no more capacity for the current Δ. Afterwards, the user may go back to step ❶ to inspect another repair.

Contributions. We present FALCON, a novel interactive data cleaning system, with the following contributions.

(1) To design data quality rules, we adopt the standard and deterministic language of SQL update statements (Section 2). We discuss how to organize the search space of candidate rules as a lattice, and its pruning principles, by leveraging the properties of the lattice (Section 3).

(2) We devise efficient algorithms for selecting candidate queries to effectively interact with the user (Section 4). In particular, in contrast to traditional traversal (one-hop) based approaches (Section 4.1), we present novel multiple-hop search algorithms such that FALCON can accurately discover useful queries in a small number of steps (Section 4.2).

(3) We describe optimization techniques to improve the efficiency of lattice maintenance (Section 5.1). We also propose *closed query sets* to compress the lattice so as to improve the search efficiency (Section 5.2).

(4) Implemented on top of an open-source data wrangling tool OpenRefine (http://openrefine.org), we have conducted experiments with real-world and synthetic data to show the effectiveness and efficiency of FALCON (Section 6).

Section 7 presents related work. Section 8 closes this paper, followed by our agenda for future work.

2. PROBLEM STATEMENT

We first introduce the rules used to repair data (Section 2.1). We then describe the search space of rules given one user update (Section 2.2) and formally define the problem studied in this paper (Section 2.3). Finally, we discuss its associated fundamental problems (Section 2.4).

2.1 SQL Update Queries: Mother Tongue

We adopt a simple and standard language to repair the database, the language of update statements in SQL (SQLU).

An SQLU statement updates records in a table T on attributes $A, B \ldots$, when some conditions hold. In this work, we restrict the language to the case where updates are done on one attribute A of table T with only boolean conjunctions:

UPDATE T SET $A = a$ WHERE boolean conjunctions

More specifically, each boolean conjunction is of the form $B = v_B$, where B is an attribute of table T and v_B is a constant value from the domain of B, *e.g.*, Molecule = "statin". Attribute B could also be the attribute to be updated (*i.e.*, $B = A$), such as Laboratory in Q_1 of Example 1.

We shall use the terms SQLU queries and *data quality rules* (or simply *rules*) interchangeably in the following. We will also treat *updates* and *repairs* equally.

Remark. SQLU queries used in this work are quite different from the integrity constraints (ICs) that are widely adopted by other data cleaning systems, such as functional dependencies [1], conditional functional dependencies [16], conditional inclusion dependencies [7], and denial constraints [12]. ICs are used to capture errors as violations, where one violation is a set of values that is not semantically coherent when putting together. In other words, ICs do not explicitly specify how to change data values to resolve violations. In contrast, SQLU statements explicitly specify how to change data values, which are thus considered to be *deterministic*. The proposed SQLU is powerful enough to support existing deterministic cleaning languages such as fixing rules [43], constant CFDs [16], and widely used ETL rules.

Note that in this work we restrict our discussion to conjunctive SQLU queries for three reasons. (1) It is easy for users to understand, which is important for interacting with users; (2) It is efficient to reason about the relationship between different queries; and (3) It is known that queries with other formulae such as disjunctions or negations can be rewritten into an equivalent conjunctive formula [1].

2.2 Search Space for One Repair

Consider a repair $\Delta : t[A] \leftarrow a'$ that changes the value of $t[A]$ from error a to its correct value a' with $a \neq a'$. We want to generalize this action so as to repair more errors.

Naturally, there exist multiple queries to interpret this repair Δ. Implicitly, for each query, the SET clause is $A \leftarrow a'$. Hence we focus on the WHERE clause. Consider a boolean condition as $B = v_B$, where B could be any attribute in relation R. In an *open-world* assumption, the constant v_B can be assigned from an infinite set of values, which is neither reasonable nor feasible in practice. Instead, we adopt a *closed-world* assumption by only using the evidence from tuple t, the tuple that is being repaired. In other words, for a query Q *w.r.t.* the above update Δ, if an attribute B appears in the WHERE condition of Q, then the boolean conjunction is $B = t[B]$, which is to bind the constant v_B to the value $t[B]$. As a special query, we consider $\varnothing$ as *no condition* being enforced in the WHERE clause. Stating in another way, it is to update all A values in T to a'.

In summary, given a repair $t[A] \leftarrow a'$ for tuple t in table T of relation R, the set $\mathcal{Q}$ of all rules for such a repair is:

UPDATE $\boxed{T}$ SET $\boxed{A = a'}$ WHERE $\boxed{X = t[X]}$

where X is an arbitrary subset of R, which can range from the empty set $\varnothing$ to all attributes in R (*i.e.*, $X = R$). Hence, there are $2^{|R|}$ possibilities of X, where $|R|$ is the arity of relation R. In other words, we can infer $2^{|R|}$ queries for each update. Consider update Δ_3 in Example 1, we can infer $2^4 = 16$ queries, where three of them are shown as Q_3, Q'_3 and Q''_3.

2.3 Problem Statement

Given a repair, one wants to find the queries that are semantically correct so as to repair the database.

Valid SQLU query. Given a repair, an SQLU query is *valid* if the query is semantically correct. Since we do not know which queries are valid in advance, we need to ask the user to either validate the query as semantically correct, or invalidate it otherwise. Naturally, we want to find all valid SQLU queries and use them to repair the database. A straightforward strategy is to ask the user to check every possible query. Of course, this method is rather expensive as there could be a large number of possible queries, for which we will use containment relationships among queries to improve the search of queries (Section 3).

Furthermore, the user normally has limited capacity for the number of queries he/she can verify. To this end, we want to find the *cost-effective queries* to maximize the number of repaired tuples based on the queries validated by the user, which is formally defined below.

Budget repair problem. Given a set $\mathcal{Q}$ of SQLU queries, a table T, and a budget B for the number of interactions the user can afford, the *budget repair problem* is to select B queries $\mathcal{Q}'$ from $\mathcal{Q}$, so as to maximize $|\bigcup_{Q \in \mathcal{Q}' \wedge \mathsf{valid}(Q)=\mathsf{T}} Q(T)|$.

Here, $\mathsf{valid}(Q)$ is a boolean function that is T (resp. F) if Q is a valid query (resp. not), and $Q(T)$ represents the set of repairs of applying query Q over table T.

Observe that in the above problem, given a query Q, the validity of Q (*i.e.*, $\mathsf{valid}(Q)$) is unknown, to be verified by the user. Such a problem is typically categorized under the framework of *online algorithms* [3], where one can process input piece-by-piece in a serial fashion (*i.e.*, the verification $\mathsf{valid}(Q)$ of some Q), without having the entire input (*i.e.*, the value $\mathsf{valid}(Q)$ for each Q in $\mathcal{Q}$) available from the start.

Offline problem. Its corresponding *offline variant* is the following. Given as input that whether each query Q in $\mathcal{Q}$ is valid or not is known, how to select B queries from $\mathcal{Q}$ to maximize the number of repaired tuples. The objective of designing an online algorithm is to get answers as accurate as the offline problem. It is easy to see that the offline problem of its online version (*i.e.*, the budget repair problem) is NP-hard, which can be readily proved by a reduction from the maximum-coverage problem [34].

On analogy of what is proved in [5], when the offline variant is NP-hard, there is no efficient algorithm for computing an optimal solution for its online algorithm. In other words, when the offline variant is intractable, there is no hope to find an optimal solution with the cost in a constant factor of the online variant (*a.k.a.* a *competitive analysis* [39]).

However, not all is lost. As will be shown later, we can organize all queries in a graphical structure, such that when the user verifies a query Q as valid or invalid, we can even generate more inputs by computing the validity of queries Q' that are related to Q (Section 3). Even better, we devise efficient algorithms to search over the above graphical structure (Section 4) and empirically show the effectiveness of the presented strategies (Section 6).

2.4 Fundamental Problems

Let $\mathcal{Q}^+$ be a set of valid queries *w.r.t.* one user update.

Termination problem. The *termination problem* determines whether a rule-based process will stop, given $\mathcal{Q}^+$ and an instance T. We can readily verify that no matter in what order the queries in $\mathcal{Q}^+$ are executed, the whole process will terminate, since the execution of each query is deterministic.

Conflicting queries. Two queries Q_1 and Q_2 are *conflicting queries* if there exists a tuple t' such that the following two sequences of SQL updates will obtain different results: (1) $Q_1(Q_2(t'))$, *i.e.*, applying Q_2 first to t followed by Q_1, and (2) $Q_2(Q_1(t'))$.

Note that, the search space *w.r.t.* one repair $\Delta : t[A] \leftarrow a'$ is a set $\mathcal{Q}$ of queries (Section 2.2), where each query $Q \in \mathcal{Q}$ is a way to generalize the action of changing $t[A]$ to a specific value a', by considering different attribute combinations. In other words, no query Q will change a tuple to a value a'' that is different from a'. Hence, conflicting queries will not be generated in one lattice.

Determinism problem. The *determinism problem* asks whether all repairing processes (with different repairing orders of the SQLU queries) end up with the same repair, given $\mathcal{Q}^+$ and an instance T.

It is easy to verify that, given $\mathcal{Q}^+$ and T, regardless of the orders of the queries in $\mathcal{Q}^+$ are applied, all data repairs are $\bigcup_{Q\in\mathcal{Q}^+} Q(T)$, where T is the original instance. Hence, any set of rules is trivially deterministic.

3. A LATTICE: FALCON SEARCH SPACE

In this section, we shall present our organization of the search space, so as to enable both efficient and effective search over the candidate rules. We start by discussing the relationship between two data quality rules.

Rule containment. For two rules Q and Q', we say that Q is *contained* by Q' (or Q' *contains* Q), denoted by $Q \preceq Q'$, if for all possible database instances T over the input schema R, the result of $Q(T)$ is a subset of the result of $Q'(T)$ (*i.e.*, $Q(T) \subseteq Q'(T)$).

Intuitively, the rule containment captures the semantic relationship among rules. In other words, no matter which database T is used, Q will update a subset of T tuples that Q' will update if $Q \preceq Q'$, since Q is more specific than Q'.

Example 2: Consider queries Q_3, Q_3' and Q_3'' in Example 1. It is straightforward to see that both Q_3 and Q_3'' are contained by Q_3' (*i.e.*, $Q_3 \preceq Q_3'$ and $Q_3'' \preceq Q_3'$), and Q_3'' is contained by Q_3 (*i.e.*, $Q_3'' \preceq Q_3$).

It is readily to verify that the query containment "$\preceq$" is a partial order over the set $\mathcal{Q}$ of all possible rules, which is reflexive, antisymmetric, and transitive. More specifically:

[Reflexivity] $Q \preceq Q$, for any $Q \in \mathcal{Q}$.
[Antisymmetry] If $Q \preceq Q'$ and $Q' \preceq Q$, then $Q = Q'$.
[Transitivity] If $Q \preceq Q'$ and $Q' \preceq Q''$, then $Q \preceq Q''$.

For a query Q, we denote by $\text{attr}(Q)$ the set of distinct attributes in its WHERE condition.

Note that for each user update, the SQLU queries have the same value constraint on the same attribute, and thus the rule containment verification is *equivalent* to a simpler condition: $Q \preceq Q'$ if $\text{attr}(Q')$ is a subset $\text{attr}(Q)$. For instance, $Q_3 \preceq Q_3'$ since $\text{attr}(Q_3') = \{\text{Molecule}\} \subseteq \{\text{Molecule}, \text{Laboratory}\} = \text{attr}(Q_3)$.

Affected tuples. For each query Q and instance T, we call the tuples in $Q(T)$ *affected tuples*, *i.e.*, the tuples that Q will repair. We also call $|Q(T)|$ the *affected number* of Q, relative to T. Consider Q_3 and T_{drug} in Example 1 for instance. The affected tuples are $Q_3(T_{\text{drug}}) = \{t_2, t_5\}$, and its corresponding affected number is $|Q_3(T_{\text{drug}})| = 2$.

We discuss next how to organize these queries to facilitate search strategies.

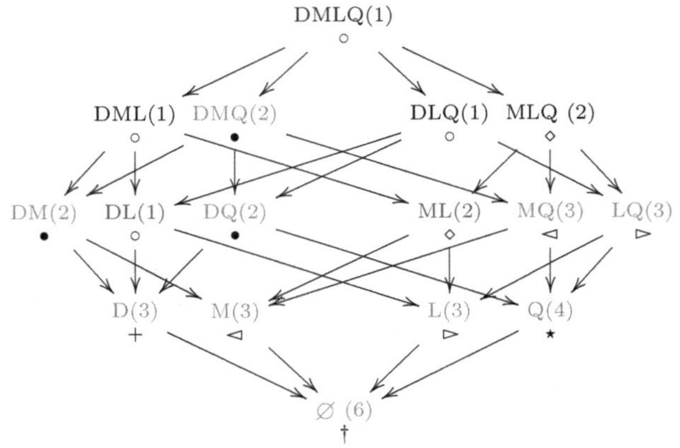

Figure 2: A sample lattice graph.

A set with a partial order is a *partially ordered set*, or *poset*. Hence, $\mathcal{Q}$ is a *poset* on the partial order $\preceq$ of rule containment. Moreover, consider any two rules Q and Q'. They have a *greatest lower bound*: the most specific query that is contained by both Q and Q'. This query, denoted by $Q \wedge Q'$, is the one *w.r.t.* $\text{attr}(Q) \cup \text{attr}(Q')$. Also, they have a *least upper bound*: the most general query that contains both Q and Q'. This query, denoted by $Q \vee Q'$, is the one *w.r.t.* $\text{attr}(Q) \cap \text{attr}(Q')$. Therefore, we can organize the queries in our search space as a *lattice*.

Query lattice. Given a repair Δ and a database instance T, we denote by $(\mathcal{Q}, \preceq, T)$ the corresponding lattice, or simply $(\mathcal{Q}, \preceq)$ when T is clear from the context. Each node in the lattice corresponds to a query $Q \in \mathcal{Q}$. Each directed edge from node Q to Q' indicates that $Q \preceq Q'$ (Q is contained in Q') and $|\text{attr}(Q)| = |\text{attr}(Q')|+1$ (with one different attribute). Moreover, the affected number associated with each query is maintained in the lattice (we will discuss how to compute the number in Section 5.1.2).

Example 3: Figure 2 depicts the lattice for dataset T_{drug} and update Δ_3 given in Example 1. Each capital letter is an abbreviation of an attribute, *e.g.*, D for Date. The node ML is for the query Q_3 on attributes Molecule and Laboratory. The edge from ML to M indicates that the query Q_3 (for ML) is contained in Q_3' (for M). The number 2 in node ML is the affected number of $|Q_3(T_{\text{drug}})|$. Moreover, the greatest lower bound (resp. lowest upper bound) of ML and DL is MDL (resp. L). We postpone the discussion of the shapes in the figure, *e.g.*, "$\rhd$", "$\star$" and "$\circ$", to Section 5.2.

Valid and maximal valid nodes. Given a lattice $(\mathcal{Q}, \preceq)$, the node relative to a rule Q is *valid* if it is semantically correct, thus should be executed to repair data. In our work, if the validity of a rule is unknown, we rely on the user to verify (see more details in Section 2.3). Fortunately, if a rule Q is known to be valid, we can infer that Q' is also valid if $Q' \preceq Q$. Moreover, the node relative to a valid rule Q is *maximal valid*, if no Q'' is valid and $Q \preceq Q''$.

Example 4: Consider the lattice in Figure 2. Assume that there are two valid queries to be applied: ML (Q_3 in Example 1); and the other query DL that represents on a certain date a certain lab works on only one molecule. All red nodes are invalid queries, *i.e.*, the queries that users will semantically invalidate. The other nodes are valid nodes. Moreover, the blue nodes DL and ML are maximal valid nodes.

One nice property of using a lattice is that it provides opportunities to prune nodes to be visited during traversal.

Lattice pruning. If a node Q is valid, by inference, all nodes Q' where $Q' \preceq Q$ are valid. On the other hand, if a node Q is invalid, by inference, all nodes Q'' where $Q \preceq Q''$ are invalid. The rationality behind the above inferences is that: if one query is valid, then any query that is more specific is also valid; conversely, if it is invalid, then any query that is more general is also invalid.

We denote by $Q^{\curlyvee}$ (*i.e.*, above Q in the lattice) the queries that Q contains, and $Q_{\curlywedge}$ (*i.e.*, below Q in the lattice) the queries that contain Q. These notations naturally extend to a set of queries, $\mathcal{Q}^{\curlyvee}$ and $\mathcal{Q}_{\curlywedge}$, such that $\mathcal{Q}^{\curlyvee} = \bigcup_{Q \in \mathcal{Q}} Q^{\curlyvee}$ and $\mathcal{Q}_{\curlywedge} = \bigcup_{Q \in \mathcal{Q}} Q_{\curlywedge}$.

Example 5: Consider again the lattice in Figure 2. During interactions with the user, if DL is validated, we can then derive that $\text{DL}^{\curlyvee}$ = {DML, DLQ, DMLQ} is valid. Consider now DQ, if DQ is invalidated, we can then derive that $\text{DQ}_{\curlywedge}$ = {D, Q, ∅} is invalid.

The notation used in this paper is summarized in Table 3 in Appendix A.

4. ALGORITHMS: FALCON IN ACTION

In this section, we first describe some traversal based algorithms to solve our budget repair problem (Section 4.1). We then present advanced algorithms to efficiently navigate the search space (Section 4.2).

When discussing the algorithms, we assume that the lattice has been built given the user provided repair. The algorithms are designed for traversing the lattice and interacting with the user. Details of constructing and maintaining the lattice will be provided in Section 5.1.

4.1 One-Hop Search: Falcon Glide

In traditional traversal algorithms of a lattice $\mathcal{L}$ the search is based on some seeds, and then neighbours of the seeds (*i.e.*, one-hop) are visited by following edge connections. For example, Breadth-first search (BFS) traverses $\mathcal{L}$, by starting at the bottom and explores the neighbor nodes first, before moving to the next level neighbors. Depth-first search (DFS) differentiates in that after visiting a node, it explores as far as possible along each branch before backtracking. A recent traversal proposal, Ducc [28], bootstraps the search with a DFS-style exploration until a node of interest is found. Then it traverses the lattice alternating visits over valid and invalid nodes, in order to identify the border between them. While the algorithm was defined to find minimal unique column combination, it can be used for any lattice traversal.

To better understand how different algorithms work, we illustrate by an example below.

Example 6: Figure 3 shows how various search algorithms work, where red nodes indicate invalid nodes, blue nodes represent maximal valid nodes, and the other nodes (*i.e.*, small circles) are valid nodes. Let $B = 3$, the number of questions the user can verify. BFS search will visit the nodes in a breadth-first fashion, *e.g.*, in the order $B1, B2, B3$. DFS search will visit the nodes in a depth-first fashion, *e.g.*, in the order $D1, D2, D3$. Different from BFS and DFS, Ducc [28] explores the graph in a zigzag fashion, which tries to pivot on valid nodes and explores their neighbors, *e.g.*, in the order $A1, A2, A3$. Since the above methods are edge based, the search paths are indicated on edges.

Now let us give some insight why traversal based algorithms fail for our problem. Nodes close to the top (resp.

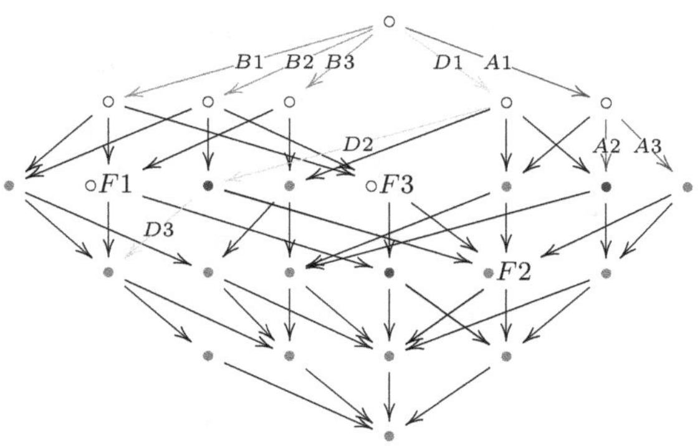

Figure 3: Lattice search algorithms. (Nodes ∘/•/• represent valid nodes/maximal valid nodes/invalid nodes. Red/green/blues edges are used to explain different search strategies: BFS/DFS/Ducc.)

bottom) are more likely to be valid (resp. invalid). Hence, if we traverse the lattice *top-down*, we have more chances to visit a valid node Q. However, since it is close to the top, the number of inferred valid nodes $Q^{\curlyvee}$ is small. On the other hand, if we traverse the lattice *bottom-up*, we have more chances to visit an invalid node Q'. However, since it is close to the bottom, the number of inferred invalid nodes $Q'_{\curlywedge}$ is small.

As shown in Example 6 and the above discussion, traversal based algorithms are locality based – they follow edge connections from visited nodes. In such a way, FALCON can only *glide* over the lattice. This is obviously not ideal when the lattice is big but the budget B is small, which is exactly the case we face. Hence, we propose new algorithms next.

4.2 Multi-Hop Search: Falcon Dive

Now that we know that traversal based algorithms are not suitable for our studied problem, we need to devise new algorithms so that FALCON can *dive* on the lattice.

4.2.1 Binary Jump

Given a budget B, our objective is to define a *divide-and-conquer* strategy that efficiently identifies nodes that are both valid and not very close to the top, so as to maximize the number of tuples to be repaired. To this purpose, we present an strategy, namely *binary jump*, inspired by classical binary search. Roughly speaking, we treat the search space as a linear space (*i.e.*, an array) by sacrificing some structural connections, and sort the nodes based on their associated affected numbers. We can then do multi-hop search to locate a candidate node to be verified with the user.

Note that conventionally, *a binary search* finds the position of a target value within a sorted array. Different from it, *binary jump* does not have a target value to be searched. In other words, binary jump is just inspired by binary search by doing half-interval style lattice traversal.

Binary jump over a path. We first discuss binary jump over a path. Consider DMLQ → DLQ → LQ → Q → ∅ in Figure 2. The ground truth of the validity of them is (T, T, F, F, F), where T means valid and F means invalid. The search algorithm does not know the ground truth, so initially we have (?, ?, ?, ?, ?). To find the truth with traversal based approaches, we need $O(N)$ questions in average, where N is the length of the path. However, using binary jump will reduce it to $O(\log N)$ questions, which is optimal, by applying inferences of finding all valid/invalid nodes.

Next we discuss the meaning of "*binary*". Straightforwardly, *binary* may refer to the offset as standard binary search. However, we need to incorporate the information of affected number. Hence, the *binary* search could refer to the median number. For instance, in Figure 2, the path DMLQ → DLQ → LQ → Q → ∅ corresponds to the affected numbers $(1, 2, 3, 4, 6)$ and the binary jump is to find the value that is closest to $\lceil (1+6)/2 \rceil = 4$.

For binary jump, we introduce a parameter d to bound the search depth, which is the number of iterations one can do binary jump before termination. Given a path $Q_1, Q_2, \cdots, Q_x$, we first ask the middle node $Q_{x/2}$. If the node is valid, we ask the next middle node between $Q_{x/2}$ and Q_x; otherwise, we ask the next middle node between Q_1 and $Q_{x/2}$. After d wrong searches, the process terminates. We refer to this search strategy as BINARYJUMP(). The rationale behind using the parameter d is that if we are following the wrong direction, we should be aware and go back to the right track, as *a fault confessed is half redressed.* We will discuss how d is set in practice in Section 6.

Note that the number of the most general query (*i.e.*, the empty set at the bottom of the lattice) will change the whole column, which makes the median number an optimistic estimation. To make it more realistic, instead, we set the binary jump using log scale to find the value that is closest to *e.g.*, $\lceil \log_2^{(1+6)} \rceil = 3$.

From a path to a lattice. In order to take the advantage of binary jump for lattice traversal, the broad intuition is to do dimension reduction from a lattice to a one-dimensional structure. That is, if we treat all nodes in the lattice uniformly, by sorting them in ascending order on their associated affected numbers, we get a sorted array similar to the one discussed above for the path.

Let $\mathcal{Q}^?$ denote a set of unvalidated nodes, $\mathcal{Q}^+$ represent a set of valid nodes, and $\mathcal{Q}^-$ indicate a set of invalid nodes. Next we present the algorithm.

Algorithm. Given a lattice $(\mathcal{Q}, \preceq)$ *w.r.t.* a repair Δ over table T, a budget B for the number of questions the user can answer, and a depth d to bound the search depth, the algorithm for binary jump is given below.

D1. [Initialization.] Let $\mathcal{Q}^- = \emptyset$, $\mathcal{Q}^+ = \{\mathsf{top}\}$ (the top node of the lattice), and $\mathcal{Q}^? = \mathcal{Q} \backslash (\mathcal{Q}^- \cup \mathcal{Q}^+)$. Also, let $\mathcal{Q}^{\checkmark}$ be the set of nodes verified by users, initially empty.

D2. [Sort.] Sort unvalidated nodes $\mathcal{Q}^?$ based on their affected numbers in ascending order.

D3. [Binary jump] Do the binary jump over $\mathcal{Q}^?$ and select one node Q, which is referred to as BINARYJUMP(). If the user still has capacity (the total number of interactions is below B), it interacts with user to verify Q, and updates $\mathcal{Q}^{\checkmark} = \mathcal{Q}^{\checkmark} \cup \{Q\}$. Otherwise, the whole process terminates. If Q is valid, it goes to step **D4**; otherwise, it goes to **D5** below, if Q is invalid.

D4. [Q is valid.] Apply Q over table T and update the affected numbers of nodes in $\mathcal{Q}$. Set $\mathcal{Q}^+ = \mathcal{Q}^+ \cup Q^{\curlyvee}$ (infer and enlarge valid nodes). Let $\mathcal{Q}^? = Q_{\curlywedge}$ and go to step **D2**.

D5. [Q is invalid.] Set $\mathcal{Q}^- = \mathcal{Q}^- \cup Q_{\curlywedge}$ (infer and enlarge invalid nodes). If the current depth is d, it goes to step **D6**. Otherwise, $\mathcal{Q}^? = Q^{\curlyvee}$ and goes to step **D2**.

D6. [New search space.] Let $\mathcal{Q}^? = \mathcal{Q} \backslash (\mathcal{Q}^{\checkmark \curlyvee} \cup \mathcal{Q}^{\checkmark}{}_{\curlywedge})$, *i.e.*, search on the nodes that are not linked to any verified node. It then goes to step **D2**.

Complexity. It is easy to see that there are up to B iterations, and the sort (**D2**) dominates the cost. Hence, the total time complexity is $O(B \cdot |\mathcal{Q}| \cdot log|\mathcal{Q}|)$. Here, budget B is typically small. Although the size of $\mathcal{Q}$ could be large for a big relation, we will discuss an optimization in Section 5.1.1 about how to ensure that the size of $\mathcal{Q}$ is easily manageable.

4.2.2 Attribute Correlation: A Good Bait

Intuitively, we want to greedily select at each step the node Q that is more likely to repair a large number of tuples. However, since we do not know what are the correct nodes until we verify them with the user, we need to estimate this information. To define the score of a node, we augment the existing information on the affected number of each query Q, *i.e.*, the number of A values Q can repair (Section 3), with the likelihood of a certain node to be related to the current attribute A.

Attribute correlations. The *attribute correlation* between two attributes A and B, denoted by $\mathsf{cor}(A, B)$, is to measure how close they are to each other.

The intuition of using attribute correlations is that, if node Q is correlated to attribute A that is being updated, then it is more likely to be semantically relevant and useful for the repair process. In general, we may get such information from data profiling tools that measure attributes correlation.

We adopt the techniques proposed in CORDS [29] to profile a database T of relation R. Specifically, CORDS computes for each attribute pair a score in $[0, 1]$. Note that (A, B) and (B, A) are different pairs. The score of an attribute pair (A, B) equals to 1 means that it is a soft FD, indicating that A approximately uniquely determines B. Otherwise, it is a score computed using χ^2 statistics by examining the attribute values in attributes A and B.

In our lattice, oftentimes, we want to estimate the correlation between the attributes in a query Q (*i.e.*, $\mathsf{attr}(Q)$) and the attribute A being updated. In other words, we need to compute the correlation between a set of attributes to a single attribute.

Using attribute correlations. We modified the algorithm presented in CORDS to compute the correlation between a set X of attributes and an attribute A, denoted by $\mathsf{cor}(X, A)$. In CORDS, an attribute pair (A, B) is a soft FD if the support value $\mathsf{sup}(A, B)$ is above a given threshold τ (see [29] for more details). Similarly, we output (X, B) as a soft FD if the support value $\mathsf{sup}(X, B) > \tau$. Otherwise, we compute the correlation score in $[0, 1]$ for (X, B) as follows.

$$\mathsf{cor}(X, B) = \frac{\chi^2}{nq} \tag{1}$$

$$\chi^2 = \sum_{v_1=1}^{m_1} \sum_{v_2=1}^{m_2} \cdots \sum_{v_k=1}^{m_k} \frac{(n_{v_1,v_2,\ldots,v_k} - e_{v_1,v_2,\ldots,v_k})^2}{e_{v_1,v_2,\ldots,v_k}} \tag{2}$$

$$e_{v_1,v_2,\ldots,v_k} = n \prod_{j=1}^{k} Pr(v_j) = n \prod_{j=1}^{k} \frac{n^j_{v_j}}{n} = \frac{n^j_{i_1} n^j_{v_2} \ldots n^j_{v_k}}{n^{k-1}} \tag{3}$$

$$q = \prod_{i=1}^{k} m_i - \sum_{i=1}^{k} m_i + k - 1 \tag{4}$$

Here, k is the number of attributes in X and m_i is the number of distinct values in the i-th attribute. Moreover, $(v_1, v_2, \ldots, v_k)$ is a tuple where the value of the j-th attribute is v_j. Also, $n_{v_1,v_2,\ldots,v_k}$ is the frequency of tuple

	Austin	N.Y.	Boston	Dubai	
$C_{16}H_{16}Cl$	1	0	0	0	1
statin	2	0	1	0	3
$C_{24}H_{75}S_6$	0	1	0	0	1
$C_{17}H_{20}N$	0	0	0	1	1
	3	1	1	1	

Table 2: A 2-way contingency table.

$(v_1, v_2, ..., v_k)$, and $e_{v_1,v_2,...,v_k}$ is the estimated frequency based on the probability of v_j appearing in the j-th attribute, *i.e.*, $n^j_{v_j}/n$, where $n^j_{v_j}$ is the frequency of v_j in the j-th attribute and n is the number of tuples.

Example 7: Consider Table 1, and a given soft FD in the traditional form: {Molecule, Laboratory} → Quantity. Naturally, we have that the correlation value for cor({Molecule, Laboratory}, Quantity) = 1, since they can be verified from the soft FD given above.

Consider now X = {Molecule} and B = Laboratory. Since there is no corresponding soft FD as {Molecule} → Laboratory, we compute its correlation value by normalizing χ^2 statistics.

To do so, we first compute contingency table (see Table 2). We then compute expected count of each symbol tuple. Consider tuple {statin,Austin}. The expected count $e_{\text{statin,Boston}} = (n^{\text{Molecule}}_{\text{stain}} \cdot n^{\text{Laboratory}}_{\text{Boston}})/n = 0.5$, and the real count $n_{\text{statin,Austin}} = 1$. Thus the difference is $(n_{\text{statin,Austin}} - e_{\text{statin,Boston}})^2/e_{\text{statin,Boston}} = 0.5$. By summing up all differences we have $\chi^2 = 12.67$, the degrees of freedom $q = 4 \cdot 4 - (4+4) + 2 - 1 = 9$, thus cor({Molecule}, Laboratory) $= 12.67/(6 * 9) = 0.235$.

We now give our greedy algorithm for multi-hop search driven by correlation and affected number.

Correlation aware binary jump (CoDive). We revise binary jump by using the correlation information, affecting **D3** in Section 4.2.1. Note that the function BINARYJUMP() will locate a node Q in the sorted list $\mathcal{Q}^?$. Instead of asking the user to verify Q, we revise it with the following methodology. (1) We pick more nodes around Q in the sorted list, with w on its left and the other w on its right. (2) For the above $2w+1$ nodes, we compute their scores (affected number multiplies correlation score) and select the one with the largest score, which will then be verified by the user. We will discuss how w is set in practice in Section 6.

5. OPTIMIZATIONS

In this section, we first discuss optimizations for maintaining the lattice (Section 5.1). We then describe a technique to compress the search space, which can be applied to all algorithms (Section 5.2). We also discuss an extension when external sources are available (Appendix B).

5.1 Lattice Maintenance

There are two main challenges when maintaining the lattice: its potential large size, and the updates of affected numbers of lattice nodes during each interaction. We address these two issues below.

5.1.1 Partial Lattice Materialization

For some dataset, the number of attributes in R can be large, such that a full materialization of the lattice is prohibitively expensive with $2^{|R|}$ nodes.

Fortunately, in our framework, the update provided by the user is a strong indicator to guide which attributes should be used. The intuition is that, given an update $t[A] \leftarrow a'$, not all attributes are relevant. Consequently, constructing a lattice by incorporating irrelevant attributes will decrease both efficiency and effectiveness. Hence, we propose to pick top-k attributes that are related to the attribute A being updated, based on the attribute correlation score discussed in Section 4.2.2. We refer to such a strategy as *partial lattice materalization*, which performs much faster than a full materialization of the entire lattice, without losing accuracy. This reduces the time complexity from $O(2^{|R|} \cdot |T|)$ to $O(2^k \cdot |T|)$ where k could be much smaller than $|R|$ in practice.

Practically, attribute correlation plays an important role in devising effective search strategies. We combine functional dependencies (FDs) and highly related attribute sets (rules) to improve the search strategy. Please see the experiment in Appendix D.1 for more details on this point.

5.1.2 Initialize and Maintain Affected Numbers

Initialization. Given an update $t[A] \leftarrow a'$, we need to compute the affected number of each query Q in the lattice. The straightforward way of executing an SQLU query for each node is very costly.

We approach the problem of *initializing affected numbers* by leveraging the containment relationships between nodes. Consider two queries Q and Q', if $Q \preceq Q'$, then given any database T, we have $Q(T) \subseteq Q'(T)$. Clearly, we can compute the result of $Q(T)$ from $Q'(T)$. This is exactly the problem of answering queries using materialized views [26]. Given the simplicity of the SQLU queries adopted in this work, the query rewriting is simply to apply a selection using a constant value.

Example 8: Consider two queries Q_3, Q'_3, and the dataset T_{drug} in Example 1. If we compute Q'_3 over T_{drug} first as $Q'_3(T_{\text{drug}})$, the result of $Q_3(T_{\text{drug}})$ is simply to select all tuples from $Q'_3(T_{\text{drug}})$ whose Laboratory values are Austin.

The above example suggests a simple way of computing affected numbers of lattice nodes in a bottom-up fashion. Indeed, only one SQLU query is needed for the bottom node of the lattice. Afterwards, in the bottom-up procedure, for each query Q, it applies the aforementioned query rewriting technique on $Q'(T)$ to compute $Q(T)$, where $Q \preceq Q'$ indicates that Q' is one level below Q.

Maintenance. Given the lattice $(\mathcal{Q}, \preceq)$ for table T and update Δ, when some rule Q is validated by the user, the tuples affected by Q will be repaired, *i.e.*, $Q(T)$ will result in a repaired database T' where $T' = T \oplus Q(T)$, *i.e.*, applying Q to T. For each yet unvalidated rule Q', the above changes should be reflected, *i.e.*, the number of affected tuples should be changed correspondingly, from $|Q'(T)|$ to $|Q'(T')|$.

The straightforward way is to execute $Q'(T')$ to refresh $|Q'(T')|$, or an optimized way of using the query rewriting technique discussed above. However, in such incremental scenarios, incremental algorithms have been developed for various applications (see [36] for a survey). For incremental algorithms, the updates are typically computed from *affected areas*, not the entire dataset. In our case, the affect area is exactly the affected tuples $Q(T)$. Next, we discuss how to compute, for each unvalidated rule Q', the new $|Q'(T')|$.

Case 1 [$Q' \preceq Q$]: $|Q'(T')| = 0$.

Case 2 [$Q \preceq Q''$]: $|Q''(T')| = |Q''(T)| - |Q(T)|$.

Case 3 [Q **and** Q''' **are disjoint**]: Neither $Q \preceq Q'''$ nor $Q''' \preceq Q$ holds. We have $|Q'''(T')| = |Q'''(T)| - |Q'''(Q(T))|$.

The above case 1 says that, if a valid rule Q is executed, then the tuples that can be affected by the queries Q' it contains have already been repaired. It is safe to set their affected numbers to 0 directly. The above case 2 tells that, for all the queries Q'' that contains Q, the set of tuples $Q(T)$ that Q'' can affect has been repaired. Hence, it is simple to reduce their affected numbers by $|Q(T)|$. In case 3, since neither $Q''' \preceq Q$ nor $Q \preceq Q'''$ holds, it first checks the number of tuples that Q''' can affect *w.r.t.* Q by executing $Q'''(Q(T))$, and then deducts its cardinality $|Q'''(Q(T))|$ from its maintained value $|Q'''(T)|$.

Time complexity. Cases 1 and 2 are clearly in constant time. For case 3, the cost is reduced from computing $Q'''(T')$ (*i.e.*, the entire table) to $Q'''(Q(T))$ (the tuples affected by Q) where $|Q(T)|$ is typically much smaller than $|T|$.

Example 9: Consider Fig. 2. Assume that during one interaction, the users validate ML (*i.e.*, query Q_3 in Example 1). The affected tuples are $Q_3(T_{\mathsf{drug}}) = \{t_2, t_5\}$ and $|Q_3(T_{\mathsf{drug}})| = 2$. One can directly set the numbers associated with DML, DLQ, and DMLQ to 0 (case 1). Moreover, it is safe to change the number with node M as $3 - 2 = 1$. Similarly, we change the number with L (resp. $\varnothing$) to 1 (resp. 4) (case 2). Consider DL and tuples $Q_3(T_{\mathsf{drug}}) = \{t_2, t_5\}$, it is easy to verify that DL can update t_2 but not t_5, hence the number with DL will be changed as $1 - 1 = 0$ (case 3).

5.2 Closed Rule Sets

A natural question, when searching a lattice, is whether there is any redundancy in the behavior of the rules, so we turn our attention now on how to identify such redundancy.

Closure operator f. Given a lattice $(\mathcal{Q}, \preceq)$ for update Δ and table T, we define a closure operator f. For any $Q \in \mathcal{Q}$, let $f(Q) = \{Q'\}$ and the following properties hold: (1) $Q \preceq Q'$; (2) $|Q(T)| = |Q'(T)|$; and (3) $\nexists Q'' \in \mathcal{Q}$ where $Q' \neq Q''$, $Q' \preceq Q''$, and $|Q'(T)| = |Q''(T)|$.

Intuitively, the closure operator f is to locate the *maximal* ancestor of a query Q that has the same effect on the number tuples they can change. Consider Fig. 2 for example, we have $f(\text{DMLQ}) = \{\text{DL}\}$, and $f(\text{DMQ}) = \{\text{DM}, \text{DQ}\}$.

Closed rule sets. Given a lattice $(\mathcal{Q}, \preceq)$, two rules Q and Q' belong to the same *closed rule set, iff* $f(Q) = f(Q')$. The smallest (minimal) closed rule set contains one rule Q, *i.e.*, $f(Q) = \{Q\}$ and no other rule Q' where $f(Q') = \{Q\}$.

Example 10: Consider Fig. 2. The shapes identify distinct closed rule sets. For example, the closed rule set for "∘" is {DMLQ, DML, DLQ, DL}, since they are connected and have the same affected numbers. Also, the closed rule set for "•" is {DMQ, DM, DQ}, similar for other shapes.

It deserves to note that the concept of closed rule sets is in the instance level, *i.e.*, queries in the same closed rule set will change the same set of tuples for the given dataset. However, they are not the same in the semantic level, *i.e.*, some of them might be valid while the others might be invalid. In order to better understand the above discussion, consider an extreme case that each lattice node can change only one tuple, which makes all candidate queries in one closed rule set. Apparently, they contain both valid and invalid rules. In other words, the closed rule set ignores the factor that whether a rule is valid or not.

Representative rule. One natural question, given a closed rule set, is which query to be verified by the user. The intuition behind our choice is that, the more specific the query is, the easier it is for the user to verify. Hence, we define the most *representative rule* in a closed rule set to be the query Q with the largest number of predicates *w.r.t.* $|\mathsf{attr}(Q)|$.

For instance, in Example 10, the representative rule for the rule set of "∘", {DMLQ, DML, DLQ, DL}, is DMLQ.

Benefits of the closed rules set. Any search algorithm over the lattice can benefit from the closed rules set. Given a node in a set, there are consequences that favor the search both if the rule is judged valid or invalid. Remember that we expose and test the representative rule. If it is true, we do not need to compute the updates for any query in the same closed rule set any more. If the answer is no, we also have a benefit in terms of pruning of the nodes, since all the nodes in the set can be safely discharged.

Example 11: Consider Figure 3 and the case that an algorithm has to test node F1. By computing the closed rule set (nodes marked with ∘), the rule at the top is tested. If the rule is valid, and therefore being executed, all the nodes marked with ∘ will have empty updates now, so we can avoid their computation. But if the rule is invalid, we can prune all the nodes in the set, which is a big benefit compared with the failed test of F1. In the latter case, we would still have to validate the remaining nodes marked with ∘, even if we can already derive that they are not valid.

The major difference of our lattice, in contrast to traditional closed item set lattice used for data mining [42], is that our lattice is dynamically changed. More specifically, for each node Q, its associated information $|Q(T)|$ might change during each interaction, such that the closed rule sets will change correspondingly.

6. EXPERIMENTAL STUDY

We implemented FALCON in Java and used PostgreSQL 9.3 as the underlying DBMS. All experiments were conducted on a MacBook Pro with an Intel i7 CPU@2.3Ghz and 16GB of memory. Our frontend extends OpenRefine.

Datasets. We used four real-world datasets and one synthetic dataset, described as follows.

❶ Soccer is a real dataset with 7 attributes and 1625 tuples about soccer players and their clubs scraped from the Web (www.premierleague.com/en-gb.html, www.legaseriea.it/en/, www.bundesliga.com/en/).

❷ Hospital is based on a dataset from US Department of Health & Human Services (http://www.medicare.gov/hospitalcompare/). It has 12 attributes and 100k tuples.

❸ BUS is one of the UK government public datasets available at http://data.gov.uk/data and deals with bus schedules and routes. It contains 15 attributes and 250K tuples.

❹ DBLP is based on the popular collection of authors, publications and venues from http://dblp.uni-trier.de/xml/. We downloaded the whole XML dataset, and translated it into a single relational table with 15 attributes. We considered instances of 1M and 5M tuples, for quality and scalability tests, respectively.

❺ Synth is a dataset we designed starting from the original Soccer dataset in order to study the scalability over the number of tuples and a larger number of attributes. The dataset has 10 attributes and we used a generator from http://www.cs.toronto.edu/tox/toxgene/ to create instances of different sizes.

Algorithms. We implemented several algorithms for the exploration of the lattice. First, we study our own proposals for multi-hop search. Dive is the binary jump algorithm presented in Section 4.2.1. CoDive is its extention to make use of the attributes correlation information, when this is available, as described in Section 4.2.2.

These are compared with one-hop search strategies (Section 4.1). Beside BFS and DFS, we have also implemented Ducc [28], which was designed to reduce the number of tests during the discovery of all the minimal unique column combinations in a given dataset. As we will show in the results, Ducc is better than BFS and DFS for extensive searches of maximal rules in the lattice, but it was not designed to deal with small values of budget B for user interactions.

In addition to these, we also compared our results with the greedy search algorithm for the off-line version of our problem. This algorithm, OffLine, is aware of the valid nodes in the lattice. Given this information, it greedily picks the node that maximizes the error coverage at each step, with the number of steps equals to the budget B.

Baselines. We compared FALCON with four baselines.

❶ *Refine*: Our proposal generalizes the transformation language of existing tools such as OpenRefine (http://openrefine.org/) and Trifacta Wrangler (https://www.trifacta.com/trifacta-wrangler/) [27]. These tools enable users to define transformations by examples exactly as in our setting. Users modify values in a cell for attribute A and the systems suggests possible transformations over the remaining tuples for A. While we do not focus on string manipulation as some of these tools, our language supports rules (*i.e.,* transformations) with look-up over any combination of columns in the relation. In fact, given an update, these tools enable the inference of only two transformations that are comparable to our language: either the single cell is updated (the top of the lattice) or the erroneous value e is replaced with the new value v for all the occurrences in the attribute. The latter corresponds to one of the nodes in our lattice. More precisely, the standardization rule is: UPDATE T SET $A = v$ WHERE $A = e$.

Given this context, a natural baseline algorithm models these transformation tools. This algorithm, namely Refine, checks for every user update the node that generalizes it to a standardization rule, or picks the rule at the top of the lattice if the validation fails.

❷ *Rule-Learning Approaches:* Many previous approaches have concentrated on learning data-quality rules (*e.g.,* [12, 17]). Therefore, we compared our algorithm with one of these methods. More specifically:

(*i*) starting from a dirty database, we asked users to clean a sample of tuples (part of the budget was used to do this);

(*ii*) based on the sample tuples, we used a CFD-miner to learn a number of SQL-updates; since it is known that rule-mining algorithms may discover semantically invalid rules (due to *"overfitting"*) we asked users to select a subset of semantically valid rules (the second part of the budget was used for this purpose); and

(*iii*) we used the set of SQL-updates to repair the dirty instance, and measured the *benefit* score (see below).

❸ *Guided Data Repairs:* To explore the impact of *active learning*, we used GDR [46]. GDR (*"Guided Data Repairs"*) is a recently proposed algorithm that relies on active learning in order to improve the quality of repairs. Given a set of rules, it will incrementally ask users to solicit the right repairs suggested by the rules. We tested an incremental variant of algorithm ❷ above, by using GDR to suggest repairs (*i.e.,* cell updates) to users. In this case, additional budget is used to answer GDR user queries.

❹ *Active Learning in Lattice Traversal:* Finally, we compared our methods to an active learning variant of our lattice-based approach that was designed *ad-hoc* for this purpose. In the active learning algorithm, we first generated some features for each node, including attribute indicator, attribute values, original value, and updated value. We then trained a support vector machine (SVM) model with labeled nodes. Finally we used active learning to select the best node to ask users in each iteration.

Errors and Metrics. Since the considered datasets are clean, we introduce noise to verify the algorithms behaviour in the cleaning process. To start, we manually defined a set of CFDs [16] and fixing rules [43] for each scenario. We used 8 rules for Soccer, 124 rules for Hospital, 8 rules for BUS, 69 rules for DBLP, and 12 rules for Synth.

Afterwards, we used an error-generation tool to inject errors into the clean instances. To make our error-generation more systematic, we relied on an open-source error generation tool by Arocena and others [6]. The tool allows users to inject various kinds of errors within a clean database, both rule-based, random and statistics-based. Being based on an open-source tool, our error generation configuration can be easily shared and reused.

We keep running an algorithm until all the introduced errors are fixed either by a rule or by the user updates. Then, we focus our attention on the *interaction cost.* We adopt natural metrics: the number of user-provided updates U, the number of users' answers for nodes validation A, and we simply add them up to get the total interaction cost T_C. Notice that the latest metric is treating both kinds of interaction with the same weight, *i.e.,* they are considered equally difficult for the user. Despite more sophisticated combinations are possible, we found that the simple sum gives a global overview of the algorithms behaviour that is close to the real overall experience of the users.

In order to have an indicator of the advantage of using interactive cleaning, we also measure the *benefit* of an algorithm in comparison to the manual update of all the errors. We first define the *cost ratio* as the number of actions divided by the number of errors. Manually updating 100 errors requires 100 user actions (updates) for a cost ratio of 1. However, by using our tool, it may be the case that 25 actions can fix 100 errors, therefore the cost ratio would be 0.25. Given an algorithm α, a dataset D, and the interaction cost T_C to obtain a set of queries $\mathcal{Q}$ covering all introduced errors, we define the *benefit* of the algorithm as $\text{BNF}_\alpha = 1 - T_C/|\mathcal{Q}(D)|$.

Finally, we measure the execution times for the algorithms in the generation of the lattice and in its maintenance.

Notice that we do not assume that users always provide correct inputs. On the contrary, the impact of user mistakes is studied in one of our experiments.

Experiments. We conducted five experiments. (*i*) Exp-1 compares benefits of the various lattice-traversal algorithms with different budget values, and show that CoDive maximizes the benefit. (*ii*) Exp-2 studies the impact of different

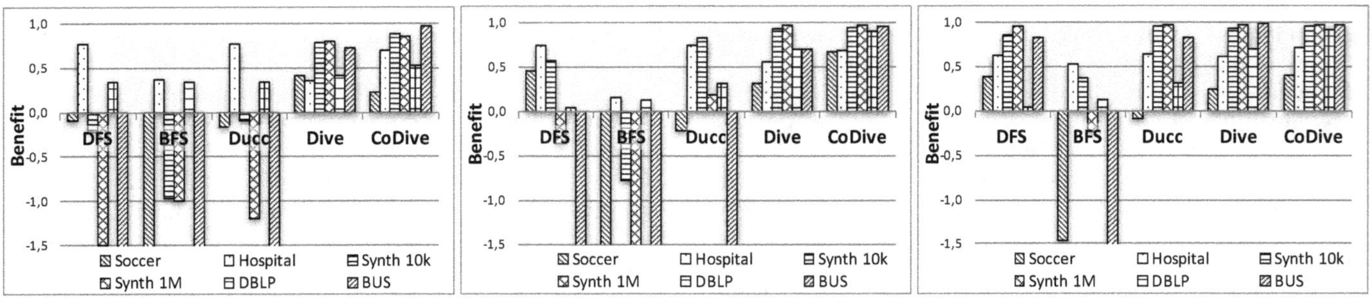

(a) Budget=2 (b) Budget=3 (c) Budget=5

Figure 4: Benefit for the various algorithms for the five datasets.

parameters of the models. In particular, we show that closed rule sets, an optimization technique discussed in Section 5.2, always reduces the cost. (*iii*) Exp-3 compares CoDive with closed rule sets to the four baselines. Interestingly, our algorithm outperforms all of the baselines. (*iv*) Exp-4 studies scalability. (*v*) Finally, Exp-5 investigates the robustness of FALCON *w.r.t.* user mistakes.

Exp-1: Lattice search algorithms. We now turn our attention to the comparison of the different search algorithms. Figure 4 reports the benefit of each algorithm for the six datasets over increasing budget B (*i.e.,* maximum number of questions after an update).

We start with the setting where the user is willing to answer only two questions (B=2) in Figure 4(a). The proposed algorithms, Dive and CoDive, consistently report a positive gain, which, for CoDive, can be interpreted as a reduction of the total user interaction cost between 22% (Soccer) and 97% (BUS). The plot also reveals that one-hop algorithms fail for the budget exploration of the lattice, with the notable exception of the Hospital dataset. This results is not surprising if we look more closely at this scenario. Hospital schema has a large number of FDs with always one or two attributes in the left hand side (LHS) of the rules. This is reflected in the CFDs that we used to introduce the errors. Rules with one or two LHS attributes are at the bottom of the lattice, and this is the most favourable setting for one-hop based algorithms, since they all start from the bottom. On the other hand, when rules start to have more attributes in the LHS, more nodes must be checked to take a decision, these algorithms fail and Dive and CoDive greatly outperform them. Similar results can be observed with B = 3 in Figure 4(b). More details are provided in Appendix D.2.

By increasing the budget to five questions, as reported in Figure 4(c), all algorithms can explore the lattice further at each update and the performance improve accordingly. This improvement is bigger for one-hop based algorithms as they are now able to get closer to the maximal rules in the traversal with a smaller number of updates.

Finally, since algorithm OffLine does not need to perform the search, for each update it is able to identify immediately the maximal rule. Therefore as expected OffLine is always able to completely fix the data with a number of steps that is equal to the number of rules used to introduce noise.

Exp-2: Closed rule sets and parameters. The results for the previous experiments have been conducted with the closed rule sets computed in the lattice. In fact, this optimization enables a reduction both in the number of updates and in the number of questions. To illustrate the impact of the closed rule sets, we executed the lattice search algorithms with and without this optimization, and we measure the difference in the number of required user updates and user answers to cover all errors on three scenarios (Soccer, Hospital and Synth 10k) (see Figure 5). All methods benefit from the optimization, with the exception of Ducc, which does not show any difference, and thus is not reported.

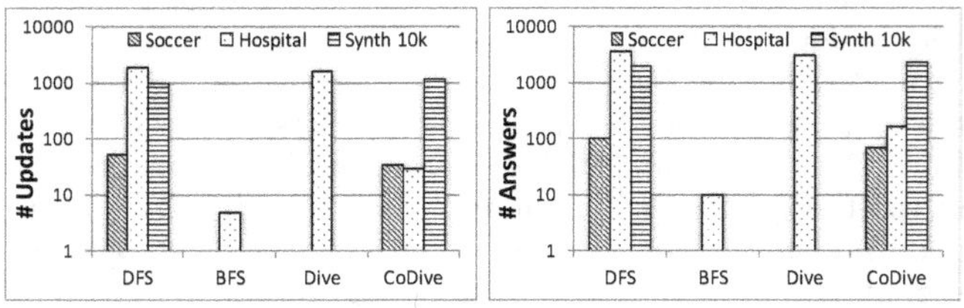

(a) Number of User Updates (b) Number of User Answers

Figure 5: Impact of closed rule sets for B = 2.

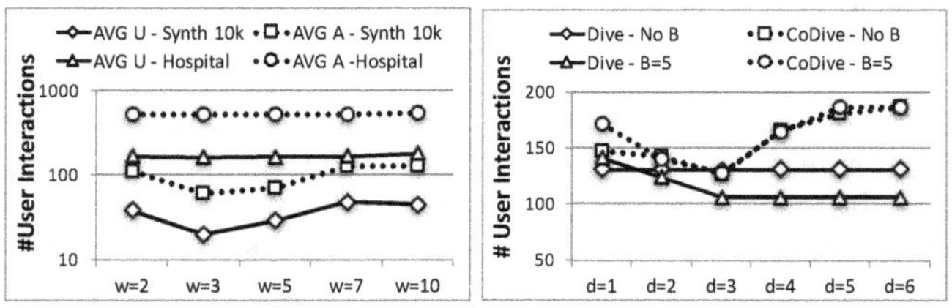

(a) Avg costs over B = 2, 3, 5 for algorithm CoDive wrt w (b) Costs for Synth 1k wrt d for B=5 and without budget

Figure 6: Effects over the interaction cost. U and A are the number of user updates and user answers.

The method that gains most benefit from this optimization is DFS. The explanation is that with low budgets, such as B = 2, DFS always reaches the level in the lattice with two attributes. While the rule corresponding to the node may be too general and therefore invalidated by the user, it may be part of a closed rule set. Therefore, the user is offered the representative rule, which is more specific and, in some cases, true. This happens also for rules with only one attribute in the LHS for Hospital, as discussed above. In fact, even BFS, which never goes beyond nodes with only one attribute in the LHS with low B values, benefits from the closed rules set for this dataset.

As shown in Exp-1, on average CoDive has higher benefit values than Dive. However, the quality of CoDive depends on the value for parameter w (Section 4.2.2). We report in Figure 6(a) the experimental results with different w values. Each reported value is the number of user updates U (user answers A) averaged over the results for B equals to 2, 3, and 5. Both for Hospital and Synth 10k the best results are observed with w = 3. The parameters does not impact the results for Soccer.

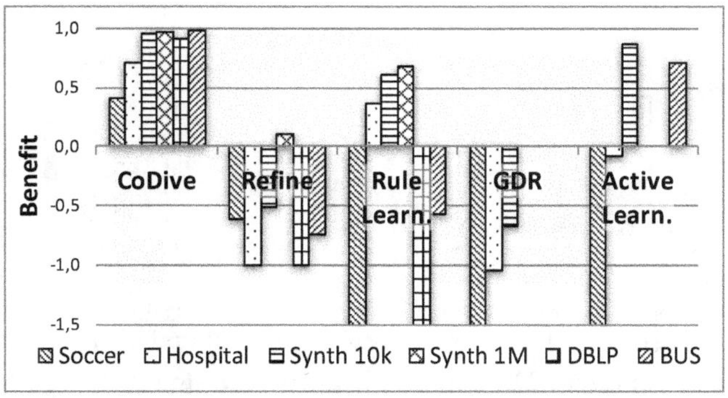

Figure 7: Benefit compared with the baselines.

We also report in Figure 6(b) the experimental results for the synthetic datasets with different values of the parameter d, as introduced for the binary jump algorithm in Section 4.2.1. Experiments over different B values and datasets also confirm that $d = 3$ leads to the best results in terms of optimization of the interaction cost.

Exp-3: Comparison to the baselines. Figure 7 reports a comparison of our CoDive algorithm to the four baselines discussed in Section 6. We fixed a timeout of two hours for all tests. Notice that not all algorithm terminated within the timeout. This accounts for the missing bars in the chart.

Our approach significantly outperforms all baselines. First, CoDive results are significantly better than those based on rule discovery. This suggests that our novel paradigm for data repairing is an improvement *w.r.t.* previous approaches in which quality rules are established upfront. Interestingly, this is confirmed also in the case in which rule discovery is coupled with an interactive algorithm, like GDR. In fact, the additional number of user interactions needed to run GDR brings to even lower benefit.

Results confirm our intuition that using user updates to lead the discovery of rules in an incremental way yields more complete and effective repairs than state-of-the-art rule-learning algorithms, which can return incomplete or redundant sets of constraints. In fact, in our experiments neither RuleLearning, nor GDR was able to repair all of errors in the data. Detailed comparison is reported in Appendix D.2.

CoDive algorithm also outperforms its active learning variant. Since ActiveLearning shares the same infrastructure as CoDive, here results are better *w.r.t.* RuleLearning and GDR. In fact, as for CoDive, whenever it terminated also ActiveLearning was able to repair all errors. ActiveLearning worked well in datasets with few rules, such as BUS and Synth 10k, while performed poorly in datasets with many rules like Hospital. Appendix C reports further details on active learning algorithm. Overall, however, benefit levels are lower. Hence, the active learning variant pays the price in terms of user-interactions of the additional training phase, which does not bring benefits *w.r.t.* CoDive.

Finally, CoDive outperforms Refine because of the less expressive language in the latter. While we discover rules using any combination of columns, Refine either generates rules for the entire column, which is unlikely to hold for data errors, or rules that update a single tuple. Single tuples updates are always correct and promptly validated, but their very small coverage leads to no benefit in using this tool.

Exp-4: Scalability. We report the performance of the lattice construction and maintenance in Figure 8. Times are reported in *ms* and the y axis is in log scale.

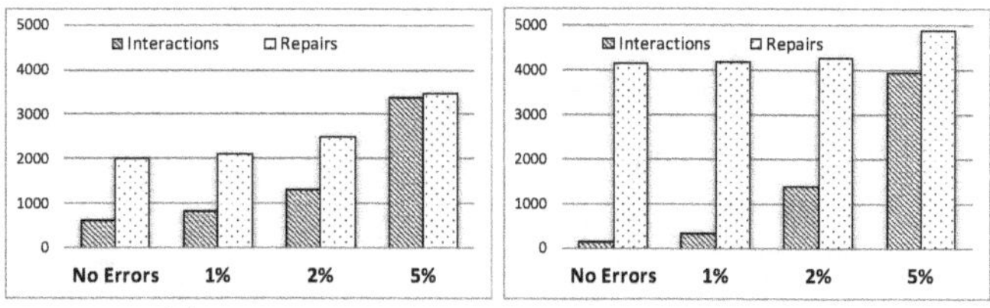

(a) Hospital (b) BUS

Figure 9: Impact of user mistakes.

We start by analyzing the impact of the techniques discussed in Section 5.1 for lattice maintenance. Figure 8(a) shows the total execution time for an update, defined as the time to create the lattice plus the time to update it with rules validated by the user in the interaction. We find it interesting to show that different updates can lead to very different execution times, because of the size of the queries involved in the lattice. Therefore, for the same scenario, we report both the execution times for the first user update, and corresponding interaction, and the times for the 4th user update. For all combinations of updates and scenarios, the incremental maintenance is 3–5 times faster than the naive solution that rebuilds the lattice for every rule validated by the user (4 times faster on average for the first five updates).

Creating the lattice requires to run queries to collect the data, and intersection over the sets of tuples to find the corresponding number of affected tuples for each node. When the dataset is large, the creation of the lattice can require a couple of seconds, as reported in Figure 8(b-c) for the average of the first ten updates. However, the creation is required only when a new user update is given, and the maintenance of the lattice in the rule validation always requires less than 20ms with our technique.

Finally, we study how the number of attributes in the dataset influences the performance. For this experiment we selected subsets of attributes of Hospital and also extended it with two more attributes by joining another table. Figure 8(d) shows the average times over the first five updates for the creation of the lattice and its maintenance with our technique. While the response time is always below 10ms, the creation of the lattice takes on average about 10 seconds, with a maximum of 30 seconds for the first user update. As discussed in Section 5.1.1, it is important to be able to identify the attributes of interest for the mining to limit the exponential explosion of the number of nodes in the lattice.

Exp-5: User Mistakes. We also tested the robustness of our approach *w.r.t.* to user-errors. That is, we do not assume that users always provide correct answers. On the contrary, assume users may sporadically make mistakes. These may be of two kinds, as follows. We notice that in both cases, our algorithm is essentially self-healing:

(i) The user performs a wrong update. This is the easier case, since we can expect that from a wrong update, only invalid rules are generated; these will be rejected by the user, and the error is fixed.

(ii) Following a valid update, the user wrongfully validates an invalid rule. This case in more delicate, since, following the wrong rule, the algorithm will indeed perform some incorrect updates. Overall, however, this will simply generate more dirtiness in the database, and the user still has a chance to correct this new dirtiness that s/he has introduced in the database in subsequent iterations.

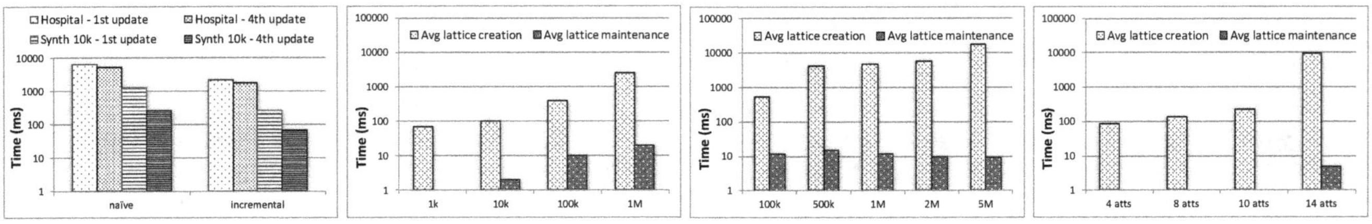

(a) Total execution time (ms) for i^{th} update: lattice creation + maintenance

(b) Avg execution time (ms) with increasing # of tuples for Synth (first 10 updates)

(c) Avg execution time (ms) with increasing # of tuples for DBLP (first 10 updates)

(d) Avg exec. time (ms) with increasing # of attributes for Hospital (first 10 updates)

Figure 8: Efficiency for the lattice creation and maintenance: Dive algorithm, unbounded B.

A key property is that the rules we discover at each step are applied only once – *i.e.,* during the step they were generated in – and therefore they can be fixed by further interaction. This requires that the user is requested to reconsider some previously updated cells. As a consequence, repair ratios decrease in case of errors. In addition, we need to prevent cyclic behaviors. To do this, the system checks updates and notifies users whenever it is updating a cell that has been repaired in previous iterations. This helps users to identify previous mistakes, and prevents cycles.

Figure 9 shows the impact of user mistakes. Assume that users made mistakes with a given probability – ranging from 1% to 5% – and compare results to the case without mistake. Experiments confirm that the system is able to recover from these errors, at the price of more user interactions.

7. RELATED WORK

Data transformation. Interactive systems for data transformation [27,37,44] also reason about the updated attribute to learn transformation rules. They mainly focus on string manipulation and reformatting at the text level. In contrast, we use more expressive SQL scripts. Consequently, we discover not only rules that contain one attribute that is being updated syntactically, but also rules that combine multiple attributes to semantically determine new repairs. Our language and algorithms can lead to smaller interaction cost, as discussed in Section 6 Exp-3.

Machine learning for cleaning. Given a set of user updates, they can be used as training data to train machine learning models, which in turn can be used to predict other repairs [41, 45]. However, ML models are typically *black-boxes* that identify updates without explanations, which are hard to be trusted by users, especially for critical applications that need repairs with guaranteed correctness. Instead, SQLU queries are declarative and are preferred for human validation. Moreover, to train a machine learning model with updates, they must be semantically consistent, *i.e.,* they refer to the same type of errors. In practice, however, this assumption does not always hold since multiple updates may refer to different types of errors. This heterogeneity may hinder the usability of the trained machine learning model for prediction. Different from them, FALCON is bootstrapped by a single update, and ensures the following interactions are related to the queries with consistent semantics.

Query by examples. Several proposals have exploited the opportunity of using examples to discover queries [2,8,9,38, 49,50], schema matchings [35,47], and schema mappings [4]. They mainly focus on finding how to join multiple tables. In contrast to them, we study how to discover SQLU queries on one table, with the main challenge of understanding the update semantics that is not considered by other approaches. From an algorithmic perspective, most of these approaches exploit active learning to validate with users informative examples; we show in Section 6 Exp-3 how other signals, such as correlation, can better guide the search in our setting.

Rule-based data cleaning. Rule-based approaches for data cleaning are divided between methods to discover the rules from clean data [11,12,17,25,40], and algorithms and systems to apply the rules over dirty data to automatically fix the detected errors [7,13,15,18,19,21,23,24,30,32,43,46]. Our proposal overcomes some of the shortcomings in these methods. In terms of rules discovery, mining on dirty data leads to a lot of useless rules, therefore most of the methods report effective results assuming a clean sample. On the contrary, we naturally start from dirty data. In terms of cleaning, we restrict our language to deterministic updates, which do no need variables or placeholders that the users ultimately have to manually verify. In terms of learning from user repairs, the closest approach to our solution is the use of previous repairs to model "repair preferences" [41]. However, this approach needs a set of rules to be given as input and it only refines them, without discovering new ones.

Closed frequent itemset. The concept of closed frequent itemset is widely used in data mining (see [48] for a survey), where it refers to a set of itemsets that are both frequent (*i.e.,* the support value is above a given threshold) and closed (*i.e.,* there is no superset that is closed). In fact, our closed rule set is inspired from closed frequent itemset, with the major difference that our data structure (*i.e.,* the lattice) keeps changing during interactions. Traditionally, the search space for closed frequent itemset in data ming is static.

8. CONCLUSION AND FUTURE WORK

We have presented FALCON, an interactive, declarative and deterministic data cleaning system. We have demonstrated that FALCON can effectively interact with users to generalize user-solicited updates, and clean-up data with a significant benefit *w.r.t.* the number of required interactions.

A number of possible future studies using FALCON are apparent. First of all, we plan to extend it by using external sources, as remarked in Appendix B. Moreover, we will leverage the information obtained from previous interactions with the user *w.r.t.* multiple data updates.

Acknowledgement. This work was partly supported by the 973 Program of China (2015CB358700), NSF of China (61422205, 61472198), Huawei, Shenzhou, Tencent, FDCT/116/2013/A3, MYRG105(Y1-L3)-FST13-GZ, National High-Tech R&D (863) Program of China (2012AA012600), and the Chinese Special Project of Science and Technology (2013zx01039-002-002).

9. REFERENCES

[1] S. Abiteboul, R. Hull, and V. Vianu. *Foundations of Databases*. Addison-Wesley, 1995.

[2] A. Abouzied, J. M. Hellerstein, and A. Silberschatz. Playful query specification with dataplay. *PVLDB*, 5(12):1938–1941, 2012.

[3] S. Albers. Online algorithms: a survey. *Math. Program.*, 97(1-2), 2003.

[4] B. Alexe, L. Chiticariu, R. J. Miller, and W. C. Tan. Muse: Mapping understanding and design by example. In *ICDE*, pages 10–19, 2008.

[5] C. Ambühl. Offline list update is np-hard. In *Algorithms - ESA 2000, 8th Annual European Symposium*, 2000.

[6] P. C. Arocena, B. Glavic, G. Mecca, R. J. Miller, P. Papotti, and D. Santoro. Messing up with BART: error generation for evaluating data-cleaning algorithms. *PVLDB*, 9(2), 2015.

[7] P. Bohannon, M. Flaster, W. Fan, and R. Rastogi. A cost-based model and effective heuristic for repairing constraints by value modification. In *SIGMOD*, 2005.

[8] A. Bonifati, R. Ciucanu, and S. Staworko. Interactive inference of join queries. In *EDBT*, 2014.

[9] A. Bonifati, R. Ciucanu, and S. Staworko. Interactive join query inference with JIM. *PVLDB*, 7(13), 2014.

[10] C. Chang and C. Lin. LIBSVM: A library for support vector machines. *ACMTIST*, 2(3):27, 2011.

[11] F. Chiang and R. J. Miller. Discovering data quality rules. *PVLDB*, 1(1), 2008.

[12] X. Chu, I. F. Ilyas, and P. Papotti. Discovering denial constraints. *PVLDB*, 6(13), 2013.

[13] M. Dallachiesa, A. Ebaid, A. Eldawy, A. K. Elmagarmid, I. F. Ilyas, M. Ouzzani, and N. Tang. NADEEF: a commodity data cleaning system. In *SIGMOD*, 2013.

[14] O. Deshpande, D. S. Lamba, M. Tourn, S. Das, S. Subramaniam, A. Rajaraman, V. Harinarayan, and A. Doan. Building, maintaining, and using knowledge bases: A report from the trenches. In *SIGMOD*, 2013.

[15] A. Ebaid, A. K. Elmagarmid, I. F. Ilyas, M. Ouzzani, J. Quiané-Ruiz, N. Tang, and S. Yin. NADEEF: A generalized data cleaning system. *PVLDB*, 6(12):1218–1221, 2013.

[16] W. Fan, F. Geerts, X. Jia, and A. Kementsietsidis. Conditional functional dependencies for capturing data inconsistencies. *ACM Trans. Database Syst.*, 33(2), 2008.

[17] W. Fan, F. Geerts, J. Li, and M. Xiong. Discovering conditional functional dependencies. *IEEE Trans. Knowl. Data Eng.*, 23(5), 2011.

[18] W. Fan, F. Geerts, N. Tang, and W. Yu. Inferring data currency and consistency for conflict resolution. In *ICDE*, 2013.

[19] W. Fan, J. Li, S. Ma, N. Tang, and W. Yu. Interaction between record matching and data repairing. In *SIGMOD*, 2011.

[20] W. Fan, J. Li, S. Ma, N. Tang, and W. Yu. Towards certain fixes with editing rules and master data. *VLDB J.*, 21(2), 2012.

[21] H. Galhardas, D. Florescu, D. Shasha, E. Simon, and C.-A. Saita. Declarative data cleaning: Language, model, and algorithms. In *VLDB*, 2001.

[22] F. Geerts, G. Mecca, P. Papotti, and D. Santoro. The LLUNATIC data-cleaning framework. *PVLDB*, 6(9), 2013.

[23] F. Geerts, G. Mecca, P. Papotti, and D. Santoro. Mapping and Cleaning. In *ICDE*, pages 232–243, 2014.

[24] F. Geerts, G. Mecca, P. Papotti, and D. Santoro. That's all folks! LLUNATIC goes open source. *PVLDB*, 7(13):1565–1568, 2014.

[25] L. Golab, H. J. Karloff, F. Korn, B. Saha, and D. Srivastava. Discovering conservation rules. In *ICDE*, 2012.

[26] A. Y. Halevy. Answering queries using views: A survey. *VLDB J.*, 10(4), 2001.

[27] J. Heer, J. M. Hellerstein, and S. Kandel. Predictive interaction for data transformation. In *CIDR*, 2015.

[28] A. Heise, J. Quiané-Ruiz, Z. Abedjan, A. Jentzsch, and F. Naumann. Scalable discovery of unique column combinations. *PVLDB*, 7(4), 2013.

[29] I. F. Ilyas, V. Markl, P. J. Haas, P. Brown, and A. Aboulnaga. CORDS: automatic discovery of correlations and soft functional dependencies. In *SIGMOD*, pages 647–658, 2004.

[30] M. Interlandi and N. Tang. Proof positive and negative in data cleaning. In *ICDE*, 2015.

[31] S. Kandel, A. Paepcke, J. M. Hellerstein, and J. Heer. Enterprise data analysis and visualization: An interview study. *IEEE Trans. Vis. Comput. Graph.*, 18(12), 2012.

[32] Z. Khayyat, I. F. Ilyas, A. Jindal, S. Madden, M. Ouzzani, J.-A. Quiane-Ruiz, P. Papotti, N. Tang, and S. Yin. BigDansing: a system for big data cleansing. In *SIGMOD*, 2015.

[33] J. Manyika. Big data: The next frontier for innovation, competition, and productivity. Technical report, McKinsey Global Institute, 2011.

[34] C. H. Papadimitriou. *Computational Complexity*. Addison Wesley, 1994.

[35] L. Qian, M. J. Cafarella, and H. V. Jagadish. Sample-driven schema mapping. In *SIGMOD*, pages 73–84, 2012.

[36] G. Ramalingam and T. W. Reps. A categorized bibliography on incremental computation. In *POPL*, 1993.

[37] V. Raman and J. M. Hellerstein. Potter's wheel: An interactive data cleaning system. In *VLDB*, pages 381–390, 2001.

[38] Y. Shen, K. Chakrabarti, S. Chaudhuri, B. Ding, and L. Novik. Discovering queries based on example tuples. In *SIGMOD*, pages 493–504, 2014.

[39] D. D. Sleator and R. E. Tarjan. Amortized efficiency of list update and paging rules. *Commun. ACM*, 28(2), 1985.

[40] S. Song and L. Chen. Efficient discovery of similarity constraints for matching dependencies. *Data Knowl. Eng.*, 87, 2013.

[41] M. Volkovs, F. Chiang, J. Szlichta, and R. J. Miller. Continuous data cleaning. In *ICDE*, 2014.

[42] J. Wang, J. Han, and J. Pei. CLOSET+: searching for the best strategies for mining frequent closed itemsets. In *SIGKDD*, 2003.

[43] J. Wang and N. Tang. Towards dependable data repairing with fixing rules. In *SIGMOD*, 2014.

[44] B. Wu and C. A. Knoblock. An iterative approach to synthesize data transformation programs. In *IJCAI*, pages 1726–1732, 2015.

[45] M. Yakout, L. Berti-Equille, and A. K. Elmagarmid. Don't be scared: use scalable automatic repairing with maximal likelihood and bounded changes. In *SIGMOD*, pages 553–564, 2013.

[46] M. Yakout, A. K. Elmagarmid, J. Neville, M. Ouzzani, and I. F. Ilyas. Guided data repair. *PVLDB*, 2011.

[47] Z. Yan, N. Zheng, Z. G. Ives, P. P. Talukdar, and C. Yu. Actively soliciting feedback for query answers in keyword search-based data integration. *PVLDB*, 6(3):205–216, 2013.

[48] M. J. Zaki and W. Meira. *Data Mining and Analysis: Fundamental Concepts and Algorithms*. Cambridge University Press, 2014.

[49] M. Zhang, H. Elmeleegy, C. M. Procopiuc, and D. Srivastava. Reverse engineering complex join queries. In *SIGMOD*, 2013.

[50] M. M. Zloof. Query by example. In *AFIPS*. ACM, 1975.

APPENDIX

A. SUMMARY OF NOTATION

We summarize the notations used in the paper in Table 3.

Symbol	Description
Q	a SQLU query, or a data quality rule
$Q(T)$	affected tuples of Q over table T
$Q_1 \preceq Q_2$	Q_1 is contained by Q_2
attr(Q)	attributes in the WHERE condition of Q
Δ: $t[A] \leftarrow a'$	an update of $t[A]$ to a'
$(\mathcal{Q}, \preceq)$ *w.r.t.* Δ	a lattice of queries $\mathcal{Q}$ on partial order $\preceq$
$Q^{\curlyvee}$ ($\mathcal{Q}^{\curlyvee}$)	the set of queries that Q (queries $\mathcal{Q}$) contains
$Q_{\curlywedge}$ ($\mathcal{Q}_{\curlywedge}$)	the set of queries that contains Q (queries $\mathcal{Q}$)

Table 3: Notations used in the paper.

Indicators				AttributeValues				Original	Updated
D	M	L	Q	D	M	L	Q	M	M
1	2	1	0	11 Nov	statin	Austin	null	statin	$C_{22}H_{28}F$

Table 4: Features of node DML.

B. USING EXTERNAL SOURCES

In this section, we discuss an extension of our system when external sources are present. Often times, external sources (*e.g.*, master data) are available and contain high quality data. Next, we shall discuss how to leverage such information by FALCON.

Consider a dirty table T with schema R and master data M with schema R_m. Assume without loss of generality that $|R| = |R_m|$, and the alignment of attribute from each attribute $A \in R$ to $A \in R'$ is given. For all other attributes in either relation that are not aligned will be ignored. Moreover, given the update $\Delta : t[A] \leftarrow a'$, we assume that $A \in R$.

UPDATE T SET $T.A = M.A'$

FROM T, M WHERE $T[X] = M[X']$

Note that, differently from the SQLU queries defined in Section 2.1, we enforce the condition that $A \notin X$. The reason is that we assume that master data contains only correct values, but not errors. In such case, the number of potential queries is $2^{|R|-1}$, which is the number of all combinations of attributes in $R\backslash\{A\}$.

From the extension, we can repair errors from instance level to schema level by using the same lattice and the same algorithms.

C. ACTIVE LEARNING APPROACH

Active learning is a special case of semi-supervised machine learning with the goal of substantially reducing the number of labelling when training a model. All the labels for learning are obtained without reference to the learning algorithm, while in active learning the learner interactively chooses which data points to label. The hope of active learning is that interaction can substantially reduce the number of labels required. The method relies on interactively querying the user for labelling the data trying to maximize the benefit for the actual learning algorithm.

We adopt a similar idea in our setting, as described below.

In order to use active learning in our problem, *i.e.*, to predict that which node (or query) in the lattice is valid or invalid, we face two main issues to be addressed.

(1) We need to generate features for nodes in the lattice, which are used to capture their characteristics.

Rank	Attributes Set	Correlation
1	{Stadium, Club Country}	1
2	{Soccer Manager, Soccer Club }	1
3	{Stadium, Soccer Club}	0.822
4	{Stadium, Soccer Manager}	0.789
5	{Stadium, Soccer Club, Soccer Manager}	0.654
...	...	...
99	{Stadium, Playercountry, Soccer Club}	0.303
100	{Stadium, Position}	0.006

Table 5: Correlation of attributes in Soccer dataset when Stadium is updated.

(2) We need to use these features to select the node with the maximum benefit to be labelled, which is then interact with users to verify the selected node.

We explain in more detail about the implementation of the above two steps below.

Feature Selection. We generate a number of features for each node Q and train a Support Vector Machine (SVM) model with LIBSVM [10]. For a node Q, the features include attribute indicator, attribute value, the original value before the update, and the updated value. Attribute indicator indicates whether the attribute is included in the node (rule): if included, the indicator is 1; 0 otherwise. While if the attribute is being updated, the indicator value is 2.

Question Generation. There are two phases in question generation. First, in the initial 20 user updates, we use Ducc to explore the lattice to label the nodes, taking the nodes (and the corresponding features) from the user labelling as the training data to train a SVM model that bootstraps the active learning. Second, in each iteration, we apply the SVM model to predict the label and corresponding probability of each node, and select the node with the highest probability of being valid (reported by SVM) to ask users. After obtaining a label from user, we use **lattice pruning** technique (discussed in Section 3) to label other nodes in the lattice and add them to existing training data to re-train the SVM model.

We illustrate by an example for the active learning method.

Example 12: Consider node DML in Figure 2. Firstly, we generate features as illustrated in Table 4. Attribute indicator of D is 1 because node DML includes attribute D, indicator of M is 2 since it is the updated attribute. Attribute values are the corresponding values taken from the update Δ_3 in Example 1. The original value and updated value for the update are shown in the table.

Secondly, in each iteration, we apply SVM model to predict the probability of being valid of each node in the lattice. Suppose node ML has the highest probability to be valid that is 0.78. We then ask the user to label node ML and, since in our example the node is valid, we label all nodes above ML, *i.e.*, {ML, DML, MLQ, DMLQ} to be valid and we add them to re-train the SVM model.

D. ADDITIONAL EXPERIMENTS

D.1 Correlation Score Results

Correlation guides the search to nodes that are likely to have a semantic connection. How to compute correlation

	Soccer		Hospital		Synth 10k		Synth 1M		DBLP		BUS	
	U	A	U	A	U	A	U	A	U	A	U	A
DFS	11	33	**129**	**387**	177	531	5094	15282	1462	4386	3646	10938
BFS	82	246	423	1269	729	2187	14035	42105	1338	4014	4172	12516
Ducc	25	75	**129**	**387**	70	210	3083	9249	1122	3036	3646	10938
Dive	15	41	219	657	29	87	**74**	**222**	462	1386	312	936
CoDive	**8**	**19**	206	412	**24**	**72**	**74**	**222**	**140**	**420**	**48**	**144**
$\|Q(T)\|$	82		2000		1640		15000		6086		4172	

Table 6: Comparison of the lattice search algorithms with $B = 3$: U is the number of user updates, A is the number of user answers, and $|Q(T)|$ is the total number of errors.

	Soccer		Hospital		Synth 10k		Synth 1M		DBLP		BUS	
	T_C	*Rep*	T_C	*Rep*	T_C	*Rep*	T_C	*Rep*	T_C	*Rep*	T_C	*Rep*
CoDive B=5	**49**	82	**567**	2000	**70**	1640	**394**	15000	**560**	6086	**96**	4172
Refine	132	82	4000	2000	2470	1640	13326	15000	12172	6086	7258	4172
Rule Learning	194	27	315	500	474	1212	4800	15000	502	0	1191	757
GDR	225	30	1025	500	1578	943	-	-	-	-	-	-
Active Learning	217	82	2157	2000	214	1640	-	-	-	-	1220	4172
$\|Q(T)\|$	82		2000		1640		15000		6086		4172	

Table 7: Comparison of the baselines. Here T_C is the total interaction cost for the user, *Rep* is the number of repaired cells, and $|Q(T)|$ is the number of errors.

is discussed in Section 4.2.2 to improve the binary jump strategy. This is crucial in order to discover set of attributes that form rules that are worth validating with the user. Note that if many null values are present, we only count non-null values, and the attributes with many null values will have low correlation score. To clarify the role of the correlation score, consider the following example.

Δ_1: t_1[Stadium] ← "Volkswagen Arena" (from "Weserstadion")

The user updates attribute Stadium. Table 5 shows a summary of the correlation scores, relative to attribute Stadium, for attributes in the Soccer dataset. Every set of attributes in the table can be seen as the left hand side attributes to form a FD. In fact, we know the conclusion of the rule for the given update (the Stadium attribute), but we do not know which attributes to use in the premise of the rule. From the correlation scores, we can deduce that each Stadium usually belongs to one Soccer Club and has one Soccer Manager, while each Stadium could have many Positions. Thus the correlation score of Stadium, SoccerClub, SoccerManager (row with rank 5) is much larger than that of Stadium and Position (row at rank 100). Our algorithm uses this intuition to guide the search strategy, and the experiment results also verify that the correlations are effective in avoiding rules that are unlikely to be validated by the user, such as the one deriving from row at rank 100.

D.2 More Details on Exp-1 and Exp-3

We now discuss in more details the different search algorithms and baselines for all datasets.

As reported in Table 6, all search algorithms, with the exception of BFS, lead to a clean dataset with a number of user updates U that is smaller than the number of errors in the data ($|Q(T)|$, reported at the bottom). When considering the user answers (A), their number is from 4 to 68 times smaller than the cost of manually fixing the errors (without any rule nor tool), when considering the best performing algorithm (numbers in bold). In particular, both for number of required updates and for number of required answers, CoDive is always the method with the lowest effort, with the exception of the Hospital dataset. In this case, DFS and Ducc perform better because of the simple rules that have been used to model the injection of the errors in the data. All rules for this dataset have only one or two attributes in the left hand side of the rules, such as Zip → State or Address, City → State. In these cases, the correct rules are at the bottom of the lattice, which is the level that DFS and Ducc explore first. On the contrary, if our algorithms miss the correct node at the bottom, they would start exploring the rest of the lattice and converge to the bottom again slowly, thus with a larger number of questions. Notice that, as discussed in Exp-2, the closed rule sets optimization shows a significant improvement on the Hospital scenario for the DFS algorithm.

We also remark that the Hospital dataset has a number of rather specific features. This dataset was created by joining several tables, originally in normal form, in order to obtain a large number of functional dependencies and redundancy in the data for testing rule-based data repair algorithms [20,22]. Given the highly denormalized table resulting from these joins, the dataset should not be considered representative of a standard data cleaning task.

Table 7 reports the results for CoDive compared with the baselines. Missing numbers denote cases for which the tool was stopped after the fixed timeout (two hours) for all tests. We observe that Rule Learning and GDR were not able to cover all errors because of the limited scope of the discovered rules. This is due to the limited size of the sample used in mining. A larger sample would lead to better results in terms of recall, but with a higher cost for the collection of the clean tuples. Refine is always able to detect all errors, but with a much larger number of interaction because of its less expressive language, compared to CoDive. Finally, active learning has worse performance *w.r.t.* CoDive because of required training data, and in two cases with large dataset it was not able to terminate before the timeout.

Sequential Data Cleaning: A Statistical Approach

Aoqian Zhang Shaoxu Song Jianmin Wang
Tsinghua National Laboratory for Information Science and Technology
KLiss, MoE; School of Software, Tsinghua University, China
{zaq13, sxsong, jimwang}@tsinghua.edu.cn

ABSTRACT

Errors are prevalent in data sequences, such as GPS trajectories or sensor readings. Existing methods on cleaning sequential data employ a constraint on value changing speeds and perform constraint-based repairing. While such speed constraints are effective in identifying large spike errors, the small errors that do not significantly deviate from the truth and indeed satisfy the speed constraints can hardly be identified and repaired. To handle such small errors, in this paper, we propose a statistical based cleaning method. Rather than declaring a broad constraint of max/min speeds, we model the probability distribution of speed changes. The repairing problem is thus to maximize the likelihood of the sequence w.r.t. the probability of speed changes. We formalize the likelihood-based cleaning problem, show its NP-hardness, devise exact algorithms, and propose several approximate/heuristic methods to trade off effectiveness for efficiency. Experiments on real data sets (in various applications) demonstrate the superiority of our proposal.

1. INTRODUCTION

Data sequences are often found with dirty or imprecise values, such as GPS trajectories or sensor reading sequences [8]. According to the survey [10], even the data of stock prices could be dirty. For instance, the price of SALVEPAR (SY) is misused as the price of SYBASE, which is denoted by SY as well in some sources. (See more examples below.)

To clean dirty data, constraint-based repairing is often employed [1]. Existing study [14] on sequential data cleaning considers the constraints on speeds of value changes, namely speed constraints. For example, the speed constraints on fuel meter values state that the fuel consumption of a crane should not be negative and not exceed 40 liters per hour. Constraint-based cleaning identifies the violations to such speed constraints and (minimally) modify the values so that the repaired results satisfy the specified speed constraints.

While speed constraints can successfully identify large spike errors (see examples below), the constraint-based cleaning repairs the dirty point to a value w.r.t. maximum/minimum speeds. As indicated in [14], the repair strategy of adjusting the value to the maximum/minimum allowed is made referring to the minimum change principle in data repairing [1]. The rationale is that people or systems try to minimize mistakes in practice. This minimum change principle is widely considered in repairing relational data [1, 3]. As the first application of the minimum change principle to sequential data [14], it unfortunately leads to the aforesaid repair strategy of choosing the maximum/minimum allowable values.

An alternative approach is to consider the average of the previous values as a repair, a.k.a. smoothing methods [2, 6]. For example, the simple moving average (SMA) [2] smooths time series data by computing the unweighted mean of the last k points. Instead of weighting equally, the exponentially weighted moving average (EWMA) [6] assigns exponentially decreasing weights over time. As indicated in [14], the problem of the smoothing methods is over-repairing, i.e., almost all the data points are modified, most of which are indeed correct originally and do not need repair.

Moreover, the speed constraints fail to identify the small errors that do not significantly deviate from the original values, and indeed satisfy the speed constraints. The small errors are particularly important in some applications. For instance, a deviation of 1m in GPS readings is prevalent and small relative to 10m large spikes. Such a small error (1m), however, is critical in car localization for automatic driving. Moreover, aggregating a large number of small errors, data mining results could be seriously misled, e.g., unable to form meaningful clusters over imprecise GPS readings with many small errors [13]. Our results in Section 6.3 also show that repairing small errors could improve the accuracy of prediction application.

Instead of considering the aforesaid max/min speeds, in this paper, we propose a novel statistical-based cleaning by introducing the likelihoods w.r.t. various speeds. Let us first illustrate a motivation example below.

Example 1. *Figure 1 presents a sequence of stock prices. Two dirty values appear at time point 1547 and 1569, respectively, in the observed sequence (in black, the corresponding true values are presented in blue).*

Existing speed constraint-based cleaning (SCREEN) [14] employs the maximum and minimum speed constraints, denoting the largest rates of allowed (stock price) value increase and decrease, respectively.

1) A violation to the speed constraints is detected at time 1547, whose value decrease exceeds the minimum speed constraint. The value of time point 1547 is thus repaired to a

SIGMOD'16, June 26-July 01, 2016, San Francisco, CA, USA

DOI: http://dx.doi.org/10.1145/2882903.2915233

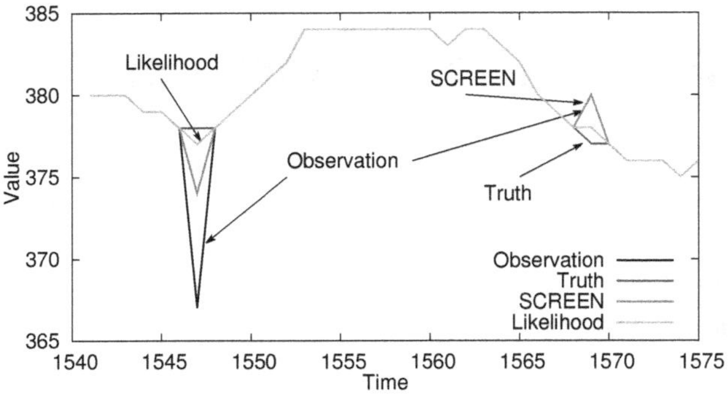

Figure 1: Speed constraint-based cleaning (SCREEN) can identify the large spike error but repair it w.r.t. the max/min speed constraints. The small error that does not significantly deviate the original values cannot be identified.

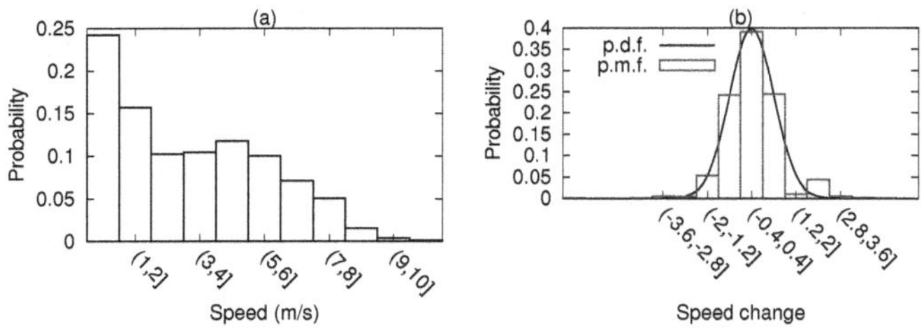

Figure 2: Probability distributions of (a) speeds and (b) speed changes, on a real GPS dataset presented in Section 6

new value w.r.t. this minimum speed constraint. Since the max/min speeds may not be reached all the time in practice, the repairs w.r.t. the max/min speed constraints could be away from the truth.

2) Moreover, the small error at time point 1569 indeed satisfies the max/min speed constraints, and thus is not detected as violations and not repaired.

By considering likelihoods w.r.t. various speeds (see detailed definition and discussion below), our proposed method computes a most likely repair , instead of a repair restricted to the max/min speed constraints.

Defining the likelihood of a repair w.r.t. various speeds is non-trivial. It is not rational by simply measuring the probabilities of speeds. The reason is that max/min speeds may also appear with considerably high probability. For example, stock prices increase in daily limit (max speed) in a period, or a car drives in its max speed in highway. As shown in Figure 2(a), the speed probabilities are almost equal, e.g., from 3 to 7. The probabilities of speeds may not be able to distinguish the likelihoods of various repairs.

Intuitively, while speeds capture the *change of values* in consecutive data points, we may also consider the relationships of speeds between data points in a sequence, i.e., modeling the *change of speeds*. The rationale behind is that the change of speeds in consecutive data points (roughly interpreted as acceleration) should not be significant. As shown in Figure 2(b), 90% speed changes are within [-1.2, 1.2].

Enlightened by the aforesaid discipline of non-significant speed changes, we employ the probability distribution of speed changes, and calculate the likelihood of a sequence w.r.t. the speed changes (see example in Figure 4 in Example 2 below). The cleaning problem is thus to find a repaired sequence with larger speed change likelihood.

Contributions

Our major contributions in this paper are summarized as:

1) We formalize the problem of repairing sequential data with the maximum likelihood (Problem 1), show its NP-hardness (Theorem 1), and introduce a pseudo-polynomial time algorithm for computing the optimal solution (Proposition 2). Efficient pruning is also devised.

2) We devise a quadratic-time constant-factor approximation algorithm (Proposition 5), again together with efficient pruning. To further accelerate the computing, a linear-time heuristic is proposed (Proposition 4).

3) We approximate the discrete probability distribution of speed changes by a continuous probability distribution, to support even faster computing. With a proper continuous probability distribution, we show that the maximum likelihood repairing problem is indeed transformed to a quadratic programming problem (Proposition 8). Efficient solvers and simple fast greedy heuristics are directly applicable.

4) We report an extensive experimental evaluation on three real datasets in different scenarios: i) To evaluate the performance over various errors, the first dataset STOCK is originally clean and injected with various errors. ii) To evaluate real errors, the second dataset collects GPS trajectories with errors naturally embedded, and the corresponding truth manually labelled. iii) To apply the methods in practice, the third experiment performs on a real dataset ENGINE with both unknown errors and unknown truth. The performance is evaluated on an application over the data with and without repairing. The results demonstrate that our proposal achieves better performance in both repair accuracy and application accuracy.

The remainder of this paper is organized as follows. We first introduce the preliminaries and problem statement in Section 2. The exact and approximate solutions are then presented in Sections 3 and 4, respectively. Section 5 develops the repairing over the continuous probability distribution. The experimental evaluation is reported in Section 6. Finally, we discuss the related studies in Section 7, and conclude the paper in Section 8. Table 3 in the Appendix lists the notations frequently used in this paper.

2. PROBLEM STATEMENT

2.1 Preliminaries

Consider a sequence $x = x[1], x[2], \ldots$, where each $x[i]$ is the value of the i-th data point from a finite domain. For brevity, we write $x[i]$ as x_i, and $x_{i\ldots j}$ denoting the subsequence $x_i, x_{i+1}, \ldots x_j$ of x.

Each x_i is associated with a timestamp t_i, and an error range θ_i. The error range, e.g., specified by engineering tolerance, denotes that the true value x'_i of i-th data point may be in the range of $[x_i - \theta_i, x_i + \theta_i]$, denoted by $x'_i \in [x_i \pm \theta_i]$. While some data sequences may have individual θ_i for each data point i, e.g., indicated as "accuracy" in GPS readings, others may specify a single $\theta_{\max}$ denoting the maximum error range for all the data points in the sequence, such as in sensor readings.

Referring to [14], the speed is defined on the *change of*

value, e.g., $v_{i-1,i} = \frac{x_i - x_{i-1}}{t_i - t_{i-1}}$ from data point $i-1$ to i. Let

$$u_i = v_{i,i+1} - v_{i-1,i} = \frac{x_{i+1} - x_i}{t_{i+1} - t_i} - \frac{x_i - x_{i-1}}{t_i - t_{i-1}} \quad (1)$$

denote the *change of speed* before and after the i-th point.

The likelihood $L(x)$ of a sequence x w.r.t. speed changes is

$$L(x) = \sum_{i=2}^{n-1} L(u_i) = \sum_{i=2}^{n-1} \log P(u_i), \quad (2)$$

where $P(u_i)$ denotes the probability of speed change u_i, and $L(u_i)$ denotes the corresponding (log) likelihood. The empirical probability distribution P on speed changes can be estimated simply by statistics on the sequence.

Example 2 (Probability distribution and likelihood computation). *Consider a sequence* $x = \{11, 12, 15, 14, 15, 15, 17\}$*, with timestamps* $t = \{1, 2, 3, 4, 5, 6, 7\}$*. Figure 3(a) illustrates the data points (in black) and Figure 4 shows the corresponding probability distribution of speed changes.*

The probability of speed change on the 3rd point (x_3) is

$$P(u_3) = P(\frac{14-15}{4-3} - \frac{15-12}{3-2}) = P(-4) = 0.1,$$

with likelihood $L(u_3) = \log(0.1) = -1.2$*. By similarly computing the likelihoods on other data points, we have the likelihood of the sequence x, i.e.,* $L(x) = \log(0.25) + \log(0.1) + \log(0.25) + \log(0.2) + \log(0.25) = -8.1$.

Indeed, the 3rd data point is dirty with error value $x_3 = 15$*. The corresponding truth value should be* $x'_3 = 13$ *instead. With this truth value, the likelihood is* $L(x') = 3 * \log(0.3) + \log(0.2) + \log(0.25) = -6.6$*, which is higher than* $L(x)$ *of the aforesaid x with dirty value.*

Referring to formula (2), the likelihood $L(x)$ is computed by the summation over the probabilities of speed changes $P(u_i)$. Consider the probability distribution of speed changes in Figure 4 for Example 2. The maximum likelihood will be reached when the probability of speed change $P(u_i)$ is maximized for each u_i, i.e., having speed change $u_i \in (-1, 1]$ with $P(u_i) = 0.3$. Consequently, the maximum likelihood is $L(x^*) = 5 * \log(0.3) \approx -6.0$.

2.2 Repair Problem

Following the intuition (presented in Figure 2 in the introduction) that speeds should not change significantly before and after a data point, we propose to find a repaired sequence x' of x such that the likelihood w.r.t. speed changes increases. On the other hand, referring to the minimum change principle in data repairing [1], a repaired sequence x' close to x is preferred. Therefore, as in [14], we also consider the repair cost from x to x'

$$\Delta(x, x') = \sum_{i=1}^{n} |x'_i - x_i|.$$

Following the same line of maximal likelihood repairing over relational data [15], we describe the problem of likelihood-based repairing over sequential data as follows. (See Section 7 for a discussion on the difference between likelihood-based relational and sequential data repairing.)

Problem 1. *Given a finite sequence x of n data points and a repair cost budget* δ*, the* maximum likelihood repair *problem is to find a repair* x' *such that* $\Delta(x, x') \le \delta$ *and the likelihood* $L(x')$ *is maximized.*

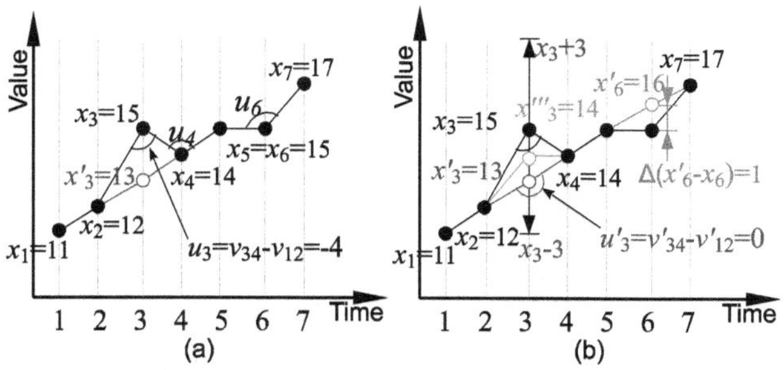

Figure 3: Possible repairs of an example sequence

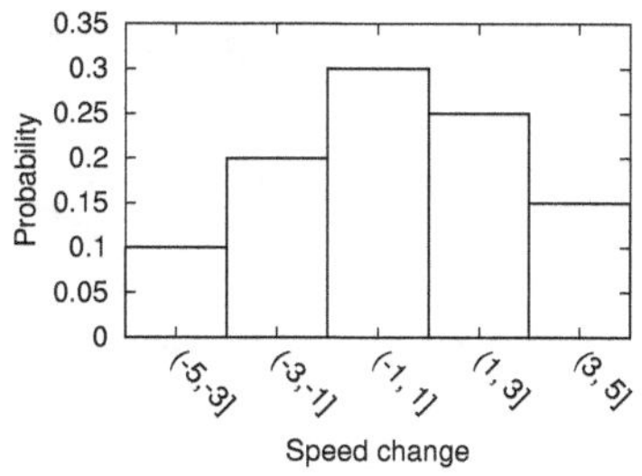

Figure 4: Probability distribution of speed changes

It is worth noting that the bound δ on repair cost is often necessary to avoid over-repaired results (see example below). As illustrated in Section 6, such a budget threshold could be practically determined by observing the likelihoods of returned repair results.

We formalize the repair problem as follows.

$$\begin{aligned} \max \quad & \sum_{i=2}^{n-1} \log P\left(\frac{x'_{i+1} - x'_i}{t_{i+1} - t_i} - \frac{x'_i - x'_{i-1}}{t_i - t_{i-1}}\right) && (3) \\ \text{s.t.} \quad & \sum_{i=1}^{n} |x'_i - x_i| \le \delta \\ & x'_i \in [x_i \pm \theta_i] && 1 \le i \le n \end{aligned}$$

Example 3 (Repair and cost). *Consider the sequence in Figure 1, a real segment from the STOCK*[1] *dataset, with probability distribution on speed changes in Figure 9(a). The error range is* $\theta_i = 12$ *for all the data points i. That is, a value in the range of* $[x_i - 12, x_i + 12]$*, simply denoted by* $[x_i \pm 12]$*, could be considered as a repair* x'_i *of* x_i.

Given a small repair cost budget, e.g., $\delta = 5$*, referring to the optimization problem in formula (3), a repair* x' *will be returned, with four points changed at time 1553, 1561, 1569 and 1573, as shown in Figure 5. It has repair cost* $\Delta(x, x') = |x_{1553} - x'_{1553}| + |x_{1561} - x'_{1561}| + |x_{1569} - x'_{1569}| + |x_{1573} - x'_{1573}| = 5 \le \delta$*, with the maximized likelihood* $L(x') = -50.1$*. It is notable that the large spike at time 1547 could not be repaired under this small budget.*

On the other hand, if the repair cost budget is too large, e.g., $\delta = 35$*, a repair* x' *with a large number of modified points is returned. The corresponding repair cost is* $\Delta(x, x') = 33 \le \delta$*, with the maximized likelihood* $L(x') = -27.0$.

Intuitively, we would consider a "proper" setting of repair cost budget, e.g., $\delta = 15$*, which is neither too small*

[1]http://finance.yahoo.com/q/hp?s=AIP.L+Historical+Prices

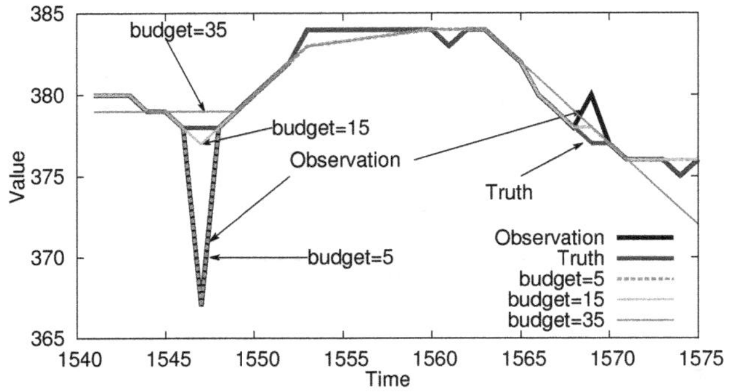

Figure 5: Example repairs with various repair cost budgets δ

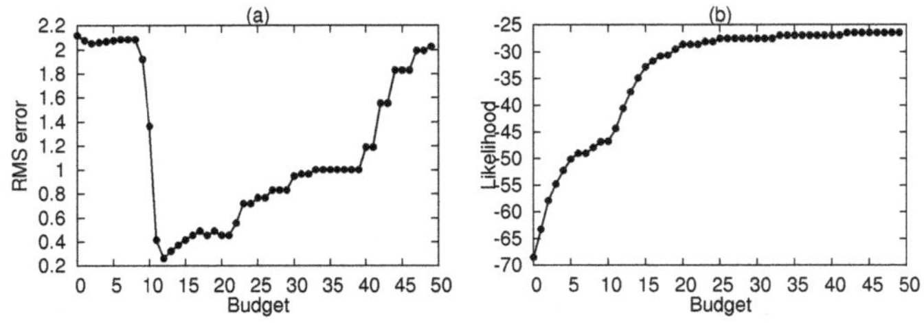

Figure 6: Repair result (a) error and (b) likelihood under various repair cost budgets δ

($\delta = 5$ with data points barely repaired and low returned likelihood) nor too large ($\delta = 35$ with data points over repaired but no significant likelihood improvement). Following this guideline, a good δ could be practically chosen by observing the repair likelihoods returned together with the repair results. For instance, the likelihood does not significantly increase by setting δ from 15 to 20 in Figure 6(b). That is, with δ in the range from 15 to 20, the data is neither insufficiently repaired (with a low likelihood) nor over-repaired (with too large repair cost budget but no much likelihood gain). Thereby, the corresponding repair result error (see Section 6.1 for formal definition) is low in Figure 6(a). (Similar results are also observed in other real datasets in Section 6, which verify again the guideline on selecting a proper repair cost budget δ.)

3. EXACT SOLUTION

In this section, we first prove the NP-hardness of the maximum likelihood repair problem, which motivates us to devise a pseudo-polynomial time algorithm based on dynamic programming in Section 3.2.

3.1 Hardness

Consider the sequence $x = \{11, 12, 15, 14, 15, 15, 17\}$ in Example 2. Suppose that the error range is $\theta_i = 3$ for all the data points i. That is, for each point x_i, there are 7 potential modifications, $x'_i = \{x_i - 3, \dots, x_i + 3\}$. A large number of 7^7 combinations could be considered as possible repairs. In particular, the repairing of x'_i is affected by the choices of x'_{i-1} and x'_{i+1} w.r.t. the speed change probability (in Figure 4). Intuitively, we can build a reduction from the 0/1 knapsack problem, by modeling the item values as the speed change probabilities, and thus show the hardness of our repairing problem.

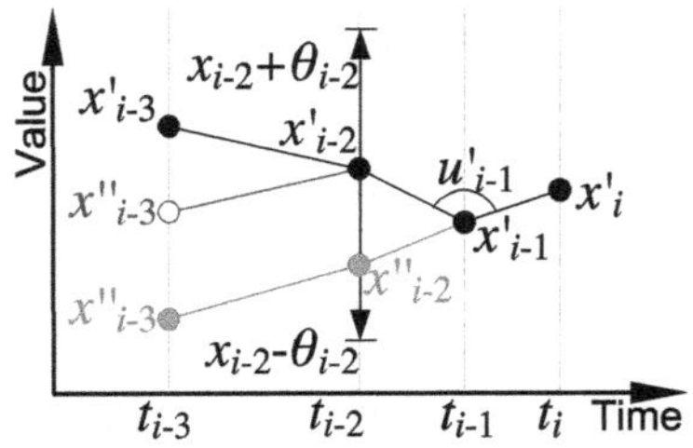

Figure 7: Recurrence equation

Theorem 1. *Given a sequence x with error range θ, repair cost budget δ, and likelihood threshold ℓ, the problem is NP-complete to determine whether exists a repair x' of x such that $\Delta(x, x') \le \delta$ and $L(x') \ge \ell$.*

3.2 Exact Algorithm

Referring to the aforesaid hardness on the maximum likelihood repair problem, we introduce a pseudo-polynomial time algorithm based on dynamic programming. Let us first illustrate the recurrence equation, upon which the dynamic programming algorithm naturally conducts. The correctness is also analyzed in the proof of Proposition 2.

3.2.1 Recurrence Equation

Intuitively, referring to formulas (1) and (2), the speed change and the corresponding likelihood on a point i are determined together with the preceding point $i-1$ and the successive point $i+1$. As illustrated in Figure 7, by considering one additional data point, say i, in the recurrence of dynamic programming, a new likelihood $L(u'_{i-1})$ defined on data point $i-1$ is introduced. Thereby, to find an optimal solution, we need to consider possible x'_{i-2}, x'_{i-1}, x'_i values in each recurrence.

Let $x'_{1\dots i}$ be a repair of the subsequence $x_{1\dots i}$ with the maximum likelihood $L(x'_{1\dots i})$, whose cost is $\Delta(x'_{1\dots i}, x_{1\dots i}) = c_i$, and the last two values of $x'_{1\dots i}$ are x'_{i-1}, x'_i, respectively. We denote this maximum likelihood $L(x'_{1\dots i})$ by $D(i, c_i, x'_{i-1}, x'_i)$.

The recurrence computation is as follows

$$D(i, c_i, x'_{i-1}, x'_i) \tag{4}$$
$$= \max_{x'_{i-2} \in [x_{i-2} \pm \theta_{i-2}]} D(i-1, c_{i-1}, x'_{i-2}, x'_{i-1}) + L(u'_{i-1})$$

where $c_{i-1} = c_i - \Delta(x'_i, x_i)$, and $u'_{i-1} = \frac{x'_i - x'_{i-1}}{t_i - t_{i-1}} - \frac{x'_{i-1} - x'_{i-2}}{t_{i-1} - t_{i-2}}$.

Initially, for $i = 2$, we have

$$D(2, c_2, x'_1, x'_2) = 0, \forall x'_1 \in [x_1 \pm \theta_1], \forall x'_2 \in [x_2 \pm \theta_2].$$

For each $i \in \{2, \dots, n\}, c_i \in \{0, \dots, \delta\}, x'_{i-1} \in [x_{i-1} \pm \theta_{i-1}], x'_i \in [x_i \pm \theta_i]$, we compute $D(i, c_i, x'_{i-1}, x'_i)$ according to the aforesaid recurrence. Algorithm 1 presents the procedure of this recurrence computation.

Let $D(n, c_n, x'_{n-1}, x'_n)$ be the maximum likelihood, among all c_n, x'_{n-1}, x'_n. By retracing all $D(i, c_i, x'_{i-1}, x'_i)$ leading to this maximum likelihood, an optimal solution x' is obtained.

Example 4 (Recurrence computing)**.** *Consider again the sequence $x = \{11, 12, 15, 14, 15, 15, 17\}$ in Example 2, with probability distribution on speed changes in Figure 4. Suppose that the repair cost budget is $\delta = 3$.*

To perform the recurrence on $D(i, c_i, x'_{i-1}, x'_i)$ in formula (4), we need to maintain a 4-dimension structure. Table 1

Algorithm 1: DP(x, θ, δ)

Data: data sequence x, error range θ, repair budget δ
Result: the maximum likelihood of the optimal repair

1 initialize $D(2, c_2, x'_1, x'_2) \leftarrow 0$ for each c_2, x'_1, x'_2;
2 **for** $i \leftarrow 3$ **to** n **do**
3   **for** $c_i \leftarrow 0$ **to** δ **do**
4   **foreach** $x'_i \in [x_i \pm \theta_i]$ **do**
5       $c_{i-1} \leftarrow c_i - \Delta(x'_i, x_i)$;
6   **foreach** $x'_{i-1} \in [x_{i-1} \pm \theta_{i-1}]$ **do**
7         $D(i, c_i, x'_{i-1}, x'_i) \leftarrow -\infty$;
8   **foreach** $x'_{i-2} \in [x_{i-2} \pm \theta_{i-2}]$ **do**
9   **if** $D(i-1, c_{i-1}, x'_{i-2}, x'_{i-1}) \neq -\infty$ **then**
10             $l \leftarrow D(i-1, c_{i-1}, x'_{i-2}, x'_{i-1}) + L(u'_{i-1})$;
11   **if** $l > D(i, c_i, x'_{i-1}, x'_i)$ **then**
12               $D(i, c_i, x'_{i-1}, x'_i) \leftarrow l$;
13   **if** $D(i, c, x'_{i-1}, x'_i) + L^u(x_{i-1\dots n}) \leq L^w(x)$ **then**
14           $D(i, c, x'_{i-1}, x'_i) \leftarrow -\infty$;
15 **return** $\max_{c_n, x'_{n-1}, x'_n} D(n, c_n, x'_{n-1}, x'_n)$

Table 1: Example of recurrence

$i \backslash c_i$	0	1	2	3	L^u_i
1					
2	x'_1=11, $x'_2 = 12$				L^u_2=-6.0
3	x''_2=12, x''_3=15, D=-1.4		x'_2=12, x'_3=13, D=-1.2		L^u_3=-4.8
4	x''_3=15, x''_4=14, D=-3.7		x'_3=13, x'_4=14, D=-2.4		L^u_4=-3.6
5		x''_4=14, x''_5=16, D=-6.0	x'_4=14, x'_5=15, D=-3.6		L^u_5=-2.4
6				x'_5=15, x'_6=16, D=-4.8	L^u_6=-1.2
7				x'_6=16, x'_7=17, D=-6.0	

illustrates two dimensions on i and c, and omits the other two dimensions of x'_i, x'_{i-1} for simplicity. Each cell, e.g., for $i = 3, c_i = 2$, presents one of the $D(3, 2, x'_2, x'_3)$.

The recurrence performs from $i = 3$ to $i = n = 7$, with $c_i \in [0, 3]$ (as $\delta = 3$). The cell of $i = 7, c_i = 3$ obtains a $D(7, 3, x'_6, x'_7) = -6.0$. with the maximum likelihood. By retracing all $D(i, c_i, x'_{i-1}, x'_i)$ leading to this maximum likelihood, an optimal solution $x' = \{11, 12, 13, 14, 15, 16, 17\}$ is obtained. It is exactly the solution x' under $\delta = 3$ in Example 3, with likelihood $L(x') = -6.0$.

Intuitively, to show the correctness of Algorithm 1, it is sufficient to illustrate that the recurrence equation in formula (4) in dynamic programming always calculates the maximum likelihood in each step.

Proposition 2. *Algorithm 1 computes the optimal solution in $O(n\theta^3_{\max}\delta)$ time with $O(n\theta^2_{\max}\delta)$ space.*

3.2.2 Pruning with Likelihood Bounds

Intuitively, $D(i, c_i, x'_{i-1}, x'_i)$ in each recurrence obtain the optimal results on the subsequence $x_{1\dots i}$. If we can obtain an upper bound of likelihood for the remaining subsequence $x_{i+1\dots n}$, efficient pruning on subsequent recurrence involving this $D(i, c_i, x'_{i-1}, x'_i)$ enables.

Given a subsequence $x_{i\dots n}$, we can quickly compute an *upper* bound of maximum likelihood for possible repair $x'_{i\dots n}$

$$L^u(x_{i\dots n}) = (n - i - 1) \cdot \log p_{\max} \geq L(x'_{i\dots n}) = \sum_{j=i+1}^{n-1} L(x'_j),$$

where $p_{\max}$ is the maximum probability of a speed change.

Let x'' be a currently known repair with $\Delta(x, x'') \leq \delta$, e.g., efficiently computed by the simple greedy method below (introduced in Section 5.2), or simply $x'' = x$. We use the likelihood $L(x'')$ as the *lower* bound $L^w(x)$ of the maximum likelihood of the optimal solution x^*

$$L^w(x) = L(x'') \leq L(x^*).$$

Proposition 3. *The recurrence on $D(i, c_i, x'_{i-1}, x'_i)$ could be pruned, if*

$$D(i, c_i, x'_{i-1}, x'_i) + L^u(x_{i-1\dots n}) \leq L^w(x).$$

As Line 14 shown in Algorithm 1, we set $D(i, c_i, x'_{i-1}, x'_i) \leftarrow -\infty$ to stop the subsequent recurrence on $D(i, c_i, x'_{i-1}, x'_i)$.

Example 5 (Pruning with likelihood). *Let us still consider the sequence x in Example 4. According to the probability distribution in Figure 4, we have $p_{\max} = \log(0.3) = -1.2$. For each level i, an upper bound of*

$$L^u(x_{i-1\dots n}) = -1.2 * (7 - i)$$

is computed, denoted by the column L^u_i in Table 1. For instance, for $i = 2$, we have $L^u_2 = L^u(x_{1\dots 7}) = -6.0$. It denotes that any repair on the (sub)sequence $x_{1\dots 7}$ will not have likelihood greater than -6.0.

Moreover, we use the likelihood of the input sequence x as the lower bound $L^w(x) = L(x) = -8.1$, which is calculated in Example 2.

Consider the cell of $i = 5$, $c_i = 1$ (in red in Table 1) with $D(5, 1, 14, 16) = -6.0$. According to $L^u_5 = L^u(x_{4\dots 7}) = -2.4$, we have $D(5, 1, 14, 16) + L^u(x_{4\dots 7}) = -6.0 - 2.4 = -8.4 < L^w(x) = -8.1$. It indicates that, given the current repair $x''_{1\dots 4} = \{11, 12, 15, 14\}$ on the processed subsequence $x_{1\dots 4}$, no matter how the remaining $x_{5\dots 7}$ is repaired, the generated result x'' will always have likelihood $L(x'')$ lower than the lower bound, and thus cannot be the optimal solution. Any subsequent recurrence on this $D(5, 1, 14, 16)$ could be pruned.

4. APPROXIMATE SOLUTION

As introduced at the beginning of Section 3, Algorithm 1 is pseudo-polynomial, whose complexity is determined by δ the budget of repair cost. Depending on the granularity of data values, there may be a huge number of possible repair costs to enumerate within δ. For instance, in bad cases, the considered repair cost budget δ could be as high as $\delta = 4500$ in Figure 14 on STOCK data, or a $\delta = 3500$ in Figure 17 for ENGINE data.

To support efficient computing, our first method (in Section 4.1) is to map the space of possible repair cost values in $[0, \delta]$ to a constant space. While this simple approximation makes Algorithm 1 runs in linear time, no guarantee on approximation performance is obtained.

To trade off the complexity for approximation performance guarantee, we devise a quadratic-time constant-factor approximation algorithm (in Section 4.2). The intuition is, rather than approximating repair cost, we approximate the likelihood instead.

4.1 Linear Time Heuristics

We map the space of granted repair cost from $[0, \delta]$ to a constant space $[0, d]$, where d is an integer constant, by introducing an approximate repair cost function. Let

$$H = \frac{\delta}{d}.$$

We define

$$\Delta'(x_i', x_i) = \lceil \frac{|x_i' - x_i|}{H} \rceil. \tag{5}$$

With this approximate repair cost function, instead of all $c_i \in \{0, \ldots, \delta\}$, we calculate only $D(i, c_i', x_{i-1}', x_i')$ for

$$c_i' \in \{H \cdot \lceil \frac{c_i}{H} \rceil \leq \delta \mid c_i \in \{0, \ldots, \delta\}\}, \tag{6}$$

with a total number $d + 1$ of possible cost values.

Moreover, instead of considering all candidates $x_i' \in [x_i \pm \theta_i]$, we only need to consider candidates in

$$x_i' \in \{x_i \pm (H \cdot j) \mid j \in [-\lfloor \frac{\theta_i}{H} \rfloor, \lfloor \frac{\theta_i}{H} \rfloor]\} \tag{7}$$

with a total number $2 \cdot \lfloor \frac{\theta_i}{H} \rfloor + 1$ of candidates. The reason is that all the candidates $x_i' \in [H \cdot j, H \cdot j + H)$ share the same approximate repair cost j, and thus are not considered.

Example 6 (Linear time computation). *Consider the sequence x in Example 2, with error range $\theta_i = 3$ for all data points i. Given a repair cost budget $\delta = 4$ and $d = 2$, we have $H = \frac{\delta}{d} = 2$.*

According to formula (6), we calculate $D(i, c_i', x_{i-1}', x_i')$ only for the repair cost values $c_i' \in \{0, 2, 4\}$ instead of all possible repair costs $c_i \in \{0, 1, 2, 3, 4\}$.

In addition, the number of candidates is also reduced. For instance, for $x_3 = 15$ with $\theta_3 = 3$, the considered candidates in the exact algorithm are $x_3' \in \{12, 13, 14, 15, 16, 17, 18\}$. In the approximate computing, according to formula (7), only the candidates $x_3' \in \{13, 15, 17\}$ are considered instead.

Proposition 4. *Algorithm 1 with approximate repair cost Δ' in formula (5) runs in $O(nd^4)$ time with $O(nd^3)$ space, where d is a fixed constant.*

While this simple approximation performs well in practice (as shown in Section 6 of experiments), unfortunately, we did not obtain a theoretical bound of approximation ratio compared to the optimal solution.

4.2 Constant-Factor Approximation

Intuitively, rather than approximating repair cost, by directly approximating the likelihood, it might be more practical to keep the approximate likelihood bounded compared to the exact one. We present below a quadratic-time (for fixed error range θ), constant-factor approximation algorithm, by approximating the likelihood. Before introducing the approximation, let us first revise the recurrence defined on likelihood (instead of defined on repair cost in Section 3.2).

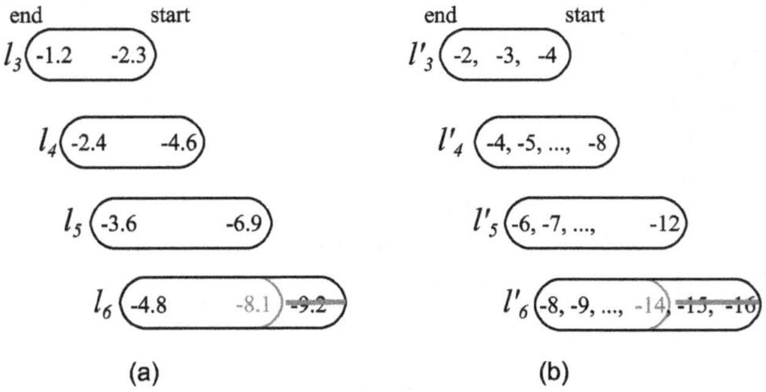

Figure 8: Space of likelihood values considered in recurrence

4.2.1 Recurrence Equation

Referring to the same intuition for the recurrence equation in formula (4), we still need to consider possible x_{i-2}', x_{i-1}', x_i' values, to address the likelihood incrementation in each recurrence.

Let $x_{1\ldots i}'$ be a repair of the subsequence $x_{1\ldots i}$, whose likelihood is $L(x_{1\ldots i}') = l_i$, the last two values of $x_{1\ldots i}'$ are x_{i-1}', x_i', respectively, and the cost $\Delta(x_{1\ldots i}', x_{1\ldots i})$ minimized. We denote this minimized cost $\Delta(x_{1\ldots i}', x_{1\ldots i})$ by $C(i, l, x_{i-1}', x_i')$.

The recurrence computation is as follows

$$\begin{aligned} & C(i, l_i, x_{i-1}', x_i') \\ = & \min_{x_{i-2}' \in [x_{i-2} \pm \theta_{i-2}]} C(i-1, l_{i-1}, x_{i-2}', x_{i-1}') + \Delta(x_i', x_i) \end{aligned} \tag{8}$$

where $l_{i-1} = l_i - L(u_{i-1}')$, and $u_{i-1}' = \frac{x_i' - x_{i-1}'}{t_i - t_{i-1}} - \frac{x_{i-1}' - x_{i-2}'}{t_{i-1} - t_{i-2}}$.

Initially, for $i = 2$, we have

$$C(2, 0, x_1', x_2') = \Delta(x_1', x_1) + \Delta(x_2', x_2),$$

$\forall x_1' \in [x_1 \pm \theta_1], \forall x_2' \in [x_2 \pm \theta_2]$.

For each i, we consider l_i in the range from l_i^{start} to l_i^{end}, where

$$\begin{aligned} l_i^{start} &= (i - 2) \cdot \log p_{\min} \\ l_i^{end} &= (i - 2) \cdot \log p_{\max} \end{aligned}$$

(See the specific l_i values considered in the range soon in Section 4.2.2.)

Example 7. *Consider again the sequence x in Example 2. Referring to the probability distribution of speed changes in Figure 4, we have $\log p_{\max} = \log(0.3) = -1.2, \log p_{\min} = \log(0.1) = -2.3$.*

Figure 8(a) illustrates the range $[l_i^{start}, l_i^{end}]$ of possible likelihoods that need to be considered for each i. For instance, we have $l_3^{start} = -2.3, l_i^{end} = -1.2$.

4.2.2 Approximation Algorithm

Intuitively, the likelihood approximation is performed by mapping the range of likelihood, from l_i^{start} to l_i^{end}, to a space presented in formula (10) below with the total number of likelihood values bounded (see the bound in the proof of Proposition 5).

Consider

$$K = -\varepsilon \cdot \log p_{\max},$$

where $\varepsilon > 0$ is an error parameter in approximation.

For each point x_i, we define approximate likelihood

$$L'(u_i') = \lfloor \frac{L(u_i')}{K} \rfloor. \tag{9}$$

In recurrence, for each i, we only need to consider the following approximate likelihood values

$$l_i' \in \{\lfloor \frac{l_i^{start}}{K} \rfloor, \lfloor \frac{l_i^{start}}{K} \rfloor + 1, \ldots, \lfloor \frac{l_i^{end}}{K} \rfloor\}, \tag{10}$$

with a total number $(i-2)\lfloor \frac{1}{\varepsilon}(\frac{\log p_{\min}}{\log p_{\max}} - 1)\rfloor$ of considered approximate likelihood values (according to formula (14) the proof of Proposition 5).

By further considering each $x_{i-1}' \in [x_{i-1} \pm \theta_{i-1}], x_i' \in [x_i \pm \theta_i]$, we compute $C(i, l_i', x_{i-1}', x_i')$ according to the aforesaid recurrence. Algorithm 2 presents the procedure of this recurrence computation with approximate likelihood.

Algorithm 2: DPC$(x, \theta, \delta, \varepsilon)$

Data: data sequence x, error range θ, repair budget δ, approximation factor ε
Result: the maximum likelihood of the optimal repair

```
K ← −ε · log p_max;
initialize C(2, 0, x'_1, x'_2) ← Δ(x'_1, x_1) + Δ(x'_2, x_2) for each x'_1, x'_2;
for i ← 3 to n do
    for l'_i ← ⌊l_i^start / K⌋ to ⌊l_i^end / K⌋ do
        foreach x'_i ∈ [x_i ± θ_i] do
            l'_{i−1} ← l'_i − L'(u'_i);
            foreach x'_{i−1} ∈ [x_{i−1} ± θ_{i−1}] do
                C(i, l'_i, x'_{i−1}, x'_i) ← ∞;
                foreach x'_{i−2} ∈ [x_{i−2} ± θ_{i−2}] do
                    if C(i − 1, l'_{i−1}, x'_{i−2}, x'_{i−1}) ≠ ∞ then
                        c ← C(i−1, l'_{i−1}, x'_{i−2}, x'_{i−1}) + Δ(x'_i, x_i);
                        if c ≤ δ and c < C(i, l'_i, x'_{i−1}, x'_i) then
                            C(i, l'_i, x'_{i−1}, x'_i) ← c;
return max_{l'_n, x'_{n−1}, x'_n} C(n, l'_n, x'_{n−1}, x'_n)
```

Let l_n' be the maximum (approximate) likelihood with $C(n, l_n', x_{n-1}', x_n') \leq \delta$, among all l_n', x_{n-1}', x_n'. By retracing all $C(i, l_i', x_{i-1}', x_i')$ leading to this $C(n, l_n', x_{n-1}', x_n')$, an approximate solution x' is obtained.

Example 8. *Consider the ranges of likelihood in Figure 8(a) in Example 7. Given $\varepsilon = 0.5$, we have $K = -\varepsilon \cdot \log(p_{\max}) = -0.5 * -1.2 = 0.6$.*

According to formula (10), for each level i, we compute a finite set of approximate likelihood values to consider in recurrence. For instance, as illustrated in Figure 8(b), we consider $l_3' \in \{-4, -3, -2\}$ for $i = 3$, where $\lfloor \frac{l_3^{start}}{K} \rfloor = \lfloor \frac{-2.3}{0.6} \rfloor = -4, \lfloor \frac{l_3^{end}}{K} \rfloor = \lfloor \frac{-1.2}{0.6} \rfloor = -2$.

Proposition 5. *Algorithm 2 with approximate likelihood L' outputs a repair x' with $L(x') \geq (1+\varepsilon) \cdot L(x^*)$, in $O(n^2\theta_{\max}^3)$ time with $O(n^2\theta_{\max}^2)$ space.*

4.2.3 Pruning

Similar to the pruning for the exact algorithm in Section 3.2.2, let us consider $L^u(x)$ and $L^w(x)$, the upper and lower bounds of the likelihood of the optimal solution.

Proposition 6. *The recurrence on $C(i, l_i, x_{i-1}', x_i')$ stops, if $l_i + L^u(x_{i-1\ldots n}) \leq L^w(x)$.*

Indeed, since $L^u(x_{i-1\ldots n}) < 0$, any $l_i \leq L^w(x)$ can be directly ignored. We can further set

$$l_i^{start} = \max\left((i-2) \cdot \log p_{\min}, L^w(x)\right). \tag{11}$$

For the approximate l_i' considered in the implementation of recurrence, the pruning condition is as follows.

Corollary 7. *The recurrence on $C(i, l_i', x_{i-1}', x_i')$ could be pruned, if*

$$K \cdot (l_i' + i - 2) + L^u(x_{i-1\ldots n}) \leq L^w(x).$$

Example 9. *Similar to Example 5, we use the likelihood of the input sequence x as the lower bound $L^w(x) = L(x) = -8.1$, which is calculated in Example 2.*

According to formula (11), for $i = 6$, we have the new $l_6^{start} = \max(-9.2, -8.1) = -8.1$, where -9.2 is the original l_6^{start}, as shown in Figure 8(a).

Referring to $K = 0.6$ in Example 8, the new $\lfloor \frac{l_6^{start}}{K} \rfloor = \lfloor \frac{-8.1}{0.6} \rfloor = -14$ is sufficient, as also illustrated in Figure 8(b).

5. FROM DISCRETE TO CONTINUOUS

Rather than approximating the computation, in this section, we approximate the discrete probability distribution P by a continuous probability distribution. The intuition is that, with a proper continuous probability distribution, the maximum likelihood repairing problem could be transformed to a quadratic programming problem (according to Proposition 12). It enables more fast computing and the application of existing efficient solvers.

5.1 Transformation

First, let us illustrate the high similarity between the discrete probability distribution observed in real datasets and the continuous probability distribution.

Example 10 (Probability distribution approximation)**.** *We study the probability distribution of speed changes over three real datasets (see Section 6 for details of these datasets), together with the corresponding probability density function of normal distribution $\mathcal{N}(\mu, \sigma)$ for approximation.*

Figure 2(a) presents the distribution over GPS dataset, together with a normal distribution $\mathcal{N}(0, 1)$. For the STOCK dataset, we plot $\mathcal{N}(0, 1.2)$ in Figure 9(a). Figure 9(b) illustrates the distribution $\mathcal{N}(0, 0.8)$ over the ENGINE dataset.

Referring to the aforesaid proximity, assume that the probability distribution u_i follows the normal distribution $\mathcal{N}(0, \sigma^2)$, having the probability density function

$$P(u_i) = \frac{1}{\sigma\sqrt{2\pi}} e^{-\frac{u_i^2}{2\sigma^2}}. \tag{12}$$

Proposition 8. *Given the probability density function in formula (12), we have $L(x') \geq L(x'')$ if and only if*

$$\sum_{i=2}^{n-1} (u_i')^2 \leq \sum_{i=2}^{n-1} (u_i'')^2,$$

where u_i', u_i'' are speed changes w.r.t. x_i', x_i'', respectively.

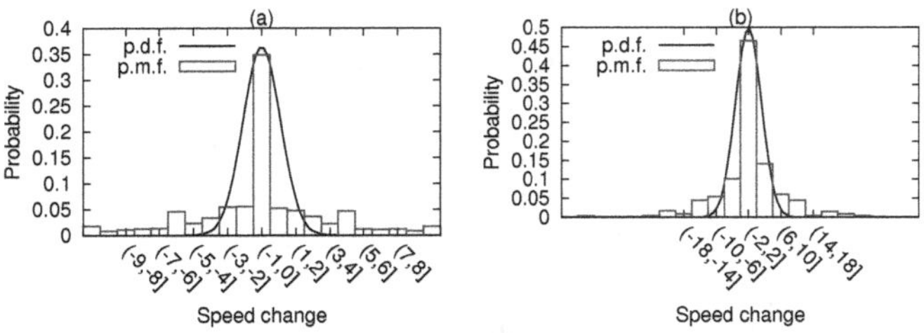

Figure 9: Probability distribution approximation over (a) STOCK and (b) ENGINE datasets

Therefore, we can rephrase Problem 1 as

$$\min \sum_{i=2}^{n-1} \left(\frac{x'_{i+1} - x'_i}{t_{i+1} - t_i} - \frac{x'_i - x'_{i-1}}{t_i - t_{i-1}} \right)^2 \tag{13}$$

$$\text{s.t.} \sum_{i=1}^{n} |x'_i - x_i| \leq \delta$$

$$x'_i \in [x_i \pm \theta_i] \qquad 1 \leq i \leq n$$

Existing tools on quadratic programming, e.g., Gurobi[2], can be directly applied.

5.2 Simple Greedy

To compute very fast a repair (e.g., for pruning in Section 3.2.2), we can use a simple greedy heuristic for the transform problem in formula (13).

Let x' be a current repair, initially $x' = x$. A natural greedy strategy is to select a x'_i with the maximum $|u'_i|$, and pay one unit cost on such x'_i towards the reduce of $|u'_i|$.

$$x'_i = \underset{x'_i \in [x'_i \pm 1] \cap [x_i \pm \theta_i]}{\arg\max} \left| \frac{x'_{i+1} - x'_i}{t_{i+1} - t_i} - \frac{x'_i - x'_{i-1}}{t_i - t_{i-1}} \right|.$$

The algorithm terminates after δ iterations or no $|u'_i|$ could be further reduced.

Example 11 (Greedy computation). *Consider again the sequence* $x = \{11, 12, 15, 14, 15, 15, 17\}$ *in Example 2. The simple greedy algorithm will first select a data point, i.e.,* $x_3 = 15$*, with the maximum* $|u_3| = 4$*. A unit cost repair will be performed on* x_3*, i.e.,* $x'_3 = 14$ *such that* $|u'_3| = 2$ *is reduced, as illustrated in Figure 10(a). It is notable that such a repair* x'_3 *on data point 3 also affects the speed changes in data points 2 and 4, having* $u'_2 = 1, u'_4 = 1$ *in the repaired sequence.*

In the next iteration, the greedy algorithm will choose the current largest $|u_i|$*, i.e., still* u'_3*. It generates a new repair with* $x''_3 = 13$*, as shown in Figure 10(b).*

The iteration carries on by further repairing $x'''_6 = 16$ *in Figure 10(c). Since all the speed changes become 0 in Figure 10(d), i.e., no* $|u'_i|$ *could be further reduced, the algorithm terminates, and returns a repaired sequence* $x''' = \{11, 12, 13, 14, 15, 16, 17\}$.

If a repair cost budget $\delta = 2$ *is given, the greedy computation will stop after two iterations. The returned repair is* $x'' = \{11, 12, 13, 14, 15, 15, 17\}$ *as illustrated in Figure 10(b).*

Proposition 9. *The greedy algorithm runs in* $O(\max(n, \delta))$ *time.*

[2]http://www.gurobi.com

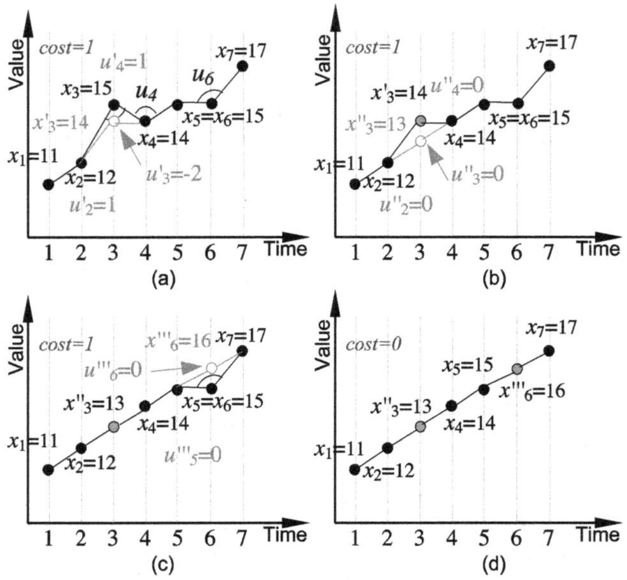

Figure 10: Simple Greedy Example

6. EXPERIMENT

In this section, we experimentally compare our proposed methods, (1) DP the exact algorithm in Section 3.2, (2) DPC the quadratic-time constant-factor approximation algorithm in Section 4.2, (3) DPL the linear time heuristic algorithm in Section 4.1, (4) QP the quadratic programming solver in Section 5.1, (5) SG the simple greedy algorithm in Section 5.2, with (6) SCREEN the state-of-the-art approach [14]. We omit reporting the other methods, such as the smoothing-based EWMA [6], or the constraint-based [7], owing to the clearly worse results (which are also observed in [14]).

The experiment runs on three real datasets and one synthetic datasets. (1) The STOCK dataset is originally clean, and errors are injected by randomly replacing the values of some data points. Thereby, the original clean data serves as the ground truth. (2) For the GPS data, collected by carrying a smartphone and walking around at campus, we manually mark the trajectory during data collection in a map and use the trajectory as the ground truth. (3) For the ENGINE data, we do not have the ground truth of sensor reading sequences. However, we have another observation (switching-count), which could be predicted from sensor readings. Therefore, instead of directly evaluating w.r.t. the ground truth of sensor readings (which are not available), we evaluate the prediction of switching-count by sensor readings with/without repairing. The switching-count observation serves as the ground truth of prediction. (4) For the SYNTHETIC data, generated by ourselves, we naturally have the ground truth.

The probability distributions of speed changes are estimated over the employed datasets. For each data point in a sequence, we calculate its speed change value before and after the point, according to formula (1). By counting the appearance of speed change values in the sequence, we estimate the probabilities of the speed changes. Figures 9(a), 2(b), 9(b) and 18 report the estimated probability distributions over the STOCK, GPS, ENGINE and SYNTHETIC datasets, respectively.

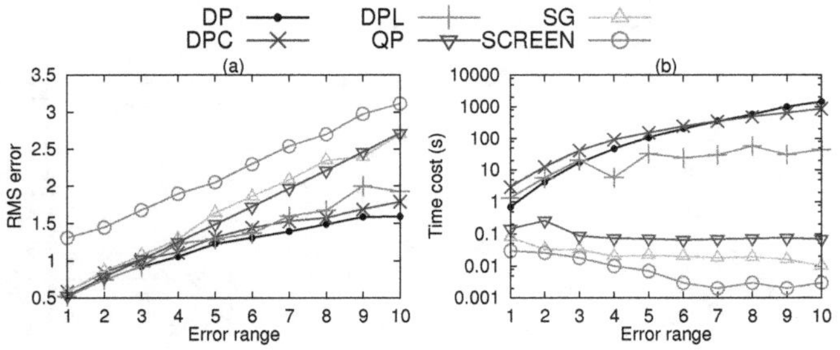

Figure 11: Varying error range θ, over STOCK with error number 600 and data size 1282

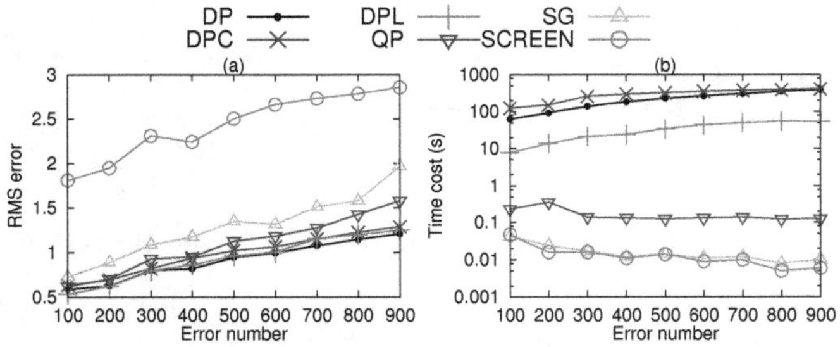

Figure 12: Varying error numbers, over STOCK with error range $\theta = 5$ and data size 2564

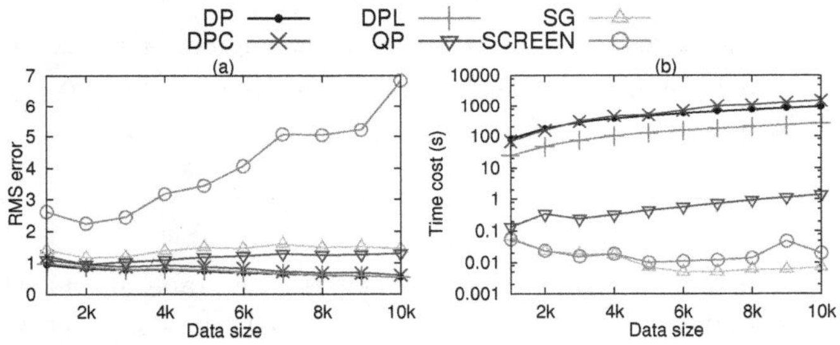

Figure 13: Scalability, over STOCK with error range $\theta = 5$ and error size 400

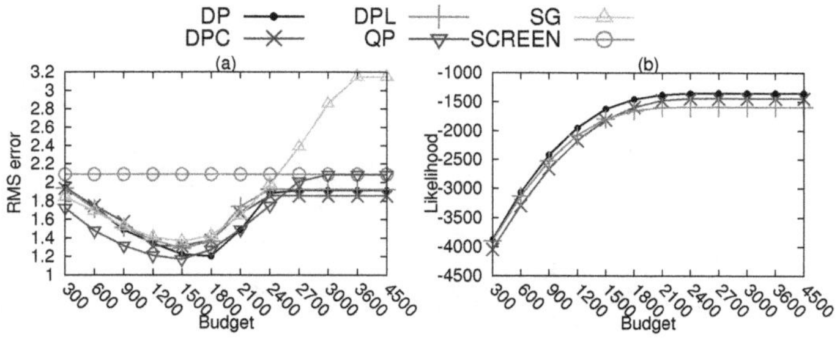

Figure 14: Varying repair cost budget δ, over STOCK with error range $\theta = 5$, error number 600 and data size 1282

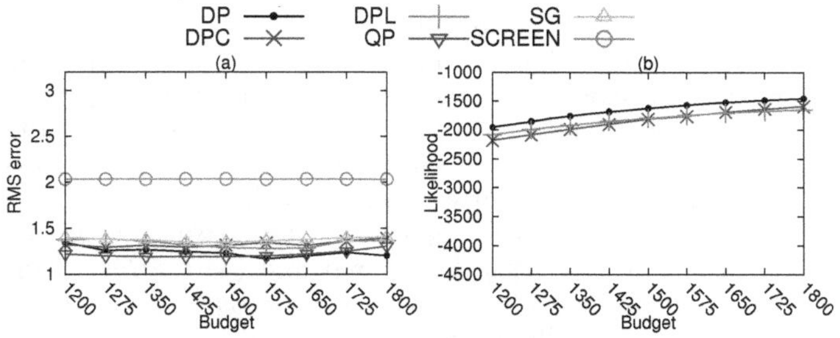

Figure 15: Detailed results with δ in the range of 1200 to 1800 in Figure 14

6.1 STOCK with Various Injected Errors

The STOCK dataset records the daily prices of a stock from 1984-09 to 2010-02, with 12826 data points in total. Since the data is originally clean, following the same line of precisely evaluating the repair effectiveness [1], errors are injected by randomly replacing the values of some data points.

Let x_{truth} be the ground truth of clean sequence, and x_{repair} be the repaired sequence. The repair accuracy is measured by root-mean-square error (RMS) [8], evaluating how close the repaired sequence x_{repair} is to the ground truth x_{truth}. The lower the RMS error is, the closer (more accurate) the repair is to the ground truth.

Besides the RMS performance on repairing accuracy, we also report the corresponding time cost and report the likelihood of repair results.

For the original clean STOCK dataset, we have error range $\theta = 0$ (i.e., no need to repair). To evaluate the repair performance, we manually inject errors in the dataset with error range $\theta > 0$. Figure 11 presents the results by varying the ranges of injected errors from $\theta = 1$ to 10. First, as shown in Figure 11(a), it is not surprising that the larger the error range is, the higher the RMS distance will be between the truth and repair results. Our exact approach DP achieves the lowest RMS measure, while its corresponding time cost is the highest in Figure 11(b). While both the approximate methods DPC (with $\varepsilon = 2$) and DPL (with $d = 1000$) also have a considerably low RMS, the time cost of the linear time heuristic DPL is significantly lower.

To evaluate the scalability, Figure 12 reports the results on various number of errors that are injected in the data, and Figure 13 presents the results over various data sizes. Generally, similar results are observed as in Figure 11. DP, DPC and DPL methods show better RMS performance, while their time costs are higher. The existing method SCREEN has worse RMS measure, but runs faster. QP and SG provide a trade-off between effectiveness and efficiency.

One interesting result is that the time cost of DP is lower than that of DPC, with small error range in Figure 11(b), or with small error number in Figure 12(b). The reason is that with a small error range, the corresponding repair budget δ needed is small as well (see results on various repair budgets below). The DP algorithm with $O(n\theta_{\max}^3\delta)$ complexity runs faster as well. For the same reason, in Figure 12(b), a larger number of errors lead to larger δ, and thus DP shows higher time cost (closer to that of DPC).

Figure 14 reports the results by varying the repair cost budget δ. As shown in Figure 14(a), if the repair cost budget is set too small, the dirty points cannot be fully repaired, with higher RMS measure. The corresponding likelihood of repair results in Figure 14(b) is low as well. On the other hand, if the repair cost budget δ sets too large, the sequence might be over-repaired. The RMS measure is high as well. Note that by further increasing the repair cost budget, the likelihood could not increase further in Figure 14(b). The reason is that the repaired sequence reaches the allowed re-

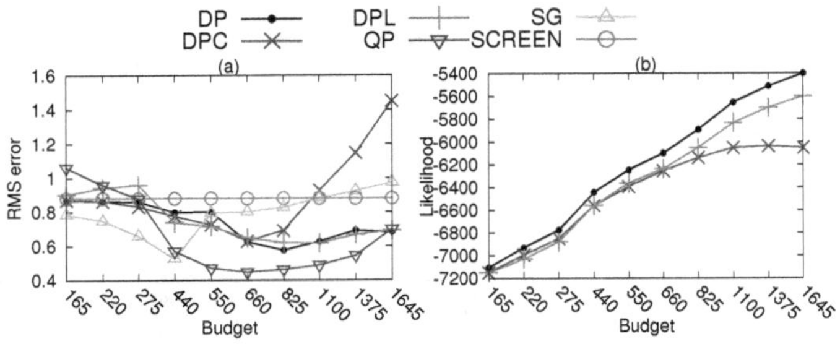

Figure 16: Varying repair cost budget δ over GPS

pair range θ. The corresponding RMS measure in Figure 14(a) does not change either.

Nevertheless, Figure 14 provides a guideline of setting the repair cost budget δ in practice. That is, by increasing δ, we observe the corresponding likelihood of results. When the likelihood does not significantly increase, e.g., with $\delta = 1500$ in Figure 14(b), the corresponding repair result is the best (with the lowest RMS). It denotes the case where the sequence is neither insufficiently repaired (with a low likelihood) nor over-repaired (with too large repair cost budget but no much likelihood gain).

It is worth noting that a range of δ could be considered, from 15 to 20 in Figure 6(b) in Example 3 as aforesaid, such that the repair error keeps low in Figure 6(a). We illustrate a very large range of δ in Figure 14 in order to verify the guideline of choosing a proper δ. Once a proper range of δ is identified, e.g., from 1500 to 1800 where the likelihood no longer significantly increases, the repair results are stable. To demonstrate the robustness, Figure 15 for the results with δ in the range of 1200 to 1800. As shown, the result appears to be less sensitive in the chosen range of δ under the aforesaid guideline.

6.2 GPS with Naturally Embedded Errors

In order to evaluate over a real dataset with *true errors* (instead of synthetically injected errors), a real GPS dataset is collected by a person carrying a smartphone and walking around at campus. Since we know exactly the path of walking, a number of 150 dirty points are manually identified (among total 2358 clear points in the trajectory). True locations of dirty points are also manually labeled, as ground truth.

Since the errors are originally embedded, we don't have experiments on various errors settings in this dataset. There is only one parameter to tune, i.e., the repair cost budget δ.

Figure 16 reports the RMS measure and likelihood of results, by varying the repair cost budget δ. Similar to Figure 14, when the budget δ is small, dirty data might not be sufficiently repaired and thus the likelihoods of results are low. By granting more budget (larger δ), while the data could be over-repaired (higher RMS error), the likelihood does not significantly increase further. The results verify again the aforesaid guideline of setting the repair cost budget δ, by observing the likelihood of results.

6.3 ENGINE without Labeled Errors and Truth

To demonstrate the effectiveness in real applications, we employ the ENGINE dataset, where neither the dirty data nor the corresponding ground truth are labeled. The ENGINE dataset collects four sequences of a crane, produced by a heavy industry company, including DT0, engine-speed, pump-volume and switching-count, which monitor the working status of the device. The meaning of variables and their domains are presented in Table 2. The total number of data points in each sequence is 464. (Link to data will be publicly available after anonymous review.)

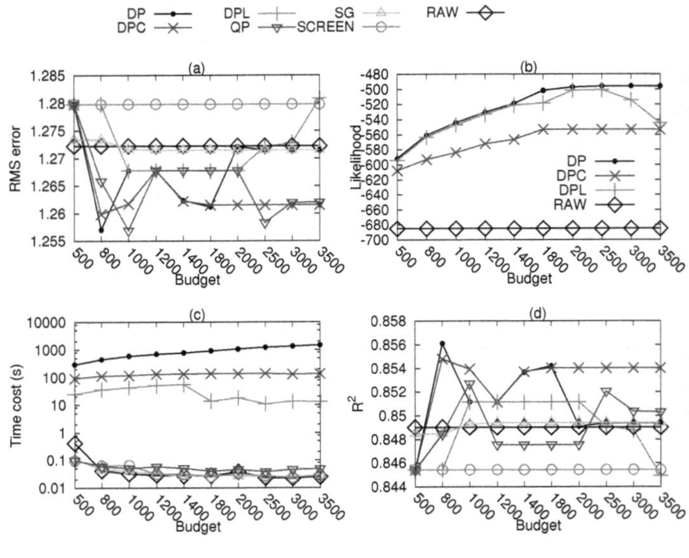

Figure 17: Varying repair budget δ over ENGINE

Table 2: ENGINE variables

Variable	Description	Domain
DT0	Current of a proportioner called DT0	[200, 800]
engine-speed	Rotate speed of the engine	[800, 2000]
pump-volume	Swept volume of the pump	[0, 100]
switching-count	Times the crane pumping per minute	[3, 27]

Owing to the sensor issues, the readings of engine-speed are often inaccurate, and thus need cleaning. Instead of directly measuring the accuracy of repairs (which is not possible since no error and truth are known in advance), we evaluate the application performance over the data with and without cleaning. Since switching-count is often missing in practice, the application is to predict switching-count according to the readings of DT0, engine-speed, pump-volume. To perform the prediction, we use the *LinearRegression Class* in WEKA[3], i.e., switching-count $= \alpha *$ pump-volume $+ \beta *$ DT0 $+ \gamma *$ engine-speed, where α, β, γ are parameters of regression.

To evaluate the application accuracy, two measures are employed, RMS reporting the closeness of the predicted values to the observed switching-count values (that are not missing) and R^2 the coefficient of determination [5]. A lower RMS error or a higher R^2 measure denotes better prediction accuracy.

Figure 17 illustrates the results by varying the repair cost budget δ. RAW denotes the results of prediction application over the raw data without performing cleaning. As shown,

[3]http://www.cs.waikato.ac.nz/~ml/weka/

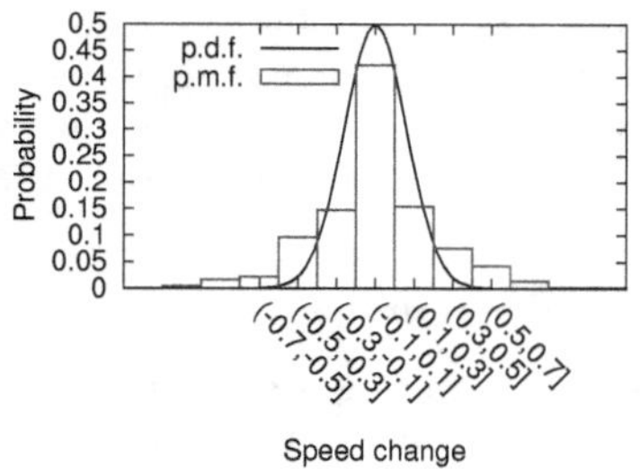

Figure 18: Probability distribution of speed changes over SYNTHETIC data

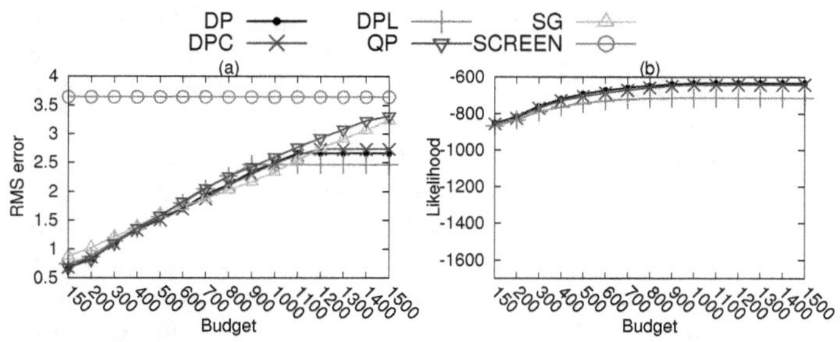

Figure 19: Repair results on various repair cost budget δ over SYNTHETIC-clean

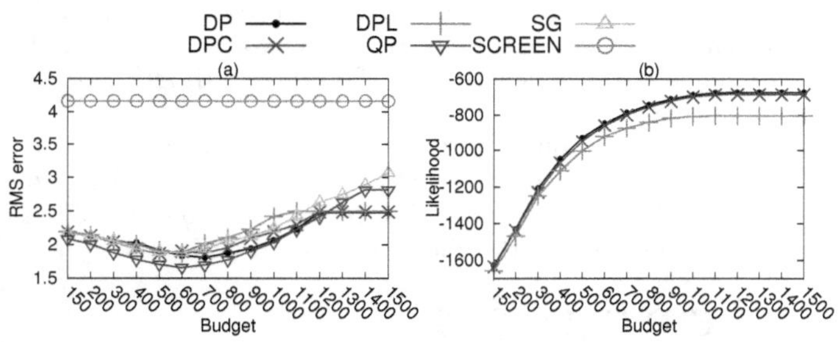

Figure 20: Repair results on various repair cost budget δ over SYNTHETIC-injected

by a proper setting of repair cost budget δ, the RMS and R^2 of prediction application improves, compared to RAW without repairing.

The RMS and R^2 measures over the application are not as stable as the RMS of repair results, owing to the prediction model. Nevertheless, as illustrated in Figure 17(b), the likelihoods of repair results are stable, which is similar to the observation in other datasets. It is also observed that a result, neither insufficiently repaired (with a low likelihood) nor over-repaired (with too large repair cost budget but no much likelihood gain), leads to better (application) effectiveness.

As shown in Figure 17(a), the existing SCREEN repair leads to higher RMS error in prediction. It is not surprising given the higher RMS error of repairing by SCREEN, e.g., in Figure 14(a) over STOCK and Figure 16(a) over GPS. The other prediction measure R^2 of SCREEN in Figure 17(d) is lower, which verifies again the results.

6.4 SYNTHETIC Evaluating False Positives

We consider two synthetic datasets, SYNTHETIC-clean and SYNTHETIC-injected. The SYNTHETIC-clean dataset

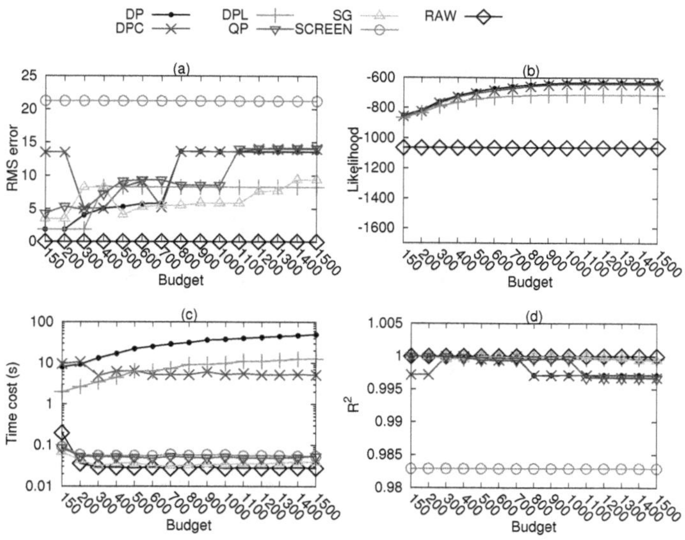

Figure 21: Prediction results on various repair cost budget δ over SYNTHETIC-clean

is generated by using speeds with changes sampled from the probabilistic model (Gaussian distribution with $\mu = 0$ and $\sigma = 0.8$) as the p.d.f. shown in Figure 18. By injecting errors into SYNTHETIC-clean data, following the same line of injection over STOCK dataset, with error range $\theta = 5$, we obtain the SYNTHETIC-injected version. Figure 18 shows the probabilistic distribution of speed changes over SYNTHETIC data.

Figures 19 and 20 present repair results over SYNTHETIC-clean and SYNTHETIC-injected, respectively. The results verify again the guideline on setting the repair cost budget δ (see Example 3 for more details about the guideline). That is, as shown in Figure 20(b) over SYNTHETIC-injected, a budget δ from 500 to 700 will be preferred, where the likelihood stops significantly increase. The RMS error of repair results under such δ is lower in Figure 20(a). Similarly, for the SYNTHETIC-clean data in Figure 19(b), no significant increase of likelihood is observed. A small δ such as 150 is sufficient, i.e., the approach prefers to make little change over the clean data. This conservative result over SYNTHETIC-clean data also demonstrates that our proposed algorithm is *not* over aggressive.

Moreover, to perform the prediction experiments (as in Section 6.3), we generate similarly other two determinant sequences plus one dependent sequence. In the SYNTHETIC-clean version without error injection, the dependent sequence could be predicted from determinant sequences, i.e., the standard baseline that always predicts the mean from the training data.

Figures 21 and 22 present the prediction results over the SYNTHETIC-clean and SYNTHETIC-injected data, respectively. Again, referring to the guideline of setting repair cost budget δ, a small $\delta = 150$ is preferred in Figure 21(b) on SYNTHETIC-clean. The corresponding prediction results are closest to the standard baseline, i.e., the prediction over the RAW clean data without repairing, in Figure 21(a). Recall that the standard baseline (on RAW over SYNTHETIC-clean) always predicts the dependent sequence with RMS error 0. Moreover, a budget δ around 600 will be chosen ac-

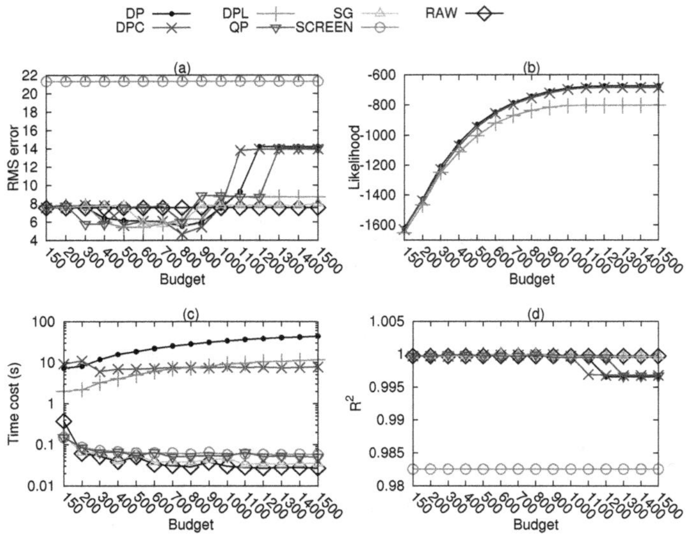

Figure 22: Prediction results on various repair cost budget δ over SYNTHETIC-injected

cording to Figure 22(b) on SYNTHETIC-injected. Again, the corresponding prediction RMS error is lower under such δ in Figure 22(a).

Summary

We list the proposed methods in the decreasing order of time cost as follows: (1) The exact DP algorithm is preferred, in order to achieve better repair accuracy (as shown in Figure 11(a)), while its time cost is high given the pseudo-polynomial time complexity $O(n\theta_{\max}^3\delta)$ in Proposition 2. (2) The DPC approximation algorithm, with time complexity $O(n^2\theta_{\max}^3)$ not directly related to δ in Proposition 5, shows better time performance when given a larger repair cost budget δ, e.g., $\delta = 3500$ in Figure 17(c). (3) The DPL approximation algorithm, with time complexity $O(nd^4)$ where d is a constant in Proposition 4, achieves even lower time cost, but its repair error could be higher, as shown in Figure 11. (4) The QP algorithm can have significantly lower time cost without losing much repair accuracy, when the exact discrete probability distribution is similar to the approximate continuous probability distribution, e.g., when the error range is small in Figure 11. (5) The simple heuristic algorithm SG always achieves the lowest time cost among the proposed methods, while its repair accuracy could not be guaranteed.

7. RELATED WORK

Constraint-based Cleaning

Besides speed constraints [14], sequential dependencies [7] also specify constraints on sequential data. Instead of concerning the speeds of value changes, sequential dependencies consider the range of value changes between two consecutive data points, while the distances on timestamps between data points are not involved. In this sense, sequential dependencies could be interpreted as a special class of speed constraints declared on time series with fixed time intervals.

With either constraint, the constraint-based cleaning identifies and repairs only the violations to the constraints, without indicating the most likely answers among all the valid repairs that satisfy the constraints. As reported in Section 6, by further revealing the likelihood of repairs, our proposal can obtain more accurate repair results than the constraint-based method.

Statistical-based Cleaning

The likelihood-based repairing over relational data has been studied in [15]. For the relation to repair, several attributes are identified with dirty values, namely *flexible* attributes, which can be modified, while the other attributes contain correct values, called *reliable* attributes. Dependencies between reliable attributes and flexible attributes are modeled and changed with flexible attributes repaired. The repairing is thus to maximize the likelihood of data replacement, given the data distribution in the relation. The difference between relational data and our studied sequential data is obvious, and thus this likelihood-based repairing over relational data [15] is not directly applicable to sequential data.

A more complex relational dependency network is introduced in [11] to model the probabilistic relationships among attribute, such as cyclic relational dependencies. Instead of maximizing the likelihood as in [15] and our proposal, the repairing in [11] performs iteratively, and observe the change of distributions before and after a repair. The cleaning process terminates when the divergence of distributions is sufficiently small. Again, without a clear dependency relationship, the relational dependency network cannot be built for single data sequences, and thus this method [11] is not applicable.

To assess the quality of a repair, a statistical distortion method is proposed in [4]. While the statistical distortion directly observes the value distribution, our considered likelihood is defined on the changes of speed (value changes).

8. CONCLUSIONS

In this study, we study the cleaning of dirty vales in a sequence. First, we show that existing speed constraint-based approach either does not precisely repair large spike errors or simply ignore small errors. Rather than restricting the repair w.r.t. max/min speed constraints, we model the likelihood of a repair by observing its speed changes. Under the discipline that speeds should not change significantly in a time point, the likelihood-based repairing is thus to maximize the likelihood on speed changes, instead of minimizing the changes in the constraint-based repairing.

To efficiently compute the maximum likelihood solution, we propose 1) a pseudo-polynomial time exact algorithm, 2) a quadratic-time constant-factor approximation algorithm, 3) a linear time heuristic algorithm, 4) a quadratic programming transformation approximation, and 5) a simple greedy heuristic. Experiments on several real datasets demonstrate the better performance of our proposal, in both repairing and application accuracies, compared to the state-of-the-art constraint-based repairing.

Acknowledgement

This work is supported in part by the Tsinghua University Initiative Scientific Research Program; Tsinghua National Laboratory Special Fund for Big Data Science and Technology; China NSFC under Grants 61572272, 61325008, 61370055 and 61202008.

9. REFERENCES

[1] P. Bohannon, M. Flaster, W. Fan, and R. Rastogi. A cost-based model and effective heuristic for repairing constraints by value modification. In *SIGMOD*, pages 143–154, 2005.

[2] D. R. Brillinger. *Time series: data analysis and theory*, volume 36. Siam, 2001.

[3] X. Chu, I. F. Ilyas, and P. Papotti. Holistic data cleaning: Putting violations into context. In *ICDE*, pages 458–469, 2013.

[4] T. Dasu and J. M. Loh. Statistical distortion: Consequences of data cleaning. *PVLDB*, 5(11):1674–1683, 2012.

[5] N. R. Draper and H. Smith. *Applied regression analysis (2. ed.)*. Wiley series in probability and mathematical statistics. Wiley, 1981.

[6] E. S. Gardner Jr. Exponential smoothing: The state of the art–part ii. *International Journal of Forecasting*, 22(4):637–666, 2006.

[7] L. Golab, H. J. Karloff, F. Korn, A. Saha, and D. Srivastava. Sequential dependencies. *PVLDB*, 2(1):574–585, 2009.

[8] S. R. Jeffery, M. N. Garofalakis, and M. J. Franklin. Adaptive cleaning for RFID data streams. In *VLDB*, pages 163–174, 2006.

[9] R. M. Karp. Reducibility among combinatorial problems. In *Proceedings of a symposium on the Complexity of Computer Computations, held at the IBM Thomas J. Watson Research Center, Yorktown Heights, New York.*, pages 85–103, 1972.

[10] X. Li, X. L. Dong, K. Lyons, W. Meng, and D. Srivastava. Truth finding on the deep web: Is the problem solved? *PVLDB*, 6(2):97–108, 2012.

[11] C. Mayfield, J. Neville, and S. Prabhakar. ERACER: a database approach for statistical inference and data cleaning. In *SIGMOD*, pages 75–86, 2010.

[12] M. D. Smucker, J. Allan, and B. Carterette. A comparison of statistical significance tests for information retrieval evaluation. In *CIKM*, pages 623–632, 2007.

[13] S. Song, C. Li, and X. Zhang. Turn waste into wealth: On simultaneous clustering and cleaning over dirty data. In *SIGKDD*, pages 1115–1124, 2015.

[14] S. Song, A. Zhang, J. Wang, and P. S. Yu. SCREEN: stream data cleaning under speed constraints. In *SIGMOD*, pages 827–841, 2015.

[15] M. Yakout, L. Berti-Equille, and A. K. Elmagarmid. Don't be scared: use scalable automatic repairing with maximal likelihood and bounded changes. In *SIGMOD*, pages 553–564, 2013.

APPENDIX

A. PROOFS

Proof of Theorem 1

Proof. The problem is clearly in NP. Given a repair x', it can be verified in polynomial time whether each point repair x'_i is in the valid range and $\Delta(x, x') \le \delta$. Besides, the likelihood $L(x')$ can also be computed in polynomial time.

To prove the NP-hardness, we show a reduction from the 0/1 knapsack problem, which is one of Karp's 21 NP-complete problems [9]. Given a set of n items numbered from 1 up to n, each with a weight w_i and a value v_i, along with a maximum weight capacity, the problem is to maximize the sum of the values of the items in the knapsack so that the sum of the weights is less than or equal to the knapsack's capacity.

We create five data points with values $x_{i1}, \dots, x_{i5}$ for each item i, having

$$\begin{aligned} x_{i1} &= b_i, & \theta_{i1} &= 0, \\ x_{i2} &= b_i, & \theta_{i2} &= 0, \\ x_{i3} &= 2b_i, & \theta_{i3} &= w_i, \\ x_{i4} &= 4b_i, & \theta_{i4} &= 0, \\ x_{i5} &= 7b_i, & \theta_{i5} &= 0, \end{aligned}$$

where $b_i = 4 * (w_1 + \cdots + w_{i-1}) + 2w_i + i$.

The probabilities of speed changes in P are defined as

$$P(u_i) = \begin{cases} 0 & \text{if } u_i = u_{i1} = 0, \\ v_i/3 & \text{if } u_i = u_{i2} = b_i + w_i, \\ v_i/3 & \text{if } u_i = u_{i3} = b_i - 2w_i \\ v_i/3 & \text{if } u_i = u_{i4} = b_i + w_i, \\ 0 & \text{if } u_i = u_{i5} = -7bi, \\ 0 & \text{otherwise} \end{cases}$$

for $i = 1, \dots, n$.

We can show that there is a subset of items with total weight W and total value V, if and only if there is a repair x' with $\Delta(x, x') = W$ and $L(x') = V$. □

Proof of Proposition 2

Proof. First, we show the correctness of the recurrence equation in formula (4) in the dynamic programming. That is, $D(i, c_i, x'_{i-1}, x'_i)$ in formula (4) always calculates the maximum likelihood $L(x'_{1\dots i})$ whose cost is $\Delta(x'_{1\dots i}, x_{1\dots i}) = c_i$, and the last two values are x'_{i-1}, x'_i.

Suppose that there is another repair x'' whose cost is also $\Delta(x''_{1\dots i}, x_{1\dots i}) = c_i$, and the last two values are also $x''_{i-1} = x'_{i-1}, x''_i = x'_i$, and $L(x'') > L(x')$.

If $x''_{i-2} \neq x'_{i-2}$, referring to $L(x'') > L(x')$, we have

$$\begin{aligned} &D(i-1, c_{i-1}, x''_{i-2}, x''_{i-1}) + L(u''_{i-1}) \\ >&D(i-1, c_{i-1}, x'_{i-2}, x'_{i-1}) + L(u'_{i-1}). \end{aligned}$$

It contradicts the condition that formula (4) takes a x'_{i-2} with the maximum $D(i-1, c_{i-1}, x'_{i-2}, x'_{i-1}) + L(u'_{i-1})$.

If $x''_{i-2} = x'_{i-2}$, we have $L(u''_{i-1}) = L(u'_{i-1})$. It follows

$$D(i-1, c_{i-1}, x''_{i-2}, x''_{i-1}) > D(i-1, c_{i-1}, x'_{i-2}, x'_{i-1}),$$

which contradicts the condition that $D(i-1, c_{i-1}, x'_{i-2}, x'_{i-1})$ is the maximum likelihood whose cost is c_{i-1}, and the last two values are $x'_{i-2}(= x''_{i-2}), x'_{i-1}(= x''_{i-1})$.

The correctness of the recurrence equation is proved.

Given the recurrence equation in formula (4), we need $O(n\theta^2\delta)$ space to maintain $D(i, c_i, x'_{i-1}, x'_i)$. By considering $2\theta + 1$ candidates for x'_{i-2} in $[x_{i-2} \pm \theta_{i-2}]$, in each calculation of $D(i, c_i, x'_{i-1}, x'_i)$, the dynamic programming runs in $O(n\theta^3_{\max}\delta)$ time. □

Table 3: Notations

Symbol	Description
x	a sequence of n data points
x'	repair of sequence x
$x[i]$ or x_i	value of i-th data point in x
$x_{i\ldots j}$	a subsequence of x from i-th to j-th data points
t_i	timestamp of i-th data point
θ	error range of each data point
δ	cost budget for repairing
u_i	speed change before and after i-th data point
P	probability distribution of speed changes
$p_{\max}, p_{\min}$	max/min probabilities in distribution P
$L(x)$	The likelihood of a sequence x w.r.t. speed changes (Equation 2)
$D(i, c_i, x'_{i-1}, x'_i)$	The maximum likelihood of the subsequence $x_{1\ldots i}$, whose cost is c_i and the last two values are x'_{i-1}, x'_i, respectively (Equation 4)
$C(i, l_i, x'_{i-1}, x'_i)$	The minimized cost of subsequence $x_{1\ldots i}$, whose likelihood is l_i and the last two values are x'_{i-1}, x'_i, respectively (Equation 8)

Proof of Proposition 3

Proof. We show that

$$\begin{aligned}
L(x') &= L(x'_{1\ldots i}) + L(x'_{i-1\ldots n}) \\
&= D(i, c_i, x'_{i-1}, x'_i) + L(x'_{i-1\ldots n}) \\
&\leq D(i, c_i, x'_{i-1}, x'_i) + L^u(x_{i-1\ldots n}) \\
&\leq L^w(x) \leq L(x^*).
\end{aligned}$$

That is, any solution x' with this $D(i, c_i, x'_{i-1}, x'_i)$ is not optimal and can be pruned. The conclusion is proved. □

Proof of Proposition 4

Proof. According to formula (6), the total number of c'_i to consider is $\frac{\delta}{H} = d$. Similarly, referring to formula (7), the total number of x'_i to consider is $2\lfloor\frac{\theta_i}{H}\rfloor + 1$. Since δ is the bound of repair cost, it follows the maximum number of x'_i to consider, $2\lfloor\frac{\delta}{H}\rfloor + 1 = 2d + 1$. Considering all $D(i, c'_i, x'_{i-1}, x'_i)$, the dynamic algorithm runs in $O(n(2d+1)^3 d)$ time with $O(n(2d+1)^2 d)$ space. The conclusion is proved. □

Proof of Proposition 5

Proof. According to formula (9), for any u'_i, we have

$$L(u'_i) \leq (L'(u'_i) + 1) \cdot K.$$

Table 4: Significance on STOCK with error number 600, data size 1282, $\theta = 5$, $\delta = 1800$

significant \ p-value	DPL	SG	SCREEN	QP
DPL	-	0.040	8.238E-10	3.989E-6
SG	yes	-	2.427E-10	2.201E-4
SCREEN	yes	yes	-	1.784E-11
QP	yes	yes	yes	-

Table 5: Significance on GPS with error number 360, data size 4712, $\theta = 38$, $\delta = 660$

significant \ p-value	DPL	SG	SCREEN	QP
DPL	-	1.348E-5	1.575E-8	7.835E-8
SG	yes	-	1.935E-5	4.282E-10
SCREEN	yes	yes	-	3.340E-15
QP	yes	yes	yes	-

Table 6: Significance on ENGINE with error number unknown, data size 464, $\theta = 20$, $\delta = 1000$

significant \ p-value	DPL	RAW	SG	SCREEN	QP
DPL	-	1.6E-12	0.015	2.2E-7	0.013
RAW	yes	-	1.1E-14	0.011	5.3E-6
SG	yes	yes	-	2.434E-6	0.007
SCREEN	yes	yes	yes	-	2.0E-6
QP	yes	yes	yes	yes	-

Let x^* denote the optimal solution. We have

$$\begin{aligned}
L(x^*) - K \cdot L'(x^*) &= \sum_{i=2}^{n-1} \left(L(u^*_i) - K \cdot L'(u^*_i)\right) \\
&\leq \sum_{i=2}^{n-1} K \\
&= (n-2) \cdot K
\end{aligned}$$

It follows

$$\begin{aligned}
L(x') &\geq K \cdot L'(x') \\
&\geq K \cdot L'(x^*) \\
&\geq L(x^*) - (n-2) \cdot K \\
&= L(x^*) + (n-2) \cdot \varepsilon \cdot \log p_{\max} \\
&\geq (1+\varepsilon) \cdot L(x^*)
\end{aligned}$$

For each i, the range of likelihood that needs to be considered is

$$l^{end} - l^{start} = (i-2) \cdot \log \frac{p_{\max}}{p_{\min}}.$$

With the approximate likelihood L' defined in formula (9), only a finite number of approximate likelihoods that need to be considered for each i, i.e.,

$$\begin{aligned}
\left\lfloor \frac{(i-2) \cdot \log \frac{p_{\max}}{p_{\min}}}{K} \right\rfloor &= (i-2)\left\lfloor -\frac{\log \frac{p_{\max}}{p_{\min}}}{\varepsilon \cdot \log p_{\max}} \right\rfloor \\
&= (i-2)\left\lfloor \frac{1}{\varepsilon}\left(\frac{\log p_{\min}}{\log p_{\max}} - 1\right) \right\rfloor
\end{aligned} \tag{14}$$

Table 7: Significance on SYNTHETIC-clean with error number 0, data size 500, $\theta = 5$, $\delta = 225$

p-value \ significant	DPL	SG	SCREEN	QP
DPL	-	8.349E-11	2.331E-12	1.315E-7
SG	yes	-	3.734E-13	7.495E-16
SCREEN	yes	yes	-	5.876E-19
QP	yes	yes	yes	-

Table 8: Significance on SYNTHETIC-inject with error number 150, data size 500, $\theta = 5$, $\delta = 225$

p-value \ significant	DPL	SG	SCREEN	QP
DPL	-	0.002	1.333E-11	3.998E-5
SG	yes	-	8.039E-11	8.179E-6
SCREEN	yes	yes	-	3.297E-12
QP	yes	yes	yes	-

Table 9: Significance on SYNTHETIC-clean prediction with error number 0, data size 500, $\theta = 5$, $\delta = 150$

p-value \ significant	DPL	RAW	SG	SCREEN	QP
DPL	-	0.005	2.7E-5	4.4E-10	1.1E-6
RAW	yes	-	7.6E-20	4.4E-12	1.1E-12
SG	yes	yes	-	4.0E-11	8.5E-9
SCREEN	yes	yes	yes	-	1.4E-10
QP	yes	yes	yes	yes	-

Table 10: Significance on SYNTHETIC-inject prediction with error number 150, data size 500, $\theta = 5$, $\delta = 600$

p-value \ significant	DPL	RAW	SG	SCREEN	QP
DPL	-	7.8E-34	4.3E-26	3.2E-9	7.4E-4
RAW	yes	-	2.1E-27	4.4E-12	1.7E-12
SG	yes	yes	-	1.9E-10	6.3E-9
SCREEN	yes	yes	yes	-	2.3E-9
QP	yes	yes	yes	yes	-

It concludes $O(n^2\theta_{\max}^3)$ time and $O(n^2\theta_{\max}^2)$ space. □

Proof of Proposition 6

Proof. For any repair x' with $C(i, l_i, x'_{i-1}, x'_i)$, we have

$$\begin{aligned} L(x') &= L(x'_{1\dots i}) + L(x'_{i-1\dots n}) \\ &= l_i + L(x'_{i-1\dots n}) \\ &\le l_i + L^u(x_{i-1\dots n}) \\ &\le L^w(x) \le L(x^*). \end{aligned}$$

That is, x' is not optimal and can be safely pruned. The conclusion is proved. □

Proof of Corollary 7

Proof. According to formula (9), for any u'_i, we have

$$L(u'_i) \le (L'(u'_i) + 1) \cdot K.$$

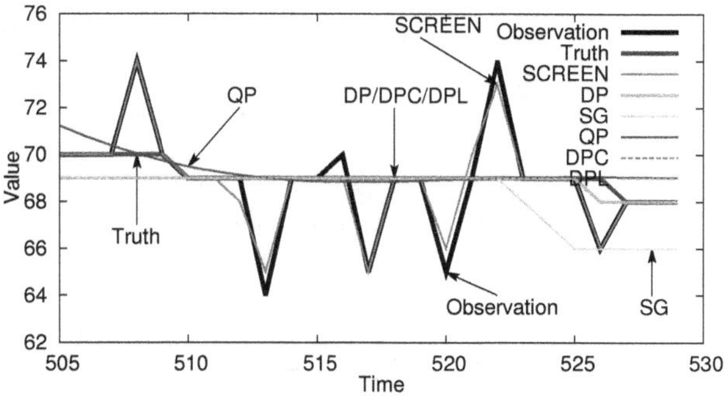

Figure 23: Case study on STOCK repair results

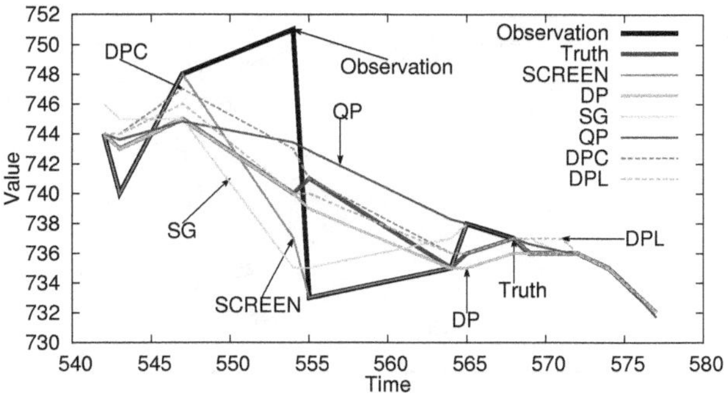

Figure 24: Case study on GPS repair results

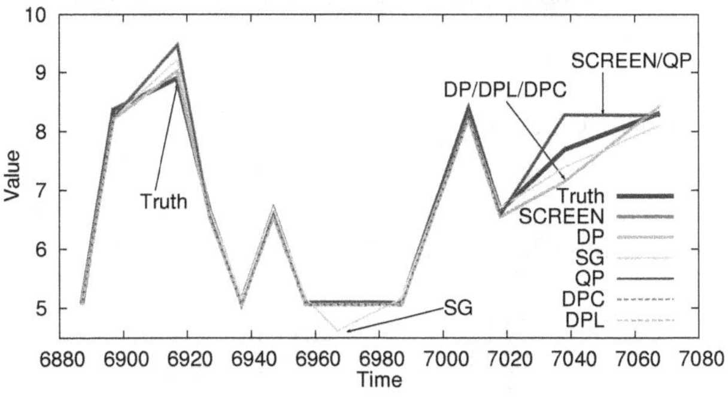

Figure 25: Case study on ENGINE prediction results

For any repair x' with $C(i, l'_i, x'_{i-1}, x'_i)$, we have

$$\begin{aligned} L(x') &= L(x'_{1\dots i}) + L(x'_{i-1\dots n}) \\ &= \sum_{j=2}^{i-1} L(u'_j) + L(x'_{i-1\dots n}) \\ &\le \sum_{j=2}^{i-1} K \cdot \left(L'(u'_j) + 1\right) + L(x'_{i-1\dots n}) \\ &= K \cdot l'_i + K \cdot (i-2) + L(x'_{i-1\dots n}) \\ &\le K \cdot (l'_i + i - 2) + L^u(x_{i-1\dots n}) \\ &\le L^w(x) \le L(x^*). \end{aligned}$$

That is, x' is not optimal and can be safely pruned. The conclusion is proved. □

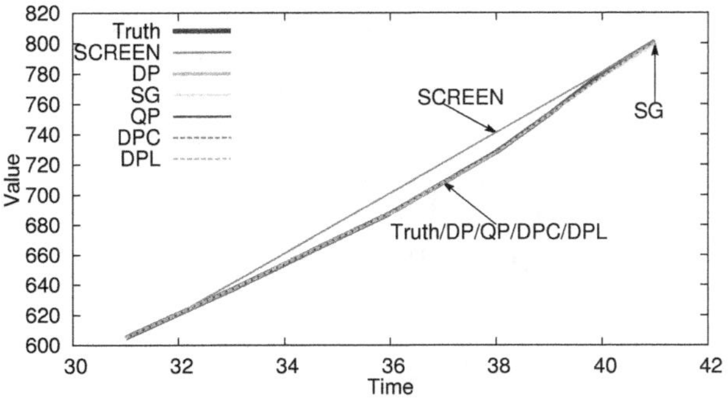

Figure 26: Case study on SYNTHETIC-clean repair results

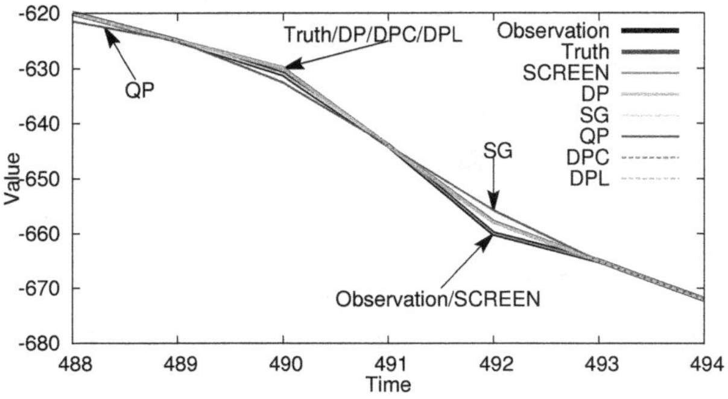

Figure 27: Case study on SYNTHETIC-injected repair results

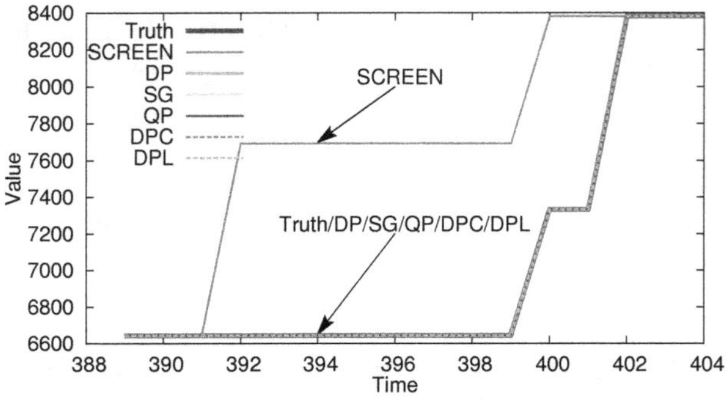

Figure 28: Case study on SYNTHETIC-clean prediction results

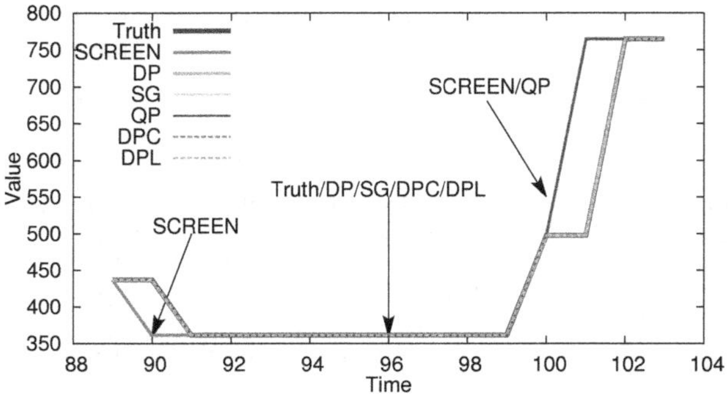

Figure 29: Case study on SYNTHETIC-injected prediction results

Proof of Proposition 8

Proof. According to formula (12), we have

$$\begin{aligned} L(x) &= \sum_{i=2}^{n-1} \log P(u_i) \\ &= \sum_{i=2}^{n-1} \log \left(\frac{1}{\sigma\sqrt{2\pi}} e^{-\frac{u_i^2}{2\sigma^2}} \right) \\ &= \sum_{i=2}^{n-1} \left(\log \frac{1}{\sigma\sqrt{2\pi}} - \frac{u_i^2}{2\sigma^2} \log e \right) \\ &= (n-2) \log \frac{1}{\sigma\sqrt{2\pi}} - \frac{\log e}{2\sigma^2} \sum_{i=2}^{n-1} u_i^2 \end{aligned}$$

It follows $L(x') - L(x'') \geq 0$ if and only if $\sum_{i=2}^{n-1}(u_i')^2 - \sum_{i=2}^{n-1}(u_i'')^2 \leq 0$, where u_i', u_i'' are speed changes w.r.t. x_i', x_i'', respectively. □

Proof of Proposition 9

Proof. The greedy computation terminates in at most δ iterations. By amortizing the likelihood values over a constant domain, data points with low likelihood could be directly obtained. The algorithm runs in $O(\max(n, \delta))$ time. □

B. STATISTICAL SIGNIFICANCE ON EXPERIMENTS

In order to demonstrate that the differences in algorithms are real in all the experiments, we report the statistical significance calculations [12]. Consider the null hypothesis that two compared algorithms are the same. Let the significance level be $\alpha = 0.05$. We run each experiment 10 times, and conduct the Student's Paired t-test by using APACHE math lib[4]. Tables 4, 5, 6, 7, 8, 9 and 10 report the calculated p-values of all the experiments, as well as the corresponding determination of whether the null hypothesis should be rejected or not. As shown, all the results are statistically significant, i.e., rejecting the null hypothesis with $p < 0.05$.

C. CASE STUDY ON EXPERIMENTS

To show the differences between the competing approaches, Figures 23, 24, 25, 26, 27, 28 and 29 present case studies on all datasets. (1) The prior method SCREEN cannot capture "small" errors, e.g., as observed at time 508 in Figure 23, since it satisfies the max/min speed constraints. (2) While SCREEN successfully detects the large spike error at time 520 in Figure 23, the max/min speed based repair makes the result only a bit closer to the truth, not as close as our proposals (DP, QP, SG, etc.). (3) Generally, the exact DP shows better performance than the approximate QP and SG, e.g., in Figure 24. (4) The difference of methods in prediction application in Figure 25 is not as significant as the results directly on repairs, which verifies the accuracy study in Figure 17. (5) For the experiments on SYNTHETIC-clean data in Figure 26, almost all the methods propose to not (or slightly) modify the data.

Learning-Based Cleansing for Indoor RFID Data

Asif Iqbal Baba[†] Manfred Jaeger[†] Hua Lu[†] Torben Bach Pedersen[†]
Wei-Shinn Ku[‡] Xike Xie[†]
[†]Department of Computer Science, Aalborg University, Denmark
[‡]Department of Computer Science and Software Engineering, Auburn University, USA
[†]{asif, jaeger, luhua, tbp, xkxie}@cs.aau.dk, [‡]weishinn@auburn.edu

ABSTRACT

RFID is widely used for object tracking in indoor environments, e.g., airport baggage tracking. Analyzing RFID data offers insight into the underlying tracking systems as well as the associated business processes. However, the inherent uncertainty in RFID data, including noise (cross readings) and incompleteness (missing readings), pose challenges to high-level RFID data querying and analysis. In this paper, we address these challenges by proposing a learning-based data cleansing approach that, unlike existing approaches, requires no detailed prior knowledge about the spatio-temporal properties of the indoor space and the RFID reader deployment. Requiring only minimal information about RFID deployment, the approach learns relevant knowledge from raw RFID data and uses it to cleanse the data. In particular, we model raw RFID readings as time series that are sparse because the indoor space is only partly covered by a limited number of RFID readers. We propose the Indoor RFID Multi-variate Hidden Markov Model (IR-MHMM) to capture the uncertainties of indoor RFID data as well as the correlation of moving object locations and object RFID readings. We propose three state space design methods for IR-MHMM that enable the learning of parameters while contending with raw RFID data time series. We solely use raw uncleansed RFID data for the learning of model parameters, requiring no special labeled data or ground truth. The resulting IR-MHMM based RFID data cleansing approach is able to recover missing readings and reduce cross readings with high effectiveness and efficiency, as demonstrated by extensive experimental studies with both synthetic and real data. Given enough indoor RFID data for learning, the proposed approach achieves a data cleansing accuracy comparable to or even better than state-of-the-art techniques requiring very detailed prior knowledge, making our solution superior in terms of both effectiveness and employability.

1. INTRODUCTION

Recently there has been a remarkable proliferation of RFID in indoor tracking and monitoring systems, e.g., airport baggage monitoring. Most RFID based applications today use low-cost passive RFID tags that are very small and require no source of power.

SIGMOD'16, June 26-July 01, 2016, San Francisco, CA, USA

DOI: http://dx.doi.org/10.1145/2882903.2882907

These tags can be attached to a person or an item. Deployed RFID readers detect such tags and thus the moving objects that they are attached to when the objects appear in the readers detection ranges. Typically, a raw RFID detection reading $\langle o, r, t\rangle$ means that object o is detected by RFID reader r at time point t.

However, the dirtiness of RFID data poses challenges to high-level RFID data querying and analysis. In this paper, we focus on cleansing *false negatives* and *false positives* in indoor RFID data.

False negatives (missing readings) occur when a reader fails to read a tag in its detection range. They are caused by power failures on a reader, tag orientation with respect to the reader, presence of metal, dielectric or water close to the tag, and other factors.

False positives (cross readings) occur when a tagged object is unexpectedly read by multiple readers simultaneously. They may result from the unexpected change of the detection range of a reader nearby. Such changes happen due to various reasons, e.g., metal items that reflect the signals or the re-direction of reader antenna(s). As a result, the object is reported by multiple readers that are placed at different positions, and thus spatial ambiguities are caused.

For illustration, we consider an example floor plan with 17 readers shown in Figure 1. A moving object with tag tag_1 moved into the building and was first detected by reader R_1 from time point t_0 to time point t_3, yielding four observations by reader R_1. The raw RFID data about tag_1 is shown in Table 1. Note that a tagged object is not continuously detected by RFID readers, which introduces uncertainties in the raw RFID data: for many time points the data does not tell where the object is.

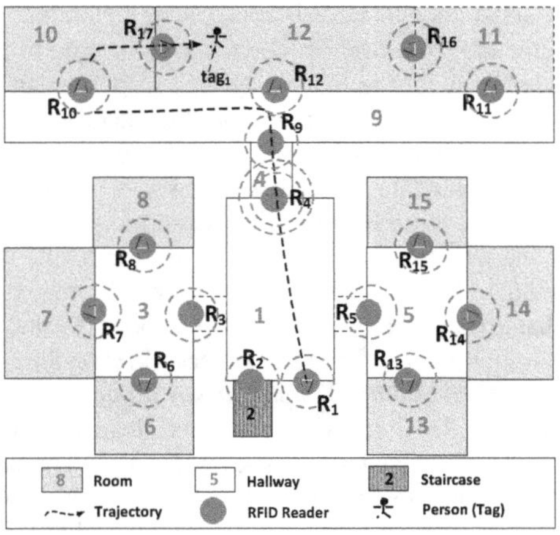

Figure 1: Example of indoor space and RFID reader deployment

At time points t_{12} and t_{13}, the moving object with tag_1 was detected by readers R_4 and R_9, due to the unexpected expansion of R_4's detection range. As a result, tag_1 seems to be present in both locations at time points t_{12} and t_{13}, thus giving rise to a false positives. It is, however, impossible that tag_1 can appear in both locations at the same time as the two readers R_4 and R_9 cover two separate locations and their detection ranges are not deployed to overlap.

After time point t_{16}, object with tag_1 was detected by reader R_{17} that kept detecting tag_1 until time point t_{29}. However, tag_1 is not supposed to be detected by R_{17} before it is detected by reader R_{10} on its way as shown in Figure 1. To enter room 12 from room 9 via room 10, tag_1 must pass R_{10}'s detection range and yield the observation. But this is not the case here: tag_1 passed through R_{10} but failed to generate any information, thus giving rise to false negatives.

tagID	readerID	t	tagID	readerID	t	tagID	readerID	t
tag_1	R_1	t_0	tag_1	R_4	t_{10}	tag_1	R_9	t_{15}
tag_1	R_1	t_1	tag_1	R_4	t_{11}	tag_1	R_9	t_{16}
tag_1	R_1	t_2	tag_1	R_4	t_{12}	tag_1	R_1	t_{26}
tag_1	R_1	t_3	tag_1	R_9	t_{13}	tag_1	R_{17}	t_{27}
tag_1	R_4	t_7	tag_1	R_4	t_{13}	tag_1	R_{17}	t_{28}
tag_1	R_4	t_8	tag_1	R_9	t_{14}	tag_1	R_{17}	t_{29}
tag_1	R_4	t_9	tag_1	R_4	t_{14}			

Table 1: Raw readings table

To support high-level RFID business logic processing, it is necessary to perform data cleansing to remove false positives and recover false negatives. Existing RFID data cleansing techniques require considerable specific prior knowledge for cleansing operations. Aiming at cleansing historical indoor RFID data, the graph model based cleansing approaches [1,2,7] rely on graphs that capture the indoor topology, the deployment of RFID readers, and multiple pertinent spatio-temporal properties such as the distances between readers and the minimum dwell time for an object to be detected by a reader. In the context of streaming RFID data, a probabilistic approach [22] demands to build four domain-specific probabilistic models before any data cleansing. In a similar online setting, another approach [20] assumes that the locations of neighboring objects are correlated to each other. In contrast, this work lifts such assumptions and needs only minimal prior knowledge about the indoor settings for which the data cleansing is to be conducted (details given in Section 3).

In this paper, we model the uncertainties in indoor RFID data by a hidden Markov model (HMM) and design methods to learn the model parameters from raw RFID data without requiring detailed prior knowledge about the indoor setting. In particular, we use a variant of the HMM [21] in finding out the exact whereabouts of a moving object from the raw indoor RFID positioning data. We transform raw RFID data into sparse time series, as objects are not under surveillance at each time point. Each moving object moves differently and may take different paths. We model the movement of an individual object as a series of state transitions outputted by an HMM that operates on a set of states. We model the indoor RFID data uncertainties and the generated object RFID readings using an *Indoor RFID Multi-variate Hidden Markov Model (IR-MHMM)*.

We model the RFID tracking and data cleansing problem by means of three connected stochastic processes. The underlying object location transition from one location to another location is a stochastic process which is not directly observable (*hidden*). A second stochastic process is the observation process, which generates (unclean) RFID observations dependent on the current object's location. A third, again unobserved, process represents the clean RFID data that ideally should have been observed given the object's location. Under suitable assumptions on the relationship between the observable unclean observation process, and the ideal clean data process, we model all three processes by means of an IR-MHMM. Using a learned IR-MHMM, we infer the clean RFID data process from the observed raw data process, and in that manner we filter out the false positives and insert the correct readings omitted as false negatives.

The paper makes the following contributions. First, we propose a general framework that models the uncertainties in indoor RFID data, which enables a cleansing service by inferring the observation states. Second, we formalize an indoor RFID multi-variate hidden Markov model (IR-MHMM) as the major building block of the cleansing service. Third, we present three different state space designs for IR-MHMM from a given indoor floor plan. Fourth, we conduct comprehensive experimental studies using both real and synthetic data. The results give insight into the design properties of the proposed IR-MHMM and demonstrate the efficiency and effectiveness of the proposed cleansing approach on indoor RFID data.

The rest of this paper is organized as follows. Section 2 covers preliminaries. Section 3 details the proposed method. Section 4 presents the evaluation approach for the proposed method. Section 5 reports the experimental results. Section 6 reviews related work, followed by the conclusion in Section 7.

2. PRELIMINARIES

We briefly recall the fundamental concepts and definitions of *Hidden Markov Models (HMMs)*. An HMM models two connected (discrete time) stochastic processes: an un-observed state transition process, and an observation process consisting of observable signals generated at each state. The underlying (hidden) state transition process is assumed to be Markovian and stationary. Formally, an HMM is a tuple $\lambda = (\mathcal{S}, \mathcal{O}, A, B, \pi)$, where:

1. $\mathcal{S} = \{s_1, \ldots, s_N\}$ is a set of (hidden) states.
2. $\mathcal{O} = \{o_1, \ldots, o_K\}$ is a set of possible observations.
3. A is an $N \times N$ transition probability matrix: $A = (a_{ij})_{i,j=1,\ldots,N}$, where a_{ij} represents the transition probability from hidden state s_i to hidden state s_j.
4. B is an $N \times K$ observation probability matrix: $B = (b_{ih})_{i=1,\ldots,N;h=1,\ldots,K}$, where b_{ih} is the probability of observing o_h when the hidden process is in state s_i.
5. π is a N-dimensional initial state probability vector: $\pi = (\pi_i)_{i=1,\ldots,N}$, where π_i is the probability that the hidden state process starts in state s_i.

An HMM defines a discrete time stochastic process over the combined state and observation space $\mathcal{S} \times \mathcal{O}$. The state of the process at time t is described by random variables $S^{(t)}$ with values in $\mathcal{S}$, and $O^{(t)}$ with values in $\mathcal{O}$, and the joint distribution of the $S^{(t)}$ and $O^{(t)}$ is defined by $P(S^{(0)} = s_i) = \pi_i$, $P(S^{(t+1)} = s_j \mid S^{(t)} = s_i) = a_{ij}$, and $P(O^{(t)} = o_h \mid S^{(t)} = s_i) = b_{ih}$.

For modeling processes where at each point in time observations of multiple variables are made, the basic HMM model has been generalized to *Multi-variate Hidden Markov Models (MHMMs)* [15]. In this model the simple observation space $\mathcal{O}$ is replaced by a multivariate observation space $\mathcal{O}_1 \times \cdots \times \mathcal{O}_M$, and at each time t one observes variables $O_1^{(t)}, \ldots, O_M^{(t)}$. In this model one can furthermore introduce the assumption that the different observations are independent given the hidden state, i.e., $P(O_1^{(t)}, \ldots, O_M^{(t)} \mid S^{(t)}) = \prod_{i=1}^{M} P(O_i^{(t)} \mid S^{(t)})$, and then parameterize the observation probability distribution given the hidden states by M

separate matrices for the distributions $P(O_i^{(t)} \mid S^{(t)})$. A customized version of this MHMM model will be the basis for our RFID data cleansing model.

3. THE IR-MHMM APPROACH

3.1 Data Transformation

To prepare the application of MHMMs to our problem, we have to transform the raw readings data as illustrated in Table 1 into a format suitable for processing by MHMMs. RFID readers continuously detect objects in their range and report in the frequency determined by their sampling rate. They thereby generate raw data entries of the form $\langle tagID, readerID, t \rangle$, which means that the object with $tagID$ is detected by the reader $readerID$ at time t.

In this paper we are concerned with cleaning the tracking data for one object at a time, so that from the raw reader data we first select all records relating to a specific tag (as already shown in Table 1). The $tagID$ then becomes a constant, and the relevant part of the records are just the pairs $\langle readerID, t \rangle$.

As a first step, we discretize the continuous timestamp data. For this, a time granularity parameter α is chosen. For an object whose tracking data spans an interval of duration $(t_e - t_s)$, where t_s and t_e are the first and last readings reported about the object, we introduce $T = \frac{(t_e - t_s)}{\alpha}$ discrete time points $0, \ldots, (T-1)$. A continuous time record $\langle readerID, t \rangle$ then is replaced by $\langle readerID, i \rangle$, where i is such that $t \in [t_s + i \cdot \alpha, t_s + (i+1) \cdot \alpha]$. The choice of α should be based on two considerations: First, it should be chosen small enough, so that the discretization does not introduce any spurious appearances of cross readings. This can be ensured when $\alpha < \Delta_{min}/2$, where Δ_{min} is the minimum absolute difference between continuous time-stamps of records with different *readerID*s. Secondly, the time granularity must be small enough, so that clean data of this granularity is sufficient for subsequent tracking and analysis purposes. Under these two constraints, α should be chosen as large as possible, to minimize the computational complexity of the cleaning process.

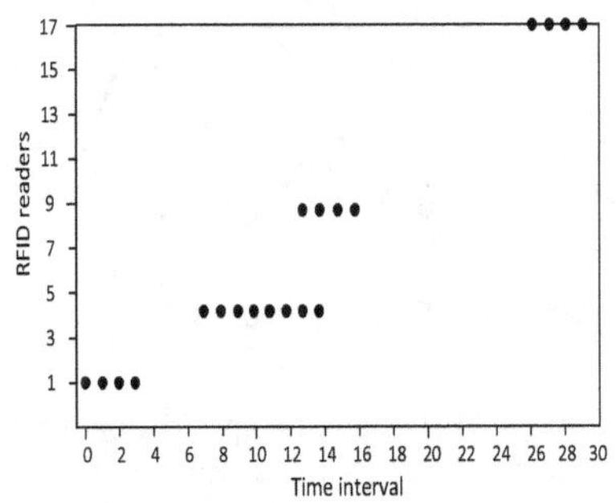

(a) Plotted

```
10000000000000000 00000000100000000
10000000000000000 00000000100000000
10000000000000000 00000000000000000
10000000000000000 00000000000000000
00000000000000000 00000000000000000
00000000000000000 00000000000000000
00000000000000000 00000000000000000
00010000000000000 00000000000000000
00010000000000000 00000000000000000
00010000000000000 00000000000000000
00010000000000000 00000000000000000
00010000000000000 00000000000000001
00010000000000000 00000000000000001
00010000100000000 00000000000000001
00010000100000000 00000000000000001
```

(b) Binary vector representation

Figure 2: Raw data of Table 1 as discrete time-series.

For illustration purposes, assume that the data in Table 1 is already discretized, i.e. t_i in this table stands for the discrete time point i. Figure 2 (a) shows an alternative representation of this data, where we plot the readings in a coordinate system with the time points on the x-axis, and the possible reader IDs on the y-axis. This time series can equivalently be encoded as a sequence of T binary vectors of length M, where M is the number of readers (Figure 2 (b)).

At the end of the transformation process, the data now consists of a sequence $\boldsymbol{V}_r^{(0)}, \ldots, \boldsymbol{V}_r^{(T-1)}$, where each $\boldsymbol{V}_r^{(t)} \in \{0,1\}^M$. The subscript r stands for *raw*, to emphasize that this still is raw data with possible false positives and false negatives. The kth component of $\boldsymbol{V}_r^{(t)}$ is denoted $V_{r,k}^{(t)}$. In the following, we will consider the $\boldsymbol{V}_r^{(t)}$ as the observations in a MHMM process, and use standard HMM learning and inference techniques to transform the $\boldsymbol{V}_r^{(t)}$ into cleaned versions $\boldsymbol{V}_c^{(t)}$. The cleaned data still takes values in $\{0,1\}^M$, but now with the condition that each $\boldsymbol{V}_c^{(t)}$ contains at most one non-zero entry (i.e., no cross readings). This cleaning process will be based on certain probabilistic modeling assumptions and computational approximations. In the following section we clarify these underlying assumptions. We do this on a more general basis than our specific data model $\boldsymbol{V}_r^{(t)}$, so that our analysis also provides a basis on which we can compare approaches taken in related work. The next section may also be skipped at a first reading, and returned to when a deeper understanding of the proposed method is desired. The concrete description of our cleaning method for the transformed data $\boldsymbol{V}_r$ continues in Section 3.3.

3.2 Probabilistic Inference for RFID Streams

In a broader sense than data cleansing alone, probabilistic methods for processing raw RFID data streams can be characterized as follows. We are given a sequence of raw readings $\boldsymbol{o}_r = o_r^{(0)}, \ldots, o_r^{(T-1)}$, where each $o_r^{(t)}$ is an observation of a random variable $O_r^{(t)}$ that takes values in a raw observation space $\mathcal{O}_r$. From $\boldsymbol{o}_r$ we want to infer a clean data sequence $\boldsymbol{o}_c = o_c^{(0)}, \ldots, o_c^{(T-1)}$ of observations of random variables $O_c^{(t)}$ that take values in a clean observation space $\mathcal{O}_c$. Based on a probabilistic model for $\boldsymbol{O}_r$ and $\boldsymbol{O}_c$ one can infer the clean from the raw data $\boldsymbol{o}_r$ by selecting the $\boldsymbol{o}_c$ that maximizes the conditional probability $P(\boldsymbol{O}_c = \boldsymbol{o}_c \mid \boldsymbol{O}_r = \boldsymbol{o}_r)$.

A straightforward approach to defining the joint distribution of $\boldsymbol{O}_r, \boldsymbol{O}_c$ is in the form of an HMM with $O_r^{(t)}$ as the observable variables, and $O_c^{(t)}$ as the hidden state variables $S^{(t)}$. This approach, however, faces two fundamental difficulties. The first difficulty lies in the fact that here the hidden state space must correspond to the clean observation space that is required for the RFID data stream processing problem at hand. On the basis of this particular hidden state space, and under the limitation of the Markov assumption for the state transition model, it may not be possible to obtain an accurate model for the joint distribution $P(\boldsymbol{O}_c, \boldsymbol{O}_r)$. To illustrate this point, consider the concrete raw and clean data models $\boldsymbol{V}_r^{(t)}, \boldsymbol{V}_c^{(t)} \in \{0,1\}^M$ we have introduced in the previous section. The clean state 0^M (no reading) would then be a hidden HMM state. Under the Markov assumption, the model could then not represent that given that currently there is no reading, the probability distribution over the next reading depends on what the most recent available reading has been. In our example of Figure 1, when currently there is no reading, then the information that the last available reading has come from reader R_1 should increase the probability that at the next point in time we observe a reading from one of R_2, R_3, R_4 or R_5.

The second difficulty arising from equating $\mathcal{S} = \mathcal{O}_c$ lies in constructing or learning an adequate model. Since now inferred hidden state sequences are the target of inference, one has to ensure that inferred hidden state values actually correspond to the relevant properties of the underlying tracking process that we want to capture with the clean data $\boldsymbol{O}_c$. When hidden HMM states are endowed in this manner with an intended meaning, we also call them *semantic states*. The construction of HMMs whose hidden states adhere to an intended semantics usually requires either manual design, or learning from labeled training data in which besides the observation variables $\boldsymbol{O}$ also the hidden states $\boldsymbol{S}$ are given.

In spite of these difficulties, most previous work that employs HMMs for RFID data stream analysis follows the $\mathcal{S} = \mathcal{O}_c$ approach [20, 22]. The first difficulty can be dealt with by a careful design of $\mathcal{S}$, whose elements must simultaneously represent the relevant information for the clean data, and some additional information to support an effective Markov model (e.g. some form of limited memory about past states). It is usually not possible to circumvent the second difficulty without taking recourse to some manual model specification, or learning from data that carries additional annotations beyond pure raw readings.

It is our goal to construct HMMs for $P(\boldsymbol{O}_c \mid \boldsymbol{O}_r)$ in a completely unsupervised manner, i.e., by learning from training data that consists of the raw observations $\boldsymbol{O}_r$ only. The hidden state space $\mathcal{S}$ then consists of *latent states*: states that have no predefined interpretation, and that are only introduced to support an adequate Markov model for the variables of interest $\boldsymbol{O}_c, \boldsymbol{O}_r$. Thus, our model will have to define a joint distribution $P(\boldsymbol{S}, \boldsymbol{O}_r, \boldsymbol{O}_c)$. Making a natural conditional independence assumption between $\boldsymbol{O}_r$ and $\boldsymbol{O}_c$ given $\boldsymbol{S}$, we can write:

$$P(\boldsymbol{S}, \boldsymbol{O}_r, \boldsymbol{O}_c) = P(\boldsymbol{S})P(\boldsymbol{O}_r \mid \boldsymbol{S})P(\boldsymbol{O}_c \mid \boldsymbol{S}). \tag{1}$$

Given the model $P(\boldsymbol{S}, \boldsymbol{O}_r, \boldsymbol{O}_c)$, the data cleaning inference task then is to compute for a given observed raw data sequence $\boldsymbol{o}_r$:

$$\underset{\boldsymbol{o}_c}{\mathit{arg\,max}}\, P(\boldsymbol{O}_c = \boldsymbol{o}_c \mid \boldsymbol{O}_r = \boldsymbol{o}_r) = \sum_{\boldsymbol{s}} P(\boldsymbol{S} = \boldsymbol{s} \mid \boldsymbol{O}_r = \boldsymbol{o}_r)P(\boldsymbol{O}_c = \boldsymbol{o}_c \mid \boldsymbol{S} = \boldsymbol{s}). \tag{2}$$

Here the sum is over all hidden state sequences $\boldsymbol{s}$ of the same length as $\boldsymbol{o}_r$. To implement this approach, two main challenges have to be met. First, one has to learn the model (1), which includes the conditional distribution $P(\boldsymbol{O}_c \mid \boldsymbol{S})$ containing only variables for which we have no observations at all. Second, the maximization problem (2) has to be solved efficiently (which precludes actual summation over all $\boldsymbol{s}$).

We tackle the first challenge by making some strong assumptions on the relationship between $\boldsymbol{O}_c$ and $\boldsymbol{O}_r$, the result of which will be that we implicitly also learn $P(\boldsymbol{O}_c \mid \boldsymbol{S})$ by learning $P(\boldsymbol{O}_r \mid \boldsymbol{S})$. Our first assumption is that the clean data space is a subset of the raw data space:

$$\mathcal{O}_c \subseteq \mathcal{O}_r. \tag{3}$$

This assumption is true in our specific data model, where $\mathcal{O}_r = \{0,1\}^M$, and $\mathcal{O}_c \subseteq \mathcal{O}_r$ consists of the vectors with at most one non-zero component.

We now make a crucial assumption on the relationship between $\boldsymbol{O}_r$ and $\boldsymbol{O}_c$. Intuitively we assume that $\boldsymbol{O}_r$ and $\boldsymbol{O}_c$ are generated by the same random process given $\boldsymbol{S}$, only that $\boldsymbol{O}_c$ is conditioned on the subset $\mathcal{O}_c$. Formally, this can be expressed by the assumption that for sequences $\boldsymbol{o}_c, \boldsymbol{s}$ (of a common length T):

$$P(\boldsymbol{O}_c = \boldsymbol{o}_c \mid \boldsymbol{S} = \boldsymbol{s}) = P(\boldsymbol{O}_r = \boldsymbol{o}_c \mid \boldsymbol{S} = \boldsymbol{s}) / P(\boldsymbol{O}_r \in \mathcal{O}_c^T \mid \boldsymbol{S} = \boldsymbol{s}). \tag{4}$$

Under assumptions (1), (3) and (4), our inference problem (2) becomes to compute

$$\underset{\boldsymbol{o}_c \in \mathcal{O}_c^T}{\mathit{arg\,max}} \sum_{\boldsymbol{s}} \frac{P(\boldsymbol{S} = \boldsymbol{s} \mid \boldsymbol{O}_r = \boldsymbol{o}_r)P(\boldsymbol{O}_r = \boldsymbol{o}_c \mid \boldsymbol{S} = \boldsymbol{s})}{P(\boldsymbol{O}_r \in \mathcal{O}_c^T \mid \boldsymbol{S} = \boldsymbol{s})} \tag{5}$$

We note that in the case where $\boldsymbol{o}_r$ already is a clean sequence, i.e., $\boldsymbol{o}_r \in \mathcal{O}_c^T$, the $\boldsymbol{o}_c$ maximizing (5) need not be equal to $\boldsymbol{o}_r$. Thus, the inference (5) can change a formally clean sequence (a sequence not containing any cross readings) by a more likely clean sequence (e.g. adding additional readings to correct likely false negatives).

The summation over all hidden state sequences $\boldsymbol{s}$ in (5) will usually be computationally infeasible. We therefore approximate the posterior distribution $P(\boldsymbol{S} = \boldsymbol{s} \mid \boldsymbol{O}_r = \boldsymbol{o}_r)$ by only considering the most probable state $\hat{\boldsymbol{s}} = \mathit{arg\,max}_{\boldsymbol{s}} P(\boldsymbol{S} = \boldsymbol{s} \mid \boldsymbol{O}_r = \boldsymbol{o}_r)$, and then computing

$$\hat{\boldsymbol{o}}_c = \underset{\boldsymbol{o}_c \in \mathcal{O}_c^T}{\mathit{arg\,max}}\, P(\boldsymbol{O}_r = \boldsymbol{o}_c \mid \boldsymbol{S} = \hat{\boldsymbol{s}}) \tag{6}$$

Note that the term $P(\boldsymbol{O}_r \in \mathcal{O}_c^T \mid \boldsymbol{S} = \hat{\boldsymbol{s}})$ now is a constant that can be omitted. In summary, our approach is characterized by making the probabilistic modeling assumptions (1), (3) and (4), and using the approximation (6) for (5).

Like most statistical assumptions, (1) and (4) are idealizations that typically will not be fully satisfied by the actual distribution $P(\boldsymbol{S}, \boldsymbol{O}_r, \boldsymbol{O}_c)$. Inferences obtained by an approach that implicitly makes these assumptions can still be accurate when the assumptions are not strictly valid (compare, e.g., the Naive Bayes classifier, whose underlying independence assumptions are hardly ever fully justified for the data that the classifier is used on).

3.3 Indoor RFID Multi-variate HMM

Based on the data transformation of Section 3.1 we implement the approach described in more general terms in Section 3.2 by a customized version of MHMMs. We define *Indoor RFID Multi-variate HMM (IR-MHMM)* as Multi-variate Hidden Markov Models $\lambda = (\mathcal{S}, \{0,1\}^M, A, B, \pi)$, where $\mathcal{S}, A, \pi$ are as in the generic (M)HMM definition, and the observation space is $\mathcal{O} = \{0,1\}^M$. Assuming that different readers are independent given the hidden state, the observation model is given by the probabilities $b_{ik} := P(V_{r,k}^{(t)} = 1 \mid S^{(t)} = s_i)$ (i.e., the probability of getting in the ith hidden state a reading from the kth reader). The observation model of the IR-MHMM now is represented by a matrix B of dimensions $N \times M$ with entries b_{ik}. Figure 3 gives a graphical representation of the model.

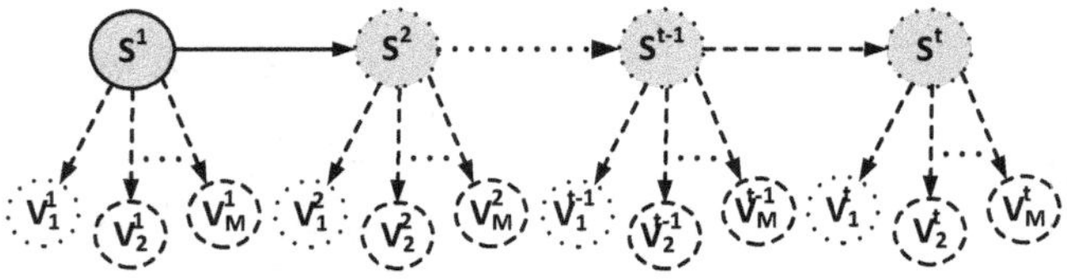

Figure 3: IR-MHMM for RFID raw data

To construct an IR-MHMM for an RFID cleaning application the model parameters N, A, B, π have to be determined (the parameter M is given by the application as the number of distinct readers). The construction is a combination of design and learning. It is our overall objective to minimize the amount of domain specific information required in the design component (such as data on spatial distances, or average travel times between readers), and to base the learning component entirely on learning from the raw data $\boldsymbol{V}_r$, without any further annotations.

In the design step, first the cardinality N of the state space is chosen. This may already complete the design component, and the probabilistic parameters A, B, π can now be learned. In this setting, the states $s_i \in \mathcal{S}$ are purely latent, without any associated semantics a-priori. Only after learning may it be possible to assign a semantic interpretation to some states. For example, if the learned value b_{ik} is much higher than other values b_{jk} ($j \neq i$), then state s_i represents that the tracked object is in the range of reader

R_k. Alternatively, one can try to associate a semantic meaning with states a-priori. It must be emphasized, however, that since learning is from raw data that does not contain information about the true nature of the hidden states, there is no guarantee that after learning the states closely adhere to their intended semantics. The best we can do is to bias the learning algorithm towards exploiting the suggested semantics of the hidden states. We do this by imposing prior constraints on the probabilistic components A and B. The following section describes three concrete designs of state spaces whose latent states are endowed with intended semantics.

3.4 State space design

We propose four different state space designs for IR-MHMMs. All our designs require as input at most some qualitative spatial information as expressed by a reader deployment graph. Designs define a set of states with associated intended semantics, such as states representing (approximate) spatial locations, or states representing some history of past transitions. The intended semantics of hidden states lead to constraints of the form $a_{ij} = 0$ (for some combinations i, j of states direct transitions will not be possible).

As a baseline, we consider the design where states are entirely latent, without associated semantics.

Unstructured-N (U-N). This design is given by the number N of hidden states alone. In our experiments for the floor plan in Figure 1, we consider the choices $N = 25, 34$ and 50, which correspond to the number of states of the three structured designs described next for a running example.

We next describe three different state space designs where states are associated with an intended semantics. We elaborated on the structure of the states spaces, and the constraints imposed on the transition model A. We defer the explanation of how the observation model B is handled to Section 3.5. The following three state space designs are illustrated in Figure 4 for the running example in Figure 1.

Minimum State Model (MSM). This design contains a state for each deployed reader R_i, and a state for each hallway or any indoor partition that is connected with more than one reader. For example, reader R_4 in Figure 1 is represented as state s_4 in the design shown in Figure 4(a). Furthermore, hallway 3 in Figure 1 is connected with four readers R_3, R_6, R_7, and R_8, and thus it is represented by a state s_{19}. The total number of states for our example scenario is $N = 25$. The transition model is constrained by setting $a_{ij} = 0$ if s_i and s_j correspond to locations that are not directly connected.

Last State Model (LSM). This design contains two states s_i and l_{si} for each deployed reader R_i. The intended meaning of s_i is that the object is within reader R_i's detection range, whereas state l_{si} represents that R_i was the last reader in whose range the object has been. The intention of this model is to alleviate the limitations of the Markov assumption by encoding a (very limited) history of previously visited states at the current state.

In this design, the non-zero transition probabilities are from states s_i to the corresponding l_{si}, and from states l_{si} to states s_j when there is a direct path from reader R_i to R_j. The state space size is $N = 2M$, i.e., $N = 34$ for our example domain of Figure 1.

In-between State Model (ISM). This design contains a state s_i for each deployed reader R_i, and a state s_{ij} for each pair of adjacent readers R_i and R_j. The intended meaning of s_{ij} is that the object is transitioning between R_i and R_j (in either direction). The transition probabilities are non-zero only between states s_i and s_{kj}, where $i \in \{k, j\}$. The design for our example domain as shown in Figure 4(c) has 50 states.

The three state space designs are applicable to any indoor space with any identification technology such as RFID, Infrared, Bluetooth, etc. The efficiency and effectiveness of the final design will, however, be dependent upon the indoor topology, target application, and the kind of data which is used to learn the parameters of the model.

3.5 Learning Parameters of IR-MHMM

Given a state space design, the unconstrained parameters (i.e., those not set to zero by the design) have to be estimated. For this we are using the standard EM algorithm (a.k.a. Baum-Welch algorithm in the HMM context), which operates on the full transition probability matrices A. Parameter constraints of the form $a_{ij} = 0$ are easy to integrate into this learning procedure: one only needs to initialize these parameters with zero values. The iterations of the EM algorithms will never turn zero values into non-zero values, so that the constraints will also be satisfied by the final solution, and the unconstrained parameters are fitted to the data.

In practice, in order to avoid division by zero errors, it is useful to initialize the constrained parameters with small values greater than 0. We therefore initialize those a_{ij} that are zero according to our state space design with values 0.01. For a fixed i, the initial values of the remaining transition probabilities a_{ij} then are set uniformly, so that $\sum_{j=1}^{N} a_{ij} = 1$. In our experiments we observe that imposing only the "soft" initial constraints $a_{ij} = 0.01$ does not lead to final solutions where the eventually learned a_{ij} parameter is significantly larger than 0. On the contrary, the parameters initialized with 0.01 typically become still much smaller during the EM iterations (usually ending with values $< 10^{-5}$ at termination) .

In all our state space designs, we have for each reader R_i a designated state s_i corresponding to locations within R_i's range. We still have to explain how we bias the learning procedure towards solutions that respect the intended semantics of these states. One could try to strictly impose the intended semantics by parameter constraints $b_{ii} = 1$ and $b_{ik} = 0$ for $k \neq i$. However, these hard constraints would preclude the possibility of cross readings. We therefore again use an initialization with a soft version of these constraints, setting $b_{ik} = 0.01$ $(k \neq i)$ and $b_{ii} = 1 - 0.01(M-1)$. Due to the presence of cross readings in the data, it may easily happen that in the final solution some b_{ik} with $k \neq i$ become significantly larger than their initial 0.01 values.

3.6 Data Cleaning

After an IR-MHMM λ has been constructed and its parameters have been learned, we use it to clean the raw RFID data as follows (cf. Algorithm 1). The input for the data cleansing procedure is raw RFID data transformed into a multi-variate binary observation sequence $\boldsymbol{v}_r = (v_{r,1}^{(t)}, \ldots, v_{r,M}^{(t)})_{t=0\ldots T-1}$, and an IR-MHMM λ.

First the standard Viterbi algorithm [23] is used to compute the most probable hidden state sequence $\hat{\boldsymbol{s}} = (\hat{s}^{(t)})_{t=0\ldots T-1}$ given $\boldsymbol{v}_r$. We then compute the most probable observation sequence $\hat{\boldsymbol{v}}_c = (\hat{v}_{c,1}^{(t)}, \ldots, \hat{v}_{c,M}^{(t)})_{t=0\ldots T-1}$ given $\hat{\boldsymbol{s}}$, under the constraint that at each t $(\hat{v}_{c,1}^{(t)}, \ldots, \hat{v}_{c,M}^{(t)})$ contains at most one non-zero entry. We denote by $\boldsymbol{e}_k \in \{0,1\}^M$ the binary vector that has value 1 at position k, and value 0 in all other components; $\mathbf{0}$ denotes the vector with value 0 in all components.

Due to the HMM structure, the most probable observation sequence given $\hat{\boldsymbol{s}}$ can be determined pointwise for each t by maximizing $P(\boldsymbol{V}_r^{(t)} = \boldsymbol{v}_r^{(t)} | S^{(t)} = \hat{s}^{(t)})$. If $\hat{s}^{(t)} = s_i$, then this probability is maximized by setting $\hat{v}_{r,k}^{(t)} = 1$ if $b_{ik} > 0.5$, and $\hat{v}_{r,k}^{(t)} = 0$ otherwise. Under the constraint that $\hat{v}_{r,k}^{(t)}$ can be nonzero for at most one k, i.e., we want to find the most probable clean observation vector $\hat{\boldsymbol{v}}_c$, this is modified to setting $\hat{v}_c^{(t)} = \boldsymbol{e}_k$ if $b_{ik} > 0.5$, and

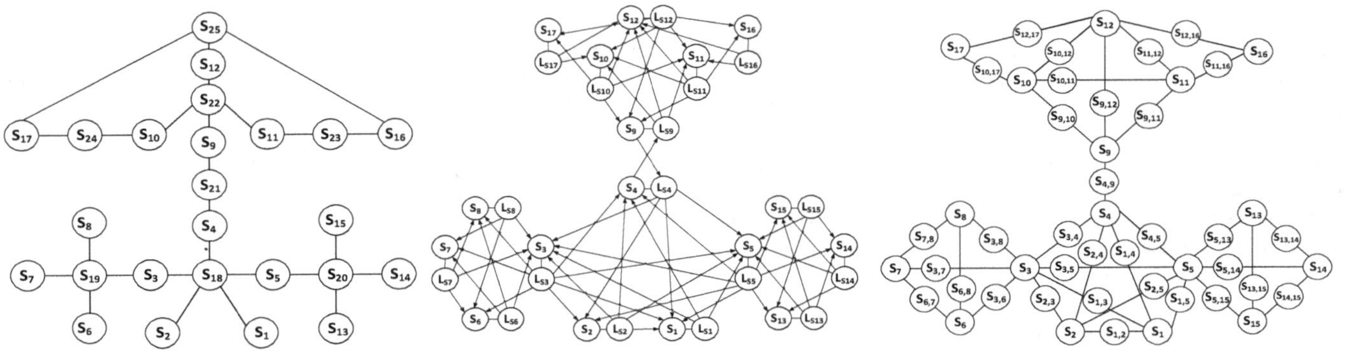

(a) Minimum state model (b) Last state model (c) In-between state model

Figure 4: State space designs

$b_{ik} > b_{ik'}$ for all $k' \neq k$ (lines 5-14). This implements (6) for our specific application.

Algorithm 1 Data Cleansing(IR-MHMM λ for M readers, Raw transformed RFID sequence $\boldsymbol{v}_r$ of length T)

1: $\hat{\boldsymbol{s}} \leftarrow$ **Viterbi** $(\boldsymbol{v}_r, \lambda)$
2: $\hat{\boldsymbol{v}}_c = \emptyset$
3: **for** $t = 0 \ldots T-1$ **do**
4:     i = state index of $\hat{s}^{(t)}$
5:     $p \leftarrow 0.5$
6:     $k_{max} = 0$
7:     **for** $k = 0 \ldots M$ **do**
8:         **if** $(b_{ik} > p)$ **then**
9:             $k_{max} \leftarrow k$
10:             $p \leftarrow b_{ik}$
11:     **if** $k_{max} > 0$ **then**
12:         $\mathbf{Concat}(\hat{\boldsymbol{v}}_c, \boldsymbol{e}_{k_{max}})$ ▷ Append $\boldsymbol{e}_{k_{max}}$ as tth component to output sequence
13:     **else**
14:         $\mathbf{Concat}(\hat{\boldsymbol{v}}_c, \mathbf{0})$ ▷ Append $\mathbf{0}$ as tth component to output sequence
15: **return** $\hat{\boldsymbol{v}}_c$

---

4. EDIT DISTANCE BASED EVALUATION

To evaluate the accuracy of inferred results, we check the similarity between the inferred observation trajectories and the corresponding ground truth trajectories. The two trajectories of the same object can be of different lengths. Since our data is not geometric but symbolic, we use a variant of edit distance [17]. It quantifies the dissimilarity between two strings by the number of operations (insert, delete, or substitute) required to transform one string into the other. When computing the edit distances, we use a slightly modified representation of the binary observation vectors. Basically, we use a sequence of reader IDs to represent an object's trajectories. If there is no reading at a time point, symbol 0 is used; if there are more than one reading at a time point, a set of reader IDs are used. Referring to the example data of object tag_1 shown in Figure 2(b), its raw trajectory (R_{traj1}) and ground truth trajectory (G_{traj1}) are shown in Figure 5.

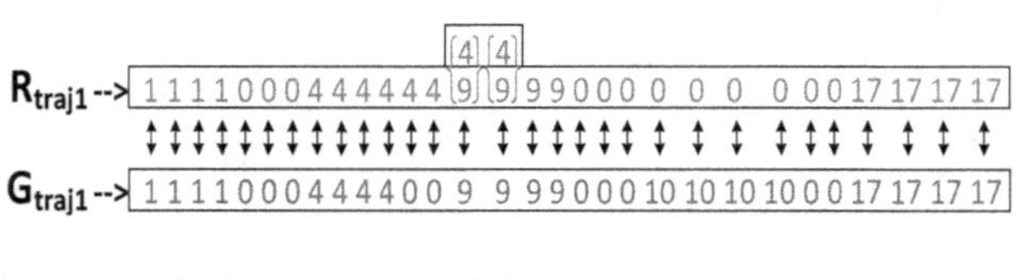

Figure 5: Example raw RFID and ground truth sequences

We use a weighted edit distance method, which allows the cost of a substitution to depend upon the symbols that are deleted or inserted. For a substitution of a symbol set $\{i, j\}$ with i or j we assign a cost of 1, whereas a substitution with $k \neq i, j$ incurs a cost of 2. Any insertion or deletion has a cost of 2. For example, in Figure 5, while comparing R_{traj1} and G_{traj1}, we compare "$\{9, 4\}$" with "9" and do the edit operation with an edit cost of 1. This way conducts a much fairer evaluation, considering that one correct observation along with one wrong observation is still better than having two completely wrong observations.

We use two methods for edit distance computation. In the first method, we apply a weighted edit distance measurement to the original inferred observation sequence and the ground truth sequence. We quantify how accurate the inferred sequence is both spatially and temporally with respect to the ground truth. We not only check if the correct observation symbol is inferred but we also check if it is correctly inferred at each time point. The edit distance score depends on how accurately our learned models infer the correct observation and how many times they infer correctly. The length of the inferred trajectory (I_{traj1}) is always equal to the length of R_{traj1} but not necessarily equal to G_{traj1}. The edit distance between G_{traj1} and R_{traj1} quantifies the amount of inaccuracies in the raw RFID sequence, and that between G_{traj1} and I_{traj1} determines how accurate the inferred results are. The difference between these two edit distances determines a learned model's effectiveness at cleansing the raw RFID data.

The ground truth trajectory G_{traj1} and inferred trajectory I_{traj1} are shown in Figure 6 for the running example. Here, R_{traj1} contains false negatives at time points 20 to 23 (reader 10 has missing readings), whereas I_{traj1} only recovers the missing reading at time point 23. This is a typical result obtained by cleaning with IR-MHMMs, due to the underlying Markov assumptions. Since there is still a discrepancy between true and inferred sequences at several time intervals, the edit distance here is still quite large at a value of 6. Measuring the error of I_{traj1} by the edit distance on the full sequences is appropriate when exact timepoints and durations of an object's presence in a reader's range are of importance. However, if the application scenario only demands to reconstruct the qualitative, spatial aspect of the trajectory, we recommend using the edit distance method on block sequences as described as follows.

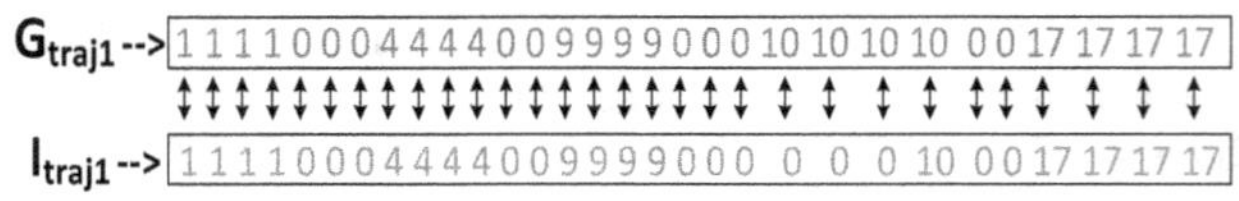

Figure 6: Edit distance on original sequences

In the second method, we treat an object's sequence of symbols as a sequence of blocks (of symbols), and we use the edit distance on the two block sequences, i.e., G_{traj1}(block) and I_{traj1}(block). The block sequences are formed from the original sequences by merging together continuous blocks of the same observation symbols. The length of the inferred block sequence depends on the accuracy of the inferred results. To illustrate, we modify the example I_{traj1} shown in Figure 6 by assuming that our model does not infer any reading at interval 23. The two corresponding block sequences are shown in Figure 7. The two block trajectories $\mathcal{G}_{traj1}$(block) and $\mathcal{I}_{traj1}$(block) are of length 9 and 7, respectively. Their edit distance 2+2=4, much less than the edit distance on original sequences.

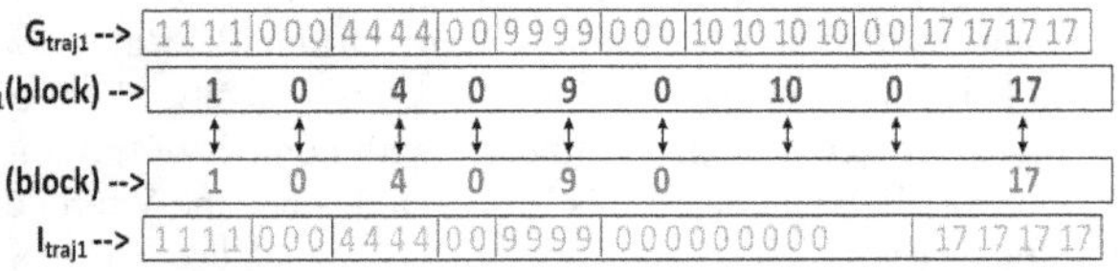

Figure 7: Edit distance on block sequences

5. EXPERIMENTAL STUDIES

In this section we report on the experimental studies that evaluate our proposed HMM-based approach for indoor RFID data cleansing. We evaluate the effectiveness, efficiency, scalability, and versatility of the approach, study the effect of reader accuracy, and compare with state-of-the-art methods. Our approach was implemented using MVNHMM [15], an open source implementation of HMM in C++. All experiments were conducted on a Linux machine with a 2.8GHz Core i7 processor and 8GB of main memory. We used both real and synthetic RFID data, as detailed below.

5.1 Settings and Performance Metrics

We performed the evaluation of learned models in two ways. 1) **Online data case:** In this case, we use two separate sets of data, one for learning the parameters of the models and the other as test data to evaluate the effectiveness of the learned models. This case is suitable for application scenarios where RFID data is continuously streamed, and incoming data is to be cleaned based on a model learned from historical data. 2) **Offline data case:** In this case, we used only one data set. We first use raw data for learning the model parameters and then use the model to clean the same data set. This case is applicable in application scenarios where a given batch of data is available off-line and needs to be cleaned. We note that we do not "overfit" by using the true results (ground truth) during training: We use only the raw data for training and the ground truth only later during testing.

To evaluate our learning and inference process, we consider two metrics: efficiency and effectiveness. The efficiency of inferring correct observations is measured using wall clock time and the effectiveness is measured by two metrics. First, the *average error* of a trajectory is defined as

$$Average\ error = \frac{\textit{sum of edit distance scores for all sequences}}{\textit{total \# of inferred symbols}}$$

The edit distance scores are calculated using the procedures described in Section 4. Second, the *error reduction ratio* between uncleaned and cleaned data is defined as

$$\textit{Error reduction ratio} = \frac{\textit{errors before cleansing - errors after cleansing}}{\textit{errors before cleansing}}$$

Table 2 summarizes the parameter settings in our experiments, with the default values in boldface. The meaning of the movement patterns is given below.

Parameters	Settings
Number of sequences	50, 100, 500, 1000, 1500, **3000**, 10000
State models	MSM, LSM, ISM
Reader accuracy	**70%**, 80%, 90%
Movement patterns	Directional-P, Directional-C, Random

Table 2: Experiment parameters

5.2 Experiments on Synthetic Data

5.2.1 *Data Generation*

We generated synthetic RFID data using a data generator that simulates object movements in an indoor space. The underlying indoor floor plan mainly used to generate the data is shown in Figure 1 (other layouts are considered later). The process of data generation to evaluation (experimental validation) is shown in Figure 8.

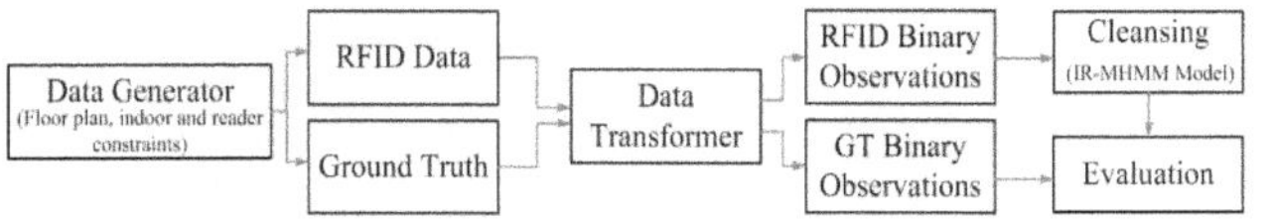

Figure 8: Simulation process

The data generator module takes an indoor RFID deployment graph and generates both raw RFID data and ground truth about the moving objects inside the given indoor space. The moving objects follow a random waypoint model [14] with a constant speed of 4km/h (1.1m/s). To generate object movements, an object in a room can move inside a room or move to any other room chosen randomly and then move along the shortest path from the source to the destination location. While moving from the current room to the destination room, an object can be detected by one or more deployed RFID readers. We generate the ground truth by recording the readings generated by the readers with 100% accuracy, by assuming that each deployed reader detects a present object for each reading cycle (epoch), which means no false negatives. Similarly, readings are generated only by the intended reader (no false positives). Later, we add inaccuracies to the RFID data. False negatives are introduced by "muting" randomly selected readers in a randomly selected path, while false positives are introduced by generating additional readings for the one or two nearest neighbors in addition to the actual reader. The data transformer module transforms the generated RFID data into multi-variate binary observation sequences, which are used to learn the model parameters. The learned model, along with the raw RFID data, is then passed to the cleansing module which is basically an inference model used to infer the true locations of the moving objects.

When generating synthetic data, we consider three typical object movement patterns *Directional-P(arallel), Directional-C(rossing) and Random*. For Directional-P and Directional-C we fix a set of source and destination locations, and objects always move along the shortest path between them. The difference is that in Directional-P, paths are *parallel*, i.e., do not overlap, while in Directional-C, they can *cross* (overlap). In Random paths, any location can be source or destination as long as they are not the same, and paths can cross/overlap.

5.2.2 *Results on Synthetic Data*

The data sets used to learn the models are generated with a default accuracy level of 70%. As an example, suppose that the fully correct raw readings table contains 100 readings. In the default case, we remove 15 readings as false negatives and add 15 readings as false positives. False negatives and false positives are equally distributed. We compute the edit distance between each pair of an inferred observation sequence and its corresponding ground truth observation sequence. We also compute the edit distance between raw RFID data (RFID) and ground truth to measure the effectiveness of the learned models.

Effectiveness: We start with evaluating the three structured models namely, *Minimum State Model* (MSM), *Last State Model* (LSM), and *In-between State Model* (ISM), and unstructured models with state spaces of 25, 34 and 50 states, respectively. We train all models using 10,000 training sequences and evaluate in the online case.

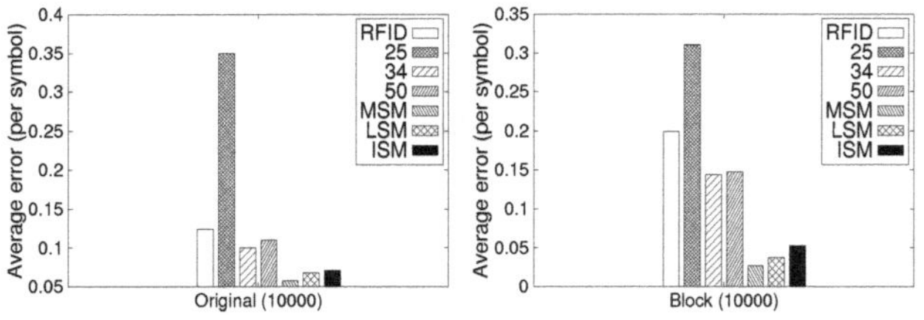

(a) Original sequences (b) Block sequences

Figure 9: Effectiveness of structured and unstructured models

Figure 9 shows that the unstructured models with 34 and 50 states manage to clean the data well, while the unstructured model with 25 states is too simple to be effective, it actually introduces more errors into the data to be cleansed. However, MSM, LSM, and ISM are significantly better than the unstructured models. Thus, it is evident that incorporating minimum knowledge about the reader deployment into the models can considerably improve the cleansing effectiveness.

Figure 10 shows results for the Directional-C data offline case. Specifically, Figure 10(a) reports results about the original inferred sequences. We see that MSM is more effective than LSM and ISM, and gets more effective when given more training sequences. With 10,000 training sequences, MSM reduces the average error by 60% over raw RFID data. Figure 10(b) show the average error estimated on the block sequences, which gives a more qualitative measure of the effectiveness of the three models. MSM is the most effective as the effectiveness increases from 60% to 90% when increasing the number of the training sequences to 10,000. LSM and ISM show a similar trend, but at a lower overall level of effectiveness.

Figure 11 shows results for the Directional-C data online case. We fixed a set of 1000 sequences as test data and learned the three models with different sets of training sequences, as shown in Table 2. In Figure 11(a), the results for original inferred sequences indicate that the learned models can reduce the average error in all cases. Again, MSM is more effective even in the online data case and the effectiveness increases with more training data. Figure 11(b) shows the results for block sequences, indicating that MSM learned with a larger number of sequences is more effective as the average error is reduced by 70-75% for 10,000 training sequences.

The results in Figure 12 are based on the Random movement offline case. Figure 12(a) gives the results for original inferred sequences. Both MSM and ISM perform better than LSM and reduce the average error with more training sequences, which implies that the more data there is available for learning, the higher the cleansing effectiveness. Figure 12(b), with results for block inferred sequences, show a similar trend, i.e., the average error shrinks with larger training sets. The likely reason for MSM to be better is its design, which represents the underlying reader deployment more closely than the other two models (ISM is a low-level abstraction of MSM). Additionally, MSM can do the learning with less states.

Results for the Random movement online case are shown in Figure 13. Here, experiments are performed on 1000 test sequences to test the effectiveness of the three models learned with a different set of data sequences. The results for both original inferred sequences and block sequences show a similar trend of increasing effectiveness with more training data. The effectiveness is slightly less than that in the offline case, but still very good. Again, MSM is the best model, achieving 50-60% error reduction.

Efficiency: For the efficiency measure, we present the time that a learned model takes to infer the results for a given data set. We use datasets with Directional-C and Random object movement with variable trajectory lengths. The results report the efficiency (inference time) of the learned models with respect to the number of sequences used to learn them. Figure 14(a) and 15(a) show the offline Directional-C and Random cases, respectively. We see that the total inference time grows linearly with number of training sequences for all the models. This is expected, since the Viterbi algorithm takes $O(|V||S|^2)$ time. Specifically, MSM takes at most 22 seconds to learn and infer for both cases, while LSM and ISM use around 38 seconds. For the online cases, Figure 14(b) (Directional-C) and Figure 15(b) (Random) report inference-only time (since the models are already learned) for inferring 1000 sequences. For Directional-C data, the inference time is stable, ranging from 1.3 to 2 seconds, with MSM being the fastest. For Random data, inference takes a little longer, from 3–7 seconds, because of the diversity and varying length of the trajectories. We omit the simple Directional-P case for brevity. In summary, learning and inference in the models are very efficient, with MSM being the fastest.

To see the effect of the movement patterns, we compare the models using a dataset of 3000 sequences with a reader accuracy of 70%. The results, in Figure 16, show that the movement pattern has a significant effect on model effectiveness and that the three models perform differently for different movement patterns. MSM is robust across all three movement patterns and as before outperforms the other two, particularly for directional movement. LSM is more effective in Directional-C, while ISM is more effective for Random movement. All three models perform better on the simple Directional-P paths.

Effect of reader accuracy: In Figure 17, we show the effectiveness of the three models with respect to reader accuracy. Reader accuracy is defined as the ability to detect an object correctly when it is inside its intended range. We use 3000 training sequences with the Directional-C movement pattern and accuracy levels of 70% (80%, 90%, resp.), i.e., 30% (20%,10%, resp.) inaccurate readings are introduced into the raw data as equal amounts of false negatives and false positives. These accuracy levels correspond both to typical real-world accuracies and the range of accuracies which is practically relevant for cleansing (close to 100% there is no need for cleansing and below 50-60% it becomes random "coin-flip" scenarios). All three models, MSM, LSM and ISM, show their effectiveness as the error reduction rate only decreases slightly when reader accuracy decreases. We see that MSM is the most effective model, as it reduces the error by more than 80% for 70% accuracy, and 90% for 90% accuracy.

Scalability: To demonstrate the scalability of the three models, we change the following parameters: 1) total number of deployed readers, 2) connectivity between readers, and 3) the length of the path (the number of readers deployed from source to destination location). We used the floor plan in Figure 1 for the 17 reader case. For the 50 and 87 reader cases, we adopted a floor plan of a multi story building, where the floors are connected by 4 staircases. For simplicity, we regard hallways and staircases as rooms, and staircase entrances as doors. We used a single floor plan for 50 readers

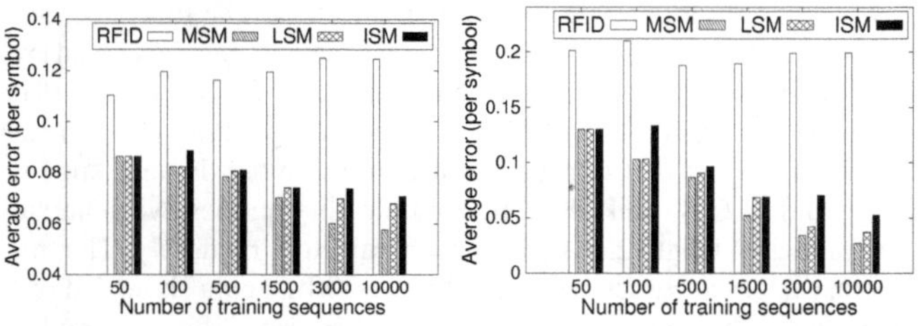

(a) Original sequences

(b) Block sequences

Figure 10: Results on Directional-C offline data

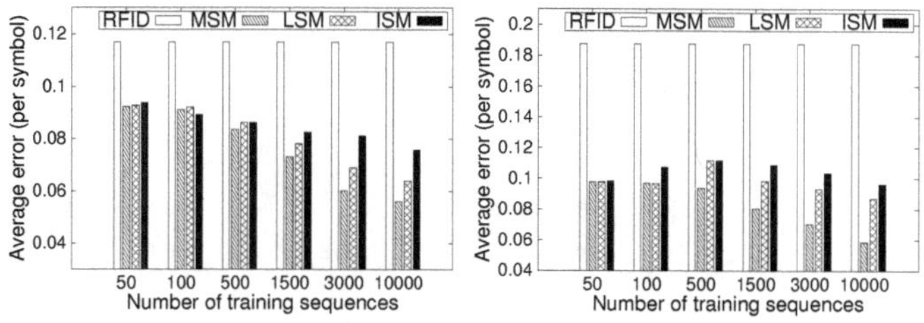

(a) Original sequences

(b) Block sequences

Figure 11: Results on Directional-C online data

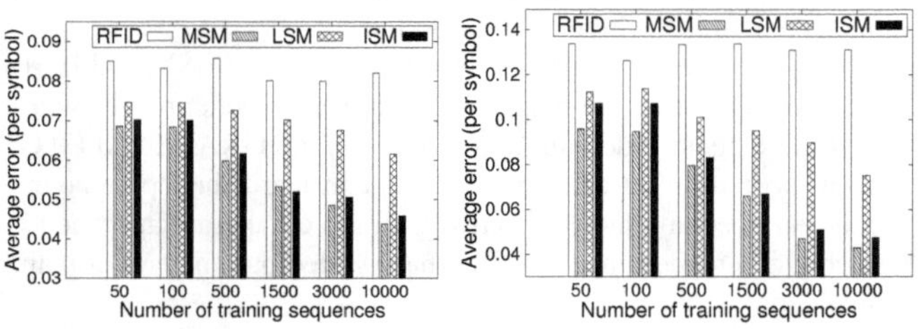

(a) Original sequences

(b) Block sequences

Figure 12: Results on Random offline data

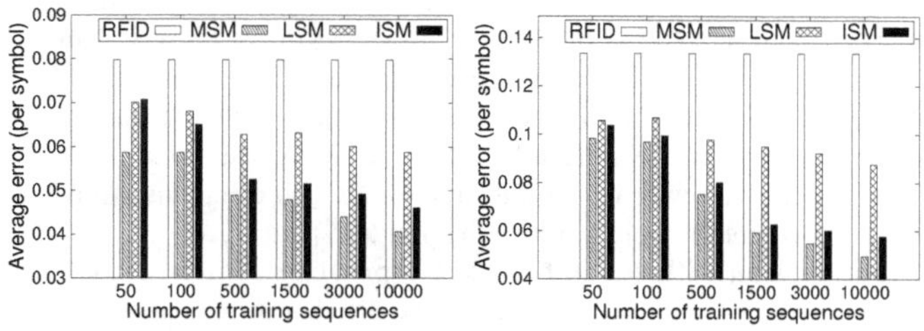

(a) Original sequences

(b) Block sequences

Figure 13: Results on Random online data

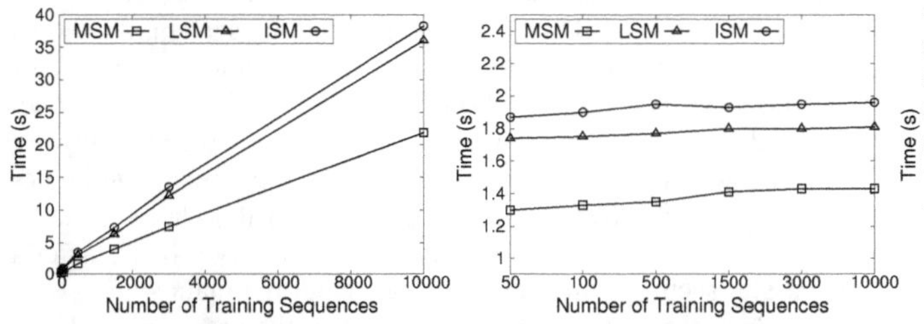

(a) Directional offline data

(b) Directional online data

Figure 14: Efficiency results on Directional-C data

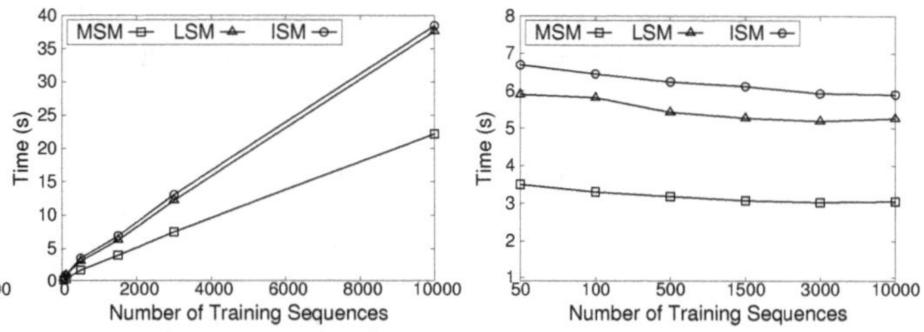

(a) Random offline data

(b) Random online data

Figure 15: Efficiency results on Random data

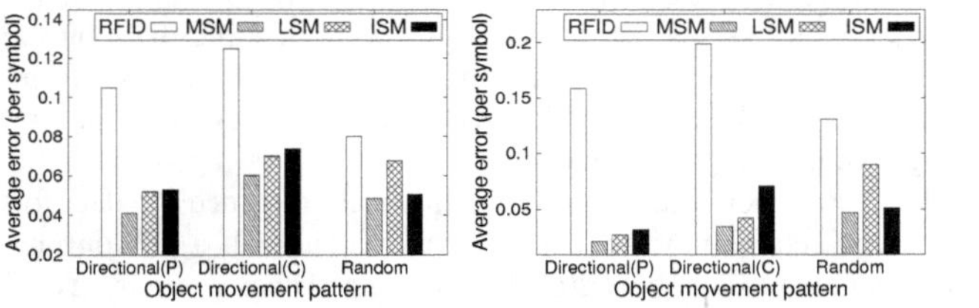

(a) Original sequences

(b) Block sequences

Figure 16: Effect of object movement patterns

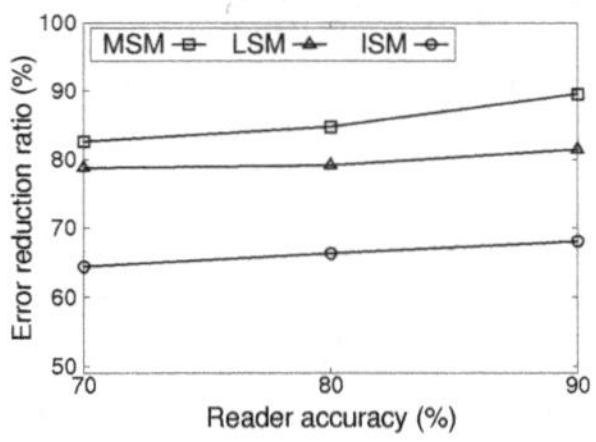

Figure 17: Effect of reader accuracy

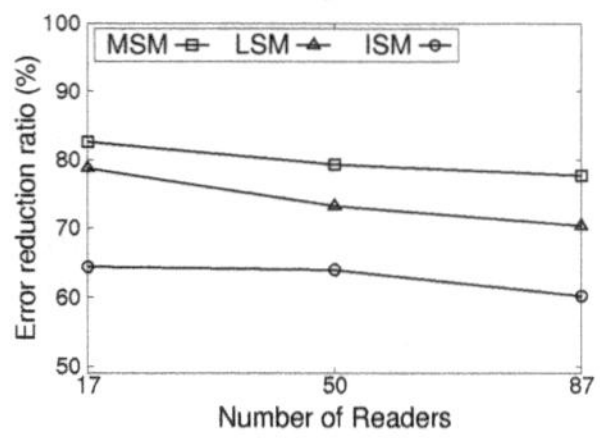

Figure 18: Effect of number of readers (state space size)

and a two floor plan for 87 readers. We generated data sets for 3000 objects with Random movement in each setting and 70% reader accuracy. We learned the models and evaluated them using the error reduction ratio defined above. The results, in Figure 18, show that our models can still achieve very good effectiveness even for large state spaces. For a deployment of 87 readers, we have 169 and 262 states for MSM and ISM, respectively. We see that both ISM and MSM achieve good effectiveness even as the number of readers increases, with MSM being the best at around 80% accuracy. Thus, our models scale well with larger reader deployments (larger state spaces). We note that these numbers of readers correspond to typical real-world deployments. Very few readers will often give good results, but less need for cleansing, while more than 100 readers are not typical even in the largest deployments.

Versatility. To evaluate their versatility, we also test the three models in different indoor environments. We consider environments which differ in aspects like floor maps, reader placements, movement patterns, and connectivity. We changed the setting of these parameters with respect to three real world environments: an office building (Figure 1), an airport scenario (Figure 21), and a warehouse scenario [16]. For the building scenario, we used Random movement data with medium connectivity; for the airport scenario, we used Directional-C movement data with low connectivity; and for the warehouse scenario, we used Random movement data with high connectivity. We used data sets of 10,000 sequences with 70% reader accuracy for the three environments, and checked the effectiveness of the models on both original and blocked sequences.

The results, in Figure 19, show that the models perform differently in the three environments. One notable thing is that all three models are relatively more effective in the airport scenario, probably due to the rather constrained Directional-C movement of the bags. MSM manage to reduce the average error by more than 90% in the airport scenario, and also show significant effectiveness for the building and warehouse scenarios. MSM is the simplest of the

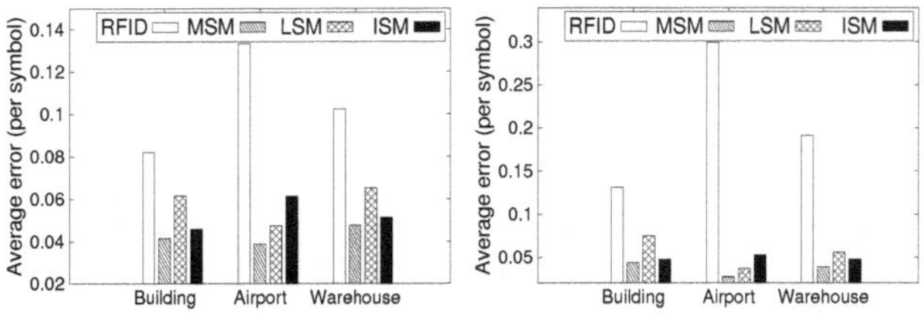

(a) Original sequences (b) Block sequences

Figure 19: Effectiveness of models in different environments

three models, which facilitates the learning with a smaller number of states. Further, MSM models the floor map more closely than the other two models. Another effective model is ISM which is almost as effective as MSM in the building and warehouse scenarios, which use Random movement data. ISM has more states, but models the paths at a lower level of abstraction, which can be useful in scenarios where the objects move in a random pattern.

Comparison with state-of-the-art approaches: We now compare our models with the two state-of-the-art cleansing approaches proposed in [1, 2], and [7]. The two approaches are close in terms of their use of constraints of the indoor settings. The proposal in [7] (denoted as CTG) does not correct errors in the raw data (as we do) but only maps the raw readings to semantic locations. Put simply, CTG works at a higher level, above the raw data level which our technique targets. Thus, we cannot use the edit distance measure for comparison with CTG, and instead use a query-based comparison, detailed below. Particularly, CTG exploits the so-called constrained trajectory graph (CTG) that represents the trajectories in presence of integrity constraints (reachability, traveling time, and latency) to distinguish valid and invalid trajectories. In contrast, the GRAPH approach [1, 2] captures the domain knowledge (distance between readers, moving speed of objects, sampling rate, etc.) in a graph and works at the (low) level of the raw RFID data, as in the present paper. Rather than discarding invalid data, false positives are filtered out and false negatives recovered. For comparison, we use the results of our three model (MSM, LSM and ISM) over the Directional-C dataset.

To measure the quality of these approaches of different natures, we use two types of queries [7]: *stay queries* and *trajectory queries*. A stay query answers where an object is at time t, whereas a trajectory query asks if an object's trajectory matches a given query pattern. A trajectory query is defined as a combination of $?^*$s, l_is, and $l_i[n]$s. Specifically, $?^*$ is a sequence of 0 or more locations, l_i is a sequence of at least one location(s), and $l_i[n]$ is a sequence of at least n l_is. The answer to a trajectory query is *"yes"* if the sequence of locations traveled by the object is the same as in the query pattern, or *"no"* otherwise. We issue the same set of queries on the outputs of CTG, GRAPH, MSM, LSM and ISM. For each, we measure the query accuracy by comparing the results with their counterparts obtained on the ground truth.

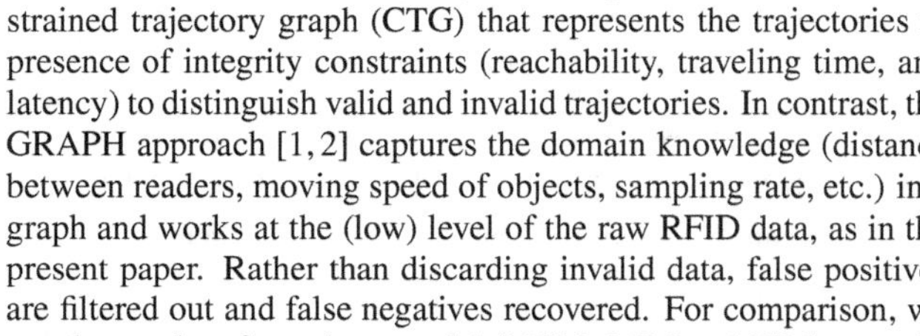

(a) Stay queries (b) Trajectory queries

Figure 20: Query quality comparison results

Each trajectory is queried with 100 stay queries, each generated by picking a random time point of the trajectory. The stay query accuracy results in Figure 20(a) show that the accuracy achieved by our three models is equal to or better than both CTG and GRAPH. A query accuracy of over 97% is achieved by MSM. This is remarkable, given that our models use only limited domain knowledge, unlike CTG and GRAPH. For trajectory queries, we generate 50 queries of length 2, 3, or 4 for each trajectory randomly. The trajectory query accuracy results, in Figure 20(b), again show that our approach is better even with trajectory queries of different lengths. The accuracy is over 90% for both MSM and ISM, even when the trajectory length is 4. As expected, trajectory query accuracy decreases slightly when the length of query gets longer, since a small mismatch marks a whole query as failed.

The performance of our learning-based models (MSM and ISM) is remarkable, since they achieve similar or even better results without using extensive domain knowledge, unlike GRAPH and CTG. Given more training data, our models can learn their parameters better, and become more effective than the competing approaches which are in some sense based on hard-coded parameters (domain knowledge).

5.3 Experiments on Real Data

Finally, we use a real data set collected from an airport that operates an automatic RFID-based baggage handling system. As shown in Figure 21, the baggage handling system features a number of specific locations (e.g., check-in desks) and RFID readers (shown with red circles). During the check-in phase, each (randomly selected) bag is attached with a passive RFID tag which is to be detected by the deployed RFID readers. From the check-in desks (CD), bags pass the screening area through conveyor belts. After a successful security screening, the bags enter the main sorting area (SO) where the sorting system ensures that the bag is pushed into a designated chute. The bags are then loaded into wagons by the baggage handling staff, before they are transported to a designated aircraft through one of the gateways (GW-1 or GW-2). Finally, bags pass through a belt-loader reader while loading them into a plane. On the other hand, arrival bags are carried by wagons from an aircraft to the arrival hall (AR) through gateway GW-2 where baggage handling staff unload the bags from the wagons onto the arrival conveyor belt. We have continuously recorded the data for two consecutive months, collecting more than half a million raw reading records for about 20,000 RFID tagged bags going from one airport to another.

We cannot use the real data directly in the evaluation, since we do not have the related ground truth (the true reading values) available. Instead, we learn the characteristics of the real RFID data, such as the time bags use to move from one reader to another, the probability with which the bags move from one reader to another, and the error characteristics. We use this information to generate "semi-real" raw data which is equivalent to the real dataset, along with ground truth. Since the data is generated by readers deployed over a baggage handling system which is mostly covered by directional conveyor belts (directional movement), and the airport layout information is available to us, the MSM model is the most appropriate to use. Alternatively, LSM and ISM could have been used if the layout information is either difficult to use (e.g., arena scenario) or is not (readily) available.

In Figure 22 we report the results on the effectiveness of MSM, learned from data generated by 20,000 moving bags with RFID tags. The results, in Figure 22, show that the average error is reduced by 65–70% when applied to original sequences and more than 90% when applied to block sequences, which validates the effectiveness of the model. Query comparison results for MSM,

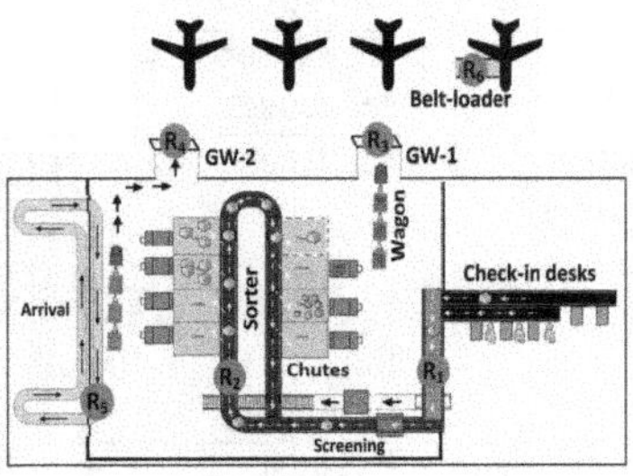

Figure 21: Airport baggage hall layout

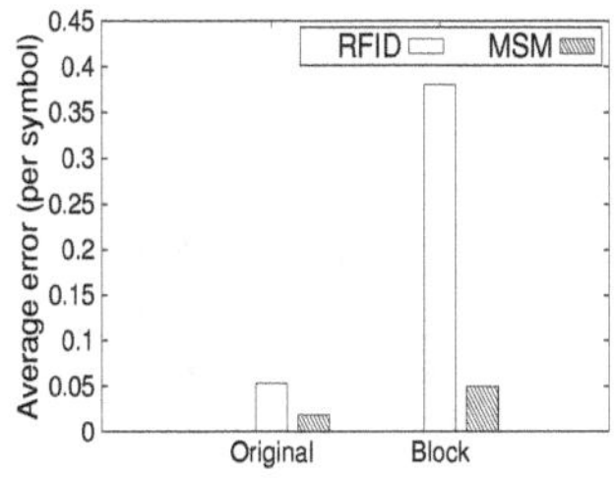

Figure 22: Effectiveness results on real data

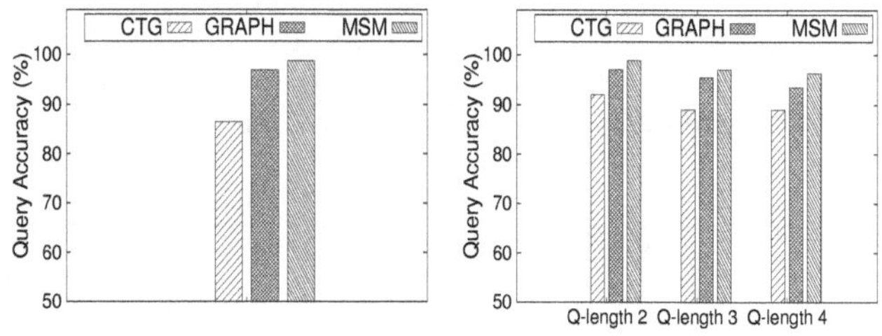

(a) Stay queries (b) Trajectory queries

Figure 23: Query quality results on real data

CTG and GRAPH, based on the stay and trajectory queries described above, are presented in Figure 23. The figure shows that MSM achieves the best accuracy results for both stay and trajectory queries. An accuracy of over 98% is achieved for stay queries, and trajectory queries of length 2. The overall results are similar to the results on synthetic data: MSM is particularly effective considered that no detailed domain knowledge is used, unlike CTG and GRAPH. This again shows that learning from larger data sets can outperform the effect of using *hard-coded parameters*.

6. RELATED WORK

In this section we briefly review the related work. We cover RFID data management/cleansing and relevant learning probabilistic models. Dealing with indoor RFID data is quite challenging. The techniques to represent RFID data along with the methods for accessing the data have been proposed in [10, 12]. In this paper, we focus on the challenge of dealing with the errors present in the RFID data and designing accurate probabilistic models.

In the past decade, considerable research interest has been seen in managing incomplete and uncertain RFID data. Chawathe et al. [4] discussed RFID data management challenges, such as inferences and online warehousing and proposed a system architecture of a distributed RFID system. Wang et al. [24] defined an expressive temporal data model for RFID data to support tracking and monitoring queries. Gonzalez et al. [10] designed a warehousing model that provides RFID data compression and path dependent aggregates. Cabenes et al. [3] used an unsupervised learning approach for mining RFID data, which allows the discovery of a topological space from a set of behavioral observations.

Because RFID data is inherently dirty, many solutions have been proposed to clean the RFID data. Jeffery et al. [13] proposed the adaptive SMURF (*Statistical sMoothing for Unreliable RFid data*) approach. Modeling the RFID data streams as statistical samples of RFID tags, SMURF uses sampling estimators to automatically adjust the filter window size. Mylyy [19] proposed a temporal smoothing filter with a fixed time window. By counting the RFID readings in the filter window and comparing them to given thresholds, this method reduces missing RFID readings from the data stream. Chen et al. [5] proposed a Bayesian inference based approach, which takes full advantage of data redundancy, for cleaning RFID raw data. The likelihood is captured by designing a state detection model. Valentine et al. [18] presented an adaptive sliding-window based approach WSTD for reducing false negative reads in RFID data streams. Yan et al. [25] proposed a Kalman filter based cleaning method, which solves false negatives and false positives from single readers. Gu et al. [11] proposed a data imputation model for RFID by efficiently maintaining and analyzing the correlations of the monitored objects. The spatio-temporal correlation between monitored objects are used to fill in the false negatives.

Baba et al. [1] [2] proposed an RFID data cleansing solution which utilizes indoor deployment graphs that capture the information about indoor settings and the deployed readers. Different versions of graphs are used to handle either false positives or false negatives. In [2] a cleansing algorithm based on distance-aware graph model is proposed to handle false positives in indoor RFID tracking data and a probabilistic graph is proposed in [1] to handle false negatives. Fazzinga et al. [7,8] proposed a probabilistic framework and a grid based filtering scheme to clean the RFID data. Their solution uses integrity constraints implied by the map and the mobility characteristics are applied to cleanse the RFID data.

Unlike the work [1, 2, 7, 8], the present work does not assume that we know the indoor space spatio-temporal constraints or the detailed characteristics of the deployed readers beforehand. Nevertheless, the proposed approach in this paper achieves essentially the same or even better results without using detailed domain knowledge and thus making it much easier to deploy in practice. The learning with larger data sets tends to improve the accuracy of learned parameters and bring forth some of the intricacies which are hidden in the data in normal views.

We presented a comparison with related HMM-based probabilistic RFID data processing solutions in Table 3. Nie et al. [20] proposed Correlated Variable Duration Hidden Markov Models to capture uncertainty and correlations of locations of tagged objects. Different from our models proposed in this paper, that probabilistic model design [20] depends on additional information apart from raw RFID data and it assumes one object's locations depend on its neighboring objects. Garcia-Valverde et al. [9] proposed a location prediction of a worker based on its destination. The RFID data used to learn the model is considered as reliable unlike our model which uses raw RFID data to learn the model parameters. Tran et al. [22] proposed a probabilistic model that captures the mobility of a reader, object dynamic, etc., and makes inference based on particle filter to infer object locations from raw RFID streams. In contrast, our model proposed in this paper does not demand such domain-specific prior knowledge about the data and environment.

As a final remark, although the possible world model [6] has been widely used in managing uncertain databases, it is not suitable for our research problem in this paper. Determined by the underlying RFID tracking system, the raw indoor RFID data we need to cleanse cannot be captured as samples with probabilities.

7. CONCLUSION AND FUTURE WORK

In this paper, we presented a learning-based approach to clean raw RFID data. Specifically, we proposed the Indoor RFID Multivariate Hidden Markov Model (IR-MHMM) to model the uncertainties present in RFID data as well as the correlation of moving object locations and RFID tagged objects. Compared to related approaches, our approach is almost entirely unsupervised: the only information needed to construct the IR-MHMM model are variants

	Training Data	Prior Knowledge	Errors Handled	Output
IR-MHMM	Raw RFID data	Indoor topology and device deployment	False positives and false negatives	Clean observation sequences
CVD-HMM [20]	Raw RFID data	Topology, device deployment, flow process of moving objects, and correlation between objects	False positives and false negatives	Inferred locations
García-Valverde et al. [9]	Clean RFID data	Indoor topology, source and destination of trajectories	–	Location predictions for fixed destination
Tran et al. [22]	Raw RFID data	Mobility information of readers, object dynamics	False positives and false negatives	Event streams

Table 3: Comparison with state-of-the-art HMM-based probabilistic RFID data processing

of basic information on the spatial reader deployment, depending on one of the proposed state space designs. Training of the model is performed using only raw RFID data; no special labeled data or ground truth trajectory data is required. We performed a comprehensive experimental study using both real and synthetic data. Results show that our approach is effective, achieving up to 90% error reduction over raw RFID data, as well as robust, scalable, and efficient. Given enough training data, it outperforms competing state-of-the-art approaches.

In future work, we plan to mitigate the limitations imposed by the Markov assumptions in our model by incorporating a probabilistic timing model to relate the travel time of objects between readers and the time objects spends at each reader. Secondly, we plan to incorporate domain-knowledge into our learning approach, which could possibly improve the effectiveness further.

Acknowledgements

This work was partly sponsored by the NILTEK project funded by European Regional Development Fund and the BagTrack project funded by the Danish National Advanced Technology Foundation under grant no. 010-2011-1.

8. REFERENCES

[1] A. I. Baba, H. Lu, T. B. Pedersen, and X. Xie. Handling false negatives in indoor RFID data. In *MDM*, pages 117–126, 2014.

[2] A. I. Baba, H. Lu, X. Xie, and T. B. Pedersen. Spatiotemporal data cleansing for indoor RFID tracking data. In *MDM*, pages 187–196, 2013.

[3] G. Cabanes, Y. Bennani, and D. Fresneau. Mining RFID behavior data using unsupervised learning. *IJAL*, 1(1):28–47, 2010.

[4] S. S. Chawathe, V. Krishnamurthy, S. Ramachandran, and S. Sarma. Managing RFID data. In *VLDB*, pages 1189–1195, 2004.

[5] H. Chen, W.-S. Ku, H. Wang, and M.-T. Sun. Leveraging spatio-temporal redundancy for RFID data cleansing. In *SIGMOD*, pages 51–62, 2010.

[6] N. N. Dalvi and D. Suciu. Efficient query evaluation on probabilistic databases. In *VLDB*, pages 864–875, 2004.

[7] B. Fazzinga, S. Flesca, F. Furfaro, and F. Parisi. Cleaning trajectory data of RFID-monitored objects through conditioning under integrity constraints. In *EDBT*, pages 379–390, 2014.

[8] B. Fazzinga, S. Flesca, F. Furfaro, and F. Parisi. Offline cleaning of RFID trajectory data. In *SSDBM*, pages 5–16, 2014.

[9] T. García-Valverde, A. García-Sola, and J. A. Botía. Improving RFID's location based services by means of hidden markov models. In *ECAI*, pages 1045–1046, 2010.

[10] H. Gonzalez, J. Han, X. Li, and D. Klabjan. Warehousing and analyzing massive RFID data sets. In *ICDE*, pages 83–92, 2006.

[11] Y. Gu, G. Yu, Y. Chen, and B. C. Ooi. Efficient RFID data imputation by analyzing the correlations of monitored objects. In *DASFAA*, pages 186–200, 2009.

[12] Y. Hu, S. Sundara, T. Chorma, and J. Srinivasan. Supporting RFID-based item tracking applications in oracle dbms using a bitmap datatype. In *VLDB*, pages 1140–1151, 2005.

[13] S. R. Jeffery, M. N. Garofalakis, and M. J. Franklin. Adaptive cleaning for RFID data streams. In *VLDB*, pages 163–174, 2006.

[14] D. B. Johnson and D. A. Maltz. Dynamic source routing in ad hoc wireless networks. In *Mobile Computing*, pages 153–181. Kluwer Academic Publishers, 1996.

[15] S. Kirshner. *Modeling of Multivariate Time Series Using Hidden Markov Models*. PhD thesis, Long Beach, CA, USA, 2005.

[16] J. S. Larson, E. T. Bradlow, and P. S. Fader. An exploratory look at supermarket shopping paths. *IJRM*, 22(4):395 – 414, 2005.

[17] V. Levenshtein. Binary Codes Capable of Correcting Deletions, Insertions and Reversals. *Soviet Physics Doklady*, 10:707, 1966.

[18] L. V. Massawe, J. Kinyua, and H. Vermaak. Reducing false negative reads in RFID data streams using an adaptive sliding window approach. In *Sensors*, pages 4187Ű–4212, 2012.

[19] O. Mylyy. RFID data management, aggregation and filtering. In *CoopIS/DOA/ODBASE*, pages 557–575, 2007.

[20] Y. Nie, Z. Li, S. Peng, and Q. Chen. Probabilistic modeling of streaming RFID data by using correlated variable-duration hmms. In *SERA*, pages 72–77, 2009.

[21] L. R. Rabiner and B. H. Juang. An introduction to hidden markov models. *IEEE ASSp Magazine*, 1986.

[22] T. T. L. Tran, C. A. Sutton, R. Cocci, Y. Nie, Y. Diao, and P. J. Shenoy. Probabilistic inference over RFID streams in mobile environments. In *ICDE*, pages 1096–1107, 2009.

[23] A. Viterbi. Error bounds for convolutional codes and an asymptotically optimum decoding algorithm. *IEEE Trans. Inf. Theory*, 13(2):260–269, Sept. 2006.

[24] F. Wang and P. Liu. Temporal management of RFID data. In *VLDB*, pages 1128–1139, 2005.

[25] W. Yan and S. B. Yan. Cleaning method of RFID data stream based on kalman filter. In *JCCS*, pages 1794–1799, 2011.

PrivateClean: Data Cleaning and Differential Privacy

Sanjay Krishnan, Jiannan Wang*, Michael J. Franklin, Ken Goldberg, Tim Kraska†
UC Berkeley, * Simon Fraser University, †Brown University
{sanjaykrishnan franklin, goldberg}@berkeley.edu †tim_kraska@brown.edu *jnwang@sfu.ca

ABSTRACT

Recent advances in differential privacy make it possible to guarantee user privacy while preserving the main characteristics of the data. However, most differential privacy mechanisms assume that the underlying dataset is clean. This paper explores the link between data cleaning and differential privacy in a framework we call PrivateClean. PrivateClean includes a technique for creating private datasets of numerical and discrete-valued attributes, a formalism for privacy-preserving data cleaning, and techniques for answering `sum`, `count`, and `avg` queries after cleaning. We show: (1) how the degree of privacy affects subsequent aggregate query accuracy, (2) how privacy potentially amplifies certain types of errors in a dataset, and (3) how this analysis can be used to tune the degree of privacy. The key insight is to maintain a bipartite graph relating dirty values to clean values and use this graph to estimate biases due to the interaction between cleaning and privacy. We validate these results on four datasets with a variety of well-studied cleaning techniques including using functional dependencies, outlier filtering, and resolving inconsistent attributes.

(a) Original Table

id	Major	Satisfaction
1	Mechanical E.	4
2	Mech. Eng.	3
3	Electrical Eng.	1
...	...	...
100	Electrical Eng.	5

(b) Private Table [Randomize Majors]

id	Major	Satisfaction
1	Mechanical E.	4
2	Mech. Eng.	3
3	Mech. Eng.	1
...	...	...
100	Electrical Eng.	5

(c) Fix Inconsistencies

id	Major	Satisfaction
1	Mech. Eng.	4
2	Mech. Eng.	3
3	Mech. Eng.	1
...	...	...
100	Electrical Eng.	5

(d) Query Result Estimation

AVG	Major
3.2	Mech. Eng.
4.9	Electrical Eng.
...	...

Figure 1: Randomly permuting a random fraction of major values can preserve the privacy of students in rare majors (Student 3 has plausible deniability). The resulting randomized table is still compatible with subsequent data cleaning (i.e., resolving inconsistencies).

1. INTRODUCTION

It is often beneficial for organizations to share user data with third parties or publish publicly available datasets. For example, the anonymous rating data shared as a part of the Netflix challenge engaged the community in developing several new recommendation algorithms [2]. While the success stories are numerous and ever growing in number, preserving the privacy of users is a fundamental obstacle [1]. Over the last few years, there have been several examples where ostensibly private data are linked to individuals through clever data mining techniques [9,32,48]. Thus, it is important to have privacy mechanisms with formal guarantees about resilience to attack without sacrificing too much utility.

Fortunately, recent advances in differential privacy make it possible to guarantee privacy against a wide range of linkage attacks while preserving the main characteristics of the data [11]. However, for reliable downstream query processing, existing models assume that the underlying data are "clean". However, raw data often requires extensive pre-processing including the extraction of named entities from textual fields [8], imputation of missing values [36], and resolution of inconsistent attributes [39]. Consequently, the burden is on the data provider to ensure that the data are completely clean before making it private, and this cost might even discourage her from sharing the data in the first place. In cleaning, the data provider has to account for every possible downstream analysis scenario, each of which may have different data quality requirements and notions of "clean".

This paper explores a differential privacy model that is compatible with several common cleaning operations and result estimation for aggregate queries after cleaning. This crucially removes much of the cleaning burden from the data provider, and analysts can clean the data as required. We propose a framework called PrivateClean, which includes a technique for creating private datasets of numerical and discrete-valued attributes, and answering `sum`, `count`, and `avg` queries after cleaning the private relation. PrivateClean supports cleaning operations that can be represented as deterministic user-defined functions over the discrete attributes that: (1) transform existing attributes, (2) create new attributes, and (3) resolve disparate attribute values to a single canonical representation. We further provide a lower bound on the amount of data required to detect the original data errors as a function of the degree of privacy and how this degree of privacy affects subsequent aggregate query accuracy.

To illustrate how this works, consider collecting college course evaluations consisting of a student's satisfaction on a scale from *1-5*, major, and some other demographic data (Figure 1a). Even

SIGMOD'16, June 26-July 01, 2016, San Francisco, CA, USA

DOI: http://dx.doi.org/10.1145/2882903.2915248

with guarantees of anonymity, students may be reluctant to provide truthful responses as it might be possible to identify an individual based on a combination of the demographic data and the major. PrivateClean extends the well-studied *Randomized Response* [45] technique where each student is given plausible deniability: (1) she flips a coin before the evaluation, (2) if heads, she reports her major/demographics truthfully, and (3) if tails, she selects an answer at random. Clearly, the likelihood of tails (p) vs. heads ($1-p$) controls the risk of identification (Figure 1b). On the other hand, increasing p (the degree of privacy) also decreases the accuracy of the analysis (i.e., the estimated average satisfaction for Mechanical Engineers).

This principle can be used to randomize any table by replacing discrete-valued attributes with probability p with another value in the domain uniformly at random; which we formalize as *Generalized Randomized Response* (GRR). The interesting technical challenges happen in query processing after randomization. By design, increasing the randomization parameter p makes rare values more common which affects the selectivity of queries and user-defined cleaning. We derive an estimate for the change in selectivity and compensate for the bias that this induces in query results. To do so, we have to maintain provenance of the values in the relation before and after the user-defined transformations using a bipartite graph (mapping dirty to clean values).

To summarize the contributions of PrivateClean:

- PrivateClean provides a mechanism for generating differentially private datasets on which the analyst can apply cleaning operations. PrivateClean maintains the necessary information to estimate query results on the cleaned private dataset. (Section 4).
- We show that directly applying `sum`, `count`, and `avg` queries with predicates produces a biased estimate where the bias is proportional to the skew in the dataset $\tilde{O}(privacy \cdot skew)$ (i.e., the selectivity in terms of distinct values vs. the selectivity in terms of actual records). We derive a corrected estimator that compensates for the bias.
- This bias is exacerbated by data cleaning operations that merge attribute values $\tilde{O}(privacy \cdot (skew + merge))$. Consequently, we leverage a graph-based provenance model to estimate and additionally compensate for the data cleaning.
- We evaluate the analysis on two synthetic and two real datasets.

2. PRIVATE CLEANING: 3 APPROACHES

This section introduces a running example to motivate private data cleaning, and discusses different approaches to clean the example dataset.

2.1 Motivating Example

M-CAFE is an online application for collecting college course evaluations [49]. Data are collected in the following relation:

$$R(id, major, section, instructor, score)$$

with a primary key id, a string attribute major, a section number, the instructor's name instructor, and a continuous numerical score for the instructor (0-5). For this example dataset, the section attribute uniquely determines the instructor with the functional dependency:

$$R[section] \mapsto R[instructor]$$

Even if the dataset is anonymous (i.e., removing the id attribute), it is not formally private. One might be able to identify individuals with rare major values, and consequently, may penalize those who left a low score. However, since these evaluations are collected via student input, they are susceptible to inconsistencies. For example, the major attribute might have alternative representations of the same logical value "Mechanical Engineering" and "Mech. Eng.". If the instructor wants to know the average score of Mechanical Engineers, she will have to resolve this inconsistency before analysis.

Consider the scenario, where we are providing this online course evaluation platform as a hosted service. We want to release the dataset to the course instructors for analysis, but we also have to provide privacy guarantees for the students. These data are potentially inconsistent, and the following describes three approaches to facilitate reliable analysis on private data. For clarity, we will use the term *provider* for the owner of the data and *analyst* to describe the recipient of the private data.

2.2 Clean First

One solution is to fully clean the dataset before making it private. However, data cleaning is often time consuming [21]. It may not be feasible to clean all of the errors before releasing a private version. Furthermore, it can be impractical or even impossible to anticipate how analysts will clean the data. For example, in our course evaluations example, suppose one student wrote "Mechanical Engineering and Math" as her major. For some types of analysis, it may be acceptable to resolve this inconsistency to "Mechanical Engineering", but there may be other cases where analysts want to process students with double majors differently. Additionally, the query workload provides valuable information about how to budget cleaning effort. For example, to calculate the average score for all students, one does not need to resolve this problem in the first place. Therefore, such transformations are best left to the discretion of the analyst.

2.3 Encryption

Another approach is homomorphic encryption that allows for data processing directly on the encrypted data [38]. The provider can encrypt all of the data and give the encrypted copy to the analyst. Essentially, homomorphic encryption is a domain transformation that obscures the values in a database. While homomorphic encryption preserves the frequencies of the distinct values, it does not preserve their actual values. In the running example, this leads to the natural issue where "Mechanical Engineering" and "Mech. Eng." are transformed to some non-human interpretable value (e.g., 0x86EF001 and 0x211415). This poses a problem for an analyst who wants to merge "Mechanical Engineering" and "Mech. Eng.". For cryptographic transformations, it is provably hard to figure out which of the encrypted values correspond to "Mechanical Engineering" and "Mech. Eng.".

2.4 PrivateClean: Solution Overview

To motivate PrivateClean, let us consider the simpler case where there are only two attributes $R(major, score)$. Suppose, we want to release a provably private relation R for analysis by the course instructors. Let M be the set of all majors, PrivateClean applies the following privacy mechanism: with probability p replace $r[major]$ with a random value from M chosen uniformly. Intuitively, if the relation is large enough (precisely characterized in Theorem 2), it is likely that the rare majors will be assigned to at least a few other students; affording some level of ambiguity. PrivateClean also needs to randomize the score attribute. Consider the case where it is known that all Civil Engineering majors gave a score of 1. Exploiting this correlation might de-privatize the result, and

PrivateClean will have to add statistical noise to all numerical attributes.

Intuitively, as the degree of privacy increases, the private dataset tends towards a uniform distribution (i.e., most ambiguous). This overestimates the prevalence of rare values, and underestimates of the prevalence of common values. Consequently, the effects of data skew get amplified by privacy, and we derive an analytic formula to compensate for this effect based on query selectivity. However, in the presence of data transformations, the original granularity of randomization may not be apparent (i.e., merging values together), and to this end, PrivateClean maintains provenance to estimate query results.

3. PROBLEM SETUP

This section describes the basic formalism for PrivateClean.

3.1 The Database Provider

A trusted provider wants to release a private relation for analysis by an untrusted analyst. Let R be the original relation, i.e., not private, destined for analysis. We consider relations of numerical attributes (real-valued or integer-valued) and discrete valued attributes (any data type). Let $A = \{a_1, ..., a_l\}$ be the set of numerical attributes, and $D = \{d_1, ..., d_m\}$ be the set of discrete-valued attributes. We assume that all user-defined data cleaning operations occur on the discrete attributes of the relation.

3.1.1 Local Differential Privacy

Given the relation R, the provider wants to release a private version of R denoted by V. We will analyze PrivateClean as a form of differential privacy [11]. A stronger variant of differential privacy, local differential privacy, is a measure of randomness in row-by-row randomized transformations. The level of privacy is parameterized by ϵ, where smaller values imply a greater degree of privacy. Intuitively, ϵ is a measure of ambiguity in a record's true value given observation of only the private value. The key consequence of Differential Privacy is that no deterministic function f applied to V can ever reduce the degree of privacy (i.e., increase ϵ).

Suppose, we are given a randomized algorithm $M : R \mapsto V$ which maps rows of R to a relation of the same schema V. We observe a result of applying this algorithm to some (unknown) row in R and call this $r_{private}$. For every element in $r_{private} \in V$, the probability of observing $r_{private}$ given an input row r is denoted by $P[r_{private} \mid r]$. M is said to be ϵ-local differentially private if for all records $r \in R$:

$$\max_{r,r'} \frac{P[r_{private} \mid r]}{P[r_{private} \mid r']} \leq \exp(\epsilon)$$

In other words, given some observed randomized result, ϵ is a bound on the ratio between the most likely input and the least likely input.

3.2 The Analyst

The analyst is given the private relation V with the same schema as R, and the analyst can apply user-defined data cleaning operations to the discrete attributes of V.

3.2.1 Data Cleaning Model

We model data cleaning operations as deterministic user-defined functions over the discrete attributes in each row. The user-defined function takes any projection g_i of D as input and returns a unique output (or output tuple), and we denote the set of all projections as $proj(D)$. Regardless of the analysts actions, privacy is preserved; even if those actions do not conform to the proposed projection/user-defined function cleaning model. However, if the analyst violates this model and attempts other types of data cleaning operations, result estimation is no longer guaranteed with PrivateClean. Formally, for each projection $g_i \in proj(D)$, a *local cleaner* can take three actions:

$\mathbf{Extract}(g_i)$ Creates a new discrete attribute d_{m+1} based the result of applying $C(v[g_i])$ for all $v \in V$. C is an arbitrary deterministic user-defined operation.

$\mathbf{Transform}(g_i)$ Replaces the values in the projection g_i with the result of applying $C(v[g_i])$ for all $v \in V$:

$$v[g_i] \leftarrow C(v[g_i])$$

$\mathbf{Merge}(g_i, Domain(g_i))$ Replaces the values in the projection g_i with some other value in the domain $Domain(g_i)$ with an arbitrary user-defined choice $C(v[g_i], Domain(g_i))$ for all $v \in V$:

$$v[g_i] \leftarrow C(v[g_i], Domain(g_i))$$

The analyst can apply an arbitrary composition of these local cleaners to the data:

$$C(\cdot) = C_1 \circ C_2 \circ ...C_k$$

These cleaners do not need to be known in advance and can be constructed through data exploration of V. The key point is that the analyst can only clean and query the private relation V. The following are examples of cleaners that can be implemented by PrivateClean:

EXAMPLE 1 (FIND-AND-REPLACE). *The analyst wants to count the number of "Electrical Engineering and Computer Sciences" majors. Suppose* major *attribute has alternative representations of the same logical value "Electrical Engineering and Computer Sciences" and "EECS". The find-and-replace operation "Electrical Engineering and Computer Sciences -> EECS" can be represented with a* **Merge** *operation.*

EXAMPLE 2 (FUNCTIONAL DEPENDENCY). *The analyst wants to compare scores across different instructors. However, suppose the functional dependency $V[section] \mapsto V[instructor]$ is violated, namely there are two students with the same section number but with different instructor names. The analyst can first apply a standard functional dependency repair algorithm (e.g., [6]), which will generate a series of updates to the records in $v_i \in V$:*

$$v_i : (section, instructor) \mapsto (section', instructor')$$

Each of these updates can be represented as a **Transform** *operation, and thus can be supported in PrivateClean.*

3.2.2 Query Processing

Let us call the resulting private relation after cleaning V_{clean}. By nature, differentially private relations preclude point queries since any given record might be randomized, but since they can answer aggregate queries since they preserve the main characteristics of the dataset. We explore a class of queries that can be answered with close-form Central Limit Theorem confidence intervals. We consider `sum`, `count`, and `avg` queries that aggregate over a single numerical attribute predicated on a single discrete attribute:

```
SELECT agg(a) FROM R WHERE cond(d)
```

where a is a numerical attribute, and d is a single discrete attribute. However, this query class is not a fundamental limitation of the technique, and we discuss extensions in Section 10.

We define accuracy with respect to the hypothetical scenario where the same sequence of cleaning operations $C(\cdot)$ was applied directly to R (non-private) resulting in $R_{clean} = C(R)$. For an aggregate query f,

$$error = |est(V_{clean}) - f(R_{clean})|$$

Bounded confidence means, that for any level of privacy, we can give a bound on $error$. Note that this definition does not consider the fact that a private relation may be harder to clean (in terms of human effort in detecting and reasoning about errors) or require more cleaning (in terms additional constraints). We treat the cleaning operations defined on the private relation by the user as ground truth and estimate the result as if those same operations were applied to the original relation.

3.3 Problem Statements

PrivateClean needs to address two issues, constructing provably private relations and query processing.

Private Relation Creation: Given a relation R with corruptions in its discrete attributes, and a privacy parameter ϵ, find a ϵ-local differentially private relation $V = T(R)$ can be cleaned with Merge, Transform, and Extract operations.

Query Processing: Let V be the private relation, $C = C_1 \circ ... \circ C_k$ be an arbitrary composition of the aforementioned data cleaning operations, and $V_{clean} = C(V)$. Let $R_{clean} = C(R)$ be the hypothetical dataset where the same transformations $C(\cdot)$ are applied to R. For an aggregate function f (`sum`, `count`, `avg`) with single attribute predicates, estimate the value of $f(R_{clean})$, using only the private cleaned relation V_{clean}.

4. GENERATING PRIVATE RELATIONS

This section presents a technique to generate private relations that allow for data cleaning.

4.1 Overview

In the generation phase, PrivateClean explores two new issues not considered prior randomized response models: (1) privacy for multiple columns and data types, and (2) analysis that describes the sufficient amount of data required before the results are meaningful. Multiple columns pose a challenge to differential privacy. This is because even one non-private column has the potential to de-randomize all of the other private columns. Even information that is not sensitive may correlate with sensitive information, and thus can be used to reverse privacy transformations. Consequently, we address (1) by proposing different randomization techniques for discrete and numerical attributes and applying this across all attributes. We address (2) using a worst-case analysis in a hypothetical highly skewed dataset, and analytically show the relationship between dataset size, the number of distinct values, and privacy.

4.2 Generalized Randomized Response

The key idea is to apply a randomized response to the partitioned discrete attributes and add random statistical noise to the numerical attributes. We propose the combination of these two "mechanisms" and call the combined technique Generalized Randomized Response (GRR)[1].

4.2.1 Discrete Attributes

For the discrete attributes, we formalize the intuition described in the introduction. Let d_i be a discrete attribute. Let $Domain(d_i)$ be the set of all the distinct values in $R[d_i]$. Then, for each d_i, we apply a randomized response mechanism:

$$r'[d_i] = \begin{cases} r[d_i] & \text{w.p } 1 - p_i \\ \mathbf{U}(Domain(d_i)) & \text{w.p } p_i \end{cases}$$

[1]All proofs are included in the Appendix

where $\mathbf{U}(\cdot)$ selects an element uniformly at random. Ignoring the other attributes, we can show that this transformation is ϵ-differentially private.

LEMMA 1 (RANDOMIZED RESPONSE MECHANISM). *The projection of each discrete attribute $\Pi_{d_i}(V)^2$ is ϵ-local differentially private, with $\epsilon = \ln(\frac{3}{p_i} - 2)$.*

PROOF SKETCH. The worst case is when there are only two values in the domain and all of the other entries in the database are one value except for one, based on the definition of differential privacy we can arrive at:

$$\epsilon = \ln(\frac{3}{p_i} - 2)$$

□

4.2.2 Numerical Attributes

However, in general, the randomized response model is not meaningful for numerical attributes. To randomize the numerical attributes, we apply a different differential privacy mechanism, the Laplace Mechanism [11]. The key idea is to add heavy-tailed, but zero-mean, statistical noise to every attribute. While this obscures outliers, the noise will average out when aggregating over a large enough dataset.

Formally, for each numerical attribute a_i,

$$r'[a_i] = \mathbf{L}(r[a_i], b_i)$$

where $\mathbf{L}(\mu, b)$ is the Laplace distribution:

$$\mathbf{L}(\mu, b) \sim \frac{1}{2b}\exp(\frac{|x - \mu|}{b})$$

The Laplace distribution is standard in the study of differential privacy. This distribution has several nice algebraic properties such as being analytically integrable, unlike the Gaussian distribution. Furthermore, it is also the maximum entropy distribution given a fixed mean value.

PROPOSITION 1 (LAPLACE MECHANISM). *The Laplace Mechanism is ϵ-local differentially private, with $\epsilon = \frac{\Delta_i}{b_i}$, where Δ_i is defined as the max difference between any two values in $\Pi_{a_i}(V)$.*

4.2.3 GRR Summary

To summarize, the GRR mechanism takes as input a set of numerical attributes A and a set of discrete attributes D. For each discrete attribute d_i there is a user-specified privacy parameter p_i which is its randomization probability, and for each numerical attribute a_i there is a parameter b_i which is the amount of Laplace noise to add. For each numerical attribute, we apply the Laplace mechanism with b_i, and for each discrete attribute partition, we apply randomized response with probability p_i. Using the composition lemma from Dwork et al. [11], we arrive at the following result:

THEOREM 1 (GENERALIZED RANDOMIZED RESPONSE). *For a set of numerical and discrete attributes, Generalized Randomized Response returns an ϵ locally differentially private mechanism with $\epsilon = \sum_{n_i} \epsilon_{n_i} + \sum_{d_i} \epsilon_{d_i}$, where ϵ_a is calculated per attribute.*

Interpretation: The basic intuition about Theorem 1 is that adding attributes (even private ones) decreases the privacy (by increasing ϵ. We can now clearly see why adding a non-randomized attribute $\epsilon_i = \infty$ de-privatizes all of the other attributes.

[2]Π denotes the standard projection relational operator.

Setting ϵ: So far, we have discussed ϵ as a given parameter from the provider. ϵ is a sum of the individual privacy factors for each attribute ϵ_i. These values can be uniformly allocated by dividing ϵ equally over the numerical attributes and the discrete attributes d_i. For numerical attributes, ϵ_i is controlled by b_i, and for discrete attribute partitions, it is controlled by p_i. Section 5 will show how to derive b_i and p_i based on the dataset size and desired query result accuracy. We formalize this into a parameter tuning algorithm listed in Appendix E.

4.3 Privacy Properties of GRR

If V is ϵ-local differentially private, then V_{clean} is ϵ differentially private, since any deterministic data manipulation is guaranteed to preserve privacy. This result is a direct consequence of Proposition 2.1 in Dwork et al. [11], which guarantees that differentially private relations are immune to post-processing.

In the discrete attributes, there is some probability that a rare value will be masked, that is, for all records that have the value the randomization will set it to a different one, and for all other records, the randomization does not choose this value. Intuitively, for a large enough database, this should be a rare occurrence. The database can regenerate the private views until this is true. Thus, we want to know how large the dataset needs to be before with high probability $(1 - \alpha)$ all of the domain values are seen after applying GRR (i.e., the expected number of re-generations is $\frac{1}{1-\alpha}$).

THEOREM 2. *For all discrete attributes d_i, let N be the number of distinct tuples in $R[d_i]$. For $p > 0$, the dataset size S has to be larger than:*

$$S > \frac{N}{p} \log \frac{pN}{\alpha}$$

for the domain is preserved probability $1 - \alpha$.

PROOF SKETCH. Assume domain value a is present once, and all other values are different. The probability that a is visible in the private relation:

$$\mathbf{P}[a] = 1 - p\frac{N-1}{N}[1 - \frac{p}{N}]^{(S-1)}$$

To extend this bound for any given value, we apply a union bound (multiplying the probability by N):

$$\mathbf{P}[all] \geq 1 - p(N-1)[1 - \frac{p}{N}]^{(S-1)}$$

The above formula can be found by solving for S and simplifying the logarithms. □

Essentially, the number of distinct values needs to be on the order of $O(\frac{S}{\log S})$ to ensure that the entire domain is preserved with high probability. This result is related to the well known result of the Coupon Collector's problem [12].

EXAMPLE 3. *For the simplified course evaluation example $R(major, score)$, let us suppose p_i is 0.25 and there are $N = 25$ distinct majors in the dirty relation. We can plug these values into Theorem 2. To have $1 - \alpha = 95\%$ confidence, we need approximately 391 records, and for $1 - \alpha = 99\%$, we need 552 records.*

5. QUERY PROCESSING

This section describes query processing on private relations without considering cleaning. Direct query processing after Generalized Randomized Response has a bias because rare values start appearing increasingly frequently. Thus, we describe how to compensate for this bias and bound the result in confidence intervals.

5.1 Overview

Given a private relation V and its non-private base relation R, we define *error* in a query result as:

$$error = \mid f(R) - f(V) \mid$$

There are two reasons why a query on V may be erroneous: Laplace privacy in the numerical attribute adding error to the aggregate and randomized response privacy in the discrete attribute adding error to the predicate.

Let us first consider an aggregate without a predicate. Since, GRR adds zero-mean statistical noise to each numerical value, and consequently `sum`, `avg`, and `count` queries can simply be estimated as:

$$f(R) \approx f(V)$$

We call this estimator the Direct estimator that is unbiased for queries without predicates. As we will see, this argument does not quite hold when there is a predicate.

5.2 Quantifying the Bias

Now, let us consider the case when there is a predicate. Let the discrete attribute d be a member of a partition g_i which has N distinct values. Every deterministic predicate $cond(d)$ can be thought of as conditioning on a subset of the N distinct values. Suppose the predicate is querying l of the distinct values. The consequence of randomized response is that there are false positives (predicate falsely true) and false negatives (ignored records). If s is the true fraction of records that satisfy the predicate, the fraction of false positive records is:

$$\text{false positive} = (1 - s)p\frac{l}{N} \tag{1}$$

and similarly, the fraction of false negative records is:

$$\text{false negative} = sp\frac{N - l}{N} \tag{2}$$

The key insight is that Equation 1 and Equation 2 are not the same, and thus, there is a bias. Accordingly, PrivateClean will estimate this bias from the observed private data and compensate for it.

PROPOSITION 2. *The Direct estimator introduces a bias w.r.t to the hypothetically cleaned non-private dataset of: $\tilde{O}(\frac{p(l-sN)}{N})$*

PROOF SKETCH. Since the Direct estimator sets two values equal, we can calculate the difference:

$$bias = (1 - s)p\frac{l}{N} - sp\frac{N-l}{N}$$

This is the fraction of tuples not accounted for, and thus, up-to some scaling this is the bias. □

What is interesting about this bias is that the term $\frac{(l-sN)}{N}$ is related to the skew in the dataset. l is the number of distinct values for which the predicate is true, s is the fraction of records selected by those distinct values. For uniform data distributions $\frac{l}{N} \approx s$. However, when this is not true, this bias is scaled by the privacy factor in the dataset. So essentially, the bias is $O(privacy \cdot skew)$.

5.3 Compensating For the Bias

To derive an estimator that compensates for this bias, there are four quantities of interest.

True Positive Probability: For a tuple t, given that the predicate is true on the original relation, the probability that predicate remains to be true on the private relation: $\tau_p = (1 - p) + p\frac{l}{N}$

False Positive Probability: For a tuple t, given that the predicate is false on the original relation, the probability that predicate is set to be true on the private relation: $\tau_n = p\frac{l}{N}$.

True Negative Probability: For a tuple t, given that the predicate is false on the original relation, the probability that predicate remains to be false on the private relation: $\gamma_p = p\frac{N-l}{N}$.

False Negative Probability: For a tuple t, given that the predicate is true on the original relation, the probability that predicate is set to be false on the private relation: $\gamma_p = (1-p) + p\frac{N-l}{N}$.

It turns out that we can derive unbiased estimators parametrized by these deterministic quantities. Given a query, we know the number of distinct values, the selectivity of the predicate l, and the privacy parameter p. Consequently, these values do not change the statistical properties of the estimation.

5.4 COUNT Estimation

Let s be the fraction of records that truly satisfy the predicate. In the private relation, there will be a fraction s_p of records that nominally satisfy the predicate. We can relate s and p with the following function:

$$s_p = s\tau_p + (1-s)\tau_n$$

We can solve for s, resulting in:

$$s = \frac{s_p - \tau_n}{\tau_p - \tau_n}$$

Therefore, we arrive at the following estimator. Let $c_{private}$ (equivalent to $S \cdot s_p$) be the count on the private view. The estimate of the true count $\hat{c}$ is:

$$\hat{c} = \frac{c_{private} - S\tau_n}{(\tau_p - \tau_n)} \tag{3}$$

Confidence Intervals: To asymptotically bound this estimate, we need to recognize that s_p is actually a random variable. Based on the Central Limit Theorem, we can bound s_p in a confidence interval where S is the size of the relation:

$$s_p \pm z_\alpha \sqrt{\frac{(1-s_p)\cdot s_p}{S}}$$

We can substitute this random variable into the above expression for s, and recognizing that τ_n is deterministic and $1-p = \tau_p - \tau_n$, it follows that the estimate is bounded by:

$$\hat{c} \pm z_\alpha \frac{1}{1-p}\sqrt{\frac{(1-s_p)\cdot s_p}{S}}$$

The confidence interval allows a user to judge a range of possible true values for the `count` query.

Parameter Tuning: However, we may be interested in knowing the error over any `count` query given a level of privacy. Interestingly enough, we can calculate a bound for this independent of the dataset properties. Over all possible queries, $\sqrt{(1-s_p)\cdot s_p}$ is bounded by $\frac{1}{4}$. Thus, for all possible count queries, the error is bounded by:

$$error < z_\alpha \frac{1}{1-p}\sqrt{\frac{1}{4S}} \tag{4}$$

This bound can be used to tune the privacy parameter p.

$$p = 1 - Z_\alpha(\sqrt{\frac{1}{4S\cdot error^2}})$$

5.5 SUM Estimation

Estimating `sum` queries will be slightly more difficult. The key challenge is correlations in the dataset. If the numerical attribute is correlated with the discrete attribute, then false positives and false negatives can lead to different mixtures of data. It is also important to note that unlike `count`, the `sum` queries also query the numerical attributes with the Laplace randomization mechanism.

Let c_{true} be the true count, μ_{true} be the average value of the true records that satisfy the predicate, and μ_{false} be the average value of the records that do not satisfy the predicate. Using this notation, we can derive the following expression for the expected private sum h_p:

$$\mathbb{E}(h_p) = c_{true}\mu_{true}\tau_p + (S - c_{true})\mu_{false}\tau_n$$

$c_{true}\mu_{true}$ is the quantity that we want to estimate.

Unlike in the `count` query case, the challenge is that there are two unknown variables $c_{true}\mu_{true}$ and μ_{false}. Thus, the problem is that there is not enough information in this equation to solve for $c_{true}\mu_{true}$. To address this, we also calculate the sum of the complement as well, that is, we invert the predicate and run the query:

$$\mathbb{E}(h_p^c) = \gamma_n c_{true}\mu_{true} + (S - c_{true})\gamma_p\mu_{false}$$

This is defines a linear system of equations which we can solve for the true sum $h_{true} = c_{true}\mu_{true}$. The resulting estimator becomes:

$$\hat{h} = \frac{(1-\tau_n)h_p - \tau_n h_p^c}{(\tau_p - \tau_n)} \tag{5}$$

Confidence Intervals: The next goal is to bound this estimate in confidence intervals. Notice, that the estimate is a weighted average of h_p and h_p^c. Therefore, it suffices to bound $h_p + h_p^c$. Let μ_p be the mean value across all of the private data and σ_p^2 be its variance:

$$\hat{h} \pm z_\alpha 2 \cdot \sqrt{\frac{s_p(1-s_p)\mu_p^2 + \sigma_p^2}{S}}$$

We can turn this into an analytic bound like before over any `sum` query. Using the fact that $\sigma_p^2 = \sigma^2 + 2b^2$, $s_p(1-s_p) \leq \frac{1}{4}$:

$$error \leq z_\alpha \frac{1}{1-p}\sqrt{\frac{\mu}{S} + 4\frac{\sigma^2 + 2b^2}{S}} \tag{6}$$

Like before, this can be used to tune the privacy parameter p and b given a desired error.

5.6 AVG Estimation

It turns out that due to a ratio of random variables problem, the intuitive estimator for `avg` $\frac{\hat{h}}{\hat{c}}$ is biased. However, empirically, this bias is small and in fact such estimates are called conditionally unbiased [17]. Confidence intervals can be computed directly from the expressions above by taking the upper confidence interval of $\widehat{h}$ and dividing it by the lower confidence interval of $\widehat{c}$, and vice versa. To get an approximate analytic form for this interval, we can apply standard error propagation techniques [34]:

$$avg \approx \frac{\widehat{h}}{\widehat{c}} \qquad error \approx \frac{1}{\widehat{c}} \cdot \frac{error_{sum}}{error_{count}} \tag{7}$$

where err denotes the width of the confidence interval. The basic intuition is this differentiates the expression and linearizes $\frac{sum}{count}$, and it holds asymptotically.

EXAMPLE 4. *In the running example dataset, suppose p is 0.25, there are 25 distinct majors in the dirty relation, and 500 records. We are interested in counting the number of engineering majors (account for 10 out of the initial 25). Suppose, the private count was* 300. *Using the formula described in Section 5.4* $est = \frac{300 - 500\times 10\times .25\times\frac{1}{25}}{.75} = 333.3$.

6. SINGLE-ATTRIBUTE CLEANING

The previous section described how to process queries on private relations, and this section will describe how to account for data cleaning in the query processing. The basic intuition is that the bias estimation in the previous section is no longer possible after data cleaning since the original distinct values are changed. To do so, we will have to keep track of provenance, i.e., the mapping between original values before data cleaning and the values after cleaning.

Recall, that the cleaning operations are deterministic user-defined operations over projections of the relation $g_i \in proj(D)$. There are two cases, single-attribute and multi-attribute, where the former is the problem where *all* cleaning operations happen on a single attribute $g_i = \{d_i\}$. The next section (Section 7) considers the multi-attribute case.

6.1 Overview

When the original relation was randomized, it was randomized on the dirty data. The key challenge in query processing after data cleaning is that data cleaning may change the number of distinct values and the selectivity of the predicate. The solution is to define a graph that keeps track of the provenance of each value in the domain and use this to find a predicate's selectivity l on the dirty data, and the number of distinct values in the dirty data N.

As in Section 5.2, where privacy amplifies the effects of skew, this discrepancy is also amplified. In other words, after cleaning l and N may change. Starting with the bias described in the previous section:

$$bias = \frac{p(l - sN)}{N}$$

However, since l and N change due to data cleaning, there is a second term accounting for the bias with respect to the new l' and N':

$$bias \leq \frac{p(l - sN)}{N} + p(\frac{l}{N} - \frac{l'}{N'})$$

The term $\frac{l}{N} - \frac{l'}{N'}$ measures the difference between the selectivity (w.r.t to the distinct values) of the query on the cleaned data vs. the original data. We call this term the "merge rate", as it describes how many of the distinct values in the predicate were merged due to data cleaning. Therefore, the resulting bias is:

$$bias = \tilde{O}(privacy \cdot (skew + merge))$$

6.2 Value Provenance Graph

We store a graph mapping dirty values to cleaned values for each attribute and use this graph to compensate for this bias. Let d_{clean} be the discrete attribute in the predicate on the cleaned private relation V_{clean}. Based on the model in Section 3.2.1, where the allowed operations are extract, merge, and transform, each d_{clean} is associated with exactly one attribute d_i. We need to understand the relationship between $Domain(V_{clean}[d_{clean}])$ and $Domain(V[d_i])$. Recall, that Section 3.2.1 makes an assumption of determinism, namely, given two records r and r', where $r[d_i] = r'[d_i]$, the operation has the same result.

Thus, the cleaning model defines a directed bipartite graph between the two domains:

$$Domain(V[g_i]) \mapsto Domain(V_{clean}[d_{clean}])$$

Let $L = Domain(V[d_i])$ be the set of distinct values of the private relation before data cleaning, and let $M = Domain(V_{clean}[d_{clean}])$ be the set of distinct values after data cleaning. Each $l \in L$ and each $m \in M$ defines a node in the bipartite graph. We add edges between L and M to represent the transformation made by a cleaner. Determinism implies a key property that this graph has many-to-one relationships but no one-to-many mappings; also implying that $|L| \geq |M|$. From a graph perspective, this graph is *fork-free* with un-weighted edges. This will be the key differentiating factor between the single-attribute case and the multiple-attribute in the next section.

6.3 Predicates as Vertex Cuts

Maintaining this graph gives us a convenient abstraction to count the number of edges affected by a predicate, and thereby, obtaining the original selectivity. Let $cond(d_{clean})$ be a predicate and each predicate can be expressed as a subset of the clean distinct values $M_{pred} \subseteq M$. Each M_{pred} will have a parent set L_{pred}, that is the set of vertices in L with an edge to exactly one $m \in M_{pred}$. Together $cut = (L_{pred}, M_{pred})$ defines a cut on the bipartite graph.

EXAMPLE 5. *Suppose we have a dirty* major *of four values "Civil Engineering", "Mechanical Engineering", "M.E", "Math". The cleaner maps the first three values to "Engineering", and the user's predicate queries "Engineering". L_{pred} is the set that contains "Civil Engineering", "Mechanical Engineering", "M.E". M_{pred} is singleton set with "Engineering".*

Let $l = |L_{pred}|$, $N = |L|$ and $r[d_i] \in L_{pred}$. We can then recompute the quantities from the previous section w.r.t to the dirty data. The estimate is parametrized by two values τ_p, τ_n, and we can calculate them as follows: The revised true positive probability and false positive probability are:

$$\tau_p = (1 - p) + p\frac{l}{N} \quad \tau_n = p\frac{l}{N}$$

The values can be plugged into the estimator described in the previous section. From a statistical estimation perspective p and l are deterministic values known to the query processing system. Therefore, τ_p, τ_n are deterministic values.

6.4 Efficiency: Linear Space, Linear Time

Of course, there is an additional space- and time-complexity overhead for materializing this graph and calculating the correction. However, we do not have to materialize the entire graph. Let $\hat{N}$ be the number of distinct values in the dirty relation affected by merge or transformation operations. Since the graph is fork-free the resulting cleaned relation will have strictly less than $\hat{N}$ values that link to those in the dirty relation. We only have to store the graph for this subset of vertices in M and L. Implemented with a hash map (cleaned value $\mapsto$ dirty value) , the space complexity of this graph is linear in $\hat{N}$, and the query complexity is linear in the distinct-value selectivity $l' = |M_{pred}|$.

PROPOSITION 3. *For an attribute that is individually cleaned with deterministic user-defined merge and transform operations. Let $\hat{N}$ be the total number of affected distinct values by these operations. The resulting provenance graph can be stored with $O(\hat{N})$ space and for a predicate with distinct-value selectivity l' can be queried in $O(l')$ time.*

7. MULTIPLE-ATTRIBUTE CLEANING

This section extends the graph cut formulation to the case when the cleaning is over multiple attributes. Since we only consider queries whose predicates are defined over single discrete attributes, it is sufficient to maintain a a single graph per-attribute. However, to understand why this case is more difficult consider the following example:

EXAMPLE 6. *Suppose g_i is (*section, instructor*). The private relation has rows "1, John Doe", "1, NULL", "2, NULL". The cleaner maps "1, NULL" to "1, John Doe" and "2, NULL" to "2, Jane Smith". The dirty distinct value $NULL$ has two possible cleaned values* `John Doe` *and* `Jane Smith`.

As illustrated in the example, the basic change from the previous section is that the provenance graph has forks, and as a result, the definition of l has to change.

7.1 Weighted Provenance Graph

As before, we need a graph to represent the relationship between $Domain(V_{clean}[d_{clean}])$ and $Domain(V[d_i])$, and we store one graph per discrete attribute. The cleaning model defines a directed bipartite graph between the two domains:

$$Domain(V[g_i]) \mapsto Domain(V_{clean}[d_{clean}])$$

Let $L = Domain(V[d_i])$ be the set of distinct values of the private relation before data cleaning, and let $M = Domain(V_{clean}[d_{clean}])$ be the set of distinct values after data cleaning. Each $l \in L$ and each $m \in M$ defines a node in the bipartite graph. We add edges between L and M to represent the transformation made by a cleaner. Let $V^{(l)}[d_i]$ denote the set of rows that have the distinct value l and $V^{(m)}_{clean}[d_i]$ denote the set of clean rows that have the distinct value m. Unlike before, we add a weight w_{lm} to each of the edges to represent the fraction of rows with the value l mapped to the value m:

$$w_{lm} = \frac{|V^{(m)}_{clean}[d_i]|}{|V^{(l)}[d_i]|}$$

In Example 6, this would assign a weight of 0.5 to both `NULL` $\mapsto$ `John Doe` and `NULL` $\mapsto$ `Jane Smith`. Intuitively, the weight captures the fraction of rows represented by the edge.

7.2 Predicate Probability Estimation

Let $cond(d_{clean})$ be a predicate and each predicate can be expressed as a subset of the clean distinct values $M_{pred} \subseteq M$. Each M_{pred} will have a parent set L_{pred}, that is the set of vertices in L with an edge to exactly one $m \in M_{pred}$. Together $cut = (L_{pred}, M_{pred})$ defines a cut on the bipartite graph. Before, we simply counted the number of vertices in L_{pred} to find l. Now, we need to account for the fraction of rows represented by the edges:

$$l = \sum_{l \in L_{pred}, m \in M_{pred}} w_{lm}$$

In the case, where the graph is fork-free this will reduce to the result in the previous section $w_{lm} \in \{0, 1\}$. Let $N = |L|$ and $r[d_i] \in L_{pred}$, then the revised true positive probability and false positive probability are:

$$\tau_p = (1-p) + p\frac{l}{N} \quad \tau_n = p\frac{l}{N}$$

The values can be plugged into the estimator described in the Section 5. This estimate is also asymptotically unbiased since the weights will tend to a fixed-point as the dataset grows in size.

7.3 Efficiency: Quadratic Space, Linear Time

Interestingly enough, the time- and space-complexity of the multi-attribute case is different from the single-attribute case. Since the graph is not fork-free the resulting attribute can have as many as $distinct(g_i)$ values that link to those in the dirty relation (follows from determinism). Let $\hat{N} \leq distinct(g_i)$ be the fraction of distinct tuple values affected by the cleaning operations. For the resulting graph implemented with a hash map (cleaned value $\mapsto$ dirty value), the space complexity of this graph is quadratic in $\hat{N}$, and the query complexity is linear in the distinct-value selectivity $l' = |M_{pred}|$.

PROPOSITION 4. *For multiple attributes cleaned with deterministic user-defined merge and transform operations. Let $\hat{N}$ be the total number of affected distinct values by these operations. The resulting provenance graph can be stored with $O(\hat{N}^2)$ space and for a predicate with distinct-value selectivity l' can be queried in $O(l')$ time.*

8. EXPERIMENTS

This section presents several experiments on real and synthetic datasets to evaluate PrivateClean. First, we show that the weighted estimator for PrivateClean is more accurate than the baseline Direct estimator, even when there are no data errors. We use a synthetic dataset and vary all of the parameters to show the tradeoffs. Next, we explore how privacy amplifies some types of data error and compare the estimates of Direct and PrivateClean. Finally, we present data cleaning and privacy applications on two real datasets.

8.1 Metrics and Setup

We implemented PrivateClean in Python 2.7 on a MacOSX i7 2.7GHZ, and the provenance algorithm was implemented using a standard Python dictionary stored in memory. To the best of our knowledge, there are no examples of a general purpose differentially private data cleaning framework in the literature. Consequently, the primary goal is to evaluate the proposed estimators for `sum`, `count`, and `avg`. We compare the following query processing approaches, both using GRR:

Direct: The Direct approach runs data cleaning on a private relation and then runs the query and returns the nominal result (no reweighting).

PrivateClean: The proposed approach in this paper including the data cleaning and weighted approximate query processing.

Error %: Let r be the result of running either PrivateClean or Direct. Let $r*$ be the result of running a query on a *cleaned non-private* dataset. The relative error % is $error = \frac{|r - r*|}{r*}$.

8.2 Datasets

We explore results on four datasets: Synthetic, TPC-DS, IntelWireless, and MCAFE.

Synthetic: This dataset includes a single numerical attribute $[0, 100]$ and a single categorical attribute $\{1, ..., N\}$. Both these attributes are drawn from a Zipfian distribution with scale parameter z. We vary N, z, and the privacy parameters to evaluate the estimation approaches. In particular, we use the synthetic dataset to validate the extremal behavior of PrivateClean and the regimes in which it performs well. In Appendix D, we list the default parameters. Unless otherwise noted, we fix the default parameters and vary one of the variables.

TPC-DS: We use this TPC-DS benchmark to construct constraint-based data cleaning use cases. We focus on a projection of one table: `customer_address(ca_city, ca_county, ca_state, ca_country)`. There are two data quality constraints on this table, one is a functional dependency:

$$[ca\_city, ca\_county] \mapsto [ca\_state]$$

There is also a matching dependency on country:

$$MD([ca\_country] \approx [ca\_country])$$

We introduce errors into the relation where we randomly replace *ca_state* and append one-character corruptions to *ca_country*. We solve for the constraints and implications using a standard repair algorithm [6]. Such algorithms are typically approximate or heuristic, and in this experiment, we measure accuracy with respect to ground truth (since the data cleaning itself may be fallible).

IntelWireless [29]: This dataset includes 2.3 million observations of sensor environment sensor measurements indexed by sensor id. It includes missing values and outliers. We simulate a task where we want to keep the sensor id private but still allow for cleaning of the outliers. This dataset is characterized by a small number of

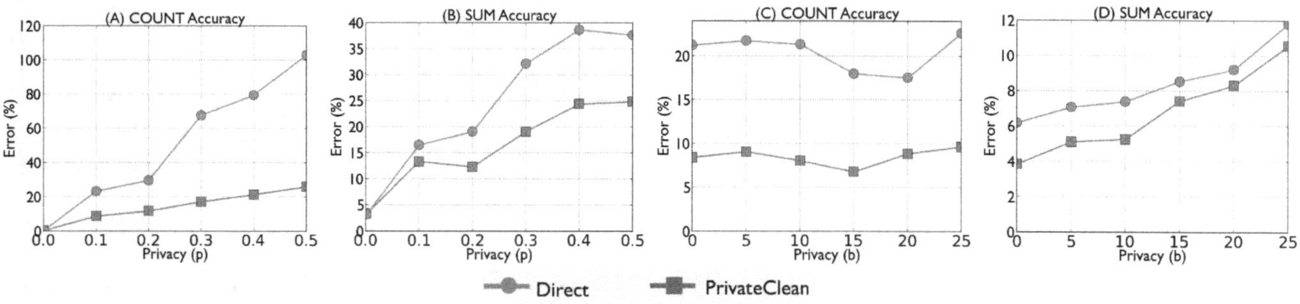

Figure 2: Relative query result error as a function of the privacy parameters (p,b). Even when there are no data errors, PrivateClean is more accurate than the Direct estimate because it accounts for data skew.

distinct discrete values (68) compared to the dataset size, which is a preferred regime of PrivateClean.

MCAFE [49]: This dataset contains 406 records of student course evaluations. We look at a numerical attribute of "enthusiasm" on a scale from 1-10, and the country code of the student. We want to keep the country codes private. We simulate a data cleaning scenario where the analyst has to merge country codes from nearby countries and remove missing values.

8.3 Synthetic Experiments

8.3.1 No Data Error

We first explore the significance of this improvement without data error and then show that the gains become more significant in the presence of data error.

Function of privacy: The two privacy parameters are p (privacy in the discrete value) and b (privacy in the numerical attribute). For a predicate with 10% selectivity and skew of $z = 2$, we first varied the categorical privacy factor p, while fixing the numerical privacy factor. Figure 2a shows how the `count` varies as a function of privacy. As predicted by the analysis the relationship is roughly linear. Even without data error, we find that when the categorical privacy factor p is high, PrivateClean has nearly a 5x reduction in query error in comparison to Direct. This is not surprising in a moderately skewed dataset given Lemma 2. Figure 2b shows how the `sum` varies as a function of privacy, and we see a similar linear relationship.

Figure 2c and Figure 2d show how the errors vary as a function of the numerical privacy factor. As expected `count` is not affected by this factor. However, there is an interesting relationship for `sum` (Figure 2d). Since the re-weighting does not affect the numerical privacy factor b, these gains w.r.t naive are diminished as the variance from the numerical privacy dominates.

Function of selectivity: The next question we explore is the how the query result error varies as a function of the selectivity. We fix the numerical and discrete privacy parameters and vary the query selectivity (defined in terms of the fraction of distinct values for which the predicate is true). Figure 3a and Figure 3b show the error % of `sum` and `count` queries for PrivateClean and Direct. PrivateClean is more accurate the Direct for low selectivity queries. The mathematical reason for this is subtle. The effects of data skew average out over more general predicates.

Function of skew: Next, we vary the skew of the data distribution by changing the Zipfian parameter z (Figure 4). PrivateClean is increasingly more accurate than Direct in skewed datasets. In fact,

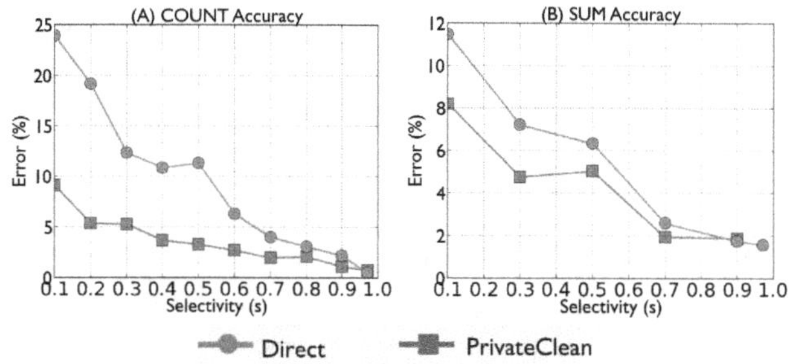

Figure 3: PrivateClean is more accurate than the Direct especially at lower selectivities.

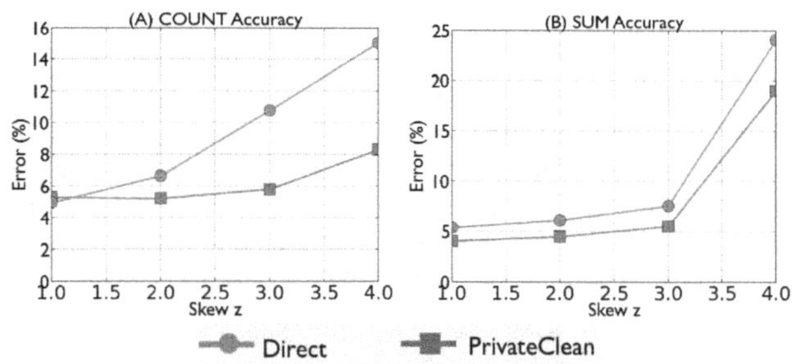

Figure 4: PrivateClean is more accurate than the Direct in skewed datasets

for count queries, there is no benefit to re-weighting results under a uniform distribution. This result is predicted by our analysis (Section 5.2).

8.3.2 Data Error

In the next set of experiments, we vary the frequency and type of data error.

Function of Error Rate: Next, we simulated data errors. For a random fraction of the distinct values mapped them to other distinct values. In Figure , we vary this fraction (error rate) while holding all of the other parameters fixed. Since Direct does not consider the provenance of the data, as the error rate increase its estimate is increasingly erroneous. On the other hand, PrivateClean keeps a constant relative error (the only error is due to the privacy factor) as the error rate is varied.

This experiment is also interesting in absolute terms. For both `sum` and `count`, PrivateClean provides a result with less than 10% error across all data error rates. This shows that in absolute

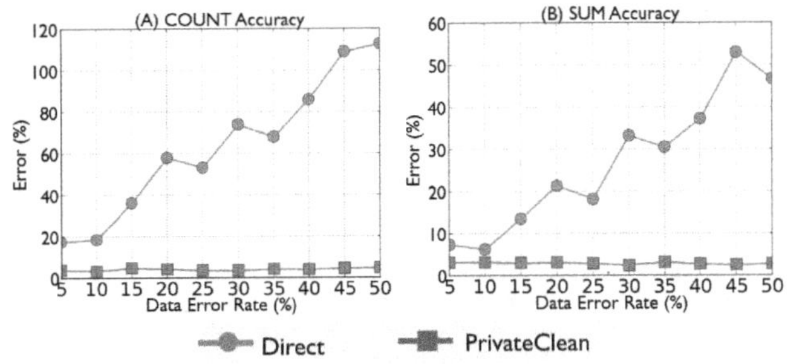

Figure 5: As the frequency of data errors increase, PrivateClean is increasingly more accurate than Direct.

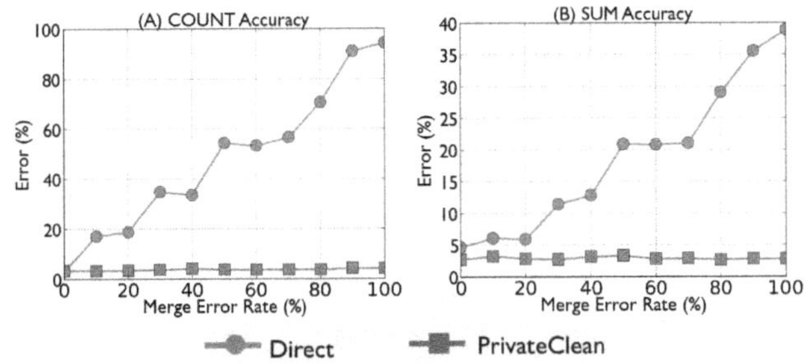

Figure 6: PrivateClean uses provenance to estimate the selectivity of queries on the original (uncleaned) data. Consequently, Direct is more sensitive to errors that "merge" distinct values.

terms the estimates from PrivateClean are useful. It also highlights a counter-intuitive property, where a query on the original dataset (no cleaning and no privacy) can be more erroneous than PrivateClean (cleaning and privacy). Privacy induces query result error while data cleaning mitigates error. This is a tradeoff that has been highlighted before in the SampleClean project [23,44].

Error Type: Of course, provenance is most valuable when the cleaned values are merged together. Next, we randomly map the distinct values to new random distinct values and other distinct values. We call this the merge rate and vary this in Figure 6. PrivateClean is more accurate than Direct when merge errors are more prevalent.

Cleaning Multiple Attributes : Figure 7 illustrates how PrivateClean to estimate results after cleaning multiple attributes. Unlike the single attribute case, we have to perform a cut on a weighted graph. We generated attribute two-attribute variant of the experiment in Figure 8.3.4a. We find that the weighted cut (PC-W) gives a more accurate result than no weighted edges (PC-U) and Direct.

8.3.3 Distinct Values

PrivateClean is designed for the setting where the number of distinct values in each discrete attribute relatively small in comparison to the dataset size. We proved a bound on the necessary dataset size to ensure that all values are visible in the private relation within probability $1-\alpha$. While this bound was necessary for the theoretical derivation of estimates and confidence intervals, it turns out that PrivateClean empirically performs well even with datasets sizes far smaller than the bound would suggest. This experiment evaluates the performance of PrivateClean as a function of the distinct fraction $\frac{N}{S}$.

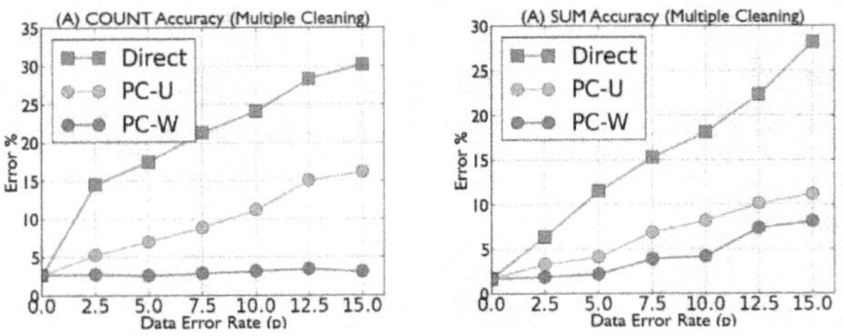

Figure 7: For cleaning operations that use information from multiple attributes, PrivateClean uses a cut on a weighted graph (PC-W) instead of an unweighted graph (PC-U).

We generated a dataset with a 5% error rate (keeping all other parameters fixed) and measure the accuracy of query results as a function of the distinct fraction. Figure 9(a-b) show the result for `sum` and `count` queries. In relative terms, PrivateClean outperforms Direct when the number of distinct values is less 50% of the dataset size. However, in absolute terms the accuracy of both methods is poor when the number of distinct values is high. Following from Figure 9, this means that as the number of distinct values increase, the relation can support (i.e., answer with the same accuracy) increasingly less selective queries.

8.3.4 Constraint-based Cleaning

Next, we evaluate PrivateClean on the constraint-based cleaning experiment with TPC-DS. We have two queries of interest that count records by the state and country:

```
SELECT count(1) FROM R GROUP BY ca_state
SELECT count(1) FROM R GROUP BY ca_country
```

In Figure 8a, we plot the results of PrivateClean as a function of the number of simulated corruptions to `ca_state`. These corruptions were fixed using a functional dependency on (`ca_city,ca_county`). Unlike before, this experiment illustrates the use of a heuristic data cleaning algorithm that does not perfectly clean the data, since it may not be possible to get a unique minimal repair. As the data error rate grows so does the error from PrivateClean, which we did not see in Figure a. As in previous experiments, we find that PrivateClean answers queries more accurately than Direct.

In Figure 8b, we plot the results of PrivateClean as a function of the number of simulated corruptions to `ca_country`. These corruptions were fixed using a matching dependency with a similarity metric using Edit Distance. Furthermore, matching dependencies can be resolved uniquely so the problems with the imperfect cleaning are not seen. We find that PrivateClean answers queries more accurately than Direct, and since this constraint merges values in the domain the difference between PrivateClean and Direct is more than in Figure 8a.

8.4 IntelWireless Experiments

Using the IntelWireless dataset, we simulate an analysis use case with PrivateClean. This dataset is a union of time series measuring environmental statistics (temperature, humidity, light) from 68 sensors (identified by a field `sensor_id`). Sensors that occasionally fail and during these failures their logs do not report a sensor id. As a result, in the `sensor_id` field there are missing or spurious values. Furthermore, during these failures statistics received from the sensor are untrustworthy. For data cleaning, we explored identifying and removing these log entries. We merged all of the spurious values to `null`.

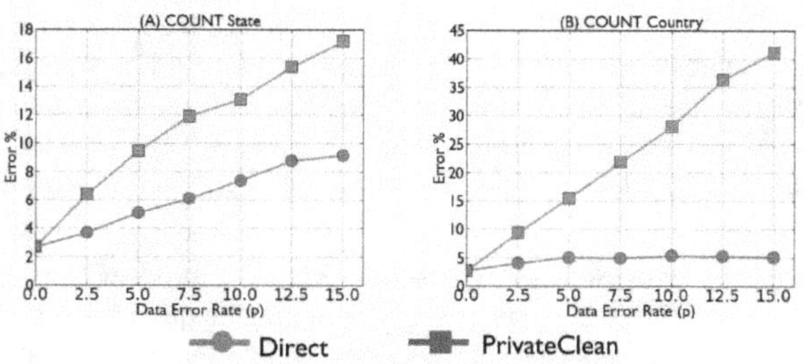

Figure 8: PrivateClean can also apply to constraint-based cleaning such using as functional dependencies and matching dependencies, and we present the results on `customer_address` table of TPC-DS.

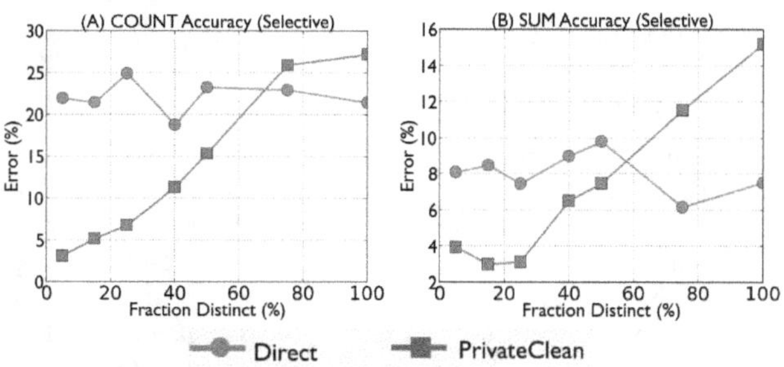

Figure 9: PrivateClean is sensitive to the number of distinct values. As the fraction of distinct values increases, the accuracy degrades. In fact, Direct becomes a more accurate estimator after a point.

We are interested in answering the following queries:

```
SELECT count(1) FROM R WHERE sensor_id != NULL
SELECT avg(temp) FROM R WHERE sensor_id != NULL
```

Figure 10 shows the query error for both queries as a function of privacy. We accordingly scale the numerical privacy parameter b such that both attributes have the same ϵ privacy parameter. As in the synthetic experiment, PrivateClean is more accurate than the Direct estimator. For reference in gray, we plot the error of the query result without data cleaning on the original dataset (without privacy). There is a counter-intuitive point at which queries on the cleaned private dataset are more accurate than queries on the dirty original dataset. Privacy introduces error while data cleaning simultaneously mitigates errors. In absolute terms, the error in these queries is relatively small $< 10\%$; demonstrating that cleaning and querying the private relation has practical utility.

8.5 MCAFE Experiments

The next experiment presents results on a much harder dataset of course evaluations. In this dataset, the number of distinct values is relatively high compared to the total number of records (21%). Consequently, the estimates for this dataset have a much larger error.

In this experiment, we demonstrate the flexibility of PrivateClean. The bipartite graph in PrivateClean can represent data transformations that go beyond traditional notions of data cleaning, such as merging together semantically similar distinct values. The MCAFE dataset has two attributes `score` and `country`. The vast majority of students are from the United States. We might be interested in aggregating students from all European countries together for comparison to the students from the United States. Like

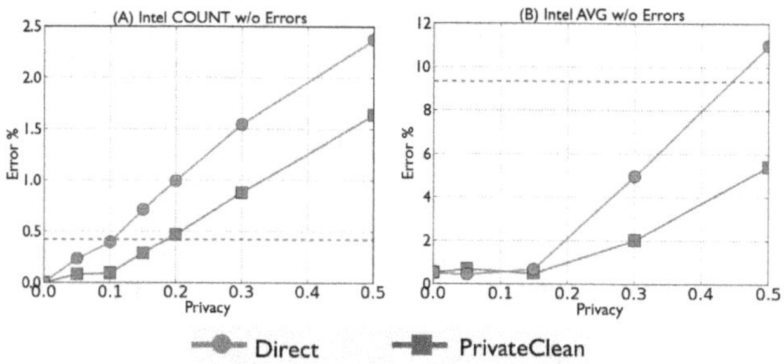

Figure 10: PrivateClean demonstrates higher accuracy in the Intel Wireless dataset validating previous results on a simulated datset.

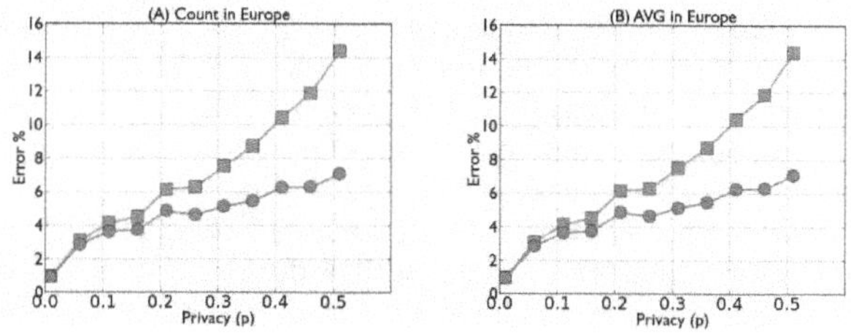

Figure 11: PrivateClean demonstrates higher accuracy on the MCAFE dataset on a data transformation task with a high fraction of distinct values.

data cleaning, this transformation is only possible if the analyst has access to the values in the private table (facilitated by GRR).

We measure the accuracy of the following queries as a function of privacy:

```
SELECT count(1) FROM R WHERE isEurope(country)
SELECT avg(score) FROM R WHERE isEurope(country)
```

The interesting point about these queries is that they cannot be answered on the untransformed data. Figure plots the error as a function of the privacy, and as in the synthetic experiments PrivateClean is more accurate than Direct. Both techniques return less than 10% query error on the private cleaned table.

9. RELATED WORK

Privacy and Data Cleaning: There have been a limited number of works that study the problem of data cleaning under privacy. However, these works do not consider differential privacy. Talukder et al. explore using cryptographic protocol to detect constraint violations in a database [43]. Similarly, Jaganathan and Wright explored using similar cryptographic protocols for secure data imputation [20].

Randomized Response: Even before the formalization of ϵ-differential privacy, statistical notions of data privacy have been well studied. Warner proposed the randomized response model in 1965 [45]. Some of the earliest work in the database community was on the topic of "data swapping" to increase privacy [40], where projections of a relation are randomly swapped. This model was the inspiration for the seminal work by Agarwal and Srikant on Privacy Preserving Data Mining (PPDM) [5]. This work led to several other results such as algorithms for classification on private data [10], statistical reconstruction of a dataset [18]. The contribution of our work, PrivateClean, is to: (1) formalize a similar mechanism using the new mathematical framework of differential privacy,

(2) understanding how data cleaning interacts with this model, (3) tight finite-sample guarantees for SQL aggregate query processing on private relations.

Privacy and Databases: In general, privacy is one of the fundamental subjects of research in the database community [19]. There are a number of surveys describing deterministic techniques for privacy preserving analytics [4,13]. These techniques include value aggregation, value suppression, and homeomorphic encryption [26,28,38,42].

Recently, the ϵ-differential privacy model [11] has renewed interest in privacy preserving analytics. McSherry proposed the seminal work of Privacy Integrated Queries (PINQ) [30]. PINQ proposed an algebra for describing privacy preserving data analytics, and ensuring the results of queries (primarily group by aggregates) would be kept differentially private. Similarly, the Airavat project studied this problem in the MapReduce setting [41]. The GUPT project explored the problem of setting ϵ (a "privacy budget") given desired accuracy guarantees [31]. Differential privacy also has been studied in a number of different contexts in databases including indexing and set-valued queries [7,27,37].

In PrivateClean, we explore the local model for ϵ differential privacy. The subtle problem of related work is that queries can only be issued a single time, and multiple runs can de-randomize a private result. On the other hand, in the local privacy model, we create a single private view of the dataset, which the analyst can query and clean an arbitrary number of times. Since the randomness is added up-front, the downside is that there are complex noise-propagation dynamics to consider. That said, PrivateClean only scratches the surface in the understanding of data error and privacy, and this is an important open problem that Getoor et al. described w.r.t entity resolution [15].

Approximate Query Processing: Approximate query processing (AQP) is a well studied problem [3,14,35] in which results of aggregate queries are approximated from samples, wavelets, or sketches. The goal of AQP is to achieve tight bounds on the results of the aggregate queries. The link between AQP and differential privacy has been studied before, and Xiao et al. [46] explore the differentially private implications of wavelet transforms. Likewise, the link between AQP and data cleaning has been studied, where Wang et al. and Krishnan et al. [23–25,44] show that samples of clean data can be used to estimate aggregate queries. PrivateClean tries to make the connection between AQP, data cleaning, and privacy. We also believe that PrivateClean will be increasingly relevant in human-in-the-loop systems as crowds are increasingly employed in data cleaning [16] and inadvertent data leaks can actually bias the crowds response [22].

10. EXTENSIONS

We highlight several points for discussion and opportunities for future work. Differential Privacy is best suited for aggregate query processing. In Section 3.2.2, we described how PrivateClean supports `sum`, `count`, `avg` queries over a single numerical attribute with predicates over a single discrete attribute. We discuss how PrivateClean can be extended to support different types of aggregate queries with more complex query structures.

Different Aggregates: PrivateClean applies additive independent Laplace random noise to each of the numerical attributes. In addition to having a mean value of 0, this noise also has a median value of 0. Therefore, it is relatively straightforward to extend PrivateClean to support `median` and `percentile` queries. Furthermore, since this noise is independent of the data, we can exploit the fact that $var(x + y) = var(x) + var(y)$ for independent random variables to also support `var` and `std` queries. For these new aggregates, calculating confidence intervals is a bit more challenging, and require an empirical method (e.g., [3,47]). However, in its current formulation PrivateClean cannot support `min` and `max` queries.

Aggregates over Select-Project-Join Views: PrivateClean can also be extended to estimate results for aggregate queries over SPJ views of differentially private relations. Since the randomization is added independently, it is easy to derive the query processing bias correction constants $\tau_n, \tau_p, \gamma_n, \gamma_p$ for such queries. For each column in the view, we essentially can calculate the constants and multiply them together, but there are some technicalities with maintaing the appropriate provenance that we defer to future work. To calcuate confidence intervals, we can use a technique like the one proposed in [33].

11. CONCLUSION

In this paper, we presented PrivateClean a framework for data cleaning and approximate query processing on locally differentially private relations. As far as we know this is the first work to marry data cleaning and local differential privacy. As a result, we hope that this initial exploration of this problem will set the stage for the exploration of more complex query processing and data cleaning models. We proposed a privacy mechanism called Generalized Randomized Response which we showed was compatible with data cleaning operations in the form of extraction, merging, and transformations. We analyzed the sufficient size of the data required for meaningful cleaning results. One of the key insights of this work is that privacy exacerbates problems of data skew, and it is crucial to estimate query selectivity for accurate query processing. However, after data cleaning apparent selectivity of a query may change, and we maintain a provenance graph to address this problem. We showed how this analysis can be inverted to select maximal privacy levels given some constraint on query accuracy. Our empirical evaluation validated the analytical results on both synthetic and real datasets.

Acknowledgements: We would like to thank Joseph Hellerstein, Joseph Gonzales, Dawn Song, and Cynthia Dwork for discussions about this work. This research is supported in part by NSF CISE Expeditions Award CCF-1139158, DOE Award SN10040 DE-SC0012463, DARPA XData Award FA8750-12-2-0331, NSERC Discovery Grant (No. 19579), and an SFU President's Research Start-up Grant (NO. 877335), and gifts from Amazon Web Services, Google, IBM, SAP, The Thomas and Stacey Siebel Foundation, Apple Inc., Arimo, Blue Goji, Bosch, Cisco, Cray, Cloudera, Ericsson, Facebook, Fujitsu, Guavus, HP, Huawei, Intel, Microsoft, Pivotal, Samsung, Schlumberger, Splunk, State Farm and VMware.

12. REFERENCES

[1] Exclusive: Apple ups hiring, but faces obstacles to making phones smarter. http://www.reuters.com/article/2015/09/07/us-apple-machinelearning-idUSKCN0R71H020150907.

[2] Netflix prize. http://www.netflixprize.com/.

[3] S. Agarwal, B. Mozafari, A. Panda, H. Milner, S. Madden, and I. Stoica. BlinkDB: queries with bounded errors and bounded response times on very large data. In *EuroSys*, 2013.

[4] C. C. Aggarwal and P. S. Yu. A general survey of privacy-preserving data mining models and algorithms. In *Privacy-Preserving Data Mining - Models and Algorithms*. 2008.

[5] R. Agrawal and R. Srikant. Privacy-preserving data mining. In *SIGMOD*, 2000.

[6] P. Bohannon, M. Flaster, W. Fan, and R. Rastogi. A cost-based model and effective heuristic for repairing constraints by value modification. In *SIGMOD*, 2005.

[7] R. Chen, N. Mohammed, B. C. M. Fung, B. C. Desai, and L. Xiong. Publishing set-valued data via differential privacy. *PVLDB*, 4(11), 2011.

[8] Z. Chen and M. J. Cafarella. Integrating spreadsheet data via accurate and low-effort extraction. In *KDD*, 2014.

[9] Y.-A. de Montjoye, C. A. Hidalgo, M. Verleysen, and V. D. Blondel. Unique in the crowd: The privacy bounds of human mobility. *Scientific reports*, 3, 2013.

[10] W. Du and J. Z. Zhan. Using randomized response techniques for privacy-preserving data mining. In *KDD*, 2003.

[11] C. Dwork and A. Roth. The algorithmic foundations of differential privacy. *Foundations and Trends in Theoretical Computer Science*, 9(3-4), 2014.

[12] P. Flajolet, D. Gardy, and L. Thimonier. Birthday paradox, coupon collectors, caching algorithms and self-organizing search. *Discrete Applied Mathematics*, 39(3), 1992.

[13] B. C. M. Fung, K. Wang, R. Chen, and P. S. Yu. Privacy-preserving data publishing: A survey of recent developments. *ACM Comput. Surv.*, 42(4), 2010.

[14] M. N. Garofalakis and P. B. Gibbons. Approximate query processing: Taming the terabytes. In *VLDB*, 2001.

[15] L. Getoor and A. Machanavajjhala. Entity resolution: Theory, practice and open challenges. *PVLDB*, 5(12), 2012.

[16] D. Haas, S. Krishnan, J. Wang, M. J. Franklin, and E. Wu. Wisteria: Nurturing scalable data cleaning infrastructure. *PVLDB*, 8(12), 2015.

[17] P. J. Haas, J. F. Naughton, S. Seshadri, and A. N. Swami. Selectivity and cost estimation for joins based on random sampling. *J. Comput. Syst. Sci.*, 52(3), 1996.

[18] Z. Huang, W. Du, and B. Chen. Deriving private information from randomized data. In *SIGMOD*, 2005.

[19] H. V. Jagadish, J. Gehrke, A. Labrinidis, Y. Papakonstantinou, J. M. Patel, R. Ramakrishnan, and C. Shahabi. Big data and its technical challenges. *Commun. ACM*, 57(7), 2014.

[20] G. Jagannathan and R. N. Wright. Privacy-preserving imputation of missing data. *Data Knowl. Eng.*, 65(1), 2008.

[21] S. Kandel, A. Paepcke, J. M. Hellerstein, and J. Heer. Enterprise data analysis and visualization: An interview study. *Visualization and Computer Graphics, IEEE Transactions on*, 18(12), 2012.

[22] S. Krishnan, J. Patel, M. J. Franklin, and K. Goldberg. A methodology for learning, analyzing, and mitigating social influence bias in recommender systems. In *RecSys*, 2014.

[23] S. Krishnan, J. Wang, M. J. Franklin, K. Goldberg, and T. Kraska. Stale view cleaning: Getting fresh answers from stale materialized views. *PVLDB*, 8(12), 2015.

[24] S. Krishnan, J. Wang, M. J. Franklin, K. Goldberg, T. Kraska, T. Milo, and E. Wu. Sampleclean: Fast and reliable analytics on dirty data. *IEEE Data Eng. Bull.*, 38(3), 2015.

[25] S. Krishnan, J. Wang, E. Wu, M. J. Franklin, and K. Goldberg. Activeclean: Interactive data cleaning while learning convex loss models. In *Arxiv: http://arxiv.org/pdf/1601.03797.pdf*, 2015.

[26] N. Li, T. Li, and S. Venkatasubramanian. t-closeness: Privacy beyond k-anonymity and l-diversity. In *ICDE*. IEEE, 2007.

[27] N. Li, W. H. Qardaji, D. Su, and J. Cao. Privbasis: Frequent itemset mining with differential privacy. *PVLDB*, 5(11), 2012.

[28] A. Machanavajjhala, D. Kifer, J. Gehrke, and M. Venkitasubramaniam. l-diversity: Privacy beyond k-anonymity. *TKDD*, 1(1), 2007.

[29] S. Madden, M. J. Franklin, J. M. Hellerstein, and W. Hong. Tinydb: an acquisitional query processing system for sensor networks. *ACM Trans. Database Syst.*, 30(1), 2005.

[30] F. McSherry. Privacy integrated queries: an extensible platform for privacy-preserving data analysis. *Commun. ACM*, 53(9), 2010.

[31] P. Mohan, A. Thakurta, E. Shi, D. Song, and D. E. Culler. GUPT: privacy preserving data analysis made easy. In *SIGMOD*, 2012.

[32] A. Narayanan and V. Shmatikov. Robust de-anonymization of large sparse datasets. In *Security and Privacy, 2008. SP 2008. IEEE Symposium on*. IEEE, 2008.

[33] S. Nirkhiwale, A. Dobra, and C. M. Jermaine. A sampling algebra for aggregate estimation. *PVLDB*, 6(14), 2013.

[34] G. W. Oehlert. A note on the delta method. *The American Statistician*, 46(1), 1992.

[35] F. Olken. *Random sampling from databases*. PhD thesis, University of California, 1993.

[36] H. Park and J. Widom. Crowdfill: collecting structured data from the crowd. In *SIGMOD*, 2014.

[37] S. Peng, Y. Yang, Z. Zhang, M. Winslett, and Y. Yu. Dp-tree: indexing multi-dimensional data under differential privacy. In *SIGMOD*, 2012.

[38] R. A. Popa, C. M. S. Redfield, N. Zeldovich, and H. Balakrishnan. Cryptdb: protecting confidentiality with encrypted query processing. In *Symposium on Operating Systems Principles, Cascais, Portugal*, 2011.

[39] E. Rahm and H. H. Do. Data cleaning: Problems and current approaches. *IEEE Data Eng. Bull.*, 23(4), 2000.

[40] S. P. Reiss, M. J. Post, and T. Dalenius. Non-reversible privacy transformations. In *PODS*, 1982.

[41] I. Roy, S. T. V. Setty, A. Kilzer, V. Shmatikov, and E. Witchel. Airavat: Security and privacy for mapreduce. In *NSDI*, 2010.

[42] L. Sweeney. Achieving k-anonymity privacy protection using generalization and suppression. *International Journal of Uncertainty, Fuzziness and Knowledge-Based Systems*, 10(5), 2002.

[43] N. Talukder, M. Ouzzani, A. K. Elmagarmid, and M. Yakout. Detecting inconsistencies in private data with secure function evaluation. 2011.

[44] J. Wang, S. Krishnan, M. J. Franklin, K. Goldberg, T. Kraska, and T. Milo. A sample-and-clean framework for fast and accurate query processing on dirty data. In *SIGMOD*, 2014.

[45] S. L. Warner. Randomized response: A survey technique for eliminating evasive answer bias. *Journal of the American Statistical Association*, 60(309), 1965.

[46] X. Xiao, G. Wang, and J. Gehrke. Differential privacy via wavelet transforms. *IEEE Trans. Knowl. Data Eng.*, 23(8), 2011.

[47] K. Zeng, S. Gao, B. Mozafari, and C. Zaniolo. The analytical bootstrap: a new method for fast error estimation in approximate query processing. In *SIGMOD*, 2014.

[48] E. Zheleva and L. Getoor. To join or not to join: the illusion of privacy in social networks with mixed public and private user profiles. In *WWW, Madrid, Spain*, 2009.

[49] M. Zhou, A. Cliff, A. Huang, S. Krishnan, B. Nonnecke, K. Uchino, S. Joseph, A. Fox, and K. Goldberg. M-cafe: Managing mooc student feedback with collaborative filtering. In *Learning@ Scale*. ACM, 2015.

APPENDIX

A. PROOFS

A.1 Proof of Lemma 1

We directly apply the definition of local differential privacy. Let $N = \mid Domain(g_i) \mid$:

$$\epsilon = \ln \frac{1 - p_i + p_i \frac{1}{N}}{p_i \frac{N-1}{N}}$$

The worst case is when there are only two values in the domain and all of the other entries in the database are one value except for one, then this gives us $N = 2$, plugging it in to the above formula:

$$\epsilon = \ln(\frac{3}{p_i} - 2)$$

A.2 Consequences of Differential Privacy

Lemma 2, Theorem 1, and Theorem 2 follow from well-established results in Differential Privacy (see [11]). We provide detailed references for the results here.

Proposition 1: This follows from Definition 3.3 in [11].

Theorem 1: This follows from Theorem 3.16 in [11].

Theorem 2: Proposition 2.1 in [11] shows that for any deterministic function applied to a differentially private result, differential privacy is preserved.

A.3 Proof of Theorem 3

For some domain value a, let us first start with the probability that a is visible in the private relation:

$$\mathbf{P}[a] = 1 - p\frac{N-1}{N}[1 - \frac{p}{N}]^{(S-1)}$$

For all domain values, we can apply a union bound:

$$\mathbf{P}[all] \geq 1 - p(N-1)[1 - \frac{p}{N}]^{(S-1)}$$

Setting $\mathbf{P}[all] = 1 - \alpha$:

$$\alpha \leq p(N-1)[1 - \frac{p}{N}]^{(S-1)}$$

With some algebra, we can show:

$$\log \frac{\alpha}{p(N-1)} \frac{1}{\log 1 - \frac{p}{N}} \leq S$$

Using the inequality $\frac{x-1}{x} \leq \log x$, we can arrive at the bound presented in the paper.

A.4 Proof of Lemma 3

We start with the predicate false positive and false negative probabilities. The false positive probability is:

$$\mathbf{P}(\text{false positive}) = (1-s)p\frac{l}{N}$$

and the false negative probability is:

$$\mathbf{P}(\text{false negative}) = sp\frac{N-l}{N}$$

For sum and count, the bias is proportional to the predicate errors. Since the Naive estimator sets two values equal, we can calculate the difference:

$$bias = (1-s)p\frac{l}{N} - sp\frac{N-l}{N}$$

$$bias = \frac{p(l - sN)}{N}$$

This value will be scaled by a constant related to the dataset size:

$$\tilde{O}(\frac{p(l-sN)}{N})$$

B. ESTIMATOR NOTATION

- $c_{private}$: Count on the private data
- c_{true}: Count on the original data
- μ_{true}: Average on the true data
- S: Dataset size
- N: Number of distinct values in the attribute partition g_i that contains the predicate attribute.
- $h_{private}$: sum on the private data
- h_{true}: sum on the true data
- $h^c_{private}$: sum on the private data (with predicate negated).
- h^c_{true}: sum on the true data (with predicate negated).

C. ESTIMATOR DERIVATIONS

COUNT: To prove this, first, we formulate an unbiased estimator:

$$\mathbb{E}(c_{private}) = c_{true}\tau_p + (S - c_{true})\tau_n$$

$$\mathbb{E}(c_{private}) = c_{true}(\tau_p - \tau_n) + S\tau_n$$

$$\frac{\mathbb{E}(c_{private}) - S\tau_n}{(\tau_p - \tau_n)} = c_{true}$$

SUM: To prove this, first, we formulate an unbiased estimator:

$$\mathbb{E}(h_{private}) = c_{true}[(1-p)+p\frac{l}{N}]\mu_{true} + (S - c_{true})(p\frac{l}{N})\mu_{false}$$

We are interested in estimating the count which is $c_{true}\mu_{true}$:

$$\mathbb{E}(h_{private}) = [(1-p)+p\frac{l}{N}]c_{true}\mu_{true} + (S - c_{true})(p\frac{l}{N})\mu_{false}$$

The challenge is that there are two unknown variables $c_{true}\mu_{true}$ and μ_{false}, so we can apply a trick where we also calculate the sum over the complement and solve:

$$\mathbb{E}(h^c_{private}) = [p\frac{N-l}{N}]c_{true}\mu_{true} + (S - c_{true})(1-p+p\frac{N-l}{N})\mu_{false}$$

This is a linear system of equations, and solving it arrives at:

$$\begin{bmatrix} h_{private} \\ h^c_{private} \end{bmatrix} = \begin{bmatrix} (1-p)+p\frac{l}{N} & (S-c_{true})(p\frac{l}{N}) \\ p\frac{N-l}{N} & (S-c_{true})(1-p+p\frac{N-l}{N}) \end{bmatrix} \begin{bmatrix} c_{true}\mu_{true} \\ \mu_{false} \end{bmatrix}$$

$$c_{true}\mu_{true} = \frac{(1-p+p\frac{N-l}{N})h_{private} - p\frac{l}{N}h_{private}}{1-p}$$

With a little bit of algebra, we can arrive at:

$$c_{true}\mu_{true} = \frac{(N-lp)h_{private} - (lp)h^c_{private}}{(1-p)N}$$

D. SYNTHETIC EXPERIMENTS DEFAULT PARAMETERS

We list the default parameters in the synthetic experiment below. Unless otherwise noted, these are the parameters which we use. For all experiments, we create 100 random instances of the private database, and for each instance we run a randomly selected query. The plots show a mean value over the 100 random instances.

Table 1: Default parameters in the synthetic experiment

Symbol	Default Value	Meaning
p	0.1	Discrete privacy parameter
b	10	Numerical privacy parameter
N	50	Number of distinct values
S	1000	Number of total records
l	5	Distinct values selected by predicate
z	2	Zipfian Skew

E. PARAMETER TUNING ALGORITHM

Following from the analysis in the paper, we derive a tuning algorithm to set ϵ by setting p_i and b_i for each attribute.

Inputs: error the user gives us the desired maximum error in any count query on the relation with $1 - \alpha$ confidence intervals.

Output: For each numerical attribute j return b_j the numerical privacy parameter, and for each discrete attribute partition g_i return a p_i the discrete privacy parameter.

1. Let $p = 1 - z_\alpha\sqrt{\frac{1}{4S \cdot error^2}}$, where z_α is the Gaussian tail parameter (e.g, $95\% \approx 1.96$).
2. For each discrete attribute partition g_i, set p_i to p.
3. For each numerical attribute j, set $b_j = \frac{\Delta_j}{\ln \frac{3}{p} - 2}$, where Δ_j is the difference between the max and min values of that attribute.

RDFind: Scalable Conditional Inclusion Dependency Discovery in RDF Datasets

Sebastian Kruse[♦] Anja Jentzsch[♦] Thorsten Papenbrock[♦]
Zoi Kaoudi[⋆] Jorge-Arnulfo Quiané-Ruiz[⋆] Felix Naumann[♦]

[♦]Hasso Plattner Institute (HPI)
Potsdam, Germany
{fistname.lastname}@hpi.de

[⋆]Qatar Computing Research Institute (QCRI)
Doha, Qatar
{zkaoudi, jquianeruiz}@qf.org.qa

ABSTRACT

Inclusion dependencies (INDs) form an important integrity constraint on relational databases, supporting data management tasks, such as join path discovery and query optimization. Conditional inclusion dependencies (CINDs), which define including and included data in terms of conditions, allow to transfer these capabilities to RDF data. However, CIND discovery is computationally much more complex than IND discovery and the number of CINDs even on small RDF datasets is intractable.

To cope with both problems, we first introduce the notion of *pertinent* CINDs with an adjustable relevance criterion to filter and rank CINDs based on their extent and implications among each other. Second, we present RDFIND, a distributed system to efficiently discover all pertinent CINDs in RDF data. RDFIND employs a lazy pruning strategy to drastically reduce the CIND search space. Also, its exhaustive parallelization strategy and robust data structures make it highly scalable. In our experimental evaluation, we show that RDFIND is up to 419 times faster than the state-of-the-art, while considering a more general class of CINDs. Furthermore, it is capable of processing a very large dataset of billions of triples, which was entirely infeasible before.

1. INCLUSIONS WITHIN RDF DATASETS

The *Resource Description Framework* (RDF) [18] is a flexible data model that shapes data as a set of subject-predicate-object triples. RDF was initially introduced for the Semantic Web. Due to its flexibility and simplicity, it is currently used in a much broader spectrum of applications ranging from databases [9,12] and data integration systems [11] to scientific applications [29,32]. As a result, very large volumes of RDF data are made available, in particular in the context of the Linked (Open) Data movement [8]. It is expected that this expansion of RDF data will perpetuate, leading to enormous amounts of large heterogeneous datasets [21].

A major particularity of RDF is that, in contrast to relational databases, its schema (ontology) is not always available, and even if it is, the data may violate the schema constraints. This impedes the use of RDF datasets, e.g., it is harder to formulate sound queries and wrong assumptions about the data might be made. *Data profiling* copes with such problems by identifying dataset properties, such as structure and integrity constraints [1].

SIGMOD'16, June 26-July 01, 2016, San Francisco, CA, USA
© 2016 ACM. ISBN 978-1-4503-3531-7/16/06...$15.00
DOI: http://dx.doi.org/10.1145/2882903.2915206

Table 1: University RDF data instance example.

	Subject s	Predicate p	Object o
t_1	patrick	rdf:type	gradStudent
t_2	mike	rdf:type	gradStudent
t_3	john	rdf:type	professor
t_4	patrick	memberOf	csd
t_5	mike	memberOf	biod
t_6	patrick	undergradFrom	hpi
t_7	tim	undergradFrom	hpi
t_8	mike	undergradFrom	cmu

One of the most important integrity constraints are *inclusion dependencies* (INDs). Basically, an IND describes the inclusion of a set of values or elements in another set. In the context of relational databases, where these sets are the values from specified columns, INDs have proven to be very useful in various data management scenarios, such as foreign key and join path discovery [33], query optimization [17], and schema (re)design [25].

Clearly, these data management operations are relevant to RDF data, too. However, in contrast to the relational model, RDF datasets do not reflect the schema of their data in terms of data structures. In fact, RDF distinguishes only *subjects*, *predicates*, and *objects* on the data structure level. These three sets are too coarse-grained to find meaningful INDs, as can be seen in the example dataset in Table 1.

However, *conditional inclusion dependencies* (CINDs) allow to refine these sets. A CIND filters the including and included sets of an IND with conditions and requires only these filtered sets to satisfy the IND. These CIND semantics allow to describe meaningful inclusions within RDF data:

EXAMPLE 1. *Assume a* CIND *stating that the set of subjects occurring in triples with predicate* rdf:type *and object* gradStudent *is a* <u>*subset*</u> *of all subjects occurring in triples with predicate* undergradFrom. *Table 1 satisfies this* CIND, *because the graduate students* patrick *and* mike *form a subset of people with an undergraduate degree, namely* patrick, tim, *and* mike.

CIND applications. CINDs of RDF datasets are useful for many applications, such as *ontology reverse engineering*, *knowledge discovery*, and *query optimization*. In the following, we exemplify this with real CINDs from DBpedia 2014[1]. More details are in Appendix B.

CINDs facilitate *ontology reverse engineering* by finding the domain and range of RDF predicates (e.g., the objects of the triples with predicate capitalPosition are included in the subjects of rdf:type gml:Feature) and revealing class hierarchies (e.g., subjects of rdf:type Leptodactylidae are a subset of the subjects of rdf:type Frog); CINDs also support *knowledge discovery* to give insights about rules that may apply to unknown RDF datasets (e.g., the subjects with areaCode 559 are included in the subjects that are partOf California).

Furthermore, CINDs can be employed for *SPARQL query optimization*. SPARQL queries very often consist of a considerable amount of self-joins [5], which negatively impacts performance. Knowing CINDs allows to remove useless query triples (i.e., query predicates) and hence to reduce the number of joins that need to be evaluated (query minimization). For example, consider the following 2-join SPARQL query on the data of Table 1 asking for the departments of graduate students and the institutes that they received their undergraduates from: `SELECT ?d ?u WHERE {?s rdf:type gradStudent . ?s memberOf ?d . ?s undergradFrom ?u .}` Note that the data in Table 1 satisfies a CIND that states that all subjects of the triples having memberOf as predicate are included in the set of subjects of rdf:type gradStudent. This CIND tells us that all department members are graduate students and allows to remove the first query triple (?s rdf:type gradStudent) without affecting the final results. As a proof of concept, we executed LUBM query Q2 [27] in RDF-3X [30] once in its original form and once CIND-optimized. Query Q2 originally contains six query triples; exploiting CINDs, we reduced Q2 to three query triples. This speeds up query execution by a factor of 3 (see Appendix B for details).

Challenges. Despite the importance and benefits of knowing CINDs in RDF datasets, the problem of CIND discovery for RDF data has not been tackled so far. A reason might be the complexity of this problem: Because each CIND involves two conditions, the search space for CINDs is quadratic in the number of possible conditions. Amongst others, equivalence conditions can be formed for each distinct value in an RDF dataset, so a few millions of values typically found in RDF datasets yield trillions of CIND candidates – only for this type of condition. This huge search space poses two major problems. First, it is difficult to maintain and explore such a large number of CIND candidates. Second, the validation of a single CIND candidate can already be very costly, let alone trillions of candidates. We acknowledge that several algorithms have been proposed for the discovery of INDs and CINDs on relational data and we discuss those as related work. However, none of them is suited or could be easily adapted to efficiently discover CINDs within RDF datasets.

Contributions and structure. We study the problem of CIND discovery in RDF data and present RDFIND, the first system to efficiently solve this problem for large datasets. Specifically, we make three main contributions:

(1) We formally define the CIND discovery problem, study its complexity and explain why the discovery of *all* CINDs is not desirable (Section 2). In response, we introduce the new class of *pertinent* CINDs, with an adjustable relevance criterion to filter and rank CINDs based on their extent and implications among each other (Section 3).

(2) We introduce RDFIND, which efficiently discovers all pertinent CINDs in a *distributed* fashion (overview in Section 4). In particular, we propose a lazy pruning approach that reduces the CIND search space in two steps; we introduce a compact representation for RDF triples that facilitates enumerating and verifying CIND candidates; and we devise algorithms for efficiently extracting CINDs (Sections 5–7).

(3) We implemented RDFIND on top of Flink[2], a distributed data processing system. We compare it against the state-of-the-art algorithm for CIND discovery using different real-world and synthetic datasets. We show that RDFIND outperforms it by a factor of 419 and scales to large datasets that other solutions cannot compute (Section 8).

We conclude the paper with related work in Section 9 and future directions in Section 10.

2. THE CIND SEARCH SPACE

Before stating the problem of finding all CINDs, we first briefly review the RDF data model [18] and present a new CIND definition for RDF.

RDF data model. An RDF *triple* is a statement of the form (s, p, o), where s is the subject, p is the predicate, and o is the object. The subject and predicate is an RDF resource (URI), while the object can also be an RDF literal, i.e., a typed value. We treat blank nodes as URIs. A set of triples is an RDF *dataset*. For a triple t, we denote with $t.s$, $t.p$, and $t.o$ the projection of the triple on the subject, predicate, and object, respectively. In the remainder of this paper, we can interchangeably use the elements of triples, s, p, and o, in most definitions and algorithms. For clarity, we thus use the symbols α, β, and γ to denote any of these three elements.

CINDs in RDF. In the relational data model, CINDs have been defined by means of an IND, which is embedded in the CIND (embedded IND) and is often partially violated, and a pattern tableau that removes the violating tuples [28]. However, the notion of embedded INDs is not appropriate for RDF data, as INDs without conditions are not meaningful. Instead, we introduce a novel and compact CIND formalism that abandons embedded INDs and instead lifts conditions as first-class selectors for the including and included sets of CINDs. As the main advantage, our definition treats CINDs similarly to INDs, which allows us to exploit algorithmic foundations of IND discovery for the CIND case. We define a CIND based on a simple concept called *capture*. Intuitively, a capture defines a projection of a triple element α over a set of triples that satisfy a *unary* or *binary condition* on some of the other two elements β and/or γ.

DEFINITION 2.1 (CONDITION). *A unary condition is a predicate* $\phi(t) := t.\beta{=}v_1$ *and a binary condition is a predicate* $\phi(t) := t.\beta{=}v_1 \wedge t.\gamma{=}v_2$ *where* t *is an* RDF *triple and* v_1 *and* v_2 *are constants, i.e., either an* RDF *resource, or literal. For simplicity, we may omit* t *and simply write* $\phi := \beta{=}v_1$ *whenever it is clear.*

DEFINITION 2.2 (CAPTURE). *A capture* $c := (\alpha, \phi)$ *combines the unary or binary condition* ϕ *with a projection attribute* α*, which must not be used in* ϕ*. The interpretation of* c *on an* RDF *dataset* T *is* $\mathcal{I}(T, c) := \{t.\alpha : t \in T \wedge \phi(t)\}$.

[1]http://wiki.dbpedia.org/Downloads2014

[2]https://flink.apache.org/

Example 2. *The binary condition ϕ := p=rdf:type $\wedge$ o=gradStudent holds for the triples t_1 and t_2 from the example dataset in Table 1. From it, we can define the capture (s, ϕ) with the interpretation {patrick, mike}.*

Having defined a capture, we can now define a CIND in a similar fashion to a relational IND. The only difference is that an IND describes the inclusion of relational attributes while a CIND describes the inclusion of captures.

Definition 2.3 (CIND). *A CIND ψ is a statement $c \subseteq c'$, where c and c' are captures. Analogous to INDs, we call c the dependent capture and c' the referenced capture. We say then that an RDF dataset T satisfies the CIND if and only if $\mathcal{I}(T, c) \subseteq \mathcal{I}(T, c')$.*

Example 3. *A valid CIND for the dataset in Table 1 is $(s, p{=}\text{rdf:type} \wedge o{=}\text{gradStudent}) \subseteq (s, p{=}\text{undergradFrom})$, because the interpretation of the dependent capture {patrick, mike} is a subset of the referenced capture's interpretation {patrick, mike, tim}.*

Naïve CIND discovery problem. A naïve formulation of the CIND discovery problem would be to discover all CINDS in the sense of Definition 2.3 that are satisfied by a given RDF dataset. However, finding all CINDs entails both a huge search space and a large solution set, which (i) renders the problem computationally extremely complex and (ii) bloats results with a sheer amount of highly specific CINDs, ineligible for the applications presented in Section 1. For instance, even one of our smallest datasets, Diseasome[3], with only 72,446 triples comprises over 50 billion CIND candidates and over 1.3 billion (!) actual CINDs. Relational CIND discovery approaches mitigate these issues by considering only a single combination of dependent and referenced projection attributes, by neglecting self-joins, and by conditioning only dependent attributes [7,16]. As a matter of fact, this reduces the CIND discovery problem to a condition discovery problem. Neither of these simplifications is appropriate for RDF data and consequently RDFIND faces new challenges. Before going into algorithmic details, we define *pertinent* CINDs in the next section to reduce the CIND search space while still covering all of its projection and condition attribute combinations. Then we revise our problem statement.

3. TAMING THE CIND SEARCH SPACE

The discovery of all CINDs in an RDF dataset must tackle two problems: First, and as explained in the previous section, the search space is enormous, so that pruning strategies are needed. Furthermore, the result space often is also enormous, making the interpretation and usage of CINDs difficult. Again, pruning strategies could help. Therefore, we narrow the search space to *pertinent* CINDs only (Section 3.1), which helps reducing both the search space and the set of result CINDs. Furthermore, we show that association rules are a special class of CINDs and help to further prune the CIND search space (Section 3.2). We then re-define the CIND discovery problem using these two concepts (Section 3.3).

3.1 Pertinent CINDs

Focusing on pertinent CINDs is crucial to significantly reduce the search space and, hence, make the CIND discovery efficient. We consider a CIND as pertinent if it is both *minimal* and *broad*. Intuitively, minimal CINDs form a non-redundant cover of all valid CINDs and broad CINDs comprise a sufficiently large number of included elements. In the following, we describe both types of CINDs in more detail.

[3]http://datahub.io/dataset/fu-berlin-diseasome

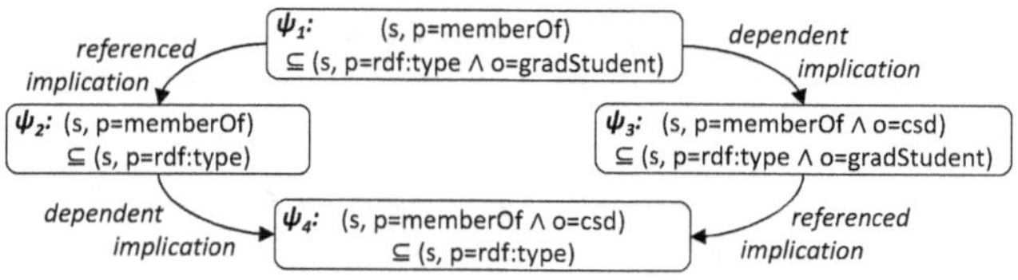

Figure 1: Extract from the CIND search space for Table 1. The nodes are CIND candidates and the arrows implications.

Minimal CINDs. As for many other integrity constraints, we can infer certain CINDs from other ones. Given a set of valid CINDs, we call those CINDs minimal that cannot be inferred from any other CIND. For example, the CIND $(s, p{=}\text{memberOf}) \subseteq (s, p{=}\text{rdf:type} \wedge o{=}\text{gradStudent})$ from Table 1 is minimal and implies various non-minimal CINDs.

Specifically, we consider two inference rules: the *dependent* and *referenced* implications [28]. Intuitively, tightening the dependent condition of a valid CIND (by making a unary condition binary) or relaxing the referenced condition (by making a binary condition unary) yields a new valid CIND. For instance, $(s, p{=}\text{memberOf} \wedge o{=}\text{csd}) \subseteq (s, p{=}\text{rdf:type} \wedge o{=}\text{gradStudent})$ and $(s, p{=}\text{memberOf}) \subseteq (s, p{=}\text{rdf:type})$ are also valid, but not minimal, because they can be inferred from the above CIND. Formally, we denote with $\phi \Rightarrow \phi'$ the fact that a binary condition ϕ implies a unary condition ϕ', i.e., the predicate of ϕ' is one of the two predicates of ϕ. For instance, $\phi := p{=}\text{memberOf} \wedge o{=}\text{csd}$ implies $\phi' := p{=}\text{memberOf}$. Consequently, $(\alpha, \phi) \subseteq (\alpha, \phi')$ is a valid CIND if $\phi \Rightarrow \phi'$. Therefore, if a CIND $(\alpha, \phi_1) \subseteq (\beta, \phi_2)$ holds in a dataset T, then: (i) a dependent implication states that any CIND $(\alpha, \phi_1') \subseteq (\beta, \phi_2)$ with $\phi_1' \Rightarrow \phi_1$ also holds in T, because $(\alpha, \phi_1') \subseteq (\alpha, \phi_1) \subseteq (\beta, \phi_2)$; and similarly (ii) a referenced implication states that any CIND $(\alpha, \phi_1) \subseteq (\beta, \phi_2')$ with $\phi_2 \Rightarrow \phi_2'$ also holds in T, because $(\alpha, \phi_1) \subseteq (\beta, \phi_2) \subseteq (\beta, \phi_2')$. Therefore, we formally define a minimal CIND $(\alpha, \phi_1) \subseteq (\beta, \phi_2)$ as that one where neither ϕ_1 (i.e., its dependent condition) can be relaxed to a condition ϕ_1' nor ϕ_2 (i.e., its referenced condition) can be tightened to a condition ϕ_2' without violating the CIND.

Example 4. *Figure 1 depicts four CINDs for the dataset from Table 1. The CIND ψ_1 implies ψ_2 and ψ_3, which in turn imply ψ_4, respectively. Hence, only ψ_1 is minimal.*

Broad CINDs. A broad CIND describes the inclusion of a sufficient number of distinct values. For instance, if we require the inclusion of at least two values, then $(s, p{=}\text{rdf:type} \wedge o{=}\text{gradStudent}) \subseteq (s, p{=}\text{undergradFrom})$ is broad. Focusing on broad CINDs avoids CINDs that (i) embed void conditions, which do not match a single triple in a given RDF dataset and which are infinite in number, (e.g., $(s, p{=}\text{memberOf} \wedge o{=}\text{geod}) \subseteq (s, p{=}\text{rdf:type} \wedge o{=}\text{professor})$) and that (ii) pertain to very few distinct values, which are neither useful to summarize nor to state the general properties of a given RDF dataset (e.g., $(o, s{=}\text{patrick} \wedge p{=}\text{rdf:type}) \subseteq (o, s{=}\text{mike} \wedge p{=}\text{rdf:type})$). We define this number of distinct values as *support*, inspired from the widely adopted measure for association rules [4]:

DEFINITION 3.1 (SUPPORT). *Given an* RDF *dataset* T, *the support of a* CIND $\psi := c \subseteq c'$ *is defined as* $supp(\psi) := |\mathcal{I}(T, c)|$.

EXAMPLE 5. *The* CIND $(s, p=\textsf{memberOf} \wedge o=\textsf{csd}) \subseteq (s, p=\textsf{undergradFrom} \wedge o=\textsf{hpi})$ *has a support of 1 in Table 1. This is because its dependent capture* $(s, p=\textsf{memberOf} \wedge o=\textsf{csd})$ *selects a single value. This implies that this* CIND *describes a rather specific insight that pertains only to* patrick.

Formally, a broad CIND has a support equal to or above a given threshold h. The choice of this threshold depends on the use case and its dataset. In our experience, h=1,000 is a reasonable choice for the query minimization use case and h=25 for the knowledge discovery use case. In Appendix B, we present some more CINDs and their support. Without any loss of generality, we assume this threshold to be given in this paper. Usually, even small support thresholds bear great pruning power. In the aforementioned Diseasome dataset, over 84 % of its 219 million minimal CINDs have a support of 1 and from the other 34.9 million CINDs, another 97.4 % have a support below 10.

3.2 CINDs as Association Rules

CINDs are natural extensions of regular INDs, but they also share some properties with exact *association rules*[4] (ARs), i.e., those with confidence 1. By interpreting RDF triples (e.g., (patrick, rdf:type, gradStudent)) as transactions ($\{s$=patrick, p=rdf:type, o=gradStudent$\}$), we can find ARs in RDF datasets, such as o=gradStudent $\rightarrow$ p=rdf:type in Table 1. Every AR $\alpha=v_1 \rightarrow \beta=v_2$ implies the CIND $(\gamma, \alpha=v_1) \subseteq (\gamma, \alpha=v_1 \wedge \beta=v_2)$, e.g., the example AR implies the CIND $(s, o=\textsf{gradStudent}) \subseteq (s, p=\textsf{rdf:type} \wedge o=\textsf{gradStudent})$. In contrast, the inverse implication is not necessarily correct, e.g., adding a triple (patrick, status, gradStudent) would invalidate the AR but not the CIND. Also note that ARs can imply CINDs of only the above mentioned kind. In particular, all example CINDs in Section 1 are not implied by ARs. Given this, ARs can replace some CINDs, thereby enhancing the result's understandability and enabling further applications, such as selectivity estimation [19]. Moreover, AR discovery is less complex than CIND discovery, so we exploit ARs to further prune the CIND search space and improve the efficiency of our CIND discovery algorithm.

3.3 Pertinent CIND Discovery Problem

We now revise the naïve problem statement from Section 2 with the above introduced concepts. For a given dataset T and a user-defined CIND support threshold h, we want to efficiently discover all pertinent CINDs that hold on T, that is, all CINDs that are both minimal and broad. Moreover, if a CIND ψ is implied by an AR r, we want to provide r instead of ψ due to its stronger semantics.

4. SYSTEM OVERVIEW

The typical scenario for RDFIND is as follows: RDFIND, which constitutes a distributable data flow, is implemented and deployed on a distributed data processing system. The input RDF datasets reside in a distributed storage engine, such as HDFS or a triple store. We do not make any further assumptions, e.g., on data partitioning.

[4]The association rules considered in this paper are different from the ones used in [3]. See Section 9 for details.

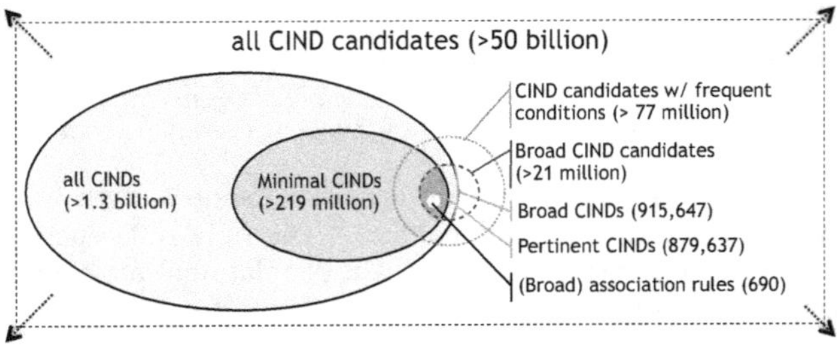

Figure 2: CIND search space for the Diseasome dataset (72,445 triples) and support threshold 10.

Let us now give the overall idea of how RDFIND efficiently discovers all pertinent CINDs in large RDF datasets. Intuitively, we need to find the sets of broad CINDs, which satisfy the user-defined support threshold, and the minimal CINDs. Then, their intersection yields the pertinent CINDs. However, in practice, the set of minimal CINDs is often considerably larger than the set of broad CINDs. For example, the Diseasome dataset has approximately 219 million minimal CINDs but fewer than 1 million broad CINDs for a support threshold of 10 (see Figure 2).

Therefore, we devise a *lazy pruning* strategy that reduces the search space in two phases. Figure 3 illustrates the overall architecture of RDFIND, which comprises three main components: the *Frequent Condition Detector* (FCDetector), the *Capture Groups Creator* (CGCreator), and the CIND *Extractor* (CINDExtractor). The first and third component are responsible for specific steps in the lazy pruning employed by RDFIND. The second component reorganizes the input data in a manner that allows for efficient CIND extraction. We briefly discuss these components next and give the algorithmic details in the remaining sections. For the implementation details, see Appendix C.

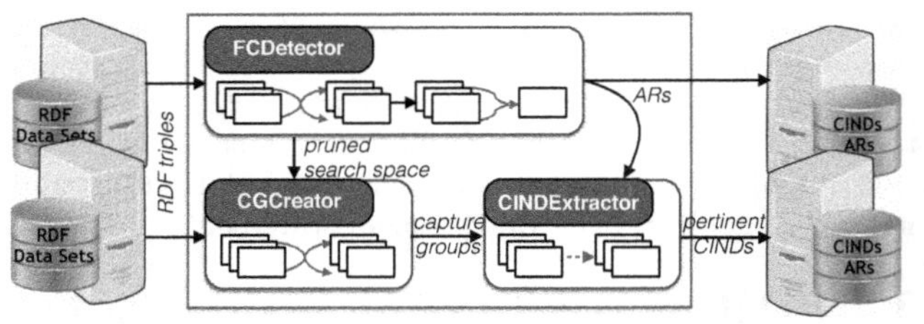

Figure 3: Overview of the RDFIND system.

FCDetector. Before initiating the actual search for CINDs, RDFIND first narrows the search space to a set of CIND candidates having *frequent conditions* only, i.e., conditions on the input dataset that are satisfied by a certain minimum number of triples. This represents the first phase of the lazy pruning. This pruning works, because all broad CINDs embed only frequent conditions (see Section 5). RDFIND also exploits frequent conditions to easily derive association rules and, consequently, to further prune the search space.

CGCreator. Next, RDFIND transforms all RDF triples in the previously pruned search space into compact representations, called *capture groups*, from which it can efficiently extract CINDs (see Section 6). A capture group is a set of captures whose interpretations have a certain value in common. For example, in Table 1 the value patrick spawns a capture group containing, amongst others, the capture $(s, p{=}\text{rdf:type}\wedge o{=}\text{gradStudent})$.

CINDExtractor. Given the capture groups, RDFIND reduces the search space of CIND candidates with frequent conditions to the set of broad CIND candidates. This is the second phase of our lazy pruning strategy. Subsequently, our system extracts the broad CINDs and their support from the capture groups. As CIND extraction is usually the most expensive step, RDFIND is equipped with several techniques, such as load balancing, to perform this step efficiently. Finally, it mines for pertinent CINDs, i.e., it searches for minimal CINDs among all discovered broad CINDs (see Section 7).

5. FREQUENT CONDITION DISCOVERY

As a start, RDFIND executes the first phase of our lazy pruning strategy and reduces the search space to the set of CIND candidates whose conditions (Definition 2.1) are frequent. Knowing frequent conditions is crucial for two main reasons: First, they allow RDFIND to significantly reduce the search space and, thus, to achieve low execution times and memory footprints. Second, they yield ARs (Section 3.2) at little cost, which improve the output usefulness. In the following, we further explain *why* frequent conditions (as well as ARs) help us to reduce the search space towards finding broad CINDs. Then, we detail *how* we discover frequent conditions and ARs.

5.1 Why Frequent Conditions?

A frequent condition is that condition whose number of satisfying triples (*condition frequency*) is not below the user-defined support threshold (Definition 3.1). The support of a CIND is tightly connected with the condition frequency of its dependent and referenced captures, as we assert in the following lemma (proof in Appendix A).

LEMMA 1. *Given a CIND $\psi := (\alpha, \phi) \subseteq (\beta, \phi')$ with support supp(ψ), the condition frequencies of ϕ and ϕ' are equal to or greater than supp(ψ).*

Frequent condition pruning. With Lemma 1 we do not need to validate CIND candidates having conditions with a frequency below a user-specified support. Indeed, finding frequent conditions drastically reduces the CIND search space. Figure 4 shows that, for real world-datasets, the vast majority of the conditions are satisfied by only very few triples. For instance, in the DBpedia dataset, 86% of the conditions have a frequency of 1, i.e., they hold only for a single triple, and 99% of the conditions have a frequency of less than 16. In practice, however, most CIND use cases require the conditions to have a high frequency.

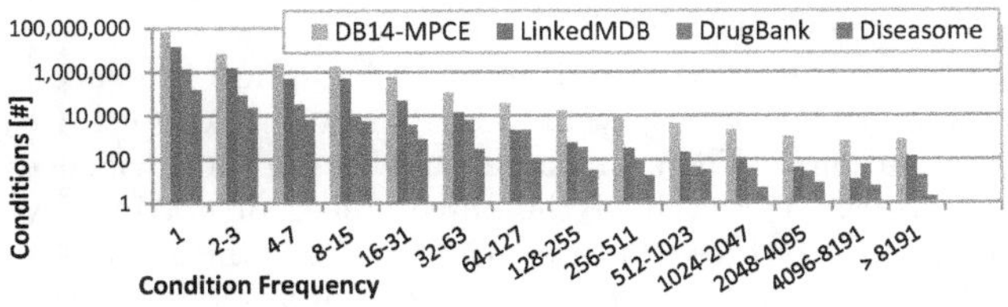

Figure 4: Number of conditions by frequency in real-world datasets of varying size from ~72*k* (Diseasome) to ~33*M* (DBP14-MPCE) triples.

Association rule pruning. In addition, frequent conditions allow RDFIND to easily derive ARs. As discussed in Section 3.2, the system can use ARs to further prune the CIND search space. The AR $\theta := \beta{=}v_1{\rightarrow}\gamma{=}v_2$ implies the CIND $\psi := (\alpha, \beta{=}v_1){\subseteq}(\alpha, \beta{=}v_1{\wedge}\gamma{=}v_2)$. For instance, Table 1 contains $o{=}\text{gradStudent} \rightarrow p{=}\text{rdf:type}$, which implies $(s, p{=}\text{rdf:type}) \subseteq (s, p{=}\text{rdf:type}\wedge o{=}\text{gradStudent})$. Therefore, RDFIND can simply keep ARs and exclude all its implied CINDs from the CIND search.

Equivalence pruning. The reverse CIND of ψ, i.e., $(\alpha, \beta{=}v_1{\wedge}\gamma{=}v_2) \subseteq (\alpha, \beta{=}v_1)$, trivially holds, because its dependent condition logically implies its referenced condition. In consequence, the AR θ implies that (the interpretations of) $(\alpha, \beta{=}v_1)$ and $(\alpha, \beta{=}v_1{\wedge}\gamma{=}v_2)$ are equal. Accordingly, our above example captures $(s, o{=}\text{gradStudent})$ and $(s, p{=}\text{rdf:type}\wedge o{=}\text{gradStudent})$ contain the exact same values, namely patrick and mike. Therefore, an AR $\beta{=}v_1 \rightarrow \gamma{=}v_2$ allows RDFIND to prune all CIND candidates involving the capture $(\alpha, \beta{=}v_1{\wedge}\gamma{=}v_2)$; they are equivalent to the candidates involving the capture $(\alpha, \beta{=}v_1)$.

5.2 Finding Frequent Conditions

We formulate the problem of finding frequent unary and binary conditions as a frequent itemset discovery problem. As such, we interpret each triple (s_1, p_1, o_1) as a transaction $\{\langle s{=}s_1\rangle, \langle p{=}p_1\rangle, \langle o{=}o_1\rangle\}$[5]. Using the state-of-the-art Apriori algorithm [4] to find all frequent unary and binary conditions, however, is inefficient as it was designed for single-node settings. Furthermore, it does not scale to large amounts of frequent itemset candidates, because it needs to keep all candidates in memory. Therefore, we devise a fully distributed algorithm that scales to arbitrary amounts of candidates by *checking candidates on-demand* using space-efficient indices. Figure 5 depicts the data flow of our algorithm to discover frequent conditions. Generally speaking, it consists of two passes over the data and an AR detection phase that takes place on the fly. In more detail, it operates in the following four main steps:

Frequent unary conditions. We assume that all triples are distributed among the RDFIND workers of a cluster, e.g., by means of a distributed triple store. Each worker can then process an independent horizontal partition of an input dataset. A worker reads each input RDF triple in its data partition and creates three unary conditions with a *condition counter* set to 1 (Step (1) in Figure 5). For instance, a worker creates the three unary condition counters $(\langle s{=}\text{patrick}\rangle, 1)$, $(\langle p{=}\text{rdf:type}\rangle, 1)$, and $(\langle o{=}\text{gradStudent}\rangle, 1)$ for the triple (patrick, rdf:type, gradStudent) in Table 1. All workers then run a global `GroupBy`[6] on the conditions of the unary condition counters and add up the counters for each resulting group (Step (2)). As this global `GroupBy` requires shuffling data through the network, RDFIND runs early-aggregations on the counters before shuffling the data, which significantly reduces the network load. After globally aggregating counters, the workers discard all non-frequent conditions with a frequency less than the user-specified support threshold.

Compacting unary frequent conditions. Once all the frequent unary conditions are found, RDFIND needs to index them for efficient containment tests both in the frequent

[5]The $\langle ...\rangle$ notation introduces its enclosed formulas as syntactical elements rather than their results.

[6]This is referred to as *reduce* on Map/Reduce-like systems.

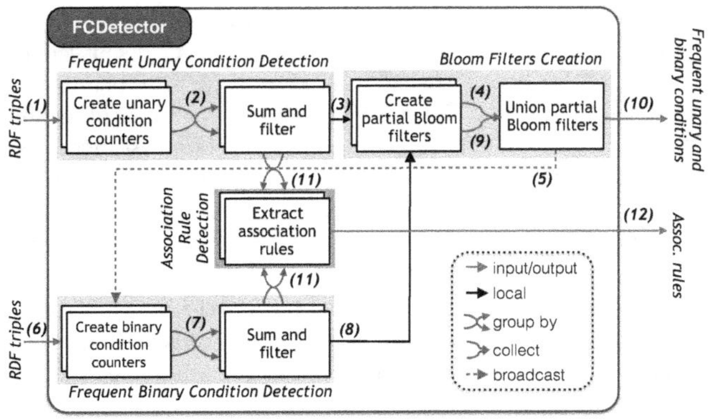

Figure 5: Data flow of the FCDetector.

binary conditions discovery and the CINDs pruning phase. RDFIND tolerates false positives in this index, so we use a Bloom filter to attain constant look-up time and a small memory footprint (tens of MB for the largest datasets). Additionally, RDFIND can create this Bloom filter in a fully distributed manner: Each worker encodes all of its locally residing frequent conditions in a Bloom filter (Step (3)). The workers then send their local Bloom filter to a single worker that unions them by calculating a bit-wise OR (Step (4)).

Frequent binary conditions. A binary condition can be frequent only if its two embedded unary conditions are frequent [4]. At this point, the original Apriori algorithm would generate all possible frequent binary condition candidates and organize them in a tree structure for subsequent counting. In RDF scenarios, however, this tree structure easily becomes too large to fit into main memory. To overcome this challenge, RDFIND never materializes the candidates and, instead, introduces on-demand candidate checking. For this, it broadcasts the previously created Bloom filter to all workers (Step (5)). Each worker runs Algorithm 1 to find the frequent binary condition candidates. In detail, each worker reads the triples from its data partition (Line 1 & Step (6)) and performs the candidate check on demand: First, it probes each unary condition embedded in the input triple against the Bloom filter (Line 2). Then, it generates all possible frequent binary condition candidates using the frequent unary conditions of the triple (Lines 3-5). For example, consider the triple (patrick, memberOf, csd) from Table 1. Knowing by means of the Bloom filter that only the two embedded unary conditions s=patrick and p=memberOf are frequent, the only candidate for a frequent binary condition is s=patrick$\wedge p$=memberOf. It then creates a binary condition counter for each frequent binary condition candidate (Line 6). As for frequent unary condition discovery, RDFIND globally aggregates the binary condition counters (Step (7)) and keeps only the frequent binary conditions.

Compacting binary frequent conditions. As for the frequent unary conditions, RDFIND encodes all frequent binary conditions in a Bloom filter in order to speed up the CIND pruning phase (Steps (8) and (9)). As a result of this process, RDFIND outputs the set of frequent unary and binary conditions, which implicitly represent the pruned CIND search space (Step (10)).

5.3 Extracting Association Rules

As in [4], our frequent conditions discovery algorithm also allows RDFIND to extract association rules at little extra

Algorithm 1: Create counters for binary conditions

Data: *RDF triples* T, *unary condition Bloom filter* B_u

1 **foreach** $t \in T$ **do**
2   probe $\langle s{=}t.s\rangle$, $\langle p{=}t.p\rangle$, and $\langle o{=}t.o\rangle$ in B_u;
3   **foreach** $(\alpha, \beta) \in \{(s,p),(s,o),(p,o)\}$ **do**
4     $v_\alpha \leftarrow t.\alpha$; $v_\beta \leftarrow t.\beta$;
5   **if** $\langle \alpha{=}v_\alpha\rangle$ *and* $\langle \beta{=}v_\beta\rangle$ *are frequent* **then**
6   forward $(\langle \alpha{=}v_\alpha \wedge \beta{=}v_\beta\rangle, 1)$;

cost. It simply performs a distributed join of the frequent unary condition counters with the frequent binary condition counters on their embedded unary conditions (Step (11)). For instance, $(\langle p$=rdf:type$\rangle, 3)$ and $(\langle o$=gradStudent$\rangle, 2)$ both join with $(\langle p$=rdf:type$\wedge o$=gradStudent$\rangle, 2)$. Then each worker checks for each pair in its partition of the join result, if the unary and binary condition counters have the same counter value. In our example, this is true for $(\langle o$=gradStudent$\rangle, 2)$ and $(\langle p$=rdf:type $\wedge$ o=gradStudent$\rangle, 2)$, hence, the responsible worker derives the association rule o=gradStudent $\rightarrow$ p=rdf:type with a support of 2. RDFIND uses the association rules to further prune the CIND search (see Section 5.1) and additionally includes them in the final result for users (Step (12)), because they are a special class of CINDs (see Section 3). In particular, the association rule support is equal to the support of its implied CINDs according to the following lemma (proof in Appendix A).

LEMMA 2. *The support* s *of the association rule* $\alpha{=}v \rightarrow \beta{=}v'$ *is equal to the support of its implied* CIND $(\gamma, \alpha{=}v) \subseteq (\gamma, \alpha{=}v \wedge \beta{=}v')$.

6. COMPACT RDF REPRESENTATION

After discovering the frequent unary and binary conditions, RDFIND transforms the RDF triples into a compact representation that allows it to efficiently create CIND candidates. We call this compact data structure *capture groups*. A capture group is a set of captures (Definition 2.2) whose interpretations have a value in common. Captures having n values in common co-occur in n capture groups. We first explain how the system creates captures groups and then demonstrate that we can obtain all broad CIND candidates from capture groups only.

6.1 Capture Groups

Our system creates capture groups in two steps. It first outputs the evidence that a certain value belongs to a capture (*capture evidence*). For this, it takes into consideration the previously found frequent conditions and ARs. Then, it groups and aggregates capture evidences with the same value creating the capture groups.

Creating Capture Evidences. A capture evidence is a statement that a certain value exists in a capture (interpretation). There are nine possible capture evidences per triple. For each of the three values of a triple, we could create three capture evidences, of which one has a binary condition and the other two have unary conditions (cf. Definitions 2.1 and 2.2). For example, the triple (patrick, memberOf, csd) entails, amongst others, the capture evidences patrick $\in$ $(s, p$=memberOf$)$ and patrick $\in$ $(s, p$=memberOf$\wedge o$=csd$)$. One might think that this is an

Algorithm 2: Creating capture evidences

Data: *triples* T, *unary condition Bloom filter* B_u, *binary condition Bloom filter* B_b, ARs AR
Result: *Evidences of relevant captures* C

1 **foreach** $t \in T$ **do**
2 $\quad C \leftarrow \emptyset$;
3 $\quad$ **foreach** $\alpha \in \{s, p, o\}$ **do**
4 $\quad\quad \{\beta, \gamma\} \leftarrow \{s, p, o\} \setminus \{\alpha\}$;
5 $\quad\quad v_\alpha \leftarrow t.\alpha$; $v_\beta \leftarrow t.\beta$; $v_\gamma \leftarrow t.\gamma$;
6 $\quad\quad$ **if** $\langle \beta = v_\beta \rangle \in B_u$ **then**
7 $\quad\quad\quad$ **if** $\langle \gamma = v_\gamma \rangle \in B_u$ **then**
8 $\quad\quad\quad\quad$ **if** $\langle \beta = v_\beta \wedge \gamma = v_\gamma \rangle \in B_b$
9 $\quad\quad\quad\quad \wedge \langle \beta{=}v_\beta \rightarrow \gamma{=}v_\gamma \rangle \notin AR$
10 $\quad\quad\quad\quad \wedge \langle \gamma{=}v_\gamma \rightarrow \beta{=}v_\beta \rangle \notin AR$ **then**
11 $\quad\quad\quad\quad\quad C \leftarrow C \cup \{\langle v_\alpha \in (\alpha, \beta{=}v_\beta{\wedge}\gamma{=}v_\gamma] \rangle\}$;
12 $\quad\quad\quad\quad$ **else** $C \leftarrow C \cup \{\langle v_\alpha \in (\alpha, \beta{=}v_\beta) \rangle, \langle v_\alpha \in (\alpha, \gamma{=}v_\gamma) \rangle\}$;
13 $\quad\quad\quad$ **else** $C \leftarrow C \cup \{\langle v_\alpha \in (\alpha, \beta{=}v_\beta) \rangle\}$;
14 $\quad\quad$ **else if** $\langle \gamma{=}v_\gamma \rangle \in B_u$ **then**
$\quad\quad\quad C \leftarrow C \cup \{\langle v_\alpha \in (\alpha, \gamma{=}v_\gamma) \rangle\}$;

expensive task as it would increase the input data volume by a factor of nine. However, remember that at this point RDFIND works on a highly pruned search space containing only frequent conditions (see Section 5). In addition, our system further reduces the number of capture evidences via implications between binary and unary conditions. For instance, consider again the triple (patrick, memberOf, csd) and its capture $(s, p{=}\text{memberOf}{\wedge}o{=}\text{csd})$. The resulting capture evidence patrick $\in (s, p{=}\text{memberOf}{\wedge}o{=}\text{csd})$ subsumes both patrick $\in (s, p{=}\text{memberOf})$ and patrick $\in (s, o{=}\text{csd})$. Hence, it suffices to keep the first binary capture evidence.

Algorithm 2 shows in detail the capture evidence creation process. Prior to its execution, the frequent condition Bloom filters and the ARs discovered by the FCDetector are broadcast, so that they are available to every worker (cf. Figure 5). As for the frequent condition discovery, each worker then processes its partition of the input triples. For each triple, it first picks a projection attribute (Line 3), e.g., $\alpha{=}s$, and two condition attributes (Line 4), e.g., $\beta{=}p$ and $\gamma{=}o$. Then, for the two emerging unary conditions ($p{=}$memberOf and $o{=}$csd), it checks whether they might be frequent using the unary Bloom filter (Lines 5–7). If so, it also checks whether the emerging binary condition ($p{=}\text{memberOf}{\wedge}o{=}\text{csd}$) is also frequent[7] (Line 8) and does not embed a known AR (Lines 9–10). In this case, it creates a capture evidence with the binary condition only (Line 11; (patrick $\in (s, p{=}\text{memberOf}{\wedge}o{=}\text{csd})$)). Otherwise, it creates the capture evidences for those of the two unary conditions that are frequent (Lines 12–14). Finally, these steps are repeated for the remaining projection attributes (p and o).

Creating capture groups. RDFIND aggregates all capture evidences with the same value using a global `GroupBy` and calculates the union of their captures in order to create *capture groups*. Again, early aggregates are calculated whenever possible to reduce network and memory pressure. Although each capture group corresponds to a certain value from the input RDF dataset, the system discards the values as they are no longer needed. For instance, for the dataset in Table 1, a support threshold of 3, and the value patrick, we have the capture evidences patrick $\in (s, p{=}\text{rdf:type})$ and patrick $\in (s, p{=}\text{undergradFrom})$. The aggregation combines them into the capture group $\{(s, o{=}\text{rdf:type}), (s, p{=}\text{undergradFrom})\}$. Note that the capture groups are distributed among the workers after this step and can be processed distributedly in the following.

[7]Notice that testing the unary conditions before the binary ones avoids some false positives from the binary Bloom filter.

6.2 From Capture Groups to Broad CINDs

Let us now show that it is possible to extract all broad CINDs from a given RDF dataset using capture groups. To this end, we exploit commonalities of the capture-based CIND definition (i.e., Definition 2.3) with the standard IND definition by extending the IND criterion described in [13]. Intuitively, if a capture group contains the referenced capture, then it also contains the dependent capture. Formally:

LEMMA 3. *Let T be an* RDF *dataset and $\mathcal{G}$ its capture groups. Then, a* CIND $\psi := c \subseteq c'$ *is valid on T iff* $\forall G \in \mathcal{G}\colon c \in G \Rightarrow c' \in G$, *with* $supp(\psi) = |\{G \in \mathcal{G}\colon c \in G\}|$.

We prove this lemma in Appendix A. Because at this step RDFIND operates in the search space of CIND candidates having frequent conditions, we infer from the above lemma that all broad CINDs can be extracted from capture groups.

THEOREM 1. *Given an* RDF *dataset T with its capture groups $\mathcal{G}$ and a support threshold h, any valid* CIND ψ *with support* $supp(\psi) \geq h$ *can be extracted from* $\mathcal{G}$.

PROOF. This trivially holds from Lemmata 1 and 3. □

7. FAST CIND EXTRACTION

As final step, in the CINDExtractor component (see Figure 6), RDFIND extracts pertinent CINDs from the previously created capture groups. Overall, it proceeds in two main steps: It first extracts broad CINDs from capture groups and then finds the minimal CINDs among the broad ones. In the following, we first show that a simple approach based on an existing IND discovery mechanism to extract broad CINDs is inadequate for RDF (Section 7.1). We then show how RDFIND extracts broad CINDs from capture groups efficiently (Section 7.2). We finally show how our system extracts the pertinent CINDs from broad CINDs (Section 7.3).

7.1 Trouble of a Direct Extraction

A simple broad CIND extraction mechanism could be based on an existing IND discovery mechanism (such as [24]). It would work as follows: Because a valid CIND's dependent capture is in the same capture groups as its referenced capture (Lemma 3), all workers enumerate all CIND candidates within their capture groups. They also initialize a support count for each CIND candidate as shown in Example 6.

EXAMPLE 6. *Consider a scenario with three capture groups:* $G_1 = \{c_a, c_b, c_c, c_d, c_e\}$, $G_2 = \{c_a, c_b\}$, *and* $G_3 = \{c_c, c_d\}$. *In this case, the naïve approach generates five* CIND candidate sets *for G_1, e.g.,* $(c_a \sqsubseteq \{c_b, c_c, c_d, c_e\}, 1)$, *and two for G_2 and G_3.*

The system then performs a global `GroupBy` on the dependent capture of the CIND candidate sets and aggregates them by intersecting all their referenced captures and summing up

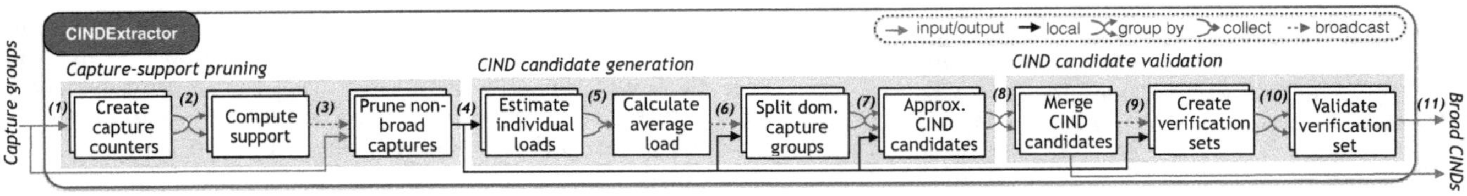

Figure 6: Data flow of the CINDExtractor.

all its supports. The aggregated CIND candidate sets represent all valid CINDs and the support count is used to retain only the broad CINDs.

The performance of this approach suffers from capture groups with a large number of captures (*dominant capture groups*). Processing a capture group with n captures yields n CIND candidate sets with up to n contained captures each, i.e., the overall number of captures in CIND candidate sets is quadratic in the size of the corresponding capture group. Therefore, dominant capture groups entail enormous memory consumption and CPU load as well as a highly skewed load distribution among workers, which severely impacts performance. Formally, inspired by [23], we consider a capture group G as dominant if its processing load, estimated by $|G|^2$, is larger than the average processing load among all w workers, $\frac{\sum_{G_i \in \mathcal{G}} |G_i|^2}{w}$. For example, assuming two workers (i.e., $w = 2$), we consider capture group G_1 in Example 6 as dominant, because $|G_1|^2 > \frac{|G_1|^2+|G_2|^2+|G_3|^2}{2}$. In practice, RDF datasets lead to several very large capture groups that emerge from frequently occurring values, such as rdf:type. This renders the above naïve solution inadequate for RDF.

7.2 Cracking Dominant Capture Groups

To efficiently cope with dominant capture groups, we enhance in the following the above simple extraction mechanism by (i) pruning the capture groups as much as possible, (ii) load balancing, and (iii) a two-phase CIND extraction strategy. Figure 6 depicts the complete process.

Capture-Support Pruning. To deal with dominant capture groups, RDFIND applies a novel *capture-support pruning* technique, which is also the second phase of our lazy pruning technique. The capture-support pruning reduces the size of all capture groups by removing some of their captures. The first phase of our lazy pruning technique (see Section 5) retains CIND candidates whose captures embed frequent conditions only. In general, however, these CIND candidates are a proper superset of the broad CIND candidates, because the support of a capture can be smaller than the frequency of its embedded condition. The capture-support pruning identifies and removes these captures from all capture groups. Basically, our system first computes all capture supports by distributedly counting their occurrences in the capture groups (Steps (1) & (2) in Figure 6), then broadcasts the prunable captures with a support less than the user-defined support threshold h to each worker, and eventually each worker removes these captures from its capture groups (Step (3)). For example, assuming that h is set to 2, we can then identify in Example 6 that c_e appears only in G_1, so its support is 1. We therefore remove it from G_1, resulting in the following capture groups: $G_1' = \{c_a, c_b, c_c, c_d\}$, $G_2 = \{c_a, c_b\}$, and $G_3 = \{c_c, c_d\}$.

CIND Candidate Generation. While the capture-support pruning significantly reduces the size of capture groups, some dominant capture groups remain and still severely impact performance. RDFIND now clears the skewed work distribution caused by them. For this purpose, each worker estimates its current load by summing the squares of its capture groups' sizes. These loads are then summed up on a single worker (Step (5)), divided by the number of workers, and the resulting average load is broadcast back to all workers (Step (6)). Then, each worker can identify its dominant capture groups and divides them into w work units and uniformly redistributes them among all workers (Step (7)). Concretely, it divides each dominant capture group G evenly into w subsets and constructs for each such subset $\hat{G}_i$ the work unit $(\hat{G}_i, G)$, whereby $\hat{G}_i$ assigns dependent captures to consider during the upcoming CIND candidate generation. For instance, the work units for G_1' are $(\{c_a, c_b\}, \{c_a, c_b, c_c, c_d\})$ and $(\{c_c, c_d\}, \{c_a, c_b, c_c, c_d\})$.

However, most of the CIND candidates enumerated by dominant capture groups are rather incidental and do not yield valid CINDs. As stated above, dominant capture groups emerge from frequent RDF-specific values, such as rdf:type. If two entities e_1 and e_2 occur with rdf:type and, thus, $(s, p{=}e_1)$ and $(s, p{=}e_2)$ are both in the capture group that corresponds to rdf:type, it is still unlikely that $(p, s{=}e_1) \subseteq (p, s{=}e_2)$ is a valid CIND. Our system exploits this observation in an approximate-validate CIND extraction approach that avoids creating a large number of these unnecessary CIND candidates. Each worker creates all CIND candidate sets for each of its capture groups and work units as discussed earlier (see Example 6). For the work units, which emerge from dominant capture groups, however, it encodes the referenced captures in a Bloom filter of constant size k instead (Step (7)). This encoding reduces the space complexity of the CIND candidate sets from $\mathcal{O}(n^2)$ to $\mathcal{O}(n)$, where n is the number of captures in a work unit. We experimentally observed that $k = 64$ bytes yields the best performance.

In Example 6, our system creates CIND candidate sets as discussed before for G_2 and G_3. In contrast, for the work units derived from G_1', it creates CIND candidate sets as follows: $(c_a \sqsubseteq Bloom(c_b, c_c, c_d), 1)^*$, where the mark $*$ indicates that this candidate comes from a dominant capture group and is *approximate*. This mark allows our system to trace back all Bloom-filter-based CIND candidates for further validation as Bloom filters may generate false positives.

CIND Candidate Validation. As in the basic extraction, our system then aggregates all the CIND candidate sets with the same dependent capture for validation (Step (8)). Algorithm 3 shows this aggregation process, where Boolean functions f_1, f_2, and f_3 mark if a candidate is approximate or not. Conceptually, the workers intersect the referenced captures, but distinguish three cases: (i) If none of the two CIND candidate sets are approximate, they are intersected

Algorithm 3: CIND candidates validation

Data: CIND *candidate set* $(c \sqsubseteq C_1, count_1)^{f_1}$, $(c \sqsubseteq C_2, count_2)^{f_2}$

Result: *merged* CIND *candidate set* $(c \sqsubseteq C_3, count_3)^{f_3}$

1 **if** $\neg$ *hasBloomFilter*(C_1) $\wedge$ $\neg$ *hasBloomFilter*(C_2) **then**
2 $\quad C_3 \leftarrow C_1 \cap C_2$;
3 **else if** *hasBloomFilter*(C_1) $\wedge$ *hasBloomFilter*(C_2) **then**
4 $\quad C_3 \leftarrow C_1$ & C_2;
5 **else**
6 $\quad C'_1 \leftarrow C_i$ where $\neg$*isBloomFilter*(C_i);
7 $\quad C'_2 \leftarrow C_j$ where *isBloomFilter*(C_j);
8 $\quad C_3 \leftarrow \{c \in C'_1 : c \in C'_2\}$;
9 $count_3 \leftarrow count_1 + count_2$;
10 $f_3 \leftarrow (f_1 \wedge f_2) \vee isEmpty(C_3)$;

as in the basic extraction (Lines 1 & 2 in Algorithm 3). As a result, the system gets *certain* CINDs (i.e., that do not require further validation); (ii) If both candidates are approximate, we calculate the bitwise AND of the Bloom filters to approximate the intersection of their elements (Lines 3 & 4); (iii) If only one of the candidates is approximate, we probe the other candidate against the Bloom filter and retain them on probing success (Lines 5–9). For instance, if we need to merge the above mentioned CIND candidate sets $(c_a \sqsubseteq Bloom(c_b, c_c, c_d), 1)^*$ and $(c_a \sqsubseteq \{c_b\}, 1)$, the result will be $(c_a \sqsubseteq \{c_b\}, 2)^*$.[8] Such CIND sets that have an approximate CIND candidate set lineage are *uncertain* and require further validation (unless the set of referenced captures is empty (Line 9)). To validate these uncertain CINDs, RDFIND broadcasts the uncertain CIND sets to each worker (Step (9)) that organize them in a map m with the dependent capture as key and referenced captures as value. Then, the workers iterate through only their work units. If a dependent capture c in a work unit is a key in m, the worker intersects the captures of the work unit with the referenced captures in $m[c]$ and issues the result as a new CIND validation set. For instance for the work unit $(\{c_a, c_b\}, G'_1)$, the respective worker finds that c_a is a key in m and creates the validation set $c_a \sqsubseteq (G'_1 \cap m[c_a])$, i.e., $c_a \sqsubseteq \{c_b\}$. Notice that the validation sets are in general much smaller in number and extent than the above explained CIND candidate sets. Finally, these validation sets are intersected as in the basic extraction (Step (10)) and the resulting CINDs complement the previously found certain CINDs, denoting then the complete set of broad CINDs (Step (11)).

7.3 From Broad to Pertinent CINDs

Once all broad CINDs are extracted, RDFIND obtains the pertinent CINDs by retaining only the minimal ones. Recall that a minimal CIND must not be implied by a further CIND, neither by dependent nor referenced implication (see Figure 1). It basically detects all implications among broad CINDs in two steps. First, it removes non-minimal CINDS with a binary dependent and a unary referenced condition ($\Psi_{2:1}$) by *consolidating* them with CINDs that either have only unary or only binary conditions ($\Psi_{1:1}$ and $\Psi_{2:2}$). Second, it then removes non-minimal CINDs from the latter two by consolidating them with CINDs that have a unary dependent condition and a binary referenced condition ($\Psi_{1:2}$).

[8]Note that in general, the result might be further aggregated with CIND candidate sets, e.g., due to early aggregation.

Table 2: Evaluation RDF datasets.

Name	Size [MB]	Triples
Countries	0.8	5,563
Diseasome	13	72,445
LUBM-1	17	103,104
DrugBank	102	517,023
LinkedMDB	870	6,148,121
DB14-MPCE	4,334	33,329,233
DB14-PLE	21,770	152,913,360
Freebase	398,100	3,000,673,968

We explain the consolidation process by example for $\psi = (s, p{=}\text{memberOf}) \subseteq (s, p{=}\text{rdf:type}) \in \Psi_{1:1}$ from Table 1. Because CINDs in $\Psi_{1:1}$ might be subject to dependent implication with CINDs in $\Psi_{1:2}$, RDFIND joins $\Psi_{1:1}$ and $\Psi_{1:2}$ on their dependent captures and referenced project attribute. In our example, this join matches ψ with $\psi' = (s, p{=}\text{memberOf}) \subseteq (s, p{=}\text{rdf:type} \wedge o{=}\text{gradStudent})$. RDFIND then finds that ψ' implies ψ and discards ψ.

8. EXPERIMENTS

We implemented RDFIND on top of Flink 0.9.0 using Scala 2.10 and exhaustively evaluate it using both real-world and synthetic datasets. We conducted our experiments with five questions in mind: (i) *How good is* RDFIND *compared to the state-of-the-art?* (ii) *How well does* RDFIND *scale?* (iii) *How well does* RDFIND *deal with different support thresholds?* (iv) *What efficiency do our pruning techniques have?* (v) *Can we start from broad* CINDs *to generate pertinent* CIND *candidates?* We provide the implementation, pointers to the datasets, and the exact measurements for repeatability purposes at https://hpi.de//naumann/projects/repeatability/data-profiling/cind-discovery-on-rdf-data.html.

8.1 Experimental Setup

Datasets. To gain comprehensive insights into RDFIND and its results, we gathered a broad range of datasets from different domains and of different sizes: seven real-world datasets and a synthetic one, summarized in Table 2.

Systems. We compare RDFIND to CINDERELLA [7], the state-of-the-art CIND discovery algorithm for relational data. CINDERELLA assumes that partial INDs were previously discovered. It basically performs left-outer joins on these partial INDs using a database to generate conditions that match only the included tuples of the partial IND. We used both MySQL 5.6 and PostgreSQL 9.3 with default settings as underlying database. Additionally, we devised an optimized version CINDERELLA* that performs more memory-efficient joins and avoids self-joins, allowing it to significantly reduce its memory footprint. Notice that we do not compare RDFIND to the PLI-variant [7], because CINDERELLA is shown to be faster, and not to *Data Auditor* [16], because it discovers only the broadest CIND for a partial IND, which is not appropriate for the RDF case. However, PLI and *Data Auditor* apply the same overall strategy as CINDERELLA and differ only in the conditions generation.

Hardware. We have conducted all experiments on a commodity hardware cluster consisting of a master node (8× 2 GHz, 8 GB RAM) and 10 worker nodes (2× 2.2 GHz, 8 GB RAM each). All nodes are interconnected via Gigabit Eth-

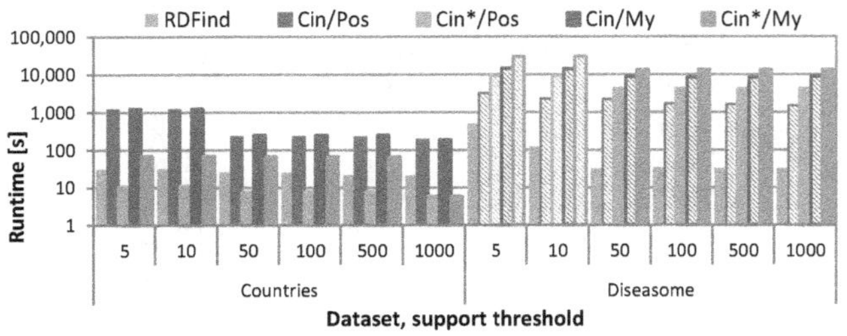

Figure 7: RDFIND vs. standard and optimized CINDERELLA on MySQL and PostgreSQL. Hollow bars indicate algorithm failures and therefore present lower bounds on the execution time.

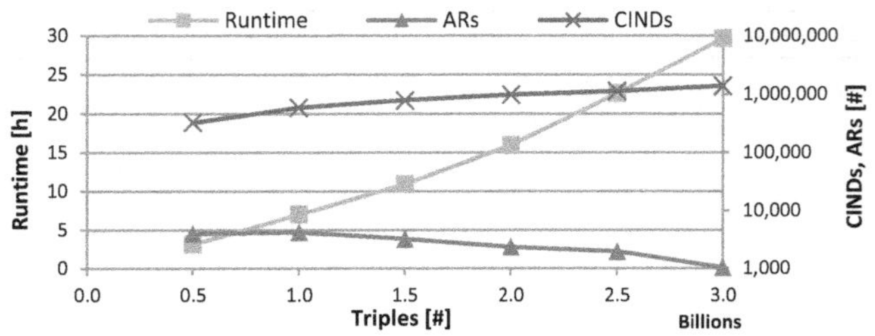

Figure 8: RDFIND when increasing the number of input triples with a support threshold of 1,000.

ernet in a star topology. Furthermore, our prototype reads RDF datasets from NTriple files distributed in HDFS. In our experiments, Flink (and hence RDFIND) was granted 4 GB of RAM on each worker node, leaving the remaining RAM to other components, such as HDFS.

8.2 RDFind vs. Cinderella

We first show that RDFIND significantly prevails over the state-of-the-art when discovering CINDs in RDF data. For this purpose, we compare the runtimes of RDFIND with CINDERELLA [7] on different datasets. As CINDERELLA is not a distributed algorithm, we ran our experiments on only the master node of our cluster, granting the algorithms 4 GB of main memory. Furthermore, due to CINDERELLA's high main memory requirements, we use only our two smallest datasets, *Countries* and *Diseasome*.

Figure 7 shows the results of this comparison with CINDERELLA. On the very small *Countries* dataset, RDFIND consistently outperforms the standard CINDERELLA by a factor from 8 to 39. However, the optimized version on PostgreSQL is up to 20 seconds faster, because RDFIND's runtime is dominated by a fix overhead, particularly Flink's start-up costs. For the larger (but still small) *Diseasome* dataset this overhead is already redeemed, though. We observe that the regular version of CINDERELLA failed for each execution and the optimized version for the support thresholds 5 and 10 due to their high memory consumption. Our system, in contrast, handles all executions flawlessly and outperforms CINDERELLA by a factor of up to 419 without considering the failed runs. This is mainly because, in contrast to CINDERELLA, which performs a join for each designated combination of projection attributes using a database (which also explains the differences among PostgreSQL and MySQL), our system covers the complete CIND search space in a single execution using optimized data structures and algorithms. Note that in contrast to RDFIND, CINDERELLA does not consider referenced conditions, which is a strong simplification of the CIND discovery problem. This increased generality, the higher efficiency, and the robustness w.r.t. main memory render RDFIND superior to CINDERELLA on RDF data. Therefore, we henceforth focus on evaluating only our system for bigger datasets that CINDERELLA cannot (efficiently) handle.

8.3 Scalability

We proceed to study the scalability of RDFIND in terms of both the number of input triples and compute machines.

Scaling the number of triples. We aim at testing RDFIND's robustness with this experiment by evaluating its efficiency when varying the number of input triples. For this experiment, we consider the Freebase dataset, which is among the largest RDF datasets: With 3 billion triples and a total size of 400 GB, it exceeds the amount of available memory in our cluster by a factor of 10. We run our system over different sample sizes of the Freebase dataset using a support threshold of 1, 000. Furthermore, we consider predicates only in conditions, because the above experiments rarely showed meaningful CINDs on predicates.

Figure 8 illustrates the runtime of RDFIND and the number of CINDs and ARs discovered for different numbers of input triples. We observe a slightly quadratic runtime behavior of our system. This is because the size of capture groups increases along with the number of input triples, and the CIND extraction runtime grows quadratically with the capture group sizes. Nevertheless, RDFIND can process the full dataset, which demonstrates its high scalability, and thereby discovers more than 1 million pertinent CINDs. Indeed, including more triples leads to more pertinent CINDs. In contrast, the number of association rules (ARs) grows to a peak at 1 billion triples and declines afterwards. ARs have stricter semantics than CINDs and hence they are more easily violated by adding triples. Although this impairs the effectiveness of our pruning with ARs, overall the system shows to scale well with the number of input triples.

Scaling out. We now evaluate the scalability of our system when increasing the number of machines. We consider the medium-size LinkedMDB dataset with a varying support threshold h and number of machines, each running a single thread. As Flink allows for parallelism in a single node through multi-threading, we consider an additional case with 10 machines, each running two threads.

Figure 9 shows the measured runtimes and the average speed-up w.r.t. a parallelism of 1. We observe that our system scales almost linearly with the number of machines. In particular, when the support threshold is low and very few capture groups dominate the runtime, the load balancing ensures high resource utilization. On average, we measured a speed-up of 8.14 on 10 machines. We also observe that the intra-node parallelism allows RDFIND to gain an additional speed-up of 1.38 on average. This shows that our system can leverage any provided additional resources.

8.4 Impact of Support Threshold

Having shown the high scalability of our system, we now focus on evaluating the efficiency of our system when the number of pertinent CINDs increases. We run an experiment with different support thresholds for a variety of datasets.

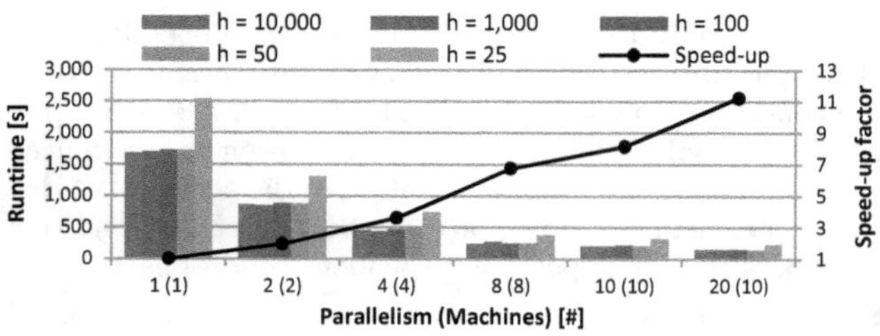

Figure 9: RDFind when increasing the number of machines on LinkedMDB with varying support threshold h.

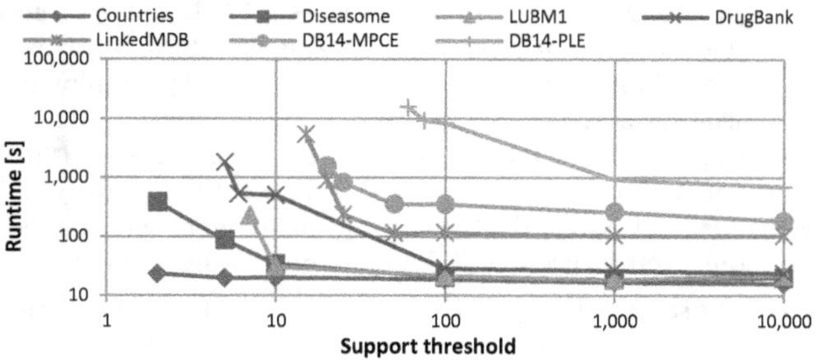

Figure 10: RDFind with different datasets and support thresholds.

Impact on runtime. We first evaluate how the support threshold impacts RDFind's runtime. Figure 10 shows the runtimes for our system when discovering pertinent CINDs on multiple datasets and different support thresholds h and reveals a pattern on all datasets: For large support thresholds, RDFind is almost indifferent to the threshold setting and provides almost a constant runtime. For instance, for LUBM1, this is the case for $h \geq 10$. In contrast, the runtime quickly rises when decreasing h below 10. The reason for this is the distribution of conditions w.r.t. their frequencies: As shown in Figure 4, most conditions in datasets hold on only very few triples. Thus, for very small support thresholds our system can prune only few conditions, which leads to more captures and, more importantly, to larger capture groups. This agrees with our observation that the CIND extraction becomes the dominating component for small support thresholds because of its quadratic complexity w.r.t. capture group sizes. However, as we show in the following experiments, low-support CINDs are also useful for specific applications.

Impact on result. We now evaluate how the support threshold impacts the result of our system. Figure 11 displays the complete number of pertinent CINDs (including ARs) that RDFind discovers for multiple support thresholds. We observe that the number of pertinent CINDs is to some extent inversely proportional to the support threshold. Decreasing the support threshold by two orders of magnitude increases the number of CINDs by three orders of magnitude in the evaluation datasets (the ARs behave similarly and usually account for 10–50% of the CINDs). In consequence, the majority of CINDs in RDF datasets have a small support, while there are only a few broad CINDs, i.e., only few CINDs are supported by a large number of triples. Still, these very broad CINDs are of high importance as they state general properties of their respective dataset. For example, we found

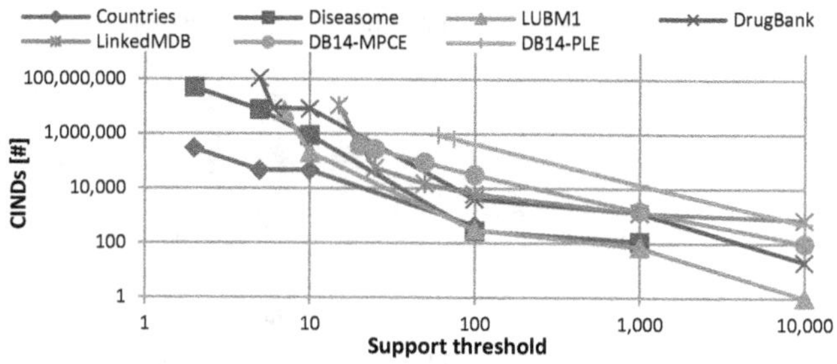

Figure 11: Number of pertinent CINDs for different datasets and supports.

that the DBpedia dataset (DB14-MPCE) embeds the two CINDs $(o, p{=}\mathsf{associatedBand}) \subseteq (o, p{=}\mathsf{associatedMusicalArtist})$ and $(s, p{=}\mathsf{associatedBand}) \subseteq (s, p{=}\mathsf{associatedMusicalArtist})$ with supports of 41,300 and 33,296, respectively. This suggests that the associatedBand predicate is a subproperty of associatedMusicalArtist and hence it is a hint to revise the ontology. On the other side, low-support CINDs are also useful to some applications. For instance, DBpedia holds the CINDs $(s, p{=}\mathsf{writer} \wedge o{=}\mathsf{Angus\_Young}) \subseteq (s, p{=}\mathsf{writer} \wedge o{=}\mathsf{Malcolm\_Young})$ and, vice versa, $(s, p{=}\mathsf{writer} \wedge o{=}\mathsf{Malcolm\_Young}) \subseteq (s, p{=}\mathsf{writer} \wedge o{=}\mathsf{Angus\_Young})$, both having a support of 26. This reveals that the AC/DC members, Angus and Malcolm Young, have written all their songs together: a new fact, that is not explicitly stated in DBpedia. These results demonstrate the relation between CIND support and CIND semantics and justify why users should set different support thresholds for different use cases.

8.5 Pruning Effectiveness

To investigate the effectiveness of our pruning techniques and algorithmic choices, we compare RDFind with two simplified versions: RDFind-*DE* (Direct Extraction) extracts CINDs from capture groups without the capture-support pruning, load balancing, and approximate-validate extraction (see Section 7.1). RDFind-*NF* (No Frequent Conditions) additionally waives any operation related to frequent conditions (see Section 5).

Figure 12 compares the three variants on our two smallest datasets. While RDFind and RDFind-DE are similarly efficient, RDFind-NF exhibits drastically inferior performance in all measurements. We conclude that the pruning techniques related to frequent conditions are highly effective, even for small datasets and low support thresholds.

We proceed to compare only RDFind and RDFind-DE on larger datasets in Figure 13. For the large support thresholds, RDFind-DE is slightly more efficient than RDFind in four of five cases. In these scenarios, the overhead for coping with dominant capture groups in RDFind is not redeemed. Still, RDFind's accumulated runtime is 4.6 minutes shorter than RDFind-DE's runtime. For the small support thresholds, RDFind is much more efficient and robust. On the three smaller dataset, it achieves an average speed-up of 5.7 over RDFind-DE. Because small support thresholds entail long runtimes, this is an absolute speed-up of 50.4 minutes. Furthermore, RDFind-DE was not able to handle the larger DB14-MPCE and DB14-PLE due to main memory requirements. These results show the improved robustness, overall higher efficiency, and the low overhead of cracking dominant capture groups of RDFind.

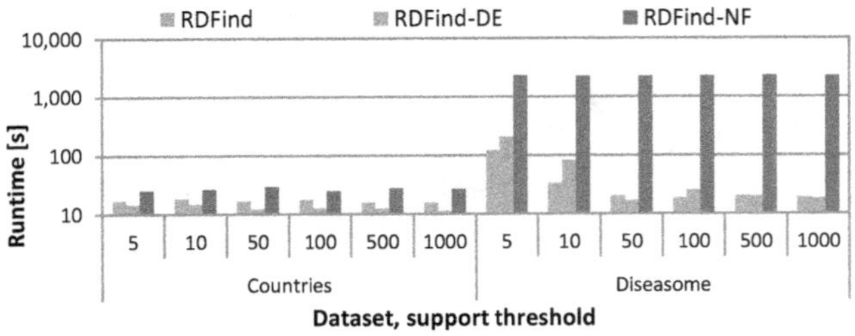

Figure 12: RDFIND vs. RDFIND-DE vs. RDFIND-NF.

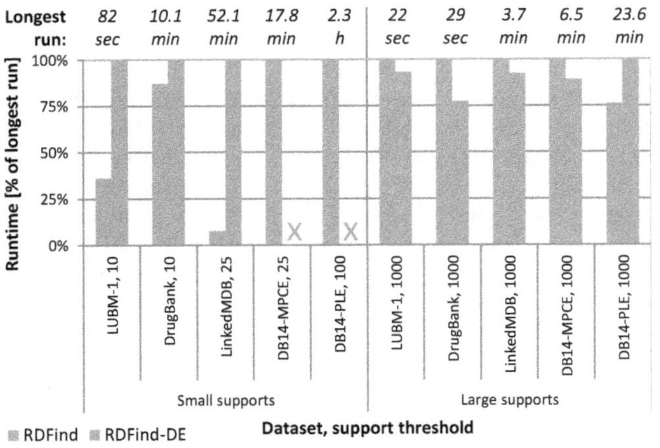

Figure 13: RDFIND vs. RDFIND-DE for small and large supports. Longest run refers to the execution time of the slower algorithm, respectively. The crosses represent algorithm failures.

8.6 Why Not Minimal CINDs First?

Recall that RDFIND finds all broad CINDs at first and then removes all non-minimal ones. It is an intriguing idea to discover only minimal CINDs at first by employing referenced and dependent implication as explained in Section 3.1. We implemented this idea by doing multiple passes over the capture groups, extracting only certain kinds of CINDs in each pass, and generating a reduced candidate set for the next pass. This strategy turned out to be up to 3 times slower even than RDFIND-DE. Usually, broader CINDs are also minimal CINDs as exemplified in Figure 2, so the overhead of this strategy is greater than its savings. This clearly shows the efficiency of the strategy we follow in RDFIND.

9. RELATED WORK

Data profiling is a well-established ongoing research area that seeks to discover different kinds of integrity constraints (ICs) and other metadata, such as functional and inclusion dependencies [1]. However, conditional ICs [10, 15] have attracted only little attention so far, even though they are a valuable extension to plain ICs [1]. We believe this is due to the additional computational complexity of condition discovery aggravating the already complex IC discovery tasks.

CIND discovery. The only existing works on CINDs discovery are the CINDERELLA/PLI algorithm [7] and *Data Auditor* [16]. However, these works differ from RDFIND, because not only do they target relational data, but also their results and algorithmic foundations are fundamentally different. As input they take a *partial* IND, that holds only on a part of the underlying data. Then, they look for conditions that select only the included tuples on the dependent side of the partial IND, potentially allowing for a certain error of the condition. In contrast to RDFIND, both algorithms are not directly taking into account conditions on the referenced side of CINDs. This is a simplification of the actual CIND discovery problem, as the choice of the referenced condition influences the set of possible dependent conditions.

IND discovery. IND discovery algorithms for relational data, in particular MIND [13], BINDER [31], and SINDY [24], find INDs by (implicitly) joining all columns in a dataset and successively extracting IND candidates with each tuple of the join product. They scale well with the number of tuples in the inspected database but not with the number of IND candidates. RDFIND also employs a (distributed) join-extract strategy (with captures instead of columns). However, we enhance and speed up this process by employing lazy pruning and using multi-pass CIND extraction. These enhancements let RDFIND scale to huge amounts of CIND candidates, which distinguishes it from all IND discovery algorithms. Moreover, RDFIND's load-balancing ensures good scale-out even in presence of dominant capture groups.

RDF data profiling. Given the recent popularity of the LOD initiative [8], there is a plethora of tools for analyzing and profiling RDF data. Most of these systems focus on either RDFS/OWL schema discovery [22, 26] or on gathering statistics of Linked Data [6, 20]. ProLOD++ [2] comprises a wider variety of data profiling and mining tasks for RDF data, such as schema discovery and key discovery. Furthermore, past research considers *association rules* (different from our ARs) on RDF data that are akin to CINDs of the form $(\alpha, \beta{=}v_1) \subseteq (\alpha, \beta{=}v_2)$ for fix, user-specified α and β [3]. This work focuses on using these rules for RDF data management tasks, such as synonym detection, but not on the discovery itself. While RDFIND's CINDs can also support these data management tasks, we show that the much broader class of CINDs can also serve many further use cases.

10. CONCLUSION & FUTURE WORK

This paper introduced the novel concept of pertinent CINDs on RDF datasets and presented the RDFIND system for their discovery. In contrast to existing CIND algorithms, which find partial INDs at first and then generate conditions for each partial IND individually, RDFIND discovers all CINDs in a single run employing efficient pruning techniques. We showed experimentally that our algorithm outperforms the state-of-the-art algorithm CINDERELLA by orders of magnitude and is robust enough to handle large RDF datasets that were not possible to handle before.

For the future, it would be helpful to (inter-)actively aid users in determining an appropriate support threshold to find the *relevant* CINDs for their applications. Also, discerning *meaningful* and *spurious* CINDs, e.g., using the local closed world assumption [14], is an interesting aspect to investigate. Finally, we have enabled new research to incorporate CINDs in many RDF data management scenarios, e.g., data integration, ontology re-engineering, knowledge extraction, and query optimization.

Acknowledgements

This research was partially funded by the German Research Society (DFG grant no. FOR 1306).

11. REFERENCES

[1] Z. Abedjan, L. Golab, and F. Naumann. Profiling relational data: A survey. *VLDB Journal*, 24(4):557–581, 2015.

[2] Z. Abedjan, T. Grütze, A. Jentzsch, and F. Naumann. Mining and profiling RDF data with ProLOD++. In *Proceedings of the International Conference on Data Engineering (ICDE)*, pages 1198–1201, 2014. Demo.

[3] Z. Abedjan and F. Naumann. Improving RDF data through association rule mining. *Datenbank-Spektrum*, 13(2):111–120, 2013.

[4] R. Agrawal and R. Srikant. Fast algorithms for mining association rules. *Proceedings of the International Conference on Very Large Databases (VLDB)*, pages 487–499, 1994.

[5] M. Arias, J. Fernández, M. Martínez-Prieto, and P. de la Fuente. An Empirical Study of Real-World SPARQL Queries. In *International Workshop on Usage Analysis and the Web of Data (USEWOD)*, 2011.

[6] S. Auer, J. Demter, M. Martin, and J. Lehmann. LODStats – an extensible framework for high-performance dataset analytics. In *Proceedings of the International Conference on Knowledge Engineering and Knowledge Management (EKAW)*, pages 353–362, 2012.

[7] J. Bauckmann, Z. Abedjan, U. Leser, H. Müller, and F. Naumann. Discovering conditional inclusion dependencies. In *Proceedings of the International Conference on Information and Knowledge Management (CIKM)*, pages 2094–2098, 2012.

[8] C. Bizer, T. Heath, and T. Berners-Lee. Linked Data - The Story So Far. *International Journal on Semantic Web and Information Systems (IJSWIS)*, 5(3):1–22, 2009.

[9] M. A. Bornea, J. Dolby, A. Kementsietsidis, K. Srinivas, P. Dantressangle, O. Udrea, and B. Bhattacharjee. Building an efficient RDF store over a relational database. In *Proceedings of the International Conference on Management of Data (SIGMOD)*, pages 121–132, 2013.

[10] L. Bravo, W. Fan, and S. Ma. Extending dependencies with conditions. In *Proceedings of the International Conference on Very Large Databases (VLDB)*, pages 243–254, 2007.

[11] D. Calvanese, G. De Giacomo, D. Lembo, M. Lenzerini, A. Poggi, M. Rodriguez-Muro, R. Rosati, M. Ruzzi, and D. F. Savo. The MASTRO system for ontology-based data access. *Semantic Web Journal (SWJ)*, 2(1):43–53, 2011.

[12] E. I. Chong, S. Das, G. Eadon, and J. Srinivasan. An efficient SQL-based RDF querying scheme. In *Proceedings of the International Conference on Very Large Databases (VLDB)*, pages 1216–1227, 2005.

[13] F. De Marchi, S. Lopes, and J.-M. Petit. Efficient algorithms for mining inclusion dependencies. In *Proceedings of the International Conference on Extending Database Technology (EDBT)*, pages 464–476. 2002.

[14] X. Dong, E. Gabrilovich, G. Heitz, W. Horn, N. Lao, K. Murphy, T. Strohmann, S. Sun, and W. Zhang. Knowledge vault: A web-scale approach to probabilistic knowledge fusion. In *Proceedings of the International Conference on Knowledge discovery and data mining (SIGKDD)*, KDD '14, pages 601–610, New York, NY, USA, 2014. ACM.

[15] W. Fan. Dependencies revisited for improving data quality. In *Proceedings of the Symposium on Principles of Database Systems (PODS)*, pages 159–170, 2008.

[16] L. Golab, F. Korn, and D. Srivastava. Efficient and Effective Analysis of Data Quality using Pattern Tableaux. *IEEE Data Engineering Bulletin*, 34(3):26–33, 2011.

[17] J. Gryz. Query folding with inclusion dependencies. In *Proceedings of the International Conference on Data Engineering (ICDE)*, pages 126–133, 1998.

[18] P. Hayes and P. F. Patel-Schneider. RDF 1.1 Semantics. W3C Recommendation, February 2014. https://www.w3.org/TR/rdf11-mt/.

[19] I. F. Ilyas, V. Markl, P. Haas, P. Brown, and A. Aboulnaga. Cords: automatic discovery of correlations and soft functional dependencies. In *Proceedings of the International Conference on Management of Data (SIGMOD)*, pages 647–658. ACM, 2004.

[20] T. Käfer, A. Abdelrahman, J. Umbrich, P. O'Byrne, and A. Hogan. Observing linked data dynamics. In *Proceedings of the Extended Semantic Web Conference (ESWC)*, pages 213–227, 2013.

[21] Z. Kaoudi and I. Manolescu. RDF in the clouds: a survey. *VLDB Journal*, 24(1):67–91, 2015.

[22] S. Khatchadourian and M. P. Consens. ExpLOD: Summary-based exploration of interlinking and RDF usage in the linked open data cloud. In *Proceedings of the Extended Semantic Web Conference (ESWC)*, pages 272–287, 2010.

[23] L. Kolb and E. Rahm. Parallel Entity Resolution with Dedoop. *Datenbank Spektrum*, 13(1):23–32, 2012.

[24] S. Kruse, T. Papenbrock, and F. Naumann. Scaling out the discovery of inclusion dependencies. In *Proceedings of the Conference Datenbanksysteme in Business, Technologie und Web Technik (BTW)*, pages 445–454, 2015.

[25] M. Levene and M. W. Vincent. Justification for inclusion dependency normal form. *IEEE Transactions on Knowledge and Data Engineering (TKDE)*, 12(2):281–291, 2000.

[26] H. Li. Data Profiling for Semantic Web Data. In *Proceedings of the International Conference on Web Information Systems and Mining (WISM)*, pages 472–479, 2012.

[27] LUBM. http://swat.cse.lehigh.edu/projects/lubm/.

[28] S. Ma, W. Fan, and L. Bravo. Extending inclusion dependencies with conditions. *Theoretical Computer Science*, 515:64–95, 2014.

[29] M. S. Marshall, R. Boyce, H. F. Deus, J. Zhao, E. L. Willighagen, M. Samwald, E. Pichler, J. Hajagos, E. Prud'hommeaux, and S. Stephens. Emerging practices for mapping and linking life sciences data using RDF - A case series. *Web Semantics: Science, Services and Agents on the World Wide Web*, 2012.

[30] T. Neumann and G. Weikum. The RDF-3X engine for scalable management of RDF data. *VLDB Journal*, 19(1):91–113, 2010.

[31] T. Papenbrock, S. Kruse, J.-A. Quiané-Ruiz, and F. Naumann. Divide & conquer-based inclusion dependency discovery. *Proceedings of the VLDB Endowment*, 8(7):774–785, 2015.

[32] N. Redaschi and UniProt Consortium. UniProt in RDF: Tackling Data Integration and Distributed Annotation with the Semantic Web. In *Proceedings of the International Biocuration Conference*, 2009.

[33] M. Zhang, M. Hadjieleftheriou, B. C. Ooi, C. M. Procopiuc, and D. Srivastava. On multi-column foreign key discovery. *Proceedings of the VLDB Endowment*, 3(1-2):805–814, 2010.

APPENDIX

A. PROOFS

Here, we provide the proofs of our Lemmata 1–3.

LEMMA 1. *Given a* CIND $\psi := (\alpha, \phi) \subseteq (\beta, \phi')$ *with support* $supp(\psi)$*, the condition frequencies of* ϕ *and* ϕ' *are equal to or greater than* $supp(\psi)$*.*

PROOF. *From the support definition, we have that the interpretation of the dependent capture* (α, ϕ) *contains* $supp(\psi)$ *values. The referenced capture* (β, ϕ')*, which is a superset, therefore contains at least* $supp(\psi)$ *values. As each value in the interpretation of a capture must be found in at least one triple and each triple yields exactly one value, the capture's embedded condition must satisfy at least as many triples as this number of values. Thus, both* ϕ *and* ϕ' *must have a condition frequency* $\geq supp(\psi)$*.* □

LEMMA 2. *The support* s *of the association rule* $\alpha{=}v \rightarrow \beta{=}v'$ *is equal to the support of its implied* CIND $(\gamma, \alpha{=}v) \subseteq (\gamma, \alpha{=}v \wedge \beta{=}v')$*.*

PROOF. *Let* s *be equal to the support of* $\alpha{=}v \rightarrow \beta{=}v'$*. By definition, the frequencies of the conditions* $\phi_1 := \alpha{=}v \wedge \beta{=}v'$ *and* $\phi_2 := \alpha{=}v$ *are also* s*. Because all triples in an* RDF *dataset are distinct, the* s *triples selected by* ϕ_1 *(and hence by* ϕ_2*) must have pairwise distinct values in* γ*. Thus, the interpretation of capture* $(\gamma, \alpha{=}v)$ *contains* s *elements.* □

LEMMA 3. *Let* T *be an* RDF *dataset and* $\mathcal{G}$ *its capture groups. Then, a* CIND $\psi := c \subseteq c'$ *is valid on* T *iff* $\forall G \in \mathcal{G}\colon c \in G \Rightarrow c' \in G$*, with* $supp(\psi) = |\{G \in \mathcal{G}\colon c \in G\}|$*.*

PROOF. *By construction of the capture groups, for each value* v *in the interpretation of a certain capture* c*,* $\mathcal{I}(T, c)$*,* c *is contained in a dedicated capture group* G_v *- and vice versa. In other words, values and capture groups are in a one-to-one relationship. In consequence, (the interpretation of)* c' *contains all values of* c *if and only if* c' *is member of all capture groups in which* c *is a member. Moreover, the number of capture group memberships of* c *is exactly the number of values in* c *and, hence, the support of* ψ*.* □

B. USE CASES

CINDs can play an important role on versatile RDF data management scenarios, as INDs do on relational databases. In the following, we demonstrate three of such use cases, namely *query minimization*, *knowledge discovery* and *ontology reverse engineering*, using examples from real-world datasets.

Query optimization. As RDF data spans a graph, queries involve many joins. With joins being a very costly operation, this impacts the performance of RDF queries. As stated in the introduction, CINDs allow to remove unnecessary joins. For instance, knowing that $(s, p{=}\text{teaching}) \subseteq (s, p{=}\text{rdf:type} \wedge o{=}\text{professor})$ would allow us to remove the second query triple in the following query: `SELECT ?s ?o WHERE {?s teaching ?o . ?s rdf:type professor}`. As a result of such a minimization, the query can be answered with a simple scan of the data, avoiding an expensive join operation. Hence, queries can obtain significant performance gains from query minimization. For example, Figure 14 demonstrates the performance improvement when minimizing and running LUBM query Q2 [27] in RDF-3X [30]. We observe that the minimized version of query $Q2$ is three times faster than the original one.

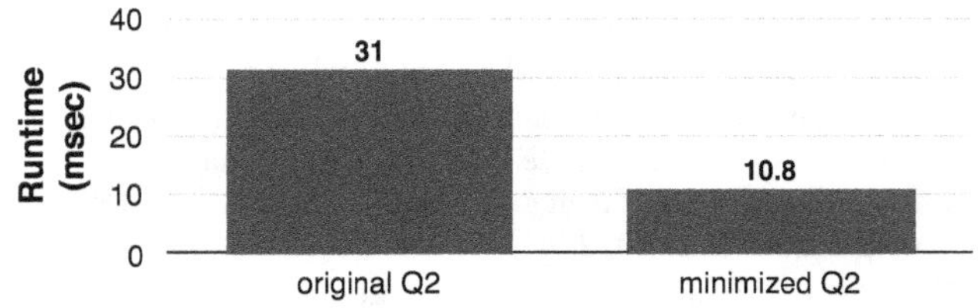

Figure 14: Effect of query minimization using CINDs.

Knowledge discovery. CINDs might reveal unknown facts about data instances that cannot be inferred from the ontology itself. As already mentioned, the DBpedia CINDs $(s, p{=}\text{writer} \wedge o{=}\text{Angus\_Young}) \subseteq (s, p{=}\text{writer} \wedge o{=}\text{Malcolm\_Young})$ (support: 26) and, vice versa, $(s, p{=}\text{writer} \wedge o{=}\text{Malcolm\_Young}) \subseteq (s, p{=}\text{writer} \wedge o{=}\text{Angus\_Young})$ (support: 26), reveal that the AC/DC members, Angus and Malcolm Young, have written all their songs together. This reveals a fact that is not explicitly stated in DBpedia. A second example is the CIND $(s, p{=}\text{areaCode} \wedge o{=}559) \subseteq (s, p{=}\text{partOf} \wedge o{=}\text{California})$ (support: 98) meaning that cities with code 559 are located in California. Another example from the DrugBank dataset is the CIND $(o, s{=}\text{drug00030} \wedge p{=}\text{target}) \subseteq (o, s{=}\text{drug00047} \wedge p{=}\text{target})$ (support: 14), which reveals that anything cured by drug00030 is also cured by drug00047. There are many more facts that can be unveiled from CINDs.

Ontology reverse engineering. RDF data is not always accompanied by an ontology and even if it is, it does not always follow the ontology constraints. CINDs can provide general insights and reveal statements not reflected by the ontology (if there is one). For instance, our ARs can be used to discover the RDF classes used in a dataset, e.g., the AR $o{=}\text{lmdb:performance} \rightarrow p{=}\text{rdf:type}$ (support: 197,271) reveals that the URI lmdb:performance is a class. Using CINDs we can also suggest to ontology engineers class and predicate relationships such as: (i) class hierarchies, (ii) predicate hierarchies, and (iii) the domain and range of predicates. For instance, the two CINDs $(s, p{=}\text{associatedBand}) \subseteq (s, p{=}\text{associatedMusicalArtist})$ (support: 33,296) and $(o, p{=}\text{associatedBand}) \subseteq (o, p{=}\text{associatedMusicalArtist})$ (support: 41,300) suggest that the associatedBand predicate is a subproperty of associatedMusicalArtist. This is because, according to the RDF semantics [18], if the predicate associatedBand is a subproperty of associatedMusicalArtist, then the set of subjects and the set of objects of the predicate associatedBand are a subset of the set of subjects and set of objects of associatedMusicalArtist, respectively. Similarly, the CIND $(s, p{=}\text{rdf:type} \wedge o{=}\text{Leptodactylidae}) \subseteq (s, p{=}\text{rdf:type} \wedge o{=}\text{Frog})$ (support: 1,010) reveals that the class Leptodactylidae could be a subclass of class Frog. The CIND $(o, p{=}\text{movieEditor}) \subseteq (s, p{=}\text{rdf:type} \wedge o{=}\text{foaf:Person})$ (support: 3,210) reveals that the range of predicate movieEditor can be the class foaf:Person. Another interesting CIND, such as $(s, p{=}\text{classificationFunction} \wedge o{=}\text{``hydrolase activity''}) \subseteq (s, p{=}\text{classificationFunction} \wedge o{=}\text{``catalytic activity''})$ (support: 812), states that the classification function hydrolase activity is a catalytic activity. This gives hints to the ontology engineer that the activities should be classes and not string literals, so that class hierarchies can be exploited.

Notice that ARs as considered in [3] cannot express all above CINDs as they contain binary conditions and different projection and selection attributes.

C. IMPLEMENTATION DETAILS

We have implemented RDFIND on top of the distributed data processing system Flink 0.9.0, which gives our prototype the flexibility both to scale up via multi-threading and scale out via distributed execution. Also, Flink's execution engine provides robust out-of-core execution for joins and aggregations. RDFIND preserves the robustness by adding only data structures with a small memory footprint, e.g., Bloom filters. This allows RDFIND to run in environments with low memory footprint, yet leveraging any available resources. Furthermore, RDFIND accepts N-Triples[9] files as inputs. For the comparison with CINDERELLA (Section 8.2) these files resided in a local filesystem. For all other experiments (Sections 8.3, 8.4, and 8.5), the files resided in Hadoop Distributed File System, specifically in HDFS 2.7, without any specific partitioning of the triples.

RDFIND uses a single Flink job, i.e., a single data flow plan, that implements all three components: FCDetector, CGCreator, and CINDExtractor. The detailed plan can be obtained from the implementation on our repeatability page (see Section 8). Here, we only want to convey the general strategy to implement RDFIND on Flink. Each operation in RDFIND, e.g., *Create unary condition counters* in Figure 5, is mostly implemented with a single Flink operator and a user-defined function that implements the respective algorithm logic. The communication between adjacent steps is handled by Flink and designated by the type of the receiving operator. We implemented our communication channels in Figures 5 and 6 as follows: (i) *local* communication using Flink's `Map` and `FlatMap` operators, (ii) *group by* using a combination of `GroupBy`, `GroupCombine`, and `GroupReduce`, (iii) *collect* using `GlobalReduce`, (iv) *joins* (multiple *group by* inputs) using a combination of `GroupBy` and `CoGroup`, and (v) *broadcast* using the `Broadcast` command. The only exception is the *group by* for load balancing of dominant capture groups. Here, we use a `FlatMap` operator to split them into work units and distribute the work units with Flink's `Repartition` operator.

[9]https://www.w3.org/TR/n-triples/

Cost-Effective Crowdsourced Entity Resolution: A Partial-Order Approach

Chengliang Chai†, Guoliang Li†, Jian Li‡, Dong Deng†, Jianhua Feng†
†Department of Computer Science, Tsinghua National Laboratory for Information Science and Technology (TNList), Tsinghua University, Beijing, China
‡Institute for Interdisciplinary Information Sciences, Tsinghua University, Beijing, China
{liguoliang, lijian83,fengjh}@tsinghua.edu.cn; {chaicl15, dd11}@mails.tsinghua.edu.cn

ABSTRACT

Crowdsourced entity resolution has recently attracted significant attentions because it can harness the wisdom of crowd to improve the quality of entity resolution. However existing techniques either cannot achieve high quality or incur huge monetary costs. To address these problems, we propose a cost-effective crowdsourced entity resolution framework, which significantly reduces the monetary cost while keeping high quality. We first define a partial order on the pairs of records. Then we select a pair as a question and ask the crowd to check whether the records in the pair refer to the same entity. After getting the answer of this pair, we infer the answers of other pairs based on the partial order. Next we iteratively select pairs without answers to ask until we get the answers of all pairs. We devise effective algorithms to judiciously select the pairs to ask in order to minimize the number of asked pairs. To further reduce the cost, we propose a grouping technique to group the pairs and we only ask one pair instead of all pairs in each group. We develop error-tolerant techniques to tolerate the errors introduced by the partial order and the crowd. Experimental results show that our method reduces the cost to 1.25% of existing approaches (or existing approaches take 80× monetary cost of our method) while not sacrificing the quality.

Categories and Subject Descriptors
H.2 [Database Management]: Database applications
Keywords: Crowdsourcing;Entity Resolution;Partial Order

1. INTRODUCTION

Entity resolution aims to find records that refer to the same entity from a collection of records. For example, consider the 11 records in Table 1. r_1, r_2 and r_3 refer to the same entity. r_4, r_5, r_6 and r_7 refer to the same entity. Entity resolution has many real-world applications, particularly in health data integration, knowledge-base construction, web search, comparison shopping, and law enforcement.

However existing machine-based methods are still far from perfect[22, 24], because the same entity may have many unpredictable representations. Crowdsourced entity resolution that leverages the crowd's ability to solve this problem has attracted significant attentions[12, 21, 23, 24, 25].

A brute-force method enumerates every pair of records and asks the crowd to check whether they refer to the same entity. This method involves huge monetary costs, especially for large datasets. To address this problem, several algorithms have been proposed to reduce the cost by pruning some pairs that do not need to be asked. Wang et al. [23] utilized the transitivity to reduce the cost, but the quality may not be guaranteed. This is because the transitivity may not hold for some records, which leads to incorrect deduction and uncontrollable error propagation. Wang et al. [24] proposed a correlation-clustering method, which adaptively assigned the records referring to the same entity into the same cluster. This method improves the quality at the expense of asking many more questions and thus involves high monetary costs. In summary, existing methods either cannot achieve high quality or involve huge monetary costs.

To address these problems, we propose Power, a partial-order based crowdsourced entity resolution framework, which significantly reduces the monetary cost while keeping high quality. The basic idea is that we define a partial order on the record pairs and prune many pairs that do not need to be asked based on the partial order. Specifically, we first define a partial order: (1) If a pair of records refer to the same entity, then the pairs preceding this pair also refer to the same entity; (2) If a pair of records refer to different entities, then the pairs succeeding this pair refer to different entities. Then we select a pair as a question and ask the crowd to check whether the records in the pair refer to the same entity. Based on the answer of this pair, we infer the answers of other pairs based on the partial order. Thus our goal is to judiciously select the pairs to ask in order to minimize the number of asked pairs. To this end, we devise effective algorithms to iteratively select pairs without answers to ask until we get the answers of all the pairs. To further reduce the cost, we propose a grouping technique to group the pairs such that we only need to ask one pair instead of all pairs in each group. Since asking only one pair in each iteration leads to a high latency, we propose effective techniques to select multiple pairs in each iteration. As both the partial order and the crowd may introduce errors, we develop error-tolerant techniques to tolerate the errors.

To summarize, we make the following contributions.

(1) We propose a partial-order based crowdsourced entity resolution framework. We define a partial order on record pairs and utilize the partial order to infer the answers of some unasked pairs so as to reduce the monetary cost.

SIGMOD'16, June 26 - July 1, 2016, San Francisco, CA, USA.

DOI: http://dx.doi.org/10.1145/2882903.2915252

(2) We construct a graph based on the partial order and utilize the graph to ask questions and infer answers. We devise efficient algorithms to construct the graph. We develop a grouping technique to group the record pairs, which can further reduce the cost. We prove that the optimal grouping is NP-hard and propose approximation algorithms.
(3) We judiciously select pairs to ask in order to minimize the number of asked pairs. We propose a path-based algorithm that asks one question in each iteration and prove that the algorithm is optimal in general. To reduce the latency, we devise a topological-sorting-based algorithm that asks multiple questions in parallel in each iteration.
(4) We develop a probability-based method to tolerate the errors introduced by the crowd and the partial order.
(5) We conduct experiments using real-world datasets on a real crowdsourcing platform. Experimental results show that our method reduces the cost to 1.25% of existing approaches (or existing approaches take more than 80 times money of our method) while not sacrificing the quality.

The rest of this paper is structured as follows. We first define the problem and review related work in Section 2 and then propose our framework in Section 3. The grouping strategy, question selection, and error-tolerant techniques are discussed in Sections 4, 5, 6 respectively. We report experimental results in Section 7 and conclude in Section 8.

2. PRELIMINARIES

2.1 Problem Definition

DEFINITION 1 (CROWDSOURCED ENTITY RESOLUTION). *Consider a table $\mathcal{T}$ with m attributes $\{\mathcal{A}_1, \mathcal{A}_2, \ldots, \mathcal{A}_m\}$ and n records $\{r_1, r_2, \ldots, r_n\}$, where each record denotes an entity. The entity resolution aims to identify the records that refer to the same entity. Crowdsourced entity resolution leverages the crowd's ability to address this problem.*

For example, Table 1 shows a table with 4 attributes and 11 records. r_1, r_2, and r_3 refer to the same entity. r_4, r_5, r_6, and r_7 refer to the same entity. Each of r_8, r_9, r_{10}, r_{11} represents a different entity. Crowdsourced entity resolution asks questions to the crowd (or workers) for identifying the records referring to the same entity. As we need to pay the workers for answering a question, the objective is to reduce the number of questions while keeping high quality.

2.2 Related Work

2.2.1 Crowdsourced Entity Resolution

Generating Questions for Workers. An important problem in crowdsourced entity resolution is to design questions for workers. A straightforward method is to generate *pair-comparison-based questions*, where each question is a pair of two records and asks workers to check whether the two records refer to the same entity. This method may generate a large number of questions. To address this problem, *clustering-based questions* are proposed [12, 22], where each question is a group of records and asks workers to classify the records into different clusters such that records in the same cluster refer to the same entity and records in different clusters refer to different entities. As the clustering-based method does not need to enumerate every pair, it can reduce the monetary cost. However, workers prefer the pair-comparison question as it is much easier to answer.
Pruning Dissimilar Pairs. Intuitively, we do not need to ask the *dissimilar pairs* that have low probabilities referring to the same entity. Wang et al. [22] proposed a similarity-based method, which computed the similarity of record pairs and pruned the pairs with small similarities. As this method can prune many dissimilar pairs without sacrificing the quality of final answers, most of existing studies used this technique to reduce the cost.
Leveraging Transitivity to Reduce The Cost. Transitivity can be used to reduce the cost: Given three records, r_1, r_2, r_3, if $r_1 = r_2$ (r_1 and r_2 refer to the same entity) and $r_2 = r_3$, we can deduce that $r_1 = r_3$ and do not need to ask whether $r_1 = r_3$. Wang et al. [23] and Vesdapunt et al. [21] studied how to utilize the transitivity to reduce the number of questions. Although this method can reduce the cost, the quality may be reduced. For example, suppose $r_1 = r_2$ and $r_2 \neq r_3$, but the crowd returns $r_1 = r_2$ and $r_2 = r_3$. Then it introduces an incorrect deduction $r_1 = r_3$.
Improving The Quality. Wang et al. [24] proposed a correlation-clustering method, which includes three steps. It first prunes dissimilar pairs with small similarities. Then, it selects some pairs to ask and divides the records into a set of clusters based on the workers' results of these asked pairs. Finally, it refines the clusters by selecting more pairs to ask, checking whether their answers are consistent with the initial clusters, and adjusting the clusters based on the inconsistencies. This method improves the accuracy at the expense of huge monetary costs.
Question Selection. A natural problem is how to select next questions to ask in order to improve the quality. Whang et al. [25] proposed a probabilistic model to select high-quality questions. Verroios et al. [20] improved the model by tolerating workers' errors. Gokhale et al. [7] studied the crowdsourced record linkage problem, which linked two records from two tables, which is different from ours as we focus on linking multiple records in the same table.

Compared with existing techniques, our model can significantly reduce the cost while not sacrificing the quality.

2.2.2 Other Related Work

Crowdsourced Operators. There are many studies on leveraging crowd's ability to improve database operators, e.g., crowdsourced selection [1, 26], crowdsourced sort[18, 2], crowdsourced max/top-k [8, 19]. They focus on trading-off monetary cost, quality and latency.
Crowdsourced Systems. Several crowdsourced databases, e.g. Deco[16, 17], Quak[13], CrowdDB[5], were proposed, aiming to implement and optimize crowdsourced operators.
Crowdsourced Quality Control. Many methods are proposed to improve the quality[9, 15, 3, 11, 27]. Most of these studies focus on devising a worker model to capture worker's quality, computing the worker's model, eliminating bad workers, assigning questions to appropriate workers, and aggregating the results from multiple workers.

3. PARTIAL-ORDER-BASED FRAMEWORK

We first define a partial order (Section 3.1) and then propose a partial-order-based algorithm (Section 3.2).

3.1 Partial Order

Record Similarity. Given two records r_i and r_j, we use p_{ij} to denote the pair (r_i, r_j) and use s_{ij}^k to denote the similarity of p_{ij} on attribute $\mathcal{A}_k$. We can utilize any similarity function to compute the similarity, e.g., edit distance, Jaccard, Euclidean distance. Here we take Jaccard and edit similarity as examples. Let $r_i[k]$ denote the value of r_i on attribute $\mathcal{A}_k$. For Jaccard, we tokenize $r_i[k]$ into a set of

	Name ($\mathcal{A}_1$)	Address ($\mathcal{A}_2$)	City ($\mathcal{A}_3$)	Flavor ($\mathcal{A}_4$)
r_1	ritz-carlton restaurant (atlanta)	181 w. peachtree st.	atlanta	european french
r_2	ritz-carlton restaurant	181 peachtree dr	atlanta	european(french)
r_3	ritz-carlton restaurant Georgia	181 peachtree st.	city of atlanta	european France
r_4	cafe ritz-carlton buckhead	3434 peachtree rd.	city of atlanta	american
r_5	cafe ritz-carlton (buckhead)	3434 peachtree rd.	city of atlanta	american
r_6	dining room ritz-carlton buckhead	3434 peachtree ave.	atlanta	international
r_7	dining room ritz-carlton (buckhead)	3434 peachtree ave.	atlanta	international
r_8	cafe claude	201 83rd st.	new york	cafe
r_9	cafe bizou (american)	13 54th st.	new york	american food
r_{10}	gotham bar & grill	12th rd.	new york	american(new)
r_{11}	mesa grill	102 5th rd.	new york	southwestern

Table 1: Eleven Records In A Real Restaurant Dataset.

p_{ij}	s^1_{ij}	s^2_{ij}	s^3_{ij}	s^4_{ij}	p_{ij}	s^1_{ij}	s^2_{ij}	s^3_{ij}	s^4_{ij}
p_{12}	0.72	0.4	1	0.88	p_{37}	0.28	0.2	0.33	0
p_{13}	0.75	0.75	0.33	0.8	p_{45}	0.92	1	1	1
p_{23}	0.77	0.5	0.33	0.69	p_{46}	0.69	0.5	0.33	0
p_{24}	0.51	0.2	0.33	0	p_{47}	0.65	0.5	0.33	0
p_{25}	0.53	0.2	0.33	0	p_{56}	0.63	0.5	0.33	0
p_{26}	0.42	0.2	1	0	p_{57}	0.71	0.5	0.33	0
p_{27}	0.45	0.2	1	0	p_{67}	0.94	1	1	1
p_{34}	0.39	0.2	1	0	p_{89}	0.33	0.2	1	0
p_{35}	0.39	0.2	1	0	$p_{10,11}$	0.5	0.25	1	0

Table 2: Record Similarity.

tokens and compute Jaccard on token sets as below.

$$s^k_{ij} = \text{JAC}(r_i[k], r_j[k]) = \frac{|r_i[k] \cap r_j[k]|}{|r_i[k] \cup r_j[k]|}, \quad (1)$$

where $|r_i[k]|$ is the token-set size of $r_i[k]$.

For edit similarity, we first compute their edit distance, which is the minimum number of edit operations (insertion, deletion, substitution) required to transform one string to the other, and then compute the edit similarity as below.

$$s^k_{ij} = \text{EDS}(r_i[k], r_j[k])) = 1 - \frac{\text{ED}(r_i[k], r_j[k])}{\max(|r_i[k]|, |r_j[k]|)}, \quad (2)$$

where EDS(ED) is the edit similarity (distance) function.

For example, we use the edit similarity on attributes $\mathcal{A}_1$ and $\mathcal{A}_4$, and Jaccard on attributes $\mathcal{A}_2$ and $\mathcal{A}_3$. For instance, $s^1_{12} = 1 - \frac{9}{33} = 0.72$, and $s^2_{12} = \frac{2}{5} = 0.4$. As discussed in Section 2.2, we do not need to consider pairs whose similarities are smaller than a similarity bound τ, as they have small probabilities to be the same entity. Formally, we only consider the *similar pair* p_{ij} such that (1) $s_{ij} = \text{JAC}(r_i, r_j) \geq \tau$ for Jaccard, where $\text{JAC}(r_i, r_j)$ is the Jaccard similarity on the token sets of r_i and r_j ; or (2) $s_{ij} = \text{EDS}(r_i, r_j) \geq \tau$ for edit similarity, where $\text{EDS}(r_i, r_j)$ is the edit similarity on records r_i and r_j. The similar record pairs with $\tau = 0.2$ are shown in Table 2. If $s^k_{ij} < \tau$, we set $s^k_{ij} = 0$ for simplicity.

Partial Order. We define a partial order on record pairs. Given two pairs $p_{ij} = (r_i, r_j)$, $p_{i'j'} = (r_{i'}, r_{j'})$, $p_{ij} \succeq p_{i'j'}$, if (r_i, r_j) has no smaller similarities than $(r_{i'}, r_{j'})$ on every attribute. $p_{ij} \succ p_{i'j'}$, if $p_{ij} \succeq p_{i'j'}$ and (r_i, r_j) has larger similarities on at least one attribute than $(r_{i'}, r_{j'})$. Formally,

$$p_{ij} \succeq p_{i'j'} \quad \text{if } s^k_{ij} \geq s^k_{i'j'} \text{ for } 1 \leq k \leq m \quad (3)$$

$$p_{ij} \succ p_{i'j'} \quad \text{if } p_{ij} \succeq p_{i'j'} \text{ and } \exists k, s^k_{ij} > s^k_{i'j'} \quad (4)$$

For example, in Table 2, $p_{34} \succeq p_{35}$, $p_{27} \succ p_{34}$, and $p_{27} \succ p_{35}$.

3.2 Graph-Based Algorithm

We model the pairs as a graph based on the partial order.

DEFINITION 2 (GRAPH MODEL). *Given a table $\mathcal{T}$, we build a directed acyclic graph $\mathcal{G} = (\mathcal{V}, \mathcal{E})$, where each vertex in $\mathcal{V}$ is a similar record pair. Given two pairs p_{ij} and $p_{i'j'}$, if $p_{ij} \succ p_{i'j'}$, there is a directed edge in $\mathcal{E}$ from p_{ij} to $p_{i'j'}$.*

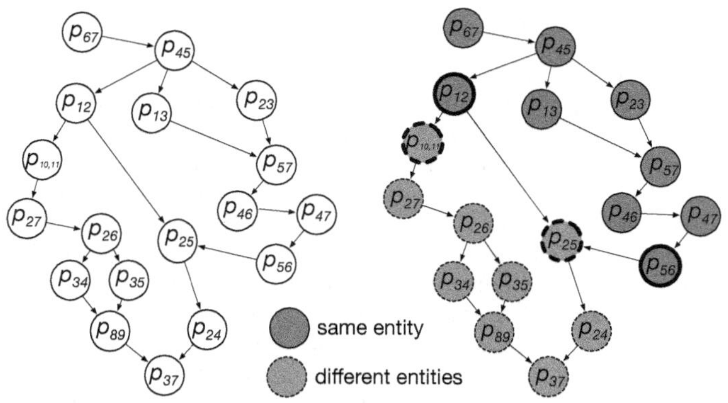

Figure 1: Partial Order and Graph Model.

Figure 1 shows the graph for the pairs in Table 1. In the figure, we do not show all the edges for illustration purpose: given two vertices, if there is already a path between them, we do not show the direct edge between them. For example, there should be an edge between p_{67} and p_{12}, but we omit it as there is already a path from p_{67} to p_{12}.

Graph Coloring. Each vertex in $\mathcal{G}$ has two possibilities: (1) they refer to the same entity and we color it GREEN; (2) they refer to different entities and we color it RED. Initially each vertex is uncolored. Our goal is to utilize the crowd to color all vertices. A straightforward method is to take the record pair on each vertex as a question and ask workers to answer the question, i.e. whether the two records in the pair refer to the same entity. If a worker thinks that the two records on the vertex refer to the same entity, the worker returns `Yes`; `No` otherwise. For each pair, to tolerate the noisy results from workers, we assign it to multiple workers, say 5. Based on the workers' results, we get a voted answer on each vertex. If majority workers vote `Yes`, we color it GREEN; otherwise we color it RED. Next, we interchangeably use vertex, pair and question if the context is clear.

Obviously this method is rather expensive as there are many vertices on the graph. To address this issue, we propose an effective coloring framework to reduce the number of questions. Algorithm 1 shows the pseudo code. It first computes the partial orders between pairs and constructs a graph (line 1). Then it selects an uncolored vertex p_{ij} (line 3) and asks workers to answer `Yes` or `No` on the vertex, (1) If majority workers vote `Yes`, we not only color p_{ij} GREEN, but also color all of its ancestors GREEN (line 5). In other words, for $p_{i'j'} \succ p_{ij}$, we also take $r_{i'}$ and $r_{j'}$ as the same entity. This is because $p_{i'j'}$ has larger similarity on every attribute than p_{ij}, and since r_i and r_j refer to the same entity (denoted by $r_i = r_j$), we deduce that $r_{i'} = r_{j'}$.
(2) If majority workers vote `No`, we not only color p_{ij} RED, but also color all of its descendants RED (line 7). In other words, for $p_{ij} \succ p_{i'j'}$, we also take $r_{i'}$ and $r_{j'}$ as different

Algorithm 1: A Partial-Order-Based Framework

```
  Input: T = {r_1, r_2 ··· , r_n}
  Output: All vertices are colored as GREEN or RED
1 Construct G = (V, E) based on partial orders;
2 while there exist uncolored vertices in V do
3     Select an uncolored vertex p_ij to ask workers;
4     if majority workers vote Yes then
5         color p_ij and p_i'j' (p_i'j' ≻ p_ij) GREEN;
6     else
7         color p_ij and p_i'j' (p_ij ≻ p_i'j') RED;
8 return colored V;
```

entities. This is because $p_{i'j'}$ has smaller similarity on every attribute than p_{ij}, and since r_i and r_j refer to different entities (denoted by $r_i \neq r_j$), we deduce that $r_{i'} \neq r_{j'}$.

If all the vertices have been colored, the algorithm terminates (line 7); otherwise, it selects an uncolored vertex and repeats the above steps (lines 2-7).

Obviously, this method can reduce the cost as we can avoid asking many unnecessary vertices. For example, consider the constructed graph in Figure 1. A naive method is to ask all eighteen pairs. However, if we first ask $p_{10,11}$, as majority workers vote No, we can color $p_{10,11}$ and its descendants p_{27}, p_{26}, p_{34}, p_{35}, p_{89} and p_{37} RED without needing to ask these descendants. Then if we select p_{56}, as majority workers vote Yes, we color p_{56} and its ancestors p_{46}, p_{47}, p_{57}, p_{23}, p_{45}, p_{67} and p_{13} GREEN without needing to ask them. In Section 5, we will show that we need to ask at least 4 questions (e.g., $p_{12}, p_{10,11}, p_{25}, p_{56}$) to color all vertices.

There are several challenges in this algorithm.

(1) Graph Construction. As there are large numbers of pairs, how to efficiently construct the graph? Can we reduce the graph size so as to reduce the number of questions?

(2) Question Selection. How to select the minimum number of vertices to ask in order to color all vertices?

(3) Error Tolerant. The coloring strategy and the workers may introduce errors. So how to tolerate the errors?

We address these challenges in the following sections.

4. GRAPH CONSTRUCTION

We first propose efficient graph-construction algorithms (Section 4.1) and then present grouping methods (Section 4.2).

4.1 Graph Construction Algorithms

Brute-Force Method. It enumerates every pair of vertices and checks whether they satisfy the partial order. If so, the algorithm adds an edge between them. The complexity of this method is $\mathcal{O}(|\mathcal{V}|^2)$. Obviously this method is rather expensive, especially if there are a large number of vertices.

Quicksort-Based Method. Quicksort is an efficient algorithm for the sorting problem and it can be extended to construct the graph. We first randomly select a vertex p_{ij} as pivot, and then split other vertices into three disjoint parts by comparing them with p_{ij}:

(1) *Parent Vertex Set:* $\mathcal{P}(p_{ij}) = \{p_{i'j'} | p_{i'j'} \succ p_{ij}\}$. For each $p_{i'j'}$ in $\mathcal{P}(p_{ij})$, we add an edge from $p_{i'j'}$ to p_{ij};

(2) *Child Vertex Set:* $\mathcal{C}(p_{ij}) = \{p_{i'j'} | p_{ij} \succ p_{i'j'}\}$. For each $p_{i'j'}$ in $\mathcal{C}(p_{ij})$, we add an edge from p_{ij} to $p_{i'j'}$;

(3) *Incomparable Vertex Set:* $\mathcal{U}(p_{ij}) = \mathcal{V} - \mathcal{P}(p_{ij}) - \mathcal{C}(p_{ij}) = \{p_{i'j'} | p_{ij} \not\succ p_{i'j'} \ \& \ p_{i'j'} \not\succ p_{ij}\}$. For each $p_{i'j'}$, there is no edge between p_{ij} and $p_{i'j'}$, as they are incomparable.

Obviously, $\forall p \in \mathcal{P}(p_{ij}), p' \in \mathcal{C}(p_{ij}), p \succ p'$, and thus we do not need to compare the pairs in $\mathcal{P}(p_{ij}) \times \mathcal{C}(p_{ij})$. Then, we consider the pairs in $(\mathcal{P}(p_{ij}) \cup \mathcal{U}(p_{ij})) \times (\mathcal{P}(p_{ij}) \cup \mathcal{U}(p_{ij}))$ and $(\mathcal{C}(p_{ij}) \cup \mathcal{U}(p_{ij})) \times (\mathcal{C}(p_{ij}) \cup \mathcal{U}(p_{ij}))$. To add edges between these pairs, we can recursively utilize the above method.[1] The worst-case complexity of this method is also $\mathcal{O}(|\mathcal{V}|^2)$ if all the vertices are incomparable. However, this method has better performance than brute-force in practice, because it can prune many unnecessary pairs (e.g., $\mathcal{P}(p_{ij}) \times \mathcal{C}(p_{ij})$).

Index-Based Method. The quicksort-based method still has poor performance for large datasets. To address this issue, we propose an index-based method. As the similarity s_{ij}^k is a numerical value, we can utilize geometric relationship to compare two pairs. For simplicity, we first assume there are two attributes ($m = 2$). So the similarity of p_{ij} has two components s_{ij}^1 and s_{ij}^2. Therefore, we can map each vertex to a point in a two-dimensional coordinate as shown in Figure 2(a).

If we want to find the child set of p_{ij}, $\mathcal{C}(p_{ij}) = \{p_{i'j'} | p_{ij} \succ p_{i'j'}\}$, we report the left-bottom vertices (i.e., vertices in the rectangle). Similarity, if we compute $\mathcal{P}(p_{ij}) = \{p_{i'j'} | p_{i'j'} \succ p_{ij}\}$, we report the top-right vertices. We can utilize the 2-dimensional range trees to achieve this goal [10].

Range Search Tree Construction. We first construct a first-level balanced binary tree based on s_{ij}^1 for all vertices as shown in Figure 2(b), where leaves are vertices in $\mathcal{V}$ and the internal nodes are guided search values. (There are multiple pairs in a node because they have the same similarity. For example, p_{34}, p_{35} are in the same node, because $s_{34}^1 = s_{35}^1 = 0.39$.) The value of a node is the largest s_{ij}^1 for all vertices in its left subtree, and thus the s_{ij}^1 values of vertices under the left subtree are not larger than the value of this node; while the s_{ij}^1 values of vertices under its right subtree are larger than the value. We can build the binary tree in a bottom-up way. For each internal node, we construct the second-level balanced binary tree based on s_{ij}^2 for vertices under this node.

Reporting $\mathcal{C}(p_{ij})$ with Range Search Tree. Given a vertex p_{ij}, we use the range search tree to report $\mathcal{C}(p_{ij})$. We first find the tree nodes whose descendants' similarities on $\mathcal{A}_1$ are not larger than s_{ij}^1 using the first-level tree. For each of such *qualified* nodes on $\mathcal{A}_1$, we visit its second-level tree and find the nodes whose descendants' similarities on $\mathcal{A}_2$ are not larger than s_{ij}^2. Then the vertices under these nodes are added into $\mathcal{C}(p_{ij})$. Next we discuss how to find such qualified nodes in the first-level tree and the same techniques can be used to search the second-level tree.

To find the qualified nodes on $\mathcal{A}_1$, we search the first-level tree from the root. For each node, (1) If its value is not larger than s_{ij}^1, (1.1) if it is a leaf, it is a qualified node; (1.2) if it is not a leaf, the similarities of all the vertices under its left child on attribute $\mathcal{A}_1$ are not larger than s_{ij}^1, and its left child is a qualified node. Next we recursively process its right child; (2) If its value is larger than s_{ij}^1, (2.1) if it is a leaf, we prune it; (2.2) if it is not a leaf, we prune its right subtree as the similarities of all the vertices under its right child on attribute $\mathcal{A}_1$ must be larger than s_{ij}^1. Next we recursively process its left child. Iteratively, we can identify all qualified nodes on $\mathcal{A}_1$. This method accesses at most $\log(|\mathcal{V}|)$ nodes in the first-level tree.

For example, suppose we want to compute $\mathcal{C}(p_{12})$ where $s_{12}^1 = 0.72$ and $s_{12}^2 = 0.4$. We first compare s_{12}^1 with the root $s_{56}^1 = 0.63$. As $s_{12}^1 > s_{56}^1$, its left child (i.e., p_{26}) is

[1] Note to avoid duplicately comparing two pairs in $\mathcal{U}(p_{ij})$, we can only select pivots from $\mathcal{C}(p_{ij})$ and $\mathcal{P}(p_{ij})$.

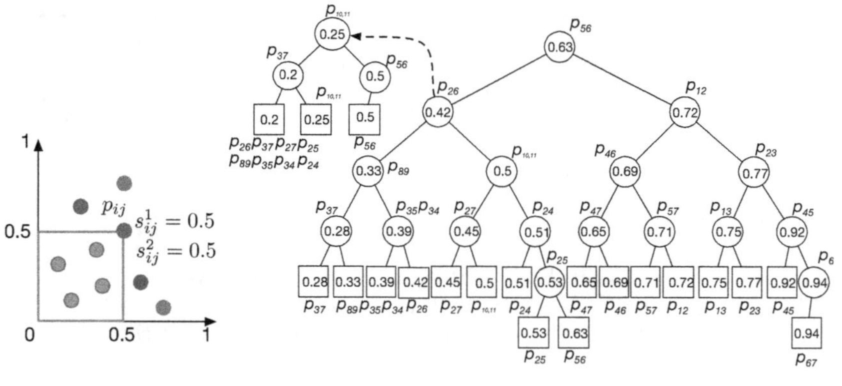

(a) $2d$ coordinate (b) Rang Search Tree

Figure 2: Index-based Graph Construction.

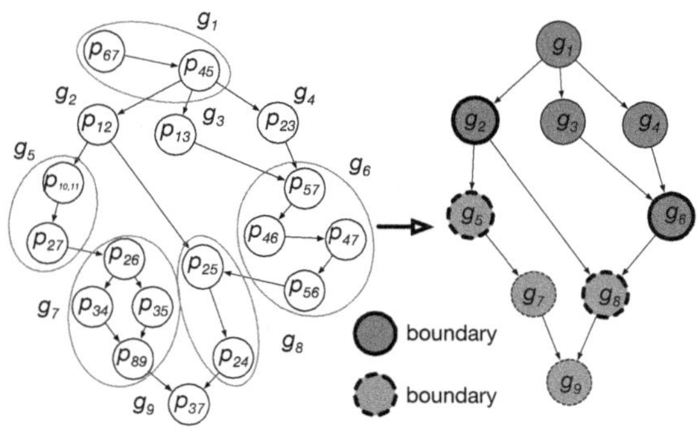

Figure 3: Vertex Grouping.

a qualified node. Next we go to the right child p_{12}. As $s^1_{12} = s^1_{12}$, we visit its left child p_{46}. As $s^1_{12} > s^1_{46}$, its left child p_{47} is a qualified node. Next we go to the right child p_{57}. As $s^1_{12} > s^1_{57}$, its left child p_{57} is a qualified node and we go to its right node p_{12}. As p_{12} is a leaf, it is a qualified node. Next for each qualified node $(p_{26}, p_{47}, p_{57}, p_{12})$, we check it on the second attribute. Take p_{26} as an example. As $s^2_{12} = 0.4$ is larger than the root's value, its left child p_{37} is a qualified node. We then visit its right child p_{56}. As $s^2_{12} \le s^2_{56}$, we go to its left child which is a leaf. As the value is larger than s^2_{12}, we prune it. Thus the pairs under node p_{37} are added into $\mathcal{C}(p_{12})$.

Building The Graph with Range Search Tree. For each vertex p_{ij}, we use the range search tree to find $\mathcal{C}(p_{ij})$ and add vertices in $\mathcal{C}(p_{ij})$ as the children of p_{ij}. Then we can build the graph. It is straightforward to generalize 2-dimensional range trees to m-dimensional range trees.

Complexity. Both the time and space complexities of constructing the tree is $\mathcal{O}(|\mathcal{V}|\log^{m-1}|\mathcal{V}|)$. The time complexity of computing $\mathcal{C}(p_{ij})$ is $\mathcal{O}(\log^m|\mathcal{V}| + |\mathcal{C}(p_{ij})|)$, where $|\mathcal{C}(p_{ij})|$ is the size of $\mathcal{C}(p_{ij})$. After using the fractional cascading technique [10], the complexity is reduced to $\mathcal{O}(\log^{m-1}|\mathcal{V}| + |\mathcal{C}(p_{ij})|)$. Thus the overall time complexity of constructing the graph is $\mathcal{O}(|\mathcal{V}|\log^{m-1}|\mathcal{V}| + |\mathcal{E}|)$.

4.2 Vertex Grouping

Note that some vertices have very close similarities and we can combine them to reduce the graph size, which not only reduces the cost but also saves the graph construction cost. For example, p_{67} and p_{45} have close similarities on the four attributes, i.e., p_{67}:(0.94, 1, 1, 1) and p_{45}:(0.92, 1, 1, 1) as shown in Table 2. Thus we can combine them as a single vertex. Next we formulate the problem.

DEFINITION 3 (VERTEX GROUP). *Given a threshold ε, a subset $g \subseteq \mathcal{V}$ is called a vertex group, if for any pairs p_{ij} and $p_{i'j'}$ in g, $|s^k_{ij} - s^k_{i'j'}| \le \varepsilon$ for $1 \le k \le m$.*

As the similarities between different pairs in a group should not have large gap, we use ε to set a constraint. For example, suppose $\varepsilon = 0.1$. $\{p_{26}, p_{34}, p_{35}\}$ is a group as the difference of their similarities on every attribute is smaller than 0.1 (p_{26}:(0.42,0.2,1,0), p_{34}:(0.39,0.2,1,0), p_{35}:(0.39,0.2,1,0)).

Next we partition the vertices into different groups.

DEFINITION 4 (GROUPING STRATEGY). *Given a set of vertices $\mathcal{V}$, a grouping strategy is a partition of $\mathcal{V}$ to generate a set of groups $g_1, g_2, \dots, g_x$, which satisfies,*
(1) Complete: For any $p_{ij} \in \mathcal{V}$, $\exists g_t, p_{ij} \in g_t$; and
(2) Disjoint: For any two groups g_i, g_j, $g_i \cap g_j = \phi$.

For example, consider the eighteen pairs in Table 1. Given threshold $\varepsilon = 0.1$, the groups $\{p_{67}, p_{45}\}$, $\{p_{12}\}$, $\{p_{13}\}$, $\{p_{23}\}$, $\{p_{10,11}, p_{27}\}$, $\{p_{57}, p_{47}, p_{46}, p_{56}\}$, $\{p_{24}, p_{25}\}$, $\{p_{26}, p_{34}, p_{89}, p_{35}\}$, $\{p_{37}\}$ satisfy the two constraints.

Partial Order on Groups. We can define the partial order on the groups. For any two groups g_i and g_j,

$$g_i \succeq g_j \quad \text{if } \forall p \in g_i, p' \in g_j, p \succeq p' \tag{5}$$
$$g_i \succ g_j \quad \text{if } \forall p \in g_i, p' \in g_j, p \succ p' \tag{6}$$

Let $g^k.l/g^k.u$ denote the smallest/largest similarity of pairs in g on $\mathcal{A}_k$, i.e., $g^k.l = \min_{p_{ij}\in g} s^k_{ij}$ and $g^k.u = \max_{p_{ij}\in g} s^k_{ij}$. We can prove that if $g^k_i.l \ge g^k_j.u$ for $1 \le k \le m$, $g_i \succeq g_j$; if $g^k_i.l \ge g^k_j.u$ and $\exists k\ g^k_i.l > g^k_j.u$, $g_i \succ g_j$. Thus we can use $g^k_i.l$ and $g^k_j.u$ to easily determine the partial orders of two groups. Given a set of groups, if $g_i \succ g_j$, we add an edge from g_i to g_j. Then we can construct a grouped graph.

DEFINITION 5 (GROUPED GRAPH). *Given a set of vertices $\mathcal{V}$ and a set of groups $g_1, g_2, \dots, g_x$ generated using the grouping strategy, we construct a grouped graph $\mathcal{G}' = (\mathcal{V}', \mathcal{E}')$, where each vertex in $\mathcal{V}'$ is a group, and there is an edge in $\mathcal{E}'$ from g_i to g_j if $g_i \succ g_j$.*

Coloring The Grouped Graph. We ask workers to color the grouped graph. If a group is selected to ask, we randomly select a pair in the group and take the answer of this pair as the answer of the group. Then we utilize our coloring algorithm (Section 3.2) to color the grouped graph.

Optimal Group Generation. There are multiple grouping strategies. We quantify how good a grouping strategy is. Obviously, the smaller the number of vertices in the grouped graph is, the lower the cost is. Thus we aim to generate the minimum number of groups.

DEFINITION 6. *(Optimal Group Generation). Given a set of vertices $\mathcal{V}$ and a threshold ε, we aim to generate the minimum number of groups.*

We can prove that the optimal group generation problem is NP-hard as proved in Theorem 1.

THEOREM 1. *The optimal group generation problem is NP-Hard. (See Appendix D.1 for the proof.)*

We propose a greedy algorithm and a heuristic algorithm.

Greedy Algorithm. The basic idea is that we first generate all the maximal groups, which are defined as below.

DEFINITION 7 (MAXIMAL GROUP). *A group g is called a maximal group if $\forall p_{ij} \in \mathcal{V} - g$, $g \cup \{p_{ij}\}$ is not a group (i.e., it does not satisfy the ε-constraint in Definition 3.).*

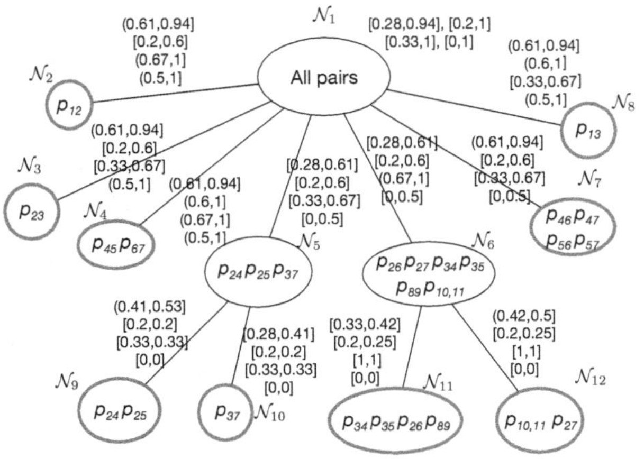

Figure 4: The Group Tree.

For example, $\{p_{26}, p_{34}, p_{35}\}$ is a group, but it is not a maximal group, because if we add p_{89}, $\{p_{26}, p_{34}, p_{35}, p_{89}\}$ is still a group satisfying Definition 3, which contradicts with Definition 7. $\{p_{26}, p_{34}, p_{35}, p_{89}\}$ is a maximal group, as we cannot add any pair to form a new group.

Next we introduce a greedy algorithm (see more details in Appendix A). We first generate the set of all maximal groups, denoted by $\mathcal{M}$. Then we greedily pick the largest group g in $\mathcal{M}$ with the maximum number of vertices. For each g_i in $\mathcal{M}$, we remove the vertices in g from g_i and update g_i to g_i-g. (If g_i-g is empty, we remove it from $\mathcal{M}$.) Next we iteratively pick the largest group from $\mathcal{M}$ until $\mathcal{M}$ is empty. This greedy algorithm has a $\ln(|\mathcal{V}|)$ approximation ratio. However it is expensive to generate the maximal groups and the complexity of this greedy algorithm is $\mathcal{O}(|\mathcal{V}|^m)$.

For example, we want to group the vertices in Figure 1. Firstly, we generate all the maximal groups $\mathcal{M} = \{\{p_{67}, p_{45}\}, \{p_{12}\}, \{p_{13}\}, \{p_{23}\}, \{p_{10,11}, p_{27}, p_{26}\}, \{p_{27}, p_{26}, p_{34}, p_{35}\}, \{p_{26}, p_{34}, p_{35}, p_{89}\}, \{p_{47}, p_{57}, p_{46}, p_{56}\}, \{p_{24}, p_{25}\}, \{p_{37}\}\}$. Then we select the largest group $\{p_{27}, p_{26}, p_{34}, p_{35}\}$ from the maximal group set as a group. Next we remove vertices in it from other maximal groups. Now $\mathcal{M} = \{\{p_{67}, p_{45}\}, \{p_{12}\}, \{p_{13}\}, \{p_{23}\}, \{p_{10,11}\}, \{p_{89}\}, \{p_{47}, p_{57}, p_{46}, p_{56}\}, \{p_{24}, p_{25}\}, \{p_{37}\}\}$. Then we select the largest group. Finally the groups are $\mathcal{M} = \{\{p_{67}, p_{45}\}, \{p_{12}\}, \{p_{13}\}, \{p_{23}\}, \{p_{10,11}\}, \{p_{27}, p_{26}, p_{34}, p_{35}\}, \{p_{89}\}, \{p_{47}, p_{57}, p_{46}, p_{56}\}, \{p_{24}, p_{25}\}, \{p_{37}\}\}$.

Split-Based Algorithm. As the greedy algorithm is expensive, we propose an efficient algorithm. The basic idea is that we first take all the pairs as a group, and if any attribute does not satisfy the threshold constraint, we partition the group based on this attribute. The pseudo code is shown in Algorithm 2. Formally, we build a tree structure and the root is $\mathcal{N}_1 = \mathcal{V}$. Let $\mathcal{N}_1^i.l/\mathcal{N}_1^i.u$ denote the minimal/maximal similarity of pairs in $\mathcal{N}_1$ on attribute $\mathcal{A}_i$. If $\mathcal{N}_1^i.u - \mathcal{N}_1^i.l > \varepsilon$, we split $\mathcal{N}_1$ based on $\mathcal{A}_i$ and generate two ranges $[\mathcal{N}_1^i.l, \frac{\mathcal{N}_1^i.l+\mathcal{N}_1^i.u}{2}]$, $(\frac{\mathcal{N}_1^i.l+\mathcal{N}_1^i.u}{2}, \mathcal{N}_1^i.u]$; otherwise, we do not split $\mathcal{N}_1$ based on this attribute. Suppose we split $\mathcal{N}_1$ based on $\mathcal{A}_{i_1}, \mathcal{A}_{i_1}, \ldots, \mathcal{A}_{i_t}$. We generate 2^t children of $\mathcal{N}_1$ by enumerating the two ranges of these attributes. For each node, we add the pairs that fall in the corresponding ranges into the node. If a node cannot be split on any attribute, it is a leaf. Finally the groups on leaves are the result.

For example, we walk through our algorithm on the records in Table 2. Suppose $\varepsilon = 0.1$. Figure 4 shows the group tree. Firstly, the root $\mathcal{N}_1$ ($[\mathcal{N}_1^1.l, \mathcal{N}_1^1.u]$,$[\mathcal{N}_1^2.l, \mathcal{N}_1^2.u]$, $[\mathcal{N}_1^3.l, \mathcal{N}_1^3.u]$, $[\mathcal{N}_1^4.l, \mathcal{N}_1^4.u]$) is denoted as ([0.28, 0.94], [0.2, 1], [0.33, 1], [0, 1]) in Figure 4. As $\mathcal{N}_1^i.u - \mathcal{N}_1^i.l > \varepsilon$ for $i \in [1, 4]$, we split $[\mathcal{N}_1^1.l, \mathcal{N}_1^1.u]$, $[\mathcal{N}_1^2.l, \mathcal{N}_1^2.u]$, $[\mathcal{N}_1^3.l, \mathcal{N}_1^3.u]$ and $[\mathcal{N}_1^4.l, \mathcal{N}_1^4.u]$ into

---

Algorithm 2: Vertex Grouping: `Split`

```
Input: G = (V, E)
Output: A set of groups g_1, g_2, ..., g_x
N_1 ← V; Priority queue Q = {N_1};
while Q is not empty do
    Pop node N_i from Q;
    for k ∈ [1, m] do
        if N_i^k.u − N_i^k.l > ε then
            Split N_i based on A_k ;
    if N_i is split by A_{i_1}, A_{i_2}, ..., A_{i_t} then
        Generate 2^t children of N_i;
        Move pairs in N_i into corresponding children;
        Add these children into Q;
    else
        N_i is a leaf and taken as a group g;
return the groups on the leaves;
```

$\langle[0.28, 0.61], (0.61, 0.94]\rangle$, $\langle[0.2, 0.6], (0.6, 1]\rangle$, $\langle[0.33, 0.67], (0.67, 1]\rangle$ and $\langle[0, 0.5]\ (0.5, 1]\rangle$ respectively. Then we move each pair in $\mathcal{N}_1$ into the 2^4 children (empty children are removed). For $i \in [1, 4]$, s_{45}^i and s_{67}^i are in the range of (0.61, 0.94], (0.6, 1], (0.67, 1], (0.5, 1], and p_{45} and p_{67} are added into $\mathcal{N}_4$. Then we calculate $\mathcal{N}_4^i.l, \mathcal{N}_4^i.u$ and get ([0.92, 0.94], [1, 1], [1, 1], [1, 1]). As each range is smaller than ε, $\mathcal{N}_4 = \{p_{45}, p_{67}\}$ is a leaf. Next, we move $\{p_{24}, p_{25}, p_{37}\}$ into $\mathcal{N}_5$ ([0.28, 0.53], [0.2, 0.2], [0.33, 0.33], [0, 0]). It is not a group and split again. As $[\mathcal{N}_5^2.u - \mathcal{N}_5^2.l] < \varepsilon$, $[\mathcal{N}_5^3.u - \mathcal{N}_5^3.l] < \varepsilon$ and $[\mathcal{N}_5^4.u - \mathcal{N}_5^4.l] < \varepsilon$, we split $\mathcal{N}_5^1$ and get two leaves $\mathcal{N}_9$ and $\mathcal{N}_{10}$. At last, we get 9 groups (as shown in Figure 3).

Complexity. The tree has at most $\log \frac{1}{\varepsilon}$ levels. Thus the time complexity of constructing the tree is $\mathcal{O}(|\mathcal{V}| \log \frac{1}{\varepsilon})$.

5. QUESTION SELECTION

An important problem is to select the minimum number of vertices as questions to color all vertices. We first formulate the question-selection problem (Section 5.1,) and then propose a serial algorithm that selects one vertex in each iteration (Section 5.2) and parallel algorithms that select multiple vertices in each iteration (Section 5.3).

5.1 Optimal Vertex Selection

We first assume that (1) if a vertex is GREEN, then all of its ancestors are GREEN; and (2) if a vertex is RED, then all of its descendants are RED. We will discuss how to support the case that the two conditions do not hold in Section 6.

DEFINITION 8 (OPTIMAL GRAPH COLORING). *Given a graph, the optimal graph coloring problem aims to select the minimum number of vertices as questions to color all the vertices using the coloring strategy.*

For example, in Figure 3, if we sequetially select vertices g_8, g_7, g_5, g_2, g_3, g_4 and g_6, we ask 7 questions. The optimal crowdsourced vertices are g_2, g_5, g_6 and g_8 (highlighted by bold circles), because the colors of these vertices cannot be deduced based on the colors of other vertices. Next we study how to identify the optimal vertices. We first introduce a notation for ease of presentation.

DEFINITION 9 (BOUNDARY VERTEX). *A vertex is a boundary vertex if its color cannot be deduced based on other vertices' colors. There are four cases: (1) all of its parents have different colors with the vertex; (2) all of its children have different colors with the vertex; (3) it has no child and its color is* GREEN*; or (4) it has no parent and its color is* RED.

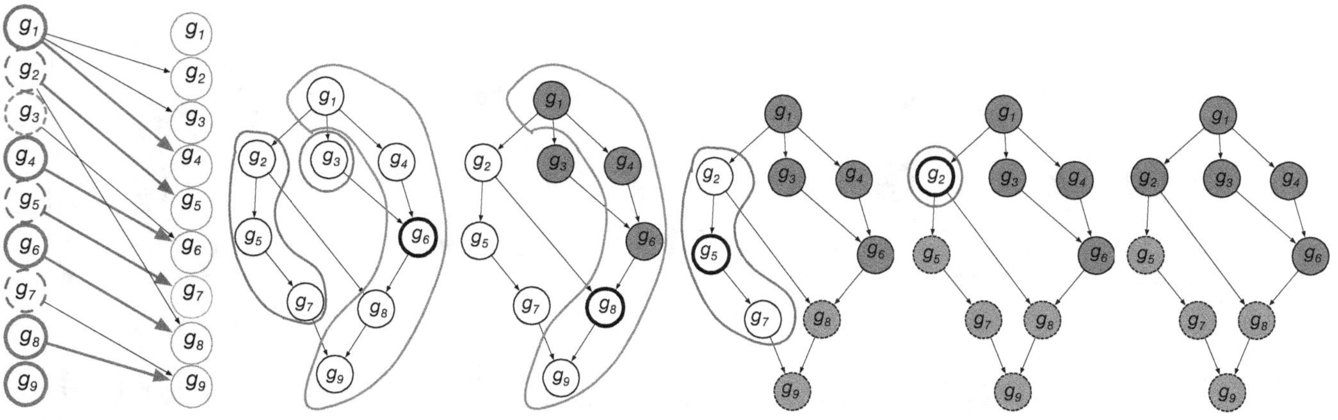

(a) Disjoint Paths (b) 3 Paths, Ask g_6 (c) Ask g_8 (d) Ask g_5 (e) Ask g_2 (f) All Colored

Figure 5: Single-Path Method.

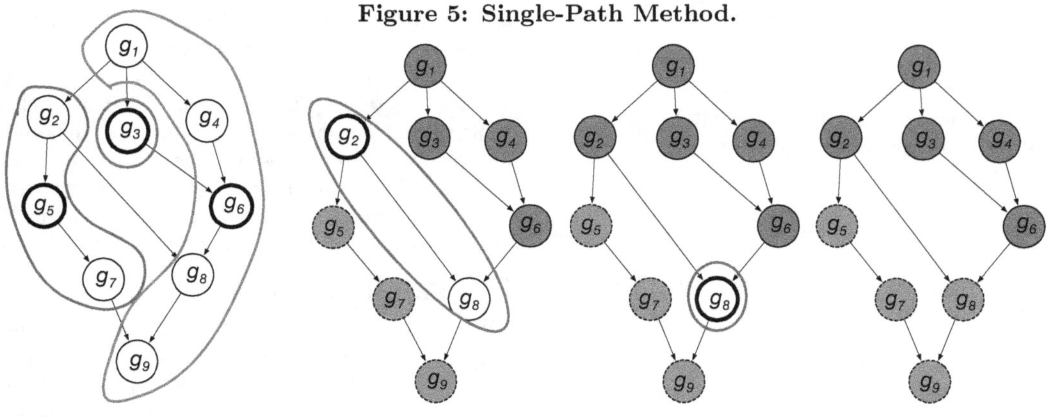

(a) Ask g_5, g_3, g_6 (b) Ask g_2 (c) Ask g_8 (d) All Colored

Figure 6: Multi-Path Method.

For example, g_6 is a boundary vertex as its child g_8 has different color with g_6. g_4 is not a boundary vertex as its child g_6 has the same color and g_4's color can be deduced based on g_6's color.

We can prove that all the boundary vertices must be asked, because their colors cannot be deduced. Thus the number of asked vertices using any algorithm is not smaller than the number of boundary vertices. However, as we do not know the ground truth, we cannot identify the boundary vertices in advance. To address this problem, we propose effective algorithms to identify the boundary vertices with theoretical guarantee.

5.2 Serial Algorithm

Comparable Vertices. Given any two vertices p_{ij}, $p_{i'j'}$, if they are *comparable*, i.e., $p_{ij} \succ p_{i'j'}$ or $p_{i'j'} \succ p_{ij}$, we may deduce p_{ij}'s color based on $p_{i'j'}$'s color, and vice versa. Obviously, two comparable vertices must be on a (directed) path in the graph, and the vertices on a path are totally ordered (i.e., any two vertices are comparable). Given a path, we can use a binary-search method to select the boundary vertices. Formally given a path, we first ask the mid-vertex on the path. (1) If the vertex is colored GREEN, its ancestors' colors can be deduced but its descendants' colors cannot be deduced, and thus we ask the mid-vertex between this vertex and the destination vertex of the path; (2) If the vertex is colored RED, its descendants' colors can be deduced but its ancestors' colors cannot be deduced, and thus we ask the mid-vertex between this vertex and the source vertex of the path. Iteratively, we can find the boundary vertices. For the path P with $|P|$ vertices, the number of asked vertices is $\mathcal{O}(\log|P|)$. This is optimal and cannot be improved in general. For example, $g_1 \rightsquigarrow g_4 \rightsquigarrow g_6 \rightsquigarrow g_8 \rightsquigarrow g_9$ is a path. We first ask the mid-vertex g_6. As g_6 is GREEN, we ask the mid-vertex between g_6 and g_9, i.e., g_8. As g_8 is RED, all the vertices are colored in the path.

Incomparable Vertices. If two vertices are incomparable, we cannot deduce one vertex's color based on the other vertex's color. Suppose there are $\mathcal{B}$ incomparable vertices (any two vertices are incomparable). We can divide the graph into $\mathcal{B}$ disjoint paths (i.e., any two paths have no common vertices). Then we can ask each path using the binary search method. As the maximum length of a path is $|\mathcal{V}|$, the number of asked vertices is $\mathcal{O}(\mathcal{B}\log|\mathcal{V}|)$. This is optimal and cannot be improved in general. This is because if $\mathcal{B} = 1$, we need to ask $\log|\mathcal{V}|$ vertices. For example, in Figure 5, we have 3 disjoint paths $g_1 \rightsquigarrow g_4 \rightsquigarrow g_6 \rightsquigarrow g_8 \rightsquigarrow g_9$, $g_2 \rightsquigarrow g_5 \rightsquigarrow g_7$, and g_3. We need to ask these paths using the binary-search algorithm.

Finding $\mathcal{B}$ Disjoint Paths. We transform the graph $\mathcal{G}$ into a bipartite graph $\mathcal{G}^b = ((\mathcal{V}_1^b, \mathcal{V}_2^b), \mathcal{E}^b)$, where $\mathcal{V}_1^b = \mathcal{V}_2^b = \mathcal{V}$ and there is an edge between $v_1 \in \mathcal{V}_1^b$ and $v_2 \in \mathcal{V}_2^b$ if there is an edge $(v_1, v_2) \in \mathcal{V}$. We find a maximal matching in $\mathcal{G}^b = ((\mathcal{V}_1^b, \mathcal{V}_2^b), \mathcal{E}^b)$, which is a maximal set of edges in $\mathcal{G}^b = ((\mathcal{V}_1^b, \mathcal{V}_2^b), \mathcal{E}^b)$ where any two edges do not share a common vertex in $\mathcal{V}_1^b$ and $\mathcal{V}_2^b$, i.e., for any two edges (v, v'), (u, u') in the matching, $v \neq u$ and $v' \neq u'$. Obviously any two edges in the matching sharing the same vertex in $\mathcal{V}$ must be on the same path, i.e., for any two edges (v, v'), (u, u') in the matching, if $v' = u$, then $v \rightsquigarrow v' = u \rightsquigarrow u'$ must be on the same path based on the partial order. Note that the maximal matching can be computed in $\mathcal{O}(\mathcal{B}|\mathcal{V}|^2)$[4]. Based

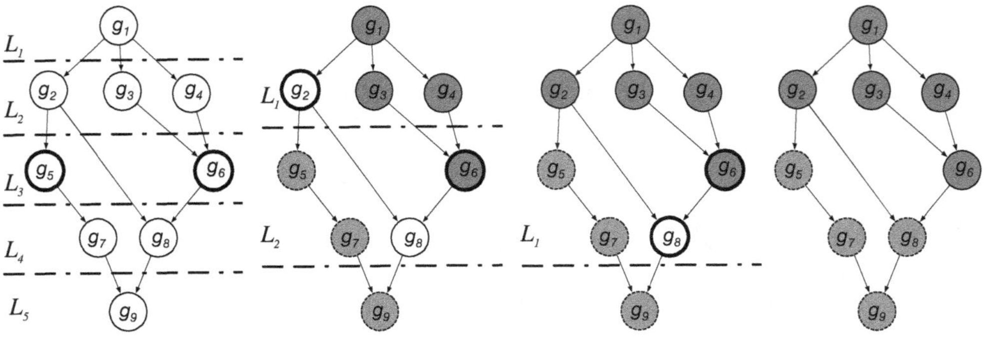

(a) Ask g_5, g_6 (b) Ask g_2 (c) Ask g_8 (d) All Colored

Figure 7: Topological-Sorting Based Method.

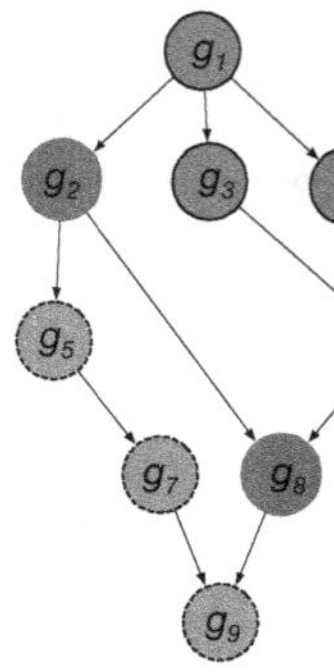

Figure 8: Error-Tolerant.

Algorithm 3: Question Selection: `SinglePath`

Input: $\mathcal{G} = (\mathcal{V}, \mathcal{E})$
Output: All vertices in $\mathcal{V}$ are colored as GREEN or RED
while *there exist uncolored vertices in* $\mathcal{V}$ **do**
  Compute disjoint paths using maximal matching;
  Color the longest path using binary search;
  Remove the colored vertices;
return *colored* $\mathcal{V}$;

---

on this idea, we utilize the maximal matching to find the $\mathcal{B}$ disjoint paths as follows.

Let $\mathcal{Y}$ denote the maximal matching, $\mathcal{Y}_1$ denote the set of the first vertices in $\mathcal{Y}$ and $\mathcal{Y}_2$ denote the set of the second vertices in $\mathcal{Y}$. Then $\mathcal{V}_2^b - \mathcal{Y}$ is the set of vertices that have no in-edges, and we can take them as the first vertex of a path. For each such vertex v, if it has an edge (v, v'), we take v' as the second vertex in the path. Then we check whether v' has an edge (v', v''). Iteratively, we can find the path starting at v. The paths computed in our method satisfy: disjoint, complete and minimal, and the correctness is guaranteed by the following theorem.

THEOREM 2. *The set of paths found by the maximal matching of $\mathcal{G}^b$ satisfy:*
(1) Disjoint: any two paths do not share a vertex;
(2) Complete: the paths contain all the vertices;
(3) Minimal: the size is exactly $\mathcal{B}$ and is not larger than the size of any other set of paths satisfying (1) and (2).

PROOF. See Appendix D.2. The proof essentially follows the Fulkerson's proof of Dilworth theorem [6]. □

For example, consider the graph in Figure 3. We construct a bipartite graph as shown in Figure 5(a). As there is an edge from g_1 to g_3 in $\mathcal{G}$, there is an edge from g_1 in $\mathcal{V}_1^b$ to g_3 in $\mathcal{V}_2^b$. Thus $\mathcal{G}$ and $\mathcal{G}^b$ have the same number of edges. Then we find a maximal matching which is the set of the colored edges. The vertices g_1, g_2 and g_3 in $\mathcal{V}_2^b$ have no in-edges in the maximal matching. We compute the disjoint paths starting from them. From g_1 we get path $g_1 \rightsquigarrow g_4 \rightsquigarrow g_6 \rightsquigarrow g_8 \rightsquigarrow g_9$; from g_2 we get $g_2 \rightsquigarrow g_5 \rightsquigarrow g_7$; and g_3 itself is a path. Thus we get 3 disjoint paths.

SinglePath Algorithm. Then we propose a path-based question-selection algorithm. The pseudo code is shown in Algorithm 3. It first computes the $\mathcal{B}$ disjoint paths. Then it asks the longest path using the binary-search method, colors the graphs, and then removes the colored vertices. Next it recomputes the disjoint paths and asks the next longest path. Iteratively it can color all vertices. The complexity of this algorithm is $\mathcal{O}(\mathcal{B}|\mathcal{V}|^2)$.

For example, in Figure 5, we first identify the minimal disjoint paths as shown in Figure 5(a). Then we select the longest path (Figure 5(b)), ask the path using binary search. We first ask g_6 and color the graph based on the answers of asked vertices (Figure 5(c)). Next we ask g_8 and get Figure 5(d). Then we recompute the disjoint paths, ask mid-vertex of the longest path $g_2 \rightsquigarrow g_5 \rightsquigarrow g_7$ (Figure 5(d)), and color the graph (Figure 5(e)). Next as there is only one vertex left, we ask it and get the final result (Figure 5(f)). This method totally asks 4 vertices and involves 4 iterations.

5.3 Parallel Algorithm

If users do not care about the latency, the single-path algorithm is a good choice. However if the latency is very crucial, the single-path algorithm is not acceptable as it needs to post one question at a time on crowdsourcing platforms, which would result in a long time latency. To address this issue, we design parallel algorithms, which select multiple vertices and ask them together in each iteration.

5.3.1 Multi-Path Algorithm

We extend the path-based algorithm to support the parallel setting. The pseudo code is illustrated in Appendix B. We first identify the $\mathcal{B}$ disjoint paths and then ask their mid-vertices in parallel. Based on the answers on these vertices, we color the graph. Next we remove the colored vertices and repeat the above step until all the vertices are colored. Figure 6 shows an example. Note that the parallel algorithm may generate conflicts. For example, if g_i is colored GREEN and g_j is colored RED, then there is a conflict on g where $g \succ g_i$ and $g_j \succ g$, because g is deduced as GREEN based on g_i and deduced as RED based on g_j. To address this issue, we can use majority voting to vote g's color.

5.3.2 Topological-Sorting-Based Algorithm

In the multi-path algorithm, the asked vertices may have ancestor-descendent relationships, and thus it may ask unnecessary questions. For example, in Figure 6(a), we do not need to ask g_3 and g_6 together, as the color of g_3 can be deduced based on the color of g_6. To address this issue, we aim to ask independent vertices in each iteration.

To this end, we perform a topological sorting on the vertices. We first identify the set of vertices with zero in-degree, denoted by $\mathcal{L}_1$. Then we delete them from the graph and find another set of vertices whose in-degrees are zero, denoted by $\mathcal{L}_2$. We repeat this step until all vertices are deleted. Suppose there are $|\mathcal{L}|$ sets, $\mathcal{L}_1, \mathcal{L}_2, \cdots, \mathcal{L}_{|\mathcal{L}|}$. Obviously vertices in each $\mathcal{L}_i$ have no in-edges (as their in-degrees are 0) and thus can be taken as an independent set. Moreover, the vertices in the sets with small subscripts (e.g., $\mathcal{L}_1, \mathcal{L}_2$) are more

Algorithm 4: Question Selection:`TopologicalSorting`

```
Input: G = (V, E)
Output: All vertices in V are colored as GREEN or RED
while there exist uncolored vertices in V do
    Do a topological sorting on the uncolored vertices in
    G and obtain |L| sets, L_1, L_2, ..., L_{|L|};
    Ask workers to color vertices in L_{(|L|+1)/2};
return colored V;
```

likely to be colored GREEN and the vertices in the sets with large subscripts (e.g., $\mathcal{L}_{|\mathcal{L}|}$) are more likely to be colored RED, and thus we cannot deduce the colors of many uncolored vertices based on them. In other words, the boundary vertices are more likely to be in the middle sets. To this end, we first ask vertices in $\mathcal{L}_{\frac{|\mathcal{L}|+1}{2}}$.

Next we design a topological-sorting-based algorithm and Algorithm 4 illustrates the pseudo code. It first computes topological-sorted sets $\mathcal{L}_1, \mathcal{L}_2, \cdots, \mathcal{L}_{|\mathcal{L}|}$. Then it asks vertices in $\mathcal{L}_{\frac{|\mathcal{L}|+1}{2}}$ in parallel. Based on the results of these vertices, it colors the graph, removes the colored vertices, and repeats the above step. Iteratively it colors all vertices.

For example, we construct the topological structure as shown in Figure 7(a). $\mathcal{L}_1 = \{g_1\}$,$\mathcal{L}_2 = \{g_2, g_3, g_4\}$,$\mathcal{L}_3 = \{g_5, g_6\}$, $\mathcal{L}_4 = \{g_7, g_8\}$,$\mathcal{L}_5 = \{g_9\}$ and $|\mathcal{L}| = 5$. So we select $\mathcal{L}_3 = \{g_5, g_6\}$ and ask the vertices. After getting their answers, we obtain Figure 7(b). Then we compute the topological sorting on the graph of the uncolored vertices. Next, $\mathcal{L}_1 = \{g_2\}, \mathcal{L}_2 = \{g_8\}$. We ask g_2. After this iteration, only g_8 is uncolored. We ask it and get the final result (Figure 7(d)). This method asks 4 vertices and has 3 iterations.

6. TOLERATING ERRORS

There are two types of possible errors in our framework. The first is caused by workers' errors and the second is introduced by our coloring strategy. For example, suppose a vertex p_{ij} is actually RED. However the workers wrongly color it GREEN. This error is caused by workers. Consider p_{ij}'s ancestor, $p_{i'j'}$, whose color is RED. Our coloring strategy will wrongly color it GREEN based on partial order. This error is caused by our coloring strategy. Next we discuss how to address these errors.

Confidence of Workers' Answers. To tolerate workers' errors, we assign each vertex to multiple workers and aggregate their answers. There are many methods to compute the confidence of workers' answers, and we take majority voting as an example and any other techniques can be integrated into our method. Suppose each vertex is assigned to z workers and $y > \frac{z}{2}$ workers vote a consensus answer (e.g, `Yes`) and $z - y$ workers vote the other answer (e.g., `No`). The confidence of the voted answer is $c = \frac{y}{z}$.

Error-Tolerant Coloring Strategy. For each crowdsourced vertex, if the confidence of workers on this vertex is high, e.g, ≥ 0.8, we use our coloring strategy to color its ancestors or descendants; otherwise, we color it BLUE and do not color its ancestors or descendants. For the GREEN and RED pairs, we take them as ground truth as their answers have large confidences. Next we utilize them to color BLUE pairs.

We first need to compute the weights of different attributes which reflect the importance in determining the colors of each pair. Let P^g denote the set of GREEN pairs. For every $p_{ij} \in P^g$, if s^k_{ij} is large, then attribute $\mathcal{A}_k$ plays an important role to determine the color of p_{ij}, and we should assign it with a large weight; otherwise it is insignificant to determine the color of p_{ij}. To this end, we assign a weight ω_k for

Algorithm 5: Error-Tolerant

```
   Input: G = (V, E)
   Output: All vertices in V are colored as GREEN or RED
1  while there exist uncolored vertices in V do
2      Select a set of uncolored vertices to ask workers;
3      for each asked p_ij with an answer do
4          if confidence >= 0.8 then
5              color p_ij and its ancestors or descendents;
6          else color p_ij BLUE;
7  Generate histogram h_i and compute Pr_i;
8  for each p_i'j' colored BLUE in h_i do
9      if Pr_i > 0.5 then color p_i'j' GREEN;
10     else color p_i'j' RED;
11 return colored V;
```

each attribute $\mathcal{A}_k$ as below

$$\omega_k = \frac{\sum_{p_{ij} \in P^g} s^k_{ij}}{\sum_{p_{ij} \in P^g} \sum_{1 \leq t \leq m} s^t_{ij}}. \tag{7}$$

Then we compute a weighted similarity of p_{ij},

$$\hat{s}_{ij} = \sum_{k \in [1,m]} \omega_k \cdot s^k_{ij}. \tag{8}$$

Coloring The Pairs in Low-Confidence Groups. We use a histogram based method to color pairs in BLUE vertices [22, 25]. We first generate equi-depth histograms based on the weighted similarities of pairs in GREEN and RED vertices. Each histogram h_i contains a set of pairs within a similarity range. We count the number of GREEN pairs in h_i and compute the probability $\mathtt{Pr}_i$ that pairs in h_i should be colored GREEN, i.e., the number of GREEN pairs to the total number of pairs in h_i. Then we assign the pairs in BLUE vertices into the histograms and color them based on probability $\mathtt{Pr}_i$. For example, if a pair falls in a histogram with high probability of GREEN, the vertex is colored GREEN; otherwise RED. Algorithm 5 shows the pseudo code. It uses the coloring strategy only for the vertices with high-confidence answers (line 5) and utilizes the histograms to color the vertices with low-confidence answers (lines 7-10).

Recall the topological-sorting method in Figure 7(b). The workers return the answer of g_2 with a low confidence, and we color it BLUE and do another topological sorting among the rest groups, i.e., g_8. g_8 is colored BLUE as workers give a low confidence answer. We get Figure 8. Then we need to color pairs in g_2 and g_8 (i.e., p_{12}, p_{24}, p_{25}) based on the colored pairs. First, we calculate the attribute weight ω based on the pairs P^g =$\{p_{12}$, p_{67}, p_{45}, p_{23}, p_{46}, p_{56}, p_{47}, $p_{57}\}$ in the colored groups. Using Equation 7, we obtain ω ={0.32, 0.28, 0.21, 0.19}. Then we build 5 histograms with width 0.2 (see Appendix C). We compute $\hat{s}_{ij}$ of each colored pair by Equation 8 and assign it into the corresponding histogram. $\{p_{67}, p_{45}\}$ are assigned into h_5 ([0.8,1]). As all of them are colored GREEN, $\mathtt{Pr}_5 = 1$. $\{p_{23}, p_{13}\}$ are assigned into h_4 ([0.6,0.8)), and $\mathtt{Pr}_4 = 1$. $\{p_{46}, p_{57}, p_{47}, p_{56}, p_{10,11}, p_{26}, p_{27}\}$ are assigned into h_3 ([0.4,0.6)), and $\mathtt{Pr}_3 = \frac{4}{7} = 0.57$. $\{p_{37}$, p_{89}, p_{34}, $p_{35}\}$ are assigned into h_2 ([0.2,0.4)), and $\mathtt{Pr}_2 = 0$. Next we compute $\hat{s}_{ij}$ of p_{12}, p_{24} and p_{25}. For instance, $\hat{s}_{12} = 0.32 \times 0.72 + 0.28 \times 0.4 + 0.21 \times 1 + 0.19 \times 0.88 = 0.72$, so we assign it into h_4 and color it GREEN due to $\mathtt{Pr}_4 > 0.5$. Similarly, we color p_{24} and p_{25} RED.

7. EXPERIMENT

In this section, we evaluate our methods and report experimental results. The goals of our experiments include (1)

	#Records	#Attr	#Pairs	#Workers/Pair
Restaurant	858	4	5010	5
Cora	997	8	29510	5
ACMPub	66,879	4	204,000	5

Table 3: Three real-world Datasets.

evaluating our proposed techniques and (2) comparing our method with state-of-the-art approaches.

7.1 Experimental Setting

Datasets. We use three real-world datasets which are widely adopted by existing works [7, 22, 23, 24]. (1) `Restaurant`[2] is a restaurant dataset consisting of 858 restaurants with 752 different entities. The dataset has four attributes, Name, Address, City and Flavor. (2) `Cora`[3] is a dataset of research papers, which contains 997 records with 191 different entities. The dataset has 8 attributes: Author, Title, Journal, Year, Pages, Publisher, Type and Editor. (3) `ACMPub`[4] is a larger publication dataset consisting of 66,879 records with 5347 different entities. It has four attributes: Author, Title, Conference and Year. Table 3 shows the details.

Similarity Functions. We use three similarity functions, Jaccard, edit similarity and bigram Jaccard. For bigram, we generate bigrams for every attribute and compute Jaccard on bigram sets as the similarity, where a bigram is a substring with length 2 and a bigram set contains all the bigrams in an attribute. We use bigram by default.

Pruning. As `ACMPub` has 66,879 records, it will generate $\frac{66879*66878}{2} = 2,236,366,881$ pairs and it is rather expensive to consider all of them. Following previous work [24, 23], we compute a similarity score for each pair of records by Jaccard and prune pairs whose similarity scores are bellow 0.3. After pruning, there are 5010, 29510 and 204000 pairs left in `Restaurant`, `Cora` and `ACMPub` datasets respectively.

AMT Setting. We use Amazon Mechanical Turk (AMT). To ensure fair comparison between different algorithms, each question should be answered by the same workers. To this end, we crowdsource all pairs in each dataset to AMT and get their answers. If different algorithms ask the same pair, they will use the same answer. We assign each question to five workers and use the weighted majority voting to integrate the answers. We pack every ten pairs in a HIT and pay 10 cents for each HIT. We vary workers' accuracy which can be specified on AMT, where the worker accuracy is computed based on workers' approval rate in history at AMT.

Comparison. We compare with state-of-the-art methods, `ACD` [23], `Trans` [24] and `GCER` [25] on the same experimental setting. We get the source codes of `ACD` and `Trans` from the authors and implement `GCER` by ourselves.

Evaluation Metrics. For different methods, we compare the quality, the number of questions, the number of iterations, and the assignment time. For quality, we use F-measure, which is a combination of precision and recall. Suppose the set of pairs that refer to the same entity is S_T, and the set of pairs that an algorithm reports as the same entity is S_P. Then the precision is $p = \frac{|S_T \cap S_P|}{|S_P|}$, the recall is $r = \frac{|S_T \cap S_P|}{|S_T|}$, and the F-measure is $\frac{2pr}{p+r}$.

7.2 Evaluating Worker Accuracy

We compare our methods (`Power` without error-tolerant techniques and `Power+` with error-tolerant techniques) with state-of-the-art approaches `ACD` [23], `Trans` [24] and `GCER` [25]. We compare the number of iterations, the number of questions, and the quality. As `GCER` requires a parameter to tune the number of asked pairs, we set this parameter the same as `ACD`, i.e., the maximum number of questions among these algorithms. `GCER` asks 100 questions in each iteration. For our two algorithms, we use the split-based grouping algorithm to group the pairs and set the grouping threshold ε as 0.1, utilize the index-based method to construct the graph, and employ the topological-sorting algorithm to select questions. We evaluate our graph construction, grouping and question-selection techniques in Appendix E.

7.2.1 Real Exp: Evaluating Worker Accuracy

Existing studies [24, 22, 7] select the workers with approval rate above 95% or passing a qualification test to avoid malicious workers. To evaluate the robustness of the algorithms, we vary the workers' accuracy. In the real crowdsourcing platforms AMT, we can specify the worker accuracy by selecting the approval rate. We select three groups of workers, 70%-80% (70% in the figure), 80%-90% (80% in the figure) and above 90% (90% in the figure) respectively. For each group of workers, we ask them to answer our questions and compare different algorithms. Figures 9-11 show the results. We make the following observations.

Quality. Firstly, `Power+` outperforms `Power`, because `Power+` can tolerate workers' errors. With the increase of worker accuracy, the improvement decreases. This is because for higher worker accuracy, there are fewer errors and `Power+` has limited room to further improve the quality. Secondly, `Power+` achieves the same quality as state-of-the-art studies and even higher. Even for low-quality workers, our methods still achieve high quality, because (1) `Power+` can tolerate errors by not coloring unconfident vertices (and thus avoid enlarging the errors by a wrong coloring vertex); and (2) few pairs invalidate the partial order. Specifically, on the `Restaurant` dataset, as the tasks are very easy, most workers can correctly compare each pair, and thus all the methods achieve high quality. On the `Cora` dataset, `Power+` and `ACD` achieve much higher quality than `Trans` and `GCER` on all three groups of workers, because this dataset is harder and workers may return noisy results. `Trans` and `GCER` cannot tolerate workers' errors and moreover they may expand the error propagation due to the transitivity rules. On the `ACMPub` dataset, `Power+` and `ACD` still outperform other methods because both of them consider crowd's errors. Thirdly, with the increase of worker accuracy, the quality of all the algorithms increase, because workers return higher quality answers. Fourthly, even for workers with different accuracy, the algorithms achieve similar quality. This is because the worker accuracy on AMT is computed based on their accuracy on history tasks but not on our tasks. A worker will give higher quality on easy datasets, e.g., `Restaurant`, and lower quality on hard datasets, e.g., `Cora`. To address this issue, we conduct a simulation experiment in Section 7.2.2.

#Questions. Firstly, our two methods `Power` and `Power+` ask fewer questions than state-of-the-art methods, even by 2 orders of magnitude. This is because we can utilize the partial order to prune many pairs that do not need to be asked and use the grouping techniques to reduce the graph size. The partial order can prune the pairs with larger similarities than a GREEN vertex and the pairs with smaller similarities than a RED vertex, while the grouping technique can prune many pairs with similar similarities close to the

[2] http://www.cs.utexas.edu/users/ml/riddle/data/restaurant.tar.gz

[3] https://www.cics.umass.edu/smccallum/data/cora-refs.tar.gz

[4] http://dbs.uni-leipzig.de/en/research/projects/object_matching/fever/benchmark_datasets_for_entity_resolution

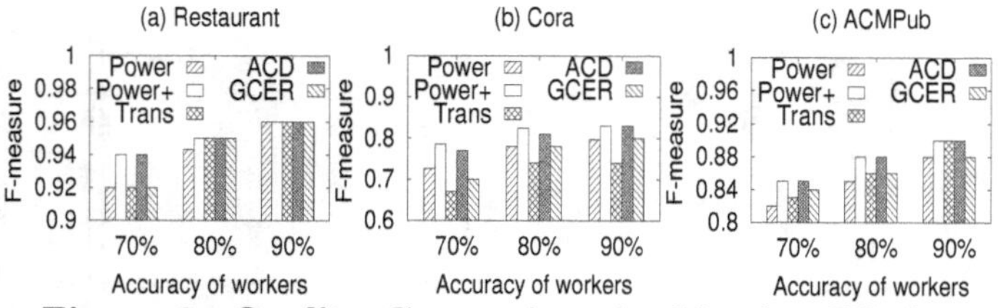

Figure 9: Quality Comparison by Varying Worker Accuracy (Real Experiments).

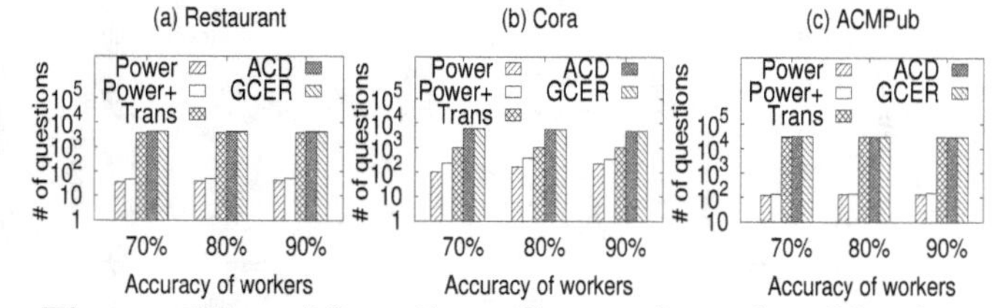

Figure 10: #Question Comparison by Varying Worker Accuracy (Real Experiments).

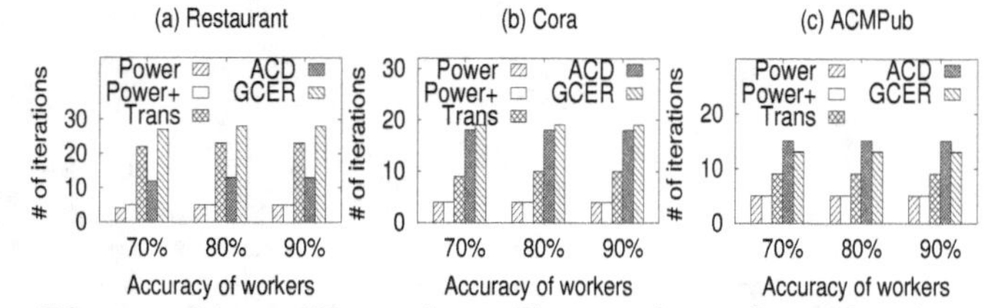

Figure 11: #Iteration Comparison by Varying Worker Accuracy (Real Experiments).

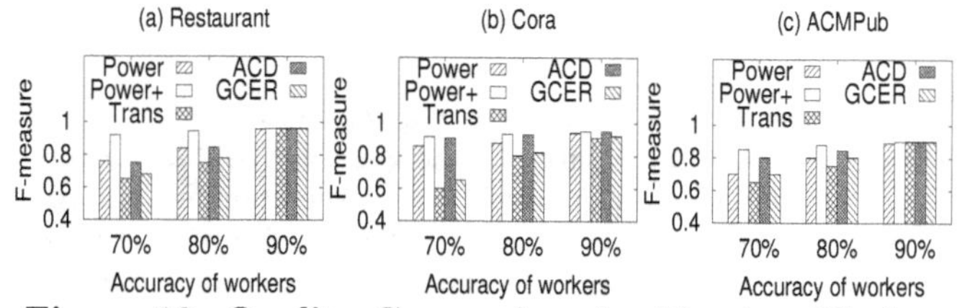

Figure 12: Quality Comparison by Varying Worker Accuracy (Simulation Experiments).

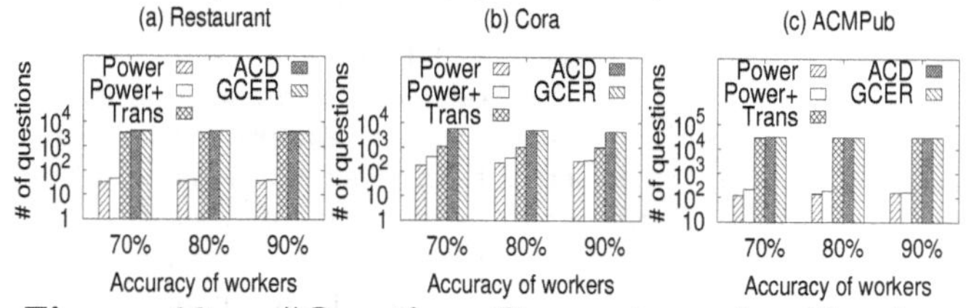

Figure 13: #Question Comparison by Varying Worker Accuracy (Simulation Experiments).

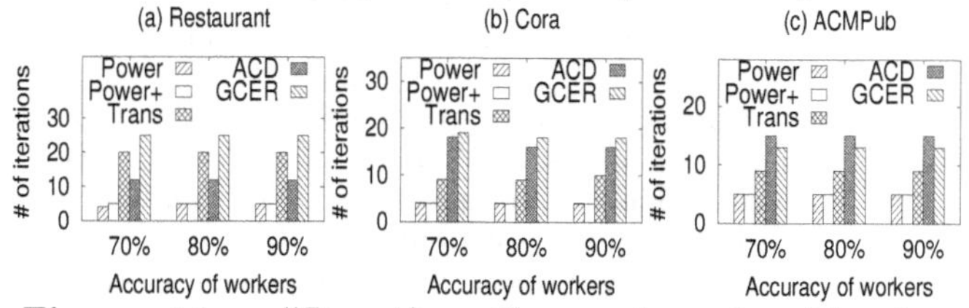

Figure 14: #Iteration Comparison by Varying Worker Accuracy (Simulation Experiments).

asked pairs. Trans can also reduce the number of questions based on transitivity at the expense of lowering down the quality. ACD and GCER achieve high quality at the expense of asking many more questions. For example, on ACMPub, ACD, GCER, and Trans ask 30,000 questions, and our methods ask 150 questions. Thus our methods can save 200× monetary cost than ACD, GCER, and Trans. On Restaurant, ACD and GCER ask 4100 questions, Trans asks 3900 questions while Power only asks 51 questions. Thus our methods save 80× monetary cost than ACD, GCER, and Trans. On Cora, ACD and GCER ask 4800 questions, Trans asks 1020 questions while our methods only ask 354 questions. Trans saves a little cost on the Restaurant dataset because only few pairs satisfy the transitivity rules. Secondly, Power+ asks a few more questions than Power to tolerate the unconfident vertices and avoid coloring their ancestors and descendants. As there are few unconfident vertices, the gap between Power+ and Power is trivial. Thirdly, the worker accuracy has little effect on the number of questions, because (1) our methods ask few questions and the question number is determined by the graph structure but not worker accuracy and (2) other methods do not consider worker accuracy to select questions.

#Iterations. Firstly, our methods involve fewer iterations than state-of-the-art approaches. This is because (1) our methods ask smaller number of questions and (2) our methods can ask many questions in parallel. For example, on the Restaurant dataset, ACD involves 13 iterations, GCER involves 28 iterations, Trans involves 23 iterations, while Power+ only involves 5 iterations. On the Cora dataset, ACD involves 18 iterations, Trans involves 10 iterations, GCER involves 19 iterations, while Power+ only involves 4 iterations. On the ACMPub dataset, ACD involves 15 iterations, Trans involves 9 iterations, GCER involves 13 iterations, while Power+ only involves 5 iterations. Thus our method saves 2-5× latency cost on the Cora dataset. Secondly, Power and Power+ nearly have the same number of iterations, because they have little difference on the number of asked questions. Thirdly, the worker accuracy has little impact on the number of iterations, because existing studies do not consider worker accuracy and our methods ask few questions.

7.2.2 Simulation Exp: Evaluating Worker Accuracy

In real experiments, we select workers based on their history accuracy on AMT. However the approval rates of workers only reflect their history accuracy when they answered other questions in history but not the accuracy on our questions. Workers may have different quality on different datasets and time. For example, on the Restaurant dataset, the problem is easy, and most workers give a correct answer even though they have a low history accuracy. On the Cora dataset, because the dataset is relative dirty and professional, many workers return wrong answers even though they have a high history accuracy. Therefore, the reason why many previous studies[7, 22, 23, 24] set a high approval rate is to filter these malicious workers, but this does not mean that most workers can give right answers under the high approval rate guarantee. To address this issue, we conduct a simulation experiment. We assume the ground truth is known and generate workers with quality in 70%-80%, 80%-90%, and above 90% respectively. Figures 12-14 show the results on the simulation experiments.

Quality. Firstly, Power+ significantly outperforms other methods for low-quality workers, e.g., 70% and 80%. This is because (1) Power+ can tolerate more errors by postponing coloring the unconfident vertices, and for low-quality workers, there are many more unconfident vertices. For example, for those wrongly answered vertices, we do not color them Green or Red immediately and also do not color their ancestors or descendants, which avoid many errors; (2) Power+ can tolerate the malicious answers by first asking middle-level vertices in the graph and thus has low possibility to wrongly label some pairs (because a high-level vertex will affect many vertices if it is colored Red and a low-level vertex will affect many vertices if it is colored Green). ACD outperforms other baselines, because it tolerates errors based on the clusters refinement (each cluster contains records referring to the same entity). However, on the `Restaurant` dataset, `ACD` has lower quality, because there are few records in each cluster and `ACD` cannot utilize this limited information to infer the answers. `Trans` and `GCER` cannot tolerate errors, and thus they have rather low quality for low worker accuracy. Secondly, for high worker accuracy, e.g., 90%, all the algorithms achieve rather high quality as there are few errors in the workers' answers. Thirdly, with the increase of worker accuracy, all the methods achieve higher quality as they can utilize high quality answers. `Power+` outperforms `ACD`, which in turns is better than other methods. For example, on the `Restaurant` dataset, in real experiments, all methods have more than 92% F-measure whatever the workers' accuracy is, because workers have high quality on this easy dataset. However, in our simulation experiment, for 70% accuracy, `Power+` achieves 92% F-measure while `Power`, `Trans`, `ACD`, and `GCER` have 76%, 65%, 77% and 75% F-measure respectively. For 80% accuracy, `Power+` still outperforms other methods, and all the methods have improvement on quality compared with 70%. For 90% accuracy, all methods can achieve high quality, e.g., 95%, because the workers return high-quality answers. On the `Cora` dataset, for 70% accuracy, `Power+` and `ACD` have high F-measure and reach 91% due to tolerating crowd's errors while `Power` has F-measure 86%. `Trans` and `GCER` expand the error propagation due to the transitivity rule, whose F-measures are 60% and 65%. For 80% accuracy, `Power+` and `ACD` improve to 93%. And `Power`, `Trans` and `GCER` are 88%, 80% and 82% respectively. For 90% accuracy, all methods improve the quality to above 90%. `Power+` and `ACD` still outperform others. On the `ACMPub` dataset, similarly to the `Restaurant` and `Cora` datasets, `Power+` and `ACD` outperform other methods when worker accuracy is low. If worker accuracy is high, all methods achieve nearly the same quality.

#Questions. Since the worker accuracy has little effect on the number of questions, there is little difference between real experiments and simulation experiments. `Power+` saves 80×, 10×, 200× monetary cost than `ACD`, `GCER`, and `Trans` on the `Restaurant`, `Cora`, and `ACMPub` datasets respectively.

#Iterations. Since the worker accuracy has little impact on the number of iterations, there is little difference between real experiments and simulation experiments. Our method still saves 2-5× latency cost on the three datasets.

7.3 Evaluating Similarity Functions

We evaluate the effect of different similarity functions. On each dataset, we respectively use Jaccard, edit similarity, and bigram on every attribute to generate the graph and compare the results for the three similarity functions. Note that on the `Restaurant` dataset, Jaccard is not a good similarity function for the Name attribute as there are only 1-2 words in the restaurant name; while on the `ACMPub` dataset, edit similarity is not a good choice for the Title attribute as there are many words in the paper title. We want to test whether our methods and state-of-the-art approaches can tolerate the noisy results generated by different similarity functions. We use the worker accuracy of 90%. Figures 15-17 show the results. We make the following observations.

Firstly, different similarity functions have little impact on the quality among all the methods, because all of these methods use a property that the pairs with large similarities have large possibility to refer to the same entity. On the real datasets, most of the similar functions satisfy this

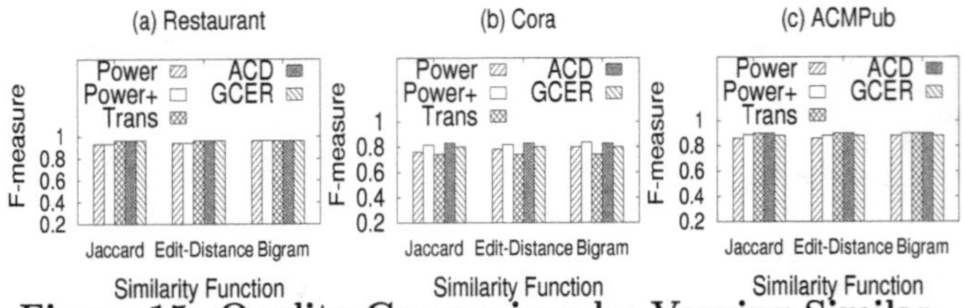

Figure 15: Quality Comparison by Varying Similarity Functions (Real Experiments).

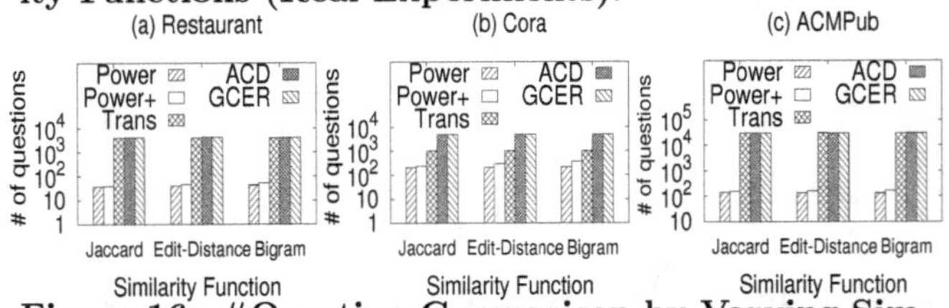

Figure 16: #Question Comparison by Varying Similarity Functions (Real Experiments).

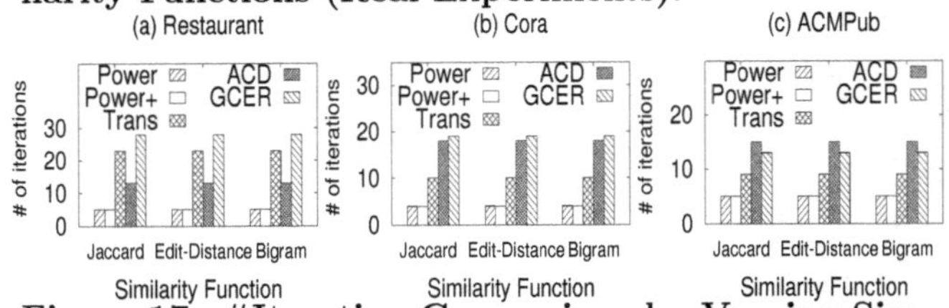

Figure 17: #Iteration Comparison by Varying Similarity Functions (Real Experiments).

property. For our methods, if the functions do not significantly invalidate the partial order, they can be used in our methods. In addition, existing methods use record-level similarity while our methods utilize attribute-level similarity to evaluate different pairs. Thus our methods can use more information to determine the partial order. Even if there exist some noisy functions on some attributes (e.g., Jaccard for Name and edit similarity for Title), our methods can utilize other similarity functions to obtain a good partial order and thus can correct the errors caused by the noisy similarity functions. Therefore our methods are robust on real datasets, even for some noisy functions. Secondly, the similarity functions have little effect on the number of questions, as the number of questions is determined by the graph structure and the graphs generated by different functions have no much difference. Thirdly, the similarity functions have little impact on the number of iterations, as the number of iterations is determined by the number of questions but not by the similarity functions.

8. CONCLUSION

We proposed a partial-order based crowdsourced entity resolution framework. We defined a partial order on record pairs based on their similarities on every attribute. We proposed a graph-based coloring strategy to deduce the answer of some pairs based on the answers of asked pairs. We devised two algorithms to construct the graph and proposed two grouping methods to reduce the graph size. We proposed effective algorithms to judiciously select pairs to ask in order to minimize the number of asked pairs. We developed error-tolerant techniques to tolerate the errors. Experimental results show that our method saves more money than existing approaches while keeping the same quality.

Acknowledgements. This work was partly supported by the 973 Program of China (2015CB358700), NSF of China (61422205, 61472198), Huawei, Shenzhou, Tencent, FDCT/116/2013/A3, MYRG105(Y1-L3)-FST13-GZ, 863 Program(2012AA012600), and Chinese Special Project of Science & Technology(2013zx01039-002-002).

Notation	Description
$\mathcal{T} = \{r_1, r_2, ..., r_n\}$	a set or records
$\mathcal{A} = \{\mathcal{A}_1, \mathcal{A}_2, ..., \mathcal{A}_m\}$	a set of attributes
$r_i[k]$	value of attribute $\mathcal{A}_k$ in record r_i
p_{ij}	(r_i, r_j)
s_{ij}^k	similarity between $r_i[k]$ and $r_j[k]$
$\mathcal{G} = (\mathcal{V}, \mathcal{E})$	a DAG of pairs in $\mathcal{T}$
$\mathcal{G}' = (\mathcal{V}', \mathcal{E}')$	a grouped DAG of $\mathcal{G} = (\mathcal{V}, \mathcal{E})$
$\succ$	partial order
$\mathcal{C}(p_{ij})$	the child vertex set of p_{ij}
$\mathcal{P}(p_{ij})$	the parent vertex set of p_{ij}
$\mathcal{B}$	the number of incomparable vertices

Table 4: Notations Used In This Paper.

9. REFERENCES

[1] C. C. Cao, J. She, Y. Tong, and L. Chen. Whom to ask? jury selection for decision making tasks on micro-blog services. *PVLDB*, 5(11):1495–1506, 2012.

[2] X. Chen, P. N. Bennett, K. Collins-Thompson, and E. Horvitz. Pairwise ranking aggregation in a crowdsourced setting. In *WSDM*, pages 193–202, 2013.

[3] J. Fan, G. Li, B. C. Ooi, K. Tan, and J. Feng. icrowd: An adaptive crowdsourcing framework. In *SIGMOD*, pages 1015–1030, 2015.

[4] S. Felsner, V. Raghavan, and J. P. Spinrad. Recognition algorithms for orders of small width and graphs of small dilworth number. *Order*, 20(4):351–364, 2003.

[5] M. J. Franklin, D. Kossmann, T. Kraska, S. Ramesh, and R. Xin. Crowddb: answering queries with crowdsourcing. In *SIGMOD*, pages 61–72, 2011.

[6] D. R. Fulkerson. Note on dilworth's decomposition theorem for partially ordered sets. *American Mathematical Society*, 7(4):701–702, 1956.

[7] C. Gokhale, S. Das, A. Doan, J. F. Naughton, N. Rampalli, J. W. Shavlik, and X. Zhu. Corleone: hands-off crowdsourcing for entity matching. In *SIGMOD*, pages 601–612, 2014.

[8] S. Guo, A. G. Parameswaran, and H. Garcia-Molina. So who won?: dynamic max discovery with the crowd. In *SIGMOD*, pages 385–396, 2012.

[9] P. G. Ipeirotis, F. Provost, and J. Wang. Quality management on amazon mechanical turk. In *SIGKDD workshop on human computation*, pages 64–67. ACM, 2010.

[10] M. Kreveld, M. Overmars, O. Schwarzkopf, M. d. Berg, and O. Schwartskopf. Computational geometry: algorithms and applications, 1997.

[11] X. Liu, M. Lu, B. C. Ooi, Y. Shen, S. Wu, and M. Zhang. CDAS: A crowdsourcing data analytics system. *PVLDB*, 5(10):1040–1051, 2012.

[12] A. Marcus, E. Wu, D. R. Karger, S. Madden, and R. C. Miller. Human-powered sorts and joins. *PVLDB*, 5(1):13–24, 2011.

[13] A. Marcus, E. Wu, S. Madden, and R. C. Miller. Crowdsourced databases: Query processing with people. In *CIDR*, pages 211–214, 2011.

[14] N. Megiddo and K. J. Supowit. On the complexity of some common geometric location problems. *SIAM journal on computing*, 13(1):182–196, 1984.

[15] W. R. Ouyang, L. M. Kaplan, and et al. Debiasing crowdsourced quantitative characteristics in local businesses and services. In *IPSN*, pages 190–201, 2015.

[16] A. G. Parameswaran, H. Park, H. Garcia-Molina, N. Polyzotis, and J. Widom. Deco: declarative crowdsourcing. In *CIKM*, pages 1203–1212, 2012.

[17] H. Park and J. Widom. Query optimization over crowdsourced data. *PVLDB*, 6(10):781–792, 2013.

[18] T. Pfeiffer, X. A. Gao, Y. Chen, A. Mao, and D. G. Rand. Adaptive polling for information aggregation. In *AAAI*, 2012.

[19] P. Venetis, H. Garcia-Molina, K. Huang, and N. Polyzotis. Max algorithms in crowdsourcing environments. In *WWW*, pages 989–998, 2012.

[20] V. Verroios and H. Garcia-Molina. Entity resolution with crowd errors. In *ICDE*, pages 219–230, 2015.

[21] N. Vesdapunt, K. Bellare, and N. N. Dalvi. Crowdsourcing algorithms for entity resolution. *PVLDB*, 2014.

[22] J. Wang, T. Kraska, M. J. Franklin, and J. Feng. Crowder: Crowdsourcing entity resolution. *PVLDB*, 2012.

[23] J. Wang, G. Li, T. Kraska, M. J. Franklin, and J. Feng. Leveraging transitive relations for crowdsourced joins. In *SIGMOD*, pages 229–240, 2013.

[24] S. Wang, X. Xiao, and C. Lee. Crowd-based deduplication: An adaptive approach. In *SIGMOD*, pages 1263–1277, 2015.

[25] S. E. Whang, P. Lofgren, and H. Garcia-Molina. Question selection for crowd entity resolution. *PVLDB*, 2013.

[26] Y. Zheng, R. Cheng, S. Maniu, and L. Mo. On optimality of jury selection in crowdsourcing. In *EDBT*, pages 193–204, 2015.

[27] Y. Zheng, J. Wang, G. Li, R. Cheng, and J. Feng. QASCA: A quality-aware task assignment system for crowdsourcing applications. In *SIGMOD*, pages 1031–1046, 2015.

APPENDIX

A. VERTEX GROUPING: GREEDY

Generating Maximal Groups. We first consider the one-dimensional case, i.e., $m = 1$. We generate all the maximal groups based on s_{ij}^1. We first sort p_{ij} based on s_{ij}^1 in a descending order, denoted by $p_1, p_2, \ldots, p_n$. For the first pair p_1, we generate a longest group $\{p_1, p_2, \ldots, p_t\}$ where $p_1 - p_t \le \varepsilon$ and $p_1 - p_{t+1} > \varepsilon$. Obviously this longest group is a maximal group. Next we generate the longest group for p_2. If the longest group of p_2 is not contained by that of p_1, it is a maximal group. Iteratively we can generate all the maximal groups. The complexity is $\mathcal{O}(|\mathcal{V}|^2)$.

For the m-dimensional case, we first generate the maximal groups $\mathcal{M}^i$ on every attribute $\mathcal{A}_i$. Then we join them to generate the maximal groups, i.e., $\mathcal{M}^1 \bowtie \mathcal{M}^2 \bowtie \cdots \bowtie \mathcal{M}^m = \{\mathcal{M}^1_{i_1} \cap \mathcal{M}^2_{i_2} \cap \cdots \cap \mathcal{M}^m_{i_m}\}$ where $1 \le i_j \le |\mathcal{M}^j|$. We prove that the generated groups contain all maximal groups. Then we utilize these groups to run the greedy algorithm.

THEOREM 3. *$\mathcal{M}^1 \bowtie \mathcal{M}^2 \bowtie \cdots \bowtie \mathcal{M}^m = \{\mathcal{M}^1_{i_1} \cap \mathcal{M}^2_{i_2} \cap \cdots \cap \mathcal{M}^m_{i_m}\}$ contains all maximal groups.*

PROOF. We prove that for any maximal group, g, there exist $\mathcal{M}^1_{i_1}$, $\mathcal{M}^2_{i_2}$, $\cdots$, $\mathcal{M}^m_{i_m}$, $g = \mathcal{M}^1_{i_1} \cap \mathcal{M}^2_{i_2} \cap \cdots \cap \mathcal{M}^m_{i_m}$. As g is a maximal group, $g_i^k.u - g_i^k.l \le \varepsilon$ for any attribute $\mathcal{A}_k$. Let $s_{ij}^k = g_i^k.l$. We generate the maximal group $\mathcal{M}^k_{i_k}$ on attribute $\mathcal{A}_k$ based on s_{ij}^k. Obviously $g \subseteq \mathcal{M}^k_{i_k}$. Thus $g \subseteq \mathcal{M}^1_{i_1} \cap \mathcal{M}^2_{i_2} \cap \cdots \cap \mathcal{M}^m_{i_m}$. As g is a maximal group, $g = \mathcal{M}^1_{i_1} \cap \mathcal{M}^2_{i_2} \cap \cdots \cap \mathcal{M}^m_{i_m}$. □

Algorithm 6 shows the pseudo code. It first generates all the maximal groups (line 1), and then greedily picks the largest group (line 3). Finally it updates other groups by removing the vertices in the largest group (line 5).

B. MULTI-PATH SELECTION ALGORITHM

Algorithm 7 shows the pseudo code. It first finds the minimal disjoint paths (line 2) and then asks their mid-vertices in parallel (lines 4-5). Next it colors the graph based on the answers and removes the colored vertices (line 6). Finally, it repeats the above step if there exist uncolored vertices in $\mathcal{V}$. For example, we first compute the three disjoint paths and asks their mid-vertices g_5, g_3 and g_6 together in Figure 6. We get the answers: g_5 is RED, and g_3 and g_6 are GREEN. We color the graph based on these three answers(Figure 6(b)). Next we generate a path: $g_2 \rightsquigarrow g_8$ and we ask g_2. The answer is: g_2 is GREEN, and we color the graph (Figure 6(c)). Iteratively we color all vertices (Figure 6(d)). This method asks 5 vertices and involves 3 iterations.

C. EXAMPLE OF ERROR TOLERANT

Recall the example in Figure 8 where g_2 and g_8 are colored BLUE as workers return low-confident answers to them. We calculate the attribute weight ω based on the pairs $P^g = \{p_{13}, p_{67}, p_{45}, p_{23}, p_{46}, p_{56}, p_{47}, p_{57}\}$ in the colored groups. Using Equation 7, we obtain $\omega = \{0.32, 0.28, 0.21, 0.19\}$.

Algorithm 6: Vertex Grouping: `Greedy`

```
Input: G = (V, E)
Output: A set of groups g_1, g_2, ..., g_x
Generate maximal groups M;
while M is not empty do
    Pick the largest group g from M;
    for each g_i in M do
        g_i = g_i - g;
```

Algorithm 7: Question Selection: `Multi-Path`

```
Input: G = (V, E)
Output: All vertices in V are colored as GREEN or RED
while there exist uncolored vertices in V do
    Compute B disjoint paths;
    for each path of these disjoint paths do
        N <- mid-vertex of the path;
    Ask N to workers in parallel and color G;
    Removed colored vertices;
return colored V;
```

Then we compute the estimated similarities based on the weight and Table 18 shows the estimated similarities. Next we divide the pairs into different histograms and Figure 19 shows the histograms. p_{12} falls in h_4 and is colored GREEN. p_{24} and p_{25} fall in h_2 and are colored RED.

p_{ij}	$\hat{s}_{ij}$	p_{ij}	$\hat{s}_{ij}$
p_{12}	0.72	p_{37}	0.21
p_{13}	0.68	p_{45}	0.97
p_{23}	0.60	p_{46}	0.43
p_{24}	0.28	p_{47}	0.42
p_{25}	0.29	p_{56}	0.41
p_{26}	0.40	p_{57}	0.44
p_{27}	0.41	p_{67}	0.98
p_{34}	0.39	p_{89}	0.37
p_{35}	0.39	$p_{10,11}$	0.44

Figure 18: Estimated Similarity $\hat{s}_{ij}$.

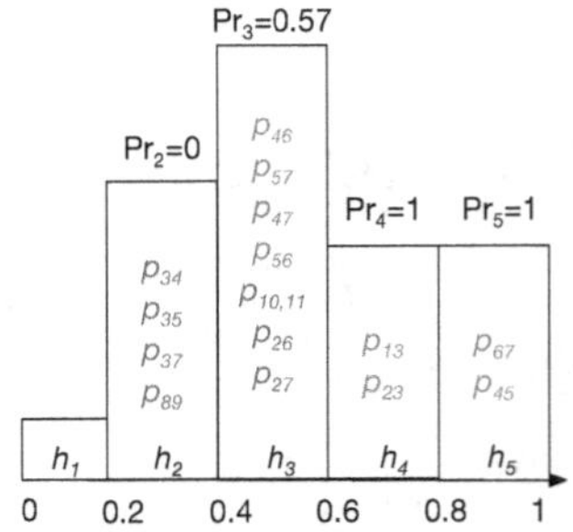

Figure 19: Equi-depth Histograms.

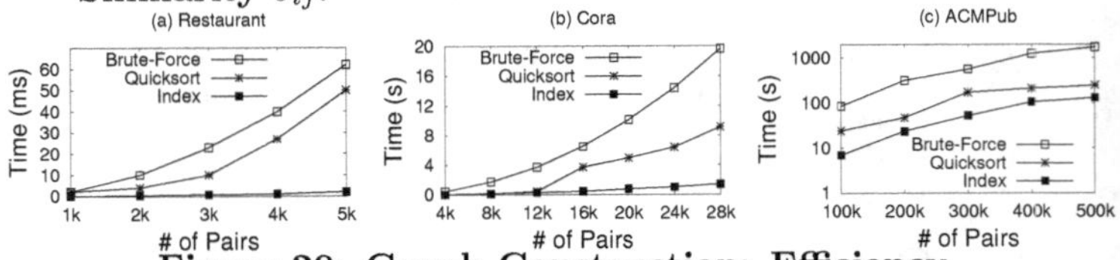

Figure 20: Graph Construction: Efficiency.

D. PROOF OF THEOREMS

D.1 Proof of Theorem 1

We prove the problem is NP-Hard even $m = 2$ by a reduction from the following rectangle cover problem. In a rectangle cover instance, we are given a set of points in the Euclidean plane $\mathbb{R}^2$. Our goal is to use the minimum number of unit squares to cover all points. The problem is known to be NP-Hard [14]. In our problem, it is easy to see a vertex group can be covered by a square of side length ϵ. We can partition the set of vertices into k groups, if and only if all vertices can be covered by k squares of side length ϵ. Therefore, our problem is equivalent to the rectangle cover problem, thus is NP-Hard as well.

D.2 Proof of Theorem 2

(1) Disjoint: If there exist two paths with common vertices, this vertex has at least two edges in the maximal matching, which contradicts with the definition of maximal matching.
(2) Complete: Consider any vertex v. If its in-degree is 0, it must be covered by a path. If its in-degree is not 0, it has an in-edge (v', v). We call v' the parent of v. If the in-degree of v' is 0, v' and v will be covered by the same path starting at v'; otherwise we find the parent of v'. Iteratively we find an ancestor of v whose in-degree is 0, and then v is covered by the path starting at this ancestor.
(3) Minimal: Let J denote the number of edges in a matching and D denote the number of disjoint paths in the graph. Fulkerson et al. [6] proved that $J + D = |\mathcal{V}|$. As $|\mathcal{V}|$ is fixed, if we find the maximal matching, then D is minimal.

E. MORE EXPERIMENTAL RESULTS

E.1 Evaluation on Graph Construction

E.1.1 Evaluation on Graph Construction Algorithms

We compare the efficiency of the three graph construction algorithms (proposed in Section 4.1). (1) `Brute-Force`: the brute-force method that compares every two pairs. (2) `QuickSort`: the quicksort-based method. (3) `Index`: the index-based method.[5] To test the scalability, on `ACMPub`, we set the bound τ as 0.18 and generate 500K pairs. Figure 20 shows the results by varying the number of pairs. We can see that `Index` significantly outperforms the other two methods, even by 1 order of magnitude. For example, on the `Cora` dataset with 28k pairs, `Brute-Force` takes 20 seconds, `QuickSort` improves it to 10 seconds, while `Index` only takes 1 second. On the larger dataset `ACMPub`, `Index` still outperforms other methods and achieves higher performance. This is because `Index` can utilize the range search tree index to efficiently find the children of a pair and can prune many unnecessary pairs (e.g., incomparable pairs). `QuickSort` outperforms `Brute-Force` because it can also remove some unnecessary pairs based on the partial order. However the improvement is not signifiant, as many vertices in the graph are not comparable based on the partial order and thus many pairs cannot be pruned. For example, in `Restaurant`, 70% pairs of records are not comparable. In `Cora`, 84% pairs of records are not comparable. In `ACMPub`, 80% pairs of records are not comparable.

E.1.2 Evaluation on Grouping

We first evaluate our two techniques `Greedy` and `Split` (proposed in Section 4.2). (1) `Greedy`: it greedily groups the vertices. (2) `Split`: it uses the split-based technique. We first compare the number of groups generated by them. Figure 21 shows the number of groups and Figure 22 shows the running time. Note that on the `ACMPub` dataset, **`Greedy` cannot report the results within 10 hours and thus we do not show `Greedy` in the figure**. We have several observations on the number of groups. Firstly, compared with the total number of pairs in `Restaurant` (5,010 pairs), `Cora` (29,510 pairs) and `ACMPub` (204,000 pairs), `Split` and `Greedy` only generate less than 150, 1300 and 700 groups. Thus the grouping technique can significantly reduce the number of vertices, and thus can reduce the time latency and the crowd cost. Secondly, `Split` generates a few more groups than `Greedy`, because `Split` uses heuristics to generate groups while `Greedy` utilizes a greedy strategy to generate high-quality groups. For example, on the `Cora` dataset with

[5]The three datasets have 4-8 attributes. As it is too complicated to construct a high dimensional range tree, we use a heuristics: we choose two important attributes in each dataset to construct 2-dimensional indexes. When we search the children of a pair, the pairs reported by the index are a superset as they may not satisfy other attributes. To addres this issue, we only need to verify them to remove the false positives based on other non-indexed attributes. In our experiment, we choose attributes Name and Address for `Restaurant`, Author and Title for `Cora`, and Author and Title for `ACMPub`.

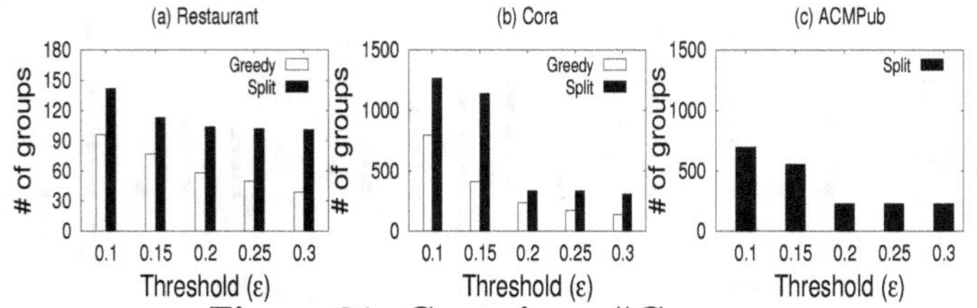

Figure 21: Grouping: #Groups.

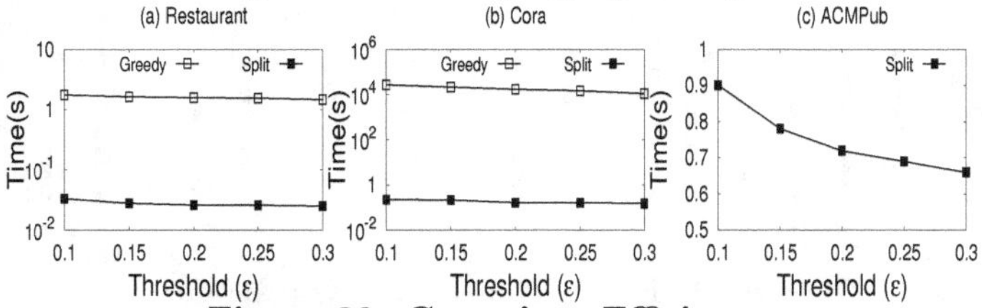

Figure 22: Grouping: Efficiency.

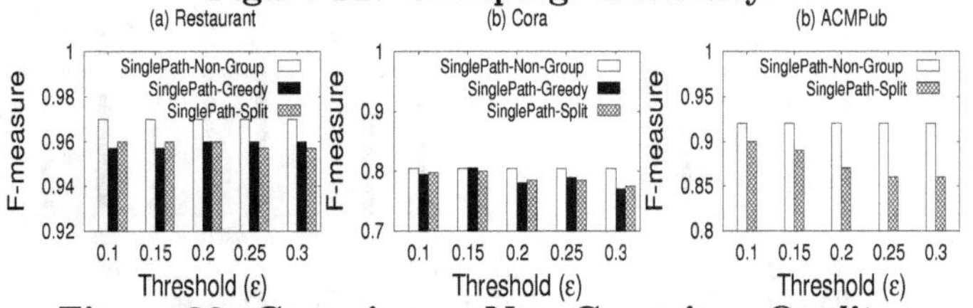

Figure 23: Grouping vs Non-Grouping: Quality.

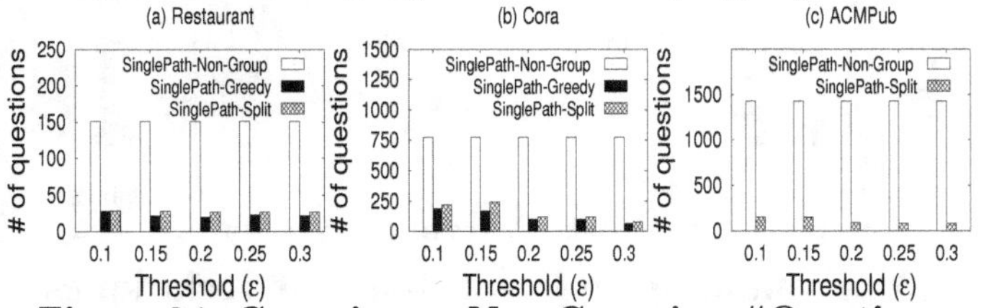

Figure 24: Grouping vs Non-Grouping:#Questions.

grouping threshold $\varepsilon = 0.1$, `Greedy` generates 800 groups and `Split` generates 1200 groups. Thus if we focus on reducing the number of groups, we can select the `Greedy` algorithm. Thirdly, with the increase of the thresholds, the number of groups decreases, because groups with larger thresholds contain more vertices. On the other hand, we can see that `Greedy` takes much longer time than `Split`, even 10000× slower on larger datasets. For example on the `Cora` dataset, `Greedy` takes more than 10000 seconds while `Split` only takes less than 1 second. Thus if we focus on high efficiency, we recommend the `Split` algorithm.

We then compare grouping with non-grouping in terms of quality and the number of questions. We compare three algorithms. (1) `SinglePath-Non-Group`, which utilizes `SinglePath` to ask questions on the original graph without grouping. (2) `SinglePath-Greedy`, which utilizes `SinglePath` to ask questions on the grouped graph generated by the `Greedy` algorithm. (3) `SinglePath-Split`, which utilizes `SinglePath` to ask questions on the grouped graph generated by the `Split` algorithm. Figure 23 shows the quality and Figure 24 shows the number of questions. Note that we do not show `SinglePath-Greedy` on the `ACMPub` dataset as it is too slow.

We have the following observations. (1) The grouping technique slightly reduces the quality by 2% than the non-grouping method. The reasons are twofold. Firstly, many pairs are grouped and we only ask one pair and utilize its answer to deduce the answer of other pairs in the group. If the pairs in the same group have different colors, this method may involve errors. Secondly, there are smaller number of edges in the grouped graph and we ask fewer questions. (2) The grouping technique significantly reduces

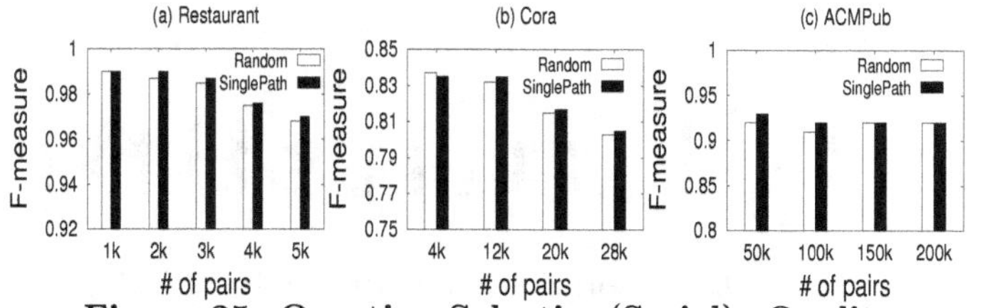

Figure 25: Question Selection(Serial): Quality.

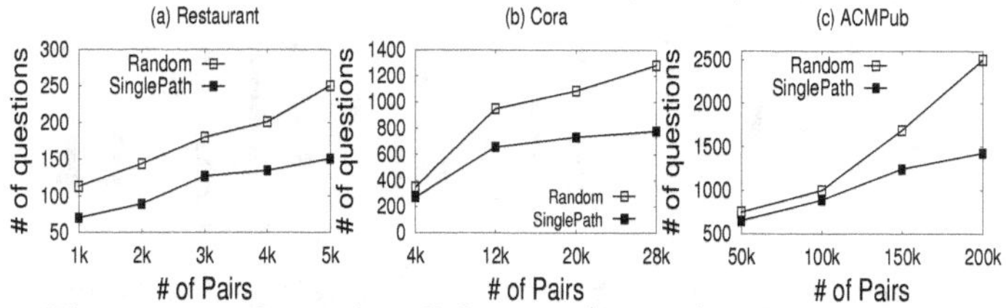

Figure 26: Question Selection(Serial): #Questions.

the number of questions. For example, on the `Cora` dataset with $\varepsilon = 0.1$, the non-grouping method asks 800 questions while the grouping method only asks 80 questions. On the `ACMPub` dataset, the non-grouping method asks 1400 questions while the grouping method asks 163 questions. This is because the grouping technique can significantly reduce the graph size. Thus we can utilize grouping techniques to reduce the cost. (3) The two grouping techniques have no large difference on the number of question as their graph sizes are very close. This verifies that we can use `Split` to generate the groups. (4) The number of questions is not only determined by the number of groups, but also the number of edges. First, fewer groups will lead to fewer questions. Second, fewer edges may lead to more questions, because the answers of many groups cannot be deduced based on the answers of other groups. With the increase of the grouping threshold, the number of groups decreases, and thus the number of questions should decrease intuitively. However, with the increase of the grouping threshold, the groups become larger and it is more difficult to add an edge between two groups. Thus there may be fewer edges in the graph and the number of questions may decrease.

E.2 Evaluation on Question Selection

E.2.1 Evaluation on Serial Algorithms

We first evaluate the serial question-selection algorithms and compare two algorithms (proposed in Section 5.2). (1) `Random`: which randomly selects a vertex in each iteration. (2) `SinglePath`: which selects a vertex from the longest path in each iteration. We compare the two algorithms on the non-grouping graphs. Figure 25 shows the quality and Figure 26 shows the number of questions. We can see that `SinglePath` outperforms `Random` and reduces the number of questions. For example, on the `Restaurant` dataset with 5000 pairs, `Random` asks 250 pairs while `SinglePath` only asks 150 pairs. On the `ACMPub` dataset, `Random` asks 2500 pairs while `SinglePath` only asks 1400 pairs. This is because `SinglePath` can effectively identify the boundary pairs using a binary search strategy. On the other hand, `SinglePath` achieves similar quality with `Random` as the question order does not significantly affect the quality. Thus we can utilize the `SinglePath` to select questions.

E.2.2 Evaluation on Parallel Algorithms

We then evaluate the parallel question-selection algorithms (proposed in Section 5.3). We compare three algorithms: (1) `SinglePath`: which selects a vertex from the longest path in each iteration. (2) `Multi-Path`: which selects multiple

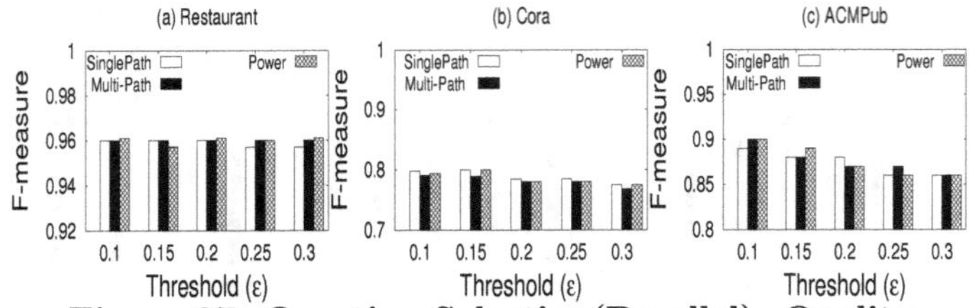

Figure 27: Question Selection(Parallel): Quality.

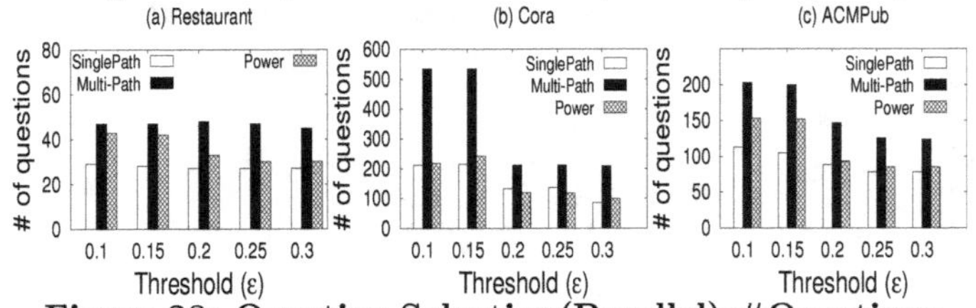

Figure 28: Question Selection(Parallel):#Questions.

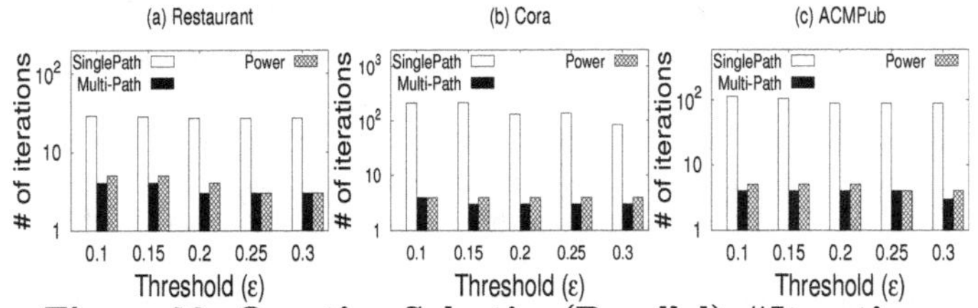

Figure 29: Question Selection(Parallel):#Iterations.

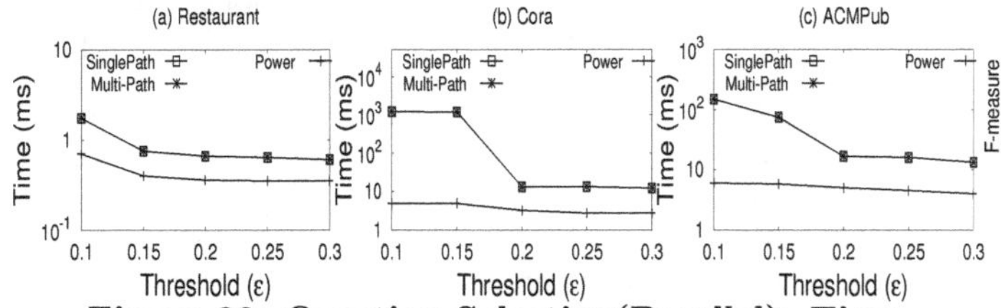

Figure 30: Question Selection(Parallel): Time.

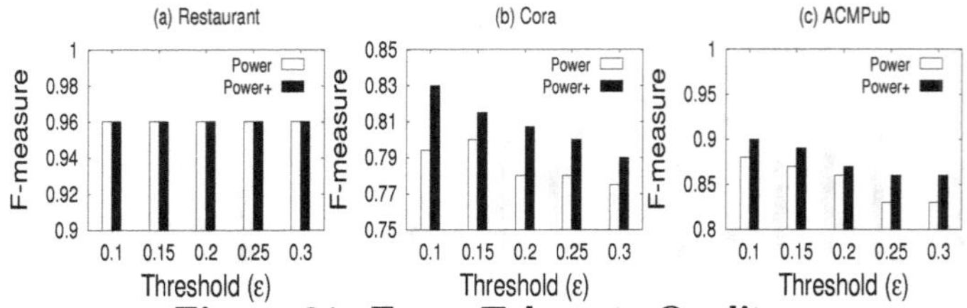

Figure 31: Error Tolerant: Quality.

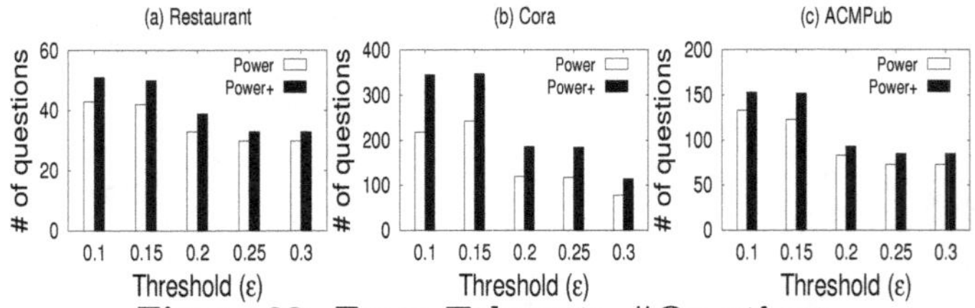

Figure 32: Error Tolerant: #Questions.

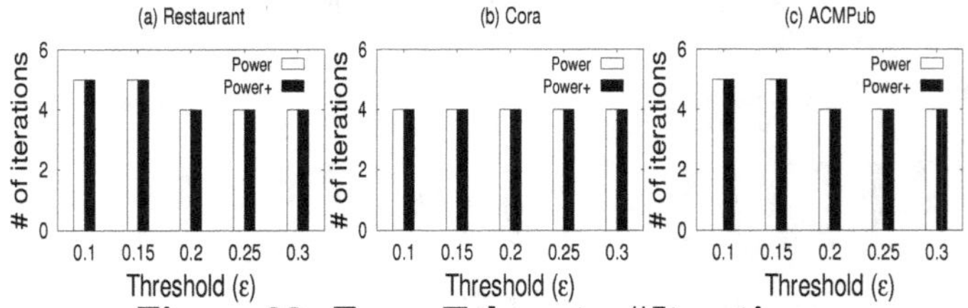

Figure 33: Error Tolerant: #Iterations.

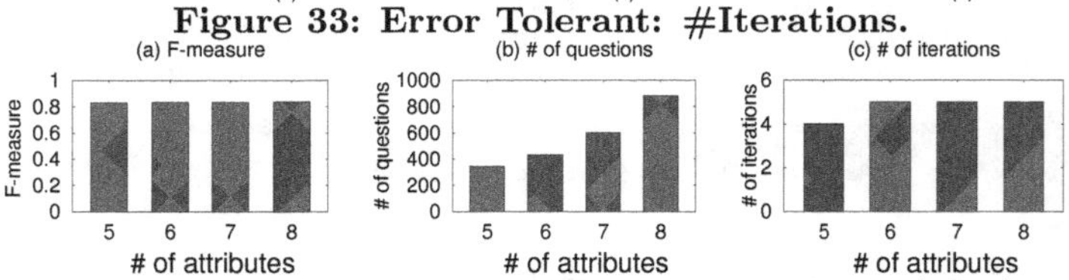

Figure 34: Evaluation by Varying #Attributes(Cora).

vertices from multiple disjoint paths in each iteration. (3) `Power`: which selects multiple independent vertices based on topological sorting in each iteration. We compare the quality, the number of questions, the number of iterations, and the assignment time in each iteration to select the questions for workers. Figures 27-30 show the results.

(1) For quality, we can see that the three methods achieve similar quality, because different question orders will not affect the quality based on the partial order. (2) For the number of questions, we can see that the two parallel algorithms `Multi-Path` and `Power` ask a few more questions than `SinglePath`. The reason is evident that `Multi-Path` may ask pairs with ancestor-descendent relationships and `Power` may ask pairs with the same descendants which can be avoided by serial algorithms based on the partial order. `Power` outperforms `Multi-Path` because `Power` asks independent questions in each iteration while `Multi-Path` may ask dependent questions. (3) For the number of iterations, the two parallel algorithms `Multi-Path` and `Power` significantly outperform `SinglePath` as they ask questions in parallel. For example, on the `Cora` dataset, `Power` and `Multi-Path` only have 4 iterations while `SinglePath` involves 200 iterations. On the `ACMPub` dataset, `Power` and `Multi-Path` have 5 iterations while `SinglePath` involves 113 iterations. Thus `Power` and `Multi-Path` can significantly reduce the latency. In practice, we need to use the parallel algorithms. (4) For assignment time, all the three algorithms can assign tasks within 1 second. `Multi-Path` and `SinglePath` take longer time than `Power` as they are expensive to find multiple independent paths using the graph matching algorithm, which is consistent with the complexity analysis, while `Power` only needs to compute the topological sorting which is efficient.

E.3 Evaluation on Error-Tolerant Techniques

We evaluate the error-tolerant techniques (proposed in Section 6) and compare two algorithms. (1) `Power`: which does not consider errors. (2) `Power+`: which extends `Power` to tolerate errors. We compare quality, the number of questions, and the number of iterations. As they have the same assignment time, we do not compare the assignment time. We build 20 histograms. Figures 31-33 show the results.

`Power+` achieves better quality than `Power`, especially on the `Cora` dataset, because it can tolerate the errors introduced by workers and the partial order. For example, on the `Cora` dataset with $\varepsilon = 0.1$, `Power` only has 79% F-measure while `Power+` improves the quality to 83%. On the `ACMPub` dataset, `Power` has 87% F-measure while `Power+` improves to 90%. On the `Restaurant` dataset, the improvement is not signifiant because the dataset is easy and `Power` already achieves 96% F-measure. On the other hand, `Power+` asks a little more questions than `Power` as `Power+` does not utilize the partial order for some pairs and thus reduces the number of deduced pairs. The two methods have the same number of iterations, because the only difference is that `Power+` does not deduce the answers for some unconfident pairs. Thus we can use the error-tolerant technique to improve the quality.

E.4 Evaluation on The Number of Attributes

We vary the number of attributes on the `Cora` dataset and Figure 34 shows the results. We can see that with the increase of attribute numbers, the number of questions increases, because it is harder to add edges between pairs for more attributes and thus the number of edges decreases. Similar to the number of questions, the number of iterations slightly increases. The quality is not affected as it is determined by the partial order and the crowd error.

Topic Exploration in Spatio-Temporal Document Collections

Kaiqi Zhao[1] Lisi Chen[2] Gao Cong[3]

Nanyang Technological University
{[1]kzhao002@e.,[2]lchen012@e.,[3]gaocong@}ntu.edu.sg

ABSTRACT

Huge amounts of data with both spatial and temporal information (e.g., geo-tagged tweets) are being generated, and are often used to share and spread personal updates, spontaneous ideas, and breaking news. We refer to such data as spatio-temporal documents. It is of great interest to explore topics in a collection of spatio-temporal documents.

In this paper, we study the problem of efficiently mining topics from spatio-temporal documents within a user specified bounded region and timespan, to provide users with insights about events, trends, and public concerns within the specified region and time period. We propose a novel algorithm that is able to efficiently combine two pre-trained topic models learnt from two document sets with a bounded error, based on which we develop an efficient approach to mining topics from a large number of spatio-temporal documents within a region and a timespan. Our experimental results show that our approach is able to improve the runtime by at least an order of magnitude compared with the baselines. Meanwhile, the effectiveness of our proposed method is close to the baselines.

1. INTRODUCTION

With the rapid development of online social media (e.g., Facebook, Flickr, Twitter, etc.) and GPS-enabled devices, huge amounts of data with both spatial and temporal information are being generated in an unprecedented scale. For example, Twitter, which allows users to compose tweets, has 320 million monthly active users who posted 500 million tweets per day, where 80% of the active users are on mobile[1]. Tweets are timestamped and they can be geo-tagged by enabling the geo-tagging functionality. Tweets are regarded as an up-to-date news source [6] and they have been analyzed for various types of human activity including execution of political actions, disaster management, crime prevention, emergency services, etc [17]. Such data can be regarded as a collection of spatio-temporal documents.

Since the spatio-temporal documents often contain information that is indicative of public views and interests [19, 12], it is of great interest to mine topics from the spatio-temporal document collections. Several studies of Online Analytical Processing (OLAP) aim at mining topics from text data (e.g., [32, 34]). Topic models, such as Probabilistic Latent Semantic Analysis (pLSA) [8], Latent Dirichlet Allocation (LDA) [4] and their variations, are proposed as one of the most effective text mining techniques and they have been successfully used for extracting topics from documents. In topic models, a document has a mixture of topics (e.g., "sport games", "entertainments", etc.) and each topic is modeled by a probabilistic distribution over a set of words (e.g., "football", "shoot", etc., for topic "sport games").

However, existing studies often neglect the fact that the location and created time of a document also play important roles in topic extraction. For example, a Twitter user in Boston may be interested in entirely different matters and news compared to a user in Hong Kong. Also, the trending topics in Boston will be different from those in U.S.A., as the trending topics in Boston may have more regional characteristics (e.g., "Boston Marathon"). Moreover, topics in June 2015 are substantially different from those in May 2015 (e.g., the emerging topic about the disease "MERS"). By finding topics in a region and a time period, many applications can be accomplished. For example, social scientists can find topics in different regions and time periods, and news providers can find breaking events from tweets within a region and a time period.

In this paper, we propose to mine topics from a collection of spatio-temporal documents within any user specified spatial region and time interval, which is to provide users with insights about events, trends, and public concerns within the specified region and time period.

Figure 1 exemplifies the problem of mining topics, where a user draws a bounded region (which is represented by the purple box on the map) and a time interval, July 4th, 2015. The blue icons indicate the spatio-temporal documents (e.g., tweets or news) containing text, location, and time information. The three topics extracted from the collection of spatial-temporal documents falling in the region on July 4th, 2015 are presented on the right. Since each topic in topic models is characterized by a probabilistic distribution over words, we use "Word Clouds" to visualize each topic. Word clouds use larger font to represent higher probability of a word in the topic. Note that for each topic we only show several words with the highest probabilities.

It is challenging to mine topics within a given region and a timespan efficiently and effectively. A straightforward method works as follows: Given a user specified region and timespan, we train a topic model on the documents falling in the region and the timespan using the existing techniques, such as LDA [4]. However, mining topics from spatio-temporal documents is very time-consuming.

[1]https://about.twitter.com/company (accessed date: Feb 9th, 2016)

SIGMOD'16, June 26-July 01, 2016, San Francisco, CA, USA

DOI: http://dx.doi.org/10.1145/2882903.2882921

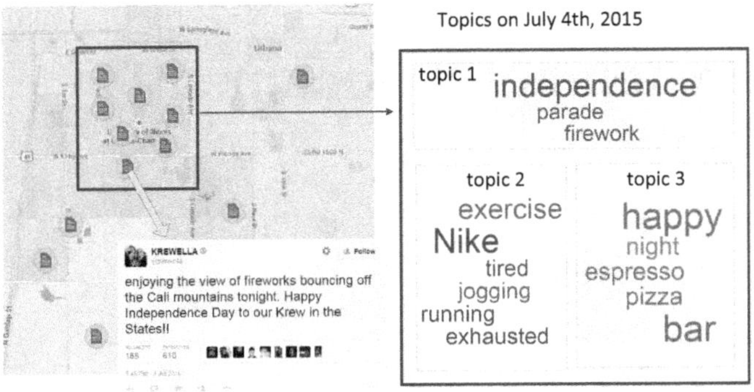

Figure 1: Topics within a Bounded Region and a Time Interval

The original problem of training topic models is NP-hard and collapsed Gibbs sampling is often used to approximately estimate the probabilistic distribution over words for each topic. However, the complexity of colllapsed Gibbs Sampling is still very high, i.e., $O(|W|KI)$, where K is the number of topics, I is the number of iterations of Gibbs sampling, and W is the set of word tokens in the document collection, which could be billions or trillions for a large document collection. For example, learning 100 topics our 3 month Twitter dataset in the New York city region, which contains 0.25 million tweets, took 8.31 minutes. As our Twitter data is a 1% sample of the geo-tagged tweet data, if we extend the result to a collection of all the 3-month geo-tagged tweets the New York city region based on the linear complexity, it would take 13.85 hours to learn 100 topics from the New York city region. Therefore, we need an efficient method to train topic models for each input of region and timespan.

To address the challenge, we propose the following new idea. We divide the collection of spatio-temporal documents into three-dimensional cells and train topic models for the documents within each cell. Then, to compute the topic models for a user specified region and timespan, we combine the topic models of the cells that are located in the specified region and timespan. To realize the idea, we propose the following novel techniques.

1. We propose a novel and efficient algorithm with a bounded error to combine two LDA topic models learnt from two document sets, both falling in the specified region and time period. Different from the existing topic modeling algorithms, our algorithm samples topics for sets of words instead of individual words. The complexity of training the LDA model on two document sets is $O((|W_1| + |W_2|)KI)$, where W_1 and W_2 are sets of word tokens in the two document sets. In contrast, our algorithm reduces the complexity to $O(K(K + |M_2| + |V_2|)I)$, where M_2 is the smaller document set and V_2 is its vocabulary. Their sizes are much smaller than W_1 and W_2.

2. We develop a new approach to partitioning the collection of spatio-temporal documents into an Octree [16], for indexing the documents. Instead of recursively partitioning the three dimensional space into equal-sized cells, we consider the word overlaps among the generated cells to determine how to perform the partitioning. Our partitioning mechanism enables our combining algorithm to achieve better accuracy, although our proposed combining algorithm works for any kind of partitioning. We also develop a mechanism to determine on which cells we pre-train topic models to guarantee a given accuracy threshold.

3. We develop a framework to find the cells whose regions and time periods fall in or overlap with the user specified region and time period. Then we employ our proposed algorithms to combine the pre-trained topic models in these cells to obtain the topics for documents in the specified region and time period.

In summary, the contributions in this study are threefold.

First, we define a practical and novel problem of extracting topics for exploration from spatio-temporal documents within a region and a timespan.

Second, we propose a novel approach comprising the aforementioned key techniques that is capable of efficiently mining topics from a large number of spatio-temporal documents within a given region and timespan.

Third, we conduct an extensive experimental study for evaluating our proposals on three large real-world datasets collected from Twitter, Meetup, and Wikipedia, respectively. Our experiments show that our proposed topic mining framework is able to improve on the runtime by at least an order of magnitude compared to LDA [4] and a variation of LDA [2] that supports online updates (online-LDA). Meanwhile, the effectiveness of the proposed topic extraction framework, measured by perplexity, is close to those of LDA and online-LDA. We also use some example topics extracted by our framework to show that the quality of the extracted topics is comparable to those of LDA and online-LDA.

The rest of this paper is organized as follows. Section 2 introduces the preliminaries and the related work. Section 3 defines the problem of mining topics given a bounded region and a timespan. Section 4 presents an overview of the proposed solution. Section 5 introduces our methods. We present the experimental studies in Section 6. Section 7 concludes the study.

2. PRELIMINARIES & RELATED WORK

Table 1: Summary of Notations

Notation	Meaning
d	a spatio-temporal document $\langle id, l, t_c, w \rangle$
$z^{(m,n)}$	topic assigned to the n-th term of the m-th document
$p(v\|k)$	probability of appearance of word v given topic k
$c^k_{*,v}$	the count that topic k is assigned to word v
$c^k_{m,*}$	the count that topic k is assigned to the m-th document
α, β	hyper parameters of LDA
R	input spatial region
$[t_b, t_e]$	input timespan

Table 1 presents the frequently used notations.

Preliminary on Topic Models. Topic models are probabilistic models for discovering "topics" in a collection of documents. Each document may contain several topics, e.g., "sports", "digital devices", etc. If a document is more likely to be a "sports" document, words such as "football", "exercise", etc., would be more likely to appear in the document than "firework" or "pizza", etc. Topic models aim to reveal such latent semantic structure of a collection of documents. In topic models, a document is modeled as a mixture of topics and each topic is represented by a multinomial distribution over words.

Latent Dirichlet Allocation (LDA) [4] is arguably the most successful topic model to date. LDA is a generative model which generates topic distribution θ_d for each document d from a Dirichlet distribution $Dir(\alpha)$ and the word distribution ϕ for each topic from another Dirichlet distribution $Dir(\beta)$. The parameters α and β are hyper parameters of LDA which are used for smoothing. For each word token v in each document d, LDA draws a topic k from θ_d and then generates v from the corresponding word distribution ϕ_k.

Estimating the parameters, i.e., word distribution for topics ϕ, in LDA is intractable, and several algorithms (e.g., variational Expectation-Maximization algorithm, collapsed Gibbs sampling, etc.) have been proposed to solve the problem. Collapsed Gibbs sampling is a commonly used method to estimate the parameters for LDA. It works as follows: 1) Randomly assign a topic (from a given number of topics K) to each word token in the document; 2) Iteratively update the topic assignment for each word token according to Eq. (1).

$$p(z^{(m,n)} = k|Z^{-(m,n)}, \alpha, \beta) \propto (c_{m,*}^{k,-(m,n)} + \alpha) \times \frac{c_{*,v}^{k,-(m,n)} + \beta}{\sum_r c_{*,r}^{k,-(m,n)} + |V|\beta}, \quad (1)$$

where $z^{(m,n)}$ denotes the topic assignment for the n-th word in document m, $Z^{-(m,n)}$ denotes the topic assignment for word tokens excluding the n-th word token in document m, $c_{m,v}^{k,-(m,n)}$ is the count of assigning topic k to word v in document m excluding the topic assignment of the n-th word token in document m, and wildcard * stands for any document/word. The set V is the set of unique words, which is also called vocabulary, in the collection of documents. Intuitively, the first part of the equation tells how prevalent is topic k in document m, while the second part tells how prevalent is word v belonging to topic k across all documents. Since Gibbs sampling updates the topic assignment for each word token (m, n) by computing Eq. (1) for K topics in each iteration, the complexity of the algorithm is $O(|W|KI)$, where W is the set of word tokens in the collection of documents, and I is the number of iterations. It could be very slow when the collection of documents is large. After Gibbs sampling, the language model of a topic (posterior word distribution given a topic) $p(v|k)$ can be estimated as:

$$p(v|k) = \frac{c_{*,v}^{k} + \beta}{\sum_{r \in V} c_{*,r}^{k} + |V|\beta}, \quad (2)$$

where $c_{*,v}^{k}$ is the count of assigning topic k to word v in all documents.

Several studies exist on parallel implementation of LDA [26, 22, 1]. The main problem in the parallel LDA systems is that the topic-word count $c_{*,v}^{k}$ in Eq. (1) is shared by all processors. To make the topic-word counts consistent, all machines need to communicate with each other at the end of each iteration of Gibbs sampling, which incurs expensive communication cost. These systems can at most achieve a sub-linear speedup and training LDA models remains expensive.

Based on LDA, several online learning algorithms are proposed for text streams [2, 28] to speed up the learning process. They aim to sample topic assignments for new documents using a topic model learnt from historical data and combine the topic assignments for new documents to construct a new topic model. Sumait et al. [2] propose an online updating method (Online-LDA) to sample new documents using the counts of topic assignments in the historical data ($c_{old,*,v}^{k}$) as a part of the prior distribution, i.e., we set $\beta' = c_{old,*,v}^{k} + \beta$. Let $c_{new,m,v}^{k,-(m,n)}$ be the count of assigning topic k to word v in the m-th new document, excluding the topic assignment for the n-th word token in the m-th new document. The update function for online-LDA is:

$$p(z_{new}^{(m,n)} = k|Z_{new}^{-(m,n)}, Z_{old}, \alpha, \beta) \propto (c_{new,m,*}^{k,-(m,n)} + \alpha) \times \frac{c_{new,*,v}^{k,-(m,n)} + c_{old,*,v}^{k} + \beta}{\sum_r c_{new,*,r}^{k,-(m,n)} + c_{old,*,r}^{k} + |V|\beta}, \quad (3)$$

where $Z_{new}^{-(m,n)}$ is the topic assignments to word tokens in the new document collection excluding the n-th word in document m, and Z_{old} is the topic assignments to word tokens in historical data.

Online-LDA has the same complexity as LDA on the set of new documents, i.e., $O(|W_{new}|KI)$, where W_{new} is the set of word tokens in the new documents. But online-LDA saves the computation for sampling topics on the old documents. Online-LDA is the state-of-the-art technique which can be used to learn topics in a given region and timespan. However, to the best of our knowledge, no existing work proposes techniques for combining two LDA topic models pre-trained from two document sets into one model as we do in this work.

Data Cube and Text Cube. Our work is inspired by the concept of data cube [7], which is widely used for Online Analytical Processing (OLAP) on multi-dimensional data with operations like slice, dice, roll-up, and drill-down. Each row in the multi-dimensional text database contains some structured dimensions (i.e., attributes) and unstructured text data. The existing work on analyzing and exploring multi-dimensional text database is closest to our problem.

Lin et al. [13] propose a text-cube model on multi-dimensional text database. Text cube is a data cube where each cell aggregates a set of documents with matching attribute values in a subset of dimensions. Based on the text cube, they study the problem of processing an IR query (i.e., a set of terms) with constraints on dimensions to retrieve relevant documents. Simitsis et al. [20] propose a keyword driven OLAP system over a collection of multidimensional text data. Operations of roll-up and drill-down can be performed efficiently and accurately based on the content and the link-structure of a dynamically selected document subset during the query time. In addition, Ding et al. [5] study the problem of finding top-k most relevant cells in text cube for a keyword query. Similarly, based on the text cube, Zhao et al. [35] develop the TEXplorer system to rank candidate dimensions and cells for a keyword query.

However, those text-cube based proposals do not consider the semantic meaning (i.e., topics) of each term in documents. They are actually orthogonal with our work, and our proposed techniques can be integrated into these proposals for exploring spatial-temporal topics of data cube. This is actually a great motivation for our work. Moreover, our proposed combining algorithm in this paper fits perfectly to support the roll-up operation for topics of a text cube.

Zhang et al. [32] develop a topic-cube model for a multidimensional text database. Specifically, the topic cube can be viewed as a standard data cube augmented by a topic dimension based on a hierarchical topic tree and the objective of the topic-cube is to support users to drill-down and roll-up the text dimension along the topic hierarchy. The topic tree in [32] is based on the topic model generated from all documents in the dataset. However, our problem requires the topic model to be generated from the documents in the user specified spatial region and time interval. Moreover, topic-cube does not support mining topics for user specified regions. Therefore, topic cube cannot be applied to our problem.

Content Exploration. Some recent work aims at developing online data exploration mechanism based on some clustering methods. Zhang et al. [33] propose MiTexCube by augmenting each cell with micro-clusters that make the online processing more efficient. More recently, Feng et al. [6] propose a system called StreamCube to explore events over the spatio-temporal Twitter stream by clustering hashtags. Each hashtag in StreamCube is represented by a vector of terms/hashtags that co-occurred with the hashtag. Consequently, the clusters are generated based on the tweets that have hashtag(s), which only take 11% tweets according to a statistical study [10]. One can use keyword extracted from the text instead of hashtags to address the sparsity problem in StreamCube. However, we focus on the problem that efficiently mines topics of a collection of documents in the user specified region and timespan, as well as the topic assignment of each selected document. The comparison of clustering and topic modeling techniques is not our focus and we leave this as future work.

Angel et al. [3] propose the Grapevine system that aims to track entities in a large scale of documents. Grapevine extracts real-word entities (e.g., Barack Obama) from a collection of text data (e.g., blog posts, news articles, and tweets) using available entity extraction algorithms (e.g., [18]). Given a temporal and demographic restriction (e.g., location, gender), the topic in Grapevine is defined by the most talked-about entities for the chosen dimensions. However, our topics are discovered from topic models where each topic is represented by a probabilistic distribution over words. In addition, Grapevine uses semantic locations (country, state, city), while we use coordinate locations.

Exploring Spatio-Temporal Information in Documents. There exists a host of work on extracting spatial or/and temporal information from text data (e.g., [23, 11]). Several studies aim at mining geographical topics from a collection of spatio-temporal documents (e.g., [30, 9, 21, 31, 36]), and they mine both geographical regions, each represented by a Gaussian distribution, and topics for the whole collection. In some proposals [2, 27], the topic models in different time slices are compared to detect burst/emerging topics. Mathioudakis et al. [15] propose an approach to monitoring trends over the Twitter stream by detecting and grouping bursty keywords from tweets. Yin et al. [29] propose a user behavior model that combines the influences of topics related to users' intrinsic interests and the topics related to temporal context. Moreover, Strötgen et al. [24] try to discover event-location pairs by considering the co-occurrence of geographical and temporal expressions in document content. However, these problems substantially differ from our problem.

3. PROBLEM STATEMENT

We introduce our data model and define the problem of mining topics over a specified region and timespan.

3.1 Data Model

Definition 1: Spatio-Temporal Document. A spatio-temporal document is denoted by a quadruple $d = \langle id, l, t_c, w\rangle$, where id is the document id, which is assigned based on t_c, the creation time of d, l is a location with latitude and longitude, and w is a sequence of word tokens from the vocabulary $V = \{v_1, v_2, ..., v_{|V|}\}$. We use $d.w[i]$ to denote the i-th token in $d.w$. □

The spatio-temporal documents in Definition 1 can be geo-tagged tweets in Twitter, geo-tagged news in news portals, geo-tagged photos with tags in Flickr, Points of Interest (POIs) and check-ins with text descriptions in Foursquare, etc. Without loss of generality, we consider each document has only one location. When a document contains more than one location, we duplicate the documents for each location. For example, if a tweet about European SuperCup is related to three locations, (e.g., Barcelona, Sevilla, and Tblisi), we generate three copies of the tweet and each copy is assigned to one location.

3.2 Problem Definition

Based on the definition of topic in Section 2, we present our problem statement.

Definition 2: Topic Mining over Documents within a Specified Region and a Timespan Query (TMRT Query). Let D be a set of spatio-temporal documents, R be a rectangular region, and $[t_b, t_e]$ be a time period. TMRT query is to mine K topics from documents in D whose locations fall in R and creation time falls in $[t_b, t_e]$, as well as the topic assignment of each selected document, based on a given topic model. □

In this paper, we use LDA to mine topics for spatio-temporal documents because it is one of the most commonly used topic models.

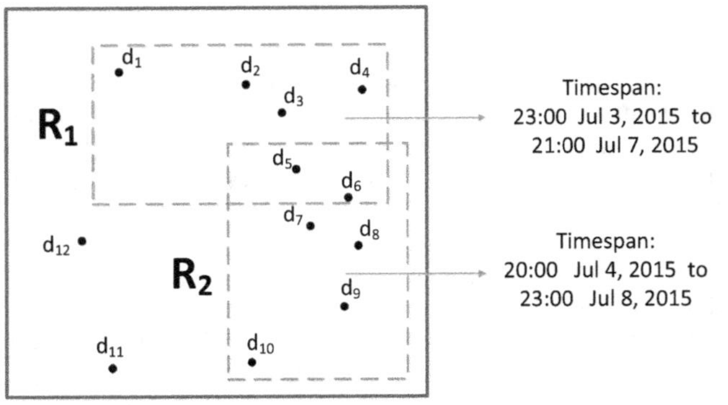

Figure 2: Example

Table 2: Information of Documents

doc	time of creation	tokens
d_1	09:42 Jul 3, 2015	yummy, pizza
d_2	10:18 Jul 6, 2015	espresso, bar, night
d_3	13:43 Jul 4, 2015	Barcelona, champion, excited
d_4	19:22 Jul 7, 2015	football, excited
d_5	17:40 Jul 6, 2015	iPhone, Nike, exercise
d_6	12:23 Jul 8, 2015	sleep, tired, holiday
d_7	22:57 Jul 3, 2015	Barcelona, sightseeing
d_8	18:41 Jul 4, 2015	marathon, exhausted
d_9	21:42 Jul 4, 2015	holiday, parade, independence
d_{10}	23:33 Jul 4, 2015	independence, firework
d_{11}	17:19 Jul 3, 2015	3D, movie, boring
d_{12}	10:40 Jul 7, 2015	sigmod, deadline

Table 3: Final Topic Assignment of R_1

document	topic of tokens
d_2	espresso (k_0), bar (k_1), night (k_1)
d_3	Barcelona (k_2), champion (k_2), excited (k_0)
d_4	football (k_2), excited (k_0)
d_5	iPhone (k_1), Nike (k_2), exercise (k_2)

Example 1: Let $D = \{d_1, d_2, ..., d_{12}\}$ be a set of spatio-temporal documents. The location of each document is presented in Figure 2. The creation time and the word tokens of each document are presented in Table 2. The two rectangles R_1 and R_2 and their corresponding timespans in Figure 2 represent two TMRT queries.

Table 4: Final Topic Assignment R_2

document	topic of tokens
d_5	iPhone (k_0), Nike (k_1) exercise (k_1)
d_6	sleep (k_0), tired (k_1), holiday (k_0)
d_9	holiday (k_0), parade (k_2), independence (k_2)
d_{10}	independence (k_2), firework (k_2)

Based on the set of documents falling in the corresponding spatial regions and timespans of R_1 and R_2, which are presented in the first column of Table 3 and Table 4, respectively, we mine LDA topic models by employing Gibbs sampling algorithm. Suppose the number of topics (i.e., "K") is set to 3, the final topic assignments for each document in R_1 and R_2 are presented in the second column of Table 3 and Table 4, respectively. The three topics of R_1 are given as follows (suppose the prior of word distribution of each topic $\beta = 0$ in LDA):

k_0: <p(excited|k_0)=0.67, p(espresso|k_0)=0.33>
k_1: <p(bar|k_1)=0.33, p(night|k_1)=0.33, p(iPhone|k_1)=0.33>
k_2: <p(Barcelona|k_2)=0.2, p(champion|k_2)=0.2, p(football|k_2)=0.2, p(Nike|k_2)=0.2, p(exercise|k_2)=0.2>.

The topics of R_2 is as follows:

k_0: <p(holiday|k_0)=0.5, p(iPhone|k_0)=0.25, p(sleep|k_0)=0.25>
k_1: <p(Nike|k_1)=0.33, p(exercise|k_1)=0.33, p(tired|k_1)=0.33>
k_2: <p(independence|k_2)=0.5, p(parade|k_2)=0.25, p(firework|k_2)=0.25>.

□

4. FRAMEWORK OVERVIEW

Based on LDA, we aim at mining K topics from a spatio-temporal document collection D for a TMRT query Q, which comprises a user specified region R and time interval $[t_b, t_e]$. In general, the collection of spatio-temporal documents is treated as a data warehouse and we conduct topic mining over a subset of documents falling in the region and time interval specified in Q. A straightforward solution would work as follows: We first find a set of documents D' such that for all $d \in D'$, d locates in R and $d.t_c \in [t_b, t_e]$. Then we learn K topics from the documents in D' using the collapsed Gibbs sampling technique [14]. However, as discussed in Section 1, it is time-consuming ($O(|W|KI)$) to train the topic model every time a TMRT query is submitted. Hence, we need a more efficient mechanism to handle the TMRT query.

An underlying idea of many approaches to performing OLAP is to organize the data into data cubes with dimensional hierarchies and summary statistics (e.g., [6, 32, 13]). With the help of data cubes, we are able to efficiently explore the data by different granularity levels [13]. Inspired by the idea of data cube, we organize the spatio-temporal documents into cells in a hierarchical index, and pre-compute topic models for a set of selected cells.

The remaining challenges of processing the TMRT query include: (1) How to leverage the pre-trained models associated with indexed cells to efficiently compute the topic model for the given query Q with region R and timespan $[t_b, t_e]$; (2) How to organize the documents into a hierarchical index, and which cells in the hierarchical index do we pre-compute topic models to help accelerate online topic mining for the TMRT query?

To address the first challenge, we propose a novel idea for efficiently combining the topic models of two cells (Section 5.1). Our idea is to accelerate the topic learning process by sampling topics for a set of word tokens instead of sampling topics for individual word tokens. We prove that our combining algorithm has a bounded error compared with the online-LDA algorithm. Based on our idea of combining topic models, we propose an online topic mining algorithm to search for cells which are completely or highly covered by the spatial region and timespan of query Q, and combine the models of these cells using our combining algorithm (Section 5.4).

To address the second challenge, we propose to organize the spatio-temporal documents based on the idea of Octree [16]. Octree is an extension of Quadtree in a three-dimensional space. It recursively partitions the space into eight equal-sized cells. Different from the traditional Octree in which a cell is partitioned into eight equal-sized subcells, we do the partitioning differently – we consider two objectives in determining how to partition a cell: 1) minimizing the word overlap among the subcells; and 2) balancing the number of documents among the subcells (Section 5.3). In addition, we propose an algorithm to determine on which cells to pre-train topic models and when to stop partitioning such that the space requirement does not exceed a specified threshold and the error of combining topic models does not exceed a predefined bound.

Figure 3 illustrates the framework of our approach. The documents are indexed by an Octree. Given a TMRT query with a rectangle and a timespan, we traverse the Octree to retrieve the topic models of the cells covered by the rectangle and the timespan. Next we combine these retrieved topic models. Finally we output the K topics of the new topic model computed by our combining algorithm.

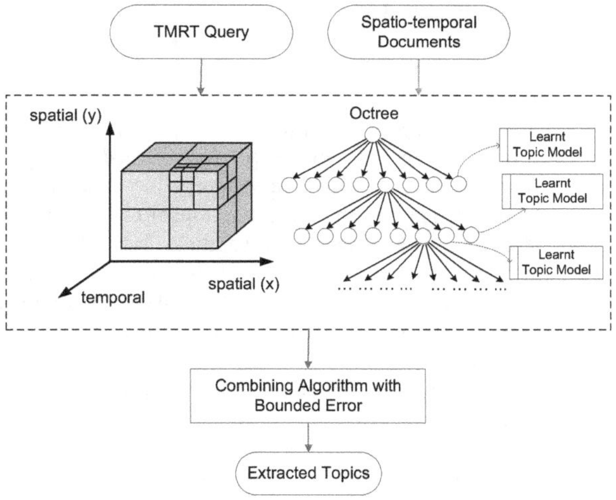

Figure 3: Framework

5. ALGORITHMS

In this section, we present the details of our algorithms for handling the TMRT queries. Specifically, we first present our sampling algorithm for combining the topic models of two Octree cells and its extension to combining multiple cells in Section 5.1. Then, we present a method to handle the cells that overlap with, but are not contained by the user specified region and timespan (Section 5.2). We present our method for partitioning the spatio-temporal documents into an Octree and the offline pre-computation for Octree cells in Section 5.3. Finally, we give our online topic learning algorithm for a TMRT query in Section 5.4.

5.1 Combining Topics of Two Octree Cells

In this subsection, we consider the case that the given region R and time interval $[t_b, t_e]$ in the TMRT problem exactly cover two Octree cells, for which we have pre-trained topic models. We will consider the general case and how to construct the Octrees in the subsequent subsections. We aim to combine the two pre-trained topic models into one topic model within R and $[t_b, t_e]$. The combining is challenging in that the topics in one model cannot be simply associated to the other model. Example 2 shows the pre-trained topics of two cells, which are represented by distribution over words. Even though k_2 in cell 1 is similar to k_1 in cell 2 (about sports), they are not exactly the same topic because their distributions are different. Moreover, a topic in one cell could be similar to multiple topics in the other cell. For example, k_0 in cell 2 is similar to k_0 and k_1 in cell 1. Due to the incompatibility of topics between the two models, we cannot simply combine them. We need to re-sample the topic models of the cells to make them compatible for combination.

Example 2: Pre-trained topics for cell 1:

k_0: <p(`iPhone`|k_0)=0.43, p(`Android`|k_0)=0.57>

k_1: <p(`bar`|k_1)=0.33, p(`night`|k_1)=0.33, p(`iPhone`|k_1)=0.33>

k_2: <p(`Barcelona`|k_2)=0.25, p(`champion`|k_2)=0.25, p(`football`|k_2)=0.25, p(`Nike`|k_2)=0.25>

Pre-trained topics for cell 2:

k_0: <p(`holiday`|k_0)=0.5, p(`iPhone`|k_0)=0.25, p(`sleep`|k_0)=0.25>

k_1: <p(`Nike`|k_1)=0.33, p(`exercise`|k_1)=0.33, p(`tired`|k_1)=0.33>

k_2: <p(`independence`|k_2)=0.5, p(`parade`|k_2)=0.25, p(`firework`|k_2)=0.25>.

□

There exist two solutions to learn the topic model for a TMRT query: 1) re-training an LDA model [4] for the spatio-temporal documents in the two cells; and 2) re-sampling the topics for one of the two Octree cells given the topic assignment of the other one using online-LDA [2]. However, both solutions suffer from high computation cost. Let the sets of word tokens in the two cells be W_1 and W_2, respectively, where W_2 is for the cell containing fewer words, i.e., $|W_2| < |W_1|$. The first solution needs to sample topics for all the documents in the two cells, and its complexity is $O((|W_1| + |W_2|)KI)$. The second solution only samples topics for documents in the cell containing fewer word tokens, and thus the training time can be reduced at least by half, i.e., $O(|W_2|KI)$. Although the second solution utilizes the pre-trained model of one cell, it fails to utilize the other pre-trained model.

To this end, we propose a combining algorithm that is able to leverage the pre-trained models of both cells. We reduce the complexity to $O((K + |M_2| + |V_2|)KI)$, where M_2 and V_2 are the set of documents and the vocabulary of the smaller cell, respectively. Note that $K + |M_2| + |V_2|$ is much smaller than $|W_2|$. We also prove that our algorithm has a bounded sampling error compared to online-LDA.

Similar to online-LDA, we use the topic assignment of one cell to re-train the model for the other cell. The significant difference is that we do not sample the topic for each word token in the documents one by one as in online-LDA. Instead, we sample the topic for word tokens that are assigned to the same topic in the pre-trained model simultaneously. Since this treatment is an approximation to online-LDA, we prove an error bound of our sampling algorithm compared to online-LDA. To the best of our knowledge, the idea is new although the topic model has attracted extensive research attention.

Let Z_1 and Z_2 be the topic assignment for the two sets of word tokens W_1 and W_2, respectively. Without loss of generality, we assume that $|W_1| > |W_2|$. We want to use the topic assignments Z_1 of the pre-trained model for cell 1 to resample Z_2. Consider the fact that the topic assignments of the pre-trained model divide the set of tokens W_2 into K subsets: $\{W_{21}, W_{22}, ..., W_{2K}\}$. Thus, we can jointly sample the word tokens of each subset according to the joint posterior distribution given the other topic assignments: $p(Z_2^{W_{2i}} = k | Z_2^{-W_{2i}}, Z_1, \alpha, \beta)$. Here, we denote $Z_2^{W_{2i}} = k$ as the event that all word tokens in W_{2i} are assigned to topic k and $Z_2^{-W_{2i}}$ as the topic assignments for the other subsets. The parameter α is prior of topic distribution and β is prior of word distribution for each topic as used in LDA.

Inference: We use collapsed Gibbs sampling to infer topics for the word tokens. Specifically, we compute the complete likelihood of the model, i.e., $p(W_2, Z_2, \Theta, \Phi | Z_1, \alpha, \beta)$, where Θ is the topic distribution and Φ is word distributions for topics. To compute the posterior distribution of assigning a topic to a set of word tokens (i.e., $p(Z_2^{W_{2i}} = k | Z_2^{-W_{2i}}, Z_1, \alpha, \beta)$), we integrate Θ and Φ out and compute the posterior as:

$$p(Z_2^{W_{2i}} = k | Z_2^{-W_{2i}}, Z_1, \alpha, \beta)$$
$$\propto \prod_{d_m \in D_{2i}} (c_{2,m,*}^{k,-W_{2i}} + \alpha)^{c_{2,m,*}^{i}} \prod_{v \in V_{2i}} \left(\frac{c_{2,*,v}^{k,-W_{2i}} + \beta'_{kv}}{\sum_r c_{2,*,r}^{k,-W_{2i}} + \beta'_{kr}}\right)^{c_{2,*,v}^{i}}, \tag{4}$$

where D_{2i} is the set of documents that contain the word tokens in W_{2i} and V_{2i} is the set of unique words in W_{2i}. The pseudo count β' is the sum of actual counts in cell 1 plus β, i.e., $\beta'_{kv} = c_{1,*,v}^{k} + \beta$, where $c_{1,*,v}^{k}$ is the count of assigning topic k to word v in cell 1. The count $c_{2,m,*}^{i}$ is the number of words in document d_m that are also in W_{2i}. Similarly, $c_{2,*,v}^{i}$ is the number of occurrences of word v in W_{2i}. The first part of Eq. (4) is the likelihood of assigning topic k to the current set of documents (D_{2i}) without considering the topic assignments on W_{2i}. The second part of Eq. (4) is the likelihood of assigning topic k to the unique words in W_{2i} by excluding the topic assignments of W_{2i}. The two parts of Eq. (4) correspond to the two parts in LDA (Eq. (1)).

Combining: To combine the topic model of two cells, we apply Eq. (4) to sample a topic for each word token set. We repeat the sampling process until the complete likelihood converges or the sampling process exceeds a large number of iterations, i.e., 1000. Let $\widetilde{c}_{2,*,v}^{k}$ be the final count of assigning topic k to word v. We combine the topic model by summing up the actual counts of the two cells: $\widetilde{c}_{*,v}^{k} = c_{1,*,v}^{k} + \widetilde{c}_{2,*,v}^{k}$. Therefore, the word distribution of each topic k for the combined model ϕ_{kv} could be estimated as:

$$\widetilde{\phi}_{kv} = \frac{\widetilde{c}_{*,v}^{k} + \beta}{\sum_r \widetilde{c}_{*,r}^{k} + |V|\beta}. \tag{5}$$

Complexity: The computation of Eq. (4) has time complexity $O(|M_{2i}| + |V_{2i}|)$ because we need to compute the production over the documents and words. We have K token sets in total and we need to compute Eq. (4) for K topics to sample the topic for each token set. Therefore, the total time complexity is $O(K^2(|M_{2i}| + |V_{2i}|)I) = O((K + |M_2| + |V_2|)KI)$, where M_2 is the set of documents and V_2 is the set of unique words in cell 2. Since $K + |M_2| + |V_2|$ is much smaller than $|W_2|$ (e.g., less than 10% of $|W_2|$ for tweets and even lower for long documents).

Sampling Error: We next prove that our algorithm has a bounded error compared to the topic models returned by online-LDA.

THEOREM 1. *Let $\phi_k^{(1,2)}$ and $\widetilde{\phi}_k^{(1,2)}$ be the language models for topic k after we combine cell 2 to cell 1 using online-LDA (Eq. (3)) and our approach (Eq. (4)), respectively. Let W_1 and W_2 be the word token sets of cell 1 and cell 2, respectively. Then, the expectation of Euclidean distance between two models $\mathbb{E}d(\phi_k^{(1,2)}, \widetilde{\phi}_k^{(1,2)}) < \sqrt{2}\frac{|W_1 \cap W_2|+|W_2|-1}{|W_1|+|W_2|}$.*

PROOF. Let $C_2^k = \sum_r c_{2,*,r}^k$, $\widetilde{C}_2^k = \sum_r \widetilde{c}_{2,*,r}^k$ and $C_1^k = \sum_r c_{1,*,r}^k$. Since the two sampling algorithms are based on the same prior α and $\beta'_{kv} = c_{1,*,v}^k + \beta$, we can assume $C_2^k \approx \widetilde{C}_2^k$. This assumption means the two algorithms will results in a similar topic proportion, i.e., the total counts for each topic is similar. Then we infer the bound as:

$$\begin{aligned}\mathbb{E}d(\phi_k^{(1,2)}, \widetilde{\phi}_k^{(1,2)})^2 &\approx \mathbb{E}\sum_{r\in W_1\cap W_2}\left(\frac{c_{2,*,r}^k - \widetilde{c}_{2,*,r}^k}{C_2^k + C_1^k + |V|\beta}\right)^2\\ &\le \mathbb{E}\sum_{r\in W_1\cap W_2}\frac{(c_{2,*,r}^k)^2 + (\widetilde{c}_{2,*,r}^k)^2}{(C_2^k + C_1^k + |V|\beta)^2}\\ &\le \frac{\mathbb{E}(\sum_{r\in W_1\cap W_2} c_{2,*,r}^k)^2 + \mathbb{E}(\sum_{r\in W_1\cap W_2}\widetilde{c}_{2,*,r}^k)^2}{(\frac{|W_1|+|W_2|}{|W_2|}C_2^k + |V|\beta)^2}.\end{aligned} \tag{6}$$

We next apply the definition of variance $\mathbb{E}(X-\bar{X})^2 = \mathbb{E}(X^2) - (\mathbb{E}X)^2$ to the inequality. Let $X = \sum_{r\in W_1\cap W_2} c_{2,*,r}^k$, then we have:

$$\begin{aligned}\mathbb{E}(\sum_{r\in W_1\cap W_2} c_{2,*,r}^k)^2 &= (\frac{|W_1\cap W_2|}{|W_2|}C_2^k)^2\\ &+ \mathbb{E}(\sum_{r\in W_1\cap W_2} c_{2,*,r}^k - \frac{|W_1\cap W_2|}{|W_2|}C_2^k)^2\\ &< (\frac{|W_1\cap W_2|}{|W_2|}C_2^k)^2 + \sum_{r\in W_1\cap W_2}\mathbb{E}(c_{2,*,r}^k - \frac{C_2^k}{|W_2|})^2.\end{aligned} \tag{7}$$

Since the maximum value of the second term appears when we assign all words to one topic, i.e., it is not hard to infer that the second term is smaller than $\frac{|W_2|-1}{|W_2|}(C_2^k)^2$. We apply similar inference on the term $\mathbb{E}(\sum_{r\in W_1\cap W_2}\widetilde{c}_{2,*,r}^k)^2$ in Eq. (6) to obtain the error bound of combining two topic models: $\sqrt{2}\frac{|W_1\cap W_2|+|W_2|-1}{|W_1|+|W_2|}$. □

According to Theorem 1, the smaller overlap of words between two cells will yield a lower error bound. Combining small cells to large cells yield a lower error bound.

Combining Multiple Cells: We extend the aforementioned method for combining two Octree cells to multiple cells. Suppose that the given region R and time interval $[t_b, t_e]$ exactly cover n cells, each having a pre-trained topic model. We can apply our combining method $n-1$ times on the n cells to learn the topic model. Next, we show that the error bound of combining multiple cells is parameterized by the number of combinings.

THEOREM 2. *Let $\phi_k^{(1,\ldots,n)}$ and $\widetilde{\phi}_k^{(1,\ldots,n)}$ be the language models for topic k obtained by combining topics of n cells according to Eq. (3) and Eq. (4), respectively. Let $W_1, \ldots, W_n$ be the sets of word tokens of n cells, respectively. Then, the expectation of Euclidean distance between two models $\mathbb{E}d(\phi_k^{(1,\ldots,n)}, \widetilde{\phi}_k^{(1,\ldots,n)}) < f(n) = \sqrt{2}\,\frac{|\cup_{i=2}^n W_i\cap W_1| + \sum_{i=2}^n |W_i| - 1}{\sum_{i=1}^n |W_i|}$.*

PROOF. Let $C_i^k = \sum_r c_{i,*,r}^k$, $\widetilde{C}_i^k = \sum_r \widetilde{c}_{i,*,r}^k$, where $1 \le i \le n$. Similar to Theorem 1, we assume $C_i^k \approx \widetilde{C}_i^k$. Then we have:

$$\begin{aligned}\mathbb{E}d(\phi_k^{(1,\ldots,n)}, \widetilde{\phi}_k^{(1,\ldots,n)})^2 &\approx \mathbb{E}\sum_{r\in\cup_{i=2}^n W_i\cap W_1}\left(\frac{\sum_{i=2}^n c_{i,*,r}^k - \widetilde{c}_{i,*,r}^k}{\sum_{i=1}^n C_i^k + |V|\beta}\right)^2\\ &\le \mathbb{E}\sum_{r\in\cup_{i=2}^n W_i\cap W_1}\frac{(\sum_{i=2}^n c_{i,*,r}^k)^2 + (\sum_{i=2}^n \widetilde{c}_{i,*,r}^k)^2}{(\sum_{i=1}^n C_i^k + |V|\beta)^2}\\ &< \frac{2(\frac{|\cup_{i=2}^n W_i\cap W_1| + \sum_{i=2}^n |W_i| - 1}{\sum_{i=2}^n |W_i|}\sum_{i=2}^n C_i^k)^2}{(\frac{\sum_{i=1}^n |W_i|}{\sum_{i=2}^n |W_i|}\sum_{i=2}^n C_i^k + |V|\beta)^2}.\end{aligned} \tag{8}$$

Thus, the error bound is $\sqrt{2}\,\frac{|\cup_{i=2}^n W_i\cap W_1| + \sum_{i=2}^n |W_i| - 1}{\sum_{i=1}^n |W_i|}$. □

5.2 Processing Partially Covered Cells

Since the given query with spatial boundary R and time interval $[t_b, t_e]$ may not cover an Octree cell completely, but only a part of it, we need to consider how to utilize the partial covered cells. Suppose the query completely covers n cells and partially covers n' cells and let $\widetilde{\phi}^{(n)}$ be the language model after combining the n completely covered cells. One solution is to apply online-LDA to the documents covered by the region and timespan of the given TMRT query in the n' partially covered cells, using $\widetilde{\phi}^{(n)}$ as the prior of language models. However, when the number of documents in the n' partially covered cells is large, it is not efficient to apply online-LDA to these n' partially covered cells.

Notice that for the cell that has a high overlap with R and $[t_b, t_e]$ (e.g., 90% of the documents are covered by R and $[t_b, t_e]$), its pre-trained topic model is often close to the one learnt from the covered documents. Therefore, it is desirable to use the pre-trained topic model of the cell to approximate the topic models learnt from the covered documents, and apply our proposed fast sampling algorithm presented in Section 5.1 to combine it to $\widetilde{\phi}^{(n)}$. In this section, we prove that there exists an error bound parameterized by the overlap using the pre-trained topic model to approximate the one learnt on covered documents.

THEOREM 3. *Let ϕ_k^{ALL} and ϕ_k^{PART} be the language models for topic k learnt on all the documents and the covered documents of a cell, respectively. Let $p \in (0,1)$ be the percentage of documents in the cell that are covered by the input spatial boundary and timespan. Then, the Euclidean distance between two models $\mathbb{E}d(\phi_k^{ALL}, \phi_k^{PART}) < \frac{\sqrt{(1+p^2)}}{p}$.*

PROOF. Let $c_{*,r}^{k,ALL}$ and $c_{*,r}^{k,PART}$ be the counts of assigning topic k to word r in all the documents and the covered documents, respectively. Let $C^{k,ALL} = \sum_r c_{*,r}^{k,ALL}$, $C^{k,PART} = \sum_r c_{*,r}^{k,PART}$. Without loss of generality, we assume the topics of tokens in the covered documents follow similar distribution of those in all the documents in the cell, i.e., $C^{k,PART} \approx pC^{k,ALL}$. Then, the following inequalities hold:

$$\begin{aligned}\mathbb{E}d(\phi_k^{ALL}, \phi_k^{PART})^2 &\approx \mathbb{E}\sum_r\left(\frac{c_{*,r}^{k,ALL} + \beta}{C^{k,ALL} + |V|\beta} - \frac{c_{*,r}^{k,PART} + \beta}{pC^{k,ALL} + |V|\beta}\right)^2\\ &< \frac{\mathbb{E}(\sum_r c_{*,r}^{k,ALL})^2 + \mathbb{E}(\sum_r c_{*,r}^{k,PART})^2}{(pC^{k,ALL} + |V|\beta)^2}\end{aligned} \tag{9}$$

Because $C^{k,PART} \approx pC^{k,ALL}$, the numerator in Eq. (9) is $(1+p^2)C^{k,PART}$. Thus, we have $\mathbb{E}d(\phi_k^{ALL}, \phi_k^{PART}) < \frac{\sqrt{(1+p^2)}}{p}$. □

According to Theorem 3, we combine the topic models of partially covered (at least τ_p percent of coverage) cells to those of completely covered cells with bounded error. Then for the remaining documents that are covered by the TMRT query, but are not in the cells covered by the query completely or at least τ_p percent, we use online-LDA to sample the topics for them.

5.3 Octree based Pre-Computation

After presenting our techniques for combining pre-computed topic models, we are now ready to present our techniques for the offline pre-computation process. The topic models built in the offline phase will be used to support our online topic mining algorithm.

In the offline pre-computation process, we need to consider two important research problems. First, how to divide the spatio-temporal documents in a large Octree cell into smaller cells to answer TMRT query efficiently and effectively, namely **Octree Cell Division** problem, which affects the accuracy and efficiency of our combining algorithm, and thus the efficiency and effectiveness of answering TMRT queries. Second, how to decide on which Octree cells we pre-train a topic model to balance the efficiency, storage, and accuracy of our approach, namely **Octree Cell Pre-Training** problem. Next, we present our approaches to solving the two problems.

Octree Cell Division: One straightforward way to divide a large Octree cell into smaller ones is to divide it equally in both spatial and temporal dimensions. However, this method is not optimized for our combining algorithm because it does not consider the word overlap between the child cells, which affects the accuracy of our algorithm for combining topic models as given in Theorem 1.

In this paper, we propose to select the division point for each dimension (latitude, longitude and time) by minimizing the word overlap between the 8 child cells divided by the division point. Specifically, suppose D_p be the set of documents in the Octree cell to be divided, $D_p^{(i)}(x)$ be the i-th child cell divided by 3-dimensional point x (latitude, longitude, and time). We optimize the following objective function:

$$\begin{aligned} \underset{x}{\text{argmin}} & \sum_{i=1}^{8} \sum_{j=1, j\neq i}^{8} |\{\cup_{d\in D_p^{(i)}(x)}\{d.w\}\} \cap \{\cup_{d\in D_p^{(j)}(x)}\{d.w\}\}| \\ s.t. \quad & \frac{|\{d|d^{(h)} > x^{(h)}, d \in D_p\}|}{|D_p|} > \sigma, \\ & \frac{|\{d|d^{(h)} \leq x^{(h)}, d \in D_p\}|}{|D_p|} > \sigma, \\ & \forall h \in \{latitude, longitude, time\}, \end{aligned} \tag{10}$$

where $d^{(h)}$ is one of the three dimensions of document d, $x^{(h)}$ is one of the three dimensions of the division point x, and σ is the threshold to control at least how many percentages of documents should be assigned to child cells on both sides of each dimension after division. This treatment is important to balance the size and overlap of the two sub-cubes. An extreme case could happen when we divide the cell into 7 empty cells and a cell that contains all the documents to achieve zero overlap. However, this division is meaningless for accelerating online topic learning. Our treatment can avoid the extreme case. More importantly, our method for Octree cell division can achieve a smaller error bound than the straightforward method of dividing a cell into eight equal-sized cells according to Theorem 1. When the division point of the straightforward method does not satisfy Eq. (10), the overlap between any two subcubes is not minimized, and thus the error bound of the straightforward method is larger than that is obtained by the optimal division point in Eq. (10) according to Theorem 1.

We solve this optimization problem as follows. Documents that fall in the cell to be partitioned comprise the set of candidate division points. We traverse these documents and select the point (document) that achieves the minimum objective score defined in Eq. (10). For each candidate point, it takes $O(|W_p'|)$ to compute Eq. (10), where W_p' is the set of word tokens in the documents within the constraints D_p'. Totally we have $|D_p'|$ candidate points, and thus the worst case time complexity is $O(|D_p'||W_p'|)$.

Octree Cell Pre-training: There exist two trade-offs in selecting the cells for topic model pre-computation. First, learning topics for cells in higher levels help improve accuracy of our method by reducing the number of combining operations if the region and timespan in the query cover the high-level cell. Nevertheless, a cell from higher levels is less likely to be completely covered by a user specified region and timespan. TMRT queries with small regions and narrow timespans may not contain the high level cells, and thus we cannot use the pre-trained topic models on high level cells to efficiently answer those TMRT queries. Second, if we build a deep Octree and pre-trained topic models for all cells, there is a better chance we can leverage the pre-trained models by our combining algorithm for a TMRT query. However, learning topic models for all cells in a deep Octree is space and time consuming.

Specifically, to make our online topic combining algorithm efficient and effective, we want to choose a group of Octree cells such that 1) the topic models built on these cells do not exceed a given space threshold τ_s; and 2) it is guaranteed that the error bound of combining topic models in the nearest descendants of these cells does not exceed a given threshold τ_e. This is because even though the TMRT query does not completely cover a high level cell, we can still combine the lower level cells covered by the query without exceeding the error threshold τ_e. To achieve this goal, we propose a greedy division algorithm for building the Octree and select the cells for pre-computation as described in Algorithm 1.

The main idea of the algorithm is to divide the Octree as finer-grained as possible within the space and accuracy threshold. We first insert all the spatio-temporal documents to the root of the Octree (line 1). Each time, we try to divide the largest cell (that contains largest number of spatio-temporal documents) into 8 subregions based on Eq. (10) (lines 5 – 6). To efficiently rank and find the largest cell, we maintain a max heap for cells to be divided with the number of spatio-temporal documents contained in each cell as the key (line 2). We invoke function `UpdateModelPos` (lines 7 – 10) to estimate the number of topic models we need to learn to guarantee the accuracy threshold τ_e. If the number of models exceeds the space threshold τ_s, we withdraw the division of current cell and stop dividing the Octree (lines 8 – 11); Otherwise, we insert the children of the current cell to the max heap to further divide them (lines 12 – 14). We repeat this process until the number of models exceeds the space threshold.

The function `UpdateModelPos` updates the number of models recursively from bottom to top. We aggregate the number of models to be learnt in the descendant cells of the current cell (lines 4 – 5). Suppose that the number of models in the descendants is $subCount$. Then we need $subCount - 1$ combining operations to construct a topic model for the current cell. We can measure the error bound of the $subCount - 1$ combining operations using a function of the number of combining operations, i.e., $f(subCount - 1)$. When the error bound is larger than the accuracy threshold τ_e, we train a topic model for the current cell to ensure that the error does not exceed the accuracy threshold (lines 6 – 8). We introduce an attribute *placeModel* to mark the cells we need to learn a topic model.

After applying Algorithm 1, we traverse the Octree and check the *placeModel* attribute of each cell. If it is true, we learn a topic model for the cell.

Algorithm 1: GreedyDivision

```
Input: A set of spatio-temporal documents D, space threshold τ_s,
       error threshold τ_e
Output: Qctree T
begin
1   Initialize T and Insert D to T;
2   Initialize max heap H, H.Insert (T);
3   modelCount ← 0;
4   while modelCount < τ_s do
5       T' ← H.DeleteTop();
6       T'.Subdivide();
7       modelCount ← UpdateModelPos(T, τ_e) ;
8       if modelCount > τ_s then
9           Withdraw the subdivision for T';
10          modelCount ← UpdateModelPos(T, τ_e);
11          return T
12      foreach T_c in T'.Children do
13          if T_c.D ∩ D ≠ ∅ then
14              H.Insert(T_c);
15  return T
Function UpdateModelPos(T, τ_e)
1   modelCount ← 0;
2   if T is not leaf then
3       subCount ← 0;
4       foreach T_c in T.Children do
5           modelCount ← subCount+
            UpdateModelPos(T_c, τ_e);
6       if f(subCount − 1) > τ_e then
7           modelCount ← modelCount + 1;
8           T.placeModel ← True;
9       else
10          modelCount ← modelCount + subCount
11          T.placeModel ← False;
12  else if T.D ∩ D ≠ ∅ then
13      modelCount ← 1;
14      T.placeModel ← True;
15  return modelCount;
```

5.4 Topic Mining within Region and Time Interval

Algorithm 2: OnlineLearning

```
Input: Octree T, spatio-temporal query Q = {R, [t_b, t_e]}, coverage
       threshold τ_p ∈ (0, 1]
Output: Topic model within Q
begin
1   N ← CellSelection(T, Q, τ_p);
2   Sort N by descending order of cell size;
3   Model ← N[0].Model;
4   for i = 1 to N.length do
5       Model ← FastSetSampling(Model, N[i].Model);
6   D_remain ← {d | d ∉ N, d ∈ Q};
7   Model ← OnlineLDA(Model, D_remain);
8   return Model
```

Algorithm 3: CellSelection

```
Input: a Octree T, spatio-temporal query Q = {R, [t_b, t_e]},
       coverage threshold τ_p ∈ (0, 1]
Output: cell set N
begin
1   N ← ∅;
2   if (|T.D ∩ Q.D| / |T.D| > τ_p) and T has pre-trained topic model then
3       N ← N ∪ {T};
4   else if T.D ∩ Q.D ≠ ∅ then
5       foreach T_c in T.Children do
6           N ← N ∪ CellSelection(T_c);
    return N;
```

Given an Octree with pre-trained topic models, we are now ready to present our online topic mining process for a TMRT query with region R and interval $[t_b, t_e]$ in Algorithm 2. We first find the cells that are covered by the given region at least τ_p percent and contain pre-trained topic models (line 1, `CellSelection`). Then, we order the returning cells in the descending order of their size (line 2) because combining smaller cells to larger cells could be more efficient as discussed in Section 5.1. Next, we combine the models of those cells using our fast word set based sampling algorithm (line 5, `FastSetSampling`). Finally, we invoke online-LDA to handle the remaining documents that are not covered by the founded cells.

In Algorithm 2, the function `CellSelection` returns cells that are completely or highly covered by the given TMRT query $Q = \{R, [t_b, t_e]\}$. When we select cells to combine, we aim to reduce the number of combining operations for 1) reducing the total combining time cost, and 2) reducing the error of combining. Therefore, we follow the greedy principle to chooses cells as large as possible (Algorithm 3). The sets $T.D$ and $Q.D$ are the sets of documents covered by the current cell T and query Q, respectively.

In Algorithm 3, we traverse the Octree tree in a breadth-first manner. We add the current cell to the result set if the cell is completely or highly covered by the given query Q (line 2). We continue to search lower levels if the current cell has overlap with Q (lines 4 – 6). We use a predefined coverage threshold τ_p to decide whether a cell is highly covered by Q and the error bound has been proven in Theorem 3.

6. EXPERIMENTAL RESULTS

We introduce the experimental setting in Section 6.1. We report the offline pre-computation cost of our framework in Section 6.2, and the experimental results in Sections 6.3 and 6.4. We show some example topics discovered by our algorithm in Appendix A.2.

6.1 Experimental Setup

Data Sets Our experiments are conducted on three real-life datasets collected from Twitter, Meetup and Wikipedia, respectively. We present our experimental results on Twitter, and Meetup in this section and the results on Wikipedia in Appendix A.1. Dataset Twitter comprises 7 million tweets posted from Aug 2012 to Oct 2012 in United States. Each tweet has text, location (latitude and longitude), and creation time, and each tweet contains 9 words on average. Dataset Meetup comprises 1.1 million events posted from Jan 2006 to Jun 2015. Each event has text description, location and creation time. and each Meetup event description has around 109 words on average. For Twitter, we randomly hold out 20% tweets of each day as test data to evaluate the accuracy of the topic models.

For Meetup, we randomly hold out 20% words of each document as documents in test data to evaluate the accuracy of the topic models. The details of the two datasets are listed in Table 5.

Table 5: Dataset Statistics

Datasets	Twitter	Meetup
# Documents	7,012,778	1,099,614
# Word Tokens	69,075,864	120,484,706
Vocabulary Size	137,141	88,004
Time Duration	Aug 2012 - Oct 2012	Jan 2006 - Jun 2015

Baseline Methods We compare our method using fast set sampling (FFS) with the following four methods.

LDA: We learn topics for the documents in the given region and timespan using LDA [4] for each TMRT query.

Online-LDA: We leverage the Octree structure in our framework to find the largest cell that is covered by the given region and timespan, and apply online-LDA [2] to sample the remaining documents based on the topic model of the largest cell.

FFS-EQ: We use our fast sampling algorithm to learn topics for TMRT queries. The difference from FFS is that FFS-EQ partitions a cell into 8 qual-sized smaller cells when building the Octree.

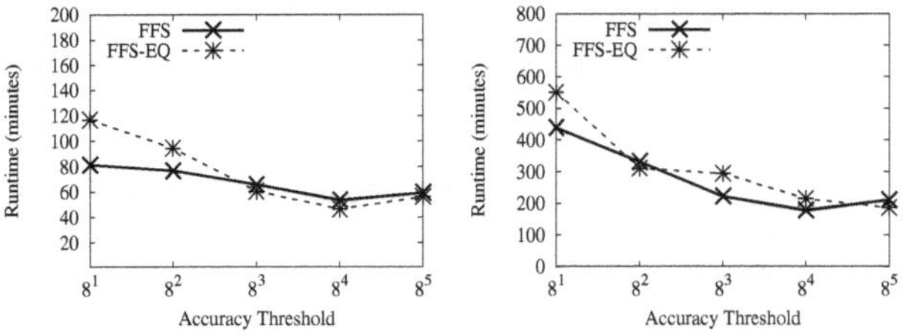

(a) Twitter (b) Meetup

Figure 4: Offline Pre-computation Cost w.r.t. Accuracy Threshold τ_e

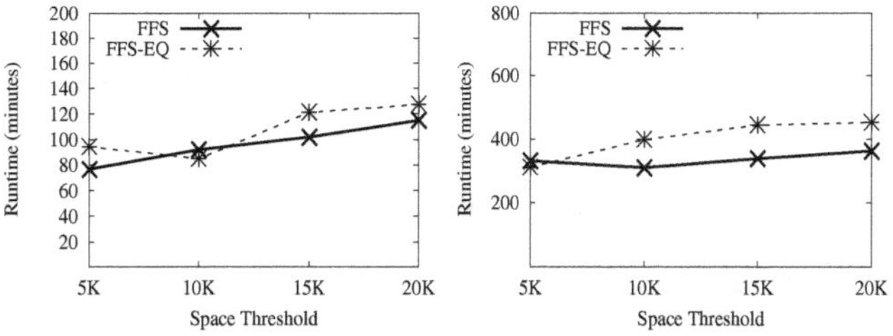

(a) Twitter (b) Meetup

Figure 5: Offline Pre-computation Cost w.r.t. Space Threshold τ_s

Evaluation Metrics To evaluate the efficiency and accuracy of the two models, we randomly generate 100 pairs of region and timespan with random size, each containing at least 100 documents in the test set for accuracy evaluation. For efficiency, we report the average runtime of the 100 pairs of region and timespan for all methods. To evaluate accuracy, we use perplexity to measure how likely we can use the model to generate the test set, which is a commonly used measure to evaluate the quality of topic models [25]. Lower perplexity means that the model has better ability of generalization. Perplexity is computed by using the probabilistic model learnt from the training set to estimate the likelihood of generating the test set.

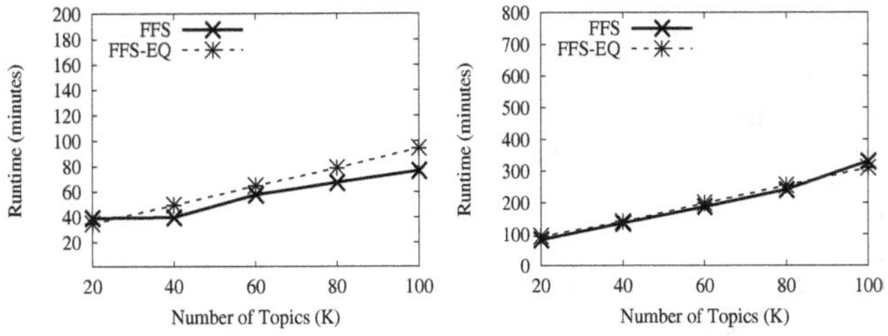

(a) Twitter (b) Meetup

Figure 6: Offline Pre-computation Cost w.r.t. Number of Topics K

Specifically, it is computed as follows:

$$perplexity(W_{test}) = exp\{-\frac{\log p(W_{test}|\Phi_{train})}{|W_{test}|}\}, \quad (11)$$

where $|W_{test}|$ is the set of word tokens in the test set, and Φ_{train} is the topic model to be evaluated. We apply the "left-to-right" method [25], which is often used for evaluating topic models, to estimate perplexity. We report the sum of perplexity of models learnt from the 100 pairs of region and timespan.

Parameter Settings We have three parameters in our framework, i.e., accuracy threshold τ_e, space threshold τ_s, and number of topics K. Note that the accuracy threshold τ_e is in fact a function of number of cells (n) to combine $f(n)$. For simplicity, we use $\tau_e = f(n)$ to denote the accuracy threshold of combining n cells. The space threshold specifies the maximum number of topic models to pre-train. We analyze the effect of these parameters by varying one parameter while fixing the others as default values. The settings of each parameter is shown in Table 6. The default settings of these parameters are $\tau_e = f(8^2)$ (i.e., learning topic models every 2 levels in the tree), $\tau_s = 5000$ and $K = 100$. We set the constraint for cell division σ in Eq. (10) at 0.3. Online-LDA and FFS-EQ use the same settings as our method (FFS).

All algorithms are implemented in C# on a workstation with Intel(R) Xeon(R) CPU E5-2680 v2 @2.80GHz and 64GB RAM.

Table 6: Parameter Settings

Parameter (notation)	Settings	Default
accuracy threshold (τ_e)	$f(8^1)$ to $f(8^5)$	$f(8^2)$
space threshold (τ_s)	5K to 20K (topic models)	5K
number of topics (K)	20 to 100	100

6.2 Pre-computation Cost

We report the pre-computation cost of FFS-EQ and our method FFS with different parameter settings. From Figure 4, we observe that the pre-computation cost is higher when the accuracy threshold τ_e is set at smaller value (corresponding to smaller error). This is because we need to learn topic models in higher level cells (which contain more documents) in the Octree to achieve better accuracy. Similarly, as the space threshold τ_s or the number of topics increases, the pre-computation costs of the three methods increase as shown in Figure 5 and Figure 6.

Our framework (FFS) with default setting takes around 100 minutes for pre-computation on Twitter data and 300 minutes on Meetup data. The pre-computation time of FFS and FFS-EQ is similar because the computation cost of pre-training topic models overwhelms the computation cost of our cell division method as described in Eq. (10).

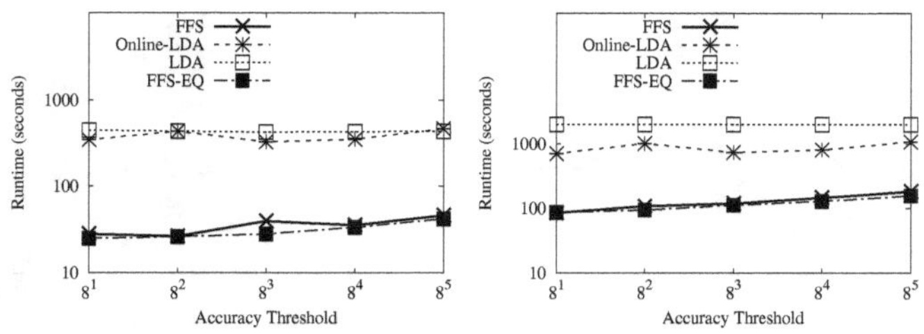

(a) Twitter (b) Meetup

Figure 7: Runtime w.r.t. Accuracy Threshold τ_e

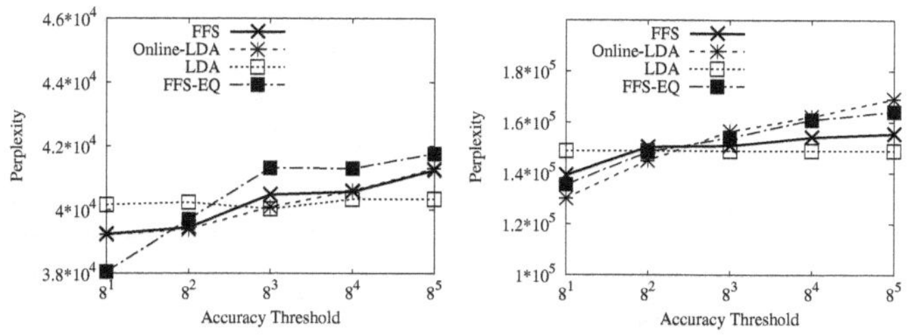

(a) Twitter (b) Meetup

Figure 8: Perplexity w.r.t. Accuracy Threshold τ_e

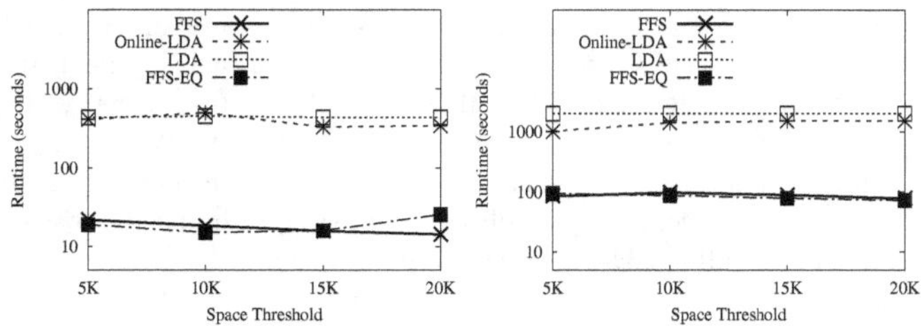

(a) Twitter (b) Meetup

Figure 9: Runtime w.r.t. Space Threshold τ_s

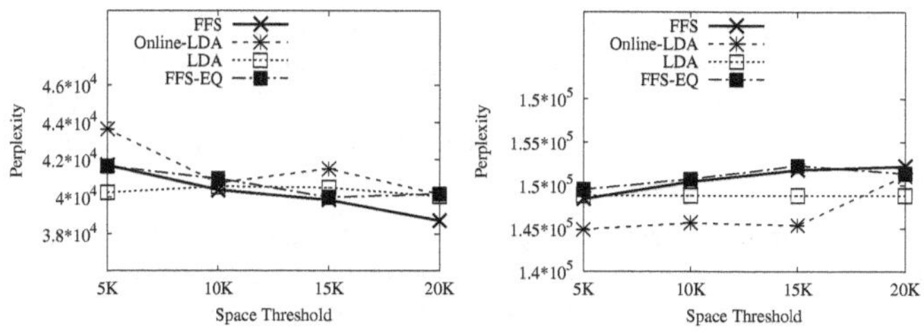

(a) Twitter (b) Meetup

Figure 10: Perplexity w.r.t. Space Threshold τ_s

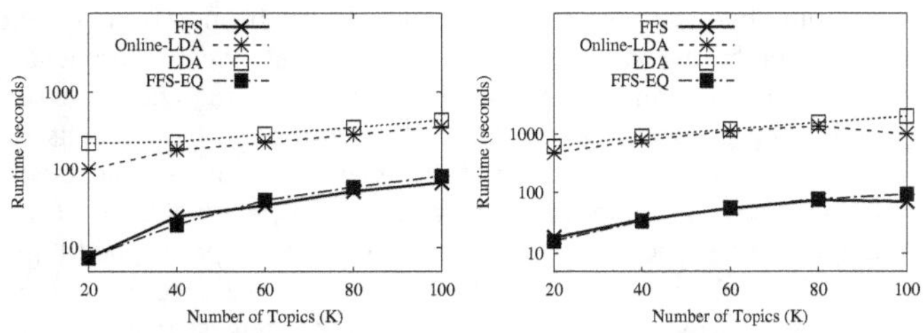

(a) Twitter (b) Meetup

Figure 11: Runtime w.r.t. Number of topics K

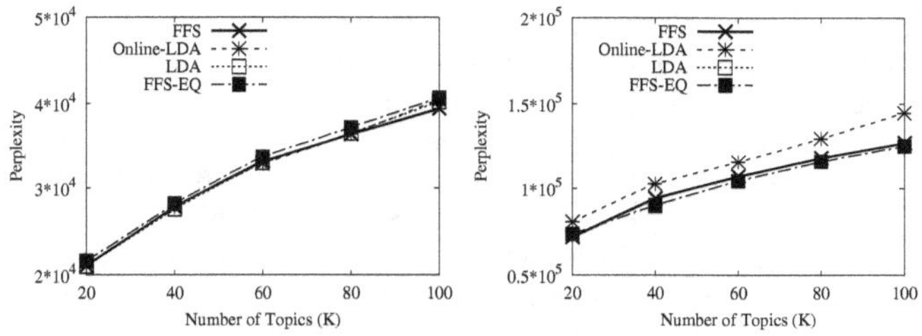

(a) Twitter (b) Meetup

Figure 12: Perplexity w.r.t. Number of Topics K

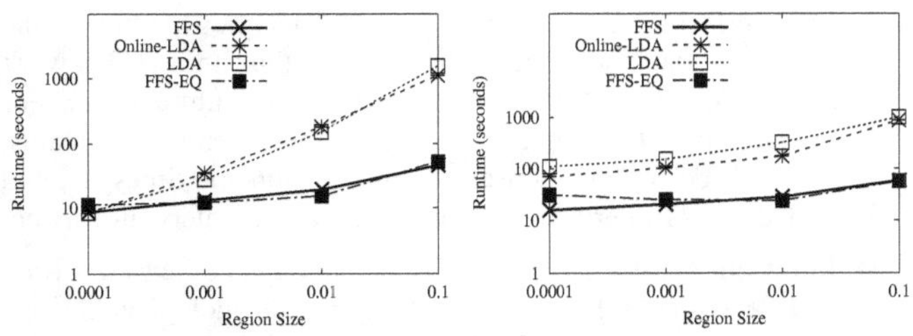

(a) Twitter (b) Meetup

Figure 13: Runtime w.r.t. Region Size

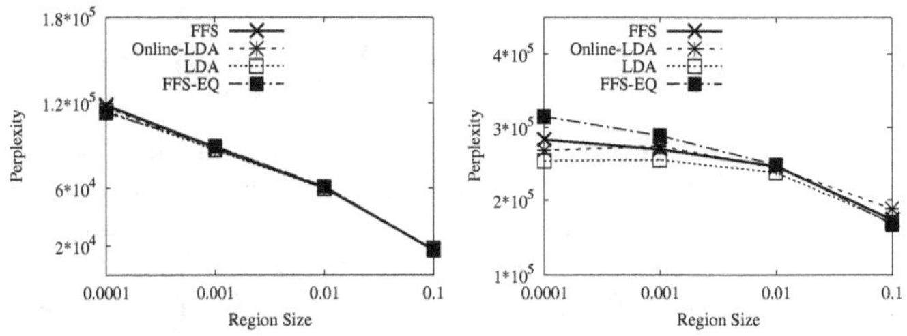

(a) Twitter (b) Meetup

Figure 14: Perplexity w.r.t. Region Size

6.3 Evaluation on Different Parameters

Varying Accuracy Threshold τ_e The accuracy threshold is used to guarantee the error bound of topic combining when we build the Octree as discussed in Section 5.3. We set the threshold as $f(8)$, $f(8^2)$, $f(8^3)$, $f(8^4)$, and $f(8^5)$, which indicates that we pre-train topic models every 1, 2, 3, 4, and 5 levels, respectively. We report the running time of learning topic models for the 100 random pairs of region and timespan in Figure 7(a) and Figure 7(b) as we vary the accuracy threshold.

Our proposed framework FFS is more than an order of magnitude faster than LDA and Online-LDA under different accuracy thresholds because our proposed sampling algorithm can efficiently combine two models without sampling all the word tokens. We also observe that with a smaller accuracy threshold (smaller τ_e), the online topic learning is slightly faster. With a lower accuracy threshold, we learn more pre-trained models for large cells in an Octree. Larger cells are more likely to cover most documents in the specified region and timespan, and thus reduce the time for combining topic models.

Figure 8(a) and Figure 8(b) show the perplexity computed on the test data for all methods. The perplexity of our proposed frame-

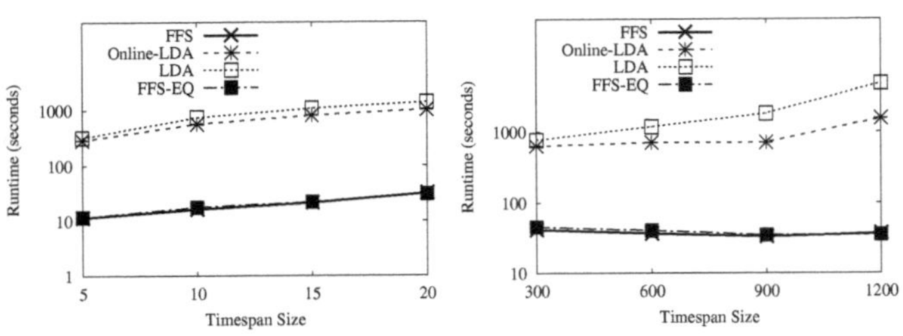

(a) Twitter (b) Meetup

Figure 15: Runtime w.r.t. Timespan Size

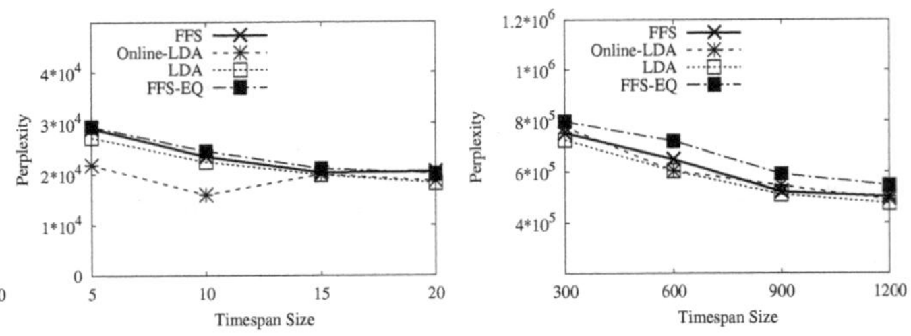

(a) Twitter (b) Meetup

Figure 16: Perplexity w.r.t. Timespan Size

work FFS is close to those of LDA and online-LDA because our algorithm combines topic models with a bounded error. Benefiting from the proposed partitioning method of Octree cells, FFS achieves higher accuracy in most cases (lower perplexity) compared with FFS-EQ.

Varying Space Threshold τ_s With a larger space threshold, we have more space for pre-trained topic models, and thus we can construct a deeper Octree. A large space threshold may help accelerate the online learning process because we can learn more pre-trained models in the Octree. As shown in Figure 9(a) and Figure 9(b), FFS and FFS-EQ outperform LDA and online-LDA by more than an order of magnitude. As shown in Figure 10(a) and Figure 10(b), FFS has better accuracy than FFS-EQ in most cases.

Varying Number of topics K The number of topics K affects both Octree based pre-computation and the running time of all methods because they all have complexity linear to K. As shown in Figure 11(a) and Figure 11(b), all methods run slower as K increases. The running time of our framework FFS increases a bit faster than LDA and Online-LDA because the complexity of our framework is quadratic to K. However, in practice K is often set to small values. As shown in Figure 12(a) and Figure 12(b), the perplexity increases when the number of K increases because there are more parameters for topic models (ϕ_k). When the number of parameters increases, the likelihood computed as the joint probability of word tokens decreases.

6.4 Evaluation on Different Regions and Timespans

We also experiment on different user specified regions and timespans. All the parameters are set as default values except the space threshold τ_s is set at 20000. Let the spatial area of the document collection be A. We vary the size of regions with the following values: $0.0001A$, $0.001A$, $0.01A$, $0.1A$ while fixing the size of timespans as 5 days on Twitter data and 300 days on Meetup data. We randomly generate 100 pairs of region and timespan for each of the four settings of region size. The efficiency results are shown in Figure 13(a) and Figure 13(b), and the perplexity results are shown in Figure 14(a) and Figure 14(b). As region size decreases, the running time decreases while the perplexity increases. The running time of our algorithm is close to or even slightly higher than LDA and online-LDA because when the region becomes smaller than the leaf cell of the Octree, our framework is equivalent to LDA. The perplexity of all methods decreases because the number of documents covered by the region increases. Without enough documents (When region size is 0.0001A), each region contains only several hundred or several thousand documents on average for both dataset, the learnt LDA model is less effective on the hold-out test data.

We also vary the timespan by 5, 10, 15, 20 days on Twitter Data and 300, 600, 900, 1200 days on Meetup data while fixing the size of regions to $0.1A$. For each of the timespan, we randomly generate 100 pairs of region and timespan. Figure 15(a) and Figure 15(b) show the efficiency of all methods in different timespans, while Figure 16(a) and Figure 16(b) show the perplexity. With a larger timespan, more documents are included, and thus it takes longer to process. The perplexity of FFS and FFS-EQ is similar to those of LDA and online-LDA as shown in Figure 16(a).

7. CONCLUSIONS AND FUTURE WORK

We study the problem of mining topics from a collection of spatio-temporal documents given a region and a time interval. Based on the LDA model, we propose an algorithm with bounded errors to combine two pre-trained topic models learnt from two document sets, each falling in a region and a time period. We also propose a method to build an Octree based indexing structure to facilitate our online topic learning algorithm. We partition the Octree cells by considering the word overlap of the generated cells to achieve better accuracy for combining two pre-trained topic models. Then we employ our proposed algorithms to combine the pre-trained topic models to obtain the topics for documents in the specified region and time period. Our experimental results suggest that our proposed framework is able to improve the runtime performance by at least an order of magnitude compared with LDA and online-LDA. Meanwhile, the effectiveness of our proposal, measured by perplexity, is close to that of LDA and online-LDA.

This work combines data management principles to improve the efficiency of machine learning/data mining algorithms. This work opens to a number of promising directions for future work. For example, exploratory topic mining from spatio-temporal streams, topic trends detection in a user specified region and timespan, and extended TMRT query with keywords as another query dimension.

Acknowledgment This research was carried out at the Rapid-Rich Object Search (ROSE) Lab at the Nanyang Technological University, Singapore. The ROSE Lab is supported by the National Research Foundation, Prime Minister's Office, Singapore, under its IDM Futures Funding Initiative and administered by the Interactive and Digital Media Programme Office. This work is also supported in part by a Tier-1 grant awarded by Ministry of Education Singapore (RG22/15). We would also like to thank the anonymous reviewers for their constructive comments and suggestions, which help us to improve the paper substantially.

8. REFERENCES

[1] A. Ahmed, M. Aly, J. Gonzalez, S. Narayanamurthy, and A. J. Smola. Scalable inference in latent variable models. In *WSDM*, pages 123–132, 2012.

[2] L. AlSumait, D. Barbará, and C. Domeniconi. On-line LDA: adaptive topic models for mining text streams with

applications to topic detection and tracking. In *ICDM*, pages 3–12, 2008.

[3] A. Angel, N. Koudas, N. Sarkas, and D. Srivastava. What's on the grapevine? In *SIGMOD*, pages 1047–1050, 2009.

[4] D. M. Blei, A. Y. Ng, and M. I. Jordan. Latent dirichlet allocation. *J. Mach. Learn. Res.*, 3:993–1022, 2003.

[5] B. Ding, B. Zhao, C. X. Lin, J. Han, C. Zhai, A. N. Srivastava, and N. C. Oza. Efficient keyword-based search for top-k cells in text cube. *IEEE Trans. Knowl. Data Eng.*, 23(12):1795–1810, 2011.

[6] W. Feng, C. Zhang, W. Zhang, J. Han, J. Wang, C. Aggarwal, and J. Huang. STREAMCUBE: hierarchical spatio-temporal hashtag clustering for event exploration over the twitter stream. In *ICDE*, pages 1561–1572, 2015.

[7] J. Han and M. Kamber. *Data Mining: Concepts and Techniques*. Morgan Kaufmann, 2000.

[8] T. Hofmann. Learning the similarity of documents: An information-geometric approach to document retrieval and categorization. In *NIPS*, pages 914–920, 1999.

[9] L. Hong, A. Ahmed, S. Gurumurthy, A. J. Smola, and K. Tsioutsiouliklis. Discovering geographical topics in the twitter stream. In *WWW*, pages 769–778, 2012.

[10] L. Hong, G. Convertino, and E. H. Chi. Language matters in twitter: A large scale study. In *Proceedings of the Fifth International Conference on Weblogs and Social Media, Barcelona, Catalonia, Spain, July 17-21, 2011*, 2011.

[11] G. Li, J. Hu, J. Feng, and K. Tan. Effective location identification from microblogs. In *ICDE*, pages 880–891, 2014.

[12] G. Li, Y. Wang, T. Wang, and J. Feng. Location-aware publish/subscribe. In *KDD*, pages 802–810, 2013.

[13] C. X. Lin, B. Ding, J. Han, F. Zhu, and B. Zhao. Text cube: Computing IR measures for multidimensional text database analysis. In *ICDM*, pages 905–910, 2008.

[14] J. S. Liu. The collapsed gibbs sampler in bayesian computations with applications to a gene regulation problem. *Journal of the American Statistical Association*, 89(427):958–966, 1994.

[15] M. Mathioudakis and N. Koudas. Twittermonitor: trend detection over the twitter stream. In *SIGMOD*, pages 1155–1158, 2010.

[16] D. Meagher. Geometric modeling using octree encoding. *Computer Graphics and Image Processing*, 19(2):129–147, 1982.

[17] N. Rehman, S. Mansmann, A. Weiler, and M. Scholl. Building a data warehouse for twitter stream exploration. In *ASONAM*, pages 1341–1348, Aug 2012.

[18] N. Sarkas, A. Angel, N. Koudas, and D. Srivastava. Efficient identification of coupled entities in document collections. In *ICDE*, pages 769–772, 2010.

[19] A. Shraer, M. Gurevich, M. Fontoura, and V. Josifovski. Top-k publish-subscribe for social annotation of news. *PVLDB*, 6(6):385–396, 2013.

[20] A. Simitsis, A. Baid, Y. Sismanis, and B. Reinwald. Multidimensional content exploration. *PVLDB*, 1(1):660–671, 2008.

[21] S. Sizov. Geofolk: Latent spatial semantics in web 2.0 social media. In *WSDM*, pages 281–290, 2010.

[22] A. Smola and S. Narayanamurthy. An architecture for parallel topic models. *PVLDB*, 3(1-2):703–710, Sept. 2010.

[23] J. Strötgen and M. Gertz. Timetrails: A system for exploring spatio-temporal information in documents. *PVLDB*, 3(2):1569–1572, 2010.

[24] J. Strötgen, M. Gertz, and P. Popov. Extraction and exploration of spatio-temporal information in documents. In *GIR*, 2010.

[25] H. M. Wallach, I. Murray, R. Salakhutdinov, and D. Mimno. Evaluation methods for topic models. In *ICML*, pages 1105–1112, 2009.

[26] Y. Wang, H. Bai, M. Stanton, W.-Y. Chen, and E. Y. Chang. Plda: Parallel latent dirichlet allocation for large-scale applications. In *AAIM*, pages 301–314, 2009.

[27] X. Yan, J. Guo, Y. Lan, J. Xu, and X. Cheng. A probabilistic model for bursty topic discovery in microblogs. In *AAAI*, pages 353–359, 2015.

[28] L. Yao, D. Mimno, and A. McCallum. Efficient methods for topic model inference on streaming document collections. In *KDD*, pages 937–946, 2009.

[29] H. Yin, B. Cui, L. Chen, Z. Hu, and Z. Huang. A temporal context-aware model for user behavior modeling in social media systems. In *SIGMOD*, pages 1543–1554, 2014.

[30] Z. Yin, L. Cao, J. Han, C. Zhai, and T. Huang. Geographical topic discovery and comparison. In *WWW*, pages 247–256, 2011.

[31] Q. Yuan, G. Cong, Z. Ma, A. Sun, and N. M. Thalmann. Who, where, when and what: Discover spatio-temporal topics for twitter users. In *SIGKDD*, pages 605–613, 2013.

[32] D. Zhang, C. Zhai, and J. Han. Topic cube: Topic modeling for OLAP on multidimensional text databases. In *SDM*, pages 1124–1135, 2009.

[33] D. Zhang, C. Zhai, and J. Han. Mitexcube: Microtextcluster cube for online analysis of text cells. In *CIDU*, pages 204–218, 2011.

[34] D. Zhang, C. Zhai, J. Han, A. N. Srivastava, and N. C. Oza. Topic modeling for OLAP on multidimensional text databases: topic cube and its applications. *Statistical Analysis and Data Mining*, 2(5-6):378–395, 2009.

[35] B. Zhao, C. X. Lin, B. Ding, and J. Han. Texplorer: keyword-based object search and exploration in multidimensional text databases. In *CIKM*, pages 1709–1718, 2011.

[36] K. Zhao, G. Cong, Q. Yuan, and K. Q. Zhu. SAR: A sentiment-aspect-region model for user preference analysis in geo-tagged reviews. In *ICDE*, pages 675–686, 2015.

APPENDIX

A. ADDITIONAL EXPERIMENTS

A.1 Evaluation on Wikipedia Data

Wikipedia contains 0.92 million geo-tagged pages, and each page contains 221 words on average. We randomly hold out 20% words of each document as documents in test data to evaluate the perplexity. Different from the two datasets in Section 6.1, Wikipedia pages do not contain temporal information. We replace Octree with Quadtree in our method to answer TMRT queries without timespan. We compare FFS, Online-LDA, and LDA by varying the size of query regions with the following values: $0.0001A$, $0.001A$, $0.01A$, $0.1A$, where A is the spatial area of the Wikipedia document collection. We use the same parameter settings as in Section 6.4. The experimental results are reported in Figure 17.

The three methods have similar efficiencies when the size of the query regions is $0.0001A$. However, as the size of the query regions increases, FFS performs much faster than Online-LDA and LDA, because more documents are covered in larger query region and our proposed method can learn the topic models by combining pre-trained models efficiently. FFS runs around an order of magnitude faster than Online-LDA and LDA, while achieves similar perplexity as the two methods.

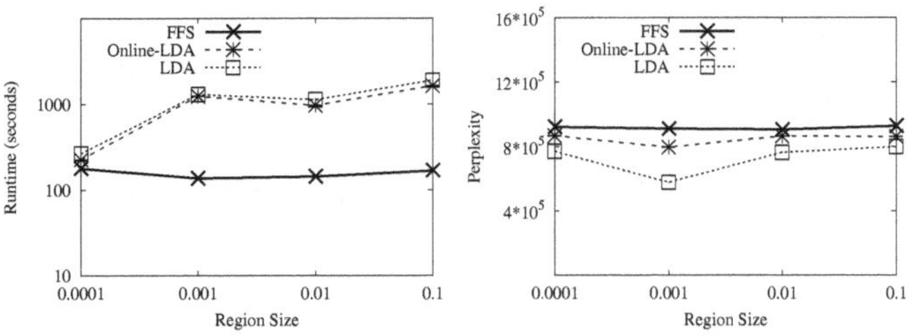

(a) Runtime (b) Perplexity

Figure 17: Runtime and Perplexity w.r.t. Region Size

A.2 Qualitative Evaluation on Extracted Topics

To exemplify the extracted topics of the three methods, we submit a TMRT problem within the region of New York city and timespan from Sep 1, 2012 to Sep 30, 2012, as shown in Figure 18. We apply FFS, LDA and Online-LDA to this TMRT problem using the default parameter setting. The number of words is 637,581, we run 1000 iterations of Gibbs sampling for the three methods. The running time of FFS, LDA and Online-LDA are 104.96 seconds, 1586.14 seconds and 1776.38 seconds, respectively.

We randomly select three topics from LDA and find three topics from the result of online-LDA and our proposed framework (FFS) that are most similar to (measured by KL divergence) the three ones of LDA, respectively. We manually name the extracted three topics as "Photo Sharing", "Politics" and "Celebration", and visualize them using "Word Cloud" in Figure 18.

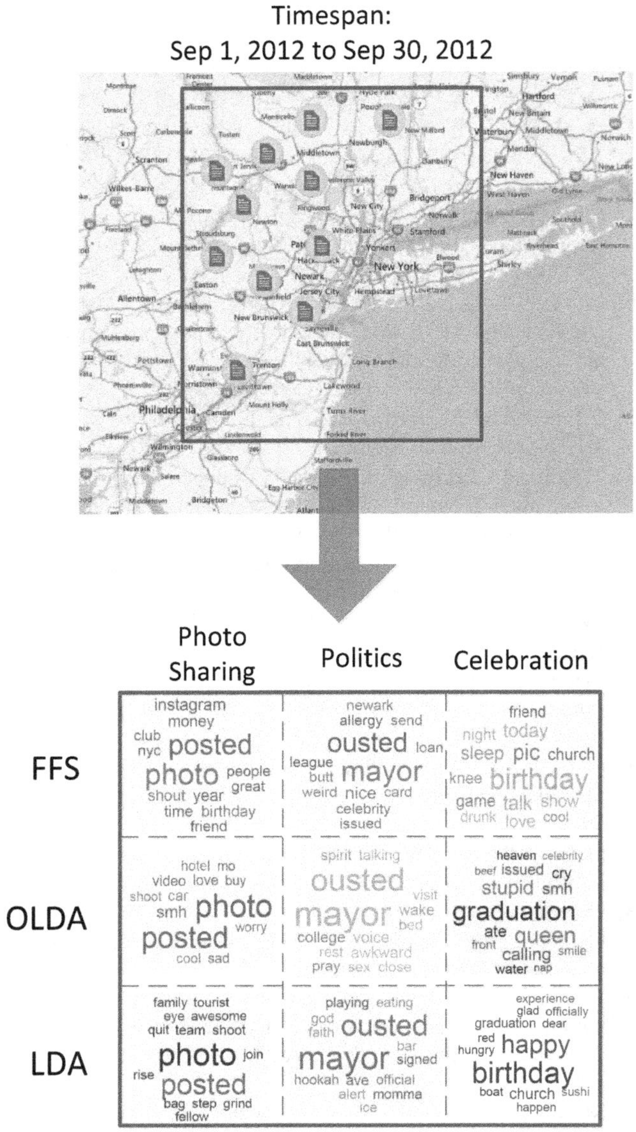

Figure 18: Topics Extracted by Different Methods

In general, the topics extracted by the three methods are similar. Surprisingly, our proposed framework can also discover some representative words for a topic (e.g., "friend" in topic "Photo Sharing" and "work", "education" in topic "Politics") that LDA and online-LDA have not discovered. Consider the quality of extracted topics and runtime efficiency, our proposed framework is more suitable to solve the TMRT problem compared to LDA and online-LDA.

ParTime: Parallel Temporal Aggregation

Markus Pilman, Martin Kaufmann, Florian Köhl
Systems Group, ETH Zürich, Switzerland
{mpilman,martinka,koehlf}@ethz.ch

Donald Kossmann
Microsoft Research, Redmond, WA, USA
donaldk@microsoft.com

Damien Profeta
Amadeus Group, Sophia Antipolis, France
damien.profeta@amadeus.net

ABSTRACT

This paper presents ParTime, a parallel algorithm for temporal aggregation. Temporal aggregation is one of the most important, yet most complex temporal query operators. It has been extensively studied in the past, but so far there has only been one attempt to parallelize this operator. ParTime supports data parallelism and has a number of additional advantages: It supports the full bi-temporal data model, it requires no a-priori indexing, it supports shared computation, and it runs well on modern hardware (i.e., NUMA machines with large main memories). We implemented ParTime in a parallel database system and carried out comprehensive performance experiments with a real workload from the airline industry and a synthetic benchmark, the TPC-BiH benchmark. The results show that ParTime significantly outperforms any other available temporal database system. Furthermore, the results show that ParTime is competitive as compared to the Timeline Index, the best known technique to process temporal queries from the research literature and which is based on pre-computation and indexing.

1. INTRODUCTION

Support for temporal data is a core feature of many data management systems. There are a number of application areas that rely heavily on temporal data. Examples are the financial industry, health care, and the travel industry. Correspondingly, the SQL standard has been mandating support for temporal data processing since 2011. As of today, most major relational database systems comply and support temporal data and queries (e.g., IBM DB2, Oracle, SAP HANA, and Teradata).

Temporal databases and the efficient implementation of temporal operators have been studied extensively since the early Nineties [22]. There are a number of different temporal operators such as time travel, temporal join, windowing, and temporal aggregation. In general, temporal databases are larger than non-temporal databases because every tuple can come in several versions. Furthermore, temporal operators are typically more complex than non-temporal operators. As a result, parallelization is important in order to achieve acceptable response times in temporal database systems.

SIGMOD'16, June 26-July 01, 2016, San Francisco, CA, USA

DOI: http://dx.doi.org/10.1145/2882903.2903732

The focus of this work is on the temporal aggregation operator. Temporal aggregation is a critical operator in many application domains. More specifically, temporal aggregation is critical in the particular workload from the travel industry that motivated this work. In that industry, for instance, analysts are interested to plot the number of available seats of all flights for a certain connection over time. It turns out that temporal aggregation is one of the most expensive temporal operators, and it has been one of the most difficult operators to optimize. As a result, there has been extensive prior work on this operator in the past; e.g., [3, 26, 16, 13] to name just a few. Because of its high cost, it is particularly important to parallelize this operator. To the best of our knowledge, however, there has been only one attempt by Gendoranoy et al. [9] to parallelize this operator. The reason is that most approaches to implement termporal aggregation are based on tree traversals and these approaches do not parallelize well as shown in Gendoranoy's work. In addition, tree-based approaches do not perform well in modern, main-memory and NUMA-aware parallel database systems as shown in [5].

This paper proposes the first parallel temporal aggregation algorithm with (almost) linear speed up, called ParTime. ParTime is a two pass algorithm that is based on the simple insight that the impact that a record has on the aggregate value can be computed independent of any other record. Based on this insight, ParTime is able to compute this impact of all records in parallel and in any given order. In the first pass, ParTime scans the whole table and computes the impact of each record at every point in time. ParTime executes this scan in parallel and there are no constraints on how the table is partitioned or the degree of parallelism. The second pass merges the results of the first pass, thereby computing the aggregation result for each point in time. This second pass works like the merge phase of an ordinary (non-temporal) sort-based `GROUP BY` operator [11]. In principle, this second pass can be parallelized, too. It turns out, however, that this second pass is cheap for most practical queries so that we propose to carry out this second pass sequentially. For completeness, we studied queries for which this second pass was not cheap with synthetic benchmarks, but we have not seen any such cases in real workloads yet.

In addition to its simplicity and embarrassing parallelism (in the first pass), ParTime has a number of other important advantages. One important advantage is that it works on any kind of bi-temporal data (i.e., databases that have multiple dimensions of business time and transaction time). In contrast, many algorithms devised in the literature only work for one time dimension. In our experience, support for the bi-temporal data model is crucial. In the airline industry, for instance, data scientists are often interested to aggregate over the time when a booking was made and the departure time of a flight. Another advantage is that ParTime integrates well into databases that were designed for modern NUMA hardware. ParTime is based on a parallel table scan that allows each core to separately and independently compute data from a different partition of the database with memory affinity. Last but not least, ParTime integrates well into any parallel database system. It is implemented by extending the scan operatior. In particular, ParTime can make use of *shared* parallel scans which are implemented in many modern parallel database systems [27, 6, 25]. As we will see, this feature is particularly important for high-throughput workloads with many concurrent non-temporal queries and updates. Due to data freshness and cost considerations, it is often not affordable to build a separate data warehouse just to execute temporal queries; instead, all queries and updates must be served by a single database system.

We implemented ParTime and integrated it into Crescando, a main-memory parallel database system deployed at Amadeus, one of the leading airline reservation systems [25]. We carried out comprehensive performance experiments with both the Amadeus workload and with a synthetic temporal database benchmark, the TPC-BiH benchmark [14]. The results confirm that Crescando with ParTime significantly outperforms any other available temporal database system. ParTime is also competitive to the best known way to implement temporal aggregation from the research literature [13]. This approach is based on the so-called Timeline Index, which effectively pre-computes the results of temporal aggregation; i.e., the Timeline Index can be seen as a materialized temporal aggregation view. The Timeline Index, thus, serves as a lower bound for the best possible performance that can be achieved and it shows that with sufficient parallelism, ParTime can reach this lower bound even without any materialization. Unfortunately, materialization and the Timeline Index are not viable for update-intensive workloads such as the Amadeus workload because of the prohibitively high cost to maintain the Timeline Index with every update; nevertheless, the Timeline Index is a great baseline to study the performance for read-only workloads.

In summary, this paper presents the following contributions:

- The ParTime method for parallel temporal aggregation. This paper shows how ParTime works for one-dimensional and multi-dimensional temporal aggregation. Additionally, we present a special optimization that is applicable to a popular class of temporal aggregation queries, so called *windowed temporal aggregation queries*.
- The implementation and integration of ParTime into Crescando, a parallel, main-memory database system. The most important contribution here is to show how the processing of temporal aggregation queries with ParTime seamlessly co-exists with the processing of other temporal and non-temporal queries and updates as part of a shared scan. It is only this embedding of ParTime into a shared scan that makes it possible to sustain the high query and update throughput of the Amadeus workload. No other database system that we are aware of is able to sustain this workload.
- The results of comprehensive performance experiments. These results study the speed-ups that can be achieved with ParTime and demonstrate the robustness of ParTime for complex and update-intensive workloads.

The remainder of this paper is organized as follows: Section 2 discusses related work. Section 3 presents the ParTime method. Section 4 shows how to integrate ParTime into Crescando. Section 5 summarizes the results of our performance experiments. Section 6 contains conclusions and possible avenues for future work.

2. RELATED WORK

Temporal databases have been the subject of extensive research since the 1990s. In particular, numerous algorithms for temporal aggregation have been devised. These algorithms often involve tree data structures which are either built on demand as an intermediate data structure or persisted as an index. Kline and Snodgrass [16] were among the first to develop sophisticated algorithms for temporal aggregation. Their best algorithm operates in two passes: In the first pass, it scans the data and builds a so-called *Aggregation Tree*. This tree encodes all the time intervals in which the aggregate function remains constant. In the second phase, this tree is traversed, thereby computing the aggregate value for each time interval. The initial work on Aggregation Trees was designed for sequential execution. Later, Gendranoy et al. studied how this approach could be parallelized and the effect of different partitioning schemes of the data, number of nodes, and placement of the intermediate results. Goa et al. [8] revisited these results for main-memory databases. The results of [8], however, show that overall the Aggregation Tree approach does not parallelize well; there is some improvement, but the speed-up is far from linear and the scalability is limited. A recent comprehensive performance study showed that even with a high degree of parallelism, the performance of the Aggregation Tree approach is not competitive [13]. From a bird's eye perspective, ParTime is similar to the original Aggregation Tree algorithm proposed in [16]: It also works in two passes and scans the table in the first pass in order to compute the affects of each tuple. However, the data structures used are different and what makes ParTime unique is the way it computes the contribution of each tuple.

One of the particular problems of the original Aggregation Tree algorithm is that the Aggregation Tree is not necessarily balanced and can degenerate into a linked list. In this case, the Aggregation Tree algorithm has quadratic complexity. To overcome this problem, Böhlen et al. [3] proposed an algorithm which is based on AVL trees for the upper and lower bounds of the time intervals stored in the Aggregation Tree. While that approach does lead to significantly improved performance and guarantees O(n * log n) complexity, [13] shows that even this approach is not competitive and is outperformed by the Timeline Index by at least one order of magnitude on modern hardware. That is why we used the Timeline Index as a baseline in the performance experiments (Section 5) and refer the interested reader to [13] for a comprehensive performance study of the most important algorithms for temporal aggregation in the research literature.

There has been a large variety of index structures for temporal databases [18]. One prominent example is the multi-version B-tree [2]. The multi-version B-tree can only index a single time dimension and it indexes both, the time dimension and a (non temporal) search key. Another example is the work by Nascimento et al. [19]. This work proposes a two-level bi-temporal indexing scheme that is based on a B+-tree on transaction time, in which every entry of a leaf node points to another tree that indexes business time. The state-of-the-art in this area, however, is the Timeline Index, which was shown to clearly outperform these indexes [13]. At the core of the Timeline Index is the *event map*, which is a pre-computed sorted list of points in time when versions of records became valid and invalid. Given this event map, computing the result of a temporal aggregation query involves only one scan of this highly compressed sorted list. To further speed the computation up, the Timeline Index features checkpoints, which materialize a bitmap with all active records for a specific point in time: This way, the scans can start at the appropriate checkpoint, rather than scanning through the whole event map from the very beginning.

The Timeline Index works particularly well for the *transaction time* dimension (see next section) which is naturally ordered. However, the Timeline Index has recently been amended to support the full bi-temporal data model [15].

In terms of query performance, the Timeline Index can be seen as a lower bound for what is possible today because it precomputes the results of temporal aggregation. Depending on checkpoints in the query interval, the Timeline Index has linear or even constant complexity. That is why we use it in Section 5 to assess the performance of ParTime for queries. However, the Timeline Index is not a viable solution for update-intensive workloads. For such workloads, maintaining the Timeline Index is prohibitively expensive. Another short-coming of the Timeline Index is that it cannot be partitioned. If the size of the Timeline Index grows beyond the size of a NUMA region or even beyond the main memory of a single machine, the performance of the Timeline Index degrades significantly.

Most vendors of commercial database systems started adding temporal features into their systems in the last few years. To the best of our knowledge, Teradata, IBM DB2, Oracle, and SAP HANA are the systems with the most advanced support for temporal database features. Of these systems, only Teradata has native support for temporal aggregation [1]. Teradata implements temporal operators with non-temporal operators. Specifically, Teradata uses the Temporal Statement Modifier approach devised by Böhlen et al. [4]. Teradata supports bi-temporal tables with at most one business time dimension. This restriction also applies to IBM DB2 [23]. HANA only supports transaction time. Oracle has been supporting temporal data for more than 10 years as part of Flashback [21]. With Oracle Version 12c, there is full support for bi-temporal tables. As shown in Section 5, ParTime significantly outperforms any commercial database system.

An important feature of ParTime is that ParTime integrates well into any system that makes use of scans and in particular shared scans. Crescando uses the ClockScan algorithm [25], but ParTime can be integrated into any other scan implementation. RedBrick was the first database system to rely heavily on shared scans in the late Nineties. In the meantime, there has been a great deal of work on shared scans; e.g., as part of MonetDB [27], Blink [20], Crescando [25], Aster Data [6], and SharedDB [10]. Based on all this work, it is widely believed that robust database performance for high-throughput workloads can only be achieved with such shared scans. To the best of our knowledge, however, ParTime is the first temporal database algorithm that tries to take advantage and integrates nicely into a shared scan.

3. PARTIME METHOD

This section presents the ParTime technique. There are two variants of the ParTime algorithm. First, a general variant that works for any kind of temporal aggregation. Second, an optimized variant that works for "windowed temporal aggregation queries." We show how both variants work for one-dimensional temporal data and for bi-temporal data with arbitrary dimensionality.

3.1 Running Examples

Figure 1 shows an example *Employee* table. For each employee, it records the *name*, *job description*, and *salary*. The *Employee* table of Figure 1 has two time dimensions, denoted as `BT` for business time (often also referred to as application time) and `TT` for transaction time (often also referred to as system time). The business time indicates when the information was true in the real world; the timestamps of the business time are set by the application. The transaction time indicates when the information was entered into

	NAME	DESCR	SALARY	START_BT	END_BT	START_TT	END_TT
Row 0	Anna	CEO	10k	01-01-1993	∞	t_0	t_7
Row 1	Anna	CEO	10k	01-01-1993	01-06-1994	t_7	∞
Row 2	Anna	CEO	15k	01-06-1994	∞	t_7	∞
Row 3	Ben	Coder	5k	01-01-1993	∞	t_0	t_7
Row 4	Ben	Coder	5k	01-01-1993	01-06-1994	t_7	∞
Row 5	Ben	Manager	5k	01-06-1994	∞	t_7	t_{11}
Row 6	Ben	Manager	8k	01-06-1994	∞	t_{11}	∞
Row 7	Chris	Coder	5k	01-08-1993	∞	t_5	t_{16}
Row 8	Chris	Coder	5k	01-08-1993	01-01-1995	t_{16}	∞

Figure 1: Temporal *Employee* Table

the database; i.e., which transaction carried out the update. The timestamps of the transaction time are set automatically by the temporal database system as a side-effect of committing transactions and creating new versions of tuples.

In Figure 1, for instance, Row 0 indicates that at the beginning (after processing Transaction t_0), the database recorded the information that Anna's salary is 10k and it has been 10k since January 1, 1993. Then, Transaction t_7 updated this information indicating that Anna had a salary increase on June 1, 1994. As a result, t_7 updates Row 0: It sets the `END_TT` timestamp of Row 0 to t_7, thereby indicating that this version of Anna's record is only valid from Version t_0 to t_7. Furthermore, t_7 creates Rows 1 and 2: Row 1 indicates that Anna's salary was 10k from January 1, 1993 to June 1, 1994. Row 2 indicates that Anna's salary has been 15k since June 1, 1994.

The bi-temporal data model that we use for this work has been described in detail in [24]. (In the literature, other definitions can be found, too.) In practice, it is not unusual to have multiple business time dimensions. In the travel industry, for instance, an application could involve a business time dimension that keeps track of when the departure of a flight was scheduled and another business time dimension that records when the flight actually departed. However, there is always only one transaction time that describes the versioning of the temporal database. In the literature, tables with only transaction time are typically denoted as *temporal tables* whereas tables with transaction time and one or several business times are denoted as *bi-temporal tables*.

There are a number of specific temporal operators that can be applied to such (bi-) temporal tables [24]. The best known operator is the so-called *time-travel operator*. This operator fixes a certain point in time for each temporal dimension. For instance, one could ask about the total payroll on June 1, 1994 given Version t_3 of the database. The result of this query applied to the table of Figure 1 is 15k because only Rows 0 and 3 existed in Version t_3 of the database. We could also ask about the total annual payroll on June 1, 1994 given the current version of the database. In our example, the result is 28k as Rows 2, 6, and 8 qualify. The time travel operator has been standardized inSQL 2011 and it has been supported for a long time in the Oracle database system.

It turns out that the time-travel operator is straightforward to implement in parallel database systems like Crescando: It is a simple selection on the time dimensions. A more involved operator is *temporal aggregation*. Temporal aggregation computes an aggregate value for every point in time. Temporal aggregation can be one or multi-dimensional. For instance, Figure 2 shows the result of asking for the total payroll in 1995 for each version of the database. This query is an example of a one-dimensional temporal aggregation query because only the transaction time is varied (the business time is fixed to 1995).

START_TT	END_TT	SUM
t_0	t_5	15k
t_5	t_7	20k
t_7	t_{11}	25k
t_{11}	t_{16}	28k
t_{16}	∞	23k

Figure 2: Example 1, Result of One-dim Temp. Aggr.
Total payroll in 1995 for each version of the database.

START_BT	END_BT	START_TT	END_TT	SUM
01-01-1993	∞	t_0	t_5	15K
01-01-1993	01-08-1993	t_5	t_7	15K
01-08-1993	∞	t_5	t_7	20K
01-01-1993	01-08-1993	t_7	t_{11}	15K
01-08-1993	01-06-1994	t_7	t_{11}	20K
01-06-1994	∞	t_7	t_{11}	25K
01-01-1993	01-08-1993	t_{11}	t_{16}	15K
01-08-1993	01-06-1994	t_{11}	t_{16}	25K
01-06-1994	∞	t_{11}	t_{16}	28K
01-01-1993	01-08-1993	t_{16}	∞	15K
01-08-1993	01-06-1994	t_{16}	∞	20K
01-06-1994	01-01-1995	t_{16}	∞	28K
01-01-1995	∞	t_{16}	∞	23K

Figure 3: Example 2, Result of Two-dim Temp. Aggr.
Total payroll for each moment in time and each version.

Figure 3 shows the result of a query that asks for all the payroll values for every point in time and all versions of the database. This is an example of a two-dimensional temporal aggregation because both the business time and the transaction time are varied. As with SQL `GROUP BY` queries, the result size of temporal aggregation grows exponentially with the number of dimensions.

Finally, Figure 4 shows the result of a query that asks for the payroll at the beginning of each year given the current state of the database (i.e., all tuples with $\text{END\_TT} = \infty$). This query is one-dimensional (transaction time is fixed, business time is varied) and an example of a *windowed temporal aggregation query*.

Snodgrass defined the semantics of the temporal aggregation operator in [16]. Due to its complexity, many algorithms have been proposed in the literature (Section 2). As we will show, ParTime is the first parallel algorithm that scales linearly, takes advantage of shared scans, and does not require any pre-computation.

3.2 General Temporal Aggregation

ParTime is a two step algorithm. The first step scans the temporal table and computes the *deltas* of each record for the time when the record became valid and for the time when the record became invalid. The first step is the most expensive step and runs in parallel. That is, each core processes a different set of tuples independently. The second step *merges* the results of Step 1. Step 2 is more difficult to parallelize (Section 3.4). Fortunately, Step 2 is cheap for most practical queries so that ParTime typically achieves linear scale-up and scale-out, even without parallelizing Step 2 (Section 5).

3.2.1 Example 1: Generating Delta Maps (Step 1)

START_BT	END_BT	SUM
01-01-1993	31-12-1993	20k
01-01-1994	31-12-1994	28k
01-01-1995	31-12-1994	23k

Figure 4: Example 3, Result of Windowed Temp. Aggr.
Total payroll by year.

	NAME	DESCR	SALARY	START_BT	END_BT	START_TT	END_TT
Row 0	Anna	CEO	10k	01-01-1993	∞	t_0	t_7
Row 1	Anna	CEO	10k	01-01-1993	01-06-1994	t_7	∞
Row 2	Anna	CEO	15k	01-06-1994	∞	t_7	∞
Row 3	Ben	Coder	5k	01-01-1993	∞	t_0	t_7
Row 4	Ben	Coder	5k	01-01-1993	01-06-1994	t_7	∞
Row 5	Ben	Manager	5k	01-06-1994	∞	t_7	t_{11}
Row 6	Ben	Manager	8k	01-06-1994	∞	t_{11}	∞
Row 7	Chris	Coder	5k	01-08-1993	∞	t_5	t_{16}
Row 8	Chris	Coder	5k	01-08-1993	01-01-1995	t_{16}	∞

Figure 5: Generating Delta Maps (Example 1)

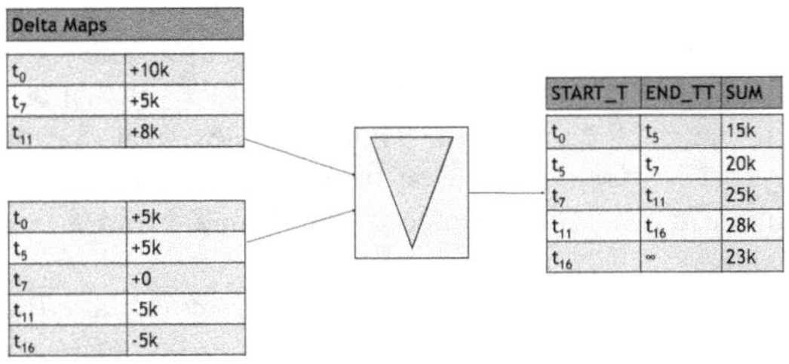

Figure 6: Merging Delta Maps (Example 1)

We illustrate the ParTime technique using the simple, one-dimensional temporal aggregation query of Example 1 (Figure 2). For the purpose of this example, we assume that we have two cores and that Core 1 processes all even rows (Rows 0, 2, 4, etc.) and Core 2 processes all odd rows (Rows 1, 3, etc.). ParTime works with any kind of partitioning; it works best if all cores process the same number of records so that *random* or *round-robin* are good partitioning schemes.

The key idea of ParTime is that every core creates a *delta map* as a result of scanning its partition of the temporal data. A *delta map* is a data structure that maps timestamps to deltas of aggregate values. That is, the delta map captures the affects of all tuples that became valid or invalid at each point in time. Furthermore, a *delta map* is ordered by timestamp, which speeds up the merge operation as part of Step 2. We used B-trees in our implementation of *delta maps*, but other data structures can be used, too, and may give even better performance.

Figure 5 shows the two delta maps that are computed for our running example and the query that asks for the total payroll for each version of the database (i.e., varying transaction time, fixing business time to 1995). To be more specific, Step 1 generates the following two deltas when processing Row 0 of Figure 1:

$$\langle t_0, +10k\rangle\langle t_7, -10k\rangle$$

These two entries indicate that at Version t_0 the total payroll needs to be increased by 10k as a result of Row 0 becoming visible in this version. Correspondingly, the payroll needs to be decreased by 10k at Version t_7 when the life time of Row 0 expires.

Because the life time of Row 2 is ∞, only one delta entry is generated for Row 2:

$$\langle t_7, +15k\rangle$$

This entry indicates that starting at Version t_7, the total payroll needs to be increased by 15k. When this entry is inserted into the delta map, it is immediately merged with the existing $\langle t_7, -10k\rangle$ entry (the delta map is indexed by timestamp). As a result, the delta map of Figure 5 shows only a single consolidated entry for t_7 that reflects the affects of both Rows 0 and 2; i.e.:

$$\langle t_7, +5k\rangle$$

```
function GENERATEDELTAMAP(chunk)
    dm ← new Btree()
    for all record in chunk do
        value ← record(column)
        validFrom ← record(validFromIdx)
        validTo ← record(validToIdx)
        DM-PUT(validFrom, value)
        if validTo ≠ ∞ then
            DM-PUT(validTo, −1 · value)
        end if
    end for
end function
```

Figure 7: Step 1 of General Aggregation (Sum)

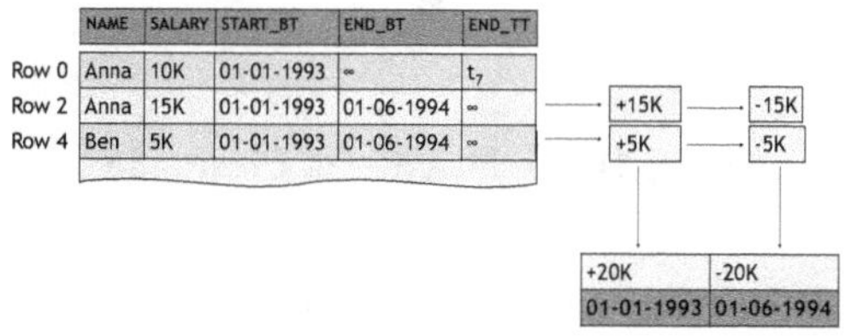

Figure 8: Generating Fixed-sized Delta Maps (Example 3)

In Example 1, Rows 1, 4, and 8 are ignored. These rows involve data that is not relevant for the query because these rows contain information for the years 1993 and 1994 only and the query asks specifically for salaries of the year 1995. Accordingly, these rows are filtered out before the ParTime algorithm takes effect and no delta entries are generated for these rows.

3.2.2 Example 1: Merging Delta Maps (Step 2)

Figure 6 shows the second step of the ParTime algorithm for general temporal aggregation; i.e., merging the delta maps generated in parallel in Step 1. This merge can be implemented in exactly the same way as a merge in a sort-based, regular (non-temporal) group-by operator [11]. That is, the timestamp is used as the group-by key and increments / decrements are simply added to generate the final payroll value for each version of the database system. Comparing Figures 6 and 2, it can be seen that the ParTime algorithm computes indeed the correct result.

3.2.3 Algorithm Description

Figure 7 gives the pseudo-code of Step 1 of the general ParTime algorithm for one-dimensional temporal aggregation if *sum* is used as an aggregate function. Assuming that B tree lookups are O(log n), the complexity of this algorithm is O(n * log n). We extended our B tree implementation to support a special *put* operation which adjusts an existing entry, if it exists, or creates a new entry, if the search key cannot be found. We omit details of Step 2 of the general ParTime algorithm because it is identical with any other merge operation (e.g., [11]).

The ParTime algorithm works very well for all aggregate functions that can be computed incrementally. Examples of such aggregate functions are *sum*, *product*, or *count*. Not all aggregate functions are incremental; e.g., *min*, *max*, or *median*. For these aggregate functions, it is not sufficient to keep a single aggregate value at all times in the delta map. Instead, the delta map keeps the set of values that became valid / invalid at each point in time. The merge step then involves keeping a priority queue to compute the aggregate value at each point in time.

```
function GENERATEDELTAMAP(chunk, size)
    dm ← new Array[size]
    for all record in chunk do
        value ← record(column)
        validFrom ← record(validFromIdx)
        validTo ← record(validToIdx)
        dm[validFrom] ← dm[validFrom] + value
        if validTo ≠ ∞ then
            dm[validTo] ← dm[validTo] − value
        end if
    end for
end function
```

Figure 9: Step 1 of Windowed Aggregation (Sum)

3.3 Windowed Queries

We will now turn to Example 3 of Section 3.1; Figure 4. In principle, this query can be executed using the very same general ParTime algorithm that was described in the previous section. However, we can do better and apply an important optimization for such windowed temporal aggregation queries.

The main observation is that the size of the result of the temporal aggregation is known in advance. This particular query asks for the total payroll at the beginning of each year. The database contains only information for three years, 1993, 1994, and 1995. This fact can be exploited to speed up the algorithm of Figure 7 significantly. Instead of maintaining the delta map as a dynamic B tree (or some other dynamic data structure), we can implement the delta map as an array and use the timestamps (i.e., years) to access the cells of this array directly. Fundamentally, the algorithm of Figure 7 is unchanged, but the *dm-put()* operations can be implemented in a much more efficient way by a simple array look-up. For completeness, Figure 9 shows the pseudo code: Compared to the algorithm of Figure 7, the only difference is that the delta map is implemented as an array instead of a B-tree.

In theory, this optimization is applicable to any temporal aggregation query, not only windowed queries. We can always calculate an upper limit for the number of versions in each time dimension. In the general case, however, this optimization is less effective because the array can become sparse and we would pay a high price in terms of memory footprint.

Figure 8 shows how windowed aggregation is applied to the third query of our running example. In this example, Row 0 is ignored because the query asks only for tuples of the *current version* of the database; i.e., records with END_TT = ∞.

3.4 Multi-dimensional Temporal Aggregation

The same two-step techniques, described in the previous two sections, can be applied to any multi-dimensional temporal aggregation query. Example 2 of Section 3.1 is a two-dimensional temporal aggregation query that varies business time *and* transaction time. The important difference to one dimensional temporal aggregation is that the deltas consider all temporal dimensions involved in the query. Another difference is that the deltas *pivot* on one temporal dimension and then capture the information along all other temporal dimensions. For instance, the ParTime algorithm generates the following two deltas for Row 0 and Example 2, if we pivot on the transaction time:

$$\langle +10k, \text{01-01-1993}, \infty, t_0\rangle, \langle -10k, \text{01-01-1993}, \infty, t_7\rangle$$

The first delta reads as follows: "At Transaction Time t_0, 10k need to be added to the total payroll for the business time duration 01-01-1993 to ∞." If we pivot for transaction time in this example,

```
function GENERATEDELTAMAP(chunk)
    dm ← new Btree()
    for all record in chunk do
        value ← record(column)
        pivotBegin ← record(idxOfBegin(0))
        pivotEnd ← record(idxOfEnd(0))
        validFrom ← array(numDimensions − 1)
        validTo ← array(numDimensions − 1)
        for i in (1..numDimensions − 1) do
            validFrom(i − 1) ← record(idxOfBegin(i))
            validTo(i − 1) ← record(idxOfEnd(i))
        end for
        fstKey ← concat(validFrom, validTo, [pivotBegin])
        DM-PUT(fstKey, value)
        if pivotEnd ≠ ∞ then
            sndKey ← concat(validFrom, validTo, [pivotEnd])
            DM-PUT(sndKey, −1 · value)
        end if
    end for
end function
```

Figure 10: Step 1 of Multi-dim. Aggregation (Sum)

ParTime generates two deltas because Row 0 expires along the transaction time dimension at t_7. If we pivot for business time, ParTime generates only one delta for Row 0 because Row 0 has no expiration date along the business time. In this case, ParTime generates the following delta. (As a convention, we keep the pivot time dimension last.)

$$\langle +10k, t_0, t_7, \text{01-01-1993} \rangle$$

This delta reads as follows which is a different yet equivalent interpretation of Row 0: "Starting at business time 01-01-1993, 10k need to be added to the total payroll for the transaction time duration t_0 to t_7." For correctness, any time dimension can be used as pivot dimension. For performance, it is best to choose the time dimension with the least distinct values (i.e., timestamps) because that will minimize the size of the delta map generated in Step 1. Typically, one of the business time dimensions has the least distinct values and our implementation of ParTime keeps statistics to pivot for the best possible time dimension.

Figure 10 shows the pseudo code for Step 1 of the multi-dimensional temporal aggregation. For simplicity, the pseudo code of Figure 10 always chooses time dimension 0 as a pivot; our implementation is more sophisticated in that regard. In Figure 10, $validFrom$ and $validTo$ are arrays that represent the start and end times for all temporal dimensions; for the pivot dimension, only the validFrom time is recorded. These times are filled in the inner loop which iterates over all temporal dimensions involved in the query. Other than that, this algorithm is the same as the one-dimensional algorithm shown in Figure 7.

Step 2 of the generalized, multi-dimensional ParTime algorithm implements the merge of delta maps in a similar way as the merge operation of a sort-merge join. Just as for the sort-merge join, Step 2 must carry out a Cartesian product for all overlapping delta entries. This Cartesian product results in the (correct) explosion of the query result of multi-dimensional temporal aggregation, as observed in Figure 3. Again, this exponential complexity in the number of time dimensions is fundamental to the temporal aggregation operator and *not* a weakness of the ParTime method, as explained in Section 3.1. Unlike the merge phase of a sort-merge join, Step 2 of the ParTime algorithm must aggregate the values of delta entries that are identical in all time dimensions.

In principle, Step 2 of the ParTime algorithm can be parallelized just as the merge phase of a sort-merge phase. For instance, this parallelization can be achieved with a multi-level merge operation as described in [11]. So far, we have not implemented such a parallel Step 2 of ParTime. The reason for this decision was that for all the temporal aggregation queries of the Amadeus workload that motivated this work, Step 2 is cheap and the cost of a temporal aggregation query is always dominated by Step 1. As shown in Section 5, however, the synthetic TPC-BiH benchmark does include cases in which Step 2 is indeed expensive and worth parallelizing. Studying how such a parallelization of Step 2 could improve performance is left for future work.

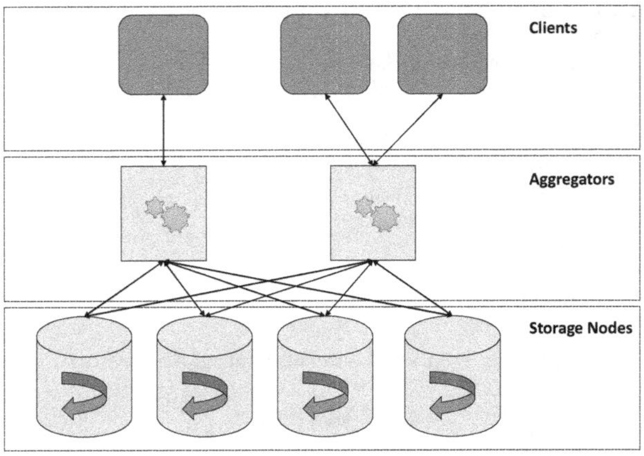

Figure 11: Architecture of Crescando

4. PARTIME AND SHARED SCANS

This section describes our implementation of ParTime in Crescando, Amadeus' parallel database system as one particular example system that can make use of ParTime. ParTime, however, can be integrated into any parallel database system: All that needs to be done is to extend the scan operator to generate delta maps and a separate operator to merge delta maps. Furthermore, the optimizer must be extended to determine the right degree of parallelism.

4.1 Overview

Figure 11 shows the architecture of Crescando; details of Crescando can be found in [25]. This architecture has been pioneered by Amazon as part of the Dynamo system [7]. Crescando is a shared-nothing database system with a two-tier architecture. At the lower layer are the storage nodes. The storage nodes persist the data. Each storage node keeps a different partition of a (temporal or non-temporal) table, thereby making use of horizontal partitioning of the data. Crescando supports any kind of partitioning scheme; in particular, it supports round-robin partitioning as used in the examples of the previous section.

Crescando is a main-memory database system. If the database grows, new storage nodes must be added. All read-requests are served completely out of main memory. Write-requests are logged to disk for crash recovery. In order to improve fault-tolerance, each storage node has a hot stand-by node (not shown in Figure 11) that fully replicates all the data and events of the storage node, thereby following state-machine replication [17].

The second tier of Crescando is composed of aggregator nodes. Crescando processes queries (and updates) in the following way: A client connects to one of the aggregators which coordinates the execution of the query. Any aggregator can be chosen for this purpose. In the default configuration, a client always connects to the same aggregator, but a round robin approach is also possible.

Query processing is then split between the storage nodes and the aggregator. Basic operations such as selections and projections are carried out by the storage nodes. Complex operations such as grouping are carried out by the aggregator. Furthermore, the aggregator collects the results from all storage nodes and produces the final query result and ships it to the client.

Depending on the partitioning scheme and the query, all or a subset of the storage nodes are involved in processing a query. For a round-robin partitioning scheme, *all* storage nodes are involved in *all* queries because it is not possible to infer that a particular storage node does not contain any relevant data that is needed to process a query. This worst-case scenario is not unusual in practice, and it is the scenario that was measured in the performance experiments reported in Section 5.

One problem of the architecture of Crescando are stragglers. If one storage node is significantly slower than all the others, then this storage node dominates the response time of all queries because the aggregator needs to wait for the results of *all* storage nodes. Crescando treats stragglers in the same way as failed nodes: It shoots them down and continues to operate with the hot stand-by node. These mechanisms are independent of ParTime and describing these mechanisms in detail is beyond the scope of this paper.

Another problem of running all queries on all storage nodes is *cost*. If the queries were executed one at a time, the storage nodes could easily become the bottleneck of the system. To address this challenge, Crescando makes heavy use of shared scans in the storage nodes. That is, a batch of queries and updates from multiple clients and aggregator nodes are processed by a storage node with a single scan, thereby processing the queries and updates on the fly. Specifically, Crescando makes use of the ClockScan algorithm described in [25] which was shown to give robust performance for demanding workloads with high update rates and complex queries. Crescando also supports indexes. For the experiments reported in Section 5, however, no indexes were used. That is, every query and update involved a full (parallel) table scan of the partition in all storage nodes. The larger the number of storage nodes, the smaller the partitions and correspondingly the faster the parallel scan.

Finally, aggregators are stateless in the architecture of Figure 11. Crescando does not make use of caching at the aggregator layer because the shared, parallel scans at the storage layer are so fast that caching does not help. When an aggregator fails, all its queries (and updates) are restarted. Furthermore, new aggregator nodes can be added at any point in time to sustain a higher load. Likewise, an aggregator can be shut down at any time if the load decreases.

4.2 Temporal Extensions

Initially, Crescando was not designed for temporal data and did not support the bi-temporal data model or temporal operators. Adding support for temporal data, however, was straightforward. As shown in Figure 1 temporal tables can be stored in the same way as regular, non-temporal tables in the storage nodes. The *start* and *end* timestamps of the temporal dimensions are stored and processed like any other column.

The time-travel operator can also be implemented in a straightforward way in Crescando. As mentioned in Section 3, time-travel involves the evaluation of range predicates on the time dimensions and range predicates were already supported in Crescando.

ParTime also fits nicely into the architecture of Figure 11. Step 1, generating the delta maps, is carried out by the storage nodes for all temporal aggregation queries. More specifically, the storage nodes generate the delta maps as part of the same shared scan that carries out all other queries and updates. Each storage node creates one delta map for each temporal aggregation query in addition to the result tuples for other queries and updates. The storage nodes generate these delta maps (and other results) in parallel independently of each other.

Step 2, merging the delta maps, is carried out by the aggregator that handles the temporal aggregation query. To this end, the aggregator waits until it has received the delta maps of all storage nodes. Since each query is assigned to exactly one aggregator, it is not easy to parallelize Step 2 in Crescando, even though Step 2 can be parallelized in principle as described in Section 3.4. Aggregation nodes also execute other complex operations such as joins, ranking and sorting, or other grouping and aggregation operations which are part of the query. It is also possible that a query involves several temporal aggregation operators. Within the aggregation nodes, the execution of the operators is pipelined using the iterator model. We are currently generalizing and improving the query processing capabilities of aggregator nodes, including parallel query operators, as part of the SharedDB project [10].

4.3 Query Optimization

Independent of ParTime, there is a need to optimize queries that involve several temporal and non-temporal operators. Query optimization is beyond the scope of this paper, but ParTime can be added to the compiler of an extensible temporal database system just like any other new algorithm [12, 11].

One special consideration for most parallel database systems is to optimize the degree of parallelism. As shown in Section 5, it is indeed advisable to carry out this optimization for ParTime, just like for any other parallel algorithm. Unfortunately, this optimization is not possible in Crescando. Crescando fixes the degree of parallelism as the number of storage nodes because every query is executed on all storage nodes. As a result, Crescando does not exploit the full flexibility and versatility of ParTime. Other parallel database systems might achieve even better performance with ParTime than Crescando by optimizing the degree of parallelism.

5. PERFORMANCE EXPERIMENTS AND RESULTS

This section studies the performance of ParTime. It compares the performance of Crescando with ParTime to two best-of-class commercial database systems and the best-known approach for temporal aggregation from the research literature. We conducted the experiments using a real workload from the travel industry and a synthetic database benchmark for bi-temporal data.

5.1 Software and Hardware Used

In order to assess the performance of ParTime, we used the following baselines in our performance experiments:

Timeline Index. [13]: The Timeline Index is the best known approach to compute temporal aggregation from the research literature. It precomputes all temporal information and keeps this information in a sorted way so that temporal aggregation can be carried out fast. We implemented the Timeline Index and the temporal aggregation algorithm based on the description of [13]. The big disadvantage of the Timeline Index is that it is a materialized view and it is costly to maintain the Timeline Index for update-intensive workloads. As a result, the Timeline Index is not practical for the Amadeus airline reservation application that motivated this work. For the purpose of this paper, the Timeline Index serves as a baseline to demonstrate the best possible query performance for read-only workloads and how close ParTime can come to that.

System D:. A commercial disk-based, general-purpose database system. We studied several general-purpose database systems and System D was the system that performed best throughout the experiments reported in this paper. We used the index advisor shipped with the product to generate indexes for the benchmark workload.

System M:. System M is a commercial main-memory database system which was specifically designed for analytics and has support for temporal data and transactions. Again, System M can be seen as the best of its class for temporal workloads and the queries and workloads studied in our experiments. By default, System M only creates indexes for the primary keys of tables. It turned out that this default was the best configuration for all our experiments.

A comprehensive performance study of other algorithms from the literature is given in [13]. Licensing agreements do not allow us to reveal the real product names of System D and System M.

We used Crescando in two modes:

- *Shared scans:* Exploit shared scans as described in Section 4. This mode is the default for Crescando.
- *No sharing:* Crescando without shared scans. In this mode, Crescando processes each query individually.

With No sharing, we could isolate the performance advantages that Crescando gets from making use of the ParTime algorithm vs. the performance advantages that Crescando has from exploiting shared scans. To the best of our knowledge, Systems D and M do not make use of shared scans. We measured throughput and response time. For all response time experiments, we ran Crescando in the No sharing mode. In all experiments reported in this paper, Crescando did not make use of any data-indexes, independent of the mode. Crescando did however use indexes on queries in sharing mode, as discribed in [25].

All experiments were carried out on a machine with 1.5 TB of main memory (DDR3, 1066MHz RAM) and four Intel Xeon E5-4650 processors with eight 2.7 GHz cores each (32 cores in total). The machine ran Linux (Kernel 3.14.17-100). In all experiments, the whole database fit in main memory and we warmed up the buffers in order to make sure that disk I/O was only required to log updates for recovery. Naturally, warming up the buffers was particularly important for System D.

Systems D and M made use of all 32 cores. To study the effectiveness of parallelization with ParTime, we varied the number of cores for Crescando. If not reported otherwise, Crescando used half of the cores to implement storage nodes and half of the cores as aggregator nodes (Figure 11). That is, in a configuration with 18 cores, Crescando used 9 cores as aggregators and partitioned the database across the other 9 cores. Temporal aggregation with the Timeline Index does not allow for parallelization so that all response time experiments with the Timeline Index were carried out with a single core. In all cases, however, we made sure that the allocated memory was close to the used cores to the extent possible. This NUMA-awareness was critical to achieve good performance for all four systems. Crescando and our implementation of the Timeline Index were in C++.

5.2 Benchmark Environment

We studied a real workload from the Amadeus airline reservation system. The results of the experiments with this workload gave insights into the end-to-end performance of a temporal database system for a complex application that includes various types of temporal queries, non-temporal queries, and a high update rate. In order to specifically study the effects of ParTime, we also carried out experiments with a synthetic benchmark.

Query	Freq.	Type	Description
ta1	1%	Temp.Aggr.	Number of Open Flights grouped by transaction time
ta2	1%	Temp.Aggr.	Number of Open Flights grouped by business time
other temporal	8%	Time Travel, Range	number of bookings at a certain time, bookings by day, etc.
other	90%	Non-temp.	e.g., number of bookings for a given flight and airline, passenger lists, etc.

Table 1: Queries of Airline Res. System

5.2.1 Amadeus Workload

Table 1 gives an overview of the queries of the Amadeus workload. In that workload, there are only two kinds of temporal aggregation queries, denoted as *ta1* and *ta2*. The first kind of these queries involves transaction time and asks, for instance, how the number of bookings for a specific flight evolved over time. The second kind of temporal aggregation queries of this system involves business time (e.g., the validity of a ticket) and queries such as the number of open and valid tickets over time. While both of these kinds of queries are quite complex, it is important to note that these queries are rare: Only about 2 percent of the queries of this workload involve temporal aggregation. 8 percent of the queries involve other temporal operators and the bulk of the queries are non-temporal (i.e., current time in all temporal dimensions).

The airline reservation workload is update-intensive. In addition to these queries, it involves 250 updates per second. These updates include inserts (e.g., new bookings) and updates (e.g., setting the frequent-flyer number, registering dietary requirements, etc.).

The database of the airline reservation system contains 2.4 Billion bookings. On average, a booking has five versions, but there is skew and some bookings are updated much more often than others. The information in the bookings table is encoded in a highly compressed way (using flags and fixed-length codes) so that the size of the database is only 300 GB (without indexes) and easily fits into main memory. Unfortunately, System D and System M were not able to execute the temporal aggregation queries on the full 2.4 Billion bookings; the queries timed out. As a result, we also carried out experiments on a 1% subset of 24 Million bookings.

5.2.2 TPC BiH Benchmark

In order to focus better on the performance of temporal operators and study a wider range of different kinds of temporal queries, we used the TPC-BiH benchmark [14]. This benchmark also allowed us to compare ParTime to the Timeline Index. We could not implement the Amadeus workload with the Timeline Index because the Amadeus workload requires a full-fledged database system with comprehensive support for the SQL standard and our prototype implementation of the Timeline Index does not have that. SAP is currently working on an implementation of the Timeline Index for HANA; however, that work has not yet been released.

Table 2 gives an overview of the queries of the TPC-BiH benchmark. All of these queries can be executed on all three systems and with our implementation of the Timeline Index. The most relevant queries for this work are queries r_1 to r_4. These are four different temporal aggregation queries that differ on whether they aggregate over transaction time and business time and that vary the time range. Queries r_1 and r_2 involve the whole database (without any selection or window), similar to Examples 1 and 2 in Section 3. Queries r_3 and r_4 are windowed temporal aggregation queries, similar to Example 3 in Section 3.

Query	Type	Description
t2	Time Travel	What was the total revenue of all orders at a given business time known as recorded at a certain previous time in history?
t3_sys	Time Travel	Compare the estimated revenue of the open orders at a given business time recorded at two different times in history?
t3_app	Time Travel	Compare the estimated revenue of the open orders at two given business times?
t6_sys	Time Travel	What is the average revenue per customer over business time, at a given time in history?
t6_app	Time Travel	What is the average order revenue per customer over history at a given point in application?
t8	Time Travel	For a given airline, how much time before the departure is the booking done in average?
t9	Time Travel	Flight Bookings per Point in System Time (time interval)
k1_sys	Key-in-Time	How did a given order as it is valid at a certain business time evolve in history?
k1_app	Key-in-Time	How did a given order as it is valid at a certain system time evolve in history?
r1	Temp.Aggr.	Which customers moved to US and still live there as registered within full system time?
r2	Temp.Aggr.	Which customers moved to US and still live there as registered within full business time?
r3	Temp.Aggr.	Which customers moved to US and still live there as registered within a system time interval?
r4	Temp.Aggr.	Which customers moved to US and still live there as registered within a business time interval?

Table 2: TPC-BiH Queries

The TPC-BiH benchmark database is created using the TPC-H benchmark database as a starting point (Version 0) and then running TPC-C style transactions in order to generate versions of the database. Each transaction creates a new version of the database. Like TPC-H, the TPC-BiH benchmark specifies a scaling factor that determines the size of the database. We used SF=1 to generate a small database of 5 GB of raw data (without indexes) and SF=100 for a large database of 312 GB of raw data. Systems D and M timed out for almost all queries on the large database so we only show the results for those systems on the small database.

5.3 Amadeus Workload

5.3.1 *Exp 1: No Sharing, Small Database*

Figure 12 shows the throughput of Systems D, M, and Crescando with ParTime for the Amadeus workload. For this experiment, we used a read-only variant of the Amadeus workload. That is, we replayed the queries from the traces we got from the airline reservation application and did not replay the updates. Furthermore, we used a small subset of the original booking database (24 Million bookings, 3 GB) because the temporal aggregation queries timed out for Systems D and M on the full 300 GB data set. Our baselines, Systems D and M, used all 32 cores throughout this experiment; both systems showed robust performance with 32 cores and we could not find a good way to vary the number of cores for these systems. For Crescando with ParTime, we varied the number of cores in order to see how it scales with the number of cores. In order to better compare ParTime with Systems D and M in this initial experiment, we ran Crescando in the No sharing mode. (The next subsection studies the importance of shared scans.)

Figure 12 shows that System M has the highest throughput and ParTime beats System D, even if ParTime runs only on two cores and System D runs on 32 cores. To better understand these results, Figure 13 shows the response times of two representative temporal

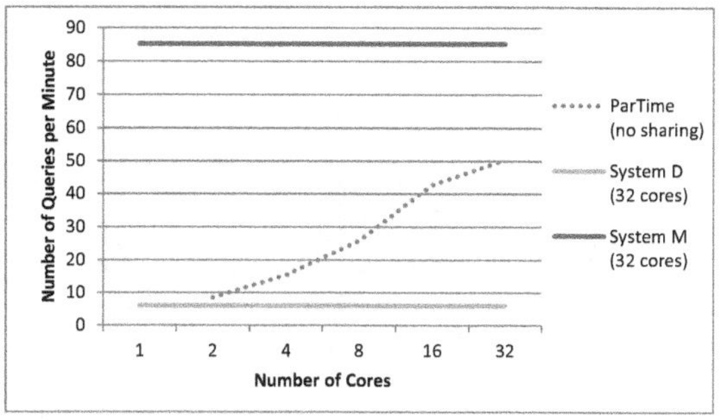

Figure 12: Tput: Amadeus, Small DB, Vary Cores, No Sharing

aggregation queries (Fig. 13a) and two non-temporal queries (Fig. 13b) of the Amadeus workload. It becomes clear that Crescando is one order of magnitude better than both System D and System M for the temporal aggregation queries; that is the effect of ParTime. Yet, Crescando is several orders of magnitude worse for the non-temporal queries for which ParTime obviously does not matter. Since the non-temporal queries are much more frequent than the temporal aggregation queries, System M outperforms Crescando in this experiment. Systems D and M outperform Crescando for the non-temporal queries because Systems D and M make use of indexes. In contrast, Crescando had to rely on a table scan for each query in this experiment which obviously resulted in poor single-query performance. Our decision to run Crescando without indexes becomes clearer in the next subsection when we show the effect of shared scans and one of the main results of this paper: ParTime helps Crescando to sustain real world workloads that no other database can handle today.

5.3.2 *Exp 2: The Importance of Sharing*

Figure 14 shows the throughput of Crescando (with and without shared scans) for the (read-only) Amadeus workload and the full database (i.e., all 2.4 Billion bookings and all their versions). No other database system that we are aware of can sustain this workload. Even though rare, the temporal aggregation queries consume so many resources in Systems D and M that the throughput virtually drops to zero. To make things worse, these temporal aggregation queries time out in Systems D and M.

Of course, ParTime's ability to process temporal aggregation queries efficiently is critical for the Amadeus workload. What this experiment, however, also demonstrates is another critical strength of ParTime: ParTime co-exists nicely with traditional (non-temporal) query processing techniques as part of a shared scan. Ultimately, that is the key to the success of ParTime for this real-world workload. With every scan through the booking table, Crescando processes a batch of up to 2000 queries. Some of these queries are cheap range queries, some of these queries are more expensive non-temporal queries, and some of them are expensive temporal aggregation queries. Unlike for Systems D and M, however, the expensive temporal aggregation queries do not slow down everybody else with ParTime. Instead, the shared scan seamlessly executes Step 1 of the ParTime algorithm. Step 2 is then carried out on dedicated aggregator nodes, again without hurting the performance of other concurrent queries.

Figure 14 also shows how nicely ParTime and Crescando scale with the number of cores. With 32 cores, the throughput is roughly 15 times as high as with 2 cores. This observation is true for Crescando in both modes. By increasing the number of cores, the size of the partition handled by each storage node gets smaller and the shared scan on each partition correspondingly requires less time. With two cores, for instance, there is only one storage node

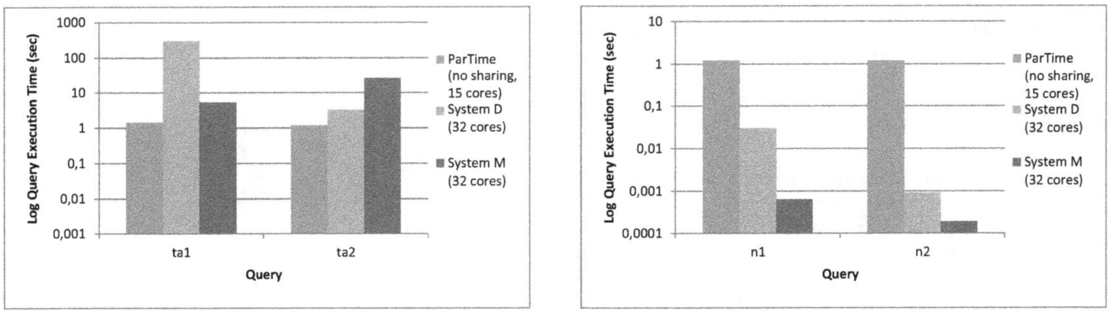

(a) Temporal Aggregation Queries

(b) Non-temporal Queries

Figure 13: Resp. Time (logscale): Amadeus, Small DB, 32 Cores (Selected Queries)

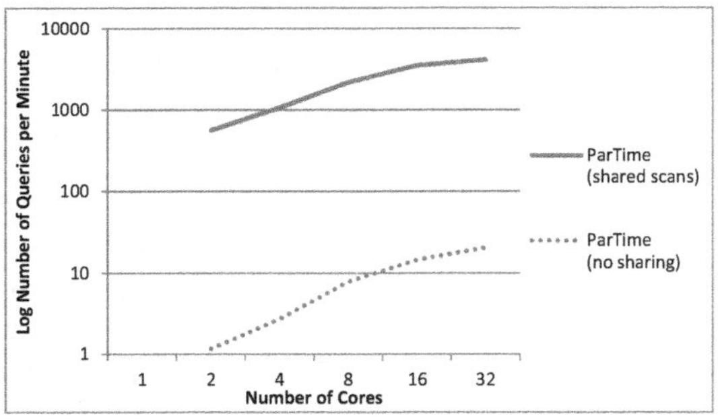

Figure 14: Tput: Amadeus, Large DB, Vary Cores

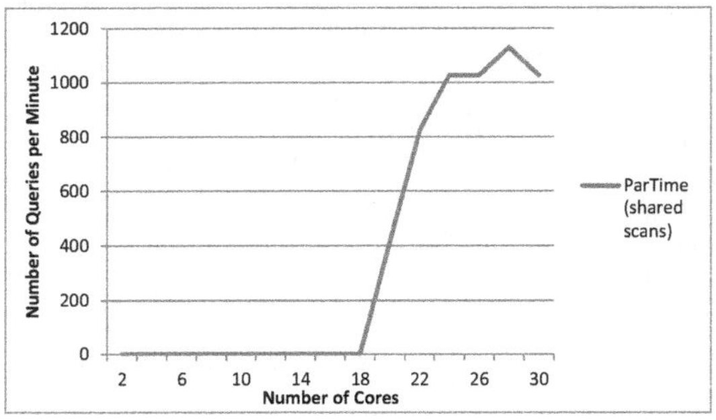

Figure 16: Tput: Amadeus, Large DB, 250 Upd/sec, Vary Cores

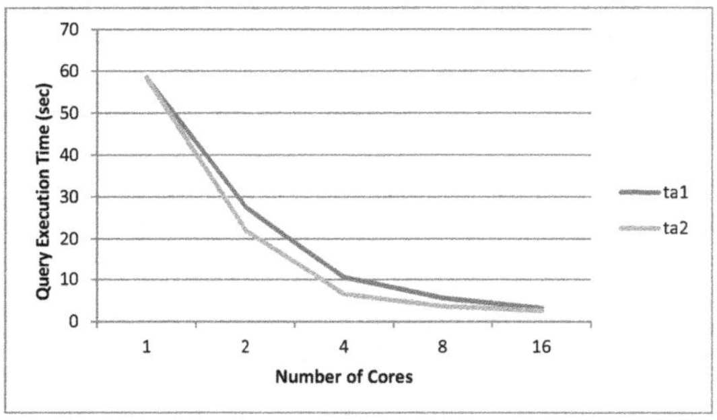

Figure 15: Resp. Time: Amadeus, Large DB, Vary Cores

(and one aggregator node) and that storage node handles the whole 300 GB database. With 30 cores, there are 15 storage nodes and each storage node needs to scan only 20 GB of data for every batch of queries.

To demonstrate the speed-up of ParTime for the temporal aggregation queries of the Amadeus workload, Figure 15 shows the response time of two selected queries with a varying number of cores. These are the same queries shown in Figure 13(a). The figure shows that ParTime has almost linear speed-up for both queries up to sixteen cores. Section 5.4 revisits the effects of parallelism and presents more response time results for a more diverse set of temporal queries of the TPC-BiH benchmark.

5.3.3 Exp 3: Updates

Experiments 1 and 2 studied the Amadeus workload without any updates; i.e., read-only workloads. Figure 16 shows the throughput of Crescando for the full Amadeus workload including 250 updates per second. For this experiment, we used the complete Amadeus database with 2.4 Billion bookings.

Figure 16 shows that Crescando requires at least 18 cores to sustain this workload. With less than 18 cores, Crescando requires all the resources to process the updates and has no more capacity to process any queries. Neither System D nor System M are able to sustain this workload, even with 32 cores and the whole database residing in main memory.

Overall, this experiment confirms the most important findings of Experiments 1 and 2: ParTime helps to handle workloads that traditional database systems cannot sustain. It is the seamless integration of processing temporal aggregation queries with ParTime into regular query processing and shared scans that makes the difference. The presence of updates does not change this basic observation. Update-intensive workloads, however, are a show-stopper for the Timeline Index, the best known approach to process temporal aggregation queries. Specifically studying the performance of ParTime vs. Timeline Index for temporal queries is the subject of the next set of experiments.

5.4 TPC-BiH Benchmark

5.4.1 Exp 4: Overview

Figures 17 and 18 give the results of Systems D, M, and ParTime for the queries of the TPC-BiH benchmark. Furthermore, these figures contain results for the Timeline Index which is directly applicable to the queries of the TPC-BiH benchmark. Again, the Timeline Index is not a good fit for the Amadeus workload because updates are extremely expensive and most queries of the Amadeus workload are non-temporal and the Timeline Index is not applicable to those queries. Furthermore, our prototype implementation of the Timeline Index was not comprehensive enough to execute all the queries and updates of the Amadeus workload.

For ParTime, we studied the response time with 2 cores (1 storage node, 1 aggregator) and with 31 cores (30 storage nodes, 1 aggregator). Systems D and M used all 32 cores in these experiments. We only show results for Systems D and M for the small

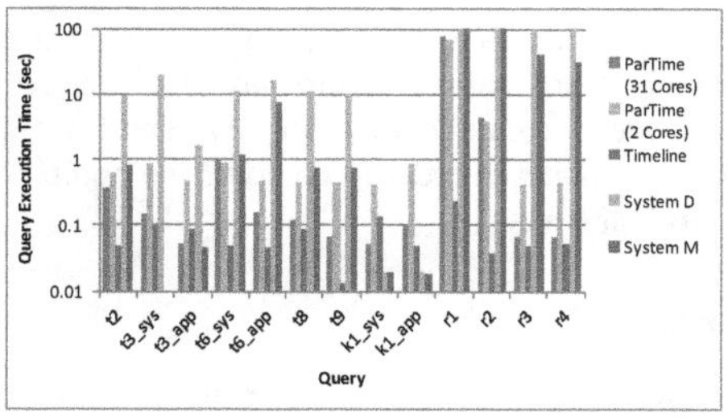

Figure 17: Resp. Time: TPC-BiH, Small DB (SF=1)

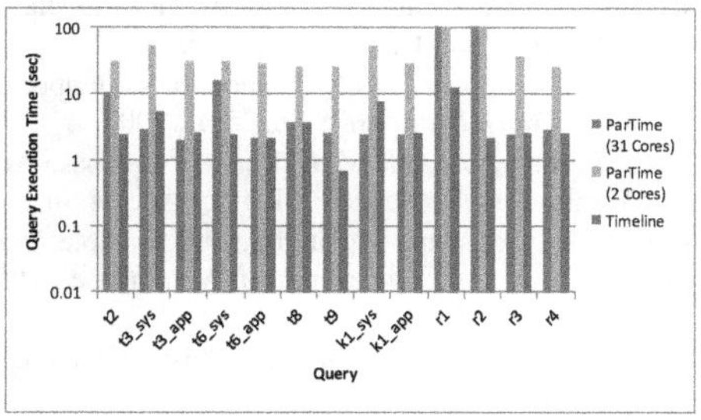

Figure 18: Resp. Time: TPC-BiH, Large DB (SF=100)

TPC-BiH database (Figure 17) because Systems D and M timed out for all queries and a large TPC-BiH database (Figure 18).

Overall, these experiments confirm all expectations. The Timeline Index is the clear winner because it precomputes all temporal information and, thus, makes the execution of temporal queries extremely fast. System D performs worst because it is a disk-based database system and cannot compete with main-memory database systems even if all the data is kept in the main-memory buffers of System D. ParTime with 31 cores outperforms System M with 32 cores because of the effectiveness of the ParTime algorithm. System M with 32 cores, however, outperforms ParTime with only 2 cores because in that configuration ParTime has no advantage from its parallelization as it runs on only one storage node.

The most interesting observation from this experiment can be made by comparing Figures 17 and 18 and focusing on the results for ParTime with 30 cores (the dark blue bars) and the Timeline Index (the red bar). We can see a good example for Amdahls law. For the small database (Figure 17), the difference between ParTime and the Timeline Index is huge: For such a small database, parallelization does not buy us much because there are a number of query processing steps that cannot be parallelized (including Step 2 of the ParTime algorithm in our implementation) and that dominate the response time. For the large TPC-BiH database (Figure 18), the dark blue and red bars are almost the same. Here, the parallelism of ParTime pays back because these queries involve scanning large volumes of data. The amazing result is that parallelization is (almost) as good as pre-computation for such large data sets. We demonstrate this effect in more detail in the next experiment.

5.4.2 *Exp 5: Parallelization*

Figure 19 shows the response time of the ParTime algorithm for two selected TPC-BiH queries, r_2 and r_4, with a varying number of cores on the large TPC-BiH database (SF=100, 320 GB of raw data). r_2 is a full temporal aggregation over the whole database on business time. r_4 is a windowed temporal aggregation over the whole database on business time.

As expected, r_4 scales almost linearly up to 16 cores (15 storage nodes, 1 aggregator). After that, it flattens out because of Amdahl's

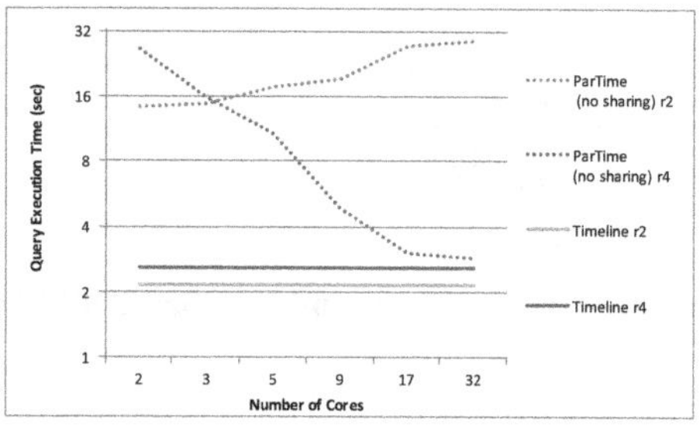

Figure 19: Resp. Time: TPC-BiH, Large DB, Vary Cores

law. For a larger database, this flattening would happen later, with more than 16 cores. This experiment confirms the results of Figure 14 and the scalability of the ParTime algorithm for the temporal queries of the Amadeus workload. The interesting observation is that due to parallelization, ParTime is competitive with the Timeline Index for r_4, even though ParTime does not precompute anything and needs to scan the whole temporal table in order to compute the temporal aggregation.

The second somewhat disappointing result of Figure 19 is that the ParTime algorithm gets worse for r_2 and a growing number of cores. The main reason for that is that the result set of this query is huge: The query result has roughly the same size as the whole temporal table. Partitioning the data does not help for this query because each partition generates a very big delta map independent of the granularity of the partition; again in the order of the size of the whole base table. With two storage nodes (3 cores), for instance, each storage node generates a big delta map and the aggregator in Step 2 merges *two* big delta maps each approximately the size of the base table. With ten storage nodes (11 cores), each storage node again generates a big delta map and the aggregator merges *ten* big delta maps that have the size of the whole base table each. Clearly, this bad behavior is an artifact of Query r_2 of the TPC-BiH benchmark which tests a specific corner case in which the temporal aggregation query virtually does not aggregate any data. Fortunately, such queries are rare in practice.

In summary, these experiments show that the degree of parallelism needs to be optimized and controlled with ParTime. As explained in Section 4, Crescando does not provide this flexibility due to its specific architecture. Other parallel database systems, however, might be able to take advantage of this additional optimization opportunity for ParTime.

5.5 Exp 6: Memory Consumption

One benefit of ParTime is that it does not need any indexes to do efficient query processing. As pointed out earlier, this allows for higher update performance. Another positive effect is that ParTime has a lower memory footprint than all the other approaches that we studied. In most data centers, main-memory footprint translates directly to cost for energy and investments into machines. Table 3 summarizes this result for the TPC-BiH database with scaling factor SF=1. Only System M beats ParTime in terms of memory footprint. The reason is that System M has much better compression than Crescando as it is the more mature main-memory database system. The Timeline Index incurs a storage overhead of almost 30 percent.

5.6 Exp 7: Bulkload Times

We also evaluated the time it takes to load the data into the system. This includes parsing of the data which was initially stored in a simple text file. Even for this relatively small data set of the

System	Size (GB)
Uncompressed Table	2.3
ParTime	2.3
Timeline	3.0
System D	2.5
System M	2.1

Table 3: Memory Consumption, Small DB (SF=1)

System	Time (minutes)
ParTime	2.5
Timeline	4
System D	220
System M	962

Table 4: Bulkload Time, Small DB (SF=1)

TPC-BiH benchmark with SF=1 (i.e., 2.3 GB), Systems D and M take a considerable amount of time. The problem is missing support for bulkloading *temporal* data. These systems are much more efficient in bulkloading non-temporal data. Crescando, in contrast, is quite fast because it bulkloads temporal data in the same way as non-temporal data. The temporal columns are no different than any other column and Crescando creates no data structures that are specific to temporal data. The Timeline Index can be constructed very fast for this small data set; however, for SF=100, it takes more than seven hours to create the Timeline Index and its storage structures whereas it takes only about three hours to bulkload the large TPC-BiH database into Crescando.

6. CONCLUSION

This paper presented ParTime, a parallel temporal aggregation algorithm. ParTime is based on a two step approach. In the first step, the temporal data is scanned, thereby computing the affects of each row in the form of deltas. In the second step, the deltas are merged to compute the result. The first step is embarrassingly parallel. The second step is more difficult to parallelize and we did not parallelize it in our implementation because it is typically cheap. Our experimental results showed that ParTime can achieve linear speed-ups for most queries found in practice. Furthermore, ParTime outperforms any existing algorithm that is not based on pre-computation. With sufficient parallelism, ParTime is even competitive to an approach that is based on a materialized temporal view (i.e., the Timeline Index). In addition to the general ParTime algorithm, this paper presented an important optimization that is applicable to a large class of temporal aggregation queries, so-called windowed temporal aggregation queries.

Arguably, parallelization is the most important feature of ParTime. In addition, ParTime has a number of other advantages. One of the most important advantages is that the first step of the ParTime algorithm integrates nicely into a shared scan. We exploited this feature and integrated ParTime in Crescando, a parallel main-memory database system that relies heavily on shared scans. This way, Crescando with ParTime was able to handle a complex workload from the travel industry with complex temporal aggregate queries and high update rates. To date, no other system is able to sustain this workload. The only way to implement this workload today is to split the workload and to carry out the temporal queries in a separate data warehouse.

There are a number of possible avenues for future work. First, we would like to generalize the ParTime technique and apply it to other temporal operators; e.g., temporal joins. Second, weplan to investigate how ParTime can co-exist with indexes such as the Timeline Index; for instance, would it be possible to partially index historic data that is not updated and to apply ParTime only to fresh and recently appended data in a hybrid way. Third, we would like to develop a cost model in order to compute the optimal degree of parallelism for ParTime.

7. REFERENCES

[1] M. Al-Kateb et al. Temporal query processing in Teradata. In *EDBT*, 2013.

[2] B. Becker et al. An asymptotically optimal multiversion B-Tree. *VLDB J.*, 1996.

[3] M. H. Böhlen, J. Gamper, and C. S. Jensen. Multi-dimensional Aggregation for Temporal Data. In *EDBT*, 2006.

[4] M. H. Böhlen, C. S. Jensen, and R. T. Snodgrass. Temporal statement modifiers. *ACM Trans. Database Syst.*, 25(4), 2000.

[5] P. A. Boncz, S. Manegold, and M. L. Kersten. Database Architecture Optimized for the New Bottleneck: Memory Access. In *VLDB*, 1999.

[6] G. Candea, N. Polyzotis, and R. Vingralek. A Scalable, Predictable Join Operator for Highly Concurrent Data Warehouses. *PVLDB*, 2009.

[7] G. DeCandia et al. Dynamo: Amazon's highly available key-value store. In *SOSP*, 2007.

[8] D. Gao et al. Main Memory-Based Algorithms for Efficient Parallel Aggregation for Temporal Databases. *Distributed and Parallel Databases*, 16(2), 2004.

[9] J. A. G. Gendrano et al. Parallel Algorithms for Computing Temporal Aggregates. In *ICDE*, 1999.

[10] G. Giannikis, G. Alonso, and D. Kossmann. SharedDB: Killing One Thousand Queries With One Stone. *PVLDB*, 5(6), 2012.

[11] G. Graefe, A. Linville, and L. D. Shapiro. Sort versus hash revisited. *IEEE Trans. Knowl. Data Eng.*, 6(6), 1994.

[12] L. M. Haas et al. Extensible query processing in starburst. In *SIGMOD*, 1989.

[13] M. Kaufmann et al. Timeline Index:A Unified Data Structure for Processing Queries on Temporal Data in SAP HANA. In *SIGMOD*, 2013.

[14] M. Kaufmann et al. TPC-BiH: A Benchmark for Bi-Temporal Databases. In *TPCTC*, 2013.

[15] M. Kaufmann et al. Bi-temporal timeline index: A data structure for processing queries on bi-temporal data. In *ICDE*, 2015.

[16] N. Kline and R. T. Snodgrass. Computing Temporal Aggregates. In *ICDE*, 1995.

[17] L. Lamport. Using Time Instead of Timeout for Fault-Tolerant Distributed Systems. *ACM Trans. Program. Lang. Syst.*, 6(2), Apr. 1984.

[18] D. B. Lomet and B. Salzberg. Access methods for multiversion data. In *SIGMOD*, 1989.

[19] M. A. Nascimento et al. M-IVTT: An Index for Bitemporal Databases. In *DEXA*, 1996.

[20] L. Qiao et al. Main-memory scan sharing for multi-core CPUs. *PVLDB*, 1(1), 2008.

[21] R. Rajamani. Oracle Total Recall / Flashback Data Archive. Technical report, Oracle, 2007.

[22] B. Salzberg and V. J. Tsotras. Comparison of Access Methods for Time-Evolving Data. *ACM Comput. Surv.*, 31(2), 1999.

[23] C. M. Saracco, M. Nicola, and L. Gandhi. A Matter of Time: Temporal Data Management in DB2 10. Technical report, IBM, 2012.

[24] R. T. Snodgrass et al. TSQL2 Language Specification. *SIGMOD Record*, 23(1), 1994.

[25] P. Unterbrunner et al. Predictable Performance for Unpredictable Workloads. *PVLDB*, 2(1), 2009.

[26] D. Zhang et al. On Computing Temporal Aggregates with Range Predicates. *ACM Trans. Database Syst.*, 33(2), 2008.

[27] M. Zukowski et al. Cooperative Scans: Dynamic Bandwidth Sharing in a DBMS. In *VLDB*, 2007.

Data Polygamy: The Many-Many Relationships among Urban Spatio-Temporal Data Sets

Fernando Chirigati*, Harish Doraiswamy*, Theodoros Damoulas★†, Juliana Freire*
* New York University ★ University of Warwick † Alan Turing Institute
{fchirigati,harishd,juliana.freire}@nyu.edu damoulas@warwick.ac.uk

ABSTRACT

The increasing ability to collect data from urban environments, coupled with a push towards openness by governments, has resulted in the availability of numerous spatio-temporal data sets covering diverse aspects of a city. Discovering relationships between these data sets can produce new insights by enabling domain experts to not only test but also generate hypotheses. However, discovering these relationships is difficult. First, a relationship between two data sets may occur only at certain locations and/or time periods. Second, the sheer number and size of the data sets, coupled with the diverse spatial and temporal scales at which the data is available, presents computational challenges on all fronts, from indexing and querying to analyzing them. Finally, it is nontrivial to differentiate between meaningful and spurious relationships. To address these challenges, we propose *Data Polygamy*, a scalable topology-based framework that allows users to query for statistically significant relationships between spatio-temporal data sets. We have performed an experimental evaluation using over 300 spatial-temporal urban data sets which shows that our approach is scalable and effective at identifying interesting relationships.

1. INTRODUCTION

Urban environments are the loci of economic activity and innovation. At the same time, most cities face huge challenges around transportation, resource consumption, housing affordability, and inadequate or aging infrastructure. The growing volumes of urban data being collected and made available [3, 19, 26, 27, 32] open up new opportunities for city governments and social scientists to engage in data-driven science to better understand cities, make them more efficient, and improve the lives of their residents.

Urban data is unique in that it captures the behavior of the different components of a city over space and time: its citizens, existing infrastructure (physical and policies), and the environment [20]. The availability of these data makes it possible to not only better understand the individual components but also obtain insights into how they interact. When an expert finds an *unexpected* pattern or feature in a data set, other related data may help explain why and under which conditions the pattern occurs. Consider the top plot in

SIGMOD'16, June 26-July 01, 2016, San Francisco, CA, USA

DOI: http://dx.doi.org/10.1145/2882903.2915245

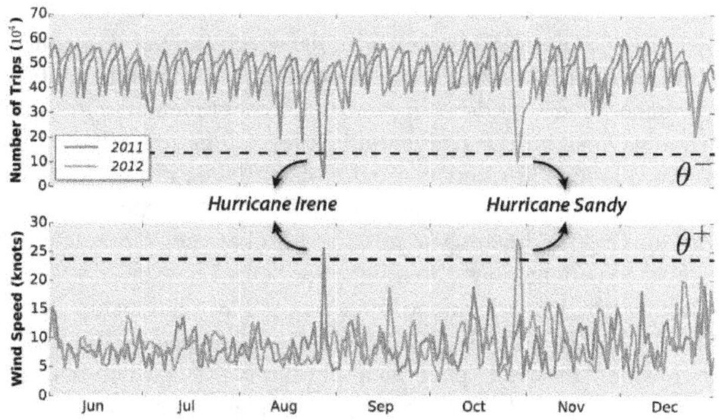

Figure 1: Variation of the number of taxi trips in NYC and its relationship with wind speed.

Figure 1, which shows the number of daily taxi trips in New York City (NYC) during 2011 and 2012. While the distribution of trips over time is very similar for the two years, we observe two large drops: one in August 2011 and another in October 2012. A natural question is what might have caused these drastic reductions. By examining wind speed data (bottom plot in Figure 1), we discover that these drops occur on days with unusually high wind speeds; here, the high wind speeds were due to hurricanes Irene and Sandy. This suggests a new hypothesis to be further investigated: high wind speed leads to significant reduction in the number of taxi trips.

Besides enabling *hypothesis generation*, studying relationships among data sets can also help with *hypothesis testing*. For instance, the difficulty in finding taxis when it is raining is a notorious problem in Manhattan. One long-standing hypothesis to explain this behavior is that taxi drivers set a daily income goal, and since there is higher demand on rainy days, they reach their goal faster and stop working earlier. Testing for the presence of such a relationship between data sets—in this case, NYC taxi data and weather data—can help experts at the NYC Taxi and Limousine Commission (TLC) frame appropriate policies to counter identified problems.

Relationship Discovery. In this paper, we define and take a first step towards addressing the problem of discovering potential *relationships* between spatio-temporal data sets. We aim to ***guide*** users in the data analysis and exploration process by allowing them to pose ***relationship queries***:

Find all data sets related to a given data set $\mathbb{D}$.

To evaluate the above query, we have to first determine *when and how two data sets are related*. Answering this question in the context of urban data sets gives rise to several challenges. Urban data can be large vertically, containing hundreds of millions to billions of data points, and horizontally, consisting of several attributes [3]. As a point of comparison, five years of taxi data contain 780 million trips [34], and the weather data set has over 200 attributes [35].

Also, there is a large number of urban data sets. NYC alone has published over 1,300 data sets in the past two years [27], and this is just a small fraction of the data collected by the city. Since a data set can be related to zero or more data sets through multiple attributes, there is a combinatorially large number of possible relationships.

This problem is compounded by the fact that these data sets contain both spatial and temporal attributes at different resolutions. For example, values for the weather attributes are collected at hourly intervals (temporal resolution) for the whole city (spatial resolution). In contrast, NYC taxi trips are associated with GPS coordinates with time precision in seconds. Other data sets use spatial resolutions at the level of neighborhoods or zip codes, and temporal resolutions as daily, weekly, and monthly intervals. Since relationships can materialize at any of these resolutions, they should be evaluated at multiple resolutions.

The data complexity coupled with the sheer number of available data sets and the combinatorially large number of possible relationships make it hard for domain experts to comprehend the information and the insights it can potentially offer. Of the several thousand possible relationships between pairs of attributes in different data sets, only a small fraction is actually informative. Unless known a priori, looking for meaningful relationships between these data sets is like, as the cliché goes, "finding a needle in a haystack."

Another challenge in identifying a possible relationship lies in defining the conditions implicating such a relationship. For example, consider the wind speed data and the NYC taxi trip data depicted in Figure 1. There is no apparent relation between the two data sets during the normal course of time: it is only when the wind speed is abnormally high (in that case, due to hurricanes) that we can see a connection with taxi trips. This is a common pattern observed across urban data sets, where relationships become visible only at *spatio-temporal regions* (locations in space and time) that behave differently compared to the regions' neighborhood.

Standard techniques, such as Pearson correlation coefficient [7] or dynamic time warping [21], do not capture these relationships because they ignore the spatio-temporal dependencies inherent in the data and operate globally over the entire data (see Section 6.4). Therefore, we need a method that captures the variation of the data over space and time at different and arbitrary resolutions.

Our Approach. To address these challenges, we propose the ***Data Polygamy*** framework. We introduce the notion of *topology-based relationships*, where two data sets are related if there is a relationship between the *salient features* of the data. A salient feature corresponds to a spatio-temporal region that exhibits an unusual behavior with respect to its neighborhood. To efficiently identify salient features, we use and extend techniques from computational topology. Topology-based techniques are naturally suited for studying properties of data involving spatial and geometric domains (e.g., see [11, 28, 38]). To give some intuition for why and how we apply topology, suppose we model a time step in an urban data set as a terrain, where the height of each point of the terrain represents the data value at that spatial location. In this case, the variation over space is captured by the peaks and valleys of this terrain. This can be extended to include time by modeling the data as a high dimensional terrain. The salient features, which as mentioned earlier correspond to spatio-temporal regions behaving differently from their neighborhood, are inherently represented as tall peaks and deep valleys. Topological methods provide *efficient algorithms to represent and compute such features*. In addition, they can identify features that have an *arbitrary spatial structure* and *straddle multiple time intervals*; they are also *generic*, in the sense that they work on data having different dimensions and resolutions without requiring any modification.

Given two data sets, to determine whether they are related, we assess how similar their corresponding terrains are, i.e., the similarities in the spatio-temporal variation patterns of the data sets. In the *Data Polygamy* framework, this is accomplished in three steps:

1. *Data Set Transformation.* Each attribute of the two data sets is transformed into a *scalar function*. A scalar function provides a mathematical representation of the terrain corresponding to a particular attribute of a data set.
2. *Feature Identification.* A topological data structure is computed for every scalar function, which provides an abstract representation of the peaks and valleys of the scalar function. This structure is used as an *index to efficiently identify salient features* in the data, which are defined based on thresholds that capture the extent of normal behavior of the scalar function. We develop a new method based on the notion of *topological persistence* [8] to automatically compute these thresholds.
3. *Relationship Evaluation.* Possible relationships are then identified based on feature similarity. Our framework filters out relationships that are *not statistically significant*. Since existing Monte Carlo methods assume independence across samples, we develop restricted Monte Carlo permutation tests that respect data dependencies due to spatial and temporal proximity.

Users can then pose relationship queries over the resulting relationships. Hypothesis generation is supported by querying for relationships among all data sets, while a given hypothesis can be tested by querying for relationships between the data sets involved in the hypothesis. Sections 2, 3, and 4 provide the formal definitions and describe the algorithms used in these stages. The end-to-end *Data Polygamy* framework is presented in Section 5.

Because we consider a large number of urban data sets, each containing many attributes, we need to compute thousands of scalar functions and derive millions of relationships. However, both salient feature identification and relationship querying are embarrassingly parallel operations. In Section 5.4, we briefly describe a map-reduce implementation of the *Data Polygamy* framework.

We demonstrate the efficiency and robustness of our framework in Section 6 through an experimental evaluation using over 300 urban data sets of varying spatio-temporal resolutions. We also present use cases demonstrating its effectiveness at identifying informative relationships.

Note that our goal is to support users in the data exploration process by helping them discover data sets that may be relevant for their task—similar to a search engine that returns a set of potentially relevant documents for a given keyword query. Users can then use the identified relationships for further analysis, such as testing for spurious relationships, testing for causality (e.g., to support a hypothesis), and generating new hypotheses.

Contributions. We define and propose a topology-based approach to the problem of identifying relationships across a large number of spatio-temporal data sets. Our main contributions are:

- We introduce the notion of *topology-based relationships* to determine whether data sets are related through salient features.
- We develop a *scalable framework* that identifies salient features based on the topology of the data, and a topology-based index that provides an *output-sensitive* strategy to compute these features: the time taken is linear in the size of the output. We also propose an *algorithm that automatically determines feature thresholds in a data-driven fashion.*
- We define the *relationship operator*, which returns the set of statistically significant relationships between two data sets. To determine whether a relationship is significant, we *develop a strategy that applies Monte Carlo permutation tests and respects data dependencies due to spatial and temporal proximity.*

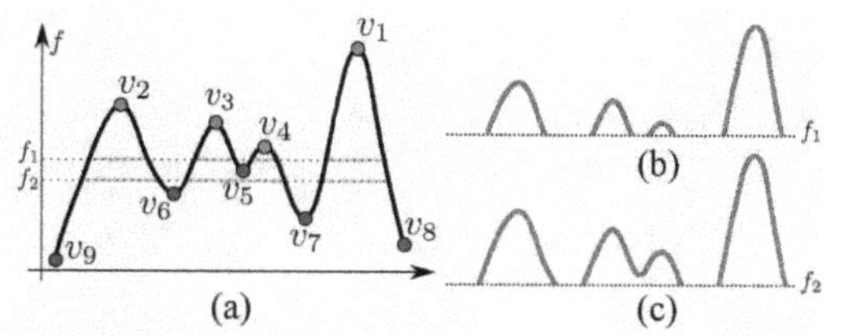

Figure 2: (a) A sample 1D scalar function. The labeled points form the set of maxima (red) and minima (blue). (b) The super-level set at f_1 consists of four components. (c) The super-level set at f_2 consists of three components.

- We describe a scalable, map-reduce implementation of the *Data Polygamy* framework.
- We perform an extensive experimental evaluation, using real and synthetic data, which shows that our framework is robust, efficient, and effective.

2. TOPOLOGY-BASED RELATIONSHIPS

In this section, we provide the required mathematical background and define the terms used in this paper, which are based on concepts from computational topology. We refer the reader to the following textbooks [13, 24] for a comprehensive discussion on these topics. We start by formally defining the concept of a topological feature and topology-based relationships. Then, we propose two measures to evaluate these relationships.

2.1 Topological Features

To discover relationships between two data sets, we first identify the set of topological features of the *scalar functions* that represent the data sets.

Scalar Functions. Let $\mathbb{D}$ be a data set, and A an attribute of $\mathbb{D}$. To identify the set of features with respect to the attribute A, we first represent the attribute as a *time-varying scalar function*.

Definition 1. A *scalar function* $f : \mathbb{S} \rightarrow \mathbb{R}$ maps points on a spatial domain $\mathbb{S}$ onto a real value.

Definition 2. A *time-varying scalar function* $f : [\mathbb{S} \times \mathbb{T}] \rightarrow \mathbb{R}$ maps points on a spatial domain across time onto a real value.

The spatial resolution of the data set $\mathbb{D}$ determines the structure of the spatial domain $\mathbb{S}$. For example, the NYC weather data set provides information on different climate attributes, such as temperature, precipitation, and wind speed. The values of these attributes correspond to an hourly time period for the entire city, i.e., all the values correspond to the same spatial point. In this case, the domain $\mathbb{S} \times \mathbb{T}$ of the time-varying scalar function is a simple time series, i.e., a 1D function (0D in space and 1D in time). Figure 2(a) and the two time series shown in Figure 1 are examples of 1D scalar functions. On the other hand, the NYC taxi data consists of a set of taxi trips, each containing the GPS coordinates for pick-up and drop-off locations. From these data, we can obtain a distribution of taxi trips over space and time by partitioning NYC into a set of polygons (e.g., neighborhoods) and counting the trips that start (or end) in each polygon at different time steps. This is a *density function*, where the spatial domain is 2D, and thus the time-varying scalar function is 3D (2D in space and 1D in time). Figure 3 shows the density function at two different spatial resolutions for one time step (i.e., one hour time period). The different scalar functions that can be used to represent a data set are discussed in Section 5.1.

Irrespective of the temporal resolution, time always contributes to one dimension in the time-varying scalar function. Unless otherwise noted, we use the term *scalar function* to refer to a time-varying scalar function corresponding to a (data set, attribute) pair.

Topological Features. Interesting features of a scalar function f are captured by the *critical points* of f.

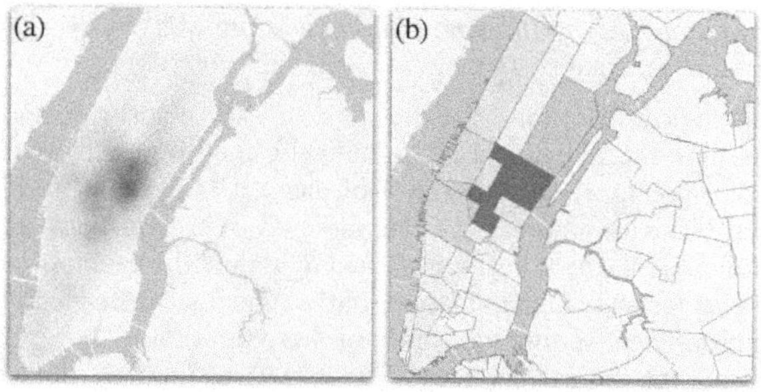

Figure 3: One time step (2D slice) of the 3D function representing the density of taxi trips in NYC at different resolutions. Dark and light regions correspond to high and low trip density, respectively. (a) NYC is represented using a high-resolution grid and the density is provided for each cell of this grid. (b) A lower resolution, at the level of neighborhood, is used.

Definition 3. Given a smooth function f, the *critical points* of f are the points where the gradient becomes zero, i.e., $\nabla f = 0$.

We assume that the scalar function f is a Morse function [24]. A Morse function has the property that (i) no two critical points have the same function value; and (ii) there are no degenerate critical points (i.e., $\nabla^2 f \neq 0$). Any continuous function f can be made Morse via a simulated perturbation of f by an infinitesimally small value such that no two points have the same function value [12]. We provide a detailed discussion on Morse functions in Appendix B.1.

We are interested in two particular types of critical points, *maximum* and *minimum*, collectively known as *extrema*. Given a Morse function, maximum and minimum points are defined as follows:

Definition 4. A point x is a *maximum* if $f(x) > f(x')$, $\forall x' \in N(x)$, where $N(x)$ defines the local neighborhood of x. Similarly, x is a *minimum* if $f(x) < f(x')$, $\forall x' \in N(x)$.

The red and blue points in Figure 2(a) correspond to the set of maxima and minima, respectively. We use the neighborhood of critical points of a function to represent the topological features of the data. The neighborhoods of the maxima and minima of f are captured by the *super-level* and *sub-level sets* of f, respectively.

Definition 5. Given a scalar function f, the *super-level set* at a real value θ is defined as $f^{-1}([\theta, \infty))$, i.e., the pre-image of the interval $[\theta, \infty)$. The *sub-level set* at θ is defined as $f^{-1}((-\infty, \theta])$.

In other words, the super-level set at a real value θ is the set of all points on the domain of f having function value greater than or equal to θ. For example, the super-level set of the function in Figure 2(a) at function value f_1 consists of 4 components (Figure 2(b)), while the super-level set at f_2 consists of 3 components (Figure 2(c)). Similarly, the sub-level set at θ is the set of all points in the domain of f having function value less than or equal to θ.

We define two types of features—positive and negative—using super-level and sub-level sets, respectively.

Definition 6. Given a feature threshold θ^+, the set of ***positive features*** is defined as the super-level set $f^{-1}([\theta^+, \infty))$.

Definition 7. Given an feature threshold θ^-, the set of ***negative features*** is defined as the sub-level set $f^{-1}((-\infty, \theta^-])$.

Feature Representation. The spatial domain $\mathbb{S}$ of $\mathbb{D}$ is represented as a set of regions $\{s_1, s_2, \ldots, s_n\}$ that partition the spatial extent of $\mathbb{D}$. Each region s_i corresponds to a polygon defined by the resolution used. For instance, the lowest resolution consists of the space represented as a single region or polygon. By using smaller polygons to partition the space, one could obtain a higher resolution representation as shown in Figure 3(a). The temporal domain $\mathbb{T}$ is represented as a set of time intervals $\{t, t+\delta, t+2\delta, \ldots\}$. The temporal resolution is defined by the value of δ. For example, when δ = 1 hour, the function is specified for hourly time steps.

Definition 8. A *spatio-temporal point* is represented by a (spatial region, time interval) pair.

Topological features of f correspond to a set of spatio-temporal points over the domain of f. Intuitively, they represent spatio-temporal points where attribute A of data set $\mathbb{D}$ deviates from its normal behavior, and capture the variation of A over both space and time. Here, the thresholds θ^+ and θ^- define the extent of normal behavior of A. Salient features of the function can be identified by appropriately setting the values of these thresholds. For example, using the indicated values of θ^+ and θ^- in Figure 1, features corresponding to the hurricanes are obtained. We describe an algorithm to identify the appropriate values for θ^+ and θ^- in Section 3.3.

2.2 Feature Relatedness

Consider two scalar functions: $f_1(\mathbb{D}_1, A_1)$ corresponding to attribute A_1 of data set $\mathbb{D}_1$, and $f_2(\mathbb{D}_2, B_1)$ corresponding to attribute B_1 of $\mathbb{D}_2$. Without loss of generality, we assume that the two functions have the same spatial and temporal resolution. Let Σ_1 and Σ_2 be the set of features of f_1 and f_2, respectively. Let $\Sigma = \Sigma_1 \bigcap \Sigma_2$ be the set of all spatio-temporal points that are features in both f_1 and f_2. The possible relationships between two functions are defined based on the relationship between their features.

Definition 9. Two functions f_1 and f_2 are *feature-related* at a spatio-temporal point $x = (s,t)$ if $x \in \Sigma$.

At points not in Σ, the two functions are not feature-related. Let $\Sigma_i^+ \subset \Sigma_i$ be a set such that $\forall x \in \Sigma_i^+, x$ is a positive feature. Similarly, let $\Sigma_i^- \subset \Sigma_i$ be the set of negative features.

Definition 10. f_1 and f_2 are *positively related* at a spatio-temporal point $x \in \Sigma$ if ($x \in \Sigma_1^+$ and $x \in \Sigma_2^+$) or ($x \in \Sigma_1^-$ and $x \in \Sigma_2^-$).

Definition 11. f_1 and f_2 are *negatively related* at a spatio-temporal point $x \in \Sigma$ if ($x \in \Sigma_1^+$ and $x \in \Sigma_2^-$) or ($x \in \Sigma_1^-$ and $x \in \Sigma_2^+$).

For instance, consider the features from Figure 1 corresponding to the indicated thresholds. At the spatio-temporal point corresponding to hurricane Sandy, there is a negative feature in the taxi density function and a positive feature in the wind speed function. The functions are therefore negatively related at that point.

2.3 Relationship Score and Strength

To assess the nature of the relationship between a given pair of functions, we define the following two measures.

Relationship Score τ. We are interested in evaluating the overall nature of the relationship between two functions, i.e., whether it is always positive, always negative, or somewhere in between. To do so, we define the *relationship score* τ between two functions f_1 $(\mathbb{D}_1, A_1)$ and f_2 $(\mathbb{D}_2, B_1)$. Let Σ_1 and Σ_2 denote the set of features of f_1 and f_2, respectively. As defined earlier, the set $\Sigma = \Sigma_1 \bigcap \Sigma_2$ denotes the feature-relations between the two functions. Let $\#p$ and $\#n$ be number of positive and negative feature relations in Σ. The relationship score is defined as

$$\tau = \frac{\#p - \#n}{|\Sigma|} \tag{1}$$

A value of τ closer to $+1$ indicates that the two functions are positively related, while a value closer to -1 indicates that the functions are negatively related.

Relationship Strength ρ. This measure is used to capture how frequently features in two functions are related: the more frequently the features are related, the stronger the relationship is. We model the set of features as binary classifiers. Consider any spatio-temporal point $x \in \Sigma_1$. If x is also present in Σ, it is considered as a true positive (tp). A point x is a false positive (fp) when $x \in \Sigma_1$ and $x \notin \Sigma$.

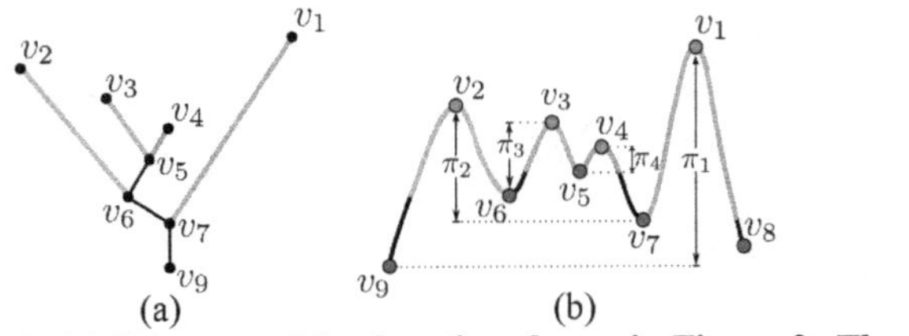

Figure 4: (a) Join tree of the function shown in Figure 2. The edges are colored based on the descending path traversed from the corresponding maxima illustrated in (b). π_i denotes the persistence of maximum v_i.

Similarly, x is false negative (fn) when $x \notin \Sigma_1$ and $x \in \Sigma$. Given these classifiers, we can compute precision and recall as

$$precision = \frac{\#tp}{\#tp + \#fp} \tag{2}$$

$$recall = \frac{\#tp}{\#tp + \#fn} \tag{3}$$

Intuitively, *precision* gives a measure of how often features in f_1 are related with features in f_2, and *recall* gives a measure of how often features in f_2 are related with features in f_1. We then use the F1 score to measure the relationship strength:

$$\rho = F_1(f_1, f_2) = 2 \times \frac{precision \times recall}{precision + recall} \tag{4}$$

A value of ρ closer to 1 indicates a strong relationship between the two functions, since a feature in one function almost always indicates a feature in the other function as well. Similarly, a value of ρ close to zero indicates a weak relationship.

3. MERGE TREE INDEX

We use a topological data structure called *merge tree* to efficiently identify salient features corresponding to a scalar function. In what follows, we give an overview of merge trees and introduce a new algorithm to compute the feature thresholds θ^+ and θ^-, a crucial step in this process.

3.1 Index Creation

Recall that a super-level set (or sub-level set) of a scalar function f at a given function value consists of multiple connected components. Therefore, decreasing or increasing the function values changes the topology, i.e., the number of connected components. A *merge tree* tracks the evolution of super-level sets or sub-level sets of f with changing function value. Formally, there are two types of merge trees.

Definition 12. The *join tree* of f tracks the connected components of the super-level sets of f with decreasing function value.

Definition 13. The *split tree* of f tracks the connected components of the sub-level sets of f with increasing function value.

Consider the 1D function shown in Figure 2(a). At the highest function value, a single super-level set component is created at v_1. As we decrease the function value, the number of components remain at one until the function value is equal to that of v_2. As we keep decreasing the function value, two more components are created at v_3 followed by v_4 (Figure 2(b)). However, when the function value reaches v_5, the components created at v_3 and v_4 merge into one component, reducing the number of components from 4 to 3 (Figure 2(c)). We stop this process when the function value goes below v_9 (the global minimum). At this point, there is a single super-level set component composed of the entire domain. The join tree tracks this evolution as a graph. Figure 4(a) shows the join tree of the 1D function from Figure 2(a). The nodes of the graph correspond to critical points where the number of components change, while an edge represents the connected super-level set component between its end points. For example, the edge (v_2, v_6) corresponds to the green connected super-level set component in Figure 4(b). The root node of a join tree is the global minimum of f, while the non-root leaf nodes correspond to the set of maxima of f. Similarly, the root node of a split tree corresponds to the global maximum and its non-root leaf nodes correspond to the set of minima of f. In order to compute merge trees, we first have to obtain a discrete representation of a scalar function, which we describe next.

Scalar Function Representation. Consider the spatial domain of a data set $\mathbb{D}$ consisting of regions $\{s_1, s_2, \dots, s_n\}$. Let the temporal domain of $\mathbb{D}$ consist of m time steps $\{t_1, t_2, \dots, t_m\}$. We create a graph $G = (V, E)$ to represent the spatio-temporal domain of $\mathbb{D}$ as follows. Vertex $v_{x,z} \in V$ represents the spatio-temporal point corresponding to region s_x at time t_z. Thus, $|V| = n \times m$. The edges $E = E_S \bigcup E_T$ are divided into two categories:

- *spatial edges*: $E_S = \{(v_{x,z}, v_{y,z}) \mid s_x \text{ adjacent to } s_y, \forall z \in [1,m]\}$
- *temporal edges*: $E_T = \{(v_{x,z}, v_{x,z+1}), \forall x \in [1,n],\ z \in [1,m)\}$

Edges in E_S connect adjacent regions of the space for each time step, and edges in E_T connect a region across adjacent time steps.

We use a piecewise linear (PL) function defined on G to represent the scalar function f: the function is defined on the vertices of G and linearly interpolated within each edge. The graph allows a single representation to be used irrespective of the dimension of the spatio-temporal domain, thus supporting different resolutions and dimensions of the data.

Merge Tree Computation. The merge tree of a PL function can be efficiently computed in $O(N \log N + M\alpha(M))$ time using the union-find data structure, where N and M are the number of vertices and edges, respectively, in G. Since the spatial domains considered in this work correspond to cities, the graph G representing these domains is planar. Thus, $M = O(N)$. The algorithm to compute join trees is given in Procedure ComputeJoinTree (for more details, see Appendix B.2). The split tree is computed analogously by using the function $f' = -f$ in this algorithm.

3.2 Querying Features

We use the join and split trees as indices to efficiently compute the set of features, i.e., the super-level sets and sub-level sets, respectively. Let θ be the feature threshold. The algorithm to compute the super-level set $f^{-1}([\theta, \infty))$ using the join tree J_T is as follows:

1. Identify the set $V^+ = \{v \mid v \text{ is a maximum and } f(v) \geq \theta\}$. This is accomplished by going over the non-root leaf nodes of J_T.
2. Set $\Sigma^+ = \emptyset$.
3. While $V^+ \neq \emptyset$
   (a) Remove v from V^+ and add to Σ^+.
   (b) Let $L^- = \{u \mid f(u) \leq f(v) \text{ and } u \text{ is adjacent to } v\}$.
   (c) Add $u \in L^-$ to V^+ if $\theta \leq f(u)$.
4. The set Σ^+ contains the vertices of G that belong to the super-level set at θ.

The algorithm performs a descending path traversal of adjacent vertices from the set of valid maxima (having function value greater than θ) until the required threshold is reached. The colored regions in Figure 4(b) indicate the descending paths followed by the algorithm starting from the different maxima of the function shown in Figure 2(a). This is analogous to traversing down the edges of the join tree. The sub-level set at θ is computed similarly, through an ascending path traversal starting from the minima of the function.

Time Complexity. Since the vertices of G are sorted when computing the join (or split) tree, the critical points of the function are also

Procedure ComputeJoinTree

```
Require: Graph G(V,E), Function f
 1: Sort V in descending order of f
 2: for each v ∈ V do
 3:     L+ = {u|(v,u) ∈ E and f(v) < f(u)}
 4:     C = {Component(u)|u ∈ L+}
 5:     if |C| = 0 then              /* v is a maximum and creator */
 6:         Create a new join component C_J
 7:         Set Head(C_J) = v, Creator(C_J) = v
 8:     else if |C| = 1 then                  /* v is not critical */
 9:         Add v to C
10:     else      /* v is a destroyer, |C| = 2 for Morse functions */
11:         Let C = {C1,C2}, f(Creator(C1)) < f(Creator(C2))
12:         Merge Components C_J = C1 ∪ C2
13:         Let u1 = Head(C1), u2 = Head(C2)
14:         Add edges (u1,v) and (u2,v) to Join Tree J_T
15:         Set Creator(C_J) = Creator(C1), Head(C_J) = v
16:         Pair Creator(C2) with destroyer v
17:     end if
18: end for
19: return Join Tree J_T
```

stored in sorted order. Thus, the number of comparisons required to identify V^+ (or V^-) is $|V^+|$ (or $|V^-|$). Each descending (or ascending) path traversal stops as soon as it reaches a vertex u that is not a feature. Thus, the number of vertices touched during querying is $O(\Sigma^+)$ (or $O(\Sigma^-)$). In other words, given the join and split trees, feature identification for a given threshold is ***output-sensitive***.

3.3 Feature Threshold Computation

Intuitively, our goal is to classify topological features not adhering to normal behavior as *salient features*. We are also interested in identifying *extreme features*, which correspond to outliers among salient features. For instance, the extremely high wind speeds during a hurricane correspond to extreme features

While users with domain knowledge can provide thresholds for computing features, this might not be feasible over all data sets. Thus, we devise a data-driven approach to identify the required thresholds, θ^+ and θ^-. Our approach is inspired by the *persistence diagram* [8], which is commonly used in scientific visualization applications to visually identify meaningful thresholds [11]. However, instead of relying on users to visually select thresholds, we develop an algorithm to automatically identify them.

Topological Persistence. Consider a sweep of the function f in decreasing order of function value. As mentioned earlier, the topology of the super-level set changes at critical points during this sweep. In particular, at a critical point, either a new super-level set component is created (maximum) or an existing super-level set component is destroyed. A critical point is a *creator* if a new component is created, and a *destroyer* otherwise. Again, consider the example in Figure 4. At critical point v_5, the components created at v_3 and v_4 are merged into one. In this case, the component created last, at v_4, is considered to be destroyed at v_5. Similarly, one can pair up each creator c_i uniquely with a destroyer d_i that destroys the topology created at c_i. Note that this pairing can be accomplished while computing the merge tree itself (Line 16 in Procedure ComputeJoinTree). The *persistence value* of c_i and d_i is defined as $|f(d_i) - f(c_i)|$, which indicates the lifetime of the feature created at c_i. Figure 4(b) illustrates the persistence values of the different critical points (as π_i) together with the creator-destroyer pairs. Intuitively, the persistence of a maximum (minimum) is equal to the height (depth) of the corresponding peak (valley).

Thresholds for Salient Features. The *persistence diagram* [8, 14] plots the maxima (or minima) of the input function as a set of points on a 2D plane, where the x and y coordinates of a feature correspond to its creation and destruction value, respectively. Figure 5(a) shows the persistence diagram of the minima of the taxi-density function from Figure 1 corresponding to one month in the data. Note that the minima are clearly split into *two groups*: those with high persistence (enclosed by the circle) and those with low persistence. This split becomes even more prominent when we plot just the persistence values (Figure 5(b)). A minimum (maximum) with a higher persistence value is considered important since the sub- (or super-) level set component created at that extremum has a longer lifetime. Our goal is to select a threshold θ^- such that all the high persistence minima are identified as salient. To do this automatically, we perform k-means clustering with $k = 2$ and use the highest value over all minima in the high persistence cluster as the threshold θ^-. This ensures that all the high-persistence minima will have function value less than or equal to θ^-, and will hence be identified as salient features. θ^+ is identified in a similar manner using the persistence of the set of maxima.

Thresholds for Extreme Features. Typically, a minimum (maximum) corresponding to an extreme feature will have function value that is significantly smaller (larger) than those corresponding to salient features. For example, in Figure 5(c), the function value of minima corresponding to the extremely low number of taxi trips in NYC between 2009 and 2013 is significantly different from the function value of other minima (corresponding to salient features). In order to identify the appropriate thresholds, we first compute the minima (or maxima) across all time steps that correspond to salient features. Next, we identify the outlier threshold from this distribution. We use the standard box plot thresholds, i.e., $Q_1 - 1.5 \times IQR$ for minima ($Q_3 + 1.5 \times IQR$ for maxima), as the required thresholds, where Q_1 and Q_3 are the first and third quartile, and IQR is the inter-quartile range. The box plot (and the corresponding outlier threshold) for the extreme negative features corresponding to the taxi density function is illustrated in Figure 5(c).

Adjusting for Seasonal Variations. Processes in a city are typically dependent on the time of year. For example, zero depth of snow during summer is normal, while this could indicate an important phenomena during the winter. Thus, it is important to take into account seasonal variations when computing features. Depending on the temporal resolution, the time range of a data set is divided into smaller intervals, and the threshold for a given interval is computed based on the persistence of the extrema present in that interval. For example, we could use monthly or quarter-yearly intervals.

4. RELATIONSHIP OPERATOR

In the previous sections, we discussed how relationships between functions are identified and measured. We now define the relationship operator, RELATION($\mathbb{D}_1, \mathbb{D}_2$), used to compute the relationship between data sets $\mathbb{D}_1$ and $\mathbb{D}_2$. Let $\mathbb{D}_1$ be represented by n functions $\{f_1, f_2, \ldots, f_n\}$, and $\mathbb{D}_2$ by m functions $\{g_1, g_2, \ldots, g_m\}$. There are $n \times m$ possible relationships between the two data sets. Since many of these relationships could be due to random chance, the relationship operator returns the set of statistically significant relationship pairs (f_i, g_j) together with their corresponding relationship score and strength.

To assess the statistical significance of a potential relationship pair (f_i, g_j), we design Generalized Monte Carlo significance tests [5, 15, 18]. Let Σ_1 and Σ_2 be the features corresponding to f_i and g_j, respectively. The null and alternative hypothesis are:

H_0: The two functions f_i, g_j are independent in their features Σ_1, Σ_2.
H_1: The two functions are dependent in their features.

We examine if we can reject the null hypothesis and accept H_1 for any pair of functions based on the identified features and their cor-

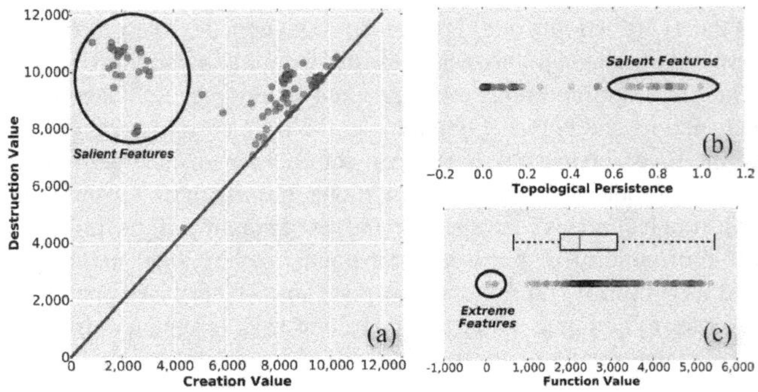

Figure 5: (a) The persistence of a minima in a persistence diagram is the height above the $x = y$ line. (b) A scatter plot of the persistence of the minima. (c) When considering only negative features across all time intervals, note that function values corresponding to extreme features (e.g., during hurricanes) are outliers of the distribution.

responding relationship score. The p-value from the Monte Carlo randomization test with test statistic x^* is given by:

$$p = P(X \leq x^* | H_0) = \frac{\sum_i^N \mathrm{I}(x_i \leq x^*)}{N} \quad \text{as } N \to \infty \tag{5}$$

where $\mathrm{I}(\cdot)$ is the indicator function and N the number of permutations on the input. Given a significance level α, the p-value is then used to define a statistically significant relationship as follows:

Definition 14. The relationship between two functions f_i and g_j is statistically significant if $p \leq \alpha$.

Urban data sets have spatial and temporal dependencies (e.g., due to neighborhood and seasonal effects) that need to be accounted for when designing randomization tests. It is well-known in the statistics literature that, if we ignore these dependencies, a simple Monte Carlo procedure for assessing statistical significance would fail and lead to erroneous claims [5, 23]. To account for the spatio-temporal correlation, a plethora of Monte Carlo and Bootstrap techniques have been developed over the last decades ranging from the block-bootstrap [22] to general restricted Monte Carlo techniques [18, 23] such as the one we propose in this paper.

Restricted Monte Carlo Tests for Spatial Correlation. We develop restricted permutation tests that respect the degree of spatial correlation of our data sources. This is typically achieved by designing toroidal shifts, where a function f is wrapped around a two-dimensional torus by connecting the margins, or spatial extents, of the data. Then, a linear map m—that maps the torus onto a rotation of itself—will yield a new randomization that still respects any horizontal interactions [18, 23].

However, given the irregular structure of a city, which is an arbitrary non-convex polygon, wrapping the spatial region over a torus is not straightforward. If we consider the spatial domain as a graph, a toroidal shift basically ensures that the adjacency of the non-boundary vertices are maintained. We make use of this observation to devise a toroidal shifting strategy that is applicable to arbitrary graphs. Given a graph G representing the spatial domain, we define the map $m_i : G \to G$ as follows. We start with a random mapping $m_i(u) = v$. The adjacent vertices of u are then assigned the vertices adjacent to v where applicable. This process is repeated in a breadth-first fashion. This process ensures that, in most cases, the distance between two vertices in G is the same as the distance between them in $m_i(G)$. Using the above mapping, the restricted Monte Carlo test now becomes:

$$p = \frac{\sum_k^{|m|} \mathrm{I}(\tau(f_i, g_j)_k \leq \tau(f_i, g_j)^*)}{|m|} \tag{6}$$

where $\tau(f_i, g_j)_k$ is the relationship score between the two functions f_i, g_j in toroidal shift k, and $|m|$ is the total number of toroidal shifts, which affects the power of the statistical test (we use $|m| = 1,000$).

Restricted Monte Carlo Tests for Temporal Correlation. For 1D functions that are purely temporal and have no spatial domain, we wrap time to a one-dimensional torus while rotating the resulting circle to obtain randomizations that respect temporal correlations [18]. We then proceed similarly to Equation 6. Unless otherwise mentioned, a relationship implies a statistically significant relationship for the remainder of the paper.

5. DATA POLYGAMY FRAMEWORK

In this section, we describe the data polygamy framework. We start by presenting the *scalar functions* that are derived from a given data set and how the framework handles different resolutions. Then, we discuss how the data is indexed and queries are evaluated. Finally, we briefly describe a map-reduce implementation of the framework.

5.1 Types of Scalar Function

Consider a data set $\mathbb{D}$ having attributes $\{K, S, T, A_1, A_2, \ldots, A_k\}$. Let K be an optional unique identifier (the data set can have zero or more identifier attributes); S and T be the spatial and temporal attributes, respectively; and $A_i, 1 \leq i \leq k$ be numerical attributes. We are interested in identifying scalar functions that capture the different properties corresponding to a given data set. For instance, when considering the taxi data, the number of taxis in different locations over time captures the activity of the taxis, while the attribute corresponding to the fare captures fare patterns over time and space. We therefore derive two types of scalar functions to represent $\mathbb{D}$: *count functions* and *attribute functions*. Extensions to other types of scalar functions are discussed in Section 8.

Count Functions. *Count functions* are used to capture the activity of the entity represented by the data set. More formally, consider a spatio-temporal point (s,t). Let Γ be the set of tuples in $\mathbb{D}$ such that $S(r) = s$ and $T(r) = t$, $\forall r \in \Gamma$. Here, S and T represent the spatial and temporal attributes of a tuple r. We define two types of count functions: *density* and *unique*. The *density function* assigns the value $|\Gamma|$ to the spatio-temporal point (s,t). For example, the density function of the taxi data assigns the number of trips originating at s during the time period t to the point (s,t). The *unique function* assigns a value equal to the number of unique identifiers of Γ to the spatio-temporal point. For instance, each tuple in the taxi data consists of an identifier corresponding to the medallion of the taxi. Thus, the number of unique medallions in Γ is essentially the number of unique taxis that are present at s during time t. Note that there is one unique function corresponding to each identifier attribute of the data set.

Attribute Functions. For a given attribute A, the *attribute function* assigns the average value of $A(r)$ over all tuples $r \in \Gamma$ to the corresponding spatio-temporal point (s,t); the function represents the variation in the properties of a given attribute over space and time.

Handling Different Data Resolutions. It is important that our framework identifies relationships that occur at different resolutions. As illustrated in Figure 6, these resolutions are represented as a directed acyclic graph (DAG), where the edges are directed from a higher resolution to a compatible lower resolution. The compatibility indicates the ability to convert the data from a higher resolution to a coarser resolution. For example, GPS resolution can be transformed into all of the other resolutions. On the other hand, neighborhood and zip-code resolutions, being incompatible, can be converted only into the city resolution. To evaluate the relationship between two functions having different resolutions, we first transform both functions into the same compatible resolution, and then evaluate the two functions at this resolution.

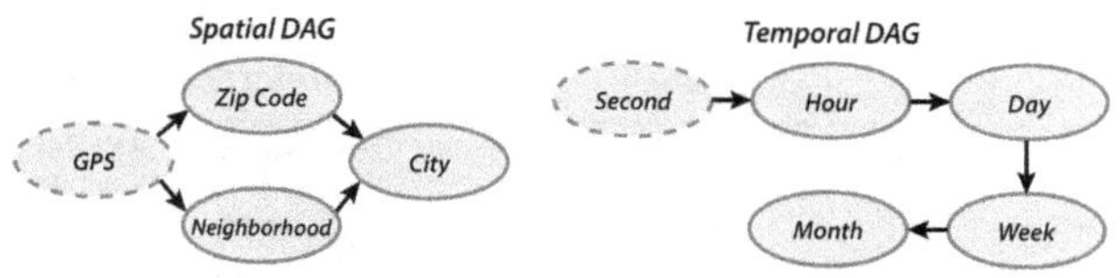

Figure 6: Hierarchical relationship for spatio-temporal resolutions represented by DAGs. Resolutions depicted using solid lines are used for evaluating relationships.

5.2 Indexing and Feature Identification

Given a data set $\mathbb{D}$, we first compute all possible scalar functions (i.e., count and attribute functions) of $\mathbb{D}$ that cover every viable spatio-temporal resolution. For example, if $\mathbb{D}$ is available at a spatial resolution of GPS locations and temporal resolution of second, then each attribute can be aggregated into 3 spatial resolutions (i.e., zip code, neighborhood, and city) and 4 temporal resolutions (i.e., hour, day, week, and month), thus resulting in a total of 12 spatio-temporal resolutions for which the scalar functions are computed. The merge tree index is then built for each scalar function. This ensures that all resolutions are considered when executing a relationship query. Recall that the computation of feature thresholds takes seasonal variations into account (Section 3.3). In particular, we use monthly and quarter-yearly intervals when the temporal resolution is hourly and daily, respectively. Since thresholds are fixed for a given function, to speed up query evaluation, we pre-compute and store the features (salient and extreme).

5.3 Query Evaluation

Let $\mathcal{D} = \{\mathbb{D}_1, \ldots, \mathbb{D}_n\}$ be the corpus of data sets that have been indexed. We support the general form of the *relationship query*:

Find relationships between $\mathcal{D}_1$ and $\mathcal{D}_2$ satisfying CLAUSE

In this query, $\mathcal{D}_1$ and $\mathcal{D}_2$ are collections of data sets such that $\mathcal{D}_1 \subseteq \mathcal{D}$ and $\mathcal{D}_2 \subseteq \mathcal{D}$. If $\mathcal{D}_2 = \emptyset$, it is assumed that $\mathcal{D}_2 = \mathcal{D}$. When a relationship query is issued, the RELATION operator is applied to all pairs $(\mathbb{D}_i, \mathbb{D}_j)$ of data sets, such that $\mathbb{D}_i \in \mathcal{D}_1$, $\mathbb{D}_j \in \mathcal{D}_2$, and $\mathbb{D}_i \neq \mathbb{D}_j$. The operator uses the pre-computed set of features to assess the relationship between the data sets. Note that, when considering a pair of functions, the relationship between them is evaluated for all possible resolutions starting with the *highest common* resolution. For example, if the spatial resolutions of two functions are neighborhood and zip code, then their relationship is evaluated at the city scale for different possible temporal resolutions. This evaluation is performed for both salient and extreme features.

Computing relationships at different resolutions is important as scalar functions may relate differently depending on how they are aggregated. For example, an hourly resolution might capture variations within a day, but could miss significant variations across different days, which can be captured using a daily resolution (see Section 6.3 for an example).

The query returns related scalar function pairs that are statistically significant, together with the resolutions for which the relationships hold. The significance level α is set at the commonly used value of 5% [15]. In the CLAUSE for a query, optional condition parameters can be specified to filter relationships satisfying a minimum score τ and/or strength ρ. Feature thresholds for computing salient and extreme features can also be optionally specified as part of the CLAUSE if the user is familiar with any of the data sets. When these thresholds are specified, features are first identified using the merge tree index before evaluating the relationship.

Table 1: Properties of the data sets in the *NYC Urban* collection.

Data Set	Data Size	# Records	Time Range	# Scalar Functions	Spatial Resolution	Temporal Resolution	Description
Gas Prices	13 KB	749	2000–2014	2	City	Week	Average gasoline price in dollars per gallon for NYC
Vehicle Collisions	47 MB	330 K	2012–2014	11	GPS	Second	Traffic collision data provided by NYPD
311 Complaints	574 MB	7.40 M	2003–2014	1	GPS	Second	Records from 311, a telephone number that provides non-emergency services to the city
911 Calls	2.2 GB	6.75 M	2012–2013	1	GPS	Second	Records from 911, a telephone number that provides emergency services to the city
Citi Bike Data	1.6 GB	10.40 M	2013–2014	5	GPS	Second	Trip data from NYC's bike sharing system
NCEI Weather Data	304 MB	64 K	2010–2014	228	City	Hour	Comprehensive weather data from NCEI
Traffic Speed	17 GB	395 M	2009–2012	2	GPS	Hour	Average speed in the streets of Manhattan
Taxi Data	108 GB	868 M	2009–2013	13	GPS	Second	Trip data from taxicabs provided by NYC TLC
Twitter	656 GB	1.10 B	2012–2014	5	GPS	Second	Data obtained from Twitter's public streams

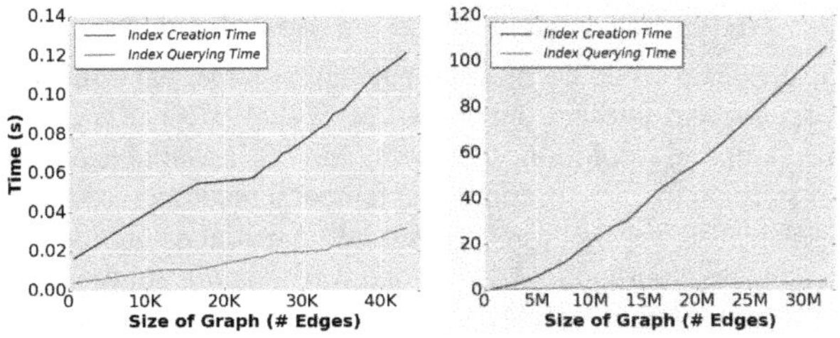

(a) City (b) Neighborhood

Figure 7: Merge tree index creation and feature querying time.

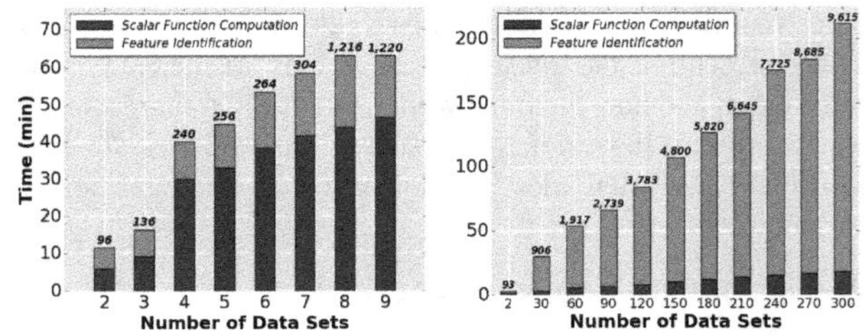

(a) *NYC Urban* (b) *NYC Open*

Figure 8: Performance of feature indexing and identification.

5.4 Implementation

Given a large number of data sets, such as the urban data sets with which we experimented (Section 6), thousands of scalar functions have to be computed, and the number of relationships to be evaluated during querying is in the order of millions. However, the indexing and querying operations can be run independently for each scalar function and scalar function pair. To leverage the *embarrassingly parallel* nature of these computations, we implemented the framework using *map-reduce*. We use three *map-reduce* jobs: (1) *Scalar Function Computation* generates all possible scalar functions at different resolutions; (2) *Feature Identification* creates the merge tree indexes and identifies the set of features of the different functions; and (3) *Relationship Computation* evaluates the relationships between the pairs of functions corresponding to a given query. Implementation details can be found in Appendix C and the released code.[1]

Space Requirements. The space required to store a scalar function for a given resolution is equal to the number of vertices in the graph G representing the domain. For a resolution at the city level and hourly intervals, this corresponds to the number of time steps, which is approximately 35 KB (365×24 float values) per year. For higher spatial resolutions, the space required to store the function is approximately $n \times 35$ KB, where n is the number of polygons used to partition the domain. For example, in NYC, for zip code and neighborhood resolutions, $n \approx 300$. Typically, the space needed to store scalar functions over all resolutions is significantly less than the original data itself. As a point of reference, the 5 years of the raw taxi data takes up 108 GB of space. In contrast, the 13 possible scalar functions over 8 resolutions uses only 417 MB. The size of the merge tree index is proportional to the number of critical points of the function. While the number of critical points is bounded by the size of the input graph in the worst case, in practice it is significantly smaller. Similarly, even the number of features, while being bounded by the size of the input graph, is usually much smaller. For example, storing all features (salient and extreme) for the taxi data over all different resolutions takes only 8 MB.

[1]`https://github.com/ViDA-NYU/data-polygamy`

6. EXPERIMENTAL EVALUATION

We have performed an extensive evaluation to assess different aspects of the *Data Polygamy* framework. We carried out a controlled experiment to quantitatively evaluate the correctness and robustness of the relationship operator, and we also used real-world data sets to study efficiency and effectiveness characteristics. Efficiency was measured to show the feasibility of computing relationships over a large number of data sets. Effectiveness was evaluated in two different ways: to demonstrate that the framework is able to prune spurious relationships, thus reducing the exploration space presented to users, and to show that our approach uncovers *interesting*, non-trivial relationships. We also analyzed the relationships obtained from standard correlation techniques and discuss their shortcomings in identifying interesting relationships.

Experimental Setup. We used Apache Hadoop 2.2.0 and Java 1.7.0. The *map-reduce* jobs were executed on a cluster with 20 compute nodes, each node having an AMD Opteron(TM) Processor 6272 (4x16 cores) running at 2.1GHz, and 256GB of RAM.

Data Sets. We used two collections of data sets in our experiments. The *NYC Urban* collection consists of nine urban data sets obtained from different NYC agencies or gathered through publicly-available APIs. These data sets have been used by various domain experts (mostly in isolation) for different analyses (see, e.g., [6, 17]) and are thus useful to evaluate the effectiveness of our framework at identifying meaningful relationships. Table 1 describes these data sets and their properties. They vary in size from a few KBs to hundreds of GBs and have different temporal and spatial resolutions.

The second collection, referred to as *NYC Open*, was primarily used to test the performance of our framework. It consists of 300 spatio-temporal data sets from NYC Open Data [27]. Even though most of these data sets are relatively small in size (less than 1 GB), the sheer number of data sets and the number of attributes they contain (on average, 8 attributes per data set) results in over 2.4 million possible relationships for a single resolution.

Each data set in these collections consists of a set of tuples having metadata about the spatial, temporal, numerical, and identifier attributes. We use this metadata to perform an additional preprocessing step that selects data corresponding to these attributes and feeds it to the scalar function computation module.

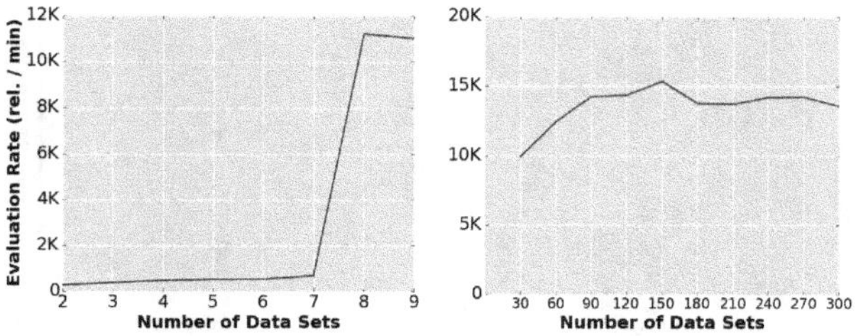

(a) *NYC Urban* (b) *NYC Open*

Figure 9: Query performance.

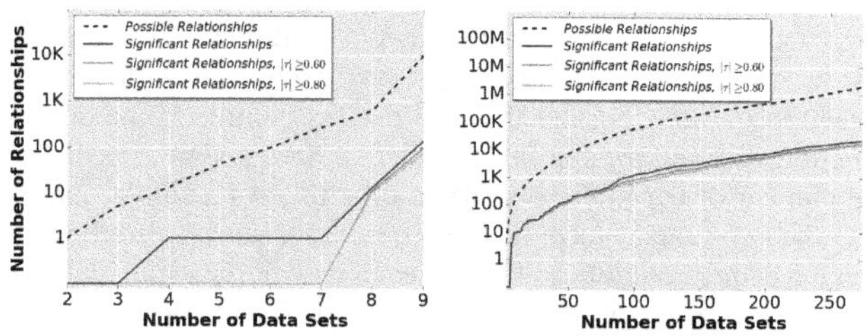

(a) *NYC Urban* (b) *NYC Open*

Figure 11: Relationship pruning.

6.1 Performance Evaluation

Indexing and Feature Identification. To assess the efficiency of feature identification and indexing, we studied the performance of the merge tree index for a single data set as well its behavior for an increasing number of data sets. Figure 7 plots the running times to create the index and query for features for the Taxi data (using its density function), for both city (1D) and neighborhood (3D) resolutions. Here, we used a single node in the cluster. The plots indicate that the time for creating the merge tree and identifying features is almost linear in the size of the function (i.e., number of edges in the spatial domain graph). Note that the indexing time includes the creation of both join and split trees, and the querying time includes the computation of thresholds as well as the identification of negative and positive features. Even for an input having more than 30 million edges, the operations took less than 2 minutes. This shows that our approach is scalable and able to handle large data sets.

The indexing component also performs well as the number of data sets increases. This is shown in Figure 8. The numbers on the bars indicate the total number of computations performed. Recall that scalar functions are computed for all attributes at different spatio-temporal resolutions. When using *NYC Urban* (Figure 8(a)), the large increase in time when moving from 3 to 4 data sets was due to the 4th data set, the Taxi data, which is not only large but also contains many attributes. It also has the highest resolution both in space and time, requiring each scalar function to be computed over different resolutions. There was also a significant increase in the number of computations when the Weather data set was introduced (the 8th data set): this data set has 228 numerical attributes. However, since it is relatively small compared to other data sets in *NYC Urban*, the running time was not significantly affected.

Given the large number of data sets in *NYC Open*, the total time taken to identify the features was significantly larger than for *NYC Urban* (Figure 8(b)). Unlike *NYC Urban*, relatively more time is spent on feature identification than on computing the scalar functions. This is due to two reasons: (1) the data sets in this collection are much smaller; (2) most of the 3D data sets in *NYC Open* are already in zip code resolution, making it faster to compute the scalar functions; in contrast, tuples in the 3D *NYC Urban* data sets are GPS points, which required additional computations to aggregate into the neighborhood or zip code resolutions. The total time taken to compute the indexes and features for all data sets in *NYC Urban* and *NYC Open* was about 1 hour and 4 hours, respectively.

Query Performance. To test the efficiency of the querying component, we executed a series of queries that identify the relationships between a fixed number of data sets. Figure 9 plots the relationship evaluation rate with increasing number of data sets. Using both collections, *NYC Urban* and *NYC Open*, we were able to consistently evaluate relationships at a rate greater than 10^4 relationships per minute. The evaluation rate stabilized once the number of relationships increased above this number, e.g., with the addition of the Weather data (data set 8) in Figure 9(a). A total of 290 thousand relationships were evaluated when the query used all data sets from *NYC Urban*; for the *NYC Open*, this number was 17.4 million. The constant rate, irrespective of the data set pairs, indicates that relationship evaluation is independent of size and resolution of the original data. This can be attributed to the abstraction of the data as functions. Note that over 90% of the querying time is spent on the statistical significance tests, which involve re-evaluating each relationship for 1,000 random spatial or temporal permutations. Also, the queries executed did not include any filtering clause. When using a clause C, the query evaluation step skips the significance test when C is not satisfied, which further improves the performance.

Scalability. To test the scalability of our framework, we computed the speedup attained by the different components with increasing number of nodes in the cluster. This experiment was performed on Amazon Web Services (AWS) using the *NYC Urban* collection. We used AWS because it allows the configurations of clusters of different sizes. Each node in the cluster had an Intel Xeon E5-2670 v2 processor (8-core) and 61GB of RAM. Figure 10 shows the speedup for the three components of the framework, which was computed against the the time taken by a single node. A relatively lower speedup was attained for identifying features and evaluating relationships than for the scalar function computation. This is primarily due to the presence of straggler reducers that deal with higher spatio-temporal resolutions, thus increasing the computation time for the randomization tests.

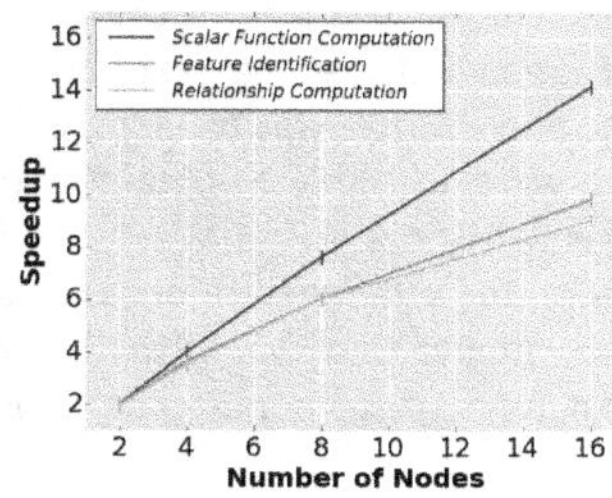

Figure 10: Speedup

Relationship Pruning. Figure 11 plots the the number of identified relationships (in log scale), when considering the (week, city) resolution, with increasing number of data sets. For the data sets in *NYC Urban* (Figure 11(a)), there was a significant decrease in the number of relationships—from 9,745 to 137, a decrease of about 98.60%. When we filtered relationships having $\tau \geq 0.6$ and $\tau \geq 0.8$, the reduction further increased to 99% and 99.20%, respectively. When handling a larger number of data sets, such as *NYC Open*, the advantages of our framework become even more evident, as Figure 11(b) shows. Given the over 2 million possible relationships for the (week, city) resolution, our framework identified 22,327 of them to be statistically significant, which corresponds to a decrease of about 98.90%. Although the number of identified relationships is still large, this is significantly better than trying to make sense of over 2 million relations. In addition, we envision that users will explore these relationships by searching, querying, and filtering them based on different attributes (e.g., τ, ρ, α, space, and time).

6.2 Correctness and Robustness

Correctness. Most urban data sets have become available only recently and work on integrating them is still incipient [3]. Since *there are no ground-truth benchmarks* that can be used to evaluate the correctness of the identified relationships, we used prior knowledge about the data sets and designed a controlled experiment to test if our technique can uncover strong relationships that are expected to occur. Consider the Taxi data in Figure 1. The density functions for taxi trips in 2011 and 2012 have a similar behavior: the number of trips in the city over time follows a similar pattern over the two years, except in specific situations, such as during extreme weather conditions. Thus, if each year of data is modeled as a function (starting at the same day and time), a strong positive relationship should be observed for the two functions. This observation was used to test our technique, which indeed identified the two functions to be strongly and significantly related across different resolutions. The relationship score and strength for the (hour, city) and the (hour, neighborhood) resolutions were ($\tau = 0.99, \rho = 0.85$) and ($\tau = 1, \rho = 0.87$), respectively.

Robustness. To assess the robustness of our technique in the presence of noise, we fixed a scalar function f, and by artificially introducing noise to f, we created a new (noisy) function f^*. We used a random Gaussian noise where the amount of noise was bounded by a fraction of the inter-quartile range of the function. Note that noise was added to every spatio-temporal point of the function domain. We then evaluated the relationship between f and f^*. Figure 12 plots the relationship scores and strengths with increasing levels of noise added to the taxi density function. Note that even when the added noise was as large as 10% of the normal function range, we were still able to obtain a strong positive relationship (which was statistically significant) between the two functions. Furthermore, the relationship score remained 1 even when the noise level was greater than 2%. This behavior can be attributed to the fact that topological persistence, which is used to identify thresholds for the salient features, is robust to noise [8]; small local maxima and minima, which are created due to the addition of noise, do not significantly affect the feature threshold.

6.3 Effectiveness: Interesting Relationships

We carried out a detailed study using *NYC Urban* to assess the effectiveness of our approach at finding interesting relationships and pruning uninformative relationships that are not statistically significant. In our evaluation, we found Weather to be the most *polygamous* data set, being related through different attributes with all data sets in the collection, except Gas Prices, indicating the impact it has on different aspects of a city. We discuss some of these relationships below (additional relationships are described in Appendix E.2). Unless otherwise noted, all relationships are with respect to salient features. Note that, while some of the results might imply the presence of a causal relationship, further analysis (not in the scope of this work) is required to ascertain causality.

Weather and Taxi. One of the relationships identified for the Taxi and Weather data sets in the (hour, city) resolution is between the number of taxis and the average precipitation, having score $\tau = -0.62$ and strength $\rho = 0.75$. The values indicate a strong negative relationship: the higher the precipitation, the lower the number of taxis in the city. As discussed in Section 1, this confirms the difficulty in finding taxis on a rainy day. When testing the hypothesis that this is due to taxi drivers being target earners, we found a positive relationship between average fare and precipitation ($\tau = 0.73, \rho = 0.7$) implying increased earnings when it rains. Note that Farber [16] refuted this hypothesis since he did not find a correlation (using OLS regression) between the drivers' earnings and rainfall. This is primarily due to two reasons: (i) he did not take into account the amount of rainfall—instead, he used a binary value indicating whether it rained or not; and (ii) more importantly, he considered the entire time period—periods with very sparse rainfall are considered equivalent to those having higher rainfall. Thus,

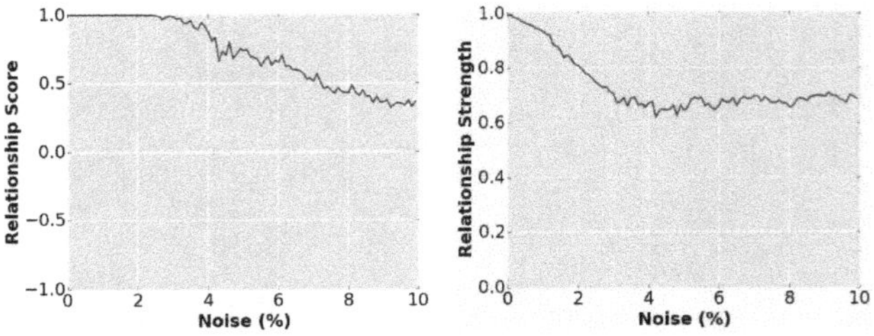

(a) Score (b) Strength

Figure 12: Robustness evaluation using the density of taxi trips.

this case study also provides evidence for the importance of looking at salient features, since they can evince relationships that are not visible when the whole data is taken into account.

While examining relationships involving extreme features, we found a negative relationship between the number of trips and the average wind speed. This relationship has a high score ($\tau = -1$) and a low strength ($\rho = 0.13$). The low strength is due to the presence of significant drops in the number of taxi trips at other periods, for example, during Thanksgiving, Christmas, and New Year [17] that are unrelated to the wind speed. However, the high score indicates that, whenever there is high wind speed, the number of taxi trips is significantly lower than usual, which is related to the impact of hurricanes in the city. We also found the same impact in the relationship between number of unique taxis and average precipitation (having $\tau = -1.0$) when considering extreme features. It is worth noting that the number of taxi trips and wind speed are not related through salient features alone (also observed from Figure 1). This demonstrates the importance of computing relationships for salient as well as extreme features.

Weather and Citi Bike. We found a positive relationship between the average snow precipitation and the average bike trip duration in the (hour, city) resolution, having $\tau = 0.61$ and $\rho = 0.16$. This implies that bike trips are longer in snowy days (or shorter when there is no snow), which is consistent with what we would expect. For a lower resolution—(day, city)—we found a negative relationship between the average snow precipitation and the active Citi Bike stations ($\tau = -0.88$ and $\rho = 0.65$), i.e., fewer bike stations are used when it snows. We believe that this is related not only to the drop in bike usage under such weather, but also because heavier snow may impact certain stations more than others: the city clears snow at different frequencies depending on the location, and some stations may get cleared faster than others. Note that the latter relationship had a low score ($\tau = 0$) when considered at the higher resolution (hour, city): the impact is usually reflected only after the snow accumulates, and such accumulation is not captured when using an hourly time step (higher resolution). This case illustrates the need for evaluating relationships at multiple resolutions.

Vehicle Collisions and Weather. We found interesting relationships between Vehicle Collisions and Weather, which correspond to the increased danger of accidents when it rains. There was a strong positive relationship between rainfall and number of motorists killed ($\tau = 0.90, \rho = 0.95$) as well as number of injured pedestrians ($\tau = 0.75, \rho = 0.66$). However, we found no significant relationship between number of accidents and rainfall, implying that, even though the number of accidents does not increase when there is heavy rain, their severity does. This leads to a new hypothesis that may explain the lack of taxis during rainfall: taxi drivers, being experienced with the possible danger during high rainfall, might return home during these periods.

Taxi and Traffic Speed. We found a positive relationship between the average taxi fare and the average traffic speed at the (hour, neighborhood) resolution with $\tau = 0.79$ and $\rho = 0.44$, implying that drivers may in fact earn less in the presence of heavy traffic. We also found strong negative relationships between the number of taxi trips and the average traffic speed in the (hour, city) resolution ($\tau = -0.90$ and $\rho = 0.65$). This is expected, especially in a city such as NYC, which has around 13,000 taxis: a larger number of trips increases the number of cars, thus slowing down the traffic.

Vehicle Collisions, 311, and Taxi. We identified relationships that involve the Vehicle Collision data set at the (hour, neighborhood) resolution: a strong positive relationship between the number of collisions and the number of 311 complaints ($\tau = 0.99, \rho = 0.86$), and a strong positive relationship between the number of collisions and number of taxi trips ($\tau = 0.99$, $\rho = 0.79$). While the implication of such relationships, especially the latter, is not clear, it provides a starting point for experts, pointing them towards data sets and attributes to be considered for further detailed analysis.

Effectiveness of Statistical Significance Test. Since there is no gold data available, to test the ability of the significance tests to remove potentially uninformative relationships, we evaluated a randomly chosen set of relationships that are not statistically significant. For instance, many relationships between the fare tax for taxi trips and different attributes from the Weather, 311, and 911 data sets were found not to be statistically significant. This indicates that, even though some of these relationship have $|\tau| > 0.60$, they are mostly random and coincidental. In fact, the tax charged in taxi trip fares does not have anything to do with different weather conditions, let alone with 311 and 911 complaints. Other examples of spurious relationships pruned by our framework include: mileage of taxi trips (Taxi) and number of injured pedestrians (Vehicle Collisions), having $\tau = 0.90$; number of bike trips (Citi Bike) and number of tweets (Twitter), having $\tau = 0.87$; and number of 311 complaints and average speed (Traffic Speed), having $\tau = 0.76$.

We also computed the statistical significance for relevant relationships using the standard Monte Carlo procedure. Many of these relationships were found to be not significant using this test, including the ones between the average snow precipitation and the average bike trip duration. This underscores the importance of taking the spatial and temporal dependencies into account while assessing statistical significance.

Note that such tests represent a best-effort approach to identify candidate relationships, and thus, they can both return spurious relationships and miss important ones. Gold data are needed to quantitatively study the trade-offs for the different techniques. Nonetheless, our initial experiments indicate that these significance tests are useful and can help guide users in the data discovery process.

6.4 Comparison against Standard Techniques

We used the *NYC Urban* collection to compare our approach against established techniques for identifying dependencies between data: Pearson correlation coefficient (PCC) [7], mutual information (MI) criterion [33], and dynamic time warping (DTW) routines [21, 31]. Some of these techniques are not naturally normalized for inter-dataset comparisons (e.g., DTW and MI) or directly extendable to spatio-temporal data. Thus, for this experiment, we proposed normalizations that provide a meaningful range of relationship score (see Appendix D for details) and focused on data represented as a time series aggregated over the city resolution.

Overall, we observed that standard approaches can identify the basic relationships that are present across the entire data. For example, the relationship between average snow precipitation and Citi Bike trip duration could be detected by PCC as well as by MI. Similarly, the relationship between number of taxi trips and average traffic speed could be found using PCC and DTW. However, these techniques did not find relationships that are only visible under certain conditions, such as the ones between rainfall and number of taxis, or wind speed and number of taxi trips. Also, relationships that take into account space, such as the ones between number of collisions and number of taxi trips, are not identified by any of the above techniques due to their inherent 1D nature. We would like to note that these approaches are orthogonal to our topology-based technique. Used in conjunction with our framework, we believe it will open new avenues in data discovery.

7. RELATED WORK

In addition to the approaches discussed in Section 6.4, other notions of relationship have also been explored by the data mining and data integration communities. Some methods focused on identifying relationships between data points *within a single* data set. Achtert et al. [1] focused on computing correlation clusters, which are composed of data points that present correlations between different attributes. Yang et al. [37] used subspace clustering, which finds different clusters of points for different subspaces of attributes, to identify relationships. Other methods have been proposed which identify different kinds of relationships. Sarma et al. [9] focused on finding candidate tables that can be unioned and joined, and considered such tables to be related. There has also been work on *data fusion*, where relationships are sought between data sets that overlap or complement each other to resolve conflicts between different sources [10, 29] and to find their derivation history [2]. These relationships are orthogonal to and can be used in conjunction with our technique to enrich the data discovery process. To the best of our knowledge, no existing method addresses the problem of identifying spatio-temporal relationships that take into account salient features in the data.

Recently, there has been a renewed interest in finding explanations for surprising results, or *outliers*, in database queries [30, 36]. Scorpion [36] focused on understanding aggregate queries over a single data set. Roy and Suciu [30] handled more complex database schemas and proposed techniques that can be used to explain relationships between different data sets. However, the thresholds for outliers must be specified by the user for each query, which becomes impractical when handling hundreds to thousands attributes and without proper knowledge about the data sets. Since our *Data Polygamy* framework generates an overview of the relationships among different data sets, the approach proposed by Roy and Suciu [30] could be used to further explore and understand the most eye-catching relationships. Thus, the techniques complement each other in the data exploration process.

Methods for comparing scalar functions use topological abstractions directly for this comparison (e.g., [4, 25]), due to which two functions are considered to be similar even if some affine transformation of the functions are similar, i.e., spatio-temporal locations of the topological features are not considered. Unlike such methods, we are interested in comparing scalar functions based on the spatio-temporal locations of their topological features.

8. DISCUSSION AND FUTURE WORK

Scalar Functions. In this work, we mainly considered data whose spatial domain has dimension up to two. However, our framework is general and can handle higher dimensions as well. For instance, data corresponding to noise in buildings can be obtained in 3D, where in addition to geo-location, the noise level varies with height. By constructing an appropriate graph to represent this spatial domain, the framework can be used as is.

While we have focused on numerical attributes, non-numerical attributes can be taken into account if they are mapped into numerical values (e.g., categorical values can be mapped to unique numbers). In addition, while we chose to use the average to represent functions, it is straightforward to extend our framework to support other functions such as *sum*, *median*, *min*, or *max*. Alternatively, users can define custom functions as well.

Types of Features. Our current feature identification approach can miss unusual patterns in the data due to its use of a single threshold. For example, a sudden increase in taxi trips in a relatively calm area and time will not be identified if the density of taxi trips does not exceed the computed threshold. Instead, we could consider the *gradient* of this density over space and time. High values of this function correspond to regions that have sudden increase/decrease of function value: the increase during a non-busy hour will show as a high-gradient region, and can thus be identified as a feature.

In future work, we plan to do a comprehensive study of the different types of scalar functions that can be derived from urban data sets, and use them to classify the types of features they identify. We will use this classification to create a taxonomy of scalar functions which can then be used by domain experts to appropriately choose the types of features and relationships in which they are interested. We will also investigate the use of a ROC curve which considers multiple thresholds. This would help users pick the operating point of interest depending on the desired sensitivity-specificity trade-off.

Spatio-Temporal Resolution. We currently support conversion from one resolution to another only when they are compatible. We plan to explore methods to support conversion between resolutions that do not have a direct translation (e.g., neighborhood and zip code) in order to help evaluate relationships directly at a higher resolution rather than moving to a lower resolution (the latter may result in loss of information).

Future Extensions. In this paper, we used salient, topological features as the basis for identifying spatio-temporal relationships across disparate data sets. One direction we would like to explore is the use of event detection techniques as an alternative to the topological features. While the topology-based approach identifies local features corresponding to maxima and minima, event detection techniques must first create a model for what constitutes normal behavior to detect events that do not follow this behavior. Even though this can be expensive computationally, especially for spatio-temporal data, it would be interesting to study the performance trade-offs of the two approaches as well as compare the quality of the relationships they derive.

With the help of domain experts, we intend to use the available open data to create a benchmark for evaluating existing and future techniques. While we are able to prune a significant number of relationships, a large number of them might still need to be explored. We plan to design a visual interface to help this exploration process. We also plan to explore techniques to identify relationships that are causal. Finally, we intend to extend the statistical significance test to use a 3-torus to incorporate both space and time together.

Acknowledgments. We thank Divesh Srivastava for his feedback on an early draft of this paper and the anonymous SIGMOD reviewers for their insightful comments and suggestions. This work was supported in part by NSF awards CNS-1229185 and CI-EN-1405927, and by the Moore-Sloan Data Science Environment at NYU. Juliana Freire is partially supported by the DARPA Memex program, and Theodoros Damoulas is partially supported by Alan Turing Institute.

9. REFERENCES

[1] E. Achtert, C. BÅąhm, H.-P. Kriegel, P. KrÅąger, and A. Zimek. Robust, Complete, and Efficient Correlation Clustering. In *SDM*, 2007.

[2] A. Alawini, D. Maier, K. Tufte, and B. Howe. Helping Scientists Reconnect Their Datasets. In *SSDBM*, pages 29:1–29:12, 2014.

[3] L. Barbosa, K. Pham, C. Silva, M. Vieira, and J. Freire. Structured Open Urban Data: Understanding the Landscape. *Big Data*, 2(3), 2014.

[4] U. Bauer, X. Ge, and Y. Wang. Measuring distance between reeb graphs. In *Proc. Symp. Comp. Geom.*, pages 464:464–464:473, 2014.

[5] J. Besag and P. Clifford. Generalized Monte Carlo Significance Tests. *Biometrika*, 76(4):633–642, 1989.

[6] A. Chohlas-Wood, A. Merali, W. Reed, and T. Damoulas. Mining 911 Calls in New York City: Temporal Patterns, Detection and Forecasting. In *AAAI Workshop On AI For Cities*, 2015.

[7] V. A. Clark, O. J. Dunn, and R. M. Mickey. *Applied Statistics: Analysis of Variance and Regression*. John Wiley, 2004.

[8] D. Cohen-Steiner, H. Edelsbrunner, and J. Harer. Stability of persistence diagrams. *Disc. Comput. Geom.*, 37(1):103–120, 2007.

[9] A. Das Sarma, L. Fang, N. Gupta, A. Halevy, H. Lee, F. Wu, R. Xin, and C. Yu. Finding Related Tables. In *SIGMOD*, pages 817–828, 2012.

[10] X. L. Dong, B. Saha, and D. Srivastava. Less is More: Selecting Sources Wisely for Integration. *PVLDB*, 6(2):37–48, 2012.

[11] H. Doraiswamy, V. Natarajan, and R. S. Nanjundiah. An Exploration Framework to Identify and Track Movement of Cloud Systems. *TVCG*, 19(12):2896–2905, 2013.

[12] H. Edelsbrunner. *Geometry and Topology for Mesh Generation*. Cambridge Univ. Press, England, 2001.

[13] H. Edelsbrunner and J. Harer. *Computational Topology: An Introduction*. Amer. Math. Soc., 2009.

[14] H. Edelsbrunner, D. Letscher, and A. Zomorodian. Topological Persistence and Simplification. *Disc. Comput. Geom.*, 28(4):511–533, 2002.

[15] M. D. Ernst et al. Permutation Methods: A Basis for Exact Inference. *Statistical Science*, 19(4):676–685, 2004.

[16] H. S. Farber. Why You Can' t Find a Taxi in the Rain and Other Labor Supply Lessons from Cab Drivers. Technical Report 20604, National Bureau of Economic Research, 2014.

[17] N. Ferreira, J. Poco, H. T. Vo, J. Freire, and C. T. Silva. Visual Exploration of Big Spatio-Temporal Urban Data: A Study of New York City Taxi Trips. *TVCG*, 19(12):2149–2158, 2013.

[18] M.-J. Fortin and G. M. Jacquez. Randomization Tests and Spatially Auto-Correlated Data. *Bulletin of the Ecological Society of America*, pages 201–205, 2000.

[19] B. Goldstein and L. Dyson. *Beyond Transparency: Open Data and the Future of Civic Innovation*. Code for America Press, 2013.

[20] B. Katz and J. Bradley. *The Metropolitan Revolution: How Cities and Metros Are Fixing Our Broken Politics and Fragile Economy*. Brookings Focus Book. 2013.

[21] E. Keogh and A. Ratanamahatana. Everything You Know About Dynamic Time Warping is Wrong. *Workshop on Mining Temporal and Sequential Data*, 2004.

[22] H. R. Kunsch. The jackknife and the bootstrap for general stationary observations. *The Annals of Statistics*, pages 1217–1241, 1989.

[23] B. F. Manly. *Randomization, Bootstrap and Monte Carlo Methods in Biology*. 1996.

[24] J. Milnor. *Morse Theory*. Princeton Univ. Press, 1963.

[25] V. Narayanan, D. M. Thomas, and V. Natarajan. Distance between extremum graphs. In *IEEE PacificVis*, pages 263–270, 2015.

[26] City of Chicago Data Portal. https://data.cityofchicago.org.

[27] NYC Open Data. https://nycopendata.socrata.com.

[28] V. Pascucci and et. al, editors. *Topological Methods in Data Analysis and Visualization*. Springer, 2010.

[29] R. Pochampally, A. Das Sarma, X. L. Dong, A. Meliou, and D. Srivastava. Fusing Data with Correlations. In *SIGMOD*, pages 433–444, 2014.

[30] S. Roy and D. Suciu. A Formal Approach to Finding Explanations for Database Queries. In *SIGMOD*, pages 1579–1590, 2014.

[31] H. Sakoe and S. Chiba. Dynamic programming algorithm optimization for spoken word recognition. *IEEE Transactions on Acoustics, Speech and Signal Processing*, 26(1):43–49, 1978.

[32] N. Shadbolt, K. O'Hara, T. Berners-Lee, N. Gibbins, H. Glaser, H. Wendy, and M. Schraefel. Linked Open Government Data:

Lessons from Data.gov.uk. *IEEE Intelligent Systems*, 27(3):16–24, 2012.
[33] Y. Su, G. Agrawal, J. Woodring, A. Biswas, and H.-W. Shen. Supporting Correlation Analysis on Scientific Datasets in Parallel and Distributed Settings. In *HPDC*, pages 191–202, 2014.
[34] TLC Trip Record Data. http://www.nyc.gov/html/tlc/html/about/trip_record_data.shtml, 2015.
[35] Weather Data. https://www.ncei.noaa.gov/, 2015.
[36] E. Wu and S. Madden. Scorpion: Explaining Away Outliers in Aggregate Queries. *PVLDB*, 6(8):553–564, 2013.
[37] J. Yang, W. Wang, H. Wang, and P. S. Yu. delta-Clusters: Capturing Subspace Correlation in a Large Data Set. In *ICDE*, pages 517–528, 2002.
[38] E. Zhang, K. Mischaikow, and G. Turk. Feature-based Surface Parameterization and Texture Mapping. *ACM TOG*, 24(1):1–27, 2005.

APPENDIX

A. TABLE OF SYMBOLS

Symbol	Description
$\mathbb{D}$	Data set
A, B	Data set attribute
f, g	Time-varying scalar function
$\mathbb{S}$	Spatial domain
$\mathbb{T}$	Temporal domain
θ	Feature threshold
θ^+	Threshold for positive features
θ^-	Threshold for negative features
Σ_i	Set of features of a scalar function
Σ	Set of feature-related points
Σ_i^+	Set of positive features of a scalar function
Σ_i^-	Set of negative features of a scalar function
G	Graph representing the spatio-temporal domain of a scalar function
τ	Relationship score
ρ	Relationship strength

B. ADDITIONAL NOTES ON TOPOLOGY

B.1 Critical Points and Morse Functions

Given a smooth, real-valued function $f : \mathbb{R}^d \rightarrow \mathbb{R}$, a critical point c_p of f is *non-degenerate* if the determinant of the *Hessian* matrix at c_p is non-singular. The function f is called a *Morse function* if it satisfies the following conditions [5]:

1. All critical points of f are non-degenerate.
2. All critical values are distinct *i.e.*, $f(p) \neq f(q)$ for all critical points $p \neq q$.

An important property of Morse functions is that critical points of such a function can be classified based on the behavior of the function within a local neighborhood [11]. In case of a PL function defined on a graph, the local neighborhood of a vertex v is defined using the *link* of that vertex.

Definition 15. The *link* of a vertex v is the sub-graph induced by the vertices adjacent on v. The *upper link* of v is the sub-graph induced by adjacent vertices having function value greater than v, while the *lower link* of v is the sub-graph induced by adjacent vertices having function value lower than v.

Banchoff [1] and Edelsbrunner et al. [9] describe a combinatorial characterization for critical points of a PL function, which are always located at vertices of the graph. Critical points are characterized by the number of connected components of the lower and upper links. The vertex is *regular* if it has exactly one lower link component and one upper link component. All other vertices are *critical*. A critical point is a *maximum* if the upper link is empty and a *minimum* if the lower link is empty. It is a *simple saddle* if it has one upper link and two lower link components, or two upper link and one lower link components. All other critical points are degenerate.

Both the conditions for a Morse function typically do not hold in practice for PL functions. In case of a degenerate critical point, it can be split into multiple simple saddles as shown by Edelsbrunner et al. [9] and Carr et al. [2]. A simulated perturbation of the function [8] ensures that no two critical values are equal. This perturbation is accomplished by adding an infinitesimally small value to the vertices such that it imposes a total order on the vertices of the graph domain. This helps in consistently identifying the vertex with the higher function value between a pair of vertices, thus ensuring that condition 2 holds. Note that in the latter case, when considering a flat local minimum (or maximum), one point in that region is identified as critical. This does not affect the identified features, since the thresholds are computed based on the persistence of the critical points, which does not change because of the location [4].

B.2 Merge Tree Computation

For completeness, we now briefly describe the algorithm to compute merge trees of a PL function. For a more detailed description, we refer the reader to the work by Carr et al. [2]. The algorithm uses the local neighborhood of a vertex in G to classify whether the vertex is a critical point or not. The merge tree is built based on this classification.

The join tree is computed by first sorting the vertices of G in decreasing order of function value. Next, for each vertex v in this sorted list, the algorithm performs the following operations:

- If v is a maximum, create a new component containing v and set v as its *head*. A vertex is a maximum if its upper link is empty [1]. This is a direct extension of Definition 4 to PL functions.
- If the vertices in the upper link belong to one component, then the vertex is not critical. Add v to this component.
- v is a critical point and not a maximum. Given a Morse function, the upper link in this case consists of 2 components [2, 9]. Add an edge between v and the head of each of the 2 components. Next, merge these components and set v as the head of the merged component.

Similarly, the split tree is computed by traversing the vertices of G in increasing order of function values and looking at the lower link of the vertices. The main operations performed in the algorithm are: (i) creating components; (ii) looking up components; and (iii) merging components. This can be efficiently accomplished using the union-find data structure [6].

Time Complexity. Let $N = |V|$ be the number of vertices in G. When computing the join / split trees, the vertices are first sorted, which takes $O(N \log N)$ time. Then, for each vertex v, a *create component* or *merge component* operation is called once, resulting in a total of N such operations. A component look up of a vertex v is executed whenever a vertex in its upper link is processed. So, the total number of look up operations is equal to $|E|/2$ (total degree over all vertices). The spatial domains considered in this work correspond to cities, which are planar. Thus, $|E| = O(N)$.

Therefore, there is a total of $O(N)$ union-find operations requiring $O(N\alpha(N))$ time, where $\alpha()$ is the inverse Ackermann function. Combining all these steps, the join and split trees can be computed in $O(N\log N + N\alpha(N))$ time.

C. IMPLEMENTATION

The number of scalar functions to be computed is proportional to the product of the total number of attributes in the data collection and the different resolutions. For the urban data sets we assessed (Section 6), thousands of scalar functions were computed, and the number of relationships evaluated during querying was in the order of millions. However, both the indexing and querying operations can be run independently for each scalar function and scalar function pair, respectively. To leverage the *embarrassingly parallel* nature of these computations, we implemented the framework using *map-reduce*. We use three *map-reduce* jobs:

- *Scalar Function Computation Job.* The map phase of the scalar function computation job maps each data point (or tuple) into the appropriate spatio-temporal points based on the resolution. The reduce phase aggregates data from each spatio-temporal point and generates all the scalar function values for that point.
- *Feature Identification Job.* The map phase splits the different scalar functions based on the spatio-temporal resolution, while the reduce phase creates the merge tree index and identifies the features for a single function. Recall that each spatio-temporal resolution of a (data set, attribute) pair is represented by one function.
- *Relationship Computation Job.* The map phase generates the different possible combinations between data sets based on the input query (including different resolutions and feature types). The reduce phase then evaluates each pair of functions based on the pre-computed set of features. To evaluate a relationship, we need to compute the intersection of feature sets. This is accomplished by representing each set of features as a bit vector, which not only reduces the memory size, but also allows us to use efficient bit operations to compute this intersection.

We use Hadoop for the *map-reduce* implementation and HDFS as the distributed file system, where the input data sets, intermediate data, and output are stored. We use compression (BZip2 or Snappy codecs) for both map and reduce outputs, and this led to significant speed ups, in particular for large data sets, as fewer bytes need to be read and written. We also use caching to speed-up future queries: when a query is issued, the framework first checks if it can be answered using the cache before invoking the *map-reduce* job. In case CLAUSE provides a threshold with respect to a data set, then features must first be identified before evaluating the relationship.

D. STANDARD APPROACHES

In Section 6.4, we compared our approach against three well-known techniques for identifying correlations: Pearson correlation coefficient (PCC) [3], mutual information (MI) [14], and dynamic time warping (DTW) [10, 12]. In what follows, we describe these approaches in detail.

Pearson's Correlation Coefficient (PCC). The Pearson's Correlation Coefficient measures the linear correlation between two variables [3]. Let X and Y be discrete random variables. The PCC score β_{PCC} can be computed as:

$$\beta_{PCC}(X,Y) = \rho_{X,Y} = \frac{\text{cov}(X,Y)}{\sigma_X \sigma_Y}$$

where *cov* is the covariance and σ is the standard deviation. The PCC score is a value between -1 and +1, where -1 indicates total negative correlation, +1 indicates total positive correlation, and 0 indicates no linear correlation.

Mutual Information (MI). In information theory, mutual information quantifies the amount of information obtained about one random variable through another random variable. Formally, the MI between two discrete random variables X and Y is given as:

$$I(X,Y) = \sum_{i\in X}\sum_{j\in Y} P(i,j)\log\frac{P(i,j)}{P(i)P(y)}$$

where $P(i,j)$ is the joint probability distribution function of X and Y, and $P(i)$ and $P(j)$ are marginal distribution functions of X and Y, respectively. Since we wanted to compare different pairs of variables, we used a normalized variant of MI (β_{MI}):

$$\beta_{MI}(X,Y) = \frac{I(X,Y)}{\sqrt{H(X)H(Y)}}$$

where $H(X)$ and $H(Y)$ are the Shannon entropies of X and Y, respectively. The MI score ranges from 0 to 1: while 0 indicates that the variables are independent, 1 specifies that variables are completely dependent.

Dynamic Time Warping (DTW). Dynamic Time Warping is a dynamic programming approach [12, 13] that is used to construct a *minimum edit-distance* between two temporal sequences. Traditionally, DTW has been used to compare different pairs of time series and perform clustering. However, since DTW distances are not naturally normalized, they cannot be directly compared across multiple time series. Therefore, we propose and employ the following normalized DTW score β_{DTW}:

$$\beta_{DTW}(X,Y) = 1 - \frac{\text{DTW}(X,Y)}{\text{DTW}(X,0)+\text{DTW}(0,Y)}$$

where 0 represents a constant line at $y = 0$, and variables X and Y are Z-normalized. This score ranges from 0 (dissimilar/uncorrelated) to 1 (identical/correlated) and allowed us to compare across DTW scores and time series distances.

E. ADDITIONAL EXPERIMENTS

E.1 Robustness Evaluation

In addition to the taxi density function, we also tested the robustness of our technique for other scalar functions of the Taxi data set, including the unique function (Figure I), the average miles function (Figure II), and the average fare function (Figure III). Similar to the result reported in Section 6.2 for the density function, we find that our technique is robust with other functions as well.

E.2 Interesting Relationships

In this section, we discuss some additional interesting and potentially informative relationships that were identified for the *NYC Urban* collection.

Weather and Taxi. A relationship between the unique number of taxi medallions and the average precipitation could also be identified in the (day, city) resolution with a higher score than in the (hour, city) resolution: $\tau = -0.81$. We also found out that the unique number of taxi medallions is positively related to the average visibility in the (day, city) resolution ($\tau = 0.7, \rho = 0.45$), and negatively related to the average snow depth in the (week, city) resolution ($\tau = -0.95, \rho = 0.95$): this might indicate that some taxi drivers avoid working when the weather conditions are not appropriate (e.g., low visibility or high snow accumulation in streets). There was also a negative relationship between the number of taxi

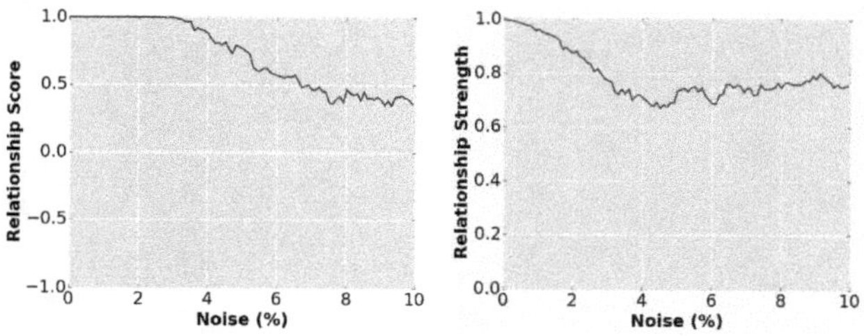

(a) Score (b) Strength

Figure I: Robustness evaluation (unique number of taxis).

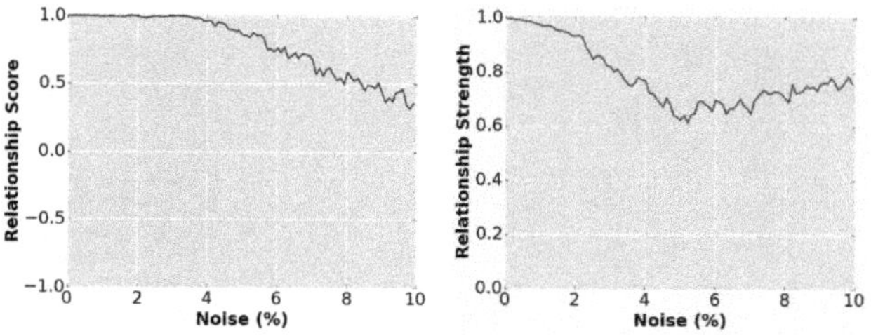

(a) Score (b) Strength

Figure II: Robustness evaluation (average of traveled miles).

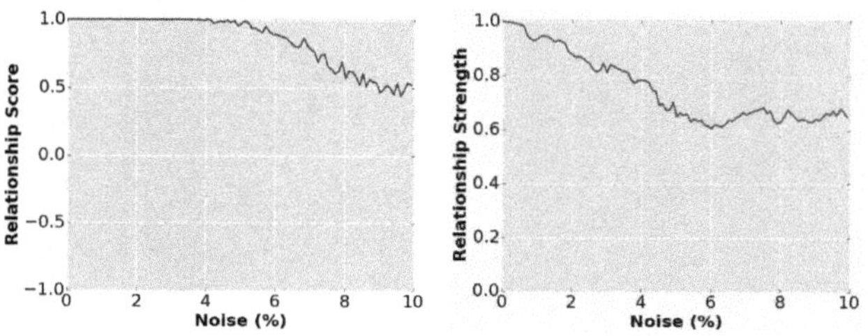

(a) Score (b) Strength

Figure III: Robustness evaluation (average of total taxi fare).

trips and the average snow precipitation in the (week, city) resolution ($\tau = -0.87, \rho = 0.82$) and in the (month, city) resolution ($\tau = -1.0, \rho = 0.07$).

Weather and Citi Bike. We identified negative relationships that involve the unique number of Citi Bikes with the average snow precipitation ($\tau = -1.0, \rho = 0.19$), the average snow depth ($\tau = -0.62, \rho = 0.45$), and rainfall ($\tau = -0.62, \rho = 0.44$), all in the (day, city) resolution. This indicates that less Citi Bikes are used when weather conditions are unpleasant.

Weather and Traffic Speed. For the Weather and Traffic Speed data sets, we found a positive relationship between the average visibility and the average traffic speed in the (week, city) resolution ($\tau = 0.75, \rho = 0.24$) and in the (month, city) resolution ($\tau = 1.0, \rho = 0.14$). Such relationships are expected: when the visibility in the streets is low (e.g., due to a foggy weather), cars tend to drive slower to avoid accidents.

Taxi and Traffic Speed. Recall that we discovered a negative relationship between the number of taxi trips and the average traffic speed in the (hour, city) resolution. This relationship was also identified in other resolutions, including (day, neighborhood) ($\tau = -0.99, \rho = 0.08$); (day, city) ($\tau = -0.84, \rho = 0.4$); and (week, city) ($\tau = -1.0, \rho = 0.16$). Additionally, there was also a negative relationship between the average taxi trip duration and the average traffic speed in the (day, city) resolution, having $\tau = -0.93$ and $\rho = 0.51$.

Taxi and Gas Prices. We found a positive relationship between the average fare and the average gas price in the (month, city) resolution, with $\tau = 1.0$ and $\rho = 0.5$: in fact, the per-mile metered taxi rate may increase when gas prices also increase [7]. We find this at a monthly resolution because it is difficult to detect the affect of gas prices at a lower resolution. Note that the Gas Prices data is available at a weekly resolution. We also found a negative relationship between the unique number of taxis and the average gas price in (week, city) resolution ($\tau = -1.0, \rho = 0.008$) and (month, city) resolution ($\tau = -1.0, \rho = 0.5$). However, the implication of this relationship is not clear.

311 and 911. There were some curious relationships between the number of 311 complaints and the number of 911 calls, in both (day, neighborhood) resolution ($\tau = 0.92, \rho = 0.27$) and (week, neighborhood) resolution ($\tau = 1.0, \rho = 0.65$). Experts can perform further analysis to better understand these relationships and find out if emergency and non-emergency calls are indeed related.

Vehicle Collisions. We identified some interesting relationships between Vehicle Collisions and other data sets. In the (day, city) resolution, there was a positive relationship between the average number of motorists injured in a vehicle crash and the average traffic speed ($\tau = 0.64, \rho = 0.46$), which might indicate that high speeds influence the occurrence of collisions that are dangerous for drivers. In the (day, neighborhood) resolution, there were relationships between the number of collisions and the number of 311 complaints ($\tau = 0.84, \rho = 0.41$), and also with the number of 911 calls ($\tau = 0.94, \rho = 0.18$). The former also showed up in the (week, neighborhood) resolution, with $\tau = 0.72$ and $\rho = 0.22$. In this resolution, there was also a positive relationship between the number of collisions and the number of taxi trips ($\tau = 0.99, \rho = 0.25$). Again, although these relationships may not have apparent implications, experts can use this information to perform further analysis and identify the reason behind them.

F. REFERENCES

[1] T. F. Banchoff. Critical Points and Curvature for Embedded Polyhedral Surfaces. *Am. Math. Monthly*, 77:475–485, 1970.

[2] H. Carr, J. Snoeyink, and U. Axen. Computing Contour Trees in All Dimensions. *Comput. Geom. Theory Appl.*, 24(2):75–94, 2003.

[3] V. A. Clark, O. J. Dunn, and R. M. Mickey. *Applied Statistics: Analysis of Variance and Regression*. John Wiley, 2004.

[4] D. Cohen-Steiner, H. Edelsbrunner, and J. Harer. Stability of persistence diagrams. *Disc. Comput. Geom.*, 37(1):103–120, 2007.

[5] K. Cole-McLaughlin, H. Edelsbrunner, J. Harer, V. Natarajan, and V. Pascucci. Loops in Reeb graphs of 2-manifolds. *Disc. Comput. Geom.*, 32(2):231–244, 2004.

[6] T. H. Cormen, C. E. Leiserson, and R. L. Rivest. *Introduction to Algorithms*. MIT Press, 2001.

[7] P. Donohue. Taxi Drivers Petition NYC for Fare Hike over Soaring Gas Prices. *NY Daily News*, April 2011.

[8] H. Edelsbrunner. *Geometry and Topology for Mesh Generation*. Cambridge Univ. Press, England, 2001.

[9] H. Edelsbrunner, J. Harer, V. Natarajan, and V. Pascucci. Morse-Smale Complexes for Piecewise Linear 3-Manifolds. In *Symp. Comput. Geom.*, pages 361–370, 2003.

[10] E. Keogh and A. Ratanamahatana. Everything You Know About Dynamic Time Warping is Wrong. *Workshop on Mining Temporal and Sequential Data*, 2004.

[11] J. Milnor. *Morse Theory*. Princeton Univ. Press, 1963.

[12] H. Sakoe and S. Chiba. Dynamic programming algorithm optimization for spoken word recognition. *IEEE Transactions on Acoustics, Speech and Signal Processing*, 26(1):43–49, 1978.

[13] S. Salvador and P. Chan. Toward Accurate Dynamic Time Warping in Linear Time and Space. *Intell. Data Anal.*, 11(5):561–580, 2007.

[14] Y. Su, G. Agrawal, J. Woodring, A. Biswas, and H.-W. Shen. Supporting Correlation Analysis on Scientific Datasets in Parallel and Distributed Settings. In *HPDC*, pages 191–202, 2014.

Distributed Evaluation of Top-k Temporal Joins

Julien Pilourdault, Vincent Leroy, Sihem Amer-Yahia
Université Grenoble Alpes - LIG, CNRS
Grenoble, France
Firstname.Lastname@imag.fr

ABSTRACT

We study a particular kind of join, coined Ranked Temporal Join (RTJ), featuring predicates that compare time intervals and a scoring function associated with each predicate to quantify how well it is satisfied. RTJ queries are prevalent in a variety of applications such as network traffic monitoring, task scheduling, and tweet analysis. RTJ queries are often best interpreted as top-k queries where only the best matches are returned. We show how to exploit the nature of temporal predicates and the properties of their associated scoring semantics to design *TKIJ*, an efficient query evaluation approach on a distributed Map-Reduce architecture. *TKIJ* relies on an offline statistics computation that, given a time partitioning into granules, computes the distribution of intervals' endpoints in each granule, and an online computation that generates query-dependent score bounds. Those statistics are used for workload assignment to reducers. This aims at reducing data replication, to limit I/O cost. Additionally, high-scoring results are distributed evenly to enable each reducer to prune unnecessary results. Our extensive experiments on synthetic and real datasets show that *TKIJ* outperforms state-of-the-art competitors and provides very good performance for n-ary RTJ queries on temporal data.

Keywords

Temporal data; Top-k; Join; Distributed processing

CCS Concepts

•**Information systems** → **Join algorithms;** *Query operators;*

1. INTRODUCTION

Temporal data is pervasive. Store receipts, tweets, traffic data, and temperature measures generated by weather sensors or by wearables, are just some examples. Such data is best represented as intervals with start and end timestamps. For instance, in a data center, large amounts of traffic requests in the form of [*IP_address,start timestamp,end timestamp,...*], are continuously generated by sensors. A system administrator who wishes to monitor traffic emanating from different countries, would formulate a query that returns pairs of requests (x, y) where x ends *before* y starts and x and y originate from different countries. In tweet analysis where intervals represent the lifespan of a hashtag, the query x *meets* y would find pairs of discussion topics where one started when the other ended.

Chronological relations between intervals are typically expressed using the Allen interval algebra [2], which defines a set of Boolean predicates such as *before, meets, starts* and *overlaps*. In this work, we argue that the ability to evaluate interval predicates *approximately* and assign scores to resulting interval pairs, appears as a natural requirement to finding interesting results. Indeed, in monitoring traffic causality, an (x, y) pair where x ends *just before* y, may be preferred to those where x ends *much earlier than* the start of y. Similarly, in tweet analysis, a Boolean interpretation of x *meets* y is likely to return an empty result and will not detect discussion topics that started *roughly* after another ended.

In this paper, we formalize n-ary Ranked Temporal Join (RTJ) queries that feature any number of temporal predicates and return the k best results. To the best of our knowledge, this is the first work that formalizes n-ary RTJ queries and devises a general-purpose distributed evaluation approach. RTJ queries raise a number of new challenges. First, an appropriate ranked semantics needs to be devised for a variety of temporal predicates in order to capture the strength of relationship between intervals as a function of the desired semantics for each predicate. Most related studies focus on a common query that involves the *intersects* predicate [7, 13, 21]. The idea is to retrieve tuples that share a common period of validity, in order to combine events whose time range has a non-empty intersection. Our semantics is richer since we are interested in any temporal predicate between intervals. For instance, we aim to capture predicates from the Allen algebra (see the three first columns of Figure 2). We illustrate that in the following example.

Network Traffic Monitoring. Consider the two interval collections C_1 and C_2 in Figure 1. Assume that each collection gathers requests from a different country. An analyst interested in monitoring traffic between two countries would seek (x, y) interval pairs, $x \in C_1$, $y \in C_2$, that form a sequence, i.e., where y starts as x ends. The best sequences are those satisfying *meets*(x, y) reflecting strict equality between the end of x and the beginning of y. In our example, only

SIGMOD'16, June 26-July 01, 2016, San Francisco, CA, USA

ISBN 978-1-4503-3531-7/16/06...$15.00

DOI: http://dx.doi.org/10.1145/2882903.2882912

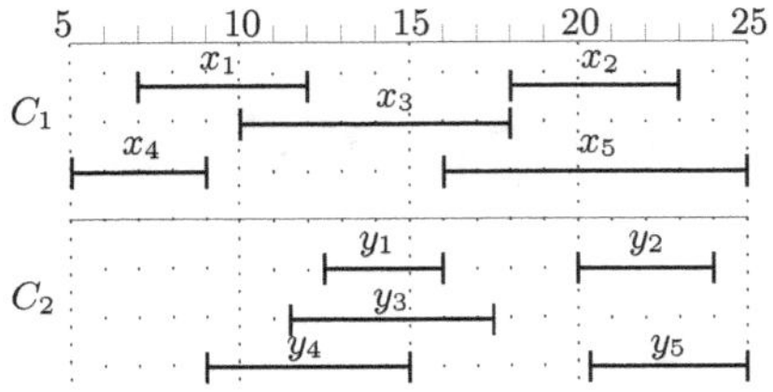

Figure 1: Motivating Example

(x_4, y_4) qualifies for a Boolean interpretation. Yet, given the uncertainty on clocks in different network equipments, a small overlap or a short free period between two consecutive tasks would be more realistic. In order to express that with Boolean semantics, a query must evaluate a disjunction of *before*, *overlaps* and *meets* and would build many useless interval pairs. A ranked semantics on the other hand, would build (x, y) pairs where x *almost meets* y, allowing a tolerance on intervals' endpoints. For instance, tuples (x, y) where x ends at most 2 timestamps before or after y starts, could be considered high-scoring. Using such a semantics, we can return the top-3 $\{(x_4, y_4), (x_1, y_3), (x_1, y_1)\}$.

A key observation we rely on is that an approximate interpretation of a predicate amounts to approximating the strength of relationship between its intervals' endpoints. That is compatible with the flexible scoring approach proposed in [12] to approximate Allen predicates [2]. It is based on associating a degree of satisfaction with equality and inequality of 2 intervals' endpoints. In this paper, we adapt this framework to allow scoring any temporal predicate. We also allow to use any monotone aggregation function to compute the score of a query result for n-ary RTJ queries. Consequently, a 3-way query involving the predicates *starts*(x, y) and *meets*(y, z) would return (x, y, z) tuples and associate to each tuple its degree of satisfaction of the query as an aggregation of individual predicate-dependent scores for each of *starts*(x, y) and *meets*(y, z).

It is important to note that, unlike existing work on returning approximate answers [4], we focus on computing exact answers of queries that make use of scored join predicates. The second challenge we tackle is to devise an efficient query evaluation strategy that guarantees to return the best answers for a variety of temporal predicates. The key difficulty here is to develop a general-purpose algorithm that works with a variety of predicates and ranked semantics and yet, that is able to exploit the nature of those predicates to devise an efficient evaluation.

The efficient processing of interval joins has been studied before [5, 7, 13, 21]. The closest to our work is the recent one by Chawda et al. [5] with a focus on processing queries on Map-Reduce [6]. However, their algorithms focus on a Boolean semantics and are not directly applicable in our case. In our work, scores constitute both a challenge and an opportunity. They are a challenge because, unlike Boolean semantics, every combination of intervals is potentially an answer. The opportunity lies in the ability to leverage statistics on input data in order to avoid computing low-scoring results. In this paper, we propose *TKIJ*, a 3-stage query evaluation approach for RTJ queries on Map-Reduce. A first offline process partitions time into granules and computes the distribution of intervals' endpoints in those granules. A second online process leverages those statistics to compute query-dependent score bounds. A third process assigns to each reducer enough high-scoring results to enable pruning unnecessary answers and hence balance the load between reducers. Each reducer executes the input RTJ query locally on the data it receives. While this query processing bears similarities to traditional *top-k* and *rank-join* processing [14, 15, 16, 20, 22], it differs greatly due to the dependence of score computation on query predicates. As a result, partial predicate-dependent scores cannot be pre-computed and each reducer relies on the score bounds produced in the statistics collection phase to avoid unnecessary computation. A final Map-Reduce job merges results obtained from each reducer.

In summary, this paper makes the following contributions:

1. We formalize n-ary RTJ queries that combine interval collections with any number of arbitrary temporal predicates and return the k best results.

2. We design *TKIJ*, an efficient query evaluation approach on Map-Reduce that leverages scores to avoid computing unnecessary results and to balance the load between reducers.

3. We run extensive experiments on synthetic and real network traffic datasets. Our experiments show the efficiency of our pruning technique and the great benefit of using scores to distribute the load between reducers. Because *TKIJ* executes only combinations that ensure to return the correct top-k answers, it scales to very large collections (up to 5M tuples per collection) and to high k values (up to 10^5).

Section 2 describes our data model and defines the problem of evaluating RTJ queries. *TKIJ* is presented in Section 3. Experiments are detailed in Section 4. We summarize the related work in Section 5 and conclude in Section 6.

2. DATA MODEL AND PROBLEM

We are given m collections of intervals $C_1, \ldots, C_m$. Each interval x has a unique identifier, a start time $\underline{x}$ and an end time $\overline{x}$.

Boolean temporal predicates. The general form of a temporal predicate between two intervals x and y is denoted $p(x, y)$ and is expressed as a Boolean conjunction of equalities and inequalities between their endpoints $\underline{x}, \overline{x}, \underline{y}, \overline{y}$. This allows to capture a wide range of predicates among which the seminal Allen algebra [2]. The first 3 columns of Figure 2 summarize Allen temporal predicates and their semantics. For example, *meets*(x, y) imposes that y starts when x finishes while *starts*(x, y) requires that x and y start at the same time and that x ends before y.

It is important to note that we aim to capture all Allen predicates but also any predicate comparing interval's endpoints. While we do not aim to provide a long list of new predicates, we discuss examples that we are using in our experiments. For example, in network traffic analysis, we introduce *justBefore*(x, y) that is satisfied iff $\underline{y} > \overline{x}$ and $\underline{y} - \overline{x} \leq AVG_z(\overline{z} - \underline{z})$. The intuition is that the elapsed time between x and y is no greater than the average interval length. A special case is the predicate *shiftMeets*(x, y) that is satisfied iff $(\underline{y} - \overline{x}) = AVG_z(\overline{z} - \underline{z})$. In tweet analysis, a possibly useful predicate would be *sparks*(x, y) which

Temporal Predicate	Boolean Interpretation	Valid answers	Scored Intepretation
$before(x, y)$	$\overline{x} < \underline{y}$	x, y	**s-before**$(x, y) = greater(\underline{y}, \overline{x})$
$equals(x, y)$	$\underline{x} = \underline{y} \wedge \overline{x} = \overline{y}$	x, y	**s-equals**$(x, y) = \min\{equals(\underline{x}, \underline{y}), equals(\overline{x}, \overline{y})\}$
$meets(x, y)$	$\overline{x} = \underline{y}$	x, y	**s-meets**$(x, y) = equals(\overline{x}, \underline{y})$
$overlaps(x, y)$	$\underline{x} < \underline{y} \wedge \overline{x} > \underline{y} \wedge \overline{x} < \overline{y}$	x, y	**s-overlaps**$(x, y) = \min\{greater(\underline{y}, \underline{x}), greater(\overline{x}, \underline{y}), greater(\overline{y}, \overline{x})\}$
$contains(x, y)$	$\underline{x} < \underline{y} \wedge \overline{x} > \overline{y}$	x, y	**s-contains**$(x, y) = \min\{greater(\underline{y}, \underline{x}), greater(\overline{x}, \overline{y})\}$
$starts(x, y)$	$\underline{x} = \underline{y} \wedge \overline{x} < \overline{y}$	x, y	**s-starts**$(x, y) = \min\{equals(\underline{x}, \underline{y}), greater(\overline{y}, \overline{x})\}$
$finishedBy(x, y)$	$\underline{x} < \underline{y} \wedge \overline{x} = \overline{y}$	x, y	**s-finishedBy**$(x, y) = \min\{greater(\underline{y}, \underline{x}), equals(\overline{x}, \overline{y})\}$

Figure 2: The Allen Algebra with Boolean and Scored Temporal Predicates.

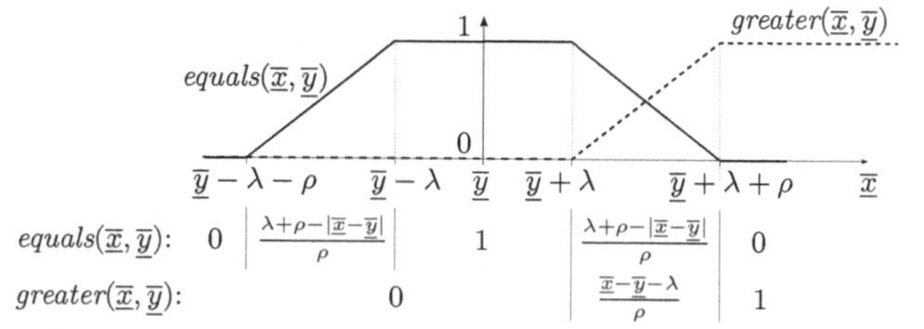

Figure 3: Approximating *equals* and *greater*. Here, $\overline{x} \in \{\underline{x}, \overline{x}\}$, $\overline{y} \in \{\underline{y}, \overline{y}\}$.

Temporal Predicate	Boolean Interpretation	Valid Answers	Scored Intepretation
$justBefore(x, y)$	$\overline{x} < \underline{y} \wedge \underline{y} - \overline{x} \leq avg$	x, avg, y	**s-justBefore**$(x, y) = \min\{equals(\overline{x}, \underline{y}), greater(\underline{y}, \overline{x})\}$ $\lambda_{greater} = \rho_{greater} = 0$, $\lambda_{equals} = avg$, $\rho_{equals} \in \mathbb{R}^+$
$shiftMeets(x, y)$	$\underline{y} = \overline{x} + avg$	x, avg, y	**s-shiftMeets**$(x, y) = equals(\overline{x} + avg, \underline{y})$
$sparks(x, y)$	$\overline{x} < \underline{y} \wedge (\overline{y} - \underline{y}) > 10 * (\overline{x} - \underline{x})$	x, l_x, y, $> 10 * l_x$	**s-sparks**$(x, y) = \min\{greater(\underline{y}, \overline{x}), greater(\overline{y} - \underline{y}, 10 * (\overline{x} - \underline{x}))\}$

Figure 4: Definition of *s-shiftMeets*, *s-justBefore* and *s-sparks*. Here, $avg = AVG_z(\overline{z} - \underline{z})$.

is satisfied iff $(\overline{y} - \underline{y}) > 10 * (\overline{x} - \underline{x})$ and $\underline{y} > \overline{x}$. As a result, the (x, y) pairs satisfying $sparks(x, y)$ would identify hashtag pairs where the preceding hashtag lasted 10 times shorter that the following. That could be useful in determining causality of long-lasting events such as finding all short-lasting hashtags before the long-lasting `#JeSuisCharlie`.

Scored temporal predicates. Since we are interested in capturing the degree at which a temporal predicate is verified by a pair of intervals, we propose to associate a score to each predicate. Here again, we aim to be general and we adopt the flexible approach for scoring Allen predicates [12] and adapt it to our settings. This approach relies on two primitive approximation comparators on intervals' endpoints. Those comparators, $equals(\overline{x}, \overline{y})$ and $greater(\overline{x}, \overline{y})$, are used to express the degree of equality or inequality of intervals' endpoints $\overline{x}$ and $\overline{y}$, where $\overline{x} \in \{\underline{x}, \overline{x}\}$, $\overline{y} \in \{\underline{y}, \overline{y}\}$ as a graded value in $[0, 1]$. They rely on two parameters λ and ρ that provide flexibility in controlling the tolerance degree when comparing intervals' endpoints. Figure 3 shows how $equals(\overline{x}, \overline{y})$ and $greater(\overline{x}, \overline{y})$ are used with λ and ρ to express that tolerance. For instance, by defining that whenever $|\overline{x} - \overline{y}| \leq \lambda$, $equals(\overline{x}, \overline{y})$ returns 1, λ sets a tolerance for exact endpoint equality. ρ, on the other hand, is used to define score values. A large ρ value defines a wide range of score values and a small ρ produces a more abrupt curve and fewer possible score values.

Since temporal predicates are expressed as equalities and inequalities on intervals' endpoints, their approximation can be achieved using a conjunction of *equals*() and *greater*() with appropriate λ and ρ values. This allows us to *associate a scored variant to each temporal predicate.* We denote that variant $s\text{-}p(x, y)$ and refer to it as *scored temporal predicate*, abusing the term "predicate" to mean "function". Indeed, while $p(x, y)$ returns a Boolean value, $s\text{-}p(x, y)$, returns a score in [0,1]. For example, we can define the scored version of $starts(x, y)$ as $s\text{-}starts(x, y) = \min\{equals(\underline{x}, \underline{y}), greater(\overline{y}, \overline{x})\}$.

We also propose to allow different values of λ and ρ for *equals*() and *greater*() for different predicates. That provides a finer control of the score values produced by each predicate. A Boolean interpretation of a predicate becomes a special case of our scored interpretation. For example, strict endpoint equality can be obtained by setting both λ_{equals} and ρ_{equals} to 0. Thus, we can define, $s\text{-}justBefore(x, y)$ with $\lambda_{greater}$ and $\rho_{greater}$ set to 0, ρ_{equals} to any value and λ_{equals} to $AVG_z(\overline{z} - \underline{z})$ (Figure 4).

Temporal join queries. We are interested in expressing n-ary join queries on interval collections $C_1, \ldots, C_m$. We express a query Q as a weakly connected oriented simple graph[1] of the form (V, E). Each each vertex $v_i \in V$ is mapped to a collection C_i. Each edge $(i, j) \in E$ between two vertices v_i and v_j is labeled with a scored temporal predicate $s\text{-}p_{(i,j)}()$ between the two collections C_i and C_j corresponding to v_i and v_j.

The evaluation of an n-ary join query Q returns a set of tuples of the form $(x_1, \ldots, x_n)$ where $x_i \in C_i$. The score of each tuple in the query result is computed using a function $\mathcal{S}$ that aggregates the partial scores assigned by each predicate $s\text{-}p_{(i,j)}()$ associated with each query edge $(i, j) \in E$. $\mathcal{S}$ could be any monotone function such as the weighted sum as it is commonly the case in ranked aggregation [15, 16, 20, 22].

For example, we can express a 3-way query that returns a tuple (x, y, z) where $x \in C_1$, $y \in C_2$ and $z \in C_3$ and the score of (x, y, z) is computed as an aggregation of its partial scores for query predicates $s\text{-}starts(x, y)$ and $s\text{-}meets(y, z)$.

Although we use the term "join" to refer to our queries, their expressivity goes beyond traditional relational joins. Our queries are compositional in the sense of a relational join

[1]no self loops and $(i, j) \in E \implies (j, i) \notin E$

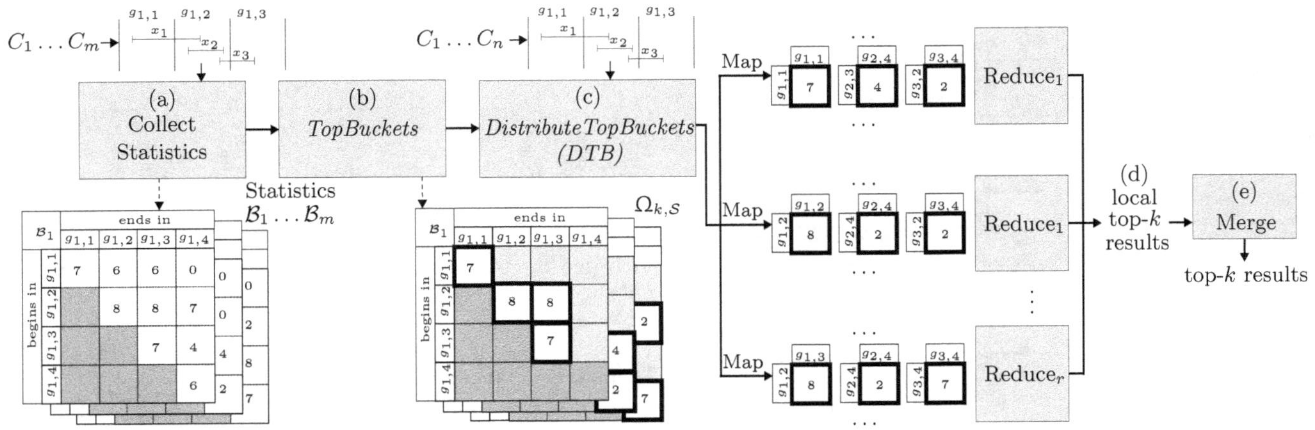

Figure 5: Overview of *TKIJ*

since their results are not intervals but tuples of any length (corresponding to the number of vertices in the query). Our queries can express any combination of interval collections with any scored predicates including chain queries and queries containing cycles.

Ranked Temporal Join (RTJ) problem. Given an n-ary temporal join query $Q = (V, E)$ expressed over a set of collections $C_1, \dots, C_m$ corresponding to query vertices in V and temporal predicates $s\text{-}p_{(i,j)}()$ associated to each edge $(i, j) \in E$, our problem is to find a top-k set of tuples of the form $(x_1, \dots, x_n)$, $x_i \in C_i$, ranked by (descending) order of $\mathcal{S}_{(i,j)\in E}(s\text{-}p_{(i,j)}(x_i, x_j))$.

3. TEMPORAL JOIN PROCESSING

We present *TKIJ*, our approach for evaluating Top-K Interval Joins, that efficiently finds the set of k *best* results for an RTJ query Q. We first provide an overview of *TKIJ*, then we give each step in detail.

3.1 Overview of TKIJ

Figure 5 summarizes *TKIJ*. Given a set of interval collections $C_1 \dots C_m$, *TKIJ* executes a query-independent preprocessing phase to collect statistics on intervals' distribution. This phase partitions time into granules and computes *buckets* for each collection (a). A bucket associated to a collection C_i corresponds to a pair of granules, and contains the number of intervals of C_i starting at one granule and ending at another. Given a query Q, these statistics are used to evaluate *bucket combinations* that should be processed in order to obtain top-k results (b). *TKIJ* relies on a constraint programming solver to compute score bounds for each bucket combination and uses those bounds to prune combinations that do not contain top-k results. The third phase is the actual join processing which relies on two Map-Reduce jobs. The first job assigns a subset of buckets to each reducer r_j (c) which then processes locally the RTJ query, returning local top-k results (d). This assignment aims at reducing data replication to limit I/O, and leverages score bounds to distribute high-scoring results evenly so that each reducer can quickly prune low-ranking results. The second Map-Reduce job merges all local results into a single query output (e).

3.2 Statistics collection

TKIJ pre-processes each dataset once in order to collect statistics which are then used to optimize the execution of any RTJ query on this dataset. These statistics maintain a matrix $\mathcal{B}_i$ representing the distribution of endpoints of intervals in each collection C_i. *TKIJ* partitions the time range of each C_i into a set of contiguous *granules*. We adopt a uniform partitioning which has been shown to be appropriate for temporal joins [5, 7, 18].

As illustrated in Figure 5a, each matrix entry records the cardinality of a bucket, where a bucket $b_{i,l,l'} = (g_{i,l}, g_{i,l'})$ contains all intervals of C_i that start in $g_{i,l}$ and end in $g_{i,l'}$: $\mathcal{B}_i[l][l'] = |b_{i,l,l'}| = |\{x \in C_i, \underline{x} \in g_{i,l} \wedge \overline{x} \in g_{i,l'}\}|$. As an example, given $g_{1,1} = [10, 20]$ and $g_{1,2} = [20, 30]$, the matrix entry for $b_{1,1,2} = (g_{1,1}, g_{1,2})$ indicates 6 intervals starting in $[10, 20]$ and ending in $[20, 30]$.

Range partitioning is a common approach in temporal join processing [5, 7, 18, 21]. The rationale is that intervals having similar endpoints are likely to satisfy similar join predicates. For example, most previous studies, that focus on *intersection* joins, leverage partitions to avoid pairs of intervals that are guaranteed not to intersect. Similarly, *TKIJ* relies on these statistics to obtain information on the distribution of intervals within buckets and prune the search space of *any* RTJ query.

Statistics are computed in a single Map-Reduce phase. Each mapper reads a fraction of the data and maintains a local matrix per collection. Matrices are then aggregated in the reduce phase, and the reducer responsible for collection C_i outputs a final matrix $\mathcal{B}_i$. While we focus in this paper on the case of statistics computed from scratch for a new dataset, we can easily handle updates by applying the same process on the inserted/deleted data.

3.3 Selection of bucket combinations

We now describe how *TKIJ* uses pre-computed statistics to estimate score bounds on candidate results. Then, we present how score bounds are used to avoid computing unnecessary results while we guarantee to return the exact top-k results. We further develop several processing strategies that aim to tackle computational costs raised by this pruning step.

Estimating score bounds

Processing an RTJ query Q requires to return the top-k tuples $(x_1, \ldots, x_n)$, $x_i \in C_i$ according to a scoring function $\mathcal{S}$. Since any tuple $(x_1, \ldots, x_n)$ is a potential answer, we investigate how to reduce the amount of data processed using scores. We use $\omega = (b_{1,l_1,l'_1}, \ldots, b_{n,l_n,l'_n})$ to denote a bucket combination, $\omega.nbRes = \prod_{i=1}^{n} |b_{i,l_i,l'_i}|$ the total number of results that can be obtained from a bucket combination ω, and Ω the set of all combinations. We define score upper and lower bounds in each ω, denoted $\omega.UB$ and $\omega.LB$.

Definition 1. The score upper-bound (resp. lower-bound) $\omega.UB$ (resp. $\omega.LB$) of a bucket combination $\omega = (b_{1,l_1,l'_1}, \ldots, b_{n,l_n,l'_n})$ is the upper-bound (resp. lower-bound) of $\mathcal{S}_{(i,j)\in E}(s\text{-}p_{(i,j)}(x_i, x_j))$ where $\underline{x_i} \in g_{i,l_i}, \overline{x_i} \in g_{i,l'_i}, \forall i \in 1 \ldots n$.

As an example, suppose that query Q features a predicate $s\text{-}meets_{(1,2)}(x, y)$ where $x \in C_1$ and $y \in C_2$, using scoring parameters $(\lambda_{equals}, \rho_{equals}) = (4, 8)$. Collected statistics show 6 intervals in bucket $b_{1,1,2} = ([10, 20], [20, 30])$ for C_1 and 7 intervals in bucket $b_{2,2,3} = ([20, 30], [30, 40])$ for C_2. We build the bucket combination $\omega = (b_{1,1,2}, b_{2,2,3})$. Then, we can derive bounds on the score $\mathcal{S}(x, y) = s\text{-}meets(x, y)$ of a result $(x, y) \in \omega$. The maximum possible score is 1 (e.g. with $(x, y) = ([12, 25], [25, 35])$), and the minimum score is 0.25 (with $(x, y) = ([15, 20], [30, 35])$). Hence, $\omega.UB = 1, \omega.LB = 0.25$. Thus, 42 results in ω have a score in $[0.25, 1]$.

TKIJ relies on a constraint programming solver as a generic approach to compute score bounds for any combination of predicates. Computing score bounds for a bucket combination requires to solve the following problem:

Bounds Problem. *Let* $\omega = (b_{1,l_1,l'_1}, \ldots, b_{n,l_n,l'_n})$. *Find* $(x_1, \ldots, x_n)$ *s.t.:*

$$\begin{aligned} \textit{max (resp. min)} \quad & \mathcal{S}_{(i,j)\in E}(s\text{-}p_{(i,j)}(x_i, x_j)) \\ \textit{s.t.} \quad & \underline{x_i} \in g_{i,l_i} \ \forall i \in 1 \ldots n \qquad (1) \\ & \overline{x_i} \in g_{i,l'_i} \ \forall i \in 1 \ldots n \qquad (2) \end{aligned}$$

Each $x_i \in C_i$ is mapped to a decision variable $\mathtt{x}_i$. For each partial score $s\text{-}p_{(i,j)}(x_i, x_j)$, we create an intermediate variable $\mathtt{s\text{-}p_{ij}}$. For all $(i, j) \in E$, we impose that the variables $\mathtt{x}_i, \mathtt{x}_j$ and $\mathtt{s\text{-}p_{ij}}$ satisfy the constraints $\{\mathtt{C}_{ij} : \mathtt{s\text{-}p_{ij}} = s\text{-}p_{(i,j)}(\mathtt{x}_i, \mathtt{x}_j)\}$. Then, we create a variable $\mathtt{score}$ and impose $\mathtt{C}_s : \mathtt{score} = \mathcal{S}_{(i,j)\in E}(\mathtt{s\text{-}p_{ij}})$. The solver then maximizes (and minimizes in the case of a lower-bound) $\mathtt{score}$ such that constraint $\mathtt{C}_s$, all constraints $\mathtt{C}_i$ and all constraints on decision variables (1)(2) are satisfied. While we virtually allow any temporal predicates, in practice, predicate implementation depends on the range of constraints supported by the server used in the implementation.

Pruning bucket combinations

TKIJ leverages computed score bounds to reduce computation cost by eliminating results that are guaranteed not to be in the top-k. To do so, it computes $\Omega_{k,\mathcal{S}} \subseteq \Omega$, a subset of the search space that is sufficient to guarantee correctness. We define $\Omega_{k,\mathcal{S}}$ as follows:

Definition 2. The set of Top Buckets $\Omega_{k,\mathcal{S}}$ is a subset of Ω satisfying the following conditions:

- $\forall \omega \in \Omega \setminus \Omega_{k,\mathcal{S}} \ \exists \Psi \subseteq \Omega_{k,\mathcal{S}}$:
  - $\forall \omega' \in \Psi \ \omega'.LB \geq \omega.UB$
  - $\sum_{\omega' \in \Psi} \omega'.nbRes \geq k$

Algorithm 1 *getTopBuckets*

Input: k, Ω list of bucket combinations with UB and LB
Output: $\Omega_{k,\mathcal{S}}$

```
 1: Sort Ω by descending LB
 2: collectedResults = 0
 3: for ω ∈ Ω
 4:     collectedResults += ω.nbRes
 5:     kthResLB = ω.LB
 6:     if collectedResults ≥ k then break
 7: Sort Ω by descending UB
 8: Ω_{k,S} ← ∅, collectedResults = 0
 9: for ω ∈ Ω
10:     if collectedResults ≥ k and ω.UB ≤ kthResLB
11:         break
12:     Ω_{k,S} ← Ω_{k,S} ∪ ω
13:     collectedResults += ω.nbRes
    return Ω_{k,S}
```

This definition ensures that whenever a bucket combination ω is pruned, there are at least k results from $\Omega_{k,\mathcal{S}}$ with a score higher than results generated from ω. Note that $\Omega_{k,\mathcal{S}}$ is not unique: given a valid set of bucket combinations, any super-set is also valid. To compute $\Omega_{k,\mathcal{S}}$, we design the *getTopBuckets* algorithm (Algorithm 1). Algorithm *getTopBuckets* uses as input a set of bucket combinations whose score bounds are pre-computed. It first computes a lower bound *kthResLB* on the score of the kth result (Lines 1-6). Then, it keeps only bucket combinations whose score upper-bound is greater than *kthResLB* (Lines 7-13). The process safely stops in Line 11 since no bucket combination outside the collected set has results with score above *kthResLB*.

Pruning unnecessary results is a two-step process, coined *TopBuckets*. A first step computes score bounds for bucket combinations using a solver. Then, a second step executes *getTopBuckets* that uses those bounds to eliminate unnecessary results. In our setting, all $(x_1, \ldots, x_n)$ combinations are potential answers, and we cannot employ traditional top-k techniques to prune the search space. *TopBuckets* addresses this challenge using pre-computed statistics to locate high-scoring answers. Still, a new challenge is to limit the overhead of *TopBuckets* due to computing score bounds for bucket combinations. In the following section, we discuss this challenge and possible solutions.

TopBuckets Strategies

A first straightforward approach to find $\Omega_{k,\mathcal{S}}$ is to build all possible bucket combinations Ω, compute their score bounds using a solver and then use *getTopBuckets* to prune useless ones. In this strategy, coined BRUTE-FORCE, a large number of n-tuples of buckets are assigned a score by the solver (with g granules per collection, $|\Omega|$ is $\mathcal{O}(g^{2n})$). Moreover, for each combination, $2n$ decision variables need to be assigned by the solver. Thus, as n or g increase, BRUTE-FORCE becomes inefficient.
To tackle that, we propose the LOOSE strategy (Algorithm 2 with the flag onePhase set true.) LOOSE first builds all bucket pairs $(b_{i,l_i,l'_i}, b_{j,l_j,l'_j})$ for each scored predicate $(i, j) \in E$ (Line 1). Score bounds are then computed by the solver (Line 3) for each pair. Then, LOOSE builds n-tuples of buckets (Lines 4-5). For each $\omega = (b_{1,l_1,l'_1}, \ldots, b_{n,l_n,l'_n})$, we obtain score bounds using bounds computed for each pair $(b_{i,l_i,l'_i}, b_{j,l_j,l'_j})$.

Algorithm 2 Strategies LOOSE, TWO-PHASE

Input: Boolean onePhase, Buckets $\{b_{i,l_i,l'_i} : i \in 1 \dots n\}$
Output: $\Omega_{k,\mathcal{S}}$
1: $L_2 \leftarrow$ all bucket pairs (b_i, b_j) s.t. $(i,j) \in E$
2: **for all** ω in L_2
3: Compute $\omega.UB$, $\omega.LB$ using solver
4: **for** ω in Ω
5: Compute $\omega.UB$, $\omega.LB$ using score bounds from $(b_i, b_j) \in L_2$
6: $L_m \leftarrow$TopBuckets(Ω)
7: **if** onePhase **then return** L_m
8: **for** $\omega \in L_m$
9: Compute $\omega.UB$, $\omega.LB$ using solver
return TopBuckets(L_m)

To calculate correct bounds, we rely on the monotonicity of $\mathcal{S}$. Without loss of generality, suppose that $\mathcal{S}$ is monotonically increasing. In the expression of $\mathcal{S}$, we replace each partial score $s\text{-}p_{(i,j)}(x_i, x_j)$ with the upper bound of the corresponding pair of bucket. Therefore $\mathcal{S}_{(i,j)\in E}((b_{i,l_i,l'_i}, b_{j,l_j,l'_j}).UB)$ is a correct upper-bound for ω. Then, LOOSE runs *getTopBuckets* on the generated bucket combinations (Line 6) and returns the selected combinations. The rationale behind LOOSE is that processing time can decrease significantly because (i) fewer bucket combinations need to be assigned a score bound (their number is $\mathcal{O}(|E| \cdot g^4)$) and (ii) the solver needs to assign only 4 variables when computing score bounds. A drawback of LOOSE is that the aggregation of bounds using $\mathcal{S}$ may result in loose bounds. We illustrate that in the following example.

Example. Figure 6 depicts a dataset with three buckets b_1, b_2, b_3 from C_1, C_2, C_3. We have $b_1 = (g_1, g_2)$, $b_2 = (g_2, g_3)$, $b_3 = (g_3, g_3)$, where $g_1 = [10, 20], g_2 = [20, 30], g_3 = [30, 40]$. Our query features scored predicates $s\text{-}starts_{(1,2)}(x, y)$ and $s\text{-}starts_{(2,3)}(y, z)$ and our aggregation function is the normalized sum. We use the scoring parameters $\{(\lambda_{equals}, \rho_{equals}), (\lambda_{greater}, \rho_{greater}) = \{(1,3), (0,4)\}$. LOOSE first computes bounds for $\omega_1 = (b_1, b_2)$. We have $\omega_1.UB = 1$ (because $s\text{-}starts_{(1,2)}(x_1, y_1) = 1$), and $\omega_1.LB = 0$ ($s\text{-}starts_{(1,2)}(x_1, y_2) = 0$). Then, LOOSE computes bounds for $\omega_1 = (b_2, b_3)$. We have $\omega_2.UB = 1$ ($s\text{-}starts_{(2,3)}(y_2, z_1) = 1$), and $\omega_2.LB = 0$ ($s\text{-}starts_{(2,3)}(y_2, z_2) = 0$). Then, LOOSE merges combinations ω_1, ω_2 in $\omega_3 = (b_1, b_2, b_3)$, and computes $\omega_3.UB = \mathcal{S}(1,1) = 1$, $\omega_3.LB = \mathcal{S}(0,0) = 0$. Yet, BRUTE-FORCE, computes $\omega_3.UB = 0.5$ because there is no (x, y, z) such that $s\text{-}starts_{(1,2)}(x, y) = s\text{-}starts_{(2,3)}(y, z) = 1$ given the buckets' bounds: it is impossible to have both $equals(\underline{x}, \underline{y}) = 1$ and $equals(\underline{y}, \underline{z}) = 1$ with $\underline{x} \in g_1, \underline{y} \in g_2$ and $\underline{z} \in g_3$. Thus, in this example, LOOSE returns an exact lower-bound and a loose upper-bound, while BRUTE-FORCE returns tight bounds.

These observations lead to propose a third strategy TWO-PHASE, that combines BRUTE-FORCE and LOOSE. TWO-PHASE is executed by Algorithm 2 when the flag onePhase is set to false. First, TWO-PHASE computes loose bounds to eliminate some bucket combinations (Lines 1-7), identically to LOOSE. Then, TWO-PHASE refines the bounds of the remaining combinations (Lines 8-9) to obtain exact bounds. The rationale behind TWO-PHASE is that its first phase may help reduce the number of bucket combinations that need to be assigned a score in the second phase, thus improving the solver's running time. Unlike LOOSE, TWO-PHASE returns tight bounds thanks to the second phase of the solver.

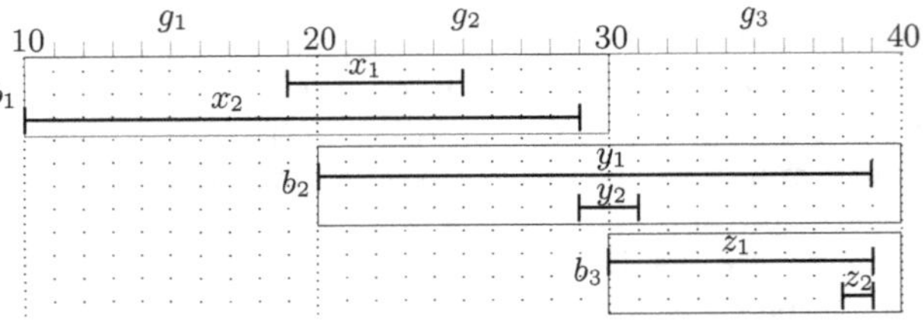

Figure 6: Example of Bucket Combinations

When selecting bucket combinations, *TKIJ* runs *TopBuckets* using one of the three strategies presented. Each strategy (i) employs the solver and (ii) executes *getTopBuckets* once or twice using loose or tight score bounds on bucket combinations.

3.4 Distributed Top-k Join Processing

The *TopBuckets* process generates $\Omega_{k,\mathcal{S}}$, a set of bucket combinations that are sufficient to accurately compute the top-k results. We now describe how *TKIJ* computes the top-k results (Steps (c)-(d)-(e) in Figure 5). We implement *TKIJ* on Map-Reduce [6]. Given a set of r reducers, *TKIJ* assigns each bucket combination $\omega \in \Omega_{k,\mathcal{S}}$ to a single reducer $r_j, j \in 1 \dots r$, that processes results in ω. The main challenge in distributed join processing is to devise an efficient workload assignment function. When performing large-scale joins, I/O often constitutes a major bottleneck. We first review existing assignment algorithms, then we consider the specifics of distributed top-k computation and show that it is essential to take scores into account when dividing the workload. We present *DistributeTopBuckets*, a novel function that focuses on assigning high-scoring results to each reducer, while minimizing I/O cost as a secondary objective. Finally, we present how an RTJ query is processed using appropriate Map-Reduce algorithms.

Existing I/O optimizations

When different reducers require the same chunk of data, this data is replicated in the shuffle phase of Map-Reduce, which increases input cost. Several distributed join algorithms, such as *RCCIS* [5] and the work of Afrati et al. [1] specifically aim at reducing that cost. In *TKIJ*, this corresponds to different reducers being assigned bucket combinations involving the same bucket. Other approaches focus on assigning a balanced load to each reducer [5, 24]. This ensures that the number of results generated by each reducer is comparable, so that no reducer will have a larger workload in output dominated tasks. Finally, some algorithms optimize both input and output costs simultaneously [30]. All these approaches are not directly applicable to our settings. They achieve optimizations for specific queries (equi-join [1], 2-way θ-join [24], m-way θ-join [30]). One close related work to ours [5] reduces I/O cost by leveraging the Boolean interpretation of Allen predicates. That is not directly applicable to scored predicates.

Top-k optimizations

TKIJ significantly differs from standard Map-Reduce-based join processes due to its ranked semantics. In *TKIJ*, each reducer processes a full RTJ query locally using the bucket combinations it receives (Figure 5d). Hence, it is important

Algorithm 3 DistributeTopBuckets (DTB)

Input: $\Omega_{k,\mathcal{S}}$
Output: M: assignments (bucket, reducer)
1: Sort $\Omega_{k,\mathcal{S}}$ by descending order of $\omega.UB$
2: $avgRes = \frac{\sum_{\omega \in \Omega_{k,\mathcal{S}}} \omega.nbRes}{r}$
3: **for all** $\omega \in \Omega_{k,\mathcal{S}}$
4: $\quad r_j = getReducer(avgRes, \omega)$
5: $\quad$ **for all** bucket $b \in \omega$ $\quad \triangleright$ Assign buckets in ω to r_j
6: $\quad\quad M \leftarrow M \cup (b, r_j)$
return M

Algorithm 4 getReducer

Input: ω bucket combination to assign, $avgRes$ average number of results per reducer
Output: reducer to which ω has to be assigned
1: $min\_\omega\_assigned = +\infty$
2: **for** $j = 1$ to r $\quad \triangleright$ Retrieve the minimum amount of bucket combinations assigned
3: $\quad$ **if** $r_j.nbRes < 2 \times avgRes$
4: $\quad\quad min\_\omega\_assigned = \min\{|\Omega_{r_j}|, min\_\omega\_assigned\}$
5: $minCost = +\infty$
6: **for** $j = 1$ to r $\triangleright$ Find the best reducer wrt $inCost(\omega, r_j)$
7: $\quad$ **if** $r_j.nbRes < 2 \times avgRes \wedge |\Omega_{r_j}| = min\_\omega\_assigned$
8: $\quad\quad$ **if** $inCost(r_j, \omega) < minCost$
9: $\quad\quad\quad$ bestReducer$=r_j$
10: $\quad\quad\quad minCost = inCost(r_j, \omega)$
return bestReducer

to ensure that each reducer quickly identifies high-scoring results as it is usually the case in top-k processing [14, 15, 16, 26]. Therefore, the assignment of bucket combinations to reducers favors an even distribution of high-scoring results.

DTB algorithm

TKIJ relies on the *DistributeTopBuckets* algorithm (Algorithm 3) to assign bucket combinations from $\Omega_{k,\mathcal{S}}$ to reducers. Following the principles described above, *DTB* increases the probability that each reducer receives a fair share of high-scoring results. This step relies on the knowledge, for each bucket combination, of the number of results generated, as well as their score bounds. *DTB* first sorts $\Omega_{k,\mathcal{S}}$ by descending order of score upper-bound (Line 1) to access them according to their likelihood of generating high-scoring results. It then assigns each bucket combination to a reducer using the *getReducer* function (Algorithm 4), which returns a reducer among the ones that were assigned the fewest bucket combinations so far.
Furthermore, *DTB* opportunistically optimizes I/O cost. First, in the worst case, a reducer evaluates all the results it is assigned. If Ω_{r_j} is the set of bucket combinations assigned to a reducer r_j, then $\sum_{\omega \in |\Omega_{r_j}|} \omega.nbRes$ would be computed. *DTB* first computes the average number of results assigned to reducers (Algorithm 3, Line 2). Then *getReducer* ensures that reducers that are already assigned more than twice the average number of results are discarded (Algorithm 4, Lines 3, 7). This heuristic limits imbalance in a worst-case scenario. In the case, where several reducers have received the same number of bucket combinations, *getReducer* selects the reducer that was already assigned the largest fraction of current ω from previous overlapping bucket combinations (Algorithm 4, Lines 8-10). For a given w, *getReducer* evaluates for each reducer r_j the input cost of assigning w to r_j using $inCost(r_j, \omega)$. We define $inCost(r_j, \omega) = \sum_{b_{i,l,l'} \in \omega} |b_{i,l,l'}| \cdot \Phi(r_j, b_{i,l,l'})$ where $\Phi(r_j, b_{i,l,l'})$ returns 1 if $b_{i,l,l'}$ was already assigned to r_j, else 0. This process favors assignments that reduce replication cost. Having selected the reducer r_j that has to be assigned the current bucket combination ω, *DTB* stores all the assignments $(b_{i,l,l'}, r_j)$ where $b_{i,l,l'} \in \omega$ (Algorithm 3, Lines 5-6). These assignments determine to which reducers buckets are communicated, ensuring both output correctness and join processing efficiency.

Join Processing

The final phase of *TKIJ* first runs *DTB* using $\Omega_{k,\mathcal{S}}$ to determine data distribution among reducers. Then, a Map-Reduce phase processes the RTJ query locally. For each input interval x, a mapper computes the bucket b_{i_x,l_x,l'_x} in which x falls. Then, x is communicated to all reducers r_j that received b_{i_x,l_x,l'_x}. That way, each reducer r_j receives its share of input data, and a list of bucket combinations $\Omega_{r_j} \subseteq \Omega_{k,\mathcal{S}}$ whose results are potential top-k candidates. Once each reducer has processed locally the RTJ query, we run an additional Map-Reduce phase (Step (e) in Figure 5), that merges local results and returns the final top-k answers.

4. EXPERIMENTS

Platform. We conduct experiments on an 8-node industrial cluster with 6 workers. Each worker has 1 Intel Xeon E5-2650L (8 cores), 32GB RAM, 5TB disk. Machines run Centos 6.6 with Cloudera 5.2.5 and Hadoop 2.5.0. All presented results are averages of 5 consecutive runs.

Statistics collection. We use the same number of granules g for each collection. We observed that only the number of interval $|C_i|$ per collection had a significant impact on statistics collection time. Statistics collection lasted between 28s for $|C_i| = 2 \times 10^5$ and 36s for $|C_i| = 5 \times 10^6$. Since this task is only executed once as a pre-processing for a given dataset, we do not include it in query evaluation time.

Selection of bucket combinations. We implement a distributed and multi-threaded version of *TopBuckets*. We split the set of buckets $\mathcal{B}_1$ into 6 equal-sized groups $\mathcal{B}_{1,j}, j \in 1 \ldots 6$. Then each worker $j \in 1 \ldots 6$ runs a local version of *TopBuckets* using buckets in $\mathcal{B}_{1,j}$ and all buckets in $\mathcal{B}_i, i \in 2 \ldots n$. Thus, each worker has as input a disjoint set of possible bucket combinations. We use Choco [25], a software for constraint programming to compute score bounds for each bucket combination. Each execution of the solver is handled in a separate thread. A second phase of *TopBuckets* merges local *TopBuckets* results on a selected worker and returns the set of best bucket combinations $\Omega_{k,\mathcal{S}}$.

Distributed join processing. We run *TKIJ* using 24 reducers. Local query execution accesses the received bucket combinations by descending order of score upper-bounds. It then uses R-Trees to access intervals in memory. For an interval x_i and a score value v, it queries the R-Tree and returns only intervals x_j s.t. $s\text{-}p_{(i,j)}(x_i, x_j) \geq v$.

Id	Scored Temporal Predicates In $\mathcal{Q}$. $x_i \in C_i \; \forall i \in 1 \ldots n$.
$\mathcal{Q}_{b,b}$	$s\text{-}before(x_1, x_2)$, $s\text{-}before(x_2, x_3)$
$\mathcal{Q}_{f,f}$	$s\text{-}finishedBy(x_1, x_2)$, $s\text{-}finishedBy(x_2, x_3)$
$\mathcal{Q}_{o,o}$	$s\text{-}overlaps(x_1, x_2)$, $s\text{-}overlaps(x_2, x_3)$
$\mathcal{Q}_{s,f,m}$	$s\text{-}starts(x_1, x_2)$, $s\text{-}finishedBy(x_2, x_3)$, $s\text{-}meets(x_1, x_3)$
$\mathcal{Q}_{s,s}$	$s\text{-}starts(x_1, x_2)$, $s\text{-}starts(x_2, x_3)$
$\mathcal{Q}_{b^*}$	$s\text{-}before(x_1, x_2), \ldots, s\text{-}before(x_1, x_n)$
$\mathcal{Q}_{o^*}$	$s\text{-}overlaps(x_1, x_2), \ldots, s\text{-}overlaps(x_1, x_n)$
$\mathcal{Q}_{m^*}$	$s\text{-}meets(x_1, x_2), \ldots, s\text{-}meets(x_1, x_n)$
$\mathcal{Q}_{f,b}$	$s\text{-}finishedBy(x_1, x_2)$, $s\text{-}before(x_2, x_3)$
$\mathcal{Q}_{o,m}$	$s\text{-}overlaps(x_1, x_2)$, $s\text{-}meets(x_2, x_3)$
$\mathcal{Q}_{s,m}$	$s\text{-}starts(x_1, x_2)$, $s\text{-}meets(x_2, x_3)$
$\mathcal{Q}_{jB,jB}$	$s\text{-}justBefore(x_1, x_2)$, $s\text{-}justBefore(x_2, x_3)$
$\mathcal{Q}_{sM,sM}$	$s\text{-}shiftMeets(x_1, x_2)$, $s\text{-}shiftMeets(x_2, x_3)$

Table 1: Queries

Id	$(\lambda_{equals}, \rho_{equals})$	$(\lambda_{greater}, \rho_{greater})$
$\mathcal{P}_1$	(4,16)	(0,10)
$\mathcal{P}_2$	(0,16)	(2,8)
$\mathcal{P}_3$	(4,12)	(0,8)
$\mathcal{P}_B$	(0,0)	(0,0)

Table 2: Scored Predicates Parameters

Queries. Tables 1 and 2 summarize queries and score parameters. We use $\mathcal{S} = \frac{\sum_{(i,j)\in E} s\text{-}p_{(i,j)}(x_i, x_j)}{|E|}$ to compute the score of a query result $(x_1, \ldots, x_n)$. Unless otherwise specified, $k = 100$.

4.1 Summary of Results

We show that *TKIJ* processes various RTJ queries efficiently on both synthetic data and real network traffic logs. *TKIJ* scales to collections of up to 5 million intervals ($|C_i| \in [1M, 5M]$) and efficiently returns the top-k results for $k \in [10, 10^5]$. We show that our workload distribution approach, *DistributeTopBuckets*, that fairly distributes high-scoring results, outperforms a more naive approach based on the *LPT* algorithm. That is particularly useful for queries that return few high-scoring results, such as those featuring equality-based predicates (e.g *starts*). We observe that the efficiency of *DistributeTopBuckets* decreases with coarser statistics. We also show that as the number of collections or the number of predicates in a query vary, *TopBuckets* efficiently prunes buckets combinations. Experiments on network traffic data show that on queries featuring *before* or *overlaps*, *TopBuckets* can select few bucket combinations guaranteeing *TKIJ* to return high-scoring results. We observe that a higher number of granules g (finer statistics) helps prune unnecessary results, which improves overall join processing time. However, it also makes pruning computation with *TopBuckets* slower. Hence, we run experiments to find a sweet-spot value for g.

4.2 Synthetic Data

To generate synthetic data, we use the same parameters as in previous work [5]. We use a pseudo-random uniform generator to get intervals' startpoints and lengths in specified ranges (respectively $s = [0, 10^5]$ and $w = [1, 100]$). Intervals' endpoints are integers. We vary the number $|C_i|$ of intervals per collection, and the number n of collections. A collection of 5M intervals measures $\approx$113MB (text format).

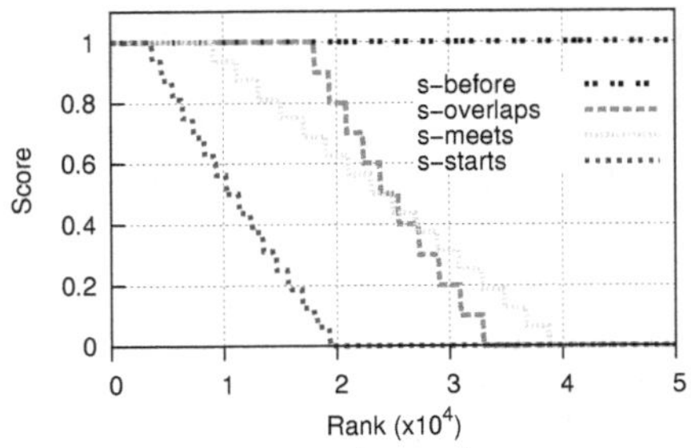

Parameters: $|C_i| = 10^4, \mathcal{P} = \mathcal{P}_1$

Figure 7: Synthetic Data - Score Distribution

4.2.1 *Score Distribution*

We conduct preliminary experiments to get an insight of the score distribution of a set of results using scored temporal predicates. Especially, we want to measure the share of results that have a high score. We want to verify that the fewer the number of high-scoring results, the less likely a worker will receive high scoring results from *DTB*. We compute all the combinations $(x_1, x_2) \in C_1 \times C_2$ and we evaluate each result with scored predicates *s-before*(x_1, x_2), *s-meets*(x_1, x_2), *s-overlaps*(x_1, x_2) and *s-starts*(x_1, x_2).

On Figure 7, we plot scores for the top-50000 results. *s-before* is the predicate with the largest number of high-scoring results (scores of top-50000 results equal 1.0), since a single inequality on endpoints is required. More high-scoring results can be found with *s-overlaps* ($\approx$ 18,000 results), that evaluates only inequality on endpoints, than with *s-meets* ($\approx$9000), where an equality is required. Fewer results are assigned a high score when *s-starts* is used since it requires both equality and inequality on endpoints. Thus, we can expect a faster join processing on queries using only inequality-based predicates where more high-scoring results can be found, since high-scoring results favor early termination of local top-k processing.

4.2.2 *Workload Distribution*

We conduct experiments to validate our workload distribution approach. We analyze executions of *TKIJ* using *DTB*, our workload distribution algorithm, and using a more straightforward algorithm.

LPT. In the context of task scheduling, the *LPT* (*Longest Processing Time*) heuristic aims to minimize scheduling time on parallel machines [11]. *LPT* executes tasks in descending order of processing time. In our context, a naive approach would minimize the maximum number of candidate join results that a reducer has to process, so as to reduce the duration of the longest task. With *LPT*, bucket combinations are analogous to tasks that we want to assign to a set of reducers. We sort the set of bucket combinations by descending order of number of results ($\omega.nbRes$) and assign each one to the least loaded reducer.

Results. Figure 8a presents the running time of the join phase on all queries, where $|C_i|$ varies from 1×10^6 to 1.6×10^6. On $\mathcal{Q}_{b,b}$, running time is identical for *LPT* and *DTB*, since a single bucket combination is selected and a large number of results with maximum score can be quickly found during the join phase. On other queries, *DTB* outperforms

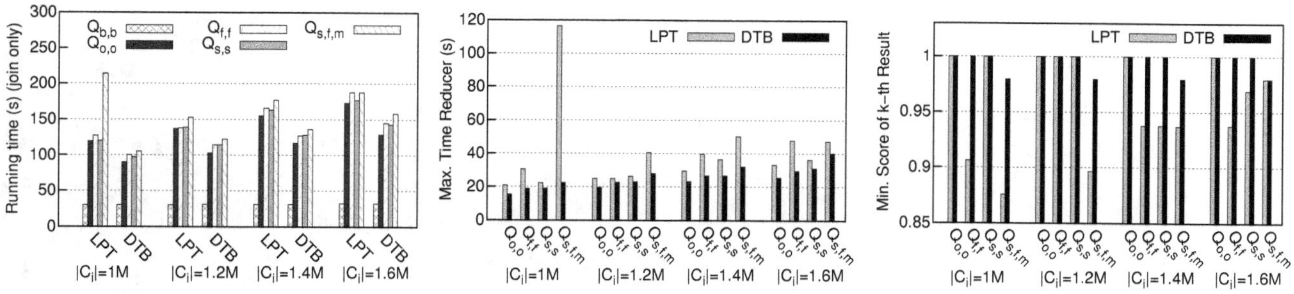

(a) Running Time (b) Max Running Time of Reducers (c) Minimum Score of k-th Result

Parameters: $g = 20, k = 1000, \mathcal{P} = \mathcal{P}_2$, *TopBuckets* : LOOSE

Figure 8: Synthetic Data - Workload Distribution

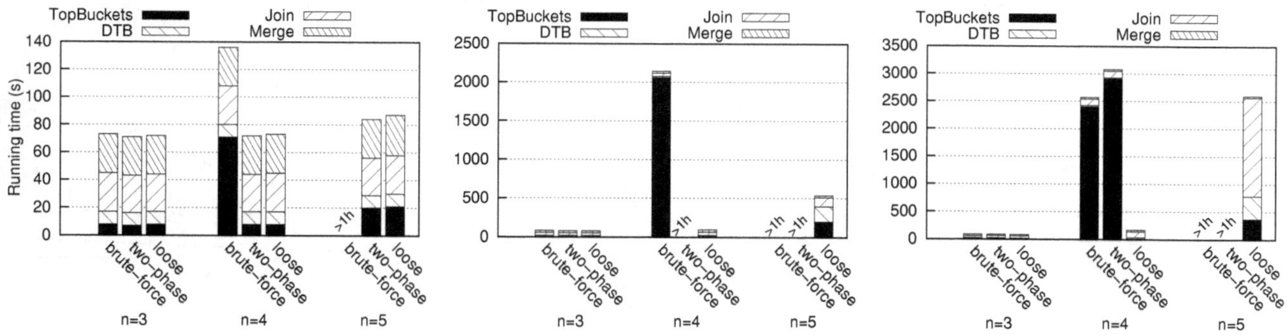

(a) $\mathcal{Q}_{b^*}$ (b) $\mathcal{Q}_{o^*}$ (c) $\mathcal{Q}_{m^*}$

Parameters: $g = 15, k = 100, |C_i| = 2 \times 10^5, \mathcal{P} = \mathcal{P}_1$

Figure 9: Synthetic Data - Detailed execution time, all *TopBuckets* strategies

LPT for two reasons. Firstly, *LPT* incurs a higher shuffle cost (on average 43% higher). When assigning a bucket combination to a reducer, *DTB* favors assignments that lessen shuffle cost. *LPT* favors the assignment of bucket combinations with a large number of results to the least loaded reducers. Hence, buckets have a higher probability to be sent to several reducers with *LPT* than with *DTB*. Secondly, *LPT* does not necessarily give a fair share of high-scoring results to each reducer. Figure 8b shows the running time of the longest reducer task (we omit $\mathcal{Q}_{b,b}$ where *LPT* and *DTB* perform equally for the reason exposed above). *DTB* always outperforms *LPT* because it increases the probability that all reduce tasks terminate early since they can all find high-scoring results. This difference is exacerbated on query $\mathcal{Q}_{s,f,m}$ with $|C_i| = 1M$. Here, the few results that satisfy best all 3 predicates featured in $\mathcal{Q}_{s,f,m}$ are better distributed using *DTB*. On Figure 8c, we represent the minimum score of the kth result among the results returned by reducers. These results support our observation: the score of returned results is higher when distribution is defined using *DTB*, while unnecessary results with lower scores are returned with *LPT*.

4.2.3 TopBuckets Strategies

We conduct experiments on the *TopBuckets* strategies exposed in Section 3.3. We vary the number of collections n using queries $\mathcal{Q}_{b^*}$, $\mathcal{Q}_{o^*}$ and $\mathcal{Q}_{m^*}$.

Figure 9 summarizes the results. We do not report results where running time exceeds 1 hour. Experiments show the inefficiency of BRUTE-FORCE and TWO-PHASE. On these strategies, n-tuples of buckets, where $n \in 3 \ldots 5$, are assigned a score bound by the solver. With BRUTE-FORCE, the running time of *TopBuckets* quickly increases (solid black box on Figure 9) with n, because the solver needs to compute score bounds for a large number of bucket combinations, each one requiring to assign $2n$ variables. The TWO-PHASE strategy only beats BRUTE-FORCE on $\mathcal{Q}_{b^*}$ (Figure 9a) where its first phase prunes a large share (more than 99% for any n) of possible bucket combinations, thus limiting the running time of the second phase, that computes exact bounds using a smaller set of bucket combinations. On others queries, TWO-PHASE does not improve running time: the first phase does not prune enough combinations (e.g. 52% on $\mathcal{Q}_{m^*}$ for $n = 4$) to lessen the cost of the second phase where remaining combinations need to be assigned tight score bounds. The LOOSE strategy is the most efficient: (i) loose bounds do not impact significantly join processing time as a large share of potential results (e.g. 81% on $\mathcal{Q}_{o^*}$ for $n = 4$) remained pruned and (ii) *TopBuckets* scales with the number of collections n. In the remainder of our experiments, we use LOOSE as the *TopBuckets* strategy.

4.2.4 Number of Granules

Since the second phase of *TKIJ* relies on collected statistics to prune the input space and distribute the workload, we expect *TKIJ* to depend on the granularity of statistics (e.g. coarse or fine-grained). We conduct experiments to validate this intuition, varying the number of granules g.

We present respectively on Figures 10a, 10b and 10c the

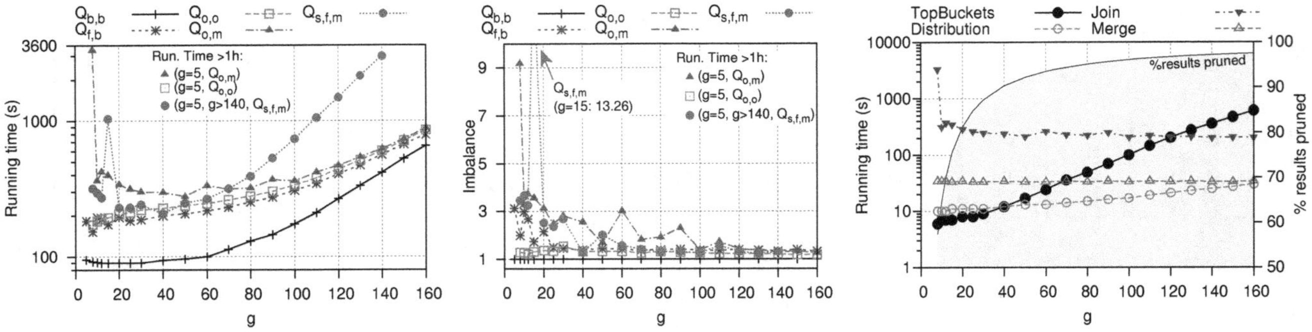

(a) Running Time (b) Imbalance (c) Detailed Running Time for $\mathcal{Q}_{o,m}$

Parameters: k = 100, $|C_i| = 2 \times 10^6$, $\mathcal{P} = \mathcal{P}_1$, *TopBuckets*: LOOSE

Figure 10: Synthetic Data - Effect of number of granules g

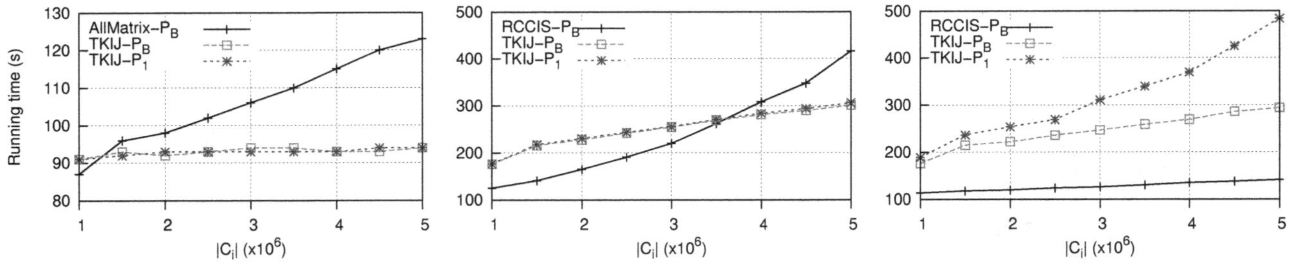

(a) $\mathcal{Q}_{b,b}$ (b) $\mathcal{Q}_{o,o}$ (c) $\mathcal{Q}_{s,m}$

Parameters: g = 40, k = 100, *TopBuckets*: LOOSE

Figure 11: Synthetic Data - Scalability

total running time of a range of queries, the load imbalance of the join phase computed using $\frac{Max\ Time\ Reducer}{Average\ Time\ Reducer}$ and the detailed running time for query $\mathcal{Q}_{o,m}$. We do not report results for executions where the total running time exceeds 1 hour. On queries that return the fewest high-scoring results ($\mathcal{Q}_{o,m}$, $\mathcal{Q}_{s,f,m}$), we observe on Figure 10a that with a lower g (coarse statistics), running time degrades. *TKIJ* suffers here from poor workload distribution. This is expected as with fewer granules, we have fewer bucket combinations and especially fewer high-scoring ones. As *TKIJ* relies on a round-robin distribution of high-scoring buckets combinations, there is a lower probability to provide each reducer high-scoring results. Hence, we can observe on Figure 10b the imbalance that is more variable when g decreases. As illustrated on Figure 10c, when g increases, the local join processing is faster, thanks to a better workload distribution and to a larger pruning of unnecessary results. 81% of potential results are pruned for $g = 20$, while it is 96% for $g = 100$ (grey filled curve on Figure 10c). Yet, the pruning process *TopBuckets* is slower when g increases and thus worsen the overall response time. Note that because it features more predicates, query $\mathcal{Q}_{s,f,m}$ requires to evaluate more bucket pairs during the *TopBuckets* process. Thus, *TopBuckets* running time increases faster with g than on others queries, hence the impact on the overall response time.
For queries $\mathcal{Q}_{b,b}$ and $\mathcal{Q}_{o,o}$, coarse statistics have nearly no effect since a large number of high-scoring results can be found during the join phase (except when g = 5 where workload distribution fails for query $\mathcal{Q}_{o,o}$: a reducer does not quickly find high-scoring results). Finally, we observe that a number of granules $g \approx 40$ provides the best trade-off for the various queries that we experimented. Future investigations include the design of benchmark approaches or the adaptation of optimization techniques [7] to compute the optimal number of granules that minimizes execution time of *TKIJ*.

4.2.5 Scalability

We vary the size of collections $|C_i|$ to evaluate the scalability of *TKIJ*. We compare *TKIJ* to state-of-the-art competitors.
As a baseline, we borrow algorithms from related work on processing interval joins on Map-Reduce [5]. In this work, algorithms *RCCIS* and *All-Matrix* are designed to process interval joins using Allen predicates. In our settings, we use these algorithms to return only results that satisfy all the Boolean predicates of a RTJ query (i.e. a subset of top-k results). We also impose reducers to stop join processing if k results are found. Then, we merge and sort local results using a final Map-Reduce phase, identically to *TKIJ*.
RCCIS handles only *colocation* predicates where intervals intersect (e.g. *overlaps, meets*). *All-Matrix* handles only *sequence* predicates (*before, after*). *RCCIS* and *All-Matrix* also partition the temporal range using contiguous granules. For *RCCIS*, we set the number of granules to 24 which implies that 24 reducers are used. For *All-Matrix*, the number of reducers depends on the number of granules and of collections. We used 4 granules with $n = 3$, yielding 20 reducers. For *TKIJ*, we conduct a first set of experiments with

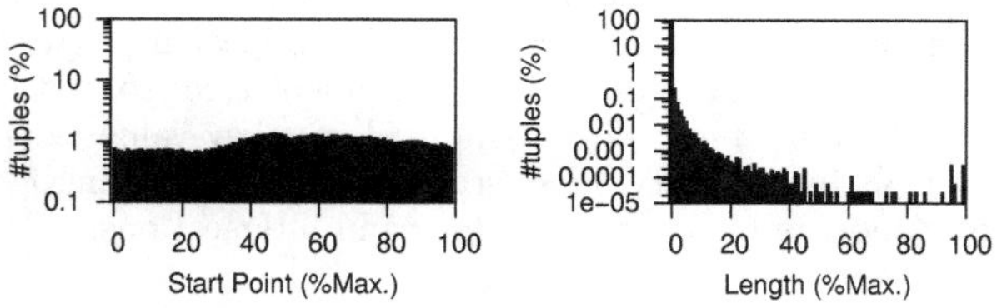

(a) Start Point (b) Length

Figure 12: Network Traffic Data Distribution

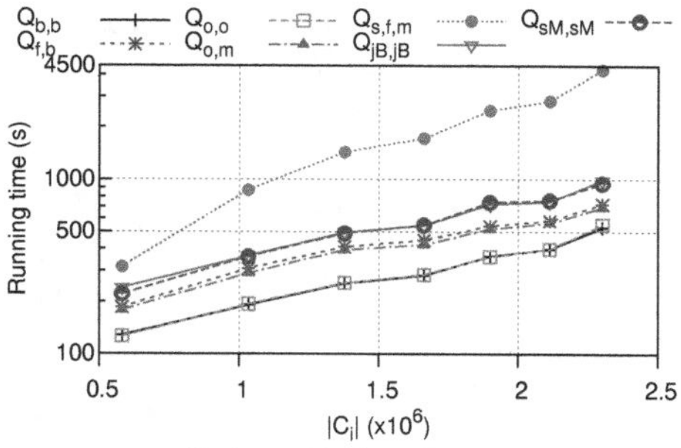

Parameters: $g = 40, k = 100, \mathcal{P} = \mathcal{P}_3$, *TopBuckets*: LOOSE

Figure 13: Network Traffic Data - Scalability

score parameters $\mathcal{P}_B = \{(0,0),(0,0)\}$ (see Table 2). We are hence using a Boolean interpretation of predicates. Because *TKIJ* must return k results, if only $k' < k$ results satisfy the Boolean predicates (with $\mathcal{S}(t) = 1.0$), $k - k'$ other results that do not satisfy at least one predicate will be returned (with $\mathcal{S}(t) < 1.0$). Thus, *TKIJ* may need to return more results than *All-Matrix* or *RCCIS*, that only return results fully satisfying all Boolean predicates. Hence, results of each algorithm are not directly comparable. For *TKIJ*, we conduct a second set of experiments using scored predicates with the score parameters $\mathcal{P}_1$.

Results. We present total running times on Figure 11. For query $\mathcal{Q}_{b,b}$ (Figure 11a), *TKIJ* remains nearly constant since *TopBuckets* returns only 1 bucket combination. Thus, *TKIJ* processes only a small share of input data. *All-Matrix* shuffles intervals belonging to all possible results, hence running time increases with $|C_i|$. For query $\mathcal{Q}_{o,o}$ (Figure 11b), *TopBuckets* selects more combinations to process. As the number of intervals per bucket increases with $|C_i|$, more data is shuffled and processed during the local join processing, hence the running time increases linearly with $|C_i|$. Figure 11b also shows that *TKIJ* outperforms *RCCIS* on $|C_i| > 3.5 \times 10^6$. In *RCCIS*, a first Map-Reduce phase builds intermediate results to determine which intervals need to be replicated to ensure output correctness in the join phase. Thus, its running time increases with $|C_i|$. Meanwhile, *TKIJ* decides which tuples should be combined on the basis of *TopBuckets*, which does not depend on $|C_i|$ and is on average 93% faster than the first phase of *RCCIS*. On $\mathcal{Q}_{s,m}$ (Figure 11c), we do not observe this phenomenon anymore: *RCCIS* first phase is faster (there are fewer intermediate results), while *TKIJ*'s join phase is longer (there are fewer high-scoring results). We observe a notable difference on query $\mathcal{Q}_{s,m}$ with scored and with Boolean predicates. The local join processing explains this difference. In the Boolean case, *TKIJ* focuses on building results where join conditions are satisfied (whose score is strictly positive), thus limiting the search space. With the approximate interpretation of predicates, more combinations need to be considered because tolerance on endpoints incurs a higher number of results with a strictly positive score. Thus, more intermediate results are computed. On query $\mathcal{Q}_{o,o}$, a large number of results have the highest score (Figure 7) which incurs major pruning. That justifies the absence of a significant difference between the scored and Boolean cases.

4.2.6 *Effect of k*

We conducted experiments where k varies in $[10, 10^5]$ on a range of queries ($\mathcal{Q}_{b,b}$, $\mathcal{Q}_{o,o}$, $\mathcal{Q}_{s,f,m}$, $\mathcal{Q}_{f,b}$, $\mathcal{Q}_{o,m}$) with $|C_i| = 2 \times 10^6$. We observed that *TKIJ* is almost constant on all queries and all values of k. Actually, a large number ($> 10^{13}$) of potential results fall in each bucket combination. Thus, the set of selected bucket combinations remains the same for $k \in [10, 10^5]$ since we can always guarantee to return the correct top-k results.

4.3 Network Traffic Data

4.3.1 *Data*

We use network traffic data collected on firewall logs of a data hosting company. Each log contains packets exchanged between servers and clients ($\approx$ 5GB, 100M packets per day). Each packet has a timestamp (seconds). We selected one log and built a list of connections by grouping packets exchanged between a pair (server, client). Only consecutive packets whose timestamps are within a time interval $[0, 60]$ are grouped. A connection [*client, server, start, end*] represents the activity of *client* on *server*, where the first packet was sent or received at timestamp *start* and the last one at timestamp *end*. The dataset obtained includes 3,636,814 intervals ($\approx$ 83MB), whose minimum, maximum, and average length are respectively 1, 86,459 and 54 seconds. Figure 12 shows the distribution of start points and lengths. Then, we copy each list of connections 3 times and process 3-way queries. We are interested in real-life scenarios occurring in network traffic analysis, hence we process queries $\mathcal{Q}_{jB,jB}$ and $\mathcal{Q}_{sM,sM}$ (Table 1). Query $\mathcal{Q}_{jB,jB}$ returns the sequences of connections that closely follow each other, while $\mathcal{Q}_{sM,sM}$ returns sequences where a delay was observed between two connections.

4.3.2 *Scalability*

We verify that *TKIJ* scales with various dataset sizes. When generating connections, we use various randomly selected samples on the log file used. We pick from 5% to 35% of input data. We obtain collections of connections whose number of intervals varies from 0.58×10^6 to 2.31×10^6.

We present total running times on Figure 13. We note that running time increases faster than what was observed on synthetic data. Here, when we use larger samples on input data, we have more buckets containing at least an interval. When $|C_i| = 0.58 \times 10^6$, there are 151 buckets containing at least an interval, while there are 296 for $|C_i| = 2.31 \times 10^6$. Thus, *TopBuckets* has to process more bucket combinations with higher $|C_i|$. On query $\mathcal{Q}_{s,f,m}$, that features more predicates, the time taken by *TopBuckets* is dominant (e.g. 82% of overall response time for $|C_i| = 1.38 \times 10^6$). Hence, overall response time increases faster on query $\mathcal{Q}_{s,f,m}$ than on all

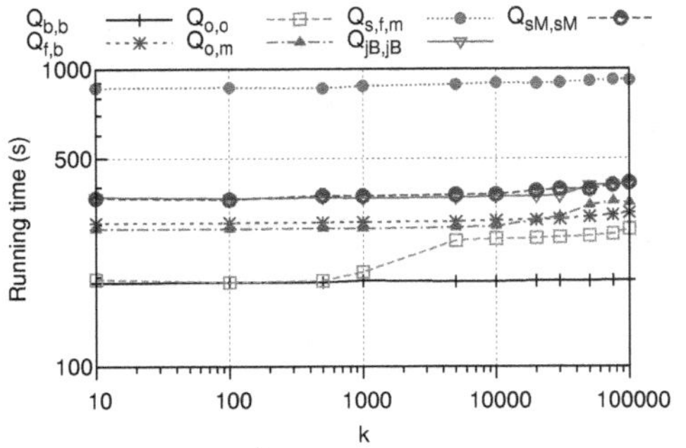

Param.: $|C_i| = 1.03 \times 10^6, g = 40, \mathcal{P} = \mathcal{P}_3$, *TopBuckets*: LOOSE

Figure 14: Network Traffic Data - Effect of k

other queries. We also observe that while $\mathcal{Q}_{o,o}$ lasts longer on synthetic data, *TKIJ* performs similarly on $\mathcal{Q}_{b,b}$ and $\mathcal{Q}_{o,o}$ on real data. That can be explained by the fact that the real dataset contains long intervals (Figure 12). These intervals fall into buckets built with granules that are far apart (e.g. $b_1 = ([2160, 4320], [19440, 21600])$ or $b_2 = ([8640, 10800], [38880, 41040])$). Thus, we can find bucket combinations (e.g. $\omega = (b_1, b_2)$) whose results (x, y) are guaranteed to have a high score *s-overlaps*(x, y). Then, *TopBuckets* returns less bucket combinations, reducing the search space while guaranteeing correctness.

4.3.3 Effect of k

We verify *TKIJ* on various values of k. We present running times on Figure 14. For all queries except $\mathcal{Q}_{o,o}$, we observe that *TKIJ* remains nearly constant when $k \leq 5000$. Then, the running time increases slowly when $k > 5000$: as more results need to be returned, more intermediate results are built before termination especially with queries having fewer high-scoring results. On $\mathcal{Q}_{o,o}$ we observe that *TKIJ* increases slightly between $k = 1000$ and $k = 5000$. That is explained by an increase (from 643 to 41,272) in the number of bucket combinations $|\Omega_{k,\mathcal{S}}|$ necessary to return the correct top-k results, which in turn increases the number of intermediate results.

5. RELATED WORK

Three research areas relate to our work, however none of them addresses the RTJ problem.

Interval Joins. The closest work to ours [5] addresses the processing of multi-way joins on Map-Reduce for Allen Boolean predicates [2]. The first algorithm, *RCCIS*, solves *colocation* queries, where all predicates require intervals to have a non-empty intersection. *RCCIS* reduces the amount of data shuffled in Map-Reduce by sending to the same reducer intervals that are most likely to be colocated. The second algorithm, *All-Matrix* handles *sequence* queries. Because such queries imply unavoidable replication, *All-Matrix* focuses on load balancing. None of those algorithms is applicable to solving the RTJ problem as they do not handle scored results.

Although flexible interpretations of Allen predicates were proposed in approximate reasoning [12, 23, 27], none of them designed join algorithms. A series of work on spatio-temporal data focused on efficiently retrieving *overlapping* objects with Boolean semantics. Objects are stored in partitions [7, 21], or tree structures [13], such as the R-Tree [3, 19] or the quadtree [17]. A more recent investigation proposed a compound index structure using segment trees to find intervals that *intersect* a query-interval in a key-value cloud-store [28]. In summary, these studies focus on reducing I/O and support only Boolean overlaps and intersections.

Top-k Processing. Instance-optimal algorithms [14, 15] were proposed for *rank-joins* ranging from centralized implementations for *HRJN* [20] and *Pull-Bound Rank Join* [26] in [16], to distributed ones in [10, 22]. Specifically, in NoSQL databases, the *BFHM* algorithm [22] places each tuple in a bucket that depends on its score. Tuples are compressed using Bloom-filters allowing to select the *best* buckets first then retrieve tuples to be joined from the database. Because a Bloom-filter yields false positives, *BFHM* may require several iterations. Our work differs in two aspects. First, our scores are predicate-dependent and are not known *a priori*. Second, reiterating join processing in our case would incur too high an overhead.

Load Balancing. Load balancing is a common concern in parallel top-k processing. RanKloud [4] computes data statistics to retrieve an estimation of the *kth* join score. Then, only the part of input data whose score is above the estimated one is uniformly distributed and processed in parallel on a set of workers. Similarly, we rely on computing statistics to avoid processing useless data. However, while RanKloud outputs approximate results, our algorithm guarantees to return exact top-k results. Another work [8] proposes a partitioning scheme on Map-Reduce based on partitioning for parallel skyline query processing [29]. The *angle-based partitioning* distributes evenly the volume that contains points near the best possible point, increasing the probability that skyline points will fall evenly in each partition. This idea is reintroduced in the context of top-k joins [8] and is shown to be superior to a cardinality-based partitioning. Although we share the same intuition, we cannot directly apply this technique since it assumes that partial scores are known *a priori* while in our case they are predicate-dependent.

6. CONCLUSION

In this paper, we introduce RTJ queries using scoring functions reflecting the degree of satisfaction of a join predicate. We design *TKIJ*, a parallel multi-way top-k interval join algorithm on Map-Reduce. *TKIJ* relies on an offline collection of statistics to prune the search space and a workload distribution scheme appropriate to top-k processing. We conduct experiments on synthetic data that validate our approach and show the efficiency of *TKIJ* on various queries. We observe the same effectiveness of *TKIJ* on real network traffic logs. Future investigations include the integration of interval attributes (e.g. IP address for a connection) in the join conditions, to build hybrid queries, similarly to previous work [5]. We also plan to pursue investigations on various distributed platforms. Although robust and scalable, Map-Reduce suffer from limitations on complex queries [9]. For instance, a field of investigation is the design of algorithms that take advantage of communication between workers.

7. ACKNOWLEDGMENTS

This work was partially funded by the Datalyse PIA project.

8. REFERENCES

[1] F. N. Afrati and J. D. Ullman. Optimizing joins in a map-reduce environment. In *EDBT*, pages 99–110, 2010.

[2] J. F. Allen. Maintaining knowledge about temporal intervals. *Commun. ACM*, 26(11):832–843, 1983.

[3] N. Beckmann, H. Kriegel, R. Schneider, and B. Seeger. The r*-tree: An efficient and robust access method for points and rectangles. In *SIGMOD*, pages 322–331, 1990.

[4] K. S. Candan, J. W. Kim, P. Nagarkar, M. Nagendra, and R. Yu. Rankloud: Scalable multimedia data processing in server clusters. *IEEE MultiMedia*, 18(1):64–77, 2011.

[5] B. Chawda, H. Gupta, S. Negi, T. A. Faruquie, L. V. Subramaniam, and M. K. Mohania. Processing interval joins on map-reduce. In *EDBT*, pages 463–474, 2014.

[6] J. Dean and S. Ghemawat. Mapreduce: Simplified data processing on large clusters. In *OSDI*, pages 137–150, 2004.

[7] A. Dignös, M. H. Böhlen, and J. Gamper. Overlap interval partition join. In *SIGMOD*, pages 1459–1470, 2014.

[8] C. Doulkeridis and K. Nørvåg. On saying "enough already!" in mapreduce. In *Cloud-I*, 2012.

[9] C. Doulkeridis and K. Nørvåg. A survey of large-scale analytical query processing in mapreduce. *VLDB J.*, 23(3):355–380, 2014.

[10] C. Doulkeridis, A. Vlachou, K. Nørvåg, Y. Kotidis, and N. Polyzotis. Processing of rank joins in highly distributed systems. In *ICDE*, pages 606–617, 2012.

[11] M. Drozdowski. *Scheduling for Parallel Processing.* Computer Communications and Networks. Springer, 2009.

[12] D. Dubois, A. HadjAli, and H. Prade. Fuzziness and uncertainty in temporal reasoning. *J. UCS*, 9(9):1168, 2003.

[13] J. Enderle, M. Hampel, and T. Seidl. Joining interval data in relational databases. In *SIGMOD*, pages 683–694, 2004.

[14] R. Fagin. Combining fuzzy information from multiple systems. In *PODS*, pages 216–226, 1996.

[15] R. Fagin, A. Lotem, and M. Naor. Optimal aggregation algorithms for middleware. In *PODS*, pages 102–113, 2001.

[16] J. Finger and N. Polyzotis. Robust and efficient algorithms for rank join evaluation. In *SIGMOD*, pages 415–428, 2009.

[17] R. A. Finkel and J. L. Bentley. Quad trees: A data structure for retrieval on composite keys. *Acta Inf.*, 4:1–9, 1974.

[18] D. Gao, C. S. Jensen, R. T. Snodgrass, and M. D. Soo. Join operations in temporal databases. *VLDB J.*, 14(1):2–29, 2005.

[19] A. Guttman. R-trees: A dynamic index structure for spatial searching. In *SIGMOD*, pages 47–57, 1984.

[20] I. F. Ilyas, W. G. Aref, and A. K. Elmagarmid. Supporting top-k join queries in relational databases. In *VLDB*, pages 754–765, 2003.

[21] H. Lu, B. C. Ooi, and K. Tan. On spatially partitioned temporal join. In *VLDB*, pages 546–557, 1994.

[22] N. Ntarmos, I. Patlakas, and P. Triantafillou. Rank join queries in nosql databases. *PVLDB*, 7(7):493–504, 2014.

[23] H. J. Ohlbach. Relations between fuzzy time intervals. In *TIME*, pages 44–51, 2004.

[24] A. Okcan and M. Riedewald. Processing theta-joins using mapreduce. In *SIGMOD*, pages 949–960, 2011.

[25] C. Prud'homme, J.-G. Fages, and X. Lorca. *Choco3 Documentation.* TASC, INRIA Rennes, LINA CNRS UMR 6241, COSLING S.A.S., 2014.

[26] K. Schnaitter and N. Polyzotis. Evaluating rank joins with optimal cost. In *PODS*, pages 43–52, 2008.

[27] S. Schockaert, M. D. Cock, and E. E. Kerre. Fuzzifying allen's temporal interval relations. *IEEE T. Fuzzy Systems*, 16(2):517–533, 2008.

[28] G. Sfakianakis, I. Patlakas, N. Ntarmos, and P. Triantafillou. Interval indexing and querying on key-value cloud stores. In *ICDE*, pages 805–816, 2013.

[29] A. Vlachou, C. Doulkeridis, and Y. Kotidis. Angle-based space partitioning for efficient parallel skyline computation. In *SIGMOD*, pages 227–238, 2008.

[30] X. Zhang, L. Chen, and M. Wang. Efficient multi-way theta-join processing using mapreduce. *PVLDB*, 5(11):1184–1195, 2012.

AT-GIS: Highly Parallel Spatial Query Processing with Associative Transducers

Peter Ogden
Imperial College London
p.ogden12@imperial.ac.uk

David Thomas
Imperial College London
d.thomas1@imperial.ac.uk

Peter Pietzuch
Imperial College London
prp@imperial.ac.uk

ABSTRACT

Users in many domains, including urban planning, transportation, and environmental science want to execute analytical queries over continuously updated spatial datasets. Current solutions for large-scale spatial query processing either rely on extensions to RDBMS, which entails expensive loading and indexing phases when the data changes, or distributed map/reduce frameworks, running on resource-hungry compute clusters. Both solutions struggle with the sequential bottleneck of parsing complex, hierarchical spatial data formats, which frequently dominates query execution time. Our goal is to fully exploit the parallelism offered by modern multi-core CPUs for parsing and query execution, thus providing the performance of a cluster with the resources of a single machine.

We describe AT-GIS, a highly-parallel spatial query processing system that scales linearly to a large number of CPU cores. AT-GIS integrates the parsing and querying of spatial data using a new computational abstraction called *associative transducers* (ATs). ATs can form a single data-parallel pipeline for computation without requiring the spatial input data to be split into logically independent blocks. Using ATs, AT-GIS can execute, in parallel, spatial query operators on the raw input data in multiple formats, without any pre-processing. On a single 64-core machine, AT-GIS provides 3× the performance of an 8-node Hadoop cluster with 192 cores for containment queries, and 10× for aggregation queries.

1. INTRODUCTION

Sources of spatial data are growing at an ever increasing rate. Crowd-sourced projects such as OpenStreetMap [21] create continuously-updated, planetary-scale datasets with 100s of millions of objects—the latest weekly OpenStreetMap snapshot is over 40 GBs compressed, 596 GBs uncompressed. High-resolution imaging, from microscopes to satellites, is another source of massive spatial data that can be analysed. In urban planning [5], transportation [52], environmental science [22] and medical image analysis [31], data scientists therefore face the task of executing spatial analytics queries over large datasets in an efficient manner. Spatial queries include selecting shapes within regions, summarising shapes that meet given criteria, and finding all intersecting or overlapping shapes. From these primitive spatial operators, more complex queries for testing for shape similarity between datasets or determining changes over time can be built.

SIGMOD'16, June 26-July 01, 2016, San Francisco, CA, USA
© 2016 ACM. ISBN 978-1-4503-3531-7/16/06... $15.00
DOI: http://dx.doi.org/10.1145/2882903.2882962

In domains with new or constantly updated spatial datasets, a key requirement is a low *data-to-query* time [2], i.e. the time to obtain a query result after the data becomes available. In pathology image analysis, in which segmented image data is queried for anomalous artefacts, it is one of the limiting factors for fast diagnosis [60]; for the OpenStreetMap dataset, this value determines how quickly new geographic features can be incorporated into any analysis.

Currently users who query large spatial datasets must either use relational database management systems (RDBMS) with spatial indexing support, such as *PostGIS* [25] or *Oracle Spatial* [45], or employ a distributed compute framework on a cluster, such as *Hadoop-GIS* [1] or *SpatialHadoop* [13]. Both approaches, however, suffer from a slow data-loading phase, which must occur before spatial queries can be run. RDBMS can only offer fast spatial query processing after the data has been fully parsed, loaded and indexed—in our experiments, loading the complete OpenStreetMap dataset into PostGIS takes over 90 minutes, with an additional 75 minutes to construct the index. Conversely, distributed frameworks with indexing support can offer good query performance, but they require substantially more computational resources than single machine deployments. To spread the load between cluster nodes, they must partition the spatial datasets, e.g. by loading it first into a distributed file system, increasing the total data-to-query time [34].

To reduce the data-to-query time for large spatial datasets, it is paramount to exploit parallelism when parsing, indexing and querying the data. If the original dataset format is simple, as it is the case for the *well-known text* (WKT) and *well-known binary* (WKB) spatial formats [42], data-parallelism can be gained from partitioning the input data into independent, fixed-sized blocks and processing them separately [58]—parsing and some spatial filtering can then be performed in parallel, while aggregation and join queries require the combination of all of the data. Unfortunately this simple partitioning approach does not work for more complex, though widely used spatial data formats, including GeoJSON [19] and XML [43]. Due to their hierarchical nature, these formats make it difficult to determine at which boundaries to split the data into independent parts without resynchronising the parser [46].

Our goal is to design a single-machine system for spatial query processing over large datasets that fully exploits the parallelism of modern multi-core CPUs. To minimise data-to-query time, our system should ingest commonly-used source data formats without any pre-processing, following the *NoDB* philosophy of executing queries over raw data [2]. The main challenge is that such a system must parallelise the parsing, indexing and spatial query execution. To scale to many CPU cores, it must thus minimise any inter-thread communication or access to global state. While the NoDB philosophy may result in increased I/O bandwidth when the input data format is complex or queries require multiple data passes, this can be mitigated through on-the-fly indexing and temporary storage.

We describe the design and implementation of **AT-GIS**, a system for highly-parallel spatial query processing on multi-core CPUs that operates on raw spatial datasets. For containment and aggregation queries, AT-GIS constructs a parallel processing pipeline that parses the data and executes the query in a single pass with constant memory. For spatial join queries, AT-GIS employs two passes, separating parsing and partitioning from the join computation.

To achieve parallelism across many CPU cores, AT-GIS uses a new computational model called **associative transducers (ATs)**. ATs allow for the data-parallel execution of otherwise sequential operations, making them a natural model for the processing of complex spatial data formats. With ATs, it is possible to separate parsing, extraction and spatial operator execution into distinct transducers that can be pipelined together. Instead of allocating a thread per transducer, which would limit the degree of parallelism and require synchronisation between them, in ATs each thread executes the entire pipeline, for separate blocks of the input data. Intermediate results in the pipeline are kept local to each thread, with only the final result synchronised and shared globally.

ATs have two features that enable them to execute multiple dependent spatial query processing stages in a data-parallel fashion: (i) they perform some degree of *speculation* during execution; and (ii) they leverage the *associativity* of spatial query operations. Parsing, data extraction and spatial operations are performed using finite and pushdown state machines, modified to support out-of-order operation through efficient speculative execution from all possible starting states. A formal model based on transducers allows multiple ATs to be pipelined while maintaining associativity. This permits AT-GIS to implement complex spatial operators using associative algorithms so that partial results can be merged.

We show experimentally that AT-GIS operates efficiently on multiple data formats: it performs spatial aggregation queries on GeoJSON or WKT-formatted OpenStreetMap data 2× faster than SpatialHadoop on the same hardware, despite not using an index; it is 10× faster than an 8-node Hadoop-GIS cluster, which has 3× the CPU cores and already pre-partitioned data. For spatial join queries, the time that AT-GIS requires to read and partition the dataset in parallel is less than 20% of the time taken to execute the join, with the total query time comparable to that of a larger cluster-based system. AT-GIS also achieves similar query performance, but with a much lower data-to-query time, as a commercial parallel DBMS with indexing for containment and aggregation queries and shows a two orders-of-magitude improvement over PostGIS.

The rest of paper is structured as follows: §2 discusses the problem and existing solutions for spatial query processing over large datasets; §3 describes the model of associative transducers for spatial queries; §4 presents the design of AT-GIS, explaining its query processing stages; §5 evaluates our prototype implementation; §6 discusses related work; and §7 concludes.

2. SPATIAL QUERY PROCESSING

We now introduce spatial queries (§2.1) and the challenges when querying large datasets (§2.2). We then discuss two approaches for large-scale spatial query processing (§2.3): spatial extensions to RDBMS and distributed systems based on the map/reduce model.

2.1 Spatial queries

As the size of data has increased, so has data that incorporates a spatial component [33]. Given that spatial searching is widely used in modern web applications [12], a common use of spatial data is in relating places on the surface of the earth. Other uses for geospatial processing are finding correlations between datasets acquired from

Listing 1: Example fragment of GeoJSON file

```
{ "type": "FeatureCollection",
  "features": [
    { "type": "Feature",
      "geometry": {
        "type": "GeometryCollection",
        "geometries": [
          { "type": "GeometryCollection",
            "geometries": [/* Shape Data */]},
          { "type": "LineString",
            "coordinates": [[1.1, 0.0],[1.2, 1.0]]}
        ]}
      "id": 1234,
      "properties": { /* User Data */ }
    }
  ]
}
```

different sources—a key component of current geospatial datastore benchmarks [16, 51]. As well as geospatial data, there is a growing use of spatial analytics in medical imaging, in particular pathology, in order to automate the process of finding a diagnosis from high-resolution digital microscopy images [31].

In this paper, we consider spatial datasets as collections of *objects*. Each object consists of a *geometry*, as defined by the Open Geospatial Consortium Standard [42], and associated *metadata*. Supported types of geometries are linestrings, polygons, multipolygons and collections. An example of a dataset consisting of one object is given in Listing 1. Here the geometry is a collection, and the metadata is both an identifier and user-provided properties.

We focus is on three classes of spatial queries:

Containment queries are the most basic primitive in spatial processing and perform a filtering operation on the data. The canonical example is finding all geometries contained within a region, but any filtering query against a defined set of reference objects can be considered as containment.

Aggregation queries are an extension of containment queries and involve some summarisation over the filtered result set. The summary can be numeric, such as the average area of all selected geometries, or spatial, e.g. computing the set-spatial union of all shapes in the set. Multiple aggregations can also be performed simultaneously, as done by `GROUP BY` SQL statements.

Join queries are one of the most expensive operations associated with spatial querying because, in the worst case, every geometry in one dataset must be compared with every geometry in another. To reduce the number of pairs of geometries for comparison and to parallelise the computation, it is common to divide the shapes into *spatial partitions* [48, 24]. Each partition contains a subset of the dataset within some defined area, and disjoint partitions can thus be processed in parallel. Partitioning allows join processing to scale to multiple CPU cores, but introduces an additional partitioning step.

2.2 Scalability challenges

The wide availability of always-connected, location-aware mobile devices is causing a massive growth in the quantity of spatial data being generated and stored [63, 61]. Crowd-sourced mapping and behavioural data has become mainstream for uses such as navigation [21] and epidemiology [23], with the number of users continuing to grow. Standards are already being developed to support the next generation of sensor and IoT systems in which updates will be continuously streamed [7], thus requiring spatial data processing systems to operate without prior offline data partitioning.

Since CPU clock speeds have remained relatively constant, multicore processing is essential for achieving fast query results [57]. For a low *data-to-query* time, all query processing stages must be parallelised. Most data querying systems now implement some form of parallelism once the data is loaded; few systems, however, consider how data can be loaded in parallel. Loading data in parallel requires the concurrent execution of two operations: *parsing* the source data format and *partitioning* or *indexing*. When the data on disk is not spatially partitioned, distributing the parsing in cluster systems causes significant I/O load as geometries are shuffled from the node responsible for parsing to the nodes with the correct spatial partitions [47]. The same is true when loading data in parallel into a single-node sharded database: here network I/O is replaced by disk I/O when moving geometries to the correct database instance.

Following a NoDB philosophy [2], a scalable spatial querying system should support the input data efficiently no matter what its format is. Many existing formats for spatial data, however, are complex to split and parse. RDBMS with spatial extensions usually handle *well-known text* (WKT) and *well-known binary* (WKB) [42] geometries contained inside comma or tab separated files. This makes splitting the data a case of searching for newlines in the dataset. Public spatial datasets, however, tend to favour more structured data formats, such as XML [43] and JSON [8], in order to simplify interoperability. These semi-structured formats do not have the same ease of splitting as database bulk formats.

As a result, we focus on *GeoJSON* [19] because it encompasses many features that make parallel processing challenging, such as a recursive definition and support for arbitrary metadata. An example fragment is given in Listing 1. Allowing geometries to contain other geometries prevents splitting based on hierarchy; supporting free-form user metadata makes splitting using known strings unsound—without full parsing, it is impossible to decide if the string indicates a hierarchy boundary or is part of the metadata. We also consider WKT- and XML-formatted data to show the flexibility of our approach in handling different input formats.

2.3 Existing solutions

Spatial DBMS. Both relational and NoSQL-style database engines have added spatial query support: *Oracle* [45], *Microsoft SQL-Server* [15] and *IBM DB2* [9] all offer spatial extensions, as well as several open-source engines, including *PostGIS* [25] and *My-SQL* [39]. RDBMS support spatial data through the use of spatial indexes, such as *R-trees* [40] (used by PostGIS) or *Quadtrees* [32] (available in Oracle). These index structures operate on the bounding boxes of geometries, providing an efficient mechanism to select possible matches. Each possible match still needs to be refined by comparing the geometries, a process often taking longer than the index search [54]. There is also the upfront cost of creating the index, which may dominate for regularly updated datasets.

In contrast, the *MonetDB* column store [59] does not have a spatial index but instead stores bounding boxes as a separate column [38]. The rationale is that the sequential access pattern of scanning a column offsets the extra computation due to the lack of an index. MonetDB can parallelise some operations, but spatial joins are sequential and require constructing the entire candidate set in memory. For containment queries, sequentially laid-out bounding boxes can achieve performance comparable to indexes for pre-filtering. This approach fails to scale to large joins because it requires sufficient memory to hold the product of the joined columns.

GeoCouch [18] supports simple filtering primitives for the CouchDB NoSQL datastore [3]. There is no join support, and the performance has so far been shown to be up to 3× worse than PostGIS on a single node [37]. By sharding documents across nodes, it may be possible for GeoCouch to scale, but this has yet to be demonstrated for geospatial data. GeoCouch also has the fewest supported spatial query operators of any of the discussed systems.

Distributed frameworks. The two main implementations for spatial query processing on clusters are *Hadoop-GIS* [1] and *Spatial-Hadoop* [13], which are both based on the Hadoop map/reduce framework [10]. While both systems perform data indexing, Hadoop-GIS assumes that index creation is inexpensive and thus can be done mostly on demand, with only the largest regions indexed statically. while SpatialHadoop is more concerned with up-front indexing. Despite the indexing support of these systems, we show that AT-GIS achieves substantially better performance without prior indexing.

Any system built on top of Hadoop requires that the data is first loaded into the HDFS distributed file system with suitable partitioning. Both systems use spatial partitioning to distribute objects between nodes. Given that an object can be part of multiple spatial partitions, each system must have a way to either eliminate duplicate objects or transfer them between nodes: Hadoop-GIS spends substantial time on boundary handling—objects are duplicated prior to parallel processing and then duplicate results are pruned; Spatial-Hadoop uses more sophisticated indexing structures to avoid this in most cases. While AT-GIS supports partitions similar to Hadoop-GIS, following a *partition-based spatial merge join* strategy [48], its single-node design eliminates expensive network I/O.

Discussion. All of the above approaches for spatial query processing require that the input data is loaded first so that indexing or partitioning can be performed. Once loaded, the data is processed in parallel using the internal data structures to create independent work units. An important requirement for a system with a low data-to-query time, however, is that it operates in parallel from the start, without assuming the existence of any ancillary data structures.

A related requirement is for the data to be left in its original form. A conversion of data into an internal representation requires at least two data passes: one pass to do the conversion, and a second pass to perform the query. For loaded data, a more compact representation may be used, which reduces I/O bandwidth for queries such as joins that require multiple passes of the data on disk; for single-pass queries, however, this may increase I/O bandwidth usage.

Finally, the system should operate on a single node in parallel. For current map/reduce-based cluster systems, significant inter-node communication is necessary during the reduce phase to handle geometries that straddle partition boundaries. By confining computation to a single multi-core node, this deduplication can be handled internally rather than being limited by the network bandwidth.

3. ASSOCIATIVE TRANSDUCERS

To execute spatial queries with a single data pass, we need a computational model that is expressive enough to represent the whole processing pipeline for spatial queries, from the parsing of the raw spatial data to the execution of spatial operators. The model must also be parallelisable and should have bounded internal state.

While *transducers* [36] have primarily been used for lexing and parsing, we introduce a new transducer class, called *associative transducers*, that can express a wide range of spatial query operations. Transducers are an inherently sequential model, but we show that, through a combination of *speculation* [41] and the properties of our new transducer class, it becomes possible to construct pipelines of transducers that can execute spatial queries with data parallelism.

First we provide a formal description of associative transducers and show how they support data-parallel operations (§3.1) while maintaining the property of compositionality required to construct complex spatial query processing pipelines (§3.2). After that, we discuss the specific types of transducers needed to support spatial querying (§3.3) and how they map to spatial query operators (§3.4). Finally, we introduce *partially-associative transducers*, an optimisation that reduces the overhead of speculation (§3.5).

3.1 Formal description

We assume a transducer T can be represented as a five-tuple $T = (Q, q_0, \Sigma, \Gamma, \delta)$ where Q is the set of states, q_0 is the starting

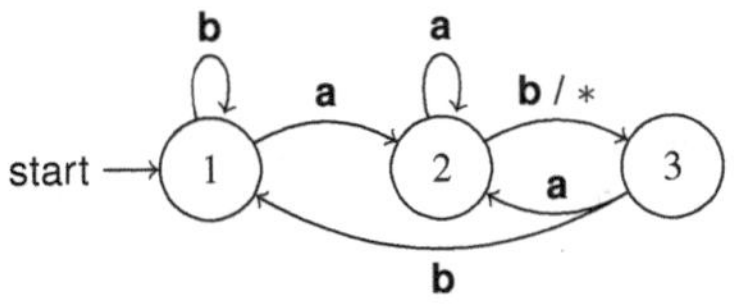

Figure 1: Transducer for matching the string ab

state, Σ is the input alphabet, Γ is the output alphabet, and δ is the transition function. We only consider deterministic transducers, making δ a function of the current state and input symbol. We do not require that Q is finite to ensure that the model can express both aggregations across infinite sets and pushdown transducers.

If we combine the state Q and output tape Γ^* of a regular transducer into a pair $p \in P = (Q \times \Gamma^*)$, we can think of execution as an operator $p \odot s \rightarrow p'$ where s is an input symbol. $\odot$ is defined as performing the state transition of T and updating the output tape. The result of processing T on a string of symbols $s_1, s_2, \cdots, s_i$ is the same as $p_0 \odot s_1 \odot s_2 \cdots \odot s_i$ where $p_0 = (q_0, \varepsilon)$. $\odot$ is clearly non-associative because it cannot operate on two symbols, relying on a left-reduction to be well-formed.

An *associative transducer* (AT), denoted as T', is a generic construction over T to support associative operations. We wish to be able to define a function $\otimes$ that has the same semantics as $\odot$ but supports associative reduction. We define ATs as having *fragments*, rather than states. A fragment f' contains a *state mapping relation* $q' \in Q' : [Q \rightarrow Q]$ that maps potential starting states to corresponding finishing states, where Q' is the set of all such relations. A fragment also contains a set of predicated output tapes $o' \in [Q \rightarrow \Gamma^*]$ to store the symbols emitted by the transducer. The predicates are needed because some output symbols may only be emitted for a subset of possible starting states.

The state mapping relation begins as the identity relation. As symbols are processed, each entry in the fragment has its finishing state updated. Merging two fragments results in the composition of the two relations. As the composition of relations is associative, the action of the AT is also associative.

Using these definitions, we can now define an operator $\bigcirc$:

$$(q', o') \bigcirc s_i \rightarrow \left(\begin{array}{l} \{(q_i, q^*) \quad | \, (q_i, q_f) \in q' \text{ and } q^* = \delta_Q(q_f, s_i)\}, \\ \{(q_i, o : o^*) \, | \, (q_i, o) \in o' \text{ and } (q_i, q_f) \in q' \text{ and} \\ \qquad o = \delta_\Gamma(q_f, s_i)\} \end{array} \right)$$

where : is string concatenation, and δ_Q and δ_Γ are defined such that $\delta(q, s_i) = (\delta_Q(q, s_i), \delta_\Gamma(q, s_i))$.

We now transform each symbol in the input into a fragment independently. We also define a function $\otimes$ to merge fragments:

$$(q'_1, o'_1) \otimes (q'_2, o'_2) \rightarrow \left(\begin{array}{l} q'_1 \circ q'_2, \\ \{(q_s, o_1 : o_2) \, | \, (q_s, o_1) \in o'_1 \text{and} \\ \qquad (q_s, o_2) \in q \circ o'_2\} \end{array} \right)$$

where $\circ$ is relation composition. As this function depends only on relation composition and string concatenation, which are both associative operations, the resulting merge function is also associative.

Rather than two relations, the fragment can be considered equivalently as a *fragment function*, which takes a starting state and returns the corresponding finishing state and output tape. Using this model, we can find efficient ways to represent the fragment function other than storing the relations directly (see §3.3).

Example (Matching transducer): Consider the simple string transducer in Fig. 1 that outputs $\star$ each time the string ab is seen. To operate on the string abab, we split the string into individual symbols and construct execution pairs for each one:

Input	a	b	a	b
Fragment	$\{1,2,3\} \rightarrow 2$	$\{1,3\} \rightarrow 1$ $\{2\} \rightarrow 3$	$\{1,2,3\} \rightarrow 2$	$\{1,3\} \rightarrow 1$ $\{2\} \rightarrow 3$
Output		$\{2\} \rightarrow \star$		$\{2\} \rightarrow \star$

The symbol b results in an execution pair that outputs a single $\star$ if the actual starting state turns out to be 2, but not if the starting state was 1 or 3. The next step is to combine the pairs associatively:

Input	ab	ab
Fragment	$\{1,2,3\} \rightarrow 3$	$\{1,2,3\} \rightarrow 3$
Output	$\{1,2,3\} \rightarrow \star$	$\{1,2,3\} \rightarrow \star$

These intermediate results show the property of *convergence*: the number of distinct finishing states in the relation decreases as data is processed. Since the transducer is deterministic, the number of distinct finishing states in a fragment cannot increase.

The final step is to merge the remaining two execution pairs to compute that, regardless of the starting state, the finishing state is 3, with $\star\star$ on the output tape.

3.2 Composition and parallel execution

By storing fragments for the next transducer in a pipeline, rather than the output tape, we can compose multiple ATs. We observe that the string concatenation operator : can be replaced by any associative operator $\otimes$ without invalidating the transformation. When two ATs are combined, the first transducer now stores a predicated set of fragments from the second transducer, rather than the output tapes. This model can be extended to a pipeline of arbitrary length.

One possible way of parallelising a pipeline would be to execute each stage concurrently, but this would limit the degree of parallelism to the number of transducers in the pipeline and require synchronisation to pass data between them. Instead, the pipeline can be executed in a *data-parallel* fashion, constructing fragments independently for blocks of data that can then be merged together. This provides greater parallelism, which is better suited to achieve scalable query processing with many CPU cores.

Example (Counting transducer): Building on the previous example, to count the number of $\star$ symbols on the tape, we can construct a simple counting transducer with $Q = \mathbb{N}$, which increments when a $\star$ is seen as input. We then compose the two transducers to count the occurrences of ab. Using the same string and the matching transducer as before, we can see below that, under b, a 1 is contained in the predicated list and a 0, otherwise.

Input	a	b	a	b
Fragment	$\{1,2,3\} \rightarrow 2$	$\{1,3\} \rightarrow 1$ $\{2\} \rightarrow 3$	$\{1,2,3\} \rightarrow 2$	$\{1,3\} \rightarrow 1$ $\{2\} \rightarrow 3$
Output	$\{1,2,3\} \rightarrow 0$	$\{1,3\} \rightarrow 0$ $\{2\} \rightarrow 1$	$\{1,2,3\} \rightarrow 0$	$\{1,3\} \rightarrow 0$ $\{2\} \rightarrow 1$

The execution proceeds analogously to the previous example except that, instead of concatenation, we add the fragments of the counting transducer. The result is that, regardless of the starting state, the finishing state of the matching transducer is 3, with 2 as the fragment of the counting transducer.

3.3 Spatial query processing

Next we explore efficient implementations of the fragment function for different types of transducers needed for spatial query processing. We identify five types of ATs that can be mapped to operations when processing spatial data:

1. *finite state transducers* for lexing the input data;
2. *deterministic pushdown transducers* for extracting the data and metadata from lexed symbols;
3. *stateless transducers* for conversions on points or aggregates;
4. *aggregation transducers* for summarising data; and
5. *periodically flushing transducers* for aggregating geometries.

We look at each in turn, grouping the conceptually similar finite and pushdown transducers together along with the stateless and aggregation transducers. To illustrate the use for each type of trans-

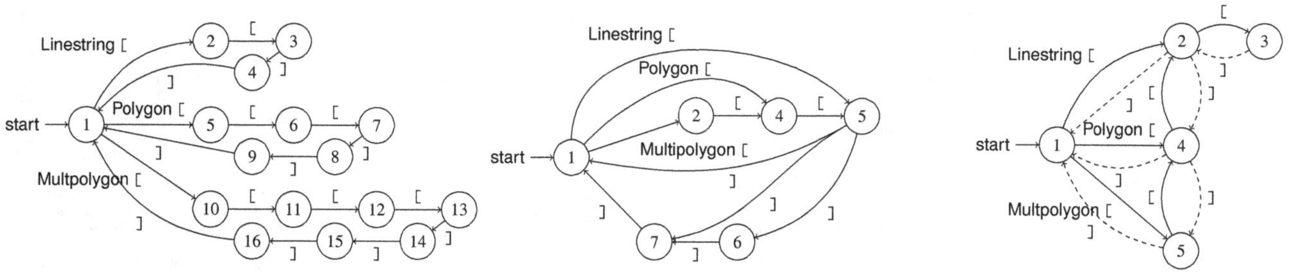

(a) Deterministic transducer (b) Non-deterministic transducer (c) Pushdown transducer

Figure 2: Three potential automata for parsing geometries

ducer, as a running example, we consider all of the stages required to divide the shapes from GeoJSON data into spatial partitions.

Finite and pushdown transducers can extract spatial data from a raw format. Finite transducers have an explicit associative form: each fragment contains the state mapping relation from all possible starting states to the corresponding finishing states and a set of output tapes predicated by the starting states. When an input symbol is processed, each entry in the relation is updated, and output symbols are appended to the output tapes.

A natural way to express these relations are as $N \times N$ binary matrices, where N is the number of states in the transducer. For a small number of states, the transitive closure under multiplication can be precomputed as a set of lookup tables. This is similar to the approach used by *simultaneous finite automata* [56] but with the addition of an output tape.

Each output tape in the fragment has a predicated set of starting states represented by a vector. By considering all output tapes formed as a vector, a matrix can be used to associate starting states with corresponding output states. The complete fragment thus holds a state relation mapping matrix, an output matrix and a vector of output tapes. This representation allows for tapes to be shared among multiple starting states after convergence was achieved.

All of the relation composition operations needed to merge execution pairs thus become precomputed matrix multiplications. Merging the output tapes from each pair thus becomes the dominant factor in performing merges. This is mitigated by limiting the number of possible starting states based on the structure of the lexer. For example, in XML, it can be guaranteed that if a block starts with a < character, there are only three possible starting states (comment, `CDATA` or neither); the **,** character in JSON can fulfil a similar purpose. This can only be done without impacting performance if the searched character is common in the input stream [41].

It is possible for the same parsing task to be implemented using different automata models. Fig. 2 shows the transition diagrams of parsers for a simplified geometry format based on GeoJSON. A deterministic finite transducer requires fewer states than either a non-deterministic or a pushdown transducer (Fig. 2a). As the cost of speculation depends on the number of states, and we do not have a formal model for a non-deterministic transducer (Fig. 2b), we choose to implement the parsing of spatial data formats using pushdown transducers (Fig. 2c).

Stateless and aggregation transducers. The stateless (SLT) and aggregation (AGT) families of transducers correspond to the functional *map/filter* and *reduce* primitives found in parallel processing [10, 26]. They are used to support mathematical and spatial transformations and aggregations in spatial queries. We exploit their associativity to provide efficient AT implementations.

A stateless transducer is one for which the set of states Q is a singleton $\perp$, i.e. there is no shared state carried over between input symbols, and each can be processed independently. The transition function δ thus takes the form $\delta(\perp, s) \rightarrow (\perp, p(s))$ where $p : \Sigma \rightarrow \Gamma^*$ is the mapping function. Each input can result in zero or more outputs, giving it the expressive power of both *map* and *filter*. A stateless transducer has a trivial associative form without any state to manage. For example, coordinate space conversion—a common operation in spatial querying—can be done by stateless transducers.

Example (Point parser): A point parser is a transducer that takes streams of point offsets and produces a stream of point values. It is used to isolate the structural parsing, performed by finite and pushdown transducers, from handling floating point values. It is stateless as each offset can be parsed into a point value independently, with no dependencies between adjacent symbols in the input data.

Aggregation transducers perform some reduction over the input data without producing output. The reduction function combines the internal state of the transducer with the input value to produce the new internal state. More formally, an aggregation transducer has a transition function $\delta(q, s) \rightarrow (a(q, t(s)), \varepsilon)$ where the *transformation function* $t : \Sigma \rightarrow Q$ converts each input symbol into a state, and an *aggregation function* $a : Q \times Q \rightarrow Q$ combines states.

An efficient AT relies on the properties of the aggregation function: if the function is associative, the transformation only needs to store one copy of the in-order state to reconstruct the whole state relation. If the aggregation function is not associative, another approach is needed, typically buffering until the aggregation can be run in-order. Aggregations can be numeric, e.g. when computing the sum of values, or spatial, e.g. when computing the set-theoretic union of a list of shapes.

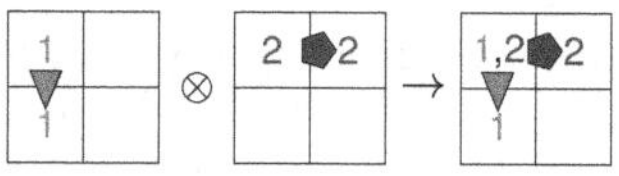

Figure 3: Partitioning expressed as an associative operation

Example (Partition): Spatial partitioning is an example of an operation that can be performed by an aggregation transducer. The state of the transducer contains a set of spatial partitions and the identifiers of the contained objects. Fig. 3 shows two partitions, each containing a single object numbered 1 and 2. The associative merge operation ($\otimes$) concatenates the list of objects in each partition.

Periodically flushing transducers are a hybrid of stateless and aggregation transducers and can perform aggregations over subsets of the input stream, e.g. computing a bounding box for each geometry.

The set of input symbols can be divided into two disjoint sets: P for processing symbols and F for flushing symbols. When a flushing symbol is received, zero or more output symbols are emitted, and the internal state resets to the starting state q_0; when a processing symbol is received, the internal state is updated but no symbols are output. Thus periodically flushing transducers perform aggregations on strings of processing symbols demarcated by flushing symbols. The processing symbols are typically points or edges, and the flushing symbols are markers for geometry boundaries.

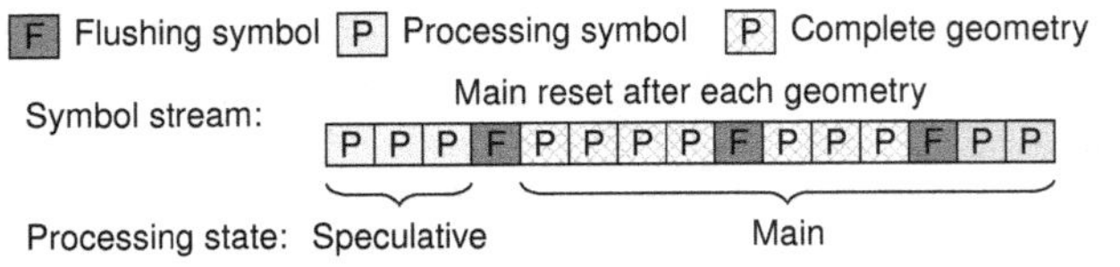

Figure 4: Data processing with a periodically flushing transducer

As with aggregation transducers, the most efficient transformations into an associative form arise when the aggregation function is itself associative. In this case, the fragment of an AT can be represented using two copies of the in-order state: the *speculative* and *main* states. Fig. 4 shows the speculative state that is used to aggregate the processing symbols before the first flushing symbol, while the main state is used for all input symbols from that point on. An additional bit is needed to record if at least one flushing symbol was seen and hence which copy of the state should be used for processing the next input symbol. Only one output tape is needed to store the results of the main state. The output from the speculative state is not determined until merging.

To merge two associative fragments, the main state at the end of the first must be merged with the speculative state at the beginning of the second. The result is a new aggregation that must be inserted into the output tape between the tapes of the two merged fragments. *Example (Polygon bounding):* A periodically flushing transducer can compute the master bounding rectangles (MBRs) of geometries. The processing symbols are the point values, and the flushing symbols are the special values marking the boundaries of geometries. MBR computation from a list of points is an associative operation as each point can be considered as its own bounding box, and an associative operation computes the union of the boxes. Merging can similarly be performed by computing the spatial union of the two partial states being merged.

3.4 Support for spatial operators

Next we consider a set of spatial operators and describe how each can be expressed as an AT. We first explain the case in which operators are used as a predicate with a single or small set of objects provided as a query parameter, and then describe how the operators can be used for joins. Finally, we address extensions, as used by PostGIS and other spatial DBMS, to provide geometry aggregation.

We focus on the spatial operators provided by the SQL option of the *Open Geospatial Consortium Simple Feature Access Specification* [42] when comparing polygons to polygons, as listed in Table 1. We split the operators into three categories: operators that (i) calculate some property on a single geometry; (ii) spatially relate two geometries; and (iii) represent set-theoretic operations on one or more geometries. Table 1 shows the mapping into transducers when one of the operands is a query parameter. We consider the case in which operators are used in a join query separately.

For each operator, we state the input and output types of the corresponding transducer as well as the type of any internal state. The class of each generated transducer (from §3.3) is also listed along with the corresponding associativity available. The most flexible form of associativity is "in shape", which allows a single shape to be distributed; "between shapes" requires that each shape is allocated to a single thread, potentially reducing parallelism.

The first category of operators contains those that operate on a single geometry to perform some form of aggregation. With the exception of `ST_IsSimple` and `ST_Boundary`, both of which must consider the geometry in its entirety, the others can be implemented as PFTs, constructing a partial aggregation and merging the two. We have already explored the case of bounding box calculation as part of the running example in the previous section.

Spatial operator	*Input*	*Output*	*Processing state*	*Transducer class*	*Associativity*
		(i) Single geometry properties			
`ST_IsEmpty`	Points	Bool	Bool	PFT	In shape
`ST_IsSimple`	Shapes	Bool	None	SLT	Between shapes
`ST_Envelope`	Edges	Boxes	Box	PFT	In shape
`ST_ConvexHull`	Points	Shapes	Shape	PFT	In shape
`ST_Boundary`	Shapes	Shapes	None	SLT	Between shapes
		(ii) Geometry relations			
`ST_Disjoint`	Edges	Bools	Bool×Bool	PFT	In shape
`ST_Intersects`	Edges	Bools	Bool×Bool	PFT	In shape
`ST_Touches`	Edges	Bools	Bool	PFT	In shape
`ST_Crosses`	Edges	Bools	Bool	PFT	In shape
`ST_Within`	Edges	Bools	Bool×Bool	PFT	In shape
`ST_Contains`	Edges	Bools	Bool×Bool	PFT	In shape
`ST_Overlaps`	Edges	Bools	Bool×Bool	PFT	In shape
`ST_Relate`	Edges	Relations	Relation	PFT	In shape
`ST_Distance`	Edges	Floats	Float	PFT	In shape
		(iii) Set-theoretic operations			
`ST_Intersection`	Shapes	Shapes	None	SLT	Between shapes
`ST_Difference`	Shapes	Shapes	None	SLT	Between shapes
`ST_Union`	Shapes	Shapes	None	SLT	Between shapes
`ST_SymDifference`	Shapes	Shapes	None	SLT	Between shapes
`ST_Buffer`	Shapes	Shapes	None	SLT	Between shapes

Table 1: Representation of spatial operators as ATs

The second category includes all those operations that perform some spatial relation. When comparing against a known reference set, these operators can be executed using an algorithm that compares each edge in turn. Using `ST_Intersects` as an example, we use an edge testing algorithm that compares each incoming edge with the edges in the reference set. Any crossing means that the geometry intersects with the reference. To handle the case in which one polygon is entirely inside another, we perform two point-in-polygon tests, one comparing the first point in the geometry against the reference set and the second comparing an arbitrary point in the reference set against the geometry. If either of these two tests matches, the geometries are intersecting.

The final category includes set-theoretic operations on shapes. As such operations require processing the entire polygon as a single entity rather than each point or edge individually, we cannot use a PFT. Instead we use transducers that operate on a stream of polygons as stateless transducers when each operation is independent, e.g. using `ST_Buffer` on a stream or `ST_Difference` on a stream of joined pairs or with a reference object. Alternatively, when the operator is used as an aggregation across a column, e.g. using `ST_Union` on a large set of geometries, we can take advantage of the associativity of set operations to use an aggregation transducer.

When a spatial predicate is used for a join between two large sets of geometries, the model used for a small reference set ceases to be effective, requiring an alternative approach. Typically some version of a plane or line-sweep algorithm can be used. Our transducer model is not a good fit for a join between two data streams, so we wrap the join into a transducer that takes sets of shapes as input and emits joined pairs as the output stream. This permits the use of transducer operations before and after the join, while having the performance of existing parallel joins. We use a *partition-based spatial merge join* [48] to perform all spatial joins between two datasets, using transducers for the initial partitioning.

3.5 Partially associative transducers

Depending on the input data, it may be possible to relax the requirement for full associativity to reduce speculation. *Partially-associative transducers* are an optimisation when the data can be split in such a way that the state at the start of a block is known. This is common in many spatial data formats, even recursive ones such as GeoJSON, if the complete schema is known in advance.

The idea for this optimisation is to introduce some logic into the splitting of the data into blocks such that block boundaries occur only at locations that result in known states: in comma- or tab-separated text files with no escaping, this is typically the end of

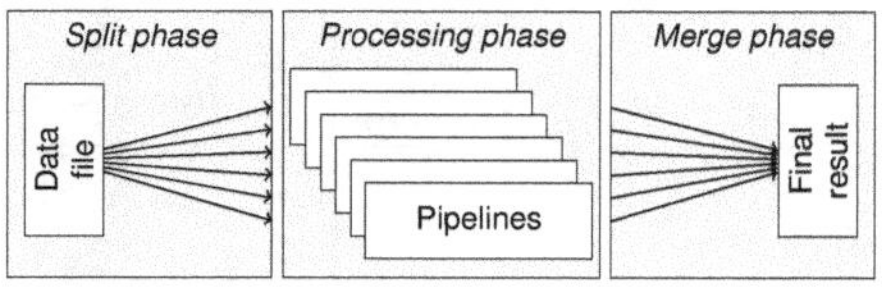

Figure 5: Phases of pipeline execution in AT-GIS

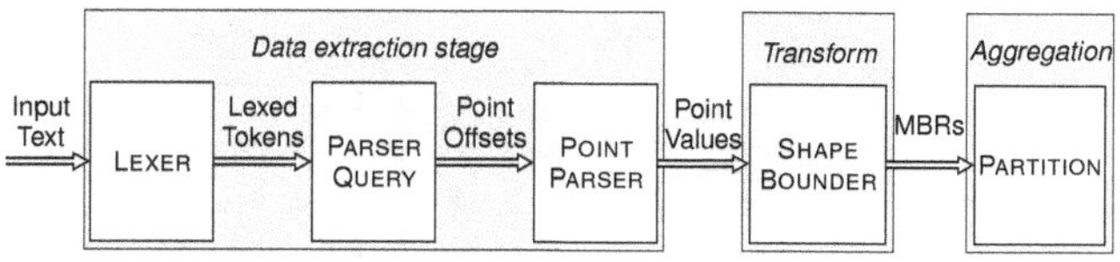

Figure 6: Pipeline for shape partitioning in a textual data format

lines; in XML or JSON, it is commonly some tag that only appears at a given point in the hierarchy and that can be used to establish the state of the parser for the block.

In some cases, it may be possible for the tag to appear at an unexpected location due to a free-form field in the input. A partially-associative transducer may then temporarily process the data incorrectly, but the inconsistency will be caught during a subsequent merge. The data would then have to be reprocessed, but it would not affect the correctness of the final result.

Example (GeoJSON parsing): For GeoJSON, the parse and querying stages can be converted into a partially-associative form by exploiting the object type field that appears within each object. If object boundaries can be found, the lexer and parser can be started in a known state, permitting the use of an optimised, off-the-shelf library without speculation. For example, it is possible to use a regular expression to search for the string `"type":"Feature"`, as seen on line 3 in Listing 1. Since the tag is not necessarily the start of an object, a parser can find the boundaries of the object.

4. AT-GIS DESIGN

In this section, we describe how AT-GIS uses associative transducers (ATs) to create parallel processing pipelines for the execution of spatial queries. First we introduce its processing model (§4.1) and present the pipelines for different query types (§4.2), explaining their physical query plans, how stages are decomposed into ATs and how the system is implemented (§4.3). After that, we focus on each pipeline stage in turn, exploring the trade-offs for performance optimisation (§4.4). We finish with a discussion of spatial joins and how they use multiple pipelines (§4.5).

4.1 Overview

AT-GIS executes spatial queries by translating a *physical query plan* into *pipelines* of transducers. The physical plan takes the form of a dataflow representation of the query [53] in which the majority of spatial operators are compiled into a single pipeline. Joins require multiple pipelines because they rely on barriers.

The construction of the physical query plan follows past work on optimising pipelined parallel query execution [6]. AT-GIS assumes a tree-shaped dataflow graph in which each spatial operator is represented by a node; edges denote the objects transfered between operators. AT-GIS supports a hierarchy of four object types, with *points* being the lowest level, followed by *edges*, *rings* and *polygons*. In general, edges should be typed with the lowest-level object supported by both sides—the lower the level, the greater the opportunity for parallelism. All but conditional and join operators have a single input and output edge.

AT-GIS then constructs a pipeline from each linear section of the dataflow graph. It makes special consideration for conditional operators (§4.4.2) to allow them to form part of a linear pipeline in spite of them not being linear. Once the pipelines have been defined, AT-GIS compiles them using an optimising compiler to reduce the overhead of the abstraction between stages.

As shown in Fig. 5, the execution of pipelines involves three *phases*: *split*, *processing* and *merge*. The split phase divides the input data into blocks. Data splitting may require incrementing a pointer (for fully-associative transducers) or executing a regular expression and lightweight parsing (for partially-associative transducers). After a data block is formed, it is placed in a work queue for the processing phase. The processing phase performs the majority of the computation by passing blocks from the work queue through the pipeline. As ATs make the tasks independent, it can be scaled to many parallel threads. The merge phase combines all of the partial results from the processing phase to compute the final query result. While the first two phases can run concurrently to reduce latency, the third phase executes only after all blocks are available.

4.2 Spatial query processing pipelines

Fig. 6 shows how a single-pass pipeline can be split into three logical *stages*: (i) parsing of the dataset and extracting the data of interest; (ii) transforming and filtering the data to answer the query; and (iii) aggregating the result. The *parsing/data extraction* stage is responsible for consuming bytes from the input file and outputting a stream of point values. If required by the query, any filtering on the metadata is also handled by this stage. Restricting metadata queries to the first stage ensures that format-specific knowledge is not needed in the rest of the pipeline. The *transformation/filtering* stage encompasses any operations that process individual geometries or points and consists primarily of periodically flushing transducers. Finally, the *aggregation* stage performs any aggregation across all the geometries. In the case of a containment query, the final stage buffers the result for output.

Each object between pipeline stages is tagged with the data offset from which it was created. Offsets are used in two ways: to enable unique identification of points and geometries; and to allow re-parsing of objects in the join pipeline. The type of the objects transfered between the transformation and aggregation stage depends on the nature of the aggregation: spatial aggregations require that the aggregation stage receives all point data, whereas numeric aggregations require only the computed result.

4.3 Pipeline implementation

Each pipeline stage is written as a C++ class template with the template parameter describing the destination for output symbols. Pipelines are thus constructed back to front, starting with the final aggregation transducer before wrapping it with the previous stages.

Using templates to perform composition rather than more commonly seen indirect function calls has two advantages: (i) there are no restrictions on the types of symbols that are passed between stages; and (ii) an optimising compiler can combine stages, using inlining to remove most of the overhead of passing symbols along the pipeline. Inlining also allows for general-purpose optimisations, such as loop unrolling, to be performed across multiple stages.

The disadvantage of a template-based approach is that the pipelines have to be known at compile time. For this reason, AT-GIS generates and compiles a pipeline prior to executing the query, creating an executable that can then be run on the raw data. While compiling templated C++ code adds some overhead compared to a traditional database engine, we show in §5.1 that the total query execution time is still much reduced compared to existing systems.

4.4 Pipeline stages

Next we describe the details of each stage. Although the structure of the pipeline is fixed for a given query, there are possible data- and query-dependent optimisations within each stage.

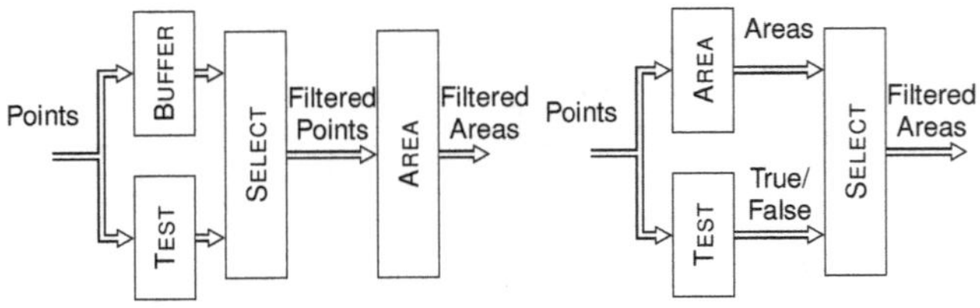

(a) Buffered (b) Streaming

Figure 7: Pipelines for selecting geometries

(1) Parsing/data extraction stage. This stage converts the input format into a list of spatial primitives suitable for the rest of the pipeline. AT-GIS supports spatial queries over GeoJSON, WKT and OpenStreetMap XML data. WKT is the most straightforward to support because it is mostly a non-nested (except for `GeometryCollections`) text-based format with all of the point data available inside the shape objects. GeoJSON adds an extra layer of complexity by allowing arbitrarily formatted metadata within the object. It thus needs a push-down parser to understand the format correctly.

OpenStreetMap XML is the most complex format to support because it separates the data into multiple sections: first it lists all the *nodes* that link a numeric identifier to a point in space; followed by the *ways* that relate multiple nodes; and finally *relations* that link nodes and ways to describe complex polygons. AT-GIS handles the separation of point and polygon data by keeping a temporary table of all points and ways on disk, which is constructed during the first data pass. When ways and relations are processed in subsequent passes, the need to re-parse the data from source is reduced.

In general, the parsing stage may use fully- or partially-associative transducers. As we show in §5.5, the type of transducer that achieves the highest throughput depends on properties of the data. Since this is not known in advance, AT-GIS leaves the selection to the user.

With partially-associative transducers, the parsing stage consists of a wrapper around an off-the-shelf parser, which inputs well-formed data blocks and outputs the stream of points, potentially filtered by some metadata. Where possible, AT-GIS uses streaming parsers, e.g. using the SAX API [55], to limit memory usage.

Fully-associative parsers are constructed from the finite and push-down transducers. For all of the supported input formats, i.e. GeoJSON, WKT and XML, AT-GIS separates the lexing and parsing and employs transducers suited for each task.

Lexing is handled by finite transducers optimised for small transition tables. As a transition must be performed after each byte, precomputation is used for all the transition tables, which reduces the overhead of the associative construction. As explained in §3.3, we use pushdown transducers to perform parsing and data extraction to reduce the required speculation.

In addition to extracting geometry and point offsets, any filtering on the accompanying metadata is also compiled into the parsing automaton. As pushdown transducers can handle XPath-style queries [49], AT-GIS supports a similar query language for JSON that filters on the structure or value of fields in the metadata.

In typical scenarios, such as our running partitioning example, the execution time of the pipeline is dominated by the parsing/data extraction stage. While exact numbers are difficult to obtain because the optimising compiler merges stages together, at least 90% of the CPU time is spent in this stage.

(2) Transformation/filtering stage. The second pipeline stage consists of periodically-flushing transducers that wrap standard geometric algorithms. AT-GIS converts between streams of edges and points to match the requirements of the algorithms. Most supported algorithms are edge-centric, such as perimeter and area calculations, and only a small number, e.g. MBR calculations, are point-centric.

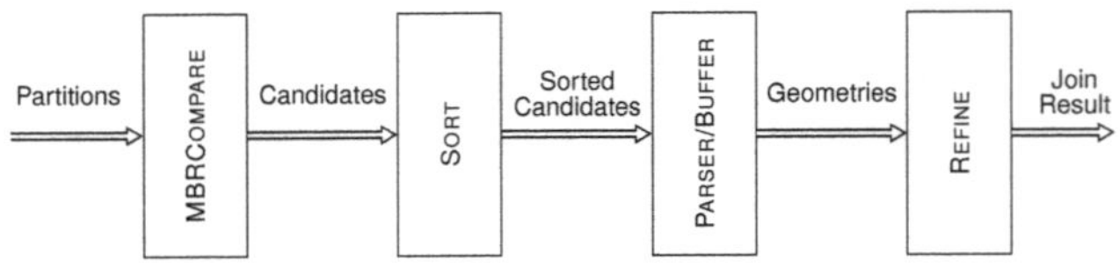

Figure 8: Join pipeline

An operation that conflicts with the requirement to perform the least amount of buffering is selecting geometries for which the point data is required later in the pipeline. An example is finding the areas of all geometries within a defined region. AT-GIS has two ways to construct a pipeline for such queries, trading off buffering against redundant computation: (i) in a buffered approach (see Fig. 7a), the geometry is stored until the result of the inclusion test is known; and (ii) in a streaming approach (see Fig. 7b), the area is computed at the same time as when the test is performed.

The most effective approach depends on the query selectivity, the expected size of the largest geometries, and the cost of the aggregation. For non-selective queries, all of the computation is necessary, so the additional buffering only adds memory overhead. For highly-selective queries, the cost of unnecessary computation outweighs the buffering overhead. We explore these trade-offs in §5.4.

(3) Aggregation and partitioning stage. The final stage in the single-pass pipeline performs aggregation. While required for aggregation queries, it is also used for containment queries to store the output of the transformation stage before returning the result.

While AT-GIS supports both spatial and numerical aggregation, it only maps numerical aggregation directly into the pipeline. Numerical aggregation consists of operations such as `sum` and `avg`, which can be mapped easily to an associative form. Spatial aggregations are operations such as spatial unions for which we have not developed a suitable associative form—AT-GIS executes them as a separate sequential phase after the executation of the pipeline.

A special form of aggregation is *partitioning*, which terminates the first pipeline when performing a spatial join. By having to concatenate multiple lists during a merge, partitioning does not have the constant-time merge property of numerical aggregations.

AT-GIS supports two data structures for partitions: arrays and linked lists. Arrays have better memory locality and a lower memory footprint at the expense of linear-time merging; linked lists achieve constant-time merging but with slower access due to cache-unfriendly patterns. To reduce the cost of merging many partitions, it is possible to perform the partitioning as a sequential step after the processing pipeline. This requires that only one list or array is merged for each block, rather than one per partition and block.

An important parameter to choose is the number of partitions. It determines the available parallelism in later processing, so a large number is desirable to improve e.g. join performance. Many partitions, however, increase the merging cost of the results of the first stage and lead to unnecessary computation when more geometries straddle partition boundaries. In §5.6, we explore this parameter choice with a large, real-world dataset.

4.5 Spatial joins

When a spatial join is part of a query, AT-GIS constructs a second pipeline that consumes partitions and emits the joined geometries. This pipeline uses a set of specialised transducers to implemented a PBSM join algorithm [48]. This permits the join to execute along-side other transducers if further selection or aggregation is needed. Since the partitions are non-disjoint, there is a possibility of duplicate results in the output, which are removed by a sequential step prior to returning the query result.

The PBSM join is realised as a *join pipeline* of ATs, operating on the spatial partitions (see Fig. 8). The partition has two lists of

Name	*Description*	*Size (GB)*	*Shapes (1000s)*
OSM-X	OpenStreetMap XML	592	187,560
OSM-G	OpenStreetMap GeoJSON	63.3	187,560
OSM-W	OpenStreetMap WKT	41.0	187,560
OSM-10G	OpenStreetMap replicated	633	1,875,600
Synth$_{n,\sigma}$	Synthetic dataset	10.0	$n/1000$

Table 2: Spatial datasets used for evaluation

MBRs and the offset in the original data of the corresponding object. Storing the offsets means that objects can be re-parsed on demand, avoiding the need to keep the entire dataset in memory.

The join pipeline first finds all MBR intersections in a partition (MBR COMPARE transducer) and passes a stream of potentially matching candidates to the SORT transducer. SORT buffers the stream until a threshold is reached, and then sorts the objects by location in the input data. The aim is to position candidates involving the same objects adjacently so that the time that objects remain in memory is bounded. As adjacency can only be achieved for one of the two sets of objects being joined, AT-GIS makes the largest set adjacent. The PARSER/BUFFER transducer re-parses objects to construct the full geometry for refinement. A hash map stores objects in the non-adjacent stream to limit repeated parsing. Once a block is processed, the hash map is cleared. Finally, the REFINE transducer performs the join test, such as geometry intersection.

Storing entire objects in memory can potentially exhaust available resources. By adjusting the threshold in SORT, the number of stored objects can be reduced. While reducing memory usage, some objects may have to be read several times when the entire partition cannot be processed as a single sorted block.

As objects can appear in multiple spatial partitions, duplicate matches may be part of the final result. To mitigate this, after the join pipeline has finished, AT-GIS sorts the result by the offsets of both objects joined and eliminates duplicates.

If additional processing is required on the joined objects, this can either be added to the end of the join pipeline or as a separate phase after duplicate elimination. As objects are only retained in memory while needed by the pipeline, running algorithms as a separate stage may require objects to be re-parsed. Executing computation inside the pipeline provides immediate access to the joined objects at the expense of potentially encountering duplicate results, which need to be removed.

5. EVALUATION

We evaluate AT-GIS experimentally: we compare its performance against other approaches (§5.1) and use synthetic and real-world datasets to explore scalability (§5.2), different data formats (§5.3), different filtering pipelines (§5.4), dataset skew (§5.5) and partitioning options (§5.6).

Datasets. Table 2 summarises our datasets. We use the OpenStreetMap dataset [44], retrieved on May 18, 2015. This is a large real-world dataset that is widely used to benchmark spatial query processing. In addition to the orignal XML file (OSM-X), we prepare two additional versions: a GeoJSON-formatted one (OSM-G) and a WKT-formatted one (OSM-W), which is used for loading into PostGIS, MonetDB and SpatialHadoop. We also create a version in a proprietary format of a commercial DBMS. In addition to the geometry, we add an object `id` into each object as metadata.

To evaluate scalability as the data sizes grow beyond the available memory, we create a larger dataset (OSM-10G) by replicating the OpenStreetMap dataset 10 times. For each replication, the geometries are kept the same but the `id` is changed to ensure uniqueness.

We also generate a synthetic dataset (Synth) that includes polygons and multi-polygons with the number of edges distributed according to a log-normal distribution. Two parameters control the number of geometries and the σ value of the distribution. The size of the geometries is scaled so that the dataset is 10 GB.

Query	*SQL*
Containment	`SELECT * FROM data WHERE ST_Intersects(geom, ref)`
Aggregation	`SELECT ST_Area(geom), ST_Perimeter(geom) WHERE ST_Intersects(geom, ref)`
Join	`SELECT * FROM data d1, data d2 WHERE d1.id < threshold AND d1.2 > threshold AND ST_Intersects(d1.geom, d2.geom)`
Combined	`SELECT ST_Area(ST_Union(d1.geom, d2.geom)) FROM data d1, data d2 WHERE ST_Perimeter(d1.geom) > t1 AND ST_Perimeter(d2.geom) < t2 AND ST_Intersects(d1.geom, d2.geom)`

Table 3: Spatial SQL queries used for evaluation

Queries. We use four types of spatial SQL queries, as shown in Table 3: a *containment* query that selects all polygons contained within some bounding box; an *aggregation* query that combines containment with a summary function over all of the matching polygons—in our case, we use the total perimeter and total area; a *join* query for which we split the input data into two disjoint subsets and which finds all intersecting pairs; and, finally, we use a *combined* query to show how AT-GIS handles more complex pipelines consisting of two containment queries to determine the input to a join, followed by an aggregation on the resulting pairs. Experiments with queries that use other geometries and predicates give similar results.

As our input data is geographic, we perform all of our computation using a spherical coordinate system. We use two methods to calculate the linear distance between points when performing perimeter calculations: by default, we use spherical projection, but, in §5.4, we also employ the more accurate but more expensive computation using Andoyer's algorithm [4].

AT-GIS implementation. Our prototype is implemented in C++. All geometric operations use the `Boost::Geometry` [17] library, other than the MBR intersection testing, which is hand-written. Aside from the partially-associative JSON parsing, which is done by *RapidJSON* [50], all other transducers are implemented by us. The created AT pipelines for a given query plan are compiled by the GNU g++ compiler. Compilation takes up to 5 seconds, which is negligible compared to the total runtime.

AT-GIS is executed using both fully- and partially-associative transducers to determine the level of optimisation available from reducing speculation: AT-GIS-FAT runs all queries using a fully-associative pipeline with no optimisation; AT-GIS-PAT uses optimised parsers when speculation can be reduced.

System comparisons. We take Hadoop-GIS [1] as an example of a distributed cluster system, which does not use stored indexes beyond the initial partitioning, and SpatialHadoop [13] as an index-based solution. We also compare to PostGIS [25], MonetDB [59] and a commercial DBMS with spatial support (DBMS-X) in terms of single-node spatial query engines. The performance results for SpatialHadoop, PostGIS, MonetDB and DBMS-X results are measured on the same machine as AT-GIS; the results for Hadoop-GIS are based on the same dataset and taken from the paper [1].

For MonetDB, the default set-up has one table with one row per object; in PostGIS, the table is manually sharded into 1000 ranged partitions; and DBMS-X uses a 1024-way spatially partitioned table. The table is indexed by the geometry and clustered by the index prior to query execution.

The experiments are performed using both bounding-box (PostGIS-B, MonetDB-B) and full-geometry comparisons (PostGIS-G,

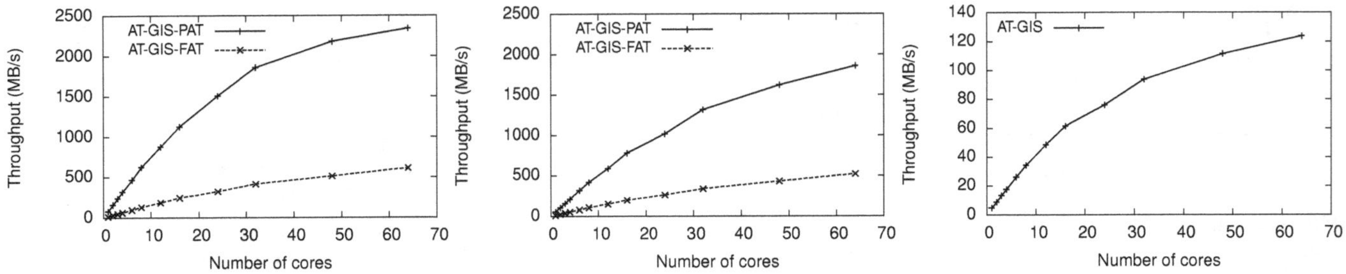

(a) Containment query (b) Aggregation query (c) Join query

Figure 9: Scaling of AT-GIS on the OpenStreetMap dataset

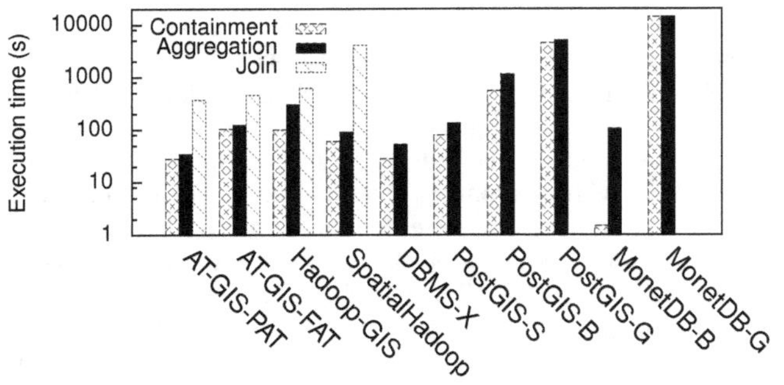

Figure 10: Comparison of query execution times

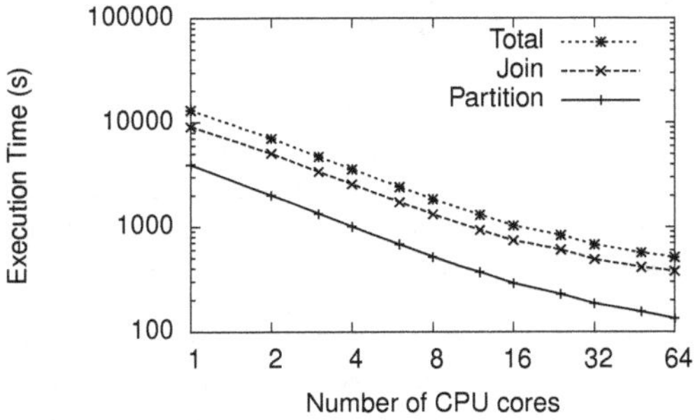

Figure 11: Partition and join query scaling to 64 CPU cores

MonetDB-G). We also manually sharded the PostGIS installation (PostGIS-S). All experiments are repeated and have low variance, which is why we omit error bars.

Experimental set-up. All experiments are performed on a quad-socket, 64-core AMD server with 128 GB RAM. Each CPU has a nominal clock speed of 2.3 GHz, with turbo mode increasing this to 2.9 GHz for small numbers of threads. To limit the effects of I/O bottlenecks, experiments using the OSM-G, OSM-W and Synth datasets read the data from a RAM disk. For experiments using the OSM-10G and OSM-X datasets, we load the data onto an SSD and ensure that the OS file cache is cleared. A second SSD is used to store any temporary data files.

5.1 Query performance

Fig. 10 shows the execution time for three of our queries on different systems.[1] Executing from RAM, AT-GIS-PAT achieves the same query execution time as DBMS-X for the containment query and takes 30% less time for aggregation queries, despite not pre-loading and indexing the data. The results also show the benefit of AT-GIS's efficient pipelining: aggregation takes only 25% longer than containment, outperforming the other comparable systems.

Of all of the RDBMS, MonetDB has the fastest query time for MBR-only queries: using a combination of sequential data access and multithreading, it outperforms the index-based PostGIS and DBMS-X as well as AT-GIS. Once full geometry comparisons are considered, however, the lack of spatial optimisations in MonetDB results in it performing the slowest of all systems.

The results also show that current RDBMS are not optimised for large spatial joins, even with hand-optimised query plans: both PostGIS and DBMS-X do not complete the join within 24 hours, and MonetDB constructs the cross-product of the input prior to joining, requiring over 17 TBs of memory. While executing on a single node, AT-GIS-PAT is $10\times$ faster than SpatialHadoop for the join query due to the latter's cluster management and communication overhead. Hadoop-GIS exhibits the closest join performance to AT-GIS, however, it is deployed on a cluster with more than $3\times$ the number of CPU cores of our server.

For the containment and aggregation queries, the communication overhead of the distributed frameworks becomes even more apparent. Hadoop-GIS requires $3\times$ longer for the aggregation query than for the containment query—the largest disparity of all systems. Taking the number of CPU cores into account, Hadoop-GIS requires $30\times$ the computation resources of AT-GIS-PAT. The upfront indexing of SpatialHadoop improves performance compared to Hadoop-GIS, but it still trails behind AT-GIS on a single node.

The difference between AT-GIS-PAT and AT-GIS-FAT for the containment and aggregation queries shows the dominance of the data parsing cost in terms of the total execution time. Note that the execution times for the other systems do not take the time to load the data into account because this may be amortised over multiple queries. Loading the data can take significant time though, ranging from 30 minutes for MonetDB to over 4 hours for DBMS-X. The data format may also need to be converted prior to loading—no system other than AT-GIS can handle raw OSM XML data.

5.2 Scalability

Next we consider how AT-GIS scales as we vary the number of CPU cores. Figs. 9a and 9b show both full and partial ATs scale to 32 CPU cores for containment and aggregation queries. There are two changes of the gradients in the scaling results: the first occurs after 16 CPU cores and is due to the overclocking of cores with few threads on the AMD CPU; the second change at 32 CPU cores is due to its micro-architecture: the CPU only has 32 FPU units shared between 64 cores. As AT-GIS executes floating-point intensive operations, the scaling beyond 32 cores becomes limited. The contention for FPUs is less of an issue for AT-GIS-FAT because it includes more integer operations when parsing the data.

[1] We do not use the combined query for comparison because the other systems exhibit excessive time or memory requirements when performing the join first.

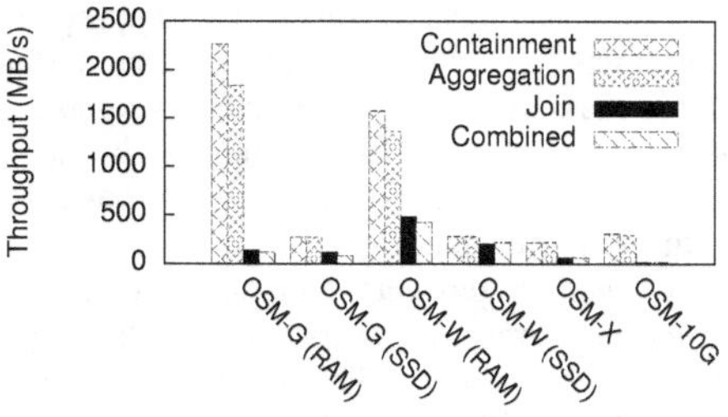

Figure 12: Performance of queries on three data formats

For join queries, Fig. 9c shows that AT-GIS scales linearly to 16 CPU cores followed by two regions (between 16 and 32 cores and greater than 32 cores) when scaling is reduced. The results are only given for AT-GIS-FAT—the parsers used in AT-GIS-PAT do not expose the per-element file offsets required for re-parsing the data in subsequent pipelines.

We explore the join query in more detail in Fig. 11 by splitting the results into the partitioning and the join computation time. It shows that the time required to perform the join dominates the time for the partitioning. The small number of partitions and the high skew between the number of candidate matches checked in each partition makes late finishing threads likely and hard to mitigate. In §5.6, we explore the impact of the number of partitions on the relative performance of the two pipelines used for joining.

5.3 Data size and format

We investigate the ability of AT-GIS to support different input data sizes and formats, in particular, when the dataset is larger than the RAM. We run all four of our queries against each of the OpenStreetMap datasets. As the data sizes on disk vary, and the expected bottleneck is SSD I/O bandwidth, we report throughput in MB/s. Where the dataset is small enough to fit into RAM, we also compare the throughput against streaming from an SSD.

Fig. 12 shows that the GeoJSON format provides superior throughput for single-pass queries because it can use optimised parsers in PAT mode. For join queries, the simpler point structure of WKT allow for faster re-parsing. The SSD results for both GeoJSON and WKT are bound by the device throughput, although OS caching reduces the cost of re-reading data during joins.

OSM-X has the lowest throughput of all single-pass queries due to the large volume of data to be parsed and the need to construct a temporary table. Despite the use of a temporary table, the quantity of data being searched and the random access patterns for finding node values further reduce the performance of joins.

Finally, the replicated dataset (OSM-10G) with single pass-queries executes almost as quickly as the SSD bandwidth allows. It suffers, however, on the join query due to the larger number of comparisons and the need to re-parse data to reduce memory usage.

5.4 Streaming vs. buffered filtering

Next we evaluate the two options for implementing filtering in a pipeline, a *streaming* approach and a *buffered* approach, as described in §4.4. In the streaming approach, the aggregation is performed concurrently with the filter test; in the buffered approach, the geometry is buffered until the result of the filter is known.

We construct a query to output the perimeters of all polygons contained partially or fully by an MBR. By varying the size of the MBR, we can change the query selectivity. The MBR at each size is chosen so that the ratio of MBR size and the number of polygons selected remains constant.

We use two different methods for computing the perimeter to assess how the computational cost affects the trade-off between the two approaches. The first method, shown in Fig. 13a, uses a spherical projection which, while efficient, can be inaccurate for high latitudes. As the ratio of shapes selected becomes less than 25%, the cost of performing the redundant computation becomes greater than that of the memory management for handling the buffers.

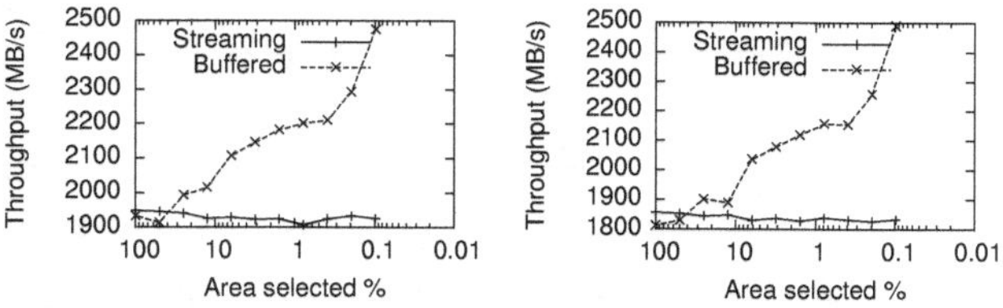

(a) Spherical projection (b) Andoyer's algorithm

Figure 13: Trade-off between different filtering approaches

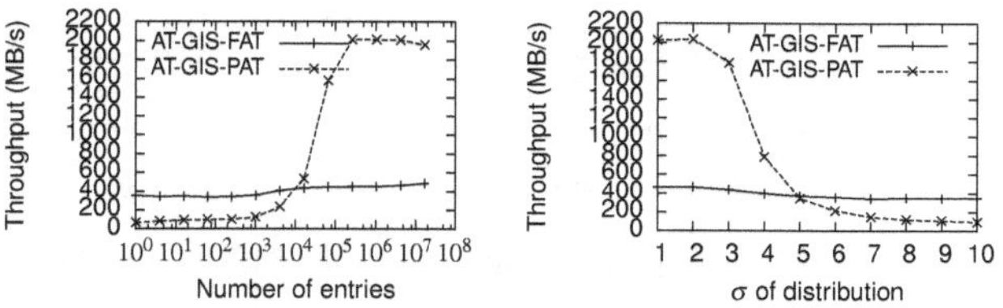

(a) Small numbers of objects (b) Skewed data distribution

Figure 14: Effect of dataset skew

The second method uses Andoyer's algorithm [4], which is more accurate at the expense of more floating-point operations. Fig. 13b shows that the cross-over point between streaming and buffered filtering stays approximately the same, but the absolute throughput of the streaming approach decreases for all selectivities. The buffered approach achieves lower throughput only for low selectivities, which is expected due to the reduced number of calculations when most geometries are rejected by the filter.

5.5 Data skew

In this section, we use a synthetic dataset to explore the limits of partially-associative transducers (AT-GIS-PAT) and the properties of datasets that require fully-associative transducers (AT-GIS-FAT) for parallel operation. We use a synthetic dataset because the objects in the OpenStreetMap dataset are distributed sufficiently, making splitting with partially-associative transducers not a bottleneck. There are two types of datasets that are difficult to split, which we evaluate separately: (i) large datasets consisting of a small number of items; and (ii) datasets with a large skew in polygon complexity.

Fig. 14a shows the processing throughput as we vary the number of objects. For a large number of objects, AT-GIS-PAT can operate around 4× faster than AT-GIS-FAT. This is due to the greater level of optimisation in the off-the-shelf JSON parser and the lack of speculation, leading to less computation. With fewer than 2000 objects, splitting of the dataset becomes the bottleneck in performing the computation—AT-GIS-FAT, which does not need to search for object boundaries, becomes faster.

We also consider the amount of skew in the data distribution. For this, we generate the number of points in each polygon in the synthetic dataset according to a log-normal distribution with a variable σ. For small amounts of skew, the splitting time is negligible, and AT-GIS-PAT performs better, as shown in Fig. 14b. For σ values beyond 5, however, the splitting cost dominates the total processing time, and AT-GIS-FAT provides a lower, more stable processing time.

While AT-GIS-FAT cannot match the speed of the off-the-shelf optimised parser used by AT-GIS-PAT, it performs better with high-skew or low-object-count data. The best of both approaches could be attained by instrumenting the splitting component in partially-associative transducers to fall back to a fully-associative pipeline if the time taken exceeds some threshold.

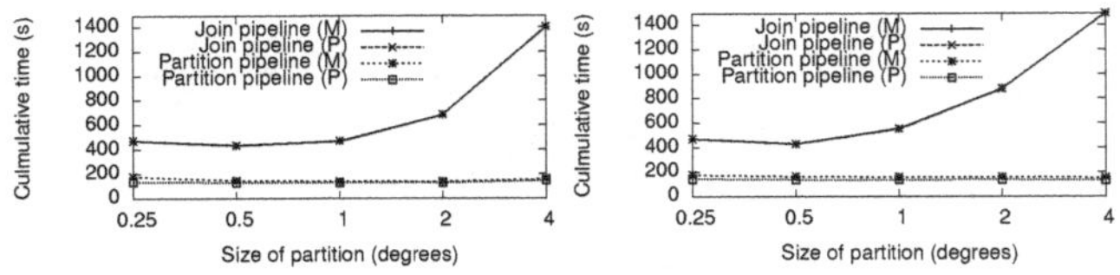

(a) Array/Associative partitioning (b) List/Associative partitioning

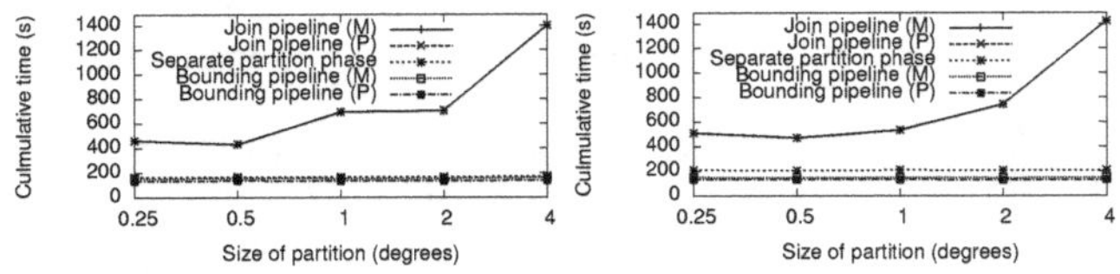

(c) Array/Separate partition phase (d) List/Separate partitioning phase

Figure 15: Effect of partition size, storage format and pipeline

5.6 Partitioning and joins

We also investigate (i) whether to run the partitioner as a separate phase or as part of the parsing associative transducer pipeline; (ii) the effect of a varying number of partitions; and (iii) the effect of the data structures used to store the partitions. These experiments are performed on the OpenStreetMap dataset, and the join query finds all intersecting polygons in subsets of the data.

As joining requires two passes, we separately time the Partition pipeline from Fig. 6 and the Join pipeline from Fig. 8. When we perform partitioning as a separate phase, we remove the PARTITION transducer from the Partition pipeline to leave a Bounding pipeline. We measure the time for the processing (P) and merge (M) phases separately for each pipeline.

We first examine the choice between using associative partitioning and a separate partitioning phase. Comparing Figs. 15a and 15c, as the number of partitions increases, there is a small but noticeable increase in the cost of the partition pipeline merge when the partitioner is associative. As would be expected, the merge time is constant when the partitioner is run non-associatively.

Next we consider the size of the partitions (defined in degrees). As can be seen in Figs. 15a–15d, if the partitions are too large, the work becomes unevenly distributed and late-finishing threads cause the total execution time to rise significantly. For small partitions, the cost of partitioning increases, but this is negligible compared to the total query time. The optimum partition size for the dataset is between 0.5 and 1 degrees—there is no further decrease in join time for smaller partitions. Using a partition size of 1 degree could allow for the first pass to employ integer rather than floating-point arithmetic, potentially resulting in a further performance increase.

Finally we consider the choice between linked lists and arrays for storing elements in a partition. Arrays allow for better data locality at the cost of linear-time merging; linked lists require more computation for each element but offer constant-time merging. By comparing Figs. 15a and 15b, we see that the difference does not affect the partitioning time significantly, but the reduced data locality increases the response time by nearly 200 seconds in the worst case. A similar pattern is revealed when comparing Figs. 15c and 15d.

6. RELATED WORK

In addition to the solutions discussed in §2.3, two areas of related work exist to our approach: *parallel automata* have been proposed for structured data parsing [35, 62, 41]; *streaming spatial processing* performs single-pass processing, but it focuses on spatio-temporal queries rather than the bulk data analytics queries as we do.

Parallel automata. The idea behind executing finite automata in parallel is to split the data into blocks and process each block independently. The most common approach, described by Johnson et al. [28] is, for each block, to construct a mapping between all possible starting states and the corresponding finishing states. Once constructed, these mappings can be combined to compute the final state. Johnson et al. have the goal to save memory when processing streams of network traffic, with packets arriving out-of-order, but they do not optimise performance.

More recently, *simultaneous finite automata* (SFA) [56] perform a static construction to improve performance at the expense of a potentially expensive compilation. The result is near-linear scaling, albeit on a limited set of benchmarks. We use ideas from both Johnson and SFA and extend them to emit symbols for the next stage in a pipeline. In particular, for all the data formats that we consider, the first stage in any pipeline is a lexer, which can be described by a deterministic finite transducer. We also reduce the size of the constructed automaton using format-specific knowledge.

There have also been other approaches to parallel lexing and parsing of structured documents [35]. Early techniques used a sequential data pre-scan to determine suitable break points; this was enhanced by exploiting special strings to guess the correct lexer state [62]. This mirrors our approach for partially associative transducers, which reduce the state space based on knowledge of the input format. Our approach goes further and can use markers in the data to specify the initial state of multiple stages in the pipeline.

Parallel pushdown transducers [41] extend parallel automata to pushdown transducers used in XML querying, with near-linear scaling for a small number of queries. The work does not explore composition, relying on sequential post-processing to perform filtering. Using composition, we present a more powerful model for parallel computation that goes beyond structural queries.

Streaming spatial query processing. There is an increasing interest in using stream processing with spatial datasets, especially with the growth of sensor networks [5, 52] and IoT use cases [11]. For example, *StreamInsight* [29] has spatial primitives to support spatial predicates over complex streams. Isenburg et al. [27] describe a number of streaming algorithms for 3D modelling and use windows to handle models that are larger than memory.

While streaming systems can answer temporal streaming queries, they are not designed for joins across an entire dataset as this is counter to their processing model over unbounded streams. In addition, single-node streaming engines typically focus on query- and not data-parallelism [20, 14]. By processing finite datasets with high parallelism, we designed a more flexible spatial engine without the windowing support of streaming systems. ATs do not presently have an efficient primitive for sliding windows [30].

7. CONCLUSION

We have described AT-GIS, a new single-node system for parallel spatial query processing that is capable of exploiting previously unavailable data parallelism using *associative transducers* (ATs). AT-GIS operates on input formats directly, avoiding expensive conversions, and thus significantly reduces data-to-query time.

AT-GIS shows good scaling behaviour for single-pass spatial queries on un-indexed data, even matching the performance of index-based systems for simple queries. Given the lack of pre-built indices, it can order filtering operations to minimise the cost of joins, while maintaining parallelism through partitioning. However, compared to large cluster-based systems, AT-GIS exhibits worse performance for large joins (>200 million elements) due to its simple partitioning scheme and the limits of single-node computation.

We have focussed on situations in which there is no knowledge of past data. Based on our experience with the XML-formatted data, our future works plans to explore how *incremental* changes in large datasets can be handled efficiently through the storage of intermediate results and lightweight index construction.

8. REFERENCES

[1] A. Aji, F. Wang, H. Vo, R. Lee, Q. Liu, X. Zhang, and J. Saltz. Hadoop-GIS: A high performance spatial data warehousing system over mapreduce. *Proc. VLDB Endow.*, 6(11), 2013.

[2] I. Alagiannis, R. Borovica, M. Branco, S. Idreos, and A. Ailamaki. NoDB: Efficient query execution on raw data files. In *SIGMOD*, 2012.

[3] J. C. Anderson, J. Lehnardt, and N. Slater. *CouchDB: The definitive guide*. O'Reilly, 2010.

[4] H. Andoyer. *Cours D'Astronomie*. 1909.

[5] M. Batty. Big data, smart cities and city planning. *Dialogues in Human Geography*, 3(3), 2013.

[6] P. A. Boncz, M. Zukowski, and N. Nes. MonetDB/X100: Hyper-pipelining query execution. In *CIDR*, volume 5, 2005.

[7] M. Botts, G. Percivall, C. Reed, and J. Davidson. OGC sensor web enablement: Overview and high level architecture. In *GeoSensor networks*. 2008.

[8] T. Bray. The JavaScript Object Notation (JSON) Data Interchange Format. RFC 7159, 2014.

[9] J. R. Davis. IBM's DB2 spatial extender: Managing geo-spatial information within the DBMS. *IBM Corporation*, 1998.

[10] J. Dean and S. Ghemawat. MapReduce: Simplified data processing on large clusters. *Communications of the ACM*, 51(1), 2008.

[11] DEBS Grand Challenge. http://www.debs2015.org/call-grand-challenge.html, 2015.

[12] M. J. Egenhofer. Toward the semantic geospatial web. In *SIGSPATIAL*. ACM, 2002.

[13] A. Eldawy and M. F. Mokbel. SpatialHadoop: A MapReduce framework for spatial data. In *ICDE*, 2015.

[14] Esper Stream Processing Engine. http://www.espertech.com/esper, 2015.

[15] Y. Fang, M. Friedman, G. Nair, M. Rys, and A.-E. Schmid. Spatial indexing in Microsoft SQL Server 2008. In *SIGMOD*, 2008.

[16] G. Garbis, K. Kyzirakos, and M. Koubarakis. Geographica: A benchmark for geospatial RDF stores. In *ISWC*. 2013.

[17] B. Gehrels, B. Lalande, M. Loskot, and A. Wulkiewicz. Boost geometry library, 2014.

[18] GeoCouch. http://github.com/couchbase/geocouch, 2015.

[19] GeoJSON specification. http://geojson.org/geojson-spec.html, 2015.

[20] V. Gulisano, R. Jimenez-Peris, M. Patino-Martinez, C. Soriente, and P. Valduriez. Streamcloud: An elastic and scalable data streaming system. *IEEE TPDS*, 23(12), 2012.

[21] M. Haklay and P. Weber. OpenStreetMap: User-generated street maps. *IEEE Pervasive Computing*, 7(4), 2008.

[22] S. E. Hampton, C. A. Strasser, J. J. Tewksbury, W. K. Gram, A. E. Budden, A. L. Batcheller, C. S. Duke, and J. H. Porter. Big data and the future of ecology. *Frontiers in Ecology and the Environment*, 11(3), 2013.

[23] S. I. Hay, D. B. George, C. L. Moyes, and J. S. Brownstein. Big data opportunities for global infectious disease surveillance. *PLoS Med*, 10(4), 2013.

[24] E. G. Hoel and H. Samet. Data-parallel spatial join algorithms. In *ICPP*, 1994.

[25] S. Holl and H. Plum. PostGIS. *GeoInformatics*, 3(2009), 2009.

[26] M. Isard and Y. Yu. Distributed data-parallel computing using a high-level programming language. In *SIGMOD*, 2009.

[27] M. Isenburg and P. Lindstrom. Streaming meshes. In *IEEE Visualization*, 2005.

[28] T. Johnson, S. Muthukrishnan, and I. Rozenbaum. Monitoring regular expressions on out-of-order streams. In *ICDE*, 2007.

[29] S. J. Kazemitabar, U. Demiryurek, M. Ali, A. Akdogan, and C. Shahabi. Geospatial stream query processing using Microsoft SQL Server StreamInsight. *Proc. VLDB Endow.*, 3(1-2), 2010.

[30] A. Koliousis, M. Weidlich, R. C. Fernandez, A. Wolf, P. Costa, and P. Pietzuch. SABER: Window-based hybrid stream processing for heterogeneous architectures. In *SIGMOD*, 2016.

[31] J. Kong, L. A. Cooper, F. Wang, D. Gutman, J. Gao, C. Chisolm, A. Sharma, T. Pan, E. G. Van Meir, T. M. Kurc, et al. Integrative, multimodal analysis of glioblastoma using TCGA molecular data, pathology images, and clinical outcomes. *IEEE Trans. on Biomedical Engineering*, 58(12), 2011.

[32] R. K. V. Kothuri, S. Ravada, and D. Abugov. Quadtree and R-tree indexes in Oracle Spatial: A comparison using GIS data. In *SIGMOD*, 2002.

[33] J.-G. Lee and M. Kang. Geospatial big data: Challenges and opportunities. *Big Data Research*, 2(2), 2015.

[34] X. Liu, J. Han, et al. Implementing WebGIS on Hadoop: A case study of improving small file I/O performance on HDFS. In *CLUSTER*, 2009.

[35] W. Lu, K. Chiu, and Y. Pan. A parallel approach to XML parsing. In *Grid Computing*, 2006.

[36] A. Meduna. Finite and pushdown transducers. In *Automata and Languages*. 2000.

[37] V. Mische. GeoCouch: A spatial index for CouchDB. *Presentation at FOSS4G*, 2010.

[38] MonetDB GeoSpatial. https://www.monetdb.org/Documentation/Extensions/GIS, 2015.

[39] MySQL 5.0 Reference Manual (11.5. Extensions for Spatial Data). https://dev.mysql.com/doc/refman/5.0/en/, 2015.

[40] T. T. Nguyen. Indexing PostGIS databases and spatial query performance evaluations. *International Journal of Geoinformatics*, 5(3), 2009.

[41] P. Ogden, D. Thomas, and P. Pietzuch. Scalable XML query processing using parallel pushdown transducers. *Proc. VLDB Endow.*, 6(14), 2013.

[42] Open Geospatial Consortium, Simple feature access specification. http://www.opengeospatial.org/standards/sfa, 2015.

[43] OpenDStreetMap XML format. http://wiki.openstreetmap.org/wiki/OSM_XML, 2015.

[44] OpenStreetMap mirror, 2015/05/18. ftp://ftp.spline.de/pub/openstreetmap/planet/2015/planet-150518.osm.bz2, 2015.

[45] Oracle Corporation. Oracle Spatial and Graph: Advanced data management. 2014.

[46] Y. Pan, Y. Zhang, and K. Chiu. Simultaneous transducers for data-parallel XML parsing. In *IPDPS*, 2008.

[47] A. Papadopoulos and Y. Manolopoulos. Parallel bulk-loading of spatial data. *Parallel Computing*, 29(10), 2003.

[48] J. M. Patel and D. J. DeWitt. Partition-based spatial-merge join. In *SIGMOD*, volume 25, 1996.

[49] F. Peng and S. S. Chawathe. XPath queries on streaming data. In *SIGMOD*, 2003.

[50] RapidJSON. https://github.com/miloyip/rapidjson, 2015.

[51] S. Ray, B. Simion, and A. Demke Brown. Jackpine: A benchmark to evaluate spatial database performance. In *ICDE*, 2011.

[52] S. Shekhar, V. Gunturi, M. R. Evans, and K. Yang. Spatial big-data challenges intersecting mobility and cloud computing. In *MobiDE*, 2012.

[53] A. Silberschatz, H. Korth, and S. Sudarshan. *Database systems concepts*. McGraw-Hill, Inc., 6 edition, 2010.

[54] B. Simion, D. N. Ilha, A. D. Brown, and R. Johnson. The price of generality in spatial indexing. In *BigSpatial*, 2013.

[55] Simple API for XML. http://sax.sourceforge.net/, 2015.

[56] R. Sinya, K. Matsuzaki, and M. Sassa. Simultaneous finite automata: An efficient data-parallel model for regular expression matching. In *ICPP*, 2013.

[57] H. Sutter. The free lunch is over: A fundamental turn toward concurrency in software. *Dr. Dobb's journal*, 30(3), 2005.

[58] O. Tange et al. Gnu parallel: The command-line power tool. *The USENIX Magazine*, 36(1), 2011.

[59] M. Vermeij, W. Quak, M. Kersten, and N. Nes. MonetDB: A novel spatial column store DBMS. In *FOSS4G*, 2008.

[60] F. Wang, J. Kong, L. Cooper, T. Pan, T. Kurc, W. Chen, A. Sharma, C. Niedermayr, T. Oh, D. Brat, A. Farris, D. Foran, and J. Saltz. A data model and database for high-resolution pathology analytical image informatics. *Journal of Pathology Informatics*, 2(1), 2011.

[61] L. Xiao and Z. Wang. Internet of things: A new application for intelligent traffic monitoring system. *Journal of networks*, 6(6), 2011.

[62] C.-H. You and S.-D. Wang. A data parallel approach to XML parsing and query. In *HPCC*, 2011.

[63] Q. Zhou and J. Zhang. Research prospect of Internet of

Towards Best Region Search for Data Exploration

Kaiyu Feng[1,2] Gao Cong[2] Sourav S. Bhowmick[2] Wen-Chih Peng[3] Chunyan Miao[1]

[1]LILY, Interdisciplinary Graduate School. Nanyang Technological University, Singapore
[2]School of Computer Engineering, Nanyang Technological University, Singapore
[3]Department of Computer Science, National Chiao Tung University, Taiwan
{kfeng002@e., gaocong@, assourav@, ascymiao@}ntu.edu.sg, wcpeng@cs.nctu.edu.tw

ABSTRACT

The increasing popularity and growth of mobile devices and location-based services enable us to utilize large-scale geo-tagged data to support novel location-based applications. This paper introduces a novel problem called the *best region search* (*BRS*) problem and provides efficient solutions to it. Given a set O of spatial objects, a submodular monotone aggregate score function, and the size $a \times b$ of a query rectangle, the *BRS* problem aims to find $a \times b$ rectangular region such that the *aggregate score* of the spatial objects inside the region is maximized. This problem is fundamental to support several real-world applications such as *most influential region* search (*e.g.,* the best location for a signage to attract most audience) and *most diversified region* search (*e.g.,* region with most diverse facilities). We propose an efficient algorithm called *SliceBRS* to find the exact answer to the *BRS* problem. Furthermore, we propose an approximate solution called *CoverBRS* and prove that the answer found by it is bounded by a constant. Our experimental study with real-world datasets and applications demonstrates the effectiveness and superiority of our proposed algorithms.

1. INTRODUCTION

Due to the prominence of mobile devices and increasing popularity of location-based services (*e.g., Foursquare* (www.foursquare.com), *Yelp* (www.yelp.com)), massive amount of geo-tagged data are being generated everyday. Nowadays, in such location-based services, users can share their geo-positions with their friends. Meanwhile, *points of interests* (POIs) are increasingly tagged with category information and textual descriptions. The availability of such large-scale geo-tagged data can facilitate understanding of users who are active in a particular region or information related to the POIs in a specific region. More importantly, such data can be leveraged to search for "best" location or region based on *certain* criteria. Consider the following motivating examples of such region search problems.

Example 1: [Most Influential Region Search] Suppose a company wishes to build a signage to market their new product. The aspiration is that when people see the advertisement in the signage, they may purchase the advertised product. More importantly, these people may also recommend the product to their friends with a certain probability. The company wants to find the *best* location for the signage to attract as many people as possible to adopt the product. How can it select such location? □

Example 2: [Most Diversified Region Search] George is planning a trip to `Rome`. Rather than visiting a region in `Rome` with a specific attraction (*e.g.,* shopping), he wishes to visit a region that has the most diverse collection of services and attractions (*e.g.,* cinemas, shopping malls, restaurants, and museums). This will enable him to experience many different attractions and services in one place without the need to travel to different regions to experience them all together. How can George select the "most diversified region" in Rome? □

Observe that in the aforementioned scenarios, it is important for a user to specify a query rectangle of size $a \times b$ that she is interested in. For instance, in Example 2, different users may prefer regions of different sizes to explore. Hence, it is desirable for a user to specify as input the query rectangle of size $a \times b$ that she is comfortable to explore. Similarly, in Example 1, the region a company wishes to advertise its product largely depends on its business goal, interest, and budget among others. Consequently, in Examples 1 and 2, there is one running theme throughout the problems encountered, despite the differences in domain: we wish to find a rectangular region with a given size from a 2-dimensional space such that the *aggregate score* of the spatial objects in the region is maximized. Specifically, in Example 1, given the query rectangle of size $a \times b$, we wish to find the *most influential region* of the given size, such that the expected number of influenced users is maximized. On the other hand, in Example 2, given the query rectangle of size $a \times b$, we wish to find the *most diversified region* of the given size, such that the number of different categories of services and attractions in the region is maximized.

In this paper we refer to the above problem as the *best region search* (*BRS*) problem. In the aforementioned problems, the two aggregate score functions are both submodular monotone set functions as the aggregate score has a "diminishing return" property[1]. Hence, given a set of spatial objects O, a query rectangle of size $a \times b$, and a submodular monotone aggregate score function f, the *BRS* problem aims to identify an $a \times b$ rectangular region r such that the aggregate score $f(O_r)$ of all spatial objects inside the region is maximized, where O_r is the set of spatial objects inside the region r. We use an example to illustrate our problem.

Example 3: Reconsider the motivating example in Example 2. Assume that each object $o \in O$ is associated with a label to in-

[1]The marginal gain from adding an element to an input set decreases as the size of the input set increases, *i.e.,* $f(S \cup v) - f(S) \geq f(T \cup v) - f(T)$ for all elements v and all pair of sets $S \subseteq T$.

SIGMOD'16, June 26-July 01, 2016, San Francisco, CA, USA

DOI: http://dx.doi.org/10.1145/2882903.2882960

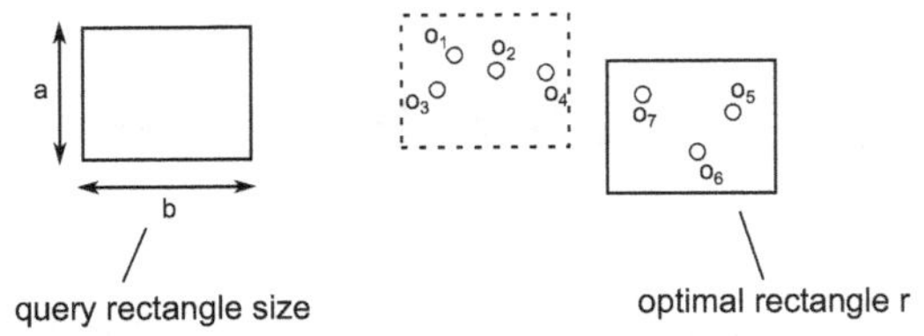

Figure 1: Example for the *BRS* problem.

dicate its category, denoted by $L(o)$. Consider the seven spatial objects $o_1, o_2, \ldots$, and o_7 shown in Figure 1 and their associated labels $L(o_1) = \ldots = L(o_5) = \{\text{Restaurant}\}$, $L(o_6) = \{\text{Mall}\}$ and $L(o_7) = \{\text{Cinema}\}$. The *BRS* problem aims to identify a most diversified region of a given size, where the diversity is measured by the number of different categories in the region. Though there are four spatial objects in the dashed-line rectangular region, all of them are restaurants and the diversity of the region is one. In the example, the solid-line rectangular region has the maximum diversity, since the spatial objects in it have three different categories. Thus, the solid-line rectangular region is an answer to the *BRS* problem. □

In the *BRS* problem, there are infinite points in the space and it is prohibitively expensive to consider all these points in the search of the best region. This is more so because submodular monotone functions are often expensive to compute [17]. Furthermore, a user may search for the best region in an *exploratory* manner. That is, she may initiate a search with a specific query rectangle as input, view the corresponding results, iteratively refine the query rectangle (by increasing or decreasing a or b) and execute the refined search until she is satisfied with the search results. Such exploratory framework demands techniques that can efficiently process the *BRS* queries over very large volumes of spatial objects.

At first glance, it may seem that the *BRS* problem can be addressed by the techniques designed to tackle the *maximizing range sum* (*MaxRS*) problem [7,12,21]. Given a set O of weighted spatial points and a rectangle r of a given size, the *MaxRS* problem aims to identify a location of r such that the sum of the weights of all the points covered by r is maximized. However, this is not the case. Consider the example shown in Figure 1, the dashed-line rectangular region is the result for the *MaxRS* problem since there are four spatial objects in the region. However, the solid-line rectangular region is the answer to our *BRS* problem. Instead of the SUM function, the *BRS* problem is a generalized problem that can employ *any* submodular monotone function. Thus, the *MaxRS* problem is a special case of the *BRS* problem (detailed in Section 2).

In this paper, we propose two novel algorithms to tackle the *BRS* problem. The first algorithm, *SliceBRS*, finds an exact answer to the *BRS* problem by reducing it to the submodular weighted rectangle intersection (*SIRI*) problem, which greatly reduces the search space. Specifically, we prove that only $O(n^2)$ candidate regions need to be considered. However, it is still inefficient to consider all $O(n^2)$ candidate regions (especially in an exploratory search environment) when the number of spatial objects is very large. This leaves us a challenge whether we can further prune the search space. The second algorithm, *CoverBRS*, assumes that slight imprecision to the solution is acceptable and finds an approximate answer to the *BRS* problem bounded by a constant. In *SliceBRS*, we propose several new concepts, including "maximal regions" and "maximal slabs" to prune the search space. Based on these concepts, we cut the space into slices and find maximal slabs in all slices. Then we prune unnecessary slices and maximal slabs to reduce the search space. It takes $O(n \times n_s)$ time to find the best point, where n is the number of spatial objects and n_s is the number of maximal slabs that we actually processed. According to our experiments, n_s is usually a very small number, which is much smaller than n. The *CoverBRS* algorithm first selects a smaller set of spatial objects T using a novel concept of *c-cover*. Then it generates a new instance of the *BRS* problem by defining a new aggregate score function and a new query rectangle on the set of spatial objects T. Lastly, it invokes the *SliceBRS* algorithm to answer the new instance. We prove that the answer to the new instance is a constant-bounded approximate answer to the original instance. The approximate ratio is determined by the parameter c.

Table 1: Table of notations

Notation	Definition
P	The 2-dimensional space
O, T	The set of spatial objects
o, p	A spatial object, a point
$a \times b$	The size of the query rectangle
$r_p^{a,b}$	The $a \times b$ rectangular region centered at p
$O_{r_p^{a,b}}$	The set of objects inside the rectangle $r_p^{a,b}$
f, f_T	The submodular monotone function on O and T
R	The set of rectangles
τ	A disjoint region
S, s	A set of maximal slabs, a maximal slab

In summary, the key contributions of this paper are as follows.

- To the best of our knowledge, this is the first work to formulate the *best region search* (*BRS*) problem for finding a rectangular region with a given size such that the submodular monotone *aggregate score* of the spatial objects inside the region is maximized.
- We develop an exact algorithm called *SliceBRS* and a constant-bounded approximate algorithm called *CoverBRS* to address the *BRS* problem.
- By applying the proposed algorithms to several real-world and synthetic datasets, we experimentally demonstrate their efficiency and effectiveness in finding the best regions in the context of most influential region search and most diversified region search problems. Furthermore, we also demonstrate how the *SliceBRS* algorithm can be adapted to address the *MaxRS* problem.

The remainder of this paper is organized as follows. The related work is reviewed in the next section. Section 3 formally introduces the best region search problem. In Section 4, we present the exact algorithm, namely *SliceBRS*. Section 5 presents the approximate algorithm *CoverBRS*. The experimental study is discussed in Section 6. Finally, the last section concludes this paper. The key notations used in this paper are given in Table 1.

2. RELATED WORK

The best region search (*BRS*) problem is related to *range aggregate query processing*, *location selection* problem, and the *region search* problem. We relate research in these areas in turn.

Range Aggregate Query Given a set O of spatial objects and a query range q, the *range aggregate* (RA) query [6,14,18,22,23] returns the total weight of the spatial objects that are inside the given query range. An RA query aim to answer "what is the total weight of objects in a given query range?" In contrast, our *BRS* problem focuses on providing answer to "where is the range of a given size such that the aggregate of objects in the range is maximized?" Clearly, these two problems are different as the queries are different. In fact, there is no systematic way to apply any method designed for RA query processing to solve the *BRS* problem. Moreover, the aggregate function used in these studies is different from the submodular monotone function used in the *BRS* problem.

Location Selection Problem Our *BRS* problem is related to the *location selection* problem.The existing work on location selection defines different optimization objectives, based on which we classify the existing work. First, Zhang *et al.* propose the *min-dist optimal-location query* [31], which takes as input a set of servers, a set of clients, and a spatial region Q. The query returns a location in Q for a new server such that the average distance from each client to its closest server is minimized. The problem is also considered in the context of road networks [5, 28] with road network distance. Second, given a set of servers and a set of clients, several efforts [9, 26] aim to find a location where a new server can maximize its influence. Zhou *et al.* [32] and Yan *et al.* [29] consider the problem with extensions to the definition of influence respectively. In addition, the problem of selecting top-k locations is also studied in the literature [11, 27, 30].

All the aforementioned types of location selection queries are fundamentally different from our *BRS* problem. Specifically, our *BRS* problem aims to find a region with the maximum aggregation value based on a submodular monotone function, which is different from the criteria used in location selection queries.

Region Search Liu *et al.* [20] study the problem of finding subject oriented top-k *hot regions* in spatial databases. Cao *et al.* [2] study the problem of finding a region with relevant objects from a road network, where the region is defined by a connected subgraph in the road network. The concept of region in these work is different from that of in the *BRS* problem.

Most germane to our work is the *maximizing range sum* (*MaxRS*) problem [7, 12, 21]. Given a set of weighted spatial objects, and a query rectangle, the *MaxRS* problem aims to find the location of a rectangle such that the sum of the weights of all spatial objects covered by the rectangle is maximized. The problem was first studied by the computational geometry community. Imai *et al.* propose an $O(n \log n)$ optimal algorithm [12] for finding the position of a rectangle of the given size enclosing the maximum number of spatial objects, where n is the number of spatial objects. This algorithm can be employed to solve the *MaxRS* problem. Later Nandy and Bhattacharya [21] propose another line-sweeping-based algorithm with the same $O(n \log n)$ cost. The *MaxRS* problem is systematically investigated by Choi *et al.* [7] where an elegant external memory algorithm based on the in-memory $O(n \log n)$ algorithm [21] is proposed. Recently, Tao *et al.* [25] extend the *MaxRS* problem to $(1-\epsilon)$-approximate *MaxRS* problem and propose efficient algorithms for answering the *MaxRS* query approximately.

The aforementioned types of region search problem are different from the *BRS* problem as they have a different definition of region. Although the *MaxRS* problem is closest to our work, it is still a different problem from our *BRS* problem. Recall that they return different results for the example in Figure 1. We shall further validate this in Section 6. The *MaxRS* problem takes SUM as the aggregate score function, while the *BRS* problem use a general submodular monotone function as the aggregate score function. In other words, the *MaxRS* problem is a special case of our *BRS* problem when the aggregate function is SUM. In addition, techniques [7, 12, 21] developed for the *MaxRS* problem cannot be deployed or adapted to solve the *BRS* problem because their pruning techniques are tightly integrated to the SUM function and hence cannot be generalized to other submodular monotone functions.

Alexander *et al.* propose Semantic Window [15] and Searchlight [16] to study the region search problem in an interactive data exploration manner for multidimensional data. In this setting, a user explores a data space by posing a number of queries to find rectangular regions that she is interested in. In contrast to our solution to the *BRS* problem, Semantic Window [15] is build on top of PostgreSQL to search the underlying data space quickly while providing online results. Searchlight [16] combines Constraint Programming machinery and DBMS to support generic search, exploration and mining over large multi-dimensional data collections.

3. BEST REGION SEARCH (BRS) PROBLEM

In this section, we formally introduce the *best region search* (*BRS*) problem that we address in this paper. We consider a set of spatial objects O in a 2-dimensional space, denoted by P. Each object $o \in O$ has a location represented by $(o.x, o.y)$ in space P. We use $r_p^{a,b}$ to denote the $a \times b$ rectangular region centered at the point $p \in P$. Without ambiguity, we also use $r_o^{a,b}$ to denote the $a \times b$ rectangular region centered at a spatial object $o \in O$. For a rectangular region $r_p^{a,b}$, we denote by $O_{r_p^{a,b}}$ the set of spatial objects in O that are located in $r_p^{a,b}$. We define submodular monotone function f as follows:

DEFINITION 1. [*Submodular monotone function [8]*]*A set function* $f : 2^{|O|} \rightarrow \mathbb{R}$, *which maps subsets of* O *to a real number is a monotone submodular function if for every* $O_i \subseteq O_j \subseteq O$ *and* $o \in O \setminus O_j$, *it satisfies: (1)* $f(O_i \cup \{o\}) - f(O_i) \geq f(O_j \cup \{o\}) - f(O_j)$; *and (2)* $f(O_i) \leq f(O_j)$.

Example 4: Assume that each object $o \in O$ is associated with a set of class labels (*e.g.*, Greek restaurant), denoted by $L(o)$. Function $f(X) = |\bigcup_{o \in X} L(o)|$ is a submodular monotone function, where $X \subseteq O$. For example, consider 3 objects o_1, o_2, and o_3 and their associated labels $L(o_1) = \{a, b, c\}$, $L(o_2) = \{a, d\}$, $L(o_3) = \{c, d\}$. Let $O_1 = \{o_2\}$, and $O_2 = \{o_2, o_3\}$. If we add o_1 into O_1, we can get an increase in the score of $f(O_1 \cup \{o_1\}) - f(O_1) = 2$. If we add o_1 into O_2, we can get an increase in the score of $f(O_2 \cup \{o_1\}) - f(O_2) = 1$. Adding o_1 to the subset O_1 can cause a higher increase in the aggregation score. □

Based on the above definition of submodular monotone function f, we now formally define the *best region search* (*BRS*) problem:

DEFINITION 2. [**BRS *problem***] *Given a set of spatial objects* O, *a submodular monotone function* $f : 2^O \rightarrow \mathbb{R}$, *and the size* $a \times b$ *of query rectangle, the* ***best region search* (BRS) *problem*** *is to find a location p from the entire space* P *such that the aggregate score of the spatial objects in the* $a \times b$ *rectangular region centered at p,* $f(O_{r_p^{a,b}})$, *is maximized:*

$$p = \arg\max_{p \in P} f(O_{r_p^{a,b}})$$

Without loss of generality, objects on the boundary of rectangles are excluded. For simplicity, we assume that no two objects have the same x coordinate or y coordinate. However, our proposed techniques can be easily extended to the case when some objects have the same x coordinate or y coordinate (detailed in Appendix A).

4. AN EXACT SOLUTION

Intuitively, the *BRS* problem requires us to select a point from infinite points in space P. However, the naive approach of scanning each point in P to find a solution to this problem is prohibitively expensive. Hence, in this section we present an efficient exact solution to the *BRS* problem to address this challenge. To this end,

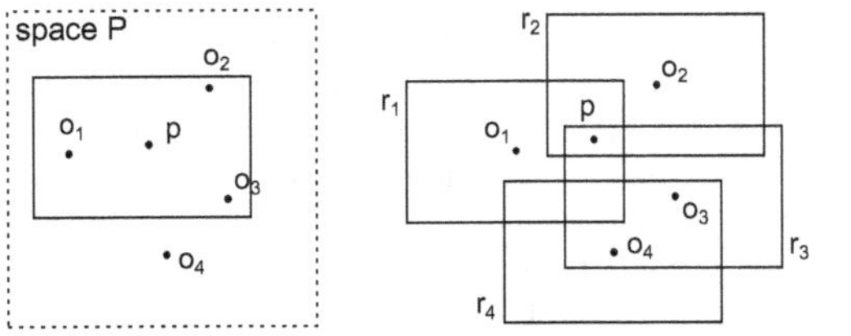

(a) The BRS problem (b) The SIRI problem

Figure 2: Reduction from *BRS* to *SIRI*.

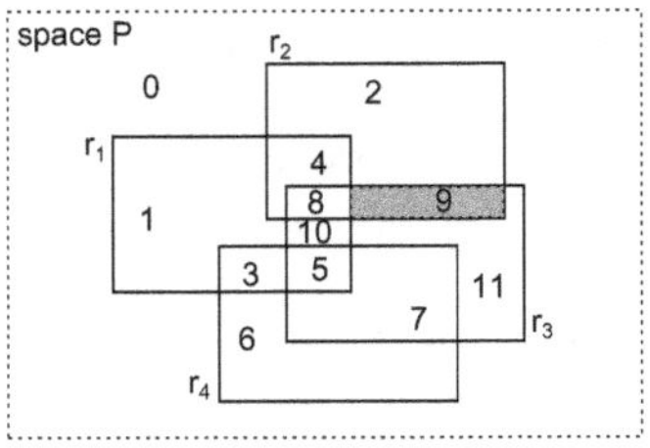

Figure 3: Disjoint regions.

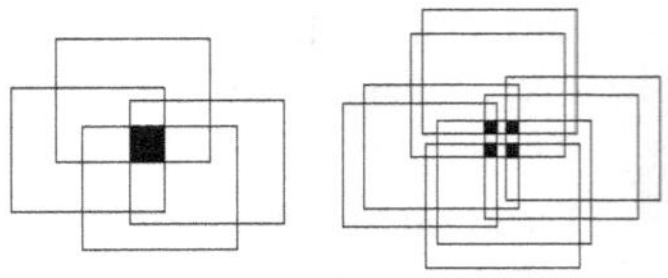

Figure 4: $O(n^2)$ maximal regions

we first introduce the ***submodular weighted rectangle intersection*** (*SIRI*) problem and show that we can reduce the *BRS* problem to the *SIRI* problem. Next, we discuss the *SliceBRS* algorithm to solve the *SIRI* problem (and thus *BRS* problem). The proofs of the theorems and the lemmas of this section can be found in Appendix B.

4.1 The SIRI Problem

We now give the formal definition of the *SIRI* problem. In the next subsection, we shall present an interesting property of the *SIRI* problem, which provides the justification behind our goal to reduce the *BRS* problem to the *SIRI* problem.

DEFINITION 3. **[SIRI *Problem*]** *Consider a set of rectangles of size $a \times b$, R, and a submodular monotone function $h : 2^R \to \mathbb{R}$ that maps a set of rectangles to a real number. We say a rectangle r is* ***affected*** *by a point p if p is inside r. We denote by $A(p)$ the set of rectangles that are* affected *by p. The* ***weight*** *of point p is defined by the submodular monotone function h on the set of rectangles $A(p)$, which is denoted by $h(A(p))$. The* **SIRI *problem*** *aims at finding a point p with the maximum weight in space P:*

$$p = \arg\max_{p \in P} h(A(p)).$$

The *BRS* problem can be reduced to the *SIRI* problem as follows. For each spatial object $o \in O$, we draw an $a \times b$ rectangle $r_o^{a,b}$ centered at o. For a set of rectangles $R_i = \{r_{o_1}^{a,b}, \ldots, r_{o_i}^{a,b}\}$, let $h(R_i) = f(\{o_1, \ldots, o_i\})$. Therefore, we get an instance of the *SIRI* problem. We illustrate the reduction with an example. Consider the example in Figure 2. In Fig 2(a), O comprises 4 spatial objects(each represented by a black dot) in space P. The size of the query rectangle is $a \times b$. To reduce the *BRS* problem to the *SIRI* problem, for each spatial object $o_i \in O, i \in [1, 4]$, we draw an $a \times b$ rectangle centered at o_i, denoted by r_i, as depicted in Fig 2(b).

To prove the answer to the *SIRI* problem is also an answer to the *BRS*, we first present the following lemma.

LEMMA 1. *Consider a point p and a spatial object o in space P. Object o is inside the $a \times b$ rectangular region $r_p^{a,b}$ iff p is inside the $a \times b$ rectangle $r_o^{a,b}$ that centers at o.*

As shown in Figure 2, point p is inside the $a \times b$ rectangle centered at o_1 and o_1 is also inside the rectangle centered at p.

Then we can have the following theorem.

THEOREM 1. *Given an instance of the* BRS *problem and the instance of the* SIRI *problem which is reduced from the* BRS *problem, an answer to the* SIRI *problem is an answer to the* BRS *problem.*

Note that the reduction is inspired by the idea of transforming the *MaxRS* problem to the rectangle intersection problem [7, 21]. The rectangle intersection problem is defined as "Given a set of weighted rectangles, find an area such that the sum of the weights of rectangles that intersect with this area is maximized." However, the techniques designed for solving the rectangle intersection problem cannot be used to solve the *SIRI* problem.

4.2 Disjoint Regions

Next, we present an interesting property of the *SIRI* problem, which also enables us to justify the reason behind the reduction of the *BRS* problem to the *SIRI* problem and solve the reduced *SIRI* problem instead of solving the *BRS* problem directly.

DEFINITION 4. **[*Disjoint Regions*]** *The edges of the rectangles in R divide the space P into regions. We say a region $\mathfrak{r}_i$ is a* ***disjoint region*** *iff: (1) $\mathfrak{r}_i$ is the intersection of a set of rectangles R_i; (2) there exists no region $\mathfrak{r}_j$ such that (a) $\mathfrak{r}_j$ is the intersection of a set of rectangles R_j, (b) $R_i \subseteq R_j$, and (c) $\mathfrak{r}_j \subseteq \mathfrak{r}_i$. We denote the set of rectangles whose intersection is $\mathfrak{r}_i$ as $\mathfrak{r}_i.R_i$.*

Example 5: Consider the example in Fig 3. There are four rectangles, r_1, r_2, r_3 and r_4 in the space. The four rectangles together divide the space into 12 disjoint regions, each is marked with an ID. Disjoint region $\mathfrak{r}_9$ (filled with grey color) is the intersection of the set of rectangles $\{r_2, r_3\}$. □

LEMMA 2. *All the points in a disjoint region can affect the same set of rectangles, whose intersection forms the disjoint region.*

THEOREM 2. *There are at most $O(n^2)$ disjoint regions, where n is the number of rectangles in R.*

Observe that for both the *BRS* problem and the *SIRI* problem, we find a point from the infinite points in space P. Lemma 2 and Theorem 2 together enable us to significantly reduce the search space. According to Lemma 2, instead of considering the infinite points in space P, we only need to consider a point for each disjoint region. Theorem 2 tells us there are at most $O(n^2)$ regions to be considered. Consequently, by reducing the *BRS* problem to the *SIRI* problem, we convert our problem from selecting a point from infinite points in space P to selecting a disjoint region from $O(n^2)$ disjoint regions.

4.3 Disjoint Region-based Solution

We proceed to present an efficient approach to solve the *SIRI* problem using the notion of disjoint region. To solve the *SIRI* problem, based on Lemma 2 and Theorem 2, a straightforward strategy is outlined as follows: we find all disjoint regions, and for each disjoint region $\mathfrak{r}_i$ and the set of rectangles, denoted by $\mathfrak{r}_i.R_i$, that are affected by points in region $\mathfrak{r}_i$, we compute its weight, denoted by $h(\mathfrak{r}_i.R_i)$. After we find the disjoint region with maximum weight, any point in the region can be an answer to the *SIRI* problem. However, there are $O(n^2)$ disjoint regions in the worst case and it is inefficient to examine every disjoint region. The question here is whether we need to examine all the disjoint regions. We next use an example to show that we do not need to examine every disjoint region.

Example 6: Consider the example in Fig 3. The points in disjoint region $\mathfrak{r}_3$ can affect $\{r_1, r_4\}$ and the points in disjoint region $\mathfrak{r}_5$ can affect $\{r_1, r_3, r_4\}$. The rectangles affected by the points in $\mathfrak{r}_3$

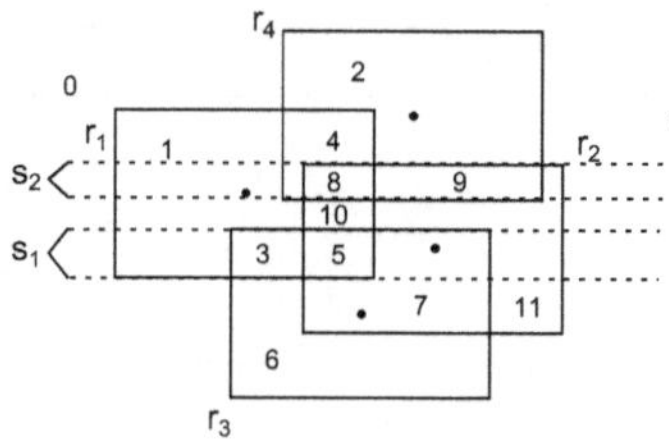

Figure 5: Example of maximal slabs.

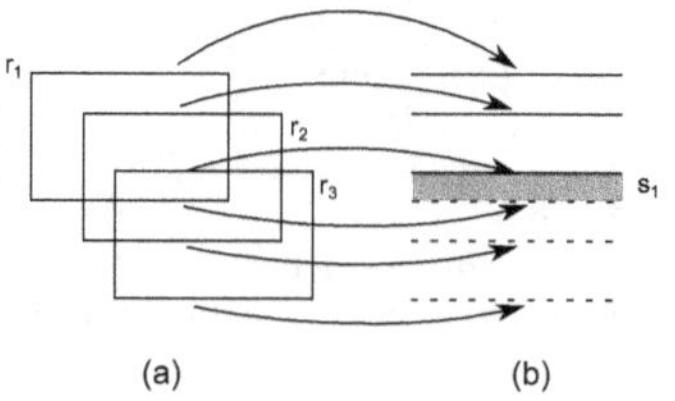

Figure 6: Find maximal slabs.

is a subset of the rectangles affected by the points in $\mathfrak{r}_5$. Since h is a submodular monotone function, $h(\{r_1, r_4\}) \leq h(\{r_1, r_3, r_4\})$ always holds. Thus there is no need to examine $\mathfrak{r}_3$. □

Inspired by the above example, we propose the notion of *maximal region* and show that we only need to check the maximal regions instead of all disjoint regions.

DEFINITION 5. [***Maximal Region***] *Consider a set of rectangles R. The edges of the rectangles divide the space into a set of disjoint regions $\mathfrak{R}$. A disjoint region $\mathfrak{r} \in \mathfrak{R}$ is defined as a* **maximal region** *if:*

(1) $\mathfrak{r}$ is a rectangular region;

(2) $\mathfrak{r}$'s left edge is part of the left edge of a rectangle in R;

(3) $\mathfrak{r}$'s right edge is part of the right edge of a rectangle in R;

(4) $\mathfrak{r}$'s top edge is part of the top edge of a rectangle in R;

(5) $\mathfrak{r}$'s bottom edge is part of the bottom edge of a rectangle in R.

Example 7: In Fig 3, $\mathfrak{r}_5$ is a maximal region because (1) it is a rectangular region; (2) its left edge is part of the left edge of rectangle r_3; (3) its right edge is part of the right edge of rectangle r_1; (4) its top edge is part of the top edge of rectangle r_4; and (5) its bottom edge is part of the bottom edge of rectangle r_1. As another example, $\mathfrak{r}_8$ is also a maximal region. However, $\mathfrak{r}_3$ is not a maximal region because its right edge is not part of the right edge of any rectangle, but is part of the left edge of rectangle r_3. As another example, $\mathfrak{r}_1$ is not a maximal region because it is not a rectangular region. □

LEMMA 3. *For any disjoint region $\mathfrak{r}_i$, there exists a maximal region $\mathfrak{r}_j$ such that $A(p_{\mathfrak{r}_i}) \subseteq A(p_{\mathfrak{r}_j})$, where $p_{\mathfrak{r}_i}$ is a point from $\mathfrak{r}_i$ and $p_{\mathfrak{r}_j}$ is a point from $\mathfrak{r}_j$.*

From Lemma 3, we know that to find a point p with maximum weight $h(A(p))$, we only need to check the points in the maximal regions instead of all disjoint regions. Usually, the number of maximal regions is much smaller than the number of disjoint regions. However, in the worst case, there are still $O(n^2)$ maximal regions.

LEMMA 4. *In the worst case, there are $O(n^2)$ maximal regions, where n is the number of rectangles.*

4.4 Maximal Slab-based Solution

Observe that the solution proposed in the preceding subsection requires us to examine all maximal regions in order to find *only one* region that is the answer to the *SIRI* problem. Thus, a natural question is whether we have to examine *all* maximal regions to find this region? In this subsection, we propose a novel approach to enable us to prune the search space of examining maximal regions.

Our idea is based on the concept of *maximal slab*. Each maximal region intersects at least one maximal slab. We show that there are at most $O(n)$ maximal slabs, where n is the number of rectangles. Furthermore, we show that we can compute an upper bound for each maximal slab and prune the maximal slabs based on the estimated upper bounds. Consequently, the maximal regions that overlap with the pruned maximal slabs are pruned.

DEFINITION 6. [***Maximal Slab***] *Consider a set of rectangles R in space P. A* **maximal slab** *is the area between two horizontal lines in the space where (1) the top horizontal line passes the top edge of a rectangle; (2) the bottom horizontal line passes the bottom edge of a rectangle; and (3) the area between the two horizontal lines does not contain top or bottom edge of any rectangle.*

Example 8: We use the example in Figure 6 to illustrate maximal slab. For each rectangle, we extend its top edge and bottom edge to get two horizontal lines, as shown in Figure 6(b). The vertical edges are ignored. We use solid line for the horizontal line passing the top edge of a rectangle and dashed for the bottom edge. The grey-filled slab s_1 in Figure 6 (b) is the only maximal slab. □

Based on the definition of maximal slab, we can derive the following lemma:

LEMMA 5. *For any maximal region $\mathfrak{r}$, there exists at least one maximal slab s such that $\mathfrak{r}$ intersects with s.*

LEMMA 6. *There are at most $O(n)$ maximal slabs, where n is the number of rectangles.*

Lemma 5 guarantees that we will not miss the answer to the *SIRI* problem if we only search inside the maximal slabs. Inspired by this, we only consider the space in all maximal slabs and search for the answer to the *SIRI* problem in each maximal slab. We can compute an upper bound for each maximal slab and prune the maximal slabs using the estimated upper bounds.

LEMMA 7. *Given a maximal slab s, let R_s denote the set of rectangles that intersect with s. For any point p in s, $h(R_s)$ is an upper bound of $h(A(p))$, denoted as $upper(s)$.*

Example 9: Consider the maximal slab s_2 in Fig 5. We compute $upper(s_2) = h(\{r_1, r_2, r_4\})$. For any point p in s_2, we have $h(A(p)) \leq upper(s_2)$. □

Approach We now present how to utilize maximal slabs to efficiently find an exact answer to the *SIRI* problem. Our approach broadly comprises two steps. First, we find the maximal slabs by using a sweep line to scan the space bottom-up to find the set S of maximal slabs together with their upper bounds. Second, we find the exact answer by checking the maximal slabs s in descending order of their upper bounds and searching for the point with maximum weight in each processed maximal slab. Once the upper bound of any remaining maximal slab in S is smaller than the best known result, we stop checking the remaining maximal slabs. We elaborate on these steps in turn.

Finding maximal slabs The main idea is to use a sweep line to scan bottom-up. While scanning, we maintain the edges that the sweep line has encountered. According to the definition of maximal slab, if the sweep line encounters a bottom edge and a top edge consecutively, then a maximal slab is found. The outline of the procedure is reported in Function `ScanSlab`. The function takes as input the set of rectangles R and returns all maximal slabs S in the space. It uses a horizontal line, denoted by l, to sweep bottom-up, and uses a queue Rec to store the rectangles that the sweep line has met. It uses $flag$ to denote whether the last edge that l met is

Function ScanSlab(R)

```
  Output: A list of maximal slabs S.
1 Rec ← ∅, S ← ∅, flag ← bottom;
2 while Sweeping the horizontal line from bottom to top do
3     if l meets the bottom edge of a rectangle r then
4         Rec ← Rec ∪ {r};
5         flag ← bottom;
6     else
          /* The sweep line meets the top edge
             of a rectangle                      */
7         if flag = bottom then
8             s ←new maximal slab, s.UB = h(Rec);
9             S ← S ∪ {s};
10        Rec ← Rec \ {r};
11        flag ← top;
12 return S;
```

Function SearchMR(R, S)

```
  Output: A point p
1 p_c ← null;
2 s ← arg max_{s∈S} s.UB;
3 while s.UB > h(A(p_c)) do
4     flag ← left, Rec ← ∅;
5     while Sweeping the vertical line l from left to right in s do
6         if l meets the left edge of a rectangle r then
7             flag ← left, Rec ← Rec ∪ {r};
8         else
9             if flag = left then
10                p ← midpoint of l ∩ s;
11                if h(A(p)) > h(A(p_c)) then
12                    p_c ← p;
13            Rec ← Rec \ {r}, flag ← right;
14    s ← arg max_{s∈S} s.UB;
15 return p_c;
```

a top edge of a rectangle or a bottom edge and $flag$ is initialized by bottom. When the sweep line l encounters a bottom edge of a rectangle r, it pushes r into Rec (line 4) and mark $flag$ as bottom (line 5). When the sweep line l encounters a top edge of a rectangle r, if $flag$ is bottom, it finds a new maximal slab with upper bound $h(Rec)$ and add it to S (lines 8–9). Next, it removes r from Rec and mark $flag$ as top (lines 10–11). The algorithm terminates when the sweep line reaches the top of the space.

Example 10: Suppose we invoke the `ScanSlab` procedure on the example shown in Figure 5(b). A horizontal line sweeps from bottom to top. It first comes across the bottom edge of r_3 and r_3 is added into the tail of Rec. The $flag$ is marked as bottom. Then the bottom edges of r_2 and r_1 are processed consequently and $Rec = [r_3, r_2, r_1]$, $flag$ = bottom. After that, the sweep line comes across the top edge of r_3. Since $flag$ = bottom, the algorithm finds a maximal slab s_1. We assume $h(\{r_1, r_2, r_3\}) = 5$. The algorithm then pushes s_1 into S. Then r_3 is removed from Rec and $Rec = [r_2, r_1]$ and $flag$ is marked as top. The sweep line keeps moving and it meets the bottom edge of r_4. The algorithm adds r_4 into Rec and mark $flag$ as bottom again. Then it meets the top edge of r_2 and $Rec = [r_2, r_1, r_4]$, $flag$ = bottom. Another maximal slab s_2 is found. We assume that $h(\{r_2, r_1, r_4\}) = 4$ and s_2 is pushed into S. The algorithm terminates when the sweep line meets the top edge of r_4. □

Finding the answer In the second step, we search for the answer iteratively. In each iteration, we pop out the maximal slab s with maximum upper bound. If the upper bound of s is smaller than the current result, we can conclude that the current result is the final result. Otherwise, we process the maximal slab as follows: We use a vertical sweep line to scan s from left to right. During the scan, we maintain the edges that the sweep line has encountered. If the sweep line encounters a left edge and a right edge consecutively, then the area between the two edges may belong to a maximal region and we check whether it has a better weight than the current result.

The formal algorithm is outlined in Function `SearchMR`. We use p_c to store the current answer to the problem and it is initialized as `null`(line 1). It keeps searching while there exists a maximal slab $s \in S$ such that $upper(s) > h(A(p_c))$ (lines 2–14). Specifically, it finds the maximal slab s with maximum upper bound in S (line 2) and uses a vertical line l to sweep from left to right (lines 5–14). The variable $flag$ is used to denote whether the last edge that the sweep line l encountered is a left edge or a right edge and it is initialized as left. The variable Rec denotes the rectangles that intersect with the sweep line l (line 4). While the vertical sweep line l meets the left edge of rectangle r, the algorithm sets $flag$ as left and adds r into Rec (lines 6–7). Otherwise, if the last edge that l met is a left edge (line 9), it takes the midpoint of segment $l \cap s$ (line 10). It then compares its weight and the current result and update p_c if it has a larger weight (lines 11–12). Then r is removed from Rec and the algorithm sets $flag$ as right (line 13). When the upper bounds of the maximal slabs in the remaining S are smaller than the current result, it returns p_c as the answer to the *SIRI* problem.

4.5 Search Space Reduction by Slicing

We next present a strategy to further reduce the search space. Our main idea can be explained as follows: We divide the space into slices with equal width along the x-axis and process each slice separately by following the divide-and-conquer strategy. We estimate an upper bound for each slice and prune the slices whose upper bound is smaller than the current result.

To realize our idea, we need to answer the following question: *How to set the width of the slices?* Observe that if the width of each slice is too small, then each rectangle will intersect with many slices. In other words, we need to consider a rectangle in many slices, which yields redundant computation. If the width of each slice is too large, then there will be fewer slices, and thus it is likely that only few slices can be pruned by our strategy. Therefore, it is important to set an appropriate width of the slices. However, if we set the width as a constant independent of the query, then given a rectangle r, the number of slices that intersect with r is dependent on the query rectangle, and is not bounded. Therefore, we may consider a rectangle unbounded number of times (for each slice that it intersects), and this incurs redundant computation. To this end, we propose to set the width of slices to be query dependent. Specifically, we set the width of each slice as θb, where b is the width of the query rectangle and θ is a positive real constant, which can be set empirically (as we shall see in Section 6).

Example 11: Consider the example in Fig 7. The width of each slice is θb and $\theta > 1$. r_3 intersects with slice 1 and slice 2. $\{r_1, r_3\}$ is the set of rectangles that intersect with slice 1. $\{r_2, r_3, r_4\}$ is the set of rectangles that intersect with slice 2. □

We can derive the following lemma:

LEMMA 8. *Let the width of each slice be θb. Each rectangle r intersects with at most $\lceil \frac{1}{\theta} \rceil + 1$ slices.*

Lemma 8 guarantees that each rectangle is processed a constant number of times if we process each slice by invoking the `ScanSlab` procedure. Thus, we further have:

Algorithm 1: SliceBRS

```
   Input: A set of objects O, query size a × b, aggregate function f
   Output: A point p
1  p_c ← null;
2  R ← the set of a × b rectangles centered at each o ∈ O;
3  Divide the space into slices with width θb;
4  for each slice i do
5  |  R_i ← the set of rectangles that intersect with slice i;
6  |  S_i ← ScanSlab(R_i);
7  while there exists a slice i s.t. max_{s∈S_i} s.UB > h(A(p_c)) do
8  |  p ← SearchMR(R_i, S_i);
9  |  if h(A(p)) > h(A(p_c)) then
10 |  |  p_c ← p;
11 return p_c;
```

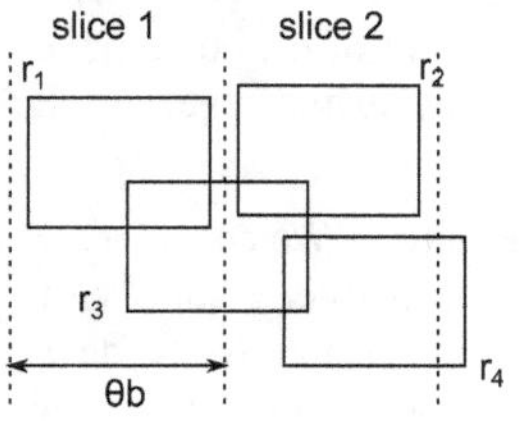

Figure 7: Equal-width slices.

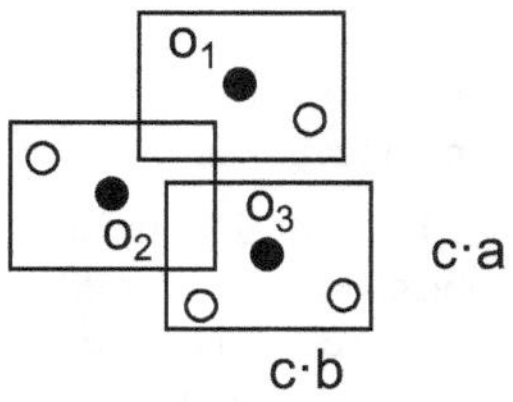

Figure 8: c-cover

LEMMA 9. *There are at most $(\lceil \frac{1}{\theta} \rceil + 1)n$ maximal slabs in all slices, where n is the number of rectangles.*

According to Lemma 9, it still takes $O(n)$ time to find maximal slabs in all slices, where n is the number of rectangles. Note that we can find the maximal slabs S_i in slice i by invoking the `ScanSlab` procedure in slice i.

4.6 The SliceBRS Algorithm

We now have all the machinery in place to discuss the *SliceBRS* algorithm to address the *BRS* problem. The key idea of the algorithm is as follows. We first transform the *BRS* problem into the *SIRI* problem and divide the space vertically into several slices with a fixed width. Next, in each slice, the algorithm performs a fast check and finds the list of maximal slabs together with their upper bounds. It uses the maximum upper bound of the slabs in a slice as the upper bound of the slice. Then, it greedily processes slices. The slice with a larger upper bound is processed first. In each slice, the algorithm searches each maximal slab greedily. A maximal slab with a larger upper bound is searched first. The algorithm terminates when the weight of the known best point is larger than the upper bound of the unprocessed slices, or all the slices have been processed.

The *SliceBRS* algorithm is presented in Algorithm 1. It takes as input a set O of spatial objects, an aggregate score function f, and the size $a \times b$ of a query rectangle. It returns the point p with maximum $h(A(p))$. It uses p_c to maintain the point with maximum weight that has currently been found and it is initialized by null (line 1). The algorithm first transforms the *BRS* problem to the *SIRI* problem by drawing an $a \times b$ rectangle centered at o for each spatial object $o \in O$ (line 2). Then it vertically divides the space into slices with width θb (line 3). After that, for each slice i, it estimates the upper bound and finds maximal slabs in the slice (lines 4–6). Based on the upper bounds, the algorithm processes the slices that are most likely to contain the best point and update p_c once a better point is found (lines 7–10). The algorithm terminates when the upper bound of the remaining slices is worse than the current result.

Complexity The *SliceBRS* algorithm comprises three phases: (1) Cutting the space into slices, (2) Scanning maximal slabs, and (3) Searching in maximal slabs. We analyse the time complexity of the three phases in turn. Let n be the number of spatial objects in O. In phase 1, it takes $O(n)$ time to cut the space into slices. In phase 2, according to Lemma 9, there are at most $(\lceil \frac{1}{\theta} \rceil + 1)n$ maximal slabs in all slices, where θ is a predefined constant. Thus, it takes Function `ScanSlab` $O(n)$ time to process all slices. In phase 3, it takes Function `SearchMR` $O(n)$ time to search one maximal slab. Since we can safely ignore the maximal slabs whose upper bounds are lower than the current result, we assume only n_s maximal slabs are actually searched by Function `SearchMR`. Thus the complexity of phase 3 is $O(n \cdot n_s)$. Putting these together, we can conclude that in the worst case, it takes $O(n + n + n \cdot n_s) = O(n \cdot n_s)$ time to find the best point.

Although n_s can be n in the worst case, n_s is usually a very small value. To have a better idea, we consider the complexity of *SliceBRS* for the following case.

LEMMA 10. *Consider a set O consisting of n spatial objects in a $W \times W$ space P. We assume that the objects in O are uniformly distributed in space P. The complexity of* SliceBRS *for this case is $O(n)$.*

In practice, according to our experiments, usually only a few of maximal slabs are actually searched and n_s is a very small value (from 30 to 3000).

5. APPROXIMATE SOLUTION

Although the *SliceBRS* algorithm can efficiently find an exact answer to the *BRS* problem, we observed that its runtime performance degrades when the number of spatial objects grows or the spatial objects in the space get denser (detailed in Section 6). Hence in this section, we present a constant-bounded approximate algorithm called *CoverBRS* for answering the *BRS* problem efficiently especially for large datasets. The proofs of the theorems and the lemmas of this section can be found in Appendix B.

5.1 Overview

The key idea behind our approximate algorithm for solving the *BRS* problem is as follows: we select a set of points, denoted by T, from the space P so that each point in T can represent some spatial objects in O. The points in T together preserve some properties of O such that the rectangle region found on the set of objects T can be an approximation of the result on O with performance guarantees. This idea has two potential benefits: (1) T contains fewer spatial objects than O; (2) The spatial objects in T are sparser than those in O. These benefits enable us to answer the *BRS* problem more efficiently.

How to select and utilize the set T such that we can achieve a bounded approximate answer? To address this challenge, we propose a novel concept called *c-cover* of O, where c is a parameter to control the approximation ratio of our proposed solution. The concept lays the foundation of our proposed algorithm called *CoverBRS*. Specifically, we first select a c-cover T of O. Next, we generate a new instance of *BRS* problem for the c-cover T by defining a new aggregate score function f_T and a new size $(1-c)a \times (1-c)b$ of the query rectangle. Lastly, we invoke the *SliceBRS* algorithm to solve the new instance and prove that the answer to the new instance of *BRS* problem is a constant-bounded approximate answer to the original one. In the subsequent subsections, we elaborate on these issues.

5.2 c-cover

We first introduce the concept of *c-cover*. Then we show some properties of c-cover which we shall use to achieve a constant-bounded approximate answer to the *BRS* problem.

DEFINITION 7. [*c-cover*] *Consider a set of spatial object O in space P and a query rectangle of size $a \times b$. Let T be a set of spatial points in P. We say T is a **c-cover** of O iff for any object $o_i \in O$, there exists one point $t \in T$ such that o_i is inside the $ca \times cb$ rectangular region centered at t.*

Hereafter, we refer to the points in T as spatial objects.

Example 12: Consider the example shown in Fig 8. The set of black and white nodes is a set of spatial objects, denoted by O. The set of black nodes $\{o_1, o_2, o_3\}$ is a c-cover of O. □

Based on the definition of c-cover, we can derive the following lemma, which is the foundation to get a constant-bounded approximate answer to the *BRS* problem. Based on this lemma, we shall establish the approximation bound of our proposed algorithm in Section 5.6.

LEMMA 11. *Consider a set of spatial objects O, a query rectangle of size $a \times b$. Let T be a c-cover of O, where $c \in (0, 1)$. For each spatial object $t \in T$, let $O_{r_t ca,cb}$ be the set of spatial objects inside the $ca \times cb$ rectangular region centered at t. Given a point p in space P, if an $(1 - c)a \times (1 - c)b)$ rectangular region centered at p can cover t, then the $a \times b$ rectangular region centered at p can cover all objects in $O_{r_t^{ca,cb}}$.*

5.3 Selection of c-cover

We next study how to select a c-cover of O. Ideally, we would like to select a minimum c-cover, on which we define a new instance of the *BRS* problem. This is because it would be more efficient for answering the new instance defined on a smaller set of spatial objects.

THEOREM 3. *Finding a minimum c-cover is NP-hard.*

Since finding the minimum c-cover is a special case of set cover problem, at first glance it may seem that we can approximate the minimum c-cover by using a greedy algorithm with an approximate ratio of $1 - 1/e$, where e is the Euler's number. Specifically, in each iteration, we select the spatial object t that can maximize the number of uncovered objects inside the $ca \times cb$ rectangular region centered at t, referred to as neighborhood of t.

Although the greedy algorithm works, unfortunately its complexity is high. It involves too many range queries in the computation. A range query in 2D space can be answered in $O(\log n + k)$ time [3], where n is the number of spatial objects and k is the number of spatial objects in the query range. In the worst case, there will be $O(n)$ iterations in the greedy algorithm and we have to perform $O(n)$ range queries in each iteration. The greedy algorithm takes $O(n^2 \log n)$ time to select a c-cover in the worst case. Thus, we need to devise a more efficient solution to select a c-cover.

Quadtree-based c-cover selection We propose a quadtree-based heuristic algorithm in order to select a c-cover efficiently. Before we present the algorithm, we first explain how we use the quadtree to index the spatial objects and give a lemma, which enables us to select a relatively small c-cover efficiently.

We use a quadtree to index all spatial objects in the space. The quadtree recursively partitions the space into four equal-sized rectangular regions[2] until each leaf node contains one spatial object.

[2]We use a minimum bounding rectangle (MBR) to enclose all spatial objects, thus we refer to the partitions as "rectangular regions" instead of "quadrants".

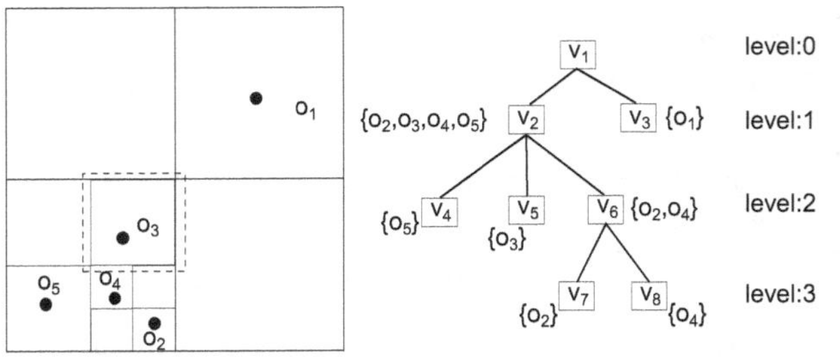

Figure 9: Selection of c-cover T.

Each node v in the quadtree corresponds to a rectangular region together with the spatial objects in the region. For each node v in the quadtree, we maintain a point, denoted by $v.t$. Specifically, if v is an internal node, let $v.t$ be the center point of the corresponding region. If v is a leaf node, let $v.t$ be the spatial object in the corresponding region.

Example 13: Consider the example in Figure 9. We consider five spatial objects $o_1, \ldots o_5$ in the space. We construct a quadtree to index these five spatial objects as shown in the figure. Node v_1 corresponds to the entire space and $v_1.t$ is the center of the entire space. Node v_3 corresponds to the top-right rectangular region. It is a leaf node and it contains spatial object o_1. Thus $v_3.t$ is spatial object o_1. □

We proceed to derive the following lemma:

LEMMA 12. *We denote by $v.l$ the level of a node v in the quadtree. Let V_l^1 be the set of maintained points of internal nodes at level l in the quadtree,* i.e., *$V_l^1 = \{v.t|v$ is an internal node $\wedge\, v.l = l\}$. Let V_l^2 be the set of maintained points of leaf nodes at any level not lower than l,* i.e., *$V_l^2 = \{v.t|v$ is a leaf node $\wedge\, v.l \geq l\}$. If the corresponding region of a node at level l can be fully covered by a $ca \times cb$ rectangle, then V_l^1 and V_l^2 together form a c-cover.*

Example 14: Consider the example in Figure 9. Let the size of the dashed-line rectangle be $ca \times cb$. The corresponding region of nodes at level 2 can be fully covered by the dashed-line rectangle. In this case, $\{o_1, o_3, o_5\}$ together with the center of the region in v_6 form a c-cover. □

Lemma 12 tells us that we can select a c-cover by retrieving V_l^1 and V_l^2 once we identify a level l such that the corresponding region of a node at level l can be fully covered by a $ca \times cb$ rectangle. However, there may exist several possible values for level l. Which value should we select? As we have discussed at the beginning of this subsection, we would like to select a c-cover with smaller number of spatial objects. The center of a higher level region can cover more spatial objects than any center of its descendant regions at lower levels. Therefore, to get a smaller c-cover, we use the highest level that can satisfy the condition in Lemma 12. Since the quadtree recursively partitions the space into four equal-sized rectangular regions, we can directly compute the level by:

$$l = \max\left(\lceil \log_2 \frac{Height}{ca} \rceil, \lceil \log_2 \frac{Width}{cb} \rceil\right). \quad (1)$$

where $Height$ and $Width$ are the height and the width of the entire space, respectively.

Now we are ready to present our quadtree-based heuristic algorithm. The algorithm comprises three steps: (1) identify the highest level l; (2) collect the centers of regions in all internal nodes at level l; and (3) collect the spatial objects in all leaf nodes at any level not lower than l. The algorithm is outlined in *Function* Select. It takes as input a set of spatial objects O and a parameter c. We use a

```
Function Select(O, c)
  Output: A set of objects T
1 QT ←the indexing quadtree;
2 T ← ∅;
3 l ← max(⌈log2 Height/(ca)⌉, ⌈log2 Width/(cb)⌉);
4 foreach internal quadtree node v s.t. v.l = l do
5   | T ← T ∪ {v.t};
6 foreach leaf quadtree node v s.t. v.l ≥ l do
7   | T ← T ∪ {v.t};
8 return T;
```

```
Algorithm 2: CoverBRS
  Input: A set of objects O, query rectangle size a × b, parameter c
  Output: A point p
1 T ← Select(O, c);
2 f_T ← New aggregate function;
3 p ← SliceBRS(T, (1 − c)a, (1 − c)b, f_T);
4 return p;
```

quadtree QT to index all spatial objects in the space (line 1). The quadtree is independent of the size of the query rectangle and is constructed in advance. Each node in the quadtree is associated with a rectangular region and each leaf node in the quadtree contains only one spatial object. Given a query rectangle of $a \times b$, in order to select a c-cover of the spatial objects O, we compute the highest level l in the quadtree using the Equation 1 (line 3). Then for each internal node at level l in the quadtree, we add the center of the associated rectangular region into T (lines 4–5). For each leaf node whose level is not lower than l in the quadtree, we add the object in the node into T (lines 6–7). Consequently, we find a c-cover of O.

Complexity We can compute the level l in $O(1)$ time. We retrieve the center of internal nodes at level l and all leaf nodes whose level is not lower than l in the quadtree. We use a list to maintain all leaf nodes sorted by their level. Thus, it takes $O(n)$ time to select a c-cover T, where n is the number of spatial objects in O. The complexity of our proposed quadtree-based algorithm is much better than the complexity of the aforementioned greedy algorithm.

5.4 Generate a New Instance of BRS

We next present how to generate a new instance of the *BRS* problem based on the generated c-cover of O, which is denoted by T. Specifically, we need to (1) define a new aggregate score function over T, and (2) define a new size of query rectangle. We first introduce how to define the aggregate function over the c-cover T.

Aggregate score function over c-cover To define a new aggregate score function, we need to represent all the objects in O by objects in T. We utilize the quadtree in *Function* Select to decide which objects in O can be represented by an object in T. Specifically, as we have presented, an object t_i in T is selected from a node v in the quadtree. We let t_i represent all spatial objects inside the region in v. Since the objects in T belongs to different nodes in the quadtree, an object o in O will be represented by exactly only one object in T.

Let $D(t_i)$ denote the set of objects represented by t_i for $t_i \in T$. Then we can define the new aggregate score function f_T for the objects in T in the new instance as follows:

DEFINITION 8. [***New aggregate score function***] *We define the new aggregate score function f_T as: $f_T : 2^T \rightarrow \mathbb{R}$, which maps a subset of T to a real number such that for any $T_i \subseteq T$ and* $T_i = \{t_1, \ldots, t_j\}$

$$f_T(T_i) = f(D(t_1) \cup \ldots \cup D(t_j))$$

One can easily verify that f_T is still a submodular monotone function.

New size of the query rectangle We next present how to define the size of new query rectangle and the intuition behind it. According to Lemma 11, we define the size of query rectangle in the new instance as $(1-c)a \times (1-c)b$. Note that if a $(1-c)a \times (1-c)$ rectangular region centered at a point p can cover an object $t_i \in T$ in the new instance, then the $a \times b$ rectangular region centered at p can cover all objects $D(t_i)$ represented by t_i in the original instance. In this way, the answer to the new instance is a good approximation of the answer to the original *BRS* problem. We shall prove later that the answer to the new instance is a constant-bounded approximate answer to the original one. Observe that once we have generated a new instance of the *BRS* problem with the newly defined aggregate score function and the size of the query rectangle, we can invoke the *SliceBRS* algorithm to solve the new instance.

5.5 The CoverBRS Algorithm

We are now ready to present the *CoverBRS* algorithm which is outlined in Algorithm 2. It takes as input a set of objects O, the size $a \times b$ of query rectangle, and a parameter c for selecting the c-cover T. It first selects a set T of spatial points from space P by invoking the `Select` procedure with the parameter c (line 1). Then it defines a new aggregate score function, denoted by f_T, based on Definition 8 for the c-cover T (line 2). Lastly, it invokes the *SliceBRS* algorithm to answer the new instance of the *BRS* problem on the subset T with aggregate function f_T and query rectangle of size $(1-c)a \times (1-c)b$.

Complexity It takes $O(n)$ for our quadtree-based heuristic algorithm to select the subset T, where n is the number of spatial objects in O. It takes $O(n^t \times n^t_s)$ time to invoke the *SliceBRS* algorithm to solve the new instance, where n^t is the number of spatial objects in T and n^t_s is the number of maximal slabs that are actually searched. Hence, the overall time complexity of the *CoverBRS* algorithm is $O(n + n^t \times n^t_s)$. Recall that the complexity of *SliceBRS* is $O(n \times n_s)$. Since the c-cover is a subset of all spatial objects and only a few maximal slabs are searched, *CoverBRS* has a better efficiency than *SliceBRS*. In our experiment, we can observe that *CoverBRS* is always more efficient than *SliceBRS*, especially when there are tens to hundreds of millions of spatial objects in the space.

5.6 Approximation Ratio

Finally, we present the approximation ratio of the answer returned by the *CoverBRS* algorithm for different values of c and also prove that the approximation ratio is tight. The proofs of the following lemma and theorems can be found in Appendix B.

LEMMA 13. *Let p be any point in the space, $O_{r_p^{a,b}}$ be the set of objects in O that are covered by $r_p^{a,b}$, and $T_{r_p^{(1-c)a,(1-c)b}}$ be the set of objects in T that are covered by $r_p^{(1-c)a,(1-c)b}$. The following holds:*

$$f_T(T_{r_p^{(1-c)a,(1-c)b}}) \leq f(O_{r_p^{a,b}})$$

THEOREM 4. *When $c = 1/3$, Algorithm* CoverBRS *returns a (1/4)-approximate answer to the optimal solution.*

THEOREM 5. *The 1/4 approximation ratio is tight for the* CoverBRS *algorithm when $c = 1/3$.*

THEOREM 6. *When* $c = 1/2$*, Algorithm 2 returns a (1/9)-approximate answer to the optimal solution.*

THEOREM 7. *The 1/9 approximation ratio is tight for the* CoverBRS *algorithm when* $c = 1/2$*.*

6. EXPERIMENTAL STUDY

In this section, we first present the setup of our experiments. Then, we study the performance of our algorithms w.r.t quality of results, efficiency, and scalability using real-world datasets and aplicaitons. All algorithms are implemented in C++ and compiled by VS 2013. All experiments are run on a Windows PC with Intel Xeon 3.70GHz CPU and 64GB memory.

6.1 Experimental Setup

Real-world applications Recall from Section 1, the *BRS* problem can be exploited to address the problem of (1) finding the most influential region and (2) finding the most diversified region. Hence, we evaluate the performance of our algorithms in the context of these two applications. Here, we briefly describe the setup for these two applications.

Application 1: Most Influential Region. Recall that the goal of this application is to find the most influential region in the context of the influence maximization problem [17]. Specifically, given the size of a region, we can apply our proposed algorithms to find the most influential region satisfying the size constraint such that the expected number of influenced users is maximized. In this application, we adopt the widely used *Independent Cascade* (IC) Model [17] to model the influence propagation. Specifically, we use a weighted directed graph to model the users and their relationships. A node in the graph represents a user. Each edge (u, v) is assigned with a propagation probability which ranges over (0,1]. In the IC model, each node is either active or inactive and a node is only allowed to turn from inactive to active, but not vice versa. By assuming that a regional marketing strategy can directly affect the people who visit the region, these people will serve as the set of seeds S in the influence propagation following the IC model. Specifically, let S_t denote the set of users activated at time step t and $S_0 = S$. At time step $t + 1$, each user $v \in S_t$ has a single chance to activate each currently inactive neighbor u with a probability $p(v, u)$. The propagation process terminates when $S_t = \emptyset$. Thus, the influence of a region is the expected number of influenced users.

Application 2: Most Diversified Region. The second application of the *BRS* problem is to find the most diversified region. Specifically, given the size of a region, we can apply our algorithms to find a region with maximum diversity. We consider a set of spatial objects, each of which is associated with a set of tags to indicate its categories, *e.g.,* "restaurant" and "bar". The *diversity* of a region is then measured by the number of different tags of the spatial objects inside the region. In this application, the submodular monotone function is $f(O_i) = |\bigcup_{o \in O_i} L(o)|$, for $O_i \subseteq O$, where O is the set of spatial objects, and $L(o)$ is the set of tags that are associated with spatial object o.

Table 2: Summary of datasets for Application 1.

Property	Brightkite	Gowalla
# of objects	693,362	1,256,692
# of check-ins	4,491,143	6,442,890
# of users	58,228	196,591
Width	314.391	495.658
Height	359.823	353.771

Table 3: Summary of datasets for Application 2.

Property	Yelp	Meetup
# of objects	48,753	589,715
# of tags/POI	48	14.7
Width	23.165	355.839
Height	123.936	180

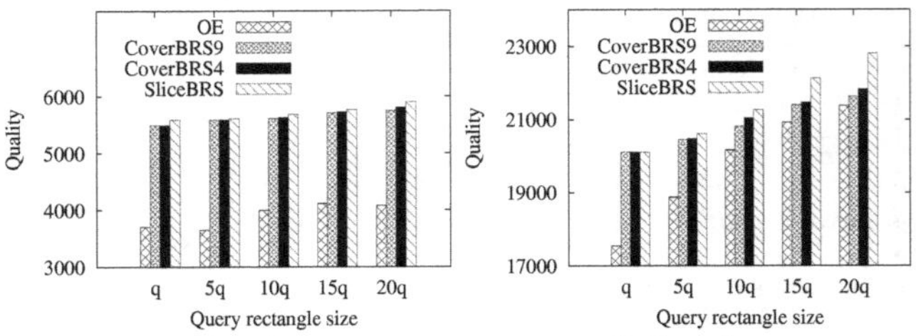

(a) Brightkite (b) Gowalla

Figure 10: Quality vs. kq.

Datasets To support evaluation of our algorithms for the first application, we use two real-life datasets[3], `Brightkite` and `Gowalla`, whose properties are given in Table 2. We use another two datasets, `Meetup` and `Yelp`[4], to evaluate our algorithms for the second application. The properties of these two datasets are reported in Table 3. In Appendix C.1, we present a more detailed description of the datasets.

Evaluated algorithms We evaluate the following algorithms. (a) *SliceBRS* algorithm; (b) *CoverBRS* algorithm with parameter $c = 1/3$, denoted as *CoverBRS4*; (c) *CoverBRS* algorithm with parameter $c = 1/2$, denoted as *CoverBRS9*, and (d) *Optimal Enclosure* algorithm proposed in [21] for addressing the *MaxRS* problem, denoted as *OE*. Recall that the *CoverBRS* algorithm returns an approximate answer to the *BRS* problem while *SliceBRS* finds the exact answer. In the *SliceBRS* algorithm, we need to partition the space into slices with fixed width. In our experiments, we set the width of each slice as b, where b is the width of the given rectangle. The *OE* algorithm is designed for the *MaxRS* problem and can be regarded as a heuristic algorithm for the *BRS* problem. Note that the aggregation of the objects in the region found by the *OE* algorithm for the *BRS* problem does not have an approximate bound to the optimal value. Due to space constraints, experiments related to the adaptation of *SliceBRS* algorithm to efficiently solve the *MaxRS* problem is reported in Appendix C.2.

Query Rectangles As the cardinality of the datasets has an influence on the efficiency of the algorithms, it is not a good idea to use the same size of query rectangle on different datasets. Therefore, we consider the cardinality of the datasets by setting $q = \frac{Height}{|O|} \times \frac{Width}{|O|}$ as the unit size of query rectangle where $Height$ and $Weight$ are the height and width of the minimum rectangular space that can include all spatial objects and $|O|$ is the number of spatial objects. Let $k \cdot q = (k \cdot \frac{Height}{|O|}) \times (k \cdot \frac{Width}{|O|})$. We vary the size of query rectangle by using different values for k.

Performance measures We consider the following performance measures: (a) The runtime of each algorithm and (b) the aggregate score of the spatial objects in rectangular region $r_p^{a,b}$, where p is the point returned by each algorithm and the aggregate score is denoted by $f(.)$ in our problem definition. In the subsequent discussion, we refer to the latter measure as "quality" of the results.

6.2 Quality and Efficiency

We first conduct a set of experiments to evaluate the performance of our algorithms in the aforementioned applications. We use the following five sizes for query rectangles, q, $5q$, $10q$, $15q$, and $20q$.

Application 1 (Most Influential Region). We first study the performance of our algorithm for Application 1, *i.e.,* finding the most influential region, in terms of both quality and runtime. Figure 10 reports the quality of the returned region for query rectangles of dif-

[3] http://snap.stanford.edu/data/index.html

[4] http://www.yelp.com.sg/dataset_challenge

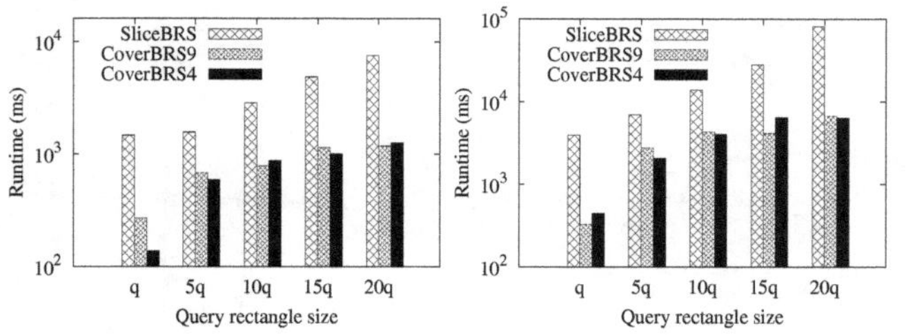

(a) Brightkite (b) Gowalla

Figure 11: Runtime vs. kq.

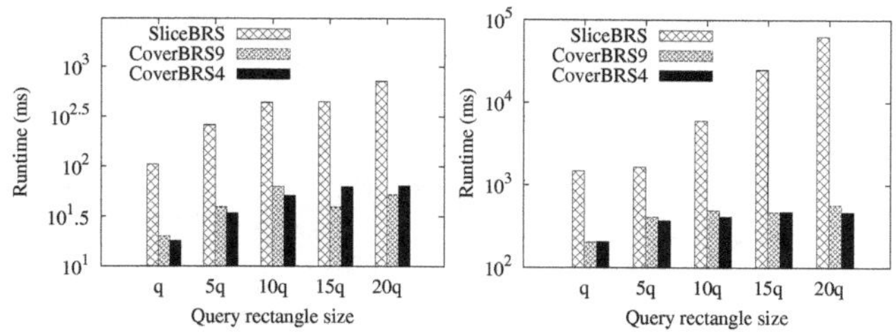

(a) Yelp (b) Meetup

Figure 13: Runtime vs. kq.

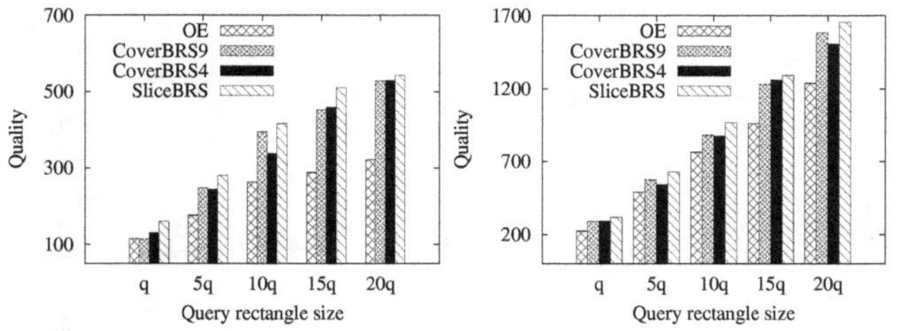

(a) Yelp (b) Meetup

Figure 12: Quality vs. kq.

Table 4: Effectiveness of maximal regions.

	Dataset	#DR	#MR
App. 1	Brightkite	38,757,062	247,332
	Gowalla	46,582,671	349,723
App. 2	Yelp	6,605,228	40,460
	Meetup	22,786,743	167,789

ferent sizes. First, we observe that the regions returned by *CoverBRS4* and *CoverBRS9* have comparable quality to the regions returned by *SliceBRS*. Second, the region returned by *OE* has the worst quality. This is because *OE* is designed for the *MaxRS* problem, which adopts different aggregate function from that used in the *BRS* problem. Thus, it is inappropriate to adopt *OE* to solve the *BRS* problem. In the subsequent discussions related to efficiency and scalability, we do not compare *OE* with our techniques.

Figure 11 depicts the runtime of our three algorithms for query rectangles of different sizes. Note that the y-axis is in logarithmic scale. Observe that although *SliceBRS* can complete in reasonable time, it is less efficient than *CoverBRS4* and *CoverBRS9*. This is due to the reasons mentioned in the preceding section: (1) the *CoverBRS* algorithm can efficiently select a c-cover T, (2) the c-cover T is sparser and has less spatial objects than the original set of spatial objects O, and (3) the new problem instance defined on T needs less computation.

Application 2 (Most Diversified Region). Next, we investigate the performance of our algorithm for Application 2. Figure 12 and Figure 13 report the quality and runtime of the evaluated algorithms, respectively. We can make similar observations as those on Figure 10 and Figure 11.

6.3 Usefulness of Optimization Strategies

We conduct several experiments to validate the usefulness of the various strategies we proposed in Sections 4 and 5 to improve efficiency of our proposed algorithms.

Usefulness of Maximal Region We first evaluate the usefulness of maximal region in improving the performance of our algorithm. We use $10q$ as the size for the query rectangle for each dataset. We compare (1) the number of disjoint regions, denoted by #DR, and (2) the number of maximal regions, denoted by #MR. The results are reported in Table 4. Observe that compared to the number of disjoint regions, the number of maximal regions is smaller. In fact, the number of maximal regions is about 1% of the number of disjoint regions. Thus, maximal regions enables us to reduce search space significantly and yield better efficiency.

Usefulness of Maximal Slab Next, we investigate the usefulness of maximal slabs in improving the efficiency of our algorithm. By using $10q$ as the size for the query rectangle, we compare (1) the number of maximal regions, denoted by #MR, (2) the number of maximal slabs, denoted by #MS, (3) the number of maximal slabs that are processed by `SearchMR`, denoted by #MSP, and (4) the number of disjoint regions (including maximal regions) that the algorithm actually process, denoted by #DRP (Note that it is possible that a non-maximal region is processed by our algorithm). The results are reported in Table5. We can see that only a small part of the maximal slabs are processed by `SearchMR`. Furthermore, compared to the number of maximal regions, only a small set of disjoint regions is processed. Note that our maximal slab-based pruning technique has a better performance on `Yelp`, `Brightkite` and `Gowalla`. This is because that two venues in `Meetup` share many common tags, the upper bound that we estimate for a maximal slab is loose. Since the upper bounds of many maximal slabs are larger than the current result, we need to keep processing these maximal slabs by invoking `SearchMR`.

Usefulness of Cutting Space into Slices In this set of experiment, we evaluate the usefulness of the idea of cutting the space into slices. We implement an algorithm, namely *SliceBRS-NoSlice*, which is the *SliceBRS* algorithm without cutting the space into slices. We use 5 sizes of query rectangles, q, $5q$, $10q$, $15q$, and $20q$ on `Brightkite` and compare the runtime of *SliceBRS* and *SliceBRS-NoSlice*. Note that *SliceBRS-NoSlice* runs out of memory when the size of query rectangle is $20q$. Figure 14 reports the runtime of the two algorithms for 4 query rectangles of different sizes, q, $5q$, $10q$ and $15q$. Notice that *SliceBRS* is orders of magnitudes faster than *SliceBRS-NoSlice*. Thus, the idea of cutting the space into slices greatly improves the efficiency of the *SliceBRS* algorithm.

Usefulness of c-cover We now evaluate the usefulness of c-cover in improving the efficiency of our algorithms. We use $10q$ as the size for the query rectangle and compare the (1) the number of spatial objects in the original set of spatial objects O, denoted by $|O|$, (2) the number of spatial objects in the c-cover, denoted by $|T|$, (3) the number of disjoint regions in the new instance, denoted by $\#DR_T$, (4) the number of maximal regions in the new instance, denoted by $\#MR_T$, and (5) the number of disjoint regions that the algorithm actually processed, denoted by $\#DRP_T$. Table 6 reports the results. We can observe that the number of spatial objects in the new instance is smaller than in the original set of spatial objects. In addition, both the number of maximal regions and the number of disjoint regions that are processed are greatly reduced compared to the original instance. Therefore, the c-cover is very useful in efficiently finding an approximate answer to the *BRS* problem.

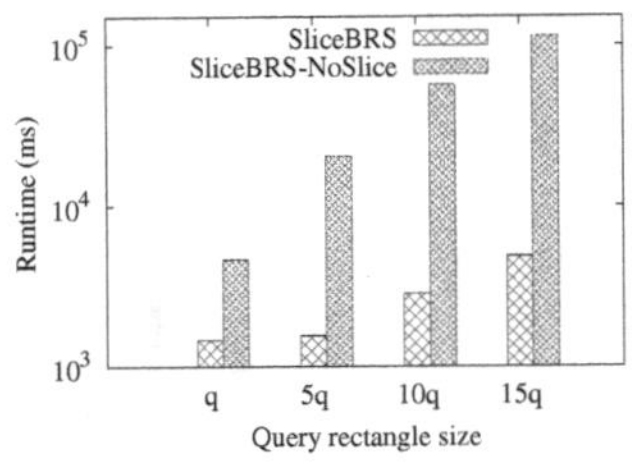

Figure 14: Runtime of *SliceBRS* with and without cutting the space into slices.

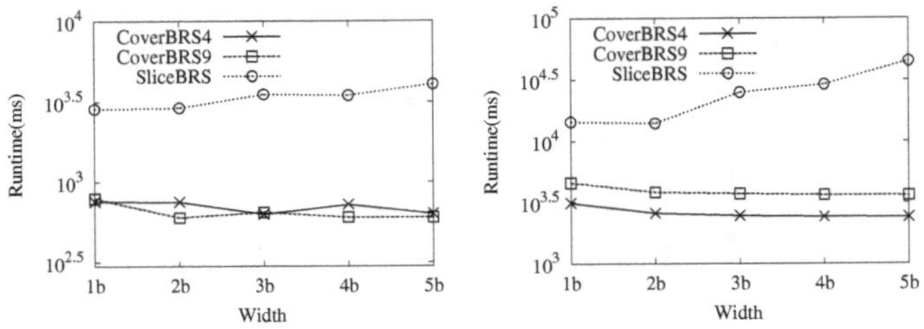

(a) Brightkite (b) Gowalla

Figure 15: Runtime vs. slice width in Application 1.

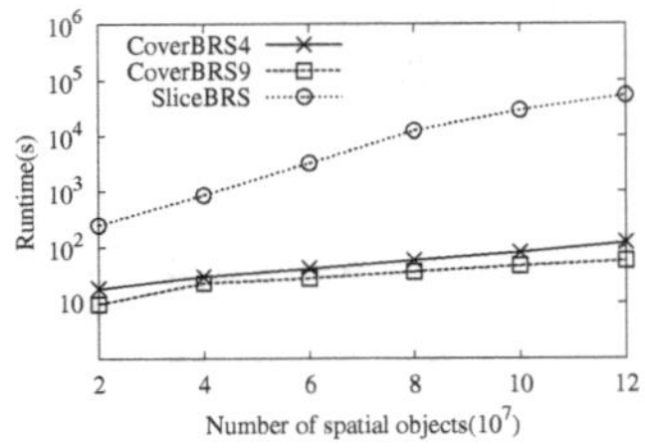

Figure 16: Runime vs. graph size.

Table 5: Effectiveness of maximal slabs.

	Dataset	#MR	#MS	#MSP	#DRP
App. 1	Brightkite	247,332	649,442	39	1,249
	Gowalla	349,723	1,206,367	132	8,417
App. 2	Yelp	40,460	33,699	170	6,342
	Meetup	167,789	516,379	3,257	199,975

Table 6: Effectiveness of c-covers.

	Dataset	$\|O\|$	$\|T\|$	#DR$_T$	#MR$_T$	#DRP$_T$
App. 1	Brightkite	693,362	91,308	223,769	39,156	8
	Gowalla	1,256,692	158,069	390,003	70,656	12
App. 2	Yelp	48,753	6,133	36,304	2,301	86
	Meetup	589,715	91,547	201,779	32,222	389

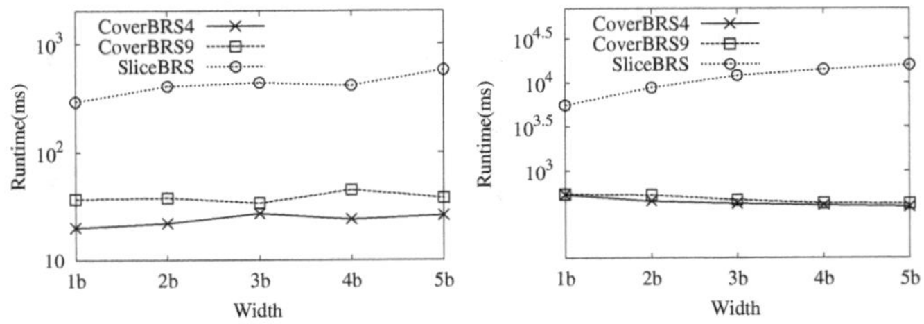

(a) Yelp (b) Meetup

Figure 17: Runtime vs. slice width in Application 2.

6.4 Effect of Parameters

Next, we investigate the effect of parameters on our proposed algorithms. Specifically, we study the effect of slice width here. Due to space constraints, the effect of the query rectangle on the performance of our algorithms is reported in Appendix C.3.

The value for θ controls the width of each slice. In this experiment, we use $10q$ as the query and vary the value of θ from 1 to 5 with an increment of 1 for each dataset in the two applications.

Application 1 (Most Influential Region). Figure 15 plots the runtime of the three algorithms with different slice widths in Application 1. Observe that as the width increases, the runtime of *SliceBRS* increases. This is because that the space will be cut into lesser slices when the slice width is larger. Consequently, there are potentially more maximal regions in a slice and lesser maximal regions can be pruned. We can also observe that *CoverBRS4* and *CoverBRS9* are less sensitive to the slice width.

Application 2 (Most Diversified Region). The results for Application 2 are reported in Figure 17. We can make similar observations as those on Figure 15.

In summary, observe that θ can be set to 1 for the aforementioned applications. More importantly, there are potentially many maximal regions can be pruned and a little redundant computation since each rectangle will only be considered in at most two slices. This set of experiments proves again that the idea of cutting space into slices greatly improves the efficiency of *SliceBRS*.

6.5 Scalability with Graph Size

Lastly, we investigate the scalability of our three algorithms. We generate synthetic datasets under Gaussian distribution for Application 2. We set the number of spatial objects of dataset to be from 20,000,000 to 120,000,000 . By following the default setting in the work that is most germane to our work [7], the spatial objects fall in a space of $10^9 \times 10^9$ and the size of the query rectangle is $10^6 \times 10^6$. For each spatial object, we randomly assign three labels from 388 categories in Foursquare. We report the runtime of the three algorithms in Figure 16. Note that the y-axis is in log-scale. From the figure we can observe that the two approximate algorithms scale well with the graph size. The exact algorithm becomes significantly slower when the number of spatial objects in the dataset gets larger.

7. CONCLUSIONS AND FUTURE WORK

The quest for high quality location-based services has become more pressing due to explosive growth of mobile devices and geo-tagged data. In this paper, we introduce the best region search (*BRS*) problem that aims to find a rectangular region with a given size such that the aggregation of the spatial objects in the region is maximized. This problem is fundamental to supporting several location-based applications such as most influential region search and most diversified region search. To this end, we propose a novel algorithm called *SliceBRS* that employs several pruning strategies to find the exact answer to the *BRS* problem. Since slight imprecision is acceptable in many real-world applications, we further propose the *CoverBRS* algorithm to find a constant-bounded answer to the *BRS* problem with a much better efficiency. The experimental study demonstrates that *SliceBRS* can find the exact answer to the *BRS* problem whereas *CoverBRS* can find a competitive answer with a better efficiency. These algorithms scale well with the number of spatial objects. As part of future work, we intend to explore efficient techniques to find *top-k regions* in the context of the *BRS* problem and explore *BRS* problem in the context of road networks.

Acknowledgments This research is supported by the National Research Foundation Singapore under its Interactive Digital Media (IDM) Strategic Research Programme, a Singapore MOE AcRF Tier 2 Grant (ARC30/12), and a Singapore MOE AcRF Tier 1 Grant (RG22/15). Wen-Chih Peng was supported in part by MOST Taiwan, Project No. 102-2221-E-009 -171 -MY3 and 104-2221-E-009 -138 -MY2.

8. REFERENCES

[1] C. Borgs, M. Brautbar, J. Chayes, and B. Lucier. Maximizing social influence in nearly optimal time. In *Proceedings of the Twenty-Fifth Annual ACM-SIAM Symposium on Discrete Algorithms*, pages 946–957, 2014.

[2] X. Cao, G. Cong, C. S. Jensen, and M. L. Yiu. Retrieving regions of interest for user exploration. *Proceedings of the VLDB Endowment*, 7(9):733–744, 2014.

[3] B. Chazelle. Filtering search: A new approach to query-answering. *SIAM J. Comput.*, 15(3):703–724, 1986.

[4] W. Chen, C. Wang, and Y. Wang. Scalable influence maximization for prevalent viral marketing in large-scale social networks. In *International Conference on Knowledge Discovery and Data Mining*, pages 1029–1038, 2010.

[5] Z. Chen, Y. Liu, R. C.-W. Wong, J. Xiong, G. Mai, and C. Long. Efficient algorithms for optimal location queries in road networks. In *International Conference on Management of Data, SIGMOD*, pages 123–134, 2014.

[6] H.-J. Cho and C.-W. Chung. Indexing range sum queries in spatio-temporal databases. *Information and Software Technology*, 49(4):324–331, 2007.

[7] D.-W. Choi, C.-W. Chung, and Y. Tao. A scalable algorithm for maximizing range sum in spatial databases. *Proceedings of the VLDB Endowment*, 5(11):1088–1099, 2012.

[8] M. Conforti and R. Rizzi. Combinatorial optimization - polyhedra and efficiency: A book review. *Quarterly Journal of the Belgian, French and Italian Operations Research Societies*, 2(2):153–159, 2004.

[9] Y. Du, D. Zhang, and T. Xia. The optimal-location query. In *Advances in Spatial and Temporal Databases*, pages 163–180. Springer, 2005.

[10] R. J. Fowler, M. S. Paterson, and S. L. Tanimoto. Optimal packing and covering in the plane are np-complete. *Information processing letters*, 12(3):133–137, 1981.

[11] J. Huang, Z. Wen, J. Qi, R. Zhang, J. Chen, and Z. He. Top-k most influential locations selection. In *Proceedings of the 20th Conference on Information and Knowledge Management*, pages 2377–2380, 2011.

[12] H. Imai and T. Asano. Finding the connected components and a maximum clique of an intersection graph of rectangles in the plane. *Journal of algorithms*, 4(4):310–323, 1983.

[13] K. Jung, W. Heo, and W. Chen. Irie: Scalable and robust influence maximization in social networks. In *International Conference on Data Mining, ICDM*, pages 918–923, 2012.

[14] M. Jurgens and H.-J. Lenz. The r a*-tree: an improved r*-tree with materialized data for supporting range queries on olap-data. In *Proceedings. Ninth International Workshop on Database and Expert Systems Applications*, pages 186–191, 1998.

[15] A. Kalinin, U. Cetintemel, and S. Zdonik. Interactive data exploration using semantic windows. In *International Conference on Management of Data, SIGMOD*, pages 505–516, 2014.

[16] A. Kalinin, U. Cetintemel, and S. Zdonik. Searchlight: enabling integrated search and exploration over large multidimensional data. *Proceedings of the VLDB Endowment*, 8(10):1094–1105, 2015.

[17] D. Kempe, J. Kleinberg, and É. Tardos. Maximizing the spread of influence through a social network. In *International Conference on Knowledge Discovery and Data Mining*, pages 137–146, 2003.

[18] I. Lazaridis and S. Mehrotra. Progressive approximate aggregate queries with a multi-resolution tree structure. In *SIGMOD Record*, volume 30, pages 401–412, 2001.

[19] B. Liu, G. Cong, Y. Zeng, D. Xu, and Y. M. Chee. Influence spreading path and its application to the time constrained social influence maximization problem and beyond. *Transactions on Knowledge and Data Engineering*, 26(8):1904–1917, 2014.

[20] J. Liu, G. Yu, and H. Sun. Subject-oriented top-k hot region queries in spatial dataset. In *Proceedings of the 20th Conference on Information and Knowledge Management*, pages 2409–2412, 2011.

[21] S. C. Nandy and B. B. Bhattacharya. A unified algorithm for finding maximum and minimum object enclosing rectangles and cuboids. *Computers & Mathematics with Applications*, 29:45–61, 1995.

[22] D. Papadias, P. Kalnis, J. Zhang, and Y. Tao. Efficient olap operations in spatial data warehouses. In *Advances in spatial and temporal databases*, pages 443–459. Springer, 2001.

[23] C. Sheng and Y. Tao. New results on two-dimensional orthogonal range aggregation in external memory. In *Proceedings of the thirtieth SIGMOD-SIGACT-SIGART symposium on Principles of database systems*, pages 129–139, 2011.

[24] Y. Tang, X. Xiao, and Y. Shi. Influence maximization: Near-optimal time complexity meets practical efficiency. In *International Conference on Management of Data, SIGMOD*, pages 75–86, 2014.

[25] Y. Tao, X. Hu, D.-W. Choi, and C.-W. Chung. Approximate maxrs in spatial databases. *Proceedings of the VLDB Endowment*, 6(13):1546–1557, 2013.

[26] R. C.-W. Wong, M. T. Özsu, P. S. Yu, A. W.-C. Fu, and L. Liu. Efficient method for maximizing bichromatic reverse nearest neighbor. *Proceedings of the VLDB Endowment*, 2(1):1126–1137, 2009.

[27] T. Xia, D. Zhang, E. Kanoulas, and Y. Du. On computing top-t most influential spatial sites. In *Proceedings of the VLDB Endowment*, pages 946–957, 2005.

[28] X. Xiao, B. Yao, and F. Li. Optimal location queries in road network databases. In *Proceedings of the 27th International Conference on Data Engineering, ICDE*, pages 804–815, 2011.

[29] D. Yan, R. C.-W. Wong, and W. Ng. Efficient methods for finding influential locations with adaptive grids. In *Proceedings of the 20th Conference on Information and Knowledge Management*, pages 1475–1484, 2011.

[30] L. Zhan, Y. Zhang, W. Zhang, and X. Lin. Finding top k most influential spatial facilities over uncertain objects. In *IEEE Transactions on Knowledge and Data Engineering*, pages 922–931, 2012.

[31] D. Zhang, Y. Du, T. Xia, and Y. Tao. Progressive computation of the min-dist optimal-location query. In *Proceedings of the VLDB Endowment*, pages 643–654, 2006.

[32] Z. Zhou, W. Wu, X. Li, M. L. Lee, and W. Hsu. Maxfirst for maxbrknn. In *Proceedings of the 27th International Conference on Data Engineering, ICDE*, pages 828–839, 2011.

APPENDIX

A. EXTENSION TO OBJECTS WITH SAME COORDINATES

In this paper, we consider the case that the coordinates of each spatial object is unique. In real-life, it is possible that several spatial objects share the same x or y coordinate. To handle the extension, we just need to assign a strict order on all spatial objects and always use this order to break ties. For example, consider two spatial objects o_i and o_j. We draw two $a \times b$ rectangles centered at o_i and o_j, denoted by r_i and r_j respectively. Assume that o_i and o_j have the same x-coordinate and we assign an order such that $o_i \succ o_j$. When we scan from left to right, the sweep-line always meets the left edge of r_i before it meets the left edge of r_j.

B. PROOFS

Proof of Lemma 1:

PROOF. If o is inside the $a \times b$ rectangular region $r_p^{a,b}$, we have, $p.x - \frac{b}{2} < o.x < p.x + \frac{b}{2}$ and $p.y - \frac{a}{2} < o.y < p.y + \frac{a}{2}$. We can easily derive: $o.x - \frac{b}{2} < p.x < o.x + \frac{b}{2}, o.y - \frac{a}{2} < p.y < o.y + \frac{a}{2}$. Thus p is inside the rectangular region $r_o^{a,b}$. Similarly, we can prove that if p is inside the $a \times b$ rectangular region $r_o^{a,b}$, then o is inside the rectangular region $r_p^{a,b}$. Putting these together, we conclude that object o is inside $r_p^{a,b}$ iff p is inside $r_o^{a,b}$. □

Proof of Theorem 1:

PROOF. Let P be the space in the *BRS* problem and the *SIRI* problem and $p \in P$ is a point in space P. According to Lemma 1, for any spatial object $o_i \in O$, we have $o_i \in O_{r_p^{a,b}}$ iff $r_{o_i}^{a,b} \in A(p)$. Thus $f(O_{r_p^{a,b}}) = h(A(p))$ holds. If $p \in P$ can maximize $h(A(p))$ in the *SIRI* problem, then it can also maximize $f(O_{r_p^{a,b}})$ in the *BRS* problem. Consequently, an answer to the *SIRI* problem is also an answer to the *BRS* problem. □

Proof of Lemma 2:

PROOF. Since each disjoint region is the intersection of a set of rectangles R_i, all points in the disjoint region can affect all rectangles in R_i. □

Proof of Theorem 2:

PROOF. We draw $2 \cdot n$ horizontal lines passing the horizontal edges of the n rectangles and $2 \cdot n$ vertical lines passing the vertical edges of the n rectangles. The horizontal lines and the vertical lines divide the space into $O(n^2)$ cells. Each disjoint region comprises at least one cell. Thus there are at most $O(n^2)$ disjoint regions. □

Proof of Lemma 3:

PROOF. We first consider two horizontally consecutive disjoint regions, $\mathfrak{r}_1$ and $\mathfrak{r}_2$. They are separated by a vertical edge from rectangle r. There are two cases:

Case 1: The vertical edge is the left edge of rectangle r, and then the points in disjoint region $\mathfrak{r}_2$ are inside rectangle r. The points in $\mathfrak{r}_2$ can affect rectangle r besides all rectangles that the points in $\mathfrak{r}_1$ can affect. In other words, the set of rectangles affected by points in $\mathfrak{r}_1$ is a subset of the rectangles affected by points in $\mathfrak{r}_2$.

Case 2: The vertical edge is the right edge of rectangle r, then the points in disjoint region $\mathfrak{r}_1$ are inside rectangle r. We can draw a similar conclusion that the set of rectangles affected by points in $\mathfrak{r}_1$ is a subset of the rectangles affected by points in $\mathfrak{r}_2$.

For two vertically consecutive disjoint regions, we have similar conclusions.

Given a disjoint region $\mathfrak{r}_i$, if it is a maximal region, then Lemma 3 holds, where $\mathfrak{r}_i = \mathfrak{r}_j$. Otherwise, we can always find a neighboring disjoint region $\mathfrak{r}_j$ of $\mathfrak{r}_i$ such that $A(p_{\mathfrak{r}_i}) \subseteq A(p_{\mathfrak{r}_j})$. Since there are finite disjoint regions, we will find a sequence of disjoint regions $< \mathfrak{r}_i, ..., \mathfrak{r}_k >$ and $\mathfrak{r}_k$ is a maximal region such that $A(p_{\mathfrak{r}_i}) \subseteq ... \subseteq A(p_{\mathfrak{r}_k})$.

Put these together, we have the conclusion. □

Proof of Lemma 4:

PROOF. We use an example to show that n rectangles can generate $O(n^2)$ maximal regions. As shown in Fig 4, the black regions are maximal regions. When there are 4 rectangles, there is $1 \times 1 = 1$ maximal region. When there are 8 rectangles, there are $2 \times 2 = 4$ maximal regions. Similarly, when there are n rectangles, there are $n/4$ maximal regions each row and there are $n/4$ rows. So there could be $n^2/16 = O(n^2)$ maximal regions in the worst case. □

Proof of Lemma 5:

PROOF. For a maximal region $\mathfrak{r}$, if there exists no horizontal line between the top and bottom edges of the region, then the area between the two horizontal lines passing through the top and bottom edges of the region is a maximal slab. If there exists horizontal lines between the top and bottom edges of the region, then there exists at least one maximal slab between the top and bottom edges of the region. □

Proof of Lemma 6:

PROOF. There are at most n horizontal lines passing the top edge of a rectangle and each of them can be paired with zero or one horizontal line passing the bottom edge of a rectangle. Thus there are at most n maximal slabs. □

Proof of Lemma 7:

PROOF. Since R_s is the set of rectangles that intersect with s, for any point p in s, we have $A(p) \subseteq R_s$. As the function h is submodular and monotone, $h(R_s) \geq h(A(p))$ holds. □

Proof of Lemma 8:

PROOF. We project each rectangle to the x-axis and get a line segment with a length of b. Similarly, we project each slice to the x-axis and get a line segment with a length of θb. A rectangle intersects with a slice iff their projections on x-axis intersect. The projection of a rectangle can intersect at most $\lceil \frac{1}{\theta} \rceil + 1$ projections of slices. Thus, each rectangle r intersects with at most $\lceil \frac{1}{\theta} \rceil + 1$ slices. □

Proof of Lemma 9:

PROOF. Since each rectangle intersects at most $\lceil \frac{1}{\theta} \rceil + 1$ slices, the top edge of a rectangle can contribute to at most $\lceil \frac{1}{\theta} \rceil + 1$ maximal slabs. Thus there are at most $(\lceil \frac{1}{\theta} \rceil + 1)n$ maximal slabs in all slices, where n is the number of rectangles. □

Proof of Lemma 10:

PROOF. Since the objects in O are uniformly distributed in space P, there are $\sqrt{n}$ spatial objects in a row and a column. The distance d_h between two horizontal adjacent spatial objects, as well as the distance d_v between two vertical adjacent objects, are given by $d_v = d_h = \frac{W}{\sqrt{n}}$. Let the size of the query rectangle be $a \times b$. We reduce the *BRS* problem to the *SIRI* problem by drawing an $a \times b$ rectangle centered at o for each object $o \in O$. We still analyse the complexity of the 3 phases of *SliceBRS* in turn: It takes $O(n)$ time to cut the space into slices in phase 1, and $O(n)$ time to find all maximal slabs in phase 2. In phase 3, we first consider the complexity

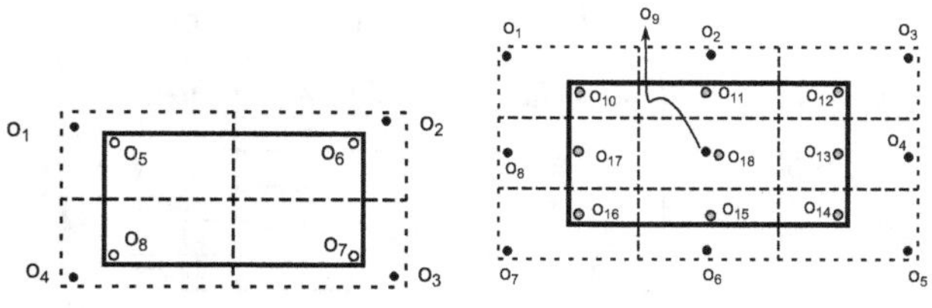

(a) $c = 1/3$. (b) $c = 1/2$.

Figure 18: Approximate Ratio.

of Function SearchMR searching one maximal slab. Recall that there are $O(\sqrt{n})$ spatial objects in a row in the space. We draw a rectangle centered at o for each spatial object o and thus there are $O(\sqrt{n})$ left edges and $O(\sqrt{n})$ right edges. Since the space is equally divided into $\frac{W}{\theta b}$ slices, there are $O(\sqrt{n} \div \frac{W}{\theta b}) = O(\frac{\theta b \cdot \sqrt{n}}{W})$ left edges and right edges in one slice. Therefore, it takes $O(\frac{\theta b \cdot \sqrt{n}}{W})$ time for Function SearchMR to process one maximal slab. There are $O(\sqrt{n})$ maximal slabs in one slice and $\frac{W}{\theta b}$ slices in the space. Thus, it takes $O(\frac{\theta b \cdot \sqrt{n}}{W} \cdot \sqrt{n} \cdot \frac{W}{b}) = O(n)$ time to find the best point. Putting these together, we can conclude that the complexity of *SliceBRS* for this case is $O(n)$. □

Proof of Lemma 11:

PROOF. Let o_i be an object in $O_{r_t^{ca,cb}}$. We have $|o_i.x - t.x| < \frac{cb}{2}$, $|o_i.y - t.y| < \frac{ca}{2}$. Since t is inside a $(1-c)a \times (1-c)b$ region centered at p, we have $|t.x - p.x| < (1-c)b/2$, $|t.y - p.y| < (1-c)a/2$. Obviously, $|o_i.x - p.x| < \frac{cb}{2}$, $|o_i.y - p.y| < \frac{ca}{2}$. Therefore, o_i is inside the $a \times b$ rectangular region centered at p. □

Proof of Theorem 3:

PROOF. Consider the geometric version of set cover problem. Given a finite set of points and a set of rectangles with predefined size in a 2 dimensional space, the problem is to find the minimum number of rectangles that cover all points. This problem is NP-hard even when the rectangles are identical squares with their sides parallel to the axes [10]. This problem is a special case of finding a minimum c-cover when the query rectangle is a square. Thus, finding a minimum c-cover is NP-hard. □

Proof of Lemma 12:

PROOF. We consider the following two cases: (1) If a spatial object o is in a leaf node whose level is not lower than l, then $o \in V_l^2$; (2) If a spatial object o is in a leaf node v whose level is lower than l, then we can traverse along the path from v to the root until we find an internal node u at level l. Spatial object o is in the corresponding region of u. Since the corresponding region of u can be fully covered by a query rectangle, object o is inside a $ca \times cb$ rectangular region centered at $u.t$.

Therefore, for any spatial object $o \in O$, there exists a $t \in V_l^1 \cup V_l^2$ such that o is inside the $ca \times cb$ rectangular region centered at t. We conclude that $V_l^1 \cup V_l^2$ is a c-cover of O. □

Proof of Lemma 13:

PROOF. We have

$$f_T(T_{r_p^{(1-c)a,(1-c)b}}) = f_T(\{t_i, \ldots, t_j\})$$
$$= f(D(t_i) \cup \ldots \cup D(t_j)) \leq f(O_{r_p^{a,b}})$$

□

Proof of Theorem 4:

PROOF. Let p_{opt} be the optimal center point for the $a \times b$ rectangular region with maximum aggregation. Let p be the point returned by the *CoverBRS* algorithm, which is the center point for the $\frac{2}{3}a \times \frac{2}{3}b$ rectangular region with maximum aggregation with respect to the set T. We can find 4 $\frac{2}{3}a \times \frac{2}{3}b$ rectangles $r_1, \ldots, r_4$ such that for any object o covered by $r_{p_{opt}}^{a,b}$, its representor is covered by $r_1 \cup \ldots \cup r_4$. Consider the Example in Figure 18a, objects $o_1, \ldots, o_4$ represent $o_5, \ldots, o_8$ respectively and $o_1, \ldots, o_4$ are covered by $r_1 \cup \ldots \cup r_4$. Thus, we can achieve the following derivation:

$$f(O_{r_{p_{opt}}^{a,b}}) \leq f_T(T_{r_1} \cup \ldots T_{r_4})$$
$$\leq f_T(T_{r_1}) + \ldots + f_T(T_{r_4}) \leq 4 f_T(T_{r_p^{\frac{2}{3}a,\frac{2}{3}b}}),$$

where T_{r_i} is the set of objects in T that are covered by rectangle r_i for $i \in [1, 4]$.

From Lemma 13, we have

$$f(O_{r_{p_{opt}}^{a,b}}) \leq 4 f(O_{r_p^{a,b}})$$

□

Proof of Theorem 5:

PROOF. We prove this with a worst case example. Consider an instance in Figure 18a where the solid-line rectangle is a $a \times b$ rectangle and the dashed-line rectangles are $\frac{2}{3}a \times \frac{2}{3}b$ rectangles. The c-cover is $T = \{o_1, o_2, o_3, o_4\}$ and they represent o_5, o_6, o_7 and o_8, respectively. We assume $f(\{o_1\}) = \ldots = f(\{o_4\}) = 1$, $f(\{o_5\}) = \ldots = f(\{o_8\}) = 1 - \beta$, where β is a small positive real number, $f(\{o_1, o_5\}) = \ldots = f(\{o_4, o_8\}) = 1$, and $f(\{o_4, \ldots, o_8\} = 4 - 4\beta$. In this case, the *CoverBRS* algorithm may choose any of $o_1, \ldots, o_4$ as the approximate solution while the optimal solution should be the center of the solid-line rectangle. Since β can be any small value, our answer is (1/4)-approximate. □

Proof of Theorem 6:

PROOF. Similar to the proof of Theorem 4, Let p_{opt} be the optimal center point for the $a \times b$ rectangle with maximum aggregation. Let p be the point returned by *CoverBRS* algorithm, which is the center point for the $\frac{1}{2}a \times \frac{1}{2}b$ rectangle with maximum aggregation with respect to the set T of spatial objects. Different from the proof of Theorem 4, we need 9 $\frac{1}{2}a \times \frac{1}{2}b$ rectangles $r_1, \ldots, r_9$ to guarantee that for any object $o \in O$ covered by $r_{p_{opt}}^{a,b}$, its representor is covered by $r_1 \cup \ldots \cup r_9$, as illustrated in Figure 18b. Thus, we can achieve the following derivation:

$$f(O_{r_{p_{opt}}^{a,b}}) \leq f_T(T_{r_1} \cup \ldots T_{r_9})$$
$$\leq f_T(T_{r_1}) + \ldots + f_T(T_{r_9}) \leq 9 f_T(T_{r_p^{\frac{1}{2}a,\frac{1}{2}b}})$$

From Lemma 13, we have

$$f(O_{r_{p_{opt}}^{a,b}}) \leq 9 f(O_{r_p^{a,b}}).$$

□

Proof of Theorem 7:

PROOF. We prove this by giving a worst case example. Consider an instance in Figure 18b where the solid-line rectangle is a $a \times b$ rectangle and the dashed-line rectangles are $\frac{1}{2}a \times \frac{1}{2}b$ rectangles. The c-cover is $T = \{o_1, \ldots, o_9\}$ and they represent $o_{10}, \ldots, o_{18}$ respectively. We assume $f(\{o_1\}) = \ldots = f(\{o_8\}) = 1$ and $f(\{o_9\}) = \ldots = f(\{o_{17}\}) = 1 - \beta$ and $f(\{o_{18}\}) = \beta$ where β is a small positive real number. We assume $f(\{o_1, o_{10}\}) = \ldots = f(\{o_8, o_{17}\}) = 1$ and $f(\{o_9, o_{18}\}) = 1 - \beta$. We also assume that $f(\{o_{10}, \ldots, o_{18}\} = 9 - 9\beta$. In this case, since the *CoverBRS* algorithm only consider the objects in the c-cover which locate at $o_1, \ldots, o_8$, we may end up choosing any one of $o_1, \ldots, o_8$

as the approximate solution. However, the optimal solution should be the center of the solid-line rectangle and it aggregation is $9 - 9\beta$. Since β can be any small positive value, our answer is (1/9)-approximate. □

C. DATASET DESCRIPTION AND MORE EXPERIMENTAL RESULTS

C.1 Datasets Description

Application 1 (Most Influential Region). Brightkite and Gowalla are from location-based social networks where users shared their locations by check-ins. Each dataset consists of a social graph, a set of points of interests, and a set of check-ins made by users. Brightkite contains 4,491,143 check-ins made in 693,362 places from 58,228 users. Gowalla contains 6,442,890 check-ins made in 1,256,692 places from 196,591 users. For each edge (u, v) in the social graph, we generate its propagation probability by a widely adopted random method [4, 13, 19], *i.e.,* the propagation probability of each edge is randomly selected from $\{0.1, 0.01, 0.001\}$. We compute the probability of a user u visiting a place p by $\frac{\text{\# of check-ins in } p \text{ of } u}{\text{\# of check-ins of } u}$, which is the ratio of the number of check-ins in p made by u to the number of check-ins made by u. We adopt the method [1, 24], referred to as the *Reverse Influence Sampling*, to approximate the influence spread of a set of users.

Application 2 (Most Diversified Region) Meetup is crawled by ourselves from an event-based social network *meetup.com* from July 2013 to Oct 2013. Each user can specify the topics that they are interested in and the website helps them to arrange a place to meet. Each spatial object represents a venue where people have held at least one event. For each venue, we select the most frequent topics of the users who have attended an event in this place and associate such topics with this venue. To generate the Yelp dataset, we collect the reviews for each POI. After removing the stop words and stemming, we collect the most frequent words in the reviews and let them be the tags of each POI.

C.2 Application to the MaxRS Problem

Recall that the *MaxRS* problem is a special case of the *BRS* problem as discussed in Section 2. Hence, our proposed algorithm can also be applied to solve the *MaxRS* problem. In this set of experiments, we compare the runtime of *OE* and an adapted version of *SliceBRS*for the *MaxRS* problem. We show that our *SliceBRS* algorithm can also be adapted to efficiently solve the *MaxRS* problem. For each dataset, we find the region of given size such that the number of POIs that are inside the region is maximized. We adapt the *SliceBRS* algorithm to make use of the SUM aggregate score function as it is used in *OE*. Specifically, in each slice, we mark all maximal slabs whose upper bounds are higher than the current result. The rectangles which do not intersect with these marked maximal slabs can be safely ignored. Then, we modify Function SearchMR to incorporate the idea of *OE* to find the point p with maximum $h(A(p))$ in the remaining maximal slabs. In this case, the complexity of *SliceBRS* is $O(n \log n)$. Note that the modification to *SliceBRS* cannot work with a general submodular monotone aggregate function. Table 7 reports the ratio of the runtime of the adapted *SliceBRS* to that of *OE*. We can see that the time cost of the adapted *SliceBRS* is about 20% to 40% of *OE*. In other words, our *SliceBRS* algorithm can also be adapted to efficiently solve the *MaxRS* problem.

Table 7: The ratio of *SliceBRS*'s runtime to *OE*'s runtime.

Query Rectangle	Brightkite	Gowalla	Yelp	Meetup
q	32.3%	29.9%	35.2%	33.5%
$5q$	22.9%	24.2%	32.1%	27.6%
$10q$	22.5%	25.1%	30%	22.4%
$15q$	23.4%	21.2%	35.2%	21.8%
$20q$	25.8%	23.9%	39.2%	22.2%

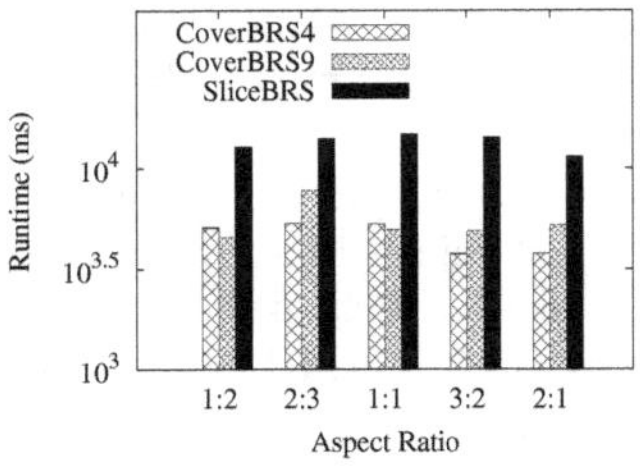

Figure 19: Effect of Aspect Ratio.

C.3 Effect of the Query Rectangle

We study the effect of the query rectangle on the performance of our algorithms from two aspects: the size and the aspect ratio.

We first study the effect of the size of the query rectangle. We use five sizes for query rectangles, q, $5q$, $10q$, $15q$, and $20q$.

Application 1 (Most Influential Region). We first study the effect of the size for the query rectangle in Application 1. Figure 10 reports the quality of the returned region when we vary the size for the query rectangle in the Application 1. We can see that as the size for the query rectangle gets larger, the gap between the quality of the region returned by *SliceBRS* and *OE* gets smaller. Figure 11 reports the runtime of our three algorithms and the *OE* algorithm when we vary the size for query rectangle. We observe that as the size of the query rectangle gets larger, the runtime of *SliceBRS* gets larger. The runtime of *CoverBRS4* and *CoverBRS9* also increase as the size of the query rectangle gets larger, but at a slower rate.

Application 2 (Most Diversified Region). Figure 12 reports the quality of the returned region when we vary the size of query rectangles in the Application 2. Figure 13 presents the runtime of the algorithms. We can make similar observations as those on Figures 10 and 11.

Lastly, we study the effect of the aspect ratio of the query rectangle. We use 5 aspect ratios, 1:2, 2:3, 1:1, 3:2, 2:1, i.e., the query rectangle varies from wide rectangle to tall rectangle. Due to the limitation of space, we only report the results on Gowalla. Similar observations can be made on other datasets. Figure 19 reports the runtime of our three algorithms for different aspect ratios. We observe that, the runtime for a square query rectangle is slightly larger than those on other rectangles. To explain this, we consider a query rectangle of size $a \times b$ where a takes a very small value. Then based on the *SIRI* problem, the rectangles centered at each object can hardly intersect with each other, yielding nearly n maximal regions. Consequently, it is likely to take more time to process a square query rectangle.

Simba: Efficient In-Memory Spatial Analytics

Dong Xie[1], Feifei Li[1], Bin Yao[2], Gefei Li[2], Liang Zhou[2], Minyi Guo[2]

[1]University of Utah [2]Shanghai Jiao Tong University

{dongx, lifeifei}@cs.utah.edu {yaobin@cs., oizz01@, nichozl@, guo-my@cs.}sjtu.edu.cn

ABSTRACT

Large spatial data becomes ubiquitous. As a result, it is critical to provide *fast, scalable, and high-throughput* spatial queries and analytics for numerous applications in location-based services (LBS). Traditional spatial databases and spatial analytics systems are disk-based and optimized for IO efficiency. But increasingly, data are stored and processed in memory to achieve low latency, and CPU time becomes the new bottleneck. We present the Simba (Spatial In-Memory Big data Analytics) system that offers scalable and efficient in-memory spatial query processing and analytics for big spatial data. Simba is based on Spark and runs over a cluster of commodity machines. In particular, Simba extends the Spark SQL engine to support rich spatial queries and analytics through both SQL and the DataFrame API. It introduces indexes over RDDs in order to work with big spatial data and complex spatial operations. Lastly, Simba implements an effective query optimizer, which leverages its indexes and novel spatial-aware optimizations, to achieve both low latency and high throughput. Extensive experiments over large data sets demonstrate Simba's superior performance compared against other spatial analytics system.

1. INTRODUCTION

There has been an explosion in the amount of spatial data in recent years. Mobile applications on smart phones and various internet of things (IoT) projects (e.g., sensor measurements for smart city) generate humongous volume of data with spatial dimensions. What's more, spatial dimensions often play an important role in these applications, for example, user and driver locations are the most critical features for the Uber app. How to query and analyze such large spatial data with low latency and high throughput is a fundamental challenge. Most traditional and existing spatial databases and spatial analytics systems are disk-oriented (e.g., Oracle Spatial, SpatialHadoop, and Hadoop GIS [11,22]). Since they have been optimized for IO efficiency, their performance often deteriorates when scaling to large spatial data.

A popular choice for achieving low latency and high throughput nowadays is to use in-memory computing over a cluster of commodity machines. Systems like Spark [38] have witnessed great success in big data processing, by offering low query latency and high analytical throughput using distributed memory storage and computing. Recently, Spark SQL [13] extends Spark with a SQL-like query interface and the DataFrame API to conduct relational processing on different underlying data sources (e.g., data from DFS). Such an extension provides useful abstraction for supporting easy and user-friendly big data analytics over a distributed memory space. Furthermore, the declarative nature of SQL also enables rich opportunities for query optimization while dramatically simplifying the job of an end user.

However, none of the existing *distributed in-memory* query and analytics engines, like Spark, Spark SQL, and MemSQL, provide native support for spatial queries and analytics. In order to use these systems to process large spatial data, one has to rely on UDFs or user programs. Since a UDF (or a user program) sits outside the query engine kernel, the underlying system is not able to optimize the workload, which often leads to very expensive query evaluation plans. For example, when Spark SQL implements a spatial distance join via UDF, it has to use the expensive cartesian product approach which is not scalable for large data.

Inspired by these observations, we design and implement the Simba (Spatial In-Memory Big data Analytics) system, which is a distributed in-memory analytics engine, to support spatial queries and analytics over big spatial data with the following main objectives: *simple and expressive programming interfaces, low query latency, high analytics throughput, and excellent scalability*. In particular, Simba has the following distinct features:

- Simba extends Spark SQL with a class of important spatial operations and offers simple and expressive programming interfaces for them in both SQL and DataFrame API.
- Simba supports (spatial) indexing over RDDs (resilient distributed dataset) to achieve low query latency.
- Simba designs a SQL context module that executes multiple spatial queries in parallel to improve analytical throughput.
- Simba introduces spatial-aware optimizations to both logical and physical optimizers, and uses cost-based optimizations (CBO) to select good spatial query plans.

Since Simba is based on Spark, it inherits and extends Spark's fault tolerance mechanism. Different from Spark SQL that relies on UDFs to support spatial queries and analytics, Simba supports such operations natively with the help of its index support, query optimizer, and query evaluator. Because these modules are tailored towards spatial operations, Simba achieves excellent scalability in answering spatial queries and analytics over large spatial data.

The rest of the paper is organized as follows. We introduce the necessary background in Section 2 and provide a system overview of Simba in Section 3. Section 4 presents Simba's programming interfaces, and Section 5 discusses its indexing support. Spatial operations in Simba are described in Section 6, while Section 7 explains

SIGMOD'16, June 26-July 01, 2016, San Francisco, CA, USA

DOI: http://dx.doi.org/10.1145/2882903.2915237

Simba's query optimizer and fault tolerance mechanism. Extensive experimental results over large real data sets are presented in Section 8. Section 9 summarizes the related work in addition to those discussed in Section 2, and the paper is concluded in Section 10.

2. BACKGROUND AND RELATED SYSTEMS

2.1 Spark Overview

Apache Spark [38] is a general-purpose, widely-used cluster computing engine for big data processing, with APIs in Scala, Java and Python. Since its inception, a rich ecosystem based on Spark for in-memory big data analytics has been built, including libraries for streaming, graph processing, and machine learning [6].

Spark provides an efficient abstraction for in-memory cluster computing called Resilient Distributed Datasets (RDDs). Each RDD is a distributed collection of Java or Python objects partitioned across a cluster. Users can manipulate RDDs through the functional programming APIs (e.g. `map`, `filter`, `reduce`) provided by Spark, which take functions in the programming language and ship them to other nodes on the cluster. For instance, we can count lines containing "ERROR" in a text file with the following scala code:

```
lines = spark.textFile("hdfs://...")
errors = lines.filter(l => l.contains("ERROR"))
println(errors.count())
```

This example creates an RDD of strings called `lines` by reading an HDFS file, and uses `filter` operation to obtain another RDD `errors` which consists of the lines containing "ERROR" only. Lastly, a `count` is performed on `errors` for output.

RDDs are fault-tolerant as Spark can recover lost data using lineage graphs by rerunning operations to rebuild missing partitions. RDDs can also be cached in memory or made persistent on disk explicitly to accelerate data reusing and support iteration [38]. RDDs are evaluated *lazily*. Each RDD actually represents a "logical plan" to compute a dataset, which consists of one or more *"transformations"* on the original input RDD, rather than the physical, materialized data itself. Spark will wait until certain output operations (known as *"action"*), such as `collect`, to launch a computation. This allows the engine to do some simple optimizations, such as pipelining operations. Back to the example above, Spark will pipeline reading lines from the HDFS file with applying the filter and counting records. Thanks to this feature, Spark never needs to materialize intermediate `lines` and `errors` results. Though such optimization is extremely useful, it is also limited because the engine does not understand the structure of data in RDDs (that can be arbitrary Java/Python objects) or the semantics of user functions (which may contain arbitrary codes and logic).

2.2 Spark SQL Overview

Spark SQL [13] integrates relational processing with Spark's functional programming API. Built with experience from its predecessor Shark [35], Spark SQL leverages the benefits of relational processing (e.g. declarative queries and optimized storage), and allows users to call other analytics libraries in Spark (e.g. SparkML for machine learning) through its DataFrame API.

Spark SQL can perform relational operations on both external data sources (e.g. JSON, Parquet [5] and Avro [4]) and Spark's built-in distributed collections (i.e., RDDs). Meanwhile, it evaluates operations lazily to get more optimization opportunities. Spark SQL introduces a highly extensible optimizer called *Catalyst*, which makes it easy to add data sources, optimization rules, and data types for different application domains such as machine learning.

Spark SQL is a full-fledged query engine based on the underlying Spark core. It makes Spark accessible to a wider user base and offers powerful query execution and optimization planning.

Despite the rich support of relational style processing, Spark SQL does not perform well on spatial queries over multi-dimensional data. Expressing spatial queries is inconvenient or even impossible. For instance, a relational query as below is needed to express a 10 nearest neighbor query for a query point $q = (3.0, 2.0)$ from the table `point1` (that contains a set of 2D points):

```
SELECT * FROM point1
ORDERED BY (point1.x - 3.0) * (point1.x - 3.0) +
           (point1.y - 2.0) * (point1.y - 2.0)
LIMIT 10.
```

To make the matter worse, if we want to retrieve (or do analyses over) the intersection of results from multiple kNN queries, more complex expressions such as nested sub-queries will be involved. In addition, it is impossible to express a kNN join succinctly over two tables in a single Spark SQL query. Another important observation is that most operations in Spark SQL require scanning the entire RDDs. This is a big overhead since most computations may not actually contribute to the final results. Lastly, Spark SQL does not support optimizations for spatial analytics.

2.3 Cluster-Based Spatial Analytics Systems

There exists a number of systems that support spatial queries and analytics over distributed spatial data using a cluster of commodity machines. We will review them briefly next.

Hadoop based system. SpatialHadoop [22] is an extension of the MapReduce framework [18], based on Hadoop, with native support for spatial data. It enriches Hadoop with spatial data awareness in language, storage, MapReduce, and operation layers. In the language layer, it provides an extension to Pig [30], called Pigeon [21], which adds spatial data types, functions and operations as UDFs in Pig Latin Language. In the storage layer, SpatialHadoop adapts traditional spatial index structures, such as Grid, R-tree and R+-tree, to a two-level index framework. In the MapReduce layer, SpatialHadoop extends MapReduce API with two new components, *SpatialFileSplitter* and *SpatialRecordReader*, for efficient and scalable spatial data processing. In the operation layer, SpatialHadoop is equipped with several predefined spatial operations including box range queries, k nearest neighbor (kNN) queries and spatial joins over geometric objects using conditions such as *within* and *intersect*. However, only two-dimensional data is supported, and operations such as circle range queries and kNN joins are not supported as well (according to the latest open-sourced version of SpatialHadoop). SpatialHadoop does have good support on different geometric objects, e.g. segments and polygons, and operations over them, e.g. generating convex hulls and skylines, which makes it a distributed geometric data analytics system over MapReduce [20].

Hadoop GIS [11] is a scalable and high performance spatial data warehousing system for running large scale spatial queries on Hadoop. It is available as a set of libraries for processing spatial queries and an integrated software package in Hive [33]. In its latest version, the SATO framework [34] has been adopted to provide different partition and indexing approaches. However, Hadoop GIS only supports data up to two dimensions and two query types: box range queries and spatial joins over geometric objects with predicates like $withind$ (within distance).

GeoSpark. GeoSpark [37] extends Spark for processing spatial data. It provides a new abstraction called Spatial Resilient Distributed Datasets (SRDDs) and a few spatial operations. GeoSpark supports range queries, kNN queries, and spatial joins over SRDDs. Besides, it allows an index (e.g. quad-trees and R-trees) to be the object inside each local RDD partition. Note that Spark allows developers to build RDDs over objects of any user-defined types outside Spark kernel. Thus essentially, an SRDD simply encapsu-

Core Features	Simba	GeoSpark	SpatialSpark	SpatialHadoop	Hadoop GIS
Data dimensions	multiple	$d \leq 2$	$d \leq 2$	$d \leq 2$	$d \leq 2$
SQL	✓	×	×	Pigeon	×
DataFrame API	✓	×	×	×	×
Spatial indexing	R-tree	R-/quad-tree	grid/kd-tree	grid/R-tree	SATO
In-memory	✓	✓	✓	×	×
Query planner	✓	×	×	✓	×
Query optimizer	✓	×	×	×	×
Concurrent query execution	thread pool in query engine	user-level process	user-level process	user-level process	user-level process
query operation support					
Box range query	✓	✓	✓	✓	✓
Circle range query	✓	✓	✓	×	×
k nearest neighbor	✓	✓	only 1NN	✓	×
Distance join	✓	✓	✓	via spatial join	✓
kNN join	✓	×	×	×	×
Geometric object	×[1]	✓	✓	✓	✓
Compound query	✓	×	×	✓	×

Table 1: Comparing Simba against other systems.

Notation	Description
R (resp. S)	a table of a point set R (resp. S)
r (resp. s)	a record (a point) $r \in R$ (resp. $s \in S$)
$\|r, s\|$	L_2 distance from r to s
$\text{maxdist}(q, B)$	$\max_{p \in B} \|p, q\|$ for point q and MBR B
$\text{maxdist}(A, B)$	$\max_{q \in A, p \in B} \|p, q\|$ for MBRs A and B
$\text{mindist}(q, B)$	$\min_{p \in B} \|p, q\|$ for point q and MBR B
$\text{mindist}(A, B)$	$\min_{q \in A, p \in B} \|p, q\|$ for MBRs A and B
$\text{range}(A, R)$	records from R within area A
$\text{knn}(r, S)$	k nearest neighbors of r from S
$R \bowtie_\tau S$	R distance join of S with threshold τ
$R \bowtie_{\text{knn}} S$	kNN join between R and S
R_i, S_j	i-th (resp. j-th) partition of table R (resp. S)
$\text{mbr}(R_i)$	MBR of R_i
cr_i	centroid of $\text{mbr}(R_i)$
u_i	$\max_{r \in R_i} \|cr_i, r\|$

Table 2: Frequently used notations.

lates an RDD of spatial objects (which can be points, polygons or circles) with some common geometry operations (e.g. calculating the MBR of its elements). Moreover, even though GeoSpark is able to use index to accelerate query processing within each SRDD partition, it does not support flexible global index inside the kernel. GeoSpark only supports two-dimensional data, and more importantly, it can only deal with spatial coordinates and does not allow additional attributes in spatial objects (e.g. strings for description). In other words, GeoSpark is *a library running on top of and outside Spark without a query engine*. Thus, GeoSpark does not provide a user-friendly programming interface like SQL or the DataFrame API, and has neither query planner nor query optimizer.

SpatialSpark. SpatialSpark [36] implements a set of spatial operations for analyzing large spatial data with Apache Spark. Specifically, SpatialSpark supports range queries and spatial joins over geometric objects using conditions like `intersect` and `within`. SpatialSpark adopts data partition strategies like fixed grid or kd-tree on data files in HDFS and builds an index (outside the Spark engine) to accelerate spatial operations. Nevertheless, SpatialSpark only supports two-dimensional data, and does not index RDDs natively. What's more, same as GeoSpark, it is also *a library running on top of and outside Spark without a query engine* and *does not* support SQL and the DataFrame API.

Remarks. Note that all the systems mentioned above does not support concurrent queries natively with a multi-threading module. Thus, they have to rely on user-level processes to achieve this, which introduce non-trivial overheads from the operating system and hurt system throughput. In contrast, Simba employs a thread pool inside the query engine, which provides much better performance on concurrent queries. There are also systems like GeoMesa and MD-HBase that are related and reviewed in Section 9. Table 1 compares the core features between Simba and other systems.

2.4 Spatial Operations

In this paper, we focus on spatial operations over *point objects*. Our techniques and frameworks also support rectangular objects (such as MBRs), and can be easily extended to support general geometric objects. Table 2 lists the frequently used notations.

Formally, consider a data set $R \subset \mathbb{R}^d$ with N records, where $d \geq 1$ is the dimensionality of the data set and each record $r \in R$ is a point in $\mathbb{R}^d$. For any two points $p, q \in \mathbb{R}^d$, $|p, q|$ denotes their L_2 distance. We consider the following spatial operations in this paper, due to their wide applications in practice [32].

Definition 1 (Range Query) Given a query area Q (either a rectangle or a circle) and a data set R, a range query (denoted as $range(Q, R)$) asks for all records within Q from R. Formally,

$$range(Q, R) = \{r | r \in R, r \in Q\}.$$

Definition 2 (kNN Query) Given a query point $q \in \mathbb{R}^d$, a data set R and an integer $k \geq 1$, the k nearest neighbors of q w.r.t. R, denoted as $\text{knn}(q, S)$, is a set of k records from R where

$$\forall o \in \text{knn}(q, R), \forall r \in R - \text{knn}(q, R), |o, q| \leq |r, q|.$$

Definition 3 (Distance Join) Given two data sets R and S, and a distance threshold $\tau > 0$, the distance join between R and S, denoted as $R \bowtie_\tau S$, finds all pairs (r, s) within distance τ such that $r \in R$ and $s \in S$. Formally,

$$R \bowtie_\tau S = \{(r, s) | (r, s) \in R \times S, |r, s| \leq \tau\}.$$

Definition 4 (kNN Join) Given two data sets R and S, and an integer $k \geq 1$, the kNN join between R and S, denoted as $R \bowtie_{\text{knn}} S$, pairs each object $r \in R$ with each of its kNNs from S. Formally,

$$R \bowtie_{\text{knn}} S = \{(r, s) | r \in R, s \in \text{knn}(r, S)\}.$$

3. Simba ARCHITECTURE OVERVIEW

Simba builds on Spark SQL [13] and is optimized specially for large scale spatial queries and analytics over multi-dimensional data sets. Simba inherits and extends SQL and the DataFrame API, so that users can easily specify different spatial queries and analytics to interact with the underlying data. A major challenge in this process is to extend both SQL and the DataFrame API to support a rich class of spatial operations *natively inside the Simba kernel*.

Figure 1 shows the overall architecture of Simba. Simba follows a similar architecture as that of Spark SQL, but introduces new features and components across the system stack. In particular, new modules different from Spark SQL are highlighted by orange boxes in Figure 1. Similar to Spark SQL, Simba allows users to interact with the system through command line (CLI), JDBC, and scala/python programs. It can connect to a wide variety of data sources, including those from HDFS (Hadoop Distributed File System), relational databases, Hive, and native RDDs.

An important design choice in Simba is to stay outside the core spark engine and only introduce changes to the kernel of Spark SQL. This choice has made a few implementations more challenging (e.g. adding the support for spatial indexing without modifying Spark core), but it allows easy migration of Simba into new version of Spark to be released in the future.

Programming interface. Simba adds spatial keywords and grammar (e.g. `POINT, RANGE, KNN, KNN JOIN, DISTANCE JOIN`) in Spark SQL's query parser, so that users can express spatial queries in SQL-like statements. We also extend the DataFrame API with a similar set of spatial operations, providing an alternative programming interface for the end users. The support of spatial operations

[1]Simba is being extended to support general geometric objects.

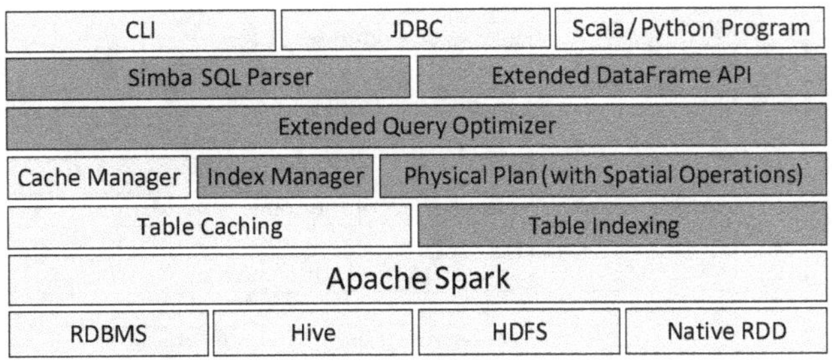

Figure 1: Simba architecture.

in DataFrame API also allows Simba to interact with other Spark components easily, such as MLlib, GraphX, and Spark Streaming. Lastly, we introduce index management commands to Simba's programming interface, in a way which is similar to that in traditional RDBMS. We will describe Simba's programming interface with more details in Section 4 and Appendix A.

Indexing. Spatial queries are expensive to process, especially for data in multi-dimensional space and complex operations like spatial joins and kNN. To achieve better query performance, Simba introduces the concept of *indexing* to its kernel. In particular, Simba implements several classic index structures including hash maps, tree maps, and R-trees [14, 23] over RDDs in Spark. Simba adopts a two-level indexing strategy, namely, *local* and *global* indexing. The global index collects statistics from each RDD partition and helps the system prune irrelevant partitions. Inside each RDD partition, local indexes are built to accelerate local query processing so as to avoid scanning over the entire partition. In Simba, user can build and drop indexes anytime on any table through index management commands. By the construction of a new abstraction called *IndexRDD*, which extends the standard RDD structure in Spark, indexes can be made persistent to disk and loaded back together with associated data to memory easily. We will describe the Simba's indexing support in Section 5.

Spatial operations. Simba supports a number of popular spatial operations over point and rectangular objects. These spatial operations are implemented based on native Spark RDD API. Multiple access and evaluation paths are provided for each operation, so that the end users and Simba's query optimizer have the freedom and opportunities to choose the most appropriate method. Section 6 discusses how various spatial operations are supported in Simba.

Optimization. Simba extends the Catalyst optimizer of Spark SQL and introduces a cost-based optimization (CBO) module that tailors towards optimizing spatial queries. The CBO module leverages the index support in Simba, and is able to optimize complex spatial queries to make the best use of existing indexes and statistics. Query optimization in Simba is presented in Section 7.

Workflow in Simba. Figure 2 shows the query processing workflow of Simba. Simba begins with a relation to be processed, either from an abstract syntax tree (AST) returned by the SQL parser or a DataFrame object constructed by the DataFrame API. In both cases, the relation may contain unresolved attribute references or relations. An attribute or a relation is called *unresolved if we do not know its type or have not matched it to an input table*. Simba resolves such attributes and relations using Catalyst rules and a `Catalog` object that tracks tables in all data sources to build logical plans. Then, the logical optimizer applies standard rule-based optimization, such as constant folding, predicate pushdown, and spatial-specific optimizations like distance pruning, to optimize the logical plan. In the physical planning phase, Simba takes a logical plan as input and generates one or more physical plans based on its spatial operation support as well as physical operators inherited

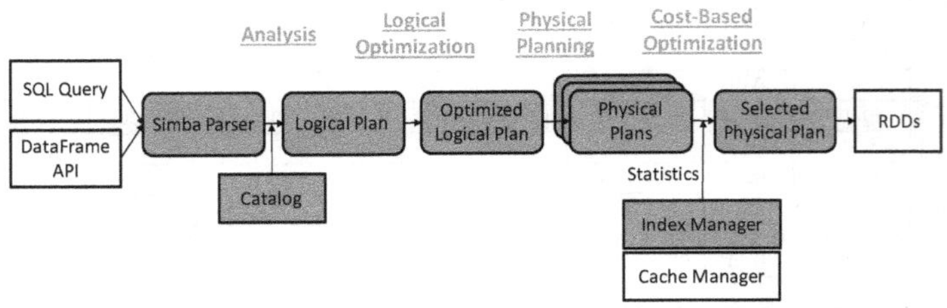

Figure 2: Query processing workflow in Simba.

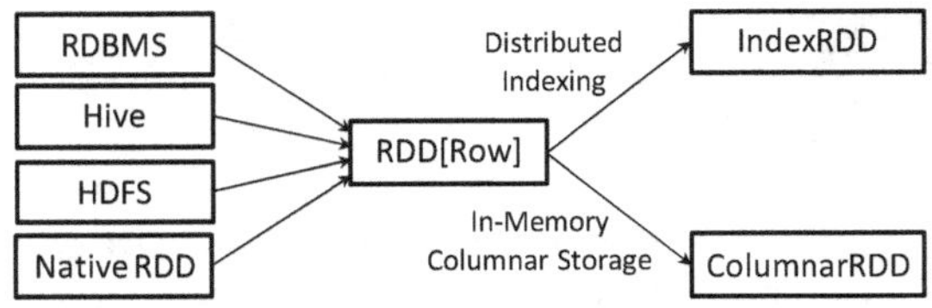

Figure 3: Data Representation in Simba.

from Spark SQL. It then applies cost-based optimizations based on *existing indexes and statistics collected in both Cache Manager and Index Manager* to select the most efficient plan. The physical planner also performs rule-based physical optimization, such as pipelining projections and filters into one Spark `map` operation. In addition, it can push operations from the logical plan into data sources that support predicate or projection pushdown. In Figure 2, we highlight the components and procedures where Simba extends Spark SQL with orange color.

Simba supports analytical jobs on various data sources such as CVS, JSON and Parquet [5]. Figure 3 shows how data are represented in Simba. Generally speaking, each data source will be transformed to an RDD of records (i.e., `RDD[Row]`) for further evaluation. Simba allows users to materialize (often referred as "cache") hot data in memory using columnar storage, which can reduce memory footprint by an order of magnitude because it relies on columnar compression schemes such as dictionary encoding and run-length encoding. Besides, user can build various indexes (e.g. hash maps, tree maps, R-trees) over different data sets to accelerate interactive query processing.

Novelty and contributions. To the best of our knowledge, Simba is the first full-fledged (i.e., support SQL and DataFrame with a sophisticated query engine and query optimizer) in-memory spatial query and analytics engine over a cluster of machines. Even though our architecture is based on Spark SQL, achieving efficient and scalable spatial query parsing, spatial indexing, spatial query algorithms, and a spatial-aware query engine in an in-memory, distributed and parallel environment is still non-trivial, and requires significant design and implementation efforts, since Spark SQL is tailored to relational query processing. In summary,

- We propose a system architecture that adapts Spark SQL to support rich spatial queries and analytics.
- We design the two-level indexing framework and a new RDD abstraction in Spark to build spatial indexes over RDDs natively inside the engine.
- We give novel algorithms for executing spatial operators with efficiency and scalability, under the constraints posed by the RDD abstraction in a distributed and parallel environment.
- Leveraging the spatial index support, we introduce new logical and cost-based optimizations in a spatial-aware query optimizer; many such optimizations are not possible in Spark SQL due to the lack of support for spatial indexes. We also exploit partition tuning and query optimizations for specific spatial operations such as kNN joins.

4. PROGRAMMING INTERFACE

Simba offers two programming interfaces, SQL and the DataFrame API [13], so that users can easily express their analytical queries and integrate them into other components of the Spark ecosystem. Simba's full programming interface is discussed in Appendix A.

Points. Simba introduces the point object in its engine, through a scala class. Users can express a multi-dimensional point using keyword `POINT`. Not only constants or attributes of tables, but also arbitrary arithmetic expressions can be used as the coordinates of points, e.g., `POINT(x + 2, y - 3, z * 2)` is a three-dimensional point with the first coordinate as the sum of attribute x's value and constant 2. This enables flexible expression of spatial points in SQL. Simba will calculate each expression in the statement and wrap them as a point object for further processing.

Spatial predicates. Simba extends SQL with several new predicates to support spatial queries, such as `RANGE` for box range queries, `CIRCLERANGE` for circle range queries, and `KNN` for k nearest neighbor queries. For instance, users can ask for the 3-nearest neighbors of point $(4, 5)$ from table `point1` as below:

```
SELECT * FROM point1
WHERE POINT(x, y) IN KNN(POINT(4, 5), 3).
```

A box range query as follows asks for all points within the two-dimensional rectangle defined by point $(10, 5)$ (lower left corner) and point $(15, 8)$ (top right corner) from table `point2` :

```
SELECT * FROM point2
WHERE POINT(x, y) IN RANGE(POINT(10, 5), POINT(15, 8)).
```

Spatial joins. Simba supports two types of spatial joins: distance joins and kNN joins. Users can express these spatial joins in a θ-join like manner. Specifically, a 10-nearest neighbor join between two tables, `point1` and `point2`, can be expressed as:

```
SELECT * FROM point1 AS p1 KNN JOIN point2 AS p2
ON POINT(p2.x, p2.y) IN KNN(POINT(p1.x, p1.y), 10).
```

A distance join with a distance threshold 20, between two tables `point3` and `point4` in three-dimensional space, is expressed as:

```
SELECT * FROM point3 AS p3 DISTANCE JOIN point4 AS p4
ON POINT(p4.x, p4.y, p4.z) IN
   CIRCLERANGE(POINT(p3.x, p3.y, p3.z), 20).
```

Index management. Users can manipulate indexes easily with index management commands introduced by Simba. For example, users can build an R-Tree index called `pointIndex` on attributes `x`, `y`, and `z` for table `sensor` using command:

```
CREATE INDEX pointIndex ON sensor(x, y, z) USE RTREE.
```

Compound queries. Note that Simba keeps the support for all grammars (including UDFs and UDTs) in Spark SQL. As a result, we can express compound spatial queries in a single SQL statement. For example, we can count the number of restaurants near a POI (say within distance 10) for a set of POIs, and sort locations by the counts, with the following query:

```
SELECT q.id, count(*) AS c
FROM pois AS q DISTANCE JOIN rests AS r
ON POINT(r.x, r.y) IN CIRCLERANGE(POINT(q.x, q.y), 10.0)
GROUP BY q.id ORDER BY c.
```

DataFrame support. In addition to SQL, users can also perform spatial operations over DataFrame objects using a domain-specific language (DSL) similar to data frames in R [10]. Simba's DataFrame API supports all spatial operations extended to SQL described above. Naturally, all new operations are also compatible with the exiting ones from Spark SQL, which provides the same level flexibility as SQL. For instance, we can also express the last SQL query above in the following scala code:

```
pois.distanceJoin(rests, Point(pois("x"), pois("y")),
                  Point(rest("x"), rest("y")), 10.0)
    .groupBy(pois("id"))
    .agg(count("*").as("c")).sort("c").show().
```

5. INDEXING

Indexing is important for the efficient processing of spatial queries and analytics, especially for multi-dimensional data and complex spatial operations such as kNN and spatial joins. In particular, indexing is a critical component towards building an effective optimizer in Simba. Since Simba is an in-memory analytical engine, reducing disk IOs is not a main focus of indexing. Rather, Simba leverages indexes to reduce query latency and improve query throughput via cutting down CPU costs. For example, indexing can help Simba prune irrelevant RDD partitions when processing a range query, which frees more CPU resources for the underlying Spark engine, leading to higher query throughput.

Simba builds (spatial) indexes directly over RDDs to speed up query processing. Specifically, tables are represented as RDDs of records (i.e., `RDD[Row]`). Thus, indexing records of a table becomes indexing elements in an RDD. However, RDDs are designed for sequential scan, thus random access is very expensive as it may become a full scan on the RDD. An extra complexity is that we want to introduce indexing support *without changing the Spark core* for the reasons explained in Section 3. To overcome these challenges, we change the storage format of an indexed table by introducing a new abstraction called `IndexRDD[Row]`, and employ a two-level indexing strategy which can accommodate various index structures to support different queries in Simba.

IndexRDD. Recall that records from a table are stored as `Row` objects (Row objects), and each tables is stored as a RDD of `Row` that contains multiple partitions. To add index support over a table, we pack all records (i.e., `Row` objects) within an RDD partition into an array, which gives each record a unique subscript as its index. Such change makes random access inside RDD partitions an efficient operation with $O(1)$ cost. To achieve this in Simba, we introduce the `IPartition` data structure as below:

```
case class IPartition[Type](Data: Array[Type], I: Index)
```

`Index` is an abstract class that we have designed, and can be instantiated as: `HashMap` (a hash index), `TreeMap` (a one-dimensional index), and `RTree` (a multi-dimensional index). `IndexRDD[Row]` is simply defined as `RDD[IPartition[Row]]` by setting `Type = Row` in the following type declaration:

```
type IndexRDD[Type] = RDD[IPartition[Type]]
```

Records from a table are partitioned by a *partitioner* (that will be described next), and then packed into a set of `IPartition` objects. Since we pack all records within a partition to an array object inside `IPartition`, Simba does introduce small space overhead which may slow down table scanning operation compared to Spark SQL's in-memory columnar storage and the original `RDD[Row]` structure. Experiments in Appendix D.3 have validated that the overhead of our design is insignificant.

Each `IPartition` object contains a *local index* over the records in that partition. Furthermore, each `IPartition` object emits the partition boundary information to construct a *global index*. In general, index construction in Simba consists of three phases: *partition*, *local index*, and *global index*, as shown in Figure 4.

Partition. In the partition phase, Simba partitions the input table (i.e., `RDD[Row]`) according to three main concerns: (1) *Partition Size.* Each partition should have a proper size so as to avoid memory overflow. (2) *Data Locality.* Records that locate close to each other (with respect to the indexing attributes) should be assigned to the same partition. (3) *Load Balancing.* Partitions should be roughly of the same size.

Spark allows users to define their own partition strategies by implementing an abstract class called `Partitioner`. A customized partitioner should specify how many partitions it will generate and how an element maps to a partition ID according to its partition

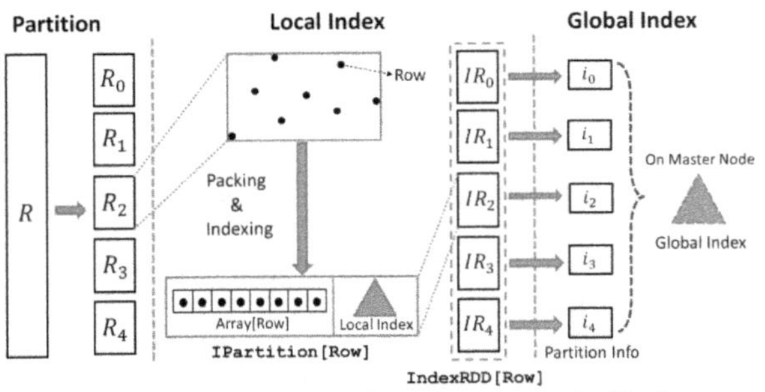

Figure 4: Two-level indexing strategy in Simba.

key. Spark provides two predefined partitioners, range partitioner and hash partitioner, which is sufficient when the partition key is one-dimensional, but does not fit well to multi-dimensional cases.

To address this problem, we have defined a new partitioner named `STRPartitioner` in Simba. `STRPartitioner` takes a set of random samples from the input table and runs the first iteration of Sort-Tile-Recursive (STR) algorithm [26] to determine partition boundaries. Note that the boundaries generated by the STR algorithm are minimum bounded rectangles (MBRs) of the samples. Thus, we need to extend theses MBRs so that they can properly cover the space of the original data set. Finally, according to these extended boundaries, `STRPartitioner` specifies which partition each record belongs to.

Simba makes no restriction on partition strategies. Instead of using `STRPartitioner`, an end user can always supply his/her own partitioner to Simba. We choose `STRPartitioner` as the default partitioner of Simba due to its simplicity and proven effectiveness by existing studies [19]. As shown in Figure 4, we assume the input table R is partitioned into a set of partitions $\{R_1, \ldots, R_m\}$ by the partitioner. The number of partitions, m, is determined by Simba's optimizer which will be discussed in Section 7.

Local index. In this phase, Simba builds a user-specified index (e.g. R-tree) over data in each partition R_i as its *local* index. It also alters the storage format of the input table from `RDD[Row]` to `IndexRDD[Row]`, by converting each RDD partition R_i to an `IPartition[Row]` object, as shown in Figure 4.

Specifically, for each partition R_i, records are packed into an `Array[Row]` object. Then, Simba builds a *local* index over this `Array[Row]`, and co-locates them in the `IPartition[Row]` object. As we can see, the storage format of the input table is no longer an RDD of `Row` objects, but an RDD of `IPartition[Row]` objects, which is an `IndexRDD` of `Row` objects by the definition above. While packing partition data and building local indexes, Simba also collects several statistics from each partition, such as the number of records and the partition boundaries, to facilitate the construction of the global index as illustrated in Figure 4.

Global index. The last phase of index construction is to build a *global* index which indexes all partitions. The global index enables us to prune irrelevant partitions for an input query *without invoking many executors* to look at data stored in different partitions.

In this phase, partition boundaries generated by the partitioner and other statistics collected in the local index phase are sent to the *master node*. Such information is utilized to bulk load an in-memory index, which is stored in the *driver program* on the master node. Users can specify different types of global indexes: When indexing one-dimensional data, a sorted array of the range boundaries is sufficient (the record count and other statistics for each partition are also stored in each array element). In multi-dimensional cases, more complex index structures, such as R-tree [14,23] or KD-tree, can be used. By default, Simba keeps the global indexes for different tables in the memory of the master node at all time (i.e., in its driver program). Nevertheless, Simba also allows users to persist global indexes and corresponding statistics to the file system.

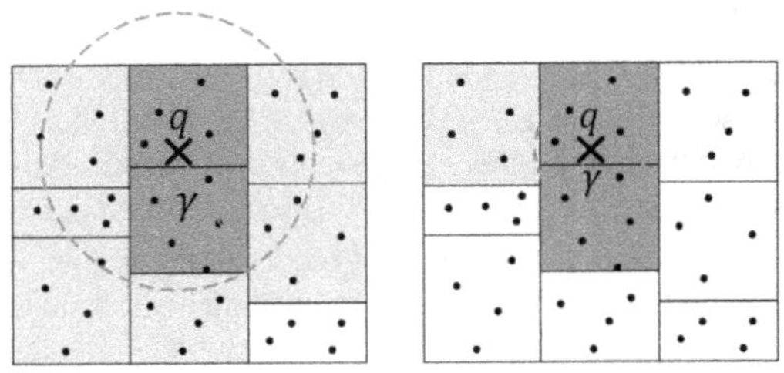

(a) Loose Pruning Bound (b) Refined Pruning Bound

Figure 5: Pruning bound for kNN query at global index.

Even for big data, the number of partitions is not very large (from several hundreds to tens of thousands). Thus, global index can easily fit in the memory of the master node. As shown in Figure 9(b) of our experiments, the global index only consumes less than 700KB for our largest data set with 4.4 billion records.

6. SPATIAL OPERATIONS

Simba introduces new *physical execution plans* to Spark SQL for spatial operations. In particular, the support for local and global indexes enables Simba to explore and design new efficient algorithms for classic spatial operations in the context of Spark. Since range query is the simplest, we present its details in Appendix B.

6.1 kNN Query

In Spark SQL, a kNN query can be processed in two steps: (1) calculate distances from all points in the table to the query point; (2) take k records with minimum distances. This procedure can be naturally expressed as an RDD action `takeOrdered`, where users can specify a comparison function and a value k to select k minimum elements from the RDD. However, this solution involves distance computation for every record, a top k selection on each RDD partition, and shuffling of large intermediate results.

In Simba, kNN queries achieve much better performance by utilizing indexes. It leverages two observations: (1) inside each partition, fast kNN selection over the local data is possible by utilizing the local index; (2) a tight pruning bound that is sufficient to cover the global kNN results can help pruning irrelevant partitions using the global index. The first observation is a simple application of classic kNN query algorithms using spatial index like R-tree [31]. The second observation deserves some discussion.

Intuitively, any circle centered at the query point q covering at least k points from R is a safe pruning bound. To get a tighter bound, we shrink the radius γ of this circle. A loose pruning bound can be derived using the global index. Simba finds the nearest partition(s) to the query point q, which are sufficient to cover at least k data points. More than one partition will be retrieved if the nearest partition does not have k points (recall global index maintains the number of records in each partition). The distance between q and a partition R_i is defined as $\mathrm{maxdist}(q, \mathrm{mbr}(R_i))$ [31]. Without loss of generality, assume the following MBRs are returned: $\{\mathrm{mbr}(R_1), \ldots, \mathrm{mbr}(R_\ell)\}$. Then $\gamma = \max\{\mathrm{maxdist}(q, \mathrm{mbr}(R_1)), \ldots, \mathrm{maxdist}(q, R_\ell)\}$ is a safe pruning bound. Figure 5(a) shows an example of this bound as a circle centered at q. The dark boxes are the nearest MBRs retrieved to cover at least k points which help deriving the radius γ. The dark and gray boxes are partitions selected by the global index according to this pruning bound.

To tighten this bound, Simba issues a kNN query on the ℓ partitions selected from the first step (i.e., two partitions with dark boxes in Figure 5(a)), and takes the k-th minimum distance from q to the $k\ell$ candidates returned from these partitions as γ. Figure 5(b) shows this new pruning bound which is much tighter in practice. Note that ℓ is small for typical k values (often $\ell = 1$), thus, this step has very little overhead.

Global index returns the partition IDs whose MBRs intersect with the circle centered at q with radius γ, Simba marks these partitions using `PartitionPruningRDD` and invokes local kNN queries using the aforementioned observation (1). Finally, it merges the k candidates from each of such partitions and takes the k records with minimum distances to q using RDD action `takeOrdered`.

6.2 Distance Join

Distance join is a θ-join between two tables. Hence, we can express a distance join $R \bowtie_{10.0} S$ in Spark SQL as:

```
SELECT * FROM R JOIN S
ON (R.x - S.x) * (R.x - S.x) + (R.y - S.y) * (R.y - S.y)
   <= 10.0 * 10.0
```

Spark SQL has to use the Cartesian product of two input tables for processing θ-joins. It then filters from the Cartesian product based on the join predicates. Producing the Cartesian product is rather costly in Spark: If two tables are roughly of the same size, it leads to $O(n^2)$ cost when each table has n partitions.

Most systems reviewed in Section 2 did not study distance joins. Rather, they studied *spatial joins*: it takes two tables R and S (each is a set of geometric objects such as polygons), and a spatial join predicate θ (e.g., `overlaps`, `contains`) as input, and returns the set of all pairs (r, s) where $r \in R$, $s \in S$ such that $\theta(r, s)$ is true; $\theta(r, s)$ is evaluated as object r 'θ' (e.g., overlaps) object s.

That said, we design the *DJSpark* algorithm in Simba for distance joins. DJSpark consists of three steps: data partition, global join, and local join, as shown in Figure 6.

Data partition. Data partition phase is to partition R and S so as to preserve data locality where records that are close to each other are likely to end up in the same partition. We also need to consider partition size and load balancing issues. Therefore, we can re-use the *STRPartitioner* introduced in Section 5. The main difference is how we decide the partition size for R and S. Simba has to ensure that it can keep two partitions (one from R and one from S) rather than one (when handling single-relation operations like range queries) in executors' heap memory at the same time.

Note that the data partition phase can be skipped for R (or S) if R (or S) has been already indexed.

Global join. Given the partitions of table R and table S, this step produces all pairs (i, j) which may contribute any pair (r, s) such that $r \in R_i$, $s \in S_j$, and $|r, s| \le \tau$. Note that for each record $s \in S$, s matches with some records in R_i *only if* $\text{mindist}(s, R_i) \le \tau$. Thus, Simba only needs to produce the pairs (i, j) such that $\text{mindist}(R_i, S_j) \le \tau$. After generating these candidate pairs of partition IDs, Simba produces a combined partition $P = \{R_i, S_j\}$ for each pair (i, j). Then, these combined partitions are sent to workers for processing local joins in parallel.

Local join. Given a combined partition $P = \{R_i, S_j\}$ from the global join, local join builds a local index over S_j on the fly (if S is not already indexed). For each record $r \in R_i$, Simba finds all $s \in S_j$ such that $|s, r| \le \tau$ by issuing a circle range query centered at r over the local index on S_j.

6.3 kNN Join

Several solutions [27,39] for kNN join were proposed on MapReduce. In Simba, we have redesigned and implemented these methods with the RDD abstraction of Spark. Furthermore, we design a new hash-join like algorithm, which shows the best performance.

6.3.1 Baseline methods

The most straightforward approach is the *BKJSpark-N* method (block nested loop kNN join in Spark).

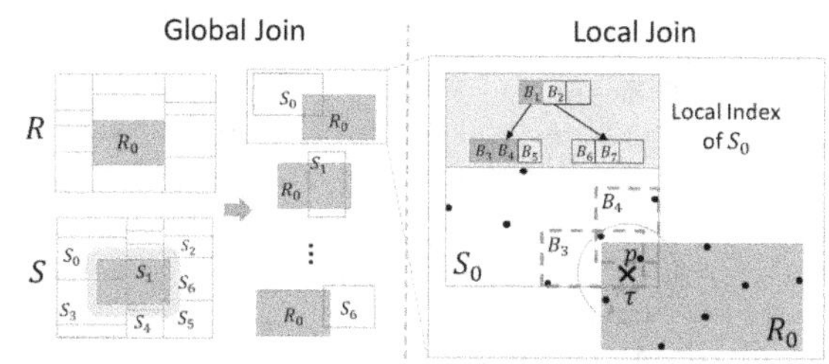

Figure 6: The DJSpark algorithm in Simba.

Producing buckets. R (and S) is divided into n_1 (n_2) equal-sized blocks, which simply puts every $|R|/n_1$ (or $|S|/n_2$) records into a block. Next, every pair of blocks, i.e., (R_i, S_j) for $i \in [1, n_1], j \in [1, n_2]$ are shuffled to a bucket (so a total of $n_1 n_2$ buckets).

Local kNN join. Buckets are processed in parallel. Within each bucket (R_i, S_j), Simba performs $\text{knn}(r, S_j)$ for every $r \in R_i$ through a nested loop over R_i and S_j.

Merge. This step finds the global kNN of every $r \in R$ among its $n_2 k$ local kNNs found in the last step (a total of $|R| n_2 k$ candidates). Simba runs `reduceByKey` (where the key is a record in R) in parallel to get the global kNN of each record in R.

A simple improvement is to build a local R-tree index over S_j for every bucket (R_i, S_j), and use the R-tree for local kNN joins. We denoted it as *BKJSpark-R* (block R-tree kNN join in Spark).

6.3.2 Voronoi kNN Join and z-Value kNN Join

The baseline methods need to check roughly n^2 buckets (when $O(n_1) = O(n_2) = O(n)$), which is expensive for both computation and communication in distributed systems. A MapReduce algorithm leveraging a Voronoi diagram based partitioning strategy was proposed in [27]. It executes only n local joins by partitioning both R and S into n partitions respectively, where the partition strategy is based on the Voronoi diagram for a set of pivot points selected from R. In Simba, We adapt this approach and denote it as the VKJSpark method (Voronoi kNN join in Spark).

Another MapReduce based algorithm for kNN join was proposed in [39], which exploits z-values to map multi-dimensional points into one dimension and uses *random shift* to preserve spatial locality. This approach also produces n partitions for R and S respectively, such that for any $r \in R_i$ and $i \in [1, n]$, $\text{knn}(r, S) \subseteq \text{knn}(r, S_i)$ *with high probability*. Thus, it is able to provide high quality approximations using only n local joins. The partition step is much simpler than the Voronoi kNN join, but it only provides approximate results and there is an extra cost for producing exact results in a post-processing step. We adapt this approach in Simba, and denote it as ZKJSpark (z-value kNN join in Spark).

6.3.3 R-Tree kNN Join

We leverage indexes in Simba to design a simpler yet more efficient method, the RKJSpark method (R-tree kNN join in Spark).

RKJSpark partitions R into n partitions $\{R_1, \ldots, R_n\}$ using the STR partitioning strategy (as introduced in Section 5), which leads to balanced partitions and preserves spatial locality. It then takes a set of random samples S' from S, and builds an R-tree T over S' in the driver program on the master node.

The key idea in RKJSpark is to derive a distance bound γ_i for each R_i, so that we can use γ_i, R_i, and T to find a subset $S_i \subset S$ such that for any $r \in R_i$, $\text{knn}(r, S) = \text{knn}(r, S_i)$. This partitioning strategy ensures that $R \bowtie_{\text{knn}} S = (R_1 \bowtie_{\text{knn}} S_1) \bigcup (R_2 \bowtie_{\text{knn}} S_2) \bigcup \cdots \bigcup (R_n \bowtie_{\text{knn}} S_n)$, and allows the parallel execution of only n local kNN joins (on each (R_i, S_i) pair for $i \in [1, n]$)).

We use cr_i to denote the centroid of $\text{mbr}(R_i)$. First, for each R_i, Simba finds the distance u_i from the furthest point in R_i to cr_i

(i.e., $u_i = \max_{r \in R_i} |r, cr_i|$) in parallel. Simba collects these u_i values and centroids in the driver program on the master node.

Next, Simba finds $\text{knn}(cr_i, S')$ using the R-tree T for $i \in [1, n]$. Without loss of generality, suppose $\text{knn}(cr_i, S') = \{s_1, \ldots, s_k\}$ (in ascending order of their distances to cr_i). Finally, Simba sets:

$$\gamma_i = 2u_i + |cr_i, s_k| \text{ for partition } R_i, \quad (1)$$

and finds $S_i = \{s | s \in S, |cr_i, s| \leq \gamma_i\}$ using a circle range query centered at cr_i with radius γ_i over S. This guarantees the desired property described above, due to:

Theorem 1 *For any partition R_i where $i \in [1, n]$, we have:* $\forall r \in R_i, \text{knn}(r, S) \subset \{s | s \in S, |cr_i, s| \leq \gamma_i\}$, *for γ_i defined in* (1).

The proof is shown in Appendix C. This leads to the design of RKJSpark. Specifically, for every $s \in S$, RKJSpark includes a copy of s in S_i if $|cr_i, s| \leq \gamma_i$. Theorem 1 guarantees that for any $r \in R_i$, $\text{knn}(r, S) = \text{knn}(r, S_i)$.

Then, Simba invokes a `zipPartitions` operation for each $i \in [1, n]$ to place R_i and S_i together into one combined RDD partition. In parallel, on each combined RDD partition, Simba builds an R-tree over S_i and executes a local kNN join by querying each record from R_i over this tree. The union of these n outputs is the final answer for $R \bowtie_{\text{knn}} S$.

7. OPTIMIZER AND FAULT TOLERANCE

7.1 Query Optimization

Simba tunes system configurations and optimizes complex spatial queries automatically to make the best use of existing indexes and statistics. We employed a cost model for determining a proper number of partitions in different query plans. We also add *new logical optimization rules* and *cost-based optimizations* to the Catalyst optimizer and the physical planner of Spark SQL.

The number of partitions plays an important role in performance tuning for Spark. A good choice on the number of partitions not only guarantees no crashes caused by memory overflow, but also improves system throughput and reduces query latency. Given the memory available on a slave node in the cluster and the input table size, Simba partitions the table so that each partition can fit into the memory of a slave node and has roughly equal number of records so as to ensure load balancing in the cluster.

Simba builds a cost model to estimate the partition size under a given schema. It handles two cases: tables with fixed-length records and tables with variable-length records. The first case is easy and we omit its details. The case for variable-length record is much harder, since it is difficult to estimate the size of a partition even if we know how many records are going into a partition. Simba resolves this challenge using a sampling based approach, i.e., a small set of samples (using sampling without replacement) is taken to build estimators for estimating the size of different partitions, where the sampling probability of a record is proportional to its length. This is a coarse estimation depending on the sampling rate; but it is possible to formally analyze the performance of this estimator with respect to a given partitioning strategy, and in practice, this sampling approach is quite effective.

Using the cost model and a specified partition strategy, Simba then computes a good value for the number of partitions such that: 1) partitions are balanced in size; 2) size of each partition fits the memory size of a worker node; and 3) the total number of partitions is proportional to the number of workers in the cluster. Note that the size of different partitions should be close but not greater than a threshold, which indicates how much heap memory Spark can reserve for query processing. In Spark, on each slave node, a fraction of memory is reserved for RDD caching, which is specified as a system configuration `spark.storage.memoryFraction`

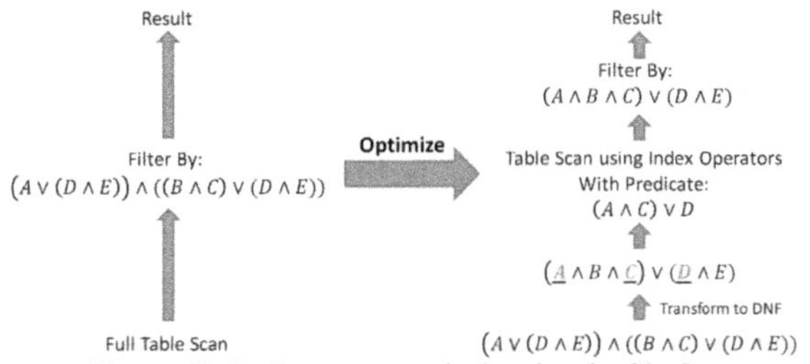

Figure 7: Index scan optimization in Simba.

(we denote this value as α). In our cost model, the remaining memory will be evenly split to each processing core.

Suppose the number of cores is c and total memory reserved for Spark on each slave node is M. The partition size threshold β is then calculated as: $\beta = \lambda((1 - \alpha)M/c)$, where λ is a system parameter, whose default value is 0.8, to take memory consumption of run-time data structures into consideration. With such cost model, Simba can determine the number of records for a single partition, and the numbers of partitions for different data sets.

To better utilize the indexing support in Simba, we add new rules to the Catalyst optimizer to select those predicates which can be optimized by indexes. First, we transform the original select condition to *Disjunctive Normal Form* (DNF), e.g. $(A \wedge B) \vee C \vee (D \wedge E \wedge F)$. Then, we get rid of all predicates in the DNF clause which cannot be optimized by indexes, to form a new select condition θ. Simba will filter the input relation with θ first using index-based operators, and then apply the original select condition to get the final answer.

Figure 7 shows an example of the index optimization. The select condition on the input table is $(A \vee (D \wedge E)) \wedge ((B \wedge C) \vee (D \wedge E))$. Assuming that A, C and D can be optimized by utilizing existing indexes. Without index optimization, the engine (e.g., Spark SQL) simply does a full scan on the input table and filters each record by the select condition. By applying index optimization, Simba works out the DNF of the select condition, which is $(A \wedge B \wedge C) \vee (D \wedge E)$, and invokes a table scan using index operators under a new condition $(A \wedge C) \vee D$. Then, we filter the resulting relation with original condition once more to get the final results.

Simba also exploits various *geometric properties* to merge spatial predicates, to reduce the number of physical operations. Simba merges multiple predicates into segments or bounding boxes, which can be processed together without involving expensive intersections or unions on intermediate results. For example, `x > 3 AND x < 5 AND y > 1 AND y < 6` can be merged into a range query on `(POINT(3, 1), POINT(5, 6))`, which is natively supported in Simba as a single range query. Simba also merges query segments or bounding boxes prior to execution. For instance, two conjunctive range queries on `(POINT(3, 1), POINT(5, 6))` and `(POINT(4, 0), POINT(9, 3))` can be merged into a single range query on `(POINT(4, 1), POINT(5, 3))`.

Index optimization improves performance greatly when the predicates are selective. However, it may cause more overheads than savings when the predicate is not selective or the size of input table is small. Thus, Simba employs a new cost based optimization (CBO), which takes existing indexes and statistics into consideration, to choose the most efficient physical plans. Specifically, we define the selectivity of a predicate for a partition as the percentage of records in the partition that satisfy the predicate.

If the selectivity of the predicate is higher than a user-defined threshold (by default 80%), Simba will choose to scan the partition rather than leveraging indexes. For example, for range queries, Simba will first leverage the local index to do a fast estimation on the predicate selectivity for each partition whose boundary intersects the query area, using *only the top levels of local indexes* for selectivity estimation (we maintain a count at each R-tree node u that is the number of leaf level entries covered by the subtree rooted at u, and assume uniform distribution in each MBR for the purpose of selectivity estimation,). Selectivity estimation for other types of predicates can be similarly made using top levels of local indexes.

CBO is also used for joins in Simba. When one of the tables to be joined is small (much smaller than the other table), Simba's optimizer will switch to *broadcast join*, which skips the data partition phase on the small table and broadcasts it to every partition of the large table to do local joins. For example, if R is small and S is big, Simba does local joins over $(R, S_1), \ldots, (R, S_m)$. This optimization can be applied to both distance and kNN joins.

For kNN joins in particular, CBO is used to tune RKJSpark. We increase the sampling rate used to generate S' and/or partition table R with finer granularity to get a tighter bound for γ_i. Simba's optimizer adjusts the sampling rate of S' according to the master node's memory size (and the max possible query value $k_{\max}$ so that $|S'| > k_{max}$; k is small for most kNN queries). Simba's optimizer can also invoke another STR partitioner *within each partition* to get partition boundaries *locally on each worker* with finer granularity without changing the global partition and physical data distribution. This allows RKJSpark to compute tighter bounds of γ_i using the refined partition boundaries, thus reduces the size of S_i's.

Lastly, Simba implements a thread-safe SQL context (by creating thread-local instances for conflict components) to support the concurrent execution of multiple queries. Hence, multiple users can issue their queries concurrently to the same Simba instance.

7.2 Fault Tolerance

Simba's fault tolerance mechanism extends that of Spark and Spark SQL. By the construction of `IndexRDD`, table records and local indexes in Simba are still encapsulated in RDD objects! They are persisted at the storage level of `MEM_AND_DISK_SER`, thus *are naturally fault tolerant because of the RDD abstraction of Spark.* Any lost data (records or local indexes) will be automatically recovered by RDD's fault tolerance mechanism (based on the lineage graph). Thus, Simba can tolerate any worker node failures at the same level that Spark provides. This also allows local indexes to be reused when data are loaded back into memory from disk, and avoids repartitioning and rebuilding of local indexes.

For the fault tolerance of the master node (or the driver program), Simba adopts the following mechanism. A Spark cluster can have multiple masters managed by zookeeper [7]. One will be elected "leader" and the others will remain in standby mode. If current leader fails, another master will be elected, recover the old master's state, and then continue scheduling. Such mechanism would recover all system states and global indexes that reside in the driver program, thus ensures that Simba can survive after a master failure.

In addition, user can also choose to persist `IndexRDD` and global indexes to the file system, and have the option of loading them back from the disk. This enables Simba to load constructed index structures back to the system even after power failures.

Lastly, note that all user queries (including spatial operators) in Simba will be scheduled as RDD transformations and actions in Spark. Therefore, fault tolerance for query processing is naturally guaranteed by the underlying lineage graph fault tolerance mechanism provided in Spark kernel and consensus model of zookeeper.

8. EXPERIMENT

8.1 Experiment Setup

All experiments were conducted on a cluster consisting of 10 nodes with two configurations: (1) 8 machines with a 6-core Intel Xeon E5-2603 v3 1.60GHz processor and 20GB RAM; (2) 2 machines with a 6-core Intel Xeon E5-2620 2.00GHz processor and 56GB RAM. Each node is connected to a Gigabit Ethernet switch and runs Ubuntu 14.04.2 LTS with Hadoop 2.4.1 and Spark 1.3.0. We select one machine of type (2) as the master node and the rest are slave nodes. The Spark cluster is deployed in standalone mode. Our cluster configuration reserved up to 180GB of main memory for Spark. We used the following real and synthetic datasets:

OSM is extracted from OpenStreetMap [9]. The full OSM data contains 2.2 billion records in 132GB, where each record has a record ID, a two-dimensional coordinate, and two text information fields (with variable lengths). We took uniform random samples of various sizes from the full OSM, and also duplicated the full OSM to get a data set 2×OSM. These data sets range from 1 million to 4.4 billion records, with raw data size up to 264GB (in 2×OSM).

GDELT stands for Global Data on Events, Language and Tone [8], which is an open database containing 75 million records in total. In our experiment, each record has 7 attributes: a timestamp and three two-dimensional coordinates which represent the locations for the start, the terminal, and the action of an event.

RC: We also generated synthetic datasets of various sizes (1 million to 1 billion records) and dimensions (2 - 6 dimensions) using *random clusters*. Specifically, we randomly generate different number of clusters, using a d-dimensional Gaussian distribution in each cluster. Each record in d-dimension contains $d+1$ attributes: namely, a record ID and its spatial coordinates.

For single-relation operations (i.e. range and kNN queries), we evaluate the performance using *throughput and latency*. In particular, for both Simba and Spark SQL, we start a thread pool of size 10 in the driver program, and issue 500 queries to the system to calculate query throughput. For other systems that we reviewed in Section 2, since they do not have a multi-threading module, we submit 20 queries at the same time and run them as 20 different processes to ensure full utilization of the cluster resources. The throughput is calculated by dividing the total number of queries over the running time. Note that this follows the same way these systems had used to measure their throughput [22]. For all systems, we used 100 randomly generated queries to measure the average query latency. For join operations, we focus on the average running time of 10 randomly generated join queries for all systems.

In all experiments, HDFS block size is 64MB. By default, $k = 10$ for a kNN query or a kNN join. A range query is characterized by its *query area*, which is a percentage over the entire area where data locate. The default query area for range queries is 0.01%. The default distance threshold τ for a distance join is set to 5 (each dimension is normalized into a domain from 0 to 1000). The default partition size is 500×10^3 (500k) records per partition for single-relation operations and 30×10^3 (30k) records per partition for join operations. The default data set size for single-relation operations is 500 million records on OSM data sets and 700 million on RC data sets. For join operations, the default data size is set to 3 million records in each input table. The default dimensionality is 2.

8.2 Cost of Indexing

We first investigate the cost of indexing in Simba and other distributed spatial analytics systems, including GeoSpark [37], SpatialSpark [36], SpatialHadoop [22], Hadoop GIS [11], and Geomesa [24]. A commercial single-node parallel spatial database system (denoted as DBMS X) running on our master node is also included. Figure 8(a) presents the index construction time of different systems on the OSM data set when the data size varies from 30 million to 4.4 billion records (i.e., up to 2×OSM). Note that DBMS X took too much time when building an R-tree index over 4.4 billion records in 2×OSM; hence its last point is omitted.

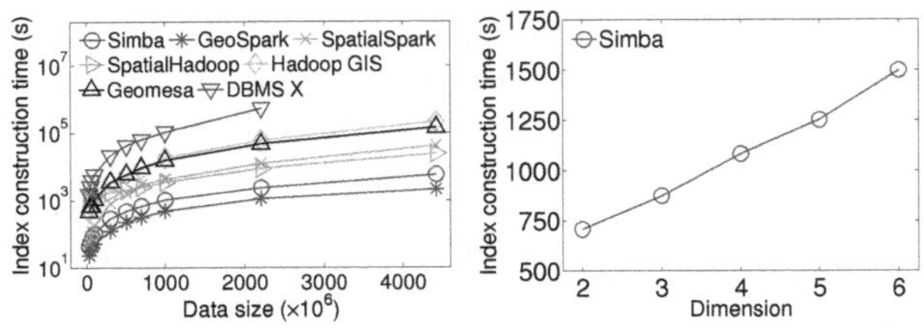

(a) Effect of data size, OSM. (b) Effect of dimension, RC.

Figure 8: Index construction time.

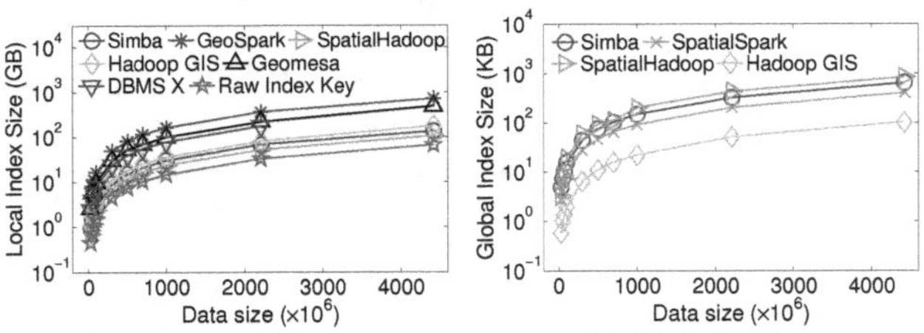

(a) Local index. (b) Global index.

Figure 9: Index storage overhead on OSM.

Simba and GeoSpark show the best index construction time, and both scale linearly to the data size. For example, Simba builds its index (which uses R-tree for both local indexes and the global index) over 1 billion records (60GB in file size) in around 25 minutes, which is 2.5x faster than SpatialHadoop, 3x faster than SpatialSpark, 12x faster than Hadoop GIS, and 15x faster than Geomesa. GeoSpark is slightly faster than Simba in building its indexes, because it uses a sampling partition strategy and it only builds a local index for each partition without building global indexes. Simba indexes RDDs natively, while Hadoop based systems index HDFS file blocks. Even though SpatialSpark is also based on Spark, it indexes HDFS files rather than native RDDs. Geomesa builds a hash based index over Apache Accumulo.

We then investigated Simba's indexing support in higher dimensions. Figure 8(b) shows the index construction time in Simba against number of dimensions on the RC data set. The cost increases linearly with the increase in dimensionality. Note that all *other systems can only support up to two dimensions.*

Next, we investigate the storage overhead (memory footprint or disk space used) of indexes in different systems, using OSM data of various sizes. Since Geomesa utilizes a hash based indexing strategy without global indexing, and DBMS X constructs its spatial index on a single node, we show their results with the local index size of the other systems in Figure 9(a), as local indexes dominate the index size of indexing in distributed systems. As a reference, we included the total size of all indexed keys (i.e., spatial coordinates) in Figure 9(a), denoted as "Raw Index Key". SpatialSpark was not included in Figure 9(a) since local indexes are not supported.

As shown in Figure 9(a), Simba, SpatialHadoop and Hadoop GIS have the lowest storage overhead in their local indexes, while those of GeoSpark, Geomesa and DBMS X are much higher (roughly 4-5x). Global indexing is only supported by Simba, SpatialSpark, SpatialHadoop and Hadoop GIS. As shown in Figure 9(b), all systems have small global index storage overhead (only in the order of KB). In particular, the global index size in Simba is very small, which can easily fit in the memory of the master node. For example, it only consumes 653KB for the largest dataset (4.4 billion records with 264GB in raw data) in Simba. This is because that the number of partitions is not a large number (in the order of hundreds to tens of thousands) even for very large data.

Overall, Simba's index storage overhead is acceptable, for example, for 1×OSM with 2.2 billion indexed keys, Simba's local indexes use only 67GB, and its global index uses only 323KB, while the raw key size is about 40GB and the data itself is 132GB.

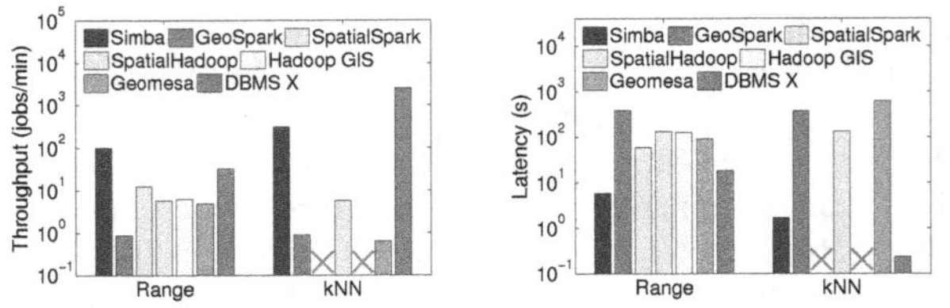

(a) Throughput (b) Latency

Figure 10: Single-relation operations on different systems.

8.3 Comparison with Existing Systems

In this section, we tested different systems using various spatial operations with the default settings described in Section 8.1 over the 0.25×OSM data set (500 million records). A red cross mark in the following bar charts indicates that the corresponding operation is *not supported* in a system.

Figure 10 shows the performance of single-relation operations on both range and kNN queries. Simba achieves 5-100x better performance (on both throughput and latency) than other existing cluster-based spatial analytics systems and the single-node parallel spatial database. Only DBMS X has outperformed Simba on kNN queries, as when k is small a single-node approach with index support is very efficient for finding kNNs. But its range query performance is worse than Simba.

Note that the performance of GeoSpark in this case is even worse than Hadoop based systems because GeoSpark has not utilized global indexes for query processing, which can help pruning large numbers of useless partitions (more than 90%) before scanning them.

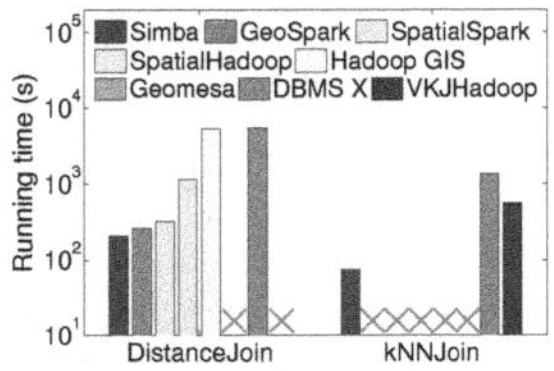

Figure 11: Join operations on different systems.

For join operations (using 3 million records in each table), as shown in Figure 11, Simba runs distance join 1.5x faster than SpatialSpark, 25x faster than Hadoop GIS, and 26x faster than DBMS X. Note that distance join over point objects is not natively supported in SpatialHadoop. Nevertheless, SpatialHadoop supports spatial joins over geometric objects. We use $RC(\tau/2) \bowtie_{\text{intersects}} SC(\tau/2)$ to work out the original distance join (by mapping two points to two circles with $\tau/2$ radius centered at them). kNN join is only supported by Simba and DBMS X. For a better comparison with existing distributed methods, we also compared Simba against the Voronoi-based kNN join implemented on Hadoop [1] (denoted as VKJHadoop). By Figure 11, Simba (using its RKJSpark algorithm) is 18x faster than DBMS X and 7x faster than VKJHadoop.

Simba is more efficient than GeoSpark [37] and SpatialSpark [36] because of its indexing support inside the query engine and its query optimizer. GeoSpark and SpatialSpark are only libraries running on top of Spark without a query engine. Compared with Hadoop based systems like SpatialHadoop [22] and Hadoop GIS [11], Simba extends the engine of Spark SQL to support spatial operations natively with a sophisticated, RDBMS-like query engine, and uses Spark for in-memory computation, hence, is much more efficient. For example, Simba provides 51x lower latency and 45x higher throughput than SpatialHadoop for kNN queries. Hadoop based systems will be useful when data is so large that they cannot fit into the cluster's memory space.

Geomesa is a distributed key-value storage system with support for spatial operations. Thus, its analytical performance is not as nearly good as Simba. DBMS X is a single-node parallel database, thus, does not scale well for expensive join operations and large datasets (as evident from its index construction cost).

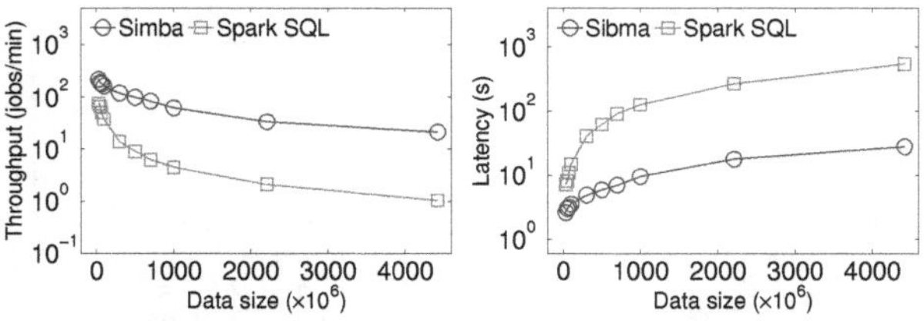

(a) Effect of data size.

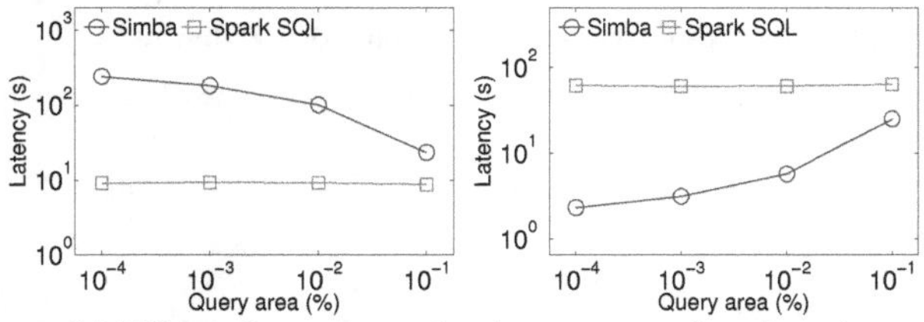

(b) Effect of query area size (percentage of total area).

Figure 12: Range query performance on OSM.

Simba is also much more user-friendly with the native support on both SQL and the DataFrame API over *both spatial and non-spatial operations within a single query*, which are *not* supported by other systems (except that SpatialHadoop supports a SQL-like query language Pigeon). Simba is a full-fledged query engine with native support for query planning, query optimization, and concurrent query processing through thread pooling. Whereas, GeoSpark and SpatialSpark are user programs running on top of Spark (i.e., Spark libraries). What's more, all these systems can only support up to two dimensions. Hence, in the following, we focus on comparing Simba with Spark SQL, which is also a full fledged analytics engine based on Spark but without native support for spatial operations, to see the benefit of extending Spark SQL to Simba for spatial analytics. We support various spatial operations in Spark SQL by directly expressing a spatial operation in its standard SQL syntax if it is possible, or using UDFs in SQL when it is not possible.

8.4 Comparison against Spark SQL

In this comparison we assume that tables are pre-loaded (i..e, we excluded the time of loading tables in both Simba and Spark SQL).

Range queries. Figure 12 shows the performance of range queries in both engines using the OSM data set. Queries are centered at random points sampled from the input data. As a result, the query workload fits well to the distribution of the data, where dense areas will be queried with higher probabilities.

Figure 12(a) shows that Simba outperforms Spark SQL by about one order of magnitude on both query throughput and query latency when data size increases from 30 million to 4.4 billion records (2×OSM). The performance of both Simba and Spark SQL drops when the data size increases while that of Simba drops much slower, which implies Simba has much better scalability. This is due to the spatial index pruning and spatial-aware optimizations in Simba: larger data size does lead to more partitions to process and larger output size, but it also brings more pruning and optimization opportunities for its indexes and optimizer. In contrast, Spark SQL has to scan the whole table regardless.

Figure 12(b) shows how throughput and latency are influenced by the size of the query area. As the query area enlarges, performance of Simba becomes closer to that of Spark SQL. The reason for this is the result size becomes so large that there are less optimization opportunities for Simba's query optimizer. Spark SQL has to scan the whole table regardless.

kNN queries. Figure 13 shows the performance of kNN queries on Spark SQL and Simba over the OSM data set, where query points are also randomly sampled from the input data as range queries.

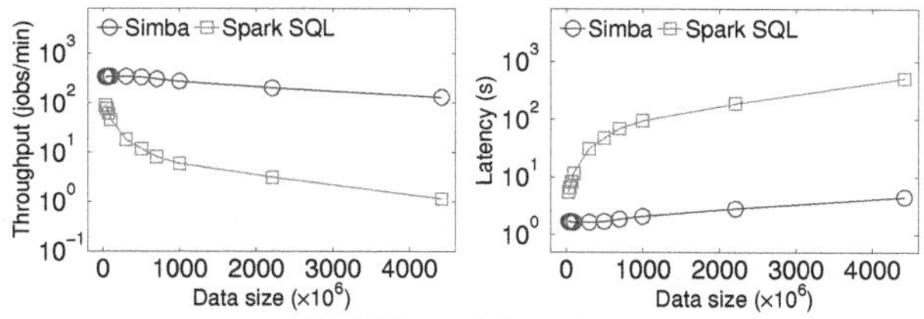

(a) Effect of data size.

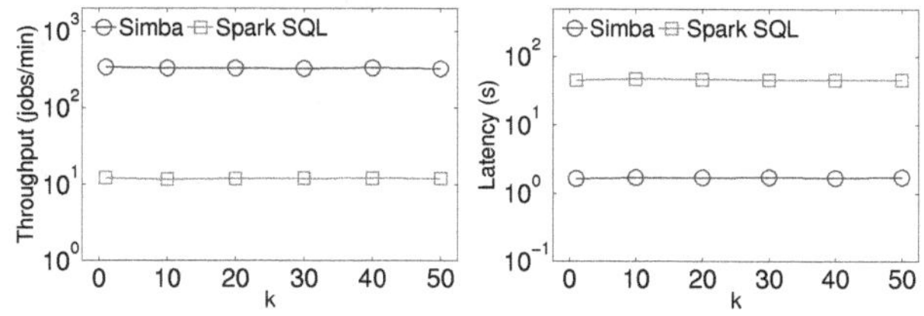

(b) Effect of k.

Figure 13: kNN query performance on OSM.

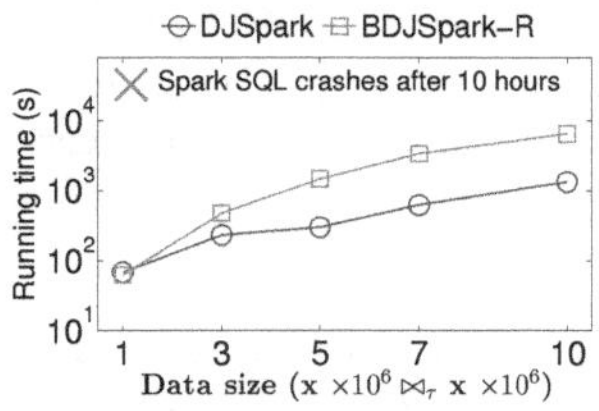

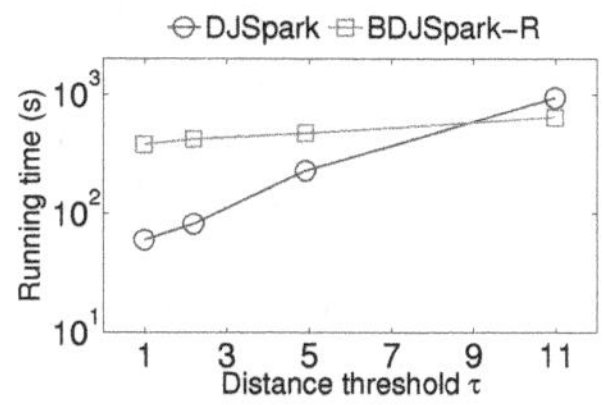

(a) Effect of data size. (b) Effect of τ.

Figure 14: Distance join performance on OSM.

Figure 13(a) measures system throughput and query latency when data size increases from 30 million to 4.4 billion records (2×OSM). Simba achieves one to two orders of magnitude better performance on both metrics. Spark SQL's performance drops significantly as the data size grows, since it requires scanning the whole table for each kNN query. In contrast, Simba's performance is almost not affected by the data size, because Simba is able to narrow the input table down quickly to just a few indexed partitions (typically one or two), which are sufficient to cover the global kNN.

Next, we study the impact of k. As k varies from 1 to 50 in Figure 13(b), Simba maintains a speedup of two orders of magnitude. Both Simba and Spark SQL's performance are not really affected by k: Spark SQL needs to scan the data regardless of k values; whereas Simba's performance will not change much when the change on k is much smaller compared with the partition size.

Distance join. Figure 14 shows the results for distance join using two tables sampled from the OSM data set. We tried expressing and running a distance join as a θ-join in Spark SQL (an example was shown in Section 6.2). However, *it did not finish in 10 hours when joining two tables of only 1 million records, and crashed, due to the expensive Cartesian product it has to perform.*

For Simba, we compared Simba's DJSpark algorithm with a nested loop join approach BDJSpark-R leveraging R-trees as local indexes (which is a simple variation of BKJSpark-R discussed in Section 6.3 by replacing each local kNN join with a local distance join).

Naturally, the cost of both algorithms increase with larger input size (Figure 14(a)) and larger distance threshold (Figure14(b)). Note that the performance of DJSpark drops fast as the distance threshold grows. This is because the power of global pruning becomes weaker, which will finally cause more overheads than savings when compared with BDJSpark-R. Nevertheless, DJSpark is always more efficient than the baseline method BDJSpark-R, unless the threshold grows to a relatively large value (say $x = 11$ in this case; roughly 1% of the space).

kNN join. It is *impossible to express kNN join in Spark SQL in a*

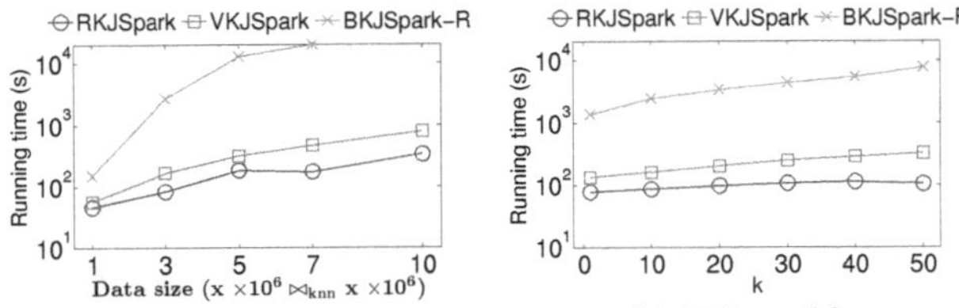

(a) Effect of data size. (b) Effect of k.

Figure 15: kNN join performance on OSM.

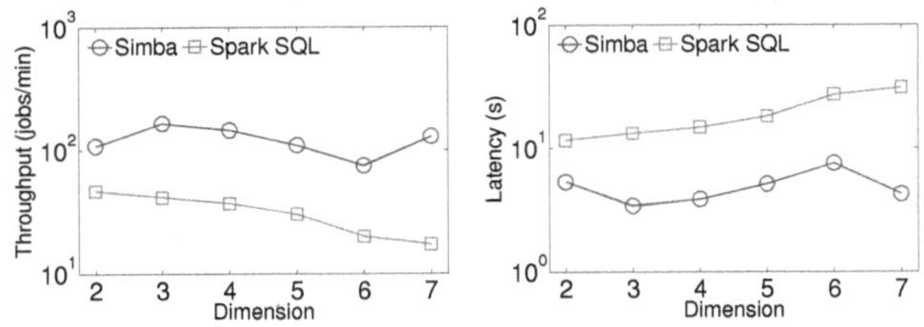

(a) Throughput (b) Latency

Figure 16: Range query performance on GDELT: dimensionality.

single SQL statement. One has to union N SQL statements where N is the number of records in the first input table, which is clearly not a practical solution for large tables. Hence, we focused on comparing different kNN join algorithms in Simba.

Figure 15 shows the performance over OSM data (default is 3 million records in each input table and $k = 10$). Clearly, RKJSpark shows the best performance and the best scalability (w.r.t. both data size and k). As an example, for a kNN join between two tables with 5 million records, RKJSpark join is 3x faster than VKJSpark and 70x faster than BKJSpark-R. Note that BKJSpark-R strictly dominates BKJSpark-N, hence, the latter is omitted.

Remarks. Spark still works when the dataset does not fit in main memory due to its disk persistence mechanism, Simba still has reasonable performance when data does not fit in memory. Clearly, performance will hurt in this case, but in principle, as long as each individual partition can fit in the heap memory of an executor, Spark is able to handle it, so is Simba (and its indexing support is even more important in these cases).

8.5 Support for Multi-Dimensions

In this section, we evaluate the performance of Simba and Spark SQL when handling data in higher dimensions. Note that other spatial analytics systems (GeoSpark, SpatialSpark, SpatialHadoop, and Hadoop GIS) *do not* support more than two dimensions.

For single-relation operations, as shown in Figures 16 and 17, both Simba and Spark SQL shows higher query latency and lower system throughput on the GDELT data set, as dimensionality increases from 2 to 6. Nevertheless, Simba outperforms Spark SQL by 1-2 orders of magnitude in all cases.

Figure 18 shows the impact of dimensionality on different join algorithms in Simba, by joining two tables with 3 million records from the RC data set as dimensionality goes from 2 to 6. DJSpark and RKJSpark remain the best performance in all dimensions.

9. RELATED WORK

We have already reviewed the most closely related systems in Sections 2 and 8, which Simba has significantly outperformed.

In addition, MD-HBase [29] extends HBase to support location services. It adds KD-tree and quad-tree indexes to HBase to support range and kNN queries. GeoMesa [24] builds a distributed spatial-temporal database on top of Apache Accumulo [3]. It uses GeoHash indexes to provide spatial queries over data stored in Apache Accumulo. Both HBase and Accumulo are modeled after Google's BigTable [16], hence, both MD-HBase and GeoMesa are essentially key-value stores with support for spatial operations. As a result, both the design and the objective of the system are very different from an in-memory spatial analytical engine like Simba.

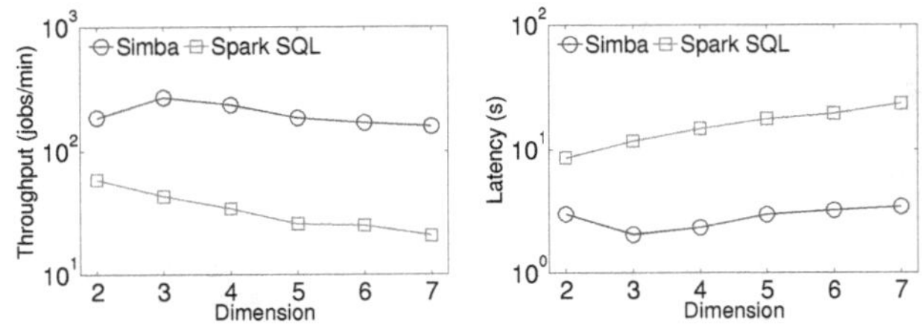

(a) Throughput (b) Latency

Figure 17: kNN query performance on GDELT: dimensionality.

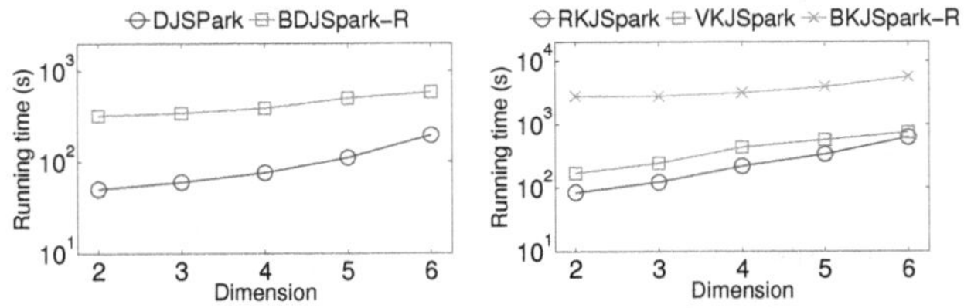

(a) Distance join (b) kNN join

Figure 18: Join operations performance on RC: dimensionality.

Most existing systems design indexing structures for the MapReduce framework (e.g., Hadoop and HDFS), and they work with indexed data from HDFS. An open source project [2] provides an approach that builds index directly on Spark's RDD abstraction. However, it only supports one-dimensional ART index [25] on key-value RDDs, which doesn't extend to spatial query processing.

In addition to system efforts, indexing and query processing for spatial data in MapReduce were explored, for example, z-value based indexing [15], range queries and kNN queries [12,28,40,40], kNN joins [27,39], and spatial join over geometric objects [41].

Various spatial partitioning strategies were explored in MapReduce (using Hadoop). A survey and performance comparison can be found in [19,34]. Simba primarily explored the Sort-Tile-Recursive (STR) partitioning scheme [26] for its indexing module, which has shown to be one of the best spatial partitioning methods (e.g., see latest results in [19]). That said, other spatial partitioning methods can be easily employed and supported by Simba.

Lastly, the general principle of Simba's query optimizer is no different from those found in classic relational query engines [17], such as selectivity estimation, CBO, and pushing down predicates. But we have to adopt those principles to an in-memory, distributed and parallel environments, and to spatial operations. The cost models developed for partitioning and cost-based spatial query evaluation in the context of Spark are new. Merging and pushing down spatial predicates based on geometric properties in such a distributed and parallel in-memory query engine was also not explored before.

10. CONCLUSION

This paper describes Simba, a distributed in-memory spatial query and analytics engine based on Spark. Simba offers simple and expressive query language in both SQL and DataFrame API. Simba extends Spark SQL with native support to spatial operations, introduces indexes on RDDs, and adds spatial-aware (logical and cost-based) optimizations to select good query plans. Extensive experiments reveal its superior performance compared to other systems.

For future work, we plan to add native support on more geometric objects (e.g., polygons) and spatial operators (e.g., spatial join over polygons), and data in very high dimensions. We will also design more sophisticated CBOs for effective auto-tuning.

11. ACKNOWLEDGMENT

Feifei Li and Dong Xie were supported in part by NSF grants 1200792, 1302663, 1443046. Bin Yao, Gefei Li, Liang Zhou, and Minyi Guo were supported by the National Basic Research Program (973 Program, No.2015CB352403), and the Scientific Innovation Act of STCSM (No.13511504200, 15JC1402400). Feifei Li and Bin Yao were also supported in part by NSFC grant 61428204.

12. REFERENCES

[1] http://www.comp.nus.edu.sg/ dbsystem/source.html.

[2] https://github.com/amplab/spark-indexedrdd.

[3] Apache accumulo. http://accumulo.apache.org.

[4] Apache avro project. http://avro.apache.org.

[5] Apache parquet project. http://parquet.incubator.apache.org.

[6] Apache spark project. http://spark.apache.org.

[7] Apache zookeeper. https://zookeeper.apache.org/.

[8] Gdelt project. http://www.gdeltproject.org.

[9] Openstreepmap project. http://www.openstreetmap.org.

[10] R project for statistical computing. http://www.r-project.org.

[11] A. Aji, F. Wang, H. Vo, R. Lee, Q. Liu, X. Zhang, and J. Saltz. Hadoop gis: a high performance spatial data warehousing system over mapreduce. In *VLDB*, 2013.

[12] A. Akdogan, U. Demiryurek, F. Banaei-Kashani, and C. Shahabi. Voronoi-based geospatial query processing with mapreduce. In *CouldCom*, 2010.

[13] M. Armbrust, R. S. Xin, C. Lian, Y. Huai, D. Liu, J. K. Bradley, X. Meng, T. Kaftan, M. J. Franklin, A. Ghodsi, et al. Spark sql: Relational data processing in spark. In *SIGMOD*, 2015.

[14] N. Beckmann, H. Kriegel, R. Schneider, and B. Seeger. The r*-tree: An efficient and robust access method for points and rectangles. In *SIGMOD*, 1990.

[15] A. Cary, Z. Sun, V. Hristidis, and N. Rishe. Experiences on processing spatial data with mapreduce. In *Scientific and Statistical Database Management*, 2009.

[16] F. Chang, J. Dean, S. Ghemawat, W. C. Hsieh, D. A. Wallach, M. Burrows, T. Chandra, A. Fikes, and R. E. Gruber. Bigtable: A distributed storage system for structured data. *TOCS*, 2008.

[17] S. Chaudhuri. An overview of query optimization in relational systems. In *PODS*, pages 34–43, 1998.

[18] J. Dean and S. Ghemawat. Mapreduce: Simplified data processing on large clusters. In *OSDI*, 2004.

[19] A. Eldawy, L. Alarabi, and M. F. Mokbel. Spatial partitioning techniques in spatial hadoop. *PVLDB*, 2015.

[20] A. Eldawy, Y. Li, M. F. Mokbel, and R. Janardan. Cg_hadoop: computational geometry in mapreduce. In *SIGSPATIAL*, 2013.

[21] A. Eldawy and M. F. Mokbel. Pigeon: A spatial mapreduce language. In *ICDE*, 2014.

[22] A. Eldawy and M. F. Mokbel. Spatialhadoop: A mapreduce framework for spatial data. In *ICDE*, 2015.

[23] A. Guttman. R-trees: A dynamic index structure for spatial searching. In *SIGMOD*, 1984.

[24] J. N. Hughes, A. Annex, C. N. Eichelberger, A. Fox, A. Hulbert, and M. Ronquest. Geomesa: a distributed architecture for spatio-temporal fusion. In *SPIE Defense+ Security*, 2015.

[25] V. Leis, A. Kemper, and T. Neumann. The adaptive radix tree: Artful indexing for main-memory databases. In *ICDE*, 2013.

[26] S. T. Leutenegger, M. Lopez, J. Edgington, et al. STR: A simple and efficient algorithm for R-tree packing. In *ICDE*, 1997.

[27] W. Lu, Y. Shen, S. Chen, and B. C. Ooi. Efficient processing of k nearest neighbor joins using mapreduce. In *VLDB*, 2012.

[28] Q. Ma, B. Yang, W. Qian, and A. Zhou. Query processing of massive trajectory data based on mapreduce. In *Proceedings of the first international workshop on Cloud data management*, 2009.

[29] S. Nishimura, S. Das, D. Agrawal, and A. El Abbadi. $\mathcal{MD}$-hbase: design and implementation of an elastic data infrastructure for cloud-scale location services. In *DAPD*, 2013.

[30] C. Olston, B. Reed, U. Srivastava, R. Kumar, and A. Tomkins. Pig latin: a not-so-foreign language for data processing. In *SIGMOD*, 2008.

[31] N. Roussopoulos, S. Kelley, and F. Vincent. Nearest neighbor queries. In *SIGMOD*, 1995.

[32] H. Samet. *Foundations of Multidimensional and Metric Data Structures (The Morgan Kaufmann Series in Computer Graphics and Geometric Modeling)*. Morgan Kaufmann Publishers Inc., 2005.

[33] A. Thusoo, J. S. Sarma, N. Jain, Z. Shao, P. Chakka, S. Anthony, H. Liu, P. Wyckoff, and R. Murthy. Hive: A warehousing solution over a map-reduce framework. In *PVDLB*, 2009.

[34] H. Vo, A. Aji, and F. Wang. Sato: A spatial data partitioning framework for scalable query processing. In *SIGSPATIAL*, 2014.

[35] R. S. Xin, J. Rosen, M. Zaharia, M. J. Franklin, S. Shenker, and I. Stoica. Shark: Sql and rich analytics at scale. In *SIGMOD*, 2013.

[36] S. You, J. Zhang, and L. Gruenwald. Large-scale spatial join query processing in cloud. In *IEEE CloudDM workshop (To Appear)*, 2015.

[37] J. Yu, J. Wu, and M. Sarwat. Geospark: A cluster computing framework for processing large-scale spatial data. In *SIGSPATIAL GIS*, 2015.

[38] M. Zaharia, M. Chowdhury, T. Das, A. Dave, J. Ma, M. McCauley, M. J. Franklin, S. Shenker, and I. Stoica. Resilient distributed datasets: A fault-tolerant abstraction for in-memory cluster computing. In *NSDI*, 2012.

[39] C. Zhang, F. Li, and J. Jestes. Efficient parallel knn joins for large data in mapreduce. In *EDBT*, 2012.

[40] S. Zhang, J. Han, Z. Liu, K. Wang, and S. Feng. Spatial queries evaluation with mapreduce. In *ICGCC*, 2009.

[41] S. Zhang, J. Han, Z. Liu, K. Wang, and Z. Xu. Sjmr: Parallelizing spatial join with mapreduce on clusters. In *IEEE ICCC*, 2009.

APPENDIX

A. FULL PROGRAMMING INTERFACE

A.1 SQL

Points. Simba introduces the point object inside the Spark SQL engine, through a scala class. Users can use keyword `POINT` followed by a list of expressions to express multi-dimensional points, where the number of expressions indicates the number of dimensions. For example, we can use `Point(x - 1, y * 2)` to express a two dimensional point with the value of $x - 1$ as the first dimension and the value of $y * 2$ as the second dimension. Note that it is easy to extend Simba with additional spatial and geometric objects by adding more scala classes inside its engine.

Range predicates. Simba supports box range query and circle range query. For a box range query, user uses the following predicate to check if points are inside a bounding box:

```
p IN RANGE(low, high)
```

In the predicate above, parameters `p`, `low` and `high` represent three point objects expressed by the grammar for points described above. Specifically, `p` indicates an input point for the predicate to check, while `low` and `high` specify the bounding box (lower-left and higher-right points) for the range query. Points `p`, `low` and `high` can reside in arbitrary dimensions.

Similarly, user specifies a circle range query as below:

```
p IN CIRCLERANGE(c, rd)
```

Note that `p` is again an input point for the predicate to check, while the point object `c` and the constant `rd` indicate a circle centered at point `c` with radius `rd` which specifies a circle range.

kNN predicates. Similar to the range query predicates, Simba provides the kNN predicate as follows:

```
p IN KNN(q, k)
```

It checks if `p` is in the set of k nearest neighbors of a query point q, with respect to an input table. The input table is indicated by the relation after the `FROM` clause. A kNN predicate is a select condition in the `WHERE` clause. A kNN predicate can also serve as the join condition for a kNN join operation.

Distance joins. User expresses a distance join between two tables `R` and `S` with a distance threshold τ as follows:

```
R DISTANCE JOIN S ON s IN CIRCLERANGE(r, τ)
```

Here `s` (resp. `r`) are points built from a record in table S (resp. R).

kNN joins. A kNN join between table `R` and table `S` is expressed as follows:

```
R KNN JOIN S ON s IN KNN(r, k)
```

Similar to distance join, s (resp. r) are built from a record in `S` (resp. `R`). User can also invoke approximate kNN join using ZKJSpark (Section 6.3.2) by replacing `KNN JOIN` with `ZKNN JOIN`.

Index management. Simba allows users to manipulate indexes easily with its index management keywords. Specifically, user is able to create an index through:

```
CREATE INDEX idx_name ON R(x1, ..., xm) USE
    idx_type
```

It builds a new index over m attributes $\{x_1, \ldots, x_m\}$ in table `R` using a specific index type as indicated by `idx_type` (which can be R-tree, tree map or hash map). The index is named as `idx_name`. User can show the indexes already built on table `R` at anytime:

```
SHOW INDEX ON R
```

In addition, user can drop an index through the index name, or drop all indexes on a table through the table name:

```
DROP INDEX idx_name ON table_name
DROP INDEX table_name
```

Lastly, Simba's SQL commands are fully integrated with Spark SQL's SQL query interface. In other words, user can easily use these keywords and commands together with arbitrary sql predicates from the standard SQL library supported by Spark SQL.

A.2 DataFrame API

Points. Simba also introduces the point object in the DataFrame API, which wraps a list of expressions into a multi-dimensional point that can be processed by Simba's query engine. For example, we can express a three dimensional point as follows:

```
Point(tb("x"), tb("y"), tb("z"))
```

Specifically, the code above wraps three attributes `x`, `y` and `z` from table `tb` into a point object for further processing.

Single-relation operations. User can apply (box or circle) range queries and kNN queries directly on data frames. Specifically, in the DataFrame API, Simba provides the following functions:

```
range(base: Point, low: Point, high: Point)
circleRange(base: Point, center: Point, r: Double)
knn(base: Point, q: Point, k: Int)
```

In the APIs described above, `base` indicates the point objects to be filtered, while the other parameters give filter conditions.

Join operations. In the DataFrame API of Simba, distance joins and kNN joins can be expressed with following functions:

```
distanceJoin(target: DataFrame, left_key: Point,
             right_key: Point, τ: Double)
knnJoin(target: DataFrame, left_key: Point,
        right_key: Point, k: Int)
```

These functions will join the current data frame with another data frame `target` using the join condition (either distance join with threshold τ, or kNN join with value k) over `left_key` (a point from the first data frame) and `right_key` (a point from the second data frame).

Index management. User can easily create and drop indexes on an input data frame through:

```
index(index_type: IndexType, index_name: String,
      attrs: Seq[Attribute])
dropIndex()
```

Finally, note that Simba's data frame API is integrated with, and can call the data frame API, from Spark SQL, and other spark-based systems that support the data frame API such as MLLib.

A.3 Limitations of the Programming Model

Simba's main programming and user interface is SQL and the DataFrame API, both of which only provide declarative semantics. As a result, Simba does not have native support for conditional branching (e.g. If. . .Else), looping (For and While loops), and recursion. That said, because Simba is based on Spark which allows users to develop and submit a customized Java or Scala program for execution, users can always overcome the aforementioned hurdles in Simba through a user program in Java or Scala and submit the program to Simba for execution.

B. RANGE QUERY

Two types of range queries are supported in Simba, namely box and circle range queries. They can be expressed by standard SQL queries in Spark SQL by using filters with properly constructed range conditions. But without Simba's programming interfaces described in Section 4, the statement becomes clumsy and error-prone. More importantly, without indexes, the engine has to scan all records, which is quite inefficient and resource intensive.

In contrast, Simba allows users to express range queries natively as shown in Section 4, and it can handle range queries using indexes (assuming that the spatial attributes are indexed):

Global filtering. In this step, Simba uses the global index to prune partitions that do not overlap with the query range. In particular, Simba inspects the global index to obtain IDs of the partitions which intersect the query area. Next, Simba calls a Spark internal developer API `PartitionPruningRDD`, which can filter partitions by ID, to mark required partitions.

Local processing. For each selected partitions from global filtering, Simba use its local index to quickly return matching records from local data. If mbr(R_i) is completely inside the query area, all records in R_i can be returned even without checking the index.

C. PROOF OF THEOREM 1

Theorem 1 *For any partition R_i where $i \in [1, n]$, we have:*

$\forall r \in R_i, \text{knn}(r, S) \subset \{s | s \in S, |cr_i, s| \leq \gamma_i\}$, *for γ_i defined in* (1).

PROOF. Recall that $\text{knn}(cr_i, S') = \{s_1, \ldots, s_k\}$ (in ascending order of their distances to cr_i), and $u_i = \max_{r \in R_i} |r, cr_i|$. Hence, for any $r \in R_i$, and for any $t \in [1, k]$, we have:

$$
\begin{aligned}
|r, s_t| &\leq |r, cr_i| + |cr_i, s_t| \quad \text{(triangle inequality)} \\
&\leq u_i + |cr_i, s_k|. \quad \text{(by construction)}
\end{aligned}
$$

This implies that a circle centered at r with radius $(u_i + |cr_i, s_k|)$ will cover at least k points (i.e., at least $s_1, s_2, s_3, ..s_k$) in $S' \subset S$. In other words, $\text{knn}(r, S) \subset S_r = \{s | s \in S, |r, s| \leq u_i + |cr_i, s_k|\}$. We denote this set as the *cover set* of record r.

For each element $e \in S_r$, we have:

$$
\begin{aligned}
|e, cr_i| &\leq |e, r| + |r, cr_i| \quad (\forall r \in R_i, \text{triangle inequality}) \\
&\leq u_i + |cr_i, s_k| + u_i \\
&= \gamma_i,
\end{aligned}
$$

which implies S_r is a subset of $\{s | s \in S, |cr_i, s| \leq \gamma_i\}$. Thus, $\forall r \in R_i, \text{knn}(r, S) \subset S_r \subset \{s | s \in S, |cr_i, s| \leq \gamma_i\}$. □

D. ADDITIONAL EXPERIMENTS

D.1 Impact of partition size

Figure 19 shows that Simba's index construction cost grows roughly linearly with respect to partition size. This is because it is more costly to build local indexes over larger partitions (which outweighs the savings resulted from processing less number of partitions).

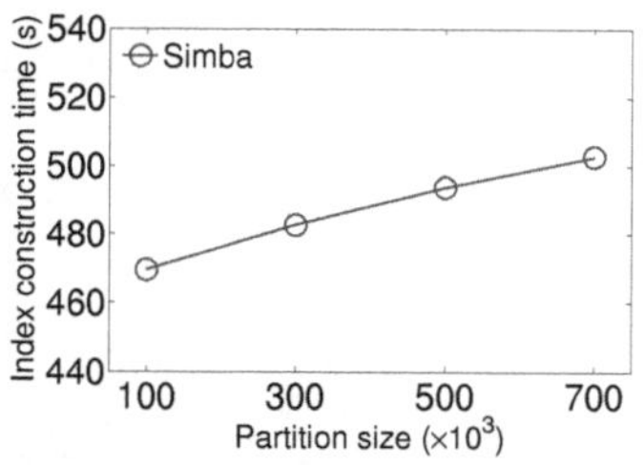

Figure 19: Index construction cost: effect of partition size.

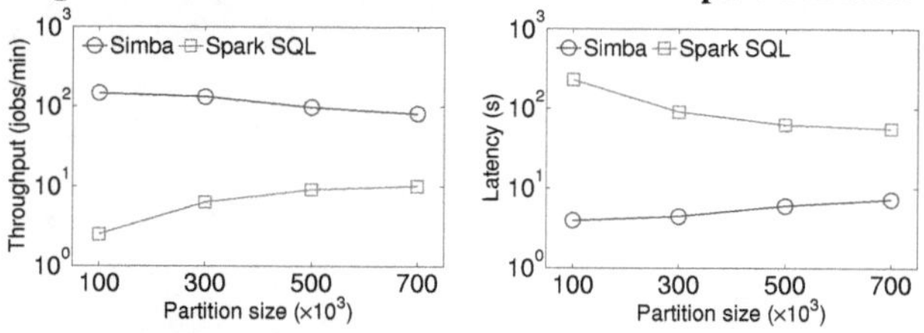

(a) Throughput (b) Latency

Figure 20: Range query performance on OSM: partition size.

Figure 20 shows the effect of partition size (from 1×10^5 to 7×10^5 records per partition). As it increases, the pruning power of global index in Simba shrinks and so does Simba's performance. Spark SQL's performance slightly increases as it requires fewer partitions to process. Nevertheless, Simba is still much more efficient due to its local indexes and spatial query optimizer.

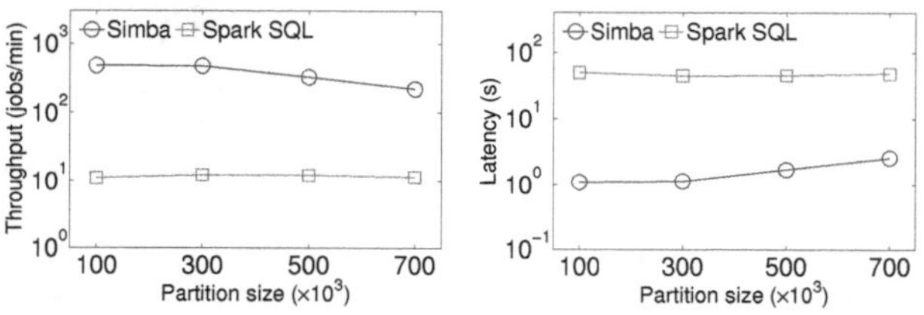

(a) Throughput (b) Latency

Figure 21: *k*NN query performance on OSM: partition size.

In Figure 21, as the partition size increases, the performance of Simba decreases as the pruning power of global index drops when the partitions become larger.

Figure 22(a) shows the effect of partition size on different distance join algorithms. As the partition size grows, the running time of DJSpark increases slightly, as the pruning power of global join phase reduces when the partition granularity is decreasing. In contrast, BDJSpark-R becomes faster because fewer local join tasks are required in the algorithm.

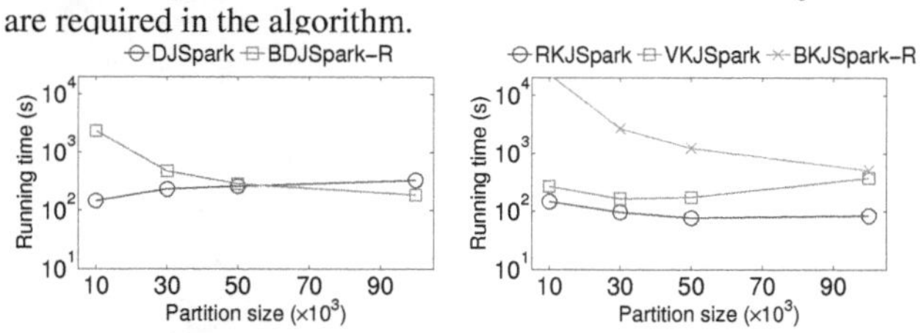

(a) Distance Join (b) *k*NN Join

Figure 22: Effect of partition size for join operations.

Figure 22(b) presents how partition size affects the performance of different *k*NN join approaches. With the increase of partition size, BKJSpark-R and RKJSpark grow faster since fewer local join tasks are required for join processing. VKJSpark becomes slightly slower as the partition size increases because the power of its distance pruning bounds weakens when the number of pivots decreases.

D.2 Influence of Dimensionality on RC

Figures 23 and 24 show the results for range and *k*NN queries when dimensionality increases from 2 to 6 on the RC data set. The trends are similar to that on the GEDLT data set as in Figures 16 and 17: Simba significantly outperforms Spark SQL in all dimensions.

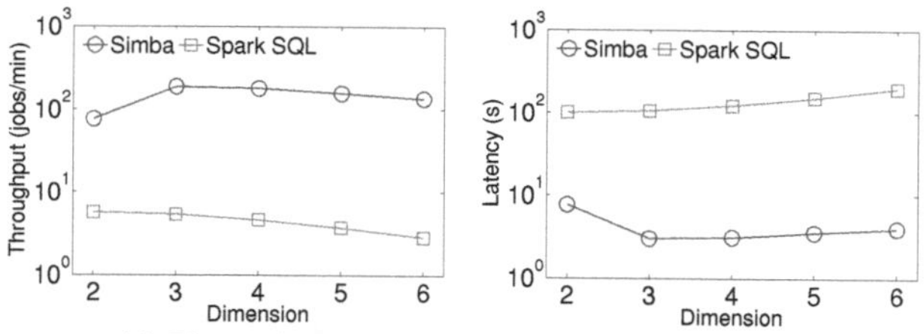

(a) Throughput (b) Latency

Figure 23: Range query performance on RC: dimensionality.

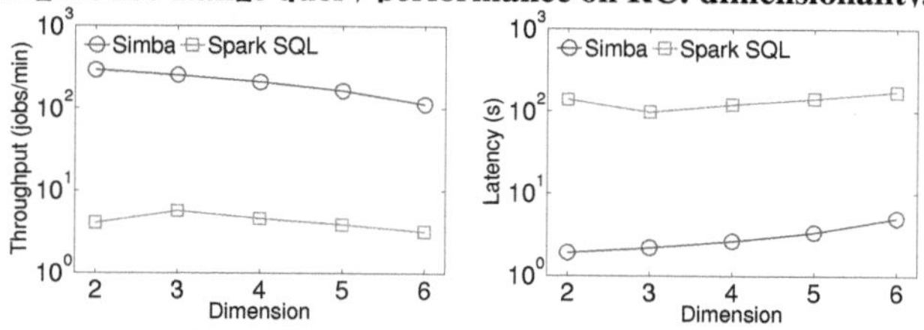

(a) Throughput (b) Latency

Figure 24: *k*NN query performance on RC: dimensionality.

D.3 Impact of the Array Structure

In this section, we experimentally validated our choice of packing all records in a partition to an array object. Specifically, we compare three different data representation strategies as below:

- Alternative 1 (A1): packing all Row objects in a partition into an array.
- Alternative 2 (A2): cache `RDD[Row]` directly.
- Alternative 3 (A3): in-memory columnar storage strategy.

We demonstrate their space consumption and scanning time on our default dataset (OSM data with 500 million records) in Figure 25. Note that these records are variable-length records (as each record contains two variable-length string attributes, the two text information fields in OSM).

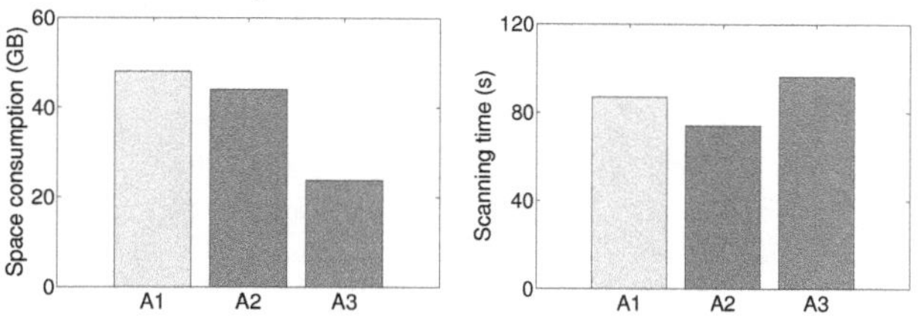

(a) Space Consumption (b) Scanning Time

Figure 25: Comparison between table representations.

Figure 25(a) shows the space consumption of different strategies. Packing all `Row` objects within a partition to an array object (A1 in Figure 25) consumes slightly more space than directly caching the `RDD[Row]` in Spark SQL (A2 in Figure 25). Such overhead is caused by additional meta information kept in array objects. On the other hand, the in-memory columnar storage (A3 in Figure 25) clearly saves space due to its columnar storage with compression.

The table scan time is shown in Figure 25(b). Caching `RDD[Row]` directly shows the best performance. The array structure adopted by Simba has slightly longer scanning time, due to the small space overhead and the additional overhead from flattening members out of the array objects. Lastly, the in-memory columnar storage gives the worst performance since it requires joining multiple attributes to restore the original `Row` object (and the potential overhead from decompression), whose overhead outweighs the savings resulted from its less memory footprint.

That said, Simba can also choose to use the in-memory columnar storage (and with compression) to represent its data.

Realtime Data Processing at Facebook

Guoqiang Jerry Chen, Janet L. Wiener, Shridhar Iyer, Anshul Jaiswal, Ran Lei
Nikhil Simha, Wei Wang, Kevin Wilfong, Tim Williamson, and Serhat Yilmaz
Facebook, Inc.

ABSTRACT

Realtime data processing powers many use cases at Facebook, including realtime reporting of the aggregated, anonymized voice of Facebook users, analytics for mobile applications, and insights for Facebook page administrators. Many companies have developed their own systems; we have a realtime data processing ecosystem at Facebook that handles hundreds of Gigabytes per second across hundreds of data pipelines.

Many decisions must be made while designing a realtime stream processing system. In this paper, we identify five important design decisions that affect their ease of use, performance, fault tolerance, scalability, and correctness. We compare the alternative choices for each decision and contrast what we built at Facebook to other published systems.

Our main decision was targeting seconds of latency, not milliseconds. Seconds is fast enough for all of the use cases we support and it allows us to use a persistent message bus for data transport. This data transport mechanism then paved the way for fault tolerance, scalability, and multiple options for correctness in our stream processing systems Puma, Swift, and Stylus.

We then illustrate how our decisions and systems satisfy our requirements for multiple use cases at Facebook. Finally, we reflect on the lessons we learned as we built and operated these systems.

1. INTRODUCTION

Realtime data processing systems are used widely to provide insights about events as they happen. Many companies have developed their own systems: examples include Twitter's Storm [28] and Heron [20], Google's Millwheel [9], and LinkedIn's Samza [4]. We present Facebook's Puma, Swift, and Stylus stream processing systems here.

The following qualities are all important in the design of a realtime data system.

- Ease of use: How complex are the processing requirements? Is SQL enough? Or is a general-purpose procedural language (such as C++ or Java) essential? How fast can a user write, test, and deploy a new application?
- Performance: How much latency is ok? Milliseconds? Seconds? Or minutes? How much throughput is required, per machine and in aggregate?
- Fault-tolerance: what kinds of failures are tolerated? What semantics are guaranteed for the number of times that data is processed or output? How does the system store and recover in-memory state?
- Scalability: Can data be sharded and resharded to process partitions of it in parallel? How easily can the system adapt to changes in volume, both up and down? Can it reprocess weeks worth of old data?
- Correctness: Are ACID guarantees required? Must all data that is sent to an entry point be processed and appear in results at the exit point?

In this paper, we present five decisions that must be made while designing a realtime stream processing system. We compare alternatives and their tradeoffs, identify the choices made by different systems in the literature, and discuss what we chose at Facebook for our stream processing systems and why.

Our main decision was that a few seconds of latency (with hundreds of Gigabytes per second throughput) meets our performance requirements. We can therefore connect all of the processing components in our system with a persistent message bus for data transport. Decoupling the data transport from the processing allowed us to achieve fault tolerance, scalability, and ease of use, as well as multiple options for correctness.

We run hundreds of realtime data pipelines in production. Four current production data pipelines illustrate how streaming systems are used at Facebook.

- Chorus is a data pipeline to construct the aggregated, anonymized voice of the people on Facebook: What are the top 5 topics being discussed for the election today? What are the demographic breakdowns (age, gender, country) of World Cup fans?
- Mobile analytics pipelines provide realtime feedback for Facebook mobile application developers. They use this data to diagnose performance and correctness issues, such as the cold start time and crash rate.

SIGMOD'16 June 26-July 01, 2016, San Francisco, CA USA
© 2016 ACM ISBN 978-1-4503-3531-7/16/06 ...$15.00.
DOI: http://dx.doi.org/10.1145/2882903.2904441.

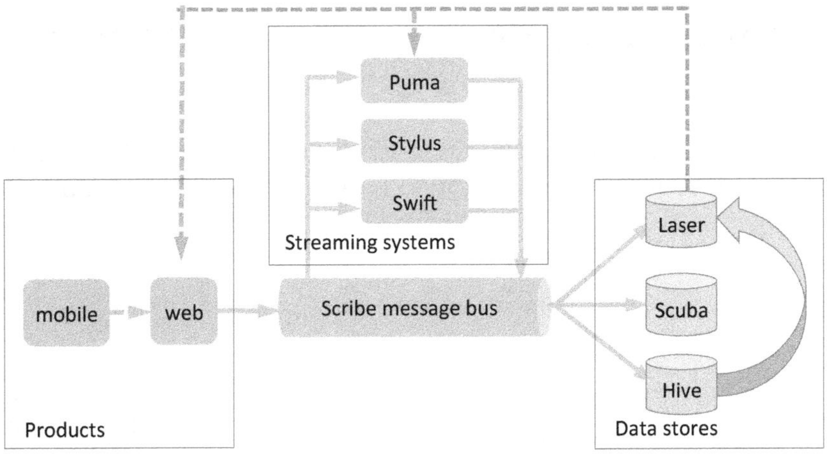

Figure 1: An overview of the systems involved in realtime data processing: from logging in mobile and web products on the left, through Scribe and realtime stream processors in the middle, to data stores for analysis on the right.

- Page insights pipelines provide Facebook Page owners realtime information about the likes, reach and engagement for each page post.
- Realtime streaming pipelines offload CPU-intensive dashboard queries from our interactive data stores and save global CPU resources.

We present several data pipelines in more detail after we describe our systems.

We then reflect on lessons we learned over the last four years as we built and rebuilt these systems. One lesson is to place emphasis on ease of use: not just on the ease of writing applications, but also on the ease of testing, debugging, deploying, and finally monitoring hundreds of applications in production.

This paper is structured as follows. In Section 2, we provide an overview of the realtime processing systems at Facebook and show how they fit together. In Section 3, we present an example application to compute trending events, which we use to illustrate the design choices in the rest of the paper. We discuss the design decisions in Section 4 and show how these decisions shaped realtime processing systems both at Facebook and in related work. We present several different streaming applications in production use at Facebook in Section 5. Then in Section 6, we reflect on lessons we learned about building and deploying realtime systems at Facebook. Finally, we conclude in Section 7.

2. SYSTEMS OVERVIEW

There are multiple systems involved in realtime data processing at Facebook. We present an overview of our ecosystem in this section.

Figure 1 illustrates the flow of data through our systems. On the left, data originates in mobile and web products. The data they log is fed into Scribe, which is a distributed data transport system. All of the solid (yellow) arrows represent data flowing through Scribe.

The realtime stream processing systems Puma, Stylus, and Swift read data from Scribe and also write to Scribe. Puma, Stylus, and Swift applications can be connected through Scribe into a complex DAG (directed acyclic graph), as needed. We overview them here and describe their differences in detail in Section 4.

On the right, Laser, Scuba, and Hive are data stores that use Scribe for ingestion and serve different types of queries. Laser can also provide data to the products and streaming systems, as shown by the dashed (blue) arrows. In this section, we describe each of the data systems.

2.1 Scribe

Scribe [5] is a persistent, distributed messaging system for collecting, aggregating and delivering high volumes of log data with a few seconds of latency and high throughput. Scribe is the transport mechanism for sending data to both batch and realtime systems at Facebook. Within Scribe, data is organized by *category*. A category is a distinct stream of data: all data is written to or read from a specific category. Usually, a streaming application consumes one Scribe category as input. A Scribe category has multiple buckets. A Scribe bucket is the basic processing unit for stream processing systems: applications are parallelized by sending different Scribe buckets to different processes. Scribe provides data durability by storing it in HDFS [23]. Scribe messages are stored and streams can be replayed by the same or different receivers for up to a few days.

2.2 Puma

Puma is a stream processing system whose applications (apps) are written in a SQL-like language with UDFs (user-defined functions) written in Java. Puma apps are quick to write: it can take less than an hour to write, test, and deploy a new app.

Puma apps serve two purposes. First, Puma provides pre-computed query results for simple aggregation queries. For these stateful monoid applications (see section 4.4.2), the delay equals the size of the query result's time window. The query results are obtained by querying the Puma app

```
CREATE APPLICATION top_events;

CREATE INPUT TABLE events_score(
  event_time,
  event,
  category,
  score
)
FROM SCRIBE("events_stream")
TIME event_time;

CREATE TABLE top_events_5min AS
  SELECT
      category,
      event,
      topk(score) AS score
  FROM
      events_score [5 minutes]
```

Figure 2: A complete Puma app that computes the "top K events" for each 5 minute time window. This app can be used for the *Ranker* in Fig 3.

through a Thrift API [8]. Figure 2 shows code for a simple Puma aggregation app with 5 minute time windows.

Second, Puma provides filtering and processing of Scribe streams (with a few seconds delay). For example, a Puma application can reduce a stream of all Facebook actions to only posts, or to only posts that match a predicate, such as containing the hashtag "#superbowl". The output of these stateless Puma apps is another Scribe stream, which can then be the input to another Puma app, any other realtime stream processor, or a data store.

Unlike traditional relational databases, Puma is optimized for compiled queries, not for ad-hoc analysis. Engineers deploy apps with the expectation that they will run for months or years. This expectation allows Puma to generate an efficient query computation and storage plan. Puma aggregation apps store state in a shared HBase cluster.

2.3 Swift

Swift is a basic stream processing engine which provides checkpointing functionalities for Scribe. It provides a very simple API: you can read from a Scribe stream with checkpoints every N strings or B bytes. If the app crashes, you can restart from the latest checkpoint; all data is thus read at least once from Scribe. Swift communicates with client apps through system-level pipes. Thus, the performance and fault tolerance of the system are up to the client. Swift is mostly useful for low throughput, stateless processing. Most Swift client apps are written in scripting languages like Python.

2.4 Stylus

Stylus is a low-level stream processing framework written in C++. The basic component of Stylus is a stream processor. The input to the processor is a Scribe stream and the output can be another Scribe stream or a data store for serving the data. A Stylus processor can be stateless or stateful. Processors can be combined into a complex processing DAG. We present such an example DAG in Figure 3 in the next section.

Stylus's processing API is similar to that of other procedural stream processing systems [4, 9, 28]. Like them, Stylus must handle imperfect ordering in its input streams [24, 10, 9]. Stylus therefore requires the application writer to identify the event time data in the stream. In return, Stylus provides a function to estimate the event time low watermark with a given confidence interval.

2.5 Laser

Laser is a high query throughput, low (millisecond) latency, key-value storage service built on top of RocksDB [3]. Laser can read from any Scribe category in realtime or from any Hive table once a day. The key and value can each be any combination of columns in the (serialized) input stream. Data stored in Laser is then accessible to Facebook product code and to Puma and Stylus apps.

Laser has two common use cases. Laser can make the output Scribe stream of a Puma or Stylus app available to Facebook products. Laser can also make the result of a complex Hive query or a Scribe stream available to a Puma or Stylus app, usually for a lookup join, such as identifying the topic for a given hashtag.

2.6 Scuba

Scuba [7, 18, 15] is Facebook's fast slice-and-dice analysis data store, most commonly used for trouble-shooting of problems as they happen. Scuba ingests millions of new rows per second into thousands of tables. Data typically flows from products through Scribe and into Scuba with less than one minute of delay. Scuba can also ingest the output of any Puma, Stylus, or Swift app.

Scuba provides ad hoc queries with most response times under 1 second. The Scuba UI displays query results in a variety of visualization formats, including tables, time series, bar charts, and world maps.

2.7 Hive data warehouse

Hive [26] is Facebook's exabyte-scale data warehouse. Facebook generates multiple new petabytes of data per day, about half of which is raw event data ingested from Scribe [15]. (The other half of the data is derived from the raw data, e.g., by daily query pipelines.) Most event tables in Hive are partitioned by day: each partition becomes available after the day ends at midnight. Any realtime processing of this data must happen in Puma, Stylus, or Swift applications. Presto [2] provides full ANSI SQL queries over data stored in Hive. Query results change only once a day, after new data is loaded. They can then be sent to Laser for access by products and realtime stream processors.

3. EXAMPLE APPLICATION

We use the example application in Figure 3 to demonstrate the design choices in the next section. This application identifies trending events in an input stream of events. The events contain an event type, a dimension id (which is used to fetch dimension information about the event, such as the language in which it is written), and text (which is analyzed to classify the event topic, such as *movies* or *babies*). The output of the application is a ranked list of topics (sorted by event count) for each 5 minute time bucket.

There are four processing nodes, each of which may be executed by multiple processes running in parallel on disjoint partitions of their input.

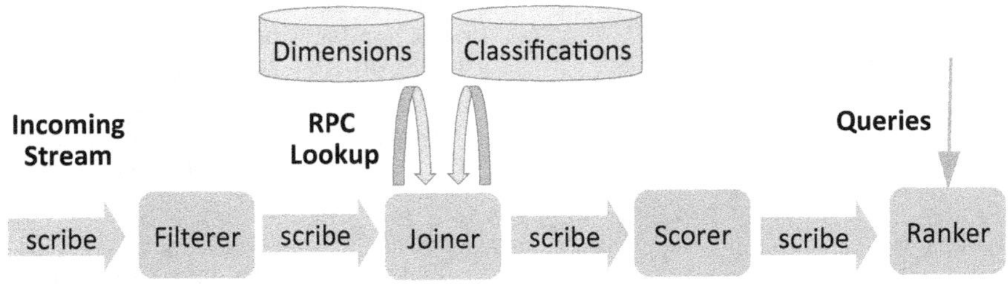

Figure 3: An example streaming application with 4 nodes: this application computes "trending" events.

1. The *Filterer* filters the input stream based on the event type and then shards its output on the dimension id so that the processing for the next node can be done in parallel on shards with disjoint sets of dimension ids.
2. The *Joiner* queries one or more external systems to (a) retrieve information based on the dimension id and (b) classify the event by topic, based on its text. Since each *Joiner* process receives sharded input, it is more likely to have the dimension information it needs in a cache, which reduces network calls to the external service. The output is then resharded by $(event, topic)$ pair so that the *Scorer* can aggregate them in parallel.
3. The *Scorer* keeps a sliding window of the event counts per topic for recent history. It also keeps track of the long term trends for these counters. Based on the long term trend and the current counts, it computes a score for each (event, topic) pair and emits the score as its output to the *Ranker*, resharded by topic.
4. The *Ranker* computes the top K events for each topic per N minute time bucket.

In this example, the *Filterer* and *Joiner* are stateless and the *Scorer* and *Ranker* are stateful. At Facebook, each of the nodes can be implemented in Stylus. Puma apps can implement the *Filterer* and *Ranker*. The example Puma app in Figure 2 contains code for the *Ranker*. Although a Puma app can join with data in Laser, the *Joiner* node may need to query an arbitrary service for the Classifications, which Puma cannot do. Swift can only be used to implement the stateless nodes.

A consumer service queries the *Ranker* periodically to get the top K events for each topic. Alternatively, the *Ranker* can publish its results to Laser and the consumer service can query Laser. Puma is designed to handle thousands of queries per second per app, whereas Laser is designed to handle millions. Querying Laser is also a better choice when the query latency requirements are in milliseconds.

4. DESIGN DECISIONS

In this section, we present five design decisions. These decisions are summarized in Table 4, where we show which capabilities each decision affects. For each one, we categorize the alternatives and explain how they affect the relevant capabilities. Then we discuss the pros and cons of our decision for Facebook's systems.

Table 5 summarizes which alternatives were chosen by a variety of realtime systems, both at Facebook and in the related literature.

4.1 Language paradigm

The first design decision is the type of language that people will use to write applications in the system. This decision determines how easy it is to write applications and how much control the application writer has over their performance.

4.1.1 Choices

There are three common choices:

- *Declarative*: SQL is (mostly) declarative. SQL is the simplest and fastest to write. A lot of people already know SQL, so their ramp-up is fast. However, the downside of SQL is its limited expressiveness. Many systems add functions to SQL for operations such as hashing and string operators. For example, Streambase [27], S-Store [21] and STREAM [12] provide SQL-based stream processing.
- *Functional*: Functional programming models [10, 30, 32] represent an application as a sequence of predefined operators. It is still simple to write an application, but the user has more control over the order of operations and there are usually more operations available.
- *Procedural*: C++, Java, and Python are all common procedural languages. They offer the most flexibility and (usually) the highest performance. The application writer has complete control over the data structures and execution. However, they also take the most time to write and test and require the most language expertise. S4 [22], Storm [28], Heron [20], and Samza [4] processors are all examples of procedural stream processing systems.

4.1.2 Languages at Facebook

In our environment at Facebook, there is no single language that fits all use cases. Needing different languages (and the different levels of ease of use and performance they provide) is the main reason why we have three different stream processing systems.

Puma applications are written in SQL. A Puma app can be written and tested in under an hour, which makes it very ease to use. Puma apps have good throughput and can increase their throughput by using more parallel processing nodes.

Swift applications mostly use Python. It is easy to prototype and it is very useful for low-throughput (tens of Megabytes per second) stream processing apps. Although it is possible to write a high performance processor with Swift, it takes a lot of effort.

Design decision	Ease of use	Performance	Fault tolerance	Scalability	Correctness
Language paradigm	X	X			
Data transfer	X	X	X	X	
Processing semantics			X		X
State-saving mechanism	X	X	X	X	X
Reprocessing	X			X	X

Figure 4: Each design decision affects some of the data quality attributes.

Design decision	Puma	Stylus	Swift	Heron	Spark Streaming	Millwheel	Flink	Samza
Language paradigm	SQL	C++	Python	Java	Functional	C++	Functional	Java
Data transfer	Scribe	Scribe	Scribe	Stream Manager	RPC	RPC	RPC	Kafka
Processing semantics	at least	at least at most exactly	at least at most	at least	best effort exactly	at least exactly	at least exactly	at least
State-saving mechanism	remote DB	local DB remote DB			limited	remote DB	global snapshot	local DB
Reprocessing	same code	same code	no batch	same DSL	same code	same code	same code	no batch

Figure 5: The design decisions made by different streaming systems.

Stylus applications are written in C++ and a Stylus processor requires multiple classes. While a script will generate boilerplate code, it can still take a few days to write an application. Stylus applications have the greatest flexibility for complicated stream processing applications.

We do not currently provide any functional paradigms at Facebook, although we are exploring Spark Streaming [32].

4.2 Data transfer

A typical stream processing application is composed of multiple processing nodes, arranged in a DAG. The second design decision is the mechanism to transfer data between processing nodes. This decision has a significant impact on the fault tolerance, performance, and scalability of the stream processing system. It also affects its ease of use, particularly for debugging.

4.2.1 Choices

Typical choices for data transfer include:

- Direct message transfer: Typically, an RPC or in-memory message queue is used to pass data directly from one process to another. For example, MillWheel [9], Flink [16], and Spark Streaming [32] use RPC and Storm [28] uses ZeroMQ [6], a form of message queue. One of the advantages of this method is speed: tens of milliseconds end-to-end latency is achievable.

- Broker based message transfer: In this case, there is a separate broker process that connects stream processing nodes and forwards messages between them. Using an intermediary process adds overhead, but also allows the system to scale better. The broker can multiplex a given input stream to multiple output processors. It can also apply back pressure to an input processor when the output processor falls behind. Heron [20] uses a stream manager between Heron instances to solve both of these problems.

- Persistent storage based message transfer. In this case, processors are connected by a persistent message bus. The output stream of one processor is written to a persistent store and the next processor reads its input from that store. This method is the most reliable. In addition to multiplexing, a persistent store allows the input and output processors to write and read at different speeds, at different points in time, and to read the same data multiple times, e.g., to recover from a processor failure. The processing nodes are decoupled from each other so the failure of a single node does not affect other nodes. Samza [4] uses Kafka [19], a persistent store, to connect processing nodes.

All three types of data transfer mechanisms connect consecutive nodes in a DAG.

There are two types of connections between consecutive nodes [31]. Narrow dependency connections link a fixed number of partitions from the sending node to the receiving node. Such connections are often one-to-one and their nodes can be collapsed. Wide dependency connections link every partition of the sender to each partition of the receiver. These connections must be implemented with a data transfer mechanism.

4.2.2 Data transfer at Facebook

At Facebook, we use Scribe [5], a persistent message bus, to connect processing nodes. Using Scribe imposes a minimum latency of about a second per stream. However, at Facebook, the typical requirement for real time stream processing is seconds.

A second limitation of Scribe is that it writes to disk. In practice, the writes are asynchronous (not blocking) and the reads come from a cache because streaming applications read the most recent data. Finally, a persistent store requires additional hardware and network bandwidth.

Accepting these limitations gives us multiple advantages for fault tolerance, ease of use, scalability, and performance.

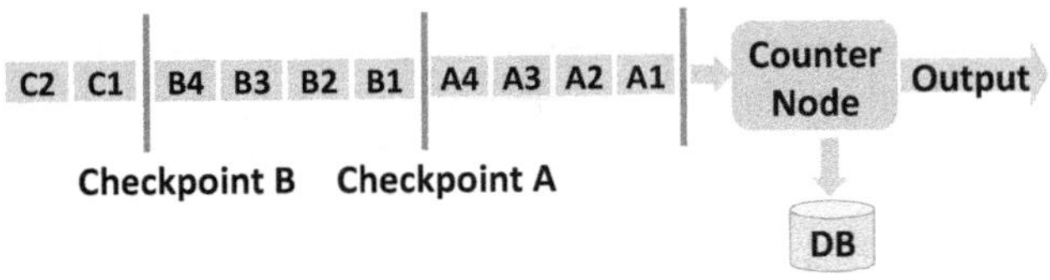

Figure 6: This Counter Node processor counts events from a $(timestamp, event)$ input stream. Every few seconds, it emits the counter value to a $(timewindow, counter)$ output stream.

- Fault tolerance: The independence of stream processing node failures is a highly desirable property when we deploy thousands of jobs to process streams.
- Fault tolerance: Recovery from failure is faster because we only have to replace the node(s) that failed.
- Fault tolerance: Automatic multiplexing allows us to run duplicate downstream nodes. For example, we can run multiple Scuba or Laser tiers that *each* read all of their input streams' data, so that we have redundancy for disaster recovery purposes.
- Performance: If one processing node is slow (or dies), the speed of the previous node is not affected. For example, if a machine is overloaded with too many jobs, we simply move some jobs to a new machine and they pick up processing the input stream from where they left off. In a tightly coupled system [9, 16, 32, 28, 20], back pressure is propagated upstream and the peak processing throughput is determined by the slowest node in the DAG.
- Ease of use: Debugging is easier. When a problem is observed with a particular processing node, we can reproduce the problem by reading the same input stream from a new node.
- Ease of use: Monitoring and alerting are simpler to implement. The primary responsibility of each node is to consume its input. It is sufficient to set up monitoring and alerts for delays in processing streams from the persistent store.
- Ease of use: We have more flexibility in how we write each application. We can connect components of any system that reads or writes data in the same DAG. We can use the output of a Puma application as the input of a Stylus processor and then read the Stylus output as input to our data stores Scuba or Hive.
- Scalability: We can scale the number of partitions up or down easily by changing the number of buckets per Scribe category in a configuration file.

Given the advantages above, Scribe has worked well as the data transfer mechanism at Facebook. Kafka or another persistent store would have similar advantages. We use Scribe because we develop it at Facebook.

4.3 Processing semantics

The processing semantics of each node determine its correctness and fault tolerance.

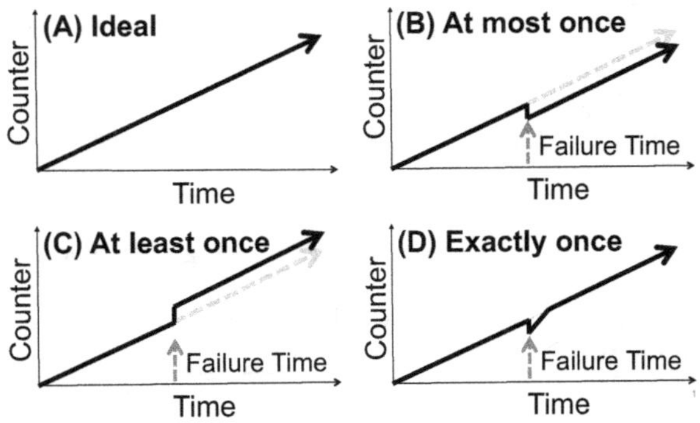

Figure 7: The output of a stateful processor with different state semantics.

4.3.1 Choices

A stream processor does three types of activities.

1. Process input events: For example, it may deserialize input events, query an external system, and update its in-memory state. These activities can be rerun without side effects.
2. Generate output: Based on the input events and in-memory state, it generates output for downstream systems for further processing or serving. This can happen as input events are processed or can be synchronized before or after a checkpoint.
3. Save checkpoints to a database for failure recovery. Three separate items may be saved:
   (a) The in-memory state of the processing node.
   (b) The current offset in the input stream.
   (c) The output value(s).

   Not all processors will save all of these items. What is saved and when determines the processor's semantics.

The implementations of these activities, especially the checkpoints, control the processor's semantics. There are two kinds of relevant semantics:

- State semantics: can each input event count at-least-once, at-most-once, or exactly-once?
- Output semantics: can a given output value show up in the output stream at-least-once, at-most-once, or exactly-once?

Stateless processors only have output semantics. Stateful processors have both kinds.

The different state semantics depend only on the order of saving the offset and in-memory state.

- At-least-once state semantics: Save the in-memory state first, then save the offset.
- At-most-once state semantics: Save the offset first, then save the in-memory state.
- Exactly-once state semantics: Save the in-memory state and the offset atomically, e.g., in a transaction.

Output semantics	State semantics At-least-once	At-most-once	Exactly-once
At-least-once	X		X
At-most-once		X	X
Exactly-once			X

Figure 8: Common combinations of state and output processing semantics.

Output semantics depend on saving the output value(s) in the checkpoint, in addition to the in-memory state and offset.

- At-least-once output semantics: Emit output to the output stream, then save a checkpoint of the offset and in-memory state.
- At-most-once output semantics: Save a checkpoint of the offset and in-memory state, then emit output.
- Exactly-once output semantics: Save a checkpoint of the offset and in-memory state and emit output value(s) atomically in the same transaction.

Figure 6 shows a stateful stream processing node, the "Counter Node", which counts events in its input and outputs the count periodically. We use the Counter Node to illustrate the different state processing semantics with at-least-once output semantics. Figure 7 shows how different semantics affect the possible counter output values after a machine or processor failure.

At-least-once output semantics allow the Counter Node to emit output as it receives events. At-least-once output semantics are desirable for systems that require low latency processing and can handle small amounts of input data duplication.

To achieve at-most-once output semantics, the Counter Node must save its checkpoint before generating output. If the processor can do side-effect-free processing of events $A1-A4$, then save checkpoint A, and then generate output, it does not need to buffer events $A1-A4$ before saving checkpoint A. This optimization also reduces the chance of losing data, since only failures that happen between checkpointing and emitting output can cause data loss. We illustrate the performance benefits of doing side-effect-free processing between checkpoints in Section 4.3.2. Photon [11] also offers options to reduce data loss with at-most-once output semantics. At-most-once state and output semantics are desirable when data loss is preferable to data duplication.

To get exactly-once output semantics, the Counter Node must save checkpoints after processing events $A1 - A4$, but atomically with emitting the output. Exactly-once output semantics require transaction support from the receiver of the output. In practice, this means that the receiver must be a data store, rather than a data transport mechanism like Scribe. Exactly-once semantics usually impose a performance penalty, since the processor needs to wait for transactions to complete.

Table 8 shows the common combinations of state and output semantics.

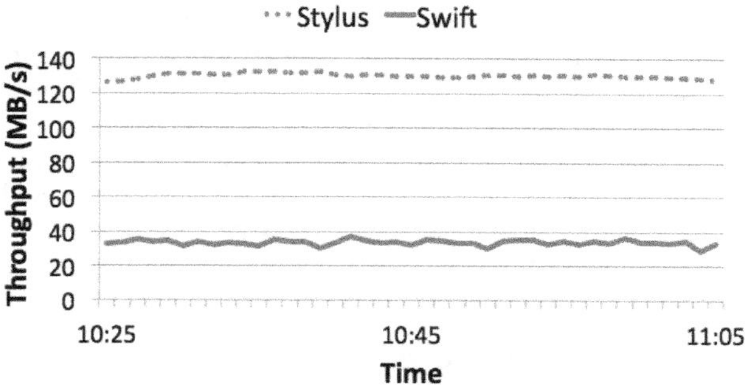

Figure 9: The Stylus implementation of this processor does side-effect-free processing between checkpoints and achieves nearly 4x as much throughput as the Swift implementation.

4.3.2 *Processing semantics used at Facebook*

In Facebook's environment, different applications often have different state and output semantics requirements. We give a few different examples.

In the trending events example in Figure 3, the *Ranker* sends its results to an idempotent serving system. Sending output twice is not a problem. Therefore, we can use at-least-once state and output semantics.

The data ingestion pipeline for Scuba [7] is stateless. Only the output semantics apply. Most data sent to Scuba is sampled and Scuba is a best-effort query system, meaning that query results may be based on partial data. Therefore, a small amount of data loss is preferred to any data duplication. Exactly-once semantics are not possible because Scuba does not support transactions, so at-most-once output semantics are the best choice.

In fact, most of our analysis data stores, including Laser, Scuba, and Hive, do not support transactions. We need to use other data stores to get transactions and exactly-once state semantics.

Getting exactly-once state semantics is also a challenge when the downstream data store is a distributed database such as HBase or ZippyDB. (ZippyDB is Facebook's distributed key-value store with Paxos-style replication, built on top of RocksDB.) The state must be saved to multiple shards, requiring a high-latency distributed transaction. Instead of incurring this latency, most users choose at-most-once or at-least-once semantics.

Puma guarantees at-least-once state and output semantics with checkpoints to HBase. Stylus offers all of the options in Figure 8 to its application writers.

We now examine the benefits of overlapping side-effect-free processing with receiving input for at-most-once output semantics. Figure 9 shows the throughput for two different implementations of the Scuba data ingestion processor. Both implementations have at-most-once output semantics. The Swift implementation buffers all input events between checkpoints, which occur approximately every 2 seconds. Then it processes those events and sends its output to the Scuba servers. While it is waiting for the checkpoint, the processor's CPU is underutilized.

The Stylus implementation does as much side-effect-free work as it can between checkpoints, including deserialization of its input events. Since deserialization is the performance bottleneck, the Stylus processor achieves much higher CPU utilization. The Stylus processor, therefore, achieves nearly four times the throughput of the Swift processor: in Figure 9 we see 135 MB/s versus 35 MB/s, respectively.

In general, separating out the side-effect-free processing and doing it between checkpoints can be implemented in custom code in any processor, if the developer has a good understanding of processing semantics. Stylus provides this optimization out of the box.

4.4 State-saving mechanisms

The state saving mechanism for stateful processors affects their fault tolerance. For example, in Figure 3, the *Scorer* maintains both long term counters and short term counters for events in order to compute the trending score. After a machine failure, we need to restore the counter values.

4.4.1 Choices

There are multiple ways to save state during processing and restore it after a failure. These solutions include:

- Replication [13]. In a replication based approach, the stateful nodes are replicated with two or more copies. This approach requires twice as much hardware, since many nodes are duplicated.
- Local database persistence. Samza [4] stores the state to a local database and writes the mutation to Kafka at the same time. After a failure, the local state is recovered from the Kafka log. The logs are compacted offline to keep log size bounded. Samza can support at-least-once but not exactly-once state and output semantics, since Kafka does not support transactions. .
- Remote database persistence. In this approach, the checkpoint and states are persisted to a remote database. MillWheel [9] saves fine-grained checkpoints to a remote database and supports exactly-once state and output semantics.
- Upstream backup. In these systems, the events are buffered in the upstream nodes and replayed after a failure [17].
- Global consistent snapshot. Flink [16] uses a distributed snapshot algorithm to maintain a globally consistent snapshot. After a failure, multiple machines must be restored to the consistent state.

4.4.2 State saving mechanisms at Facebook

At Facebook, we have different demands for fault tolerance for stream processing systems. Puma provides fault tolerance for stateful aggregation. Stylus provides multiple out-of-the-box fault tolerant solutions for stateful processing.

We implemented two state-saving mechanisms in Stylus: a local database model and a remote database model. In this section, we will focus only on our general local database implementation and our implementation of a remote database model for monoid processors, defined below.

Saving state to a local RocksDB [3] database is attractive for many users at Facebook. It is easy to set up. The local database writes are fast when a flash or memory-based file system (such as tmpfs) is used, since there is no network cost.

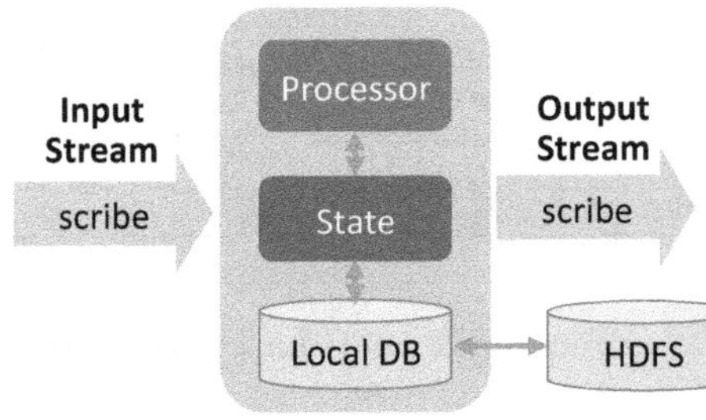

Figure 10: Saving state using a RocksDB local database and HDFS for remote backup.

It also supports exactly-once state and output semantics for stateful processing.

The *Scorer* node in Figure 3 is a good candidate for saving its state to a local database: the overall state is small and will fit into the flash or disk of a single machine.

Figure 10 illustrates RocksDB embedded in the same process as the stream processor and its state. The in-memory state is saved to this local database at fixed intervals. The local database is then copied asynchronously to HDFS at a larger interval using RocksDB's backup engine. When a process crashes and restarts on the same machine, the local database is used to restore the state and resume processing from the checkpoint. If the machine dies, the copy on HDFS is used instead.

HDFS is designed for batch workloads and is not intended to be an always-available system. If HDFS is not available for writes, processing continues without remote backup copies. If there is a failure, then recovery uses an older snapshot. We can parallelize reading from HDFS at recovery time so that HDFS read bandwidth is not a bottleneck.

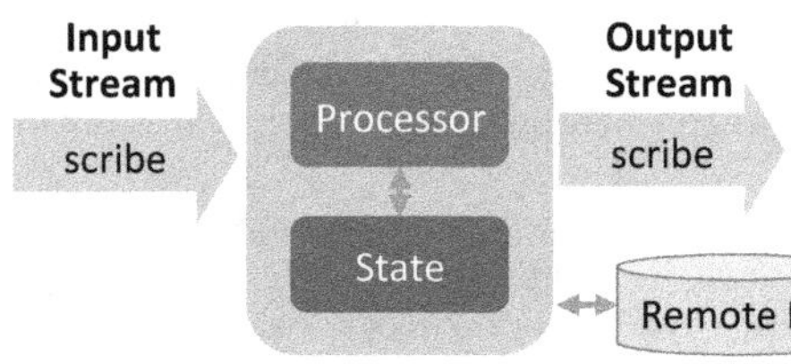

Figure 11: Saving state using a remote database.

A remote database can hold states that do not fit in memory. A remote database solution also provides faster machine failover time since we do not need to load the complete state to the machine upon restart. Often, a distributed database serves as the store for the output of the stream processing system. The same remote database can be used for saving state.

Figure 11 illustrates saving state in a remote database. When an event is received from the input stream, the state is updated. If the needed state is not in memory, it is read from the remote database, modified, and then saved back to the database. This read-modify-write pattern can be optimized if the states are limited to monoid processors.

A monoid [1, 14] is an algebraic structure that has an identity element and is associative. When a monoid processor's application needs to access state that is not in memory, mutations are applied to an empty state (the identity element).

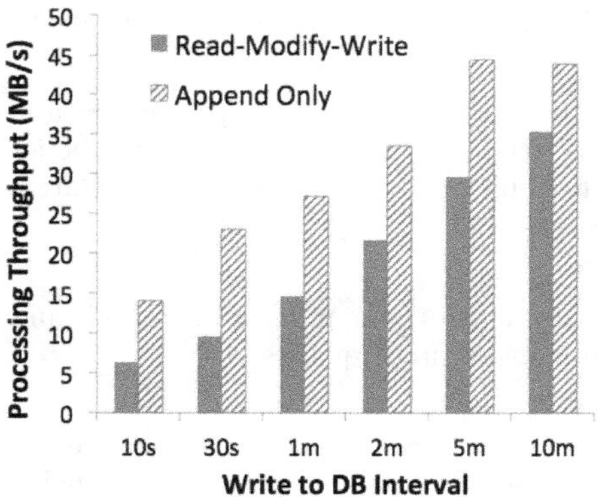

Figure 12: Saving state: read-modify-write vs append-only remote database write throughput.

Periodically, the existing database state is loaded in memory, merged with the in-memory partial state, and then written out to the database asynchronously. This read-merge-write pattern can be done less often than the read-modify-write.

When the remote database supports a custom merge operator, then the merge operation can happen in the database. The read-modify-write pattern is optimized to an append-only pattern, resulting in performance gains.

RocksDB and ZippyDB support custom merge operators. We illustrate the performance gains in Figure 12, which compares the throughput of the same Stylus stream processor application, configured with and without the append-only optimization. The application aggregates its input events across many dimensions, which means that one input event changes many different values in the application state. The remote database is a three machine ZippyDB cluster. Since different applications may have different requirements for how often to save their state remotely, we varied the interval for flushing to the remote database. Figure 12 shows that the application throughput is 25% to 200% higher with the append-only optimization.

The aggregation functions in Puma are all monoid. In Stylus, a user application declares that it is a monoid stream processor. The application appends partial state to the framework and Stylus decides when to merge the partial states into a complete state. This flexibility in when to merge — and the resulting performance gain — is the main difference between our remote database approach and that of Millwheel.

4.5 Backfill processing

We often need to reprocess old data, for several reasons.

- When a user develops a new stream processing application, it is good to test the application against old data. For example, in Figure 3, it is useful to run the trending algorithm on a known events stream and see if it identifies the expected trending events.
- For many applications, when we add a new metric, we want to run it against old data to generate historical metric data.
- When we discover a logging or processing bug, we need to reprocess the data for the period with the bug.

4.5.1 Choices

There are a few approaches to reprocessing data.

- Stream only. In this approach, the retention of the data transport mechanism must be long enough to replay the input streams for reprocessing.
- Maintain two separate systems: one for batch, and one for stream processing. For example, to bootstrap the long term counters in Figure 3, we could develop a separate batch pipeline to compute them. This approach is challenging: it is hard to maintain consistency between two different systems. Summingbird [14] uses a high level DSL to convert one processor specification to each system automatically, but still needs to maintain consistency between two different processing system implementations.
- Develop stream processing systems that can also run in a batch environment. Spark Streaming and Flink are good examples of this approach, which is also the one we take.

4.5.2 Reprocessing data at Facebook

We configure Scribe to store data for a short time. For longer retention, we store input and output streams in our data warehouse Hive. Our approach is different from Spark Streaming and Flink. They use similar fault tolerance and data transfer mechanisms for both their batch and stream processing.

To reprocess older data, we use the standard MapReduce framework to read from Hive and run the stream processing applications in our batch environment. Puma applications can run in Hive's environment as Hive UDFs (user-defined functions) and UDAFs (user-defined aggregation functions). The Puma app code remains unchanged, whether it is running over streaming or batch data.

Stylus provides three types of processors: a stateless processor, a general stateful processor, and a monoid stream processor. When a user creates a Stylus application, two binaries are generated at the same time: one for stream and one for batch. The batch binary for a stateless processor runs in Hive as a custom mapper. The batch binary for a general stateful processor runs as a custom reducer and the reduce key is the aggregation key plus event timestamp. The batch binary for monoid processors can be optimized to do partial aggregation in the map phase.

5. FACEBOOK APPLICATIONS

In this section, we describe several different realtime applications in production use at Facebook. We show how these applications use the different components available to achieve their particular goals.

5.1 Chorus

The Chorus data pipeline [25, 29] transforms a stream of individual Facebook posts into aggregated, anonymized, and annotated visual summaries (that do not reveal any private information). This pipeline enables Facebook's communications and insights teams to report to the public about realtime conversations, as they happen, without needing to know about the underlying data stores or queries. New posts show up in query results in seconds: for example, during the 2015 Superbowl, we watched a huge spike in posts containing the hashtag "#likeagirl" in the 2 minutes following the TV ad. http://insights.fb.com/2015/02/02/the-big-gathering-xlix/ contains an analysis of Superbowl 2015 conversation in the U.S.

There are many steps in this pipeline. We would like to call attention to two things.

First, this pipeline contains a mix of Puma and Stylus apps, with lookup joins in Laser and both Hive and Scuba as sink data stores for the results. All data transport is via Scribe. The data flow is similar to the example in Figure 3.

Second, this pipeline has evolved substantially over the last two years. The original pipeline had only one Puma app to filter posts. The laser joins were added with custom Python code to perform the join. Later still, a Stylus app replaced the custom code. At each step in the pipeline's evolution, we could add or replace one component at a time and test and deploy incrementally.

5.2 Dashboard queries

Dashboards are popular for observing trends and spotting anomalies at a glance. They run the same queries repeatedly, over a sliding time window. Once the query is embedded in a dashboard, the aggregations and metrics are fixed. Stream processing apps compute their query results as the data arrives. They are ideal for dashboard queries.

Scuba was designed for interactive, slice-and-dice queries. It does aggregation at query time by reading all of the raw event data. When we realized that queries from dashboards consumed much Scuba CPU, we built a framework to migrate dashboard queries from Scuba to Puma.

There were a few challenges. First, Puma apps could read the Scuba input from Scribe, but needed new code to compute Scuba UDFs that were defined in Scuba's visualization layer.

Second, Puma was designed for apps with millions of time series in their results. Those Puma apps shard their data by time series. Most Scuba queries have a limit of 7: it only makes sense to visualize up to 7 lines in a chart. They can not be sharded by time series into $N > 7$ processes: the processes must use a different sharding key and compute partial aggregates. One process then combines the partial aggregates.

Third, while exporting queries to dashboards, people experiment with different queries. We need to detect dead dashboard queries in order to avoid wasting CPU. Overall, the migration project has been very successful. The Puma apps consume approximate 14% of the CPU that was needed to run the same queries in Scuba.

In general, there is a tradeoff between processing at read time, such as Scuba does, and processing at write time, such as the stream processors Puma and Stylus do. Read time processing is much more flexible – you don't need to choose the queries in advance – but generally more CPU intensive.

5.3 Hybrid realtime-batch pipelines

Over half of all queries over Facebook's data warehouse Hive are part of daily query pipelines. The pipelines can start processing anytime after midnight. Due to dependencies, some of them complete only after 12 or more hours. We are now working on converting some of the earlier queries in these pipelines to realtime streaming apps so that the pipelines can complete earlier.

Interesting challenges in these conversions include:

- Validating that the realtime pipeline results are correct. Correct realtime results may not be identical to batch results. For example, the boundaries between days may differ.
- Adding enough common Hive UDFs to Puma and Stylus to support most queries.
- Making the conversion process self-service, so that teams can convert, test, and deploy without help from the Puma and Stylus teams.

In multiple cases, we have sped up pipelines by 10 to 24 hours. For example, we were able to convert a portion of a pipeline that used to complete around 2pm to a set of realtime stream processing apps that deliver the same data in Hive by 1am. The end result of this pipeline is therefore available 13 hours sooner.

6. LESSONS LEARNED

We have learned a lot while building our ecosystem of realtime data systems, as much from comparing them as from building any single system. Many of the lessons below are about service management: it is not enough to provide a framework for users to write applications. Ease of use encompasses debugging, deployment, and monitoring, as well. The value of tools that make operation easier is underestimated. In our experience, every time we add a new tool, we are surprised that we managed without it.

6.1 Multiple systems let us "move fast"

There is no single stream processing system that is right for all use cases. Providing a set of systems at different points in the ease of use versus performance, fault tolerance, and scalability space has worked well in Facebook's culture of "move fast" and "iterate". We have seen multiple applications start out in Puma or Swift and then move to Stylus (weeks or months later) as they needed more expressiveness or higher throughput. Writing a simple application lets our users deploy something quickly and prove its value first, then invest the time in building a more complex and robust application.

Similarly, evolving our own systems has been important. Every major piece of Puma has been rewritten at least once. Using a high-level language allows us to modify the underlying implementation without requiring changes to Puma apps.

Covering more points in the design space has also been beneficial. We can and do create stream processing DAGs that contain a mix of Puma, Swift, and Stylus applications, which gives us a lot of flexibility in satisfying the requirements for each node individually.

Finally, connecting nodes with Scribe streams makes it easy not just to replace a node with a faster or more expressive node, but also to reuse the output of that node in another data pipeline (DAG). We have been able to save developer time and system resources by reusing the same processor output for different purposes.

6.2 Ease of debugging

Databases typically store data and enable users to run queries on it. Such an environment is very conducive to an iterative development process. A user can program one processing stage and run it. If it doesn't yield the right results, they can modify the processing logic and rerun it on the same data.

When working with stream processing systems, it is harder to iterate during development because the data is not stored. When you update a stream processing operator, it begins running on new streaming data, not the same data as before, so the results may be different. Moreover, you have to handle delayed data. With persistent Scribe streams, we can replay a stream from a given (recent) time period, which makes debugging much easier.

6.3 Ease of deployment

Writing a new streaming application requires more than writing the application code. The ease or hassle of deploying and maintaining the application is equally important.

Laser and Puma apps are deployed as a service. Stylus apps are owned by the individual teams who write them, but we provide a standard framework for monitoring them.

Laser apps are extremely easy to setup, deploy, and delete. There is a UI to configure the app: just choose an ordered set of columns from the input Scribe stream for each of the key and value, a lifetime for each key-value pair, and a set of data centers to run the service. The UI then gives you a single command to deploy an app and another command to delete it.

A Puma app is almost as easy to deploy and delete as a Laser app, but requires a second engineer: the UI generates a code diff that must be reviewed. The app is deployed or deleted automatically after the diff is accepted and committed.

Puma apps were not always this easy to deploy. Originally, a member of the Puma team had to deploy each new app, which created a bottleneck for both the Puma team and the teams that wrote the apps. Making Puma deployment self-service let us scale to the hundreds of data pipelines that use Puma today.

6.4 Ease of monitoring and operation

Once an app is deployed, we need to monitor it. Is it using the right amount of parallelism? With Scribe, changing the parallelism is often just changing the number of Scribe buckets and restarting the nodes that output and consume that Scribe category. However, guessing the right amount of parallelism before deployment is a black art. We save both time and machine resources by being able to change it easily; we can get started with some initial level and then adapt quickly.

We then use alerts to detect when an app is processing its Scribe input more slowly than the input is being generated. We call that "processing lag". The Puma team runs processing lag alerts for all Puma apps, because the Puma service is maintained by the Puma team. Stylus provides its application developers with processing lag alerts. These alerts notify us to adapt our apps to changes in volume over time.

In the future, we would like to provide dashboards and alerts that are automatically configured to monitor both Puma and Stylus apps for the teams that use them. We would also like to scale the apps automatically.

6.5 Streaming vs batch processing

Streaming versus batch processing is not an either/or decision. Originally, all data warehouse processing at Facebook was batch processing [26]. We began developing Puma and Swift about five years ago. As we showed in Section 5.3, using a mix of streaming and batch processing can speed up long pipelines by hours.

Furthermore, streaming-only systems can be authoritative. We do not need to treat realtime system results as an approximation and batch results as the "truth." It is possible to create streaming systems that do not miss data (so counts and sums are exact). Good approximate unique counts (computed with HyperLogLog) are often as actionable as exact numbers.

7. CONCLUSIONS

In the last few years, real time processing has proliferated at Facebook. We have developed multiple, independent yet composable systems. Together, they form a comprehensive platform to serve our diverse needs.

In this paper, we discuss multiple design decisions we made and their effects on ease of use, performance, fault tolerance, scalability, and correctness. We would like to conclude with three points.

First, targeting seconds of latency, not milliseconds, was an important design decision. Seconds is fast enough for all of the use cases we support; there are other systems at Facebook to provide millisecond or microsecond latency in our products. Seconds latency allows us to use a persistent message bus for data transport. This data transport mechanism then paved the way for fault tolerance, scalability, and multiple options for correctness in our stream processing systems Puma, Swift, and Stylus.

Second, ease of use is as important as the other qualities. In our culture of hacking, where "move fast" is printed on posters, having systems available with the right learning curves lets us get prototype applications up and running in hours or days, not weeks. We can then test and iterate. In addition, making debugging, deployment, and operational monitoring easy has greatly increased the adoption rate for our systems, and we plan to continue making it even easier.

Third, there is a spectrum of correctness. Not all use cases need ACID semantics. By providing choices along this spectrum, we let the application builders decide what they need. If they need transactions and exactly-once semantics, they can pay for them with extra latency and hardware. But when they do not – and many use cases are measuring relative proportions or changes in direction, not absolute values – we enable faster and simpler applications.

Our systems continue to evolve to serve our users better. In the future, we plan to work on scaling our system infrastructure. For example, we want to improve the dynamic load balancing for our stream processing jobs; the load balancer should coordinate hundreds of jobs on a single machine and minimize the recovery time for lagging jobs. We are also considering alternate runtime environments for running stream processing backfill jobs. Today, they run in Hive. We plan to evaluate Spark and Flink. We hope to bridge the gap between realtime and batch processing at Facebook.

8. ACKNOWLEDGMENTS

Many people contributed to our systems. KC Braunschweig, Matt Dordal, Li Fang, Eric Hwang, Brett Proctor, Sam Rash, Assaf Sela, Brian Smith, Chong Xie, and Alexander Zhavnerchik built Scribe. Ankur Goenka, Yuhan Hao, Alex Levchuk, Abhishek Maloo, Yuan Mei, Sam Rash, and Gautam Roy contributed to Puma. Ajoy Frank, Daniel Marinescu, and Adam Radziwonczyk-Syta built the predecessor of Stylus. Neil Kodner, Danny Liao, and Jason Sundram provided valuable feedback as they developed Chorus.

9. REFERENCES

[1] Monoid. https://en.wikipedia.org/wiki/Monoid.

[2] Presto. http://prestodb.io.

[3] Rocksdb. http://rocksdb.org.

[4] Samza. http://samza.apache.org.

[5] Scribe. https://github.com/facebook/scribe.

[6] Zeromq. https://zeromq.org/.

[7] L. Abraham, J. Allen, O. Barykin, V. Borkar, B. Chopra, C. Gerea, D. Merl, J. Metzler, D. Reiss, S. Subramanian, et al. Scuba: diving into data at facebook. In *PVLDB*, pages 1057–1067, 2013.

[8] A. Agarwal, M. Slee, and M. Kwiatkowski. Thrift: Scalable cross-language services implementation. Technical report, Facebook, 2007.

[9] T. Akidau, A. Balikov, K. Bekiroğlu, S. Chernyak, J. Haberman, R. Lax, S. McVeety, D. Mills, P. Nordstrom, and S. Whittle. Millwheel: Fault-tolerant stream processing at internet scale. *PVLDB*, 6(11):1033–1044, Aug. 2013.

[10] T. Akidau, R. Bradshaw, C. Chambers, S. Chernyak, R. J. Fernández-Moctezuma, R. Lax, S. McVeety, D. Mills, F. Perry, E. Schmidt, and S. Whittle. The dataflow model: A practical approach to balancing correctness, latency, and cost in massive-scale, unbounded, out-of-order data processing. *PVLDB*, 8(12):1792–1803, Aug. 2015.

[11] R. Ananthanarayanan, V. Basker, S. Das, A. Gupta, H. Jiang, T. Qiu, A. Reznichenko, D. Ryabkov, M. Singh, and S. Venkataraman. Photon: fault-tolerant and scalable joining of continuous data streams. In *SIGMOD*, pages 577–588, 2013.

[12] A. Arasu, B. Babcock, S. Babu, J. Cieslewicz, M. Datar, K. Ito, R. Motwani, U. Srivastava, and J. Widom. Stream: The stanford data stream management system. Technical Report 2004-20, Stanford InfoLab, 2004.

[13] M. Balazinska, H. Balakrishnan, S. R. Madden, and M. Stonebraker. Fault-tolerance in the borealis distributed stream processing system. *ACM TODS*, 33(1):3:1–3:44, Mar. 2008.

[14] O. Boykin, S. Ritchie, I. O'Connell, and J. Lin. Summingbird: A framework for integrating batch and online mapreduce computations. *PVLDB*, 7(13):1441–1451, Aug. 2014.

[15] N. Bronson, T. Lento, and J. L. Wiener. Open data challenges at facebook. In *ICDE*, pages 1516–1519, 2015.

[16] P. Carbone, G. Fóra, S. Ewen, S. Haridi, and K. Tzoumas. Lightweight asynchronous snapshots for distributed dataflows. *CoRR*, abs/1506.08603, 2015.

[17] R. Castro Fernandez, M. Migliavacca, E. Kalyvianaki, and P. Pietzuch. Integrating scale out and fault tolerance in stream processing using operator state management. In *SIGMOD*, pages 725–736, 2013.

[18] A. Goel, B. Chopra, C. Gerea, D. Mátáni, J. Metzler, F. Ul Haq, and J. L. Wiener. Fast database restarts at Facebook. In *SIGMOD*, pages 541–549, 2014.

[19] J. Kreps, N. Narkhede, and J. Rao. Kafka: A distributed messaging system for log processing. In *SIGMOD Workshop on Networking Meets Databases*, 2011.

[20] S. Kulkarni, N. Bhagat, M. Fu, V. Kedigehalli, C. Kellogg, S. Mittal, J. M. Patel, K. Ramasamy, and S. Taneja. Twitter heron: Stream processing at scale. In *SIGMOD*, pages 239–250, 2015.

[21] J. Meehan, N. Tatbul, S. Zdonik, C. Aslantas, U. Cetintemel, J. Du, T. Kraska, S. Madden, D. Maier, A. Pavlo, M. Stonebraker, K. Tufte, and H. Wang. S-store: Streaming meets transaction processing. *PVLDB*, 8(13):2134–2145, Sept. 2015.

[22] L. Neumeyer, B. Robbins, A. Nair, and A. Kesari. S4: Distributed stream computing platform. In *IEEE Data Mining Workshops*, pages 170–177, 2010.

[23] K. Shvachko, H. Kuang, S. Radia, and R. Chansler. The Hadoop distributed file system. In *Mass Storage Systems and Technologies (MSST)*, pages 1–10, 2010.

[24] M. Stonebraker, U. Çetintemel, and S. B. Zdonik. The 8 requirements of real-time stream processing. *SIGMOD Record*, 34(4):42–47, 2005.

[25] J. Sundram. Developing data products. Big Data Spain, 2015. https://www.youtube.com/watch?v=CkEdD6FL7Ug.

[26] A. Thusoo, Z. Shao, S. Anthony, D. Borthakur, N. Jain, J. Sen Sarma, R. Murthy, and H. Liu. Data warehousing and analytics infrastructure at facebook. In *SIGMOD*, pages 1013–1020, 2010.

[27] R. Tibbetts, S. Yang, R. MacNeill, and D. Rydzewski. Streambase liveview: Push-based real-time analytics. *StreamBase Systems (Jan 2012)*, 2011.

[28] A. Toshniwal, S. Taneja, A. Shukla, K. Ramasamy, J. M. Patel, S. Kulkarni, J. Jackson, K. Gade, M. Fu, J. Donham, N. Bhagat, S. Mittal, and D. Ryaboy. Storm@twitter. In *SIGMOD*, pages 147–156, 2014.

[29] J. L. Wiener. Understanding realtime conversations on Facebook. QCON San Francisco, 2015. https://qconsf.com/sf2015/speakers/janet-wiener.

[30] Y. Yu, M. Isard, D. Fetterly, M. Budiu, Ú. Erlingsson, P. K. Gunda, and J. Currey. Dryadlinq: A system for general-purpose distributed data-parallel computing using a high-level language. In *OSDI*, volume 8, pages 1–14, 2008.

[31] M. Zaharia, M. Chowdhury, T. Das, A. Dave, J. Ma, M. McCauley, M. J. Franklin, S. Shenker, and I. Stoica. Resilient distributed datasets: A fault-tolerant abstraction for in-memory cluster computing. In *NSDI*, pages 2–2, 2012.

[32] M. Zaharia, T. Das, H. Li, T. Hunter, S. Shenker, and I. Stoica. Discretized streams: Fault-tolerant streaming computation at scale. In *SOSP*, pages 423–438, 2013.

SparkR: Scaling R Programs with Spark

Shivaram Venkataraman[1], Zongheng Yang[1], Davies Liu[2], Eric Liang[2], Hossein Falaki[2]
Xiangrui Meng[2], Reynold Xin[2], Ali Ghodsi[2], Michael Franklin[1], Ion Stoica[1,2], Matei Zaharia[2,3]
[1]AMPLab UC Berkeley, [2] Databricks Inc., [3] MIT CSAIL

ABSTRACT

R is a popular statistical programming language with a number of extensions that support data processing and machine learning tasks. However, interactive data analysis in R is usually limited as the R runtime is single threaded and can only process data sets that fit in a single machine's memory. We present SparkR, an R package that provides a frontend to Apache Spark and uses Spark's distributed computation engine to enable large scale data analysis from the R shell. We describe the main design goals of SparkR, discuss how the high-level DataFrame API enables scalable computation and present some of the key details of our implementation.

Keywords

Spark; R; Statistical Computing;

1. INTRODUCTION

Recent trends in big data analytics indicate the growing need for interactive analysis of large datasets. In response to this trend, a number of academic [12, 32, 8] and commercial systems [18] have been developed to support such use cases. However, data science surveys [1] show that in addition to relational query processing, data scientists often use tools like R to perform more advanced analysis on data. R is particularly popular as it provides support for structured data processing using data frames and includes a number of packages for statistical analysis and visualization.

However, data analysis using R is limited by the amount of memory available on a single machine and further as R is single threaded it is often impractical to use R on large datasets. Prior research has addressed some of these limitations through better I/O support [35], integration with Hadoop [13, 19] and by designing distributed R runtimes [28] that can be integrated with DBMS engines [25].

In this paper, we look at how we can scale R programs while making it easy to use and deploy across a number of workloads. We present SparkR: an R frontend for Apache Spark, a widely deployed [2] cluster computing engine. There are a number of benefits to designing an R frontend that is tightly integrated with Spark.
Library Support: The Spark project contains libraries for running SQL queries [10], distributed machine learning [23], graph analytics [16] and SparkR can reuse well-tested, distributed implementations for these domains.
Data Sources: Further, Spark SQL's data sources API provides support for reading input from a variety of systems including HDFS, HBase, Cassandra and a number of formats like JSON, Parquet, etc. Integrating with the data source API enables R users to directly process data sets from any of these data sources.
Performance Improvements: As opposed to a new distributed engine, SparkR can inherit all of the optimizations made to the Spark computation engine in terms of task scheduling, code generation, memory management [3], etc.

SparkR is built as an R package and requires no changes to R. The central component of SparkR is a distributed data frame that enables structured data processing with a syntax familiar to R users [31](Figure 1). To improve performance over large datasets, SparkR performs lazy evaluation on data frame operations and uses Spark's relational query optimizer [10] to optimize execution.

SparkR was initially developed at the AMPLab, UC Berkeley and has been a part of the Apache Spark project for the past eight months. SparkR is an active project with over 40 contributors and growing adoption [6, 7]. We next outline the design goals of SparkR and key details of our implementation. Following that we outline some of the efforts in progress to improve SparkR.

2. BACKGROUND

In this section we first provide a brief overview of Spark and R, the two main systems that are used to develop SparkR. We then discuss common application patterns used by R programmers for large scale data processing.

2.1 Apache Spark

Apache Spark [2] is a general purpose engine for large scale data processing. The Spark project first introduced Resilient Distributed Datasets (RDD) [34], an API for fault tolerant computation in a cluster computing environment. More recently a number of higher level APIs have been developed in Spark. These include MLlib [23], a library for large scale machine learning, GraphX [16], a library for processing large graphs and SparkSQL [10] a SQL API for analytical queries. Since the above libraries are closely integrated with the core API, Spark enables complex workflows where say SQL queries can be used to pre-process data and the results can then be analyzed using advanced machine learning algorithms. SparkSQL also includes Catalyst [10], a distributed query optimizer that improves performance by generating the optimal physical plan for a given query. More recent efforts [9] have looked at developing a high level distributed DataFrame API for structured data processing. As queries on DataFrames are executed using the SparkSQL query optimizer, DataFrames provide both better usabil-

SIGMOD'16, June 26-July 01, 2016, San Francisco, CA, USA

DOI: http://dx.doi.org/10.1145/2882903.2903740

ity and performance compared to using RDDs [4]. We next discuss some of the important characteristics of data frames in the context of the R programming language.

2.2 R Project for Statistical Computing

The R project [26] consists of a programming language, an interactive development environment and a set of statistical computing libraries. R is an interpreted language and provides support for common constructs such as conditional execution (`if`) and loops (`for`, `while`, `repeat`) etc. R also includes extensive support for numerical computing, with data types for vectors, matrices, arrays and libraries for performing numerical operations.

Data frames in R: In addition to numerical computing, R provides support for structured data processing through data frames. Data frames are tabular data structures where each column consists of elements of a particular type (e.g., numerical or categorical). Data frames provide an easy syntax for filtering, summarizing data and packages like `dplyr` [31] have further simplified expressing complex data manipulation tasks on data frames. Specifically, `dplyr` provides a small number of *verbs* for data manipulation and these include relational operations like selection, projection, aggregations and joins. Given its popularity among users, the concept of data frames has been adopted by other languages like Pandas [21] for Python etc. Next, we look at some of the common workflows of data scientists who use R as their primary programming language and motivate our design for SparkR based on these workflows.

2.3 Application Patterns

Big Data, Small Learning: In this pattern, users typically start with a large dataset that is stored as a JSON or CSV file. Data analysis begins by joining the required datasets and users then perform data cleaning operations to remove invalid rows or columns. Following this users typically aggregate or sample their data and this step reduces the size of the dataset. The pre-processed data is then used for building models or performing other statistical tasks.

Partition Aggregate: Partition aggregate workflows are useful for a number of statistical applications like ensemble learning, parameter tuning or bootstrap aggregation. In these cases the user typically has a particular function that needs to be executed in parallel across different partitions of the input dataset and the results from each partition are then combined using a aggregation function. Additionally in some cases the input data could be small, but the same data is evaluated with a large number of parameter values.

Large Scale Machine Learning: Finally for some applications users run machine learning algorithms on large datasets. In such scenarios, the data is typically pre-processed to generate features and then the training features, labels are given as input to a machine learning algorithm to fit a model. The model being fit is usually much smaller in size compared to the input data and the model is then used to serve predictions.

We next present SparkR DataFrames and discuss how they can be used to address the above use cases.

3. DESIGN

In this section we present some of the design choices involved in building SparkR. We first present details about the DataFrames API and then present an overview of SparkR's architecture.

3.1 SparkR DataFrames API

The central component of SparkR is a distributed data frame implemented on top of Spark. SparkR DataFrames have an API similar to dplyr or local R data frames, but scale to large datasets using Spark's execution engine and relational query optimizer [10].

```
1  # Load the flights CSV file using 'read.df'
2  df <- read.df(sqlContext, "./nycflights13.csv",
3                "com.databricks.spark.csv")
4
5  # Select flights from JFK.
6  jfk_flights <- filter(df, df$origin == "JFK")
7
8  # Group and aggregate flights to each destination.
9  dest_flights <- agg(
10     groupBy(jfk_flights, jfk_flights$dest),
11     count = n(jfk_flights$dest))
12
13 # Running SQL Queries
14 registerTempTable(df, "table")
15 training <- sql(sqlContext,
16   "SELECT distance, depDelay, arrDelay FROM table")
```

Figure 1: Example of the SparkR DataFrame API

```
dest_flights <- filter(df, df$origin == "JFK") %>%
    groupBy(df$dest) %>%
    summarize(count = n(df$dest))
```

Figure 2: Chaining DataFrame operators in SparkR

DataFrame Operators: SparkR's DataFrame supports a number of methods to read input and perform structured data analysis. As shown in Figure 1, SparkR's `read.df` method integrates with Spark's data source API and this enables users to load data from systems like HBase, Cassandra etc. Having loaded the data, users are then able to use a familiar syntax for performing relational operations like selections, projections, aggregations and joins (lines 6–11). Further, SparkR supports more than 100 pre-defined functions on DataFrames including string manipulation methods, statistical functions and date-time operations. Users can also execute SQL queries directly on SparkR DataFrames using the `sql` command (lines 15–16). SparkR also makes it easy for users to chain commands using existing R libraries [11] as shown in Figure 2. Finally, SparkR DataFrames can be converted to a local R data frame using the `collect` operator and this is useful for the big data, small learning scenarios described earlier.

Optimizations: One of the main advantages of the high-level DataFrame API is that we can tightly integrate the R API with the optimized SQL execution engine in Spark. This means that even though users write their code in R, we do not incur overheads of running interpreted R code and can instead achieve the same performance as using Scala or SQL. For example, Figure 4 compares the performance of running group-by aggregation on 10 million integer pairs on a single machine using Spark with R, Python and Scala. From the figure we can see that SparkR's performance is similar to that of Scala / Python and this shows the benefits of separating the logical specification in R from the physical execution.

3.2 Architecture

SparkR's architecture consists of two main components as shown in Figure 3: an R to JVM binding on the driver that allows R programs to submit jobs to a Spark cluster and support for running R on the Spark executors. We discuss both these components below.

3.2.1 Bridging R and JVM

One of the key challenges in implementing SparkR is having support for invoking Spark functions on a JVM from R. The main requirements we need to satisfy here include (a) a flexible approach where the JVM driver process could be launched independently by say a cluster manager like YARN (b) cross-platform support on

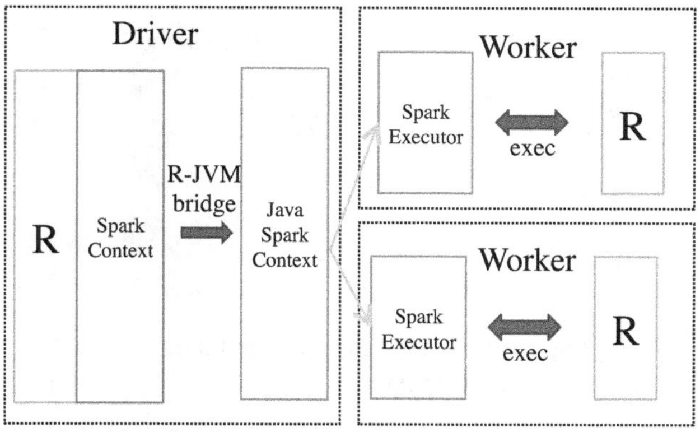

Figure 3: SparkR Architecture

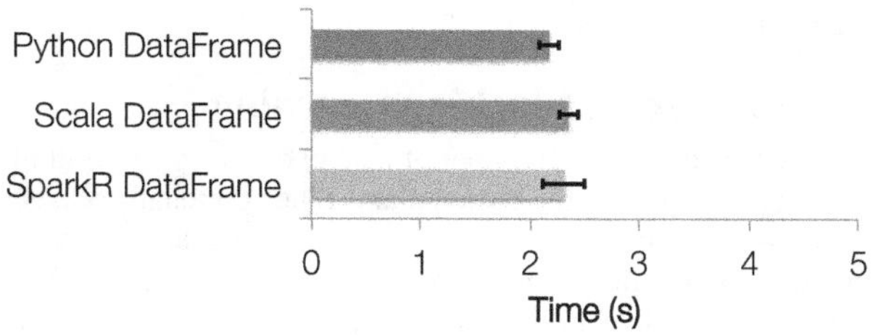

Figure 4: SparkR Performance Comparison with Python, Scala APIs

Windows, Linux, etc. (c) a lightweight solution that does not make it cumbersome to install SparkR. While there are some existing packages which support starting an in-process JVM [27] we found that these methods do not meet all our requirements.

Thus we developed a new socket-based SparkR internal API that can be used to invoke functions on the JVM from R. Our high level design is inspired by existing RPC or RMI-based systems [29] and we introduce a new SparkR JVM backend that listens on a Netty-based socket server. Our main reason for using sockets is that they are supported across platforms (in both Java and R) and are available without using any external libraries in both languages. As most of the messages being passed are control messages, the cost of using sockets as compared other in-process communication methods is not very high.

There are two kinds of RPCs we support in the SparkR JVM backend: method invocation and creating new objects. Method invocations are called using a reference to an existing Java object (or class name for static methods) and a list of arguments to be passed on to the method. The arguments are serialized using our custom wire format which is then deserialized on the JVM side. We then use Java reflection to invoke the appropriate method. In order to create objects, we use a special method name `init` and then similarly invoke the appropriate constructor based on the provided arguments. Finally, we use a new R class 'jobj' that refers to a Java object existing in the backend. These references are tracked on the Java side and are automatically garbage collected when they go out of scope on the R side.

3.2.2 Spawning R workers

The second part of SparkR's design consists of support to launch R processes on Spark executor machines. Our initial approach here was to fork an R process each time we need to run an R function. This is expensive because there are fixed overheads in launching the

```
# Query 1
# Top-5 destinations for flights departing from JFK.
jfk_flights <- filter(flights, flights$Origin == "JFK")
head(agg(group_by(jfk_flights, jfk_flights$Dest),
         count = n(jfk_flights$Dest)), 5L)

# Query 2
# Calculate the average delay across all flights.
collect(summarize(flights,
                  avg\_delay = mean(flights$DepDelay)))

# Query 3
# Count the number of distinct flight numbers.
count(distinct(select(flights, flights$TailNum)))
```

Figure 7: Queries used for evaluation with the flights dataset

R process and in transferring the necessary inputs such as the Spark broadcast variables, input data, etc. We made two optimizations which reduce this overhead significantly. First, we implemented support for coalescing R operations which lets us combine a number of R functions that need to be run. This is similar to operator pipelining used in database execution engines. Second, we added support for having a daemon R process that lives throughout the lifetime of a Spark job and manages the worker R processes using the `mcfork` feature in `parallel` package [26]. These optimizations both reduce the fixed overhead and the number of times we invoke an R process and help lower the end-to-end latency.

4. EVALUATION

In this section we evaluate some of our design choices described in the previous sections and also study how SparkR scales as we use more machines. The dataset we use in this section is the airline on-time performance dataset[1] that is used to evaluate existing R packages like dplyr [30]. This dataset contains arrival data for flights in USA and includes information such as departure and arrival delays, origin and destination airports etc. We use data across six years (2009-2014) and overall our input has 37.27M rows and 110 columns. The queries we use to evaluate SparkR are listed in Figure 7. The queries make use of filtering, aggregation and sorting and are representative of interactive queries used by R users. We use a cluster of 32 `r3.xlarge` machines on Amazon EC2 for our evaluation. Each machine consists of 2 physical cores, 30GB of memory and 80GB of SSD storage. All experiments were also run using Apache Spark 1.6.0 and we used the `spark-csv`[2] package for reading our input.

4.1 Strong Scaling

We first study the scaling behavior of SparkR by executing the three queries in Figure 7 and varying the number of cores used. In this experiment, the input data is directly processed from HDFS and not cached in memory. The time taken for each query as we vary the number of cores from 8 to 64 is shown in Figure 5. From the figure we can see that SparkR achieves near-linear scaling with the time taken reducing from around 115 seconds with 8 cores to around 20 seconds with 64 cores. However waiting for 20 seconds is often sub-optimal for interactive queries and we next see how caching data in memory can improve performance.

4.2 Importance of Caching

For studying the benefits of caching the input table in memory we fix the number of cores used as 64 and measure the time taken

[1]http://www.transtats.bts.gov/Tables.asp?DB_ID=120
[2]http://github.com/databricks/spark-csv

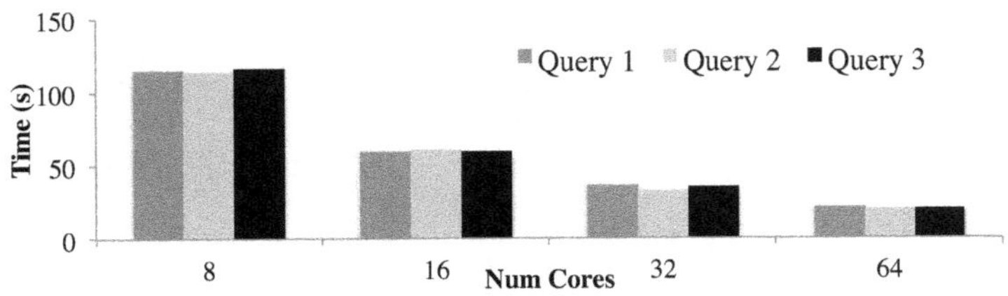

Figure 5: Query performance as we scale the number of cores used for three queries from Figure 7

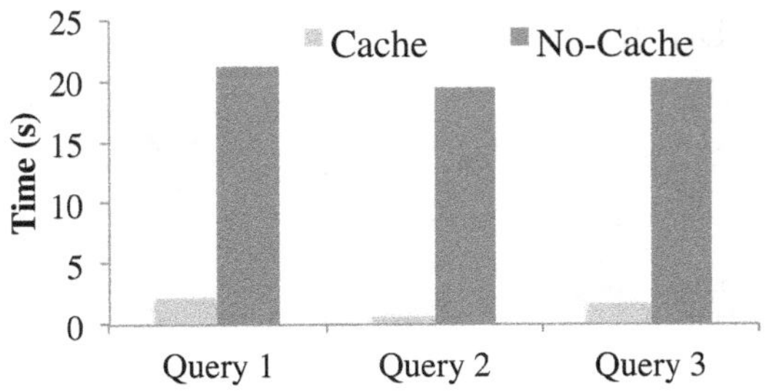

Figure 6: Effect of caching input data

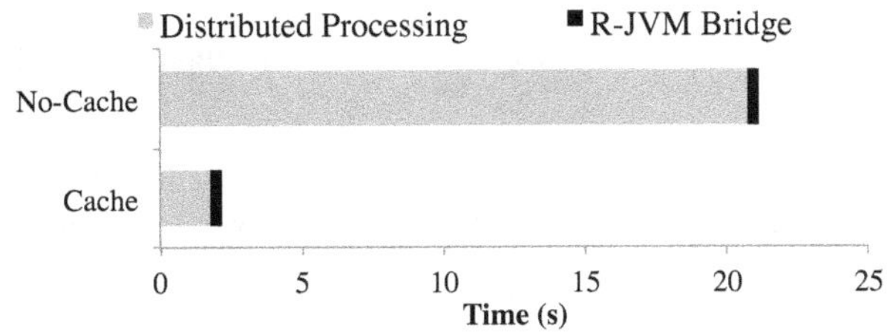

Figure 8: Breakdown of time taken R-to-JVM bridge and distributed processing Spark for Query 1 from Figure 7

```
# Train a GLM model
model <- glm(arrDelay ~ depDelay + distance,
             family = "gaussian", data = training)

# Print model summary
summary(model)

# Compute predictions using model
preds <- predict(model, training)
```

Figure 9: Building Generalized Linear Models in SparkR

by each query when the input data is cached. Results from this experiment are shown in Figure 6. We see that caching the data can improve performance by $10x$ to $30x$ for this workload. These results are in line with previous studies [34, 10] that measured the importance of caching in Spark. We would like to note that the benefits here come not only from using faster storage media, but also from avoiding CPU time in decompressing data and parsing CSV files. Finally, we can see that caching helps us achieve low latencies (less than 3 seconds) that make SparkR suitable for interactive query processing from the R shell.

4.3 Overhead of R-JVM binding

We next evaluate the overhead of using our socket-based R to JVM bridge discussed in Section 3.2.1. To do this we use query 1 from Figure 7 and run the query with both caching enabled and disabled on 64 cores. Using the performance metrics exported by Spark, we compute the time taken to run distributed computation and the time spent in the R-JVM bridge. In Figure 8, we see that the R-JVM bridge adds a constant overhead around 300 milliseconds irrespective of whether the data is cached or not. This overhead includes the time spent in serializing the query and in deserializing the results after it has been computed. For interactive query processing we find having an overhead of a few hundred milliseconds does not affect user experience. However, as the amount of data shipped between R and JVM increases we find that the overheads become more significant and we are exploring better serialization techniques in the R-JVM bridge to improve this.

5. ONGOING WORK

We are continuing work on SparkR in many areas to improve performance and enable more use cases. The two main areas we discuss here relate to large scale machine learning by integration with MLlib [23] and supporting partition aggregate workflows using user-defined functions (UDFs).

5.1 Large Scale Machine Learning

R includes support for a number of machine learning algorithms through the default `stats` package and other optional packages like `glmnet` [14], `cluster` [20] etc. The machine learning algorithms typically operate directly on data frames and use C or Fortran linkages for efficient implementations. One of the most widely used machine learning functions in R is the `glm` method that fits Generalized Linear Models. The `glm` method in R lets users specify the modeling of a response variable in a compact symbolic form using *formulas*. For example, the formula $y \sim a + b$ indicates the response y is modeled linearly by variables a and b. `glm` also lets users specify the loss function to use and can thus be to used to implement linear regression, logistic regression etc. The `glm` method returns a model trained using the input data and users typically use the `summary` function in R to print a number of statistics computed about the model.

To support large scale distributed machine learning in SparkR, we are working on integrating Spark's MLlib API with SparkR DataFrames. Our first focus is `glm` and to provide an intuitive interface for R users, we extend R's native methods for fitting and evaluating models as shown in Figure 9. We support a subset of the R formula operators in SparkR. These include the $+$ (inclusion), $-$ (exclusion), : (interactions) and intercept operators. SparkR implements the interpretation of R model formulas as an MLlib [23] feature transformer and this integrates with the ML Pipelines API [22]. This design also enables the same RFormula transformer to be used from Python, Scala and thereby enables an R-like succinct syntax for GLMs across different Spark APIs.

We are also working on implementing support for model summaries in SparkR to compute (a) minimum and maximum deviance residuals of the estimation (b) the coefficient values for the estimation (c) the estimated standard errors, t-values and p-values. Currently we have implemented these metrics for Gaussian GLMs trained using weighted least squares and we are working towards extending support for such metrics across different different families (Poisson, Gamma etc.) and link functions (logit, probit etc.) using iteratively re-weighted least squares (IRWLS).

5.2 User Defined Functions

To support the partition aggregate usage pattern discussed before, we are working on providing support for running user-defined functions (UDFs) in parallel. Spark supports UDFs written in Scala, Python and these APIs allow UDFs to run on each row of the input DataFrame. However, a number of R packages operate on local R data frames and it would be more user-friendly to support UDFs where R users can directly make use of these packages. In SparkR we plan to support UDFs that operate on each partition of the distributed DataFrame and these functions will in turn return local R columnar data frames that will be then converted into the corresponding format in the JVM.

In addition to the above UDF-based API, we find that for some use cases like parameter tuning, the input dataset is small but there are a number of parameter values that need to be evaluated in parallel. To support such workflows we are working on a parallel execution API, where we take in a local list, a function to be executed and run the function for each element of the local list in one core in the cluster. Finally one of the main features that we aim to support with UDFs is closure capture or support for users to refer to external global variables inside their UDFs. We plan to implement this using R's support for reflection and one of the challenges here is to ensure that we only capture the necessary variables to avoid performance overheads.

5.3 Efficient Data Sharing

One of the main overheads when executing UDFs in SparkR is the time spent serializing input for the UDF from the JVM and then deserialzing it in R. This process is also repeated for the data output from the UDF and thus adds significant overhead to the execution time. Recent memory management improvements [3] have introduced support for off heap storage in Spark and we plan to investigate techniques to use off heap storage for sharing data efficiently between the JVM and R. One of the key challenges here is to develop a storage format that can be parsed easily in both languages. In addition to the serialization benefits, off heap data sharing can help us lower the memory overhead by reducing the number of data copies required.

6. RELATED WORK

A number of academic (Ricardo [13], RHIPE [17], RABID [19]) and commercial (RHadoop [5], BigR [33]) projects have looked at integrating R with Apache Hadoop. SparkR follows a similar approach but inherits the functionality [23] and performance [3] benefits of using Spark as the execution engine. The high level DataFrame API in SparkR is inspired by data frames in R [26], dplyr [31] and pandas [21]. Further, SparkR's data sources integration is similar to pluggable backends supported by dplyr. Unlike other data frame implementations, SparkR uses lazy evaluation and Spark's relational optimizer to improve performance for distributed computations. Finally, a number of projects like DistributedR [25], SciDB [24], SystemML [15] have looked at scaling array or matrix-based computations in R. In SparkR, we propose a high-level DataFrame API for structured data processing and integrate this with a distributed machine learning library to provide support for advanced analytics.

7. CONCLUSION

In summary, SparkR provides an R frontend to Apache Spark and allows users to run large scale data analysis using Spark's distributed computation engine. SparkR has been a part of the Apache Spark project since the 1.4.0 release and all of the functionality described in this work is open source. SparkR can be downloaded from `http://spark.apache.org`.

Acknowledgments: We would like to thank the anonymous reviewers and our shepherd Tyson Condie for their feedback. We would also like to thank Sun Rui, Yu Ishkawa, Chris Freeman, Dan Putler, Felix Cheung, Hao Lin, Antonio Piccolboni, Yanbo Liang, and all other contributors to the open source SparkR project. This research is supported in part by NSF CISE Expeditions Award CCF-1139158, DOE Award SN10040 DE-SC0012463, and DARPA XData Award FA8750-12-2-0331, and gifts from Amazon Web Services, Google, IBM, SAP, The Thomas and Stacey Siebel Foundation, Adatao, Adobe, Apple, Inc., Blue Goji, Bosch, Cisco, Cray, Cloudera, EMC, Ericsson, Facebook, Guavus, HP, Huawei, Informatica, Intel, Microsoft, NetApp, Pivotal, Samsung, Schlumberger, Splunk, Virdata and VMware.

8. REFERENCES

[1] 2015 data science salary survey. https://www.oreilly.com/ideas/2015-data-science-salary-survey.

[2] Apache Spark Project. http://spark.apache.org.

[3] Project Tungsten: Bringing Spark Closer to Bare Metal. https://databricks.com/blog/2015/04/28/project-tungsten-bringing-spark-closer-to-bare-metal.html.

[4] Recent performance improvements in Apache Spark: SQL, Python, DataFrames, and More. https://goo.gl/RQS3ld.

[5] Rhadoop. http://projects.revolutionanalytics.com/rhadoop.

[6] Spark survey 2015. http://go.databricks.com/2015-spark-survey.

[7] Visual Analytics for Apache Spark and SparkR. http://goo.gl/zPje2i.

[8] A. Alexandrov, R. Bergmann, S. Ewen, J.-C. Freytag, F. Hueske, A. Heise, O. Kao, M. Leich, U. Leser, V. Markl, et al. The Stratosphere platform for big data analytics. *VLDB Journal*, 23(6):939–964, 2014.

[9] M. Armbrust, T. Das, A. Davidson, A. Ghodsi, A. Or, J. Rosen, I. Stoica, P. Wendell, R. Xin, and M. Zaharia. Scaling spark in the real world: performance and usability. *Proceedings of the VLDB Endowment*, 8(12):1840–1843, 2015.

[10] M. Armbrust, R. S. Xin, C. Lian, Y. Huai, et al. Spark SQL: Relational data processing in Spark. In *SIGMOD*, pages 1383–1394, 2015.

[11] S. M. Bache and H. Wickham. *magrittr: A Forward-Pipe Operator for R*, 2014. R package version 1.5.

[12] M. Barnett, B. Chandramouli, R. DeLine, S. Drucker, D. Fisher, J. Goldstein, P. Morrison, and J. Platt. Stat!: An interactive analytics environment for big data. In *SIGMOD 2013*, pages 1013–1016.

[13] S. Das, Y. Sismanis, K. S. Beyer, R. Gemulla, P. J. Haas, and J. McPherson. Ricardo: integrating R and Hadoop. In *SIGMOD 2010*, pages 987–998. ACM, 2010.

[14] J. Friedman, T. Hastie, and R. Tibshirani. Regularization paths for generalized linear models via coordinate descent. *Journal of Statistical Software*, 33(1):1–22, 2010.

[15] A. Ghoting, R. Krishnamurthy, E. Pednault, B. Reinwald, et al. SystemML: Declarative machine learning on MapReduce. In *ICDE*, pages 231–242. IEEE, 2011.

[16] J. E. Gonzalez, R. S. Xin, A. Dave, D. Crankshaw, M. J. Franklin, and I. Stoica. Graphx: Graph processing in a distributed dataflow framework. In *OSDI 2014*, pages 599–613.

[17] S. Guha, R. Hafen, J. Rounds, J. Xia, J. Li, B. Xi, and W. S. Cleveland. Large complex data: Divide and Recombine (d&r) with RHIPE. *Stat*, 1(1):53–67, 2012.

[18] M. Kornacker, A. Behm, V. Bittorf, T. Bobrovytsky, C. Ching, A. Choi, J. Erickson, M. Grund, D. Hecht,

M. Jacobs, et al. Impala: A modern, open-source SQL engine for Hadoop. In *CIDR 2015*.

[19] H. Lin, S. Yang, and S. Midkiff. RABID: A General Distributed R Processing Framework Targeting Large Data-Set Problems. In *IEEE Big Data 2013*, pages 423–424, June 2013.

[20] M. Maechler, P. Rousseeuw, A. Struyf, M. Hubert, and K. Hornik. *cluster: Cluster Analysis Basics and Extensions*, 2015.

[21] W. McKinney. Data Structures for Statistical Computing in Python . In S. van der Walt and J. Millman, editors, *Proceedings of the 9th Python in Science Conference*, pages 51 – 56, 2010.

[22] X. Meng, J. Bradley, E. Sparks, and S. Venkataraman. ML Pipelines: A New High-Level API for MLlib. https://goo.gl/pluhq0, 2015.

[23] X. Meng, J. K. Bradley, B. Yavuz, E. R. Sparks, et al. MLlib: Machine Learning in Apache Spark. *CoRR*, abs/1505.06807, 2015.

[24] Paradigm4 and B. W. Lewis. *scidb: An R Interface to SciDB*, 2015. R package version 1.2-0.

[25] S. Prasad, A. Fard, V. Gupta, J. Martinez, J. LeFevre, V. Xu, M. Hsu, and I. Roy. Large-scale predictive analytics in vertica: Fast data transfer, distributed model creation, and in-database prediction. In *SIGMOD 2015*.

[26] R Core Team. *R: A Language and Environment for Statistical Computing*. R Foundation for Statistical Computing, Vienna, Austria, 2015.

[27] S. Urbanek. *rJava: Low-Level R to Java Interface*, 2015. R package version 0.9-7.

[28] S. Venkataraman, E. Bodzsar, I. Roy, A. AuYoung, and R. S. Schreiber. Presto: Distributed Machine Learning and Graph Processing with Sparse Matrices. In *Eurosys 2013*, pages 197–210.

[29] J. Waldo. Remote Procedure Calls and Java Remote Method Invocation. *IEEE Concurrency*, 6(3):5–7, 1998.

[30] H. Wickham. *nycflights13: Data about flights departing NYC in 2013.*, 2014. R package version 0.1.

[31] H. Wickham and R. Francois. *dplyr: A Grammar of Data Manipulation*, 2015. R package version 0.4.3.

[32] R. S. Xin, J. Rosen, M. Zaharia, M. J. Franklin, S. Shenker, and I. Stoica. Shark: SQL and rich analytics at scale. In *SIGMOD 2013*.

[33] L. Yejas, D. Oscar, W. Zhuang, and A. Pannu. Big R: Large-Scale Analytics on Hadoop Using R. In *IEEE Big Data 2014*, pages 570–577.

[34] M. Zaharia, M. Chowdhury, T. Das, A. Dave, et al. Resilient distributed datasets: A fault-tolerant abstraction for in-memory cluster computing. *NSDI*, 2012.

[35] Y. Zhang, W. Zhang, and J. Yang. I/O-efficient statistical computing with RIOT. In *ICDE 2010*, pages 1157–1160.

VectorH: Taking SQL-on-Hadoop to the Next Level

Andrei Costea‡ Adrian Ionescu‡ Bogdan Răducanu‡ Michał Świtakowski‡ Cristian Bârcă‡
Juliusz Sompolski‡ Alicja Łuszczak‡ Michał Szafrański‡
Giel de Nijs‡ Peter Boncz§
Actian Corp.‡ CWI§

ABSTRACT

Actian Vector in Hadoop (VectorH for short) is a new SQL-on-Hadoop system built on top of the fast Vectorwise analytical database system. VectorH achieves fault tolerance and storage scalability by relying on HDFS, and extends the state-of-the-art in SQL-on-Hadoop systems by instrumenting the HDFS replication policy to optimize read locality. VectorH integrates with YARN for workload management, achieving a high degree of elasticity. Even though HDFS is an append-only filesystem, and VectorH supports (update-averse) ordered tables, trickle updates are possible thanks to Positional Delta Trees (PDTs), a differential update structure that can be queried efficiently. We describe the changes made to single-server Vectorwise to turn it into a Hadoop-based MPP system, encompassing workload management, parallel query optimization and execution, HDFS storage, transaction processing and Spark integration. We evaluate VectorH against HAWQ, Impala, SparkSQL and Hive, showing orders of magnitude better performance.

1. INTRODUCTION

Hadoop, originally an open-source copy of MapReduce, has become the standard software layer for Big Data clusters. Though MapReduce is losing market share as the programming framework of choice to an ever-expanding range of competing options and meta-frameworks, most prominently Spark [26], Hadoop has established itself as the software base for a variety of technologies, thanks to its evolution which decoupled the YARN resource manager from MapReduce and the wide adoption of its distributed file system HDFS, which has become the de-facto standard for cheap scalable storage for on-premise clusters. *SQL-on-Hadoop systems* allow to connect existing SQL-based business applications with the results of "big data" pipelines, adding to their worth, further accelerating the adoption of Hadoop in commercial settings. This paper describes **VectorH**, a new SQL-on-Hadoop system with advanced query execution, updatability, YARN, HDFS and Spark integration.

SIGMOD '16, June 26–July 1, 2016, San Francisco, California, USA.

ISBN 978-1-4503-1247-9/12/05...$15.00

DOI: http://dx.doi.org/10.1145/2882903.2903742

SQL-on-Hadoop=MPP DBMS? A SQL-on-Hadoop system shares certain characteristics with an analytical parallel DBMS, such as Teradata. First of all, these so-called MPP systems are used in *analytical* workloads, which consist of relatively few very heavy queries – compared to transactional workloads – that perform heavy scans, joins, aggregations and analytical SQL, such as SQL'2003 window functions based on PARTITION BY, ROLL UP and GROUPING SETS. That said, these workloads are by no means read-only, and systems must also sustain a continuous stream of voluminous updates under limited concurrency.

In the past decade, analytical database systems have seen the rise of (i) *columnar stores* – which reduce the amount of IO and memory bandwidth needed in query processing further boosted by (ii) integrated *data compression* and (iii) facilities that allow *data skipping* in many queries, e.g. through lightweight index structures like MinMax indexes that exploit natural orders and correlations in the data. Such modern analytical database systems typically (iv) use a query engine that is (re)designed to exploit modern hardware strengths. Two approaches for this are popular. Vectorwise [27] developed the first fully *vectorized* query engine where all operations on data are performed on vectors of values, rather than tuple-at-a-time, reducing query interpretation overhead, increasing data and code CPU cache locality and allowing to use SIMD instructions. The competing approach is to use Just-In-Time (JIT) compilation, such that a SQL query is translated into assembly instructions – see Impala [24].

A commonality between SQL-on-Hadoop and MPP systems is that both run on a cluster of nodes; both systems must distribute data in some way over this cluster and when a single query is run it must ideally parallelize over all nodes – and all their cores – in this cluster. While this shared goal is obvious, it requires a lot of technical excellence in data placement, query optimization and execution to achieve near-linear parallel scalability on complex SQL queries. Both kinds of system, finally, must be prepared for nodes or links between them to go down (un)expectedly, and thus replicate data and take measures to achieve fault tolerance.

SQL-on-Hadoop≠MPP DBMS. There are also significant differences between SQL-on-Hadoop and MPP systems. MPP systems typically run on a dedicated cluster, and sometimes even on specific hardware (database machines), whereas SQL-on-Hadoop systems share a Hadoop cluster with other workloads. The task of dividing the hardware resources between concurrent parallel queries is already hard in MPP, but when other Hadoop jobs also take cores, memory, network and disk bandwidth, this becomes even harder.

In order to counter this problem, all members of the Hadoop ecosystem should coordinate their resource usage through a resource manager such as YARN.

By basing data storage on HDFS, SQL-on-Hadoop systems leverage scalability and fault-tolerance for a large part from their Hadoop infrastructure; whereas MPP systems must introduce specific and proprietary mechanisms for fault tolerance (e.g. for adding and removing hardware, reacting gracefully to failures, monitoring status). MPP systems are typically more expensive, not only in upfront software and hardware cost, but also in terms of administration cost; the required expertise is more rare than that for maintaining a Hadoop cluster, which has become a standard in this space.

In some analysis scenarios, raw data first needs to be processed with methods and algorithms that cannot be expressed in SQL, but better in a programming language. MPP systems have introduced proprietary UDF (User Defined Function) interfaces with differing degrees of expressive power in an attempt to address this, whereas in SQL-on-Hadoop it is more natural to use parallel programming frameworks like Spark for such tasks. The advantage of this approach is that Spark is more powerful and flexible than any UDF API, and is open, so re-use in creating UDFs is more likely. SQL-on-Hadoop systems thus must fit seamlessly into "big data" pipelines, either through integrated APIs or through an ability to read and write large datasets in a number of standard formats (text, binary, ORC, Parquet) stored via HDFS on the cluster.

VectorH Features and Contributions. VectorH is a SQL-on-Hadoop system whose prime contribution is (i) to provide vastly superior query processing *performance*. This higher performance is based on a combination of a truly vectorized query engine, compressed columnar data formats with better lightweight compression methods than those used in common Hadoop formats, and better data skipping statistics than these common formats. Its SQL technology is mature, which is especially visible in the query plan quality produced by its cost-based query optimizer, but is also observed in its robust SQL support including analytical SQL, encryption, authentication, and user role management.

A second system-level contribution is that VectorH (ii) instruments the HDFS block placement policy to determine where its compressed columnar blocks are replicated – by HDFS default on 3 nodes. VectorH uses this locality to always guarantee local IO, even if the cluster composition changes, e.g. due to hardware failures. This tight *integration with HDFS* is a novelty in SQL-on-Hadoop systems.

VectorH also pioneers (iii) *elasticity* features in Hadoop, by tightly integrating with YARN; it is able to scale up and down its memory usage and core footprint, in order to accommodate fluctuating workloads needs on a Hadoop cluster that is shared with many other users and job types.

VectorH further (iv) allows *fine-grained updates* (inserts, deletes, modifications) to its columnar compressed tables by leveraging the Vectorwise's Positional Delta Tree [12] data structure, without updates affecting the high performance of read queries – which still work on the latest up-to-date state. Integrating its column storage formats and PDTs in the append-only HDFS environment is another system-level contribution of the system. Finally, the *Spark integration* of VectorH allows it to read all common Hadoop formats with full HDFS locality and also enables running user code in parallel on VectorH-resident data efficiently.

2. FROM VECTORWISE TO VECTORH

In this section we first summarize the most relevant features of the Vectorwise system, the performance-leading[1] single-server **Actian Vector** product. Then, we provide a short overview of how this technology was used to architect the new shared-nothing **Actian VectorH** SQL-on-Hadoop product, which also serves as roadmap for the paper.

Relevant Vectorwise Features. Vectorized processing performs any operation on data at the granularity of *vectors* (mini-columns) of roughly 1000 elements. This dramatically reduces the overhead typically present in row-based query engines that interpret query plans tuple-at-a-time [4]. Additionally, instruction cache locality increases as the interpreter stays longer in each function, and memory bandwidth consumption is reduced as all vectors reside in the CPU data cache. Vectorized execution exposes possibilities to leverage features of modern CPUs like SIMD instructions in database workloads and increases analytical query performance by an order of magnitude. The vectorized execution model has been adopted by analytical subsystems such as IBM BLU [20] and SQLserver column indexes [17]; and it is also being deployed in new releases of Hive [13].

Vectorwise introduced the compression schemes PFOR, PFOR-DELTA and PDICT, designed to achieve good compression ratios even with skewed frequency value distributions, as well as high decompression speed [28]. PDICT is dictionary compression, PFOR is zero prefix compression when representing values as the difference from a block-dependent base (the Frame Of Reference). PFOR-DELTA compresses deltas between subsequent tuples using PFOR, and has been adopted by the Lucene system to store its inverted text index. These schemes represent values as thin fixed-bitwidth codes packed together, but store infrequent values uncompressed as "exceptions" later in the block. The letter P in these stands for "Patched", since decompression first inflates all values from the compressed codes; then in a second phase patches the values that were exceptions by hopping over the decompressed codes starting from the first exception, treating these codes as "next" pointers. Thus, the data-dependent part of decompression is separated in a short second phase while most work (code inflation) is SIMD-friendly and branch-free. These decompression formats were recently re-implemented in Vectorwise in AVX2, yielding a function that decompresses 64 or 128 consecutive values in a typically less than half a CPU cycle per value. The Hadoop formats ORC and Parquet, while clear improvements over predecessor formats such as sequence and RCfile, have not been designed for branch-free SIMD decompression and are much slower to parse [25].

In data warehouses, fact table order is often time-related, so date-time columns typically are correlated with tuple-order. Vectorwise automatically keeps so-called *MinMax* statistics on all columns. These MinMax indexes store simple metadata about the values in a given range of records, and allow quick elimination of ranges of records during scan operations (skipping), saving both IO and CPU decompression cost. Both ORC and Parquet adopted this idea, but Parquet often cannot avoid IO as it stores MinMax information at a block position that can only be determined while parsing the header – forcing the block to be read [25].

[1] See www.tpc.org/downloaded_result_files/tpch_results.txt

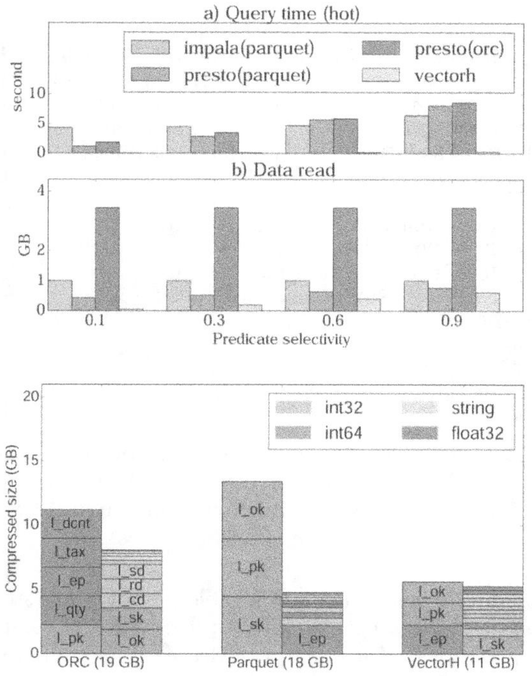

Figure 1: Data Format Micro-Benchmarks.

Storage Format Micro-Benchmarks. We performed micro-benchmarks on the SF=100 TPCH `lineitem` table that was sorted on the `l_shipdate` column, to corroborate our belief that the Vectorwise data storage is more efficient than ORC and Parquet implementations. The *topmost* chart of Figure 1 shows that Vectorwise is faster on: `SELECT max(l_linenumber) FROM lineitem WHERE l_shipdate<X` queries, where `X` is varied to test different selection percentages. Such queries can profit strongly from MinMax skipping, given the table order on `l_shipdate`. While the time differences can be partly explained by the higher efficiency of the query processing engine of VectorH, and specifically its vectorized decompression (whereas the Parquet and ORC readers decode value-at-a-time), the *middle* chart shows that it is also touching much less data. Impala does not do MinMax skipping at all while Presto does, but it reads more data than needed[2] (for example, at 90% selectivity data read is even bigger than the total size of the columns). Parquet/ORC split row groups by row count, so compressible columns may be split into too small chunks [14]. In contrast, VectorH's format allows these thin columns to occupy full 512KB blocks. For example, one VectorH block might contain the whole column while with Parquet/ORC this column could be split into thousands of small pieces depending on the compressability of the other columns.

A small part of the reduced data reading is in fact not due to better skipping, but because the PFOR schemes used in VectorH compress better than both the ORC and Parquet formats do, as shown by the *lowest* chart[3]. Vectorwise data is almost twice smaller, though Parquet could be close were it not for its inefficient handling of 64-bits integers.

Vectorwise Physical Design Options. Vectorwise tables can be stored unordered or as a "clustered index". Rather than creating some kind of B-tree, this means that Vectorwise stores the table sorted on the index key. It also provides unclustered indexes (i.e. real index trees), which can help queries that access a few tuples to avoid a table scan. Vectorwise supports horizontal table partitioning by hash, which can be combined with indexing.

The main benefit of a clustered index is data skipping in scans for queries with range-predicates on the index keys. When a clustered index is declared on a foreign key, treatment is special as the tuple order then gets derived from that of the referenced table, making the tables *co-ordered*. This allows merge-joins between them, and is very similar on the physical storage level to nested Hadoop data formats such as ORC and Parquet (where, say, an `order` object may contain nested `lineitems`). In the columnar layout used by ORC and Parquet, this means a table consists of columns with the same tuple order, and nested tables are co-ordered and merge-joinable using an also co-ordered "repeat-count" column. Such a tight, co-ordered, layout is difficult to insert/delete in, a problem solved in Vectorwise with "PDTs".

Compressed, columnar, ordered, data formats are read-optimized and direct modifications on these would be costly. Vectorwise allows high-performance updates nevertheless, using a differential update mechanism based on *Positional Delta Trees* (PDT) [11]. Positional Delta Trees are *counting* B+-trees that store updates (insert, delete, modify) in their leaves, where the interior nodes count the amount of inserts minus the amount of deletes in the sub-tree below them. PDTs can quickly translate back-and-forth between the old position of a tuple (the SID - stable ID) and its current position (RID). PDTs allow to update ordered tables (i.e. clustered indexes) as well a co-ordered tables (clustered index on a foreign key) with logarithmic complexity [11]. Their primary goal is *fast merging* of differences in a scan, which happens for each and every query. Merging in differences from a PDT is fast because it identifies tuples by position, rather than by primary key, which saves both key-comparisons (CPU) and scan work on the key (IO).

VectorH & Paper Roadmap. VectorH is a YARN-based cluster version of Vectorwise relying on HDFS for storage and fault-tolerance. HDFS is a global cluster filesystem where all nodes can read all data, but in order to achieve good performance, one must read local data mostly. The VectorH integration with HDFS is discussed in Section 3.

To determine on which nodes VectorH can run, given data locality but also Hadoop resource availability, it integrates with YARN, as discussed in Section 4.

The foundation of shared-nothing parallel Vectorwise was laid by a MSc project [7]. It created a MPP system consisting of Vectorwise processes, adding a MPI-based parallel query processing infrastructure, "exchange" operators, and a parallel rewriter. This prototype was significantly extended in the VectorH product as described in Section 5.

HDFS is an append-only filesystem, but this restriction does not hinder Vectorwise's PDT update structure. Section 6 describes transaction handling in VectorH, including distributed logging and 2PC. Section 7 outlines the VectorH-Spark integration that allows users to run code near their data in parallel, but also to read and write data in Hadoop data formats with high performance. VectorH is evaluated against Impala, Hive, HAWQ and SparkSQL on a 1000GB TPC-H database in Section 8. We then discuss related work in Section 9 before concluding in Section 10.

[2]Profile information showed that the Presto ORC reader does not skip IO, but it does skip decompression CPU work.
[3]We omitted `l_comment` from the comparison as it is not compressible with lightweight schemes.

3. STORAGE AFFINITY WITH HDFS

The storage layer of Vectorwise was modified in VectorH to use the `libhdfs` JNI library instead of a normal filesystem, for its persistent table storage, and its write-ahead log (WAL). HDFS files are split into fixed size blocks (typically 128MB to 1GB) which are automatically replicated across the datanodes in the cluster (by default at R=3 locations) to provide fault-tolerance. VectorH may optionally also use HDFS for temporary storage spilling operators though then it overrides the replication degree to just 1. Vectorwise has a *predictive buffer manager* that not only handles immediate page requests but tries to keep concurrent scan queries busy by prefetching [23]. Whereas on standard filesystems Vectorwise uses asynchronous direct IO, for HDFS a thread pool was added to perform parallel synchronous HDFS block reads. HDFS provides an efficient way to read local data called *short-circuit* reads, through which files can be read directly from disk, bypassing the datanode. This provides reasonable performance (say 30% overhead compared to direct IO). VectorH in general achieves the situation that all table IOs are short-circuited. Its IO scheduler uses HDFS *block location tracking* to decide which thread makes each IO request, with the goal of keeping all local disks busy.

Original Layout. In Vectorwise, the unit of table storage is a block of fixed compressed size (default 512KB). For IO efficiency, writing is done in groups of consecutive blocks (by default 8 groups per block). This makes the effective IO unit bigger (4MB by default) which is better suited for rotational disks. Blocks are stored consecutively in files, where by default one file is used for each column in a table partition. Each block has a number which determines its position in a file (e.g. block 0 will be at position 0, block 1 at position 512KB). In memory, a column is a list of blocks, not necessarily with the same ordering as in the file. This is because the file space of freed blocks can be reused.

Blocks can be freed as a result of updates (delete, drop column, etc.) and subsequently reused. However, this requires writing in the middle of a file, which is not supported by HDFS. In the original layout, space could therefore only freed by rewriting the table fully elsewhere and deleting its files – either triggered manually, or automatically in case when differential updates in PDTs exceed a RAM threshold and *update propagation* is triggered. For clustered (ordered) tables, all updates (delete, insert, modify) go to PDTs, while for unordered tables inserts are handled as appends. Thus, workloads consisting of consecutive deletes (which are compact in the PDT) and inserts can lead to significant wasted disk space. A second problem is that appending to a table requires opening many files. For example, a table with 100 columns and 10 partitions, at a replication degree R=3, requires 3000 open files.

File-per-partition Layout. It is noteworthy that Hadoop formats such as ORC and Parquet store data of all columns in the same file; their column orientation is to be understood as PAX [1] with a huge block size. For instance, ORC uses 1GB chunks that represent a table slice, in which different segments store the various columns – OLAP queries only need to read these files partially and skip over the column segments that are not needed. Even though the HDFS block size is 128MB or larger, (short-circuit) reads occur on the actual granularity of the IO, i.e. more fine-grained.

To better suit HDFS, a *file-per-partition* VectorH layout

node1	node2	node3	node4
R01 R02 R03	**R04 R05 R06**	**R07 R08 R09**	**R10 R11 R12**
S01 S02 S03	**S04 S05 S06**	**S07 S08 S09**	**S10 S11 S12**
R10a R11a R12a	R01a R02a R03a	R04a R05a R06a	R07a R08a R09a
S10a S11a S12a	S01a S02a S03a	S04a S05a S06a	S07a S08a S09a
R07b R08b R09b	R10b R11b R12b	R01b R02b R03b	R04b R05b R06b
S07b S08b S09b	S10b S11b S12b	S01b S02b S03b	S04b S05b S06b

after node4 failure:

node1	node2	node3	
R01a R02a **R03**	**R04 R05** R06a	**R07 R08 R09**	
S01a S02a **S03**	**S04 S05** S06a	**S07 S08 S09**	
R10 R11 R12	**R01 R02** R03a	R04a R05a **R06**	
S10 S11 S12	**S01 S02** S03a	S04a S05a **S06**	
R07b R08b R09b	R10b R11b R12b	R01b R02b R03b	
S07b S08b S09b	S10b S11b S12b	S01b S02b S03b	
R04b R05b R06b	R07a R08a R09a	R10a R11a R12a	*re-replicated*
S04b S05b S06b	S07a S08a S09a	S10a S11a S12a	*partitions*

Figure 2: Partition Affinity Mapping for the 12 partitions of table R,S before (top) & after (bottom) node4 failure. Responsible partitions in bold; a/b are the second/third copy (R=3).

was introduced: all columns of a table partition are stored in the same file. So, for example, a table with 100 columns and 10 partitions, at a replication degree R=3 leads to 30 HDFS files.

To reclaim unused space VectorH data files are split horizontally, into fixed-size chunks consisting of 1024 blocks, similar to Parquet RowGroups. Each block chunk is stored in a separate HDFS file. Only one block chunk file is open for writing at a time. Block chunks make it possible to write in the middle of a table partition, although only at block chunk boundaries. Thus it becomes possible to free space by deleting a block chunk file when all (or most) of the blocks in it are unused. At the end of an append, though, the last blocks are typically only partially filled. Since blocks are written to files at fixed offsets, these partially filled blocks would use as much space as full blocks. As a solution to this, partial blocks are written to a partial chunk file. A subsequent append merges these blocks with new data into new blocks and then frees the previous partial chunk file.

Instrumenting HDFS Replication. HDFS by default replicates data in R=3 locations, and the default replication policy is that the first copy is stored on the datanode that issues the write, and the two others are determined by the namenode – if the cluster is large and topology information is present, one replica may be in the same rack and the third in a different rack. The HDFS replication policy determines this placement *per file*, hence all the blocks in one file get spread over the same R=3 datanodes. While all SQL-on-Hadoop systems so far have left block placement to HDFS, VectorH specifically influences this.

In VectorH each table partition at any time has one *responsible node*. This assignment is currently semi-static and is changed when a node fails or when the administrator changes the set of nodes across which VectorH is deployed. VectorH strives for a responsibility assignment where all data files of a partition are local to the HDFS datanode which is responsible for it. VectorH tries to achieve this by issuing appends only from the responsible datanode, as by default the first copy ends up with the writer. However, if this datanode goes down or for some other reason is no longer available to VectorH, we have to access the second or third copy of these chunk files, and given the default HDFS replication policy these could be anywhere. Therefore, node failures or changes in the node set used by a SQL-on-Hadoop system will degrade data affinity whenever using the default policy.

To get control over data placement, VectorH instruments the HDFS replication policy for its own files. HDFS allows to register a `BlockPlacementPolicy` class for this, whose method `chooseTarget()` gets a filename as a parameter and delivers a list of datanode names where replicas should be stored. It is called when a client initiates a file append, but also during HDFS re-replication and re-balancing initiated in the background by the namenode. The current VectorH replication policy initially establishes the *affinity* between partitions and nodes by assigning table partitions to all datanodes running VectorH in such a way that each partition gets stored evenly at R different datanodes. Each such partition assignment means that all chunk files of the partition are stored at that particular datanode. Figure 2 shows a *partition affinity mapping* example of tables R and S with 12 partitions (R04 in bold is the primary copy and R04a and R04b its two replicas). As can be seen, the initial affinity mapping performed at table creation forms a round-robin pattern – we discuss node failures in the next section.

Another benefit of explicit locality control is the co-location of table partitions that refer to each other over a declared foreign key. This can be done when the partitioning key of one table includes a foreign key, and the partitioning key of the other table includes the primary key that it refers to, and both tables have the same amount of partitions. In such cases, the foreign key join between these two tables can be performed by just joining the matching partitions, and if these matching partitions happen to be stored on the same HDFS datanodes, no network communication is needed. Indeed, in Figure 2 one can see that matching partitions of tables R,S are always co-located such that the `WHERE R.key = S.key` join in SQL queries can be executed by joining the corresponding partitions on their responsible node.

4. ELASTICITY WITH YARN

Workers and Master. VectorH consists of a set of N Vectorwise processes, called the *worker set* that run on the datanodes of a Hadoop cluster. The VectorH administrator maintains a *list of viable machines* in a configuration file to identify these – this may just be a subset of the whole Hadoop cluster so one can use a set of machines which have the same hardware, as this leads to better parallel query load balancing. Before actually starting these processes, VectorH needs to negotiate with YARN's resource manager where to run, and it ends up using a subset of these machines as its worker set. One of the workers becomes the *session-master*, however this node does not possess any specific data structures, so this role can be easily interchanged. The session master has a coordinating role in transactions, and performs parallel query optimization which includes running a query *scheduler* that performs DBMS workload management, determining the amount of cores and memory it can use. Currently, this is done using a policy where table partition scans are performed at their responsible nodes, and the available amount of cores is divided equally among them.

Out-of-band YARN. The YARN resource manager (RM) administers RAM and CPU resources on a Hadoop cluster, for this purpose a NodeManager (NM) daemon runs on each datanode. Clients communicates with the RM, to start a first process as their ApplicationMaster (AM). Typically, the AM starts further containers (processes) on other nodes by communicating with the NMs, following negotiated resource demands in terms of minimum and maximum (desired) amounts of RAM and cores. YARN can use different scheduling policies, namely the `FairScheduler` and `CapacityScheduler` where the latter assigns resources to multiple queues having different priorities. Newly arriving high-priority jobs may cause running jobs to be *pre-empted* by YARN, first by asking their AMs to decrease resource usage and after a timeout by killing their containers.

While YARN is a great step forward for Hadoop and native applications, SQL-on-Hadoop systems still struggle to fit into its concepts because they are usually long-running processes. Equating YARN job submission to query submission, is not viable because a DBMS needs to run a query on threads in the already active server processes, rather than spawn a separate new process for each query, and furthermore the latency of the YARN protocols is high and would eclipse interactive query running times. Also, even if a Vectorwise process would run in a YARN container, the problem would be that YARN does not allow yet to modify the resources of a container. Stopping and re-starting a Vectorwise container just to e.g. increase its RAM budget would interrupt the running application for tens of seconds and lose the contents of its buffer pool to much performance detriments.

Therefore, VectorH runs processes *out-of-band*, i.e. separate from its containers. The actual containers are dummies that sleep almost constantly, monitoring once in a while the co-located VectorH processes to ping back their live status to YARN and implicitly to VectorH, i.e. VectorH runs a dbAgent process that acts as its YARN client. Instead of running a single container on each datanode with all its RAM and core resources, it typically runs multiple AMs with corresponding containers on the worker set, each allocating a slice of its resources. Hereby, it can gradually increase and decrease its resource usage (start or stop new AMs/slices) over time. YARN pre-emption can even kill containers in which case dbAgent notices this event and then instructs the session master to adjusts its own resource usage accordingly, by changing the configuration of the DBMS workload management (e.g. making queries use less cores and memory, possibly leading to spilling operators).

Min-cost Flow Network Algorithms. When VectorH initially starts, or when it recovers from node failures[4] its dbAgent must select those N machines with most data locality (stored blocks), out of all nodes which are on the viable machine list and which have enough free memory and core resources. To get cluster resource information, dbAgent asks YARN for the *cluster node reports*, and for finding VectorH table partition locality it queries the HDFS Namenode to retrieve *block locations* for the corresponding chunk files. It may happen that there are no such nodes available, in which case the worker set shrinks, which is also the case in the below part of Figure 2.

After establishing the worker set, dbAgent checks which partitions are already local to them. Not all partitions may

[4]Typical VectorH deployments are maximally a few co-located racks, so node failures are rare and recovery is kept simple: the system silently restarts, though users will notice at most a minute of non-responsiveness plus transaction aborts.

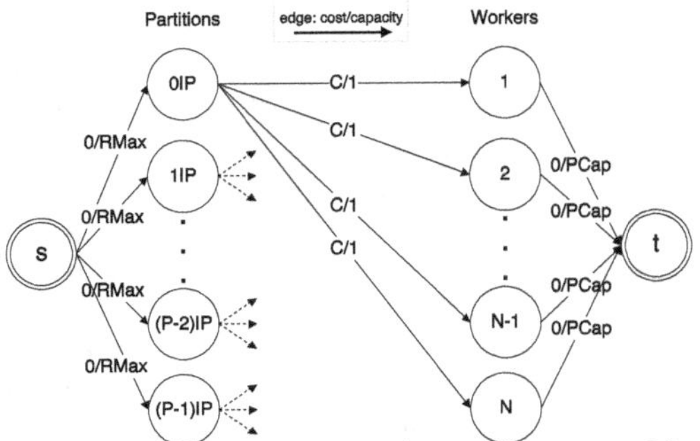

Figure 3: The flow network (bipartite graph) model used to determine the responsibility assignment.

be represented R times already, so the question is which partitions should go where – the resulting *partition affinity map* steers the behavior of the instrumented HDFS `BlockPlacementPolicy` class (and hence re-replication). Figure 2 shows an outcome where partitions 10-12 that were on node4 are re-replicated to node3, 7-9 to node2 and 4-6 to node1.

This mapping can be computed by solving a min-cost matching problem on a network flow where the left side represents the table partitions and the right side the workers, as illustrated in Figure 3 (a related approach was proposed in [15]). From the source (s) to each partition, we create edges with cost 0 and capacity equal to the HDFS replication degree (RMax=R), and we create edges from each partition to each worker with capacity 1 and cost C=0 for local partitions, otherwise C=1. We then create edges from the workers to the destination node (t), assigning a cost 0 and a capacity equal to the amount of partitions each node should store (PCap = #partitions/N).

A final step for dbAgent is to compute the responsibility assignment: which worker is responsible for each partition (i.e. which partitions should be in bold in Figure 2). To assign responsibilities to worker nodes, it runs the same min-cost flow algorithm, with the only difference that the edges from source (s) to each partition have cost 0 and capacity 1. The lower part of Figure 2 shows an example result of this, were node1 becomes responsible for partitions 3,10-12; node2 for 1-2,4-5 and node3 for 6-9 (in bold).

More details about the min-cost algorithms used for (i) worker set selection, (ii) creating the data affinity mapping, (iii) responsibility assignment, and even (iv) run-time query resource scheduling can be found in [5].

Dynamic Resource Management. While VectorH runs, the amount of cores and memory it uses in the query scheduler may change over time – though the worker set currently must stay the same. At startup, VectorH will negotiate with YARN to get to its configured *target* of resources, if this is not possible, it will start nevertheless as long as it gets above a configured minimum. If there are higher-priority jobs, YARN will pre-empt VectorH and reduce its resources, but VectorH will periodically negotiate with YARN to go back to its target resource footprint. Using the *automatic footprint* option, VectorH can also self-regulate its desired core/memory footprint depending on the query workload. In a future release, we intend to also allow to grow and shrink the worker set (not only cores/RAM) dynamically.

In Figure 2 one can see that after the failure of node4, and assuming these nodes have 24 cores, a maximal resource query plan can run on 3x24 cores processing a join query between R and S[5]. If in a future release VectorH would support dynamic shrinking of the worker set, in an idle workload VectorH could shrink to a minimum resource footprint of $\lceil \#nworkers/R \rceil$ and *still* have all table partitions local at the active workers. In the scenario of Figure 2 we could imagine that the partition responsibility assignment is changed such that node1 becomes responsible for all its partitions (all in bold), and node2 and 3 for none of theirs (all a/b versions), as they become inactive workers. A minimal-resource query plan could just use *one thread* at node1 – 72 times fewer resources than the maximal plan.

5. PARALLELISM WITH MPI

The shared-nothing parallelism in VectorH builds on the infrastructure for multi-core parallelism in Vectorwise [2], which is based on *Exchange* (`Xchg`) operators [10]. An `Xchg` operator does not modify the data that streams in and out of it, but only redistributes these streams. It thus encapsulates parallelism, allowing other query operators (scan, select, join, aggregation) to be unaware of it. The different `Xchg` operator flavors are characterized by specific constraints on the numbers of producer/consumer streams and the type of data redistribution performed. For example, `XchgHashSplit` hash-partitions the data from n producer streams to m consumer streams, while `XchgUnion` has a single consumer and there is no data partitioning involved. We also implement `XchgMergeUnion`, `XchgBroadcast` and `XchgRangeSplit`. In our system a stream corresponds to a separate thread that executes some part of an operator pipeline. Consequently, an `Xchg` operator acts as a synchronization point among a number of producer and consumer threads.

This "Volcano" model with `Xchg` operators was adopted in the 1990s by relational DBMS products, which in those days added multi-CPU parallel capabilities to their existing designs, allowing all existing query processing operators to be used as-is. In recent years, new single-server multi-core systems have been presented [20, 19] that have advocated an approach where all relational operators are redesigned to be explicitly aware of parallelism. Ingredients to such designs are fine-grained shared-memory work-queues, NUMA affinity, and lock-avoidance with atomic instructions or -elision with hardware transactional memory. However, when considering MPP parallelism, these approaches do not apply and `Xchg` is still a solid basis for MPP parallelism.

Distributed Exchange. Figure 4 depicts the implementation of a generic Distributed Exchange (`DXchg`) operator with two producer nodes (`n1` and `n2`) and two consumer nodes (`n3` and `n4`). On `n4` there are two threads. For network communication we use MPI (Message Passing Interface), which is extensively used in the high performance computing community and offers a rich and well-defined API for collective and point-to-point communication. It provides a good balance between efficiency (low latency, high throughput), portability across various network fabrics found in Hadoop clusters (e.g. Ethernet, Infiniband) and ease of development and maintenance. Specifically, we use the Intel MPI library, which provides good multi-threading support and in our experience outperforms all alternatives, particularly

[5]Even though each node has 4 primary matching join partitions, these joins can be parallelized 6-way each, over multiple cores to keep all 24 threads busy.

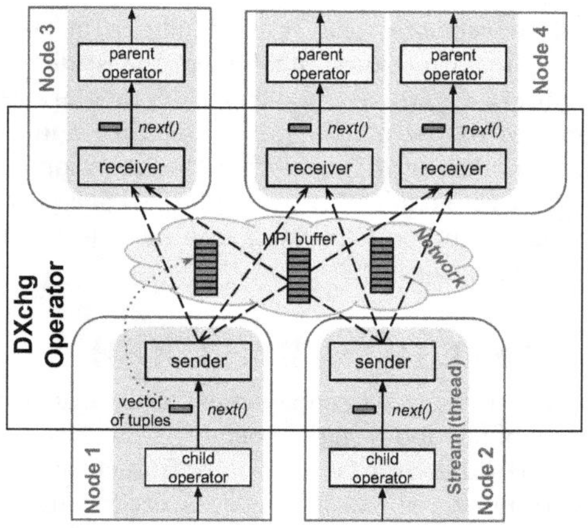

Figure 4: DXchg Operator Implementation

on high-speed Infiniband networks (where MPI provides a native binding, avoiding slow TCP/IP emulation).

`DXchg` producers send messages of a fixed size (>= 256KB for good MPI throughput) to consumers and use double-buffering, such that communication overlaps with processing (i.e. partitioning + serialization). Tuples are serialized into MPI message buffers in a PAX-like layout, such that Receivers can return vectors directly out of these buffers with minimal processing and no extra copying.

It is often the case that the sets of producer and consumer nodes are overlapping, or even the same. As an optimization, for intra-node communication we only send pointers to sender-side buffers in order to avoid the full `memcpy()` that MPI would otherwise need to do behind the scenes.

For the two partitioning `DXchg` variants, `DXchgHashSplit` (DXHS) and `DXchgRangeSplit` (DXRS), the original implementations, described in [7], used a *thread-to-thread* approach. Each `DXchg` sender partitions its own data with a fanout that is equal to the total number of receiver threads across all nodes. For senders to operate independently, they each require *fanout* private buffers. Typically, the nodes in the cluster are homogeneous (same *num_cores*). Hence, the partitioning fanout equates to $num\_nodes * num\_cores$, and considering double-buffering and the fact that each node has *num_cores* `DXchg` threads active, this results in a per-node memory requirement of $2 * num\_nodes * num\_cores^2$. As VectorH gets deployed on larger systems with typically tens and sometimes more than 100 nodes, each having often around 20 cores, partitioning into 100*20=2000 buffers becomes more expensive due to TLB misses. More urgently, this could lead to buffering many GBs ($2*100*20^2*256$KB = 20GB). Not only is this excessive, but the fact that the buffers are only sent when full or when the input is exhausted (the latter being likely in case of 20GB buffer space per node, leading also to small MPI message sizes) can make `DXchg` a materializing operator, reducing parallelism.

Therefore, we implemented a *thread-to-node* approach, where rather than sending MPI messages to remote threads directly, these get sent to a node, reducing the fanout to *num_nodes* and the buffering requirements to $2*num\_nodes*num\_cores$. The sender includes a one-byte column that identifies the receiving thread for each tuple. The exchange receiver lets consumer threads selectively consume data from incoming buffers using the one-byte-column. The *thread-to-node* `DXchg` is more scalable than the default implementation, yet on low core counts and small clusters the *thread-to-thread* implementation is still used as it has a small performance advantage there.

Query Optimization. Currently it is the session-master which parallelizes incoming queries. In the future, it will be relatively easy to distribute this work over all worker nodes at least for read-queries, but given that updates need some form of central coordination, and the fact that analytical workloads have only a limited query throughput, we settled for this centralized approach for now. Most query optimization changes were made in the Parallel Rewriter that already existed in Vectorwise for single-server query parallelization [2]. It performs cost-based optimization using a dynamic programming algorithm, and a simple cost model based on the cardinality estimates taken from the serial plan. A *state* in this search space is a tuple consisting of a physical operator label x, some structural properties sp and a current level of parallelism pl: $s = (x, sp, pl)$. For each such state, we define as $c(s)$ the best (estimated) cost of a parallel query plan for the sub-tree rooted at x that satisfies the structural data properties sp such that exactly pl[6] streams consume the output of x. The structural properties used in VectorH are partitioning (guarantees that two tuples with the same value on a set of keys will be output by the same stream) and sorting (guarantees that tuples from each stream are sorted on some other keys). The aim is thus to find $c(s = (root, \emptyset, 1))$ where *root* is the full query tree.

The Parallel Rewriter contains a collection of rewrite rules that transform a state in a different state. We give three examples for *MergeJoin*. The first adds an *XchgHashSplit* on top and from a state $s_1 = (mj, partitioned[keys], pl)$ recurses into $s'_1 = (mj, \emptyset, pl)$, relaxing the requirement for partitioning since *XchgHashSplit* (on [*keys*]) takes care of it. The second adds an *XchgUnion*[pl] when at a state $s_2 = (mj, \emptyset, 1)$ and therefore recurses into $s'_2 = (mj, \emptyset, pl)$. A final transformation just recurses into mj's children from $s_3 = (mj, \emptyset, 1)$ into $s'_3 = (child_1, sorted[keys], 1)$ and $s''_3 = (child_2, sorted[keys], 1)$. More details on the dynamic programming algorithm to traverse this search space is in [2].

The initial MPP prototype of VectorH [7] modified the Parallel Rewriter to (i) make *pl* a list (instead of an integer) that contains the current parallelism level per node, (ii) adapting transformations to introduce *distributed* `Dxchg` rather than local `Xchg` operators and (iii) adapting the cost model for these operators. This was sufficient since the initial prototype assumed the presence of a global distributed file system without table partitioning, where everybody can read everything at equal IO cost. This was a simplifying assumption only, and is invalid in HDFS even though that *is* a global distributed filesystem, since tables have affinities to datanodes. Moreover, with the introduction of hash-partitioned tables in VectorH there appeared a number of new optimization opportunities, e.g. certain group by/join queries on the partition key can be executed without `Dxchg` operations. The Parallel Rewriter aims to avoid communication at all cost, and appropriately adds a high cost for `Dxchg` operators in its model. Finally, with the addition of trickle updates on partitioned tables, ensuring data locality for update operators becomes a requirement rather than an optimization opportunity as will be discussed in Section 6.

Detecting locality. We will illustrate some of the VectorH-

[6]This number is always smaller than the maximum level of parallelism granted to a query by the scheduler.

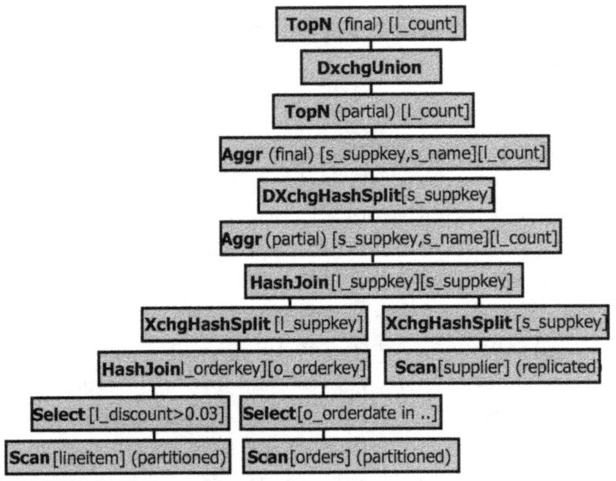

Figure 5: Example Distributed Query Plan

specific transformations through a query on the TPC-H schema, on tables `lineitem` partitioned by `l_orderkey`, `orders` partitioned by `o_orderkey` and `supplier` non-partitioned (i.e. replicated):

```
SELECT FIRST 10 s_suppkey, s_name, count(*) as l_count
FROM   lineitem, orders, supplier
WHERE l_orderkey=o_orderkey AND l_suppkey=s_suppkey AND
      l_discount>0.03 AND
      o_orderdate BETWEEN '1995-03-05' AND '1997-03-05'
GROUP BY s_suppkey, s_name
ORDER BY l_count
```

The distributed plan that VectorH generates is shown in Figure 5. The only network communication is high up in the query tree (the `DXchg` operator), namely splitting *s_suppkeys* that match all the predicates and communicating partial results before selecting the top 10 suppliers. The Parallel Rewriter finds this plan using transformations like:

- **local join**: the opportunity to `HashJoin` the matching partitions of `lineitem` and `orders` is detected by tracking the origins the join keys, detecting that the tables are partitioned on the join key.
- **replicate build side of a join**: in the `HashJoin` with `supplier`, we detect that the build side of the join operates entirely on replicated tables, and thus splits both sides of the join only *locally* (between threads on the same node). A variant of this would be to forgo splitting and build a shared hash table – the decision between these is made based on cost.
- **partial aggregation**: before the `DXchgHashSplit` required by the `Aggr` on `s_suppkey` (and `s_name` but Vectorwise knows it is functionally determined), it is often better to aggregate locally first. Rather than letting each thread aggregate its stream locally, on medium-cardinality aggregations, inserting a local `Xchg` has the effect of bringing together more duplicate keys, and thus further reducing the amount of data that needs to be sent. This strategy is detected here, but VectorH also detects that a `XchgHashSplit` does not need to be inserted below the `Aggr` as the stream is already partitioned on `s_suppkey` at that point.

With all three rules applied, on a 6-node cluster with Infiniband 40Gbit/s for TPC-H SF-500 VectorH runs the example query in 5.02s. Without partial aggregation this is 5.64s; and without replication in the build 5.67s. The biggest effect is from local joins: without this, performance deteriorates to 25.51s; whereas without any of these rewrites it is 26.14s.

Some of the changes that were made to accommodate these new transformations augmented the state structure by (i) adding a *replicated* boolean field to mark that the entire sub-tree rooted at the state's operator will be replicated on all nodes, by (ii)extending the partitioning structural property to include also a mapping of each partition to streams/nodes[7] and (iii) marking whether the partitioning property is partial or not.

6. TRANSACTIONS IN HADOOP

Vectorwise transaction management is described in [12], and consists of the following elements:

- as described in Section 3, updates (insert,modify,delete) are administered as differences, stored in a Positional Delta Tree (PDT) that is kept for each table (partition) in RAM. Not all updates go to PDTs, large inserts to unordered tables are appended directly on disk.
- PDTs can be stacked (differences on differences on .. on a table). Isolation is provided by sharing among all queries a slow-moving large *Read-PDT* that contains direct differences to a persistent table and stacked on that a smaller *Write-PDT* that contains differences to the Read-PDT. When it starts, a transaction creates an empty private *Trans-PDT* stacked on top it all.
- while a transaction runs, it gathers changes w.r.t. the transaction start in the Trans-PDT. This provides *snapshot isolation*, since commits by concurrent transactions make a copy-on-write of the master Write-PDT. If such a situation occurs, the old master Write-PDT is freed as soon as all transactions referencing it finish.
- when a transaction commits, its Trans-PDT is *serialized* to the global database state, which may have advanced in the meantime. PDT serialization not only transforms the Trans-PDT contents but implements *optimistic concurrency control* as it will detect write-write conflicts at the tuple granularity. Such conflicts, if present, force the transaction to abort.
- during commit, which happens atomically (globally locked), the serialized Trans-PDT is written into a Write Ahead Log (WAL) for persistence, and its changes are *propagated* into the master Write-PDT; this makes the system reach the new database state that new incoming transactions will see. The changes from Write-PDT are propagated to the Read-PDT when the size of the Write-PDT reaches a certain threshold.

Vectorwise uses a single, global, WAL that is also used to log other meta-data, such as DDL commands, the creation and deletion of blocks in column files, and changes to the contents of MinMax indexes.

Distributed Transactions in VectorH. We now summarize how VectorH builds on this for distributed transaction management. Since the PDTs store all committed updates in RAM and grow over time, holding them in memory on all nodes would not scale. Rather than a single WAL, VectorH uses table partition-specific WALs, and only the node that is *responsible* for a table partition (see Sections 3 and 4) reads

[7]Was needed to ensure correctness in situations where responsibilities change over time or where the number of threads allocated to a query does not match the number of table partitions. This also has the added benefit of being flexible in concurrency scenarios, i.e. #partitions is not strongly tied to parallelism level

this WAL at startup, keeps the respective PDTs in memory, and writes to it as part of the commit sequence. Update queries get a distributed query plan that ensures that each table partition is updated at its responsible node, and hence modifies PDTs on the right node, or if applicable, performs HDFS appends to the right datanode.

VectorH introduces 2PC (2-Phase Commit) to ensure ACID properties for distributed transactions, where a much-reduced global WAL is written to by the session-master, who coordinates transaction processing. The fact that HDFS is a distributed filesystem, and any worker can read (and potentially write) this global WAL means that the role of session-master can be taken over by any other worker in case of session-master failure.

Log Shipping. Not all VectorH tables are partitioned: typically, small tables will not use partitioning and these can be scanned and cached in the buffer pool by all workers (therefore we consider them as "replicated"). All workers need to read their PDTs from their WALs on startup (replicated PDTs) and keep them in RAM in order to ensure that table scans on these see the latest image. The commit protocol was extended with *log-shipping* for these replicated tables, such that all changes to them are broadcast during transaction processing to all workers, who then can apply the changes (i.e., to the replicated PDTs). We could alternatively have forced a query plan that executes updates on replicated tables to replicate this work on all nodes. However, log-shipping consumes less resources and, in the future, we plan to allow nodes that have a table partition HDFS-local but are *not* responsible for it, to also participate in query processing – for increased parallelism and better load-balancing. For this functionality, the responsible node will have to ship its log actions to the (R-1) nodes that also store the table-partition. Hence, log-shipping is useful. The log actions sent over the network use the same format as in the on-disk transaction log, and are applied in a manner similar to the replay of transaction log on startup, allowing reuse of existing code and the testing infrastructure.

Update Propagation. The in-memory PDT structures cannot grow forever. Vectorwise implements a background process called *update propagation* that is responsible for flushing PDTs to the compressed column store. Update propagation is triggered based on the size of PDTs as well as the fraction of tuples that reside in memory. The latter policy cares for high performance of table scans, which are affected by merging of the on-disk data with PDT data. The internal storage of PDTs is column-wise, as this improves memory access locality and saves bandwidth in table scans. We found that in practice inserts account for most of the PDT volume. To make update propagation more efficient, VectorH introduces an algorithm that is able to separate tail inserts from other types of updates. It also provides a query option whereby inserts to unordered tables, which normally would be direct appends, get buffered as PDT inserts, as for very small inserts this provides better performance (no IO). In a future release, this decision should become automatic. Deletes are stored efficiently in PDTs, especially for contiguous ranges of deleted tuples, while modifies often concern only one column. Flushing tail inserts only creates new data blocks and does not modify existing ones. Other kinds of updates require re-compression of existing blocks and can be flushed with a lower frequency. In future releases we will exploit the horizontally fragmented table partitions, in block chunk files (see Section 3); making the decision for each chunk-file to either (i) re-write it in a new file with the PDT changes applied and delete the old one or (ii) to avoid rewriting it if there are few updates on it – moving these updates to the new PDTs, rather than fully emptying them.

Referential Integrity. The ability to perform concurrent updates is provided for schemas with an enforced unique key or foreign key constraint as well. It must not be allowed for two transactions to insert the same key if an unique key is defined. If the table is partitioned and the partition key is a subset of the unique key, VectorH verifies such constraints by performing node-local verification only. Foreign key constraints also prohibit inserting keys that do not exist in the referenced table or have been concurrently deleted from the referenced table. If one of the involved tables is non-partitioned (i.e. replicated), typically the smaller referenced side, all nodes have a replica of committed PDTs and it is possible to find possible conflicts if all nodes execute the verification. If both tables are partitioned, and co-located at their responsible nodes, VectorH again performs quick node-local verification. The default policy for integrity constraints that cannot be checked without communication is to reject concurrent updates – though this policy may be refined in a future release. However, this policy covers all typical cases, as it is the most natural to partition data on the primary key and the foreign key referencing it.

MinMax Indexes. MinMax indexes are small table summaries kept for each table partition; it conceptually divides a table in a limited number of large tuple ranges, where for each range it keeps the Min and Max value of each column. Whereas ORC and Parquet store this information inside their file format, VectorH stores this information separately as part of the WAL. The rationale is that MinMax information is intended to help prevent data accesses, therefore it is better to store it separately from that data. Because on VectorH only the responsible nodes have this information, yet during query optimization this information is consulted (e.g. by the Parallel Rewriter), a MPI network interface was developed to allow MinMax indexes to be consulted remotely. This interface was engineered such that it is possible to resolve all MinMax information needed for an entire query (which may involve multiple selection predicates on multiple tables) in a single network interaction. MinMax information is relatively easy to maintain: deletes are ignored, and for inserts and modifies the Min and Max extremes can just be widened using the new values, without need to scan the old values in the table. MinMax indexes are rebuilt from scratch as part of update propagation, which happens in distributed fashion in VectorH already.

7. CONNECTIVITY WITH SPARK

Vectorwise has a `vwload` loader utility for bulk-loading. It provides a range of features enabling users to load from a variety of input files and handle errors in a flexible way. For example, it allows to specify custom delimiters, load only a subset of columns from the input file, perform character set conversion, use custom date formats, skip a number of errors, log rejected tuples to a file, etc. VectorH extends `vwload` with a capability to load data from HDFS in parallel. To achieve high efficiency its functionality was moved into a *vwload* operator that runs directly inside the VectorH server.

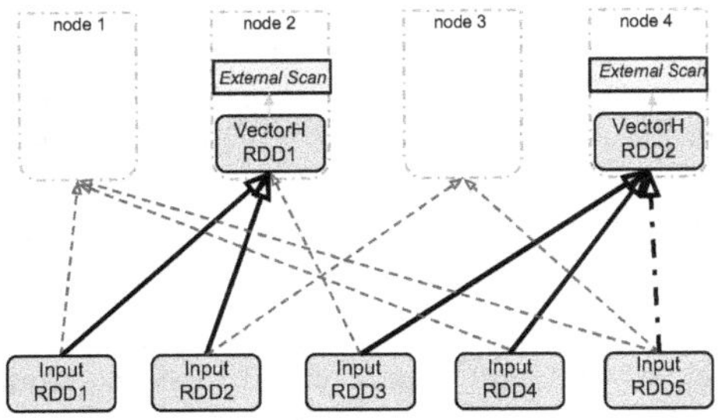

Figure 6: Mapping Spark RDDs to VectorH RDDs and ExternalScan operators

Spark-VectorH Connector. SparkSQL [3] is a module built on top of Apache Spark that enhances it with relational processing capabilities. It has seen increasing popularity among data scientists because of its versatility and tight integration with various systems from the Hadoop ecosystem, Parquet, Avro or Hive to name a few. In early 2015, its Data Source API was released, providing users with the ability to develop their own data source that can export data into SparkSQL, but that can also ingest data from SparkSQL into another database system.

For this connector some new operators were needed in VectorH: `ExternalScan` is an operator that is able to process binary data coming from multiple network sockets (in parallel) and `ExternalDump` that is able to output binary data in parallel through network sockets. Using these operators, we were able to implement (i) the `insert()` and the (i) `buildScan()` methods of the `BaseRelation` interface exposed by the Data Source API. A prerequisite for improved performance was to implement our own `VectorH RDD` which extended Spark's RDD (Resilient Distributed Dataset) interface. This new RDD has exactly as many partitions as `ExternalScan/ExternalDump` operators and overrides the `getPreferredLocations()` method in order to specify the affinity of each RDD partition to the location (hostname) of its corresponding `ExternalScan/ExternalDump` operator. Consequently, we instruct Spark's scheduler where to process those `VectorH RDD` partitions to get local Spark-VectorH transfers. Finally, we add a `NarrowDependency` between the `VectorH RDD` and its parent RDD that defines the mapping between parent RDD partitions and `VectorH RDD` partitions, using an algorithm similar to Hopcroft-Karp's matching in bipartite graphs. Figure 6 shows an Input RDD with 5 partitions mapped to 2 VectorH `ExternalScan` operators on 4 nodes. Each input partition has an affinity to exactly two nodes (e.g. HDFS blocks in a scenario where replication is set to R=2). The dashed arrows represent these affinities, the solid arrows represent assignments that respect affinity, while the dot-dash arrow represent assignments that are forced to ignore affinity information (and therefore possibly incur network communication).

We are currently able to ingest data into VectorH coming from arbitrary Spark sources: files stored in formats like Parquet, Avro, ORC, etc, but also perform complex computation in Spark and only load the transformed data into VectorH. Furthermore, a SparkSQL user can perform computations in Spark on data read (and possibly filtered) from VectorH. A benefit of loading data into VectorH from Spark is that Spark(SQL) creates one RDD partition per input HDFS block. In scenarios where VectorH and Spark run on the same set of nodes, we can instrument assignments in such a way that all blocks are read locally with short-circuit HDFS reads. This is in contrast with the standard `vwload` utility, which typically reads remote blocks over HDFS.

Performance. We tested loading 650GB in 72 CSV input files with 10 uniformly distributed integer columns into VectorH on the same 6-node cluster used for the experiment in Figure 5. Using the `vwload` utility this takes 1237 seconds. However, by distributing the CSV input files in HDFS such that each node has 12 of them local and tweaking with the parameter order in `vwload` to make the VectorH load operators only read local files, this is reduced to 850 seconds. Using the Spark-VectorH Connector, this works out-of-the-box in 892 seconds, which is impressive given that the data is read and parsed in a different process.

8. EVALUATION IN TPC-H SF1000

We evaluated the performance of VectorH on a Hadoop cluster on the TPC-H dataset benchmark scale-factor 1000[8] and compare it with the latest version of Impala, Apache Hive, HAWQ and SparkSQL. The cluster consists of 10 nodes with Hadoop 2.6.0 (Cloudera Express 5.5.0) installed. One node runs runs the Hadoop namenode and other services (Cloudera Manager, etc), so we used the remaining 9 machines for the SQL-on-Hadoop experiments. The nodes all have two Intel Xeon E5-2690 v2 CPUs, at 3.00GHz, totaling 20 real cores (40 hyper-threading) and have 256GB RAM (1866 MT/s). Each node has a 10Gb Ethernet card, 24 magnetic disks of 600GB (2.5inch 10K RPM) one holding the OS (CentOS 6.6) and the others for data/HDFS.

VectorH. We tested a pre-release version of VectorH 5.0, built with Intel MPI 5.1.1. Our DDL resembles that used in previous audited TPC-H runs of Vectorwise (Actian Vector): it declares all primary and foreign keys, except for a PK on `lineitem`. Clustered indexes are defined for `region` and `part` on their primary keys; `orders` is clustered on `o_orderdate`, and `lineitem`, `partsupp` and `nation` are clustered on their foreign keys `l_orderkey`, `ps_partkey` and `n_regionkey`, respectively. We also partition `lineitem` and `orders` on `l_orderkey` and `o_orderkey` respectively, as well as `part` and `partsupp` on `p_partkey` and `ps_partkey` respectively, as well as `customer` on `c_custkey` This partitioning scheme, which in all cases uses 180 partitions, means that joins between `lineitem` and `orders` as well as `part` and `partsupp` are co-located mergejoins. The clustered indexes cause selections on date (of any kind) to enable data skipping thanks to MinMax indexes. Total data size was 327GB (in between Parquet at 347GB and ORC at 327GB – both using snappy compression), and thus I/O plays no role. VectorH is CPU-bound on TPC-H, though in Q16 we measured 45% network cost, in Q2,5,10,14,15 around 30% and in Q13,20,22 around 20%, caused by exchange operators with all-to-all communication.

Impala. We tested Impala 2.3 with the official Cloudera TPC-H queries[9], which are more recent than those used in [8]. `lineitem` and `orders` were partitioned by `l_shipdate` and `o_orderdate`, respectively, to trigger Impala's partition

[8]This evaluation does not represent an official score, is not audited, and we omit overall TPC-H metrics. All DDLs and SQL queries are at: **https://github.com/ActianCorp/VectorH-sigmod2016**

[9]github.com/cloudera/Impala/blob/34dc5bd210ddb7af23735f831033d769b0134821/testdata/workloads/tpch

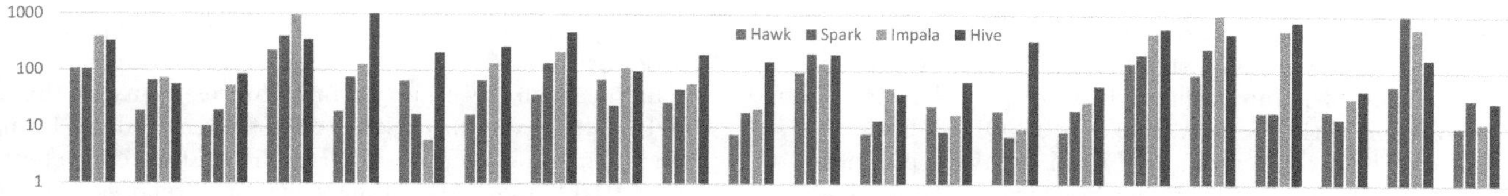

	Q1	Q2	Q3	Q4	Q5	Q6	Q7	Q8	Q9	Q10	Q11	Q12	Q13	Q14	Q15	Q16	Q17	Q18	Q19	Q20	Q21	Q22
VectorH	**1.5**	**1.14**	**3.16**	**0.17**	**1.94**	**0.31**	**2.75**	**1.31**	**11.11**	**1.21**	**1.69**	**0.34**	**3.66**	**0.83**	**1.63**	**1.68**	**1.24**	**0.99**	**1.32**	**2.15**	**1.48**	**2.84**
HAWQ	158.2	21.46	32.06	38.21	36.38	20.19	44.74	48.38	766.4	32.97	12.48	31.75	27.97	19.47	31.58	14.17	173.2	87.08	24.82	42.84	84.7	29.44
SparkSQL	155.4	74.98	62.38	68.27	146.5	5.1	180.2	174.6	264.0	56.62	30.28	66.97	47.65	6.92	11.16	33.81	244.9	254.7	24.89	31.56	1614	91.18
Impala	585.4	81.81	167.7	163.18	242.5	1.81	369.0	276.2	1242.9	69.97	35.04	45.67	180.8	13.95	15.19	47.52	581.53	1234	714.7	74.25	880.8	34.81
Hive	490.1	63.57	266.6	59.08	DNF	63.63	721.8	625.6	1077	230.5	246.1	65.78	140.7	53.23	556.5	92.51	711.7	454.5	1010	100.5	247.7	81.11
after executing updates: Hive: RF1=34s RF2=112s **GeoDiff=138.2%** - VectorH: RF1=17.8s RF2=8.4s **GeoDiff=102.8%**																						
VectorH	1.68	0.94	3.21	0.23	1.9	0.27	2.74	1.4	11.62	1.21	1.44	0.37	3.9	0.81	1.57	1.64	1.27	0.95	1.5	2.25	1.78	2.82
Hive	608.4	80.8	335.7	205.4	DNF	128.0	690.7	719.8	1150	334.4	218.7	170.5	143.8	130.7	596.7	101.4	891.2	594.6	1167	153.3	275.6	67.85

Figure 7: Table: TPC-H SF1000 results (seconds). Chart: How many times faster is VectorH?

pruning. In Q19 predicate pushdown is not working, which appears to be a known issue.

Hive. We tested Apache Hive 1.2.1 using all available performance optimizations such as the Tez execution engine, vectorization, predicate pushdown, cost-based optimizer and correlation optimizer [13]. We used ORC file with Snappy compression. Partitioning with *bucketing* allows Hive to use local joins and improves performance of a number of queries. The tables are bucketed by the same keys as in the VectorH schema, which leads to the same co-locations. We tuned Tez and YARN, so the number of containers is equal to the number of cores and all RAM is used. Also, we tuned the split size: one mapper is scheduled per container, so the map phase ends in a single wave. The reduce phase uses Hive's auto reducer parallelism feature.

We found some problems: Q5 did not finish in 2 hours, and in Q17 the correlation optimization did not trigger, so lineitem gets scanned twice. Finally, we found that decimal types in columns such as `l_extendedprice`, `l_discount` and `l_tax` are much slower than 32-bit floats; however we used decimals to be fair with the other systems and because the rounding errors inherent to floating point arithmetic are not acceptable in business queries on monetary values.

HAWQ. We tested Apache HAWQ 1.3.1, with 10 segments per node, each with 21GB vmem limit, 12GB for work memory, 6GB for query statements, 256MB shared buffers; merge join optimizations were also enabled. The table schemas were taken from Pivotal[10], in which Parquet storage with snappy compression for the `LINEITEM` and `ORDERS` tables is used. We tried to further improve the performance by partitioning `LINEITEM` and `ORDERS` on dates with 1 month intervals, but this just slowed down many queries.

SparkSQL. We tested SparkSQL 1.5.2 with Parquet storage and snappy compression, and partitioned on `o_orderdate` and `l_shipdate`. SparkSQL was configured to cache tables in RM when possible. Most queries had to be re-written to avoid IN/EXISTS/NOT EXISTS subqueries. Also, some of the queries generated Cartesian Products and had to be manually rewritten to explicitly define the join order.

Results. The total database sizes achieved are 340GB (ORC), 347GB (Parquet) and 364GB (VectorH); showing that applying general-purpose compression to all data (ORC and Parquet use Snappy), which adds significant decompression cost to all table scans, does not provide much extra space savings over doing this only for non-dictionary compressed string columns (VectorH uses LZ4 in this case). VectorH provides interactive performance on TPC-H and is at least one order of magnitude faster than the competition, but sometimes two or even three. HAWQ has the richest physical design options, and is a bit faster than the other competitors (nearest is SparkSQL). We attribute the large difference to VectorH to its PostgreSQL-based query engine, which cannot compete with a modern vectorized engine in terms of CPU efficiency (e.g. see Q1). Impala performance mostly suffers from its single-core join and aggregation processing.

Impact of Updates. Apart from VectorH only Hive allows updates; this results behind-the-scenes in additional delta tables for deletions, insertions, and modifications that must be merged transparently during *all subsequent queries*. This merging can have a cost, which we measure by comparing the geometric mean of the 22 queries before and after ("GeoDiff") the TPC-H refresh functions RF1 (inserts) and RF2 (deletes). Hive query performance after these updates deteriorates to be 38% slower than before. In VectorH, the GeoDiff is 2.8%, which is in range of noise. Therefore, thanks to PDTs, query performance remains unaffected by updates.

9. RELATED WORK

VectorH builds on previous work in high-performance vectorized query engine [27], parallel query optimization using `Xchg` operators [2], the preceding Vectorwise MPP project [7], and a study into creating an elastic DBMS in YARN [5].

The Hadoop formats ORC and Parquet, borrow some ideas from Vectorwise's PFOR, PFOR-DELTA and PDICT compression schemes [28], but are also influenced by Google's Dremel [18] which popularized a nested object format – nested columnar formats as these allow fast mergejoin-like navigation, and putting multiple tables in one file makes colocation easy in distributed environments. An interesting future direction is to use the join-index update algorithms described in the Positional Delta Trees thesis [11] to support updates on such nested columnar formats efficiently. Our micro-benchmarks as well as source-code inspection of the ORC and Parquet readers across the tested systems found these to be unnecessarily inefficient, in their implementation of skipping as well as decompression (e.g., routine use of expensive general-purpose compression such as Snappy as well as tuple-at-a-time bitwise value decoding instead of doing so in vectorized manner exploiting SIMD) [25].

VectorH is the first SQL-on-Hadoop system that instruments HDFS block placement to ensure co-located table par-

[10]github.com/pivotalguru/demos/tree/master/TPC-H%20Benchmark

titions even as HDFS block distribution evolves over time – though the idea of instrumenting HDFS was proposed to co-locate separate column files in [9]. HAWQ [6] has in common with VectorH that it is a SQL-on-Hadoop system that evolved from an analytical database product (i.e. Greenplum). It provides richer SQL feature support and a more mature optimizer [22] than the "from-scratch" efforts SparkSQL[3], Impala [24] and Hive [13]. However, HAWQ cannot do deletes and modifications to HDFS-resident data as it lacks a differential update mechanism like PDTs, and while all other tested systems can deal with failing nodes quite transparently, manual segment recovery is needed in HAWQ. Our performance tests with these competing systems conform with those in [8], though the newer versions of Hive and Impala we tested need fewer reformulated SQL queries to run TPC-H, showing optimizer progress.

Impala shares certain virtues of VectorH, such as out-of-band YARN integration through its Llama component [16], and a modern query engine – in its case using JIT compilation [24]. Here, each operator is compiled in isolation and passes *tuple buffers* from its child-, and to its parent-operators in the pipeline, on each `next()` call. Similar to vectorization, these `next()` calls are thus amortized over many tuples, and intermediate data is stored in memory – posssibly CPU cache resident. Impala's *operator-template-based* JIT compilation is much easier to write, test and maintain than the more efficient *data centric* compilation proposed in HyPer [19] that fuses all operators in a pipeline into a single tight loop, avoiding in-memory materialization of intermediates – these stay in CPU registers. Further, Impala does not have co-located table partitioning, or control over HDFS placement, regularly suffers from low-quality query optimization, and lacks multi-core parallelism.

Recently, an early version of VectorH [11] was benchmarked on TPC-H SF100 against a distributed version of HyPer [21], that proposes full communication multiplexing, where all threads funnel their outgoing data through a single multiplexer, to spread the data according to destination and push it onto a high-speed RDMA network. The experimental results differ from our measurements here due to the small dataset and early demo version of VectorH used, yet such work in the direction of network shuffling optimization is of immediate interest for VectorH, whose scalability sweetspot we soon intend to improve from tens to hundreds of machines. We did not benchmark against distributed HyPer here because it does not work in Hadoop – where high-end RDMA network hardware is seldomly available.

10. CONCLUSION

VectorH is a new SQL-on-Hadoop system built on the fast analytical Vectorwise technology. It raises the bar in SQL-on-Hadoop systems in terms of mature SQL support on many dimensions, elasticity in full cooperation with YARN, updatability powered by Positional Delta Trees (PDTs) and absolute performance. In our TPC-H evaluation against Impala, Hive, HAWQ and SparkSQL on TPC-H, VectorH proved to be 1-3 orders of magnitude faster, thanks to a combination of lightweight compression, effective MinMax skipping, vectorized execution, data partitioning and clustered indexing, control over HDFS block locality, a well-tuned query optimizer and efficient multi-core parallel execution.

In the future, we aim to integrate elements of the VectorH data layout in existing open-source Hadoop formats. For the integration of VectorH in the Hadoop ecosystem beyond HDFS and YARN, the focus is on extending the Spark-VectorH connector into a seamless external tables, UDF and query pushdown facility integrated with Spark.

[11]The development code-name of VectorH was "Vortex" – this name is used to identify the system in [21].

11. REFERENCES

[1] A. Ailamaki, D. DeWitt, M. Hill, and M. Skounakis. Weaving relations for cache performance. In *PVLDB*, 2001.

[2] K. Anikiej. Multi-core parallelization of vectorized query execution. *MSc thesis, VU University*, 2010.

[3] M. Armbrust, R. Xin, et al. Spark SQL: Relational data processing in Spark. In *SIGMOD*, 2015.

[4] P. Boncz, M. Zukowski, and N. Nes. MonetDB/X100: hyper-pipelining query execution. In *CIDR*, volume 5, 2005.

[5] C. Bârcă. Dynamic Resource Management in Vectorwise on Hadoop. *MSc thesis, VU University Amsterdam*, 2014.

[6] L. Chang, Z. Wang, T. Ma, L. Jian, L. Ma, A. Goldshuv, L. Lonergan, et al. HAWQ: a massively parallel processing SQL engine in hadoop. In *SIGMOD*, 2014.

[7] A. Costea and A. Ionescu. Query optimization and execution in Vectorwise MPP. *MSc thesis, VU University*, 2012.

[8] A. Floratou, U. F. Minhas, and F. Özcan. SQL-on-Hadoop: Full circle back to shared-nothing database architectures. *PVLDB*, 7(12), 2014.

[9] A. Floratou, J. Patel, E. Shekita, and S. Tata. Column-oriented storage techniques for mapreduce. *PVLDB*, 4(7), 2011.

[10] G. Graefe. *Encapsulation of parallelism in the Volcano query processing system*, volume 19. 1990.

[11] S. Héman. *Updating Compressed Column Stores*. PhD thesis, VU University, 2015.

[12] S. Héman, M. Zukowski, N. J. Nes, L. Sidirourgos, and P. Boncz. Positional update handling in column stores. In *SIGMOD*, 2010.

[13] Y. Huai, A. Chauhan, A. Gates, G. Hagleitner, E. Hanson, et al. Major technical advancements in Apache Hive. In *SIGMOD*, 2014.

[14] Y. Huai, S. Ma, R. Lee, O. O'Malley, and X. Zhang. .. table placement methods in clusters. *PVLDB*, 6(14), 2013.

[15] M. Isard, V. Prabhakaran, J. Currey, U. Wieder, K. Talwar, and A. Goldberg. Quincy: fair scheduling for distributed computing clusters. In *SOSP*, 2009.

[16] M. Kornacker et al. Impala: A modern, open-source sql engine for hadoop. In *CIDR*, 2015.

[17] P.-Å. Larson, C. Clinciu, E. Hanson, A. Oks, S. Price, S. Rangarajan, A. Surna, and Q. Zhou. SQL server column store indexes. In *SIGMOD*, 2011.

[18] S. Melnik, A. Gubarev, J. Long, G. Romer, S. Shivakumar, M. Tolton, and T. Vassilakis. Dremel: interactive analysis of web-scale datasets. *PVLDB*, 3(1-2), 2010.

[19] T. Neumann. Efficiently compiling efficient query plans for modern hardware. *PVLDB*, 4(9), 2011.

[20] V. Raman et al. DB2 with BLU acceleration: So much more than just a column store. *PVLDB*, 6(11), 2013.

[21] W. Rödiger, T. Mühlbauer, A. Kemper, and T. Neumann. High-speed query processing over high-speed networks. *PVLDB*, 9(4), 2015.

[22] M. A. Soliman et al. Orca: a modular query optimizer architecture for big data. In *SIGMOD*, 2014.

[23] M. Świtakowski, P. Boncz, and M. Zukowski. From cooperative scans to predictive buffer management. *PVLDB*, 5(12), 2012.

[24] S. Wanderman-Milne and N. Li. Runtime code generation in cloudera impala. *DEBULL*, 37(1), 2014.

[25] S. Whoerl. Efficient relational main-memory query processing for Hadoop Parquet Nested Columnar storage with HyPer and Vectorwise. *MSc thesis, CWI/LMU/TUM/U. Augsburg*, 2014.

[26] M. Zaharia, M. Chowdhury, M. Franklin, S. Shenker, and I. Stoica. Spark: cluster computing with working sets. In *USENIX*, volume 10, 2010.

[27] M. Zukowski. *Balancing Vectorized Query Execution with Bandwidth-Optimized Storage*. PhD thesis, 2009.

[28] M. Zukowski, S. Héman, N. Nes, and P. Boncz. Super-scalar RAM-CPU cache compression. In *ICDE*, 2006.

Appendix

For the perusal of the reader, we provide a graphical performance profile for the SF1000 evaluation by VectorH of TPC-H Q1. This query has a simple plan: **Scan** of **lineitem** followed by **Select** that evaluates a date constraint (99% of tuples qualify) then performs computations in a **Project** on **l_tax**, **l_discount**, **l_extendedprice** etc. followed by GROUP BY aggregation in **Aggr** which produces just 4 groups.

This query is parallelized by putting a **DXchgUnion** (DXU 180:1) on top and then aggregating again.

Between the operators we see arrows with the amount of produced tuples plotted. In the detail-boxes for each operator we also see the amount of tuples going in and out of the operator, as well as the time spent evaluating the operator itself (time) and all time spent in the operator and its children together (cum_time).

Below the DXU there are 180 threads, above just one. The parallel operations in the profile show for each thread the time, cum_time and number of produced tuples, in a graph where on the X-axis every point is a thread (notation **Nxx@yy** means: node **xx**, thread **yy**). Here we see that the query spends most time in the lower **Aggr**, **Project** and **MScan**, which is expected, and there is a slight load balancing problem: cum_time in the parallel **Aggr** varies between 2.95G cycles and 3.64G cycles (20%). Still, the overall performance penalty for this is less than 15%.

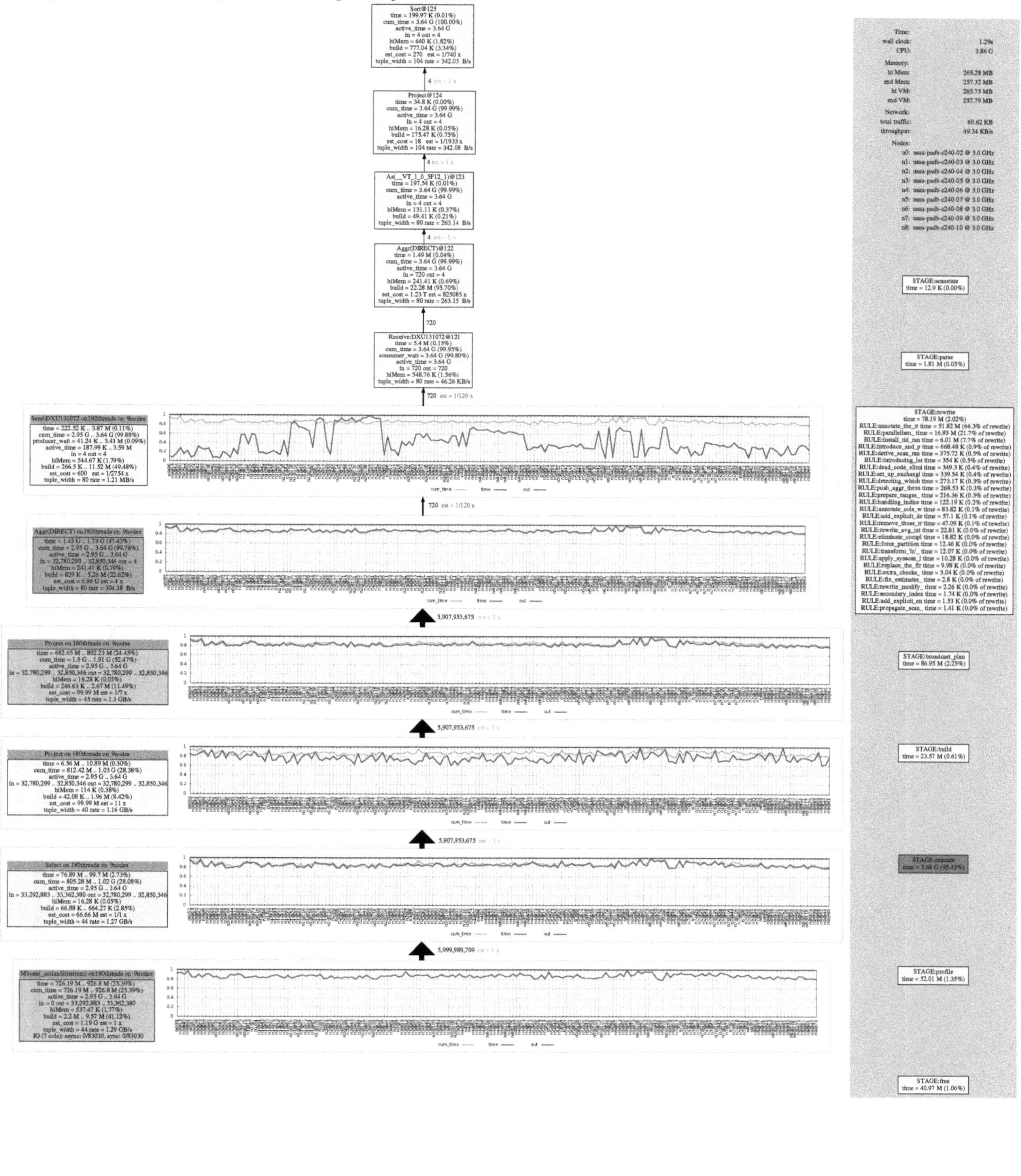

Adaptive Logging: Optimizing Logging and Recovery Costs in Distributed In-memory Databases

Chang Yao[‡] Divyakant Agrawal[♯] Gang Chen[§] Beng Chin Ooi[‡] Sai Wu[§]
[‡]National University of Singapore [♯]University of California at Santa Barbara [§]Zhejiang University
[‡]{yaochang,ooibc}@comp.nus.edu.sg [♯]agrawal@cs.ucsb.edu [§]{cg,wusai}@zju.edu.cn

ABSTRACT

By maintaining the data in main memory, in-memory databases dramatically reduce the I/O cost of transaction processing. However, for recovery purposes, in-memory systems still need to flush the log to disk, which incurs a substantial number of I/Os. Recently, command logging has been proposed to replace the traditional data log (e.g., ARIES logging) in in-memory databases. Instead of recording how the tuples are updated, command logging only tracks the transactions that are being executed, thereby effectively reducing the size of the log and improving the performance. However, when a failure occurs, all the transactions in the log after the last checkpoint must be redone sequentially and this significantly increases the cost of recovery.

In this paper, we first extend the command logging technique to a distributed system, where all the nodes can perform their recovery in parallel. We show that in a distributed system, the only bottleneck of recovery caused by command logging is the synchronization process that attempts to resolve the data dependency among the transactions. We then propose an adaptive logging approach by combining data logging and command logging. The percentage of data logging versus command logging becomes a tuning knob between the performance of transaction processing and recovery to meet different OLTP requirements, and a model is proposed to guide such tuning. Our experimental study compares the performance of our proposed adaptive logging, ARIES-style data logging and command logging on top of H-Store. The results show that adaptive logging can achieve a 10x boost for recovery and a transaction throughput that is comparable to that of command logging.

1. INTRODUCTION

While in-memory databases have been studied since the 80s, recent advances in hardware technology have re-generated interest in hosting the entirety of the database in memory in order to provide faster OLTP and real-time analytics. Simply replacing the storage layer of a traditional disk-based database with memory does not satisfy the real-time performance requirements because of the retention of the complex components from traditional database systems, such as the buffer manager, latching, locking and logging [12, 38, 42]. This calls for re-examination and re-design of many core system components [20, 41]. In this paper, we focus on logging and recovery efficiency in distributed in-memory databases.

SIGMOD'16 June 26 - July 01, 2016, San Francisco, CA, USA

ACM ISBN 978-1-4503-3531-7/16/06.

DOI: http://dx.doi.org/10.1145/2882903.2915208

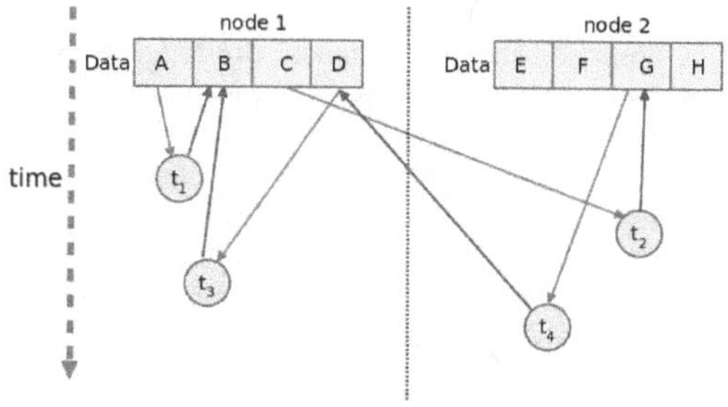

Figure 1: Example of logging techniques

Recovery is an indispensable and expensive process of database systems that ensures updates made by committed transactions before any system crash are reflected in the database after recovery, while updates made by uncommitted transactions are ignored. In an OLTP system, logging for the purpose of recovery affects the system throughput, and recovery affects the system availability and hence its overall throughput. Therefore, efficient logging and recovery are important to the overall performance of an OLTP system. While node failures are infrequent, an increasingly large number of compute nodes in a distributed system inevitably leads to an increase in the probability of node failures [30, 32, 36]. Consequently, increasing number of failed nodes results in higher failure costs as more recoveries are needed. Therefore, providing an effective failure recovery strategy is as imperative as efficient logging for distributed database systems.

The most widely used logging method in conventional databases is the write-ahead log (e.g., ARIES log [23]). The idea is to record how tuples are being updated by the transactions, and we refer to it as the data log in our discussion. Let us consider Figure 1 as an example. There are two nodes processing four concurrent transactions, t_1 to t_4. All the transactions follow the same format:

$$f(x, y) : y = 2x$$

So $t_1 = f(A, B)$, indicating that t_1 reads the value of A and then updates B as $2A$. Since different transactions may modify the same value, a locking mechanism is required. Based on their timestamps, the correct serialized order of the transactions is t_1, t_2, t_3 and t_4. Let $v(X)$ denote the value of parameter X. The ARIES data log of the four transactions are listed as in Table 1.

ARIES log records how the data are modified by the transactions, and supports efficient recovery using the log data when a failure occurs. However, the recovery process of in-memory databases is

Table 1: ARIES log

timestamp	transaction ID	parameter	old value	new value
100001	t_1	B	v(B)	2v(A)
100002	t_2	G	v(G)	2v(C)
100003	t_3	B	v(B)	2v(D)
100004	t_4	D	v(D)	2v(G)

sightly different from that of their disk-based analog. It first loads the database snapshot recorded in the last checkpoint and then replays all the committed transactions in ARIES log. For uncommitted transactions, no roll-backs are required as the corresponding updates are not persistent onto disk yet.

ARIES log is a "heavy-weight" logging method, as it incurs high overhead. In conventional databases, where I/Os for processing transactions dominate the performance, the logging overhead is a small fraction of the overall cost. However, in an in-memory database where all the transactions are processed in memory, logging cost dominates the overall cost.

To reduce the logging overhead, a command logging approach [22] is proposed to only record the transaction information with which transaction can be fully replayed during failure recovery. In H-Store [16], each command log records the ID of the corresponding transaction and the stored procedure that has been applied to update the database along with the input parameters. As an example, the command logging records for Figure 1 are simplified in Table 2.

Table 2: Command log

transaction ID	timestamp	stored procedure pointer	parameters
1	100001	p	A, B
2	100002	p	C, G
3	100003	p	D, B
4	100004	p	G, D

Since all four transactions follow the same routine, we only keep a pointer p to the details of stored procedure: $f(x,y) : y = 2x$. For recovery purposes, we also need to maintain the parameters for each transaction, so that the system can re-execute all the transactions from the last checkpoint when a failure happens. Compared with ARIES-style log, a command log is much more compact and hence reduces the I/O cost for materializing it onto disk. It has been shown that command logging can significantly increase the throughput of transaction processing in in-memory databases [22]. However, the improvement is achieved at the expense of much longer recovery time after a failure since transactions have to be re-executed to recreate the database state.

When there is a node failure, all the transactions have to be replayed in the command logging method, while ARIES-style logging simply recovers the value of each column. Throughout the paper, we use "attribute" to refer a column defined in the schema and "attribute value" to denote the value of a tuple in a specific column. For example, to fully redo transaction t_1, command logging needs to read the value of A and update the value of B, whereas for ARIES logging, we just need to set B's value as $2v(A)$ as recorded in the log file. More importantly, command logging does not support parallel recovery in a distributed system. In command logging [22], command logs of different nodes are merged at the master node during recovery. To guarantee the correctness of recovery, transactions must be reprocessed in a serialized order based on their timestamps. For example, even in a cluster consisting of two nodes, the transactions have to be replayed one by one due to their possible contentions. In the previous example, transaction t_3 and t_4 cannot be concurrently processed by node 1 and 2 respectively, because both transactions need to lock the value of D. There is no such limitation in the ARIES-style logging that actually partitions the log data into different nodes. In Table 1, log records of t_1, t_3 and t_4 are stored in node 1, while the record of t_2 is maintained by node 2. Both nodes can start their recovery process concurrently and independently. All contentions can be resolved locally by each node.

In command logging, a single-node failure will trigger a complete recovery process because we do not know which parts of the updates are lost. For example, if node 2 in Figure 1 fails, both node 1 and node 2 need to roll back and replay transaction t_1 to t_4. Suppose an in-memory database is hosted over hundreds of nodes [1, 3, 26], where failures cannot be assumed as exceptions, command logging could adversely affect the overall system throughput. If ARIES-style log is applied instead, each node maintains all data updates in its local log file. Therefore, we only need to recover the failed node using its own log data and no global recovery is required. In summary, command logging reduces the I/O cost of processing transactions, but incurs a much higher cost for recovery than ARIES-style logging, especially in a distributed environment. To this end, we propose a new logging scheme that achieves a comparable performance as command logging for processing transactions, while enabling a much more efficient recovery. Our logging approach also allows the users to tune the parameters to achieve a preferable trade-off between transaction processing and recovery.

In this paper, we first propose a distributed version of command logging. In the recovery process, before redoing the transactions, we first generate the dependency graph by scanning the log data. Transactions that read or write the same tuple will be linked together. A transaction can be reprocessed only after all its dependent transactions have been committed. On the other hand, the transactions that do not have dependency relationship can be concurrently processed. Based on this principle, we organize the transactions into different processing groups. Transactions inside a group have dependency relationship, while transactions of different groups can be processed concurrently.

While the distributed version of command logging effectively exploits the parallelism among the nodes to speed up recovery, some processing groups could be rather large, causing a few transactions to block the processing of many others. We subsequently propose an adaptive logging approach that adaptively makes use of the command logging and ARIES-style logging. Specifically, we identify the bottlenecks dynamically based on a cost model and resolve them using ARIES logging. We materialize the transactions identified as bottlenecks in ARIES log so that transactions depending on them can be recovered more efficiently. In an extreme case, if all the transactions are identified as bottlenecks, our method spends the same I/O cost as the ARIES logging. However, this will definitely increase the cost of transaction processing. Therefore, our adaptive logging method selectively creates ARIES logs using a cost model based on a given budget. The budget is used as a parameter in adaptive logging for users to tune the trade-off between transaction processing and recovery.

It is indeed very challenging to classify the transactions into the ones that may cause bottleneck and those that will not, because we have to make a real-time decision on adopting either command logging or ARIES logging. During transaction processing, we do not know the impending distribution of transactions, and even if the dependency graph of impending transactions is known beforehand, the optimization problem of log creation remains to be NP-hard. Hence, we propose both offline and online heuristic approaches to derive approximate solutions, by estimating the importance of each transaction based on the access patterns of existing transactions. The offline approach provides the ideal logging plan and is used mainly for comparison in our performance study, while our system uses the online approach.

Finally, we implement our two proposed methods, namely distributed command logging and adaptive logging, on top of H-Store [16] and compare them with `ARIES` logging and command logging. Experimental results show that adaptive logging can achieve a comparable performance for transaction processing as command logging, while it performs 10x faster than command logging for recovery in a distributed system.

The remainder of the paper is organized as follows. We present our distributed command logging method in Section 2 and the new adaptive logging method in Section 3. The experimental results are presented in Section 4 and we review some related work in Section 5. The paper is concluded in Section 6.

2. DISTRIBUTED COMMAND LOGGING

As described earlier, command logging only records the transaction ID, stored procedure and its input parameters [22]. Once failure occurs, the database can restore the last snapshot and redo all the transactions in the command log to re-establish the database state. Command logging operates at a much coarser granularity and writes much fewer bytes per transaction than `ARIES`-style logging. However, the major concern of command logging is its recovery performance.

In H-Store [16] and its commercial successor, VoltDB[1], command logs of different nodes are shuffled to the master node that merges them based on the timestamp order. Since command logging does not record how the data are manipulated in each page, all the transactions must be redone sequentially, incurring a high recovery overhead. An alternative solution is to maintain multiple replicas, so that data on the failed nodes can be recovered from other replicas. However, the drawback of such an approach is twofold. First, maintaining the consistency among replicas incurs a high synchronization overhead and as a consequence slows down the transaction processing. Second, given a limited amount of memory, it is too expensive to maintain replicas in memory, especially when processing large scale dataset. This is confirmed by a performance study of a replication-based technique in Appendix C. In this paper, we shall therefore focus on the log-based approaches.

Even with command logging, it is unnecessary to replay all committed transactions by examining the correlations among transactions. Our intuition is to design a distributed command logging method that enables all nodes to start their recovery in parallel and replay only the necessary transactions.

We first define the correctness of recovery in our system. Suppose the data are partitioned to N cluster nodes. Let $\mathcal{T}$ be the set of transactions since the last checkpoint. For a transaction $t_i \in \mathcal{T}$, if t_i reads or writes a tuple on node $n_x \in N$, n_x is marked as a participant of t_i. Specifically, we use $f(t_i)$ to denote all those nodes involved in t_i and use $f^{-1}(n_x)$ to represent all the transactions in which n_x has participated. In a distributed system, each transaction has a coordinator, typically the node that minimizes the data transfer for processing the transaction. The coordinator schedules the data accesses and monitors how its transaction is processed. Hence, the command log entry is usually created in the coordinator [22]. We use $\theta(t_i)$ to denote t_i's coordinator. Obviously, we have $\theta(t_i) \in f(t_i)$.

Given two transactions t_i, $t_j \in \mathcal{T}$, we define an order function $\prec$ as: $t_i \prec t_j$, only if t_i is committed before t_j. When a node n_x fails, a set of transactions $f^{-1}(n_x)$ need to be redone. But these transactions may compete for the same tuple with other transactions. Let $s(t_i)$ and $c(t_i)$ denote the submission time and commit time of a transaction t_i respectively.

[1]http://voltdb.com/

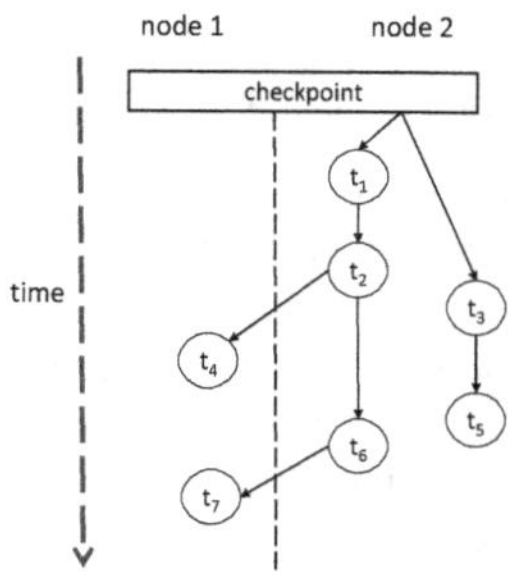

txn	submission time	commit time	stored procedure	parameters
1	1	2	$f_1(p_1)$: $p_1=p_1+1$	x_1
2	2	4	$f_2(p_1,p_2)$: $p_1=p_1-1$, $p_2=p_1+2$	x_1,x_3
3	3	4	$f_3(p_1)$: $p_1=2*p_1$	x_4
4	4	5	$f_4(p_1)$: $p_1=\log(p_1)$	x_3
5	4	5	$f_5(p_1, p_2)$: $p_1=2*p_2$	x_4, x_5
6	5	6	$f_5(p_1, p_2)$: $p_1=2*p_2$	x_6, x_1
7	6	7	$f_1(p_1)$: $p_1=p_1+1$	x_6

Figure 2: A running example

DEFINITION 1. **Transaction Competition**
Transaction t_i competes with transaction t_j, if the two conditions below are satisfied.

1. $s(t_j) < s(t_i) < c(t_j)$.
2. *t_i and t_j read or write the same tuple.*

Accordingly, transaction competition is defined as a unidirectional relationship: t_i competes with t_j, and t_j may compete with the others that may modify the same set of tuples and commit before it. We further let $\odot(t_i)$ be the set of all the transactions that t_i competes with, and define function g for transaction set $\mathcal{T}_j$ as:

$$g(\mathcal{T}_j) = \bigcup_{\forall t_i \in \mathcal{T}_j} \odot(t_i)$$

To recover the database from n_x's failure, an initial recovery set $\mathcal{T}_0^x = f^{-1}(n_x)$ is created and set $\mathcal{T}_{i+1}^x = \mathcal{T}_i^x \cup g(\mathcal{T}_i^x)$. As the number of committed transactions is limited, there exists a minimum number L such that when $j \geq L$, $\mathcal{T}_{j+1}^x = \mathcal{T}_j^x$, and there are no other transactions accessing the same set of tuples since the last checkpoint. We call $\mathcal{T}_L^x$ the complete recovery set for n_x.

Next, we define the correctness of recovery in the distributed system as:

DEFINITION 2. **Correctness of Recovery**
When node n_x fails, all the transactions in its complete recovery set need to be redone by strictly following their commit order, i.e., if $t_i \prec t_j$, then t_i must be reprocessed before t_j.

To recover from a node's failure, our approach needs to retrieve its complete recovery set. For this purpose, it builds a dependency graph.

2.1 Dependency Graph

Dependency graph is defined as a directed acyclic graph $G = (V, E)$, where each vertex in V is a transaction t_i, containing the information about its timestamps ($c(t_i)$ and $s(t_i)$) and coordinator $\theta(t_i)$. t_i has an edge to t_j, if and only if

1. $t_i \in \odot(t_j)$
2. $\forall t_m \in \odot(t_j), c(t_m) < c(t_i)$

For a specific order of transaction processing, there is one unique dependency graph as shown in the following theorem.

THEOREM 1. *Given a transaction set $\mathcal{T} = \{t_0, ..., t_k\}$, where $c(t_i) < c(t_{i+1})$, there exists a unique dependency graph for $\mathcal{T}$.*

PROOF. Since the vertices represent transactions, we always have the same set of vertices for the same set of transactions. We only need to prove that the edges are also unique. Based on the definition, edge e_{ij} exists, only if there exists one set of tuples that are accessed by t_j and updated by t_i and no other transactions that have been committed between t_i and t_j would update the same set of tuples. Therefore, edge e_{ij} is a unique edge between t_i and t_j. □

A running example that illustrates the idea is shown in Figure 2. There are seven transactions since the last checkpoint, aligned based on their coordinators: node 1 and node 2. The transaction IDs, submission times, commit times, stored procedures and parameters are also shown in the table. Based on the definition, transaction t_2 competes with transaction t_1, as both of them update x_1. Transaction t_4 competes with transaction t_2 on x_3. The complete recovery set for t_4 is $\{t_1, t_2, t_4\}$. Note that although t_4 does not access the attribute that t_1 updates, t_1 is still in t_4's recovery set because of the transitive dependency among t_1, t_2 and t_4. After having constructed the dependency graph and generating the recovery set, the failed node can then be recovered adaptively. For example, to recover node 1, we do not have to reprocess transactions t_3 and t_5.

2.2 Processing Group

In order to generate the complete recovery set efficiently, we organize transactions as processing groups. Algorithm 1 and 2 illustrate how the groups are generated from a dependency graph. In Algorithm 1, we start from the root vertex that represents the checkpoint to iterate over all the vertices in the graph. The neighbors of the root vertex are transactions that do not compete with the others. We create one processing group for each of them (line 3-7). *AddGroup* is a recursive function that explores all reachable vertices and adds them into the group. One transaction may exist in multiple groups if more than one transactions compete with it.

Two indexes are built for each processing group. One is an inverted index that supports efficient retrieval of the participating groups of a given transaction. The other index creates a backward link from each transaction to the transactions it competes with. Using these two indexes, it is efficient to generate the complete recovery set for a specific transaction.

Algorithm 1 `CreateGroup(DependencyGraph` G`)`

```
1: Set S = ∅
2: Vertex v = G.getRoot()
3: while v.hasMoreEdge() do
4:     Vertex v0 = v.getEdge().endVertex()
5:     Group g = new Group()
6:     AddGroup(g, v0)
7:     S.add(g)
8: return S
```

Algorithm 2 `AddGroup(Group` g`, Vertex` v`)`

```
g.add(v)
while v.hasMoreEdge() do
    Vertex v0 = v.getEdge().endVertex()
    AddGroup(g, v0)
```

2.3 Algorithm for Distributed Command Logging

When a failure on node n_x is detected, the system stops the transaction processing and starts the recovery process. One new node is started to reprocess all the transactions in n_x's complete recovery set. Since some transactions are distributed transactions involving multiple nodes, the recovery algorithm runs as a distributed process.

Algorithm 3 shows the basic idea of recovery. First, it retrieves all the transactions that do not compete with the others since the last checkpoint (line 3). These transactions can be processed in parallel. Therefore, they would be forwarded to the corresponding coordinators for processing. At each coordinator, Algorithm 4 is invoked to process a specific transaction t. t first waits until all the transactions in $\odot(t)$ are processed. Then it would be processed and all its neighbor transactions are retrieved by following the links in the dependency graph. If t's neighbor transactions are also in the recovery set, *ParallelRecovery* function would be invoked recursively to process them.

THEOREM 2. *Distributed command logging algorithm guarantees the correctness of the recovery.*

PROOF. In Algorithm 3, if two transactions t_i and t_j are in the same processing group and $c(t_i) < c(t_j)$, t_i must be processed before t_j, as we follow the links of dependency graph. The complete recovery set of t_j is the subset of the union of all the processing groups that t_j joins. Therefore, we will redo all the transactions in the recovery set for a specific transaction as in Algorithm 3. □

As an example, suppose node 1 fails in Figure 2. The recovery set is $\{t_1, t_2, t_4, t_6, t_7\}$. t_1 on node 2 is the only transaction that can run without waiting for the other transactions. It will be redone first. Note that although node 2 does not fail, t_1 still needs to be reprocessed, because it affects the correctness when reprocessing the committed transactions on node 1. After t_1 and t_2 commit, the new node that replaces node 1 will reprocess t_4. Simultaneously, node 2 will process t_6 in order to recover t_7. The example shows that compared with the original command logging method, our distributed command logging has the following two advantages:

1. Only the involved transactions need to be reprocessed. Therefore, the recovery processing cost is reduced.

2. Different processing nodes can perform the recovery process concurrently, leveraging the parallelism to speed up the recovery.

Algorithm 3 `Recover(Node` n_x`, DependencyGraph` G`)`

```
1: Set S_T = getAllTransactions(n_x)
2: CompleteRecoverySet S=getRecoverySet(G,S_T)
3: Set S_R = getRootTransactions(S)
4: for Transaction t ∈ S_R do
5:     Node n = t.getCoordinator()
6:     ParallelRecovery(n, S_T, t)
```

2.4 Footprint of Transactions

To reduce the overhead of transaction processing, a dependency graph is built offline. Before a recovery process starts, the dependency graph is built by scanning the logs. For this purpose, we introduce a light weight write ahead footprint log for the transactions. Once a transaction is committed, we record the transaction ID and the involved tuple IDs as its footprint log.

Figure 3 illustrates the structure of footprint log and `ARIES` log. `ARIES` log maintains the detailed information about a transaction, including partition ID, table name, modified column, original value

Algorithm 4 `ParallelRecovery(Node` n_x`, Set` S_T`, Transaction` t`)`

```
while wait(⊙(t)) do
    sleep(timethreshold)
if t has not been processed then
    process(t)
    Set S_t = g.getDescendant(t)
    for ∀t_i ∈ S_t ∩ S_T do
        Node n_i = t.getCoordinator()
        ParallelRecovery(n_i, S_T, t_i)
```

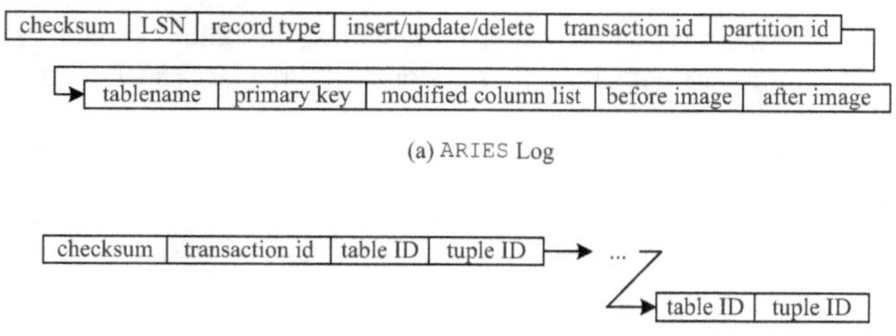

(a) ARIES Log

(b) Footprint Log

Figure 3: ARIES log versus footprint log

and updated value, based on which we can correctly redo a transaction. On the contrary, a footprint log only records IDs of those tuples that are read or updated by a transaction. It consumes less storage space than ARIES log (on average, each record in ARIES log and footprint log require 3KB and 450B respectively on the TPC-C benchmark). The objective of maintaining footprint log is not for recovering the lost transactions, but for building the dependency graph.

3. ADAPTIVE LOGGING

The bottleneck of distributed command logging is caused by the dependencies among the transactions. To ensure consistency [5], transaction t is blocked until all the transactions in $\odot(t)$ have been processed. In an ideal case, where no transactions compete for the same tuple, the maximal parallelism can be achieved by recovering all transactions in parallel. Otherwise, transactions that compete with each other must be synchronized, which significantly slows down the recovery process. If the dependencies among the transactions are fully or partially resolved, the cost of recovery could be effectively reduced.

3.1 The Key Concept

As noted in the introduction, ARIES log allows each node to recover independently. If node n_x fails, all the updates since the last checkpoint would be redone by scanning its log. Recovery with ARIES log does not need to take transaction dependency into account, because the log completely records how a transaction modifies the data. Hence, the intuition of our adaptive logging approach is to combine command logging and ARIES logging. For transactions that are highly dependent on the others, ARIES logs are created to speed up their reprocessing during the recovery. For other transactions, command logging is applied to reduce the logging overhead at runtime.

For the example shown in Figure 2, if ARIES log has been created for t_7, there is no need to reprocess t_6 during the recovery of node 1. Moreover, if ARIES log has been created for t_2, the recovery process just needs to redo t_2 and then t_4 rather than starting from t_1. For the recovery of node 1, only three transactions, namely $\{t_2, t_4, t_7\}$, need to be re-executed. To determine whether a transaction depends on the results of other transactions, we need a new relationship in addition to the transaction competition to describe the causal consistency [5].

DEFINITION 3. **Time-Dependent Transaction**
Given two transaction t_i and t_j, t_j is t_i's time-dependent transaction, if and only if

1. $c(t_i) > c(t_j)$
2. *t_j updates an attribute a_x of tuple r that is accessed by t_i*
3. *there is no other transaction with commit time between $c(t_i)$ and $c(t_j)$ that also updates $r.a_x$*

Let $\otimes(t_i)$ denote all the time-dependent transactions of t_i. For transactions in $\otimes(t_i)$, their time-dependent transactions can also be found recursively, denoted as $\otimes^2(t_i) = \otimes(\otimes(t_i))$. This process continues until it finds the minimal x satisfying $\otimes^x(t_i) = \otimes^{x+1}(t_i)$. $\otimes^x(t_i)$ represents all the transactions that must run before t_i to guarantee the causal consistency. In a special case, if transaction t_i does not compete with the others, it does not have time-dependent transactions (namely, $\otimes(t_i) = \emptyset$) either. $\otimes^x(t_i)$ is a subset of the complete recovery set of t_i. Instead of redoing all the transactions in the complete recovery set, t_i can be recovered correctly by only reprocessing the transactions in $\otimes^x(t_i)$.

If some transactions in $\otimes^x(t_i)$ are adaptively selected to create ARIES logs, the recovery cost of t_i can be effectively reduced. In other words, if ARIES log is created for transaction $t_j \in \otimes^x(t_i)$, $\otimes(t_j) = \emptyset$ and $\otimes^x(t_j) = \emptyset$, because t_j can now be recovered by simply loading its ARIES log since it does not depend on the results of the other transactions.

More specifically, let $A = \{a_0, a_1, ..., a_m\}$ denote the attributes that t_i needs to access. These attributes may come from different tuples. Let $\otimes(t_i.a_x)$ represent the time-dependent transactions of t_i that have updated a_x. Therefore, $\otimes(t_i) = \otimes(t_i.a_0) \cup ... \cup \otimes(t_i.a_m)$. To formalize the usage of ARIES log in reducing the recovery cost, we introduce the following lemmas.

LEMMA 1. *If an ARIES log has been created for $t_j \in \otimes(t_i)$, transactions t_l in $\otimes^{x-1}(t_j)$ can be discarded from $\otimes^x(t_i)$, if*

$$\nexists t_m \in \otimes(t_i), t_m = t_l \vee t_l \in \otimes^{x-1}(t_m)$$

PROOF. The lemma states that all the time-dependent transactions of t_j can be discarded, if they are not time-dependent transactions of the other transactions in $\otimes(t_i)$, which is obviously true. □

The above lemma can be further extended for an arbitrary transaction in $\otimes^x(t_i)$.

LEMMA 2. *Suppose an ARIES log has been created for transaction $t_j \in \otimes^x(t_i)$ that updates attribute set $\bar{A}$. Transaction $t_l \in \otimes^x(t_j)$ can be discarded, if*

$$\nexists a_x \in (A - \bar{A}), t_l \in \otimes^x(t_i.a_x)$$

PROOF. Since t_j updates $\bar{A}$, all the transactions in $\otimes^x(t_j)$ that only update attribute values in $\bar{A}$ can be discarded without violating the correctness of causal consistency. □

Lemma 2 shows that the time-dependent transactions of t_j are not necessary in the recovery process, if they are not time-dependent transactions of any attribute in $(A - \bar{A})$. Recovery of the values of attribute set $\bar{A}$ for t_i can start from t_j's ARIES log by redoing t_j, and then all the transactions with timestamps falling in the range $(c(t_j), c(t_i))$ that also update $\bar{A}$. To simplify the presentation for the time being, we use $\phi(t_j, t_i, t_j.\bar{A})$ to denote these transactions.

Finally, we summarize our observations as the following theorem, based on which we design our adaptive logging and the corresponding recovery algorithm.

THEOREM 3. *Suppose* ARIES *logs have been created for transaction set $\mathcal{T}_a$, to recover t_i, it is sufficient to redo all the transactions in the following set.*

$$\bigcup_{\forall a_x \in (A - \bigcup_{\forall t_j \in \mathcal{T}_a} t_j.\bar{A})} \otimes^x(t_i.a_x) \cup \bigcup_{\forall t_j \in \mathcal{T}_a} \phi(t_j, t_i, t_j.\bar{A})$$

PROOF. t_i can be recovered correctly by redoing all its time-dependent transactions from the latest checkpoint. Based on Lemma 1 and Lemma 2, the number of redoing transactions can be reduced by creating ARIES logs. The first term of the formula represents all the transactions that are required to recover attribute values in $(A - \bigcup_{\forall t_j \in \mathcal{T}_a} t_j.\bar{A})$, while the second term denotes all those transactions that we need to recover from ARIES logs following the timestamp order. □

3.2 Logging Strategy

By combining ARIES logging and command logging into a hybrid logging approach, the recovery cost can be effectively reduced. Users should first specify an I/O budget $B_{i/o}$ according to their requirements. With a given I/O budget $B_{i/o}$, our adaptive approach selects the transactions for ARIES logging to maximize the recovery performance. This decision of which type of logs to create for each transaction has to be made during transaction processing. However, since the distribution future of transactions cannot be known in advance, it is impossible to generate an optimal selection. In fact, even if we know all the future transactions, the optimization problem is still NP-hard.

Let $w^{aries}(t_j)$ and $w^{cmd}(t_j)$ denote the I/O costs of ARIES logging and command logging for transaction t_j respectively. We use $r^{aries}(t_j)$ and $r^{cmd}(t_j)$ to represent the recovery cost of t_j regarding to the ARIES logging and command logging respectively. If an ARIES log is created for transaction t_j that is a time-dependent transaction of t_i, the recovery cost is reduced by:

$$\Delta(t_j, t_i) = \sum_{\forall t_x \in \otimes^x(t_i)} r^{cmd}(t_x) - \sum_{\forall t_x \in \phi(t_j, t_i, t_j.\bar{A})} r^{cmd}(t_x) - r^{aries}(t_j) \quad (1)$$

If ARIES logs are created for more than one transactions in $\otimes^x(t_i)$, $\Delta(t_j, t_i)$ should be updated accordingly. Let $\mathcal{T}_a \subset \otimes^x(t_i)$ be the set of transactions with ARIES logs. We define an attribute set:

$$p(\mathcal{T}_a, t_j) = \bigcup_{\forall t_x \in \mathcal{T} \wedge c(t_x) > c(t_j)} t_x.\bar{A}$$

$p(\mathcal{T}_a, t_j)$ represent the attributes that are updated after t_j by the transactions with ARIES logs. Therefore, $\Delta(t_j, t_i)$ is adjusted as

$$\Delta(t_j, t_i, \mathcal{T}_a) = \sum_{\forall t_x \in \otimes^x(t_i) - \mathcal{T}_a} r^{cmd}(t_x) - r^{aries}(t_j) - \sum_{\forall t_x \in \phi(t_j, t_i, t_j.\bar{A} - p(\mathcal{T}_a, t_j))} r^{cmd}(t_x) \quad (2)$$

DEFINITION 4. **Optimization Problem of Logging Strategy** *For transaction t_i, find a transaction set $\mathcal{T}_a$ to create* ARIES *logs so that:*

$$\textit{maximize} \sum_{\forall t_j \in \mathcal{T}_a} \Delta(t_j, t_i, \mathcal{T}_a) \text{ s.t. } \sum_{\forall t_j \in \mathcal{T}_a} w^{aries}(t_j) \le B_{i/o}$$

We note that the single transaction optimization problem is analogous to the 0-1 knapsack problem, while the more general case is similar to the multi-objective knapsack problem. It becomes more complicated when function Δ is also determined by the correlations of transactions. We therefore design both offline and online heuristic methods to derive approximate solutions.

3.2.1 *Offline Algorithm*

We first introduce our offline algorithm designed for the ideal case, where the impending distribution of transactions is known. The offline algorithm is only used to demonstrate the basic idea of adaptive logging, while our system employs its online variant. $\mathcal{T}$ is used to represent all the transactions from the last checkpoint to the point of failure.

For each transaction $t_i \in \mathcal{T}$, the benefit of creating ARIES log is computed as:

$$b(t_i) = \sum_{\forall t_j \in \mathcal{T} \wedge c(t_i) < c(t_j)} \Delta(t_i, t_j, \mathcal{T}_a) \times \frac{1}{w^{aries}(t_i)}$$

Initially, $\mathcal{T}_a = \emptyset$.

The transactions are sorted based on their benefit values. The one with the maximal benefit is selected and added to $\mathcal{T}_a$. All the transactions update their benefits accordingly based on Equation 2. This process continues until

$$\sum_{\forall t_j \in \mathcal{T}_a} w^{aries}(t_j) \le B_{i/o}$$

Algorithm 5 outlines the basic idea of the offline algorithm.

Algorithm 5 `Offline(TransactionSet` $\mathcal{T}$`)`

```
Set T_a = ∅, Map benefits;
for ∀t_i ∈ T do
    benefits[t_i] = computeBenefit(t_i)
while getTotalCost(T_a)< B_i/o do
    sort(benefits)
    T_a.add(benefits.keys().first())
return T_a
```

Since Algorithm 5 needs to re-sort all the transactions after each update to $\mathcal{T}_a$, the complexity of the algorithm is $O(l^2)$, where l is the number of transactions. In practice, full sorting can be avoided in most of the cases, because $\Delta(t_i, t_j, \mathcal{T}_a)$ should be recalculated only if both t_i and t_j update a value of the same attribute.

3.2.2 *Online Algorithm*

Our online algorithm is similar to the offline algorithm, except that it must choose either ARIES logging or command logging in real-time. Since the distribution of future transactions is unknown, we use a histogram to approximate the distribution. In particular, for all the attributes $A = (a_0, ..., a_k)$ involved in transactions, the number of transactions that read or write a specific attribute value is recorded. The histogram is used to estimate the probability of accessing an attribute a_i, denoted as $P(a_i)$. Note that attributes in A may come from the same tuple or different tuples. For tuple v_0 and v_1, if both $v_0.a_i$ and $v_1.a_i$ appear in A, they will be recorded as two different attributes.

In the previous discussion, we use $\phi(t_j, t_i, t_j.\bar{A})$ to denote the transactions that commit between t_j and t_i and also update some attributes in $t_j.\bar{A}$. We are now ready to rewrite it as:

$$\phi(t_j, t_i, t_j.\bar{A}) = \bigcup_{\forall a_i \in t_j.\bar{A}} \phi(t_j, t_i, a_i)$$

Similarly, let $S = t_j.\bar{A} - p(\mathcal{T}_a, t_j)$. The third term in Equation 2 can be computed as:

$$\sum_{\forall t_x \in \phi(t_j, t_i, S)} r^{cmd}(t_x) = \sum_{\forall a_x \in S} \Big(\sum_{\forall t_x \in \phi(t_j, t_i, a_x)} r^{cmd}(t_x) \Big)$$

During the processing of transaction t_j, the number of the future transactions that are affected by the results of t_j and the cost of recovering a future transaction using command log are both unknown. Therefore, we use a constant R^{cmd} to denote the average recovery cost of command logging. Then the above Equation can be simplified as:

$$\sum_{\forall t_x \in \phi(t_j, t_i, S)} r^{cmd}(t_x) = \sum_{\forall a_x \in S} (P(a_x) R^{cmd}) \quad (3)$$

The first term in Equation 2 estimates the cost of recovering t_j's time-dependent transactions using command logging. It can be efficiently computed in real-time if we maintain the dependency graph. Therefore, by combining Equation 2 and Equation 3, the benefit $b(t_i)$ of a specific transaction can be estimated during online processing. Supposing ARIES logs already have been created for the transactions in $\mathcal{T}_a$, the benefit should be updated based on Equation 2.

The last problem is how to define a threshold γ to trigger the creation of ARIES log for a transaction when its benefit is greater than the threshold. Let us consider an ideal case. Suppose the node fails while processing t_i and an ARIES log for t_i has been created. This log achieves the maximal benefit that can be estimated as:

$$b_i^{opt} = (\mathbb{N} R^{cmd} \sum_{\forall a_x \in A} P(a_x) - R^{aries}) \times \frac{1}{W^{aries}}$$

where $\mathbb{N}$ denotes the number of transactions committed before t_i, and R^{aries} and W^{aries} are the average recovery cost and I/O cost of an ARIES log respectively.

Suppose the occurrence of failure arbitrarily follows a Poisson distribution with parameter λ. That is, the expected average failure time is λ. Let $\rho(\lambda)$ be the number of committed transactions before the failure. So the possibly maximal benefit is:

$$b^{opt} = (\rho(\lambda) R^{cmd} \sum_{\forall a_x \in A} P(a_x) - R^{aries}) \times \frac{1}{W^{aries}}$$

We define our threshold as $\gamma = \alpha b^{opt}$, where α is a tunable parameter.

Given an I/O budget, approximately $\frac{B_{i/o}}{W^{aries}}$ ARIES log records can be created. As failures may happen randomly at anytime, the log should be evenly distributed over the timeline. More specifically, the cumulative distribution function of the Poisson distribution is

$$P(fail\_time < k) = e^{-\lambda} \sum_{i=0}^{\lfloor k \rfloor} \frac{\lambda^i}{i!}$$

Hence, at the k-th second, we can maximally create

$$quota(k) = P(fail\_time < k) \frac{B_{i/o}}{W^{aries}}$$

ARIES log records. At runtime, the system should check whether it still has the quota for ARIES log. If not, no more ARIES logs will be created.

Finally, the idea of online adaptive logging scheme is summarized in Algorithm 6.

Algorithm 6 Online(Transaction t_i, int $usedQuota$)

```
int q = getQuota(s(t_i))- usedQuota
if q > 0 then
   Benefit b=computeBenefit(t)
   if b > τ then
      usedQuota++
      createAriesLog(t_i)
   else
      createCommandLog(t_i)
```

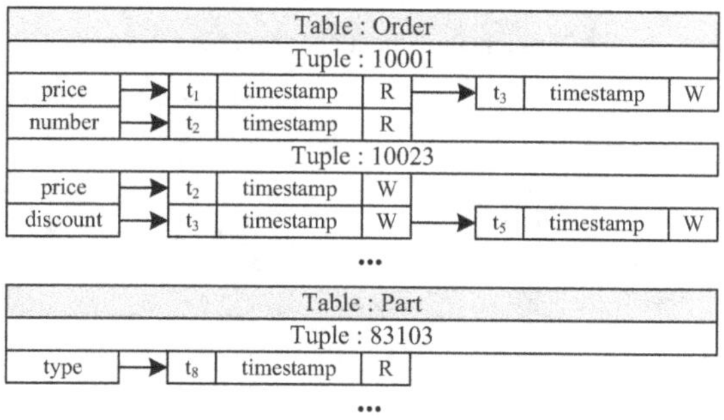

Figure 4: In-memory index

3.3 In-Memory Index

To help compute the benefit of each transaction, an in-memory inverted index is created in our master server. Figure 4 shows the structure of the index. The index entries are organized by table ID and tuple ID. For each specific tuple, we record the transactions that read or write its attributes. As an example, in Figure 4, transaction t_2 reads the *number* of tuple 10001 and updates the *price* of tuple 10023.

By using the index, the time-dependent transactions of a transaction can be efficiently retrieved. For transaction t_5, let A_5 be the attributes that it accesses. The recovery process searches the index to retrieve all the transactions that update any attribute in A_5 before t_5. In Figure 4, because the *discount* value of tuple 10023 is updated by t_5, we check its list and find that t_3 updates the same value before t_5. Therefore, t_3 is a time-dependent transaction of t_5. In fact, the index can also be employed to recover the dependency graph of transactions.

When a transaction is submitted to the system, its information is inserted into the in-memory index. We maintain the index in memory for the following reasons.

1. The index construction should not slow down the transaction processing.

2. The index is small as it only records the necessary information for causal consistency.

3. If the master server fails and the index is lost, system can retain the correctness of transaction processing unaffected, but the performance may be affected. We evaluate such performance impact in Appendix E.1.

Since the in-memory index is used mainly for estimation purpose, it is unnecessary to enforce the index in the master node to be strictly consistent. Therefore, in our current implementation, each processing node caches its in-memory index which is synchronized with that in the master node periodically. We provide more detailed discussion in Appendix D.5.

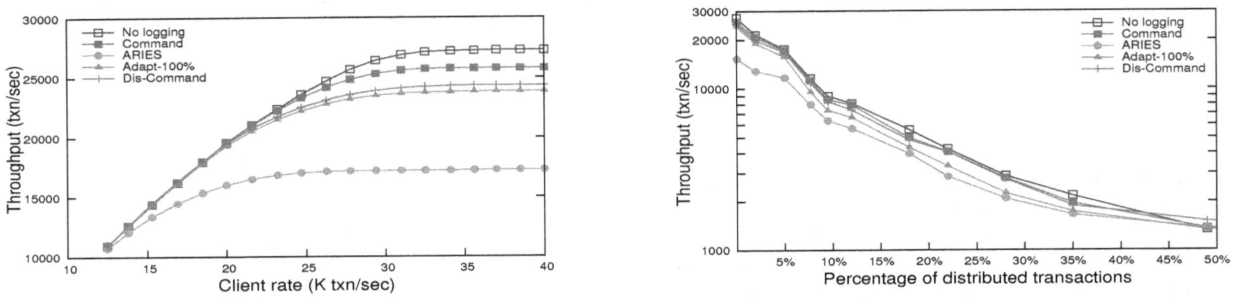

(a) Throughput without distributed transactions

(b) Throughput with distributed transactions (with log scale on y-axis)

Figure 5: Throughput evaluation on the TPC-C benchmark

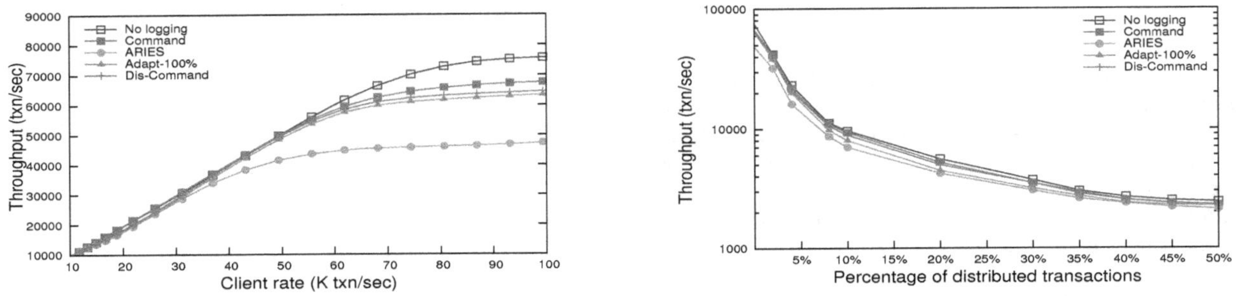

(a) Throughput without distributed transactions

(b) Throughput with distributed transactions (with log scale on y-axis)

Figure 6: Throughput evaluation on the Smallbank benchmark

4. EXPERIMENTAL EVALUATION

In this section, we conduct a runtime cost analysis of our proposed adaptive logging, and compare its query processing and recovery performance against two existing logging methods. Since both traditional ARIES logging and command logging are already supported by H-Store, for consistency, we implement our distributed command logging and adaptive logging methods on top of H-Store as well. For ease of explanation, we adopt the following notations to represent the methods used in the experiments.

- **ARIES** – ARIES logging.
- **Command** – command logging proposed in [22].
- **Dis-Command** – distributed command logging method proposed in Section 2.
- **Adapt-x** – adaptive logging method proposed in Section 3. The x indicates the percentage of distributed transactions for which ARIES logs are created. There are two special cases. For x = 0%, adaptive logging is the same as distributed command logging. For x = 100%, adaptive logging adopts a simple strategy: ARIES logging for all distributed transactions and command logging for all single-node transactions.

All the experiments are conducted on an in-house cluster of 17 nodes. The head node is a powerful server equipped with an Intel(R) Xeon(R) 2.2 GHz 24-core CPU and 64 GB RAM. The compute nodes are blades, each with an Intel(R) Xeon(R) 1.8 GHz 4-core CPU and 8 GB RAM. H-Store is deployed on a cluster of 16 compute nodes with the database being partitioned evenly. Each node runs a transaction site. As a default setting, only eight sites in H-Store are used in all the experiments, except in the scalability experiment (and the replication experiment in Appendix C). We use the TPC-C benchmark[2] and the Smallbank benchmark [6], with 100 clients running concurrently in the head node and each submitting its transaction requests one by one.

[2]http://www.tpc.org/tpcc/

4.1 Throughput

We first compare the costs of different logging methods at runtime. For the TPC-C benchmark, we use the number of New-Order transactions processed per second as the metric to evaluate the impact of different logging methods on the system throughput. To study the behavior of different logging methods, we adopt two workloads: one contains local transactions only, and the other contains the mix of local and distributed transactions.

Figure 5a and Figure 6a show the throughput with different logging methods when only local transactions are involved. The client rate is defined as the total number of transactions submitted by all the clients per second. It varies from 10,000 transactions per second to 40,000 (resp. 100,000) transactions per second with the TPC-C (resp. SmallBank) workload in Figure 5a (resp. Figure 6a). When the client rate is low (e.g., 10,000 transaction per second), the system is not saturated and all the incoming transactions can be completed within a bounded waiting time. Although different logging methods incur different I/O costs, all the logging methods show a fairly similar performance due to the fact that I/O is not being the bottleneck. However, as the client rate increases, the system with ARIES logging saturates at around the input rate of 20,000 transactions per second for the TPC-C benchmark and around 60,000 transactions per second for the Smallbank benchmark. The other three methods, namely adaptive logging, distributed logging and command logging, reach the saturation point at around 30,000 transactions per second and 90,000 transactions per second on the TPC-C benchmark and the Smallbank benchmark respectively, which are slightly lower than the ideal case (represented as the no logging method). The throughput of distributed command logging is slightly lower than that of command logging. This is primarily due to the overhead of footprint log used in distributed command logging.

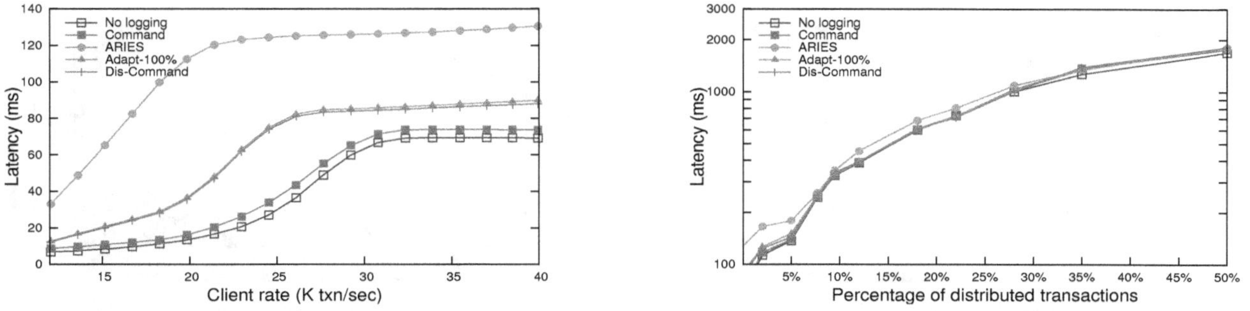

(a) Latency without distributed transactions

(b) Latency with distributed transactions (with log scale on y-axis)

Figure 7: Latency evaluation on the TPC-C benchmark

Figure 5b and Figure 6b show the throughput variation (with log scale on y-axis) when distributed transactions are involved. We saturate the system by setting the client rate to 30,000 and 90,000 transactions per second for the TPC-C benchmark and the Smallbank benchmark respectively. Meanwhile, we vary the percentage of distributed transactions from 0% to 50% so that the system performance is affected by both network communications and logging. To process distributed transactions, multiple sites have to cooperate with each other, and as a result, the coordination cost rises with the increased amount of participating sites. To guarantee the correctness at the commit phase of distributed transaction processing, all the methods adopt the two-phase commit protocol implemented in H-Store. Unlike the pure local transaction processing as shown in Figure 5a and Figure 6a, the main bottleneck of distributed processing gradually shifts from logging to network communication. Compared with a local transaction, a distributed transaction incurs additional network overhead and this reduces the effect of the logging cost.

As shown in Figure 5b, when the percentage of distributed transactions is less than 30%, the throughput of the three other logging strategies are still 1.4x higher than ARIES logging. In this experiment, the threshold x of adaptive logging is set to 100%, where the ARIES logs are created for all the distributed transactions. This is for evaluating the throughput in the worst case when adaptive logging is adopted.

As a matter of design, command logging is more suitable for local transactions with multiple updates, while ARIES logging is preferred for distributed transaction with few updates [22]. However, since the workload may change over time, neither command logging nor ARIES logging can fully satisfy all the access patterns. In contrast, our proposed adaptive logging can adapt to the dynamic change of the workload properties (e.g., distribution of the local/distributed transactions).

4.2 Latency

The average latency of different logging methods is expected to increase along the increment of client rate. Figure 7a shows that the latency of distributed command logging is slightly higher than that of command logging. However, it still performs much better than ARIES logging. Like other OLTP systems, H-Store first buffers the incoming transactions in a transaction queue, and then its transaction engine dequeues and processes them in order. H-Store adopts the single-threaded transaction processing mechanism, where each thread is responsible for a distinct partition so that no concurrency control needs to be enforced for the local transactions within the partition. When the system becomes saturated, newly arrived transactions need to wait in the queue, leading to the increment of latency.

Typically, before a transaction commits at the server side, all its log entries have to be flushed to disk; after it commits, the server sends the response information back to the client. Similarly, our proposed distributed command logging materializes the command log entries and footprint log before a transaction commits. Once a transaction completes, it compresses the footprint log, which contributes to a slight delay in response. However, the penalty becomes negligible over a large number of distributed transactions as the network overhead dominates the cost. This is confirmed by the results shown in Figure 7b (with log scale on y-axis), that with an increasing number of distributed transactions, the impact on latency contributed by logging becomes secondary.

4.3 Recovery

In the next set of experiments, we evaluate the recovery performance with respect to different logging methods. We simulate two scenarios of failures. In the first scenario, we run the system for one minute and then shut down an arbitrary site to trigger the recovery process. In the second scenario, each site processes at least 30,000 transactions before a random site is purposely terminated so that the recovery algorithm can be invoked. In both scenarios, we measure the time span for recovering the failed site.

The recovery times of all methods except ARIES logging are affected by two factors, namely the number of committed transactions and the percentage of distributed transactions. Figure 8 and Figure 9 show the recovery times of the four logging methods. Intuitively, the recovery time is proportional to the number of transactions that must be reprocessed upon a failure. For the first scenario of failure and its corresponding results shown in Figure 8a and Figure 9a, we observe that as the percentage of distributed transactions increases, fewer transactions are completed within a given unit of time. The reduction in the number of distributed transactions per fixed unit of time provides an offset to the more expensive recovery of distributed transactions. Consequently, as shown in Figure 8a and Figure 9a, the percentage of distributed transactions does not adversely affect the recovery time. For the second scenario of failure, we require all sites to complete at least 30,000 transactions each, and its results are shown in Figure 8b and Figure 9b. We observe that a higher recovery cost is incurred when there is an increase in the percentage of distributed transactions.

In both scenarios, ARIES logging shows the best recovery performance and is not affected by the percentage of distributed transactions, whereas command logging is always the worst performer. Our distributed command logging significantly reduces the recovery overhead of command logging, achieving a 5x improvement. The adaptive logging further improves the performance by tuning the trade-off between the recovery cost and the transaction processing cost. We provide the detailed analysis as follows.

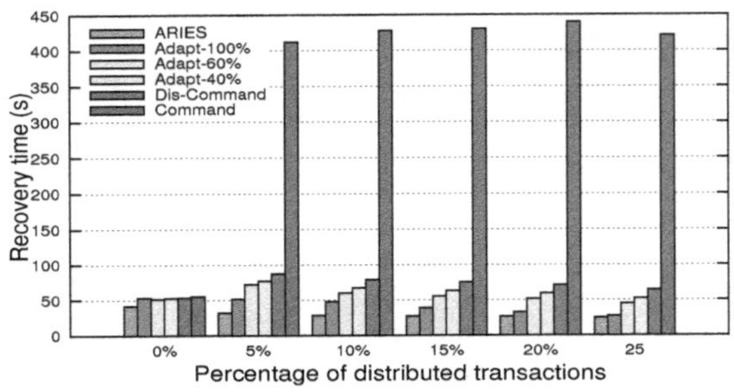

(a) 1 minute after the last checkpoint

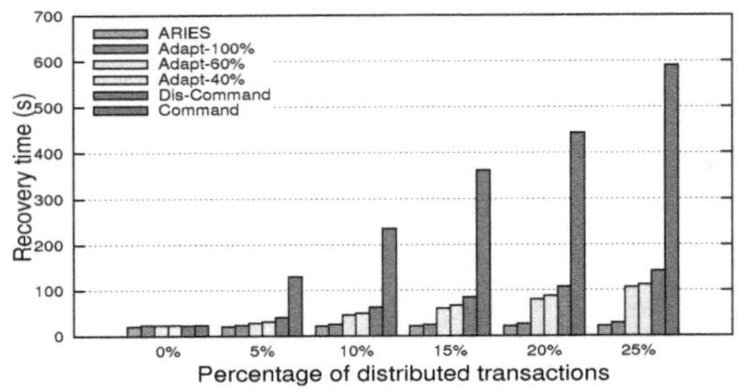

(b) After 30,000 transactions committed at each site

Figure 8: Recovery evaluation on the TPC-C benchmark

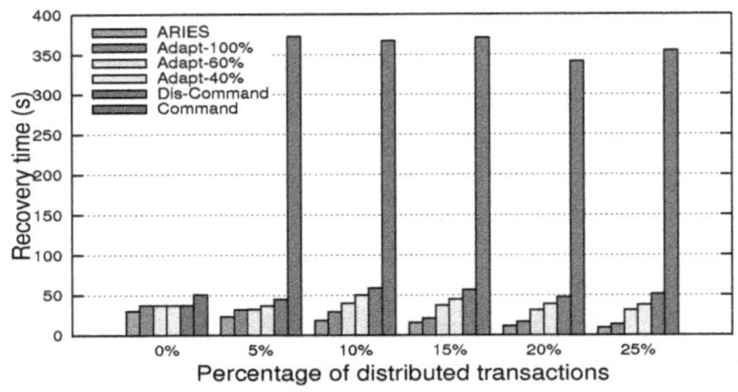

(a) 1 minute after the last checkpoint

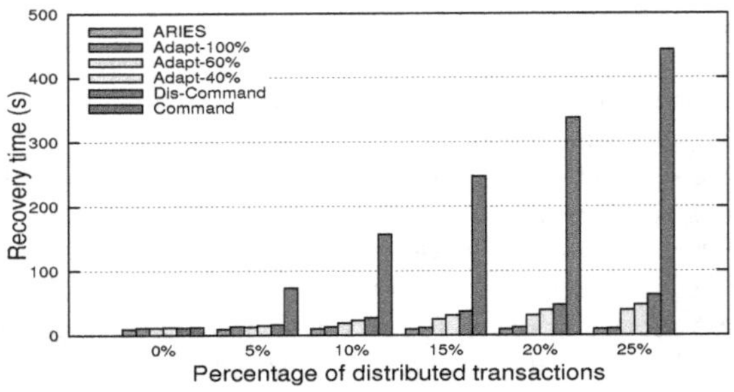

(b) After 30,000 transactions committed at each site

Figure 9: Recovery evaluation on the Smallbank benchmark

Table 3: Number of reprocessed transactions during recovery after 30,000 transactions committed at each site

Percentage of distributed transactions	Total number of committed transactions before failure	Command	Dis-Command	Adapt-40%	Adapt-60%	Adapt-100%
0%	240031	240031	30015	30201	30087	30076
5%	239321	239321	35642	33742	32483	29290
10%	240597	240597	39285	36054	34880	30674
15%	240392	240392	42979	39687	37496	32201
20%	239853	239853	48132	43808	40912	33994
25%	240197	240197	57026	50465	46095	35617

ARIES logging supports independent parallel recovery, since each ARIES log entry contains one tuple's data image before and after each operation. Intuitively, the recovery time of ARIES logging should be less than the time interval between the checkpointing and the failure time, since read operations and transaction logics are not required to be redone during the recovery. As ARIES logging is not affected by the percentage of distributed transactions and the workload skew, its recovery time is therefore proportional to the number of committed transactions.

Command logging incurs a much higher overhead during a recovery that involves distributed transactions (even for a small proportion, e.g., 5%). This is reflected in Figure 10 , which shows the recovery time of command logging with one failed site after each site has at least 30,000 committed transactions since the last checkpoint. If no distributed transactions are involved, command logging can reach the recovery performance similar to the other methods, because transaction dependencies can be resolved within each site. Otherwise, the overhead of synchronization during recovery severely affects the recovery performance of command logging.

Distributed command logging, as illustrated in Figure 8a and Figure 9a, effectively reduces the recovery time that is required by command logging. The results in Figure 8b and Figure 9b further show that the performance of distributed command logging is less sensitive to the percentage of distributed transactions compared with command logging. However, distributed command logging

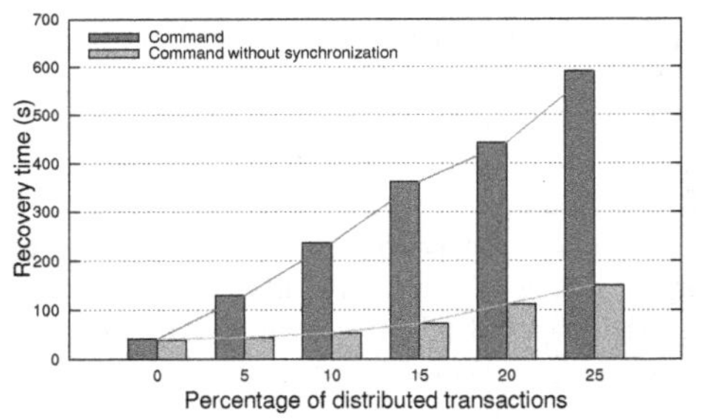

Figure 10: Synchronization cost of command logging on TPC-C benchmark

incurs the cost of scanning the footprint logs for building the dependency graph. For a one-minute TPC-C workload, the time for building the dependency graph increases from 2s to 5s when the percentage of distributed transactions increases from 5% to 25%. Nevertheless, when the total recovery cost is taken into consideration, the time spent on the dependency graph construction is relatively small.

Adaptive logging selectively creates ARIES logs and command logs. To reduce the I/O overhead of adaptive logging, we set a threshold $B_{i/o}$ in our online algorithm. As a result, at most $\mathbb{N} = \frac{B_{i/o}}{W_{aries}}$ ARIES logs can be created. In this experiment, we use a dynamic threshold, by setting $\mathbb{N}$ as x percentage of the total number of distributed transactions. In Figure 8 and 9, x is set as 40%, 60% or 100% to tune the recovery cost and transaction processing cost. The results show that the recovery performance of adaptive logging is much better than command logging in all the settings. It only performs slightly worse than ARIES logging. As x increases, more ARIES logs are created by adaptive logging, resulting in the reduction of recovery time. In the extreme case, when x = 100%, ARIES log is created for every distributed transaction. As a consequence, all dependencies of distributed transactions during recovery can be resolved using ARIES logs, and each site can process its recovery independently.

Figure 11 shows the recovery performance of adaptive logging (Adapt-x) with different x values. When x = 100%, the recovery times are almost the same for all distributions, regardless of the percentage of distributed transactions. This is because all the dependencies have been resolved using ARIES log. On the contrary, adaptive logging degrades to distributed command logging when x = 0%. In this case, more distributed transactions result in higher recovery cost.

Table 3 shows the number of transactions that are reprocessed during the recovery in Figure 8b. Compared with command logging and distributed command logging (Adapt-0%), adaptive logging methods significantly reduce the number of transactions that need to be reprocessed.

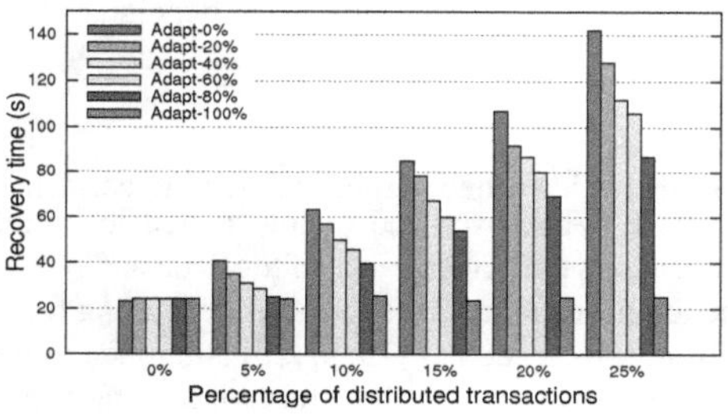

Figure 11: Recovery performance of Adapt-x on the TPC-C benchmark

4.4 Overall Performance

When commodity servers are used in a large number, failures are no longer an exception [39]. Therefore, the system must be able to recover efficiently when a failure occurs and provide a good overall performance. In this set of experiments, we measure the overall performance of different methods. In particular, we run the system for three hours and intentionally shut down a node chosen at random with a predefined failure rate. The system iteratively processes transactions and performs recovery, and creates a checkpoint every 10 minutes. Then, the total throughput of the entire system is measured as the average number of transactions processed per second over the three hours period.

Figure 12 shows the effects of failure interval on the throughput over three different distributions of distributed transactions. ARIES logging is superior to the other methods when the failure rate is very high (e.g., one failure per 5 minutes). When the failure rate is low, distributed command logging exhibits the best performance, because it is just slightly slower than command logging for transaction processing, but recovers much faster than command logging. As the failure interval drops, Adapt-100% cannot provide a comparable performance to command logging, because Adapt-100% creates an ARIES log for every distributed transaction, which is too costly in transaction processing.

4.5 Scalability

In this experiment, we evaluate the scalability of the logging methods. The percentage of distributed transactions is set to 10%, which are uniformly distributed among all the sites. Each site processes at least 30,000 transactions before we randomly terminate one site and the other sites will detect it as a failed site. It can be observed from Figure 13 that command logging does not scale. Its recovery time is positively correlated to the number of sites, because all the sites need to reprocess their committed transactions from the last checkpoint. The recovery cost of distributed command logging, which starts with a lower base compared with command logging, increases by about 50% when the number of sites is increased from 2 to 16. This is because the processing groups are larger when there are more sites involved.

The other logging methods show a scalable recovery performance. Adaptive logging selectively creates ARIES logs to break the dependency relations among the compute nodes. Therefore, the number of transactions required to be reprocessed is greatly reduced during recovery.

4.6 Cost Analysis

To study the overhead of different methods, we conduct a cost analysis using the TPC-C workload, where 5% of the generated transactions are distributed transactions. In both Figure 14 and Figure 15, the cost is presented as the percentage of CPU cycles.

Figure 14 shows the cost at runtime. The results show that the overhead of thread blocking due to distributed transactions is the major cost in all the logging methods. For adaptive logging, online decisions can be made even when the partition is blocked by distributed transactions. So the cost of online decisions does not add much burden to the system. Similarly, footprint logging only contributes a small cost to distributed command logging and adaptive logging. The logging and footprint costs of adaptive logging slightly increase when adaptive logging uses more data logs to break dependency links. As expected, compared with the other methods, ARIES logging takes more time to construct and write the logs.

We next analyze the recovery cost of different logging methods. Figure 15 shows that command logging spends the most amount of time in performing synchronization during recovery. With adaptive logging, the composition of command logs and data logs could be controlled. The synchronization process is reduced as Adapt-x increases its x value from 0% to 100%. The clever use of data logs in breaking dependency links among distributed transactions at runtime reduces the synchronization cost during recovery. More importantly, adaptive logging is able to exploit the strengths of both ARIES and command logging to cater to different workloads.

5. RELATED WORK

ARIES logging [23] is widely adopted for recovery in traditional disk-based database systems. As a fine-grained logging strategy, ARIES logging needs to construct log records for each modified tuple. Similar techniques are applied to in-memory database systems [9, 13, 14, 43].

To reduce the overhead of logging, [34] proposed to reduce the log size by only recording the incoming statements. In [22], the authors argue that for in-memory systems, since the whole database is maintained in memory, the overhead of ARIES logging can be a bottleneck. Consequently, they proposed a different kind of coarse-grained logging strategy called command logging. It only records the transaction identifier and parameters instead of concrete tuple modification information.

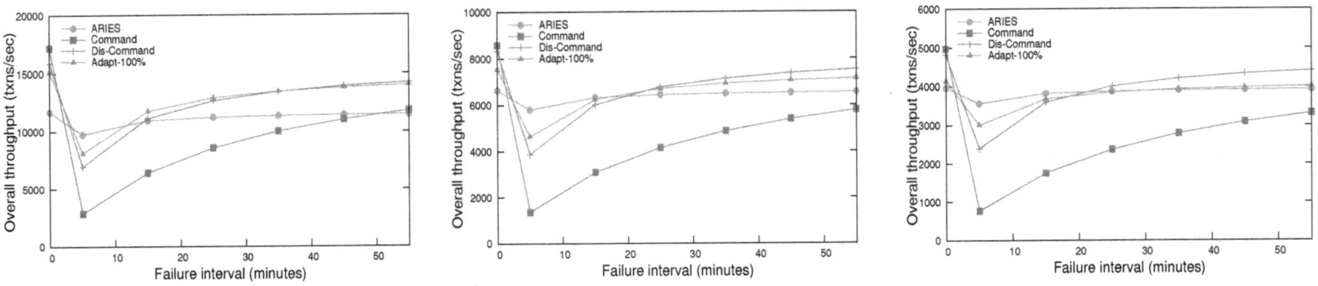

(a) Overall throughput with 5% distributed transactions

(b) Overall throughput with 10% distributed transactions

(c) Overall throughput with 20% distributed transactions

Figure 12: Overall performance evaluation on the TPC-C benchmark

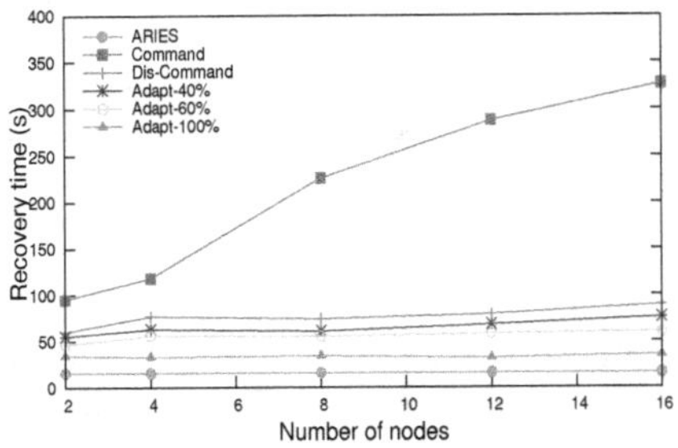

Figure 13: Scalability of logging methods on recovery for the TPC-C becnmark with 10% of distributed transactions

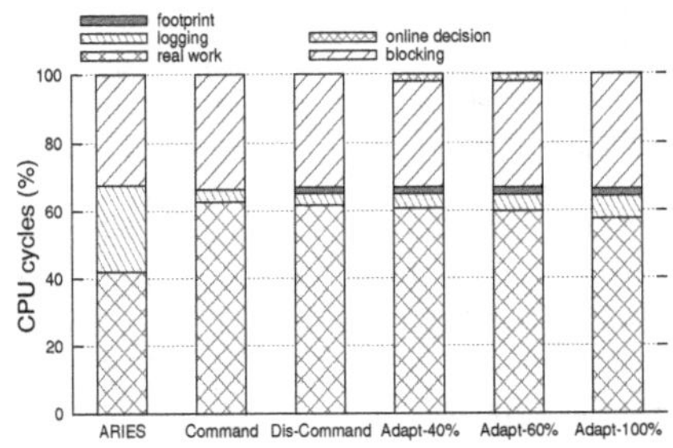

Figure 14: Runtime cost analysis on the TPC-C benchmark

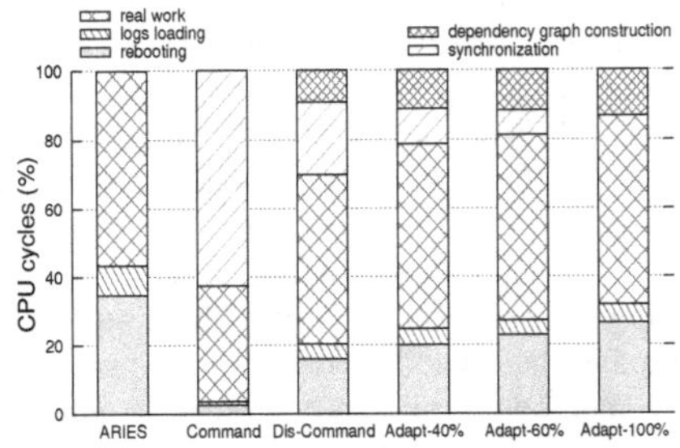

Figure 15: Cost analysis during recovery on the TPC-C benchmark

ARIES log records contain the before and after images (i.e., old and new values) of tuples. Dewitt et al [8] proposed to reduce the log size by writing only the new values to log files. However, log records without old values cannot enable the undo operation. So it needs large enough stable memory which can hold the complete log records for active transactions. They also proposed to write log records in batches to optimize the disk I/O performance. Similar techniques such as group commit [11] have also been explored in modern database systems.

Asynchronous commit strategy [2] allows transactions to complete without waiting for the log writing to finish. This strategy can reduce the overhead of log flush to some extent. However, it sacrifices the durability guarantee, since the states of the committed transactions may lose when failures happen.

Lomet et al [21] proposed a logical logging strategy. The recovery phase of ARIES logging combines physiological redo and logical undo. This extends ARIES to work in a logical setting, and the idea has been used to make ARIES logging more suitable for in-memory database system. Systems such as [16, 17] adopt this logical strategy.

If non-volatile RAM is available, database systems [4, 10, 19, 25, 29, 40] can use it to reduce the runtime overhead and speedup the recovery. With non-volatile RAM, recovery algorithms proposed by Lehman and Carey [18] could be applied.

There have been many research efforts [7, 8, 31, 33, 34, 43] devoted to efficient checkpointing for in-memory database systems. Recent works such as [7,43] focus on fast checkpointing to support efficient recovery. Usually the checkpointing techniques need to collaborate with the logging techniques and complement each other to actualize a reliable recovery process. Salem et al [35] surveyed many checkpointing techniques, which cover both inconsistent and consistent checkpointing with different logging strategies.

Johnson et al [15] identified logging-related impediments to database system scalability. The overhead of log related locking/latching contention decreases the performance of the database systems, since each transaction needs to hold the locks while waiting for its log to be materialized. Works such as [15, 27, 28] attempted to make logging more efficient by reducing the effects of locking contention.

RAMCloud [24], a key-value store for large-scale applications, replicates node's memory across nearby disks. It supports very fast recovery by carefully reconstructing the failed data from the survival nodes. However, RAMCloud does not support transactional operations that involve multiple keys. Moreover, the replication-based techniques are orthogonal to adaptive logging.

6. CONCLUSION

In the context of in-memory databases, command logging [22] shows a much better performance than ARIES logging [23] (a.k.a. write-ahead logging) for transaction processing. However, the trade-off is that command logging can significantly increase the recovery time in the case of a failure. The reason is that command logging redoes all the transactions in the log since the last checkpoint in a serial order. To address this problem, we first extend command logging to a distributed setting and enable all the nodes to perform their recovery in parallel. We identify the transactions involved in the failed node by analyzing the dependency relations and only redo the necessary transactions to reduce the recovery cost. We find that the recovery bottleneck of command logging is the synchronization process for resolving data dependency. Consequently, we design a novel adaptive logging method to achieve an optimized trade-off between the runtime performance of transaction processing and the recovery performance upon failures. Our experiments on H-Store show that adaptive logging can achieve a 10x boost for recovery while its runtime throughput is comparable to command logging.

Acknowledgments

We would like to thank Qian Lin for his suggestions that help improved the paper. We also thank the reviewers for their valuable comments. This work was in part supported by the National Research Foundation, Prime Minister's Office, Singapore under its Competitive Research Programme (CRP Award No. NRF-CRP8-2011-08). Gang Chen and Sai Wu's work was partially supported by the National Basic Research Program of China 973 (No. 2015CB-352400).

APPENDIX

A. REFERENCES

[1] MemSQL. http://www.memsql.com.

[2] Postgresql 8.3.23 documentation,chapter 28. reliability and the write-ahead log. http://www.postgresql.org/docs/8.3/static/wal-async-commit.html. Accessed: 2015-6-06.

[3] SAP HANA Wrings Performance from New Intel Xeons. http://www.enterprisetech.com/2014/02/19/sap-hana-wrings-performance-new-intel-xeons/.

[4] J. Arulraj, A. Pavlo, and S. R. Dulloor. Let's talk about storage & recovery methods for non-volatile memory database systems. In *SIGMOD*, pages 707–722. ACM, 2015.

[5] P. Bailis, A. Ghodsi, J. M. Hellerstein, and I. Stoica. Bolt-on causal consistency. In *SIGMOD*, pages 761–772, 2013.

[6] M. J. Cahill, U. Röhm, and A. D. Fekete. Serializable isolation for snapshot databases. In *TODS*, 34(4):20, 2009.

[7] T. Cao, M. A. V. Salles, B. Sowell, Y. Yue, A. J. Demers, J. Gehrke, and W. M. White. Fast checkpoint recovery algorithms for frequently consistent applications. In *SIGMOD*, pages 265–276, 2011.

[8] D. J. DeWitt, R. H. Katz, F. Olken, L. D. Shapiro, M. Stonebraker, and D. A. Wood. Implementation techniques for main memory database systems. In *SIGMOD*, pages 1–8, 1984.

[9] M. H. Eich. Main memory database recovery. In *Proceedings of 1986 ACM Fall joint computer conference*, pages 1226–1232. IEEE Computer Society Press, 1986.

[10] R. Fang, H.-I. Hsiao, B. He, C. Mohan, and Y. Wang. High performance database logging using storage class memory. In *ICDE*, pages 1221–1231. IEEE, 2011.

[11] R. B. Hagmann. Reimplementing the cedar file system using logging and group commit. In *SOSP*, pages 155–162, 1987.

[12] S. Harizopoulos, D. J. Abadi, S. Madden, and M. Stonebraker. OLTP through the looking glass, and what we found there. In *SIGMOD*, pages 981–992, 2008.

[13] H. V. Jagadish, D. F. Lieuwen, R. Rastogi, A. Silberschatz, and S. Sudarshan. Dalí: A high performance main memory storage manager. In *VLDB*, pages 48–59, 1994.

[14] H. V. Jagadish, A. Silberschatz, and S. Sudarshan. Recovering from main-memory lapses. In *VLDB*, pages 391–404, 1993.

[15] R. Johnson, I. Pandis, R. Stoica, M. Athanassoulis, and A. Ailamaki. Aether: A scalable approach to logging. In *PVLDB*, 3(1):681–692, 2010.

[16] R. Kallman, H. Kimura, J. Natkins, A. Pavlo, A. Rasin, S. B. Zdonik, E. P. C. Jones, S. Madden, M. Stonebraker, Y. Zhang, J. Hugg, and D. J. Abadi. H-store: a high-performance, distributed main memory transaction processing system. In *PVLDB*, 1(2):1496–1499, 2008.

[17] A. Kemper and T. Neumann. Hyper: A hybrid oltp&olap main memory database system based on virtual memory snapshots. In *ICDE*, pages 195–206, 2011.

[18] T. J. Lehman and M. J. Carey. A recovery algorithm for A high-performance memory-resident database system. In *SIGMOD*, pages 104–117, 1987.

[19] X. Li and M. H. Eich. Post-crash log processing for fuzzy checkpointing main memory databases. In *ICDE*, pages 117–124. IEEE, 1993.

[20] Q. Lin, P. Chang, G. Chen, B. C. Ooi, K.-L. Tan, and Z. Wang. Towards a non-2pc transaction management in distributed database systems. In *SIGMOD*. ACM, 2016.

[21] D. B. Lomet, K. Tzoumas, and M. J. Zwilling. Implementing performance competitive logical recovery. In *PVLDB*, 4(7):430–439, 2011.

[22] N. Malviya, A. Weisberg, S. Madden, and M. Stonebraker. Rethinking main memory OLTP recovery. In *ICDE*, pages 604–615, 2014.

[23] C. Mohan, D. J. Haderle, B. G. Lindsay, H. Pirahesh, and P. M. Schwarz. ARIES: A transaction recovery method supporting fine-granularity locking and partial rollbacks using write-ahead logging. In *TODS*, 17(1):94–162, 1992.

[24] D. Ongaro, S. M. Rumble, R. Stutsman, J. K. Ousterhout, and M. Rosenblum. Fast crash recovery in ramcloud. In *SOSP*, pages 29–41, 2011.

[25] I. Oukid, W. Lehner, T. Kissinger, T. Willhalm, and P. Bumbulis. Instant recovery for main-memory databases. In CIDR, 2015.

[26] J. Ousterhout, P. Agrawal, D. Erickson, C. Kozyrakis, J. Leverich, D. Mazières, S. Mitra, A. Narayanan, D. Ongaro, G. Parulkar, et al. The case for ramcloud. In *Communications of the ACM*, 54(7):121–130, 2011.

[27] I. Pandis, R. Johnson, N. Hardavellas, and A. Ailamaki. Data-oriented transaction execution. In *PVLDB*, 3(1):928–939, 2010.

[28] I. Pandis, P. Tözün, R. Johnson, and A. Ailamaki. PLP: page latch-free shared-everything OLTP. In *PVLDB*, 4(10):610–621, 2011.

[29] S. Pelley, T. F. Wenisch, B. T. Gold, and B. Bridge. Storage management in the nvram era. In *PVLDB*, 7(2):121–132, 2013.

[30] E. Pinheiro, W.-D. Weber, and L. A. Barroso. Failure trends in a large disk drive population. In *FAST*, pages 17–23, 2007.

[31] C. Pu. On-the-fly, incremental, consistent reading of entire databases. In *Algorithmica*, 1(1-4):271–287, 1986.

[32] F. Roos and S. Lindah. Distribution system component failure rates and repair times–an overview. In *NORDAC*. Citeseer, 2004.

[33] D. J. Rosenkrantz. Dynamic database dumping. In *SIGMOD*, pages 3–8, 1978.

[34] K. Salem and H. Garcia-Molina. Checkpointing memory-resident databases. In *ICDE*, pages 452–462, 1989.

[35] K. Salem and H. Garcia-Molina. System M: A transaction processing testbed for memory resident data. In *TKDE*, 2(1):161–172, 1990.

[36] B. Schroeder, G. Gibson, et al. A large-scale study of failures in high-performance computing systems. In *TDSC*, 7(4):337–350, 2010.

[37] M. Stonebraker, D. J. Abadi, A. Batkin, X. Chen, M. Cherniack, M. Ferreira, E. Lau, A. Lin, S. Madden, E. O'Neil, et al. C-store: a column-oriented dbms. In *VLDB*, pages 553–564, 2005.

[38] K.-L. Tan, Q. Cai, B. C. Ooi, W.-F. Wong, C. Yao, and

H. Zhang. In-memory databases: Challenges and opportunities from software and hardware perspectives. In *ACM SIGMOD Record*, 44(2):35–40, 2015.

[39] K. V. Vishwanath and N. Nagappan. Characterizing cloud computing hardware reliability. In *SoCC*, pages 193–204. ACM, 2010.

[40] T. Wang and R. Johnson. Scalable logging through emerging non-volatile memory. In *PVLDB*, 7(10):865–876, 2014.

[41] C. Yao, D. Agrawal, P. Chang, G. Chen, B. C. Ooi, W.-F. Wong, and M. Zhang. Exploiting single-threaded model in multi-core systems. *arXiv preprint arXiv:1503.03642*, 2015.

[42] H. Zhang, G. Chen, B. C. Ooi, K. Tan, and M. Zhang. In-memory big data management and processing: A survey. In *TKDE*, 27(7):1920–1948, 2015.

[43] W. Zheng, S. Tu, E. Kohler, and B. Liskov. Fast databases with fast durability and recovery through multicore parallelism. In *OSDI*, pages 465–477, Oct. 2014.

B. IMPLEMENTATION

Our distributed command logging and adaptive logging are implemented on top of H-Store [16] , a distributed in-memory database system, which supports the basic ARIES logging and command logging.

Recovery time of an in-memory database is proportional to the number of transactions recorded in the log since the last checkpoint. To reduce recovery overhead, in-memory database systems typically perform periodical checkpointing to create a snapshot in disk. Consequently, log records before the snapshot can be discarded. In our implementation, the checkpointing thread runs concurrently with the transaction processing threads, and flushes only the "dirty tuples" (i.e., tuples that have been updated since the last checkpoint) to disk. The interval of checkpointing is set to 180 seconds.

For command logging, we added one bit in its log record to indicate whether it is a distributed transaction or not. When recovering using command logging, we must synchronize the recovery process to guarantee the causal consistency. This is implemented differently in H-Store. In the single-thread architecture, a distributed transaction is intentionally blocked until all its time-dependent transactions commit, while in the single-site case, the transaction could be directly sent to the corresponding coordinator site which helps to synchronize the processing.

To build the dependency graph, our distributed command logging creates a small footprint log for each transaction, which is saved as a separate log file at each site. The footprint log is a light-weight write-ahead log which must be flushed to disk before a transaction commits. During the recovery process, one transaction may participate in multiple processing groups. However, as indicated in Algorithm 4, each transaction is recovered at most once. No redundant work is performed, and the write sets of transactions involved in multiple groups are buffered to avoid duplicated execution.

Adaptive logging makes an online decision between distributed command logging and ARIES logging. To this end, we implemented a *Decision Manager* at the transaction processing engine. The decision manager collects the statistics about transactions and maintains their dependencies. For each incoming transaction, the decision manager returns a decision to the engine which adaptively invokes different logging methods.

To further improve the performance of transaction processing in H-Store, we incorporate the following optimizations in our implementation.

1. Group commits: transactions need to flush their logs to disk before committing. Group commit batches several such flush requests together to achieve a higher I/O performance. It can also reduce the logging overhead for each transaction.
2. Dirty Column Tracking: ARIES logging records the modified tuples' old image and new image in its log records. Obviously, for tables with wide rows, it is costly to record the whole tuple. Only saving the data of those modified columns can effectively reduce the size of ARIES log. The same strategy is also adopted in our adaptive logging method.
3. Compression: it is a common technique to reduce the log size. In our implementation, the footprint log is compressed as follows. We collect the footprint log of each transaction in the form of $(txnId, tableName, tupleId)$. The information about table name and tuple ID will be duplicated in many records. So after one transaction commits, we aggregate its footprint log as $(txnId, tableName, tupleId_1, ..., tupleId_n)$. This simple operation can efficiently reduce the size of the footprint log.
4. Checkpoints: we use the checkpointing component of H-Store to do a non-blocking transaction-consistent checkpointing.

C. EFFECTS OF K-SAFETY

K-safety [37] is a replication-based technique that is often used to provide high availability and fault tolerance in the database cluster. However, it always incurs high synchronization overhead to achieve strong consistency. While this is orthogonal to the focus of the paper, it may be used to enhance logging approaches. Therefore, we conduct an experiment to study the effects of replication.

Since H-Store does not provide the K-safety feature, we measure the effects of K-safety using H-Store's commercial version VoltDB with the TPC-C benchmark. Figure 16 shows the results with different numbers of replicas. In the experiment, the cluster consists of 8 nodes and each node maintains 3 sites. We find that when K=1 (i.e., one replica is used), the throughput degrades by 46% and latency increases by 63% compared to the one without replicas. When K=7 (i.e., system could provide availability even there is only one healthy node remaining), the throughput degrades by 82.6% and the latency increases by 483%. In summary, system's performance degrades significantly when replication is enabled.

In terms of availability, K-safety shows good performance. However, it still depends on logs to recover when more than K nodes fail simultaneously. We conducted experiments to measure the availability in Appendix E.2 and Appendix E.3.

D. RUNTIME ANALYSIS

In this set of experiments, we conduct a cost analysis of the online algorithm and the in-memory index in our proposed adaptive logging.

D.1 Online Algorithm Cost of Adaptive Logging

In Figure 17, we analyze the computation cost of every minute by showing the percentage of time taken for making online decisions and processing transactions. Overheads of the online algorithm increase when the system runs for a longer time, because more transaction information is being maintained in the in-memory index. However, we observe that it takes only 5 seconds to execute the online algorithm in the 8th minute, and the main bulk of the time is still spent on transaction processing. In practice, the online decision cost would not grow in an unlimited manner as it is

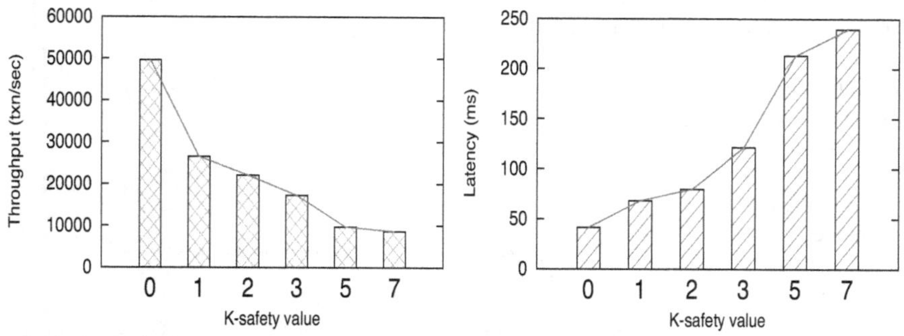

(a) Throughput evaluation

(b) Latency evaluation

Figure 16: Effects of K-safety on the TPC-C benchmark

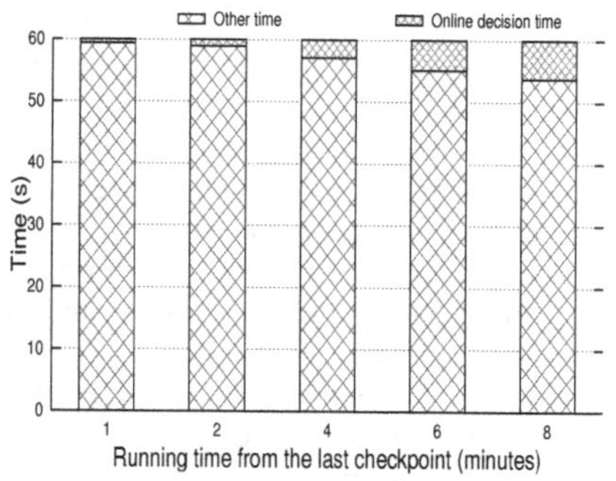

Figure 17: Cost of online decision algorithm on the TPC-C benchmark

bounded by the checkpointing interval. Since the online decision is made before the execution of a transaction, we could multitask the computation of online decisions while the transaction is waiting in the transaction queue to further reduce the latency.

D.2 Online Algorithm vs Offline Algorithm

The offline algorithm assumes that the distribution of transactions is known upfront, and such information can be used to generate an optimal logging strategy for performance comparison purposes. The offline algorithm can be considered as the ideal case, but it is not realistic in real implementation. For the online algorithm, we exploit historical statistics to predict the distribution of future transactions so that the system can dynamically make a decision on a logging plan.

We compare the performance of the online and offline algorithms in Figure 18. In this experiment, we disabled the checkpoints. For the offline algorithm, we ran the same workload twice. For the first run, we recorded the transaction distribution information, which is used as priori knowledge in the second run. As shown in Figure 18, the throughput of the online algorithm slightly decreases when the system runs for a longer time, since more information is maintained in the in-memory index, causing the overhead of logging selection to increase. It degrades about 6.24% at the 8th minute after about 3.8 million transactions are processed. In practice, the online decision cost will not keep growing as it is bounded by the checkpointing interval.

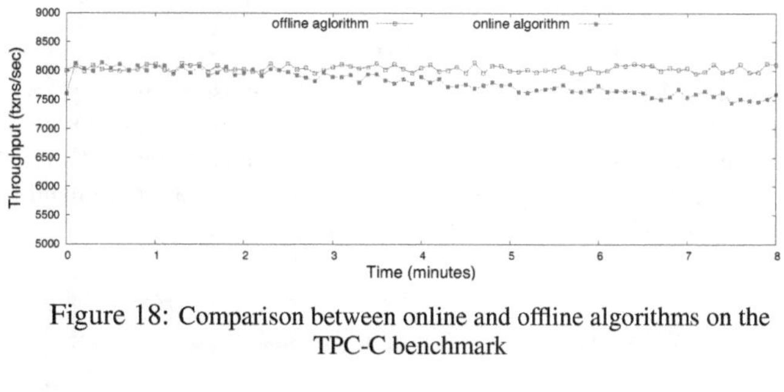

Figure 18: Comparison between online and offline algorithms on the TPC-C benchmark

D.3 Accuracy of the Online Algorithm

In Figure 19, we evaluate the accuracy of online algorithm by comparing with the ideal offline algorithm and a random algorithm. The result of the offline algorithm which assumes that it knows all the transactions is used as the ground truth in the comparison. For the random algorithm, if system still has I/O budget, it chooses the ARIES log or command log at random; otherwise, it sticks to command logging. The approximate estimation of our online algorithm is able to produce logging plans that are similar to those produced by the offline algorithm. If the I/O budget can only support building ARIES logs for 20% distributed transactions, the approximate online algorithm achieves 80% prediction accuracy.

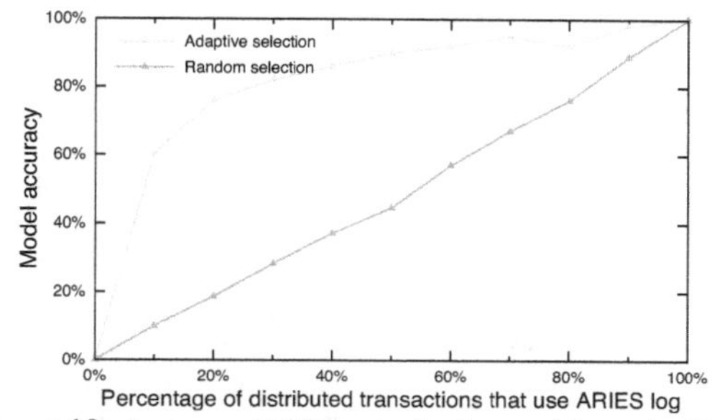

Figure 19: Accuracy of different selection models on the TPC-C benchmark

D.4 Effects of Transaction Pattern

We next conduct experiments on the TPC-C benchmark to evaluate the effects of transaction pattern on our logging selection algorithm. After the system becomes saturated, we change the hot item set at the 10th minute. In Figure 20, we measure the accuracy of our online algorithm as well as the random algorithm. As expected, the accuracy of the proposed online algorithm drops significantly when the transaction pattern changes dramatically, since it uses a wrong (old) statistical distribution. In our implementation, adaptive logging updates the statistical distribution every minute. As can be observed, the online algorithm continues to provide a good prediction as soon as it is able to use the new statistical distribution (after the update).

D.5 Effects of the In-memory Index

The main purpose of the in-memory index is for estimating the cost/benefit of using either the ARIES log or the command log.

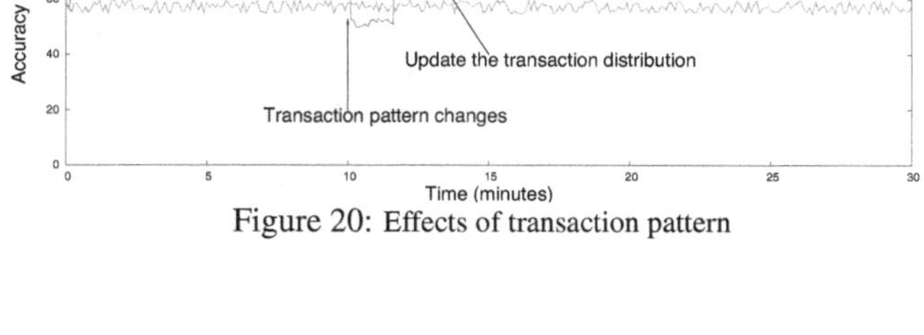

Figure 20: Effects of transaction pattern

Asynchronous update of the in-memory index is used to reduce the maintenance overhead. Indexes of a batch of transactions are cached locally and periodically synchronized with the master node. Since the in-memory index is used mainly for estimation, it is unnecessary to require the index in the master node to be strictly consistent (eventual consistency is sufficient).

We have also conducted experiments on the TPC-C benchmark to show the benefits of asynchronous update by comparing the two strategies: asynchronous update and synchronous update. Synchronous update requires the transaction to update the in-memory index in the master node before it commits. For asynchronous update, transaction only updates the cached indexes in the processing nodes. The processing nodes will synchronize the indexes in the master node periodically. As shown in Figure 21, synchronous update is very costly and dramatically affects the performance of transaction processing. Further, synchronous update only leads to a marginal improvement in the recovery process. This observation confirms that the asynchronous approach is a more efficient approach.

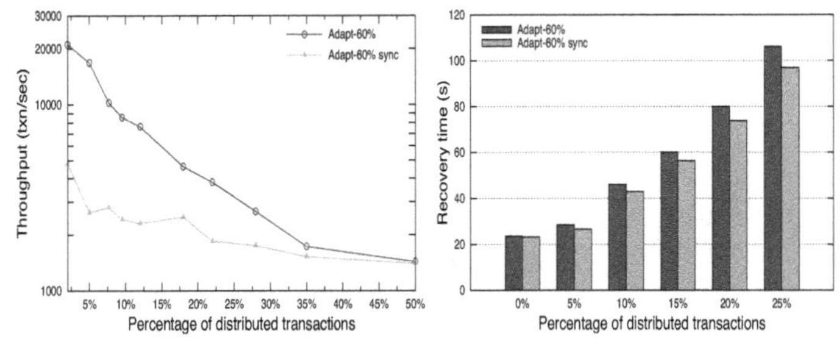

(a) Throughput at runtime

(b) Recovery time when 30,000 transactions commit at each site

Figure 21: Effects of asynchronous update on in-memory index

E. RECOVERY ANALYSIS

We conduct a set of experiments to evaluate the system performance in different failure scenarios.

E.1 Master-Node Failure

The master node maintains the in-memory index which is used to help estimate the cost/benefit of using the ARIES log and command log. If the master fails and the in-memory index is lost, adaptive logging always sticks to command logging, because our adaptive logging model enforces a constraint such that ARIES log will not be preferred unless the benefit of building the ARIES log is larger than a predefined threshold. If the in-memory index is absent, it is hard to retrieve transaction's time-dependent transactions, all ARIES logs are estimated to be not beneficial enough. To address the issue, our system caches the in-memory index in each processing node. It can be updated in an asynchronous manner. In the event when the master node fails, the system can still switch between the two logging approaches.

As discussed in Appendix D.5, the in-memory index is updated in an asynchronous manner. As shown in Figure 22, when the master node fails, the transaction coordinator can still apply the adaptive approach to select a logging strategy using its local copy of in-memory index. The throughput slightly increases because there is no communication between the master and slave nodes. After a new master node is elected, all nodes will synchronize their local indexes with the new master node, which incurs high communication cost and leads to the throughput drop. The index synchronization only lasts for a few seconds. After the index in the master node is synchronized and the system is fully recovered, the throughout increases until it becomes steady.

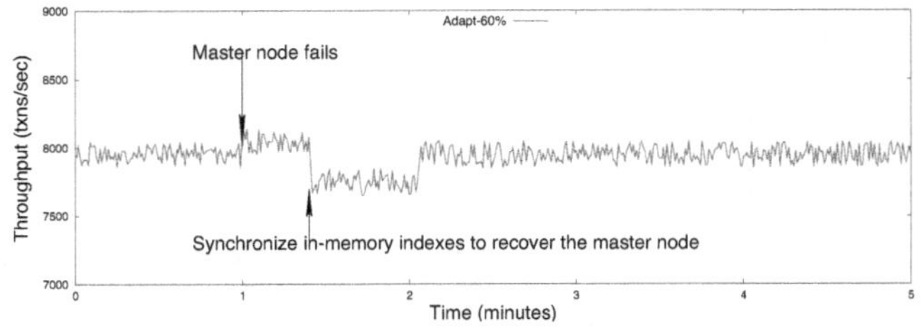

Figure 22: Throughput evaluation on TPC-C benchmark when the master node fails

E.2 Single-Node Failure

In Figure 23, we simulate a single-node failure by randomly selecting a node and killing its running processes. Systems with ARIES logging and command logging have to halt (the throughput drops to zero) until the failed node is fully recovered. On the contrary, system with K-safety can continue the transaction processing. Its throughput even slightly increases, since the number of replicas that needs to be synchronized decreases. System with adaptive logging can process new transactions and do the recovery simultaneously. As discussed in Section 2.4, the system first constructs the dependency graphs based on the lightweight footprint log. With the dependency graphs, the database in the failed node can be recovered on demand while the surviving nodes continue with the processing. The throughput gradually increases as the database in the failed node is being recovered.

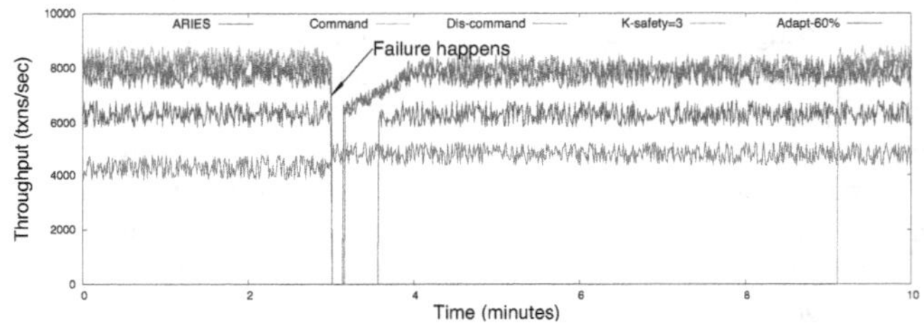

Figure 23: Throughput evaluation on the TPC-C benchmark when a single node fails

E.3 Entire-Cluster Failure

Figure 24 shows the results when the entire cluster fails. Unlike the case of a single-node failure, system with K-safety cannot retain system availability and durability if the entire cluster fails. Thus, it still has to rely on logs to perform the recovery (e.g., command logging is enabled for K-safety in this experiment).

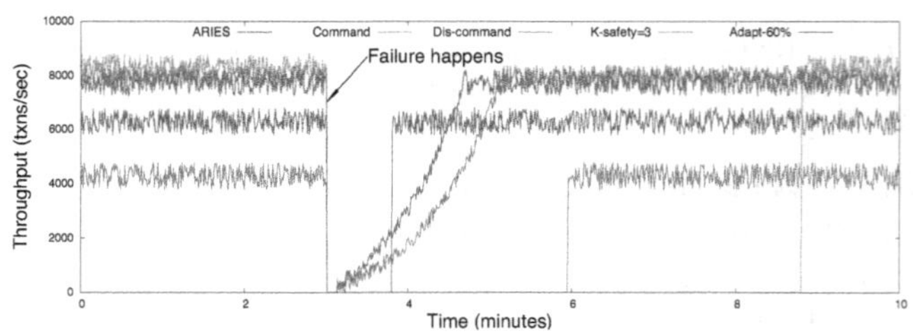

Figure 24: Throughput evaluation the TPC-C benchmark when the entire cluster fails

Big Data Analytics with Datalog Queries on Spark

Alexander Shkapsky Mohan Yang Matteo Interlandi Hsuan Chiu
Tyson Condie Carlo Zaniolo
University of California, Los Angeles
{shkapsky, yang, minterlandi, cherylautumn, tcondie, zaniolo}@cs.ucla.edu

ABSTRACT

There is great interest in exploiting the opportunity provided by cloud computing platforms for large-scale analytics. Among these platforms, Apache Spark is growing in popularity for machine learning and graph analytics. Developing efficient complex analytics in Spark requires deep understanding of both the algorithm at hand and the Spark API or subsystem APIs (e.g., Spark SQL, GraphX). Our BigDatalog system addresses the problem by providing concise declarative specification of complex queries amenable to efficient evaluation. Towards this goal, we propose compilation and optimization techniques that tackle the important problem of efficiently supporting recursion in Spark. We perform an experimental comparison with other state-of-the-art large-scale DATALOG systems and verify the efficacy of our techniques and effectiveness of Spark in supporting DATALOG-based analytics.

Keywords

Datalog, Recursive Queries, Monotonic Aggregates, Spark

1. INTRODUCTION

Over the past decade, the demand for analytics has driven both researchers and industry to build cluster-based data analysis systems. Initially, the focus was on batch analysis and both research and industry proposed systems [3, 20, 26, 35] and languages [32, 51] supporting this endeavour. Recently, demand has exploded for analytics over graphs and networks. This has led researchers to refocus on providing scalable systems for machine learning and graph analytics. Among these systems is Apache Spark [4, 62], which is attracting a great deal of interest as a general platform for large-scale analytics, particularly because of its support for in-memory iterative analytics.

Some might think as a system designed for iterative applications, Spark would also be well suited for recursive applications such as shortest paths computations, and link and graph structure analysis. However this ignores three decades worth of recursive query evaluation and optimization techniques. Spark's support of recursion through iteration is inefficient: in an iterative Spark application, a new job is submitted for every iteration and thus the system has only limited visibility over an application's entire execution. From a programming perspective, the development of efficient recursive applications in Spark requires the programmer to have (1) deep understanding of the algorithm being implemented, (2) extensive knowledge of the Spark API, and (3) mastery of Spark internals. Nevertheless, Spark is a promising system for recursive applications because it provides many features essential for recursive evaluation, including dataset caching and low task startup costs. Along those lines, to examine how Spark can be made to efficiently support recursive applications we implement a recursive query language on Spark. Specifically, we implement DATALOG, a well known recursive query language. New interest has recently re-emerged around DATALOG for a wide spectrum of knowledge-oriented applications including distributed programming [25], AI [27], and distributed data management [64], as well as analytics on single-node systems [47, 49]. The fact that DATALOG is also well suited to declaratively support large-scale analytics was recently recognized by [48, 54].

In this paper we present BigDatalog, a full DATALOG language implementation on Apache Spark developed under the ***D****eductive* ***A****pplication* ***L****anguage* ***S****ystem* (*DeALS*) project [7] at UCLA. The *DeALS* project seeks to (1) design a unified logical language that enables the concise and declarative expression of analytics [41, 42], and (2) provide a system that optimizes execution over diverse platforms including sequential implementations [49], multi-core machines [59], and clusters (with BigDatalog). BigDatalog supports relational algebra, aggregation, and recursion, as well as a host of declarative optimizations. It also exploits semantic extensions for programs with *aggregation in recursion* [41, 42]. As a result, the Spark programmer can now implement complex analytics pipelines of relational, graph and machine learning tasks in a single language, instead of stitching together programs written in different APIs, i.e., Spark SQL [16], GraphX [33] and MLlib. Furthermore, BigDatalog employs techniques to identify and evaluate recursive programs that are *decomposable* and can be evaluated without communication [46, 57], leading to efficient distributed evaluations.

Motivating Example. As an example of the performance improvement that BigDatalog achieves for the evaluation of recursive queries consider Figure 1. This figure shows the execution time required to compute a 100 million vertex pair transitive closure of a graph using a highly optimized hand-

SIGMOD'16, June 26-July 01, 2016, San Francisco, CA, USA
© 2016 ACM. ISBN 978-1-4503-3531-7/16/06...$15.00
DOI: http://dx.doi.org/10.1145/2882903.2915229

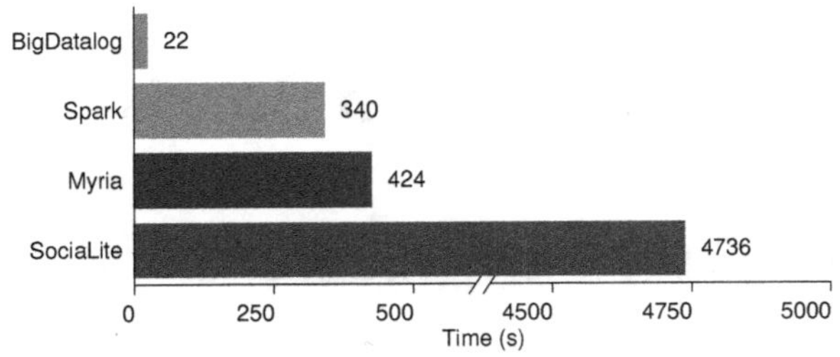

Figure 1: Example Recursive Query Performance.

written Spark program versus the BigDatalog version (cluster specs. in Section 6). This example shows how BigDatalog is both considerably better than its host framework and also performant *w.r.t.* large-scale DATALOG systems, namely, Myria [54] and SociaLite [48]. This orders of magnitude speed-up is achieved by employing the efficient evaluation techniques and optimizations of DATALOG in Spark.

Contributions. We make the following contributions:

- We design and implement the BigDatalog compiler. We show how BigDatalog programs are compiled into recursive physical plans for Spark.
- We present a parallel evaluation technique for distributed DATALOG evaluation on Spark. We introduce recursion operators and data structures to efficiently implement the technique in Spark.
- We propose physical planning and scheduler optimizations for recursive queries in Spark, including techniques to evaluate decomposable programs.
- We present distributed monotonic aggregates, and accompanying evaluation technique and data structures to support DATALOG programs with aggregates on Spark.
- We provide experimental evidence that a generic declarative system can compete with a special-purpose graph system.

Spark as a runtime for BigDatalog. In addition to its popularity and healthy ecosystem, Spark is a general data processing system and provides a SQL API; therefore, it is conducive to supporting a DATALOG compiler and DATALOG evaluation. Moreover, Spark's large and active user community helps to ease engineering effort. BigDatalog both benefits from and is limited by Spark's generality and overall system design principles. These tradeoffs will be discussed throughout the paper. Lastly, BigDatalog is designed for general analytical workloads, and although we will focus much of the discussion and experiments on graph queries and recursive program evaluation, we do not claim that Spark is the best platform for graph workloads in general. In fact, BigDatalog can also be backed by other general dataflow systems, including Naiad [44] and Hyracks [20], and many of the optimization techniques presented in this paper will also apply. This is the benefit of employing a declarative language, and comparing and analyzing the performance tradeoffs between different backend systems and/or computation models on various workloads would be an interesting future work.

Outline. In Section 2, we review DATALOG and Spark. Section 3 introduces BigDatalog and the distributed evaluation technique used to evaluate BigDatalog programs, and shows how BigDatalog programs are compiled into physical plans for execution on Spark. Section 4 presents evaluation, physical plan and job scheduling optimizations. Section 5 describes our aggregate design and implementation. Section 6 presents experimental results, including comparisons of BigDatalog with other large-scale DATALOG systems. Section 7 reviews related works. Section 8 presents conclusions and plans for future work.

2. PRELIMINARIES

In this section, we first provide background on DATALOG and then briefly review Spark. We will then tie the two together with an example and discuss challenges for using Spark as a DATALOG runtime.

2.1 Datalog

A DATALOG program is a finite set of rules. A *rule* r has the form $h \leftarrow b_1, \ldots, b_n$, where h is the *head* of r and $b_1, \ldots, b_n$ is the *body*. h and each b_i are *literals* with the form $p_i(t_1, \ldots, t_j)$ where p_i is a *predicate* and $t_1, \ldots, t_j$ are *terms* which can be *constants*, *variables* or *functions*. We say r is a rule of predicate h, unless it has an empty body, and then it is a *fact*. The comma separating literals in a body is a logical conjunction (AND). A successful assignment of all variables in the body produces a fact for the head's predicate. Predicates are also considered *relations* and WLOG throughout the paper we will use the terms predicate and relation interchangeably. A *query* indicates the desired predicate to evaluate. As a convention, predicate and function names begin with lower case letters, and variable names begin with upper case letters.

Datalog by Example. We continue our review of DATALOG with the *Transitive Closure* (TC) program. Program 1 recursively produces all pairs of vertices that are connected by some path in a graph.

PROGRAM 1. *Transitive Closure*

```
r1. tc(X,Y) ← arc(X,Y).
r2. tc(X,Y) ← tc(X,Z), arc(Z,Y).
```

Program 1 is explained as follows. *r1* is an *exit rule* because it serves as a base case of the recursion. In *r1*, the `arc` predicate represents the edges of the graph – `arc` is a *base relation*[1]. *r1* produces a `tc` fact for each `arc` fact. *r2* is a *recursive rule* since it has the `tc` predicate in both its head and body. *r2* will recursively produce `tc` facts from the conjunction[2] of previously produced `tc` facts and `arc` facts. The query to evaluate TC is of the form `tc(X,Y)`. Lastly, this program uses a *linear* recursion in *r2*, since there is a single recursive predicate literal, whereas a *non-linear* recursion will have multiple recursive literals in its body. The number of iterations required to evaluate Program 1 is, in the worst case, equal to the longest simple path in the graph.

2.2 Datalog Evaluation

DATALOG is a declarative language and therefore rules are independent of the operators used to implement them (e.g., type of join used). Furthermore, rules are independent of the particular evaluation order and technique used as long as the monotonic *w.r.t.* set-containment[3], and least fixpoint,

[1]For readers not familiar with DATALOG, base relations can be seen as tables stored in a relational DBMS.

[2]In relational terminology, `tc` is joined with `arc` on `Z` – which is positionally interpreted as where the second argument of `tc` equals the first argument of `arc`.

[3]With set-containment monotonicity, evaluation only grows a predicate's set of facts.

semantics of DATALOG is maintained. Lastly, the order of literals in a rule body provides no semantic meaning and most implementations, including this work, evaluate literals in a left-to-right fashion.

A *naïve* evaluation of Program 1 will execute *r1* and then repeatedly evaluate *r2*, joining `arc` facts with already discovered `tc` facts in each iteration, until no new facts are produced – a *fixpoint* has been reached. This approach will inefficiently re-produce known facts in every iteration. We can instead use the well-known *Semi-Naïve evaluation* (SN) [18] which is efficient and produces no duplicates. Both naïve and SN evaluations are *bottom-up* evaluation techniques, which start from the initial database and perform a repeated application of the rules until a fixpoint is reached. Although SN is a centralized evaluation method, since it serves as the basis for the evaluation method used in this paper (cf. Section 3.3) we walk through an application of SN using Program 1 as our target. To enable SN, a (symbolic) rewriting [63] is applied to the rules of the original program to produce a new recursive rule that maintains program correctness. In the specific case of Program 1, the new rule only evaluates facts of the recursive predicate (`tc`) produced during the previous iteration (indicated with δ) and has the form $\texttt{tc(X,Y)} \leftarrow \delta\texttt{tc(X,Z)},\ \texttt{arc(Z,Y)}$.

Algorithm 1 Semi-Naïve Evaluation of Program 1

1: $\delta\texttt{tc} := \texttt{arc(X,Y)}$
2: $\texttt{tc} := \delta\texttt{tc}$
3: **do**
4: $\quad\delta\texttt{tc}' := \pi_{\texttt{X,Y}}(\delta\texttt{tc(X,Z)} \bowtie \texttt{arc(Z,Y)}) - \texttt{tc}$
5: $\quad\texttt{tc} := \texttt{tc} \cup \delta\texttt{tc}'$
6: $\quad\delta\texttt{tc} := \delta\texttt{tc}'$
7: **while** $(\delta\texttt{tc} \neq \varnothing)$
8: **return** `tc`

Algorithm 1 shows the SN evaluation for Program 1. Note that the rules have been converted to a relational operator form (lines 1,4). In Algorithm 1 `tc` is the set of all facts produced for the recursive predicate and $\delta\texttt{tc}$ ($\delta\texttt{tc}'$) is the set of facts produced for `tc` during the previous (current) iteration. In SN, exit rules are evaluated first. The facts of `arc` become the initial set of facts for both $\delta\texttt{tc}$ (line 1) and `tc` (line 2). Then, SN iterates until a fixpoint is reached (line 7). Each iteration begins by joining $\delta\texttt{tc}$ with `arc` and projecting `X, Y` terms to produce candidate `tc` facts (line 4). These facts are then set-differenced with `tc` to eliminate duplicates and produce $\delta\texttt{tc}'$ (line 4), which is unioned into `tc` (line 5) and becomes $\delta\texttt{tc}$ (line 6).

2.3 Apache Spark

Spark provides a language-integrated Scala API enabling the expression of programs as *dataflows of transformations* (e.g., `map`, `filter`) on *Resilient Distributed Datasets* (RDD) [62]. An RDD is a distributed shared memory abstraction representing a partitioned dataset; RDDs are immutable, and transformations are coarse-grained and thus apply to all items in the RDD to produce a new RDD. Spark executes transformations lazily: a *job* is submitted for execution only when *actions* such as `count` or `reduce` are called by the user's program. Once a job is submitted, the scheduler groups transformations that can be pipelined (e.g., `map` over a `join`) into a single *stage*. The stages composing a dataflow are executed *synchronously* in a topological order: a stage will not be scheduled until all stages it is dependent upon

```
1  var tc = sc.parallelize(graph, numPartitions)
2  val arcs = tc.map(x => (x._2, x._1)).cache()
3  var deltaTC = tc
4  do {
5    deltaTC = deltaTC.join(arcs)
6      .map(x => (x._2._2, x._2._1))
7      .subtract(tc).distinct().cache()
8    tc = tc.union(deltaTC).cache()
9  } while (deltaTC.count() > 0)
10 tc
```

Figure 2: Semi-naïve TC Spark Program.

have finished successfully. Between stages, Spark *shuffles* the dataset to *repartition* it among the nodes of the cluster. When a stage can be run, the scheduler creates a set of *tasks* (i.e., execution units) consisting of one task for each input *partition*, and launches the tasks on *worker nodes*.

RDDs can be explicitly cached by the programmer in memory or on disk at workers. Fault tolerance is provided by recomputing the sequence of transformations for the missing partition(s). Spark has libraries for structured data processing (Spark SQL), stream processing (Spark Streaming), machine learning (MLlib), and graph processing (GraphX).

Spark SQL. Spark's structured data and relational processing module, supports a subset of SQL. Spark SQL provides logical and physical relational operators. Spark SQL physical operators use a pipelined iterator model and are implemented as functions applied over the iterator from an upstream operator. The Catalyst framework [16] supports the compilation and optimization of Spark SQL programs into physical plans. In this work, we use and extend Spark SQL operators. We also propose BigDatalog operators that are implemented using the Catalyst framework so BigDatalog can use Catalyst planning features on recursive plans.

Iterative Spark Programs. Spark iterative applications are implemented by having a *driver program* iterate over a sequence of transformations terminated by an action. Each iteration is a new job that operates on cached RDD(s) produced by the previous iteration. Iteration terminates after a user-defined number of iterations or based on a user-defined predicate that determines when convergence is reached. Examples of algorithms supported by this approach include PageRank, logistic regression, and the semi-naïve transitive closure shown in Figure 2, and explained as follows. After some initial setup including distributing the graph among nodes of the cluster (line 1) and preparing the edges of the graph for joins (line 2), the program enters a `do-while` loop. It will iterate by executing a new job for each `count` action, until an iteration produces no new results (line 9). In each iteration, the program will join facts from the previous iteration (`deltaTC`) with `arcs` (line 5), project the pair of vertices (line 6), and eliminate duplicates (line 7). The set of all previously produced pairs is then combined with the newly produced pairs (line 8). Reused RDDs are cached.

Note the simplicity of the DATALOG program in Program 1 compared to the Spark program in Figure 2. Spark requires the programmer (1) be familiar with semi-naïve evaluation, (2) directly express a dataflow's physical plan composed of properly ordered operations and (3) handle memory management (RDD caching) to obtain better performance. Instead, BigDatalog enables high-level specification amenable to optimizations and rescues the programmer from extensive coding, debugging and maintenance effort.

Challenges for Datalog on Spark. The three main challenges we face with implementing DATALOG on Spark are:

1. Acyclic Plans: Supporting compilation, optimization and evaluation of DATALOG programs on Spark requires features not currently supported. A recursive, rule-based syntax requires a different compiler front-end than Spark SQL language queries. Spark SQL lacks recursion operators, operators are designed for acyclic use, and the Catalyst optimizer is targeted for non-recursive plans.

2. Scheduling: Spark's synchronous stage-based scheduler issues tasks for a stage only after all tasks of the previous stages have completed. For (monotonic) DATALOG programs, like the ones studied in this paper, this can be seen as unnecessary coordination because monotonic DATALOG programs are eventually consistent [15, 34].

3. RDD Immutability & Memory Utilization: An iteration of recursion will produce a new RDD to represent the updated recursive relation. This RDD will contain both new facts and all the facts produced in earlier iterations, which are already contained in earlier RDDs. If poorly managed, recursive applications on Spark can experience memory utilization problems.

3. BIGDATALOG

BigDatalog programs are expressed as DATALOG rules, then compiled, optimized and executed on Spark. BigDatalog will manage the persistence of datasets and make partitioning decisions. BigDatalog supports recursion, non-monotonic aggregation (min, max, sum, count, average) and aggregation in recursion with monotonic aggregates (Section 5).

3.1 Benchmark Programs

In this paper, we focus on monotonic (positive) programs which include classical recursive queries from the literature as well as aggregate queries, some of which are long studied (e.g., shortest paths) and others studied more recently (connected components) [48, 54].

Classical Recursive Queries

- **Transitive Closure** (TC)
- **Same Generation** (SG) identifies pairs of vertices where both are the same number of hops from a common ancestor.
- **Reachability** (REACH) produces all nodes connected by some path to a given source node.

Aggregation in Recursion Queries

- **Single-Source Shortest Paths** (SSSP) computes the length of the shortest path from a source vertex to each vertex it is connected to.
- **Connected Components** (CC) identifies connected components in the graph.

3.2 BigDatalog API By Example

The program snippet shown in Figure 3 computes the size of the transitive closure of the graph using the BigDatalog API for Spark. In a driver program, the user first gets a `BigDatalogContext` (line 1), which wraps the `SparkContext` (`sc`) – the entry point for writing and executing Spark programs. The user then specifies a database schema definition for base relations and program rules (lines 2-4). Lines 3-4 implement TC from Program 1. The database definition and rules are given to the BigDatalog compiler which loads

```
1 val bdCtx = new BigDatalogContext(sc)
2 val program = "database({arc(X:Integer, Y:Integer}})."
3   + "tc(X,Y) <- arc(X,Y)."
4   + "tc(X,Y) <- tc(X,Z), arc(Z,Y)."
5 bdCtx.datalog(program)
6 bdCtx.datasource("arc", filePath)
7 val tc = bdCtx.query("tc(X,Y).")
8 val tcSize = tc.count()
```

Figure 3: BigDatalog Program for Spark.

the database schema into a relation catalog (line 5). Next, the data source (e.g., local or HDFS file path, or RDD) for the `arc` relation is provided (line 6). Then, the query to evaluate is given to the `BigDatalogContext` (line 7) which compiles it and returns an execution plan used to evaluate the query. As with other Spark programs, evaluation is lazy – the query is evaluated when `count` is executed (line 8).

3.3 Parallel Semi-naïve Evaluation on Spark

BigDatalog programs are evaluated using a parallel version of SN we call *Parallel Semi-naïve evaluation* (PSN). PSN is an execution framework for a recursive predicate and it is implemented using RDD transformations. Since Spark evaluates synchronously, PSN will evaluate one iteration at a time, where an iteration will not begin until all tasks from the previous iteration have completed.

The two types of rules for a recursive predicate – the exit rules and recursive rules – are compiled into separate *physical plans* (plans) which are then used in the PSN evaluator. Physical plans are composed of Spark SQL and BigDatalog operators that produce RDDs. The exit rules plan is first evaluated once, and then the recursive rules plan is repeatedly evaluated until a fixpoint is reached. Note that as with SN, PSN will also evaluate symbolically rewritten rules (e.g., $\texttt{tc(X,Y)} \leftarrow \delta\texttt{tc(X,Z)},\ \texttt{arc(Z,Y)}.$).

Algorithm 2 is the psuedocode for the PSN evaluator. The **exitRulesPlan** (line 1) and **recursiveRulesPlan** (line 5) are plans for the exit rules and recursive rules, respectively. We use `toRDD()` (lines 1,5) to produce the RDD for the plan. Each iteration produces two new RDDs – an RDD for the new results produced during the iteration (`delta`) and an RDD for all results produced thus far for the predicate (`all`). The `updateCatalog` (lines 3,8) stores new `all` and `delta` RDDs into a catalog for plans to access. The exit rule plan is evaluated first. The result is de-duplicated (`distinct`) (line 1) to produce the initial `delta` and `all` RDDs (line 2), which are used to evaluate the first iteration of the recursion. Each iteration is a new job executed by `count` (line 9). First, the **recursiveRulesPlan** is evaluated using the `delta` RDD from the previous iteration. This will produce an RDD that

Algorithm 2 PSN Evaluator with RDDs

```
1: delta = exitRulesPlan.toRDD().distinct()
2: all = delta
3: updateCatalog(all, delta)
4: do
5:     delta = recursiveRulesPlan.toRDD()
6:         .subtract(all).distinct()
7:     all = all.union(delta)
8:     updateCatalog(all, delta)
9: while (delta.count() > 0)
10: return all
```

is set-differenced (`subtract`) with the `all` RDD (line 6) and de-duplicated to produce a new `delta` RDD. With lazy evaluation, the union of `all` and `delta` (line 7) from the previous iteration is evaluated prior to its use in `subtract` (line 6).

We have implemented PSN to cache RDDs that will be reused, namely `all` and `delta`, but we omit this from Algorithm 2 to simplify its presentation. Lastly, in cases of mutual recursion, when two or more rules belonging to different predicates reference each other (e.g., A ← B, B ← A), one predicate will "drive" the recursion with PSN and the other recursive predicate(s) will be an operator in the driver's recursive rules plan.

3.4 Compilation and Planning

For BigDatalog we have extended the *DeALS* compiler [49, 50], which was originally designed for sequential program evaluation, and we optimized and re-targeted it for parallel, distributed bottom-up evaluation of DATALOG programs. The input for the compiler is a database schema definition, a set of rules and a query. From this, the compiler creates a logical plan for the program, which is optimized using database techniques such as projection pruning. The logical plan for a non-recursive BigDatalog query is mapped into a Spark SQL plan and executed accordingly. Logical plans for recursive queries are converted to BigDatalog physical plans.

3.4.1 Logical Plans

Here, we use Program 1 (TC) to describe how the compiler produces a logical plan. Given the query `tc(X,Y)`, the program is first compiled into a Predicate Connection Graph (PCG) to identify the exit rules (*r1*) and recursive rules (*r2*) of the `tc` recursive predicate. The PCG is a type of AND/OR tree where OR nodes represent predicate occurrences in rule bodies and AND nodes represent rule heads [17]. From the PCG, the logical query plan is produced by mapping it into a tree of relational and recursion (i.e., fixpoint) operators. A recursion operator has two child logical (sub)plans: one plan for the predicate's exit rules and the other for the predicate's recursive rules. Figure 4(a) is the logical plan produced by the BigDatalog compiler for Program 1. The left side of Figure 4(a) is the exit rules plan with only the `arc` relation, representing *r1*. The right side of Figure 4(a) is the recursive rules plan made up of relational operators to produce one iteration of *r2*.

PROGRAM 2. *Same Generation*

r1. `sg(X,Y)` ← `arc(P,X)`, `arc(P,Y)`, `X != Y`.
r2. `sg(X,Y)` ← `arc(A,X)`, `sg(A,B)`, `arc(B,Y)`.

Consider Program 2, the same generation (SG) program. The exit rule *r1* produces all `X,Y` pairs with the same parents (i.e. siblings) and the recursive rule *r2* produces new `X,Y` pairs where both `X` and `Y` have parents of the same generation. For PSN, *r2* is (symbolically) rewritten as `sg(X,Y)` ← `arc(A,X)`, δ`sg(A,B)`, `arc(B,Y)`. The left side of Figure 4(b) is the exit rules plan with a self-join of `arc` to find siblings. The right side of Figure 4(b) is the recursive rules plan which includes a three-way join of δ`sg` and `arc`.

3.4.2 Physical Plans

BigDatalog translates logical plans into physical plans comprised of Spark SQL and BigDatalog physical operators. Like Spark SQL operators, BigDatalog operators use the Spark SQL `Row` type. Most logical-to-physical operator mapping is

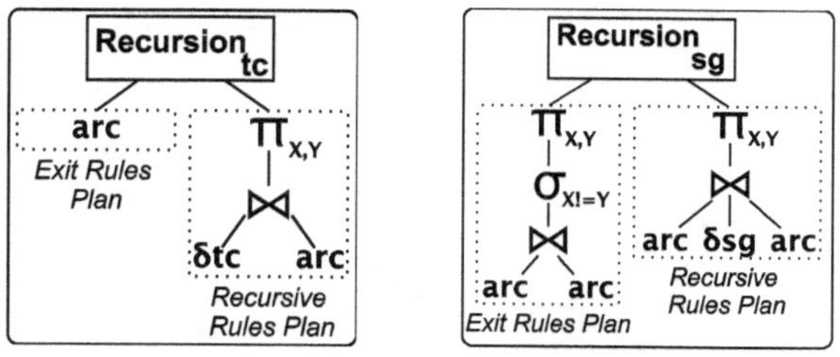

(a) TC (b) SG

Figure 4: BigDatalog Logical Plans.

straightforward, however *recursion*, *join* and *shuffle* operators require discussion.

Recursion Operators. The *Recursion Operator* (RO) is a special driver operator that runs on the master and executes PSN, i.e., the psuedocode from Algorithm 2. An RO has two child physical (sub)plans, the *Exit Rules Plan* (ERP) and the *Recursive Rules Plan* (RRP). A *Recursive Relation* operator represents a recursive predicate in the RRP and produces the recursive relation when evaluated (i.e., the plan version of a recursive predicate body literal).

Join Operators. BigDatalog uses binary hash join operators. We convert a multi-way join from logical plans into a hierarchy of binary join operators, in a left-to-right fashion. In a linear recursion, where only one join input is a recursive relation, the non-recursive input is loaded into lookup tables and the recursive relation is streamed. For instance, from the logical plan for TC in Figure 4(a), the RRP will have a join where δ`tc` is streamed and `arc` is loaded into lookup tables. To help explain our approach for non-linear recursions, we use the following non-linear program. In this program, *r2* creates new `tc` facts of the form `(X,Y)` by joining `tc` facts of the form `(X,Z)` with `tc` facts of the form `(Z,Y)`.

PROGRAM 3. *Non-Linear Transitive Closure*

r1. `tc(X,Y)` ← `arc(X,Y)`.
r2. `tc(X,Y)` ← `tc(X,Z)`, `tc(Z,Y)`.

In Program 3, *r2* will be (symbolically) rewritten for SN, as `tc(X,Y)` ← δ`tc(X,Z)`, `tc(Z,Y)`. Since both inputs to the join are recursive relations, δ`tc` will be loaded into lookup tables and `tc` will be streamed. We choose this approach because loading the smaller of the two into lookup tables is less expensive and after a few iterations, `tc` is likely to be much larger than δ`tc`.

Shuffle Operators. After mapping the logical operators into physical operators, the last step to produce a physical plan for execution is to add *shuffle operators* for distributed evaluation. Shuffle operators are used to repartition the dataset when there is a mismatch between an operator's required input partitioning and a child operator's output partitioning. For example, a shuffle operator is needed to repartition an input to a join if the input is not partitioned on the join keys. We use a Catalyst feature to analyze the physical plan and add shuffle operators where needed. We use hash partitioning and a static number of partitions throughout evaluation. Future work is to investigate dynamically adjusting the number of partitions during evaluation.

Example Plans. The physical plans produced for Program 1 (TC) and Program 2 (SG) are displayed in Figure 5(a) and 5(b), respectively. Using Figure 5(a) as our point of

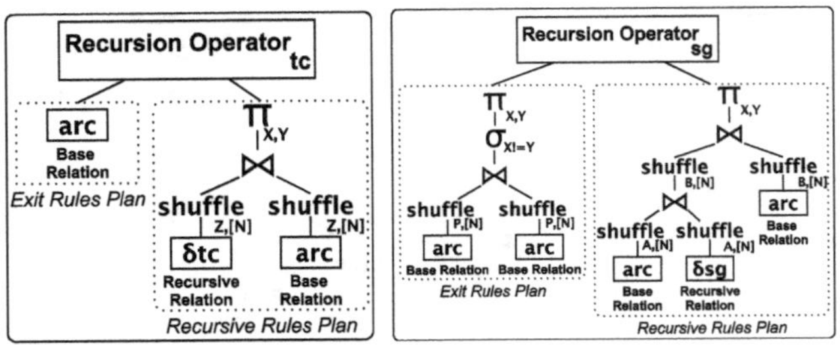

(a) TC (b) SG

Figure 5: BigDatalog Physical Plans.

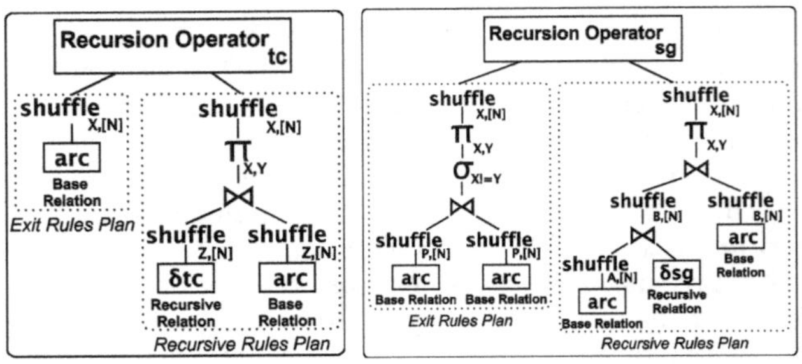

(a) TC (b) SG

Figure 6: PSN with SetRDD Physical Plans.

reference, we explain how our operators from above are used in plans. The root of the plan is the RO for the `tc` recursive predicate. In the RRP, δ`tc` is a `Recursive Relation` and when evaluated will produce `tc`'s facts from the previous iteration. Both inputs to the binary hash join are shuffled. The subscript `Z`, [`N`] indicates the partitioning key is the `Z` argument (from the rule), and there will be `N` partitions. Here `Z` is the join argument so that tuples of `arc` and δ`tc` having the same key will be co-located on the same worker.

4. OPTIMIZATIONS

This section presents optimizations to improve the performance of BigDatalog programs. Details on the datasets used in experiments in this section can be found in Section 6.

4.1 Optimizing PSN

As shown with Algorithm 2, PSN can be implemented with RDDs and transformations such as `subtract`, `distinct` and `union`. However, using standard RDD transformations is inefficient because each iteration the results of the recursive rules are set-differenced with the entire recursive relation (line 6 in Algorithm 2), which is growing each iteration, and thus expensive data structures must be created each iteration. We propose instead to use the *SetRDD*, a specialized RDD for storing distinct `Rows` and tailored for set operations needed for PSN. Each partition of a SetRDD is a set data structure.

Monotonicity and RDD Immutability. We can apply an optimization enabled by DATALOG set-containment semantics to efficiently produce a new SetRDD from the union transformation. Although an RDD is intended to be immutable, we make SetRDD mutable under the union operation. The `union` mutates the set data structure of each SetRDD partition and outputs a new SetRDD comprised of these same set data structures. If a task performing union fails and must be re-executed, this approach will not lead to incorrect results because union is monotonic and facts can be added only once. This design saves system memory because only one set exists per partition across all iterations.

Table 1 displays the results of evaluating TC and SG with both PSN and PSN with SetRDD. PSN with SetRDD outperforms PSN significantly in all cases.

Table 1: PSN vs. PSN with SetRDD Performance

Time (s)	TC			SG		
	Tree17	Grid150	G10K	Tree11	Grid150	G10K
PSN	244	OOM	208	OOM	230	1129
PSN with SetRDD	41	134	20	59	61	130

4.2 Partitioning

The initial version of PSN used RDD transformations (e.g., `distinct`, `subtract`) that performed the necessary shuffling operations. That approach was sufficient to produce a correct result, but could be inefficient to evaluate. Now, SetRDD's `diff` and `union` transformations are designed to require properly partitioned input (i.e., they will not shuffle). Therefore, none of the transformations used in PSN will repartition inputs so shuffle operators need to be placed into ERP and RRP to produce properly partitioned output for PSN transformations. This approach allows for a simplified and generalized PSN evaluator and brings the insertion of shuffle operators to the workflow under the control of the BigDatalog compiler. With full control over shuffle operator placement, (i.e., communication decisions), BigDatalog can produce very efficient evaluations.

Earlier DATALOG research showed a good *partitioning strategy* (i.e., the arguments on which to partition) for a recursive predicate was important for efficient parallel evaluation [23, 30, 31, 56]. In general, we seek a partitioning strategy that limits shuffling. The default partitioning strategy employed by BigDatalog is to partition the recursive predicate on the *first argument.* Now we can produce plans for PSN that will terminate with a shuffle operator if the output of the plan does not match the partitioning strategy of the predicate. Figure 6(a) is the plan for Program 1 for PSN with SetRDD. With the recursive predicate (`tc`) partitioned on the first argument notice how both the ERP and RRP terminate with a shuffle operator.

User-Defined Partitioning. In the plan in Figure 6(a) δ`tc` requires shuffling prior to the join since it is not partitioned on the join key (`Z`) because the default partitioning is the first argument (`X`). However, if the second argument were instead made the default, the inefficiency with Figure 6(a) would be resolved but then other programs such as SG in Figure 6(b) would suffer (δ`sg` would require a shuffle prior to the join). Therefore, to support programs where the default partitioning will lead to inefficient execution, BigDatalog allows the user to define a recursive predicate's partitioning via a configuration option. For instance, by overriding the default partitioning and making `tc`'s second argument the partitioning strategy, the shuffle for δ`tc` before the join in Figure 6(a) will not be inserted to the plan. Table 2 shows the results of TC evaluated with the plan in Figure 6(a) versus the same plan, but using the second argument as `tc`'s partitioning strategy. In fact, on all graphs from Table 6, the plan using the second argument matched or outperformed the other.

Table 2: Comparison of TC with Different Partitioning

Time (s)	Tree17	Grid250	G10K
1st Argument	41	370	20
2nd Argument	26	265	19

Table 3: Join Optimizations for Linear Recursion

Time (s)	TC		SG	
	Tree17	Grid250	Tree11	Grid250
Shuffle join no caching	26	265	59	107
Shuffle join caching	17	196	56	81
Broadcast join	53	197	45	54

4.3 Join Optimizations for Linear Recursion

Input Caching. Since we use a static number of partitions and because non-recursive inputs do not change during evaluation, for a *shuffle join* implementing a linear recursion, the non-recursive join input can be cached. This can lead to significant performance improvement since input partitions no longer have to be shuffled and loaded into lookup tables prior to the join each iteration. Table 3 shows the improved performance of caching. For TC on Tree17, the time for shuffling and loading lookup tables each iteration is significant even though there are only 17 iterations. Grid250 also benefits from caching because although the dataset is smaller, evaluation requires 500 iterations.

Broadcast Joins. For linear recursions, instead of shuffle joins, each partition of a recursive relation can be joined with an entire relation (*broadcast join*[4]). For both types of joins, the non-recursive input is loaded into a lookup table. For a broadcast join, the cost of loading the entire relation into a lookup table is amortized over the recursion because the lookup table is cached and then reused every iteration.

Figure 7 shows an RRP for Program 2 (SG) where the three-way join from the logical plan (Figure 4(b)) has been converted to a two-level broadcast join. In the event that a broadcast relation is used multiple times in a plan, as in Figure 7, BigDatalog will broadcast it once and share it among all broadcast join operators joining the relation.

Table 3 shows the results of using broadcast joins compared to shuffle joins for TC and SG. SG benefits on both graphs from using broadcast joins because three shuffles are eliminated from the plan and these graphs require minimal broadcast time. However, broadcast joins proved inefficient for Tree17 for TC — the job to load and broadcast the lookup table takes as long as the entire execution using shuffle joins. Nevertheless, broadcast join is the default join operator for linear recursion, and shuffle join can be selected via configuration setting.

4.4 Decomposable Programs

Previous research on parallel evaluation of DATALOG programs determined some programs are *decomposable* and thus evaluable in parallel without redundancy (a fact is only produced once) and without processor communication or synchronization [57]. Techniques for evaluating decomposable programs are appealing for BigDatalog because data-parallel systems like Spark can scale to large numbers of cpu cores. Furthermore, mitigating the cost of synchronization and shuffling can lead to significant execution time speedup. However, even if a program is decomposable, the system still

[4]Broadcast joins are supported with Spark's broadcast variable infrastructure.

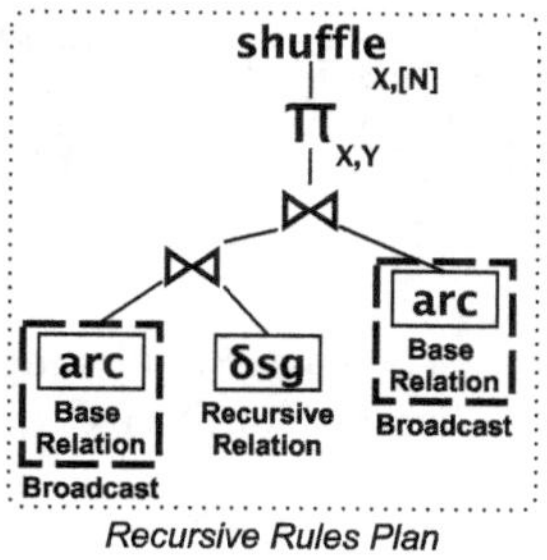

Figure 7: SG with Broadcast Joins.

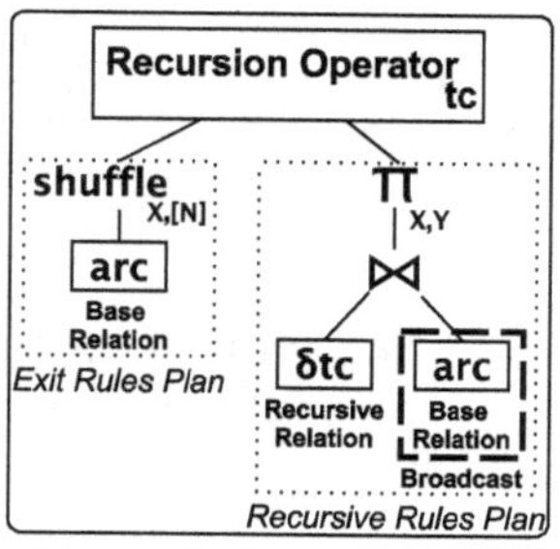

Figure 8: Decomposable TC Plan.

needs to be able to produce physical plans to evaluate it as such. We consider a BigDatalog physical plan decomposable if RRP has no shuffle operators.

Program 1 (linear TC) is a decomposable program [57] however, its physical plan shown in Figure 6(a) has shuffle operators in RRP. BigDatalog will produce a decomposable physical plan for Program 1 by partitioning `tc` on the first argument and using a broadcast join. The partitioning strategy (first argument) divides the recursive relation so each partition can be evaluated independently and without shuffling, and the broadcast join allows each partition of the recursive relation to join with the *entire* `arc` base relation. Figure 8 is the decomposable physical plan for Program 1. Since we do not pre-partition base relations, the ERP has a shuffle operator to repartition the `arc` base relation into `N` partitions by `arc`'s first argument `X`. Table 4 displays the execution times using the shuffle join plan and the decomposable plan (Figure 8). With the exception of Tree17, the decomposable plan greatly outperforms.

Table 4: Shuffle vs. Decomposable TC Plans

Time (s)	Tree17	Grid250	G10K	G10K-0.01	G20K
Shuffle	26	265	19	121	101
Decomposable	49	55	7	22	19

Identifying Decomposable Programs. BigDatalog identifies decomposable programs via syntactic analysis of program rules using techniques presented in the *generalized pivoting* work [46]. The authors of [46] show that the existence of a *generalized pivot set* (GPS) for a program is a sufficient condition for decomposablility and present techniques to identify GPS in arbitrary DATALOG programs. We have implemented the techniques described in [46] to determine the GPS for BigDatalog programs. When a BigDatalog program is submitted to the compiler, the compiler will apply the generalized pivoting solver to determine if the program's recursive predicates have GPS. If they indeed do, we now have a partitioning strategy and in conjunction with broadcast joins we efficiently evaluate the program with these settings. For example, Program 1 has a GPS which says to partition the `tc` predicate on its first argument.

Note that this technique is enabled by using DATALOG and allows BigDatalog to analyze the program at the logical level. The Spark API alone is unable to provide this support since programs are written in terms of physical operations.

4.5 Job Optimizations

Lineage. Since RDDs produced during an iteration are input for the next iteration, RDD lineage can grow long for

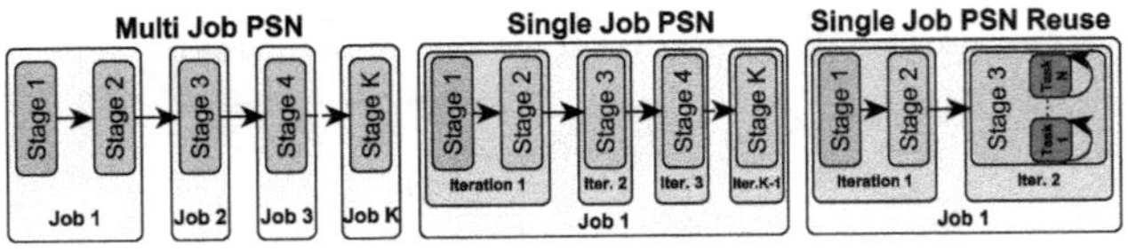

Figure 9: Program 1 (TC) Scheduling Options. ShuffleMapStages are orange; ResultStages are gray; FixpointStages are blue. Job 0 broadcasts the `arc` base relation.

recursive programs. Since lineage is inspected frequently during execution, for long running recursions we found this can result in a stack overflow. The standard solution is to checkpoint the RDD which clears the lineage after the RDD is written to disk. To optimize this, we implement a technique for cached RDDs that will clear lineage, but does not checkpoint. We sacrifice some degree of fault tolerance in favor of execution time performance, although this technique can still utilize cache replication. Otherwise, we leverage the standard fault tolerance mechanisms provided by Spark.

Scheduler-Aware Recursion. With PSN as shown in Algorithm 2, the scheduler is unaware that subsequent iterations could be required and therefore is unable to optimize recursive execution. To address this, we investigate pushing the recursion into the scheduler so recursive queries are supported as *Single-Job PSN*. We extend the Spark scheduler to use a special stage for recursion (*FixpointStage*) and support a *fixpoint job*, which is different from normal jobs in that 1) each iteration, the scheduler evaluates a new RDD over the previous iteration's results and 2) the scheduler will issue iterations until evaluation of the RDD results in an empty RDD indicating a fixpoint has been reached. We now refer to the original PSN (job per iteration) as *Multi-Job PSN*. To support checkpointing an iteration in Single-Job PSN, checkpointing is also pushed into the scheduler.

Optimizing Single-Job PSN. With Single-Job PSN, the scheduler is now aware that multiple iterations could be required. If a program is partitioned such that it does not require shuffling in the recursion, the scheduler will not create stages with shuffle operators. When the scheduler detects this situation, it configures the stage's tasks to iterate on workers and execute the same RDD until a fixpoint is reached. To support reusing the same RDD, the RDD partitions in the local cache from the previous iteration are overwritten with the RDD partitions produced during the current iteration. We call this *Single-Job PSN Reuse*. This approach eliminates the cost of scheduling and task creation for subsequent iterations. Figure 9 depicts the three different scheduling approaches for Program 1 (TC) evaluated with the plan from Figure 8.

Table 5 displays results of the execution times of TC and SG using the Multi-Job PSN, Single-Job PSN and Single-Job PSN Reuse. For datasets that require many iterations, such as `Grid250`, the performance improvement is substantial.

Table 5: Comparison of PSN Job Strategies

Time (s)	TC		SG	
	Tree17	Grid250	Tree11	Grid250
Multi-Job PSN	51	111	53	75
Single-Job PSN	49	55	53	53
Single-Job PSN Reuse	45	26	N/A	N/A

Note that this scheduler optimization is used on decomposable programs. Being able to identify a decomposable program (i.e., generalized pivoting) is independent from this optimization and thus this can be used in general to evaluate a decomposable plan, not just by BigDatalog.

5. AGGREGATES

BigDatalog supports non-monotonic aggregates (e.g., traditional SQL aggregates) **min**, **max**, **sum**, **count**, **avg**. As an example, consider Program 4, the BigDatalog program which counts the triangles in a graph, an important program in network analysis. In this non-recursive program, *r1* performs self-joins of **arc** to produce triangle occurrences which are then counted by *r2*. Lastly, note that although this program is expressed as two DATALOG rules, this program is a 50+ line GraphX program.

PROGRAM 4. *Triangle Counting*

$r1.\ \mathtt{triangles(X,Y,Z)} \leftarrow \mathtt{arc(X,Y), X < Y, arc(Y,Z), Y < Z, arc(Z,X)}.$
$r2.\ \mathtt{count\_triangles(count\langle\_\rangle)} \leftarrow \mathtt{triangles(X,Y,Z)}.$

However, non-monotonic aggregates cannot be used in recursion. Researchers have recently proposed aggregates that are monotonic w.r.t. set containment, the same monotonicity used by standard DATALOG, meaning these aggregates can be used in recursive rules and evaluated using techniques such as SN and magic sets [41, 42]. We have presented a sequential version of these aggregates in [49], whereas in this paper, we present a distributed version of the aggregates.

BigDatalog supports four monotonic aggregates - **mmin**, **mmax**, **mcount**, **msum**. The declarative semantics allows the aggregates inside the recursion so long as monotonicity w.r.t. set containment is maintained. Therefore, during evaluation the monotonic aggregates can produce new higher (**mmax**, **mcount**, **msum**) or lower (**mmin**) values with each input fact and thus an outer non-monotonic aggregate (**min** or **max**) is necessary to produce only the final value. An example of this can be seen in Program 5, the single-source shortest paths program (SSSP). Note, BigDatalog uses aggregates functions in rule heads with the non-aggregate arguments as the grouping arguments.

PROGRAM 5. *Single-Source Shortest Paths*

$r1.\ \mathtt{sssp2(Y,mmin\langle D\rangle)} \leftarrow \mathtt{Y = 1, D = 0}.$
$r2.\ \mathtt{sssp2(Y,mmin\langle D\rangle)} \leftarrow \mathtt{sssp2(X,D1), arc(X,Y,D2), D = D1 + D2}.$
$r3.\ \mathtt{sssp(X,min\langle D\rangle)} \leftarrow \mathtt{sssp2(X,D)}.$

The SSSP program computes the length of the shortest path from a source vertex to all vertices it is connected to. This program uses a `mmin` monotonic aggregate. Here the `arc` predicate in *r2* denotes edges of the graph (`X, Y`) with edge cost `D2`. *r1* seeds the recursion with starting vertex 1. Then, *r2* will recursively produce all new minimum cost paths to a node `Y` though node `X`. Lastly, *r3* produces only the minimum cost path for each node `X`, however in our actual implementation, we do not have to evaluate *r3* since at the completion of the recursion, `sssp2`'s relation will contain the shortest path from 1 to each vertex.

Evaluation and Implementation. Programs with monotonic aggregates in recursive rules are evaluated with an aggregate version of PSN we call *Parallel Semi-naive - Aggregate* (PSN-A). Compared with PSN, PSN-A is a simpler evaluator. Since new facts are only produced when a greater (`mmax`, `mcount`, `msum`) or lesser (`mmin`) value than the previous value for the (aggregate) group is produced, de-duplication is unnecessary. Furthermore, the union is unnecessary because new results are added to the aggregate relation during aggregate evaluation. We implement PSN-A in an aggregate version of an RO. Also, we use a specialized RDD called an *AggregateSetRDD*, in which each partition is a key value map where each entry represents a unique group and its current value. Caching AggregateSetRDD avoids the expense of reloading key value maps each iteration for aggregate. Additionally, since the aggregate functions are monotonic, as with SetRDD's `union` operation, AggregateSetRDD is mutable under aggregate evaluation. AggregateSetRDD will reference the same maps as its creator. Should a task fail during evaluation, any changes to the aggregate partition will not result in incorrect results since a value can only be updated if it is higher (`mmax`, `mcount`, `msum`) or lower (`mmin`) than previously computed values.

6. EXPERIMENTS

Experimental Setup. Our experiments are conducted on a 16 node cluster. Each node runs Ubuntu 14.04 LTS and has an Intel i7-4770 CPU (3.40GHz, 4 core/8 thread), 32GB memory and a 1 TB 7200 RPM hard drive. Nodes of the cluster are connected with 1Gbit network. Our implementation is in Spark 1.4.0 and uses Hadoop 1.0.4.

Table 6: Parameters of Synthetic Graphs

Name	Vertices	Edges	TC	SG
Tree11	71,391	71,390	805,001	2,086,271,974
Tree17	13,766,856	13,766,855	237,977,708	—
Grid150	22,801	45,300	131,675,775	2,295,050
Grid250	63,001	125,500	1,000,140,875	10,541,750
G5K	5,000	24,973	24,606,562	24,611,547
G10K	10,000	100,185	100,000,000	100,000,000
G10K-0.01	10,000	999,720	100,000,000	100,000,000
G10K-0.1	10,000	9,999,550	100,000,000	100,000,000
G20K	20,000	399,810	400,000,000	400,000,000
G40K	40,000	1,598,714	1,600,000,000	1,600,000,000
G80K	80,000	6,399,376	6,400,000,000	6,400,000,000

Table 7: Parameters of Real World Graphs

Name	Vertices	Edges	Source
livejournal	4,847,572	68,993,773	[9, 58]
orkut	3,072,441	117,185,083	[10, 58]
arabic	22,744,080	639,999,458	[5, 19]
twitter	41,652,231	1,468,365,182	[36]

Datasets. Table 6 shows the synthetic graphs used for TC and SG experiments. We use these graphs to understand how BigDatalog evaluates TC and SG on graphs exhibiting specific structural properties. `Tree11` and `Tree17` are trees of height 11 and 17 respectively, and the degree of a non-leaf vertex is a random number between 2 and 6. `Grid150` is a 151 by 151 grid while `Grid250` is a 251 by 251 grid. The G*n*-*p* graphs are *n*-vertex random graphs (Erdős-Rényi model) generated by randomly connecting vertices so that each pair is connected with probability *p*. G*n*-*p* graph names omitting *p* use default probability 0.001. Note that although these graphs appear small in terms of number of vertices and edges, TC and SG are capable of producing result sets many orders of magnitude larger than the input dataset, as shown by the last two columns in Table 6.

We perform experiments on REACH (Program 7), CC (Program 8) and SSSP (Program 5) using both real world and synthetic graphs. The real world graphs are displayed in Table 7. The synthetic graphs, `RMAT`-n for $n \in \{1M, 2M, 4M, 8M, 16M, 32M, 64M, 128M\}$, are generated by the RMAT graph generator [8] with parameters $(a, b, c) = (0.45, 0.25, 0.15)$. `RMAT`-$n$ has n vertices and $10n$ directed edges with uniform integer weights range from $[0, 100)$.

6.1 Benchmark Comparison

In this section, we report experimental results over the benchmark programs of Section 3.1. We compare BigDatalog with other distributed DATALOG systems, namely *Myria* [54] and *SociaLite* [48], and with options available in the Spark stack. The purpose of this comparison is two-fold. Firstly, it shows how the enhancements and optimizations proposed in this paper enable Spark to serve as an efficient runtime for DATALOG. Secondly, it shows how our BigDatalog implementation performs *w.r.t.* to other DATALOG systems.

For each system, one machine was dedicated as the master and each of the 15 worker nodes was allowed 30 GB RAM and 8 CPU cores (120 total cores). Myria was configured with one instance of Myria and PostgreSQL per node, since each node has one disk, which was confirmed as appropriate by an author of [54]. For Spark programs and BigDatalog, we evaluate with one partition per available CPU core. BigDatalog uses Single-Job PSN with SetRDD.

6.1.1 TC and SG Experiments

For TC, BigDatalog uses Program 1 with the decomposed plan from Figure 8. We use the Program 1 equivalent in Myria and Socialite, and a hand-optimized semi-naïve program written in the Spark API which is implemented to minimize shuffling. For SG, BigDatalog uses Program 2 with the plan with broadcast joins whose RRP is shown in Figure 7. We use the Program 2 equivalent in Myria and Socialite, and we also implement a hand-optimized semi-naïve program in the Spark API that attempts to minimize shuffling.

BigDatalog is the only system that finishes the evaluation for TC and SG on all graphs in Table 6, except SG on `Tree17` since the size of the result is larger than the total disk space of the cluster. Figure 10 shows the evaluation time for all four systems, while the results for graphs that only BigDatalog is capable of handling are not displayed. We now go into details for each program.

TC. BigDatalog has the fastest execution time on six of the seven graphs for TC; on four of the graphs it outperforms the other systems by an order of magnitude. The BigDatalog plan only performs an initial shuffle of the dataset, and then evaluates the recursion without shuffling, and proves very efficient. In the case of `Grid150`, which is the smallest graphs used in this experiment, in terms of both edges and transitive closure size, Myria outperforms BigDatalog. This is explained as the evaluation requires many iterations (300), where each iteration performs very little work, and therefore the overhead of scheduling in BigDatalog takes a significant portion of execution time. Note however that if BigDatalog instead evaluates `Grid150` with Single-Job PSN Reuse (Section 4.5), the execution time drops to thirteen seconds.

The Spark program is also affected by the overhead of scheduling on `Grid150` and `Grid250`, which requires 300 and 500 iterations, respectively, but also suffers memory utilization issues related to dataset caching and therefore runs out of memory. For the remaining five graphs, the Spark program is slower compared with BigDatalog due to the over-

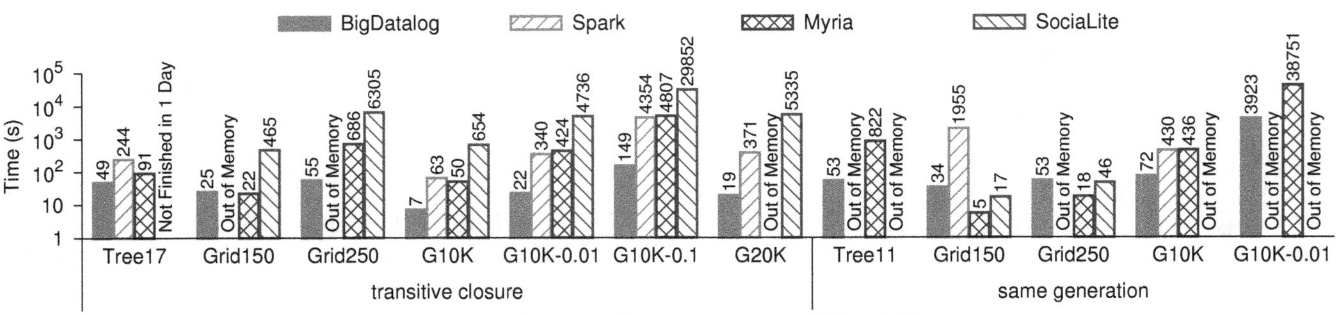

Figure 10: System Comparison using TC and SG.

head of shuffling. The same amount of data is also transmitted via shuffling or message passing for both Myria and SociaLite, but their performance is less stable compared with Spark. More specifically, Myria runs out of memory on `G20K` and SociaLite is always more than 10X slower. We believe this is, in part, because the implementation of their communication subsystem is less robust compared to Spark's.

SG. BigDatalog outperforms the other systems on the three graphs with the largest result sets for SG. Although evaluation of `Grid150` and `Grid250` produces the two smallest intermediate results and two smallest final results of our test graphs, because there is little work to be performed each iteration, Myria and SociaLite outperform BigDatalog on both of these graphs due to the overhead of scheduling in BigDatalog and differences in the generated physical plan. For instance, recall the RRP for SG in Figure 7. The two joins can generate a massive amount of intermediate duplicate results, however de-duplication occurs after the shuffle (in PSN). Therefore, to prevent a large amount of disk writes for the shuffle, we place a **`distinct`** operator into the plan immediately before the shuffle, much like a map-side combiner. However, this has a negative impact on execution time for the smaller graphs (`Grid150` and `Grid250`), but allows BigDatalog to support larger graphs. This optimization, along with Spark's robust shuffling implementation, helps to explain why BigDatalog is faster than Myria and SociaLite on `Tree11`, `G10K` and `G10K-0.01`.

For SG, BigDatalog outperforms the handwritten Spark programs on all graphs tested. Unlike with TC, the handwritten Spark program finishes the evaluation on `Grid150` as the amount of data it caches in memory for SG is much less than it does for TC. However it is over 50X slower compared with BigDatalog since BigDatalog only requires a single shuffle per iteration, whereas the Spark program has to shuffle between nested-loop joins. The handwritten Spark program runs out of memory on three graphs due to dataset caching.

6.1.2 REACH, CC *and* SSSP *Experiments*

We perform experiments comparing the execution time of BigDatalog for REACH, CC and SSSP programs with Myria, SociaLite and GraphX programs on both the RMAT graphs and the real world graphs of Table 7. For these experiments, we use programs for GraphX [33], Spark's graph processing module that implements Pregel [40], instead of handwritten Spark programs. GraphX outperforms native Spark on these types of programs [33], which we validated in our experimental environment. Lastly, these results also help us understand how BigDatalog scales on different programs as the graph sizes increase. Further scaling experiments are reported in Appendix B.

Let n, m and d be the number of vertices, number of edges, and diameter of a graph; the number of intermediate results produced during evaluation is $O(m)$, $O(dm)$ and $O(nm)$ for REACH, CC and SSSP, respectively. Figures 11 and 12 show the experimental results for the RMAT graphs and the real world graphs, respectively. For each system, we report the total time of evaluation starting from loading the data from persistent storage, i.e., from PostgreSQL for Myria and from HDFS for the remaining three systems, until the evaluation completes. For CC, each point represents the average evaluation time on the test graph over five runs. For REACH and SSSP, each point represents the average time over ten randomly selected vertices, run five times each. A point is not reported in a figure if a system runs out of memory for the experiment for all vertices. In general we noticed that for all three programs on our test graphs, SociaLite spends most of the time on the loading and initialization of base relations, and its implementation expects a fast network connection to load large datasets efficiently, as suggested by an author of [48]. Lastly, although both systems evaluate on Spark, BigDatalog requires storing less auxiliary data in memory than GraphX. We will now detail the results of each program.

REACH. The REACH program finds all vertices connected by some path to a given source vertex using a simple linear recursion. REACH can be found in Appendix A. Figure 11(a) shows that Myria performs the best on all graph instances for REACH. Although Myria significantly outperforms on the smaller graphs, as the graph size increases, and thus the amount of communication required increases, BigDatalog is able to narrow the gap in performance. Similar behavior appears also in Figure 12. On all test graphs, BigDatalog outperforms GraphX for REACH.

CC. The connected component program is depicted in Program 8 of Appendix A. It uses a label propagation approach for determining the lowest vertex id a vertex is connected to, thus establishing membership in a component. This program is interesting because it uses a monotonic **`mmin`** aggregate in recursion. The Myria and SociaLite programs are expressed similarly and we use the connected components program packaged with the GraphX distribution.

For the RMAT graphs, as the amount of communication increases, BigDatalog outperforms Myria starting from `RMAT`-8M for CC. BigDatalog is roughly 20% faster than GraphX for the RMAT graphs. SociaLite exhibits poor relative performance due to slow dataset loading times. For the real world graphs, we observed that BigDatalog outperforms Myria and Socialite on all four graphs, and outperforms GraphX on three graphs, the exception being **`arabic`**.

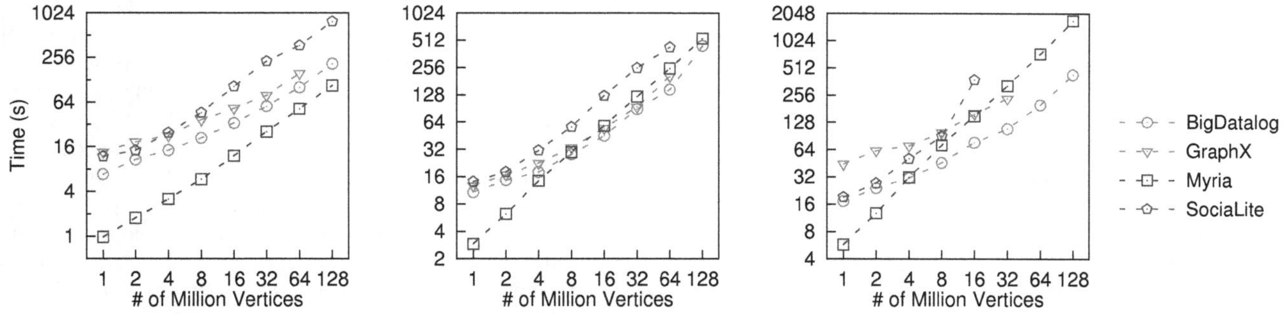

(a) REACH (b) CC (c) SSSP

Figure 11: Performance comparison on RMAT Graphs. The x-axis represents test graphs from RMAT-1M to RMAT-128M.

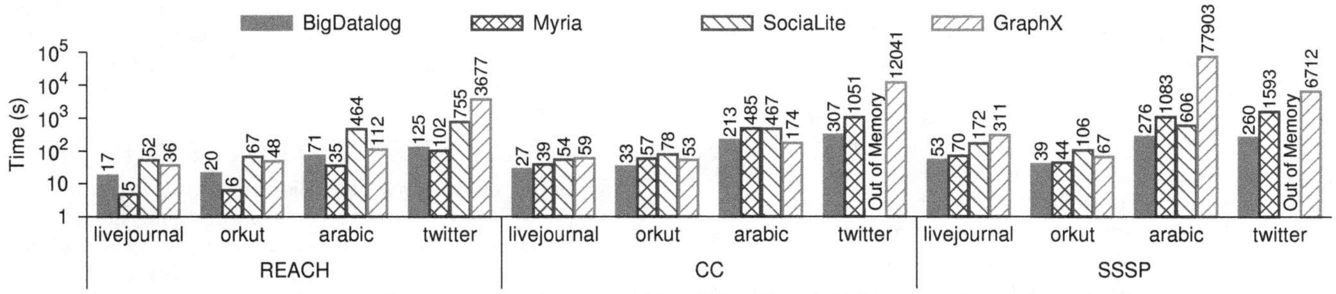

Figure 12: Performance comparison of REACH, CC and SSSP on real world graphs.

SSSP. This program was introduced in Program 5 and uses a `mmin` aggregate and a linear recursion. The Myria and SociaLite programs are expressed similarly. We have implemented SSSP in GraphX. As shown in Figure 11(c) and 12, BigDatalog outperforms all the systems on both synthetic and real world graph, except for Myria on the two smallest RMAT instances (1M, 2M). On all test graphs, BigDatalog outperforms GraphX.

6.2 Complex Data Analytics

In this section, we report experimental results on two data analytics programs, where each represents a complex data-processing pipeline of mixed graph and relational workloads. For each program, we compare BigDatalog against (1) a regular Spark implementation; and (2) an implementation that uses a mixture of GraphX (for graph computations) and Spark SQL (for the relational part of the queries). The later is the implementation that an expert programmer will design to be able to exploit system-specific optimizations.

People You May Know (PYMK) is a feature of LinkedIn that helps members to grow their network by recommending other people to connect with [6]. One important component used in PYMK is based on the idea that a member is likely to know the people that share many common connections with him/her. This is also known as *triangle closing.* Program 9 in Appendix A contains our implementation of PYMK. Specifically, we count for a given member `X`, the number of common connections with each member `Y` that is not already connected to `X`. We then display to `X` the members with top-k ranked count values together with their basic information. The member information are stored in a 200GB table produced using the PigMix dataset generator [11]. The query evaluation is depicted in Figure 13(a), where we used each of the four real world graphs in Table 7 as the member connection graph. This query is not recursive, therefore BigDatalog generates a plan that is the same as the regular Spark SQL plan. As the experiments show, the performance of BigDatalog is competitive to that of the GraphX/Spark SQL implementation of the query.

Multi-Level Marketing Network Bonus Calculation (MLM). Many companies use a multi-level marketing model to sell a variety of products [1]. The MLM query, as shown in Program 10 of Appendix A, computes the net profit of a company embracing a Multi-Level Marketing model after paying bonuses to members. A bonus is distributed to each member based on his/her personal sales, and the sales of each member of the network he/she directly/indirectly sponsored. The database contains the following tables:

- `sponsor(M, NM)` stores the sponsorship information. A new member `NM` is sponsored by a member `M` that is already part of the marketing network;
- `sales(M, S, P)` stores the transaction records, where member `M` sold some products for `S` dollars, and the gross profit of the transaction is `P`;
- `schedule(LS, RS, BP)` stores the bonus schedule, which is used to determine the bonus for making a sales of `S` dollars, i.e., the bonus is `BP` $\times$ `S` if `S` $\in$ [`LS`, `RS`).

We generate tables under a setting akin to the TPC-H benchmark [13]: for a given scale factor (SF), `sponsors` contains a forest of ten random recursive trees [12] with 150K $\times$ SF vertices in total, and `sales` contains 1.5M $\times$ SF

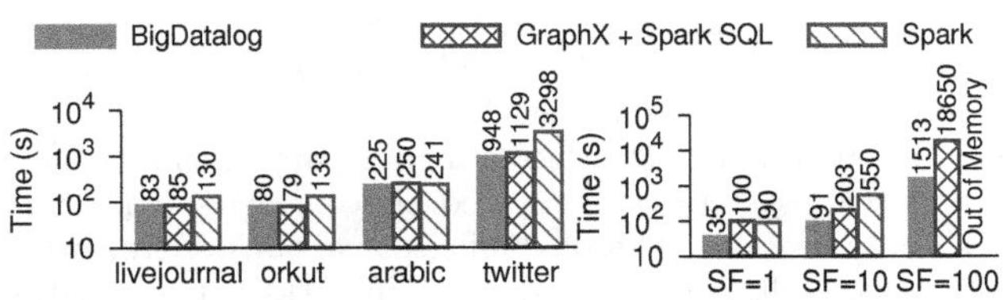

(a) PYMK (b) MLM

Figure 13: Comparison of complex data analytics programs.

records. `schedule` always contains 12 records. Figure 13(b) shows the experimental results on scale factors 1, 10 and 100; BigDatalog is consistently at least 2 times faster than Spark and GraphX/Spark SQL.

7. RELATED WORKS

Datalog Implementations. The Myria [54] runtime supports DATALOG evaluation using a pipelined, parallel, distributed execution engine that evaluates a graph of operators. Datasets are sharded and stored in PostgreSQL instances at worker nodes. SociaLite [48] is a DATALOG language implementation for social network analysis. SociaLite programs are evaluated by parallel workers that use message passing to communicate. Both SociaLite and Myria support monotonic aggregation inside recursion using aggregate semantics based on the lattice-semantics of Ross and Sagiv [45]. This semantics was shown to be not general and difficult to use in practice [53]. Furthermore, although operational semantics of their monotonic aggregate programs is provided, no declarative semantics is given. Instead, BigDatalog bases its monotonic aggregate (operational and declarative) semantics on works [41, 42] that use monotonic *w.r.t.* set-containment semantics, and therefore maintain the least fixpoint semantics of DATALOG.

Parallel Datalog Evaluation and Languages. Previous research on parallel evaluation of DATALOG programs determined that some programs are evaluable in parallel without redundancy and without processor communication or synchronization [57]. Such programs are called decomposable. BigDatalog identifies decomposable programs via syntactic analysis of program rules using the generalized pivoting work [46]. To our knowledge BigDatalog is the only current DATALOG system providing such a feature.

Many works produced over twenty years ago focused on parallelization of bottom-up evaluation of DATALOG programs, however they were largely of a theoretical nature. For instance [52] proposed a message passing framework for parallel evaluation of logic programs. Techniques to partition program evaluation efficiently among processors [56], the tradeoff between redundant evaluation and communication [30, 31] and classifying how certain types of DATALOG programs can be evaluated [23] were also studied. A parallel semi-naïve fixpoint has been proposed for message passing [56] that includes a step for sending and receiving tuples from other processors during computation. The PSN used in this work applies the same program over different partitions and shuffle operators in place of processor communication.

Among the distributed DATALOG languages, it is noteworthy to mention *OverLog* [24, 38], used in the P2 system to express overlay networks, and *NDlog* [37] for declarative networking. The $Bloom^L$ [25] distributed programming language uses various monotonic lattices, also based on the semantics of [45], to identify program elements not requiring coordination. [21] showed how XY-stratified DATALOG can support computational models for large-scale machine learning, although no full DATALOG language implementation on a large-scale system was provided. Recent works on recursive query evaluation showed efficient versions of transitive closure for multi-core [60] and distributed [14] settings, however these works did not address how to convert arbitrary programs to these desirable evaluation forms.

Systems for Large Scale Data Analysis. Spark [62] has recently gained much attentions as a general platforms for large-scale analytics. The Spark stack provides APIs for relational queries [16], graph analytics [33], stream processing and machine learning. DryadLINQ [61], REX [43], and SCOPE [66] provide high level languages for data analysis and support iteration. Extended MapReduce system designs providing API support include Haloop [22], PrIter [65], and Twister [28]. Incremental iterations were integrated into Stratosphere to support iterative algorithms with sparse computational dependencies [29]. ScalOps [55] supports a loop construct to include iteration in a recursive query plan executed on Hyracks [20], a distributed dataflow engine. Naiad [44] uses a time-based dataflow computational model to support iterative workflows and incremental updates. Distributed systems providing a vertex-centric API for graph analytics workloads include Pregel [40], Giraph [2] and GraphLab [39].

8. CONCLUSION AND FUTURE WORK

In this paper, we presented BigDatalog, a DATALOG language implementation on Apache Spark. Using our system Spark programmers can now benefit from using a declarative, recursive language to implement their distributed algorithms, while maintaining the efficiency of highly optimized programs. On our large test graph instances BigDatalog outperforms other state-of-the-art DATALOG systems on the majority of our tests. Moreover, our experimental results confirmed that among Spark-based systems BigDatalog outperforms both GraphX and native Spark for recursive queries.

Addressing our Challenges. We addressed the challenges for using Spark as a DATALOG runtime as outlined in Section 2.3 as follows: now with BigDatalog, recursive queries are compiled and optimized for efficient evaluation on Spark, which was verified by our experimental results (Challenge 1). BigDatalog is able to identify and produce physical plans for evaluating decomposable programs. In addition, we propose a new type of job for recursive programs to allow the scheduler greater control over iterations (Challenge 2). Lastly, we propose specialized RDDs (SetRDD/AggregateSetRDD) that utilize DATALOG semantics to support memory-efficient recursive evaluation (Challenge 3).

Future Work. In the course of this research we have identified several opportunities for exciting new directions. One first direction is to extend BigDatalog to support XY-DATALOG and realize the vision of [21] to use DATALOG to support complex machine learning analytics such as logistic regression over a massively parallel system. Another area is to investigate system extensions for provenance and fault tolerance enabled by monotonic DATALOG constructs.

For the latest updates on the BigDatalog project, see [7].

9. ACKNOWLEDGEMENTS

This work was supported by NSF grants IIS-1218471, IIS-1302698 and CNS-1351047, U54EB020404 awarded by the NIBIB through funds provided by the NIH BD2K initiative, and generous gifts from IBM Research, Symantec and Intel. We thank our reviewers for their thoughtful comments and insights. We very much appreciate the time and effort they put forth to make this a better paper. We thank Jingjing Wang and Jiwon Seo for their assistance with the experimental comparison.

10. REFERENCES

[1] Amway Business Reference Guide. https://www.amway.com/en/ResourceCenterDocuments/Visitor/ops-amw-gde-v-en--BusinessReferenceGuide.pdf.

[2] Apache Giraph. http://giraph.apache.org.

[3] Apache Hadoop. http://hadoop.apache.org.

[4] Apache Spark. http://spark.apache.org.

[5] arabic-2005 network. http://law.di.unimi.it/webdata/arabic-2005/.

[6] Big Data Ecosystem at LinkedIn. http://www.slideshare.net/mitultiwari/big-data-ecosystem-at-linkedin-keynote-talk-at-big-data-innovators-gathering-at-www-2015. Keynote talk at Big Data Innovators Gathering at WWW 2015.

[7] Deductive Application Language System (DeALS). http://wis.cs.ucla.edu/deals/.

[8] GTgraph. http://www.cse.psu.edu/~kxm85/software/GTgraph.

[9] LiveJournal social network. http://snap.stanford.edu/data/com-LiveJournal.html.

[10] Orkut social network. http://snap.stanford.edu/data/com-Orkut.html.

[11] PigMix. https://cwiki.apache.org/confluence/display/PIG/PigMix.

[12] Recursive tree. https://en.wikipedia.org/wiki/Recursive_tree.

[13] TPC-H. http://www.tpc.org/tpch/.

[14] F. N. Afrati and J. D. Ullman. Transitive closure and recursive datalog implemented on clusters. In *EDBT*, pages 132–143, 2012.

[15] T. J. Ameloot, F. Neven, and J. Van den Bussche. Relational transducers for declarative networking. In *PODS*, pages 283–292, 2011.

[16] M. Armbrust, R. S. Xin, C. Lian, Y. Huai, D. Liu, J. K. Bradley, X. Meng, T. Kaftan, M. J. Franklin, A. Ghodsi, and M. Zaharia. Spark SQL: Relational Data Processing in Spark. In *SIGMOD*, pages 1383–1394, 2015.

[17] F. Arni, K. Ong, S. Tsur, H. Wang, and C. Zaniolo. The deductive database system ldl++. *TPLP*, 3(1):61–94, 2003.

[18] F. Bancilhon. Naive evaluation of recursively defined relations. In *On Knowledge Base Management Systems*, pages 165–178. Springer-Verlag, 1986.

[19] P. Boldi, B. Codenotti, M. Santini, and S. Vigna. UbiCrawler: A Scalable Fully Distributed Web Crawler. *Software: Practice & Experience*, 34(8):711–726, 2004.

[20] V. R. Borkar, M. J. Carey, R. Grover, N. Onose, and R. Vernica. Hyracks: A flexible and extensible foundation for data-intensive computing. In *ICDE*, pages 1151–1162, 2011.

[21] Y. Bu, V. R. Borkar, M. J. Carey, J. Rosen, N. Polyzotis, T. Condie, M. Weimer, and R. Ramakrishnan. Scaling datalog for machine learning on big data. *CoRR*, abs/1203.0160, 2012.

[22] Y. Bu, B. Howe, M. Balazinska, and M. D. Ernst. The haloop approach to large-scale iterative data analysis. *The VLDB Journal*, 21(2):169–190, 2012.

[23] S. Cohen and O. Wolfson. Why a single parallelization strategy is not enough in knowledge bases. In *PODS*, pages 200–216, 1989.

[24] T. Condie, D. Chu, J. M. Hellerstein, and P. Maniatis. Evita raced: metacompilation for declarative networks. *PVLDB*, 1(1):1153–1165, Aug. 2008.

[25] N. Conway, W. R. Marczak, P. Alvaro, J. M. Hellerstein, and D. Maier. Logic and lattices for distributed programming. In *SoCC*, 2012.

[26] J. Dean and S. Ghemawat. Mapreduce: Simplified data processing on large clusters. In *OSDI*, pages 137–150, 2004.

[27] J. Eisner and N. W. Filardo. Dyna: Extending datalog for modern ai. In *Datalog Reloaded*, pages 181–220, 2010.

[28] J. Ekanayake, H. Li, B. Zhang, T. Gunarathne, S.-H. Bae, J. Qiu, and G. Fox. Twister: a runtime for iterative mapreduce. In *HPDC*, pages 810–818, 2010.

[29] S. Ewen, K. Tzoumas, M. Kaufmann, and V. Markl. Spinning fast iterative data flows. *PVLDB*, 5(11):1268–1279, 2012.

[30] S. Ganguly, A. Silberschatz, and S. Tsur. A framework for the parallel processing of datalog queries. In *SIGMOD*, pages 143–152, 1990.

[31] S. Ganguly, A. Silberschatz, and S. Tsur. Parallel bottom-up processing of datalog queries. *The Journal of Logic Programming*, 14(1):101–126, 1992.

[32] A. Gates, O. Natkovich, S. Chopra, P. Kamath, S. Narayanam, C. Olston, B. Reed, S. Srinivasan, and U. Srivastava. Building a highlevel dataflow system on top of mapreduce: The pig experience. *PVLDB*, 2(2), 2009.

[33] J. E. Gonzalez, R. S. Xin, A. Dave, D. Crankshaw, M. J. Franklin, and I. Stoica. Graphx: Graph processing in a distributed dataflow framework. In *OSDI*, pages 599–613, 2014.

[34] M. Interlandi and L. Tanca. On the CALM principle for BSP computation. In *AMW*, 2015.

[35] M. Isard, M. Budiu, Y. Yu, A. Birrell, and D. Fetterly. Dryad: distributed data-parallel programs from sequential building blocks. In *EuroSys*, pages 59–72, 2007.

[36] H. Kwak, C. Lee, H. Park, and S. Moon. What is twitter, a social network or a news media? In *WWW*, pages 591–600. ACM, 2010.

[37] B. T. Loo, T. Condie, M. N. Garofalakis, D. E. Gay, J. M. Hellerstein, P. Maniatis, R. Ramakrishnan, T. Roscoe, and I. Stoica. Declarative networking: language, execution and optimization. In *SIGMOD*, pages 97–108. ACM, 2006.

[38] B. T. Loo, T. Condie, J. M. Hellerstein, P. Maniatis, T. Roscoe, and I. Stoica. Implementing declarative overlays. In *SOSP*, pages 75–90. ACM, 2005.

[39] Y. Low, D. Bickson, J. Gonzalez, C. Guestrin, A. Kyrola, and J. M. Hellerstein. Distributed graphlab: A framework for machine learning and data mining in the cloud. *PVLDB*, 5(8):716–727, 2012.

[40] G. Malewicz, M. H. Austern, A. J. Bik, J. C. Dehnert, I. Horn, N. Leiser, and G. Czajkowski. Pregel: A system for large-scale graph processing. In *SIGMOD*, pages 135–146, 2010.

[41] M. Mazuran, E. Serra, and C. Zaniolo. A declarative

extension of horn clauses, and its significance for datalog and its applications. *TPLP*, 13(4-5):609–623, 2013.

[42] M. Mazuran, E. Serra, and C. Zaniolo. Extending the power of datalog recursion. *The VLDB Journal*, 22(4):471–493, 2013.

[43] S. R. Mihaylov, Z. G. Ives, and S. Guha. Rex: Recursive, delta-based data-centric computation. *PVLDB*, 5(11):1280–1291, July 2012.

[44] D. G. Murray, F. McSherry, R. Isaacs, M. Isard, P. Barham, and M. Abadi. Naiad: A timely dataflow system. In *SOSP*, pages 439–455, 2013.

[45] K. A. Ross and Y. Sagiv. Monotonic aggregation in deductive databases. In *PODS*, pages 114–126, 1992.

[46] J. Seib and G. Lausen. Parallelizing datalog programs by generalized pivoting. In *PODS*, pages 241–251, 1991.

[47] J. Seo, S. Guo, and M. S. Lam. Socialite: Datalog extensions for efficient social network analysis. In *ICDE*, pages 278–289, 2013.

[48] J. Seo, J. Park, J. Shin, and M. S. Lam. Distributed socialite: A datalog-based language for large-scale graph analysis. *PVLDB*, 6(14):1906–1917, 2013.

[49] A. Shkapsky, M. Yang, and C. Zaniolo. Optimizing recursive queries with monotonic aggregates in deals. In *ICDE*, pages 867–878, 2015.

[50] A. Shkapsky, K. Zeng, and C. Zaniolo. Graph queries in a next-generation datalog system. *PVLDB*, 6(12):1258–1261, 2013.

[51] A. Thusoo, J. S. Sarma, N. Jain, Z. Shao, P. Chakka, S. Anthony, H. Liu, P. Wyckoff, and R. Murthy. Hive - a warehousing solution over a map-reduce framework. *PVLDB*, 2(2):1626–1629, 2009.

[52] A. Van Gelder. A message passing framework for logical query evaluation. In *SIGMOD*, pages 155–165, 1986.

[53] A. Van Gelder. Foundations of aggregation in deductive databases. In *DOOD*, pages 13–34, 1993.

[54] J. Wang, M. Balazinska, and D. Halperin. Asynchronous and fault-tolerant recursive datalog evaluation in shared-nothing engines. *PVLDB*, 8(12):1542–1553, 2015.

[55] M. Weimer, T. Condie, and R. Ramakrishnan. Machine learning in scalops, a higher order cloud computing language. In *BigLearn*, December 2011.

[56] O. Wolfson and A. Ozeri. A new paradigm for parallel and distributed rule-processing. In *SIGMOD*, pages 133–142, 1990.

[57] O. Wolfson and A. Silberschatz. Distributed processing of logic programs. In *SIGMOD*, pages 329–336, 1988.

[58] J. Yang and J. Leskovec. Defining and evaluating network communities based on ground-truth. *Knowledge and Information Systems*, 42(1):181–213, 2015.

[59] M. Yang, A. Shkapsky, and C. Zaniolo. Parallel bottom-up evaluation of logic programs: DeALS on shared-memory multicore machines. In *Technical Communications of ICLP*, 2015.

[60] M. Yang and C. Zaniolo. Main memory evaluation of recursive queries on multicore machines. In *IEEE Big Data*, pages 251–260, 2014.

[61] Y. Yu, M. Isard, D. Fetterly, M. Budiu, Ú. Erlingsson, P. K. Gunda, and J. Currey. Dryadlinq: A system for general-purpose distributed data-parallel computing using a high-level language. In *OSDI*, pages 1–14, 2008.

[62] M. Zaharia, M. Chowdhury, T. Das, A. Dave, J. Ma, M. McCauley, M. J. Franklin, S. Shenker, and I. Stoica. Resilient distributed datasets: A fault-tolerant abstraction for in-memory cluster computing. In *NSDI*, 2012.

[63] C. Zaniolo, S. Ceri, C. Faloutsos, R. T. Snodgrass, V. S. Subrahmanian, and R. Zicari. *Advanced Database Systems*. Morgan Kaufmann, 1997.

[64] V. Zaychik Moffitt, J. Stoyanovich, S. Abiteboul, and G. Miklau. Collaborative access control in webdamlog. In *SIGMOD*, pages 197–211, 2015.

[65] Y. Zhang, Q. Gao, L. Gao, and C. Wang. Priter: A distributed framework for prioritized iterative computations. In *SOCC*, pages 13:1–13:14, 2011.

[66] J. Zhou, N. Bruno, M.-C. Wu, P.-A. Larson, R. Chaiken, and D. Shakib. Scope: Parallel databases meet mapreduce. *The VLDB Journal*, 21(5):611–636, Oct. 2012.

APPENDIX

A. ADDITIONAL QUERIES

PROGRAM 6. *Who will attend the party?*

```
r1. cntComing(Y, mcount⟨X⟩) ← attend(X), friend(Y, X).
r2. attend(X) ← organizer(X).
r3. attend(X) ← cntComing(X, N), N ≥ 3.
```

Program 6 is the ATTEND program which identifies people who will attend a party if they are an organizer or at least three of their friends are attending. A version of this program was originally proposed in [45]. This program is explained as follows. The **friend(Y,X)** predicate instance represents that person Y is a friend of X. *r1* uses the **mcount** monotonic aggregate inside the recursion to count the number of friends X that each person Y knows who is going to the party. *r2* says that organizers attend the party. *r3* determines X is going to the party if they have at least three friends already attending.

There are two attributes of the ATTEND program worth noting. Firstly, this program has a mutual recursion between the **attend** and **cntComing** recursive predicates. The query to evaluate the program will be of the form **attend(X)** so BigDatalog will make the **attend** predicate the RO, and thus the driver of the recursion, and **cntComing** will be a non-driver recursion operator in **attend**'s RRP. Second, the comparison $N \geq 3$ in *r3* provides an example of a monotonic arithmetic and monotonic boolean expression[5], the only type of expressions allowed on the result of a monotonic aggregate. If instead of ≥, equality was used, this comparison would only be true at three and then become false at higher counts and thus introduce non-monotonicity. □

PROGRAM 7. *Reachability*

```
r1. reach(Y) ← Y = $ID.
r2. reach(Y) ← reach(X), arc(X, Y).
```

[5]Once a monotonic boolean expression evaluates to true, it stays true for evaluations on subsequent values.

The reachability (REACH) program identifies all nodes reachable from the given source node $ID. It has a linear recursion and a unary (single argument) recursive predicate (**reach**). *r1* initializes the recursion from $ID. Then, in *r2* previously computed **reach** facts are joined to **arc** to find new vertices reachable from $ID. □

PROGRAM 8. *Connected Components*

```
r1. cc2(X, mmin⟨X⟩) ← arc(X, _).
r2. cc2(Y, mmin⟨Z⟩) ← cc2(X, Z), arc(X, Y).
r3. cc(X, min⟨Y⟩) ← cc2(X, Y).
```

The connected components (CC) program is used to identify the connected components of a graph. This program works by initially assigning the node's id to itself (*r1*), and then propagating a new lower node id for any edge the node is connected to. *r3* is necessary to select only the minimum node id Y for each X found in cc2. □

PROGRAM 9. *People You May Know*

```
r1. uarc(X, Y) ← arc(X, Y).
r2. uarc(Y, X) ← arc(X, Y).
r3. cnt(Y, Z, count⟨X⟩)) ←uarc(X, Y), uarc(X, Z), Y!= Z, ~uarc(Y, Z).
r4. pymk(X, W9, topk⟨10, Z⟩) ← cnt(X, $ID, Z), pages(X, W2, ..., W9).
```

The people you may know (PYMK) program is for helping members to grow their network by recommending other people to connect with. Let **arc(X, Y)** be the member connection graph. We assume the input graph to be undirected, but **arc** only keeps pairs (X, Y) that satisfy X < Y in order to save space. *r1* and *r2* construct the full undirected graph from **arc**, and *r3* counts the number of shared connections between each pair (Y, Z) such that Y and Z are not directly connected by an edge in the graph. In BigDatalog syntax, Y!= Z means Y is not equal to Z, and ~uarc(Y, Z) means that tuple (Y, Z) is not in **uarc**. For a given member $ID, *r4* first finds all the tuples (X, $ID, Z) in **cnt**, i.e., X is a candidate member to recommend to $ID, and Z is the number of shared connections between X and $ID; then finds the user information for each candidate member X, which is stored in the last column of **pages**. Finally, *r4* returns the top 10 candidate members (together with their infos) by number of shared connections. In BigDatalog, **topk⟨X, Y⟩** is a special "aggregate" function returning the top X tuples ordered by the Y-term. □

PROGRAM 10. *Multi-Level Marketing Network Bonus Calculation*

```
r1. networkTC(M, M) ← sponsor(M, _).
r2. networkTC(M, M) ← sponsor(_, M).
r3. networkTC(M, M2) ← networkTC(M, M1), sponsor(M1, M2).
r4. memberTotalSales(M, sum⟨S⟩) ← networkTC(M, NM),
                                  memberSales(NM, S).
r5. memberBonusSelf(M, B) ← memberSales(M, ST),
         memberTotalSales(M, S), schedule(LS, RS, BP),
         S >= LS, S < RS, B = ST * BP.
r6. memberBonusFrontline(M, sum⟨B⟩) ← sponsor(M, NM),
         memberTotalSales(NM, S), schedule(LS, RS, BP),
         S >= LS, S < RS, B = S * BP.
r7. bonus(sum⟨B⟩) ← memberBonusSelf(M, B1),
           memberBonusFrontline(M, B2), B = B1 + B2.
r8. grossProfit(sum⟨P⟩) ← sales(_, _, P).
r9. netProfit(NP) ← grossProfit(P), bonus(B), NP = P − B.
```

The multi-level marketing network bonus calculation (MLM) program computes the net profit of a company embracing a multi-level marketing model, after paying bonuses to members. **sponsor** is a directed acyclic graph that represents the sponsorship relation. *r1*, *r2*, and *r3* computes the transitive closure of **sponsor**, such that **networkTC** contains all the tuples (M, NM) where M directly/indirectly sponsors NM. For each member M, *r4* computes the total sales for the network where the members in the network are directly/indirectly sponsored by M. The bonus of each member M consists of the following two parts: (1) the bonus from his/her own personal sales (*r5*); and (2) the bonus derived from the sales of each NM directly sponsored by M (*r6*). Bonuses are computed by multiplying the related sales figures with a factor BP determined by the **schedule**. Finally, *r7* computes the total bonus paid by the company, *r8* computes the gross profit of the company, and *r9* computes the net profit for the company. □

B. MORE SCALING EXPERIMENTS

Here we report additional experimental results of how BigDatalog scales over different cluster and dataset sizes.

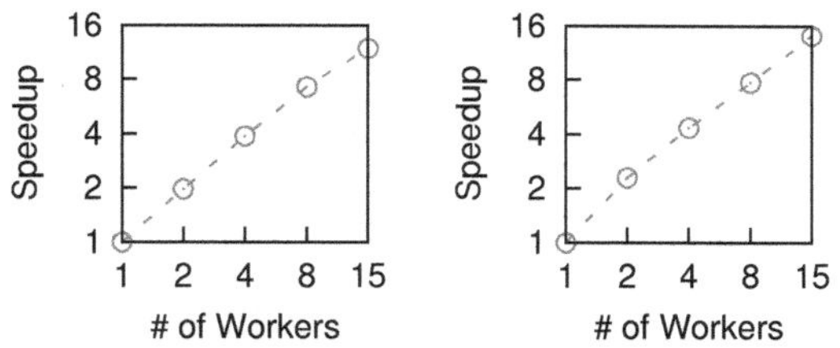

(a) TC on G20K (b) SG on G10K

Figure 14: Scaling-out Cluster Size.

Scaling-out. In this set of experiments we use the largest Gn-p graphs that could be evaluated on all cluster sizes. Figure 14(a) shows the speedup for TC on G20K as the number of workers increases from one to 15 (all with one master) *w.r.t.* using only one worker, and Figure 14(b) shows the same experiment run for SG with G10K. Both figures show a linear speedup, with the speedup of using 15 workers is 12X and 14X for TC and SG, respectively.

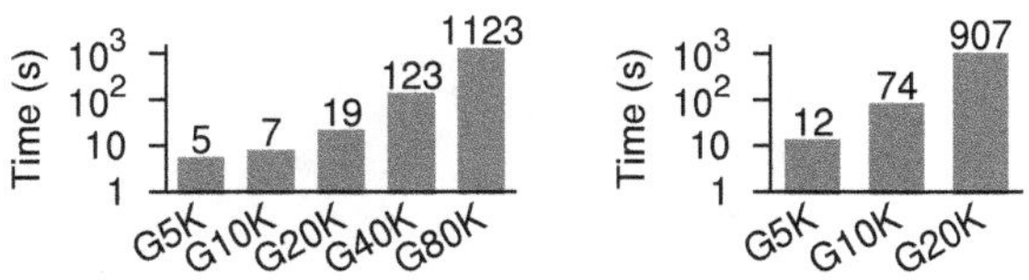

(a) TC (b) SG

Figure 15: Scaling-up on Random Graphs.

Scaling-up. We use the full cluster to see how BigDatalog scales over graphs of increasing sizes for TC and SG. We use Gn-p graphs from Table 6. For TC in Figure15(a) the smaller G5K and G10K graphs take roughly the same time to evaluate. From G20K, we observe the increase in runtime matches the number of intermediate facts produced, which should be viewed as the work the system must perform, rather than the increases in the size of the transitive closure. For example from G40K to G80K, the size of the transitive closure increases 4X, while the size of the intermediate results increases over 10X. We observe a similar result with SG. For example from G10K to G20K we observe a 4X increase in the size of the SG result set, but a nearly 16X increase in intermediate facts produced.

An Efficient MapReduce Cube Algorithm for Varied Data Distributions

Tova Milo
Tel-Aviv University
Tel-Aviv, Israel
milo@post.tau.ac.il

Eyal Altshuler
Tel-Aviv University
Tel-Aviv, Israel
eyalalts@post.tau.ac.il

ABSTRACT

Data cubes allow users to discover insights from their data and are commonly used in data analysis. While very useful, the data cube is expensive to compute, in particular when the input relation is very large. To address this problem, we consider cube computation in MapReduce, the popular paradigm for distributed big data processing, and present an efficient algorithm for computing cubes over large data sets. We show that our new algorithm consistently performs better than the previous solutions. In particular, existing techniques for cube computation in MapReduce suffer from sensitivity to the distribution of the input data and their performance heavily depends on whether or not, and how exactly, the data is skewed. In contrast, the cube algorithm that we present here is resilient and significantly outperforms previous solutions for varying data distributions. At the core of our solution is a dedicated data structure called the *Skews and Partitions Sketch* (SP-Sketch for short). The SP-Sketch is compact in size and fast to compute, and records all needed information for identifying skews and effectively partitioning the workload between the machines. Our algorithm uses the sketch to speed up computation and minimize communication overhead. Our theoretical analysis and thorough experimental study demonstrate the feasibility and efficiency of our solution, including comparisons to state of the art tools for big data processing such as Pig and Hive.

1. INTRODUCTION

Data cube [23] is a powerful data analysis tool, allowing users to discover insights from their data by computing aggregate measures over all possible dimensions. Imagine an analyst that is given a database relation describing products sold by a company in various cities in the world over the years. Using the data cube, it is possible to group the data by every combination of attributes and compute the aggregate over the different groups (e.g. product, year, location, and subsets thereof) and discover interesting trends as well as anomalies.

SIGMOD'16, June 26-July 01, 2016, San Francisco, CA, USA

DOI: http://dx.doi.org/10.1145/2882903.2882922

While very useful, the data cube is expensive to compute, in particular when the input relation is large. Consequently, much research has been devoted for developing efficient algorithms for cube computation [15, 22, 31, 36, 30]. Such efficient computation becomes even more intricate and more critical in a big data scenario, where information is spread over many machines in dedicated platforms employed for enabling parallel computation over huge amounts of data. New cube algorithms that best exploit the properties of these platforms must be developed. Our work focuses on one such popular platform - MapReduce [19]. *We present here a new efficient algorithm for computing data cubes over large data sets in MapReduce environments and show that it consistently performs better than the previous solutions.*

Before describing our results, let us briefly explain how the MapReduce framework operates and what are the weaknesses of previously developed cube algorithms for this framework. MapReduce programs use two functions, map and reduce, that are executed in a cluster in two phases. In the first phase, all machines run the map function and generate intermediate data which is delivered to the appropriate reducers. Then, in the second phase, all machines run the reduce function on their input to compute output. A MapReduce algorithm is typically built using a series of such MapReduce rounds. The key difficulty in efficient programming in MapReduce is to minimize network traffic between the machines while at the same time balancing their workload. This is particularly challenging in cube computation because some of the aggregated groups as well as the computed cube itself may be very large and thus balancing computation and avoiding the generation of large intermediate data is not trivial.

Several algorithms for data cube using MapReduce have been developed, e.g. [26, 8, 33, 25]. Some have even been implemented in Pig [5] and Hive [4] - engines that provide a database interface over MapReduce and allow users to query data in an SQL-like syntax. For instance, Pig implements the data cube algorithm from [26]. However, to our knowledge, all previous solutions, including those in Pig and Hive, suffer from sensitivity to the distribution of the input data and their performance heavily depends on whether or not, and how exactly, the data is skewed. Intuitively, skews yield large groups that need to be aggregated. For example, if an extremely large number of laptops were sold in 2012, they may not all fit (e.g. for their costs to be aggregated) in a single machine's main memory. Managing the aggregation of such big groups alongside many smaller ones is challenging. While some of these algorithms, e.g. [26], make an attempt to handle skews, the solution that they propose (to be explained later) is insufficient, and still existence of skewed groups affects the performance.

In contrast, our new cube algorithm gracefully handles mixtures of skewed and non skewed groups and consistently outperforms previous solutions for varying data distributions. The key idea underlying our solution is that to optimize performance, data must be analyzed at the *group* granularity. Note that by the definition of the cube, every subset of tuples that agree on the value of some group-by attributes contributes (after aggregation of its measure attribute) one tuple to the cube. We call each such tuple a *cube group* (c-group for short). While skewed c-groups have many tuples belonging to them, this large data is "compressed" by the aggregation and yields relatively small output. On the other hand, non-skewed c-groups are each small, but the cube computation may generate very many of them. To reduce network traffic it is thus beneficial to perform as much of the aggregation of skewed c-groups already at the map phase, whereas for non skewed ones it is better to postpone their materialization to the reduce phase. Our algorithm employs careful optimization to factorize, when possible, the computation across multiple c-groups, determine which c-groups should be computed where, and partition the work in a balanced manner among the available machines.

To support this we have developed a novel data structure called the *Skews and Partitions Sketch* (SP-Sketch for short). The SP-Sketch has two nice properties. On the one hand, it is very compact in size and fast to compute. On the other hand, it captures all needed information for identifying skewed c-groups and for effectively partitioning the processing of skewed and non skewed c-groups between the machines.

To understand the novelty of our approach, let us briefly contrast with the state of the art algorithm in [26]. The algorithm in [26] also uses sampling to obtain information about the data properties. However, a major disadvantage is that it makes a decision about the existence of skews *at the granularity of a full cuboid.* If a skewed group is detected, it aborts computation for the cuboid that contains this group, and recursively splits the cuboid. It then checks again, at each recursive iteration, for skews *at the granularity of the full given partition*, and if detected aborts the computation and splits the data again, and so on. The number of rounds thus depends of the skewness level, which makes the algorithm sensitive to data distribution. In contrast, our novel approach, and the use of SP-Sketch, allows us to determine, *in a single round*, skewness *at the c-group granularity*, for all c-groups in all cuboids. Neither recursion nor aborts are thus required by our algorithm, making it faster and resilient to any data distribution. The crux of our efficient solution is that we managed to prove that the for practical settings the number of skewed c-groups is in fact bounded and information on all of them can be kept simultaneously in main memory. While working at the c-group granularity was indeed mentioned in [26] as a desirable future direction that may allow for performance improvement, it is only this result of ours that made this idea practically feasible. The SP-Sketch, our use of it for data partitioning, the particular split of work between mappers and reducers, as well as factorized processing *at the c-group granularity* in the reducers, are all novel ideas.

Our main contributions are the following:

Formal Model. Our first contribution is a formal model defining the notion of (skewed) c-groups. We highlight the challenges that must be addressed by an efficient cube algorithm by analyzing a naive MapReduce algorithm. We formally define the notion of (skewed) c-groups and show why skewed c-groups need to be specially treated and why the relationship between c-groups must be exploited to avoid redundant network traffic.

SP-Sketch. Our second contribution is a novel data structure called SP-Sketch, that summarizes the important information for efficiently computing the cube. We start by presenting a utopian view of the SP-sketch, which is too expensive to compute. Then we describe an algorithm for building an approximated variant of the SP-Sketch. The algorithm is based on data sampling and is used to efficiently compute an approximated variant of the SP-Sketch. *We prove the sketch to have high accuracy as well as being small enough to entirely fit in a single machine main-memory.*

SP-Cube Algorithm. Our third contribution is an efficient algorithm that utilizes the previosly computed SP-Sketch, to efficiently split work between mappers and reducers: mappers will perform partial aggregation of skewed c-groups and determine which non-skewed c-groups may be processed together (and by which reducer). Reducers then process efficiently their assigned non-skewed c-groups and globally aggregate the (partially aggregated) skews.

Theoretical analysis. Our fourth contribution is a theoretical demonstration of the efficiency of our algorithm in terms of the size of machines' memory and the intermediate data transferred between the mappers and the reducers. We show that in an extreme (synthetic) case the amount of data that is transferred may be exponential in the number of cube dimensions. However, we prove that in common cases the size of the transferred data is only polynomial in the number of dimensions thereby enabling efficient processing. Regarding memory, we prove that the SP-Cube workload is balanced between the machines.

Experimental Analysis. Our fifth contribution is a thorough experimental analysis that matches our theoretical results. We experiment with two real-life data sets as well as synthetic data and examine the various steps of our algorithm and its performance as a whole. We compare the performance of SP-Cube to existing algorithms implemented in Pig and Hive. Working on varying data distributions, we show that SP-Cube consistently outperforms other algorithms, achieving between 20%-300% better running time and smaller network traffic.

Throughout the paper, assume the aggregate function to be applied is *count*, i.e the cardinality of every c-group . In Section 7 we discuss different types of aggregate functions to charactierize our algorithm in the general case.

Outline. We start in Section 2 by providing the necessary background and definitions. Section 3 then highlights the challenges in cube computation via a naive cube algorithm. Section 4 presents the SP-Sketch and analyzes it. Section 5 then describes our SP-Cube algorithm that uses the sketch and studies its properties. Our experimental study is presented in Section 6 and related work is discussed in Section 7. Finally, we conclude is Section 8. For space constraints, some proofs and experiments are deferred to the Appendix.

2. PRELIMINARIES

We start by providing the basic definitions for data cube and the additional notions that will be used in the rest of the paper.

2.1 Data Cube, Cuboids, and Cube Groups

Given a domain $\mathcal{A}$ of attribute names, consider a relation $R(A_1, A_2, \ldots, A_d, B)$ with a set $A = \{A_1, \ldots, A_d\} \subseteq \mathcal{A}$ of attributes called *dimensions*, and an additional disjoint attribute $B \in \mathcal{A}$ called the *measure* attribute. W.l.o.g we will assume that the set of attributes names in R is ordered, and denote a tuple in R by $t = (a_1, \ldots, a_d, b)$, meaning that the value of attribute A_i (resp. B) in t is a_i (b). We also assume that the measure attribute takes a numeric value. Finally, we assume that the value of the attributes (as well as computed aggregates over the measure attribute) can fit in a fixed number of memory bytes, and take this as a constant in our complexity analysis.

We will often be interested in only a subset $A' \subseteq A$ of the dimensions, and then replace the attribute names of R that are not in A' by $*$. Similarly, we will often be interested in the projection of a tuple t to a subset A' of the dimensions. We will then replace the value of the dimension attributes not in A' by $*$ and omit the measure value b.

EXAMPLE 2.1. *As a simple running example, we consider a relation R describing the products sold by a company in various cities in Europe over the years. R has three dimension attributes:* $A_1 = name$, $A_2 = city$, $A_3 = year$, *and a measure attribute* $B = sales$. *A tuple in R records the number of sales for a given product name, in a specific city and year. For instance, the tuple* $t = (laptop, Rome, 2012, 2000)$ *describes the fact that that* 2000 *laptops where sold in Rome at* 2012. *The projection of t to the dimensions name and year is denoted* $(laptop, *, 2012)$.

First introduced in [23], the *data cube* of a relation R is a set of relations, capturing of all possible group-by's that can be computed over a subset $A' \subseteq A$ of the dimensions of R, w.r.t some given aggregate function. Examples of common aggregate functions include *sum*, *count*, and *max*.

The result of each such group-by is given in a separate table called a *cuboid*. We often overload notation and denote a given cuboid by the set A' of dimensions on which its group-by was performed. Each subset of tuples in R that agree on the value of the group-by attributes contributes (after aggregation of its measure attributes) one tuple to the cuboid. We call each such tuple a *cube group* (c-group for short). For a given c-group g, we will often be interested only in the values of its dimension attributes, and will then denote g by its projection to these attributes. Finally, we refer to the set of tuples of R that was grouped together to generate g as *the set of g*, denoted $set(g)$. We say that a tuple t in R contributes to a cube group g if $t \in set(g)$. Note that by definition each tuple t contributes to multiple such cube groups, each corresponding to a projection over some subset of its dimension attributes.

EXAMPLE 2.2. *To continue with our running example, the data cube of R consists of* 8 *cuboids, including for instance the cuboids* $C_1 = (name, *, year)$ *and* $C_2 = (*, *, *)$. *The cuboid* C_1 *is obtained by grouping the tuples in R by product name and year, applying the aggregation function to the measure attribute of each group. Two c-groups in* C_1 *may be* $c_1 = (laptop, *, 2012)$ *and* $c'_1 = (laptop, *, 2015)$. c_1 *(resp.* c'_1*) is generated by aggregating the set of tuples* $set(c_1)$ *(resp.* $set(c'_1)$*) of R that includes all tuples describing laptop sales in* 2012 *(*2015*). The cuboid* C_2 *consists of a single value* c_2 *obtained by aggregating the measure attribute of the all tuples in R. Here* $set(c_2)$ *consists of all the tuples in R. Note that the tuple* $t = (laptop, Rome, 2012, 2000)$ *contributes to both* c_1 *and* c_2.

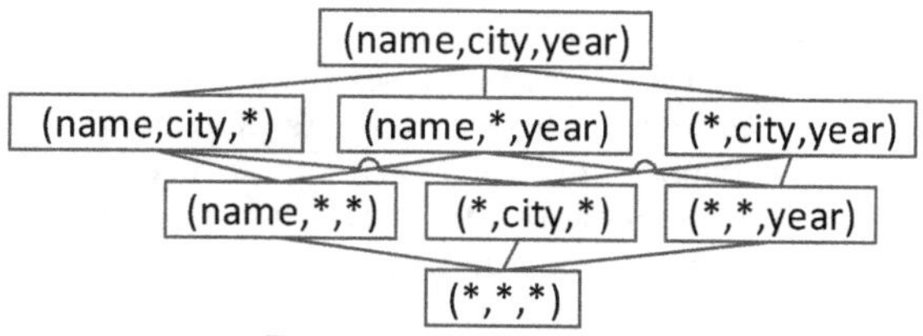

Figure 1: Cube lattice

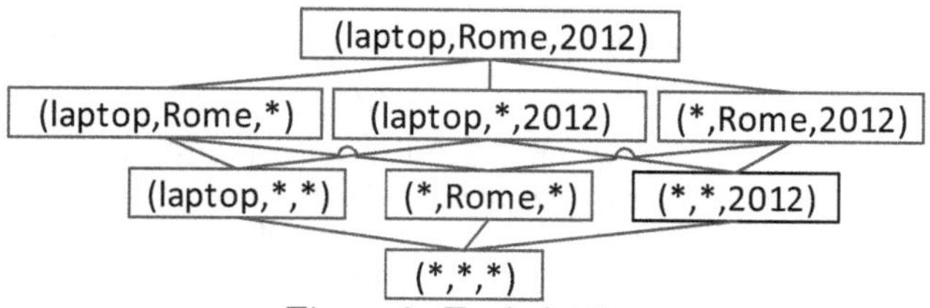

Figure 2: Tuple lattice

2.2 The Cube and Tuple Lattices

Inspired by [12] we employ here two notions of a lattice graph - the *cube lattice* and the *tuple lattice*, that capture respectively the relationships between different cuboids and cube groups.

DEFINITION 2.3 (THE CUBE LATTICE). *Given a relation R, the nodes of the cube lattice -* $lattice(R)$ *are the cuboids of R. In this lattice, a cuboid* C' *is a descendant of a cuboid C iff its set of group-by attributes is obtained from that of C by omitting one attribute. We say that C is an ancestor of* C' *iff* C' *is a descendant of C.*

An example of the cube lattice for the relation in our running example is given in Figure 1.

DEFINITION 2.4 (THE TUPLE LATTICE). *Given a tuple t in R, the nodes of the tuple lattice -* $lattice(t)$ *are all possible projections of t on subsets of the dimension attributes. A projection* t'' *is a descendant of a projection* t' *iff* t'' *is obtained from* t' *by omitting one attribute.* t' *is an ancestor of* t'' *iff* t'' *is a descendant of* t'.

Consider the tuple $t = (laptop, Rome, 2012, 2000)$. The lattice for t is given in Figure 2. Note that the nodes in the tuple lattice correspond precisely to the c-groups to which t contributes.

Two simple observations on theses lattices will be helpful in the sequel. The first, used already in previous work [26], concerns the cube lattice.

OBSERVATION 2.5. *For each cuboid C in the lattice and each descendant* C' *of C, C can be easily derived from the tuple sets of the cube groups in* C' *by partitioning the tuples in each set w.r.t the added attribute of* C'*, then generating one aggregated tuple per partition.*

This observation is the basis for the traditional BUC data cube algorithm [15], which processes the lattice bottom up, computing each cuboid from one of its descendants. The specific descendant from which each cuboid is computed is chosen using some heuristics for optimizing performance.

We observe here that an analogous situation holds for the tuple lattice.

OBSERVATION 2.6. *For every c-group g in the tuple lattice and every descendant g' of g, the set of tuples that is aggregated for generating g, is a subset of the set used to generate g'. Namely, $set(g) \subseteq set(g')$.*

This observation will be useful in our group-focused algorithm. Recall that each node in $latice(t)$ corresponds to some c-group g to which t contributes. If all tuples that contribute to a given cube group g (tuples in $set(g)$) are sent to the same machine (e.g. the tuples in $set((laptop, *, *))$), the machine can also use them to compute locally the ancestors c-groups in the lattice ($(laptop, *, 2012)$, $(laptop, Rome, *)$, and $(laptop, Rome, 2012)$), using e.g. the BUC algorithm, applied locally to the given tuples subset.

2.3 MapReduce Settings

We specify here the MapReduce cluster settings that will be used in the rest of the paper. Consider a relation R with n tuples and $d+1$ attributes. Working in a distributed environment, suppose we have k machines, and assume each one can run a single map or a single reduce function in every map or reduce phase, respectively. We assume that the n tuples of the input are equally loaded to the machines at the beginning of the algorithm. We additionally assume that the machines have a main memory that is in the order of their input size. We mark $m = \frac{n}{k}$ and assume that a machine main memory size is $O(m)$. In addition, we assume that all machines share a distributed file system, in which R is read from and to which the output data cube will be written. To conclude this section, we formally define skewed c-groups in terms of their freuquency relative to a machine memory size.

DEFINITION 2.7. *a c-group g is* skewed *if the cardinality of its tuples set is larger than m, namely $|set(g)| > m$.*

Note that the threshold of skewed c-groups depends on a machine memory size, m. For performance considerations, we generally want c-groups to be computed in main memory. As skewed c-groups do not fit in a single machine main memory, efficient treatment for them is challenging, and we explain later in the paper how our novel algorithm overcomes these difficulties.

3. GUIDELINES FOR EFFICIENT CUBE COMPUTATION WITH MAPREDUCE

Before presenting our algorithm for cube computation, let us first consider a naive basic MapReduce-based algorithm, and then use it to highlight the challenges addressed by our solution. Note that the naive algorithm we present has been improved by previous work, but our goal here is not to serve as baseline but rather, because of its simplicity, for highlighting the challenges that a good algorithm needs to address.

3.1 MapReduce Cubing - Naive Approach

We assume that the tuples of the relation R are read from a distributed file system and are equally split among the given set of mappers in an arbitrary manner. A pseudo code of the naive cube algorithm is shown in Algorithm 1.

Algorithm 1: Naive MapReduce Cubing Algorithm

```
1 Map(t)
2     groups = Nodes(lattice(t))
3     measure = measure-attribute(t)
4     for g ∈ groups do
5         emit(g,measure);
6     end
7 Reduce(g,values)
8     result = agg(values)
9     emit(g,result)
```

The algorithm starts by a map phase (lines 1-6) where each tuple t is projected on every subset of its dimensions. This is done by constructing the tuple lattice $lattice(t)$ and retrieving its nodes, which are precisely these projections (line 2). For each such projection, a (key,value) pair is emitted (line 5), where the key is the projected tuple and the value is the measure attribute of t (retrieved by the $measure - attribute$ function). All pairs are then sent to a reducer that is in charge on all tuples with the same key. Observe that by this construction all tuples belonging to a given cube group are sent to the same reducer. The specific reducer for each group is implicitly chosen by the MapReduce framework, by hashing the key (c-group value).

Next, in the reduce phase (lines 7-9), for every c-group, the reducer that received its corresponding tuples applies the aggregate function on the set and writes the resulting tuple (the c-group and its corresponding aggregate value) - back to the distributed file system (line 9). Note that for simplicity of presentation, the algorithm writes the c-groups to the distributed file system in an arbitrary order. If one wishes to generate one file per cuboid, the code can be slightly modified so that tuples of distinct cuboids are written to distinct files (with the files generated by the different reducers concatenated to form the full cuboid). We omit this here.

Let us discuss the problems with this naive algorithm.

3.2 Skews

The first problem with the naive algorithm is its sensitivity to heavy skews in the data. Consider a relation R where many tuples agree on the value of some subset of the attributes. For instance, suppose that many tuples have the value $(*, Paris, 2010)$ when projected on the *city* and *year* attributes. If the cube group for $(*, Paris, 2010)$ is larger than what can fit in a reducer's main memory, the corresponding reducer will not be able to perform the aggregation in main-memory and performance will suffer.

As we have stated, m denotes the machines' partial input size. Recall that a c-group g is *skewed* if the cardinality of its tuples set is larger than m. Since skewed groups cannot fit in the reducer main memory, the computation in the reduce phase will involve I/Os between main-memory and disk, making the overall computation slower. To avoid this delay, our optimized algorithm detects all skewed groups and partially aggregates them already at the map phase, before being sent to the relevant reducer. Interestingly, we will show that the number of skewed groups is not large, and thus this partial aggregation does not weigh heavily on the mappers. The formal upper bound for the number of skewed groups is proved in Section 4.

3.3 Load Balancing

In the MapReduce framework, work is distributed among reducers by implicitly applying some partitioning function to the *key* of each (*key*, *value*) pair and directing it to the resulting reducer. This can be a generic hash function, but also a pluggable customized one. Whether the resulting load is balanced or not depends on the compatibility of the partitioning function and the keys distribution. To alleviate the sensitivity to data distribution and assure that work is always evenly distributed, our optimized algorithm plugs a partitioning function that exploits the lexicographical order of cube groups. Intuitively, for a given cuboid, the relation tuples are (virtually) partitioned into k partitions of equal size, k being the number of reducers, such that the tuples in partition i, when projected on the cuboid dimensions, are lexicographically smaller than those of partition $i+1$. The (projected) tuples of partition i are then assigned to reducer i. We will explain in the next two sections how (together with skews detections) this partitioning is efficiently achieved and exploited by our algorithm for load balancing the reducers work.

3.4 Network Traffic

The naive algorithm treats each c-group independently and does not exploit the relationships between different groups. Indeed, for each of the n tuples of the input relation, Algorithm 1 generates 2^d projections, d being the number of dimensions, yielding an overall number of $n \cdot 2^d$ key-value pairs, sent over the network to the relevant reducers. As we will show in Section 5, much of this redundant communication may be avoided by exploiting the Observation 2.6. Intuitively, projections whose corresponding cube groups may be computed from descendants in the tuple lattice, need not be resent and instead can be computed by the reducer assigned to the smallest (non-skewed) descendant. We will explain this in more details in Section 5.

4. THE SP-SKETCH

We present our optimized cube algorithm in two steps. First we describe in this section the SP-Sketch data structure used by our algorithm. The sketch contains information that allows to (1) identify *skewed* cube groups (in section 3.2 we defined that a group g is skewed if $|set(g)| > m$) and (2) *partition* the relation tuples for balancing the reducers workload. Hence the name SP-sketch. Then, in the following section we explain how the SP-sketch is used by our cube algorithm to ensure efficient computation with reduced network traffic.

We start by presenting a utopian view of the SP-sketch, which is too expensive to compute. Then we describe an approximated yet accurate enough variant, that can be efficiently computed. We note that the SP-Sketch captures the properties of the input relation and is independent of the aggregate function to be used. Consequently, once constructed, the same SP-Sketch can be used to efficiently compute multiple aggregated functions.

4.1 Data Partitioning

We first define some useful auxiliary notions. Consider a relation R and a cuboid C of R. For two tuples t_1, t_2 in R, we say that $t_1 <_C t_2$ (resp. $t_1 =_C t_2$) if, when restricted to the dimension attributes of C, t_1 is lexicographically smaller than t_2 (resp. equals t_2). We denote by *sorted*(R, C) a *sorted* version of R where the tuples are ordered w.r.t $<_c$ (equal tuples are ordered arbitrarily). Let n be the number of tuples in R, let k be the number of available machines and let m be the size of a machine's memory. Recall that we assume that $m \geq \frac{n}{k}$, namely that the relation tuples can altogether fit in the memories of the given k machines. We can partition the tuples in R into k subsets, using the $k-1$ *partition elements* in *sorted*(R, C). We now define the partition elements of every cuboid.

DEFINITION 4.1. *The* partition elements *of* R *w.r.t* C *are the tuples in positions* $i\frac{n}{k}$, $i = 1 \dots k-1$, *in* *sorted*(R, C).

Given partition elements $t_1, \dots, t_{k-1}$, the first partition contains all tuples t s.t. $t \leq t_1$. The ith partition, $i = 2 \dots k-2$, contains the tuples t s.t. $t_i < t \leq t_{i+1}$. Finally, the kth partition contains the tuples t s.t. $t_{k-1} < t$. The resulting split has two nice properties that will be useful in the sequel.

PROPOSITION 4.2. *The following two properties hold -*

1. *For each non-skewed c-group* g *in* C*, all its tuples fall in the same partition, and*
2. *Omitting the members of skewed c-groups , all partitions are of size* $O(m)$.

In our algorithm, each partition (excluding its skewed groups) is assigned to a machine. The first property will guarantee that for each c-group all its tuples will be sent to the same machine, while the second guarantees bounded machines load.

4.2 Building the SP-Sketch

The (utopian) **SP-Sketch** is a graph with a structure similar to the cube lattice described in Section 2. For each cuboid node C in the lattice, the SP-sketch records two items: The first, denotes *skews*(C), records the set of skewed c-groups in this cuboid. The second, denoted *partition − elements*(C) records the partitions elements of R w.r.t C.

EXAMPLE 4.3. *Figure 3 depicts the SP-Sketch for our running example. It details part of the information kept for three of the cuboids. For each of the three cuboids we see (part of) its skewed c-groups and partition elements. Note that as the cuboid* $(*, *, year)$ *is a descendant of the cuboid* $(name, *, year)$*, all instances of a skewed c-group in the latter are also instances of the corresponding c-group in the former, making it skewed as well. For instance, the groups* $(keyboard, *, 2009)$, $(printer, *, 2011)$ *and* $(television, *, 2012)$ *are skewed c-groups in the cuboid* $(name, *, year)$*, and thus* $(*, *, 2009)$, $(*, *, 2011)$ *and* $(*, *, 2012)$ *are also skewed in the cuboid* $(*, *, year)$ *(which also as an additional skewed c-group -* $(*, *, 2014)$*).*

A naive but too expensive algorithm for building the SP-Sketch would build *sorted*(R, C) for all cuboids, then derive from the sorted lists the skewed cube groups and the partition elements.

Instead, we adopt here sampling techniques from [32] and [26] to build an approximated version to the SP-sketch. We

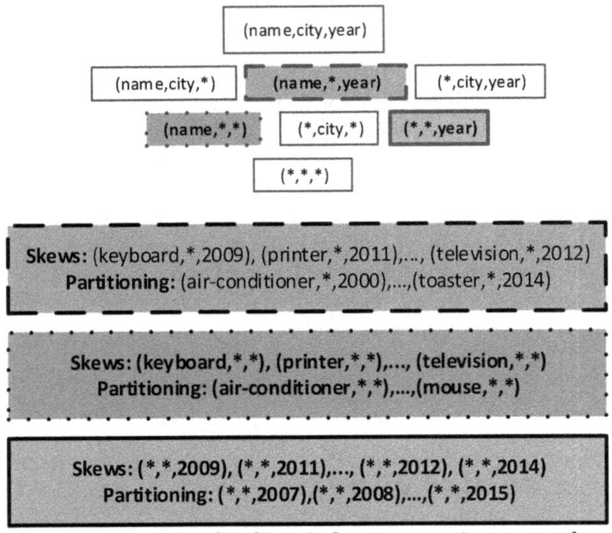

Figure 3: The SP-Sketch for our running example

sample tuples from R with probability α (to be defined below) for each tuple, independently of the others. Then, we build the SP-sketch based on this data sample. The sampling technique in [32] is a standard technique for sketching a data using uniform sampling. However, our use of the sample is novel. We use the sample to detect the skewed groups and partition elements of each cuboid (for building the SP-Sketch), whereas [32] uses the sketch to find bucketing elements for sorting. Algorithm 2 is a MapReduce-based implementation of this approximation algorithm, which we run in the first round in our cube algorithm (to be presented in the next section).

In the map phase (lines 2-5) the relation tuples are loaded from the distributed file system, equally split among the k mappers. Each mapper samples its tuples, and each tuple is taken into the sample independently of the others, with probability $\alpha = \frac{1}{m}ln(nk)$ (α is the probability to pass the *if* test in line 4). The specific value of $\alpha = \frac{1}{m}ln(nk)$ is chosen for ensuring a small sample size, for in-memory computations. However, we need the sample to be as informative as possible, as we use it to build the sketch. Therefore, it should contain enough tuples from the original data. Our mathematical development (see the proofs of Propositions 4.4, 4.5, and 4.6) have led us to derive that this chosen value of α achieves this desired tradeoff. The entire sample is then delivered to a single reducer that builds the SP-sketch (lines 7-10). Namely, this MapReduce algorithm uses k machines in the map phase, but only one is needed in the reduce phase. In the reduce phase, the SP-Sketch is built over the sample. The invoked *build-sketch* procedure (not detailed in the figure) implements a brute-force approach for building the SP-sketch, using in-memory computation, as follows (We will prove later that the sample is small enough to allow this):

Skews: For determining the skewed c-groups , we compute a cube over the sample and employ *count* as the aggregate function.[1] We then record as skewed the c-groups whose count value is larger than $\beta = ln(nk)$. Our choice of β is justified using the following tradeoff. If its value is too large, we might miss some skewed groups. If it is too small, we

[1]Our implementation employs here the classic BUC algorithm [15] but any cube algorithms will do.

Algorithm 2: Approximated SP-Sketch

```
1  // k mappers
2  Map(t)
3  |  pick at random α ∈ [0, 1]
4  |  if α ≤ (1/m) ln(nk) then
5  |  |  emit(0,t);
6  // 1 reducer, only 0 key, values - sampled tuples
7  Reduce(key,values)
8  |  sample = values
9  |  sketch = build-sketch(sample)
10 |  emit(0,sketch)
```

might consider too many groups as skewed, and the sketch would be too large to fit in a machine main memory. Our particular choice of β was designed such the SP-Sketch successfully captures all skewed groups in the cube (with high probability), but is still small to fit in all machines main memory. Its specific chosen value is formally justified in the proof of Proposition 4.5.

Partitions: For determining the partition elements, we sort the sampled tuples w.r.t to each cuboid C, and compute for each sorted list its $k-1$ partition elements: If n' is the number of samples, then the partition elements here are the tuples in positions $i\frac{n'}{k}$, $i = 1 \ldots k-1$.

Once computed, the SP-Sketch is stored in the distributed file system (to be later cached, in the second MapReduce phase of our cube algorithm, by all machines).

4.3 SP-Sketch Properties

We conclude this section by analyzing the size of the sample and the generated sketch, as well as its accuracy.

As mentioned above, the sampling technique that we use is inspired by [32] and [26]. [32] uses sampling to devise efficient sorting in MapReduce, whereas [26] uses samples to determine whether a given cuboid contains some skews. Our use of the samples, as dictated by the needs of the SP-Sketch, is slightly different - we only wish to partition the data and not to fully sort it, and we are interested in identifying all skewed c-groups and not just in determining whether some exist. Nevertheless, we can adapt some of the proofs from [32, 26] to our context, as we show below.

We first show that with high probability, the sample size is small enough to fit entirely in a machine's memory. Recall that we use n to denote the number of tuples in R, k the number of machines and m the size of a machine's memory.

PROPOSITION 4.4. *Assume every tuple is independently taken into the sample with probability* $\alpha = \frac{1}{m}ln(nk)$. *Then, with probability of at least* $1 - O(\frac{1}{n})$ *the sample size is* $O(m)$.

The proof follows the same simple probabilistic analysis as in [32] where elements are sampled independently with the same probability α. We thus omit this here.

We next show that the SP-sketch generated from the sample has high accuracy. The first proposition shows that the SP-Sketch successfully captures skewed groups.

PROPOSITION 4.5. *Let d be the number of dimensions and assume* $2^d \cdot k = O(m)$. *Then, with probability of at least* $1 - O(\frac{1}{k})$, *the algorithm detects all skewed groups.*

We note that the assumption that $2^d * k = O(m)$ is reasonable and typically holds in a MapReduce environment:

The memory of a reducer, m, is in the order of Gigabytes, whereas d is a small constant, and k, the number of machines, is in the order of hundreds or thousands.

The second proposition shows that the SP-Sketch successfully captures the partitioning elements of every cuboid.

PROPOSITION 4.6. *Let d be the number of dimensions and assume $2^d \cdot k = O(m)$. Then, with probability of at least $1 - O(\frac{2^d}{n})$, omitting the members of skewed c-groups , all partitions are of size $O(m)$.*

Finally, we show that the computed SP-sketch is small enough and can entirely fit in the main memory of every machine in the cluster.

PROPOSITION 4.7. *Let d be the number of dimensions and assume $2^d * k = O(m)$. Then, with probability of at least $1 - \frac{1}{k}$, the SP-sketch size is $O(m)$.*

5. THE SP-CUBE ALGORITHM

We are now ready to describe our cube algorithm, called *SP-Cube*. The algorithm is composed of two MapReduce rounds. In the first round, the SP-Sketch is built. In the second round the cube is computed efficiently using the sketch. We now explain this second round.

Recall that the SP-Sketch records k partitions for each cuboid, k being the given number of machines. Correspondingly, when sent to reducers, tuples from the ith partition, $i = 1 \dots k$, of any cuboid will be assigned to reducer i. For simplicity of presentation, we assume an additional given reducer, numbered 0, that will be in charge of aggregating the partial aggregates of skewed groups. (Otherwise this work can be assigned to one of the existing reducers).

Note that the SP-Sketch captures all requruired information for the algorithm to decide whether a c-group is skewed or not. This is implemented by maintaining a hash table in which items correspond to the skewed c-groups. The key for each item in the hash table is the (concatenated) value of the dimension attributes of the group. For each such key, the associated value is the c-group partial aggregated value. Then, to know whether a group is skewed or not, the SP-Cube algorithm checks whether the groups's key (concatenated value its the dimension attributes) appears in the table.

5.1 Algorithm Overview

The pseudo-code of our algorithm is depicted in Algorithm 3. We first explain what mappers do, then the reducers.

Map. The mappers process the tuples in the relation R as follows. For each tuple t assigned to the mapper, the tuple lattice $lattice(t)$ is built (line 4). Recall that each node in the lattice corresponds to one cuboid c-group to which the tuple belongs. The nodes in the lattice are traversed bottom up, in BFS (breadth first search) order (line 5). For each unmarked lattice node (initially all nodes are unmarked) we check, in the corresponding cuboid node in SP-Sketch node, whether the tuple's c-group is skewed or not. If it is skewed then we perform local aggregation, adding the tuple's measure value to the c-group (local) aggregated value, and mark the node as processed (lines 6-8). Otherwise, if the c-group is not skewed, we check (again, using the sketch) to which partition the c-group belongs. We send the tuple to the corresponding reducer, mark the node *and all its ancestors and their ancestors recursively* (lines 9-13) as processed, and continue with the next not marked node in the BFS traversal.

Note that if the given c-group is not skewed so are all its ancestors in the tuple lattice. Furthermore, following Observation 2.5, the reducer to which the tuple is sent will have all the needed information not only for computing the given c-group but also all its ancestors. This is why the ancestors are recursively marked as well and skipped (thereby reducing communication overhead).

Finally, once all tuples are processed, the mapper sends its partial aggregates of skewed c-groups to reducer in charge on skewed c-groups (lines 16-20).

EXAMPLE 5.1. *To illustrate the Map phase, let us consider the tuple $t = (laptop, Rome, 2012, 2000)$ and assume that the aggregate function is sum. The tuple lattice of t, depicted in figure 2, is constructed and traversed bottom up in BFS order, starting from the node $(*, *, *)$. As this c-group aggregates the values of all database tuples, it will be found in the SP-sketch as skewed, and thus the mapper performs local aggregation for the c-group and adds t's measure attribute (2000) to the so-far-computed sum. The node is marked and the mapper continues to $(laptop, *, *)$ - the next node in the BFS order.*

Assume this c-group is not skewed and that, according to the $(name, *, *)$ of the SP-Sketch, the tuple belongs to the second partition (as $(laptop, *, *)$ is lexicographically between $(keyboard, *, *)$ and $(printer, *, *)$). Thus it is sent to reducer 2 and $(laptop, *, *)$ as well as its ancestors in the lattice - $(laptop, Rome, *)$, $(laptop, *, 2012)$, and $(laptop, Rome, 2012)$ - are marked as processed.

Next the mapper continues to $(*, Rome, *)$. Assume this c-group is also not skewed. Then the tuple is sent to the reducer in charge of the corresponding partition, and both the c-group $(*, Rome, *)$ and its (non marked so far) ancestor $(*, Rome, 2012)$ are marked. Finally the mapper processes $(*, *, 2012)$. Assume this c-group is skewed (as it appears in the skewed c-groups list of $(*, *, year)$ in Figure 3), and thus the algorithm adds 2000 to the local partial sum maintained for $(*, *, 2012)$.

Once all tuples are processed, local partial sums computed e.g. for $(*, *, *)$, and $(*, *, 2012)$ are sent to reducer 0.

Reduce. We are now ready to describe what reducers do. For skewed c-groups , the responsible reducer aggregates the local aggregated values it received from the mappers (lines 24-27). For instance, to continue with the above example, it sums up, respectively, the partial sums obtained for each of the c-groups $(*, *, *)$ and $(*, *, 2012)$.

Note that for every skewed group, there are at most k values of partially aggregated tuples coming from the k mappers. The actual aggregation computation performed by the reducer depends on the aggregate function. If, for instance, as in the above example, the aggregate function is *sum*, then the reducer should simply compute the sum of the partial sums. For another example, if the aggregate function is *avg*, then the reducer should get from each mapper both the local *sum* and *count* and combine them to compute the global average, summing the partial sums and dividing the result by global sum of the local counts.

For non-skewed c-groups the reducer computes, given the set of tuples of a c-group g, not only the aggregate value for g but also of its ancestor c-groups, using a standard cube

Algorithm 3: Cube computation

```
// k mappers, SP-Sketch in main-memory
Map(t)
    for t ∈ mapper-input do
        L = lattice(t)
        for g = NextUnmarkedBFS(L) do
            if skewed(g,SP-Sketch) then
                partially-aggregate(g)
                mark g
            else
                key = partition(g,SP-Sketch)
                emit(key,measure(t))
                mark g and its ancestors (recursively)
            end
        end
    end
    for g ∈ partially-aggregated-groups do
        key = 0
        value = Pair(g,aggregate-value(g))
        emit(key,value)
    end

// k+1 reducers , SP-Sketch in main memory
Reduce(key,values)
    if skewed-group-reducer then
        g = decode-group(values)
        value = aggregate-func(values)
        emit(g,value)
    else
        key = decode-group(key)
        compute BUC over ancestors
    end

```

algorithm (we use BUC [15] in our implementation). For instance, the reducer responsible for $(laptop, *, *)$ computes also the aggregated values for the c-groups $(laptop, Rome, *)$, $(laptop, *, 2012)$, and $(laptop, Rome, 2012)$.

Note however that some optimization is required to avoid redundant processing. Some c-groups have common ancestors, and so we should avoid computing these common ancestors multiple times. We thus assign the computation of each c-group to its smallest (in the BFS traversal order) non-skewed descendant. For instance, in our running example $(laptop, rome, *)$ is an ancestor of both $(laptop, *, *)$ and $(*, rome, *)$. $(laptop, *, *)$ preceded $(*, rome, *)$ in our lattice BFS traversal and thus $(laptop, rome, *)$ and is computed as part of the cube computation for $(laptop, *, *)$.

We conclude the presentation of our algorithm by analyzing its efficiency in terms of the size of the intermediate data transferred between the mappers and the reducers.

5.2 Intermediate Data Transfer

By the definition of the cube, the size of the output may be exponential in the number of dimensions, and so is not surprising that in extreme cases the amount of data that is transferred may be exponential as well. However, we show that in common cases the transferred data size is polynomial in the number of dimensions thereby enabling efficient processing (recall that in the Naive algorithm presented in Section 3 the transferred data is exponential in the dimensions number). This will also be confirmed by our experiments on real-life as well as synthetic data. For space constraints, all proofs are deferred to the Appendix.

We start by considering skewed c-groups . The proof of the following proposition (as well as of the other results in this section) can be found in the Appendix.

PROPOSITION 5.2. *Assume $2^d \cdot k = O(m)$. Then, with probability of at least $1 - O(\frac{1}{k})$, the amount of data transferred for computing skewed c-groups is $O(dn)$.*

From now on, assume Proposition 5.2 holds. We next consider non-skewed c-groups. We first show that in the worse case, data transfer may be exponential in the number of dimensions.

THEOREM 5.3. *There exists a relation on which the SP-Cube algorithm generates network traffic size of $\theta(2^d \cdot n)$*

However, such extreme situations are unlikely to occur in practice. We prove that in common cases the transferred data size is polynomial in the number of dimensions.

We start by defining some useful notions. Consider a c-group g. By definition, if g is skewed, then every subset of g must be skewed as well. However, the opposite is not necessarily true. Namely, it may be the case that all subset of g are skewed, whereas g itself is not. We call relations where such situations do not occur **skewness-monotonic**.

DEFINITION 5.4. *A relation R is **skewness-monotonic** if for every c-group g, g is skewed if and only if all of its sub-groups are skewed. For databases without skews, the definition of skewness-monotonic is vacuously true.*

We show the following.

PROPOSITION 5.5. *For every **skewness-monotonic** relation R, the amount of network traffic generated by SP-Cube when applied to R is $O(d^2 \cdot n)$*

Even for databases that are not skewness-monotonic, traffic is still often bounded. Consider a database in which attributes values are taken independently from some skewed distribution. Namely, for every attribute, it has some given probability of having a skewed value. Then, there is a smaller probability for having skews in higher levels of the cube lattice. Therefore, in such databases, there are instances of non-skewed c-groups that all of their sub-groups are skewed.

PROPOSITION 5.6. *Let R be a relation and consider its cube. Assume all attributes in R are independently distributed. Let c be a cuboid of l attributes. Let $t \in R$ be a tuple. If the probability that t contributes to a skewed group in c is at most $\frac{l+\sqrt[1]{d}}{d}$, then the total network traffic of the SP-Cube algorithm is bounded by $O(d^3 \cdot n)$.*

In accordance with the above results, our experiments on both real-life and synthetic data always exhibit moderate data transfer. They show that the intermediate data size was always significantly smaller than that of the competitor algorithms. We leave for future work the full characterization of relations over which traffic is guaranteed to be polynomial.

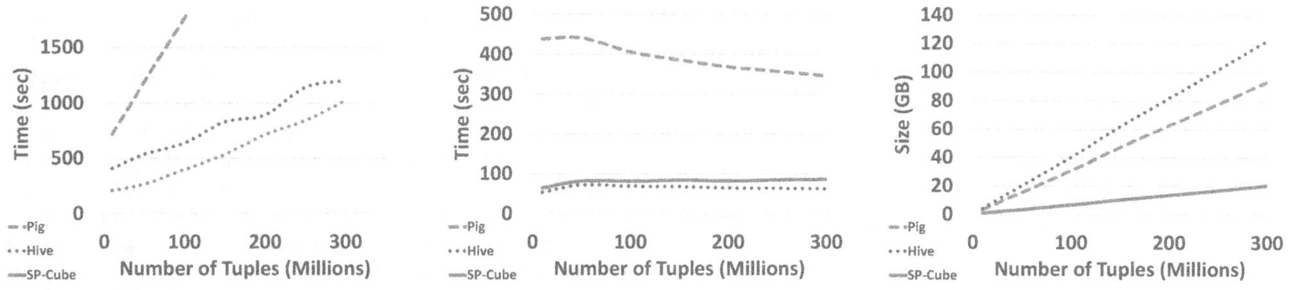

(a) running times comparison (b) reduce time comparison (c) map output comparison

Figure 4: The Wikipedia Statistics dataset

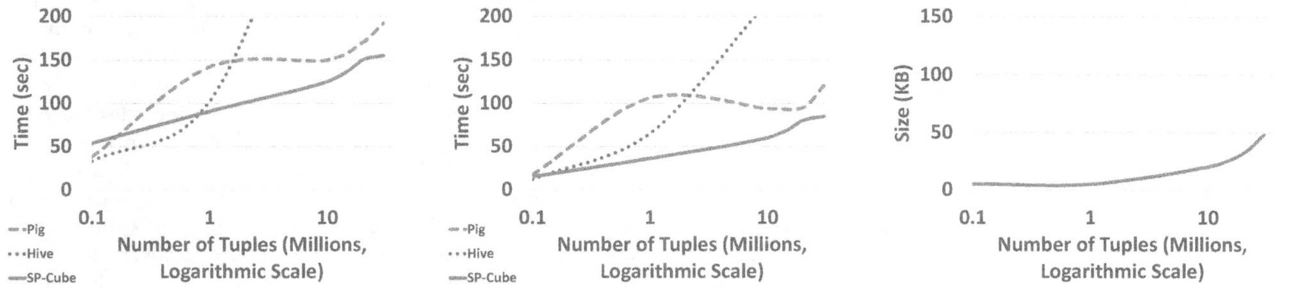

(a) running times comparison (b) map time comparison (c) SP-Sketch size

Figure 5: The USAGOV dataset

6. EXPERIMENTS

We tested the performance of the SP-Cube algorithm in an extensive series of experiments. We ran the experiments on Amazon's cloud environment, AWS [2]. We rented a cloud of 20 virtual machines of type m3.xlarge, each machine having 4 cores, a memory of size 15GB, and a 80GB of SSD. In the experiments we used two real-life datasets and two synthetic datasets that we have generated. We wrote our algorithm in Java and ran it on top of Hadoop [3], version 2.4.0. We ran our algorithm against Apache Pig Cube algorithm, version 0.12.0 and Apache Hive Cube algorithm, version 0.13.1. To assure that we compete against a good, optimized implementation of the competitors, we chose to run against the code developed by the actual authors of the competing algorithms. The [26] authors directed us to use Pig cube operator. Their algorithm is shipped as a feature in Pig since version 0.11.0. In [26], the algorithm's performance is demonstrated and shown to outperform previous cube algorithms implemented on top of MapReduce and we therefore do not compare SP-Cube to them. Regarding Hive cube algorithm, as any algorithm in Hive, it is compiled into a query plan that is computed according to some Hive policies, for instance having heuristics for map-side aggregations and choosing which aggregates should be computed before others. We refer below to the two cube algorithms as Pig ad Hive respectively.

The measures that we use to present our results are the total running time, the average running time of a mapper and a reducer in a single job, and the intermediate data size, which is the size of traffic in the cluster that is delivered between mappers and reducers. Note that in every experiment we computed all measures however we omit some of the graphs. In all cases where omitted a graph, this is because it showed similar trends to previous graphs, and thus for space constraints we just point to a previous graph to see the trend.

6.1 Real World Datasets

We use two real datasets for checking the performance of the algorithms on real-world data distributions. The use of two distinct datasets from different sources allows to examine different real-life data distributions. One dataset that we use is large while the other one is smaller. This allows us to examine what effect the data size has on the relative performance of the algorithms. In addition, to have a closer look at the affect of data size within each data distribution, we also considered for each of the two datasets subsets of varying sizes, selected by random sampling.

The first dataset that we use is the Wikipedia Traffic Statistics Dataset [7] containing statistics about user browser requests to Wikipedia pages. The dataset is 150GB in size, and contains about 12 billion records. We run our experiments on a random sample of 300 million records of it. The dataset has 4 dimension attributes and we calculate the cube over them. In retrospect we have found approximately 180 million c-groups in the data, and around 50 of them were skewed, of cardinality 5%-30% of the original tuples number.

The second dataset is the USAGOV dataset [1], containing log files of all clicks of users entering USA government websites between the years 2011-2013. This dataset is of size 22GB and we run our experiments on random sample of 30 million records out of it. We have found that this dataset contains around 30 of groups were skewed with cardinality of 2-8 million (6%-25% of the original tuples number). The total number of c-groups in this dataset was around 20 million. The dataset has 15 dimension attributes. As we wanted to compare the results to what was obtained for the Wikipedia dataset we built our cubes over 4 of them with similar settings to the Wikipedia traffic dataset. We also experimented with building cubes for more than 4 attributes, and the algorithms showed similar trends.

Wikipedia Traffic dataset. To examine the effect of the data size on the algorithm behavior, we took random samples of varying sizes out of the 300 million tuples, and analyzed the performance of the algorithm as the data grows. We further examined additional parameters that may explain the behavior. The results are depicted in Figure 4. Regarding running time, SP-Cube was 20% faster than Hive and 300% faster than Pig. This is shown in Figure 4a. (The Pig curve is shown here only partially as it ran out of scale for larger datasets).

Trying to explain the results, we examined closely the map and reduce times in the different algorithms. The average reduce times are shown in Figure 4b. We can see that Pig's average reduce time is both longer than those of SP-Cube and Hive. Hive's reduce time is close to that SP-Cube (and even slightly shorter). However, its map time was much larger than that of SP-Cube. The average map time shows a trend similar to what seen in Figure 4a and thus omitted.

We additionally examined the size of the intermediate data size. As can be seen in Figure 4c, much less data is transferred between the machines in SP-Cube compared to Pig and Hive. The growth rate of intermediate data size of SP-Cube is the slowest, and for 300 million tuples it is 5 times smaller than Pig and 6 times smaller than Hive. As we previously explained, in MapReduce, the amount of network traffic highly influences the running time of the algorithms. Regarding the SP-Sketch size, it was 6 orders of magnitudes smaller than the original dataset size, and we omit its graph due to space constraints.

USAGOV dataset. Here again we examine the algorithm behavior for growing data sizes. The results are shown in Figure 5. Figure 5a shows that, again, the SP-Cube algorithm performs significantly better than its competitors. In this experiment, Hive performs worse and we see a 300% relative speedup for CP-Cube even on small subsamples of the order of ten million tuples. We also see that SP-Cube has a speedup of 30% compared to the Pig algorithm. (The Hive curve is partial as it ran out of scale for larger datasets).

We tracked some measurements in the experiment and found that the exhibited running time is highly affected by the average map time. This is shown in Figure 5b. In this graph, we see that the Pig and Hive algorithms have a longer average map time as data size grows. The Pig algorithm map time is worse than that of our SP-Cube by almost 30%, whereas the Hive map time is much longer, which explains the long time for running Hive on this dataset. As it turns out, the SP-Cube optimized computation not only reduces data transfer but also allows the mappers to save work (and time) by not scanning redundant cube groups. Regarding the average reduce time, there was no significant difference between all three algorithms.

Looking closer at the Wikipedia and USGOV datasets, and in particular at the algorithms running time for subsets of similar sizes (10M-30M), we can note that unlike Pig and Hive that behave very differently on the two data sets, SP-Cube demonstrates similar performance (around 150 seconds) for two data distributions.

Finally, we have also examined the size of the SP-Sketch computed for the two datasets. As the trend is similar we show here only the results for USAGOV. In our implementation, the sketch is implemented as a java class, and we use java serialization engine to create a serialized stream of bytes for representing the sketch object. This file is delivered to all machines using the distributed file system. Each machine de-serializes the file and thus getting the sketch object. Figure 5c shows the sketch size as a function of the number of tuples. We see that the size grows linearly with a small gradient. It is worth mentioning that the growth is due to the fact that more skewed c-groups are identified. However, in all of the experiments, the sketch size is negligible compared to the original dataset size. Where the data is in the order of tens of Gigabytes, the sketch size is in the order of tens of Kilobytes, thus smaller by 6 orders of magnitude.

Note that the running time of SP-Cube includes the construction of the SP-Sketch and the actual cube computation. While the construction of the SP-Sketch is negligible compared to the cube computation time for large data sets, it is more noticeable for small data and this yields the slightly slower performance of SP-Cube. Note however that such small size of data is anyhow not a practical candidate for MapReduce computation, as the cube could be computed by a single machine using standard algorithms, and we show these results here only for completeness. In general, we conclude from our experiments that the SP-Cube consistently outperforms both Pig and Hive, with the performance gain increasing significantly for large datasets.

6.2 Synthetic Datasets

The next set of experiments involves two synthetic datasets that allow to isolate the effect of different properties of the data, and in particular examine the sensitivity of the algorithms to the data distribution. We name the the datasets *gen-binomial* and *gen-zipf*. We describe below the generation process of each dataset and then explain some interesting insights obtained from running the three algorithms on it. We ran the experiments for datasets with varying number of dimension attributes. As the trends were similar we show here a sample of the results for cubes with 4 dimension attributes. This allows to relate them to the results obtained for the real-life datasets.

gen-binomial dataset. The generation process for this dataset is as follows. Tuples were generated independently with the following probabilities. With probability p, We uniformly pick a number $i \in 1, \dots, 20$, and create a tuple having i in all of its attributes (namely the tuples $(1, 1, \dots, 1), (2, 2, \dots, 2)$, and so on). With probability $1 - p$, we draw each attribute uniformly as a 32-bit integer. Intuitively, in the generated dataset, a fraction p of the tuples contribute to skews in each cuboid. The other $1 - p$ of the tuples are likely not to form skews. We ran two sets experiments using these settings. In the first set of experiments, we fixed the size of the database and measured the algorithms performance for varying values of the probability p. We describe below a representative sample of the results.

Figure 6 shows the results for a dataset containing 300 million tuples with four dimension attributes and varying p values. Running time results are shown in Figure 6a. We

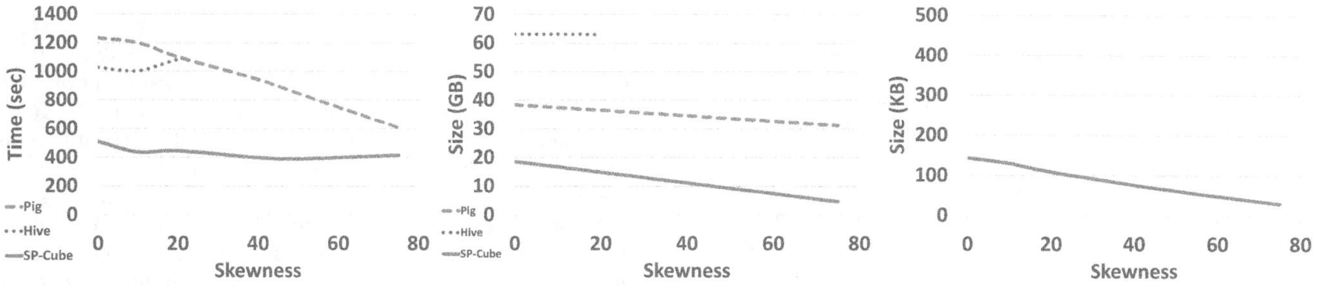

(a) running times comparison (b) map output size comparison (c) SP-Sketch size

Figure 6: gen-binomial: Varying skewness

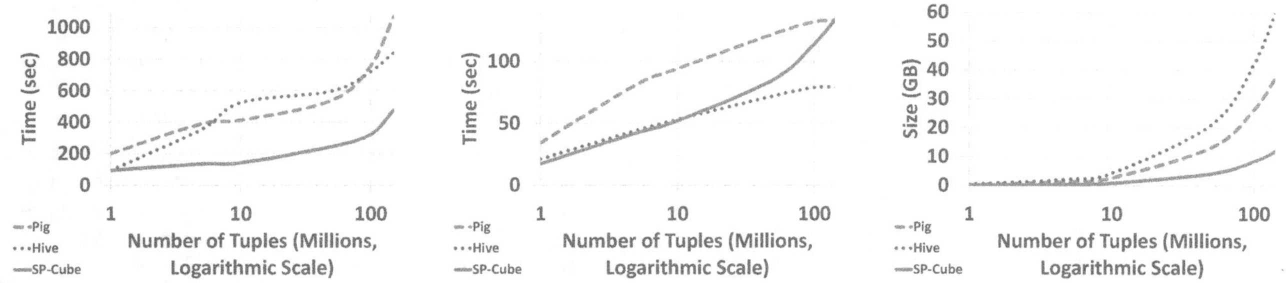

(a) running times comparison (b) average reduce time comparison (c) map output size comparison

Figure 7: gen-zipf: Zipfian Distribution

can see that SP-Cube outperforms Pig and Hive and shows stable running time. Regarding Hive, it did not manage to handle heavy skews in the data: For $p \geq 0.4$ it got stuck as some reducers got out of memory. For Pig we found that it is highly affected by the value of p. Its performance decreased by a factor of 2 as p grows form 0 to 0.75.

These results can be explained by examining the size of the intermediate data, shown in Figure 6b. We can see that the map output in Pig is larger for non skewed data and is in general much larger than that of SP-Cube. The size of intermediate data decreases as p grows in both Pig and SP-Cube because the total number of c-groups is getting smaller. Hive's intermediate data is the largest and it appears that when p is large there are reducers that get too much information, and therefore get stuck. We also examined the average map and reduce times; their trend is similar to what we see for the size of the intermediate data and we therefore omit the graphs.

Finally, the SP-Sketch sizes for this experiment are depicted in Figure 6c. We can see that the sketch size is always very small and always less than 200KB (approximately 6 orders of magnitude smaller than the input data size). It gets smaller for large values of p as most of the data contributes to the given set of predefined skews and thus fewer additional ones are generated.

In the second set of experiments we fixed p, and changed the database size. We got similar trends. Due to space constraints, these results are shown in the Appendix.

gen-zipf dataset. In the gen-zipf experiment we tested the SP-Cube performance against a data with attributes drawn from a Zipfian distribution. We generated 150 million tuples independently. Inside each tuple all attributes were also drawn independently. Two of the attributes were generated using a zipf data generator, with 1000 elements and an exponent factor of 1.1. The other two attributes were drawn from a uniform distribution having 1000 elements. In this experiment we had groups of various sizes. Namely, for some cuboids, there were c-groups with a cardinality of 30 million (20% of the tuples) together with c-groups that created from a small number of tuples (dozens of tuples). We checked the algorithm behavior on subsamples of this dataset. Some of the results are shown in Figure 7. In 7a we show an improvement of 100% over Hive and 150% over Pig. We explain the behavior on smaller sets as in previous experiments - the preprocessing time of computing the sketch becomes more dominant. In this experiment, the map average time had a similar trend to the running time graph and thus omitted. The results of the average reduce time are shown in Figure 7b. Note that in this measure Hive performs the best, and SP-Cube and Pig perform quite similarly. However, we have found that the most dominant measure here was the map output size, that is presented in Figure 7c, in which SP-Cube has an improvement of 400% over Pig and 600% over Hive, and therefore had the best running times. Regarding SP-Sketch, its size was always bounded by 200KB, a 6 orders of magnitudes smaller than the original data. This graph is omitted as it has similar trends to previously presented sketch graphs.

We conclude by mentioning the performance of SP-Cube in terms of parallelism. In all of our experiments, SP-Cube achieved a good balancing between reducers, with the reducers' output data files being of similar sizes.

7. RELATED WORK

Sequential Cube Algorithms. The Cube Operator was originally presented in [23]. Many efficient sequential cube algorithms have been developed over the years, e.g. [12, 22, 31, 24, 30, 34]. The cube lattice is often used in these algorithms. Some employ bottom up traversal over the lattice, as BUC [15], whereas others prefer top-down traversal [12]. We adopt the bottom up approach as it allowed us to achieve a two phases MapReduce algorithm, compared to previous top down MapReduce algorithm [25] that computes the cube using multiple rounds (to be further explained below). As the size of the cube may be exponential in the size of the input, some algorithms deal with full materialization of the cube, whereas others deal with partial materialization of the data and on-demand computation of cuboids [22].

Parallel Cube Algorithms and MapReduce. The fact that the data cube is expensive to compute, in particular when the input relation is large, has motivated the study of parallel algorithms for cube computation. [27] presented some parallel algorithms for cube computation that work for small clusters. More recently, dedicated platforms such as MapReduce are employed for enabling parallel computation over huge amounts of data, with much work dedicated to their implementation and efficiency [20, 28, 21]. The implementation of database operators over MapReduce has received much attention, suggesting efficient algorithms for *Join* [11, 35, 10, 16] and *cartesian product* [29]. Skewed data has been shown to be challenging for the computation of such operators as well [14]. Our work follows this line of works and proposes an efficient MapReduce algorithm for cube computation, that is resilient to data distribution. A complementary line of work considers MapReduce as a parallelized computational model and defines measurements for an efficient MapReduce algorithm [32, 9]. Among them, balanced workload and small communication overhead are the measurements that our work adopts.

MapReduce is implemented as an open source framework in Hadoop [3]; a very popular implementation that is highly used for massive computation. The Pig [5] and Hive [4] projects were developed on top of Hadoop, and give an abstraction of a database and an SQL-like query engine on top of it. As previously mentioned, the cube algorithm from [26] is shipped as a feature for implementing the cube in Pig. Both [26] and SP-Cube follow a bottom up approach and they both use sampling. However, as explained in the introduction a key disadvantage is that it makes decisions about the existence of skews in the granularity of a full cuboid and tails recursion and aborts that yield inferior performance. Note that the Pig framework adds to the original algorithm the use of combiners [19] but, as we show the result is still sensitive to the data distribution.

Another MapReduce cube algorithm is [25] that takes top-down traversal approach parallelizing the Pipesort algorithm [12]. This algorithm finds top-down computation paths in the lattice. This yieds a series of MapReduce rounds. Note that the more MapReduce rounds, the more are the ram-to-disk transactions and thus performance is inferior to previously mentioned algorithms. Furthermore, this algorithm suffers from the skews problem mentioned in Section 3. In case of a skewed c-group , the assigned reducer will be heavily loaded and parallelism will not be utilized. Thus, we did not include it in the experiments section.

Finally, we mention [33] which describes a LinkedIn system that contains implementation of cube on top of MapReduce. The algorithm is embedded in an internal system and exploits the system's data types and thus unlike SP-Cube cannot be run on unprocessed data in a generic platform.

Types of Aggregate Functions. Aggregation functions are traditionally divided into three classes [23]: distributive functions, such as count and sum, where partial aggregation can be merged to the full one; algebraic functions, like average, where multiple partial aggregates can be combined to obtain the result (e.g. partial sums and counts can be used for computing the full average using division); and holistic functions (like top-k most frequent) that in general cannot be computed from partial aggregates. [26] defines a subset of holistic measures called partially algebraic measures, which are functions whose computation can be partitioned according to one of their attributes' value. By its behavior, SP-Cube supports all distributive and algebraic aggregate functions, and all partially algebraic functions in which the generated partitions are not skewed. The support of efficient computation of arbitrary holistic aggregate functions for skewed c-groups is a challenging future work.

Sketching. Sampling-based sketches over large data sets are used for scalable computation of data properties such as top-k, distance measures, distinct counting, and various aggregates [13, 18, 17, 32, 26]. As previously mentioned, the sampling approach we use for building our SP-Sketch is inspired by [32, 26] and we adapt some of their proofs to show it is both small and accurate. The sampling technique adapted from [32] is a standard technique for sketching a data using uniform sampling. However, our use of the sample is novel. We use the sample to detect skewed groups and partition elements of each cuboid (for building the SP-Sketch), whereas [32] uses it to find bucketing elements for sorting.

8. CONCLUSIONS

In this paper, we present an efficient algorithm, SP-Cube, for cube computation over large data sets in MapReduce environments. Our algorithm is resilient to varied data distribution and consistently performs better than the previous solutions. At the core of our solution is a compact data structure, called SP-Sketch, that records all needed information for detecting skews and effectively partitioning the workload between the machines. Our algorithm uses the sketch to speed up computation and minimize communication overhead. Our theoretical analysis and experimental study demonstrate the feasibility and efficiency of our solution compared to the state of the art alternatives.

We focus here on aggregate functions that are distributive or algebraic. The support of arbitrary holistic aggregate functions is a challenging future work. Another challenge is exact theoretical characterization of data sets for which network traffic is guaranteed to be polynomial in the number of dimension attributes. Skews are problematic also for other common database operators such as joins. It is interesting to see whether some of the ideas presented here can be used to reduce network traffic and speed up computation for such operators. Finally, optimizing cube computation in other big data processing frameworks, such as Spark [6], is an intriguing future work.

Acknowledgements We are grateful to Yael Amsterdamer and the anonymous reviewers for their insightful comments. This work has been partially funded by the European Research Council under the FP7, ERC grant MoDaS, agreement 291071.

9. REFERENCES

[1] 1.usa.gov data. http://www.usa.gov/About/developer-resources/1usagov.shtml.

[2] Amazon web services. http://aws.amazon.com.

[3] Apache hadoop. http://hadoop.apache.org.

[4] Apache hive. http://www.hive.com.

[5] Apache pig. https://pig.apache.org/.

[6] Apache spark. https://spark.apache.org.

[7] Wikipedia page traffic statistic v3. http://aws.amazon.com/datasets/6025882142118545.

[8] A. Abelló, J. Ferrarons, and O. Romero. Building cubes with mapreduce. In *DOLAP*, pages 17–24, 2011.

[9] F. N. Afrati, A. D. Sarma, S. Salihoglu, and J. D. Ullman. Upper and lower bounds on the cost of a map-reduce computation. *PVLDB*, 6(4):277–288, 2013.

[10] F. N. Afrati and J. D. Ullman. Optimizing joins in a map-reduce environment. In *EDBT*, pages 99–110, 2010.

[11] F. N. Afrati and J. D. Ullman. Optimizing multiway joins in a map-reduce environment. *IEEE*, 23(9):1282–1298, 2011.

[12] S. Agarwal, R. Agrawal, P. Deshpande, A. Gupta, J. F. Naughton, R. Ramakrishnan, and S. Sarawagi. On the computation of multidimensional aggregates. In *VLDB*, pages 506–521, 1996.

[13] Z. Bar-Yossef, T. S. Jayram, R. Kumar, D. Sivakumar, and L. Trevisan. Counting distinct elements in a data stream. In *RANDOM*, pages 1–10, 2002.

[14] P. Beame, P. Koutris, and D. Suciu. Skew in parallel query processing. In *PODS*, pages 212–223, 2014.

[15] K. S. Beyer and R. Ramakrishnan. Bottom-up computation of sparse and iceberg cubes. In *SIGMOD*, pages 359–370, 1999.

[16] S. Chu, M. Balazinska, and D. Suciu. From theory to practice: Efficient join query evaluation in a parallel database system. In *SIGMOD*, pages 63–78, 2015.

[17] E. Cohen. All-distances sketches, revisited: HIP estimators for massive graphs analysis. In *PODS*, pages 88–99, 2014.

[18] E. Cohen and H. Kaplan. Leveraging discarded samples for tighter estimation of multiple-set aggregates. In *SIGMETRICS/Performance*, pages 251–262, 2009.

[19] J. Dean and S. Ghemawat. Mapreduce: Simplified data processing on large clusters. In *OSDI*, pages 137–150, 2004.

[20] I. Elghandour and A. Aboulnaga. Restore: Reusing results of mapreduce jobs. *PVLDB*, 5(6):586–597, 2012.

[21] M. Y. Eltabakh, Y. Tian, F. Özcan, R. Gemulla, A. Krettek, and J. McPherson. Cohadoop: Flexible data placement and exploitation in hadoop. *PVLDB*, 4(9):575–585, 2011.

[22] M. Fang, N. Shivakumar, H. Garcia-Molina, R. Motwani, and J. D. Ullman. Computing iceberg queries efficiently. In *VLDB*, pages 299–310, 1998.

[23] J. Gray, A. Bosworth, A. Layman, and H. Pirahesh. Data cube: A relational aggregation operator generalizing group-by, cross-tab, and sub-total. In *Proceedings of the Twelfth International Conference on Data Engineering, February 26 - March 1, 1996, New Orleans, Louisiana*, pages 152–159, 1996.

[24] V. Harinarayan, A. Rajaraman, and J. D. Ullman. Implementing data cubes efficiently. In *SIGMOD*, pages 205–216, 1996.

[25] S. Lee, J. Kim, Y. Moon, and W. Lee. Efficient distributed parallel top-down computation of ROLAP data cube using mapreduce. In *Data Warehousing and Knowledge Discovery - 14th International Conference, DaWaK 2012, Vienna, Austria, September 3-6, 2012. Proceedings*, pages 168–179, 2012.

[26] A. Nandi, C. Yu, P. Bohannon, and R. Ramakrishnan. Data cube materialization and mining over mapreduce. *IEEE Trans. Knowl. Data Eng.*, 24(10):1747–1759, 2012.

[27] R. T. Ng, A. S. Wagner, and Y. Yin. Iceberg-cube computation with PC clusters. In *SIGMOD*, pages 25–36, 2001.

[28] T. Nykiel, M. Potamias, C. Mishra, G. Kollios, and N. Koudas. Mrshare: Sharing across multiple queries in mapreduce. *PVLDB*, 3(1):494–505, 2010.

[29] A. Okcan and M. Riedewald. Processing theta-joins using mapreduce. In *SIGMOD*, pages 949–960, 2011.

[30] K. A. Ross and D. Srivastava. Fast computation of sparse datacubes. In *VLDB*, pages 116–125, 1997.

[31] S. Sarawagi, R. Agrawal, and N. Megiddo. Discovery-driven exploration of OLAP data cubes. In *EDBT*, pages 168–182, 1998.

[32] Y. Tao, W. Lin, and X. Xiao. Minimal mapreduce algorithms. In *SIGMOD*, pages 529–540, 2013.

[33] S. Vemuri, M. Varshney, K. Puttaswamy, and R. Liu. Execution primitives for scalable joins and aggregations in map reduce. *PVLDB*, 7(13):1462–1473, 2014.

[34] D. Xin, J. Han, X. Li, and B. W. Wah. Star-cubing: Computing iceberg cubes by top-down and bottom-up integration. In *VLDB*, pages 476–487, 2003.

[35] X. Zhang, L. Chen, and M. Wang. Efficient multi-way theta-join processing using mapreduce. *PVLDB*, 5(11):1184–1195, 2012.

[36] Y. Zhao, P. Deshpande, and J. F. Naughton. An array-based algorithm for simultaneous multidimensional aggregates. In *SIGMOD*, pages 159–170, 1997.

APPENDIX

Proofs: We provide below the proofs for Sections 4 and 5.

PROOF PROPOSITION 4.5. As in [26] we start by bounding the probability that our algorithm does not detect a single skewed group. Let g be a skewed c-group , and assume its size is s. The expected size of g in the sample is $\Omega(ln(nk)) = C{*}ln(nk)$ for some constant C. Using Chernoff Bound-

$$\begin{aligned} Pr(s < (1-\delta) * C * ln(nk)) < \\ exp^{-C*ln(nk)\frac{\delta^2}{2}} = \\ O(\frac{1}{n}) \end{aligned} \tag{1}$$

The last transition is due to the fact that C, δ are small constants and k is very small compared to n. Now, we need to consider all c-groups . Each cuboid contains at most $O(k)$ skewed groups, as the size of a skewed groups is at least m and the database contains n tuples. Therefore, the total number of skewed groups in D is bounded by $2^d \cdot k = O(m)$, summing over all cuboids. Using union bound, with probability of at least $1 - O(\frac{1}{k})$, the algorithm detects all skewed groups and keeps them in the sketch. □

PROOF PROPOSITION 4.6. In [32], a bucketing argument shows that sorting a set of n items, then with probability of at least $1-\frac{1}{n}$, the partitioning elements divide the input into partitions of size $O(m)$ each. We apply the same argument in our case. Then, for a single cuboid, with probability of at least $1-\frac{1}{n}$, its partitioning elements kept in the SP-Sketch divide the cuboid (its non-skewed groups) into partitions of size $O(m)$. Thus, using union bound, the event happens for all cuboids with probability of at least $1-\frac{2^d}{n}$. □

PROOF PROPOSITION 4.7. As stated in Proposition 4.5, with probability of at least $1-\frac{1}{k}$ the algorithm detects all skewed c-groups. As we have stated earlier, there are at most k skewed c-groups at each node in the lattice, and $k-1$ partition elements. Putting it all together, we get that data size at each node in the SP-Sketch is $O(k)$. Since there are 2^d nodes, then the lattice size is bounded by $O(2^d \cdot k) = O(m)$. □

PROOF PROPOSITION 5.2. We use here Proposition 4.5 which shows that with probability of at least $1 - O(\frac{1}{k})$ the SP-Cube algorithm detects all skewed c-groups. The size of the key-value pair generated for every such skewed c-group is $O(d)$. (Recall that the size of attribute values and computed aggregates are taken as a constant). Each mapper locally aggregates at most $O(m)$ skewed c-groups. As there are k mappers, we obtain that they all create an intermediate data for skewed c-groups of size at most $O(dmk) = O(dn)$ □

PROOF THEOREM 5.3. We describe how to build such a relation R. R has d dimension attributes, and we describe how to build them (the value of the measure attribute is not important). Mark $w = m+1$, and mark by $S_{\frac{d}{2}}$ the set of all sets of $\frac{d}{2}$ numbers between 1 and d. For every $s \in S_{\frac{d}{2}}$, we add w identical tuples to R, each of the tuples having the value 1 in all attributes that their index is in s, and 0 in the other attributes. By definition of w, each cuboid in level $\frac{d}{2}$ contains a skewed group, which is the group of ones in the cuboid attribute indexes. In addition, no cuboid of size $\frac{d}{2}+1$ contains a skewed group as there are no $s_1, s_2 \in S$ that share the same values in any subset of $\frac{d}{2}+1$ attributes. Therefore, for every tuple, the algorithm consideres each of the c-groups of $\frac{d}{2}+1$ attributes as unmarked and non-skewed. For each such c-group, an intermediate data is generated. Summing over all tuples, the network traffic size for R is $\theta(2^d * n)$. □

PROOF PROPOSITION 5.5. Intuitively, such databases are handled very efficiently by our algorithm: In case there are no skews other than the most general $(*, *, \ldots, *)$ c-group, all c-groups are generated using the reducers assigned to the single attribute c-groups, so each tuple is sent at most d times. For instance, all c-groups of the tuple $t = (laptop, Paris, 2013, 700)$ are handled using the reducers of c-groups $(laptop, *, *)$, $(*, Paris, *)$, and $(*, *, 2013)$. When skews do exist, they are all "catched" using the sketch, and then the remaining c-groups can still be efficiently computed as above. We make this argument more formal below.

We have seen that all skews are computed using $O(dn)$ intermediate data. Let $t \in D$. *lattice*(t) contains 2^d nodes. We can ignore all of the nodes that their groups are skewed. Because D is skewness-monotonic, all attributes that are skewed, must be skewed together. All other attributes which are non-skewed, cover the rest of the lattice. As the number of non-skewed attributes is $O(d)$, each tuple generates at most $O(d)$ key-value pairs, each of size $O(d)$. Summing over all tuples, we have $O(d^2 \cdot n)$ intermediate data. Additionally to the data sent for skewed groups, we get a total size of $O(d^2 \cdot n)$. □

PROOF PROPOSITION 5.6. We have seen that handling of skewed groups requires intermediate data of size $O(dn)$. We compute the amount of traffic needed for the rest of the groups. Let t be a tuple. Denote by $C(t)$ the number of non-skewed c-groups in *lattice(t)* for which the algorithm generates intermediate data. These are the groups that the mapper sends to reducers. Other non-skewed c-groups are treated in the reduce phase using BUC, and need not a special traffic. As t is an arbitrary tuple, $C(t)$ is a random variable. It depends on which projections of t are skewed and which are not. We compute $\mathrm{E}(C(t))$. Denote by $C_i(t)$ the indicator random variable of the i'th node in *lattice(t)*. Then -

$$C_i(t) = \begin{cases} 1 & \text{c-group in node i not skewed, sent to a reducer} \\ 0 & \text{elsewhere} \end{cases}$$

Note that for $C_i(t) = 1$ for non-skewed c-groups that have a single attribute, or that all of their descendants in *lattice(t)* are skewed. We express $C(t)$ as a sum of the 2^d indicator random variables, of the nodes in *lattice(t)*, and get by linearity of expectation -

$$\mathrm{E}(C(t)) = \mathrm{E}(\sum_{i=1}^{2^d} C_i(t)) = \sum_{i=1}^{2^d} \mathrm{E}(C_i(t))$$

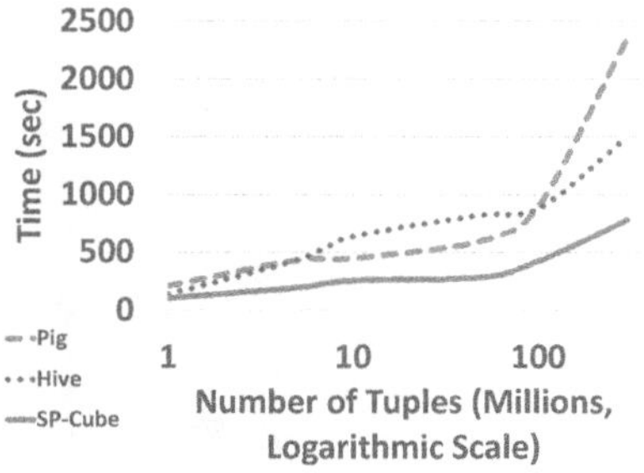

(a) running times comparison

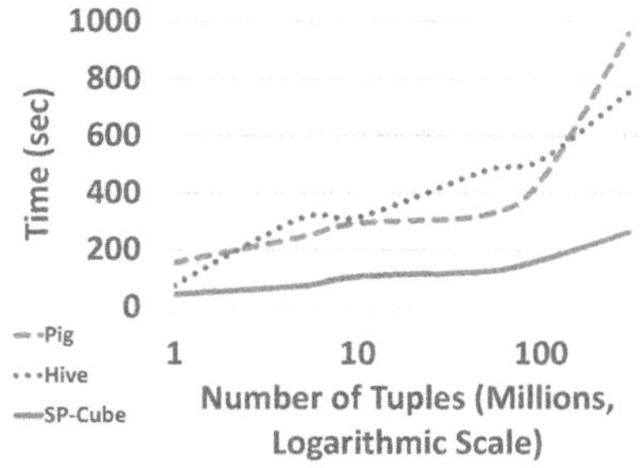

(b) average map time comparison

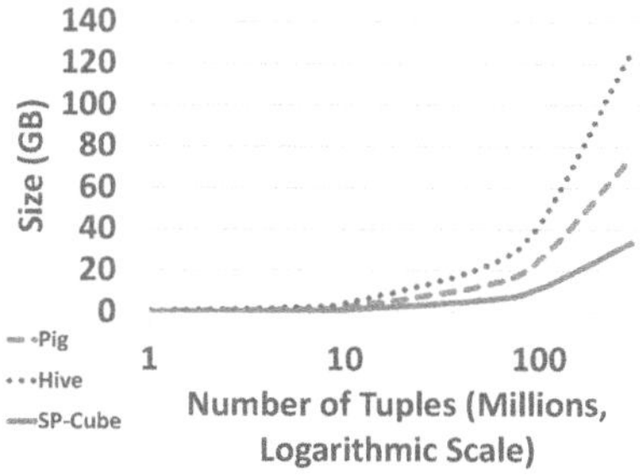

(c) map output size comparison

Figure 8: gen-binomial: Varying data size

We compute the expectation of a single indicator variable. Assume a specific indicator of a node $v \in lattice(t)$, and assume v has $l \geq 2$ attributes (we later handle $l = 1$). We mark by g_t the c-group of t in v, and denote by A the event that all of g_t descendants in *lattice(t)* are skewed c-groups. Then-

$$\begin{aligned} \Pr(C_v(t) = 1) &= \Pr(C_v(t) = 1 \mid A) * \Pr(A) \\ &\leq \Pr(A) \end{aligned} \tag{2}$$

We use the law of total probability, and the fact that if g_t has a non-skewed descendant in *lattice(t)*, then g_t is not sent to a reducer. As v's descendants are all cuboids of $l-1$ attributes, and the attributes in R are independently distributed, we get-

$$\begin{aligned} \Pr(A) &\leq \cap_{p \,\in\, descendants(g_t)} \Pr(p \textit{ is skewed}) \\ &\leq \left(\frac{d^{\frac{1}{l}}}{d}\right)^l \\ &= \frac{d}{d^l} \\ &= \frac{1}{d^{l-1}} \end{aligned} \tag{3}$$

Therefore, $E(C_v(t)) \leq \frac{1}{d^{l-1}}$. Recall that the number of nodes having l attributes is $\binom{d}{l} = O(d^l)$. Therefore, for every $l \geq 2$, the expected number of non-skewed c-groups with l attributes that are sent to reducers is bounded by $O(d)$. Summing over the lattice levels from 2 to d, we get that the expected number for the entire lattice (except from level 1) is bounded by $O(d^2)$. For the case of $l = 1$, the number of c-groups in *lattice(t)* with one attribute is d, and therefore the number of non-skewed c-groups that are sent to reducers is $O(d)$. We thus get that for (an arbitrary tuple) t, the expected number of non-skewed c-groups that are sent to a reducer is at most $O(d^2)$. Namely, $E(C(t)) = O(d^2)$. As the information sent for each non skewed c-group is of size $O(d)$, we get that the expected size of network traffic that the algorithm is sending for (an arbitrary tuple) t is $O(d^3)$. Therefore, the entire network for all of the tuples is at most $O(d^3 \cdot n)$. □

Experiments: We now provide our results of the second set of experiments on the synthetic *gen-binomial.*

In the second set of experiments we fixed p, and checked the algorithms performance for varying database size. Figure 8 illustrates the results for $p = 0.1$. Regarding running time, we can again see in Figure 8a that SP-Cube outperforms Pig and Hive. We can also see compatibility with the results obtained for the real-life datasets. On samples of size 50 million, for instance, Hive is worse than Pig similarly to the USAGOV dataset. For samples of size 300 million, Pig is worse than Hive, similarly to the Wikipedia dataset.

However, the gaps are dramatically larger in this experiment. For 300 million tuples, SP-Cube achieves a speedup of about 200% compared to Hive and 300% compared to Pig. These gaps follow from similar gaps in the average map time and map output sizes, shown in the graphs in Figure 8b and 8c, respectively. In this experiment the reduce average times behaved similarly to the total running time, and the sketch size was bounded by hundreds of Kilobytes, similarly to previous experiments.

In the second set of experiments we fixed p, and checked the algorithms performance for varying database size. Figure 8 illustrates the results for $p = 0.1$. Regarding running time, we can again see in Figure 8a that SP-Cube outperforms Pig and Hive. We can also see compatibility with the results obtained for the real-life datasets. On samples of size 50 million, for instance, Hive is worse than Pig similarly to the USAGOV dataset. For samples of size 300 million, Pig is worse than Hive, similarly to the Wikipedia dataset.

However, the gaps are dramatically larger in this experiment. For 300 million tuples, SP-Cube achieves a speedup of about 200% compared to Hive and 300% compared to Pig. These gaps follow from similar gaps in the average map time and map output sizes, shown in the graphs in Figure 8b and 8c, respectively. In this experiment the reduce average times behaved similarly to the total running time, and the sketch size was bounded by hundreds of Kilobytes, similarly to previous experiments.

Diversified Top-k Subgraph Querying in a Large Graph

Zhengwei Yang Ada Wai-Chee Fu Ruifeng Liu
The Chinese University of Hong Kong
{zwyang,adafu,rfliu}@cse.cuhk.edu.hk

ABSTRACT

Subgraph querying in a large data graph is interesting for different applications. A recent study shows that top-k diversified results are useful since the number of matching subgraphs can be very large. In this work, we study the problem of top-k diversified subgraph querying that asks for a set of up to k subgraphs isomorphic to a given query graph, and that covers the largest number of vertices. We propose a novel level-based algorithm for this problem which supports early termination and has a theoretical approximation guarantee. From experiments, most of our results on real datasets used in previous works are near optimal with a query time within 10ms on a commodity machine.

Keywords

subgraph isomorphism; top-k; diversity; maximum k-coverage

1. INTRODUCTION

Graph databases have been found useful in social networks, RDF, and many other applications. An important processing for graph data applications is that of the subgraph isomorphism search. Given a data graph and a query graph, the querying returns subgraphs in the data graph that are isomorphic to the query graph. Though this is an NP-hard problem, it has been found to be solvable with good response time for many real data graphs [6, 16, 26, 35, 21, 15]. The problem is manageable since the query graph is quite small in most applications. However, as data graphs are growing in size, the number of isomorphic subgraphs in such a graph can be excessively large. Most existing works stop their computation when a fixed number of subgraphs are found. Unfortunately, the resulting subgraphs are often highly overlapping and not very representative, whilst more interesting solutions may be missed. Such an observation has been made in [10]. They advocate the importance of diversity in the search results. Let us illustrate with an example based on the motivating application in [10].

EXAMPLE 1. A fraction of a collaboration network is shown as G' in Figure 1(b). In this graph, each node represents a person, with a label for the job of the person. The label "a" stands for project manager (PM), "b" for programmer (PRG), "c" for database developer (DB), and "d" for software tester (ST). A company issues a graph query to find a team consisting of a PM, a PRG, a DB, and an ST, such that there is a link between the PM and each of the PRG and DB, the PRG is linked to the DB, and both the PRG and DB are linked to the ST. These requirements are given by the query graph Q in Figure 1(a). There are many matching subgraphs in G'. We limit the number of resulting matchings to a small number k. In this example, let us set $k = 2$. The question is which set of two matchings is better. If we return $(v3, v8, v7, v12)$ and $(v3, v8, v9, v12)$ as matchings for $(u1, u2, u3, u4)$, we have the same PM, PRG and ST in both answers. This limits the choices for the company, since if any of the PM, PRG or ST is not available or not suitable, both results will not be useful. Instead, the disjoint matchings of $(v1, v5, v4, v10)$ and $(v2, v6, v7, v12)$ form a better solution set. Hence, in selecting the top k matchings we aim to reduce the overlapping information among the matchings. That is, the matchings should be diversified.

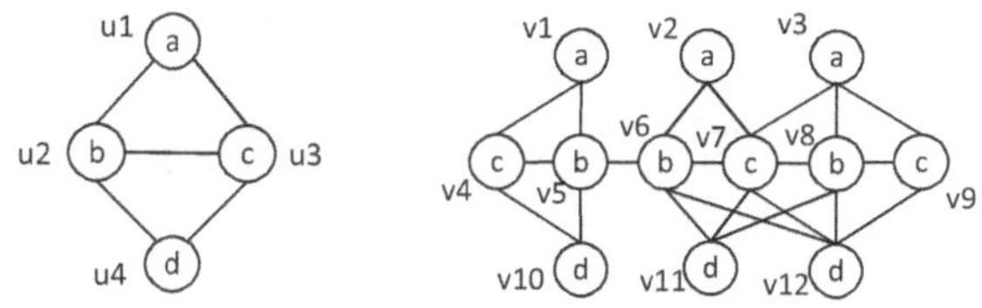

(a) query graph Q (b) part of the data graph, G'

Figure 1: Diversified subgraph matching; the meanings of the vertex labels are: a - project manager; b - programmer; c - database developer; d - software tester.

The above example shows that top-k diversified subgraph querying (DSQ) can rectify the issues caused by an excessive number of matchings in existing subgraph querying algorithms. Diversity is measured by the number of vertices covered by all the subgraphs in the result. The problem is to find at most k isomorphic subgraphs with a maximum coverage. Diversity has been proposed in [10], but their problem is to search for vertices that match with a single query node, say $u1$ in our example, and they consider graph simulation instead of isomorphism. In Figure 1, for example, [10] considers that $(v2, v6, v7, v11, v12)$ is also a matching to the query graph. To our knowledge, this is the first study to consider DSQ. However, to solve for DSQ, there are some major challenges:

(1) As the number of isomorphic subgraphs is potentially exponential, existing algorithms typically stop after generating around a thousand matchings. With DSQ, we may need to generate many more matchings for selecting the diversified results.

(2) Assuming that we can generate and store all isomorphic sub-

SIGMOD'16, June 26-July 01, 2016, San Francisco, CA, USA
© 2016 ACM. ISBN 978-1-4503-3531-7/16/06...$15.00
DOI: http://dx.doi.org/10.1145/2882903.2915216

graphs for a query, the remaining problem then becomes maximum k-coverage, which is also NP-hard. Though a simple greedy algorithm provides an approximation ratio guarantee of over 0.63, it requires scanning all the isomorphic subgraphs k times. However, generating all matchings may already be prohibitively costly.

(3) From the above discussion, a scalable algorithm would need an early termination mechanism so as to return k matchings without an exhaustive search, while having a good approximation guarantee.

Contributions. We study the above challenges and propose a solution for DSQ. Our contributions are summarized as follows.

(1) We propose to study the diversified subgraph querying problem where we ask for top-k diversified isomorphic subgraphs.

(2) We propose a novel solution, called DSQL, for DSQ. DSQL is based on a level-wise subgraph search, where **level** refers to the overlapping size of a newly selected subgraph with a set of collected subgraphs. DSQL has the following desirable properties: (a) an approximation ratio guarantee of $0.25(1 + \max(\frac{1}{k}, \frac{1}{q}))$, where q is the number of vertices in the query graph; (b) supports early termination when k results are obtained.

(3) We propose optimization strategies which greatly improve the performance of DSQL. Two of the strategies can also be used for the subgraph querying problem.

(4) We empirically verify the efficiency and effectiveness of our algorithm. Our experiments show that DSQL often generates near optimal solutions with a fast response time.

(5) Our study leads to some new results for the Maximum k-coverage problem. We propose a multi-scanning technique for a better approximation guarantee, which is asymptotically 0.5. We improve the approximation guarantee of existing streaming algorithms to $0.25(1 + \max(\frac{1}{k}, \frac{1}{q}))$, where q is the number of vertices in the query graph.

The rest of this paper is organized as follows. Section 2 states the problem definition and describes existing methods for related problems. Section 3 gives an overview of our two-phase solution DSQL. Section 4 describes the first phase of DSQL. Section 5 is about the optimization of DSQL. Section 6 is about the second phase of DSQL. The experimental results are given in Section 7. Related works are summarized in Section 8. We conclude in Section 9.

2. PROBLEM DEFINITION AND EXISTING WORKS

Existing work on subgraph querying (SQ) motivates our study. Some preliminary definitions concerning SQ are given below.

Data Graph. We define a data graph as an undirected, vertex-labeled graph $G = (V, E, \Sigma, L)$, where
(1) V is the set of data vertices;
(2) $E \subseteq V \times V$ is a set of undirected edges;
(3) Σ is a set of vertex labels;
(4) for each vertex $v \in V$, $L(v) \in \Sigma$ is the label of v.

Subgraph. A graph $G_s = (V_s, E_s, \Sigma_s, L_s)$ is a *subgraph* of G if $V_s \subseteq V$, $E_s \subseteq E$, $\Sigma_s \subseteq \Sigma$, for each edge $e = (v, v') \in E_s$, $v \in V_s$ and $v' \in V_s$, and for each $v \in V_s$, $L_s(v) = L(v)$.

Query Graph. A query graph is an undirected, vertex-labeled graph $Q = (V_Q, E_Q, \Sigma_Q, L_Q)$, where (1) V_Q, E_Q, and Σ_Q are the sets of query vertices, edges, and vertex labels, respectively; (2) for each vertex $u \in V_Q$, $L_Q(u) \in \Sigma_Q$ is the label of u. Let $q = |Q| = |V_Q|$.

Subgraph Isomorphism (or embedding). Given a data graph $G = (V, E, \Sigma, L)$ and a query graph $Q = (V_Q, E_Q, \Sigma_Q, L_Q)$, a *subgraph isomorphism* is an injective function $f : V_Q \to V$ such that (1) $L_Q(u) = L(f(u))$ for any vertex $u \in V_Q$; (2) for each edge $(u_i, u_j) \in E_Q$, there exists an edge $(f(u_i), f(u_j)) \in E$.

If an embedding f exists, let G' be the subgraph in G consisting of the vertices $f(u)$ for $u \in V_Q$, and the edges $(f(u_i), f(u_j))$ in (2) above, then we say that G' **is isomorphic to** Q and vice versa. We also say that G' is the subgraph for the embedding f, and that G' is an isomorphic subgraph.

DEFINITION 1 (SUBGRAPH QUERYING -**SQ**). *Given a data graph G and a query graph Q, the subgraph querying problem (SQ) is to find all embeddings of Q in G.*

DEFINITION 2 (COVERAGE). *Given a set $S = \{s_1, ..., s_i\}$ of subgraphs of G, where $s_i = (V_i, E_i)$, the cover set of S, denoted by $C(S)$, is the vertex set $V_C = V_1 \cup V_2 \cup ... \cup V_i$. The coverage of S is given by $|C(S)|$.*

DEFINITION 3 (DIVERSIFIED SUBGRAPH QUERYING - **DSQ**). *Given a data graph G, a query graph Q, and an integer k, the diversified subgraph querying problem (DSQ) is to select a set S of no more than k subgraphs in G that are isomorphic to Q, and such that S has the largest coverage among all such selections of k or less subgraphs.*

Given a data graph G, a query Q and an integer k, diversified subgraph querying returns k subgraphs that are isomorphic to Q and that cover the largest number of vertices possible in G. Unfortunately this problem is NP-hard, a proof of which is given in the appendix.

THEOREM 1. *The problem of DSQ is NP-hard.*

Notice that two embeddings may select the same vertex sets from the data graph G, with different matchings to the query graph. Duplicated vertex sets will not increase the coverage, and thus need not appear in a solution for DSQ. Hence, we are only interested in a set of embeddings with distinct vertex sets.

We overload the term **embedding** to also refer to the vertex set of the subgraph for an embedding isomorphic to Q. Given a set of embeddings, $S = \{s_1, s_2, ..., s_m\}$, for some integer m, denote the set of vertices $s_1 \cup s_2 \cup ... \cup s_m$ as $V(S)$. $C(S) = V(S)$ is the cover set of S. We say that the coverage of S is $|C(S)| = |V(S)|$. For better clarity, we refer to vertices in the query Q as **nodes** and those in the data graph G as **vertices**.

2.1 Disjoint Embeddings

From the definition of DSQ, the best possible coverage for k subgraphs is attained when the subgraphs are disjoint. Therefore, it is interesting to consider an algorithm that returns a maximum number of disjoint isomorphic subgraphs. If the number of returned subgraphs is k or more, we have an optimal solution for DSQ. This problem is also NP-hard, since Maximum 3-dimensional matching is a special case of the problem.

THEOREM 2. *The problem of maximum disjoint isomorphic subgraphs is NP-hard.*

However, a maximum disjoint set may not be necessary for our problem. Instead, a maximal disjoint set of isomorphic subgraphs is already an optimal solution, once there are at least k such subgraphs. This observation is key in our proposed solution, though we generalize it to optimistically look for subgraphs with as little overlapping as possible, progressively relaxing the restriction on the overlapping size.

Algorithm 1: EXISTING SQ FRAMEWORK: QSearch(S,...)

```
if |S| = |V_Q| then return S ;
u ← nextQueryNode(...);
cand(u) ← refineCandidates(u, cand(u), ...);
foreach v ∈ cand(u) and v that is not matched do
    if IsJoinable(S, u, v) then
        Update(S, u, v); QSearch(S, ...); Restore(S, u, v);
```

2.2 Existing Subgraph Querying Algorithms

DSQ can be solved by first generating all embeddings and then selecting k embeddings with the best coverage. In such a way, DSQ is related to the problems of subgraph querying, SQ, and maximum k-coverage. Here we consider known solutions for SQ. In known applications, query graphs are very small, and a very large number of matching subgraphs are typically obtained from a large data graph. In known existing works for SQ, the search is terminated when k embeddings are found, where k is 1000 in [16, 35] and 1024 in [27, 15]. We also observe that many of the resulting subgraphs with known algorithms are highly overlapping. The best known mechanisms follow the basic scheme by Ullmann in [28], which is a recursive backtracking scheme. This scheme computes the solutions by incrementally enumerating and verifying partial solutions. Its worst case time complexity is $\Theta(|V|!\,|V|^2)$ [6]. This generic framework for the SQ problem is shown in Algorithm 1.

Algorithm 1. The algorithm begins with $S = \emptyset$ and recursively explores any matching for the query graph Q one node at a time. $cand(u)$, where $u \in V_Q$, is the set of vertices in V_G that have label $L_Q(u)$. Subroutine $IsJoinable$ determines if the edges between u and the already matched nodes in Q have matching edges between v and already matched vertices of G in S. If so, it updates the set S with the inclusion of v, and the newly matched edges. The recursion continues with $QSearch$; i.e., $QSearch$ is triggered within $QSearch$ to search for the next query vertex. When the recursive call returns, we restore S and continue with other candidates in $cand(u)$. $refineCandidate$ differs in different algorithms, ranging from simple degree checking to filtering by the neighborhood information of u. It is often the case that vertices that are near to each other are searched consecutively, which gives rise to many overlapping subgraphs in the solution.

Adapting Algorithm 1 for DSQ. A simple adaptation of this framework for DSQ is to consider all the candidate vertices for the first query node in the above framework and to try to retrieve embeddings in a random manner from these starting points. It is hoped that since the first candidates are dispersed, they may lead to diversified embeddings. However, our empirical studies show that this is not the case and the resulting coverage is not high. This is because although the first candidate vertices are distinct, the search paths may converge to common vertices in the remaining candidate matching. E.g. in Figure 1, let the first query node be $u3$, we may select $v7$ and $v9$ for $u3$. For the remaining searches, they may converge to $v3$ for $u1$, $v8$ for $u2$, and $v12$ for $u4$. Thus, the two embeddings returned will overlap at $v3$, $v8$, and $v12$.

2.3 Existing Maximum k-coverage Solutions

For DSQ, when all the embeddings (matchings) are given, the remaining problem is a special case of the maximum k-coverage problem with a subset size of $|Q|$. This well-studied problem is NP-hard, and we may adopt some known approximation algorithms.

GreedyDSQ. Given the set of all embeddings, GreedyDSQ keeps selecting the next embedding that gives the maximum gain in coverage, until k embeddings are obtained. GreedyDSQ has an approximation threshold of $(1-1/e) \approx 0.632$, which is the best possible guarantee for a polynomial time algorithm as shown in [12]. However, since the number of embeddings can be very large [1], the cost to generate and store all embeddings can be prohibitive.

Streaming Algorithms: SWAP0, SWAP1, SWAP2, SWAP$_A$. In the following, we describe four streaming algorithms which keep only a collection A_{curr} of k candidate embeddings at any time. The matching embeddings are scanned once, each newly scanned embedding may be swapped with an embedding in the current collection. The algorithms differ mainly in the swapping conditions. SWAP0 swaps the next embedding with an embedding in A_{curr} whenever it increases the coverage. However, this may result in a poor approximation. For a better guarantee we may swap embeddings based on the criterion in [25], resulting in algorithm SWAP1, or that in [3], resulting in algorithm SWAP2. Informally, SWAP1 swaps embedding s with a new s' when the benefit of adding s' is at least twice the loss of removing s in the coverage. SWAP2 swaps s with new s' when the coverage of the set of collected embeddings after swapping is $(1 + 1/k)$ times that of the current collection. Another algorithm SWAP$_A$ can be seen as a hybrid of SWAP1 and SWAP2, where a weighted combination of their swapping conditions is adopted [32]. Each of SWAP1, SWAP2, and SWAP$_A$ is a 0.25 approximate algorithm [25, 3, 32]. The streaming algorithms are still prohibitively costly since they require a feeding stream from the set of all embeddings. The preprocessing to generate all embeddings is required at query time and typically will take an excessive amount of time.

Use of SWAP2 in Diversified Clique Search. Diversified top-k maximal clique search is considered in [33]. This problem is similar to DSQ since diversity is also defined based on the coverage. [33] utilizes SWAP2 so that only a selection of k cliques is maintained at any time. With such a streaming algorithm, an initial set of k cliques need to be generated. The initialization step of [33] selects a set of k maximal cliques greedily for better pruning power. We also utilize a streaming algorithm. However, in our solution, the initialization step becomes a first phase, which is the more important phase since in most cases it returns the solution directly. A highly effective indexing, PNP, is proposed in [33] for the swapping phase. We adapt this index for DSQ in our implementation.

3. SOLUTION OVERVIEW

As discussed in Section 2.3, existing approximation algorithms for maximum k-coverage require the generation and scanning of all embeddings. Let us first assume that we can adopt an existing algorithm to generate all embeddings and that they can be stored and scanned. We shall remove this assumption later in this section. As pointed out in Section 2.1, if we aim for totally disjoint embeddings and succeed, we raise the approximation ratio to 1. Based on this idea, our first attempt is a simple multi-scanning approach starting with a zero overlapping constraint, and relaxing the overlap constraint level by level. We call this algorithm DSQ_{NS} (DSQ with No Swapping). It works as follows. We maintain a solution set T, and starting with $T = \emptyset$, we perform up to $|Q|$ scans of the embeddings. At the $i+1$-th scanning, a new embedding is selected if it contributes $|Q| - i$ new vertices to the coverage after this scan. DSQ_{NS} terminates when $|T| = k$. We denote the set of vertices in a set of embeddings S as $C(S)$. $|C(S)|$ is the coverage of S. Let us compare the solution of DSQ_{NS} with an optimal solution OPT. Clearly, $|C(OPT)| \le k|Q|$. Suppose $|T| = k$ in the i-th scanning, then it is easy to see that $\frac{|C(T)|}{|C(OPT)|} \ge \frac{|Q|-i}{|Q|}$. If $i = 0$,

Algorithm 2: DSQL-P1 Framework: Phase 1 (no swapping)

```
begin
    i ← 0; T ← ∅;
    while i < |Q| do
        Generate a maximal set of embeddings S s.t. for any x ∈ S,
        |x ∩ V(T)| = i and ∀x, y ∈ S, x ∩ y ⊆ V(T);
        T ← T ∪ S;
        if |T| ≥ k then return T and i;
        i ← i + 1;
    return T and i;
```

T is optimal. Next consider the case where $|T| < k$ after the i-th scanning where $i = |Q| - 1$. In this case, each embedding o in OPT that is not chosen by the algorithm cannot contribute any new vertex to the solution T. That is, for each embedding o in OPT, it is either included in T, or all the vertices in o are already in $C(T)$. Thus, T is also optimal: $\frac{|C(T)|}{|C(OPT)|} = 1$.

While DSQ_{NS} has good approximate guarantee when it terminates early, there are two problems: (1) Typically, it is excessively costly to generate and scan all embeddings; (2) the worst case approximation guarantee is $1/|Q|$, which is below that of the swapping algorithms SWAP1 and SWAP2 if $|Q| > 4$.

We propose a novel level-based solution called DSQL (DSQ with Level-wise coverage) preserving the benefits of DSQ_{NS} while avoiding the above problems.

1. To avoid generating all embeddings, DSQL will selectively generate embeddings as the input to a mechanism that resembles DSQ_{NS}. Our study shows that the diversity objective can help to restrict the search scope significantly. The embedding generation process of DSQL is based on the recursive backtracking scheme of Algorithm 1.
2. To achieve a better guarantee than SWAP1, we propose a two phase algorithm. The first phase is non-swapping and resembles DSQ_{NS}. For the second phase we propose a multi-scan swapping algorithm called SWAP$_\alpha$. The embedding generation process remains level-wise and selective. The two phases are summarized in the following.

[**Non-swapping Phase**(DSQL-P1)]: The first phase of our solution is called DSQL-P1. The framework is shown in Algorithm 2. The solution set is collected in T, beginning with $T = \emptyset$. Initially we are at level 0. We collect a maximal set of disjoint embeddings in T and move on to level 1. Let T_i be the set of embeddings T immediately after level i. At level $i+1$, we try to add a maximal set of embeddings to T where each new embedding contains exactly $i+1$ vertices in $V(T_i)$, and all remaining vertices are distinct. When k embeddings are collected in T at any point at any level, the algorithm terminates, thereby simulating the effects of DSQ_{NS}.

[**Swapping Phase** (DSQL-P2)]: After Phase 1, to improve the approximate guarantee, we may continue with the second phase based on the swapping mechanism SWAP$_\alpha$. The swapping phase resumes the level-wise embedding generation, continuing at the level at which Phase 1 ends. Each generated embedding may swap with an embedding in T. Our swapping condition (Inequality (2)) allows us to set up an early termination criterion for this phase, which can significantly improve efficiency.

Some main properties of DSQL are summarized in the following.

LEMMA 1 (MAXIMALITY). *After the level i iteration in DSQL-P1, if $|T| < k$, then any embedding s that is not in T must overlap with the union of embeddings in T at $i+1$ or more vertices.*

THEOREM 3. *Let OPT be an optimal solution. If DSQL-P1 stops at the i-th iteration then the result A has an approximation ratio of $\frac{|C(A)|}{|C(OPT)|} \geq \frac{|Q|-i}{|Q|} + \frac{i}{k|Q|}$, which is tight for any i and k. If it terminates at the $|Q|-1$-th iteration and result A has size $|A| < k$, then A is optimal, i.e. $|C(A)|/|C(OPT)| = 1$.*

THEOREM 4. *Let OPT be an optimal solution. The approximation ratio of the solution SOL of DSQL is lower bounded by*

$$\frac{|C(SOL)|}{|C(OPT)|} \geq \max\left(\frac{1}{4}\left(1+\frac{1}{k}\right), \frac{1}{4}\left(1+\frac{1}{q}\right)\right)$$

We list below the meaning of some of the terms we use.

T	the current collection of embeddings
$V(T)$	set of vertices belonging to the embeddings in T
$candS(u)$	initial set of candidate vertices for u
$qList$	a list storing the rankings of query nodes
$Qovp$	set of query nodes that overlap with T
$ovpEmb$	a partial embedding (with -1 for non-overlap nodes)
$TcandS$	set of $candS(u) \cap T$ for $u \in V_Q$
$qfList$	list of ranked query nodes with father nodes
$Rcand$	candidate vertex sets as restricted by localized search
$pEmb$	a partial embedding as a set of (u, v) matching pairs

4. PHASE ONE OF DSQL: DSQL-P1

DSQL-P1 proceeds from level 0 up to level $|Q| - 1$, with possible early termination. A set T is used to collect embeddings. Algorithm 3 is the pseudocode for DSQL-P1.

Algorithm 3: DSQL-P1: the non-swapping phase

```
    Input  : candidates sets candS, k
    Output : embedding set T, i (level number)
1   begin
        // Let Q, G, T, candS be global variables
2       qList ← Order(Q, candS);
3       T ← ∅;
        // Q1Search updates T
4       Q1Search(qList, ∅);
5       if |T| == k then
6           return T, k;
7       foreach i ∈ {1, ..., |Q| − 1} do
8           QoverlapList ← { i-subsets of qList };
9           TcandS ← { TcandS[u] from T | u ∈ V_Q };
            // TcandS[u] = candS[u] ∩ V(T)
10          foreach Qovp ∈ QoverlapList do
                // get i-overlap partial embeddings
11              while
                ovpEmb = getNextOvpEmb(TcandS, Qovp) do
12                  Q1Search(qList, ovpEmb);
13                  if |T| == k then
14                      return T, i;
15      return T, i;
```

T is initially empty. New embeddings are added to T at each level. The value of i at Line 7 is the level number. When $|T| = k$, or when no more embeddings can be added, DSQL-P1 terminates. Let $V(T)$ be the set of vertices that belong to the embeddings in T. Let T_i be the value of T after the level i processing. At level i, a new embedding to be selected should overlap with $V(T_{i-1})$ at i vertices. To find an embedding, we first set i query nodes as **overlap nodes**, and the matching data vertices of these query nodes are selected from $V(T_{i-1})$. For the other query nodes, vertices in $V_G \backslash V(T_{i-1})$ are matched. Each vertex in $V_G \backslash V(T_{i-1})$ is matched at most once at level i. When such a new embedding is added into T, it brings $|Q| - i$ new vertices to T.

An index is pre-computed for looking up the set of vertices with a given label. We also use indices for **degree and neighborhood signature filtering** for candidates as in previous works such as [16]. Before running DSQL, we first generate a candidate set $candS(u)$ for each $u \in V_Q$ based on these filters. For better selectivity, DSQL ranks the query nodes and stores the ranking in a list $qList$ based on $|candS(u)|/degree(u)$, where $candS(u)$ is the set of data vertices with the same label as u, and $degree(u)$ is the degree of u in Q. DSQL-P1 next calls subroutine $Q1Search$ to get disjoint embeddings at Line 4 (we will describe $Q1Search$ in Section 4.1), resulting in T_0. If k embeddings are found, DSQL terminates. Otherwise, DSQL-P1 continues to search for embeddings with overlap (number of vertices that are already in current T) from size 1 to $|Q| - 1$ (Lines 7-14), in a level-wise manner. The algorithm terminates once k embeddings are found.

When the overlap size is i (Level i), each i-subset of V_Q is a possible set of overlap nodes, we denote such a set of query nodes as $Qovp$. Each $Qovp$ is sorted based on the ranking in $qList$, and is kept in $QoverlapList$ (Line 8). For each $Qovp$, DSQL-P1 finds matching data vertices for the overlap nodes in $Qovp$. For every query node $u \in V_Q$, we derive the candidate set $TcandS[u]$, where $TcandS[u] = candS[u] \cap V(T)$ (Line 9). For every $Qovp$, we find a match v for every node $u \in Qovp$ by picking a vertex in $TcandS[u]$, resulting in a valid **partial embedding**, $ovpEmb$, in which only the overlap nodes are matched (Line 11). These partial embeddings, $ovpEmb$, are passed to $Q1Search$ one by one to form any complete embedding. Let $qList = (u_1, ..., u_q)$, a partial embedding can be denoted by an ordered list of $(a_1, ..., a_q)$ where $a_i = v_i$ if v_i is the vertex matched to the overlap node u_i, and $a_i = -1$ (null) otherwise, i.e. -1 signifies an non-overlap node u_i that has not been matched.

4.1 Subgraph Search Function Q1Search

$Q1Search$ (Lines 4 and 12 in Algorithm 3) is similar to the recursive backtracking function of $QSearch$ in Algorithm 1 in Section 2.2, with three major differences:

(1) Some query nodes in $qList$ have been matched in the given partial embedding $ovpEmb$; there is no need to search for matchings for these nodes. The remaining nodes are searched in the order of $qList$; the candidate set for u is $candS(u) \setminus V(T)$.

(2) For each given $ovpEmb$, the only overlapping nodes should be the ones in $ovpEmb$. Once an embedding that matches all the null (-1) entries in $ovpEmb$ is found, there is no need to generate any more embeddings that match $ovpEmb$. This avoids the generation of many embeddings when compared to $QSearch$.

(3) Any data vertex matched in any full embedding is marked so that it will not be matched again for non-overlap nodes in other embeddings.

EXAMPLE 2. *Consider Figure 2. Let* $k = 6$. *Algorithm 3 ranks the query nodes in Q as qList* $= (u1, u2, u3)$. *First, it searches the candidates of* $u1$, *which are* $\{v1, v7, v14, v16\}$, *and get embeddings without overlap in* $T = \{(v1, v2, v3), (v7, v8, v9)\}$. *Since* $K = 6$, *and* $|T| = 2 < k$, *we continue to search for embeddings with overlapping vertices with T. We move on to Level 1 (see Figure 2(d)). The overlap size is set to 1; the ordered QoverlapList =* $(\{u1\}, \{u2\}, \{u3\})$. *From T, derive* $TcandS = (u1 : \{v1, v7\}, u2 : \{v2, v8\}, u3 : \{v3, v9\})$. *For each Qovp in QoverlapList, generate partial embeddings ovpEmb one by one and pass on to Q1Search. When Qovp =* $\{u1\}$, *we get ovpEmbs* $(v1, -1, -1)$, $(v7, -1, -1)$. *For ovpEmb =* $(v1, -1, -1)$, *we get embedding* $(v1, v5, v6)$. *After processing all entries in QoverlapList, T contains* $(v1, v2, v3)$, $(v7, v8, v9)$, $(v1, v5, v6)$, $(v14, v2, v15)$, *and* $(v16, v17, v3)$, $|T| = 5 < 6$. *We continue with Level 2 (see*

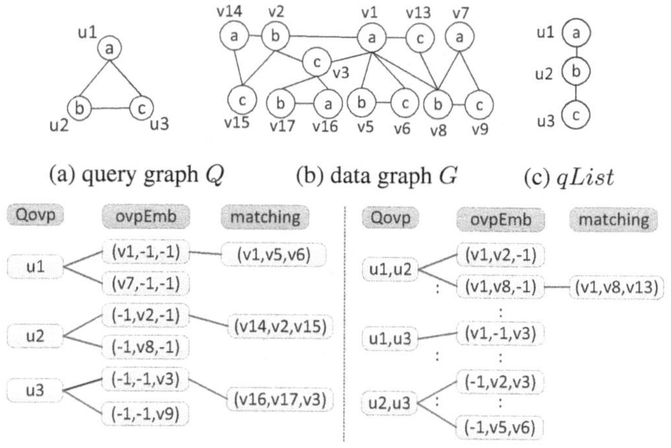

(a) query graph Q (b) data graph G (c) $qList$

(d) Level 1 (e) Level 2

Figure 2: (a) Q, (b) G, (c) $qList$, (d) $Qovp, ovpEmb$ and embeddings generated at Level 1 of DSQL-P1, (e) some $ovpEmb$s at Level 2 if $T = \{(v1, v2, v3), (v7, v8, v9), (v1, v5, v6), (v14, v2, v15), (v16, v17, v3)\}$.

Figure 2(e)) to search for embeddings with overlap size 2 ($i = 2$). *Now, QoverlapList =* $(\{u1, u2\}, \{u1, u3\}, \{u2, u3\})$, *and TcandS =* $(u1 : \{v1, v7, v14, v16\}, u2 : \{v2, v5, v8, v17\}, u3 : \{v3, v6, v9, v15\})$. *Q1Search gets a new embedding* $(v1, v8, v13)$. *Now* $|T| = 6$, *so DSQL-P1 terminates. The results are* $(v1, v2, v3)$, $(v7, v8, v9)$, $(v1, v5, v6)$, $(v14, v2, v15)$, $(v16, v17, v3)$, *and* $(v1, v8, v13)$.

4.2 Indexing and Properties of DSQL-P1

DSQL-P1 requires the indices of $candS$, vertex degrees and neighborhood signatures for filtering candidates (see Line 3 of Algorithm 1). The **neighborhood signature** of a vertex v, denoted by $NS(v)$, is the set of labels of the neighbors of v. $NS(v) = \{\ell : (v, v') \in E \text{ and } L(v') = \ell\}$. The storage requirement is thus $O(|V| + |E|)$.

At each level i, Lemma 1 says that we generate a maximal set of new embeddings. An approximation guarantee for this phase is given in Theorem 3. The proofs are shown in the appendix.

5. OPTIMIZING DSQL-P1

The efficiency of DSQL-P1 can be greatly improved if we consider some properties of the diversity requirement. We introduce some optimization strategies in this section. The first two strategies prune partial embeddings by restricting the candidate sets for query nodes. The next two strategies avoid unnecessary subgraph search in the backtracking process. All four strategies require very little extra storage and are easy to implement.

5.1 Localized Subgraph Search

When we are given partial embeddings, some query nodes are already matched. We may greatly improve the performance by limiting the search scope to the neighborhood of the matched vertices. In Algorithm 3, we order the query nodes in $qList$ according to their selectivity. With this strategy, we reorder the vertices by giving higher ranks to matched nodes. We record essential information in a new data structure *qfList*. The elements of *qfList* are of the form (u, u_f), where u is a query node, and u_f is a designated **father node** for u. $u_f = -1$ for the first element in *qfList*. A father node u_f for node u is a query node that is processed before u and there is an edge linking u_f to u in the query graph Q. If (u, f) is the r-th entry in *qfList*, we say that the **rank** of u, $rank(u) = r$. We refer to u as *qfList*$[r].node$, and f as *qfList*$[r].father$.

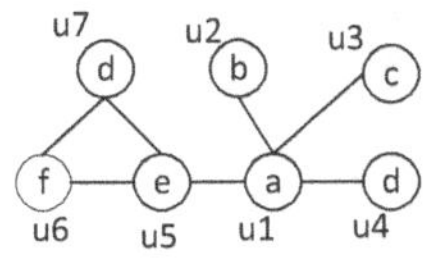

(a) query graph Q

u	u1	u5	u6	u7	u3	u2	u4
u_f	-1	u1	u5	u5	u1	u1	u1

(b) *qfList*

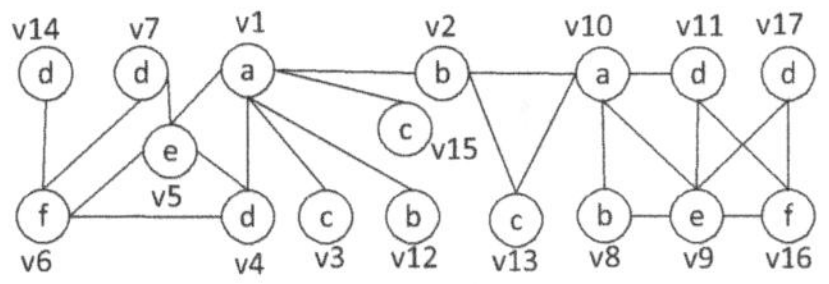

(c) data graph G

Figure 3: Query graph Q, *qfList*, and data Graph G

EXAMPLE 3. *Figure 3 shows a query graph and its qfList. (The initial ordering in qList is given by $u1, u5, u6, u7, u3, u2, u4$.) Suppose that currently $u1$ is matched to $v1$ in the data graph in Figure 3 (c). Q1iSearch in Algorithm 4 follows the order in qfList, thus, $u5, u4, u2, u3$ will be searched after $u1$. Since $u1$ is matched to $v1$, the search is localized in the neighborhood of $v1$. In qfList, the "father" of each of $u5, u4, u2, u3$ is $u1$. The candidates for $u5, u4, u2, u3$ will be limited to the neighbors of $v1$, which are $\{v5\}$, $\{v4\}$, $\{v2, v12\}$, $\{v3, v15\}$, respectively.*

This strategy is similar to that of candidate region exploration, which is a main idea proposed in [15]. However, compared to [15], we have a more powerful localization condition since we limit the search scope by T_0 based on the following lemma, which can be easily proved as a corollary of Lemma 1.

LEMMA 2. *For any level i, $i > 0$, let T_i be the value of T after Level i of DSQL-PL. Each embedding in $T_i - T_{i-1}$ must overlap with embeddings in T_0, and $|T_0| \leq k$.*

For this strategy, we introduce two subroutines as follows.

[Subroutine reSort($Q, qList, Qovp$)]
$reSort$ scans the nodes in $qList$ until the first matched node u ($u \in Qovp$) is found. $(u, -1)$ is entered as the first element in *qfList*. Next, for each neighbor u' of u in Q, if the father node of u' has not been set, it is set to be u, and (u', u) is added to *qfList*. After this, $(u, -1)$ is marked in *qfList*. We scan *qfList* until we come to the first unmarked element, and repeat a similar process as that for u. This is repeated until $|qfList| = |Q|$. Finally we shift the entries (u, u_f) to the end of *qfList* if $degree(u) = 1$ in Q.

[Subroutine setCandidates($u_j, u_f, pEmp, Qovp$)]
$setCandidates$ sets the candidate data vertices for a given query node u_j, given its father node u_f in *qfList*. Let the result be $Rcand$. First set $Rcand = candS[u_j]$. Next, do the following.

1. If u_f is matched to some vertex v_f in $pEmb$, set $Rcand$ to be the set of neighbors of v_f in G with the same label as u_j.

2. (1) If $u_j \in Qovp$: then further restrict $Rcand$ to vertices in T. Thus, $Rcand \leftarrow Rcand \cap V(T)$. (2) If $u_j \notin Qovp$: then, $Rcand \leftarrow Rcand \setminus V(T)$.

DSQL-P1 (Algorithm 3) is modified accordingly as follows. Function reSort is triggered initially after $qList$ is built at Line 2 and also in each level for each $Qovp$ after Line 10. We call the improved search function **Q1iSearch** (see **Algorithm 4**), passing the parameter of *qfList* instead of $qList$. We do not generate $ovpEmp$ at Line 11, but instead pass an empty set to *Q1iSearch* for the partial embedding. *Q1iSearch* will also search for the partial embedding matchings, *pEmb*. setCandidates is triggered in the beginning of *Q1iSearch* at Line 5, when a node u_j is to be matched and the father u_f is retrieved from *qfList*. In *Q1iSearch*, ***QSearchD*** is triggered when we encounter the first query node that is not in $Qovp$ (Line 16). $QSearchD$ is similar to *Q1iSearch* except that it returns true if an embedding is found and will not search for more embeddings, and $QSearchD$ will only trigger $QSearchD$ recursively.

5.2 Single Embedding Search Mode

Consider the example in Figure 2 again. If at level 1, $Qovp = \{u1\}$ and $ovpEmb = \{v1, -1, -1\}$, then suppose we assign a candidate $v5$ to match with $u2$. Next, we can only select a single embedding that contains $v1$ and $v5$, otherwise the overlap size will not be 1. Thus we enter the single embedding search mode with $pEmb = \{v1, v5, -1\}$. This search mode is handled by function $QSearchD$ in Algorithm 4. Recall that $QSearchD$ is triggered when we encounter the first query node that is not in $Qovp$. Since we only need to find a single embedding in the single embedding search mode, we further restrict the candidate set for query nodes. For this purpose we define $labelRm$ and $neighborRm$ for each query node when *qfList* is updated, the use of which will be explained shortly. $labelRm(u)$ is the number of higher ranked nodes in *qfList* that has label $L(u)$. $neighborRm(u)$ is the number of higher ranked nodes in *qfList* linked to u by an edge in Q. That is, $labelRm(u) = |\{u' : rank(u') > rank(u) \wedge L(u') = L(u)\}|$ $neighborRm(u) = |\{u' : rank(u') > rank(u) \wedge (u, u') \in E_Q\}|$.

query node	u1	u5	u6	u7	u3	u2	u4
labelRm	0	0	0	1	0	0	0
neighborRm	4	2	1	0	0	0	0

EXAMPLE 4. *The above table shows the values of $labelRm$ and $neighborRm$ for the example in Figure 3. For $u1$, no query node after $u1$ in qfList has label $L(u1) = a$, hence $labelRm(u1) = 0$. $neighborRm(u1) = 4$, since $u1$ is linked to $u5, u2, u3, u4$.*

For a query node u_j, if $neighborRm(u_j) = 0$, we randomly retain only $labelRm(u_j)+1$ valid vertices in $Rcand$, where a valid vertex is a vertex joinable to the matched vertices. In $QSearchD$, a candidate is matched if it is joinable to the vertices that are already matched. If $neighborRm(u_j) = 0$, the matching of u_j will not disqualify that for the higher ranked nodes in *qfList* due to this join criteria, so the matching for u_j can be randomly selected. The matching for u_j may affect other nodes with the same label, say u_k, since u_j may take up a good candidate for u_k. By choosing $labelRm(u_j)+1$ candidates we allow for one additional candidate that avoids such conflict. The enhanced $QSearchD$ has a stronger pruning power than $Q1Search$ since it restricts the candidate set and will not continue the search if no embedding is found after exhausting the candidates.

EXAMPLE 5. *Let us consider the case in Example 4. Since $neighborRm(u2) = 0$ and $labelRm(u2) = 0$, the number of candidates for $u2$ is limited to 1. In Figure 3, if $u1$ is matched to $v1$, according to qfList, the candidates of $u2$ are the neighbors of $v1$ with label b, namely, $v2, v12$. Hence, we randomly pick $v2$ to be the single candidate for $u2$, and $v12$ will not be matched. For* *u7, neighborRm(u7) = 0 and labelRm(u7) = 1, we pick 2 candidates from the neighbors of v5, namely, v4 and v7. We need to pick 2 candidates since if we pick v4 only, we cannot form the embedding with v5, for v4 should be matched to u4.*

5.3 Skipping Query Nodes in Backtracking

For our next enhancement strategy, the idea is to skip the processing of certain query nodes under some condition to speed up the backtracking process in the $Q1iSearch$ or $QSearchD$ recursions. Let $pEmb$ be a set of matching pairs (u, v), where u is a query node, and v is a data vertex. When $pEmb$ contains a pair (u, v) for each vertex u in V_Q, it is a full embedding. In $Q1iSearch$ (Algorithm 4), $pEmb$ records the current partial embedding. $pEmp$ is initially empty on the first call of $Q1iSearch$, but grows as more matching pairs are found. Given two query nodes u_i and u_j, during the computation, when the current partial embedding is $pEmb$, we say that u_j **conflicts with** u_i if either of the followings holds:

1. u_j is linked to u_i by an edge in Q.
2. v_j has been matched to u_j in the current partial embedding, i.e. $(u_j, v_j) \in pEmb$. Also, v_j is a valid candidate for u_i, i.e. $L(v_j) = L_Q(u_i)$ and v_j passes the degree and neighborhood signature filters for u_i.

We use a **conflict table** to record the above conflict relationships. A conflict table is a boolean array of size $|Q|$. We construct a static conflict table for every $u \in V_Q$ as $CT(u, *)$, with an entry in $CT(u, *)$ for each query node. If u is connected with u' in Q, then the entry of u' in $CT(u, *)$ is set as true (1), otherwise it is set as false (0). When matching query node u_i, we construct a dynamic conflict table for u_i, $CT(u_i, \beta)$, where β is the current partial embedding, and first, we initialize all entries to false. If a candidate v passes the degree and neighborhood signature filter of u_i, but it is matched to u_j in β, then u_j conflicts with u_i, and we mark the entry of u_j of $CT(u_i, \beta)$ as true.

[Skipping Non-conflict Nodes]. We say that DSQL fails at u_i when it cannot find a vertex to match with u_i. If DSQL fails at u_i, it returns the conflict table $CT(u_i, \beta)$, where β is the current partial embedding. When backtracking to u_k, the algorithm checks tables $CT(u_i, \beta)$ and $CT(u_i, *)$. If the corresponding elements of u_k in both tables are false, then there is no conflict, and the algorithm skips u_k and backtracks to a higher level. Otherwise it continues with the next candidate for u_k.

[Correctness]. Suppose u_k is skipped by the strategy after failing at u_i and backtracking to u_k. This implies that u_k does not conflict with u_i, thus, u_k is not a neighbor of u_i in Q. Note that by the construction of *qfList*, the parent node of u_i will be encountered before its other ancestor nodes in the backtracking. Thus, the only way that the matching of u_k to a vertex v_k may affect the success or failure of matching u_i is when v_k is a valid candidate for u_i. This is because if we have not selected v_k for u_k, it can be matched to u_i, and may result in a success instead of a failure. However, since u_k does not conflict with u_i, v_k is not a valid candidate for u_i. Thus, we can safely skip u_k.

EXAMPLE 6. *Consider the example in Figure 4. The querying order for Q is u_1, u_2, u_3, u_4. $Q1iSearch$ matches v_1 to u_1 and v_2 to u_2, and gets partial embedding $\beta_1 = \{(u_1, v_1), (u_2, v_2)\}$. We continue to try to match u_3; candidates v_2, v_5, v_7 to v_{1007} all fail the degree filter test. So we fail at u_3, returning $CT(u_3, \beta_1)$. We backtrack to u_2. u_2 does not conflict with u_3 in both $CT(u_3, \beta_1)$ and $CT(u_3, *)$, so we directly backtrack to u_1 and use v_6 to match u_1. Note that without node skipping, the backtracking will process v_5, v_7,...,v_{1007} to map u_2, and fail to find any embedding. Thus, a large number of useless node searches are saved.*

Algorithm 4: Q1iSearch (to replace Q1Search in DSQL-P1)

```
Input  : TcandS, qfList, start, Qovp, pEmb
Output : T, candS, and matched are updated
begin
    if |pEmb| = |Q| then return;
    j ← start;
    u_j ← qfList[j].node, u_f ← qfList[j].father;
    Rcand ← setCandidates(u_j, u_f, pEmp, Qovp);
    foreach v ∈ Rcand following its ordering do
        if u_j ∉ Qovp and matched[v] == true then
            continue;
        if v fails to pass the degree or neighborhood filters then
            candS[u_j] ← candS[u_j] \ {v}; continue;
        if isJoinable(pEmb, u_j, v) then
            pEmb ← pEmb ∪ {(u_j, v)};
            matched[v] = true;
            if u_j ∈ Qovp then
                Q1iSearch(TcandS, qfList, j+1, Qovp, pEmb);
            else if
            QSearchD(TcandS, qfList, j + 1, Qovp, pEmb)
            then
                T ← T ∪ pEmb;
                if |T| == k then return;
                continue;
            if u_j ∉ Qovp then matched[v] ← false;
            pEmb ← pEmb \ {(u_j, v)};
```

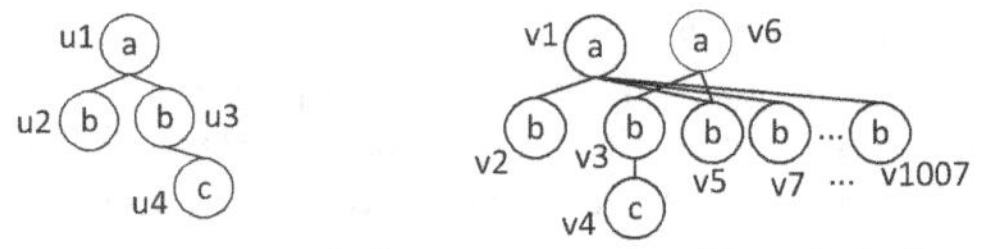

(a) query graph Q (b) data graph G

u1	u2	u3	u4
1	0	0	1

(c) $CT(u_3, *)$

u1	u2	u3	u4
0	0	0	0

(d) $CT(u_3, \beta_1)$

u1	u2	u3	u4
0	1	0	0

(e) $CT(u_3, \beta_2)$

Figure 4: (a) Q, (b) G, and node conflict tables: (c) static conflict table (d) partial embedding is $\beta_1 = \{(u_1, v_1), (u_2, v_2)\}$ (e) partial embedding is $\beta_2 = \{(u_1, v_6), (u_2, v_3)\}$

To continue, we match v_6 to u_1, and v_3 to u_3, The current partial embedding is $\beta_2 = \{(u_1, v_6), (u_2, v_3)\}$. We proceed to match u_3. However, the candidate v_3 is already mapped to u_2. Because of this, u_2 conflicts with u_3. After failing at u_3, we backtrack to u_2. Since u_2 conflicts with u_3, we cannot skip u_2, and match u_2 with the next candidate v_5. With further recursions, we get the embedding (v_6, v_5, v_3, v_4).

5.4 Skipping Data Vertices in Backtracking

When the average degree in the data graph is relatively high, there may be many vertices sharing the same or similar neighborhood. Failure with such vertices may incur many duplicated computations. [24] rewrites vertices with the same neighborhood as a super node, thus reducing the costs. Our algorithm simply keeps track of "bad" vertices to a similar effect.

Let the query nodes be processed in the order of $u_1, ..., u_q$, i.e., we assume the following ranking in *qfList*: $rank(u_1) < ... <$

$rank(u_q)$. Suppose we match a data vertex v_i for u_i, but we could find no match for u_{i+1}, then we mark v_i as a **"bad" vertex**. These markings of vertices are only kept for one layer: when we backtrack to the parent of u_i, all "bad" vertices marked at the matching for u_{i+1} are unmarked. When the subgraph search fails at query node u_i, we backtrack to the first query node u_j that conflicts with u_i. We examine the query node u_{j-1} before u_j. If u_{j-1} does not conflict with u_i, the data vertex for u_j is marked as a "bad" vertex. When we backtrack to the query node u_{j-1}, the processing of u_{j-1} will skip the "bad" vertices for the matching of u_j next time. We illustrate the effects of this strategy with the following example.

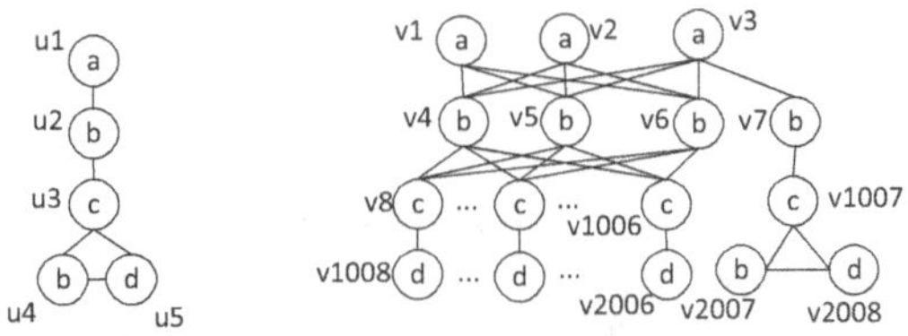

(a) query graph Q (b) data graph G

Figure 5: An example of a denser data graph

EXAMPLE 7. *Given G and Q in Figure 5. Consider the case when the partial embedding* $pEmb = \{(u_1, v_1), (u_2, v_4)\}$ *and we try to match* u_3. *The next candidate is* v_8. *Since there is no matching for* u_4, *the algorithm marks* v_8 *as "bad". Similarly,* $v_9, ..., v_{1006}$ *are marked as "bad" vertices. When the algorithm chooses* v_5 *for* u_2, *it will directly skip "bad" vertices, i.e.* $v_8, ..., v_{1006}$. *Then there is no matching for* u_3, *so* v_5 *is marked as "bad". The algorithm continues this process. Finally, when* v_3 *is mapped to* u_1, v_5 *and* v_6 *are all marked as "bad" vertices, the algorithm directly checks* v_7 *and finally finds one matching* $(v_3, v_7, v_{1007}, v_{2007}, v_{2008})$.

Note that v_{1006} *will be marked as a "bad" vertex when there is no matching for* u_4, *as it is searched after matching* v_6 *to* u_2. *However, when we move up to* u_1, v_{1006} *will be unmarked.*

LEMMA 3. *The strategy of skipping "bad" vertices is correct.*

A proof is given in the appendix. Note that this strategy and the previous strategy are also applicable for subgraph querying, SQ.

6. PHASE TWO OF DSQL: DSQL-P2

Phase two of DSQL continues the search from phase one, with the objective of enhancing the result by swapping embeddings and providing a better worst case approximate guarantee.

6.1 SWAPα: Multi-Scan with Swapping

To simplify our discussion, we assume again that we first have all the embeddings generated by an SQ mechanism. Then in Section 6.2 we shall remove this assumption. The streaming algorithms described in Section 2.3 are 0.25-approximate. In this subsection, we show that multiple embedding scannings can lead to better guarantees. The main results in this section are: (1) we propose a multi-scan algorithm SWAPα, and derive the parameter settings for progressive improvements on the approximation bound, which is asymptotically 0.5. (2) We introduce a new swapping condition in SWAPα which allows for early stopping. (3) We improve the approximation bound of the known algorithms of SWAP1, SWAP2, and SWAP$_A$ to $0.25 \times \max((1 + 1/k), (1 + 1/q))$, which also applies to SWAPα.

6.1.1 *Swapping Criterion for Each Scan*

Let $h = (V_h, E_h)$ be an embedding of G, $C(h) = V_h$, $|C(h)|$ stands for the coverage of h. Let $F = \{g_1, g_2, ..., g_k\}$ be a set of k embeddings of G, where $g_i = (V_i, E_i)$, $C(F) = \bigcup_i V_i$, $|C(F)|$ is the coverage of F. We assume that we are given a list of all embeddings. SWAPα consists of multiple passes, and in each pass, all embeddings are scanned once. Let the embedding list be $S = s_1, s_2, ..., |S| \geq k$.

In each pass, a collection F of k embeddings for the current best selections is maintained. We swap embeddings in the collection with a newly scanned embedding when the swapping criterion is satisfied. The first collection of k embeddings for the first pass is $F_0 = \{s_1, .., s_k\}$. The final collection generated by the t-th pass is the first collection of the $t+1$-th pass.

The coverage loss of an embedding f w.r.t. an embedding set F containing f is the coverage that is lost if f is deleted from F:

$$L(f, F) = |C(f) \setminus C(F \setminus f)| \tag{1}$$

The coverage benefit of an embedding h w.r.t. a set F of embeddings is the gain in coverage if h is added to F:

$$B(h, F) = |C(h) \setminus C(F)|$$

[**Swapping Criterion**] In general, we swap the next candidate h with any candidate $f^* \in F$ if for a certain parameter $\alpha \geq 0$,

$$B(h, F) \geq (1 + \alpha)L(f^*, F) \tag{2}$$

The loss function $L(f, F)$ above differs from the loss measurement in [25], which is given by $L^+(f, h, F) = |C(f) \setminus C(F \cup h \setminus f)|$. In our empirical studies, we show that the two loss functions result in similar performance in efficiency and quality for maximum k-coverage. However, $L(f, F)$ is independent of the new embedding h, which allows us to introduce an early stopping strategy in our algorithm for DSQ, as will be shown in the proof of Lemma 4 in Section 6.2.

6.1.2 *Progressive Gain with Multiple Scans*

The question is how to set the value of α in Equation (2) in each scan. Let α_t be the value of α used for the t-th scan of the embeddings. γ_t is a lower bound for the approximation ratio of the resulting collection of embeddings in the t-th scan. For a scanning of the embeddings, let F_0 be the initial embedding collection, and F_i be the embedding collection when f_i is removed from it, where f_i is the i-th embedding swapped out by the algorithm. Hence $f_i \in F_i$ and $f_i \notin F_{i+1}$. Let F_{final} be the final collection. We set γ_t as the value of $|C(F_{final})|/|C(OPT)|$ for the $t-1$-th scan or the value of $|C(F_0)|/|C(OPT)|$ for the t-th scan, where OPT is an optimal solution. Our main result on the setting of α and the coverage guarantee is the following:

THEOREM 5. *At the t-th scanning of SWAPα, if* $\gamma_{t-1} < 0.5$, *then by setting*

$$\alpha_t = 1 - 2\gamma_{t-1} \tag{3}$$

the approximation ratio of the embedding collection after the scanning is lower bounded by

$$\gamma_t = 0.25(1/(1 - \gamma_{t-1})) \tag{4}$$

A proof of Theorem 5 is given in the appendix. From Equations (3) and (4), if $\gamma_0 = 0$, $\alpha_1 = 1$, $\gamma_1 = 0.25$, $\alpha_2 = 0.5$, $\gamma_2 = 1/3$, $\alpha_3 = 1/3$, $\gamma_3 = 3/8$, $\alpha_4 = 1/4$, $\gamma_4 = 0.4$, $\alpha_5 = 0.2$, $\gamma_5 \approx 0.416$, $\alpha_6 = 1/6$, $\gamma_6 \approx 0.428$, $\alpha_7 \approx 0.114$, $\gamma_7 \approx 0.437$ ...

It can be shown that $\gamma_0, \gamma_1, ...$ converges to the fixed point of 0.5.

6.1.3 A Better Bound for the Swapping Mechanism

For the first scan, we can get a better bound if we do not simply pick the first k scanned embeddings for F_0. Instead, we begin with an empty F_0, and add the next scanned embedding h if the swapping criterion is met, assuming that an empty fictitious embedding f is swapped out. Since the loss $L(f,T) = 0$, the next embedding is added whenever there is non-zero additional coverage. This is repeated until k embeddings are collected in F_0. After that the algorithm continues as before. We refer to this as *the progressive initialization step*. We prove the following in the appendix.

THEOREM 6. *For DSQ, let SOL be the solution of any of the one-pass algorithms SWAP1, SWAP2, SWAP$_A$ and SWAPα with $\alpha = 1$, with the progressive initialization step,*

$$\frac{|C(SOL)|}{|C(OPT|)} \geq \max\left(\frac{1}{4}\left(1+\frac{1}{k}\right), \frac{1}{4}\left(1+\frac{1}{q}\right)\right)$$

E.g. if $k = 2$, $\gamma_1 = 0.375$, if $q = 5$, then $\gamma_1 = 0.3$.

This is a better bound compared to 0.25 derived in [25] and [32]

The result holds also for the maximum k-coverage problem when the given subsets are of the same size, q.

6.2 DSQL-P2

SWAPα assumes an input stream of embeddings. We now relax the seemingly necessary requirement to generate all embeddings. As in DSQL-P1, in DSQL-P2, we generate embeddings in a level-based approach and supply the embeddings to a SWAPα based algorithm, with an early stopping technique that can attain the same approximation guarantee without generating all embeddings.

After Phase 1 of DSQL, we obtain an embedding set T and also a level number i. T and i are input to the second phase, DSQL-P2. There are two possibilities:
(1) $i = |Q| - 1$ and $|T| < k$. From Theorem 3, the solution T is an optimal solution. Thus, we terminate without triggering Phase 2.
(2) Otherwise, $|T| = k$. This is because $|T| = k$ is the termination criteria at any level below $|Q| - 1$. There are two subcases:
(2a) The embeddings in T are disjoint. In this case, the algorithm has an optimal solution and is terminated.
(2b) Otherwise, if the approximation ratio of T is ≥ 0.5, return T as the solution. Else, trigger Phase 2, DSQL-P2.

We terminate at an approximation ratio[1] of 0.5 or above since the guarantee of SWAPα is bounded by 0.5. Note that at the beginning of Phase 2, $|T| = k$. DSQL-P2 is shown in Algorithm 5. The first step in DSQL-P2 is to save the input T as $T1$. In $Q2Search$, we generate embeddings as in the first phase except for a main difference: we always use $T1$ instead of T in the generation of $TcandS$. When an embedding h is found, we check if the swapping condition of Inequality (2) is satisfied for any embedding f in T: $B(h,T) \geq (1+\alpha)L(f,T)$. If it is satisfied then we swap h with f. Next, we check if DSQL-P2 can be terminated. The termination condition is described below.

[Early Termination]: The swapping phase is terminated if both of the following two conditions hold:

(1) $V(T1) \subseteq V(T)$;

(2) For each embedding $f \in T$, $L(f,T) \geq (q-i)/(1+\alpha)$.

If the above conditions do not hold, we continue with the generation of the next embedding. When all level i embeddings have been generated, and if $i < |Q|$, we continue with the next level of $j = i + 1$. This recursive process continues until either we can terminate early or $j = |Q| - 1$. The following lemma is proved in the appendix.

[1]The approximation ratio is taken to be $|C(T)|/kq$.

Algorithm 5: Swapping Phase: DSQL-P2(T,i)

Input : $Q, G, candS, k, qList, T, i$ (level number)
Output : top k embeddings (T)

```
begin
    T1 ← T;
    // Q, G, T, candS, k are global
    foreach j ∈ {i, ..., |Q| − 1} do
        QoverlapList ← {subset of qList of size j};
        TcandS ← {TcandS[u] from T1|u ∈ V_Q};
        foreach Qovp ∈ QoverlapList do
            while
            ovpEmb = getNextOvpEmb(TcandS, Qovp) do
                if ¬Q2Search(qList, 0, ovpEmb, T1) then
                    return T;
```

LEMMA 4. *The early termination for DSQL-P2 is correct.*

Initially $T = T1$, therefore if for all $f \in T1$, $L(f,T1) \geq (q - i)/(1+\alpha)$, the swapping process can be terminated. The overall approximation guarantee of DSQL is given by Theorem 4, a proof of which is included in the appendix.

7. EMPIRICAL STUDY

In this section, we present our experimental results. All our experiments are conducted on a machine with 3.4Ghz Intel Core i7-4770 CPU and 16 GB RAM, running Ubuntu 12.04 LTS Linux OS. All algorithms are implemented in C++. For existing algorithms we use the coding provided by the authors of [24] for BoostIso over $Turbo_{ISO}$, and for $Turbo_{ISO}$.

Datasets. We use 9 real datasets in our experiments: Human, Yeast, Youtube, Wordnet, DBLP, Epinion, USpatent, Dbpedia, and IMDB. The first six sets are used in [24], USpatent is used in [27], and DBpedia and IMDB are used in [18]. Dbpedia is an RDF graph crawled from Wikipedia[2]. We choose the person dataset and their links to build the graph. Epinion is a who-trust-who online social network[3]. The IMDB data set contains rich information of movies and TV series. We extract the relationship among movies, TV series, actors, actresses and directors to build the whole graph. Each of these datasets is one data graph. For Youtube, Epinion, DBLP, and Dbpedia, there are no given labels, as in [24], we have assigned a label for each vertex from a synthetic label set of sizes 100, 50, 50, and 100, respectively, with a uniform random distribution. The details are shown in Table1.

Query Set. Except for the special queries used in Section 7.2, we generate query graphs by randomly selecting connected subgraphs of G, using the query generator coding from the authors of [24]. There are 1000 query graphs in one query set with the same query size (the number of edges). The query size ranges from 1 to 10. Let the query size be z. The generator begins with an empty Q, and randomly picks a vertex u from G, puts it into Q, and continues to randomly choose an edge $e = (u,v)$ incident to a vertex u in Q from E, and adds v and e to Q, until there are z edges in Q. We vary k from 10 to 50. The default query size is 5 and the default k value is 40.

Measurements. In our experiments, we measure the runtime, which is by taking the average time per query after running 1000

[2]http://dbpedia.org/
[3]http://snap.stanford.edu/data/

Dataset(G)	$\|V\|$	$\|E\|$	$\|\Sigma\|$	Avg. degree
Yeast	3101	12519	31(184)	8.07
Human	4675	86282	90	36.92
Wordnet	76854	213308	5	5.55
Epinion	75879	405741	50*	10.69
DBLP	317080	1.04M	50*	6.62
Youtube	1.1M	2.9M	100*	5.26
Dbpedia	809597	3.72M	100*	9.19
IMDB	4.49M	7.49M	123	3.34
USpatent	3.77M	16.5M	388	8.75

Table 1: Statistics of datasets (* indicates synthetic labels)

random queries. We also measure the coverage, which is an average value taken over 1000 queries. Let A be a solution for DSQ. $|C(A)|$ is the coverage of A. If the optimal solution size, $|C(OPT)|$, is known, then the *approximation ratio* is given by $|C(A)|/|C(OPT)|$. Otherwise, the approximation ratio is set to $|C(A)|/kq$, where q is the query size in number of vertices, in which case, it is actually a lower bound on $|C(A)|/|C(OPT)|$. Again, we take the average value over the query set. Note that we set the time limit to 5 hours, if the algorithm cannot finish the 1000 queries, we would terminate the program.

7.1 Results with Existing Methods

Our first study computes the total number of embeddings for the real datasets when the query size is 5 and $k = 40$. We used the coding of BoostIso over $Turbo_{ISO}$ for generating the embeddings. The results are shown in Table 2. The average per query is taken over 1000 random queries for DBLP and 50 queries for the other datasets, since 50 queries already take many hours. We have no result for the remaining datasets as they take more than 5 hours for 50 queries. The numbers are very large except for DBLP, which is due to the smaller data size and average degree, and the more even distribution of labels in DBLP. This result shows that enumerating all embeddings leads to very large answer sets. In addition, the time to enumerate all embeddings is not scalable to large graphs.

	Yeast	Epinion	DBLP	Youtube	Others
average	123389.6	666387.4	412.3	36.3M	–
worst case	19.33M	1.02M	13559	1925.45M	–
time(sec)	121.75	11.28	1.32	775.46	–

Table 2: Total number of embeddings and query time by best known SQ method (per query) with $|E_Q| = 5$

Next, we adopt a known SQ method and take the first k generated embeddings as the result. We apply the state-of-the-art algorithm of BoostIso on top of $Turbo_{ISO}$. The results are shown in Table 3. The coverages are small because the first k matchings are trapped in local areas, creating much overlapping. Thus, this approach cannot provide a well diversified solution.

	Yeast	Epinion	DBLP	Youtube	Others
$coverage$	21.05	21.76	39.07	25.82	–
approx ratio	0.105	0.091	0.168	0.108	–

Table 3: Results of best known SQ method, $|E_Q| = 5, k = 40$

7.2 Some Query Results with IMDB

Next we evaluate the performance of DSQL. We compare $DSQL$ with an interleaving search method adapted from a SQ solution. We call this method COM. We also apply our localized subgraph search and skipping strategies to this method. COM first sorts the query to form $qList$. Then for every candidate v_i of the first node in $qList$, it maintains a list of recursive iterators where each iterator traverses the candidates of every query node, and explores a search region rooted at v_i. COM processes the results in an interleaving manner. Once it finds an embedding in a search region rooted by v_i, it saves the states of the iterators for v_i, and then randomly jumps to another region rooted at another candidate v_j. When COM next jumps back to the search region rooted by v_i, it restores the states for continuing searching. COM terminates when k embeddings are found.

Query Graph A Subgraph Result

For IMDB, we build an edge if an actor/actress/director takes part in a movie/TV series. We label the movies and TV series by the rank and genre information, e.g., *Adventure3* stands for an excellent (rank $\geq$ 8.5) adventure movie. We examine the results of the query in the above figure, which resembles our motivating example. With the default setting of $k = 40$, COM gets a coverage of 97, while DSQL gets a coverage of 150. E.g. DSQL retrieves "Prison Break" for u_4, while COM does not. The figure above shows an interesting result returned by DSQL. Another interesting result is the following:

{Welliver_Titus, Scarwid_Diana, Beesley_Matt_Earl, Prison Break, Lost}

7.3 Performance of DSQL

In this subsection, we compare the runtime and coverage of DSQL and COM. For the comparison of each dataset, we vary the values of k from 10 to 50 and measure both the runtime and the coverage. We repeat this by varying the value of $|E_Q|$ from 1 to 10, following the settings of [24]. The results are shown in Figure 6. Here the number of nodes (# Nodes) refers to $|C(A)|$, where A is the resulting set of embeddings, for both DSQL and COM. To see how close the coverage is to the optimal result, we also plot a MAX value for comparison. With DSQL, we may discover an optimal solution if we get k disjoint embeddings or the number of embeddings in the solution is below k (see Theorem 3). In such cases, MAX is set to $|C(A)|$ if A is the solution set. Otherwise, MAX is set equal to $|V_Q| \times k$, which upper bounds the optimal coverage. Thus, we can compare the value of $|C(A)|$ for our solution A with MAX.

In general, the coverage increases with both k and $|E_Q|$, since more embeddings collected increase the number of covered vertices. Typically, a larger query size also leads to more covered vertices. COM covers much fewer vertices compared to DSQL. Even though it adopts an interleaving approach and randomly jumps between search regions, there is no mechanism to avoid overlapping as in DSQL. The coverage is generally very high for DSQL because it can avoid being trapped in a local area as it targets embeddings with limited overlapping.

For IMDB the label distribution is highly skewed, 90% of the labels are actor, actress or director, so the matchings can be highly numerous in some regions, and if a search enters such a region it can be very costly irrespective of the query size. Hence, we see some fluctuations in the runtime.

Since COM returns the first k embeddings found, it is quite fast when query size is small. When the data graph or query size is large, COM may not finish within our time limit of 5 hours. This happens with Wordnet when the query size is large than 9, and with IMDB when the query size is 6 or above. This is because COM may run into some deep recursion that involves many redundant computations without yielding any result. DSQL performs much

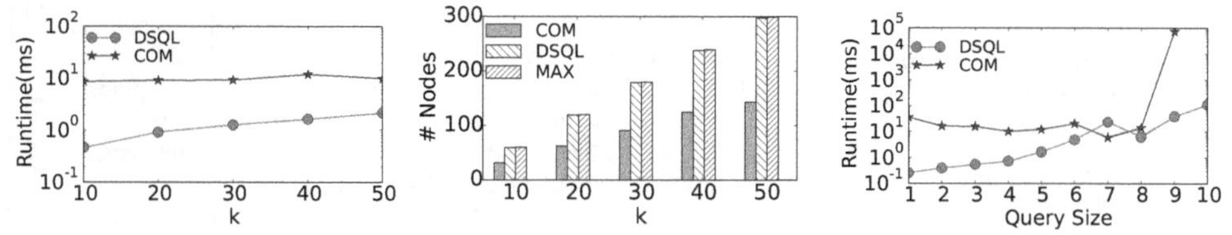

(a) query time and coverage for Wordnet

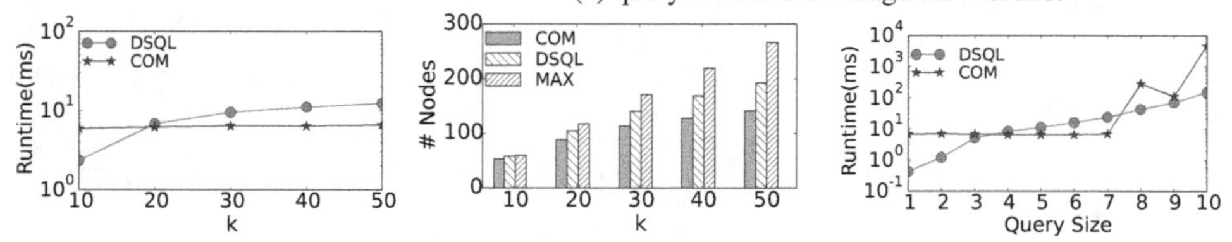

(b) query time and coverage for DBpedia

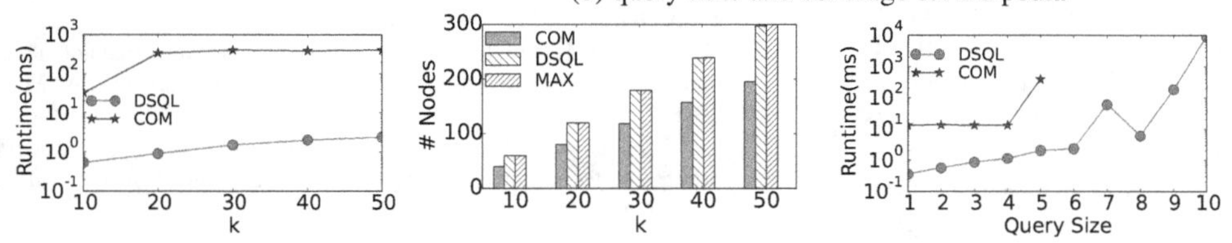

(c) query time and coverage for IMDB

Figure 6: Comparing DSQL with an interleaving search method, COM

better since the single embedding search stops searching when no match is found for a restricted set of candidates. DSQL also limits the exploration of search space within the single required embedding for each overlap pattern.

7.4 Effects of Varying the Label Set Size

We study the performance of DSQL with different label densities. Here we define label density as $\frac{|\Sigma|}{|V|}$. We consider datasets DBLP and Youtube with synthetic labels. For each graph, we vary the label density from $0.05 * 10^{-3}$ to $0.2 * 10^{-3}$.

In Figure 7, the bars labeled Youtube and DBLP show the coverages of DSQL algorithm, while MYoutube and MDBLP are their MAX values, respectively.

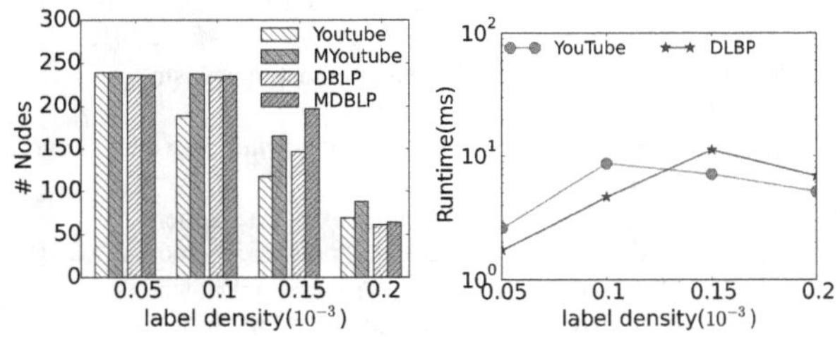

Figure 7: Effects of the label set size, k=40, $|Q|$=5

From the result, the coverage of DSQL is always close to MAX. As the label density increases, the approximation ratio would first decrease then increase, while the running time first increases then decreases.

The reason for these trends is the following. When label density is relatively small, there exist many matches in the data graph so that DSQL finds diversified results easily within a very short time. As the label density increases, there exists less matches. DSQL would terminate at higher levels, so the approximation ratio would decrease and more time is needed. As the label density grows even larger, there may not be enough k matches in the data graph, so DSQL often quickly terminates at the last level, and the coverage is close to MAX.

8. RELATED WORK

Subgraph isomorphism problem is an NP-complete problem[5]. A lot of effort has been devoted to solving it in a reasonable time for real datasets. Ullmann proposed the first practical algorithm for solving subgraph isomorphism problem [28]. It is a recursive backtracking algorithm which computes the solutions by incrementally enumerating and verifying partial solutions. In recent years, many works such as VF2[6], QuickSI[26], GraphQL[16], SPath[35] and TurboIso[15] have been proposed based on the backtracking framework. They improve the performance of the Ullmann algorithm by using vertex matching order strategies, adding powerful filters to prune invalid candidates early and choosing proper join orders. The best known complexity of an algorithm for this problem is that of VF2, which is $\Theta(|V|!\,|V|)$ [6], however, VF2 has been shown to be less efficient than variants of the Ullmann algorithm in later works. In [1], the number of subgraphs of G isomorphic to a given graph H is shown to be $O(|E_G|^{|V_H|})$ for finite simple graphs. BoostIso[24], TurboIso[15], and RBSub[11] solve the graph matching problem by graph compression. They exploit an equivalence relationship between vertices and the structure of the query graph to compress the data graph. Efficient RDF querying based on the properties of RDF data is studied in [19].

The indexing method that we use exploiting neighborhood information to prune candidate set of vertices has been used in previous works including GraphQL[16], SPath[35], and STwig[27]. The indexes are used as filters, so these algorithms are all under the backtracking framework in Section 2.2. An in-depth study is made in [21] comparing such methods and it is found that excessive indexing may lower the performance because of the overhead and limited filter effects. We adopt the best indexing strategy as noted in [21], which is that of the neighborhood signatures. For the study of querying a large set of relatively small graphs, indexes have been used as the filters of candidate graphs, some previous works are gIndex[30], FG-index[4], Tree+δ[36], and SwiftIndex[26]. A distributed algorithm STwig is proposed in [27] for solving subgraph isomorphism problem in billion-node graphs. Subgraph enumeration in MapReduce is considered in [20].

Approximate matching in large graphs is studied in SAPPER[34], where matching with bounded edit distance from the query graph is considered. [22] proposes the notion of strong simulation, with a tractable time complexity in the computation. Based on strong simulation, [11, 9] apply graph compression strategies to do efficient graph querying. [37, 10, 14] also study the problem of ranking the results. [37, 14] exploit the weights of nodes or edges, while [10] ranks the matched subgraphs based on their structure and diversity. [11] studies personalized social search in directed graphs where a query contains a particular person node.

The more general problem of diversity in search results has received much attention. A survey of top-k querying techniques in relational database systems is given in [17]. Three categories of diversity are identified in [7], namely, content based, novelty, and coverage. Algorithms of swapping heuristics and greedy selection have been used in diversifying recommendations for web tagging sites [31]. Efficient data access for diversity-aware search of relevant documents is studied in [2], and that for vector objects in [13]. A diversity measure based on distances among data objects is proposed in [8]. Redundancy-aware maximal clique searching is studied in [29]. Diversified top-k clique search proposes to find k maximal cliques in a data graph with the maximum coverage [33]. Another related work is [23], which reformulates a given query graph into a number of supergraphs to enrich the search results, and the search results are diversified.

9. CONCLUSION

We study the problem of diversified subgraph querying (DSQ) in a large graph, which is to find k subgraphs isomorphic to a given query graph with maximum coverage. We propose a novel level-based algorithm called DSQL with an approximation guarantee. DSQL proceeds from low to high levels. The level number refers to the number of common vertices of a newly selected subgraph with the collected subgraphs. Our experiments show that DSQL can generate highly diversified solutions with a quick response time.

10. ACKNOWLEDGEMENTS

We would like to thank the authors of [24] for kindly sharing their source code with us, Janet Yung for help in the proof-reading, and the reviewers for helpful comments. This research is supported in part by the Hong Kong RGC/GRF research grant 412313 Project ID 2150758.

11. REFERENCES

[1] N. Alon. On the number of subgraphs of presribed type of graphs with a given number of edges. *Israel Journal of Mathematics*, 38(1-1):116–130, 1981.

[2] A. Angel and N. Koudas. Efficient diversity-aware search. In *SIGMOD*, 2011.

[3] G. Ausiello, N. Boria, A. Giannakos, G. Lucarelli, and V. T. Paschos. Online maximum k-coverage. *Discrete Applied Mathematics*, 160(13-14):1901–1913, 2012.

[4] J. Cheng, Y. Ke, W. Ng, and A. Lu. Fg-index: towards verification-free query processing on graph databases. In *SIGMOD*, 2007.

[5] S. A. Cook. The complexity of theorem-proving procedures. In *Proceedings of the third annual ACM symposium on Theory of computing*, pages 151–158. ACM, 1971.

[6] L. P. Cordella, P. Foggia, C. Sansone, and M. Vento. A (sub) graph isomorphism algorithm for matching large graphs. *IEEE Transactions on Pattern Analysis and Machine Intelligence*, 26(10):1367–1372, 2004.

[7] M. Drosou and E. Pitoura. Search result diversification. *SIGMOD Record*, 39(1):41–47, 2010.

[8] M. Drosou and E. Pitoura. Disc diversity: Result diversification based on dissimilarity and coverage. In *VLDB*, 2013.

[9] W. Fan, J. Li, X. Wang, and Y. Wu. Query preserving graph compression. In *SIGMOD*, pages 157–168. ACM, 2012.

[10] W. Fan, X. Wang, and Y. Wu. Diversified top-k graph pattern matching. *VLDB*, 6(13):1510–1521, 2013.

[11] W. Fan, X. Wang, and Y. Wu. Querying big graphs within bounded resources. In *SIGMOD*, pages 301–312. ACM, 2014.

[12] U. Feige. A threshold of ln n for approximating set cover. *JACM*, 45(4):634–652, 1998.

[13] P. Fraternali, D. Martinenghi, and M. Tagliasacchi. Top-k bounded diversification. In *SIGMOD*, 2012.

[14] M. Gupta, J. Gao, X. Yan, H. Cam, and J. Han. Top-k interesting subgraph discovery in information networks. In *ICDE*, pages 820–831. IEEE, 2014.

[15] W.-S. Han, J. Lee, and J.-H. Lee. Turbo iso: towards ultrafast and robust subgraph isomorphism search in large graph databases. In *SIGMOD*, pages 337–348. ACM, 2013.

[16] H. He and A. K. Singh. Graphs-at-a-time: query language and access methods for graph databases. In *SIGMOD*, pages 405–418. ACM, 2008.

[17] I. F. Ilyas, G. Beskales, and M. A. Soliman. A survey of top-k query processing techniques in relational database systems. *ACM Comput. Surv.*, 40(4), 2008.

[18] A. Khan, Y. Wu, C. C. Aggarwal, and X. Yan. Nema: Fast graph search with label similarity. In *VLDB*, 2013.

[19] J. Kim, H. Shin, and W.S.Han. Taming subgraph isomorphism for RDF query processing. In *VLDB*, 2015.

[20] L. Lai, L. Qin, X. Lin, and L. Chang. Scalable subgraph enumeration in mapreduce. In *VLDB*, 2015.

[21] J. Lee, W.-S. Han, R. Kasperovics, and J.-H. Lee. An in-depth comparison of subgraph isomorphism algorithms in graph databases. In *VLDB*, volume 6, pages 133–144. VLDB Endowment, 2012.

[22] S. Ma, Y. Cao, W. Fan, J. Huai, and T. Wo. Capturing topology in graph pattern matching. *VLDB*, 5(4):310–321, 2011.

[23] D. Mottin, F. Bonchi, and F. Gullo. Graph query reformulation with diversity. In *SIGKDD*, 2015.

[24] X. Ren and J. Wang. Exploiting vertex relationships in speeding up subgraph isomorphism over large graphs. *VLDB*, 8(5), 2015.

[25] B. Saha and L. Getoor. On maximum coverage in the streaming model and application to multi-topic blog-watch. In *SDM*, 2009.

[26] H. Shang, Y. Zhang, X. Lin, and J. X. Yu. Taming verification hardness: an efficient algorithm for testing subgraph isomorphism. *VLDB*, 1(1):364–375, 2008.

[27] Z. Sun, H. Wang, H. Wang, B. Shao, and J. Li. Efficient subgraph matching on billion node graphs. *VLDB*, 5(9):788–799, 2012.

[28] J. R. Ullmann. An algorithm for subgraph isomorphism. *Journal of the ACM (JACM)*, 23(1):31–42, 1976.

[29] J. Wang, J. Cheng, and A. Fu. Redundancy-aware maximal cliques. In *KDD*. ACM, 2013.

[30] X. Yan, P. S. Yu, and J. Han. Graph indexing: a frequent structure-based approach. In *SIGMOD*, pages 335–346. ACM, 2004.

[31] C. Yu, L. Lakshmanan, and S. Amer-Yahia. It takes variety to make a world: Diverisification in recommender systems. In *EDBT*, 2009.

[32] D. Yuan, P. Mitra, H. Yu, and C. Giles. Updating graph indices with a one-pass algorithm. In *SIGMOD*, 2015.

[33] L. Yuan, L. Qin, X. Lin, L. Chang, and W. Zhang. Diversified top-k clique search. In *ICDE*, 2015.

[34] S. Zhang, J. Yang, and W. Jin. Sapper: subgraph indexing and approximate matching in large graphs. *VLDB*, 3(1-2):1185–1194, 2010.

[35] P. Zhao and J. Han. On graph query optimization in large networks. *VLDB*, 3(1-2):340–351, 2010.

[36] P. Zhao, J. X. Yu, and P. S. Yu. Graph indexing: tree+ delta<= graph. In *VLDB*, pages 938–949. VLDB Endowment, 2007.

[37] L. Zou, L. Chen, and Y. Lu. Top-k subgraph matching query in a large graph. In *Proceedings of the ACM Ph. D. workshop in CIKM*, pages 139–146. ACM, 2007.

APPENDIX

A. SOME PROOFS

Some theorems and lemmas are proved in this section.

A.1 Proof of Theorem 1

PROOF. We prove by showing that the decision problem of DSQ is NP-complete. In the decision problem of DSQ, we are given a data graph G, a query graph Q, and two values k and c. The question is whether there exists a set S of k embeddings of Q in G where $|C(S)| \geq c$. This problem is in NP since we can guess S and check its validity in polynomial time. It is NP-complete because we can transform the decision version of maximum disjoint isomorphic subgraphs, let us call it DMDIS (see Theorem 2), to this problem by first equating k in the DSQ problem to the required number of disjoint subgraphs in DMDIS, and then setting the value of c to $k|Q|$. □

A.2 Properties of DSQL-P1

In DSQL-P1, let T_i be the currently collected set of embeddings, stored in T, after the $(i+1)$-th iteration. Note that T_0 contains disjoint embeddings. Let us restate Lemma 1:

LEMMA 1. *(restated) At the end of the i-th iteration of Algorithm DSQL-P1, $0 \leq i \leq q-1$, if $|T_i| < k$, then any embedding s that is not included in T_i must overlap with the union of embeddings in T_i at $i+1$ or more vertices.*

PROOF. We prove by induction. Consider the base case for the 1-st iteration. $T_0 = M$ is a maximal set of non-overlapping subgraphs. For any other embedding s, s must overlap with at least one of the embeddings in M, otherwise M would not be maximal, since s can be added to M. Thus, the base case holds.

At the beginning of $i+1$-th iteration, T_{i+1} is set to be equal to T_i. By the induction hypothesis, any remaining embedding s overlaps with T_i at $i+1$ or more vertices. Suppose s overlaps with T_i at vertices $w_1, ..., w_{i+1}, ...$. An $ovpEmb$ containing $w_1, ..., w_{i+1}$ will be generated in the $i+1$-th iteration (at Line 11 of Algorithm 3) and s is examined in Q1Search. There are 2 possible outcomes: (1) s does not overlap at any other vertex with the current T_{i+1}, it is included into T_{i+1}; (2) $|V(s) \cap V(T+i+1)| \geq i+2$. Since T_{i+1} grows monotonically, at the end of the iteration, s still has at least $i+2$ overlapping vertices with T_{i+1}. Thus, after the i-th iteration, all remaining subgraphs must overlap with T_{i+1} at $i+2$ or more vertices. □

[Proof of Theorem 3]:

PROOF. Let $q = |Q|$. Clearly, $|C(OPT)| \leq kq$. Suppose DSQL-P1 stops at the i-th iteration and gets a solution A. If $|A| = k$, let n_j embeddings be added to the solution at iteration j for $0 \leq j \leq i$, we have $|A| = \sum_{j=0}^{i} n_j = k$. The first n_0 embeddings are disjoint and introduce qn_0 vertices. At the j-th iteration, the overlap size is j, every newly generated embeddings adds $q-j$ new vertices to $C(T_j)$, so we have $|C(A)| = qn_0 + \sum_{j=1}^{i} n_j(q-j) \geq qn_0 + \sum_{j=1}^{i} n_j(q-i) = qn_0 + (\sum_{j=1}^{i} n_j)(q-i)$. Since $n_0 \geq 1$, $\frac{|C(A)|}{|C(OPT)|} \geq \frac{q+(k-1)(q-i)}{qk} = \frac{q-i}{q} + \frac{i}{kq}$.

To prove that the above bound is tight for any i and k, construct a circle query Q with distinct labels and $|Q| = ik$. We set $q = ik$, so Q is a ring with $(u_1, u_2, ..., u_q)$. Let the data graph contain $k+1$ such circles, where one of the circle with vertices $(v_1, v_2, ..., v_q)$ overlaps at i unique vertices with other k circles. We denote this circle as C_0, and the other circles as $C_1, C_2, ..., C_k$. More specifically, $C_0 \cap C_i = \{v_{(i-1)q+1}, ..., v_{iq}\}$. Suppose DSQL first picks C_0 and then $C_1, ...C_{k-2}$, and returns T, then $|C(T)| = q + (q-i)(k-1) = (q-i)k + i$. Clearly the optimal solution OPT is $\{C_1, C_2, ..., C_k\}$, and so the approximation ratio is exactly $\frac{q-i}{q} + \frac{i}{kq}$.

If $|A| < k$, then after the $i = q-1$ iteration, DSQL-P1 still cannot get k embeddings. According to Lemma 1, any embedding s that is not included in A overlaps with the union of embeddings of A at q nodes. Let OPT be an optimal solution. In this case, each embedding o in OPT cannot contribute any new vertex to A. That is, for each embedding o in OPT, either $o \in A$, or all the vertices in o are already in A. Thus $\frac{|C(A)|}{|C(OPT)|} = 1$. □

Next we show that DSQL-P1 does not miss any embedding since it effectively scans all embeddings in the given graph. Here, *effectively scanning an embedding* h means either including h in the solution, or dismissing h since it will not increase the coverage.

THEOREM 7. *After the $q-1$-th iteration, DSQL-P1 effectively scans all embeddings.*

Theorem 7 holds because Lemma 1 says that after the $q-1$-th iteration, any embedding that is not included in T_{q-1} must overlap with T_{q-1} at q vertices.

A.3 Proof of Lemma 3

Lemma 3 is about the correctness of the strategy of skipping "bad" vertices, which is introduced in Section 5.4.

PROOF. Consider the order of nodes in a query Q as shown in the figure below. The wavy line between u_0 and u_{j-1} means that some nodes may exist between u_0 and u_{j-1}.

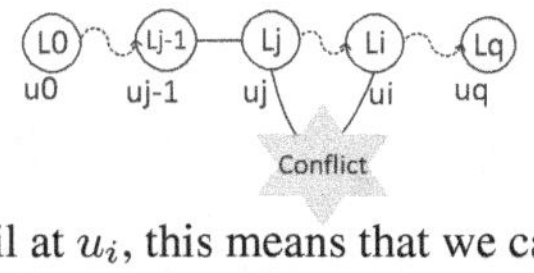

Suppose we fail at u_i, this means that we cannot find a matching vertex for u_i. Let the nearest conflict node of u_i preceding u_i in $qList$ be u_j. Let the current partial embedding be $pEmb_1 = \{(u_0, v_0), ..., (u_{j-1}, v_{j-1}), (u_j, v_j), ..., (u_{i-1}, v_{i-1})\}$. We can see that for $j < k < i$, u_k is not a neighbor of u_i because u_k does not conflict with u_i. Based on the strategy in Section 5.3, we backtrack from u_i to u_j, skipping the non-conflict nodes. Suppose u_{j-1} is not a conflict node of u_i. We mark the candidate v_j for u_j as a "bad" vertex. Having tried v_{j-1} for u_{j-1}, we consider the next candidate v'_{j-1} and get $pEmb_2 = \{(u_0, v_0), ..., (u_{j-1}, v'_{j-1})\}$. The lemma says that we can skip any "bad" candidate v_j for u_j. We prove by contradiction that this holds. Assume on the contrary that this skipping is not correct, so that when we match v_j to u_j, we can eventually find a match v'_i for u_i, resulting in $pEmb_3$.
Let $pEmb_0 = \{(u_0, v_0), ..., (u_{j-2}, v_{j-2})\}$.
$pEmb_3 = pEmb_0 \cup \{(u_{j-1}, v'_{j-1}), (u_j, v_j), ..., (u_i, v'_i)\}$.
Let $pEmb_4 = \{(u_{j+1}, v_{j+1}), \dots, (u_{i-1}, v_{i-1})\}$. Thus,
$pEmb_1 = pEmb_0 \cup (u_{j-1}, v_{j-1}) \cup (u_j, v_j) \cup pEmb_4$.

$pEmb_3$ shares with $pEmp_1$ the matchings in $pEmb_0$ and (u_j, v_j). Denote the set of neighbors of u_i which appear earlier than u_i in the query order as NS_{u_i}. So, we have $NS_{u_i} \subseteq \{u_0, u_1, ..., u_{j-2}, u_j\}$ = $\{u(pEmb_0) \cup u_j\}$, where $u(pEmb_0)$ is the set of query nodes that appear in $pEmb_0$. Since $(u_i, v'_i) \in pEmb_3$ and $pEmb_0 \cup (u_j, v_j) \subseteq pEmb_3$, then (u_i, v'_i) could also be used to extend $pEmb_1$. This is because all the neighbors of u_i are in $u(pEmb_0) \cup u_j$ and the other query nodes in $pEmb_1$ do not conflict with u_i. This contradicts the fact that there is no match for u_i when the current partial embedding is $pEmb_1$. □

A.4 Proof of Theorem 5

We first introduce a lemma that will be useful.

LEMMA 4. *For a scan, assume that the coverage of the initial set of k embeddings, given by $|F_0|$, is lower bounded by $\gamma|C(OPT)|$, i.e., $|C(F_0)| \geq \gamma|C(OPT)|$.*

$$(2 + \tfrac{1}{\alpha} + \alpha)|C(F_{final})| \geq (1 + \tfrac{\gamma}{\alpha})|C(OPT)| \quad (5)$$

PROOF. Our proof is based on the concepts of set charge and element charge as used in [25] and [32]. The analysis is based on tracking the coverage $|C(OPT)|$ of an optimum solution OPT as embeddings in OPT are examined. For each embedding o in OPT, if o is not selected, a set charge is computed. If it is selected, then an element charge is computed for each vertex in o. We ensure that the total charge is an upper bound of $|C(OPT)|$.

[**Set Charge**] Let $\beta = 1 + \alpha$. For an embedding o_i in OPT, let H_i be the collection of k embeddings when o_i is examined. If o_i is not selected, then $\forall f \in H_i, B(o_i, H_i) < \beta \times L(f, H_i)$, hence

$$kB(o_i, H_i) < \beta \sum_t L(f_t, H_i)$$

It is easy to see that $\sum_t L(f_t, H_i) \leq |C(H_i)|$,

$$kB(o_i, H_i) < \beta|C(H_i)|$$

Set charge for each element in H_i is given by

$$\tfrac{B(o_i,H_i)}{|C(H_i)|} < \tfrac{\beta}{k}$$

Note also that $|C(F_{final})| \geq |C(H_i)|$.

Total set charge for all embeddings in OPT is less than

$$\sum_{i=1}^{k} |C(H_i)| \times \frac{\beta}{k} = \sum_{i=1}^{k} \frac{\beta|C(H_i)|}{k} \leq \beta|C(F_{final})|$$

[**Element Charge**] Let F_i be the embedding collection when f_i is removed from it, where f_i is the i-th embedding swapped out by the algorithm. Hence $f_i \in F_i$ and $f_i \notin F_{i+1}$. Let F_{final} be the final collection. The element charge is to keep track of the coverage of vertices in embeddings in OPT that have been selected, which may either appear in F_{final} or be swapped out. The total element charge is at most $|C(F_{final})| + \sum_{i\geq 0} |L(f_i, F_i)|$, where f_i is the i-th removed embedding.

$$\begin{aligned}|C(F_{i+1})| - |C(F_i)| &\geq B(h_i, F_i) - L(f_i, F_i)\\ &\geq (\beta - 1)L(f_i, F_i)\end{aligned}$$

$$\begin{aligned}\textstyle\sum_{i\geq 0} |L(f_i, F_i)| &\leq \tfrac{1}{\beta-1} \textstyle\sum_{i\geq 0}(|C(F_{i+1})| - |C(F_i)|)\\ &= \frac{1}{\beta - 1}(|C(F_{final}) - |C(F_0)|)\end{aligned}$$

[**Total Charge**] Summing up the set charges and element charges, we get $\beta|C(F_{final})|+|C(F_{final})|+\frac{1}{\beta-1}(|C(F_{final})| - |C(F_0)|)$

Clearly, this sum upper bounds $|C(OPT)|$. Since $\beta = 1 + \alpha$,

$$(2 + \tfrac{1}{\alpha} + \alpha)|C(F_{final}) - \tfrac{1}{\alpha}|C(F_0)| \geq |C(OPT)|$$

If the coverage of the initial set of k embeddings is lower bounded by $\gamma|C(OPT)|$, i.e., $|C(F_0)| \geq \gamma|C(OPT)|$, we have

$$(2 + \frac{1}{\alpha} + \alpha)|C(F_{final})| \geq (1 + \frac{\gamma}{\alpha})|C(OPT)|$$

□

[**Proof of Theorem 5**]: From Inequality (5) in Lemma 4, we have

$$\frac{|C(F_{final})|}{|C(OPT)|} \geq \frac{1 + \frac{\gamma}{\alpha}}{2 + \frac{1}{\alpha} + \alpha} = \frac{\alpha + \gamma}{(\alpha + 1)^2} \quad (6)$$

Differentiate w.r.t. α and set the result to zero, we get an optimal value for α for the swapping condition.

$$\alpha = 1 - 2\gamma \quad (7)$$

From Equations (6) and (7),

$$\begin{aligned}\alpha_{t+1} &= 1 - 2\gamma_t\\ \gamma_{t+1} = \frac{\alpha_{t+1} + \gamma_t}{(\alpha_{t+1} + 1)^2} &= \frac{1}{4(1 - \gamma_t)}\end{aligned}$$

□

Similar proof arguments will show that a similar theorem applies with $L^+(f, h, F)$ replacing $L(f, F)$. Note that in [25], α_1 is set to 1, which follows Equation (3) in Theorem 5, assuming $\gamma_0 = 0$.

At the fixed point of Equation (4), $4\gamma(1 - \gamma) = 1$. Solving for the equation of $4\gamma^2 - 4\gamma + 1 = 0$, we obtain the fixed point value of $\gamma_\infty = 0.5$. If $f(x) = \frac{1}{4(1-x)}$, $f'(x) = \frac{1}{4(1-x)^2}$, and $f'(0.5) = 1$. Thus the sequence of $\gamma_0, \gamma_1, ...$ converges to the fixed point of 0.5.

A.5 Asymptotic Tightness of SWAP$_\alpha$

Consider an online model of DSQ where embeddings are released one at a time. An online algorithm under such a model is allowed to keep at most k candidate embeddings at any time. We say that an online algorithm is greedy if the coverage of the collected embeddings can only increase.

LEMMA 5. *Any deterministic greedy online algorithm for DSQ cannot have an approximation ratio guarantee above 0.5.*

PROOF. Let the embedding size be Δ. Suppose the adversary first generates the following sequence of embeddings, $G_1, ..., G_{k''}$, where each G_i contains a common subset of R and also a subset X_i that is distinct for each G_i. $|R| = \Delta - 1$, $|X_i| = 1$.

Suppose that the algorithm keeps $k' \leq k$ such embeddings, let the embeddings be $R \cup A_1$, $R \cup A_2$, ..., $R \cup A_{k'}$, and dismisses embeddings $R \cup B_1$, ..., $R \cup B_j$, $j = k'' - k'$.

There must be a point when $j \geq k - \lceil k'/\Delta \rceil$. At this point, the adversary submits the following embeddings: $A_1 \cup A_2 ... \cup A_\Delta$, $A_{\Delta+1} \cup ... \cup A_{2\Delta}$, ...

The optimal solution covers $A_1, ..., A_{k'}, R, B_1, ..., B_{k-\lceil k'/\Delta \rceil}$, the coverage is $\Delta - 1 + k' + k - k'/\Delta = \Delta - 1 + k'(1 - 1/\Delta) + k$.

The solution from the algorithm covers $R, A_1, A_2, .., A_{k'}$, the coverage is $\Delta - 1 + k'$. Approximation ratio $\gamma = \frac{\Delta-1+k'}{\Delta-1+k'(1-1/\Delta)+k}$. This function increases with the value of k', and $0 \leq k' \leq k$. Thus, we have the greatest ratio when $k' = k$.

If $k' = k$, $\gamma = \frac{\Delta-1+k}{\Delta-1+k(2-1/\Delta)}$, which approaches 1/2 if k is large. □

A similar proposition is proved in [3], however their proof requires that Δ is a multiple of $\sqrt{k} + 1$, i.e., $\Delta/(\sqrt{k} + 1) \in \mathbb{N}$, which may not hold in our case since our query size, Δ, can be smaller than $\sqrt{k} + 1$. Our proof avoids this assumption.

For the case of multiple scans, if the only information that is passed from one scan to the next is the solution set, then this can be seen as passing the embeddings in the solution sets as the prefix in the embedding stream to the next scan. For the example used in the above proof, the solution contains only embeddings of the first type, namely $R \cup A_i$. Thus, arguments in the above can be used to show that for any greedy multi-scan online algorithm, the best approximation ratio guarantee approaches 0.5 as k is large.

A.6 Proof of Theorem 6

PROOF. Consider the algorithm of SWAP$_\alpha$. If F_0 is returned by the progressive initialization step, clearly, $|C(F_0)| \geq q + k - 1$. Since $|C(OPT)| \leq kq, q \geq |C(OPT)|/k$ and $k \geq |C(OPT)|/q$. We have $|C(F_0)| \geq \max(|C(OPT)|/k, |C(OPT)|/q)$. Thus, $\gamma_0 \geq \max(1/k, 1/q)$, and Inequality (6) follows from Theorem 5.

Since the initialization is altered, we need to prove that we get the same result as the original algorithms with a certain input stream. Let $F_0 = \{f_1, f_2, ..., f_k\}$ after the progressive initialization step. Let $g_1, ..., g_t$ be the embeddings that are dismissed in the initialization. Let F^i be the collection when g_i is examined. Clearly, $B(g_i, F^i) = 0$, since otherwise, the swapping condition is satisfied as the loss of swapping out a fictitious empty embedding is 0. Hence, $C(g_i) \setminus C(F^i) = \emptyset$. Since $C(F^i) \subseteq C(F_0)$, $C(g_i) \setminus C(F^i) = \emptyset$, thus, $B(g_i, F_0) = 0$. Therefore, F_0 is also obtained after $f_1, ..., f_k$, and $g_1, ..., g_t$ are scanned if the algorithm collects the first k embeddings, and the input stream begins with $f_1, ..., f_k, g_1, ..., g_t$.

Similar results can be readily derived for SWAP1, SWAP2, and SWAP$_A$. In particular, that for $SWAP_A$ can be derived by setting $\beta = \beta_1 + \beta_2, \beta_1 = (1 - \alpha_i)$ and $\beta_2 = (1 + \alpha_i)$ in Inequality (23) in [32]. □

A.7 Proof of Lemma 4

PROOF. We need to show that early termination does not affect the result. In the following, *effectively scanning* an embedding h means either including h in T, or dismissing h since it does not qualify for swapping. Let DSQL-P2 begin at level i. Similar to Lemma 1, we can show that at the end of the level j iteration of Algorithm DSQL-P2, $j \geq i$, any embedding that has not been effectively scanned must overlap with $V(T1)$ at $j+1$ or more vertices. Thus, at level i, the overlap size with $T1$ for any newly scanned embedding h is at least i. If $V(T1) \subseteq V(T)$, then for any new embedding h, the benefit of h is at most $q - i$, i.e., $B(h, T) \leq q - i$. If in the current T, for each embedding $f \in T$, $L(f, T) > (q-i)/(1+\alpha)$, hence, $B(h, T) < (1+\alpha)L(f, T)$. Thus, there will not be any new embedding with a benefit that satisfies the swapping criteria of Inequality (2). Hence DSQL-P2 can be terminated without affecting the result. □

A.8 Proof of Theorem 4

PROOF. With DSQL-P2 we consider the swapping for each embedding with possible gain in the coverage. The algorithm is the same as SWAP$_\alpha$ except that we are given an initial set of k embeddings from DSQL-P1, and early termination may take place. From Lemma 4, we know that the early termination does not change the result. It remains to show that the initial collection F of k embeddings from DSQL-P1 is a possible set of first k embeddings for F_0 as constructed by the process described in Section 6.1.3. This is true if for each embedding s added to T in DSQL-P1, there is non-zero benefit $B(s, T)$. This is guaranteed by DSQL-P1, since when an embedding s is added to T at level i in DSQL-P1, $|Q| - i$ vertices in s are not in $V(T)$, and $i \leq |Q| - 1$. Thus, DSQL has the guarantee as stated in Theorem 6. □

B. MORE EXPERIMENTAL RESULTS

In this section, we include some additional experimental results.

B.1 Some Query Results with DBpedia

For DBpedia in this experiment, we extract the occupation information from the dataset and use it as the label for every person vertex. We obtain 195 major occupations from the data and name the remaining occupations as *Other*. So there are 196 distinct labels in total.

Assume that we are interesting to find politicians who are connected with scientists and physicists, thus we submit the following query graph for DBpedia.

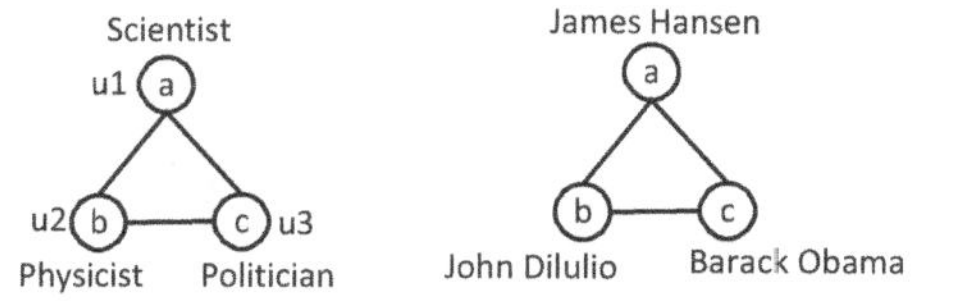

query graph a result subgraph

For this query, with $k = 40$, DSQL obtains the above result subgraph that is about the current US President. Some other interesting results are:
{{Anatoli_Blagonravov}{Thomas_O._Paine}{Richard_Nixon}}
{{Michael_Faraday}{Joseph_Priestley}{Richard_Sharp }}

Note that Richard Nixon was the US President presiding over the Apollo 11 moon landing. Richard Sharp was a British Member of Parliament that was known for founding the London Institute.

B.2 Comparison of Swapping Strategies

For the comparison of the swapping strategies, we first generate all embeddings for DBLP. We tried two generators: using the coding of BoostIso [24] on TurboIso [15], and that of TurboIso provided by the author of [24]. The results are shown in Table 4. We apply the greedy algorithm GreedyDSQ (Greedy in the table) and also different swapping algorithms (single scan) on the set of all embeddings. For swapping and GreedyDSQ, t is the time for generating the embeddings. GreedyDSQ takes more time since it requires k scans, and the coverage is a little better compared to the other swapping algorithms. Our swapping condition with SWAPα has similar diversity result compared to other swapping conditions. BoostIso is more efficient than TurboIso (with runtime t), with slightly smaller coverages. Also, if we compare the coverages with the results in Table 3, we can see that applying maximum k-coverage techniques can greatly improve the diversity. Finally, DSQL has the best results in both time and coverage.

	SWAP1	SWAP2	SWAP$_A$	SWAPα	Greedy	DSQL
time (ms)	22.68+t	26.57+t	3.31+t	9.03+t	251.61+t	10.06
$coverage$	114.76	115.56	112.57	114.64	118.42	127.4

(a) results of running BoostIso on TurboIso ($t = 116.00$)

	SWAP1	SWAP2	SWAP$_A$	SWAPα	Greedy	DSQL
time (ms)	165.11+t	170.06+t	8.36+t	28.02+t	451.02+t	10.06
$coverage$	121.66	122.55	119.85	119.95	127.5	127.4

(b) results of running TurboIso ($t = 217.95$)

Table 4: Comparing the time and coverage of GreedyDSQ, swapping algorithms, and DSQL for DBLP, $|E_Q| = 5, k = 40$

We have compared the coverage results from multiple scans. The results show that the coverage improvement is not big with additional scans. Note that the approximation ratios are above 0.5, the asymptotic theoretical bound. Also note that in our experiments with DSQL (see Section 7.3), there is little scanning in DSQL-P2 due to early termination.

B.3 More Results on Comparison with COM

We show the results for the datasets of Yeast, Human, and US-patent in Figure 8. We compare our proposed method with COM, the interleaving method described in Section 7.3 in terms of query time and coverage in the number of nodes.

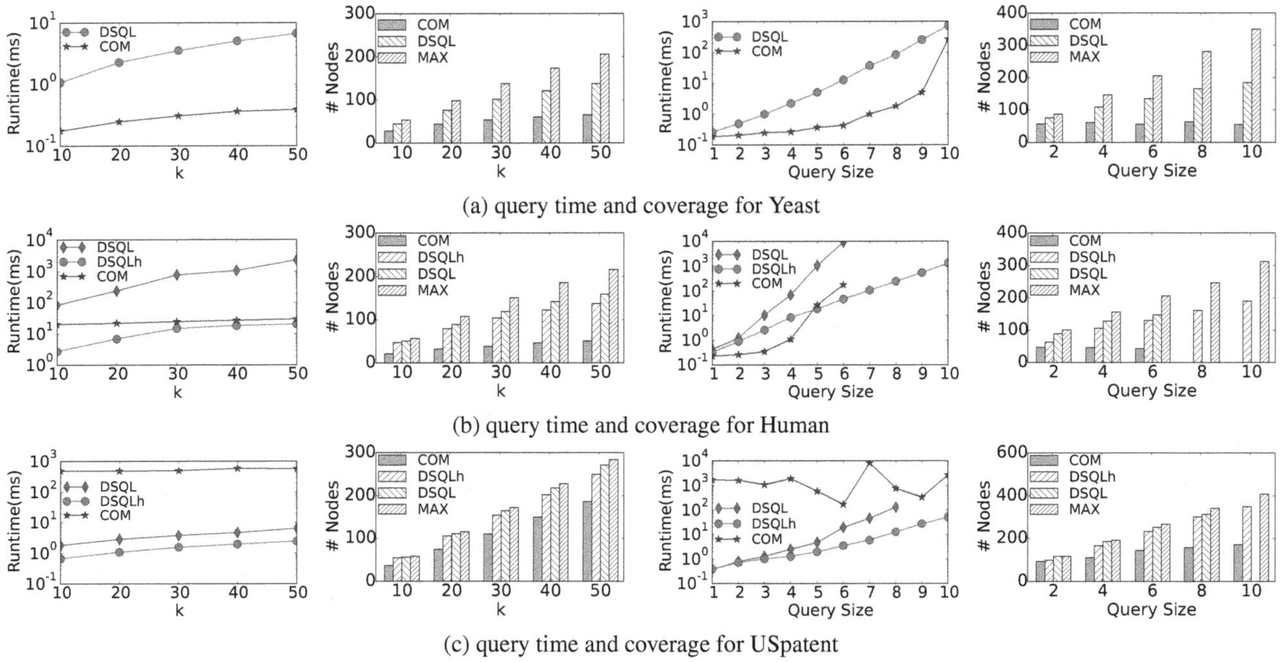

(a) query time and coverage for Yeast

(b) query time and coverage for Human

(c) query time and coverage for USpatent

Figure 8: Comparing the performances of DSQL, DSQLh, and COM

The trends are similar to that for the other datasets reported in Section 7.3. COM runs faster for smaller query and dataset sizes, but becomes inefficient as query size increases or dataset is large.

For Human and USpatent, both DSQL and COM cannot finish the query batches of 1000 queries of large query sizes within 5 hours, we thus introduce a variation of DSQL, called DSQLh. It differs from DSQL in the strategy of skipping bad vertices. We try to match u with its candidates. (1) If we cannot find any match for u, then as in DSQL in Section 5.4, we fail at u and backtrack to u_c, the closest conflict node of u. If u_{c-1} does not conflict with u, we mark the corresponding matched vertex v_c as "bad". (2) If we can find matches for u, but the matches are "bad" vertices, then we regard the matching of u as a failure, and begin the backtracking process of u as in (1). This deviates from DSQL where we would check the node u_p preceding u in *qfList*, and if u_p does not conflict with u, we mark matched v_p as "bad", and try to match u_p with the next vertex. With this variation, more skipping is allowed and there is more impact by "bad" vertices. A smaller coverage may be returned, but it can be much more efficient for denser data graphs. Our results show that DSQLh is efficient with both Human and USpatent. In summary, DSQL returns a solution within 10ms on average in most datasets, the coverage of DSQL is close to MAX and is much higher than that of COM.

B.4 Different Strategies of DSQL

Next we study the effects of the proposed optimization strategies. The following variations of DSQL are evaluated:

◇ DSQL0: Most primitive method, only using the localized subgraph searching strategy (see Section 5.1).

◇ DSQL1: Combining DSQL0 and the single embedding search strategy using $labelRm$ and $neighborRm$ (see Section 5.2).

◇ DSQL2: Combining DSQL0 and the conflict table strategy in Section 5.3.

◇ DSQL3: Combining DSQL2 and the "bad" vertex skipping strategy in Section 5.4.

◇ DSQLh: The variation of DSQL equipped with the relaxed skipping strategy introduced in Section B.3.

Still we set the time limit for 1000 queries to 5 hours. The default setting is a query size of 5, and $k = 40$. The results in Figure 9 show that every strategy can help reduce the runtime, since DSQL0 has a much longer runtime in comparison. DSQL1 is almost as good as DSQL in Figure 9(a). The single embedding search is effective because it controls the overlap size and avoids getting trapped in a local search area.

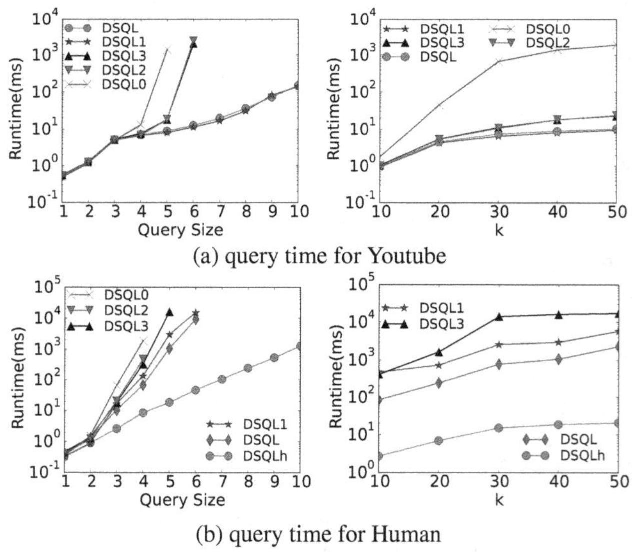

(a) query time for Youtube

(b) query time for Human

Figure 9: Effects of the optimization strategies

From Figure 8(a), DSQL2 and DSQL3 are not as effective as DSQL1 for Youtube. The skipping strategies are useful for denser graphs. This is demonstrated by the results with Human in Figure 9(b). DSQLh, based on DSQL2 and DSQL3, greatly reduces the runtime while the coverage is still close to MAX (see Figure 8(b)). In the last graph, DSQL0 and DSQL2 are not shown since the runtime is too long.

Graph Indexing for Shortest-Path Finding over Dynamic Sub-Graphs

Mohamed S. Hassan
Purdue University
West Lafayette, IN, USA
msaberab@cs.purdue.edu

Walid G. Aref
Purdue University
West Lafayette, IN, USA
aref@cs.purdue.edu

Ahmed M. Aly
Purdue University
West Lafayette, IN, USA
aaly@cs.purdue.edu

ABSTRACT

A variety of applications spanning various domains, e.g., social networks, transportation, and bioinformatics, have graphs as first-class citizens. These applications share a vital operation, namely, finding the shortest path between two nodes. In many scenarios, users are interested in filtering the graph before finding the shortest path. For example, in social networks, one may need to compute the shortest path between two persons on a sub-graph containing only family relationships. This paper focuses on dynamic graphs with labeled edges, where the target is to find a shortest path after filtering some edges based on user-specified query labels. This problem is termed the *E*dge-*C*onstrained *S*hortest *P*ath query (or ECSP, for short). This paper introduces *E*dge-*D*isjoint *P*artitioning (EDP, for short), a new technique for efficiently answering ECSP queries over dynamic graphs. EDP has two main components: a dynamic index that is based on graph partitioning, and a traversal algorithm that exploits the regular patterns of the answers of ECSP queries. EDP partitions the graph based on the labels of the edges. On demand, EDP computes specific sub-paths within each partition and updates its index. The computed sub-paths are cached and can be leveraged by future queries. To answer an ECSP query, EDP connects sub-paths from different partitions using its efficient traversal algorithm. EDP can dynamically handle various types of graph updates, e.g., label, edge, and node updates. The index entries that are potentially affected by graph updates are invalidated and are re-computed on demand. EDP is evaluated using real graph datasets from various domains. Experimental results demonstrate that EDP can achieve query performance gains of up to four orders of magnitude in comparison to state of the art techniques.

1. INTRODUCTION

The ubiquity of location-based services, social networks, and other graph-dependent systems calls for ongoing research efforts in graph data management systems. One of the most important operations performed over graphs is finding a shortest path. Many applications require filtering the underlying graph first before computing a shortest path. To illustrate, let $\sigma_{predicate}(G)$ be a relational select operator that yields a sub-graph $\acute{G}$ as a result of filtering Graph G using some select predicate. Let $\S_{s,d}(\acute{G})$ be an operator that finds the shortest path from Node s to Node d in Graph $\acute{G}$. The following example queries illustrate useful applications of these operators when interacting together:

Biological networks: One may need to find the shortest path (that acts as a relatedness measure) between two proteins, say p_1 and p_2, under stable or covalent interactions among these proteins [22]. This can be expressed by $\S_{p_1,p_2}(\sigma_{interaction\ in(stable,\ covalent)}(\mathit{ProteinNetwork}))$. In this example, a shortest-path computation needs to be performed on a subset graph that is dynamically specified at query time. Hence, any preprocessing on the original graph will be useless as only a subset of the graph is of interest to the shortest-path operation.

Road networks: A traveler from Location loc_1 to Location loc_2 may be interested in the shortest distance route with certain types of roads, e.g., avoid roads with construction work to prevent delays, or avoid toll roads. The latter can be expressed by $\S_{loc_1,loc_2}(\sigma_{roadtype \neq toll}(\mathit{RoadNetwork}))$. Again, only the subset of the graph that is specified at query time is needed for the shortest-path operation, hence invalidating any preprocessing that took place on the entire graph.

Social networks: Some graph analysis techniques compute the shortest path between two persons, say p_1 and p_2, where the returned path has to use certain types of relationships (e.g., family relationships). This can be expressed by $\S_{p_1,p_2}(\sigma_{relation\ =\ family}(\mathit{SocialNetwork}))$.

This paper introduces a new technique for finding the shortest path on a sub-graph, say G_{sub}, that is dynamically selected at query time. G_{sub} is selected by a predicate that uses a set of labels, say A, so that each edge in G_{sub} is labeled by at least one label in A. We term this query the *E*dge-*C*onstrained *S*hortest-*Path* query (or ECSP, for short). An ECSP query, say Q, is expressed as $Q(s,\ d,\ A)$, where s is the source vertex, d is the destination vertex, and A is the set of allowed labels.

A straightforward approach to answer an ECSP query is to use Dijkstra's algorithm [11]. During the traversal of the graph, we check the label for each edge, say e, on the fly. e is processed only if it satisfies the filtering predicates, or otherwise is discarded. Although this approach leads to a correct answer to the query, it does not leverage any preprocessing, and hence can be inefficient as it may traverse a large portion of the graph. This calls for novel techniques that can efficiently answer ECSP queries.

Several existing techniques address unconstrained shortest-path finding (e.g., [5,7,15,19]). However, these techniques are not directly applicable to ECSP queries because they rely on indexes that do not assume any constraints on the graph edges. To illustrate, consider the ECSP query $Q(1,\ 6,\ \{Blue, Red\})$ using the graph in Figure 1, where Vertex 1 is the source vertex, Vertex 6 is the

SIGMOD'16, June 26-July 01, 2016, San Francisco, CA, USA

DOI: http://dx.doi.org/10.1145/2882903.2882933

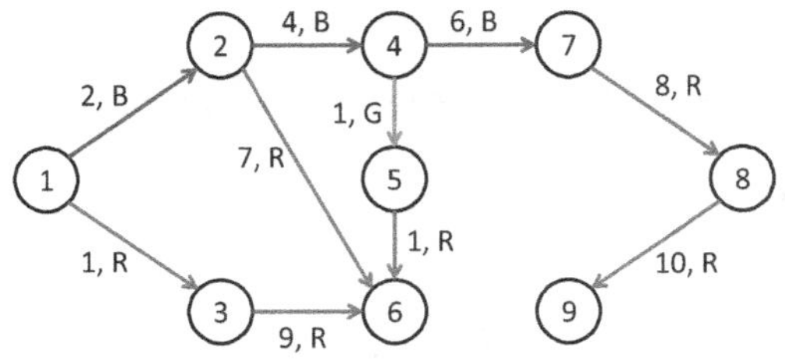

Figure 1: Edge-labeled Graph G with each edge having two values: $Weight$, $Label$. R, G, and B refer to the labels Red, $Green$ and $Blue$, respectively.

destination vertex, and $\{Blue, Red\}$ is the set of allowed edge labels. A typical index that pre-computes the shortest paths without considering the labels will find a shortest path from Vertex 1 to Vertex 6 with cost 8, i.e., the path given by $1 \rightarrow 2 \rightarrow 4 \rightarrow 5 \rightarrow 6$. However, this path is useless for Q (except for acting as a lower-bound). The reason is that the green edge from Vertex 4 to Vertex 5 is not allowed by Q. The correct answer to an ECSP query should be a feasible path with the least cost. The answer to Q is the path of cost 9 given by $1 \rightarrow 2 \rightarrow 6$.

This paper introduces *E*dge-*D*isjoint *P*artitioning (EDP, for short), a new technique that provides an exact answer to ECSP queries. EDP exploits regular expressions over the labels in the ECSP query-answers. Refer to Figure 1. Consider the ECSP Query $Q_j(1, 9, \{Blue, Red\})$. The shortest path P of Q_j is $1 \rightarrow 2 \rightarrow 4 \rightarrow 7 \rightarrow 8 \rightarrow 9$. P has the following edge labels in order: $Blue$, $Blue$, $Blue$, Red, Red. The regular expression $(Blue{*}\ Red{*})$ matches the ordered labels of P's edges, i.e., P begins with three $Blue$ edges followed by two Red edges. In general, Let Q_i be an ECSP query whose predicates allow only Labels $\{L_1, L_2, ..., L_k\}$. The labels for Q_i's correct answer should match the regular expression *(L_1 | L_2 | ... | L_k)**. Specifically, EDP optimizes for paths of the form *(L_1* | L_2* | ... | L_i* | ... | L_k*)+*, i.e., the paths that have consecutive edges of the same label. We term each sub-path L_i* of the same label a *monochrome* sub-path. EDP supports fast access to the monochrome sub-paths corresponding to each label in the graph. For example, Path P has a monochrome sub-path that consists of three consecutive $Blue$ edges: $1 \rightarrow 2 \rightarrow 4 \rightarrow 7$. EDP provides fast access to this monochrome sub-path to construct Path P efficiently.

EDP realizes an incremental index to evaluate ECSP queries efficiently. During preprocessing, the input graph is partitioned so that any monochrome sub-path is constructed by consulting only one partition, i.e., each partition has edges of the same label. Incrementally, EDP maintains monochrome shortest sub-paths within each partition in a fixed-size cache. These sub-paths are shortcuts to efficiently answer future ECSP queries. However, these sub-paths are not aggressively precomputed for each partition. Instead, EDP applies a *build-as-you-go* mechanism that distributes the cost of the precomputations over all ECSP queries. To illustrate, assume that a shortest path, say P_i, of a query has a certain monochrome sub-path, say P_{ij}, and that P_{ij} has already been computed and cached for a previously answered query. Instead of recomputing P_{ij}, EDP directly reuses the cached index entry for P_{ij}. In other words, each sub-path, if needed, is computed only once unless it is invalidated by an update operation or is removed from the cache. Also, EDP uses an efficient traversal algorithm to build an ECSP from its monochrome sub-paths. EDP's fixed-size cache puts a cap on the storage size designated for the stored sub-paths, and hence avoids the quadratic growth in space requirements (see Section 5.4).

To the best of our knowledge, only two research efforts [8, 18] study ECSP queries. Bonchi et al. [8] compute an approximate answer to the problem. In contrast, EDP can compute an exact answer in a sub-millisecond. Rice et al. [18] present CHLR, an exact answer to ECSP queries. CHLR is tailored to road-network graphs as CHLR extends the contraction hierarchies technique [15]. In contrast, EDP is not tailored to any specific graph domain. As demonstrated in Section 8, EDP outperforms CHLR by up to four orders-of-magnitude w.r.t. query-processing time. Both [8,18] supports only static graphs, i.e., if the graph is updated by inserting or deleting edges or nodes, or by changing edge labels or weights, the indexes in [8, 18] need to be rebuilt. EDP is the first technique to process ECSP queries over dynamic graphs. Furthermore, EDP outperforms the state-of-the-art techniques on static graphs.

The contributions of this paper are as follows:

- We introduce EDP, a new technique for answering ECSP queries that is applicable to any graph domain. We present its complexity analysis as well as a proof of its correctness.
- We demonstrate how EDP handles graph updates efficiently.
- We present a dynamic indexing mechanism that amortizes the indexing cost by incrementally building the index of EDP. We introduce a fixed-size cache in EDP to cache and reuse already computed monochrome shortest sub-paths. Use of this cache puts a cap on the worst-case storage requirements for the stored sub-paths.
- We present an efficient index traversal algorithm that exploits the regular expressions in the answers of ECSP queries.
- We conduct extensive experiments using six real datasets including the Tiger dataset [3] and other graphs from different domains. Results demonstrate that EDP can achieve more than four orders-of-magnitude enhancement in query performance compared to CHLR, the state-of-the-art technique. Moreover, EDP's performance is stable and robust, as its variance when applying 95% confidence intervals is small for all reported speedup measurements.

2. EDGE-CONSTRAINED SHORTEST-PATH QUERIES

2.1 Problem Definition

Let $G = (V, E, L, l, w)$ be a directed weighted graph, where V is a set of vertexes, E is a set of positively weighted edges, L is a set of labels (that can be viewed as colors), l is a function that assigns a label to each edge, and w is a function that assigns a weight to each edge (i.e., $\forall e \in E, \exists l(e) \in L$ and $\exists w(e) \in \mathbb{R}^+$). Let $Q(s, d, A)$ be an edge-constrained shortest-path (ECSP) query, where $s \in V$ is the source vertex, $d \in V$ is the destination vertex, and $A \subseteq L$ is the set of allowed labels by Q. Q searches for a path $P = (e_1, e_2, \ldots, e_c)$ from s to d that uses only edges with labels from A (i.e., $\forall\, e \in P \mid l(e) \in A$) such that the summation $\sum_{e \,\in\, P} w(e)$ is minimized. Refer to Table 1 for a listing of the notations used in this paper.

2.2 Straightforward Approaches

One way to answer an ECSP query is to use an index, e.g., as in [5, 7, 15], that is designed for the unconstrained shortest-path problem (no restricted edges). This can be achieved by building $2^{|L|}$ indexes, where L is the set of labels of the underlying graph G (i.e., the powerset of L). To answer a query, one of the $2^{|L|}$ indexes that corresponds to the labels permitted by the query is selected. Clearly, the exponential space of the required indexes

Notation	Description
G	A directed, weighted, and labeled graph
V	A set of vertexes
E	A set of edges
L	A set of labels
$w(e)$	Weight of Edge e
$l(e)$	Label of Edge e, e can be represented by the vertex-identifiers of its endpoints
$Q_i(s, d, A)$	ECSP Query Q_i from Vertex s to Vertex d with the allowed Labels-set A
$I(G)$	Edge-disjoint index for Graph G
$sp(s, d)$	Unlabeled shortest path from Vertex s to d
$CP(P)$	Contracted sub-paths of Path P
$Pr_i(v)$	Vertex v in Partition Pr_i

Table 1: Frequently used notations

makes this approach impractical. Also, this approach cannot handle graph updates efficiently.

Another straightforward approach is to modify any traditional shortest path algorithm (e.g., Dijkstra) to consider only the allowed edges of an ECSP query. The main drawback of this approach is that it may explore most of the graph edges if the query has low selectivity (i.e., most of the labels are allowed by the query). Moreover, this approach will perform an exhaustive traversal if the destination is not reachable from the source using the allowed labels. Hence, this approach is unlikely to scale for large graphs.

3. RELATED WORK

Since the 1950s, the problem of finding the shortest path has gained extensive attention (e.g., see [20,21]). Tremendous research efforts have been conducted to support shortest-path querying (e.g., see [5,7,15,19]). In this section, we discuss two main categories of related work: 1) existing approaches for answering unconstrained shortest-path queries that can be modified to support ECSP queries, and 2) existing approaches for answering ECSP queries.

In the first category, several techniques have been proposed to preprocess a graph, say G, to enable fast computation of unconstrained shortest-path queries. Goldberg et al. [16] present a two-hop approach for answering unconstrained shortest-path queries. The main idea is to select a set of landmark vertexes $LM \subseteq G.V$ such that for any shortest path, say $sp(u, v)$, where $u, v \in G.V$, $\exists$ a vertex, say $w \in LM$, that lies on $sp(u, v)$. The two-hop approach is not directly applicable to ECSP queries as the shortest paths from/to the vertexes of LM do not consider any labels. One modification to this approach is to build a separate graph G_{sl} for each possible set of labels sl. G_{sl} will contain only edges of G with labels in sl. Unfortunately, this modified approach requires $O(2^{|L|})$ space and time complexities as the number of different subsets of labels is $O(2^{|L|})$, and hence it will not scale.

In [9], the idea of landmarks is extended to dynamic graph settings, where the weights of the edges may change. However, the techniques in [9] consider only unconstrained shortest path queries. One approach to answer ECSP queries using the techniques in [9] is as follows. Given a query, we set the weights of all the disallowed edges to positive infinity, and re-adjust these weights to their original values after the query is answered. Clearly, this approach is not scalable to large graphs especially if the queries are highly selective (many graph updates will be performed).

In the second category, Bonchi et al. [8] present approximate answers for ECSP queries based on landmark vertexes. They propose two types of indexes, namely, PowCov and ChromLand that exhibit interesting trade-offs between index size and accuracy. However, both indexes are not suitable for applications that require exact shortest-path computations.

CHLR [18] is the state-of-the-art technique that can answer ECSP queries exactly. CHLR has been extended to support more flexible edge restrictions [14]. CHLR adopts Contraction Hierarchies (CH, for short) [15] to provide an exact answer to the following query: Given a source, say s, a destination, say d, and a set of restricted labels, say R, retrieve the shortest path from s to d that avoids all the edges with labels in R. An ECSP Query $Q(s, d, A)$ can be answered by CHLR after computing the complement of Set A. The main idea of CHLR is similar to that in [15]. The main difference is that CHLR considers edge-labels while contracting the underlying graph nodes. In particular, when contracting a node, say v, and there is a sub-path passing through the vertexes u, v, and w (i.e., $u \rightsquigarrow v \rightsquigarrow w$) such that a shortcut ($u \rightsquigarrow w$) is added, the shortcut ($u \rightsquigarrow w$) is labeled by the labels of the sub-paths ($u \rightsquigarrow v$) and ($v \rightsquigarrow w$). Labeling the shortcuts with labels enables CHLR to avoid these shortcuts if they contain any restricted label.

CH is originally designed for road-network graphs, and so is CHLR as it uses CH at its core. Consequently, CH has assumptions that are not valid for other networks. For example, CH assumes that the average fan-out of the vertexes is small (e.g., 2). The small fan-out assumption is valid for road networks, but is invalid for graphs from other domains. For example, an average fan-out of 15 is common in biological networks. In CHLR, when contracting a vertex with high fan-out, many shortcuts will be added. Adding many shortcuts by CHLR negatively affects its performance as the sparsity of the traversed graph will decrease. EDP, as proposed in this paper, performs up to four orders-of-magnitude faster than CHLR. Moreover, EDP supports dynamic graphs and is not tailored to road networks. To the best of our knowledge, EDP is the first technique that processes ECSP queries over dynamic graphs, and yet outperforms the state-of-the-art on static graphs by up to four orders-of-magnitude.

Variants for finding Regular-Language-Constraint-Paths (RLCP) have been studied [6, 10, 17]. An RLCP query works on edge-labeled graphs where the concatenation of the labels of the found path satisfies a query-specified regular expression. Unlike ECSP, RLCP queries assume that the user knows the exact order of the labels. Hence, RLCP queries are orthogonal to ECSP queries because ECSP queries do not impose any order on the allowed labels.

4. OVERVIEW OF EDP

A monochrome sub-path consists of edges with the same label. We define a contracted path of an ECSP query answer P as follows:

DEFINITION 1. *The* **contracted path** *of Path P, denoted by $CP(P) = (P_1, P_2, \ldots, P_i, \ldots, P_m)$, is an ordered list of monochrome sub-paths that, if concatenated, will produce P. A monochrome sub-path $P_i \in CP(P)$ is the maximum contraction of a set of consecutive edges with the same label.*

To illustrate how a contracted path is formulated, let $Q_i(v_a, v_f, \{L_1, L_2\})$ be an ECSP query. Assume that the answer P' to Q_i is represented by the edges $((v_a, v_b), (v_b, v_c), (v_c, v_d), (v_d, v_e), (v_e, v_f))$, where the labels of these edges are $(L_1, L_1, L_1, L_2, L_2)$, respectively. Then, $CP(P') = ((P'_1(v_a \rightsquigarrow v_d), P'_2(v_d \rightsquigarrow v_f))$ represents the contracted sub-paths of P', namely P'_1 and P'_2, such that each sub-path is monochrome and contains the maximum possible number of consecutive edges with the same label.

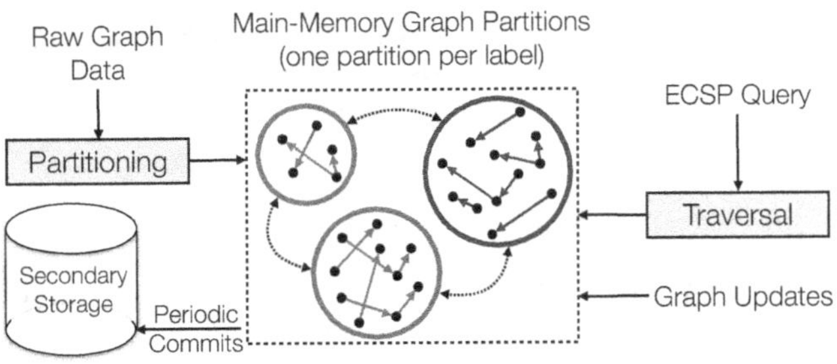

Figure 2: An Overview of EDP.

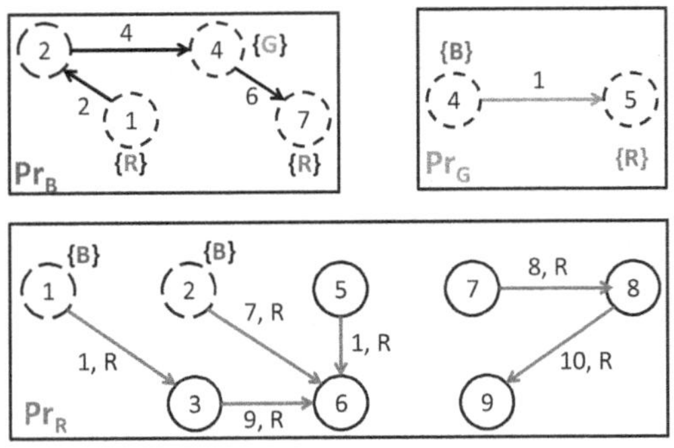

Figure 3: Edge-disjoint partitioning of the graph in Figure 1.

EDP consists of two main components:

1. **Indexing:** treats the contracted sub-paths of any ECSP query as independent tuples, and indexes these tuples.
2. **Traversal:** connects the appropriate contracted sub-paths efficiently to form the answer of any ECSP query.

Figure 2 gives a high-level overview of EDP. First, a raw graph is partitioned so that constructing any monochrome sub-path is doable by consulting only one partition. Thus, EDP constructs one partition per graph label. A partition corresponding to Label L_i hosts all the graph edges with Label L_i. Given an ECSP query, say Q, the traversal algorithm visits the partitions necessary to produce Q's answer. Each partition computes local shortest sub-paths. These local shortest sub-paths are cached in main memory to be leveraged by future queries (as explained in Section 6). To process graph updates, EDP assigns timestamps to each index entry. These timestamps help decide if some index entries need to be recomputed. EDP periodically commits the cached shortest sub-paths to secondary storage to avoid recomputing them upon system restart.

5. INDEX CONSTRUCTION

For a directed weighted graph G, the index $I(G)$ can be viewed as two integrated components: 1) a set of graph partitions, and 2) a set of lookup tables, where some shortest monochrome sub-paths are stored. The lookup tables are continuously updated as queries arrive. Section 5.1 discusses the graph partitioning of EDP while Section 5.2 describes the lookup tables of the shortest sub-paths.

5.1 Graph Partitioning

EDP partitions an input graph so that any two edges of different labels cannot co-exist in the same partition. Thus, each graph label, say c, has a corresponding partition, say Pr_c, that holds all the graph edges with Label c. The intuition behind this partitioning is twofold. First, only the partitions corresponding to a given set of query labels are considered and all the other partitions are safely discarded. This reduces the traversal search space. Second, any contracted sub-path, say p_i, that is part of the query answer will be computed using only the edges of the partition corresponding to the label of p_i (recall that a contracted sub-path is monochrome). Thus, each partition can cache all the contracted sub-paths it computes so that they can be leveraged by future queries. Hence, a contracted sub-path is computed once from scratch unless it is potentially affected by a graph update (see Section 7). Afterwards, it is recalled from the cache as needed.

Algorithm 1 constructs an edge-disjoint index I for a given graph G. Let L be the set of graph labels in G. Algorithm 1 creates a partition for each label and assigns an integral identifier to it (Lines 2-4). Each Label $i \in \{0, 1, ..., |L| - 1\}$ has a corresponding Partition Pr_i. The edges in Pr_i are defined by $Pr_i.E = \{(u, v) \in G.E \mid l(u, v) = i\}$, i.e., Pr_i contains all the edges of G that are labeled with Label i. To assign edges to each partition, the graph edges E are scanned only once (Lines 5-18). The $|L|$ partitions form an edge-disjoint partitioning of G.

To illustrate Algorithm 1, we partition Graph G of Figure 1 into the partitions of $I(G)$ in Figure 3. G has three labels. Thus, Algorithm 1 creates 3 partitions and assigns an integer identifier to each label, say $\{R = 0, B = 1, G = 2\}$. Thus, we have the 3 partitions Pr_R, Pr_B, and Pr_G that contain the red, blue, and green edges, respectively. As we explain in Section 6, the traversal algorithm traverses only $I(G)$ and not G. Thus, $I(G)$ should preserve all the connections of G. To preserve the connectivity of G, Algorithm 1 annotates some vertexes with properties as defined below.

DEFINITION 2. **Bridge Vertex:** Given Partitions Pr_i and Pr_j, a vertex $v \in Pr_i$ is termed a bridge vertex in Pr_i if and only if $\exists$ an edge, say $(v, u) \in Pr_j$ where $i \neq j$.

In Figure 3, bridge vertexes are marked with dashed circles. For instance, Vertex 5 in Partition Pr_G is a bridge vertex because Vertex 5 has an outgoing edge hosted by another partition (i.e., Pr_R). However, Vertex 5 in Partition Pr_R is not a bridge vertex because there are no outgoing edges from Vertex 5 that are hosted by a partition other than Pr_R. We denote a vertex instance v hosted by Partition Pr_i by $Pr_i(v)$.

DEFINITION 3. **OtherHosts List:** Given a bridge vertex, say $v \in Pr_i$ (i.e., $Pr_i(v)$), the OtherHosts list of $Pr_i(v)$ is the set of label identifiers of all the outgoing edges of $v \in G$ not equal to the identifier of Label i, where i is the label identifier of Partition Pr_i. Formally, $Pr_i(v).OtherHosts = \{j | \exists (v, u) \in G.E(l(v, u) = j \wedge j \neq i)\}$.

In Figure 3, the OtherHosts list of each bridge vertex is listed in curly braces. For instance, the bridge vertex $Pr_G(5)$ has its OtherHosts list set to $\{R\}$, where R is the label identifier of the red label. The reason is that Vertex 5 in G (as in Figure 1) has an outgoing Red edge to Vertex 6. Notice that there is a one-to-one mapping between a label identifier, say R, and its corresponding partition, say Pr_R. Hence, the OtherHosts list of $Pr_G(5)$ indicates that Partition Pr_R hosts an outgoing Red edge of Vertex $Pr_G(5)$. In Algorithm 1, Lines 9-13 flag the bridge vertexes and set their OtherHosts lists. The OtherHosts lists are used by the traversal algorithm to connect contracted sub-paths of different labels to form the requested shortest path (see Section 6). Notice that if a vertex, say v, is replicated in more than one partition, v keeps the same local identifier in each hosting partition. However, each vertex instance in a partition has a global identifier consisting of its local identifier as well as the partition identifier hosting that instance.

Algorithm 1 EDP-Partitioning ($G < V, E, L, l, w >$)

```
I.PlainGraph ← G
for each label identifier i ∈ G.Labels do
    I.CreatePartition(i)
end for
for each edge (u, v) ∈ E do
    Partition ← I.getPartition(l(u, v))
    for each vertex a ∈ {u, v} do
        if !Partition.Contains(a) then
            isBridge ← false
            OtherHosts ← {l(a, b) ∈ E | l(a, b) ≠ l(u, v)}
            if OtherHosts ≠ ∅ then
                isBridge ← true
            end if
            Partition.addVertex(a, isBridge, OtherHosts)
        end if
    end for
    Partition.addEdge(u, v, w(u, v))
end for
return I
```

Observe that it is possible that the partitions become unbalanced, e.g., some partitions have most of the edges while the other partitions are almost empty. This unbalance does not affect the efficiency of EDP. In fact, in some cases, it is beneficial to have large partitions because we will be able to precompute more effective shortcuts in these partitions. These shortcuts are leveraged by the traversal algorithm. The only disadvantage for having large partitions is the inflation in the number of reachable bridge vertexes from the partition's vertexes. We address this issue in Section 6.2.

5.2 Repository for Shortest Sub-Paths

EDP stores a set of shortest paths in each partition. These shortest paths are used by the traversal algorithm as monochrome sub-paths to construct the final query answer. Index traversal is discussed in detail in Section 6.1. For a given ECSP Query $Q(s,\ d,\ A)$, the traversal algorithm keeps a current vertex instance, say $Pr_i(v)$. When $Pr_i(v)$ is the current vertex instance, EDP needs to be aware of only the following two types of paths in Pr_i, if any exists: 1) the shortest path from $Pr_i(v)$ to Destination d if d is hosted by Pr_i, 2) the shortest paths from $Pr_i(v)$ to the bridge vertexes in Pr_i. The latter allows EDP to consider other possible sub-paths hosted by other partitions.

DEFINITION 4. **Bridge Shortcut Edge:** Given any two vertexes hosted by the same partition, say $Pr_i(u)$ and $Pr_i(v)$, where $Pr_i(v)$ is a bridge vertex, if there is a monochrome shortest path of Label i from $Pr_i(u)$ to $Pr_i(v)$, that path is termed a bridge shortcut edge, or **bridge edge**, for short.

For example, consider the two vertexes $Pr_B(1)$, and $Pr_B(7)$ in Partition Pr_B of Figure 3. Vertex $Pr_B(7)$ is a bridge vertex that has an incoming monochrome shortest path from Vertex $Pr_B(1)$ (call it $P = 1 \rightarrow 2 \rightarrow 4 \rightarrow 7$). P is a bridge edge and is represented as a shortcut edge from $Pr_B(1)$ and $Pr_B(7)$ in Figure 4.

So, each partition in EDP holds a set of shortest paths stored in hash tables. Each vertex in a partition can possibly be a source, destination, or an intermediate node in a shortest path. This suggests that we might need a comprehensive list of all the shortest paths between all the possible pairs in any partition in order to support any query. Although this process can be performed as part of Algorithm 1 when constructing the index, this does not scale for large partitions. The space complexity of a partition's shortest-path lookup will be quadratic w.r.t. the number of the partition's vertexes ($O(|V|)$); also the pre-processing time for computing the all-pairs shortest paths will be $O(|V| * (|E| + |V| log(|V|))$. Fortunately, EDP does not have to aggressively precompute these comprehensive shortest paths. Instead, EDP builds incrementally the shortest-paths repository in response to the queries received. Also, EDP limits the index size so that it does not exceed a user-specified size. EDP may replace some existing index-entries by new entries in order not to exceed the index maximum size (See Section 5.4).

A comprehensive construction of all-pairs shortest paths of a partition's vertexes assumes that all the vertexes in that partition will be used as sources and destinations for queries. However, usually not all the vertexes in a partition are queried as sources and destinations. For example, on a road network, we may have hotspot vertexes (as destinations) to which the shortest paths need to be computed, while many other vertexes are unlikely to be queried as destinations (e.g., a vertex on a highway that does not represent any point of interest). Hence, we construct a partition's shortest-paths list as queries arrive. The computations performed to serve a query, say Q_i, can serve a future query, say Q_j. Thus, the cost to update the index by computing a shortest path, say sp, is amortized over all the queries that use sp as part of their path discovery process.

5.3 Index Operations

EDP supports the following index operations:

isBridge(pr, v): Returns true if Vertex $pr(v)$ is marked as a bridge vertex. This operation takes constant time.

getCost(pr, v, u): Returns the cost of the shortest path from Vertex v to Vertex u inside Partition pr. If one or both of u and v are not hosted by pr, or they are both hosted by pr but not connected in pr, positive infinity is returned, and an index entry is added to flag that $pr(v)$ and $pr(u)$ are not connected. $getCost$ uses a hash table to store and retrieve a path cost. The key of the hash table is a function of both v and u.

getBridgeEdges(pr, v): Returns all the bridge edges from Vertex $pr(v)$ to all the reachable bridge vertexes in pr. The returned list is sorted in ascending order by the cost of the edges in a hash table. Section 6.2 explains how $getBridgeEdges$ is implemented as a non-blocking operator, i.e., a caller to $getBridgeEdges$ will not be suspended until the whole list is computed.

5.4 Index Size

Although EDP replicates some vertexes in more than one partition (e.g., Vertex 1 is replicated in Pr_R and Pr_B of Figure 3), the replicated vertexes are *light-weight*, i.e., only the vertex identifier and some connectivity information are replicated, but not the whole vertex's objects that are stored in G.

For Graph G, let n be the number of vertexes, m be the number of edges, c be the number of labels, and a be the number of vertexes that have outgoing edges of different labels. Assume that the maximum fan-out of vertexes in G is f. Then, the number of bridge vertexes in Index $I(G)$ is $O(af) = O(nf)$ in the worst-case, when all the vertexes are bridge vertexes. For the partitions component of the index, in the worst case, the space complexity is $O(m + nfc)$. Observe that the term (nfc), has the factor c because, in the worst-case, a bridge vertex will be replicated in c partitions. As the edges are distributed among the partitions without replication, the space complexity of the index has the term m.

The repository for shortest sub-paths determines the size of EDP's index, however, this size is query-driven. Notice that the repository for shortest sub-paths does not store full query answers. Instead, monochrome sub-paths are stored to help construct answers of different queries. Although the number of queries that vary only in the source/destination vertexes is $O(n^2)$, the number of index entries in practice does not reach $O(n^2)$ for two reasons: 1) EDP does not store full paths, and 2) Not all the vertexes of ECSP queries are designated as sources/destinations. To avoid any chance of quadratic space-growth, EDP limits the index size by adopting a least-recently-used (LRU) replacement policy. Section 8.4 shows that EDP's index does not exceed a few gigabytes after processing millions of queries over real large graphs. The replacement policy of EDP tracks the index entries usage by a doubly linked list to quickly determine the LRU entries. Although the index of EDP has a light memory-footprint (see Section 8.4), EDP regularly monitors the hit-rate of the index and writes it into an event log. Writing the hit-rate into the event log helps an administrator decide if the limit of the index needs to increase according the current query-workload.

6. QUERY PROCESSING

EDP's query processing algorithm (termed EDP-QP, for short) follows a greedy traversal approach. The greedy traversal connects the source vertex to the vertexes with least cost. The traversal continues until reaching the destination vertex. Once the destination vertex is reached, the shortest cost is obtained, and the shortest path can be determined.

6.1 EDP Index Traversal

Given an ECSP Query $Q(s,\ d,\ A)$ over Graph G, EDP-QP uses Index $I(G)$ to answer Q. As EDP-QP traverses I(G), all the vertexes referenced by EDP-QP are identified by their global identifiers (e.g., $Pr_i(v)$ to refer to the instance of Vertex v hosted in Partition Pr_i). When EDP-QP traverses Partition Pr_i, it only traverses the shortcut edge to the destination node if hosted by Pr_i as well as some bridge edges of Pr_i. When processing Query Q, only the partitions corresponding to the allowed labels of Q are considered; the other partitions are ignored.

EDP-QP uses a min-priority Queue PQ of vertexes whose final shortest-path weights from the source vertex have not been determined yet. The structure of PQ is keyed by the 2D global vertex-identifiers of EDP (i.e., partition Id and vertex Id). An element in PQ has the following attributes: 1) Pr: a partition's identifier, 2) v: the vertex's identifier that is reachable from the source and is hosted by Pr, and 3) $cost$: the least cost observed so far that connects the source vertex to Vertex $Pr(v)$, where the elements in the min-priority queue are ordered by $cost$. Two additional attributes in the queue will be introduced in Section 6.2.

EDP-QP uses a two-dimensional $cost$ table to maintain the least-costs observed so far to connect the source vertex to the visited vertexes of $I(G)$ (regardless of whether the visited instances of vertexes are dequeued or not). A key of the $cost$ lookup table is identified by: 1) a partition identifier, and 2) a vertex identifier. For a given key of the $cost$ table, say k, the value that corresponds to k is a structure holding k as well as the least-cost observed so far to reach the vertex identified by k from the source vertex.

Algorithm 2 outlines the traversal Algorithm EDP-QP that returns only the cost of the shortest path. Constructing the actual path is straightforward (see Appendix B). Given an ECSP Query $Q(s,\ d,\ A)$ and $I(G)$, the partitions of $I(G)$ are traversed in a greedy way to find a feasible path with minimum cost if one exists. At any point in time, Algorithm 2 will have a current vertex, say $Pr_i(v)$. Algorithm 2 checks if there is a sub-path in Partition Pr_i that reaches Destination d from Vertex $Pr_i(v)$. If this sub-path exists, Algorithm 2 will have a feasible path, say P_i, that can be a shortest path. To consider other feasible paths that can be shorter than P_i, Algorithm 2 considers other allowed edges hosted by other partitions. Edges of other allowed partitions can be reached through the bridge vertexes of Partition Pr_i. Algorithm 2 uses the bridge

Algorithm 2 EDP-QP(I, s, d, A)

```
1:  PQ ← ∅, cost(p, v) ← ∅
2:  if s and d have edges labeled by at least one label of A then
3:      PQ.Insert(getPr(s, A), s, 0))
4:  end if
5:  while PQ.NotEmpty() do
6:      t ← PQ.ExtractMin()
7:      if t.v = d then
8:          return t.Cost
9:      end if
10:     PQ.InsertIfRelaxed(t.Pr, d, t.Cost + I.w(t, d)))
11:     if I.isBridge(t) then
12:         for each pr ∈ t.v.OtherHosts ∩ A do
13:             PQ.InsertIfRelaxed(pr, t.v, t.Cost)
14:         end for
15:     end if
16:     for each e ∈ I.getBridgeEdges(t.Pr, t.v) do
17:         for each pr ∈ e.To.OtherHosts ∩ A do
18:             PQ.InsertIfRelaxed(pr, e.To, t.Cost + e.getWeight())
19:         end for
20:     end for
21: end while
22: return ∞
```

vertexes of Partition Pr_i that are reachable from Vertex $Pr_i(v)$ to explore other feasible shorter paths. To explore other feasible paths from Vertex $Pr_i(v)$ through a bridge vertex, say $Pr_i(b)$, the $OtherHosts$ list of Bridge Vertex $Pr_i(b)$ is intersected with the allowed query labels (i.e., $Q.A$). The intersection of the label sets $Pr_i(b).OtherHosts$ and $Q.A$ determines partitions that can form other feasible paths.

Algorithm 2 does not explore all possible feasible paths. As soon as the current vertex instance of Algorithm 2 is a destination vertex instance, Algorithm 2 yields the shortest-path cost and terminates. To illustrate all the logical branches of Algorithm 2, we use two query examples using the partitions in Figure 3.

Consider Query $Q_1(1,\ 6\ \{R\})$. EDP-QP tests if a feasible path can exist. No feasible path exists if the source vertex has no outgoing edge labeled by Label R. Q_1 passes this necessary-but-not-sufficient test (Lines 2-4), and the vertex $Pr_R(1)$ will be added to Priority Queue PQ with cost zero. EDP-QP traverses $I(G)$ as long as the shortest path is not determined and PQ is not empty (Lines 5-21). For Q_1, the initial status of PQ is $((Pr_R,\ 1,\ 0))$. After extracting $(Pr_R,\ 1,\ 0)$ from PQ, the current vertex will be $Pr_R(1)$. As the current partition Pr_R hosts an instance of the destination Vertex 6, EDP-QP will compute the shortest path $Pr_R(1) \rightsquigarrow Pr_R(6)$, and will relax (decrease) the cost to the destination Vertex $Pr_R(6)$. Initially, the cost of reaching all the vertexes except the source is positive infinity. Relaxing the cost of reaching $Pr_R(6)$ will update $cost(Pr_R,\ 6)$ to 10, and will add $Pr_R(6)$ with the updated cost to PQ (Line 10). The status of PQ becomes $((Pr_R,\ 6,\ 10))$. As only red edges are allowed, EDP-QP will not explore other partitions. In the next iteration, the current vertex becomes $Pr_R(6)$. As $Pr_R(6)$ corresponds to the Destination Vertex 6, EDP-QP returns the shortest cost of 10 (Line 8).

To illustrate how EDP-QP traverses different partitions, consider Query $Q_2(1,\ 6\ \{R,\ B\})$. Q_2 uses the Index $I(G)$ of Figure 3. The edges traversed to answer Q_2 are given in Figure 4. The dashed edges in Figure 4 do not physically exist. They are there to illustrate the sequence of traversing the different partitions to answer Q_2. As the source Vertex 1 has two allowed partitions hosting two instances of Vertex 1, one instance should be selected to start the traversal. Procedure $getPr$ (Line 3) selects a partition hosting an allowed outgoing edge of Vertex 1 with the minimum edge cost. For Q_2, $getPr$ selects Partition Pr_R as it hosts an outgo-

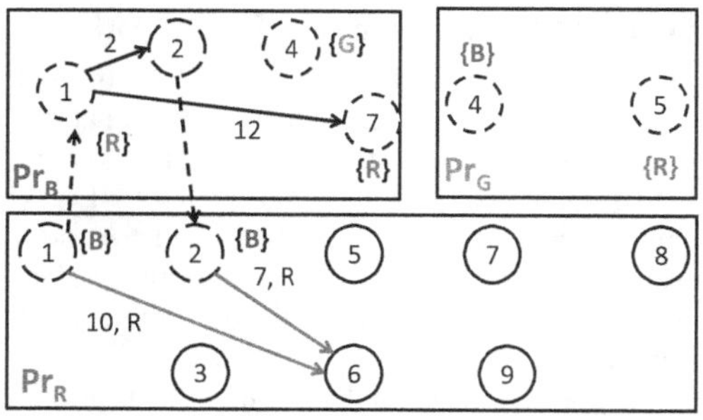

Figure 4: Index traversal for the shortest path from Vertex 1 to Vertex 6 using only Red and Blue edges.

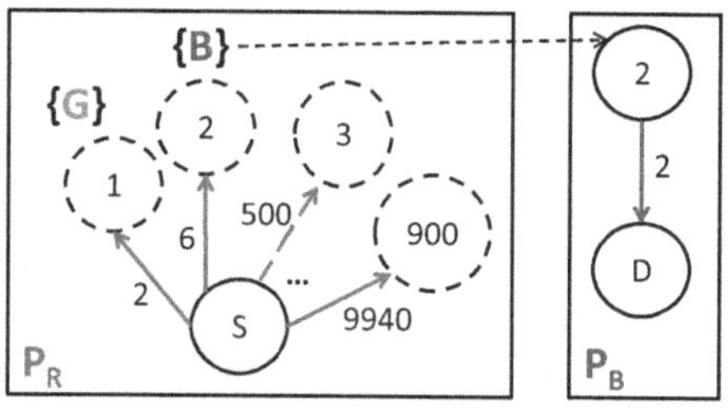

Figure 5: Example of a vertex with many reachable bridge vertexes (Vertex S). Dashed vertexes are bridge vertexes.

ing edge of Vertex 1 with the least cost (see Figure 1). So, PQ is initially set to $((Pr_R,\ 1,\ 0))$. At the beginning of the traversal, the current Vertex becomes $Pr_R(1)$. As the destination Vertex 6 is hosted by Pr_R and is reachable from the current vertex, the shortest Red path from $Pr_R(1)$ to $Pr_R(6)$ is retrieved from the index, and PQ is updated to $((Pr_R,\ 6,\ 10))$. As $Pr_R(1)$ is a bridge vertex, its $OtherHosts$ list is intersected with the allowed labels $\{R,\ B\}$); the set intersection determines other partitions hosting outgoing edges of the current vertex that are allowed by Q_2. The bridge vertex logic handling (Lines 11-15) causes the following update to PQ $((Pr_B,\ 1,\ 0),\ (Pr_R,\ 6,\ 10))$. Notice that the entry corresponding to $Pr_R(6)$ in PQ imposes an upper bound of 10 to the query answer. In the next iteration, $Pr_B(1)$ becomes the current vertex. Although $Pr_B(1)$ is a bridge vertex, its $OtherHosts$ list will not cause any cost relaxation, i.e., the cost of $Pr_R(1)$ is already zero. Thus, Lines 11-15 will not update PQ. EDP-QP will not find Vertex 6 in Pr_B. However, EDP-QP will try to leave Partition Pr_B searching for the destination vertex. As in Figure 4, leaving Pr_B is possible through the bridge vertexes $Pr_B(2)$, $Pr_B(4)$ and $Pr_B(7)$ that are reachable from $Pr_B(1)$. Edges $(Pr_B(1),\ Pr_B(2))$, $(Pr_B(1),\ Pr_B(4))$ and $(Pr_B(1),\ Pr_B(7))$ are called the bridge edges of Vertex $Pr_B(1)$. As the $OtherHosts$ list of the Bridge-vertex $Pr_B(4)$ does not contain allowed labels, the Bridge-vertex $Pr_B(4)$ is discarded. However, $Pr_B(2)$ and $Pr_B(7)$ have allowed labels in their $OtherHosts$ list. Lines 16-20 handle the bridge edges of the current node and cause the following update to PQ $((Pr_R,\ 2,\ 2),\ (Pr_R,\ 6,\ 10),\ (Pr_R,\ 7,\ 12))$. In the next iteration, the current vertex becomes $Pr_R(2)$ that can reach the destination Vertex $Pr_R(6)$. Relaxing the cost of reaching $Pr_R(6)$ from $Pr_R(2)$ (Line 10) causes the following status of PQ $((Pr_R,\ 6,\ 9),\ (Pr_R,\ 6,\ 10),\ (Pr_R,\ 7,\ 12))$. The following iteration will have $Pr_R(6)$ as the current vertex. Hence, EDP-QP will return the exact shortest cost 9 for Q_2.

Notice that any computed bridge edges of a vertex (e.g., bridge edges of Vertex $Pr_B(1)$ computed by Q_2) will be computed from scratch only once unless it is invalidated by a recent graph-update. Other queries that need any saved bridge edges will leverage them from the index to avoid any recomputations as long as they are not out-of-date (see Section 7). As we explain in Section 6.2, EDP-QP computes bridge edges by a non-blocking operator that runs on a separate thread. This allows the traversal algorithm to continue traversing $I(G)$ while the bridge edges are still being computed.

6.2 Handling Large Bridge Vertexes

For large graph datasets, the partitioning scheme formed by Algorithm 1 may lead to many bridge vertexes in one partition. The disadvantage of this case is the increased fan-out of the vertexes (recall that the traversal algorithm can explore all the outgoing bridge edges of a given vertex). EDP handles this issue by not exploring all the possible transitions at once, i.e., the bridge edges of the current node are not relaxed all together. To illustrate the intuition behind this handling, consider a road-network graph. If the current node is a commuter's location on a highway, and EDP wants to compute a toll-free exit to a certain destination, it is not wise to consider all the possible reachable exits from the current position (some of them will be very far and not of interest). The intuition is to consider a small near subset of all the possible exits, and the commuter will most likely reach his/her destination by a cost less than the cost of reaching other far exits (i.e., bridge vertexes that are reachable by high costs).

For example, in Figure 5, Vertex S has 900 bridge edges. If we insert all 900 reachable bridge vertexes in PQ, we will issue 900 insertion operations in PQ. Moreover, ExtractMin on PQ will be a function of an enlarged number of elements in PQ. Thus, we modify the way Algorithm 2 handles bridge vertexes. Instead of performing a breadth exploration when processing a current node (e.g., S in Figure 5), EDP follows a hybrid traversal approach without losing the correctness of Algorithm 2. Recall that the outgoing bridge edges of any vertex are sorted by the edge weights. EDP defines a system parameter, termed $MaxBreadth$, that is set to a positive integer. EDP sets $MaxBreadth$ to the average fan-out of the vertexes in G having at least two edges with different labels (in order not to increase the average fan-out observed by the traversal algorithm). $MaxBreadth$ ensures that at any iteration of the main while loop of Algorithm 2 (Lines 5-21), the maximum number of explored outgoing edges of the current vertex is not going to exceed the value of $MaxBreadth$.

To preserve the correctness of EDP-QP, we add two new attributes to the structure of elements of PQ (namely, $edgeId$ and $costRank$). An element PQ becomes a tuple having the following five attributes: 1) Pr: a partition's identifier, 2) v: the identifier of a vertex that is reachable from the source and hosted by Pr, 3) $cost$: the least cost observed so far that connects the source vertex to Vertex v, 4) $edgeId$: the identifier of the outgoing edge of Vertex v that should be investigated when the element is dequeued (initialized to zero), and 5) $costRank$: the key of the PQ element (initialized to the same value of cost); $costRank$ has the same domain as the $cost$ attribute, but its value may differ.

We describe the modifications required for Algorithm 2 to handle the possibility of having many reachable bridge vertexes from the current vertex. In particular, we describe the modifications to Lines 16-20. Before the for-loop at Line 16, EDP-QP defines a counter that starts at 0 and that is incremented at each iteration of the for-loop. The body of the for-loop will have an extra check using the defined counter and the value of $MaxBreadth$. If EDP-QP already investigated $MaxBreadth$ outgoing edges of the current vertex, it performs these steps:

Step 1: Update the $edgeId$ and $costRank$ attributes of the current

element t so that t can be safely re-enqueued into PQ. Notice that EDP-QP should remember the id of the edge, say e, at which the investigation stops as well as the potential cost if e is relaxed. For example, if the last investigated outgoing edge of the current vertex has index k (w.r.t. the sorted list of outgoing bridge edges from the current vertex), we set $edgeId$ to $k + 1$ and set $costRank$ to $t.Cost$ + the cost of the $(k + 1)^{th}$ edge.
Step 2: Insert Element t to PQ again with an updated $costRank$ (to ensure that we do not lose a potential path).
Step 3: At every investigation of the outgoing bridge edges of a current vertex, EDP-QP starts from the edge specified by $t.edgeId$ (edges with id less than t.edgeId have been already investigated).

Refer to Figure 5. Let $MaxBreadth$ be equal to 2. PQ is initialized to $((P_R, S, 0, 0, 0))$. Then, we relax up to 2 outgoing bridge edges. So, PQ becomes $((P_R, 1, 2, 0, 2), (P_R, 2, 6, 0, 6), (P_R, S, 0, 2, 500))$. Notice that only two elements are added to PQ plus the element $(P_R, S, 0, 2, 500)$ (name it $delayedEntry$) instead of adding 900 elements. The $delayedEntry$ indicates that EDP-QP should consider refetching Vertex $P_R(S)$ from PQ to explore its third outgoing edge with $costRank$ 500 ($edgeId$ is zero-based). The cost of the $delayedEntry$ does not change as we have not reached Vertex 3 yet. However, costRank is set to 500 as EDP-QP should keep the correct order of resuming the processing of Vertex $P_R(S)$ (500 is the cost of reaching Vertex $P_R(3)$ from Vertex $P_R(S)$).

In the figure, Element $(P_R, 1, 2, 0, 2)$ will not be further explored as it does not have allowed access paths (marked as having only outgoing edge(s) with Label G), and hence will be ignored. Entry $(P_R, 2, 6, 0, 6)$ causes a transition to Partition P_B. Now, PQ contains $((P_B, 2, 6, 0, 6), (P_R, S, 0, 2, 500))$. Element $(P_B, 2, 6, 0, 6)$ gets processed in the next iteration and PQ will then include: $((P_B, D, 8, 0, 8), (P_R, S, 0, 2, 500))$. EDP-QP reaches the destination node when extracting the first element of PQ. Hence, a minimum cost of 8 is returned without exploring the delayed outgoing edges of S.

Non-blocking Operator for Computing Bridge-edges. Recall that the bridge edges of any vertex, say $Pr(v)$, are computed from scratch only once. Assume that EDP-QP needs $Pr(v)$'s bridge-edges for the first time. If $Pr(v)$ has many bridge-edges, EDP-QP would block until all bridge-edges are computed, and the query response time would increase. EDP-QP handles this issue by computing the bridge-edges of $Pr(v)$ by a non-blocking operator, namely $BridgeEdgesOp$. Recall that EDP-QP asks for a maximum of $MaxBreadth$ bridge-edges at any iteration. So, when EDP-QP calls $BridgeEdgesOp$ to compute $Pr(v)$'s bridge-edges, a separate thread is initiated. This thread runs Dijkstra's algorithm to search for the shortest paths from $Pr(v)$ to all the bridge-vertexes in Partition Pr. Dijkstra's algorithm finds the bridge-edges in increasing order of their cost. So, once a bridge-edge is computed, $BridgeEdgesOp$ pipelines it to EDP-QP that can then resume its traversal. The thread running $BridgeEdgesOp$ computes all bridge-edges even if all the requests of EDP-QP are satisfied. The computed bridge-edges are stored in EDP's index. This avoids any recomputations of the bridge-edges in the future. EDP-QP runs a separate thread for the first request to compute a bridge-edges set from scratch. To address synchronization issues among concurrently executing queries that attempt to simultaneously build the bridge-edges of the same vertex, EDP-QP follows a many-consumer-one-producer synchronization model. In other words, each bridge-edges set, say Set_i, can be requested by more than one query (consumers). However, only one thread (producer) is responsible for computing Set_i.

6.3 Time Analysis of EDP Traversal

In this section, we analyze the time complexity of the traversal algorithm EDP-QP, and we present some strategies that make EDP-QP fast (e.g., parallel execution). For an underlying graph, say G, recall that EDP-QP traverses Index $I(G)$ and not G. Let n' and m' be the number of vertexes and edges of G, and let n and m be the number of vertexes and edges of $I(G)$, respectively. We analyze Algorithm 2, and then discuss the implications of the modification presented in Section 6.2 on the time analysis.

EDP uses a Fibonacci heap implementation for its priority queue, and hence insertion into the priority queue, and decreasing the key of an entry are $O(1)$ operations, however, the ExtractMin operation is $O(\log n)$, where n is the number of vertexes in the priority queue [13]. In Algorithm 2, the number of iterations of the While loop in Lines 5-21 is bounded by $O(n)$, and the most costly operation (i.e., ExtractMin) is $O(\log n)$. As each bridge edge is examined at most once (Lines 11-20), Algorithm 2 runs in $O(m + n \log n)$. The number of vertexes of $I(G)$, n, can be expressed as $n = n' + \sum_{v \in G.V} (l(v) - 1)$, where n' is the number of vertexes in G, and $l(v)$ is the number of distinct labels of the outgoing edges of Vertex v. Similarly, the number of edges of $I(G)$, m, can be expressed as $m = \sum_{p \in I.P} \sum_{c \in p.C} |c.V| \times |c.BV|$, where $I.P$ represents the partitions of Index I, $p.C$ represents the disconnected components of Partition p, $|c.V|$ represents the number of vertexes in Component c, and $|c.BV|$ represents the number of bridge vertexes in c. This formula is a theoretical upper bound. In practice, not all the vertexes of a component are connected to all the bridge vertexes of that component. Also, notice that the bridge edges are computed on demand based on the query workload.

Observe that the bridge edges in $I(G)$ are path contractions of the edges in G. This means that $I(G)$ has a smaller diameter than G, and hence traversing $I(G)$ is faster than traversing G. Also, in order not to increase the average fan-out of $I(G)$ observed by the traversal algorithm, Algorithm 2 is modified as discussed in Section 6.2. The modification described in Section 6.2 may add the current vertex to the priority queue again in order not to explore all its bridge edges all at once. This may lead to $k = \sum_{v \in I.V} \frac{|v.BE|}{MaxBreadth}$ priority-queue insertions, where $|v.BE|$ is the number of bridge edges emerging from Vertex v. Thus, the worst-case time-complexity of the modified algorithm is $O(m + k \log n)$.

In practice, not all the bridge edges of a node are examined. The main reason is that bridge edges have high-variability in their costs (e.g., in a road network, the bridge edges from a restaurant to all the highways will have costs with high variance). Hence, in practice, it is unlikely to scan all the bridge edges of a graph before finding the shortest path. In addition, the number of bridge edges m is query-workload dependent. This is because the bridge edges are computed only on demand according to the received queries. Also, recall that the modified algorithm allows parallel computation of the bridge edges if they are not cached (see Section 6.2).

In addition to the parallel computation of bridge edges, Algorithm 2 early computes (in parallel) some shortest paths that may be required by the main traversal thread. Recall that Line 10 checks the cost between the current node and the destination node if the destination is hosted by the same component hosting the current node. EDP uses parallel execution and caching so that Line 10 can run in constant amortized time. When a new vertex, say v, is added to the priority queue, a thread from an active thread-pool computes the distance between v and the destination node. This computation is cached to be ready if Vertex v becomes the current node. In many cases, this distance is marked as infinity in $O(1)$ when the destination node is not hosted by the component hosting Vertex v.

7. GRAPH UPDATES

The ubiquity of dynamic graphs calls for indexing techniques that can handle graph updates efficiently. For example, the roads of a road network have dynamic travel-costs that vary with time (e.g., long travel-times during rush hours). Also, roads are sometimes closed for maintenance/accidents. Similarly, other graph types like social networks are dynamic in nature (e.g., new relationships are added with time). To the best of our knowledge, EDP is the first work to answer ECSP queries on dynamic graphs.

Graph updates can be categorized into two categories: 1) topological updates (e.g., adding or removing an edge), and 2) non-topological updates (e.g., updating an edge's weight). EDP supports all kind of updates on the underlying graph, i.e., topological and non-topological updates.

7.1 Timestamp Approach

A straightforward approach for EDP to handle updates is to invalidate the pre-computations that are only affected by the updates. However, determining exactly the pre-computations to invalidate for each update is time consuming and does not scale for online applications. Hence, EDP adopts a timestamp-based approach to decide whether an indexed monochrome sub-path needs to be re-computed or not.

After the graph partitioning phase (see Section 5.1), EDP finds the disconnected components of each partition. The main idea is to host any index entry by a single component. As a result, EDP can invalidate a component instead of invalidating its index entries individually. The process of finding the disconnected components in EDP places any two nodes that are connected by any path in the same component. EDP uses a variation of Tarjan's algorithm [24] to find the disconnected components in linear time. For example, the partitioned graph in Figure 3 is processed to find the disconnected components of each partition as shown in Figure 6. Each disconnected component is given an identifier that is unique with respect to the hosting partition. For instance, in Figure 6, Partition Pr_R has two disconnected components: C_1 and C_2.

Each disconnected component, say C_i, holds Timestamp $TS(C_i)$. Also, each indexed monochrome sub-path in Component C_i, say P_{ij}, has Timestamp $TS(P_{ij})$. The timestamp values in EDP are assigned values from a global clock. The global clock is advanced by each update operation. Each update results in advancing the timestamp of the affected components. Also, each indexed monochrome sub-path, say P_{ij}, is associated with a timestamp that stores the value of the global clock at the time of computing P_{ij}. Whenever the traversal algorithm asks for Sub-path P_{ij}, the timestamps of the Sub-path and its hosting component are compared to decide if P_{ij} needs to be recomputed, i.e., if $TS(P_{ij})$ is less than $TS(C_i)$, Sub-path P_{ij} is recomputed and is assigned a new higher timestamp.

Notice that adding a new edge may lead to the merge of two components. Also, deleting an existing edge may cause a component to split into two disconnected components. EDP does not perform the merging/splitting operations instantly to support online updates and querying. Delaying the merging/splitting operations in these cases clearly do not affect the correctness of EDP. However, there is a thread pool that run periodically in the background to perform the merge/split operations if necessary.

For each update type, the global clock is advanced, and EDP maintains the timestamp of the affected components as follows:

Update edge weight: On updating the weight of an edge, its hosting component, say C_i, is determined and its timestamp (i.e., $TS(C_i)$) is set to the value of the global clock.

Update edge label: On updating an edge's label, its original hosting component, say C_o, and its new hosting component in the new partition, say C_n, are determined. The edge is removed from Component C_o and is added to Component C_n (new vertexes may be added to the new hosting component). The timestamps $TS(C_o)$ and $TS(C_n)$ are updated.

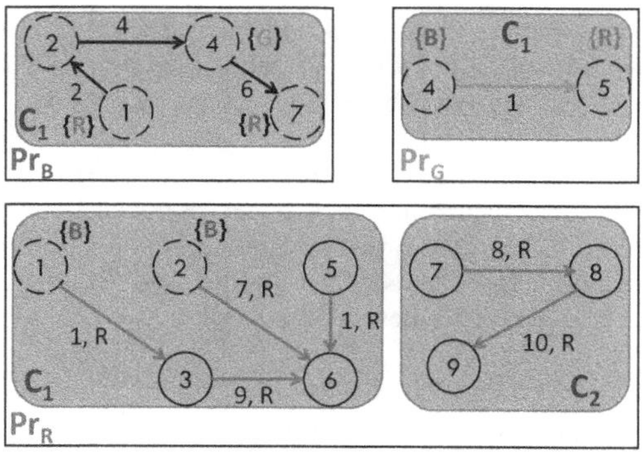

Figure 6: Disconnected Components of the graph in Figure 1.

Add edge: On adding a new edge, say e, the label of Edge e determines the hosting partition. The endpoint vertexes of Edge e can be either hosted by one or two components. After adding Edge e, the timestamp of the affected component(s) is updated. If the endpoint vertexes of Edge e is hosted by different components, EDP adds an entry to a system hash-table that these components are connected.

Delete edge: After deleting the edge, the timestamp of its hosting component is updated.

Add vertex: Nothing takes place until an edge connected to this vertex is added.

Delete vertex: On deleting a vertex, say v, all its instances in all the partitions are determined. For each instance of v, all the incoming/outgoing edges of that instance are deleted and the timestamp of the affected components are updated.

EDP performs any graph-update operation in $O(1)$ time except when deleting a vertex, which takes linear time in the number of partitions hosting that vertex's instances, and the number of their in/out edges. Recall that an indexed monochrome sub-path, say P_{ij}, hosted by a component, say C_i, is associated with a timestamp. On demand, P_{ij} is recomputed only if $TS(P_{ij})$ is less than $TS(C_i)$.

8. EXPERIMENTAL EVALUATION

In this section, we experimentally evaluate the performance of EDP against that of CHLR [18] that is the state-of-the-art technique. Mainly, we measure the average speedup in query-time that EDP achieves in comparison to CHLR. Our experiments are conducted on a machine running Linux kernel 3.17.7 on 32 cores of Intel Xeon 2.90 GHz and 192 GB of main-memory. Our implementation is based on Java 1.8. For fair comparison with CHLR, we implement all the optimizations mentioned in [18] and [14], e.g., the node ordering for the contraction algorithm.

8.1 Datasets

We use six real graph datasets: Tiger [3], BioGrid [4], BioMine [12], String [2], DBLP [1], and Youtube [23]. Table 2 summarizes the properties of the datasets. Tiger is a road network dataset covering the entire U.S., where the labels describe the types of roads (e.g., primary road, ramp, alley). The BioGrid and String datasets are protein-interaction networks, where the vertexes represent proteins, the edges represent interactions among the proteins, and the labels represent the interaction types. The BioMine dataset is a network that captures a set of relationships among biological entities. DBLP and Youtube datasets are subsets of the popular co-authorship network, and the popular video sharing service, respectively. In DBLP, the vertexes represent authors, the edges represent co-authorship, and the labels represent publication topics as described in [8]. For the Youtube dataset, the vertexes represent users, the edges represent user relationships, and the edges are labeled by relation types as described in [23].

8.2 Preprocessing Time

The preprocessing overhead performed by EDP is much less than that of CHLR (see Table 2). EDP builds $I(G)$ by scanning the edges of G in one pass. In contrast, during preprocessing, CHLR performs many shortest path computations, i.e., it is workload-independent. On the other hand, EDP computes shortcut edges on-demand according to the query workload received. The preprocessing time of EDP is affected by the size and the density of the graph as well as the number of bridge vertexes to be created (see Table 2). For example, the time for preporocessing BioGrid is greater than the time for preprocessing Tiger because the average fan-out of BioGrid is greater than that of Tiger by an order-of-magnitude. Also, the maximum fan-out for Tiger is 7, while BioGrid has a maximum fan-out of 36987.

For static graphs, EDP computes any shortcut edge, say e, only once. afterwards, other queries can leverage e. However, the first query that asks for e pays the cost of its computation. In order to have a tangible measure of the cost to answer shortest path queries by EDP using a fresh index (i.e., one that has no precomputations), in our experiments, we run EDP on the query workload twice. We refer to the first run as cold-run, where we measure the performance of EDP without having any precomputations in its cached index. The second run, called warm-run, assumes that all the required shortcuts are already computed in the first run.

8.3 Effect of the Number of Query Labels

We study the effect of the number of labels specified in the query on the speedup of EDP compared to CHLR. For each dataset, we generate random queries with $1 \cdots |L|$ labels. For each label size and using $1000 * |L|$ random source nodes, we generate more than one million random queries. From these queries, we select 1000 queries randomly for each label Size s.

Figure 7 gives the speedup of EDP when changing the query label set size for each dataset. Figure 7 also gives the 95%-confidence interval bars. Notice that the speedup of EDP downgrades as the query label set size increases. In this case, EDP explores more partitions and traverses a larger number of bridge edges.

EDP achieves the highest speedup when the query has only one label. For example, the Tiger dataset shown in Figure 7(a) reaches a warm-run speedup of 2068 ± 211 with a 95% confidence-interval. The speedup downgrades as more labels are considered. The lowest warm-run speedup is 61 ± 14 when all the labels are considered. For the cold-run, when no precomputations exist in EDP's index, the best speedup is 152 ± 19 and the lowest speedup is 10.4 ± 0.78. For the Tiger dataset, EDP provides answers in a sub-millisecond on average during the warm-runs.

Graph Updates: Figure 7 also gives query-performance for dynamic graphs. After performing the cold and warm runs, we run a set of random updates on the graph, and then measure the speedup using the same queries. For each edge in the graph, an update is selected based on the following probability distribution: 40% no-update, 40% weight-update, 10% label-update, 5% edge deletion, and 5% random edge addition. These probabilities are based on the occurrence-likelihood of the update types in real applications. From Figure 7, EDP achieves significant speedups on dynamic graphs without any downtime for index reconstruction in contrast to CHLR which requires rebuilding its index from scratch (and may lead to downtimes of several hours). In this experiment, EDP performs an update operation in 3.43 ± 1.2 microseconds on average with a 95% confidence interval for the Tiger dataset. The other datasets experience similar behavior as EDP handles any graph-update operation in $O(1)$ time. Figure 7 illustrates the effectiveness of the EDP's timestamp invalidation approach, and demonstrates that EDP can handle dynamic graphs efficiently. Note that the after-update speedup curve is constantly better than the cold-run curve that outperforms CHLR.

In contrast to CHLR, EDP is not tailored to road networks. For instance, in the case of the BioGrid dataset in Figure7(b), EDP achieves up to four orders-of-magnitude speedup over CHLR for static graphs, and up to three orders-of-magnitude speedup for dynamic graphs. EDP shows significant speedups of 14305 ± 2718 in the best case and 11.7 ± 6.4 in the worst case compared to CHLR with 95% confidence intervals.

Observe that CHLR and the contraction hierarchies are originally designed for road-network graphs, and hence they have assumptions that are not valid for other networks. For instance, it is assumed that the graph vertexes can be placed in hierarchies based on their importance. Also, it is assumed that the average fan-out of the vertexes is small (e.g., 2). However, these assumptions are invalid for graphs of other domains (e.g., a protein-interaction network). For example, the Tiger dataset has an average fan-out of 1.2, but the BioGrid dataset has an average fan-out of 14. Moreover, the maximum fan-out for the Tiger dataset is 7 in contrast to a maximum fan-out of 36987 for the BioGrid dataset.

One of the reasons of the superiority of EDP over CHLR is that CHLR's shortcuts are not sufficient to answer ECSP queries and they have to be combined with edges from the original graph. In contrast, the shortcuts of EDP are sufficient to discover any ECSP query shortest path. Moreover, EDP prunes the irrelevant portions of the search space at low-cost. The reason is that the graph is partitioned, and all the partitions corresponding to disallowed labels are discarded from the search space.

8.4 Index Size

In this set of experiments, we measure the size of EDP's index as queries are processed. We also measure the effect of varying the maximum index size on the query performance.

To measure the index size of EDP, we process millions of randomly generated queries and measure the index size. Because the total number of different queries is exponential (i.e., $2^{|L|} \times n^2$), we use a workload of 10 millions random queries. The number of labels per query is fixed to half of the number of the labels in each dataset. Figure 8 shows the size of EDP's index grows linearly with the number of processed queries. The reason is that the precomputations added to EDP's index after processing ECSP queries are reused by newly arriving queries. The figure also demonstrates that EDP can process millions of random queries using few gigabytes of main memory, which can be easily provided by commodity servers. We observe that the main factor of the index size corresponding to the Tiger dataset is the indexed monochrome sub-paths with long lengths, while for the other graphs (e.g., BioMine), the main factor of the index size was the computed bridge edges in response to the processed queries.

Figure 9 (cold-run curves) shows the effect of limiting the index size (i.e., cache) on the query-time speedup using the same

Dataset	# Vertexes	# Edges	# Labels	Avg. Fan-out	% Bridge Vertexes	EDP Preprocessing	CHLR Preprocessing
Tiger	24412259	58698439	32	1.2	4%	46 seconds	6.9 hours
BioGrid	56395	1578358	7	14	34%	3.6 minutes	5.1 hours
String	35423	444331	6	13	63%	14 seconds	70 minutes
BioMine	47175	286372	7	3	56%	3 seconds	16 minutes
DBLP	47598	252881	8	6	66%	6 seconds	15 minutes
Youtube	15088	13628895	5	909	73%	9 minutes	10.7 hours

Table 2: The datasets used and the preprocessing time of EDP and CHLR.

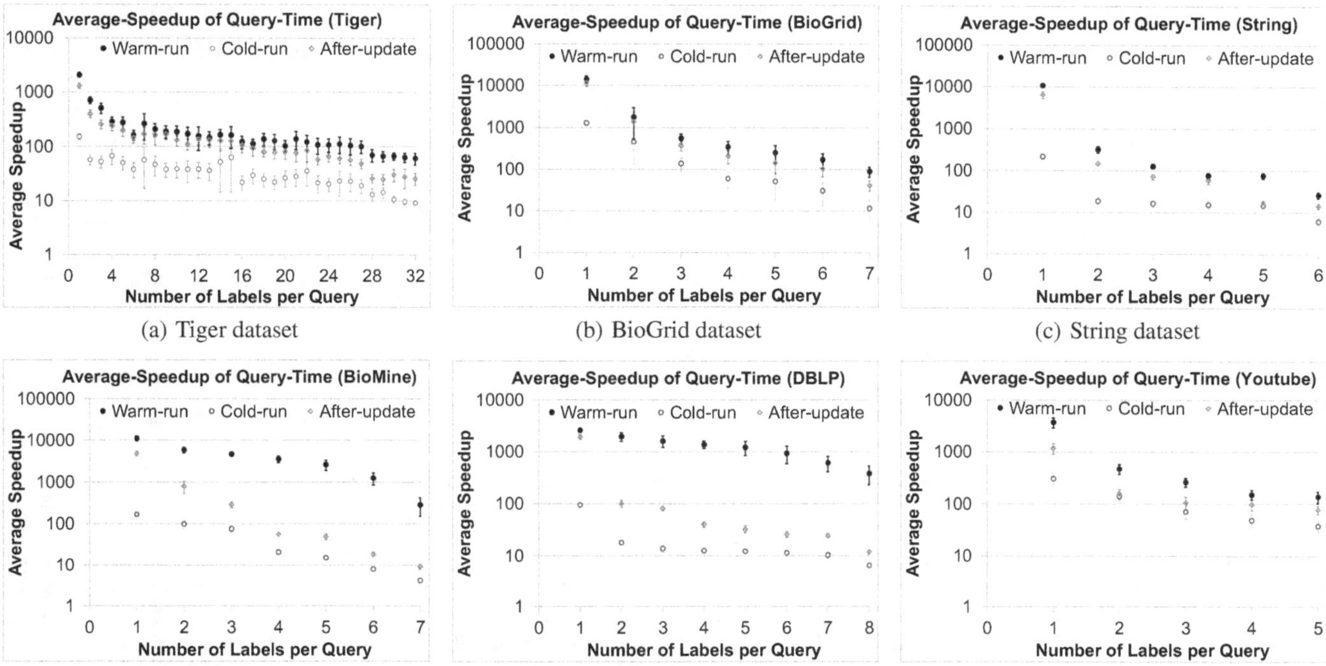

(a) Tiger dataset (b) BioGrid dataset (c) String dataset

(d) BioMine dataset (e) DBLP dataset (f) Youtube dataset

Figure 7: Query-Time Speedup of EDP vs. CHRL with 95% confidence intervals w.r.t. the number of labels per query.

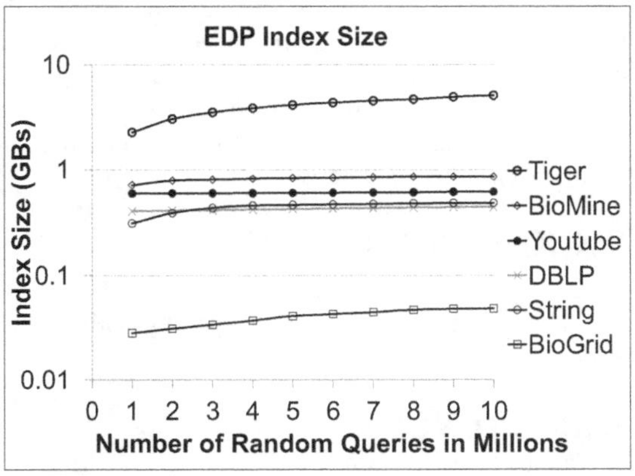

Figure 8: Index Size of EDP w.r.t number of processed queries.

query workload described above. In this experiment, we measure the average query-time speedup of processing 10 million randomly generated ECSP queries using both EDP and CHLR. For EDP, we run the queries for different maximum index-size values (according to Figure 8). EDP has significant speedup for limited cache sizes. For instance, in Figure 9(a) for the Tiger dataset, EDP achieves a speedup of 8.79 ± 1.7 with 95% confidence interval when using only 500 MB of memory (i.e., 9% of the total memory required after processing the entire workload), and an order-of-magnitude speedup is achieved when limiting the index-size to just one GB.

8.5 Interleaving Updates

In this experiment, we monitor the performance of EDP when graph updates are interleaved with ECSP queries. Recall that the index entries of EDP are invalidated based on the level of the disconnected components of a partition (see Section 7.1). So, after processing 10 million random queries, and after ensuring that the cache is full, we select a workload of 1000 ECSP queries, say QS. We run a graph-update workload associated with a percentage value, say p, to ensure that p% of the components serving QS are updated, and hence, these components will be invalidated. Determining the components serving an ECSP query is straightforward as the monochrome sub-paths forming the query answer are associated with their hosting components identifiers. After running the graph-update workload, we measure the average query-time speedup when executing QS. We interleave this process three time for three different values of p, specifically 10%, 25%, and 50%. For instance, in Figure 9, the curve corresponding to 10% updates means that 10% of the components serving QS are updated.

As Figure 9 shows, EDP has significant speedup for different

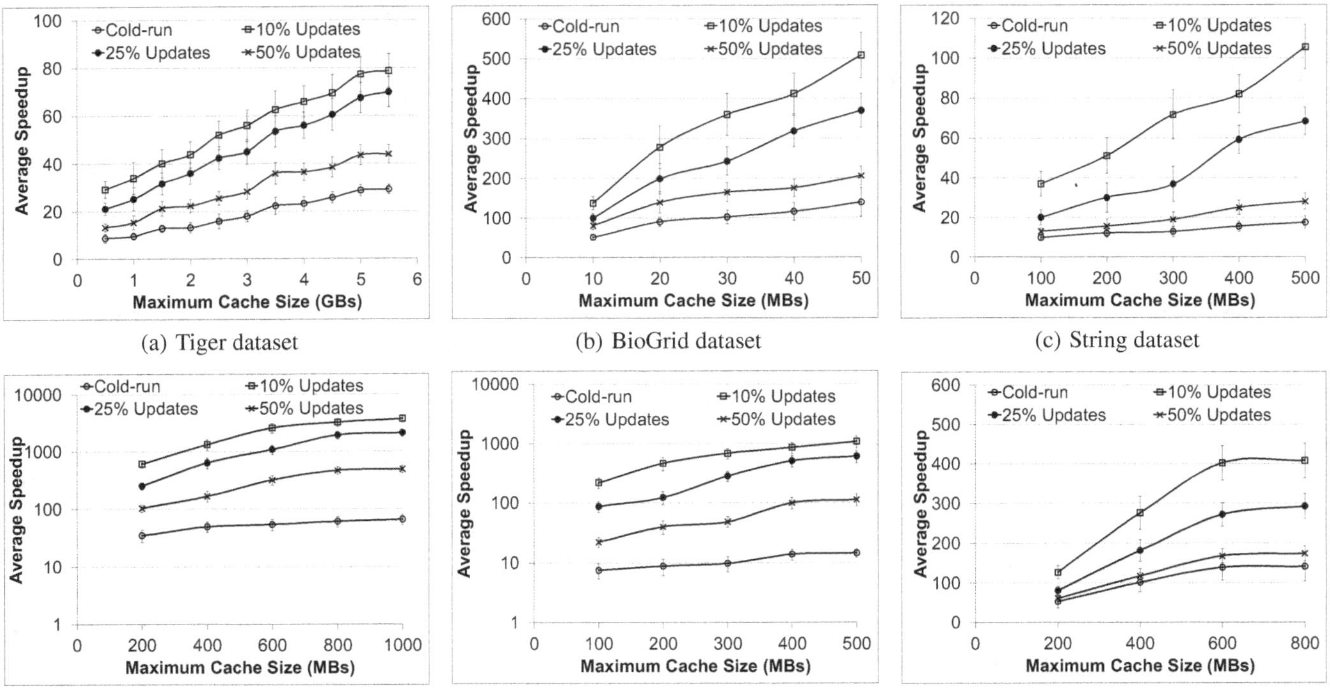

(a) Tiger dataset (b) BioGrid dataset (c) String dataset

(d) BioMine dataset (e) DBLP dataset (f) Youtube dataset

Figure 9: Query-Time Speedup with interleaved updates w.r.t maximum cache size.

graph-updates frequencies under limited cache sizes. Observe that, the 10% update curves show the highest speedups because the queries of these curves have high probabilities of being partially served from the cache (i.e., similar to a warm-run). The speedup decreases as the graph-updates frequency increases, however, at the worst case, the queries will experience a performance similar to that of a cold-run. Recall that a cold-run of EDP still outperforms CHLR, and that a cache entry is replaced in $O(1)$ time.

Discussion

EDP outperforms CHLR due to EDP's natural partitioning based on edge labels. A query processed by EDP visits only the partitions of interest based on the query labels. Another reason for EDP's good performance is that it only uses shortcuts to discover a shortest path. EDP uses the original graph edges to create a shortcut for the first time only (cold-run). Hence, the added shortcuts of EDP would not much decrease the sparsity of the underlying graph. Also, by using the $MaxBreadth$ parameter as described in Section 6.2, EDP does not necessarily investigate the whole shortcuts of a vertex visited during the traversal. While limiting the index-size of EDP, EDP still achieves orders-of-magnitude speedup as it efficiently frees space for new index-entries, besides the afore-mentioned reasons of why EDP performs well on cold-runs. EDP executes online graph updates efficiently in $O(1)$ time by flagging the affected components as invalidated. An index entry in an invalidated component will be computed on demand based on the query-workload. Hence, with no downtime, EDP presents query-time speedups that lie between warm-run and cold-run speedups for dynamic graphs.

9. CONCLUSION

EDP is a technique for answering edge-constrained shortest path queries (ECSP). It assumes a dynamic graph where each edge has one label. EDP also works for multi-graphs with edges having multiple labels. EDP has two components: an index and a traversal algorithm. We exploit the notion of contracted monochrome sub-paths of any ECSP shortest path to design the index for EDP. We illustrate how to decrease recomputations of monochrome sub-paths by caching them once computed. Thus, the costs of on-demand computation of these sub-paths are amortized over all future queries that use the already constructed shortcuts. Moreover, we demonstrate that the cache size needed is small. The monochrome sub-paths are only re-computed on demand if they are potentially affected by some graph updates. We present EDP's traversal algorithm and provide its proof of correctness. The experimental study over real six graphs spanning different domains show up to four orders-of-magnitude speedup compared to the state-of-the-art with 95% confidence intervals.

10. ACKNOWLEDGMENTS

We would like to thank Engy M. Abdallah for her help in editing this paper. This research was supported in part by National Science Foundation under Grant IIS 1117766.

11. REFERENCES

[1] http://dblp.uni-trier.de/xml/.

[2] http://string-db.org/.

[3] https://www.census.gov/geo/maps-data/data/tiger.html.

[4] http://thebiogrid.org.

[5] I. Abraham, D. Delling, A. V. Goldberg, and R. F. F. Werneck. Hierarchical hub labelings for shortest paths. In *Algorithms - ESA 2012 - 20th Annual European Symposium, Ljubljana, Slovenia, September 10-12, 2012. Proceedings*, pages 24–35, 2012.

[6] C. Barrett, K. Bisset, R. Jacob, G. Konjevod, and M. V. Marathe. Classical and contemporary shortest path problems

in road networks: Implementation and experimental analysis of the transims router. In *Proceedings of the 10th Annual European Symposium on Algorithms*, ESA '02, 2002.

[7] H. Bast, S. Funke, D. Matijevic, P. Sanders, and D. Schultes. In transit to constant time shortest-path queries in road networks. In *Proceedings of the Nine Workshop on Algorithm Engineering and Experiments, ALENEX 2007, New Orleans, Louisiana, USA, January 6, 2007*, 2007.

[8] F. Bonchi, A. Gionis, F. Gullo, and A. Ukkonen. Distance oracles in edge-labeled graphs. In *Proc. 17th International Conference on Extending Database Technology (EDBT), Athens, Greece, March 24-28, 2014.*, pages 547–558, 2014.

[9] D. Delling and D. Wagner. Landmark-based routing in dynamic graphs. In *Experimental Algorithms, 6th International Workshop, WEA 2007, Rome, Italy, June 6-8, 2007, Proceedings*, pages 52–65, 2007.

[10] J. Dibbelt, T. Pajor, and D. Wagner. User-constrained multimodal route planning. *J. Exp. Algorithmics*, 19, Apr. 2015.

[11] E. W. Dijkstra. A note on two problems in connection with graphs. *Numerical Mathematics*, 1:269–271, 1959.

[12] L. Eronen and H. Toivonen. Biomine: Predicting links between biological entities using network models of heterogeneous database. In *BMC Bioinformatics*, pages 13–119, 2012.

[13] M. L. Fredman and R. E. Tarjan. Fibonacci heaps and their uses in improved network optimization algorithms. *J. ACM*, 34(3):596–615, July 1987.

[14] R. Geisberger, M. N. Rice, P. Sanders, and V. J. Tsotras. Route planning with flexible edge restrictions. *ACM Journal of Experimental Algorithmics*, 17(1), 2012.

[15] R. Geisberger, P. Sanders, D. Schultes, and D. Delling. Contraction hierarchies: Faster and simpler hierarchical routing in road networks. In *Experimental Algorithms, 7th International Workshop, WEA 2008, Provincetown, MA, USA, May 30-June 1, 2008, Proceedings*, pages 319–333, 2008.

[16] A. V. Goldberg, H. Kaplan, and R. F. F. Werneck. Better landmarks within reach. In *Experimental Algorithms, 6th International Workshop, WEA 2007, Rome, Italy, June 6-8, 2007, Proceedings*, pages 38–51, 2007.

[17] A. O. Mendelzon and P. T. Wood. Finding regular simple paths in graph databases. *SIAM J. Comput.*, 24(6), Dec. 1995.

[18] M. N. Rice and V. J. Tsotras. Graph indexing of road networks for shortest path queries with label restrictions. *PVLDB*, 4(2):69–80, 2010.

[19] H. Samet, J. Sankaranarayanan, and H. Alborzi. Scalable network distance browsing in spatial databases. In *Proceedings of the ACM SIGMOD International Conference on Management of Data, SIGMOD 2008, Vancouver, BC, Canada, June 10-12, 2008*, pages 43–54, 2008.

[20] A. Shimbel. Applications of matrix algebra to communication nets. *Bulletin of Mathematical Biophysics*, 13:165–78, 1951.

[21] A. Shimbel. Structural parameters of communication networks. *Bulletin of Mathematical Biophysics*, 15:501–507, 1953.

[22] S. N. Simões, D. C. Martins-Jr, H. Brentani, and R. Fumio. Shortest paths ranking methodology to identify alterations in ppi networks of complex diseases. In *Proceedings of the ACM Conference on Bioinformatics, Computational Biology and Biomedicine*, BCB '12, pages 561–563, 2012.

[23] L. Tang, X. Wang, and H. Liu. Community detection via heterogeneous interaction analysis. *Data Min. Knowl. Discov.*, 25(1):1–33, July 2012.

[24] R. Tarjan. Depth first search and linear graph algorithms. *SIAM Journal on Computing*, 1972.

APPENDIX

A. CORRECTNESS OF EDP

THEOREM 1. The traversal Algorithm EDP-QP finds a correct shortest path if one exists.

Proof. The proof for this theorem follows very closely the proof of correctness of Dijkstra's algorithm. Recall that $I(G)$ preserves the connectivity of G by construction (refer to Section 5.1). Hence, a shortest path that exists in G also exists in $I(G)$. To prove the correctness of EDP-QP, we need only to prove that when a vertex, say $pr_m(u)$, is dequeued from PQ, the cost of $pr_m(u)$ in the *cost* table is the cost of the shortest path from the source vertex to Vertex $pr_m(u)$. This can be proven by contradiction.

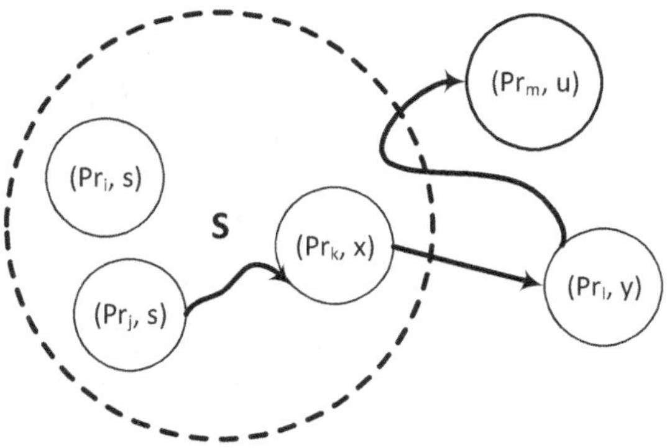

Figure 10: Proof of correctness for EDP-QP. The big dashed circle encloses the set S of dequeued elements. A vertex is represented by a pair (pr, v) indicating Vertex v in Partition pr.

Let S be the set of all $I(G)$ vertexes that are extracted from PQ. We claim that the following invariant holds till the termination of Algorithm 2: $\forall$ element $e \in S$, we have $cost(e) = \delta(s, e.v)$, where s is the source vertex and $\delta(s, e.v)$ is the cost of the shortest path from s to $e.v$. Notice that when a bridge vertex is visited, all of its copies in other allowed partitions are added to PQ with the same cost of the visited bridge-vertex. For the sake of contradiction, assume that $e = (pr_m, u)$ in Figure 10 is the first element added to S, where cost(e) $\neq \delta(pr_j(s), pr_m(u))$. $pr_m(u)$ cannot represent $pr_j(s)$ because $cost(pr_j, s) = 0$. Hence, there must be a path from (pr_j, s) to (pr_m, u). Otherwise, $cost(pr_m, u)$ would be infinity and it would not appear in S. If a path exists from (pr_j, s) to (pr_m, u), then a shortest one is there.

At the time, say t, when (pr_k, x) gets added to S, $cost(pr_k, x)$ equals $\delta(pr_j(s), pr_k(x))$ (recall our hypothesis that $pr_m(u)$ is the first element that violates the claimed invariant). Also, $cost(pr_l(y)) = \delta(pr_j(s), pr_l(y))$ (because edge $(pr_k(x), pr_l(y))$ has been relaxed at Time t). Then, $cost(pr_l(y)) = \delta(pr_j(s), pr_l(y)) \leq \delta(pr_j(s), pr_m(u)) \leq cost(pr_m(u))$. However, as both vertexes $pr_m(u)$ and $pr_l(y)$ were not in S when $pr_m(u)$ was chosen, it follows that $cost(pr_m(u)) \leq cost(pr_l(y))$. Then, the previous inequality relation becomes equality as follows: $cost(pr_l(y)) =$

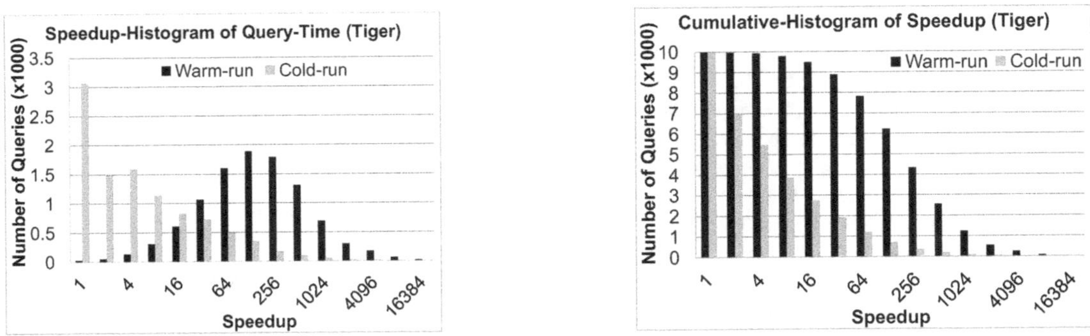

(a) Speedup Histogram of EDP vs. CHLR

(b) Cumulative Speedup of EDP vs. CHLR

Figure 11: Speedup of EDP vs. CHLR for the Tiger dataset

$\delta(pr_j(s),\ pr_l(y)) = \delta(pr_j(s),\ pr_m(u)) = cost(pr_m(u))$. Consequently, $cost(pr_m(u)) = \delta(pr_j(s),\ pr_m(u))$, which contradicts our choice of $pr_m(u)$. Therefor, this proves that $cost(pr_m(u)) = \delta(pr_j(s),\ pr_m(u))$ when $pr_m(u)$ is added to S, and this equality is maintained afterwards. Hence, when Line 10 of Algorithm 2 extracts a PQ entry that corresponds to a destination vertex instance, then its associated cost is the cost of the shortest path cost.

B. SHORTEST PATH CONSTRUCTION

In this section, we illustrate how EDP-QP builds the actual shortest path. Each entry in the $cost$ lookup table used by EDP-QP keeps an attribute called $parent$. Whenever EDP-QP relaxes the cost of an edge, say $(pr_i(u), pr_j(v))$, it sets the parent attribute of $cost(pr_j(v))$ to $pr_i(u)$'s $cost$ entry. When the cost of the shortest path is found, the chain of entries ending at $cost(pr_k(d)).parent$ is constructed by a backward traversal (d is the final destination vertex). The constructed chain indicates the vertex/partition pairs that construct the shortest path in order. This chain gives the contracted monochrome sub-paths $CP(P)$ and not P. Using $I(G)$, the details of each monochrome sub-path in $CP(P)$ are to form the final shortest path P. The complexity of this construction algorithm is $O(|CP(P)|)$, where $|CP(P)|$ is the number of monochrome sub-paths in P.

C. MULTI-GRAPHS AND MULTI-LABELS SUPPORT

A multi-graph is a graph where any two vertexes can have more than one edge connecting them. EDP can safely handle multi-graphs. EDP has an edge disjoint partitioning. Given any two vertexes u, v with multi-edges, each of these edges, say e, is hosted by a separate partition based on e's label. EDP treats each edge independently and the semantics of an ECSP query does not change. However, if a certain edge has more than one label, an ECSP query can have two different but valid semantics.

Let $Q(s,\ d,\ A)$ be an ECSP query. Given a labeled graph G' where an edge $e \in G'.E$ can have multi-labels (i.e., $l(e) \subseteq G'.L$), Q can have two different possible semantics:

- **Semantic 1:** An edge in $|G'|$ is allowed if its labels contain at least one query label (i.e., $\forall$ e $\in sp(s,\ d,\ A) \mid l(e) \cap Q.A \neq \Phi$).
- **Semantic 2:** An edge in $|G'|$ is allowed if all its labels are in the query labels (i.e., $\forall$ e $\in sp(s,\ d,\ A) \mid l(e) \subseteq Q.A$).

ECSP supports $Semantic$ 1 by viewing a multi-labeled edge as a set of independent edges. If interested in $Semantic$ 2, the user may transform the graph to have single label edges, if possible.

D. EXCLUSION LOGIC AND QUERY REWRITING

Given a labeled graph where each edge has only one label, an ECSP Query $Q(s,\ d,\ A)$ can take one of the following two forms:

- **Inclusion logic form:** Labels in A are allowed in the shortest path.
- **Exclusion logic form:** Labels in A are not allowed in the shortest path, and hence the labels in $overline A$ are allowed.

The inclusion logic form is suitable for social network graphs, e.g., a query will most likely include only a small subset of the edge labels, e.g., two or three social relation types. In contrast, the exclusion logic form is suitable for road network graphs, e.g., avoiding toll roads. The two forms are equivalent for graphs with single-label edges, and can be transformed to each other easily. EDP supports both forms and can rewrite a query accordingly, e.g., rewrite $Q_i(s,\ d,\ A)$ into $Q_e(s,\ d,\ \overline{A})$ to support the exclusion semantics based on a simple yet effective cost model.

D.1 Query Rewriting

EDP-QP can process an ECSP query in either of the inclusion and exclusion forms. It can choose the form that makes the processing faster. For example, since the $OtherHosts$ list of the index $I(G)$ is fixed w.r.t. any query, being a frequent operation, the intersection operation between $OtherHosts(Pr(v)) \cap Q.A$ for every visited bridge-edge $Pr(v)$ will depend on the size of $Q.A$. Clearly, some queries are better written in a particular form over the other depending of the size of A vs. $L - A$. Hence, we can rewrite the query to be in either the inclusion or the exclusion-forms, and Algorithm 2 adapts its edge selection logic, accordingly (e.g., the comparison logic of Line 18 in Algorithm 2).

When executing an ECSP Query, say Q, a query-rewrite step takes place, and an attribute is set for Q, say $Q.Type$, to indicate its logic-form. If $Q.Type$ is inclusion and $|Q.A| > |L$ - $Q.A|$, $Q.Type$ is changed to exclusion and $Q.A$ is reset to L - $Q.A$. Similarly, if $Q.Type$ is exclusion and $|Q.A| > |L$ - $Q.A|$, $Q.Type$ is changed to inclusion and $Q.A$ is rest to L - $Q.A$. When EDP-QP processes Q, it checks $Q.Type$ to perform the right label filtering.

E. EDP FOR NON-DIRECTED GRAPHS

As every non-directed graph can be represented by an equivalent directed graph, EDP easily supports non-directed graphs. EDP takes a parameter to indicate if the input graph is directed or non-directed. If the input graph is non-directed, then an edge, say e, is stored only once. However, at each of the endpoint vertexes of

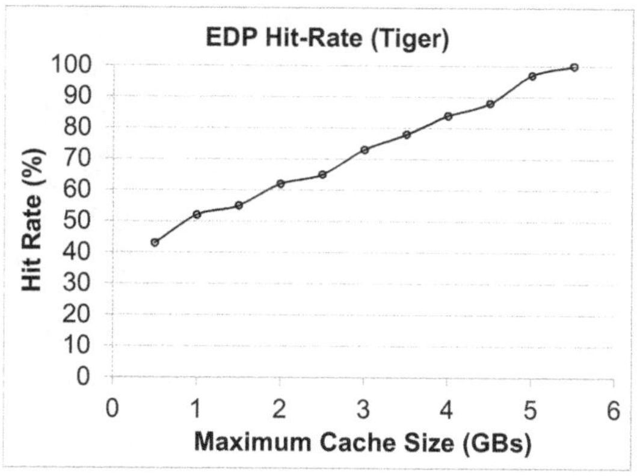

Figure 12: Hit Rate of EDP w.r.t. Maximum Cache Size.

Edge e, EDP stores the identifier of Edge e in both the "InEdges" and "OutEdges" lists of its endpoints. Hence, in a non-directed graph, each vertex is aware of all of its edges.

F. ADDITIONAL EXPERIMENTS

F.1 Fixing Query-Label Size

In this experiment, we fix the query label size, and study the performance speedup of individual queries. We generate more than 50K random queries such that each query has $|L|/2$ allowed labels. The reason for setting the number of labels per query to $|L|/2$ is to cancel the effect of the query labels size on both EDP and CHLR. Recall that for a given ECSP query with allowed labels A, we compute a restricted set $R = L - A$ as the input to the CHLR technique. So we choose A so that $|A| = |L| / 2$ to give CHLR a query with restricted labels R where $|R|$ is of size $|L| / 2$. This cancels the effect of query labels-set size when comparing EDP to CHLR.

From the 50K queries generated, we execute $10,000$ random queries, measure the running time of EDP and CHRL per query, and compute the speedup. Figure 11(a) gives a histogram of the results. The x-axis indicates buckets of speedup ranges and the y-axis indicates the number of queries out of the 10,000 queries that fall in each bucket of the x-axis.

As shown in Figure 11(a), EDP and CHLR perform similarly in the warm-run for only 31 queries out of the 10k queries (i.e., there is no speedup for only 0.3% of the random queries). However, for the remaining 99.7% random queries, EDP has a speedup of more than two over CHLR. For the cold-run, where the precomputation time is added to each query, there is no speedup for 30% of the random queries while 70% of the queries experience a speedup of at least two. Figure 11(b) gives the cumulative distribution of the speedups. About 95% of the queries have at least a speedup of one order-of-magnitude for the warm-run while, for the cold-run, near 38% of the queries experience at least an order-of-magnitude speedup.

F.2 Cached-Index Hit-Rate

In this experiment, we measure the hit rate of EDP's cached-index w.r.t. different index-size limits. This experiment uses the 10 millions randomly-generated ECSP queries used before to measure the index size. Although the workload is random and EDP uses an LRU replacement-policy, the hit rate is still a good measure to represent the likelihood of finding an index entry in the cache when needed by new ECSP queries.

Starting from a maximum index-size of 500 MBs to 5.5 GBs, we measure the hit rate of EDP's cached index after processing the entire workload. As Figure 12 shows, the hit rate increases linearly when increasing the maximum index-size. EDP achieves a hit rate of more than 50% when using only 1 GB cache, and a hit rate of 84% when using 4 GBs cache. Figure 12 shows that EDP has a high potential of not missing requested index-entries even when limiting the index size by small values (e.g., 500 MBs).

Efficient Subgraph Matching by Postponing Cartesian Products

Fei Bi[†], Lijun Chang[†], Xuemin Lin[†], Lu Qin[‡], Wenjie Zhang[†]

[†]University of New South Wales, Australia

[‡]University of Technology, Sydney, Australia

f.bi@student.unsw.edu.au, {ljchang,lxue,zhangw}@cse.unsw.edu.au, lu.qin@uts.edu.au

ABSTRACT

In this paper, we study the problem of subgraph matching that extracts all subgraph isomorphic embeddings of a query graph q in a large data graph G. The existing algorithms for subgraph matching follow Ullmann's backtracking approach; that is, iteratively map query vertices to data vertices by following a matching order of query vertices. It has been shown that the matching order of query vertices is a very important aspect to the efficiency of a subgraph matching algorithm. Recently, many advanced techniques, such as enforcing connectivity and merging similar vertices in query or data graphs, have been proposed to provide an effective matching order with the aim to reduce unpromising intermediate results especially the ones caused by redundant Cartesian products. In this paper, for the first time we address the issue of unpromising results by Cartesian products from "dissimilar" vertices. We propose a new framework by postponing the Cartesian products based on the structure of a query to minimize the redundant Cartesian products. Our second contribution is proposing a new path-based auxiliary data structure, with the size $O(|E(G)| \times |V(q)|)$, to generate a matching order and conduct subgraph matching, which significantly reduces the exponential size $O(|V(G)|^{|V(q)|-1})$ of the existing path-based auxiliary data structure, where $V(G)$ and $E(G)$ are the vertex and edge sets of a data graph G, respectively, and $V(q)$ is the vertex set of a query q. Extensive empirical studies on real and synthetic graphs demonstrate that our techniques outperform the state-of-the-art algorithms by up to 3 orders of magnitude.

1. INTRODUCTION

In recent years, graph analysis has been playing an increasingly important role in the area of data analytics. Subgraph matching is one of the most fundamental problems in graph analysis. Given a query graph q and a large data graph G, the problem of subgraph matching is to extract all *subgraph isomorphic embeddings* of q in G. Subgraph matching has a wide range of applications including protein interaction network analysis [13], social network analysis [17], and chemical compound search [20].

Despite the NP-completeness of subgraph matching [5], recent research efforts lead to significant advances in developing computing paradigms to conduct subgraph matching [4, 8, 14, 15, 22]. A key issue is to reduce the number of unpromising intermediate results when iteratively mapping vertices one by one from a query graph to a data graph, especially to prevent generating unpromising immediate results caused by redundant Cartesian products. VF2 [4] and QuickSI [15] propose to enforce the connectivity to reduce redundant Cartesian products; that is, prevent generating an intermediate embedding, in a data graph for a query graph q, from two disjoint subgraphs q_1 and q_2 of q such that there are no edges connecting a vertex in q_1 and another vertex in q_2. To further reduce the chance of unnecessarily enumerating Cartesian products, Turbo$_{\mathsf{ISO}}$ [8] proposes to merge together the *similar* vertices in a *query graph* q (i.e., the vertices with the same labels and the same neighborhoods), and [14] significantly extends the work of [8] to compress a *data graph* G by merging together the similar vertices in G to boost the performance of the technique in [8].

The second key issue is to generate an effective matching order for iteratively mapping vertices one by one from a query graph to a data graph with the aim to minimize the total number of intermediate results. QuickSI [15] proposes to generate a matching order based on the *infrequent-labels* first strategy. SPath [22] proposes to generate a matching order based on the *infrequent-paths* first strategy to resolve the limitations of only considering vertices and edges in [15]. The technique Turbo$_{\mathsf{ISO}}$ in [8] proposes to exactly enumerate all paths to overcome the limitations in [22] that possibly overestimates the join cardinality by an estimation formula.

Challenges and Our Approaches. Our initial empirical study demonstrated that Turbo$_{\mathsf{ISO}}$ [8] and its boost [14] can be very inefficient when the size of a query graph gets larger. This motivates us to develop new, more efficient and scalable techniques to conduct subgraph matching. Below are the two challenges that we will deal with in the paper.

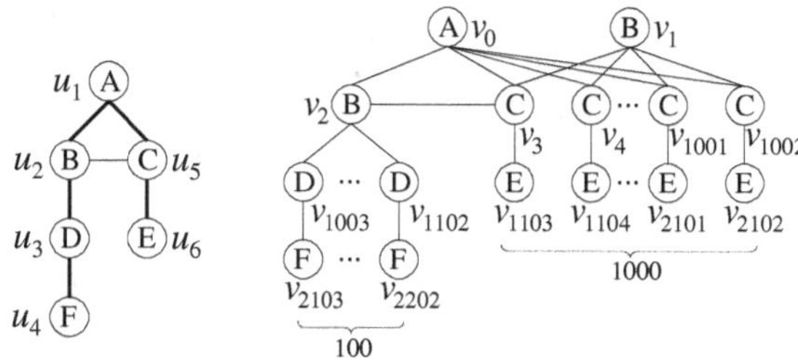

(a) Query q (b) Data graph G

Figure 1: Challenge 1

Challenge 1: Redundant Cartesian Products by Dissimilar Vertices. Consider the query q in Figure 1(a) and the data graph G in Figure 1(b). It is immediate that q and G cannot be compressed by the techniques in [8] and [14], respectively, since *there are no sim-*

SIGMOD'16, June 26-July 01, 2016, San Francisco, CA, USA

© 2016 ACM. ISBN 978-1-4503-3531-7/16/06...$15.00

DOI: http://dx.doi.org/10.1145/2882903.2915236

ilar vertices in q or G (i.e., no vertices with the same labels and the same neighborhoods). Note that the recent techniques [8, 14, 15, 22] are all based on iteratively extending a mapping (i.e., embedding) from q to G along a spanning tree of q and also checking the non-tree edges adjacent to a newly extended vertex in q. Suppose that the spanning tree q_T of q is as depicted by thick lines in Figure 1(a); that is, (u_1, u_2), (u_2, u_3), (u_3, u_4), (u_1, u_5), and (u_5, u_6). The state-of-the-art edge-based ordering (i.e., QuickSI) and path-based ordering (i.e., $\mathsf{Turbo_{ISO}}$) techniques will both choose the matching order in q_T as $(u_1, u_2, u_3, u_4, u_5, u_6)$. Consequently, the 100 partial mappings $(v_0, v_2, v_{1000+i}, v_{2100+i})$ $(3 \leq i \leq 102)$ of (u_1, u_2, u_3, u_4) have to be combined with the 1000 partial mappings (v_0, v_j) $(3 \leq j \leq 1002)$ of (u_1, u_5) before checking the mapping of the non-tree edge (u_2, u_5). Clearly, in this case the Cartesian product of $(100000 - 100)$ partial mappings are false positive and redundant.

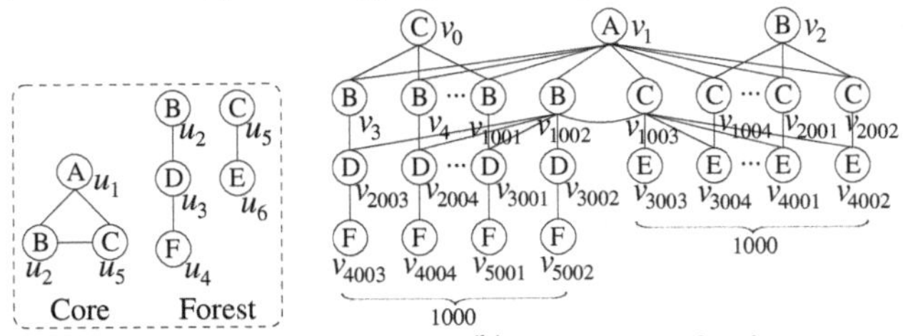

(a) Decomposition of q (b) Another Data Graph

Figure 2: Our Approach

Our Approach: Postpone Cartesian Products. Regarding the above example, if we use the matching order $(u_1, u_2, u_5, u_3, u_4, u_6)$, then we can avoid this Cartesian product of 100×1000 partial mappings. In fact, the second matching order leads to only 100 + 1000 partial mappings since an early checking of the non-tree edge (u_2, u_5) can eliminate the 999 partial mappings (v_0, v_j) $(4 \leq j \leq 1002)$ of (u_1, u_5) before extending the mapping to u_3 in q. This can be generalized into a new framework by decomposing a query graph into a dense subgraph (i.e., *core*) and a *forest* such that we process the core first; for example, Figure 2(a) illustrates such a decomposition of the query graph in Figure 1(a). Note that a dense query subgraph has a stronger pruning power (thus, reduces the number of unpromising partial mappings) while a forest potentially may have more mappings in G. Therefore, processing core first potentially postpones Cartesian products and thus reduces the chance to generate redundant Cartesian products.

Moreover, we can further postpone possible redundant Cartesian products by processing all leaf (i.e., degree-one) vertices (if exist) of a query in the last. For example, suppose that now the data graph is the one in Figure 2(b), we process the leaf vertices u_4 and u_6 of q in the last. In this case, the 1000 partial mappings of the subgraph of q induced by (u_1, u_2, u_5, u_3) will be generated. Nevertheless, we will leave their Cartesian product with the 1000 mappings of (u_5, u_6) to the last. The advantage of doing this is that such Cartesian product could be redundant if the query graph in Figure 1(a) has additional parts; thus it should be postponed, to be avoided.

Challenge 2: Exponential Size of The Path-based Data Structure in $\mathsf{Turbo_{ISO}}$. The state-of-the-art approach, $\mathsf{Turbo_{ISO}}$ [8], outperforms the other approaches due to its accurate calculation of join cardinality of a root-to-leaf query path in a spanning tree of a query q and the materialization of all embeddings in a data graph for each of such query paths so that they can be used to generate subgraph isomorphic embeddings. This immediately results in the exponential size $O(|V(G)|^{|V(q)|-1})$ of such path embeddings in the worst case, where $|V(G)|$ and $|V(q)|$ are the number of vertices in a data graph G and a query graph q, respectively (see Section 4.1 for more details). To resolve this, $\mathsf{Turbo_{ISO}}$ [8] in its implementation only materializes k embeddings for each root-to-leaf query path to compute the matching order of query vertices, if we only retrieve k subgraph isomorphic embeddings for q. Note that such a materialization cannot always guarantee to generate k subgraph isomorphic embeddings for q. Thus, more path embeddings may be materialized on demand when enumerating subgraph isomorphic embeddings. Moreover, if we want to retrieve all subgraph isomorphic embeddings, then we have to materialize all path embeddings; that is, the worst-case exponential size is unavoidable in $\mathsf{Turbo_{ISO}}$. As a result, $\mathsf{Turbo_{ISO}}$ cannot scale to large queries or large data graphs.

Our Approach: Compact Path-based Data Structure with Polynomial Size. As shown in [8], the auxiliary path-based data structure can greatly speed up the computation of subgraph matching. To resolve the issue of the exponential size of the path-based data structure in $\mathsf{Turbo_{ISO}}$, in this paper we propose not to enumerate and materialize all embeddings of query paths. Instead, we compute a data structure, called compact path-index (CPI), to store the candidates of embeddings of each query path. Since we generate subgraph isomorphic embeddings from CPI, it is immediate that the smaller the size of CPI, the more efficient conducting subgraph matching. We can show that while minimizing the size of CPI is NP-hard, the size of the CPI generated by our techniques is polynomial $O(|E(G)| \times |V(q)|)$ and our CPI construction algorithm runs in $O(|E(G)| \times |E(q)|)$ time, where $|E(G)|$ and $|E(q)|$ are the number of edges in G and q, respectively.

Moreover, in this paper we also propose to compute a matching order of query vertices based on a cost model and the CPI. Our experiments demonstrate that our ordering technique significantly outperforms the existing techniques.

Contributions. Our main contributions are summarized as follows.

- We develop a new framework with the aim to postpone Cartesian products. The new framework decomposes a query graph into a core and a forest for subgraph matching and proposes to deal with all leaf vertices of a query (if exist) in the last. We also develop an effective technique to compress the mappings of leaf vertices on the fly to avoid generating redundant Cartesian products.
- We design a compact auxiliary path-based data structure CPI with size $O(|E(G)| \times |V(q)|)$ for accurately estimating the number of embeddings of query paths and for generating subgraph isomorphic embeddings.
- While showing that minimizing CPI is NP-hard, we propose an efficient heuristic to build CPI in $O(|E(G)| \times |E(q)|)$ time.
- We develop efficient and effective algorithms for conducting subgraph matching.

Our extensive experiments on various dataset and query settings demonstrate that our techniques outperform the state-of-the-art techniques [8, 14] by up to 3 orders of magnitude, even excluding the cases when $\mathsf{Turbo_{ISO}}$ [8] and its boost [14] cannot terminate.

Organization. The rest of the paper is organized as follows. A brief overview of related work follows immediately. Section 2 defines the problem of subgraph matching. Section 3 presents our new framework to postpone Cartesian products. We propose our CPI-based techniques in Section 4, while CPI construction techniques are presented in Section 5. Experimental results are reported in Section 6. We give a conclusion in Section 7. *Proofs are omitted due to space limits and can be found in Section A.1 in the Appendix.*

Related Works. Related works are categorized as follows.

1) Subgraph Matching over a Single Large Data Graph. The problem of subgraph matching over a single large graph has been studied for decades. The first result is Ullmann's algorithm [19] proposed in 1976, which iteratively maps vertices one by one from a query graph q to a data graph G by following the input order of query vertices. To enhance the performance, *connected matching order* is used in VF2 [4] and QuickSI [15] that propose to generate the matching order by selecting a vertex connected to one of the already selected vertices rather than a random selection; this enables to prune false-positive candidates at an early stage, especially those caused by redundant Cartesian products. QuickSI [15] proposes to further remove false-positive candidates by first processing vertices and edges of q that are infrequent in G. GraphQL [9] and SPath [22] focus on reducing the candidates of query vertices by exploiting neighborhood-based filtering. As mentioned earlier, $\text{Turbo}_{\text{ISO}}$ [8] and the boost technique in [14] propose to merge similar vertices (i.e., vertices with the same labels and the same neighborhoods) in q and G, respectively. In this paper, we propose new efficient and effective techniques to scalably conduct subgraph matching. Firstly, we for the first time address the issue of unpromising results by Cartesian products from "dissimilar" vertices, in addition to that from similar vertices [8, 14]. Secondly, we propose to compute a connected matching order of query vertices based on a cost model and a compact path-based data structure rather than simple edge-frequencies in [15]. Thirdly, we propose a new light-weight candidate filtering technique to reduce the candidates of query vertices, in addition to the existing ones in [9, 22].

While the above techniques are based on the *depth-first paradigm* that is shown as the most efficient strategy to conduct subgraph matching on a single computer, the problem of subgraph matching has also been investigated in a distributed environment [11, 16, 18], where the *join paradigm* has been demonstrated as the most popular strategy. The goal of this paper is to develop novel techniques on a single computer to resolve the scalability issues in the existing techniques. Recently, the problem of similarity subgraph matching, which is to retrieve all subgraphs from a large data graph that are similar to a query graph, is also studied in the database community (e.g., [21, 24]). Our contributions in this paper may also be useful to study the problem of similarity subgraph matching.

2) Subgraph Containment Search over a Graph Database. The problem of subgraph containment search over a graph database is to identify the data graphs (from a graph database) that contain a query graph. This involves performing the subgraph isomorphism search over a graph database. To efficiently conduct this, many graph-feature based approaches have been proposed, following the filtering-and-verification framework, and can be classified into two categories: *frequent subgraph mining based approaches* (e.g., gIndex [20], Tree+Δ [23], and FG-Index [3]) and *exhaustive enumeration based approaches* (e.g., gCode [25], CT-Index [10] GraphGrepSX [2], and Grapes [7]). Although both subgraph containment search and subgraph matching involve subgraph isomorphism search, they are inherently different; the problem of subgraph matching, the problem we study in the paper, is harder since it requires enumerating all embeddings.

2. PRELIMINARIES

In this paper, we focus on a *vertex-labeled undirected graph* $g = (V, E, l, \Sigma)$. Here, V is the set of vertices, $E \subseteq V \times V$ is the set of edges, Σ is the set of labels, and l is a labelling function that assigns each vertex $v \in V$ a label in Σ (denoted $l_g(v)$). The number of vertices and the number of edges in g are denoted by $|V(g)|$ and $|E(g)|$, respectively. The set of neighbors of $v \in V(g)$ in g is denoted by $N_g(v) = \{v' \in V(g) \mid (v, v') \in E(g)\}$, and the degree of v, denoted $d_g(v)$, is the number of neighbors of v (i.e., $d_g(v) = |N_g(v)|$). Given a subset V_s of V, the subgraph of g induced by V_s is $g[V_s] = (V_s, \{(u, v) \in E \mid u, v \in V_s\}, l, \Sigma)$. In the following, for ease of presentation we simply refer a vertex-labeled undirected graph as a graph. Note that, our techniques can be readily extended to handle edge-labeled and directed graphs.

Definition 2.1: Given graphs $q = (V(q), E(q), l, \Sigma)$ and $G = (V(G), E(G), l, \Sigma)$, q is **subgraph isomorphic** to G if and only if there exists an *injective* mapping M from $V(q)$ to $V(G)$ such that $\forall u \in V(q)$, $l_q(u) = l_G(M(u))$ and $\forall (u, u') \in E(q)$, $(M(u), M(u')) \in E(G)$, where $M(u)$ is the vertex to which u is mapped. □

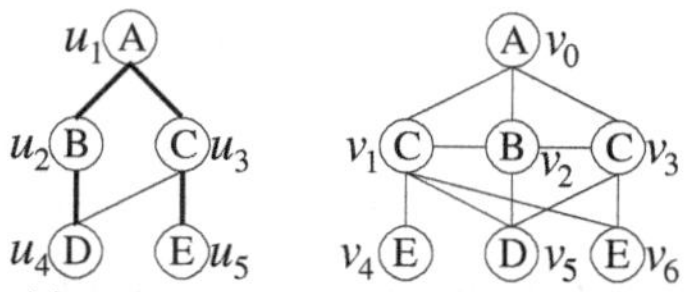

(a) Query q (b) Data graph G

Figure 3: Subgraph Matching

We call an injective mapping from vertices of q to vertices in G as a *subgraph isomorphic embedding* of q in G. For example, consider the graph q in Figure 3(a) and the graph G in Figure 3(b) where {A, B, C, D, E} is the set of vertex-labels, q is subgraph isomorphic to G since there is a subgraph isomorphic embedding $M(u_1 \to v_0, u_2 \to v_2, u_3 \to v_3, u_4 \to v_5, u_5 \to v_6)$.

Problem Statement. Given a query q and a large data graph G, in this paper we study the problem of *subgraph matching* which efficiently extracts all subgraph isomorphic embeddings of q in G.

For example, for the query graph q in Figure 3(a) and the data graph G in Figure 3(b), there are three subgraph isomorphic embeddings of q in G, which maps $(u_1, u_2, u_3, u_4, u_5)$ to $(v_0, v_2, v_1, v_5, v_4)$, $(v_0, v_2, v_1, v_5, v_6)$ and $(v_0, v_2, v_3, v_5, v_6)$, respectively.

In the remaining of this paper, we use the term "embedding" to refer to "subgraph isomorphic embedding" for simplicity when there is no ambiguity, and we may use *embedding* and *mapping* interchangeably. We also simplify $l_g(v)$, $N_g(v)$ and $d_g(v)$ as $l(v)$, $N(v)$ and $d(v)$, respectively, when the context is clear. We assume that both the query graph q and the data graph G are connected.

Notation	Description
q and G	Query and data graph
$V(q)$ and $E(q)$	Vertex set and edge set of q
$V(G)$ and $E(G)$	Vertex set and edge set of G
$l_g(v)$, $N_g(v)$ and $d_g(v)$	Label, neighbors and degree of v in g
V_C, V_T and V_I	Core-set, forest-set and leaf-set of q
q_T and r	Rooted (BFS) spanning tree of q and its root
CPI	Auxiliary data structure (compact path-index)
$u.C$	Candidates of a query vertex u in CPI
$N_u^{u'}(v)$	Adjacency list of v regarding (u', u) in CPI

Table 1: Notations

Frequently used notations are summarized in Table 1.

2.1 Existing Subgraph Matching Algorithms

The study of subgraph matching is initiated by Ullmann's backtracking algorithm [19], which iteratively maps vertices one by one from a query graph q to a data graph G by following the input order of query vertices. To enhance the performance, later algorithms in [4, 8, 14, 15] all enforce connectivity of the matching sequence/order. That is, given a spanning tree q_T of q, the matching order, $(u_1, \ldots, u_n)$, of q_T is constructed such that, for each vertex u_i except u_1, its parent $u_i.p$ in q_T is always before u_i in the matching order. This is called a *connected matching order*. For example, assume the spanning tree of the query graph in Figure 3(a) consists of edges (u_1, u_2), (u_2, u_4), (u_1, u_3), and (u_3, u_5), then a possible connected matching order is $(u_1, u_2, u_3, u_4, u_5)$ where $u_4.p = u_2$.

A subgraph matching algorithm grows an embedding M by mapping each query vertex u_i of q, according to the matching order, to a data vertex in G. When mapping u_i, the algorithm iteratively tries each data vertex v that is adjacent to the mapping $M(u_i.p)$ of $u_i.p$ as a candidate mapping of u_i; v is a *successful mapping* of u_i if 1) v has not been used in the current *partial embedding* and 2) it satisfies all the connection requirements specified by *non-tree edges* in the query (i.e., for each $(u_j, u_i) \in E(q)$ with $j < i$, $(M(u_j), v) \in E(G)$). A *full embedding* is obtained if every query vertex is mapped to a data vertex. For example, consider the above matching order for q and the data graph G in Figure 3(b). Assume a partial embedding M maps u_1, u_2, u_3, and u_4 to v_0, v_2, v_1, and v_5, respectively. Then, for mapping u_5, the algorithm iteratively tries v_4 and v_6 which are adjacent to $M(u_5.p)$ $(= M(u_3) = v_1)$, to extend M.

Cost Model for Subgraph Matching Algorithms. In this paper, we adopt the cost model in [15] for computing our matching order; that is, the total cost of a backtracking algorithm for subgraph matching is $T_{iso} = B_1 + \sum_{i=2}^{n} \sum_{j=1}^{B_{i-1}} d_i^j (r_i + 1)$. Here, B_i (called the *search breadth*) is the total number of embeddings in G for the subgraph of q induced by $\{u_1, \ldots, u_i\}$, d_i^j is the number of neighbors of $M_{i-1}^j(u_i.p)$ in G with the same label as u_i where M_{i-1}^j is the j-th embedding in G for the subgraph induced by $\{u_1, \ldots, u_{i-1}\}$ and $M_{i-1}^j(u_i.p)$ is the vertex to which the parent $u_i.p$ of u_i in q_T maps, and r_i is the number of non-tree edges between u_i and vertices before u_i in the matching order. Intuitively, a partial embedding M_{i-1}^j of $(u_1, \ldots, u_{i-1})$ in G is extended by mapping u_i to each vertex v in G that is adjacent to $M_{i-1}^j(u_i.p)$ and has the same label as u_i (there are d_i^j such vertices); v is a successful mapping of u_i if it satisfies all connection requirements specified by the r_i non-tree edges of u_i.

Example 2.1: Given the matching order $(u_1, u_2, u_3, u_4, u_5)$ of q in Figure 3(a), $r_3 = 0$ while $r_4 = 1$. $M_2^1 = \{u_1 \to v_0, u_2 \to v_2\}$, then the neighbors of $M_2^1(u_3.p)$ $(= v_0)$ are v_1 and v_3 and thus $d_3^1 = 2$. □

3. A NEW FRAMEWORK

In this paper, we propose a new framework for subgraph matching aiming at postponing the Cartesian products. We first decompose a query graph into three substructures, and then conduct subgraph matching in a substructure-by-substructure manner. In the following, we first define the core-forest-leaf decomposition.

Core-Forest-Leaf (CFL) Decomposition. The core-forest-leaf decomposition consists of core-forest decomposition and forest-leaf decomposition.

Core-Forest Decomposition. Edges of q can be categorized into two categories regarding a spanning tree q_T of q: edges in q_T are called *tree edges* while edges of q that are not in q_T are called *non-tree edges* regarding q_T. Our core-forest decomposition is to compute a small dense subgraph containing all non-tree edges regarding any spanning tree, which is defined as follows.

Definition 3.1: Given a query q, the **core-forest decomposition** of q is to compute the *minimal connected* subgraph g of q that contains all non-tree edges of q regarding any spanning tree of q; g is called the *core-structure* of q. □

The subgraph of q consisting of all other edges not in the core-structure is called the *forest-structure* of q, denoted T. We prove in Lemma 3.1 that the core-structure of q is exactly the 2-core of q, where a 2-core of q is the maximal subgraph of q such that every vertex in the subgraph has at least two neighbors in the subgraph. Note that, 2-core of q is a vertex-induced subgraph of q, and it is connected and unique [1].

Lemma 3.1: *The core-structure of q is the 2-core of q.* □

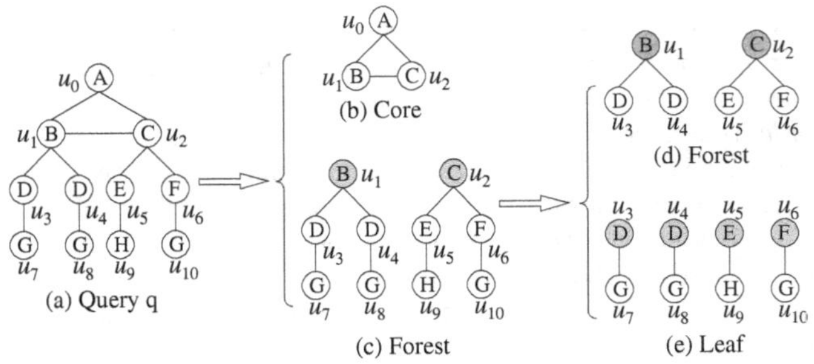

Figure 4: Core-Forest-Leaf Decomposition

We call the vertex set of the core-structure as the *core-set* and denote it as V_C; then, the core-structure is $q[V_C]$. One most important feature of the core-forest decomposition is that the core-structure is the minimal connected subgraph containing all non-tree edges of q regarding any spanning tree of q. As illustrated by *Challenge 1* in Introduction, a good matching order for q needs to conduct all non-tree edge checkings as early as possible, which will not only prune unpromising partial mappings but also reduce the total number of non-tree edge checkings. Thus, we put all vertices of V_C at the beginning of the matching order. Note that, the core-structure is a connected subgraph which is required to generate a connected matching order; this is vital for efficient subgraph matching [4, 15].

Compute Core-Forest Decomposition. Following Lemma 3.1, we compute the core-set V_C by *iteratively* removing all degree-one vertices from q, and the final set of remaining vertices is V_C. This process of iteratively removing degree-one vertices can be implemented in linear time regarding the query size (i.e., in $O(|E(q)|)$ time) [1]. For example, Figures 4(b) and 4(c) show the result of the core-forest decomposition for the query in Figure 4(a). Initially, $\{u_7, u_8, u_9, u_{10}\}$ is the set of degree-one vertices, and its removal creates new degree-one vertices $\{u_3, u_4, u_5, u_6\}$ which are then also removed. Finally, the core-set is $V_C = \{u_0, u_1, u_2\}$ as shown in Figure 4(b). Note that if q itself is a tree, the core-set is simply the root vertex of q, whose selection is discussed in Section A.6 in Appendix; it is possible that the entire query q is the core-structure.

One thing to notice is that, *the forest-structure consists of a set of connected trees and each connected tree in the forest-structure T shares exactly one vertex with the core-structure.* The shared vertex acts as the connection vertex between the tree and the core-structure. For example, u_1 and u_2 are shared by the core-structure and the two connected trees in Figure 4(c), respectively.

Forest-Leaf Decomposition. As illustrated by *Challenge 1* in Introduction, a good matching order also needs to postpone the Cartesian products caused by the candidates of all leaf vertices. Thus, we further decompose the forest-structure T, obtained by the core-forest decomposition, to a *forest-set* V_T and a *leaf-set* V_I, and put all vertices of V_I to the end of the matching order.

Definition 3.2: Given the forest-structure T, the **forest-leaf decomposition** is to compute the set V_I of leaf vertices of T by rooting each tree of T at its connection vertex. The set of other vertices of q not in $V_C \cup V_I$ is called the *forest-set* of q, denoted V_T. □

Thus, $V(q) = V_C \cup V_T \cup V_I$ and $V_C \cap V_T = V_C \cap V_I = V_T \cap V_I = \emptyset$. For example, Figures 4(d) and 4(e) are the results of the forest-leaf decomposition for the forest-structure T in Figure 4(c). In the following, we simply call the subgraph of T after removing all vertices of V_I and their associated edges from T the *forest-structure*.

The CFL-Decomposition based Framework. From the above core-forest-leaf decomposition for a query q, we obtain three vertex sets, the core-set V_C, the forest-set V_T, and the leaf-set V_I. We define a macro ordering of query vertices of q as (V_C, V_T, V_I); that is, we first map vertices of V_C, then vertices of V_T, and finally vertices of V_I, to data vertices. Thus, we propose a new framework towards efficient and scalable subgraph matching, and its pseudocode is shown in Algorithm 1, denoted CFL-Match.

Algorithm 1: CFL-Match

```
Input: a query q and a data graph G
Output: the set M of all embeddings of q in G
1 (V_C, V_T, V_I) ← CFL-Decompose(q);
2 CPI ← CPI-Construct(q, G, V_C);
3 M ← ∅;
4 for each core embedding M_C in Core-Match(V_C, CPI, G) do
5     for each forest embedding M_T in Forest-Match(V_T, CPI, M_C) do
6         M ← M ∪ ({M_C} × {M_T} × Leaf-Match(V_I, CPI, M_C ∪ M_T));
7 return M;
```

Given a query q, we first compute its core-forest-leaf decomposition (V_C, V_T, V_I) (Line 1), which has been discussed in above. Then, we build an auxiliary data structure, called compact path-index (CPI), for the query q regarding the data graph G (Line 2); the details of the CPI construction will be discussed in Section 5. Finally, based on the constructed CPI, we conduct core-match (Line 4), forest-match (Line 5), and leaf-match (Line 6), respectively; the details of these matching algorithms will be discussed in Section 4. Note that, each time when we invoke Core-Match or Forest-Match or Leaf-Match, it returns the next embedding; that is, to save memory space, only one embedding is generated each time.

Benefits of the CFL-Decomposition based Framework. Consider the query q in Figure 1(a) and the data graph G in Figure 1(b) in Introduction. For the matching order $(u_1, u_2, u_3, u_4, u_5, u_6)$ with $u_5.p = u_1$, the search breaths (see Section 2.1) are $B_1 = 1$, $B_2 = 1$, $B_3 = 100$, $B_4 = 100$, and $B_5 = 100$. Since only u_5 has a non-tree edge, the total cost (see Section 2.1) of subgraph matching regarding this matching order is $T_{iso} = B_1 + B_1 \times 1 \times 1 + B_2 \times 100 \times 1 + B_3 \times 1 \times 1 + B_4 \times 1000 \times 2 + B_5 \times 1 \times 1 = 200302$. Our core-forest-leaf decomposition based framework will generate the matching order $(u_1, u_2, u_5, u_3, u_4, u_6)$ which conducts the non-tree edge checkings at an earlier stage, then the cost becomes $T'_{iso} = 2302$ which is significantly smaller than T_{iso}. Moreover, it is immediate that the Cartesian products caused by leaf query vertices are put to the end of the subgraph matching process by our new framework.

4. OUR APPROACHES

In this section, we propose a new auxiliary data structure, called compact path-index (CPI), for efficiently conducting subgraph match. In the following, we first define the compact path-index (CPI) in Section 4.1, and then give our CPI-based core-match, forest-match, and leaf-match in Sections 4.2, 4.3, and 4.4, respectively, while the CPI construction algorithm will be presented in Section 5.

4.1 Auxiliary Data Structure

To compactly encode all possible embeddings of a query in a data graph, we propose a new auxiliary data structure, called compact path-index (CPI). CPI not only prunes false-positive candidates of query vertices, but also serves for the purpose of computing an effective matching order (see Section 4.2).

CPI Structure. Given a query q and a data graph G, CPI is defined regarding a *BFS tree* q_T of q and has the same structure as q_T. To differentiate the vertices of CPI from the vertices of q and G, we call vertices of CPI as *nodes*. Each node u in CPI carries the same label (i.e., $l_q(u)$) as in q_T. Similar to the parent-child relationships in q_T, any two adjacent nodes in CPI also have a parent-child relationship.

The structure of CPI is as follows.

- Each node u of CPI has a *candidate set*, denoted $u.C$, which stores all vertices of G to which u can be mapped.
- There is an edge between $v \in u.C$ and $v' \in u'.C$ for adjacent nodes u and u' in CPI if and only if (v, v') exists in G.

Thus, constructing CPI is equivalent to computing a candidate set $u.C$ for every query vertex u of q.

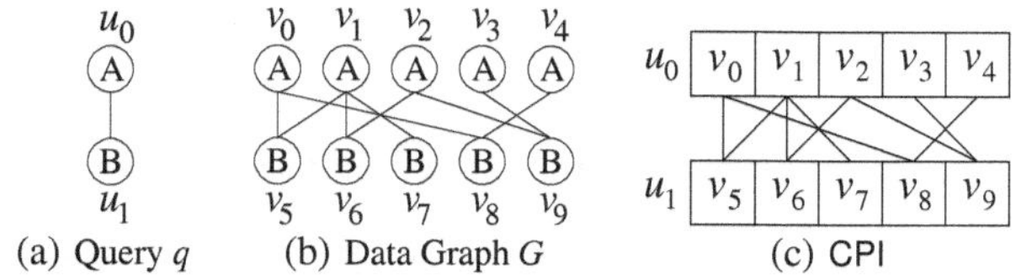

(a) Query q (b) Data Graph G (c) CPI

Figure 5: Example CPI

For example, Figure 5(c) shows the CPI constructed for the query q in Figure 5(a) over the data graph G in Figure 5(b). The candidate sets of u_0 and u_1 are $u_0.C = \{v_0, \ldots, v_4\}$ and $u_1.C = \{v_5, \ldots, v_9\}$, respectively. The edges between vertices in $u_0.C$ and vertices in $u_1.C$ are exactly the same as in the data graph, as shown in the CPI in Figure 5(c). One thing to notice is that, a data vertex of G may appear in the candidate sets of multiple nodes in CPI. Our storage representation of CPI is discussed in Section A.2 in Appendix.

Soundness. Our goal is to directly use the CPI, constructed for a query q over a data graph G, for computing all embeddings of q in G. The data graph G is only probed for non-tree edge checkings (i.e., check whether there exists an edge in G between the mappings of the two end-points of a non-tree edge). To achieve this, the CPI must satisfy the following *soundness requirement*:

- *For every node u in* CPI, *if there is an embedding of q in G that maps u to v, then v must be in $u.C$.*

A CPI is *sound* if it satisfies the soundness requirement. Note that, although in the soundness requirement we only consider candidates of query vertices, the edges between candidates of parent-child query vertices are automatically included based on our CPI definition. Regarding a sound CPI, we have the following theorem.

Theorem 4.1: *Given a sound* CPI, *all embeddings of q in G can be computed by traversing only the* CPI *while G is only probed for non-tree edge checkings.* □

The Size of A Sound CPI. *A naive sound* CPI *can be constructed by letting $u.C$ to be the set of all vertices of G with label $l_q(u)$.* The naive CPI will contain a lot of false-positive candidates for query vertices, which will greatly affect the running time of a subgraph matching algorithm due to generating many partial embeddings that are eventually pruned. One natural goal is to build a minimum and sound CPI; that is, the total size of the candidate sets of query vertices in the CPI is minimum. However, this is NP-hard as shown in the lemma below.

Lemma 4.1: *It is NP-hard to build a minimum and sound* CPI. □

Nevertheless, the worst-case size of the CPI built for a query q over a data graph G is $O(|V(q)| \times |E(G)|)$, though there can be exponential number of embeddings of q in G. This is because, i) the size of the candidate set for a query vertex is at most $|V(G)|$, ii) for any pair (u, u') of parent-child nodes in CPI, the size of all the adjacency lists $N^u_{u'}(\cdot)$ is at most $|E(G)|$ since there is no duplicate edges, and iii) there are $|V(q)|$ query vertices and $(|V(q)| - 1)$ pairs of parent-child nodes. Moreover, for a data graph G with $|\Sigma|$ different labels, the average worst-case size of CPI is $O(\frac{|V(q)| \times |E(G)|}{|\Sigma|^2} + \frac{|V(q)| \times |V(G)|}{|\Sigma|})$. This is because the average size of the candidate set of a query vertex is $|V(G)|/|\Sigma|$, and the average total size of all adjacency lists corresponding to a pair of parent-child query vertices is $|E(G)|/|\Sigma|^2$ since

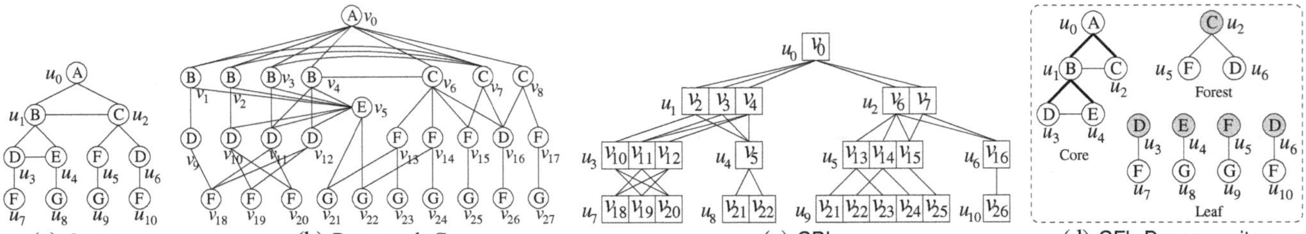

(a) Query q (b) Data graph G (c) CPI (d) CFL-Decompositon

Figure 6: A Running Example

the probability for an edge of G to be in an adjacency list in CPI is $1/|\Sigma|^2$.

In this paper, we aim to build a *small and sound* CPI, which will be discussed in detail in Section 5. For example, Figure 6(c) shows the CPI constructed by our algorithm for the query in Figure 6(a) over the data graph in Figure 6(b).

Remark. Turbo$_{\text{ISO}}$ [8] also proposes an auxiliary data structure to store all path embeddings in a data graph for all root-to-leaf paths of a spanning tree of the query. However, CPI is inherently different. One major difference is that, the data structure in Turbo$_{\text{ISO}}$ can be of exponential size (i.e., with space complexity $O(|V(G)|^{|V(q)|-1})$), and thus the construction time is also exponential. To resolve this, Turbo$_{\text{ISO}}$ [8] only materializes k embeddings for each root-to-leaf query path, where k is the number of subgraph isomorphic embeddings to be reported, when computing the matching order of query vertices; more path embeddings may be materialized on demand when enumerating subgraph isomorphic embeddings. However, we still have to materialize all path embeddings if we want to retrieve all subgraph isomorphic embeddings; that is, the worst case exponential size is unavoidable in Turbo$_{\text{ISO}}$. As a result, Turbo$_{\text{ISO}}$ cannot scale to large queries or large data graphs. Please see Section A.3 in Appendix for a detailed discussion about these issues.

4.2 CPI-based Core-Match

Given a sound CPI for a query q over a data graph G, all embeddings of q in G can be computed by traversing CPI while G is only used for non-tree edge checkings. Here, for presentation simplicity, we assume q itself is the core-structure; otherwise, we only consider the part of CPI corresponding to the core-structure of q. In the following, we first present our CPI-based matching order selection, and then describe the embedding enumeration approach.

4.2.1 CPI-*based Matching Order Selection*

Our algorithm for computing a matching order of query vertices is a *path-based ordering*. Recall that, CPI corresponds to a BFS tree of q, from which we can get a set of root-to-leaf paths $\{\pi_1, \ldots, \pi_k\}$ with all k paths sharing the root node of CPI. Our goal is to compute an effective ordering of the k paths.

The matching order *seq* of query vertices can be obtained from the ordering of paths as follows. Assume the paths are ordered as $(\pi_1, \ldots, \pi_k)$. We initialize *seq* as π_1, and then iteratively add vertices of π_i to *seq* for $i = 2, \ldots, k$. When adding vertices of $\pi_i = (v_{i_1}, \ldots, v_{i_y})$ to *seq*, it is easy to see that π_i shares a prefix with *seq*; we call the last shared vertex v_{i_x} as the *connection vertex* of π_i, and denoted $\pi_i.p$ in analogy to $u.p$ as discussed in Section 2.1. Then, we add vertices $v_{i_x+1}, \ldots, v_{i_y}$ of π_i to *seq*. For example, for the CPI in Figure 6(c), the BFS tree of the core-structure consists of three paths $\pi_1 = (u_0, u_1, u_3), \pi_2 = (u_0, u_1, u_4)$ and $\pi_3 = (u_0, u_2)$. Assume the ordering of paths is (π_2, π_1, π_3), then the matching order of query vertices is $(u_0, u_1, u_4, u_3, u_2)$.

Cost Analysis of Subgraph Matching via Path-based Ordering. Recall from Section 2.1 that, the total cost of a subgraph matching algorithm based on the matching order $(u_1, \ldots, u_n)$ is $T_{iso} = B_1 + \sum_{i=2}^{n} \sum_{j=1}^{B_{i-1}} d_i^j (r_i + 1)$ [15]. For a path-based ordering $(\pi_1, \ldots, \pi_k)$, assume the matching order is $(u_1, \ldots, u_n)$ and the position of the leaf (i.e. last) vertex of π_i in the matching order is l_i. Then, the matching cost is rewritten as,

$$
\begin{aligned}
T_{iso} &= B_1 + \textstyle\sum_{i=2}^{l_1} \sum_{j=1}^{B_{i-1}} d_i^j + \sum_{x=2}^{k} \sum_{i=l_{x-1}+1}^{l_x} \sum_{j=1}^{B_{i-1}} d_i^j (r_i + 1) \\
&\approx \textstyle\sum_{i=1}^{l_1} B_i + \sum_{x=2}^{k} \sum_{i=l_{x-1}+1}^{l_x} B_i (r_i + 1) \\
&\approx B_{l_1} + \textstyle\sum_{i=2}^{k} B_{l_i} (r_{l_i} + 1)
\end{aligned}
$$

where the first equation follows from the fact that there is no non-tree edge among vertices on the same root-to-leaf path in a BFS tree, and the next two equations follow from two assumptions: 1) $\sum_{j=1}^{B_{i-1}} d_i^j \approx B_i$, and 2) $\sum_{i=l_{x-1}+1}^{l_x} B_i (r_i + 1) \approx B_{l_x} (r_{l_x} + 1)$. Note that, with the help of CPI, given a partial mapping $(v_1, \ldots, v_{i-1})$ of query vertices $(u_1, \ldots, u_{i-1})$, the partial mapping is extended by considering each vertex $v \in N_{u_i}^{u_j}(v_j)$ in CPI as a candidate of u_i, where u_j is the parent of u_i in CPI. The first assumption says that each extension of an embedding of $(u_1, \ldots, u_{i-1})$ based on $N_{u_i}^{u_j}(v_j)$ in CPI will lead to an embedding of $(u_1, \ldots, u_i)$; this is based on the fact that the pruning of non-tree edges has already been exploited in building the CPI (see Section 5). The second assumption naturally follows from the path-based ordering strategy; that is, we assume that the largest cost of mapping vertices of a query path determines the cost of mapping the path.

Greedy Approach to Ordering Paths. Note that the number of non-tree edges (i.e., r_i) between u_i and vertices before u_i in the matching order depends on the actual matching order. Since the total number of configurations of r_is is exponential (i.e., $O(|V(q)|!)$), it will be too expensive to optimize T_{iso} on the fly by considering r_i. Thus, we instead minimize an approximation of T_{iso}, $\tilde{T}_{iso} = \sum_{i=1}^{k} B_{l_i}$ (i.e., the total size of the search breadths of leaf vertices of q_T). Nevertheless, this is still a hard problem. We propose a greedy approach for ordering paths aiming to minimize $\tilde{T}_{iso}$.

The first path is the one with the minimum number of embeddings (i.e., $\arg\min_{\pi \in \mathcal{P}} c(\pi)$), where $\mathcal{P}$ is the set of all paths and $c(\pi_1, \ldots, \pi_i)$ is the number of embeddings in CPI for the tree formed by these paths. Given a set of chosen paths P, the next path is the one that together with P have the minimum number of embeddings (i.e., $\arg\min_{\pi \in \mathcal{P} \setminus P} c(P \cup \pi)$, or equivalently $\arg\min_{\pi \in \mathcal{P} \setminus P} \frac{c(P \cup \pi)}{c(P)}$). Here, $\frac{c(P \cup \pi)}{c(P)}$ can be estimated as $\frac{c(\pi^u)}{|u.C|}$, where $u = \pi.p$ is the connection vertex of π to P and π^u is the suffix of π starting from u. Intuitively, each embedding of P can be extended to $\frac{c(\pi^u)}{|u.C|}$ embeddings of $P \cup \pi$.

Estimate $c(\pi)$. Recall that π is a query path in CPI. Although the embeddings of π are not explicitly stored in CPI, we can estimate the number of such embeddings by a dynamic programming algorithm. We illustrate the dynamic programming algorithm by an example. Consider estimating the number of embeddings of the path $\pi = (u_0, u_1, u_3, u_7)$ in Figure 6(c). For each vertex $v \in u.C$ with $u \in \pi$, we compute $c_u(v)$, the number of embeddings in CPI for the subgraph of q induced by the suffix of π starting from u such that

u is mapped to v. Initially, $c_u(v) = 1$ for the leaf vertex u; that is, $c_{u_7}(v_{18}) = c_{u_7}(v_{19}) = c_{u_7}(v_{20}) = 1$. Then, we compute such numbers in a bottom-up fashion, $c_u(v) = \sum_{v' \in N^u_{u'}(v)} c_{u'}(v')$; for example, $c_{u_3}(v_{10}) = c_{u_7}(v_{19}) + c_{u_7}(v_{20}) = 2$. Finally, $c(\pi) = \sum_{v \in u.C} c_u(v)$ where u is the first vertex of π. The running time is linear to the total size of all adjacency lists corresponding to edges of π.

The Greedy Algorithm. The greedy algorithm for ordering all root-to-leaf paths in the BFS tree q_T of q is shown in Algorithm 2. The first path is the path with the minimum number of embeddings discounted by the number of non-tree edges of vertices on the path (Lines 2–3). Then, we iteratively select the next path, which is the one minimizing $\frac{c(\pi^u)}{|u.C|}$ where $u = \pi.p$ is the connection vertex of π to seq (i.e., the last shared vertex between π and seq) (Lines 4–6).

Algorithm 2: Matching-Order

Input: A BFS tree q_T of q and the corresponding CPI
Output: The matching order of query vertices

```
1 𝒫 ← all root-to-leaf paths in q_T;
2 π* ← arg min_{π∈𝒫} c(π)/|NT(π)|; /* NT(π): non-tree edges of π */;
3 Add vertices of π* to seq; 𝒫 ← 𝒫\{π*};
4 while 𝒫 ≠ ∅ do
5     π* ← arg min_{π∈𝒫} c(π^u)/|u.C|;          /* u = π.p */;
6     Add vertices of π* to seq; 𝒫 ← 𝒫\{π*};
7 return seq;
```

Time Complexity. Let $\bar{N}^u_{u'}$ denote the average total size of adjacency lists corresponding to each pair of parent-child nodes in CPI. Then, the time complexity of Algorithm 2 is $O(\bar{N}^u_{u'} \times (\sum_{\pi \in \mathcal{P}} |\pi|))$, where $\mathcal{P}$ is the set of all root-to-leaf paths in CPI and $|\pi|$ is the number of edges in π. Note that $\sum_{\pi \in \mathcal{P}} |\pi|$ is guaranteed to be at most the number of leaf nodes in CPI multiplied by the height of CPI. This time complexity can be achieved by computing $c(\pi^u)$ for each suffix of $\pi \in \mathcal{P}$ in a bottom-up fashion, as described in *Estimate* $c(\pi)$ in above.

Example 4.1: Consider the CPI in Figure 6(c) and the core-structure in Figure 6(d). There are three root-to-leaf paths, $\pi_1 = (u_0, u_1, u_3)$, $\pi_2 = (u_0, u_1, u_4)$, and $\pi_3 = (u_0, u_2)$, with $c(\pi_1) = 4$, $c(\pi_2) = 3$, and $c(\pi_3) = 2$. Since $|NT(\pi_1)| = |NT(\pi_2)| = 2$ and $|NT(\pi_3)| = 1$, the first path is π_2. Then, $\pi_1.p = u_1$, $\pi_3.p = u_0$, $c(\pi_1^{u_1}) = 4$, and $c(\pi_3^{u_0}) = 2$. Thus, the second path is π_1 with $c(\pi_1^{u_1})/|u_1.C| = 4/3$. The third path is π_3, and the matching order is $(u_0, u_1, u_4, u_3, u_2)$. □

4.2.2 CPI-*based Embedding Enumeration*

Given a CPI and a matching order $(u_1, \ldots, u_{|V(q)|})$, the embeddings of q in G are enumerated by Core-Match, where the pseudocode is shown in Section A.4 (Algorithm 5) in Appendix. We iteratively map each query vertex u_i to a data vertex regarding the matching order. 1) If all query vertices are mapped (i.e., $i = |V(q)| + 1$), then we output the embedding. 2) If this is the first query vertex (i.e., $i = 1$), then we map u_1 to a data vertex $v \in u_1.C$ in CPI. 3) Otherwise, u_i has a parent $u_i.p$ in the matching order, and $u_i.p$ has been mapped to $M(u_i.p)$; the candidates of u_i are obtained from the adjacency list $N^{u_i.p}_{u_i}(M(u_i.p))$ in CPI, and we map u_i to each candidate each time and proceed to the next query vertex u_{i+1}.

Remark. We do not compress the core-structure by the query graph compression technique in $\text{Turbo}_{\text{ISO}}$ [8]. This is because for randomly generated queries as tested in our experiments, their core-structures can hardly be compressed; for example, the core-structures can only be reduced on average by less than 1 vertex (i.e., most core-structures cannot be compressed); see Table 4 in Appendix.

4.3 CPI-based Forest-Match

Our CPI-based forest-match is similar to the core-match in Section 4.2, except that the forest-structure may consist of multiple connected trees. Also note that the forest-structure has no non-tree edges. Following the path-ordering strategy in Section 4.2, we first estimate the number of embeddings in CPI for each connected tree, and then order the connected trees in increasing order regarding their number of embeddings; the root-to-leaf paths in each connected tree are then ordered by Algorithm 2. In this way, we obtain the matching order of query vertices in the forest-structure.

The embedding enumeration algorithm for forest-structure is similar to Core-Match in Algorithm 5 except that we do not need to conduct non-tree edge checkings. Thus, *the data graph G is not probed for forest-match.* We omit the details of these algorithms.

Remark. We do not compress the forest-structure by the compression technique in $\text{Turbo}_{\text{ISO}}$ [8], because the forest-structure in a query q cannot be compressed based on the lemma below.

Lemma 4.2: *The compression technique in* $\text{Turbo}_{\text{ISO}}$ *[8] for compressing a query q cannot compress the forest-structure of q. That is, there is no two vertices in the forest-set that have the same labels and the same neighborhoods.* □

4.4 CPI-based Leaf-Match

In this subsection, we propose an efficient technique for enumerating all embeddings of the leaf-set V_I, given an embedding M_C of the core-set V_C and an embedding M_T of the forest-set V_T. Note that, $V_C \cup V_T \cup V_I = V(q)$.

Based on M_C and M_T, we first compute a candidate set $C(u)$ for each query vertex $u \in V_I$. Specifically, $C(u) = N^{u.p}_u(M(u.p)) \backslash (M_C \cup M_T)$; that is, $C(u)$ is the set of vertices in the adjacency list of $N^{u.p}_u(v)$ excluding those vertices being used in $M_C \cup M_T$, where $v = M(u.p)$ is the data vertex to which $u.p$ maps in $M_C \cup M_T$. Note that, $C(u) \subseteq u.C$ where $u.C$ is the set of candidates of u in CPI. For example, in Figure 6, $V_I = \{u_7, u_8, u_9, u_{10}\}$. Assume u_3 $(= u_7.p)$, u_4 $(= u_8.p)$, u_5 $(= u_9.p)$, u_6 $(= u_{10}.p)$ are mapped to $v_{12}, v_5, v_{13}, v_{16}$, respectively, then $C(u_7) = \{v_{18}, v_{19}\}$, $C(u_8) = \{v_{21}, v_{22}\}$, $C(u_9) = \{v_{21}, v_{23}\}$, $C(u_{10}) = \{v_{26}\}$.

Then, our technique is based on the following lemma.

Lemma 4.3: *For any two query vertices, u and u′, in V_I, if the labels of u and u′ are different (i.e., $l_q(u) \neq l_q(u')$), then $C(u) \cap C(u') = \emptyset$.* □

Thus, we partition query vertices of V_I into label classes depending on their labels. A *label class* with label a, denoted S_{a}, consists of all vertices of V_I with label a, and we denote the set of label classes of V_I by $\mathcal{S}$. After generating all embeddings of each label class S_{a} in $\mathcal{S}$, the embeddings of V_I can be obtained as a Cartesian product of embeddings for all different label classes. For example, continue the above example, there are two label classes, $S_{\mathsf{G}} = \{u_8, u_9\}$ and $S_{\mathsf{F}} = \{u_7, u_{10}\}$. After generating embeddings for these two label classes, $\mathcal{M}(u_8, u_9) = \{(v_{21}, v_{23}), (v_{22}, v_{21}), (v_{22}, v_{23})\}$ and $\mathcal{M}(u_7, u_{10}) = \{(v_{18}, v_{26}), (v_{19}, v_{26})\}$, we obtain $|\mathcal{M}(u_8, u_9)| \times |\mathcal{M}(u_7, u_{10})| = 3 \times 2 = 6$ embeddings of V_I.

Generate Embeddings for a Label Class. Firstly, we merge all vertices of S_{a} that have the same parents into neighborhood equivalence class (NEC) vertices. Note that, these NEC vertices are exactly the same as that obtained by the compression technique in $\text{Turbo}_{\text{ISO}}$ [8]; that is, a degree-one vertex can only be in the same NEC with another degree-one vertex. Moreover, all vertices in the same NEC have the same set of candidates. Thus, we will be dealing with this updated label class S_{a} which contains NEC vertices.

We sort all vertices of S_a in increasing order according to their numbers of candidates (i.e., $|C(u)|$), and then iteratively map each query vertex u to a data vertex in $C(u)$ according to this order. Note that, for an NEC vertex u' of cardinality $|u'|$ (i.e., containing $|u'|$ query vertices), we map u' to a combination, instead of a permutation, of $|u'|$ vertices from $C(u')$. The set of all embeddings can be obtained if needed, by permuting the mappings for query vertices in each NEC vertex.

Compared with the compression technique in Turbo$_{ISO}$ [8], we not only consider NEC vertices but also put all leaf query vertices with the same label together (i.e., label class). Note that, only query vertices with the same label may conflict with each other; that is, two query vertices with the same label are not allowed to be mapped to the same data vertex in the same mapping. Thus, by putting query vertices with the same label together, we are able to prune unpromising partial embeddings at early stages.

Remark. Note that, the concept of leaf-set V_l can be generalized to an *independent-set* (i.e., there is no edge between any two vertices in the independent-set) of query vertices of q. Nevertheless, we show that the leaf-set V_l is the maximal possible independent-set of the forest-structure of q; details are in Section A.5 in Appendix.

5. CPI CONSTRUCTION

In this section, we develop efficient techniques for constructing a small and sound CPI. Since constructing the smallest sound CPI is NP-hard as proved in Lemma 4.1, we propose a heuristic approach for constructing CPI in two phases: top-down construction (see Section 5.2) and bottom-up refinement (see Section 5.3), where both tree edges and non-tree edges are exploited to prune false-positive candidates of query vertices (see Section 5.4). In the following, we first present the general idea of our CPI construction algorithms in Section 5.1.

5.1 General Idea

The CPI is constructed regarding a BFS tree q_T of q. The selection of the root vertex r of q_T is discussed in Section A.6 in Appendix. Then, vertices of q are partitioned according to their BFS levels where the BFS level of a vertex of q_T is one plus its distance to r in q_T; edges of q are partitioned into tree edges and non-tree edges. The non-tree edges are further categorized as follows.

Definition 5.1: For a non-tree edge (u, u') in q regarding q_T, if u and u' are at the same BFS levels in q_T, then (u, u') is called a **same-level non-tree edge (S-NTE)**; otherwise (u, u') is called a **cross-level non-tree edge (C-NTE)**. □

For example, consider the query q in Figure 7(a). Assume u_0 is the root vertex, the BFS tree q_T is shown in Figure 7(b), and the non-tree edges are (u_1, u_2) and (u_2, u_3), where (u_1, u_2) is a S-NTE and (u_2, u_3) is a C-NTE.

Following Section 4.1, the general idea of our CPI construction is to compute the candidate set $u.C$ for each vertex u in q, while the induced edges in G between $v \in u.C$ and vertices of $u'.C$ are stored as an adjacency list $N^u_{u'}(v)$ in CPI, regarding the tree edge (u, u') of q_T. Thus, the main issue is to construct a sound CPI such that $u.C$ is as small as possible for each $u \in V(q)$. However, we proved in Lemma 4.1 that this is NP-hard. Thus, we propose a heuristic approach for constructing a small CPI based on the following idea.

- *A data vertex v can be pruned from $u.C$ if there exists a neighbor u' of u in q such that $u'.C$ contains none of the neighbors of v in G (i.e., $u'.C \cap N_G(v) = \emptyset$).*

Equivalently, $u.C$ can be obtained as the intersection of the sets of neighbors, with label $l_q(u)$, of vertices in $u'.C$ for all $u' \in N_q(u)$. Thus, following the above general idea, we propose to construct the CPI in two phases: top-down construction, and bottom-up refinement, as will be discussed in the following two subsections.

5.2 Top-Down Construction

Given a BFS tree q_T of the query q, the CPI is constructed by visiting query vertices level-by-level in a top-down manner, in which we also utilize the pruning power of non-tree edges to prune unpromising candidates. The algorithm is shown in Algorithm 3.

Firstly, we obtain the candidates for the root query vertex r, which are the vertices in G that have label $l_q(r)$ and degree at least $d_q(r)$ and also pass the candidate-verification (CandVerify) (Lines 1–2). CandVerify basically verifies whether a data vertex conforms with the local features of the query vertex, which is discussed in Section A.6 in the Appendix. We mark r as visited and set $v.cnt$ to be 0 for all vertices v in G (Line 3), where $v.cnt$ will later be used to determine whether a vertex is qualified to be a candidate.

Then, we process query vertices level-by-level (Lines 4–28) and for query vertices at the same level, we 1) firstly generate their sets of candidates in the forward processing, 2) then prune unpromising candidates in the backward processing, and 3) finally construct the adjacency lists corresponding to query vertices and their parents in q_T. Assume the set of vertices at level lev is V_{lev}.

1) Forward Candidate Generation. In the forward processing, we process query vertices according to their order in V_{lev}. In processing query vertex u, let $u.N$ denote the set of visited neighbors of u in q, and $u.UN$ denote the set of unvisited neighbors of u in q that are at the same BFS level as u in q_T. $u.UN$ is obtained at Lines 7–9, and will be used in the backward processing (see Line 20). The set $u.C$ of candidates of u is generated from the sets of candidates of vertices in $u.N$ (Lines 11–16). Intuitively, *a data vertex v is in $u.C$ only if for each $u' \in u.N$, there is a data vertex $v' \in u'.C$ that is adjacent to v.* To achieve this, we maintain a counter $v.cnt$ for each data vertex in G to count the number of visited query neighbors of u that have a candidate v' adjacent to v. The counters of vertices (i.e., $v.cnt$) are updated at Lines 11-13, and Cnt records the number of query vertices in $u.N$ (Line 14). The candidate $u.C$ is the set of vertices satisfying $v.cnt = Cnt$ and also passing CandVerify (Lines 15–16), following Lemma 5.1. Then we mark u as visited, and reset $v.cnt$ to be 0 for every vertex v that has a positive count (i.e., $v.cnt > 0$) (Line 17). Note that, to reset $v.cnt$, we only need to access those vertices with positive counts, which are stored when we change $v.cnt$ at Line 13.

Lemma 5.1: *Through lines 6–14 of Algorithm 3, a data vertex v with label $l_q(u)$ has a neighbor in $u'.C$ for every $u' \in u.N$ if and only if $v.cnt = Cnt$ (i.e., Line 15).* □

2) Backward Candidate Pruning. In the backward processing, we apply Lemma 5.1 again to filter candidates for each query vertex u based on its set of unvisited neighbors (i.e., $u.UN$), which were not exploited in the forward processing. In contrast to the forward processing, now we process query vertices V_{lev} in reverse order (Lines 18–23). For each $u \in V_{lev}$, we apply Lemma 5.1; a vertex $v \in u.C$ is pruned if $v.cnt \neq |u.UN|$ (Lines 21–22).

3) Adjacency List Construction. After every query vertex $u \in V_{lev}$ has been assigned a set $u.C$ of candidates, the adjacency lists corresponding to tree edge (u_p, u), where $u_p = u.p$ is the parent of u in q_T, is constructed (Lines 26–28). For each data vertex $v \in u_p.C$, an adjacency list $N^{u_p}_u(v)$ is constructed, which is the set of data vertices in $u.C$ that are connected to v; that is, $N^{u_p}_u(v) = \{v' \in u.C \mid (v, v') \in E(G)\}$ (Lines 27–28). Note that, $u_p.C$ has already been constructed in the iteration for processing query vertices at level $lev - 1$.

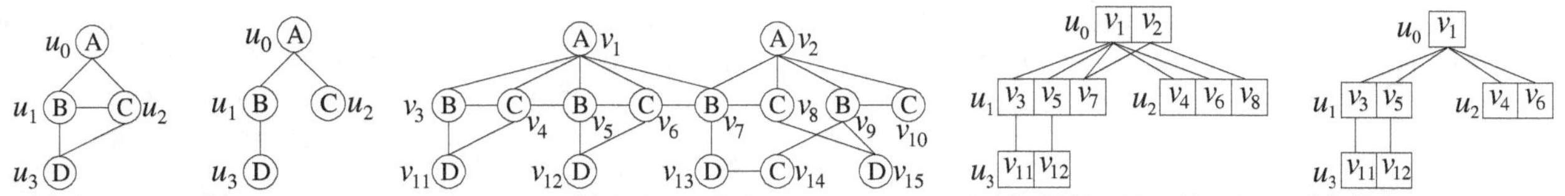

(a) Query q (b) BFS tree q_T (c) Data graph G (d) CPI by Algorithm 3 (e) CPI by Algorithm 4

Figure 7: Example CPI Construction

Algorithm 3: Top-Down Construction

```
Input: A query q and its root vertex r, and a data graph G
Output: the CPI of q over G

1  for each v in G with label l_q(r) and degree at least d_q(r) do
2      if CandVerify(v, r) then r.C ← r.C ∪ {v};
3  Mark r as visited; Set v.cnt ← 0 for all v in G;
4  for each level lev from 2 to max_level do
       /* Lines 5-17: Forward Candidate Generation */
5      for each query vertex u at level lev do
6          Cnt ← 0;
7          for each query vertex u' ∈ N_q(u) do
8              if u' is unvisited and (u', u) is a S-NTE then
9                  u.UN ← u.UN ∪ {u'};
10             else if u' is visited then
11                 for each vertex v' ∈ u'.C do
12                     for each vertex v ∈ N_G(v') with label l_q(u) and
                       degree at least d_q(u) do
13                         if v.cnt = Cnt then v.cnt ← v.cnt + 1 ;
14                 Cnt ← Cnt + 1;
15         for each vertex v in G with v.cnt = Cnt do
16             if CandVerify(v, u) then u.C ← u.C ∪ {v};
17         Mark u as visited; Reset v.cnt ← 0 for all v in G s.t. v.cnt > 0;
       /* Lines 18-23: Backward Candidate Pruning */
18     for each query vertex u at level lev in reverse order do
19         Cnt ← 0;
20         for each query vertex u' ∈ u.UN do Same as Lines 11–14;
21         for each vertex v ∈ u.C do
22             if v.cnt ≠ Cnt then Remove v from u.C;
23         Reset v.cnt ← 0 for all v in G s.t. v.cnt > 0;
       /* Lines 24-28: Adjacency List Construction */
24     for each query vertex u at level lev do
25         u_p ← u.p;
26         for each vertex v_p ∈ u_p.C do
27             for each vertex v ∈ N_G(v_p) with label l_q(u) do
28                 if v ∈ u.C then N_u^{u_p}(v_p) ← N_u^{u_p}(v_p) ∪ {v};
29 return CPI;
```

Example 5.1: Consider the query q in Figure 7(a) with the BFS tree in Figure 7(b) where u_0 is the root vertex. Then, vertices of q are partitioned into three levels, with u_0 at level 1, $\{u_1, u_2\}$ at level 2, and u_3 at level 3. Firstly, we process vertices at level 1 (i.e., u_0). The set of candidates of u_0 is assigned as $u_0.C = \{v_1, v_2\}$.

Secondly, we consider vertices at level 2 (i.e., u_1 and u_2). *1) In the forward processing*, we first process u_1 with $u_1.N = \{u_0\}$ and $u_1.UN = \{u_2\}$; $u_1.C$ is assigned to be the set of vertices with label $l_q(u_1)$ that are adjacent to a vertex in $u_0.C$, and $u_1.C = \{v_3, v_5, v_7, v_9\}$. Then, we process u_2 with $u_2.N = \{u_0, u_1\}$ and $u_2.UN = \emptyset$; $u_2.C$ is assigned as $\{v_4, v_6, v_8\}$. Note that, although v_{10} also satisfies the requirement specified by Lemma 5.1, v_{10} is pruned by the CandVerify due to having no neighbor with label D which is required by u_2. *2) In the backward processing*, v_9 is also pruned from $u_1.C$ due to having no neighbor in $u_2.C$; recall that $u_1.UN = \{u_2\}$. *3) In adjacency list construction*, the adjacency lists corresponding to (u_0, u_1) and to (u_0, u_2) are constructed as shown in Figure 7(d).

Finally, we process vertices at level 3 (i.e., u_3). Since there is only one query vertex at this level, we only have the *forward processing*; $u_3.N = \{u_1, u_2\}$, and $u_3.C = \{v_{11}, v_{12}\}$. Vertices v_{13} and v_{15} are pruned due to having no neighbors in $u_2.C$ or in $u_1.C$, respectively. The adjacency lists corresponding to $(u_3.p, u_3)$ (i.e., (u_1, u_3)) are constructed as shown in Figure 7(d). □

5.3 Bottom-Up Refinement

Note that the top-down construction algorithm in Section 5.2 only considers the ancestors (i.e., parent, parent of parent, $\cdots$) in q_T of a query vertex u to construct $u.C$. Thus, it is possible that a candidate vertex $v \in u.C$ does not have any neighbor in $u'.C$, where u' is a child of u in q_T. For example, in Figure 7(d), v_7 in $u_1.C$ does not have any neighbor in $u_3.C$; or equivalently, $N_{u_3}^{u_1}(v_7) = \emptyset$. In this subsection, we propose a bottom-up refinement approach for further refining the candidates of query vertices.

Algorithm 4: Bottom-Up Refinement

```
Input: A query q and its root vertex r, a data graph G, and a CPI
Output: The refined CPI

1  for each query vertex u of q in a bottom-up fashion do
       /* Lines 2-7: Candidate Refinement */
2      Cnt ← 0;
3      for each lower-level neighbor u' of u in q do
4          Same as Lines 11–14 of Algorithm 3;
5      for each vertex v ∈ u.C do
6          if v.cnt ≠ Cnt then Remove v from u.C and remove all
           adjacency lists of v from the CPI;
7      Reset v.cnt ← 0 for all v in G s.t. v.cnt > 0;
       /* Lines 8-11: Adjacency List Pruning */
8      for each vertex v ∈ u.C do
9          for each child u' of u in the BFS tree of q do
10             for each vertex v' ∈ N_{u'}^u(v) do
11                 if v' ∉ u'.C then N_{u'}^u(v) ← N_{u'}^u(v)\{v'};
12 return CPI;
```

The pseudocode of bottom-up refinement is shown in Algorithm 4. We process query vertices of q in a bottom-up fashion regarding q_T (Line 1). Note that, here the order of query vertices at the same BFS level can be arbitrary since we do not consider the S-NTE in this bottom-up refinement process. Firstly, in *candidate refinement*, similar to Lines 18–23 of Algorithm 3 we exploit the candidate sets of lower-level neighbors of u to prune unpromising candidates from $u.C$ (Lines 2–7). Then, in *adjacency list pruning*, we remove from each adjacency list $N_{u'}^u(v)$ those vertices that are not in $u'.C$ (Lines 8–11).

Example 5.2: Continuing Example 5.1, we refine the candidates for query vertices of q in a bottom-up fashion regarding q_T; assume they are processed in the order of u_3, u_2, u_1, u_0. Firstly, u_3 has no lower-level neighbors, and we do nothing. In processing u_2, we refine the candidates $u_2.C$ of u_2 by the candidates $u_3.C$ of u_3; v_8 is pruned from $u_2.C$ since it has no neighbors in $u_3.C$. Next, in processing u_1, v_7 is pruned from $u_1.C$, and the adjacency lists of v_7 are also removed, as shown in Figure 7(e). Finally, we process u_0;

v_2 is pruned from $u_0.C$ due to the same reason, and the adjacency lists of v_2 are removed. Moreover, we also need to remove v_7 from the adjacency list $N_{u_1}^{u_0}(v_1)$ of v_1, since v_7 is no longer a candidate of u_1. The final CPI after refinement is shown in Figure 7(e). □

5.4 Analysis of CPI Construction

Pruning Power of Tree Edges and Non-Tree Edges. In our CPI construction (i.e., Algorithms 3 and 4), we exploit both tree edges and non-tree edges as well as both directions of these edges to refine candidates for query vertices. That is, for a query edge (u, u') in q, we exploit the candidates $u.C$ of u to refine the candidates $u'.C$ of u' as well as exploit $u'.C$ to refine $u.C$; for example, if a candidate $v \in u.C$ has no neighbors in $u'.C$, then v is pruned from $u.C$. The directions of query edges that are utilized for pruning in different processing stages are summarized in Table 2, where the direction (e.g., $\rightarrow$, $\leftarrow$, $\downarrow$, $\uparrow$) indicates the direction of a unidirectional edge regarding an ordered BFS tree; for example, in Figure 7(a), $u_1 \rightarrow u_2$, $u_2 \leftarrow u_1$, $u_1 \downarrow u_3$, and $u_3 \uparrow u_1$. More details and an example are given in Section A.7 in Appendix.

Algorithms	Query Edges	Directions
Top-down construction (Algorithm 3)	Tree edges & C-NTEs	$\downarrow$
	S-NTEs	$\rightarrow$, $\leftarrow$
Bottom-up refinement (Algorithm 4)	Tree edges & C-NTEs	$\uparrow$

Table 2: Directions of Query Edges Utilized in Pruning

Correctness. We prove the correctness of our CPI construction (i.e., Algorithms 3 and 4) by the following two lemmas.

Lemma 5.2: *For a data vertex $v \in V(G)$ and a query vertex $u \in V(q)$, if there is an embedding M of q in G that maps u to v, then after running Algorithm 3, v is a candidate of u (i.e., $v \in u.C$). That is, the* CPI *constructed by Algorithm 3 is sound.* □

Lemma 5.3: *Given a sound* CPI*, after the bottom-up refinement (i.e., running Algorithm 4), the* CPI *is still sound.* □

Time Complexity. The time complexities of Algorithms 3 and 4 are shown in the following theorem.

Theorem 5.1: *Both Algorithm 3 and Algorithm 4 take time $O(|E(G)| \times |E(q)|)$.* □

6. EXPERIMENTS

We conduct extensive performance studies to evaluate the efficiency of our core-forest-leaf decomposition based framework and our CPI-based matching algorithms. Specifically, the following existing algorithms are evaluated.

- QuickSI: the algorithm in [15].
- Turbo$_{\text{ISO}}$: the state-of-the-art algorithm in [8].
- Turbo$_{\text{ISO}}$-Boost: the Turbo$_{\text{ISO}}$ algorithm boosted by the data graph compression techniques in [14].

We also evaluate the following variants of our algorithms.

- CFL-Match: our core-forest-leaf decomposition based algorithm (see Section 3) with the proposed CPI constructed by Algorithms 3 and 4 (see Section 5) (i.e., *our best algorithm*).
- CFL-Match-Boost: the CFL-Match algorithm boosted by the data graph compression techniques in [14].
- CFL-Match-Naive: the CFL-Match algorithm where the CPI is naively constructed (see Section 4.1).
- CFL-Match-TD: the CFL-Match algorithm where the CPI is constructed by Algorithm 3 in Section 5.2.
- CF-Match: the core-forest decomposition based algorithm (see Section 3) with the proposed CPI (see Section 5); that is, the forest-leaf decomposition is not applied.
- Match: the subgraph matching algorithm without query decomposition and with the proposed CPI; that is, apply the core-match algorithm in Section 4.2 on the entire query q.

All algorithms are implemented in C++ and compiled with GNU GCC with the -O3 flag; source codes of the existing algorithms, QuickSI [15], Turbo$_{\text{ISO}}$ [8], and Turbo$_{\text{ISO}}$-Boost [14], are obtained from their authors, respectively. Experiments are conducted on a machine with an Intel i5 3.20GHz CPU and 8GB memory.

Datasets. We evaluate the performance of the tested algorithms on both real and synthetic graphs as follows.

Real Graphs. We evaluate the algorithms on three real graphs, HPRD[1], Yeast, and Human, which are widely used in existing works [8, 12, 14, 22]. All the three graphs are protein interaction networks where vertex labels are generated under the *Gene Ontology Term*. *HPRD* contains 37,081 edges, 9,460 vertices with an average degree 7.8, and 307 distinct labels. *Yeast* contains 12,519 edges, 3,112 vertices with an average degree 8.1, and 71 distinct labels. *Human* is a dense graph of human protein interactions, which contains 86,282 edges, 4,674 vertices with an average degree 36.9, and 44 distinct labels. We also tested the algorithms on WordNet and DBLP (see Eval-A-II in Appendix), and get similar results.

Synthetic Graphs. We also generate large synthetic data graphs to evaluate the algorithms. We first randomly generate a spanning tree and then randomly add edges to the spanning tree, while vertex labels are added following the power-law distribution. The default settings of synthetic graphs are: $|V(G)| = 100k$ *(i.e., 10^5 vertices)*, $d(G) = 8$ *(i.e., the average degree is 8), and* $|\Sigma| = 50$ *(i.e. the number of distinct labels is 50).* Note that the smaller the number of distinct labels, the more challenging. The following synthetic data graphs are generated to test the scalability of our algorithms.

- *Vary $|V(G)|$*: We generate 3 data graphs denoted by G_{100k}, G_{500k}, and G_{1000k}, where each G_{ik} has ik $(= i \times 10^3)$ vertices with the default settings of $d(G)$ and $|\Sigma|$.
- *Vary $d(G)$*: We generate 4 data graphs denoted by $G_{d=4}$, $G_{d=8}$, $G_{d=16}$, and $G_{d=32}$, where each $G_{d=i}$ has an average degree of i with the default settings of $|V(G)|$ and $|\Sigma|$.
- *Vary $|\Sigma|$*: We generate 4 data graphs denoted by $G_{L=25}$, $G_{L=50}$, $G_{L=100}$, $G_{L=200}$, where each $G_{L=i}$ contains i distinct vertex labels with the default settings of $|V(G)|$ and $d(G)$.

Data graphs	Query Sets	Default
HPRD, Yeast, Synthetic	q_{25S}, q_{25N}, q_{50S}, q_{50N} q_{100S}, q_{100N}, q_{200S}, q_{200N}	q_{50S}, q_{50N}
Human	q_{10S}, q_{10N}, q_{15S}, q_{15N} q_{20S}, q_{20N}, q_{25S}, q_{25N}	q_{15S}, q_{15N}

Table 3: Default Query Sets

Query Graphs. A query graph is generated as a connected subgraph of the data graph, by conducting random walk on the data graph. For each data graph, we generate 8 query sets, each containing 100 query graphs of the same size, as summarized in Table 3. In specific, for HPRD, Yeast, and Synthetic graphs, we generate query sets q_{25S}, q_{25N}, q_{50S}, q_{50N}, q_{100S}, q_{100N}, q_{200S}, and q_{200N}, where q_{iS} and q_{iN} denote query sets with i vertices and, respectively, average degree ≤ 3 (i.e., **S**parse) and > 3 (i.e., **N**on-sparse); q_{50S} *and* q_{50N} *are default query sets.* For Human which is a harder data graph for subgraph matching due to a higher average degree and fewer distinct labels, we generate smaller query sets q_{10S}, q_{10N}, q_{15S}, q_{15N}, q_{20S}, q_{20N}, q_{25S}, and q_{25N}, with q_{15S} *and* q_{15N} *being the default.*

[1] http://www.hprd.org/download/

#Embeddings. We vary the number of embeddings to be reported, from 10^3 to 10^5 and 10^8 with *#embeddings* = 10^5 *being the default.* Note that, the total number of embeddings can be much larger.

Metrics. For each testing, we run an algorithm for a query set, containing 100 query graphs, three times, and *report the average CPU time in milliseconds for processing each query graph.* Note that, we set the time limit for processing a query set to 5 hours (i.e., 1.8×10^7 ms). If an algorithm cannot finish within the time limit, then we plot its processing time as "INF".

6.1 Comparing with Existing Techniques

In this subsection, we evaluate CFL-Match against the existing algorithms, QuickSI, $\text{Turbo}_{\text{ISO}}$, and $\text{Turbo}_{\text{ISO}}$-Boost. Note that, we also ran $\text{Turbo}_{\text{ISO}}$-Boost for our queries on the tested graphs using the source code provided by the authors in [14]; however, it cannot finish within the time limit for most of the queries, and even for the cases that it can finish, it is much slower than $\text{Turbo}_{\text{ISO}}$ (see Figure 21 in Appendix). Apparently, there are some implementation issues in the source code of $\text{Turbo}_{\text{ISO}}$-Boost. We have communicated with the authors in [14] through email and the problem cannot be solved. Thus we omit $\text{Turbo}_{\text{ISO}}$-Boost in the following comparisons to be fair to the authors in [14]. Nevertheless, we implemented the techniques in [14] in combination with our techniques as the boosted version of CFL-Match and evaluate it in **Eval-IV**.

Eval-I: Against Existing Algorithms by Varying $|V(q)|$. We evaluate CFL-Match against existing algorithms by varying $|V(q)|$ regarding the *total processing time, embedding enumeration time,* and *query vertex ordering time.* Embedding enumeration time is the time to enumerate embeddings after obtaining a matching order of query vertices, while query vertex ordering time is the time to compute the matching order and other auxiliary data structures that are required for computing the matching order.

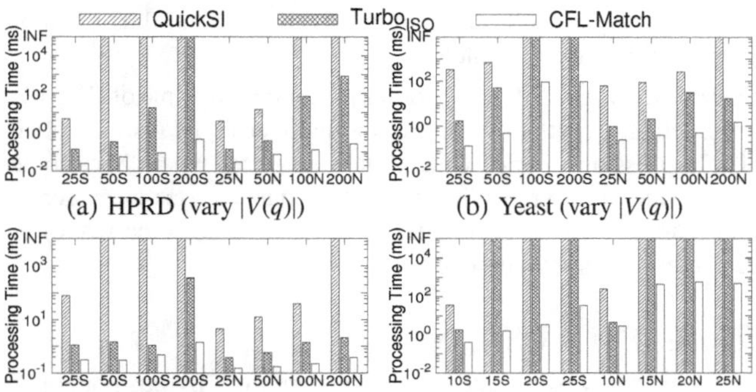

(a) HPRD (vary $|V(q)|$) (b) Yeast (vary $|V(q)|$)

(c) Synthetic (vary $|V(q)|$) (d) Human (vary $|V(q)|$)

Figure 8: Against Existing Algorithms (total processing time)

Total Processing Time. Figure 8 shows the average total processing time for each query graph. In general, all three algorithms run slower for larger queries, and QuickSI and $\text{Turbo}_{\text{ISO}}$ may not finish within the time limit for large queries (denoted as "INF" in the figures). CFL-Match consistently outperforms $\text{Turbo}_{\text{ISO}}$ which then performs better than QuickSI. This is due to our new framework by postponing the Cartesian products and also our CPI-based effective ordering of queries vertices. Our CFL-Match algorithm improves upon the state-of-the-art algorithm, $\text{Turbo}_{\text{ISO}}$, by over 3 orders of magnitude (see query q_{200N} in Figure 8(a)), even excluding the cases when $\text{Turbo}_{\text{ISO}}$ cannot finish within the time limit.

Embedding Enumeration Time. Figure 9 shows the embedding enumeration time of the three algorithms on HPRD and Synthetic graph. We omit the results on Yeast and Human due to QuickSI and $\text{Turbo}_{\text{ISO}}$ cannot finish within the time limit for most of the queries on these two graphs (see Figure 8). CFL-Match consistently out-

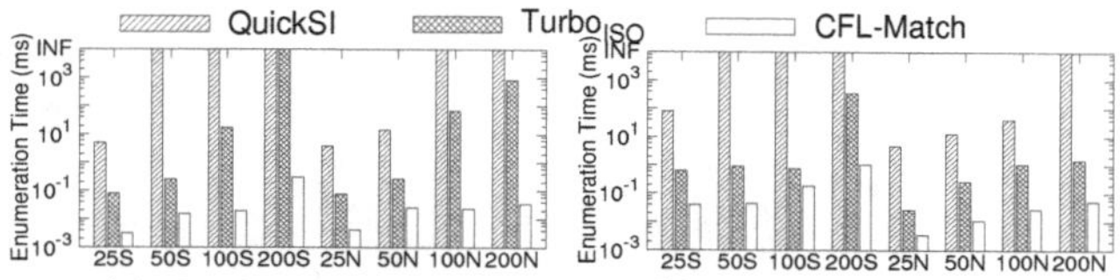

(a) HPRD (vary $|V(q)|$) (b) Synthetic (vary $|V(q)|$)

Figure 9: Against Existing Algorithms (enumeration time)

performs $\text{Turbo}_{\text{ISO}}$ across all queries for enumerating embeddings, and the improvement can be over 4 orders of magnitude (see query q_{200N} on HPRD); QuickSI runs the slowest. This confirms the advantage of our new framework, by postponing the Cartesian products (see Section 3), over the existing algorithms.

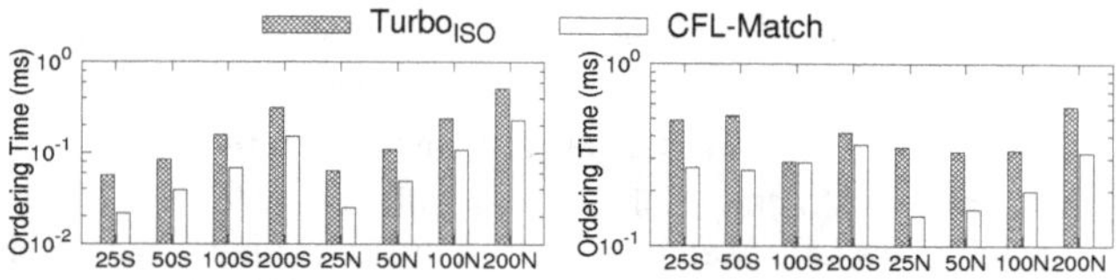

(a) HPRD (vary $|V(q)|$) (b) Synthetic (vary $|V(q)|$)

Figure 10: Against Existing Algorithms (ordering time)

Query Vertex Ordering Time. We illustrate the query vertex ordering time of $\text{Turbo}_{\text{ISO}}$ and CFL-Match on HPRD and Synthetic graph in Figure 10. Note that, the query vertex ordering time of QuickSI is negligible since the ordering is directly based on the edge frequencies; thus, we omit QuickSI in Figure 10. We can see that the query vertex ordering time of CFL-Match is much smaller than that of $\text{Turbo}_{\text{ISO}}$, due to the $O(|E(q)| \times |E(G)|)$ time complexity of CFL-Match for CPI construction. Although $\text{Turbo}_{\text{ISO}}$ has a worst-case exponential time complexity for constructing its data structure due to possibly exponential number of path embeddings, the number of path embeddings in these two graphs are small. Thus, $\text{Turbo}_{\text{ISO}}$ also performs well regarding query vertex ordering time.

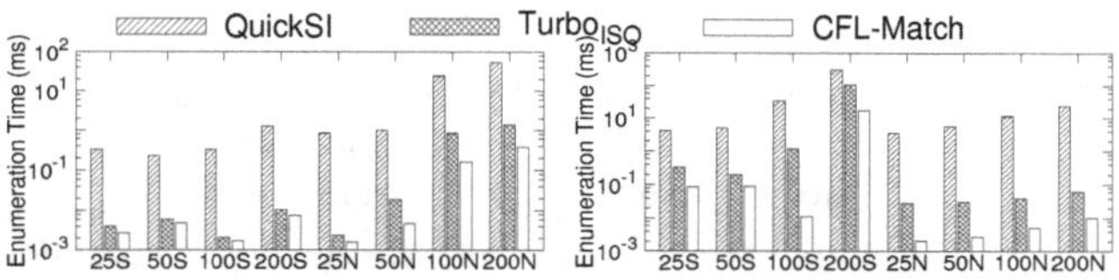

(a) HPRD (enumeration time) (b) Synthetic (enumeration time)

Figure 11: Enumeration Time for Core-Structures (Vary $|V(q)|$)

Eval-II: Evaluating Enumeration Time for Core-Structures of Queries. In this testing, we evaluate the enumeration time of the algorithms for processing core-structures of queries. That is, our core-forest-leaf decomposition based framework has no effect on the running time; CFL-Match is equivalent to the Core-Match algorithm in Section 4.2. The results are shown in Figure 11. Different from Figure 9, both QuickSI and $\text{Turbo}_{\text{ISO}}$ can now finish within the time limit. This is because, 1) the size of a core-structure is smaller than that of the original query in Figure 9, and 2) the number of embeddings of a core-structure is usually smaller than that of a general query. The embedding enumeration time of CFL-Match is much smaller than that of $\text{Turbo}_{\text{ISO}}$; this confirms the better matching order computed by our greedy path-ordering approach based on the cost model in Section 4.2.1.

Eval-III: Varying #Embeddings. Figure 12 shows the results of the algorithms by varying *#embeddings*. As expected, the processing time of all three algorithms increases when more embeddings are generated. Nevertheless, CFL-Match consistently outperforms $\text{Turbo}_{\text{ISO}}$ with QuickSI performing the worst.

Eval-IV: Evaluating The Boost Technique in [14]. The results of applying the boost technique in [14], which compresses the data

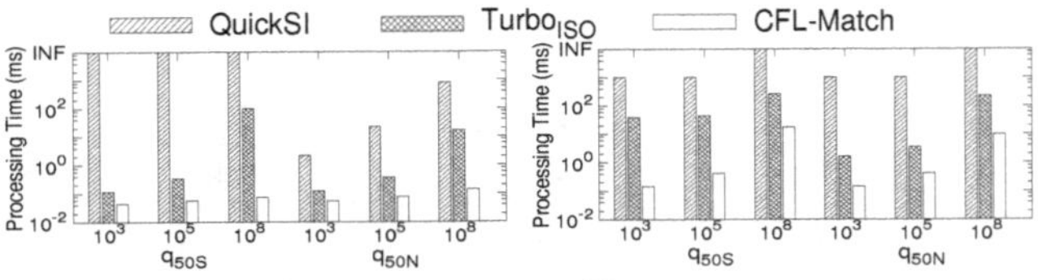

(a) HPRD (vary *#embeddings*) (b) Yeast (vary *#embeddings*)

Figure 12: Evaluating *#embeddings*

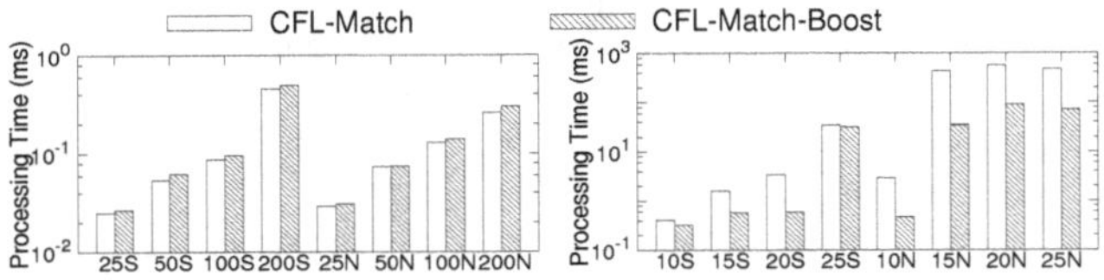

(a) HPRD (vary $|V(q)|$) (b) Human (vary $|V(q)|$)

Figure 13: Evaluating The Boost Technique

graph, to CFL-Match are shown in Figure 13. The boost technique improves CFL-Match on Human due to the high data graph compression ratio (i.e., about 40%). However, CFL-Match-Boost performs a little slower than CFL-Match on HPRD, due to the low compression ratio of HPRD (i.e., < 5%); note that the query-dependent compression has overheads. Thus, *the boost technique may not always help; we omit* CFL-Match-Boost *in the following*.

6.2 Effectiveness of New Framework

In this subsection, we evaluate the effectiveness of our proposed techniques in reducing the overall processing time, and the scalability of our CFL-Match algorithm. We run variants of CFL-Match on different graphs for query sets q_{50S} (average degree ≤ 3, denoted Sparse) and q_{50N} (average degree > 3, denoted Non-Sparse).

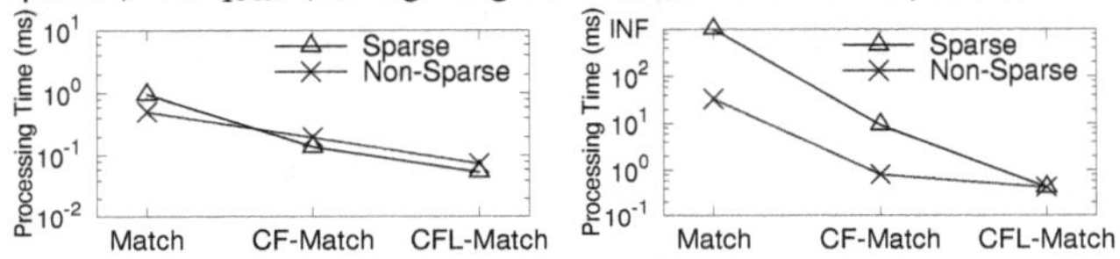

(a) HPRD (vary algorithms) (b) Yeast (vary algorithms)

Figure 14: Evaluating Our Framework

Eval-V: Evaluating Our Framework. We compare CFL-Match with CF-Match and Match to evaluate the effectiveness of our core-forest-leaf decomposition based framework. The results on HPRD and Yeast are shown in Figure 14. We can see that, the core-forest decomposition based framework (i.e., CF-Match) improves upon a non-decomposition based framework (i.e., Match), and the forest-leaf decomposition based framework (i.e., CFL-Match) further improves CF-Match by postponing the Cartesian products. The improvement of the core-forest-leaf decomposition based framework on Yeast is more significant due to more candidates for each query vertex in CPI (thus, more Cartesian products).

Eval-VI: Evaluating the Effectiveness of CPI Construction Strategies. The evaluation results of the effect of different CPI construction strategies on the total processing time of our CFL-Match algorithm are illustrated in Figure 15. The naively constructed CPI (see Section 4.1) significantly degrades the performance of CFL-Match due to lots of false-positive candidates for query vertices in CPI. CFL-Match-TD improves upon CFL-Match-Naive by constructing the CPI in a top-down fashion (see Section 5.2), which also exploits the non-tree edges for candidate pruning. Finally, the bottom-up refinement of CPI (see Section 5.3) further reduces the candidates of query vertices, thus leads to the best performance of CFL-Match. Note that, due to very few candidates of query vertices in CPI constructed by the top-down algorithm for HPRD, the improvement of CFL-Match over CFL-Match-TD is insignificant in Figure 15(a).

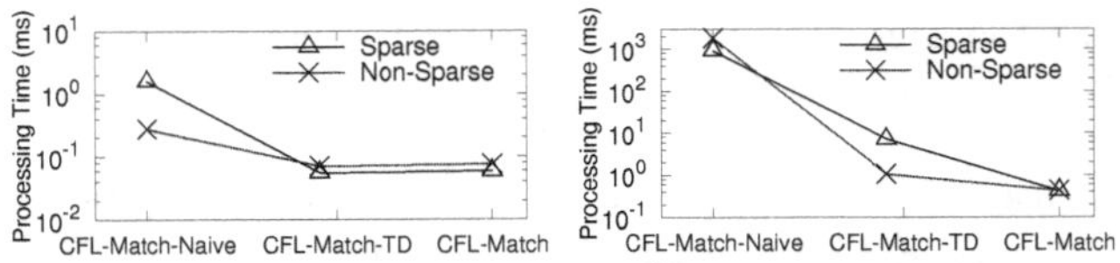

(a) HPRD (vary algorithms) (b) Yeast (vary algorithms)

Figure 15: Evaluating CPI Construction Strategies

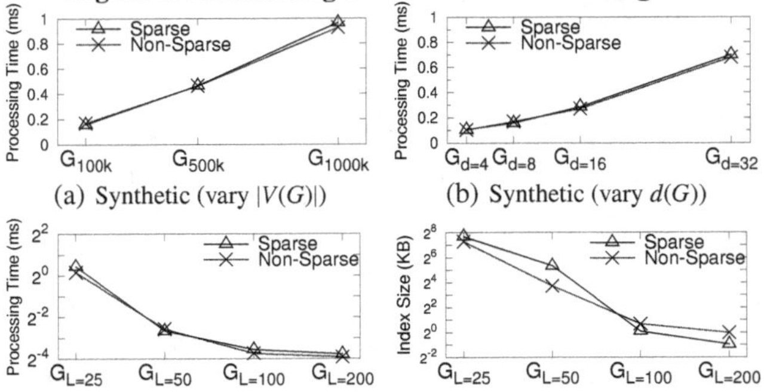

(a) Synthetic (vary $|V(G)|$) (b) Synthetic (vary $d(G)$)

(c) Synthetic (vary $|\Sigma|$) (d) Index Size (vary $|\Sigma|$)

Figure 16: Scalability Testing of CFL-Match

Eval-VII: Scalability Testing. We test the scalability of CFL-Match on Synthetic graphs by varying $|V(G)|$, $d(G)$, and $|\Sigma|$.

Varying $|V(G)|$. The results of varying $|V(G)|$ are illustrated in Figure 16(a). The processing time of CFL-Match increases linearly with respect to $|V(G)|$. This is because, for Synthetic graphs, the query vertex ordering time dominates the embedding enumeration time as shown in Figures 9(b) and 10(b). The time for CPI construction, $O(|E(G)| \times |E(q)|)$, is the dominating factor in the query vertex ordering time, and it increases linearly regarding $|V(G)|$.

Varying $d(G)$. Figure 16(b) shows the results of varying the average degree $d(G)$ of Synthetic graphs. The processing time of CFL-Match increases almost linearly regarding $d(G)$. This is because the larger $d(G)$, the more edges in CPI, and thus the more running time of CFL-Match.

Varying $|\Sigma|$. Figure 16(c) illustrates the processing time of CFL-Match on Synthetic graphs by varying the number $|\Sigma|$ of distinct labels. The processing time of CFL-Match decreases when $|\Sigma|$ becomes larger, due to fewer candidates for each query vertex as evidenced in Figure 16(d) where the index size (i.e., y-axis) is the size of the CPI constructed by our algorithm.

7. CONCLUSION

In this paper, we proposed a new framework by postponing the Cartesian products based on the core-forest-leaf decomposition of a query to minimize the redundant Cartesian products. We are the first to address the issue of unpromising results by Cartesian products from "dissimilar" vertices. We proposed a new path-based auxiliary data structure, of size $O(|E(G)|\times|V(q)|)$, to generate matching order and conduct subgraph matching, which significantly reduces the exponential size $O(|V(G)|^{|V(q)|-1})$ of the existing data structure in [8]. Extensive empirical studies on real and synthetic graphs demonstrate that our techniques outperform the state-of-the-art algorithm by up to 3 orders of magnitude. As a possible future work, extending our core-forest-leaf decomposition to a hierarchical decomposition of the core-structure (e.g., compute k-core, $(k$-1)-core, ...) might be an interesting issue to be investigated.

Acknowledgements. Lijun Chang is supported by ARC DE150100563 and ARC DP160101513. Xuemin Lin is supported by NSFC61232006, ARC DP140103578 and ARC DP150102728. Lu Qin is supported by ARC DE140100999, and ARC DP160101513. Wenjie Zhang is supported by ARC DP150103071 and ARC DP150102728.

8. REFERENCES

[1] V. Batagelj and M. Zaversnik. An o(m) algorithm for cores decomposition of networks. *CoRR*, cs.DS/0310049, 2003.

[2] V. Bonnici, A. Ferro, R. Giugno, A. Pulvirenti, and D. Shasha. Enhancing graph database indexing by suffix tree structure. In *Proc. of PRIB'10*, 2010.

[3] J. Cheng, Y. Ke, W. Ng, and A. Lu. Fg-index: towards verification-free query processing on graph databases. In *Proc. of SIGMOD'07*, 2007.

[4] L. P. Cordella, P. Foggia, C. Sansone, and M. Vento. A (sub)graph isomorphism algorithm for matching large graphs. *IEEE Trans. Pattern Anal. Mach. Intell.*, 26(10), 2004.

[5] M. R. Garey and D. S. Johnson. *Computers and Intractability: A Guide to the Theory of NP-Completeness*. W. H. Freeman, 1979.

[6] A. Gibbons. *Algorithmic Graph Theory*. Cambridge University Press, 1985.

[7] R. Giugno, V. Bonnici, N. Bombieri, A. Pulvirenti, A. Ferro, and D. Shasha. Grapes: A software for parallel searching on biological graphs targeting multi-core architectures. *PLoS ONE*, 8(10), 10 2013.

[8] W. Han, J. Lee, and J. Lee. Turbo$_{\text{iso}}$: towards ultrafast and robust subgraph isomorphism search in large graph databases. In *Prof. of SIGMOD'13*, 2013.

[9] H. He and A. K. Singh. Graphs-at-a-time: query language and access methods for graph databases. In *Proc. of SIGMOD'08*, 2008.

[10] K. Klein, N. Kriege, and P. Mutzel. Ct-index: Fingerprint-based graph indexing combining cycles and trees. In *Proc. of ICDE'11*, 2011.

[11] L. Lai, L. Qin, X. Lin, and L. Chang. Scalable subgraph enumeration in mapreduce. *PVLDB*, 8(10), 2015.

[12] J. Lee, W. Han, R. Kasperovics, and J. Lee. An in-depth comparison of subgraph isomorphism algorithms in graph databases. *PVLDB*, 6(2), 2012.

[13] N. Przulj, D. G. Corneil, and I. Jurisica. Efficient estimation of graphlet frequency distributions in protein-protein interaction networks. *Bioinformatics*, 22(8), 2006.

[14] X. Ren and J. Wang. Exploiting vertex relationships in speeding up subgraph isomorphism over large graphs. *PVLDB*, 8(5), 2015.

[15] H. Shang, Y. Zhang, X. Lin, and J. X. Yu. Taming verification hardness: an efficient algorithm for testing subgraph isomorphism. *PVLDB*, 1(1), 2008.

[16] Y. Shao, B. Cui, L. Chen, L. Ma, J. Yao, and N. Xu. Parallel subgraph listing in a large-scale graph. In *Proc. of SIGMOD'14*, 2014.

[17] T. A. B. Snijders, P. E. Pattison, G. L. Robins, and M. S. Handcock. New specifications for exponential random graph models. *Sociological Methodology*, 36(1), 2006.

[18] Z. Sun, H. Wang, H. Wang, B. Shao, and J. Li. Efficient subgraph matching on billion node graphs. *PVLDB*, 5(9), 2012.

[19] J. R. Ullmann. An algorithm for subgraph isomorphism. *J. ACM*, 23(1), 1976.

[20] X. Yan, P. S. Yu, and J. Han. Graph indexing: A frequent structure-based approach. In *Proc. of SIGMOD'04*, 2004.

[21] S. Zhang, J. Yang, and W. Jin. SAPPER: subgraph indexing and approximate matching in large graphs. *PVLDB*, 3(1), 2010.

[22] P. Zhao and J. Han. On graph query optimization in large networks. *PVLDB*, 3(1), 2010.

[23] P. Zhao, J. X. Yu, and P. S. Yu. Graph indexing: Tree + delta >= graph. In *Proc. of VLDB'07*, 2007.

[24] G. Zhu, X. Lin, K. Zhu, W. Zhang, and J. X. Yu. Treespan: efficiently computing similarity all-matching. In *Proc. of SIGMOD'12*, 2012.

[25] L. Zou, L. Chen, J. X. Yu, and Y. Lu. A novel spectral coding in a large graph database. In *Proc. of EDBT'08*, 2008.

A. APPENDIX

A.1 Proofs of Lemmas and Theorems.

Proof Sketch of Lemma 3.1. Firstly, we prove that the 2-core of q contains all non-tree edges of q regarding any spanning tree of q. It is easy to see that the set of non-tree edges regarding any spanning tree of q is exactly the set of edges in simple cycles [6] in q, and all vertices in a simple cycle have exactly two neighbors in the cycle. Thus, the 2-core will include all such simple cycles (i.e., include all non-tree edges regarding any spanning tree of q).

Secondly, we prove that the 2-core of q is the minimal connected subgraph of q containing all non-tree edges of q regarding any spanning tree of q, by contradiction. Assume there is a smaller connected subgraph g' of q that contains all non-tree edges of q regarding any spanning tree of q. Denote the 2-core of q as g. Then, there must be an edge (u_1, u_2) of g that is not in g'. Since g' contains all non-tree edges of q regarding any spanning tree of q, there will be no simple cycle of q containing (u_1, u_2), which means that (u_1, u_2) is a bridge of q [6]. Then, the set of all simple cycles in q will form at least two connected components in the subgraph of q by removing (u_1, u_2); otherwise, g will not contain (u_1, u_2). This contradicts that g' is connected and does not contain (u_1, u_2).

Thus, the lemma holds. □

Proof Sketch of Theorem 4.1. Firstly, it is easy to see that there will be no false positives. This is because every edge between two candidate vertices in the CPI is also an edge in the data graph.

Now, we give a constructive proof to show that there is no false negative; that is, every embedding of q in G will be computed by traversing CPI. Consider an embedding $M = (v_0, \ldots, v_n)$ of $q = (u_0, \ldots, u_n)$. Without loss of generality, assume u_0 is the root node in CPI, and the parent node of u_i ($i \neq 0$) in CPI is $u_i.p$ and it is mapped to $v_i.p$ by M. Then, v_0 must be in $u_0.C$, and moreover, for each u_i ($i \neq 0$), v_i must be in both $u_i.C$ and $N_{u_i}^{u_i.p}(v_i.p)$, since CPI is sound. Thus, the embedding $(v_0, \ldots, v_n)$ will be generated by traversing CPI, and it will also survive all non-tree edge checkings.

Hence, the theorem holds. □

Proof Sketch of Lemma 4.1. We reduce the problem of checking subgraph isomorphism to the problem of determining whether a minimum and sound CPI is empty. We prove that, given graphs q and G, q is subgraph isomorphic to G, which is NP-complete [5], if and only if a minimum and sound CPI is non-empty.

($\Longrightarrow$). If q is subgraph isomorphic to G, assume the subgraph isomorphic embedding is M, then for each $u \in V(q)$, the mapping $M(u)$ of u must be in $u.C$ in the sound CPI. Thus, the minimum and sound CPI is non-empty.

($\Longleftarrow$). It is easy to see that, if a minimum and sound CPI is non-empty, then there must be an embedding of q in G. □

Proof Sketch of Lemma 4.2. Note that, each vertex in the forest-structure and not in V_C has at least two-neighbors in q; recall that, all the degree-one vertices are put in the leaf-set V_I (see Section 3).

We prove the lemma by contradiction. Assume there are two vertices u and u' from the forest-structure that have the same labels and the same neighborhoods, and u_1 and u'_1 are the (common) neighbors of u and u'. Then, (u, u_1, u', u'_1) forms a cycle in q, which means that u and u' cannot be in the forest-structure. We reach a contradiction. Thus, the lemma holds. □

Proof Sketch of Lemma 4.3. This lemma directly follows from the fact that each vertex in G has a single label. Any vertex $v \in C(u)$ with label $l_G(v) = l_q(u)$ is not in $C(u')$ since $l_q(u') \neq l_q(u)$. □

Proof Sketch of Lemma 5.1. We prove the lemma by induction. Obviously, the lemma holds for $|u.N| = 1$ (i.e., $Cnt = 1$). Now, let's consider $u.N = \{u_1, \ldots, u_k\}$. We assume the lemma holds after processed the first $(k-1)$ visited neighbors of u. That is, a data vertex v with label u has a neighbor in $u_i.C$ for $1 \leq i \leq k-1$ if and only if $v.cnt = k-1$; let V_{k-1} denote the set of all such vertices $\{v\}$. Then, after checking $v.cnt = k-1$ at Line 13, only those vertices from V_{k-1} will satisfy this requirement. Moreover, a vertex $v \in V_{k-1}$ have $v.cnt = k$ after processing u_k if and only if there is a vertex from $u_k.C$ that is adjacent to v. Thus, the lemma holds. □

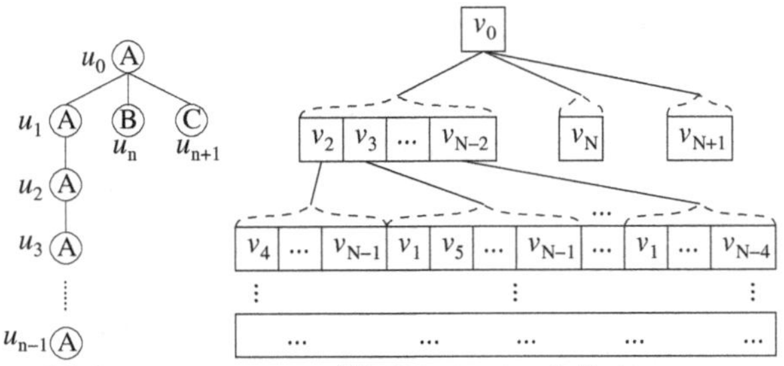

(a) Query q (b) Data structure in $\text{Turbo}_{\text{ISO}}$

Figure 17: Example Data Structure in $\text{Turbo}_{\text{ISO}}$

Proof Sketch of Lemma 5.2. We prove the lemma by contradiction. Firstly, it is easy to see that, if v is in $u.C$ for every processed query vertex u before running *backward candidate pruning* (i.e., Lines 18–23), then v is still in $u.C$ afterwards. This is because for every query vertex $u' \in u.UN$, $M(u')$ is in $u'.C$.

Now, we assume u is the first query vertex according to the processing order defined by Lines 4–5 of Algorithm 3 such that $v \notin u.C$ with $v = M(u)$. Then, v must satisfy $v.cnt \neq Cnt$ at Line 15. However, since u is the first such query vertex, $M(u')$ must be in $u'.C$ for every $u' \in u.N$. Then, according to Lemma 5.1, $v.cnt = Cnt$. We reach a contradiction. Thus, the lemma holds. □

Proof Sketch of Lemma 5.3. Let's consider an arbitrary embedding M of q in G, we prove that $M(u) \in u.C$ in CPI for every $u \in V(q)$. Since this condition holds before running Lines 2–10 of Algorithm 4, $M(u).cnt = Cnt$ holds afterwards according to Lemma 5.1. Thus $M(u) \in u.C$, and the lemma holds. □

Proof Sketch of Theorem 5.1. Firstly, we consider Algorithm 3, we show that Lines 6–17 for a specific u take time $O(|E(G)| \times |u.N|)$. In particular, for each vertex $v' \in u'.C$, Lines 12–13 take $O(d_G(v'))$ time; thus, for all vertices in $u'.C$, Lines 12–13 take time $O(\sum_{v' \in u'.C} d_G(v')) = O(|E(G)|)$. Similarly, Lines 19–23 for u take time $O(|E(G)| \times |u.UN|)$ time and Lines 25–28 for u take time $O(|E(G)|)$ time. Thus, the total time for a specific u is $O(|E(G)| \times (|u.N| + |u.UN|)) = O(|E(G)| \times d_q(u))$, and the total running time of Algorithm 3 is $O(\sum_{u \in V(q)} |E(G)| \times d_q(u)) = O(|E(G)| \times |E(q)|)$.

The time complexity of Algorithm 4 can be proved similarly. □

A.2 Storage Representation of CPI

In representing a CPI, we store the candidate set for each node in CPI as an array of vertex ids; for example, $u_0.C = \{v_0, v_1, v_2, v_3, v_4\}$ is stored as an array of five elements in Figure 5(c). For each pair of parent-child (i.e., adjacent) nodes u and u' in CPI with u being the parent, we store the edges between each vertex $v \in u.C$ and vertices of $u'.C$ as an adjacency list of v corresponding to the query edge (u, u'), denoted $N^u_{u'}(v)$. For example, $N^{u_0}_{u_1}(v_0) = \{v_5, v_8\}$.

In order to support fast traversal of a CPI by following vertices' adjacency lists, instead of directly storing vertex ids we store their positions (i.e., offsets) in the corresponding candidate set of the child node, into the adjacency lists. For example, the adjacency list of v_0 becomes $N^{u_0}_{u_1}(v_0) = \{1, 4\}$ meaning that the adjacency list of v_0 contains the first (i.e., v_5) and fourth (i.e., v_8) vertices in $u_1.C$. Consequently, the adjacency lists of v_5 and v_8 can be directly obtained, as the first and forth adjacency lists among all adjacency lists stored in u_1 regarding each child of u_1 in CPI, without the help of a hash-structure. Nevertheless, for presentation simplicity, in the paper we still use vertex ids instead of positions/offsets in the representation of the contents of adjacency lists in CPI.

A.3 Analysis of The Data Structure in $\text{Turbo}_{\text{ISO}}$

Exponential Size of The Auxiliary Data Structure in $\text{Turbo}_{\text{ISO}}$. The auxiliary data structure in $\text{Turbo}_{\text{ISO}}$ [8] can be of exponential size. For example, consider the spanning query tree q in Figure 17(a) and a data graph G with $N + 2$ vertices, where the subgraph of G induced by the first N vertices, $(v_0, \ldots, v_{N-1})$, form a near-clique and all have label A, edges (v_0, v_{N-1}) and (v_i, v_{i+1}) for each $0 \leq i < N - 1$ are absent from G, and v_0 is connected to v_N and v_{N+1}, respectively, with labels B and C.[2] The data structure built by $\text{Turbo}_{\text{ISO}}$ is shown in Figure 17(b). u_0 has only one candidate, v_0. For u_1, there are $(N - 3)$ candidates $\{v_2, \ldots, v_{N-2}\}$; note that v_0 is not a candidate because it has been used in the mapping of u_0, and v_1 and v_{N-1} are also not candidates because they are not connected to v_0 (the map of the parent of u_1, i.e., u_0) in G. For u_2, there are $(N - 3) \times (N - 4)$ candidates; that is, regarding each candidate v_i of u_1 (i.e., the parent of u_2), there are $(N - 4)$ candidates for u_2. In general, u_i has $\prod^{i}_{j=1}(N - j - 2)$ candidates for $1 \leq i \leq n - 1$ (assume $n < N$). Thus, the total size of the data structure is at least $\prod^{n-1}_{i=1}(N - i - 2) > (\frac{N-3}{e})^{n-1}$, which is exponential to the size of the query; here e is a mathematical constant and is approximately equal to 2.71828. Note that, if there is a non-tree edge between u_2 and u_n in q in Figure 17(a), then there will be no embeddings of q in G; that is, all these generated candidates in the data structure will be finally pruned during embedding enumeration.

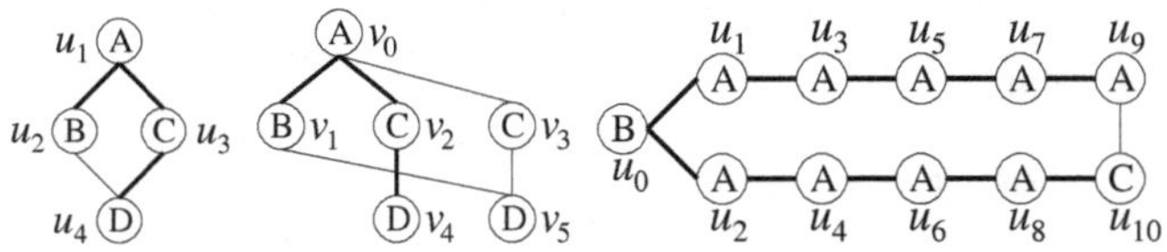

(a) Query q (b) Data Graph G (c) Another Query q'

Figure 18: Restrict to k (= 1) Path Embeddings

Restrict to k Path Embeddings. To resolve the issue of possible exponential size of the auxiliary data structure, $\text{Turbo}_{\text{ISO}}$ only materializes k embeddings for each root-to-leaf query path *in its implementation* when computing the matching order of query vertices, if we only retrieve k subgraph isomorphic embeddings for q. However, such a materialization cannot always guarantee to generate k subgraph isomorphic embeddings for q from the data structure. For example, consider the query q in Figure 18(a) and the data graph G in Figure 18(b), where the BFS tree q_T of q is illustrated by thick edges. Assume $k = 1$, the materialized auxiliary data structure in $\text{Turbo}_{\text{ISO}}$ may only contain the embedding of q_T in G as illustrated by the thick edges in Figure 18(b). Then, from the data structure, we cannot generate the embedding of q in G that maps u_1 to v_0.

To generate k embeddings of q in G, $\text{Turbo}_{\text{ISO}}$ materializes more path embeddings on demand in enumerating subgraph isomorphic embeddings, when needed. For example, in Figure 18(b), the path embedding (v_0, v_3, v_5) will be materialized in enumerating subgraph isomorphic embeddings. Thus, the size of the data structure in $\text{Turbo}_{\text{ISO}}$ can still be exponential in the worst case. We tested $\text{Turbo}_{\text{ISO}}$ on the query q' in Figure 18(c) and a data graph with 103 vertices, where the vertices $v_0, \ldots, v_{99}$ with label A form a near-clique as above, v_{100} with label B is connected to v_i for $0 \leq i \leq 99$, and v_{101} with label C is connected to v_0 and also connected to v_{102} with label A; the spanning tree of q is chosen as indicated by thick edges in Figure 18(c), $k = 1$, $\text{Turbo}_{\text{ISO}}$ crashes due to the exponential size of the data structure constructed when enumerating subgraph isomorphic embeddings; note that, there actually is no result for this query on this data graph.

Moreover, if we want to retrieve all subgraph isomorphic embeddings, then we have to materialize all path embeddings; that is, the worst case exponential size is unavoidable using $\text{Turbo}_{\text{ISO}}$. As a result, $\text{Turbo}_{\text{ISO}}$ cannot scale to large queries or large data graphs.

[2]Note that neither the query q nor the data graph G can be compressed by the techniques in [8] or [14].

A.4 Pseudocode of Core-Match

Algorithm 5: Core-Match

```
Input: Matching index i, matching order (u_1, ..., u_|V(q)|), a CPI, and a
       data graph G
Output: All embeddings of q in G

if i = |V(q)| + 1 then  Output M as an embedding of q in G;
else if i = 1 then
    for each data vertex v ∈ u_i.C do
        M(u_i) ← v;  Mark v as visited;
        Core-Match(i + 1);  Mark v as unvisited;
else for each data vertex v ∈ N_{u_i}^{u_i.p}(M(u_i.p)) do
    if v is unvisited and ValidateNT(v, u_i, G) then
        Same as Lines 4–6;
```

The pseudocode of Core-Match is shown in Algorithm 5, where ValidateNT(v, u_i, G) validates non-tree edges. That is, for each non-tree edge $(u_j, u_i) \in E(q)$ with $j < i$ and $u_j \neq u_i.p$ in the matching sequence/order, it checks whether $(M(u_j), v) \in E(G)$. Note that, for simplicity, we present Algorithm 5 in a recursive form by recursively invoking Core-Match; however, for efficiency consideration, our implementation of Algorithm 5 is non-recursive.

A.5 Generalize Leaf-Set to Independent-Set

It is immediate that a leaf-set is an independent-set. However, the reverse is not true. Thus, we can generalize the forest-leaf decomposition in Section 3 to a *forest-IS (independent-set) decomposition*; that is, compute the maximal independent-set of the forest-structure T. Intuitively, we want the independent-set to be as large as possible (or equivalently, the forest-set V_T as small as possible); moreover, we also need the subgraph $q[V_C \cup V_T]$ to be connected to obtain a connected matching order of $V_C \cup V_T$. This is to compute the Connected Minimum Vertex Cover (cMVC) that is also connected to the core-structure $q[V_C]$, for each connected tree in T; that is, we need the connection vertex of the connected tree to be in the cMVC. In general, computing cMVC is NP-hard for a graph [5]. The good news is that we are dealing with trees. Moreover, we require the connection vertex between the tree and the core-structure to be in the cMVC (e.g., u_1 and u_2 in Figure 4(c) need to be in the cMVC). Therefore, it is easy to verify that the set of vertices with degree at least two and the connection vertex is the cMVC; thus, V_T is the set of vertices with degree at least two and excluding the connection vertices, and V_I *is the set of degree-one vertices excluding the connection vertices*. That is, the leaf-set is maximal possible independent-set we can get from the forest-structure T.

Discussion. It is, in principle, also possible to compute an independent set from the core-structure $q[V_C]$ of q and put the independent set at the end of the matching order. However, this will put some of the non-tree edge checkings at the end of the matching, which is not a good idea as shown in the Introduction. This is because we have proved in Lemma 3.1 that the core-structure $q[V_C]$ is the minimal connected subgraph containing all possible non-tree edges regarding any spanning tree of q. For example, consider a query q where the core-structure consists of a cycle, then every edge in the core-structure is a possible non-tree edge. Thus, we do not compute the independent set for the core-structure.

A.6 Root Selection and Candidate Filtering

Root Vertex Selection for a Query. To build the CPI, we first need to construct a BFS tree of the query q, which is to choose a root vertex for q. Recall that, in our core-forest-leaf decomposition based framework (see Section 3), we put all query vertices from the core-structure at the beginning of the matching order. Moreover the root vertex will be the first vertex in a matching order. Thus, the root vertex is chosen from the core-set V_C.

Intuitively, we favor the root vertex to have a small number of candidates and to have a large degree; fewer candidates means fewer partial embeddings being generated, while larger degree means more chance to prune partial embeddings at early stages. Similar to [8], we choose the root vertex r as $r \leftarrow \arg\min_{u \in V(q)} \frac{|C(u)|}{d_q(u)}$ where $C(u)$ is the set of candidates in G of u. There are different strategies for obtaining $C(u)$, and different strategies will have different costs. Thus, we first use a light-weight strategy to obtain $C(u)$ based on only the label $l_q(u)$ and degree $d_q(u)$ of u; that is, $C(u)$ is the set of vertices in G with label $l_q(u)$ and degree at least $d_q(u)$. Top-3 vertices are obtained based on the computed $C(u)$. Then, we compute a reduced (i.e., more accurate) set $C(u)$ of candidates for the selected top-3 vertices, by using the candidate filtering techniques (i.e., CandVefiry) which will be described in below; the vertex with the smallest $|C(u)|/d_q(u)$ is selected as the root vertex. For example, for the query q in Figure 7(a) and the data graph G in Figure 7(c), u_0 is chosen as the root, because $d_q(u_0) = 2$ and $C(u_0) = \{v_1, v_2\}$ and $|C(u_0)|/d_q(u_0) = 1$ is the smallest among all query vertices.

Candidate Filtering. To reduce the size of candidate sets of query vertices, many *candidate filtering techniques* have been proposed [4, 8, 15, 19, 22, 24] by exploiting the local features of query vertices, such as vertex label filter [19], vertex degree filter [19], and Neighborhood Label Frequency (NLF) filter [24]. In Algorithm 3, we retrieve the candidates for a query vertex based on the vertex label filter and vertex degree filter (see Lines 1,12). Applying the NLF filter is time-consuming; that is, verifying one candidate vertex v for a query vertex u takes $O(|L_N(u)|)$ time, where $L_N(u)$ is the set of unique labels of u's neighbors. In order to reduce the number of invokings of the expensive NLF filter, we propose the *maximum neighbor-degree* filter, which can be verified in constant time for each candidate data vertex.

Definition A.1: The **maximum neighbor-degree** of a vertex u in a graph g, denoted $mnd_g(u)$, is the maximum degree of all its neighbors (i.e., $mnd_g(u) = \max_{u' \in N_g(u)} d_g(u')$). □

We verify candidates for query vertices by the lemma below.

Lemma A.1: *Given a query q and a data graph G, a data vertex $v \in V(G)$ is not a candidate of $u \in V(q)$ if $mnd_G(v) < mnd_q(u)$.* □

Proof Sketch: We prove the lemma by contradiction. Assume v is a candidate of u with $mnd_G(v) < mnd_q(u)$; that is, there is an embedding M that maps u to v. Let u' be the neighbor of u with the maximum degree among all neighbors of u (i.e., $d_q(u') = mnd_q(u)$), and v' be the vertex to which u' maps in M. Then, $d_G(v') \leq mnd_G(v) < mnd_q(u) = d_q(u')$, and u' cannot be mapped to v' due to degree violation. We reach a contradiction. Thus, the lemma holds. □

Algorithm 6: CandVerify

```
Input: A potential candidate vertex v for a query vertex u
Output: true if v is a candidate of u, and false otherwise

1 if mnd_G(v) < mnd_q(u) then  return false;
2 for each label l ∈ L_N(u) do
3     if d(v, l) < d(u, l) then
4         return false;
5 return true;
```

Then, CandVerify is shown in Algorithm 6. We check the light-weight (i.e., constant-time) filter (Line 1) before applying the more expensive NLF filter (Lines 2–4), where $d(v, l)$ denotes the number of neighbors of v with label l.

A.7 Pruning Power in CPI Construction

As shown in Table 2 in Section 5, both directions of S-NTEs are exploited in the top-down construction algorithm. The direction of $\rightarrow$ is exploited in the forward processing of Algorithm 3, while the direction of $\leftarrow$ is exploited in the backward processing. The direction of $\downarrow$ (i.e., from upper-level vertices to lower-level vertices) for tree edges and C-NTEs is exploited in the forward processing of Algorithm 3, while the direction of $\uparrow$ is exploited in Algorithm 4. Therefore, both directions of every query edge in q are exploited for reducing the size of candidates of query vertices.

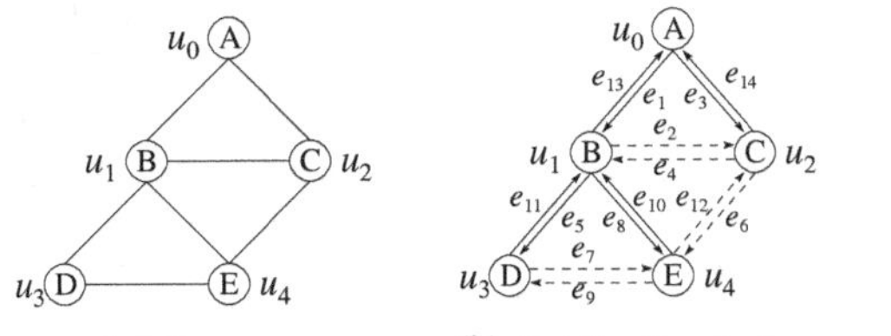

(a) Query q (b) Unidirectional edges

Process order	Vertex	Edges	Algorithm phase
1	u_1	e_1	Algorithm 3 – Forward
2	u_2	e_2, e_3	Algorithm 3 – Forward
3	u_1	e_4	Algorithm 3 – Backward
4	u_3	e_5	Algorithm 3 – Forward
5	u_4	e_6, e_7, e_8	Algorithm 3 – Forward
6	u_3	e_9	Algorithm 3 – Backward
7	u_2	e_{12}	Algorithm 4
8	u_1	e_{10}, e_{11}	Algorithm 4
9	u_0	e_{13}, e_{14}	Algorithm 4

(c) Pruning power of edges exploited

Figure 19: Exploit Both Directions of Query Edges in Pruning

Example 1.1: Figure 19 illustrates exploiting the pruning power of both directions of query edges at different algorithm phases. Figure 19(b) shows the unidirectional edges of the query q in Figure 19(a); each undirected edge of q is replaced by two unidirectional edges, and solid edges are tree edges while dashed edges are non-tree edges. Query vertices of q are processed in the order shown in the first column of Figure 19(c); the last column shows the different phases of the algorithms, while the third shows the set of unidirectional edges exploited in candidates generation or pruning. Thus, each edge is exploited twice, once in each direction. □

A.8 Additional Experimental Results

Eval-A-I: Additional Results for Section 6. Firstly, we show some additional results for the testings in Section 6.

Effectiveness of Compressing Core-Structures. Table 4 shows the average number (i.e., Avg) of reduced vertices by the query graph compression technique (NEC) in [8] for compressing core-structures of queries, and the number (i.e., #R) of queries whose core-structures are compressed by NEC for each query set containing 100 queries.

Query	HPRD		Yeast		Synthetic		Human	
	Avg	#R	Avg	#R	Avg	#R	Avg	#R
q_{25S}/q_{10S}	0.09	8	0.41	33	0.02	2	0.62	41
q_{50S}/q_{15S}	0.16	13	0.46	34	0.03	3	0.45	32
q_{100S}/q_{20S}	0.41	28	0.41	33	0	0	0.31	25
q_{200S}/q_{25S}	0.35	27	2.3	83	0.01	1	0.65	39
q_{25N}/q_{10N}	0.1	9	0.41	33	0.01	1	0.83	39
q_{50N}/q_{15N}	0.21	16	0.34	21	0	0	1.37	49
q_{100N}/q_{20N}	0.68	47	0.61	38	0.01	1	1.39	49
q_{200N}/q_{25N}	1.29	67	0.89	44	0	0	0.86	43

Table 4: Avg: average number of reduced vertices by NEC [8]; #R: number of queries compressed by NEC [8]

Enumeration/Ordering Time by Varying #embeddings. Figure 20 shows the results of splitting the total processing time in Figure 12 into enumeration time and ordering time. The query vertex ordering time of CFL-Match remains the same when varying *#embeddings* since our ordering time is independent of *#embeddings*. However, the query vertex ordering time of $\text{Turbo}_{\text{ISO}}$ increases when more embeddings need to be reported. This is because, $\text{Turbo}_{\text{ISO}}$ heuristically restricts to only generate and materialize *#embeddings* embeddings in a data graph for query paths (see Section A.3).

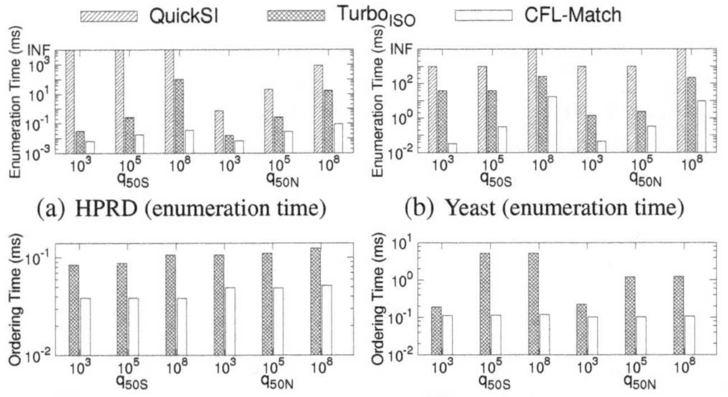

(a) HPRD (enumeration time) (b) Yeast (enumeration time)

(c) HPRD (ordering time) (d) Yeast (ordering time)

Figure 20: Enumeration/Ordering Time (vary *#embeddings*)

Eval-A-II: Additional Datasets and Queries. In the following, we report the experiment results on another two large real graphs, DBLP[3] and WordNet[4]. WordNet contains 133,445 edges, 82,670 vertices with an average degree 3.3, and 5 distinct labels; DBLP contains 1,049,866 edges, and 317,080 vertices with an average degree 6.6. Vertices in DBLP have no labels, we randomly assign a label out of 100 distinct labels to each vertex.

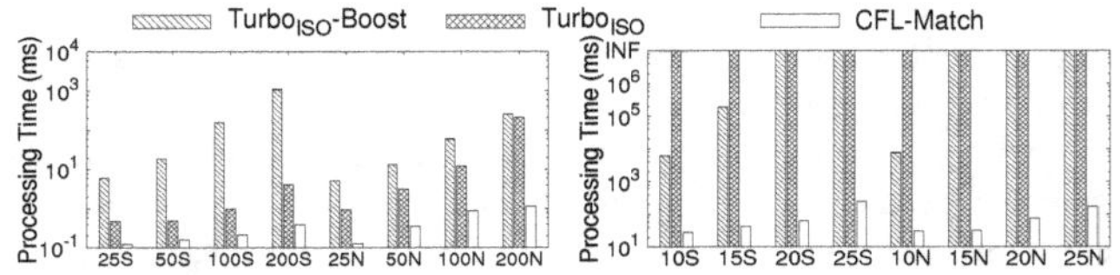

(a) DBLP (vary $|V(q)|$) (b) WordNet (vary $|V(q)|$)

Figure 21: Evaluating $\text{Turbo}_{\text{ISO}}$-Boost

Total Processing Time of $\text{Turbo}_{\text{ISO}}$-Boost. Figure 21 shows the processing time of $\text{Turbo}_{\text{ISO}}$-Boost against other algorithms on DBLP and WordNet. $\text{Turbo}_{\text{ISO}}$-Boost is faster than $\text{Turbo}_{\text{ISO}}$ for queries $q_{10S}, q_{15S}, q_{10N}$ on WordNet, but slower for other settings. Nevertheless, CFL-Match significantly outperforms both algorithms.

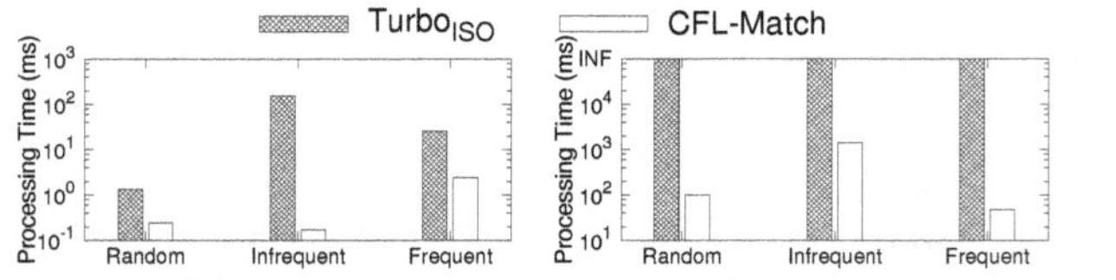

(a) DBLP (b) WordNet

Figure 22: Frequent Query vs Infrequent Query

Frequent/Infrequent Queries. In addition to random queries as tested in Section 6, we also consider frequent queries (*#embeddings* $>$ 10^4 for DBLP and $> 10^8$ for WordNet), and infrequent queries (*#embeddings* $< 10^3$ for DBLP and $< 10^8$ for WordNet). The results are shown in Figure 22. CFL-Match is much faster than $\text{Turbo}_{\text{ISO}}$ for all 3 query sets (frequent/infrequent/random queries). CFL-Match is faster for frequent queries than infrequent queries on WordNet since it is easier to reach *#embeddings* results for frequent queries as a result of the permutation effect; however, it runs faster for infrequent queries on DBLP since the number of candidates for query vertices in infrequent queries is much smaller.

[3]https://snap.stanford.edu/data/

[4]http://vlado.fmf.uni-lj.si/pub/networks/data/

Adding Counting Quantifiers to Graph Patterns

Wenfei Fan[1,2] Yinghui Wu[3] Jingbo Xu[1,2]
[1]University of Edinburgh [2]Beihang University [3]Washington State University
{wenfei@inf, jingbo.xu@}.ed.ac.uk, yinghui@eecs.wsu.edu

ABSTRACT

This paper proposes quantified graph patterns (QGPs), an extension of graph patterns by supporting simple counting quantifiers on edges. We show that QGPs naturally express universal and existential quantification, numeric and ratio aggregates, as well as negation. Better still, the increased expressivity does not come with a much higher price. We show that quantified matching, *i.e.*, graph pattern matching with QGPs, remains NP-complete in the absence of negation, and is DP-complete for general QGPs. We show how quantified matching can be conducted by incorporating quantifier checking into conventional subgraph isomorphism methods. We also develop parallel scalable algorithms for quantified matching. As an application of QGPs, we introduce quantified graph association rules defined with QGPs, to identify potential customers in social media marketing. Using real-life and synthetic graphs, we experimentally verify the effectiveness of QGPs and the scalability of our algorithms.

CCS Concepts

•**Theory of computation** → *Pattern matching;*

Keywords

Quantified graph patterns; graph association rules

1. INTRODUCTION

Given a graph pattern $Q(x_o)$ and a graph G, *graph pattern matching* is to find $Q(x_o, G)$, the set of matches of x_o in subgraphs of G that are isomorphic to Q. Here "query focus" x_o is a designated node of Q denoting search intent [9]. Traditionally, pattern Q is modeled as a (small) graph in the same form as G. This notion of patterns is used in social group detection and transportation network analysis.

However, in applications such as social media marketing, knowledge discovery and cyber security, more expressive patterns are needed, notably ones with counting quantifiers.

Example 1: (1) Consider an association rule for specifying regularities between entities in social graphs:

SIGMOD'16, June 26-July 01, 2016, San Francisco, CA, USA

DOI: http://dx.doi.org/10.1145/2882903.2882937

- *If (a) person x_o is in a music club, and (b) among the people whom x_o follows, at least 80% of them like an album y, then the chances are that x_o will buy y.*

Its antecedent specifies conditions (a) and (b). If these two conditions hold, then we can recommend album y to x_o. This is an example of social media marketing, which is predicted to trump traditional marketing. Indeed, empirical studies suggest that "90% of customers trust peer recommendations versus 14% who trust advertising" [1], and "the peer influence from one's friends causes more than 50% increases in odds of buying products" [8].

The antecedent is specified as a *quantified graph pattern* (QGP) $Q_1(x_o)$ shown in Fig. 1, where x_o is its query focus, indicating potential customers. Here edge follow(x_o, z) carries a *counting quantifier* "$\geq 80\%$", for condition (b) above. In a social graph G, a node v_x matches x_o in Q_1, *i.e.*, $v_x \in Q_1(x_o, G)$, if (a) there exists an isomorphism h from Q_1 to a subgraph G' of G such that $h(x_o) = v_x$, *i.e.*, G' satisfies the topological constraints of Q_1, and (b) among all the people whom v_x follows, 80% of them account for matches of z in $Q_1(G)$, satisfying the counting quantifier.

The following association rules are also found useful in social media marketing, with various counting quantifiers:

- *If for all the people z whom x_o follows, z recommends Redmi 2A (cell phone), then x_o may buy a Redmi 2A.*
- *If among the people followed by x_o, (a) at least p of them recommend Redmi 2A, and (b) no one gives Redmi 2A a bad rating, then x_o may buy Redmi 2A.*

The antecedents of these rules are depicted in Fig. 1 as QGPs $Q_2(x_o)$ and $Q_3(x_o)$, respectively. Here Q_2 uses a *universal* quantification ($= 100\%$), while Q_3 carries numeric aggregate ($\geq p$) and *negation* ($= 0$). In particular, a node v_x in G matches x_o in Q_3 only if there exists *no* node v_w in G such that follow(v_x, v_w) is an edge in G and there exists an edge from v_w to Redmi 2A labeled "bad rating". That is, counting quantifier "$= 0$" on edge follow(x_o, z_2) enforces negation.

(2) Quantified graph patterns are also useful in knowledge discovery. For example, QGP $Q_4(x_o)$ of Fig. 1 is to find

- *all people who (a) are professors in the UK, (b) do not have a PhD degree, and (c) have at least p former PhD students who are professors in the UK.*

It carries negation ($= 0$) and numeric aggregate ($\geq p$). □

These counting quantifiers are not expressible in traditional graph patterns. Several questions about QGPs are open. (1) How should QGPs be defined, to balance their expressive power and complexity? (2) Can we efficiently conduct graph pattern matching with QGPs in real-life graphs,

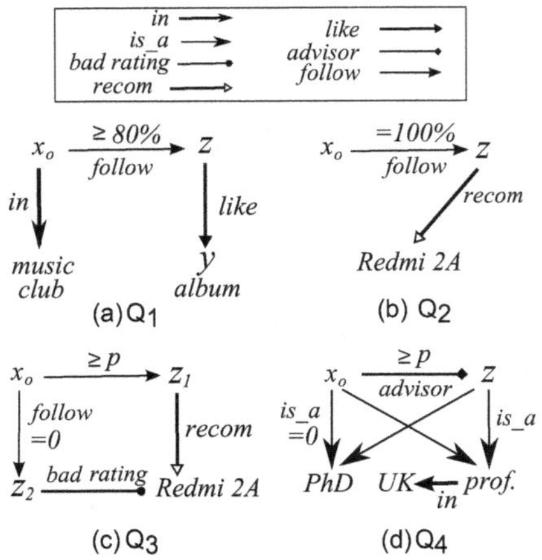

Figure 1: Quantified graph patterns

which may have trillions of nodes and edges [20]? (3) How can we make use of QGPs in emerging applications? The need for studying these is highlighted in, *e.g.*, social marketing, knowledge discovery and cyber security.

Contributions. This paper aims to answer these questions.

(1) We propose QGPs (Section 2). Using simple counting quantifiers, QGPs uniformly support numeric and ratio aggregates, universal and existential quantification, and negation. We formalize *quantified matching, i.e.*, graph pattern matching with QGPs, by revising the traditional semantics of pattern matching to incorporate counting quantifiers.

(2) We establish the complexity of quantified matching (Section 3). We show that despite their increased expressivity, QGPs do not make our lives much harder: quantified matching is NP-complete in the absence of negation, the same as subgraph isomorphism; and it is DP-complete otherwise.

(3) We provide a quantified matching algorithm (Section 4). The algorithm unifies conventional pattern matching and quantifier verification in a generic search process, and handles negation by novel incremental evaluation IncQMatch. As opposed to conventional incremental settings, IncQMatch acts in response to changes in patterns, not in graphs, and is *optimal* by performing only necessary verification.

(4) We develop parallel algorithms for quantified matching (Section 5). We identify a practical condition under which quantified matching is *parallel scalable, i.e., guaranteeing* provable reduction in sequential running time with the increase of processors. Under the condition, we develop graph partition and QGP matching algorithms, both parallel scalable, by exploring inter and intra-fragment parallelism.

(5) As an application of QGPs, we introduce quantified graph association rules (QGARs; Section 6). QGARs help us identify potential customers in social graphs, and (positive and negative) correlations in knowledge graphs. We propose support and confidence metrics for QGARs, a departure from their conventional counterparts. We also show that the (parallel) quantified matching algorithms can be readily extended to identify interesting entities with QGARs.

(6) Using real-life and synthetic graphs, we experimentally verify the effectiveness of QGPs and the scalability of our algorithms (Section 7). We find the following. (a) Quantified matching is feasible on large graphs. It takes 125 seconds on graphs of 150 millions nodes and edges by using 4 processors, and 42.3 seconds with 20 processors. (b) Our matching (resp. partition) algorithm is parallel scalable: it is on average 2.8 (resp. 3.5) and 3.2 (resp. 2.5) times faster on real-life social and knowledge graphs, respectively, when the number of processors increases from 4 to 20. (c) QGARs capture behavior patterns in social and knowledge graphs that cannot be expressed with conventional graph patterns.

We contend that QGPs and QGARs are useful in emerging applications such as social marketing and knowledge discovery. Despite the increased expressivity, they yield practical tools over large real-world graphs, which can be built upon existing (parallel) graph analytic systems.

Proofs and optimization strategies are given in Appendix.

Related work. We categorize the related work as follows.

Quantified graph querying. The need for counting in graph queries has long been recognized. SPARQLog [28] extends SPARQL with first-order logic (FO) rules, including existential and universal quantification over node variables. Rules for social recommendation are studied in [30], using support count as constraints. QGRAPH [10] annotates nodes and edges with a counting range (count 0 as negated edge) to specify the number of matches that must exist in a database. Set regular path queries (SRPQ) [31] extends regular path queries with quantification for group selection, to restrict the nodes in one set connected to the nodes of another. For social networks, SocialScope [5] and SNQL [32] are algebraic languages with numeric aggregates on node and edge sets.

The study of QGPs is to strike a balance between the expressivity and the complexity. It differs from the prior work in the following. (1) Using a uniform form of counting quantifiers, QGPs support numeric and ratio aggregates (*e.g.*, at least p friends and 80% of friends), and universal (100%) and existential quantification (≥ 1). In contrast, previous proposals do not allow at least one of these. (2) We focus on graph pattern queries, which are widely used in social media marketing and knowledge discovery; they are beyond set regular expressions [31] and rules of [30]. (3) Quantified matching with QGPs is DP-complete at worst, slightly higher than conventional matching (NP-complete) in the polynomial hierarchy [33]. In contrast, SPARQL and SPARQLog are PSPACE-hard [28], and SRPQ takes EXPTIME [31]; while the complexity bounds for QGRAPH [10], SocialScope [5] and SNQL [32] are unknown, they are either more expensive than QGPs (*e.g.*, QGRAPH is a fragment of FO(count)), or cannot express numeric and ratio quantifiers [5,32]. (4) No prior work has studied parallel scalable algorithms for its queries.

Parallel pattern matching. A number of (parallel) matching algorithms have been developed for subgraph isomorphism [22,27,35]. None of these addresses quantifiers. In contrast, (1) in the same general framework [27] used by these methods, our sequential quantified matching algorithms cope with quantifiers and negated edges without incurring considerable cost; and (2) our parallel scalable algorithms exploit both inter and intra-fragment parallelism for effective quantifier verification in QGP evaluation.

Various strategies have been studied for graph partition [6,11,23]. This work differs from the prior work in the following. (1) We propose a d-hop preserving partition scheme such that the d-hop neighbor of each node is contained in a fragment, and that all fragments have an even size, with an approximation bound. Closest to ours is the n hop-guarantee partition [22]. However, [22] provides no approximation bound to ensure both d-hop preserving and balanced fragment sizes, especially for nodes with a high degree. (2) We propose a partition algorithm that is parallel scalable, a property that is not guaranteed by the prior strategies.

Quantified association rules. Association rules [3] are traditionally defined on relations of transaction data. Over relations, quantified association rules [38] and ratio rules [25] impose value ranges or ratios (*e.g.,* the aggregated ratio of two attribute values) as constraints on *attribute values.* There has also been recent work on extending association rules to social networks [30,36] and RDF knowledge bases, which resorts to mining conventional rules and Horn rules (as conjunctive binary predicates) [17] over tuples with extracted attributes from social graphs, instead of exploiting graph patterns. Closer to this work is [16], which defines association rules directly with patterns without quantifiers.

Our work on QGARs differs from the previous work in the following. (1) As opposed to [3,25,38], QGARs extend association rules from relations to graphs. They call for topological support and confidence metrics, since the conventional support metric is not anti-monotonic in graphs. (2) QGARs allow simple yet powerful counting quantifiers to be imposed on matches of graph patterns, beyond attribute values. In particular, rules of [25,38] cannot express universal quantification and negation. When it comes to graphs, (3) the rules of [16] cannot express counting quantifiers, and limits their consequent to be a single edge, and (4) applying QGPs and QGARs becomes an intractable problem, as opposed to PTIME for conventional rules in relations.

2. QUANTIFIED GRAPH PATTERNS

We next introduce quantified graph patterns QGPs. To define QGPs, we first review conventional graph patterns.

2.1 Conventional Graph Pattern Matching

We consider labeled, directed *graphs*, defined as $G = (V, E, L)$, where (1) V is a finite set of nodes; (2) $E \subseteq V \times V$ is a set of edges, in which (v, v') denotes an edge from node v to v'; and (3) each node v in V (resp. edge e in E) carries $L(v)$ (resp. $L(e)$), indicating its label or content as commonly found in social networks and property graphs.

Two example graphs are depicted in Fig. 2.

We review two notions of subgraphs. (1) A graph $G' = (V', E', L')$ is a *subgraph of* $G = (V, E, L)$, denoted by $G' \subseteq G$, if $V' \subseteq V$, $E' \subseteq E$, and for each edge $e \in E'$ (resp. node $v \in V'$), $L'(e) = L(e)$ (resp. $L'(v) = L(v)$). (2) We say that G' is *a subgraph induced by* a set V' of nodes if $G' \subseteq G$ and E' consists of all the edges in G whose endpoints are in V'.

Patterns. A *graph pattern* is traditionally defined as a graph $Q(x_o) = (V_Q, E_Q, L_Q)$, where (1) V_Q (resp. E_Q) is a set of pattern nodes (resp. edges), (2) L_Q is a function that assigns a node label $L_Q(u)$ (resp. edge label $L_Q(e)$) to each pattern node $u \in V_Q$ (resp. edge $e \in E_Q$), and (3) x_o is a node in V_Q, referred to as the *query focus* of Q, for search intent.

Pattern matching. A *match* of pattern Q in graph G is a *bijective function* h from nodes of Q to nodes of a subgraph G' of G, such that (a) for each node $u \in V_Q$, $L_Q(u) = L(h(u))$, and (b) (u, u') is an edge in Q if and only if $(h(u), h(u'))$ is an edge in G', and $L_Q(u, u') = L(h(u), h(u'))$. From h, subgraph G' can be readily deduced.

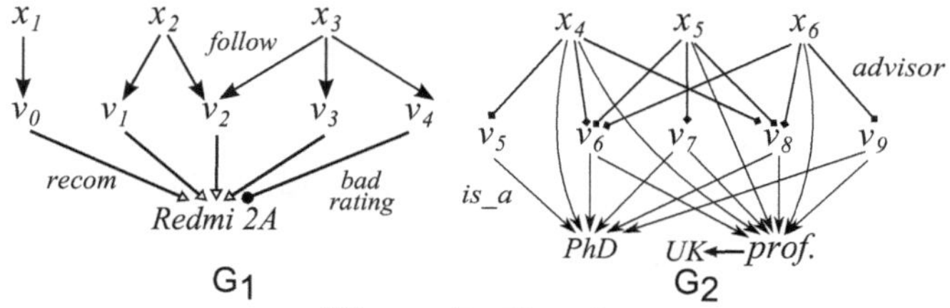

Figure 2: Graphs

We denote by $Q(G)$ *the set of matches* of Q in G, *i.e.,* the set of bijective functions h that induce a match of Q in G. *Query answer* is the set of all matches of x_o in $Q(G)$.

Given $Q(x_o)$ and G, *graph pattern matching* is to compute $Q(x_o, G)$, *i.e.,* all matches of query focus x_o in G via Q.

2.2 Quantified Graph Patterns

We next define QGPs, by extending conventional graph patterns to express quantified search conditions.

Syntax. A *quantified graph pattern* (QGP) $Q(x_o)$ is defined as (V_Q, E_Q, L_Q, f), where V_Q, E_Q, L_Q and x_o are the same as their traditional counterparts, and f is a function such that for each edge $e \in E_Q$, $f(e)$ is a predicate of

- a *positive form* $\sigma(e) \odot p\%$ for a real number $p \in (0, 100]$, or $\sigma(e) \odot p$ for a positive integer p, or
- $\sigma(e) = 0$, where e is referred to as a *negated edge.*

Here $\odot$ is either $=$ or $\geq$, and $\sigma(e)$ will be elaborated shortly. We refer to $f(e)$ as the *counting quantifier* of e, and $p\%$ and p as *ratio* and *numeric aggregate*, respectively.

Counting quantifiers express logic quantifiers as follows:

- *negation* when $f(e)$ is $\sigma(e) = 0$ (*e.g.,* Q_3 in Example 1);
- *existential quantification* if $f(e)$ is $\sigma(e) \geq 1$; and
- *universal quantifier* if $f(e)$ is $\sigma(e) = 100\%$ (*e.g.,* Q_2).

A conventional pattern Q is a special case of QGP when $f(e)$ is $\sigma(e) \geq 1$ for all edges e in Q, *i.e.,* if Q has existential quantification only. We leave out $f(e)$ if it is $\sigma(e) \geq 1$.

We call a QGP Q *positive* if it contains no negated edges (*i.e.,* edges e with $\sigma(e) = 0$), and *negative* otherwise.

Example 2: Graph patterns Q_1–Q_4 given in Example 1 are QGPs with various counting quantifiers, *e.g.,* (1) edge (x_o, z) in Q_1 has a quantifier $\sigma(x_o, z) \geq 80\%$; (2) Q_2 has a universal quantifier $\sigma(x_o, z)$=100% on edge (x_o, z), and an existential quantifier for edge $(z$, Redmi 2A); and (3) Q_3 has a negated edge (x_o, z_2) with $\sigma(x_o, z_2) = 0$. Among the QGPs, Q_1 and Q_2 are positive, while Q_3 and Q_4 are negative. □

Remark. To strike a balance between the expressive power and the complexity of pattern matching with QGPs in large-scale graphs, we assume a predefined *constant* l such that on any simple path (*i.e.,* a path that contains no cycle) in $Q(x_o)$, (a) there exist at most l quantifiers that are not existential, and (b) there exist no more than one negated edge, *i.e.,* we exclude "double negation" from QGPs.

The reason for imposing the restriction is twofold. (1) Without the restriction, quantified patterns would be able to express first-order logic (FO) on graphs. Indeed, FO sentences $P_1X_1 \ldots P_lX_l\ \varphi$ can be encoded in such a pattern, where P_i is either $\forall$ or $\exists$, φ is a logic formula, and l is unbounded. Such patterns inherit the complexity of FO [29], in addition to #P complication. Then even the problem for deciding whether there exists a graph that matches such a pattern is beyond reach in practice. As will be seen shortly, the restriction makes QGPs discovery and evaluation feasible in

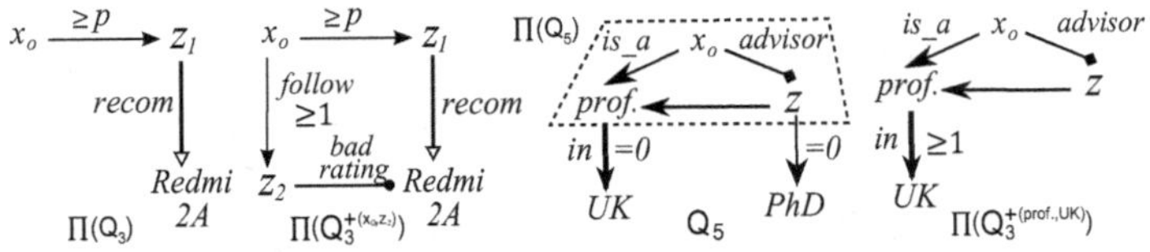

Figure 3: Negative QGPs

large-scale graphs. (2) Moreover, we find that QGPs with the restriction suffice to express quantified patterns commonly needed in real-life applications, for *small* l. Indeed, empirical study suggests that l is at most 2, and "double negation" is rare, as "99% of real-world queries are star-like" [18].

One can extend $f(e)$ to support $>$, $\neq$ and $\leq$ as $\odot$, and conjunctions of predicates. To simplify the discussion, we focus on QGPs $Q(x_o)$ in the simple form given above.

Semantics. We next give the semantics of QGPs. We consider positive QGPs first, and then QGPs with negation.

Positive QGPs. We use the following notations. Striping all quantifiers $f(e)$ off from a QGP $Q(x_o)$, we obtain a conventional pattern, referred to as the *stratified pattern* of $Q(x_o)$ and denoted by $Q_\pi(x_o)$. Consider an edge $e = (u, u')$ in $Q(x_o)$, a graph G and nodes v_x and v in G. When x_o is mapped to v_x, we define *the set of children of* v *via* e *and* Q, denoted by $M_e(v_x, v, Q)$ when G is clear from the context:

$$\{v' \mid h \in Q_\pi(G), h(x_o) = v_x, h(e) = (v, v')\},$$

i.e., the set of children of v that match u' when u is mapped to v, subject to the constraints of Q_π. Abusing the notion of isomorphic mapping, $h(e) = (v, v')$ denotes $h(u) = h(v)$, $h(u') = h(v')$, $(v, v') \in G$ and $L_Q(u, u') = L(v, v')$.

We define $M_e(v) = \{v' \mid (v, v') \in G, L(v, v') = L_Q(e)\}$, the set of the children of v connected by an e edge.

For a positive QGP $Q(x_o)$, *a match* $h_0 \in Q(G)$ satisfies the following conditions: for *each* node u in Q and *each* edge $e = (u, u')$ in Q,

- if $f(e)$ is $\sigma(e) \odot p\%$, then $\frac{|M_e(h_0(x_o), h_0(u), Q)|}{|M_e(h_0(u))|} \odot p\%$, in terms of the ratio of the number of children of v via e and Q to the total number of children of v via e; and
- if $f(e)$ is $\sigma(e) \odot p$, then $|M_e(h_0(x_o), h_0(u), Q)| \odot p$, in terms of the number of children of v via e and Q.

That is, $\sigma(e)$ is defined as ratio $\frac{|M_e(h_0(x_o), h_0(u), Q)|}{|M_e(h_0(u))|}$ or cardinality $|M_e(h_0(x_o), h_0(u), Q)|$, for $p\%$ or p, respectively. Intuitively, $\sigma(e)$ requires that at least $p\%$ of nodes or p nodes in $M_e(v)$ are matches for u' when v is mapped to u. A match in $Q(G)$ must satisfy the topological constraints of Q_π and moreover, the counting quantifiers of Q. Note that the counting quantifier on edge $e = (u, u')$ is applied at *each match* $h_0(u)$ of u, to enforce the semantics of counting.

We denote by $Q(u, G)$ the set of matches of a pattern node u, *i.e.*, nodes $v = h(u)$ induced by all matches h of Q in G. The *query answer* of $Q(x_o)$ in G is defined as $Q(x_o, G)$.

Example 3: For graph G_1 in Fig. 2 and QGP Q_2 of Example 1, $Q_2(x_o, G_1) = \{x_1, x_2\}$. Indeed, 100% of the friends of x_1 and x_2 recommend Redmi 2A. More specifically, for pattern edge e = follow(x_o, z), when x_o is mapped to x_1 via h_0, $M_e(h_0(x_o), x_1, Q) = \{v_0\}$, which is the set $M_e(x_1)$ of all people whom x_1 follows; similarly when x_o is mapped to x_2. In contrast, while x_3 matches x_o via the stratified pattern of Q_2, $x_3 \notin Q_2(x_o, G_1)$ since at least one user whom x_3 follows (*i.e.*, v_4) has no recom edge to Redmi 2A. □

symbols	notations
$Q(x_o)$	QGP, defined as (V_Q, E_Q, L_Q, f)
$Q(x_o, G)$	query answer, the set of matches of x_o
$Q_\pi(x_o)$	stratified pattern of Q by removing quantifiers
$G' \subseteq G$	G' is a subgraph of G
$M_e(v_x, v, Q)$	$\{v' \mid h \in Q_\pi(G), h(x_o) = v_x, h(e) = (v, v')\}$, $e = (u, u')$
$M_e(v)$	$\{v' \mid (v, v') \in G, L(v, v') = L_Q(e)\}$
$\sigma(e) \odot p\%$	$\frac{\lvert M_e(h_0(x_o), h_0(u), Q)\rvert}{\lvert M_e(h_0(u))\rvert} \odot p\%$, $e = (u, u')$, $h_0 \in Q(G)$
$\sigma(e) \odot p$	$\lvert M_e(h_0(x_o), h_0(u), Q)\rvert \odot p$, $e = (u, u')$, $h_0 \in Q(G)$
$\Pi(Q)$	$Q(x_o)$ excluding nodes with negated edges
Q^{+e}	by positifying a negated edge e in Q
$R(x_o)$	QGAR $Q_1(x_o) \Rightarrow Q_2(x_o)$

Table 1: Notations used in the paper

Negative QGPs. To cope with QGP $Q(x_o)$ with negated edges, we define the following: (1) $\Pi(Q)$: the QGP induced by those nodes in $Q(x_o)$ that are connected to x_o (via a path from or to x_o) with non-negated edges in $Q(x_o)$, *i.e.*, $\Pi(Q)$ excludes all those nodes connected via at least one negated edge; (2) Q^{+e}, obtained by "positifying" a negated edge e in Q, *i.e.*, by changing $f(e)$ from $\sigma(e) = 0$ to $\sigma(e) \geq 1$; and (3) E_Q^-, the set of all negated edges in Q.

Then in a graph G, *query answer* to $Q(x_o)$ is defined as

$$Q(x_o, G) = \Pi(Q)(x_o, G) \setminus \left(\bigcup_{e \in E_Q^-} \Pi(Q^{+e})(x_o, G)\right).$$

That is, we enforce negation via set difference. One can verify that for *each* node u in Q and *each* negated edge $e = (u, u')$ in Q, $|M_e(h_0(x_o), h_0(u), Q)| = 0$.

Example 4: Consider G_1 and Q_3 of Example 1 with p=2. Pattern $\Pi(Q_3)$, which excludes the negated edge $e = (x_o, z_2)$ in Q_3, and $\Pi(Q_3^{+e})$, which"positifies" e in Q_3, are shown in Fig. 3. One can verify the following: (1) $\Pi(Q_3)(x_o, G_1)$ is $\{x_2, x_3\}$; note that x_1 is not a match since only 1 user whom x_1 follows recommends Redmi 2A, and hence violates the counting quantifier $\geq p$; and (2) $\Pi(Q_2^{+e})$ is $\{x_3\}$, which is a "negative" instance for Q_3. Hence, $Q_3(x_o, G_1)$ is $\{x_2\}$, where x_3 is excluded since he follows v_4 who gave a bad rating on Redmi 2A, *i.e.*, violating the negation $\sigma(e) = 0$.

Similarly, for QGP Q_4 and graph G_2 of Fig. 2, when p=2, $Q_4(x_o, G_2)$ is $\{x_5, x_6\}$. Note that node x_4 matches the stratified pattern of Q_4, but it violates the negation on (x_o, PhD), which requires that matches of x_o must not be a PhD.

As another example, consider $Q_5(x_o)$ with two negated edges e_1 = (Prof, UK) and e_2 = (z, PhD). It is to find non-UK professors who supervised students who are professors but have no PhD degree. As shown in Fig. 3, $\Pi(Q_5)$ finds professors who supervised students who are professors. In contrast, $\Pi(Q_5^{+e_1})$ finds such professors in the UK, and $\Pi(Q_5^{+e_2})$ (not shown) retrieves professors with students who are professors and have a PhD. In a graph G, $Q(x_o, G) = \Pi(Q_5)(x_o, G) \setminus (\Pi(Q_5^{+e_1})(x_o, G) \cup \Pi(Q_5^{+e_2})(x_o, G))$. □

The notations of this paper are summarized in Table 1.

3. THE COMPLEXITY OF QUANTIFIED MATCHING

In the next three sections, we study *quantified matching*:

- *Input*: A QGP $Q(x_o)$ and a graph G.
- *Output*: $Q(x_o, G)$,

to compute the set of all matches of query focus x_o of Q in G. We start with its complexity in this section.

Decision problem. Its decision problem, referred to as *the quantified matching problem*, is stated as follows.

- *Input*: A QGP $Q(x_o)$, a graph G and a node v in G.

∘ *Question*: Is $v \in Q(x_o, G)$?

When $Q(x_o)$ is a conventional pattern, the problem is NP-complete. When it comes to QGPs, however, ratio aggregates $\sigma \odot p\%$ and negation $\sigma = 0$ increase the expressive power, and make the analysis more intriguing. To handle $\sigma \odot p\%$, for instance, a brute-force approach invokes an NP algorithm that calls a #P oracle to check the ratio aggregate.

We show that while the increased expressive power of QGPs comes with a price, their complexity bound does not get much higher. In particular, #P is not necessary.

Theorem 1: *The quantified matching problem remains* NP-*complete for positive* QGPs, *and it becomes* DP-*complete for (possibly negative)* QGPs. □

Here DP is the class of languages recognized by oracle machines that make a call to an NP oracle and a call to a coNP oracle. That is, L is in DP if there exist languages $L_1 \in$ NP and $L_2 \in$ coNP such that $L = L_1 \cap L_2$ [33].

That is, adding positive quantifiers to conventional graph patterns does not increase the complexity, although ratio aggregates add extra expressive power. Note that such positive patterns alone are already useful in practice. In contrast, the presence of negation makes quantified matching harder, but it remains low in the polynomial hierarchy [33].

The proof is nontrivial. Below we present lemmas needed.

The lower bounds follow from the stronger results below, which are in turn verified by reductions from SUBGRAPH ISOMORPHISM and EXACT-CLIQUE, which are NP-complete and DP-complete, respectively (cf. [33]).

Lemma 2: *For* QGPs *with numeric aggregates only, the quantified matching problem is* NP-*hard for positive* QGPs, *and* DP-*hard for (possibly negative)* QGPs. □

The upper bounds are verified by the next two lemmas. In particular, Lemma 4 shows that ratio aggregates can be encoded as numeric aggregates by transforming *both* query Q and graph G, in PTIME. This explains why positive QGPs with ratio aggregates retain the same complexity as conventional patterns, despite their increased expressivity.

Lemma 3: *For* QGPs *with numeric aggregates only, the quantified matching problem is in* NP *for positive* QGPs, *and is in* DP *for (possibly negative)* QGPs. □

Lemma 4: *Any* QGP $Q(x_o)$ *and graph* G *can be transformed in* PTIME *to* QGP $Q_d(x_o)$ *with numeric aggregates only and graph* G_d*, respectively, such that* $Q(x_o, G) = Q_d(x_o, G_d)$. □

Remark. As QGPs with quantifiers bearing $\leq, \neq$ and $<$ subsume the case when $\sigma(e) = 0$, quantified matching is DP-hard for such QGPs. Due to the space limit, we focus on $\geq, =, >$ and leave a full treatment to future work.

4. ALGORITHMS FOR QUANTIFIED MATCHING

We next provide an algorithm, denoted by QMatch, for quantified matching. It takes a QGP $Q(x_o)$ and a graph G as input, and computes $Q(x_o, G)$ as output. It extends existing algorithms $\mathcal{T}$ for conventional subgraph isomorphism, to incorporate quantifier checking and process negated edges.

Generic graph pattern matching. We start by reviewing a generic procedure for subgraph isomorphism, denoted by Match and shown in Fig. 4, slightly adapted from [27] to output $Q(x_o, G)$ for query focus x_o. As observed in [27],

```
Algorithm Match
Input: pattern Q(x_o), graph G
Output: the answer set Q(x_o, G)
1.  Q(x_o, G):= ∅; Q(G):=∅; M := ∅;
2.  for each u of Q do
3.     C(u):=Filtercandidate(Q, G, u);
4.     if C(u)=∅ then return ∅;
5.  SubMatch(Q, G, M, Q(G));
6.  for each isomorphic mapping h ∈ Q(G) do
7.     Q(x_o, G):=Q(x_o, G) ∪ {h(x_o)};
8.  return Q(x_o, G);

Procedure SubMatch(Q, G, M, Q(G))
1.  if Verify(M) then
2.     Q(G):=Q(G) ∪ {h}; /*h: the isomorphism defined by M*/
3.  else u:=SelectNext(Q);
4.        for each v ∈ C(u) not matched in M do
5.           if IsExtend(Q, G, M, u, v) then
6.              M := M ∪ {(u, v)};
7.              SubMatch(Q, G, M, Q(G));
8.              Restore(M, u, v);
9.  return;
```

Figure 4: Generic search procedure Match

state-of-the-art graph pattern matching algorithms $\mathcal{T}$ typically adopt Match, and differ only in how to optimize key functions (*e.g.,* SelectNext, IsExtend; see below). Given a traditional pattern $Q(x_o)$ and a graph G, Match initializes $Q(x_o, G)$, as well as a partial match M as a set of node pairs (line 1). Each pair (u, v) in M denotes that a node from G matches a pattern node u in Q. It identifies a candidate match set $C(u)$ for each pattern node u in Q (lines 3-4) (FilterCandidate). If there exists a pattern node u with no candidate, it returns $\emptyset$ (line 4). Otherwise, it invokes SubMatch to compute *all matches* (isomorphic mappings) $Q(G)$ (lines 5). It then computes and returns query answer $Q(x_o, G)$ from mappings $h \in Q(G)$ (lines 6-8).

Procedure SubMatch recursively extends partial match M by using three key functions. (1) It picks a pattern node u from Q that has no match yet (SelectNext, line 3). (2) It then checks whether a candidate v of u not yet in M matches u (IsExtend), and if so, it adds (u, v) to M (lines 4-6). (3) It recursively calls SubMatch to extend M with steps (1) and (2) (line 7), and restores it when SubMatch backtracks (line 8). If M is a valid isomorphism (Verify, line 1), it adds M to $Q(G)$ (line 2). This continues until $Q(G)$ is completed.

4.1 Quantified Graph Pattern Matching

Algorithm QMatch revises the generic Match to process quantifiers. (1) It first adopts a *dynamic selection and pruning strategy* to compute $\Pi(Q)(x_o, G)$. The dynamic search picks top p promising neighbors based on a potential score, with p adapted to the corresponding quantifiers. (2) It then employs *optimal incremental evaluation* to process negated edges, which maximally reuses cached matches for $\Pi(Q)$ when processing Q^{+e} for positified e, instead of recomputing $Q^{+e}(G)$ starting from scratch. The strategies are supported by optimized data structures and key functions from Match.

Auxiliary structures. QMatch maintains auxiliary structures for each node v in $C(u)$ as follows: (1) a Boolean variable $X(u, v)$ indicating whether v is a match of u via isomorphism from $\Pi(Q)$ to G, and (2) a vector T, where entry $T(v, e)$ for an edge $e{=}(u, u')$ in Q is a pair $\langle c(v, e), U(v, e)\rangle$, in which c (resp. U, initialized as $M_e(v)$) records the current size (resp. an estimate upper bound for) $|M_e(v_x, v, Q)|$.

Algorithm QMatch
Input: a QGP $Q(x_o)$, graph G
Output: the answer set $Q(x_o, G)$

```
1.  Q(x_o, G) := ∅; M := ∅; Π(Q)(x_o, G) := ∅; Π(Q)(G) := ∅;
2.  for each u of Q do
3.      initializes C(u) and auxiliary structures;
4.  Π(Q)(x_o, G) := DMatch(Π(Q), G, M, Π(Q)(G));
5.  for each negative edge e in E_Q^- do
6.      Q^{+e}(x_o, G) := IncQMatch(Π(Q)(x_o, G), Q^{+e});
7.  Q(x_o, G) := Π(Q)(x_o, G) \ ∪_{e∈E_Q^-} Q^{+e}(x_o, G);
8.  return Q(x_o, G);
```

Figure 5: Algorithm QMatch

Algorithm. Algorithm QMatch (outlined in Fig. 5) revises Match to process QGP $Q(x_o)$ in three steps. (1) It first initializes the candidate set and auxiliary structures with a revised Filtercandidate (lines 1-3). For each pattern node u in $Q(x_o)$, it initializes (a) $C(u)$ with nodes v of the same label, and (b) $X(u, v) = \perp$, $c(v, e)$=0 and $U(v, e) = |M_e(v)|$ for each e=(u, u') in Q. It removes v from $C(u)$ if $U(v, e)$ does not satisfy the quantifier of e. (2) It next invokes a procedure DMatch revised from SubMatch in Fig. 4 to compute $\Pi(Q)(x_o, G)$ (line 4). (3) It then processes each negated edge e by constructing its positified pattern Q^{+e}, and computes $Q^{+e}(x_o, G)$ with an incremental procedure IncQMatch (lines 5-6). (4) It computes $Q(x_o, G)$ by definition (line 7). We next present DMatch, and defer IncQMatch to Section 4.2.

Example 5: Given Q_3 with p=2 (Fig. 1) and G_1 (Fig. 2), QMatch first computes $\Pi(Q_3)(x_o, G_1)$ (Fig. 3). It initializes variables for nodes in G_1, partially shown below ($i \in [0, 4]$).

	X	c	U
x_1	$X(x_o, x_1)$=$\perp$	$c(x_1, (x_o, z_1))$=0	$U(x_1, (x_o, z_1))$=1
x_2	$X(x_o, x_2)$=$\perp$	$c(x_2, (x_o, z_1))$=0	$U(x_2, (x_o, z_1))$=2
x_3	$X(x_o, x_3)$=$\perp$	$c(x_3, (x_o, z_1))$=0	$U(x_3, (x_o, z_1))$=3
v_i	$X(x_o, v_i)$=$\perp$	$c(v_i, (z_1,$Redmi$))$=0	$U(v_i, (z_1,$ Redmi$))$=1

At this stage, since $U(x_1, (x_o, z_1))$=1 $\leq$ 2, x_1 fails the quantifier of (x_o, z_1), and is removed from $C(x_o)$. □

Procedure DMatch. Given positive QGP $\Pi(Q)$, DMatch revises SubMatch (Fig 4) by adopting dynamic search. To simplify the discussion, we consider numeric $\sigma(e) \odot p$ first.

(1) Given a selected pattern node u' (line 3 of SubMatch), a candidate $v \in C(u)$, and an edge e=(u, u') with quantifier $\sigma(e) \odot p$, DMatch *dynamically* finds p best nodes (recorded in a heap $S_P(u')$) from $C(u')$ that are children of v (lines 4-5 of SubMatch, IsExtend), using selection and pruning rules (see Appendix B). Denote as $P(v')$ the parent set of v' in G, the *potential* of a match $v' \in C(u')$ is defined as:

$$(1 + \frac{|P(v') \cap C(u)|}{|C(u)|}) * \Sigma_{\forall e=(u', u'')} \frac{U(v', e)}{p_e},$$

where p_e is the number in $\sigma(e) \odot p_e$ for edge e=(u', u''). It favors those candidates that (a) benefit the verification of more candidates during future backtracking, and (b) have high upper bounds *w.r.t.* p (hence more likely to be a match itself). We select candidates with the highest scores.

DMatch then updates M by including (u, v), and recursively conducts the next level of search by forking p verifications in the order of the selected p candidates (line 7, SubMatch). It keeps a record of M and a cursor to memorize the candidates in S_P for backtracking, using a stack.

(2) When backtracking to a candidate $v \in S_P(u)$ from a child v' of v, DMatch restores M and the cursor (Restore, line 8 of SubMatch). It next dynamically updates $S_P(u)$. (a) If $X(u', v')$=false, it reduces $U(v, e)$ by 1. (b) It applies the selection and pruning rules to $C(u)$ using the *updated* potentials *w.r.t.* the changes in (a). If the upper bound $U(v, e)$ fails the quantifier of e, v is removed from $C(u)$ and $S_P(u)$ *without* further verifying its other children. Otherwise, it picks a new set $S_P(u)$ of candidates with top potentials.

(3) When M is complete, *i.e.*, each node u in $\Pi(Q)$ has a match in M, DMatch checks whether M is an isomorphic mapping. If so, it updates $X(u, v)$=true for each pair $(u, v) \in M$, and increases the counter $c(v, e)$. It then checks whether the counters *satisfy the quantifiers* of $\Pi(Q)$. If so, it adds v_x to $Q(x_o, G)$. Otherwise, it proceeds. DMatch terminates when all the candidates of x_o are checked.

Example 6: Continuing with Example 5, given $C(x_o) = \{x_2, x_3\}$, DMatch selects x_2, and extends M with (x_o, x_2). In contrast to Fig 4, DMatch picks top 2 best candidates $S_P(z_1)$ = $\{v_2, v_1\}$ from $C(z_1)$ following edge e=(x_o, z_1). This adds (z_1, v_2) to M, and (Redmi 2A, Redmi 2A) for the next round. At verification, it finds M a complete isomorphism, and updates $X(v_o, x_2)$=true and $c(x_2, e)$=1. As x_2 cannot be verified as a match via $\Pi(Q_3)$ yet, DMatch next verifies v_1, and sets $c(x_2, e)$=2. As x_2 is a match and has a counter satisfying the quantifier, it is added to $\Pi(Q_3)(x_o, G_1)$. The updated variables for candidates of $C(x_o)$ are as follows.

	X	c	U
x_2	$X(x_o, x_2)$=True	$c(x_2, (x_o, z_1))$=2	$U(x_2, (x_o, z_1))$=2
x_3	$X(x_o, x_3)$=$\perp$	$c(x_3, (x_o, z_1))$=2	$U(x_3, (x_o, z_1))$=3

DMatch next verifies x_3. It starts by selecting top 2 candidates $S_P(x_3)$=$\{v_2, v_3\}$. Once v_3 is processed, it finds that x_3 is in an isomorphism with $c(x_3, e)$=2, and hence is a match. It returns $\{x_2, x_3\}$ as $\Pi(Q_3)(x_o, G_1)$. □

One can readily verify the following (see Appendix A).

Lemma 5: DMatch *computes* $\Pi(Q)(x_o, G)$ *by (a) verifying no more candidates than any* Match*-based subgraph isomorphism algorithm* $\mathcal{T}$*, and (b) with space cost* $O(p_m|Q| + |V|)$*, where* p_m *is the largest constant in all quantifiers of* Q. □

That is, quantified matching can be evaluated following conventional $\mathcal{T}$ without incurring significant extra time and space cost. The performance of DMatch is further improved by selection and pruning rules presented in Appendix B.

Ratio aggregates. DMatch can be readily extended to process ratio aggregates. Indeed, for each pattern e=(u, u') with $\sigma(e) \odot p\%$ and at a candidate v of u, DMatch "transforms" the quantifier to its equivalent numeric counterpart $\sigma(e) \odot p'$ as follows. (a) DMatch computes $|M_e(v)|$ by definition. (2) It sets $p' = \lfloor |M_e(v)| * p\% \rfloor$. The transformation for e preserves all the exact matches for ratio quantifiers by definition, and takes a linear scan of G (in $O(|G|)$ time). In addition, QMatch easily extends to QGPs with quantifiers $\sigma(e) > p$, by replacing it with $\sigma(e) \geq p + 1$.

4.2 Incremental Quantified Matching

If $\Pi(Q)(x_o, G)$ is nonempty, QMatch proceeds to compute $\Pi(Q^{+e})(x_o, G)$ for each negated edge $e \in E_Q^-$ (lines 5-6, Fig. 5). Observe the following: (1) $\Pi(Q^{+e})$=$\Pi(Q) \oplus \Delta E$, *i.e.*, $\Pi(Q^{+e})$ "expands" $\Pi(Q)$ with a set ΔE of positive edges; and (2) for any node u in $\Pi(Q)$, $\Pi(Q^{+e})(u, G) \subseteq \Pi(Q)(u, G)$, since $\Pi(Q^{+e})$ adds more constraints to $\Pi(Q)$.

This observation motivates us to study a novel *incremental quantified matching* problem. Given a graph G, a QGP Q, computed matches $Q(u, G)$ for each u in Q, and a new QGP $Q'=Q \oplus \Delta E$, it is to compute $Q'(x_o, G) = Q(x_o, G) \oplus \Delta O$, *i.e.*, to find changes ΔO in the output. It aims to make maximum use of cached results $Q(u, G)$, instead of computing $Q'(x_o, G)$ from scratch. As opposed to conventional incremental problems [15, 34], we compute ΔO in response to changes in *query* Q, rather than to changes in graph G.

As observed in [34], the complexity of incremental graph problems should be measured in the size of *affected area*, which indicates the amount of work that is necessarily performed by any algorithm for the incremental problem. For pattern matching via subgraph isomorphism, the number of verifications is typically the major bottleneck. Below we identify affected area for quantified matching, to characterize the optimality of incremental quantified matching.

Optimal incremental quantified matching. Given Q and $\Pi(Q^{+e})$, the *affected area* is defined as

$$\mathsf{AFF} = \bigcup C(u_i) \cup \{N(v) \mid v \in C(u_i)\},$$

where (1) u_i is in edge $e_i=(u_i, u_i')$ or (u_i', u_i) for each $e_i \in \Delta E$; (2) $C(u_i)$ includes (a) the match sets cached after DMatch processed $\Pi(Q)$; and (b) the candidate sets initialized by QMatch (line 3 of Fig 5) for new nodes u_i introduced by $\Pi(Q^{+e})$, which have to be checked; and (c) $N(v)$ is the set of nodes in cached $C(\cdot)$ that are reachable from (or reached by) v, via paths that contains only the nodes in $C(\cdot)$.

An incremental quantified matching algorithm is *optimal* if it incurs $O(|\mathsf{AFF}|)$ number of verifications. Intuitively, AFF is the set of nodes that are necessarily verified in response to ΔE, for any such algorithms to find exact matches.

Proposition 6: *There exists an incremental algorithm that computes each $\Pi(Q^{+e})(x_o, G)$ by conducting at most $|\mathsf{AFF}|$ rounds of verification.* □

As a proof, we present an optimal algorithm IncQMatch.

Procedure IncQMatch. Algorithm IncQMatch (used in line 6, Fig. 5) incrementally computes $\Pi(Q^{+e})(x_o, G)$ by reusing the cached match sets and the counters computed in the process of DMatch for $\Pi(Q)$. It works as follows.

(1) IncQMatch initializes $\Pi(Q^{+e})(u, G)$ for each u with the cached matches $\Pi(Q)(u, G)$. It then computes the edge set ΔE in $\Pi(Q^{+e})(x_o, G)$ to be "inserted" into $\Pi(Q)$.

(2) IncQMatch then iteratively processes the edges $e=(u, u')$ in ΔE. It first identifies those cached matches that are *affected* by the insertion. It considers two possible cases below.

- Both u and u' are in $\Pi(Q)$. For each match $v \in \Pi(Q)(u, G)$, IncQMatch adds v to AFF and verifies whether v matches u via isomorphism following DMatch. If $X(u, v)$=true, it counts $c(v, e)$ as the number of v's children v' that are matches of u' and checks the quantifier of e. If $c(v, e)$ satisfies the quantifier, no change happens. Otherwise ($c(v, e)$ fails the quantifier) IncQMatch removes v from $\Pi(Q^{+e})(u, G)$.
- One or both of nodes u and u' are not in $\Pi(Q)$. For the new node u (or u'), IncQMatch treats e as a single edge pattern and verifies each candidate v_1 in $C(u)$. Since $\Pi(Q)$ is a "sub-pattern" of $\Pi(Q^{+e})$ and $\Pi(Q^{+e})$ is connected, we need only to inspect those matches v_1 reachable from some nodes in cached $C(.)$, *i.e.*, $v_1 \in N(v_2)$ for some cached v_2; hence $v_1 \in \mathsf{AFF}$.

For each v removed in the steps above, QMatch then propagates the impact recursively by (a) reducing all the counters of v's parents by 1, and (b) removing invalid matches due to the updated counters and adds them to AFF, following the same backtracking verification as in DMatch, until a fixpoint is reached, *i.e.*, no more matches can be removed.

Example 7: Continuing with Example 6, QMatch invokes IncQMatch to process $\Pi(Q_3^{+(x_o, z_2)})$, with $\Delta E = \{(x_o, z_2), (z_2, \text{Redmi 2A})\}$ (see Fig. 3) as follows.

(1) IncQMatch first initializes the candidate sets as the cached matches in DMatch (shown below). For node z_2 not in $\Pi(Q)$, IncQMatch finds $C(z_2)$ as initialized in QMatch.

pattern node	$C(\cdot)$
x_o	$C(x_o)=\{x_2, x_3\}$
z_1	$C(z_1)=\{v_1, v_2, v_3\}$
z_2	$C(z_2)=\{v_4\}$
Redmi	C(Redmi 2A)={Redmi 2A}

(2) It starts with edge (z_2, Redmi 2A), and initializes AFF as $C(z_2) \cup C$(Redmi 2A)=$\{v_4$, Redmi 2A$\}$. It next checks whether v_4 and Redmi 2A remain matches with counter satisfying the quantifiers. In this process, it only visits the two cached matches x_3 and v_3 following the pattern edges. As both nodes are matches, no change needs to be made.

(3) IncQMatch next processes edge (x_o, z_2). It adds the set $C(x_o)=\{x_2, x_3\}$ to AFF, and checks whether x_2 and x_3 remain matches. As x_2 has no edge to v_4, $X(x_o, x_2)$ is updated to false, and x_2 is removed from $C(x_o)$. It next finds that x_3 is a valid match, by visiting v_2, v_3, Redmi 2A, and v_4.

As no more matches can be removed, IncQMatch stops the verification. It returns $\Pi(Q_3^{+(x_o, z_2)})(x_o, G_1)$ as $\{x_3\}$. After the process, AFF contains $\{v_4, x_2, x_3, v_2, v_3$, Redmi 2A$\}$. It incurs in total 3 rounds of verification for v_4, x_2 and x_3. □

Contrast IncQMatch with DMatch. (1) IncQMatch only visits the cached matches and their edges, rather than the entire G. (2) IncQMatch incurs at most $|\mathsf{AFF}|$ rounds of verifications; hence it is *optimal w.r.t.* incremental complexity.

Analysis of QMatch. Algorithm QMatch correctly computes $Q(x_o, G)$ following the definition of quantified matching (Section 2.2). For its complexity, observe the following.

(1) If Q is positive, *i.e.*, $E_Q^- = \emptyset$, IncQMatch is not needed. Then QMatch and a conventional Match-based algorithm $\mathcal{T}$ for subgraph isomorphism have the same complexity. Quantifier checking is incorporated into the search process.

(2) If E_Q^- is nonempty, IncQMatch invokes at most $|E_Q^-|$ rounds of incremental computation by *optimal* IncQMatch, while $|E_Q^-| \leq |Q|$ and Q is typically small in practice. For each round, the overall time taken is bounded by $|\mathsf{AFF}| * K$, where K is the cost of a single verification.

Put together, QMatch takes $O(t(\mathcal{T}) + |E_Q^-||\mathsf{AFF}| * K)$ time in total, where $t(\mathcal{T})$ is the time complexity of a Match-based algorithm $\mathcal{T}$ for conventional subgraph isomorphism. We find in our experiments that QMatch and $\mathcal{T}$ have comparable performance, due to small $|E_Q^-|$ and $|\mathsf{AFF}|$. Moreover, existing optimization for $\mathcal{T}$ can be readily applied to QMatch.

Algorithm QMatch also makes use of graph simulation [21] to filter candidates and reduce verification cost. We defer this optimization strategy to Appendix-B.

5. PARALLEL QUANTIFIED MATCHING

Quantified matching – in fact even conventional subgraph isomorphism – may be cost-prohibitive over big graphs G.

This suggests that we develop a parallel algorithm for quantified matching that guarantees to scale with big G. We develop such an algorithm, which makes quantified matching feasible in real-life graphs, despite its DP complexity.

5.1 Parallel Scalability

To characterize the effectiveness of parallelism, we advocate a notion of *parallel scalability* following [16, 26]. Consider a problem I posed on a graph G. We denote by $t(|I|, |G|)$ the running time of the best *sequential algorithm* for solving I on G, *i.e.*, one with the least worst-case complexity among all algorithms for I. For a parallel algorithm, we denote by $T(|I|, |G|, n)$ the time it takes to solve I on G by using n processors, taking n as a parameter. Here we assume $n \ll |G|$, *i.e.*, the number of processors does not exceed the size of G; this typically holds in practice as G often has trillions of nodes and edges, much larger than n [20].

Parallel scalability. An algorithm is *parallel scalable* if

$$T(|I|, |G|, n) = O(\frac{t(|I|, |G|)}{n}) + (n|I|)^{O(1)}.$$

That is, the parallel algorithm achieves a linear reduction in sequential running time, plus a "bookkeeping" cost $O((n|I|)^l)$ that is *independent of* $|G|$, for a constant l.

A parallel scalable algorithm *guarantees* that the more processors are used, the less time it takes to solve I on G. Hence given a big graph G, it is feasible to efficiently process I over G by adding processors when needed.

5.2 Parallel Scalable Algorithm

Parallel scalability is within reach for quantified matching under certain condition. We first present some notations. For a node v in graph G and an integer d, the *d-hop neighbor* $N_d(v)$ of v is defined as the subgraph of G induced by the nodes within d hops of v. The *radius* of a QGP $Q(x_o)$ is the longest shortest distance between x_o and any node in Q.

The main result of the section is as follows.

Theorem 7: *There exists an algorithm* PQMatch *that given* QGP $Q(x_o)$ *and graph* G, *computes* $Q(x_o, G)$. *It is parallel scalable for graphs* G *with* $\sum_{v \in G} |N_d(v)| \leq C_d * \frac{|G|}{n}$, *taking* $O(\frac{t(Q,G)}{n} + n)$ *time, where* d *is the radius of* $Q(x_o)$, C_d *is a predefined constant, and* $t(Q, G)$ *is the worst-case running time of sequential quantified matching algorithms.* □

The condition is practical: 99% of real-life patterns have radius at most 2 [18], and the average node degree is 14.3 in social graphs [12]; thus $|N_d(v)|$ is often a small constant. In addition, we will show that PQMatch can be adapted to evaluate QGPs Q with radius larger than d.

As a proof, below we present PQMatch. The algorithm works with a coordinator S_c and n workers (processors) S_i. It utilizes two levels of parallelism. (a) At the *inter-fragment parallelism* level, it creates a partition scheme of G over multiple processors *once for all*, so that quantified matching is performed on all these fragments in parallel. The same partition is used for all QGPs $Q(x_O)$ within radius d. (b) At the *intra-fragment* level, local matching within each fragment is further conducted by multiple threads in parallel.

Hop preserving partition. We start with graph partition. To maximize parallelism, a partition scheme should guarantee that for any graph G, (1) each of n processors manages a small fragment of approximately equal size, and (2) a query can be evaluated locally at each fragment without incurring inter-fragment communication. We propose such a scheme.

Given a graph $G = (V, E, L)$, an integer d and a node set $V' \subseteq V$, a *d-hop preserving partition* $\mathcal{P}_d(V')$ of V' distributes G to a set of n processors such that it is

(1) *balanced*: each processor S_i manages a fragment F_i, which contains the subgraph G_i of G induced by a set V_i of nodes, such that $\bigcup V_i = V'$ ($i \in [1, n]$) and the size of F_i is bounded by $c * \frac{|G|}{n}$, for a small constant $c < C_d$; and

(2) *covering*: each node $v \in V'$ is *covered* by $\mathcal{P}_d(V')$, *i.e.*, there exists a fragment F_i such that $N_d(v)$ is in F_i.

We say that $\mathcal{P}_d(V')$ is *complete* if $|V'| = |V|$.

One naturally wants to find an optimal partition such that the number $|V'|$ of covered nodes is maximized. Although desirable, creating a balanced d-hop preserving partition is NP-hard. Indeed, conventional balanced graph partition is a special case when d=1, which is already NP-hard [6].

Parallel d-hop preserving partition. We provide an approximation algorithm for d-hop preserving partition with an approximation ratio. Better still, it is parallel scalable.

Lemma 8: *If* $\sum_{v \in G} |N_d(v)| \leq C_d * \frac{|G|}{n}$, *for any constant* $\epsilon > 0$, *there is a parallel scalable algorithm with approximation ratio* $1 + \epsilon$ *to compute a d-hop preserving partition.* □

Below we present such an algorithm, denoted by DPar. Given a graph G stored at the coordinator S_c, it starts with a base partition of G, where each fragment F_i has a balanced size bounded by $c * \frac{|G|}{n}$. This can be done by using an existing balanced graph partition strategy (*e.g.*, [23]). DPar then extends each fragment F_i to a d-hop preserving counterpart.

(1) It first finds the "border nodes" $F_i.O$ of F_i that have d-hop neighbors not residing in F_i, by traversing F_i in parallel.

(2) Each worker S_i then computes and loads $N_d(v)$ for each $v \in F_i.O$, by "traversing" G via disk-based parallel breadth-first search (BFS) search [24]. Moreover, DPar uses a balanced loading strategy (see below) to load approximately equal amount of data to each worker in the search. The process repeats until no fragments can be expanded.

Balancing strategy. DPar enforces a balanced fragment size $c * \frac{|G|}{n}$. It conducts a d-hop preserving partition $\mathcal{P}_d(V')$ with approximation ratio $1 - \epsilon$ subject to the bound, for any given ϵ. That is, if the size of nodes covered by the optimal d-hop partition in G is $|V^*|$, then $\mathcal{P}_d(V')$ has $|V'| \geq (1 - \epsilon)|V^*|$.

More specifically, at the BFS phase, for each $v \in \bigcup F_i.O$, DPar assigns $N_d(v)$'s to workers by reduction to *Multiple Knapsack problem* (MKP) [13]. Given a set of weighted items (with a value) and a set of knapsack with capacities, MKP is to assign each item to a knapsack subject to its capacity, such that the total value is maximized. DPar treats each $N_d(v)$ as an item with value 1 and weight $|N_d(v)|$, and each fragment as a knapsack with capacity $c * \frac{|G|}{n} - |F_i|$, with the number of covered nodes as the total value. It solves the MKP instance by invoking the algorithm of [13], which computes an assignment with approximation ratio $1 + \epsilon$ for any given ϵ, in $O(|V'|^{\frac{1}{\epsilon}})$ time. Each worker S_i then loads its assigned $N_d(v)$. This gives us a d-hop preserving partition $\mathcal{P}_d$ with ratio $1 + \epsilon$ (see Appendix A for the reduction).

Partition $\mathcal{P}_d$ may not be complete, *i.e.*, not every node in V is covered. To maximize inter-fragment parallelism, DPar "completes" $\mathcal{P}_d$ while preserving the balanced partition size.

Algorithm PQMatch

Input: QGP $Q(x_o)$, graph G, coordinator S_c, n workers $S_1, \ldots, S_n$
Output: the answer set $Q(x_o, G)$.

1. DPar(G); /*Preprocessing*/

/*executed at coordinator S_c*/

2. $Q(x_o, G) := \emptyset$; post Q to each worker;
3. **if** every worker S_i returns answer $Q(x_o, F_i)$ **then**
4. $\quad Q(x_o, G) := \bigcup Q(x_o, F_i)$;
5. **return** $Q(x_o, G)$;

/*executed at each worker in parallel*/

6. $Q(x_o, F_i) :=$ mQMatch(b, Q, F_i); /* b: the # of threads*/
7. **return** $Q(x_o, F_i)$;

Figure 6: Algorithm PQMatch

For each uncovered node v, it assigns $N_d(v)$ to a worker S_i that minimizes estimated size difference $|F_{max}| - |F_{min}|$, where F_{max} (resp. F_{min}) is the largest (resp. smallest) fragment *if* $N_d(v)$ is merged to F_i. Since $\sum |N_d(v)| \leq C_d * \frac{|G|}{n}$, this suffices to make $\mathcal{P}_d$ both complete and d-preserving.

Example 8: Consider graph G_2 of Fig. 2 and a set $V' = \{v_5, \ldots, v_9\}$. Assume a base partition distributes $\{v_5\}$ to worker S_1, $\{v_7, v_9\}$ to S_2, $\{v_6, v_8\}$ to S_3, respectively. DPar creates a 1-hop preserving partition $\mathcal{P}_1$ for V' as follows. (1) Each S_i identifies its border nodes $F_i.O$ by a local traversal, *e.g.*, $v_5 \in F_1.O$. (2) Each S_i traverses G_2 at S_c and finds $N_1(v)$ for $v \in F_i.O$, in parallel. At the end, S_c keeps track of the nodes (edges) "requested" by workers as follows.

node	requested by
x_4	S_1, S_3
x_5, x_6, **prof.**	S_2, S_3
PhD.	S_1, S_2, S_3

DPar next determines which site to send the border nodes by solving an MKP instance, shown as follows.

site	$N_1(\cdot)$	(estimated) $\lvert F_i \rvert$
S_1	$N_1(v_5)$, $N_1(v_9)$	14 ($\lvert N_1(v_5)\rvert = 6$, $\lvert N_1(v_9)\rvert = 8$)
S_2	$N_1(v_7)$	8
S_3	$N_1(v_8)$	15

Here $N_1(v_5)$ includes three nodes x_4, v_5, PhD, and three edges (x_4, v_5), $(v_5$, PhD) and $(x_4$, PhD); similarly for the others. This induces a 1-hop preserving partition $\mathcal{P}_1$ that covers $\{v_5, v_7, v_8, v_9\}$. To complete $\mathcal{P}_1$, DPar selects S_2 to load $N_1(v_6)$, where $|N_1(v_6)| = 15$. This minimizes the estimated size $|F_{max}| - |F_{min}| = 19 - 14 = 5$. Here $|F_{max}|$ is estimated as the sum of $|F_2| = 8$ and 11 additional nodes and edges in $N_1(v_6)$ that are not "requested" by S_2 (*e.g.*, (x_4, v_6), $(v_6$, PhD)). The completed $\mathcal{P}_1$ covers V' with fragment size 14, 19 and 15 for S_1, S_2 and S_3, respectively. □

Parallel algorithm. Using DPar, we next develop algorithm PQMatch. As shown in Fig. 6, PQMatch takes as input a QGP $Q(x_o)$ of radius at most d, and a graph G distributed across n workers by DPar, where fragment F_i of G resides at worker S_i. It works as follows. (1) The coordinator S_c posts $Q(x_o)$ to each worker S_i (line 2). (2) Each worker S_i then invokes a procedure mQMatch to compute local matches $Q(x_o, F_i)$ (line 7), where mQMatch implements QMatch using multi-threading (see below). Once verified, $Q(x_o, F_i)$ is sent to S_c (line 6). (3) Once all the workers have sent their partial matches to S_c, the coordinator computes $Q(x_o, G)$ as the union of all $Q(x_o, F_i)$ (lines 3-4).

Procedure mQMatch. Procedure mQMatch is a multi-threading implementation of PQMatch (Section 4), supporting inter-fragment level parallelism. For pattern edge $e = (u, u')$ with quantifier $\sigma(e) \odot p$ and a candidate v in $C(u)$, it spawns p threads to simultaneously verify the top p selected candidates, one for each. Each thread i maintains local partial matches (in its local memory). When all the p threads backtrack to v, the local partial matches are merged, and the local counter of u is updated by aggregating the local storage of each thread i (see Appendix B for more details).

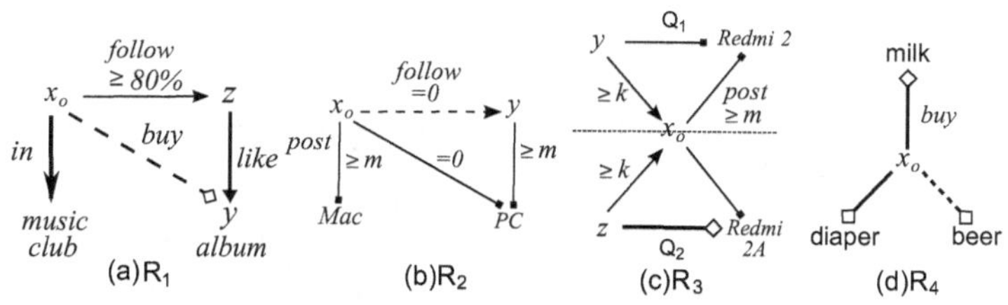

Figure 7: QGARs

From Lemma 8 and Lemma 9 below, Theorem 7 follows (see Appendix A for a proof). We remark that G is partitioned *once* by using a d-hop preserving partition process. Then for all QGPs with radius within d, *no re-partitioning* is needed. That is, condition $\sum |N_d(v)| \leq C_d * \frac{|G|}{n}$ is needed only for d-hop preserving partition to be parallel scalable.

Lemma 9: *Given G distributed over n processors by a d-hop preserving partition $\mathcal{P}_d$, (1) $Q(x_o, G) = \bigcup_{i \in [1,n]} Q(x_o, F_i)$, and (2)* mQMatch *is parallel scalable for all* QGPs *$Q(x_o)$ with radius bounded by d.* □

Remark. Algorithm PQMatch can be easily adapted to dynamic query load and graphs. (1) For a query with radius $d' > d$, each worker S_i incrementally computes $N_{d'-d}(v)$ for each node $v \in F_i.O$, via the balanced parallel BFS traversal. (2) When G is updated, coordinator S_c assigns the changes (*e.g.*, node/edge insertions and deletions) to each fragment. Each worker then applies incremental distance querying [15] to maintain $N_d(v)$ of all affected $v \in F_i.O$ for $i \in [1, n]$.

6. QUANTIFIED ASSOCIATION RULES

As an application of QGPs, we introduce a set of graph association rules (QGARs) with counting quantifiers, to identify regularity between entities in graphs in general, and potential customers in social graphs in particular.

QGARs. A *quantified graph association rule* $R(x_o)$ is defined as $Q_1(x_o) \Rightarrow Q_2(x_o)$, where Q_1 and Q_2 are QGPs, referred to as the *antecedent* and *consequent* of R, respectively.

The rule states that for all nodes v_x in a graph G, if $v_x \in Q_1(x_o, G)$, then the chances are that $v_x \in Q_2(x_o, G)$.

Using QGPs, QGAR R can express *positive and negative* correlations [40] and social influence patterns with statistical significance [19], which are useful in targeted advertising. (1) If Q_2 is a positive QGP, $R(x_o)$ states that if x_o satisfies the conditions in Q_1, then "event" Q_2 is likely to happen to x_o. For instance, $Q_2(x_o)$ may be a single edge buy(x_o, y) indicating that x_o may buy product y. In a social graph G, $R(x_o, G)$ identifies potential customers x_o of y. (2) When Q_2 is, *e.g.*, a single negated edge buy(x_o, y), $R(x_o)$ suggests that no v_x in $Q_1(x_o, G)$ will likely buy product y.

Example 9: A positive QGAR $R_1(x_o)$: $Q_1(x_o) \Rightarrow$ buy(x_o) is shown in Fig. 7, where Q_1 is the QGP given in Example 1, and Q_2 is a single edge buy(x_o) (depicted as a dashed edge). It states that if x_o is in a music club and if 80% of people whom x_o follows like an album y, then x_o will likely buy y.

A negative QGAR R_2 is also shown in Fig. 7, where Q_2 is a single negative edge $\mathsf{follow}(x_o, y)$. The QGAR states that if x_o and y actively ($\geq k$) tweet on competitive products (*e.g.,* "Mac" vs "PC"), then x_o is unlikely to follow y. Intuitively, R_2 demonstrates "negative" social influence [19].

As another example, R_3 of Fig. 7 is a rule in which Q_2 consists of multiple nodes. Here Q_1 in R_3 specifies users x_o who actively promote mobile phone Redmi 2 and influence other users; and Q_2 predicts the impact of x_o on other users for a new release Redmi 2A. Putting these together, R_3 states that if x_o is influential over an earlier version, then x_o is likely to promote the selling of a new release [4]. Intuitively, Q_1 identifies x_o as "leaders" [19], who are often targeted by companies for promotion of a product series [4].

To the best of our knowledge, these QGARs are not expressible as association rules studied so far (*e.g.,* [16, 17]).

QGARs also naturally express conventional association rules defined on itemsets. For instance, milk, diaper $\Rightarrow$ beer is depicted as QGAR $R_4(x_o)$ in Fig. 7. It finds customers x_o who, if buy milk and diaper, are likely to purchase beer. □

For real-world applications (*e.g.,* social recommendation), we consider practical and nontrivial QGARs by requiring: (a) Q_1 and Q_2 are connected and *nonempty* (*i.e.,* each of them has at least one edge); and (b) Q_1 and Q_2 do not overlap, *i.e.,* they do not share a common edge. We treat R as a QGP composed of both Q_1 and Q_2 such that in a graph G,

$$R(x_o, G) = Q_1(x_o, G) \cap Q_2(x_o, G).$$

Interestingness measure. To identify interesting QGARs, we define the support and confidence of QGARs.

Support. Given a QGAR $R(x_o)$ and a graph G, the *support* of R in G, denoted as $\mathsf{supp}(R, G)$, is the size $|R(x_o, G)|$, *i.e.,* the number of matches in $Q_1(x_o, G) \cap Q_2(x_o, G)$. We justify the support with the result below, which shows its *anti-monotonicity* for both pattern topology *and* quantifiers.

Lemma 10: *For any extension R' of R by (1) adding new edges (positive or negative) to Q_1 or Q_2, or (2) increasing p in positive quantifiers, $|\mathsf{supp}(R', G)| \leq |\mathsf{supp}(R, G)|$.* □

Confidence. We follow the local close world assumption (LCWA) [14], assuming that graph G is locally complete, *i.e.,* either G includes the complete neighbors of a node for any known edge type, or it has no information about these neighbors. We define the confidence of $R(x_o)$ in G as

$$\mathsf{conf}(R, G) = \frac{|R(x_o, G)|}{|Q_1(x_o, G) \cap X_o|},$$

where X_o is the set of candidates of x_o that are associated with an edge of the same type for every edge $e{=}(x_o, u)$ in Q_2. Intuitively, X_o retains those "true" negative examples under LCWA, *i.e.,* those that have every required relationship of x_o in Q_2 but are not a match (see Appendix C for justification).

Quantified entity identification. We want to use QGARs to identify entities of interests that match certain behavior patterns specified by QGPs. To this end, we define the set of entities identified by a QGAR $R(x_o)$ in a (social or knowledge) graph G with confidence η as follows:

$$R(x_o, \eta, G) = \{v_x \mid v_x \in R(x_o, G), \mathsf{conf}(R, G) \geq \eta\},$$

i.e., entities identified by R if its confidence is above η.

We study the *quantified entity identification* (QEI) problem: Given a QGAR $R(x_o)$, graph G, and a confidence threshold $\eta > 0$, it is to find all the entities in $R(x_o, \eta, G)$.

The QEI problem is DP-hard, as it embeds the quantified matching problem, which is DP-hard (Theorem 1). However, the (parallel) quantified matching algorithms for QGPs can be extended to QEI, *without* incurring substantial extra cost. Denote as $t(|Q|, |G|)$ the cost for quantified matching of QGP Q in G. Then we have the following (Appendix A).

Corollary 11: *There exist (1) an algorithm to compute $R(x_o, \eta, G)$ in $O(t(|R|, |G|))$ time; and (2) a parallel scalable algorithm to compute $R(x_o, \eta, G)$ in $O(\frac{t(|R|, |G|)}{n} + n)$ time with n processors, under the condition of Theorem 7.* □

7. EXPERIMENTAL STUDY

We conducted three sets of experiments to evaluate (1) the scalability and (2) parallel scalability of our quantified matching algorithms, and (3) the effectiveness of QGAR for identifying correlated entities in large real-world graphs.

Experimental setting. We used two real-life graphs: (a) *Pokec* [2], a social network with 1.63 million nodes of 269 different types, and 30.6 million edges of 11 types, such as *follow, like*; and (b) *YAGO2*, an extended knowledge base of YAGO [39] that consists of 1.99 million nodes of 13 different types, and 5.65 million links of 36 types.

We also developed a generator to produce synthetic social graphs $G = (V, E, L)$, controlled by the numbers of nodes $|V|$ (up to 50 million) and edges $|E|$ (up to 100 million), with L drawn from an alphabet $\mathcal{L}$ of 30 labels. The generator is based on GTgraph [7] following the small-world model.

Pattern generator. For real-life graphs we generated QGPs Q controlled by $|V_Q|$ (size of pattern nodes), $|E_Q|$ (pattern edges), $p\%$ (in quantifiers) and $|E_Q^-|$ (size of negated edges). (1) We first mined frequent features, including edges and paths of length up to 3 on each of *Pokec* and *YAGO2*. We selected top 5 most frequent features as "seeds", and combined them to form the stratified pattern Q_π of $|V_Q|$ nodes and $|E_Q|$ edges. (2) For frequent pattern edges $e{=}(u, u')$, we assigned a positive quantifier $\sigma(e) \geq p\%$, where $p\%$ is initialized as 30% unless otherwise specified. This completes the generation of $\Pi(Q)$. (3) We added $|E_Q^-|$ negated edges to $\Pi(Q)$ between randomly selected node pairs (u, u'), to complete the construction of Q. For synthetic graphs, we generated 50 QGPs with labels drawn from $\mathcal{L}$.

We denote by $|Q| = (|V_Q|, |E_Q|, p_a, |E_Q^-|)$ the size of QGP Q, where p_a is the average of p in all its quantifiers.

Algorithms. We implemented the following, all in Java.

(1) Algorithm QMatch, versus (a) QMatch_n, a revision of QMatch that processes negated edges using DMatch, not the incremental IncQMatch, and (b) Enum, which adopts a state-of-the-art subgraph isomorphism algorithm [35] to enumerate all matches first, and then verify quantifiers. The algorithm in [35] is verified to outperform conventional counterparts, *e.g.,* VF2, by 3 orders of magnitude.

(2) Algorithm PQMatch, versus (a) $\mathsf{PQMatch}_s$, its single-thread counterpart, (b) $\mathsf{PQMatch}_n$, the parallel version of QMatch_n, and (c) PEnum, a parallel version of Enum, which first invokes a parallel subgraph listing algorithm [37] to enumerate all matches, and then verifies quantifiers. We also implemented (d) DPar for d-hop preserving partition.

We deployed the parallel algorithms over n processors for $n \in [4, 20]$. Each processor has 2.6GHz 4vCPU with 16G

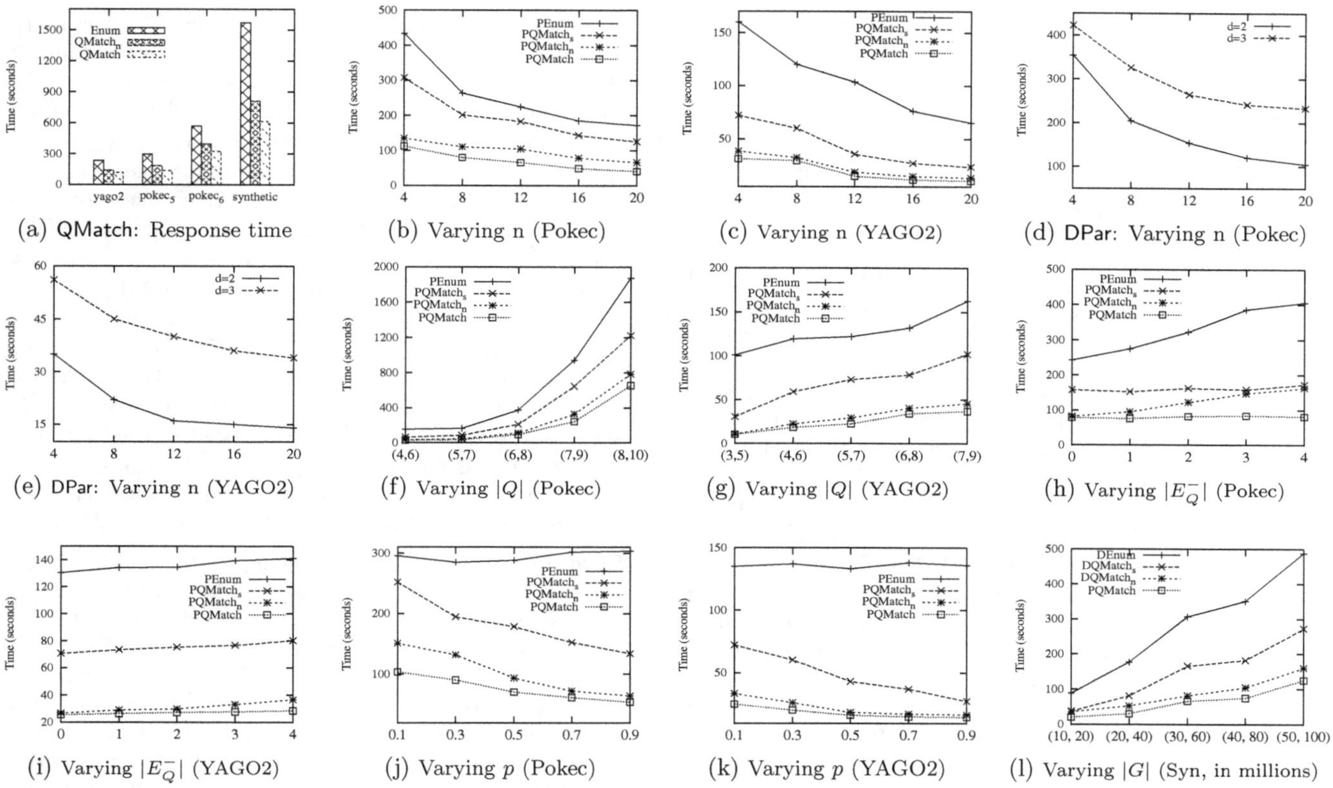

(a) QMatch: Response time (b) Varying n (Pokec) (c) Varying n (YAGO2) (d) DPar: Varying n (Pokec)

(e) DPar: Varying n (YAGO2) (f) Varying $|Q|$ (Pokec) (g) Varying $|Q|$ (YAGO2) (h) Varying $|E_Q^-|$ (Pokec)

(i) Varying $|E_Q^-|$ (YAGO2) (j) Varying p (Pokec) (k) Varying p (YAGO2) (l) Varying $|G|$ (Syn, in millions)

Figure 8: Performance evaluation

memory, and 128GB SSD storage. Each experiment was run 5 times and the average is reported here.

Experimental results. We next report our findings.

Exp-1: Performance of QMatch. We first evaluated the performance of QMatch versus QMatch$_n$ and Enum. Fixing $|Q|$=$(5, 7, 30\%, 1)$, *i.e.,* patterns with 5 nodes and 7 edges, p_a = 30% and one negative edge, Figure 8(a) reports the performance of QMatch over two real-world graphs *Pokec* (denote the result as *Pokec*$_5$) and *YAGO2*, and a larger synthetic graph G_s of 50 million nodes and 100 million edges. We find the following. (1) QMatch outperforms the other algorithms. It is on average 1.2 and 2.0 times faster than QMatch$_n$ and Enum over *YAGO2*, 1.3 and 2.0 times faster over *Pokec*, and 1.3 and 2.6 times faster over G_s, respectively. This verifies that our optimization strategies effectively reduce the verification cost. (2) QMatch works reasonably well over real-world social and knowledge graphs. It takes up to 150 (resp. 116) seconds over *Pokec* (resp. *YAGO2*), comparable to conventional subgraph isomorphism without quantifiers. Moreover, it takes longer time for larger $|Q|$ (*e.g.,* with size $(6, 8, 30\%, 1)$, the result is denoted as *Pokec*$_6$), as expected.

Exp-2: Scalability of PQMatch. This set of experiments evaluated the scalability of parallel algorithm PQMatch, compared to PQMatch$_n$, PQMatch$_s$, and PEnum. In these experiments, we fixed $|Q| = (6, 8, 30\%, 1)$, $d = 2$ for d-hop preserving partition and $b = 4$ for the number of threads in intra-fragment parallelism, unless stated otherwise.

*Varying n (*PQMatch*).* We varied the number n of processors from 4 to 20. As shown in Fig. 8(b) (resp. Fig. 8(c)) over *Pokec* (resp. *YAGO2*), (1) PQMatch and PQMatch$_s$ scale well with the increase of processors: for PQMatch, the improvement is 2.8 (resp. 3.2) times when n increases from 4 to 20; this verifies Theorem 7; (2) PQMatch is 3.8 (resp. 5.8) times faster than PEnum; and (3) with optimization strategies (incremental evaluation and multi-threads), PQMatch outperforms PQMatch$_n$ and PQMatch$_s$ by 1.5 (resp. 1.1) times and 2.8 (resp. 2.3) times, respectively. (4) PQMatch works reasonably well on large graphs. With 20 processors, it takes 40.3 (resp. 10.2) seconds on *Pokec* (resp. *YAGO2*).

*Varying n (*DPar*).* We also evaluated the scalability of DPar for d-hop preserving partition, with $d = 2$ and $d = 3$. Here DPar incrementally computed the partition when d is changed from 2 to 3 (see Section 5.1). As shown in Figures 8(d) and 8(e), (1) DPar scales well with n: when d=2, the improvement is 3.5 (resp. 2.5) times when n increases from 4 to 20 over *Pokec* (resp. *YAGO2*). (2) The fragments are well balanced: the "skew" (the ratio of the size of the smallest fragment to the largest one) is at least 80% when n=8, for both *Pokec* and *YAGO2*. (3) DPar effectively updates the partition when d is increased.

These justify the parallel scalability of DPar andPQMatch.

Varying $|Q|$. Fixing p_a = 30%, $|E_Q^-| = 1$ and $n = 8$, we varied $(|V_Q|, |E_Q|)$ from (4, 6) to (8, 10) (resp. (3, 5) to (7, 9)) on *Pokec* (resp. *YAGO2*). As shown in Figures 8(f) and 8(g), (1) the larger $|Q|$ is, the longer time is taken by all the algorithms, as expected. (2) PQMatch works well on real-life queries. For queries of size $(5, 7)$ (close to real-world queries), it takes up to 35 (resp. 16.3) seconds over *Pokec* (resp. *YAGO2*). It works better on more sparse *YAGO2*. (3) PQMatch outperforms the other algorithms, which is consistent with the results shown in Figures 8(b) and 8(c).

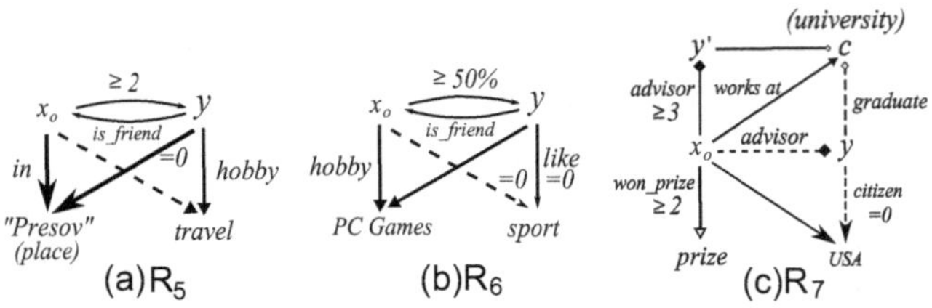

Figure 9: Real-world QGARs

Varying $|E_Q^-|$. We also studied the impact of the number of negated edges. The purpose of this test is to evaluate the effectiveness of incremental matching strategy IncQMatch.

Fixing $n = 8$, $(|V_Q|, |E_Q|) = (6, 8)$ and $p_a = 30\%$, we varied $|E_Q^-|$ from 0 to 4 by selecting $|E_Q^-|$ edges e and "negating" them by setting $\sigma(e) = 0$. As shown in Figures 8(h) and 8(i), (1) PQMatch and PQMatch$_s$ are rather indifferent to the change of $|E_Q^-|$, which incurs small extra cost due to their incremental strategy (IncQMatch). (2) In contrast, PQMatch$_n$ and PEnum are more sensitive to the increment of $|E_Q^-|$. Both algorithms, without IncQMatch, always recompute the matches of pattern Q^{+e} for each negated edge $e \in E_Q^-$, and hence take more time over larger $|E_Q^-|$. The improvement of PQMatch over PQMatch$_n$ and PEnum becomes more significant (from 1.1 to 2 times, and 3.1 to 5 times) with larger $|E_Q^-|$ (from 1 to 4) over *Pokec*. These results verify the effectiveness of IncQMatch.

Varying p_a. Fixing n=8, $|E_Q^-| = 1$ and $(|V_Q|, |E_Q|) = (6, 8)$ (resp. (5, 7)) for *Pokec* (resp. *YAGO2*), we evaluated the impact of aggregates by varying p_a from 10% to 90%. As shown in Figures 8(j) and 8(k), (1) with larger p_a, PQMatch, PQMatch$_s$ and PQMatch$_n$ take less time, since more candidates are pruned in the verification process. (2) In contrast, PEnum is indifferent to the change of p_a, since it always enumerates all the matches regardless of p_a. This verifies the effectiveness of the pruning strategies of PQMatch.

Observe that PQMatch is less sensitive than PQMatch$_n$ to p_a. When p_a is small, the overhead of PQMatch$_n$ incurred by the recomputation of Q^{+e} for negated edges e is larger, since a large number of candidates need to be verified. With larger p_a (more strict quantifiers), the overhead reduces due to the effective pruning of candidates by PQMatch$_n$. This explains the comparable performance of PQMatch and PQMatch$_n$ when p_a is large (*e.g.*, p_a=0.9).

Varying $|G|$. Fixing $n = 4$, we varied $|G|$ from $(10M, 20M)$ to $(50M, 100M)$ using synthetic social graphs. As shown in Fig. 8(l), (1) PQMatch scales well with $|G|$ and is feasible on large graphs. It takes 125 seconds when $|G| = (50M, 100M)$. (2) PQMatch is 1.5, 2.3 and 4.7 times faster than PQMatch$_n$, PQMatch$_s$ and PEnum on average, respectively.

Exp-3: Effectiveness of QGAR. We also evaluated the effectiveness of QGARs. We developed a simple QGAR mining algorithm by extending the algorithm of [16] for mining graph pattern association rule (GPARs). GPARs are a special case of QGARs $Q_1(x_o) \Rightarrow Q_2(x_o)$ that have no quantifiers and restrict Q_2 to a single edge. (1) We mined a set of top GPARs using [16] over *Pokec* and *YAGO2*, for confidence threshold $\eta = 0.5$. For each GPAR R, we initialized a QGAR R'. (2) We extended Q_2 in each R' by adding frequent edges whenever possible, and by gradually enlarging p_a for frequent edges by increment 10% (1 for numeric aggregates). We stopped when the confidence of R' got below η. We show three QGARs in Fig. 9, illustrated as follows.

(1) R_5 (*Pokec*) says that if a user has "long-distance" friends, *i.e.*, at least two of her friends do *not* live in the same city "Presov" where she lives, then the chances are that they share the hobby of traveling. We found 50 matches in *Pokec*.

(2) R_6 (*Pokec*; confidence 0.8) demonstrates a negative pattern: for a user x_o, if more than half of his friends share the same hobby "PC Games", and none of them like sports, then it is likely x_o does not like sports. R_6 has support 4000.

(3) R_7 (*YAGO2*; confidence 0.75) states that if a US professor (a) won at least two academic prizes, and (b) graduated at least 4 students, then the chances are that at least one of her/his students is not a US citizen. It discovers scientists such as Marvin Minsky (Turing Award 1969) and Murray Gell-Mann (Nobel Prize Physics 1969) from *YAGO2*. Here Q_2 in R_7 has three (dashed) edges, as opposed to GPARs [16].

These QGARs demonstrate quantified correlation between the entities in social and knowledge graphs, which cannot be captured by conventional association rules and GPARs [16].

Summary. We find the following. Over real-life graphs, (1) quantified matching is feasible: PQMatch (with 20 processors) and QMatch took 40.3s and 342s on *Pokec*, and 10.2s and 116s on *YAGO2*, respectively. (2) Better still, PQMatch and DPar are parallel scalable: their performance is improved by 3 times on average with workers increased from 4 to 20. (3) Our optimization techniques improve the performance of QMatch and PQMatch by 1.27 and 1.3 times on average, and 2.2 and 4.5 times over Enum and PEnum, respectively. (4) QGARs capture behavior patterns that cannot be expressed with conventional graph patterns.

8. CONCLUSION

We have proposed quantified matching, by extending traditional graph patterns with counting quantifiers. We have also studied important issues in connection with quantified matching, from complexity to algorithms to applications. The novelty of this work consists in quantified patterns (QGPs), quantified graph association rules (QGARs), and algorithms with provable guarantees (*e.g.*, optimal incremental matching and parallel scalable matching). Our experimental study has verified the effectiveness of QGPs and the feasibility of quantified matching in real-life graphs.

We will study practical extensions of QGPs to more general graph patterns (*e.g.*, bounded simulation with regular path constraints) and other built-in predicates ($<, \leq, \neq$). Another topic concerns QGAR discovery. It calls for a nontrivial extension of prior pattern mining algorithms (*e.g.*, [16, 17]) to accurately identify quantifiers.

Acknowledgments. Fan and Xu are supported in part by ERC 652976, 973 Program 2014CB340302 and 2012CB316200, NSFC 61133002 and 61421003, EPSRC EP/J015377/1 and EP/M025268/1, NSF III 1302212, Shenzhen Peacock Program 1105100030834361, Guangdong Innovative Research Team Program 2011D005, Shenzhen Science and Technology Fund JCYJ20150529164656096 and Guangdong Applied R&D Program 2015B010131006.

9. REFERENCES

[1] Nielsen global online consumer survey. *http://www.nielsen.com/content/dam/corporate/us/en/newswire/uploads/2009/07/pr_global-study_07709.pdf.*

[2] Pokec social network. *http://snap.stanford.edu/data/soc-pokec.html.*

[3] R. Agrawal, T. Imieliński, and A. Swami. Mining association rules between sets of items in large databases. *SIGMOD Record*, 22(2):207–216, 1993.
[4] W. Amaldoss and S. Jain. Research note-trading up: A strategic analysis of reference group effects. *Marketing science*, 27(5):932–942, 2008.
[5] S. Amer-Yahia, L. V. S. Lakshmanan, and C. Yu. Socialscope: Enabling information discovery on social content sites. In *CIDR*, 2009.
[6] K. Andreev and H. Racke. Balanced graph partitioning. *Theory of Computing Systems*, 39(6):929–939, 2006.
[7] D. A. Bader and K. Madduri. Gtgraph: A synthetic graph generator suite.
[8] R. Bapna and A. Umyarov. Do your online friends make you pay? A randomized field experiment in an online music social network. *NBER working paper*, 2012.
[9] M. Bendersky, D. Metzler, and W. Croft. Learning concept importance using a weighted dependence model. In *WSDM*, 2010.
[10] H. Blau, N. Immerman, and D. Jensen. A visual language for querying and updating graphs. *University of Massachusetts Amherst Computer Science Technical Report*, 37:2002, 2002.
[11] F. Bourse, M. Lelarge, and M. Vojnovic. Balanced graph edge partition. In *SIGKDD*, pages 1456–1465, 2014.
[12] P. Burkhardt and C. Waring. An NSA big graph experiment. Technical Report NSA-RD-2013-056002v1, U.S. National Security Agency, 2013.
[13] C. Chekuri and S. Khanna. A PTAS for the multiple knapsack problem. In *SODA*, pages 213–222, 2000.
[14] X. Dong et al. Knowledge vault: A web-scale approach to probabilistic knowledge fusion. In *KDD*, 2014.
[15] W. Fan, X. Wang, and Y. Wu. Incremental graph pattern matching. *TODS*, 38(3):18, 2013.
[16] W. Fan, X. Wang, Y. Wu, and J. Xu. Association rules with graph patterns. *PVLDB*, 2015.
[17] L. A. Galárraga, C. Teflioudi, K. Hose, and F. Suchanek. AMIE: association rule mining under incomplete evidence in ontological knowledge bases. In *WWW*, 2013.
[18] M. A. Gallego, J. D. Fernández, M. A. Martínez-Prieto, and P. de la Fuente. An empirical study of real-world SPARQL queries. In *USEWOD workshop*, 2011.
[19] A. Goyal, F. Bonchi, and L. V. Lakshmanan. Discovering leaders from community actions. In *CIKM*, 2008.
[20] I. Grujic, S. Bogdanovic-Dinic, and L. Stoimenov. Collecting and analyzing data from e-government facebook pages. In *ICT Innovations*, 2014.
[21] M. R. Henzinger, T. Henzinger, and P. Kopke. Computing simulations on finite and infinite graphs. In *FOCS*, 1995.
[22] J. Huang, D. J. Abadi, and K. Ren. Scalable SPARQL querying of large RDF graphs. *PVLDB*, 4(11), 2011.
[23] G. Karypis. Metis and parmetis. In *Encyclopedia of Parallel Computing*, pages 1117–1124. 2011.
[24] R. E. Korf. Minimizing disk I/O in two-bit breadth-first search. In *AAAI*, pages 317–324, 2008.
[25] F. Korn, A. Labrinidis, Y. Kotidis, and C. Faloutsos. Ratio rules: A new paradigm for fast, quantifiable data mining. In *VLDB*, 1998.
[26] C. P. Kruskal, L. Rudolph, and M. Snir. A complexity theory of efficient parallel algorithms. *TCS*, 71(1), 1990.
[27] J. Lee, W.-S. Han, R. Kasperovics, and J.-H. Lee. An in-depth comparison of subgraph isomorphism algorithms in graph databases. In *PVLDB*, volume 6, 2012.
[28] C. Ley, B. Linse, and O. Poppe. SPARQLog: SPARQL with rules and quantification. *Semantic Web Information Management: A Model-Based Perspective*, page 341, 2010.
[29] L. Libkin. *Elements of Finite Model Theory.* Springer, 2004.
[30] W. Lin, S. A. Alvarez, and C. Ruiz. Collaborative recommendation via adaptive association rule mining. *Data Mining and Knowledge Discovery*, 6:83–105, 2000.
[31] V. Liptchinsky, B. Satzger, R. Zabolotnyi, and S. Dustdar. Expressive languages for selecting groups from graph-structured data. In *WWW*, 2013.
[32] M. Martın, C. Gutierrez, and P. Wood. SNQL: A social networks query and transformation language. In *AMW*, 2011.
[33] C. H. Papadimitriou. *Computational Complexity.* Addison-Wesley, 1994.
[34] G. Ramalingam and T. Reps. On the computational complexity of dynamic graph problems. *TCS*, 158(1-2), 1996.
[35] X. Ren and J. Wang. Exploiting vertex relationships in speeding up subgraph isomorphism over large graphs. *PVLDB*, 8(5):617–628, 2015.
[36] C. Schmitz, A. Hotho, R. Jäschke, and G. Stumme. Mining association rules in folksonomies. In *Data Science and Classification*, pages 261–270. 2006.
[37] Y. Shao, B. Cui, L. Chen, L. Ma, J. Yao, and N. Xu. Parallel subgraph listing in a large-scale graph. In *SIGMOD*, 2014.
[38] R. Srikant and R. Agrawal. Mining quantitative association rules in large relational tables. In *SIGMOD*, 1996.
[39] F. M. Suchanek, G. Kasneci, and G. Weikum. Yago: a core of semantic knowledge. In *WWW*, pages 697–706, 2007.
[40] X. Wu, C. Zhang, and S. Zhang. Efficient mining of both positive and negative association rules. *TOIS*, 22(3), 2004.

Appendix A: Proofs

Proof of Theorem 1

It is easy to see that Theorem 1 follows from Lemmas 2, 3 and 4. Below we verify these lemmas.

Lemma 2: Lower bounds. We first prove the lower bounds of quantified matching, for positive and negative QGPs.

(1) NP-hardness. The quantified matching for positive QGPs with numeric aggregates is already NP-hard. This can be verified by constructing a polynomial time reduction from subgraph isomorphism (**subISO**), where a QGP Q is constructed by adding quantifiers $\delta(e) \geq 1$ for all the edges e in a graph pattern Q' in an instance of **subISO**. As **subISO** is NP-hard (cf. [33]), so is quantified matching.

(2) DP-hardness. We next prove that quantified matching for (possibly) negative QGPs is DP-hard by reduction from EXACT-CLIQUE, which is DP-complete (cf. [33]). Given a graph G and a natural number k, EXACT-CLIQUE is to determine whether the largest clique of G has size exactly k. Given an instance of EXACT-CLIQUE, We construct a QGP $Q(x_o)$ that consists of a k-clique Q_1, a $k+1$-clique Q_2 such that x_o has a unique match v_o in G', there is an edge e from x_o to each node in q_1 with $\sigma(e) \geq 1$, and to a single node v' in Q_2 via a negated edge. The transformation is obviously in PTIME. Moreover, the largest clique of G has size k if and only if $v_o \in Q(x_o, G')$. Therefore, the transformation above is a reduction. As EXACT-CLIQUE is DP-complete, quantified matching with (possibly) negative QGPs is DP-hard.

Lemma 3: Upper bounds. We next prove the upper bounds for quantified matching. We first consider positive QGPs Q with numeric aggregates $\sigma(e) \odot p$ only (Lemma 3). We then extend the result to ratio aggregates $p\%$ (Lemma 4).

(1) Given a QGP $Q(x_o)$, we construct a traditional graph pattern $Q_e(x_o)$ without quantifiers, by (a) stripping off all quantifiers from Q, and (b) for each edge $e(u, u')$ associated with $\sigma(e) \odot p$, if $p > 1$, we make p copies of u' in Q_e as children of u, along with copies of edges from u' and so on. Then one can easily verify the following: (a) for any

graph G, $Q(x_o, G) = Q_e(x_o, G)$, and (b) the time for constructing Q_e and hence $|Q_e|$ are both a polynomial in $|Q|$; this is because on each simple path in Q, there are at most k non-existential quantifiers, for a predefined constant k. These make a PTIME reduction from quantified matching with positive numeric aggregates to conventional subgraph isomorphism. Since the latter is in NP, so is the former.

(2) We next prove that the quantified matching for (possibly) negative QGPs is in DP. Following [33], it suffices to construct two languages L_1 and L_2, such that a node v_x is in $Q(x_o, G)$ if and only if v_x is in $L_1 \cap L_2$.

We consider two languages below:

- L_1, the set $\Pi(Q)(x_o, G)$, and
- L_2, the set of "yes" instances for a node v_x that is not a match of x_o for $\bigcup_{e \in E_Q^-}(\Pi(Q^+)(x_o, G)$.

One can verify that (1) $L_1 \in$ NP, (2) $L_2 \in$ coNP, and (3) a node v_x is in $Q(x, G)$ if and only if v_x is in $L_1 \cap L_2$, by the definition of QGPs. Thus quantified matching is in DP.

Lemma 4: Ratio aggregates. Given a QGP Q that contains ratio aggregates $\sigma(e) \odot p\%$, we construct a QGP Q_d and graph G_d in PTIME such that Q_d consists of numeric aggregates only, and $Q_d(x_o, G_d) = Q(x_o, G)$. To simplify the discussion, we consider *w.l.o.g.* positive Q. For negated edges e, by the definition of $Q(x_o, G)$, e is positified in Q^{+e}. Hence, it suffices to consider positive edges.

(a) We transform G to a graph G_d as follows. For each node v with g child in G, we add $(1-p\%)(d-g)$ dummy children with a label that does not match any pattern node in Q, and $p\%(d-g)$ dummy children that complete a dummy subgraph G_Q at v that is isomorphic to Q_π of Q.

(b) We transform Q to Q_d such that for each edge e with quantifier $\sigma(e) \odot p\%$, we replace $p\%$ with a constant $p\% * d$.

One may verify that a node $v_x \in \mathcal{Q}(x_o, G)$ if and only if its G_d-counterpart $v_d \in Q_d(x_d, G_d)$. Moreover, the transformation is obviously in PTIME. Since quantified matching for all numeric quantified Q_d is in NP by Lemma 3, so is its counterpart for QGPs Q with ratio quantifiers. □

This completes the proof of Theorem 1.

Proof of Lemma 5

To show the correctness of DMatch, first observe that DMatch always terminates. Indeed, DMatch follows the verification process of conventional subgraph isomorphism algorithm. The process, in the worst case, enumerates all possible isomorphism mappings from the stratified pattern Q_π to G, which are finitely many. Hence DMatch terminates.

We next show that DMatch correctly verifies whether a candidate v_x is a match of x_o in $\Pi(Q)$ via an isomorphism $h_0 \in \Pi(Q)(G)$. It suffices to show that (1) h_0 is a match in $Q_\pi(G)$, and (2) for each u in $\Pi(Q)$ and each edge $e{=}(u, u')$, $|M_e(h_0(x_o), h_0(u), Q)| \odot p$ for $f(e) = \sigma(e) \odot p$.

(1) When DMatch terminates, for each $u \in \Pi(Q)$ and every candidate v in $C(u)$ with $X(u, v)$=true, $v = h(u)$ for some $h \in Q_\pi(G)$, guaranteed by the correctness of Match.

(2) For each edge (u, u') in $\Pi(Q)$ and a node v with $X(u, v)$=true, DMatch correctly verifies the quantifiers by checking the updated local counter of v that keeps track of the current $|M_e(h_0(x_o), h_0(u), Q)|$. In addition, DMatch *waits* until either v is determined not a valid match due to that the upper bound fails the quantifier (by the local pruning rule, Appendix B), or the lower bound satisfies the quantifier (in the verification). Hence, v_x is a match if and only if $v_x \in \Pi(Q)(x_o, G)$ when DMatch terminates.

For the space complexity, it takes $O(|V|)$ space to store the auxiliary structures for the nodes in G. During the search, DMatch keeps, at each level of the search, at most p_m best matches to be verified, where p_m is the largest constant in quantifiers. Since there are in total $|\Pi(Q)| \leq |Q|$ levels of search, it takes in total $O(p_m|Q| + |V|)$ space. □

Proof of Proposition 6

We prove Proposition 6 by giving the correctness and complexity analysis of IncQMatch below.

Correctness. Given a QGP $\Pi(Q^{+e})$, algorithm IncQMatch correctly computes $\Pi(Q^{+e})(x_o, G)$ by processing ΔE one edge at a time. At any time, the newly formed pattern Q' contains $\Pi(Q)$ as a subgraph. It is easy to verify that $\Pi(Q)(u, G) \subseteq \Pi(Q^{+e})(u, G)$, for any $u \in \Pi(Q)$. Hence, IncQMatch only needs to determine the nodes to be removed from the cached matches/candidates from QMatch.

We next show that IncQMatch removes a node v from $C(u)$ if and only if it is not a match in $\Pi(Q^{+e})(u, G)$, for any node u in $\Pi(Q^{+e})$. (1) If v is not a match, then either v is not in an isomorphism mapping, or v fails the quantifier of at least one edge (u, u'). IncQMatch captures both cases by the isomorphism checking and quantifier verification. Hence it guarantees to remove all the v that are not match. (2) Assume by contradiction that IncQMatch removes a node v that is a match. Then either v is not a match via isomorphism, or v fails the counter for an edge (u, u'). Both contradict the assumption that v is a match. Hence, IncQMatch only removes the nodes that are not matches in $\Pi(Q^{+e})(u, G)$.

Complexity. During the process, IncQMatch visits and verifies the following sets of nodes: (1) $C(u)$, including the cached matches and candidates of u if u is not in $\Pi(Q)$, where u is in edge $e = (u, u')$ or $e{=}(u', u)$, for each $e \in \Delta E$; and (2) those nodes reachable from (or can be reached by) those nodes in (1) via a sequence of cached matches/candidates including those nodes in (1). The number of verification hence is bounded by the size of the set combining (1) and (2), which is in total at most |AFF|. □

Proof of Theorem 7

We prove Theorem 7 by providing the correctness and complexity analysis below for algorithm PQMatch.

Correctness. Given graph G distributed over n processors by a d-hop preserving partition $\mathcal{P}_d$, PQMatch computes $Q(x_o, G)$ as $\bigcup Q(x_o, F_i)$ ($i \in [1, n]$), for any QGP $Q(x_o)$ with radius bounded by d. It suffices to show Lemma 9(1).

Lemma 9(1). Observe the following. (1) For any match $v_x \in Q(x_o, F_i)$, QMatch only needs to visit $N_d(v_x)$ to verify whether v_x is a match. (2) For every candidate $v_x \in C(x_o)$, there exists a fragment F_i, such that $N_d(v_x) \subseteq F_i$ (including v_x) (by d-hop preservation). Hence, any match of x_o must be from at least one match set $Q(x_o, F_i)$ evaluated at fragment F_i. (3) For every match $v_x \in Q(x_o, F_i)$ locally computed at F_i, v_x is a match of x_o guaranteed by the correctness of QMatch. Hence PQMatch correctly computes $Q(x_o, G)$ as $\bigcup$ $Q(x_o, F_i)$ ($i \in [1, n]$) over a d-hop preserving partition.

Complexity. Algorithm PQMatch consists of three steps: (1) the distribution of Q and construction of d-hop preserving partition, (2) the parallel evaluation, and (3) assembling of partial matches. The time for step (2) and (3) are in $O(\frac{t(Q,G)}{n})$ and $O(n)$, respectively, *i.e.*, are parallel scalable.

Hence it suffices to focus on the parallel scalability of step (1), by proving Lemma 8 and Lemma 9(2).

Lemma 8 (Parallel scalability of DPar*)*. We first show that procedure DPar is parallel scalable. We will show the approximation ratio of DPar separately in the next proof.

Observe the following. (1) For each worker S_i managing a fragment F_i in the base partition, the border nodes $F_i.O$ can be computed via a linear scan of F_i. Hence the overall time is in $O(|C_d * \frac{|G|}{n}|)$ by the condition of Lemma 8. (2) Given $V'{=}\bigcup F_i.O$, DPar applies the $(1{+}\epsilon)$ approximation algorithm of [13], which computes an assignment in time $O(|V'|^{\frac{1}{\epsilon}})$. For ϵ small enough for a good approximation, *e.g.*, $\epsilon{=}1$, the time cost is $O(|V'|)$. Since $|V'|{=}\sum F_i.O{\leq} \sum N_d(v)$ ($v \in V'$), and $\sum N_d(v)$ is bounded by $O(C_d * \frac{|G|}{n})$, the process takes time in $O(C_d * \frac{|G|}{n}){=}\ O(\frac{|G|}{n})$. (3) For each border node $v \in F_i.O$, each S_i fetches $N_d(v)$ from G in parallel. In the worst case, each worker takes in total $O(\sum|N_d(v)|)$ time for all the border nodes $v \in F_i.O$. As the fetch process is bounded by $O(C_d * \frac{|G|}{n})$ at each fragment, the overall parallel partition time is bounded by $O(C_d * \frac{|G|}{n}){=}O(\frac{|G|}{n})$. Hence, DPar is parallel scalable.

Lemma 9(2) (Parallel scalability of mQMatch). Procedure mQMatch is conducted locally in parallel at each worker. From the correctness of Lemma 9(1), each worker only performs local matching without the need to communicate with others once DPar terminates. Hence, the overall time complexity is $O(\frac{t(Q,G)}{n})$. The time cost for merging the answers is in $O(n)$ time. Putting these together, PQMatch is in $O(\frac{t(Q,G)}{n}){+}O(n)$ time. Lemma 9(2) thus follows, and so does the parallel scalability of PQMatch. □

Lemma 8 (Approximation). The d-hop preserving partition problem at the coordinator S_c is to find an assignment for each $N_d(v)$ to a worker S_i, such that (a) $\sum|N_d(v_i)| \leq c * \frac{|G|}{n}$ for all $N_d(v_i)$ assigned to S_i, and (b) $|V_c|$ is maximized, where V_c refers the nodes covered in V'. We show that the problem is $1+\epsilon$-approximable, by constructing an approximation preserving reduction (APR) [13] to the multiple knapsack problem (MKP) as follows.

- **function** f: (a) for each $v \in V'$, construct an item u_i with value 1 and weight $|N_d(v)|$; and (b) for each worker S_i, construct a bin B_i with capacity $c * \frac{|G|}{n} - |F_i|$.
- **function** g: for each item u_i packed to a bin B_i in $s(I_2)$, g maps u_i to v_i, and B_i to S_i.

We next show that the transformation above is an APR. Indeed, (1) f is in PTIME, and (2) for a feasible solution $s(I_2)$, $g(s(I_1))$ is also a feasible solution, since the packing does not exceed the capacity constraints in $s(I_2)$ if and only if the assignment $g(s(I_1))$ does not exceed the capacity of each fragment. (3) Assume $s(I_2) \geq \frac{s^*(I_2)}{1+\epsilon}$ (α=1). One can verify that $|s^*(I_1)|{=}\ |V_c|$ (the size of covered nodes) $= |g(s^*(I_2)|$ (the size of packed items), $|s(I_1)| = |g(s(I_2)|$. Hence $g(s(I_2)){=}s(I_1){\geq}\ \frac{s^*(I_2)}{1+\epsilon}{=}\frac{g(s^*(I_2))}{1+\epsilon}$. Thus, the transformation is an APR. As a result, from [13] it follows that d-hop preserving partition is $1+\epsilon$ approximable.

Remarks. We use a balanced bound for all fragments. This guarantees the correctness of the reduction to MKP. The choice of MKP is to get a balanced fragment bound and at the same time, to minimize synchronization cost. Our experimental study shows that this leads to quite balanced fragments (Exp-2), with minimum communication cost.

Proof of Lemma 10

Assume that $R'(x_o)$: $Q'_1(x_o) \Rightarrow Q'_2(x_o)$ is extended from $R(x_o)$: $Q_1(x_o) \Rightarrow Q_2(x_o)$. It suffices to prove that $R'(x_o, G) \subseteq R(x_o, G)$ for any G. Consider two cases below.

(1) If Q'_1 is extended by adding new edge (either positive or negative) to Q_1, then $Q'_1(x_o, G) \subseteq Q_1(x_o, G)$ (see Section 4.2). Hence, $R'(x_o, G){=}Q'_1(x_o, G){\cap}Q_2(x_o, G) \subseteq Q_1(x_o, G) \cap Q_2(x_o, G){=}R(x_o, G)$.

(2) Assume that Q'_1 is obtained by increasing p in a positive quantifier of an edge $e{=}(u, u')$ in Q_1. Assume that there exists a node $v \in R'(x_o, G)$ that is not a match in $R(x_o, G)$. Then there must exist a positive edge (x_o, u) with quantifier $\sigma(e) \odot p$ for which v does not have enough matches in its children. Nevertheless, for any positive quantifier $\sigma(e) \odot p$ in R and its counterpart $\sigma(e) \odot p'$ in R', $p' \geq p$. As v is a match of $R'(x_o, G)$, this contradicts the assumption that v is in $R(x_o, G)$. Hence $R'(x_o, G) \subseteq R(x_o, G)$.

The same argument applies to the case when Q'_2 is revised from Q_2. Hence Lemma 10 follows. □

Proof of Corollary 11

As a constructive proof, we outline two algorithms for computing $R(x_o, \eta, G)$ with the desired complexity as follows.

Sequential quantified entity matching. Given a QGAR R, confidence threshold η and G, the first algorithm, denoted as garMatch, (1) invokes QMatch to compute $Q_1(x_o, G)$ and $Q_2(x_o, G)$, respectively; (2) computes $R(x_o, G) = Q_1(x_o, G) \cap Q_2(x_o, G)$; and (3) verifies whether $\mathsf{conf}(R){=}\frac{|R(x_o,G)|}{|Q_1(x_o,G)\cap X_o|} \geq \eta$. If so, it returns $R(x_o, G)$.

The correctness and complexity of garMatch follow from their QMatch counterparts (Lemmas 5 and 6).

Parallel quantified entity matching. We introduce a parallel algorithm, denoted as dgarMatch, for parallel quantified entity matching. It follows the generic steps of PQMatch. The only difference is as follows: (a) each worker evaluates two patterns Q_1 and Q_2 in parallel, and (b) the coordinator S_c assembles the results to evaluate the confidence of R.

Algorithm dgarMatch starts with a set of base partitions. (1) It constructs a d-hop preserving partition, where d is a predefined upper bound of the largest radius Q_1 and Q_2 in R. (2) Each worker then computes local match $Q_1(x_o, F_i)$ and $Q_2(x_o, F_i)$ in parallel. It also computes the local set X_{oi}. (3) Each worker returns the local matches to the coordinator S_c. Then dgarMatch computes $R(x_o, G)$ as $(\bigcup Q_1(x_o, F_i)) \setminus (\bigcup Q_2(x_o, F_i))$, and computes the confidence $\mathsf{conf}(R, G)$ as $\frac{|R(x_o,G)|}{|\bigcup Q_1(x_o,F_i) \cap \bigcup X_{oi}|}$. It next verifies whether $\mathsf{conf}(R, G) \geq \eta$ and if so, returns $R(x_o, G)$. Otherwise, it returns $\emptyset$.

The correctness and complexity of dgarMatch follow from their PQMatch counterparts. □

Appendix B: Optimization Techniques

Selection and Pruning Rules (Section 4)

We show that the number of verification in algorithm QMatch can be further reduced, by applying the following selection and pruning rules.

(1) **[pruning rules]**. The pruning rules are applied *each time* when DMatch backtracks from a candidate $v' \in S_P(u')$ to a match $v \in S_P(u)$ for an edge $e=(u, u')$.

(a) *local pruning rule*: If the dynamically maintained upper bound $U(v_x, e)$ of each $v_x \in C(x_o)$ fails the quantifier of e (because of a verified non-match v' as its child), then removes v from $C(u)$ and $S_P(u)$.

(b) *global pruning rule*: monitors the size of current candidates $C(u')$, excluding those nodes verified to be non-matches (*i.e.*, $X(u', u) = \mathsf{false}$).

The lemma below justifies these pruning rules.

Lemma 12: *Node x_o in $\Pi(Q)$ has a match only if for every node u' in $\Pi(Q)$, $|C(u')| \geq p_m$, where $p_m = \max\{p'\}$ for p' ranging over p in $\sigma(u, u') \geq p$ for all u''s parent u.* □

If $C(u') < p_m$ for some pattern node u', QMatch terminates and returns the current $\Pi(Q)(x_o, G)$.

(2) **[selection rule]**. The selection rule is applied *each time* when DMatch extends the search to a next level, at a match $v \in S_P(u)$ for edge $e=(u, u')$. Denote as $P(u')$ the parent set of u' in G, the *potential* of a match $v' \in C(u')$ is

$$(1 + \frac{|P(v') \cap C(u)|}{|C(u)|}) * \Sigma_{\forall e=(u',u'')} \frac{U(v', e)}{p_e}$$

The rule picks candidates with highest potential scores.

Example 10: Consider Q_4 with p=3 (Fig. 2) and a revised G_2 (Fig. 2) by changing "UK" to "US". QMatch terminates early without verifying all the nodes, in contrast to Match. As the potential of the candidates x_4, x_5 and x_6 for x_o are all 1, QMatch starts with *e.g.*, x_5. (1) Following edge $e=(x_o, z)$, the potentials of candidates v_8, v_6, v_7 and v_9 are $2*(1+\frac{3}{3})=4$, 4, $\frac{5}{3}$, and $\frac{4}{3}$, respectively. Hence QMatch selects v_6, v_8 and v_7 as top 3 candidates, starting with v_6. (2) When backtracking to v_6, QMatch finds v_6 not a match; so it reduces the upper bound of x_4-x_6 for edge e by 1. QMatch next backtracks to x_5. By the local pruning rule, it finds $U(x_5, e)$ smaller than 3; thus v_5 is not a match. (3) Applying the global pruning rule, the size $C(z)$ ($\{v_7, v_9\}$) is already smaller than 3. Hence QMatch returns $\emptyset$ without further checking. □

Proof of Lemma 12

Proof: We show Lemma 12 by contradiction. Assume that a node $v_x \in C(x_o)$ is a match of x_o, and there exists a node u' in $\Pi(Q)$ that $|C(u')| < p_m$, where p_m is the largest constant in the positive quantifier from edges (u, u'). (1) Since v_x is a match of x_o, there exists a node $v' \in C(u')$ that is a match for u'. As v' is a valid match for u', it must have a parent v that matches u in an isomorphic mapping, and satisfies the quantifier of edge $e_i=(u_i, u')$, for every parent u_i of u'. (2) This indicates that v' must have at least p_i children that match u' with size at least p_i, for e_i with quantifier $\sigma(e_i) \odot p_i$, *i.e.*, $|C(u')| \geq p_i$. (3) Since (2) holds for every edge (u_i, u'), $|C(u')| \geq p_m$. This contradicts the assumption that $|C(u')| < p_m$. Hence Lemma 12 follows. □

Optimization For QMatch (Section 4)

We leverage graph simulation [21] to further reduce verification. A node v in G simulates a query node u in Q, *i.e.*, (u, v) is in a simulation relation R if v and u have the same label, and for each u's child u' connected via edge e, v has a child v' connected via edge e' having the same label of e such that $(u', v') \in R$. It is known that R can be computed in quadratic time [21]. One can verify the following.

Lemma 13: *For any edge $e=(u, u')$ in $\Pi(Q)(x_o)$ and its quantifier $\sigma(e) \odot p$, v is a match of u in Q when x_o is mapped to v_x only if (1) v_x simulates x_o, (2) v simulates u, and (3) $|R(v_x, v, G)|$ (resp. $\frac{|R(v_x,v,F_i)|}{|M_e(v)|}$) $\odot\, p$ (resp. $p\%$).* □

Here $R(v_x, v, G)$ is the set of children of v simulating u'. Indeed, one may verify that $|R(v_x, v, G)|$ is an upper bound of $|M_e(h_0(x_o), h_0(u), Q)|$ for positive edges e. The result above suggests that we can use simulation as preprocessing, and remove invalid candidates early by following Lemma 13.

Proof of Lemma 13

One may verify that v is a match for u via isomorphism only if v can simulate u. Indeed, If a node v cannot simulate u, then either $v \notin C(u)$, or no descendant u' of u s in $C(u')$. Both indicates that v cannot match u via an isomorphism. Assume that v is a match of u when v_x is matched with x_o. (1) If v_x (resp. v) does not simulate x_o (resp. u), then v_x (resp. v) cannot match x_o (resp. u) via isomorphism. (2) If $|R(v_x, v, F_i)|$ fails the quantifier e, then the number of possible matches in v's children fails the quantifier. Both contradict the assumption. Lemma 13 thus follows. □

Multi-thread Quantified Matching (Section 5)

Given $Q(x_o)$ and fragment F_i, mQMatch follows QMatch to verify the candidates in $C(x_o)$. It dynamically spawns p threads to simultaneously verify the top p selected candidates v for each pattern edge $e=(u, u')$, one for each candidate. For a candidate $v \in C(u)$, the thread i for v spawns a thread for each of the top p candidates $v' \in C(u')$ to be verified. As multi-threading can be expensive when d is large, mQMatch utilizes *thread blocking* to avoid the overhead: (1) it only spawns at most b threads, and "sequentializes" the rest $p - b$ verification with a single thread, and (2) it only spawns threads for the first two search levels.

Appendix C: Confidence of QGARs (Section 6)

One might be tempted to define the confidence of $R(x_o)$ as $\frac{|R(x_o,G)|}{|Q_1(x_o,G)|}$, following traditional association rules [38]. However, this does not work well in incomplete graphs.

Example 11: For QGAR R_1, consider two matches v_1 and v_2 in $Q_1(x_o, G)$, where user v_1 has *no* edge labeled buy. Since G is usually incomplete, it is an overkill to assume that v_1 is a negative example as a potential customer of books, since some of its buy edges may possibly be missing from G. □

To accommodate incomplete graphs, we follow the local close world assumption (LCWA) [14], which assumes that G is locally complete, *i.e.*, either G includes the complete neighbors of a node for any existing edge type, or it knows nothing about the neighbors. We define $\mathsf{conf}(R, G)$, the confidence of $R(x_o)$ in G under LCWA, as $\frac{|R(x_o,G)|}{|Q_1(x_o,G) \cap X_o|}$.

Continuing with Example 11, user v_2 is retained in X_o but v_1 is excluded due to missing buy edges. Hence, v_1 is no longer considered to be a negative match under LCWA.

DUALSIM: Parallel Subgraph Enumeration in a Massive Graph on a Single Machine

Hyeonji Kim ‡
hjkim@dblab.postech.ac.kr

Juneyoung Lee ‡
jylee@dblab.postech.ac.kr

Sourav S. Bhowmick †
assourav@ntu.edu.sg

Wook-Shin Han ‡*
wshan@dblab.postech.ac.kr

JeongHoon Lee ‡
jhlee@dblab.postech.ac.kr

Seongyun Ko ‡
syko@dblab.postech.ac.kr

Moath H.A. Jarrah ‡
moath@dblab.postech.ac.kr

‡Pohang University of Science and Technology (POSTECH), Korea
†Nanyang Technological University, Singapore

ABSTRACT

Subgraph enumeration is important for many applications such as subgraph frequencies, network motif discovery, graphlet kernel computation, and studying the evolution of social networks. Most earlier work on subgraph enumeration assumes that graphs are resident in memory, which results in serious scalability problems. Recently, efforts to enumerate all subgraphs in a large-scale graph have seemed to enjoy some success by partitioning the data graph and exploiting the distributed frameworks such as MapReduce and distributed graph engines. However, we notice that all existing distributed approaches have serious performance problems for subgraph enumeration due to the explosive number of partial results. In this paper, we design and implement a disk-based, single machine *parallel subgraph enumeration solution* called DUALSIM that can handle massive graphs without maintaining exponential numbers of partial results. Specifically, we propose a novel concept of the *dual approach* for subgraph enumeration. The dual approach swaps the roles of the data graph and the query graph. Specifically, instead of fixing the matching order in the query and then matching data vertices, it fixes the data vertices by fixing a set of disk pages and then finds all subgraph matchings in these pages. This enables us to significantly reduce the number of disk reads. We conduct extensive experiments with various real-world graphs to systematically demonstrate the superiority of DUALSIM over state-of-the-art distributed subgraph enumeration methods. DUALSIM outperforms the state-of-the-art methods by up to orders of magnitude, while they fail for many queries due to explosive intermediate results.

Keywords

Subgraph enumeration; dual approach; graph analytics

*corresponding author

SIGMOD'16, June 26-July 01, 2016, San Francisco, CA, USA

DOI: http://dx.doi.org/10.1145/2882903.2915209

1. INTRODUCTION

Given an unlabeled query graph q and an unlabeled data graph g, the subgraph enumeration finds all occurrences of q in g. Subgraph enumeration is important for several applications such as subgraph frequencies [31], network motif discovery [2, 12, 18, 22, 34, 35], graphlet kernel computation [25], and studying the evolution of social networks [16]. Furthermore, triangle enumeration, a special case of the subgraph enumeration, facilitates applications such as clustering coefficient computation [33] and community detection [32].

1.1 Motivation

Most of the earlier work on subgraph enumeration assumes that graphs are resident in memory [7, 12], which encounters serious scalability problems. Recently, efforts to enumerate all subgraphs in a large-scale graph have seemed to enjoy some success by partitioning the data graph and exploiting distributed frameworks such as MapReduce [1, 20] and distributed graph engines [24]. Afrati et al. [1] propose a seminal work for subgraph enumberation using single map-reduce round method. In order to do this, the method duplicates edges several times in multiple machines at the map phase so that each machine can perform a multi-way join independent of other machines. Although this multi-way join based method requires one map-reduce round, it is very likely to keep almost the entire graph in memory of each machine if the query graph becomes complex. In order to avoid expensive join operations, Shao et al. [24] proposed an enhanced method called PSGL which generates partial subgraph results level-by-level using the parallel breadth-first search (BFS) without performing join. Those partial results (a.k.a, *partial solutions*) are stored in the main memory of each machine. However, we show that the size of partial solutions grows exponentially as the number of query vertices increases. Thus, as we shall see later, this method fails to handle even moderate-size graphs for most of the queries we tested. More recently, Lai et al. [20] present Hadoop-based TWINTWIGJOIN, which is an enhanced map-reduce method that executes a left-deep join tree where each vertex in the tree corresponds to either a single edge or two incident edges of a vertex. However, this join-based approach can also be viewed as a variant of parallel BFS search. Thus, it is bound to generate an explosive number of partial solutions. As we shall show later, all existing distributed approaches have serious performance problems for subgraph enumeration.

Furthermore, although distributed computing resources are readily available through the Cloud nowadays, large-scale graph com-

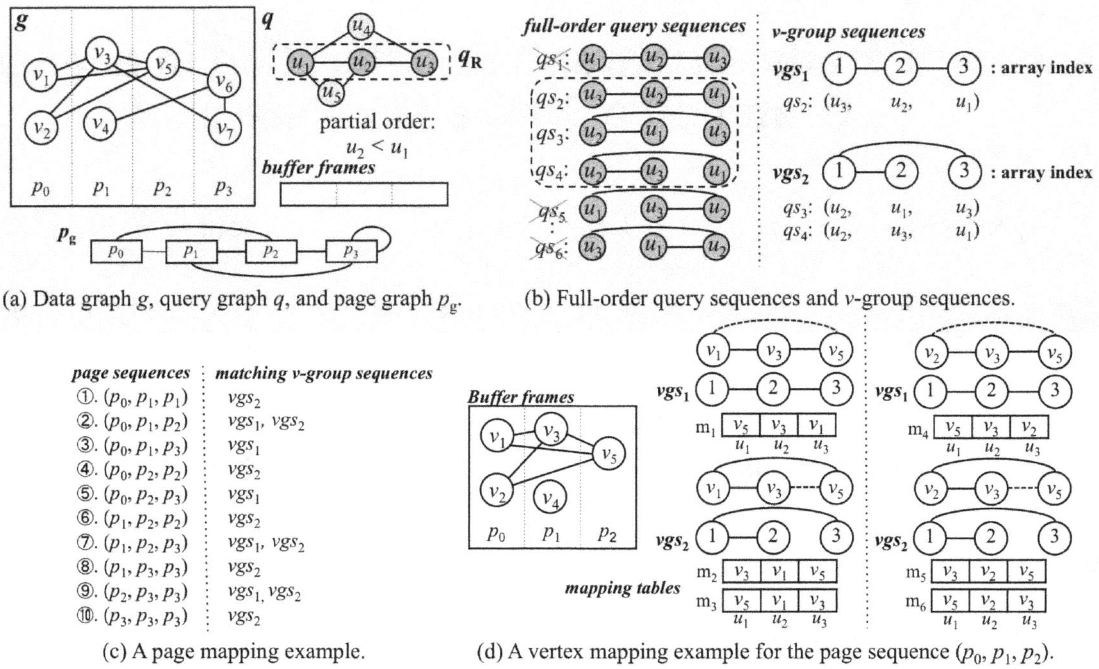

(a) Data graph g, query graph q, and page graph p_g. (b) Full-order query sequences and v-group sequences. (c) A page mapping example. (d) A vertex mapping example for the page sequence (p_0, p_1, p_2).

Figure 1: A running example.

putation often demands judicious partitioning of the graph across cluster machines that minimizes communication between the machines, which is known to be a hard problem [21]. From the end users' perspective, debugging and optimizing distributed algorithms is hard [19]. Additionally, it is financially expensive for ordinary users or a small research group to purchase and maintain such cluster nodes. For example, it is highly unlikely that a biologist would invest in a distributed framework to discover motifs in a protein-protein interaction (PPI) network.

A natural question, therefore, is whether it is possible to devise a scalable and efficient *disk-based solution to the subgraph enumeration problem in a single machine?* In this paper, we provide an affirmative answer to this question. Specifically, we design and implement a disk-based, single machine *parallel subgraph enumeration* solution called **DUALity-based Subgraph EnumeratIon on a Single Machine** (DUALSIM) that can handle massive graphs without maintaining exponential numbers of partial results.

1.2 Overview & Contributions

At first glance, it may seem that the depth-first search (DFS) strategy used in existing in-memory subgraph matching algorithms [7, 12] could be adopted to address the aforementioned excessive partial solution problem. Specifically, DFS-based subgraph matching algorithms fix the matching order of query vertices and recursively match one query vertex with data vertices one at a time, requiring minimal space to store the current partial solution. However, this strategy may incur considerable redundant disk reads since those data vertices are scattered across pages in disk. To illustrate this problem, consider the data graph g in Figure 1(a) composed of 7 vertices and 9 edges and the query graph q. Observe that g is stored in four disk pages (p_0 to p_3) but we have only three memory frames available in the buffer. Each vertex in the *page graph* p_g represents a page, and each edge (p_i, p_j) in p_g represents the fact that there is at least one edge across two pages. We assume that the subgraph q_R in q having only three vertices u_1, u_2, and u_3 is used for graph traversal. Consequently, we need to evict loaded disk pages whenever necessary by following a buffer replacement policy. As a result, this strategy will incur many disk page accesses to enumerate all occurrences of q_R!

In order to solve this challenging problem, we propose the novel concept of the *dual approach* for subgraph enumeration. The key feature of dual approach is that it swaps the roles of the data graph and the query graph. Specifically, instead of fixing the matching order in the query and then matching data vertices, it fixes the data vertices by fixing a set of disk pages and then finds all subgraph matchings in these pages (*i.e.,* matching query vertices). This enables us to significantly reduce the number of disk reads.

In the dual approach, before enumerating data subgraphs, we first need to enumerate all possible query sequences, each of which matches an ordered data sequence, thus making the data sequence fixed. These query sequences are called *full-order query sequences*. The full-order query sequence $(u_{i_1}, u_{i_2}, \cdots, u_{i_k})$ matches only with ordered data sequence $(v_{j_1}, v_{j_2}, \cdots, v_{j_k})$ such that $j_1 < j_2 < \cdots < j_k$. For example, in Figure 1(b), there are six full-order query sequences (qs_1 to qs_6). Suppose that we have a partial order constraint, $u_2 < u_1$. Then, qs_1, qs_5, and qs_6 are pruned. When a full-order query sequence matches a page sequence $(p_{j_1}, p_{j_2}, \cdots, p_{j_k})$, the condition $j_1 \leq j_2 \leq \cdots < j_k$ must be satisfied. This is because a page can contain more than one data vertex.

The dual approach groups full-order query sequences by their topology in order to minimize CPU time. This group sequence is called a *v-group sequence*. Figure 1(b) shows examples of two v-group sequences vgs_1 and vgs_2.

Next, the dual approach traverses the data graph stored in pages based on v-group sequences. Figure 1(c) shows a series of page sequences for the two v-group sequences. First, the page sequence (p_0, p_1, p_1) matches vgs_2, and p_0 and p_1 are now in the buffer. Next, the page sequence (p_0, p_1, p_2) matches both vgs_1 and vgs_2. In this way, we match the page sequence with a set of v-group sequences.

After matching a page sequence with v-group sequences, we find valid data vertex mappings for each v-group sequence. For each valid mapping, we enumerate all full-order query sequences in the

v-group sequence and generate data vertex mappings for them. For example, in Figure 1(d), a page sequence (p_0, p_1, p_2) matches vgs_1 and vgs_2. Thus, in the vertex level mapping, we can find a vertex-level matching sequence (v_1, v_3, v_5). Since there is only one full-order query sequence in vgs_1, a full solution $\{(u_3, v_1), (u_2, v_3), (u_1, v_5)\}$ is obtained. Similarly, since there are two full-order query sequences in vgs_2, two full solutions $\{(u_2, v_1), (u_1, v_3), (u_3, v_5)\}$, $\{(u_2, v_1), (u_3, v_3), (u_1, v_5)\}$ are obtained. Similarly, for the vertex-level matching sequence (v_2, v_3, v_5), we also generate three solutions.

Another interesting issue we need to consider is how to select a subset of query vertices for efficient graph traversal. Note that this has a similar flavor to the external triangulation problem where only two query vertices are used for matching data vertices in a database [15, 17]. Specifically, reducing the number of query vertices for graph traversal should reduce the number of disk accesses. This is because in order to match the remaining query vertices, we can utilize the adjacent lists which are already retrieved from disk. For example, reconsider Figure 1(a). Suppose that query vertices u_1 and u_2 are being matched with data vertices v_i and v_j, respectively. Then, we can identify data vertices for u_5 by intersecting the adjacent lists of v_1 and v_2.

In order to handle this issue, we propose the concept of the *red-black-ivory (*RBI*) graph* which is a vertex-colored graph where a color is assigned to a query vertex according to the operational semantics. If a query vertex u is colored *r*ed, we need to *r*etrieve the adjacency list of a data vertex for matching. If u is adjacent to m (>1) red query vertices, u is colored *i*vory. Consequently, in order to identify corresponding data vertices for u, we need to perform an (m-way) *i*ntersection of the adjacency lists of data vertices for the m red query vertices. If u is adjacent to only one red query vertex, u is colored *b*lack. In order to identify corresponding data vertices for u, we need to *b*rowse (or scan) the adjacency list of the data vertex corresponding to the red query vertex. For example, in Figure 1(a), we have 5 query vertices and 6 edges. In this case, only u_1, u_2, and u_3 are colored red (also called *red query graph*) and are used for graph traversal. The other two query vertices u_4 and u_5 are colored ivory. Thus, we need to perform 2-way intersections for identifying corresponding data vertices for u_4 and u_5. For example, once the two adjacency lists for u_1 and u_3 are obtained, we can obtain corresponding data vertices for u_4 by intersecting the two adjacency lists.

In summary, this paper makes the following key contributions.

- We propose an efficient and scalable disk-based subgraph enumeration method in a single machine for large-scale graphs. Unlike existing methods, DUALSIM does not maintain explosive partial solutions resulting in robust performance.
- We propose the novel concept of *dual approach* for subgraph enumeration. The dual approach uses novel concepts of *v-group sequence* and *v-group forest* in order to minimize processing time for subgraph enumeration. In addition, in order to realize the dual approach with a limited buffer size, we propose novel concepts of *candidate page sequence* and *current page window*. In order to overlap CPU processing with I/O processing, we propose novel concepts of *internal and external subgraphs*. All of these new concepts together lead to the concrete implementation of DUALSIM.
- We propose a technique that transforms a query graph to a RBI *query graph*, which enables us to lower the number of disk reads by matching part of the query graph only and utilizing their associated adjacency lists.
- We conduct exhaustive experiments using various real-world graphs to systematically demonstrate the superiority of DUALSIM over the-state-of-the-art subgraph enumeration methods. Specifically, DUALSIM using a single machine significantly outperforms TWINTWIGJOIN using a single machine by up to 866.61 times. Note that, TWINTWIGJOIN fails to process queries generating enormous partial solutions, while DUALSIM handles all queries without maintaining such explosive partial solutions. DUALSIM using a single machine also outperforms both PSGL and TWINTWIGJOIN using 51 machines by up to 35.04 and 903.47 times, respectively. Note that PSGL failed for 46.6% of experiments we tested due to enormous partial solutions.

1.3 Paper Organisation

The rest of the paper is organized as follows. In Section 2, we introduce fundamental graph concepts and formally define the subgraph enumeration problem addressed in this paper. We introduce the notions of the RBI query graph and the red query graph in Section 3 and explain how they are generated from a query graph. In Section 4, we introduce the dual approach using v-group sequence and v-group forest. In Section 5, we describe the algorithm of DUALSIM in detail. We present experimental results in Section 6 and review related work in Section 7. We conclude in Section 8.

2. BACKGROUND

A data graph $g(V, E)$ is modeled as an undirected and unlabeled graph where V is the set of vertices, and E ($\subseteq V \times V$) is the set of edges. A subgraph g' of $g(V, E)$ is a graph such that $V(g') \subseteq V(g)$ and $E(g') \subseteq E(g)$. Given a vertex v, we denote the degree of v as $d(v)$. $adj(v)$ denotes the adjacency list of v. $id(v)$ denotes the id of v. $P(v)$ denotes the page ID of the data vertex v. A query graph $q(V', E')$ is an undirected, unlabeled, and connected graph. We use u_i and v_j to represent the i-th query vertex and the j-th data vertex, respectively.

A graph $q(V', E')$ is *isomorphic* to a subgraph of a data graph $g(V, E)$ if there is an injection (or an embedding) $m : V \rightarrow V'$ such that $\forall (u_i, u_j) \in E, (m(u_i), m(u_j)) \in E'$.

When storing adjacency lists of data vertices in disk, we use the slotted page format, which is widely used in database systems. That is, each $(v, adj(v))$ for $v \in V$ is stored in pages. When the size of an adjacency list is larger than the page size, the adjacency list is broken into multiple sublists, and each sublist is stored in a page.

Following the convention in [15,17,20,24], we use the following *total order* $\prec$ for data vertices in g. For any two data vertices v_i and v_j, $v_i \prec v_j$ if and only if $d(v_i) < d(v_j)$ or $d(v_i) = d(v_j)$ and $id(v_i) < id(v_j)$. We rearrange the vertices in g according to $\prec$.

A *vertex cover* of an undirected graph $q(V_q, E_q)$ is a subset of vertices $V'_q \subset V_q$ such that for any edge $(u_i, u_j) \in E_q$, $u_i \in V'_q$, or $u_j \in V'_q$, or both [8]. For example, consider the query graph q in Figure 2. The vertex-covers of this graph are $\{u_1, u_4\}$, $\{u_2, u_3\}$, $\{u_1, u_2, u_3\}$, $\{u_1, u_2, u_4\}$, $\{u_2, u_3, u_4\}$, $\{u_1, u_3, u_4\}$, and $\{u_1, u_2, u_3, u_4\}$. A minimum vertex cover (MVC) is a vertex cover having the smallest number of vertices. A connected vertex cover is a vertex cover V'_q such that the induced subgraph using V'_q is connected [28]. If the size of a connected vertex cover is the minimum among all possible connected covers for q, the connected vertex cover is called a minimum connected vertex cover (MCVC) [28]. Reconsidering the above example, the vertex cover $\{u_1, u_2, u_3\}$ is an MCVC whereas $\{u_1, u_4\}$ is not.

In order to generate each subgraph exactly once, we need to eliminate the automorphism of a query graph q. Here, an automorphism of q is a graph isomorphism from q to itself [20]. Suppose that an embedding m is found. Then for any $u_i < u_j$ in *partial orders*, $m(u_i) \leq m(u_j)$ should be satisfied. Note that a set of partial or-

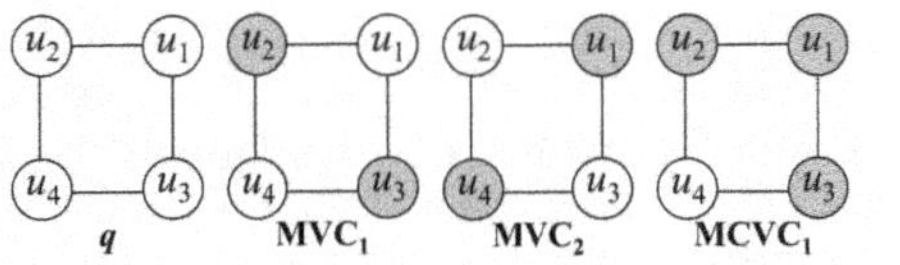

Figure 2: A query graph q, and two MVCs, and one MCVC.

ders can be obtained by breaking the automorphism of q [20, 24]. For example, if we have a triangle-shaped query having u_1, u_2, and u_3 as query vertices, partial orders $u_1 < u_2 < u_3$ can be obtained.

Definition 1. ***[Problem Statement]*** *Given a data graph g stored in disk, a query graph q, and a set PO of partial orders, the subgraph enumeration problem identifies all mappings of g that are isomorphic to q such that each mapping satisfies all partial orders in PO.*

3. RBI QUERY GRAPH

In order to minimize the number of disk reads, we need to use a minimum number of query vertices during graph traversal. Once adjacency lists for a subset of query vertices are retrieved from disk, we can match the remaining query vertices with only the adjacency lists retrieved. We realize this strategy by transforming the query graph q to an RBI *query graph* q_{RBI} by *coloring* its vertices.

In order to handle this issue, we propose the *red-black-ivory (*RBI*) query graph* which is a vertex-colored graph where a color is assigned to a vertex according to the operational semantics. If u is colored red, we need to retrieve the adjacency list of a data vertex for matching. If u is colored ivory, it is adjacent to m (>1) red query vertices. Consequently, in order to identify corresponding data vertices for u, we need to perform an (m-way) intersection of the adjacency lists of data vertices for the m red query vertices. If u is colored black, it is adjacent to only one red query vertex. Then, in order to identify corresponding data vertices for u, we need to browse (or scan) the adjacency list of data vertices for the red query vertex. Figure 3 depicts two examples of query graphs and RBI query graphs. In Figure 3(a), u_1 and u_2 are colored red. The query vertices u_4 and u_5 are colored ivory because they are adjacent to two red query vertices u_1 and u_2. On the other hand, u_3 is colored black because it is adjacent to u_2 only. In Figure 3(b), u_1, u_2, and u_3 are colored red. There is no black colored vertex because u_4 and u_5 are both connected to two red query vertices.

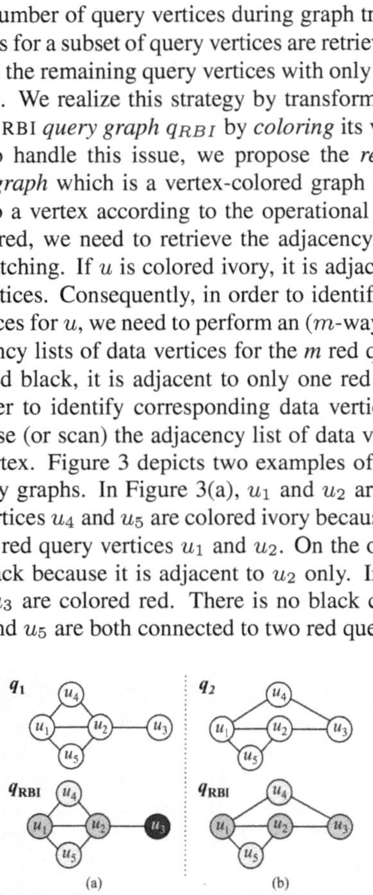

Figure 3: Two examples showing a query graph q and its RBI query graph q_{RBI}.

A *red query graph*(RQG) $q_R(V_R, E_R)$ is an induced subgraph of the red query vertices in $q_{RBI}(V_Q, E_Q)$ where $V_R \subset V_Q$ and $E_R \subset E_Q$. For example, in Figure 3(a), the RQG is an induced subgraph of query vertices $\{u_1, u_2\}$ and in Figure 3(b), it is an induced subgraph of query vertices $\{u_1, u_2, u_3\}$.

In order to select the smallest number of red query vertices, we can use the MVC. That is, all query vertices in a selected MVC are colored red. We can color the other query vertices based on the description above. Although the number of red query vertices increases slightly, we prefer to use the MCVC in this paper. This approach enables us to access data vertices reachable from the data vertices corresponding to the first red query vertex selected. Otherwise, we have to scan all vertices regardless of their reachability. This issue corresponds to the join versus cartesian product in relational databases. Although we use MCVC in this paper, the extension to support MVC is straightforward. Note that, while finding an MVC/MCVC is NP-hard, $|V_q|$ is generally very small, so its exponential complexity is not a problem in reality. We may use an approximate algorithm when $|V_q|$ is large [26].

A keen reader may observe that a query graph may contain more than one MCVC (or RQG). In this case, which one do we choose as a red query graph? In the following, we propose two rules which leverage partial orders and MCVCs, which can affect I/O time as well as CPU time.

Given a set of partial orders PO, a query graph $q(V_Q, E_Q)$ and an RQG (V_R, E_R), a partial order $(u_1 < u_2) \in PO$ is *an internal partial order* if $u_1 \in V_R$ and $u_2 \in V_R$.

Rule 1. *Given any two* RQG*s, we choose the* RQG *which has more internal partial orders.*

Rule 2. *If there is a tie in Rule 1, we choose a denser* RQG. *That is, we choose the* RQG *which has more edges.*

As shown in Figure 1(b), internal partial orders can prune full-order query sequences. Thus, Rule 1 can reduce candidate data vertices during graph exploration. Rule 2 can also reduce the CPU processing time during red vertex matching if one RQG has more edges than the other RQG.

4. DUAL APPROACH

Recall that in the dual approach, we swap the roles of the data graph and the query graph. Specifically, instead of fixing the matching order in the query and then matching data vertices, it fixes the data vertices by fixing a set of disk pages and then finds all subgraph matchings in these pages (*i.e.*, matching query vertices). This enables us to significantly reduce the number of disk reads.

Full-order query sequence. Before enumerating data subgraphs, the dual approach first must enumerate all possible query sequences, each of which matches an *ordered* data sequence, thus making the data sequence fixed. These query sequences are called *full-order query sequences*, which is formally defined below.

Definition 2. ***[Full-order query sequence]*** *Given an* RQG $q_R(V_R, E_R)$ *and a set of partial order PO, a full-order query sequence qs is a permuted sequence of vertices in* V_R *such that PO is a subset of the full order* $(qs[1] < qs[2] < \cdots < qs[|V_R|])$ *among query vertices in qs.*

Property 1 states that a full-order query sequence matches an ordered data sequence of size $|V_R|$ element by element.

Property 1. *Given an* RQG $q_R(V_R, E_R)$, *when a full-order query sequence qs matches a data vertex sequence of size* $|V_R|$ *using a mapping (injection) m,* $m[qs[1]] \prec m[qs[2]] \prec \cdots \prec m[qs[|V_R|]]$.

Lemma 1. *Suppose that vertices are stored in pages according to* $id(\cdot)$. *Given an* RQG $q_R(V_R, E_R)$, *when a full-order query sequence qs matches a data vertex sequence of size* $|V_R|$ *using an injection m,* $P(m[qs[1]]) \leq P(m[qs[2]]) \leq \cdots \leq P(m[qs[|V_R|]])$.

PROOF. Refer to Appendix C. □

This way, we fix the page sequence of size $|V_R|$ in a non-decreasing order, varying all full-order query sequences. There can be many full-order query sequences of q_R, and hence, finding subgraph mappings for each such sequence may lead to a redundant matching process. To tackle this issue, we utilize the notion of *v-group sequence*.

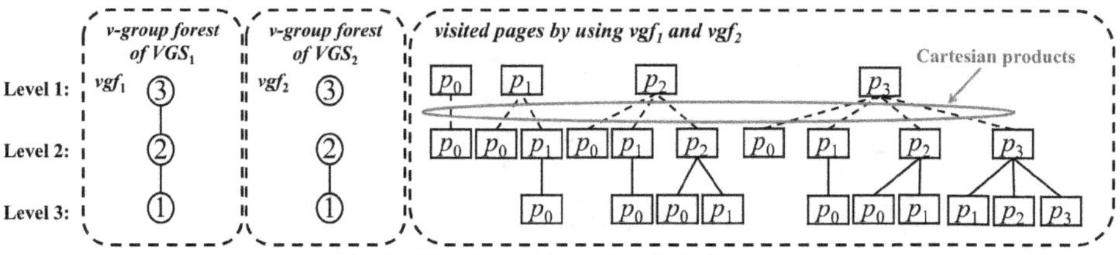

(a) Global matching order: (3, 2, 1).

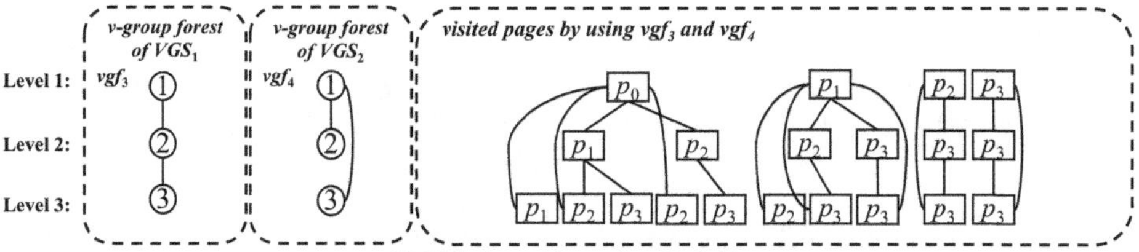

(b) Global matching order: (1, 2, 3).

Figure 4: An example of v-group forests.

v-group sequence. We first group the full-order query sequences by their topology based on *equivalence* of query sequences as defined below.

Definition 3. *[Query Sequence Equivalence] Let QS be the set of all full-order query sequences for an* RQG $q_R(V_R, E_R)$. *Let $\cong$ be an equivalent relation over QS such that $qs_i \cong qs_j$ if and only if $\forall 1 \leq k, k' \leq |V_R|$, if $(qs_i[k], qs_i[k']) \in E_R$, $(qs_j[k], qs_j[k']) \in E_R$.*

The equivalent class of qs_i is a set of full-order query sequences which are equivalent to (*i.e.,* $\cong$) qs_i. This class is called a *v-group sequence*, since all full-order query sequences in a v-group sequence match the same data vertices. For example, in Figure 1, $qs_3(u_2, u_1, u_3)$ and $qs_4(u_2, u_3, u_1)$ constitute a v-group sequence. Thus, when (v_1, v_3, v_5) matches qs_3, it also matches qs_4.

Once all v-group sequences are obtained, we need to determine a matching order for each of them in order to traverse the data graph, *i.e.,* pages in the database. Since there can be multiple v-group sequences, we may traverse the data graph as many times as the number of v-group sequences. Thus, we provide a method for determining a global matching order which is used to traverse the data graph (*i.e.,* pages in disk) based on all v-group sequences. The term vgs_i denotes the i-th v-group sequence, and $\{vgs_i\}$ is a set of all v-group sequences.

v-group forest. In order to solve the explosive partial solution size problem, when we traverse the data graph, we maintain candidate vertices for each red query vertex rather than saving all possible partial solutions. For this, we construct an acyclic traversal structure called a *v-group forest* for each v-group sequence. This way, the total size of partial solutions for each v-group sequence is bounded by $O(|V_R| * |V_G|)$. If we use a bitmap, its size is significantly smaller than the graph size.

Intuitively, each node in a v-group forest stores an array index for the v-group sequences. Each node is associated with its level. At each level, we have only one node. Thus, the number of levels is equal to $|V_R|$. Note that the array index is also used to enforce the total order in the v-group sequences. Figure 4(a) shows the v-group forest for vgs_1 when the global matching order of array indexes is (3, 2, 1). There is only one tree in this forest having two edges, while the v-group forest for vgs_2 consists of two trees. In the second v-group forest, the node storing 2 as the array index is not connected from the node storing 3. The node storing 1 as the array index can be a child of the other two nodes; thus, we choose the one which is farthest from its root node with respect to the length of the path from the root node. The term vgf_i denotes the v-group forest for vgs_i, and $\{vgf_i\}$ is a set of all v-group forests. The term $vgf_i[j]$ denotes the node at level j of vgf_i.

Data graph traversal. Given a global matching order, we explain how we traverse the data graph considering the matching order as well as the topology information of every v-group forest. In order to do this, for each v-group forest, we first determine a set of candidate pages to explore at level l by considering its topology. Then, a set of pages to explore at level l should be a union of the sets of candidate pages for the nodes at level l of all v-group forests. Figure 4(a) shows the visited pages by using two v-group forests, vgf_1 and vgf_2. At the first level, we can match any page (p_0 to p_3) in the database. For each page at the first level, we need to access pages in the next level, considering the topologies of both v-group forests. If we consider only the first v-group forest, we only need to access pages connected from the page at the first level. However, if we consider the second v-group forest, we need to consider all pages for each page retrieved in the first level, incurring a Cartesian product. Note that the dotted lines between pages represent the Cartesian product. Thus, the set of pages to retrieve at the second level should be a union of candidate pages from both v-group forests. Note that, even in this case, we can still exploit the total order in each v-group sequence. Therefore, in this example, p_0 at level 1 does not match p_1, p_2, p_3 at level 2, while p_3 at level 1 matches p_0 to p_3. Figure 4(b) shows the visited pages by using vgf_3 and vgf_4 derived from the global matching order (1, 2, 3). In contrast to Figure 4(a), there is no Cartesian product needed when we traverse the data graph.

Now, we explain how to select a global matching order. Different matching orders can generate different numbers of Cartesian products. Thus, we enumerate all possible matching orders and choose the one generating the least number of Cartesian products. Since the number of red query vertices is very small, such enumeration cost is negligible compared to the subgraph enumeration itself.

5. DUALITY-BASED SUBGRAPH ENUMERATION

DUALSIM traverses the data graph level by level. However, due to the limited buffer size, we can load a subset of pages in memory for each level. Here, we need to ensure that the same sets of pages are loaded only once in order to minimize the number of disk I/Os. For this purpose, we propose novel concepts of *current vertex/page*

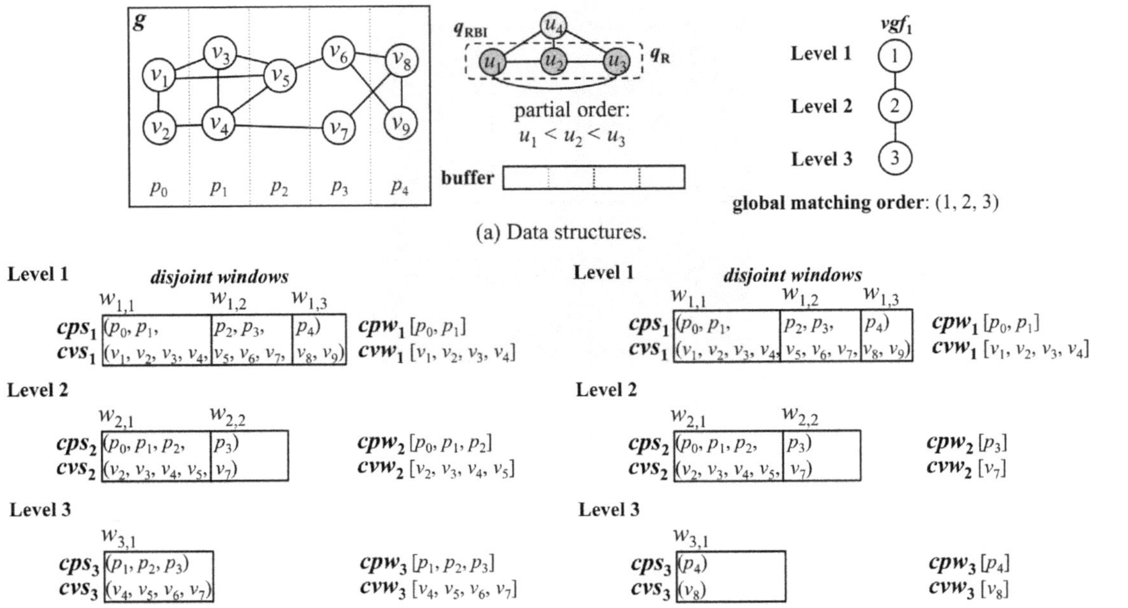

(a) Data structures.

(b) When current page windows for $w_{1,1}$, $w_{2,1}$, $w_{3,1}$ are chosen. (c) When current page windows for $w_{1,1}$, $w_{2,2}$, $w_{3,1}$ are chosen.

Figure 5: An example of candidate vertex/page sequences and current vertex/page windows.

window and *candidate vertex/page sequence* in Section 5.1, which are used together with the concept of v-group forest in Section 4. When we load a set of pages for each level, we issue page requests in a sequential scan fashion without incurring random disk page accesses. This strategy is important especially when we use HDDs.

Subgraph enumeration is a CPU intensive task. Thus, the important issue is how to overlap CPU processing with I/O processing effectively. Specifically, as soon as a page is loaded at the last level, we issue I/O requests for the next pages and execute subgraph enumeration using pages in memory at the same time. This is how our overlapping strategy can effectively hide the I/O cost. For this purpose, we propose novel concepts of *internal and external subgraphs* under the dual approach in Section 5.2.

5.1 Candidate Sequence and Current Window

We traverse the data graph based on the v-group forest by retrieving vertices/pages level-by-level. Suppose that m_j buffer frames are allocated for the j-th level in vgf_i. Assume that there is one v-group forest for ease of explanation and then explain how to handle multiple v-group forests.

Candidate sequence and current window. A vertex/page window currently in the buffer for processing is called the current vertex window (CVW) and current page window (CPW). The candidate vertex/page sequence (CVS and CPS) for $vgf_i[j]$ is recursively defined as an ordered sequence of vertices/pages connected from the current vertex/page window corresponding to the parent node of $vgf_i[j]$. As a base case, the candidate vertex/page sequence at level 1 is defined as a sequence of all vertices/pages.

Now, we explain how we load a subset of pages, i.e., the current page window, from the candidate page sequence at each level so that we can ensure that the same arrangement of page sets for all levels is made only once. For this purpose, we divide the sequence into disjoint windows. Since some vertices/pages in the sequence can be in the buffer already, disjoint windows can be variably sized. Once disjoint windows are identified, we can iterate over them one by one. When we load a set of pages for each level, we issue page requests in a sequential scan fashion without incurring random disk page accesses.

Figure 5 shows an example of the current vertex window and the current page window at each level. The data graph is stored in five pages $p_0 \sim p_4$, while we have four memory buffer frames. Due to the partial order ($u_1 < u_2 < u_3$), we have only one v-group sequence and, accordingly, one v-group forest vgf_1. Consider Figure 5(b). At level 1, we need to retrieve all vertices. Thus, the candidate vertex sequence (denoted as cvs_1) is $(v_1, v_2, \cdots, v_9)$, while the candidate page sequence (denoted as cps_1) is $(p_0, p_1, \cdots, p_4)$. Suppose that two memory frames are allocated for the first level. Then, we load the first two pages p_0 and p_1 in the buffer. Thus, the current page window (cpw_1) is (p_0, p_1), while the current vertex window is (v_1, v_2, v_3, v_4). Once p_0 and p_1 are loaded, we can identify cps_2 and cvs_2. Here, cps_2 is (p_0, p_1, p_2, p_3), and cvs_2 is $(v_2, v_3, v_4, v_5, v_7)$. Suppose that we allocate one memory frame for the second level. Then, the current page window at the second level (cpw_2) is (p_0, p_1, p_2), while the second page window is p_3. Note that p_0 and p_1 in cpw_2 are already in the buffer. After loading cpw_2, we can identify the candidate vertex/page sequences at the last level. Figure 5(c) shows CPSs, CVSs, CPWs, and CVWs at each level, when $w_{1,1}$, $w_{2,2}$, and $w_{3,1}$ are chosen as current page windows.

Merged sequence and current merged window. In general, there can be multiple v-group forests. Thus, if we process these v-group forests one by one, we are unable to ensure that the same arrangement of page sets for all levels is made only once. In order to avoid this problem, for each level, we first find all candidate sequences for all v-group forests and merge them into one sorted sequence, called *merged sequence*, removing any duplicate in the merged sequence. We then divide this merged sequence by disjoint windows called *merged window*. After loading a merged, disjoint window, we assign loaded vertices/pages to relevant v-group forests accordingly. This way, we can avoid repeated loading of pages from disk.

Figure 6 shows an example of merged vertex/page sequences and their windows at each level using g in Figure 5(a). Now we have two v-group forests vgf_1 and vgf_2 as shown in Figure 6(b). Figure 6(c) and Figure 6(d) represent CPSs and CVSs for each v-group forest and their current page windows. Consider Figure 6(e). The

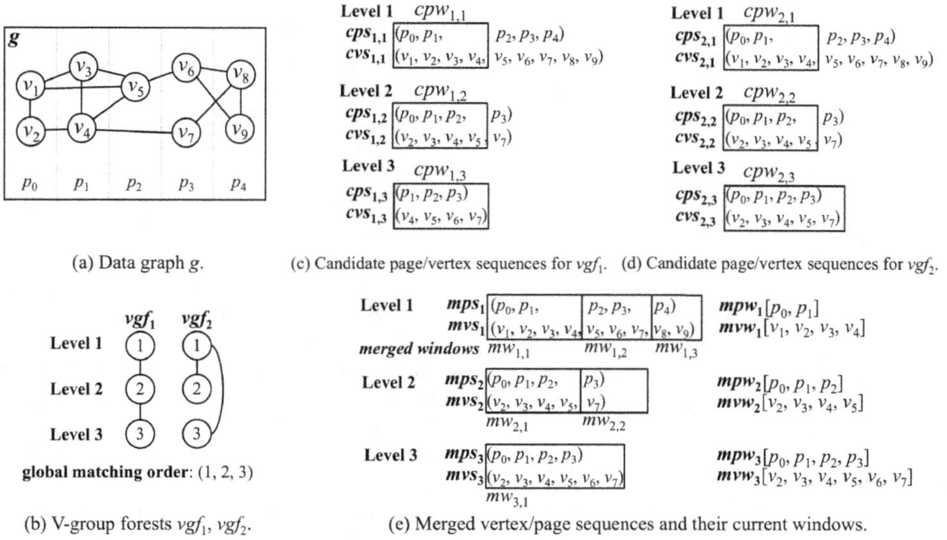

(a) Data graph g. (b) V-group forests vgf_1, vgf_2. (c) Candidate page/vertex sequences for vgf_1. (d) Candidate page/vertex sequences for vgf_2. (e) Merged vertex/page sequences and their current windows.

Figure 6: An example of merged vertex/page sequences and their windows.

merged vertex sequence for level i (denoted as mvs_i) is a merged sequence using $cvs_{1,i}$ and $cvs_{2,i}$. The merged page sequence for level i (denoted as mps_i) is a merged sequence using $cps_{1,i}$ and $cps_{2,i}$. Suppose that two memory frames are allocated for level 1. The current merged page window (denoted as mpw_1) is (p_0, p_1), while the current merged vertex window (mvw_i) is (v_1, v_2, v_3, v_4). Once p_0 and p_1 are loaded, we can identify $cps_{1,2}$, $cps_{2,2}$, and $cps_{2,3}$. All three candidate page sequences are (p_0, p_1, p_2, p_3) in this case, and thus mps_2 is (p_0, p_1, p_2, p_3). We can also identify $cvs_{1,2}$, $cvs_{2,2}$, and $cvs_{2,3}$ as $(v_2, v_3, v_4, v_5, v_7)$. Accordingly, mvs_2 is $(v_2, v_3, v_4, v_5, v_7)$. Suppose that we allocate one memory frame for level 2. Then, the current merged page window (mpw_2) is (p_0, p_1, p_2) since p_0 and p_1 are already in the buffer. After loading mpw_2, we can identify the candidate vertex/page sequences at the last level of vgf_1 ($cvs_{1,3}$ and $cps_{1,3}$). If we allocate one memory frame for level 3, the current merged page window (mpw_3) is (p_0, p_1, p_2, p_3) since $p_0 \sim p_2$ are already in the buffer.

5.2 Internal and External Subgraphs

In order to support overlapped and parallel subgraph enumeration in our dual approach, we define concepts of *internal and external subgraphs*, which are generalized concepts of internal and external triangles [17]. Before introducing the concepts in detail, we first explain how we overlap CPU processing with I/O processing at a high-level. DUALSIM achieves two types of overlapping: 1) Once the current window at level 1 is loaded, we can start to find data subgraphs within the window (i.e., internal subgraphs). At the same time, we find subgraphs connected from the vertices in the current window at level 1 by traversing the data graph level by level as we explain in the previous section. Those subgraphs are called external subgraphs. 2) As soon as we load a page at the last level, we can find subgraphs using pages in memory. At the same time, we can issues I/O requests for the next pages at the last level. DUALSIM splits the buffer by the number of levels of the v-group forest. The j-th area in the buffer consists of m_j memory frames. The first area, corresponding to level 1, is called *internal area* while all the other areas together are called *external area*.

We assume that the adjacency list of each vertex can be loaded in each buffer area. This assumption is called the small-degree assumption [15]. However, what if we have vertices whose adjacency lists are larger than an area? This can easily be handled by using [15]. First, identify all such vertices. For each large-degree vertex u, load as many edges of u as the first area can hold. Then, we report all subgraphs that involve at least one edge in the first area. The key issue here is how to identify candidate vertex/page sequences from a partly loaded adjacency list. This can be achieved by scanning the incoming edges of all vertices in the data graph. If we can identify the candidate vertex/page sequence, we can use the dual approach. We then remove all edges in the first area from the data graph. We repeat this process until no large-degree data vertices remain.

We now define the concept of the internal subgraph and the external subgraph. If a data subgraph which matches the RQG is in the internal area, then such a subgraph is called an *internal subgraph*. The data subgraph matching the RQG is called *external subgraph* if there is at least one data vertex in the internal area and there is at least one data vertex in the external area. We assume that, after finding subgraphs which match the RQG, we further match the other query vertices. Figure 7 shows internal subgraphs and external subgraphs when the query graph is q in Figure 1. Suppose that $v_1 \prec v_2 \prec v_3$. The first two cases correspond to internal subgraphs while the others correspond to external subgraphs.

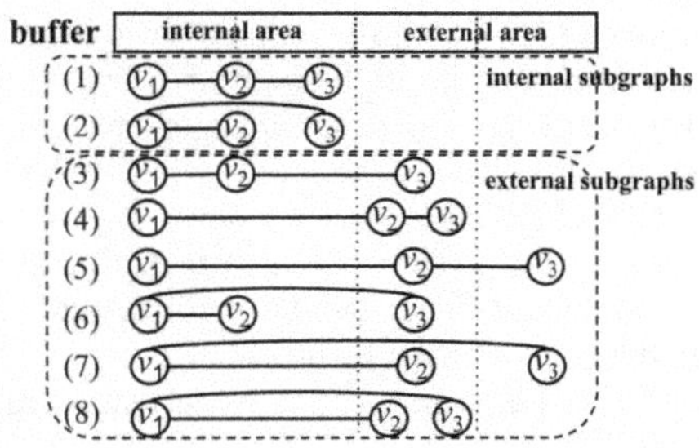

Figure 7: An example of internal and external subgraphs.

Note also that DUALSIM is a true generalization of the-state-of-the art triangulation [17], which handles the triangle-shaped query having two red query vertices. Thus, in our framework, the buffer space is divided into two areas. Like OPT [17], DUALSIM also supports overlapped and parallel subgraph enumeration. That is, as soon as a subset of disk pages is loaded into the internal area, we overlap internal subgraph enumeration with external subgraph enumeration. The internal subgraph enumeration finds all internal subgraphs in the pages loaded into the internal area, while the external subgraph enumeration finds all external subgraphs. Since we can use any in-memory subgraph enumeration algorithm for finding internal subgraphs, we focus on enumerating external subgraphs.

More importantly, during the external subgraph enumeration, we overlap CPU processing with I/O processing. That is, as soon as a page for the last level of the v-group forest is loaded from disk, DUALSIM finds external subgraphs using pages in memory, and issues asynchronous I/O requests for the next pages at the same time. This way, DUALSIM effectively hides I/O cost.

5.3 The DualSim Algorithms

DUALSIM consists of two steps: 1) the preparation step and 2) the execution step. Algorithm 1 summarizes how DUALSIM works. The elapsed time for the preparation step is at most 1 msec. for all queries we tested, which is negligible.

Algorithm 1. DUALSIM

```
    Input: A data graph g, A query graph q
    /* 1.  Preparation step                                              */
1:  PO ← FINDPARTIALORDERS(q);
2:  ⟨q_RBI, q_R⟩ ← GENERATERBIQUERYGRAPH(q, PO);
3:  {vgs_i} ← FINDVGROUPSEQUENCES(q_R, PO);
4:  mo_g ← FINDGLOBALMATCHINGORDER({vgs_i});
5:  {vgf_i} ← BUILDVGROUPFORESTS({vgs_i}, mo_g);
    /* 2.  Execution step                                                */
6:  INITIALIZECANDIDATESEQUENCES(root nodes in {vgf_i});
7:  foreach (merged vertex/page window (mvw_1, mpw_1) from {vgf_i[1]}) do
8:      foreach (page id pid ∈ mpw_1) do
9:          AsyncRead(pid, COMPUTECANDIDATESEQUENCES(pid,
              {cvw_{i,1}}, all child nodes of {vgf_i[1]});
10:     end
11:     wait until COMPUTECANDIDATESEQUENCES executions are finished
12:     level ← 2;
13:     DELEGATEEXTERNALSUBGRAPHENUMERATION(level, q_RBI,
          {vgs_i}, {vgf_i}, {mvw_j}, {mpw_j});
14:     INTERNALSUBGRAPHENUMERATION(mvw_1, mpw_1);
15:     UNPINPAGES(mpw_1);
16:     CLEARCANDIDATESEQUENCES(the children of {vgf_i[1]});
17: end
```

In the preparation step, DUALSIM first finds a set PO of partial orders using the symmetry-breaking algorithm [12] (Line 1). Then, it generates q_{RBI} and q_R using PO (Line 2). Next, it finds all v-group sequences (Line 3). It then finds a global matching order considering all v-group sequences (Line 4). It next constructs a v-group forest for each v-group sequence using the global matching order (Line 5).

In the execution step, DUALSIM initializes candidate vertex/page sequences for all root nodes in the v-group forests (Line 6). This initialization makes every root node correspond to all vertices/pages. Then, we traverse the data graph level-by-level with the v-group forest by using the concept of merged vertex/page window (Lines 7 $\sim$ 16). Here, we use COMPUTECANDIDATESEQUENCES$(\cdot)$ (in Appendix A) to compute the candidate vertex/page sequences for each page in the current merged window.

Specifically, DUALSIM first obtains the current, merged vertex/page window at level 1, mvw_1/mpw_1 (Line 7). For each page p in mpw_1, we asynchronously read the page (Line 8 $\sim$ Line 10). Note that we can pass a callback function when we request an asynchronous I/O. Here, the callback function, COMPUTECANDIDATESEQUENCES$(\cdot)$ is invoked as soon as the requested page is loaded into the buffer. Since the current level is set to 1, the callback function computes the candidate vertex/page sequences for level 2. We need to wait until all requested pages are loaded in the buffer. Then, we invoke a recursive function, DELEGATEEXTERNALSUBGRAPHENUMERATION$(\cdot)$ in order to find all external subgraphs connected from the current, merged vertex window (Line 13). This way, the main thread delegates the external subgraph enumeration to other threads. The main thread executes internal subgraph enumeration using the pages loaded in the internal area (Line 14). When either internal subgraph enumeration or external subgraph enumeration ends, then we perform *Thread Morphing* [17], which assigns the available threads to the unfinished subgraph enumeration. Execution of thread morphing is omitted in Algorithm 1 due to space limitation. This is how we overlap the internal subgraph enumeration with the external subgraph enumeration.

For example, consider Figure 6. mpw_1 of the first iteration (Line 8) is (p_0, p_1), and mvw_1 of the first iteration is (v_1, v_2, v_3, v_4). At the first iteration, two pages p_0 and p_1 in mpw_1 are loaded in the internal area by calling AsyncRead. COMPUTECANDIDATESEQUENCES$(\cdot)$ is invoked when each of the requested pages is loaded into the buffer. Then, COMPUTECANDIDATESEQUENCES$(\cdot)$ computes $cvs_{1,2}$ with $adj(v)$ and $cps_{1,2}$ with $\{P(v')|v' \in adj(v)\}$ for each v in $cvw_{1,1}$. This function also computes $cvs_{2,2}$, $cps_{2,2}$, $cvs_{2,3}$, and $cps_{2,3}$. We then delegate the external subgraph enumeration to the other threads by calling DELEGATEEXTERNALSUBGRAPHENUMERATION$(\cdot)$. After delegation of external subgraph enumeration, the main thread invokes INTERNALSUBGRAPHENUMERATION$(\cdot)$. After executions for both functions are finished, the pages p_0 and p_1 are unpinned for page replacement. These steps are repeated until all merged vertex/page windows are processed.

Now, we explain DELEGATEEXTERNALSUBGRAPHENUMERATION$(\cdot)$. The inputs to this function are l, q_{RBI}, $\{vgs_i\}$, $\{vgf_i\}$, mvw_l, and mpw_l: Here, l is the current level to process: We have a loop over merged vertex/page windows. At each iteration, we identify the current, merged vertex/page window, mvw_l, and mpw_l. If l is the last level, we invoke read requests with the callback EXTVERTEXMAPPING$(\cdot)$ (in Appendix A), which finds all vertex-level mappings using data vertices loaded in the buffer. That is, once the current vertex window at every level is loaded in the buffer, we can find the external subgraphs using EXTVERTEXMAPPING$(\cdot)$. At the same time, by invoking AsynRead$(\cdot)$ calls for the next pages, we can overlap CPU processing of EXTVERTEXMAPPING$(\cdot)$ with I/O processing. Here, since all internal subgraphs are enumerated in the internal area, this function avoids matching all red query vertices with data subgraphs in the internal area in order not to generate duplicate results. Instead, for each page in mpw_l, we request an asynchronous I/O with the callback function COMPUTECANDIDATESEQUENCES$(\cdot)$. Then, we recursively invoke DELEGATEEXTERNALSUBGRAPHENUMERATION$(\cdot)$ for the next level.

For example, consider Figure 6. Here, l is set to 2. Thus, at level 2, we compute the current merged vertex/page sequence, mpw_2 ($= (p_0, p_1, p_2)$) and mvw_2 ($= (v_2, v_3, v_4, v_5)$). We then request three asynchronous reads with the callback function COMPUTECANDIDATESEQUENCES$(\cdot)$ for p_0, p_1, and p_2. We recursively delegate external subgraph enumeration to available threads. When DELEGATEEXTERNALSUBGRAPHENUMERATION$(\cdot)$ is called at level 3 (the last level in this example), we request asynchronous reads with another callback function EXTVERTEXMAPPING$(\cdot)$ so that we can find external subgraphs, starting from each page loaded at level 3.

I/O Cost of DualSim. Now, we analyze the I/O cost of DUALSIM. Let $|E|$ be the number of edges in the data graph, M be the memory buffer size, and B be the page size. We assume that each edge is stored in one memory word, and M is equally divided into ($|V_R|$-1) regions. Note that we need only one memory frame for scanning pages at the last level. This additional memory frame is not considered in the asymptotic analysis. s_j represents the average reduction factor ($0 \leq s_j \leq 1$) for level j. Since we access only pages con-

Algorithm 2. DELEGATEEXTERNALSUBGRAPHENUMERATION

```
Input: Current level l, RBI query graph q_RBI, v-group sequences {vgs_i},
       v-group forests {vgf_i}, merged current vertex windows {mvw_j},
       merged current page windows {mpw_j}

foreach (merged vertex/page window (mvw_l, mpw_l) from {vgf_i[l]}) do
    if (l < |G_R|) then
        foreach (page id pid in mpw_l) do
            AsyncRead(pid, COMPUTECANDIDATESEQUENCES(pid,
                {cvw_{i,l}}, children of {vgf_i[l]});
        wait until COMPUTECANDIDATESEQUENCES executions are
            finished;
        DELEGATEEXTERNALSUBGRAPHENUMERATION(l+1, q_RBI,
            {vgs_i}, {vgf_i}, {mvw_j}, {mpw_j});
        UNPINPAGES(mpw_l);
        CLEARCANDIDATESEQUENCES(the children of {vgf_i[l]});
    else
        foreach (pid in mpw_l) do
            AsyncRead(pid, EXTVERTEXMAPPING(pid, q_RBI, {cvw_i},
                {vgs_i}, {vgf_i}));
    end
end
```

nected from the pages loaded at level 1. Then, at level l, DUALSIM requires $s_1(=1) \times \frac{|E|}{\frac{M}{|V_R|-1}} \times s_2 \times \frac{|E|}{\frac{M}{|V_R|-1}} \times \cdots \times s_l \times \frac{|E|}{B}$ disk I/Os. Thus, the total I/O cost is the summation of disk I/Os for each level as follows.

$$\sum_{1 \le l \le |V_R|} \prod_{i=1}^{l} s_i \times \left(\frac{|E|}{\frac{M}{|V_R|-1}}\right)^{l-1} \times \frac{|E|}{B} \quad (1)$$

Buffer allocation strategy. Until now, we assume that the buffer is divided into equal-sized memory frames. We propose a better buffer allocation strategy where only two buffer frames * # of threads are allocated for the last level, and two third of the remaining buffer frames are allocated for the first level and one third are equally divided for the other levels. One buffer frame is used when we load a page at the last level, while the other buffer frame is used for asynchronous I/O processing. When the number of red vertices is 2 (i.e., triangulation), all the remaining buffer frames are allocated for the first level. This allocation enables the effective overlapping of CPU processing with I/O processing. By using this strategy, the number of iterations for the first level is much smaller than the equal-sized allocation strategy, which is very effective especially when we use HDDs. We use this buffer allocation strategy for all experiments in Section 6. Experimental results show that DUALSIM effectively hide the expensive I/O cost for subgraph enumeration using either SSDs or HDDs.

6. EXPERIMENTS

In this section, we present the performance of DUALSIM. Specifically, the key goals of this experimental study are as follows. Additional performance results are reported in Appendix B due to space constraints.

- We show the insensitivity of the elapsed time of DUALSIM to varying buffer size (Section 6.2.2).
- We show the linear speedup of DUALSIM with an increasing number of CPU cores (Appendix B.1).
- We show significantly better performance of DUALSIM compared to the state-of-the art subgraph enumeration methods in a *single* machine (Section 6.2.3).
- We show significantly better performance of DUALSIM in a single machine compared to the state-of-the art distributed methods using 51 machines (Section 6.2.4). We also show that DUALSIM is the only method to enumerate subgraphs in massive graphs.

Table 1: Statistics of Datasets.

	WG	WT	UP	LJ	OK	WP	FR	YH
$\|V\|$	$0.9M$	$2.4M$	$3.8M$	$4.8M$	$3.1M$	$25M$	$66M$	$1.4B$
$\|E\|$	$8.6M$	$9.3M$	$33M$	$86M$	$234M$	$234M$	$3610M$	$12.9B$
$Size$	$115MB$	$140MB$	$504MB$	$1.28GB$	$3.47GB$	$4.07GB$	$66.9GB$	$263GB$

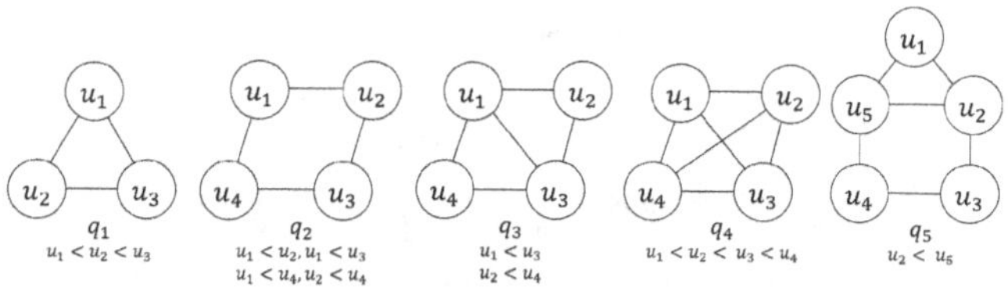

Figure 8: Queries.

6.1 Experimental Setup

Datasets/Queries. Eight real-world graph datasets were used in the experiments (WebGoogle (WG), WikiTalk (WT), USPatents (UP), LiveJournal (LJ), Wikipedia (WP), Friendster (FR), Yahoo (YH), and Orkut (OK)). All datasets can be downloaded from their original web sites. In order to show the performance over varying graph sizes, we generated different sizes by choosing 20%, 40%, 60%, 80%, and 100% of vertices from Friendster. Table 1 summarizes the statistics of these datasets. We use the same queries as in [24]. Figure 8 depicts the five queries.

Competitors. We compare the performance of DUALSIM with two state-of-the-art distributed subgraph enumeration frameworks, PSGL [24] and TWINTWIGJOIN [20]. We use binary files obtained from the authors of both methods. Note that since TWINTWIGJOIN is based on Hadoop, it can run in a single machine. PSGL failed in most experiments in a single machine environment due to memory overruns. Hence, we only discuss its performance in a distributed setting. In addition, we implemented two variants of TWINTWIGJOIN using PostgreSQL (TTJ-PG) and Spark SQL [4] (TTJ-SparkSQL) for comprehensive performance comparison. That is, DUALSIM is compared to TTJ-PG for single machine experiments and to TTJ-SparkSQL for cluster experiments. We also added experimental results using the Samsung 850 Pro 1TB SSD when DUALSIM is investigated in a distributed framework.

Running Environments. In our experiments, we use either a single-machine environment or distributed environment. In the single machine environment, we conducted experiments using two machines having identical hardware – an Intel Core i7-3930K CPU (6 CPU cores), 24GB RAM, and one 1TB HDD (Western Digital VelociRaptor). DUALSIM was executed on Windows 7, while TWINTWIGJOIN was executed on Linux since DUALSIM currently supports the Windows platform only, while TWINTWIGJOIN currently supports the Linux platform only. Note that due to a faster file system support in Linux, binaries executed on Linux are typically faster than those executed on Windows [14, 17]. In the distributed environment, we conducted experiments on a cluster of 51 machines, one master and 50 slaves, interconnected by an InfiniBand 40G network. Each machine has two Intel Xeon E5-2650 CPUs (a total of 16 cores), 32GB RAM, and one 300GB HDD (Hitachi Ultrastar). We use one machine in the cluster to execute DUALSIM. Note that using a high speed network is important for boosting the performance of distributed frameworks. Whenever we load a database page from disk, we bypass OS cache. Thus, every access to the database incurs a real disk I/O. This holds true even if we use small datasets.

Measure. To measure the cost, the elapsed time is used. To measure the parallelization effect, the speed-up is used, which is the elapsed time of the single thread execution over that of the multiple thread execution.

6.2 Experimental Results

We now report the performance of DUALSIM. Table 2 shows the various parameter values used for our experiments. Unless specified otherwise, values in boldface are used as default parameters in each experiment.

Table 2: Parameters used in the experiments.

Parameter	Description	Values Used
DS	data graphs	**WebGoogle**, **WikiTalk**, USPatents, **LiveJournal**, Orkut, Wikipedia, Friendster, Yahoo
q	query graphs	$\mathbf{q_1}$, q_2, q_3, $\mathbf{q_4}$, q_5
t	# of threads	1, 2, 3, 4, 5, **6** (single machine) **16** (cluster)
buf	buffer size (% of data graph size)	5, 10, **15**, 20, 25 (single machine)
s	# of slaves	8, 16, 32, **50** (cluster)

6.2.1 *Preprocessing Cost*

We first study the impact of preprocessing cost associated with subgraph enumeration techniques. Note that all existing subgraph enumeration methods use the degree-based ordering [1,20,24]. Table 3 reports the results for different datasets. Note that this preprocessing incurs an external sort of the original database, whose I/O cost is $O(n_p log n_p)$ where n_p is the number of pages in the database. At the last level in external-merge sort, we also update adjacency lists of all reordered vertices before they are finally written to disk. Thus, the preprocessing cost is theoretically cheaper than the cost for q_1. In fact, the preprocessing time is significantly smaller compared to the execution time of complex query patterns. For example, the processing time is 8.5 times smaller than processing q_4 for the FR dataset.

Table 3: Elapsed time of preprocessing (in sec.).

	WG	WT	UP	LJ	OK	WP	FR	YH
Preprocessing time	0.892	1.280	4.126	9.423	26.70	28.54	439.6	1951

Even if we consider dynamic graphs, we can still sort the database whose cost is typically smaller than the cost for processing q_1. Once we have a database and have small updates to the database, we do not need to reorder the whole database. In order to simulate evolving graphs, we make 95% of vertices fully sorted, and append 5% of them to the database. We tested with FR dataset using queries $q1$ and $q4$. The performance degradation is only 14.7% to 15.9%. Thus, in order to process complex queries (*e.g.*, q_4 and q_5), we always reorder the database as the reordering cost is significantly smaller than the cost for processing queries. Regarding q_1, we do not need to reorder the database until there is a significant number of changes to the database.

6.2.2 *Varying the Buffer Size*

To see the effect of the memory buffer size on the elapsed time, we varied it from 5% of the graph size to 25% in 5% increments. We measure the relative elapsed time of DUALSIM with a given memory buffer size compared to that with 25% of the graph size.

Figure 9 plots the relative elapsed times of DUALSIM using q_1 and q_4 for LJ and OK. DUALSIM showed almost constant performance except in the case where the buffer is very small (5% of the graph size). Specifically, for q_1, the relative elapsed times of DUALSIM remain 1 over varying buffer sizes. For the query q_4, when

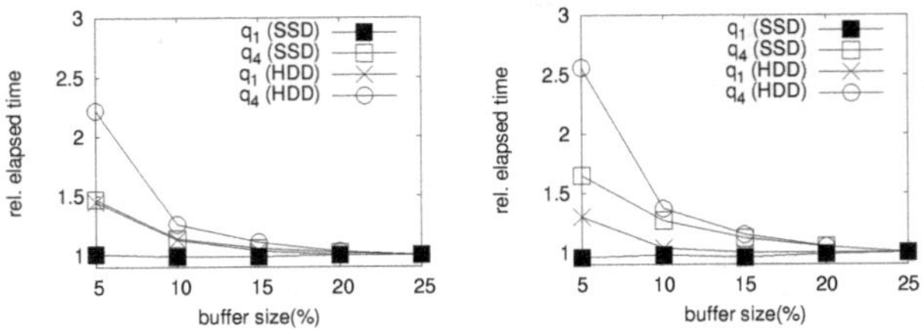

(a) LJ. (b) OK.

Figure 9: Relative elapsed times for varying the buffer size.

we reduce the buffer size from 25% to 5% (5 times), DUALSIM shows 2.22 and 2.56 times performance degradation. Overall, DUALSIM achieves robust performance even under the limited memory budget. When we use the SSD instead of the HDD, DUALSIM shows almost no performance degradation for q_1 while it shows at most 1.65 times the performance degradation for q_4 when the buffer size is set to 5% of the graph size.

6.2.3 *Comparison in a Single Machine Environment*

We now compare DUALSIM with TWINTWIGJOIN, which can execute subgraph enumeration in a single machine. Note that DUALSIM is configured to use a limited size of memory buffer (15% of the graph size), while TWINTWIGJOIN uses all available memory (*i.e.,* 24G memory size). We follow experimental parameters for TWINTWIGJOIN as in [24].

Varying datasets. Figure 10 shows the elapsed times of DUALSIM and TWINTWIGJOIN for q_1 and q_4 on different datasets. DUALSIM consistently shows better performance than TWINTWIGJOIN for all datasets. Specifically, DUALSIM outperforms both variants of TWINTWIGJOIN by up to 318.34 times even if DUALSIM uses much less memory. Also, note that TWINTWIGJOIN failed to process all queries on the largest data set (*i.e.,* YH).

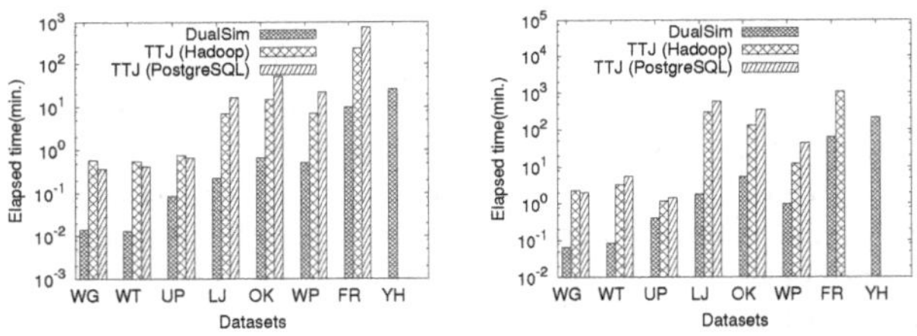

(a) Query q_1. (b) Query q_4.

Figure 10: Varying datasets in a single machine.

The performance gain of DUALSIM is primarily due to two key causes. First, it enables significant reduction in CPU processing time using efficient graph traversal with the dual approach rather than expensive join operations. Second, it achieves significant reduction in the number of disk I/Os since DUALSIM does not need to write enormous partial results to disk at all. We shall report the estimated and actual sizes of partial results of TWINTWIGJOIN and PSGL in Appendix B.4. Although accurate estimation of intermediate result sizes is an interesting future research topic, it is beyond the scope of this paper; Table 5 in Appendix B.4 uses estimation formulae in [20, 24] in order to estimate the number of intermediate results. However, due to unrealistic assumptions, we will see that these formulae lead to significant estimation errors.

Note that PostgreSQL uses merge join extensively and hence must sort intermediate results. Consequently, if these results are stored in memory, TTJ-PG outperforms the Hadoop-based TWINTWIGJOIN, while it performs slower than the latter if the intermediate results need to be spilled to disk, which leads to external sort.

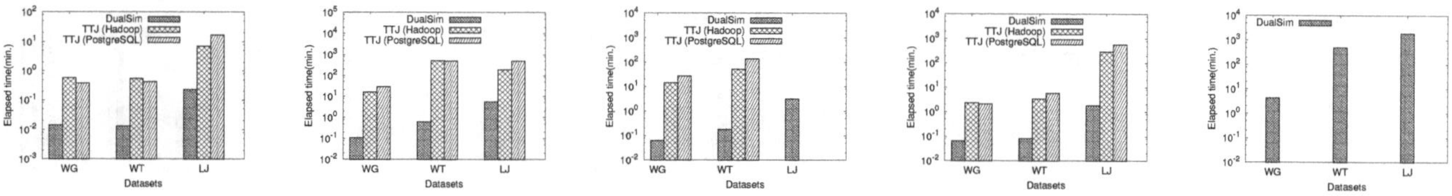

(a) Query q_1. (b) Query q_2. (c) Query q_3. (d) Query q_4. (e) Query q_5.

Figure 11: Varying queries in a single machine.

Varying queries. We now vary queries by fixing datasets. Figure 11 reports the elapsed times in a single machine for all queries using WG, WT, and LJ. Observe that DUALSIM shows much shorter elapsed times compared to TWINTWIGJOIN. DUALSIM outperforms TWINTWIGJOIN by up to 77.83, 866.61, 779.39, and 318.34 times for q_1, q_2, q_3, and q_4 respectively. Note that the binary executable of TWINTWIGJOIN fails to handle q_5.

It is worthwhile to note that DUALSIM significantly outperforms TWINTWIGJOIN as the number of solutions increases. For example, DUALSIM outperforms TWINTWIGJOIN by 866.61 times in WT using q_2. DUALSIM efficiently traverses the graph using the dual approach while TWINTWIGJOIN generates excessive partial solutions so that the join cost for them is very expensive. There is a relatively small number of solutions in UP for q_4. Thus, DUALSIM outperforms TWINTWIGJOIN by 3.54 times. Since WP is a bipartite graph, there is no solution for q_4 using WP. Even in this case, DUALSIM outperforms TWINTWIGJOIN by 44.23 times due to efficient graph traversal based on the dual approach. Lastly, observe that TWINTWIGJOIN fails to complete q_3 on LiveJournal. This is due to spill failure in Hadoop since TWINTWIGJOIN generates excessive partial results.

Varying graph size. Lastly, we demonstrate the scalability of DUALSIM in a single machine over varying graph sizes. In order to vary the number of vertices, we generate datasets by randomly sampling 20%, 40%, 60%, and 80% vertices from the original FR dataset according to [24]. Note that we choose FR over YH in this experiment because TWINTWIGJOIN failed to process queries on the latter dataset.

Figure 12 shows the performance over varying graph sizes. DUALSIM outperforms TWINTWIGJOIN in all cases. Furthermore, the performance gap between DUALSIM and TWINTWIGJOIN increases as the graph size increases. Regarding q_1, the performance gaps are 20.25, 46.17, 17.26, 75.35, and 24.13 respectively. TWINTWIGJOIN fails in several cases again. For q_2 and q_3, TWINTWIGJOIN fails to report results whenever the graph size is larger than 40% of the original FR.

6.2.4 *Comparison on Distributed Environment*

We now compare the performance of DUALSIM to the state-of-the-art distributed subgraph enumeration methods (PSGL and TWINTWIGJOIN). Recall that both distributed methods use 51 machines, while DUALSIM use only a single machine.

Varying datasets. Figure 13 plots the elapsed times of DUALSIM, PSGL, and TWINTWIGJOIN for various real graphs. In all cases, DUALSIM significantly outperforms competitors. Specifically, DUALSIM is faster than PSGL and TWINTWIGJOIN by up to 6.53 and 162.05 times for q_1, respectively. Regarding q_4, DUALSIM outperforms PSGL and TWINTWIGJOIN by up to 12.96 and 24.64 times, respectively.

Observe that TTJ-SparkSQL typically performs better than Hadoop-based TWINTWIGJOIN when intermediate results can be stored in memory. Otherwise, the former performs slower than the latter when queries generate large intermediate results as Spark SQL

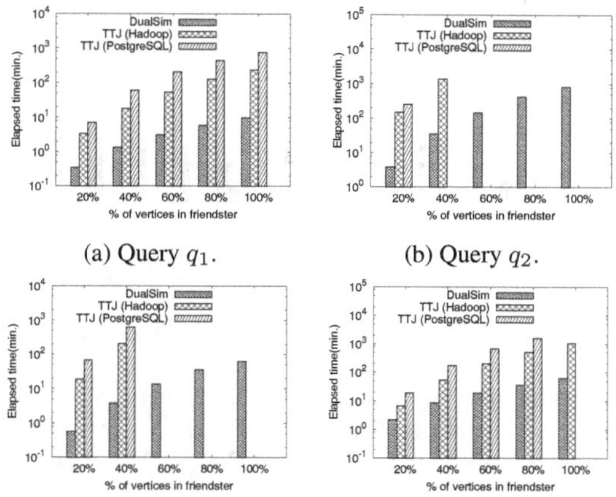

(a) Query q_1. (b) Query q_2.

(c) Query q_3. (d) Query q_4.

Figure 12: Varying graph size in a single machine.

must spill those results into disk. Importantly, TTJ-SparkSQL fails for some queries which generate a large size of intermediate results, where those results are divided into partitions across machines in a cluster. Specifically, it fails to process if the size of a partition block becomes larger than 2 GB. A typical workaround for this problem is to manually set a larger number of partition blocks. However, if we arbitrarily increase the number of partition blocks, the performance would significantly decrease. For instance, when on FR dataset, TTJ-SparkSQL fails with the default number of partition blocks. Even when we increase the number of partition blocks by up to 3200, it still fails due to the same problem. Both PSGL and all variants of TWINTWIGJOIN implementations fails to process this Yahoo dataset due to the out of memory problem.

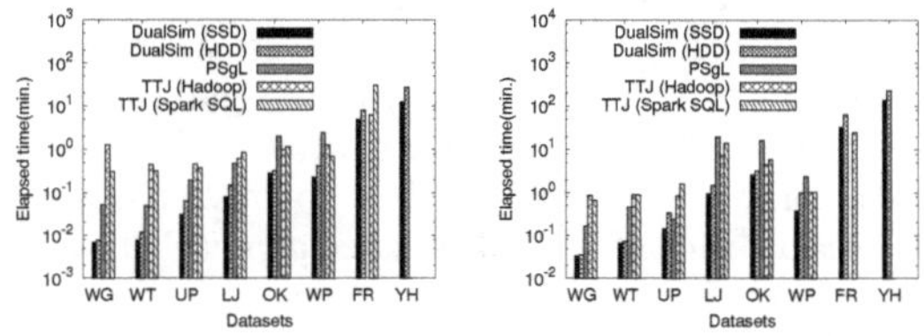

(a) Query q_1. (b) Query q_4.

Figure 13: Varying datasets in a cluster.

Varying queries. Figure 14 shows elapsed times of DUALSIM, TWINTWIGJOIN, and PSGL for all queries using WG, WT, and LJ. Again, DUALSIM outperforms its competitors for all queries. Specifically, it outperforms TWINTWIGJOIN by up to 162.05, 903.47, 144.40, and 24.64 times for q_1, q_2, q_3, and q_4, respectively. DUALSIM outperforms PSGL by up to 6.53, 8.88, 23.87, and 12.96 times for q_1, q_2, q_3, and q_4, respectively. Recall that TWINTWIGJOIN cannot handle q_5. Furthermore, since PSGL maintains partial solutions in memory, PSGL fails to process q_2 and q_3 for LJ, and q_5 for all three datasets. In these cases, the sizes of partial solutions are enormous.

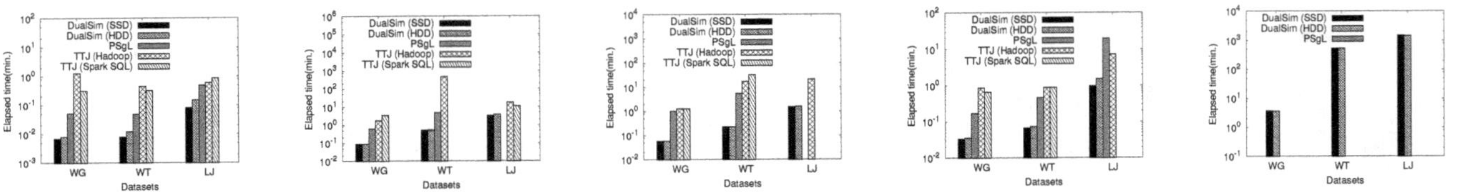

(a) Query q_1. (b) Query q_2. (c) Query q_3. (d) Query q_4. (e) Query q_5.

Figure 14: Varying queries in a cluster.

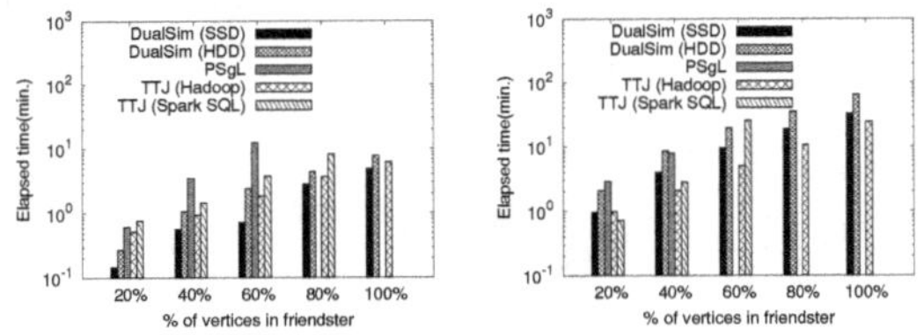

(a) Query q_1. (b) Query q_4.

Figure 15: Varying graph size in a cluster.

Varying graph size. Figure 15 shows elapsed times with varying the number of vertices in the data graph. DUALSIM outperforms PSGL and TWINTWIGJOIN by up to 5.34 and 2.86 times, respectively, for q_1. TWINTWIGJOIN using 51 machines shows better performance than DUALSIM using a single machine for q_4 since (a) TWINTWIGJOIN is optimized to process clique queries and (b) there are relatively small numbers of results for FR. Specifically, TWINTWIGJOIN requires two join operations for a clique query while DUALSIM requires three-level graph traversal. PSGL fails to complete queries for q_1 using 80% and 100% datasets, and fails to answer for q_4 using 60%, 80% and 100% datasets, respectively.

We also perform experiments using q_2 and q_3 for varying graph sizes (detailed in Appendix B.3). Note that all state-of-the-art techniques fail as the graph size increases whereas DUALSIM successfully processes all queries and outperforms TWINTWIGJOIN and PSGL by up to 5.27 and 35.04 times.

7. RELATED WORK

In-memory Methods. Most of the previous work on subgraph enumeration assumes that the graph would fit in main memory. [7] proposes a simple edge-searching based method with the time complexity of $O(\alpha(g)|E|)$ for three query shapes, where $\alpha(g)$ is the arboricity of the data graph g. [7] may incur significant disk reads if it is applied to external subgraph enumeration. [12, 34] propose enhanced algorithms compared to [7]. In contrast, in this paper we propose a scalable and efficient disk-based approach to address the subgraph enumeration problem.

Disk-based Methods. Many external triangulation methods [15, 17, 19, 29] have been proposed. However, all these methods only deal with triangle enumeration, a special case of the subgraph enumeration. [17] proposes an overlapped and parallel, disk-based triangulation framework, OPT. In this paper, we generalize OPT using the concept of the dual approach so that we can support any shaped queries efficiently.

Distributed Methods. Subgraph enumeration on a large-scale graph is computationally expensive, and thus various, distributed approaches have been proposed.

[23] proposes SGIA-MR, which is based on an edge-based join. However, a reducer can run out of memory since it could generate a large number of intermediate results [23]. [1] proposes a single map-reduce round method for subgraph enumeration. The method duplicates edges in multiple machines at the map phase so that each machine can perform independent subgraph enumeration. However, when the query graph is complex, it can cause out-of-memory error [20] due to the large amount of intermediate results. [20] is the-state-of-the-art map-reduce algorithm. It first partitions a query graph into a set of of TwinTwigs, each of which is an edge or two incident edges. It then constructs a left-deep join plan. [20] shows its superiority compared with [1,23], but it still suffers from a large number of partial solutions.

[24] proposes a distributed subgraph enumeration method which is based on Apache Giraph. At each superstep, it expands partial subgraph instances. This method stores all partial solutions in memory. Thus, it easily fails for many queries due to memory overruns.

Our disk-based DUALSIM algorithm not only employs a novel dual approach on a *single machine* instead of a distributed setup to address the subgraph enumeration problem but also addresses the limitation of explosive intermediate result size effectively.

There are several, distributed triangulation methods. [11] proposes a method based on PowerGraph, while [3] proposes an MPI-based distributed algorithm. [30] proposes a map-reduce triangulation. [9] presents a distributed triangulation method using efficient external memory access.

Approximate Methods. There are several methods [2, 5, 6, 10, 36] which can estimate the number of subgraphs for a given query. Although they are efficient for massive graphs, such approximate counts may lead to erroneous conclusions [24].

8. CONCLUSION

In this paper, we proposed an efficient and scalable, disk-based subgraph enumeration framework, DUALSIM, in a single machine. For this framework, we proposed a novel notion of the dual approach for subgraph enumeration, which completely solves the notorious, excessive partial solution size problem. In order to efficiently traverse the data graph, we proposed the novel concepts of v-group forest and candidate data/page sequence. The dual approach together with these concepts minimizes the number of disk I/Os while it uses a bounded storage space for saving candidate results. We also proposed the concept of v-group sequence in order to avoid repeated pattern matching in the dual approach. We then proposed detailed parallel algorithms for DUALSIM which support overlapped and parallel subgraph enumeration under the dual approach. We also derived the cost model for DUALSIM. Experiments using various real datasets showed that DUALSIM significantly outperformed the-state-of-the-art methods both in a single machine and in a distributed environment. DUALSIM showed robust performance for all queries, while the-state-of-the-art methods failed for many queries we tested. Overall, we believe our overlapped and parallel subgraph enumeration provides comprehensive insight and a substantial framework for future research.

9. ACKNOWLEDGMENTS

This work was supported in part by an industrial gift from Microsoft. This work was also supported by the National Research Foundation of Korea(NRF) grant funded by the Korea government (MSIP) (No. NRF-2014R1A2A2A01004454), the MSIP(Ministry of Science, ICT and Future Planning), Korea, under the "ICT Consilience Creative Program" (IITP-2015-R0346-15-1007) supervised by the IITP(Institute for Information & communications Technology Promotion), and Next-Generation Information Computing Development Program through the National Research Foundation of Korea(NRF) funded by the Ministry of Science, ICT & Future Plannig (NRF-2012M3C4A7033342). Sourav S Bhowmick was supported by the Singapore-MOE AcRF Tier-1 Grant RG24/12.

10. REFERENCES

[1] F. N. Afrati, D. Fotakis, and J. D. Ullman. Enumerating subgraph instances using map-reduce. In *ICDE*, pages 62–73, 2013.

[2] N. Alon, P. Dao, I. Hajirasouliha, F. Hormozdiari, and S. C. Sahinalp. Biomolecular network motif counting and discovery by color coding. In *ISMB*, pages 241–249, 2008.

[3] S. Arifuzzaman, M. Khan, and M. V. Marathe. PATRIC: a parallel algorithm for counting triangles in massive networks. In *CIKM*, pages 529–538, 2013.

[4] M. Armbrust, R. S. Xin, C. Lian, Y. Huai, D. Liu, J. K. Bradley, X. Meng, T. Kaftan, M. J. Franklin, A. Ghodsi, and M. Zaharia. Spark SQL: Relational Data Processing in Spark. In *SIGMOD*, pages 1383–1394, 2015.

[5] I. Bordino, D. Donato, A. Gionis, and S. Leonardi. Mining large networks with subgraph counting. In *ICDM*, pages 737–742, 2008.

[6] L. S. Buriol, G. Frahling, S. Leonardi, A. Marchetti-Spaccamela, and C. Sohler. Counting triangles in data streams. In *PODS*, pages 253–262, 2006.

[7] N. Chiba and T. Nishizeki. Arboricity and subgraph listing algorithms. *SIAM J. Comput.*, 14(1):210–223, 1985.

[8] B. Escoffier, L. Gourvès, and J. Monnot. Complexity and approximation results for the connected vertex cover problem in graphs and hypergraphs. *J. Discrete Algorithms*, 8(1):36–49, 2010.

[9] I. Giechaskiel, G. Panagopoulos, and E. Yoneki. Pdtl: Parallel and distributed triangle listing for massive graphs. Technical Report, University of Cambridge, 2015, https://www.cl.cam.ac.uk/techreports/UCAM-CL-TR-866.pdf.

[10] M. Gonen, D. Ron, and Y. Shavitt. Counting stars and other small subgraphs in sublinear time. In *SODA*, pages 99–116, 2010.

[11] J. E. Gonzalez, Y. Low, H. Gu, D. Bickson, and C. Guestrin. Powergraph: Distributed graph-parallel computation on natural graphs. In *OSDI*, pages 17–30, 2012.

[12] J. A. Grochow and M. Kellis. Network motif discovery using subgraph enumeration and symmetry-breaking. In *RECOMB*, pages 92–106, 2007.

[13] J. Lee, W. Han, R. Kasperovics, and J. Lee. An In-depth Comparison of Subgraph Isomorphism Algorithms in Graph Databases. *PVLDB*, 6(2):133–144, 2012.

[14] W. Han, S. Lee, K. Park, J. Lee, M. Kim, J. Kim, and H. Yu. Turbograph: a fast parallel graph engine handling billion-scale graphs in a single PC. In *KDD*, pages 77–85, 2013.

[15] X. Hu, Y. Tao, and C. Chung. Massive graph triangulation. In *SIGMOD*, pages 325–336, 2013.

[16] S. R. Kairam, D. J. Wang, and J. Leskovec. The life and death of online groups: predicting group growth and longevity. In *WSDM*, pages 673–682, 2012.

[17] J. Kim, W. Han, S. Lee, K. Park, and H. Yu. OPT: a new framework for overlapped and parallel triangulation in large-scale graphs. In *SIGMOD*, pages 637–648, 2014.

[18] W. Kim, M. Li, J. Wang, and Y. Pan. Biological network motif detection and evaluation. *BMC Systems Biology*, 5(S-3):S5, 2011.

[19] A. Kyrola, G. E. Blelloch, and C. Guestrin. Graphchi: Large-scale graph computation on just a PC. In *OSDI*, pages 31–46, 2012.

[20] L. Lai, L. Qin, X. Lin, and L. Chang. Scalable subgraph enumeration in mapreduce. *PVLDB*, 8(10):974–985, 2015.

[21] J. Leskovec, K. J. Lang, A. Dasgupta, and M. W. Mahoney. Community structure in large networks: Natural cluster sizes and the absence of large well-defined clusters. *Internet Mathematics*, 6(1):29–123, 2009.

[22] R. Milo, S. Shen-Orr, S. Itzkovitz, N. Kashtan, D. Chklovskii, and U. Alon. Network motifs: Simple building blocks of complex networks. *Science*, 298(5594):824–827, 2002.

[23] T. Plantenga. Inexact subgraph isomorphism in mapreduce. *J. Parallel Distrib. Comput.*, 73(2):164–175, 2013.

[24] Y. Shao, B. Cui, L. Chen, L. Ma, J. Yao, and N. Xu. Parallel subgraph listing in a large-scale graph. In *SIGMOD*, pages 625–636, 2014.

[25] N. Shervashidze, S. V. N. Vishwanathan, T. Petri, K. Mehlhorn, and K. M. Borgwardt. Efficient graphlet kernels for large graph comparison. *AISTATS*, pages 488–495, 2009.

[26] J. Cardinal and E. Levy. Connected vertex covers in dense graphs. *Theor. Comput. Sci.*, 411(26–28):2581–2590, 2010.

[27] F. N. Afrati and J. D. Ullman. Optimizing Multiway Joins in a Map-Reduce Environment. *TKDE*, 23(9):1282–1298, 2011.

[28] M. R. Garey and D. S. Johnson. The rectilinear Steiner tree problem is NP-complete. *SIAM Journal of Applied Mathematics*, 32(4), 826–834, 1977.

[29] S. Chu and J. Cheng. Triangle listing in massive networks and its applications. In *KDD*, pages 672–680, 2011.

[30] S. Suri and S. Vassilvitskii. Counting triangles and the curse of the last reducer. In *WWW*, pages 607–614, 2011.

[31] J. Ugander, L. Backstrom, and J. M. Kleinberg. Subgraph frequencies: mapping the empirical and extremal geography of large graph collections. In *WWW*, pages 1307–1318, 2013.

[32] J. Wang and J. Cheng. Truss decomposition in massive networks. *PVLDB*, 5(9):812–823, 2012.

[33] D. J. Watts and S. H. Strogatz. Collective dynamics of 'small-world' networks. *nature*, 393(6684):440–442, 1998.

[34] S. Wernicke. Efficient detection of network motifs. *IEEE/ACM Trans. Comput. Biology Bioinform.*, 3(4):347–359, 2006.

[35] E. A. Wong and B. Baur. On network tools for network motif finding: a survey study, 2010.

[36] Z. Zhao, M. Khan, V. S. A. Kumar, and M. V. Marathe. Subgraph enumeration in large social contact networks using parallel color coding and streaming. In *ICPP*, pages 594–603, 2010.

[37] P. Erdös and A. Rényi. On the evolution of random graphs. *Publ. Math. Inst. Hungar. Acad. Sci*, 5:17–61, 1960.

APPENDIX

A. ALGORITHMS DETAILS

COMPUTECANDIDATESEQUENCES($\cdot$) computes the candidate vertex/page sequences for all child nodes of $\{vgf_i[cur]\}$. It first pins page pid (Line 1). Then, for each v-group forest, for each data vertex v in page pid, we check if v is in the current vertex window, $cvw_{i,cur}$ (Lines 2 $\sim$ 4). If so, we compute candidate vertex/page sequences for all child nodes of $vgf_i[cur]$ (Lines 5 $\sim$ 7). All pinned pages in this function are unpinned in Algorithm 1 (for level 1) or Algorithm 2 (for the other levels except the last level).

Algorithm 3. COMPUTECANDIDATESEQUENCES

Input: page ID pid, the current vertex windows for current level $\{cvw_{i,cur}\}$, all child nodes of $\{vgf_i[cur]\}$

1: Pin page pid;
2: **foreach** (vgf_i) **do**
3:     **foreach** (v in data vertices of page pid) **do**
4:         **if** $(v \in cvw_{i,cur})$ **then**
5:             **foreach** (the child node n_c of $vgf_i[cur]$) **do**
6:                 add $adj(v)$ to cvs for n_c;
7:                 add $\{P(v')|v' \in adj(v)\}$ to cps for n_c;
8:             **end**
9:         **end**
10:     **end**
11: **end**

EXTVERTEXMAPPING($\cdot$) enumerates the vertex mappings for all possible external subgraphs, starting from page pid loaded at the last level. It first pins page pid (Line 1). Then, for each v-group forest, for each data vertex v in page pid, we check if v is in the current vertex window, $cvw_{i,cur}$ (Lines 2 $\sim$ 4). If so, we map v to the corresponding node $vgf_i[|V_R|]$ (Line 5). Note that we use another mapping m_{vgs} which can be used for enumerating all full-order query sequences in the v-group sequence. Then, we recursively map data vertices in the buffer to the remaining nodes in vgf_i by invoking RECEXTVERTEXMAPPING (Line 7). At the end of EXTVERTEXMAPPING, we unpin page pid (Line 12).

Algorithm 4. EXTVERTEXMAPPING

Input: Page id pid, RBI query graph q_{RBI}, current vertex windows cvw, v-group sequences $\{vgs_i\}$, v-group forests $\{vgf_i\}$

1: Pin page pid;
2: **foreach** (vgf_i) **do**
3:     **foreach** (data vertex v in page pid) **do**
4:         **if** $(v \in cvw_{i,|V_R|})$ **then**
5:             $m_{vgs}[vgf_i[|V_R|]] \leftarrow v$;
6:             $idx \leftarrow 2$; `// idx represents the index in the matching order.`
7:             ; RECURSIVEEXTVERTEXMAPPING$(idx, m_{vgs}, q_{RBI}, cvw_i, vgs_i, vgf_i)$;
8:             $m_{vgs}[vgf_i[|V_R|]] \leftarrow$INVALID;
9:         **end**
10:     **end**
11: **end**
12: Unpin page pid;

RECEXTVERTEXMAPPING($\cdot$) recursively maps data vertices in the buffer to the remaining nodes in vgf_i. It basically follows GenericQueryProc in [13] using the matching order qo_i. The main differences are that 1) RECEXTVERTEXMAPPING maps all red query vertices to the corresponding data vertices, and then maps non-red query vertices and 2) RECEXTVERTEXMAPPING uses two-

Algorithm 5. RECEXTVERTEXMAPPING

Input: Current matching index idx, v-group sequence mapping m_{vgs}, RBI query graph q_{RBI}, vgf_i's current vertex window cvw_i, v-group sequence vgs_i, v-group forest vgf_i

1: $U_{CON} \leftarrow adj(qo_i[idx]) \cap qo_i[1 : idx - 1]$;
2: **foreach** (v in $\bigcap_{n \in U_{CON}} adj(m_{vgs}[qo_i[n]])$) **do**
3:     **if** (IsJoinable$(qo_i[idx], v, m_{vgs}, vgs_i, cvw_i)$) **then**
4:         $m_{vgs}[qo_i[idx]] \leftarrow v$;
5:         **if** $(idx < |q_R|)$ **then**
6:             RECEXTVERTEXMAPPING$(idx + 1, m, q_{RBI}, vgs_i, vgf_i)$;
7:         **else**
8:             **foreach** $(qs \in vgs_i)$ **do**
9:                 $m \leftarrow \emptyset$;
10:                 **for** $(1 \le j \le |V_R|)$ **do**
11:                     $m[qs[j]] \leftarrow m_{vgs}[qo_i[k]]$ where the array index of the $qo_i[k]$ is j;
12:                 **end**
13:                 NONREDVERTEXMATCHING(m);
14:             **end**
15:         **end**
16:         $m_{vgs}[qo_i[idx]] \leftarrow$ INVALID;
17:     **end**
18: **end**

level mapping functions (m_{vgs} and m) to reduce the CPU processing time. U_{CON} represents a set of query vertices where each query vertex is already matched and connected from $qo_i[idx]$.

B. ADDITIONAL EXPERIMENTAL RESULTS

B.1 Varying the Number of Threads

The purpose of this experiment is to assess the CPU parallelization effect. We measure the elapsed times and speed-ups by varying the number of execution threads. In order to simulate hot-run, we preload the whole graph in memory so that the speed up due to CPU parallelism can be measured. Figure 16 plots the speed-ups of DUALSIM in LJ by varying the number of execution threads from 1 to 6. DUALSIM achieves almost linear speed-up. Specifically, the speed-up using 6 threads for q_1 is 5.46 while the speed-up for q_4 is 5.53. The experimental results substantiate that DUALSIM fully utilizes multi-core parallelism.

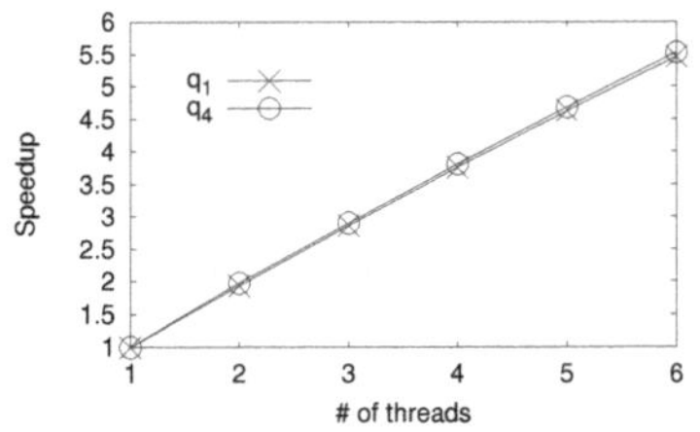

Figure 16: Varying the number of execution threads.

B.2 Comparison to OPT

We compare DUALSIM with OPT [17], a state-of-the-art disk-based triangulation. We use LJ, FR and YH datasets to this end. Figure 17 shows the results demonstrating superiority of DUALSIM for enumerating triangles. DUALSIM is a generalization of OPT but outperforms OPT since DUALSIM has a better buffer allocation strategy where most of buffer frames are allocated for internal triangulation and only two buffer frames * # of threads are allocated for external triangulation. By using this strategy, the number of iterations for the first level is much smaller than OPT, which is very effective when we use HDDs.

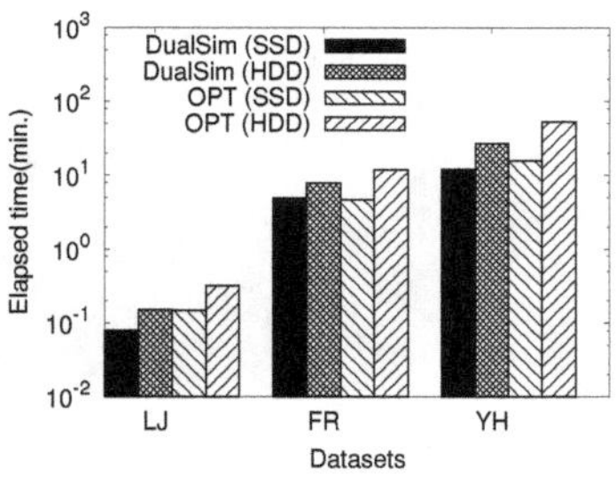

Figure 17: Comparison to OPT.

B.3 Varying Graph Size for Q2 and Q3

Figure 18 shows experimental results for $q2$ and $q3$ in a distributed enviroment. Regarding q_2 and q_3, DUALSIM outperforms TWINTWIGJOIN and PSGL by up to 5.27 and 35.04 times. TWINTWIGJOIN (Hadoop), TWINTWIGJOIN (Spark SQL), and PSGL fail to process q_2 when the input graph reaches 80%, 60%, and 40% of the original FR, respectively. Regarding q_3, they fail when the input graph reaches 60% of the original graph size. We also note that PSGL successfully processes q_3 for 40% of vertices but fails to process for 20% of vertices, since one slave machine has three times more intermediate results even if the dataset size is smaller, depending on partitioning results.

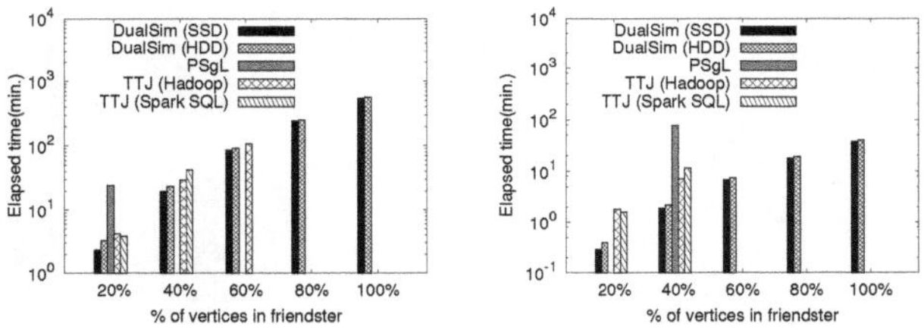

(a) Query q_2.

(b) Query q_3.

Figure 18: Varying graph size in a cluster.

B.4 Intermediate Result Size

Table 4 shows the *actual* number of intermediate results generated by TWINTWIGJOIN and PSGL for q_1 and q_4 across different datasets. As remarked earlier, the massive number of these results have significant adverse impact on the performances of these approaches.

Table 4: The actual number of intermediate results.

	TWINTWIGJOIN		PSGL	
	q_1	q_4	q_1	q_4
WG	17 728 487	120 080 516	14 267 638	80 638 724
WT	13 986 397	161 379 149	11 597 979	132 275 038
UP	24 233 735	30 466 127	11 290 035	10 776 978
LJ	330 307 042	20 761 697 361	290 581 577	19 871 938 971
OK	760 453 448	8 495 795 053	631 448 564	6 450 113 417
WP	135 418 732	42 568 284	26 134 800	25 236 087
FR	6 338 480 209	32 419 482 939	**fail**	**fail**
YH	**fail**	**fail**	**fail**	**fail**

Table 5 shows the *estimated* number of intermediate results using the estimation formulae in [20, 24]. We observe that there are significant estimation errors in their estimation. In [24], when a query vertex u is selected to match a data vertex v, it assumes that every data vertex in $adj(v)$ can be mapped to any non-matched query vertex in $adj(u)$. However, some vertices in $adj(v)$ could have been matched with query vertices already. Thus, this assumption leads to over-estimation. In [20], the estimation model assumes the Erdös-Rényi random graph model. However, this model does not capture characteristics of real-world graphs. Furthermore, neither formula takes into account of bloom filters or partial orders in their estimation. Even if we do not use bloom filters or partial orders, their estimation still leads to significant errors due to the aforementioned, unrealistic assumptions. Accurate estimation of intermediate result sizes would be an interesting future research topic.

Table 5: The estimated number of intermediate results.

	TWINTWIGJOIN		PSGL	
	q_1	q_4	q_1	q_4
WG	89 647 379	255 985 479	728 292 937	40 912 661 890
WT	40 923 518	108 792 088	8 300 949 511	137 340 284 542
UP	305 676 473	867 478 443	339 556 041	11 701 483 501
LJ	1 595 424 330	4 656 266 644	7 274 351 324	930 439 994 468
OK	17 995 274 430	53 668 127 117	45 628 539 012	6 177 760 914 437
WP	2 475 955 253	7 061 648 888	355 660 021 848	2 156 268 223 798
FR	200 675 735 441	596 618 192 868	720 720 573 330	137 456 527 555 023
YH	123 599 731 090	351 495 517 035	13 589 362 651 547	132 438 400 752 902

B.5 Preparation Cost

Table 6 shows elapsed time for the preparation step for varing queries. The preparation step takes at most 1 msec, which is negligible.

Table 6: Elapsed time of preparation step (in msec.).

query	q_1	q_2	q_3	q_4	q_5
time	0	0	0	1	1

C. PROOF TO LEMMA 1

PROOF. According to Property 1, $m[qs[1]] \prec m[qs[2]] \prec .. \prec m[qs[|V_R|]]$. Vertices are stored according to $id(\cdot)$. Thus, if $id(v_i) < id(v_j)$, $P(v_i) \leq P(v_j)$. Therefore, the condition, $P(m[qs[1]]) \leq P(m[qs[2]]) \leq \cdots \leq P(m[qs[|V_R|]])$, is satisfied. $\square$

Distributed Set Reachability

Sairam Gurajada
Max-Planck-Institute for Informatics
Campus E1.4
66123 Saarbrücken, Germany
gurajada@mpi-inf.mpg.de

Martin Theobald
University of Ulm
James-Franck-Ring O27
89069 Ulm, Germany
martin.theobald@uni-ulm.de

ABSTRACT

In this paper, we focus on the efficient and scalable processing of set-reachability queries over a distributed, directed data graph. A *set-reachability query* is a generalized form of a reachability query, in which we consider two sets S and T of source and target vertices, respectively, to be given as the query. The result of a set-reachability query are all pairs of source and target vertices (s, t), with $s \in S$ and $t \in T$, where s is reachable to t (denoted as $S \leadsto T$). In case the data graph is partitioned into multiple, edge- and vertex-disjoint subgraphs (e.g., when distributed across multiple compute nodes in a cluster), we refer to the resulting set-reachability problem as *distributed set reachability*. The key goal in processing a distributed set-reachability query over a partitioned data graph both efficiently and in a scalable manner is (1) to avoid redundant computations within the local compute nodes as much as possible, (2) to partially evaluate the local components of a set-reachability query $S \leadsto T$ among all compute nodes in parallel, and (3) to minimize both the size and number of messages exchanged among the compute nodes.

Distributed set reachability has a plethora of applications in graph analytics and for query processing. The current W3C recommendation for SPARQL 1.1, for example, introduces a notion of *labeled property paths* which resolves to processing a form of generalized graph-pattern queries with set-reachability predicates. Moreover, analyzing dependencies among *social-network communities* inherently involves reachability checks between large sets of source and target vertices. Our experiments confirm very significant performance gains of our approach in comparison to state-of-the-art graph engines such as Giraph++, and over a variety of graph collections with up to 1.4 billion edges.

1. INTRODUCTION

1.1 Background & Motivation

The reachability problem in directed graphs is one of the most fundamental problems in terms of both graph theory and applications: for a directed graph $G = (V, E)$ with vertices V and edges E, given a source vertex $s \in V$ and a target vertex $t \in V$, determine whether there is a consecutive path of edges from s to t over E.

To avoid redundant computations, many graph applications in fact require an extension of this basic reachability problem, where entire *sets* S, T *of source and target vertices*, respectively, need to be processed "at once". The resulting reachability problem, which we then coin *set reachability*, aims to retrieve all pairs of source and target vertices (s, t), with $s \in S$ and $t \in T$, where s is reachable to t. Moreover, in case the data graph is partitioned into multiple, edge- and vertex-disjoint subgraphs (e.g., when distributed across multiple compute nodes in a cluster), we refer to the resulting set-reachability problem as *distributed set reachability* (or "DSR" for short). The key goal in processing a DSR query over a partitioned data graph both efficiently and in a scalable manner is (1) to avoid redundant computations within the local compute nodes as much as possible, (2) to partially evaluate the local components of a set-reachability query $S \leadsto T$ among all compute nodes in parallel, and (3) to minimize both the size and number of messages exchanged among the compute nodes.

State-of-the-art indexing techniques for reachability queries [12, 16, 18, 25, 28, 32, 33, 34, 36] are largely limited to a centralized setting and thus address only point (1) of the above objectives. As for (2) and (3), we are currently aware of only one approach that specifically tackles the problem of distributed reachability queries for single-source, single-target queries [9]. For multi-source, multi-target (i.e., actual *set-*) reachability queries, we are aware of just two centralized approaches [12, 30] that provide suitable indexing and processing strategies. Both are based on a notion of *equivalence sets* among graph vertices which effectively resolves to a preprocessing and indexing step of the data graph to predetermine these sets. Efficient centralized approaches, however, are naturally limited to the main memory of a single machine and usually do not consider a parallel—in this case multi-threaded—execution of a reachability query.

Distributed graph engines, such as Google's Pregel [22], Berkeley's GraphX [35] (based on Spark [37]), Apache Giraph [1] and IBM's very recent Giraph++ [31], on the other hand, allow for the scalable processing of graph algorithms over massive, distributed data graphs. All of these provide generic API's for implementing various kinds of algorithms, including multi-source, multi-target reachability queries. However, a principal assumption we follow in this work is that set-reachability queries are *selective*. That is,

SIGMOD'16, June 26-July 01, 2016, San Francisco, CA, USA

DOI: http://dx.doi.org/10.1145/2882903.2915226

for any given sets S, T of source and target vertices, both S and T are usually much smaller than V, while the set of reachable pairs in turn usually is much smaller than the cross-product $S \times T$. Just like in relational approaches, an efficient processing of set-reachability queries thus calls for the aforementioned usage of indexing strategies that take advantage of the salient properties of the data graph. Graph indexing and the processing of selective queries however breaks the *node-centric computing* paradigm of Pregel and Giraph, where major amounts of the graph are successively shuffled through the network in each of the underlying MapReduce iterations (the so-called "supersteps").

Giraph++ is a very recent approach to overcome this overly myopic form of node-centric computing, which led to a new type of distributed graph processing that is coined *graph-centric computing* in [31]. By exposing intra-node state information as well as the inter-node partition structure to the local compute nodes, Giraph++ is a great step towards making these graph computations more context-aware. However, index structures that specifically tackle the iterative communication rounds required for the supersteps are difficult to accomplish even here, such that a direct implementation of a reachability query may still result in as many iterations (and hence communication rounds) as the diameter of the graph in the worst case.

Finally, the set-reachability problem has a plethora of applications in graph analytics and query-processing tasks. With its recent update, SPARQL 1.1, for example, underwent a major revision in which the usage of *labeled property paths* [2] allows a user to formulate transitive reachability constraints among the query variables. Since both the source and target variables of a property path may become bound to multiple RDF constants at query processing time, the processing of property paths in SPARQL 1.1 resolves to processing set-reachability queries. Another interesting application of set-reachability is *community analysis in social networks*. That is, given sets of source and target vertices, each representing social-net users such as on Twitter or Facebook, we may want to efficiently detect which communities are densely connected. For example, consider two communities—billionaires and non-profit organizations—, it would be interesting to find the list of billionaires who are also involved in philanthropic activities.

1.2 Contributions

We summarize the contributions of our work as follows.

- We formalize the problem of *distributed set reachability* (DSR) over a partitioned, and hence distributed, directed data graph. To our knowledge, our approach is the first to specifically tackle this problem.
- We develop a graph-based index structure that allows us to strictly restrict the communication protocol among the compute nodes to a *single round of message exchange* in order to resolve the results of any DSR query posed against a given partitioning of the data graph. This guarantee holds regardless of the properties of the data graph (such as its diameter and partition structure) and the properties of the query (such as the distribution of source and target vertices among the graph partitions).
- Our indexing strategy allows for *incremental updates* of the underlying data graph, with an efficient support for vertex and edge insertions and a principle support for respective deletions.
- Our approach is also *extensible* in the sense that any existing, centralized reachability index can be "plugged-in" at the local compute nodes. We report the results of our distributed approach in combination with a plain DFS search [6], the MS-BFS approach of [30], and FERRARI [28] as local search strategies.
- Moreover, we provide an *extensive experimental evaluation* of our approach over a variety of both small and large graphs and in comparison to different extensions of Giraph++. We also investigate two application scenarios of our approach for processing SPARQL 1.1 queries with property paths and for detecting dependencies among social-network communities.

2. PRELIMINARIES

We start by formally defining our data and query model. This section also serves to establish the notation we will use through the rest of the paper.

DEFINITION 1. *A* **data graph** $G(V, E, L, \phi)$ *is a directed graph consisting of vertices V and edges $E \subseteq V \times V$. Further, we assume a unique label (i.e., an identifier) for each vertex in the graph to be given by a bijective mapping $\phi : V \to L$ from vertices V to labels L.*

Given two vertices $s, t \in V$, a *path* P from s to t is denoted by a consecutive set of edges $\{(s := u_0, u_1), (u_1, u_2), \ldots, (u_{n-1}, u_n =: t)\}$ such that each $(u_i, u_j) \in E$. Two vertices s and t are called *reachable*, denoted as $s \rightsquigarrow t$, iff there exists at least one path $P \subseteq E$ from s to t.

Graph Partitioning. To scale a reachability query $s \rightsquigarrow t$ to a very large data graph, which may not necessarily fit into the main-memory of a single compute node, we allow the graph to be partitioned into k edge- and vertex-disjoint subgraphs. Formally, a *subgraph* $G_i(V_i, E_i, L, \phi)$ of a data graph $G(V, E, L, \phi)$ is a vertex-induced subgraph of G, such that $V_i \subseteq V$ and $E_i = \{(u, v) \mid u \in V_i, v \in V_i \text{ and } (u, v) \in E\}$. We refer to $\mathcal{G} = \{G_1, G_2, \ldots, G_k\}$ as the *partitioning* of G and to $C(V_C, E_C, L, \phi)$ as the *cut* of G, respectively. Here, k denotes the number of partitions of G and each partition G_i (including C) denotes a subgraph of G. Moreover, C is a subgraph of G such that, for a given graph partitioning $\mathcal{G}$, $E_C = \{(u, v) \mid (u, v) \in E, u \in V_i, v \in V_j \text{ and } i \neq j\}$ with vertices $u, v \in V_C$, iff edge $(u, v) \in E_C$.

DEFINITION 2. *Given a partitioning $\mathcal{G} = \{G_1, G_2, \ldots, G_k\}$ and the respective cut $C(V_C, E_C, L, \phi)$ of a data graph G, a* **DSR query***, denoted as $S \rightsquigarrow T$, returns all pairs of source and target vertices (s, t), with $s \in S$ and $t \in T$, where $s \rightsquigarrow t$.*

DEFINITION 3. *For a given graph partitioning $\mathcal{G}$ and implied cut C of a data graph G, we define the set of* **in-boundaries** *I_i for partition G_i as $I_i = \{v \mid v \in V_i, \exists(u, v) \in E_C, u \in V_j \text{ and } i \neq j\}$, i.e., as the set of vertices in G_i that have an incoming edge from the cut C.*

Conversely, we define the set of **out-boundaries** *$O_i = \{v \mid v \in V_i, \exists(v, u) \in E_C, u \in V_j \text{ and } i \neq j\}$ as the set of vertices in G_i that have an outgoing edge into the cut C.*

Partitioning Function. We denote by $\rho : V \mapsto \mathbb{N}_0^+$ the *partitioning function* that determines to which of the compute nodes (i.e., "slaves") in a cluster architecture each graph vertex $v \in V$ is distributed. Without loss of generality, and to simplify notation for the following presentation, we assume a simple partitioning strategy by distributing every

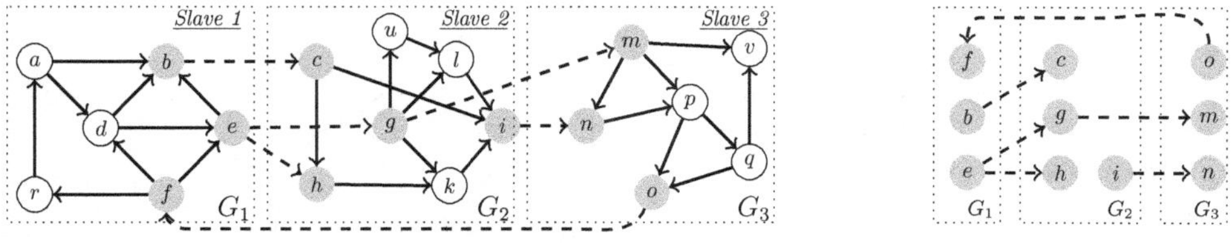

(a) Graph G (b) Cut C

Figure 1: (a) Graph G with partitions $\mathcal{G} = \{G_1, G_2, G_3\}$ and (b) respective cut C

vertex $v \in V_i$ to slave i (i.e., $\rho(v) = i$ for each $v \in V_i$). We will thus refer to a graph partition and a slave interchangeably. To increase concurrent executions (e.g., when using multi-threading at the local compute nodes), an "overpartitioning" strategy may be employed instead, by assigning multiple graph partitions to each of the slaves.

EXAMPLE 1. *Figure 1(a) shows an example graph G with three partitions $\mathcal{G} = \{G_1, G_2, G_3\}$ which are stored at three slaves. Its corresponding cut C is shown in Figure 1(b). In- and out-boundaries are $I_1 = \{f\}, O_1 = \{b, e\}$, $I_2 = \{c, g, h\}$, $O_2 = \{i\}$, and $I_3 = \{m, n\}$, $O_3 = \{o\}$, respectively.*

Distributed Reachability. Our approach for processing DSR queries uses a similar setting as described by Fan et al. [9]. In [9], a distributed (single-source, single-target) reachability query $s \rightsquigarrow t$ over a master-slave architecture is evaluated as follows. The master receives $s \rightsquigarrow t$ and communicates it to all slaves. At partition G_i, containing the source s, a local evaluation of the reachability of s to each vertex in the set of out-boundaries O_i is computed first. Similarly, at partition G_j containing the target t, a local evaluation of the reachability of each vertex in the set of in-boundaries I_j is computed next. Additionally, a local computation of the reachability between all in-boundaries I_i and out-boundaries O_i is computed at each partition $G_1, \ldots, G_k$ and hence at all slaves $i = 1..k$ in the compute cluster *in parallel*.[1]

The resulting local reachability information is encoded into sets of Boolean formulas, where each such set represents the local connectivities between the in-boundaries I_i (including the source s, if present) with the out-boundaries O_i (including the target t, if present) at partition G_i. All of these formulas are communicated back to a single master node for the final evaluation. A query-specific *global dependency graph* is constructed at this master node for $s \rightsquigarrow t$ using the Boolean formulas and the static cut C. A reachability algorithm is then run over the dependency graph to answer $s \rightsquigarrow t$ via substitution of the variables that are reversely connected to the target vertex t. The overall algorithm provided in [9] can be implemented with a simple communication protocol and, for example, be executed in a single MapReduce iteration among all compute nodes.

EXAMPLE 2. *Consider the distributed reachability query $d \rightsquigarrow q$ over the graph partitioning shown in Figure 1. The local evaluation at each partition results in the following Boolean representation of partial reachability information: $\{d = b \vee e, f = b \vee e\}@G_1$, $\{c = i, g = i, h = i\}@G_2$, $\{m = q \vee o, n = q \vee o\}@G_3$. By including the edges in the cut C (Figure 1(b)), the global dependency graph (Figure 2(a)) is constructed at the master node to finally resolve $d \rightsquigarrow q$. By running a reachability algorithm (such as backward DFS)*

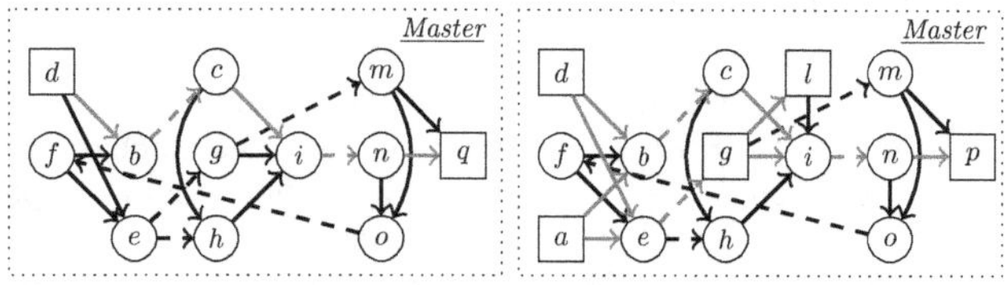

(a) Single Reachability (b) Set Reachability

Figure 2: Dependency graph as constructed in [9] for a single reachability query (a) and an extension to set reachability (b)

over the dependency graph, one can find that $d \rightsquigarrow q$ is indeed true *(the red path in Figure 2(a)).*

3. DISTRIBUTED SET REACHABILITY

3.1 Naïve Approach

A *naïve approach* to extend the distributed reachability problem to sets of vertices S, T would be to simply invoke a separate reachability query $s \rightsquigarrow t$ for every pair (s, t), with $s \in S$ and $t \in T$. However, an obvious reason for the limited efficiency of this approach, even for reasonably-sized sets S and T, is that this approach does not exploit the assumption we made earlier, namely that queries are *selective*, i.e., that by far not all pairs in $S \times T$ are reachable. Consequently, this approach can also not reuse any intermediate computations and thus likely performs many redundant computations.

3.2 DSR with a Dynamic Dependency Graph

An *improved approach* to extend the distributed reachability algorithm provided in [9] to sets is as follows. Let $S \rightsquigarrow T$ be the query received at the master. First, we partition $S \rightsquigarrow T$ into subqueries $S_1 \rightsquigarrow T_1$, $S_2 \rightsquigarrow T_2$, $\ldots$, $S_k \rightsquigarrow T_k$, where k is the number of graph partitions, such that each $S_i \subseteq V_i$ and $T_i \subseteq V_i$ contains only vertices that are local to partition G_i. Next, a local evaluation at each slave i involves finding the reachability among all pairs of vertices from the sets $S_i \cup I_i$ and $O_i \cup T_i$, respectively. These can again be run *in parallel* across all slaves. The resulting reachability information, again represented as sets of Boolean formulas, is then communicated from all slaves to the master node for the final evaluation. At the master node, the query-specific dependency graph for the sets S, T is constructed as described in Section 2, and a local reachability algorithm is then used at the master node to emit all reachable pairs (s, t), with $s \in S$ and $t \in T$.

EXAMPLE 3. *Consider the DSR query $S \rightsquigarrow T$ with $S = \{a, d, g\}$ and $T = \{l, p\}$ over the cut C shown in Figure 1(b). The sets of Boolean formulas obtained after the local evaluation at each slave are as follows: $\{a = b \vee e, d = b \vee e, f = b \vee e\}@G_1$, $\{c = i, g = i \vee l, h = i\}@G_2$, $\{m = p \vee o, n = p \vee o\}@G_3$. At the master node, after evaluating $S \rightsquigarrow T$ over the global dependency graph shown in Figure 2(b), we obtain the following reachable pairs of source and target vertices: $\{(a, l), (a, p), (d, l), (d, p), (g, l), (g, p)\}$.*

[1] Note that we follow a slightly different definition of in- and out-boundaries than in [9]. However, the algorithm in [9] directly translates to the one outlined above.

3.2.1 Discussion

Although the second algorithm provides a more viable solution of the DSR problem than the naïve approach, it still leaves a number of disadvantages that limit both its efficiency and scalability.

- First, the query-dependent, global dependency graph is generated "from scratch" for each query $S \rightsquigarrow T$, although both the cut C and the local reachability information $I_i \rightsquigarrow O_i$ among the in- and out-boundaries at each graph partition G_i are in fact static.
- Second, the approach does not leverage any distributed computation in its second step, as the final reachability computation $S \rightsquigarrow T$ over the global dependency graph is performed only by a single master node.
- Third, since the global dependency graph is generated dynamically for each query $S \rightsquigarrow T$, a reachability index for the static cut C and the local $I_i \rightsquigarrow O_i$ components cannot be constructed, which restricts the final reachability computation to either a simple BFS or DFS strategy over the dependency graph.

3.3 DSR with a Static Reachability Index

In *our approach*, instead of computing the global dependency graph for each incoming query from scratch at the master node, we precompute a partition-specific variant thereof, called the "boundary graph", only once and store this in the form of a static reachability index at each slave. This strategy provides multiple benefits. First, it avoids repeated computations of the boundary graph for each query. Second, since each slave has the complete reachability information among the boundary vertices of all other slaves available, finding the reachability of any two vertices (s, t) in the entire data graph G resolves to a local reachability computation at at most two slaves, which is irrespective of the diameter of the graph and the distribution of the source and target vertices of a set-reachability query (see Theorems 1 and 2). Additionally, an index can be built over the static boundary graph to accelerate this processing. Third, storing a (compacted version of the) boundary graph at each slave allows for a fully distributed processing of a set-reachability query and thus avoids the single-node bottleneck of previous approaches. We next formally define how we generate the boundary graph and its derived index structures.

3.3.1 Precomputed Index Structures

Boundary Graph. A *boundary graph* is a directed graph that represents the reachability information among the in- and out-boundaries of all graph partitions $\mathcal{G} = \{G_1, \ldots, G_k\}$ with respect to a given cut C.

Definition 4. *Let $G_i^B(V_i^B, E_i^B, L, \phi)$ denote the **boundary graph** we compute for partition G_i, such that the following holds:*

- *The vertices $V_i^B = \bigcup_{i=1..k} I_i \cup O_i$ consist of the union of all in- and out-boundaries of all partitions $G_1, \ldots, G_k$.*
- *There exists an edge $(u, v) \in E_i^B$, iff*
  - *$(u, v) \in E_C$, or*
  - *$u \in I_j$ and $v \in O_j$, for $j \neq i$, and $u \rightsquigarrow v$ (i.e., u and v are both located at another partition G_j and there exists a path from u to v in G_j).*

That is, the boundary graph for partition G_i merges the static cut C with the static reachability information $I_j \rightsquigarrow O_j$ among all the remaining graph partitions G_j (for $i \neq j$) into a new, precomputed graph G_i^B. The resulting boundary graphs are thus partition-specific.

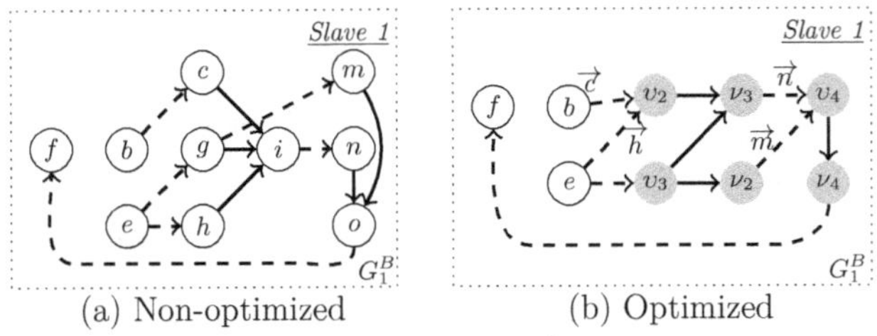

Figure 3: Boundary graph G_1^B for partition G_1

Example 4. *For our graph G with partitions G_1, G_2, G_3 and respective cut C as shown in Figure 1, the boundary graph G_1^B for partition G_1 is shown in Figure 3(a). Here, the dashed edges refer to edges in the cut C, while the solid edges denote the transitive reachability $I_j \rightsquigarrow O_j$ (for $j \neq 1$).*

Complexity. The construction of the boundary graph requires us to materialize the pairwise reachability $I_i \rightsquigarrow O_i$ among the in- and out-boundaries for each partition G_i. Using a simple BFS/DFS-based approach, the time complexity of this computation is $\mathcal{O}((|V_i|+|E_i|) \cdot |I_i| \cdot |O_i|)$ per partition. This can be further improved to $\mathcal{O}(1 \cdot |I_i| \cdot |O_i|)$ when using a sophisticated, local reachability index for this operation. On the other hand, the (worst-case) space complexity for storing the boundary graph at partition i is $\mathcal{O}(\sum_{j=1}^{k} |I_j| \cdot |O_j| + |E_C|)$, for $j \neq i$. From this, one can deduce that both the time and space complexity of the boundary graph computation strongly depend on the amounts of in- and out-boundaries we obtain from the cut C.

Min-k-Cut Partitioning. A standard approach to reduce this number of boundary vertices is to reduce the number of edges in the cut C, while trying to keep the sizes of the partitions $G_1, \ldots, G_k$ balanced. Although finding an optimal such *min-k-cut* partitioning is a well-known NP-complete problem [6], current graph libraries such as METIS [17] are capable of achieving very good approximations even for graphs with hundreds of millions of edges.

Equivalence Sets. Even for a given cut C, we can further reduce the size of the boundary graph by grouping the in- and out-boundary vertices into *equivalence sets* of vertices, thus continuing the idea presented in [12] to a distributed setting. Specifically, we achieve this by grouping the boundary vertices into *forward-* and *backward-equivalent sets* according to the following definition.

Definition 5. *Two in-boundaries b_1, b_2 are called **forward-equivalent** with respect to subgraph G_i, i.e., $b_1 \equiv^f b_2$, iff for any vertex $v \in V_i - I_i$ and $b_1 \rightsquigarrow v$, it holds that $b_2 \rightsquigarrow v$.*

*Conversely, two out-boundaries b_1, b_2 are called **backward-equivalent** with respect to subgraph G_i, i.e., $b_1 \equiv^b b_2$, iff for any vertex $v \in V_i - O_i$ and $v \rightsquigarrow b_1$, it holds that $v \rightsquigarrow b_2$.*

That is, once the forward- and backward-equivalent sets of vertices are identified for each subgraph G_i, each such set is replaced by a new *in-virtual vertex* υ (for a forward-equivalent set) and a new *out-virtual vertex* ν (for a backward-equivalent set), respectively.

Example 5. *Following the above definition of equivalence for the partitioning $\mathcal{G} = \{G_1, \ldots, G_3\}$ of G shown in Figure 1(a), we can obtain the following, partition-specific equivalence sets: $\{\upsilon_1 = \{f\}\}@G_1$, $\{\nu_1 = \{b, e\}\}@G_1$; $\{\upsilon_2 =$*

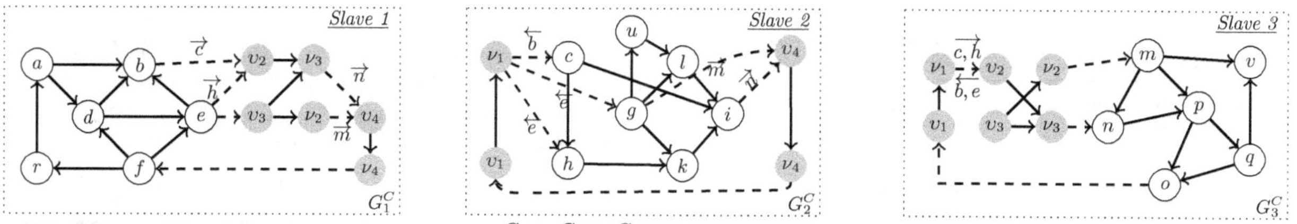

Figure 4: Final compound graphs G_1^C, G_2^C, G_3^C constructed for graph G with cut C of Figure 1

$\{c,h\}, \upsilon_3 = \{g\}\}@G_2$, $\{\nu_2 = \{g\}, \nu_3 = \{i\}\}@G_2$; $\{\upsilon_4 = \{m,n\}\}@G_3$, $\{\nu_4 = \{o\}\}@G_3$.

Next, the in- and out-boundaries are redefined with respect to the new virtual vertices. That is, I_i comprises of all in-virtual vertices and O_i comprises of all out-virtual vertices. The optimized boundary graph for partition G_1 is shown in Figure 3(b). Note that we attach additional labels to the cross-edges in the boundary graph to obtain a lossless representation of the boundary graph with respect to the partitions $G_1, \ldots, G_k$. For example, the cross-edge (b,c) is represented by connecting the vertex b and the in-virtual vertex υ_2 with the label $\overrightarrow{c}$ to denote that b is connected to only c in υ_2. The forward arrow denotes that this connection is valid only for a forward exploration. This is required, since vertices c, h are forward-equivalent, i.e., $c \equiv^f h$, with respect to partition G_2 only.

Computing Equivalence Sets. According to Definition 5, two in-boundaries $b_1 \in I_i$ and $b_2 \in I_i$ are forward-equivalent if they are reachable to exactly the same set of vertices in $V_i - I_i$. To determine the sets of forward-equivalent boundaries, we need to (1) compute all reachable pairs from I_i to $V_i - I_i$ and then (2) group the vertices in I_i into these equivalence sets. For large sets I_i and $V_i - I_i$, this computation may be prohibitively expensive. To address (1) and thus reduce the input that needs to be considered for (2), we apply the following optimizations.

- b_1, b_2 can only be forward-equivalent with respect to partition G_i if both belong to the same *strongly connected component* (SCC) in G_i. We thus condense G_i into a more compact DAG by computing the SCCs over G_i.
- Instead of considering all target vertices $V_i - I_i$, we consider only the *direct successors* $S(I_i)$ of I_i, and hence $S(I_i) - I_i$, to check for forward-equivalence. The intuition for considering only successors is that if two boundaries b_1, b_2 are reachable to the same set of vertices in $S(I_i) - I_i$, then b_1, b_2 also are reachable to the same set of vertices in $V_i - I_i$.

A similar construction then holds also for backward-equivalence, except that *predecessors* $P(O_i)$ are considered instead.

EXAMPLE 6. *Consider partition G_3 with in-boundary set $I_3 = \{m,n\}$ to compute the sets of forward-equivalent vertices in I_3. In this case, this requires us to only verify whether $m \equiv^f n$, since m, n are the only in-boundaries in I_3. First, we run the SCC algorithm to condense G_3 into the DAG G'_3. In this example, $G'_3 = G_3$, and we see that m, n do not belong to the same SCC. We then check their forward-equivalence based on the sets of vertices in $V_3 - I_3$ that are reachable from both m and n. To compute these reachable sets of vertices, we consider only the direct successors $S(I_3) - I_3 = \{p,v\}$ instead of considering all of $V_3 - I_3 = \{p,o,q,v\}$. Thus, the reachable set of vertices of both m and n is $\{p,v\}$, and hence we have $m \equiv^f n$.*

A compact algorithm for computing these equivalence sets is depicted in Appendix 8.1.

Compound Graph. After compacting the partition-specific boundary graphs G_i^B by replacing both the forward- and backward-equivalent sets of vertices with their in- and out-virtual counterparts, we perform one more step to obtain our final graph index for evaluating DSR queries. To do so, we merge the partition-specific boundary graphs with the local partitions into a *compound graph* G_i^C for each partition G_i. These compound graphs will facilitate the processing of DSR queries via a combination of local reachability computations and a single filtering step among these local results.

DEFINITION 6. *Let $G_i^C(V_i^C, E_i^C, L, \phi)$ denote the* ***compound graph*** *we compute for partition G_i, such that the following holds:*

- *The vertices $V_i^C = V_i \cup V_i^B$ consist of the union of vertices in the local subgraph G_i and boundary graph G_i^B.*
- *The edges $E_i^B = E_i \cup E_i^B$ consist of the union of edges in the local subgraph G_i and boundary graph G_i^B.*

Figure 4 shows the compound graphs for the initial data graph G from Figure 1(a).

Forward- and Backward-Lists. Our last precomputation step consists of storing the forward- and backward-lists, F_i and B_i, of boundaries which are non-local to each partition G_i. These will serve for routing messages to only those partitions G_j which are connected to G_i. Specifically, the *forward-list* $F_i = \bigcup_{j \neq i} \{\upsilon \mid \upsilon$ *is in-virtual vertex of* $G_j\}$ is the set of all vertices that are non-local to G_i and are in-virtual vertices of another partition G_j. Similarly, the *backward-list* $B_i = \bigcup_{j \neq i} \{\nu \mid \nu$ *is out-virtual vertex of* $G_j\}$ consists of all out-virtual vertices that are non-local to G_i. For instance, for partition G_1 shown in Figure 4, we have $F_1 = \{\upsilon_2, \upsilon_3, \upsilon_4\}$ and $B_1 = \{\nu_2, \nu_3, \nu_4\}$.

3.3.2 Evaluating DSR Queries

Given these precomputed index structures, i.e., the compound graphs G_i^C and respective forward- and backward-lists, F_i and B_i, evaluating a DSR query now becomes straightforward. We again begin with a discussion of the single-source, single-target case and then explain how it generalizes to the multi-source, multi-target case.

A. Single Reachability. Consider the reachability query $s \rightsquigarrow t$. The algorithm for processing the query is shown in Algorithm 1. Given a data graph G with partitioning $\mathcal{G}$, we evaluate the query as follows. If both s and t belong to same partition G_i, then the reachability $s \rightsquigarrow t$ is confined to only slave i which stores the compound graph G_i^C. Since the compound graph G_i^C augments each G_i with the global reachability information among all boundary vertices, we can safely evaluate the reachability of $s \rightsquigarrow t$ on G_i^C by calling any centralized reachability algorithm via the function localSetReachability(.) (Lines 11-13). A formal justification for this is provided by the following theorem.

THEOREM 1. *Let s, t both be local vertices of partition i, i.e., $s,t \in V_i$. Then the evaluation of the reachability*

Algorithm 1: Distributed Reachability Processing

Input: Compound graphs: $\{G_1^C, G_2^C, ..., G_k^C\}$, Query: $s \rightsquigarrow t$
Output: true/false

1 **Master:**
2 $rank_s := \rho(s)$ ▷ i.e., $s \in V_i$ and G_i is at Slave $\rho(i)$
3 $rank_t := \rho(t)$ ▷ i.e., $t \in V_j$ and G_j is at Slave $\rho(j)$
4 $result :=$ false
5 **foreach** $rank$ **do**
6     $result := result \vee$ compute$(s, rank_s, t, rank_t)$
      ▷ invokes parallel computations at all ranks
7 **return** $result$

8 Slave i:
9 **method** compute(s, $rank_s$, t, $rank_t$) :
10 $rset := \emptyset$
11 **if** $rank_s = i$ *and* $rank_t = i$ **then**
      ▷ invoke local reachability evaluation
12   **if** localSetReachability$(\{s\}, \{t\}) \neq \emptyset$ **then**
13   **return** true
14 **else if** $i = rank_s$ **then**
15     $j := rank_t$
16     $\Upsilon_s^j :=$ localSetReachability$(\{s\}, F_i^j)$;
      ▷ $F_i^j \subseteq F_i$ is the set of in-virtual vertices local to j
17     $rset[s] := \Upsilon_s^j$
18   sendMessage(j, $rset$)
19   **return** false
20 **else if** $i = rank_t$ **then**
21   receiveMessage(i, $rset$)
22     $\Upsilon_s^i := rset[s]$
23   **for** v *in* Υ_s^i **do**
24         $b := v.rep$ ▷ b is a member vertex in eqset v
25   **if** localSetReachability$(\{b\}, \{t\}) \neq \emptyset$ **then**
26   **return** true
27 **return** false

$s \rightsquigarrow t$ *over graph* G *can be answered entirely locally over the compound graph* G_i^C *without requiring any message exchange among the compute nodes.*

PROOF. See Appendix 8.2.1. □

EXAMPLE 7. *Consider the query* $b \rightsquigarrow f$. *Both vertices* b, f *are local to partition* G_1. *By considering only the subgraph* G_1, *one cannot find that* f *is reachable from* b. *But by considering the whole graph* G, *we see that* $b \rightsquigarrow f$ *is* true *via the path* $b \to c \to i \to n \to p \to o \to f$. *However, using the local compound graph* G_1^C *(see Figure 4), we can indeed find that* $b \rightsquigarrow f$ *is* true *via the path* $b \to v_2 \to \nu_3 \to v_4 \to \nu_4 \to f$.

If, on the other hand, s and t are located at two different partitions G_i, G_j, with $i \neq j$, the evaluation of a reachability query works as follows (Lines 14-25). Starting at partition G_i, we find the reachability from s to all the forward-boundaries $v \in F_i^j \subseteq F_i$ (Line 15) which are located at another partition G_j. Let $\Upsilon_s^j \subseteq F_i$ be the set of in-virtual vertices located at partition G_j (and hence stored by slave j as per our assumption) which are reachable from s. The message rset[s]:=$\langle s, \Upsilon_s^j \rangle$ is then communicated to slave j. At slave j, we consider each $v \in \Upsilon_s^j$ and replace it with any one of its members b, after which we evaluate the reachability from b to the local target vertex t. If there exists one such $b \in v \in \Upsilon_s^j$ with $b \rightsquigarrow t$, we report that $s \rightsquigarrow t$ is *true* (Lines 22-25).

THEOREM 2. *Let* $s \in V_i$ *and* $t \in V_j$, *with* $i \neq j$. *Then, the evaluation of the reachability* $s \rightsquigarrow t$ *can be answered over the two compound graphs* G_i^C *and* G_j^C *by using a single step of message exchange from slave* i *to slave* j.

PROOF. See Appendix 8.2.2 □

EXAMPLE 8. *Consider the query* $a \rightsquigarrow q$, *where* a *is located at partition* G_1 *and* q *is located at partition* G_3. *At partition* G_1, *we compute the reachability from* a *to the single forward-boundary* $\{v_4\}$ *which is located at* G_3. *From the compound graph* G_1^C *(shown in Figure 4), we have* $\Upsilon_a^3 = \{v_4\}$ *since* $a \rightsquigarrow v_4$. Υ_a^3 *is then communicated to slave* 3. *At slave* 3, *we expand the actual vertices represented by the virtual vertex* v_4 *(say* m, *since* $m \in v_4$*) and find the reachability from* m *to* q. *Since* $m \rightsquigarrow q$, *we thus find that* $a \rightsquigarrow q$ *is* true.

B. Set Reachability. An actual DSR query $S \rightsquigarrow T$, which is received by the master node, is processed in our approach as shown in Algorithm 2. First, $S \rightsquigarrow T$ is partitioned into subqueries $S_1 \rightsquigarrow T_1$, $S_2 \rightsquigarrow T_2, \ldots$, $S_k \rightsquigarrow T_k$, where k is again the number of graph partitions. The partitioning of the query into these subqueries is determined such that each source vertex $s_i \in S_i$ and target vertex $t_i \in T_i$ resides locally at partition G_i (Line 2).

Step 1. (Lines 13-19) A local evaluation at partition G_i involves processing the pairwise reachability among the vertices from S_i to T_i and from S_i to F_i at *all slaves* $i = 1..k$ *in parallel.* This operation generates two types of reachable pairs: (s_i, t_i) and (s_i, v_j). The first type denotes the reachability between both a local source $s_i \in S_i$ and a local target $t_i \in T_i$. The second type denotes the reachability between a local source $s_i \in S_i$ and a forward-boundary $v_j \in F_i$, which is represented by an in-virtual vertex located at slave j.

Step 2. (Lines 21-32) The communication of the remotely reachable pairs, each of the form (s_i, v_j), is performed from slave i to slave j among *all pairs of slaves* $i, j = 1..k$ *in parallel.* In order to reduce the overhead of communicating individual pairs, each slave buffers its partial reachability information and communicates this buffer at once. Each buffer sent from slave i to slave j is of the form $\{\langle s_i, \Upsilon_{s_i}^j \rangle\}$ for all $s_i \in S_i$. For easier processing, the messages received at slave i from all other slaves are stored in an inverted index $\mathcal{I}_i(\Upsilon_*^i, L_i)$, where Υ_*^i is the aggregated set of in-virtual vertices (local to slave i). For each in-virtual vertex $v \in \Upsilon_*^i$, its aggregated non-local source set $S_v \subseteq S$ is stored in L_i. That is, for $s \in S_v$ and $v \in \Upsilon_*^i$, we already know that $s \rightsquigarrow v$.

Step 3. (Lines 34-39) A final local evaluation involves processing the set reachability $\Upsilon_*^i \rightsquigarrow T_i$ from the in-virtual vertices Υ_*^i to the target sets T_i at *all slaves* $i = 1..k$ *in parallel.* For each in-virtual vertex $v \in \Upsilon_*^i$ and original vertex b represented by v, we evaluate the reachability from b to all targets $t \in T_i$. If $b \rightsquigarrow t$ is *true*, then for each $s \in S_v$, we report that $s \rightsquigarrow t$ is *true*.

EXAMPLE 9. *Consider again the graph* G *with partitions* G_1, G_2, G_3 *in Figure 1(a). The respective compound graphs* G_1^C, G_2^C, G_3^C *are shown in Figure 4. Let* $S = \{d, l, p\} \rightsquigarrow T = \{a, k, q\}$ *be the DSR query received at the master node. The query is partitioned into* $\{d\} \rightsquigarrow \{a\}$, $\{l\} \rightsquigarrow \{k\}$, $\{p\} \rightsquigarrow \{q\}$. *At partition* G_1, *we find the set-reachability (Step 1) between* $\{d\}$, $\{v_2, v_3, v_4, a\}$, *thus returning the reachable pairs* $\{(d, v_2), (d, v_3), (d, v_4), (d, a)\}$. *We perform the same operation in parallel at slaves* 2 *and* 3 *and communicate the results to all other slaves (Step 2). At slave* 1, *we receive*

Algorithm 2: Distributed Set-Reachability Processing

```
Input: Compound graphs {G_1^C, G_2^C, ..., G_k^C}, Query: S ⇝ T
Output: R {(s,t) | s ∈ S, t ∈ T and s ⇝ t}

Master:
partition S, T into {(S_1, T_2), (S_2, T_2), ..., (S_k, T_k)}
    ▷ where S_i ⊆ V_i and T_i ⊆ V_i
result := ∅
for i = 1...k do
    result := result ∪ compute(S_i, T_i)
return result

Slave i:
method compute(S_i, T_i) :
local_rset := ∅
remote_rset := ∅
result := ∅
// Step 1:
local_rset := localSetReachability(S_i, T_i)
remote_rset := localSetReachability(S_i, F_i)
for s in S_i do
    for t in local_rset[s] do
        result := result ∪ {(s,t)}
    for v in remote_rset[s] do
        Υ_s^j := Υ_s^j ∪ v
        ▷ v is an in-virtual vertex of partition j
// Step 2:
for j = 1 to k do
    if j ≠ i then
        msg := ∅
        for s in S_i do
            msg := msg ∪ {⟨s, Υ_s^j⟩}
        sendMessage(j, msg)
I_i(Υ_*^i, L_i) = ∅
for j = 1 to k do
    receiveMessage(j, msg)
    for ⟨s, Υ_s^i⟩ in msg do
        for v in Υ_s^i do
            I_i[v] := I_i[v] ∪ {s}
// Step 3:
for v in Υ_*^i do
    b := v.rep
    local_rset := localSetReachability({b}, T_i)
    for s in I_i[v] do
        for t ∈ local_rset[b] do
            result := result ∪ {(s,t)}
return result
```

the following reachability information: $\{(v_1, [l,p])\}$. *Similarly, at slave* 2, *we receive* $\{(v_2, [d,p]), (v_3, [d,p])\}$*; and at slave* 3, *we receive* $\{(v_4, [d,l])\}$. *At the end of the local evaluation from boundaries to the final targets (Step 3), by replacing virtual vertices with each of their represented vertices (at slave* 1, v_1 *is replaced with* f*), the sets* $\{(d,a),(l,a),(p,a)\}@G_1$, $\{(d,k),(l,k),(p,k)\}@G_2$ *and* $\{(d,q),(l,q),(p,q)\}@G_3$ *of reachable pairs are generated at the partitions.*

Local Reachability Evaluation. Algorithms 1 and 2 both require partial reachability processing at each slave via the function localSetReachability(.). For this, any centralized reachability index (see, e.g., [6, 28, 12, 36]) can be plugged into our framework. We abstract this by calling localSetReachability(.) in our algorithms whenever a local (set-)reachability operation is invoked.

Forward vs. Backward Processing. Our above discussion focused on starting from the source vertices and ending at the target vertices. If there are less targets than sources, one may also start from the target vertices and search backwards to the source vertices to arrive at the same results. We therefore maintain both forward- and backward-lists, F_i and B_i, to facilitate these two directions of searching.

3.3.3 Incremental Updates

Insertions. Insertions over the SCC-condensed compound graphs G_i^C can be implemented *without* storing the original (i.e., uncondensed) compound graphs.

Let (u,v) denote a new edge that is to be inserted into the graph G. First, assume both u and v belong to the same graph partition i. Further, if u, v belong to the same SCC, then adding (u,v) to G_i would not change the local compound graph G_i^C (nor any other) at all and thus can be safely ignored. If, on the other hand, u, v belong to two different SCCs, then a series of update actions are required. First, we add the new edge to the local compound graph G_i^C and locally recompute the SCCs and equivalence sets. Next, new connections among the local in- and out-boundaries, I_i and O_i, are communicated to all other partitions j (for $j \neq i$) as additional edges. These can be incrementally merged into all the compound graphs G_j^C by updating their SCCs as well. Second, if u and v belong to two different partitions i and j, then this means we have a new edge in the cut C, which however does not affect the reachability within partitions i and j. Thus, (u,v) can directly be merged into the distributed compound graphs as described above.

Let n, m denote the number of vertices and edges in the condensed compound graph G_i^C, and let $|I_i|$, $|O_i|$ be the number of in- and out-boundaries for partition i, respectively. By adding a local edge to partition i, a partial or full recomputation of the connections among vertices from I_i to O_i is required. Thus the worst-case time complexity of this step is $\mathcal{O}((n+m) \cdot |I_i| \cdot |O_i|)$, which is asymptotically optimal [7]. The SCC recomputation at each compound graph has a time complexity of $\mathcal{O}(n' + m')$, where n' and m' are the numbers of vertices and edges in the new G_i^C's.

Deletions. Deletions over the SCC-condensed compound graphs G_i^C, on the other hand, result in a decremental maintenance of the SCCs, which requires either storing the original (i.e., uncondensed) compound graphs or organizing the SCCs in a hierarchical manner [19]. In our implementation, we resort to storing the uncondensed compound graphs along with the condensed compound graphs G_i^C, albeit approaches like [19] may be employed for further optimizations.

A deletion of a local edge (u,v) in partition i is processed over the condensed compound graph G_i^C as follows. If the vertices u, v belong to the same SCC, then we expand this SCC into its original edges and reconnect these edges to the remaining SCCs in G_i^C. Moreover, in case of deletions, some of the existing boundaries may not be connected anymore. We identify such pairs of boundaries and communicate these to the other compute nodes. After receiving this list of deleted boundary edges, we reconstruct the local compound graphs G_j^C (for $j \neq i$) analogously to the insertion case. If, on the other hand, the vertices u, v belong to two different SCCs, then we expand both of them.

Here, the worst-case time complexity to maintain the local boundary edges is $\mathcal{O}((|V_i| + |E_i|) \cdot |I_i| \cdot |O_i|)$, which is the same as for rebuilding the local boundary graphs (see Section 3.3.1). The new compound graphs are condensed via SCC computation, whose worst-case time complexity is $\mathcal{O}(n' + m')$, where n' and m' again are the numbers of vertices and edges in the new G_i^C's.

4. EVALUATION

We next present a detailed empirical evaluation of our proposed indexing and updating strategies for DSR queries. Specifically, we compare the following approaches:

- our DSR approach with a static reachability index (coined "*DSR*"), as described in Section 3.3;
- a naïve enumeration of all pairs of source and target vertices (coined "*DSR-Naïve*"), as described in Section 3.1;
- a generalization of the algorithm described by Fan et al. (coined "*DSR-Fan*") [9] to sets of source and target vertices, as described in Section 3.2;
- an implementation of DSR queries in Apache Giraph (coined *"Giraph"*) [1], as depicted in Appendix 8.4.1;
- an implementation of DSR queries in Giraph++[2] (coined *"Giraph++"*) [31], as depicted in Appendix 8.4.2;
- an extended version of Giraph++ with equivalence sets (coined "*Giraph++wEq*"), as depicted in Appendix 8.4.3.

Further, for *"DSR"*, we report the results in combination with the following local reachability indexes:

- a plain depth-first-search (DFS) strategy which requires no additional index structures except for those described in Section 3.3 (coined *"DSR-DFS"*);
- the multi-source-breath-first-search (MS-BFS) algorithm described by Then et al. [30] which also requires no additional index structures except for those described in Section 3.3 (coined *"DSR-MSBFS"*);
- using FERRARI [28] as a local reachability index that is generated on top of the compound graphs described in Section 3.3 (coined *"DSR-FERRARI"*).

Unless stated otherwise, we report the combination of our DSR index with DFS as the default local search strategy.

Datasets. The list of graph collections we consider for our evaluation is shown in Table 1. All the smaller graphs (including the two Live Journal versions) are obtained from the Stanford Snap[3] project. For our evaluation over larger graphs, we used the real-world Freebase[4] and Twitter[5] snapshots. In addition, we also used the widely popular synthetic LUBM RDF benchmark, which we generated using the UBA 1.7[6] data generator.

Small Graphs	|V|	|E|	Large Graphs	|V|	|E|
Amazon	0.4M	3.3M	LiveJ-68M	4.8M	68.9M
BerkStan	0.7M	7.6M	Twitter-1.4B	41.7M	1,468.4M
Google	0.9M	5.1M	Freebase-500M	97.3M	499.9M
NotreDame	0.3M	1.5M	Freebase-1B	156.6M	999.9M
Stanford	0.3M	2.3M	LUBM-500M	115.6M	500.0M
LiveJ-20M	2.5M	20.0M	LUBM-1B	222.2M	961.4M

Table 1: Graph datasets and sizes

General Setup. We implemented the DSR variants in C++ using GCC-4.7.2 with Boost-1.55 and compiled with -O3 optimization. We used MPICH2-1.4.1 for communication among the compute nodes, using a cluster of 10 nodes which are connected via a 10GBit LAN. Each node has 64GB of RAM and an Intel X5650@2.67GHz quadcore CPU with HT enabled. Giraph and its variants are implemented in Java, where we used Hadoop v0.20 for running Giraph [1]. Appendix 8.4 depicts our actual implementation of DSR queries for the three Giraph variants.

[2]https://issues.apache.org/jira/browse/GIRAPH-818
[3]http://snap.stanford.edu
[4]http://freebase.com
[5]http://an.kaist.ac.kr/traces/WWW2010.html
[6]http://swat.cse.lehigh.edu/projects/lubm/

	DSR			DSR-Fan	DSR-Naïve
	Compound graph			*Dep.graph*	*Dep.graph*
Graphs	**Original** *(#edges)*	**DAG** *(#edges)*	**Size** *(MB)*	*(#edges)*	*(#edges)*
Amazon	1.0M	34.7K	206	622.3M	622.2M
BerkStan	2.1M	0.5M	383	2.2M	2.1M
Google	1.2M	0.2M	302	43.6M	43.6M
NotreDame	0.8M	68.9K	123	4.7M	4.7M
Stanford	0.8M	41.2K	122	1.2M	1.2M
LiveJ-20M	13.7M	1.0M	1,553	861.4M	n/a
LiveJ-68M	44.1M	0.3M	928	n/a	n/a
Freebase-1B	460.4M	241.6M	64,141	n/a	n/a
Twitter-1.4B	1,285.0M	8.2M	20,053	n/a	n/a
LUBM-1B	891.8M	891.3M	107,608	n/a	n/a

Table 2: Index sizes for DSR variants

4.1 Efficiency

For this experiment, we considered several real-world data graphs (both small and large) and the synthetic LUBM graph. We fixed the compute cluster to 6 nodes (i.e., to 5 slaves and 1 master). We randomly selected 10 source and 10 target vertices from all datasets (except LUBM-1B) as queries, thus resulting in 100 reachability comparisons. For LUBM-1B, which is very sparsely connected, we randomly chose 1,000 sources and 1,000 targets, of which only 131 pairs turned out to be reachable.

Table 2 shows the maximum (i.e., per node) uncondensed ("*Original*") and SCC-condensed ("*DAG*") compound-graph sizes as well as the total byte size ("*Size*") for our DSR index in comparison to the dependency-graph sizes for DSR-Fan and DSR-Naïve. In DSR-Fan, for a given DSR query $S \rightsquigarrow T$, all of S and T are used "at once" to generate the dependency graph. In DSR-Naïve, which generates the dependency graph per (s, t) pair, the sizes represented in Table 2 are the average dependency-graph sizes over 100 pairs. SCC compression, which is not feasible for the dynamically generated dependency graph, drastically reduces the sizes of the compound graphs stored at each slave. For example, for the Twitter-1.4B graph, which is highly connected, the size of each compound graph stored at the slaves initially is comparable to the size of the original graph. Applying SCC compression condenses these graphs by a factor of about 150. Also for LiveJ-68M, the SCC compression leads to a much smaller DAG size than for LiveJ-20M, such that our query times are actually lower for LiveJ-68M than for LiveJ-20M.

Table 3 shows our query-processing results. For both the small and large graphs, our approach clearly demonstrates efficiency improvements of several orders of magnitude when compared to the three Giraph variants as well as to DSR-Fan and DSR-Naïve. Even with a single round of communication, DSR-Fan and DSR-Naïve exhibit a considerable overhead in generating the dynamic dependency graph for each query. Specifically, we observed that for LiveJ-20M, DSR-Fan generates a dependency graph of about 861 million edges even when the data graph is partitioned by METIS [17] in order to minimize the cut. Our DSR approach, which benefits from the optimizations we apply when constructing the compound graphs, avoids the repeated generation of a large dependency graph at the master node and therefore is able to achieve very significant performance gains over DSR-Fan and DSR-Naïve. Giraph++ and Giraph++wEq, on the other hand, perform better than the native Giraph implementation, as the former benefit from their local updates of neighboring vertices. This drastically reduced the number of supersteps required for processing a set-reachability query. The equivalence-sets optimization for Giraph++wEq further reduced the communication but only marginally improved the query processing times.

Graphs	Indexing Time DSR	Query Size |S|	|T|	Query Time DSR	Giraph++	Giraph++wEq	Giraph	DSR-Fan	DSR-Naïve
(a) Small Graphs (times in seconds)									
Amazon	2.380	10	10	**0.008**	12.250	11.348	55.034	72.111	855.159
BerkStan	3.048	10	10	**0.009**	44.180	5.680	779.006	2.219	38.036
Google	3.194	10	10	**0.060**	60.154	11.426	53.614	25.210	114.078
NotreDame	1.089	10	10	**0.057**	11.085	12.320	94.787	1.800	50.598
Stanford	1.511	10	10	**0.008**	7.808	8.922	341.976	0.468	6.211
LiveJ-20M	44.536	10	10	**0.227**	19.888	19.262	28.075	521.569	n/a
(b) Large Graphs (times in seconds)									
LiveJ-68M	144.981	10	10	**0.090**	64.728	61.940	93.253	n/a	n/a
Freebase-1B	1,938.670	10	10	**67.849**	1,371.423	1,014.442	1,857.124	n/a	n/a
Twitter-1.4B	6,963.730	10	10	**1.119**	3,065.483	3,046.450	n/a	n/a	n/a
LUBM-1B	2,083.190	1,000	1,000	**1.340**	146.864	142.142	154.407	n/a	n/a

Table 3: Efficiency evaluation (indexing and query times) of DSR approaches for small and large graphs

4.2 Scalability

Next, we evaluated our approach in comparison to the Giraph variants under both strong and weak scaling. We dropped DSR-Fan and DSR-Naïve from these comparisons, as they could not scale to the larger graphs anymore. We considered LiveJ, Freebase, Twitter and the synthetic LUBM graph for our scalability evaluation. We used METIS to partition the graphs and distributed the partitions to up to 10 compute nodes (one of which used as master), and we considered 10 random source and 10 random target vertices as queries. Figures 5(d)(h)(l)(p) also show the robustness of our approach with respect to larger query sets.

Live Journal: Figures 5(a)-(d) depict the scalability evaluation of our approach and the Giraph variants for LiveJ-68M. Figure 5(a) shows the results for a strong scaling. Here, we can observe that DSR scales very well and performs significantly better than the Giraph variants. We also observe that Giraph++ and Giraph++wEq perform slightly better than Giraph by leveraging the node locality and equivalence-sets optimization, respectively. This observation is confirmed further by Figure 5(b), where Giraph communicates about two orders of magnitude more messages compared to Giraph++and Giraph++wEq. Figure 5(c) shows the weak scalability for the 10 by 10 DSR queries.

Freebase: The scalability results for Freebase-1B are shown in Figures 5(e)-(h). We can observe that our approach scales well on average, even when the graph sometimes is rather unevenly partitioned as a result of using METIS. This uneven partitioning also is the reason for the runtime increase from 7 to 8 slaves. By leveraging node locality in Giraph++ and the equivalence-sets optimization in Giraph++wEq, both approaches continue to show performance gains over Giraph, but this time with a more visible difference in the communication costs among the three variants as shown in Figure 5(f). Figure 5(g) shows the weak scalability.

Twitter: We next performed a similar scalability evaluation over Twitter, consisting of more than 1.4 billion edges and more than 41 million vertices. METIS this time resulted in a very skewed partitioning, with one partition containing almost half of the edges and almost one third of the edges being cut edges. This constituted a challenge for our approach, because we compute the boundary graph along with the cut edges. However, since vertices in Twitter are densely connected, the resulting compound graphs at all slaves can very well be condensed using SCC compression, which led to very small graph indexes at the slaves (with a compression factor of more than 150). Without this optimization, Giraph was able to load the Twitter graph but failed to process the set-reachability query, returning an "out of memory" exception. The strong and weak scalability of our approach and the Giraph variants are shown in Figures 5(i) and 5(k).

LUBM: As the final scalability experiment, we considered the synthetic LUBM-1B dataset whose results are shown Figures 5(m)-5(p). Most of the RDF-based LUBM graph is acyclic and sparsely connected. Thus, our SCC condensation for the compound graphs has very low effect on the overall query processing. Figure 5(m) shows the strong scalability of our approach versus the Giraph variants. Figure 5(n) shows the communication costs for different variants of Giraph and our approach. Again, our DSR approach, which evaluates a set-reachability query in a single round of communication, exchanges a very low amount of messages compared to the iterative Giraph variants.

4.3 Updates

We considered the six smaller graphs plus the LiveJ-68M dataset (see Table 1) for updates. We distinguish two principal kinds of incremental update workloads, which we call *bulk updates* and *progressive updates*, respectively.

- For bulk insertions, we start with 60% of randomly chosen edges of the original graph and then increment the graph by 5% of the remaining edges, until we reach the original graph. For bulk deletions, we start with the original graph and decrement the graph in 5% steps.
- For progressive insertions, we randomly pick x% (say, 5%) of edges from the original graph and measure the time to insert these into an index built over the remaining $(100 - x)$% (say, 95%) of edges. We increment x in 5% steps. For progressive deletions, we decrement the original graph by a progressive amount of edges.

We used the same queries as described in Section 4.1 to measure the effect of these update steps on the query times.

Insertions. Figures 6(a)(e) show the update and respective query times for our bulk insertions. It can be observed that the time needed for bulk insertions remains almost constant for each 5% step. Query performance, which depends on the final DAG size, however varied considerably with each update. Next, we considered progressive insertions. From Figure 6(b), it can be clearly seen that the update times are only a fraction of the total rebuild time (see Table 2). Query performance, shown in Figure 6(f), increased marginally at each step, as expected, although also this depends on the final DAG size as a result of the update operation.

Deletions. Deletions are generally more costly in our setting and took almost the same time as building the index from scratch (see Table 2) for both bulk and progressive updates. Figures 6(c)(g) depict the update and respective query times for bulk deletions. While deletion times show a downward trend, query times tend to increase as the graphs become more sparsely connected, thus leading to larger DAG sizes. This is especially visible for the LiveJ-68M dataset. For the case of progressive deletions, as shown

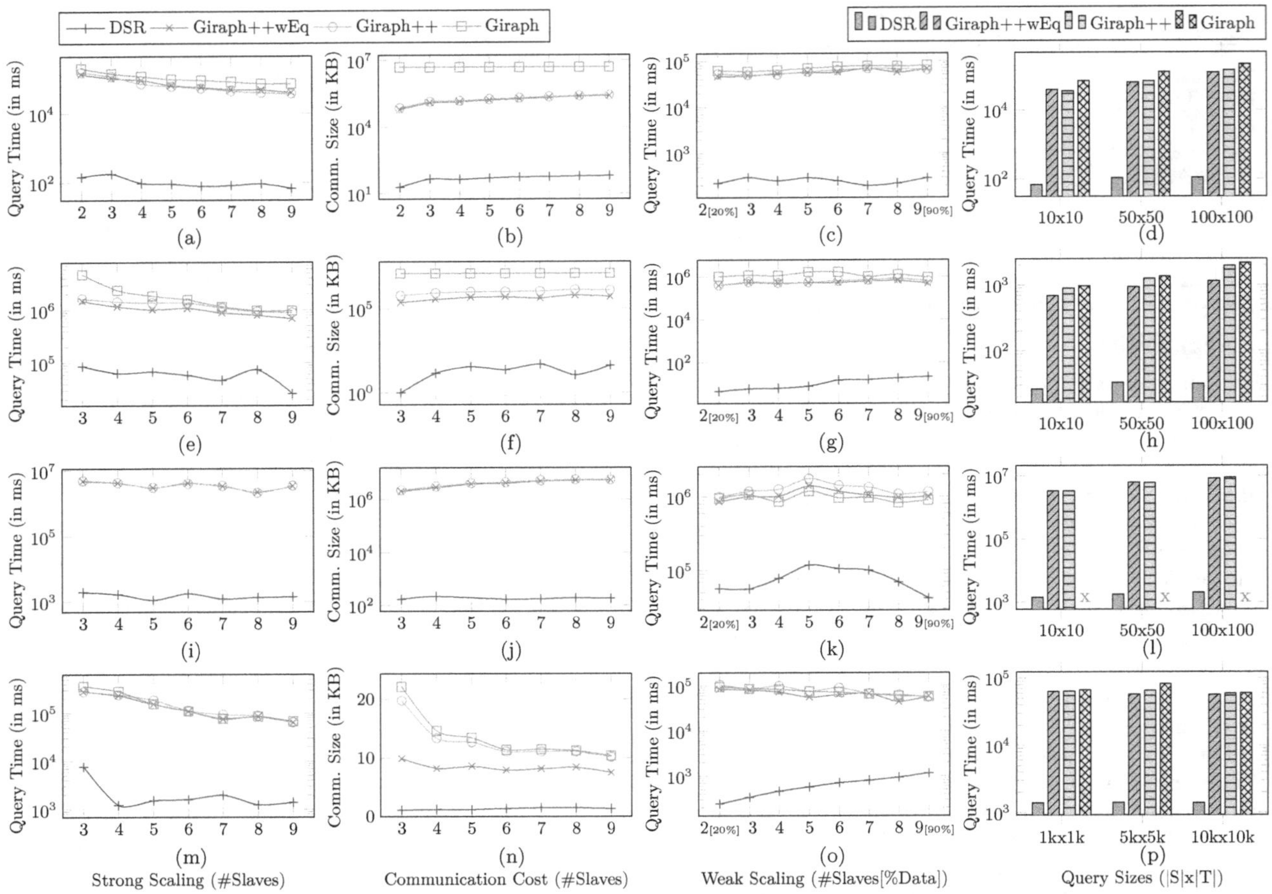

Figure 5: Scalability evaluation for LiveJ-68M (a-d), Freebase-1B (e-h), Twitter-1.4B (i-l), LUBM-1B (m-p)

in Figures 6(d)(h), we observe similar trends in terms of update and query times.

4.4 Parameters

A. Local Reachability Indexes. We next measured our DSR approach in conjunction with three centralized strategies. For all three cases, we condense the local compound graphs via computing SCCs. DSR-DFS uses a standard DFS strategy [6] for processing a DSR query, where no additional index is built over the compound graphs. For each source s and target t in the given DSR query, we perform a DFS to evaluate the reachability $s \rightsquigarrow t$. MS-BFS [30] caches, for each vertex v that is visited during a graph traversal, the reachability of v to all its targets. Thus, if v is another source in the query, we avoid recomputing the reachability and thus save a graph traversal. FERRARI [28] finally provides a tunable tradeoff between index size and query performance. We set both the number of intervals per vertex and the number of seed vertices to 1,000.

Figure 7 shows the effects on query performance when using different local search strategies. For this experiment, we again considered 10 nodes of which one was the master node. We used two real-world datasets, LiveJ-68M and Freebase-1B, for this evaluation. We considered different query sizes to demonstrate the strengths and weaknesses of the three approaches. Figure 7(a) shows the results for LiveJ-68M. We can observe that DSR-DFS takes longer compared to the other two baselines as it requires one graph traversal (in the worst case) for each source. DSR-FERRARI, with its compact reachability index, demonstrates significant performance gains over the other two baselines for different query sizes. On the other hand, for large query sizes, the DSR-MSBFS approach benefits from its memoization and less redundant graph traversal and tends to close the gap to FERRARI. The three strategies show similar trends also for the larger Freebase-1B dataset (see Figure 7(b)).

B. Equivalence-Sets Optimization. By computing equivalence sets among in- and out-boundaries, we are able to reduce both the boundary-graph sizes as well as the number of reachability computations required per slave. Table 4 shows the benefits of this optimization. Figure 8 shows a comparison for the query performance and communication costs with and without equivalence sets in Giraph.

	Query Time (*times in sec.*)		Boundary-Graph Sizes (*#forward; #backward*)	
Graph	**Non-Opt.**	**Opt.**	**Non-Opt.**	**Opt.**
Amazon	0.101	0.008	900; 530	18; 5
BerkStan	0.157	0.110	20,750; 49,462	3,916; 4,981
Google	1.416	1.003	47,822; 98,955	3,759; 6,287
NotreDame	1.085	0.768	16,771; 6,899	2,481; 37
Stanford	0.061	0.038	5,411; 13,942	183; 475

Table 4: Equivalence-sets optimization in DSR

C. Partitioning Strategy. We next considered the effect of the partitioning strategy on the performance of our approach. For this, we used two partitioning strategies: a random hash-partitioning and METIS [17]. We used a cluster of 6 nodes (one of which was dedicated as the master) and evaluated the strategies using a set-reachability query with 10 sources and 10 targets. Table 5 shows the performance comparison of the two partitioning strategies over several real-world graphs. It can be clearly observed that the choice of the partitioning strategy influences the performance of our approach. Hash partitioning (i.e., "random

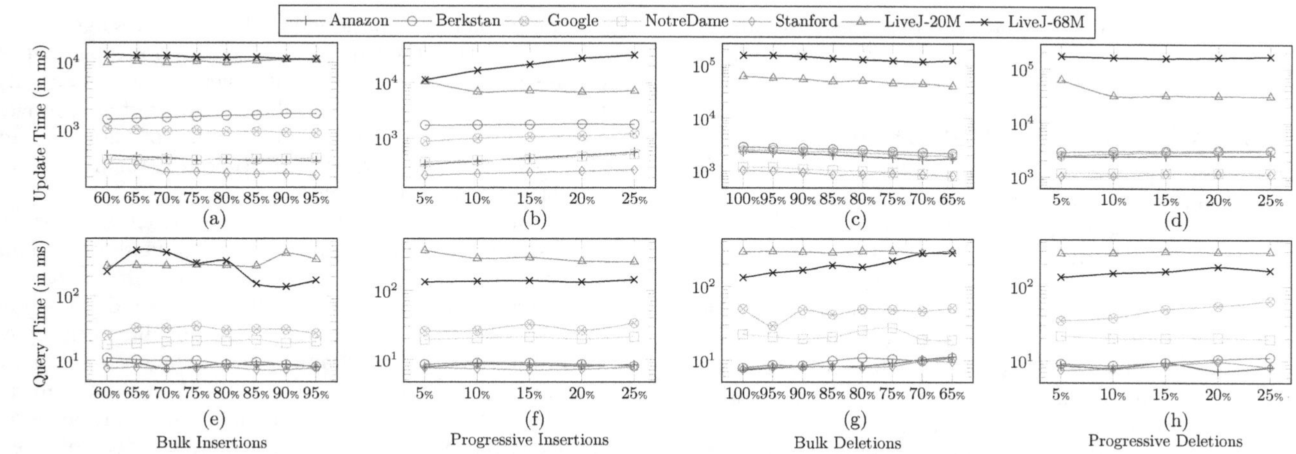

Figure 6: Update evaluation (both insertions and deletions) for various graph collections

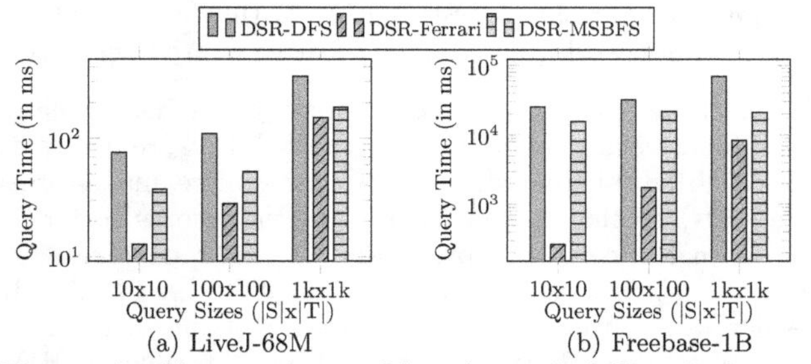

Figure 7: Comparison of local reachability indexes

sharding") usually results in a drastic increase of cut edges and thus in a lower query performance. METIS partitioning in turn helps in minimizing this cut, which significantly improves the query performance.

Graph	Hash	METIS
	Partitioning (query times in sec.)	
Amazon	0.009	0.008
BerkStan	0.016	0.009
Google	0.330	0.060
NotreDame	0.085	0.057
Stanford	0.009	0.008
LiveJ-20	0.524	0.227
LiveJ-68	0.188	0.090

Table 5: Impact of hash vs. METIS partitioning

4.5 Applications

A. SPARQL 1.1 with Property Paths. For this experiment, we considered the LUBM-500M and Freebase-500M datasets (both in RDF format). We augmented a distributed RDF store [15] with our DSR approach by modifying its query processor to handle property paths via our new index structures. To evaluate the performance of our approach in processing SPARQL 1.1 queries, we compared against the commercial Virtuoso RDF store [8]. The results are shown in Table 6, while the customized SPARQL queries we used for this evaluation are depicted in Appendix 8.3

B. Social-Network Communities. As another DSR application, we detected connectivities among communities in a social network. This problem is a basic step in many graph-analytics tasks. That is, given two communities C_1 and C_2 together with a set of representative members for each community $S \subseteq C_1$, $T \subseteq C_2$, find all pairs s, t, with $s \in S$ and $t \in T$, such that $s \rightsquigarrow t$. We considered two social network datasets, LiveJ-68M and Twitter-1.4B, for this experiment. We employed the iterative community-detection algorithm by Blondel et al. [3] to identify communities. We then randomly picked two communities, and from each we picked 10 to 1,000 members as representatives. We then

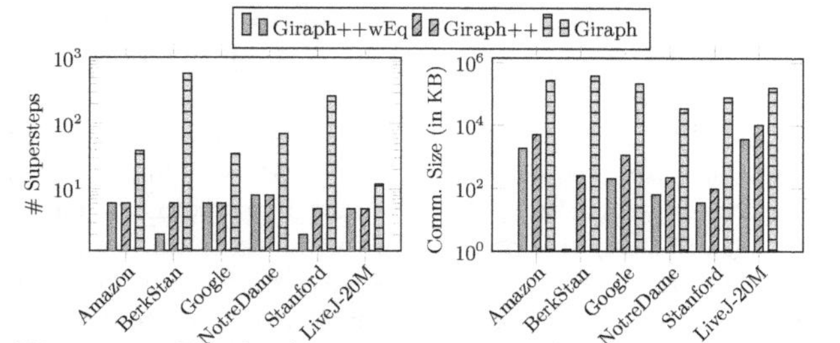

Figure 8: Equivalence-sets optimization in Giraph

ran our DSR approach to identify all reachable pairs among these representatives. The results are shown in Table 7.

(a) LUBM-500M *(query times in sec.)*	#Slaves	L1	L2	L3	Geo.-Mean
DSR	1	6.437	0.331	42.681	4.497
DSR	5	**1.250**	**0.162**	**8.516**	**1.199**
Virtuoso (cold)	1	10.050	12.624	57.776	19.425
Virtuoso (warm)	1	4.963	5.452	56.603	11.527
(b) Freebase-500M *(query times in sec.)*	**#Slaves**	**F1**	**F2**	**F3**	**Geo.-Mean**
DSR	1	1.084	1.568	0.677	1.048
DSR	5	**0.356**	0.642	**0.423**	0.459
Virtuoso (cold)	1	6.590	4.112	13.809	7.206
Virtuoso (warm)	1	1.196	**0.002**	5.601	**0.238**

Table 6: SPARQL 1.1 queries with property paths

Query Size (|S|x|T|)	LiveJ-68M *#Communities: 5,032* Query Time *(in sec.)*	#Pairs	Twitter-1.4B *#Communities: 17,121* Query Time *(in sec.)*	#Pairs
10x10	0.065	81	1.339	63
100x100	0.164	8,184	2.476	8,526
1kx1k	0.717	784,947	10.175	712,725

Table 7: Community connectedness using DSR

4.6 Summary of Results

Our experiments confirm the significantly improved efficiency (with a gain in query times of several orders of magnitude) of our DSR index compared to iterative approaches such as Apache Giraph and variants of [9]. Moreover, we are also able to demonstrate the good update support of our index structure, which—in particular for insertions—behaves much better in practice than suggested by the worst-case bounds we provide in Section 3.3.3. We believe that insertions are the much more likely use-case for managing large, dynamic graphs (e.g., Twitter streams), while deletions, which are costly to handle for any kind of graph-compression technique, are much more uncommon in practice. Also, there is also hardly any support for updates in the centralized approaches (such as [28]), which restricts our local search strategy to a simple DFS or BFS in this case.

Further experiments demonstrate the robustness of our approach under different parameters and show its viability for various large-scale graph-analytics tasks.

5. RELATED WORK DISCUSSION

Centralized Approaches. The reachability problem in directed graphs is one of the most fundamental graph problems and thus has been tackled by a plethora of *centralized indexing techniques* [5, 12, 16, 18, 25, 28, 32, 33, 34, 36] (just to name a number of recent approaches). All of these aim to find tradeoffs among query time and indexing space which, for a directed graph $G(V, E)$, are in between $\mathcal{O}(|V|+|E|)$ for both query time and space consumption when no indexes are used, and $\mathcal{O}(1)$ query time and $\mathcal{O}(|V|^2)$ space consumption when the transitive closure is fully materialized.

Recently, Gao et al. [12] proposed a suitable, but centralized indexing strategy, based on a notion of *equivalence sets* of graph vertices that have the same reachability properties. [30], on the other hand, focused on the *query-time optimization* of multi-source BFS searches. However, there exist hardly any works so far on distributed reachability queries [9]. Fan et al. [9] recently discussed distributed, but single-source, single-target reachability algorithms for partitioned graphs and also provide performance guarantees. For a directed graph and given cut, [9] uses a partially iterative and partially indexing-based evaluation to find the reachability for a given pair of vertices over a classical master-slave architecture. In Section 3, we therefore provide a detailed review of the techniques proposed in [9], while the query-time processing we perform based on equivalence sets to a large extent resembles also the techniques described in [12, 30] for a centralized setting. However, unlike in [12], we do not enumerate the actual path sequences.

Distributed Graph Engines. Distributed graph engines such as Pregel [22], GraphX [35], GraphLab [20], Trinity [29], PowerGraph [21], Giraph [1] and Giraph++ [31] are either based on MapReduce [22, 35, 21], or they implement their own, proprietary communication protocols via Message Passing [13, 20, 29]. Giraph, for example, offers the `sendMessage(.)` and `compute(.)` methods as generic API functions to implement various kinds of graph algorithms (including BFS and DFS). To implement a *single-source, single-target reachability query* over a directed graph, each iteration over the `compute(.)` method (as it is required for a single BFS/DFS step), however, results in a new call of the Map function or so-called "superstep". Among two such supersteps, messages are communicated among all compute nodes, which is a strategy that—due to the a-priori unknown amount of iterations—usually does not permit for interactive query response times. For *multi-source, multi-target queries*, on the other hand, this approach scales well with the query size due to the possibility to implement shared computations in the `compute(.)` method.

A similar observation holds for GraphLab [21], Trinity [29] and PowerGraph [13] which implement asynchronous protocols based on the Message Passing Interface (MPI) [11]. PowerGraph, for example, which is specifically tuned for skewed graphs, implements a judiciously chosen schedule of exchanged messages, but also here the worst-case amount of iterations remains equal to the diameter of the graph. The very recently proposed Giraph++ [31] framework (built on top of Giraph) provides further optimizations by shifting from a purely node-centric to a more graph-centric ("think like a graph") compute paradigm. All (local) messages among the vertices within the same graph partition are performed inside a superstep, while other messages are processed only between two such supersteps. This significantly improves the performance by minimizing the number of messages but also gives a much higher degree of freedom in the implementation of various graph algorithms.

Thus, on the one hand, the generic abstraction layers of these distributed graph engines make it difficult to exploit shared computations and yet to fully benefit from the underlying distribution scheme. On the other hand, these engines generally do not support graph-indexing techniques known from the centralized approaches, which could ideally be employed to even completely avoid iterative communication rounds among the compute nodes. Since Giraph++ offers the most flexible API among the aforedescribed engines, we extensively compared our approach against two principle implementations of DSR queries in the very recent Giraph++ framework (including one native Giraph version).

Processing SPARQL 1.1 Property Paths. Finally, combining relational joins with reachability predicates in SPARQL 1.1 inherently leads to a multi-source, multi-target (i.e., set-) reachability problem. Very few works so far focused on the combined processing of relational joins with additional graph-reachability predicates [4, 10, 14, 27]. In earlier works, the bisimulation-based indexing of path expressions for XML trees [23] has been extended to RDF graphs [24], but the latter did not yet consider property paths. Likewise, [4] proposed an index structure that is limited to DAGs obtained from XML/XLink(s). [26] finally investigated an initial approach to evaluate property paths via MapReduce. Also here, we are aware of only one RDF engine that is available for processing property paths in SPARQL 1.1, namely Virtuoso [8], against which we compared our approach experimentally.

6. CONCLUSIONS

We investigated a generalized form of the well-known reachability problem in directed graphs, which (1) considers both sets of source and target vertices as queries, and (2) allows the underlying graph to be partitioned and hence be distributed across multiple compute nodes. The DSR problem is a basic building block and thus has a plethora of applications in graph analytics and query-processing tasks. As our core contribution, we presented an efficient and scalable framework for processing DSR queries and also studied its formal properties. By precomputing and materializing the reachability information among vertices along the cut of a partitioned data graph, our approach is guaranteed to require at most one round of communication among the compute nodes to resolve any DSR query. Our approach exhibits a very good support for incremental vertex and edge insertions, while our current implementation resorts to just a basic support for respective deletions. Moreover, any state-of-the-art centralized reachability index may be applied to the local graph partitions to further accelerate query-processing times. Our evaluation over both real-world and synthetic graphs and in comparison to very recent iterative approaches also empirically demonstrated the viability of our approach. As a future work, we aim to explore more types of reachability problems with additional length restrictions and regular expressions over path labels as constraints.

7. REFERENCES

[1] http://giraph.apache.org/.

[2] http://www.w3.org/TR/sparql11-property-paths/.

[3] V. D. Blondel, J.-L. Guillaume, R. Lambiotte, and E. Lefebvre. Fast unfolding of communities in large networks. *Journal of Statistical Mechanics: Theory and Experiment*, 2008(10):P10008, 2008.

[4] J. Cheng, J. X. Yu, and B. Ding. Cost-Based Query Optimization for Multi Reachability Joins. In *DASFAA*, pages 18–30, 2007.

[5] E. Cohen, E. Halperin, H. Kaplan, and U. Zwick. Reachability and distance queries via 2-hop labels. In *SODA*, pages 937–946, 2002.

[6] T. H. Cormen, C. E. Leiserson, R. L. Rivest, and C. Stein. *Introduction to Algorithms*. The MIT Press, 3rd edition, 2009.

[7] C. Demetrescu and G. F. Italiano. Dynamic shortest paths and transitive closure: Algorithmic techniques and data structures. *Journal of Discrete Algorithms*, 4(3):353 - 383, 2006.

[8] O. Erling and I. Mikhailov. Virtuoso: RDF Support in a Native RDBMS. In *SWIM*, pages 501–519, 2009.

[9] W. Fan, X. Wang, and Y. Wu. Performance guarantees for distributed reachability queries. *PVLDB*, 5(11):1304–1315, 2012.

[10] W. Fan, X. Wang, and Y. Wu. Answering graph pattern queries using views. In *ICDE*, pages 184–195, 2014.

[11] T. M. Forum. MPI: A Message Passing Interface, 1993.

[12] S. Gao and K. Anyanwu. PrefixSolve: efficiently solving multi-source multi-destination path queries on RDF graphs by sharing suffix computations. In *WWW*, pages 423–434, 2013.

[13] J. E. Gonzalez, Y. Low, H. Gu, D. Bickson, and C. Guestrin. PowerGraph: Distributed Graph-Parallel Computation on Natural Graphs. In *OSDI*, pages 17–30, 2012.

[14] A. Gubichev, S. J. Bedathur, and S. Seufert. Sparqling Kleene: fast property paths in RDF-3X. In *GRADES*, pages 14:1–14:7, 2013.

[15] S. Gurajada, S. Seufert, I. Miliaraki, and M. Theobald. TriAD: a distributed shared-nothing RDF engine based on asynchronous message passing. In *SIGMOD*, pages 289–300, 2014.

[16] R. Jin, N. Ruan, Y. Xiang, and H. Wang. Path-tree: An efficient reachability indexing scheme for large directed graphs. *TODS*, 36(1):7, 2011.

[17] G. Karypis and V. Kumar. A Fast and High Quality Multilevel Scheme for Partitioning Irregular Graphs. *SIAM J. Sci. Comput.*, 20(1):359–392, 1998.

[18] A. Kyrola, G. Blelloch, and C. Guestrin. GraphChi: Large-Scale Graph Computation on Just a PC. In *OSDI*, pages 31–46, 2012.

[19] J. Łącki. Improved deterministic algorithms for decremental reachability and strongly connected components. *ACM Trans. Algorithms*, 9(3):27:1–27:15, 2013.

[20] Y. Low, J. Gonzalez, A. Kyrola, D. Bickson, C. Guestrin, and J. M. Hellerstein. GraphLab: A New Framework For Parallel Machine Learning. In *UAI*, pages 340–349, 2010.

[21] Y. Low, J. Gonzalez, A. Kyrola, D. Bickson, C. Guestrin, and J. M. Hellerstein. Distributed GraphLab: A Framework for Machine Learning in the Cloud. *PVLDB*, 5(8):716–727, 2012.

[22] G. Malewicz, M. H. Austern, A. J. C. Bik, J. C. Dehnert, I. Horn, N. Leiser, and G. Czajkowski. Pregel: a system for large-scale graph processing. In *SIGMOD*, pages 135–146, 2010.

[23] T. Milo and D. Suciu. Index structures for path expressions. In *ICDT*, pages 277–295, 1999.

[24] F. Picalausa, Y. Luo, G. H. L. Fletcher, J. Hidders, and S. Vansummeren. A structural approach to indexing triples. In *ESWC*, pages 406–421, 2012.

[25] V. Prabhakaran, M. Wu, X. Weng, F. McSherry, L. Zhou, and M. Haradasan. Managing large graphs on multi-cores with graph awareness. In *USENIX*, pages 41–52, 2012.

[26] M. Przyjaciel-Zablocki, A. Schätzle, T. Hornung, and G. Lausen. RDFPath: Path query processing on large RDF graphs with MapReduce. In *ESWC*, pages 50–64, 2011.

[27] M. Sarwat, S. Elnikety, Y. He, and M. F. Mokbel. Horton+: A distributed system for processing declarative reachability queries over partitioned graphs. *PVLDB*, 6(14):1918–1929, 2013.

[28] S. Seufert, A. Anand, S. J. Bedathur, and G. Weikum. FERRARI: flexible and efficient reachability range assignment for graph indexing. In *ICDE*, pages 1009–1020, 2013.

[29] B. Shao, H. Wang, and Y. Li. Trinity: a distributed graph engine on a memory cloud. In *SIGMOD*, pages 505–516, 2013.

[30] M. Then, M. Kaufmann, F. Chirigati, T. Hoang-Vu, K. Pham, A. Kemper, T. Neumann, and H. T. Vo. The more the merrier: Efficient multi-source graph traversal. *PVLDB*, 8(4):449–460, 2014.

[31] Y. Tian, A. Balmin, S. A. Corsten, S. Tatikonda, and J. McPherson. From "think like a vertex" to "think like a graph". *PVLDB*, 7(3):193–204, 2013.

[32] S. Trißl and U. Leser. Fast and practical indexing and querying of very large graphs. In *SIGMOD*, pages 845–856, 2007.

[33] S. J. van Schaik and O. de Moor. A memory efficient reachability data structure through bit vector compression. In *SIGMOD*, pages 913–924, 2011.

[34] R. R. Veloso, L. Cerf, W. M. Jr., and M. J. Zaki. Reachability queries in very large graphs: A fast refined online search approach. In *EDBT*, pages 511–522, 2014.

[35] R. S. Xin, J. E. Gonzalez, M. J. Franklin, and I. Stoica. GraphX: a resilient distributed graph system on Spark. In *GRADES*, 2013.

[36] H. Yildirim, V. Chaoji, and M. J. Zaki. GRAIL: Scalable Reachability Index for Large Graphs. *PVLDB*, 3(1-2):276–284, 2010.

[37] M. Zaharia, N. M. M. Chowdhury, M. Franklin, S. Shenker, and I. Stoica. Spark: Cluster Computing with Working Sets. Technical Report UCB/EECS-2010-53, UC Berkeley, 2010.

8. APPENDIX

8.1 Computing Equivalence Sets

Algorithm 3 computes the forward-equivalent sets of vertices in each graph partition G_i as follows. Given a graph partition G_i with in-boundaries I_i, the forward-equivalent sets EQ_i^f are computed as follows. First, the graph is condensed into its DAG representation G_i' by computing the strongly connected components of G_i. Next, the target vertices $S(I_i) - I_i$ are chosen as the successors of the in-boundaries I_i. We define a Boolean array rep[] (for "representative"), whose truth value for a given boundary b_m denotes whether a forward-equivalent set (i.e., an in-virtual vertex) v is formed with any other boundary b_l, for $m > l$. The rep[] array is initially set to "true" for all boundaries. A boundary b_l is equivalent to b_m, iff either b_l and b_m belong to same SCC (Lines 11-14) or have the same reachability set rset (Lines 17-19). rset[j] for the jth boundary denotes the set of vertices from $S(I_i) - I_i$ that are reachable from b_j. The computed equivalence set v starting at boundary b_l, where rep[b_l]:=true, is added to EQ_i^f at the end of each iteration (outer loop). With minor modifications from $S(I_i) - I_i$ to $P(O_i) - O_i$ (thus using predecessors instead of successors), the algorithm can similarly be adapted to compute the backward-equivalent sets EQ_i^b of out-boundaries.

Algorithm 3: Computing Forward-Equivalent Sets

Input: Subgraph G_i, In-boundaries I_i
Output: Forward-equivalent sets EQ_i^f

```
1  EQ_i^f := ∅
2  G'_i := condense(G_i)              ▷ graph condensation via SCC computation
3  S(I_i) := successors(I_i, G'_i)
4  rep[1..|I_i|] := true
5  rset[k] := ∅
6  for l = 1...|I_i| do
7      if rep[l] then
8          v := {b_l}
9          if rset[b_l] = ∅ then
10             rset := localSetReachability({b_l}, S(I_i) − I_i)
11         for m = l + 1...|I_i| do
12             if scc(b_l) = scc(b_m) then
13                 v := v ∪ {b_m}
14                 rep[m] := false
15             else
16                 rset := localSetReachability({b_m}, S(I_i) − I_i)
17                 if rset[b_l] = rset[b_m] then
18                     v := v ∪ {b_m}
19                     rep[m] := false
20         EQ_i^f := EQ_i^f ∪ v
```

8.2 Proofs of Theorems

8.2.1 *Proof of Theorem 1*

PROOF. Let $P = \{(s, u_1), \ldots, (u_m, u), (u, v), (v, v_n), \ldots, (v_1, t)\}$ denote the set of edges along a path from source s to target t. Then the following holds: edge $(u, v) \in P$, with $u \in V_i, v \in V_j$, can either be (1) a *cut edge* iff $i \neq j$, (2) a *local edge* in partition i iff $i = j$, or (3) a *non-local edge* with respect to partition k iff $i = j$ and $i \neq k$.

<u>Case A:</u> Let all edges in P be either local to partition i (1) or be a cut edge (2) among partitions i, j. Then, from Definition 6 of the compound graph $G_i^C = (V_i^C, E_i^C)$, it follows that $P \subseteq E_i^C$. That is, the reachability $s \rightsquigarrow t$ can be computed entirely locally at partition i using E_i^C.

<u>Case B:</u> Let $(u, v) \in P$ such that (u, v) is a non-local edge (3) to partition i but a local edge (1) to another partition j, with $i \neq j$. That is, $(u, v) \in E_j^C$ but $(u, v) \notin E_i^C$. From this, it follows that $\exists p, q$ such that the edges (u_{p-1}, u_p), $(v_q, v_{q-1}) \in P$ are cut edges (2), where u_p, $v_q \in V_j$ with $1 \leq p \leq m$ and $1 \leq q \leq n$. Next, we choose (u_{p-1}, u_p), $(v_q, v_{q-1}) \in P$ as the edges with the largest indices of p, q for which this property holds. This choice ensures that a path from u_p to v_q via (u, v) resides entirely in partition j. Then, vertex u_p forms an in-boundary while vertex v_p forms an out-boundary of partition j, and the edges of the sub-path $\{(u_{p-1}, u_p), \ldots, (u_m, u), (u, v), (v, v_n), \ldots, (v_q, v_{q-1})\} \subseteq P$ reside in partition j. In this case, by the construction of the boundary graph $G_i^B = (V_i^B, E_i^B)$, we added a reachability edge (u_p, v_q) to E_i^B (see Definition 4). This means, in the optimized E_i^B, we add an edge (v, ν), where $u_p \in v$ is an in-virtual vertex and $v_q \in \nu$ is an out-virtual vertex. Since $E_i^B \subseteq E_i^C$ (see Definition 6), there exists a path $\{(s, u_1), (u_1, u_2), \ldots, (u_{p-1}, v), (v, \nu), (\nu, v_{q-1}), \ldots, (v_1, t)\}$ in partition i, thus again ensuring that the reachability of $s \rightsquigarrow t$ can be computed entirely locally at partition i using E_i^C. □

8.2.2 *Proof of Theorem 2*

PROOF. The proof is simple and leverages the result of Theorem 1. Let $P = \{(s, u_1), (u_1, u_2), \ldots, (u_{p-1}, u_p), \ldots, (u_n, t)\}$ denote the set of edges along the path from source s to target t, where $s \in V_i, t \in V_j$. If $i \neq j$, then there exists an edge $(u_{p-1}, u_p) \in P$ which is a cut edge (1). That is, $u_{p-1} \in V_k$, $u_p \in V_j$ and $k \neq j$. Next, we choose the largest index p such that the subpath $\{(u_p, u_{p+1}), \ldots, (u_n, t)\}$ resides entirely at partition j. Since (u_{p-1}, u_p) is a cut edge and $u_p \in V_j$, u_p forms an in-boundary of partition j. We next choose the smallest q such that $\{(s, u_1), \ldots, (u_{q-1}, u_q)\}$ resides entirely at partition i. Note that in the optimized boundary graph, we actually use virtual vertices instead of the regular ones, which we omit here for simplicity.

Path P can be thus written as a concatenation of subpaths $P_1 = \{(s, u_1), \ldots, (u_{q-1}, u_q)$, $P_2 = (u_q, u_{q+1}) \ldots (u_{p-1}, u_p\}$, and $P_3 = \{(u_p, u_{p+1}), \ldots, (u_n, u_t)\}$. According to Theorem 1, P_1 and P_3 can be computed entirely at partition i and j, respectively. u_q and u_p thus are an out- and in-boundary of partition i and j, respectively, i.e., $u_q, u_p \in V_C$. As per the construction of the local compound graphs (see Definition 6), P_2 can be evaluated at either partition i or j. Thus, the reachability problem $s \rightsquigarrow t$ is reduced to two reachability problems: (a) $s \rightsquigarrow u_p$ at partition i and (b) $u_p \rightsquigarrow t$ at partition j. To find such a u_p, we iterate over all in-boundaries b of partition j residing at partition i. We then compute the reachability $s \rightsquigarrow b$ and communicate the reachable in-boundaries to partition j. Thus, answering $s \rightsquigarrow t$, where $s \in V_i$ and $t \in V_j$, with $i \neq j$, requires a local processing at two partitions i, j and involves only a single step of message exchange from partition i to partition j. □

8.3 SPARQL 1.1 Queries with Property Paths

A. LUBM Queries

```
@prefix rdf: <http://www.w3.org/1999/02/22-rdf-syntax-ns#>
@prefix ub: <http://www.lehigh.edu/~zhp2/2004/0401/univ-bench.owl#>
L1: SELECT * WHERE { ?x rdf:type ub:ResearchGroup .
    ?x ub:subOrganizationOf* ?y. ?y rdf:type ub:University. }
```

L2: SELECT * WHERE { ?x rdf:type ub:FullProfessor. ?x ub:headOf ?d. ?d ub:subOrganizationOf* ?y. ?y rdf:type ub:University.}

L3: SELECT * WHERE { ?r1 rdf:type ub:ResearchGroup . ?r1 ub:subOrganizationOf* ?y. ?y rdf:type ub:University . ?r2 rdf:type ub:ResearchGroup. ?r2 ub:subOrganizationOf* ?y.}

B. Freebase Queries

@prefix rdf: <http://www.w3.org/1999/02/22-rdf-syntax-ns#>
@prefix fb: <http://rdf.freebase.com/ns>

F1: SELECT * WHERE { ?p fb:people.person.place_of_birth ?city . ?city fb:location.location.containedby* ?state. ?country fb:location.location.contains ?state. }

F2: SELECT * WHERE { ?p fb:people.person.place_of_birth ?city . ?city fb:location.location.containedby* ?state. ?country fb:location.location.contains ?state. ?p fb:award.award _winner.awards_won ?prize. ?p rdf:type fb:government.us _president. }

F3: SELECT * WHERE {?p fb:award.award_winner.awards_won ?prize. ?prize rdf:type* ?z . ?z fb:award.award_honor.ceremony> ?c. ?p fb:people.person.sibling_s* ?p1. ?p1 fb:award.award_winner.awards_won> ?prize. }

8.4 Giraph Implementations of DSR Queries

8.4.1 Giraph

The following program code illustrates our implementation of DSR queries in Giraph. In superstep 0, all source vertices are first added to a newSources array. Thus, the function isSource(.) returns true if the vertex is a source. In the subsequent supersteps, newSources represents the additional sources from which the current vertex v is reachable. If newSources is not empty, then we iteratively propagate these sources to all neighbors of vertex v.

Distributed Set Reachability in Giraph

```
public void compute(Vertex v, Iterable m){
  ArrayList<Integer> newSources = new ArrayList<Integer>();
  if(getSuperStep() == 0){
    if(isSource(v))
      newSources.add(v.getId().get());
    v.getValue().clearSources()
  }else
    for(IntWritable msg : m)
      newSources.add(m.get());

  newSources.removeAll(v.getValue().getSources());
  if(newSources.size() > 0){
     v.addSources(newSources);
      for(Edge<IntWritable, NullWritable> e : v.getEdges()){
        IntWritable nb = e.getTargetVertexId();
        for(int src: newSources)
          sendMessage(nb,new IntWritable(src));  } } }
}
```

8.4.2 Giraph++

Unlike in Graph, the Giraph++ API exposes the underlying partitioning information along with each call of the compute(.) function. The code for DSR processing is similar to Giraph, except that the vertices that are local to the current source vertices are directly updated using a centralized local reachability computation via localProcess(.). After the local processing, for each vertex we again communicate its reachable list of vertices to the remote neighbors.

Distributed Set Reachability in Giraph++

```
public void compute(Partition p){
   ArrayList<Integer> q_sources = new ArrayList<Integer>();
   ArrayList<Integer> newSources = new ArrayList<Integer>();
   if(getSuperStep() == 0){
     if(isSource(v))
       sources.add(v.getId().get();
   }else{
     MessageStore<IntWritable, IntWritable> mstore
            = getCurrentMessageStore();
     for(Vertex v : p.getVertices()){
       if(mstore.hasMessagesForVertex(v.getId())){
         newSources.clear();
         for(IntWritable message :
            mstore.getVertexMessages(v.getId()))
            newSources.add(message.get());
         newSources.removeAll(v.getValue().getSources());
         if(newSources.size() > 0){
           q_sources.add(v.getId());
           v.getValue().addNewSources(newSources);
         } } }
   }
   localProcess(p,q_sources);
   for(Vertex v : p.getVertices()){
     if(v.getValue().getNewSources().size() > 0){
       for(Edge<IntWritable, NullWritable> edge
                  : v.getEdges()){
         int nb = edge.getTargetVertexId().get();
         if(!p.contains(nb)
           for(int src : v.getValue().getNewSources())
             sendMessage(nb,new IntWritable(src));
       }
       v.getValue().addSources(v.getValue().getNewSources());
       v.getValue().getNewSources().clear();}
   }
}
```

8.4.3 Giraph++wEq

The following code depicts our DSR implementation in Giraph++wEq, including our proposed equivalence-sets optimization. We first compute equivalence sets in our DSR system and prepare an adjacency graph as input to Giraph. For each vertex v in the input graph, in addition to its adjacent neighbors, we also add their equivalence sets (our in-virtual vertices) as counterparts. This graph is loaded into Giraph using a custom input reader. The below code shows the DSR computation. The implementation shares a major part of the code with the Giraph++implementation, where the only difference lies in the communication of the reachable sets of vertices in each superstep. After the local processing, we iterate over each vertex and send its reachable list of sources to only the in-virtual vertices instead of all neighbors.

Distributed Set Reachability in Giraph++wEq

```
public void compute(Partition p){
   ArrayList<Integer> q_sources = new ArrayList<Integer>();
   ArrayList<Integer> newSources = new ArrayList<Integer>();
   if(getSuperStep() == 0){
     if(isSource(v))
       sources.add(v.getId().get();
   }else{
     MessageStore<IntWritable, IntWritable> mstore
            = getCurrentMessageStore();
     for(Vertex v : p.getVertices()){
       if(mstore.hasMessagesForVertex(v.getId())){
         newSources.clear();
         for(IntWritable message :
            mstore.getVertexMessages(v.getId()))
            newSources.add(message.get());
         newSources.removeAll(v.getValue().getSources());
         if(newSources.size() > 0){
           q_sources.add(v.getId());
           v.getValue().addNewSources(newSources);
         } } }
   }
   localProcess(p,q_sources);
   for(Vertex v : p.getVertices()){
     if(v.getValue().getNewSources().size() > 0){
       for(int eq_nb : v.getEqList())
         for(int src : v.getValue().getNewSources())
        sendMessage(new IntWritable(eq_nb),new IntWritable(src));
       v.getValue().addSources(v.getValue().getNewSources());
       v.getValue().getNewSources().clear();}
   }
}
```

Fast Multi-Column Sorting in Main-Memory Column-Stores*

Wenjian Xu[§] Ziqiang Feng[§] Eric Lo[†]
[§]Department of Computing, The Hong Kong Polytechnic University
[†]Department of Computer Science and Engineering, The Chinese University of Hong Kong
[§]{cswxu, cszqfeng}@comp.polyu.edu.hk [†]ericlo@cse.cuhk.edu.hk

ABSTRACT

Sorting is a crucial operation that could be used to implement SQL operators such as GROUP BY, ORDER BY, and SQL:2003 PARTITION BY. Queries with multiple attributes in those clauses are common in real workloads. When executing queries of that kind, state-of-the-art main-memory column-stores require one round of sorting per input column. With the advent of recent fast scans and denormalization techniques, that kind of *multi-column sorting* could become a bottleneck. In this paper, we propose a new technique called "code massaging", which manipulates the bits across the columns so that the overall sorting time can be reduced by eliminating some rounds of sorting and/or by improving the degree of SIMD data level parallelism. Empirical results show that a main-memory column-store with code massaging can achieve speedup of up to 4.7X, 4.7X, 4X, and 3.2X on TPC-H, TPC-H skew, TPC-DS, and real workload, respectively.

1. INTRODUCTION

In modern main-memory column-stores like SAP HANA [13], MonetDB [8], Vectorwise [42], and Oracle Exalytics [34], queries are read-mostly, data columns are encoded [30, 29] for memory efficiency, and their performance goal is to support real-time analytic.

Sorting, which could be used to implement SQL operators such as `GROUP BY`, `ORDER BY`, and `PARTITION BY`[1], is a crucial operation in main-memory column-stores. There are a plethora of works in main-memory databases on making sorting run faster. Works including [21] and [10] pioneered the discussion of accelerating sorting on modern CPU architectures by leveraging SIMD (Single Instruction Multiple Data) instruction set (e.g., SSE 128-bits, AVX2 256-bits), whose instructions can execute one multi-operand operation per cycle (each operand is b bits, where b, the *bank size*, equals 8, 16, 32, or 64 in AVX2). Subsequent works further improved the efficiency of in-memory sorting by reducing memory access through multi-way merging [37], increasing IPC (instructions per cycle) through bitonic merge network [26], and enhancing scalability on multi-core through partitioning [3, 5, 36]. In what follows, we refer any SIMD-enabled sorting implementation as *SIMD-sort*.

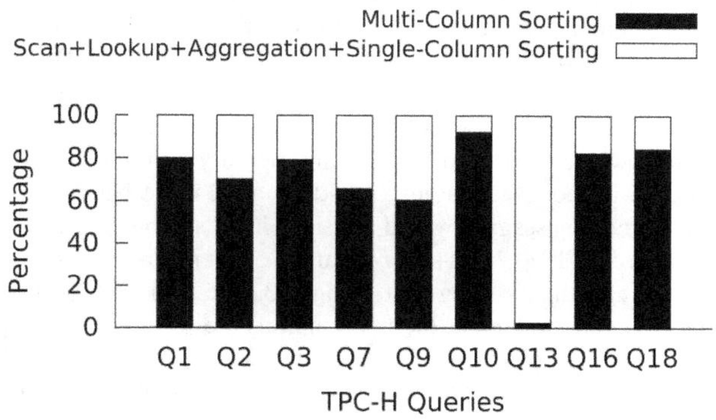

Figure 1: Time breakdown of TPC-H queries with ByteSlice [14] fast scans and WideTable [31] implemented. Queries with multiple attributes in their `GROUP BY` and/or `ORDER BY` clauses. 10GB data. Time spent on multi-column sorting is significant in general, except one exceptional case (Q13).

In state-of-the-art column-store implementations, when there are more than one column needed to be sorted, they are typically sorted *column-at-a-time*. Consider a TPC-H query with an `ORDER BY order_date, retail_price` clause. Column-stores like MonetDB [8] would first sort column `order_date` in the first round; then in the second round, it sorts column `retail_price` for each group of (tied) `order_date` values. With the recent advent of denormalization techniques that eliminate joins [31, 29] and fast scan techniques that perform filtering with early stopping [30, 14], that kind of *multi-column sorting* could take up a significant portion of the query execution time. Figure 1 shows the time breakdown of executing TPC-H queries that have multiple attributes in their `GROUP BY` and/or `ORDER BY` clauses, which can trigger multi-column sorting (experimental setting is given in Section 6). In that experiment, WideTable denormalization [31, 29] and ByteSlice [14] fast scan were used, and we used one of the most efficient SIMD-sort implementations to-date: merge-sort with sorting-network kernel [5]. We see that **the time spent on multi-column sorting is significant** — taking up 60% (Q9) to 92% (Q10) of time in general, except for Q13, which carries out a multi-column sorting after `GROUP BY` on a single attribute (so that the

*This work is partly supported by the Research Grants Council of Hong Kong (GRF 521012, 15200715), Hong Kong Polytechnic University, and Research Committee of CUHK.

[†]Work done while at Hong Kong Polytechnic University.

[1]`PARTITION BY` is part of SQL:2003 standard for the use of window functions.

SIGMOD'16, June 26-July 01, 2016, San Francisco, CA, USA

DOI: http://dx.doi.org/10.1145/2882903.2915205

query execution is actually dominated by the single-column sorting instead).

In this paper, we take the first step to study the issues of optimizing multi-column sorting in main-memory column-stores. Queries that could get benefit include all those containing `GROUP BY`, `ORDER BY`, or `PARTITION BY` clauses with multiple attributes, which are not uncommon in real workloads. In TPC-H, we found 9 out of 22 such queries. In TPC-DS benchmark, we found 71 out of 99 such queries.

Our key technique is called **code massaging**, which leverages the properties of multiple available bank sizes in SIMD instructions and forms sort keys that best utilize SIMD's data parallelism. Using the encoding scheme in [30], the TPC-H attributes `order_date` and `retail_price` can be respectively encoded as 12-bit column and 17-bit column. For the example query above, state-of-the-art main-memory column-store implementations would carry out sorting in two rounds: first sort `order_date` using SIMD-sort with 16-bit banks (i.e., $b = 16$); then sort `retail_price` using SIMD-sort with 32-bit banks (i.e., $b = 32$), as `retail_price` column is wider than 16 bits. A main-memory column-store, if equipped with code massaging, could do a lot more better. For example, code massaging would consider first "stitching" the two columns as one (12+17)-bit super-column "`order_date-retail_price`" and then sorting that using a 32-bit bank SIMD-sort. In that *code massage plan*, the two columns are sorted in one go, thereby eliminating one round of sorting. Code massaging would also allow "bit-borrowing" among columns. For example, another feasible plan is column `order_date` "borrows" one bit from column `retail_price` so that the query execution engine can first sort the (12+1)-bit `order_date` column using a 16-bit bank SIMD-sort , and then sort the (17–1)-bit `retail_price` column using another 16-bit bank SIMD-sort. While this plan still requires two rounds of sorting, a 16-bit bank SIMD-sort is used in place of a 32-bank SIMD-sort in the second round, attaining 2X data parallelism there.

To the best of our knowledge, this is the first work to pinpoint and tackle the issue of multi-column sorting, which is emerging as a time significant phase in recent main-memory column-store implementations. This paper makes four contributions around this new issue. The principal contribution is code massaging, a technique that manipulates the bits across the columns to accelerate multi-column sorting. In order to choose the most promising code massage plan, our second contribution is an *architectural-aware cost model* that quantifies the cost of different code massage plans, with various architectural-sensitive parameter values (e.g., latency of a cache miss) calibrated from controlled experiments. Our third contribution is a *round-based greedy plan search algorithm*, which efficiently explores the huge search space to identify the most promising plan. Our last contribution is the integration of code massaging into a column-store prototype and the experimental evaluation on TPC-H, TPC-H Skew, TPC-DS and real data. Empirical results report a query speedup of up to 4.7X, 4.7X, 4X, 3.2X on TPC-H, TPC-H Skew, TPC-DS, and real workload, respectively.

The remainder of this paper is organized as follows: Section 2 presents some essential background information and discusses the related work. Section 3 presents our code massaging technique. Section 4 presents an architectural-aware cost model. Section 5 presents the plan search algorithm. Section 6 presents our experimental results. Section 7 contains our concluding remarks. For easy reading, Table 3 in the Appendix summarizes the most frequently used symbols in this paper.

2. BACKGROUND AND RELATED WORK

SIMD SIMD instructions interact with S-bit SIMD registers as a *vector of banks*. A bank is a continuous section of b bits. In AVX2, $S = 256$ and b is 8, 16, 32, or 64. We adopt these values in this paper but remark that our techniques can be straightforwardly extended to other models (e.g., 512-bit AVX-512 [24] and Larrabee [38]). The choice of b, the *bank width*, is on per instruction basis. A SIMD instruction carries out the same operation on the vector of banks simultaneously. For example, the `_mm256_add_epi32()` instruction[2] performs an 8-way addition between two SIMD registers, which adds eight pairs of 32-bit integers simultaneously. Similarly, the `_mm256_add_epi16()` instruction performs 16-way addition between two SIMD registers, which adds sixteen pairs of 16-bit short integers simultaneously. The degree of such *data-level parallelism* is S/b.

Column Encoding In modern main-memory column-stores, data is often stored in an encoded form [6, 12, 13, 27]. For example, in dictionary encoding, native column values are compressed as fixed-length order-preserving *codes*. All data types including numeric and strings are encoded as unsigned integer codes. For example, strings are encoded by building a sorted dictionary of all strings in that column [7, 27]. Floating point numbers with limited precision can be scaled to integers by multiplication with a certain factor [12]. From now on, we adopt fixed-length encoding and use the terms **code** and **value** interchangeably.

Fast Scan/Lookup and Denormalization Scan and lookup are two core operations in main-memory column-stores. A scan operation scans a column and returns a result bit vector that indicates which records satisfy a filter. Once a column scan is completed, the result bit vector is converted into a list of record numbers, which is then used to look up values from other columns of interest for a query. Recent studies [25, 30, 14] discuss how to carry out scans at the speed of the processing core. Their main idea is to pack multiple codes from the same column into the same CPU word so as to leverage SIMD to carry out parallel predicate evaluation. The latest work is ByteSlice [14], which chops codes into multiple bytes, so that scans can be executed very efficiently through early stopping while lookups can still be very efficient through byte stitching.

A recent trend of main-memory column-stores is to pre-join tables upfront and materialize join results as one or more *WideTables* [31, 29]. Queries on the original database, even complex join queries, can then be handled by fast scans on WideTables. Such a denormalization approach would not incur much storage overhead because of the various effective encoding schemes enabled by columnar storage [31, 29].

Sorting Sorting is known to be both computational and memory intensive in main-memory column-stores and has attracted great attention in optimizing its performance. This line of works started with [21] and [10], which pioneered the discussion of SIMD-enabled sorting. Then, sorting had been revisited in the context of *sort merge join* [26, 37, 3, 5]. It was first shown that a merge-sort implementation based on bitonic sorting network and bitonic merge yields superior performance [26, 37]. Later, merge-sort implementations based on multi-way merge and data partitioning for NUMA architectures were introduced [3, 5]. Recently, to mitigate data skew, a merge-sort implementation with range-partitioning and sampling was proposed [36]. All these works are based on the merge-sort framework because the structure of the merge-sort is intrinsi-

[2]Technically, it is a C function supported by SIMD instructions. We use the C function names in place of the SIMD instructions for simplicity.

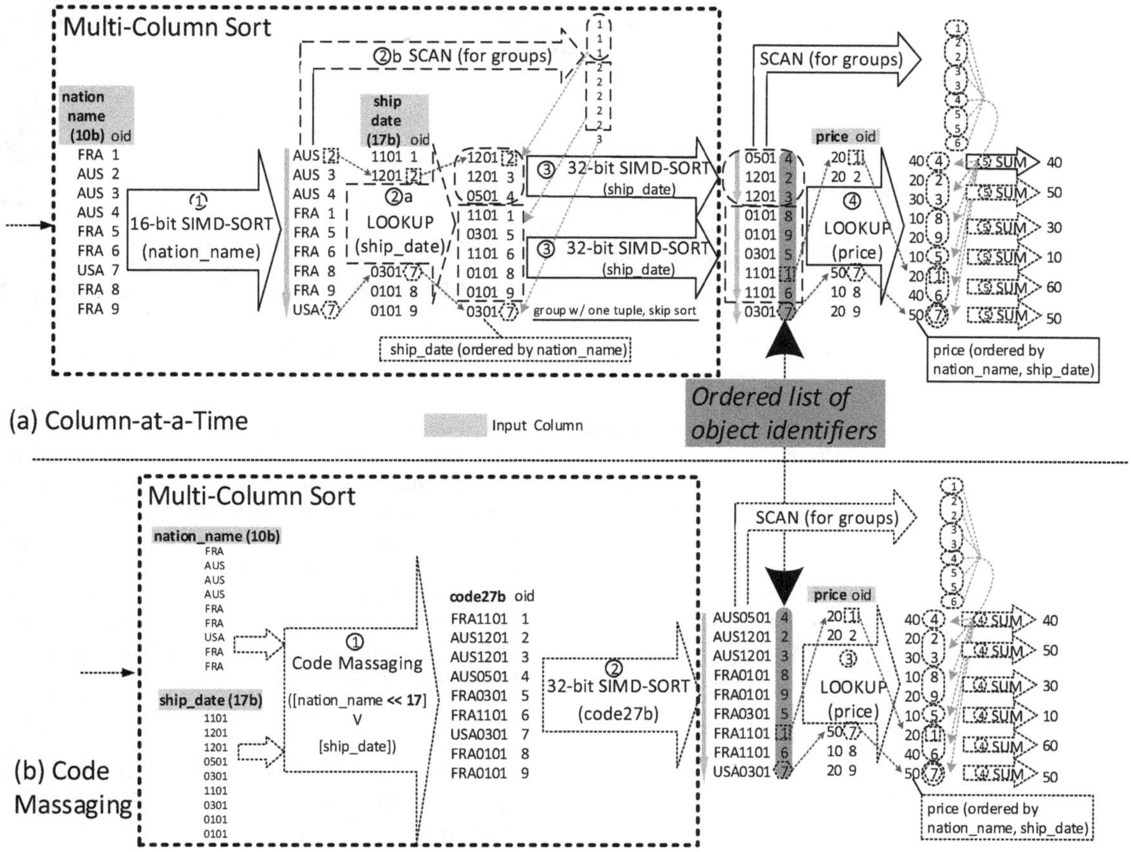

Figure 2: Multi-column sorting. Labels ①, ②, ... denote the execution sequences. Steps with the same label mean they can be executed in parallel. (a) Without code massaging (column-at-a-time) (b) With code massaging (1 round)

cally easy to be parallelized on multi-cores, compared with other comparison-based sorts. The internal sorting operation of merge-sort is usually based on *sorting network*, as sorting networks can be implemented as a series of branch-free SIMD `min/max` instructions, thereby minimizing branch mis-predictions. Non-comparison based sorting such as radix-sort had also been discussed [37, 11, 36, 22]. These works focused on exploiting SIMD to parallelize radix calculation, and using streaming load/store instructions to reduce cache pollution.

Overall, the performances of merge-sort and radix-sort are data-dependent and comparable [37, 36]. Recently, the discussion of sorting has also been extended to sorting an array of structures [22]. In [35], the discussion of sorting has been extended to the emerging MIC (many integrated core) platforms (e.g., Intel Xeon Phi).

Multi-Column Sorting State-of-the-art column-store implementations sort multiple columns column-at-a-time [39, 13, 20, 42, 34]. Figure 2a illustrates an example of that. The example illustrates the execution of the query below $Q1$, whose result is listed on the right:

```
SELECT SUM(price) //Query Q1
FROM ...
GROUP BY nation_name, ship_date
```

nation _name	ship_date	SUM (price)
AUS	0501	40
AUS	1201	50
...	...	...
USA	0301	50

In the example, the first round of sorting is carried out on column `nation_name` (Step ①). Then, the list of (rearranged) object identifiers (oid's) of the sorted column is extracted and passed to a lookup operator, which aims to rearrange the codes in the other column, `ship_date`, based on the order predefined by sorted `nation_name` (Step ②a). Based on the grouping information obtained by scanning the sorted `nation_name` (Step ②b), the second round of sorting is carried out on column `ship_date` per `nation_name` group (e.g., AUS) (Step ③). After that round of sorting, each ⟨`nation_name`, `ship_name`⟩ group (e.g., ⟨AUS,0501⟩) invokes the lookup operator to fetch the values belonging to that group from column `price` (Step ④). Finally, price values within each group are aggregated through the SUM operator (Step ⑤).

3. CODE MASSAGING

The goal of code massaging is to speed up multi-column sorting triggered by the existence of `ORDER BY`, `GROUP BY`, or `PARTITION BY` clauses in a SQL query. Its key idea is to manipulate the bits across the columns to be sorted to form new sort keys.

For correctness, we have to ensure that sorting multiple columns with code massaging would return the same ordered list of object identifiers as with the one without using code massaging (i.e., sorting m columns in m rounds). Without loss of generality, we focus on sorting in ascending order. Denote C_i as a column/attribute, w_i as the code width of C_i, and $t.C_i$ as the code/value of attribute C_i in tuple t. For an `ORDER BY` C_1, C_2, ..., C_m clause, the correct sorting order of two tuples t_1 and t_2 is defined as $t_1 \prec t_2$, where $t_1.C_k < t_2.C_k$ for some $1 \leq k \leq m$ and $t_1.C_i = t_2.C_i$ for all $i < k$.

Now, let us denote $y||z$ as the code formed by concatenating code y and code z, and $|x|$ be the width of code x. For instance, given $y = (111)_2$ and $z = (0000)_2$, $y||z = (1110000)_2$. So,

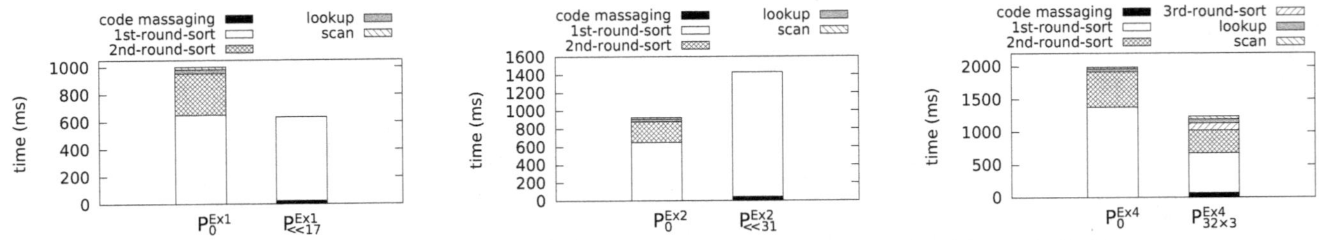

(a) [Example Ex1]
`ORDER BY` 10-bit-column, 17-bit column

(b) [Example Ex2]
`ORDER BY` 15-bit-column, 31-bit column

(c) [Example Ex4]
`ORDER BY` 48-bit-column, 48-bit column

Figure 3: Performance of Various Code Massage Plans

given two tuples $t_1 = \langle x_1, y_1 || z_1 \rangle$ and $t_2 = \langle x_2, y_2 || z_2 \rangle$, where $|x_1| = |x_2|, |y_1| = |y_2|, |z_1| = |z_2|$, we have:

LEMMA 1 (CORRECTNESS OF CODE MASSAGING).

$$\begin{aligned} & t_1 \prec t_2 \\ \Leftrightarrow & \langle x_1, y_1 || z_1 \rangle \prec \langle x_2, y_2 || z_2 \rangle \\ \Leftrightarrow & \langle x_1 || y_1, z_1 \rangle \prec \langle x_2 || y_2, z_2 \rangle \end{aligned}$$

PROOF. If $\langle x_1, y_1 || z_1 \rangle \prec \langle x_2, y_2 || z_2 \rangle$, then there are two possible relationships between x_1 and x_2: either $x_1 < x_2$ or $x_1 = x_2$.

Case 1 ($x_1 < x_2$):

$$\begin{aligned} & x_1 < x_2 \\ \Rightarrow & x_1 || y_1 < x_2 || y_2 \\ \Rightarrow & \langle x_1 || y_1, z_1 \rangle \prec \langle x_2 || y_2, z_2 \rangle \end{aligned}$$

Case 2 ($x_1 = x_2$):

Then there must be $y_1 || z_1 < y_2 || z_2$. Hence two possible relationships between y_1 and y_2: either $y_1 < y_2$ or $y_1 = y_2$.

Case 2a: ($y_1 < y_2$):

$$\begin{aligned} & x_1 = x_2, y_1 < y_2 \\ \Rightarrow & x_1 || y_1 < x_2 || y_2 \\ \Rightarrow & \langle x_1 || y_1, z_1 \rangle \prec \langle x_2 || y_2, z_2 \rangle \end{aligned}$$

Case 2b: ($y_1 = y_2$):

$$\begin{aligned} & y_1 || z_1 < y_2 || z_2, y_1 = y_2 \\ \Rightarrow & z_1 < z_2 \\ & x_1 = x_2, y_1 = y_2, z_1 < z_2 \\ \Rightarrow & x_1 || y_1 = x_2 || y_2, z_1 < z_2 \\ \Rightarrow & \langle x_1 || y_1, z_1 \rangle \prec \langle x_2 || y_2, z_2 \rangle \end{aligned}$$

The proof of the opposite direction is similar. □

Lemma 1 essentially states that for `ORDER BY` clause, the sort order remains intact even though we shift the bits across the columns.

[Example Ex1] Figure 2b shows an example based on query $Q1$. With code massaging, the two columns `nation_name` (10-bit) and `ship_date` (17-bit) are "stitched" together as one 27-bit column. Concretely, the code massaging process first left-shifts ($\ll$) column `nation_name` by 17 bits, and then carries out a bitwise-OR ($\vee$) with column `ship_date` to form the 27-bit new column. From the figure, we see that we can sort the 27-bit column using one round, and by Lemma 1 we see that the ordered list of object identifiers *is the same as* the one obtained through two rounds of sorting in Figure 2a.

Figure 3a shows the performance results for this example (experimental setting is given in Section 6). In this experiment and the rest of this section, we generated $N = 2^{24}$ tuples and a w-bit column with 2^{13} distinct values[3] uniformly distributed on a $[0, 2^w - 1]$ domain. Since the steps after sorting are the same no matter code massaging is used or not (e.g., see Step ④/③ in Figure 2a/b), we only report the running time up to the point where all sortings are done. We use the notation R_i: $w/[b]$ to denote that a b-bit-bank SIMD-sort is used to sort a w-bit column in the i-th round of sorting. So, we denote the original column-at-a-time plan, which sorts the two columns `nation_name` (10-bit) and `ship_date` (17-bit) in two rounds, as plan

$$P_0^{Ex1} = \{R_1 : 10/[16], R_2 : 17/[32]\}$$

The code massage plan, which stitches the two columns into one by left-shifting 17-bits from the right column to the left, is denoted as $P_{\ll 17}^{Ex1}$=$\{R_1$: 27/[32]$\}$.

From Figure 3a, we observe that $P_{\ll 17}^{Ex1}$ has improved the performance of such multi-column sorting by 44%. That attributes to not only the elimination of one round of sorting, but also the eliminations of one lookup operation and one scan operation (Steps ②a and ②b in Figure 2a). From Figure 3a, we also observe that the bitwise and memory operations required by code massaging (Step ① in Figure 2b) incur insignificant cost. □

Code massaging is not as simple as always stitching all input columns together. One obvious example is that we cannot stitch all input columns together when their total code width W exceeds 64 bits, the maximum bank width of AVX2. Another example is as follows.

[Example Ex2] Figure 3b shows the performance results of a multi-column sorting on a 15-bit column and a 31-bit column. We see that a reckless stitch of the two columns as a 46-bit column would result in a degraded performance. Originally, the two columns could be sorted by one 16-bit SIMD-sort and one 32-bit SIMD-sort (Plan $P_0^{Ex2} = \{R_1 : 15/[16], R_2 : 31/[32]\}$). Stitching them together (Plan $P_{\ll 31}^{Ex2} = \{R_1 : 46/[64]\}$) would require one 64-bit SIMD-sort instead. 64-bit SIMD-sort has a relatively weaker data parallelism. That outweighs the benefit of eliminating one round of sorting, explaining why P_0^{Ex2} is better than $P_{\ll 31}^{Ex2}$ for this specific instance. □

Code massaging actually involves a huge space of plan choices in addition to the original column-at-a-time plan and the simple "stitch-all" plan. In the following, we illustrate that with two more examples.

[Example Ex3] This example is a multi-column sorting on a 17-bit column and a 33-bit column. Figure 4a shows the performance of all possible massage plans for that. The plans $P_{\ll 33}^{Ex3}$ and $P_{\gg 17}^{Ex3}$ at the two extremes are referring to the same "stitch-all" plan: $P_{\ll 33}^{Ex3}$

[3] If $w < 13$, then 2^w distinct values are generated instead.

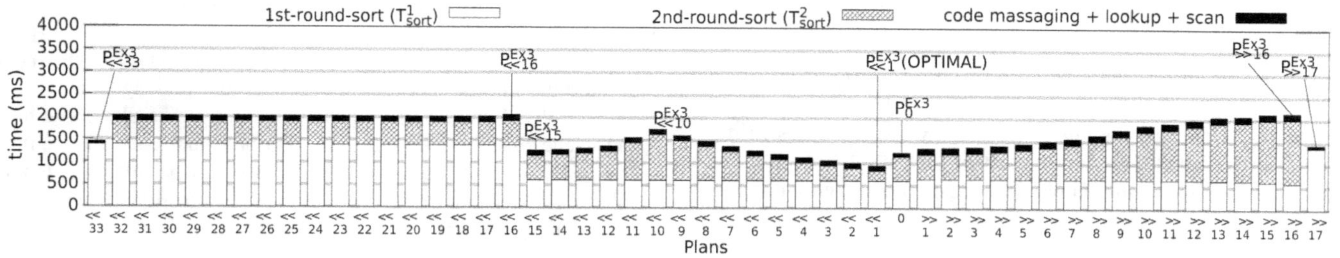

(a) Time breakdown of various code massage plans

Shifted Bits	$P^{Ex3}_{\ll 32} \sim P^{Ex3}_{\ll 16}$	$P^{Ex3}_{\ll 15}$	$P^{Ex3}_{\ll 13}$	$P^{Ex3}_{\ll 11}$	$P^{Ex3}_{\ll 10}$	$P^{Ex3}_{\ll 2}$	$P^{Ex3}_{\ll 1}$	P^{Ex3}_{0}	$P^{Ex3}_{\gg 1}$	$P^{Ex3}_{\gg 10}$	$P^{Ex3}_{\gg 16}$
num. SIMD-sort (N_{sort})	2.0e06	2.1e06	2.9e06	4.4e06	4.6e06	**31756**	**15878**	8192	7235	64	2
num. groups (N_{group})	1.45e07	1.43e07	1.31e07	0.96e07	0.67e07	**31756**	**15878**	8192	7235	64	2
avg. group size ($\overline{N}^i_{code}$)	1.15	1.17	1.27	1.73	2.47	**528**	**1056**	2048	2318	0.26e6	0.84e6

(b) Factors in first round sorting that influence the time cost of second round sorting T^2_{sort}

Figure 4: [Example Ex3] `ORDER BY` **17-bit-column, 33-bit-column**

shows the result of shifting all bits of the 33-bit column to the left and forming a single 50-bit super column while $P^{Ex3}_{\gg 17}$ shows the result of shifting all bits of the 17-bit column to the right and forming the same 50-bit super column. Both plans require only one round of 64-bit SIMD-sort. From Figure 4a, we observe that $P^{Ex3}_{\ll 33}$ and $P^{Ex3}_{\gg 17}$ are slightly inferior to the original column-at-a-time plan P^{Ex3}_{0} for the same reason that we explained in Example Ex2.

Figure 4a indeed contains observations that are more intriguing. First, we see that by left-shifting one bit from the original plan P^{Ex3}_{0}={R_1: 17/[32], R_2: 33/[64]}, the optimal plan $P^{Ex3}_{\ll 1}$={R_1: 18/[32], R_2: 32/[32]} is found. $P^{Ex3}_{\ll 1}$ is superior in terms of using 32-bit SIMD-sort in both rounds when compared with P^{Ex3}_{0}.

Second, as we further left-shift the bits from $P^{Ex3}_{\ll 1}$, we observe a time hill with plan $P^{Ex3}_{\ll 10}$={R_1: 27/[32], R_2: 23/[32]} as the peak, plan $P^{Ex3}_{\ll 15}$={R_1: 32/[32], R_2: 18/[32]} as the left tail, and the optimal plan $P^{Ex3}_{\ll 1}$ as the right tail. We explain that starting from the right tail, i.e., $P^{Ex3}_{\ll 1}$. Referring to Figure 4b, as we left-shift one bit from $P^{Ex3}_{\ll 1}$ and result in plan $P^{Ex3}_{\ll 2}$={R_1: 19/[32], R_2: 31/[32]}, that would:

(a) *increase the number of groups N_{group}* formed by the tied values in the first round from 15878 to 31756, since the width of the first column has increased by one and *more distinct values* are found in that column;

(b) *increase the number of SIMD-sort invocations N_{sort}* in the second round from 15878 to 31756, because each group formed in the first round would invoke one SIMD-sort;

(c) *decrease the number of codes for sorting N^i_{code} in each group* i in the second round from 1056 to 528, because now there are more groups.

Therefore, the time cost T^k_{sort} of the k-th round of sorting can be captured by:

$$T^k_{sort} = \sum_{i=1}^{N_{sort}} T_{sort}(N^i_{code}, b) \quad (1)$$

where $T_{sort}(N^i_{code}, b)$ is the time spent by a b-bit SIMD-sort to sort N^i_{code} codes. Assume the implementation of merge-sort with sorting-network kernel [5] is used, then:

$$T_{sort}(N^i_{code}, b) = C_{overhead} + T_{mergesort}(N^i_{code}, b) \quad (2)$$

where $C_{overhead}$ is the overhead of memory allocation and initialization of a merge-sort function call, and $T_{mergesort}(N^i_{code}, b)$ is the cost of running a SIMD-enabled merge-sort.

So, following the discussion above, $P^{Ex3}_{\ll 2}$ has a *larger* N_{sort} but a *smaller* N^i_{code} when compared with $P^{Ex3}_{\ll 1}$. That means $P^{Ex3}_{\ll 2}$ has to carry out *more SIMD-sort* in round 2 but each SIMD-sort in that round *has a smaller input size*. With the existence of $C_{overhead}$ per SIMD-sort, the increase of N_{sort} would increase the overall overhead in T^2_{sort}, and that outweighs the decrease of per-merge-sort running time caused by the decrease of N^i_{code}. That explains the uphill from $P^{Ex3}_{\ll 1}$ to the peak $P^{Ex3}_{\ll 10}$.

The downhill from the peak $P^{Ex3}_{\ll 10}$ to the left-tail $P^{Ex3}_{\ll 15}$ can be explained similarly, but in a different angle. Referring to Figure 4b, we observe a *decrease* in the number of SIMD-sort (N_{sort}) in round 2 starting from $P^{Ex3}_{\ll 11}$. That is because as we continue to shift more bits to the left, more groups are generated in the first round, and each group has fewer tuples. Eventually, some groups would contain just one tuple. Notice that *groups with one tuple do not require sorting*. So, when we proceed from $P^{Ex3}_{\ll 10}$ to $P^{Ex3}_{\ll 15}$, while N_{group} would increase, more singleton groups are generated, causing fewer SIMD-sorts are called (i.e., N_{sort} would decrease). That explains the downhill from the peak $P^{Ex3}_{\ll 10}$ to $P^{Ex3}_{\ll 15}$. In Figure 4a, T^1_{sort}, the time cost of the first round of sorting, remain steady throughout the whole hill because all plans between the left-tail $P^{Ex3}_{\ll 15}$ and right-tail $P^{Ex3}_{\ll 1}$ use the same 32-bit SIMD-sort to sort the same amount $N = 2^{24}$ of codes in the first column.

Let us move forward to observe the consequence of further left-shift one more bit from the left-tail $P^{Ex3}_{\ll 15}$ ={R_1: 32/[32], R_2: 18/[32]} of the hill to $P^{Ex3}_{\ll 16}$={R_1: 33/[64], R_2: 17/[32]}. There, we observe an increase in cost. That is because $P^{Ex3}_{\ll 16}$ has to use a 64-bit SIMD-sort in place of a 32-bit SIMD-sort to sort a 33-bit column in the first round. From $P^{Ex3}_{\ll 16}$ to $P^{Ex3}_{\ll 17}$={R_1: 34/[64], R_2: 16/[16]} we observe a minor decrease in cost. That is due to the switch of using a 16-bit SIMD-sort in round 2.[4] The relatively stable performance between $P^{Ex3}_{\ll 17}$ and $P^{Ex3}_{\ll 32}$={R_1: 59/[64], R_2:

[4]In current generation of SIMD, i.e., AVX2, we find that 16-bit SIMD-merge-sort only outperforms its 32-bit counterpart slightly. That is because some SIMD functions available for 32-/64-bit banks are not available for 8-/16-bit banks. So, they have to be simulated with more primitive instructions. That is also the reason why we do not use 8-bit bank SIMD-merge-sort in this paper.

oid	A	B
x	2	**5**
y	2	1
z	7	4

(a) Input

oid	A‖B
x	2 5
y	2 1
z	7 4

→

oid	sort(A‖B)
y	2 1
x	2 5
z	7 4

(b) Wrong

oid	A‖B^c
x	2 **2**
y	2 6
z	7 3

→

oid	sort(A‖B^c)
x	2 2
y	2 6
z	7 3

(c) Correct

Figure 5: Code massaging `ORDER BY` **with attributes in different orders: (a) input and result of** `ORDER BY A ASC, B DESC`**; (b) without complement (wrong); (c) complement before stitch (correct)**

1/[16]} is due to the consistent use of 64-bit SIMD-sort in round 1 and 16-bit SIMD-sort in round 2.

Let us wrap up this long example by explaining the increasing cost from P_0^{Ex3} to $P_{\gg 16}^{\text{Ex3}}$, which involves *right*-shifting bits from the 17-bit first column to the 33-bit second column. We observe an increasing cost trend there because of the decrease of the number of groups N_{group} and thus the increase of average group size $\overline{N}^i_{code}$. When $\overline{N}^i_{code}$ reaches a certain value, the increase in $\overline{N}^i_{code}$ manifests the cost $T_{mergesort}(\overline{N}^i_{code}, b)$, which has $\Theta(\overline{N}^i_{code} \log \overline{N}^i_{code})$ complexity, dominates $\mathcal{C}_{overhead}$. That explains the increasing trend from P_0^{Ex3} to $P_{\gg 16}^{\text{Ex3}}$. □

[Example Ex4] This last example is a multi-column sorting on two 48-bit columns, which contains another important observation. The original column-at-a-time plan P_0^{Ex4}={R_1: 48/[64], R_2: 48/[64]} requires two rounds of sorting. Figure 3c shows the performance of P_0^{Ex4} and a code massaged plan, $P_{32\times 3}^{\text{Ex4}}$={$R_1$: 32/[32], R_2: 32/[32], R_3: 32/[32]}. It shows that the time to sort two 48-bit columns can be reduced by *increasing the number of rounds*! In this case, the performance improvement is brought by the better utilization of SIMD parallelism in three rounds, compared with a waste of 64–48=16 bits in two rounds of sorting. That implies code massaging should also consider increasing the number of sorting rounds. □

We close this section by presenting four more aspects about code massaging.

First, unlike `ORDER BY`, multi-column sorting incurred by `GROUP BY` and `PARTITION BY` requires no specific sorting sequence among the columns. That is, while the result of `ORDER BY A, B` is different from the result of `ORDER BY B, A`, the results between `GROUP BY A, B` and `GROUP BY B, A` are the same. `PARTITION BY` exhibits the same property as with `GROUP BY` in this aspect. Therefore, the plan space of multi-column sorting incurred by `GROUP BY` and `PARTITION BY` could be $m!$ times larger than the plan space incurred by `ORDER BY` (where m is the number of attributes involved in the clause).

Second, it is legitimate to massage the bits across *non-adjacent* columns for `GROUP BY` and `PARTITION BY` clauses. For example, consider a query with `GROUP BY A, B, C` and a tuple $\langle a_1||a_2, b, c_1||c_2\rangle$. The end results would remain correct even though the tuple is massaged as $\langle a_1||c_1||a_2, b, c_2\rangle$. Nevertheless, we do not consider this option in this paper to avoid space explosion.

Third, code massaging needs an extra step if the attributes in an `ORDER BY` clause specify different sorting orders. Consider a query with `ORDER BY A ASC, B DESC` that ensures all tuples are sorted in ascending order according to column A but sorted in descending order according to column B for tied values. Code massaging has to carry out a complement on column B before it stitches them together. Figure 5 illustrates that with an example. The input data is listed in Figure 5a. Coincidentally, the result of `ORDER BY A ASC, B DESC` is identical to its input. Prior to stitching the two columns together, code massaging has to carry out a complement operation on column B first (Figure 5c)[5]. Otherwise, an incorrect result would be obtained (Figure 5b).

Lastly, we note that the code massaging process is very lightweight because the column access pattern during code massaging is *highly sequential* and *branchless*, allowing efficient superscalar execution and cache line pre-fetching. We also note that code massaging can easily support multi-threading — we can partition the input columns evenly and each thread massages partitions from every column independently.

4. COST MODEL

In this section, we present a cost model that estimates the execution time of an instance of multi-column sorting problem under a specific code massage plan P. The cost model takes as inputs a code massage plan P and basic statistics about the data such as the number of tuples (i.e., number of codes per column) N, the column width w_i, and the value distribution of a column (e.g., a histogram). The cost model could be used by any cost-based plan search algorithm in quest of a low-cost code massaging plan.

Cost modeling in main-memory databases is still an active topic. One popular direction is to develop cache-aware cost models (e.g., [32, 15]) that estimate the number of cache misses of a specific database operation. Cache misses are highly correlated with the total CPU cycles in database access methods because the primary action of these access methods is to retrieve values from memory [15]. Multi-column sorting, however, includes not only data access but also computational demanding sorting operations. Recent work shows that a *calibrated* cost model [16, 40] can provide good estimates of query execution time. Therefore, we provide a cache-aware cost model that captures both computational and data access costs, with values of various architectural-dependent parameters (e.g., the latency of a cache miss) calibrated based on running controlled experiments on the column-store hardware platform.

Given a code massage plan P and basic statistics about the data, the cost model aims to compute, T_{mcs}, the CPU time to execute multi-column sorting according to P. Referring to Section 3 and Figure 2, T_{mcs} is composed of four major subcosts:

(a) **Lookup** (T_{lookup}): Time spent on reordering a column based on another column's sorting order (e.g., Step ②a in Figure 2a);

(b) **Code massaging** ($T_{massage}$): Time spent on massaging the input columns to form new columns (e.g., Step ① in Figure 2b);

(c) **SIMD-sort** (T_{sort}): Time spent on sorting N codes by SIMD-sort (e.g., Step ② in Figure 2b);

(d) **Scan** (T_{scan}): Time spent on scanning a column to form groups based on the tied values (e.g., Step ②b in Figure 2a);

In the following, we elaborate on each subcost:

[Estimating T_{lookup}] T_{lookup} gives the cost of using the lookup operator to reorder a w-bit column C with N codes. This lookup process is essentially issuing N random accesses to the column. Let $size(w)$ be $2^{\lceil log_2 \lceil w/8 \rceil \rceil}$, which gives the size (in bytes) of the smallest data type that can hold a code in C, e.g., $size(15) = 2$ (`int16`) and $size(17) = 4$ (`int32`). Then, $N \cdot size(w)$ is the memory footprint of column C. Further, let M_{LLC} be the size (in bytes) of the last level cache, which is given by the hardware specification. So, we model the *cache hit ratio* as $\frac{M_{LLC}}{N \cdot size(w)}$. Let $\mathcal{C}_{cache}$ be the access latency of a data item in cache (usually in tens

[5]Example of complement: let $x.B = 5 = (101)_2$, so complement of $x.B$ is: $x.B^c = (101)_2^c = (010)_2 = 2$.

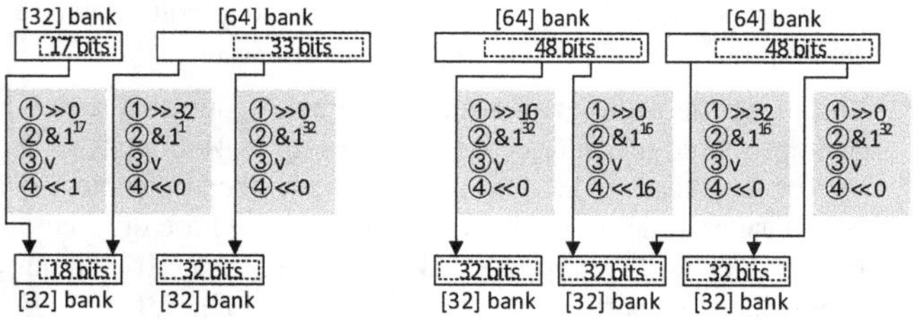

(a) $P^{\mathsf{Ex3}}_{\ll 1}$ (b) $P^{\mathsf{Ex4}}_{32\times 3}$

Figure 6: Code Massaging Implementation

of cycles) and $\mathcal{C}_{mem}$ is the access latency of a data item in memory (usually in hundreds of cycles), we can therefore model T_{lookup} as:

$$T_{lookup} = N \cdot \left(\mathcal{C}_{cache} \cdot \frac{M_{LLC}}{N \cdot size(w)} + \mathcal{C}_{mem} \cdot (1 - \frac{M_{LLC}}{N \cdot size(w)})\right) \quad (3)$$

which is essentially the number of cycles of random accessing N items with a cache hit ratio of $\frac{M_{LLC}}{N \cdot size(w)}$.

To obtain the values of $\mathcal{C}_{cache}$ and $\mathcal{C}_{mem}$, we use a linear system based calibration method similar to [40]. In this method, we calibrate the values of $\mathcal{C}_{cache}$ and $\mathcal{C}_{mem}$ simultaneously instead of micro-benchmark them individually. This approach has the advantage of calibrating parameters that are correlated. Otherwise, it would be difficult to micro-benchmark the cost of memory access without cache access.

The calibration process is as follows. We generated an array of N_{cal} w-bit integers and an array of random permuted oid's. Then we carried out the lookup procedure on the array based on the oid array and measured the execution time $T_{measured}$. After that, we plugged $T_{measured}$, N_{cal}, w along with M_{LLC} (obtained from the hardware specification) into T, N, w and M_{LLC} of Equation 3, respectively, to form an instantiation of the equation containing two unknowns: $\mathcal{C}_{cache}$ and $\mathcal{C}_{mem}$. Since there are two unknowns, we need two instantiations of the equation in order to solve them. So, we used two different N_{cal} values and generated two instantiations of Equation 3 (with two different $T_{measured}$), and then solved $\mathcal{C}_{cache}$ and $\mathcal{C}_{mem}$ as a linear system. By default, we used two N_{cal} values that lead to a cache hit ratio (i.e., $\frac{M_{LLC}}{N \cdot size(w)}$), of 0.1 and 0.9, respectively. Alternatively, we can use more than two N_{cal} values to generate more than two instantiations of Equation 3 and use statistical methods (e.g., linear regression) to obtain the best fit values.

[Estimating $T_{massage}$] $T_{massage}$ gives the cost of massaging the input columns according to a specific code massage plan P. The code massaging process, in a specific sense, consists of multiple invocations of a *four-instruction program (FIP)*: (1) shift ($\ll$ / $\gg$), (2) mask, (3) bitwise-OR ($\vee$), and (4) shift ($\ll$ / $\gg$).[6]

Figure 6 illustrates the four-instruction program (FIP) in the code massaging process for plan $P^{\mathsf{Ex3}}_{\ll 1}$={R_1: 18/[32], R_2: 32/[32]} in example Ex3 and the code massage plan $P^{\mathsf{Ex4}}_{32\times 3}$={$R_1$: 32/[32], R_2: 32/[32], R_3: 32/[32]} in example Ex4. We see that the former goes through that FIP *three* times whereas the latter goes through that FIP *four* times. Let $\mathcal{C}_{massage}$ be the number of CPU cycles of executing an FIP. Then, we can model $T_{massage}$ as:

$$T_{massage} = \mathcal{I}_{FIP} \cdot \mathcal{C}_{massage} \cdot N \quad (4)$$

where $\mathcal{I}_{FIP}$ is the number of invocations of the FIP. $\mathcal{I}_{FIP} = 3$ for $P^{\mathsf{Ex3}}_{\ll 1}$ and $\mathcal{I}_{FIP} = 4$ for $P^{\mathsf{Ex4}}_{32\times 3}$. The value of $\mathcal{I}_{FIP}$ is the number of elements in the union of two prefix sum sequences:

$$\mathcal{I}_{FIP} = |\{s_1, s_2, ...\} \cup \{s'_1, s'_2, ...\}|$$

where $\{s_1, s_2, ...\}$ is the prefix sum of the widths w_1, w_2, ... of the input columns involved, and $\{s'_1, s'_2, ...\}$ is the prefix sum of the widths w'_1, w'_2, ... of the columns after massaging. For plan $P^{\mathsf{Ex3}}_{\ll 1}$={R_1: 18/[32], R_2: 32/[32]} that sorts a 17-bit column and a 33-bit column in example Ex3:

$$\mathcal{I}_{FIP} = |\{17, 50\} \cup \{18, 50\}| = |\{17, 18, 50\}| = 3$$

To obtain the value of $\mathcal{C}_{massage}$, we carried out calibration based on generating N_{cal} random codes using the massage plans in Examples Ex1 to Ex4[7]. We measured the average time of executing code massaging according to selected code massage plan and divide that by $N_{cal} \cdot \mathcal{I}_{FIP}$ to get an estimation of $\mathcal{C}_{massage}$.

[Estimating T_{sort}] T_{sort}, or more specifically, $T_{sort}(N, b)$, is the time spent by a b-bit SIMD-sort to sort N codes, captured by Equation 2. The constant $\mathcal{C}_{overhead}$ in Equation 2 is the number of CPU cycles spent on initial function call and memory allocation, and how to calibrate this value would be discussed after we have introduced the other constants. The cost $T_{mergesort}(N, b)$ is specific to the implementation. Assume the implementation of merge-sort with sorting-network kernel [5] is used, then $T_{mergesort}(N, b)$ can be represented as:

$$\begin{aligned} &T_{mergesort}(N, b) = \\ &\quad T_{\textit{in-register}}(N,b) + T_{\textit{in-cache}}(N, b) + T_{\textit{out-of-cache}}(N, b) \end{aligned} \quad (5)$$

Specifically, the merge-sort implementation in [5] is composed of three phases:

(a) **In-register sorting** ($T_{\textit{in-register}}$): Using SIMD instructions with bank size b and S-bit registers, in-register sorting reads in $(S/b)^2$ codes each time, executes S/b sorting networks in parallel, and generates as outputs S/b sorted runs. Each sorted run contains S/b values, and each value is $b/8$ bytes. We call each sorted run as an *in-register sorted run* because it has a size of $S/8$ in bytes, which fits into a (SIMD) CPU register. So, if we denote $\mathcal{C}^b_{\textit{sort-network}}$ as the number of cycles of running in-register sort per code under bank size b, then

$$T_{\textit{in-register}}(N, b) = \mathcal{C}^b_{\textit{sort-network}} \cdot N \quad (6)$$

(b) **In-cache merging** ($T_{\textit{in-cache}}$): This phase recursively merges in-register sorted runs from the first phase to form larger sorted runs that fit into half L2 cache. The merging is carried out by bitonic merge networks, which can also be parallelized by SIMD. Let M_{L2} be the size (in bytes) of the L2 cache. Each *in-cache merged run* is therefore $0.5M_{L2}$ in bytes and holds $0.5M_{L2}/(b/8)$ values. As each in-register sorted run holds S/b values, each in-cache merged run is therefore merged from $\frac{0.5M_{L2}/(b/8)}{(S/b)}$ in-register sorted runs in $\lceil \log_2(\frac{0.5M_{L2}/(b/8)}{(S/b)}) \rceil$ passes. So, if we denote $\mathcal{C}^b_{\textit{in-cache-merge}}$ as the number of cycles spent on merging $\frac{0.5M_{L2}/(b/8)}{(S/b)}$ in-register sorted runs divided by the number of values being merged ($0.5M_{L2}/(b/8)$), then we have:

$$T_{\textit{in-cache}}(N, b) = \mathcal{C}^b_{\textit{in-cache-merge}} \cdot N \quad (7)$$

[6]For ORDER BY clause with different sorting orders, the program needs to do complement as well.

[7]For Example Ex3, the optimal plan $P^{\mathsf{Ex3}}_{\ll 1}$ is used for calibration.

(c) **Out-of-cache merging** ($T_{out\text{-}of\text{-}cache}$): This final phase merges the in-cache merged runs from the second phase recursively until a single sorted run is produced. In order to reduce cache misses, instead of a binary merge, a merge tree with a larger fanout F is used. Since the second phase will generate $\frac{Nb/8}{0.5M_{L2}}$ in-cache merged runs, merging them requires $\lceil \log_F \frac{Nb/8}{0.5M_{L2}} \rceil$ passes. So, if we denote $C^b_{out\text{-}of\text{-}cache\text{-}merge}$ as the number of cycles per tuple of merging F in-cache merged runs, we have:

$$T_{out\text{-}of\text{-}cache}(N, b) = C^b_{out\text{-}of\text{-}cache\text{-}merge} \cdot N \cdot \lceil \log_F \frac{Nb/8}{0.5M_{L2}} \rceil \quad (8)$$

Calibrating the constants We calibrate $C_{overhead}$, $C^b_{sort\text{-}network}$, $C^b_{in\text{-}cache\text{-}merge}$ and $C^b_{out\text{-}of\text{-}cache\text{-}merge}$ in a batch by treating them as four unknowns to a linear system. By putting Equations 1, 2, 5, 6, 7, and 8 together, we obtain a linear equation for T^k_{sort} containing the above four unknowns. We generated an array of N_{cal} b-bit random integers and an array of N_{cal} entries to hold the group information. After that we executed the sorting algorithm multiple times based on data with different N_{group} values (1, 2, 4, ..., N_{cal}) to obtain different T^k_{sort} values. Then we can solve the linear system with the four constants as the unknowns. By default, we set N_{cal} such that $N_{cal} \cdot b/8$ is 100X in size of the last level cache and uniformly distributed the integers to N_{group} groups. Finally, the above steps are repeated for b equals to 16, 32 and 64, respectively.

[Estimating T_{scan}] T_{scan} gives the cost of a sequential scan of a sorted column to extract the grouping information. Thus,

$$T_{scan} = C_{scan} \cdot N \quad (9)$$

where C_{scan} is the average cost of sequentially scanning N values and filling in the grouping information to another array. Since modern processors are very efficient in hiding *sequential* memory access latency through prefetching, here we do not distinguish between cache hit and cache miss as we do for estimating T_{lookup} (which incurs *random* memory access).

To obtain the value of C_{scan}, we generated an array of N_{cal} sorted integers and pre-allocated another array with N_{cal} entries to hold the grouping information. Then we executed the scan procedure to scan the array and fill the grouping information array and measured the average cycles per row. By default, we set N_{cal} such that the data size is 100X in size of the last level cache.

5. PLAN SEARCH

We begin this section with a quantification of the size of the whole code massage plan space $\mathcal{P}$. Let $W = \sum_1^m w_i$ be sum of the column widths $w_1, w_2, \ldots, w_m$ of m input columns involved. The code massage plan space $\mathcal{P}$ is equivalent to the integer compositions problem [19], i.e., enumeration of all ways of writing W as the sum of a sequence of (strictly) positive integers. Hence, $|\mathcal{P}| = 2^{W-1}$. For multi-column sorting problems incurred by `GROUP BY` and `PARTITION BY`, the sorting order among the columns does not matter. So, their plan spaces are $m!$ times larger, although m is usually a small number in real workload (e.g., the largest m in TPC-H is 7).

In the following, we present our round-based greedy plan search algorithm. By round-based we mean the algorithm searches for the optimal plan from candidate plans that are restricted to have only one round of sorting, then from candidate plans that are restricted to have only two rounds, and so on. By greedy, we mean, given a restricted plan space (e.g., when considering plans only with three rounds), the algorithm greedily assigns a certain column width to the first round, then to the second round, and so on.

Bounding the number of rounds Normally, our plan search algorithm should consider candidate plans up to W rounds of sorting for not missing the optimal plan (remember Example Ex4?). So, consider a multi-column sorting instance, whose original plan $P_0 = \{R_1 : 17/[32], R_2 : 30/[32], R_3 : 12/[16]\}$ requires three rounds of sorting, the plan $P_{1\times 59} = \{R_1 : 1/[16], R_2 : 1/[16], \ldots, R_{59} : 1/[16]\}$ that requires $W = 17 + 30 + 12 = 59$ rounds is actually viable. In the following, we show that plans with more than $\lfloor \frac{2(W-1)}{b_{min}} \rfloor + 1$ rounds (where b_{min} is minimum bank size used by the available SIMD-sort implementations) are dominated by plans with fewer than or equal to $\lfloor \frac{2(W-1)}{b_{min}} \rfloor + 1$ rounds in cost. Therefore, for the example above, our plan search algorithm would only consider plans that require at most $\lfloor \frac{2\cdot(59-1)}{16} \rfloor + 1 = 8$ rounds of sorting, when we have 16/32/64-bit SIMD-sort implementations available.[4]

LEMMA 2. *Plans with more than* $\lfloor \frac{2(W-1)}{b_{min}} \rfloor + 1$ *rounds are dominated by plans with fewer than or equal to* $\lfloor \frac{2(W-1)}{b_{min}} \rfloor + 1$ *rounds in cost.*

PROOF. Consider a candidate/original plan P with K rounds (where $K \le W$). If we stitch two columns C_i and C_j in P, we get a new plan P' with $K - 1$ rounds and a column C' of size $w' = w_i + w_j$. When (a) C_i and C_j are adjacent, i.e., $C_j = C_{i+1}$ and (b) $w' \le b_i$, where b_i is the minimum bank size that is enough to hold C_i, we can conclude that P' is better than P in cost [8]. As an example, consider plan $P_{1\times 59}$ above, whose $K = 59$. If we stitch columns C_1 and C_2 to be column C', we get a new plan P' with K–1=58 rounds. Note that as $w' = 2 \le b_1 = 16$, so P' would use the same b_1-bit SIMD-sort to sort C' but with one round fewer than $P_{1\times 59}$. Therefore, P' must be better than $P_{1\times 59}$ in cost. In other words, for each candidate plan P with K rounds, if we are able to find two columns C_i and C_j that satisfy (a) and (b), that implies all plans with K rounds can be dominated by some plans with $K - 1$ rounds. Hence, all candidate plans with K rounds can be pruned.

In contrast, consider $P_0 = \{R_1 : 17/[32], R_2 : 30/[32], R_3 : 12/[16]\}$ above, whose $K = 3$. If we stitch columns C_1 and C_2 to be column C', we get a new plan P' with $K - 1 = 2$ rounds. However, as $w' = 17 + 30 = 47 \not\le b_1 = 32$, column C' has to be sorted using a 64-bit SIMD-sort, which has a lower degree of parallelism. Likewise when we try to merge C_2 and C_3. Therefore, P' may not be better than P_0 in this case. In other words, plans with $K = 3$ rounds should be retained for the sake of not discarding any competitive plans.

Summing up the above, when considering plans with K rounds, denoted as $\mathcal{P}^K$, if we stitch any two adjacent columns in a plan $P \in \mathcal{P}^K$ (condition (a) holds) and the resulting plan P' may not be better than P, then we shall retain plans with K rounds in the search space for costing. The only reason that the resulting plan P' may not be better than P when condition (a) holds is: *condition (b) is violated.* So, that gives us:

$$\begin{cases} w_1 + w_2 & > b_1 \\ w_2 + w_3 & > b_2 \\ \ldots & \ldots \\ w_{K-1} + w_K & > b_{K-1} \end{cases}$$

$$\Longrightarrow 2\sum_{i=1}^{K} w_i - w_1 - w_K > \sum_{i=1}^{K-1} b_i$$

[8] A formal proof of this is given as Property 1 in Appendix A.

$$2W - w_1 - w_K > \sum_{i=1}^{K-1} b_i$$

$$2W - 2 \geq 2W - w_1 - w_K > \sum_{i=1}^{K-1} b_i \quad \because w_1 \geq 1, w_K \geq 1$$

$$2W - 2 \geq \sum_{i=1}^{K-1} b_i$$

$$2W - 2 > \sum_{i=1}^{K-1} b_i \geq \sum_{i=1}^{K-1} b_{min} \quad \because \forall_i b_i \geq b_{min}$$

$$2W - 2 > \sum_{i=1}^{K-1} b_{min} = (K-1) b_{min}$$

$$K < \frac{2(W-1)}{b_{min}} + 1$$

$$K \leq \lfloor \frac{2(W-1)}{b_{min}} \rfloor + 1 \qquad (10)$$

Tracing backward, when $K \leq \lfloor \frac{2(W-1)}{b_{min}} \rfloor + 1$, condition (b) is violated, then we should retain plans with that value of K for the sake of not discarding any competitive plans. In other words, our round-based plan search algorithm can skip plans with more than $\lfloor \frac{2(W-1)}{b_{min}} \rfloor + 1$ rounds. ☐

Round-based enumeration and greedy costing Our round-base enumeration strategy is to first enumerate and cost candidate plans with $k = 1$ round, then candidate plans with $k = 2$ rounds, and so forth. The last set of candidate plans to be considered are those with $\lfloor \frac{2(W-1)}{b_{min}} \rfloor + 1$ rounds.

When enumerating candidate plans that are restricted to only k round(s) of sorting, it first partitions the subspace according to various bank size combinations. Then, for each subspace under a specific bank size combination, it assigns a_j-bits to the j-th bank based on minimizing T^{j+1}_{sort}, the time cost of the $(j+1)$-th round of sorting, starting from j equals 1, till j equals $k-1$; remaining bits are assigned to k-th round.

For example, consider $P_0 = \{R_1 : 17/[32], R_2 : 30/[32], R_3 : 12/[16]\}$. Our plan enumeration strategy would first enumerate candidate plans that are restricted to only one round of sorting, then to only two rounds, and finish until it has enumerated plans with $\lfloor \frac{2 \cdot (59-1)}{16} \rfloor + 1 = 8$ rounds. Specifically, when $k = 1$, only one valid bank size combination is available — the use of one 64-bit bank because $64 > W = 59 > 32$. Therefore, candidate plans are in the form of $\mathcal{P}^1 = \{R_1 : a_j/[64]\}$ and then the goal is to cost all valid plans in $\mathcal{P}^1$. In this example, the only valid plan is $\{R_1 : 59/[64]\}$, i.e., $a_j = 59$, so this plan would be costed. Next, our plan enumeration strategy would consider $k = 2$, i.e., plans with only two rounds of sortings. When $k = 2$, valid candidate plans $\mathcal{P}^2$ are in the form of:

$\{R_1 : a_1/[16], R_2 : a_2/[64]\}$ $\{R_1 : a_1/[32], R_2 : a_2/[32]\}$
$\{R_1 : a_1/[32], R_2 : a_2/[64]\}$

Note that candidate plans in the form of $\{R_1 : a_1/[16], R_2 : a_2/[16]\}$, $\{R_1 : a_1/[16], R_2 : a_2/[32]\}$, $\{R_1 : a_1/[32], R_2 : a_2/[16]\}$ are *invalid* because the two banks are insufficient to hold $W = 59$ bits. Candidate plans in the form of $\{R_1 : a_1/[64], R_2 : a_2/[16]\}$, $\{R_1 : a_1/[64], R_2 : a_2/[32]\}$, $\{R_1 : a_1/[64], R_2 : a_2/[64]\}$ are *pruned* for the same reason given by Property 1 of Lemma 2.

Given a valid bank size combination, our plan enumeration strategy would then further trim the search plan by considering only plans that are in compliance with the input instances. For example, consider plans in the form of $\{R_1 : a_1/[16], R_2 : a_2/[64]\}$, the plan $\{R_1 : 1/[16], R_2 : 63/[64]\}$ would not be enumerated because the two columns would be wider than $W = 59$ bits. So, for this example, the subspace consists of plans instantiated with $(a_1 = 1, a_2 = 58), (a_1 = 2, a_2 = 57), \ldots, (a_1 = 16, a_2 = 43)$. These 16 plans would be costed.

When $k \geq 3$, each subspace formed by a valid bank size combination alone has size $O(\binom{W-1}{k-1})$. To avoid plan explosion, we thus enumerate only the subspace with a chosen a_j value that gives the $(j+1)$-th round the lowest sorting cost T^{j+1}_{sort}.

Consider a specific subspace $\{R_1 : a_1/[16], R_2 : a_2/[16], R_3 : a_3/[16], R_4 : a_4/[16]\}$ when $k = 4$. The value of a_1, the number of bits to assigned to the $(j = 1)$-th bank, is determined based on minimizing T^2_{sort}, the time spent on the $(j+1)$-th round of sorting. Recall from Equation 1 that different a_1 values would lead to different N_{sort} and N^i_{code} values. So, among 16 different values for a_1 (from 1, 2, ..., 16), the one that gives the lowest T^2_{sort} would be greedily chosen as the value of a_1.

Assuming $a_1 = 5$ gives the lowest T^2_{sort} , the enumeration would proceed to determine the value of a_2 recursively. Specifically, with $a_1 = 5$, the enumeration would focus on plans in the form of $\{R_1 : 5/[16], R_2 : a_2/[16], R_3 : a_3/[16], R_4 : a_4/[16]\}$ and choose a value for a_2 that minimizes T^3_{sort}, so on and so forth.

Finally, among plans that have been enumerated and costed, the one that minimizes T_{mcs} is chosen and returned.

Pseudocode and time-bound optimization Algorithm 1 depicts the pseudocode of the plan search algorithm. The pseudocode is self-explanatory and mainly summarizes what we have discussed

Algorithm 1 Plan Search Algorithm

Input: original column-at-a-time plan P_0
Input: cost model $T(\cdot)$
Input: input statistics (number of rows, etc.)
Input: time threshold ρ
Output: P^*: plan with the lowest cost

1: $W = \sum_i P_0.w_i$ ▷ Total num of bits
2: $P^* = P_0$ ▷ Initialize global optimal
3: Start stopwatch Ω
4: **for** $k = 1 \ldots \lfloor \frac{2(W-1)}{b_{min}} \rfloor + 1$ **do**
5:   **for** each valid bank size combination $(b_1, \ldots, b_k) \in \mathcal{B}^k$ **do**
6:     **if** $\Omega > \rho \cdot T_{mcs}(P^*)$ **then**
7:       **return** P^* ▷ Time's up
8:     $\hat{P} = \emptyset$ ▷ Initialize local optimal
9:     **for** $i = 1 \ldots k-1$ **do**
10:       **for** each possible a bits assigned to R_i **do**
11:         Estimate T^{i+1}_{sort} given $\hat{P} \cup \{R_i : a/[b_i]\}$
12:       **end for**
13:       $\hat{a} = \text{argmin}_a T^{i+1}_{sort}$ given $\hat{P} \cup \{R_i : a/[b_i]\}$
14:       $\hat{P} = \hat{P} \cup \{R_i : \hat{a}/[b_i]\}$ ▷ Greedy construction
15:     **end for**
16:     Assign the remaining bits to R_k
17:     **if** $T_{mcs}(\hat{P}) < T_{mcs}(P^*)$ **then**
18:       $P^* = \hat{P}$ ▷ Update global optimal
19:   **end for**
20: **end for**
21: **if** handling `GROUP BY` or `PARTITION BY` **then**
22:   Generate next permutation of P_0 then repeat Lines 4 – 20
23: **return** P^*

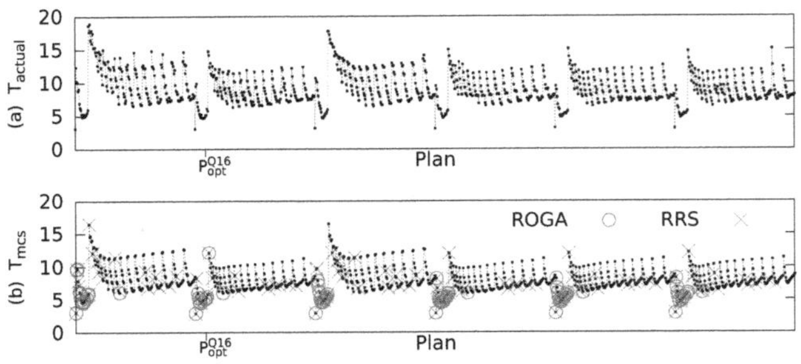

Figure 7: Q16 in TPC-H: (a) perfect cost model $\mathcal{A}_{16}$ based on exhaustively enumerating and executing all feasible plans; (b) our cost model. Both ROGA and RRS find the actual optimal plan P^{Q16}_{opt}.

Table 1: Cost Model and Plan Quality

Measure	TPC-H		TPC-H Skew		TPC-DS		Real Data	
	ROGA	RRS	ROGA	RRS	ROGA	RRS	ROGA	RRS
(a) $\overline{rank}$	4.8	110.8	5.2	72.7	6	47	8	43.2
(b) Best Rank	1	1	1	1	1	1	1	1
(c) Worst Rank	48	1206	58	576	53	223	36	169
Cost Model MRE	0.42		0.57		0.36		0.4	

above, so we do not give it a full walkthrough here. The only issue worth noticing is that we introduce a time threshold ρ (line 6) to the whole optimization process. One reason is that multi-column sorting, if accelerated by code massaging, could be executed *really* fast. Another reason is that the optimization would take a longer time when the total code width W is really very large. Therefore, we have to ensure that the searching process itself would not be a bottleneck. So, the algorithm starts a stopwatch at the beginning of the optimization process, and the algorithm terminates once the elapsed time Ω has exceeded a percentage ρ of the cost of the best plan so far. Nevertheless, since our algorithm is round-based (incrementing k one-by-one) and the optimal plans are usually those with small k values, such early stopping never discards any optimal plans in our experiments.

6. EXPERIMENTAL EVALUATION

The techniques used and proposed in this paper can be integrated into any main-memory column-store. The implementation can be done by (i) modifying the *storage manager* to support ByteSlice data layout [14]; (ii) adding four physical operators into the *query execution engine*: `ByteSlice-Scan` and `ByteSlice-Lookup` that respectively execute fast scans and lookups on ByteSlice data as proposed in [14]; `SIMD-Sort` that carries out (single-column) SIMD sorting as proposed in [5] with multi-threading support; and `Code-Massage` that carries out code massaging as depicted in Figure 6; (iii) modifying the *query optimizer* to include our cost model (Section 4), our plan search algorithm (Section 5), and WideTable query rewriting [31]. We note that changes to these components can be done in any typical relational column-stores. In this paper, we present results based on our own column-store prototype. Appendix B presents a reference implementation based on open-source MonetDB.

We run our experiments on two hardware platforms. The first is a server with a 2.60GHz Intel Xeon E5-2660 v3 10-core processor, and 32GB DDR3 memory. Each core has 32KB L1i cache, 32KB L1d cache and 256KB L2 unified cache. All cores share a 25MB L3 cache. The second is a PC with a 3.40GHz Intel i7-4770 quad-core processor, and 16GB DDR3 memory. Each core has 32KB L1i cache, 32KB L1d cache and 256KB L2 unified cache. All cores share an 8MB L3 cache. Both CPUs are based on Haswell microarchitecture which supports AVX2 instruction set. Due to space limit, we mainly present Xeon experimental results and but include i7 results when necessary.

All implementations are done in C++ and compiled using g++ 4.9 with optimization flag -O3. We use Intel Performance Counter Monitor [23] to collect the performance profiles. All experiments are run in a single process with a single thread by default. We discuss multi-thread experiments in Section 6.4.

We evaluate our techniques based on TPC-H, TPC-H skew [9] (skew factor $zipf = 1$), TPC-DS, and real data. There are 9 out of 22 TPC-H queries and 71 out of 99 TPC-DS queries require multi-column sorting. As TPC-H queries do not have `PARTITION BY` clauses, we complement that by selecting TPC-DS queries that include `PARTITION BY` clauses. Among 12 eligible TPC-DS queries, 8 of them include moving window, which is not yet supported by our prototype. So, we can only include 4 TPC-DS queries in the experiments. A scale factor of one is used by default. The real data is the Airline Origin and Destination Survey dataset released by Bureau of Transportation Statistics in US. The dataset is 4G in size and is publicly available at [1]. Table 4 and Table 5 in the Appendix list the table schema and the five queries that require multi-column sorting extracted from a real application on top of that dataset.

6.1 Quality of Plans

The effectiveness of code massaging depends on (i) the accuracy of the cost model and (ii) the quality of the plan search algorithm.

Recent works that focus on query latency prediction [2, 40] employ mean relative error (MRE) to measure *the accuracy of the cost model*. In this paper, we also report the MRE of our cost model for a query workload $\mathcal{Q}$. The last row of Table 1 shows that our cost model has MRE between 0.36 and 0.57 for all workloads, which is good enough even in the context of latency prediction [28, 40].

Define $P^{Q_i}_{opt}$ as the optimal plan for a query Q_i returned by a plan search algorithm based on our cost model. We report *the quality of a plan search algorithm for a workload* $\mathcal{Q}$ as

$$\overline{rank} = \frac{1}{|\mathcal{Q}|}\sum_{i=1}^{|\mathcal{Q}|} rank(P^{Q_i}_{opt}, \mathcal{A}_i)$$

where (i) $\mathcal{A}_i$ is the perfect cost model based on exhaustively enumerating all feasible plans for Q_i and measuring their actual running times (yes, it took us weeks to obtain $\mathcal{A}_i$'s); and (ii) $rank(P^{Q_i}_{opt}, \mathcal{A}_i)$ is the rank of $P^{Q_i}_{opt}$ with respect to $\mathcal{A}_i$. For example, if the plan $P^{Q_i}_{opt}$ chosen by a plan search algorithm is the second best plan based on $\mathcal{A}_i$, then $rank(P^{Q_i}_{opt}, \mathcal{A}_i) = 2$. In other words, if a plan search algorithm is always able to find the actual optimal plan for a given workload $\mathcal{Q}$ based on our cost model, then $\overline{rank} = 1$. So, while MRE focuses on the difference between the actual execution cost of a multi-column sorting instance T_{actual} and its estimated cost T_{mcs}, the metric $\overline{rank}$ focuses on the *reliability of the cost model and the plan search algorithm.*

Figure 7 shows an example of how $\overline{rank}$ complements MRE. Figure 7a plots the actual execution costs T_{actual} of all feasible plans for TPC-H query Q16, which has 3 attributes in its `GROUP BY` clause. Figure 7b plots the estimated costs T_{mcs} of all feasible plans based on our cost model. If we simply look at the MRE, our cost model reports an MRE of 0.42 for TPC-H workload (Table 1). However, we can see that our cost model indeed captures the

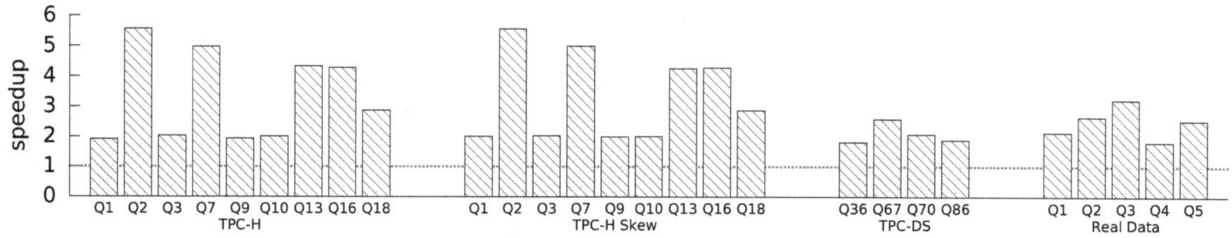

Figure 8: Speedup of Multi-column Sorting.

Table 2: Percentage of Time Used by ROGA in Multi-column Sorting

Workload	TPC-H									TPC-H Skew									TPC-DS				Real Data				
	Q1	Q2	Q3	Q7	Q9	Q10	Q13	Q16	Q18	Q1	Q2	Q3	Q7	Q9	Q10	Q13	Q16	Q18	Q36	Q67	Q70	Q86	Q1	Q2	Q3	Q4	Q5
%	0.002	0.09	0.07	0.04	0.06	0.1	0.07	0.01	0.1	0.004	0.08	0.08	0.05	0.05	0.1	0.06	0.02	0.1	0.09	0.1	0.05	0.01	0.08	0.02	0.01	0.09	0.07

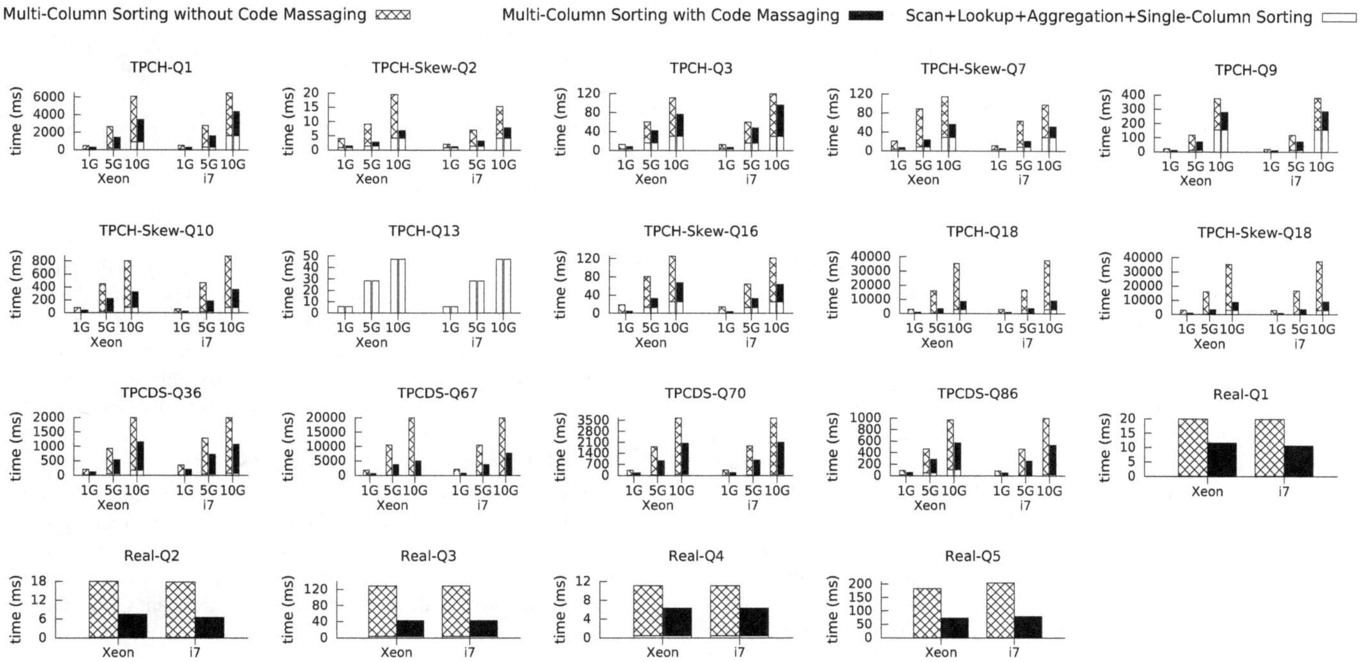

Figure 9: Query Execution Time (1G, 5G, and 10G data)

actual behavior very well. Figure 7b also shows all the plans (in circles ◯) enumerated by our round-based greedy algorithm (ROGA for short). For comparison, Figure 7b also shows all the plans (in crosses ×) enumerated by a recursive random search (RRS) algorithm [41] that searches the plan space based on our cost model. RRS is a powerful technique developed to solve black-box optimization problems. It first samples the subspace randomly to identify promising regions that contain the optimal setting with high probability. It then samples recursively in these regions which either move or shrink gradually to local-optimal settings based on the samples collected. RRS then restarts random sampling to find a more promising region to repeat the recursive search. RRS has been adopted as a plan search algorithm in a number of recent works (e.g., [17, 18]). For TPC-H query Q16, our cost model is actually reliable enough to allow both our plan search algorithm ROGA and RRS to find the actual optimal plan, i.e., $rank(P_{opt}^{Q_{16}}, \mathcal{A}_{16}) = 1$ for both ROGA and RRS, despite an MRE of 0.42 for the whole query workload is reported. In the experiments, the default time threshold ρ for ROGA is 0.1%, meaning ROGA would not spend more than 0.1% of the optimal plan (estimated) execution time to find the plan. For fairness, we stop RRS when ROGA stops.

Table 1 also reports the quality of the plan search algorithms in terms of rank. We see that ROGA consistently returns higher quality plans than RRS. For example, the $\overline{rank}$ of ROGA is 4.8 on TPC-H data (see row (a)), meaning the 5-th best actual plan is found for all involved TPC-H queries on average. In contrast, the $\overline{rank}$ of RRS is only 110.8 on TPC-H data. We notice that both ROGA and RRS can find out the actual optimal plan for some queries in the workloads (see row (b)). Worst cases happen when working on TPC-H skew data (see row (c)). Nevertheless, ROGA can find out the 58-th best actual plan. In contrast, RRS can only find the 576-th best actual plan in the same experiment.

6.2 Multi-Column Sorting Speedup

Figure 8 shows the speedup of multi-column sorting time by using code massaging for eligible TPC-H, TPC-DS, and real queries.

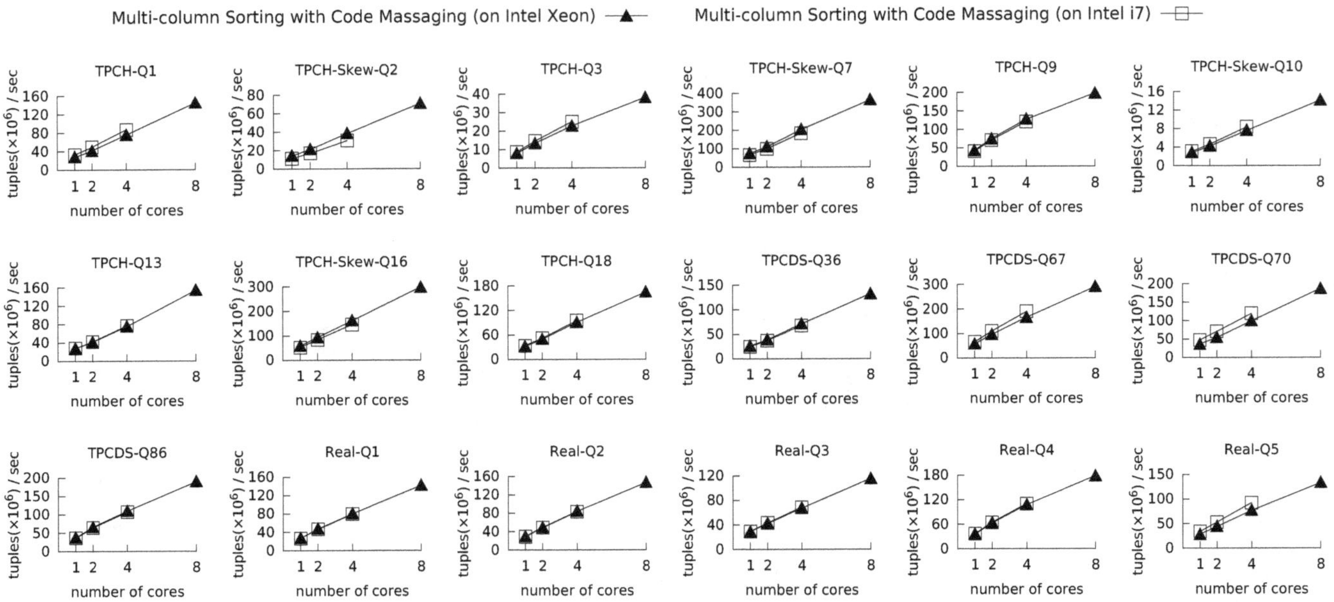

Figure 10: Throughput: Varying Number of Cores.

When code massaging is disabled, multi-column sorting is carried out using the column-at-a-time plan. When code massaging is enabled, multi-column sorting is carried out using the best plan among the column-at-a-time plan and a variety of enumerated code massage plans, returned by ROGA. From Figure 8, we observe that multi-column sorting with code massaging yields at least 1.8X speedup (real query Q4) and up to 5.5X speedup (TPC-H Q2). We also observe that the time used by ROGA to find a good code massage plan is negligible (see Table 2). Indeed, under $\rho = 0.1\%$, 22 out of all 27 queries (9 TPC-H queries on uniform and skewed data + 4 TPC-DS queries + 5 real queries) completed the whole plan search process before the deadline. In Appendix C, we present experiments of varying ρ values on different workloads and hardware platforms. We see that $\rho = 0.1\%$ is a sufficiently good threshold in general because it gives ROGA (usually more than) enough time to find a very high quality plan, without making itself as a bottleneck. In general, we recommend $\rho = 0.1\%$ based on our empirical results above. Finding ρ automatically is feasible and we discuss that in Appendix C.

6.3 Overall Query Speedup

Figure 9 shows the execution times of TPC-H, TPC-DS, and real queries on both Xeon and i7 CPUs. TPC-H and TPC-DS datasets have three scale factors 1, 5 and 10. In TPC-H, 9 queries Q1, Q2, Q3, Q7, Q9, Q10, Q13, Q16, Q18 require multi-column sorting. However, for space reasons, we only selectively present the results of Q1, Q3, Q9, Q13, Q18 on TPC-H *dbgen* data, Q2, Q7, Q10, Q16, Q18 on TPC-H skewed data, all 4 eligible queries on TPC-DS data, and all 5 eligible queries on real data.

From the experimental results, we observe that query execution with code massaging enables a query speedup of up to 4.7X (Q18; 5G; i7) on TPC-H, 4.7X (Q18; 10G; i7) on TPC-H skew, 4X (Q67; 10G; Xeon) on TPC-DS, and 3.2X (Q3; i7) on real data. TPC-H query Q13 is an exception. TPC-H Q13 has a `GROUP BY` clause on a single attribute `C_COUNT` and an `ORDER BY` clause on two attributes `CUSTDIST` and `C_COUNT`. During evaluation, the `GROUP BY` clause is first evaluated. So, the `ORDER BY` clause, which requires a multi-column sorting, is actually working on each individual group. In this case, the time percentage spent by multi-column sorting is actually insignificant (see Figure 1). Therefore, the 4.2X speedup brought by code massaging (see Figure 8 TPCH-Q13) is insignificant with respect to the whole query execution. Despite that, we observe from Figure 9 that code massaging consistently yields promising query speedup on data in different scales.

6.4 Varying Number of Cores

Figure 10 shows the throughput (in terms of the number of million tuples per second) of selected queries when code massaging is enabled with different number of threads. Each thread is pinned to a distinct physical core in the processor. Linear core/thread scalability is observed across all workloads and two different CPU models.

7. CONCLUSION

Recently, there is a resurgence of interest in main-memory analytic databases because of the large RAM capacity of modern servers (e.g., Intel Xeon E7 v2 servers can support 6TB of RAM) and the increasing demand for real-time analytic platforms. With the advent of recent fast scans and denormalization techniques, we observe that multi-column sorting would become a bottleneck for queries possessing multiple attributes in their `GROUP BY`, `ORDER BY`, or `PARTITION BY` clauses. Queries of that kind are not uncommon in real workloads. This paper therefore provides the first solution, namely, code massaging, to this emerging problem. Code massaging reduces the time of multi-column sorting by manipulating the bits across input columns so that the overall sorting time can be reduced through fewer sorting rounds and/or higher degree of SIMD data parallelism. Experiments on TPC and real workloads show that a main-memory column-store with code massaging can achieve up to 4.7X speedup in query execution. Our future work is to include radix-sort [11] into our study. The performance of in-memory radix-sort depends on the size (number of bits) of the radix, which is a parameter. Code massaging would allow a careful choice of the radix size when radix-sorting multiple columns, thereby improving the performance of multi-column sorting with a different flavor.

8. REFERENCES

[1] Airline Origin and Destination Survey Batabase. http://www.transtats.bts.gov/.

[2] M. Akdere, U. Çetintemel, M. Riondato, E. Upfal, and S. B. Zdonik. Learning-based query performance modeling and prediction. In *ICDE*, 2012.

[3] M.-C. Albutiu, A. Kemper, and T. Neumann. Massively parallel sort-merge joins in main memory multi-core database systems. *PVLDB*, 2012.

[4] C. Balkesen, G. Alonso, J. Teubner, and M. T. Özsu. Parallel Joins on Multi-Core. http://www.systems.ethz.ch/projects/paralleljoins.

[5] C. Balkesen, G. Alonso, J. Teubner, and M. T. Özsu. Multi-core, main-memory joins: Sort vs. hash revisited. *Proceedings of the VLDB Endowment*, 2014.

[6] R. Barber, P. Bendel, M. Czech, O. Draese, F. Ho, N. Hrle, S. Idreos, M.-S. Kim, O. Koeth, J.-G. Lee, et al. Business analytics in (a) blink. *IEEE Data Eng. Bull.*, 2012.

[7] C. Binnig, S. Hildenbrand, and F. Färber. Dictionary-based order-preserving string compression for main memory column stores. In *SIGMOD*, 2009.

[8] P. A. Boncz, M. Zukowski, and N. Nes. MonetDB/X100: Hyper-Pipelining Query Execution. In *CIDR*, 2005.

[9] S. Chaudhuri and V. Narasayya. Program for TPC-D data generation with skew, 2012.

[10] J. Chhugani, A. D. Nguyen, V. W. Lee, W. Macy, M. Hagog, Y.-K. Chen, A. Baransi, S. Kumar, and P. Dubey. Efficient implementation of sorting on multi-core SIMD CPU architecture. *PVLDB*, 2008.

[11] M. Cho, D. Brand, R. Bordawekar, U. Finkler, V. Kulandaisamy, and R. Puri. PARADIS: an efficient parallel algorithm for in-place radix sort. *PVLDB*, 2015.

[12] W. Fang, B. He, and Q. Luo. Database compression on graphics processors. *PVLDB*, 2010.

[13] F. Färber, N. May, W. Lehner, P. Große, I. Müller, H. Rauhe, and J. Dees. The SAP HANA Database–An Architecture Overview. *IEEE Data Eng. Bull.*, 2012.

[14] Z. Feng, E. Lo, B. Kao, and W. Xu. ByteSlice: Pushing the envelop of main memory data processing with a new storage layout. In *SIGMOD*, 2015.

[15] M. Grund, J. Krüger, H. Plattner, A. Zeier, P. Cudre-Mauroux, and S. Madden. HYRISE: a main memory hybrid storage engine. *PVLDB*, 2010.

[16] B. He, M. Lu, K. Yang, R. Fang, N. K. Govindaraju, Q. Luo, and P. V. Sander. Relational query coprocessing on graphics processors. *ACM Trans. Database Syst. (TODS)*, 2009.

[17] H. Herodotou and S. Babu. Profiling, what-if analysis, and cost-based optimization of mapreduce programs. *PVLDB*, 2011.

[18] H. Herodotou, F. Dong, and S. Babu. No one (cluster) size fits all: automatic cluster sizing for data-intensive analytics. In *ACM Symposium on Cloud Computing*, 2011.

[19] S. Heubach and T. Mansour. *Combinatorics of compositions and words*. CRC Press, 2009.

[20] S. Idreos, F. Groffen, N. Nes, S. Manegold, K. S. Mullender, and M. Kersten. MonetDB: Two decades of research in column-oriented database architectures. *IEEE Data Eng. Bull.*, 2012.

[21] H. Inoue, T. Moriyama, H. Komatsu, and T. Nakatani. AA-Sort: A new parallel sorting algorithm for multi-core SIMD processors. In *PACT*, 2007.

[22] H. Inoue and K. Taura. SIMD- and cache-friendly algorithm for sorting an array of structures. *Proceedings of the VLDB Endowment*, 2015.

[23] Intel. Intel Performance Counter Monitor. https://software.intel.com/en-us/articles/intel-performance-counter-monitor/.

[24] Intel. Intel architecture instruction set extentions programming reference, 2013.

[25] R. Johnson, V. Raman, R. Sidle, and G. Swart. Row-wise parallel predicate evaluation. *PVLDB*, 2008.

[26] C. Kim, T. Kaldewey, V. W. Lee, E. Sedlar, A. D. Nguyen, N. Satish, J. Chhugani, A. Di Blas, and P. Dubey. Sort vs. hash revisited: Fast join implementation on modern multi-core CPUs. *PVLDB*, 2009.

[27] J. Krueger, C. Kim, M. Grund, N. Satish, D. Schwalb, J. Chhugani, H. Plattner, P. Dubey, and A. Zeier. Fast updates on read-optimized databases using multi-core CPUs. *PVLDB*, 2011.

[28] J. Li, R. V. Nehme, and J. Naughton. Gslpi: A cost-based query progress indicator. In *Data Engineering (ICDE), 2012 IEEE 28th International Conference on*, 2012.

[29] Y. Li, C. Chasseur, and J. M. Patel. A padded encoding scheme to accelerate scans by leveraging skew. In *SIGMOD*, 2015.

[30] Y. Li and J. M. Patel. Bitweaving: Fast scans for main memory data processing. In *SIGMOD*, 2013.

[31] Y. Li and J. M. Patel. WideTable: An accelerator for analytical data processing. *PVLDB*, 2014.

[32] S. Manegold, P. Boncz, and M. Kersten. Optimizing main-memory join on modern hardware. *Knowledge and Data Engineering, IEEE Transactions on (TKDE)*, 2002.

[33] S. Manegold, M. L. Kersten, and P. Boncz. Database architecture evolution: mammals flourished long before dinosaurs became extinct. *PVLDB*, 2009.

[34] Oracle Exalytics In-memory Machine. http://www.oracle.com/us/solutions/ent-performance-bi/business-intelligence/exalytics-bi-machine/overview/index.html.

[35] O. Polychroniou, A. Raghavan, and K. A. Ross. Rethinking SIMD vectorization for in-memory databases. In *SIGMOD*, SIGMOD, 2015.

[36] O. Polychroniou and K. A. Ross. A comprehensive study of main-memory partitioning and its application to large-scale comparison-and radix-sort. In *SIGMOD*, 2014.

[37] N. Satish, C. Kim, J. Chhugani, A. D. Nguyen, V. W. Lee, D. Kim, and P. Dubey. Fast sort on CPUs and GPUs: a case for bandwidth oblivious simd sort. In *SIGMOD*, 2010.

[38] L. Seiler, D. Carmean, E. Sprangle, T. Forsyth, M. Abrash, P. Dubey, S. Junkins, A. Lake, J. Sugerman, R. Cavin, R. Espasa, E. Grochowski, T. Juan, and P. Hanrahan. Larrabee: A many-core x86 architecture for visual computing. In *ACM SIGGRAPH*, 2008.

[39] M. Stonebraker, D. J. Abadi, A. Batkin, X. Chen, M. Cherniack, M. Ferreira, E. Lau, A. Lin, S. Madden, E. O'Neil, et al. C-store: a column-oriented DBMS. In *PVLDB*, 2005.

[40] W. Wu, Y. Chi, S. Zhu, J. Tatemura, H. Hacigumus, and J. F. Naughton. Predicting query execution time: Are optimizer cost models really unusable? In *ICDE*, 2013.

[41] T. Ye and S. Kalyanaraman. A recursive random search algorithm for large-scale network parameter configuration. *ACM SIGMETRICS*, 2003.

[42] M. Zukowski, M. van de Wiel, and P. Boncz. Vectorwise: A vectorized analytical DBMS. In *ICDE*, 2012.

APPENDIX

A. STITCHING COLUMNS C_K AND C_{K+1} WITH $W_K + W_{K+1} \leq B_K$ YIELDS BETTER PLAN

PROPERTY 1. *Stitching columns C_k and C_{k+1} with $w_k+w_{k+1} \leq b_k$ yields better plan.*

PROOF. Without loss of generality, assume the plan P before stitching has n rounds. Then if we are allowed to stitch C_k and C_{k+1} of P as stated to form a new plan P', the plans would look like:

Table 3: Major notations in this paper

Notation	Meaning
P	A code massage plan
P_0	The original column-at-a-time plan (no massaging)
$R_i : w/[b]$	The i-th round of a plan, containing w bits of data and using a b-bit bank SIMD-sort
C_i	The i-th column of a plan/tuple
w_i	The number of bits of the C_i
b_i	The bank size used in the i-th round of a plan
m	The number of input columns to be sorted
T_{mcs}	The total cost of multi-column sorting based on our cost model
T^i_{sort}	The sorting subcost of the i-th round
$\mathcal{C}$	Calibrated constant used in cost model
M_{LLC}, M_{L2}	The capacity (in bytes) of the last level cache (LLC) / L2 cache
N	Input size (number of rows) to a multi-column sort program
$\mathcal{A}_i$	The perfect cost model based on exhaustively enumerating all feasible plans for query Q_i and measuring their actual running times
$\mathcal{Q}$	A query workload

$$\begin{aligned}P = \{\ & R_1 : w_1/[b_1], \cdots \\ & \mathbf{R_k} : \mathbf{w_k}/[\mathbf{b_k}], \qquad \mathbf{R_{k+1}} : \mathbf{w_{k+1}}/[\mathbf{b_{k+1}}], \\ & \cdots, R_n : w_n/[b_n]\} \\ P' = \{\ & R_1 : w_1/[b_1], \cdots \\ & \mathbf{R_k} : (\mathbf{w_k} + \mathbf{w_{k+1}})/[\mathbf{b_k}], \quad \mathbf{R_{k+1}} : \emptyset, \\ & \cdots, R_n : w_n/[b_n]\}\end{aligned}$$

The resulted plan P' should have $\mathbf{n-1}$ rounds. For the sake of proof, we insert a dummy "empty round" ($\emptyset$) at the $(\mathbf{k+1})$-th round above to make both P and P' have the form of $\mathbf{n}$ rounds. It can be seen that any R_i for $i < k$ and $i > k+1$ of both plans are identical.

Referring to Figure 2 and Section 4, three types of subcosts are incurred for *each* round: T_{lookup}, T^k_{sort} and T_{scan}, while $T_{massage}$ is incurred upfront. Let's define $cost(P.R_i)$ be the sum of T_{lookup}, T^i_{sort} and T_{scan} in the i-th round. We can therefore represent the total cost T_{mcs} of plan P and plan P' as:

$$T_{mcs}(P) = T_{massage}(P) + \sum_{i=1}^{n} cost(P.R_i) \qquad (11)$$

$$T_{mcs}(P') = T_{massage}(P') + \sum_{i=1}^{n} cost(P'.R_i) \qquad (12)$$

Now we are going to prove $T_{mcs}(P) - T_{mcs}(P') > 0$.

We first perform a **round-wise** comparison based on our cost model, to show that $\sum_{i=1}^{n} cost(P.R_i) - \sum_{i=1}^{n} cost(P'.R_i) = cost(P.R_{k+1})$:

1. When $i < k$, $cost(P.R_i) = cost(P'.R_i)$

   Intuitively, both plans behave identically from the first round until the k-th round. To quantify that, let us compare $P.R_i$ and $P'.R_i$. Note that the following of both are the same when $i < k$: (a) input size; (b) SIMD-sort bank size; (c) group information. Referring to our cost model in Section 4, these parameters suffice to determine T_{lookup}, T^k_{sort} and T_{scan}. As a result, all subcosts of the i-th round remain the same and thus $cost(P.R_i) = cost(P'.R_i)$.

2. $cost(P.R_k) = cost(P'.R_k)$

   Note the three factors (a), (b) and (c) above still remain the same for the k-th round. It is straightforward to see both (a) input size and (b) bank size remain the same. For (c), note the important fact that the group information fed to the i-th round is determined by **the number of bits prior to the i-th round**. Hence, though the bits allocated to $P.R_k$ and $P'.R_k$ are different, they both have $\sum_{j=1}^{k-1} w_j$ bits prior to them, so their costs are equal based on our cost model.

3. $cost(P.R_{k+1}) - cost(P'.R_{k+1}) = cost(P.R_{k+1})$

   This is obvious as $cost(P'.R_{k+1}) = cost(\emptyset) = 0$.

4. When $i > k+1$, $cost(P.R_i) = cost(P'.R_i)$.

   The reasoning is akin to (2). Although the bits allocated to R_k and R_{k+1} are different, the number of bits **prior to** R_i for $i > k+1$ are $\sum_{j=1}^{i-1} w_j$ in both plans. So all factor of (a), (b) and (c) are the same for both $P.R_i$ and $P'.R_i$.

Summarizing above, we have:

$$\begin{aligned}&\sum_{i=1}^{n} cost(P.R_i) - \sum_{i=1}^{n} cost(P'.R_i) \\ &= \sum_{i=1}^{n} \left(cost(P.R_i) - cost(P'.R_i)\right) \\ &= cost(P.R_{k+1})\end{aligned} \qquad (13)$$

Now let's consider $T_{massage}$. It is actually possible for P' to incur a higher $T_{massage}$ by introducing more invocations of the four-instruction program ($\mathcal{I}_{FIP}$, cf. Section 4). However, the increase of $\mathcal{I}_{FIP}$ is bounded by 1 (i.e., $\mathcal{I}_{FIP}(P') - \mathcal{I}_{FIP}(P) \leq 1$), as we can always form columns of P' by carrying out one more FIP that stitches C_i and C_{i+1} of P. So,

$$\begin{aligned}&T_{massage}(P') - T_{massage}(P) \\ &= \mathcal{I}_{FIP}(P') \cdot \mathcal{C}_{massage} \cdot N - \mathcal{I}_{FIP}(P) \cdot \mathcal{C}_{massage} \cdot N \\ &= (\mathcal{I}_{FIP}(P') - \mathcal{I}_{FIP}(P)) \cdot \mathcal{C}_{massage} \cdot N \\ &\leq \mathcal{C}_{massage} \cdot N\end{aligned} \qquad (14)$$

Putting Equations 11, 12, 13, 14 together, we have:

$$T_{mcs}(P) - T_{mcs}(P') \geq cost(P.R_{k+1}) - \mathcal{C}_{massage} \cdot N \qquad (15)$$

In reality, $\mathcal{C}_{massage} \cdot N$ is always at least one order of magnitude smaller than $cost(P.R_{k+1})$, because the former only includes the cost of carrying out one FIP for N codes, while the latter includes the costs of lookup, sorting and scanning N codes. So $T_{mcs}(P) - T_{mcs}(P') > 0$.

In summary, we can conclude P' is a better plan than P by stitching adjacent columns as stated. □

B. MONETDB REFERENCE IMPLEMENTATION

Figure 11 shows a reference system architecture if implementing the techniques mentioned in this paper into MonetDB (modified/added components are shaded). Specifically:

- We shall add a *ByteSlice storage manager* that implements ByteSlice [14] column-store layout.
- We shall add four BAT[9] algebra operators to the MonetDB execution engine (aka. Gorblin Database Kernel [20]), including `ByteSlice-Scan` and `ByteSlice-Lookup` that execute fast scans and lookups on ByteSlice data as proposed in

[9]Binary Association Table, the primitive data structure used in MonetDB's execution engine.

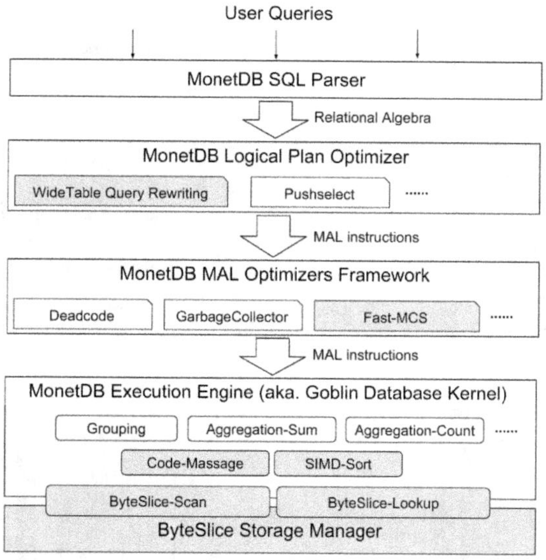

Figure 11: Implementing Code Massaging into MonetDB

[14], `SIMD-Sort` adapted from [4] that carries out (single-column) sorting with SIMD and multi-threading support, and `Code-Massage` that carries out code massaging process described in Figure 6. Other operators in MonetDB shall leave intact because operations other than scan and lookup manipulate intermediate data structures (BAT in this case) instead of base column storage [14].

- We shall add a `Fast-MCS` (fast multi-column sorting) module in the MonetDB MAL[10] optimizers framework. In MonetDB, an MAL plan is optimized by a series of modules in an *optimizer pipeline* [33]. Each module takes an MAL plan as input and transforms it into a more efficient one. For example, the `garbageCollector` module takes as input an MAL plan and injects calls to the garbage collector to free up space. Similarly, the `Fast-MCS` module shall (a) examine an input MAL plan and identifies the MAL instructions carrying out multi-column sorting, then (b) invoke the plan search algorithm (cf. Algorithm 1) to find an optimal massaging plan, finally (c) re-write the MAL instructions for multi-column sorting with code massaging. For example, a simplified set of MAL instructions to sort column a and column b with 16-bit bank would be:

```
(permuted_oid, group_info):=
          SIMD-Sort(a, 16, NULL)
permuted_b :=
          Lookup(b, permuted_oid)
(final_oid,final_group_info):=
          SIMD-Sort(permuted_b, 16, group_info)
```

Assume stitching these two columns as one and sorting it with 32-bit bank turns out to be the optimal plan in this case, the MAL plan re-written by `Fast-MCS` module would be:

```
super_column :=
          Code-Massage(a,b,'stitch')
(final_oid,final_group_info):=
          SIMD-Sort(super_column,32, NULL)
```

[10]MonetDB Assembly Language, the language to express a physical plan to be interpreted by the execution engine.

- We shall add a `WideTable Query Rewriting` module in the MonetDB logical plan optimizer. In MonetDB, the logical plan parsed from SQL is optimized using domain-specific rules. For example, `Pushselect` optimizes the logical plan by pushing down selections. So, the `WideTable Query Rewriting` module shall translate the logical plans into WideTable aware plans (i.e., to remove joins from the plans and use denormalized tables).

C. VALUE FOR TIME THRESHOLD ρ

Our experiments use $\rho = 0.1\%$ by default. Figures 12a, 12b and 12c show the time breakdown and the rank of resulted plan of one TPC-H, one TPC-DS, and one real query under various ρ on both Xeon and i7. We have the following findings. First, ROGA is so efficient that its running time is not observable in the figures. Second, we see that ROGA can complete even we do Not Set (N/S) any time threshold. Third, the effectiveness of ROGA is indeed not sensitive to ρ unless a really stringent value (e.g., 0.01%) is given. Indeed we found 22 such queries out of all 27 queries (9×2 TPC-H queries on uniform and skewed data + 4 TPC-DS queries + 5 real queries) that follow the findings above.

For the remaining 5 out of 27 queries, their total code width W is larger than 87, which may require up to 11 rounds of sorting (cf. Equation 10). Figures 12d, 12e, and 12f show the time breakdown of three of them. For those queries, we still see $\rho = 0.1\%$ is a good choice because that gives ROGA sufficient time to find a very competitive plan, without making itself as a bottleneck.

So, overall, we generally recommend $\rho = 0.1\%$. In general, we believe such an empirical approach is sufficient to determine the value of ρ. As a future work, we will study the following two approaches that can automate the process of finding ρ:

- **Offline calibration**: In this approach, the system uses a collection of sample queries and invokes the plan search algorithm (Algorithm 1) on each query with different ρ values. It uses a wide range of possible ρ values, from very stringent (e.g., 0.01%) to very loose (e.g.,10%, ρ higher than this is considered unacceptable anyway). For each query, we will record a list of estimated cost (T_{mcs}) with their corresponding ρ. We mark the "best" plan for each query as the one with the lowest estimated cost (T_{mcs}), which is usually obtained at the highest ρ. As observed in Figure 12, many queries find their best plans much earlier before using the largest ρ. So we find the smallest threshold ρ_0 that allows every query to reach its best plan. In other words, no query would obtain better plans with lower estimated cost if we increase ρ beyond ρ_0. Note that in this approach, the system only invokes the cost model to estimate the costs without actually executing the queries. So the process is fast and incurs very little overhead.
- **Online calibration**: In this approach, the optimizer assigns different ρ values to different queries online. Specifically, the plan search algorithm starts with setting $\rho = \rho_{low}$, where ρ_{low} is a low watermark. When time is up, we check whether the best plan found so far (P^*) has been updated. If yes, we anticipate further improvement is possible and extend the time limit by, say, $\rho \leftarrow \rho \times 2$. When the new time limit is reached, we check whether P^* has been updated again and increase ρ conditionally. To prevent ρ from growing infinitely, we cap it with a high watermark ρ_{high}. When ρ grows above ρ_{high}, we stop the plan search algorithm anyway. ρ_{low} and ρ_{high} can be set upfront as sufficiently small and large values respectively, for example, 0.01% and 10%.

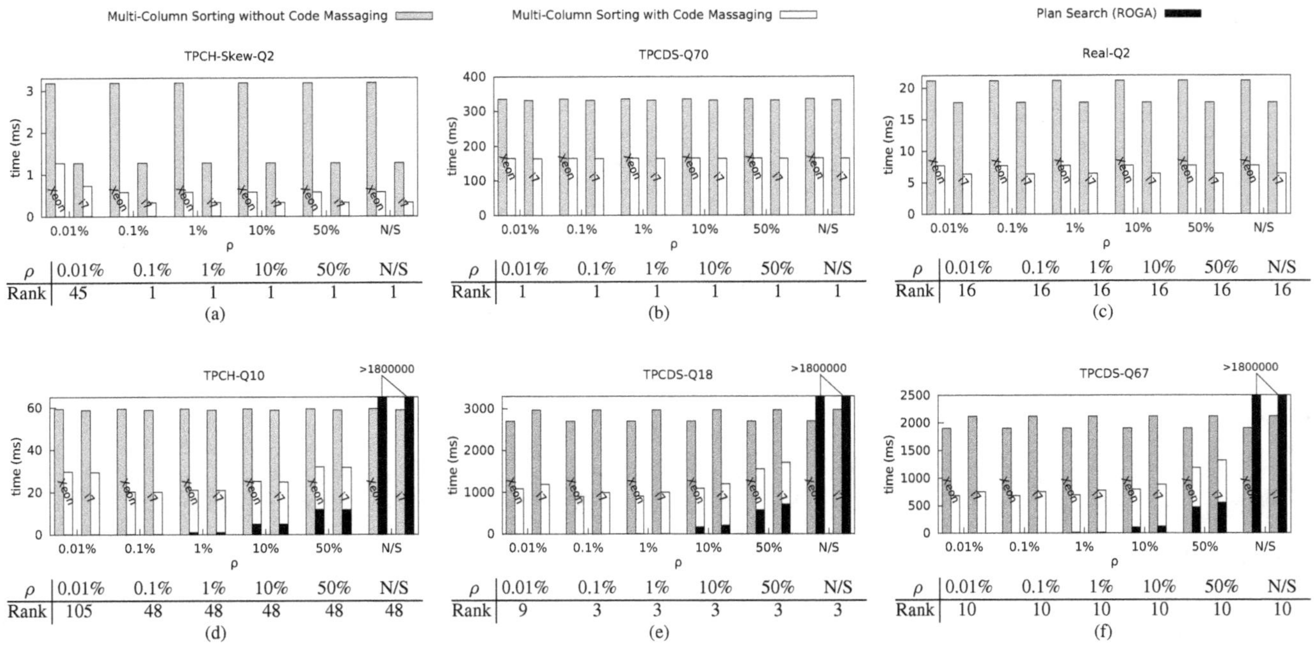

(a)

ρ	0.01%	0.1%	1%	10%	50%	N/S
Rank	45	1	1	1	1	1

(b)

ρ	0.01%	0.1%	1%	10%	50%	N/S
Rank	1	1	1	1	1	1

(c)

ρ	0.01%	0.1%	1%	10%	50%	N/S
Rank	16	16	16	16	16	16

(d)

ρ	0.01%	0.1%	1%	10%	50%	N/S
Rank	105	48	48	48	48	48

(e)

ρ	0.01%	0.1%	1%	10%	50%	N/S
Rank	9	3	3	3	3	3

(f)

ρ	0.01%	0.1%	1%	10%	50%	N/S
Rank	10	10	10	10	10	10

Figure 12: Sorting time breakdown with various time threshold; N/S: do not set any time threshold

Table 4: Schema of the real dataset

Attribute name of relation `Ticket`	Description	Attribute name of relation `Market`	Description
ItinID	Itinerary ID	ItinID	Itinerary ID
Year	Year	MktID	Market ID
Quarter	Quarter (1-4)	Year	Year
OriginAirportID	Origin airport ID	Quarter	Quarter (1-4)
OriginCountry	Country of origin airport	OriginAirportID	Origin Airport ID
OriginStateName	State name of origin airport	DestAirportID	Destination Airport ID
RoundTrip	Round Trip Indicator (1=Yes)	OpCarrier	Operating carrier
DollarCred	Dollar Credibility Indicator	Passengers	Number of passengers
ParePerMile	Itinerary Fare Per Miles Flown in Dollars	MktFare	Market fare (yield per itinerary mile × miles flown)
RPCarrier	Reporting Carrier	MktDistance	Market distance (including ground transport)
Passengers	Number of passengers	MktDistanceGroup	Distance group, in 500 Mile intervals
Distance	Itinerary distance (including ground transport)	MktMilesFlown	Market Miles flown (Track Miles)
DistanceGroup	Distance group, in 500 Mile intervals	ItinGeoType	Itinerary geography type
ItinGeoType	Itinerary geography type (1=Non-contiguous Domestic)		

Table 5: Queries on the real dataset

Query ID	SQL	Semantic
Q1	`SELECT OriginAirport, DollarCred, FarePerMile FROM Ticket WHERE OriginStateName = 'Texas'` **`ORDER BY DollarCred, FarePerMile`**	Check the relationship between credibility and fare per mile in a given state.
Q2	`SELECT OriginAirportID, DistanceGroup, Passengers,` **`RANK() OVER (PARTITION BY OriginAirportID, DistanceGroup ORDER BY Passengers)`** `FROM Ticket WHERE ItinGeoType = 1`	For each origin airport and distance group, obtain number of passengers in order.
Q3	`SELECT RPCarrier, OriginState, RoundTrip, DistanceGroup, AVG(Passengers)` **`FROM Ticket GROUP BY RPCarrier, OriginState ,RoundTrip, DistanceGroup`**	For each carrier, calculate the average number of passengers per state, per trip type, and per distance group.
Q4	`SELECT OriginAirportID, DestAirportID, AVG(MktFare) FROM Market WHERE OpCarrier = 'B6'` **`GROUP BY OriginAirportID, DestAirportID`**	Retrieve the average fare between each pair of airport.
Q5	`SELECT OpCarrier, MktFare,` **`RANK() OVER (PARTITION BY OpCarrier, ItinGeoType ORDER BY MktFare)`** `FROM Market WHERE MktDistanceGroup = 1`	For each carrier and itinerary type, check its rank of market fare.

Elastic Pipelining in an In-Memory Database Cluster

Li Wang[§‡], Minqi Zhou[§]*, Zhenjie Zhang[‡], Yin Yang[⊥], Aoying Zhou[§], Dina Bitton[†]
[§]Institute for Data Science and Engineering, East China Normal University, China
[‡]Advanced Digital Sciences Center, Illinois at Singapore Pte. Ltd., Singapore
[⊥]College of Science and Engineering, Hamad Bin Khalifa University, Qatar
[†]Bitton Consulting, USA
{wang.li, zhenjie}@adsc.com.sg, {mqzhou,ayzhou}@sei.ecnu.edu.cn, yyang@qf.org.qa, dinabitton@cs.wisc.edu

ABSTRACT

An in-memory database cluster consists of multiple interconnected nodes with a large capacity of RAM and modern multi-core CPUs. As a conventional query processing strategy, pipelining remains a promising solution for in-memory parallel database systems, as it avoids expensive intermediate result materialization and parallelizes the data processing among nodes. However, to fully unleash the power of pipelining in a cluster with multi-core nodes, it is crucial for the query optimizer to generate good query plans with appropriate intra-node parallelism, in order to maximize CPU and network bandwidth utilization. A suboptimal plan, on the contrary, causes load imbalance in the pipelines and consequently degrades the query performance. Parallelism assignment optimization at compile time is nearly impossible, as the workload in each node is affected by numerous factors and is highly dynamic during query evaluation. To tackle this problem, we propose *elastic pipelining*, which makes it possible to optimize intra-node parallelism assignments in the pipelines based on the actual workload at runtime. It is achieved with the adoption of new *elastic iterator model* and a fully optimized *dynamic scheduler*. The elastic iterator model generally upgrades traditional iterator model with new dynamic multi-core execution adjustment capability. And the dynamic scheduler efficiently provisions CPU cores to query execution segments in the pipelines based on the light-weight measurements on the operators. Extensive experiments on real and synthetic (TPC-H) data show that our proposal achieves almost full CPU utilization on typical decision-making analytical queries, outperforming state-of-the-art open-source systems by a huge margin.

1. INTRODUCTION

In-memory database achieves promising performance by keeping all tables and intermediate results entirely inside RAM, eliminating costly I/Os in traditional DBMSs. Query processing engines in the in-memory databases are designed to minimize the CPU cycles and memory access overhead in the query evalutaions. Such database systems were known to run well on high-end servers equipped with large RAM as well as newer-generation CPUs with many cores, large processor caches and super-scalar / SIMD capabilities. Although centralized in-memory databases are fast, the scalability is inherently limited by the amount of RAM and the number of cores within a single server, while in-memory parallel databases on a cluster of servers promise to overcome this limitation by distributed data storage and parallel data processing with multiple nodes [26]. Designing new query processing methods that fully utilize the power of a high-end server cluster, however, is highly challenging. Existing systems have focused on optimizing specific aspects of an in-memory cluster such as in-memory query optimizations [4, 8, 20, 23, 27, 30] and inter-node communication minimization [26]. The basic query processing framework still largely relies on existing solutions for traditional parallel databases.

We observe that traditional distributed query processing methods are designed based on very different assumptions, leading to potential waste on computation resource when used in an in-memory database cluster. Specifically, in these methods, a node usually materializes intermediate results before they are sent to other nodes over the network. However, in an in-memory database cluster, materialization is usually not considered as a good option due to its high memory consumption. Moreover, materialization increases query response time and incurs high memory access overhead by polluting the CPU cache [23].

Pipelined execution [7] enabled by the iterator model [13], in which a node immediately sends its result tuples through network to its consumer node(s) for execution without concrete materialization, saves the overhead and memory usage in materialization. Pipelined execution also effectively reduces the query response time by parallelizing the data processing on the producer and consumer nodes and the network data transmission between them. However, pipelined execution is challenging, since it results in tight data synchronization between the query nodes in a pipeline. To fully unleash the power of pipelined execution on modern multi-core hardware, the system is expected to exploit the hardware resources, e.g., CPU cores and network bandwidth, and balance all the producer-consumer speeds in the pipelines. This is unfortunately nearly impossible under existing iterator model, due to the unpredictable and fluctuating workload on each node and the nature of static parallelism in the traditional iterator model. In the following, we illustrate the problems with a motivating example.

Figure 1 shows an example SQL query in a financial data warehouse system and its corresponding query plan. Assume that both tables are distributed across multiple nodes, and only S is partitioned based on the join attribute *acct_id*. A popular join algorithm used in today's in-memory clusters is repartition join [6], with two phases: shuffle and local-join. Clearly, if materialization is adopted in query processing, huge amounts of intermediate results,

*Minqi Zhou is the corresponding author.

SIGMOD'16, June 26-July 01, 2016, San Francisco, CA, USA
© 2016 ACM. ISBN 978-1-4503-3531-7/16/06...$15.00
DOI: http://dx.doi.org/10.1145/2882903.2882904

```
SELECT  sec_code, acct_id,
        sum(trade_volume),
        sum(entry_volume)
FROM    Trades T, Securities S
WHERE
T.trade_date = "2010-10-30" AND
S.entry_date = "2010-10-30" AND
T.acct_id = S.acct_id
GROUP BY T. sec_code, S.acct_id;
```

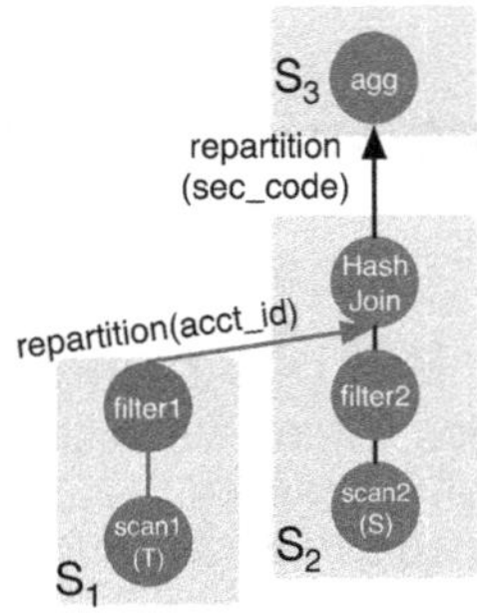

(a) Sql query (b) Query plan

Figure 1: An example SQL query in a financial warehouse system.

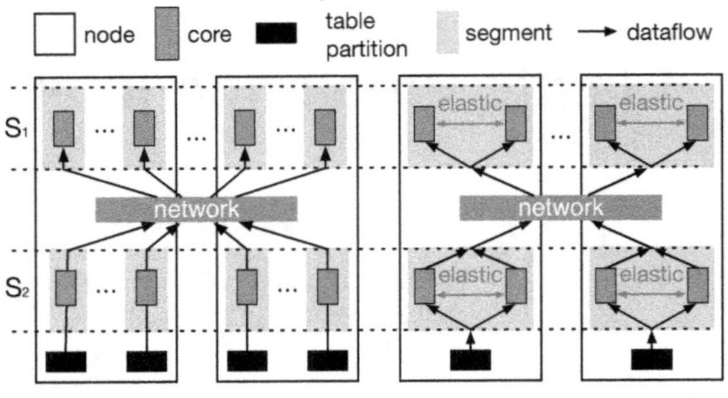

(a) Static pipeline (b) Elastic pipeline

Figure 2: Different parallelism mechanisms in traditional iterator model and elastic iterator model

e.g. shuffled partitions, are generated and kept in main memory. By employing pipelined execution, as shown in Figure 1(b), the SQL query is evaluated by an execution plan with two pipelines. The red arrow and the black arrow represent the two pipelines $P1$ and $P2$ respectively, which can be further decomposed into three segments, S_1, S_2 and S_3.

Let us zoom in on the first pipeline as shown in Figure 2(a). During its execution, both segment S_1 and segment S_2 are running simultaneously. In S_1, tuples from T satisfying $filter1$ are hash-partitioned on the join attribute and are sent to S_2. At the same time, S_2 receives the tuples from S_1 and constructs the hash table on-the-fly. One node in the in-memory database cluster could run multiple instances of S_1 and S_2 to achieve intra-node parallelism. As each segment instance works exclusively on a partitioned dataflow, this scheme results in a static pipeline, in which the intra-node parallelism must be determined at the compile time and hence cannot be modified on-the-fly. The main problem arises here: before query processing, the system must accurately estimate the throughput of the segments and generate query plan with proper intra-node parallelism in order to balance the workload in the pipeline and fully utilize the CPUs and network bandwidth. For example, too low parallelism of S_2 may lead to slow hash table construction, consequently blocking S_1 and under-utilizing CPU cycles and network bandwidth; conversely, too many cores on the instances of S_2 may exhaust S_1 or the network, leading to idle cores. Since the segment throughputs are affected by many factors such as operator selectivity, data distribution, implementation algorithms, and hardware features, it is very challenging for the query optimizer to foresee all those factors and generate query plans with optimal parallelism. Even worse, for a large dataset, the workload of each operator may fluctuate during runtime. In such case, the query processing with static parallelism can never be optimal. For instance, consider that tuples in T are roughly ordered by their insertion time, which correlates with attribute *entry_time*. The filter operator initially discards all tuples in T whose dates are before the selection criterion "2010-10-30", meaning no inputs for S_2. Accordingly, most cores should be given to S_1. Later on, the filter reaches a hotspot where almost all tuples match the selection criterion, causing a sudden burst of inputs for S_2. Thus, the core allocation should be dynamically adjusted to increase the speed of the join, and decrease that of the filter.

In this paper, we propose elastic pipelining (EP) to address the above challenges. The elastic pipelining consists of a novel elastic iterator model and a dynamic scheduler. The elastic iterator model enables query processing with dynamic intra-node parallelism as shown in Figure 2(b) and hence exempts the query optimizer from deciding the error-prone intra-node parallelism at compile time. The dynamic scheduler keeps tracks of the workload for each running segment and makes dynamic parallelism assignment to the segments in order to balance the workload in pipelines and fully leverage the available CPU cores and network bandwidth. Extensive experiments, using both a real financial dataset and synthetic TPC-H data, demonstrate that EP is highly effective: 5X faster than static pipelining. Meanwhile, our in-memory database cluster system implementing EP also outperforms Impala and Shark, two popular open-source distributed SQL query engines, by a huge margin. The main contributions of the paper are listed below:

1. We propose elastic pipelining to support online parallelism adjustment for query processing in the in-memory database cluster.
2. We introduce an elastic iterator model to add new elasticity functionalities to existing iterator model.
3. We design online scheduler algorithms to run lightweight resource scheduling on segments in the pipelines. uu
4. We evaluate the advantages of our proposal on both synthetic and real database workloads.

The rest of this paper is organized as following. Section 2 introduces the scenario we focus, shows the limitations of static pipelining and existing adaptive parallelism methods, and highlights the design philosophy of our elastic pipelining. Section 3 presents the elastic iterator model behind our elastic pipelining system. Section 4 discusses the dynamic scheduling strategy used in the system. Second 5 evaluates our proposal with experimental studies. Section 6 reviews the existing and related works in the literature, and Section 7 finally concludes the paper and highlight future works.

2. PRELIMINARIES

In this paper, we focus on query processing for in-memory parallel database systems running on clusters of servers with shared-nothing architecture, each of which is equipped with multicore processor(s) under CMP, SMP or NUMA architectures. The servers in the cluster, called *nodes* in the rest of the paper, are connected by local network. One node acts as the *master* to manage other *salve* nodes in the cluster. The master node is also responsible to query optimization and physical execution plan generation. The input tables are partitioned and distributed across the slave nodes, and entirely reside in main memory during query processing.

2.1 Iterator Model and Its Parallelism

In this part of the section, we introduce the core concepts in the traditional iterator model. We use the query plan in Figure 3 as the running example to explain these concepts.

Iterator: The iterator model [13] has been widely used in state-of-the-art database systems, because of its excellent generality and

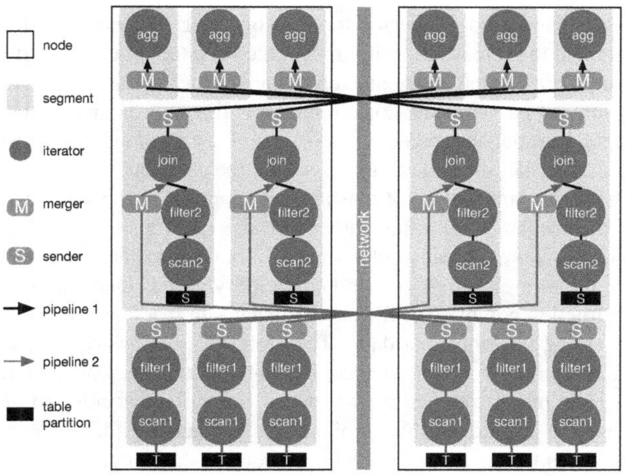

Figure 3: An example of iterator model and parallel execution

extensibility. All operators under iterator model follow a unified data-oriented interface, with basic functionalities of `open`, `next`, and `close` for input data manipulation. Every iterator is associated with a *state*, which maintains the runtime status and the important structure of the iterator. For hash join operator, for example, the state of the iterator maintains a hash table for the tuples from one of its input dataflow. For scan operator, for another example, the state of the iterator maintains a reference to the input file and the current reading cursor. The `open` function is responsible for state construction, such that the iterator is ready to emit output tuples when its `next` function is called. Some iterators, including hash join, aggregate and sort, are called *blocking iterators* or *pipeline breakers*, as they need to consume the entire dataflow on at least one input side to construct their state. Other iterators are called *non-blocking iterators*. The dataflow among iterators running on different nodes are connected by data exchange operator [13], which consists of *senders* and *mergers*. Senders and mergers are both non-blocking iterators.

Pipeline: Based on the concept of blocking iterators, an algebraic query plan is decomposed into pipelines, such that each pipeline forms a chain in the query plan tree and ends at certain pipeline breaker. In Figure 3, for example, there are two pipelines for the original query plan, including workflows as $(scan1, filer1, join)$ and $(scan2, filter2, join, agg)$ respectively.

Segment: To achieve *horizontal parallelism*, a fragment of a query plan can be duplicated into several identical *segment instances* or *segments* for short, each of which is responsible for a partition of the input dataflow for the pipeline and thus independently evaluated. The set of identical segments is called *segment group*. In Figure 3, for example, $(scan1, filter1)$ has three identical segments on each node to achieve intra-node parallelism. Those segments receiving data from network are called *producer segments*, while those segments sending result tuples via network are called *consumer segments*. *Pipelined parallelism* is achieved by running the producer and the consumer segments simultaneously.

Stage: A pipeline may cover more than one segment. Within a pipeline, the set of iterators in the same segment is called a *local stage*, or *stage* for short. For instance, the iterators within the first pipeline in Figure 3 consists of two types of stages: $\{scan1, filter1, sender\}$ and $\{merger, join\}$. Similarity, a segment may belong to multiples pipeline and thus consists of several stages. When a segment is running, only one stage is active at a given time. In the active stage, the dataflow is release from the *stage beginner* and ends at the *stage ender*.

After the decomposition of the query execution plan on the segment level, each result segment is assigned to a node in the distributed system. As reported in [33], grouping tuples into blocks and block-at-a-time processing turns more efficient than tuple-at-a-time processing. In the rest of the paper, we assume the data blocks as the basic processing units in the system, although all of our proposals work well with tuple-at-a-time processing.

2.2 System Design Principles

In this part of section, we discuss the design principles for efficient in-memory query processing systems, especially from the perspective of desirable system features. In particular, we believe the following system features are important to maximize the computation utilization of the cluster and minimize the query response time.

DESIDERATA 1. ***Materialization-Free*** *property avoids any materialization of intermediate results during query processing.*

Materialization-free property allows the in-memory cluster to save unnecessary memory consumption and materialization overhead. This property is essentially important when a large amount of intermediate results are generated and transmitted across different nodes in the cluster.

DESIDERATA 2. ***CPU Efficiency*** *property minimizes CPU idle rate and maximizes query throughput per CPU cycle.*

In the in-memory database cluster, the response time for a given query largely depends on the CPU utilization and efficiency. When the CPUs are idle-free and processing the query in an effective manner, the query response time is minimized, especially when the queries are computation-intensive. This requirement is generally difficult to meet in distributed system, since it usually involves heavy synchronization among computation nodes in the cluster. As motivated in the introduction section, the workloads of querying processing logic is nearly unpredictable and varies at different phases, which leads to the third requirement below.

DESIDERATA 3. ***Self-Tuning*** *property allows the in-memory cluster to dynamically reallocate computation tasks based on the instantaneous workload of the system.*

Table 1: Comparisons on distributed processing techniques

Technique	Material.-Free	CPU Efficiency	Self-Tuning
[7, 19, 24]	✓	×	✓
[22]	✓	✓	×
Shark [31]	×	✓	✓
EP	✓	✓	✓

Table 1 classifies known methods according to the above desirable properties. [24] creates more query threads than the number of hardware cores and relies on the operating system to schedule them. However, this method keeps high CPU utilization at the expense of low CPU-efficiency, as it inevitably introduces expensive context switches and cache thrashing. [7, 19] decompose the queries into fine-grained, self-maintained executable units, each of which can be executed by a thread independently. Once a thread has processed one unit, it picks up another one based on a specific pickup algorithm to achieve desirable parallelism assignment. However, when using the methods to balance the workload in pipelines in our settings, the pickup algorithm will be much more complicated and time-consuming than its original design, leading to expensive scheduling overhead. [22] estimates the producing rate of operators, based on which the system allocates the optimal parallelism to achieve load balance. However, this method is not self-tuning. It leads to low CPU utilization when the workload within the pipelines is imbalanced due to the estimation errors or workload changes. In

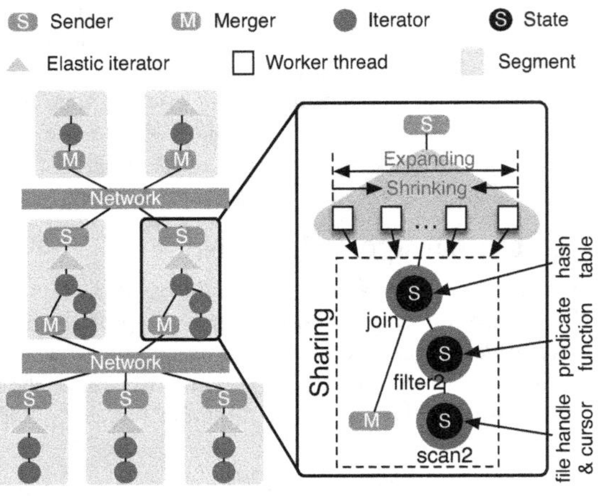

Figure 4: Overview of the elastic iterator model

Shark [31], materialization is run on the producer side to eliminate the necessity of synchronization among computation nodes, which simplifies the scheduling algorithm and improves the CPU utilization. However, materialization incurs high RAM consumption and inhibits pipelined parallelism.

As a conclusion of this section, to meet all these three requirements for distributed in-memory SQL query engine, it is essential to support *pipelining* with *dynamic parallelism* scheduling on the operators in the pipeline. In this paper, we will introduce *elastic pipelining* as a holistic solution.

2.3 Framework Overview of Elastic Pipelining

The system design principles in previous subsection motivate us to propose the framework of elastic pipelining. It consists of *elastic iterator model* and *dynamic scheduler*.

(1) The elastic iterator model is a set of implementation techniques to enable query processing with dynamic parallelism on the segment level. It generally updates the traditional iterator model with two functionalities *expand* and *shrink*, allowing the system to freely update the parallelism on each query segments on-the-fly. The elastic iterator model is introduced in Section 3.

(2) The runtime dynamic scheduler monitors the online status of all the running segments and makes decisions on parallelism update, in order to minimize the overall query response time and avoid computation resource waste. If one of the segments overproduces, i.e. generating tuples too fast for the network bandwidth or throughput of its producer/consumer segments, the scheduler calls the segment to shrink its parallelism. On the other hand, if a slow segment is identified as the performance bottleneck of the whole query, the scheduler calls the segment to expand parallelism, for the purpose of overall performance optimization. The dynamic scheduler is discussed in Section 4.

3. ELASTIC ITERATOR MODEL

In traditional iterator model, the input data flow is partitioned based on segments, such that each segment independently processes one of the partitions. Parallelism update on segment level is extremely difficult, since any insertion or removal of the segment involves state construction, destruction and migration across segments. In Figure 4, we present the internal structure of a segment from the query evaluation plan in Figure 3. Each segment is bound to an instance of iterator, within which the iterator state may contain a huge hash table for join operator, the predicate function for filter operator and file cursor for scan operator. If a new segment is created to increase the parallelism, the hash table must be redistributed among the segments accordingly. Such iterator state migration can be very time-consuming. It is thus more reasonable to support parallelism update within segment, by dynamically adjusting the number of worker threads within the segment.

An important feature of elastic iterator model is the state sharing mechanism among the worker threads. During state initialization, all worker threads collaboratively build the states, e.g. the hash table in Figure 4, in a unified memory space. Once the state construction completes, all worker threads can read the state when processing its own input data. Therefore, if a new worker thread is added into the elastic iterator, the initialization cost of the new thread is minimized. Similarly, when the system decides to decrease the parallelism by terminating a worker thread, the target thread can terminate quickly without iterator state migration. This feature enables the database query processing engine to revise the parallelisms of any running segment in milliseconds at runtime.

In the remainder of this section, we introduce the semantics of elastic iterator (Section 3.1) and optimizations used in the implementation of elastic iterator model on modern multi-core hardware (Section 3.2).

3.1 Semantics of Elastic Iterator

The elastic iterator is an extension to the conventional open-next-close protocol. In open-next-close protocol, all instances of iterators have the same data processing interface, by calling the `open`, `next` and `close` functions. There are two new functions in elastic iterator model, i.e. *expand* and *shrink*, to support runtime parallelism adjustment. This part of the section introduces the new semantics of the generic functions in the elastic iterator, to reflect the new support to elasticity.

Figure 5(a) illustrates the overall working mechanism of the elastic iterators. The execution of each segment is run by the corresponding elastic iterator, represented by a triangle in the segment. Generally speaking, the `open` function of the elastic iterator creates a number of worker threads for the segment and initializes a joint data buffer for all worker threads. The threads collaboratively process in parallel and insert the output blocks into the data buffer. The `next` function of the elastic iterator returns one data block from data buffer at a time, if there is any data block available; otherwise, the `next` function is blocked, until new data blocks arrive or *end-of-file* is reached. Data buffer connects the dataflow between the worker threads and the thread calling `next`, in an asynchronous way. Similar to the traditional iterator model, `close` function frees all the resource within the iterator and recursively calls `close` of its child iterators to terminate the entire iterator subtree.

The worker threads first call the `open` function of the child iterator to recursively construct the state of each iterator in parallel. Figure 5(b) and (c) demonstrate the process of state construction for a non-blocking iterator and a blocking iterator respectively. After the completion of state construction for all the iterators, the worker threads call the `next` function of the child iterator to retrieve an output data block at a time, and insert result data blocks into the data buffer, as demonstrated in Figure 5(d). To guarantee the completeness and accuracy of the query results, all the iterators support the thread-safe version of `open` and `next` functions. The pseudocode and revisions over traditional iterators for these functions are available in the appendix of the paper.

Before delving into the details of expansion and shrinkage operations, we first introduce the concepts regarding the status of the worker threads. Specifically, the worker threads in an active segment are in one of the following three statuses at any time. (S1)

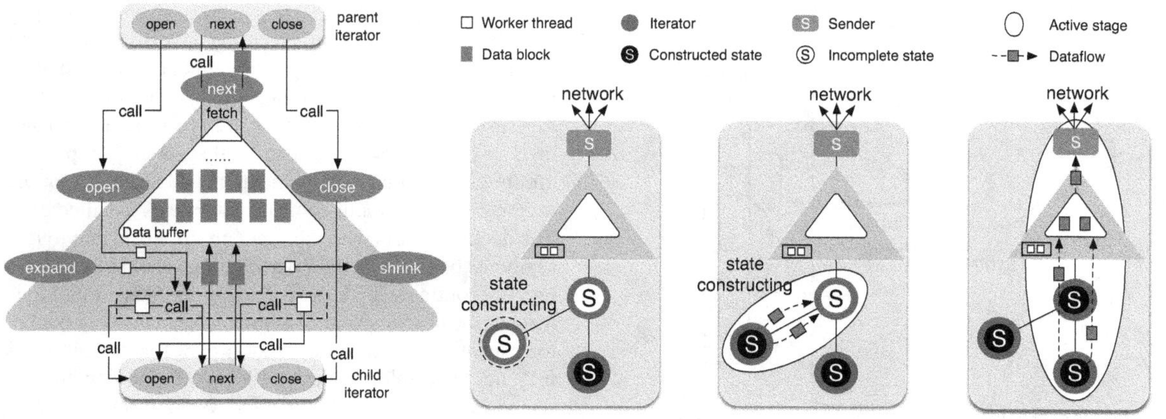

(a) Elastic Iterator (b) State construction for non-blocking iterator (c) Parallel state construction for blocking iterator (d) Parallel data generation for the elastic iterator

Figure 5: Structure and work mechanism of the elastic iterator model

The worker thread is constructing the state of a non-blocking iterator's state as demonstrated in Figure 5(b). (S2) The worker thread is constructing the state of a blocking iterator's state as shown in Figure 5(c). (S3) The worker thread is processing the data for the elastic iterator's buffer as shown in Figure 5(d). The logics of the expansion and shrinkage operations rely on the status of the involved worker threads, as described below.

Expand: When expansion is called, the elastic iterator creates a new worker thread. As the new worker thread shares all the iterators' states with existing threads, it can immediately participate in the processing, either parallel state construction for the segment or parallel output data generation. To be specific, when the existing worker threads are in S1 or S2, the newly added worker thread joins the state construction work. For the hash table for join operator, for example, the new worker thread immediately reads the data and insert the tuples into the hash table based on the hash value of the keys. When existing worker threads are in S3, all worker threads are processing input data to generate output data blocks. In such case, the new worker thread simply calls the `next` function of its child iterator and inserts result data blocks to elastic iterator's buffer.

Shrink: When shrinkage is called, the elastic iterator chooses one of its worker threads to terminate. As the states of the iterators are shared by the worker threads, the terminating thread does not need to transfer the states to any other threads; instead, it only needs to guarantee that its termination does not introduce inconsistency to the states of the iterator. In particular, when the target worker thread is in S2 or S3, the data flow is fetched from the stage beginner (by calling the stage beginner's `next` function) and is fed into the state of the stage ender (or the buffer of the elastic iterator resp.). Therefore, once the thread has finished his current data block from the stage beginner, it can be terminated safely when the current data block is completely processed and the results are written to the state of the stage ender (or the buffer of the elastic iterator resp.). When the thread is in S1, it can terminate once the current state construction is completed. In our model, this termination strategy is achieved by adding checking operations at the beginning of each iterator's `open` function.

3.2 Implementation Optimizations

The implementation of the elastic iterators involves a variety of optimizations. Some of the techniques are borrowed from existing in-memory algorithms designed for multi-core processors, e.g. in-memory radix join [20], sort-merge join [3], NUMA-aware aggregation [30]. In the following, we list three novel methods, which are crucial for the performance of the parallel in-memory database.

(1) *Context Reuse.* Some iterators require each worker thread to maintain a private structure for auxiliary information, called *context*. In private/hybrid hash aggregation, for example, each worker thread contains a private hash table for partial aggregation results. When expansions and shrinkages are frequently called on these operators, the expensive reconstruction of these contexts is the nightmare for the parallel database system. To alleviate the potential problem, we do not destroy the context of the worker thread when it terminates. Instead, the context is kept, for the purpose of *context reuse*. When a new worker thread starts its operation, it first tries to find and reuse one of the existing contexts to skip the tedious context initialization. Each iterator is allowed to choose one from three different strategies of context maintenance, i.e. *void* mode, *processor* mode and *core* mode. In void mode, the locality is not considered and the available context can be reused by any worker thread. In processor mode, the worker thread can only reuse the contexts created by the cores on the same processor. This mode could potentially avoid remote memory access when reading the in-memory context in a NUMA architecture, if the context is still resident in the last level cache. In core mode, the worker thread can only reuse the context allocated by the same core, which provides opportunities of reusing the context resident in private CPU cache. For each iterator, the context maintenance strategy is selected according to the storage size of its context.

(2) *Order Preservation:* It is desirable for the elastic iterator model to have order preserving properties such that the tuple order in the dataflow produced by multiple threads is the same as that produced by a single thread. Without such property, elastic iterators cannot be used before any iterator that requires sorted data, limiting the usage of elastic iterator model. To do this, each block released from the stage beginner is given a unique sequence number according to its original order. After the data blocks are inserted into the elastic iterator's buffer, elastic iterator reorders them based on their sequence number, before they are later fetched by the parent iterator (typically the sender). The reordering is extremely fast, as it operates on the data blocks instead of tuples. However, it forces the iterator to be a pipeline breaker. To solve this problem, we implement stage beginner in such a way that data blocks taken by the same worker thread are in their original order. By doing this, the sequence numbers of data blocks inserted into the data buffer by the same worker threads are in increasing order. As a result, the elastic iterator only needs to merge the sorted data blocks generated

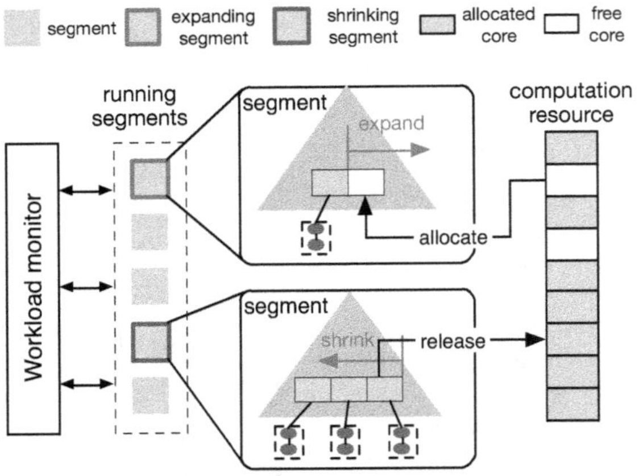

Figure 6: The interaction between segments and scheduler on a slave node.

Table 2: Table of Notations

notation	description
k	the number of nodes in the system
m	the number of CPU cores on a node
n	the number of segments
S_i	a segment
λ	the throughput of the pipeline
D_i	the service demand of S_i
V_i	the average visit rate of S_i
T_i	the processing rate of S_i
R_i	the normalized processing rate of S_i
δ_i	the selectivity of S_i
t_{ij}	the estimated processing rate of S_i with j worker threads

by different worker threads, which resolves the risk of becoming pipeline breaker.

(3) *NUMA Awareness:* In a NUMA architecture, it is more efficient to read data in local memory. Our elastic iterator model can easily achieve NUMA-awareness. When a worker thread asks for a data block from stage beginner for processing, the thread prefers to get a data block on the local memory, such that the subsequent data processing on that data block does not go through expensive remote memory access.

4. DYNAMIC SCHEDULER

In this section, we focus on the design and implementation of the dynamic scheduler, which is run on each slave node in the cluster to manage the runtime resource allocation. Figure 6 presents a concrete example of the scheduler on a slave node. The scheduler is run as an independent process on the slave node, on which it maintains a list structure for all active segments on the node. When a segment turns active, it is added to the end of the list, waiting for core assignment by the scheduler. The scheduler collects metrics from the threads and the corresponding segments, and keeps these statistical numbers in its own memory space. The scheduler evaluates possible performance improvement by core reassignment periodically. If the performance model identifies a better core assignment, the scheduler calls `shrink` on a segment to remove a core and calls `expand` on another segment to add the core. In the rest of the section, we will present the mathematical problem formulation of the scheduler (Section 4.1), introduce the basic optimization approach (Section 4.2), and discuss the metric collection procedure in the system (Section 4.3 and 4.4).

4.1 Problem Formulation

Assume that the parallel in-memory database system consists of k nodes, i.e. $\{N_1, N_2, \ldots, N_k\}$, each of which is equipped with m CPU cores. Given an executing plan for a query, there are a number of segment groups. Each segment group contains segments with identical processing logic, which are bound to different nodes for execution. We assume there are n concrete segments, denoted by $\mathbb{S} = \{S_1 \ldots, S_n\}$, running in all segment groups. The segment group without producer segments is called *input group*, while the segment group without consumer segments is called *output group*. The dataflow starts with the input group, flows into to its consumer segments based on certain partitioning scheme for execution. This process continues with the following segments, until the data flow reaches the output group. A segment is exclusively bound to a node for execution, based on execution plan for the query. Each node may host multiple segments. We use G_i to denote the segments bound to i-th node in the parallel system, such that $G_i \cap G_j = \emptyset$ for any $i \neq j$, and $\cup_i G_i = \mathbb{S}$.

The exact number of cores assigned to a particular segment S_i is called its *parallelism*, i.e. p_i for segment S_i. The throughput of the pipeline, denoted by $\lambda(p_1, \ldots, p_n)$ is measured as the aggregated processing rate of the segments in the input group, given the parallelism assignment $\{p_1, \ldots, p_n\}$. The goal of dynamic scheduling is to find an optimal core-to-segment assignment such that λ is maximized, under the constraint of valid core assignment to the segments, i.e.

$$\begin{aligned} \text{Maximize: } & \lambda(p_1, p_2, \ldots, p_n) \\ \text{s.t } & p_i \geq 0 \\ & \forall G_j \, , \sum_{S_i \in G_j} p_i \leq m \end{aligned} \tag{1}$$

Basically, the total number of cores assigned to local segments with each node is no larger than m. In the rest of the section, we will study the connection between λ and $\{p_1, \ldots, p_n\}$, as well as the solution to the optimization program above.

4.2 Scheduling Algorithm

According to [18] and [12], the active pipeline forms an open queuing system, such that the generation and processing of intermediate results in pipelines are modeled as queues for service. When there are n basic processing units running (segments in our setting) at the same time, regardless of the overall topology, the overall throughput of the system λ is determined by

$$\lambda = \frac{1}{\max\limits_{1 \leq i \leq n} D_i} \tag{2}$$

In Equation (2), D_i is called *service demand* and can be calculated as $D_i = V_i / T_i$, where V_i and T_i are the *average visit rate* and the *processing rate* of segment S_i respectively. Specifically, the average visit rate is the average number of tuples received by segment S_i for each original input tuple at the input segment. The processing rate is the number of tuples the segment can process within a unit time. The details on the collections of these two types of metrics are available in Section 4.3 and Section 4.4.

Given the metrics $\{(S_i, V_i, T_i)\}$ available to the scheduler, by simple manipulation over Equation (2), we have:

$$\lambda = \min_{1 \leq i \leq n} \frac{T_i}{V_i} \tag{3}$$

In Equation 3, T_i / V_i is called the *normalized processing rate*, denoted by R_i, of the segment S_i, in which $1/V_i$ is also known as the normalization factor. Equation (3) shows that λ is purely decided by the bottleneck segment, i.e., the segment with the smallest

Algorithm 1: Scheduling Algorithm

Input: the overall throughput λ, the segment set G on the node, penalty factor Δ

Construct a segment set $U \subseteq G$ with normalized processing rate close to λ;
Construct a segment set $O = G - U$ with normalized processing rate significantly higher than λ;
Retrieve the parallelism of each segment $S_i \in G$;
Initialize an empty array A;
for $(S_i, S_j) \in U \times O$ **do**
    Evaluate the new normalized processing rates on T_i' and T_j' by Equation 4;
    if $T_i' \geq \lambda + \Delta$ *and* $T_j' \geq \lambda + \Delta$ **then**
        Insert (S_i, S_j, T_i', T_j') in A;
if A *is not empty* **then**
    Select a pair of (S_i, S_j) with maximal throughput improvement;
    Adjust the parallelism for S_i and S_j by calling the functions in iterators;

normalized processing rate. This observation also simplifies the scheduling algorithm. It is unnecessary to conduct global parallelism assignment across nodes in the system. Instead, if all nodes are aware of the overall throughput λ of the whole system, they only need to run local optimization independently, simply to ensure the normalized processing rates of all the local segments are better than λ.

On the other hand, it is equally important to estimate the normalized processing rate under specified parallelism for each segment S_i. Fortunately, the average visit rate V_i also depends on the processing logic of precedent segments. It is thus sufficient to collect the statistics from the segments to generate accurate estimation on V_i. The processing rate T_i is obviously dependent of the parallelism p_i for segment S_i. The scheduler on a node maintains a scalability vector $(t_{i1}, t_{i2}, \ldots, t_{im})$, each entry t_{ij} in which is an estimation on the processing rate T_i on segment S_i when there are j cores assigned to S_i. We leave the discussions on the generation of these statistics to the following subsections.

Given all the statistics available to the scheduler, the pseudo codes of the scheduling algorithm are listed in Algorithm 1. Given the global throughput λ, the scheduler firstly partitions all its segments into two parts. The first segment set U contains underperforming segments with normalized processing rate close to λ, while the second segment set O contains over-performing segments with normalized processing rate significantly larger than λ. The algorithm then tests for all paris of $(S_i, S_j) \in U \times O$. For each (S_i, S_j), it evaluates the potential improvement to the throughput by moving one worker thread from S_j to S_i. The evaluation is based on the estimation of new normalized processing throughputs on S_i and S_j that

$$T_i' = \frac{t_{i(p_i+1)}}{V_i} \qquad T_j' = \frac{t_{j(p_j-1)}}{V_j} \tag{4}$$

After enumerating all possible paris, the algorithm finally selects the best pair with the largest potential improvement.

4.3 Measurements on Average Visit Rate

In general, average visit rate is propagated through the pipeline

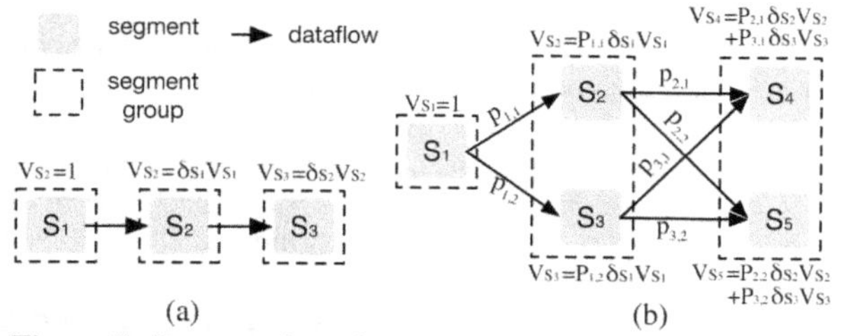

Figure 7: Propagation of average visit rates in the dataflow

along with the dataflow, from one segment to another. Apparently, the average visit rate for any segment in the input group is 1. Consequently, if we are aware of how the values are propagated among the segments, then we are able to obtain the average visit rate for each segment in the pipeline. In the following, we first discuss the method to calculate the average visit rate in the simplified cases where each segment group has only one segment, and then extend the method to the general ones.

Consider a pipeline as demonstrated in Figure 7(a), in which each segment group has only one segment. There is no partitioning on the dataflow; the output dataflow generated by a segment is entirely sent to one consumer segment for execution. Consequently, for any segment S_i, the average visit rate of its consumer segment is $\delta_i \cdot V_i$, in which δ_i is the selectivity of S_i, i.e., the ratio of the number of output tuples to the number of input tuples consumed.

Now we extend our method to the general cases, in which a segment group might contain several segments as shown in Figure 7(b). For a segment S_i with multiple consumer segments, the output dataflow is partitioned based on a certain partitioning scheme, e.g., hash partition. The contribution of average visit rate that S_i makes to its j-th consumer segment is $p_j \cdot \delta_i V_i$, where p_j is the percentage of output dataflow S_i sends to its jth consumer segment. Similarity, for a segment S_j with multiple producer segments, its average visit is the sum of the average visit rates that all its producer segments contribute to it.

In our implementation, in order to obtain the average visit rates without introducing explicit communication among segments and nodes, we integrate instantaneous values of average visit rates in the dataflow. In particular, in the tail of each data block, we maintain the value of average visit rate for the tuples within the data block. The value is updated when the data block is processed by each segment or partitioned across the network. For a segment, it is kept updated to its instantaneous value of the average visit rate by reading tail information of its input data blocks.

4.4 Measurements on Processing Rate

The prediction of throughput plays an important role in the optimization procedure called by the scheduler. However, accurate prediction is very challenging, as the throughput of a segment is affected by numerous factors and is dynamic during the query execution. In this subsection, we present our method to achieve accurate, scalable estimation on the throughput with minimal efforts.

Our system maintains a data structure, called *scalability vector*, in the memory of the nodes. For each segment S_i, there is a vector, with the j-th entry in the vector as a value pair (t_{ij}, l_{ij}), in which t_{ij} is the measured instantaneous processing rate of S_i with j parallel worker threads and l_{ij} is the timestamp when the latest metric is recorded. During the execution of S_i, we periodically detect the instantaneous data processing rate and update the corresponding entry in the scalability vector, if the measured data processing rate is not under-estimated, i.e., the processing rate of S_i is not limited by that of other segments or the network bandwidth. As the scalability for a segment varies when running different stages, before the start of the execution of a stage, each entry in the scalability vector is initialized to be invalid, indicating that the actual value is not known.

At system time l, when estimating the processing rate of a segment S_i with a target parallelism p_i, the system checks the p_i-the entry in the scalability vector. If t_{ip_i} is valid and l_{ip_i} is a fresh record, i.e. $\|l_{ip_i} - l\| \leq \theta$ under the specified threshold θ, the system directly uses t_{ip_i} as the estimation of the processing rate. Otherwise, there is no existing record on the processing rate for direct estimation use. The system then uses the neighbor record in the scalability vector, as the current parallelism for S_i is either $p_i - 1$ or $p_i + 1$ before the scheduler tries a new round of optimization. The estimation on the processing rate is simply proportional to the number of cores, based on either $(p_i + 1)$-th record or $(p_i - 1)$-th record in the scalability vector. Note that such estimation may not be accurate but does not incur much assignment problem, as the scheduler only reassigns one core each time and inaccurate estimation could be quickly identified and corrected when next round of optimization comes into operation.

5. EXPERIMENT

5.1 Environment & Dataset

We implement the framework of elastic pipelining in CLAIMS [1], our in-memory parallel database prototype, tailored for efficient data analysis on clusters of shared-nothing multi-core servers. The system accepts SQL queries and employs an internal query optimizer to convert queries into physical execution plans with minimized cost. We employ block-at-a-time processing strategy in our elastic iterator model, with a block size of 64 KB to fit the L2 cache size on CPUs.

All the experiments run on a cluster with 10 identical nodes. The detailed hardware specifications of the nodes are listed in Table 3. The servers are inter-connected by a Gigabyte switch. The operating system is Redhat Enterprise 6.3 with kernel version 2.6.32.

Table 3: Hardware specifications of the server

Number of sockets	2
Number of physical (logical) Cores	12 (24)
Size of DRAM per NUMA socket	32 GB
L1 / L2 cache size (private)	32 / 256 KB
L3 cache size (shared within a NUMA socket)	15 MB

The evaluations are done over a synthetic dataset and a real dataset. The synthetic dataset is generated with TPC-H benchmark with scale factor at 100. The real-life dataset contains transactional records in Stock Exchange (SSE) in three months of year 2010. These transactional records are stored in two tables under schemas: Securities(*order_no*, *acct_id*, *sec_code*, *entry_date*, *entry_volume*) and Trades(*acct_id*, *sec_code*, *trade_date*, *trade_time*, *order_price*, *trade_volume*). Each table contains more than 840 million records. Without otherwise specification, all the tables in both datasets are hash-partitioned and kept on 10 nodes based on their primary key(s). Besides the standard TPC-H queries, we also test with another 5 synthetic queries, i.e. (S-Q1 - S-Q5), for TPC-H dataset, as well as 4 real queries (i.e., SSE-Q6 - SSE-Q9) commonly used on Stock Exchange dataset, to better demonstrate the properties of our proposals:

```
S-Q1: SELECT * FROM orders
      WHERE o_comment not like "%[word1]%[word2]";
S-Q2: SELECT * FROM orders
      WHERE o_orderdate < "[date]";
S-Q3: SELECT l_returnflag, l_linestatus,
             sum(l_quantity), avg(l_discount)
      FROM lineitem
      GROUP BY l_returnflag, l_linestatus;
S-Q4: SELECT l_commitdate, sum(l_quantity),
             avg(l_discount)
      FROM lineitem
      GROUP BY l_commitdate;
S-Q5: SELECT * FROM orders, lineitem
      WHERE l_orderkey=o_orderkey;
SSE-Q6: SELECT count(*)
        FROM  Trades T, Securities S
        WHERE S.sec_code = 600036  AND
        T.trade_date = "2010-10-30" AND
        S.acct_id = T.acct_id;
SSE-Q7: SELECT acct_id, sum(trade_volume)
        FROM Trades
        GROUP BY acct_id;
SSE-Q8: SELECT acct_id, sec_code sum(trade_volume)
        FROM Trades
        WHERE trade_date = "2010-10-10"
        GROUP BY acct_id, sec_code;
SSE-Q9: SELECT sec_code, acct_id,sum(trade_volume)
               sum(entry_volume)
        FROM Trades T, Securities S
        WHERE T.trade_date = "2010-10-30" AND
        S.entry_date= "2010-10-30" AND
        T.acct_id = S.acct_id
        GROUP BY T.sec_code, S.acct_id;
```

5.2 Elastic iterator model

Scalability: To evaluate the scalability of intra-segment parallelism enabled by our elastic iterator model, we run the synthetic queries (i.e., S-Q1 - S-Q5) on the TPC-H dataset and present the results in Figure 8. S-Q1 and S-Q2 filter tuples over the *orders* table. S-Q1 is computation-intensive because of the LIKE operator, while S-Q2 is data-intensive. S-Q3 and S-Q4 contain aggregations with group-by cardinalities of 4 and 250 million respectively in terms of the generated TPC-H dataset. S-Q5 evaluates equal join between two large tables. To evaluate the real scalability of a segment regardless of the network communication or workloads of other segments, we run this micro-benchmark over a non-partitioned TPC-H dataset on a single node, such that the query plan for each of the 5 queries contains only one segment .

Figure 8(a) illustrates the scalability of the filter operator (S-Q1 and S-Q2). For computation-intensive workload, e.g. S-Q1, the throughput of the filter operator increases almost linearly. In contrast, for data-intensive queries, e.g. S-Q2, the performance is no longer improved when the parallelism exceeds 8, due to the memory bandwidth limitation. Figure 8(b) presents the scalability of the hash aggregation operator (S-Q3 and S-Q4). S-Q3 and S-Q4 are evaluated under both shared-aggregation and independent aggregation algorithms, respectively. Due to the hash table contention caused by small group-by cardinality, S-Q3 scales poorly in shared aggregation algorithm. In contrast, as hash table contention rarely happens, S-Q3 with independent aggregation and S-Q4 with both algorithms scale well when hyper-threading is not involved. Figure 8(c) shows the scalability of join operator (S-Q5). As hash join is mainly data-intensive and lock-free structures are employed in hash table to avoid the latching cost, the query scales well both in building phase and probing phase without hyper-threading.

The above results confirm the good scalability of our elastic iterator model when the algorithms are properly configured. The results also show that the optimal parallelism for a given query relies on the query workload, data distribution and underlying algorithm implementation. They further imply the high risk of suboptimal query plan with poor thread parallelism chosen at compile time.

Overhead of expansion and shrinkage: We then evaluate the delay caused by expansion and shrinkage functions. The overhead determines the efficiency of parallelism adjustment and response to workload variance. The overhead of expansion is the time duration between worker thread creation and its beginning of data processing. The overhead of shrinkage is the time duration between the termination request on a worker thread and the complete termination of the thread. Figure 9(a) shows the average overhead with vary-

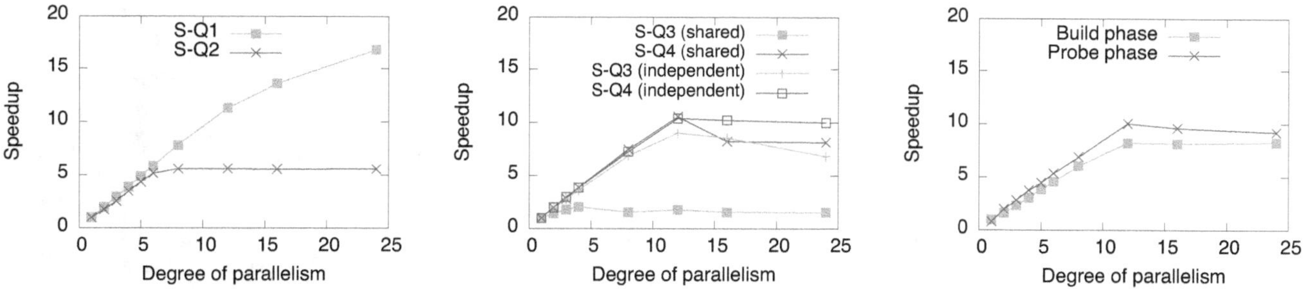

(a) *filter* operator (b) *hash aggregation* operator (c) *hash join* operator

Figure 8: Scalability of intra-segment parallelism of the elastic iterator model

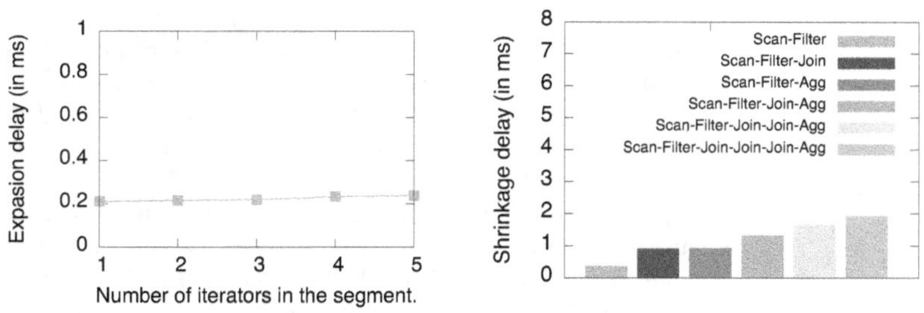

(a) overhead of expansion (b) overhead of shrinkage

Figure 9: The efficiency of expansion and shrinkage operations

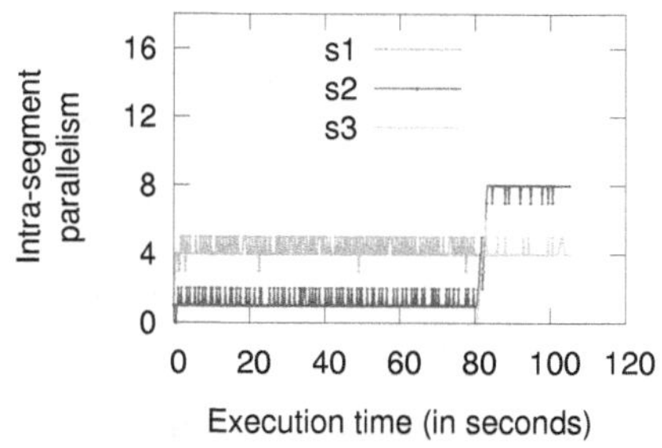

Figure 10: Parallelism dynamics of elastic pipelining on SSE-Q9

ing numbers of running iterators in the segments. As expected, the overhead of expansion is negligible and only slightly affected by the number of iterators in the segment. That is because the newly created thread does not need to process any data before catching up with other existing ones. In contrast, the overhead of shrinkage shown in Figure 9(b) depends on the number of iterators in the segment and their types. Before termination, the terminating thread must ensure its corresponding data block are finished by all the iterators in the active stage. Consequently, the overhead of shrinkage grows when the termination target is more time-consuming operators (e.g. join and aggregation) or a larger number of iterators are active in the segment. Nevertheless, the overhead of shrinkage is sufficiently small to support high flexibility of online parallelism adjustment.

5.3 Dynamic Scheduler

In this part of experiments, we show how our dynamic scheduler adaptively updates the parallelism for segments by an in-depth case study on SSE-Q9, which is daily issued to generate reports for Stock Exchange database. Table T is partitioned across 10 nodes on attribute "sec_code", while table S is partitioned on attribute "acct_id". As the equal hash join is run on attribute "acct_id", the dataflow of T has to be repartitioned on "acct_id" before joining with S. The query plan is generated after query optimization, as shown in Figure 1(b). In this query plan, there are two pipelines $P1$ and $P2$, and three segments S_1, S_2 and S_3, each of which runs on all of the 10 nodes. Without specific clarification, the initial intra-segment parallelism is set to 1.

Dynamic intra-segment parallelism: We keep track of the intra-segment parallelism for each stage on a randomly chosen node and show the results in Figure 10. When pipeline $P1$ begins to execute, S_1 is the performance bottleneck of this query due to the low selectivity of $filter1$. The scheduler detects such workload on-the-fly and lets S_1 expand to accelerate the data processing. As a consequence, the throughput of S_1 is improved and the new performance bottleneck moves to S_2, which will be expanded by the scheduler sequentially. As the throughput of data processing in S_1 and S_2 increases, the network communication between S_1 and S_2 finally becomes the performance bottleneck which prevents S_1 and S_2 from benefiting from further parallelism growth. The scheduler detects the network bottleneck and keeps S_1 and S_2 around the appropriate parallelism, such that the data processing rate of the two segments matches the network bandwidth. After the hash table construction, the query steps into pipeline $P2$. The scheduler quickly detects the workload on S_2 and S_3 and adjusts their parallelism for high CPU-efficiency and excellent load balancing.

Resilient to workload variance: To evaluate the adaptivity of our dynamic scheduler, we reorder the tuples in each partition of $Trade$ on attribute "trade_date" in ascending order, to simulate fluctuating selectivity on $filter1$ during query processing. The results for SSE-Q9 are shown in Figure 11. At the beginning of the query evaluation, the selectivity of $filter1$ is 0, as the dates of the data are all way before the date "2010-10-30" in filter condition. The scheduler detects that S_1 is under-producing and expands S_1. It also shrinks segment S_2 as there is no input data available for processing. As the query evaluation goes on, the selectivity of $filter1$ jumps to 1 when the tuples on "2010-10-30" are coming into the system. At this moment, S_1 turns over-producing due to the large selectivity of $filter1$, and is requested to shrink by the scheduler to ensure a proper producing rate matching the network bandwidth. Moreover, the scheduler starts to expand the "hibernating" segment S_2, as huge amount of tuples are flooding into S_2.

During the query evaluation, we run a CPU-intensive program periodically on each of the nodes to slow down the overall data processing throughput. We run SSE-Q9 again and monitor how our dynamic scheduler acts in such dynamic processing throughput. To better understand the behavior of the scheduler in response to workload variance, we let the program sleep 20 seconds for every 40 seconds. The parallelism of each segment during the query on a randomly chosen node is shown in Figure 12. When the inference program turns active, the scheduler immediately detects the low throughput of the segments and ask them to shrink for better CPU

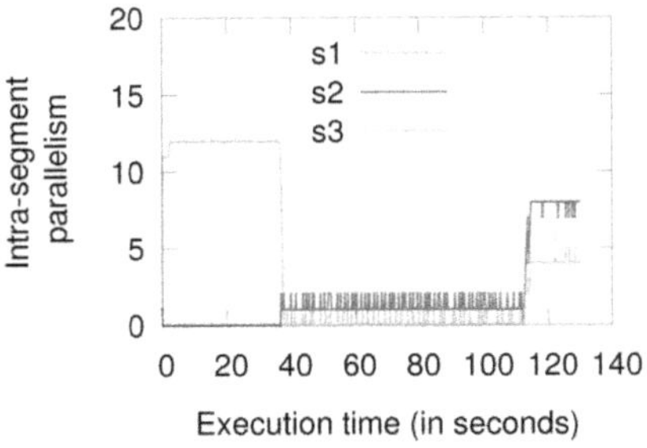

Figure 11: The adaptivity of dynamic scheduler to the selectivity fluctuation

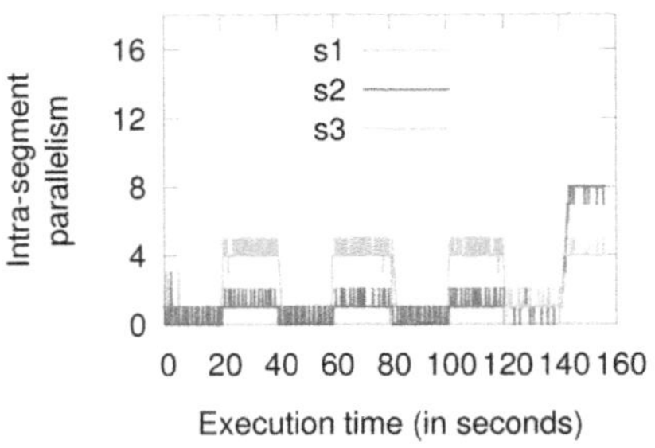

Figure 12: The adaptivity of dynamic scheduler to the interfering program

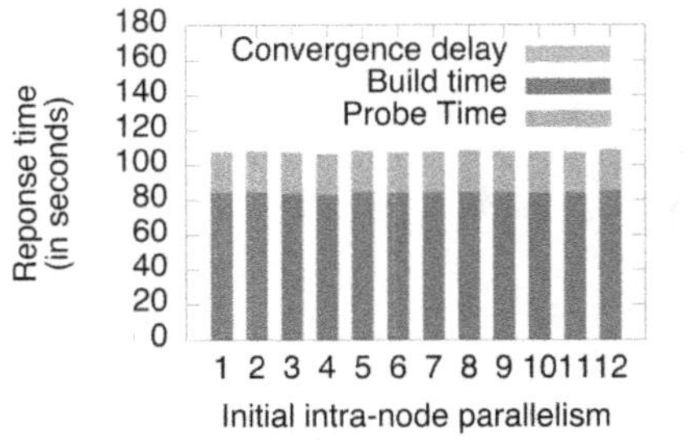

Figure 13: The robustness to the initial parallelism assignment

Table 4: Comparison on memory consumption (in GB)

	SSE-Q6	SSE-Q7	SSE-Q8	SSE-Q9
EP	3.56	1.41	2.0	2.3
SP	3.7	1.4	2.2	2.4
ME	23.4	4.2	11.3	16.5

utilization. In contrast, whenever the inference program pauses, the dynamic scheduler immediately identifies the potentials on the scalability of the segments, and expands them accordingly to leverage computation resource of CPUs.

Fast convergence and robustness to initial parallelism: To confirm the fast convergence of our dynamic scheduler in refining the parallelism and the robustness to the initial parallelism assignment specified at the beginning of query processing, we run SSE-Q9 with different initial intra-segment parallelism and report the complete query response time and convergence delays in Figure 13. The results show that as the query begins to evaluate or steps into a new stage, our scheduler can respond to the varying workload and readjusts to the optimal parallelism with a very short convergence delay. The results also demonstrate that the initial intra-segment parallelism does not obviously affect the query response time, which confirms the self-tunning feature of our elastic pipelining.

5.4 End-to-End evaluation

Comparison against static pipelining and materialized execution: The superiority of our elastic pipelining (EP) is verified by comparing with both static pipelining (SP) and materialized execution (ME). In ME, all the tuples generated by a segment are fully materialized before they are sent to the consumer segment(s) via network. Table 4 presents the memory consumption during query processing under the three processing frameworks. Due to space limitations, we only give the results on SSE dataset. As expected, ME consumes much more RAM compared with pipelined execution due to the materialization.

Table 7 shows the query response time of various queries under these three settings, respectively. As the query response time in SP and ME is significantly affected by the parallelism assignment, its efficiency is underestimated if the query optimizer fails to generate a query plan with the optimal parallelism. To avoid such underestimation, we manually register 10 different constant parallelism for each query and report only the best result as the strawman to our EP approach. In the parallelism assignment, we try to assign each segment with the optimal parallelism such that the segment is allocated with proper cores to accelerate data processing and to match the data processing rate of its downside/upside segments. The results show that SP outperforms ME, with benefits from pipelined parallelism among segments and the skip of materialization. However, the performance improvement by pipelined parallelism is no larger than 20% in most queries. That is because the imbalanced generating rates among consumer segments and producer segments in static pipelining severely discount the benefits of pipelining. In contrast, parallelism of each segment in elastic pipelining is dynamically adapted to the runtime workload for load balance within pipelines, which enhances the utilization of CPU cores and the network bandwidth. Consequently, elastic pipelining outperforms static pipelining by a huge margin.

Comparison to adaptive parallelism scheduling methods: We compare our elastic pipelining (EP) with two existing parallelism scheduling methods, namely implicit scheduling (IS) [24] and morsel-driven-parallelism (MDP) [19]. As the codes of their systems used in their experiments are not publicly available, we implement IS and MDP in our own system. In our IS implementation, each query plan consists of multiple segments on each node. One segment is bound to one thread for execution and the operating system is responsible for scheduling on the worker threads. In our MDP implementation, query segments are decomposed into fine-grained executable units, which are inserted to a waiting list and can be executed concurrently. A set of worker threads are created to process the executable units. Once a worker thread has processed a unit, it randomly picks up the next available one. We also implemented MDP$^+$, an enhanced version over MDP, in which each worker thread picks up the next unit based on our dynamic scheduling strategy that considers the scalability of the segments and the load balance among nodes. The aim of MDP$^+$ is to show how we can improve the performance of MDP by using a better scheduling strategy tailored to the in-memory database cluster. For MDP, we test a variety of executable unit sizes to find the optimal unit size at 64KB. We thus use 64KB as the executable unit size in our comparisons. To avoid the CPU under-utilization and reduce context switch cost, we test various concurrency levels for IS, MDP and MDP$^+$ respectively, as suggested in [24]. Concurrency level, denoted as c, is the ratio of worker threads to the number of hardware cores. We run all the SSE and TPC-H queries with these four methods respectively, and show the average response times under each method in Table 5 of all queries. To get a better perspective of the performance variances, we also report the average CPU utilization rate, cache miss ratio, context switches and scheduling overhead. CPU utilization rate is measured on the cores allocated to the query threads. Cache miss ratio is the average of L1, L2 and L3 data cache miss ratio, measured by Intel PCM. Context switch counts are obtained from the linux process profile. For MDP, MDP$^+$ and EP, the scheduling overhead is measured as the ratio of the aggregate scheduling CPU time to the query response time. As IS is scheduled by the OS, the scheduling overhead is not available.

The results show that IS and MDP perform poorly when c=1 (one thread per core), due to the low CPU utilization. Using more worker threads, e.g., c=5, helps to keep CPU busy, because if one thread is blocked due to imbalanced workload or inefficient network bandwidth, the thread can yield its core to another waiting

Table 5: Comparison with three baseline scheduling methods

	IS			MDP			MDP$^+$(unit size=64K)			MDP$^+$(unit size=8K)			EP
	c=1	c=2	c=5	c=1	c=2	c=5	c=1	c=2	c=5	c=1	c=2	c=5	c=1
CPU utilization rate(%)	27.0	53.5	88.2	36.2	66.9	93.5	59.6	76.4	97.3	87.2	99.5	99.6	99.6
context switches / second ($\times$1000)	0.2	8.3	18.0	0.2	3.0	10.0	0.1	2.9	6.9	0.1	2.6	6.2	0.2
scheduling overhead (%)	n/a	n/a	n/a	0.21	0.92	1.54	0.49	1.27	2.82	3.36	6.22	17.41	0.20
cache miss ratio	0.41	0.52	0.75	0.42	0.54	0.76	0.46	0.52	0.75	0.21	0.56	0.73	0.41
response time (s)	202.3	144.7	123.4	172.2	131.4	120.7	138.1	121.3	111.9	145.4	131.1	122.7	54.3

thread. Unfortunately, using more worker threads may bring more context switches and hence ruins cache locality. Consequently, the benefits of higher CPU utilization brought by using more worker threads are discounted severely. Compared with IS and MDP, MDP$^+$ has better CPU utilization and better performance. That is because MDP$^+$ is equipped with our scheduling algorithm, which is capable of reassigning the cores from blocked segments to under-producing segments. It is interesting to find that MDP$^+$ always outperforms the other two methods, when IS, MDP and MDP$^+$ have the similar CPU utilization. Such phenomenon is due to our scheduling policy on MDP$^+$ with consideration on the scalability of segments. When a free core is available for multiple segments, the scheduling algorithm prefers to assign the core to the most scalable segment. Note that in MDP$^+$, if a thread is blocked by the network I/O, it cannot switch to another unit until the current unit is completely processed. As a result, a large unit size will cause delays in parallelism adjustment, which explains the relatively low CPU utilization for a large unit size. Using a smaller unit size could effectively improve the CPU utilization. However, as shown in Table 5, smaller unit size introduces expensive scheduling overhead, limiting the query performance. Although MDP$^+$ and EP use our dynamic scheduling strategy, EP is superior on cache locality and scheduling overhead, and thus significantly cuts the query response time. In our EP approach, CPU cores are always focusing on the data processing in their assigned segments until they are notified by the scheduler to migrate, which helps to retain good cache locality. Instead of running the time-consuming scheduling algorithm for each individual worker thread to make decision on a subsequent processing unit, our scheduling strategy in EP is called at much lower frequency while remains sensitive to workload change. This guarantees instantaneous response to changes on query processing with minimal scheduling overhead.

From another perspective, a key advantage of EP over baseline methods is that it always tries to improve the hardware utilization by revising the parallelism assignment according to the runtime workload, until the executing query reaches the limitation of the available hardware. To verify this claims, we divide the query execution time into slices and monitor the hardware utilization for each time slice. A time slices is called *high-utilized* if its average utilization of either CPU or network reaches a threshold, e.g., θ_u=0.95. The high utilization rate of a query is the percentage of high-utilized time slices. Table 6 presents the high utilization rates and the response times for the queries. Due to space limitation, we only show the results for TPC-H-Q1, TPC-H-Q9 and TPC-H-Q14, which respectively represent computing-intensive queries, network-intensive queries and mixed-workload queries. The results show that EP can always fully leverage the hardware resource, which partially explains the superior performance of EP over other methods.

Comparison to state-of-the-art systems: Finally, we compare the performance of elastic query processing engine with Impala and Shark, two state-of-the-art distributed SQL query engines in the open source community. For Impala and Shark, Parquet is used as the table format, which is reported to be the best option [11]. For

Table 6: Comparison with baselines on hardware utilization

	high utilization rate (%)			Query response time (s)		
Queries	IS	MDP	EP	IS	MDP	EP
TPC-H-Q1	28.9	21.3	96.5	19.5	9.6	4.8
TPC-H-Q9	38.6	33.2	95.4	256.4	203.7	105.1
TPC-H-Q14	19.3	18.4	89.2	112.3	87.3	20.6

sake of fair comparison on these systems, we carefully configure the setup in Impala and Shark to avoid disk I/O during the query evaluations. In particular, HDFS cache is enabled and all the tables are read before conducting comparison so that Impala and Shark can query over the cached data. Note that although Impala writes query results onto disk, this does not noticeably increase the query response time due to the very small output results size (smaller than 100KB) for the queries evaluated in our experiments. Also, we ensure that the intermediate results materialization in Shark is buffered by operating system cache with minimal disk I/Os, which is verified by monitoring Linux Process profile. Table 7 shows the query response times for a variety of queries on these three systems. Due to the limitation of our query engine, some TPC-H queries are not supported in CLAIMS and hence the results for those queries are not shown in the table. Largely due to the efficient data processing features in Impala, such as code generation, SIMD instructions etc., it outperforms Shark by a huge margin. However, with the huge benefits from scalable intra-segment parallelism as well as the sophisticated parallelism assignment enabled by elastic pipelining, CLAIMS is consistently 5 times faster than Impala in most cases.

We hereby emphasize that, although the framework of elastic pipelining is proven to be efficient, it is possible to improve the performance by including other orthogonal optimization techniques. Firstly, since network data transmission is the major bottleneck in our settings, significant performance enhancement is expected by employing high-speed interconnect devices, such as InfiniBand. Second, we can further enhance the query performance of CLAIMS by integrating code generation features into the query engine. For instance, our recent investigations on our system show that filter operators gain a speedup by up to two orders of magnitude by simply employing LLVM [17] to generate query-specific code.

6. RELATED WORK

Centralized In-Memory Database. By maintaining data and intermediate results completely in main memory, in-memory databases employ new techniques to resolve new bottlenecks in query processing and exploit multi-core architecture and memory hierarchy for performance improvement. The existing studies can be generally classified into three categories, based on their targets and assumptions on the systems.

The first category covers research attempts with better data placement and organization in main memory. [10] shows column store is helpful to alleviate the memory access bottleneck. Light-weight data compression is introduced in [25] to reduce the data access overhead. The second category includes research works trying to improve cache behavior of database operators. Manegold et al. [21] propose radix join algorithm to accelerate in-memory equal join. Wang et al. [30] validates the possibility of improvement for

Table 7: **Response time (in seconds) of various queries in CLAIMS, Shark and Impala**

Queries	CLAIMS ME	SP	EP	Shark	Impala
TPC-H-Q1	38.3	35.0	4.8	102.7	35.1
TPC-H-Q2	25.4	28.4	5.4	76.5	28.4
TPC-H-Q3	172.3	76.6	28.0	231.0	150.9
TPC-H-Q5	323.2	200.9	68.8	412.9	321.0
TPC-H-Q6	62.5	58.7	15.1	120.2	46.0
TPC-H-Q7	223.1	203.3	62.3	325.3	243.3
TPC-H-Q8	312.7	284.1	58.5	421.2	256.2
TPC-H-Q9	398.8	363.2	105.1	512.6	410.4
TPC-H-Q10	188.0	175.0	65.0	342.4	183.0
TPC-H-Q12	91.2	85.7	16.7	78.5	43.2
TPC-H-Q14	94.5	61.1	20.6	130.3	78.3
SSE-Q6	38.0	33.9	10.3	56.6	35.2
SSE-Q7	25.2	21.1	3.5	48.2	27.9
SSE-Q8	26.3	20.34	2.4	35.3	20.5
SSE-Q9	58.3	53.2	28.4	203.7	147.4

in-memory database by running aggregation queries under NUMA architecture. Albutiu et al. [3] propose extensive optimizations to achieve scalable sort-merge join in NUMA architectures. [15] revisits the parallel sort-merge join and hash join run over modem hardware. [5] further exploits the parallel join algorithms and shows the competitiveness of non-partitioning join. The third category contains research studies on data processing model and sophisticated compilation techniques. MonetDB and Vectorwise prove the power of column-at-a-time and block-at-at-a-time data processing model respectively to improve the code efficiency. Krikellas et al. show that query performance can be significantly improved by generating query-specific C code [16]. HyPer [23] and Impala [2] leverage LLVM [17] to generate specific, optimized code for a given query.

All these studies above are designed for centralized in-memory database running on one single machine. We hereby emphasize that, all those techniques are generally orthogonal to the proposal in this paper, and applicable in our prototype system for further performance improvement.

In-Memory Parallel Database. Recently, the research efforts on parallel relational query processing is shifting from disk-based architecture to the new in-memory processing paradigm, to keep the pace with the quick advances of cloud computing, abundance of RAMs in modern servers and the interactive querying requirements from real applications. A number of new systems are emerging in recent years, with new technologies to better address such demands. Shark [31], for example, processes queries on top of Apache Spark, with a data-centric computation resource allocation mechanism. It materializes huge amount of data for fault tolerance purpose and thus potentially wastes CPU cycles and memory space, to gain the benefits on efficient failure recovery. Imapla [2], known as the top performer in a wide group of tests [9] against Hive [28] and Presto [29], supports query processing under the massive parallel processing (MPP) paradigm. However, Impala does not fully exploit the computation power in modern multi-core hardware, as it uses single-threaded algorithms to process joins and aggregations [11]. In the following, we discuss two specific and general challenges for in-memory parallel database systems.

Firstly, inter-node data and intermediate result transmission becomes one of the major bottlenecks in multi-node in-memory parallel databases, due to the relative slow network bandwidth. There is extensive work on reducing the network communication. A general coloring theory is introduced in [14] to dispatch operators over the distributed nodes in order to minimize network communication. [32] minimizes the data repartitioning cost by reducing data repartitioning in the query plans. [26] proposes optimal data partition assignment strategy, to leverage data co-location for smaller network transmission cost. Our elastic pipelining technique assumes that the query execution plan on the distributed nodes is already optimized. The elasticity feature on the pipelines provides additional performance enhancement by fully utilizing the CPU cycles and network bandwidth.

Secondly, the workload imbalance among the pipelines significantly hinders the query processing efficiency. Manish et al. [22] propose a model on data producing rate of operators, together with intra-operator parallelism assignment strategy for load balancing. However, their method may not be applicable to the in-memory database cluster, as the data producing rates are more sensitive than traditional disk-based databases. In this paper, we simplify the load balance problem by adjusting the intra-segment parallelism at runtime rather than fixing the parallelism at compile time. There are also several adaptive parallelism methods proposed for online load balance in pipelined execution. [24] relies on the operating system scheduler to decide the runtime parallelism of the queries. It may result in expensive context switch cost and cache miss penalty. Our dynamic scheduler avoids the context switch cost by allocating one query thread per core and dynamically provisioning cores to segments based on the runtime workload. [19] achieves adaptive parallelism by decomposing query into self-contained, small-sized units. However, their method does not fully address the potential problem of parallel in-memory database. Our proposal provides a complete solution even when the operators interact via network connection.

7. CONCLUSION AND FUTURE WORK

In this paper, we propose elastic pipelining as a new approach to unleash the huge performance potential of pipelining framework for in-memory database clusters. We present elastic iterator model, as an extended version of traditional iterator model, to support runtime intra-segment parallelism update in a generic way. A dynamic scheduler is designed to monitor the workload of query execution, wisely choose the appropriate parallelism for each segment, which dramatically improves the overall throughput on data processing and minimizes the query response time. Extensive experiments on the real dataset and TPC-H dataset validate the great flexibility of our iterator model and effectiveness of our scheduling strategy.

In the future, we plan to explore the following directions for more performance improvement over the current system. Firstly, it is promising to allow runtime segment movement across nodes in the database cluster. Currently, the segment-to-node assignment is pre-defined and fixed during query execution. In extreme cases, the workloads on the nodes can be highly skewed. More flexibility on segment movement will enable the system to achieve better workload balancing for higher processing throughput. Secondly, the scheduling method can be further extended to handle multiple queries running at the same time. When there are a number of query executions running on the nodes, the scheduling strategy needs to be updated, in order to address the demands on the overall response time minimization on all queries.

8. ACKNOWLEDGMENT

This study is partially supported by National Science Foundation of China under grant No.61332006 and 863 Key project under grant No. 2015AA015303, the research grant for the Human-Centered Cyber-physical Systems Programme at the Advanced Digital Sciences Center from Singapore's A*STAR, and Infosys.

9. REFERENCES

[1] https://github.com/dase/claims.git.

[2] https://www.cloudera.com/products/apache-hadoop/impala.html.

[3] M.-C. Albutiu, A. Kemper, and T. Neumann. Massively parallel sort-merge joins in main memory multi-core database systems. *PVLDB*, 5(10):1064–1075, 2012.

[4] C. Balkesen, G. Alonso, J. Teubner, and M. T. Ozsu. Multi-core, main-memory joins: Sort vs. hash revisited. *PVLDB*, 7(1), 2013.

[5] S. Blanas, Y. Li, and J. M. Patel. Design and evaluation of main memory hash join algorithms for multi-core cpus. In *SIGMOD*, pages 37–48, 2011.

[6] S. Blanas, J. M. Patel, V. Ercegovac, J. Rao, E. J. Shekita, and Y. Tian. A comparison of join algorithms for log processing in mapreduce. In *SIGMOD*, pages 975–986, 2010.

[7] L. Bouganim, D. Florescu, P. Valduriez, et al. Dynamic load balancing in hierarchical parallel database systems. In *VLDB*, pages 436–447, 1996.

[8] J. Cieslewicz and K. Ross. Adaptive aggregation on chip multiprocessors. In *VLDB*, pages 339–350, 2007.

[9] J. Erickson, M. Kornacker, and D. Kumar. New sql choices in the apache hadoop ecosystem: Why impala continues to lead. http://blog.cloudera.com/blog/2014/05/new-sql-choices-in-the-apache-hadoop-ecosystem-why-impala-continues-to-lead.

[10] F. Färber, S. K. Cha, J. Primsch, C. Bornhövd, S. Sigg, and W. Lehner. Sap hana database: data management for modern business applications. *ACM Sigmod Record*, 40(4):45–51, 2012.

[11] A. Floratou, U. F. Minhas, and F. Ozcan. Sql-on-hadoop: Full circle back to shared-nothing database architectures. *PVLDB*, 7(12):1295–1306, 2014.

[12] T. Z. J. Fu, J. Ding, R. T. B. Ma, M. Winslett, Y. Yang, and Z. Zhang. Drs: Dynamic resource scheduling for real-time analytics over fast streams. In *ICDCS*, pages 411–420, 2015.

[13] G. Graefe. Volcano-an extensible and parallel query evaluation system. *IEEE Trans. Knowl. Data Eng.*, 6(1):120–135, 1994.

[14] W. Hasan. *Optimization of SQL queries for parallel machines*. PhD thesis, Stanford University, 1995.

[15] C. Kim, T. Kaldewey, V. W. Lee, E. Sedlar, A. D. Nguyen, N. Satish, J. Chhugani, A. Di Blas, and P. Dubey. Sort vs. hash revisited: Fast join implementation on modern multi-core cpus. *PVLDB*, 2(2):1378–1389, 2009.

[16] K. Krikellas, S. D. Viglas, and M. Cintra. Generating code for holistic query evaluation. In *ICDE*, pages 613–624, 2010.

[17] C. Lattner and V. Adve. Llvm: A compilation framework for lifelong program analysis & transformation. In *CGO*, pages 75–86, 2004.

[18] E. D. Lazowska, J. Zahorjan, G. S. Graham, and K. C. Sevcik. *Quantitative system performance: computer system analysis using queueing network models*. Prentice-Hall, Inc., 1984.

[19] V. Leis, P. Boncz, A. Kemper, and T. Neumann. Morsel-driven parallelism: A numa-aware query evaluation framework for the many-core age. In *SIGMOD*, pages 743–754, 2014.

[20] S. Manegold, P. Boncz, and M. Kersten. Optimizing main-memory join on modern hardware. *IEEE Trans. Knowl. Data Eng.*, 14(4):709–730, 2002.

[21] S. Manegold, P. A. Boncz, and M. L. Kersten. Optimizing database architecture for the new bottleneck: memory access. *VLDB Journal*, 9(3):231–246, 2000.

[22] M. Mehta and D. J. DeWitt. Managing intra-operator parallelism in parallel database systems. In *VLDB*, pages 382–394, 1995.

[23] T. Neumann. Efficiently compiling efficient query plans for modern hardware. *PVLDB*, 4(9):539–550, 2011.

[24] I. Psaroudakis, T. Scheuer, N. May, and A. Ailamaki. Task scheduling for highly concurrent analytical and transactional main-memory workloads. In *ADMS@ VLDB*, pages 36–45, 2013.

[25] V. Raman, G. Attaluri, R. Barber, N. Chainani, D. Kalmuk, V. KulandaiSamy, J. Leenstra, S. Lightstone, S. Liu, G. M. Lohman, et al. Db2 with blu acceleration: So much more than just a column store. *PVLDB*, 6(11):1080–1091, 2013.

[26] W. Rodiger, T. Muhlbauer, P. Unterbrunner, A. Reiser, A. Kemper, and T. Neumann. Locality-sensitive operators for parallel main-memory database clusters. In *ICDE*, pages 592–603, 2014.

[27] J. Teubner and R. Mueller. How soccer players would do stream joins. In *SIGMOD*, pages 625–636. ACM, 2011.

[28] A. Thusoo, J. S. Sarma, N. Jain, Z. Shao, P. Chakka, S. Anthony, H. Liu, P. Wyckoff, and R. Murthy. Hive: a warehousing solution over a map-reduce framework. *PVLDB*, 2(2):1626–1629, 2009.

[29] M. Traverso. Presto: Interacting with Petabytes of Data at Facebook. https://www.facebook.com/notes/facebook-engineering/presto-interacting-with-petabytes-of-data-at-facebook/10151786197628920.pdf, 2014.

[30] L. Wang, M. Zhou, Z. Zhang, M. S. Shan, and A. Zhou. Numa-aware scalable and efficient in-memory aggregation on large domains. *IEEE Trans. Knowl. Data Eng.*, 27(4):1071–1084, 2015.

[31] R. S. Xin, J. Rosen, M. Zaharia, M. J. Franklin, S. Shenker, and I. Stoica. Shark: Sql and rich analytics at scale. In *SIGMOD*, pages 13–24, 2013.

[32] J. Zhou, P.-A. Larson, and R. Chaiken. Incorporating partitioning and parallel plans into the scope optimizer. In *ICDE*, pages 1060–1071, 2010.

[33] M. Zukowski, M. van de Wiel, and P. Boncz. Vectorwise: A vectorized analytical dbms. In *ICDE*, pages 1349–1350, 2012.

APPENDIX

A. IMPLEMENTATION DETAILS

In this section, we introduce the implementation details of iterators in our elastic iterator model.

A.1 Elastic Iterator

Algorithm 2 presents the concrete workflow of the worker thread. When a new worker thread is started, it immediately calls child iterator's `open` function to initialize the entire sub-iterator tree. The new worker thread checks the returned status of `open` function. If the status is TERMINATED, it means that the expanded thread has received a terminate request during calling its child iterator's open. Then the thread exits to complete the shrinkage. Otherwise, the thread will repeatedly get data blocks from child iterator by calling `next` of child iterator and inserts the newly obtained data blocks into the data buffer until the calling of `next` returns status other than SUCCESS, which means either the input dataflow has been entirely consumed or the thread receives a terminate request.

Algorithm 2: Pseudocodes of the worker thread.

```
open_status=child_iterator.open()
if open_status=TERMINATED then
    /*open terminated due to terminal requrest*/
    return SHRINK_SUCCESS
/*open is successful, and call next*/
while true do
    next_ret=child_iterator.next()
    if next_ret=block then
        /*successfully get a block*/
        insert block to the buffer.
    else if next_ret=TERMINATED then
        /*received terminate request*/
        return SHRINK_SUCCESS
    else if next_ret=FINISH then
        /*child iterator is exhausted*/
        return FINISH
```

A.2 Modification to Existing Iterators

Before delving into the details, we first give the basic rules of revision over traditional iterator model to support the multi-threaded calling of `open` and `next` functions. Then we introduce our implementation of synchronization barriers, which is a fundamental function widely used in the implementation of elastic iterator model, to guarantee the correctness of multi-threaded query processing. Finally, we present the details of modification over existing iterators.

A.2.1 Modification Sketch

Implementation of `open`: The `open` function has two major tasks, including (a) calling the child iterator's `open` if necessary, and (b) initializing the state. For the first task, the corresponding code of traditional iterators does not need to be modified, as it is the responsibility of the child iterator to handle the multi-threaded calling of `open`. For the second task, the code should be carefully designed such that the state initialization is correct in case of multi-threaded calling of `open`. The way of handling multi-threaded calling of `open` depends on whether the workload of constructing its state is heavy enough such that multi-threaded processing is deserved.

For the non-blocking iterators such as filter and scan, they do not need to consume any data from the child iterator to construct their states, and hence the state construction is light-weighed and can be finished instantly. For instance, to construct the state of a filter iterator, the thread only needs to initialize the references to the predicate functions. For such operators, we only need to slightly modify the codes, such that only the worker thread first arriving at the initialization code is responsible for the state construction while other worker threads arriving later all wait at the synchronization barrier until the completion of state construction.

Blocking iterators, i.e., pipeline breakers, build their states with the data blocks obtained by calling child iterator's `next`. Compared with non-blocking iterator, the state construction in the blocking iterator is very heavy and deserves multi-threaded processing. Consequently, we let all the worker threads construct the state in parallel. As the child iterator is responsible for handling the multi-threaded calling of `next`, the blocking iterator only needs to achieve thread safety on `open` function, when the obtained data blocks are fed into the state by multiple threads concurrently. For instance, in the hash join iterator's `open`, it is necessary to protect the hash table only, by employing locks or atomic instructions.

Implementation of `next`: Recall that `next` function consumes data either from the iterator's state or from the child iterator, processes the data, and returns the processed data block to its caller each time. The way of supporting multi-threading in the `next` depends on whether the calling of `next` updates the state of the iterator.

For some iterators, such as filter and hash join, the codes in `next` only get access to iterator states in a read-only mode, and hence worker threads work independently of each other. Consequently, the `next` function under this category does not require any modification to support multi-threaded calling.

For the other iterators, such as scan, aggregation, and sort, the calling of `next` updates the states. `next` should be implemented in such a way that the updates to the state are thread-safe. Take hash aggregation iterator as an example. After state construction in `open`, the aggregated results are stored in hash table. `next` will return a block of tuples in hash table at a time. The update to the cursor that records the current read position in the hash table should be thread-safe by using locking or atomic instructions.

A.2.2 Synchronization Barriers

Synchronization barriers are widely used in our iterator implementation. A synchronization barrier forces multiple threads (the caller to the barrier) to wait until a specified number of threads have reached the particular point of execution where the barrier is injected. As the number of worker threads might change during query execution due to shrinkage and expansion operations, the barriers should be updated appropriately when a worker thread is terminated or created. To achieve this in our implementation, each barrier maintains a value, called $thread\_count$. The threads waiting at the barrier are blocked until the number of waiting threads reaches $thread\_count$. The initial value of $thread\_count$ is set to 0. When a newly created thread calls `open` of an iterator, it will call *registerToAllBarriers()* to increase the $thread\_count$ of all the barriers in this iterator by 1 such that the other worker threads have to wait this new thread if they arrived at any of the barriers. When a thread terminates, it will call *boradcastExitToAllBarriers()* to decrease the $thread\_count$ of all the barriers by 1 such that other threads waiting at the barriers will not wait this thread.

A.2.3 Modification Details

In the rest of this subsection, we will introduce the implementation details for the iterators one by one.

Scan: Algorithm 3 presents the mechanism of $scan$ iterator. $Scan$'s `open` initializes the read cursor for the target table. The workload in $scan$ is light-weight and can be finished by a single thread instantly. Consequently, only the worker thread who first calls $scan$'s `open` is responsible for initializing the read cursor. After `open` is finished, `next` will be called. Then the iterator gets one block from the read cursor and moves the cursor to the next reading position. To support multi-threaded calling of $scan$'s `next`, the movement of the read cursor should be atomic, either by locking or more efficient compare-and-swap (CAS) instruction. To achieve NUMA-awareness in a NUMA architecture, $scan$ maintains multiple read cursors, each pointing to a partition of the table on a NUMA socket. When $scan$'s `next` is called by a worker thread, $scan$ iterator prefers to return a block in local socket. As $scan$ is a pipeline beginner, if it detects a termination request when `next` is called, it will immediately return TERMINATE to its parent iterator such that the worker thread can terminate when all the tuples derived from the $scan$ iterator is processed properly.

Algorithm 3: Pseudocodes of the *scan* iterator.

```
def open ()
    registerToAllBarriers ();
    if isFirstWorkerThread () then
        initialize the read cursor;
    Barrier->arrive ();
def next ()
    if detectedTerminateRequest () then
        return TERMINATE;
    /*get a data block, preferring blocks on local memory.*/
    if getBlockFromCursoe (block) =SUCCESS then
        return block;
    else
        return end-of-file;
```

Sender: Algorithm 4 presents the mechanism of *sender* iterator. *Sender* iterator is responsible for sending the data blocks from its segment to consumer (upside) segments. In our elastic iterator model, *sender* is always the parent of expander iterator, thus it is never called by multiple threads. *Sender*'s `open` creates sending thread, which sends data block in the buffer to the *mergers* of the upside segments according to a specified partitioning schema. After the sending thread is created, the *sender* gets data blocks from elastic iterator and inserts the obtained data blocks to the sending buffer. *Sender*'s `next` returns end-of-file when all the blocks have been sent.

Algorithm 4: Pseudocodes of the *sender* iterator.

```
def open ()
    create sending thread;
    child->open ();
    while child->next (block) =SUCCESS do
        insert block into sending buffer;
def next ()
    blocked until all the blocks in sending buffer are sent;
    return end-of-file;
```

Merger: Algorithm 5 presents the mechanism of *merger* iterator. A *merger* is responsible for receiving data from the *senders* of its downside segments. The first worker thread calling *merger*'s `open` is responsible for creating a merging thread. The merging thread receives data blocks from *senders*, and stores them in the *merger*'s buffer. In the NUMA architecture, *merger*'s buffer is split into several partitions, each of which is stored on a NUMA socket. And the data blocks received from *senders* are inserted into each partition in a round-robin manner, for the purpose of balancing the workload among NUMA sockets. Note that creating a new merging thread is important in our elastic iterator model, because it guarantees that the *merger* is able to receive data blocks when all worker threads have been terminated. When *merger*'s `next` is called, it gets a data block from its buffer, preferring to the data blocks on local socket. As *merger* is the pipeline beginner in a segment, the termination code is inserted at the beginning of `next`.

Filter: The `open` of *filter* iterator initializes the filter function. Similar to *scan* iterator, the state can be constructed by a single work thread instantly. *Filter* iterator's `next` does not modify its state when being called, thus *Filter*'s `next` is the same as traditional iterator.

Hash Join: Algorithm 6 presents the mechanism of *join* iterator. *Join* iterator has two input iterators, say L and R. In *join* iterator's `open`, the tuples obtained by calling L's `next` are inserted into the hash table. To guarantee the correctness of building hash table by multiple threads, tuple insertion to the hash table should be atomic, by locking or CAS instruction. When L's `next` returns TERMINATE, it means that the worker thread received a terminate request. In such cases, the thread stop building the hash table and is terminated in Line 9.

Algorithm 5: Pseudocodes of the *merger* iterator.

```
def open ()
    registerToAllBarriers ();
    if isFirstWorkerThread () then
        create merging thread;
    Barrier->arrive ();
def next ()
    if detectedTerminateRequest () then
        return TERMINATE;
    /*get a data block, preferring blocks on local memory.*/
    if getBlockFromBuffer (block) =SUCCESS then
        return block;
    else
        return end-of-file;
```

Algorithm 6: Pseudocodes of the *join* iterator.

```
1  def open ()
2      registerToAllBarriers ();
3      left_child->open ();
4      while left_child->next (block) =SUCCESS do
5          foreach tuple ∈ block do
6              atomic insert tuple into its corresponding hash bucket;
7      if detectedTerminateRequest () then
8          broadcastExitToAllBarriers ();
9          return TERMINATE;
10     right_child->open ();
11     Barrier->arrive ();
12 def next ()
13     while right_child->next (block) =SUCCESS do
14         foreach tuple ∈ block do
15             insert all the matching tuples in hash table to
               result_block;
16         return result_block;
17     return end-of-file;
```

After the hash table is built, *join*'s `next` will be called by multiple worker threads to get the join results. Once *join* iterator's `next` is called by a worker thread, the thread asks for data blocks by calling R's `next`. By probing the hash table with the tuples from R, *join* iterator returns join results in form of data blocks to its parent iterator. Once the tuples in R are exhausted, the iterator returns end-of-file. As the probe in equal join never modifies the hash table, it does not need any synchronization under multiple thread workers.

Hash Aggregation: Algorithm 7 presents the mechanism of *aggregation* iterator. The `open` of *aggregation* iterator reads data blocks from child iterator and updates the results of the corresponding entries in the hash table. As the same as *join* iterator, aggregation is expensive and deserves multi-threaded processing. For multi-threaded aggregation, the updates to hash table should be protected by an atomic instruction or a lock. We provide two aggregation implementations, denoted as shared aggregation and hybrid aggregation. In shared aggregation, all the worker threads directly update the hash table, which is efficient when the group-by cardinality is large. In hybrid aggregation, a small private hash table is allocated to each worker thread to buffer the partial aggregation results, from which the overflowing entries are flushed into the global hash table. In hybrid aggregation, before a worker thread terminates, it stores its private hash table in the iterator's context for reuse. When a new worker arrives at the aggregation's `open`, it tries to get a unused private hash table allocated by the same core. By dong so, the hash table initialization cost can be avoided by reusing the context if the private hash table is still in cache. This feature is important to keep a short shrinkage delay. To improve the performance under NUMA architectures, the private hash table for each thread is allocated on the local NUMA socket, while the global hash table is partitioned across all the NUMA sockets for better load balance.

Algorithm 7: Pseudocodes of the *aggregation* iterator.

```
def open()
    registerToAllBarriers();
    child->open();
    if isHybridAggregation() then
        /*try to reuse private hash allocated by
        the same core*/
        private_hashtable=getOrCreateContext()(core
        mode);
    while child->next(block) =SUCCESS do
        foreach tuple ∈ block do
            atomically aggregate tuple into the global/private hash
            table;
    if detectedTerminateRequest() then
        broadcastExitToAllBarriers();
        if isHybridAggregation() then
            storeContext(private_hashtable);
        return TERMINATE;
    foreach private hash table pht in the context do
        atomically remove pht from context and flush the result into
        hash table.;
    Barrier->arrive();
def next()
    if detectedTerminateRequest() then
        broadcastExitToAllBarriers();
        return TERMINATE;
    if atomicGetBlockFromHashTable(block) =SUCCESS
    then
        return block;
    else
        return end-of-file;
```

After the `open` function of *aggregation* iterator finishes, the aggregation results are stored in the hash table. When *aggregation*'s `next` is called by a worker thread (from the parent iterator), the iterator organizes a data block from hash table and returns it to the parent iterator. The updates to the read cursor recording the current read position in the hash table should be thread-safe, again by employing locking or CAS instructions. As *aggregation* is a pipeline beginner, the worker thread return TERMINATION if it receives a terminate request, which is similar to *scan* iterator.

Sort: Algorithm 8 presents the mechanism of *sort* iterator. In *sort*'s `open`, the worker thread first calls the child iterator's `open`, and then repeatedly calls `next` function of the child iterator and inserts the obtained data blocks into its buffer. After all the data

Algorithm 8: Pseudocodes of the *sort* iterator.

```
def open()
    registerToAllBarriers();
    child->open();
    while child->next(block) =SUCCESS do
        insert block into buffer;
    if detectedTerminateRequest() then
        broadcastExitToAllBarriers();
        return TERMINATE;
    while getChunkFromBuffer(&chunk) =SUCCESS do
        local sort chunk and add chunk into the
        sorted_chunk_list;
        if detectedTerminateRequest() then
            broadcastExitToAllBarriers();
            return TERMINATE;
    Barrier1->arrive();
    if isFirstWorkerThread() then
        compute the global separators keys and assign them to each
        worker thread;
    Barrier2->arrive();
    merge the data into sorted_buffer according to assigned
    separators keys;
    Barrier3->arrive();
def next()
    if detectedTerminateRequest() then
        broadcastExitToAllBarriers();
        return TERMINATE;
    if getBlockFromSortedBuffer(block) =SUCCESS then
        return block;
    else
        return end-of-file;
```

blocks from child iterator are inserted to the buffer, the worker thread gets one chunk from the buffer at a time, sorts the chunk, and inserts the sorted chunk into a list. Before the worker thread tries to obtain the next chunk to sort, it terminates if terminate request is detected. The chunk size is a trade-off between the shrinkage delay and the merging cost, which can be easily configured by empirical results in practice. After all the chunks are sorted, one worker thread is responsible for computing the global separators and assigns them to each worker thread such that each work can merge the data without synchronization. When *sort*'s `next` is called by a worker thread, the iterator returns a data block from the sorted buffer and updates the read cursor with locking or CAS instruction employed.

Page As You Go: Piecewise Columnar Access In SAP HANA

Reza Sherkat, Colin Florendo, Mihnea Andrei, Anil K. Goel, Anisoara Nica, Peter Bumbulis
Ivan Schreter, Günter Radestock, Christian Bensberg, Daniel Booss, Heiko Gerwens
SAP SE
<*firstname.lastname*>@sap.com

ABSTRACT

In-memory columnar databases such as SAP HANA achieve extreme performance by means of vector processing over logical units of main memory resident columns. The core in-memory algorithms can be challenged when the working set of an application does not fit into main memory. To deal with memory pressure, most in-memory columnar databases evict candidate columns (or tables) using a set of heuristics gleaned from recent workload. As an alternative approach, we propose to reduce the unit of load and eviction from column to a contiguous portion of the in-memory columnar representation, which we call a *page*. In this paper, we adapt the core algorithms to be able to operate with partially loaded columns while preserving the performance benefits of vector processing. Our approach has two key advantages. First, partial column loading reduces the mandatory memory footprint for each column, making more memory available for other purposes. Second, partial eviction extends the in-memory lifetime of partially loaded columns. We present a new in-memory columnar implementation for our approach, that we term *page loadable column*. We design a new persistency layout and access algorithms for the encoded data vector of the column, the order-preserving dictionary, and the inverted index. We compare the performance attributes of page loadable columns with those of regular in-memory columns and present a use-case for page loadable columns for cold data in *data aging* scenarios. Page loadable columns are completely integrated in SAP HANA, and we present extensive experimental results that quantify the performance overhead and the resource consumption when these columns are deployed.

Categories and Subject Descriptors

H.2.4 [**Database Management**]: Systems—*Query processing*

Keywords

In-Memory columnar databases; Data aging

SIGMOD'16, June 26-July 01, 2016, San Francisco, CA, USA

DOI: http://dx.doi.org/10.1145/2882903.2903729

1. INTRODUCTION

Modern in-memory database systems achieve extreme performance for analytical workloads by taking advantage of recent trends in hardware technology, including affordable large dynamic random-access memory (DRAM) and the instruction level parallelism of register vector processing, e.g. Advanced Vector Extensions (AVX) processor capabilities [7, 23, 27]. For in-memory columnar databases, dictionary based compression schemes produce uniform representation and in-memory layout for each column. The memory layout can be optimized for extremely fast basic database operations, such as scan and search [8, 17, 26].

With the rapid growth in the variety of applications that want to combine business data with the emerging Internet of Things (IoT) and/or social media data, there is an important need to also provide very high performance for very large datasets while optimizing the use of precious main memory for low value or low density data. To reduce overall systems memory pressure and to achieve optimal total cost of ownership (TCO), an application may intelligently analyze its workload, and keep only an active subset of data in memory at a given time. As Plattner indicated in [21], SAP HANA optimally serves business applications by being aware of the lifecycle of business data. As data ages, it is rarely accessed and can be moved in the cold store. Unlike the hot store containing the current data, which offers extreme performance, the cold store has a performance−TCO tradeoff biased towards TCO reduction. Another example is an Enterprise Resource Planning (ERP) system which may have two extreme data subsets. On one side lie the frequently accessed columns needed to generate high value reports for decision making. On the other extreme are rarely accessed columns needed for infrequent or low value queries and activities.

In order to achieve optimal memory utilization, an adaptive workload-aware strategy may keep an active subset of columns in memory, and may decide to evict some columns under critical memory pressure. However, loading and unloading columns completely in this way poses two important performance challenges. First, each on-demand access to a column needs a fully memory resident column, even if the access needs to read only a portion of the column (e.g. a single row). Second, the loading of infrequently accessed columns can trigger the eviction of another column, which may be needed again soon. The common root cause of these challenges is the *granularity* of column loading and eviction. Ideally, the memory overhead of each column must be correlated with the portion of the column which is accessed during a workload while limiting the resulting loss of performance as compared to highly optimized in-memory access methods. Therefore, for infrequently accessed columns, we advocate for piecewise columnar presence in memory. To support this, we implemented a new type of column in SAP HANA which we termed *page loadable column*.

A page loadable column is logically treated as a regular column, with one key physical difference. A regular column fully resides in memory during access while one or more fractions of a page loadable column may be evicted from (or never be loaded into) memory. This physical difference is, however, invisible to applications and is reminiscent of pagination in classic database buffer pool implementations. In SAP HANA, each column is associated with three data structures, namely an encoded data vector, a dictionary, and an optional inverted index. We carefully designed page loadable columns in a way that every data structure pertaining to a column becomes page loadable. This design provides for some unique advantages for page loadable columns. For instance, instead of the complete dictionary, only sections of it may be loaded during late materialization [11] of the result of a query on a page loadable column. As another advantage, only a section of a paged inverted index may get loaded corresponding to the search criteria of a scan on a page loadable column. In summary, page loadable columns extend the properties of in-memory column-store databases [3, 25] with support from classic paged buffer pool concepts. The preferred loading behavior of a column is specified at creation time as being loaded either fully or piecewise. Once created, page loadable columns can be manipulated by the same SQL statements as regular columns in SAP HANA. The access layer implements algorithms for piecewise loading of column data structures. The resource manager evicts portions of data structures of a page loadable column.

Our main contributions are:

- We study fine granular columnar accesses for a modern in-memory database system. Our solution provides adaptive flexibility for an extreme performant in-memory column store database with selective and judicious techniques from traditional page-based database system without losing the core advantages of modern in-memory vector processing for scans.
- We propose physical layouts and on-demand access algorithms for data structures of a page loadable column, i.e. its data vector, its order preserving dictionary, and its inverted index for a hybrid implementation.
- We present an overview of our memory management component, which balances system memory allocation by reactive and proactive piecewise column eviction mechanisms.
- We present a use case for page loadable columns in a data aging scenario, and demonstrate the benefits of our solution.
- We present an experimental evaluation of page loadable columns in a large database, and report on runtime overhead and memory footprint reduction.

Roadmap: Section 2 is the background. Section 3 presents page loadable data structures. Section 4 demonstrates data aging as a use case of page loadable columns. Section 5 presents an overview of our memory manager. Section 6 reports our experimental study. Related work is surveyed in Section 7 followed by future research directions in Section 8. Finally, we conclude in Section 9.

2. COLUMN STORE IN SAP HANA

We present an overview of SAP HANA's column store. The architecture of SAP HANA is described in [7, 23]. Each columnar table is composed of a set of columns. Every column has a read optimized section, referred to as its *main* fragment and a write optimized section known as its *delta* fragment. Inserting new rows or updating existing rows are both regarded as changes. Changes do not physically modify existing rows (i.e. no in-place update) but append new rows into delta fragments. During the delta merge operation, all committed row changes from the delta fragment are moved into a newly constructed main fragment. Each query on a column is evaluated independently on the main and on the delta fragment of the column. The two result sets are joined and returned, with some rows removed after applying proper row visibility rules.

As for any in-memory database, both the main and the delta fragments of each column are kept in memory during query processing. To achieve a compact in-memory representation which allows for efficient CPU access patterns when processing a column, each data fragment of a column is encoded using dictionary encoding which assigns a unique value identifier to each value. The value identifier vector for each column fragment is termed its *data vector*. The value identifiers in each data vector are assigned using the value dictionary of the corresponding fragment. Each fragment may also have a memory resident inverted index, to support efficiently finding of all row positions given a value identifier. Every loaded fragment has its data vector, its dictionary, and its inverted index fully loaded in memory. The memory consumption of each column is the total sum of the memory footprints of its two fragments. Because delta merge regularly moves most of the data in a column from the delta fragment to the main fragment, in general, the main fragment of a column consumes more memory than the corresponding delta fragment.

The construction phase of value dictionaries for delta and main are inherently different. The former is built while inserts arrive and identifiers are being appended at the end of the data vector of the delta. To be optimized for write operations, it would be costly to keep the dictionary for delta fragment in a way that the order between values remain consistent with the order between value identifiers. The main dictionary, however, is created during delta merge. During delta merge, the set of possible values for the new main fragment is known. Therefore, it is possible to assign value identifiers in the same sorted order as that of keys in main dictionary. The data vector, the order−preserving dictionary, and the inverted index for main fragment remain unchanged between two consecutive delta merge operations.

3. PAGE LOADABLE COLUMNS

We present our solutions to partially load data vector (Section 3.1), dictionary (Section 3.2), and inverted index (Section 3.3) for the main fragment of a column. Table 1 summarizes our notations.

3.1 Paged Data Vector

In SAP HANA, the data portion of main fragments are stored in memory as value identifier vectors. For large columns, the memory footprint of these vectors can be significant even after compression with algorithms such as sparse encoding [15]. In this section, we introduce partially loadable

Table 1: List of Notations

Notations	Description
$pDataVector$	paged data vector containing, for each row, its encoded value identifier
$pDataVector[p, rpos]$	$O(1)$ operation on $pDataVector[p, \_]$ to retrieve the vid for a given row position stored on page p
$ipDataVector$	paged inverted index on data vector
$ipDataVector[vid]$	find in $ipDataVector$ all row positions having vid as value identifier
$pDict$	the paged dictionary of a column
$pDict[p, vid]$	$O(1)$ operation on $pDict[p, \_]$ to retrieve the value encoded with vid from page p
$ipDict_{ValueId}$	the sparse helper index on $pDict$ with one entry (vid, p) per page p of $pDict$: vid is the last id stored on page p
$ipDict_{ValueId}[vid]$	binary search operation on $ipDict_{ValueId}$ to find the page p where vid is stored
$ipDict_{Value}$	the sparse helper index on $pDict$ with one entry $(value, p)$ per page p of $pDict$: $value$ is the last stored on page p
$ipDict_{Value}[value]$	binary search operation on $ipDict_{Value}$ to find the page p where vid encoding $value$ is stored

value identifier vectors. We first present the physical layout for a paged data vector (Section 3.1.1) and algorithms that use a stateful iterator to read from a paged data vector (Section 3.1.2) followed by performance enhancements (Section 3.1.3).

3.1.1 Physical layout

The value identifiers in a paged data vector $pDataVector$ are encoded using uniform n-bit compression where n is equal to the number of bits needed to encode the largest value identifier in the entire vector. Paged vectors are split into chunks of exactly 64 identifiers and stored as a chain of disk resident pages. Each page contains an integral number of chunks. We denote the vector of value identifiers stored on page p with $pDataVector\ [p, \_]$. Storing 64 identifiers per chunk ensures that each chunk consists of an integral number of bytes[1] independent of n. Our choice of uniform compression supports efficient mapping from row position to logical page number in $pDataVector$'s page chain (Section 3.1.2). Also, it enables vectorized implementations of the primitive iterator operators (Section 3.1.3).

3.1.2 Algorithms

One type of logical access operation on paged data vector is to find all row positions having a given value identifier vid. The general algorithm (Alg. 1) loads one page at a time, decodes each value identifier on the page, and searches each vector $pDataVector[p, \_]$ for specified vid[2]. To implement the basic operations of decoding a value identifier for a given row position and searching in a range of row positions given a set of value identifiers, we use an iterator based access to paged data vector, in order to perform paging as part of the iterator's functionality. The iterator implements two decode methods and a set of search methods: $get(rpos)$ decodes the value identifier in $pDataVector$ at the given row position $rpos$, and $mget(rpos_{from}, rpos_{to})$ decodes the set of value identifiers that appear in the given row position range.

There are four varieties of the method *search(set of row positions, set of value identifiers)* which takes a set of row positions (e.g., a range, a bitmap) and a search predicate specified as a set of value identifiers, and returns a set of row positions for which the predicate is true. For all iterator methods, the iterator is provided with a range of row positions which is used to selectively load pages from $pDataVector$'s page chain. Finding the right set of pages to load can be achieved because of the uniform value identifier encoding. More specifically, the iterator can identify the chunk(s) that contain the value identifiers in the specified row position range. In order to read the chunks, the iterator must load $pDataVector$'s pages that contain the desired chunks. The iterator can use the constant chunk size (in bytes) and the page size, to find the logical page number of pages where the desired chunks belong to. The iterator loads the pages associated with the logical page number(s) (e.g., a page p) and executes the desired functionality (e.g., $mget(rpos)$) on page level (e.g. on $pDataVector\ [p, \_]$). The iterator may need more than one chunk from the same page, in which case it pins the page in memory to make sure the page does not get evicted by the resource manager when it is being read. On the other hand, the iterator may need to read more than one page. In this case, it pins each new page after releasing the handle to the previous page during page reposition. Our design choice of *preventing each value identifier from spanning more than one chunk* guarantees that the iterator has stable access to each chunk, and that the page is never evicted by the resource manager while being accessed by an iterator. Using uniform n-bit packing simplifies associating row position to corresponding encoded value identifier.

Algorithm 1 $findByValueID(pDataVector, vid)$

```
rposs ← ∅
for all p a page of pDataVector do
    load page p of pDataVector if not loaded
    for all row position rpos in page p do
        if pDataVector[p, rpos] == vid then
            rposs ← rposs ∪ {rpos}
return rposs
```

3.1.3 Optimizations

Having chunks of uniformly encoded value identifiers enables us to vectorize most of the primitive operators used to implement the paged data vector's iterator [26]. We take advantage of the platform provided by Single Instruction Multiple Data (SIMD) instruction set (AltiVec on IBM Power, SSE4 and AVX2 on Intel 64) and attempt to minimize both CPU cache misses and branch misprediction. Fig. 1 shows micro benchmark results (average time per symbol) for the *mget* and *search* operators on n-bit encoded data vectors. In particular, on current Intel server processors, the search primitive is bottlenecked by the memory read bandwidth available to a single core; improving search performance is not possible without reducing the amount of data scanned. For example, performance could be improved for some queries by using a representation like vertical bitweaving with early pruning [17] but only at the expense of noticeably worse performance for the remaining queries. Optimizations higher up in the iterator call stack include cache awareness: both ensuring that intermediate results do not exceed the Last Level Cache (LLC) size and processing data in cache line sized units.

[1] More precisely, 64-bit words.

[2] An optimization of Alg. 1 may prune loading and examining pages using column-level metadata information.

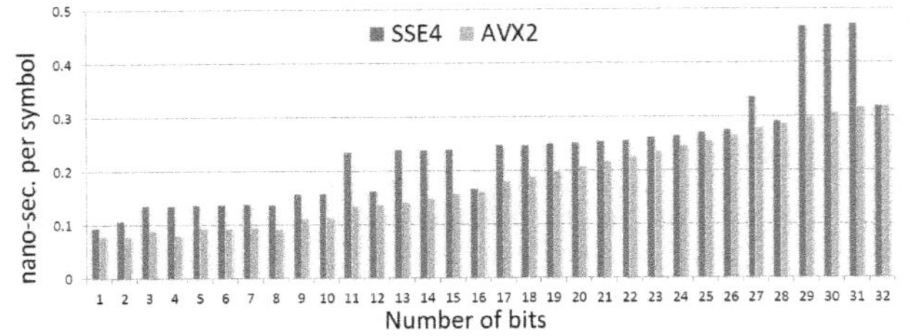

(a) *mget*

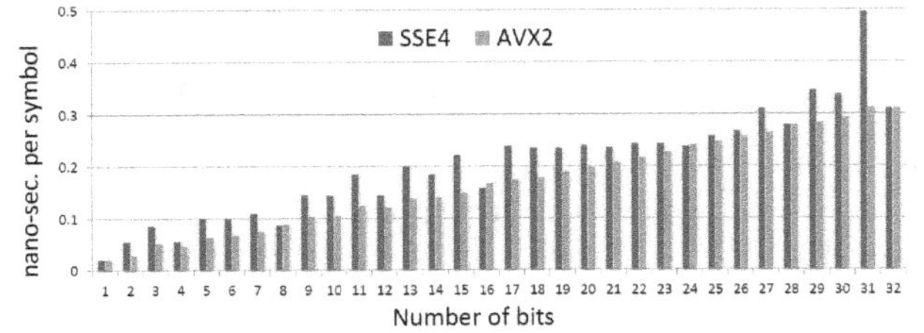

(b) *search*

Figure 1: Average time (nano-second) per symbol: varying number of bits n used for n-bit compression. Micro benchmarks conducted on a server with Intel(R) Xeon(R) CPU E5-2697 v3 @ 2.60GHz

3.2 Paged Dictionary

Even with paging less frequently accessed data vectors, the memory footprint can be large due to tables with a large number of columns with memory resident dictionaries, specifically for columns with large strings. Often an active subset of a dictionary needs to be accessed for page loadable columns. The subset could be expressed explicitly in the query predicate[3]. Alternatively, dictionary access might be needed to retrieve the values, given a set of value identifiers for the result set of a query. To reduce the memory footprint of dictionaries in page loadable columns, we propose a hybrid representation for a dictionary (Section 3.2.1) which has an in memory data structure, always loaded, and a physical page loadable representation. Our goal is to reduce the memory footprint with minimum overhead to the read performance. As for the paged data vector, we apply our solution to the main fragment of page loadable columns (i.e. the read only section of a column) as opposed to the delta fragment. This is mainly because performing regular delta to main merge guarantees that the memory footprint of the main dominates that for the delta section of a column. We hide the details of loading and unloading dictionary pages via paged dictionary iterators as described in Section 3.2.2. Iterators take advantage of transient data structures and physical layout of dictionary pages.

3.2.1 Physical layout and transient structure

This section presents the physical and the transient data structures for paged dictionary, denoted by *pDict*. We focus on data types for which the memory footprint for dictionary is noticeable (CHAR and VARCHAR), as opposed to basic data types such as INTEGER and FLOAT. Therefore, in this section, we use the term *string* to refer to a value encoded in a paged dictionary. The dictionary for the main fragment is

[3]E.g., in SELECT * FROM T WHERE Name='Mike', we first find the value identifier *vid* for the value 'Mike' by consulting the dictionary of column Name; then the data vector is used to find all row positions for *vid*.

prefix length	block length	string suffix (the new piece in this block)			*on-page section* ←
# of logical pointers	logical pointer 1	...	logical pointer n	total length	*off-page section* ←

Figure 2: Prefix-encoded string

created during the delta merge. The strings in main dictionary are sorted and its value identifiers are assigned using the same order of strings. Often consecutive strings in main dictionary have a prefix in common. We take advantage of this redundancy and use prefix encoding to reduce space for paged dictionary page. We group every 16 consecutive strings in a single string value block. We use the format shown in Fig. 2 to store each string in a value block. First, we store the length of the common prefix with the preceding string in the same value block, or zero for the first string in a value block. Then we store the block length, followed by the string suffix (i.e. the string minus the common prefix). For large strings, the size of each string can exceed the size of a dictionary page. Therefore, we store each string in two sections; an *on-page* piece (stored literally in the block) and an *off-page* piece. The off-page section contains references to sections of the large string, each stored on a separate dictionary page. We keep a set of logical pointers per string, where each logical pointer refers to a piece of the string, in a different dictionary page. This enables re-constructing large strings. Meanwhile it reduces the memory footprint of the dictionary pages with large strings, for instance when the page is loaded to materialize only one large string during single dictionary lookup. We store value blocks (along with their offsets on page) on each dictionary page.

A paged dictionary is stored as a chain of dictionary pages, with two helper dictionaries to support search. The first helper dictionary $ipDict_{ValueId}$ is the value identifier directory, a sparse index having one entry of the form (vid, p) for each dictionary page, where *vid* is the *last* value identifier stored on the page p of *pDict*. This index is organized into a set of directory blocks. Each directory block stores a list of value identifiers. Each identifier in a directory block corresponds to the identifier of the *last* string of a dictionary page. The second helper dictionary $ipDict_{Value}$ is the value separator directory, indexing entries of the form $(value, p)$, one entry per page p of the dictionary *pDict*, where *value* is the *last* value stored on page p. This index contains a set of separator blocks, each such block stores the last string in each dictionary page. If the string has an off-page component, we store the logical pointers to the off-page components in a separator block for large strings.

Besides the physical structures of *pDict*, we construct a transient data when a dictionary page gets loaded. The transient data contains a vector of pointers to string value blocks stored on the *in-memory* representation of the page. The transient data is registered to the corresponding dictionary page during load, and is unloaded (i.e. destroyed) when either the column is unloaded or the dictionary page is unloaded by the resource manager (see Section 5).

3.2.2 Algorithms

We implemented an iterator based access to paged dictionary, to hide the paging of the dictionary from the consumers of the dictionary functionality. The paged dictionary iterator implements two methods, *findByValue* and

Algorithm 2 *findByValue*$(pDict, ipDict_{Value}, value)$

```
p ← binary_search(ipDict_Value, value)
load page p of pDict if not loaded
vid ← binary_search(pDict[p, _], value)
return vid
```

Algorithm 3 *findByValueID*$(pDict, ipDict_{ValueId}, vid)$

```
p ← binary_search(ipDict_ValueId, vid)
load page p of pDict if not loaded
value ← pDict[p, vid]
return value
```

findByValueID[4]. The former method finds the value identifier encoding a given value, whereas the latter method finds the value corresponding to the given value identifier.

For a fully loaded dictionary, *findByValue* can perform a binary search as strings in main dictionary are always sorted and available in memory (even the large strings). For a paged dictionary, *findByValue* (Alg. 2) first needs to load the right dictionary page. For this purpose, the separator helper dictionary (i.e. $ipDict_{Value}$) is used to find the logical page number of dictionary page, given the search string value. Because the strings in the separator dictionary are sorted, the probe is done by performing a binary search. Once it is determined that the query string maybe in the dictionary, the logical page number p is retrieved from the separator dictionary. If page p is not in memory, it is loaded and its transient data is constructed for the iterator. A second binary search is performed on the transient data, to identify the value block which may contain the search string. For small strings, only the on-page content is compared against the search string. For large strings, however, the off-page contents are compared against the search string by incrementally loading each off-page piece. *findByValue* terminates in a value block when either a match with query string is found or there is no match.

Similarly, *findByValueID* (Alg. 3) takes a two phase approach. It first uses the directory helper dictionary to find the logical dictionary page given a *vid*. Because the value identifiers are assigned the same order as dictionary strings, the logical page number on directory can be found using binary search. It loads the dictionary page into memory, and from the block header of the loaded dictionary page and the value identifier, it extracts the offset for the the value block corresponding to the query value identifier. The sought after string is constructed incrementally by scanning the value block, and loading the off-page sections of at most one string.

Apart from the helper dictionaries, the memory footprint of paged dictionary for the invocation of *findByValue* and *findByValueID* methods is one dictionary page (which contains the target value block) and, for large strings, a set of dictionary pages containing the off-page contents. We typically choose the pages in dictionary page chain to be 1MB, except the last dictionary page, which is large enough to hold the value blocks and offsets in the last dictionary page. In practice, the number of pages in helper dictionaries is small, and the memory footprint of the helper dictionaries is negligible.

3.2.3 Optimizations

In the lifetime of a paged dictionary iterator, we may need to load the same page multiple times, for different string values and value identifiers. This, for instance, can happen during a batch lookup for a set of ordered strings or value identifiers. In this scenario, it makes sense to keep pages loaded during the lifetime of the iterator, and prevent the resource manager to unload the pages, until the iterator gets out of scope. For this purpose, we create a handle cache for each iterator as follows. For each logical page number that we are requested to load after probing helper dictionaries, we update the handle cache if the handle for the corresponding logical page is invalid (i.e. not set yet), then load the page spanning the dictionary block and update the handle. Otherwise, we reuse the page handle. The iterator cache is destroyed and its handles are released when the iterator gets out of scope. Keeping handles to dictionary pages prevents the resource manager from unloading these pages during the lifetime of the iterator. Each of the helper dictionaries has a single value per dictionary page. Because a search on helper dictionaries is the first step in both *findByValue* and *findByValueID*, we pre-load the page chains of the helper dictionaries on the first access to a paged dictionary. This improves the performance of probing helper dictionaries to find logical page numbers for paged dictionaries.

3.3 Paged Inverted Index

Retrieving all rows which satisfy a search predicate is a common query task performed on a column. This involves dictionary lookups to find the encoding value identifiers for the predicate, and then find all the row positions in the data vector (Alg. 4). Unfortunately, a full scan of paged data vector to find row positions that fulfill search predicate would trigger the load of *all* data vector pages, even those that do not have any eligible row. One may keep a summary of each data vector page in a transient data structure. The summary can be used to filter some *pDataVector* pages without loading them. An example summary may keep the minimum and the maximum of the encoded values per page [2]. The summary can be used to determine whether a page contains value identifiers within a range without actually loading the *pDataVector* page. However, if the search value identifier range overlaps with the summary, page load is required to prune false positives. This approach is effective when the range per summary is compact.

To alleviate the large memory overhead and CPU cost, we use a secondary *paged* data structure (its inverted index) which is built from *pDataVector*. A classic inverted index provides a mapping from each *vid* to the set of row positions observing the *vid*, we call this set the *postinglist* for *vid*). We denote such index by *ipDataVector*. The inverted index can efficiently answer *which row positions of the data vector have a given vid*. However, the size of the inverted index is linearly proportional to the size of the corresponding data vector. The size factor makes a fully loaded inverted index a prohibitive solution for in-memory database systems. We optimize the physical layout (Section 3.3.1) and iterator based access algorithms (Section 3.3.2) to support on-demand load of fractions of inverted index with a memory footprint proportional to query result size.

3.3.1 Physical layout

An inverted index of a dictionary encoded data vector is composed of two data structures; a directory of offsets (directory) and a vector of row positions (postinglist). The

[4]For brevity, we only discuss primitive search types, and do not discuss high level search operations, e.g. LIKE.

Algorithm 4 *findByValue(pDataVector, ipDataVector, pDict, ipDict$_{Value}$, value)*

```
vid ← findByValue(pDict, ipDict_Value, value)
rposs ← findByValueID(pDataVector, ipDataVector, vid)
return rposs
```

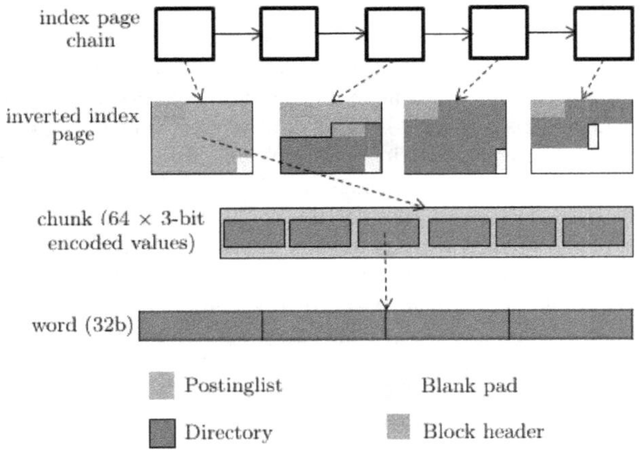

Figure 3: Layout of paged inverted index

postinglist is a rearrangement of the data vector such that row positions are ordered based on the value identifier they contain. This property ensures that row positions with the same value identifiers are grouped together in the posting list. The directory provides the offset of the first occurrence of a value identifier in the postinglist.

For in-memory columns, both directory and postinglist are kept in memory as compressed vectors. For page loadable columns, we store postinglist and directory in *one* chain of *index* pages (Fig. 3). The chain contains a set of index pages for postinglist, at most one mixed page (described shortly), and a set of index pages to persist the directory vector. Each index page is composed of one or more index blocks. Each index block can represent a section of either a postinglist or a directory. Each index block is composed of an index block header, followed by a set of one or more index block chunks. An index block chunk contains 64 n-bit encoded values. In a chunk of postinglist index block, each value is a row position. In a chunk of a directory index block, each value is an offset to the postinglist. Naturally, the number of bits required to encode a row position can be different from that of an offset in directory block. The mixed index page contains a postinglist index block, followed by a directory index block. For unique columns, each value appears in a single row position, meaning that the directory vector becomes an identity vector. Because of this, for unique indexes we save the space for storing directory.

3.3.2 Algorithms

We implemented an iterator based access to paged inverted index, to hide the paging details for postinglist and directory from the consumers of iterator's functionality. This iterator is used, for example, for the logical operation $rposs \leftarrow ipDataVector[vid]$ in Alg. 5. The paged index iterator implements $getFirstRowPos$(vid) and $getNextRowPos()$ methods. These methods are in charge of loading and pinning the right pages from the index page chain, and returning the correct row position, given a value identifier which

Algorithm 5 *findByValueID(pDataVector, ipDataVector, vid)*

```
if ipDataVector exists then
    rposs ← ipDataVector[vid]
else
    /* Sequential scan of pDataVector data vector */
    rposs ← findByValueID(pDataVector, vid)
return rposs
```

is in the main dictionary. $getFirstRowPos$ finds the index page containing the directory section corresponding to *vid*. This page is loaded, if it is not already in memory. Then, $getFirstRowPos$ reads the first offset of *vid*'s first row position in the postinglist. Let b be the logical page number of the mixed index page in the index page chain. If there is no mixed page, then b is the page number of the first directory page. Let v_{first} and v_{page} be, respectively, the number of encoded offsets on the first directory index page (which can be a mixed page) and a full directory page. Because offsets in the directory are all encoded using the same number of bits, the logical page number of the directory page which contains the offset of *vid* is

$$p = \begin{cases} b & \text{if } vid \le v_{first} \\ b + \lfloor \frac{vid - v_{first}}{v_{page}} \rfloor & \text{otherwise.} \end{cases} \quad (1)$$

The offset of *vid* in the postinglist is the kth n-bit encoded offset on the directory index block on page p, where

$$k = \begin{cases} vid & \text{if } vid \le v_{first} \\ (vid - v_{first}) \bmod v_{page} & \text{otherwise.} \end{cases} \quad (2)$$

After reading the offset, one more page access is required to read the first row position in $getFirstRowPos$. To achieve this, the logical page number and the location of the encoded row position on its postinglist block needs to be computed. This computation can be performed in a similar way as in Eq. 1 and Eq. 2. Next is to load an index page (with the computed logical page number) and decode the row position (with the computed row position location). Invoking $getFirstRowPos$ is often followed by several calls to $getNextRowPos$. The index iterator keeps the offset to postinglist as its *state*, as well as the offset of the last row position to read. Therefore, each call to $getNextRowPos$ only needs to read from a postinglist block. However, the postinglist block to read from might be already cached in memory, by a previous call to $getNextRowPos$ which has loaded and pinned the required index page. The iterator keeps a handle to the postinglist page, which prevents the unload of the page, until either the iterator gets out of scope, or a reposition of the iterator brings in a new postinglist page and unloads the previously loaded index page. Having handle to the postinglist block prevents the unload of the corresponding index page being used by the iterator. Thus, in consecutive calls of $getNextRowPos$ for the same *vid*, there is high chance that the corresponding postinglist page is already loaded with a chunk cached. The memory footprint for the index of a paged data vector is bounded by the number of pages that are loaded by corresponding index iterator. At each call of $getFirstRowPos$ and $getNextRowPos$, the iterator brings in at least one page (if both row position and offset are in one mixed index page) and at most two index pages. If the index iterator is created for many value identifiers, then without proper memory management many directory and postinglist pages may stay in memory. In Section 5, we explain how we can effectively limit this issue.

4. DATA AGING USING PAGE LOADABLE COLUMNS

Business data is typically accessed frequently in the beginning of its life-cycle, when the corresponding business processes are still active. After some time, dependent on its status, the data is not accessed as part of the regular working set any more. However, it may happen that the old data becomes interesting again, for example when running analysis over multiple years, when accessing the order history of a customer, or during an audit. This observation is often characterized with the data temperature metaphor. Operationally relevant data is called *hot*, and data that is no longer accessed during normal operation is called *cold*. The data temperature can be used to horizontally partition the application data for optimizing resource consumption and performance. The process of moving data between the different partitions (i.e. from hot to cold) is called *data aging*.

In SAP HANA, aging is different from archiving in the sense that cold data is still kept within the SAP HANA database and remains accessible via SQL in the very same table as the hot data (yet in another partition). Aging does not necessarily replace archiving, although it is enables the system to keep data longer in the database before it is being archived. The goal of aging is to both reduce the main memory footprint and speed up database queries by only keeping operationally relevant (hot) data in main memory. In contrast to this, cold data may be stored, loaded and accessed differently, but remaining accessible via SQL. Business objects often span multiple tables, for example *header* and *lineitem* tables. These objects have statuses, e.g an order's fulfillment. However, such a status might only be set in one of the tables. Using a status as partitioning column is therefore usually neither sufficient nor always possible as partitioning always relates to the columns of a single table where the tuple is stored in. To maintain a brace for the tables that make up a business object and to be backwards compatible, for applications including customer code, we have introduced an artificial temperature column for aging-aware tables. The application actively sets values in this column to a date to indicate that the object is closed and the row shall be moved to the cold partition(s). It does so consistently for all related tables of the same business object, or even for a group of related business objects.

4.1 Storage for Cold Data

The main goal of aging is to remove huge volumes of historical data from main memory and to place it on less expensive storage. There is a direct trade-off between performance and cost. Requirements for access to cold partitions may vary, so do access patterns. Some applications may do OLAP-intensive operations on them, others may access only individual rows using a primary key lookup. A proper sizing and gauging has to take place to find ideal settings in terms of what data is classified as cold and how to store data to accommodate for a given scenario. Cold partitions may reside *externally* as a whole in a separate database, e.g. a federated disk-based database that belongs to the same database image. An orthogonal option is to store cold partition within the same database. For this, there are two possible options:

Default columns. The default behavior of SAP HANA is to load columns entirely into memory upon first access. In case of partitioned tables, only the columns of relevant partitions are touched. A built-in least recently used (LRU) algorithm unloads columns upon memory pressure. A higher unload priority may be used as a weight in the LRU algorithm so that cold partitions are evicted from memory earlier than hot partitions or other memory artifacts of the same age. The drawback of this storage, in the context of aging, is that it causes a long wait time for the first access to cold partitions caused by the load of complete columns. This is not ideal from user perspective. Moreover, huge quantities of memory get loaded that may come into conflict with hot partitions despite a higher unload priority. In an extreme case, a cold partition is read with a fully specified primary key, but the entire column gets loaded into memory.

Page Loadable columns. With cold partitions stored as page loadable columns, only requested pages are being loaded into memory, allowing a lower overall memory consumption. Page loadable columns also facilitate a finer loading granularity. This results in a quicker response to many types of OLTP-like queries, especially for the first access to cold partitions. The pages of columns in cold partitions are loaded into a page pool separate from the pool for other database objects. As described in Section 5, the page pool is associated with a tunable upper and lower boundary. When the upper boundary is reached, pages are unloaded until the lower boundary is reached. Query performance on cold partitions is better when more pages of a column are already loaded. Therefore, the configurable size of the page pool is again a direct trade-off between performance and cost.

The advantage of using page loadable columns rather than any federated database are: 1) it works seamlessly in the existing engine, using the same operators and engines on top without losing any engine features; and 2) the management of memory resources, compared with the default columns, can be done in finer granularity.

4.2 Working with Aging-aware Tables

Aging is an optional feature that may be switched on in the application on business object level, thus effecting the underlying tables. When doing so, typically a non-partitioned table is re-interpreted as a partitioned table with only one partition, which is the hot partition. Another option is that the table is already partitioned, for example with Hash partitioning. Then a logical second level of partitioning is added; Range partitioning with just one defined range for the hot partition. Further, cold partitions will be added when needed with an explicit ADD PARTITION. The cold partitions will typically have page loadable columns enabled from the very beginning.

In summary, enabling aging for a table can be conducted in all straightforward cases without a downtime; all relevant partitioning operations run in constant time, without reorganizing the data layout of the already existing data. The process which moves data from the hot partition to the cold partition(s) is implemented as an update on the partitioning column which triggers a move of the corresponding rows. The rows are being inserted into the delta fragment of the cold partitions as updates. During the asynchronous delta merge step, the data is eventually written into the main fragment of the cold partition, as page loadable columns. Because new data is always written first into the delta fragment, there is no performance impact when using page loadable columns. As the data movement from hot to cold is inherently an ordinary DML operation, it does not block any other operations on the same table.

5. MEMORY MANAGEMENT

Memory management in SAP HANA differs from traditional database buffer manager implementations, as SAP HANA manages memory used by logical resources rather than just physical pages. As an in-memory database, SAP HANA generally requires an entire logical structure, such as a column or index, to be present in contiguous memory. Although the contiguous memory may be allocated as traditional memory pages, the cache policy for these pages is controlled as part of the entire logical structure rather than the pages themselves.

In SAP HANA, the fully-in-memory structures are typically not disk-compatible, meaning the in-memory representation of the logical structure is different than the on-disk representation. In most cases, the in-memory representation must be built and managed as a separate memory resource from the on-disk pages themselves. With page-wise accessible structures described here, each page of the logical structure is registered as a separate resource, whereas completely memory resident structures are registered as a single resource. Unlike buffer caches in traditional database systems, SAP HANA manages page caching for not only pageable data structures, but also the memory resources for fully memory resident structures. These are typically managed by a separate heap manager in most traditional database systems.

SAP HANA uses a weighted LRU (Least Recently Used) strategy to evict unused resources, e.g. columns, persistent pages, and many other cached but currently unused memory objects. To solve a low memory situation, SAP HANA unloads currently unused resources in descending order of $\frac{t}{w}$, where t is the time since the last touch of the resource and w is the weight associated with the *disposition* of the corresponding in-memory page. A resource disposition categorizes the cache eviction policy for each resource. For instance, the objects loaded with *temporary* disposition are expected to be unloaded by the resource manager as soon as they are not needed any more, whereas resources loaded with *non-swappable* disposition cannot be unloaded at all. Every resource of a page loadable column is loaded with *paged attribute* disposition. The resource might be a column page, a dictionary page, or an inverted index page. These pages are unloaded by either the *reactive* or the *proactive* mechanism. The LRU strategy gives higher priority for eviction to resources that are not touched recently and have a smaller disposition weight, compared with other resources.

In case of low memory situation, paged attribute resources are unloaded if they consume more memory than specified by the *lower limit* threshold; we call this the reactive unload. If paged resources consume more memory than specified by the *upper limit* threshold, then these resources are evicted by the LRU strategy until the lower limit is reached – even if plenty of memory is still available. We call this mechanism the proactive unload. The weight of resources does not play any role neither in the reactive approach nor in the proactive approach of unloading paged attribute resources. The proactive unload is executed asynchronously, meaning that it does not block the creation of new paged attribute resources if needed (e.g. loading a piece of a column). As a consequence, the total size of paged attributes resources may exceed the upper limit threshold until the proactive unload strategy is completely executed.

Table 2: Notations used for experiments

T_b	The base table
T_p	Same schema and data as T_b, with all non-primary key columns in T_p designated to be PAGE LOADABLE
T_{pp}	Same schema and data as T_b, with only the primary key column in T_{pp} designated to be PAGE LOADABLE
T_b^i	T_b with one inverted index per column
T_p^i	T_p with one inverted index per column
Q_{pk}^{num}	Select a numeric column, for a random row: SELECT C_{num} FROM T WHERE C_{pk}=value
Q_{pk}^{str}	Select a string column, for a random row: SELECT C_{str} FROM T WHERE C_{pk}=value
Q_{pk}^{*}	Select all columns, for a random row: SELECT * FROM T WHERE C_{pk}=value
Q_{num}^{count}	Select total count, for random rows where numeric column is equal to a value: SELECT COUNT(*) FROM T WHERE C_{num}=value
Q_{str}^{count}	Select total count, for random rows where string column is equal to a value: SELECT COUNT(*) FROM T WHERE C_{str}=value
Q_{pk}^{rid}	Select row identifier for a random row: SELECT ROWID() FROM T WHERE C_{pk}=value
$Q_{\sigma_{pk}}^{*}$	Select all columns for a range query on the primary key column with a given selectivity SELECT * FROM T WHERE $v_1 \leq C_{pk} \leq v_2$
$Q_{\sigma_{pk}}^{sum}$	Select sum of a numeric column for a range query on the primary key column with given selectivity SELECT SUM(C_{num}) FROM T WHERE $v_1 \leq C_{pk} \leq v_2$
$t(q,T)$	runtime to evaluate query q on table T

6. EXPERIMENTAL EVALUATIONS

We report the performance and the memory footprint for SAP HANA's default columns, which are always fully loaded vs. the page loadable columns. We first inspect the impact of paging on each data structure individually (Section 6.2) followed by an end-to-end evaluation (Section 6.3).

6.1 Dataset and Metrics

We used an in-house data generator to create a realistic dataset for our study. Our generator produces tables that are very similar to those in a real ERP system. Our base dataset is a columnar table T_b with 100 million records and 128 columns of types INTEGER, DECIMAL, DOUBLE, CHAR, and VARCHAR. Column cardinalities ranged from 1 to 10M. In T_b, 112 columns have less than 100 distinct values and 14 columns have more than 1,000 distinct values. For each experiment, we created a modified table with the same schema and data as T_b, but with a subset of the columns designated as being page loadable and possibly some inverted indexes. Table 2 summarizes the notations for modified tables and query workloads. We compared paged and fully resident columns along two key metrics. First, we monitored system memory when queries were executed. A smaller memory footprint is more desirable. Second, for each test, we measured the time ratio of running a query against the modified table with page loadable columns, over the processing time of the same query on the reference table. A smaller time ratio is more desirable. Every experiment was conducted after a cold system start, to avoid having already cached pages. We set the page loadable limits to default values. All experiments were performed on a server with two CPU sockets, eight cores per socket, and two threads per core, with 256GB of RAM. The machine had SUSE Linux Enterprise Server 11 with a single instance of SAP HANA SPS11.

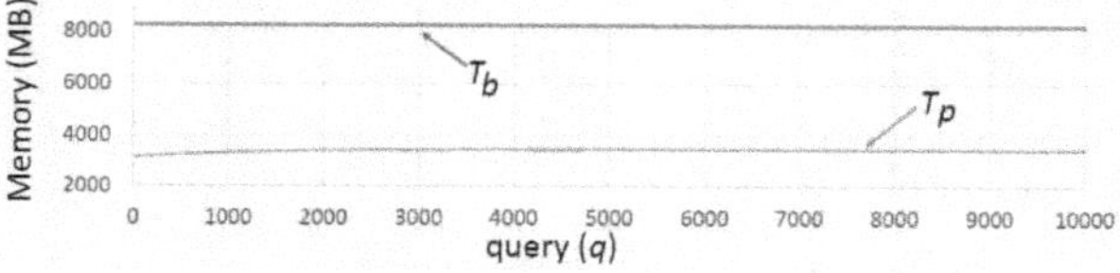

(a) memory footprint varying q

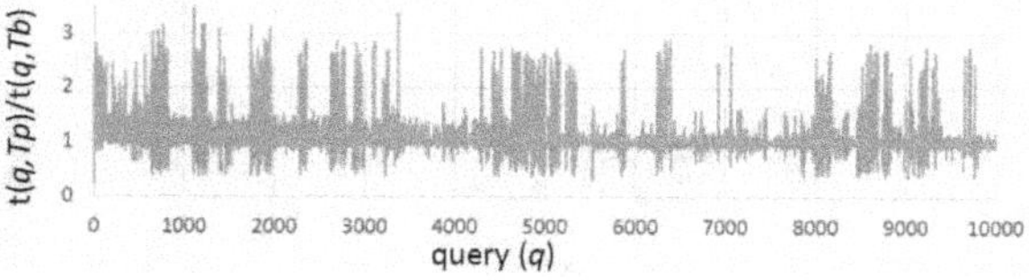

(b) run-time ratio varying q

Figure 4: Single read of C_{num} paged data vector: $q = Q_{pk}^{num}$

6.2 The Impact of Paging Data Structures

6.2.1 *Paging Data Vector*

We created 10,000 random queries of type Q_{pk}^{num} and measured the system memory footprint and the query run-time ratio on T_p over T_b. We picked the query type Q_{pk}^{num} in order to exercise the code path for paging data vector only. In this experiment, the numeric column doesn't have a paged dictionary and there is no access to inverted index of any result column. As Fig. 4 shows, the system memory footprint reduced significantly (from 8.2GB to 3.6GB) when page loadable column was used. As more random queries were processed, more pieces of data vector were pulled into memory. Therefore, the memory footprint for T_p grew while processing more queries. With loading new pieces of the data vector, spikes appear in query run-time ratio (Fig. 4b). The memory resident columns suffer from this performance drop only once, during their complete load. The load time for a full column is significantly larger than for a piece of a page loadable column (43.5 seconds vs. 9.6 seconds). The average query run-time ratio is 1.07, with 90% confidence interval of 0.29. This means accessing paged data vector does not cause a large performance impact for single point queries that do not touch the paged dictionary or the paged inverted index.

6.2.2 *Paging Dictionary*

We created 10,000 random queries of type Q_{pk}^{str} on T_b and T_p. Each query in Q_{pk}^{str} returns a (random) string column value for one random row. There is one access to paged data vector, to read the value identifier for the random row, one access to dictionary directory, and one access to one dictionary page. Except for the primary key column, no other inverted index was defined on T_b nor T_p. As Fig. 5a demonstrates, the system memory footprint is again smaller in the page loadable scenario. Notice that at the 1621th query, we observe a 1.2GB increase in the memory footprint for T_b. The query touches one particular column for the first time. Such an access could trigger a column eviction, if the system is under memory pressure. However, we do not observe a memory jump of this magnitude for T_p. From the performance point of view (Fig. 5b), we observe a run-time degradation for T_p whenever either a required paged data vector or a needed dictionary piece – either a directory or a dictionary page – is not in memory. Loading a page has an I/O cost which is much higher than accessing an in-memory data structure. The degradation is often larger than

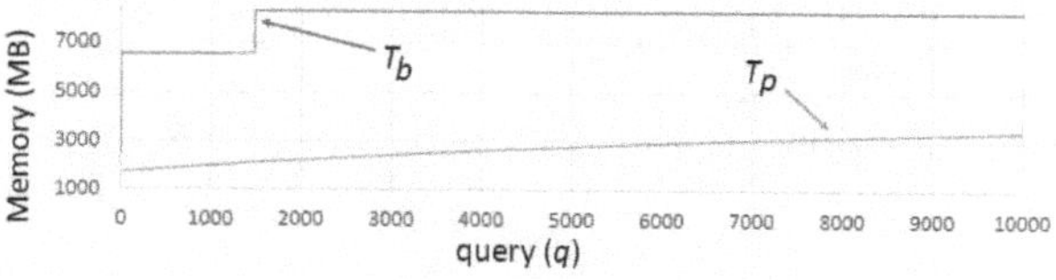

(a) memory footprint varying q

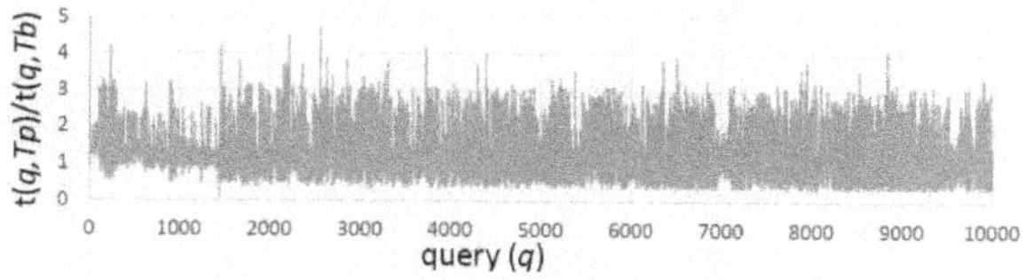

(b) run-time ratio varying q

Figure 5: Single read of C_{str} paged dictionary and paged data vector: $q = Q_{pk}^{str}$

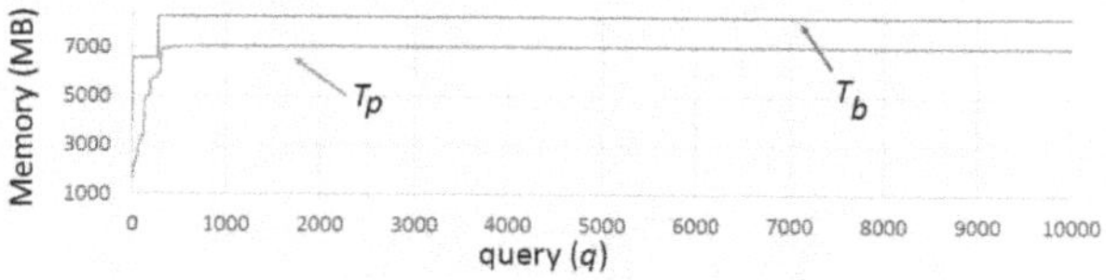

(a) memory footprint varying q

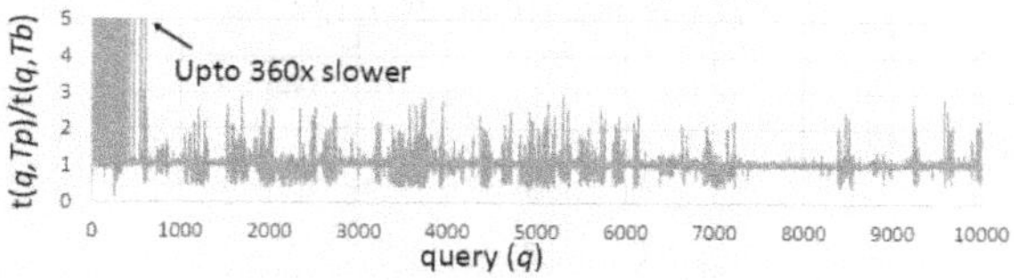

(b) run-time ratio varying q

Figure 6: Multiple reads of C_{str} paged dictionary: $q = Q_{str}^{count}$

that for a paged data vector[5] because here there is demand for paged data vector and paged dictionary. However, the gap between the run-times of T_p and T_b reduces when the requested dictionary pages are already loaded.

We next created 10,000 random queries of type Q_{str}^{count} on T_b and T_p. Each query of type Q_{str}^{count} exercises search by value and accesses pages from the helper separator index dictionary on value, and the paged dictionary. Searching paged dictionary, in general, requires more pages to be loaded from the helper dictionaries, as well as the paged dictionary itself. Therefore, as depicted in Fig. 6a, the memory footprint for T_p increased very fast for the first 400 queries. The burst in pulling pages is characterized as significant performance degredation (up to 360X) in the run-time ratio of Fig. 6b. After this point, the memory footprint becomes stable in T_p. As in earlier experiments, we see spikes in query run-time ratio when pages are loaded. As the helper dictionaries are key interfaces needed for both $findByValue$ and $findByValueID$, it would be more effective to have these auxiliary dictionaries always loaded in memory, or in a very fast storage (e.g. Non-Volatile Memory).

6.2.3 *Paging Inverted Index*

We created 10,000 random queries of type Q_{num}^{count} and evaluated on T_b^i and T_p^i, to only exercise the code path for paged inverted index. As shown in Fig. 7a, the paged inverted index had smaller memory footprint than the loaded inverted index (note, our test here does not include the primary key

[5]Average ratio is 1.24, with 90% confidence interval of 0.69.

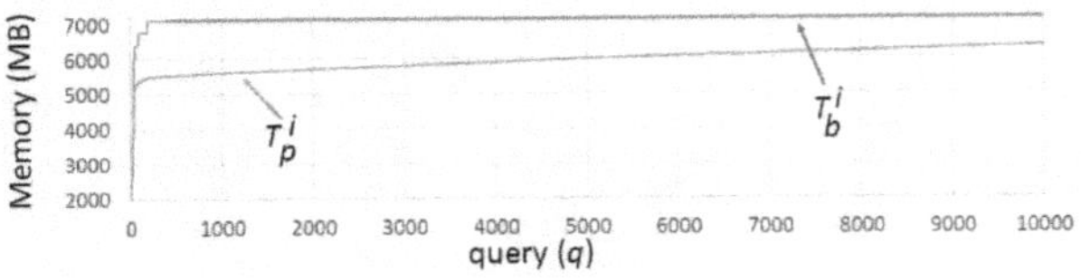

(a) memory footprint varying q

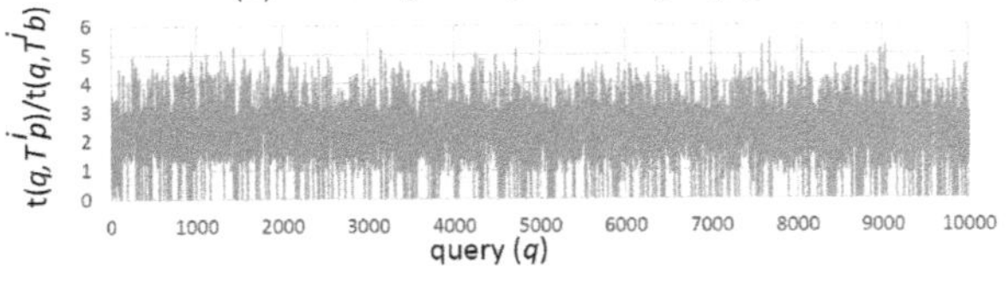

(b) run-time ratio varying q

Figure 7: Multiple reads of C_{num} paged inverted index: $q = Q^{count}_{num}$

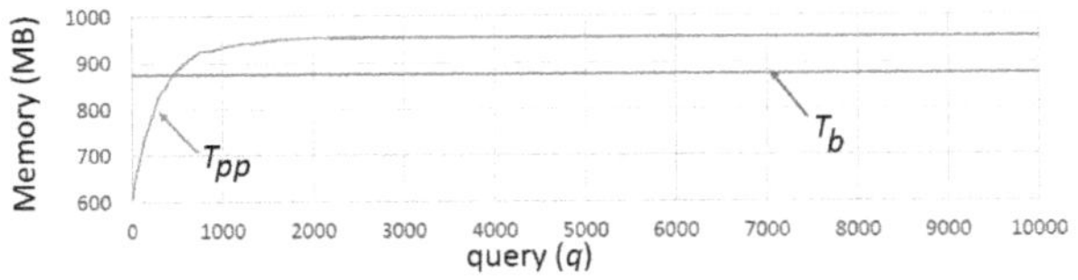

(a) memory footprint varying q

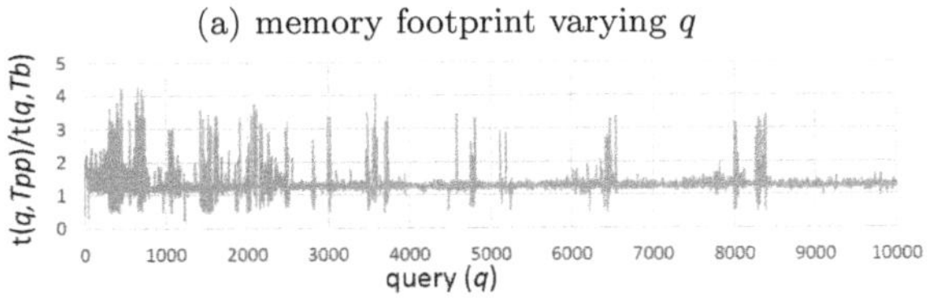

(b) run-time ratio varying q

Figure 8: Single read of C_{pk} paged unique inverted index: $q = Q^{rid}_{pk}$

column which is VARCHAR). As most of the columns in T^i_b and T^i_p are sparse, each paged inverted index has a mixed page of postinglist and directory for each column, and no index page which contains just the directory. In the mixed page, searching inverted index is not as catastrophic as the early phase of searching paged dictionary (i.e. Fig. 6b). However, because each search on the paged index requires at most two page accesses (if the index page is not loaded), the overall performance for the paged inverted index is between that of the paged data vector (Fig. 4b) and paged dictionary (Fig. 6b). To evaluate the unique paged inverted index, we created 10,000 Q^{rid}_{pk} queries on T_b and T_{pp}. Search by primary key requires to decode only one value in the postinglist, thus the run-time gets closer to the non-paged index (Fig. 8b) with fewer spikes. Access to paged inverted index is on average 29% slower than non-paged inverted index. However, as shown in Fig. 8a, the memory consumption of a paged inverted index is larger than that of a non-paged inverted index; both indexes store only the postinglist vector but the minimum size for the paged inverted index is one page.

6.3 Putting It All Together

We generated 10,000 random Q^*_{pk} queries on T^i_p and T^i_b. This resembles random single point queries on aged data (e.g. data auditing). Each query does a single read of the paged inverted index of the primary key column, and, to construct the result set, a single read of each column's paged dictionary and paged data vector. As shown in Fig. 9a, the memory footprint is smaller when page loadable columns were used. For the first 1,000 queries, the run-time ratio is

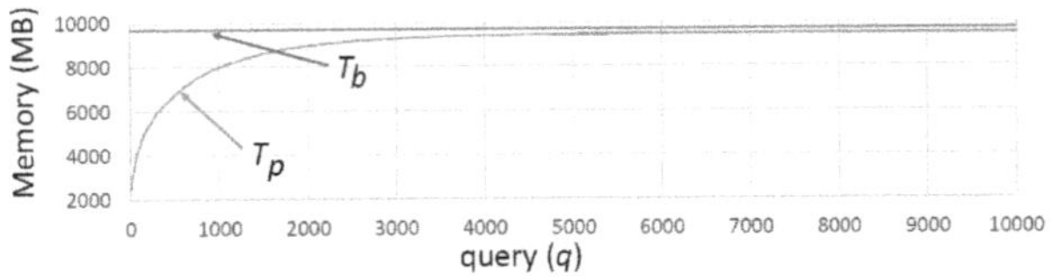

(a) memory footprint varying q

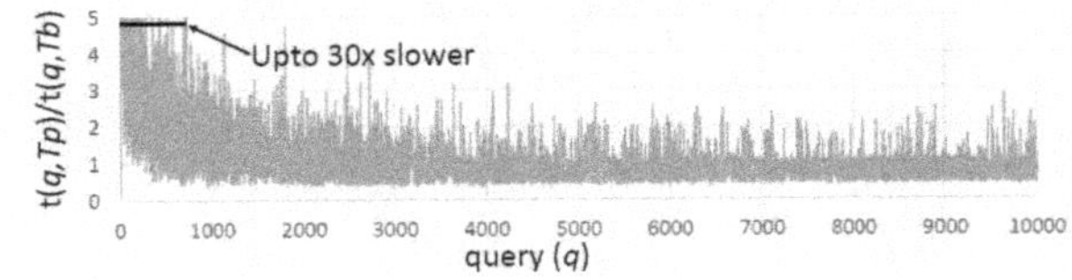

(b) run-time ratio varying q

Figure 9: Single read of a random row, $q = Q^*_{pk}$

Table 3: Memory saving and average run-time ratio, after 10 times repeating 1,000 queries of types $Q^*_{\sigma_{pk}}$, $Q^{sum}_{\sigma_{pk}}$

		rows accessed in T			
		1 row	0.01%	0.1%	1%
Memory reduction (GB)	$Q^*_{\sigma_{pk}}$	5.1	4.9	4.3	2.3
	$Q^{sum}_{\sigma_{pk}}$	4.8	4.6	4.6	4.6
Average run-time ratio	$Q^*_{\sigma_{pk}}$	1.29	1.82	1.62	1.65
	$Q^{sum}_{\sigma_{pk}}$	1.01	1.33	1.15	1.11

large (Fig. 9b); it was rare that all pages required for the first 1,000 queries are loaded in memory. However, as the queries are random, the run-time degradation was not as severe as that for searching the paged dictionary (Fig. 6b). The run-time ratio, after processing 2̃,000 queries gets very close to one, with average 1.09 and 90% confidence interval of 1.25. However, as exactly same query is almost never rerun, these results do not show run-time if all pages needed to evaluate a query on page loadable columns were already loaded. We designed another experiment which runs queries of types $Q^*_{\sigma_{pk}}$ and $Q^{sum}_{\sigma_{pk}}$ on T^i_b and T^i_p, once after a database restart (cold run) followed by 10 runs of the exactly same workload (hot run). This evaluates the impact of paging on query time when data is already loaded. As Table 3 reports, page loadable columns offer significant reduction in memory footprint, especially for very selective queries. The overhead of using iterators to read from page loadable columns degrades performance up to 82% when 0.01% of rows are selected in $Q^*_{\sigma_{pk}}$. However, when only a single row of a page loadable column is accessed, the performance remains very close to fully loaded column. On the other hand, while page loadable columns often come with a performance overhead, they can be used to keep performance critical columns fully loaded and avoid their eviction.

7. RELATED WORK

There is an extensive history of research on in-memory databases [27] and a growing interest in column oriented DBMS products, e.g. VectorWise [29], MonetDB [18], Vertica [14], IBM DB2 BLU [22], and ParAccel [1], to name a few. The first approach, when the dataset size is slightly larger than the available memory, is to further compress data (i.e. on top of dictionary encoding). Lemke et al. [15] propose sparse encoding of columns along with a number of size specific optimizations. Column reordering has been suggested [16] to be applied on top of existing optimizations to further reduce memory footprint when columns have clusters of adjacent value identifiers. Funke et al. [9] propose to compact the immutable data and optimize it for efficient, memory-consumption friendly snapshotting. This is to free up as much as possible space for having mutable data loaded, thus having minimum impact on mission critical OLTP throughput. They assign a *temperature* to data at Virtual Memory (VM) page granularity, and optimize the layout of the frozen pages for OLAP.

There has been research to improve the performance of cold data handling, mostly for in-memory databases optimized for OLTP. HyPer [13] takes advantage of processor-inherent support for VM management such as address translation, caching, and copy on update. Stoica et al. [24] log data access at tuple level, and compute scores for operating system's VM pages, and evict cold pages. DeBrabant et al. [5] propose *anti-caching* to move cold data from memory to disk in a transactionally safe manner. Under memory pressure, anti-caching gathers the coldest tuples and flush them to disk. Fine grained eviction (at tuple level) is the key advantage of anti-caching, over techniques that rely on OS level VM paging (e.g. [13]). As empirically evaluated recently by Zhang et al. [28], most application semantic is available to user-space approaches that offer finer granularity (e.g. at tuple level) eviction. However, kernel-space approaches (e.g. VM based) can integrate better with the operating system and directly take advantage of CPU, hardware features, and low-level system measurements. Zhang et al. [28] propose a hybrid method to exploit both kernel-level and application level anti-caching. Our approach is similar to anti-caching, in the sense that our internal memory manager keeps track of the resource usage at the granularity of paged column pieces, and decides eviction in cooperation with statistics collected from page usage and operating system. Eldawy et al. [6] propose Siberia as a framework to manage cold data in Microsoft Hekaton main memory engine, optimized for OLTP. For cold data, they propose compact in-memory data structures (bloom filter and range filters) to reduce the number of accesses to cold data for point and range queries. The key difference from our approach with Siberia is that our focus is the main fragment i.e. the read only piece of page loadable column. Siberia guarantees transactional consistency for updates to hot and cold data. However, in SAP HANA, updates are only applied to the delta fragment and applied to cold data during delta merge operation.

Graefe et al. [10] adapt the buffer pool design by replacing page identifiers with specialized pointers. This saves one level of redirection to convert from page identifier to page address. Using this technique, they report in-memory performance for disk based databases, when the working dataset fits completely in the database buffer pool. A number of in-memory database systems avoid the overhead of disk based systems by providing the best performance for memory resident data [19, 18]. There are other commercial systems that do not make this assumption. For instance, the second generation of IBM DB2 BLU [22, 4] provides a buffer pool supported access to relational data. Each DB2 BLU table is partitioned into column groups. Column groups are persisted in pages. Each page contains a header, a section with page-specific compression dictionaries and compressed columns. Fine-grain in-memory synopses and a specialized probabilistic buffer pool protocol for scans were implemented to reduce disk access with aggressive prefetching. SAP HANA is architecturally different from IBM DB2 BLU as SAP HANA applies changes to delta fragments only. Furthermore, SAP HANA uses uniform encoding of n-bit packed columns to efficiently find, prefetch, and load the pieces of each column on demand for page loadable columns.

8. FUTURE RESEARCH DIRECTION

Our current implementation of page loadable columns is based on the classical in-memory columnar database architecture where all the data structures for the main fragment of a logical column are rebuilt during delta-merge operation which brings delta fragment into the main fragment, practically rebuilding the whole main fragment and resetting the delta fragment to an empty state. For page loadable columns, the order-preserving paged dictionary, its helper sparse indexes on the paged dictionary, the paged data vector, and its paged inverted index are all fully rebuilt and persisted during delta-merge operation. A promising new extension to page loadable design is to selectively rebuild and persist, during delta-merge, only the critical data of the main fragment, and employ adaptive and partial rebuilding for non-critical data, all driven by the current workload.

For page loadable columns, the *critical data* is the data stored in the paged dictionary and the data stored in the paged data vector. All other data structures are considered *non-critical data* as they can be recovered and rebuilt from critical data. Based on the workload immediately before a delta-merge operation, it can be decided if the helper indexes on dictionary should be built based on their usage in the past. The same decisions are made for inverted indexes. After the delta-merge operation, driven by the current workload, these structures can be dynamically rebuilt and refined as more queries are executed which access a page loadable column. For example, for a column which is always accessed just by full scan or by set of row identifiers, only the helper index dictionary on value identifier $ipDict_{ValueId}$ is needed. However, if point queries are the norm, all non-critical data structures are used and they are needed to achieve maximum performance. For instance, the usual search on data vector ($findByValueID$) can dynamically rebuild $ipDataVector$ entries driven by the queries being executed.

Recent developments, such as the announcement by Intel and Micron of the new non-volatile memory technology and the addition of persistent memory support to the Intel 64 instruction set [12], hint that Storage Class Memory (SCM) might become a reality in the not too distant future. SCM promises byte addressable persistence with memory-like performance and storage-like capacity, endurance, and cost. The expectation is that SCM will have read and write latencies only within an order of magnitude of DRAM [20], low enough to be masked by prefetching for sequential access patterns. One line of research that we are investigating is improving performance by moving latency sensitive disk-based data structures to SCM, accessing them directly rather than via a DRAM cached copy. In particular, we are considering to move to SCM those non-critical data structures that can be rebuilt from other primary data structures. This mitigates the concern that the contents of SCM can become unavailable if the server hosting the SCM suffers a hardware failure. For paged loadable columns, the most promising candidate data structures are the inverted indexes. and the helper sparse dictionary indexes as their performance determines the performance of paged dictionaries.

9. CONCLUSION

We proposed piecewise implementation of the columnar data structures and access methods for SAP HANA. Instead of having columns fully loaded in main memory, we partially load pieces as they are needed. Our experiments confirm that page loadable columns reduce the memory footprint of a system, especially when only a small fraction of each column is accessed. The small loss of performance may be acceptable for accessing small portion of cold data (e.g. auditing aged data). There are still additional scenarios particularly when dealing with huge datasets where additional online and offline storage hierarchies are still warranted beyond the use of page loadable columns. Page loadable columns are the main driver for reducing the memory footprint in data aging scenarios; they not only reduce the total cost of ownership of large ERP systems, but also leave more memory available to keep performance-critical columns always in memory. Thus, indirectly contribute to the overall database performance.

Acknowledgments

We thank the anonymous reviewers for the comments and suggestions, which contributed to improving significantly the presentation of this paper. We give special thanks to all colleagues and contributors to the paged loadable column project, including Manbeen Kohli, Carsten Thiel, Chaitanya Gottipati, Steffen Geißinger, Christian Lemke, Sebastian Seifert, Robert Schulze, and Mohammed Junaid Azad.

10. REFERENCES

[1] The ParAccel analytic database: A technical overview. http://www.paraccel.com/ Whitepaper, 2009.

[2] [RFC] Minmax indexes. A. Herrera's email to Pg Hackers, 2013.

[3] D. Abadi, P. A. Boncz, S. Harizopoulos, S. Idreos, and S. Madden. The design and implementation of modern column-oriented database systems. *Foundations and Trends in Databases*, 5(3):197–280, 2013.

[4] R. Barber, G. M. Lohman, V. Raman, R. Sidle, S. Lightstone, and B. Schiefer. In-memory BLU acceleration in ibm's DB2 and dashdb: Optimized for modern workloads and hardware architectures. In *ICDE*, 2015.

[5] J. DeBrabant, A. Pavlo, S. Tu, M. Stonebraker, and S. B. Zdonik. Anti-caching: A new approach to database management system architecture. *PVLDB*, 6(14):1942–1953, 2013.

[6] A. Eldawy, J. Levandoski, and P. Larson. Trekking through siberia: Managing cold data in a memory-optimized database. *PVLDB*, 7(11), 2014.

[7] F. Färber, N. May, W. Lehner, P. Große, I. Müller, H. Rauhe, and J. Dees. The SAP HANA database – an architecture overview. *IEEE Data Engineering Bulletin*, 35(1):28–33, 2012.

[8] Z. Feng, E. Lo, B. Kao, and W. Xu. Byteslice: Pushing the envelop of main memory data processing with a new storage layout. In *ACM SIGMOD*, 2015.

[9] F. Funke, , A. Kemper, and T. Neumann. Compacting transactional data in hybrid oltp&olap databases. *PVLDB*, 5(11), 2012.

[10] G. Graefe, H. Volos, H. Kimura, H. Kuno, J. Tucek, M. Lillibridge, and A. Veitch. In-memory performance for big data. *PVLDB*, 8(1), 2014.

[11] S. Idreos, M. L. Kersten, and S. Manegold. Self-organizing tuple reconstruction in column-stores. In *ACM SIGMOD*, 2009.

[12] Intel 64-bit instruction set. https://software.intel.com/sites/default/files/managed/07/b7/319433-023.pdf.

[13] A. Kemper and T. Neumann. Hyper: A hybrid oltp&olap main memory database system based on virtual memory snapshots. In *ICDE*, 2011.

[14] A. Lamb, M. Fuller, R. Varadarajan, N. Tran, B. Vandier, L. Doshi, and C. Bear. The vertica analytic database: C-store 7 years later. *PVLDB*, 5(12), 2012.

[15] C. Lemke, K. Sattler, F. Faerber, and A. Zeier. Speeding up queries in column stores - A case for compression. In *DAWAK*, 2010.

[16] C. Lemke, K. Sattler, and F. Färber. Kompressionstechniken für spaltenorientierte bi-accelerator-lösungen. In *BTW*, 2009.

[17] Y. Li and J. M. Patel. BitWeaving: Fast Scans for Main Memory Data Processing. In *SIGMOD*, 2013.

[18] Monetdb. https://www.monetdb.org/.

[19] Oracle timesten. http://www.oracle.com/technetwork/products/timesten.

[20] I. Oukid, W. Lehner, T. Kissinger, T. Willhalm, and P. Bumbulis. Instant recovery for main memory databases. In *CIDR*, 2015.

[21] H. Plattner. The impact of columnar in-memory databases on enterprise systems. *PVLDB*, 7(13):1722–1729, 2014.

[22] V. Raman, G. K. Attaluri, R. Barber, N. Chainani, D. Kalmuk, V. KulandaiSamy, J. Leenstra, S. Lightstone, S. Liu, G. M. Lohman, T. Malkemus, R. Müller, I. Pandis, B. Schiefer, D. Sharpe, R. Sidle, A. J. Storm, and L. Zhang. DB2 with BLU acceleration: So much more than just a column store. *PVLDB*, 6(11):1080–1091, 2013.

[23] V. Sikka, F. Färber, W. Lehner, S. K. Cha, T. Peh, and C. Bornhövd. Efficient transaction processing in SAP HANA database: the end of a column store myth. In *ACM SIGMOD*, 2012.

[24] R. Stoica and A. Ailamaki. Enabling efficient os paging for main-memory oltp databases. In *DaMon*, 2013.

[25] M. Stonebraker, D. J. Abadi, A. Batkin, X. Chen, M. Cherniack, M. Ferreira, E. Lau, A. Lin, S. Madden, E. J. O'Neil, P. E. O'Neil, A. Rasin, N. Tran, and S. B. Zdonik. C-store: A column-oriented DBMS. In *VLDB*, 2005.

[26] T. Willhalm, N. Popovici, Y. Boshmaf, H. Plattner, A. Zeier, and J. Schaffner. Simd-scan: Ultra fast in-memory table scan using on-chip vector processing units. *PVLDB*, 2(1):385–394, 2009.

[27] H. Zhang, G. Chen, B. C. Ooi, K. Tan, and M. Zhang. In-memory big data management and processing: A survey. *IEEE TKDE*, 27(7):1920–1948, 2015.

[28] H. Zhang, G. Chen, B. C. Ooi, W. Wong, S. Wu, and Y. Xia. "anti-caching"-based elastic memory management for big data. In *ICDE*, 2015.

[29] M. Zukowski and P. A. Boncz. Vectorwise: Beyond column stores. *IEEE Data Eng. Bull.*, 35(1), 2012.

Hybrid Garbage Collection for Multi-Version Concurrency Control in SAP HANA

Juchang Lee [#]
juc.lee@sap.com

Hyungyu Shin [‡]
hgshin@dblab.postech.ac.kr

Chang Gyoo Park [#]
chang.gyoo.park@sap.com

Seongyun Ko [‡]
syko@dblab.postech.ac.kr

Jaeyun Noh [#]
jaeyun.noh@sap.com

Yongjae Chuh [#]
yongjae.chuh@sap.com

Wolfgang Stephan [†]
wolfgang.stephan@sap.com

Wook-Shin Han [‡*]
wshan@dblab.postech.ac.kr

[#]SAP Labs Korea, Korea
[‡]Pohang University of Science and Technology (POSTECH), Korea
[†]SAP SE, Germany

ABSTRACT

While multi-version concurrency control (MVCC) supports fast and robust performance in in-memory, relational databases, it has the potential problem of a growing number of versions over time due to obsolete versions. Although a few TB of main memory is available for enterprise machines, the memory resource should be used carefully for economic and practical reasons. Thus, in order to maintain the necessary number of versions in MVCC, versions which will no longer be used need to be deleted. This process is called garbage collection. MVCC uses the concept of *visibility* to define garbage. A set of versions for each record is first identified as candidate if their version timestamps are lower than the minimum value of snapshot timestamps of active snapshots in the system. All such candidates, except the one which has the maximum version timestamp, are safely reclaimed as garbage versions. In mixed OLTP and OLAP workloads, the typical garbage collector may not effectively reclaim record versions. In these workloads, OLTP applications generate a high volume of new versions, while long-lived queries or transactions in OLAP applications often block garbage collection, since we need to compare the version timestamp of each record version with the snapshot timestamp of the oldest, long-lived snapshot. Thus, these workloads typically cause the in-memory version space to grow. Additionally, the increasing version chains of records over time may also increase the traversal cost for them. In this paper, we present an efficient and effective garbage collector called HybridGC in SAP HANA. HybridGC integrates three novel concepts of garbage collection: timestamp-based group garbage collection, table garbage collection, and interval garbage collection. Through experiments using mixed OLTP and OLAP workloads, we show that HybridGC effectively and efficiently collects garbage versions with negligible overhead.

Keywords

Garbage collection; multi-version concurrency control; SAP HANA

1. INTRODUCTION

Commercial database management systems (DBMSs) including SAP HANA employ multi-version concurrency control (MVCC) due to robust and better performance for various workloads [10]. In MVCC, updates (including deletes) by a transaction to a record generate new versions rather than updating the existing record in place, and thus, a series of versions are maintained for each record.

SAP HANA supports snapshot isolation [3], which is a popular MVCC protocol where a transaction can read a snapshot of committed versions, i.e., a snapshot of the versions that were created by committed transactions. There are two variants of snapshot isolation supported in SAP HANA [19]: statement-level snapshot isolation (Stmt-SI) and transaction-level snapshot isolation (Trans-SI). In Stmt-SI, which is the default isolation level of SAP HANA and widely used by the vast majority of enterprise applications of SAP, all reads logically occur at the beginning of the statement. In Trans-SI, all reads logically occur at the beginning of the transaction. In Stmt-SI, each statement has its own snapshot associated with a new snapshot timestamp, while, in Trans-SI, each transaction has its own snapshot with a new snapshot timestamp.

While MVCC supports fast and robust performance, it has the potential problem of a growing number of versions over time due to obsolete versions. Although a few TB of main memory is available for enterprise machines, the memory resource should be used carefully for economic and practical reasons [2]. Thus, in order to maintain the necessary number of versions in MVCC, versions which will no longer be used need to be deleted. This process is called *garbage collection*.

*corresponding author

SIGMOD'16, June 26-July 01, 2016, San Francisco, CA, USA

ISBN 978-1-4503-3531-7/16/06...$15.00

DOI: http://dx.doi.org/10.1145/2882903.2903734

MVCC uses the concept of *visibility* to define garbage. Specifically, in typical commercial DBMSs supporting MVCC, a set of versions for each record is first identified as a candidate if their version timestamps are lower than the minimum value (a.k.a. the global minimum timestamp) of snapshot timestamps of active snapshots in the system. All such candidates, except the one which has the maximum version timestamp, are safely reclaimed as garbage versions. One can guarantee that such record versions will no longer be visible to any active snapshots. Figure 1 shows how the typical garbage collector identifies garbage versions. First, the global minimum timestamp is set to 3. Thus, the conventional garbage collector identifies v_{11} *only* as garbage, since its version timestamp (=1) is lower than 3, and there exists v_{12} whose version timestamp 2 is also lower than 3. However, notice that both v_{13} and v_{14} are invisible to any active transaction, and thus, they should be subject to being "garbage collected."

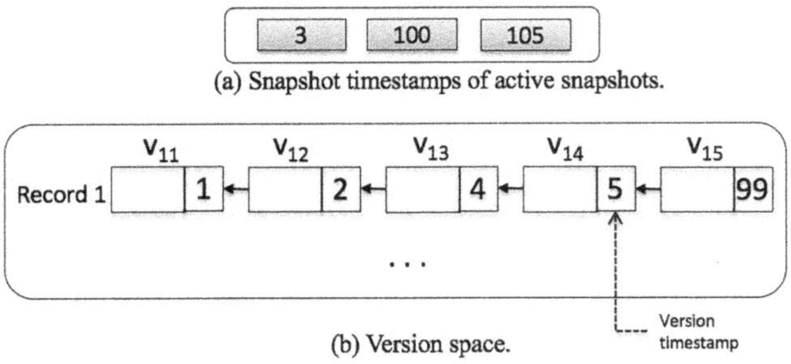

Figure 1: An example of record versions.

In mixed OLTP and OLAP workloads, the typical garbage collector may not effectively reclaim record versions. In these workloads, OLTP applications generate a high volume of new versions, while long-lived queries (under Stmt-SI) or transactions (under Trans-SI) in OLAP applications often block garbage collection, since we need to compare the version timestamp of each record version with the snapshot timestamp of the oldest, long-lived snapshot. Thus, these workloads typically cause the in-memory version space to grow. Additionally, the increasing version chains of records over time may also increase the traversal cost for them. We also observe other types of garbage collection blockers in real customer systems. Long-duration cursors or Trans-SI transactions due to either application logic or developers' mistakes can easily block garbage collection. For example, we collected statistics on cursor durations from a real ERP system. Out of 408,664 distinct queries executed in the system, the life times of six cursors were more than one hour!

Figure 2 shows the impact of the long-lived snapshot when there exists no optimized garbage collector. This real screen shot is taken from the HANA system load view, which visualizes the status of key performance indicators in the system over time. Especially, the light blue color, marked as "Active Commit ID Range", denote the difference between the last CID value and the minimum global snapshot timestamp value. If the value increases, this means that there is at least one long-live snapshot in the system. The number of record versions, marked as "Active Versions" in blue color, keeps increasing over time. As a result, the system's memory consumption, marked as "Used Memory" with green color, keeps growing.

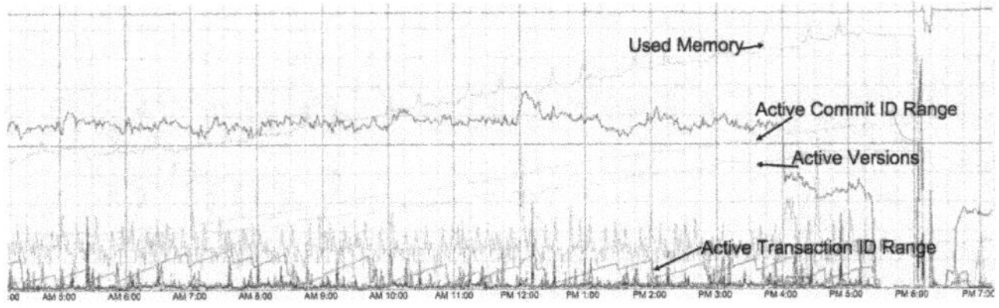

Figure 2: A real example of version space overflow problem.

Conventional workarounds for this version space overflow problem are as follows. 1) The system flushes old versions out to disk. 2) The system closes problematic cursors or Trans-SI transactions by force and returns errors to clients. This is implemented in SAP HANA, especially to handle application developers' mistakes. 3) The system implicitly closes cursors earlier than the explicit cursor close request; as soon as the query results are materialized or the system can guarantee that there is no more request to access the version space, the system implicitly closes cursors. This workaround is also supported in SAP HANA for a limited set of cases.

In order to collect more garbage versions, unlike the traditional garbage collector which uses the global minimum timestamp, we propose an *interval garbage collector* that uses *visible intervals* among consecutive timestamps of each record version. Here, the visible interval $[s, e)$ for a record v represents a set of snapshot timestamps to which v can be visible. The traditional garbage collector uses the global minimum timestamp and is thus unable to collect record versions which are invisible to any active or future snapshots. For example, v_{13}, and v_{14} are invisible to any active transactions. Visible intervals for the record 1 of Figure 1 are {[1, 2), [2, 4), [4, 5), [5, 99), [99, ∞)}. Consider the interval for v_{13}, [4, 5). No active snapshot timestamp is included in this interval. Thus, v_{13} is invisible to any active snapshot and can be reclaimed as garbage. Similarly, v_{14} whose visible interval is [5, 99) is also reclaimed as garbage if we use this interval-based decision.

Garbage collection may incur non-negligible overhead for normal transaction processing. In order to efficiently collect garbage, we propose the concept of the *group garbage version* collector. Typically, a set of versions generated by the same transaction can form a group, and thus, the garbage collector checks whether this group can be reclaimed as a whole. The group garbage collector can also be implemented using either the timestamp-based decision or the interval-based decision.

Figure 3 shows the taxonomy of 4-quadrants of garbage collectors containing two dimensions. Along the dimension of garbage granularity, a garbage version can be either a single record version or a group version. Along the dimension of comparison unit, there exist timestamp-based and interval garbage collectors. Thus, we can have four types of garbage collectors (ST, SI, GT, and GI). Note that existing garbage collectors belong to ST.

In addition to granularity and comparison unit, we can exploit semantic optimization for efficiently collecting garbage versions. Under Stmt-SI or some special cases of Trans-SI (e.g. pre-compiled stored procedures), one can reclaim more garbage versions by identifying the tables which are not relevant to the currently long-running snapshots. In this paper,

Granularity		Comparison unit: Timestamp	Comparison unit: Interval
	Single version	ST	SI
	Group version	GT	GI

Figure 3: The taxonomy of garbage collectors.

this type of garbage collector is called the *table garbage collector* (TG).

In order to execute effective and efficient garbage collection, we propose the novel concept of *hybrid garbage collector* which executes GT, TG, and SI in this order. GT is a light-weight garbage collector since it examines group garbage versions only. TG is also effective under Stmt-SI and relatively lighter than SI. Although the SI can reclaim more garbage versions, it can be heavier than the others. Thus, we propose an efficient algorithm for SI to identify garbage versions using visible intervals.

In summary, this paper makes the following key contributions.

- We propose the novel concept of *interval garbage collection*. For this, we formally model the garbage collection problem as the consecutive interval intersection problem. Then, we provide an efficient merge-based solution to this problem.
- We propose the novel concept of *group garbage collection*. This granular garbage collection enables us to efficiently determine a set of record versions as garbage. Furthermore, this concept can be applied to typical, minimum snapshot timestamp-based garbage collection as well as interval garbage collection.
- We propose the novel concept of *table garbage collection*. This exploits the semantic information that versions in tables which are irrelevant to current snapshots can be reclaimed at any time.
- We present a hybrid garbage collector which combines three different flavors of garbage collectors. Thus, we can effectively and efficiently collect garbage versions with negligible performance overhead.
- We implement the hybrid garbage collector in SAP HANA and perform extensive experiments using a modified TPC-C benchmark which includes long-running queries. Experimental results confirm that the hybrid garbage collector effectively collects garbage versions and considerably reduces the latency of long-running OLAP queries.

The rest of this paper is organized as follows. Section 2 reviews some background information in SAP HANA. In Section 3, we propose the concept of the interval garbage collector. Section 4 presents the concepts of the group garbage version, table garbage collection, and the hybrid garbage collection for SAP HANA. In Section 5, we present the results of performance evaluations, and Section 6 reviews related work. Section 7 concludes the paper.

2. PRELIMINARIES

In this section, we first explain the architecture of SAP HANA. We then explain how SAP HANA manages the version space.

2.1 SAP HANA In-memory Database

SAP HANA is an ACID-compliant and in-memory relational DBMS, designed to efficiently handle both of OLTP and OLAP workloads together in a single system [16,18,19]. SAP HANA has both an in-memory column store and an in-memory row store for high-performance OLAP and high-performance OLTP, respectively.

In order to seamlessly integrate the column store and row store from transaction and query processing perspectives, the unified transaction manager and the unified query processor are built on top of the two different stores. For example, the unified transaction manager provides durability based on logging and checkpointing to a common persistency, and it also provides snapshot isolation based on the common commit timestamp.

For supporting snapshot isolation, the transactions across the row store and the column store are centrally controlled by the unified transaction manager although each store has its own version space layout. While the garbage collection scheme proposed in this paper can also be applied to the column store, the rest of this paper is described based on its implementation at the row store for convenience of the description.

2.2 Version Management in HANA RowStore

The in-memory area in the SAP HANA row store consists of the table space and the version space. Since the row store implements the snapshot isolation based on MVCC, the newly added version is appended to the version space, instead of performing the in-place update directly to the table space. Later on, by garbage collection, the added data is moved to the table space once it is certain that there is no potential reader to the original data maintained in the table space. In this way, the table space maintains the oldest versions of the existing records while the version space maintains newer record versions until they are reclaimed or their record images are copied to the table space by a garbage collector.

In particular, on every INSERT/UPDATE/DELETE operation, a *record version* (or a *version entry*—we use the terms interchangeably) is created at the version space. A single record version consists of a version header and its payload. The version header stores the creator's operation type, the changed record's identifier (RID), the table ID which the record belongs to, and a few pointers to maintain version chains. The payload stores the new record image for the UPDATE operation. For the INSERT operation, the new record image is directly inserted into the table space since there is no older image for the particular record.

In the version space, the record versions having the same RID are linked with each other in the latest-first order. Differently from organizing the version entries in the oldest-first order, the *latest-first* ordering in the version chain can reduce the cost of traversing version chains for future queries and transactions. This is more likely to access more recent versions by the nature of snapshot isolation. The pointer to the latest record version of each version chain is maintained by a central hash table, called *RID hash table*, for

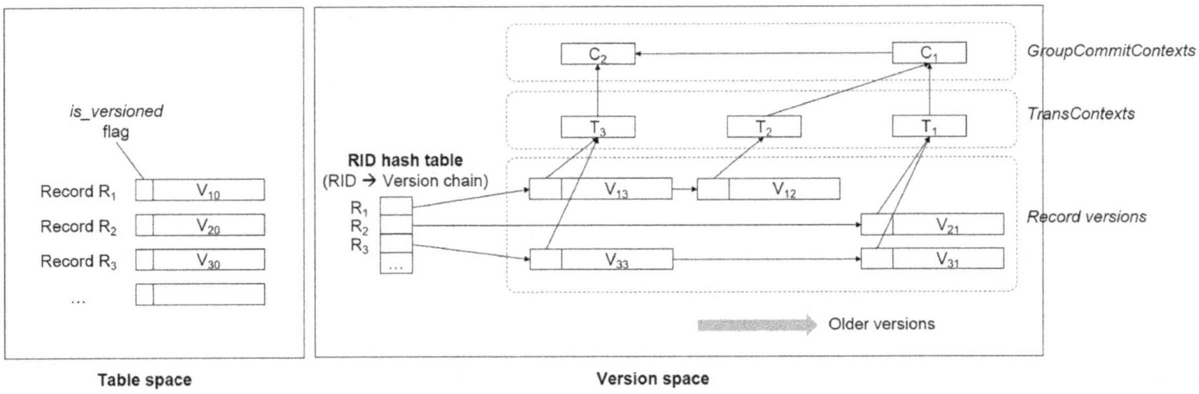

Figure 4: Version management in the HANA row store.

fast RID-to-version-chain lookup. In order to reduce the cost of checking whether a particular record has its own version chain, each record in the table space stores the so-called *is_versioned* flag. This flag is set only when the record in the table space has additional record versions in the version space. If this flag is not set, looking up the hash table can be skipped.

The RID hash table is implemented as a chained hash structure. Basically, it is an array of hash buckets, each of which stores the pointer to the corresponding version chain. However, if multiple version chains are associated to a single hash bucket, the hash bucket creates additional linked list to maintain the pointers to the multiple version chains. As the result, if a single hash bucket contains 10 version chains, then the query accessing the hash bucket may encounter 5 additional pointer traversals in average and 10 additional pointer traversals in the worst case just to find the corresponding version chain. Since every pointer traversal in this additional chain may lead to hardware-level cache misses, this cost can significantly affect the overall performance, especially for short-running queries and transactions where the version space access cost takes a non-trivial portion of its execution time. Remark that the row store is currently implemented using the RID hash table, considering that an efficient garbage collector can reduce the probability of the hash collisions. The detailed experimental analysis on the performance impact of such hash collisions is given in Section 5.

The record versions created by the same transaction are associated as a group by pointing to the same data object, called *TransContext*. When a transaction issues a write operation for the first time, it creates a TransContext object. All the next record versions created by the transaction point to the same TransContext object. The TransContext object points to NULL until the corresponding transaction starts to commit. On transaction commit, once the set of write transactions to be committed together is decided by the *group commit* logic, another object called *GroupCommitContext* is created, and thus the TransContext objects for all concurrent transactions committing together point to the same GroupCommitContext object. After that, if the commit ID (CID) is decided for the group commit operation, the CID is written to the GroupCommitContext object, and the CID becomes immediately visible to all related TransContext objects and version entries which share the same CID value. This atomic, indirect CID assignment scheme is more efficient than the approach of directly copying the CID values to the record versions. The indirect CID assignment is done in an atomic way without relying on any latch or lock, and thus is efficient.

The expected penalty in the atomic indirect CID assignment is that the accessing the CID value of a record version may have to follow an additional pointer, but this cost can be minimized by asynchronously propagating the CID value from the GroupCommitContext object to the individual record versions. For efficient backward CID propagation, backward links from the GroupCommitContext object to individual record version are also maintained.

Figure 4 illustrates the version space management scheme in the row store. We assume the records R_1, R_2, and R_3 are already in a user table. The transaction T_1 generates the record versions V_{21} and V_{31} and commits with creating TransContext T_1. The transaction T_2 generates the record versions V_{12} and commits with creating TransContext T_2. Since T_1 and T_2 are committed together by the same group commit operation, they share the same GroupCommitContext C_1. Then, the transaction T_3 generates the record version V_{13} and V_{33} and commits with creating TransContext T_3 and GroupCommitContext C_2.

3. VARIANTS OF GARBAGE COLLECTOR

In the paper, we classify garbage collectors into four variants according to the comparison unit and the granularity.

3.1 Timestamp vs Interval Garbage Collector

Conventional, timestamp-based garbage collectors identify a version record by comparing its timestamp with active snapshot timestamps. Specifically, a set of versions for each record is first identified as a candidate if their version timestamps are lower than the global minimum timestamp in the system. All such candidates, except the one which has the maximum version timestamp, are safely reclaimed as garbage versions. Such record versions will no longer be visible to any active snapshots.

Before we explain interval garbage collectors, we formally model the interval-based garbage collection as the consecutive interval intersection problem. First, we define some terminology and introduce the consecutive intersection problem. We then propose an efficient merge-based solution to this problem.

Consider an integer t and an ordered sequence S of integers. Without loss of generality, we assume that S always contains a number which is larger than or equal to any t. Then, the *least greater number* (LGN) for t with respect to S is defined as the smallest number in S such that the number is greater than or equal to t. We denote the least greater number by LGN(t,S). Suppose that t=10, and S = [1, 4, 6, 8, 12, 14]. Then, LGN(t,S) $= min\{12, 14\} = 12$. If t =15, LGN(t,S) $= \infty$.

Definition 1 (Consecutive interval intersection). *Given two ordered sequences of integers, S and T, find the subset $T_\cap$ of T satisfying the following condition.*

$$T_\cap = \{t | t \in T, \text{LGN}(t+1, T) \leq \text{LGN}(t, S)\} \square \quad (1)$$

Consider S = [90, 92, 95, 96, 99] and T = [91, 93, 94, 95, 98]. We can compute LGN($t+1, T$) and LGN(t,S) for each t. Finally, we can compute $T_\cap = \{93, 94\}$.

Suppose that S is an ordered sequence of snapshot timestamps, and T is an ordered sequence of record versions for a record. Then, the elements in $T_\cap$ are identified as garbage. Here, $[t, \text{LGN}(t+1, T))$ is called *visible interval* for t.

Now, we explain how to compute $T_\cap$. The naive way to compute $T_\cap$ uses nested loops. That is, for each record version t, we perform a set intersection operation for every snapshot timestamp in S. Then, the time complexity is $O(|T| \times |S|)$.

In order to minimize the garbage collection overhead, we now propose a merge-based solution. Algorithm 1 shows a merge-based garbage collector. It computes $T_\cap$ in Eq. (1) in $O(|T| + |S|)$. We denote the i-th element of T by $T[i]$. In order to merge two ordered sequences, we maintain two index variables, i and j. For each element $T[i]$, we move j until $S[j] \geq T[i]$ (Lines 3 ~ 4). Then, $S[j]$ should be LGN($T[i], S$). If $S[j] \geq T[i+1]$, then $T[i]$ is identified as garbage. Otherwise, we skip $T[i]$ by incrementing i since it is not garbage.

Algorithm 1 MergeBasedGC(S, T)

Input: Two ordered sequence of integers S, T.
Output: $T_\cap$.

```
1:  i ← 0, j ← 0
2:  while i < |T|-1 do
3:      if S[j] < T[i] then
4:          j ← j + 1
5:      else if T[i + 1] ≤ S[j] then
        /*T[i + 1] represents LGN(T[i] + 1, T).*/
6:          T∩ ← T∩ ∪ T[i]
7:          i ← i + 1
8:      else
9:          i ← i + 1
10:     end if
11: end while
12: return T∩
```

3.2 Single vs Group Garbage Collector

The granularity for garbage collectors can be either a single record version or a group of record versions. All record versions generated by transactions belonging to the same GroupCommitContext have the same version timestamp. Thus, if we group record versions by their timestamp, we can efficiently check whether a (version) group is reclaimed as garbage. That is, we can directly apply the timestamp-based garbage collector to both the single version and the version group. Such garbage collectors are classified as ST and GT, respectively.

Now, we explain how we can apply the interval garbage collector to the version group. For this purpose, we propose the novel concept of *immediate successor subgroup.*

The immediate successor subgroup in a group G_i consists of record versions in G_i which have the immediate successors in the next group G_{i+1}. Then, we can apply the interval garbage collector to an ordered sequence of immediate successor subgroups. In this scheme, we need an efficient, systematic mechanism to move a record version in G_i to form its immediate successor subgroup, which is beyond of the scope of our paper and would be an interesting future topic of research.

Figure 5 shows an ordered sequence of k groups. Each group G_i has one immediate successor subgroup denoted by sg_i. Note that the version v_1 belongs to sg_1 since its immediate successor is in G_2, while the version v_2 does not. However, if we generate the immediate successor of v_2 and insert the successor into G_2, then v_2 belongs to sg_1. Note that sg_k does not contain any record version since G_k is the last group in the ordered sequence.

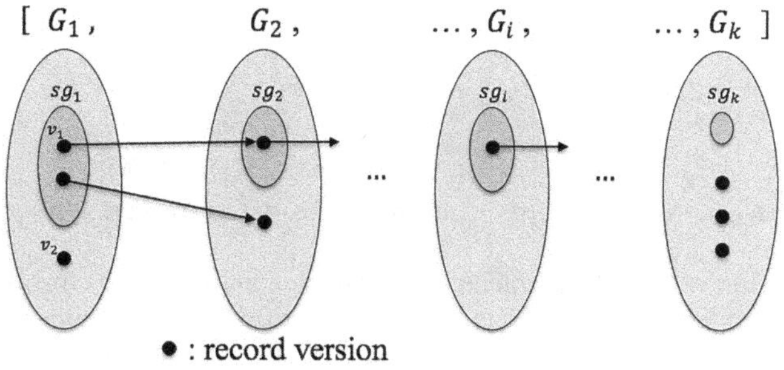

Figure 5: An ordered sequence of k groups containing immediate successor subgroup.

Now, we can apply the interval garbage collector to both the single version and the version group. Such garbage collectors are classified as SI and GI, respectively. In the next section, we explain how these garbage collectors are implemented in SAP HANA.

4. IMPLEMENTATION IN SAP HANA

This section describes how the proposed interval garbage collector and the group garbage collector are implemented in SAP HANA together with the additional practical optimizations. Specifically, we describe GT, SI, and the table garbage collectors implemented in SAP HANA.

4.1 Global Group Garbage Collector

GT is implemented as the global garbage collector in SAP HANA, considering the following two optimization strategies: (1) efficiently select the minimum global snapshot timestamp value and (2) efficiently detect a group of garbage versions.

As the first optimization strategy, the so-called *global snapshot timestamp tracker* (global STS tracker) is maintained globally in the system. The global STS tracker is an ordered list of reference-counted snapshot timestamp values. When a snapshot starts, it acquires its snapshot timestamp value from the transaction manager according to the definition of snapshot isolation. If the acquired snapshot timestamp value is already in the tracker, we simply increment the reference count of the corresponding snapshot timestamp object by one. Otherwise, a new snapshot timestamp object is inserted into the tracker. Then, if the snapshot associated with a query or a transaction finishes its processing, the reference count of the corresponding snapshot timestamp decrements by one. When the reference count becomes zero, the corresponding snapshot object is deleted from the global STS tracker. Since each active snapshot maintains a pointer to the corresponding snapshot timestamp object in the global STS tracker as shown in Figure 6, we can directly access the snapshot timestamp object without scanning the entire list in the tracker. Note that the snapshot timestamp values in the global STS tracker are maintained in increasing order. When the global garbage collector needs to find the global minimum snapshot timestamp value at a certain time point, accessing the head of the list without scanning the entire tracker is sufficient.

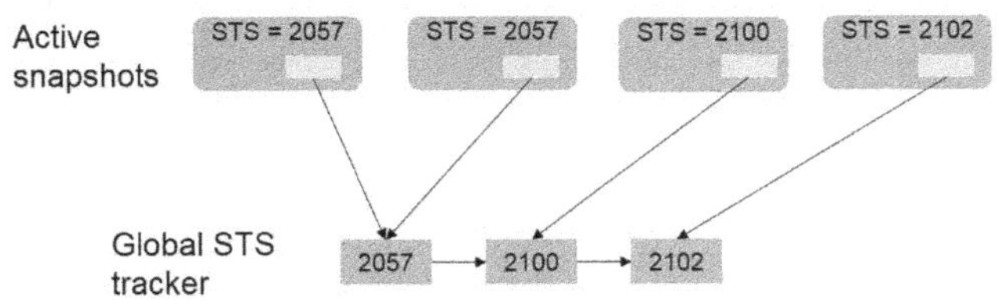

Figure 6: Global Snapshot Timestamp Tracker.

As the second optimization strategy, we exploit the GroupCommitContext and the TransContext objects, described in Section 2. Since (1) record versions created by the same transaction are associated with the same TransContext object, and (2) the transactions which are committed together and share the same CID value are associated as a group with the same GroupCommitContext object, we can efficiently find the group of record versions that share the same CID by just accessing the GroupCommitContext object. The GroupCommitContext objects are also maintained by an ordered list of their CID values as shown in Figure 7. Then, the global group garbage collector can identify a set of garbage versions as a group by just checking the GroupCommitContext object list without traversing the individual record versions. If the global garbage collector encounters a GroupCommitContext object which has a larger CID value than the minimum global snapshot timestamp, then the global garbage collector finishes its iteration of the GroupCommitContext object list. After the group garbage collector finishes the identification of groups of garbage versions, the corresponding record versions, TransContext objects, and GroupCommitContext objects are physically deleted in the background.

4.2 Interval Garbage Collector

For the simplicity of implementation in SAP HANA, the group garbage collector uses only the timestamp-based decision, while the single garbage collector uses only the interval-based decision. The interval garbage collector consists of

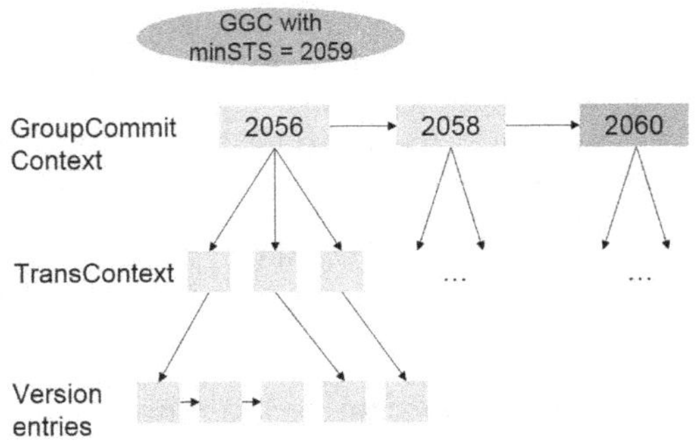

Figure 7: Global Group Garbage Collection.

the following four steps. (1) The full set of active snapshot timestamps is retrieved by scanning the whole snapshot timestamp values maintained by the global STS tracker. Let's denote the ordered set of active snapshot timestamp values by S (following the same notation at Definition 1). (2) At the second step, the interval garbage collector scans the existing GroupCommitContext objects and finds GroupCommitContext objects whose CID values are larger than the minimum value of S and smaller than the maximum value of S. We denote the set of the identified GroupCommitContext objects by P. (3) At the third step, by iterating GroupCommitContext objects in P in the highest-CID-first order, the interval garbage collector accesses the record versions reachable from the GroupCommitContext objects. (4) Finally, for each reachable record version, the interval garbage collector identifies (and reclaim, if exists) garbage versions in its version chain, following Algorithm 1. The CID values in the version chain compose T in Algorithm 1, and the interval garbage collector reclaims the record versions whose CID values exist in $T_\cap$.

Instread of accessing version chains starting from the available GroupCommitObject list as described above, it is an alternative implementation option to reach to the version chains starting from the RID hash table, which is more useful when we need to logically partition the version space to execute the interval garbage collector by multiple threads in parallel.

4.3 Table GC: Semantic Optimization

In addition to the interval garbage collector and group garbage collector, we present another optimization dimension for garbage collection by exploiting semantic information of executed snapshots. In this optimized garbage collection, called *table garbage collection* (TG), TG leverages the target tables that will be accessed by a given snapshot a priori. In general, it is not possible to predict the complete set of the tables to be accessed by the snapshot at the time when a snapshot timestamp is assigned to it. However, under Stmt-SI, which is the default isolation mode in SAP HANA and widely used in SAP enterprise applications, the complete set of the accessed tables within that snapshot can be retrieved by just accessing its compiled query plan. Even under Trans-SI, in certain scenarios (e.g. pre-compiled stored procedure execution), it is possible to identify the tables to be accessed within the snapshot a priori. Therefore, it is possible to restrict the negative impact of long-live snapshots only to their relevant tables.

If a table garbage collector is invoked, it performs the following three steps: (1) discovering long-lived snapshots and their scopes, (2) moving snapshot timestamp objects from the global STS tracker to relevant, per-table STS trackers, (3) reclaiming versions by traversing the version space based on the per-table minimum snapshot timestamps. In the first step, it checks whether there is any long-lived (determined based on the pre-defined time threshold) snapshot in the system by accessing the system monitor which keeps track of every active snapshot's status If any long-live snapshot is found, then it checks again whether the complete set of the target tables of the detected long-lived snapshots is already determined. In the second step, the snapshot timestamp of the classified snapshot is copied to one or more relevant *per-table snapshot timestamp trackers* (per-table STS trackers), each of which maintains only the timestamps of the snapshots relevant to the given table. Then, the snapshot timestamp of such snapshot is removed from the global STS tracker. Finally, the table garbage collector decides the minimum snapshot timestamps from the available per-table STS trackers and then, based on the per-table minimum snapshot timestamp, the table garbage collector is able to reclaim versions which could not be reclaimed by the global garbage collector alone. During this visibility check, depending on the table ID stored in the record version, it is determined which minimum snapshot timestamp is compared with the record version's CID.

In the example of Figure 8, suppose that the snapshots S_1 and S_2 are identified as long-lived snapshots. Assume that their scopes are Table 1 and Table 2, respectively. For the record versions which are not relevant to Table 1 and Table 2, 2100 is used as the minimum snapshot timestamp. For the record versions relevant to Table 1 or Table 2, 2057 is used as the minimum snapshot timestamp.

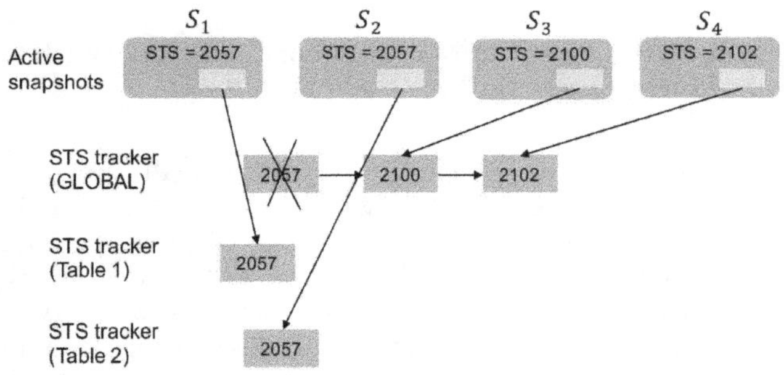

Figure 8: Per-table snapshot timestamp trackers for table garbage collection.

Although it is also possible to apply this semantic optimization to a finer-granular object such as partitions (by additionally leveraging the partition-pruning results of the queries), only the table-level semantic optimization is implemented in SAP HANA for now. In practice, this table garbage collection is used more widely even for Trans-SI, particularly for internal transactions, because there is an API that application programmers can explicitly declare which tables will be accessed by the transactions. If the transaction tries to access a non-declared table object, an error is reported to the transaction. In addition to the internal transaction case, if a Trans-SI transaction is used in a pre-compiled stored procedure, it is also possible to identify the tables to be accessed within the snapshot a priori.

For mixed OLTP and OLAP workload, the table garbage collector is particularly useful in a database system such as SAP HANA which uses separate row and column stores. By the table garbage collection, the long-lived OLAP queries running on column store tables do not affect the garbage collection of the other row store tables which deals with a large number of versions rapidly created by the OLTP workloads.

4.4 HybridGC: Putting It Altogether

Finally, we propose a hybrid garbage collector which combines the global group garbage collector, the table garbage collector, and the interval garbage collector. The three garbage collectors are invoked independently, having its own invocation period. When the table garbage collector or the interval garbage collector is invoked, it internally executes the global group garbage collector first. For the remaining versions after the implicitly invoked group garbage collection, the table garbage collector or the interval garbage collector tries to reclaim them.

Figure 9 shows three regions of the version space by the three different version garbage collectors in HybridGC. The set of versions marked by the region A is reclaimed at once by the global group garbage collector. The region B is inspected by the table garbage collector, while the region C is inspected by the interval garbage collector. While the interval-garbage collector eventually scans all existing version chains which are available when the interval garbage collector starts, the table garbage collector scans only a subset of the GroupCommitContext objects whose commit timestamps are less than the minimum value of the global STS tracker. Note that the global garbage collector and the interval garbage collector need to be slightly changed when they are used together with the table garbage collector because the table garbage collector could move some snapshot timestamp values from the global STS tracker to the per-table STS trackers. That is, the global garbage collector should calculate its global minimum snapshot timestamp by considering not only the global STS tracker but also the existing per-table STS trackers. The interval garbage collector also needs to consider existing per-table STS trackers as well as the global STS tracker. To deal with the situation where there are too many per-table STS trackers, the union of the global STS tracker and the available per-table STS trackers is pre-materialized and maintained separately to fast extract the minimum value for the global garbage collector or the entire snapshot timestamp set for the interval garbage collector.

All the proposed garbage collectors can be easily executed in parallel by multiple threads. For example, by logically partitioning the GroupCommitContext object list or by logically partitioning the version space based on table ID or RID.

5. EXPERIMENTS

We evaluate the performance of three different garbage collectors, which are implemented in SAP HANA row store The garbage collectors considered are as follows: (1) GT, a global group garbage collector which uses the timestamp-based decision; (2) GT+TG, a garbage collector that uses the combination of GT + TG; (3) HG(=HybridGC in Sec-

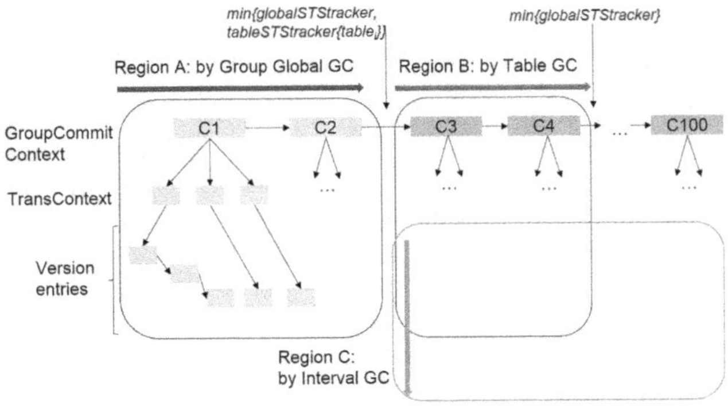

Figure 9: Hybrid garbage collection.

tion 4.4), the hybrid garbage collector which executes the three garbage collectors GT+TG+SI in this order.

Our main objective is to show that the hybrid garbage collector 1) effectively collects garbage and 2) efficiently works with negligible overhead. The detailed goals of the experiment are as follows:

- HG reclaims the version space more effectively than the two alternatives (Section 5.2).
- HG improves the OLTP performance especially for the SAP HANA row store by reducing the number of hash collisions in the version space (Section 5.3).
- HG improves query performance during incremental query processing (Section 5.4).
- HG effectively collects garbage in the presence of Trans-SI transactions, while the other alternatives do not. (Section 5.5).
- The overhead of HG is negligible (Section 5.6).

5.1 Experiment Setup

We used the TPC-C benchmark with 100 warehouses with the following minor modifications: 1) In order to avoid network performance effect, the TPC-C logic was embedded inside the database server using HANA SQLScript, which is the stored procedure supported by SAP HANA. 2) In order to see the behaviors of the garbage collectors while the record versions are generated rapidly, we allocated a dedicated worker thread for each warehouse and let the thread access the home warehouse only. Note that this modification does not simplify the work of garbage collectors because the worker thread information or the database partition information is not exploited by the garbage collectors in this experiment. 3) In order to emulate mixed OLTP and OLAP workloads, we added an emulated OLAP workload by using a long-duration cursor (under Stmt-SI) or long-duration transactions (under Trans-SI).

All TPC-C transactions were executed under the Stmt-SI mode except the experiment in Section 5.5. In all the experiments, the garbage collectors are triggered periodically with 1 second for GT, 3 seconds for TG, and 10 seconds for SI. The impact of the garbage collection period is discussed in Section 5.6. In order to measure how effective garbage collectors are, we use the number of record versions. We use the throughput (=committed statements/sec) for measuring efficiency of each garbage collector.

All the experiments were performed on a single 4-socket machine having 1TB of main memory and 60 physical CPU cores in total (120 logical cores with hyper-threading).

5.2 Impact on Version Space Size

To see the impact of a long-duration cursor to the version space size, we executed a simple scan query on the STOCK table without closing its cursor until the TPC-C benchmark finishes (each worker thread terminates after executing a fixed number of iterations in TPC-C). We measured the number of record versions maintained by each garbage collector.

Figure 10 shows the number of record versions existing in the version space over time. While the number of record versions keeps growing for GT and GT+TG, the number of record versions in HG remained almost constant in spite of the long-duration cursor. This indicates that SI effectively collects garbage versions while the other two do not in the presence of the long-lived query. GT+TG reclaims more record versions than GT alone because the long-duration cursor is defined only for the table STOCK in this experiment.

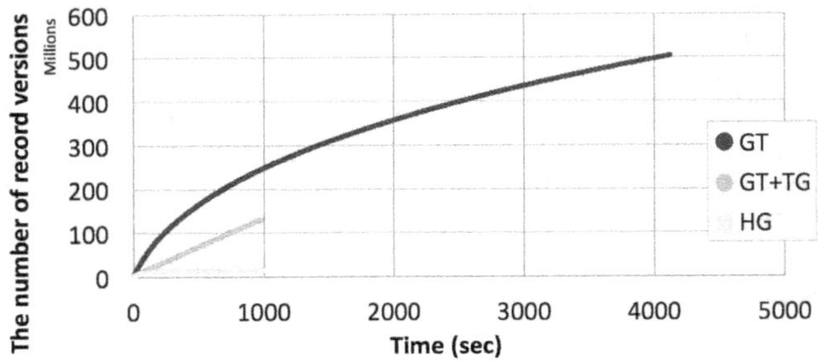

Figure 10: The number of record versions with a long-duration cursor.

Remark that the version growth ratio in GT decreases over time while GT+TG shows almost linear growth in terms of the number of the record versions. This was because the version generation speed from the TPC-C benchmark decreased as the number of the hash collisions at the version space increases. This issue will be discussed in detail in Section 5.3. Similarly, the graphs of HG and GT+TG terminate earlier than GT because the given number of TPC-C iterations at HG or GT+TG finishes earlier than GT.

Figure 11 shows the accumulated number of record versions reclaimed by each of GT, TG and SI when HG is used in the experiment of Figure 10. Due to the long-duration cursor, GT did not reclaim any record version but TG and SI respectively reclaimed 379 million versions and 118 million versions during the 1000 seconds of the TPC-C run time. The number of reclaimed versions by SI in Figure 11 is equivalent to the number of remaining versions at GT+TG in Figure 10 and this indicates that HG could reclaim more versions than GT+TG by the work of SI.

5.3 Impact on OLTP Performance

In order to see the impact of the long-duration cursor to the OLTP performance, we measured the throughput of the

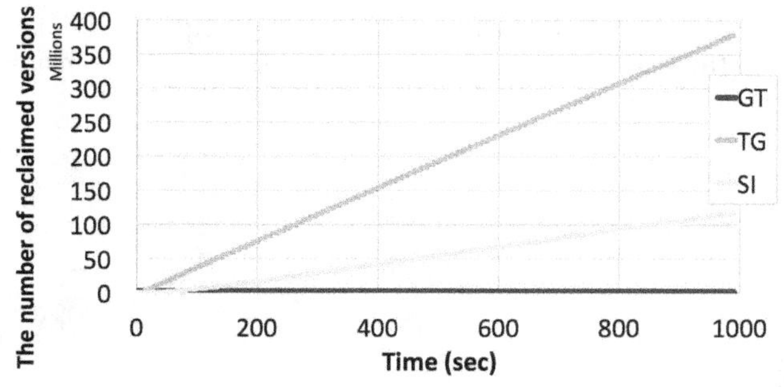

Figure 11: The accumulated number of reclaimed versions per garbage collector under HG.

TPC-C transactions in the same experiment with the one in Section 5.2.

Figure 12 shows the throughput of the TPC-C transactions in terms of the number of executed statements per second. The overall performance using GT alone dropped over time while the long-duration cursor is available for the table STOCK. This is due to the characteristics of the chained hash implementation in SAP HANA row store. As explained in Section 2, if the number of the version chains in the version space increases, the chained hash need to maintain additional hash entries in a separate linked list, which incurs the additional navigation cost to find the corresponding version chain for a given RID.

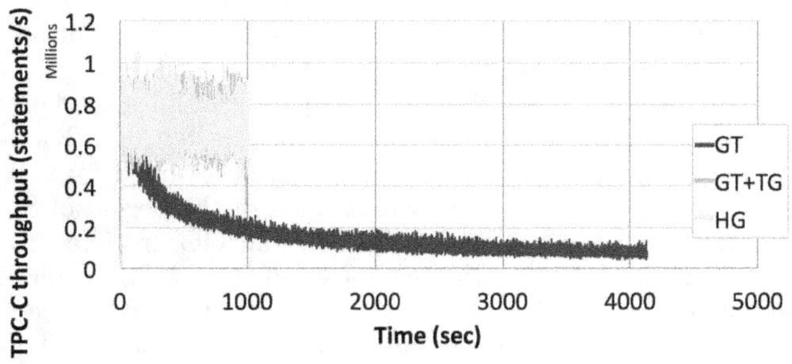

Figure 12: TPC-C throughput with a long-duration cursor.

To confirm the correlation between the TPC-C throughput drop and the hash collision ratio, we additionally measured the hash collision ratio during the same experiment with the one in Figure 13. The hash collision ratio is defined as the number of the version chains assigned to a single hash bucket on average. For example, the hash collision ratio of 10 means that 10 version chains are assigned to a single bucket in the hash table on average. The TPC-C transactions are relatively short, and thus, the increase in the hash collision ratio affected the overall performance significantly. Note that, in GT+TG, the number of the record versions keeps increasing as shown in Figure 10, but it does not lead to the increase of the collision ratio at the version space hash because TPC-C generates only the UPDATE workload to the STOCK table and the UPDATE record version does not create a new version chain.

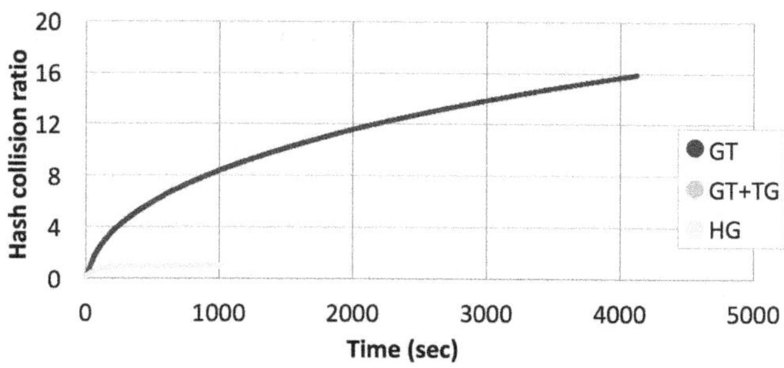

Figure 13: Hash collision ratio in the experiment of Figure 12.

5.4 Impact to Incremental Query Processing Performance

In this section, we check whether the garbage collectors affect the performance of the incremental query processing. In order to emulate incremental query processing, the long-duration cursor incrementally and periodically fetches its query results to the client. While the query is supposed to return 5 million result records in total and eventually, 10 thousands of the result records are returned to the client at a time by the FETCH call of the returned cursor. The next FETCH operation is called after 5 seconds of sleep time, emulating the application-side processing logic for the received chunk of the result records.

Figure 14 shows the latency of the individual FETCH operations of a cursor over time. HG showed almost constant latency even though FETCH operations are repeated within a cursor while the latency increased over time in GT or GT+TG. It is expected that two performance penalties are involved in case of GT and GT+TG: (1) the hash collision in the RID hash table and (2) the cost of traversing the record versions within a single version chain. Unlike OLTP-style workloads which access more recent record versions (the time gap between the snapshot timestamp assignment operation and the version access operation is relatively short), the second cost could become more prominent for long-running, incremental query processing because it should access older record versions as its own snapshot timestamp becomes relatively older.

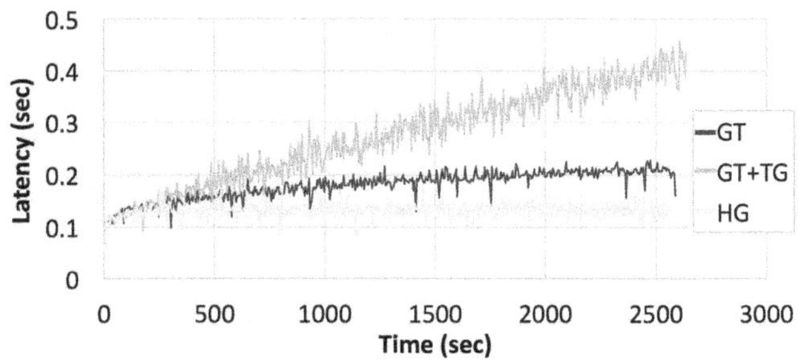

Figure 14: Latency of individual FETCH operations in a cursor.

To verify our analysis, we also measured the number of the record versions traversed by a single FETCH operation. Figure 15 shows as a similar trend as Figure 14. This confirms that the latency of an individual FETCH operation is mostly affected by the number of record versions traversed for the FETCH operation.

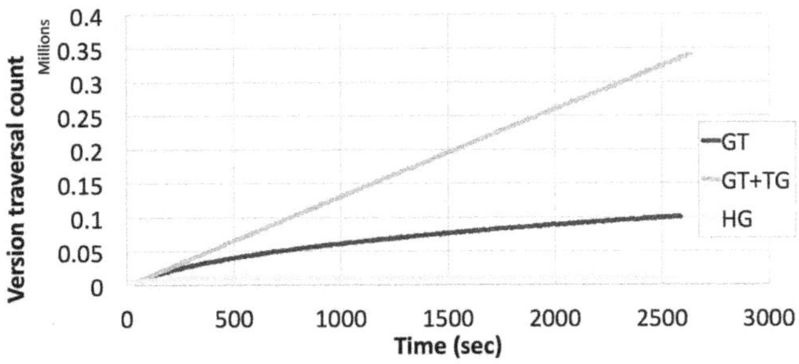

Figure 15: The number of the record versions traversed by individual FETCH operations in a cursor.

By the similar reason, not only for the incremental query processing, we can expect the same performance impact for the queries executed within Trans-SI transactions because the snapshot timestamp is assigned at the time of the transaction start but the queries can be executed later with the assigned snapshot timestamp. This will be further discussed in Section 5.5.

5.5 Impact of Trans-SI Transactions

So far, we have run the experiments only under Stmt-SI. To see the impact of Trans-SI transaction, instead of using the long-duration cursor as in the previous experiments, we ran the following Trans-SI transaction repeatedly: (1) start a Trans-SI transaction, (2) sleep 10 minutes (emulating other query processing or application logic inside the transaction boundary), (3) execute the simple scan-based query for the STOCK table, (4) commit the transaction.

Figure 16 shows the latency of the query executed within the Trans-SI transaction. TG did not show any gain compared with GT since TG was unable to predict the target tables that the Trans-SI transaction would access, as explained in Section 4. On the contrary, SI can effectively collect garbage versions regardless of whether GT is blocked by Stmt-SI cursors or Trans-SI transactions. As a result, HG performs the best, showing the shortest query latency among the three.

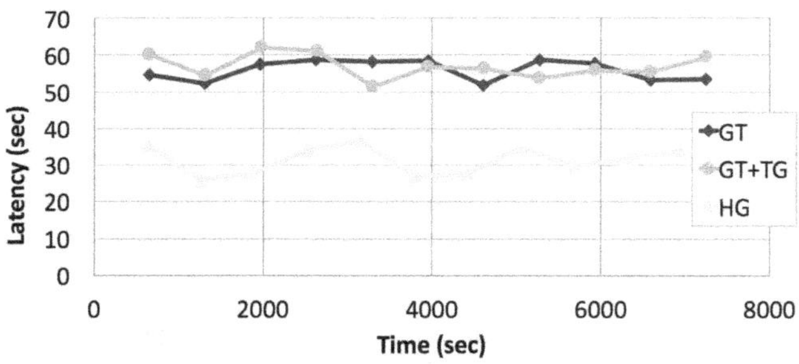

Figure 16: The latency of the queries executed in the Trans-SI transactions.

Figure 17 shows the number of record versions in the version space. There are three saw-like plots in the figure. This experiment confirms that HG maintains the smallest number of record versions in the version space. Note that the number of the record versions drops sharply almost periodically (approximately, every 10 minutes(=every 600 seconds)) since the global snapshot timestamp is reclaimed from the global snapshot timestamp tracker at the transaction end time under Trans-SI.

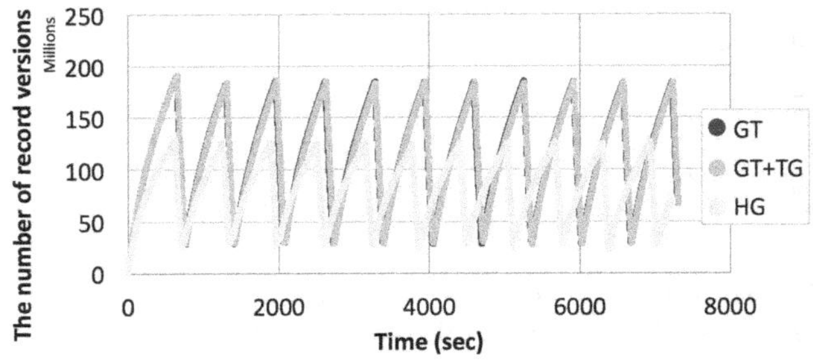

Figure 17: The number of record versions.

5.6 Overhead of Garbage Collection

Finally, to check the amount of overhead incurred by HG, we measure the TPC-C transaction throughput while varying the invocation period of the three different garbage collectors. Figure 18 and Figure 19 show the TPC-C transaction throughput in terms of the executed statements per second with increasing the garbage collectors' invocation period from 1 second, which is the minimum value configurable in SAP HANA. Note that the period of TG was varied by fixing the GT's period as 1 second under the configuration GT+TG, while the period of SI was varied by fixing the GT's period to 1 second and the TG's periods to 3 seconds under the configuration HG. Figure 18 represents experiments without any long-duration snapshot and Figure 19 represents the experiment with the long-duration cursor for the table STOCK.

In Figure 18, when there is no long-duration snapshot, varying the period of SI or TG did not affect the TPC-C throughput because most of versions are reclaimed by GT which is running by 1 second regardless of the period of SI or TG. When the periods of SI, TG, and GG are fixed to 1 second (as shown in the left-most point of each graph), HG showed about 0.8% of performance overhead compared to GT and GG+TG showed about 0.3% of overhead. This is because, compared to GT, SI or TG additionally checks whether there is any long-duration cursor or whether there is any intermediate record versions that can be reclaimed by them. Remark that, as the triggering period of GT increases, the overall performance sharply dropped due to the hash collision issue already discussed in Section 5.3.

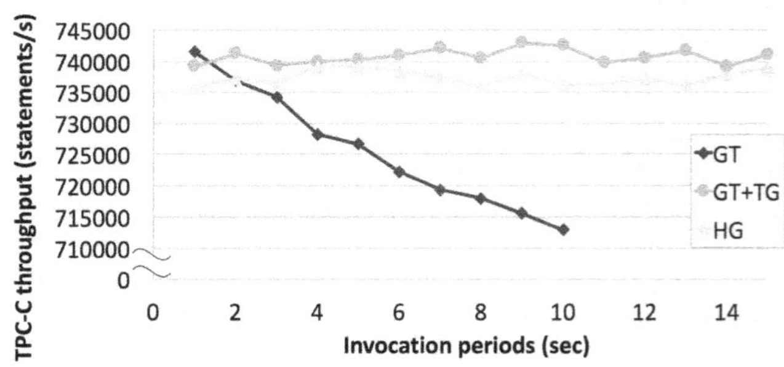

Figure 18: TPC-C throughput with varying the garbage collectors' invocation periods (without any long-duration snapshot).

In Figure 19, when there is a long-duration cursor on the table STOCK, GT almost failed to reclaim. Thus, the throughput under GT remained almost constant regardless of its invocation period. If TG were called less frequently, then the performance under GT+TG would eventually converge to the performance of GT. This is why the throughput under GT+TG slowly decreased over time. Under HG, the TPC-C throughput was almost insensitive to its invocation period.

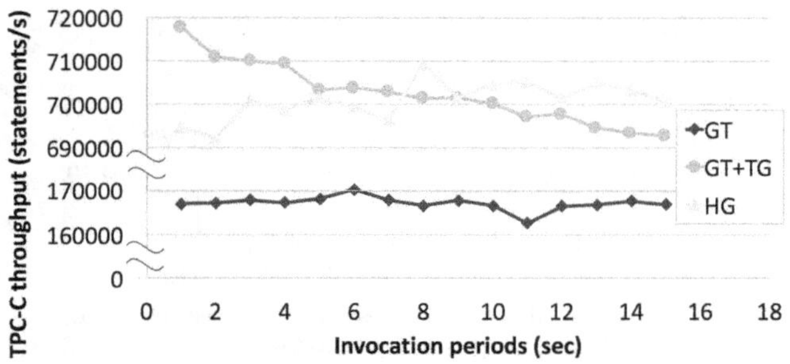

Figure 19: TPC-C throughput with varying the garbage collectors' invocation periods (with a long-duration cursor)

6. RELATED WORK

We first review existing garbage collection schemes in multi-version concurrency control. Then, we explain the fundamental difference between garbage collector for MVCC and those for programming languages. We finally explain the current implementation status and future plan for garbage collection in SAP HANA.

6.1 Garbage Collection in MVCC Database Systems

HyPer [15], one of the most recent in-memory database implementations, updates data in-place, i.e., the latest record image is directly applied into a table space. It also stores versions as before-image deltas in undo buffers which can be used for transaction rollback as well as for reconstructing a needed record version. HyPer also provides for light-weight lock-free garbage collection of versions within a transaction's undo log buffers comparing each transaction's commit timestamp with the oldest transactionID. This, however, is a variant of GT where each group corresponds to only a single transaction.

In Hekaton [6], there is no distinction between the table space and the version space. All the record versions are maintained at a single space. The versions of the same record are linked with each other but in the oldest-first order according to the figure in the paper (differently from HANA row store or Hyper). Regarding garbage collection, the paper describes "any version whose end timestamp is less than the current oldest active transaction in the system is not visible to any transaction and can be safely discarded." This indicates that their garbage collector belongs to ST. In addition to its background garbage collection process, Hekaton uses a cooperative mechanism [6] where the threads running the transaction workload can try to reclaim garbage versions when the thread traverses version chains. Compared to the latest-first version chain maintenance, it seems that this cooperative garbage collection mechanism could make more sense in their oldest-first version chain maintenance scheme because there is a higher probability of encountering garbage versions until the right version entry is found during the query processing.

Silo [20] uses a variant of single-version concurrency control which supports read-only snapshot transactions by additionally maintaining per-epoch snapshot versions. Because versions in a snapshot are claimed only when its epoch precedes the oldest transaction's epoch. This can be regarded as a variant of GT where each group corresponds to a set of transactions within an epoch.

Loesing et al. [12] propose a shared-data architecture in a distributed environment. They also use load-link and store-conditional primitives to implement efficient MVCC. The paper mentions potential growth of garbage records. However, again, [12] also uses the minimum snapshot timestamp. Thus, their garbage scheme also belongs to ST.

To the best of our knowledge, most of well-known DBMSs employing the multi-version concurrency control rely on the global garbage collection. It appears that the need and the concept of SI are already known to some implementors [9,17]. However, the algorithm available in [17] is more expensive than the merge-based SI presented in this paper because [17] requires linear search on the active snapshot timestamps whenever it checks the visibility of a given version. [9] describes the need of SI but we could not find any further information about its implementation.

6.2 Garbage Collection under Programming Language Runtime

In the area of programming language runtime, there have been a number of research studies seeking to achieve lock-free access to shared objects by creating multiple versions of them if the object is being read by one or more threads. The created old versions can be reclaimed only after all the pre-existing readers finish their access to the old versions. That is, in this context, the garbage versions are defined as versions that are not referred to from anywhere or by the term of the "reachability" [6]. For example, in order to identify not-referenced object versions, [1,5,21] maintain *reference counters* to individual versions. [14] proposed the so-called *hazard pointers* to bookkeep the set of active references instead of using the reference counters. [7,13] suggested to decide the reachability to an object version by checking whether all the active threads have reached a *quiescence point* [13] or a sufficient number of *epochs* [7].

Differently from the garbage collection in programming language runtime, the garbage collection under the database multi-version concurrency control relies on the concept of *visibility* rather than *reachability* because it must consider the set of versions which can potentially be accessed by the active statements or transactions in the future, not only the versions currently being accessed. Thus, the detailed mechanism is inherently different.

6.3 SAP HANA In-Memory Row Store

The MVCC implementation of SAP HANA row store was inherited from P*TIME [4,8] since P*TIME is used as one of the key components of SAP HANA. As SAP HANA keeps evolving into a platform to handle both OLTP and OLAP workloads together, its garbage collection scheme has been revisited and optimized as presented in this paper. Among the proposed garbage collection optimizations, GT and TG have already been available in the product versions [11] while SI was only available in a pre-production version at the time of writing this paper. For HANA column store, TG is already incorporated and the other optimizations are also to be applied.

7. CONCLUSION

In this paper, we presented an efficient and effective garbage collector called HYBRIDGC in SAP HANA. We empirically showed that HYBRIDGC effectively reclaimed garbage versions while incurring negligible overhead.

We first proposed the novel notion of interval-based garbage collection by formally modelling the garbage collection problem as the consecutive interval intersection problem. We then proposed an efficient, merge-based solution to this problem. We next proposed the novel notion of group garbage collection, which enables us to efficiently determine a set of record versions as garbage. We also explained how this granular garbage collection can be applied to the timestamp-based garbage collector as well as the interval-based garbage collector. We next proposed the novel notion of table garbage collection, which exploits semantic information such that versions in tables irrelevant to current active snapshots can be reclaimed at any time. We finally proposed HYBRIDGC which combines these three different flavours of garbage collectors.

Through experiments using mixed OLTP and OLAP workloads, we showed that HYBRIDGC effectively and efficiently collected garbage versions. Overall, we believe that our comprehensive study for garbage collection lays a foundation for future research in various MVCC systems.

8. ACKNOWLEDGMENTS

The authors would like to acknowledge Sang Kyun Cha, who lead the development of P*TIME and SAP HANA row store and thus provided the foundation for the research presented in this paper. The authors would like to appreciate Sangyong Hwang, Ki Hong Kim, and Sung Heun Wi who implemented the initial version of MVCC of P*TIME, which became the basis of this research. The authors would like to thank the anonymous reviewers for their valuable comments.

9. REFERENCES

[1] S. Ashwin, P. Roy, S. Seshadri, A. Silberschatz, and S. Sudarshan. Garbage collection in object oriented databases using transactional cyclic reference counting. In *VLDB Conference*, pages 366–375, 1997.

[2] R. Barber, G. M. Lohman, V. Raman, R. Sidle, S. Lightstone, and B. Schiefer. In-memory BLU acceleration in IBM's DB2 and dashDB: Optimized for modern workloads and hardware architectures. In *ICDE Conference*, pages 1246–1252, 2015.

[3] H. Berenson, P. Bernstein, J. Gray, J. Melton, E. O'Neil, and P. O'Neil. A critique of ANSI SQL isolation levels. In *SIGMOD Conference*, pages 1–10, 1995.

[4] S. K. Cha and C. Song. P*TIME: Highly scalable OLTP DBMS for managing update-intensive stream workload. In *VLDB Conference*, pages 1033–1044, 2004.

[5] D. L. Detlefs, P. A. Martin, M. Moir, and G. L. Steele Jr. Lock-free reference counting. *Distributed Computing*, 15(4):255–271, 2002.

[6] C. Diaconu, C. Freedman, E. Ismert, P.-A. Larson, P. Mittal, R. Stonecipher, N. Verma, and M. Zwilling. Hekaton: SQL server's memory-optimized OLTP engine. In *SIGMOD Conference*, pages 1243–1254. ACM, 2013.

[7] K. Fraser. *Practical lock-freedom*. PhD thesis, University of Cambridge, 2004.

[8] S. Y. Hwang, K. H. Kim, S. H. Wi, and S. K. Cha. Dual access to concurrent data in a database management system. US Patent 7930274, issued in 2009.

[9] InnoDB. A feature request to InnoDB. https://bugs.mysql.com/bug.php?id=74919.

[10] P. Larson, S. Blanas, C. Diaconu, C. Freedman, J. M. Patel, and M. Zwilling. High-performance concurrency control mechanisms for main-memory databases. In *VLDB Conference*, pages 298–309, 2011.

[11] J. Lee, C. G. Park, Y. Chuh, J. Noh, and M. Muehle. Version garbage collection using snapshot lists. US Patent 13/750,204, issued in 2015.

[12] S. Loesing, M. Pilman, T. Etter, and D. Kossmann. On the design and scalability of distributed shared-data databases. In *SIGMOD Conference*, pages 663–676, 2015.

[13] P. E. McKenney and J. D. Slingwine. Read-copy update: Using execution history to solve concurrency problems. In *Parallel and Distributed Computing and Systems*, pages 509–518, 1998.

[14] M. M. Michael. Hazard pointers: Safe memory reclamation for lock-free objects. *Parallel and Distributed Systems, IEEE Transactions on*, 15(6):491–504, 2004.

[15] T. Neumann, T. Mühlbauer, and A. Kemper. Fast serializable multi-version concurrency control for main-memory database systems. In *SIGMOD Conference*, pages 677–689, 2015.

[16] H. Plattner. A common database approach for OLTP and OLAP using an in-memory column database. In *SIGMOD Conference*, pages 1–2, 2009.

[17] RocksDB. A code snippet from RocksDB. https://github.com/facebook/rocksdb/blob/master/db/compaction_iterator.cc#L204.

[18] SAP. SAP HANA In-memory Platform. http://go.sap.com/solution/in-memory-platform.html.

[19] V. Sikka, F. Färber, W. Lehner, S. K. Cha, T. Peh, and C. Bornhövd. Efficient transaction processing in SAP HANA database: the end of a column store myth. In *SIGMOD Conference*, pages 731–742, 2012.

[20] S. Tu, W. Zheng, E. Kohler, B. Liskov, and S. Madden. Speedy transactions in multicore in-memory databases. In *ACM Symposium on Operating Systems Principles*, pages 18–32, 2013.

[21] J. D. Valois. Lock-free linked lists using compare-and-swap. In *ACM Symposium on Principles of Distributed Computing*, pages 214–222, 1995.

UpBit: Scalable In-Memory Updatable Bitmap Indexing

Manos Athanassoulis
Harvard University
manos@seas.harvard.edu

Zheng Yan*
University of Maryland
zhengyan@cs.umd.edu

Stratos Idreos
Harvard University
stratos@seas.harvard.edu

ABSTRACT

Bitmap indexes are widely used in both scientific and commercial databases. They bring fast read performance for specific types of queries, such as equality and selective range queries. A major drawback of bitmap indexes, however, is that supporting updates is particularly costly. Bitmap indexes are kept compressed to minimize storage footprint; as a result, updating a bitmap index requires the expensive step of decoding and then encoding a bitvector. Today, more and more applications need support for both reads and writes, blurring the boundaries between analytical processing and transaction processing. This requires new system designs and access methods that support general updates and, at the same time, offer competitive read performance.

In this paper, we propose scalable in-memory **Up**datable **Bit**map indexing (UpBit), which offers efficient updates, without hurting read performance. UpBit relies on two design points. First, in addition to the main bitvector for each domain value, UpBit maintains an update bitvector, to keep track of updated values. Effectively, every update can now be directed to a highly-compressible, easy-to-update bitvector. While update bitvectors double the amount of uncompressed data, they are sparse, and as a result their compressed size is small. Second, we introduce *fence pointers* in all update bitvectors which allow for efficient retrieval of a value at an arbitrary position. Using both synthetic and real-life data, we demonstrate that UpBit significantly outperforms state-of-the-art bitmap indexes for workloads that contain both reads and writes. In particular, compared to update-optimized bitmap index designs UpBit is $15-29\times$ faster in terms of update time and $2.7\times$ faster in terms of read performance. In addition, compared to read-optimized bitmap index designs UpBit achieves efficient and scalable updates ($51-115\times$ lower update latency), while allowing for comparable read performance, having up to 8% overhead.

1. INTRODUCTION

Bitmap indexing is a popular indexing technique for large data sets. It leverages fast bitwise operations [9, 10, 20, 21, 32], and is commonly used for a number of applications ranging from scientific data management [33] to analytics and data warehousing [11, 19, 24, 26, 27, 36]. Bitmap indexes are used by several popular database systems, including open-source systems like PostgreSQL and commercial systems like Oracle [25], SybaseIQ [19, 21], and DB2 [7].

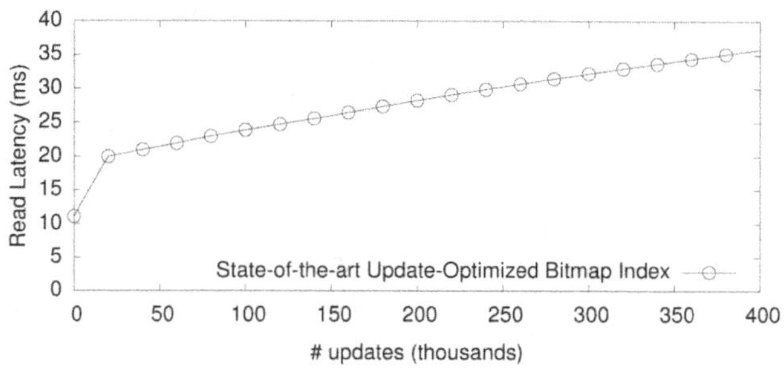

Figure 1: The problem: Read latency of the state-of-the-art update-optimized bitmap index UCB [8] does not scale with # of updates.

Bitmap indexes demonstrate significant benefits especially for equality or low selectivity queries as we can quickly get all qualifying rowIDs. In addition, they efficiently support analytical queries that include logical operations in the `where` clause, as well as ad-hoc queries with multiple selections. Bitmap indexes are also useful for counting values, as well as counting NULLs, something typically not supported by other indexes.

A basic bitmap index consists of multiple bitvectors[1]; one for each distinct value of the domain of the indexed attribute A. The k_{th} position of a bitvector corresponding to value v is set to one if the k_{th} position of the attribute A is equal to v. While without compression the storage requirements for a bitmap index are very high (the space required is proportional to the product of the relation size multiplied by the domain cardinality of the indexed column), several compression techniques have been proposed to greatly reduce bitmap index size [1, 13, 14, 15, 16, 18, 34]. Typically these techniques apply variations of run-length encoding in order to reduce the size down to the same order of magnitude as the indexed column. Hence, every read operation requires a bitvector decode while every update operation requires a decode followed by an encode.

The Problem: Scalability for Updates. The major drawback of bitmaps indexes is offering updates. This is exacerbated by the increasing need of applications to require support for both efficient reads and updates, to deliver both good read performance and data freshness [2, 3, 5, 17, 22, 30].

Read-optimized bitmap index designs are not suitable for updates. The reason is that updating a bitmap index requires a series

*Work done while the author was a year-long intern at Harvard University.

[1]We use the term *bitmap index* for the access method and *bitvector* for its building block throughout this paper.

SIGMOD '16, June 26–July 01, 2016, San Francisco, CA, USA

DOI: http://dx.doi.org/10.1145/2882903.2915964

of decoding and encoding actions on the individual bitvectors that correspond to the old and new values. In order to efficiently support updates, a bitmap index ideally should avoid repetitive decodings and re-encodings.

Update Conscious Bitmaps [8] (UCB) is the state-of-the-art design for update-optimized bitmap indexes. The core idea of UCB design is the auxiliary *existence bitvector*[2] (EB) [21] that stores information about whether specific bits in the actual bitvectors are valid or not. A significant drawback of UCB is that read performance does not scale with updates. Figure 1 shows that the read latency of UCB increases by more than 2× as updates are applied to the bitmap index. In other words, as more updates arrive, read queries become increasingly more expensive (the graph and the experimental setup is further discussed in Section 4).

UpBit: Scalable Updates in Bitmap Indexing. We present UpBit, a scalable in-memory **Up**datable **Bit**map index design. UpBit achieves both (i) efficient reads, similar to read-optimized indexes, and (ii) lower update time than both read-optimized and update-optimized bitmap indexes. UpBit read performance remains stable as more updates, deletes, or inserts are applied.

Similar to read-optimized bitmap indexes, for every value v of the domain of the indexed attribute, UpBit maintains a *value bitvector* (VB). Each value bitvector stores a bit set to one at the positions having value v for the indexed column, and zero otherwise. UpBit introduces two new design elements to achieve efficient updates and to maintain good read performance as updates accumulate.

First, for every value bitvector, UpBit introduces a corresponding *update bitvector* (UB). Every incoming update results in two changes, one in the update bitvector corresponding to the old value, and another in the update bitvector of the new value. The aggregate size of the uncompressed bitvectors for UpBit is twice as much as for a read-optimized bitmap index, however, at any point in time each update bitvector has only a small number of bits set to one. This allows for negligible storage and CPU decoding overhead. In order to maintain high compressibility the update bitvectors are periodically merged with value bitvectors and re-initialized. When queried, UpBit combines – through a bitwise XOR – the value bitvector and the corresponding update bitvector. When updated, UpBit only needs to flip two bits, one in the UB of the new value and on in the UB of the old value.

Second, UpBit introduces *fence pointers* to allow efficient retrieval of arbitrary values. Fence pointers allow direct access to any position of a compressed bitvector. As a result, fence pointers help to avoid unnecessary decodings by allowing a read query to jump directly to the relevant area and decode only a small part of the bitvector that contains the target information. Using fence pointers as pivot elements also enables efficient multi-threaded decoding of a bitvector during querying with minimal synchronization needed during reconstruction.

While the use of multiple update bitvectors seems like more work than updating in-place or simply having a single existence bitvector, it allows UpBit to achieve drastically better read and update performance, following the intuition of the RUM Conjecture [4], because: (i) there is no single bitvector that receives all updates, hence compressibility is higher and updating does not create a single bottleneck on the auxiliary bitvectors; the cost is distributed to multiple update bitvectors, (ii) fence pointers minimize decoding and encoding action when updating and reading from the update bitvectors, and (iii) UpBit maintains a threshold of compressibility after which value bitvectors and update bitvectors are merged, and update bitvectors are reset. When the number of updates stored in an update bitvector exceeds this threshold, UpBit performs the merge operation during the following read query on the corresponding domain value, which involves this particular bitvector. Each read query decodes and on-the-fly merges the corresponding value and update bitvectors, hence, in the merge-back operation the read query initiates a write-back as well. Since UpBit maintains one update bitvector per value of the domain, each pair of VB and UB can be independently merged in a query-driven fashion, without having to alter the structure of the entire bitmap index.

UpBit for Modern Data Stores. A bitmap index can be beneficial for a modern data system, regardless of whether the physical data organization is a single column, or groups of columns. UpBit's design is orthogonal to the underlying data layout, and it benefits the read latency in either case. The benefit of using UpBit is pronounced when data is organized in groups of columns, as using a secondary index avoids reading more data.

Contributions. In summary, we make the following contributions.

- We introduce UpBit, an updatable bitmap index that allows fast updates without sacrificing read performance. UpBit is based on two design points:
  - We introduce *update bitvectors*, a set of additional auxiliary bitvectors (one per value of the domain), that distribute the update burden.
  - We introduce *fence pointers* for compressed bitvectors as a way to avoid decoding entire bitvectors and efficiently access only their relevant parts. Fence pointers also enable efficient multi-threaded bitvector decoding when querying.
- We show that we can achieve scalability in terms of the number of updates by periodically merging the changes to make sure the compressibility of the auxiliary bitvectors is high.
- Through experimentation with synthetic and real data we demonstrate the efficiency of UpBit in a variety of scenarios varying update rate, data size, and cardinality of the indexed column. We show that UpBit offers consistently negligible or small read latency overhead when compared with a read-optimized bitmap index. In addition, when compared with a state-of-the-art update-optimized bitmap index, UpBit achieves significantly lower update cost and much faster reads, scaling with the number of updates.

2. BITMAP INDEXES & UPDATES

In this section, we provide background on bitmap index literature and we motivate our work by showing that existing bitmap indexes are not suitable for workloads with frequent updates.

Bitmap Indexes. Initially designed for static analytic workloads, bitmap indexes have been used in a variety of applications, targeting both equality and range queries. A general binary representation of the content of a column was first introduced using a variable number of bits per value [32], however, typically today bitmap indexes use a single bit per row [20, 21], and one bitvector per value containing ones for rows that are equal to this value and zeros otherwise. An unencoded bitmap index is depicted in Figure 2. The figure shows a column with three different values, and three bitvectors, each containing a bit set to one when the corresponding position is equal to the value each stores.

Keeping Bitvectors Small. Bitvectors contain a lot of redundant data (a bit for every value of the domain for every position of the

[2]Called *existence bitmap* in prior work; here we use *existence bitvector* to maintain consistent terminology throughout the paper.

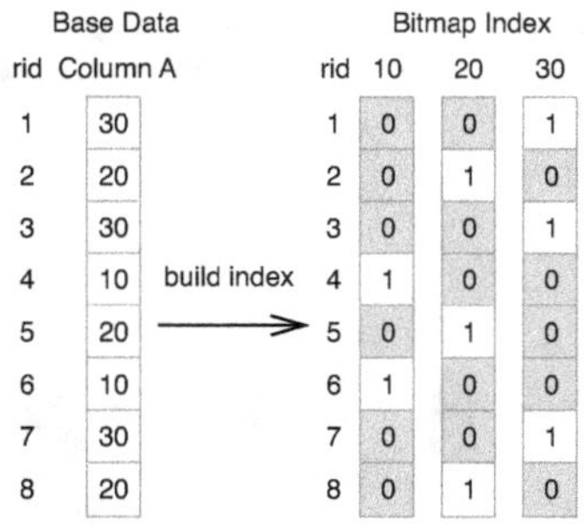

Figure 2: Read-Optimized Bitmap Index.

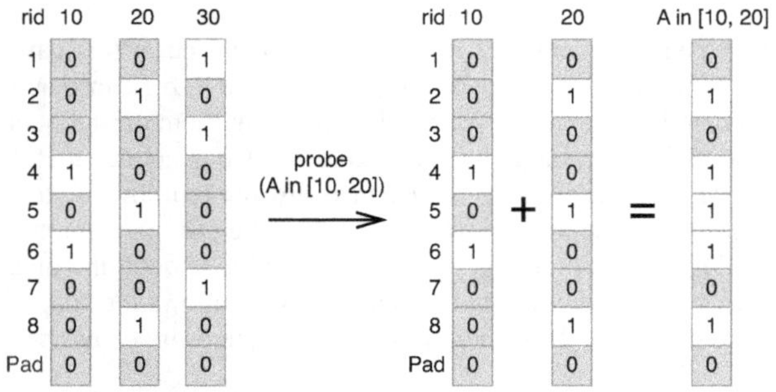

Figure 3: Searching a Bitmap Index for $A \in [10, 20]$.

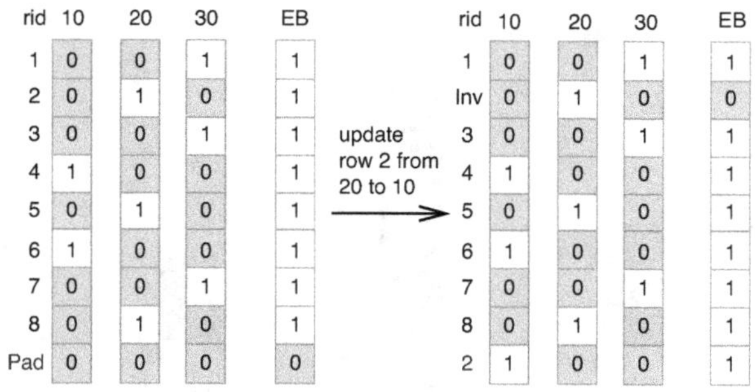

(a) Update value of second row from 20 to 10 using UCB.

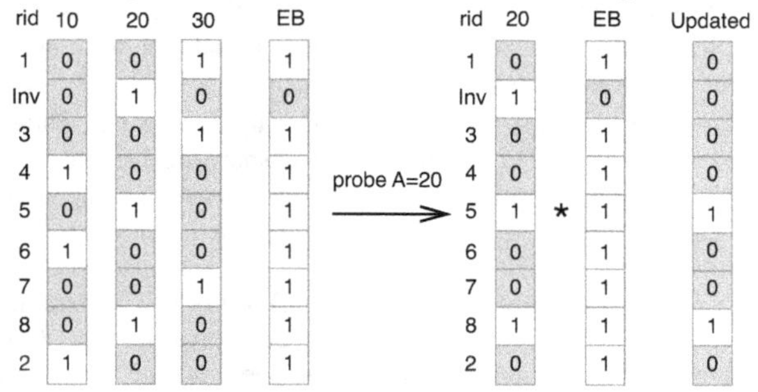

(b) Probe for value B using UCB.

Figure 4: Illustration of Update Conscious Bitmaps [8].

column). This redundancy can be easily reduced by employing appropriate encoding schemes [9, 10]. In the case of range queries, bitmap indexes either perform bitwise OR operations between the corresponding bitvectors, as shown in Figure 3, or employ a different encoding scheme (range encoding), which however, has much greater space requirements [10]. Read performance is further improved by using compression in conjunction with encoding. The first such design was Byte-aligned Bitmap Compression (BBC) [1]. Word-Aligned Hybrid (WAH) [34] encoding applies run-length encoding and has a few follow-up variations. To ensure memory-alignment on modern architectures, WAH splits bits into words (32 bits each), which become the unit of compression. Using this encoding, a maximum run of 2^{32} identical bits can be represented by a single WAH fill word. However, in practice runs with identical bits are shorter and require less bits to be encoded. This was addressed by follow-up proposals which use a few bits per word to signify a long run of identical bits, or a specific pattern interleaved with long runs. CONCISE [13] and Position List Word Aligned Hybrid (PLWAH) [14] improve compression ratio when a single bit or a short pattern interrupts a long run. In this work we use the bitvector implementation of FastBit [33] which relies on WAH compression [34].

Updates. Traditionally, bitmap indexes have been built for read-intensive workloads, and as a result they are not well-suited for updates [9, 32]. This happens because in-place updates cause a costly decoding of the whole bitvector and a re-encoding to store its updated version. For example to update rowID k from value v_1 to value v_2 we would need to go to position k in the value bitvector for value v_1 and set the bit to zero, and then set the k_{th} bit of the value bitvector for v_2 equal to one. Both bitvectors need to be decoded in order to find the bits to be updated. The decoding begins at the very beginning of the bitvector, and after the update the bitvector needs to be encoded as a whole anew. On the contrary, handling new rows is easier as new bitvectors can be appended at the end of the current ones without the costly decode-then-encode cycle.

Update-Conscious Bitmaps. To handle the update problem, a number of approaches have been proposed. The state of the art for update-optimized bitmap index is the Update Conscious Bitmaps (UCB) [8], which supports efficient deletes. Updates are treated as a delete-then-insert using the new delete mechanism, while the new value is appended in the end of the bitvector and a mapping between the invalidated position and the appended value is kept.

Update Conscious Bitmaps use – in addition to a bitvector for each value of the domain – a bitvector to store whether a given row of the indexed column has been updated, called the existence bitvector (EB) [21]. When a position x in EB is 0, the corresponding rows of all value bitvectors are invalidated. When a bit of EB is 1, the bitmap index can be accessed as usual. That way, every delete is performed by setting to 0 the bit of the EB corresponding to the deleted row. In-place updates are transformed to delete-then-append operations (Figure 4a). By avoiding decoding and encoding the value bitvectors at the time of an update, UCB offers faster updates than other approaches, and particularly efficient deletes.

Reading from UCB, however, requires an additional AND operation between the value and the existence bitvector (Figure 4b). When all value bitvector positions are valid, and hence, every bit of the existence bitvector is set to one, this bitwise AND is very efficient. As more updates or deletes are applied, however, the existence bitvector becomes less compressible because it contains more bits that have been set to zero. Figure 1 plots the average read latency of UCB as updates are applied over a relation with 100M values of synthetic data in an in-memory setup (more details about the experimental setup are in Section 4.1). The y-axis plots the read latency as a function of the updates cumulatively applied on UCB, shown on the x-axis. UCB read performance does not scale with the number of updates. The reason is three-fold. First, the scattered updates deteriorate the compressibility of the bitvectors. Second, every update initiates both a decode and re-encode operation. Third, in order to support updates, UCB uses an additional level of indirection maintaining the mapping of rowIDs for which the values stored in the bitvector has been invalidated.

Figure 5 shows the average query latency in the same experiment presented in Figure 1, when compared with a read-optimized bitmap index that supports in-place updates. The black bars corre-

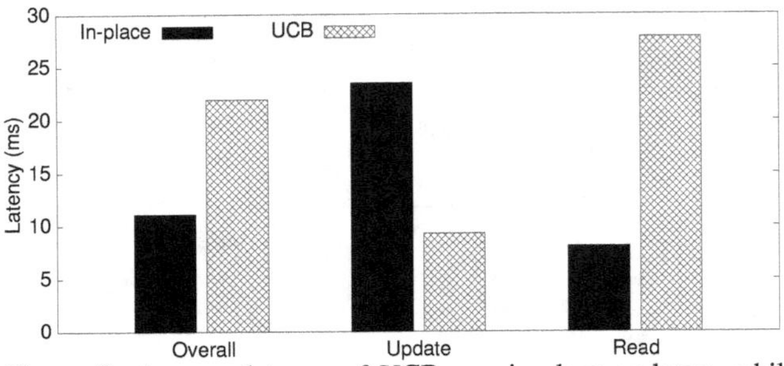

Figure 5: Average latency of UCB vs. in-place updates: while UCB offers 2.88x faster execution for updates, searching with a read-optimized bitmap index that employs in-place updates is 3.57x faster, leading to a 2x overall performance degradation for a mixed workload, with 10% updates.

spond to a bitmap index with naïve in-place updates and the pattern bars correspond to UCB. The first two bars show the average query latency for the full workload (90% read queries and 10% updates). The second pair of bars shows the average *update* latency for the in-place updates and UCB, and the third pair shows the average *read* latency for the two approaches. While UCB offers 2.57× faster update performance when compared to in-place updates, both UCB's read latency (3.45×), and overall average query latency (1.98×) is significantly higher than in-place updates. When answering a read query, UCB needs to perform an additional AND operation with the existence bitvector which, in turn, needs to decode the entire value bitvector. In addition, UCB needs to consult a translation table for every invalidated row, and consequently do another AND operation. The fast update operation – just update a single bit in a highly compressible bitvector to begin with – is not enough to address the slow query time. This behavior is exacerbated as more updates accumulate, as shown in Figure 1.

In order to better understand why UCB degrades as more updates are accumulated, Figure 6 shows the breakdown of the response time of equality queries and updates for UCB. In particular, Figure 6 presents the breakdown of the response time of equality queries and updates when we use the UCB design, (i) after the first update, (ii) after 1K updates, (iii) after 10K updates, (iv) after 200K updates, and, (v) after 1M updates. The cost to update in-place does not depend on the number of past updates, while both costs to update and to read using UCB depends heavily on the past updates. Further, UCB initially minimizes the updating cost because it only changes one bit in a highly compressible bitvector and completely avoids the update cost by updating the existence bit. This approach leads to very fast updates as long as there are only a few bits in the existence bitvector that are set to zero, and as a result, the existence bitvector is highly compressible. As we have more updates, however, the existence bitvector becomes less compressible, hence, updating it becomes more expensive, leading to higher overall update cost. During a read query, UCB always has to pay the price of decoding the bitvector corresponding to the search predicate, as would any design. Decoding the value bitvectors is a fixed cost that is not affected by the number of updates. UCB, however, requires the additional step of the bitwise AND operation between the bitvectors and the EB, creating a cost factor which increases as more updates accumulate (and EB becomes less compressible).

Updating Bitmap Indexes With Low Impact on Read Performance. Figure 6 helps us pinpoint what should be optimized in order to offer efficient updates. The update cost of UCB contains the cost of updating the existence bitvector. While this cost is negligible for up to 10k updates, as more updates are applied it increases exponentially. In addition, the read time due to the bitwise AND between the value and the existence bitvector is the

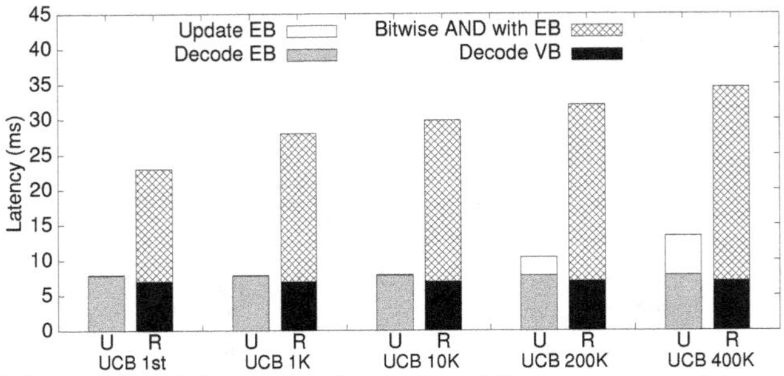

Figure 6: Breakdown of update and read time: as more updates accumulate UCB spends more time in updating the EB when updating and ANDing VB with EB when querying.

most expensive operation. The approach proposed in this paper, UpBit, aims at addressing these two factors. First, by using multiple update bitvectors and periodically merging them during query time with the corresponding value bitvector, we guarantee that the cost to update the auxiliary bitvector is always kept low. Second, by distributing the update overhead to multiple UB (as opposed to one EB) we have higher compressibility and we bound the query cost as well. In addition, having multiple UBs allows the adaptive reconstruction of VB by merging them on a query-driven basis.

3. UpBit: EFFICIENT READS AND WRITES FOR BITMAP INDEXES

In this section, we present UpBit in detail, and describe how it can offer efficient updates without compromising read query performance. UpBit shifts the update burden from a single bitvector (the existence bitvector of UCB) to multiple update bitvectors, and builds an efficient way to search the value of a specific position of an encoded bitvector by introducing fence pointers.

We begin by introducing the notation and the UpBit structure. Then we describe each operation: probing the index, deleting a row, updating a value, inserting new data, and any auxiliary operation needed to support these actions.

3.1 UpBit Data Structure

Notation. UpBit is a bitmap index over an attribute A of a table T. The domain of A has d unique values, hence UpBit contains d value bitvectors $VB = \{V_1, V_2, ..., V_d\}$ and d update bitvectors, $UB = \{U_1, U_2, ..., U_d\}$.

The Internals of UpBit. For every value of the domain of the indexed attribute, UpBit stores a value bitvector showing which rows contain the corresponding value. For example, Figure 7a shows the three bitvectors corresponding to the attribute A values 10, 20, and 30, respectively. Rows 4 and 6 are equal to 10, rows 2, 5 and 8 are equal to 20, and rows 1, 3, and 7 are equal to 30, and as a result, the value bitvectors have the corresponding bits set to one. In addition, UpBit uses one additional bitvector per value, termed the update bitvector (UB). Each update bitvector is initialized with zeros with size equal to the one of the value bitvectors of the index. The update bitvectors are used to mark which bits of the value bitvector are changed. In particular, the current value of a row of the UpBit is given by the XOR between the corresponding position of the value and the update bitvectors. The update bitvectors distribute the burden of each update to multiple bitvectors, keeping the update cost low, and, at the same time, the compressibility of these bitvectors high in order to have minimal impact on read performance.

Value-Bitvector Mapping (VBM). A common operation in any bitmap index is to locate the bitvector, V_i, corresponding to a specific value, v, of the domain. Any query that needs to search the

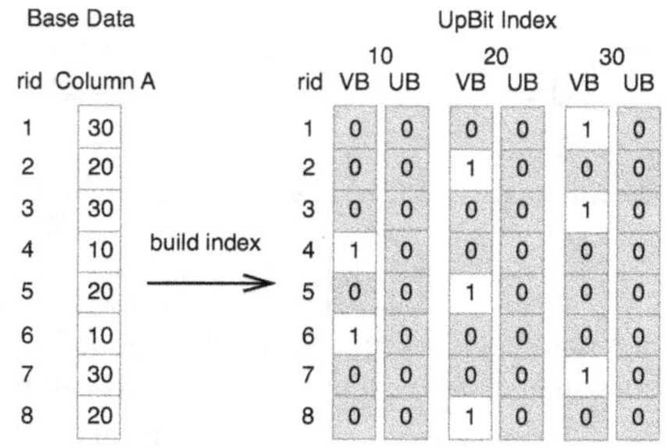

(a) The internals of UpBit.

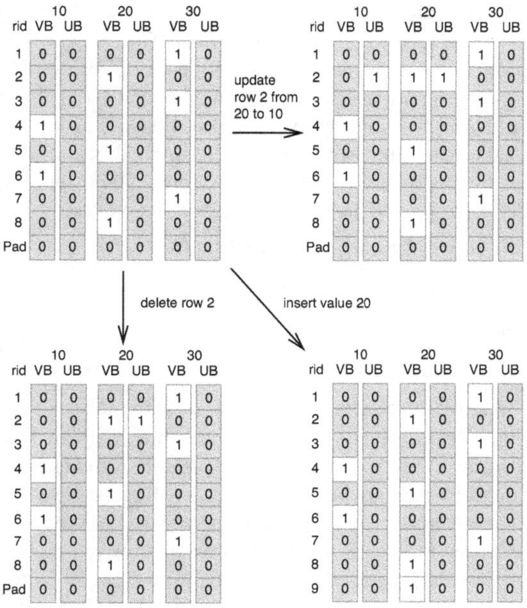

(b) Updating, deleting, and inserting using UpBit.

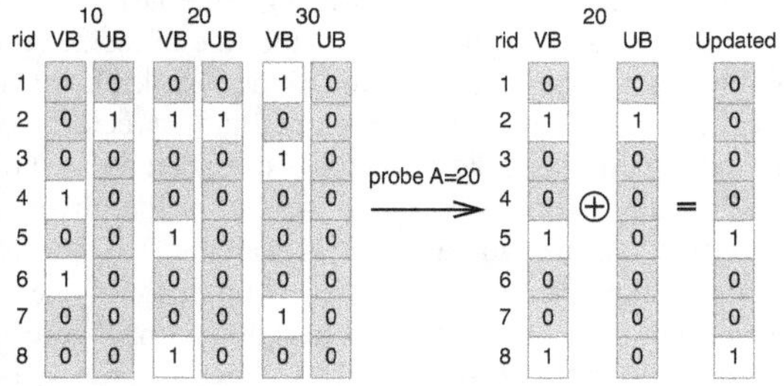

(c) Search for a single value with UpBit.

Figure 7: Illustration of UpBit.

bitmap index performs this action. This is typically implemented using a dictionary which returns the bitvector id i, given v.

No Space Overhead. The update bitvectors are initially empty, thus, they can be very efficiently compressed as 0-Fill words. In the beginning of UpBit's operation, the update bitvectors are practically single words, hence, they have negligible impact on the overall size of the index.

Interpreting Update Bitvectors. In order to return the value of the position of any value bitvector, UpBit performs a bitwise XOR between this value bitvector and the corresponding update bitvector, as shown in Figure 7c. When a column is indexed with UpBit the update bitvectors are initialized to zero (shown in Figure 7a). Effectively, the XOR between the VB and UB at the initial state of the index will always result to the VB itself. As an optimization, we always maintain a counter of the number of bits set to one in each update bitvector and if it is equal to zero, we can avoid performing the XOR altogether.

3.2 UpBit Operations

Let us now consider, in detail, how each of the probe, delete, update, and insert operations are designed using UpBit.

Searching. We first discuss how UpBit is probed for exact match queries; that is, how we find whether a value, *val*, exists in the indexed column, and in which position.

The first step is to find the bitvector i that corresponds to *val*, using the VBM which links values to bitvectors. The next step is to check whether any updates have occurred that are marked on U_i. If all bits in U_i are unset then no updates exist; more specifically, there have been no updates on *val*. Otherwise, if even a single bit is set, then updates on *val* exist and UpBit has to account for them. In order to return the right bitvector UpBit performs a bitwise XOR between V_i and U_i.

search (index: *UpBit*, **value:** *val*)

```
Find the i bitvector that val corresponds to
if U_i contains only zero then
    return V_i
else
    return V_i ⊕ U_i
end if
```

Algorithm 1: Searching UpBit for value *val*.

For example, in Figure 7c we probe for value equal to 20. In this case we first check the update bitvector for value 20 and if not all bits are set to zero, UpBit performs a XOR between U_i and V_i in order to get the positions that contain 20 (Algorithm 1).

Deleting a Row. We continue with how UpBit handles the deletion of a row. In this case we assume that the workload consists of the delete of a specific row, k.

delete_row (index: *UpBit*, **row:** *k*)

```
1: Find the val of row k
2: Find the i bitvector that val corresponds to
3: U_i[k] = ¬U_i[k]
```

Algorithm 2: Deleting row k with UpBit.

In order to make sure that the index will never return row k as an answer to any query, we first need to retrieve the value of this row (line 1 of Algorithm 2), and then find the update bitvector corresponding to this value B_i (line 2 of Algorithm 2). The first operation constitutes one of the main challenges when supporting general updates in bitmap indexes: *retrieve the value of an arbitrary row*. The last step of deleting a row is to negate the contents of the selected update bitvector for row k: $U_i[k] = \neg U_i[k]$. The whole process is shown by Algorithm 2, and is depicted in Figure 7b in the bottom left part. In prior work, deletes are supported through the existence bitvector which invalidates the whole row [8, 21], in order to avoid the costly retrieval of the value of an arbitrary position. Here, we discuss how to efficiently do so.

get_value (index: *UpBit*, **row:** *k*)

```
for each i ∈ {1,2,...,d} do
    temp_bit = V_i.get_bit(k) ⊕ U_i.get_bit(k)
    if temp_bit then
        Return val_i
    end if
end for
```

Algorithm 3: Get value of row k using UpBit.

Retrieving the Value of a Row. Algorithm 3 shows how to retrieve the value of row k. Instead of going to base data which may be on disk, we search all bitvectors. This operation can be aggressively parallelized as it is embarrassingly parallel: each bitvector search can run independently. In fact, for every bitvector we run Algorithm 4 using a small amount of additional metadata to avoid decoding the whole bitvector, effectively reducing the decoding cost.

get_bit (bitvector: *B*, row: *k*)

```
pos = fence_pointer.nearest(k)
while pos < k do
    if isFill(B[pos]) then
        value, length = decode(B[pos])
        if (pos + length) * 31 < k then
            pos+ = length
        else
            Return value
        end if
    else
        if pos * 31 - k < 31 then
            Return B[pos]&(1 << (k%31))
        else
            pos++
        end if
    end if
end while
```

Algorithm 4: Get k_{th} bit of a bitvector using UpBit.

Reducing Decoding Cost. A large fraction of the time to get the value of the k_{th} row goes to decoding the bitvectors before the XOR operation, and reading the k_{th} bit. The reason why this cost is high, is that in order to access the k_{th} bit we need to decode all previous bits; there is no way to decode a subset of the bitvector knowing in which position the decoding starts with the existing encoding schemes. We address this performance limitation by adding *fence pointers* which enable efficient partial decoding close to any arbitrary position[3]. Both encoded and not encoded bitvectors are organized in words. The words of a not encoded bitvector contain its raw bits, while the words of an encoded bitvector may represent multiple unencoded words. The metadata of fence pointers form a small separate index of the encoded bitvector which allows direct access to the encoded words corresponding at known positions of the not encoded bitvector. Fence pointers have a predefined granularity on the not encoded bitvector, g. For a bitvector with n not encoded words, fence pointer i stores the offset of the encoded word that contains the unencoded word $i \cdot g: \ i = 1, 2, ..., \frac{n}{g}$. Every encoded word is aligned to an unencoded word (the reverse is not always true, i.e., a single encoded word encodes multiple unencoded words). As a result the granularity g is only approximate. Figure 8 details such an example. The array on the top contains the unencoded word id (fence) and the offset of the encoded word that starts with the contents of the said word id. An encoded word always starts at the beginning of a not encoded word, which in turn always contains 31 bits. In this example we are looking for the position of bit 62073, this will be in the $62073 \div 31 = 2002$ unencoded word, in position 62073 mod 31 = 11. Using the fence pointer index we find that we need to decode $w97$ to retrieve unencoded word 2002, and then look for the 11th bit. If we were looking for the position of bit 62150 we would probably need to decode more than one word (e.g., continue to word $w98$) depending on the exact distribution of the bits. In general, fence pointers help to avoid both unnecessary CPU processing (decoding) and memory consumption (storing the unnecessary parts of the decoded bitvector). However, if the granularity becomes too fine (g becomes too small) the overhead of maintaining fence pointers increases; we effectively use more space to index the same information. In Sections 4.4 and 4.6 we show what granularity is beneficial through extensive experimentation.

Updating a Row. The most challenging operation is updating the value of a row. We assume that the operation requests to change the

[3]The existence bitvector of UCB can also benefit from fence pointers; UCB needs to checks whether a position is valid.

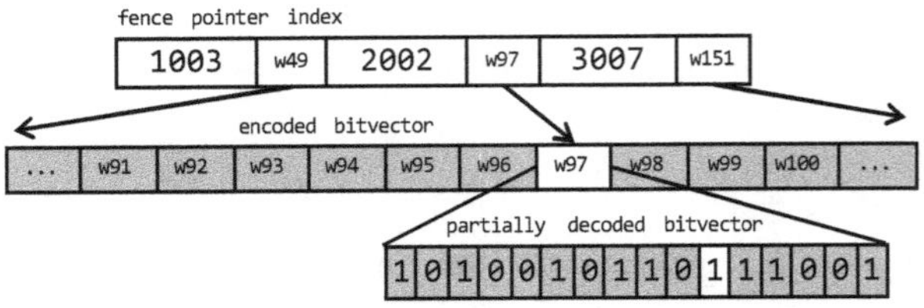

Figure 8: Fence pointers allow efficient partial decoding by storing a mapping between encoded and unencoded words of the bitvector.

value of row k to val. The top part of Figure 7b depicts the update operation of row 2 from 20 to 10.

In order to indicate the new value, UpBit flips the bit of position k of the bitvector corresponding to val (U_i). However, this is not enough, because we need to negate the bit of position k of the bitvector corresponding to the old value as well (U_j). Since we do not necessarily know the old value of position k, we need to retrieve this value similarly to what we described before. The last two steps are the negation of the corresponding bits: $U_i[k] = \neg U_i[k]$, and $U_j[k] = \neg U_j[k]$. Algorithm 5 describes this process.

update_row (index: *UpBit*, row: *k*, value: *val*)

```
Find the i bitvector that val corresponds to
Find the old value old_val of row k
Find the j bitvector that old_val corresponds to
U_i[k] = ¬U_i[k]
U_j[k] = ¬U_j[k]
```

Algorithm 5: Update row k to val with UpBit.

Inserting a Row. The last operation with a bitmap index is inserting a new row. This operation does not require to update existing values, hence, we do not need to decode any bitvectors; we extend the current bitvectors so there is some necessary bookkeeping.

We first need to find the bitvector corresponding to val (U_i). Following Fastbit implementation of WAH, we use active words [34, 35] to append at the end of the bitvectors. The last word stores two variables: the literal value and the number of bits. Hence, we do not need to fully decode the bitvector to get the last word. Typically, the new bit can be appended, and the size of the bitvector is increased without a physical expansion of the encoded bitvector. In rare cases, the last word is not enough and the bitvector needs to be extended. In this case, the bitvector is extended by a word and additional padding space is added in the end of the bitvector for future inserts. Once the padding space is available, we increase the U_i size by one element and we set the new bit equal to one on the B_i bitvector. For example, in the bottom right part of Figure 7b we see how inserting value 20 is handled. The overall process is also described in Algorithm 6.

insert_row (index: *UpBit*, value: *val*)

```
Find the i bitvector that val corresponds
if U_i does not have enough empty padding space then
    Extend U_i padding space
end if
U_i.#elements++
U_i[#elements] = 1
```

Algorithm 6: Insert new value, val.

While the insertion can happen directly at V_i as well, we select to use U_i because it is typically smaller and more compressible, hence every operation is more efficient. In addition, we follow a merging policy between value and update bitvectors during read queries to exploit existing processing as we discuss in Section 3.3. A major difference of our approach when compared against prior work [8] is that because it does not invalidate rows, there is no need for keeping a mapping when the value of a row is updated. However, as updates or deletes accumulate update bitvectors become less compressible and need to be merged back with the main value bitvectors.

3.3 Scaling With the Number of Updates

As UpBit accumulates updates, deletes and inserts, its update bitvectors become unavoidably less compressible, leading to expensive bitwise operations and decodings. We address this problem by merging each update bitvector with the corresponding value bitvector, when their size is larger than a threshold.

The decision whether the two bitvectors are going to be merged is based on the number of accumulated updates. We describe in Section 4.4 how to tune the merging threshold. Once the threshold is determined to T updates, UpBit can start merging the update and the value bitvector as follows: it monitors the number of updates applied to each bitvector independently and when the accumulated updates are more than T, the corresponding update bitvector is marked as "to be merged". In the next search operation involving this bitvector the merging between the value and the update bitvector will happen in order to produce the result expected by the user ($V_i \oplus U_i$). This result will also be saved as the new value bitvector while the update bitvector will be re-initialized. This process is described in Algorithm 7.

merge (index: *UpBit*, bitvector: *i*)

```
V_i = V_i ⊕ U_i
comp_pos = 0
uncomp_pos = 0
last_uncomp_pos = 0
for each i ∈ {1,2,...,length(V_i)} do
    if isFill(V_i[pos]) then
        value,length+ = decode(V_i[pos])
        uncomp_pos+ = length
    else
        uncomp_pos++
    end if
    if uncomp_pos − last_uncomp_pos > THRESHOLD then
        FP.append(comp_pos,uncomp_pos)
        last_uncomp_pos = uncomp_pos
    end if
    comp_pos++
end for
U_i ← 0s
```

Algorithm 7: Merge UB of bitvector *i*.

After the update threshold is met, we perform the merge during a subsequent query evaluation. The reason is that at this point we calculate anyway the result of the XOR between the value and the update bitvector to return it as a result of the read query. Hence, by writing back after a read query we avoid the unnecessary overhead of performing bitwise XOR during updates. When the bitvectors are merged, U_i is reset to zeros, while V_i is updated and its fence pointers are recalculated during encoding. Last but not least, UpBit's multiple update bitvectors allow the merging mechanism to happen in a bitvector-by-bitvector case. On the contrary, prior work UCB uses the existence bitvector, and as a result it needs to perform a merge operation of the existence bitvector with all value bitvectors at once, increasing the merging overhead drastically.

4. EXPERIMENTAL ANALYSIS

In this section we provide a detailed experimental analysis of UpBit against state-of-the-art updatable bitmap indexes and state-of-the-art read-optimized bitmap indexes. We show that UpBit brings drastically faster overall workload execution. When compared to the update-optimized bitmap index UpBit achieves both faster updates and faster reads. On the other hand, when compared to read-optimized bitmap indexes it achieves similar read performance and much faster update performance.

4.1 Experimental Methodology

Infrastructure. Our experimentation platform is a server running Debian "Wheezy" with kernel 3.18.11. The server is equipped with four sockets each with an Intel Xeon CPU E7-4820 v2, running at 2GHz. Each processor has 16MB L3 cache, and supports 8 hardware threads, and 8 hyper-threading threads, for a total of 64 hardware contexts with HT enabled. The main memory is 1TB, corresponding to 256GB per socket, and the storage is based on a RAID-5 configuration of 300GB 15KRPM SAS hard disks.

Implementation. The implementation of UpBit is a standalone implementation in C++. A key component in UpBit is the design of bitvectors. For this, we built on top of the FastBit bitvector [33] which we modified to support update bitvectors, fence pointers, and multi-threading. In order to parallelize the search of different bitvectors we use C++11 threads.

Tested Approaches. We compare UpBit with both state-of-the-art update-aware bitmap indexes and read-optimized indexes. Specifically we compare *UpBit* against (i) read-optimized bitmap indexes supporting *in-place updates*, for which we modify FastBit, and (ii) *UCB*, which we reimplemented using FastBit in order to provide a more efficient implementation and to use the same underlying bitvector logic for a fair comparison.

Select Operator API. We design and we test UpBit as a drop-in replacement for a select operator in a modern system. Its input is a column where we want to perform a selection and its output is a set of qualifying positions in the column. This is equivalent to a standard scan or index scan operator. We also compare against a modern hardware optimized scan (with multi-core, SIMD and tight for-loops) as a sanity check.

Workloads. We experiment with both synthetic and real-life data sets. We generate synthetic integer data varying two key parameters for the performance of a bitmap index: the size of the data set, n, and the cardinality of the domain, d. The distribution of the values follow either the uniform or the zipfian distribution. We further test with the Berkeley earth data [6] and with TPC-H [28].

Performance Metrics. Experiments showing response time always show the average of ten runs with standard deviation below 3% while throughput experiments show real-time behavior using a moving average of a small fraction of the experiment duration. We show both complete workload performance – that is, a mix of reads and writes – and also individual read and write performance.

4.2 Scalable Updates With UpBit

Read Performance. The first experiment demonstrates the scalability of UpBit in terms of the number of updates. The experiment has the same setup as the one shown in Figure 1. The initial dataset consists of $n = 100$M tuples, with domain cardinality $d = 100$. The workload contains equal number of updates and equality queries, both uniformly distributed across the domain (we discuss range queries later on). Figure 9 shows the results for UCB and UpBit. While UCB read latency increases unsustainably, UpBit scales, offering stable latency as more updates are applied.

Impact of Updates. Next, we show that the average read latency of a workload with updates is minimally impacted, and that the update latency is much faster than any previous approach. We show these observations for a variable percentage of updates in the workload.

We experiment with a synthetic data set consisting of $n = 100$M values, taken from a domain with $d = 100$ unique values. We present average read and update time for three different workloads: one that contains 1% updates in the query mix, one that contains 5% of updates, and finally one that contains 10% updates in the query mix of 100k operations.

Figures 10 and 11 show the results. The white bars correspond to a read-optimized bitmap index that employs in-place updates,

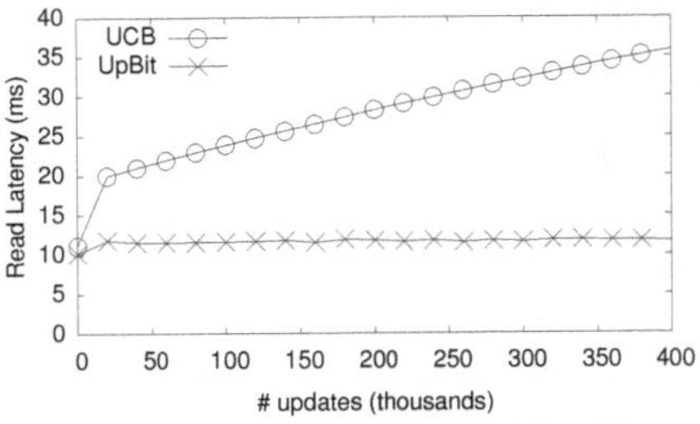

Figure 9: When stressing UpBit with updates, it delivers scalable read performance, addressing the most important limitation observed for UCB.

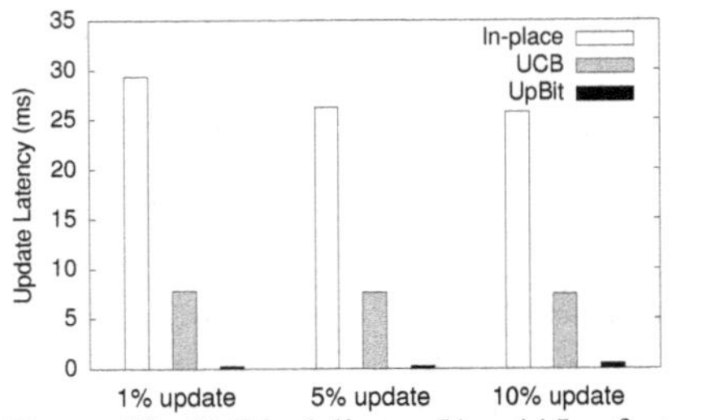

Figure 10: UpBit delivers $51-115\times$ faster updates than in-place updates and $15-29\times$ faster updates than state-of-the-art update-optimized bitmap index UCB.

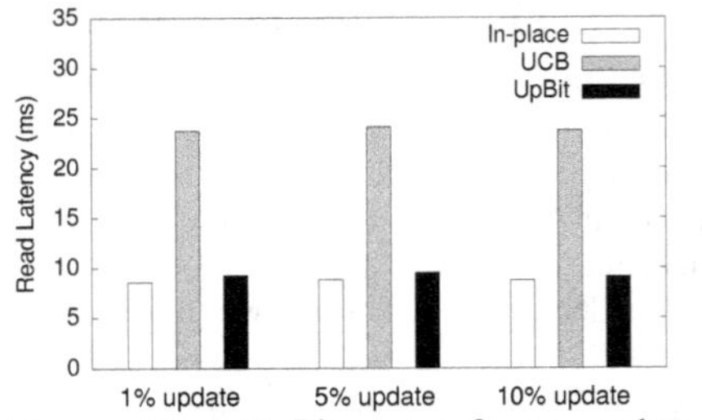

Figure 11: UpBit outperforms update-optimized indexes by nearly $3\times$ in terms of read performance while it loses only 8% compared to read-optimized indexes.

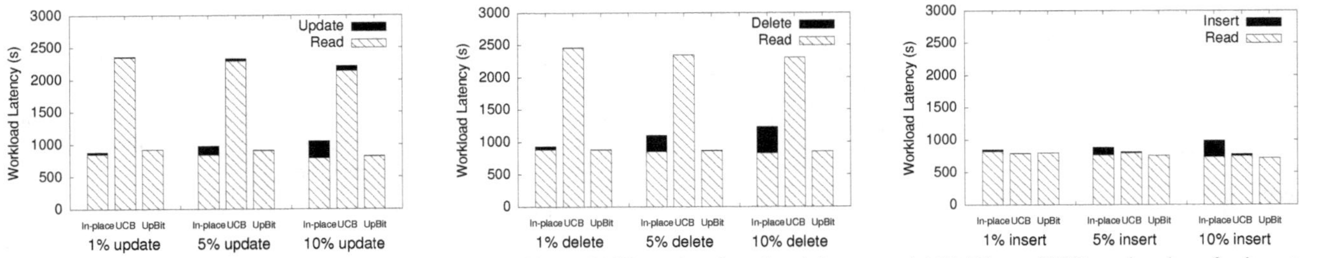

(a) UpBit vs. UCB vs. in-place for updates. (b) UpBit vs. UCB vs. in-place for deletes. (c) UpBit vs. UCB vs. in-place for inserts.

Figure 12: As we vary the percentage of updates, deletes or inserts from 1% to 10%, UpBit has the lowest overall workload latency when compared with any other setup. UpBit achieves similar read performance to a read-optimized bitmap index and drastically better updates (a) and deletes (b) than both read-optimized and update-optimized indexes. When inserting new values (c) all approaches have a similar low overhead on read performance. In-place updates cannot gradually absorb the new values, hence, inserting cost does not scale.

the grey bars to UCB and the black bars to UpBit. UCB delivers $3.43-3.77\times$ faster update latency than in-place updates. Our approach is significantly faster delivering $51-115\times$ faster update time than in-place updates ($15-29\times$ faster than UCB). The biggest factor of in-place updates is to actually decode and then encode the corresponding value bitvectors, while for UCB it is decoding and updating the existence bitvector. On the other hand, UpBit updates two highly compressible update bitvectors leading to much lower update latency. Figure 11 shows the impact in read latency. The read latency of the approach with in-place updates is effectively the ideal read latency of a bitmap index because there is no auxiliary bitvectors or other data to read from. UCB on the other hand merges the existence bitvector with the value bitvector when answering each query leading to a $2.71-2.77\times$ performance degradation in read latency. UpBit, however, delivers read latency with at most 8% overhead which accounts for combining with XOR the relevant parts of the value and the update bitvectors.

Figure 12a shows the overall workload latency of the previous experiment as we vary the percentage of updates in the workload. We see that the update overhead for in-place updates is very low for a very small number of updates while it drastically increases as we have more updates in the workload. On other hand, UCB has small update cost in all cases but the read cost is prohibitively high, leaving UpBit as the approach that combines low update cost scaling with updates and very low read performance overhead, leading to faster workload latency against both in-place updates and UCB.

Impact of Deletes. Next, we repeat the above experiment replacing updates with deletes. Figure 12b shows the overall workload latency of 100k operations where 1%, 5%, or 10% of them are deletes and the rest lookups. Similarly to the previous experiments, in-place updates have a drastically increasing overhead as the percentage of deletes increases and UCB has very high read overhead. On the other hand, UpBit has $1.06-1.44\times$ lower workload latency than in-place deletes by combining low read overhead and very efficient deletes.

Impact of Inserts. Figure 12c compares in-place updates, UCB, and UpBit when only inserting new values, using the same setup as the previous experiments. Since inserts are treated differently than updates and deletes (using the available padded space of the value and the update bitvectors to append new values) we expect different performance as well. Except for in-place updates that suffer as the percentage of inserts increases, UCB and UpBit perform almost the same because appending new values in the bitvectors is treated in a similar way using active words.

Mixed Workload. Figure 13 puts everything together, using a workload that write requests consist equally of Updates, Deletes and Inserts (UDI). We vary the aggregate percentage of UDI operations between 1% and 10% as in our previous experiments. The impact of updates dominates, and UpBit is the approach with the fastest workload latency. As the percentage of UDI increases the performance of in-place degrades, while UCB is slower but maintains stable performance. UpBit outperforms both approaches.

We repeat similar experiments varying a number of parameters, one at a time, to shed light on UpBit's behavior. We vary the cardinality of the indexed column, the data size, and the data distribution. Lastly, we experiment with a real-life data set which typically uses bitmap indexing.

Scaling With Cardinality. Domain cardinality is a critical parameter for bitmap indexes as it defines the number of maintained bitvectors. In this experiment we study the effect of cardinality. Figure 14 shows the overall workload latency of 100K queries over a relation with $n = 100$M values, which has a domain with $d = 1000$ unique values. On average each bitvector has now $10\times$ fewer bits set to one, and as a result, read time is about $10\times$ faster than the corresponding experiment with $d = 100$ (Figure 13). The update cost, however, remains similar to the previous experiment, and the gain when compared with the in-place updates is much bigger.

Scaling With Data Size. The behavior of all three approaches remains the same when we increase data size. Figure 15 shows the same experiment with 10K queries, repeated with $n = 1$B values

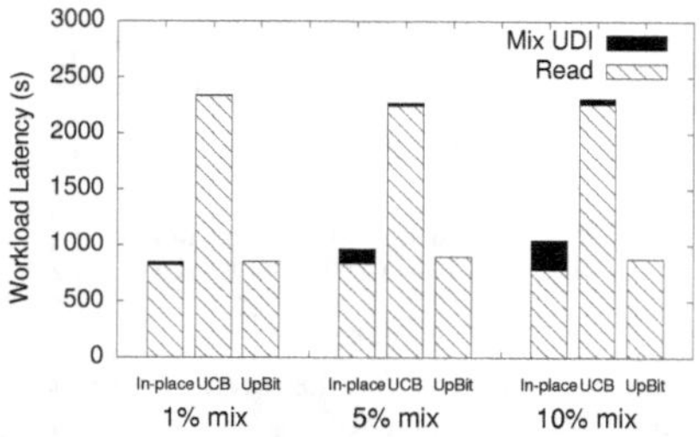

Figure 13: For general UDI workload, the overhead of maintaining a gradually less compressible EB overwhelms UCB, while UpBit offers faster workload execution than both approaches.

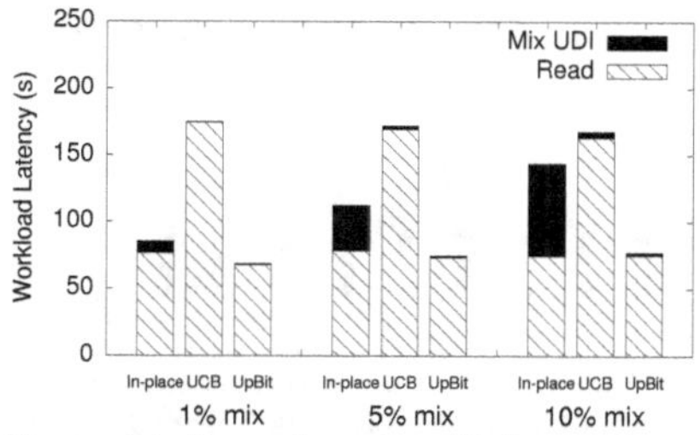

Figure 14: For a data set with larger domain cardinality ($d = 1000$) the update cost is relatively higher, and UpBit has a bigger benefit over in-place updates for the same number of updates.

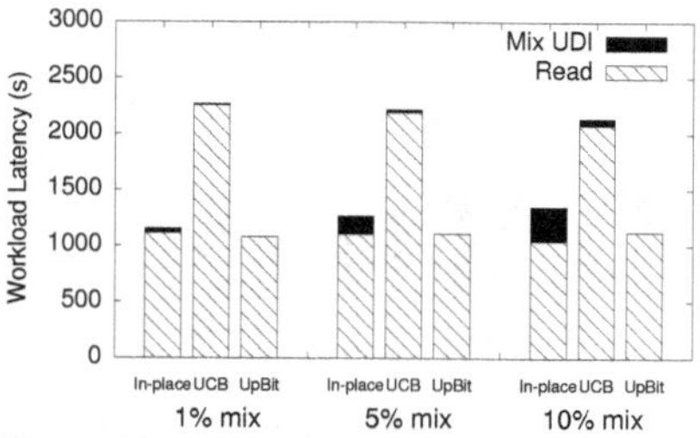

Figure 15: When increasing the data set size ($n = 1B$, $d = 100$), the qualitative behavior of all approaches remain the same. The average latency increases linearly with the data set size.

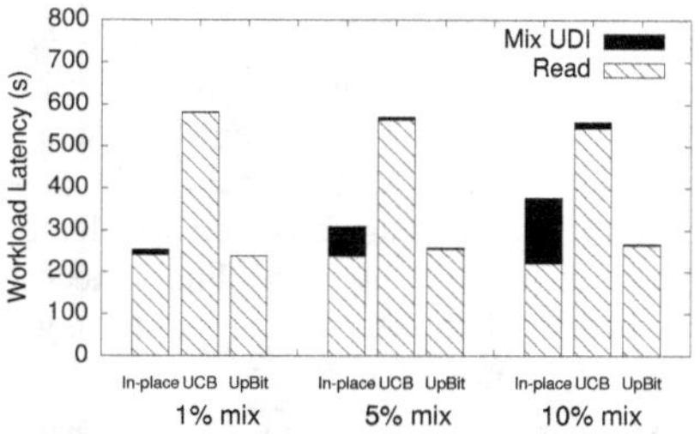

Figure 16: For skewed data (zipfian with $S = 1.5$), the latency decreases as most bitvectors are nearly empty. UpBit faces a small overhead because it has the same distribution of FPs in all VBs.

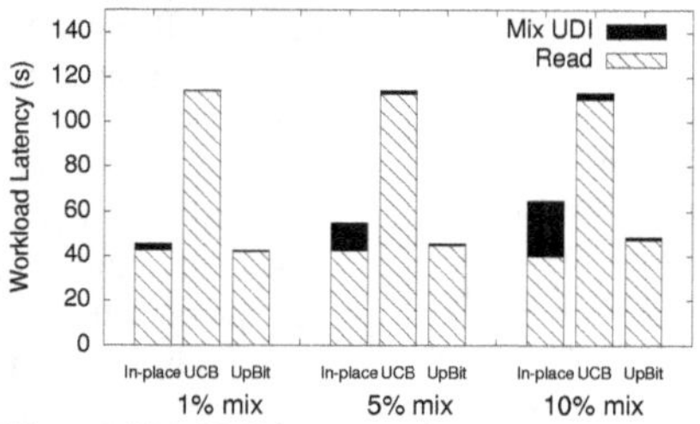

Figure 17: UpBit outperforms all other approaches with real data as well (Berkeley Earth data set with $n = 31$M values, and domain cardinality $d = 114$) for a workload with 1%, 5% or 10% updates.

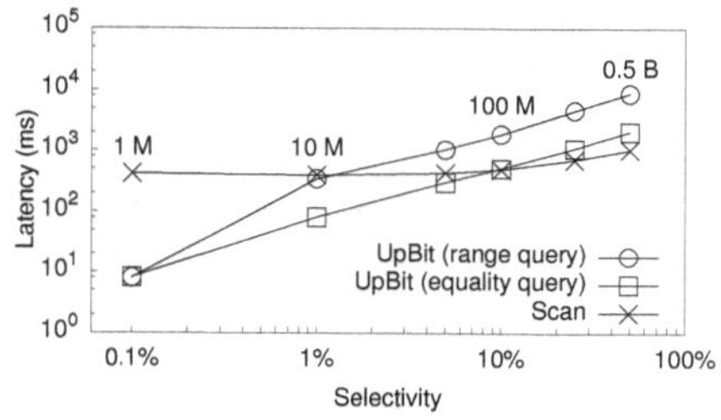

Figure 18: Compared with a fast scan, UpBit is faster for range queries with up to 1% selectivity. Equality queries with similar selectivity are much more efficient because we avoid the bitwise OR between VBs.

and the domain cardinality as in the initial experiment ($d = 100$). Figure 15 looks almost identical to Figure 13. The data size does not affect the performance trends and the relative behavior of different bitmap index designs. As we index more data over the same attribute we have more bits per bitvector, maintaining, however, the same number of value and update bitvectors. As a result, the relative performance of the different approaches is the same, and the absolute performance increases linearly with the data set size.

Zipfian Distribution. The distribution of the data affects the behavior of all approaches in different ways. In a uniform distribution all bitvectors get the same number of bits set to one, and as a result, they have similar compressibility. In distributions with skew, some bitvectors will contain more ones and others will be almost empty, leading to very fast querying. Figure 16 shows the overall workload latency of an experiment with $n = 100$M and $d = 100$, when the data follow the zipfian distribution ($S = 1.5$; about 40% of the items have the two most popular values, and the remaining are uniform in the domain). Read and update requests are uniformly distributed over the domain. We observe that all approaches are faster than the case where the distribution is uniform, because most bitvectors contain very few bits set to one and are highly compressible. The update cost, however, remains approximately the same as in the previous case because we still have to decode and then encode the update values. As a result, the contribution of the update cost is now increasing faster as the number of updates increases. UpBit is slightly slower than the read-optimized bitmap index, because having bitvectors with drastically different number of bits set equal to one would require a different granularity of fence pointers in each value bitvector. This would incur more translation overheads since UpBit would have to keep multiple mappings of fence pointers and positions; one for each value bitvector.

Berkeley Earth Data Set. Finally, we use UpBit to index the Berkeley earth data set showing significant performance benefits over both in-place updates and UCB. The data set contains measurements from 1.6 billion temperature reports, and is used for several climate studies. It contains information about temperature, date of measurement, and location (longitude and latitude). We use binning to query based on rounded temperature. Figure 17 shows that UpBit offers up to 1.34× smaller workload latency than in-place updates and 2.33× than UCB.

4.3 UpBit vs Modern Fast Scans

Here we compare UpBit with an in-house modern fast scan which uses tight for-loops, and exploits the available processing in terms of multi-core and SIMD implementing standard practices from the literature [23, 31, 37, 38]. Figure 18 shows the latency of a select operator over a synthetic data set of $n = 1$B values and $d = 1000$ when executed with UpBit and the modern scan, while varying the selectivity on the x-axis between 0.1% and 50%. We observe that UpBit is 65× faster than the modern scan for selecting 0.1% of the column. Since we are selecting from a column with one billion values, 0.1% values still correspond to 10^6 elements. The speedup drops sharply to 1.09× for selectivity 1%, and the break-even point is at 1.52%. When selecting 5% or more of the data UpBit is anywhere between 2.4× and 8.7× slower than the scan. We observe very similar behavior for different data sizes. Figure 18 also plots a line corresponding to the UpBit when each read query is an equality query. In this case, even though the queries have different selectivity, they all address only one bitvector; for every query the domain cardinality is different. Similar to what we observed before, UpBit is 65× faster than the scan for selectivity 0.1%. UpBit's benefits remains for 1% selectivity (4.6×) and 5% (1.4×), while for 10% selectivity UpBit and the scan have virtually the same performance. For higher selectivity the scan is more efficient: 1.5× for 25% selectivity and 1.99× for 50% selectivity. The difference between a range and an equality query with the same selectivity is the additional cost to perform the bitwise OR between the value bitvectors.

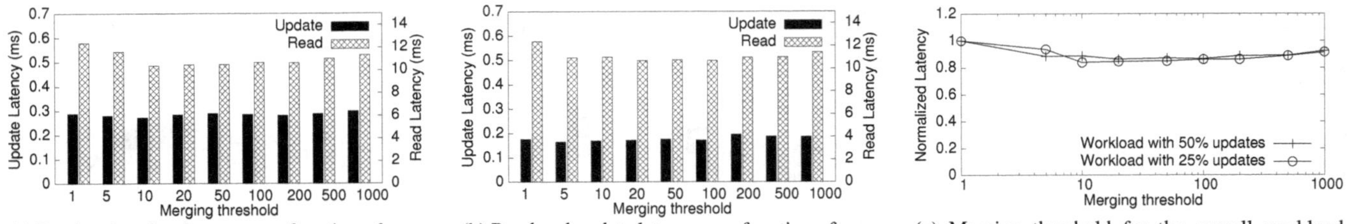

(a) Read and update latency as a function of merging threshold for a workload with 20% updates. (b) Read and update latency as a function of merging threshold for a workload with 50% updates. (c) Merging threshold for the overall workload combining reads and updates.

Figure 19: In workloads that have both read and update queries the optimal threshold of bits set to one before merging is 10. For lower threshold we merge too often and for higher threshold we disturb the compressibility of the update bitvectors.

4.4 Tuning UpBit

Merging UBs to VBs. As updates are being stored in the update bitvector they become less compressible, hurting the overall performance. Hence, UpBit merges value and update bitvectors, as described in Section 3.3. Figures 19a and 19b show the average update and read latency as we vary the merging threshold on the x-axis, for two different workloads; Figure 19a corresponds to a workload with 20% updates and Figure 19b to a workload with 50% updates. Note that the update latency uses the y-axis on the left hand-side and the read latency the y-axis on the right hand-side. For both workloads, we observe a small increase in update time as the merging threshold increases, since the updated bitvectors are becoming less compressible. This trend, however, is almost hidden because the update latency is dominated by the cost to get the old value of the updated row (about 93% of the execution time of an update goes to the *get_value* operation for our experiment with domain cardinality $d = 100$). Using merging threshold equal to one result in the most expensive read latency, since every read has to merge all pending updates (a cost more pronounced in Figure 19b where indeed every read is merging the previous update), but it drops sharply for threshold between 10 and 20. For higher threshold values the read cost gradually increases as we operate on less compressible UBs. In order to make the correct decision about what threshold value we should choose we look at the overall workload latency. Figure 19c shows the workload latency for both experiments, normalized by the slowest setup; which is for threshold equal to one. In this case, the expensive read latency dominates. On the other hand, the normalized workload latency is 15% faster for threshold equal to 10 or 20 for both workloads. For bigger thresholds the overall workload latency gradually increases, and eventually reaches 0.92 for merging every 1000 updates. A merging threshold of 10 updates leads experimentally to the fastest workload execution, hence, it is used in rest of our experimentation.

Fence Pointers. Fence pointers help in reading only the useful part of the bitvectors, however, as their granularity becomes finer they have a substantial space overhead. Here we vary the granularity of the fence pointers and we show the achieved read latency and the corresponding size overhead. Figure 20 shows the overall system performance as we vary the granularity of fence pointers, in particular, the number of bits between two consecutive fence pointers. In this experiment we have 100 million rows with 100 distinct values and we show the average latency sustained, with a workload having 10% updates and 90% read queries. The x-axis shows the granularity of the fence pointers, while the last bar shows the performance of UpBit when no fence pointers are employed. The solid line shows the space overhead as a ratio of the size of the overall bitmap index. On the left hand-side we have a fence pointer after every value effectively paying the price of having the data uncompressed, leading to very expensive reads, however, as we make the fence pointers granularity coarser there is a sweet-spot that has minimum latency and small size overhead. This optimization fits the test data set ($n = 100$M, $d = 100$). For each data set a similar optimization experiment is executed.

Parallel Bitvector Reading. A key operation to support efficient updates on bitmap indexes is to be able to efficiently read an arbitrary value of the column from the bitmap index in order to decide which bitvector will need to be updated. Algorithm 3 can be parallelized in a way that different bitvectors are accessed simultaneously. In addition, with fence pointers we avoid reading unnecessary parts of the bitvectors. Figure 21 shows how getting the value at an arbitrary position scales with number of threads.

UpBit Scaling With Hardware Contexts. In addition to parallel bitvector reading, UpBit employs multi-threaded execution of read queries. All approaches decode bitvectors using multiple threads. Figure 22 shows how the average read and update latency of in-place updates, UCB, and UpBit scales with the number of threads for a workload with $n = 1$B values and domain cardinality $d = 100$. The solid lines show the average update time and the dotted lines show the average read time. Both in-place and UpBit read performance scales for up to 8 threads, at which point, the overhead of on-the-fly merging the value bitvector with the update bitvector for UpBit dominates the read latency, while UCB cannot take advantage of multiple threads. The update latency for in-place updates scales for up to 32 threads (which is the number of physical cores of the machine used). Updates with UpBit scale up to 8 threads. The update bitvectors are sparse and have up to 10 bits set to one at any point of time because of the periodic merge with the value bitvectors. Hence, breaking an update bitvector to more than 8 partitions does not help read performance. On the contrary, it requires more bookkeeping and increased overhead of result distributing and collecting, leading to an overall increase in update latency.

Tuning Summary. UpBit has three major parameters that are exposed for tuning: (i) the UB-VB merging threshold, (ii) the fence pointer granularity, and (iii) the level of parallelism used. Statically defined values deliver robust performance for various workloads. UpBit, however, allows fine tuning of these knobs in the case of a workload that may require different tuning.

4.5 The Impact of UpBit Design Elements

In order to more clearly understand the performance benefit of the two main design elements of UpBit, we evaluate UpBit performance when only fence pointers are enabled (UpBit-FP). We measure the impact of fence pointers with different granularity, when there is only one update bitvector, similar to the existence bitvector employed by UCB. When updating this bitvector, instead of decoding the whole bitvector we can use the fence pointers to decode only the literal word containing the bit we are about to update. That way we avoid the initial unnecessary decoding, but we may still have to decode and then encode until the end of the existence bitvector if the update changes the overall size of the encoding.

Figure 23 shows how UpBit-FP performs in an experiment with

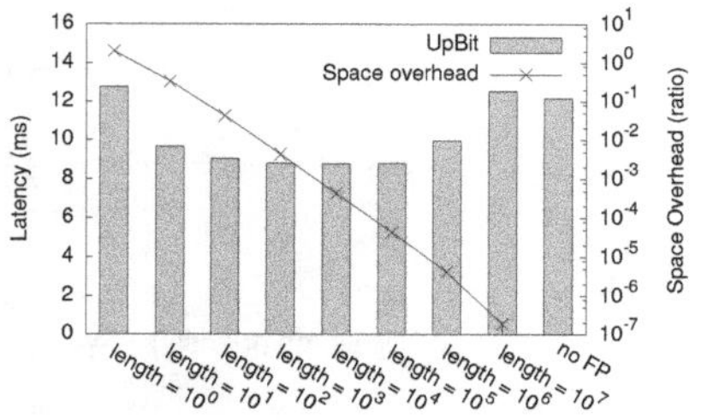

Figure 20: UpBit's optimal behavior needs fence pointers every 10^3-10^5 values having less than 0.5% space overhead.

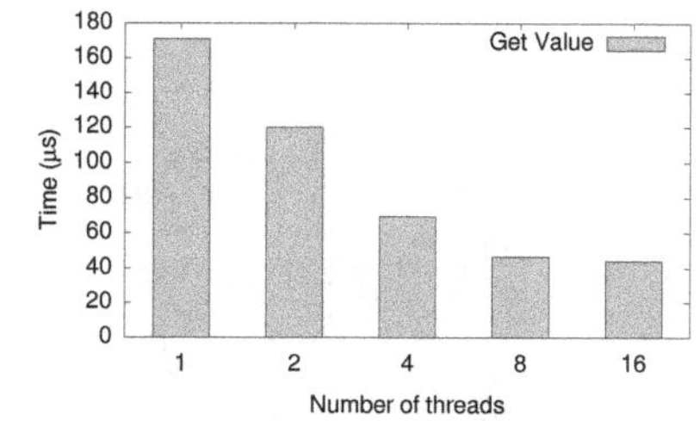

Figure 21: Bitvectors parallel scans scale with number of threads, leading to 3.9× improvement in *get_value*.

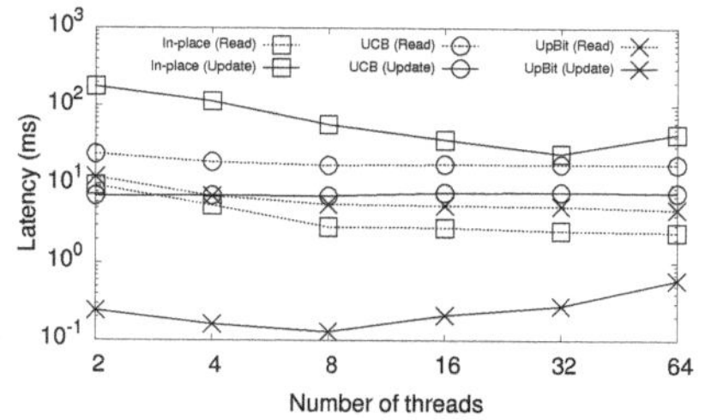

Figure 22: Updates with UpBit are two orders of magnitude faster than other approaches and scale for up to 8 threads.

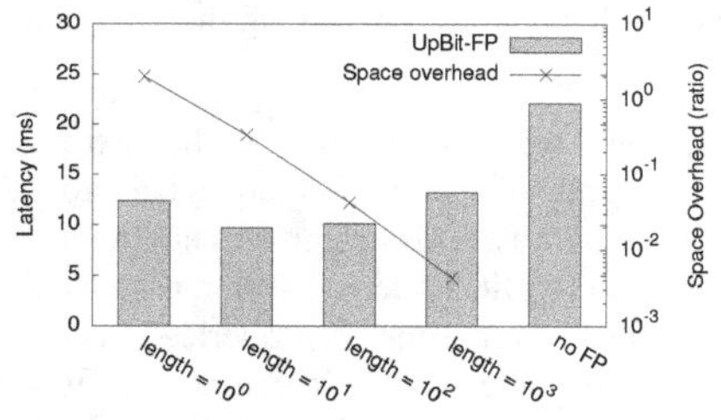

Figure 23: Fence pointers alone offer more than 2× better performance, having less than 10% space overhead.

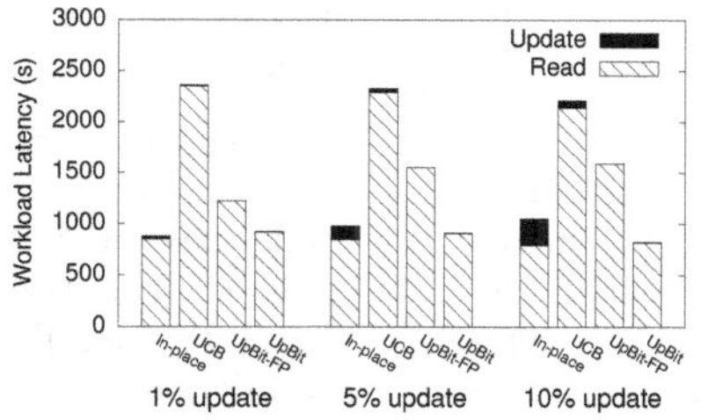

Figure 24: Both fence pointers, and update bitvectors contribute towards the overall performance gains of UpBit.

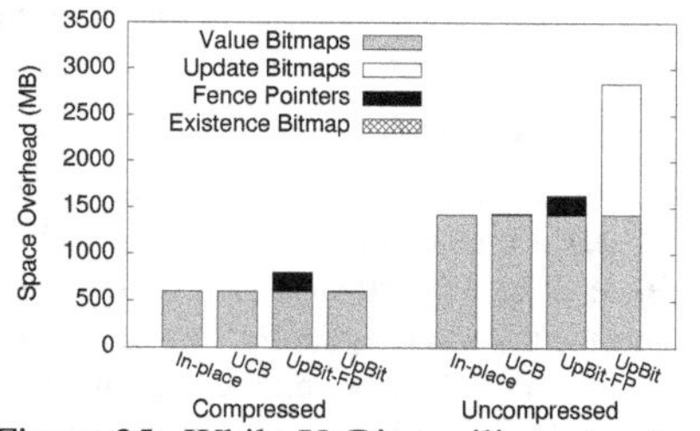

Figure 25: While UpBit auxiliary structures add a lot of raw space, when compressed the space overhead of UpBit is negligible.

data size $n = 100$M rows, cardinality $d = 100$, and a workload with 10% updates and 90% read queries. We observe that fence pointers can indeed help to decrease average latency by 2.29×, requiring, however, significant space overhead of about 15%. Almost the same benefit (2.18×), can be achieved for only 4% space overhead.

Full UpBit Design. We now put the whole design together. We repeat the same experiment as in Figure 12a but now we also include UpBit-FP. Figure 24 shows that the performance gains of UpBit is due to both design decisions of introducing (i) update bitvectors, and (ii) fence pointers. The efficiency of UpBit is the result of the combination of the two design elements. Fence pointers on the existence bitvector alone would be less effective because as we accumulate updates the auxiliary bitvector does not maintain compressibility. On the other hand, a system with update bitvectors like UpBit needs fence pointers to amortize their cost.

4.6 Read-Update-Memory Tradeoff

UpBit is an updatable bitmap index which makes use of additional metadata to support fast updates with low overhead on read queries. Naturally, it is interesting to find out at what cost we achieve this performance tradeoff. Figures 20 and 23 highlight the tradeoff between read performance and memory size. In addition, Figure 25 shows the breakdown of the size of the four update-aware approaches used in our experimentation. Update bitvectors result in doubling the uncompressed size of the bitmap index. However, they can be efficiently compressed because they are sparse. Similarly, the fence pointers add about 0.5% for UpBit, but they result in more space overhead to have the maximum performance gain if they are not used with update bitvectors (UpBit-FP). Finally, the auxiliary bitvector employed in UCB and UpBit-FP approaches has negligible size. UpBit maintains low space overhead by periodically merging update bitvectors with value bitvectors. The high compressibility of the sparse update bitvectors due to efficient encoding, allows for low update and merging overhead.

We further analyze the average latency of UpBit as we vary the granularity of fence pointers separately for read and update queries, for an experiment with $n = 100$M values and domain cardinality $d = 100$. In particular, Figure 26 shows the average read latency, update latency, and memory overhead when we vary the fence pointers granularity between one for every single value, and one every 10^7 values, which is virtually identical with what we observe when we have no fence pointers. Figure 26 shows a triangular tradeoff between read latency, update latency, and memory overhead. For very dense fence pointers both read and update latency are high and, of course, memory overhead is very high, resulting in no benefits. As we make the fence pointers sparser we observe that both read and update latency drop. The minimum read latency is achieved when we store a fence pointer every 10^5 values, and the minimum update latency when we store a fence pointer every 10^3 values. As we further decrease the granularity of fence pointers updates become very expensive as we have to decode larger parts of each bitvector. In summary, we want to minimize all three values: read latency, update latency, and memory overhead. If we have hard requirements (e.g., in read latency or memory size) we will have a specific range of values that we can select. In any case, we can select a "sweet spot" corresponding to the requirements of the application at hand. For example, depending on how many update and read queries comprise the workload, we select the appropriate fence pointer granularity to minimize the overall workload latency.

4.7 UpBit on TPC-H

We now continue to demonstrate that UpBit is effective on full queries with the standard TPC-H benchmark (scale factor 100). We integrate UpBit in an in-house column-store prototype system that supports full select-project-join queries. We experiment using as select operator, either UpBit or an optimized scan. The workload consists of a variation of TPC-H Q6; the selectivity of the `l_quantity` clause is varied from 2% to 100%, and we index on the `l_quantity` column. Q6 has two more select predicates, hence the overall query selectivity is between 0.08% to 3.9%, accordingly (more details about query generation can be found in Appendix B).

Figure 27 shows that UpBit achieves significant benefits compared to the scan-based execution. For query selectivity between 0.08% and 2.4%, (indexed column selectivity 2% – 60%), UpBit is up to 6× faster, while for higher query selectivity (2.4% – 3.9%, indexed column selectivity > 60%), the scan approach is up to 1.4× faster. Using UpBit for full SQL queries on larger data sets results in similar behavior as observed earlier (e.g., Figure 18).

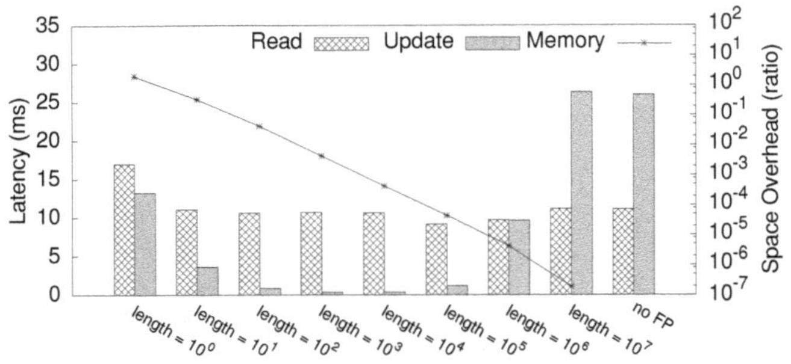

Figure 26: In order to decide fence pointer granularity we analyze the expected workload to get the best combination of performance and memory overhead.

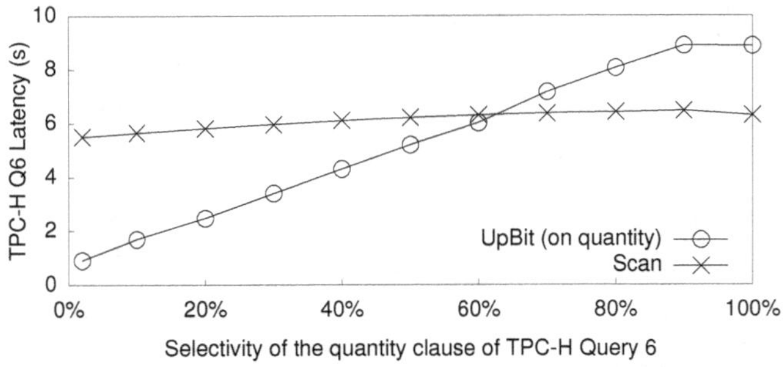

Figure 27: UpBit achieves significant benefits up to 6× compared to the scan-based execution of TPC-H Q6, when varying the selectivity of the `l_quantity` clause.

4.8 Discussion

Designing Bitmap Indexes. The analysis of UpBit leads to three core observations about designing bitmap indexes. First, introducing fence pointers mitigates one of the most important costs of bitmap indexes when updating: decoding and re-encoding bitvectors. In addition, distributing the cost of updating to several highly compressible update bitvectors allows for (i) very efficient updates, (ii) efficient on-the-fly merges during reads, and (iii) query-driven absorption of the updates. Finally, both fence pointers and update bitvectors increase the memory requirement of the index by a small fraction, however, we show that we can keep the memory overhead low and that we can fine-tune it based on the expected workload.

Protecting Updates. While in this paper we focus on serial execution, UpBit is ideally situated to absorb concurrent updates compared to past work. The introduction of one update bitvector per value of the domain means that UpBit can operate in parallel for queries that update or read different values. Locking can happen in a fine grained way at the granularity of each individual value/update bitvector, providing maximum flexibility for concurrency compared to state-of-the-art techniques that essentially have a single point of access for all queries (e.g., either in-place updates or a single existence bitvector).

5. RELATED WORK

Updating Bitmap Indexes. The state of the art in update-friendly bitmap indexes is Update Conscious Bitmaps (UCB) [8]. USB supports updates by using an existence bitvector (EB) [21] which is updated when a row is deleted. Updates in this context are handled by a delete-then-insert operation. In order to efficiently support inserts UCB bitvectors are expanded by a single synthetic 0-fill-pad fill word which can represent very large bitvectors comprised only of zeros. In an event of an insert, or of a delete-then-insert, the new values are stored in the additional words. UCB, however, needs to store the mapping information when physical rows get invalidated. In addition to that, EB becomes less compressible as updates arrive because more bits are set to one, and there are fewer opportunities for space efficient encoding. UCB offers very low update times for a small number of updates, however, both update time and read time increases as updates accumulate.

In this paper we address this limitation by introducing UpBit with two key design elements. First, UpBit employs update bitvectors (one per value of the domain) to distribute the update burden from the single bitvector that UCB employs, the existence bitvector. The difference now is that the auxiliary bitvectors can maintain their compressibility which is the main cost factor when querying using a bitmap index. The way to maintain auxiliary bitvector compressibility is by merging the update bitvectors and the value bitvectors based on a threshold. In particular, when a performance-driven threshold of bits set in an update bitvector is reached, it is marked for merging in the next read query. Then, in the next read query for the given value the update bitvector is merged back to the value bitvector in a query-driven way. This design was not practical with UCB because, contrary to UpBit, a query-driven merge would result into updating all bitvectors for some read queries. Second, UpBit introduces fence pointers in the update bitvectors to allow for efficient reads of arbitrary positions of each bitvector without decoding them entirely. This design reduces unnecessary decodings, and offers both better update time and query time when compared with the state of the art.

HICAMP Bitmap Index. HICAMP bitmap index [29] uses the DAG structure of HICAMP memory prototype [12]. HICAMP (Hierarchical Immutable Content-Addressable Memory Processor) offers architectural support for efficient concurrency safe shared structured data accesses. The HICAMP bitmap index uses HICAMP memory in order to efficiently deduplicate bitvectors. When any part of a bitvector is updated the memory management unit of HICAMP memory delivers efficient deduplication, in order to offer both space and update optimizations. HICAMP bitmap can be updated with $O(log(n))$ cost, and the read cost is $O(m \cdot log(n))$ where m is related to the number of non-zero words of the bitvector.

HICAMP bitmap index, orthogonally to UCB and UpBit, offers efficient concurrency-safe bitmap indexing with aggressive deduplication building directly on top of the HICAMP prototype memory which is not yet available outside hardware simulation. UpBit can take advantage of the deduplication support of HICAMP memory to store for free most of the update bitvectors and potentially absorb more updates before merging update and value bitvectors.

6. CONCLUSIONS

In this paper, we show that state-of-the-art bitmap indexes suffer in terms of update performance, and they do not scale with the number of updates. We introduce UpBit, a new bitmap index which allows for both efficient reads and writes and scales with the number of updates without hurting read performance.

Instead of updating bitvectors directly, when an update query arrives, UpBit buffers the update allowing multiple updates at the same time while supporting fast response times for read queries, having access to the latest updates with negligible overhead. UpBit uses dedicated *update bitvectors* for every value of the domain to buffer inserts, deletes and updates. At the same time it uses *fence pointers* across these bitvectors to allow for fast navigation by minimizing decoding. We demonstrate that UpBit achieves faster workload latency compared with both state-of-the-art read and update-optimized bitmap indexes, combining the best of both worlds.

Acknowledgments. We thank the reviewers and the DASlab group for their valuable feedback. This work is supported by SNSF Grant No. P2ELP2_158936 and by NSF Grant No. IIS-1452595.

7. REFERENCES

[1] G. Antoshenkov. Byte-aligned Bitmap Compression. In *Proceedings of the Conference on Data Compression (DCC)*, pages 476–476, 1995.

[2] M. Athanassoulis, S. Chen, A. Ailamaki, P. B. Gibbons, and R. Stoica. MaSM: Efficient Online Updates in Data Warehouses. In *Proceedings of the ACM SIGMOD International Conference on Management of Data*, pages 865–876, 2011.

[3] M. Athanassoulis, S. Chen, A. Ailamaki, P. B. Gibbons, and R. Stoica. Online Updates on Data Warehouses via Judicious Use of Solid-State Storage. *ACM Transactions on Database Systems (TODS)*, 40(1), 2015.

[4] M. Athanassoulis, M. S. Kester, L. M. Maas, R. Stoica, S. Idreos, A. Ailamaki, and M. Callaghan. Designing Access Methods: The RUM Conjecture. In *Proceedings of the International Conference on Extending Database Technology (EDBT)*, pages 461–466, 2016.

[5] J. Becla and K.-T. Lim. Report from the first workshop on extremely large databases (XLDB 2007). *Data Science Journal*, 7, feb 2008.

[6] Berkeley. Berkeley Earth Data. *http://berkeleyearth.org/data/*.

[7] M. Cain and K. Milligan. IBM DB2 for i indexing methods and strategies. *IBM White Paper*, 2011.

[8] G. Canahuate, M. Gibas, and H. Ferhatosmanoglu. Update Conscious Bitmap Indices. In *Proceedings of the International Conference on Scientific and Statistical Database Management (SSDBM)*, pages 15–25, 2007.

[9] C.-Y. Chan and Y. E. Ioannidis. Bitmap index design and evaluation. *ACM SIGMOD Record*, 27(2):355–366, 1998.

[10] C.-Y. Chan and Y. E. Ioannidis. An efficient bitmap encoding scheme for selection queries. *ACM SIGMOD Record*, 28(2):215–226, 1999.

[11] S. Chaudhuri and U. Dayal. An Overview of Data Warehousing and OLAP Technology. *ACM SIGMOD Record*, 26(1):65–74, 1997.

[12] D. R. Cheriton, A. Firoozshahian, A. Solomatnikov, J. P. Stevenson, and O. Azizi. HICAMP: Architectural Support for Efficient Concurrency-safe Shared Structured Data Access. In *Proceedings of the International Conference on Architectural Support for Programming Languages and Operating Systems (ASPLOS)*, pages 287–300, 2012.

[13] A. Colantonio and R. Di Pietro. Concise: Compressed 'N' Composable Integer Set. *Information Processing Letters*, 110(16):644–650, 2010.

[14] F. Deliège and T. B. Pedersen. Position list word aligned hybrid: optimizing space and performance for compressed bitmaps. In *Proceedings of the International Conference on Extending Database Technology (EDBT)*, pages 228–239, 2010.

[15] F. Fusco, M. Vlachos, X. Dimitropoulos, and L. Deri. Indexing million of packets per second using GPUs. In *Proceedings of the Conference on Internet Measurement Conference (IMC)*, pages 327–332, 2013.

[16] F. Fusco, M. Vlachos, and M. P. Stoecklin. Real-time creation of bitmap indexes on streaming network data. *The VLDB Journal*, 21(3):287–307, 2011.

[17] A. Gupta, F. Yang, J. Govig, A. Kirsch, K. Chan, K. Lai, S. Wu, S. G. Dhoot, A. R. Kumar, A. Agiwal, S. Bhansali, M. Hong, J. Cameron, M. Siddiqi, D. Jones, J. Shute, A. Gubarev, S. Venkataraman, and D. Agrawal. Mesa: Geo-replicated, Near Real-time, Scalable Data Warehousing. *Proc. VLDB Endow.*, 7(12):1259–1270, 2014.

[18] G. Guzun, G. Canahuate, D. Chiu, and J. Sawin. A Tunable Compression Framework for Bitmap Indices. In *Proceedings of the IEEE International Conference on Data Engineering (ICDE)*, pages 484–495, 2014.

[19] R. MacNicol and B. French. Sybase IQ Multiplex - Designed For Analytics. In *Proceedings of the International Conference on Very Large Data Bases (VLDB)*, pages 1227–1230, 2004.

[20] P. E. O'Neil. Model 204 Architecture and Performance. In *Proceedings of the International Workshop on High Performance Transaction Systems (HPTS)*, pages 40–59, 1987.

[21] P. E. O'Neil and D. Quass. Improved query performance with variant indexes. *ACM SIGMOD Record*, 26(2):38–49, 1997.

[22] Oracle. Oracle Database 12c for Data Warehousing and Big Data. *Oracle White Paper*, 2013.

[23] L. Qiao, V. Raman, F. Reiss, P. J. Haas, and G. M. Lohman. Main-memory scan sharing for multi-core CPUs. *Proceedings of the VLDB Endowment*, 1(1):610–621, 2008.

[24] P. Russom. High-Performance Data Warehousing. *TDWI Best Practices Report*, 2012.

[25] V. Sharma. Bitmap Index vs. B-tree Index: Which and When? *Oracle White Paper*, 2005.

[26] K. Stockinger. Bitmap Indices for Speeding Up High-Dimensional Data Analysis. In *Proceedings of the International Conference on Database and Expert Systems Applications (DEXA)*, pages 881–890, 2002.

[27] M. Stonebraker, D. J. Abadi, A. Batkin, X. Chen, M. Cherniack, M. Ferreira, E. Lau, A. Lin, S. R. Madden, E. J. O'Neil, P. E. O'Neil, A. Rasin, N. Tran, and S. Zdonik. C-Store: A Column-oriented DBMS. In *Proceedings of the International Conference on Very Large Data Bases (VLDB)*, pages 553–564, 2005.

[28] TPC. Specification of TPC-H benchmark. *http://www.tpc.org/tpch/*.

[29] B. Wang, H. Litz, and D. R. Cheriton. HICAMP Bitmap: Space-Efficient Updatable Bitmap Index for In-Memory Databases. In *Proceedings of the International Workshop on Data Management on New Hardware (DAMON)*, pages 1–7, 2014.

[30] C. White. Intelligent business strategies: Real-time data warehousing heats up. *DM Review*, 2002.

[31] T. Willhalm, N. Popovici, Y. Boshmaf, H. Plattner, A. Zeier, and J. Schaffner. SIMD-Scan: Ultra Fast in-Memory Table Scan using on-Chip Vector Processing Units. *Proceedings of the VLDB Endowment*, 2(1):385–394, 2009.

[32] H. K. T. Wong, H.-F. Liu, F. Olken, D. Rotem, and L. Wong. Bit Transposed Files. In *Proceedings of the International Conference on Very Large Data Bases (VLDB)*, pages 448–457, 1985.

[33] K. Wu, S. Ahern, E. W. Bethel, J. Chen, H. Childs, E. Cormier-Michel, C. Geddes, J. Gu, H. Hagen, B. Hamann, W. Koegler, J. Lauret, J. Meredith, P. Messmer, E. J. Otoo, V. Perevoztchikov, A. Poskanzer, O. Rübel, A. Shoshani, A. Sim, K. Stockinger, G. Weber, and W.-M. Zhang. FastBit: interactively searching massive data. *Journal of Physics: Conference Series*, 180(1):012053, 2009.

[34] K. Wu, E. J. Otoo, and A. Shoshani. Optimizing Bitmap Indices with Efficient Compression. *ACM Transactions on Database Systems (TODS)*, 31(1):1–38, 2006.

[35] K. Wu, E. J. Otoo, A. Shoshani, and H. Nordberg. Notes on Design and Implementation of Compressed Bit Vectors. Technical report, Lawrence Berkeley National Laboratory, 2001.

[36] M.-C. Wu and A. P. Buchmann. Encoded Bitmap Indexing for Data Warehouses. In *Proceedings of the IEEE International Conference on Data Engineering (ICDE)*, pages 220–230, 1998.

[37] J. Zhou and K. A. Ross. Implementing database operations using SIMD instructions. In *Proceedings of the ACM SIGMOD International Conference on Management of Data*, pages 145–156, 2002.

[38] M. Zukowski, P. A. Boncz, and S. Héman. MonetDB/X100 - A DBMS In The CPU Cache. *IEEE Data Engineering Bulletin*, 28(2):17–22, 2005.

APPENDIX

A. IMPLEMENTATION

UpBit is implemented as a standalone prototype access method in C++. A key component for efficient bitmap indexing is the design of bitvectors. For this, we built on top of the state-of-the-art bitmap representation when it comes to read performance using the bitvectors implementation of FastBit [33]. We have modified FastBit to support existence bitvectors (to implement UCB), update bitvectors, fence pointers, and multi-threading.

A key challenge when implementing UpBit is how to find the old value of a given row (`get_value`) in order to set the corresponding bit in the update bitvector. We parallelize this process using C++11 threads. We take advantage of the available hardware parallelism (number of cores) in order to concurrently search all value bitvectors for the given row. Fence pointers are particularly helpful because we do not need to decode the bitvectors in their entirety.

A.1 Integration

UpBit can be easily integrated to a full database system. UpBit exposes a traditional secondary index interface, allowing for initial build, point query, range query, delete, update, and insert operations. The space management is currently independent from a database system since it is more efficient to store the encoded bitvectors contiguously. In our prototype column-store implementation integrating UpBit has minima overhead, since it can directly use a column as input and can also separately manage the storage used for storing the index durably. Finally, we augment the implementation of UpBit with a method to convert the final bitvector after querying a column using the index to a list of rowIDs.

B. TPC-H QUERY 6

Here we discuss in detail how we generated the TPC-H queries used in the experiment presented in Section 4.7. In this experiment we use a modified TPC-H Query 6, where we vary the selectivity. The SQL code of Q6 is shown in Listing 1. The value of the parameter `DATE` is the first of January of a randomly selected year within $[1993, 1997]$. The dates of the TPCH data span the year 1992 to 1998 for a total of 7 years. The parameter `DISCOUNT` is randomly selected within $[0.02, 0.09]$, where the possible values are distributed in the range $[0, 0.1]$, in increments of 0.01, having, as a result, 11 evenly distributed distinct values. Finally, the value of the parameter `QUANTITY` is either 24 or 25, while all possible values of the domain are the integers in the range $[1, 50]$, distributed uniformly. As a result, an average Query 6 selects the rows corresponding to 1 of the 7 years, 3 of 11 possible values of discount, and 24 or 25 of 50 possible values of quantity, leading to selectivity $\frac{1}{7} \cdot \frac{3}{11} \cdot \frac{24.5}{50} \approx 1.91\%$. In our experimentation (Figure 27) we index the `l_quantity` column and we vary the selectivity of on this column from 2% (`l_quantity < 1`) to 100% (`l_quantity < 50`). As a result, the overall Q6 selectivity varies between $\frac{1}{7} \cdot \frac{3}{11} \cdot \frac{1}{50} \approx 0.08\%$ and $\frac{1}{7} \cdot \frac{3}{11} \cdot \frac{50}{50} \approx 3.9\%$.

Listing 1: TPCH Q6

```
SELECT
    sum(l_extendedprice * l_discount)
        as revenue
FROM
    lineitem
WHERE
    l_shipdate >= date '[DATE]'
    AND l_shipdate <
        date '[DATE]' + interval '1' year
    AND l_discount between
        [DISCOUNT] - 0.01 AND [DISCOUNT] + 0.01
    AND l_quantity < [QUANTITY];
```

FluxQuery: An Execution Framework for Highly Interactive Query Workloads

Roee Ebenstein Niranjan Kamat Arnab Nandi
Computer Science & Engineering
The Ohio State University
{ebenstei,kamatn,arnab}@cse.osu.edu

ABSTRACT

Modern computing devices and user interfaces have necessitated highly interactive querying. Some of these interfaces issue a large number of dynamically changing and continuous queries to the backend. In others, users expect to inspect results *during* the query formulation process, in order to guide or help them towards specifying a full-fledged query. Thus, users end up issuing a fast-changing workload to the underlying database. In such situations, the user's query intent can be thought of as being *in flux*.

In this paper, we show that the traditional query execution engines are not well-suited for this new class of highly interactive workloads. We propose a novel model to interpret the variability of likely queries in a workload. We implemented a cyclic scan-based approach to process queries from such workloads in an efficient and practical manner while reducing the overall system load. We evaluate and compare our methods with traditional systems and demonstrate the scalability of our approach, enabling thousands of queries to run simultaneously within interactive response times given low memory and CPU requirements.

1. INTRODUCTION

Interactive experiences using modern devices such as netbooks, iPads, smart watches, Google Glass, etc. have become increasingly popular. Constructing a query interactively is common whether it be autocompletion [27], instant search for search engines, using gestures on iPads and touch-based devices [26,35], or through image analysis in augmented reality interfaces [43,48]. In such cases, the user's intent (and the final query) is not explicitly clear to the system *during* the construction of the query. The query input terminates when the user finalizes her actions and is happy with the constructed query. Current systems typically do not aid the user during this query construction or specification process; the user does not get result feedback for each exploratory query formulation. This makes it hard for the user to verify the impact of each query clause, or if the constructed query yields the *intended* query results. User studies have found that this type of query construction occurs over query specification sessions that take in the order of tens of seconds [35], and that *interactive*-level latency necessitates response to the user within the sub-second range [8,10,19,31,34,42]. Thus, the interface can provide a preview of the results *while* the query is being formulated, thereby, assisting to formulate the final query. Since the traditional database paradigm is that of "query→result", the concept of interactive-level feedback *during* the construction of a query is challenging. As shown in the following sections, it is difficult to handle these tasks at the application layer, and thus requires rethinking of the underlying database design.

SIGMOD'16, June 26-July 01, 2016, San Francisco, CA, USA

ISBN 978-1-4503-3531-7/16/06...$15.00

DOI: http://dx.doi.org/10.1145/2882903.2882945

1.1 Interactivity & Ambiguous Query Intent

Often, the user is not completely aware of the data, the schema, or the query language. This presents a challenge to the user *during* the process of specifying her *query intent* – the process in which the system finds the user-intended query out of all the possible queries, going through a process which can be simply given as "ambiguous intent → unambiguous query". Once an articulated query exists, the query can be executed – "query→result". While decades of work exist in database systems towards query processing, the challenge of aiding a user to articulate her intent is comparatively novel.

Providing the user with an instantaneous/interactive feedback allows her to understand the result space better, which in turn aids the query specification process. For a complex database, the space of possible queries is large. Executing all these simultaneously, while considering large data size, is often expensive, and thus hinders exploratory querying abilities. Clients have limited resources, therefore a solution is needed at the engine level. As highly interactive workloads become increasingly common, this need intensifies.

1.2 Applications

Consider the case of performing an exploratory equijoin using hand gestures on a visual query interface running on a multitouch touch screen, a well-motivated scenario detailed in [35]. Here, while the system helps the user in specifying a query, it is unclear which tables and columns the user wishes to join until the user approves of the system's recognition. A preview of the query results enables the user to express her intent faster, allowing her to continuously skim resultsets of multiple queries rapidly – a use case which requires queries to continue execution after each preview is stopped being viewed. In addition, once the intended query has been identified, a part of the result is already available for processing, and the rest can be continuously processed. We focus on simple equijoins for the illustrative examples, the system works similarly for other types of joins (including outer joins) – the join criteria is orthogonal to the methods presented here.

Our exploratory join scenario is quite common for the query formulation process – real-world databases sometimes lack the documentation or primary / foreign key relationships explicitly annotated on schema. Let the two tables to be joined be denoted by T_1 and T_2. Thus, the queries at hand are denoted by:

$$\tilde{Q}_{gesture} = T_1 \tilde{\bowtie} T_2 \quad (1)$$

where the conditions on the JOIN are determined by the user. During the gestural query articulation process, as the user drags columns of each of the tables close to each other by using a touch screen, the system is not certain of what the final user query would be, and shows a preview of the results for the most likely intended queries. Assuming the two tables T_1 and T_2 have c_1 and c_2 columns respectively, in the worst case, there can be $c_1 \times c_2$ different joins possible, and hence $\tilde{\bowtie}$ is used to denote that the join is *in "ux*. Although not all join options have high likelihood, in an expansive schema, the number of queries can be big enough to overload current systems. We have experienced that systems become overloaded once the number of queries becomes greater than twice the number of cores. Since touch screens encourage a high level of interactivity, the rate of exploration increases – the user can consider each of the combinations in a rapid and arbitrary manner resulting in a rapid fluctuation of the probabilities of each query to be the user-intended one. Further exacerbating the situation is that tables might be huge, resulting in each join taking a long time to complete. As the user explores through all possible combinations, she settles on one of the JOIN combination as her final intended query.

This example is merely an illustrative example of a highly interactive application, and not the only use case. A similar use case can be found in web exploratory searches [36]. In addition, visual analytics tools, scientific data exploration tools, etc. are moving towards providing highly interactive experiences, which we expect will result in similar workloads.

Furthermore, orthogonal research, such as query expansions [32] and query recommendations [20], requires database engines to respond well to in-flux queries, and assume they do. Both produce in-flux queries, and the engines can use the concepts presented here to decrease the dependence of the techniques on the limitations of the underlying databases.

1.3 Challenges

Interactive querying provides us with numerous challenges. As shown in Tables 4-6 in the evaluation section, current databases are unable to provide interactive response time under heavy workloads.

- **Number of Queries:** The number of possible queries can be large. Even in the case of a single column equijoin between 2 tables T_1 and T_2 having c_1 and c_2 columns respectively, the maximum number of queries equals $c_1 \times c_2$. Processing even a relatively small fraction of these can get unwieldy for large tables. The user expects interactive response times and executing each query as the user transitions between them would overwhelm most existing systems.
- **Query Variability:** The number of different queries produced (or *churn*) in an interactive setting can be large. During the query specification process, the space of possible queries is initially large, and includes all the $c_1 \times c_2$ join options. The user may consider numerous queries before finalizing her intent, decreasing the space to a single query at the end. Thus, the rate of issuing (and canceling) queries poses a serious challenge.
- **Response Time vs. Throughput:** While increasing the throughput of the joins has been researched thoroughly, decreasing the response time has not been studied at the same depth. Current research primarily focuses on decreasing the overall query execution time, at the expense of responsiveness. Interactivity requires a short response time, while throughput is a secondary concern.
- ***Highly* Interactive Querying:** Interactive querying often refers to short response time, in the order of seconds or at the most minutes. Highly Interactive Querying, on the other hand, requires: 1. response time within milliseconds at the most (here, we use $500ms$ as a binary interactivity threshold); 2. responsiveness - the system should provide immediate feedback for each user request; 3. adequate number of results for the user to explore (we use 500 results as the threshold). Current systems are not intended to be used within such constraints, and as shown later often do not respond well.

1.4 Contributions and Outline

We make the following contributions:

- We introduce a novel *query intent* model that allows us to properly represent highly interactive query workloads (Section 2).
- We describe *FluxQuery*, our framework for interactive query execution, based on a novel cyclic join approach (Sections 3- 4).
- We provide algorithms for scheduling and executing highly interactive query workloads (Section 4), including novel join algorithms – the *FluxJoin* and the *Fast FluxJoin*.
- We experimentally demonstrate that unlike traditional databases, our implementation can successfully handle highly interactive query workloads within interactive response times (Section 5).

2. THE QUERY INTENT MODEL

The set of valid queries that can be issued to the database at any given time is considered as the **intent space**. Thus, the **query intent** is defined as the likelihood of each query in that space, represented by a probability distribution function (PDF) over all possible queries in the intent space. The determination of the query PDF is external to our system – we do not control it, but need to satisfy all the query constraints it demands. Without any input, the PDF is uniform – all queries are equally likely. At the end of the query specification, all but one of the queries are ruled out (i.e. probability set to 0) and the probability of the unambiguous intended query is set to 1.0.

During the user's interaction (such as the touch-based dragging gesture), the user starts with a perfectly ambiguous query and each action results in a change in the likelihood of the queries. We can formalize this concept by

$$\tilde{Q} = \{PDF_{t=1..TT}(Q_{1..q(t)}(T_{1..k}))\} \quad (2)$$

where $\tilde{Q}$, the **query intent transition**, is the set of all speculative queries and their probabilities during the lifetime of the specification of the query; $T_{1..k}$ are the tables on which the interactive query acts; and $t = 1..TT$ are the points in time through the query intent transition. The most difficult scenario to handle is if all queries change, e.g. all queries in $t = n$ do not appear in $t = n + 1$, etc. Fluxquery is designed to limit the effect such a churn has on the system. The PDF holds the first order Markovian property, i.e. the PDF at time $t + 1$ depends only on the PDF at time t and the user interaction – the function of change in the query likelihoods is smooth, with the gradient and current state determining the next.

Throughout this paper, we will consider and demonstrate using a simple single-column equijoin to be the running example, since it is the most challenging and critical component of highly interactive querying. However, as we will see the model can be extended to most of the query types.

In Figure 1, we demonstrate the *trembling* effect, similar to the one discussed in [28]. It demonstrates the likelihood of a query to be the intended one over time. Deciding the user-intended query becomes challenging because of the observed fluctuations. The consequences of stopping query execution and restarting it later are severe; therefore, we accommodate execution strategies which helps us in deciding when to start, stop, and re-start queries.

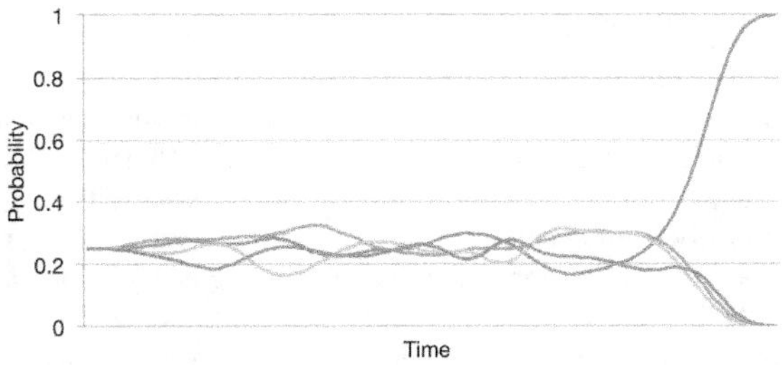

Figure 1: Query intent transition comprising 4 queries, during an interactive query specification task. All possible queries are equally likely at the start of the query specification, and 1 query emerges as the unambiguous query at the end.

2.1 Execution Strategies

Given that the query intent transition represents rapidly changing likelihoods of possible *queries*, the goal of the database is to provide useful results for all user queries during this process, pruning query options that are not probable while executing the rest. Considering the *bursty* and rapid changing of query probabilities, we list two execution strategies for deciding which queries to continuously execute and which to stop.

Full Query List Execution: In cases where all likely queries need to be executed, a tremendous load is put on the database. We consider this as *full execution*, where the database engine has to execute all the queries in the query intent space, i.e., all nonzero probability queries at any given time. We note that this workload refers to the queries we execute, not to the query results. We assume that all query results produced by the join execution while the query is registered are needed. FluxQuery is allowed to remove a query from the query execution list only if it completed its execution – the query list is client-controlled.

Query List Top-k Execution: In applications such as the multi-touch gestural join, due to the *pdf* Markovian property, it is possible to save some computing resources by using the *top-k* strategy. Since only the most probable queries are likely to be previewed to the user, there is lesser value in executing unlikely queries, other than because they might become likely later. Selecting the right *k* is a difficult task – a low *k* value would result in bursts of queries being sent to the engine, while a high value of *k* would behave like the full execution approach and is an interesting topic for future research. In this scenario, FluxQuery is allowed to stop and restart queries based on likelihood. We note that the top-k refers to the k *queries* with the highest likelihood, and not to the top-k results.

3. THE FLUXQUERY FRAMEWORK

3.1 System Architecture

We propose a centralized main-memory execution engine based on the idea of continual *circular clock scans* [4, 5, 12, 52], where concurrent queries register to ongoing scans, much like passengers getting on and off a cyclic elevator. This family of scan strategies allows reduction in latency, and prioritization of buffer page loads, and is ideal for **interactive query execution** based on the workloads presented in Section 2. The most likely subset of queries the user might intend to execute are registered for execution, using the strategies presented in Subsection 2.1, and share scans if possible.

Figure 2 shows the system architecture. A client builds a query and sends it to the server, which executes all queries simultaneously and returns results gradually. Each client has an optional server process within the DB engine, which transfers the client commands to the engine. The server process is optional since if the client process is given access to the internal DBMS API, it becomes unnecessary to hold a dedicated server process (similar to *Shared Servers* [29]).

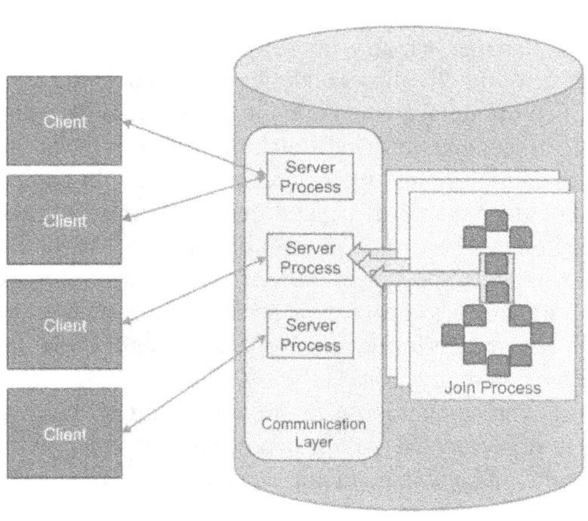

Figure 2: FluxQuery Architecture

A single server process handles requests from multiple clients. Its responsibility is to transfer client commands to the appropriate join process for both query registration and query execution. A significant effect of this design is the ability to issue commands while the client is waiting for results of previously issued queries, resulting in a *many-to-many* relationship between queries and sessions (session is a connection between a client and a database server).

Each join process performs a cyclic join, enabling resource sharing between queries in order to provide the users their results as quickly as possible, minimizing the overall system overhead.

A major design decision was to send the results directly from the join process to the client, instead of through the server process. This architecture nullifies the need for result queues for inner server communication between the server process and the join process, which is done in the *Shared Servers* architecture.

We consider two key query operators in the interactive setting – selection and join. Although our approach is similar to that of Crescando [17] and SharedDB [16], we cover joins in depth and provide techniques to decrease the response time by allowing queries to begin execution sooner.

3.2 System Design

Current commercial and traditional research DBMS systems are based on a threading model that assumes each process requires a latch, a short synchronization mechanism used to protect memory structures, on the data it uses. However, one of the basic concepts introduced in this paper is sharing latches and table scans among different queries. This design limitation leads us to write storage and query execution modules that allows the necessary sharing. While designing the storage structure, we used ideas for table and block design presented in [2, 12].

FluxQuery uses two main engines - Storage Engine (SE), and a Query Execution Engine (QEE), both were written in C++ (~6,000 lines) using pre-optimized libraries, e.g. Boost. The storage engine manages memory and disk space. When creating a new object, the SE assigns storage to the object. Each object is structured from a set of "database blocks" (or "blocks") each of which is a sequential memory structure of a configurable block size. Each object can have a different block size, but all the blocks of a specific object are of the same size. The object size changes dynamically. Each database block contains records of variable sizes depending on the object definition. Blocks can be synchronized with the disk by using a buffer manager, which is not fully implemented in our system. The interface of the SE allows adding rows and deleting rows – the disk and memory management are obfuscated from the user.

The SE implements efficient latching and row locks, assuring that clients can query and modify records safely. In addition, the SE also provides "snapshot" capabilities for queries – allowing implementing multiple transaction visibility options. We used a block structure similar to the one employed by commercial systems in order to confidently compare their performances, and as shown in the evaluation, the performance of our naïve algorithms is similar to that of the commercial ones.

The QEE implementation uses streaming and pipelining. Each operator is implemented within a process that receives a set of streams and emits a single stream. Processes can be pipelined together to form the user's query, e.g., 3 queries that join over two tables using the same join criteria will use the same join process. If for two queries additional subsetting is required using different conditions, an additional subsetting process will be created that will serve both. Architecturally, this scenario sums up to a join process that executes two queries - one resultset is sent to the user, while the other one is sent to an additional server process. The additional subsetting process executes both subsettings, although each is on a different column, and streams resultsets to the clients.

The system is agnostic to the number of incoming streams to each server process - each server process reads from multiple streams. Although we implemented a proof of concept for multi-table joins (join over three or more tables), we have not throughly researched its behavior and performance. We have not implemented a query optimizer. The execution engine accepts an already parsed execution plan for DMLs, data modifications, and queries.

3.3 Preliminaries

Multiple ways exist to share resources such as latches, connections, processes, etc. We favor two techniques – Shared Servers [29] and Shared Scans [16, 17].

As opposed to previous work, we focus on providing initial results within interactive response times. In the Shared Server approach, the CPU is assumed to be the congested resource and, hence, the access to it is controlled by the Shared Server processes by sharing the session among different processes; However, the data is not shared between different queries or sessions. It results in a decreased and controlled load on the system at the expense of increased response time. On the other hand, Shared Scans utilize the same table scan for multiple queries to provide results within a predictable interval. It introduces a significant delay between the query being introduced in the system and starting execution. Both approaches have drawbacks with respect to interactivity since the start of a query is delayed in both approaches.

An important challenge we face is improving interactivity without harming the overall query performance. We propose using shared latches within cyclic scans, with an interactive client-server communication protocol. Although the time a latch is held while a block is joined is linearly dependent on the number of queries, the duration of joining two blocks for one query or thousands of queries was less than $1ms$ in our setting (32KB block size, approximately 256 rows in each block). On the other hand, the time taken to obtain a latch varies from $1ms$ to $200ms$ (averages to $20ms$) – due to contention, the time taken to obtain a latch increases with bigger system loads. Therefore, the main performance bottleneck is block latching, and not the join itself.

Shared latches, although developed for Cyclic Scans, can also be used to reduce the number of latches in a generic DBMS, helping to avoid contention problems while increasing the system stability and performance, issues that are hard to address.

3.4 Cyclic scan

The most commonly used joins are *Nested Loop Join (NL)* and *Hash Join (HJ)*, which we focus on in this paper and base our cyclic scan engines on. Using the cyclic scan approach [6, 16, 17, 21, 29, 52] reduces contentions and improves query response times, and can be easily implemented for join algorithms that scan the relations linearly. These approaches enable creating new join operators that fit the interactive scenarios better than current ones.

In our cyclic approach, a single thread in a cyclic manner continuously scans the *external table* (chosen by an optimizer). For each block of the external table, each block of the internal table is scanned or the relevant hashmap searched. When a query is issued, it does not start execution immediately. Instead, it registers itself in a pending queue of future queries to run. Query modifications such as cancellations and priority changes are performed in a similar fashion – the modification frequency is controlled by the client or the execution strategy used (Section 2). Depending on the granularity of the *safe points* (elaborated in Section 4.4, safe points can be briefly described as the logical points to modify the list of queries the join process operates on), we check if there are any pending queries that can start execution. If such queries exist, we start the execution of the new query from the current scan position, where its execution will also be stopped.

Algorithm 1 Naïve Algorithm

```
1: procedure NAÏVEINTERACTIVEJOIN
2:     while true do
3:         for Each block of external table do
4:             for Each block of internal table do
5:                 for Each external block row do
6:                     for Each internal block row do
7:                         Safe point - modify query execution list
8:                         for Each query in current query set do
9:                             Latch the blocks
10:                            Perform join
```

The naïve algorithm, Algorithm 1, demonstrates the basic ideas of the cyclic join. A discussion regarding the placement of the safe point can be found in Subsection 4.4. An important optimization is obtaining the block latches for every block combination (between Lines 4 and 5), instead of for every row and query combination (Line 9). As noted before, the time taken to get a latch often greater than the time to scan the data, making it more practically efficient to obtain the latches for blocks instead of for rows.

The API (presented in Table 1), which is part of the protocol for our cyclic scan engine, and based on the interactivity requirements shown in Section 2, primarily consists of the following methods: RegisterQuery, ReadResult, ModifyQuery, and StopQuery. The commands RegisterQuery, ModifyQuery, and StopQuery are asynchronous and return control to the client almost immediately.

API	Description
RegisterQuery(q)	Registers the query q in the system for execution using the relevant join process.
ReadResult(q, s)	Reads the next result. If there are no results, the system waits for a result for s seconds.
ModifyQuery(q, m)	Modifies properties of q, such as priority and maximum number of tuples to send. m is a map of properties to modify.
StopQuery(q)	Removes query q from the execution list.

Table 1: FluxQuery API

4. ALGORITHMS

Algorithm	Description
Algorithm 2	Full execution thread for CNL
Algorithm 3	Full execution thread of CHJ
Algorithm 4	FluxJoin main concept
Algorithm 5	Fast FluxJoin main concept
Algorithm 6	Complex communication protocol for query registration for CHJ
Algorithm 7	The safe point of CHJ. Demonstrates the communication protocol

Table 2: Algorithm List

We introduce four different algorithms - *CNL* (Cyclic Nested Loop Join), *CHJ* (Cyclic Hash Join), FJ (FluxJoin), and a variation of it, FFJ (Fast FluxJoin). FJ and FFJ draw from both CNL and CHJ. They have a lower response time compared with CHJ, and a lower total execution time compared with CNL. Both are based on the observation that multiple queries can share the same hashtables/hashmaps built over the internal table, avoiding multiple scans of the internal table data for different queries. Instead of scanning over the internal table blocks to match rows to an external table block, we build a hashtable over the queried columns of the internal block to speed up lookup for matching rows, decreasing response time.

The query lists and the hashmaps are accessed only by the join execution thread. Hence, latches are only needed for data blocks and safe points (Subsection 4.4) on the thread executing the join.

Algorithm 2 Cyclic Nested Loop - Execute

```
procedure EXECUTE JOIN
    start:
    ▷ Waits for a new query to register from parallel threads
    PendingQueriesSemaphore.Wait()
    while true do
        for Each external table block exb do
            for Each internal table block inb do
                ▷ This is a safe point for modifying objects
                CNLSafePoint()
                ▷ Execution of Nested Loop:
                LatchAsReader(exb);
                LatchAsReader(inb);
                for Each row er in exb do
                    for Each row ir in inb do
                        for Each query q in Queries do
                            if q.Join(er, ir) then
                                emit q.JoinResults to client
                                q.TotalResults += 1
                ReleaseLatch(inb);
                ReleaseLatch(exb);
```

In Algorithm 2, we show the CNL algorithm execution process. The algorithm demonstrates that in the absence of queries, the execution thread sleeps, while during query execution, the basic NL algorithm is executed for each query. The fact that each query begins and ends execution at the correct location is guaranteed by the safe point (Subsection 4.4).

In Algorithm 3, we show the execution thread for CHJ. In CHJ, the internal table blocks are not accessed directly as in CNL – the rows are accessed through the hashmaps. Thus, it does not iterate over the internal table. The hashmaps needed are assured to be available due to the safe point – the hashmaps are built within the safe point since multiple queries might use the same hashmaps (see later discussion).

Algorithm 3 Cyclic Hash Join - Execute

```
procedure EXECUTE JOIN
    start:
    ▷ Waits for a new query to register from parallel threads
    PendingQueriesSemaphore.Wait()
    while true do
        for Each external table block exb do
            ▷ This is a safe point for modifying objects
            CHJSafePoint()
            ▷ Execution of Hash Join:
            LatchAsReader(exb);
            for Each row er in exb do
                for Each query q in Queries do
                    map = CurrentHashMaps.get(q.HashmapCol)
                    if q.Join(er, map) then
                        emit q.JoinResults to client
                        q.TotalResults += q.JoinResults.size
            ReleaseLatch(exb);
```

4.1 FJ - The FluxJoin

FluxJoin is designed to be used in a cyclic fashion. FJ is based on the observation that the Nested Loop Join is extremely responsive, but slow, while the Hash Join is fast, but slower to respond. Furthermore, data blocks are independent of each other but are ordered for the purpose of a table scan. We developed a combination of the two algorithms, Nested Loop Join and Hash Join, that allows the usage of hashmaps for accelerating the Nested Loop Join – FJ. This was done by changing the granularity of the hashmap from being on the full table to being on a block.

We reuse the block-hashmaps only for each external-internal block combination, and do not cache them in order to limit the memory dependency. Therefore, it is able to handle the cases where CHJ cannot fit all the hashmaps in memory. We have not considered using multiple blocks for building the block hashmaps – an optimization option that might be beneficial. Determining the optimal number of blocks for such a scenario can be done using a variety of methods such as auto-tuning [25] or workload profiling, and is ideal future work.

In FJ, as seen in Algorithm 4, we execute a modified CNL, in which in the innermost iteration, we do not iterate over each row within the block. Instead, we build hashmaps on the current inner block for each column that is queried, and search it using the external block rows. We reuse the same hashmaps for all the queries on the same column, as done in CHJ. Maps are held only for the duration of the internal iteration.

Figure 3 illustrates the steps taken by FJ. We assume that 3 queries are running and join using 2 columns of the inner table. While the cyclic scan is executing (Step 1), we build a set of hashmaps on all the queried columns for the current internal table block (Step 2). After the hashmaps are built, all the queries are executed (Step 3). Next, the blocks are switched and the process repeats (Step 4).

For q queries that use c distinct columns, if the outer relation has o blocks with m rows each and the inner relation has i blocks with n rows each, the complexity for CNL would be $O(o \times m \times i \times n \times q)$, while for FJ the complexity would be $O(o \times i \times (n \times c + m \times q))$. Thus, we can see that in the case where numerous queries use the same columns, the performance gain of FJ is greater than that of

Algorithm 4 The FluxJoin

```
procedure EXECUTEFJ
    start:
    ▷ Waits for a new query to register from parallel threads
    PendingQueriesSemaphore.Wait()
    while true do
        for Each block of external table eb do
            for Each block of internal table ib do
                ▷ This is a safe point for modifying objects
                CNLSafePoint()
                ▷ Execution of FluxJoin:
                LatchAsReader(exb);
                LatchAsReader(inb);
                maps = BuildMapsForBlock(ib, Queries)
                for Each row in eb do
                    for Each query in Queries do
                        Join row with column map
                        Emit Results
                ReleaseLatch(inb);
                ReleaseLatch(exb);
                Free(maps)
```

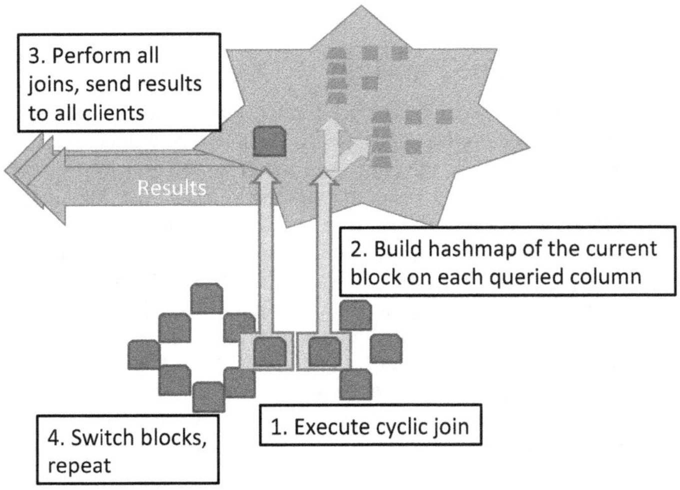

Figure 3: FluxJoin Walkthrough

CNL. In the worst case where $c = q$, FJ's performance is similar to that of CNL because m and n are small and limited.

In contrast with Hash Join and Nested Loop Join, assuming the number of rows in each block of both the tables are similar (most databases use the same block size for all tables), it is not important if the internal table, the one on which we build the hashmaps, is the smaller table or the bigger table. In both cases, the complexity and response time are not affected.

FJ consumes a constant and low amount of memory compared with Hash Join. The size of all hashmaps for a data block cannot be greater than the size of nine data blocks and would rarely exceed the size of two data blocks. Each distinct value that appears in a data block will occupy its size in the hashmap, and in addition the hashmap holds a set of pointers to the data within the data block. Assuming that in the worst case there are no repetitions of any values, the values would require at most the size of one data block. Each value will also have a pointer. Supposing each value is at least one byte and a pointer is at most eight bytes, the hashmap size will not exceed the size of nine data blocks. This worst case analysis is extreme, since most values held are bigger than a byte. Further, due to repeating values in databases, the size of the FJ hashmaps would often be equal to the size of one to two data blocks.

FJ's memory overhead is negligible and fits well within the different levels of system caches. The performance of FJ is similar to that of CNL when a single query is executed, yet, when multiple joins execute using the same column, the performance improvement is linear with regards to the number of executing queries thanks to hashmap sharing. FJ cannot perform as well as HJ due to repeated creation of hashmaps for the inner table blocks. However, our experiments show that when thousands of joins are executed over the same set of columns, FJ's performance is closer to that of HJ than to that of NL because of the hashmaps reuse. Considering that FJ emits results nearly as fast as NL, it is ideal for interactivity.

4.2 FFJ - The Fast FluxJoin

FJ does not reuse hashmaps across different external blocks, and thus can be optimized further. In FFJ we assume all hashmaps can fit in memory, and build full hashmaps for each queried column while FJ executes and emits results – preserving its CNL-like low response time for initial results and achieving CHJ-like low total execution time. After the full hashmap is built on each column, which happens at the second external table block after adding a query, the join process can use it instead of scanning the internal table. This limits the number of internal table scans to the number of columns, in the worst case.

Algorithm 5 The Fast FluxJoin

```
procedure EXECUTEFFJ
    for Each block of external table eb do
        Execute a Safe Point
        for Each query with prepared hashmap do
            map = FullMaps[column]
            Emit results of eb joined with map
        if maps need to be built then
            for Each block of internal table ib do
                Execute a Safe Point
                for Each column that needs a hashmap do
                    map = BuildMapForBlock(ib, column)
                    FullMaps[column].merge(map)
                    for Each query on column do
                        Emit results of eb joined with map
                    Free(map)
```

In Algorithm 5, for brevity, we show the high-level design of the Fast FluxJoin (FFJ) algorithm, and have not shown sleeping or latching mechanisms. In FFJ, when a new query begins execution, the hashmap needed for it on the internal table either exists or does not. If the needed hashmap is fully built, we execute Cyclic Hash Join. If not, we execute FluxJoin and while doing so, we build a full hashmap that will be used for later hashjoins. The safe point has to be modified in this situation for considering the case where a hashtable is partially built.

In the case of partially built hashmap, within the safe point we execute Hash Join by using the partially built map, and then continue executing FluxJoin using the rest of the internal table blocks – together the entire internal table is scanned for the specific external block. Starting with the next external table block, the fully built hashmap will be used. This behavior is similar to that of the Ripple Hash Join [22], jumping back to already scanned data for deferred joining with the already seen data, yet both are substantially different as follows – 1. FFJ scans both tables linearly, and the *jump* to previous already scanned data is limited only for the internal relation, using a hashmap. 2. The usage of the partially built hashmap will happen at most once for a query, and only while the hashmap is not yet built.

The benefits of this approach are substantial, and as shown later, the performance is similar to CHJ, while providing interactive response time. In FJ, for each block of the internal table, we have to build the hashmaps repeatedly. In comparison, in FFJ, we scan each block of the internal table once for each queried column.

The complexity of FFJ for the average case is (as given before, there exist q queries, c distinct columns, outer relation has o blocks with m rows each, and inner relation has i blocks with n rows each) $O(c \times i \times n + i \times m \times q + o \times m \times q)$. The first term indicates the cost of building the hashmaps on the internal tables. The second term shows the complexity of joining the first external table block with every block in the internal table (note the term o that appeared in the complexity for FJ is missing here). The last term indicates the cost of joining the rest of the external table blocks with the fully built hashmaps. Thus, we can note that by having enough memory to hold the entire hashmaps, we are able to achieve execution times similar to those of CHJ while obtaining CNL-like response time.

4.3 Comparison between Join Algorithms

Each join algorithm mentioned above will be useful for a different scenario. Here we summarize the preferred use case for each:

- CHJ is preferable when all results are necessary, and there is no constraint on response time. CHJ builds a full hashmap on one of the tables, if it wasn't built and cached earlier, and until this step is completed no results will be emitted. The caching of the hashmaps results in excess memory consumption, and if memory is limited it is not feasible.
- CNL produces results in an extremely low response time. Yet, FJ or FFJ are nearly always preferable over CNL since both always perform the same, or better, than CNL.
- FJ is preferable when memory is limited and interactive response time is needed.
- FFJ is preferable when memory is not limited, but an interactive response time is needed. This algorithm builds hashmaps and caches these similarly to CHJ.

4.4 Safe points

We define a safe point to be the place within the cyclic join where we can freeze the join execution process and modify the list of executing queries safely – add a query, remove a query, or change query properties.

The optimal place for the safe point is just before latching the data blocks since it shortens the latch times – the safe point is entered often enough for query modifications to not delay the query execution start substantially and barely affects already running queries (a delay of less than $5ms$ for query to start, and less than $3ms$ for currently executing queries).

Since query registration requires the join process itself to freeze in order to prevent data races, we execute the safe point on the same thread as the join itself – a design that allows us to use safe *change lists* and unsafe, fast, join process internal lists. There are two obvious places to freeze the join execution in order to register queries– the switch of a block in the external table, which we define as Outer Registration Window (ORW), and the switch of a block in the internal table, which we define as Inner Registration Window (IRW).

In IRW, for every internal-external block combination, before executing the join for the already registered queries, we freeze the join and check whether any new queries exist that can start execution, or if any query exists that has completed a full cycle.

In ORW, instead of freezing the join process in order to check for new queries and scan completions for every outer-inner block combination, we do so only for outer blocks. Therefore, we scan the entire internal table before registering the pending queries.

Thus, we can see that in IRW, each query starts running virtually immediately after its registration - but the external table scan is paused more often. However, in ORW it takes a full scan for the internal table, in the worst case, for a query to be scheduled to run. This results in fewer stalls for the already executing queries. The choice between using IRW and ORW is therefore based on the tradeoff between providing interactivity and reducing the overall query execution time.

It is trivial that IRW is preferable for CNL (it reduces the delay between query registration and execution). Yet, ORW is preferable for CHJ because of the extremely short lookup time of records in the hashmap and the limited number of rows in a database block.

Algorithm 6 Cyclic Hash Join - Add Query

```
procedure ADD QUERY(query)
    col = Column that should be hashed by the query
    CAS_Lock(ColumnsHavingHashes)
    if !ColumnsHavingHashes.Contains(col) then
        if !CurrentlyBeingBuilt.Contains(col) then
            SafeAddToList(CurrentlyBeingBuilt, col)
            CAS_Unlock(ColumnsHavingHashes)
            map = CreateHashmap(col)
            SafeAddQueue(PendingMaps, map)
        else
            CAS_Unlock(ColumnsHavingHashes)
            sem = new Semaphore
            SafeAddQueue(PendQuerySem[col], sem)
            sem.wait()
    else
        CAS_Unlock(ColumnsHavingHashes)
    SafeAddQueue(QueriesToAdd, query)
    CAS_Lock(QueriesToRemove)
    if CAS_Read(ExecutingQueriesCounter) == 0 then
        PendingQuerySemaphore.Post()
    CAS_Unlock(QueriesToRemove)
```

In Algorithms 6 (CHJ Add Query) and 7 (CHJ Safe Point), we demonstrate the communication protocol between a client request to add a query and the server process. In the Add Query algorithm, there are three scenarios that need to be considered – the hashmap needed for the query exists, it does not exist and needs to be built, or it is currently in the process of being built. If the hashmap exists, we simply use it. If the hashmap does not exist, the first client thread that needs the hashmap builds it. After the hashmap is built, it is added to the pending hashmap list (the modification of the actual hashmap list is done by the join thread itself within the safe point as demonstrated in Algorithm 7, to avoid the need for latching). If the query to be registered needs a hashmap that is currently being built, the thread that needs it goes to sleep after registering itself as pending for that specific hashmap. This allows the join executer thread, within the safe point, to wake up the sleeping thread when the hashmap is ready. For simplicity, we have presented a synchronous algorithm for adding queries, although, as mentioned before, it can be easily modified to be asynchronous.

In addition to the complex hashmap management, this protocol allows the process which executes the join to *sleep* while waiting for requests. A part of the Add Query algorithm, and its synchronization with the safe point itself, allows waking up the executer thread if no query was executing, saving system resources.

Algorithm 7 Cyclic Hash Join - Safe Point

```
1: procedure CHJSAFEPOINT
2:     for Each query in Queries do
3:         ▷ Remove queries that are done
4:         if query.ResultsCount >= MaxResults OR
5:                 query.ShouldStop(exb) then
6:             SafeAddQueue(QueriesToRemove, query)
7:     if !QueriesToAdd.empty() then
8:         ▷ Queries are waiting to be added to the run queue
9:         Lock(QueriesToAdd)
10:        while map = SafeDequeue(PendingMaps) do
11:            col = Column the HashMap hash is on
12:            CurrentHashMaps.add(col, map)
13:            for Each semaphore in PendQuerySem[col] do
14:                semphore.Post()
15:        while !QueriesToAdd.empty() do
16:            query = SafeDequeue(QueriesToAdd)
17:            AddToList(Queries, query)
18:            CAS_Add(ExecutingQueriesCounter, 1);
19:        Unlock(QueriesToAdd)
20:    if !QueriesToRemove.empty() then
21:        ▷ Queries are queued to finish
22:        Lock(QueriesToRemove)
23:        while !QueriesToRemove.empty() do
24:            query = SafeDequeue(QueriesToRemove)
25:            RemoveFromList(Queries, query)
26:            CAS_Sub(ExecutingQueriesCounter, 1);
27:        Unlock(QueriesToRemove)
28:        if ExecutingQueriesCounter == 0 then
29:            go to start
```

Line 5 of Algorithm 7 decides if a query should stop execution based only on *exb*, the external block. This signifies that this specific CHJ algorithm implements ORW. For CNL implementing IRW this method would require the internal block, *inb*, as well.

The safe point protocol for CNL is much simpler than the one demonstrated here. Although it implements IRW, the "Add Query" only includes adding a pending query while the safe point itself only manages the execution list from within the safe point itself – there is no need to manage hashmaps there.

Currently, we keep the hashmaps in memory until the join process terminates – the safe point does not clear hashmaps with completion of queries. It is possible to release a hashmap from memory or save it to disk after all the queries that use it have completed, which we plan to do in the future by using different eviction policies such as LRU, ARC, etc. FluxJoin, presented in subsection 4.1, avoids memory exhaustion and is ideal in settings requiring both - limited memory and interactivity.

An optimistic method to test for pending queries, first without latches, and then with latches on the internal data structures and queues, improves performance and makes the check for the pending modifications nearly free. The correctness of this approach lies in memory fences imposed by the latches on the data blocks. The penalty for using the optimistic approach is that in the worst case, a registered query would have to wait for two block cycles, instead of one. Paying this price is reasonable since block switches in a scan are more frequent than query modifications, and the stall duration is short and lasts for at most a few milliseconds.

Our preliminary experimental results aligned with our intuition and both directed us to these conclusions:

- For CNL, the safe point should implement IRW. The performance penalty is relatively small compared to the delay in start of query execution, which ORW imposes.
- For CHJ, the safe point should be at ORW.
- For FJ, the safe point should be at IRW, similarly to CNL.
- For FFJ, the safe point should depend on the current state - while building the hashmaps, IRW should be implemented, after the hashmaps are built, ORW is preferred.
- An optimistic method for modification of the execution list needs to be implemented for allowing safe point to be executed often at a low cost.

5. EVALUATION

We evaluate our system's scalability and response time, i.e. interactivity. We measure our system performance over increasing datasets (table content of between 10KB and 100GB) and increasing number of queries (between 1 to 2048), while determining whether each experiment met the interactivity constraints. We demonstrate the scalability of our system – all our algorithms successfully process thousands of simultaneous queries, while FJ and FFJ provide results in interactive response time.

5.1 Experimental Setup

We performed our experiments on the following configurations: MACHINE_{244GB} : RedHat (kernel 2.6), Intel(R) Xeon(R) CPU E5-2670 v2 @ 2.50GHz x 4 (32 cores), 20 MB L2 cache with 244 GB of RAM (`EC2 r3.8xlarge`),
MACHINE_{4GB} : CentOS (kernel 2.6), Intel(R) Xeon(R) CPU X3210 @ 2.13GHz x 1 (4 cores), 8 MB L2 cache with 4 GB of RAM.

Datasets: Since a benchmark for interactivity with large datasets does not exist, we synthesized data in such a way as to control join selectivity. In Table 3, we provide the selectivity for some data sets, all based on TPC-DS [40] – between 3% to 10%. The *Selectivity* describes the percent of data selected from each joined table, while the *Cartesian selectivity* denotes the selectivity of the resultset compared to a cartesian multiplication of both tables. Unless reported otherwise, the number of columns in each table is set to 16. Between table sizes of 10 KB to 100 GB, our experiments cover the entire spectrum of expected requirements from in-memory DBMS's.

Selectivity	100MBx10MB	1GBx1GB	100GBx100GB
Table	4.11%	4.11%	2.05%
Cartesian	0.1%	0.01%	0.005%

Table 3: Data Sets Sizes Selectivity Setting

Workloads: The workloads determine how many queries will be executed in parallel and when each begins and ends execution. The workload is orthogonal to the size of resultset – there is no limitation on the resultset size. We constructed 2 workloads based on different burstiness behaviors (Section 2.1) of joins involving 2 tables– WORKLOAD_{FULL} (default) and WORKLOAD_{TOPK}. We also experimented with a real workload, provided by the authors of [35], WORKLOAD_{REAL}. In this workload, users gesturally interact with their system to build simple queries.

The probabilities that the *TOPK* algorithm uses are based on real users interaction with a demo system, described later in Subsection 5.3.5. The *PDF* changes over time based on the user interaction with the system.

Baseline DBMS: We compared our system with System X, a commercial DBMS system; System Y, a commercial vector based DBMS system based on [5]; and PostgreSQL 9.3. We focused on these systems since they are intended to be used in data warehouses and represent the majority of research and commercial systems.

Although System Y outperformed System X for queries involving a single relation, System X outperformed System Y in every experiment involving joins. Hence, we have not reported the performance of System Y.

We were unable to obtain neither implementation, source code, nor executables of research DBMS engines more closely related to ours despite multiple attempts to contact authors of multiple papers. As a solution, we discuss the design principles for all related work in the absence of these specific implementations.

5.2 Metrics

Each experiment was repeated 3 times, after a warm-up run, and we report the average of the 3 runs in logarithmic scale. We report the standard deviation (*stdev*) where applicable. In all Hash Join experiments, the hashes are neither cached nor re-used across runs.

Interactivity Constraint Criteria: For each experiment, we tested whether the results were returned within an interactive response time limit, set to 0.5 Seconds. This value was chosen as the *interactive time* criteria since it has been shown to be the average human response time [41] and the detrimental effects of latencies over $500ms$ have been well demonstrated [31].

We set the minimum number of results to be returned to be 500 in order to consider a system as interactive so as to make sure that a reasonable number of tuples are available for the user to skim – unlike most related work, which sets it at a single tuple. Although the interactivity criteria requires us to deliver limited amount of results in limited time, we do not stop query execution after these were produced unless the clients requests so.

Time for Completion: For each experiment, we report the execution time for all queries in seconds, which represents the time between the client issuing its first query and receiving all the results for all issued queries. This time is unrelated to the interactivity criteria, which is a binary criterion.

5.3 Experiments

5.3.1 Scale Of Simultaneous Queries

Traditional systems are limited in the amount of parallel computations they can provide since different clients use separate threads. These systems utilize the idle time spent waiting for resources needed by a user to process other requests. If idle time is unavailable, they get overloaded. In our experiments, PostgreSQL and System X could not process more than 128 and 512 parallel requests respectively. In contrast, our system was able to reach the maximum available threads allowed by the operating system.

In Figures 4 and 5, we compared the query execution times for different relation sizes with increasing number of concurrent queries. We have not reported the performance of NL or CNL here since they are much slower than CHJ. We have presented the execution times for FJ and FFJ only for $\text{Data}_{100MB \times 10MB}$, since for $\text{Data}_{1GB \times 1GB}$ adding FJ distorts the graph due to a scale change – the experiments provided later compare the cyclic algorithms specifically, while Figure 5 compares hash join only.

The *stdev* of the execution times across the different runs differs based on the data set. For $\text{Data}_{1GB \times 1GB}$, the *stdev*s of CHJ, System X, and PostgreSQL are 0.05s, 223.13s, and 326.95s respectively. For $\text{Data}_{100MB \times 10MB}$, the *stdev*s of CHJ, FFJ, FJ, and System X are 1.10s, 11.61, 16.03s, and 281.01s respectively. The *stdev* increases with increasing number of threads for all experiments due to increase in both the query execution times as well as the overall system load.

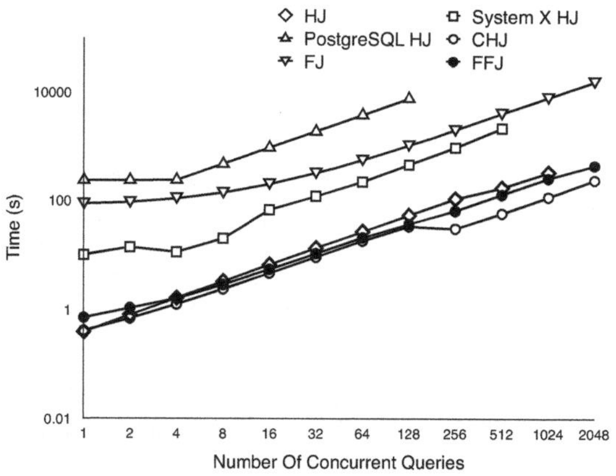

Figure 4: Time To Completion, $\text{Data}_{100MB \times 10MB}$, Machine_{4GB}. Here, CHJ has the least execution time, while FJ scales the best (smallest slope).

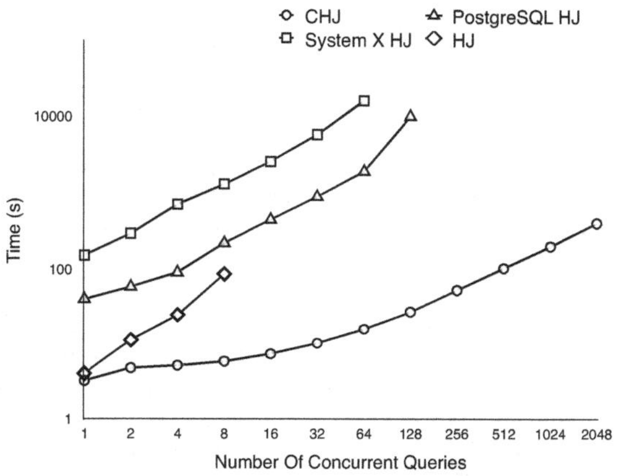

Figure 5: Time To Completion, $\text{Data}_{1GB \times 1GB}$, Machine_{4GB}. Here, CHJ is the only algorithm that scales, while having the least execution time.

We conclude:

- CHJ offers the best scalability.
- The performance of FJ is comparable to some of the hash join implementations.
- The performance of FFJ is closer to CHJ than to any of the other cyclic join algorithms.
- The cyclic algorithms have better performance predictability (lower *stdev*).

5.3.2 Impact of Data Size

We report whether each algorithm can be considered as interactive in Tables 4, 5, and 6 based on the interactivity criteria (Section 5.2) for data sizes ranging from 10 MB to 100 GB. '✓' and '✗' specify whether the experiment held the criteria or not respectively. '·' denotes that the underlying DBMS failed execution.

HJ does not provide interactive response times in most of the cases, while FJ, FFJ, and NL usually do (for our engine, NL, CNL, and FJ always provides interactive response times, while some of the systems we compared to did not). The cyclic versions of all

Threads	16	32	64	128	256	512	$1K$	$2K$
HJ	✓	✗	✗	✗	✗	✗	✗	✗
System X HJ	✗	✗	✗	✗	✗	✗	·	·
PostgreSQL HJ	✗	✗	✗	✗	·	·	·	·
CHJ	✓	✓	✗	✗	✗	✗	✗	✗
System X NL	✓	✓	✓	✓	✓	✓	·	·
PostgreSQL NL	✗	✗	✗	✗	·	·	·	·
NL	✓	✓	✓	✓	✓	✓	✓	✓
CNL	✓	✓	✓	✓	✓	✓	✓	✓
FJ	✓	✓	✓	✓	✓	✓	✓	✓
FFJ	✓	✓	✓	✓	✓	✓	✓	✓

Table 4: Interactivity Over Data$_{100MB\times 10MB}$, Machine$_{4GB}$ for simultaneous queries (threads). Here, NL, CNL, FJ and FFJ are the only interactive algorithms.

Threads	16	32	64	128	256	512	$1K$	$2K$
HJ	✗	✗	✗	✗	✗	·	·	·
System X HJ	✗	✗	✗	✗	✗	✗	·	·
CHJ	✗	✗	✗	✗	✗	✗	✗	✗
System X NL	✓	✓	✗	✗	✗	✗	·	·
NL	✓	✓	✓	✓	✓	✓	✓	✓
FJ	✓	✓	✓	✓	✓	✓	✓	✓
FFJ	✓	✓	✓	✓	✓	✓	✓	✓

Table 5: Interactivity Over Data$_{1GB\times 1GB}$, Machine$_{4GB}$ for simultaneous queries (threads). Here, NL, FJ, and FFJ are the only interactive algorithms.

the algorithms were able to handle a heavy load (up to $16K$ simultaneous queries), while their simplistic counterparts, the HJ and NL, failed much earlier. Interestingly, when HJ failed, the reuse of cached hashmaps allowed CHJ to complete.

All the hash joins (including FFJ) require additional memory during execution. This has a detrimental effect on the experiments performed using Data$_{100GB\times 100GB}$ even on machines such as Machine$_{244GB}$ – the entire memory is consumed and the hash join execution fails. In comparison, CNL does not consume additional memory, while FJ requires limited additional amount of memory. As seen in our experiments, FJ and FFJ always provide interactive response time.

We conclude:

- The cyclic versions are preferable over the non-cyclic ones for both performance as well as interactivity.
- FJ, FFJ, and CNL are always interactive.

5.3.3 Impact of Workload Strategy

We set a limit of 10 seconds for an interaction with the system to complete, i.e. after 10 seconds, only the user-intended query remains. On Data$_{100GB\times 100GB}$, both CNL and FJ provide response within interactive times, although the user query took more than 10 minutes to complete. CHJ and FFJ could not finish execution since they required more memory than was available.

	CHJ	FFJ	FJ	CNL
Workload$_{TOPK}$	1.97S	16.94	29.97S	404.25
Workload$_{FULL}$	2.07S	16.85	32.79S	6168.36

Table 7: Impact of workload on execution time, Data$_{100MB\times 10MB}$, K=512. Here, Workload$_{TOPK}$ has better performance than Workload$_{FULL}$.

Threads	64	128	256	512	$1K$	$4K$	$8K$	$16K$
HJ	·	·	·	·	·	·	·	·
System X HJ	✗	✗	✗	✗	✗	·	·	·
CHJ	·	·	·	·	·	·	·	·
System X NL	✓	✓	✗	✗	✗	·	·	·
NL	✓	✓	✓	✓	✓	·	·	·
CNL	✓	✓	✓	✓	✓	✓	✓	✓
FJ	✓	✓	✓	✓	✓	✓	✓	✓
FFJ	✓	✓	✓	✓	✓	✓	✓	✓

Table 6: Interactivity Over Data$_{100GB\times 100GB}$, Machine$_{244GB}$ for simultaneous queries (threads). Here, CNL, FJ, and FFJ are the only algorithms that scale for large relations, while being interactive.

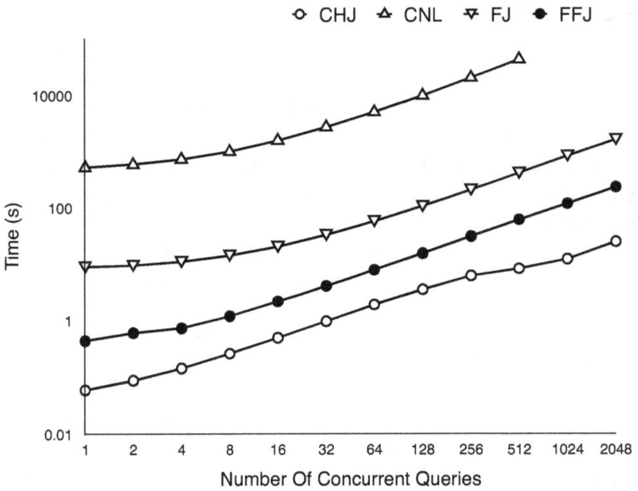

Figure 6: Join Types Comparison, Data$_{10MB\times 10MB}$, Machine$_{4GB}$. Here, FJ and FFJ represent a good trade-off between CHJ (non-interactive) and CNL (interactive).

In Table 7, we show the impact of the execution strategy on the execution time. All queries returned results within our interactive time limit. K was chosen to enable high query load as well as high query flux (queries are added and removed from the top-k list frequently, approximately every $10 - 100$ms).

Using the TOP-K technique reduces the system overhead for CHJ and FJ, while holding the interactivity criteria, saving approximately 10% of the total execution time. Although a larger number of queries are sent to the DBMS in the top-K approach (since some queries need to be stopped and restarted), the performance of these algorithms improves. FFJ was expected to execute slower for the Top-K workload, because query removals and additions make it fluctuate between CHJ and FJ – an expensive operation. However, no substantial performance change was observed.

We conclude:

- Top-K workloads improve performance for CHJ, FJ, and CNL.
- FFJ is not susceptible to the workload in use, whereas CNL is greatly affected.

5.3.4 Impact of Fast FluxJoin and FluxJoin

We compare the behavior of FJ and FFJ with CNL and CHJ using Data$_{10MB\times 10MB}$ to allow all the queries to finish execution.

In Figure 6, we show FJ is exponentially faster than CNL, yet slower than CHJ - making it a good intermediate point between the two when interactivity is needed. FFJ performs similarly to CHJ, and has the same performance pattern. Due to long execution

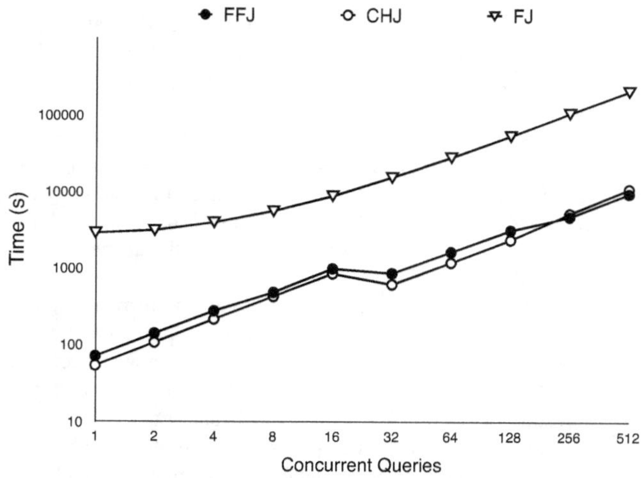

Figure 7: Join Types Comparison, Data$_{1024MB\times100MB}$ on Machine$_{244GB}$. Here, FFJ is ideal for interactivity.

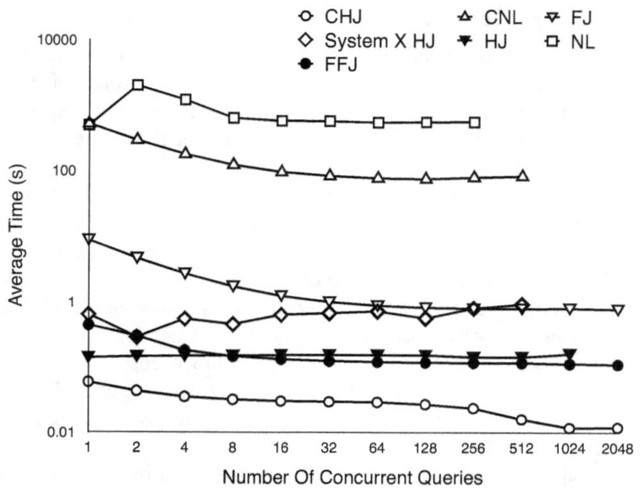

Figure 8: Average Query Time, Data$_{10MB\times10MB}$, Machine$_{4GB}$. Here, the average query time of FJ and FFJ are closer to the HJ family than the NL one, while FFJ is within the same scale as HJ and close to CHJ.

time, we ran CNL for select few configurations. In Figure 7, we show that FFJ performs nearly as well as CHJ, and better than FJ. Yet, FFJ provides interactive response time like FJ does, while CHJ does not. Figure 8 shows that cyclic joins have lower average query execution time than traditional joins due to resource sharing. The results using bigger data sets followed a similar pattern.

We conclude:

- All cyclic methods improve the execution time with increasing load for interactive workloads.
- FJ and FFJ are preferable over CNL since its performance is at worst similar to NL, when hashmaps cannot be reused.
- When memory is not limited, FFJ is the ideal algorithm - based on response time and performance.
- CHJ always has the least execution time.

5.3.5 *Real workload*

We experimented using WORKLOAD$_{REAL}$ with table sizes varying from 10 KB to 100 GB and number of columns from 3 to 16. Since the systems we compared to rarely returned any results during the interaction, we only report our system's performance.

CHJ did not provide results within interactive times in any of the experiments with table sizes bigger than 100 MB, although it was always the fastest overall. FFJ performed similarly to CHJ, but held the interactive response time criteria. CNL, FJ, and FFJ were interactive for all queries in all the experiments, including the one involving two 16 column tables of size 100GB each.

The response time for the first 500 results across all the experiments for CNL, FJ, and FFJ was lesser than the interactive response time limit (average being 0.26s for CNL and FFJ, and 0.27 for FJ). For this workload as well, CNL and FJ have similar performance while running a single query and FJ performs better when it can reuse hashmaps, as the case of multiple queries (through the interaction duration). FFJ performs similarly to CHJ, but little slower.

Join Type	CHJ	FFJ	CNL	FJ
Increase Times	491.7%	385.9%	81.9%	81.8%

Table 8: Increase Percent Average. Additional queries add a heavy load to CHJ and FFJ, compared with CNL and FJ.

In Table 8, we present the average of the time difference across all data sizes, while varying the number of columns in the internal table from 3 to 16. Increasing the number of columns in a table results in decreased number of rows since the table size remains constant. We can see that the performance of CHJ worsened when the number of columns increases, while the performance of both CNL and FJ improved. FFJ performance is similar to that of CHJ, which deteriorated since more hashmaps were needed to be built, whereas FJ was able to reuse the hashmaps and CNL was better since it had to process a fewer number of rows. We conclude:

- The overhead of CHJ is high. When the number of columns increases, CHJ takes longer to execute while CNL and FJ perform better.
- FJ and CNL behave similarly when a single query is executed. As shown before, the advantages of FJ are more noticeable when multiple queries use the same hashmaps.
- FFJ has similar overhead to CHJ, yet provides interactive response time for the initial resultset.
- After user interaction ends, the performance of each cyclic algorithm is similar to its underlying algorithm, showing that the overhead of the cyclic implementation itself is low.

6. RELATED WORK

Interactive queries have been explained in [8,24] and in [45,46], the authors delve into details regarding the need for this type of queries in more depth than here. An interactive engine challenges the current state of the art systems with additional requirements such as limited response time and in-flux queries [14,23,50]. The current state of the art developments can be divided into two research areas – parallel scans and shared scans.

Parallel scans [3,15,18,49,51] aim to improve the resource utilization. The main idea is to reduce the system response time by using available resources that are not utilized. Although we have not explored parallelization, a parallel cyclic scan, or a parallel join on latched blocks, it is an interesting avenue for future work.

Shared Servers [29] allow different queries to execute within the same host server process. It also enables transactions to be executed on different server processes while preserving ACID requirements. It is implemented using queues that register queries for execution. Each query sequentially uses the Shared Server process. In Shared Servers, one query executes at a time within each Shared Server process. When the current query completes, the next query is dequeued and begins execution. In contrast with Shared Servers,

FluxQuery executes all the queries simultaneously, sharing the table scans, and not only the hosting process. The similarity between our approach and Shared Servers is mostly related to the queue for communication between the client and the execution process.

Shared scan, introduced explicitly in [16, 17] and based on [6, 21, 29, 52], introduces the ability to share a table scan for processing multiple queries. We adopted the shared scan approach since it is well suited for providing interactivity. The shared scan, as presented before, aims to provide system predictability in OLTP environments, whereas we focus on data warehouse environments. It originally targets a response time of $2s$, which is greater than interactive thresholds of at most $0.5s$. We add to the existing work a thorough discussion regarding joins including Cyclic Hash Join and FluxJoin, hitherto missing. We demonstrate how sharing latches in addition to scans can further speed-up query execution. In addition, we utilize the client for some of the server process operations (for example, building hashmaps). Furthermore, we start executing queries at the granularity of data blocks as opposed to the entire relation.

Multi-Column Joins are an interesting avenue to pursue. The techniques shown in [37] allow implementing one join process that enables two or more column join. The same approach, as presented there can be extended to more than three columns, therefore we believe the expansion of our CHJ/CNL algorithms to join more than two columns is feasible, and can be targeted in future work.

We implemented 4 different cyclic join algorithms: CNL, CHJ, FJ, and FFJ. Other join types such as sort-merge joins, etc. and aggregation types exist, which might also benefit from our approach. Some, for example ripple joins [22], cannot be implemented in a cyclic manner since data is not scanned linearly in both tables.

The database engines, objects, and operators change over time as shown in [30, 37]. Our objects are built in a manner that allows tunneling an output resultset stream into another operator (pipelining), allowing our system to use techniques shown in [53]. Cyclic scans need to be researched in more depth with regards to pipelining. We find query vectorization and pipelining techniques, presented in MonetDB [5], useful towards that goal.

In Eddies [1], *moments of symmetry* is introduced which has resemblance with our notion of *Safe Points*. Both are similar in the action they perform - enforcing a halt of the main algorithm for communication (in Safe Points, query list modifications, in "Eddies" for join data intended for processing). However, the intention and implementation are vastly different. Safe Points are meant for internal lists modifications, and are used for assuring consistency of memory structures, allowing multiple simultaneous queries execution while lowering performance hit. *Moments of Symmetry* are meant for synchronization of data between nodes processing a singular distributed join assuring result correctness.

Shared Operators have been introduced before in the context of continuous queries over streams [33]. Assuming the subsetting criteria is identical, Shared operators allow executing specific filters simultaneously for multiple queries. In our work, not only are the join criteria different, but the columns the joins are on differ as well - preventing us from using Shared Operators. Our system is structured for using different subsettings and join criteria while sharing the table scans.

7. CONCLUSION

In this paper, we formalized the concept of an in-flux interactive query. We discussed the different aspects and expectations a user might have from an interactive engine such as response time limits, system load, etc.

We introduced new techniques for joining tables while also sharing the data and the latches. We developed protocols for adding queries to the shared join process, while other queries are executed, at a low cost.

We proposed a hybrid join strategy called the FluxJoin which reduces the complexity of the Nested Loop Join, while using limited memory and maintaining the short response time necessary for interactive queries. Fast FluxJoin, a variant of FluxJoin, which results in lower execution time at the cost of additional memory, is shown as well.

We showed our system provides significant performance gain. The systems we compared with crashed when pressured with a heavy load. On the other hand, our engine's average execution time scaled sub-linearly with increasing number of queries – more queries results in a larger degree of resource sharing.

The methods introduced in this paper can be implemented as optional elements in a full-featured database system, enabling clients to choose sharing the scan resources in exchange for interactivity, thus, reducing the system load.

8. FUTURE WORK

The query intent model has been introduced and not presented in great depth since the cyclic scan based system is the focus of this paper. It helps us motivate our problem setting and helps explain some of the FluxQuery design choices. The model deserves work with sole focus on it.

In the current implementation, we execute the join within the same process for all of the registered queries. Some of this work can be parallelized, such as emitting the results to the client, or performing the join itself for different queries.

When numerous results are produced rapidly, a *slow reader* should not exhaust the server resources, which in our case is the memory. Multiple solutions exist such as freezing sending of results to a slow reader until its buffer is cleared, improving the result stream object, or sending the most *interesting* results to the client, which decreases the required buffer size.

A major performance bottleneck was the transfer of the result set to the client. Work related to processing data streams [13, 47] can be used for handling this issue. It can be mitigated using sampling as well [9, 11, 38, 39, 44, 54]. Fault tolerance and scale out streams [7] are also relevant to our work.

Multi-table and multi-column joins are an interesting avenue of future work. Currently, multi-table joins can be implemented by pipelining multiple join processes while multi-column join can be implemented by one join process and additional pipelined subsettings. An interesting goal of implementing multi-table and multi-column joins within one process will be targeted in the future.

There is a clear need to research optimization of cyclic engines. In this paper, we have assumed that an optimizer, which builds execution plans for such engines exists, and we would like to work on it in the future – we currently manually built the execution plans.

There are multiple aspects of sampling that can be used in the context of interactive query execution. It is clear that a row sampled while keeping a particular join combination in consideration is usually not useful for another join combination and, thus, sampling rows with multiple join criteria in mind is an interesting avenue for future work. Finding samples that would be relevant for all possible join and subsetting criteria is both challenging and interesting.

Acknowledgements

We acknowledge the generous support of Amazon's AWS Cloud Credits for Research Program and the U.S. National Science Foundation under awards IIS-1422977 and CAREER IIS-1453582.

9. REFERENCES

[1] R. Avnur and J. M. Hellerstein. Eddies: Continuously adaptive query processing. In *SIGMOD*. ACM, 2000.

[2] E. Bakke. Schema-independent DB UI. *CIDR*, 2011.

[3] D. Bayliss et al. Query scheduling in a parallel-processing database system, 2007. US Patent 7,185,003.

[4] J. Bernet. *Dictionary compression for a scan-based, main-memory database system*. PhD thesis, Master thesis, Eidgenössische Technische Hochschule, 2009-2010, 2010.

[5] P. A. Boncz, M. Zukowski, and N. Nes. Monetdb/x100: Hyper-pipelining query execution. *CIDR*, 2005.

[6] L. Bouganim, F. Fabret, C. Mohan, et al. Dynamic query scheduling in data integration systems. *ICDE*, 2000.

[7] R. Castro Fernandez, M. Migliavacca, et al. Integrating scale out and fault tolerance in stream processing using operator state management. *SIGMOD*, 2013.

[8] G. Chatzopoulou et al. Query recommendations for interactive database exploration. *SSDBM*, 2009.

[9] S. Chaudhuri, R. Motwani, and V. Narasayya. On random sampling over joins. *SIGMOD*, 1999.

[10] K. Church, B. Smyth, K. Bradley, et al. A large scale study of european mobile search behaviour. *MobileHCI*, 2008.

[11] W. G. Cochran. *Sampling techniques*. John Wiley & Sons, 2007.

[12] C. Cook. Database architecture: The storage engine, 2001.

[13] A. Das, J. Gehrke, and M. Riedewald. Approximate join processing over data streams. *SIGMOD*, 2003.

[14] M. C. Ferreira de Oliveira et al. From visual data exploration to visual data mining: A survey. *TVCG*, 2003.

[15] M. N. Garofalakis and Y. E. Ioannidis. Parallel query scheduling and optimization with time-and space-shared resources. *SORT*, 1997.

[16] G. Giannikis, G. Alonso, and D. Kossmann. Shareddb: killing one thousand queries with one stone. *VLDB*, 2012.

[17] G. Giannikis et al. Crescando. *SIGMOD*, 2010.

[18] J. Giceva, G. Alonso, T. Roscoe, and T. Harris. Deployment of query plans on multicores. *VLDB*, 2014.

[19] S. L. Greene, L. M. Gomez, and S. J. Devlin. A cognitive analysis of database query production. *HFES*, 1986.

[20] J. Guo, X. Cheng, G. Xu, and H. Shen. A structured approach to query recommendation with social annotation data. In *CIKM*. ACM, 2010.

[21] A. Gupta, S. Sudarshan, and S. Vishwanathan. Query scheduling in multi query optimization. *IDEAS*, 2001.

[22] P. J. Haas and J. M. Hellerstein. Ripple joins for online aggregation. *SIGMOD*, 1999.

[23] J. Hellerstein, R. Avnur, A. Chou, C. Hidber, et al. Interactive Data Analysis: The Control Project. *Computer*, 1999.

[24] J. M. Hellerstein et al. Adaptive query processing: Technology in evolution. *IEEE Data Eng. Bull.*, 2000.

[25] S. Idreos. Database cracking: Towards auto-tuning database kernels. *CWI and University of Amsterdam*, 2010.

[26] S. Idreos and E. Liarou. dbtouch: Analytics at your fingertips. *CIDR*, 2013.

[27] S. Ji, G. Li, C. Li, and J. Feng. Efficient interactive fuzzy keyword search. *WWW*, 2009.

[28] L. Jiang and A. Nandi. Snaptoquery: providing interactive feedback during exploratory query specification. *VLDB*, 2015.

[29] M. Lai et al. System and procedure for concurrent database access by multiple user applications through shared connection processes, 1997. US Patent 5,596,745.

[30] J. J. Levandoski, D. B. Lomet, and S. Sengupta. The bw-tree: A b-tree for new hardware platforms. *ICDE*, 2013.

[31] Z. Liu and J. Heer. The effects of interactive latency on exploratory visual analysis. *TVCG*, 2014.

[32] Z. Liu, S. Natarajan, and Y. Chen. Query expansion based on clustered results. *VLDB*, 2011.

[33] S. Madden, M. Shah, et al. Continuously adaptive continuous queries over streams. *SIGMOD*, 2002.

[34] D. Maxwell and L. Azzopardi. Stuck in traffic: how temporal delays affect search behaviour. *IIix*, 2014.

[35] A. Nandi et al. Gestural query specification. *VLDB*, 2014.

[36] G. Neumann and S. Schmeier. Exploratory search on the mobile web. In *ICAART (1)*, 2012.

[37] H. Q. Ngo et al. Skew strikes back: New developments in the theory of join algorithms. *SIGMOD*, 2014.

[38] F. Olken and D. Rotem. Random sampling from databases: a survey. *Statistics and Computing*, 1995.

[39] B.-H. Park, G. Ostrouchov, N. F. Samatova, et al. Reservoir-based random sampling with replacement from data stream. *SDM*, 2004.

[40] M. Poess, B. Smith, et al. Tpc-ds, taking decision support benchmarking to the next level. *SIGMOD*, 2002.

[41] A. Polonsky, R. Blake, J. Braun, et al. Neuronal activity in human primary visual cortex correlates with perception during binocular rivalry. *Nature neuroscience*, 2000.

[42] P. Reisner. Human factors studies of database query languages: A survey and assessment. *CSUR*, 1981.

[43] J. Rekimoto. Matrix: A realtime object identification and registration method for augmented reality. *CHI*, 1998.

[44] J. Ren, W. Jiang, and C. Huo. Random sampling over streaming window joins. *ISDPE*, 2007.

[45] B. Shneiderman. Response time and display rate in human performance with computers. *CSUR*, 1984.

[46] B. Shneiderman, C. Williamson, et al. Dynamic queries: Database searching by direct manipulation. *SIGCHI*, 1992.

[47] U. Srivastava and J. Widom. Memory-limited execution of windowed stream joins. *VLDB*, 2004.

[48] G. Takacs et al. Outdoors augmented reality on mobile phone using loxel-based visual feature organization. *MIR*, 2008.

[49] A. Thusoo, J. S. Sarma, N. Jain, Z. Shao, et al. Hive-a petabyte scale data warehouse using hadoop. *ICDE*, 2010.

[50] Q. T. Tran et al. Query by output. *SIGMOD*, 2009.

[51] P. Unterbrunner, G. Alonso, and D. Kossmann. High availability, elasticity, and strong consistency for massively parallel scans over relational data. *VLDB*, 2014.

[52] P. Unterbrunner, G. Giannikis, G. Alonso, et al. Predictable performance for unpredictable workloads. *VLDB*, 2009.

[53] T. Urhan and M. J. Franklin. Dynamic pipeline scheduling for improving interactive query performance. *VLDB*, 2001.

[54] F. Xu, C. Jermaine, and A. Dobra. Confidence bounds for sampling-based group by estimates. *TODS*, 2008.

iOLAP: Managing Uncertainty for Efficient Incremental OLAP

Kai Zeng
Cloud and Information Services Lab, Microsoft
kaizeng@microsoft.com

Sameer Agarwal
Databricks Inc.
sameer@databricks.com

Ion Stoica
University of California, Berkeley
istoica@cs.berkeley.edu

ABSTRACT

The size of data and the complexity of analytics continue to grow along with the need for timely and cost-effective analysis. However, the growth of computation power cannot keep up with the growth of data. This calls for a paradigm shift from traditional batch OLAP processing model to an *incremental OLAP processing model*. In this paper, we propose `iOLAP`, an incremental OLAP query engine that provides a smooth trade-off between query accuracy and latency, and fulfills a full spectrum of user requirements from approximate but timely query execution to a more traditional accurate query execution. `iOLAP` enables interactive incremental query processing using a novel mini-batch execution model—given an OLAP query, `iOLAP` first randomly partitions the input dataset into smaller sets (mini-batches) and then incrementally processes through these mini-batches by executing a *delta update query* on each mini-batch, where each subsequent delta update query computes an update based on the output of the previous one. The key idea behind `iOLAP` is a novel delta update algorithm that models delta processing as an uncertainty propagation problem, and minimizes the recomputation during each subsequent delta update by minimizing the uncertainties in the partial (including intermediate) query results. We implement `iOLAP` on top of Apache Spark and have successfully demonstrated it at scale on over 100 machines. Extensive experiments on a multitude of queries and datasets demonstrate that `iOLAP` can deliver approximate query answers for complex OLAP queries orders of magnitude faster than traditional OLAP engines, while continuously delivering updates every few seconds.

1. INTRODUCTION

Over the last few years, there has been a significant increase in the amount of data that is being collected and analyzed every day to support various data-driven decisions. A major challenge in processing these massive amounts of data comes from the fact that the underlying hardwares cannot get fast or cheap quickly enough to keep up with the data growth[1], which in turn means that cost of decision making will keep increasing. As OLAP queries usually touch a significant amount of data, this mismatch between data growth and computation power shows clearly that the batch processing model used by traditional OLAP processing is no longer suitable for many OLAP applications.

Furthermore, data-driven applications pose a wide variety of requirements on query latency and accuracy—on one hand, business-critical analysis usually requires perfect accuracy, while on the other, time-critical analysis (such as system diagnosis/log processing) value timeliness of query results over perfect accuracy. More recently there is an increasing need for interactive human-driven exploratory analysis, whose desired accuracy or the time-criticality cannot be known *a priori* and change dynamically based on unquantifiable human factors (such as insights gained during the analysis). However, existing OLAP engines either always deliver a perfectly accurate result which may incur long query latency, or intentionally trade off accuracy for latency by only delivering approximate answers on samples of data [7, 9, 12, 17, 34]. No existing OLAP engine can provide a single system that can fulfill the variety of requirements by giving a smooth trade-off between accuracy and latency.

In this paper, we propose a new system—`iOLAP` (for *incremental* OLAP)—to tackle this performance mismatch, by replacing the traditional batch processing model with a more interactive *incremental query processing model*. The core idea behind `iOLAP` is fairly intuitive—given an OLAP query, the system presents the user an *approximate* result with an associated error estimate (e.g., confidence intervals), as soon as it has processed a small portion of the whole dataset. At the same time, the system keeps crunching a larger and larger fraction of the whole dataset, refining the approximate query results and updating the user. This process continues until either the user is satisfied with the accuracy of the query results and stops the query, or the system has processed all the data (in which case it delivers accurate query results just as a traditional DBMS). This approach gives the user a smooth control over query execution and the flexibility to make the accuracy-latency trade-off on the fly, and provides a unified system that covers the whole spectrum, from approximate but timely query answers to perfectly accurate query answers with a larger latency. As an example, compared to a traditional OLAP engine, `iOLAP` can deliver an approximate answer with a 95% accuracy 15× faster, an answer with a 98% accuracy 7× faster, and a perfectly accurate answer by executing the query on the entire dataset at a comparable performance (see Section 8). Last but not least, this approach simplifies the design of existing sampling-based approximate query processing (S-AQP) systems [7, 9, 12, 17, 34] by removing the requirements of pre-generating and maintaining samples.

A limited form of incremental query processing for simple SPJA[2] queries was proposed in Online Aggregation (OLA) [26]. More gen-

[1] According to one recent report [3], data is expected to grow by 64% every year.

[2] SPJA queries are those that consist of any combinations of select, project and join operators followed by an aggregation operator.

SIGMOD '16, June 26–July 1, 2016, San Francisco, CA, USA.
© 2016 ACM. ISBN 978-1-4503-3531-7/16/06... $15.00
DOI: http://dx.doi.org/10.1145/2882903.2915240

erally, incremental query processing has also been extensively studied in the context of delta view maintenance [18, 25, 25, 31, 10]. An underlying limitation of these existing techniques is that they cannot efficiently support anything beyond simple (in most cases, flat SPJA) queries. This implies that for complex queries, such as those with nested comparison subqueries, none of these techniques can incrementally process the query efficiently. In a separate context, incremental processing has also been studied in the context of data stream systems. These systems either rely on manually programming the delta update logic [6, 22, 30, 35] (something that's nontrivial and error-prone for complex OLAP queries) or use progressive models [28, 15, 16] for query processing. While these models are very powerful for modeling delta updates, they often cause a lot of recomputation for complex queries, and hence share the same set of performance bottlenecks as other incremental view maintenance techniques.

As an example, consider a simplified `Sessions` log, storing the web sessions of users accessing a video-sharing website, with three columns: `session_id`, `buffer_time`, `play_time`. The "Slow Buffering Impact" (`SBI`) query (Example 1) can be used to find out how a longer (than average) buffering time impacts user retention on the website. While `SBI` is a fairly straightforward nested aggregate query, it is very costly to incrementally process it. This is because as the query executes on larger and larger portions of the `Sessions` table, any refinement of the inner aggregate `AVG(buffer_time)` could result in recomputing the whole outer query on all previously-processed data from `Session`.

Example 1 (SBI: Slow Buffering Impact).

```
SELECT AVG(play_time)
FROM Sessions
WHERE buffer_time > ( SELECT AVG(buffer_time)
                      FROM Sessions )
```

In this paper we propose `iOLAP`, a framework that addresses these set of challenges around performance and generality with a novel incremental query processing technique based on uncertainty propagation. `iOLAP` significantly generalizes incremental query processing to complex queries with arbitrary nested subqueries, user-defined functions (UDFs) and user-defined aggregate functions (UDAFs). `iOLAP` has been demonstrated [38] to scale to more than a 100 machines while crunching terabytes of data in parallel. This paper focuses on the theory and implementation details behind the system. `iOLAP` uses a novel *mini-batch* execution model for incremental query processing: Given an OLAP query, `iOLAP` automatically rewrites the query into an enhanced delta query, randomly partitions the dataset into smaller batches, and processes through them by repeatedly executing the enhanced delta query on each mini-batch of data one at a time. Each delta query in the sequence computes a fast delta update of the previous query.

The key idea behind `iOLAP` is a new delta update algorithm based on *uncertainty propagation*. In particular, we propose a novel perspective on the incremental processing problem by treating the changes that could happen in partial results of any operator during incremental processing—either tuple attributes or tuple multiplicities—as *uncertainties*. Note that these uncertainties need to be recomputed during delta updates. Therefore, the problem of efficient delta updates boils down to precisely figuring out uncertainties that *would* change from those that *would not* change at a very fine-grained level. Based on this, `iOLAP` focuses on minimizing the recomputation on uncertainties that would change.

Specifically, we introduce a formal uncertainty propagation theory that categorizes uncertainties into attribute uncertainty (changing attribute) and tuple uncertainty (changing multiplicity), annotate these uncertainties for each tuple, and track their propagation through a relational query plan. **For tuple uncertainties**, we quantify how likely each tuple uncertainty would change, and prune those that would not change. For instance, in Example 1, after executing the query on a certain portion of data, if we were to know that `AVG(buffer_time)` falls within the range [21.1, 53.9], we know that with a very high probability, `buffer_time = 58` will be always greater than the average, and can be selected in the inner filter. **For attribute uncertainty**, we carry lineage information for each uncertain attribute (i.e., the values used to compute the attribute) within the tuple itself, and compute the up-to-date values of the uncertain attributes in place by only referencing the carried lineage. This avoids generating tuples from scratch during recomputation, and thus maximizes the re-use of previous computation.

In summary this paper claims to make the following contributions:

- We present an uncertainty analysis framework for partial results produced in incremental query processing that provides a dichotomy of the uncertainties in partial results, and reveals how relational operators propagate uncertainties through a query plan. (Section 4)
- Based on the uncertainty propagation theory, we developed a novel delta update algorithm that estimates uncertainties and minimizes delta update recomputation at a tuple/attribute granularity using the lineage-based lazy evaluation.
- We implemented `iOLAP` using a mini-batch execution model that can be easily integrated with existing database engines, and fit well with distributed computing environment. We also conducted an extensive performance study of `iOLAP`.

In the rest of the paper, we firstly define the query model and semantics of `iOLAP` in Section 2. We then demonstrate the limitation of existing delta processing techniques in Section 3. In Section 4, we propose a novel uncertainty propagation theory to model the delta processing problem, develop a delta update algorithm based on that, and discuss the ideas for optimizing tuple uncertainty and attribute uncertainty. We detail the tuple uncertainty optimization and the attribute uncertainty optimization in Section 5 and 6 respectively. We cover the implementation details of `iOLAP` in Section 7, and evaluate the performance in Section 8.

2. QUERY MODEL

When the user submits a query Q on a dataset D, `iOLAP` randomly partitions D into p batches $\Delta D_1, \cdots, \Delta D_p$. It then iteratively crunches through these partitions by processing a single batch as input at a time, i.e., at the i-th ($1 \leq i \leq p$) batch, it processes ΔD_i and delivers to the user a partial query result. As these partial results are computed on samples and thus are approximations of the true query result that is computed on the whole dataset, `iOLAP` also presents an error estimate (e.g., a confidence interval) associated with the partial results. As more and more data is processed, the partial result gets refined periodically with better and better accuracy. Similar to the `POSTGRES-OLA` implementation [26], the users can stop the execution at any time when the result meets their desired accuracy criterion.

In order to provide statistically meaningful approximate answers to queries, `iOLAP` assumes that each batch of data contains a random subset of the entire dataset. By default, `iOLAP` supports block-wise randomness by randomly partitioning data blocks into batches. This works well when the attributes needed in the query are not correlated with the blocks. However, if this assumption does not hold, `iOLAP` also provides data pre-processing tools to randomly shuffle the entire input dataset. Furthermore, `iOLAP` also gives precise control to users in specifying which input relations need to be processed in an online fashion. For example, if the `SBI` query were to contain more than one input relations, the user could explicitly specify to stream through a large *fact* table like `Sessions` while reading smaller dimension tables in entirety.

Query Semantics. In this paper, we use the relational algebra with bag semantics, but generalize it to tuple multiplicities that are real numbers (see Appendix A for a formal definition). Semantically, given a query Q, the partial query result given by `iOLAP` at batch i is equivalent to computing Q on all the data seen in the first i batches (and scaled appropriately). In other words, let us denote the data processed up to batch i by $D_i = \bigcup_{j=1}^{i} \Delta D_j$, the partial query result delivered in batch i is equivalent to computing Q on D_i where each tuple is annotated with a multiplicity of $m_i = |D|/|D_i|$. This means that seeing a tuple in D_i is roughly equivalent to seeing it m_i times in D. We denote this partial query result by $Q(D_i, m_i)$. Clearly, $Q(D_i, m_i)$ is an approximation to the true query result $Q(D)$. For the sake of simplicity, we use $Q(D_i)$ and $Q(D_i, m_i)$ interchangeably throughout the paper.

Error Estimation. Since $Q(D_i, m_i)$ is an approximation to the true query result $Q(D)$, `iOLAP` also associates an error estimation with the partial answer. In our implementation, we use *bootstrap* [21] to estimate the error of $Q(D_i)$ with respect to $Q(D)$. Bootstrap is a simple Monte-Carlo procedure that repeatedly carries out a subroutine called a *trial*. Each trial generates a simulated database, say $\hat{D}_{i,j}$, which is of the same size as D_i (by sampling $|D_i|$ tuples i.i.d. from D_i *with* replacement), and then computes query Q on $\hat{D}_{i,j}$. The collection of the query results $\{Q(\hat{D}_{i,j})\}$ obtained from all the bootstrap trials form an empirical distribution, based on which an error measure can be computed. Bootstrap can be efficiently piggybacked with the normal query execution [8, 39].

3. OVERVIEW

To achieve low latency in each batch, the guiding design principle behind `iOLAP` is to take full advantage of delta computation to minimize recomputation (and hence maximizes the reuse of prior work). In other words, instead of computing $Q(D_i)$ from scratch for each batch i, we utilize the fact that $D_i = D_{i-1} + \Delta D_i$, and update $Q(D_{i-1})$ from the previous batch by a delta query $\Delta Q(D_{i-1}, \Delta D_i)$, that is defined by $\Delta Q(D_{i-1}, \Delta D_i) = Q(D_i) - Q(D_{i-1})$. The intuition is that computing $\Delta Q(D_{i-1}, \Delta D_i)$ would be much faster than directly computing $Q(D_i)$. Similar intuition is shared by online aggregation (OLA) [26] and incremental view maintenance [10, 25, 31], with slight differences in the definition of ΔD: For OLA and `iOLAP`, ΔD is insertion of new sample tuples to the previous accumulated sample relation; while for delta view maintenance and streaming systems, ΔD can also include deletion of old tuples.

3.1 Limitations of Existing Approaches

Delta query processing is a well-studied area. Yet, previous approaches can only provide efficient delta update algorithms for simple SPJA queries, and thus fall short in generalizing to complex queries. In particular, we argue that previous delta update techniques are *static* and *coarse-grained*. Specifically, previous approaches generate delta update rules by only utilizing "static" information—the query structure. Such delta update rules (as shown in Figure 1) only exploit the strong compositionality of the relational algebra, but do not consider the relations which the query is evaluated on. As a result, these delta update rules are also "coarse-grained", in the sense that the delta queries in the rules are expressed as a function of the previous relations and the delta relations. Consequently, the rules cannot distinguish which subset of columns–or even more fine-grained, which columns of which subset of tuples–in the final and any intermediary query result are subject to change due to the update. Without fine grained updates, for complex OLAP

- `SELECT`: $\Delta(\sigma_\theta R) = \sigma_\theta(\Delta R)$
- `PROJECT`: $\Delta(\pi_{\bar{A}} R) = \pi_{\bar{A}}(\Delta R)$
- `JOIN`: $\Delta(R_1 \bowtie R_2) = (\Delta R_1 \bowtie R_2) \cup (R_1 \bowtie \Delta R_2) \cup (\Delta R_1 \bowtie \Delta R_2)$
- `UNION`: $\Delta(R_1 \cup R_2) = (\Delta R_1) \cup (\Delta R_2)$
- `AGGREGATE`[3]: $\Delta\gamma_{\bar{A},\Psi=sum} R = \gamma_{\bar{A},\Psi=sum}(\Delta R)$

Figure 1: Delta update rules for simple SPJA queries

queries (such as those with evolving nested aggregates in θ and Ψ), a large fraction of the query, sometimes even an entire subquery, needs to be re-evaluated from scratch every time, incurring a lot of overhead. Recently DBToaster [10] proposes to use higher-order delta queries to alleviate these limitations. But it still relies on the delta rules to generate the higher-order queries, and thus shares similar limitations.

As an illustration, let us revisit the `SBI` query (Example 1). Figure 2(a) depicts its query plan. Assume we evaluate the `SBI` query incrementally on the dataset shown in Figure 2(b), where the `Sessions` relation is partitioned into p mini-batches $\{\Delta D_1, \cdots, \Delta D_p\}$, each of size n (e.g., for $n = 3$, $\Delta D_1 = \{t_1, t_2, t_3\}$ and $\Delta D_2 = \{t_4, t_5, t_6\}$ and so on). As we can see, operator ② produces a different `AVG(buffer_time)` with new data added in each batch. This in turn affects ⑤ (that filters tuples using the current value of `AVG(buffer_time)`), and ⑥ (that aggregates the filtered tuples), and requires them to be re-evaluated on all previously-processed tuples in every iteration. Based on the delta update rules in Fig. 1, the delta update query for `SBI` can be written as follows:

$$\Delta\overset{⑥}{\gamma}(\overset{⑤}{\sigma}(D_i \overset{④}{\bowtie} \overset{②}{\gamma}(D_i))) = \overset{⑥}{\gamma}(\overset{⑤}{\sigma}(D_i \overset{④}{\bowtie} (\overset{②}{\gamma}(D_{i-1}) \oplus \overset{②}{\gamma}(\Delta D_i)))) \quad ^4$$

showing that we can only reuse subquery ② (i.e., $\gamma(D_{i-1})$), but have to recompute the subquery involving operators ③, ④, ⑤, ⑥ in Figure 2(a) every iteration. Note that since these static delta update algorithms do not keep track of the distributions of data that has already been *seen*, all recomputations on the same data are performed again and again regardless of whether it is really necessary. For example, let us look into the first two mini-batches. As `AVG(buffer_time)` at ② evaluates to 37 in batch 1 and 35.3 in batch 2, operator ⑤ makes conflicting decisions about tuple t_1: t_1 is filtered out in batch 1 and selected in batch 2. Therefore t_1 needs to be evaluated in batch 2. However, as the `buffer_time` of t_2 (t_3) is much less (greater) than the `AVG(buffer_time)` in both batches, operator ⑤ makes consistent decisions, and thus t_2 and t_3 do not need to be ideally re-evaluated. Due to the coarse-grained delta update rules, existing engines repeatedly re-evaluate ③ to ⑥ on t_2 and t_3 regardless of the above observation incurring significant costs in each batch. Quantitatively, the delta update cost increases linearly with batches, hindering continuous update. Roughly, processing through all the p mini-batches will process $n \cdot O(p^2)$ data in total, which could be much larger than the original dataset of size $p \cdot n$.

3.2 Our Approach

On the contrary, we propose a novel delta update technique that is both *dynamic* and *fine-grained*. Specifically, we treat the changes that could happen in the partial query results as uncertainties in the results, and explicitly track the uncertainty at a much fine-grained level—per column within specific tuples. Based on this tracking, we develop a delta update algorithm that is much more targeted and efficient.

[3] $\gamma_{\bar{A},\Psi}$ represents an `AGGREGATE` operator with group-by column $\bar{A}$ and aggregate function Ψ.

[4] We annotate the equation with their corresponding operators in Figure 2(a). $\oplus$ represents the delta update function for `AVG` aggregate based on the running sum and running count.

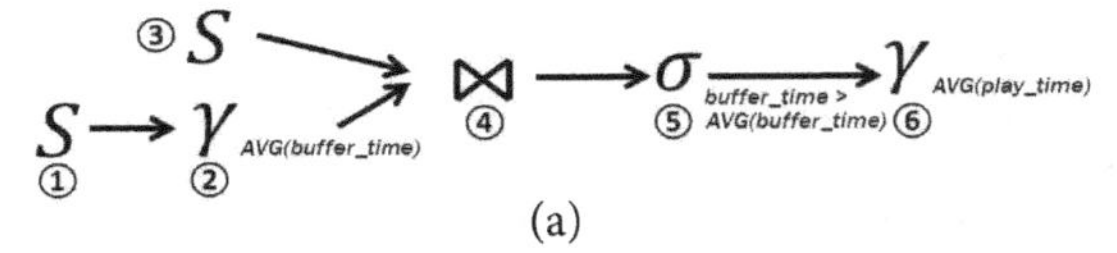

(a)

		session_id	buffer_time (s)	play_time (s)
ΔD_1	t_1	id_1	36	238
	t_2	id_2	58	135
	t_3	id_3	17	617
ΔD_2	t_4	id_4	56	194
	t_5	id_5	19	308
	t_6	id_6	26	319
...		...	...	...

(b) *Sessions*

Figure 2: (a) The query plan of the SBI query (Example 1), and (b) an example of the Sessions relation.

Let us revisit the SBI query in Figure 2(a) as an example. By tracking uncertainty, we can identify that—as a result of aggregating incomplete data—the column AVG(buffer_time) is uncertain at ②; despite this uncertain column, the columns outputted by ④ are deterministic as the (empty) join key is deterministic; the selection decisions at ⑤ are uncertain (as they're affected by AVG(buffer_time) which is uncertain); finally, ⑥ aggregates on a deterministic column of an uncertain set of tuples. Furthermore, such uncertainty can be tagged with a different confidence level on a per-tuple basis by exploiting the "dynamic" information collected at runtime—for instance, the data statistics of the uncertain columns in any intermediary and final query results. To be specific, if we could measure that AVG(buffer_time) obtained at ②, although *uncertain*, falls with a given range (say [21.1, 53.9]) with a very high probability, we can confidently say that tuples like t_2 (t_3) which have buffer_time far greater (less) than the range are always selected (filtered) with high probability across batches. And thus, we can avoid re-evaluating t_2 and t_3 in batch 2 (and all the following batches), leading to more efficient delta updates.

3.3 Supported Queries

In this paper, we limit the discussion of the iOLAP delta update algorithm to positive relational algebra queries, i.e., any query that can be composed using relational operators SELECT, PROJECT, JOIN[5], UNION, and AGGREGATE. Additionally we do not consider queries that have approximate join/group-by keys under sampling. Generalization to relational algebra including set differences, and queries with approximate join/group-by keys under sampling, are out of the scope of this paper, and would be ideal future directions. iOLAP delta update algorithm relies on efficient error estimation of uncertain columns. We use recent advances in bootstrap-based error estimation, which can be applied to arbitrary user-defined aggregate functions as long as they are Hadamard differentiable, or more intuitively *smooth*[6] under sampling-based approximation, that are common pre-conditions to apply sampling to approximate queries. For instance, MIN/MAX aggregates are not Hadamard differentiable, and thus are usually not approximated through sampling approach.

4. UNCERTAINTY AND DELTA UPDATE

As mentioned earlier, iOLAP treats the changes that could happen in the partial results of any operator in a query as *uncertainties*. In this section, we first categorize these uncertainties that exist in delta processing, and study how they propagate through a query plan in Sec. 4.1. Based on this uncertainty propagation theory, we then develop a new delta update algorithm to compute partial results efficiently in Sec. 4.2. Please note that the uncertainty propagation theory introduced in this section is a slightly conservative version that does not fully utilize statistics collected at runtime, but the delta update algorithm built on top of it already subsumes the existing delta update rules in Figure 1. Finally, in Sec. 4.3, we discuss the ideas for optimizing the uncertainty propagation and the delta update algorithm, by utilizing the statistics collected at runtime (Sec. 5) and leveraging the query lineage (Sec. 6).

4.1 Uncertainty Dichotomy and Propagation

Given an operator in a positive relational query, the difference between the partial result R_i produced by the operator at batch i and the true final query result R of the operator can be characterized by two basic properties: (1) their tuple multiplicities and (2) the attribute values of the tuples in the result. On one hand, some tuples that should be part of the true result (i.e., appear in R) are not included in R_i, while on the other, some tuples that are not part of R appear in the partial result R_i. We refer to this mismatch of tuple multiplicities in the partial result as *tuple uncertainty*. Furthermore, even for same tuples, some of them in R_i can have different attribute values than those in R. We refer to this mismatch in attributes as *attribute uncertainty*. To summarize, there are two types of uncertainties in partial results R_i: (1) the *tuple uncertainty*, and (2) the *attribute uncertainty*. Furthermore, please note that these uncertainties are not just limited to the query result and can exist in the output of all intermediate query operators, while propagating through the query plan.

Next we discuss how each relational operator propagates these two types of uncertainties in the query plan. For each relation R at a particular batch i, we define two types of tagging functions $u_\#$ (for tuple uncertainty) and u_A (for attribute uncertainty), that map tuples in R to $\{T, F\}$:

- $u_\#$ tags each tuple $t \in R$ with whether the multiplicity of t is uncertain or not, where $u_\#(t) = T$ indicates that the multiplicity of t is uncertain, and $u_\#(t) = F$ when it is not.
- For each attribute A of R, u_A tags each tuple $t \in R$ with whether the value of attribute A in t is uncertain or not, where $u_A(t) = T$ indicates that $t.A$ is uncertain, and $u_A(t) = F$ when it is not.

For any input relation R at the leaf level of a query plan, all its attributes are deterministic, i.e., $u_A(t) = \text{T}$ for any attribute A in R. For the tuple uncertainty, if R is not streamed in, $u_\#(t) = F$. Otherwise, the multiplicity of each tuple t is defined by $s(t;i)$ where $s(\cdot;i)$ is the accumulated sampling function for the i-th batch. $s(\cdot;i) = 1$ indicates that a tuple has been *seen* (i.e., processed) in the first i batches while $s(\cdot;i) = 0$ indicates that it is not. Given that we always process a new batch of data in each iteration, $s(\cdot;\cdot)$ has an property that $s(t;j) \geq s(t;i)$ for $j \geq i$. Thus, if $s(t;i) = 1$ at batch i, we know that the multiplicity of t will not change in subsequent batches and can mark $u_\#(t) = F$. On the other hand, if $s(t;i) = 0$, we mark $u_\#(t) = T$. We denote the attributes referenced in f, which is either a tuple function or an aggregate function, by $attr(f)$. The following rules describe the uncertainty propagation in a query plan[7].

- SELECT: SELECT propagates the attribute uncertainty of its input relation, but could incur tuple uncertainty if the selection predicate is applied on uncertain attributes. That is, if u'_x

[5]By JOIN we mean natural join throughout the paper. Outer joins are not considered part of classical relational algebra, and require set difference to express them.

[6]See [33] by Pol and Jermaine for an intuitive definition of smooth queries.

[7]We use the SQL version of PROJECT and UNION which are without duplicate elimination. Duplicate elimination can be expressed using AGGREGATE, and thus not explicitly discussed here.

are the tagging functions of R, then the tagging functions u_x of $(\sigma_\theta R)$ are defined by

$$\begin{cases} u_A(t) = u'_A(t) \\ u_\#(t) = u'_\#(t) \vee \bigvee_{B \in attr(\theta)} u'_B(t) \end{cases}$$

- `PROJECT`: `PROJECT` propagates the tuple uncertainty of its input relation, but could generate uncertain attributes if the projection functions are applied on uncertain attributes. That is, if u'_x are the tagging functions of R, then the tagging functions u_x of $(\pi_{\overline{A_i=\psi_i}} R)$ are defined by

$$\begin{cases} u_A(t) = \bigvee_{B \in attr(\psi)} u'_B(t') \\ u_\#(t) = u'_\#(t') \end{cases}$$

  where $t.A_i = \psi_i(t')$ for $\forall i$.
- `JOIN`: JOIN propagates the attribute uncertainty and tuple uncertainty of its input relations. Specifically, if u^1_x and u^2_x are the tagging functions of R_1 and R_2 respectively, then the tagging functions u_x of $(R_1 \bowtie R_2)$ are defined by

$$\begin{cases} u_A(t) = u^i_A(t_i) \\ u_\#(t) = u^1_\#(t_1) \vee u^2_\#(t_2) \end{cases}$$

  where $A \in$ schema U_i of R_i, and $t_j = t$ on schema U_j for $j = 1, 2$.
- `UNION`: UNION propagates the attribute uncertainty and tuple uncertainty of its input relations. Specifically, if u^1_x and u^2_x are the tagging functions of R_1 and R_2 respectively, then the tagging functions u_x of $(R_1 \cup R_2)$ are defined by

$$\begin{cases} u_A(t) = u^i_A(t) \\ u_\#(t) = u^i_\#(t) \end{cases}$$

  where $i = 1$ or 2 and $t \in R_i$.
- `AGGREGATE`: `AGGREGATE` is a bit complicated. Both of the attribute uncertainty and tuple uncertainty of its input relation could result in attribute uncertainty in its output; on the contrary, an output tuple has tuple uncertainty only if all input tuples within a group have tuple uncertain. Formally, if u'_x are the tagging functions of R, then the tagging functions u_x of $(\gamma_{\bar{A},\Psi} R)$ are defined by

$$\begin{cases} u_A(t) = \bigvee_{t'=t \text{ on } \bar{A}} u'_A(t') \text{ and} \\ \quad u_\Psi(t) = \bigvee_{t'=t \text{ on } \bar{A}} (\bigvee_{B \in attr(\Psi)} (u'_B(t') \vee u'_\#(t'))) \\ u_\#(t) = \bigwedge_{t'=t \text{ on } \bar{A}} u'_\#(t') \end{cases}$$

As we can see, the attribute uncertainty and the tuple uncertainty can *cause* each other, propagating and interleaving through a query plan. Take the `SBI` query (Example 1) and its query plan depicted in Figure 2(a) as an example. Figure 3 shows the uncertainty annotations on the outputs of selected operators in the plan. Since the input dataset to `AVERAGE` ② is streamed in and thus has tuple uncertainty, the `AVG(buffer_time)` attribute in ②'s output is uncertain. This attribute uncertainty further causes the tuple uncertainty in the output of `SELECT` ⑤, which subsequently causes attribute uncertainty and tuple uncertainty in `AGGREGATE` ⑥.

4.2 Delta Update Algorithm

The uncertainty propagation theory identifies subsets of partial results of the query operators that are subject to change across batches. At each batch, all the uncertain values from the previous batch, both attributes and tuple multiplicities, need to be recomputed and brought up-to-date with the new data. Therefore, delta updating a query simply boils down to the problem of updating values with uncertainties in the output relations of the query operators. Before diving into the detailed delta update rules, we first

	session_id	buffer_time	play_time	#
t_1	$id_1(F)$	$36(F)$	$238(F)$	$1(F)$
t_2	$id_2(F)$	$58(F)$	$135(F)$	$1(F)$
t_3	$id_3(F)$	$17(F)$	$617(F)$	$1(F)$
t_4	$id_4(F)$	$56(F)$	$194(F)$	$0(T)$
...	...	...	...	...

(a) Outputs of ① and ③/ Inputs for ② and ④

AVG(buffer_time)	#
$37(T)$	$1(F)$

(b) Output of ②/ Input for ④

	buffer_time	play_time	AVG(buffer_time)	#
t_1	$36(F)$	$238(F)$	$37(T)$	$1(F)$
t_2	$58(F)$	$135(F)$	$37(T)$	$1(F)$
t_3	$17(F)$	$617(F)$	$37(T)$	$1(F)$

(c) Output of ④/ Input for ⑤

	buffer_time	play_time	AVG(buffer_time)	#
t_1	$36(F)$	$238(F)$	$37(T)$	$0(T)$
t_2	$58(F)$	$135(F)$	$37(T)$	$1(T)$
t_3	$17(F)$	$617(F)$	$37(T)$	$0(T)$

(d) Output of ⑤/ Input for ⑥

AVG(play_time)	#
$135(T)$	$1(T)$

(e) Output of ⑥

Figure 3: Uncertainty annotations of the `SBI` query (shown in Figure 2(a)) on the outputs of selected operators in batch 1. Note that for ① we show tuples t_4 and so on conceptually (and thus are grayed out) to demonstrate the annotation. Physically these tuples have not been processed and thus have multiplicity = 0 at batch 1.

introduce Principle 1 to handle and update the tuple and attribute uncertainties.

Principle 1 (Delta Update Principle).

- ***Tuple Uncertainty****. Tuples with tuple uncertainty may change their participation in the outputs. Therefore, tuple uncertainty should be updated as early as possible—at the first operator that causes this tuple uncertainty—in order to minimize unnecessary computation on the corresponding tuple.*
- ***Attribute Uncertainty****. Uncertain attributes should be updated as late as possible, only when its value is used. The core intuition is to avoid updating attributes that are never used, and to maximize the reuse of computation on the corresponding tuple.*

As some tuples need to be remembered and re-evaluated in the next batch, we name the collection of tuples that needs to be remembered (and preferably cached) by an operator, as the *state* of that operator. Next, we devise the delta update rules for each relational operator according to Principle 1.

- `SELECT`. `SELECT` could incur tuple uncertainty if the predicate is computed on uncertain attributes. Therefore, `SELECT` saves each input tuple t into its operator state if t has no tuple uncertainty at the input, but has tuple uncertainty in the output. For instance, ⑤ in Figure 2(a) saves all tuples in Table 3(c) in its state after batch 1. All the uncertain attributes in the state are then updated in the next batch.
- `PROJECT` and `UNION`. These operators do not change tuple uncertainty. In other words, the operator states for `PROJECT` and `UNION` are always $\varnothing$.
- `AGGREGATE`. `AGGREGATE` accumulates all the tuples seen so far in order to deliver the correct running results. Thus, `AGGREGATE` constructs its state by saving the state from the previous batch, along with all input tuples without tuple uncertainty in the current batch. In practice, all the tuples in the state can be compressed into a *sketch state*, which is much more

space-efficient. For instance, to compute the average, in batch 1, ② in Figure 2(a) saves the running sum and running count of all the tuples in Table 3(a) in its state. In general, any aggregate function that can be computed using sub-linear space can maintain the state of AGGREGATE space-efficiently using sketches. However, if the aggregated column is uncertain, the state cannot be compressed into a sketch, instead each uncertain attribute need to be updated in the next batch.

- JOIN. New incoming tuples from each input relation need to be joined with all the previous tuples in the other input relation to produce the correct join result. Thus, for each side of the join, if the other side have tuples with tuple uncertainty, JOIN constructs its state by augmenting its state from the previous batch with all its input tuples in the current batch without tuple uncertainty, which in turn can greatly reduce the intermediate operator state for JOIN. For instance, in batch 1, ④ in Figure 2(a) saves Table 3(b) in its state but does not need to save tuples in Table 3(a) in the state since the other side of the join—Table 3(b)—does not have tuple uncertainty. All the uncertain attributes in the state are then updated in the next batch. In practice, many workloads join a large *fact* table with smaller *dimension* table(s). Therefore, if we only sample and stream the larger *fact* table, we only need to keep the smaller *dimension* table in the JOIN operator's state.
- SINK. We add a virtual operator SINK at the end of every query plan. SINK reconstructs its from the state from the previous batch, along with all input tuples without tuple uncertainty in the current batch. All the uncertain attributes in the state are updated in the next batch.

One can easily verify that this delta update algorithm subsumes the delta update rules used in previous work as in Figure 1. Some viewlet transformation optimizations proposed in DBToaster [10] can also be applied to our delta update algorithm (as shown in Appendix B. In combination, this conservative version of our delta update algorithm can achieve the same higher-order delta update rules of DBToaster [10].

4.3 Optimizing Delta Update

The uncertainty propagation theory in Section 4.1 only utilizes static information like the query structure and the monotonicity of the sampling process, but does not exploit any dynamic information, e.g., statistics collected at runtime about uncertain attributes (as discussed in Section 3.2). Therefore, it always conservatively tags all the tuples in the same relation indifferently with the same uncertainty property, incurring unnecessary recomputation overhead.

The key idea to optimize the uncertainty propagation, and thus the delta update algorithm, is to introduce an even more fine-grained partitioning of both per-row and per-column uncertainty, where: (1) **per-row**, we partition tuple uncertainty based on how *confident* we are about whether a given tuple is uncertain; (2) **per-column**, we only recompute uncertain attributes by leveraging lineage-based lazy evaluation techniques.

Tuple Uncertainty. The techniques used by iOLAP to handle tuple uncertainty are based on an important observation: *The tuple uncertainties, although in the same relation, may not be equally uncertain. By exploiting dynamic information at query time, we can identify tuples that are not likely to change their multiplicities across batches.*

Specifically, we can use data statistics collected at runtime, to estimate the distribution of uncertain attributes and get insights into tuple uncertainty that is caused by attribute uncertainty. This can allow us to carefully partition the tuples with uncertain multiplicities into two parts—the *non-deterministic* and the *near-deterministic* sets. The key intuition is that although tuples in the near-deterministic set has tuple uncertainty, with very high probability they are unlikely to change their multiplicities in the following batches. In contrast, the non-deterministic set of tuples are likely to change their multiplicities. Therefore, we only need to save the tuples in the non-deterministic set in the operator state, that will be recomputed in the next batch. We will explain this optimization in detail in Section 5.

Attribute Uncertainty. As discussed in Section 4.2, uncertain attributes in operator states need to be updated with the latest values in the next batch. The previous delta processing techniques usually interpret value update as deleting the old tuple followed by inserting a tuple. However, this approach is inefficient, as generating a new tuple requires going through the entire plan. The intuition of iOLAP is that although the uncertain attributes in a tuple need to be recomputed, many computations involved in generating the tuple can be avoided. Such computations include I/O operation (reading the input tuples from disk), shuffling the tuple according to a deterministic key, and evaluating the deterministic attributes. iOLAP achieves this by propagating the lineage information along with each uncertain attribute, and thus enables fine-grained update targeting only the uncertain attributes. This avoids re-generating the whole tuple from scratch, and maximize the reuse of previous computations.

5. TUPLE UNCERTAINTY PARTITION

In this section, we describe the optimization technique to handle tuple uncertainty.

5.1 Discovering Certainty in Uncertainty

As discussed in Section 4.1, the attribute uncertainty is first brought into a query by evaluating an AGGREGATE on incomplete data. Due to the blocking nature of the AGGREGATE operators, the running results for aggregate functions (on samples of data) are approximate and uncertain. This makes complex OLAP queries with nested aggregates non-monotonic, making simple delta maintenance techniques inefficient. However, there is a key principle behind all S-AQP techniques—running aggregate results will eventually converge to the *true result* (i.e., the aggregate result computed on the full dataset) as the sample size increases. Therefore, as the query engine processes through these batches, the running aggregate results will concentrate in a relatively small range around the true results, and this range will shrink as more and more data is processed. In general, as the attribute uncertainty propagates through a query plan, any uncertain attribute in the outputs of operators in a query plan also shares this convergence property. iOLAP leverages this convergence property of uncertain attributes. Before we dive into details of the algorithm, let's first make an observation using an example.

EXAMPLE 2. *Assume that all the intermediate results of AVG(buffer_time) throughout its online processing are within the range of 37 ± 16.9 (Example. 1/Table 2(b)). This implies that across all batches, tuple t_2 (with buffer_time = 58) will be selected, while tuple t_3 (with buffer_time = 17) will be filtered out. For these tuples, the decisions made by the query engine will never change across all batches. Thus, if we know this fact a priori, we can prune these near-deterministic tuples during online processing.*

From the above example, we can see that by utilizing the convergence property of uncertain attributes, the tuple uncertainty of different tuples can be classified according to how confident we are of the filter decisions we made on the uncertain attributes. And for the decisions we are quite confident of, we can classify those tuples as "not having tuple uncertainty", and thus eliminate the recomputation on them.

Formally, for an uncertain attribute u in an intermediate tuple, we define its *variation range* as the set of all the possible values that u may take during the online execution, denoted by $\mathfrak{R}(u)$. For simplicity, we uniformly define the variation range of a deterministic value d as itself, i.e., $\mathfrak{R}(d) = \{d\}$. Next, for simplicity, we will explain the delta-maintenance algorithm using fine-grained tuple uncertainty by first assuming that these variation ranges are given, and then explain how these variation ranges can be approximated in practice. In batch i, at any predicate $x\ \vartheta\ y$ involving uncertain values,[8] `iOLAP` classifies the input tuples into two sets: the *non-deterministic* set U_i in which tuples satisfy $\mathfrak{R}(x) \cap \mathfrak{R}(y) \neq \emptyset$, and the *near-deterministic* set C_i in which tuples satisfy $\mathfrak{R}(x) \cap \mathfrak{R}(y) = \emptyset$. For instance, if $\mathfrak{R}($`AVG(buffer_time)`$) = [21.1, 53.9]$, then $t_2, t_3 \in C_1$, while $t_1 \in U_1$. Clearly, for the tuples in U_i, the predicate may evaluate to different answers in different batches, while for the tuples in C_i, the predicate will evaluate to the same answer across all batches. Therefore, in batch $(i-1)$, we save U_{i-1} in the state; and in batch i, instead of evaluating $Q(D_i)$ from scratch by recomputing both U_{i-1} and C_{i-1}, `iOLAP` only needs to compute a delta update based on U_{i-1} and ΔD_i.

Of course, the variation ranges cannot be known until we have finished the query. In practice, `iOLAP` approximates the variation ranges using running estimates. Next we will explain how we can approximate the variation range using bootstrap. Note that bootstrap can be substituted with other error estimation methods.

Recall that we use bootstrap to estimate the accuracy of the running query results. As a by-product of this process, we can obtain a set of bootstrap outputs $\hat{u}$ for each uncertain value u, where $\hat{u}$ is shown to be an accurate approximation of the true distribution of u[9]. In practice,

- We use the range defined by $\hat{\mathfrak{R}}(u) = [min(\hat{u}) - \varepsilon \cdot stdev(\hat{u}), max(\hat{u}) + \varepsilon \cdot stdev(\hat{u})]$ to approximate $\mathfrak{R}(u)$, where ε is a slack variable that can be controlled by the user.
- $\hat{\mathfrak{R}}(u)$ may fail in the sense that some running value of u or a bootstrap output in $\hat{u}$ exceed the variation range in some batches, which will result in incorrect query answers. Thus, to check the integrity of $\hat{\mathfrak{R}}(u)$. we keep the history of $\hat{\mathfrak{R}}(u_i)$ at each batch i. At a new batch $(i+1)$, we check the integrity of $\hat{\mathfrak{R}}(u_i)$, or in other words, detect the *failure*, by checking $[min(\hat{u_{i+1}}), max(\hat{u_{i+1}})] \subseteq \hat{\mathfrak{R}}(u_i)$.
- If the check succeeds, $\hat{\mathfrak{R}}(u)$ is updated by setting $\hat{\mathfrak{R}}(u_{i+1}) = [min(\hat{u_{i+1}}) - \varepsilon \cdot stdev(\hat{u_{i+1}}), max(\hat{u_{i+1}}) + \varepsilon \cdot stdev(\hat{u_{i+1}})] \cap \hat{\mathfrak{R}}(u_i)$. If the check fails, we trace up the history of $\hat{\mathfrak{R}}(u_i)$, pick the last batch j where $\hat{\mathfrak{R}}(u_{i+1}) \subseteq \hat{\mathfrak{R}}(u_j)$, and recover the correct query result by recomputing the query on the data from batch $(j+1)$ to i.

THEOREM 1. *At batch i, the above algorithm delivers the same query result as* $Q(D_i)$*, i.e., the result of evaluating a query Q on* D_i.

PROOF. We give a brief sketch-proof by induction for Theorem 1. It holds obviously at batch 1. Assume that it holds up to batch i. If $[min(\hat{u_{i+1}}), max(\hat{u_{i+1}})] \subseteq \hat{\mathfrak{R}}(u_i)$ for any x and y in predicate $x \vartheta y$, then $\mathfrak{R}(x_{u_{i+1}}) \cap \mathfrak{R}(y_{u_{i+1}}) \subseteq \mathfrak{R}(x_{u_i}) \cap \mathfrak{R}(y_{u_i})$, which implies that the non-deterministic sets $U_{i+1} \subseteq U_i$. As we will re-evaluate U_i in batch $(i+1)$, we can guarantee to deliver the correct query result as $Q(D_{i+1})$. The proof follows similarly for the case where the integrity check fails and we recover the correct query result. Note that each bootstrap trial can be viewed as evaluating the query on the same set of input tuples with different multiplicities. Thus, the bootstrap estimation is also guaranteed to be correct. □

[8] ϑ is some comparison operator.

[9] We refer interested readers to [8] for the implementation details of bootstrap.

	buffer_time	play_time	AVG(buffer_time)	#
t_1	36(F)	238(F)	37, $\mathfrak{R}$ = [21.1, 53.9](T)	1(F)
t_2	58(F)	135(F)	37, $\mathfrak{R}$ = [21.1, 53.9](T)	1(F)
t_3	17(F)	617(F)	37, $\mathfrak{R}$ = [21.1, 53.9](T)	1(F)

(a) Output of ④

	buffer_time	play_time	AVG(buffer_time)	#
t_1	36(F)	238(F)	37, $\mathfrak{R}$ = [21.1, 53.9](T)	0(T)
t_2	58(F)	135(F)	37, $\mathfrak{R}$ = [21.1, 53.9](T)	1(F)
t_3	17(F)	617(F)	37, $\mathfrak{R}$ = [21.1, 53.9](T)	0(F)

(b) Output of ⑤

AVG(play_time)	#
135, $\mathfrak{R}$ = ···(T)	1(F)

(c) Output of ⑥

Figure 4: Uncertainty annotation of the `SBI` query (shown in Figure 2(a)) at selected operators in batch 1, using the new uncertainty propagation rules.

The user can also decrease the chance of failure-recover by setting a larger ε (at the cost of increasing the size of the non-deterministic set). In practice, setting ε to 2× the standard deviation of $\hat{u}$ achieves a good balance in controlling the probability of failure-recover and reducing the size of the non-deterministic sets (See Section 8).

5.2 Propagation of Non-Deterministic Sets

In this subsection, we summarize how the new tuple uncertainty propagates through the query plan, and elaborate the delta processing using non-deterministic sets. We modify the tagging functions by introducing per-row partitioning. In general, the new uncertainty propagation rules are the same as those discussed in Section 4.1, but are different for tuple uncertainty in `SELECT`.

- `SELECT`. A tuple t in $(\sigma_\theta R)$ does not have tuple uncertainty if tuple t does not have tuple uncertainty in R, and $\theta = true$ for all possible values of uncertain attributes in θ. That is, assuming $\theta = x\ \vartheta\ y$ where ϑ is some comparison operator, and the tuple uncertainty tagging function for relation R is $u'_{\#}$, the tuple uncertainty tagging function $u_{\#}$ of $(\sigma_\theta R)$ is defined by

$$u_{\#}(t) = u'_{\#}(t) \vee (\mathfrak{R}(x) \cap \mathfrak{R}(y)) \neq \emptyset)$$

Figure 4 demonstrates the uncertainty annotation of the `SBI` query in batch 1. Note that ④ now annotates `AVG(buffer_time)` with its variation range $\mathfrak{R}$, which in turn is used by ⑤ to prune the tuple uncertainty of t_2 and t_3, yielding $u_{\#}(t_2) = u_{\#}(t_3) = F$ by following our new `SELECT` rule. As a result, the output of ⑥ is marked without tuple uncertainty, as at least t_2 is contributing to the aggregate result.

Delta Update Rules. The new uncertainty propagation rules significantly optimize the states maintained by operators. By following the new uncertainty annotation, `SELECT` ⑤ in Figure 2(a) now only saves t_1 (marked in dark shade in Figure 4) in the state, while t_2 and t_3 are pruned from the state because they are not marked with tuple uncertainty; `AGGREGATE` ⑥ saves the running sum and running count of t_2 (marked in light shade in Figure 4) in its state.

6. LINEAGE AND LAZY EVALUATION

As discussed in Section 4.2, `iOLAP` requires all uncertain attributes in states of the previous batch to be updated with the latest values in the current batch, in order to correctly compute the delta update. Take the `SBI` query as an example. During batch 1, t_1 is classified in U_1 and thus saved in the state of ⑤ (as in Figure 5(a)). During batch 2, since ② updates the inner aggregate `AVG(buffer_time)` to 35.3 (as in Figure 5(b)), t_1 in Figure 5(a) has to be updated to 35.3 in order to evaluate the predicate correctly.

As discussed in Section 4.3, it is obviously a waste to regenerate a tuple from scratch just in order to update a couple of uncertain attributes. Additionally, since the cached data is just a subset of the running result set, regenerating the tuples from scratch would require random I/O access to the input relations. However, the following example reveals an important observation that can help us avoid such wasteful recomputation.

EXAMPLE 3. *Consider the SBI query plan shown in Figure 2(a). In the input relation of SELECT ⑤, although attribute AVG(buffer_time) is uncertain, attribute `play_time` is deterministic. Furthermore, the join relationship between tuples from ② and ③ is also deterministic. Therefore, we should avoid re-evaluating JOIN and re-generating the `play_time` attribute from scratch.*

The key idea here is to *locally* recompute and update the uncertain attributes, without touching other deterministic attributes. The recomputation is local in the sense that each operator can update its own saved state without referencing other operators.

To achieve this local update algorithm, `iOLAP` uses two techniques: (1) **Lineage Propagation.** `iOLAP` propagates with each tuple the information about how its uncertain attributes are computed, i.e., its *lineage*. (2) **Lazy Evaluation**. During delta update, `iOLAP` updates the saved state by re-evaluating the carried lineage information, without re-generating the whole tuple from scratch. This evaluation is done lazily only when the corresponding uncertain values are accessed. Next, we will discuss these two techniques in detail.

6.1 Lineage Propagation

A natural first step is to decide *the lineage information that needs to be propagated.* Intuitively, we can model the computation used to generate an uncertain attribute u as a lineage function, i.e., $u = f(\bar{x})$. The function definition f and the input parameter $\bar{x}$ are enough to recompute u. Note that f is static and shared by all tuples in the relation, and thus is extracted at compile time (i.e., it does not need to propagated with each tuple). Thus, `iOLAP` only propagates $\bar{x}$, defined as *Lineage*:

DEFINITION 1 (LINEAGE). *We define the lineage for attribute A of tuple t output by a query plan P, denoted by $\mathcal{L}_{t.A}()$, inductively as:*

- *Base Relation. The lineage function of a base relation R is defined by $\mathcal{L}_A(t) = \{t.A\}$.*
- *SELECT. If $\mathcal{L}'$ is the lineage function of R, then the lineage function of $\sigma_\theta(R)$ is defined by $\mathcal{L}_A(t) = \mathcal{L}'_A(t)$.*
- *PROJECT. If $\mathcal{L}'$ is the lineage function of R, then the lineage function of $\pi_{\overline{A_i=\psi_i}}(R)$ is defined by $\mathcal{L}_A(t) = \bigcup_{B_i \in attr(\psi_i)} \mathcal{L}'_{B_i}(t')$ where $t.A_i = \psi_i(t')$ for $\forall i$.*
- *JOIN $R_1 \bowtie R_2$. If $\mathcal{L}^1$ and $\mathcal{L}^2$ are the lineage functions of R_1 and R_2 respectively, then the lineage function of $(R_1 \bowtie R_2)$ is defined by $\mathcal{L}_A(t) = \mathcal{L}^i_A(t_i)$ where $A \in$ schema U_i of R_i and $t_j = t$ on schema U_j for $j = 1, 2$.*
- *UNION. If $\mathcal{L}^1$ and $\mathcal{L}^2$ are the lineage functions of R_1 and R_2 respectively, then the lineage function of $(R_1 \cup R_2)$ is defined by $\mathcal{L}_A(t) = \mathcal{L}^i_A(t_i)$ where $i = 1$ or 2 and $t \in R_i$.*
- *AGGREGATE. If $\mathcal{L}'$ is the lineage function of R, then the lineage function of $\gamma_{\bar{A},\Psi}(R)$ is defined by $\mathcal{L}_A(t) = \bigcup_{t'=t \text{ on } \bar{A}} \mathcal{L}'_A(t')$ and $\mathcal{L}_\Psi(t) = \bigcup_{t'=t \text{ on } \bar{A}} \bigcup_{B \in attr(\Psi)} \mathcal{L}'_B(t')$.*

Block-wise Lineage. Note that since aggregates are computed from a large set of values, propagating the lineage of aggregates will cause an explosion in the storage and networking overhead. We optimize the lineage propagation by dividing a query into multiple *lineage blocks*. A lineage block is a maximal subtree of the query plan that is an SPJA block, i.e., a subtree consisting of any combinations of select, project and join operators followed by an aggregation operator. It is maximal in the sense that extending the subtree with any

	buffer_time	play_time	AVG(buffer_time)	#
t_1	$36(F)$	$238(F)$	$37, \mathfrak{R} = \cdots\ (T)$	$0(T)$

(a) State of ⑤ at Batch 1

AVG(buffer_time)	#
$35.3, \mathfrak{R}' = \cdots\ (T)$	$1(F)$

(b) Output of ② at Batch 2

	buffer_time	play_time	AVG(buffer_time)	#
t_1	$36(F)$	$238(F)$	$37, \mathfrak{R} = \cdots, \mathcal{L} = \{(②, \text{key=\_})\}\ (T)$	$0(T)$

(c) State of ⑤ at Batch 1 with Lineage

Figure 5: Lineage propagation and lazy evaluation of `iOLAP`.

node in the query plan will violate this requirement. As an example, the query plan shown in Figure 2(a) can be divided into two lineage blocks: {①, ②}, {③, ④, ⑤, ⑥}. `iOLAP` propagates lineage within each lineage block, while simply propagating the aggregate results along with their corresponding group-by keys between lineage blocks, thus bounding the overall cost of lineage propagation. Formally, Definition 1 is modified as:

- `AGGREGATE`. If $\mathcal{L}'$ is the lineage function of R, then the lineage function of $\gamma_{\bar{A},\Psi}(R)$ is defined by $\mathcal{L}_A(t) = \{(rel(\gamma), t.key)\}$, where $rel(\gamma)$ is a unique reference to the output relation of $\gamma_{\bar{A},\Psi}(R)$ and $t.key$ is the group-by key of t.

Figure 5(c) shows the state of ⑤ with lineage. We can see that AVG(`buffer_time`) in t_1 is annotated with the lineage "computed from the aggregate of group (key=_) in the output of ②".

Folding deterministic value. We can fold deterministic part of the lineage function into a single attribute, and therefore reduce of the size of the lineage propagated with each tuple. Here *deterministic* means that the subexpressions do not involve uncertain attributes and thus remain unchanged across batches. For instance, in $sum(x) + y + 3$, we can fold $y + 3$ into a single expression z, and propagate z instead of $y + 3$.

6.2 Lazy Evaluation

It is straightforward to lazily evaluate an uncertain attribute if its propagated lineage does not involve aggregates. However, it is less obvious when the lineage involves aggregates. As we only propagate a reference to the aggregate results, along with their group-by keys across lineage block boundaries, we need to join the up-to-date aggregate results with the propagated lineage information in order to update the corresponding uncertain values. For example, to update AVG(`buffer_time`) of t_1 (as in Figure 5(c)) at batch 2, one needs to join it with the output of ② in Figure 5(b) to retrieve the latest AVG(`buffer_time`). Formally, if the lineage of t is defined as $\mathcal{L}_A(t) = \{(rel, key)\}$, lazy evaluation of t requires natural joining t with the relation rel on column key and projecting onto column $rel.A$, i.e., $\Pi_{rel.A}(\{t\} \bowtie_{key} rel)$. Joining t and rel is non-trivial and often requires shipping data, because t and rel are usually distributed according to different shuffle keys, especially in a distributed SQL engine like SparkSQL. However, in practice the aggregate relation rel is usually very small, and it is often very efficient to broadcast-join t and rel by broadcasting rel to all the machines. Finally, we conclude this section with an important observation. Note that this update process is modeled as a join query, and is thus able to be optimized using the underlying SQL optimization framework by choosing the most cost-effective way to deliver the lineage information.

7. IMPLEMENTATION

In this section, we present the implementation details of `iOLAP`.

Mini-Batch Execution Model. We use a mini-batch execution model to implement `iOLAP`. As shown in Figure 6(a), the mini-

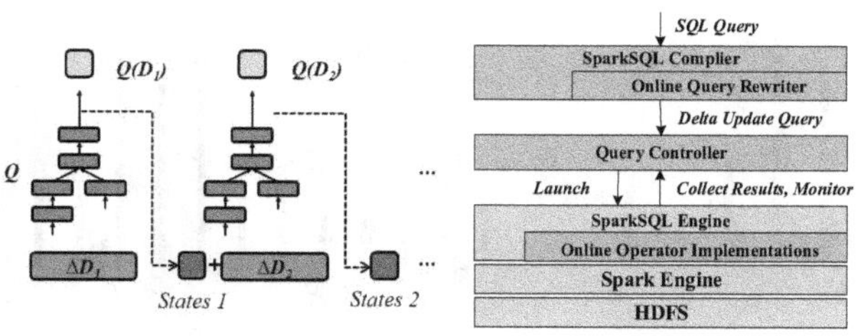

(a) (b)

Figure 6: (a) and (b) The mini-batch execution model and system architecture of `iOLAP`.

Workload	Batch Size	# of Tuples Per Batch
TPC-H (`lineorder`)	11.5GB	86, 000, 000
TPC-H (`partsupp`)	7.5GB	80, 000, 000
TPC-H (`customer`)	2.5GB	15, 000, 000
Conviva	25.6GB	10, 600, 000

Table 1: Batch sizes used for the relations that are streamed in

batch model treats the iterative query processing of `iOLAP` as a series of short and independent jobs. At each batch, the job takes the new incoming data and the states from the previous batch as input, and produces the query results and a set of states for the next batch. The mini-batch execution model can easily utilize the distributed computation resources, handle fault tolerance and stragglers, and better integrate with existing batch-oriented database systems. Last but not least, it is worth noting that `iOLAP` can be implemented using other execution models—such as the streaming operator model commonly used in existing streaming and online aggregation systems [26, 32, 6, 22, 30, 35].

System Architecture. We have implemented `iOLAP` in SparkSQL [4], a distributed OLAP engine built on top of Spark. `iOLAP` is open-sourced [2]. Figure 6(b) depicts the system architecture of `iOLAP`. `iOLAP` extends SparkSQL in three modules:

(1) *Online Query Rewriter.* The online query rewriter rewrites the query into a delta update query, which when plugged with different mini-batches of data, turns into a series of mini-batch queries. This rewriting includes (1) adding columns for bootstrap and lineage; (2) replacing operators with their online counterparts; (3) modifying plans to support lazy evaluation. We have a detailed discussion about query rewriting in Appendix C. The online query rewriter simply consists of a set of plan rewriting rules. It can be easily integrated into a relational query compiler.

(2) *Online Operator Implementations.* We modify the SparkSQL engine with implementations of online operator. Compared to the standard relational operators, these online operators can store and load states as in Section 4.2.

(3) *Query Controller.* The query controller partitions the input data into mini-batches, schedules the delta update query on each mini-batch and collects query results. The controller also monitors the correctness of all the variation ranges, and schedules recomputing jobs to recover the query result when a failure is detected. The query controller is implemented as a thin user application in Spark driver.

8. EXPERIMENTAL STUDY

In this section, we evaluate the effectiveness and efficiency of `iOLAP`. All the experiments are performed on a EC2 cluster of 20 r3.2xlarge machines (each with 8 vCPU[10], 61GB of RAM and 160GB SSD). All the data is stored on S3. Our experiments are conducted on both synthetic and real-world workloads:

- A synthetic 1TB dataset from the TPC-H benchmark [5]. As real-life large scale OLAP usually use denormalized relation schema to avoid expensive distributed joins, we project the TPC-H relation onto a schema similar to the SSB benchmark. Specifically, we join table `lineitem` and `orders` into a single relation `lineorder`, but keep other relations unchanged. We choose a subset of the TPC-H benchmark queries which include all the queries with nested subqueries structures (Q11, Q17, Q18, Q20, Q22), and a representative subset of the rest which are all simple SPJA queries. We used the same TPC-H queries as in [39].
- A 2TB subset of a 17TB anonymized real-world video content distribution workload from Conviva Inc. [1], comprising of a de-normalized fact table. We compose a query workload based on the real analysis used in [29, 20] on the same dataset, which involves simple SPJA queries (C3, C5, C11, C12), complex queries with nested subqueries and `HAVING` clauses (C1, C2, C4, C6, C7, C8, C9, C10), UDF (C6, C7) and UDAF (C8, C9, C10). The queries with nested subqueries are similar to those in the TPC-H benchmark.

During the experiments, we always stream in the fact table or the largest table (`lineorder`, `partsupp` or `customer` in TPC-H) used in the queries, and use bootstrap with 100 trials for error estimation. Unless specified, we use the batch sizes as shown in Table 1, and the default slack parameter = 2.0 for `iOLAP` throughout the experiments. We compare the performance of `iOLAP` with existing online processing techniques in OLA [26] and incremental view maintenance work [10, 25, 31], specifically DBToaster [10], which is the state-of-the-art delta processing algorithm. We implement the higher-order delta update algorithm of DBToaster (referred to as `HDA`) without code generation and indexes on SparkSQL, as code generation and indexes are outside the scope of this paper.

8.1 End-to-End Performance

In this section, we evaluate the effectiveness of incremental OLAP interface for interactive analysis by comparing `iOLAP` with the batch processing model of a traditional OLAP engine (named the *baseline*), i.e., answering the query on the original dataset using unmodified SparkSQL. The results are shown in Figure 7(a), 7(b) and 7(c).

Figure 7(a) demonstrates a typical query processing in `iOLAP` using C8 from the Conviva workload. As one can see, any traditional query engine will only be able to deliver an answer after processing the entire dataset, which in this case, would incur 10.7 minutes latency (marked by the vertical bar). On the other hand, `iOLAP` can deliver an approximate answer in 39.4 secs (i.e., only in about 6.1% of the whole query time). Furthermore, `iOLAP` continuously refines the answer at a very user-friendly pace of roughly every 10 seconds. It is worth noting that while `iOLAP` incurs an additional 50% overhead in processing the whole dataset as compared to the baseline (primarily due to the error estimation overheads and scheduling multiple mini-batch jobs), it enables the user to make a smooth trade-off between error and latency by allowing her to stop the query execution at any time. For instance, if the user is satisfied with an accuracy of say, 2% relative standard deviation, she can stop the query at 1.6 minutes, which is almost 7× faster than a batched execution.

Figure 7(b) and 7(c) plot more results on all the TPC-H and Conviva queries. For the sake of presentation, we only plot (1) the query time of the baseline to process all the data (denoted by *baseline*), (2) the query time of `iOLAP` to process all the data (denoted by *iOLAP*), (3) the query time of `iOLAP` to process a 5% sample (denoted by *iOLAP on 5% data*), and (4) the query time of `iOLAP` to process a 10% sample (denoted by *iOLAP on 10% data*). For clarity, we also mark the relative ratio between *iOLAP* and *baseline* in the figures.

[10]Each vCPU is a hyperthread of an high frequency Intel Xeon E5-2670 Processor.

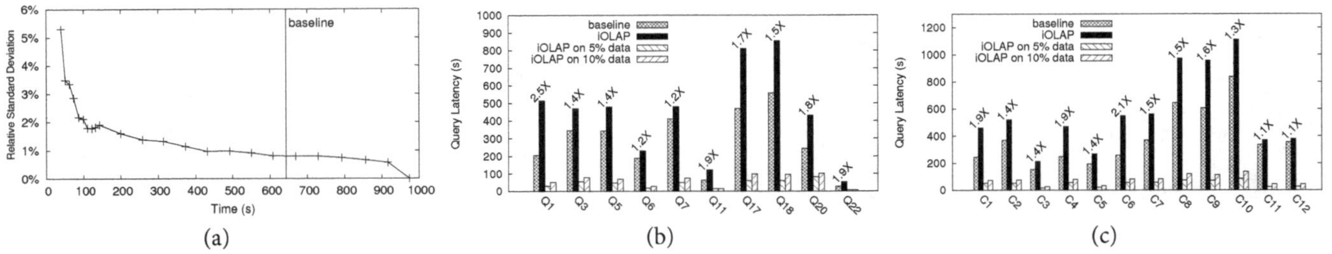

Figure 7: (a) The relative standard deviation vs. query time curve delivered by iOLAP on Conviva C8. We plot the values for the first 10 mini-batches, and then for brevity, every 5 mini-batches after that. (b) and (c) The query times of the baseline, iOLAP to deliver approximate results on 5% and 10% samples, and the iOLAP to process all the data for TPC-H and Conviva workloads respectively.

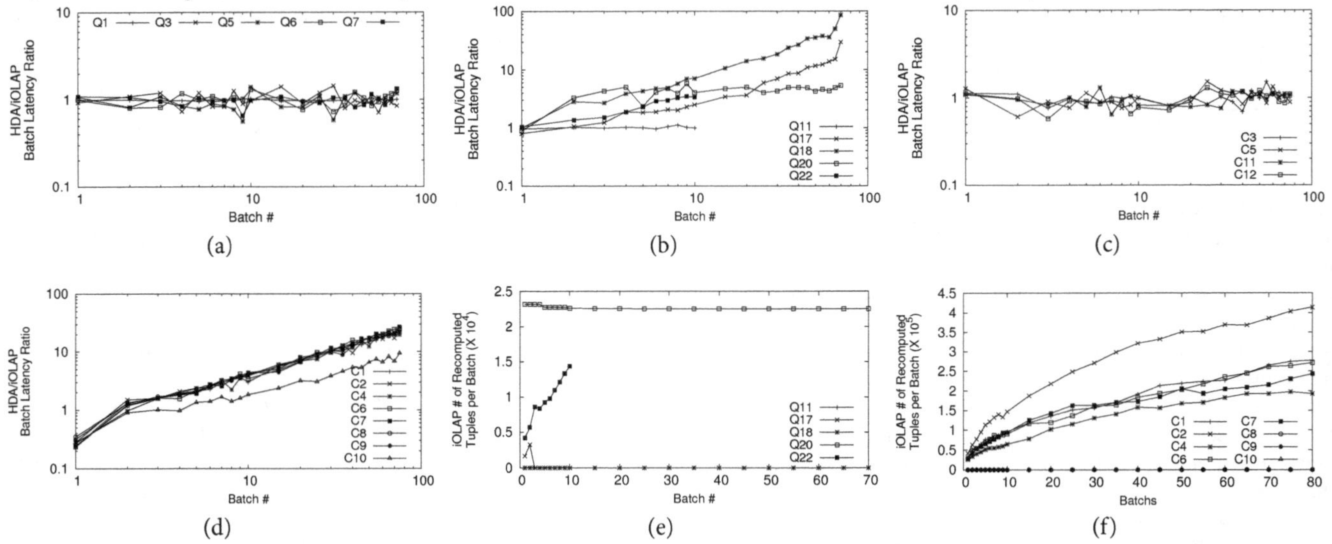

Figure 8: (a)-(d) The ratio of query times of iOLAP and HDA in the first 10 batches, and for brevity every 5 mini-batches after that, for TPC-H ((a) and (b)) and Conviva ((c) and (d)) workloads respectively. (e) and (f) The number of tuples recomputed by iOLAP in the first 10 batches, and for brevity every 5 mini-batches after that, for TPC-H and Conviva workloads respectively.

When processing the whole dataset, iOLAP incurs 60% overhead on average, and at most cases the overhead is below 100%. Again, these overheads are primarily due to the use of bootstrap for error estimation and the scheduling cost of multiple mini-batch jobs. Moreover, at query time, especially in a distributed environment, the majority of the query latency is spent on shuffling data, computing joins, etc., compared to which the relative overhead incurred by iOLAP is small. It is also worth noting that iOLAP is able to deliver approximate answers much faster than the baseline, e.g., if an approximate answer computed on a 10% sample is all that is needed, iOLAP usually takes only 10% to 20% of the baseline latency.

8.2 Delta Processing of iOLAP

In this subsection, we study the performance of the delta maintenance algorithms used by iOLAP for incremental query processing. We compare iOLAP with HDA. In this section, we focus on breakdown experiments that shed light on the performance benefits brought by iOLAP. We have more experiments showing end-to-end performance comparison between iOLAP and HDA in Appendix D.

Delta Update Latency. We compare the query latency per batch used by iOLAP and HDA. We plot the ratio of the query times spent by HDA and iOLAP for each batch in Figure 8(a)-8(d). For clarity, we plot both the X and Y axes using log scale. We can observe that the trends of the per-batch latency ratios in general fall into two classes: For simple SPJA queries (shown in Figure 8(a) and 8(c)), the performance of iOLAP and HDA is comparable, this clearly demonstrates that the delta processing techniques of iOLAP boil down to the classical delta processing techniques, as discussed at the beginning of Section 5. On the other hand, for complex queries with nested subqueries (shown in Figure 8(b) and 8(d)), iOLAP significantly outperforms the classical delta-maintenance algorithms. Specifically, iOLAP performs slightly slower than HDA in the first batch (because iOLAP need extra work on caching uncertainty sets, caching input relations for joins etc. as discussed in Section 5.2), but is much faster than HDA in the following batches. Furthermore, the per-batch query latency ratio grows linearly in general, which shows that the performance of HDA degrades with more data processed; on the contrary, iOLAP achieves almost constant query time for each batch. This is because that in the classical algorithms, every update on an inner aggregate subquery causes the engine to recompute the outer query on the entire data that was previously processed, while iOLAP could effectively limit the recomputation needed in each batch. Unlike other queries, the curves of TPC-H Q11 and Q20 flatten out. This is because their outer queries join two aggregate subqueries which are small in size, and thus are less expensive to be recomputed. Even though, iOLAP outperforms HDA in batch latency for Q20, as it avoids most of the recomputation of the outer query.

Number of Tuples Recomputed. We further look into the delta processing by studying the number of tuples recomputed in each mini-batch in iOLAP. Figure 8(e) and 8(f) depict the number of tuples recomputed in each batch. We only plot the curves for complex queries with nested subqueries as simple SPJA queries do not have recomputation. Recall that we use the default batch sizes in Table 1. The numbers of tuples recomputed per batch shown in the figures are almost negligible compared to the average number of incoming tuples per batch (some of which are even 0), which incurs very little recomputation overhead. It is also worth noting that for almost all the queries, the number of tuples recomputed grows sub-linearly across batches, which demonstrates the efficiency of the tuple uncertainty partitioning technique in iOLAP.

Optimization Breakdown. To better understand the delta update algorithms used in iOLAP, we conducted an experiment to study the effectiveness of the two major optimizations: (1) tuple uncertainty partitioning, denoted by OPT1, and (2) lineage propagation and lazy evaluation, denoted by OPT2. We gradually turned off the optimizations until fall back to HDA. We show the breakdown results of C2 from Conviva as an example in Figure 9(a). As we can see, the tuple uncertainty partitioning limits the recomputation to the non-deterministic sets, which reduces the query latency of each mini-batch to almost 25% of that of HDA. However, we still need to recompute the non-deterministic set from scratch. The lineage propagation and lazy evaluation maximize reusing of the computation for the tuples that need to be recomputed, bringing down the query latency per batch by another 18%.

8.3 Memory Utilization of iOLAP

In this section, we study the memory utilization of iOLAP. Due to space limit, we only show the experiment results on the TPC-H workload. The results on the Conviva workload are similar and are available in Appendix D.

We plot the memory overhead caused by keeping states for operators in Figure 9(b). Since JOIN only save states in the first batch (due to the fact that all joins in the experiments are between a streamed fact table and dimension tables) but other operators save states every batch, we show the states of JOIN and other operators separately. As shown, iOLAP only need to keep states of a few hundreds MBs for most queries. Exceptions are Q3, Q5, Q7, Q11, Q18 and Q20, which have a large JOIN states (5-50GB) because they have many joins due to a snowflake schema. However, it is worth noting that these JOIN states are already optimized to only keep the small dimension tables (see Section 4.2), as shown by the fact that the JOIN states are much smaller than the total amount of data shipped by the baseline. Moreover, the JOIN states in memory can always be spilled to disk.

We also study the data footprint overhead of bootstrap and lineage propagation of iOLAP. These techniques require expanding the intermediate query results with extra columns, incurring a larger data footprints than the baseline. As iOLAP is built on SparkSQL, which uses a pipeline implementation, these data footprints are eventually reflected on the data shipped across network (shuffled or broadcasted) at query time. Figure 9(c) compare the data shipped by the baseline and iOLAP. As different operator has different data footprint overhead (e.g., the overhead can go up to 100× for AGGREGATE, but much smaller for other operators), we divide the queries into two categories: (1) Queries that only ship AGGREGATE results (e.g., Q1, Q6, Q20, Q22), which only ship a small amount (< 10GB) of data (2) Queries that ship results of a mixed operators (e.g., Q3, Q5, Q7, Q11, Q17, Q18), which ship > 10GB data in our experiments. This classification can be verified by the data shipped by the baseline. As shown, iOLAP-Total has a small overhead for both categories compared to the baseline (100MB-9GB for (1) and 23%-45% for (2)). Additionally the data footprint of iOLAP-Per-Batch is 1-2 orders of magnitude smaller than that of the baseline, which implies that the user would shuffle much less data if she stops the query early.

8.4 Parameter Tuning

We next study tuning the parameters of iOLAP, i.e., the slack parameter and batch sizes in practice. We show the experiment results on Conviva. The results on TPC-H are similar and can be found in Appendix D.

Slack Parameter. As discussed in Section 5, the approximate algorithm to estimate the variation ranges has a tunable knob—the slack parameter, that directly impacts (1) the probability of failure-recovery happening at query time, and (2) the size of the non-deterministic set. In short, a larger slack parameter will decrease the probability of failure-recovery, but increase the size of the non-deterministic set and thus increase the recomputation per batch, and vice versa. Therefore, the user needs to tune this parameter to make the optimal trade-off in practice. We study the impact of this slack parameter by varying it from 0 to 2.5, and measuring the probability of failure-recovery and the size of the non-deterministic set. The results are shown Figure 9(d). Interestingly, we find out that setting a slightly bigger slack can significantly reduce the probability of failure-recovery. With the slack increasing, the probability of failure-recovery quickly goes to 0. For instance, setting slack = 0.5 reduces the failure probability by 7 − 8× on average compared to the extreme case (slack = 0); when slack = 2.0, all queries have no failure-recovery. On the other hand, increasing the slack parameter can increase the size of the non-deterministic set. But in practice, even a very small sample contains enough data to make the variation range concentrate in a very small range. Thus, the non-deterministic set does not increase much. The results are shown in Figure 9(e). All in all, we find out that slack = 2.0 leads to a good trade-off in practice.

Batch Size. Another tunable knob of iOLAP is the batch size. In practice, the batch size depends on two factors: (1) how interactive the user wants to get updates on the query results, and (2) how much latency of the whole query processing the user can tolerate. Smaller batch sizes will reduce the query latency spent in each mini-batch, but increase the number of mini-batches and thus increase the overhead of scheduling more mini-batch jobs. Figure 9(f) and 9(g) show how per-batch latency and overall latency change with varying the batch size. Clearly, with a larger batch size, the per-batch latency increases linearly, but the overall latency decreases linearly.

9. RELATED WORK

Online Aggregation. Online aggregation [26] and its successors [19, 32] proposed the idea of allowing users to observe the progress of aggregation queries and control the execution on the fly. The users can trade accuracy for time in a smooth manner. However, online aggregation is limited to simple SPJA queries without any support for nested aggregation subqueries.

Sampling-based Approximate Query Processing. There has been substantial work on using sampling to provide approximate query answers, many of which [7, 9, 12, 17, 34] focus on constructing the optimal samples to improve query accuracy. STRAT [17], SciBORQ [34], Babcock et al. [12] and AQUA [7] construct and/or pick the optimal stratified samples given a fixed time budget, but do not allow users to specify an error bound for a query. BlinkDB [9] supports sample selection given user-specified time or accuracy constraints. Such selection relies on an error-latency profile, which is built for a query by repeatedly trying out the query on smaller sample sizes and extrapolating the points. iOLAP relies on simulation-based bootstrap techniques used by BlinkDB to estimate the variation ranges of uncertainty attributes. Therefore, modulo the stratified sampling building phase, a first iteration of iOLAP is the same as BlinkDB. Different from BlinkDB-like AQP systems that provides near-instantaneous approximate result output, iOLAP can provide progressively approximate results over time. iOLAP does not require preparing a fixed sized sample beforehand, which simplifies the design of AQP systems. Additionally, given a query and a user-defined error bound, BlinkDB relies on an estimation module to pick a sample size. If the answer on this sample isnÕt accurate, or it doesnÕt

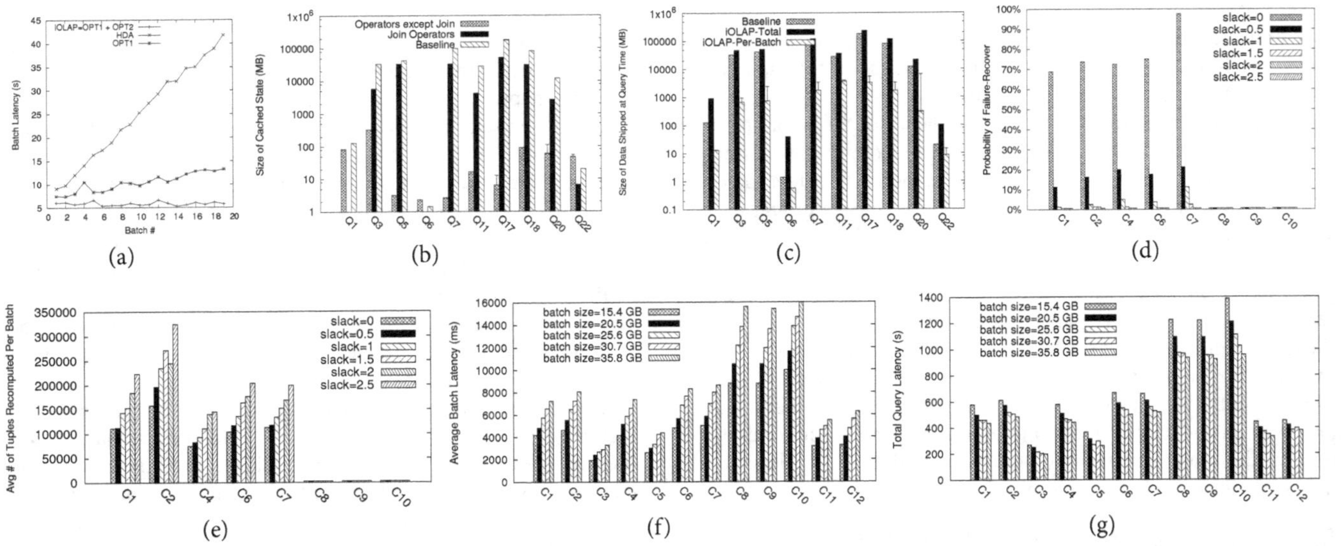

Figure 9: (a) Breakdown results of the delta processing optimization techniques used in iOLAP for C2. (b) The state sizes saved by iOLAP for TPC-H. We plot the all-batch total state sizes across all batches for JOIN, and the average and max (as error bars) per-batch state sizes for other operators. We also plot the data size shuffled/broadcasted by the baseline as a reference. (c) The size of data shipped by the baseline and iOLAP for TPC-H. We plot the all-batch total data size (iOLAP-Total), and the average and max (as error bars) per-batch data size (iOLAP-Per-Batch). (d)-(g) The relationship of the slack parameter vs. the probability of failure-recovery, the slack parameter vs. the size of non-deterministic set, the batch size vs. the query latency per mini-batch, and the batch size vs. the total query latency on Conviva workload respectively.

satisfies the userÕs requirements, BlinkDB then has to rerun the full query from scratch on a larger sample size. On the contrary, iOLAP just needs to compute a delta update query on the new delta input. ABM [39] is an analytical bootstrap method which is much faster than simulation-based bootstrap. The analytical bootstrap work is orthogonal to iOLAP. iOLAP can use the analytical bootstrap proposed in analytical bootstrap instead of simulation-based bootstrap to estimate the variation ranges, achieving better performance.

Incremental View Maintenance. Incremental view maintenance (IVM) is a very important topic in database view management, and has been studied for over three decades. IVM focuses on a similar problem—computing a *delta update* query when the input data is updated. Maintaining SQL query answers have been studied in both the *set* [13, 14] and *bag* [18, 25] semantics. [23, 24] proposed a $\mathbb{Z}$-relation model for annotating relations for incremental view maintenance. iOLAP utilizes this relational model to model the propagation of uncertainties in a relational query. Computing the delta update query has been studied for query with aggregates [25, 31] and temporal aggregates [37]. However, majority of work in this area only focuses on simple SPJA queries without nested and correlated aggregation subqueries. More recently, DBToaster [10] has investigated higher-order IVM and support for nested queries. However, for queries with nested aggregates, the *delta update* query obtained by higher-order IVM is often no simpler than the original query. iOLAP's delta-maintenance technique doesn't have this limitation. [27] models incremental view maintenance as a sample clean problem, and use the view on a cleaned sample to infer the view on the whole dataset. While [27] focuses more on how to maintain a statistically sound sample for a view definition, and how to maintain the view approximately, iOLAP focus on how to exactly maintain the result of a query given uniform sample updates.

Data Stream Processing. Data stream processing [6, 22, 30, 35] combines (1) incremental processing (e.g., sliding windows) and (2) sublinear space algorithms for handling updates. These techniques mainly rely on manual programming and composing, and thus have limited adoption and generalization. More recent works on stream processing [28, 15, 16] use a progressive model to model incremental processing. Tuples are augmented with progressive intervals, and operators are aware of progressive intervals. This model can automatically achieve the delta update rules in Figure 1, but also share the same performance limitation on complex queries beyond SPJA queries. In particular, [16] also uses the progressive model to model different sampling schemes, but still relies on the user to code the data flow query in order to deliver meaningful result under sampling, e.g., scaling a SUM aggregate according to the sampling rate. In contrast, iOLAP provides a meaningful semantics for uniform sampling by default without user intervention, and can be extended to incorporate stratified sampling. There has also been work on one-pass streaming algorithms [11, 36] for single layer of nested aggregate queries that rely on building correlated aggregate summaries on streams of data. However, it is non-trivial to automatically build these summaries for queries with arbitrary levels of nesting and/or user defined aggregates. iOLAP on the other hand provides automatic incremental processing to general SQL queries, including those with multiple levels of nesting and arbitrary aggregates.

10. CONCLUSION

This paper presented iOLAP, an incremental OLAP query engine that uses a mini-batch execution for interactive incremental query processing. iOLAP uses a novel delta update algorithm that is built on top of an uncertainty propagation theory. We experimentally validated the effectiveness and efficiency of iOLAP. The delta processing techniques of iOLAP could benefit other related fields in general, e.g., delta view maintenance and streaming systems.

Acknowledgments

This research is supported in part by NSF CISE Expeditions Award CCF-1139158, LBNL Award 7076018, and DARPA XData Award FA8750-12-2-0331, and gifts from Amazon Web Services, Google, SAP, The Thomas and Stacey Siebel Foundation, Adatao, Adobe, Apple, Inc., Blue Goji, Bosch, C3Energy, Cisco, Cray, Cloudera, EMC, Ericsson, Facebook, Guavus, Huawei, Informatica, Intel, Microsoft, NetApp, Pivotal, Samsung, Splunk, Virdata and VMware.

11. REFERENCES

[1] Conviva Inc. http://www.conviva.com/.

[2] iOLAP Github repository. https://github.com/amplab/iolap.

[3] Knowledge Management. http://www.globalgraphics.com/technology/knowledge-management/.

[4] Spark and SparkSQL. http://spark.apache.org/.

[5] TPC-H Benchmark. http://www.tpc.org/tpch/.

[6] D. J. Abadi, Y. Ahmad, M. Balazinska, U. Cetintemel, M. Cherniack, J.-H. Hwang, W. Lindner, A. Maskey, A. Rasin, E. Ryvkina, et al. The design of the borealis stream processing engine. In *CIDR*, volume 5, pages 277–289, 2005.

[7] S. Acharya, P. B. Gibbons, V. Poosala, and S. Ramaswamy. The aqua approximate query answering system. In *SIGMOD Record*, volume 28, pages 574–576, 1999.

[8] S. Agarwal, H. Milner, A. Kleiner, A. Talwalkar, M. I. Jordan, S. Madden, B. Mozafari, and I. Stoica. Knowing when you're wrong: building fast and reliable approximate query processing systems. In *SIGMOD*, pages 481–492, 2014.

[9] S. Agarwal, B. Mozafari, A. Panda, H. Milner, S. Madden, and I. Stoica. Blinkdb: queries with bounded errors and bounded response times on very large data. In *EuroSys*, pages 29–42, 2013.

[10] Y. Ahmad, O. Kennedy, C. Koch, and M. Nikolic. Dbtoaster: Higher-order delta processing for dynamic, frequently fresh views. *PVLDB*, 5(10):968–979, 2012.

[11] R. Ananthakrishna, A. Das, J. Gehrke, F. Korn, S. Muthukrishnan, and D. Srivastava. Efficient approximation of correlated sums on data streams. *IEEE Trans. Knowl. Data Eng.*, 15(3):569–572, 2003.

[12] B. Babcock, S. Chaudhuri, and G. Das. Dynamic sample selection for approximate query processing. In *SIGMOD*, pages 539–550, 2003.

[13] J. A. Blakeley, P.-A. Larson, and F. W. Tompa. Efficiently updating materialized views. In *SIGMOD*, volume 15, pages 61–71, 1986.

[14] O. P. Buneman and E. K. Clemons. Efficiently monitoring relational databases. *TODS*, 4(3):368–382, 1979.

[15] B. Chandramouli, J. Goldstein, M. Barnett, R. DeLine, J. C. Platt, J. F. Terwilliger, and J. Wernsing. Trill: A high-performance incremental query processor for diverse analytics. *PVLDB*, 8(4):401–412, 2014.

[16] B. Chandramouli, J. Goldstein, and A. Quamar. Scalable progressive analytics on big data in the cloud. *PVLDB*, 6(14):1726–1737, 2013.

[17] S. Chaudhuri, G. Das, and V. Narasayya. Optimized stratified sampling for approximate query processing. *TODS*, 32(2):9, 2007.

[18] S. Chaudhuri, R. Krishnamurthy, S. Potamianos, and K. Shim. Optimizing queries with materialized views. In *ICDE*, pages 190–190, 1995.

[19] T. Condie, N. Conway, P. Alvaro, J. M. Hellerstein, J. Gerth, J. Talbot, K. Elmeleegy, and R. Sears. Online aggregation and continuous query support in mapreduce. In *SIGMOD*, pages 1115–1118, 2010.

[20] F. Dobrian, V. Sekar, A. Awan, I. Stoica, D. A. Joseph, A. Ganjam, J. Zhan, and H. Zhang. Understanding the impact of video quality on user engagement. In *Proceedings of the ACM SIGCOMM 2011 Conference on Applications, Technologies, Architectures, and Protocols for Computer Communications, Toronto, ON, Canada, August 15-19, 2011*, pages 362–373, 2011.

[21] B. Efron and R. J. Tibshirani. *An Introduction to the Bootstrap*. Chapman & Hall, New York, 1993.

[22] T. M. Ghanem, A. K. Elmagarmid, P.-Å. Larson, and W. G. Aref. Supporting views in data stream management systems. *TODS*, 35(1):1, 2010.

[23] T. J. Green, Z. G. Ives, and V. Tannen. Reconcilable differences. *Theory Comput. Syst.*, 49(2):460–488, 2011.

[24] T. J. Green, G. Karvounarakis, and V. Tannen. Provenance semirings. In *Proceedings of the Twenty-Sixth ACM SIGACT-SIGMOD-SIGART Symposium on Principles of Database Systems, June 11-13, 2007, Beijing, China*, pages 31–40, 2007.

[25] T. Griffin and L. Libkin. Incremental maintenance of views with duplicates. In *ACM SIGMOD Record*, volume 24, pages 328–339, 1995.

[26] J. M. Hellerstein, P. J. Haas, and H. J. Wang. Online aggregation. In *SIGMOD*, pages 171–182, 1997.

[27] S. Krishnan, J. Wang, M. J. Franklin, K. Goldberg, and T. Kraska. Stale view cleaning: Getting fresh answers from stale materialized views. *PVLDB*, 8(12):1370–1381, 2015.

[28] J. Li, K. Tufte, V. Shkapenyuk, V. Papadimos, T. Johnson, and D. Maier. Out-of-order processing: a new architecture for high-performance stream systems. *PVLDB*, 1(1):274–288, 2008.

[29] X. Liu, F. Dobrian, H. Milner, J. Jiang, V. Sekar, I. Stoica, and H. Zhang. A case for a coordinated internet video control plane. In *ACM SIGCOMM 2012 Conference, SIGCOMM '12, Helsinki, Finland - August 13 - 17, 2012*, pages 359–370, 2012.

[30] R. Motwani, J. Widom, A. Arasu, B. Babcock, S. Babu, M. Datar, G. Manku, C. Olston, J. Rosenstein, and R. Varma. Query processing, approximation, and resource management in a data stream management system, 2002.

[31] T. Palpanas, R. Sidle, R. Cochrane, and H. Pirahesh. Incremental maintenance for non-distributive aggregate functions. In *PVLDB*, pages 802–813, 2002.

[32] N. Pansare, V. R. Borkar, C. Jermaine, and T. Condie. Online aggregation for large mapreduce jobs. volume 4, pages 1135–1145, 2011.

[33] A. Pol and C. Jermaine. Relational confidence bounds are easy with the bootstrap. In *SIGMOD*, pages 587–598, 2005.

[34] L. Sidirourgos, M. L. Kersten, and P. A. Boncz. Sciborq: Scientific data management with bounds on runtime and quality. In *CIDR*, volume 11, pages 296–301, 2011.

[35] H. Thakkar, N. Laptev, H. Mousavi, B. Mozafari, V. Russo, and C. Zaniolo. SMM: A data stream management system for knowledge discovery. In *ICDE*, pages 757–768, 2011.

[36] S. Tirthapura and D. P. Woodruff. A general method for estimating correlated aggregates over a data stream. In *ICDE*, pages 162–173, 2012.

[37] J. Yang and J. Widom. Incremental computation and maintenance of temporal aggregates. In *ICDE*, pages 51–60, 2001.

[38] K. Zeng, S. Agarwal, A. Dave, M. Armbrust, and I. Stoica. G-OLA: generalized on-line aggregation for interactive analysis on big data. In *SIGMOD*, pages 913–918, 2015.

[39] K. Zeng, S. Gao, B. Mozafari, and C. Zaniolo. The analytical bootstrap: A new method for fast error estimation in approximate query processing. In *SIGMOD*, pages 277–288, 2014.

APPENDIX

A. RELATIONAL ALGEBRA WITH BAG SEMANTICS

In this paper, we generalize multiset relations to tuple multiplicities that are real numbers. Formally, a multiset relation R maps all tuples with schema U (we denote this set of tuples as U-Tup) to tuple multiplicities, i.e., $R : U\text{-Tup} \to \mathbb{R}$. That is, $R(t)$ represents the multiplicity of tuple t in relation R. We focus on positive relational algebra, i.e., queries that can be composed using operators `SELECT`, `PROJECT`, `JOIN`, `UNION` and `AGGREGATE`. Note that we use the SQL version of `PROJECT` and `UNION` which are without duplicate elimination. Duplicate elimination can be expressed using `AGGREGATE`, and thus not explicitly discussed here.

- `SELECT`: If $R : U\text{-Tup} \to \mathbb{R}$ and the selection predicate θ maps each tuple to either 0 or 1, then $\sigma_\theta R : U\text{-Tup} \to \mathbb{R}$ is defined by

$$(\sigma_\theta R)(t) = R(t) \cdot \theta(t)$$

- `PROJECT`: If $R : U\text{-Tup} \to \mathbb{R}$ and ψ_i is a tuple function, then $\pi_{\overline{A_i = \psi_i}} R : U\text{-Tup} \to \mathbb{R}$ is defined by

$$(\pi_{\vec{A}} R)(t) = R(t')$$

where $t.A_i = \psi_i(t')$ for $\forall i$.

- `JOIN`: If $R_i : U_i\text{-Tup} \to \mathbb{R}$ for $i = 1, 2$, then $R_1 \bowtie R_2 : U\text{-Tup} \to \mathbb{R}$ is defined by

$$(R_1 \bowtie R_2)(t) = R_1(t_1) \cdot R_2(t_2)$$

where $t_i = t$ on schema U_i for $i = 1, 2$.

- `UNION`: If $R_1, R_2 : U\text{-Tup} \to \mathbb{R}$, then $R_1 \cup R_2 : U\text{-Tup} \to \mathbb{R}$ is defined by

$$(R_1 \cup R_2)(t) = R_i(t)$$

where $i = 1$ or 2 and $t \in R_i$.

- `AGGREGATE`: If $R : U\text{-Tup} \to \mathbb{R}$ and Ψ is an aggregate function, then $\gamma_{\bar{A},\Psi} R : U\text{-Tup} \to \mathbb{R}$ is defined by

$$(\gamma_{\bar{A},\Psi} R)(t) = \sum_{t'=t \text{ on } \bar{A}} R(t')$$

B. OPTIMIZING DELTA UPDATE STATES

The optimizations of viewlet transformation proposed in DBToaster [10] can be translated into a set of query rewriting rules, By applying these query rewriting rules, we can rewrite a query into an equivalent query, which can reduce the size of the states maintained by our delta update algorithm proposed in Section 4.2. Using the query rewriting rules in combination with our delta update rules, we can achieve the same higher-order view maintenance ideas as in DBToaster. Below are the equivalent query rewriting rules of the viewlet transformation rules as listed in Figure 2 of [10].

- **Query Decomposition**

$$\gamma_{\bar{A}\bar{B},\Psi=sum(f_1 \times f_2)}(Q_1 \bowtie Q_2) = \gamma_{\bar{A}\bar{B},\Psi_3=sum(\Psi_1 \times \Psi_2)}(\gamma_{\bar{A},\Psi_1=sum(f_1)}(Q_1) \bowtie \gamma_{\bar{B},\Psi_2=sum(f_2)}(Q_2)) \quad (1)$$

where Q_1 and Q_2 have no common columns; $\bar{A}$ and $\bar{B}$ are the group-by terms of each.

This optimization rule pushes group-by `AGGREGATE` below `JOIN`, which can help reduce the state of `JOIN`. For instance, assuming Q_2 has tuple uncertainties, before rewriting, we need to save all tuples from Q_1 without tuple uncertainty in the state, which is of size $|Q_1|$; in contrast, after rewriting, the state is reduced to all tuples from $\gamma_{\bar{A},\Psi_1=sum(f_1)}(Q_1)$ without tuple uncertainty, whose size is the number of distinct $\bar{A}$ in Q_1.

- **Factorization and Polynomial Expansion**

$$(Q \bowtie Q_1) \cup (Q \bowtie Q_2) \cup \cdots = Q \bowtie (Q_1 \cup Q_2 \cup \cdots) \quad (2)$$

This optimization rule can pull common subexpressions out of `UNION`. When $Q_1, Q_2, \cdots$ have tuple uncertainties, instead of keep Q as the state for each `JOIN` in the left hand size of Equation 2, we only need to save Q as the state for the only `JOIN` in the right hand side.

- **Input Variables**

$$\gamma_{\bar{A},\Psi=sum(f(\overline{BC}))}(\sigma_{\theta(\overline{BC})}(Q)) = \gamma_{\bar{A},\Psi_2=sum(f(\bar{B}\bar{C}))}(\sigma_{\theta(\bar{B}\bar{C})}(\gamma_{\bar{A}\bar{B},\Psi_1=sum(1)}(Q))) \quad (3)$$

where f, θ are functions over columns; $\bar{B}$ is the columns in Q used by f, θ; $\bar{C}$ is a column that do not appear in Q.

This optimization rule push `AGGREGATE` below `SELECT`, which can reduce the state of `SELECT`. If the predicate θ causes tuple uncertainty, this rewriting rules can compress multiple tuples in the state that are from Q and with the same $\bar{A}\bar{B}$ columns into a single tuple from $\gamma_{\bar{A}\bar{B},\Psi_1=sum(1)}(Q)$.

- **Nested Aggregates and Decorrelation**

$$\gamma_{\bar{A},\Psi=sum(f)}(\sigma_{\theta(\bar{B},\bar{C})}(Q_O \bowtie Q_N)) = \gamma_{\bar{A},\Psi_2=sum(1)}(\sigma_{\theta(\bar{B},\bar{C})}(\gamma_{\bar{A}\bar{B},\Psi_1=sum(f)}(Q_O) \bowtie Q_N)) \quad (4)$$

where Q_N is a nested non-grouping aggregate subquery; f, θ are functions over columns; $\bar{A}$ is columns from Q_O; $\bar{B}$ is the columns in Q_O used by f, θ; $\bar{C}$ is the columns in Q_N used by θ; Q_O and Q_N have no common columns.

This optimization rule works similarly to the input variable rule above, by pushing `AGGREGATE` below `SELECT`. This rule reduces the state of `SELECT` by compressing multiple tuples in the state which are from $Q_O \bowtie Q_N$ and with the same $\bar{A}\bar{B}$ columns into a single tuple from $\gamma_{\bar{A}\bar{B},\Psi_1=sum(f)}(Q_O) \bowtie Q_N$.

Next we show an example to demonstrate how these rewriting rules work.

EXAMPLE 4. *Given two relations R (of two columns AB) and S (of two columns CD), and query*

```
SELECT SUM(A * D)
FROM R, S
WHERE B = C
```

Assume that both R and S are streamed in, and thus we need to keep all the tuples seen so far from both R and S as the state of `JOIN`. By applying Query Decomposition rule, we can rewrite the above query into $\gamma_{AB,\Psi_3(\Psi_1 \times \Psi_2)}(\gamma_{B,\Psi_1=sum(A)}(R) \bowtie_{B=C} \gamma_{C,\Psi_2=sum(D)}(S))$. After the rewriting, for `JOIN`, we only need to save $\gamma_{B,\Psi_1=sum(A)}(R)$ and $\gamma_{C,\Psi_2=sum(D)}(S))$ as the state, which is equivalent to the higher order view $\Delta_R(S)$ and $\Delta_S(R)$ in [10]'s terminology.

C. IMPLEMENTATION OF IOLAP

Given a query, `iOLAP` automatically rewrites it into a delta query. The delta query is a normal SQL query, but enhancing the original query with error estimation, uncertainty tagging, lineage propagation, and lazy evaluation. The rewriting consists of 4 steps:

1. At compile time, the compiler analyzes the query plan, tagging each attribute (including the multiplicity column) with its corresponding uncertainty by following the propagation rules in Section 4.1.
2. After that, we add bootstrap into the query plan to support error estimation. We use a poissonized bootstrap implementation proposed in [8]. Specifically, we insert columns representing bootstrap-generated multiplicities after scanning the streamed relations. These multiplicity columns take random values from a $Poisson(1)$ distribution, and are propagated downstream. Consequently, all the downstream `AGGREGATE` operators are modified to use these multiplicity columns, and thus all the uncertain attributes throughout the plan are duplicated to multiple instances, each one corresponding to one bootstrap trial.
3. After modifying the plan for bootstrap, we further add uncertainty propagation and lineage propagation support into the plan. For each operator that may produce tuple uncertainty, we insert a new column in its output to keep the tuple uncertainty, and propagate it to downstream operators. For each operator whose output has uncertain attributes, we insert the lineages of the uncertain attributes as columns into its output, and propagate them through the plan.
4. The compiler then replaces the operators in the plan with their online counterparts, and inserts join and project operators to implement lazy evaluation as described in Section 6.

D. MORE EXPERIMENTS

D.1 End-to-End Performance

We study the performance of `iOLAP` and `HDA` by comparing the query latency used by them to process (1) all the data, (2) a 5% sample, and (3) a 10% sample. The results on TPC-H and Conviva are de-

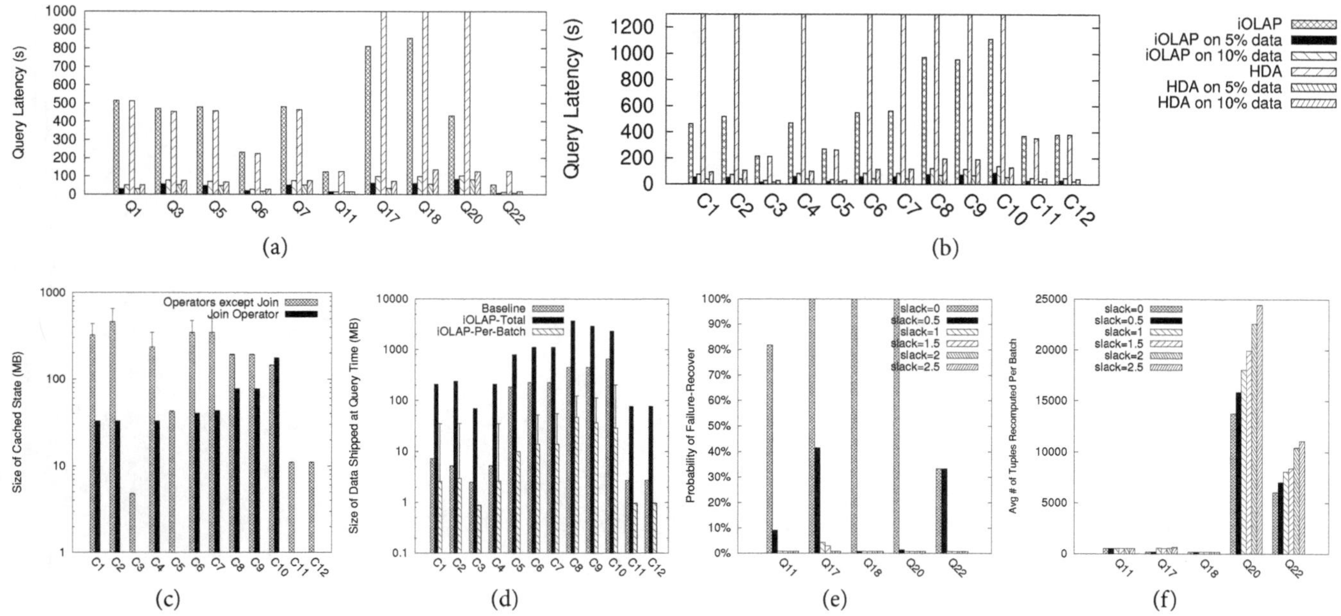

Figure 10: (a) and (b) The query times of iOLAP and HDA to deliver approximate results on all the data, as well as 5% and 10% samples for TPC-H and Conviva workloads respectively. (c) The state sizes saved by iOLAP for Conviva. We plot the all-batch total state sizes across all batches for JOIN, and the average and max (as error bars) per-batch state sizes for other operators. (d) The size of data shipped by the baseline and iOLAP for Conviva. We plot the all-batch total data size (iOLAP-Total), and the average and max (as error bars) per-batch data size (iOLAP-Per-Batch). (e) and (f) The relationship of the slack parameter vs. the probability of failure-recover, and the slack parameter vs. the size of non-deterministic set on TPC-H respectively.

picted in Figure 10(a) and 10(b) respectively. As we can see, for simple SPJA queries, such as TPC-H Q1, Q3, Q5, Q6, Q7, Q11, Q22, and Conviva C3, C5, C11, C12, iOLAP and HDA have comparable performance. For complex queries with nested subqueries, HDA's overhead quickly accumulate up: The query latencies of HDA on 10% samples have already exceeded those of iOLAP. When processing all the data, HDA took much longer time than iOLAP. Actually most of the complex queries did not finish in a reasonable time, and the bars get cut off in the figures.

D.2 Memory Utilization of iOLAP

We study the memory overhead caused by keeping states for various operators on Conviva. The results are plotted in Figure 10(c), which shows that all the operators, including JOIN, keep only a few hundreds of MBs states across all iterations.

We study the data footprint overhead of the bootstrap and lineage propagation of iOLAP on Conviva, as shown in Figure 10(d). Because the Conviva dataset has a single fact table, all Conviva queries fall into the category of queries that only ship AGGREGATE results . It is clear that iOLAP-Total has a < 5GB overhead compared to the baseline. And the data footprint of iOLAP-Per-Batch is 1-2 orders of magnitude smaller than that of the baseline.

D.3 Parameter Tuning

We experiment with different slack parameter settings to see how it impact the probability of failure-recovery and the size of non-deterministic set on the TPC-H workload. We plot the results in Figure 10(e) and 10(f). Similar to the results on Conviva, with the slack increasing, the probability of failure-recovery quickly decrease to 0; in contrast, the size of non-deterministic sets increases slowly.

Dynamic Prefetching of Data Tiles for Interactive Visualization

Leilani Battle
MIT
Cambridge, MA 02139
leilani@csail.mit.edu

Remco Chang
Tufts University
Medford, MA 02155
remco@cs.tufts.edu

Michael Stonebraker
MIT
Cambridge, MA 02139
stonebraker@csail.mit.edu

ABSTRACT

In this paper, we present ForeCache, a general-purpose tool for exploratory browsing of large datasets. ForeCache utilizes a client-server architecture, where the user interacts with a lightweight client-side interface to browse datasets, and the data to be browsed is retrieved from a DBMS running on a back-end server. We assume a detail-on-demand browsing paradigm, and optimize the back-end support for this paradigm by inserting a separate middleware layer in front of the DBMS. To improve response times, the middleware layer fetches data ahead of the user as she explores a dataset.

We consider two different mechanisms for prefetching: (a) learning what to fetch from the user's recent movements, and (b) using data characteristics (*e.g.*, histograms) to find data similar to what the user has viewed in the past. We incorporate these mechanisms into a single prediction engine that adjusts its prediction strategies over time, based on changes in the user's behavior. We evaluated our prediction engine with a user study, and found that our dynamic prefetching strategy provides: (1) significant improvements in overall latency when compared with non-prefetching systems (430% improvement); and (2) substantial improvements in both prediction accuracy (25% improvement) and latency (88% improvement) relative to existing prefetching techniques.

1. INTRODUCTION

Exploratory browsing helps users analyze large amounts of data quickly by rendering the data at interactive speeds within a viewport of fixed size (*e.g.*, a laptop screen). This is of particular interest to data scientists, because they do not have the time or resources to analyze billions of datapoints by hand. One common interaction pattern we have observed in data scientists is that they analyze a small region within a larger dataset, and then move to a nearby region and repeat the same analysis. They initially aggregate or sample these regions when looking for a quick answer, and zoom into the raw data when an exact answer is needed. Thus, we focus on supporting a detail-on-demand browsing paradigm, where users can move to different regions within a single dataset, and zoom into these regions to see them in greater detail.

While users want to be able to drill down into specific regions of a dataset, they also want their actions within the browsing tool to be fluid and interactive. Even one second of delay after a pan or zoom can be frustrating for users, hindering their analyses and distracting them from what the data has to offer [17, 15]. Thus, the goal of this project is to make all user interactions extremely fast (*i.e.*, 500 ms or less), thereby providing a seamless exploration experience for users. However, although modern database management systems (DBMS's) allow users to perform complex scientific analyses over large datasets [20], DBMS's are not designed to respond to queries at interactive speeds, resulting in long interaction delays for browsing tools that must wait for answers from a backend DBMS [2]. Thus, new optimization techniques are needed to address the non-interactive performance of modern DBMS's, within the context of exploratory browsing.

In this paper, we present ForeCache, a general-purpose tool for interactive browsing of large datasets. Given that data scientists routinely analyze datasets that do not fit in main memory, ForeCache utilizes a client-server architecture, where users interact with a lightweight client-side interface, and the data to be explored is retrieved from a back-end server running a DBMS. We use the array-based DBMS SciDB as the back-end [23], and insert a middleware layer in front of the DBMS, which utilizes prefetching techniques and a main-memory cache to speedup server-side performance.

When the user performs zooms in ForeCache, she expects to see more detail from the underlying data. To support multiple levels of detail, we apply aggregation queries to the raw data. However, complex scientific analyses take time, and may not execute at interactive speeds in the DBMS. To ensure that zooms are fast in ForeCache, we compute each level of detail, or *zoom level*, beforehand, and store them on disk. A separate materialized view is created for each zoom level, and we partition each zoom level into equal-size blocks, or *data tiles* [16].

The user cycles through the following steps when browsing data in ForeCache: (1) she analyzes the result of the previous request, (2) performs an action in the interface to update or refine the request (*e.g.*, zooms in), and then (3) waits for the result to be rendered on the screen. ForeCache eliminates step 3 by prefetching neighboring tiles and storing them in main memory while the user is still in step 1, thereby providing the user with a seamless browsing ex-

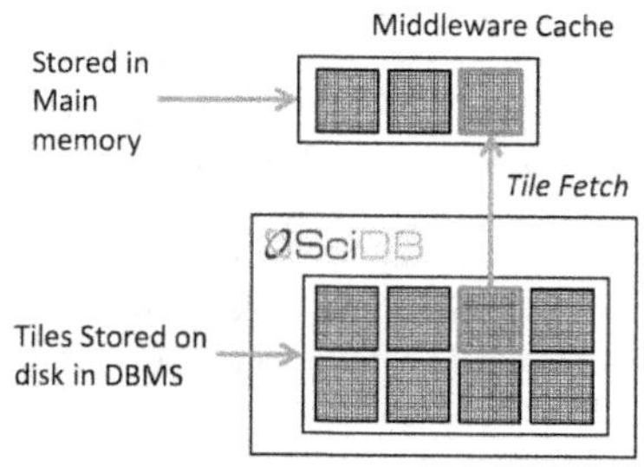

Figure 1: A diagram of ForeCache's tile storage scheme.

SIGMOD'16, June 26-July 01, 2016, San Francisco, CA, USA

DOI: http://dx.doi.org/10.1145/2882903.2882919

perience. At the middleware level, we incorporate a main-memory cache for fetching computed tiles, shown in Figure 1. When tiles are prefetched, they are copied from SciDB to the cache. However, in a multi-user environment, there may be too little space on the server to cache all neighboring tiles for every user. Furthermore, we may only have time to fetch a small number of tiles before the user's next request. Thus, we must rank the tiles first, and fetch only the most likely candidates.

While prefetching is known to be effective, ForeCache needs access to the user's past interactions with the interface to predict future data requests. We have observed that the client has extensive records of the user's past interactions, which we can leverage to improve our prefetching strategy. For example, the client knows what regions the user has visited in the past, and what actions she has recently performed. One straightforward optimization is to train a Markov model on the user's past actions, and to use this model to predict the user's future actions [6, 8]. We refer to these prediction techniques as *recommendation models* throughout this paper.

However, the user's actions are often too complex to be described by a single model (which we will show in Section 5). Thus, existing models only cover a fraction of possible analysis goals, leading to longer user wait times due to prediction errors. A comprehensive approach is needed, such that we can consistently prefetch the right tiles over a diverse range of high-level analysis goals.

To address the limitations of existing techniques, we have designed a new two-level prediction engine for our middleware. At the top level, our prediction engine learns the user's current *analysis phase* (i.e., *her current frame of mind*), given her most recent actions. The user's analysis phase hints at her current analysis goals, and thus provides context for which actions in the interface she may use to reach her goals. We provide examples of analysis phases in the following paragraph. Furthermore, users frequently employ several low-level browsing patterns within each analysis phase (*e.g.,* panning right three times in a row). Therefore at the bottom level, our prediction engine runs multiple recommendation models in parallel, each designed to model a specific low-level browsing pattern. Using this two-level design, our prediction engine tracks changes in the user's current analysis phase, and updates its prediction strategy accordingly. To do this, we increase or decrease the space allotted to each low-level recommendation model for predictions.

Taking inspiration from other user analysis models [19], we have observed that the space of user interaction patterns can be partitioned into three separate analysis phases: Foraging (analyzing individual tiles at a coarse zoom level to form a new hypothesis), Sensemaking (comparing neighboring tiles at a detailed zoom level to test the current hypothesis), and Navigation (moving between coarse and detailed zoom levels to transition between the previous two phases). The user's goal changes depending on which phase she is currently in. For example, in the Navigation phase, the user is shifting the focus of her analysis from one region in the dataset to another. In contrast, the user's goal in the Foraging phase is to find new regions that exhibit interesting data patterns.

We consider two separate mechanisms for our low-level recommendation models: (a) learning what to fetch based on the user's past movements (*e.g.,* given that the the user's last three moves were all to "pan right," what should be fetched?) [8]; and (b) using data-derived characteristics, or *signatures*, to identify neighboring tiles that are similar to what the user has requested in the past. We use a Markov chain to model the first mechanism, and a suite of signatures for the second mechanism, ranging from simple statistics (*e.g.,* histograms) to sophisticated machine vision features.

To evaluate ForeCache, we conducted a user study, where domain scientists explored satellite imagery data. Our results show that ForeCache achieves (near) interactive speeds for data exploration (*i.e.,* average latency within 500 ms). We also found that ForeCache achieves: (1) dramatic improvements in latency compared with traditional non-prefetching systems (430% improvement in latency); and (2) higher prediction accuracy (25% better accuracy) and significantly lower latency (88% improvement in latency), compared to existing prefetching techniques.

In this paper, we make the following contributions:

1. We propose a new three-phase analysis model to describe how users generally explore array-based data.
2. We present a tile-based data model for arrays, and architecture for enabling interactive exploration of tiles in SciDB,
3. We present our two-level prediction engine, with an SVM classifier at the top level to predict the user's current analysis phase, and recommendation models at the bottom to predict low-level interaction patterns.
4. We present the results from our user study. Our results show that our approach provides higher prediction accuracy and significantly lower latency, compared to existing techniques.

1.1 Background

ForeCache relies on a diverse set of prediction components and user inputs. Here, we provide an overview of the main concepts utilized in ForeCache, some of which were introduced in Section 1.

User Interactions/Moves: The user's interactions with ForeCache are the actions she makes in the front-end interface to explore her data. We also refer to these interactions as *moves*.

User Session: A user session refers to a single session for which the user has logged into ForeCache and explored a single dataset.

Data Model: The ForeCache data model defines: (1) the structure and layout of data tiles, and (2) how to build data tiles. We explain the ForeCache data model in detail in Section 2.

Analysis Model: Our analysis model is defined by our three analysis phases, and how these phases interact with each other. We explain our analysis model in detail in Section 4.2.

Analysis Phase: The user's current analysis phase represents her frame of mind while exploring data in ForeCache (*i.e.,* Foraging, Navigation, or Sensemaking). Analysis phases can be inferred through the user's interactions; we explain how we predict analysis phases in Section 4.2.2.

Browsing Patterns: Low-level browsing patterns are short chains of interactions repeated by the user (*e.g.,* zooming in three times). We explain how we predict these patterns in Section 4.3.

Recommendation Model: A recommendation model is an algorithm used to predict low-level browsing patterns (*e.g.,* Markov chains). ForeCache employs two kinds of recommendation models: Action-Based (Section 4.3.2) and Signature-Based (Section 4.3.3).

2. DATA MODEL

In this section, we describe the kinds of datasets supported by ForeCache, and our process for building zoom levels and data tiles.

2.1 Datasets Supported by ForeCache

The datasets that work best with ForeCache share the same properties that make SciDB performant: (a) the majority of column types are numerical (integers, floats, etc.), and (b) the relative position of points within these columns matters (*e.g.,* comparing points in time, or in latitude-longitude position). These properties ensure that the underlying arrays are straightforward to aggregate, partition, and visualize in ForeCache. The following three example datasets share these properties: geospatial data (*e.g.,* satellite im-

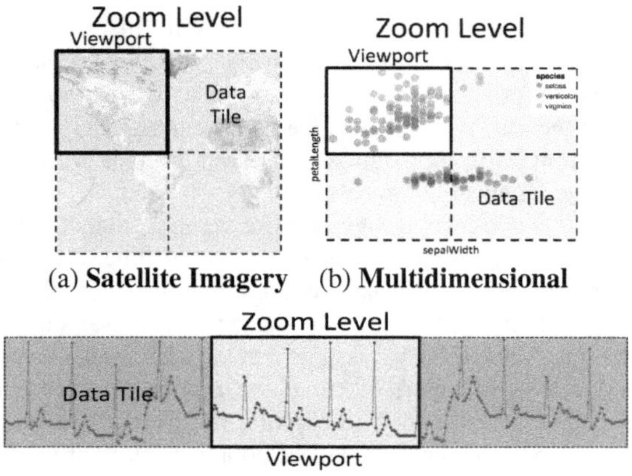

(a) **Satellite Imagery** (b) **Multidimensional**

(c) **Timeseries (Heart rate Monitoring)**

Figure 2: Potential tiling schemes for three types of data.

agery in Figure 2a), multidimensional data (*e.g.,* iris flower classification in Figure 2b), and time series data (*e.g.,* heart rate monitoring in Figure 2c). Beyond these three examples, SciDB has also been used for efficiently analyzing genomics data [24] and astronomy data [22]. Given its extensive support for complex analytics over multidimensional datasets, we use SciDB as the back-end DBMS in ForeCache.

Consider Figure 2a, where the user is exploring an array of snow cover measurements computed from satellite imagery. Each array cell has been mapped to a pixel, where orange and yellow pixels correspond to snow. We have partitioned the current zoom level along the array's two dimensions (latitude and longitude), resulting in four data tiles. The user's current viewport is located at the top left data tile; the user can move to other tiles by panning in the client-side interface. The user can also zoom in or out to explore different zoom levels.

2.2 Interactions Supported by ForeCache

In this paper, we focus on supporting data exploration through two-dimensional (2D) views, where exploration means that the user can browse, but not modify the underlying dataset. In addition, we assume that users are interacting with the data using consistent, incremental actions that only retrieve a fraction of the underlying dataset. For example, if the user wants to go from zoom level 0 to 4 in ForeCache, she must go through levels 1, 2, and 3 first. Otherwise, users are essentially performing random accesses on the underlying data, which are generally difficult to optimize for any back-end DBMS (*e.g.,* "jumping" to any location in the dataset).

These assumptions define a specific class of exploration interfaces, characterized by the following four rules: (a) the interface supports a finite set of interactions (*i.e.,* no open-ended text boxes); (b) these interactions cannot modify the underlying dataset; (c) each interaction will request only a small fraction of data tiles; and (d) each interaction represents an incremental change to the user's current location in the dataset (*i.e.,* no "jumping"). Note that given rule (c), ForeCache does not currently support interactions that force a full scan of the entire dataset, such as searches (*e.g.,* find all satellite imagery pixels with a snowcover value above 0.7).

2.3 Building Data Tiles

To improve performance, ForeCache builds all data tiles in advance, and stores them on disk in SciDB. In this section, we explain how ForeCache builds zoom levels and data tiles in advance, which is done in three steps: (1) building a separate materialized view for each zoom level; (2) partitioning each zoom level into non-overlapping blocks of fixed size (*i.e.,* data tiles); and (3) computing any necessary metadata (*e.g.,* data statistics) for each data tile. The most detailed zoom level (*i.e.,* highest resolution) is just the raw data without any aggregation.

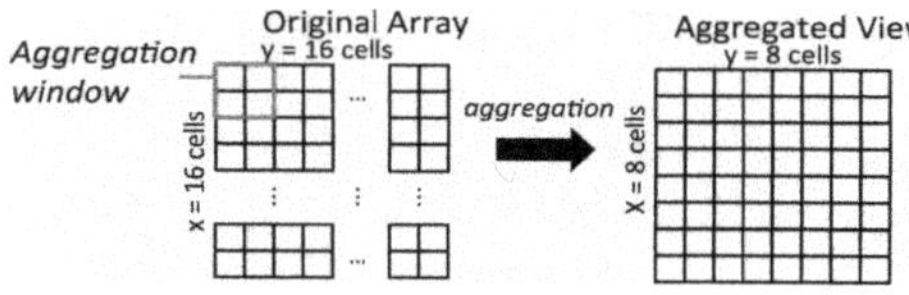

Figure 3: A 16x16 array being aggregated down to an 8x8 array with aggregation parameters $(2,2)$.

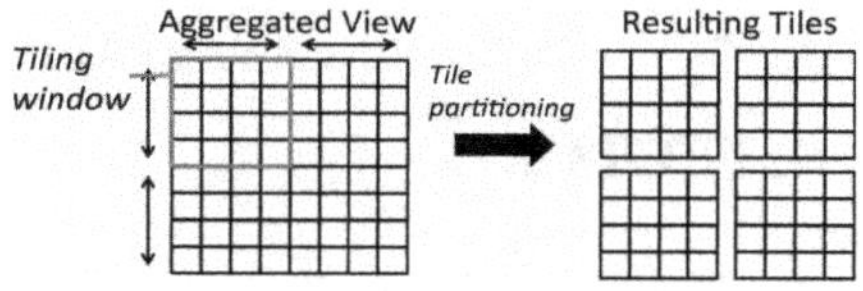

Figure 4: A zoom level being partitioned into four tiles, with tiling parameters $(4,4)$.

Building Materialized Views: To build a materialized view, we apply an aggregation query to the raw data, where the aggregation parameters dictate how detailed the resulting zoom level will be. These parameters form a tuple $(j_1,j_2,...,j_d)$, where d is the number of dimensions. Each parameter j specifies an aggregation interval over the corresponding dimension, where every j array cells along this dimension are aggregated into a single cell. Consider Figure 3, where we have a 16x16 array (on the left), with two dimensions labeled x and y, respectively. Aggregation parameters of $(2,2)$ correspond to aggregating every 2 cells along dimension x, and every 2 cells along dimension y (*i.e.,* the red box in Figure 3). If we compute the average cell value for each window in the 16x16 array, the resulting array will have dimensions 8x8 (right side of Figure 3).

Partitioning the Views: Next, we partition each computed zoom level into data tiles. To do this, we assign a tiling interval to each dimension, which dictates the number of aggregated cells contained in each tile along this dimension. For example, consider our aggregated 8x8 view in Figure 4. If we specify a tiling window of $(4,4)$, ForeCache will partition this view into four separate data tiles, each with the dimensions we specified in our tiling parameters (4x4).

We choose the aggregation and tiling parameters such that one tile at zoom level i translates to four higher-resolution tiles at level $i+1$. To do this, we calculated our zoom levels bottom-up (*i.e.,* starting at the raw data level), multiplying our aggregation intervals by 2 for each coarser zoom level going upward. We then applied the same tiling intervals to every zoom level. Thus, all tiles have the same dimensions (*i.e.,* tile size), regardless of zoom level.

Computing Metadata: Last, ForeCache computes any necessary metadata for each data tile. For example, some of our recommendation models rely on data characteristics, or signatures, to be computed for each tile, such as histograms or machine vision features (see Section 4 for more detail). As ForeCache processes each tile and zoom level, this metadata is computed and stored in a shared data structure for later use by our prediction engine.

Choosing a Tile Size: Pre-computing tiles ensures that ForeCache provides consistently fast performance across zoom levels. However, choosing a bad tile size can negatively affect performance. For example, increasing the tile size reduces the number of tiles that can be stored in the middleware cache (assuming a fixed cache size), which could reduce ForeCache's prefetching capabilities. In our evaluation (Section 5), we take this into account by varying the number of tiles that are prefetched by ForeCache in our experiments. We plan to perform an in-depth study of how tiling parameters affect performance as future work.

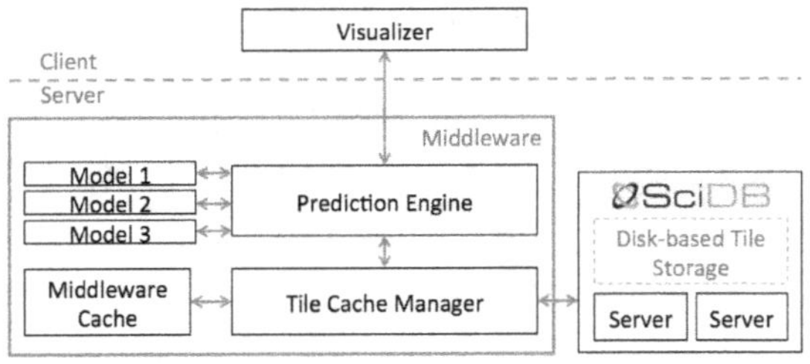

Figure 5: Overview of the ForeCache architecture.

3. ARCHITECTURE

ForeCache has four primary components, illustrated in Figure 5: a web-based visualization interface on the client; a prediction engine; a tile cache manager; and the back-end DBMS. The visualizer sends tile requests to the tile prediction engine, and the prediction engine then sends these requests to the cache manager for retrieval. To anticipate the user's future requests, the prediction engine sends predictions to the cache manager to be fetched ahead of time. The cache manager stores predicted tiles in the middleware tile cache, and retrieves tiles requested by the client from either the middleware cache or SciDB. We elaborate on the first three components of the ForeCache architecture in the rest of this section.

Front-End Visualizer: ForeCache is agnostic to the front-end visualizer, which can be implemented in any language or platform on the client. The only requirement is that the visualizer must communicate with the back-end through tile requests. For our experiments, we implemented a lightweight visualizer that runs in a web browser on the client machine (see Section 5 for more details).

Prediction Engine: The purpose of the prediction engine is to manage ForeCache's tile requests, which consists of two major tasks: responding to tile requests from the client; and managing both the high-level (analysis phase classifier) and low-level (recommendation models) predictions used to infer the user's future requests. To fulfill existing tile requests, the prediction engine retrieves requested tiles from the cache manager, and sends them back to the client for visualization. This component also manages ForeCache's predictions. At the top-most level, this component runs an SVM classifier that predicts the user's current analysis phase. At the lower level, the prediction engine manages several tile recommendation models running in parallel. These recommendation models make suggestions for what data tiles to fetch, and the actual fetching of the tiles is left to the cache manager. After each user request, the prediction engine retrieves a separate list of predictions from each recommender, and forwards these predictions to the cache manager for further processing. We describe our SVM classifier and recommendation models in detail in Section 4.

Tile Cache Manager: The cache manager decides which tiles will be stored in the main-memory middleware cache. Each recommendation model is allotted a limited amount of space in this cache to make predictions. The remaining space in the middleware cache is used to store the last n tiles requested by the interface. We refer to the allocations made to our recommendation models as the cache manager's current *allocation strategy*. This allocation strategy is reevaluated after each request to ensure that space is allocated efficiently across all models. We explain how we update these allocations in Section 4. The cache manger then uses the tile recommendations from the prediction engine to fill the cache once the allocations have been updated.

4. PREDICTION ENGINE DESIGN

The goal of our prediction engine is to identify changes in the user's browsing patterns, and update its prediction strategy accordingly. In this way, our prediction engine ensures that the most relevant prediction algorithms are being used to prefetch data tiles. To do this, our prediction engine makes predictions at two separate levels. At the top level, it learns the user's current analysis phase. At the bottom level, it models the observed analysis phase with a suite of recommendation models.

We chose a two-level design because we have found that users frequently switch their browsing patterns over time. In contrast, recommendation models make strict assumptions about the user's browsing patterns, and thus ignore changes in the user's behavior. For example, Markov chains assume that the user's past moves will always be good indicators of her future actions. However, once the user finds a new region to explore, the panning actions that she used to locate this region will be poor predictors of the future zooming actions she will use to move towards this new region. As a result, we have found that recommendation models only work well in specific cases, making any individual model a poor choice for predicting the user's entire browsing session.

However, if we can learn what a user is trying to do, we can identify the analysis phase that best matches her current goals, and apply the corresponding recommendation model(s) to make predictions. To build the top level of our prediction engine, we trained a classifier to predict the user's current analysis phase, given her past tile requests. To build the bottom level of our prediction engine, we developed a suite of recommendation models to capture the different browsing patterns exhibited in our analysis phases. To combine the top and bottom levels, we developed three separate allocation strategies for our middleware cache, one for each analysis phase.

In the rest of this section, we formalize the general prediction problem solved by ForeCache, explain the top and bottom level designs for our prediction engine, and discuss how we combine the two levels using our allocation strategies.

4.1 Prediction Formalization

Here, we provide definitions for all inputs to and outputs from ForeCache, and a formalization of our general prediction problem.

User Session History: The user's last n moves are constantly recorded by the cache manager and sent to the prediction engine as an ordered list of user requests: $H = [r_1, r_2, ..., r_n]$. Each request $r_i \in H$ retrieves a particular tile T_{ri}. Note that n (*i.e.,* the history length) is a system parameter set before the current session starts.

Training Data: Training data is used to prepare the prediction engine ahead of time, and is supplied as a set of traces: $\{U_1, U_2, ...\}$. Each trace U_j represents a single user session, and consists of an ordered list of user requests: $U_j = [r_1, r_2, r_3, ...]$.

Allocation Strategy: The cache manager regularly sends the current allocation strategy to the prediction engine: $\{k_1, k_2, ...\}$, were k_1 is the amount of space allocated to recommendation model m_1.

General Prediction Problem: Given a user request r for tile T_r, a set of recommender allocations $\{k_1, k_2, ...\}$, and session history H, compute an ordered list of tiles to prefetch $P = [T_1, T_2, T_3, ...]$, where each tile $T_i \in P$ is at most d moves away from T_r. The first tile (T_1) has highest priority when prefetching tiles. d is a system parameter set before the current session starts (default is $d = 1$).

Only a few of these prediction parameters must be specified by the user: allocation strategies for the tile cache (Section 4.4); distance threshold d (Section 4.3.1); user history length n (Section 4.3.2); and user traces as training data (Sections 4.2.2-4.3.2).

4.2 Top-Level Design

In this section, we explain the three analysis phases that users alternate between while browsing array-based data, and how we use this information to predict the user's current analysis phase.

Table 1: Input features for our SVM phase classifier, computed from traces from our user study (see Section 5 for more details).

Feature Name	Information Recorded	Accuracy for this Feature
X position (in tiles)	X position	0.676
Y position (in tiles)	Y position	0.692
Zoom level	zoom level ID	0.696
Pan flag	1 (if user panned), or 0	0.580
Zoom-in flag	1 (if zoom in), or 0	0.556
Zoom-out flag	1 (if zoom out), or 0	0.448

4.2.1 Learning Analysis Phases

We informally observed several users browsing array-based data in SciDB, searching for common interaction patterns. We used these observed patterns to define a user analysis model, or a general-purpose template for user interactions in ForeCache. Our user analysis model was inspired in part by the well-known Sensemaking model [19]. However, we found that the Sensemaking Model did not accurately represent the behaviors we observed. For example, the Sensemaking model does not explicitly model navigation, which is an important aspect of browsing array data. Thus, we extended existing analysis models to match these observed behaviors. We found that our users alternated between three high-level analysis phases, each representing different user goals: Foraging, Sensemaking, and Navigation. Within each phase, users employed a number of low-level interaction patterns to achieve their goals. We model the low-level patterns separately in the bottom half of our prediction engine, which we describe in detail in Section 4.3.

In the Foraging phase, the user is looking for visually interesting patterns in the data and forming hypotheses. The user will tend to stay at coarser zoom levels during this phase, because these levels allow the user to scan large sections of the dataset for visual patterns that she may want to investigate further. In the Sensemaking phase, the user has identified a region of interest (or ROI), and is looking to confirm an initial hypothesis. During this phase, the user stays at more detailed zoom levels, and analyzes neighboring tiles to determine if the pattern in the data supports or refutes her hypothesis. Finally, during the Navigation phase, the user performs zooming operations to move between the coarse zoom levels of the Foraging phase and detailed zoom levels of the Sensemaking phase.

4.2.2 Predicting the Current Analysis Phase

The top half of our two-level scheme predicts the user's current analysis phase. This problem is defined as follows:

Sub-Problem Definition: given a new user request r and the user's session history H, predict the user's current analysis phase (Foraging, Sensemaking, or Navigation).

To identify the current analysis phase, we apply a Support Vector Machine (SVM) classifier, similar to the work by Brown *et al.* [3]. SVM's are a group of supervised learning techniques that are frequently used for classification and regression tasks. We used a multi-class SVM classifier with a RBF kernel. We implemented our classifier using the LibSVM Java Library[1].

To construct an input to our SVM classifier, we compute a feature vector using the current request r, and the user's previous request $r_n \in H$. The format and significance of each extracted feature in our feature vector is provided in Table 1. Because this SVM classifier only learns from interaction data and relative tile positions, we can apply our classification techniques to any dataset that is amenable to a tile-based format. To build a training dataset for

[1] https://github.com/cjlin1/libsvm

Algorithm 1 Pseudocode to update the last ROI after each request.

Input: A user request r for tile T_r
Output: ROI, a set of tiles representing the user's last visited ROI.

```
1: ROI ← {}
2: temp_ROI ← {}
3: inFlag ← False
4: procedure UPDATEROI(r)
5:     if r.move = "zoom-in" then
6:         inFlag ← True
7:         temp_ROI ← {T_r}
8:     else if r.move = "zoom-out" then
9:         if inFlag = True then
10:            ROI ← temp_ROI
11:        inFlag ← False
12:        temp_ROI ← {}
13:    else if inFlag = True then
14:        add T_r to temp_ROI
15:    return ROI
```

the classifier, we collected user traces from our user study. We then hand-labeled each user request from the user traces with its corresponding analysis phase. We describe our user study and evaluate the accuracy of the analysis phase classifier in Section 5.

4.3 Bottom-Level Design

Once the user's current analysis phase has been identified, ForeCache employs the corresponding recommendation model(s) to predict specific tiles. ForeCache runs these models in parallel, where each model is designed to predict specific low-level browsing patterns. These recommendation models can be categorized into two types of predictions: (a) *Action-Based (AB)*: learning what to predict from the user's previous moves (*e.g.*, pans and zooms); and (b) *Signature-Based (SB)*: learning what to predict by using data characteristics, or *signatures*, from the tiles that the user has recently requested (*e.g.*, histograms). For an individual recommendation model m, the prediction problem is as follows:

Sub-Problem Definition: given a user request r, a set of candidate tiles for prediction C, and the session history H, compute an ordering for the candidate tiles $P_m = [T_1, T_2, ...]$. The ordering signifies m's prediction of how relatively likely the user will request each tile in C. The prediction engine trims P_m as necessary, depending on the amount of space allocated to m.

Here, we describe: (1) the inputs and outputs for our recommendation models; (2) how the individual models were implemented; and (3) how we allocate space to each model per analysis phase.

4.3.1 General Recommendation Model Design

Our Signature-Based recommendation model requires one additional input in order to make predictions: the last location in the dataset that the user explored in detail, which we refer to as the user's most recent *Region of Interest*, or ROI. Here we explain how we derive C, and the user's most recent ROI.

Candidate Tiles for Prediction: We compile the candidate set by finding all tiles that are at most d moves away from r. For example, $d = 1$ represents all tiles that are exactly one move away from r.

Most Recent ROI: We represent the user's most recent ROI as a set of data tiles, and use a simple heuristic to compute this set; the pseudocode is provided in Algorithm 1. When a new user request is received, the prediction engine calls UPDATEROI to update the user's most recent ROI. To find the most recent ROI, this heuristic searches through H for a match to the following pattern: one *zoom-in*, followed by zero or more *pan*'s, followed by one *zoom-out*. In lines 5-7 of Algorithm 1, a *zoom-in* triggers the collection of a new temporary ROI ($temp_{ROI}$), and the requested tile T_r is added to $temp_{ROI}$ (line 7). We track *zoom-in*'s using the $inFlag$ variable

Algorithm 2 Pseudocode showing the Markov chain transition frequencies building process.

Input: For PROCESSTRACES, a set of user traces, and sequence length n.
Output: F, computed transition frequencies.

1: **procedure** PROCESSTRACES($\{U_1, U_2, ..., U_j, ...\}$, n)
2: $F \leftarrow \{\}$
3: **for** user trace U_j **do**
4: $V_j \leftarrow$ GETMOVESEQUENCE(U_j)
5: $F \leftarrow$ UPDATEFREQUENCIES(V_j, F, n)
6: **return** F
7: **procedure** GETMOVESEQUENCE(U_j)
8: $V_j \leftarrow [\,]$
9: **for** $i = 1, 2, ...,$ where $i \leq |V_j|$ **do**
10: $V_j[i] \leftarrow U_j[i].move$
11: **return** V_j
12: **procedure** UPDATEFREQUENCIES($V_j = [v_1, v_2, v_3, ...]$, F, n)
13: **for** $i = n+1, n+2, ...,$ where $n < i \leq |V_j|$ **do**
14: $F[sequence(v_{i-n}, v_{i-(n-1)}, v_{i-(n-2)}, ..., v_{i-1}) \rightarrow v_i]$ += 1
15: **return** F

(line 6). In contrast, an observed *zoom-out* tells the prediction engine to stop adding tiles to $temp_{ROI}$ (lines 8-12). If the $inFlag$ was set while the zoom-out occurred, we replace the user's old ROI with $temp_{ROI}$ (lines 9-10). Then, $temp_{ROI}$ is reset (line 12). Last, if $r.move = pan$ while the $inFlag$ is true, T_r (*i.e.,* the requested tile) is added to $temp_{ROI}$ (lines 13-14).

4.3.2 Actions-Based (AB) Recommender

As the user moves to or from ROI's, she is likely to consistently zoom or pan in a predictable way (*e.g.,* zoom out three times). Doshi *et al.* leverage this assumption in their Momentum model, which predicts that the user's next move will match her previous move [8]. We expand on this idea with our AB recommender, which builds an n-th order Markov chain from users' past actions.

To build the Markov chain, we create a state for each possible sequence of moves, where we only consider sequences of length n (*i.e.,* the length of H). For example, if $n = 3$, then the following are two sequences that would have their own states in the Markov chain: panning left three times (*i.e.,* $left$, $left$, $left$), and zooming out twice and then panning right (*i.e.,* out, out, $right$). After creating our states, we create an outgoing transition from each state for every possible move the user can make in the interface. In the $n = 3$ case, if the user is in state ($left$, $left$, $left$) and then decides to pan right, we represent this as the user taking the edge labeled "*right*" from the state ($left$, $left$, $left$) to the state ($left$, $left$, $right$).

We learn transition probabilities for our Markov chains using traces from our user study; the traces are described in Section 4.1. Algorithm 2 shows how we calculate the transition frequencies needed to compute the final probabilities. For each user trace U_j from the study, we extract the sequence of moves observed in the trace (lines 7-11). We then iterate over every sub-sequence of length n (*i.e.,* every time a state was visited in the trace), and count how often each transition was taken (lines 12-15). To do this, for each sub-sequence observed (*i.e.,* for each state observed from our Markov chain), we identified the move that was made immediately after this sub-sequence occurred, and incremented the relevant counter (line 14). To fill in missing counts, we apply Kneser-Ney smoothing, a well-studied smoothing method in natural language processing for Markov chains [7]. We used the BerkeleyLM [18] Java library to implement our Markov chains.

4.3.3 Signature-Based (SB) Recommender

The goal of our SB recommender is to identify neighboring tiles that are visually similar to what the user has requested in the past.

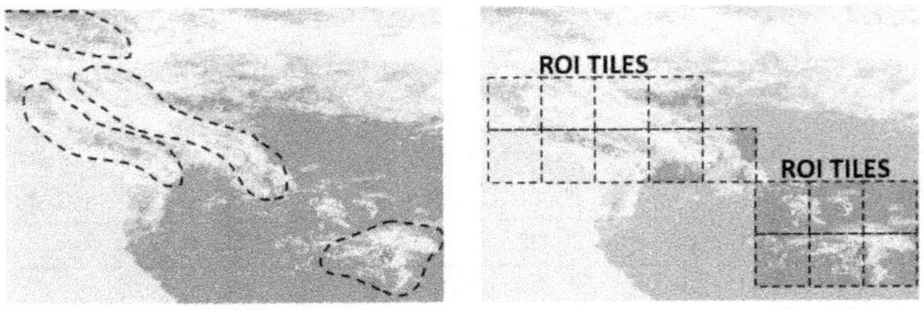

(a) **Potential snow cover ROI's in the US and Canada.** (b) **Tiles in the user's history, after visiting ROI's from (a).**

Figure 6: Example ROI's in the US and Canada for snow cover data. Snow is orange to yellow, snow-free areas in green to blue. Note that (a) and (b) span the same latitude-longitude range.

Table 2: Features computed over individual array attributes in ForeCache to compare data tiles for visual similarity.

Signature	Measures Compared	Visual Characteristics Captured
Normal Distribution	Mean, standard deviation	average position/color/size of rendered datapoints
1-D histogram	histogram bins	position/color/size distribu- -tion of rendered datapoints
SIFT	histogram built from clustered SIFT descriptors	distinct "landmarks" in the visualization (*e.g.,* clusters of orange pixels)
DenseSIFT	same as SIFT	distinct "landmarks" *and* their positions in the visualization

For example, in the Foraging phase, the user is using a coarse view of the data to find new ROI's to explore. When the user finds a new ROI, she zooms into this area until she reaches her desired zoom level. Each tile along her zooming path will share the same visual features, which the user depends on to navigate to her destination. In the Sensemaking phase, the user is analyzing visually similar data tiles at the same zoom level. One such example is when the user is exploring satellite imagery of the earth, and panning to tiles within the same mountain range.

Consider Figure 6a, where the user is exploring snow cover data derived from a satellite imagery dataset. Snow is colored orange, and regions without snow are blue. Thus, the user will search for ROI's that contain large clusters of orange pixels, which are circled in Figure 6a. These ROI's correspond to mountain ranges.

Given the user's last ROI (*i.e.,* the last mountain range the user visited), we can look for neighboring tiles that look similar (*i.e.,* find more mountains). Figure 6b is an example of some tiles that may be in the user's history if she has recently explored some of these ROI's, which we can use for reference to find new ROI's.

We measure visual similarity by computing a diverse set of tile *signatures*. A signature is a compact, numerical representation of a data tile, and is stored as a vector of double-precision values. Table 2 lists the four signatures we compute in ForeCache. All of our signatures are calculated over a single SciDB array attribute. The first signature in Table 2 calculates the average and standard deviation of all values stored within a single data tile. The second signature builds a histogram over these array values, using a fixed number of bins.

We also tested two machine vision techniques as signatures: the scale-invariant feature transform (SIFT), and a variant called denseSIFT (signatures 3 and 4 in Table 2). SIFT is used to identify and compare visual "landmarks" in an image, called *keypoints*. Much like how seeing the Statue of Liberty can help people distinguish pictures of New York city from pictures of other cities, SIFT key-

Algorithm 3 Computes the visual distance of each candidate tile, with respect to a given ROI.

Input: Signatures S_1-S_4, candidate tiles, ROI tiles
Output: A set of distance values D
1: **for** Signature S_i, $i = 1 - 4$ **do**
2: $d_{i,MAX} \leftarrow 1$
3: **for** each candidate tile T_A **do**
4: Retrieve signature $S_i(T_A)$
5: **for** each ROI tile T_B **do**
6: Retrieve signature $S_i(T_B)$
7: **for** each candidate/ROI pair (T_A,T_B) **do**
8: $d_{i,A,B} \leftarrow 2^{d_{manh}(T_A,T_B)-1}[dist_{S_i}(S_i(T_A),S_i(T_B))]$
9: $d_{i,MAX} \leftarrow max(d_{i,MAX}, d_{i,A,B})$
10: **for** each candidate/ROI pair (T_A,T_B) **do**
11: $d_{i,A,B} \leftarrow \frac{d_{i,A,B}}{d_{i,MAX}}$
12: **for** each candidate/ROI pair (T_A,T_B) **do**
13: $d_{A,B} \leftarrow \frac{\sqrt{\sum_{S_i} w_i(d_{i,A,B})^2}}{d_{physical}(A,B)}$
14: **for** each candidate tile T_A **do**
15: $d_A \leftarrow \sum_B d_{A,B}$
return $D = \{d_1, d_2, ..., d_A, ...\}$

points help ForeCache compare visual landmarks in two different visualizations (*e.g.,* two satellite imagery heatmaps with similar clusters of orange pixels, or two line charts showing unusually high peaks in heart-rate signals). We used the OpenCV library to compute our SIFT and denseSIFT signatures[2].

Algorithm 3 outlines how we compare candidate tiles to the user's last ROI using these signatures. We first retrieve all four signatures for each candidate tile (lines 3-4). We also retrieve these four signatures for each ROI tile on lines 5-6. Then we compute how much each candidate tile (T_A) deviates from each ROI tile (T_B), with respect to each signature (lines 7-8). To do this, a distance function for the signature is applied to the candidate tile and ROI tile (denoted as $dist_{S_i}$ in Algorithm 3). Since our signatures do not automatically account for the physical distance between T_A and T_B, we apply a penalty to our signature distances based on the Manhattan distance between the tiles. Since all four of our current signatures produce histograms as output, we use the Chi-Squared distance metric as the distance function for all signatures. We then normalize the computed distance values (lines 10-11).

To produce a single distance measure for a given candidate-ROI pair, we treat the four resulting distance measures as a single vector, and compute the ℓ^2-norm of the vector (lines 12-13). To adjust how much influence each signature has on our final distance measurements, we can modify the ℓ^2-norm function to include weights for each signature. All signatures are assigned equal weight by default, but the user can update these weight parameters as necessary.

$$\ell^2_{weighted}(A,B) = \sqrt{\sum_{S_i} w_i(d_{i,A,B})^2}$$

At this point, there will be multiple distance values calculated for each candidate tile, one per ROI tile. For example, if we have four ROI tiles, then there will be four distance values calculated per candidate tile. We sum these ROI tile distances, so we have a single distance value to compare for each candidate tile (lines 14-15). We then rank the candidates by these final distance values.

Note that it is straightforward to add new signatures to the SB recommender. To add a new signature, one only needs to add: (1) an algorithm for computing the signature over a single data tile, and (2) a new distance function for comparing this signature (if the Chi-Squared distance is not applicable).

[2]http://opencv.org

4.4 Cache Allocation Strategies

In this section, we describe the recommendation models generally associated with each analysis phase, and how we use this information to allocate space to each recommender in our tile cache.

In the Navigation phase, the user is zooming and panning in order to transition between the Foraging and Sensemaking phases. Thus, we expect the AB recommendation model to be most effective for predicting tiles for this phase, and allocate all available cache space to this model.

In the Sensemaking phase, the user is mainly panning to neighboring tiles with similar visual features. Therefore, we expect the SB recommendation model to perform well when predicting tiles for this phase, and allocate all available cache space to this model.

In the Foraging phase, the user is using visual features as cues for where she should zoom in next. When the user finds a ROI that she wants to analyze, the tiles she zooms into to reach this ROI will share the same visual properties. Thus, the SB model should prove useful for this phase. However, the user will also zoom out several times in a row in order to return to the Foraging phase, exhibiting a predictable pattern that can be utilized by the AB model. Therefore, we allocate equal amounts of space to both models for this phase.

5. EXPERIMENTS

Although the goal behind ForeCache is to reduce user wait times, we will demonstrate in Section 5.5 that there is a linear (constant factor) correlation between latency and the accuracy of the prediction algorithm. As such, we claim that we can improve the observed latency in ForeCache by reducing the number of prediction errors that occur when prefetching tiles ahead of the user. Our aim in this section is to show that ForeCache provides significantly better prediction accuracy, and thus lower latency, when compared to existing prefetching techniques.

We validate our claims about user exploration behavior through a user study on NASA MODIS satellite imagery data, and evaluate the prediction accuracy of our two-level prediction engine using traces collected from the study. To validate our hypothesis that prediction accuracy dictates the overall latency of the system, we also measured the average latency observed in ForeCache for each of our prediction techniques.

To test the accuracy of our prediction engine, we conducted three sets of evaluations. We first evaluate each prediction level separately. At the top level, we measure how accurately we can predict the user's current analysis phase. At the bottom level, we measure the overall prediction accuracy of each recommendation model, with respect to each analysis phase, and compare our individual models to existing techniques. Then we compare the accuracy of the full prediction engine to our best performing individual recommendation models, as well as existing techniques. Last, we evaluate the relationship between accuracy and latency, and compare the overall latency of our full prediction engine to existing techniques.

5.1 MODIS Dataset

The NASA MODIS is a satellite instrument that records imagery data. This data is originally recorded by NASA in a three-dimensional array (latitude, longitude and time). Each array cell contains a vector of wavelength measurements, where each wavelength measurement is called a MODIS "band."

One use case for MODIS data is to estimate snow depths in the mountains. One well-known MODIS snow cover algorithm, which we apply in our experiments, is the Normalized Difference Snow Index (NDSI) [21]. The NDSI indicates whether there is snow at a given MODIS pixel (*i.e.,* array cell). A high NDSI value (close to 1.0) means that there is snow at the given pixel, and a low value (close to -1.0) corresponds to no snow cover. The NDSI uses two MODIS bands to calculate this. We label the two bands used in the NDSI as VIS for visible light, and SWIR for short-wave infrared. The NDSI is calculated by applying the following function to each cell of the MODIS array. It is straightforward to translate this transformation into a user-defined function (UDF) in SciDB:

$$NDSI = \frac{(visible\ light\ -\ short\ wave\ infrared)}{(visible\ light\ +\ short\ wave\ infrared)}.$$

5.1.1 *Modifications for User Study*

Our test dataset consisted of NDSI measurements computed over one week of raw NASA MODIS data, where the temporal range of the data was from late October to early November of 2011. We downloaded the raw data directly from the NASA MODIS website[3], and used SciDB's MODIS data loading tool to load the data into SciDB. We applied the NDSI to the raw MODIS data as a user-defined function, and stored the resulting NDSI calculations in a separate array. The NDSI array was roughly 10TB in size when stored in SciDB.

To ensure that participants could complete the study in a timely manner, we chose to simplify the dataset to make exploring it easier and faster. Prior to the study, The NDSI dataset was flattened to a single, one-week window, reducing the total dimensions from three (latitude, longitude, time) to two (latitude and longitude only). The NDSI dataset contained four numeric attributes: maximum, minimum and average NDSI values; and a land/sea mask value that was used to filter for land or ocean pixels in the dataset. ForeCache's tile computation process resulted in nine total zoom levels for this dataset, where each level was a separate layer of data tiles.

5.1.2 *Calculating the NSDI in SciDB*

In this section, we explain how to compute the NSDI in SciDB. We assume that we already have a NDSI UDF written in SciDB, which we refer to as "ndsi_func".

Let S_{VIS} and S_{SWIR} be the SciDB arrays containing recorded data for their respective MODIS bands. We use two separate arrays, as this is the current schema supported by the MODIS data loader for SciDB [20]. S_{VIS} and S_{SWIR} share the same array schema. An example of this schema is provided below.

$$S_{VIS/SWIR}(\text{reflectance})[latitude, longitude].$$

The array attributes are denoted in parentheses (reflectance) and the dimensions are shown in brackets (latitude and longitude). The attributes represent the MODIS band measurements recorded for each latitude-longitude coordinate.

The following is the SciDB query we execute to compute the NDSI over the S_{VIS} and S_{SWIR} arrays:

Query 1: SciDB query to apply the NDSI.

```
1 store(
2     apply(
3         join(S_VIS, S_SWIR),
4         ndsi,
5         ndsi_func(S_VIS.reflectance,
6             S_SWIR.reflectance)
7     ),
8     NDSI
9 );
```

We first perform an equi-join, matching the latitude-longitude coordinates of the two arrays (line 3). Note that SciDB implicitly joins on dimensions, so latitude and longitude are not specified in the query. We then apply the NDSI to each pair of joined array cells by calling the "ndsi_func" UDF (lines 5-6). We pass the reflectance attribute of S_{VIS} and the reflectance attribute of S_{SWIR} to the UDF. We store the result of this query as a separate array in SciDB named *NDSI* (line 8), and the NDSI calculations are recorded in a new "ndsi" attribute in this array (line 4).

[3]http://modis.gsfc.nasa.gov/data/

5.2 Experimental Setup

5.2.1 *Hardware/Software setup*

The ForeCache front-end for the study was a web-based visualizer. The D3.js Javascript library was used to render data tiles. We describe the interface in more detail below.

The data was partitioned across two servers running SciDB version 13.3. Each server had 24 cores, 47GB of memory, and 10.1 TB of disk space. Both servers ran Ubuntu Server 12.04. The first server was also responsible for running the ForeCache middleware (prediction engine and cache manager), which received tile requests from the client-side interface.

5.2.2 *Measuring Accuracy*

The number of cache misses (*i.e.,* prediction accuracy) directly impacts whether delays occur in ForeCache, and thus also determines the length of user wait times (*i.e.,* the latency). Therefore, we used prediction accuracy as one of our primary metrics for comparison, similar to Lee *et al.* [12]. To compute this, we ran our models in parallel while stepping through tile request logs, one request at a time. For each requested tile, we collected a ranked list of predictions from each of our recommendation models, and recorded whether the next tile to be requested was located within the list.

We simulated space allocations in our middleware cache by varying k in our accuracy measurements. Thus measuring prediction accuracy becomes equivalent to measuring the hit rate of our tile cache. For example, $k = 2$ meant that ForeCache only had space to fetch two tiles before the user's next request. We varied k from 1 to 8 in our experiments. At $k = 9$, we are guaranteed to prefetch the correct tile, because the interface only supports nine different moves: zoom out, pan (left, right, up, down), and zoom in (users could zoom into one of four tiles at the zoom level below).

Given that ForeCache prefetches new tiles after every request, we found that having ForeCache predict further than one move ahead did not actually improve accuracy. Therefore, predicting beyond the user's next move was irrelevant to the goals of these experiments, and we only considered the tiles that were exactly one step ahead of the user. We leave prefetching more than one step ahead of the user as future work.

5.2.3 *Comparing with Existing Techniques*

To compare our two-level prediction engine with existing techniques, we implemented two models proposed in [8], the "Momentum" and "Hotspot" models. Several more recent systems, such as ATLAS [6] and ImMens [16] apply very similar techniques (see Section 7 for more information).

Momentum: The Momentum model assumes that the user's next move will be the same as her previous move. To implement this, the tile matching the user's previous move is assigned a probability of 0.9, and the eight other candidates are assigned a probability of 0.0125. Note that this is a Markov chain, since probabilities are assigned to future moves based on the user's previous move.

Hotspot: The Hotspot model is an extension of the Momentum model that adds awareness of popular tiles, or *hotspots*, in the dataset. To find hotspots in the NDSI dataset, we counted the number of requests made for each tile visited in our user study, and chose the tiles with the most requests. When the user is not close to any hotspots, the Hotspot model defaults to the behavior of the Momentum model. When a hotspot is nearby, the Hotspot model

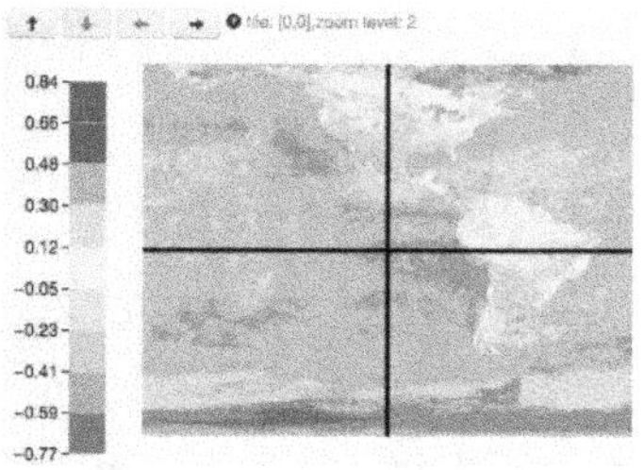

Figure 7: ForeCache browsing interface.

assigns a higher ranking to any tiles that bring the user closer to that hotspot, and a lower ranking to the remaining tiles. We trained the Hotspot model on trace data ahead of time. This training process took less than one second to complete.

5.3 User Study

To ascertain whether prefetching was a viable strategy for exploring multidimensional scientific datasets, we worked directly with earth and ocean scientists at the University of California Santa Barbara (UCSB) and the University of Washington (UW) to: (1) choose a use case of interest to our collaborators (MODIS snow cover); and (2) develop a set of search tasks for this use case that domain scientists with diverse backgrounds and skill sets could complete during the study. In this section, we outline the study design, and validate whether our analysis phases are an appropriate classification of user behavior using results from the study. We avoided biasing the behavior of our study participants by caching all data tiles in main memory while the study was being conducted. This prevented our participants from choosing their movements based on response time (*e.g.,* avoiding zooming out if it is slower than other movements). This also ensured that all study participants had the same browsing experience throughout the study.

5.3.1 *Study Participants*

The study consisted of 18 domain scientists (graduate students, post doctoral researchers, and faculty). Most of our participants were either interested in or actively working with MODIS data. Participants were recruited at UW and UCSB.

5.3.2 *Browsing Interface*

Figure 7 is an example of the client-side interface. Each visualization in the interface represented exactly one data tile. Participants (*i.e.,* users) used directional buttons (top of Figure 7) to move up, down, left, or right. Moving up or down corresponded to moving along the latitude dimension in the NDSI dataset, and left or right to the longitude dimension. Each directional move resulted in the user moving to a completely separate data tile. User's left clicked on a quadrant to zoom into the corresponding tile, and right clicked anywhere on the visualization to zoom out.

Directional buttons ensured that users' actions mapped to specific data tiles. Though different from existing geospatial interfaces (*e.g.,* Google Maps), our browsing interface provides clear and efficient button-based navigation through the dataset. Furthermore, study participants commented that this navigation design is useful when selecting specific data ranges for further analysis.

5.3.3 *Browsing Tasks*

Participants completed the same search task over three different regions in the NDSI dataset. For each region, participants were asked to identify four data tiles (*i.e.,* four different visualizations) that met specific visual requirements. The tasks were as follows:

1. Find four data tiles in the continental United States at zoom level 6 with the highest NDSI values.

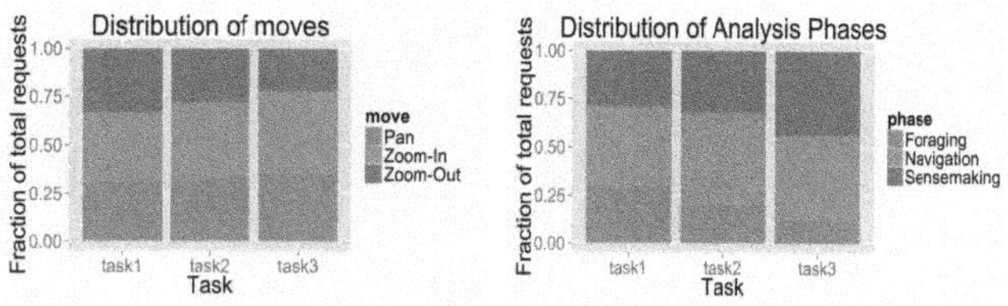

(a) **Disribution of moves** (b) **Distribution of Phases**

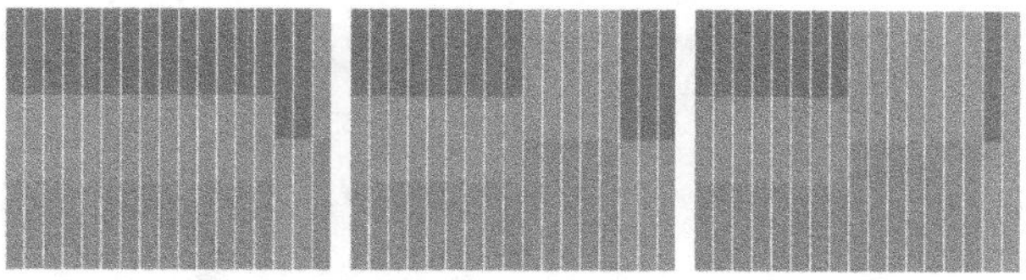

(c) **Moves (Task1)** (d) **Moves (Task 2)** (e) **Moves (Task3)**

Figure 8: Distribution of moves (a) and phases (b), averaged across users, partitioned by task; distribution of moves for individual users for Task 1 (c), Task 2 (d), and Task 3 (e). In Figures (c), (d), and (e): panning is red, zooming in is green, and zooming out is blue; users with similar move distributions are grouped together.

2. Find four data tiles within western Europe at zoom level 8 with NDSI values of .5 or greater.
3. Find 4 data tiles in South America at zoom level 6 that contain NDSI values greater than .25.

A separate request log was recorded for each user and task. Therefore, by the end of the study we had 54 user traces, each consisting of sequential tile requests.

5.3.4 *Post-Study: General Observations*

The most popular ROI's for each task were: the Rocky Mountains for Task 1, Swiss Alps for Task 2, and Andes Mountains for Task 3. The average number of requests per task are as follows: 35 tiles for Task 1, 25 tiles for Task2, and 17 tiles for Task 3. The mountain ranges in Tasks 2 and 3 (Europe and South America) were closer together and had less snow than those in task 1 (US and Southern Canada). Thus, users spent less time on these tasks, shown by the decrease in total requests.

We also tracked whether the request was a zoom in, zoom out, or pan. Figure 8a shows the distribution of directions across all study participants, recorded separately for each task. We see that for all tasks, our study participants spent the most time zooming in. This is because users had to zoom to a specific zoom level for each task, and did not have to zoom back out to the top level to complete the task. In tasks 1 and 2, users panned and zoomed out roughly equally. In task 3, we found that users clearly favored panning more than zooming out. We also found that large groups of users shared similar browsing patterns, shown in Figures 8c-8e. These groupings further reinforce the reasoning behind our analysis phases, showing that most users can be categorized by a small number of specific patterns within each task, and even across tasks.

5.3.5 *Evaluating Our Three Analysis Phases*

To demonstrate some of the patterns that we found in our user traces, consider Figure 9, which plots the change in zoom level over time for one of our user traces. The coarsest zoom level is plotted at the top of Figure 9, and the most-detailed zoom level was plotted at the bottom. The x-axis represents each successive tile request made by this user. A downward slope corresponds to the user moving from a coarser to a more detailed zoom level; an

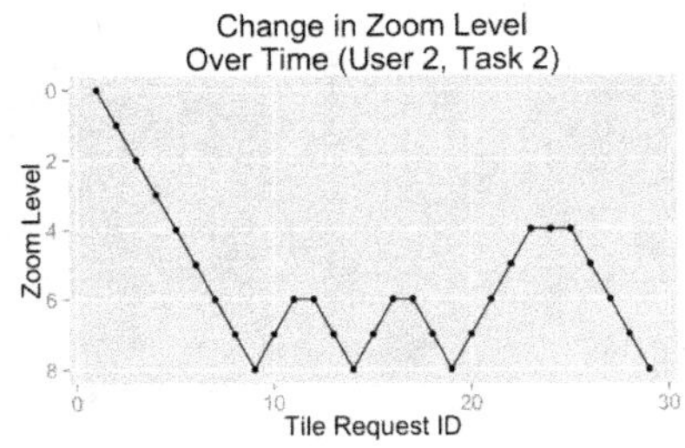

Figure 9: Change in zoom level per request as study participant 2 completed task 2.

upward slope corresponds to the reverse; and a flat line (*i.e.*, slope of 0) to the user panning to tiles at the same zoom level.

We see that the user alternates between zooming out to a coarser zoom level, and zooming into more detailed zoom levels. We know that the coarser views were used to locate snow, and the high-resolution views to find specific tiles that satisfied task 2 (hence the four tile requests specifically at zoom level 8).

We see in Figure 9 that this user's behavior corresponds directly to the three analysis phases described in Section 4.2.1. The user's return to coarser views near the top of Figure 9 correspond to the user returning to the Foraging phase (*e.g.*, request ID's 20 to 23). The user's zooms down to the bottom half of the plot correspond to the user moving to the Sensemaking phase, as they searched for individual tiles to complete the task. Furthermore, we found that 13 out of 18 users exhibited this same general exploration behavior throughout their participation in the study. 16 out of 18 users exhibited this behavior during 2 or more tasks. Furthermore, we found that only 57 out of the 1390 total requests made in the study were not described adequately by our exploration model.

Therefore, we conclude that our three analysis phases provide an accurate classification of how the vast majority of users actually explored our NDSI MODIS dataset.

5.4 Evaluating the Prediction Engine

Now that we have established that our three analysis phases provide a comprehensive labeling scheme for user behavior, we move on to evaluating our two-level prediction engine. In particular, we evaluated each level of our prediction engine separately, and then compared the complete prediction engine to the existing techniques described in our experimental setup.

At the top level of our prediction engine, we measured how accurately we could predict the user's current exploration phase. At the bottom level, we measured the accuracy of each recommendation model, with respect to each analysis phase.

The following experiments apply *leave-one-out cross validation* [11], a common cross-validation technique for evaluating user study data. For each user, the models were trained on the trace data of the other 17 out of 18 participants, and tested on the trace data from the remaining participant that was removed from the training set. After evaluating each user individually, we averaged the results across all users to produce our final accuracy calculations.

5.4.1 *Predicting the User's Current Analysis Phase*

The goal was to measure how accurately we could predict the user's current analysis phase. To build a training and testing set for this experiment, we manually labeled each request in our request logs with one of our 3 analysis phases. Figure 8b shows the distribution of phase labels. We see that users spent noticeably less time in the Foraging phase for tasks 2 and 3 (*i.e.*, looking for new ROI's), which is consistent with our user study observations.

To test our SVM classifier, we performed leave-one-out cross validation (see above), where all requests for the corresponding user were placed in the test dataset, and the remaining requests were placed in the training set. Training the classifier took less than one second. We found that our overall accuracy across all users was 82%. For some users, we could predict the current analysis phase with 90% accuracy or higher.

5.4.2 *Accuracy of Recommendation Models*

To validate the accuracy of our individual recommenders, we conducted two sets of experiments, where we: (1) compared the accuracy of our AB recommender to existing techniques, and (2) measured the prediction accuracy of our SB recommender separately for each of our four tile signatures. The goal of these experiments was two-fold. First, we wanted to find the phases where existing techniques performed well, and where there was room for improvement. Second, we wanted to test whether our AB and SB models excelled in accuracy for their intended analysis phases. To do this, we evaluated how accurately our individual models could predict the user's next move, for each analysis phase.

Action-Based (AB) Model: To evaluate the impact of history length on our AB recommender, we implemented a separate Markov chain for $n = 2$ to $n = 10$, which we refer to as Markov2 through Markov10, respectively. Each Markov chain only took milliseconds to train. We found that $n = 2$ was too small, and resulted in worse accuracy. Otherwise, we found negligible improvements in accuracy for lengths beyond $n = 3$, and thus found $n = 3$ (*i.e.*, Markov3) to be most efficient Markov chain for our AB model.

Figure 10a shows the prediction accuracy of our AB model compared to the Momentum and Hotspot models, with increasing values of k. Note that k represents the total space (in tiles) that each model was given for predictions (see Section 5.2.2 for more information). In Figure 10a, we see that for the Foraging and Sensemaking phases, our AB model matches the performance of existing techniques for all values of k. Furthermore, we found that our AB model achieves significantly higher accuracy during the Navigation phase for all values of k. This validates our decision to use the AB model as the primary model for predicting the Navigation phase.

Signature-Based (SB) Model: Figure 10b shows the accuracy of each of our individual signatures, with respect to analysis phase. To do this, we created four separate recommendation models, one per signature. Amongst our signatures, we found that the SIFT signature provided the best overall accuracy. We expected a machine vision feature like SIFT to perform well, because users are comparing images when they analyze MODIS tiles.

We found that the denseSIFT signature did not perform as well as SIFT. denseSIFT performs worse because it matches entire images, whereas SIFT only matches small regions of an image. Here, relevant visualizations will contain clusters of orange snow pixels, but will not look similar otherwise. For example, the Rockies will look very different from the Andes, but they will both contain clusters of snow (orange) pixels. Thus, many relevant tiles will not appear to be similar with regards to the denseSIFT signature.

5.4.3 *Evaluating the Final Prediction Engine*

We used the accuracy results for our phase predictor and best individual recommendation models as inputs to our final two-level prediction engine. Our prediction engine only incorporated two recommenders, the AB recommender with $n = 3$ (*i.e.*, Markov3) and the SIFT SB recommender. Note that we updated our original allocation strategies based on our observed accuracy results. When the Sensemaking phase is predicted, our model always fetches predictions from our SB model only. Otherwise, our final model fetches

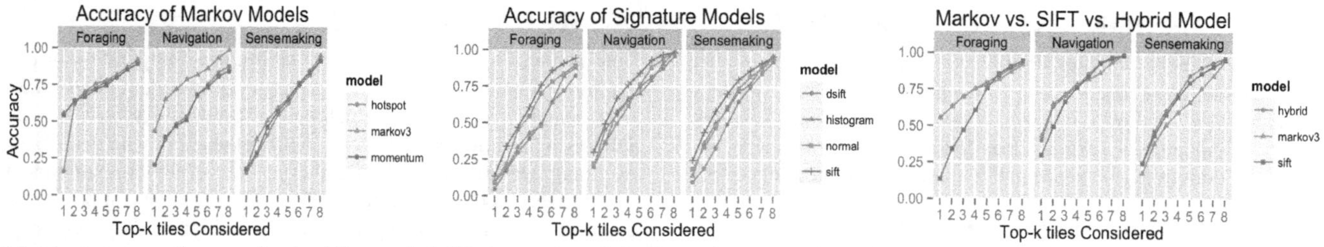

(a) **Accuracy of our best AB model (Markov3) and existing models.** (b) **Accuracy of the four signatures in our SB model.** (c) **Accuracy of our final engine (hybrid) and our best individual models.**

Figure 10: Accuracy of our AB model, SB model, and final prediction engine (*i.e.,* hybrid model).

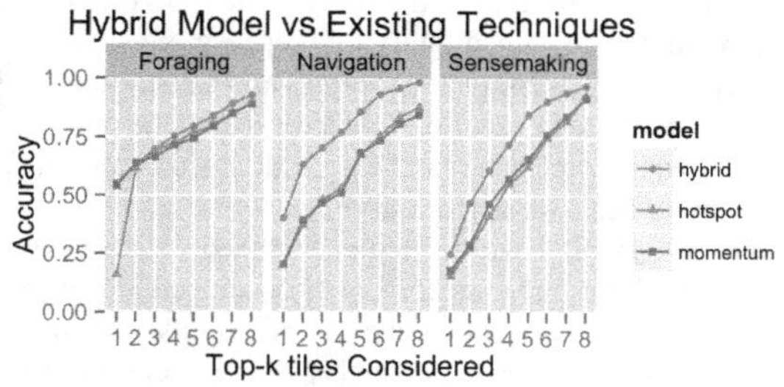

Figure 11: Accuracy of the hybrid model compared to existing techniques.

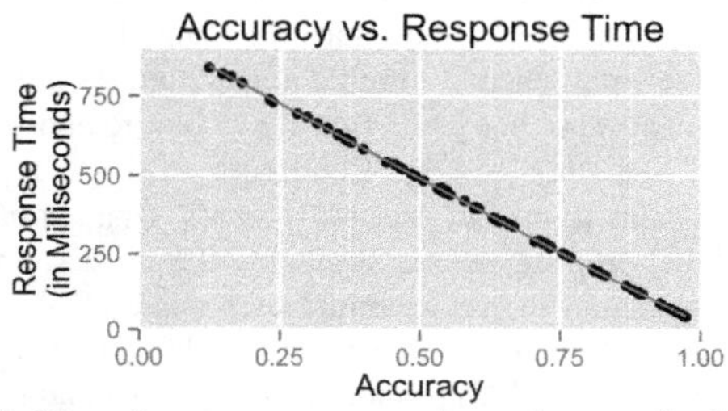

Figure 12: Plot of average response time given prefetch accuracy, for all models and fetch sizes (linear regression: Adj R^2=0.99985, Intercept=961.33, Slope=-939.08, P=1.1704e-242.

the first 4 predictions from the AB model (or less if $k < 4$), and then starts fetching predictions from the SB model if $k > 4$.

Figure 10c shows that our final prediction engine successfully combined the strengths of our two best prediction models. It was able to match the accuracy of the best recommender for each analysis phase, resulting in better overall accuracy than any individual recommendation model. We also compared our final prediction engine to existing techniques, shown in Figure 11. We see that for the Foraging phase, our prediction engine performs as well (if not better) than existing techniques. For the Navigation phase, we achieve up to 25% better prediction accuracy. Similarly for the Sensemaking phase, we see a consistent 10-18% improvement in accuracy.

5.5 Latency

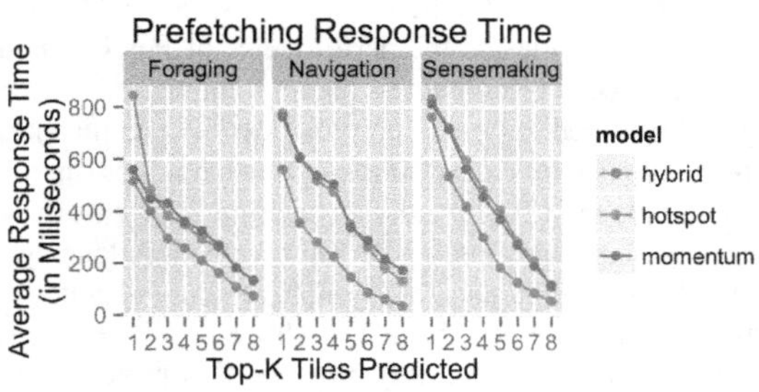

Figure 13: Average prefetching response times for hybrid model and existing techniques.

We used the same setup from our accuracy experiments to measure latency. To measure the latency for each tile request, we recorded the time at which the client sent the request to the middleware, as well as the time at which the requested tile was received by the client. We calculated the resulting latency by taking the difference between these two measurements. On a cache hit, the middleware was able to retrieve the tile from main memory, allowing ForeCache to send an immediate response. On a cache miss, the middleware was forced to issue a query to SciDB to retrieve the missing tile, which was slower. On average, the middleware took 19.5 ms to send tiles for a cache hit, and 984.0 ms for a cache miss.

To evaluate our claim that accuracy dictates latency, we plotted the relationship between prefetching accuracy and average response time (*i.e.,* average latency), shown in Figure 12. Accuracy and response times were plotted for all models and fetch sizes. We see a strong linear relationship between accuracy and response time, where a 1% increase in accuracy corresponded to a 10ms decrease in average response time (adjusted $R^2 = 0.99985$). Given this constant accuracy-latency factor, we found that the higher prediction accuracy of our hybrid algorithm translates to a time savings of 150-250ms per tile request, when compared with existing prefetching techniques. The difference in latency is plotted in Figure 13, where we calculated the average response times for three models. We found that our hybrid model reduced response times by more than 50% for $k \geq 5$, compared with existing techniques.

This latency evaluation indicates that ForeCache provides significantly better performance over not only traditional systems (*i.e.,* exploration systems without prefetching), but also existing systems that enable prefetching (*e.g.,* [8, 6, 16]). Specifically, as shown in Figure 13, with a prefetch size of 5 tiles ($k = 5$), our system demonstrates a 430% improvement over traditional systems (*i.e.,* average latency of 185ms vs. 984ms), and 88% over existing prefetching techniques (average latency of 185 ms vs. 349 ms for Momentum, and 360 ms for Hotspot).

In addition, ForeCache provides a much more fluid and interactive user experience than traditional (no prefetching) systems. As shown in HCI literature, a 1 second interaction delay is at the limit of a user's sensory memory [4]. Delays greater than 1 second make users feel like they cannot navigate the interface freely [17, 15]. In this regard, traditional systems (*i.e.,* a constant latency of 1 second per request) are not considered interactive by HCI standards.

In contrast, ForeCache remains highly interactive during most of the user's interactions with the interface, with only 19.5ms of delay per tile request. As shown in Figure 11, with a fetch size of 5 tiles ($k = 5$), the prediction algorithm succeeds the vast majority of the time (82% of the time), making a cache miss (and the full 1 second delay) an infrequent event. Thus our techniques allow systems with limited main memory resources (*e.g.,* less than 10MB of prefetching space per user) to operate at interactive speeds, so that many users can actively navigate the data freely and in parallel.

6. DISCUSSION AND FUTURE WORK

While ForeCache provides significantly better performance over other systems, there is still room for improvement. Here, we discuss extending the ForeCache prediction engine beyond two dimensions, and present several ideas for further improvements to ForeCache both in performance and applicability to other datasets.

6.1 Prediction Beyond 2D datasets

The current ForeCache system focuses on 2D visualization. To support multidimensional exploration (*e.g.,* 3D datasets), we can employ a *coordinated view* design, where tiles are represented by several visualizations at the same time. For example, to extend our snowcover example to three dimensions (latitude, longitude and time), we could create two navigable views: (1) a snowcover heatmap (*e.g.,* Figure 7); and (2) a line chart showing maximum snow cover over time for the current tile. To navigate via latitude and longitude, the user moves in the heatmap. To navigate via time, the user moves in the line chart.

However, the number of tiles grows exponentially with the number of dimensions, increasing the search space and making prediction more challenging. One solution is to insert a pruning level between our phase classifier and recommendation models to remove low-probability interaction paths. A second solution is to restrict the number of possible interactions ahead of time by having the user choose only two dimensions to explore at a time. This technique reduces the user's range of possible actions, enabling ForeCache to still make accurate predictions. We plan to implement 3D visualizations and pruning in ForeCache, and plan to conduct a new user study on higher-dimensionality datasets to evaluate the accuracy and response time benefits provided by these new techniques.

6.2 Future Work

We describe three future directions for ForeCache: (1) extending our tiling scheme; (2) implementing more signatures; and (3) new prediction and caching techniques for multi-user environments.

Our proposed tiling scheme works well for arrays. However, when considering other types of data (*e.g.,* social graphs or patient health records), it is unclear how to map these datasets to tiles. We plan to develop a general-purpose tiling mechanism for relational datasets. We also plan to study how tiling parameters affect performance for array and non-array datasets.

We manually identified four signatures for our SB recommender, and found that SIFT works best for the NDSI dataset. However, other features may be more appropriate for different datasets. For example, counting outliers or computing linear correlations may work well for prefetching time series data. We plan to build a general-purpose signature toolbox with more of these signatures, and plan to extend ForeCache to learn what signatures work best for a given dataset automatically.

To evaluate ForeCache's new tiling scheme and signature toolbox, we plan to conduct a user study on non-array-based datasets. For example, we plan to support the MIMIC II medical dataset, which provides hospital data recorded for thousands of patients and many data types (*e.g.,* unstructured text, tabular, and array data).

In addition, our prediction framework does not currently take into account potential optimizations within a multi-user scheme. For example, it is unclear how to partition the middleware cache to make predictions for multiple users exploring different datasets, or how to share data between users exploring the same dataset. We plan to extend our architecture to manage coordinated predictions and caching across multiple users.

7. RELATED WORK

Many systems use online computation, pre-computation or prefetching techniques to support exploratory browsing of large datasets. The ScalaR system [2] computes aggregates and samples in the DBMS at runtime to avoid overwhelming the client with data. However, aggregation and sampling queries are too slow to complete at interactive speeds. Fisher *et al.* [9] combine online sampling with running summaries to improve response times. However, users must still wait for queries to complete if they want accurate results.

Several systems instead build pre-computed data reductions to speed up query execution. BlinkDB [1] builds stratified samples over datasets as they are loaded into the DBMS, and provides error and latency guarantees when querying these samples. The DICE system [10] utilizes pre-computed samples and a distributed DBMS environment to shorten execution times for data cube queries. The techniques used in ForeCache can be used alongside sampling techniques to further improve performance.

Two recent systems have created specialized data structures to support data exploration. Lins *et al.* [14] developed new data cube structures, which they call nanocubes, to efficiently visualize large datasets. However, the entire nanocubes data structure must fit in memory. Thus, nanocubes do not scale easily to larger datasets. Similar to our approach, the imMens system [16] builds data tiles in advance, and fetches these tiles from the backend at runtime. However, users must build the data tiles manually, and imMens does not utilize comprehensive prediction techniques to fetch tiles.

A number of systems use prediction algorithms to boost prefetching accuracy. Lee *et al.* [12] and Cetintemel *et al.* [5] propose using Markov chains to predict user movements. Chan *et al.* [6] and Doshi *et al.* [8] propose several strategies–the most sophisticated being Markov chains–to predict future user requests. We compare with two of these strategies, Momentum and Hotspot, in our experiments. Yesilmurat *et al.* [25] propose techniques similar to the Momentum model for prefetching geospatial data. Li *et al.* [13] combine the Hotspot model with Markov chains to further improve performance. ForeCache builds on these existing techniques with new signature-based prediction algorithms and a novel adaptive framework for running multiple algorithms in parallel.

8. CONCLUSION

In this paper, we presented ForeCache, a general-purpose exploration system for browsing large datasets. ForeCache employs a client-server architecture, where the user interacts with a lightweight client-side interface, and the data to be explored is retrieved from a back-end server running a DBMS. We inserted a middleware optimization layer in front of the DBMS that uses a two-level prediction engine and main-memory cache to prefetch relevant data tiles given the user's current analysis phase and recent tile requests. We presented results from a user study we conducted, where 18 domain experts used ForeCache to explore NASA MODIS satellite imagery data. We tested the performance of ForeCache using traces recorded from our user study, and presented accuracy results showing that our prediction engine provides: (1) significant accuracy improvements over existing prediction techniques (up to 25% higher accuracy); and (2) dramatic latency improvements over current non-prefetching systems (430% improvement in latency), and existing prediction techniques (88% improvement in latency).

Acknowledgements: We thank Bill Howe and James Frew for their feedback and support on this project. This project was supported by NSF awards IIS-1452977 and IIS-1218170, and the Intel Science and Technology Center (ISTC) for Big Data.

9. REFERENCES

[1] S. Agarwal, B. Mozafari, A. Panda, H. Milner, S. Madden, and I. Stoica. Blinkdb: queries with bounded errors and bounded response times on very large data. In *Proc. EuroSys 2013*, pages 29–42, New York, NY, USA, 2013. ACM.

[2] L. Battle, M. Stonebraker, and R. Chang. Dynamic reduction of query result sets for interactive visualizaton. In *IEEE BigDataVis Workshop*, pages 1–8, 2013.

[3] E. Brown, A. Ottley, H. Zhao, Q. Lin, R. Souvenir, A. Endert, and R. Chang. Finding Waldo: Learning about Users from their Interactions. *IEEE TVCG*, 20(12):1663–1672, Dec. 2014.

[4] S. K. Card, G. G. Robertson, and J. D. Mackinlay. The Information Visualizer, an Information Workspace. In *Proceedings of the SIGCHI Conference on Human Factors in Computing Systems*, CHI '91, pages 181–186, New York, NY, USA, 1991. ACM.

[5] U. Cetintemel, M. Cherniack, J. DeBrabant, Y. Diao, K. Dimitriadou, A. Kalinin, O. Papaemmanouil, and S. B. Zdonik. Query steering for interactive data exploration. In *CIDR*, 2013.

[6] S.-M. Chan, L. Xiao, J. Gerth, and P. Hanrahan. Maintaining interactivity while exploring massive time series. In *VAST*, 2008.

[7] S. F. Chen and J. Goodman. An empirical study of smoothing techniques for language modeling. *Computer Speech & Language*, 13(4):359–394, Oct. 1999.

[8] P. Doshi, E. Rundensteiner, and M. Ward. Prefetching for visual data exploration. In *Proc. DASFAA*, 2003.

[9] D. Fisher. Incremental, approximate database queries and uncertainty for exploratory visualization. In *LDAV*, 2011.

[10] N. Kamat, P. Jayachandran, K. Tunga, and A. Nandi. Distributed interactive cube exploration. *ICDE*, 2014.

[11] R. Kohavi et al. A study of cross-validation and bootstrap for accuracy estimation and model selection. In *Ijcai*, volume 14, pages 1137–1145, 1995.

[12] D. H. Lee, J. S. Kim, S. D. Kim, K.-C. Kim, Y.-S. Kim, and J. Park. Adaptation of a Neighbor Selection Markov Chain for Prefetching Tiled Web GIS Data. ADVIS '02, pages 213–222, London, UK, UK, 2002. Springer-Verlag.

[13] R. Li, R. Guo, Z. Xu, and W. Feng. A Prefetching Model Based on Access Popularity for Geospatial Data in a Cluster-based Caching System. *Int. J. Geogr. Inf. Sci.*, 26(10):1831–1844, Oct. 2012.

[14] L. Lins, J. Klosowski, and C. Scheidegger. Nanocubes for real-time exploration of spatiotemporal datasets. *IEEE TVCG*, 2013.

[15] Z. Liu and J. Heer. The Effects of Interactive Latency on Exploratory Visual Analysis. *IEEE TVCG*, 20(12):2122–2131, Dec. 2014.

[16] Z. Liu, B. Jiang, and J. Heer. immens: Real-time visual querying of big data. *Proc. EuroVis*, 32, 2013.

[17] J. Nielsen. Powers of 10: Time Scales in User Experience, Oct. 2009.

[18] A. Pauls and D. Klein. Faster and smaller n-gram language models. HLT, pages 258–267, Stroudsburg, PA, USA, 2011.

[19] P. Pirolli and S. Card. The sensemaking process and leverage points for analyst technology as identified through cognitive task analysis. In *Proc. International Conference on Intelligence Analysis*, volume 2005, pages 2–4, 2005.

[20] G. Planthaber, M. Stonebraker, and J. Frew. Earthdb: Scalable analysis of modis data using scidb. In *BigSpatial*, pages 11–19, New York, NY, USA. ACM.

[21] K. Rittger, T. H. Painter, and J. Dozier. Assessment of methods for mapping snow cover from modis. *Advances in Water Resources*, 51(0):367 – 380, 2013.

[22] E. Soroush, M. Balazinska, S. Krughoff, and A. Connolly. Efficient Iterative Processing in the SciDB Parallel Array Engine. In *Proceedings of the 27th International Conference on Scientific and Statistical Database Management*, SSDBM '15, pages 39:1–39:6, New York, NY, USA, 2015. ACM.

[23] M. Stonebraker, P. Brown, A. Poliakov, and S. Raman. The architecture of scidb. In *SSDBM*, pages 1–16. Springer, 2011.

[24] R. Taft, M. Vartak, N. R. Satish, N. Sundaram, S. Madden, and M. Stonebraker. GenBase: A Complex Analytics Genomics Benchmark. In *Proceedings of the 2014 ACM SIGMOD International Conference on Management of Data*, SIGMOD '14, pages 177–188, New York, NY, USA, 2014. ACM.

[25] S. Yesilmurat and V. Isler. Retrospective Adaptive Prefetching for Interactive Web GIS Applications. *Geoinformatica*, 16(3):435–466, July 2012.

Expressive Query Construction through Direct Manipulation of Nested Relational Results

Eirik Bakke
MIT CSAIL
ebakke@csail.mit.edu

David R. Karger
MIT CSAIL
karger@csail.mit.edu

ABSTRACT

Despite extensive research on visual query systems, the standard way to interact with relational databases remains to be through SQL queries and tailored form interfaces. We consider three requirements to be essential to a successful alternative: (1) query specification through direct manipulation of results, (2) the ability to view and modify any part of the current query without departing from the direct manipulation interface, and (3) SQL-like expressiveness. This paper presents the first visual query system to meet all three requirements in a single design. By directly manipulating nested relational results, and using spreadsheet idioms such as formulas and filters, the user can express a relationally complete set of query operators plus calculation, aggregation, outer joins, sorting, and nesting, while always remaining able to track and modify the state of the complete query. Our prototype gives the user an experience of responsive, incremental query building while pushing all actual query processing to the database layer. We evaluate our system with formative and controlled user studies on 28 spreadsheet users; the controlled study shows our system significantly outperforming Microsoft Access on the System Usability Scale.

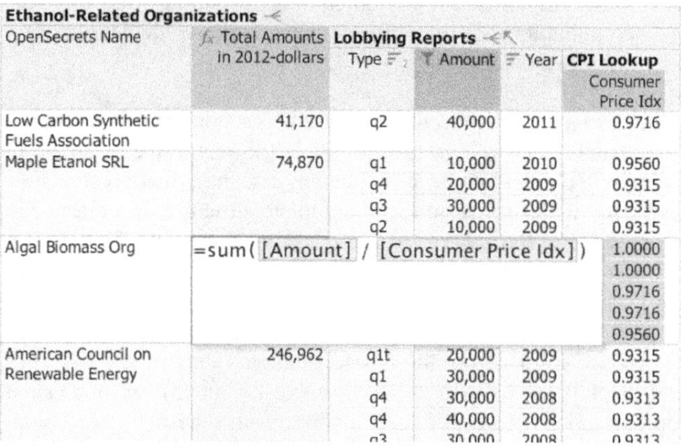

Figure 1: Spreadsheet-style formula editing in a nested relational result. The query structure is encoded in the table header, which shows three joined table instances (bold labels), one-to-many relationships (-<), sorting (⩶), active filters (▼, ↖), and a formula (f_x).

1. INTRODUCTION

Four decades after Query by Example [61], the broad problem of Making Database Systems Usable [30] remains open. Technical users still interact with relational data through hand-coded SQL, while non-technical users rely on restrictive form- and report-based interfaces tailored, at great cost, for their specific database schema [37, 32, 4]. Queries that involve "complex aggregates, nesting, correlation, and several other features remain on a tall pedestal approachable only by the initiated" [28]. Simple report queries traversing one-to-many relationships in the database schema, such as retrieving "a list of parts, and for each part a list of suppliers and a list of open orders", are painful to define for programmers and largely inaccessible to end users.

Meanwhile, users from a wide range of backgrounds seem happy, indeed eager, to interact with their data if it is served to them in spreadsheet form. "Export to Excel", the joke goes, "is the third most common button in data and business intelligence apps... after OK and Cancel" [18]. Spreadsheets lack basic database functionality such as joins and views, but demonstrate the great value of usable, general-purpose data manipulation tools [4].

SIGMOD'16, June 26-July 01, 2016, San Francisco, CA, USA

ISBN 978-1-4503-3531-7/16/06...$15.00

DOI: http://dx.doi.org/10.1145/2882903.2915210

Shneiderman [50] attributes the usability of the spreadsheet to its nature as a *direct manipulation* interface. The properties of such an interface include "visibility of the object of interest", "rapid, reversible, incremental actions", and "replacement of complex command language syntax by direct manipulation of the object of interest". Shneiderman paraphrases Harold Thimbleby: "The display should indicate a complete image of what the current status is, what errors have occurred, and what actions are appropriate."

We agree with Liu and Jagadish [41] that a successful solution to the visual query language problem must come in the form of a spreadsheet-like direct manipulation interface. In particular, we consider three requirements that have yet to be met in a single user interface design:

R1. *Query specification through direct manipulation of results.* The user should build queries incrementally through a sequence of operations performed directly on the data in the database, as seen through the result of each intermediate query [41]. In Shneiderman's terms, the *object of interest* is not the query, but the data, as when working with a spreadsheet.

R2. *The ability to view and modify any part of the current query, including operations performed many steps earlier, without redoing subsequent steps or departing from the direct manipulation interface.* This is tricky in light of R1, because the user will be looking at and manipulating the *result* of a query rather than an actual query expression. The mapping between the two is not obvious. [41]

R3. *SQL-like expressiveness from within the direct manipulation interface.* R1 and R2 can be trivially met if only simple queries are allowed. For example, Excel's *filter* feature works by direct manipulation of results, and allows its complete state to be viewed and modified from within the same interface, but supports only basic selection queries. To compete with SQL, a visual query system should allow the user to express any query commonly supported by SQL implementations, including arbitrary (multi-block) combinations of operations such as joins, calculations, and aggregations.

In this paper, we present SIEUFERD (pronounced *soy-fird*), the first visual query system to meet all of the requirements above in a single user interface design. The key insight is that given a suitable data model for results, the complete structure of a query can be encoded in the schema of the query's own result. This in turn allows the user interface to display the query and its result in a single visual representation, which can then be manipulated directly to modify any part of the query. Specifically, we allow queries to produce results from the nested relational data model [29, 38], and display results using a nested table layout [5]. In our visual representation, the header area of the result's nested table layout encodes the structure of the query, which can then be manipulated using spreadsheet idioms such as formulas and filters. The use of nested results affords a natural visualization of operations such as joins and aggregation, and allows the user to see, in context, intermediate tuples produced in any part of the query.

Using our system, the user can express a relationally complete [17] set of query operators plus calculation, aggregation, outer joins, sorting, and nesting (see Appendix A for details). This covers the full set of query operators generally considered as the minimum to model SQL [6, 26], and expresses, for example, all SELECT statements valid in SQL-92. Furthermore, the ability to produce nested results makes our system suitable for complex report creation tasks that would otherwise require multiple SQL queries and custom programming to merge and format results. Our Java-based prototype gives the user an experience of responsive, incremental query building while pushing all query processing to the database layer.

In an initial formative user study, 14 participants were able to solve complex query tasks with a minimal amount of training, with many expressing strong levels of satisfaction with the tool. In a second, controlled study, another 14 participants rated both SIEUFERD and the query designer found in Microsoft Access on the System Usability Scale (SUS) [8] after doing a series of tasks on each. Users rated SIEUFERD 18 points higher on average than Access. This corresponds to a 46 percentage point difference on a percentile scale of other studies in the Business Software category.

2. RELATED WORK

Visual query systems have been surveyed by Catarci et al. [11] and, recently, El-Mahgary and Soisalon-Soininen [21]. Systems discussed in this section include, in particular, those that employ direct manipulation, nested results, or optimizations for traversing relationships in the database. We omit systems that rely entirely on text-based languages for query construction. Table 1 categorizes systems by query representation style, and provides an assessment of each system against the requirements set forth in the introduction.

Direct Manip.	*Query Representation*	*Year*	*System*		*R1*	*R2*	*R3*	*Unrestricted Nested Results*
Yes	Overlaid on Result	2014	GBXT	[2]	X	X		X
		2012	DataPlay	[1]	X	X		X
		2006	Tabulator	[7]	X	X		X
		2002	Polaris/Tableau	[54]	X	X		
	Spreadsheet Formulas	2016	Object Spreads.	[43]	X	X		X
		2010	Spreads. as DB	[57]	X	X		
		2005	A1	[35]	X	X		X
		1997	OOF Spreads.	[16]	X	X		X
		1994	Forms/3	[9]	X	X		
	Exposed Algebraic	2013	Mashroom	[25]	X		X	X
		2011	Wrangler	[34]	X		X	
		1991	TableTalk	[22]	X		X	X
	Hidden Algebraic	2016	Gneiss	[13]	X		X	
		2013	GestureDB	[45]	X		X	
		2010	CRIUS	[48]	X			X
		2009	SheetMusiq	[41]	X			
		2008	AppForge	[60]	X			X
		1989	R^2	[27]	X		X	X
No	Diagram-based	2014	VisualTPL	[15]				X
		2009	App2You	[36]				X
		2005	QBB	[47]				
		2002	QURSED	[46]				X
		1990	QBD	[3]				
	Form-based	2008	Form Cust.	[33]				
		1998	QBEN	[42]				X
		1997	ESCHER	[59]				X
		1989	PERPLEX	[52]				
		1977	QBE	[61]				

Table 1: Summary of related systems, evaluated as visual query interfaces. R1 is indicated where some class of queries can be initially specified by direct manipulation of results. R2 is indicated where all parts of such queries can subsequently be modified through similar means. R3 is indicated where the same class of queries is relationally complete and supports aggregation in arbitrary multi-block queries.

Besides our core requirements, Table 1 also indicates which systems support nested results, i.e. a graphical equivalent of a hierarchical data model such as XML, JSON, or nested relations. This handles report-style queries that encode multiple parallel one-to-many relationships in a single result, as when retrieving "a list of parts, and for each part a list of suppliers and a list of open orders" [5]. Systems that base their result representation on a single flat table of primitive values, such as Tableau [54], are unable to express such queries. The same tends to hold for any system that takes its input from a single joined SQL query, since multivalued dependencies [23] in the flattened result (PARTS↠SUPPLIERS and PARTS↠ORDERS in the preceding example) would interact to produce a pathological number of tuples for even small inputs. Some systems, like Tableau and Gneiss [13], support a restricted form of nesting, where an otherwise flat result table can be grouped into a single-branch hierarchy, or a finite set of such (a *dashboard* in Tableau, or a set of *hierarchical tables* in Gneiss). This still does not handle PARTS↠SUPPLIERS/ORDERS-type queries from the example above. Tableau, as well as other systems based on the pivot table concept, produce cross-tabulated rather than nested results; these concepts are orthogonal. Besides their use in visual query systems, nested data models have been used both in optimization [53, 10] and expressiveness analysis [40] of query languages with aggregate functions.

We first discuss visual query systems that do not fall in the direct manipulation category. *Form-based* systems originated with Query by Example (QBE) [61], where the user populates a set of empty *skeleton tables* with conditions, variables (*examples*), and output

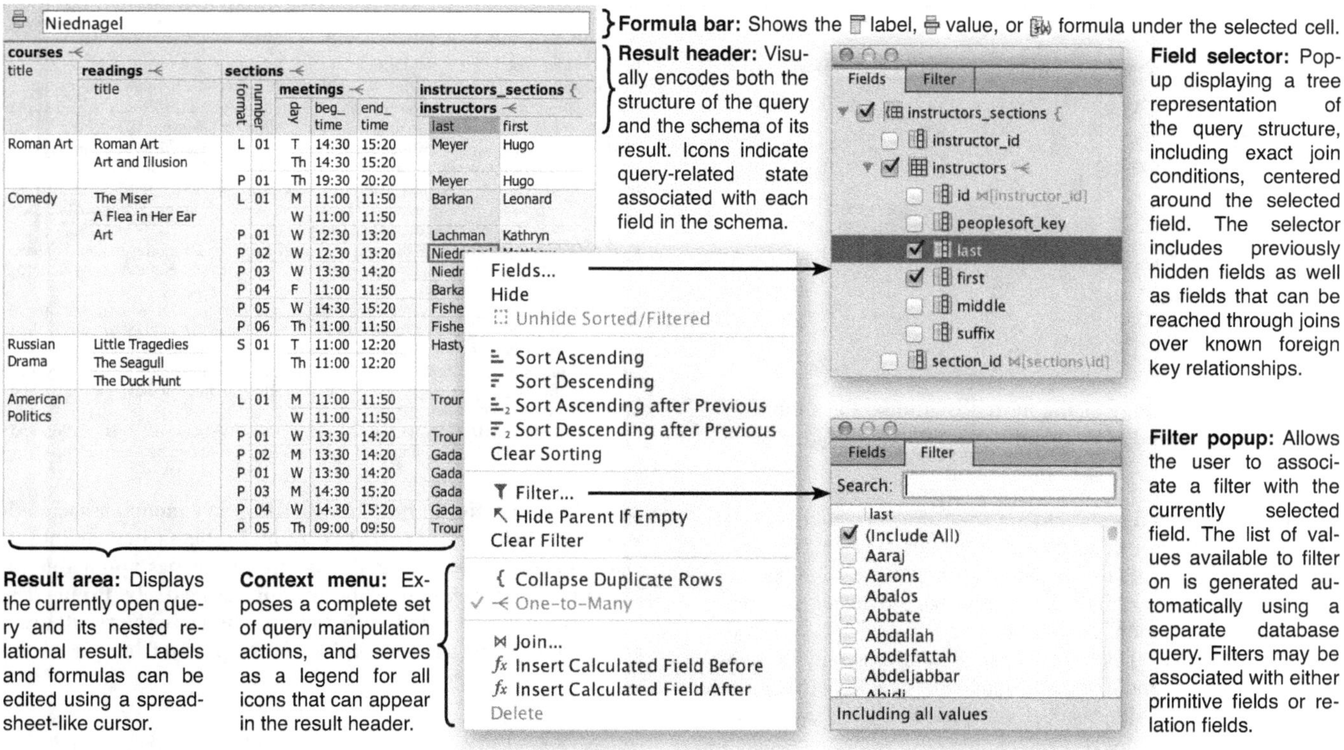

Figure 2: The SIEUFERD query interface. To create queries, users start from a simple tabular view of a table in the database and add filters, formulas, and nested relations. The integrated result and query representation is displayed continuously as the user interacts with the data. The particular query above instantiates six database tables (one per nested relation), contains five joins (each child relation against its parent), and is evaluated using five generated SQL queries (one for each one-to-many relationship ⤙). This query was constructed purely by checking off the appropriate fields and foreign key relationships in the field selector.

indications. ESCHER [59] and QBEN [42] extend QBE to support nested results, while PERPLEX [52] supports general-purpose logic programming. The ubiquitous search forms of commercial database applications can be seen as restricted versions of QBE tailored for a specific schema; Form Customization [33] generalizes such forms by considering the form designer as part of the query system. In *diagram-based* systems, the user manipulates queries for example through a schema tree or schema diagram, as in Query by Diagram (QBD) [3], Query by Browsing (QBB) [47], QURSED [46], and App2You [36], or through a diagrammatic query plan, as in VisualTPL [15]. The diagram-based query building style is common in commercial tools–Microsoft Access, Navicat, pgAdmin, dbForge, Alteryx etc. The general problem with both form-based and diagram-based interfaces is that users must manipulate queries through an abstract query representation that is divorced from the actual data that is being retrieved. To construct and understand queries, the user must look back and forth between the query representation on one side of the screen and a separate result representation on the other. Thus we do not consider these systems to be direct manipulation interfaces (requirement R1).

In the direct manipulation category, we now consider *algebraic* user interfaces. In such systems, the user builds queries by selecting, one step at a time, a series of operations to be applied to the currently displayed result. Each operation is applied to the result of all previous operations. Formal expressiveness is easy to achieve in algebraic interfaces, since the relevant relational operators can simply be exposed to the user directly. The main problem with algebraic interfaces is that the user has no direct way to, in the words of Liu and Jagadish, "modify an operation specified many steps earlier without redoing the steps afterwards" [41] (requirement R2). For example, in GestureDB [45], the user has no way to modify a filter on a column that was subsequently used in an aggregation or removed with a projection. Similar problems exist in R^2 [27], AppForge [60], CRIUS [48], and Gneiss [13]. SheetMusiq [41] provides a partial solution by using an algebra where certain operators can commute out of a complex expression for subsequent modification; however, the technique breaks down for expressions enclosed in binary operators such as joins, set union, or set difference. In other systems, the underlying algebraic expression is exposed directly, as in the procedural *data manipulation scripts* of Wrangler [34], the XQuery-like *mashup scripts* of Mashroom [25], or the diagram-based representation in TableTalk [22]. Thus, only the initial query specification can be done through direct manipulation; tweaking and examination of existing queries must be done with a separate, indirect interface.

With clever use of formulas, Tyszkiewicz [57] shows that existing spreadsheet products can be considered expressive enough to formulate arbitrary SQL queries. If we consider Excel as a query system, however, only a subset of such queries could be said to be constructible by direct manipulation. Heavy reliance on set-based formula functions such as INDEX, MATCH, and SUMPRODUCT means that spreadsheet formulas soon take the role of a text-based query language, with a vocabulary far removed from that of typical query tasks. This would also be the case for spreadsheet programming systems such as Forms/3 [9], Object Oriented Functional Spreadsheets [16], A1 [35], and Object Spreadsheets [43].

Last, we consider direct manipulation systems that *overlay* their query representation on the result of the same query, with the structure of the query reflecting the visual structure of the result. This solves the mapping problem of requirement R2. The problem is

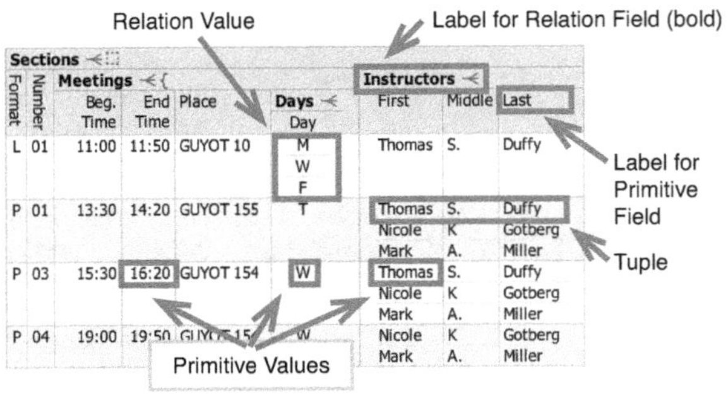

Figure 3: Terminology of the nested relational data model, illustrated on a nested table layout.

P R	**Visible.** Whether this field should be visible in the result layout.
P R	**Label.** Presentation label for the field; default is technical column/table name.
P R	**⏷ Filter.** A filter condition. Filters are stored in a format that can be generated from and restored to a spreadsheet-style filter selection UI.
P R	**Sort.** An optional ordinal indicating the position of this field among the parent relation's sort terms, plus an ascending/descending flag.
P	**⋈ JoinedOn.** An optional reference to a primitive child field of the parent relation's parent relation. This denotes an equijoin condition between this field and the referenced field.
P	***fx* ColumnDefinition.** Either the technical name of a column in the database table specified by InstantiatedTable, or a formula expression over fields in the query model.
R	**InstantiatedTable.** The technical name of a database table to instantiate at this level. Allowed to be absent, in which case semantics are equivalent to instantiating a single-tuple, zero-column table.
R	**{ CollapseDuplicateRows.** False by default, in which case the primary key fields of InstantiatedTable are projected in intermediate and retrieved results even if not Visible.
R	**↖ HideParentIfEmpty.** If true, an inner join is used between this relation and its parent. Set automatically by the filter UI, but can be overridden.

Table 2: Properties in the SIEUFERD query model, associated with each field in the nested relational schema that defines a visual query. P, R, and P R indicate properties applicable to primitive fields, relation fields, or both, respectively. Properties with icons correspond directly to icons shown in the result area and actions in the user-accessible context menu from Figure 2.

that current such representations are not expressive enough to support arbitrary queries (requirement R3). For example, the direct manipulation interfaces of Tabulator [7] and GBXT [2] support filters and joins over schema relationships, but are unable to express calculation, aggregation, general-purpose joins, or other binary operators. In DataPlay [1], direct manipulation is used only to choose between universal and existential qualifiers. Tableau [54] allows a large class of two-dimensional visualizations to be created and manipulated through direct manipulation of table headers and corresponding axis *shelves*; however, queries involving calculations or binary operators must be configured using a separate interface rather than through direct manipulation. Our own system is the first to achieve SQL-like expressiveness from within a direct manipulation interface based on an overlaid query/result representation.

3. SYSTEM DESCRIPTION

3.1 Overview

Our core query building interface is shown in Figure 2. All user interactions are initiated from the *result area*, which shows the current query's nested relational result, formatted using a nested table layout. In a nested table layout, the table's *header* area visually encodes the schema of the nested result, including which fields are nested under others in the hierarchical schema. Because our system maps all query-related state to specific fields in the result schema, the result's table header simultaneously becomes a visual representation of the query that generated it. A set of icons, carefully designed to allow every aspect of the query state to be represented in the header, is used to augment the information that can be derived from the names and positions of fields.

Starting from any selection of fields (columns) in the result area, the user may open a *context menu* of query-related actions, which also serves as a legend for icons that may appear in the result header. Query actions modify the query state, not the data in the database. Whenever a visual query is modified, the system generates and executes one or more corresponding SQL queries to evaluate it, merges the returned flat results into a single nested result, and displays the latter to the user. At the same time, the fields and iconography in the new result's header reflect the updated state of the modified query.

To keep the result layout compact, several aspects of the query state are indicated with icons in the header but are not displayed in full until the user requests it. In these cases we leverage well-established spreadsheet idioms to expose the underlying state. A filter icon (⏷) next to a field label indicates the presence of a filter on that field, which can be manipulated by opening the *filter popup* from the context menu. A formula icon (*fx*) indicates that the primitive field in question is a calculated field with an associated spreadsheet-style formula. The actual formula can be edited using the *formula bar* above the result area, or directly in any non-header cell belonging to the field's column, as illustrated in Figure 1. Finally, as in a spreadsheet, our system allows fields (columns) to be hidden from view and later recalled for inspection. If the hidden field was used for filtering or sorting, or is referenced from a formula, a dashed cell icon (⁞⁞) is shown for the relevant dependent field to indicate that the visible result depends on a hidden portion of the query. Hidden fields can be recalled using the *field selector* popup, which shows an expandable list of available fields, centered around the field it was opened for. The field selector also serves to suggest new joins over known foreign key relationships, modeled as pre-existing hidden fields, and to display exact join conditions.

For the remainder of this paper, we will use the following terminology when referring to concepts in the nested relational data model: A *value* is either a *primitive* or a *relation*, where a relation is defined as a set of *tuples*, each containing a set of *fields* identified by *labels*, each containing a value, recursively. The *schema* of a value either defines the value to be a primitive, or defines the value to be a relation, with schemas further specified for each of the latter's fields, recursively. See Figure 3.

3.2 Query Model

We now discuss the specific structure of queries in our system. A visual query is modeled as a nested relational schema that has been annotated with query- and presentation-related properties on each field. See Table 2. We refer to the annotated schema as the SIEUFERD *query model*. When SQL queries are generated from a visual query and flat result sets have been assembled into a nested relational result, the schema of the nested result is identical to the schema in the query model. This correspondence makes it straightforward to translate high-level user interactions on the visualized query result to concrete modifications on the underlying query model, and conversely, to indicate the state of the query model in the table header of the visualized result.

Table instantiation. As a basic rule, each relation in the query model gets to retrieve data from one concrete table in the underlying database; that relation is said to *instantiate* the database table.

The following is a simple query that instantiates the table called COURSES and displays a selection of its fields:

courses ≺					
id	area _id	title	may_ pdf	may_ audit	exam_type
56	2	Roman Art	N	Y	Other
177	2	Comedy	Y	Y	Final
845	2	Russian Drama	N	N	Other
1795	4	American Politics	Y	Y	Final
2566		Junior Seminars	N	N	Other
3921	4	Judicial Politics	Y	Y	Final

In the SIEUFERD query model, the query above is represented as a nested relational schema whose root relation references the COURSES table from its INSTANTIATEDTABLE property, with primitive child fields storing the technical name of each table column in their respective COLUMNDEFINITION properties. Similar encodings are used for all query states that will be discussed in this section; see Table 2 for details.

Nesting and joins. Queries need to be able to incorporate data from multiple tables. Commonly, tables need to be equijoined together, for example when the user wishes to examine data spread across foreign key relationships in a normalized database schema. In the SIEUFERD query model, the introduction of a new table instance can be done by defining a *nested relation*, optionally constrained by an equijoin condition against its parent relation:

courses ≺									
id	area _id	title	may_ pdf	may_ audit	exam_ type	readings ≺			
						id	⋈ course _id	author_ name	title
56	2	Roman Art	N	Y	Other	44	56	Ramage	Roman Art
						8,838	56	Gombrich	Art and Illusion
177	2	Comedy	Y	Y	Final	4,998	177	Moliere	The Miser
						12,138	177	Feydeau	A Flea in Her Ear
						16,878	177	Reza	Art
845	2	Russian Drama	N	N	Other	603	845	Pushkin	Little Tragedies
						9,207	845	Chekhov	The Seagull
						12,366	845	Vampilov	The Duck Hunt
1795	4	American Politics	Y	Y	Final				
2566		Junior Seminars	N	N	Other	9,935	2566	Pierre Loti	India
3921	4	Judicial Politics	Y	Y	Final	2,570	3921	Rosenberg, Gerald	The Hollow Hope
						17,629	3921	Lazarus, Edward	Closed Chambers

In the query above, the nested relation READINGS instantiates the database table with the same name, and equijoins itself against its parent relation COURSES on the COURSE_ID field, as indicated by the join icon (⋈) on the latter. The other side of the equijoin condition is the ID field in the COURSES relation. The latter information is omitted from the result layout to save space, but is displayed in the field selector (Figure 2). The one-to-many icon (≺) on the READINGS relation indicates that our system decided the latter may contain more than one tuple for each corresponding tuple in COURSES, the parent relation.

The joins described here have different semantics than the traditional flat joins encountered in SQL and most other visual query tools. Rather than duplicating tuples on one side of the operator for each occurrence of a matching tuple on the other, each tuple from the parent side of the join has a nested relation added to it holding zero or more matching tuples from the child side. This operator is known formally as a *nest equijoin* [53], though we will simply use the term *join* when unambiguous. One convenient property of nest equijoins is that tuples on the left-hand side of the operator do not disappear when the join fails to find matching tuples on the right; this can be seen in the query above for the course AMERICAN POLITICS, which has no books in its reading list.

It is often desirable to hide technical primary key fields, fields made redundant by equijoin conditions (e.g. COURSE_ID), or otherwise uninteresting fields, for presentation purposes. Continuing the example above, our query model allows us to hide several fields without altering the query semantics:

courses ≺					
title	may_ pdf	may_ audit	exam_ type	readings ≺	
				author_name	title
Roman Art	N	Y	Other	Ramage	Roman Art
				Gombrich	Art and Illusion
Comedy	Y	Y	Final	Moliere	The Miser
				Feydeau	A Flea in Her Ear
				Reza	Art
Russian Drama	N	N	Other	Pushkin	Little Tragedies
				Chekhov	The Seagull
				Vampilov	The Duck Hunt
American Politics	Y	Y	Final		
Junior Seminars	N	N	Other	Pierre Loti	India
Judicial Politics	Y	Y	Final	Rosenberg, Gerald	The Hollow Hope
				Lazarus, Edward	Closed Chambers

The hidden fields could be recalled at any time using the field selector. As before, the field selector can also be used to see the exact join conditions between READINGS and COURSES.

Nested relations can be used very effectively to display data spread over many tables in a database schema. In the following example, we pull data from five database tables to see more information about each university course:

courses ≺									
area		title	readings ≺		sections ≺				
title	code		author_ name	title	type	num	meetings ≺		
							day	start	end
Literature and the Arts	LA	Roman Art	Ramage	Roman Art	L	01	T	14:30	15:20
			Gombrich	Art and Illusion			Th	14:30	15:20
					P	01	Th	19:30	20:20
Literature and the Arts	LA	Comedy	Moliere	The Miser	L	01	M	11:00	11:50
			Feydeau	A Flea in Her Ear			W	11:00	11:50
					P	01	W	12:30	13:20
			Reza	Art	P	02	W	12:30	13:20
					P	03	W	13:30	14:20
					P	04	F	11:00	11:50
					P	05	W	14:30	15:20
					P	06	Th	11:00	11:50
Literature and the Arts	LA	Russian Drama	Pushkin	Little Tragedies	S	01	T	11:00	12:20
			Chekhov	The Seagull			Th	11:00	12:20
			Vampilov	The Duck Hunt					

Notice that tuples in the READINGS relation occur independently of tuples in the SECTIONS relation; this kind of visualization can not be constructed in tools based on flat tabular results (see Related Work). Also notice the absence of the of the one-to-many icon (≺) on the AREA relation: because the latter relation was joined on its instantiated table's primary key, our system deduced that at most one tuple can exist in AREA for each parent tuple in COURSES.

Sorting. Each nested relation can be sorted on a sequence of its direct child fields, indicated by subscripted sort icons ($\equiv_{123}$) on the latter. In the following example, the root-level COURSES relation is sorted ascending on the MAX_ENROLL field, while individual sets of READINGS are sorted by AUTHOR_NAME, then by TITLE:

courses ≺								
title	≡ max _enroll	readings ≺		sections ≺				
		author_ name ≡	title $\equiv_2$	type	num	meetings ≺		
						day	start	end
Russian Drama	0	Chekhov	The Seagull	S	01	T	11:00	12:20
		Pushkin	Little Tragedies			Th	11:00	12:20
		Vampilov	The Duck Hunt					
Junior Seminars	12	Pierre Loti	India	S	01	M	13:30	16:20
Judicial Politics	24	Lazarus, Edward	Closed Chambers	L	01	W	11:00	11:50
						F	11:00	11:50
		Rosenberg, Gerald	The Hollow Hope	P	01	Th	14:30	15:20
				P	02	W	13:30	14:20
				P	04	W	11:00	11:50
				P	03	T	11:00	11:50
Roman Art	25	Gombrich	Art and Illusion	L	01	T	14:30	15:20
		Ramage	Roman Art			Th	14:30	15:20
				P	01	Th	19:30	20:20

It is possible to sort on both primitive and relation fields, though we omit the exact semantics of the latter case here. Following any explicit sort terms, our system automatically sorts every relation on a tuple-identifying subset of its retrieved fields. This ensures that all query results are retrieved in a deterministic order. The automatic sort is usually on an indexed primary key; see *set projection* below.

Filter. Using the filter popup (Figure 2), a filter can be defined on any field, indicated by the filter icon (▼). Filters on relation fields restrict the set of tuples retrieved in that relation, while filters on primitive fields restrict the tuples of the parent relation. In the following example, the MEETINGS relation is filtered to show only tuples for which the DAY is W:

courses title	max_enroll	readings author_name	readings title	sections type	num	meetings day	start	end
Comedy	99	Moliere	The Miser	L	01	W	11:00	11:50
		Feydeau	A Flea in Her Ear	P	01	W	12:30	13:20
				P	02	W	12:30	13:20
		Reza	Art	P	03	W	13:30	14:20
				P	05	W	14:30	15:20
American Politics	78			L	01	W	11:00	11:50
				P	01	W	13:30	14:20
				P	01	W	13:30	14:20
				P	04	W	14:30	15:20
Judicial Politics	24	Rosenberg, Gerald	The Hollow Hope	L	01	W	11:00	11:50
				P	02	W	13:30	14:20
		Lazarus	Closed	P	04	W	11:00	11:50

By default, the effect of a filter in a nested relation is propagated all the way to the root of the query by means of a HIDE PARENT IF EMPTY setting on each intermediate relation, indicated by the arrow-towards-root icon (↖) on the SECTIONS and MEETINGS relations above. In the example, the courses ROMAN ART and RUSSIAN DRAMA have disappeared because they do not have any Wednesday sections. If, rather than retrieving "a list of courses with at least one Wednesday section", we wanted to retrieve "a list of all courses, showing sections on Wednesday only", we could deactivate HIDE PARENT IF EMPTY on the SECTIONS relation:

courses title	max_enroll	readings author_name	readings title	sections type	num	meetings day	start	end
Roman Art	25	Ramage	Roman Art					
		Gombrich	Art and Illusion					
Comedy	99	Moliere	The Miser	L	01	W	11:00	11:50
		Feydeau	A Flea in Her Ear	P	01	W	12:30	13:20
				P	02	W	12:30	13:20
		Reza	Art	P	03	W	13:30	14:20
				P	05	W	14:30	15:20
Russian Drama	0	Pushkin	Little Tragedies					
		Chekhov	The Seagull					
		Vampilov	The Duck Hunt					
American Politics	78			L	01	W	11:00	11:50
				P	01	W	13:30	14:20
				P	01	W	13:30	14:20
				P	04	W	14:30	15:20
Junior Seminars	12	Pierre Loti	India					
Judicial Politics	24	Rosenberg	The Hollow	L	01	W	11:00	11:50

Formulas. An important part of the expressiveness offered by SQL is the ability to include scalar and aggregate computations over primitive values in any part of the query. In the SIEUFERD query model, both kinds of calculations are supported by means of *calculated fields*. A calculated field is a primitive field, added to any relation by the user, that takes its value from a *formula* rather than from a particular column in an instantiated database table. Like other fields, calculated fields can be sorted or filtered on.

SIEUFERD formulas are syntactically similar to spreadsheet formulas, but belong to and reference entire columns of field values rather than hard-coded ranges of cells. This allows SIEUFERD queries, like SQL queries, to be defined independently of the exact data that might reside in a database at any given time. Without this design, the user might have to rewrite formulas if the data in the underlying data source changes, or if other parts of the query are changed in such a way as to add or remove tuples in the result. Forgetting to update formulas when input data is changed is a common kind of error in spreadsheets [31, 12], which we avoid.

The restriction that calculated fields always be primitive fields is an important one; we do not wish formulas to take the role of a textual query language embedded within the visual one. Formulas do not provide a relational algebra, but rather allow simple computations over primitive values.

Continuing the course catalog example, we can calculate the duration of each meeting of a course section:

`=minutes([end] - [start])`

courses title	sections type	num	meetings day	start	end	fx duration
Roman Art	L	01	T	14:30	15:20	50
			Th	14:30	15:20	
	P	01	Th	19:30	20:20	50
Comedy	L	01	M	11:00	11:50	50
			W	11:00	11:50	50
	P	01	W	12:30	13:20	50
	P	02	W	12:30	13:20	50
	P	03	W	13:30	14:20	50
	P	04	F	11:00	11:50	50
	P	05	W	14:30	15:20	50
	P	06	Th	11:00	11:50	50
Russian Drama	S	01	T	11:00	12:20	80
			Th	11:00	12:20	80

The calculated field DURATION, marked with the formula icon (***fx***), is evaluated once for each tuple in MEETINGS, its containing relation. Using another calculated field, we can add up the durations as well, at the level of each course:

`=sum([duration])`

courses title	fx total duration	sections type	num	meetings day	start	end	fx duration
Roman Art	150	L	01	T	14:30	15:20	50
				Th	14:30	15:20	50
		P	01	Th	19:30	20:20	50
Comedy	400	L	01	M	11:00	11:50	50
				W	11:00	11:50	50
		P	01	W	12:30	13:20	50
		P	02	W	12:30	13:20	50
		P	03	W	13:30	14:20	50
		P	04	F	11:00	11:50	50
		P	05	W	14:30	15:20	50
		P	06	Th	11:00	11:50	50
Russian Drama	160	S	01	T	11:00	12:20	80
				Th	11:00	12:20	80

When using aggregate functions such as SUM or COUNT, the relation in which the calculated field is defined determines the level at which aggregate values are grouped. In the example above, because the TOTAL DURATION field is a child of the COURSES relation, a total is calculated for each course rather than, say, for each section. Each course includes in its total only tuples from the MEETINGS relation that are descendants of that course's tuple in the COURSES relation.

It is permitted for a formula to reference fields outside its own containing relation, as in the following example:

`=100 * [duration] / [total duration]`

courses title	fx total duration	sections type	num	meetings day	start	end	fx duration	fx percent
Roman Art	150	L	01	T	14:30	15:20	50	33.33
				Th	14:30	15:20	50	33.33
		P	01	Th	19:30	20:20	50	33.33
Comedy	400	L	01	M	11:00	11:50	50	12.50
				W	11:00	11:50	50	12.50
		P	01	W	12:30	13:20	50	12.50
		P	02	W	12:30	13:20	50	12.50
		P	03	W	13:30	14:20	50	12.50
		P	04	F	11:00	11:50	50	12.50
		P	05	W	14:30	15:20	50	12.50
		P	06	Th	11:00	11:50	50	12.50
Russian Drama	160	S	01	T	11:00	12:20	80	50.00
				Th	11:00	12:20	80	50.00

Here, the formula in the PERCENT field references the TOTAL DURATION field of the outer COURSES relation. This is analogous to a correlated subquery in SQL. Such *outward* references are not crucial to our query model's expressiveness; we eliminate them using a decorrelation technique like that described by Van den Bussche and Vansummeren [58, p. 8].

Filters and aggregate functions. When an aggregate function references a relation with a filter applied to it, the filter is evaluated before the aggregate. In the following example, the SECTIONS relation is filtered to only include lecture-type sections. The TOTAL DURATION for each course changes accordingly:

courses								
title	fx total duration	sections		meetings				
		type	num	day	start	end	fx duration	fx percent
Roman Art	100	L	01	T	14:30	15:20	50	50.00
				Th	14:30	15:20	50	50.00
Comedy	100	L	01	M	11:00	11:50	50	50.00
				W	11:00	11:50	50	50.00
Russian Drama	0							
American Politics	100	L	01	M	11:00	11:50	50	50.00
				W	11:00	11:50	50	50.00
Junior Seminars	0							
Judicial Politics	100	L	01	W	11:00	11:50	50	50.00
				F	11:00	11:50	50	50.00

It is equally valid to define a filter on the output side of an aggregate, e.g. on TITLE or TOTAL DURATION in the example above.

Flat joins. Traditional flat joins can be expressed by referencing a descendant relation from a formula without enclosing the reference in an aggregate function. In the following example, each course title is repeated once for each distinct author name in the reading list, because the AUTHOR REFERENCE field in the COURSES relation references the READINGS relation without the use of an aggregate function:

courses				
title	exam_type	author reference fx	readings	
			author_name	title
Roman Art	Other	Gombrich	Gombrich	Art and Illusion
Roman Art	Other	Ramage	Ramage	Roman Art
Comedy	Final	Feydeau	Feydeau	A Flea in Her Ear
Comedy	Final	=[author_name]		The Miser
Comedy	Final	Reza	Reza	Art
Russian Drama	Other	Chekhov	Chekhov	The Seagull
Russian Drama	Other	Pushkin	Pushkin	Little Tragedies
Russian Drama	Other	Vampilov	Vampilov	The Duck Hunt
American Politics	Final			
Junior Seminars	Other	Pierre Loti	Pierre Loti	India
Judicial	Final	Lazarus	Lazarus, Edward	Closed Chambers

The actual behavior is that of a left join, with a null value being returned for the course AMERICAN POLITICS, which has no readings in its reading list. To express an inner join instead, the HIDE PARENT IF EMPTY setting could be enabled on the READINGS relation. The left join semantics of these *inward* formula references help our visual query language maintain some desirable properties. In particular, the mere introduction of a new calculated field (e.g. AUTHOR REFERENCE) will never cause tuples to disappear from said field's containing relation (COURSES).

Set projection. By default, tuples retrieved for a relation always include the primary key fields of the relation's instantiated table, even if the user has hidden those fields from view. This allows our system to keep result tuples in a stable order as the user hides or shows fields, and to keep a one-to-one relationship between tuples on the screen and tuples in instantiated database tables. It also allows us to generate more efficient SQL queries, for example by avoiding expensive `SELECT DISTINCT` statements. The automatic inclusion of primary key fields in the projection of a particular relation can be avoided by means of the HIDE DUPLICATE ROWS option, indicated by the bracket icon (**{**):

courses		
title	sections	
	type	status
Roman Art	L	O
	P	X
Comedy	L	O
	P	O
	P	O
	P	O
	P	O
	P	X
	P	X
Russian Drama	S	O

courses		
title	sections {	
	type	status
Roman Art	L	O
	P	X
Comedy	L	O
	P	O
	P	X
Russian Drama	S	O
American Politics	L	O
	P	X
Junior Seminars	S	O
Judicial Politics	L	O

3.3 Query Building

Having explained the query model, we now show how the user would actually build queries using our direct manipulation interface. We do this by means of an example query building session. The user is an investigative journalist who is writing a story about ethanol biofuel lobbying [20]. She has compiled, in the table PLANTS_OS, a list of major ethanol producers[1], and would like to find the total lobbying expenditures of each. Another table, LOBBYING, contains quarterly lobbying reports from US corporations in the years 1998 through 2012 (727,927 tuples)[2].

Base table. The user starts by opening the table of ethanol producers as a template for the new query:

plants_os					
id	company	noplants	loccountry	feedstock	nameplate_cap_mgy
1	New Energy Corp	1	United States	Corn	102.0
2	Maple Etanol SRL	1	Peru	Sugar Cane	35.0
3	Gevo Inc	1	United States	Corn	21.0
4	Patriot Renewable Fuels	1	United States	Corn	100.0
5	Tate & Lyle North American Sugars	1	United States	Corn	105.0
6	AG Processing	1	United States	Corn	52.0

Join. To add another table to the query, the user selects the column or columns to join on and invokes the JOIN action from the context menu. This opens a dialog box for selecting the table to join with, in this case LOBBYING, and for selecting the corresponding columns from the latter to be matched in an equijoin constraint. The user joins the PLANTS_OS and LOBBYING tables on the COMPANY and ULTORG fields, respectively:

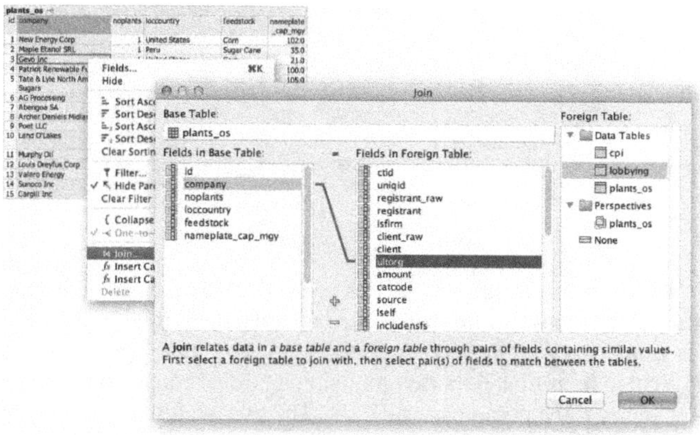

In cases where the database defines explicit foreign key relationships between tables, use of the above JOIN dialog is unnecessary; instead, all available joins will be available as hidden relations in the field selector. The effect is a schema navigation capability analogous to that of QBB [47], AppForge [60], and App2You [36].

Hide fields. After the join, a lot of columns are shown, so the user selects a few of them and invokes the HIDE action:

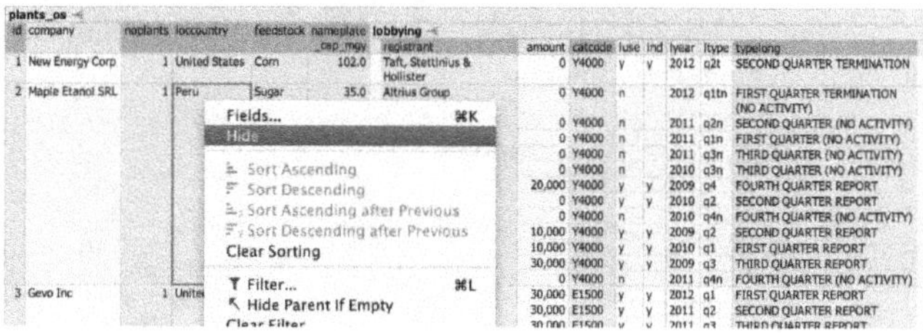

It is now easier to get a sense of the data. We have a new child relation field, called LOBBYING, containing the lobbying reports for each company:

[1]Renewable Fuels Association/Maple Etanol SRL (2012)
[2]The Center for Responsive Politics (2012) https://www.opensecrets.org

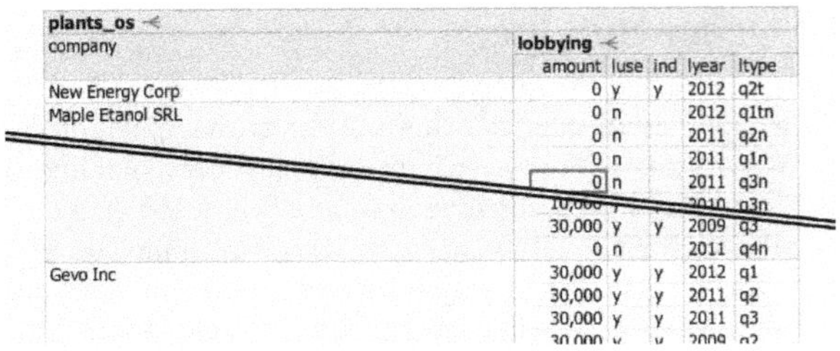

Sort. The user decides to sort the lobbying reports for each company most-recent-first, invoking the SORT DESCENDING action on the LYEAR field and then invoking the SORT DESCENDING AFTER PREVIOUS action on the LTYPE field. This sorts individual LOBBYING relations by year (⩧) and then by quarter (⩧$_2$):

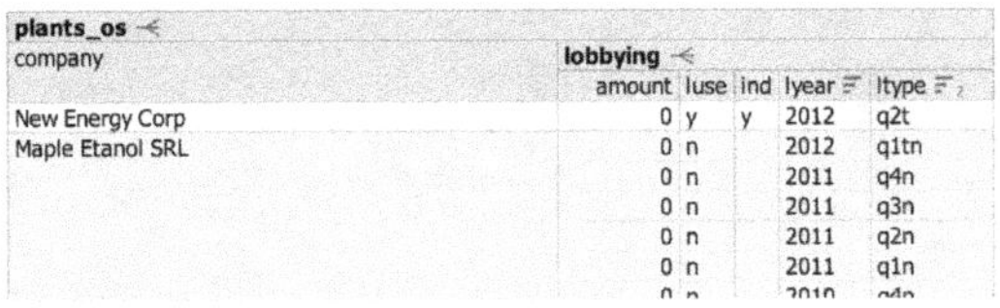

Aggregate formula. The user would now like to calculate a total lobbying amount for each company. She invokes the INSERT CALCULATED FIELD AFTER action to insert a calculated field (***fx***) next to the COMPANY field, and enters the name SUM OF AMOUNTS in the new column's label cell. She then moves the cursor to one of the column's value cells, and enters a sum formula, clicking the AMOUNT column to insert the column reference:

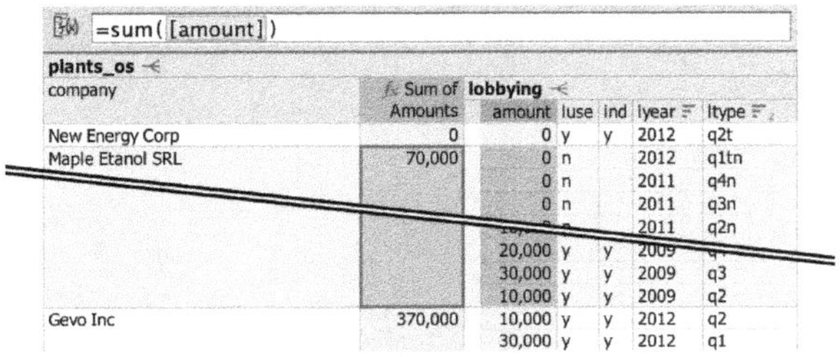

Unlike in a spreadsheet, there is no need to "drag down" the sum formula; it is always evaluated once for each tuple in PLANTS_OS, its parent relation.

Scalar formula. Reported lobbying amounts come from different years, some going back to 1998. The user would like to calculate inflation-corrected totals. A separate table CPI contains yearly Consumer Price Index values normalized for 2012. The user performs another JOIN, this time between LOBBYING and CPI, on the LYEAR and CYEAR fields, respectively. This brings the CPIV value for each lobbying report's year into the nested result. The user then adds another calculated field, this time under the same relation as the existing AMOUNT field, and enters a formula that calculates the inflation-adjusted amount for each report. We here have a useful example of an inward formula reference (to CPIV) that is not enclosed in an aggregate function:

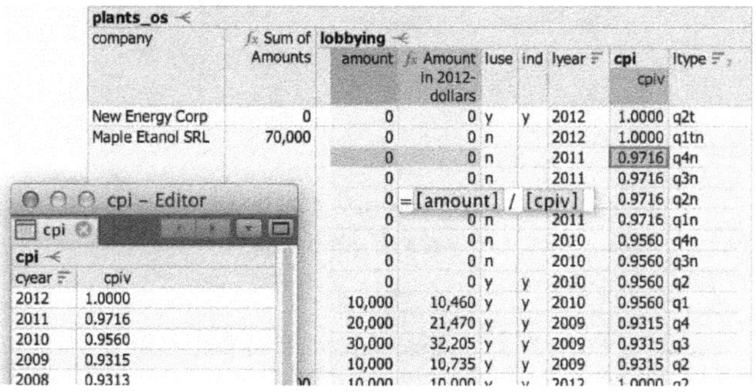

A new inflation-adjusted total can now be added as a calculated field at the PLANTS_OS level, shown adjacent to the existing non-adjusted sum:

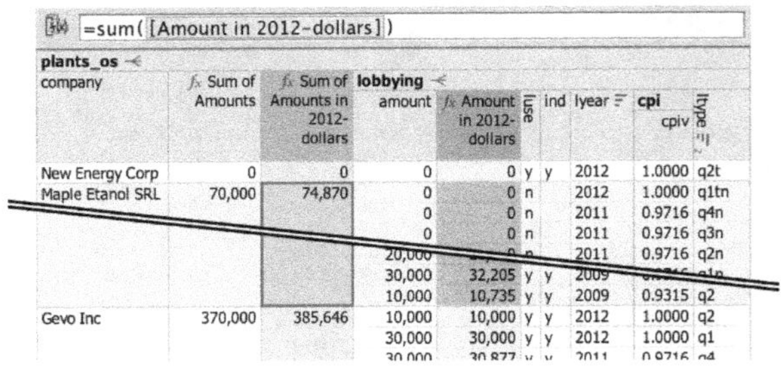

Filter. Lobbying reports may sometimes be amended, in which case the superseded reports should be excluded from totals to avoid double counting. The user can look for superseded reports by invoking the FILTER action on the LUSE field and selecting the value N:

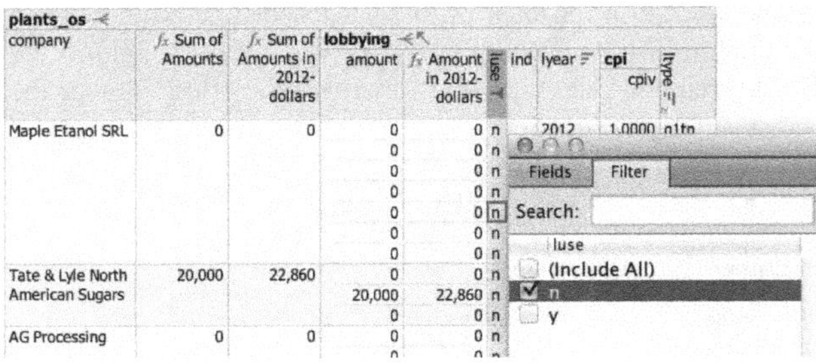

The user sees that there are superseded reports in the database with non-zero dollar amounts, and inverts the filter to exclude them.

Select fields. The user now decides to hide the individual reports altogether and instead reintroduce some of the fields that were hidden from the PLANTS_OS relation before, using the field selector:

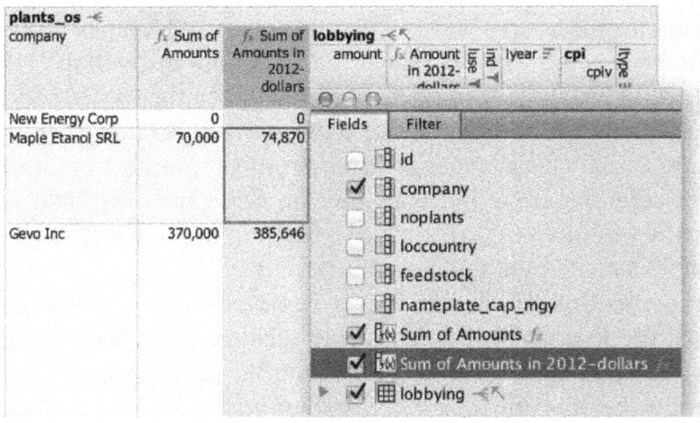

Final touches. The user edits the field labels to make them a bit more readable, and sorts the companies by their lobbying totals. The underlying SQL column names can still be seen in the field selector. The user also enables a formatting option on the last column to produce a bar chart visualization. The result now looks presentable:

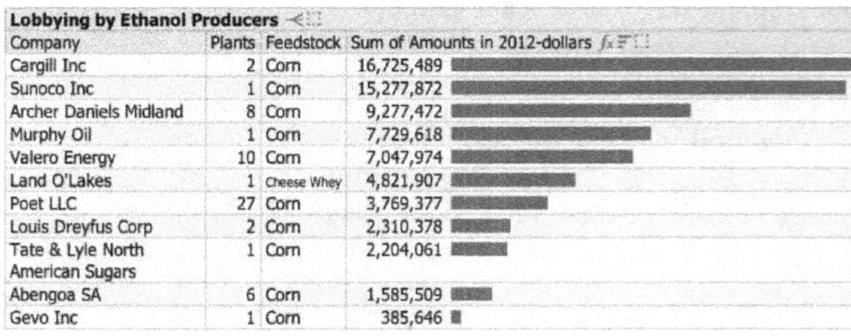

While the LOBBYING relation that feeds into the aggregate formula is now hidden, the user could easily make it visible again from the field selector, like she did for the previously hidden PLANTS and FEEDSTOCK fields. There are also shortcuts for unhiding hidden fields referenced from the formula, or the hidden filter, indicated by the dashed cell icons (⬚).

3.4 Architecture

Our visual query system allows a large class of queries to be expressed by end users. As a necessary consequence, we can make few assumptions about how fast results can be computed. In many cases, even though the final query desired by the user may be cheap to compute, intermediate or explorative queries generated during interactive query building may be expensive. Intermediate queries may even contain user errors, such as circular dependencies in formulas. A key requirement of our system is to avoid getting the user stuck in such states, and to keep the query building interface responsive and up to date even when expensive or incorrect queries are encountered.

Our system's basic architectural decision is to defer all query processing to a relational database backend, generating SQL queries over JDBC and retrieving a complete new result every time the user modifies the query model. This produces transactionally consistent results while avoiding complicated incremental evaluation logic. We then provide the necessary smoke and mirrors to give the user an experience of responsive, incremental query building. The key features to this effect are as follows:

Visual stability. Our query semantics ensure that nested result tuples from successive steps of a visual query building process remain in the same order by default, and that the set of logical tuples in a relation does not usually change as fields are hidden or shown. The presentation properties of result layouts, such as table column widths, are based on average and confidence interval values that do not change once a target number of unique sample values have been collected from observed query results. Text breaking and font sizing is done to ensure that even exceptionally long string values can be displayed at a given visual width. Thus, even though an entirely new result set is generated every time the user modifies the query, the visual transition from the old to the new result appears seamless. The generation of compact nested table layouts is done using our previously described system for visualization of structured hierarchical reports [5].

Decoupled query and result updates. The display of a nested table header, which our system uses to communicate query state, need not be postponed until a query returns with actual results. Better yet, upon a change to the query model, we can immediately render a new table layout whose structure and indications are based on the updated query model, but whose data is taken from whichever query completed most recently. For fields not present in the old result, we show a placeholder icon (···) where data values would normally appear. Meanwhile, updated SQL queries run while a non-modal progress indication is shown in the toolbar area. Once the query completes, the result layout is rendered again with actual results. The user does not need to wait for the query to complete before making new changes.

For example: When unhiding a previously hidden field, the user sees the result layout immediately update to accommodate the new table column, already at the correct width, with placeholder icons seamlessly being replaced by data values as soon as the updated query completes.

Interruptable queries. If the user modifies the query before the previous query has finished executing, the previous query is automatically interrupted using the database backend's preferred mechanism. This is crucial for letting the user escape from long-running queries, and also allows the user to perform multiple modifications

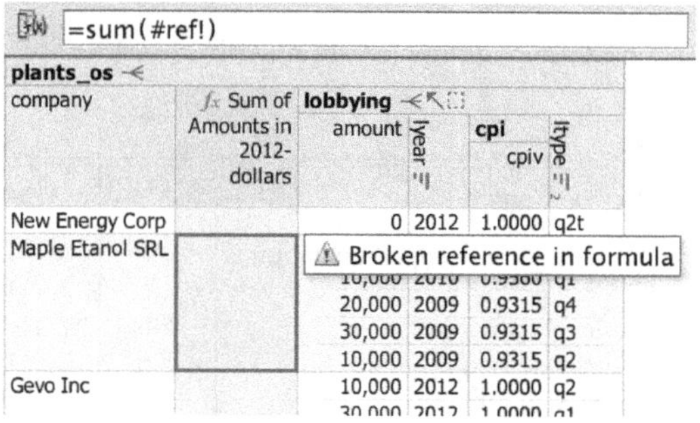

Figure 4: High-level error handling. A referenced field was deleted, so the formula can no longer be evaluated. The system shows a warning while evaluating the rest of the query normally.

to the query without waiting for the exact result of each step to appear. The on-screen layout remains undisturbed by the automatic interruption and restarting of queries in the background. Note that even long-running queries can be constructed with responsive result feedback if the user can manage to temporarily filter the dataset down to a smaller size during query construction.

Automatic query limiting. All generated SQL queries include an automatic LIMIT clause, retrieving initially 100 tuples total for each relation field. This populates the visible part of a typical result window. If the user scrolls far enough down to see the end of the result layout, and there are more tuples left, the query is re-executed using a limit twice as large as before. This allows the user to reach tuple N in $O(N)$ time. Infinite scrolling appears seamless.

High-level error handling. User-defined formulas introduce a variety of possible error conditions, including circular references, broken references, type errors, and arithmetic runtime errors. Our system detects and handles many such errors at a high level. In the result layout, formulas with errors are highlighted in yellow, with a tooltip showing specific error messages if the cursor is moved to the highlighted area. For query evaluation purposes, erroneous formulas are replaced by null values, ensuring that the rest of the query can still be evaluated normally. See Figure 4.

Complete high-level error handling requires the set of functions and data types available in formulas to be known to the system. It may also require functions such as arithmetic division to be rewritten to return null instead of triggering runtime errors on, say, division by zero. SIEUFERD includes a standardized set of formula functions that can be compiled to the dialects of various database backends, currently PostgreSQL, MySQL, and Oracle. Standardizing functions and data types allows a single unit test suite and online documentation set to be used for all backend dialects.

Undo/redo. Undo/redo can be easily supported by storing successive states of the modified query model; a similar technique is used in Tableau [55, p. 90]. Like other kinds of query modifications, undo/redo benefits from several of the previously mentioned features, e.g. interruptable queries.

4. FORMATIVE USER STUDY

We conducted a formative user study with 14 participants (5 male, median age 42) from a variety of technical and professional backgrounds; see Table 5 (appendix) for a demographic summary.

In the first part of the study, done by users A-I, users were given standardized tasks aimed at assessing the initial learnability of our tool. No prior training was given; instead, initial tasks were designed to act as training tasks for subsequent ones. In the sec-

Table 3: Tasks and timings for standardized tasks used as part of the formative user study. Error bars show the standard error of the mean.

#	Task		Training for task	N	Mean time to complete task (s)
1a	Lobbying Totals	Manual join	2a	7	274
1b		Formula	2b	7	672
2a	Inflation Correction	Manual join		7	123
2b		Formula		7	109
3	Single-level auto join		4-6	7	96
4	Multi-level auto join		5-6	7	101
5	Filter via auto join			7	107
6	Multi-level auto join, again			6	94

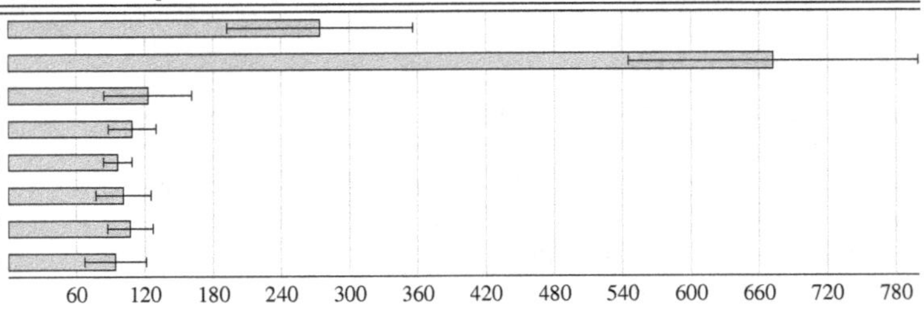

Tasks done: Tasks 1-2 were done by users A-G. Tasks 3-6 were given to users B-I, with some exceptions. **Task order:** User F did tasks 1-2 last. Order is otherwise as indicated. **Hints:** Training tasks included hints as necessary. In task 2a, users D and G were told that they would need to use the JOIN feature.

ond part of the study, and as time permitted during earlier sessions, users were given a chance to do more open-ended tasks on datasets we provided, including some datasets from the users' own organization. Here, we gave participants demos and instructions for operating our tool, in order to gather higher-level observations than would be possible during pure learning tasks.

From screen and voice recordings of each user study session, we collected detailed observations that were later coded and categorized, as well as timing data for standardized tasks.

4.1 Standardized Tasks

This section describes tasks and timings for the standardized portion of our study. We designed the standardized tasks to assess the initial learnability of our system's basic query operators, likely to cover a range of common queries. Tasks designated as training tasks reflect the user's first encounter with a particular feature, with few upfront instructions given on how to proceed. If a user got stuck during a training task, hints were given and any relevant observations noted, ensuring that the user progressed to the corresponding follow-up task. See Table 3.

Formulas and manual joins. Tasks 1 and 2 correspond to the lobbying example from Section 3.3, in two parts. In task 1, which functions as a training task, the user is started off with a fresh query showing only the PLANTS_OS table, and is asked to find the total amount spent on lobbying by each organization. A minimal schema diagram is provided on paper, showing the two tables involved and the fields to be matched in the join condition. The user will have to discover that the operation called JOIN is needed, and then figure out how to use a formula to calculate totals. In task 2, the user is asked to modify the existing query to calculate inflation-corrected totals, using consumer price index values from the CPI table and features that have already been used. The user now has to realize that another join is needed, followed by one or two additional formulas. This task tests whether the user, after only a single training task, has developed enough of a mental model of how joins and formulas work to combine the two features to arrive at a single result.

Task 1, the training task, took users about 16 minutes on average, with 70% of the time spent after users figured out the initial manual join. Task 2, a strictly harder task using the same features as task 1, took only about 4 minutes, 4.1 times faster. The difference is statistically significant ($p = 0.009$ with two-tailed Welch's t-test). Comparing only times spent on the join portion of the tasks vs. times spent on the formula portion of the tasks, the difference is only statistically significant for the latter ($p = 0.004$). In this case, users solved the second formula task 6.2 times faster than the first.

Auto joins and filters. Tasks 3-6 involve automatic joins over known foreign key relationships (*auto joins*), starting again from a fresh query showing a single base table. Users are given a schema diagram on paper, with the relevant joins marked, and told that because the system already knows about the relationships between the tables, it will not be necessary to use the manual JOIN action. Tasks 3 and 4 ask the user to produce a report-style query similar to the course catalog shown in Figure 2, first adding a table related to the base table via a single join (e.g. READINGS), and then adding a table related to the base table via multiple joins (SECTIONS, INSTRUCTORS_SECTIONS, INSTRUCTORS). In task 5, the user is asked to filter the result on a field in a table that has not yet been joined into the current query, specifically to "show only courses offered in Spring 06-07", where semester names are stored in a separate table. This allows us to assess the user's expectations wrt. interactions between nested joins and filters. In task 6, the user is started off with a fresh new query, starting from a different base table (INSTRUCTORS). Having previously produced a course catalog showing a list of instructors for each course, the user is now asked to show a list of courses taught by each instructor. This repeats task 4, but from the opposite end of the schema.

4.2 Observations

We now discuss a specific observations gathered from both the standardized and the open-ended portions of the study.

Manual joins. The manual join dialog, quoting user C, was "actually very easy to use"; most users moved through it quickly and correctly on their first attempt. Still, users preferred auto joins once introduced to them, see below. Users CEJ wanted to visually verify that the equijoin condition was satisfied, and were briefly confused because our system automatically hid the redundant constrained field on the nested side of the join. Users performing task 2 had no problems with the join portion of the task; only users DG required a hint that they would need to use the JOIN feature again, while the rest realized this on their own.

Formulas. When first attempting to perform a sum aggregation, users BCDE started by looking for an explicit sum action, as would be found in Excel's toolbar. Users CGK looked for an Excel-style formula builder. Having eventually realized that they needed to insert a calculated field and enter a formula themselves, users DEFK had initial trouble learning how to physically enter the formula, trying for example to enter the formula in an already-existing column, or in the column header.

In Excel, sums can be produced either using formulas or pivot tables. The two interfaces are largely separate, with users often preferring one or the other. Our system follows the formula approach. Users CH commented that they thought of pivot tables when first trying to compute a sum, while users BEI thought of pivot tables during other tasks.

A significant difference between spreadsheet formulas and SIEUFERD formulas is that the latter, like SQL queries, reference entire columns of values rather than an explicit range of cells. Users ABCFH expected this on their first attempts to insert a reference in a sum formula. Users DEGN expected the spreadsheet model, initially attempting to select a range of cells. A related challenge was to understand the level at which a calculated field should be inserted in order for sums to be grouped in the right way. The fact that the position of a formula in the relation hierarchy determines the grouping of aggregate functions is a further deviation from the spreadsheet model, while the lack of an explicit GROUP BY clause may be confusing to SQL users. User H tried to specify the set of columns to group by in the aggregate function itself, as in the formula =SUM([NAME],[AMOUNT]), while user F tried to hide every field other than the one to be summed. User G attempted to invoke the HIDE DUPLICATE ROWS action. Users CFGH also tried placing the calculated field next to the value to be summed rather than at the parent level. The latter has the trivial effect of producing sums each over only a single input value. User G, who spent 20 minutes on Task 2b, thought aloud:

"Wouldn't it be fantastic if there was a way simply to operate at that group level rather than these individual entries? [After creating a new formula at the correct level:] Is it doing it that way? Oh, that's perfect. ... That is meeting my heart's desire. But I wouldn't have the cue for that."

Despite initial difficulty with formulas in training task 1b, users applied them quickly and accurately in follow-up task 2b. This is despite the follow-up task requiring more steps (a join, a scalar function, and an aggregate function). This suggests users are able to apply formulas effectively after first learning them, but that there is significant potential for improved learnability. We agree with users AM, who suggested adding an explicit sum action like that of Excel. This feature would automatically generate a sum formula above the nearest one-to-many relationship, which would then serve as an example to the user to learn from.

After initial learning, users appreciated the behavior of formulas. Users CEGK noted explicitly that the behavior of aggregate functions, including grouping and subtotaling behavior, made sense. Users ILK also commented that the all-column nature of formula references made sense and was an advantage over Excel's range-style references. User K noted:

"I just feel like I have a truer sense of what I'm adding up, or what's being considered in this format vs. the traditional Excel. Because [in Excel] you could be pulling from the wrong places, you can be getting weird numbers, you could accidentally hit a field that now ends up in your calculation."

Field selection; auto joins. Users performing tasks 3-6, or similar tasks on other datasets, were generally able to use the auto join feature without trouble. The exception was user N, who had a hard time because of the lack of visible indications in the result area that more fields could be shown. User G also noted this issue. Users IKN specifically looked for an action named "Unhide", like in Excel. This suggests that our user interface needs a more visible affordance for accessing hidden fields. We expect hidden fields to be far more common in SIEUFERD than in Excel, since a typical database query projects only a small subset of columns available from instantiated database tables. The design of an improved unhide affordance should take this into account.

Users EGHJKL reacted particularly enthusiastically to the auto join feature, using words such as "fantastic", "wow", "damn", and "amazing". User E noted:

"Yes, the manual join made sense, but that was a very simple situation. I wouldn't want to have done the joins on this [more complicated database]. The fact that I was just able to double-click and expand it out, that meant, it dumbed the task down to the level that I was happy performing it."

Field selection; efficiency. One important problem was that of poor defaults for which fields should be visible immediately after a new relation is introduced into the current query. For manual joins, all (non-redundant) fields in the foreign table would be visible in the nested relation; this made it hard to grasp the overall structure of the query without first going through the step of hiding a number of irrelevant columns, usually necessitating horizontal scrolling. For auto joins, in contrast, only primary key fields were displayed by default. This also turned out to be a poor choice, because primary key fields often consist of purely technical identifiers that neither help the user identify an entity in the database nor its type. An example would be the relation EMPLOYEES(ID, FIRST_NAME, LAST_NAME), where the database identifies each tuple by the technical primary key ID (maybe a number, like "16") but where the user would rather like to see the first and last names of each employee—despite the theoretical possibility that two employees might have the same name. Showing only primary key fields by default made auto joins harder to work with than necessary, requiring users to click four or five times in the field selector in order to introduce a new relation and show a reasonable set of fields from that relation.

Post-study, in response to the problem of poor field visibility defaults, we modified our system to allow a subset of columns from each database table to be marked as human-readable heading fields. These are the fields that will initially be visible whenever the table in question is introduced into a query. As suggested by users MN, various heuristics can be used to configure this setting automatically. Several proposed attribute ranking algorithms [19, 44] could be suitable. For now, we simply look for column names containing the words "title" or "name". Summarization may even be useful in the vertical direction, with several techniques available [14, 51].

For databases containing a large number of fields per table, navigating the field selector became cumbersome. This was noted by users EJM, who got a chance to try our tool on a real data warehouse schema containing 22 interconnected tables with up to 40-73 fields each (19 on average). User L also pointed this out for the smaller course catalog schema. User E explains:

"You've got massive lists, and they're not ordered alphabetically. You've got table names, and field names, and sometimes they are not very English."

One part of the problem is that users spent a significant amount of time scanning up and down looking for specific field names. A search box in the field selector, like that of the filter popup, would help mitigate this, as suggested by users JM. A separate problem is the fact that the multitude of primitive fields in the field selector obscures the overall structure of relation fields in the query, including those accessible via auto joins. Users JM also commented that they would have liked to see a schema diagram of some sort on-screen. In the future, we may consider adding a second kind of field selector that shows relation fields only in a tree representation that is fully expanded by default; this would provide a compact way to see the entire foreign key structure of the database schema as reachable from the current query.

4.3 General Sentiment

At the end of the session, users CDHIJK expressed that they had a high degree of understanding of the tool. User K, who had 2-300 hours of experience with SQL from their previous job, noted:

"It's probably fair to say that I am as comfortable with this as I am with SQL right now, just because I haven't used SQL that often

in the recent past. Given 2 hours, I think I could make an accurate report in this, allowing for mistakes, and fixing my mistakes. Take that same period in SQL, and I think I would still be at sea."

Users EJKL rated SIEUFERD favorably compared to existing commercial tools they are familiar with.

User J: *"It took me a lot longer to get anything useful out of Access after I first started using that. So that's huge. This is more intuitive than either Excel or Access. I think, for the novice that doesn't know what they're doing, this can be very powerful."*

5. CONTROLLED USER STUDY

In a second user study, we aimed to get a more precise idea of how users might rate our system compared to an existing industry tool. We chose the "Query Design" facility of Microsoft Access 2016 as a control. Being part of the Office Professional suite, it is one of the most common visual query tools available. It is also a good example of a query builder that uses a diagram-based approach rather than direct manipulation of results (see Related Work).

The controlled study was a within-subjects counterbalanced design, measuring usability using the System Usability Scale (SUS) [8]. Tullis and Stetson [56] recommend sample sizes of 12-14 users to get reasonably representative results from within-subjects studies based on the SUS survey; we collected data from 14 users (5 male, median age 36). See Table 5 (appendix) for a demographic summary. Only users OTÆ had prior experience with the Access query designer. We met with each user for a single study session, structured as follows:

1. Complete demographic/background survey.
2. Briefly discuss the sample database that will be used for tasks, consulting a schema diagram on paper. The paper diagram remains available to the user during the tasks that follow.
3. Work through some standardized tasks to evaluate Tool 1. Stop after about 20 minutes. The first tool is SIEUFERD for half of the users and Microsoft Access for the other half, randomized.
4. Complete SUS survey for Tool 1.
5. Work through the same tasks in Tool 2, under otherwise identical conditions. Stop after about 20 minutes.
6. Complete SUS survey for Tool 2.
7. Discussion and feedback.

The standardized tasks, all done on the 7-table "Northwind" example database that shipped with older versions of Microsoft Access, are intended to be realistic examples of queries that a user might want to run on such a database. They incorporate joins, filters, sorting, scalar calculations and aggregates, but are limited to queries that can be expressed in Microsoft Access' visual query designer; this excludes queries requiring nested results as well as multi-block queries (e.g. aggregates used as inputs to other aggregates). The exact tasks are listed in Table 6 (appendix). In both tools, we configured foreign key relationships upfront so that the user would not have to manually specify exact join constraints between tables. The first five tasks are guided training tasks, intended to expose the user to all features, in both tools, that are needed to complete the subsequent unguided tasks. The guided tasks tended to take about half of the 20 minutes that users had available to try each tool. After the guided tasks, users were asked to try solving four unguided tasks without help. Since the main purpose of tasks was to give the user enough of an impression of each system to complete the subsequent SUS survey, we gave hints during unguided tasks whenever users reported being stuck.

The results of the study are shown in Table 4. The raw SUS score is reported along with separate Learnability and Usability scores

Table 4: Mean SUS survey results for the controlled study, using various standard scales. Higher scores are better. Error bars show the standard error of the mean.

Scale	*Tool*	*Score (0-100)*
Raw SUS	Access	50
	Sieuferd	68
Learnability	Access	49
	Sieuferd	64
Usability	Access	50
	Sieuferd	69
Percentile	Access	6
	Sieuferd	52

as defined by Lewis and Sauro [39], as well as a percentile rating among 30 other studies in the B2B (Business Software) category as detailed by Sauro [49]. The difference in raw SUS scores between Access and SIEUFERD is statistically significant ($p = 0.0019$ with two-tailed paired t-test).

Interpreting the results, with the caveat that these observations are based on only 20-minute interactions with each tool, we see that SIEUFERD significantly outperformed Microsoft Access in terms of usability. Most of the difference can be attributed to the poor performance of Microsoft Access, considering its low ranking on the percentile scale; SIEUFERD simply achieved an average rating compared to other business software. This supports the original hypothesis of our paper: database querying is hard, but can be made significantly easier using a direct manipulation interface. SIEUFERD still has significant potential for improved usability. In conversations with users, the main requests for future design improvements were (1) the ability to get an overview of the complete database schema from within the query interface and (2) reduced dependency on formulas during query building. This is consistent with observations from the formative study.

6. CONCLUSION

SIEUFERD is a visual query system that achieves SQL-like expressiveness from a pure direct manipulation interface. Whereas previous direct manipulation systems either sacrifice expressiveness or hide the actual query from the user, SIEUFERD integrates the query and its result into a single interactive visualization, using spreadsheet concepts like filters and formulas to expose the complete state of the current query. Compared with the diagram-based query designer of Microsoft Access 2016, users greatly preferred our direct manipulation interface, with the latter scoring 46 percentiles higher on a SUS-based percentile scale. For data-minded people of all professions, we believe SIEUFERD's interaction style holds promise as an alternative to hand-coded SQL.

7. FUTURE WORK

In the current query interface, some queries are expressible yet awkward to construct; examples include range filters, grouping on custom attributes, and `UNION`-type queries. Here, the interface could be improved without significant changes to the underlying query model. See for example the proposed syntactic sugar for union queries in Figure 7 (appendix). Other future work will focus on expanding the ways in which results can be displayed; our query model is well-suited for the retrieval of data for visualizations such as dashboards, crosstabs, calendars, forms, and reports. Already supported are crosstabs, see Figure 5 (appendix), and form/report layouts [5]. Finally, we hope to incorporate *editing* of data; this will allow SIEUFERD to act as a complete schema-independent end user front-end for relational databases.

8. REFERENCES

[1] A. Abouzied, J. Hellerstein, and A. Silberschatz. DataPlay: Interactive tweaking and example-driven correction of graphical database queries. In *Proceedings of the 25th annual ACM symposium on User interface software and technology (UIST '12)*, pages 207–218, New York, NY, USA, 2012. ACM.

[2] S. Achler. GBXT: A gesture-based data exploration tool for your favorite database system. In *Model and Data Engineering*, pages 224–237. Springer International Publishing, Cham, Switzerland, 2014.

[3] M. Angelaccio, T. Catarci, and G. Santucci. Query by Diagram: A fully visual query system. *Journal of Visual Languages & Computing*, 1(3):255–273, 1990.

[4] E. Bakke and E. Benson. The schema-independent database UI: A proposed holy grail and some suggestions. In *Proceedings of the 5th Biennial Conference on Innovative Data Systems Research (CIDR '11)*, 2011.

[5] E. Bakke, D. R. Karger, and R. C. Miller. Automatic layout of structured hierarchical reports. *IEEE Transactions on Visualization and Computer Graphics*, 19(12):2586–2595, December 2013.

[6] E. Baralis and J. Widom. An algebraic approach to static analysis of active database rules. *ACM Transactions on Database Systems (TODS)*, 25(3):269–332, September 2000.

[7] T. Berners-Lee, Y. Chen, L. Chilton, D. Connolly, R. Dhanaraj, J. Hollenbach, A. Lerer, and D. Sheets. Tabulator: Exploring and analyzing linked data on the semantic web. In *Proceedings of the 3rd International Semantic Web User Interaction Workshop (SWUI '06)*, 2006.

[8] J. Brooke. SUS: A quick and dirty usability scale. In *Usability evaluation in industry*, pages 189–194. Tailor & Francis, London, UK, 1996.

[9] M. Burnett, J. Atwood, R. Walpole Djang, J. Reichwein, H. Gottfried, and S. Yang. Forms/3: A first-order visual language to explore the boundaries of the spreadsheet paradigm. *Journal of Functional Programming*, 11:155–206, March 2001.

[10] B. Cao and A. Badia. SQL query optimization through nested relational algebra. *ACM Transactions on Database Systems (TODS)*, 32(3):18, 2007.

[11] T. Catarci, M. F. Costabile, S. Levialdi, and C. Batini. Visual query systems for databases: A survey. *Journal of Visual Languages & Computing*, 8(2):215–260, 1997.

[12] J. P. Caulkins, E. L. Morrison, and T. Weidemann. Spreadsheet errors and decision making: Evidence from field interviews. *Journal of Organizational and End User Computing*, 19(3):1, 2007.

[13] K. S.-P. Chang and B. A. Myers. Using and exploring hierarchical data in spreadsheets. In *Proceedings of the 34th Annual ACM Conference on Human Factors in Computing Systems (CHI '16)*, New York, NY, USA, 2016. ACM.

[14] S. Chaudhuri, G. Das, V. Hristidis, and G. Weikum. Probabilistic ranking of database query results. In *Proceedings of the 30th International Conference on Very Large Data Bases (VLDB '04)*, pages 888–899. VLDB Endowment, 2004.

[15] W.-K. Chen and P.-Y. Tu. VisualTPL: A visual dataflow language for report data transformation. *Journal of Visual Languages & Computing*, 25(3):210–226, 2014.

[16] C. Clack and L. Braine. Object-oriented functional spreadsheets. In *Proceedings of the 10th Glasgow Workshop on Functional Programming (GlaFP '97)*, 1997.

[17] E. F. Codd. Relational completeness of data base sublanguages. In *Database Systems*, pages 65–98. Prentice Hall, 1972.

[18] R. Collie. The 3rd most common button in data apps is... http://www.powerpivotpro.com/2012/03/the-3rd-most-common-button-in-data-apps-is, March 2012.

[19] G. Das, V. Hristidis, N. Kapoor, and S. Sudarshan. Ordering the attributes of query results. In *Proceedings of the 2006 ACM SIGMOD International Conference on Management of Data*, pages 395–406, New York, NY, USA, 2006. ACM.

[20] E. Díaz-Struck. Ethanol industry battles to keep incentives, May 2013. Investigation for the New England Center for Investigative Reporting and Connectas, available at http://eye.necir.org/2013/05/26/ethanol-industry-battles-to-keep-incentives.

[21] S. El-Mahgary and E. Soisalon-Soininen. A form-based query interface for complex queries. *Journal of Visual Languages & Computing*, 29:15–53, 2015.

[22] R. G. Epstein. The TableTalk query language. *Journal of Visual Languages & Computing*, 2(2):115–141, 1991.

[23] R. Fagin. Multivalued dependencies and a new normal form for relational databases. *ACM Transactions on Database Systems (TODS)*, 2(3):262–278, 1977.

[24] H. Garcia-Molina, J. D. Ullman, and J. Widom. *Database Systems: The Complete Book*. Pearson Prentice Hall, Upper Saddle River, NJ, USA, 2nd edition, 2009.

[25] Y. Han, G. Wang, G. Ji, and P. Zhang. Situational data integration with data services and nested table. *Service Oriented Computing and Applications*, 7(2):129–150, 2013.

[26] L. Hella, L. Libkin, J. Nurmonen, and L. Wong. Logics with aggregate operators. *Journal of the ACM (JACM)*, 48(4):880–907, July 2001.

[27] G.-J. Houben and J. Paredaens. A graphical interface formalism: Specifying nested relational databases. In *Proceedings of the IFIP TC2 Working Conference on Visual Database Systems*, pages 257–276, 1989.

[28] Y. E. Ioannidis. Visual user interfaces for database systems. *ACM Computing Surveys (CSUR)*, 28(4es), 1996.

[29] G. Jaeschke and H. J. Schek. Remarks on the algebra of non first normal form relations. In *Proceedings of the 1st ACM SIGACT-SIGMOD Symposium on Principles of Database Systems (PODS '82)*, pages 124–138, New York, NY, USA, 1982. ACM.

[30] H. V. Jagadish, A. Chapman, A. Elkiss, M. Jayapandian, Y. Li, A. Nandi, and C. Yu. Making database systems usable. In *Proceedings of the 2007 ACM SIGMOD international conference on Management of data*, pages 13–24, New York, NY, USA, 2007. ACM.

[31] D. Janvrin and J. Morrison. Using a structured design approach to reduce risks in end user spreadsheet development. *Information & management*, 37(1):1–12, 2000.

[32] M. Jayapandian and H. V. Jagadish. Automated creation of a forms-based database query interface. *Proceedings of the VLDB Endowment*, 1:695–709, August 2008.

[33] M. Jayapandian and H. V. Jagadish. Expressive query specification through form customization. In *Proceedings of the 11th International Conference on Extending Database Technology (EDBT '08)*, pages 416–427, New York, NY, USA, 2008. ACM.

[34] S. Kandel, A. Paepcke, J. Hellerstein, and J. Heer. Wrangler: Interactive visual specification of data transformation scripts. In *Proceedings of the 2011 annual conference on Human Factors in Computing Systems (CHI '11)*, pages 3363–3372, New York, NY, USA, 2011. ACM.

[35] E. Kandogan, E. Haber, R. Barrett, A. Cypher, P. Maglio, and H. Zhao. A1: End-user programming for web-based system administration. In *Proceedings of the 18th Annual ACM Symposium on User Interface Software and Technology (UIST '05)*, pages 211–220, New York, NY, USA, 2005. ACM.

[36] K. Kowalzcykowski, A. Deutsch, K. W. Ong, Y. Papakonstantinou, K. K. Zhao, and M. Petropoulos. Do-It-Yourself database-driven web applications. In *Proceedings of the 4th Biennial Conference on Innovative Data Systems Research (CIDR '09)*, 2009.

[37] D. Król, J. Oleksy, M. Podyma, and B. Trawiński. The analysis of reporting tools for a cadastre information system. In *Proceedings of the 9th International Conference on Business Information Systems (BIS '06)*, pages 150–163, 2006.

[38] M. Levene. *The Nested Universal Relation Database Model*, volume 595 of *Lecture Notes in Computer Science*. Springer Berlin/Heidelberg, 1992.

[39] J. R. Lewis and J. Sauro. The factor structure of the system usability scale. In *Proceedings of the 1st International Conference on Human Centered Design (HCD '09)/HCI International 2009*, pages 94–103, Berlin, Heidelberg, 2009. Springer-Verlag.

[40] L. Libkin and L. Wong. On the power of aggregation in relational query languages. In S. Cluet and R. Hull, editors, *Proceedings of the 6th International Workshop on Database Programming Languages*

(DBPL '97), Lecture Notes in Computer Science, pages 260–280. Springer Berlin/Heidelberg, 1998.

[41] B. Liu and H. V. Jagadish. A spreadsheet algebra for a direct data manipulation query interface. In *Proceedings of the IEEE 25th International Conference on Data Engineering (ICDE '09)*, pages 417–428, April 2009.

[42] N. Lorentzos and K. Dondis. Query by Example for Nested Tables. In *Database and Expert Systems Applications*, pages 716–725. Springer, 1998.

[43] R. M. McCutchen, S. Itzhaky, and D. Jackson. Initial report on Object Spreadsheets. Technical Report MIT-CSAIL-TR-2016-001, MIT Computer Science and Artificial Intelligence Laboratory, January 2016.

[44] M. Miah, G. Das, V. Hristidis, and H. Mannila. Standing out in a crowd: Selecting attributes for maximum visibility. In *Proceedings of the 24th International Conference on Data Engineering (ICDE '08)*, pages 356–365, Washington, DC, USA, April 2008. IEEE Computer Society.

[45] A. Nandi, L. Jiang, and M. Mandel. Gestural query specification. *Proceedings of the VLDB Endowment*, 7(4):289–300, 2013.

[46] Y. Papakonstantinou, M. Petropoulos, and V. Vassalos. QURSED: Querying and reporting semistructured data. In *Proceedings of the 2002 ACM SIGMOD International Conference on Management of Data*, pages 192–203, New York, NY, USA, 2002. ACM.

[47] S. Polyviou, G. Samaras, and P. Evripidou. A relationally complete visual query language for heterogeneous data sources and pervasive querying. In *Proceedings of the 21st International Conference on Data Engineering (ICDE '05)*, pages 471–482, Washington, DC, USA, 2005. IEEE Computer Society.

[48] L. Qian, K. LeFevre, and H. V. Jagadish. CRIUS: User-friendly database design. *Proceedings of the VLDB Endowment*, 4(2):81–92, 2010.

[49] J. Sauro. *A practical guide to the System Usability Scale: Background, benchmarks & best practices*. Measuring Usability LLC, 2011.

[50] B. Shneiderman. Direct Manipulation: A step beyond programming languages. *IEEE Computer*, 16(8):57–69, 1983.

[51] M. Singh, A. Nandi, and H. V. Jagadish. Skimmer: Rapid scrolling of relational query results. In *Proceedings of the 2012 ACM SIGMOD International Conference on Management of Data*, pages 181–192, New York, NY, USA, 2012. ACM.

[52] M. Spenke and C. Beilken. A spreadsheet interface for logic programming. In *Proceedings of the SIGCHI Conference on Human Factors in Computing Systems (CHI '89)*, pages 75–80, New York, NY, USA, 1989. ACM.

[53] H. J. Steenhagen, P. M. G. Apers, and H. M. Blanken. Optimization of nested queries in a complex object model. In *Proceedings of the 4th International Conference on Extending Database Technology (EDBT '94)*, pages 337–350, New York, NY, USA, 1994. Springer New York.

[54] C. Stolte, D. Tang, and P. Hanrahan. Polaris: A system for query, analysis, and visualization of multidimensional databases. *Communications of the ACM*, 51(11):75–84, November 2008.

[55] C. R. Stolte. *Query, analysis, and visualization of multidimensional databases*. PhD thesis, Stanford University, Stanford, CA, USA, 2003.

[56] T. S. Tullis and J. N. Stetson. A comparison of questionnaires for assessing website usability, 2004. Usability Professionals Association (UPA) 2004 Conference.

[57] J. Tyszkiewicz. Spreadsheet as a relational database engine. In *Proceedings of the 2010 International Conference on Management of Data (SIGMOD '10)*, pages 195–206, New York, NY, USA, 2010. ACM.

[58] J. Van den Bussche and S. Vansummeren. Translating SQL into the relational algebra. Course notes, Hasselt University and the Free University of Brussels, retrieved April 2016. http://cs.ulb.ac.be/public/_media/teaching/infoh417/sql2alg_eng.pdf.

[59] L. Wegner, S. Thelemann, J. Thamm, D. Wilke, and S. Wilke. Navigational exploration and declarative queries in a prototype for visual information systems. In C. Leung, editor, *Visual Information Systems*, volume 1306 of *Lecture Notes in Computer Science*, pages 199–218. Springer Berlin/Heidelberg, 1997.

[60] F. Yang, N. Gupta, C. Botev, E. F. Churchill, G. Levchenko, and J. Shanmugasundaram. WYSIWYG development of data driven web applications. *Proceedings of the VLDB Endowment*, 1(1):163–175, 2008.

[61] M. M. Zloof. Query-by-Example: A data base language. *IBM Systems Journal*, 16(4):324–343, 1977.

APPENDIX

A. EXPRESSIVENESS

Like Liu and Jagadish [41], we demonstrate relational completeness of our visual query language by defining a translation from a *complete set* of operators in the relational algebra ($\sigma\pi\times\cup-$) to queries in our visual language. We also translate outer joins as well as the *extended projection* and *grouping* operators [24, p. 213]; the latter two formalize scalar and aggregate calculations, respectively. Assume set semantics in the relational algebra.

Notation. Let e, e_a, and e_b be relational algebra expressions. Let $N(e)$ be the number of attributes in e. Assume that the attribute names of any relational algebra expression e are $e[1], ..., e[N(e)]$. Define a *formula*, notated $\langle ... \rangle$, to be a functional expression over attribute names. Formulas are used both in the relational algebra and in the SIEUFERD query model. Properties in the query model are used as defined in Table 2.

Translation from relational algebra. Let $t(e)$ be a translation from a relational algebra expression e to a relation field in the SIEUFERD query model. We define $t(e)$ recursively as follows:

- *Constants.* If $e = U$, where U is a constant relation, then $t(e)$ is a relation field with INSTANTIATEDTABLE $= U$. It has primitive child fields named $e[1], ..., e[N(e)]$ with COLUMNDEFINITION set to the technical column names $U[1], ..., U[N(e)]$, respectively.
- *Selection.* If $e = \sigma_C(e_a)$, where C is a boolean formula, then $t(e)$ is a relation field with the following child fields:
  - A relation field $t(e_a)$.
  - Primitive fields named $e[1], ..., e[N(e)]$ having COLUMNDEFINITION $= \langle e_a[1] \rangle, ..., \langle e_a[N(e)] \rangle$, respectively.
  - A primitive field with COLUMNDEFINITION $= C$, VISIBLE turned off, and FILTER set to include only values of TRUE.
- *Inner/outer joins, and Cartesian product.* If $e = e_a \bowtie_C e_b$, where $\bowtie$ is either an inner join or left outer join and C is a boolean formula over attribute names in e_a and e_b, then $t(e)$ is a relation field with the following child fields:
  - A relation field $t(e_a)$.
  - A relation field $t(\sigma_C(e_b))$ having HIDEPARENTIFEMPTY turned on iff $\bowtie$ is an inner join. The translation for $\sigma_C(e_b)$ applies even though C may reference attributes outside of e_b.
  - Primitive fields named $e[1], ..., e[N(e)]$ having COLUMNDEFINITION $=$ $\langle e_a[1] \rangle, ..., \langle e_a[N(e_a)] \rangle, \langle e_b[1] \rangle, ..., \langle e_b[N(e_b)] \rangle$, respectively.

  The Cartesian product ($\times$) is an inner join with $C = \langle \text{TRUE} \rangle$. A full outer join is the union of two left joins.

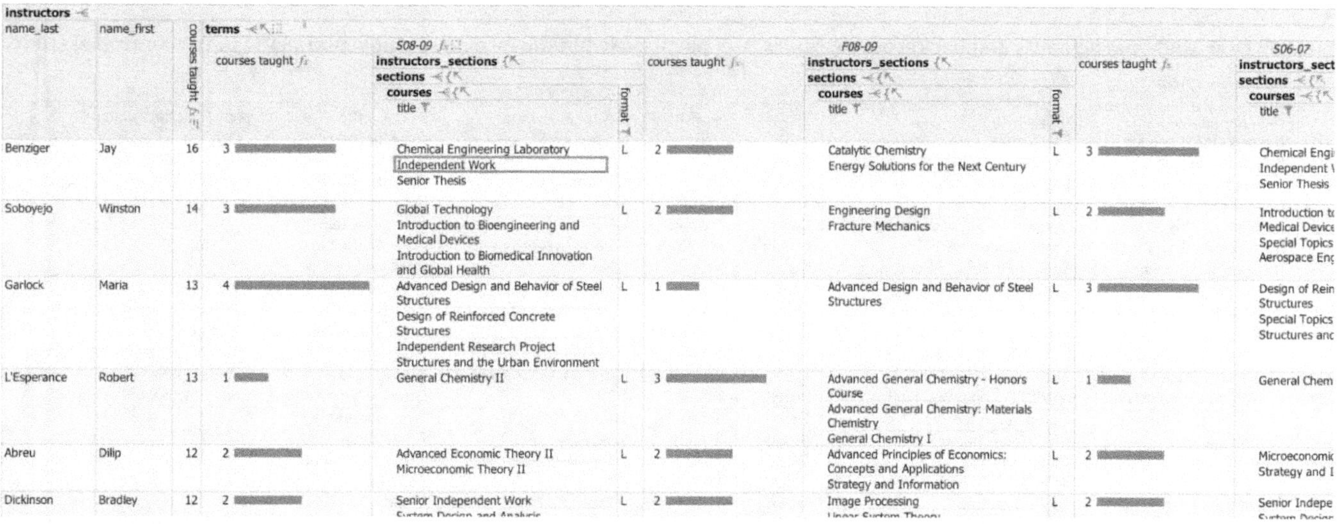

Figure 5: A crosstab, shown as an example of one of the many alternative layouts that can be used to render data retrieved using the SIEUFERD query interface. The query shown here is identical to that of Figure 6, but has a crosstab formatting option enabled on the TERMS relation. All the usual query interface actions remain available from the crosstab layout.

- *Extended projection.* If $e = \pi_{F_1 \to e[1], \ldots, F_n \to e[n]}(e_a)$ where each of $F_1, \ldots, F_n$ is a formula over attribute names in e_a, then $t(e)$ is a relation field with the following child fields:
  - A relation field $t(e_a)$.
  - Primitive fields named $e[1], \ldots, e[n]$, with COLUMNDEFINITION set to formulas $F_1, \ldots, F_n$, respectively.
- *Grouping (aggregation).* If $e = \gamma_{A_1, \ldots, A_n}(e_a)$, where each of $A_1, \ldots, A_n$ is either a grouping attribute name or an aggregation operator applied to an attribute name in e_a, then we can use the same translation as for extended projection by permitting aggregate functions in formulas. In this case, $t(e) = t(\pi_{\langle A_1 \rangle \to e[1], \ldots, \langle A_n \rangle \to e[n]}(e_a))$.
- *Set union.* A conditional formula can be used with a Cartesian product to produce the desired effect. If $e = e_a \cup e_b$, with $n = N(e)$, then $t(e) = t(\pi_{F_1 \to e[1], \ldots, F_n \to e[n]}(e_a \times e_b \times V))$ where V is the constant relation $\{(\text{FALSE}), (\text{TRUE})\}$ and F_i denotes the formula $\langle V[1] \mathbin{?} e_a[i] : e_b[i] \rangle$. In the future, we might introduce an explicit UNION function as syntactic sugar for this kind of construction; see Figure 7 for an example.
- *Set difference.* Here, we can filter for null values generated by a left join. If $e = e_a - e_b$, with $n = N(e)$, then $t(e) = t(\pi_{\langle e_a[1] \rangle \to e[1], \ldots, \langle e_a[n] \rangle \to e[n]}(\sigma_{\langle M \text{ IS NULL} \rangle}(e_a \ltimes_C e'_b)))$ where $\ltimes$ is a left outer join, $C = \langle e_a[1] = e'_b[1] \wedge \ldots \wedge e_a[n] = e'_b[n] \rangle$, and e'_b adds an arbitrary non-nullable attribute M to e_b, e.g. $e'_b = \pi_{\langle e_b[1] \rangle \to e'_b[1], \ldots, \langle e_b[n] \rangle \to e'_b[n], \langle 42 \rangle \to M}(e_b)$. Another approach would be to COUNT values in e_b and filter for zero.

In the query model translations above, except when mentioned, the FILTER, SORT, JOINEDON, and INSTANTIATEDTABLE properties are cleared, while the VISIBLE, COLLAPSEDUPLICATEROWS, and HIDEPARENTIFEMPTY properties are TRUE.

Note that queries created by the fully general translation above can usually be simplified, e.g. by combining selection, projection, and table instantiation in a single relation field, or by using the JOINEDON property instead of filters on formula fields.

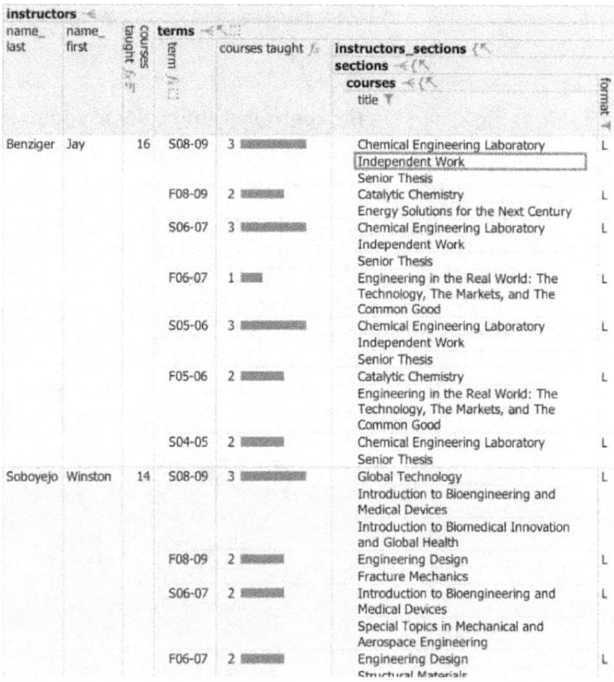

Figure 6: Input data for the crosstab example in Figure 5, shown here in a regular nested table layout. The field COURSES TAUGHT has a formatting option enabled on it to display numbers using a bar chart visualization.

Table 5: User study participants and backgrounds. Users A-N participated in the formative study, users O-Ø in the controlled study.

#	*Professional Area*	*Educational Background*	*Technical Background/Tools Used* *Excel*	*SQL*	*Programming*	*Other Tools*
A	Data journalism	Journalism	Daily	Weekly	A bit of Python	Access often, Tableau/OpenRefine occasionally
B	Business intelligence	Linguistics	Daily	Daily	Some PHP	BrioQuery daily
C	Business intelligence	Psychology	Daily	No	No	Spotfire daily, BrioQuery occasionally
D	Financial	Philosophy, Research Adm.	Daily	No	Learning basic Python	Some SAPGUI
E	IT decision-making	Computer Science	Weekly	In 1992	Java/VB years ago	Some R
F	Business intelligence	Operations Mgmt., Business	Daily	Frequently	VB.net	BrioQuery daily
G	CS research, teaching	CS, Commun., Art Hist., Lit.	Monthly	Monthly	Java/C years ago	R a long time ago
H	Business intelligence	Sociology, Higher Education	Daily	No	No	BrioQuery daily
I	Health policy	Sociology	Weekly	No	No	Access for survey entry once, SPSS in school
J	Investigative journalism	English, Business/Econ. Journ.	Daily	No	Very basic Python	Access weekly, e.g. for joins before continuing in Excel
K	Publishing	Writing, Literature & Publishing	Daily	Frequently*	No	Crystal Rep. frequently*, 2 industry-specific systems
L	Health policy, research	Public Health, Public Policy	Daily*	No	No	Access for data entry*, knows SAS/Stata/SPSS/ArcGIS
M	Engineering data analytics	Finance, Management	Daily	Frequently*	Python/VB years ago	Access/Crystal Rep. frequently*; now Tableau, Alteryx
N	University administration	Math & Economics, Higher Ed.	Daily	No	No	BrioQuery for canned reports, internal CRUD apps
O	IT	Computer Science	Daily	Yearly	Java/VB/Perl*	Access monthly*
P	Bioinformatics	CS, Bioinformatics	Monthly	Weekly	Weekly	R monthly
Q	Electrical eng./research	Electrical Eng., Systems Eng.	Weekly	Tried once	C/Java/Fortran*	MATLAB frequently*
R	Medicine	MD, Adm. & Management	Weekly	No	No	Electronic medical records
S	Bioinformatics/research	Bioinformatics	Weekly	Tried twice	Daily	R daily, MATLAB
T	Bioinformatics/research	Bioinformatics	Daily	Monthly	Daily (Python, JS)	Access monthly*, Spotfire daily*, R weekly
U	Biomedical/data science	Chemical Eng./Statistics	Monthly	Daily	Some Python	R weekly, Access for data entry*
V	Student	Neuroscience	Weekly	No	Some Python	Some MATLAB, SPSS, Access for data entry
W	Library adm./info science	Biology	Weekly	No	No	BrioQuery monthly*, SAP, FileMaker
X	Student	Electrical Engineering & CS	Monthly	Once	Daily	R once, MATLAB
Y	Student	Journalism	Monthly	One course	One course (Java)	N/A
Z	Student	Journalism	Weekly	No	No	N/A
Æ	Journalism, teaching	Journalism, Law	Weekly	Monthly	No	Access*/OpenRefine/Tableau monthly, many others
Ø	Research	Electrical Engineering	Weekly	No	Weekly (Python, C++)	MATLAB, Access for data entry*, R/SAS/SPSS

*In previous job.

Table 6: Tasks used in the controlled study. Some additional bonus tasks were also available to users who finished quickly.

Type	#	*Task*	*Operations involved*
Guided	1	Show a list of products with the PRODUCTNAME and DISCONTINUED fields visible.	Field selection
	2	Find the total quantity sold of each product, via the quantities in the ORDERDETAILS table.	Join, aggregate
	3	Find the total sales for each product. This involves a UNITPRICE $*$ QUANTITY calculation.	Scalar formula, aggregate
	4	Include in totals only orders shipped outside the US.	Join, pre-aggregate filter
	5	Show the products with the most revenue first, hiding any order details if still visible.	Sorting
Unguided	6	Show customers and all their orders, sorted by customer.	Field selection, join, sorting
	7	For each of the customers' orders, show the total dollar amount for that order.	Join, scalar formula, aggregate
	8	Show the name and phone number of the shipping company serving each order.	Join, field selection
	9	Show only orders assigned to employee Margaret Peacock.	Join, filter

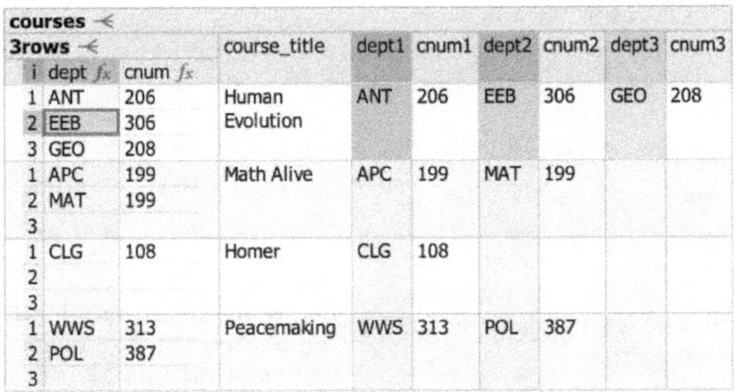


```
[dept]  =if([i] = 1, [dept1], if([i] = 2, [dept2], [dept3]))
        =union([dept1], [dept2], [dept3])

[cnum] =if([i] = 1, [cnum1], if([i] = 2, [cnum2], [cnum3]))
        =union([cnum1], [cnum2], [cnum3])
```

Figure 7: A union query. Following a classic schema design antipattern, the COURSES table stores course codes using numbered table columns. To facilitate subsequent operations such as filtering by course code, the query collects course codes under a single nested relation via the helper table 3ROWS = {(1), (2), (3)}. An explicit UNION function, as proposed above, would make the expression of such queries more elegant.

Shasta: Interactive Reporting At Scale

Gokul Nath Babu Manoharan[α], Stephan Ellner[α], Karl Schnaitter[α], Sridatta Chegu[α], Alejandro Estrella-Balderrama[α], Stephan Gudmundson[α], Apurv Gupta[α], Ben Handy[α], Bart Samwel[α], Chad Whipkey[α], Larysa Aharkava[α], Himani Apte[α], Nitin Gangahar[α], Jun Xu[α], Shivakumar Venkataraman[α], Divyakant Agrawal[α], Jeffrey D. Ullman[β*]

[α]Google, Inc. [β]Stanford University

ABSTRACT

We describe Shasta, a middleware system built at Google to support interactive reporting in complex user-facing applications related to Google's Internet advertising business. Shasta targets applications with challenging requirements: First, user query latencies must be low. Second, underlying transactional data stores have complex "read-unfriendly" schemas, placing significant transformation logic between stored data and the read-only views that Shasta exposes to its clients. This transformation logic must be expressed in a way that scales to large and agile engineering teams. Finally, Shasta targets applications with strong data freshness requirements, making it challenging to precompute query results using common techniques such as ETL pipelines or materialized views. Instead, online queries must go all the way from primary storage to user-facing views, resulting in complex queries joining 50 or more tables.

Designed as a layer on top of Google's F1 RDBMS and Mesa data warehouse, Shasta combines language and system techniques to meet these requirements. To help with expressing complex view specifications, we developed a query language called RVL, with support for modularized view templates that can be dynamically compiled into SQL. To execute these SQL queries with low latency at scale, we leveraged and extended F1's distributed query engine with facilities such as safe execution of C++ and Java UDFs. To reduce latency and increase read parallelism, we extended F1 storage with a distributed read-only in-memory cache. The system we describe is in production at Google, powering critical applications used by advertisers and internal sales teams. Shasta has significantly improved system scalability and software engineering efficiency compared to the middleware solutions it replaced.

1. INTRODUCTION

Many business applications at Google aim to provide interactive data-rich UIs, allowing users such as advertisers, publishers and video content creators to manage and analyze their data. It is not uncommon for such applications to combine interactive reporting (OLAP) and update (OLTP) functionality in the same UI.

*Work performed while at Google, Inc.

SIGMOD/PODS'16 June 26 - July 01, 2016, San Francisco, CA, USA

ACM ISBN 978-1-4503-3531-7/16/06.

DOI: http://dx.doi.org/10.1145/2882903.2904444

For a representative example, consider AdWords, Google's search advertising product: In a Web UI, advertisers configure their campaigns. Campaign configurations are stored in the F1 database [13] in hundreds of normalized tables backed by Spanner storage [5]. Google serves ads based on these configurations, and log aggregation systems [1] use ad server logs to continuously update hundreds of metrics tables stored in Mesa [8], tracking the performance of the running ad campaigns in near real-time. Deeply integrating OLTP and OLAP functionality, the AdWords Web UI allows advertisers to view interactive reports with campaign performance metrics and to make changes to campaign configurations. Corresponding SOAP developer APIs allow advertisers to interact with their campaign and reporting data programmatically.

A challenge in scaling such applications in practice are vast database schemas with hundreds of tables, placing significant transformation logic between stored data and user-facing concepts. This "concept gap" tends to be particularly wide for OLAP functionality, posing non-trivial questions for application designers:

- **How to encapsulate complex data transformations?** Without proper abstractions, business logic tends to leak into inappropriate parts of the system or get duplicated, creating problems for code ownership, readability, consistency, and release velocity.

- **How to express the transformations?** Even if business logic is encapsulated well, the right paradigm to express it is non-obvious. Procedural languages such as Java or C++ are powerful, but can be cumbersome for expressing complex query operations on top of vast database schemas, e.g., joins of 50 tables. SQL on the other hand naturally captures relational operations, but doesn't scale gracefully to code artifacts of thousands of lines of code. Furthermore, applications that allow users to interactively change data visualization parameters such as column selection, segmentations, and filters require that developers express queries with a large degree of dynamic variation in query operations such as joins, aggregations, and filters.

- **How to compute the transformations?** Deciding during which phase of data processing to compute the transformations poses awkward tradeoffs. A common data warehousing approach is to rely on precomputation, maintaining a "read-friendly" denormalized copy of transactional data optimized for OLAP workloads [4]. If the denormalized copy is stale with respect to database updates, it tends to not satisfy applications with a high bar for fresh and consistent data, and the necessary offline pipelines tend to make systems more stateful and operationally complex. Transactionally updated materialized views on the other hand increase the cost of writes. Finally, computing most transformations as part of online queries makes achieving interactive (sub-second) latencies challenging, especially if queries read from multiple data stores with different performance characteristics.

In this paper we describe Shasta, a middleware system built at Google to power interactive reporting functionality in critical business applications. Using a combination of techniques in language and system design, Shasta addresses the challenges listed above at scale. Shasta encapsulates the transformation logic between stored data and user-facing concepts and hides it from applications by providing an abstraction similar to denormalized views over diverse data stores. To its clients, *Shasta views* are parameterized virtual read-only tables that are significantly easier to understand and query than the underlying schemas. Shasta's system components power several critical business applications at Google, including the AdWords Web UI and corresponding developer APIs. Figure 1 shows Shasta as part of the AdWords data processing architecture.

What makes Shasta quite different from common approaches to data warehousing is how its views are expressed and computed. First, Shasta views are expressed in RVL, a declarative language that combines SQL-like functionality with limited but powerful procedural constructs, designed to succinctly capture the dynamic nature of interactive applications. RVL code is dynamically compiled to SQL. Second, Shasta does not rely heavily on precomputation to minimize query time transformations, although view definitions are highly complex. Rather, many view queries "go all the way" from normalized data storage to user-facing concepts. This stateless and dynamic approach enables rich interactive UIs, with fresh and consistent data everywhere, yet without the burden of maintaining separate denormalized storage dedicated to query workloads. Shasta uses F1's distributed SQL engine to execute complex generated queries over multiple data sources. With key extensions – including a cache that leverages spatial and temporal locality of data accessed by application users – F1 runs the resulting interactive workloads reliably at low latency and scales well to more data-intensive workloads.

The contributions of this paper are:

- We introduce an integrated language and system approach to designing application middle tiers for interactive reporting applications. The approach is unusual in its heavy reliance on online data transformations.
- We show how, using a new SQL templating language, we have made the maintenance of complex business logic on top of vast legacy schemas by large engineering teams more efficient.
- We show how, thanks to F1's distributed query execution architecture, our approach achieves a high degree of operational simplicity and data freshness, keeps interactive query latencies low, and scales to more data-intensive workloads.
- We describe an implementation of this approach, our experience with it, its benefits, and its limitations.

The rest of the paper is structured as follows: Section 2 lists Shasta's system requirements, Section 3 presents the overall architecture, and Sections 4-6 describe the major components in more detail. In Section 7 we report from our experience running Shasta in production at Google. Section 8 summarizes related work.

2. SYSTEM REQUIREMENTS

The design of Shasta was driven by the following requirements of critical interactive business applications at Google:

Data stores are diverse. Generally, user-facing business applications at Google depend on multiple data stores. Data transactionally updated by users, or dimensions, is often stored in the F1 RDBMS, which is backed by Spanner storage. On the other hand, performance metrics, or facts, may be stored in systems like Mesa, where they can be continuously updated by Google's internal systems. In AdWords for instance, advertiser-provided campaign configurations are stored in F1, and financially critical metrics about ad campaign performance are stored in Mesa. Completing the picture, some application state is stored in Bigtable [3] for legacy reasons. Intuitively, different data stores have different performance characteristics. Mesa supports high throughput updates by batching them and low latency reads by virtue of its sophisticated data versioning, its storage format, and other techniques [8]. On the other hand, system parameters and schemas in F1 deployments tend to be optimized more for write latency and less for read latency, in order to mitigate the overhead (50–150ms) of cross-region two-phase commits [13].

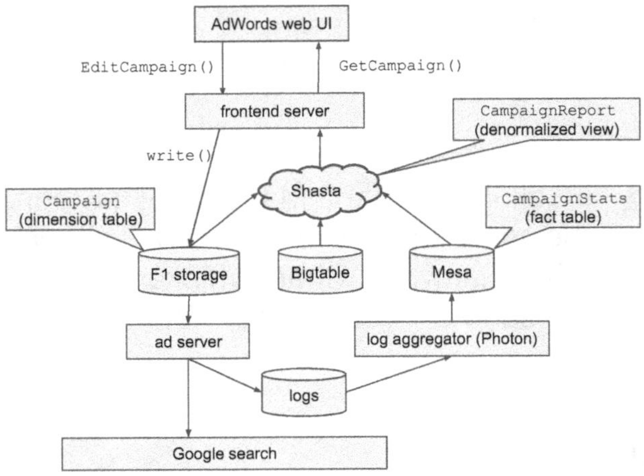

Figure 1: Simplified AdWords data-processing architecture.

View computations are complex. For schema design and legacy reasons, there is often a large gap between the concepts shown to application users and the schemas of underlying data stores. For instance, computing the main table in the AdWords UI "Campaigns" tab involves joining and aggregating approximately 20 F1 tables and 20 Mesa tables, with intricate business logic applied to the scanned data. Furthermore, interactive reporting UIs often display multiple pivots of the same data next to each other, e.g., a table breaking down metrics per campaign, a chart showing the same metrics over time, and a single row summarizing the table metrics. In order to power such UIs efficiently and ensure that different pivots are fully consistent, shared query portions should be computed only once. Given these complexities, view computations tend to be expensive and difficult to formulate.

Views must reflect data updates immediately. To be truly interactive, applications allow users to explore performance metrics *and* modify their business data. The AdWords Web UI is a good example, allowing advertisers to explore how their campaigns are performing and update campaign configurations inline, in the same tables. Consider a scenario where a table in the UI shows that an ad campaign's budget is exhausted. In response, the advertiser may decide to increase the budget, which is easily done in the same UI table row. Any future rendering of the table must then consistently reflect the budget change. Due to the complexity of view definitions, a user changing a single cell in a sorted UI table can induce subtle changes to other columns in the same row and the application may choose to recompute the entire table immediately after the write. In AdWords, advertiser changes to campaign data result in writes to F1, bypassing Shasta. Immediately after the write, the frontend server may request table data for the given Shasta view and expect subsequent queries to return fresh and consistent data, taking into account the most recent update by the user.

View queries from interactive UIs must be fast. Shasta queries are on the critical path to rendering pages in user-facing applications with sub-second latency targets. Importantly, interfaces and APIs in such applications are often scoped to an individual user's business data, so that typical Shasta queries process only a modest subset of data in underlying data stores. Still, individual fully optimized queries can scan gigabytes of raw data from 50 or more physical tables, and the transformations required for a query can be computationally demanding. Fortunately, interactive applications tend to be used in user sessions, allowing Shasta to leverage temporal and spatial locality of accessed data.

View definitions are parameterized. To its clients, Shasta views are parameterized virtual tables, which provide access to denormalized data while hiding complex storage schemas with hundreds of tables. Issuing a Shasta query is straightforward: The client specifies a view name, a list of column names, a simple specification for how to filter and sort resulting rows, and more ad-hoc parameters that customize the view semantics. To answer a given Shasta query, Shasta then needs to compute the view in the context of the given parameters. In practice, parameter values can have a major effect on the semantics of a view. For instance, depending on whether the user is part of a feature whitelist, a Shasta view may require data to be read from different tables and joined in a different structure.

View implementation must be manageable. In practice, hundreds of software engineers across different teams need to modify shared view definitions and schemas. Resulting changes need to be released to production multiple times per week, without downtime. In order to achieve these goals, Shasta needs a view definition format that helps developers easily reason about and modify views, and this format needs to scale to complex and highly parameterized view definitions. Ideally, view definitions should be mostly declarative, but views must be allowed to invoke some application code written in a procedural language such as C++ or Java.

3. SYSTEM ARCHITECTURE

In principle, it would be reasonable to express Shasta view transformations using SQL and leverage F1's distributed query engine for scalable query execution, since the transformations required by Shasta views are a natural fit for SQL. However, it is challenging in practice to define Shasta views in terms of SQL and meet the latency requirements of interactive applications, given the complex nature of queries. Shasta's system architecture overcomes these two challenges, thus allowing query execution to be handled by F1.

In order to push all computation to F1, Shasta needs to translate each client query into a single SQL query. This is difficult due to the complexity of data transformations, paired with a wide variety of queries corresponding to different view parameter values. The Shasta architecture simplifies the task of SQL generation: View definitions are expressed in a new language called RVL and are translated to SQL using a just-in-time compiler. The syntax of RVL is SQL-like, but extended with higher-level constructs which make it easier to define Shasta views concisely while accounting for dynamic view parameters. RVL supports user-defined functions (UDFs), allowing Shasta view definitions to invoke procedural application code.

The following extensions to the F1 query engine were made to meet the needs of Shasta:

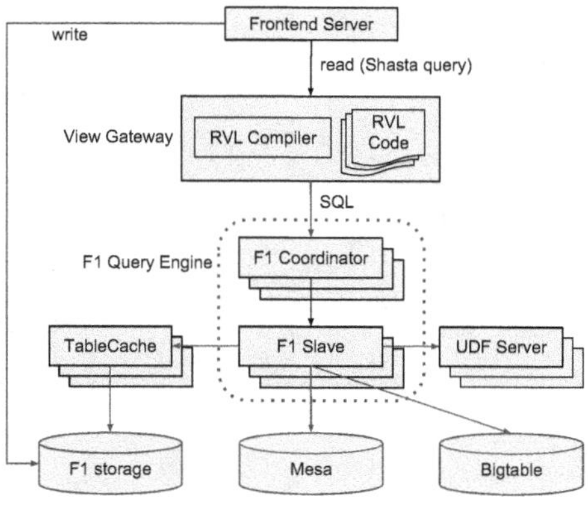

Figure 2: Shasta architecture.

- We improved support for UDFs in F1. Specifically, we added a component called UDF server to F1, which supports safe evaluation of compiled C++ and Java UDFs with high throughput.

- In order to meet the latency constraints of Shasta, we added an in-memory read-only cache between F1 storage and query engine, called TableCache. Shasta uses TableCache to access consistent snapshots of F1 data significantly faster than reading from F1 storage directly. The cache is kept up-to-date using a light-weight protocol based on F1's Change History feature. For Shasta applications, maintaining similar caches for other data sources such as Mesa and Bigtable has proven either less critical or too expensive in practice.

Figure 2 shows how the components of Shasta fit together to answer queries. A query issued by the application's frontend server specifies a view name, columns to query, and view parameters such as application user ID or feature ID. In addition, the client often specifies a timestamp, which tells Shasta to use F1 data which is consistent with the snapshot at that timestamp. Exposing the list of available view schemas to application developers is typically done via shared code repositories. The *view gateway* receives the Shasta query and invokes the RVL compiler with view parameter bindings to generate a potentially large SQL string. The F1 query engine executes the generated SQL, using UDF servers to evaluate any UDFs in the query. TableCache accelerates access to F1 storage during query execution, while the query engine reads directly from data sources other than F1 such as Mesa and Bigtable. F1 supports access to such "external" data sources using a plugin API [13], allowing for tight integration with the query engine. F1 pushes filters and projections to external data sources where possible, performing other computations itself. Optimizations that would delegate more complex query operations to external data sources [9] are left as future work.

It is worth noting that Shasta does not rely on precomputation and materialization of intermediate view query results. Although precomputation may improve the latency of Shasta queries, it tends to be a poor fit for Shasta applications, especially when dealing with financial user data: Keeping materialized results synchronized with user-issued changes to underlying data stores makes writes more expensive, which is often not an option. It would also be impractical to use stale materializations while satisfying freshness requirements, due to the complexity of Shasta views. These drawbacks can be avoided by evaluating queries on raw data.

The following sections provide more details on RVL (Section 4), Shasta's use of the F1 query engine and UDF servers (Section 5), and TableCache (Section 6).

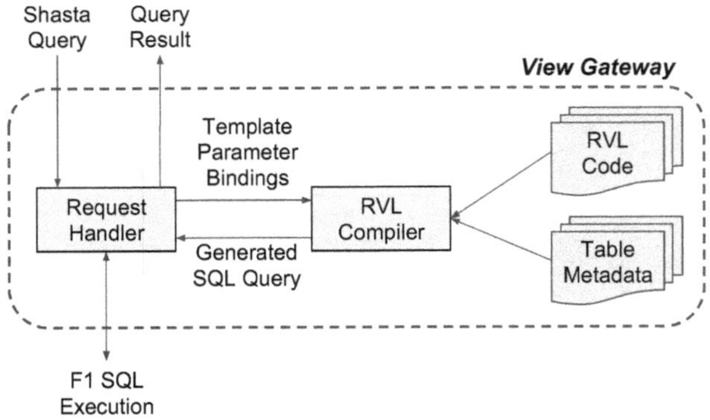

Figure 3: Using the RVL compiler in Shasta.

4. RVL: RELATIONAL VIEW LANGUAGE

As described in Section 3, Shasta uses a language called RVL (Relational View Language) to define Shasta views, and compiles RVL into equivalent SQL which can be executed in the F1 query engine. RVL helps view definition authors focus on the specifics of each view and to not concern themselves with the problem of generating SQL. The features of RVL can be summarized as follows:

- At the core of RVL is a self-contained query language. The syntax of the query language is similar to SQL, but with important differences in semantics. In particular, RVL uses information in the schema to automatically aggregate data when columns are projected, which makes it easier for developers to express the complex aggregation logic of Shasta views.
- RVL embeds its query language in higher-level constructs called view templates. A view template specifies a dynamic query using replaceable parameters. Within each template, a query can be built as a sequence of subquery assignment statements. Each subquery in a template may refer to template parameters and instantiate other view templates. Overall, composable templates and sequential query construction allow a view's implementation to be factored into manageable and reusable pieces.

RVL code is structured as a collection of view templates. In order to actually generate SQL, the RVL compiler requires one template to be specified as an entry point, along with parameter bindings for that template. Figure 3 illustrates the role of the RVL compiler in the view gateway of Shasta. When Shasta receives a query, the request handler first translates that query into parameter bindings to pass to the RVL compiler, which returns generated SQL. The request handler then executes the SQL query on F1 and forwards the query results back to the Shasta client.

In this section, we provide an overview of RVL. We start by describing the query language in isolation, and then show how the query language is embedded in view templates. We next describe the most interesting aspects of RVL compilation and conclude with an end-to-end RVL example.

4.1 Query Language

RVL includes a query language to specify data transformations. The syntax and semantics are similar to SQL, with one fundamental difference: RVL automatically determines how to aggregate query results. As we show in examples below, automatic aggregation can help simplify the specification of view queries for reporting applications built on Shasta. To take advantage of automatic aggregation, the metadata of each column may optionally specify an *implicit aggregation function*. If a column has an implicit aggregation function, we refer to that column as an *aggregatable column*. Otherwise, it is a *grouping column*. When a query operation is performed in RVL, the result will only preserve the unique values of the grouping columns, and the aggregatable columns are implicitly aggregated for each row based on the associated aggregation function. In other words, the grouping columns always form a unique key for a relation in RVL, and the aggregatable columns represent measures associated with values of the unique key. In the special case where all columns are grouping columns, the behavior of RVL is consistent with relational algebra on sets. In practice, Shasta applications specify implicit aggregation functions as overlays on an existing database schema and include this information in the table metadata given to the RVL compiler. RVL also supports syntax to modify or remove implicit aggregation functions assigned to the columns of a relation (see Section 4.4).

RVL queries may use several syntactic constructs borrowed from SQL such as SELECT, FROM, WHERE, JOIN, and UNION. The behavior of these operations is similar to SQL, except that implicit aggregation is applied after each operation to yield a set of unique rows. There is no GROUP BY clause in RVL, since aggregation is implicit for each SELECT. RVL also makes extensions to SQL in order to help with large-scale code maintenance, as described in Section 4.2.

We can illustrate the behavior of RVL queries on the following two tables representing information about employees and buildings of a company:

Employee table:

EmpId	*DeptId*	*BldgId*	*Salary* [SUM]
I	A	X	20
J	A	Y	30
K	B	Y	40
L	B	Z	50

Building table:

BldgId	*CityId*	*Capacity* [SUM]
X	M	100
Y	N	200
Z	N	300

The columns for salary and capacity have the [SUM] annotation to indicate that they use SUM as their implicit aggregation function.

An application may need to derive the total salary or capacity for a variety of grouping columns. Using RVL, we can start by combining the tables with a left join, and let `Q0` denote this subquery:

```
Q0 = SELECT *
     FROM Employee LEFT JOIN Building USING (BldgId);
```

This provides a list of employees and information about their building, if known. We may use this subquery to write a very simple query for the total salary in each department:

```
Q1 = SELECT DeptId, Salary FROM Q0;
```

Evaluating `Q1` will return the unique DeptId values and automatically compute the sum of salaries in each department, yielding the final result:

DeptId	*Salary* [SUM]
A	50
B	90

This could be expressed in SQL using an explicit SUM and GROUP BY clause:

```
SELECT DeptId, SUM(Salary) FROM Employee
GROUP BY DeptId;
```

The RVL compiler will actually generate this SQL for `Q1`. The join with the Building table can be pruned since none of the Building columns are required. Join pruning is a key feature of RVL, which we discuss in Section 4.3.

Implicit aggregation becomes more interesting when data is requested from both tables. For example:

```
Q2 = SELECT CityId, Salary, Capacity FROM Q0;
```

This will return the unique CityId values and automatically compute the total salaries of employees in each city, along with the capacity of the buildings in that city:

CityId	*Salary* [SUM]	*Capacity* [SUM]
M	20	100
N	120	500

The RVL compiler generates the following SQL representation of Q2 which adds two GROUP BY steps:

```
SELECT CityId, SUM(Salary) AS Salary,
       SUM(Capacity) AS Capacity
FROM
  (SELECT BldgId, SUM(Salary) AS Salary
   FROM Employee GROUP BY BldgId)
  LEFT JOIN Building USING (BldgId))
GROUP BY CityId;
```

Observe that the inner subquery removes EmpId and DeptId, in order to aggregate the remaining columns of the Employee table before the join. The inner aggregation ensures that the capacity is computed correctly. If we naively removed all unwanted columns after the join and performed the aggregation in a single step, the capacity values would be multiplied by the number of employees in each building. Our desired result should only count the capacity of each building once. We will revisit this example and the RVL compiler's strategy for arranging GROUP BY clauses in Section 4.3.

The value of RVL can be seen by comparing Q1 and Q2 to the corresponding SQL representations. In RVL, we can define a single subquery Q0 such that Q1 and Q2 can be expressed as simple projections over Q0. In contrast, the SQL representations of Q1 and Q2 have drastically different structure. RVL also makes it easy to derive meaningful aggregate values from Q0 for many other combinations of grouping columns. A direct SQL representation of all possible projections over the join would need to account for all the potential arrangements of GROUP BY clauses and invocations of aggregation functions. In practice, real Shasta queries can be more complex, requiring dozens of tables to be joined. It becomes challenging for developers to formulate the correct aggregation semantics using SQL directly whereas formulating queries using RVL makes it much more simple and intuitive.

4.2 View Templates

As described above, the RVL query language provides implicit aggregation to help developers express aggregation semantics when the set of requested columns is not fixed. However, implicit aggregation does not solve all the challenges of implementing Shasta views. In particular:

- The parameters of a Shasta view may have a large impact on the RVL query. For instance, the view parameters may change the tables used in joins or the placement of filters in the query. RVL needs to be more dynamic in order to capture this wide range of possible query structures.
- An RVL query could grow quite large with many column transformations and deeply nested joins. A typical Shasta view would require 100s of lines of code, and expressing that as a single large query can be difficult to read and maintain.

RVL *view templates* solve these problems. View templates allow large queries to be constructed dynamically from smaller pieces which can be composed and reused by multiple Shasta views. A view template takes input parameters which are used to represent the dynamic aspects of a query (e.g., list of requested columns), and returns a corresponding RVL query using the parameter values. In other words, for any fixed choice of parameter values, a view template is shorthand for an RVL query (similar to the traditional notion of a view).

A view template may be referenced in the FROM clause of RVL queries by passing values for its input parameters, and the reference will be replaced with the query generated by the view template. The following values may be bound to view template parameters:

- *RVL text:* A string containing valid RVL syntax can be bound to a view template parameter, and that parameter can be referenced in places where it would be valid to inject the RVL syntax string. For example, a template parameter bound to the string "X,Y" could be referenced in a SELECT clause, and the template parameter reference will behave exactly as if "X,Y" were written directly in the query.
- *Nested dictionary:* A template parameter can be bound to a dictionary of name-value pairs, where the values can either be another dictionary, or RVL text. Intuitively, a nested dictionary is a collection of RVL text parameters with hierarchical names.
- *Subquery:* A template parameter can be bound to an RVL subquery, and referenced anywhere a table can be referenced. A subquery value differs from RVL text values, in the sense that subquery values are substituted in a purely logical manner which is independent of the syntax used to create the subquery. In contrast, an RVL text value is purely a text injection, which allows any variables in the RVL text to be interpreted based on the context where the parameter is referenced.

RVL text values allow RVL parameters to be more flexible than traditional SQL runtime parameters, since RVL allows parameters to represent large substructures of queries. However, RVL text values do not allow for arbitrary code injection. In order to make view templates less error-prone, an RVL text value is only allowed to contain a few specific syntactic forms, such as scalar expressions, expression lists, and base table names. There are also strict rules controlling the locations where each syntactic form can be substituted.

We use the following example to illustrate the basic template syntax and semantics:

```
view FilterUnion<input_table, params> {
  T1 = SELECT $params.column_name FROM $input_table;
  T2 = SELECT $params.column_name FROM Employee;
  T = T1 UNION T2;
  return SELECT * FROM T
         WHERE $params.column_name >= $params.min_value;
}
```

The view template contains three assignment statements which give aliases to subqueries, and the fourth statement returns the final query. There are two template parameters:

- input_table can be bound to a table name or subquery. It is referenced in the first FROM clause as $input_table.
- params must be bound to a nested dictionary. In this example, $params.column_name should be the name of a column in $input_table, and $params.min_value is a lower bound that we want to apply to that column.

The behavior of the view template is intuitive: The first two statements fetch a dynamically chosen column from the $input_table parameter as well as the Employee table, the third statement combines the two sets of values, and the final statement applies a lower bound to the values before returning them.

A view template can be designated as an entry point in the RVL code, in which case it is called a *main view template*. RVL provides an API to invoke a main view template, with a nested dictionary as a parameter. The main view template can use one or more output statements to specify the desired result. For example, using the previous FilterUnion view template:

```
main OutputValues<params> {
  b = SELECT * FROM Building;
  all_values = SELECT * from FilterUnion<@b, $params>;
  output all_values AS result;
}
```

The output statement specifies a table to produce as the final result when the main view template is invoked, as well as an alias for that table. If there are multiple output statements, the aliases must be unique so that the Shasta view gateway can distinguish the results. Multiple output statements can reference the same RVL subquery by name which is useful when applications need to display multiple pivots of the same shared view computation. To achieve consistency between different data pivots within a view query, RVL guarantees that each named subquery is only executed once.

In Section 4.4 we present a larger RVL example which uses additional syntax features. Most interestingly, RVL view templates may use control structures written as if/else blocks to dynamically choose between two or more subqueries.

4.3 RVL Compiler and Query Optimization

The RVL compiler generates SQL which will produce the output tables specified by a main view template, given the required parameter bindings. Shasta executes the generated SQL using the F1 query engine, taking advantage of F1's query optimizations and distributed execution. In order to perform SQL generation, the RVL compiler first resolves references to view templates and named subqueries, producing an algebraic representation of an RVL query plan that includes all outputs of the invoked main view template. The RVL compiler performs some transformations to optimize and simplify the query plan before translating it to SQL. In this section, we describe some details of RVL query optimization and explain why it is important.

The RVL compiler optimizes query plans using a rule-based engine. Each rule uses a different strategy to simplify the plan based on algebraic structure, without estimating cost. In practice, rule-based optimization is sufficient because the only goal is to simplify the generated SQL, rather than determine all details of query execution. We avoid using cost-based optimization because a cost model would tie the RVL compiler to a specific SQL engine and make it less generic.

The intuitive reason to optimize an RVL query plan before generating SQL (as opposed to relying on F1 for all optimizations) is to take advantage of RVL's implicit aggregation semantics. Several optimization rules are implemented in the RVL compiler relying on properties of implicit aggregation to ensure correctness. The RVL compiler also implements optimization rules which do not depend directly on implicit aggregation, because they interact with other rules that do depend on implicit aggregation and make them more effective. We describe a few of the more interesting rules below.

Column Pruning: Recall the Employee/Building example earlier in this section. Our SQL representation of `Q2` performed a projection and aggregation before the join, which differs from the order of operations in the RVL for `Q2`. The join and aggregation steps are reordered by an RVL optimization rule called *column pruning*. Without column pruning, the equivalent SQL representation of `Q2` would be:

```
SELECT CityId, SUM(Salary) AS Salary,
       SUM(Capacity) AS Capacity
FROM
  (SELECT BldgId, CityId,
          SUM(Salary) AS Salary, Capacity
   FROM Employee LEFT JOIN Building USING (BldgId)
   GROUP BY BldgId, CityId, Capacity)
GROUP BY CityId;
```

Observe that this SQL representation performs two stages of aggregation after the join, in order to compute correct aggregate values for both salary and capacity. A sufficiently advanced SQL optimizer may be able to optimize this query by pushing the inner aggregation below the join, but this is a difficult optimization to generalize in the context of SQL [16]. For larger RVL queries, the SQL representation may become much more complicated when computing aggregate values after joining. In the worst case, an implicit aggregation may require aggregatable columns to be computed in a temporary table and joined back into the original query. That pattern in particular is extremely difficult for a SQL engine to optimize, so column pruning is needed in order to simplify the task of the F1 query optimizer. Moreover, the logic for pruning columns in the RVL compiler is straightforward due to implicit aggregation semantics. For all these reasons, the RVL compiler aggressively prunes unneeded columns and performs aggregations before joins whenever possible.

Filter Pushdown: In a SQL database, filter pushdown could be considered one of the most basic optimizations, where the goal is to filter data as early as possible in the query plan. At first glance, it might seem unnecessary for RVL to push down filters, since the F1 query optimizer is fully capable of performing this optimization. However, filter pushdown can improve the effectiveness of the column pruning optimization. For example, if there is a filter on a column which is not part of the final result, the filter will prevent column pruning from removing the column before the filter is applied. It is crucial for the filter to be pushed down as early as possible in the query plan, so that the column can be pruned early as well.

Left Join Pruning: In RVL, if a left join does not require any of the columns from its right input, the right input can be removed from the query plan. In a general SQL database, this optimization is less obvious and less likely to apply, since a left join may duplicate rows in the left input. Consider the following example of a SQL left join, using the example Employee and Building tables:

```
SELECT EmpId, SUM(Salary)
FROM Employee LEFT JOIN Building USING (BldgId);
```

If it is known that each Employee row will join with at most one row in the Building table, the join can be pruned, resulting in:

```
SELECT EmpId, SUM(Salary) FROM Employee;
```

A SQL optimizer might be able to perform this optimization if it knows that BldgId is a unique key of the Building table. The optimization would become more difficult to do if the Building table were replaced with a complex subquery. On the other hand, the left join in RVL is trivial to prune, since the inputs of the join are always guaranteed to be sets, and the column pruning optimization will prune all Building columns except BldgId.

The join pruning optimization makes RVL programming more convenient. A user can add many left joins to their view templates to fetch columns which might not be required, and they can be confident that the RVL compiler will know which joins can be skipped.

4.4 Example View Template

Figure 4 shows example schemas for F1 and Mesa tables, using advertising concepts from the AdWords application. The example

Customer(root table)

CustomerId	CustomerInfo
20	{ name: "flowers" }

BudgetSuggestionV1

CustomerId	**BudgetId**	SuggestionInfo
20	200	{ suggested_amount: 120 }

BudgetSuggestionV2

CustomerId	**BudgetId**	SuggestionInfo
20	200	{ suggested_amount: 118 }

Campaign

CustomerId	**CampaignId**	CampaignInfo
20	100	{ name: "Rose" status: "ENABLED" budget_id: 200 }
20	101	{ name: "Tulip" status: "ENABLED" budget_id: 200 }
20	102	{ name: "Daisy" status: "ENABLED" budget_id: 201 }

Budget

CustomerId	**BudgetId**	BudgetInfo
20	200	{ amount: 100 }
20	201	{ amount: 50 }

CampaignStats

CustomerId	**CampaignId**	**Device**	Impressions	Clicks	Cost
20	100	'Desktop'	20	5	3
20	100	'Tablet'	10	3	1
20	101	'Mobile'	30	4	2
20	102	'Desktop'	40	10	5

CampaignConversionStats

CustomerId	**CampaignId**	**Device**	**ConversionType**	Conversions
20	100	'Desktop'	'Purchase'	2
20	100	'Desktop'	'Wishlist'	1
20	101	'Mobile'	'Wishlist'	2

Figure 4: Example storage schema. Bolded column names refer to primary keys.

```
view CampaignDimensions<params> {
  campaign = SELECT *,
    CampaignInfo.name AS Name,
    CampaignInfo.budget_id AS BudgetId
    FROM Campaign;
  budgets = SELECT *,
    BudgetInfo.amount AS BudgetAmount
    FROM Budget;
  budget_suggestion_table =
    if ($params.use_budget_suggestion_v2) {
      BudgetSuggestionV2;
    } else {
      BudgetSuggestionV1;
    }
  budgets_with_suggestion = SELECT *
    FROM budgets LEFT JOIN budget_suggestion_table
    USING CustomerId, BudgetId;
  return SELECT *,
    ComputeCampaignStatus(CampaignInfo, BudgetInfo,
                          BudgetSuggestionInfo) AS Status
    FROM campaign LEFT JOIN budgets_with_suggestion
    USING CustomerId, BudgetId;
}
view CampaignFacts<params> {
  return SELECT *,
    MakePair(Impressions, Clicks)
      AS ClickThroughRate [aggregation = "RateAgg"]
    FROM CampaignStats FULL JOIN CampaignConversionStats;
}
main CampaignReport<params> {
  campaign_report = SELECT $params.main_table_columns
    FROM CampaignDimensions<$params>
         LEFT JOIN CampaignFacts<$params>
         USING CustomerId, CampaignId;
  output SELECT *
    FROM campaign_report
    WHERE $params.filters
    ORDER BY $params.order_by_columns
    LIMIT $params.limit as top_k_table;
  output SELECT $params.summary_columns
    FROM campaign_report as summary;
}
```

Figure 5: CampaignReport RVL code.

uses F1 dimension tables Customer, Campaign, Budget, BudgetSuggestionV1, and BudgetSuggestionV2, using CustomerId as the root ID BudgetSuggestionV1 and BudgetSuggestionV2 tables capture a case that often comes up in practice: The application is migrating from an older to a newer, higher quality representation of budget suggestions. The application may want to use the new suggestions for only a small whitelist of advertisers initially, and ramp up slowly to all customers. We therefore maintain both versions during the transition period. Since different teams maintain the respective backend pipelines, separate tables help clarify ownership.

The example also uses Mesa fact tables CampaignStats and CampaignConversionStats. Impressions, Clicks, Cost, and Conversions columns use SUM for implicit aggregation. CampaignConversionStats is a separate table because conversions can be broken down by the additional dimension ConversionType.

Abstracting over the complex storage schema, Shasta exposes a flat denormalized view CampaignReport. The view schema exposes the following columns: CustomerId, CampaignId, Name, Status, BudgetAmount, Device, Impressions, ClickThroughRate, Clicks, and Conversions. RVL code for CampaignReport is shown in Figure 5. The following aspects are worth noting:

- The CampaignDimensions view template performs a join of F1 tables. The input parameter `use_budget_suggestion_v2` indicates which version of budget suggestion to use. The Status column is computed with a user-defined function (UDF).
- The CampaignFacts view template performs a join of Mesa tables. ClickThroughRate is made explicitly aggregatable by a user-defined aggregation function (UDAF) RateAgg. No explicit GROUP BY is specified, as the RVL compiler generates the correct GROUP BY clauses based on the request context.
- The main view template CampaignReport joins data from CampaignDimensions and CampaignFacts. The two view outputs `top_k_table` and `summary` share the `campaign_report` subquery, ensuring consistency of the two data pivots.
- `params.filters` typically contains a filter on CustomerId, but it can also contain filters on aggregatable columns like Impressions. The RVL code filters the data after projecting the final columns, but the RVL compiler may move filters to be applied earlier when possible.

Figure 6 illustrates the entire flow of a sample Shasta query with (i) a specific Shasta query issued by a Shasta client against the "CampaignReport" Shasta view, (ii) RVL template parameters generated from the Shasta query by the view gateway, and (iii) the Shasta query result. Note the result contains only two campaigns because of the "limit: 2" clause in the query, while the summary row contains aggregate stats for all campaigns.

5. QUERY EXECUTION ON F1

F1's SQL query engine has been described in [13]. It supports both *centralized* and *distributed* execution of queries. Centralized execution can deliver low latencies for simple queries with input data volumes that are easily processed on a single F1 server, and distributed F1 queries are a natural fit for workloads with larger in-

Shasta query

```
view_name: CampaignReport
columns: CampaignId, Name, Status, Budget, Impressions,
         Clicks, ClickThroughRate, Conversions
sort order: Clicks Descending
limit: 2
summary: on
application_params: CustomerId=20, BudgetSuggestionVersion=2
```

RVL template parameters

```
main_table_columns: CampaignId, Name, Status, BudgetAmount,
                    Impressions, Clicks, ClickThroughRate, Conversions
filters: CustomerId = 20
order_by_columns: Clicks DESC
limit: 2
summary_columns: Impressions, Clicks, ClickThroughRate, Conversions
use_budget_suggestion_v2: true
```

Query result

CampaignId	Name	Status	BudgetAmount	Impressions	Clicks	ClickThroughRate	Conversions
102	Daisy	Enabled	50	40	10	0.25	0
100	Rose	BudgetThrottled	100	30	8	0.27	3
Summary				100	22	0.22	5

Figure 6: Shasta view invocation.

puts and less stringent latency requirements, e.g., queries scanning all rows in a large F1 or Mesa table. Shasta represents a novel use of F1's query engine as it places heavily distributed query execution at the heart of latency sensitive and business-critical applications. While Shasta queries are typically scoped to a modest subset of data in underlying databases (e.g., a single advertiser's campaign configurations and performance metrics), the combination of remote input data, diverse data stores, data freshness requirements, and complexity of query logic make it challenging to achieve low latencies reliably using centralized execution, in Google's production environment based on shared commodity hardware. In the remainder of this section, we describe core F1 query engine features that were critical for the Shasta workload, our approach to supporting user-defined functions in F1, and how we tuned the distributed query processing pipeline for low latency.

5.1 Engine Features Critical for Shasta

In distributed F1 query execution, a *query coordinator* receives the incoming SQL query. The query is parsed and an execution plan is laid out as a directed acyclic graph (DAG) of potentially hundreds of *plan parts*. Each plan part is a tree of operators like scan, filter, project etc. Data flows from the leaves of the DAG towards the coordinator. F1 aims to maximize streaming of data between operators and to minimize pipeline stalls. Each plan part is annotated with the degree of parallelism at which it is to be run. The coordinator schedules plan parts to run on *F1 slaves* and configures the data flow between them as per the plan's DAG structure.

Hash-based repartitioning: The F1 query engine was designed for settings where co-partitioning of data between storage and query processing is not feasible, and where storage systems such as Spanner apply effectively arbitrary partitioning of data. To this end, F1 supports hash-based repartitioning of data during query execution. This support is critical for Shasta workloads, where input data stores are diverse and often not read-optimized. Hash-based repartitionings are used for co-partitioining in joins and for distributed aggregations. Shasta prefers to arrange large numbers of joins and aggregations in shallow, bushy trees to reduce latency and to allow for increased parallelism. As a result, latency depends more on tree depth than on the number of joins. Using SQL hints, skew-sensitive joins to small tables are often executed by broadcasting the smaller input, leaving the distribution of the larger input unchanged.

DAG-structured query plans: It is idiomatic in RVL to assign variable names to subqueries and then refer to them multiple times in subsequent RVL code. For instance, an RVL template may output a table and a summary row as different pivots of the same named subquery. For data consistency and computational efficiency, the underlying query engine should compute the subquery only once and feed results into multiple downstream computations. F1 supports such common table expressions using standard SQL WITH syntax. F1 internally represents multiple references to the same subquery as a DAG structure in which the subquery has multiple parent operators. Buffering mitigates the case of parent operators consuming result rows from the shared subquery at different rates.

External Data Sources: Shasta queries commonly scan and join data from storage systems as diverse as Spanner, F1 TableCache, Mesa, and Bigtable. Using a plugin framework for federated querying, the F1 query engine supports these data sources and several others. Central to the plugin framework is the abstraction of a *ScanOperator*. For every supported data source, a ScanOperator implementation translates between the data source API and the F1 SQL runtime. ScanOperator implementations can be carefully tailored to peculiarities of each data store. The resulting deep integrations between query engine and data stores were key in meeting the latency and scalability requirements in Shasta query workloads. A prime example for this is how F1 determines the degree of parallelism for distributed table scans, a fundamental feature of distributed query processing. The appropriate degree of parallelism for a table scan depends on how much data the table scan is expected to return, which in turn depends on the given query and data source. For each supported data source, the F1 ScanOperator plugin implements a GetPartitions() function. The F1 query planner calls this function to retrieve cardinality information in the context of a specific query. GetPartitions() implementations are naturally tailored to each data store. For instance, the Mesa ScanOperator's GetPartitions() implementation leverages precise Mesa-internal metadata only accessible by issuing Mesa RPCs, while the GetPartitions() implementation for TableCache uses metadata stored by an offline job in F1 storage. Compared to F1 maintaining cardinality metadata for all data sources centrally, the GetPartitions() protocol allows for more precise and up-to-date cardinality information. Federated ownership of metadata for different data stores also tends to be more scalable operationally.

5.2 UDF Servers

RVL code can invoke user-defined functions (UDFs) written in procedural languages such as C++ or Java. Motivations include sharing critical procedural code between RVL definitions and other systems processing the same data, re-use of subtle legacy code, and expressivity. UDFs are a common feature in SQL engines. However, UDF support in F1 allows users to deploy compiled C++ or Java UDF code in custom binaries called UDF servers that run in production alongside the F1 query engine, as separate processes and under client teams' credentials. In order to be able to register with the F1 query engine, UDF server binaries must implement a standard RPC API defined by F1. F1 provides "glue" libraries that make building a compliant UDF server trivial, given just a library of C++ or Java functions written by the client team. During execution of queries with UDF calls, F1 slaves issue RPCs to appropriate UDF servers, which in turn invoke corresponding UDF code. Compared to dynamically loading UDF libraries in F1 processes, this model provides the same release schedule flexibility but significantly stronger system isolation and security properties: UDF code never runs using F1's credentials and the F1 SQL runtime is protected from crashes or memory corruptions introduced by bugs in C++ UDFs, and from garbage collection spikes or exceptions introduced by Java UDFs.

One challenge in this decoupled approach is to minimize the latency costs that often come with turning function calls into RPCs. We have managed to largely mitigate these costs using two techniques. First, F1 slaves and UDF servers have independent degrees of parallelism: While F1 slaves use a single thread to process each plan part, an F1 slave thread calling a UDF can distribute rows across hundreds of UDF servers. Second, matching other parts of the F1 query engine, we heavily leverage batching and pipelining for UDF calls: As rows stream through the CallUdf operator, the operator maintains a queue of UDF server RPCs and blocks on results only if more than a certain threshold of RPCs are in-flight. RPC results are processed out-of-order if possible, reducing the impact of slow RPCs in a batch and hence reducing tail latency.

5.3 Distributed Execution Improvements

We highlight two distributed execution improvements that were key in meeting Shasta's low latency and scalability requirements.

Query Planning: During query planning, the query coordinator needs to determine the degree of parallelism for each plan part. Choosing this parameter well is key in scaling queries to different input sizes. Using GetPartitions() as explained above, we determine the degree of parallelism for scan plan parts (i.e., leaves), aiming to assign each scan partition to a different slave. For non-leaves, parallelism information is propagated up the DAG. For each plan part, the degree of parallelism is set to the maximum value among its children. This ensures that each internal plan part's parallelism takes input data size into account, improving scalability.

Query scheduling: After query planning, the coordinator assigns plan parts to specific F1 slave jobs and connects them with each other as sources and sinks per the query plan's DAG structure. Common Shasta queries have hundreds of plan parts. Instead of delaying the start of query execution until all plan parts are scheduled, scheduling is done in a bottom-up fashion: Leaf plan parts are scheduled first and can start working while their sink plan parts are still being scheduled. Once the sinks are scheduled, leaf parts are updated to use the respective sinks. This approach is used all the way up the DAG. By interleaving scheduling and execution in this way, we reduced query latency by tens of milliseconds.

6. F1 TABLECACHE

TableCache is a distributed in-memory read-through cache for data stored in F1, situated between F1 storage and the F1 query engine. As Shasta applications access data in per-user sessions, TableCache is designed for workloads where individual queries are scoped to one specific root ID. In F1, a *root ID* is the primary key of the root in a hierarchy of tables, and application users are identified by a root ID in typical F1 schemas. Given (table, root ID, timestamp) triples, TableCache serves data to the F1 query engine faster and at significantly higher throughput compared to raw F1 storage. For advertiser sessions in the AdWords Web UI for example, TableCache often achieves 20 times higher read throughput. TableCache is multi-versioned and provides the same snapshot read semantics as F1, but only for a moving window of timestamps from "just committed" to a few minutes in the past. TableCache does not support reads across root IDs or for timestamps further in the past.

The intuition behind TableCache is that, for F1 storage backed by Spanner, there is a natural tension between optimizing the database for reads vs. for writes: write latencies tend to benefit from keeping the number of shards per Spanner directory modest, to minimize participants in transactions. Read throughput on the other hand benefits from a larger number of smaller shards. A distributed read-only in-memory cache can avoid this tension: Read throughput can be dramatically increased by serving data from RAM and by using shard sizes and data structures solely optimized for reads. However, as important Shasta applications cannot tolerate stale data with respect to recent user updates, the cache must be kept consistent and fresh without significant negative impact on write or read latencies. TableCache achieves this using F1 Change History.

The following subsections describe TableCache's design in three parts. First, we divide F1 rows for (table, root ID) pairs into small table shards using periodic offline analysis. Second, a set of potentially hundreds of distributed in-memory cache servers lazily load and evict table shards. The cache server API is designed to work well as a data source for distributed F1 SQL queries, and a hash-based protocol balances table shards across cache servers. Finally, loaded table shards are versioned based on F1 timestamps. If a shard is not fresh enough for a given query, we update it by incrementally applying changes from F1 Change History.

6.1 Sharding of Cached Data

To allow for more read parallelism compared to reading from F1 directly, we divide F1 rows for a given (table, root ID) into *table shards* significantly smaller than shards at the F1 storage level, often 10x smaller. A periodic offline job stores TableCache sharding metadata in an F1 system table, mapping each (table, root ID) pair to a list of table shard boundary keys and size estimates. The sharding algorithm aims to create small yet evenly sized shards, maximizing read throughput yet minimizing input data skew during F1 query processing. The offline job reruns its analysis for root IDs with a significant number of recent changes, which can be determined easily in F1 using a Change History SQL query. We describe TableCache's use of F1 Change History in more detail later in this section.

6.2 Cache Serving

TableCache was designed to be used as a data source in distributed F1 SQL queries such as the following:

```
DEFINE TABLE tablecache_Campaign(format='tablecache',
                                 table_name='Campaign');
SELECT * FROM tablecache_Campaign WHERE CustomerId = 20;
```

The F1 query engine works best with external data sources that support separate RPCs for dynamic cardinality estimation and for reading data. TableCache servers therefore expose two RPCs. Both are called from within the F1 ScanOperator implementation – i.e., query engine plugin – for TableCache.

- GetPartitions(table, root_id) returns to the F1 coordinator a list of shard split points.
- Read(table, root_id, read_timestamp, shard_id) returns to an F1 slave an ordered list of F1 rows for one table shard.[1]

Table shards are not statically mapped to cache servers – any cache server will readily load any table shard for which it receives a re-

[1]In practice, F1 can push down additional filters to TableCache.

quest. Rather, the client (the F1 query engine) is responsible for distributing table shards evenly across cache servers, by issuing Read() requests for specific shards to specific cache servers. To decide which server to talk to, TableCache clients use the deterministic hash based function GetServer which maps a table shard (table, root_id, shard_id) to a specific cache server.[2] GetServer tends to return different cache servers for different table shards, balancing table shards evenly across cache servers. Using the (table, root_id) pair (Campaign, 20) from the SQL query above and assuming the query client requests data as of F1 snapshot timestamp T_{Query}, a TableCache scan is executed in F1 as follows.

The F1 coordinator issues a GetPartitions RPC to the cache server determined by GetServer(Campaign, 20, 0). Note shard_id is always set to 0 for GetPartitions calls. The cache server looks up and returns shard split points stored by the offline job in F1 for (Campaign, 20). The coordinator schedules one F1 slave to issue a Read RPC for each table shard as determined by GetPartitions. Each slave then issues the RPC Read(Campaign, 20, T_{Query}, shard_id) to the cache server determined by GetServer(Campaign, 20, shard_id). The cache servers now need to load the requested table shards, if not yet present in RAM. Before loading, each server confirms that there is enough RAM available or evicts other table shards, using an LRU-based replacement policy. The server then reads the CampaignId range corresponding to the shard split points for shard_id from F1.Campaign at timestamp (T_{Query} – 15 minutes). "15 minutes" is a system parameter, configuring the moving window of consistent data versions that TableCache supports. The server stores read F1 rows in a modified B-tree data structure and records the checkpoint $T_{\text{Cache}} = T_{\text{Query}} - 15\text{m}$ to mark how fresh the cache for this table shard currently is. Clearly the cache is not fresh enough yet to answer queries at timestamp T_{Query}. The process of updating the cache immediately after loading a table shard or later in a session is essentially the same, and we describe that next.

6.3 Updating the Cache

TableCache heavily leverages F1's Change History feature as described in [13]. We give a brief overview of the feature before explaining how data loaded in TableCache is kept up-to-date.

Unlike traditional DBMSs, F1 provides a user-queryable change log called Change History. This log is maintained by the database system itself, not by application business logic, so it is guaranteed to capture all changes to change-tracked tables, including manually applied emergency data changes. Whether an F1 table is change-tracked or not is configured in the schema. Every F1 transaction that writes to a change-tracked table creates one or more ChangeBatch Protocol Buffers, which include the primary key and before and after values of changed columns for each updated row. These ChangeBatch records are then written to a Change History table, the primary key of which includes the associated root ID and transaction commit timestamp. Change History tables are first-class tables in F1, meaning they are tunable in the schema and queryable by F1 clients like any other F1 table. Based on the primary keys in Change History tables, clients can process Change History entries strictly ordered by root ID and commit timestamp of the corresponding F1 transactions and build a precise image of F1 data physically outside F1. This can be done using a relatively simple protocol based on checkpoints and before/after values contained in Change History records. A good example for this is how F1 TableCache keeps loaded data up-to-date.

[2] In practice, GetServer returns a specific permutation of the list of available cache servers, and clients iterate through the list, for failover in case of unhealthy cache servers.

Whenever a loaded table shard's timestamp T_{Cache} is older than the requested timestamp T_{Query}, the cache server updates the table shard by querying F1 Change History at snapshot time T_{Query}, retrieving all change records for (table, root ID) with a commit timestamp > T_{Cache}. Our system and schema are optimized to make this read fast enough to be placed on the latency critical path of interactive applications. For every returned change record, if the changed CampaignId is in range for the given table shard, the cache server applies the change to its in-memory representation, but preserving older versions within the configured moving window of snapshots supported. Once all changes are applied, the table shard's checkpoint is updated to T_{Query}, and the read request can be satisfied.

Using this protocol, TableCache achieves a powerful property: As long as queries are grouped into user sessions by root ID so that the cost of loading table shards from F1 storage is amortized over subsequent cache reads, TableCache can provide an order of magnitude higher read throughput to an application that expects 100% fresh data in requests issued immediately after writes to F1. Still, TableCache's design is relatively simple, especially when compared to alternatives such as write through caches: TableCache never needs to invalidate and reload an entire data set in response to writes. Furthermore, the write path at the database level can be unaware of the existence of the cache. This is critical, as putting cache updates on the critical path of F1 writes would re-introduce the tension we described above: Cache writes would have to be applied across shards and across geo-replicated regions, and to keep those fast, fewer and larger cache shards would be needed, in turn hurting reads.

7. PRODUCTION EXPERIENCE

Shasta powers multiple critical interactive reporting applications at Google. In this section, we report on our experience using Shasta for an important advertiser-facing application. Before Shasta, the views in this application were defined in C++ and computed using a custom query engine. When compared to this legacy system, Shasta has made software engineering more efficient, while also improving the performance and scalability of the system.

Software engineering efficiency: The design of the legacy system followed a common pattern for domain-specific backends, starting as a fairly simple C++ server and evolving into a mix of complex view definitions and query processing code. Without the strong boundaries that come with a declarative language like RVL, the query processing "engine" code overlapped with the code for view definitions, making it infeasible to separate ownership of the two pieces. As a result, feature development was bottlenecked on 15 engineers who had sole expert knowledge of both the custom engine and approximately 100 view definitions. Using Shasta's RVL view declarations, more than 200 code contributors across multiple teams now share view development, concentrating solely on business logic, while a smaller, separate team focuses on engine and compiler work. We replaced around 130k lines of C++ view definition code with 30k lines of RVL and 23k lines of C++ UDF code. The new code encapsulates all the logic of view transformations without relying on additional precomputed results for performance. This stateless design simplifies rollout of application changes and adds to the software engineering benefits of Shasta. For instance, changing a Shasta view column definition does not require updating data materializations previously stored using the old definition.

Relative system performance: The legacy reporting system was tailored for a particular storage schema, with limited support for query planning and distributed processing. Figures 7 and 8 show performance of Shasta relative to the legacy system for two views

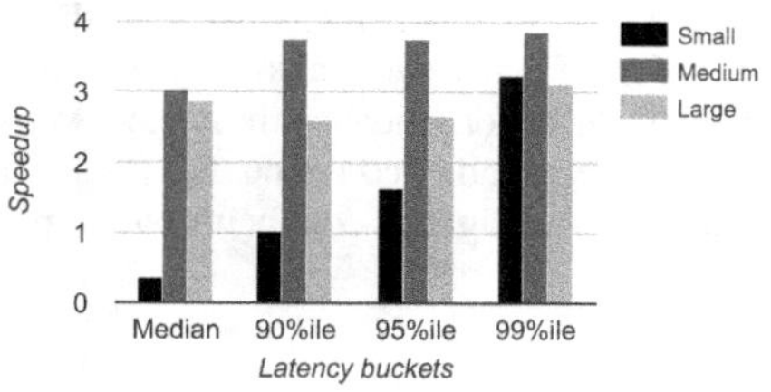

Figure 7: Speedup of Shasta vs. legacy system for View 1.

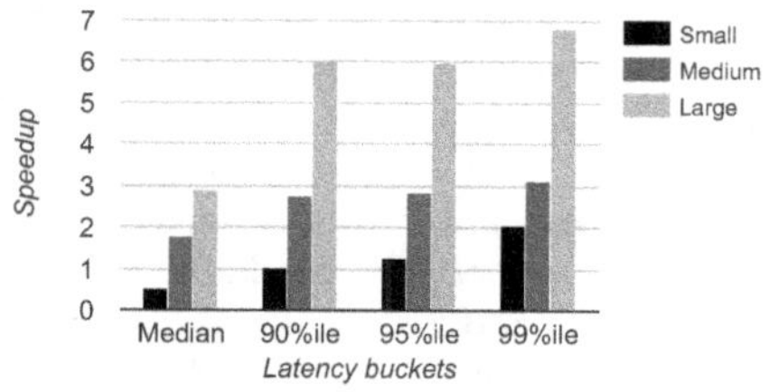

Figure 8: Speedup of Shasta vs. legacy system for View 2.

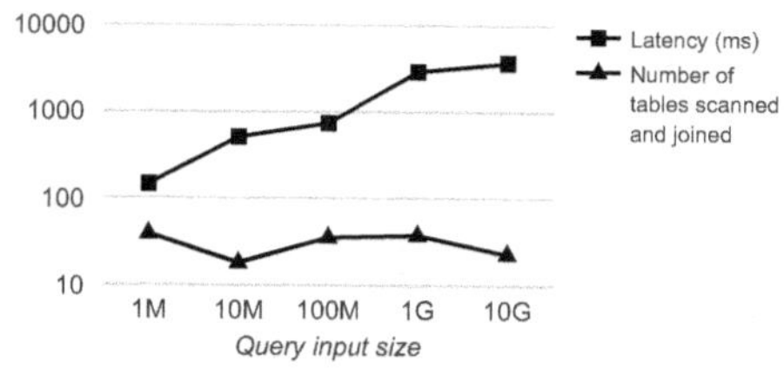

Figure 9: System scalability.

used in production. A "Speedup" value of 2 means Shasta is two times faster than the legacy system, 1 means latency is on par, and 0.5 means Shasta is two times slower. For each view, performance is compared for different query input data sizes (small, medium, large) which for this interactive workload are at most a few gigabytes per query. The views have varying business logic and query plan structures, yet the performance pattern is the same: Shasta is 2.5x to 7x faster for large queries and 2x to 4x faster for medium queries, thanks to more parallelism and data balancing via dynamic repartitioning available in F1's query engine. Only at the median for small queries does the legacy system consistently outperform Shasta. This is due to overhead inherent in the Shasta architecture, incurred by parsing and optimizing RVL code, generating SQL strings, parsing and planning SQL in F1 and scheduling query plans for execution. The overhead is typically modest in absolute terms (10s of ms), and not the majority portion of user-perceived latency, which includes network latency and latency from other systems higher in the stack. For larger and higher percentile queries on the other hand, the speedups achieved by Shasta were significant in terms of user-perceived latency. Future work may further reduce planning overhead using techniques such as prepared queries.

System scalability: While underlying tables in storage can be terabyte scale, Shasta queries issued by interactive applications are typically scoped to a single user's data. Carefully structured indexes in Mesa and data clustering by F1 root ID in TableCache then allow F1 queries to scan modest amounts of input – at most a few gigabytes for queries that run at interactive latencies. On the other hand, query plan complexity is high: important individual queries scan data from 50 tables and perform 60 join operations.

Despite the fact that input data size for most interactive queries is relatively modest, we made a conscious design decision to place highly distributed query processing at the core of the Shasta architecture, for two reasons. First, achieving reliably interactive latencies for workloads with the query complexities outlined above on single machines is challenging in Google's production environment, where commodity hardware shared between different services is the norm. Second, we find that in practice, sophisticated business applications are not truly limited to interactive queries with modest input sizes: As businesses evolve, data sizes and schema complexity tend to increase in ways that are hard to predict. Furthermore, applications tend to become *platforms*, offering to users not only interactive UIs, but also powerful programmatic developer APIs where query input sizes are larger and interactive latencies are less critical, yet where data freshness and consistency requirements are just as stringent. Shasta scales naturally to this setting and is used as a shared layer powering vastly different application interfaces of such platforms, guaranteeing fully consistent concepts and semantics in the different interfaces.

Combining data measured across one such platform at Google, Figure 9 illustrates the scalability of Shasta. As the size of input data increases, query latency has sublinear growth, made possible by F1's distributed query processing. Using statistical regression analysis, we found that the latency follows a trend of $O(n^{0.36})$ when n bytes are scanned. The chart also illustrates that structural query complexity – measured by the number of tables scanned and joined in the query – is largely constant across different input sizes. In Shasta applications, query input size tends to be determined by view parameters such as date ranges and the size of the given user's account, whereas query plan complexity is a function of schema complexity and application design, so the two are orthogonal.

Impact of TableCache: TableCache is critical for achieving low query latencies. The F1 query engine achieves at least 20x higher throughput reading from TableCache compared to reading from F1 storage directly. This is primarily due to the fact that TableCache partitions data much more finely, allowing much higher read parallelism, and leverages read-optimized data structures.

8. RELATED WORK

When comparing RVL to other query languages, one interesting feature to consider is implicit aggregation. The support for implicit aggregation has parallels to the MDX language [15] for querying OLAP data cubes. Dimensions and measures in the schema used by MDX are analogous to grouping columns and aggregatable columns in RVL, since measures are automatically aggregated for any selection of dimensions. RVL provides more flexibility than MDX, by supporting automatic aggregation on arbitrary joins. This makes RVL more readily applicable to existing SQL databases.

We can also compare RVL's view templates and sequential assignment statements to the features of other languages. The support for sequential subquery assignments has become particularly popular in query languages, as this syntax comes naturally to many developers. The scripting languages SCOPE [17] and Pig Latin [12] have support for assignment statements and output statements similar to RVL. The view templates of RVL allow blocks of assignment statements to be grouped together and reused with dynamic parameters, which can help developers organize a large code base. Spark SQL [2] supports the DataFrame API which can be used in various programming languages to formulate queries as a sequence of steps. Using DataFrames, a developer may create dynamic and reusable subqueries using constructs of the programming language (e.g., Java methods). RVL is intended to combine the best aspects of these approaches, allowing dynamic and reusable subqueries to be specified in one unified language.

TableCache acts as an extra layer of caching between the F1 query engine and F1 storage backed by Spanner. It can be compared to the usage of buffer pools in traditional database architectures [14, 6] since the goal is to exploit database access patterns to accelerate I/O. However, TableCache is read-only, which allows the design to be optimized for the read path without sacrificing write performance. In particular, TableCache uses fine-grained sharding to perform many small reads in parallel, and transactional writes become more expensive with higher degrees of parallelism. Also, TableCache provides a higher-level abstraction than traditional block-based caches, where data from a table is accessed based on root ID and timestamp. Oracle TimesTen [10] can be deployed as a read-only cache in a similar way, but without timestamp-based access. We may also compare TableCache to the in-memory data management used by the scale-out extension (SOE) of SAP HANA [7], which allows reads at specific timestamps. The Shasta architecture differs from the SAP HANA SOE since the cache is decoupled from the query processing nodes, which allows TableCache to communicate directly with other server processes. Maintaining the freshness of TableCache is facilitated by F1 Change History which is conceptually based on the classical notion of write-ahead logging [11] in commercial DBMS engines. However, the implementation of F1 Change History is very different in that it is exposed as a first-class database entity which can be operated upon as a regular database table.

9. CONCLUDING REMARKS

Exposing interactive reporting and data analysis to users is crucial in business applications. For UIs to be truly interactive, user query latency must be low, and query results must provide fresh data that always include the most recent user updates. Data stores holding the transactional truth of underlying business data often have vast and complex schemas, placing significant transformation logic between stored data and user-facing concepts. The necessary data transformations often have to access data from multiple data stores, not all of which are read-optimized. In order to provide fresh data to applications while allowing for agile application development, it is ideal to avoid relying on precomputation and perform all transformations at query time. This results in two significant challenges: First, complex data transformations must be expressed in a way that scales to large engineering organizations and supports dynamic generation of online queries, based on rich query-time parameters. Second, the resulting online queries are complex – e.g., queries read from diverse data stores and join 50 or more tables – yet need to be executed reliably at interactive latencies.

Shasta takes an integrated approach to solving these challenges, using both language-level and system-level advances. In particular, Shasta provides a hybrid language interface to its users via RVL. RVL combines SQL-like functionality with limited but powerful procedural constructs. Using RVL, user queries can be stated succinctly and view definitions can naturally capture the dynamic nature of applications. At the system level, Shasta leverages a caching architecture that mitigates the impedance mismatch between stringent latency requirements for reads on the one hand and the underlying data store being mostly write-optimized on the other. Shasta also extends F1's distributed query processing framework to support user-defined function (UDF) calls at low latency yet with strong system isolation. As a result, Shasta incurs low latencies in computing complex views with little reliance on view materialization and without compromising on data freshness.

10. ACKNOWLEDGEMENTS

We would like to thank all current and past members of the Shasta team, especially Tuan Cao, Kelvin Lau, Patrick Lee, Wei-Hsin Lee, Curtis Menton, Aditi Pandit, Shashank Senapaty, Alejandro Valerio, and Junxiong Zhou. We'd also like to thank members of application teams that migrated to RVL, including Dmitry Churbanau, Daniel Halem, Raymond Ho, Anar Huseynov, Sujata Kosalge, Luke Snyder, and Andreas Sterbenz. We are grateful to the F1 team, including Brian Biskeborn, John Cieslewicz, Daniel Tenedorio, and Michael Styer, and to the Mesa team, including Mingsheng Hong, Kevin Lai, and Tao Zou. Finally, we thank Ashish Gupta, Sridhar Ramaswamy, and Jeff Shute for guidance throughout various stages of Shasta's development, and Nico Bruno, Ian Rae, Jeff Shute, and SIGMOD reviewers for insightful comments on our paper draft.

11. REFERENCES

[1] R. Ananthanarayanan, V. Basker, S. Das, A. Gupta, H. Jiang, T. Qiu, A. Reznichenko, D. Ryabkov, M. Singh, and S. Venkataraman. Photon: Fault-tolerant and scalable joining of continuous data streams. In *SIGMOD*, pages 577–588, 2013.

[2] M. Armbrust, R. S. Xin, C. Lian, Y. Huai, D. Liu, J. K. Bradley, X. Meng, T. Kaftan, M. J. Franklin, A. Ghodsi, et al. Spark SQL: Relational data processing in Spark. In *SIGMOD*, pages 1383–1394, 2015.

[3] F. Chang, J. Dean, S. Ghemawat, W. C. Hsieh, D. A. Wallach, M. Burrows, T. Chandra, A. Fikes, and R. E. Gruber. Bigtable: A distributed storage system for structured data. *TOCS*, 26(2):4, 2008.

[4] S. Chaudhuri and U. Dayal. An overview of data warehousing and OLAP technology. *ACM SIGMOD Record*, 26(1):65–74, 1997.

[5] J. C. Corbett, J. Dean, M. Epstein, A. Fikes, C. Frost, J. J. Furman, S. Ghemawat, A. Gubarev, C. Heiser, P. Hochschild, et al. Spanner: Google's globally distributed database. *TOCS*, 31(3):8, 2013.

[6] W. Effelsberg and T. Haerder. Principles of database buffer management. *TODS*, 9(4):560–595, 1984.

[7] A. K. Goel, J. Pound, N. Auch, P. Bumbulis, S. MacLean, F. Färber, F. Gropengiesser, C. Mathis, T. Bodner, and W. Lehner. Towards scalable real-time analytics: An architecture for scale-out of OLxP workloads. *PVLDB*, 8(12):1716–1727, 2015.

[8] A. Gupta, F. Yang, J. Govig, A. Kirsch, K. Chan, K. Lai, S. Wu, S. G. Dhoot, A. R. Kumar, A. Agiwal, S. Bhansali, M. Hong, J. Cameron, M. Siddiqi, D. Jones, J. Shute, A. Gubarev, S. Venkataraman, and D. Agrawal. Mesa: Geo-replicated, near real-time, scalable data warehousing. *PVLDB*, 7(12):1259–1270, 2014.

[9] L. M. Haas, D. Kossmann, E. L. Wimmers, and J. Yang. Optimizing queries across diverse data sources. In *VLDB*, pages 276–285, 1997.

[10] T. Lahiri, M.-A. Neimat, and S. Folkman. Oracle TimesTen: An in-memory database for enterprise applications. *IEEE Data Eng. Bull.*, 36(2):6–13, 2013.

[11] C. Mohan, D. J. Haderle, B. G. Lindsay, H. Pirahesh, and P. M. Schwarz. ARIES: A transaction recovery method supporting fine-granularity locking and partial rollbacks using write-ahead logging. *TODS*, 17(1):94–162, 1992.

[12] C. Olston, B. Reed, U. Srivastava, R. Kumar, and A. Tomkins. Pig Latin: A not-so-foreign language for data processing. In *SIGMOD*, pages 1099–1110, 2008.

[13] J. Shute, R. Vingralek, B. Samwel, B. Handy, C. Whipkey, E. Rollins, M. Oancea, K. Littlefield, D. Menestrina, S. Ellner, J. Cieslewicz, I. Rae, T. Stancescu, and H. Apte. F1: A distributed SQL database that scales. *PVLDB*, 6(11):1068–1079, 2013.

[14] M. Stonebraker. Operating system support for database management. *Communications of the ACM*, 24(7):412–418, 1981.

[15] P. Vassiliadis and T. Sellis. A survey of logical models for OLAP databases. *ACM SIGMOD Record*, 28(4):64–69, 1999.

[16] W. Yan and P.-A. Larson. Performing group-by before join. In *ICDE*, pages 89–100, 1994.

[17] J. Zhou, N. Bruno, M.-C. Wu, P.-A. Larson, R. Chaiken, and D. Shakib. SCOPE: Parallel databases meet MapReduce. *VLDB Journal*, 21(5):611–636, 2012.

Datometry Hyper-Q: Bridging the Gap Between Real-Time and Historical Analytics

Lyublena Antova, Rhonda Baldwin, Derrick Bryant, Tuan Cao, Michael Duller, John Eshleman, Zhongxian Gu, Entong Shen, Mohamed A. Soliman, F. Michael Waas
Datometry Inc.
795 Folsom St #100, San Francisco, CA 94107, U.S.A.
www.datometry.com
⟨first.last⟩@datometry.com

ABSTRACT

Wall Street's trading engines are complex database applications written for time series databases like kdb+ that uses the query language Q to perform real-time analysis. Extending the models to include other data sources, e.g., historic data, is critical for backtesting and compliance. However, Q applications cannot run directly on SQL databases. Therefore, financial institutions face the dilemma of either maintaining two separate application stacks, one written in Q and the other in SQL, which means increased IT cost and increased risk, or migrating all Q applications to SQL, which results in losing the inherent competitive advantage on Q real-time processing. Neither solution is desirable as both alternatives are costly, disruptive, and suboptimal.
In this paper we present Hyper-Q, a data virtualization platform that overcomes the chasm. Hyper-Q enables Q applications to run natively on PostgreSQL-compatible databases by translating queries and results on the fly. We outline the basic concepts, detail specific difficulties, and demonstrate the viability of the approach with a case study.

1. INTRODUCTION

The financial services industry has long been a pioneer in data processing. Real-time databases and special purpose query languages have fundamentally transformed trading desks in the past twenty years. Today's trading engines are elaborate database applications that implement complex mathematical models in the form of queries. The advent of Big Data technology over the past years presents a significant opportunity not only to integrate new data sources but also to extend existing models to incorporate substantial amounts of historical data.

Unfortunately, the mismatch between data models and query languages makes this kind of data integration a difficult undertaking and institutions so far faced the choice of either (1) committing to one specific solution as a compromise and migrate their entire application ecosystem to that technology or (2) maintaining multiple copies of the application stack, one for each technology, e.g., one for in-memory, one for SQL databases, one for archival NoSQL systems. Either choice is associated with high implementation cost. Either choice may also result in suboptimal operational performance or, in the case of multiple stacks, high maintenance cost of an inherently error-prone process. The underlying problem has been referred to as the Holy Grail of historical data processing [5] by practitioners in this space: a unified solution will have significant financial implications as it allows trading applications to take advantage of additional data and thus outperform competitors, but also avoids the penalty of high maintenance cost.

In this paper we present a unique solution that avoids the aforementioned compromise but rather keeps the application layer intact while enabling the use of real-time and archival database systems side by side. Building on the basic concept of Adaptive Data Virtualization (ADV) [1], we present Hyper-Q, an actual implementation of a platform that abstracts the backend database and translates queries and data exchange on the fly. The use-case we present in this paper shows how applications originally written for real-time systems using the programming language Q can seamlessly access SQL databases, as Hyper-Q provides a full-featured Q interface on top of an MPP database or a NoSQL system.

During the development of Hyper-Q we had to master a number of hard challenges including the mapping of different data types, reconciliation of different semantics around operators and functions, as well as operational challenges like emulation of management or authentication mechanisms.

Note that at this stage of our project we address the challenge of *accessing* data from native applications using emulated APIs. We rely on the assumption that all relevant data is loaded into the underlying systems independently. In practice, we found transferring the data to be much less of a problem. We consider adding tools that perform data movement and the mapping of schemas in the future; we expect that development to be greatly simplified by Hyper-Q's capabilities.

The remainder of this paper is organized as follows: In Section 2 we provide background on the technologies we leverage in our work. Section 3 gives an architectural deepdive of Hyper-Q. Section 4 is a discussion of implementation details. We present a case-study on an actual deployment of Hyper-Q in Section 5. Our experimental evaluation is in Section 6. We discuss related work in Section 7. Finally, Section 8 summarizes the paper with concluding remarks.

SIGMOD'16, June 26-July 01, 2016, San Francisco, CA, USA
© 2016 ACM. ISBN 978-1-4503-3531-7/16/06...$15.00
DOI: http://dx.doi.org/10.1145/2882903.2903739

2. BACKGROUND

In this section, we briefly survey background needed for the developments in the rest of this paper. First, in Section 2.1, we present the approaches adopted by the industry for supporting real-time and historical analytics. Then, we give an overview in Section 2.2 on the kdb+ system and its Q language, which provide the main motivating application of our framework.

2.1 Real-time and Historical Analytics

In this section, we give background on the building blocks and problems associated with integrating real-time and historical data analytics in financial services.

Financial services utilize specialized environments and proprietary algorithms to perform stock trading at large scale. Stock trading is a highly competitive business. Entities that have the fastest access to information and the most sophisticated trading algorithms are at an advantage.

Market data is the time-series data produced by an entity like a stock exchange. For specification and samples, we refer the reader to the New York Stock Exchange Trades and Quotes (NYSE's TAQ) dataset [17]. Market data is used in real-time to make time-sensitive decisions about trading equities and is also used for historical data applications like predictive modeling, e.g., projecting pricing trends, calculating market risk and backtesting of trading strategies.

Real-time databases have held a strong presence in capital markets for two main reasons; low-latency query processing and query language expressiveness. Query response times must be sub-second and systems achieve this by utilizing columnar data organization, in-memory query processing, and avoiding the typical RDBMs bottlenecks such as locking and synchronization overheads. Expressiveness and terseness of the query language to perform time-series analytics was also a major advantage over early RDBMs systems.

Recently, retention and analysis of data beyond short horizons have become increasingly important and a competitive differentiator within the financial services industry. Organizations are confronted with finding a way of continuing to do the analysis their business run on today within the tight SLAs as well as extend that analysis to include larger time windows of data.

The approaches that are typically adopted to run both real-time and historical analytics in financial services are the following: (1) scaling real-time databases, (2) migration to a scale-out analytical database, or (3) using a hybrid of real-time and analytical databases. We highlight the main limitations of these different approaches.

Scaling Real-time Databases. Adding more real-time database servers could allow analytical financial services to scale to some extent. However, this approach can be prohibitively expensive because of multiple reasons:

1. Cost: The hardware costs associated with expanding real-time systems can easily exceed the cost of conventional RDBMS technology on commodity hardware.

2. Compute Power: Most real-time databases are single machine and sometimes even single CPU. The slowdown of Moore's law against ever increasing data volumes means that the compute power in these systems could not catch up with workloads as data volumes increase.

3. Tools: Real-time database systems are built for a very different use case than analytics on historical data. They often lack the compliance, management utilities, and tools required by enterprises when storing massive volumes of historical data, which RDBMS vendors have taken 20-30 years to perfect.

Migration to Analytical Databases. Analytical databases, such as Massively Parallel Processing (MPP) databases, are effective at scaling to very large data sizes. Migrating real-time database applications/workloads to use an analytical database can address the historical data challenge.

However, latency overhead in analytical databases, especially for short-running queries, is typically larger than the traditional RDBMs overhead. This is mainly attributed to the large system scale and the need to optimize and dispatch query fragments over a cluster of machines. Consequently, analytical databases cannot typically meet the real-time SLAs that financial applications needs. Furthermore, migrating applications and workloads that are fine-tuned over years from real-time database to analytical database is an overwhelming undertaking. This process is known to be error-prone and has no clear quality guarantees. In some settings, database queries could be automatically generated by libraries, packages, web services, etc. This makes changing the query language very difficult.

A Hybrid of Real-Time and Analytical Databases. Building a hybrid system that deploys both real-time and historical database comes with its own problems. Most organizations find it straightforward to handle the data schema and loading of data between the two systems. Beyond that they quickly run into many challenges that must be overcome:

1. Training costs and challenge of finding qualified personnel who are adept at writing financial analytic algorithms in both the real-time database language, typically vector oriented, as well as in the historical database language, typically set oriented.

2. Once analytics are written for both systems, how does an organization vet and prove that they give the same or compatible results in both places. What configuration management practices must they employ to ensure that they stay compatible over time as minor modifications must be made?

3. Having to write analytics in both places slows down the pace of innovation and ability for the organization to continue to innovate and remain competitive.

An alternative solution would leverage investments in existing applications by keeping the real-time database applications, while allowing a choice of runtime execution environment. In this scenario, the application layer is kept intact, while the underlying data processing layer is virtualized such that the same query language can be used to query both real-time and analytical databases. This paper advocates for the viability and value of this novel solution.

2.2 kdb+

This section gives a high-level overview of the kdb+ system and is primarily meant to highlight the challenges involved in translating queries written in the query language Q into a relational language, such as SQL. A more complete documentation can be found at [14].

kdb+ is a columnar database specifically designed for real-time analytics. Its premier application area is in-memory query processing although it can operate over on-disk data. The system lacks many of the features found in classical relational database systems such as ACID transactions. Like other special purpose database systems, kdb+ accomplishes isolation through serialization, i.e., the main server loop executes a single request at a time. Concurrent requests are queued to be executed serially. Atomicity, consistency and durability are the application's responsibility, if desired. For historical reasons, kdb+ had no need for access control or sophisticated security mechanisms. Similarly, kdb+ does not provide built in support for data replication. Disaster recovery or high-availability are accomplished through external tooling.

kdb+ is queried using Q, a highly domain-specific query language. Q is distinguished by its terse syntax. It is rich in idioms that are specifically tailored to the financial analytics use case. The highly compressed syntax is often lauded for eliminating room for error: a single line of Q may correspond to an entire page of SQL, the correctness of which is usually much harder to ascertain.

Q pre-dates most of the OLAP extensions found in recent SQL standard which initially gave it a unique competitive advantage over relational database languages. More recently, the SQL standard has caught up and provides sufficient language constructs to implement equivalent functionality. Unlike relational databases, Q is not based on a tabular calculus. Rather, Q is a list processing language that supports, besides scalar data types, several compound types such as dictionaries or tables, which are made up of lists. Lists are, by definition, ordered, which in turn greatly facilitates time series analysis in Q.

As a recent addition to the language, Q features several SQL-like constructs even though their semantics often diverge from relational dialects in surprising ways. For example, UPDATE operation in Q simply replaces columns in the query output instead of changing any persisted state.

To illustrate the expressiveness of Q consider the following example:

> **Example 1** A standard point-in-time query to get the prevailing quote as of each trade:

```
aj[`Symbol`Time;
   select Price from trades
   where Date=SOMEDATE, Symbol in SYMLIST;
   select Symbol, Time, Bid, Ask from quotes
   where Date=SOMEDATE]
```

This query is one of the most commonly used queries by financial market analysts [9]. It can be used to measure the difference between the price at the time users decide to buy and the price paid at actual execution, i.e. the fill message reported by the broker. The *as-of-join* (aj) is a unique built-in function in Q which natively supports time-series queries. In this query, *Symbol* and *Time* are the columns to join on, *trades* is a reference table and *quotes* is a table to be looked up.

The performance of this query largely depends on the size of the *quotes* table. If the data is small enough so that the underlying database has one partition per date, this *as-of-join* achieves very good performance. Instead of reading the entire Symbol, Time, Bid, and Ask columns into memory to perform the lookup, it can search through the memory map of the *quotes* table. However, if the *quotes* table is large, and there are multiple partitions per date, all partitions need to be read into memory to perform the lookup since rows with the same symbol could occur in multiple partitions. To work around this, Q programmers often need to manually rewrite the above query to do *as-of-join* on each partition and then aggregate the result from each partition. The rewrite is very complex and requires deep knowledge of the structure of the underlying database [9].

kdb+ does not have a query optimizer. A query is executed in reverse order of its components. Q programmers have to determine join orders explicitly in their queries and have to be aware of how individual operations such as a lookup-join are executed. Mistakes in crafting the query may have severe consequence for the performance of a query or even crash the server process due to out-of-memory conditions.

In many ways, performance is achieved by exposing to users how data is actually stored so that users can take advantages of this while constructing queries. For example, Q allows marking a list as having all occurrences of a value occurring in a sequential block. This allows the creation of a lookup table from each distinct value to its first occurrence, then all occurrences of that value can be found in one sequential read. As a consequence, Q programmers often need to understand how underlying data is structured in order to write optimal queries [7].

Due to considerable differences in query language and data model, building a virtualized system allowing Q application to run on top of a SQL database involves multiple challenges:

- Q applications communicate with kdb+ using specific wire protocol which is usually very different from the wire protocol of the underlying SQL database. While SQL databases typically implement protocols that stream individual rows, Q uses an object-based protocol that communicates a query results as a single message. In order to run Q applications seamlessly on an SQL database, we need to convert the packets in Q wire format to the underlying database wire format and vice versa. This conversion includes the transformation of data types and values as well as the pivoting of database rows into the object-based format that is to be presented to the application.

- While SQL is based on set/bag semantics, in which order of rows in a table is not defined, Q is based on *ordered-list* semantics, in which ordering is the first class citizen for all complex data structures, such as tables and dictionaries. In particular, each Q table has an implicit order column. Providing implicit ordering using SQL requires database schema changes and imposes challenges on query generation.

- Q is *column-oriented*, i.e., it stores tables as columns and can apply operations to entire column. In contrast to Q, SQL is not column-oriented. Even in columnar SQL databases, the support is mainly implemented in the underlying storage and execution engines. Therefore, query constructs that express column-wise operations cannot be easily specified in SQL.

- Q uses a *two-valued logic* in contrast to SQL's *three-valued logic*. Operations on null values have very different semantics in Q and in SQL. For example, two nulls compare as equal in Q, while the result is undefined/unknown in SQL. Imposing these semantics on SQL queries requires careful composition of query constructs to maintain correctness of the results.

- Unlike SQL which is statically typed, Q is dynamically typed where the type of a variable is determined by its value. Consider an expression x+y, if x and y are not statically defined then their types are determined by the values assigned to them at runtime. In particular, if x and y are assigned scalar values then x and y have scalar type; if x and y are assigned as lists then x and y have list type. Translating a dynamic-typed language to a static-typed language requires significant amount of runtime support. If not done efficiently, type inference may add a considerable overhead to the query latency.

- Q expressions are evaluated strictly *right-to-left* with no operator precedence, reflecting the implementation of the underlying execution engine. This is considerably different from expression evaluation using SQL.

Q programmers are often unwilling to switch to SQL and its verboseness. A single line of Q code may be semantically equivalent to a large snippet of SQL. It can be challenging to reason about the correctness of such transformation by eyeballing. Manual migration of complex applications quickly becomes infeasible. Additional challenges arise from operational aspects such as using advanced authentication mechanisms (e.g., Kerberos).

3. HYPER-Q PLATFORM

Hyper-Q bridges the gap between real time and historical data analytics by virtualizing the data processing layer. Using Hyper-Q, applications and workloads written in the Q language can run unchanged while using a PostgreSQL (PG) compatible database for running data analytics.

Q to SQL translation is only one of the problems that need to be addressed to enable such communication. Other problems include (i) network communication, where queries and results need to be parsed, transformed and packaged according to the wire protocols of the two end systems, and (ii) state management, where a variable may be defined and reused across multiple queries.

The choice of translating Q queries into PG-compatible SQL was driven by customer requirements. Many analytical database systems are based on some version of PG. Examples include Greenplum [20], HAWQ [3], Vertica [2], Aster Data [24] and Redshift [8]. Many of these systems maintain, to a large extent, PG-compatible query language, query clients and communication protocols. This makes supporting PG query language (which closely follows SQL standard) and PG communication protocol a plausible path to enable many customers to run Q applications through Hyper-Q.

Figure 1 shows a high-level architectural diagram of the Hyper-Q platform illustrating the interaction between a Q application and a PG database.

Query Life Cycle. A connection request is sent from a Q application to Hyper-Q. The connection message is encoded according to the **Q-I**nter **P**rocess **C**ommunication (QIPC) wire protocol. Once authenticated, the Q application uses

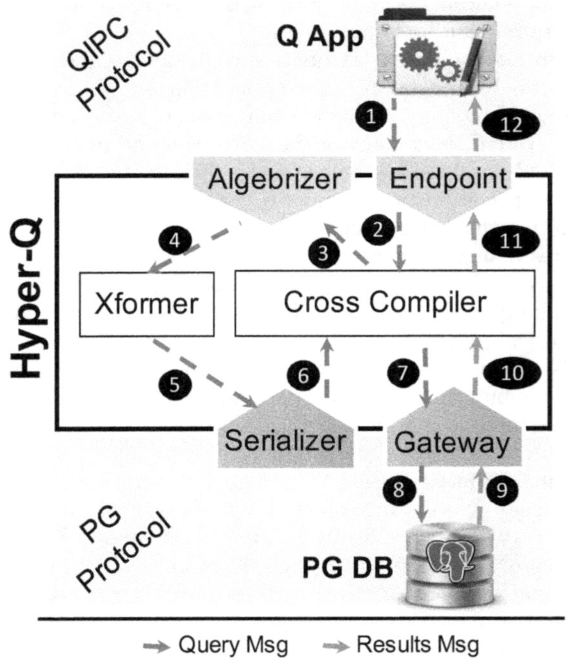

Figure 1: The Hyper-Q platform

the Hyper-Q connection to send Q query messages to Hyper-Q (Section 3.1). The Algebrizer component parses the incoming Q query and transforms it into an extensible relational algebra expression (Section 3.2). The Xformer component then modifies the algebraic expression by applying a series of transformations to guarantee correct query semantics and optimize query performance (Section 3.3). The end algebraic expression is then translated into one or more SQL query messages encoded using the PG v3 wire protocol. The SQL queries are sent to PG database for processing. Query results are translated back into the QIPC data format before getting sent to the Q application. These operations are managed by the Cross Compiler (XC) component (Section 3.4). System-specific plugins are used for handling network communication, parsing messages exchanged between the Q application and the database, as well as generating query messages.

Hyper-Q virtualizes access to different databases by adopting a plugin-based architecture and using version-aware system components. For example, the Algebrizer component triggers parsing rules based on the type and version of the database system that client application is designed to work with. Similarly, the Xformer component triggers transformations based on the type and version of the backend database system. This flexibility allows Hyper-Q to support Q applications that were designed to run on top of specific versions of the kdb+ system, as well as PG-based database systems that have deviated in functionality or semantics from the core PG database. Non-PG database systems can be supported by adding a plugin to the platform that enables query and result transformation as well as network protocol support for the desired database system. In the next sections we describe the components of the Hyper-Q platform that enable Q clients to work with a PG-compatible databases.

3.1 Network Communication

kdb+ uses TCP/IP for inter-process communication. The QIPC wire protocol describes message format, process handshake, and data compression. Messages can be of different types including connection open/close and synchronous/asynchronous calls. PG uses its own message-based protocol for communication between applications and servers. The PG wire protocol is supported over TCP/IP as well as Unix domain sockets.

The two previous protocols are widely different in terms of message format and process handshakes. The network packets transmitted from Q applications cannot be directly parsed by PG servers. To enable such communication, Hyper-Q acts as a bridge between the two protocols. Hyper-Q takes over kdb+ server by listening to incoming messages on the port used by the original kdb+ server. Q applications run unchanged while, under the hood, their network packets are routed to Hyper-Q instead of kdb+.

An incoming message to Hyper-Q includes a Q query. The Endpoint component in Figure 1 is a kdb+-specific plugin we implemented for handling the communication between Q application and Hyper-Q. The Endpoint component parses the incoming message, extracts the query text and passes it to the Algebrizer component (cf. Section 3.2) for subsequent processing.

Hyper-Q transforms incoming Q queries into semantically equivalent SQL queries, compatible with the backend PG database. The Gateway component in Figure 1 is a PG-specific plugin we implemented for handling the communication between Hyper-Q and PG database.

The Gateway component packs a SQL query into a PG formatted message and transmits it to PG database for processing. After query execution is done, the query results are transmitted back from PG server to Hyper-Q. Hyper-Q extracts the row sets from result messages and packs them into messages with the same format that a Q application expects (i.e., using the QIPC protocol). The formatted messages are sent to the Endpoint component, which in turn forwards the results back to the Q application.

Some of the previous operations could be performed using a database driver (e.g., ODBC/JDBC driver). However, integrating a third party driver in our data pipeline adds further complexity and comes with performance overhead. Processing network traffic natively is key for high throughput in Hyper-Q.

3.2 Algebrizer

The Algebrizer component translates a Q query into an eXTended Relational Algebra (XTRA) expression. XTRA is the internal query representation in Hyper-Q. It uses a general and extensible algebra to capture the semantics of query constructs, and make the generation of SQL queries a systematic and principled operation.

The Algebrizer operates in two steps. In the first step, the Q query text is parsed into a Q abstract syntax tree AST. In the second step, the AST is bound to an XTRA tree by resolving all variable references through metadata lookup and translating Q operators to semantically equivalent XTRA tree nodes. We describe the parsing and the binding steps using the following example:

Example 2 Consider the following Q query, which computes the so called *as-of-join* (`aj`) of two tables `trades` and `quotes`. For each record in `trades`, `aj` returns a matching value of `Symbol` column in `quotes`. A match occurs based on an implicit range condition on the `Time` column. If no match is found, a null value is returned.

```
aj[`Symbol`Time; trades; quotes]
```

The algebrization result of Example 2 is shown in Figure 2. We discuss how algebrization is done in the next sections.

3.2.1 *Parsing*

The parser converts Q query text to an AST. In contrast to traditional relational query languages like SQL, the data model of Q allows for stand-alone table, scalar, list, or dictionary queries to be expressed in the query language. Variables are dynamically typed based on the values they are bound to. Moreover, the query syntax does not restrict the type of the result. To illustrate, consider the following Q language examples:

```
x:  1
x:  1 2 3
x:  select from trades
```

The first statement assigns a scalar value 1 to variable `x`. The second statement redefines `x` to be a list, while the third statement redefines `x` again to be a table expression. The type of `x` depends on the value it is bound to. Global variables are stored in kdb+ server's memory, and they can be redefined and used from different Q query clients.

The Q query `x+y` could be interpreted as arithmetic addition of two scalars or a pairwise addition of list elements. It could also raise an error if `x` and `y` are two lists of different length.

The previous query semantics are different from SQL, where a query clause restricts the type of expressions that can appear in some context. For example, the SQL `FROM` clause restricts the following expression to be a table expression.

Dynamic typing in Q can yield a complicated parser design since we need to inspect a large number of possible parse trees. In Hyper-Q, determining a variable type may require a round trip to the PG database for metadata lookup. For example, when a Q query refers a variable `x`, the parser may need to know if `x` is a table in the PG database. Due to these considerations, we have decided to design a lightweight parser in Hyper-Q whose only role is to create an abstract representation of the query in memory, and delegate the type inference and verification to the binder component (cf. Section 3.2.2).

The parser constructs an AST, consisting of the following main elements:

- literals: constant expressions such as integers (e.g., `1i`) and symbols (e.g., `` `GOOG ``).
- variables: expressions that reference a named entity (e.g., `trades`).
- monadic and dyadic operators: operations on one or two arguments, respectively.
- join operators: different types of Q joins such as the `aj` operator in Example 2.

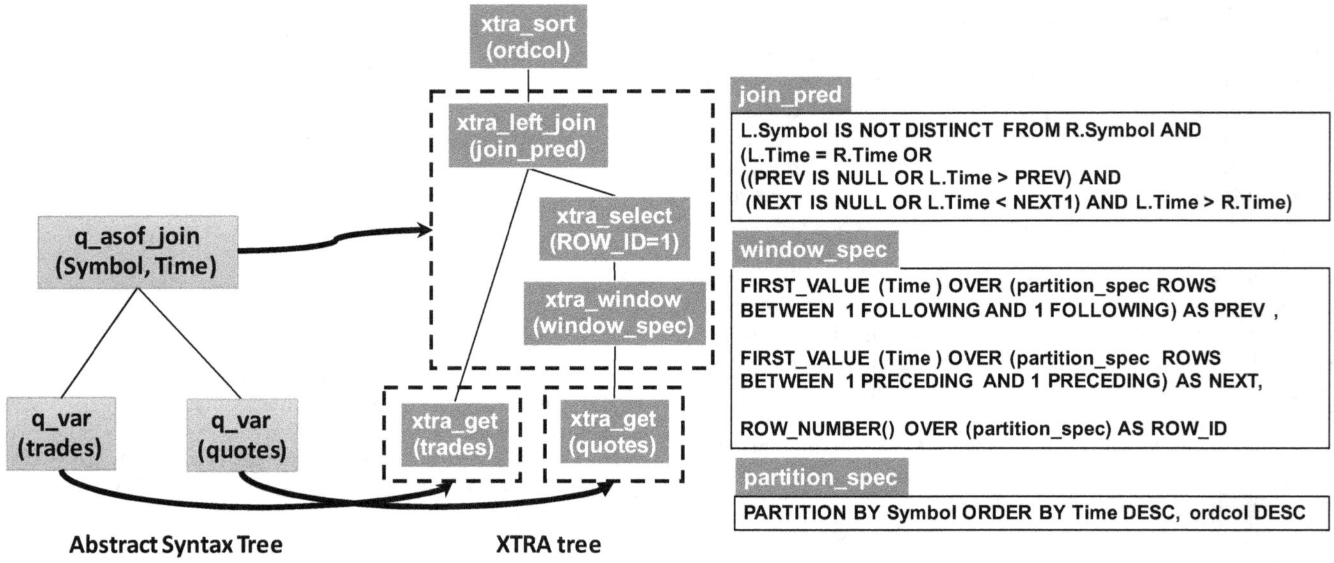

Figure 2: Algebrization of query in Example 2

- variable assignments: expressions of the form `var:expression`.

The AST for Example 2 is shown in Figure 2. The parser does not attempt to decide on the types of the variable references `trades`, and `quotes` since in the general case, they may be expressions of any type.

3.2.2 Binding

After parsing is done, the binder performs semantic analysis of the resulting AST and binds it to XTRA, the internal query representation in Hyper-Q. Binding Q queries into XTRA expressions is based on the fact that, although Q and SQL data models are different, the vast majority of Q operators can be mapped to corresponding (but sometimes more complicated) relational algebra expressions. Hyper-Q provides an extensible framework to build and compose such mapping rules to achieve the largest possible coverage of the Q language. The framework also allows using more sophisticated methods, such as UDFs in SQL databases, to capture the Q language constructs that cannot be directly mapped to relational algebra expressions.

Binding is a recursive operation that is done in a bottom-up fashion, where for each Q operator in the AST, the binder processes the operator's inputs, derives and checks input properties, and then maps the operator to its corresponding XTRA representation in the following way:

- Literals get bound to scalar const operators `xtra_const`, where the Q type of the literal is mapped to Hyper-Q's type system. For example, int types get mapped to equivalent integer types, symbol type gets mapped to varchar, whereas string literals get mapped to text constants.

- Variable references are resolved by looking up their definition through the metadata interface. Table variable references get bound to a relational get operator `xtra_get`. For example, in Figure 2, `q_var(trades)` is bound to `xtra_get(trades)`.

- When binding each operator, operator's properties are derived in the resulting XTRA tree. For relational operators, derived properties include the output columns with their names and types, keys, and order. For scalar operators, derived properties include the output type and whether the expression has side effects.

- After binding the inputs of an operator, the binder first checks whether the inputs are valid for the given operator by accessing their properties derived at the previous step. For example, the `aj` operator expects its two inputs to be table expressions and the right input to be a keyed table. Also, the join columns must be included in the output columns of input operators. If property checking succeeds, the operator is bound to its XTRA representation. In Figure 2, the `aj` operator is bound to a left outer join operator that computes a window function on its right input. The results need to be ordered at the end to conform with Q ordered lists model.

3.2.3 Metadata lookup

The binder resolves variable references by looking up associated metadata in the metadata store. In the basic case, where Q variables are mapped to PG tables, this corresponds to executing a query against PG catalog to retrieve various properties of the searched object. For tables, the retrieved metadata include columns, keys and sort order, while for functions, the retrieved metadata include function arguments and return type. Q also allows the definition of in-memory variables. A computation result can be stored to a variable that gets referenced in subsequent queries. Consider the following example:

> **Example 3** Consider the following Q function, which returns max price of `trades` matching a given symbol `Sym`:

```
f:
{ [Sym]
  dt:  select Price from trades where Symbol=Sym;
```

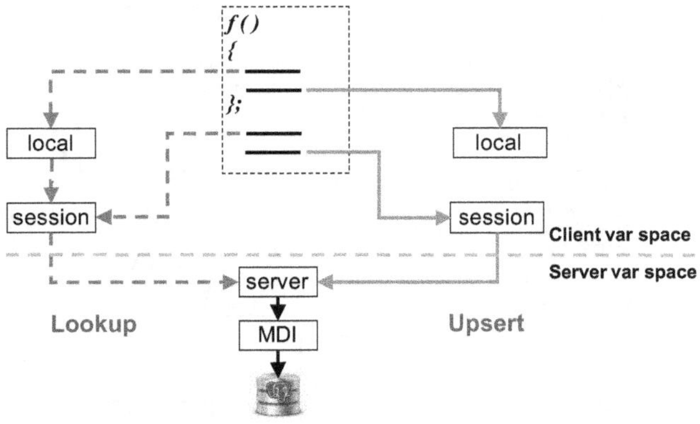

Figure 3: Hierarchy of variable scopes in Hyper-Q.

```
    :select max Price from dt;
  };
  f[`GOOG];
```

Example 3 defines a function `f`, which assigns a computed table to variable `dt`, while applying a filter to `Symbol` column using the function argument `Sym`. The function returns the maximum `Price` in the computed table `dt`. The last statement in Example 3 calls `f` while passing the symbol (`` `GOOG``) as an argument.

Q distinguishes between two main types of variables: (i) local variables defined in function bodies like `dt` in Example 3, and (ii) global (server) variables like the function `f` itself. Local variables are only visible in the scope where they are defined, whereas global variables are visible to all Q query clients connected to the same kdb+ server.

Local variables shadow global variables with the same name. In Example 3, after the program is executed, the function `f` becomes accessible by any client connected to the server. If `f` is invoked later in the same session, there is no guarantee that the function definition would still be the same, since it may have been overwritten in the meantime by another query client.

Hyper-Q needs to maintain the aforementioned behavior for Q applications. The backend PG database is used to store and materialize global server variables in publicly accessible schemas. Shadowing of global variables by local variables with the same names is implemented using a hierarchy of variable scopes, as depicted in Figure 3. The hierarchy has three variable scopes:

1. Local scope stores local function variables.
2. Session scope stores variables defined within session.
3. Server scope stores global variables.

Figure 3 shows a query session with a function `f` and two statements outside `f`. The first statement in `f` looks up a variable. The lookup has to be performed in the *local* scope first. If the variable is not locally defined, the lookup operation follows the scopes hierarchy. The first statement outside `f` also looks up a variable. In this case, lookup is directed to the *session* scope, since we are now outside the function `f`. The bottom-most scope corresponds to retrieving variable definition, such as tables and functions, through PG MetaData Interface (MDI).

Figure 3 also shows how variable upsert (definition/redefinition) operation takes place. The second statement in `f` upserts a variable (e.g., through variable assignment). This upsert call can only be executed in the *local* scope since, according to Q semantics, local upsert calls never get promoted to higher scopes. The second statement outside `f` is making another upsert call. In this case, the call is directed to *session* scope. Session variables are promoted to global (server) variables after upsert call is processed. This is done as part of the session scope destruction.

3.3 Xformer

The Xformer component is responsible for applying transformations to the XTRA expression before serializing it into a SQL query. Transformations are used in Hyper-Q for three main purposes:

- **Correctness.** Data models and query languages in kdb+ and PG systems are widely different with implicit assumptions on each side. For example, null values in Q assume 2-valued logic, while in SQL, null values assume 3-valued logic. To bridge this gap in semantics between the two languages, a transformation is used to replace strict equalities in XTRA expressions with `Is Not Distinct From` predicate, which provides the needed 2-valued logic for null values when serializing the outgoing SQL query.

- **Performance.** The XTRA expression holds relational and scalar properties that are used to optimize the serialized SQL. For example, each node in the XTRA tree is annotated with all columns it can produce. The requested columns at each node may be however a small subset of the available columns. A transformation that prunes the columns of each XTRA node, to keep only the needed columns, is used to avoid bloating the serialized SQL with unnecessary columns, which may negatively impact query performance.

- **Transparency.** Ordering is a first-class citizen in Q. However, this is not the case in SQL. To maintain Q ordering semantics in the serialized SQL query, ordering criteria may need to be automatically added to the SQL query constructs generated by Hyper-Q. This operation is implemented via a transformation. Each relational XTRA operator can declare an implicit order column and an order preservation property that indicates whether the XTRA operator can preserve the order in its output or not. This property is used by the Xformer to ignore ordering in some cases. For example, consider a nested query in which the outer query performs a scalar aggregation on the result of the inner query. In this case, the Xformer can remove the ordering requirement on the inner query. The Xformer may also generate implicit order columns by injecting window functions in the transformed expressions.

3.4 Cross Compiler

The XC component is responsible for driving the translation of incoming queries written in the Q language into PG SQL, as well as the reverse translation of query results produced by PG database into the result format expected

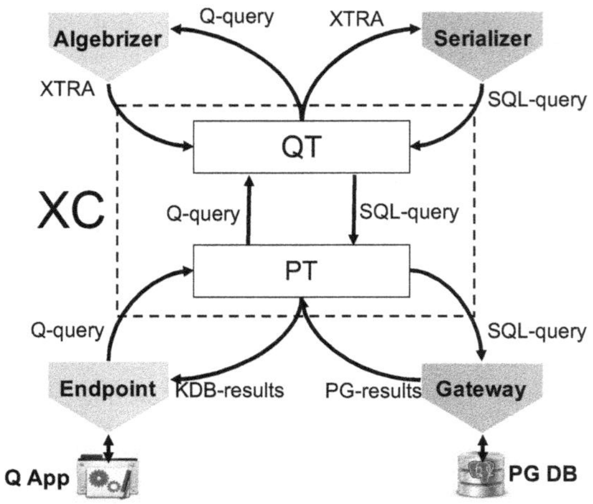

Figure 4: XC architecture

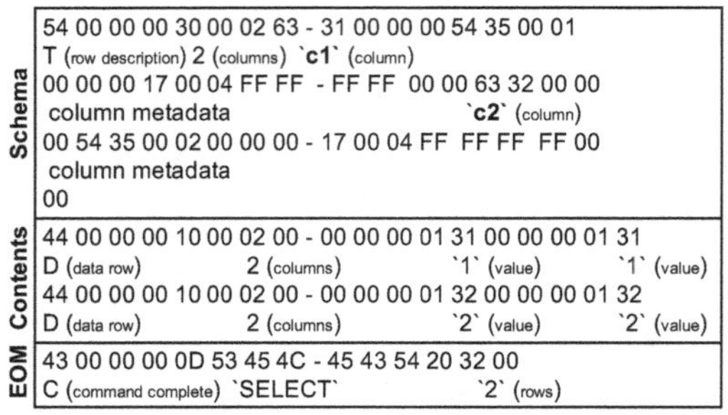

(a) PG v3

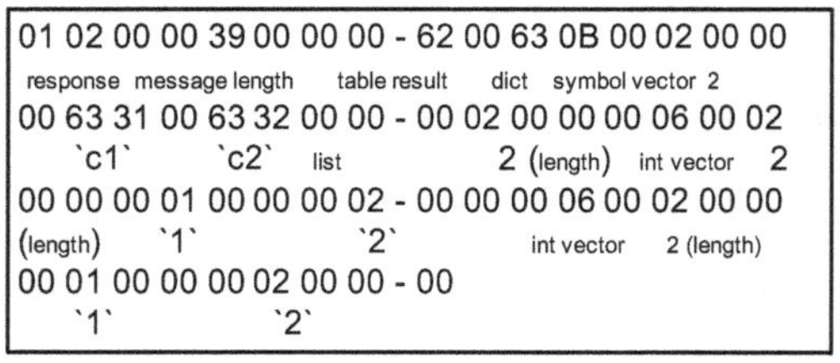

(b) QIPC

Figure 5: Representation of {(1, 1), (2, 2)} result set

by Q application. Figure 4 gives an overview of XC architecture:

- **Protocol Translator (PT).** This layer is the DB protocol handler of Hyper-Q. PT is responsible for cross translation of messages sent to and received from the two end-point systems (Q application and PG database). Parsing DB protocol messages to extract queries as well as creating messages that hold queries and query results are handled by this layer.

- **Query Translator (QT).** This layer is the query language handler of Hyper-Q. QT is responsible for driving the translation of Q queries into XTRA, the internal query representation of Hyper-Q, serializing XTRA expressions into equivalent SQL statements, and communicating the generated SQL statements to PT to be sent to the PG database for execution. QT communicates with the Algebrizer and Serializer components to perform these tasks.

The interface between PT and QT is as simple as sending out a Q query from PT, and receiving back an equivalent SQL query from QT.

The design of XC abstracts the implementation details of PT and QT into two separate processes. Each translator process is designed as a Finite State Machine (FSM) that maintains translator internal state while providing a mechanism for code re-entrance. This is particularly important because operations performed by the translators may entail heavy processing, such as serializing large SQL statements or executing PG queries. FSMs allow firing asynchronous events that kick-off backend processing, as well as defining function callbacks that get automatically triggered when events occur. For example, when the results of a PG query are ready for translation, an FSM callback is automatically triggered to process the results and generate the required translation.

4. DISCUSSION

In this section, we discuss some of the implementation details of Hyper-Q platform.

4.1 Erlang

We chose Erlang as the programming language to build Hyper-Q. The decision to use Erlang was motivated by the requirement of building an efficient and highly available virtualization system. Erlang is a programming environment that combines powerful abstractions of parallel primitives and is natively able to manipulate network traffic, while providing high availability and massive data throughput. Building on the Erlang parallelism and networking libraries greatly improves our productivity while building Hyper-Q.

4.2 Database Systems Protocols

To communicate with both Q applications and PG databases, Hyper-Q uses several methods to extract information from network messages, package information into messages, and implement process handshake and message flow needed to establish connections with both ends.

When establishing a connection using QIPC specifications, a client sends Hyper-Q a null-terminated ASCII string "username:passwordN" where N is a single byte denoting client version. If Hyper-Q accepts the credentials, it sends back a single byte response. Otherwise, it closes the connection immediately. After the connection is established, the client sends queries in the form of raw text. Hyper-Q sends back query result messages encoding both result type and contents as defined in [22].

When communicating using PG v3 protocol, Hyper-Q exchanges different types of messages with PG database to handle start-up, query, function call, copy data, and connection shutdown requests. An authentication server is used during connection start-up to support authentication mechanisms such as clear text password, MD5, and Kerberos. A PG v3 message starts with a single byte denoting message type, followed by four bytes for message length. The remainder of the message body is reserved for storing contents [18,19].

A key point to enable two-way communication between a Q application and PG database is handling the different representations of queries and results in the two protocols. PG v3 protocol allows streaming of query results. An initial message describes the schema of the results. Each row in the results is then transmitted in the following messages. At the end, an end-of-content message is sent. On the other hand, QIPC forms the result set in a column-oriented fashion and sends it as a single message back to the client.

Figure 5 shows the raw byte representation of a tabular result set, with two columns `c1` and `c2` and two rows $\{(1, 1), (2, 2)\}$, using both QIPC and PG v3 protocols. To send query results back to Q application, Hyper-Q buffers the query result messages received from the PG database until an end-of-content message is received. The results are then extracted from the messages, and a corresponding QIPC message is formed and sent back to the Q application.

The incompatibility of result set formats between QIPC (column-oriented) and PG v3 (row-oriented) poses a challenge when transmitting large data sets: Hyper-Q needs to buffer the entire result set before it transmits the corresponding QIPC messages. A possible solution is materializing the result set in the PG database (as a temporary table), and then extracting column by column to form the QIPC messages. This problem does not exist when the two end systems use compatible formats, since Hyper-Q can stream the results directly after translation.

4.3 Eager Materialization

This section discusses the need to implement eager materialization of intermediate results during query cross-compilation in Hyper-Q. We use Example 3 for illustration. The function `f` gets interpreted only when it is invoked, e.g., when issuing the query ``f[`GOOG]``. When algebrizing the definition of `f` in Hyper-Q, we store the function definition as plain text in the current variable scope (cf. Section 3.2.3). When `f` is invoked, the textual definition is retrieved from the current variable scope and it gets algebrized.

The first statement of `f` assigns a computed table to an in-memory variable `dt`. Before algebrizing the rest of the function's body, the definition and metadata of `dt` must be stored in the current variable scope, so that the following statements that refer to `dt` can be successfully algebrized. In general, a Q variable assignment statement may need to be physically executed before algebrizing the following statements. The reason is that a variable assignment in Q could have side effects (e.g., modifying other tables). In Hyper-Q, materialization of Q variables into PG objects may need to be done in situ to maintain a behavior consistent with the behavior of Q applications with kdb+.

The previous semantics trigger the need to implement eager materialization of Q variables into PG objects during query translation. In some cases, only logical materialization (e.g., using PG views, or maintaining the variable definition for scalar variables in Hyper-Q's variable store) is sufficient. In other cases, physical materialization (e.g., using temporary PG tables) is necessary for correctness. To illustrate, Hyper-Q generates the following SQL queries when translating the Q query ``f[`GOOG];`` in Example 3 using the physical materialization approach:

```
CREATE TEMPORARY TABLE HQ_TEMP_1 AS
SELECT ordcol, Price FROM trades
WHERE Symbol IS NOT DISTINCT FROM `GOOG`::varchar
ORDER BY ordcol;

SELECT `1`::int AS ordcol, MAX(Price)
FROM HQ_TEMP_1 ORDER BY ordcol;
```

Note that in the presence of variable assignment multiple Q statements may be folded into a single SQL statement, where each variable reference is replaced by its definition.

5. CASE STUDY

The broad vision behind Hyper-Q is to provide full functional compatibility between kdb+ and PG. Naturally, due to the technical challenges associated with an automated solution, there has been some skepticism about the feasibility of our approach.

We describe our experience delivering on this vision and providing real business value in deploying Hyper-Q at one of our early adopters - a large Wall Street investment bank. This customer had a pressing need to migrate some of their workloads into a PG-compatible MPP database (while still keeping the real-time analytics on kdb+). We started this engagement by collecting representative query workloads, which helped us shape our backlog and attack the features in order of importance. In order to achieve a tight feedback loop, we provided the customers with monthly release drops, gathered their feedback and prioritized features for the upcoming releases.

The following summarizes our lessons learned throughout the course of deploying Hyper-Q at the customer:

- The customer was easily able to perform the schema mapping and data movement part of the migration into their MPP database. This reaffirmed our belief that while most automated solutions focus on this step, the real challenge is elsewhere.
- The backup and disaster recovery solution, as well as increased concurrency provided by the target MPP system was critical to the customer's IT department. This further validated our hypothesis that different data processing environments match customer requirements better, and providing a seamless integration between these environments is important to success.
- Since Hyper-Q is a man-in-the-middle technology, one of the initial challenges when operationalizing Hyper-Q was around security. We worked closely with the customer to resolve Kerberos authentication issues and provided them with a solution.
- As we implemented features from the customer workload, we needed a way to ensure the exact same behavior to the application as before. For this purpose we built a side-by-side testing framework, which can be used for internal testing of features, and also used by the customers in their staging environments to ensure correctness of operation.
- In certain cases Hyper-Q improves on the user experience provided by kdb+. For example, error messages in Hyper-Q are more verbose and informative than those provided by kdb+, which can increase productivity especially for system administrators and analysts new to Q and kdb+.

One of the most important insights from this engagement was that while Q as a whole is rather large, customer queries use only a fraction of the language. As a result, we have achieved a sufficiently large coverage of the kdb+ functional surface to make Hyper-Q useful in practical customer use cases, including in workloads with a large variety of Q operators, local and global variables, and unrolling a large class of Q user-defined functions without the need to create user-defined functions in PG. The latter is important as the data analyst using Hyper-Q may not have sufficient rights to create objects at the backend system.

Since Hyper-Q is still under active development, it has certain limitations, which can be broadly summarized in the following categories:

1. Missing common language features, which have a corresponding SQL representation. Naturally, we will close this gap as we move forward.
2. Missing features for which PG does not provide the same built-in capabilities as kdb+, for example kdb+ data types that do not exist in PG. We have not seen many of these in current customers' workloads, but it is possible that they become important in the future. We plan on attacking these limitations through PG's extensibility mechanism, that is, providing customers with a "toolbox" of PG's user-defined types and functions to achieve the desired behavior. Since Q includes complex query language constructs such while-loops and recursion, just-in-time compilation to SQL stored procedure may be required in certain cases.

In addition, there are also certain cases where Hyper-Q enhances the kdb+ experience without breaking application code in areas like configurable concurrency and improved error logging. Despite all roadblocks, we have demonstrated that an automated solution for integrating real-time and historical analytics systems is possible. We have built a system, which solves real customer use cases for a large set of application scenarios. In the future, we plan to continue working closely with customers to prioritize our development according to their use cases.

6. EXPERIMENTS

In this section, we present our experimental evaluation of Hyper-Q. Since Hyper-Q sits between the application and data processing layers, one obvious question that arises is what is the overhead introduced by Hyper-Q?

We focus on evaluating the efficiency of query translation in Hyper-Q. Evaluating end-to-end query performance is outside the scope of this paper, since it mainly depends on the relative performance and capabilities of kdb+ and the analytical databases, which is orthogonal to this work. The goal of our evaluation is to demonstrate that the overhead introduced by Hyper-Q is typically minimal. We also illustrate the feasibility of adding new features in Hyper-Q to cover the language surface of Q.

All experiments are conducted on an *Analytical Workload* driven from customer use-cases. The workload is representative of actual production settings and consists of 25 queries that involve three or more wide tables (e.g., tables with more than 500 columns), joins, and various kinds of analytical aggregate functions. We use Greenplum [20, 23], a massively parallel database system, as the backend database. All experiments are done on a dual core machine with 3GHz Intel Core i7 processor and 16 GB RAM.

Query translation goes through the following stages: algebrization of Q queries to XTRA, optimization by applying XTRA transformations, and finally serialization of XTRA expressions to SQL queries. During algebrization, Hyper-Q needs to lookup metadata (e.g., table definitions) in the PG database catalog to bind parse trees into XTRA expressions. Typically, metadata do not have frequent updates. Hyper-Q provides a configurable metadata caching mechanism with configurable invalidation policies and cache expiration time. Our experiments are conducted with metadata caching enabled.

Figure 6 shows the total time consumed by query translation for the Analytical Workload. On average, the time consumed is around 0.5% of the total query execution time. The maximum query translation time is 4% of the query execution time. Queries # 10, 18, 19, and 20 involve more tables to join compared to other queries. Hence, it takes longer time to algebrize these queries, lookup the required metadata, and serialize them into final SQL queries.

Figure 7 shows the split of translation time across different stages. The optimization and serialization stages consume most of the time in the shown results. This is because the processing done in these stages for analytical queries typically involves multi-table joins and aggregate functions that generate XTRA expressions resulting in multi-level subqueries. During optimization, multiple transformations need to be invoked to prepare the XTRA expressions for SQL serialization (cf. Section 3.3). For example, the generated columns in these expressions need to be processed to prune the unused ones before serializing the final query.

The extensibility of Hyper-Q framework allows building support for the surface of the Q language at a consistent speed. While building the framework has been a challenging task, the payoffs from having an extensible framework are substantial. Typically, supporting a new Q query type in Hyper-Q requires adding parsing routines, AST nodes and query transformations. The Hyper-Q framework handles all the details of establishing the data pipeline, representing new query constructs in the XTRA world, firing up the relevant transformations and exchanging messages in the right formats with the two endpoint systems. By building on the powerful infrastructure provided by Hyper-Q, we have been able to support many customer feature requests out-of-the-box, and provide short turnaround times for missing features. Driven by customer requirements, we expect reaching parity with the bulk of the Q language surface in the very near future.

Hyper-Q machine-generated queries go through extensive correctness and quality assurance checks. The equivalent manually migrated queries pose a much higher risk of bugs and semantic inconsistencies. Adding a new feature in Hyper-Q starts with finding a safe translation, and then, based on customer feedback, adding further optimizations.

7. RELATED WORK

In [1] we have proposed the concept of *Adaptive Data Virtualization* (ADV) and identified the primary requirements for the success of an ADV platform. This paper presents Hyper-Q, the first implementation of an ADV platform. Data virtualization has initially been proposed 30

Figure 6: Efficiency of query translation

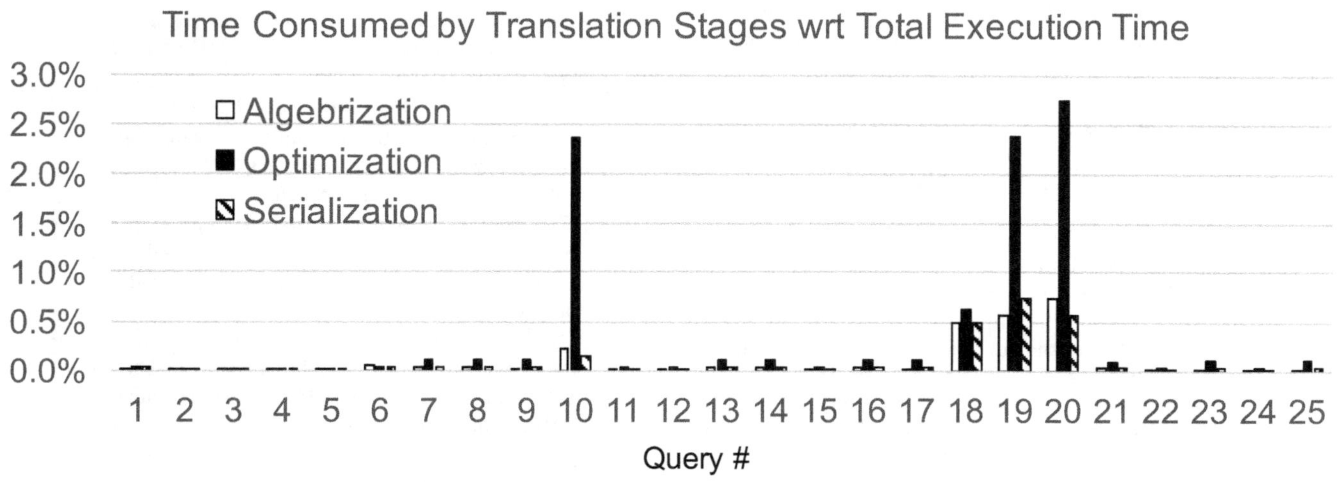

Figure 7: Query translation stages

years ago [10]. Recently it has become an alternative to ETL for business intelligence applications [21] with a number of vendors like, e.g., Informatica [13], Denodo [4], and IBM [11]. Adaptive Data Virtualization extends traditional Data Virtualization to also include applications. In addition to data and the machines it is hosted on, applications also remain unmodified and are transparently adapted by the platform.

The trading algorithms of the financial industry are written for time-series databases like KDB [25]. They focus on low-latency processing of large volumes of real time trade ticks. To meet the timing requirements, the query processing engines manage and process data directly in main memory and in columnar format. Their capacity is restricted by main memory and scalability constraints, limiting the data that can be analyzed and processed to a couple of days. Massively parallel processing database systems (MPPs) like, e.g., SQL Server PDW [16], Amazon Redshift [8], Greenplum [20], and IBM dashDB [12], on the other hand, scale well in data size and compute capacity. Their shared-nothing architecture and feature set suits Big Data analytics workloads well, enabling processing of very large amounts of data. However, they lack the ability to process complex queries on time-series data in real time.

Real-time warehousing solutions like MemSQL [15] combine one or more of the aforementioned technologies (data virtualization or integration of transactional processing in one system to avoid ETL, in-memory processing for better performance) to provide fast analytics. They cannot close the gap between real time processing and Big Data analytics, though, leaving the financial trading applications to the specialized systems built for them.

[6] raises the concern that vendors become "locked in" to outdated costly technologies, despite various options to use faster and lower cost execution engines. [6] introduced Musketeer, a proof-of-concept workflow manager to map workflows expressed in high-level query languages to various query engine executions. In particular, high-level query language operators are translated into an intermediate representation from which it generates jobs for query execution

engines. However, the intermediate representation is limited to SQL-like operators and depends on user-defined functions to translate the remaining high-level operators.

By tackling the integration of existing applications with different kinds of data management system, adaptive data virtualization enables businesses to leverage the advantages each system provides and combine them seamlessly in their existing applications.

8. SUMMARY

Adaptive Data Virtualization is the broad vision of decoupling applications from the underlying database systems in a way that is completely transparent and non-intrusive. In this paper, we presented Hyper-Q, an initial implementation of this vision. Hyper-Q enables applications written for one specific database to run on a wide variety of alternative database systems – fully transparently and without requiring changes to the application. Effectively liberating enterprises from vendor lock-in, Hyper-Q provides businesses with unprecedented flexibility to adopt database technology and modernize their data infrastructure.

The financial use case of bridging real-time and analytics has proven a great starting point for our development as it required us to address differences between systems on all conceivable levels. As a result, our framework matured substantially over the past 12 months; great care has been taken to delineate platform and plugins cleanly. The resulting system clearly demonstrates the feasibility of our vision. Our initial experience in implementing this platform has been very encouraging and additional plugins for other languages are currently under development.

While Hyper-Q as it stands today is not a data integration or a federated system, it can be used as a building block in this context. For example, in a federated system which delegates parts of queries to different systems, Hyper-Q can be used to translate the query to the language of the corresponding backend system, and convert the results back into the format expected by the federated system.

9. REFERENCES

[1] L. Antova *et al.*, "An Integrated Architecture for Real-Time and Historical Analytics in Financial Services," in *BIRTE*, 2015.

[2] C. Bear, A. Lamb, and N. Tran, "The Vertica Database: SQL RDBMS for Managing Big Data," in *Proceedings of the 2012 Workshop on Management of Big Data Systems*, 2012.

[3] L. Chang *et al.*, "HAWQ: A Massively Parallel Processing SQL Engine in Hadoop," in *Proceedings of the 2014 ACM SIGMOD International Conference on Management of Data*, 2014.

[4] Denodo. [Online]. Available: http://www.denodo.com/

[5] S. Garland, "Big Data Analytics: Tackling the Historical Data Challenge," *Wired Magazine, Innovation Insights*, 2014.

[6] I. Gog *et al.*, "Musketeer: all for one, one for all in data processing systems," in *Proceedings of EuroSys*, 2015.

[7] C. Gorman. [Online]. Available: http://www.firstderivatives.com/downloads/q_for_Gods_Mar_2013.pdf

[8] A. Gupta *et al.*, "Amazon Redshift and the Case for Simpler Data Warehouses," in *Proceedings of the 2015 ACM SIGMOD International Conference on Management of Data*, 2015.

[9] J. Hanna. [Online]. Available: http://www.firstderivatives.com/downloads/q_for_Gods_Oct_2012.pdf

[10] D. Heimbigner and D. McLeod, "A Federated Architecture for Information Management," *ACM Transactions on Information Systems*, vol. 3, pp. 253–278, 1985.

[11] IBM. [Online]. Available: http://www.ibm.com/

[12] IBM. IBM dashDB. [Online]. Available: http://www-01.ibm.com/software/data/dashdb/

[13] Informatica. [Online]. Available: https//www.informatica.com/

[14] kdb+. [Online]. Available: http://kx.com/software.php

[15] MemSQL. [Online]. Available: http://www.memsql.com/

[16] Microsoft. Microsoft Analytics Platform System. [Online]. Available: http://www.microsoft.com/en-us/server-cloud/products/analytics-platform-system/

[17] NYSE Market Data. [Online]. Available: http://www.nyxdata.com/Data-Products

[18] PGv3 Message Formats. [Online]. Available: http://www.postgresql.org/docs/9.2/static/protocol-message-formats.html

[19] PGv3 Protocol Flow. [Online]. Available: http://www.postgresql.org/docs/9.2/static/protocol-flow.html

[20] Pivotal Software. Pivotal Greenplum Database. [Online]. Available: http://greenplum.org/

[21] L. J. Pullokkaran, "Analysis of Data Virtualization and Enterprise Data Standardization in Business Intelligence," Ph.D. dissertation, Massachusetts Institute of Technology, 2013.

[22] QIPC. [Online]. Available: http://code.kx.com/wiki/Reference/ipcprotocol

[23] M. A. Soliman *et al.*, "Orca: A modular query optimizer architecture for big data," in *Proceedings of the 2014 ACM SIGMOD International Conference on Management of Data*, 2014.

[24] Teradata Aster Big Data Analytics. [Online]. Available: http://www.teradata.com/Teradata-Aster/

[25] A. Whitney and D. Shasha, "Lots o' Ticks: Real-Time High Performance Time Series Queries on Billions of Trades and Quotes," in *Proceedings of the 2001 ACM SIGMOD International Conference on Management of Data*, 2001.

Time Adaptive Sketches (Ada-Sketches) for Summarizing Data Streams

Anshumali Shrivastava*
Dept. of Computer Science
Rice University
Houston, TX, USA
anshumali@rice.edu

Arnd Christian König
Microsoft Research
Redmond
WA 98052, USA
chrisko@microsoft.com

Mikhail Bilenko
Microsoft
Redmond
WA 98052, USA
mbilenko@microsoft.com

ABSTRACT

Obtaining frequency information of data streams, in limited space, is a well-recognized problem in literature. A number of recent practical applications (such as those in computational advertising) require temporally-aware solutions: obtaining historical count statistics for both time-points as well as time-ranges. In these scenarios, accuracy of estimates is typically more important for recent instances than for older ones; we call this desirable property *Time Adaptiveness*. With this observation, [20] introduced the HOKUSAI technique based on count-min sketches for estimating the frequency of any given item at any given time. The proposed approach is problematic in practice, as its memory requirements grow linearly with time, and it produces discontinuities in the estimation accuracy. In this work, we describe a new method, *Time-adaptive Sketches*, (ADA-SKETCH), that overcomes these limitations, while extending and providing a strict generalization of several popular sketching algorithms.

The core idea of our method is inspired by the well-known digital Dolby noise reduction procedure that dates back to the 1960s. The theoretical analysis presented could be of independent interest in itself, as it provides clear results for the time-adaptive nature of the errors. An experimental evaluation on real streaming datasets demonstrates the superiority of the described method over Hokusai in estimating point and range queries over time. The method is simple to implement and offers a variety of design choices for future extensions. The simplicity of the procedure and the method's generalization of classic sketching techniques give hope for wide applicability of Ada-sketches in practice.

1. INTRODUCTION AND MOTIVATION

"Scaling Up for High Dimensional Data and High Speed Data Streams" has been recognized one of the top 10 challenging problems in data mining research [25]. Mining big data streams brings three major challenges: *volume, velocity* and *volatility* [18]. Volume and velocity require processing a high volume of data in limited time. Consider the case of click-through probability prediction, a central problem for online advertising, which is estimated to be a \$230 billion dollar industry[1]. This industry relies on tracking and responding to the behavior of billions of users, to whom large platforms must serve tens of millions of ad impressions per hour with typical response times under 50ms per request [15]. Moreover, it is essential to rapidly update predictive models as new clicks and non-clicks are observed [21]. Maximizing predictive accuracy demands keeping track of the counts of many combinations of events (such as clicks and impressions broken down by country, IP, advertiser, or ad-type), leading to a blow-up in the number of items under consideration. Volatility, on the other hand, corresponds to a dynamic environment with ever-changing patterns, making the scale of the problem even worse. A major reason for volatility is the drift in the distributions of patterns of interest over time, and constant churn of users, advertisers and content providers [18].

Obtaining frequency information, or statistical patterns of interest, from data streams is an important problem in this context. Count-based features are commonly used in practice for many predictive tasks. For example, features such as counts of number of clicks on "Amazon.com", given specific user characteristics, in the past hour, are common in click-through probability prediction. In particular, there is a need to estimate the count of a given item i (or event, or combinations thereof) during some specified time t, or in some $[t_1, t_2]$ range [23, 20, 16]. Since the number of possible combinations is enormous, we end up with the classical problem of counting under memory and time constraints over streaming data in one pass. Note that in the streaming setting, we only see increments in counts over time, and hence cannot store all items seen, which makes estimation with limited resources a challenging problem.

Typically, items with highest counts, commonly known as *heavy hitters*, are of most interest. However, identifying heavy hitters in streaming data is a non-trivial task with limited memory. There has been a strong line of work in computing limited-memory summaries, popularly called *sketches* [13] of data streams, allowing approximate estimation of the counts [12, 1, 14, 6, 22, 10, 2], even over dynamic temporal streams [8, 17]. Sketches allow high-accuracy estimation of heavy hitters. Notable among them is the Count-Min Sketch [7], an accurate technique widely popular due to its simplicity and parallelizability.

*Work done while visiting Microsoft.

[1]Source: http://www.emarketer.com/, Dec. 2014

SIGMOD'16, June 26-July 01, 2016, San Francisco, CA, USA
© 2016 ACM. ISBN 978-1-4503-3531-7/16/06...\$15.00
DOI: http://dx.doi.org/10.1145/2882903.2882946

With more than 30 years of active research, existing data stream sketching techniques can reasonably address the challenges of volume and velocity. However, the volatility aspect of the problem has received little attention. With changing patterns, drift in distributions over time is commonly observed in data streams, sometimes with high variance in so-called bursty data streams. In a drifting distribution, as was pointed out in [18], "old data is of limited use, even if it could be saved and processed again later". This is because, in most applications, recent patterns have more predictive power compared to patterns in the past. For instance, most recent variations in credit history are much stronger indicators of a person's ability to make loan payments compared to variations in credit history from distant past.

Thus, given a limited resource budget, if we have to trade off errors effectively, we need to be more accurate in estimating the recent statistics (or counts) compared to the older ones [20]. In particular, we need sketches that are "time adaptive". Classical sketching techniques are oblivious to time, and hence do not provide this smarter trade-off. The focus of this paper is developing sketches for accurate estimation that provide such desired time adaptability.

An obviously tempting and reasonable attempt to achieve time adaptability is to allocate resources to different time periods disproportionately. More specifically, if we create large-size sketches to handle recent events, and use small-size sketches for older intervals, we can immediately achieve time adaptability, as sketch size directly translates to accuracy for reasonable algorithms. The key challenge lies in designing algorithms that dynamically adjust per-interval sketch sizes and reallocate them in streaming fashion as time passes. Addressing this problem was the key insight of the recently proposed HOKUSAI algorithm [20] for item aggregation.

An open problem for HOKUSAI algorithm lies in its allocation of a fixed-size sketch for each time point t, regardless of the number of distinct items contained in it. Let us consider a "bursty" data distribution, where a million items arrived at a single time point t', with many fewer arriving at subsequent times. In order to represent this data with high accuracy, HOKUSAI must allocate sketches with $O(10^6)$ cells not only to the time point t', but also to every time point $t > t'$, even though most of the space in sketches for subsequent times will be wasted.

As described in Section 2.6, discontinuities in the degradation of HOKUSAI estimates with time is a significant problem. Such issues are inherent to any approach that associates a sketch with every time instance t. As an alternative, we provide a *time-adaptive* solution based on a very different approach motivated by the noise reduction literature, which avoids the limitations of HOKUSAI, while yielding significantly higher accuracy at the same time.

Our Contributions: We present *Time-adaptive Sketches* (ADA-SKETCH) for estimating the frequency of any given item i at given time t, or over a time interval $[t_1, t_2]$, using limited space. Ada-sketches provide a strict generalization of several well-studied sketching algorithms in the data streams literature for obtaining temporal estimates. The proposed generalization, while retaining the counts of heavy hitters with good accuracy, also provides provable time-adaptive estimation guarantees. In particular, the estimate of the count of item i during time t is more accurate compared to the estimate of same item i during time t' for all $t' \leq t$. The key idea in our proposed technique is the use of pre-emphasis and de-emphasis transformations analogous to those used in the popular Digital Dolby systems for noise reduction.

We demonstrate that the method can provide a variety of desired time-adaptive estimates by appropriately engineering the choice of pre-emphasis and de-emphasis transformations. More formally, the problem of finding the right sketch for the application at hand reduces to solving a given set of simultaneous equations and finding the appropriate pre-emphasis and de-emphasis transformations. This reduction could be of independent theoretical interest in itself.

We provide theoretical analysis and quantifications of error bounds with Ada-sketches for both point and range queries. The analysis confirms the adaptive nature of errors with time. An experimental evaluation on two real streaming datasets supports the theoretical claims: estimation accuracy shows time-adaptive behavior for both point and range queries, as expected from our analysis. Experimental comparisons also clearly show the advantages of the described method over the previously proposed HOKUSAI [20] temporally-aware sketches.

Ada-sketches simultaneously address and allow trading off the three key challenges of data stream algorithms: *volume, velocity* and *volatility*. Holistically addressing these challenges has been called out as an important yet understudied research direction [18], and we hope that this work will lead to further exciting developments in the area.

2. REVIEW

2.1 Notation

We assume the usual turnstile streaming model with positive updates [22]. The set of all items will be denoted by $I = \{1, 2, ..., N\}$. Time starts from $t = 0$, and the current time will be denoted by $T > 0$. The total increment to item i during time instance (or interval) t will be denoted by c_i^t, which is an aggregation of many streaming updates arriving at t. The results in this paper, without loss of any generality and for notational convenience, will use c_i^t to refer to the current update. We consider t to be a discrete timestamp or time interval of some fixed length and appropriate granularity. $C^t = \sum_{i \in I} c_i^t$ denotes the total increment of all items during time t. We define stream moments as

$$\mathcal{M}^T = \sum_{t=0}^{T} C^t; \qquad \mathcal{M}_2^T = \sum_{t=0}^{T} (C^t)^2$$

2.2 Count-Min Sketch (CMS)

The *Count-Min Sketch* (CMS) [7] algorithm is a generalization of Bloom filters [4] that is a widely popular in practice for estimating counts of items over data streams. CMS is a data structure with a two-dimensional array of counter cells M of width w and depth d, shown in Figure 1. It is accessed via d pairwise-independent hash functions $h_1, h_2, ..., h_d : \{1, 2, ..., N\} \mapsto \{1, 2, ..., w\}$. Each counter is initialized with zero, and every update c_i^t is added for all d rows to counters $M(j, h_j(i))$, where $j = \{1, 2, ..., d\}$. A query for the count of item i reports the minimum of the corresponding d counters i.e., $\min_{j \in \{1,2,...,d\}} M(j, h_j(i))$. This simple algorithm has strong error guarantees and is very accurate for estimating heavy hitters over entire streams,

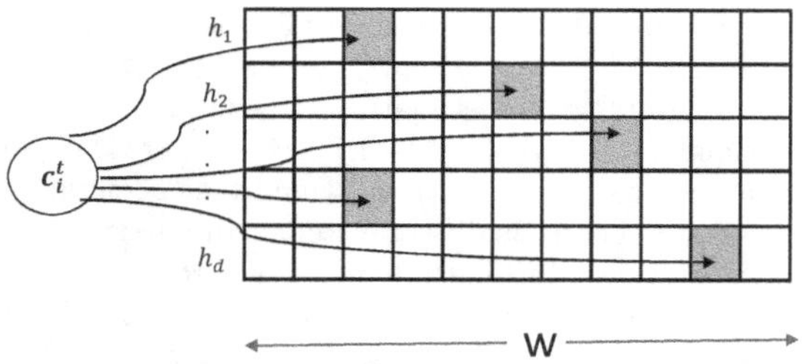

Figure 1: Count-Min Sketch Data Structure

with its simplicity and easy parallelization contributing to its wide adoption.

2.3 Lossy Counting (LC)

Lossy Counting [19] is another popular algorithm for counting frequent items over data streams. The algorithm keeps a fixed-size map of items and their counts seen so far. Whenever an update c_i^t arrives, the algorithm increments the map's counter corresponding to item i by c_i^t, if item i is present in the map. If the map does not contains item i, the algorithm allocates memory for i. When the map reaches its capacity, the algorithm simply deletes all items with counts below a specified threshold from the map, creating space for new items. The algorithm is motivated by the expectation that frequent items will survive periodic deletions. Despite the method's simplicity, it has near optimal theoretical guarantees for estimating heavy hitters with limited space [19].

2.4 The Need for Time Adaptive Sketches

In most applications that involve temporal data, most recent trends tend to be most informative for predictive purposes [18, 20]. For instance, in clickthrough predictions, recent click history provides best estimates of future clicks compared to logs from the more distant past. At the same time, old heavy hitters (or old but significant trends) also must be preserved, especially in the absence of more recent frequent occurrences of an item. With limited space, we can tolerate some error on counts of items in distant history, but would like to obtain highly accurate counts for recently seen items. While existing sketches, such as CMS and LC, are very good in retaining accurate information about heavy hitters, they do not take into account this temporal disparity in desired accuracy. It is possible to use straightforward extensions (discussed later) to existing sketching techniques to encode the temporal information; however, this results in error guarantees that are *independent* of time, and not adaptive to item recency. In this paper, we present adaptive variants of these sketches that achieve the desired time adaptability. To the best of our knowledge, only one technique has been designed specifically to capture frequency information over time, which we describe in the following:

2.5 Existing Method: Hokusai

In [20], the authors presented two modifications of CMS for aggregating information over temporal data streams. The first algorithm, referred to as *time aggregation*, aggregates information only in dyadic time intervals, i.e., intervals of the form $[t2^k + 1, ..., (t+1)2^k]$. However, this method does not provide (*item, time*) estimation for individual items. Moreover, in order to retain efficiency, the method incurs deterministic over-counting which can make the errors unpredictable. Hence, the focus of our comparison is on the *item aggregation* algorithms (Algorithm 3 in [20]) proposed for constructing time-adaptive sketches. This method provides general (*item, time*) estimation. Throughout this paper we will refer the item aggregation algorithms of [20] as the HOKUSAI (name of the paper) algorithm.

HOKUSAI uses a set of Count-Min sketches for different time intervals, to estimate the counts of any item for a given time or interval. To adapt the error rate temporally in limited space, the algorithm uses larger sketches for recent intervals and sketches of smaller size for older intervals, as illustrated in Figure 2. In a streaming setting, this setup creates additional overhead of tracking time intervals and shrinking the sketch size for older ones as time progresses. To efficiently achieve such sketch shrinking, [20] utilize an elegant insight: the size of count-min sketches can be halved simply by adding one half of the sketch to the other half, as shown in Algorithm 1. This operation also requires halving the hash function ranges, which can be easily accomplished using modulo 2 operation. Thus, it is possible to maintain sketches of varying sizes as shown in Figure 2 and dynamically adjust them as time progresses.

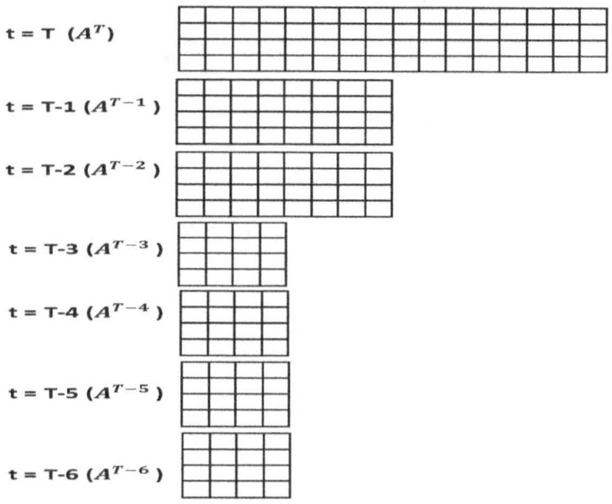

Figure 2: Hokusai

Algorithm 1 *Hokusai [20]*

$t \leftarrow 0$
while data arrives **do**
  Receive data in Sketch M for this t (**Modify M**)
  $t \leftarrow t+1$
  $A^t = M$ (**Copy**)
  for $k = 1$ **to** $\lfloor \log_2 t \rfloor$ **do**
    $\forall\ i, j$ in sketch A^{t-2^k}
    $A^{t-2^k}[i,j] = A^{t-2^k}[i,j] + A^{t-2^k}[i, j+2^{m-k}]$
    Shrink to size 2^{m-k}
  end for
end while

2.6 Shortcomings of Hokusai

Because Count-Min sketch accuracy depends on size, with HOKUSAI, we expect counts for recent time instances (that use larger sketches) to be more accurate than counts corresponding to older time intervals (that use smaller sketches).

Although this idea of having different-sized sketches for different time intervals is reasonable and yields accuracies that are time-adaptive, it comes with several inherent shortcomings which are summarized in the following subsections.

1. Discontinuity: Observe that in Algorithm 1, whenever t increments, we halve the size of sketches for $\log_2 t$ time instances. This abruptly doubles the errors for all items in those time instances, and happens at every transition from t to t+1. Even if the current time interval t is empty (or nearly empty), i.e., we do not add anything to the data structure, we still shrink sketches, unnecessarily reducing the accuracy of count estimates for many items. For instance, in a temporal stream, if the current time t has very few or no items, we still double our errors for time interval $t-1$, as well as many preceding it. This is undesirable and unnecessary, as we show below. In practice, such burstiness in data streams over time is very common, with some intervals adding many more counts than others. Owing to this discontinuity, we see oscillating accuracy over time with HOKUSAI. Ideally, accuracy for past counts should decrease smoothly as more items are included.

2. Too many sketches: We are keeping sketches for all the time instances $t \in \{0, 1, 2, ..., T\}$. In practice, the total time range T can be very large. If we keep sketches for all time points up to T, we cannot avoid using $O(T)$ memory, even if most of these intervals are "empty" and not associated with any items at all. When keeping time at a fine granularity, the $O(T)$ memory requirement can be become prohibitively expensive, making memory overhead of $O(\log T)$ highly desirable. If we force the total sketch size to be $O(\log T)$ while using the HOKUSAI approach, at least $T-O(\log T)$ time instances will have sketches of size zero, with all information corresponding to them lost.

3. Inflexibility: Algorithm 1 is inflexible, as all $t \in [t-2^i, t-2^{i+1}]$ use sketches of same size. With every time step, the size reduction in sketches also happens by a fixed amount which is half. With every transition of time from t to $t+1$, Hokusai doubles the error for specific time instances. There is not much flexibility in terms of the error distribution. Because we often do not know beforehand what error distribution over time is needed, having error tolerance that is flexible temporally would be very useful.

4. Overhead for shrinking: Whenever t increments, we need to shrink $\log t$ sketches by half, which involves one pass over all counters for those sketches.

Nonetheless, the key insight of HOKUSAI – shrinking sketch size with time – is a natural solution for achieving time adaptability. In subsequent sections, we demonstrate that there is an alternative approach, formulated in Section 4, that achieves time adaptability while rectifying the issues summarized above.

3. CMS FOR TEMPORAL QUERIES

CMS is a widely popular technique for summarizing data streams where typically we are interested in accurately estimating the heavy hitters (or items with significant counts). Before we describe our proposal, we argue that there is a trivial modification of CMS using which we can keep track of items over time without worrying about time adaptability. Our time adaptive variants will then build upon this modification.

We are interested in estimating the counts of items during any specified interval of time. To use existing CMS (or even LC) for such task, we can treat same items occurring in different time intervals as different items. In particular, we can distinguish item i during time instance t from the same item i during a different time instance t'. After this distinction, we can keep track of all distinct items over time, $N \times T$ of them, using the vanilla CMS (or LC). We need hash functions that hash both time and item, i.e. our hash functions will be

$$h_1, h_2, ..., h_d : \{1, 2, ..., N\} \times \{0, 1, 2, ..., T\} \mapsto \{1, 2, ..., w\}.$$

Effectively, we only increase the total number of items. The total number of items will be $N \times T$ which can be a very large number, because both T and N are huge in practice. Even space requirements of $O(N)$ or $O(T)$ are prohibitive and so handling $N \times T$ items is clearly still a concern.

Given the near optimality of the existing sketches, we cannot hope to be able to decrease the errors for all items consistently for all the time. However, there is a room for smartly distributing the errors to achieve the desired time adaptability described in the next section.

4. OUR PROPOSAL: TIME ADAPTIVE SKETCHES (ADA-SKETCHES)

We present Adaptive Count-Min Sketch (Ada-CMS) and Adaptive Lossy Counting (Ada-LS), which are time adaptive variants of Count-Min Sketch (CMS) and Lossy Counting (LC) respectively. The idea behind these adaptive sketches is analogous to the widely popular noise reduction process used in Dolby[2] via *pre-emphasis* and *de-emphasis*.

4.1 Short Detour: Dolby Noise Reduction, Pre-Emphasis and De-Emphasis

In Dolby systems, while recording the signal, a pre-emphasis transformation is applied, which artificially inflates certain frequencies in the signal relative to the tape's overall noise levels. This preserves the inflated signals with lesser distortion while recording on the tape. During playback an opposite transformation de-emphasis is applied which reduces back the inflated signals canceling the effect of artificial pre-emphasis. In the process, noise is attenuated more sharply. Please refer to [9, 24] for more details.

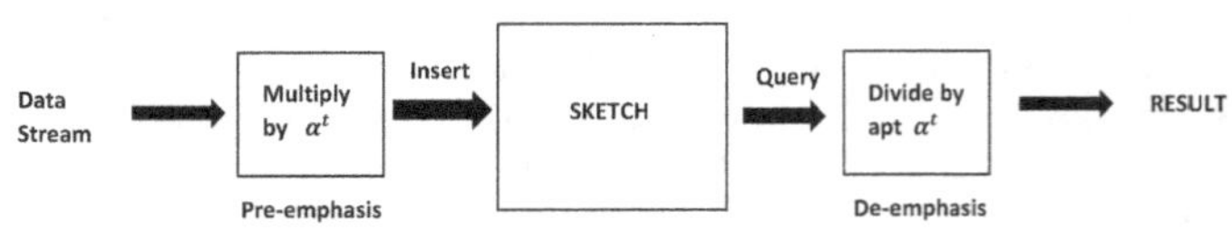

Figure 3: Adaptive Sketching via Pre-emphasis and De-emphasis analogous to Dolby Noise Reduction Procedure

We exploit the fact that Count-Min Sketch (CMS) and Lossy Counting (LS) have better accuracy for heavy hitters as compared to the rest of the items. While updating

[2] http://en.wikipedia.org/wiki/Dolby_noise-reduction_system

the sketch we apply pre-emphasis and artificially inflate the counts of more recent items compared to older ones, i.e., we make them heavier with respect to the older items. This is done by multiplying the updates c_i^t with $f(t)$, which is any monotonically increasing function of time t. Thus, instead of updating the sketch with c_i^t we update the sketch with $f(t) \times c_i^t$. The tendency of the sketch is to preserve large values. This inflation thus preserves the accuracy of recent items, after artificial inflation, compared to the older ones. While querying, we apply the de-emphasis process, where we divide the results by $f(t)$, to obtain the estimate of item i at time instance t. The procedure is simple and summarized in Figure 3. In this process, as we show later, the errors of the recent counts are decreased more than the errors of the older counts.

To understand why the pre-emphasis and de-emphasis defined in previous paragraph works, consider the case of CMS with only one hash function h_k, i.e. $d = 1$ and only a one row sketch as shown in Figure 4. The vanilla update procedure is simply adding c_i^t at location $h_k(i,t)$ for every increment c_i^t. During estimation of counts for item i in time interval t we simply report the value of $h_k(i,t)$.

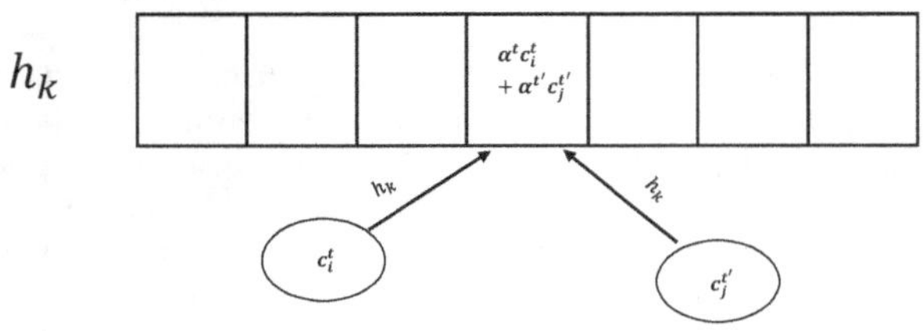

Figure 4: Toy illustration of a collision after Pre-emphasis

Now consider the case when we apply the artificial pre-emphasis and later de-emphasis to cancel it. When there are no collisions, just like the old sketches, we estimate the counts c_i^t exactly. Pre-emphasis and de-emphasis cancel each other and have no effect. Errors occur when there are collisions. For illustration, assume that $h_k(i,t) = h_k(j,t')$, i.e. both c_i^t and $c_j^{t'}$ collide and go to the same location. Suppose we have $t > t'$. The estimate of both c_i^t and $c_j^{t'}$ using vanilla CMS would be simply $c_i^t + c_j^{t'}$ because they both go to the same location and we simply return the counter. Note, we have only one row, and so the minimum is over one value. For the adaptive variant, based on the pre-emphasis and de-emphasis using a monotonic sequence $f(t)$ the estimates of c_i^t and $c_j^{t'}$ would be

$$\widehat{c_i^t} = \frac{f(t)c_i^t + f(t')c_j^{t'}}{f(t)} = c_i^t + \frac{f(t')}{f(t)}c_j^{t'}$$

$$\widehat{c_j^{t'}} = \frac{f(t)c_i^t + f(t')c_j^{t'}}{f(t')} = c_j^{t'} + \frac{f(t)}{f(t')}c_i^t.$$

Since $t > t'$, we will have $f(t) > f(t')$ because of monotonicity of $f(t)$ with respect to t. With vanilla CMS we overestimate c_i^j by $c_j^{t'}$ whereas the overestimation after pre-emphasis and de-emphasis is $\frac{f(t')}{f(t)}c_j^{t'}$ which is strictly smaller than $c_j^{t'}$. On the other hand, the error in $c_j^{t'}$ is $\frac{f(t)}{f(t')}c_i^t$ which is greater than c_i^t, the error with vanilla CMS. Thus, whenever there is a collision, the recent items suffer less compared to older items. This achieves the desired time adaptability in errors, given the same amount of space. The whole idea works for any sequence $f(t)$ which is monotonic in t. We now make this notion more rigorous.

4.2 Adaptive Count-Min Sketch (Ada-CMS)

Ada-CMS requires a monotonically increasing sequence $\{f(t); t \geq 0\}$ for performing the pre-emphasis and de-emphasis. Monotonicity implies $f(t) \geq f(t') \forall t > t'$. Similar to CMS we have a two dimensional cell with depth d and width w. The overall procedure is summarized in Algorithm 2.

Algorithm 2 *Adaptive Count-Min Sketch*

Input: Any monotonic sequence $\{f(t); t \geq 0\}$
$w \leftarrow \lceil \frac{e}{\epsilon} \rceil$
$d \leftarrow \log \frac{1}{\delta}$
$M \leftarrow d \times w$ array initialized to 0

Update c_i^t
for $j = 1$ **to** d **do**
  $M(j, h_j(i,t)) \leftarrow M(j, h_j(i,t)) + f(t)c_i^t$
end for

Query for counts of item i **during** t
$\widehat{c_i^t} \leftarrow \min_{j \in \{1,2,\ldots,d\}} \frac{M(j,h_j(i,t))}{f(t)}$
return $\widehat{c_i^t}$

Just like the vanilla CMS described in Section 3, we hash both item and time simultaneously, i.e., our hash functions are from the product of time and items to $[1, w]$. The update and the query use the pre-emphasis and de-emphasis as described in Section 4. Other than this simple modification, the overall algorithm is same. Thus, clearly we have no additional overhead. If we make $f(t) = 1$, then we recover the vanilla CMS algorithm. Thus, Algorithm 2 is a strict generalization of CMS. This simple modification, as we show later, is very powerful and achieves the desired functionality of time adaptability. Furthermore, as shown in Section 4.2.3, we obtain many design choices, which can be tailored for different applications.

4.2.1 Analysis

The analysis follows similar lines with the analysis of vanilla CMS [7] except that we have to deal with the pre-emphasis and de-emphasis factor $f(t)$.

THEOREM 1. *For $w = \lceil \frac{e}{\epsilon} \rceil$ and $d = \log \frac{1}{\delta}$, given any (i,t) we have*

$$c_i^t \leq \widehat{c_i^t} \leq c_i^t + \epsilon\beta^t\sqrt{\mathcal{M}_2^T}$$

with probability $1 - \delta$. Here $\beta^t = \frac{\sqrt{\sum_{t'=0}^{T}(f(t'))^2}}{f(t)}$ is the time adaptive factor monotonically decreasing with t.

Intuition Behind the Proof: We will start by analyzing errors under just one hash function. Note, that if there are no collisions, then the estimation is exact. Collisions are bad events that cause errors (overestimation), but with large enough values of w, random collisions have small probability. This small probability will make the expectations of error small. Furthermore, repeating the process with d independent hash functions, and finding the best (minimum) count among d repetitions of the experiment, will give the required high probability of concentration.

PROOF. Given i and t, define indicator variable $\mathbb{I}_{k,j}^{t'}$ as

$$\mathbb{I}_{k,j}^{t'} = \begin{cases} 1, & \text{if } (i,t) \neq (j,t') \text{ and } h_k(i,t) = h_k(j,t') \\ 0 & \text{otherwise} \end{cases} \tag{1}$$

$$\mathbb{E}[\mathbb{I}_{k,j}^{t'}] = Pr\left(h_k(i,t) = h_k(j,t')\right) = \frac{1}{w}. \tag{2}$$

Let us consider a single row estimate of c_i^t corresponding to hash function h_k, i.e. row k, call it $\widehat{c_{k,i}^t}$.

$$\widehat{c_{k,i}^t} = \frac{1}{f(t)}\left[f(t)c_i^t + \left[\sum_{t'=0}^{T}\left(f(t') \times \sum_{j=1}^{N}\mathbb{I}_{k,j}^{t'}c_j^{t'}\right)\right]\right] \geq c_i^t. \tag{3}$$

$\widehat{c_{k,i}^t} > c_i^t$ is true for all k and hence also true for the minimum. For the other side of the bound we have,

$$\mathbb{E}[\widehat{c_{k,i}^t} - c_i^t] = \frac{1}{f(t)}\mathbb{E}\left[\sum_{t'=0}^{T}\left(f(t) \times \sum_{j=1}^{N}\mathbb{I}_{k,j}^{t'}c_j^{t'}\right)\right] \tag{4}$$

$$= \frac{1}{f(t)}\sum_{t'=0}^{T}\left(f(t') \times \sum_{j=1}^{N}\frac{1}{w}c_j^{t'}\right) - \frac{c_i^t}{w} \tag{5}$$

$$\leq \frac{1}{wf(t)}\sum_{t'=0}^{T} f(t')C^{t'} \tag{6}$$

$$\leq \frac{1}{w}\left(\frac{\sqrt{\sum_{t'=0}^{T}(f(t'))^2}}{f(t)}\right)\sqrt{\mathcal{M}_2^T} = \frac{\beta^t}{w}\sqrt{\mathcal{M}_2^T} \tag{7}$$

In getting Equation 5 we used linearity of expectation. Since $\mathbb{I}_{k,i}^t = 0$, it created a hanging term $\frac{c_i^t}{w}$, dropping which gives the next inequality instead of equality. The next step is Cauchy-Schwartz and the definition of $\mathcal{M}_2^T$. From Markov's inequality we have:

$$Pr\left(\widehat{c_{k,i}^t} - c_i^t \geq \epsilon\beta^t\sqrt{\mathcal{M}_2^T}\right) \leq \frac{1}{\epsilon}\frac{1}{w} \leq e \tag{8}$$

Our final estimate is the minimum over d estimates which are independent because of pairwise independence of h_k. So for the final estimate $\widehat{c_i^t}$ we have

$$Pr\left(\widehat{c_i^t} - c_i^t \leq \epsilon\beta^t\sqrt{\mathcal{M}_2^T}\right) \geq 1 - e^d = 1 - \delta. \tag{9}$$

as required. The monotonicity of β^t follows directly from the monotonicity of $f(t)$ in the denominator. □

Remarks on Theorem 1: We can see that since β^t is monotonically decreasing the upper bound on errors, given by Theorem 1, decreases as time t increases. Thus, for point queries we obtain time adaptive error guarantees. For a vanilla CMS sketch we can get the upper bound in terms of the L_1 norm (see [7] for details) which is simply the sum Σ^t. Here, we get the upper bound in terms of weighted sum (Equation 6) which is further upper bounded by $\sqrt{\mathcal{M}_2^T}$ due to Cauchy-Schwartz inequality.

Dealing with Overflows: Due to artificial pre-emphasis, it is possible that the counters in the sketch can overflow sooner (particularly in the exponential) than vanilla CMS. A simple way to deal with this occasional overflow is to periodically divide all counters by a constant to keep the overflow under control. If we know beforehand a safe constant to divide by, we can always divide even before adding elements to the sketch. During estimation we can multiply the outputs by those known constants.

Before we look into choices of $f(t)$ and start contrasting Ada-CMS with standard CMS for time adaptive data summarization, we emphasize why Ada-CMS is free from the set of shortcomings, inherent to Hokusai, described in Section 2.6.

4.2.2 *Advantages of Ada-CMS over Hokusai*

Since Ada-CMS only keeps one sketch and use pre-emphasis and de-emphasis to achieve time adaptability we automatically get rid of the first problem mentioned in Section 2.6. If certain time interval t is empty then there is no addition to the Ada-CMS sketch. Therefore, there are no extra collisions. The previous counters and hence their accuracies are unchanged. We do not have any shrinking overhead. The update and the estimation complexity of Ada-CMS is exactly same as that of CMS.

As argued in Section 3, we are dealing with $N \times T$ distinct items. The error guarantee shown in Theorem 1 holds for any point query with probability $1-\delta$. To ensure this upper bound for all $N \times T$ items with probability $1 - \delta$, we need to choose $d = \log\frac{NT}{\delta}$ instead of $\log\frac{1}{\delta}$ and further take the union bound. Thus, with Ada-CMS we only need

$$dw = O(\frac{e}{\epsilon} \times \log\frac{NT}{\delta}) = O\left(\frac{(\log N + \log T - \log\delta)}{\epsilon}\right)$$

space to answer all possible point queries with provable time adaptive guarantees. On the other hand, Hokusai needs one sketch for every time instance t making it scale linearly with time $O(T)$, which is prohibitively expensive in practice.

We will further see in the next Section that we can handle a variety of design choices by exploiting the flexibility that we have in choosing the monotonic sequence $f(t)$. Later during evaluation, in Section 6, we will observe that the errors of Ada-CMS are smooth over time unlike Hokusai which abruptly changes errors over time.

4.2.3 *Comparison with Vanilla Count-Min Sketch and Design Choices*

Our aim is to distribute errors more smartly than CMS which has no information about time. In particular, we want errors for the recent counts to be very accurate while for the older counts we are ready to tolerate extra errors. In this section, we show that by appropriately choosing the sequence $f(t)$ we can obtain a variety of error distributions.

One major question that we are interested in is "Given a fixed space and current state of time T, what are the values of time $t \leq T$ where Ada-CMS is more accurate than vanilla CMS ?" We know that if we put $f(t) = 1$ for all t in Ada-CMS, then we recover the vanilla CMS algorithm. This observation comes handy for theoretical comparisons and leads to the following corollary:

COROLLARY 1. *For same w and d, the expected error in c_i^t with Ada-CMS is less than the expected error of Vanilla*

CMS if and only if

$$\sum_{t'=0}^{T} \frac{f(t')}{f(t)} C^{t'} \leq \sum_{t'=0}^{T} C^{t'} \tag{10}$$

PROOF. Immediate from combining Equation 5 with the fact that the final estimate is simply the minimum. □

Due to the monotonicity of $f(t)$ the condition is always true for $t = T$. For $t < T$, the left hand term is weighted sum and $\frac{f(t')}{f(t)} < 1 \ \forall t' < t$. Thus, for t close to T the left hand side is likely to be smaller.

To get a sense of quantifications, a convenient way for comparison is to compare the upper bounds i.e., β^t. For Vanilla CMS we simply substitute $f(t) = 1$ and get $\beta^t = \sqrt{T}$. Therefore, for all time instance $\geq t$ such that

$$\frac{\sqrt{\sum_{t'=0}^{T}(f(t'))^2}}{f(t)} \leq \sqrt{T} \text{ or } \frac{\sum_{t'=0}^{T}(f(t'))^2}{T} \leq (f(t))^2 \tag{11}$$

we get a better upper bound on errors with Ada-CMS for c_i^t compared to vanilla CMS. For instance, if we choose $f(t) = t + 1$ the above condition becomes

$$t \geq \sqrt{\frac{(T+1)(2T+1)}{6}} \geq \sqrt{\frac{1}{3}}T \simeq 0.57T \tag{12}$$

Thus, for recent half of the time we are more accurate than vanilla CMS.

Another interesting choice is exponential, i.e. $f(t) = a^t$ for some $a > 1$. With this we achieve better accuracy than CMS for all (assuming $a^{T+1} \gg 1$)

$$t \geq \frac{\log \frac{a^{T+1}-1}{(a-1)T}}{2\log a} \simeq \frac{T+1}{2} - \frac{\log T + \log(a-1)}{2\log a} \tag{13}$$

We can achieve finer control by more complicated choices of $f(t)$. To illustrate a reasonable scenario, suppose we want the errors with Ada-CMS to be never off by a factor γ away from that of vanilla CMS $\forall\, t$. This ensures that we guarantee accuracy within factor γ of what the original CMS would achieve to even very old heavy hitters. In addition, we want to be more accurate than CMS on all recent time $t > K$, for some desirable choice of K. Note that $\beta^t = \sqrt{T}$ for CMS. All these can be translated into the following constraints

$$\beta^t \leq \gamma\sqrt{T} \quad \forall t > 0 \text{ and } \beta^t \leq \sqrt{T} \quad \forall t > K. \tag{14}$$

Because β^t is monotonically decreasing, the above condition is also satisfied if

$$\beta^0 = \gamma\sqrt{T}; \quad \beta^K = \sqrt{T} \quad \text{or}$$

$$\frac{\sum_{t'=0}^{T}(f(t'))^2}{T} = \gamma^2(f(0))^2; \quad \frac{\sum_{t'=0}^{T}(f(t'))^2}{T} = (f(K))^2$$

To simplify let us choose $f(t) = \sqrt{at^2 + bt + 1}$, and after expansion we are left with the following system of simultaneous equation for a and b.

$$a\left[\frac{1}{6}(T+1)(2T+1)\right] + b\left[\frac{1}{2}(T+1)\right] = \gamma^2 - 1 \tag{15}$$

$$a\left[\frac{1}{6}(T+1)(2T+1) - K^2\right] + b\left[\frac{1}{2}(T+1) - K\right] = 0 \tag{16}$$

This system leads to the following choice of a and b

$$a = \frac{(\gamma^2-1)(B-K)}{K(BK-A)}; \quad b = \frac{(\gamma^2-1)(A-K^2)}{K(A-BK)} \tag{17}$$

$$A = \frac{(T+1)(2T+1)}{6}; \quad B = \frac{T+1}{2} \tag{18}$$

We require one more condition that $at^2+bt+1 > 0$, which is always true if $a > 0$ and $b > 0$. These two conditions is satisfied if $\gamma > 1$ and $\sqrt{\frac{(T+1)(2T+1)}{6}} > K > \frac{T+1}{2}$. $\gamma > 1$ is a very natural condition because $\gamma < 1$ would mean that we are universally better, than vanilla CMS for all time t. We cannot hope to achieve that, given the near optimality of CMS sketches.

Some Remarks: We have shown that there is significant room of distributing the errors in CMS more smartly using the idea of pre-emphasis and de-emphasis. The flexibility in engineering the monotonic sequence $f(t)$ makes it applicable to a wide variety of situation at hand. The choice of pre-emphasis and de-emphasis transformations along with the sketching parameters, thus, unifies the trade-off between memory, accuracy and "time adaptability" in a single generalized framework, which is very exciting.

Here, we have focused on giving importance to the more recent time interval t. The idea of pre-emphasis and de-emphasis is more general and not just limited to time. For instance, if we want to estimate more accurately a set of items coming from some important source, the idea of pre-emphasis and de-emphasis is naturally applicable, as well.

4.2.4 Extension to Other Popular Sketches

There are two major variants of CMS in literature: (i) CMS with conservative updates [11] and (ii) CMS with skipping [3]. These two variants can be naturally extended with the idea of pre-emphasis and de-emphasis. Count Sketches [6] which predate CMS is another popular algorithm in practice and it is very much similar in nature to CMS. The idea of pre-emphasis and de-emphasis is directly applicable to Count Sketches as well for obtaining adaptive error guarantees. The details and analysis is analogous to Ada-CMS and so we do not repeat them here. To demonstrate the generality of pre-emphasis and de-emphasis idea, we provide time adaptive variant of Lossy Counting (LC) which is a very popular deterministic algorithm for counting heavy hitters, and it is very different in nature from CMS.

4.3 Adaptive Lossy Counting (Ada-LC)

In line with Ada-CMS we can use pre-emphasis and de-emphasis idea to obtain an adaptive variant of the popular lossy counting (LC) algorithm. Ada-LC, just like vanilla LC, needs one map M of size l. To perform pre-emphasis and de-emphasis, for obtaining adaptability over time, we again need a monotonically increasing sequence $f(t)$.

Just like Ada-CMS, before adding an element c_i^t to the map we multiply it by $f(t)$. If the map is full then we remove the minimum element from the map to create space. While estimating c_i^t, we just report the count of the element in the map divided by $f(t)$ (de-emphasis). The overall procedure is summarized in Algorithm 3. A more practical algorithm is to delete all elements which are less than minimum plus some predefined threshold.

Algorithm 3 *Adaptive Lossy Counting*

Requirement: Any monotonic sequence $\{f(t); t \geq 0\}$
$l \leftarrow \lceil \frac{1}{\epsilon} \rceil$
$M \leftarrow Empty$
$min \leftarrow 0$

```
Update c_i^t
M[(i,t)] ← M[(i,t)] + f(t)c_i^t
if M is Full then
  min = min_{a∈M} M[a]
  for a ∈ M do
    if M[a] = min then
      Delete M[a]
    end if
  end for
end if
```

```
Query for counts of item i during t
if M contains (i,t) then
  return ĉ_i^t = M[(i,t)] / f(t)
else
  return 0
end if
```

4.3.1 Analysis

The intuition why pre-emphasis and de-emphasis work for Ada-LC is easy to see. Since recent counts are inflated during pre-emphasis they are unlikely to be deleted compared to the older counts and hence their values are preserved more accurately in the map. This simple idea is also amenable to analysis and gives provable time adaptive error bounds.

Unlike the Ada-CMS, Ada-LC is deterministic and so the analysis does not involve probability.

THEOREM 2. *If* $l = \lceil \frac{1}{\epsilon} \rceil$ *then the Ada-LC returns an estimate* $\widehat{c_i^t}$ *such that*

$$c_i^t \geq \widehat{c_i^t} \geq c_i^t - \epsilon\beta^t\sqrt{\mathcal{M}_2^T}$$

where $\beta^t = \frac{\sqrt{\sum_{t'=0}^{T}(f(t'))^2}}{f(t)}$ *is the time adaptive factor and it is same as in Theorem 1.*

PROOF. The total amount of increment to M is all items in the stream along with the pre-emphasis $\sum_{t=0}^{T} f(t)C^t$. Let $min_{i,t}$ be the minimum value after the insertion of c_i^t. Then in the worst case all counters can be $min_{i,t}$ and we decrement $l \times min_{i,t}$ in this iteration. Thus, the maximum possible total decrement is $l\sum_{t=0}^{T}\sum_{i=1}^{N} min_{i,t}$. Since, the total decrement is less than the total increment we have

$$\sum_{t=0}^{T} f(t)C^t - l\sum_{t=0}^{T}\sum_{i=1}^{N} min_{i,t} \geq 0 \quad or$$

$$\sum_{t=0}^{T}\sum_{i=1}^{N} min_{i,t} \leq \frac{1}{l}\sum_{t=0}^{T} f(t)C^t \leq \epsilon\left(\sqrt{\sum_{t'=0}^{T}(f(t'))^2}\right)\sqrt{\mathcal{M}_2^T}$$

The last step is Cauchy-Schwartz. Thus, every counter has decreased by at most $\epsilon\left(\sqrt{\sum_{t'=0}^{T}(f(t'))^2}\right)\sqrt{\mathcal{M}_2^T}$. Since we always decrement any count in the map and increment c_i^t as $f(t)c_i^T$, we have

$$f(t)c_i^t \geq M[(i,t)] \geq f(t)c_i^t - \epsilon\left(\sqrt{\sum_{t'=0}^{T}(f(t'))^2}\right)\sqrt{\mathcal{M}_2^T}$$

Dividing by $f(t)$ leads to the desired expression. □

Since the error bound has the time adaptive expression equal to $\epsilon\beta^t\sqrt{\mathcal{M}_2^T}$ which is same as the expression for the Ada-CMS, we can directly borrow all the design choices shown in Section 4.2.3 for choosing $f(t)$.

5. RANGE QUERIES

In practice, we are typically interested in range queries over time. For example, count-based features are common in click-through rate prediction, such as counts of clicks in past 24 hours on a given ad. Define $c_i^{[t_1,t_2]}$ to be the count of item i during any specified time interval $[t_1, t_2]$. One naive estimate of this range query is simply the sum of all point estimates leading to a crude estimator:

$$\widehat{c_i^{[t_1,t_2]}} = \sum_{t=t_1}^{t_2} \widehat{c_i^t} \tag{19}$$

An obvious problem with this estimator is that the summation involves too many terms. The errors grow linearly with the length of the interval.

A well know solution [7] is to store multiple sketches for different size of dyadic intervals. The idea is to keep $\log T$ sketches, one each for the intervals of the form $[t2^k+1, ..., (t+1)2^k]$ (of size 2^k) with $k = 0, 1, ..., \log T$. When $k = 0$ this consists of the usual sketch for every time instance t or the interval $[t, t]$, when $k = 1$, these sketches keep estimates of two consecutive time intervals $[t, t+1]$, etc. The key observation, made in [7], is that any interval $[t_1, t_2]$ can be decomposed as a sum of at most $2\log T$ dyadic intervals. For instance interval $[10, 20]$ can be decomposed into union of four disjoint dyadic intervals $[10, 10]$, $[11, 12]$, $[13, 16]$, $[17, 20]$. Thus, to estimate $c_i^{[10,20]}$, we only need 4 point queries compared to 11 with the crude estimator given by equation 19. The errors in the worst case grow as $O(\log T)$ instead of linearly in the length of the interval (or range). The price that we pay in terms of time and memory, for answering any range query, is an increase of a factor of $O(\log T)$. The overall complexity is still logarithmic in both total time T and total items N.

The idea of pre-emphasis and de-emphasis for range queries is quite straightforward except for one subtlety. We need to keep $\log T$ different adaptive sketches, one for each type of dyadic range, and use the same idea of decomposing ranges into at most $2\log T$ intervals. However, we need to ensure that every time instance $t \in [t2^k+1, ..., (t+1)2^k]$, for sketches corresponding to this type of dyadic interval, gets the same pre-emphasis and later de-emphasis. For example, if we are keeping sketches to count intervals of size 2, i.e. of the form $[2t+1, 2t+2]$, we have to give same pre-emphasis to $2t+1$ and $2t+2$. This is because we cannot have a well defined de-emphasis for recovering $c_i^{[2t+1,2t+2]} = c_i^{2t+1} + c_i^{2t+2}$ from $f(2t+1)c_i^{2t+1} + f(2t+2)c_i^{2t+2}$ unless $f(2t+1) = f(2t+2)$. Implementation wise this is very simple: we only need to make $2t+1$ and $2t+2$ indistinguishable by changing t to $t' = \lceil t/2 \rceil$ (in general $t' = \lceil t/2^i \rceil$ for sketches corresponding to dyadic interval $[t2^i+1, ..., (t+1)2^i]$).

5.1 Analysis

We focus our analysis on range queries with Ada-CMS, a very similar analysis applies to Ada-LC.

Define $t^k = \lceil \frac{t}{2^k} \rceil$. With this distinction, all $t \in [t2^k + 1, ..., (t+1)2^k]$ have can be denoted by the same value t^k. We keep one Ada-CMS sketch for intervals of form $[t2^k + 1, ..., (t+1)2^k]$ (of size 2^k) with $k = 0, 1, ..., \log T$. The point queries for this sketch $c_i^{t^k}$ directly give the count of interval $[t2^k + 1, ..., (t+1)2^k]$. With slight abuse of notation we will also use $t^k = [t2^k + 1, (t+1)2^k]$ to denote any dyadic range.

With a similar line of analysis as Theorem 1 it can be shown that if $w = \lceil \frac{e}{\epsilon} \rceil$ and $d = \log \frac{1}{\delta}$, then with probability $1 - \delta$ the following holds, for a sketch corresponding to any dyadic range of the form $[t2^k + 1, ..., (t+1)2^k]$:

$$c_i^{t^k} \leq \widehat{c_i^{t^k}} \leq c_i^{t^k} + \epsilon \beta^{t^k} \sqrt{\mathcal{M}_2^T}, \qquad (20)$$

where

$$\beta^{t^k} = \frac{\sqrt{\sum_{t=0}^{T} (f(t))^2}}{f(t^k)} = \frac{\sqrt{\sum_{t=0}^{\lceil \frac{T}{2^k} \rceil} 2^k (f(t^k))^2}}{f(t^k)} \qquad (21)$$

is a monotonically decreasing function of t^k.

Let $I_{dyd}^{[t_1,t_2]}$ be the set of all dyadic intervals that are contained in $[t_1, t_2]$. Formally,

$$I_{dyd}^{[t_1,t_2]} = \{[x, y] : [x, y] \subseteq [t_1, t_2] \;\&\; [x, y] = [t2^k + 1, (t+1)2^k]\} \qquad (22)$$

for some $t \in \mathbb{Z}$ and $k \in \{0, 1, ..., \log T\}$.

We now define

$$B^{[t_1,t_2]} = \max_{t^k \in I_{dyd}^{[t_1,t_2]}} \beta^{t^k}. \qquad (23)$$

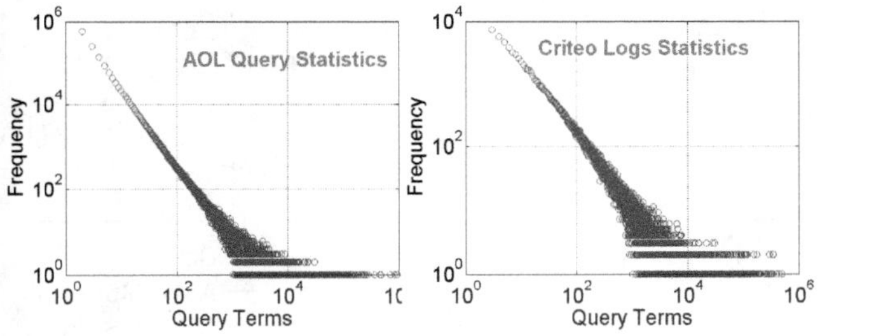

Figure 5: Frequency of items observed over the entire stream. The trends clearly depicts a power law as expected in real environments. The x-axis display items grouped by Matlab's tabulate function.

With this $B^{[t_1,t_2]}$ we have the following:

THEOREM 3. *Given* $w = \lceil \frac{e}{\epsilon} \rceil$ *and* $d = \log \frac{1}{\delta}$, *then with probability* $1 - \delta$ *we have for any given range* $[t_1, t_2]$

$$c_i^{[t_1,t_2]} \leq \widehat{c_i^{[t_1,t_2]}} \leq c_i^{[t_1,t_2]} + 2\epsilon B^{[t_1,t_2]} \sqrt{\mathcal{M}_2^T} \log T \qquad (24)$$

PROOF. The proof follows from the fact that any interval $[t_1, t_2]$ can be written as union of at most $2 \log T$ disjoint dyadic intervals. For each of those dyadic intervals t^k we must have $t^k \subseteq [t_1, t_2]$. The error for estimating that dyadic range is upper bounded by $\epsilon \beta^{t^k} \sqrt{\mathcal{M}_2^T} \leq \epsilon B^{[t_1,t_2]} \sqrt{\mathcal{M}_2^T}$. This follows from the definition of $B^{[t_1,t_2]}$. The lower bound is trivial because we always overestimate. □

Remarks: The factor of $\log T$ appears in the upper bound along with some constants. This is analogous to upper bounds for range queries with vanilla CMS [7].

6. EXPERIMENTAL EVALUATION

Code: Algorithms were implemented in C#, with all experiments performed on an Intel Xeon 3.10 GHz CPU.

Datasets: Two real-world streaming datasets were used, *AOL* and *Criteo*, covering two important applications: online search and advertisement.

AOL: AOL query logs consist of 36 million search queries collected from 650 thousand users over 3 months. The dataset is comprised of search queries with associated timestamps, containing 3.8 million unique terms.

Criteo: Criteo conversions dataset contains feature values and conversion feedback for clicked display ads sampled over a two-month period [5]. Every ad is associated with a timestamp and 9 categorical terms hashed for anonymity, for a total of 150k unique hashed categorical terms.

Figure 5 plots the frequency of terms for both datasets in decreasing order on log-log scale. We use the Matlab tabulate function, which automatically computes the frequency and groups the plots. The plots reveal the power-law phenomenon common among real-world frequency distributions. An important problem in a variety of real applications is to keep track of the counts of important terms over time, in a streaming setting under a memory budget.

In these experiments, we focus on *time adaptability*: methods are compared by their accuracy on more recent counts, while we expect them to permit higher error rates for counts in distant past.

Competing Methodologies: Count-min sketching (CMS) is a widely popular algorithm in industrial practice. Our aim is to evaluate the effects of pre-emphasis and de-emphasis on CMS and compare it with HOKUSAI [20] algorithm that aims to make error rates time-adaptive. Since HOKUSAI is also built on CMS, we focus our comparison on the novel variants of CMS proposed in this paper. We omit comparisons to Lossy Counting in this section because, unlike CMS and Hokusai, it is deterministic, slow, and difficult to parallelize, due to the repeated linear-space-complexity creation step that executes every time when the map is full (see Algorithm 3 and Section 6.2). Therefore, for clarity, we defer the comparisons of Lossy Counting to its adaptive variants to Appendix C.

For comparisons, we keep track of all discrete items of interest (3.8 million in case of AOL and 150k for Criteo) over time using the following variants of CMS sketching schemes:

1. **Hokusai:** this algorithm was proposed in [20] for time-adaptive counting, based on CMS of different sizes for each time instance, described in Algorithm 1 and Section 2.5.

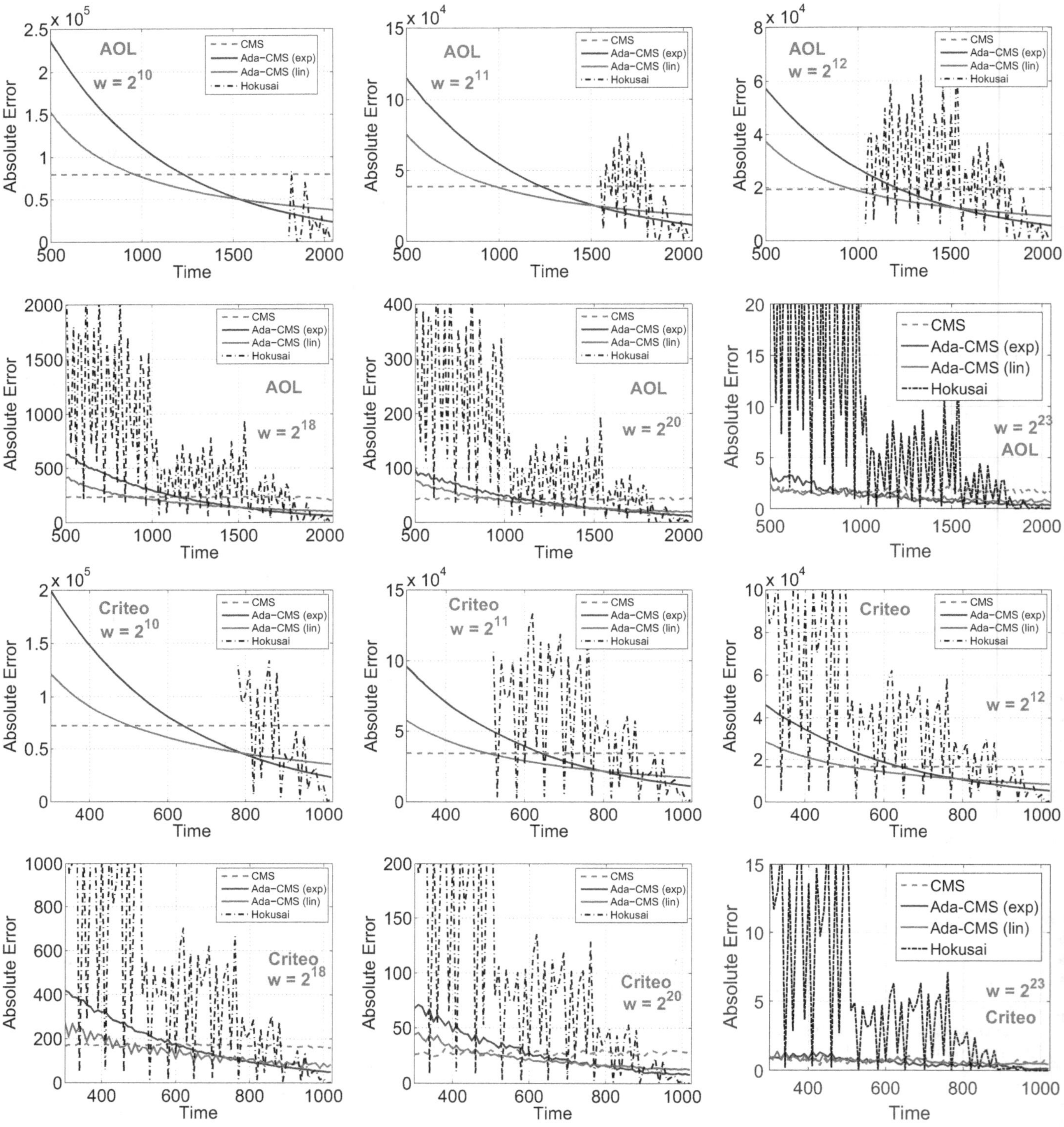

Figure 6: Average absolute error over time for different sketching scheme with varying sizes of range w (memory). A value of $d = 4$, (also used in [20]), was fixed in all the experiments. We ensured that all algorithms take exactly the same amount of memory while comparisons. CMS does not have any time adaptability. Hokusai keeps different sketches for all time intervals and therefore the error fluctuates. For smaller w ($w \leq 2^{12}$), Hokusai does not have enough sketches for all t. Both variants of Ada-CMS show the desired time adaptability, validating our claims, and is significantly better than Hokusai.

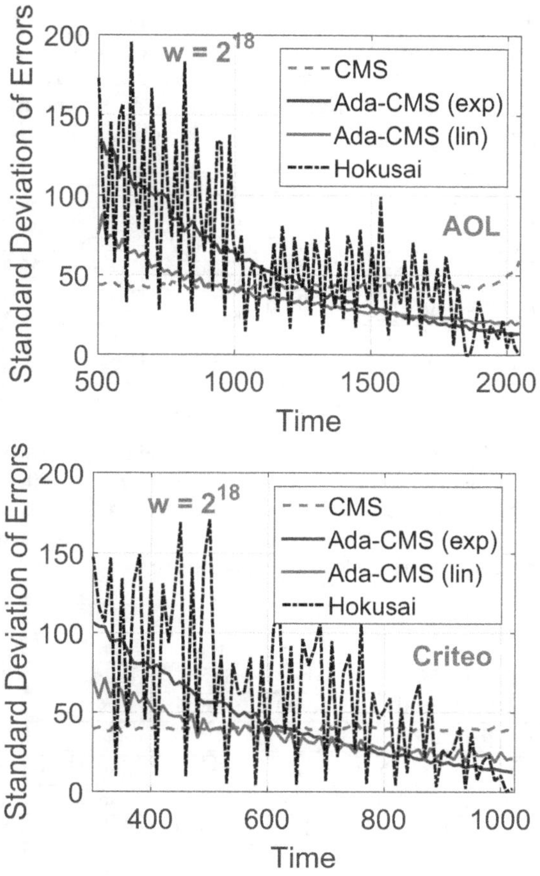

Figure 7: Standard deviation of errors for $w = 2^{18}$.

2. **CMS:** the basic CMS with the modification described in Section 3. Because it is not time-adaptive, it will serve as a baseline for the other algorithms.

3. **Ada-CMS (lin):** the proposed adaptive variant of CMS with pre-emphasis and de-emphasis using linearly increasing sequence $f(t) = a \times t$ for a fixed a. Please see Algorithm 2 and Section 4.2 for more details. All experiments used $a = 0.5$.

4. **Ada-CMS (exp):** the proposed adapative variant of CMS with pre-emphasis and de-emphasis using exponentially increasing sequence $f(t) = a^t$ for a fixed a. All experiments used $a = 1.0015$.

We use time granularity of one hour, thus each time instance t covers an hour of data. This yields around 2000 time instances for the AOL dataset, and around 1000 time instances for Criteo. We use the four competing algorithms to summarize the datasets. For *AOL* consisting of 3.8 million terms over more than 2000 time instances, the effective number of items is around $3.8M \times 2000 \simeq 8 \times 10^9$ which is a reasonably big number. For *Criteo*, the effective number of items is around $150k \times 1000 \simeq 1.5 \times 10^8$.

6.1 Accuracy-Memory Trade-off

Approximate counting algorithms provide a trade-off between estimation accuracy and the amount of space used. A superior algorithm provides a better tradeoff between accuracy and memory. Therefore, we compare the accuracies of all the algorithms for a fixed amount of space.

In the experiments, we kept the sketch depth of $d = 4$ fixed, following the setup used in [20]. This choice fixes the value of probability guarantee $1 - \delta$ to a constant value of $1 - \frac{1}{e^d}$ for all the four sketching schemes. To see the effect of variations on the sketch sizes, we varied the value of sketch width w in $\{2^{10}, 2^{11}, ..., 2^{23}\}$. For HOKUSAI, we chose the sketch size for each time instance so that the total amount of memory (the total size of all sketches) is exactly the same as the amount of memory used by the other algorithms. To ensure reasonable estimate quality, we verified that every time instance gets sketch size of $w \geq 4$, otherwise it simply returns the sum of stream over that time period. In some cases, ($w \leq 12$ for AOL and $w \leq 11$ for Criteo) we cannot have enough sketches, of any reasonable size, for all time spans. For such cases, we only report time instances for which Hokusai can make predictions. This is one of the shortcomings of Hokusai in that it requires a large number of sketches to keep track of all time instances because it needs one sketch for each of them.

In real settings, we are interested in estimates for items with high counts. For generating queries, we chose the top 1000 terms from both datasets based on their frequencies over the entire stream as items of interest. We then estimate the counts of these 1000 items for all the time intervals (2000 for AOL and 1000 for Criteo) by issuing point queries to the sketches. We compare the estimates of these counts with the true (gold standard) counts. The plot of the mean absolute error, of 1000 frequent items, over time for all the four competing schemes, is shown in Figure 6. We only highlight $w = \{2^{10}, 2^{11}, 2^{12}, 2^{18}, 2^{20}, 2^{23}\}$ to illustrate accuracy trends for high memory (2^{18-23}), as well as for low memory (2^{10-12}) regions. It should be noted that each of the plots shows accuracy for a given, fixed amount of memory for all the algorithms. In addition, we also illustrate the statistical significance of these numbers by showing the standard deviation of error estimates over time for $w = 2^{18}$ for both the datasets in figure 7. The standard deviation plots for other values of w exhibit analogous behavior.

Observations: the plots clearly show that the errors (both mean and standard deviation) for HOKUSAI fluctuate with time, producing significantly worse estimtes than the alternative sketches for both datasets. The fluctuations are expected because HOKUSAI keeps different CMS sketches for each time instance. Such fluctuations were also observed in [20]. It is known than the accuracy of CMS decreases with the total number of items added to the sketch. Therefore, for a busy time interval we can expect bad accuracy compared to non-busy intervals, leading to fluctuation in errors over time. With limited space $w \leq 2^{12}$, it is not possible to keep any reasonable sized sketch for all time intervals. For instance, when $w = 2^{10} \leq T \simeq 2000$, we cannot allocate any reasonable memory for all the time intervals. For such cases, we only report the time intervals we can track with HOKUSAI. Therefore, for those cases ($w < 2^{12}$), we do not see any values with HOKUSAI for all time instances t.

Baseline CMS does not provide any time adaptability, thus its error rates stay constant over time as expected. In contrast, the ADA-CMS results clearly demonstrate the time adaptive behavior for both mean and standard deviation. For recent time intervals, it is significantly more accurate compared to CMS and thereafter errors grow smoothly with decrease in time. Since CMS and Ada-CMS has only one sketch, we do not see the undesirable fluctuations in the errors observed with Hokusai.

The difference between ADA-CMS (lin) and ADA-CMS (exp) clearly demonstrates the effect of choosing different forms for $f(t)$. With ADA-CMS (exp), the errors for the recent time intervals are better than those of ADA-CMS (lin) but grow faster than ADA-CMS (lin) with time on both the datasets. This clearly demonstrates that, in addition to time adaptability of errors, we have control over the rate of growth of errors over time. We have only shown linear and exponentially increasing sequences for demonstration, but can obtain a whole spectrum of errors by choosing various forms of $f(t)$. Irrespective of the growth rate, the errors and standard deviations with ADA-CMS are significantly less those of HOKUSAI for all experiments.

As we double the memory provided to the algorithms, the errors halve as expected. It is clear that with more memory the algorithms become more accurate, but ADA-CMS retains advantage over HOKUSAI, demonstrating a consistent trend. CMS and its variants are almost exact for $w = 2^{23}$, whereas HOKUSAI loses accuracy, especially for older counts.

6.2 Performance Comparisons

One of the major concern with Hokusai, as mentioned in Section 2.6, is the overhead of the shrinking operations. Not only does (the *item aggregation* scheme of) Hokusai requires one Count-min Sketch A^t for every time instance t but every transition of time from t to $t+1$ requires halving the size of $\log t$ many sketches. The halving of a sketch A^t requires a linear scan of all the cells in A^t, leading to poor scaling of HOKUSAI with the growing sketch sizes.

In this section, we compare the computational overheads of inserting streaming data into the sketches. Table 1 and Table 2 summarize the average running time, in seconds, of insertion for the *AOL* and *Criteo* datasets, respectively, using different sketching schemes. The averages are taken over 10 independent runs. Lower times indicate faster processing rate (throughput) of the sketching scheme. To further illustrate the effect of memory consumption (sketch size), we performed independent experiments with varying memory sizes. Results are shown for sketch widths $w = \{2^{20}, 2^{22}, 2^{25}, 2^{27}, 2^{30}\}$.

The results reveal how slow Lossy Counting (LC) is in general. To create space for the incoming items, once the map gets full, low-count elements must be purged; if we only remove the minimum element as suggested by the classical algorithm, then the algorithm insertion does not even finish in 2 -3 days. We therefore implemented a more practical version, in which, once the map gets full, we remove the items having smallest 10% of counts from the map. With this modification, LC and Ada-LC run in reasonable time.

The numbers clearly show the poor scalability of HOKUSAI with increasing sketch size. As the sketches increase, shrinking overhead in Hokusai with every increment in t makes the algorithm extremely slow. In contrast, for CMS and ADA-CMS, increases in sketch size have negligible affect on the processing time, which is not surprising given that the sketch size has no effect on the insertion time of the algorithm.

LC and its adaptive variants shows the opposite trend. LC and Ada-LC are deterministic algorithms (no hashing is used) that are hard to parallelize. When memory is reduced, the map quickly runs out of space and requires removal of smaller elements, a linear time operation. Therefore, under smaller memory budget, LC and Ada-LC are very slow. As the memory increases, space creation is less frequent, and LC and Ada-LC exhibit faster running times.

Table 1: Time (seconds) of summarizing the full *AOL* dataset using the respective sketches of different widths w. The numbers are averaged over 10 independent runs. Lower time indicates faster processing rate (throughput) of the sketching scheme.

	2^20	2^22	2^25	2^27	2^30
CMS	44.62	44.80	48.40	50.81	52.67
Hoku	68.46	94.07	360.23	1206.71	9244.17
ACMS_lin	44.57	44.62	49.95	52.21	52.87
ACMS_exp	68.32	73.96	76.23	82.73	76.82
LC	1334.843	578.70	268.67	267.48	253.40
ALC_lin	3184.40	1576.46	326.23	289.54	284.09
ALC_exp	1789.07	955.29	286.50	283.14	272.98

Table 2: Time (seconds) of summarizing the full *Criteo* dataset using sketches of different widths w. The numbers are averaged over 10 independent runs. Lower time indicates faster processing rate (throughput) of the sketching scheme.

	2^20	2^22	2^25	2^27	2^30
CMS	40.79	42.29	45.81	45.92	46.17
Hoku	55.19	90.32	335.04	1134.07	8522.12
ACMS_lin	39.07	42.00	44.54	45.32	46.24
ACMS_exp	69.21	69.31	71.23	72.01	72.85
LC	794.45	415.15	393.27	390.15	385.85
ALC_lin	3074.51	1472.34	432.14	398.21	393.10
ALC_exp	1291.82	821.27	388.06	372.15	365.18

CMS is popular in practice due its ease, parallelization and small overhead. All these properties are mimicked by the ADA-CMS variants proposed in the paper, which are strict generalization of CMS. By performing time-adapative sketching via pre-emphasis and de-emphasis, ADA-CMS avoids the overheads of HOKUSAI, and yields significant improvements in ability to trade off accuracy and memory, as shown in Section 6.1.

7. CONCLUSIONS

We found a mathematical opportunity that makes two widely popular sketching techniques temporally adaptive, thereby making them more suitable for massive data streams with drift over time. Our proposed technique, Ada-sketch, provides time-adaptive sketching that integrates the powerful idea of pre-emphasis and de-emphasis of with existing sketching techniques. As a result, we obtain strict generalization of classic sketching algorithms, unifying the trade-off between memory, accuracy and time adaptability in a single framework. This generalization comes with no additional overhead, and our proposal is simple to implement.

The proposed integration of sketches with pre-emphasis and de-emphasis, as we demonstrate, posseses strong theoretical guarantees on errors over time. Experiments on real datasets support our theoretical findings and show significantly superior accuracy and runtime overhead compared to the recently proposed Hokusai algorithm. We hope that our proposal will be adopted in practice, and it will lead to further exploration of the pre-emphasis and de-emphasis idea for solving massive data stream problems.

8. REFERENCES

[1] N. Alon, Y. Matias, and M. Szegedy. The space complexity of approximating the frequency moments. In *Proceedings of the twenty-eighth annual ACM symposium on Theory of computing*, pages 20–29. ACM, 1996.

[2] B. Babcock, S. Babu, M. Datar, R. Motwani, and J. Widom. Models and issues in data stream systems. In *Proceedings of the twenty-first ACM SIGMOD-SIGACT-SIGART symposium on Principles of database systems*, 2002.

[3] S. Bhattacharyya, A. Madeira, S. Muthukrishnan, and T. Ye. How to scalably and accurately skip past streams. In *Data Engineering Workshop, 2007 IEEE 23rd International Conference on*, pages 654–663. IEEE, 2007.

[4] B. H. Bloom. Space/time trade-offs in hash coding with allowable errors. *Communications of the ACM*, 13(7):422–426, 1970.

[5] O. Chapelle. Modeling delayed feedback in display advertising. In *Proceedings of the 20th ACM SIGKDD international conference on Knowledge discovery and data mining*, pages 1097–1105. ACM, 2014.

[6] M. Charikar, K. Chen, and M. Farach-Colton. Finding frequent items in data streams. In *Automata, Languages and Programming*, pages 693–703. Springer, 2002.

[7] G. Cormode and S. Muthukrishnan. An improved data stream summary: the count-min sketch and its applications. *Journal of Algorithms*, 55(1):58–75, 2005.

[8] G. Cormode, S. Tirthapura, and B. Xu. Time-decayed correlated aggregates over data streams. *Statistical Analysis and Data Mining: The ASA Data Science Journal*, 2(5-6):294–310, 2009.

[9] R. Dolby. Noise reduction systems, Nov. 5 1974. US Patent 3,846,719.

[10] C. Estan and G. Varghese. Data streaming in computer networking.

[11] C. Estan and G. Varghese. *New directions in traffic measurement and accounting*, volume 32. ACM, 2002.

[12] P. Flajolet and G. N. Martin. Probabilistic counting algorithms for data base applications. *Journal of computer and system sciences*, 31(2):182–209, 1985.

[13] P. B. Gibbons and Y. Matias. Synopsis data structures for massive data sets.

[14] A. C. Gilbert, Y. Kotidis, S. Muthukrishnan, and M. Strauss. Surfing wavelets on streams: One-pass summaries for approximate aggregate queries. In *VLDB*, volume 1, pages 79–88, 2001.

[15] T. Graepel, J. Q. Candela, T. Borchert, and R. Herbrich. Web-scale bayesian click-through rate prediction for sponsored search advertising in microsoft's bing search engine. In *Proceedings of the 27th International Conference on Machine Learning (ICML-10)*, pages 13–20, 2010.

[16] D. Hillard, S. Schroedl, E. Manavoglu, H. Raghavan, and C. Leggetter. Improving ad relevance in sponsored search. In *Proceedings of the third ACM international conference on Web search and data mining*, pages 361–370. ACM, 2010.

[17] O. Kennedy, C. Koch, and A. Demers. Dynamic approaches to in-network aggregation. In *Data Engineering, 2009. ICDE'09. IEEE 25th International Conference on*, pages 1331–1334. IEEE, 2009.

[18] G. Krempl, I. Žliobaite, D. Brzeziński, E. Hüllermeier, M. Last, V. Lemaire, T. Noack, A. Shaker, S. Sievi, M. Spiliopoulou, et al. Open challenges for data stream mining research. *ACM SIGKDD Explorations Newsletter*, 2014.

[19] G. S. Manku and R. Motwani. Approximate frequency counts over data streams. In *Proceedings of the 28th international conference on Very Large Data Bases*, pages 346–357. VLDB Endowment, 2002.

[20] S. Matusevych, A. Smola, and A. Ahmed. Hokusai-sketching streams in real time. In *UAI*, 2012.

[21] H. B. McMahan, G. Holt, D. Sculley, M. Young, D. Ebner, J. Grady, L. Nie, T. Phillips, E. Davydov, D. Golovin, et al. Ad click prediction: a view from the trenches. In *KDD*, 2013.

[22] S. Muthukrishnan. *Data streams: Algorithms and applications*. Now Publishers Inc, 2005.

[23] M. Richardson, E. Dominowska, and R. Ragno. Predicting clicks: estimating the click-through rate for new ads. In *Proceedings of the 16th international conference on World Wide Web*, pages 521–530. ACM, 2007.

[24] S. V. Vaseghi. *Advanced digital signal processing and noise reduction*. John Wiley & Sons, 2008.

[25] Q. Yang and X. Wu. 10 challenging problems in data mining research. *International Journal of Information Technology & Decision Making*, 2006.

APPENDIX

A. RECONSTRUCTION EXPERIMENTS

In response to reviewer's feedback we will demonstrate the ability of Ada-CMS to preserve a signal in this section and use of Ada-CMS sketches for the reconstruction of time series. We use the same sketches used to summarize the whole AOL and Criteo dataset from the Experiments in Section 6. For illustration, we summarize the whole dataset using Ada-CMS with $w = 2^{21}$ and then reconstruct the counts of top 3 heavy hitter over time. We plot the actual counts and the estimated counts for both the dataset in Figure 8. We can clearly see that the two plots, despite burstiness, are almost indistinguishable from each other, showing near perfect reconstruction.

B. EVALUATION OF RANGE QUERIES

In this section we evaluate the four sketching schemes for estimating the counts over a range of given time interval $c_i^{[t_1,t_2]}$ as described in Section 5. We use the dyadic interval idea to decompose any given range $[t_1, t_2]$ into at most $2 \log T$ point queries. We need to store $\log T$ different sketches for answering range queries. We used the same values of parameters as before. From the previous section, we knew that small w is not sufficient for Hokusai to keep track of all time intervals. Therefore we only varied w in $\{2^{13}, 2^{14}, ..., 2^{20}\}$. Given a fixed value of w, we ensured that the total memory used by any of the four algorithms is same to ensure fair comparisons.

We again chose the same top 1000 frequent terms, used for point query experiments, as items of interest. This time we are interested in keeping track of the counts of terms per day

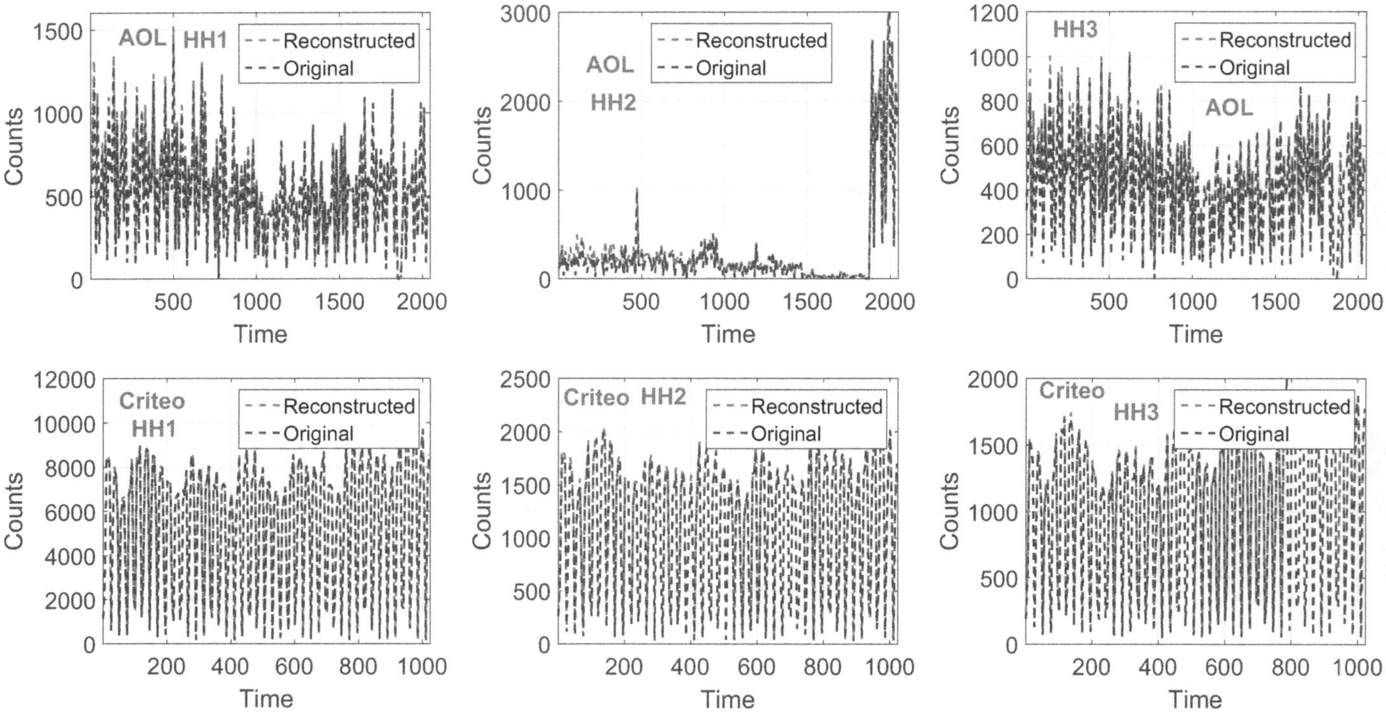

Figure 8: Actual and reconstructed counts of top 3 heavy hitters (HH) over time for both the datasets. The plots almost overlap.

for over 80 days with AOL and around 40 days with Criteo. We again set the time granularity of one hour, thus every t denotes an hour. So for estimating the counts of a given day, we are estimating intervals of size 24. We computed the gold standard error and plot the mean absolute error of the estimates returned by the four sketching schemes of interest. The mean was taken over the chosen 1000 terms of interest. The result is summarized in Figure 9. The errors with Hokusai are significantly higher than the errors of all other techniques, making it difficult to visualize the difference between CMS and Ada-CMS in the same graph; therefore we show the results of CMS and Ada-CMS in a separate Figure 10 to make the difference more visible.

Observations: We can clearly see that the errors with Hokusai are significantly worse with range queries compared to CMS and Ada-CMS on both the datasets. This is expected because range query estimate is sum of many point query estimates. Therefore, the errors add up. We know from the previous section that Hokusai is worse for point queries and this difference blows up for range queries. Ada-CMS again, as expected, shows the adaptive behavior, which clearly supports our claims. Also, we have the additional option to choose different $f(t)$ for different dyadic ranges but to keep things simple we only use the same values of $f(t)$, as used for point queries, in this experiment for all the sketches.

We can see that there are small fluctuations with CMS and Ada-CMS for range queries. It should be noted that the upper bounds shown in Theorem 3 comes from the fact that every interval can be decomposed into at most $2 \log T$ dyadic intervals. The term $2 \log T$ is the worst case and in many cases it is less, depending on the interval itself. For example, the intervals of size 10 $[9, 18]$ can be decomposed into just two dyadic ranges $[9, 16]$ and $[17, 18]$, whereas $[10, 19]$ has decomposition into 4 intervals $[10, 10]$, $[11, 12]$, $[13, 16]$, $[17, 18]$ and $[19, 19]$. The error estimates of each interval sum up. This explains the fluctuation in the Figure 10 for estimating range queries with CMS and Ada-CMS, which is universal for the dyadic interval trick. The global trend in errors is clearly adaptive.

C. MEMORY VS ACCURACY TRADEOFF FOR LC AND ADA-LC

In this section, we compare the accuracy of LC and its adaptive variants Ada-LC (lin) and Ada-LC (exp), over time, with a given fixed amount of memory. The experimental setup is same as described in Section 6.1, except that we replace the CMS variants of sketching algorithms with their LC counterparts. We also used the same $f(t)$ for linear and exponential variants. It should be noted that LC and Ada-LC keep a map for $(item, time)$ pairs. If the pair is present, then the estimation is very accurate for this $(item, time)$ pair, otherwise LC returns zero. LC and its variant always underestimate the counts, whereas with CMS and its variants we always overestimate. As noted in Section 6.2, LC and its variants are very slow. We use a more practical implementation in which we remove smallest 10% of elements from the map to make it run in reasonable time.

After summarizing the dataset with the LC and Ada-LC sketches, we compare the estimates of counts of 1000 frequent items over time with the corresponding true gold standard counts. The plot of the mean absolute error over time for LC and Ada-LC schemes, is shown in Figure 11. To show the variation with respect to memory we show plots for three different values of $w = \{2^{16},\ 2^{17},\ 2^{18}\}$.

Observations: We can see that Ada-LC, on an average, gets more hits for recent time interval compared to LC. For very old time instances, LC is better on an average.

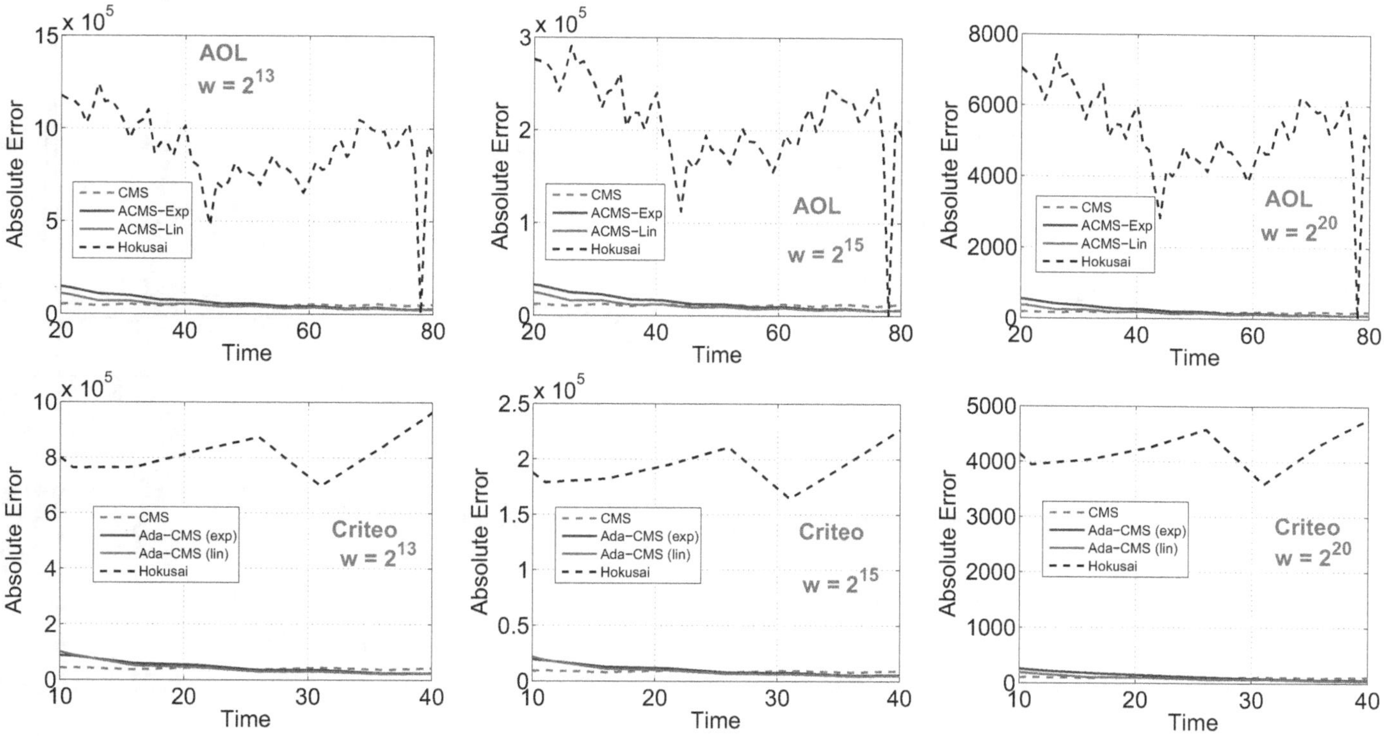

Figure 9: Average absolute error for estimating range queries with time for all the four competing schemes. Hokusai has significantly worse errors. See Figure 10 for a better visualization of comparisons between the errors of CMS and Ada-CMS.

This clearly demonstrates the adaptive nature of the Ada-LC compared to LC. The trends are consistent. Again Ada-LC (exp) is more aggressive than Ada-LC (lin) as expected. Thus, the adaptive variants, which are strict generalization of classical LC algorithm, achieve the desired time adaptability, which is not surprising given our theoretical results.

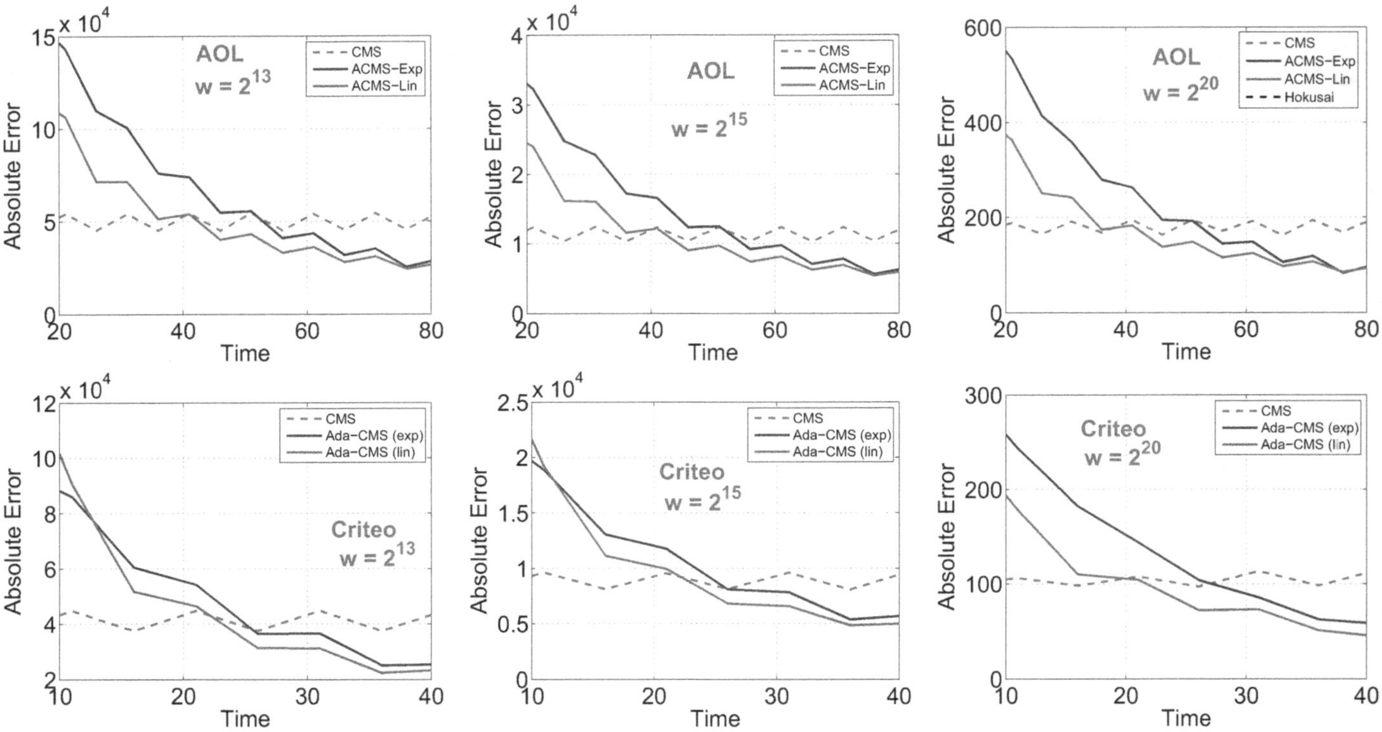

Figure 10: Average absolute error over time, for estimating range queries, with CMS and Ada-CMS. The global trend clearly shows the adaptive nature of Ada-CMS with time

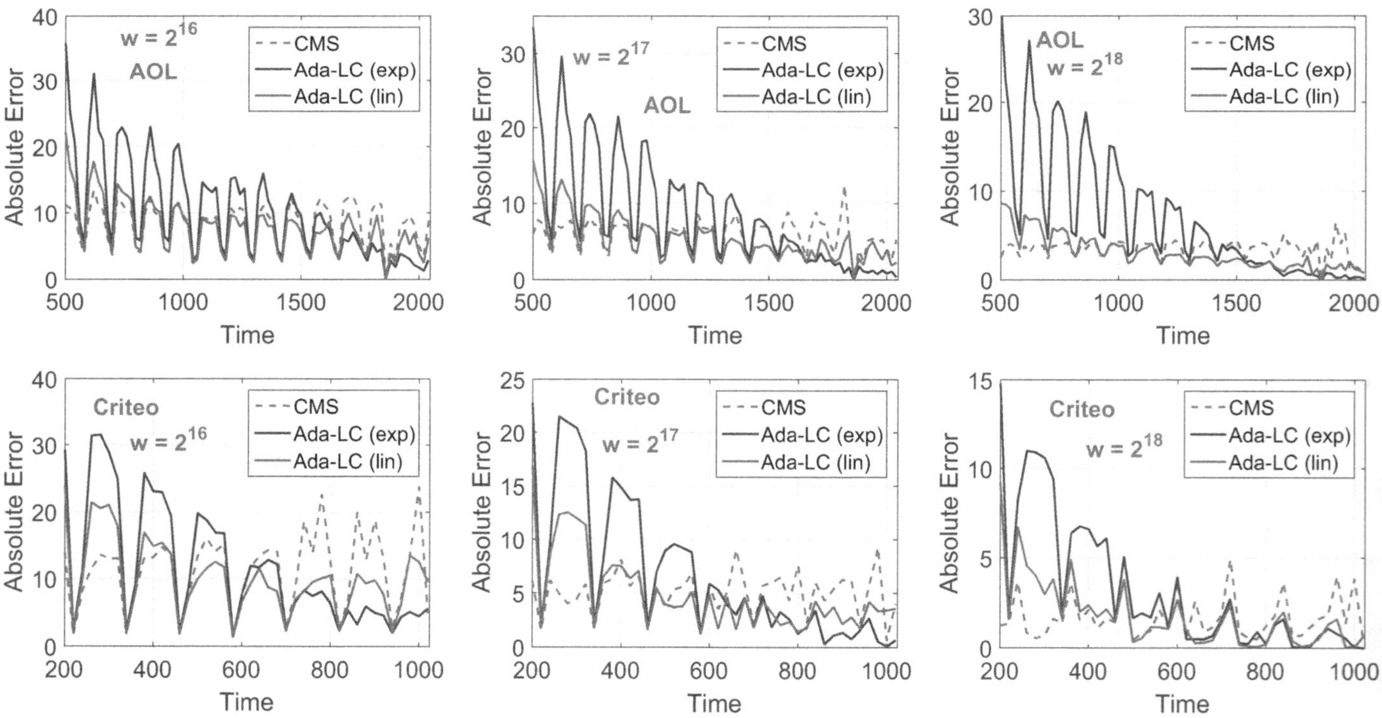

Figure 11: Average absolute error for estimating range queries with time for LC and its adaptive variants. On an average Ada-LC clearly shows adaptive behaviors.

Streaming Algorithms for Robust Distinct Elements

Di Chen*
Hong Kong Univ. of Science and Technology
Clear Water Bay, Kowloon
Hong Kong
dchenad@cse.ust.hk

Qin Zhang†
Indiana University Bloomington
Bloomington, IN 47401
United States
qzhangcs@indiana.edu

ABSTRACT

We study the problem of estimating distinct elements in the data stream model, which has a central role in traffic monitoring, query optimization, data mining and data integration. Different from all previous work, we study the problem in the *noisy* data setting, where two different looking items in the stream may reference the same entity (determined by a distance function and a threshold value), and the goal is to estimate the number of distinct *entities* in the stream. In this paper, we formalize the problem of robust distinct elements, and develop space and time-efficient streaming algorithms for datasets in the Euclidean space, using a novel technique we call bucket sampling. We also extend our algorithmic framework to other metric spaces by establishing a connection between bucket sampling and the theory of locality sensitive hashing. Moreover, we formally prove that our algorithms are still effective under small distinct elements ambiguity. Our experiments demonstrate the practicality of our algorithms.

1. INTRODUCTION

Estimating the number of distinct elements is a fundamental problem in the streaming model [18, 2], where a single machine is observing a sequence of data items of unknown size arriving over time, and it would like to compute the number of distinct elements of this data sequence by a single left-to-right scan using a memory space that is much smaller than the size of the input sequence. The distinct elements problem was first studied by Flajolet and Martin [18] in 1985, and has attracted a significant attention in the past three decades, due to its central importance in traffic monitoring, query optimization, data mining and integration. In this paper we try to attack a more difficult question:

> *What if the dataset is noisy? More precisely, if two different looking data items may reference to the same entity, can we effectively and efficiently estimate the number of distinct entities in the streaming model?*

Here we define an entity in a broad sense: it can be an atomic real-world entity; it can also be a topic (e.g., images can be partitioned into cats, dogs, cars, etc.). In general, given a pairwise distance function between items, and a threshold value α, we say two items reference to the same entity if their distance is no more than α; we call these two items *near-duplicates.* One can view the distinct elements problem in the noise-free case as setting $\alpha = 0$.

Motivation. Our problem is motivated by the fact that real-world datasets are inherently noisy. A few examples:

- Images of the same content uploaded to Flickr may look differently due to different formats, compressions, rescales, photoshop edits, etc.
- Twitter messages are re-distributed with small edits.
- Queries of the same meaning are sent to Google under different keywords combinations.

In this paper we study the distinct elements problem on such noisy datasets in the streaming model. The streaming model is relevant since (1) items (images, messages, query keywords) typically come in a streaming fashion; and (2) a single scan of the dataset using a small working memory is much faster than randomly accessing data in the disk.

We note that one cannot run the streaming algorithms designed for noise-free datasets in the noisy setting since an algorithm for noise-free datasets will treat 100 near-duplicated items as 100 different elements, and then the resulting number of distinct elements will be 100 instead of 1.

The universal needs of handling noisy datasets have fueled an extensive research activity in the past few decades. The line of research that is closest to ours is called data *de-duplication* (or *entity resolution*, *record linkage*, etc.). We refer readers to [25, 14, 21, 12] for introductions to this subject. Unfortunately, in the streaming model it is impossible to perform entity de-duplication thoroughly, simply because we cannot store the whole dataset, even spending only 1 bit for each item in the stream.

One may wonder if we can adapt the previous techniques for noise-free streaming data. Indeed, if we can design a *magic* hash function h which can hash items referencing to the same entity (different entities) to the same element (different elements), then we can simply adopt any existing algorithm for distinct elements in the hashing space. However,

*Work supported in part by HKRGC grants GRF-621413 and GRF-16211614. Part of the work was done when the author was visiting Indiana University Bloomington.
†Work supported in part by NSF CCF-1525024, and IU's Office of the Vice Provost for Research through the FRSP.

SIGMOD'16, June 26-July 01, 2016, San Francisco, CA, USA

ISBN 978-1-4503-3531-7/16/06...$15.00
DOI: http://dx.doi.org/10.1145/2882903.2882915

such a magic hash function is unlikely to be constructed and stored in a small space (say, logarithmic in terms of the stream length), simply due to the fact that the number of such mappings is exponentially large.

One who is familiar with locality sensitive hashing (LSH) [22, 3] may think if LSH functions can be used as magic hash functions. We notice that LSHs can only guarantee that similar items are mapped into the same bucket with a certain probability, while not-so-similar items may also be mapped into the same bucket with a certain probability. One can use the "AND-OR" trick[1] to sharpen these probabilities, but the "OR" part cannot be implemented in the streaming setting, because unlike "AND" it does not create a well-defined hash value for each point. However, the theory of LSH is still very useful to our problem, and we will discuss it in detail in Section 4.

Similarly, all linear sketching algorithms in the streaming literature cannot be used in the noisy data setting, simply because items referencing to the same entity may be mapped into different coordinates of the sketching vectors.

One who is familiar with clustering may wonder if this problem has any connection with the *streaming k-center* problem (e.g., [20]), in which we want to cluster items to k groups so that the maximum group diameter is minimized. Indeed, an algorithm called `Baseline` that we used for comparison in the experiments can be thought as a streaming algorithm for k-center. The issue of formulating our robust distinct elements problem as a clustering problem is that in our case, the number of clusters, that is the "k", can potentially be linear in the number of distinct entities, and thus the space usage will be at least linear in the worst case.

Problem Definition. Now we formally define our robust distinct elements (F_0) problem.

DEFINITION 1 (ROBUST F_0). *Let $d(\cdot,\cdot)$ be a distance function, and α be a threshold value. The robust F_0 of a dataset S, denoted by $F_0(S,\alpha)$ in this paper, is the size of the* minimum-cardinality *partition $\mathcal{G} = \{G_1, G_2, \ldots, G_n\}$ of S so that for each pair of points p, q that belong to the same group G_i, $d(p,q) \le \alpha$; in other words, the diameter of each group G_i is at most α.*

In the analysis part of this paper we assume that α is given, which can often be obtained by domain knowledge or deduced from a small sample of labelled items. In the experiments (Section 5) we will also give a method to handle the case where we do not know the value of α.

When clear from the context, we omit α and/or S and simply write F_0 , $F_0(S)$, or $F_0(\alpha)$. Note that the definition of robust F_0 is *monotonic*, that is, $F_0(A) \le F_0(B)$ if $A \subseteq B$ and $F_0(\alpha_0) \le F_0(\alpha_1)$ if $\alpha_0 \ge \alpha_1$.

We next introduce a notion of *well-shaped* datasets.

DEFINITION 2 ((α,β)-SPARSITY AND SEPARATION RATIO). *Let $S \subseteq U$ be a dataset, $d : U \times U \to [0,\infty)$ be a distance function, and α be a threshold value. We say S is (α,β)-*sparse *for some $\beta \ge \alpha$ if for any pair of items $u, v \in S$, we have*

$$\text{either} \quad d(u,v) \le \alpha, \quad \text{or} \quad d(u,v) > \beta. \qquad (1)$$

We call $\max_\beta \beta/\alpha$ be the separation ratio *of S, where β runs over all values that (1) holds.*

[1]http://en.wikipedia.org/wiki/Locality-sensitive_hashing

Intuitively, if S is (α,β)-sparse, then all pairs of items that belong to the same group have distance at most α (consistent with the definition of robust F_0), and all pairs that belong to different groups have distance at least β.

DEFINITION 3 (WELL-SHAPED DATASET). *If S is (α,β)-sparse with $\beta/\alpha \ge 2$, then items in S can naturally be partitioned into a set of groups such that the* intra-*group distance (diameter) is at most α, and the* inter-*group distance is more than β. We call such datasets* well-shaped.

To see the natural partition, note that for any three points u, v, w, if $d(u,v) \le \alpha$ and $d(v,w) \le \alpha$, by the triangle inequality we must have $d(u,w) \le 2\alpha \le \beta$. Now since S is (α,β)-sparse, we must have $d(u,w) \le \alpha$ (by (1)).

It is also easy to see that if S is well-shaped, then the natural partition achieves the minimum, and it can be computed easily offline: we just group items within distance α in a greedy fashion. However, for a general dataset, computing $F_0(S)$ as an optimization problem is difficult even in the RAM model, not mentioning the more restrictive streaming model. To handle general datasets we introduce a notion we call *F_0-ambiguity*, which characterizes how far a dataset is from well-shapedness. This parameter will be used in our F_0 approximation guarantees for general datasets (Section 3.1).

DEFINITION 4 (F_0-AMBIGUITY). *Let $S \subseteq U$ be a dataset, and let $d : U \times U \to [0,\infty)$ be a distance function. The F_0-ambiguity of S is the minimum δ ($\delta \in [0,1)$) such that there exists $T \subseteq S$ satisfying the followings:*

- *$S \backslash T$ is well-shaped.*
- *$F_0(S \backslash T) \ge (1-\delta) \cdot F_0(S)$,*

We use $\delta(S)$ (or simply δ when there is no confusion) to denote the F_0-ambiguity of S.

Note that if $\delta = 0$, then S is well-shaped. Conversely, if S is not well-shaped, then $\delta > 0$. Also note that T is just used for defining how *ambiguous* the dataset is; we are not dropping items in T – the final robust F_0 still takes items in T into account.

We comment in advance that our algorithms are designed to handle datasets with *small* F_0-ambiguities. We believe that it is hard to handle datasets with high F_0-ambiguities in the streaming model since a comprehensive entity-resolution (in particular, identifying two point clouds connected by a bridge point as a single group) cannot be done using a small memory space. For applications mentioned in the motivation, we expect that the F_0-ambiguities of the datasets are small given carefully chosen distance functions and threshold α's. We will show how to automatically determine good α's in the Euclidean metric in Section 5.

Our Contributions. We have made the following contributions in this paper.

1. We have given a first study of the robust F_0 problem in the streaming model, and have obtained *provable* theoretical guarantees. Our space upper bounds for well-shaped datasets in $O(1)$-dimensional Euclidean spaces even match (up to a logarithmic factor) the lower bound in the noise-free setting. This upper bound is obtained using a new technique called *bucket sampling* which may be of independent interest. These are presented in Section 2.1.

2. We have *quantitatively* shown that our algorithms also work well for general datasets in the Euclidean space with small F_0-ambiguity. This is presented in Section 3.

3. We have proposed an algorithm framework for the robust F_0 problem in a general metric space, and established a connection between our bucket sampling framework and the theory of locality sensitive hashing (LSH). More precisely, if a metric space admits an efficient LSH scheme satisfying an additional natural property, then we immediately obtain a streaming algorithm for estimating robust F_0 in that metric space. This is presented in Section 4.

4. We have implemented our algorithms for the Euclidean metric and run them on image data. The experiments have demonstrated the effectiveness of our robust F_0 algorithms in accuracy, space usage and running time. This is presented in Section 5.

Related Work. The distinct elements problem in the noise-free setting has been studied extensively in the streaming literature, due to its numerous applications in network traffic monitoring [15], query planning [27], data mining in graph databases [26], data integration [8] and data warehousing [1]. The first streaming algorithm to $(1+\epsilon)$-approximate distinct elements was proposed by Flajolet and Martin [18], followed by a long line of research in the past several decades ([4, 5, 13, 17, 19], etc.), culminated in an optimal algorithm with $O(1/\epsilon^2 + \log u)$ bits (u is the item universe size) by Kane et al. [24]. However, all these algorithms cannot be used to handle noisy datasets simply because they will consider each item in a group as a different element. As a toy example, if the dataset contains 10000 near-duplicates belonging to the same group, these algorithms will give values close to 10000 which is far away from the true robust F_0 which is 1.

As far as we have concerned, the distinct element problem has not been studied in the noisy streaming data setting. Very recently, statistical estimations for noisy well-shaped datasets have been studied in the distributed setting for several basic problems, including distinct elements, ℓ_0-sampling, frequency moments, heavy hitters and empirical entropy [30], in the general metric space, but the algorithms in [30] cannot be applied to the streaming setting since all of them need a "second look" at the dataset. On the other hand, our streaming algorithms can be trivially translated to algorithms for distributed data: k parties process their local datasets using the streaming algorithm in turn following a fixed order, and then send their memory configurations to their successors; the last party outputs the answer. In particular, by such a translation we can obtain a distributed robust F_0 algorithm with communication cost of $O(k/\epsilon^2)$ words for datasets in the Euclidean space, improving the generic algorithm in [30] by a factor of $1/\epsilon \cdot \text{poly} \log m$ ($m = |S|$ is the length of the stream).

Preliminaries. We use $[t]$ to denote $\{1, \ldots, t\}$. Let $U = [u]$ be the item universe. We say n' is a $(1+\epsilon)$-approximation of n if $n' \in [(1-\epsilon)n, (1+\epsilon)n]$. All log's are base of 2.

We will need a few mathematical tools including Markov Inequality, Chebyshev's inequality and Chernoff bound. Due to the space constraints we leave them in Appendix C

We summarize the main notations in this paper in Table 1.

Symbol	Description
m	length of the stream
n	number of groups, that is, robust F_0
U	item universe
S	set of items in the stream, $\|S\| = m$
$\mathcal{G}/G$	set of groups / a group in $\mathcal{G}$
C	a grid cell in the Euclidean space; also denote the set of points in the cell
$\mathcal{C}$	set of non-empty grid cells;
$\mathcal{G}_C$	set of groups intersecting cell C
$w(G)$	number of non-empty cells group G intersects
δ	F_0-ambiguity
ϵ	multiplicative approximation ratio
α	threshold of group diameter
cell(p)	cell where point p is located

Table 1: List of notations

2. WELL-SHAPED DATASETS IN THE EUCLIDEAN SPACE

In this section we consider the case where data items are points in the Euclidean space, which is a very useful metric since many objects, such as documents and images, can be mapped into vectors/points in the Euclidean spaces.

We will focus on well-shaped datasets, that is, those with separation ratio $\beta/\alpha > 2$. The general datasets will be studied in Section 3. W.l.o.g., we assume that $\alpha = 1$, since we can always rescale all distances between points in $S \subset \mathbb{R}^2$ by a factor of α.

2.1 Constant Dimensional Euclidean Spaces

In this section we consider points in constant dimensional Euclidean spaces. We present our algorithms in the 2D case, but they can be literally carried over to any $O(1)$-dimensional spaces.

For a well-shaped dataset $S = \{p_1, \ldots, p_m\}$, let $\mathcal{G} = \{G_1, \ldots, G_{F_0}\}$ be the natural minimum-cardinality group partition of S (we of course do not know F_0 which is the objective that we are going to compute). We post a random grid $\mathbb{G}$ of side length $1/\sqrt{2}$ on $\mathbb{R}^2$, and call a grid cell simply a *cell*. Note that such a random grid can be specified by a pair of two offsets $(\Delta_x, \Delta_y) \in [0, 1/\sqrt{2})^2$ from the origin, and thus can be stored in $O(1)$ words. We assume all points have x, y-coordinates in the range $[-\text{MAX}, \text{MAX}]$, and thus we only need to consider the portion of the grid $\mathbb{G}$ in this range, and consequently $|\mathbb{G}|$ is finite and can be computed in advance. For simplicity, we assume that points do not fall onto the boundary of cells, because this probability will be zero if the grid is random.

Let $\mathcal{C}$ be the collection of non-empty cells, that is, $\mathcal{C} = \{C \in \mathbb{G} \mid C \cap S \neq \emptyset\}$. See Figure 1 for an illustration. In this section $d(p,q)$ denotes the Euclidean distance between points p, q. For a cell C and a point p, let $d(p, C) = \min_{q \in C} d(p,q)$; define $d(p, C) = 0$ if $p \in C$. For a $p \in S$, let cell(p) be the cell where p is located.

2.1.1 The Algorithm

The Idea. We start by giving some general ideas of our algorithm. For each cell C in the grid $\mathbb{G}$, let $\mathcal{G}_C$ be the set of groups intersecting C, that is,

$$\mathcal{G}_C = \{G \in \mathcal{G} \mid G \cap C \neq \emptyset\}.$$

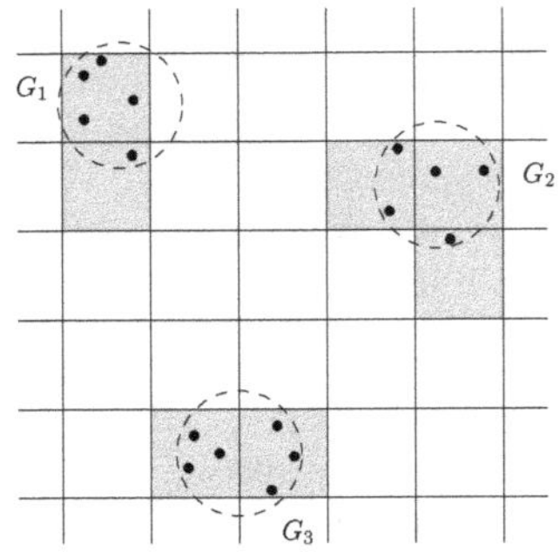

Figure 1: A well-shaped point set. Non-empty cells $\mathcal{C}$ are in gray.

Note that if the dataset is $(1, \beta)$-sparse with $\beta \geq 2$ and $\mathbb{G}$ has side length $1/\sqrt{2}$, then $|\mathcal{G}_C| = 1$ for each non-empty cell $C \in \mathcal{C}$. Let G_C denote this unique intersecting group. Taking Figure 1 for example, the G_C for the left top two cells is G_1; the G_C for the bottom two cells is G_3; and the G_C for the right three cells is G_2.

We define the weight of a group G to be the number of non-empty cells $C \in \mathcal{C}$ it intersects, that is,

$$w(G) = |\{C \in \mathcal{C} \mid C \cap G \neq \emptyset\}|,$$

and define the weight of a non-empty cell $C \in \mathcal{C}$ to be

$$w(C) = \frac{1}{w(G_C)}. \tag{2}$$

For example, in Figure 1, the weights of the left top two cells 1/2; the weights of the bottom two cells are 1/2; and the weights of the right three cells is 1/3. It is easy to see that the sum of weights of all cells is F_0:

$$\begin{aligned} \sum_{C \in \mathcal{C}} w(C) &= \sum_{G \in \mathcal{G}} \sum_{C : C \cap G \neq \emptyset} w(C) \\ &= \sum_{G \in \mathcal{G}} \left(w(G_C) \cdot \frac{1}{w(G_C)} \right) \\ &= F_0. \end{aligned} \tag{3}$$

To obtain a small-space $(1+\epsilon)$-approximation of F_0, a natural idea is to sample a sufficiently large subset of cells $\mathcal{C}' \subseteq \mathcal{C}$, compute their weights, and then add up all weights and rescale to obtain an approximation of F_0.[2] However, at first glance it seems difficult to implement this idea in the streaming model, for the following reasons.

1. The weight of each cell C is determined by how many cells the group G_C intersects, and thus we need to know the information about C's non-empty neighboring cells which intersect group G_C; call them *important* neighboring cells. This suggests us to fix the sampled cells before the stream of points come, since otherwise we risk discarding the information of important neighboring cells when sampling a cell at a later stage of the one-pass scan. Note that we cannot store all the cells due to the small working space constraint.
2. On the other hand, most grid cells will be empty at the end of the streaming process. If we sample cells at the very beginning, then most sampled cells will be empty at the end thus are not in the set $\mathcal{C}$, and consequently cannot be used to approximate F_0. In other words, to get enough non-empty sampled cells at the end we need to sample a much larger number of cells, and thus need a much larger working space.

[2]We comment that up to this point, at the high level, our idea is similar to Algorithm 2 in [30] in the distributed model, but there is an important difference which is used to save the space usage by a factor of $\max_{G \in \mathcal{G}} |G|$: we operate on *cells* instead of *individual items*. Our algorithm after this point will be very different from that in [30], mainly because in the streaming model we are not allowed to scan the input for a second time.

These two observations seem to contradict each other. That is, the first suggests to sample cells at the beginning of the streaming process, while the second suggests to sample a cell until we know it is not empty (i.e., until an input point in S falls into that cell). To handle this dilemma, we propose a method we call *bucket sampling*, which we will explain in the rest of this section.

Bucket Sampling. Our key idea is to sample *collections* of cells in the grid, and only keep information about non-empty and neighboring non-empty cells for each sampled collection, which can be done at the runtime when an input point in S falls into a cell. We can use a hash function to sample collections of cells at the beginning of the streaming process, and then we do not need to explicitly maintain the IDs of each cell in a sampled collection (which cannot be done in a small space), but just use the hash function to test their "memberships" (i.e., whether they are in a sampled collection) when needed. Since we have employed a hash function to solve the dilemma, we call each collection a bucket, and this sampling process bucket sampling.

We maintain a random hash function $h : \mathbb{G} \to [R]$, where R is a carefully chosen value such that

$$\mathbf{Pr}[|\{C \in \mathcal{C} \mid h(C) = 1\}| \in [1000/\epsilon^2, 20000/\epsilon^2]] \geq 0.99.$$

Note that the cardinality of $\mathcal{C}$ will increase during the streaming process, therefore we need to update(double) the value of R once in a while (see Line 10 in Algorithm 1). Every time R doubles, we also need to update h. At the beginning we set $h(x) = 1$ for all x, and when R is updated we reset $h(x) = (ax + b \bmod \kappa \bmod R) + 1$, where κ is an arbitrary but fixed prime in $[|\mathbb{G}|, 2|\mathbb{G}|]$, and a, b are randomly chosen from $\{0, \ldots, \kappa - 1\}$ conditioned on $a \neq 0$.

We now choose the set of sampled cells to be $\mathcal{C}' = \{C \in \mathcal{C} \mid h(C) = 1\}$. Thus by our choice of R,

$$\mathbf{Pr}\left[|\mathcal{C}'| \in [1000/\epsilon^2, 20000/\epsilon^2]\right] \geq 0.99. \tag{4}$$

To maintain the value R, we can use any off-the-shelf streaming algorithm for distinct elements on *noise-free* datasets to maintain a number z which is a $(1+\epsilon)$-approximation to the number of non-empty cells $|\mathcal{C}|$, and double R when $z \geq 6000R/\epsilon^2$. Algorithm 1 shows how to maintain the value R, the hash function h, and the set of sampled cells $\mathcal{C}'$. In this paper in the theory part we use the algorithm by Kane et al. [24] to maintain z, denoted as `CountNonEmptyCells`(p), where p is a streamed-in point. While in the experiments we will use the algorithm by Bar-Yossef et al. [4] which is simpler to implement, though its theoretical performance is a bit worse. The formal analysis to show (4) will be given in Section 2.1.2.

Point Storage. During the streaming process we will store a set of center points, denoted by Γ initialized to be $\emptyset$. At

Algorithm 1 Maintain the Set of Sampled Cells $\mathcal{C}'$

1: z is a global variable which is a $(1+\epsilon)$-approximation of $|\mathcal{C}|$
2: $h : \mathbb{G} \to [R]$ is the global random hash function with R initialized to be 1.
3: κ is an arbitrary but fixed prime between $|\mathbb{G}|$ and $2|\mathbb{G}|$. a is randomly sampled from $\{1, \ldots, \kappa - 1\}$ and b is randomly sampled from $\{0, 1, \ldots, \kappa - 1\}$.
4: **procedure** MaintainSampledCells(p)
5:     **if** $h(\text{cell}(p)) = 1$ **then**
6:         $\mathcal{C}' := \mathcal{C}' \cup \{\text{cell}(p)\}$
7:     **end if**
8:     $z :=$ `CountNonEmptyCells`(p)
9:     **if** $z \geq 6000R/\epsilon^2$ **then**
10:         $R := 2R$ ▷ Double the range of h
11:         set $h(x) = (ax + b \bmod p \bmod R) + 1$
12:         $\mathcal{C}' := \{C \in \mathcal{C}' \mid h(C) = 1\}$ and discard stored point centers (Algorithm 2) in cells that are no longer in $\mathcal{C}'$ ▷ Re-sample each cell in $\mathcal{C}$ with probability 1/2
13:     **end if**
14: **end procedure**

Algorithm 2 Store Point Centers for Sampled Cells $\mathcal{C}'$

1: **procedure** StoreCenter(p)
2:     **if** $\exists C \in \mathbb{G}$ *s.t.* $h(C) = 1 \wedge d(p, C) \leq 1$ **then**
3:         **if** ($\nexists q \in \Gamma$ *s.t.* $\text{cell}(p) = \text{cell}(q)$) **then**
4:             insert p to Γ ▷ Keep a new center
5:         **end if**
6:     **end if**
7: **end procedure**

the end of the streaming process we will use Γ to recover the weight of each sampled cell. The algorithm for processing and storing each input point is described in Algorithm 2. In words, it maintains all streamed-in points p that are in or within distance 1 to a cell in $\{C \in \mathbb{G} \mid h(C) = 1\}$, given that no other point in $\text{cell}(p)$ has already been stored in Γ.

We illustrate the "sample and store" procedure in Figure 2. Cells with red heavy strokes are sampled cells in $\mathcal{C}$; points in red are stored point centers.

We comment that in Algorithm 2 it could be the case that a stored point p is within a distance of 1 to a sampled cell $C \in \mathbb{G}$ that is not in $\mathcal{C}$; in other words, C will be empty at the end of the streaming process and thus will be ignored. In such a case p may not be used to compute the weights for any sampled $C \in \mathcal{C}'$ at the end (in Algorithm 3), and is thus *wasted*. However, in the analysis we will show that such an overhead will not affect the asymptotic storage cost.

Post-processing and the Full Algorithm. At the end of the streaming process, we use Algorithm 3 to compute the weight for each sampled cell $C \in \mathcal{C}'$. We simply find all groups that intersect C using the stored point centers, and then for each such group compute its weight. The weight of the sampled cell will be the sum of the inverse of these group weights. Note that in the setting considered in this section each cell only intersects at most one group, and thus the *while* iteration at Line 7 will only run once. In Section 2.2 when we consider higher dimensional Euclidean spaces, a cell may intersect multiple groups.

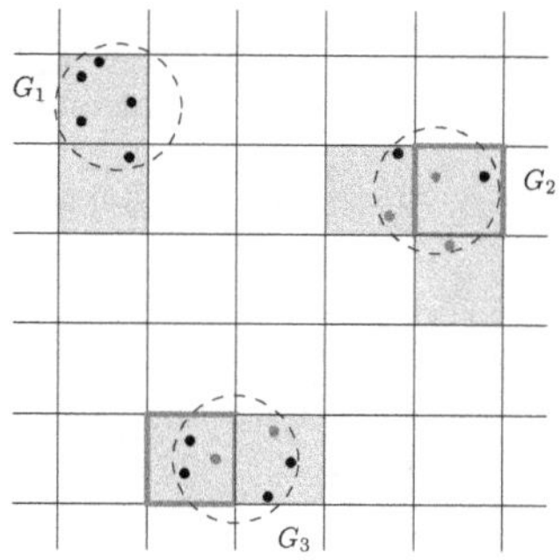

Figure 2: Cells with red stroke are sampled cells in $\mathcal{C}$; points in red are stored point centers.

Algorithm 3 Computing Weights of Sampled Cells

1: Γ is the set of points stored by calling StoreCenter( )
2: **procedure** ComputeWeight( )
3:     $W := 0$
4:     $\Gamma' = \Gamma$ ▷ Backup of Γ
5:     **for** each $C \in \mathcal{C}'$ **do**
6:         $w := 0$
7:         **while** $\exists p \in \Gamma$ *s.t.* $d(p, C) \leq 1$ **do**
8:             pick any such $p \in \Gamma$ ▷ Consider a group in G intersecting C
9:             $K := \{\text{cell}(p)\}$
10:             **for** each $q \in \Gamma$ *s.t.* $d(q, p) \leq 1$ **do**
11:                 **if** $\text{cell}(q) \notin K$ **then**
12:                     $K := K \cup \{\text{cell}(q)\}$ ▷ K is the set of cells the considered group G intersects
13:                 **end if**
14:                 delete q from Γ
15:             **end for**
16:             $w := w + \frac{1}{|K|}$ ▷ Compute the weight of cell C
17:             delete p from Γ
18:         **end while**
19:         $W := W + w$ ▷ Compute total weights of sampled cells
20:         $\Gamma := \Gamma'$ ▷ Restore Γ
21:     **end for**
22:     **return** W
23: **end procedure**

We describe the final one-pass streaming algorithm in Algorithm 4.

2.1.2 The Analysis

We now show the correctness of our algorithm and analyze its efficiency. We need the following lemma in [24] to maintain the value z at Line 8 in Algorithm 1.

Lemma 1 ([24]). *There is an algorithm that computes a $(1+\epsilon)$-approximation of $|\mathcal{C}|$ with probability 0.99, using $O(1/\epsilon^2 + \log u)$ bits space and $O(1)$ processing time per item.*

Correctness. Let $F_0 = F_0(S, 1)$ be the number of groups in S, which is the value we are going to compute. First, notice that

$$1 \leq |\mathcal{C}|/F_0 \leq 9. \tag{5}$$

The left hand side inequality is due to the fact that each non-empty cell intersects at most one group in our setting.

Algorithm 4 Computing Robust F_0 in $\mathbb{R}^2$

```
C' is the set of sampled cells, maintained by MaintainSampledCells( )
z is a global variable which is a (1+ε)-approximation of |C|
Streamed input points p_1, ..., p_m
while a new input point p_i comes do
    MaintainSampledCells(p_i)
    StoreCenter(p_i)
end while
w := ComputeWeight( )                       ▷ Post-processing
Output z/|C'| · w                 ▷ Rescale to compute robust F_0(S)
```

The right hand side inequality holds since the side length of the grid is $1/\sqrt{2}$, while the diameter of each group is at most 1, as a consequence each group intersects at most 9 grid cells.

Second, we show that Inequality (4) holds. Recall that at Line 9, 10 in Algorithm 1, R is maintained such that

$$\frac{3000R}{\epsilon^2} \le z \le \frac{6000R}{\epsilon^2},$$

where z is a $(1+\epsilon)$-approximation of $|\mathcal{C}|$. Therefore

$$\frac{|\mathcal{C}|}{R} \in \left[\frac{2000}{\epsilon^2}, \frac{12000}{\epsilon^2}\right]. \tag{6}$$

Write $\mathcal{C}$ as $\{C_1, \ldots, C_{|\mathcal{C}|}\}$. For each $C_i \in \mathcal{C}$, define $Y_i = 1$ if $h(C_i) = 1$, and $Y_i = 0$ otherwise. Let $Y = \sum_{i \in [|\mathcal{C}|]} Y_i$, thus $Y = |\mathcal{C}'|$. We have $\mathbf{E}[Y] = \frac{|\mathcal{C}|}{R}$. By a Chernoff bound,

$$\begin{aligned}\mathbf{Pr}\left[|\mathcal{C}'| \in \left[\frac{|\mathcal{C}|}{2R}, \frac{3\,|\mathcal{C}|}{2R}\right]\right] &= \mathbf{Pr}\left[|Y - \mathbf{E}[Y]| \le \frac{\mathbf{E}[Y]}{2}\right] \\ &\ge 1 - 2e^{-\frac{|\mathcal{C}|}{12R}} \ge 1 - 2e^{-\frac{2000}{12\epsilon^2}} \\ &\ge 0.99.\end{aligned}$$

Consequently,

$$\begin{aligned}\mathbf{Pr}\left[|\mathcal{C}'| \in \left[\frac{1000}{\epsilon^2}, \frac{20000}{\epsilon^2}\right]\right] &\overset{\text{by (6)}}{\ge} \mathbf{Pr}\left[|\mathcal{C}'| \in \left[\frac{|\mathcal{C}|}{2R}, \frac{3\,|\mathcal{C}|}{2R}\right]\right] \\ &\ge 0.99,\end{aligned}$$

proving Inequality (4).

Now let $t = |\mathcal{C}'|$ be the number of sampled cells. Define X_i ($i \in [t]$) be the random variable representing the weight of the i-th sampled cell $C_i \in \mathcal{C}'$, and let $X = \frac{1}{t}\sum_{i \in [t]} X_i$. Since each cell in $\mathcal{C}'$ is sampled from the set of non-empty cells $\mathcal{C}$ independently uniformly at random, we have

$$\mathbf{E}[X_i] = \frac{F_0}{|\mathcal{C}|} \quad \text{for each } i \in [t],$$

$$\text{and} \qquad \mathbf{E}[X] = \mathbf{E}\left[\frac{1}{t}\sum_{i \in [t]} X_i\right] = \frac{F_0}{|\mathcal{C}|}. \tag{7}$$

We next compute their variances. For each $i \in [t]$.

$$\begin{aligned}\mathbf{Var}[X_i] &= \mathbf{E}[X_i^2] - \mathbf{E}^2[X_i] \le \mathbf{E}[X_i^2] \\ &= \cdot \frac{1}{|\mathcal{C}|}\sum_{C \in \mathcal{C}} (w(C))^2 \\ &\le \frac{1}{|\mathcal{C}|} \cdot F_0 \overset{\text{by (7)}}{=} \mathbf{E}[X],\end{aligned}$$

where the last inequality is by the fact that $w(C) \le 1$ for any $C \in \mathcal{C}$, and $\sum_{C \in \mathcal{C}} w(C) = F_0$ (by (3)).

Since X_i ($i \in [t]$) are i.i.d. samples, we have

$$\mathbf{Var}(X) = \frac{1}{t^2}\sum_{i \in [t]} \mathbf{Var}(X_i) \le \frac{\mathbf{E}[X]}{t}. \tag{8}$$

Finally, by a Chebyshev's inequality, we have

$$\mathbf{Pr}[|X - \mathbf{E}[X]| > \epsilon \mathbf{E}[X]] \le \frac{\mathbf{E}[X]}{t \cdot \epsilon^2 \mathbf{E}^2[X]} \le 0.01, \tag{9}$$

where the last inequality is due to $\mathbf{E}[X] = \frac{F_0}{|\mathcal{C}|} \ge 1/9$ (by (5)) and $t = |\mathcal{C}'| \ge 1000/\epsilon^2$ (by (4)). Therefore, $X \cdot |\mathcal{C}|$ is a $(1+\epsilon)$-approximation of F_0 with probability at least 0.99. Finally, in Algorithm 4 we have $w = X \cdot t$, and z is a $(1+\epsilon)$-approximation of $|\mathcal{C}|$, thus zw/t is a $(1+\epsilon)^2 \le (1+3\epsilon)$-approximation of F_0. Note that the constant 3 in the approximation ratio can be removed by setting $\epsilon' = 3\epsilon$ and adjusting relevant constants in the analysis.

To sum up, the final success probability is $1 - 0.01 - 0.01 - 0.01 = 0.97$, where the first error term 0.01 is introduced by (4), the second error term 0.01 is introduced by (9), and the third error term 0.01 is introduced by Lemma 1.

Space and Time Complexities. Now we analyse the performance of Algorithm 4.

For the space usage, the dominating cost is the storing of point centers in Γ. Note that each cell C will have at most one point center, which is stored only if $h(C) = 1$ or $h(C') = 1$ where C' is any of C's neighboring cells. Thus each $C \in \mathcal{C}$ will have a point center stored with probability at most $9/R = O(1/(\epsilon^2\,|\mathcal{C}|))$. Therefore the total stored point centers can be bounded by $O(1/\epsilon^2)$ with probability $1 - o(1)$ by a Chernoff bound. The costs for storing other random variables in Algorithm 4 and its subroutines, the grid and the hash functions are negligible.

For each new input point p, storing p using Algorithm 2 can be done in $O(1)$ time, since we can locate the cell $h(p)$ and then search/check its neighboring sampled cells in constant time. By Lemma 1, `MaintainSampledCells`(p) can be done in $O(1)$ time. Therefore the total processing time per item is $O(1)$. At the end, Algorithm 4 calls `ComputeWeight`() to post-process the stored information and then return the answer. It is easy to see that `ComputeWeight`() can be done in $O(1/\epsilon^2)$ time since each stored center point and each sampled cell will be considered at most $O(1)$ times.

We can in fact avoid a separate post-processing step by maintaining the weights of each cell and their sum during the streaming process. This will not change the $O(1)$ processing time per item since each item will only affect the weights of an $O(1)$ number of neighboring cells.

As mentioned, our algorithm and analysis can be literally carried to any $O(1)$-dimensional space (by appropriately adjusting constant parameters). We sum up this section with the following theorem. Note that our space upper bound even matches (up to a logarithmic factor) the $\Omega(1/\epsilon^2)$ bits space streaming lower bound for distinct elements in the noise-free data setting [23].

THEOREM 1. *There is a streaming algorithm that given a well-shaped dataset S in the $O(1)$-dimensional Euclidean space, outputs a $(1+\epsilon)$-approximation to robust $F_0(S)$ with probability* 0.96*, using $O(1/\epsilon^2)$ words of space and $O(1)$ processing time per item.*

2.2 High Dimensional Euclidean Spaces

In this section we consider points in the d-dimensional Euclidean space for $d > 2$.

Following the ideas in Section 2.1.1, we employ a d-dimensional grid but with side length d to partition $\mathbb{R}^d$ to cells. We first discuss the case when $\beta \geq d^{3/2}$, which guarantees that each cell intersects at most one group of points. We will show that in this case our algorithm for the 2D case (with the grid size replaced by d) can still produce a $(1+\epsilon)$-approximation to $F_0(S)$. We then extend it to general well-shaped datasets (i.e., $(1, \beta)$-sparse with $\beta \geq 2$).

2.2.1 $(1, \beta)$-sparse Datasets with $\beta \geq d^{3/2}$

Correctness. Compared with the 2D case discussed in Section 2.1, the main difference in the d-dimensional case with a random grid of side length d is that each group can intersect up to 2^d grid cells in the worse case. Note that we cannot simply use 2^d to replace the constant "9" in Equation (5) in the 2D case, because the number of sampled cells $|\mathcal{C}'|$ and the final space usage will be proportional to this intersection value, and will consequently be exponential in d. Fortunately, we can show that *on average* each group will intersect $\Theta(1)$ cells, which is enough for keeping the correctness of Algorithm 4.

LEMMA 2. *Let S be a $(1, \beta)$-sparse dataset in the d-dimensional Euclidean space with $\beta \geq d^{3/2}$, let $\mathbb{G}$ be a random grid of side length d, let $\mathcal{C} = \{C \in \mathbb{G} \mid C \cap S \neq \emptyset\}$, and let $\mathcal{G} = \{G_1, \ldots, G_{F_0}\}$ be the natural minimum-cardinality group partition of S. Then $1 \leq |\mathcal{C}| / F_0 \leq 300$ with probability 0.99.*

Due to the space constraints, we delay the technical proof to Appendix B.1.

It is easy to see that if we use Lemma 2 to replace Inequality (5), the rest of correctness proof in Section 2.1.2 still holds (by appropriately adjusting constant parameters).

Space and Time Complexities. We next analyze the space and time costs of our algorithm in the d-dimensional Euclidean space. For a group $G \in \mathcal{G}$, let $\mathsf{B}(G)$ be a ball of diameter 3 that contains all unit balls centered at some point $q \in G$. Let ν be the probability that $\mathsf{B}(G)$ is cut by the boundaries of grid cells, which can be bounded by $\nu \leq 3/d$. Let N_G be the number of grid cells group G intersects; let M_G be the number of grid cells that group G adjoin, i.e.,

$$M_G = |\{C \mid \exists p \in G \text{ } s.t. \text{ } d(p, C) \leq 1\}|.$$

Obviously $N_G \leq M_G$. Similar to (23) (in Appendix B.1), by replacing μ with ν, we can show that

$$\mathbf{E}[M_G] = O(1). \tag{10}$$

Note that a non-empty cell $C \in \mathcal{C}$ will have a point stored only if at least one cell in M_{G_C} has been sampled. We thus can upper bound the total number of point centers stored in Γ by

$$Z = \sum_{G \in \mathcal{G}} (N_G \cdot \chi(\text{one of cells in } M_G \text{ is sampled})),$$

where $\chi(A) = 1$ if event A holds, and $\chi(A) = 0$ otherwise.

We now bound the expectation of Z.

$$\begin{aligned}
\mathbf{E}[Z] &= \sum_{G \in \mathcal{G}} \mathbf{E}[N_G \cdot \chi(\text{one of cells in } M_G \text{ is sampled})] \\
&\leq \sum_{G \in \mathcal{G}} \mathbf{E}[M_G \cdot \chi(\text{one of cells in } M_G \text{ is sampled})] \\
&\leq \sum_{G \in \mathcal{G}} \sum_{i=0}^{d} 2^i \binom{d}{i} \nu^i (1-\nu)^{d-i} \cdot \frac{2^i}{R} \\
&= \frac{F_0}{R} \cdot (4\nu + (1-\nu))^d \\
&\leq O\left(\frac{1}{\epsilon^2}\right) \cdot (1 + 9/d)^d = O\left(\frac{1}{\epsilon^2}\right),
\end{aligned}$$

where the first inequality is due to the fact that $N_G \leq M_G$ (by definitions); in the second inequality, $2^i/R$ is the probability that one of cells in M_G is sampled (recall that R is the range size of the random hash function used in the bucket sampling; see Section 2.1.1); the last inequality is due to $|\mathcal{C}| \geq F_0$ and Equation (6) (constants need to be adjusted for the high dimensional case). Therefore by a Markov inequality, $Z = O(1/\epsilon^2)$ with probability 0.99.

We next consider the processing time per item. Compared with the 2D case, the difference is that in `StoreCenter`(p), in the worst case one needs to test up to 2^d adjacent cells to see if any of them are sampled. Fortunately by (10) we can upper bound the total processing time by

$$T = \sum_{G \in \mathcal{G}} (|G| \cdot M_G).$$

Taking the expectation,

$$\begin{aligned}
\mathbf{E}[T] &= \sum_{G \in \mathcal{G}} (|G| \cdot \mathbf{E}[M_G]) \\
&\overset{\text{by (10)}}{\leq} O(1) \cdot \sum_{G \in \mathcal{G}} |G| = O(m).
\end{aligned}$$

Therefore $T = O(m)$ with probability 0.99 by a Markov inequality. Thus on average, for each inserted point we only need to check $O(1)$ adjacent cells.

Finally, the cost of the post-processing step can again be amortized into each insertion step. We thus arrive at the following theorem.

THEOREM 2. *There is a streaming algorithm that given a $(1, \beta)$-sparse dataset S with $\beta \geq d^{3/2}$ in the d-dimensional Euclidean space, outputs a $(1+\epsilon)$-approximation to robust $F_0(S)$ with probability 0.9, using $O(d/\epsilon^2)$ words of space and amortized $O(d)$ processing time per item.*

2.2.2 Well-shaped Datasets

For general well-shaped datasets in $\mathbb{R}^d$ $(d > 2)$ and a grid with side length d, it is possible that a grid cell intersects multiple groups of points. While the high level idea of sampling cells and add up their weights still apply, we need to modify the definition of the weight of a non-empty cell $C \in \mathcal{C}$ (Equation (2)) to be

$$w(C) = \sum_{G \in \mathcal{G} : G \cap C \neq \emptyset} 1/w(G).$$

Algorithms presented in Section 2.1 can still be used for this case. However, once a cell intersects multiple groups, its weight can no longer be bounded by a constant. Thus it is not clear how to use rigorous theoretical analysis to determine the least number of cells we need to sample in order to obtain a $(1+\epsilon)$-approximation of $F_0(S)$, since the variance of the weights of cells can be very high. We leave this to future work.

3. GENERAL DATASETS IN CONSTANT DIMENSIONAL EUCLIDEAN SPACES

In this section we consider a general dataset which is possibly not well-shaped. That is, it has an F_0-ambiguity $\delta > 0$. We can rigorously show that Algorithm 4 still performs well if δ is small. Ideally, we would also like to have an algorithm to estimate the F_0-ambiguity δ of a dataset, so that we can filter out those inputs that have a large δ, on which Algorithm 4 may not perform well; in other words, we can declare that the value returned by Algorithm 4 may not be very accurate due to the fact that the dataset is "too noisy" (call such a dataset a *bad* input). Unfortunately, we noticed that one needs $\Omega(m)$ (recall that $m = |S|$ is the length of the stream) space to differentiate whether $\delta = 0$ or $1/2$.

3.1 Approximation Guarantees under Small F_0-ambiguity

In this section we prove the following theorem, which shows that Algorithm 4 still performs well when F_0-ambiguity is small.

THEOREM 3. *There is a streaming algorithm that given a dataset S with F_0-ambiguity δ in the $O(1)$-dimensional Euclidean space, outputs a $(1 + \Theta(\delta + \epsilon))$-approximation to robust $F_0(S)$ with probability 0.9, using $O(1/\epsilon^2)$ words of space and $O(1)$ processing time per item.*

The proof for this theorem is very technical, and we delay it to Appendix A due to the space constraints. The idea of the proof is as follows. Let T be the set of "outliers" defined in Definition 4, such that S/T is well-shaped and $F_0(S\backslash T) \geq (1 - \delta) \cdot F_0(S)$. If the F_0-ambiguity δ is small, then we can think the optimal grouping is the natural grouping for $S\backslash T$ plus some balls[3] of diameter α covering points in T. Note that in $O(1)$-dimensional Euclidean space, a ball of diameter 2α can be covered by $O(1)$ balls of diameter α. Thus in the optimal solution the balls that are used to cover T are *evenly spread* across the (natural) groups formed by $S\backslash T$. Since our algorithms use *near-uniform* group samplings (the probability of sampling each group differs by at most a constant), if δ is small then only a small fraction of our sampled groups will be relevant to points in T. Consequently, the outliers T will not affect much of our estimation of $F_0(S\backslash T)$, which is close to $F_0(S)$ by the definition of T.

3.2 Estimating F_0-ambiguity is Theoretically Hard

The problem of estimating the F_0-ambiguity is closely related to the problem of computing the diameter of a point set, that is, given a set of points S in the Euclidean space, try to find $\max_{p,q \in S} d(p, q)$. It has been shown that to compute the diameter exactly in the streaming model, we need $\Omega(|S|) = \Omega(m)$ space [16].

The connection between computing the diameter of the point set and estimating its F_0 ambiguity is as follows. Again rescale $\alpha = 1$. If the diameter of the dataset is 1, then all the points will be in one group, that is, (robust) $F_0 = 1$; otherwise if the diameter is $1 + \iota$ for an arbitrarily small $\iota > 0$, then F_0 will be at least 2. By the hardness of the diameter problem we cannot differentiate whether $F_0 = 1$ or 2 unless using $\Omega(m)$ space, equivalently, we cannot differentiate whether $\delta = 0$ or $1/2$ without using $\Omega(m)$ space.

[3]This is not very precise since a group of diameter 1 may not be covered by a ball of diameter 1, but they are close.

4. A SOLUTION FRAMEWORK FOR GENERAL METRIC SPACE

So far we have discussed datasets in the Euclidean space. In this section we show that our algorithmic framework in Section 2 can also be used for datasets in other metric spaces.

Recall our high level ideas for datasets in the Euclidean space in Section 2. First, we use a random grid to partition the item universe U to cells so that each group of items only adjacent to a small number of grid cells. Second, we reduce the problem of approximating robust $F_0(S)$ to sampling cells and adding up their weights (and rescaling at the end). Third, to solve the dilemma on the timing of the samplings we employ a technique we call bucket sampling.

The observation is that the second and third steps can be applied to any metric spaces, while in the first step the random grid can be thought as a "hash function", which is generalized to the following concept.

DEFINITION 5 (SMART HASH FUNCTION). *We say a hash function h is ρ-*smart *on an (α, β)-sparse ($\beta \geq 2\alpha$) dataset S and its natural minimum-cardinality group partition if it satisfies the followings:*

- *(Low "image distance"). Each group is adjacent to ρ cells on average, where we say a group G is adjacent to a hash cell C if there exists a pair of items $p, q \in S$ such that $p \in G, h(q) = C$ and $d(p, q) \leq \alpha$. We call ρ the* image distance *of the smart hash function.*
- *(No false-positive). Items from different groups will be hashed into disjoint buckets.*

Obviously, the smaller the ρ, the better the performance of the smart hash function. When $\rho = 1$, we get a magic hash function, which is however unlikely to exist (see our discussion in the introduction).

4.1 Locality Sensitive Hashing as Smart Hash Functions

As we have shown, a random grid can be used as a smart hash function for the Euclidean space. In fact, a random grid can be seen as a *locality sensitive hash* (LSH) function, whose general form is as follows:

DEFINITION 6 (LSH). *(see, e.g., [22, 3]) Let U be the item universe, and $d(\cdot, \cdot)$ be a distance function. We say a hash family $\mathcal{H}$ is (ℓ, u, p_1, p_2)-sensitive if for any two items $p, q \in U$,*

1. *if $d(p, q) \leq \ell$ then $\mathbf{Pr}_{h \in_r \mathcal{H}}[h(p) = h(q)] \geq p_1$,*
2. *if $d(p, q) \geq u$ then $\mathbf{Pr}_{h \in_r \mathcal{H}}[h(p) = h(q)] \leq p_2$,*

where $h \in_r \mathcal{H}$ means picking h randomly from $\mathcal{H}$.

Under this definition, the random grid we used in Section 2.1 (in $\mathbb{R}^2$, of side length $1/\sqrt{2}$) can be thought as a $\left(\ell, u, \frac{1}{\sqrt{2}} - \ell, \frac{(1-u)^2}{2}\right)$-sensitive LSH. In this section we show that a locality sensitive hash function for *any* metric space, if satisfies an additional natural property, can be used as a smart hash function for that space, and thus can be used to compute robust F_0.

Definition 7 (Concentrated Hash Function). *Let $S \subseteq U$ be a dataset and let $\mathcal{G} = \{G_1, \ldots, G_{F_0}\}$ be the natural minimum-cardinality partition of S. A hash function h is called η-concentrated on S if for any $G \in \mathcal{G}$,*

$$|\{h(x) \mid \exists y \in G \text{ s.t. } d(x, y) \leq \alpha\}| \leq \eta.$$

We say an LSH family that is η-concentrated on S if for any $h \in \mathcal{H}$, h is η-concentrated on S.

In fact, many popular LSHs are of low concentration, as we will see shortly.

Definition 8 (k-fold Hash Function). *Let $\mathcal{H}$ be a hash family. We say $\mathcal{F}$ is a k-fold hash family of $\mathcal{H}$ if*

$$\mathcal{F} = \{F = (h_1, \ldots, h_k) \mid h_i \in \mathcal{H} \text{ for any } i \in [k]\},$$

For any $x, y \in U$, we define $F(x) = F(y)$ if and only if $h_i(x) = h_i(y)$ for any $i \in [k]$.

The following lemma reveals the connection between LSHs and smart hash functions. The proof can be found in Appendix B.2.

Lemma 3. *Let $\beta \geq 2\alpha$. Let $S \subseteq U$ be an (α, β)-sparse dataset consisting of m items. Let $\mathcal{G}$ be the natural minimum-cardinality partition of S. Let $\mathcal{H}$ be a $(2\alpha, \beta, p_1, p_2)$-sensitive LSH family that is η-concentrated on S. Let $\mathcal{F}$ be a k-fold hash family of $\mathcal{H}$ and let $f \in_r \mathcal{F}$. Then f is $100(\eta(1-p_1)+p_1)^k$-smart on S with probability at least $(0.99 - m^2 p_2^k)$.*

We next show two examples on how use Lemma 3 together with some well-known LSHs to construct smart hash functions with low image distances for data in corresponding metric spaces.

Gaussian LSH for Euclidean Metric. For a point set $S \subseteq \mathbb{R}^d$ ($|S| = m$) in the Euclidean space that is $(\frac{1}{2}, \beta)$-sparse (rescale α to $\frac{1}{2}$ for technical convenience), we can use the Gaussian LSH [10]. Let γ a parameter. Define Gaussian LSH family $\mathcal{H}_G$ be the set of functions $h_{\vec{a},b}(\vec{x}) : \mathbb{R}^d \to \mathbb{N}$ mapping a d-dimensional vector $\vec{x}$ onto the set of integers, where $\vec{a}$ is a vector chosen from the unit sphere $\mathcal{S}^{d-1}$, and b is a scale parameter in the range $[0, \gamma)$. More precisely,

$$h_{\vec{a},b}(x) = \left\lfloor \frac{\vec{x} \cdot \vec{a} + b}{\gamma} \right\rfloor.$$

It was shown in [10] that $\mathcal{H}_G$ is $(1, \beta, p(1), p(\beta))$-sensitive where

$$p(x) = 1 - 2\Phi\left(-\frac{\gamma}{x}\right) - \frac{2}{\sqrt{2\pi}\gamma/x}\left(1 - e^{-\frac{\gamma^2}{2x^2}}\right),$$

where $\Phi(\cdot)$ is the cumulative distribution function for the standard Gaussian distribution $\mathcal{N}(0,1)$. Now we choose $\beta = \log m$ and $\gamma = \log m$, and then

- $\eta = 2$ since each group, when projecting to a line by an $h \in \mathcal{H}$, has a diameter at most 1, and thus can adjacent at most 2 cells;
- $p_1 = p(1) \geq 1 - 2/\log m$;
- $p_2 = p(\beta) = 1 - 2\Phi(-1) - \frac{2}{\sqrt{2\pi}}(1 - e^{-1/2}) < 0.4$.

Finally let $\mathcal{F}$ be a k-fold hash family of $\mathcal{H}$ with $k = 2\log m$. By Lemma 3 we have that for an $f \in_r \mathcal{F}$, f is $\Theta(1)$-smart on S with probability at least 0.98.

To plug-in the algorithm framework in Section 2, we need to define for a point p and a hash bucket C the distance $d(p, C)$ so that we can test $d(p, C) \leq \alpha$ (in Section 2 w.l.o.g. we have assumed $\alpha = 1$). Note that LSH buckets *partitions* the item universe. In the case of Gaussian LSH for Euclidean Metric, the set of the points in $\mathbb{R}^d$ (denoted by $S(C)$) hashed into the same bucket C is the intersection of $2k = O(\log m)$ half-spaces. We define $d(p, C) = \min_{q \in S(C)} d(p, q)$, which can be computed by measuring the Euclidean distances between p and the boundaries of the $2k$ half-spaces.

The following theorem summarizes the performance of Gaussian LSH on estimating robust F_0 in the Euclidean metric. The analysis is very similar to that for high dimensional Euclidean space in Section 2.2, and is omitted here.

Theorem 4. *There is a streaming algorithm that given a dataset S with separation ratio $\Omega(\log m)$ in the d-dimensional Euclidean space, outputs a $(1 + \epsilon)$-approximation to robust $F_0(S)$ with probability 0.9, using $O(\log m/\epsilon^2)$ words of space and amortized $O(d \log m)$ processing time per item.*

Random Projection LSH for Cosine Metric. The cosine distance function is defined as follows: given two vectors $\vec{a}, \vec{b} \in \mathbb{R}^d$, the cosine distance is defined to be $d(\vec{a}, \vec{b}) = 1 - \langle \vec{a}, \vec{b} \rangle / (\|\vec{a}\| \, \|\vec{b}\|)$. This distance function is used extensively in information retrieval and text mining, in particular, in comparing the similarity between two documents [28].

For a set of vectors S ($|S| = m$) in $\mathbb{R}^d$ under the cosine distance, we can use the random projection LSH [9]. Define random projection LSH family $\mathcal{H}_P$ be the set of functions $h_{\vec{a}}(\vec{x}) : \mathbb{R}^d \to \{+1, -1\}$ mapping a d-dimensional vector $\vec{x}$ onto signs $\{+1, -1\}$, where $\vec{a}$ is a vector chosen from the unit sphere $\mathcal{S}^{d-1}$. Concretely,

$$h_{\vec{a}}(\vec{x}) = \begin{cases} +1 & \text{if } \langle \vec{a}, \vec{x} \rangle > 0 \\ -1 & \text{otherwise,} \end{cases} \tag{11}$$

It is shown in [9] that $\mathcal{H}_P$ is $(2\alpha, \beta, 1 - 2\alpha/\pi, 1 - \beta/\pi)$-sensitive. Obviously $\eta = 2$ since the range of each hash function in $\mathcal{H}_P$ only consists of two numbers $\{+1, -1\}$.

Let $\mathcal{F}$ be a k-fold hash family of $\mathcal{H}$ with $k = \frac{3\log m}{\log(1-\pi/\beta)}$. By Lemma 3, for any parameter α, β with $\alpha \leq \frac{1}{\log m}$ and $\Omega(1) \leq \beta < \pi$, we have that for an $f \in_r \mathcal{F}$, f is $\Theta(1)$-smart on S with probability at least 0.98.

Similar to Gaussian LSH, the set of the vectors/points in $\mathbb{R}^d$ hashed into the same Random Projection LSH bucket is the intersection of $k = O(\log m)$ half-spaces. Thus $d(p, C)$ can again be computed by measuring the cosine distances between p and the boundaries of the k half-spaces.

We have the following theorem for random projection LSH for the cosine metric. The analysis is again similar as before and is omitted.

Theorem 5. *Let α, β be parameters such that $\alpha \leq \frac{1}{\log m}$ and $\Omega(1) \leq \beta < \pi$. There is a streaming algorithm that given an (α, β)-sparse dataset S in $\mathbb{R}^d$ under the cosine distance, outputs a $(1 + \epsilon)$-approximation to robust $F_0(S)$ with probability 0.9, using $O(\log m/\epsilon^2)$ words of space and amortized $O(d \log m)$ processing time per item.*

At the end of this section, we would like to remark that not all LSH functions can be used as smart hash functions with a small image distance. We delay the details of this remark to Appendix B.3 due to the space constraints.

5. EXPERIMENTS

We will refer to our algorithm as `Sketch` in this section. Our theoretical analysis has shown that `Sketch` has good accuracy guarantees, and is both space and time efficient. We now show how these theoretical expectations interact with practice.

We note that our theoretical analysis focuses on a fixed, known α (i.e. group diameter). We explore in this section how one can deal with unknown α, and propose a heuristic that reliably complements `Sketch` under realistic circumstances.

5.1 The Setup

Datasets. We derive our test data from a set of images, denoted by `Images`, which contains 4 million images taken from ImageNet [11]. These images serve as the *ground truth.*

To study the scalability of `Sketch`. We take subsets `Images` with sizes 4, 000, 000 (whole set), 512, 600, 100, 000 and 10, 000, denoted by `I4m`, `I500k`, `I100k` and `I10k` respectively. The sizes are chosen to differ by magnitudes, to contrast the effects of the resource usage.

For each image in `I500k`, `I100k` and `I10k`, we introduce an average of 100 perturbed duplicates, producing test datasets `I500k100x`, `I100k100x` and `I10k100x`, which contain approximately 50 million, 10 million and 1 million images, respectively. For `I500k`, we also generate another dataset `I500k10x`, where an average of 10 duplicates are generated for each ground truth image.

To test our algorithms on datasets with low duplication ratios, we introduce an average of 2 perturbed duplicates to `I4m`, `I500k`, with number of duplications for each image following the *power-law* distribution, this gives datasets `I4m2x` and `I500k2x`.

Finally, we map each image to a signature in a feature space. Each image is mapped to a point, i.e. a *signature* of the image, in $\mathbb{R}^5$, $\mathbb{R}^{10}$ or $\mathbb{R}^{20}$. Our final test datasets are

- `I500k100x5d`, `I100k100x5d`, `I10k100x5d` for basic tests.
- `I4m2x5d`; `I500k2x5d` for low duplication ratio tests.
- `I4m2x10d`; `I4m2x20d` for high dimensionality tests.

The duplicates are generated through resizing images in the ground truth set; each image is randomly resized to between 300 and 500 in width and/or length. Resizing introduces interpolation errors, which are usually small but can sometimes be large, serving as a realistic source of noise.

To map an image to a point in $\mathbb{R}^d$, we first convert an image into grayscale, and then take the color histogram with d buckets as a d-dimensional vector, and rescale so that its ℓ_1 norm is 100, 000. The final rescaling effectively normalizes each signature to that of an image with 100, 000 pixels. We note that our datasets are not well-shaped (i.e., they have non-zero F_0-ambiguities), which is expected for real datasets.

Parameters and resources. We use the grid as our smart hash function, and the ℓ_2 norm as the distance function.

We use the distinct elements algorithm in [4] (for the noise-free data setting) to approximate the number of non-empty cells for `Sketch`. The storage space is fixed at 500 words, which is accurate enough for our purpose. This space cost is negligible compared with the other parts of our sketching algorithm, and thus is neglected for simplicity.

We run our experiments on a desktop PC with 8GB of RAM and a 4-core 3.40GHz Intel i7 CPU. Single-threaded running times are recorded.

5.2 Reference Algorithms

We compare `Sketch` with two alternative methods. The first one is `Baseline`, corresponding to a non-sampling version of our sketching algorithm (thus needs at least *linear* space in the worst case). In `Baseline`, we scan through points in S in an arbitrary order, during which we maintain a set $\hat{\Gamma}$ of balls with radius α, initialized to $\emptyset$. When a point p is not covered by the union of balls in $\hat{\Gamma}$, we add to $\hat{\Gamma}$ the ball with radius α centered at p. At the end, we output $|\hat{\Gamma}|$.

It is easy to see that `Baseline` stores up to F_0 balls, outputs $F_0(S, \alpha)$ if S is well-shaped, and otherwise outputs a value between $(1 - \delta(S))F_0$ and F_0 (recall that $\delta(S)$ is the F_0-ambiguity of the dataset S). `Baseline` is used to demonstrate the validity of our data model, measure the accuracy of `Sketch`, and serve as a baseline for the space usage. Note that in the worst case it will use a linear amount of space. In some sense it represents the clustering-based algorithms and the full space de-duplication algorithms (but can be done much faster in one scan).

The second one, `CellCount`, simply counts the number of non-empty cells in the grid. As the grid can be considered an LSH, this method corresponds to grouping elements simply by LSH. We show that `CellCount` is not suitable for estimating robust F_0 by contrasting it to `Sketch` and `Baseline`.

As mentioned in the related work, all the state-of-the-art streaming algorithms for distinct elements for noise-free datasets are just infeasible to handle noisy datasets – they will simply output values that are approximations to the total number of items instead of groups; for example, on `I100k100x5d` their outputs will be values close to 10 million, which is far-away from the ground truth 100, 000. We thus do not compare them in our experiments.

5.3 Finding Group Diameters

We first consider the case where α is not known a priori. Our idea is to run `Sketch` on parallel guesses α' for α, and make use of the assumption that the dataset has a good separation ratio.

Recall that once we fix S, $F_0(\alpha')$ decreases monotonically as α' increases. In particular, if $\alpha' < \alpha$, then $F_0(\alpha') \geq F_0(\alpha)$, as ground truth groups will be broken down into smaller groups; on the other hand if $\alpha' > \beta$, we will have $F_0(\alpha') \leq F_0(\alpha)$, because small groups may be merged into a few larger groups. However, if the dataset is (α, β)-sparse with a reasonably large separation ratio β/α, then there will be a range of values of $\alpha' \in [\alpha, \beta]$ for which $F_0(\alpha') = F_0(\alpha)$.

Of course, real-world datasets rarely have large well-defined separation ratios; it could be the case that some groups are too close to each other, though the overall distribution is spatially sparse. In the case when the separation ratio is not large, we can still expect there is a region where the change in $F_0(\alpha')$ is very small as we vary α', unless in extreme cases.

Suppose that our trials use $\alpha' = \alpha_0, \alpha_1, \ldots, \alpha_l$ where α_i's form a geometric sequence, finding the appropriate value for α reduces to searching for a region with a low gradient in

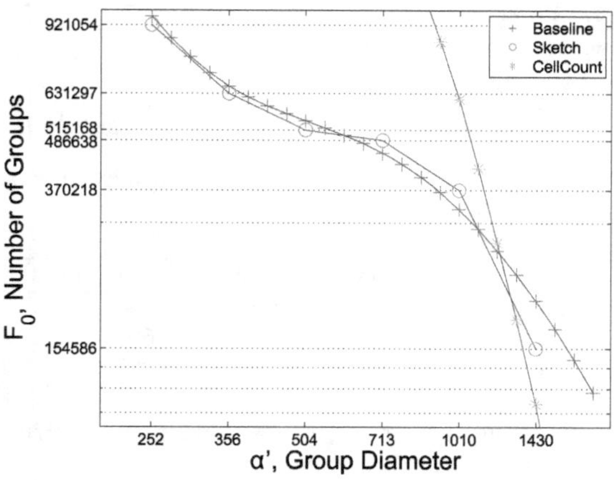

Figure 3: $F_0(\alpha')$ against α' on dataset `I500k100x5d`, with log-log plots.

the log-log plot of F_0 against α. Our heuristic simply finds an i $(0 < i \leq l)$ that minimizes the absolute value of the slope of the corresponding piece-wise linear plot, that is:

$$\left| \frac{\log F_0(\alpha_i) - \log F_0(\alpha_{i-1})}{\log \alpha_i - \log \alpha_{i-1}} \right|. \tag{12}$$

This is equivalent to finding two adjacent values α' that make the least percentage change in $F(\alpha')$. We then take $\tilde{F_0} = (F_0(\alpha_i) + F_0(\alpha_{i-1}))/2$ as the estimator for the true F_0. We call this the *saddle point heuristic*. We will see that, given an algorithm that computes $F_0(\alpha')$ accurately, this allows us to identify appropriate ranges for α' which is close to or contains α, and the corresponding $F_0 = F_0(\alpha)$.

For `Baseline`, to demonstrate that this heuristic is viable, we try values of α' in smaller steps in factors of $2^{\frac{1}{8}}$ to build a fine-grading graph. For `Sketch`, since we need to reduce the space usage, we have to narrow down the search range for a good α'. Our idea is to determine the smallest and largest values of α' that we are going to try, denoted by $\alpha_{\min}$ and $\alpha_{\max}$, which can be done by sampling a small number of labelled data points. We then step from $\alpha_{\min}$ to $\alpha_{\max}$ by increasing α' by factors of $\sqrt{2}$.

5.4 Results - Unknown Group Diameters

Figure 3 shows a log-log plot for `Baseline`, `Sketch` and `CellCount` on dataset `I500k100x5d`, with $F_0(\alpha')$ against α'.

First of all, it can be seen that `Sketch`, with larger steps, interpolates `Baseline` well.

For `Baseline`, one can see that the gradient decreases as one approaches from both sides near the interval $504 \leq \alpha' \leq 713$, where $F_0(\alpha')$ is very close to the ground truth. This is in accordance to the intuition of the heuristic. In particular, the segment $504 \leq \alpha' \leq 599$ minimizes the slope (Equation (12)). Similarly, for `Sketch`, the slope is the smallest for the segment $504 \leq \alpha' \leq 713$, and the F_0 values at the endpoints are both close to the ground truth 512,600.

It is easy to see that no such thing can be said for `CellCount`. The output is wildly high for lower cell lengths, rapidly drops to very low values in the graph, encompassing a large range of guesses at F_0 without hinting at any plausible way to detect the ground truth graphically. This suggests modelling robust F_0 directly using LSH is not a good idea.

	Full-info	`Baseline`	`Sketch`
Space (million points)	51	3.2	0.43
Average Error	–	4.8%	7.3%

Table 2: Unknown α; saddle point heuristic on 6 α' values for both `Baseline` and `Sketch`; over 10 runs.

Samples:	200	400	800	1,600
Space (pts):	1,500	3,000	6,000	12,000
`I500k100x5d`	27.3%	19.7%	11.6%	9.3%
`I500k10x5d`	25.8%	21.1%	10.4%	8.8%
`I100k100x5d`	22.6%	18.2%	8.9%	7.5%
`I10k100x5d`	17.1%	14.5%	8.2%	7.6%

Table 3: Average error over 20 runs; single sketch; known α. *Samples* refers to number of sampled buckets; *space* denotes the total number of points stored.

We note that the cost for the unknown α case is high even for a non-streaming algorithm, since we still have to guess different α' values in parallel. In Figure 3, we used small steps in `Baseline` to figure out the best α, during which we also had to allocate space for each run of `Baseline`.

We compare `Sketch` to two alternatives: one is `Baseline` but we use the same 6 α' values as that for `Sketch`; the other is simply storing the entire dataset and process offline. For `Baseline` we randomize the order of points in the data streams, so the answer may vary due to the F_0-ambiguity.

Table 2 summarizes the space usage and accuracy. `Sketch` uses 6 sketches each with a space bound of 12,000 points, and 6 values of α' are tried in parallel. The total space is thus 432,000 (points). The corresponding space usage for `Baseline` is 3,200,000. The space saving of `Sketch` over `Baseline` is about a magnitude, at a small cost of accuracy. We expect the space savings to grow as the size of the dataset grows further.

5.5 Results - Known Group Diameters

We next consider the case where α is known, e.g. using domain knowledge.

Table 3 shows average error percentages over 20 trials for datasets `I500k100x5d`, `I500k10x5d`, `I100k100x5d` and `I10k100x5d`, run against different space allowances (in terms of number of points stored), using α' determined by the saddle point heuristic. Table 4 summarizes the error percentages by taking the median of outputs of 6 parallel sketches, again average over 20 trials. All results are compared with the corresponding exact values $F_0(\alpha')$ outputted by `Baseline`.

We notice that the error percentages correlate relatively weakly with the numbers of duplicates and the numbers of groups. In contrast to magnitude differences in data size, the error percentages display much smaller changes.

We next look at the effects of using different numbers of duplicates. The observation is that the datasets `I500k10x5d` and `I500k100x5d` do not require significantly different space budgets to achieve similar accuracies, despite the magnitude difference in the number of duplicates. This shows that the choice of the length of our grid is good at limiting the number of cells that a group can intersect, and hence bounding the variance of the estimator.

Table 5 summarizes the average processing times for various datasets, for `Sketch` under different space budgets, and

Space (pts)	9,000	18,000	36,000	72,000
I500k100x5d	22.8%	10.6%	8.3%	6.6%
I500k10x5d	15.8%	9.2%	6.7%	5.7%
I100k100x5d	12.7%	8.4%	5.5%	3.5%
I10k100x5d	10.8%	8.8%	3.6%	3.0%

Table 4: Average error over 20 runs; median output of 6 sketches; known α.

Samples:	200	400	800	1,600	
Space (pts):	1,500	3,000	6,000	12,000	Baseline
I500k100x5d	0.45	0.47	0.49	0.46	1.45
I500k10x5d	0.42	0.50	0.52	0.46	1.42
I100k100x5d	0.48	0.44	0.48	0.53	1.38
I10k100x5d	0.42	0.48	0.51	0.50	1.35

Table 5: Average processing time (seconds) per 10,000 pts

for Baseline. We observe that in Sketch the average time to process each point is almost a constant, which is consistent with our theoretical analysis. Baseline is a bit slower, but the time is still linear in the number of points.

5.6 Datasets with Low Duplication Ratios and/or High Dimensionality

In fact, in all of our experiments above, for the sake of a "stress test", the ambiguity we injected into the raw dataset Images is on the high end – the average number of duplicates we generated is between 10 to 100, while for many real-world datasets this ratio can be below 2. For example, the duplication ratios of the document datasets in the Internet studied by Broder [7] are between 1.4 to 1.8. Similar phenomenon has been observed by Wang et al. [29] on Internet images.

We thus also test our algorithms in datasets with low duplication ratios. In datasets I500k2x5d and I4m2x5d, the number of duplications of images follow a *power-law* distribution scaled to an expectation of 2 (to better model the real-world image duplications).

Table 6 shows that under the same ground truth $F_0 = 512,600$, the performance of Sketch becomes better when the duplication ratio becomes smaller. The error does not increase much when we increase the robust F_0 to 4 million while keeping the same sketch size.

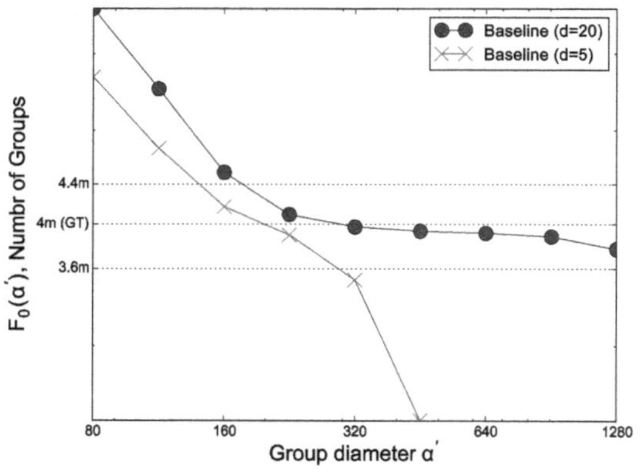

Figure 4: $F_0(\alpha')$ against α' on dataset I4m2x20d and I4m2x5d, with log-log plots. GT stands for *ground truth.*

No. pts	9,000	18,000	36,000	72,000
I500k100x5d	22.8%	10.6%	8.3%	6.6%
I500k10x5d	15.8%	9.2%	6.7%	5.7%
I500k2x5d	5.2%	3.0%	2.8%	2.2%
I4m2x5d	6.0%	3.5%	3.3%	2.4%

Table 6: Vary duplication ratio; average error over 20 runs; median output of 6 sketches; known α.

No. pts	9,000	18,000	36,000	72,000	144,000
I4m2x5d	6.0%	3.5%	3.3%	2.4%	1.7%
I4m2x10d	5.8%	4.2%	3.4%	2.6%	1.5%
I4m2x20d	6.4%	4.4%	3.6%	2.0%	1.3%

Table 7: Vary dimensionality; average error over 20 runs; median output of 6 sketches; known α.

Finally we test how the dimensionality of the feature space affects the performance of Sketch. Table 7 shows the performance of Sketch when the dimensionality varies. One can see that under the same number of sampled points, the performance of Sketch is roughly the same on the three datasets. The reason is that when mapping images to points in $\mathbb{R}^5$, the dataset I4m2x5d has already exhibit a good separation ratio; see the α-curve for I4m2x5d in Figure 4. Further increasing the dimensionality indeed gives better separation ratio; see the α-curve for I4m2x20d in Figure 4. However, it does not give much advantage in terms of accuracy. The main reason is that the variance generated in the sampling step of Sketch is larger in higher dimensions. On the other hand, points in higher dimensions cost more storage space and processing time (note that datasets in Table 7 are compared under the same number of samples points, not the total space). To conclude, our experiments suggest that we should use the least necessary number of features that exhibit a good separation ratio.

6. CONCLUSION

In this paper we present a set of streaming algorithms for computing the number of distinct elements for noisy datasets. We have shown that our algorithm for well-shaped noisy datasets in constant dimensional Euclidean spaces is theoretically optimal. We have also rigorously proved that our algorithms still work well on datasets with small F_0-ambiguities, and proposed a method to detect datasets with high F_0-ambiguities. Furthermore, we have proposed an algorithm framework for datasets in a general metric space using the theory of locality sensitive hashing. The effectiveness of our algorithms have been verified experimentally on image data (or rather, point sets in the Euclidean space). Future work includes designing algorithms for computing robust F_0 for datasets in high dimensions with provable guarantees and extending our experiments to other metrics and similarity functions.

7. REFERENCES

[1] S. Acharya, P. B. Gibbons, V. Poosala, and S. Ramaswamy. The aqua approximate query answering system. In *SIGMOD*, pages 574–576, 1999.

[2] N. Alon, Y. Matias, and M. Szegedy. The space complexity of approximating the frequency moments. *J. Comput. Syst. Sci.*, 58(1):137–147, 1999.

[3] A. Andoni and P. Indyk. Near-optimal hashing algorithms for approximate nearest neighbor in high dimensions. *Comm. of the ACM*, 51(1):117, 2008.

[4] Z. Bar-Yossef, T. Jayram, R. Kumar, D. Sivakumar, and L. Trevisan. Counting distinct elements in a data stream. In *Randomization and Approximation Techniques in Computer Science*, pages 1–10. Springer, 2002.

[5] K. Beyer, P. J. Haas, B. Reinwald, Y. Sismanis, and R. Gemulla. On synopses for distinct-value estimation under multiset operations. In *Proceedings of the 2007 ACM SIGMOD international conference on Management of data*, pages 199–210. ACM, 2007.

[6] A. Z. Broder. On the resemblance and containment of documents. In *Compression and Complexity of Sequences 1997. Proceedings*, pages 21–29. IEEE, 1997.

[7] A. Z. Broder. Identifying and filtering near-duplicate documents. In *Proceedings of the 11th Annual Symposium on Combinatorial Pattern Matching*, COM '00, pages 1–10, London, UK, UK, 2000. Springer-Verlag.

[8] P. Brown, P. J. Haas, J. Myllymaki, H. Pirahesh, B. Reinwald, and Y. Sismanis. Toward automated large-scale information integration and discovery. In *Data Management in a Connected World*, pages 161–180, 2005.

[9] M. Charikar. Similarity estimation techniques from rounding algorithms. In *STOC*, pages 380–388, 2002.

[10] M. Datar, N. Immorlica, P. Indyk, and V. S. Mirrokni. Locality-sensitive hashing scheme based on p-stable distributions. In *SoCG*, pages 253–262, 2004.

[11] J. Deng, W. Dong, R. Socher, L. Li, K. Li, and F. Li. Imagenet: A large-scale hierarchical image database. In *2009 IEEE Computer Society Conference on Computer Vision and Pattern Recognition (CVPR 2009), 20-25 June 2009, Miami, Florida, USA*, pages 248–255, 2009.

[12] X. L. Dong and F. Naumann. Data fusion: resolving data conflicts for integration. *Proceedings of the VLDB Endowment*, 2(2):1654–1655, 2009.

[13] M. Durand and P. Flajolet. Loglog counting of large cardinalities. In *Algorithms-ESA 2003*, pages 605–617. Springer, 2003.

[14] A. K. Elmagarmid, P. G. Ipeirotis, and V. S. Verykios. Duplicate record detection: A survey. *IEEE Trans. Knowl. Data Eng.*, 19(1):1–16, 2007.

[15] C. Estan, G. Varghese, and M. Fisk. Bitmap algorithms for counting active flows on high-speed links. *IEEE/ACM Trans. Netw.*, 14(5):925–937, Oct. 2006.

[16] J. Feigenbaum, S. Kannan, and J. Zhang. Computing diameter in the streaming and sliding-window models. *Algorithmica*, 41(1):25–41, 2004.

[17] P. Flajolet, É. Fusy, O. Gandouet, and F. Meunier. Hyperloglog: the analysis of a near-optimal cardinality estimation algorithm. *DMTCS Proceedings*, (1), 2008.

[18] P. Flajolet and G. N. Martin. Probabilistic counting algorithms for data base applications. *J. Comput. Syst. Sci.*, 31(2):182–209, 1985.

[19] S. Ganguly. Counting distinct items over update streams. *Theoretical Computer Science*, 378(3):211–222, 2007.

[20] S. Guha. Tight results for clustering and summarizing data streams. In *ICDT*, pages 268–275, 2009.

[21] T. N. Herzog, F. J. Scheuren, and W. E. Winkler. *Data quality and record linkage techniques*, volume 1. Springer, 2007.

[22] P. Indyk and R. Motwani. Approximate nearest neighbors: Towards removing the curse of dimensionality. In *STOC*, pages 604–613, 1998.

[23] P. Indyk and D. P. Woodruff. Tight lower bounds for the distinct elements problem. In *FOCS*, pages 283–288, 2003.

[24] D. M. Kane, J. Nelson, and D. P. Woodruff. An optimal algorithm for the distinct elements problem. In *PODS*, pages 41–52, 2010.

[25] N. Koudas, S. Sarawagi, and D. Srivastava. Record linkage: similarity measures and algorithms. In *SIGMOD*, pages 802–803. ACM, 2006.

[26] C. R. Palmer, P. B. Gibbons, and C. Faloutsos. Anf: a fast and scalable tool for data mining in massive graphs. In *SIGKDD*, pages 81–90, 2002.

[27] P. G. Selinger, M. M. Astrahan, D. D. Chamberlin, R. A. Lorie, and T. G. Price. Access path selection in a relational database management system. In *SIGMOD*, pages 23–34, 1979.

[28] A. Singhal. Modern information retrieval: A brief overview. *IEEE Data Eng. Bull.*, 24(4):35–43, 2001.

[29] X. Wang, L. Zhang, and C. Liu. Duplicate discovery on 2 billion internet images. In *IEEE Conference on Computer Vision and Pattern Recognition, CVPR Workshops 2013, Portland, OR, USA, June 23-28, 2013*, pages 429–436, 2013.

[30] Q. Zhang. Communication-efficient computation on distributed noisy datasets. In *Proceedings of the 27th ACM on Symposium on Parallelism in Algorithms and Architectures, SPAA 2015, Portland, OR, USA, June 13-15, 2015*, pages 313–322, 2015.

APPENDIX

A. PROOF OF THEOREM 3

In this section we prove Theorem 3. We first consider the 2-dimensional Euclidean space.

Given a dataset S with F_0-ambiguity δ, let $n_1 = F_0(S)$ and $n_2 = F_0(S \backslash T)$ where $T \subseteq S$ is the corresponding subset such that $S \backslash T$ is well-shaped. By the monotonicity of the robust $F_0(\cdot)$ function and the second item of Definition 4,

$$(1-\delta)n_1 \leq n_2 \leq n_1. \tag{13}$$

Let $\mathcal{G} = \{G_1, \ldots, G_{n_1}\}$ be the minimum-cardinality partition of S. We will show that if we run Algorithm 4 (call it $\mathcal{A}$) on S, then with a good probability the following holds:

$$(1 - O(\delta + \epsilon))n_1 \leq \mathcal{A}(S) \leq (1 + O(\delta + \epsilon))n_1. \tag{14}$$

In other words, $\mathcal{A}(S)$ produces a $(1+O(\delta+\epsilon))$-approximation to $F_0(S)$.

Let $\mathcal{C}_1$ and $\mathcal{C}_2$ be the sets of non-empty cells corresponding to S and $S \backslash T$ respectively. Obviously $\mathcal{C}_2 \subseteq \mathcal{C}_1$. By the second item of Definition 4, and the fact that a group intersects at most 9 grid cells under the settings in Section 2.1, we have

$$|\mathcal{C}_1 \backslash \mathcal{C}_2| \leq 9\delta\,|\mathcal{C}_1|\,, \tag{15}$$

We now run $\mathcal{A}$ on S, and let $\mathcal{C}_1' \subseteq \mathcal{C}_1$ be the whole set of sampled items. Let $\mathcal{C}_2' \subseteq \mathcal{C}_1'$ be the set of cells sampled from $\mathcal{C}_2$. Since $\mathcal{C}_1'$ is sampled uniformly at random from $\mathcal{C}_1$, by (15) and a Chernoff bound, we have with probability $1-o(1)$ that

$$|\mathcal{C}_1' \backslash \mathcal{C}_2'| \leq 10\delta\,|\mathcal{C}_1'|\,. \tag{16}$$

Moreover, observe that

$$\forall C \in \mathcal{C}_1, w(C) = \Theta(1). \tag{17}$$

This follows from the simple geometry fact that each cell can intersect at most $O(1)$ unit-diameter groups under the condition that $F_0(S)$ is defined on the group partition with the minimum size, since otherwise some groups can be merged to produce a group partition of a smaller size.

By (15), (16) and (17), we have with probability $1-o(1)$,

$$\begin{aligned} & (1-O(\delta))\frac{|\mathcal{C}_1|}{|\mathcal{C}_1'|}\cdot\sum_{C\in\mathcal{C}_1'} w(C) \\ \leq\ & \frac{|\mathcal{C}_2|}{|\mathcal{C}_2'|}\cdot\sum_{C\in\mathcal{C}_2'} w(C) \\ \leq\ & (1+O(\delta))\frac{|\mathcal{C}_1|}{|\mathcal{C}_1'|}\cdot\sum_{C\in\mathcal{C}_1'} w(C). \end{aligned} \tag{18}$$

The idea to finish the proof is the following: Suppose we run Algorithm (4) on $S\backslash T$ only, since $\mathcal{C}_2'$ is a uniformly random sample on $\mathcal{C}_2$, we know by the analysis in Section 2.1 that with probability 0.96,

$$\frac{|\mathcal{C}_2|}{|\mathcal{C}_2'|}\sum_{C\in\mathcal{C}_2'} w(C) \in [(1-\epsilon)n_2, (1+\epsilon)n_2]. \tag{19}$$

And then by (13), (18) and (19), it holds with probability $1-o(1)-0.04 > 0.95$ that

$$(1-O(\delta+\epsilon))n_1 \leq \frac{|\mathcal{C}_1|}{|\mathcal{C}_1'|}\sum_{C\in\mathcal{C}_1'} w(C) \leq (1+O(\delta+\epsilon))n_1, \tag{20}$$

proving (14).

The cavity of the above argument is that (19) does not necessarily hold since points from T may interfere the value of $w(C)$ for a cell $C \in \mathcal{C}_2'$. Fortunately, we can show that such an interference is negligible.

For a cell $C \in \mathcal{C}_2$, we say it is *contaminated* if there exists a cell $C' \in \mathcal{C}_1\backslash\mathcal{C}_2$ and a group $G \in \mathcal{G}$ such that both C and C' intersect with G. Let $\mathcal{C}_3 \subseteq \mathcal{C}_2$ denote the set of contaminated cells, and let $\mathcal{C}_3' \subseteq \mathcal{C}_2'$ be the set of sampled contaminated cells. Note that $w(C)$ will only decrease if cell C is contaminated. Now observe that each cell in $\mathcal{C}_1\backslash\mathcal{C}_2$ can contaminate at most $O(1)$ cells in $\mathcal{C}_2$ in the Euclidean plane. Together with (16) and a Chernoff bound, we have with probability $1-o(1)$ that

$$|\mathcal{C}_3'| \leq O(\delta)\cdot|\mathcal{C}_2'|\,. \tag{21}$$

Therefore by (17), (21) and the analysis in Section 2.1, it holds with probability $1-o(1)-0.04$ that,

$$\begin{aligned} \frac{|\mathcal{C}_2|}{|\mathcal{C}_2'|}\sum_{C\in\mathcal{C}_2'} w(C) &\in \left[(1-\epsilon)n_2\left(1-O\left(\frac{|\mathcal{C}_3'|}{|\mathcal{C}_2'|}\right)\right), (1+\epsilon)n_2\right] \\ &\subseteq [(1-O(\epsilon+\delta))n_2, (1+\epsilon)n_2]. \end{aligned} \tag{22}$$

Finally replacing (19) with (22), we can show that (20) still holds, and thus (14) also holds. Therefore, the probability that (14) holds is $1-o(1)-o(1)-0.04 > 0.95$, where the two $o(1)$ error terms are introduced by Chernoff bounds (for deducting (16) and (21)), and the 0.04 error term is introduced by using the analysis in Section 2.1.

The above analysis can be literally carried to any constant dimensional Euclidean space (one only needs to slightly adjust some constant parameters).

B. OTHER MISSING PROOFS

B.1 Proof for Lemma 2

Proof: First, note that if $\beta \geq d^{3/2}$, then each cell can intersect at most one group. Thus $|\mathcal{C}| \geq F_0$.

Second, since the grid $\mathbb{G}$ is random and each group has diameter at most 1, the probability that the convex hull $\mathsf{CH}(G)$ of a group of points G is *cut* by the boundaries of grid cells in each dimension is at most $\mu = 1/d$. If $\mathsf{CH}(G)$ is cut by grid boundaries in i dimensions, then G intersects (at most) 2^i grid cells. Therefore the expectation of the number of cells each group G intersects, denoted by N_G, can be bounded by

$$\begin{aligned} \mathbf{E}[N_G] &\leq \sum_{i=0}^{d} 2^i \binom{d}{i}\mu^i(1-\mu)^{d-i} \\ &= (2\mu + (1-\mu))^d \\ &= (1+1/d)^d < 3. \end{aligned} \tag{23}$$

By the linearty of expectation, $\mathbf{E}[\mathcal{C}] \leq \sum_{G\in\mathcal{G}} \mathbf{E}[N_G] \leq 3F_0$. Therefore $|\mathcal{C}| \leq 300F_0$ with probability at least 0.99 by a Markov inequality.

□

B.2 Proof for Lemma 3

We investigate the two items in the definition of a smart hash function (Definition 5). Let f be a random hash function sampled from $\mathcal{F}$. For each pair $x, y \in S$ that are in different groups, the probability that $f(x) \neq f(y)$ is at least $1 - p_2^k$ by the definitions of LSH and k-fold hash function. By a union bound, with probability $1 - m^2 p_2^k$, we have for all pairs $x, y \in S$ that are in different groups, $f(x) \neq f(y)$.

Let $f(x) = (h_1(x), \ldots, h_k(x))$ where $h_i \in_r \mathcal{H}$. We next consider each group $G \in \mathcal{G}$. We say G is *cut* by h_i if there exist two items $x \in G$ and $y \in U$ such that $d(x,y) \leq \alpha$ but $h_i(x) \neq h_i(y)$. Thus if G is cut by j hash functions, then the cardinality of the $\{f(x) \mid \exists y \in G\ s.t.\ d(x,y) \leq \alpha\}$ can be bounded by η^j since $\mathcal{H}$ is η-concentrated. The probability that G is cut by h_i can be bounded by p_1 since $\mathcal{H}$ is $(2\alpha, \beta, p_1, p_2)$-sensitive and Diameter$(G) \leq \alpha$ (S is (α,β)-sparse). We thus can upper bound

$$\mathbf{E}[\rho] \leq \sum_{j=0}^{k} \eta^j \binom{k}{j}(1-p_1)^j p_1^{k-j},$$

which is $(\eta(1-p_1)+p_1)^k$. By a Markov inequality $\rho \leq 100(\eta(1-p_1)+p_1)^k$ with probability 0.99.

B.3 A Remark on LSH and Smart Hash Function

We note that not all LSH functions can be used as smart hash functions with a small image distance. We use the MinHash [6] for example.

Given a set $A = \{a_1, \ldots, a_t\} \subseteq U$, the MinHash is defined to be

$$h(A) = \min\{g(a) \mid a \in A\},$$

where $g : U \to \mathbb{N}$ is a random hash function. MinHash is an $(\alpha, \beta, 1-\alpha, 1-\beta)$-sensitive LSH for the Jaccard distance function $J(\cdot,\cdot)$, which is defined as follows: Given two sets $A, B \subseteq U$,

$$\text{JDist}(A, B) = 1 - \frac{|A \cap B|}{|A \cup B|}.$$

For any $x \in U \backslash A$, let $A_x = A \cup \{x\}$. It is easy to see that even for the small threshold $\alpha = 1/(t+1)$, A_x $(x \in U \backslash A)$ are in the same group, but $|h(A_\ell) \mid \ell \in [t]| \approx |U|/t$ which could be very large.

On the other hand, in practice, when given any query point, one often chooses to only search a much smaller number of buckets than $|U|/t$ for near neighbors, giving a *de facto* bound on the 'image distance', and the techniques in this paper may still be applied.

C. MATHEMATICAL TOOLS

We will need the following mathematical tools.

LEMMA 4 (MARKOV INEQUALITY). *Let $X \geq 0$ be a random variable. Then for all $a > 0$, $\mathbf{Pr}[X \geq a] \leq \frac{\mathbf{E}[X]}{a}$.*

LEMMA 5 (CHEBYSHEV'S INEQUALITY). *Let $X \geq 0$ be a random variable. Then for all $a > 0$,*

$$\mathbf{Pr}[|X - \mathbf{E}[X]| \geq a] \leq \frac{\mathbf{Var}[X]}{a^2}.$$

LEMMA 6 (CHERNOFF BOUND). *Let $X_1, \ldots, X_k \in [0, 1]$ be independent random variables, and let $X = \sum_{i=1}^{k} X_i$.*

$$\mathbf{Pr}[|X - \mathbf{E}[X]| \geq \epsilon \mathbf{E}[X]] \leq 2e^{-\frac{\epsilon^2 \mathbf{E}[X]}{3}}.$$

Augmented Sketch: Faster and More Accurate Stream Processing

Pratanu Roy[*]
Systems Group Computer Science
ETH Zurich
pratanu@inf.ethz.ch

Arijit Khan[†]
School of Computer Engineering
NTU Singapore
arijit.khan@ntu.edu.sg

Gustavo Alonso
Systems Group Computer Science
ETH Zurich
alonso@inf.ethz.ch

ABSTRACT

Approximated algorithms are often used to estimate the frequency of items on high volume, fast data streams. The most common ones are variations of Count-Min sketch, which use sub-linear space for the count, but can produce errors in the counts of the most frequent items and can misclassify low-frequency items. In this paper, we improve the accuracy of sketch-based algorithms by increasing the frequency estimation accuracy of the most frequent items and reducing the possible misclassification of low-frequency items, while also improving the overall throughput.

Our solution, called Augmented Sketch (ASketch), is based on a pre-filtering stage that dynamically identifies and aggregates the most frequent items. Items overflowing the pre-filtering stage are processed using a conventional sketch algorithm, thereby making the solution general and applicable in a wide range of contexts. The pre-filtering stage can be efficiently implemented with SIMD instructions on multi-core machines and can be further parallelized through pipeline parallelism where the filtering stage runs in one core and the sketch algorithm runs in another core.

Keywords

data streams; sketch; approximated algorithms; data structures; stream summary

1. INTRODUCTION

In scenarios such as real-time IP traffic, phone calls, sensor measurements, web clicks and crawls, massive amounts of data are generated as a high-rate stream [10, 26]. Processing of such streams often requires approximation through succinct synopses created in a single-pass [8]. These synopses summarize the streams to give an idea of the frequency of items, using a small amount of space, while allowing to process the stream fast enough. Due to the smaller size of the synopsis compared to the original stream size, there is a trade-off among space, accuracy, and efficiency: reducing the space increases the efficiency but affects accuracy.

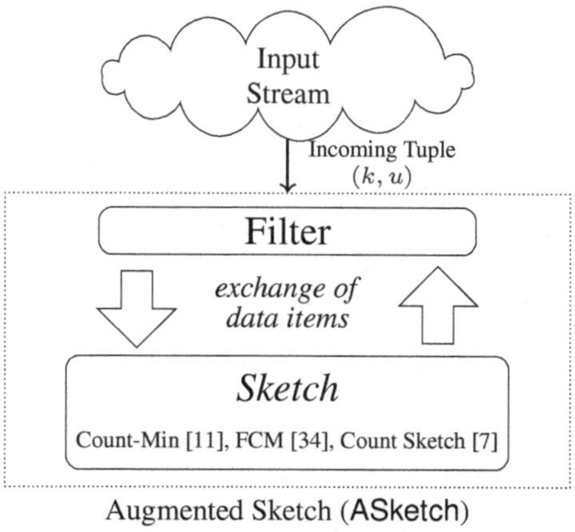

Figure 1: ASketch exchanges data items between the filter and the sketch such that high-frequency items are kept in the filter.

In this paper, we study the problem of frequency estimation over data streams that require summarization: given a data item as a query, we estimate the frequency count of that item in the input stream. In the literature, sketch data structures [3, 7, 11, 12, 18, 22] are the solution of choice to address this problem. By using multiple hash functions, sketches summarize massive data streams within a limited space. However, due to summarization, the approach can give inaccurate results. First, it can give an inaccurate count for the most frequent items. Second, it can misclassify low-frequency items and report them as high-frequency ones. Since the high-frequency items are usually more relevant in many applications including load-balancing and heavy-hitter queries [9, 35], it is important to estimate the frequency of the most frequent items *as accurately as possible*. In the literature, there are many examples of where lower accuracy on the frequency estimation impacts the subsequent analysis of the data. For instance, it was shown in [35] that due to the lower accuracy provided by traditional sketches, an algorithm trying to balance the load will result in biases and unbalanced job distribution. Similarly, in case of natural language processing (NLP) applications such as sentiment analysis, a typical application of sketches is to compute the pointwise mutual information (PMI), and subsequently find the top-k positive and negative words [19]. Without an accurate ranking, words can easily be misclassified, leading to wrong interpretations. To find out the level of accuracy of existing solutions, we constructed a Count-Min sketch summary of size 128KB from a real-world *IP-trace* stream data, originally containing 461M tuples. This results in the estimated frequency of the most frequent item to be 18 018 217, whereas its

[*]Author's new affiliation: Oracle Labs, Zurich, Email: pratanu.r.roy@oracle.com.
[†]This work has been done while the author was at ETH Zurich.

SIGMOD'16, June 26-July 01, 2016, San Francisco, CA, USA

DOI: http://dx.doi.org/10.1145/2882903.2882948

	Stream Processing Throughput Updates/milisecond	*Frequency-Estimation Query Throughput* Queries/milisecond	*Frequency-Estimation Error* Observed error (%)
Count-Min [11]	6481	6892	0.0024
Frequency-Aware Count [34]	6165	7551	0.0013
Holistic UDAFs [10]	17508	6319	0.0025
ASketch [this work]	**26739**	**30795**	**0.0004**

Table 1: ASketch vs. other sketch-based methods: ASketch is implemented on top of Count-Min with a filter capacity of 32 items. All methods are allocated 128KB of space. The stream size is 32M, and the number of distinct data items is 8M. The stream data has a Zipf frequency distribution with skew 1.5. For details about various parameters, query setting, and evaluation metrics, see Section 7.

true frequency is 17 978 588. Similar margin of errors also occur for other high-frequency items in the *IP-trace* stream, as well as in other stream datasets that we experimented with. Although the error may seem small, it can create problems in applications checking thresholds, doing bookkeeping, and establishing ranking as just discussed.

In addition, due to the *one-sided error guarantee* (i.e., the estimated frequency of an item is at least as high as its true frequency) ensured by many sketches, a low-frequency item can misleadingly appear as a high-frequency item in the sketch synopsis. This is indeed the case found in our empirical evaluation. When we constructed a 16KB Count-Min synopsis of a synthetic stream having a Zipf frequency distribution, we find that 27 low-frequency items are misclassified as very high-frequency items, with an average relative error in the order of 10^5 for these misclassified items. Such misclassifications can be detrimental to various machine learning applications. For instance, it was shown in [36] that since frequent items mining is the first step of frequent itemsets mining, even a small number of misclassified items leads to a large number of false-positive itemsets, which makes effective frequent itemsets mining from summarized streams difficult. A similar situation arises in sketch-based clustering and classifications, often used in suspicious events detection, where a slight improvement in prediction accuracy can result in a huge improvement [1, 2].

In this paper, we propose a way to solve these problems by complementing existing techniques and without requiring a radically different solution. ASketch (Augmented Sketch) is a stream processing framework, applicable over many sketch-based synopses, and coupled with an adaptive pre-filtering and early-aggregation strategy. It utilizes the skew[1] of the underlying stream data to improve the frequency estimation accuracy for the most frequent items by filtering them out earlier. It also improves the overall throughput — while using *exactly* the same amount of space as traditional sketches. The idea of ASketch is illustrated in Figure 1. All items in the stream pass through a filtering stage. The filter retains the high-frequency items and the sketch processes the tail of the distribution. The throughput improvement comes from the skewed distribution and extremely fast lookup time of the filter (e.g., with *vector instructions*). Catching high-frequency items with a filtering stage also improves the accuracy of the frequency estimation for the frequent items. For example, ASketch of size 128KB reports the estimated frequency of the most frequent item to be exactly 17 978 588 in the *IP-trace* stream. At the same time, separation of high frequency items from the sketch reduces misclassifications. In our experiments, we do not find any instance of misclassified low frequency items, when using an ASketch synopsis of the same size.

Our contributions can be summarized as follows.

- We explore the use of a filter to catch heavy hitters earlier and remove them from the subsequent sketch data structure. The resulting design, ASketch, shows how to implement such filter efficiently so that not only *accuracy improves* but also *overall throughput* (Section 5).
- Since introducing a filter in front of a sketch data structure changes the properties of the latter, we provide an extensive analysis of ASketch, and how the different parameters of the design affect accuracy and performance (Section 4).
- Modern hardware offers several possibilities for increasing the efficiency of the filtering stage. In the paper, we explore possible parallel implementations using separate cores, using SIMD instructions, and in an SPMD (single program, multiple data) parallel model (Section 6).
- The performance analysis showing the advantages of ASketch, also shed light on the differences between existing solutions and how the filter interacts with different forms of sketches. We compare ASketch with Count-Min [11], Holistic UDAFs [10], Frequency-Aware Counting [34], and Space Saving [27] (Section 7).

[1] Manerikar et. al. [26] reported Zipf skew $z \geq 1.4$ in real-world datasets.

2. RELATED WORK

The problem of synopsis construction has been studied extensively [8] in the context of a variety of techniques such as sampling [15], wavelets [16, 17], histograms [20], sketches [3, 7, 11, 12, 18, 22], and counter-based methods, e.g., Space Saving [27] and Frequent [9]. Among all these techniques, sketches and counter-based approaches are widely used for stream data summarization. Sketches are typically used for frequency estimation. Counter-based data structures are designed for finding the top-k frequent items. Sketches keep approximate counts for all items, counter-based approaches maintain approximate counts only for the frequent items. Sketches can support top-k queries with an additional heap [7] or a hierarchical data structure [8]. However, counter-based approaches achieve faster update throughput than sketches for the top-k estimation [9], as they do not count the frequency of all items.

Several systems have been proposed either to improve the stream processing throughput of sketches, e.g., Holistic UDAFs [10], or to improve their query processing accuracy, e.g., Frequency-Aware Counting [34] and gSketch [37]. ASketch improves both accuracy and throughput with the help of pre-filtering and early-aggregation of high frequency items. Approaches like Holistic UDAFs and Frequency-Aware Counting use additional data structures, increasing the overall storage requirement, which is often significant with respect to small-space sketch data structures. As an example, we empirically compare in Table 1 the efficiency and accuracy of ASketch with several existing techniques, e.g., Count-Min [11], Holistic UDAFs [10], and Frequency-Aware Counting [34], while allocating the same amount of space. The results demonstrate the advantages of ASketch.

The idea of separating high-frequency items from skewed data distribution is not new [15]. Modern processors employ caches on top of main memory to capture the locality of access and to improve

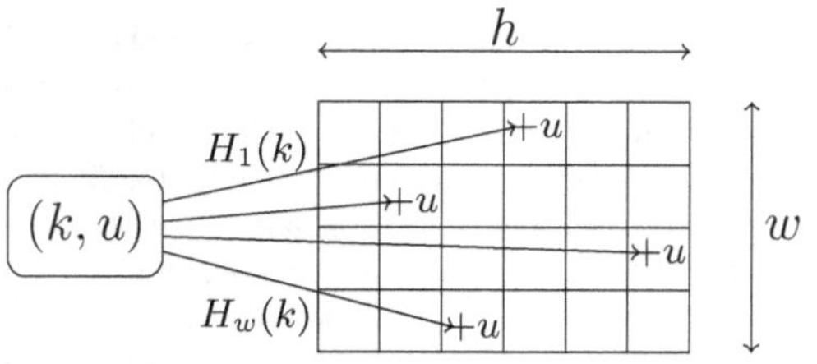

Figure 2: Count-Min.

the overall throughput. Skimmed Sketch [14] observed that major part of the error in join size estimation with sketches appears due to the collisions of high frequency items with low frequency items, and therefore, proposed to skim-off the high frequency items in a post-processing manner with the help of a heap [7].

The pre-filtering and early-aggregation strategy has been effectively used in many applications, e.g., duplicate elimination [23], external merge sort [5], Space Saving synopsis construction [32], etc. String matching techniques are utilized to improve XML pre-filtering so that the memory consumption and processing time decreases [21]. In [24], pre-filtering has been effectively used to prune irrelevant events from the ones that are being monitored in a complex event detection application. In both of these cases [21, 24], pre-filtering is used to eliminate data. ASketch uses a pre-filtering strategy to separate common items from the less common ones for sketch data structures.

3. PRELIMINARIES

A data stream of running length n is a sequence of n tuples. The t-th tuple is denoted as (k_t, u_t), where k_t is a data-item key used for hashing and u_t is a frequency value associated with the data item. Usually the values for k_t are drawn from a large domain (e.g, IP addresses, URLs, etc.) and the value u_t is a positive number[2,3]; hence, the frequency counts of data items increase monotonically.

Sketches are a family of data structures for summarizing data streams. Sketches bear similarities to Bloom filters [6, 31] in that both employ hashing to summarize data; however, they differ in how they update the hash buckets and use these hashed data to derive estimates. Among the various sketches available [3, 7, 11, 13, 18, 22, 25], it has been shown [9, 33, 34] that Count-Min [11] achieves the best update throughput in general, as well as high accuracy on skewed distributions. Therefore, we shall discuss ASketch on top of Count-Min. Nevertheless, ASketch *is generic and can be applied in combination with other sketches.* To demonstrate it, we also evaluate the performance of ASketch with other underlying sketches. Next, for the ease of presentation, we introduce Count-Min.

Count-Min. In Count-Min, hashing is used to approximately maintain the frequency counts of a large number of distinct items in a data stream. We use w pairwise independent hash functions, each of which maps onto uniformly random integers in the range $[0 \dots h-1]$. The data structure itself consists of a 2-dimensional array with $w \cdot h$ cells of length h and width w. Each hash function corresponds to one of w 1-dimensional arrays with h cells. The hash functions are used to update the counts of different cells in this 2-dimensional data structure (Figure 2).

In order to *estimate* the count of an item, we determine the set of w cells to which each of the w hash-functions maps onto, and compute the minimum value among all these cells. Let c_t be the true value of the count being estimated. The estimated count is at least equal to c_t, since we are dealing with non-negative counts only, and there may be an over-estimation because of collisions among hash cells. As it turns out, a probabilistic upper bound to the estimate can be determined [11]. For a data stream with N as the sum of the counts of the items received so far, the estimated count is at most $c_t + (\frac{e}{h})N$ with probability at least $1 - e^{-w}$. Here, e is the base of the natural logarithm.

4. MOTIVATION FOR FILTERING AND AGGREGATING FREQUENT ITEMS

We analytically compare the frequency estimation error, frequency estimation time, and stream processing throughput of both Count-Min and ASketch. Let us denote by N the aggregate of the counts of all items in the data stream.

Count-Min Properties. Consider a Count-Min with w pairwise independent hash functions, each of which maps onto uniformly random integers in the range $[0 \dots h-1]$. The time required to insert an item in Count-Min is $t_s = \mathcal{O}(w)$. This is also same as the time required to answer a frequency estimation query. The expected error in the frequency estimation [11] is at most $(\frac{e}{h})N$, with probability at most e^{-w}, where e is the base of the natural logarithm.

How is a Filter Accommodated in an ASketch? ASketch augments the traditional Count-Min with a filter. Let us assume that the filter consumes s_f space, while the time required to insert an item (as well as query an item) in the filter is t_f. Usually, s_f is very small and due to the hardware conscious implementation of the filter (explained in Section 6.1), $t_f << t_s$. To accommodate the filter in ASketch, the space from the underlying sketch data structure is reduced so that the overall space for ASketch stays the same as that of the Count-Min alone. Reduction of space from the underlying sketch can be achieved either by reducing the number of hash functions, or by reducing the range of each hash function, or by both. More specifically, let w' and h' be the number of hash functions and the range of each hash function in ASketch, respectively. Then, we have: $s_f + w'h' = wh$. In our implementation, we fix $w' = w$, and reduce h' to $(h - \frac{s_f}{w})$, due to two reasons: (1) Usually, $h > w$. Hence, for the same amount of change in h or w, the former will have a lower impact in reduction of storage space consumed by the underlying sketch. Therefore, updating h is more flexible to accommodate various sizes of filter in ASketch. (2) By having the same w number of hash functions for both Count-Min and ASketch, we keep the error bound probability e^{-w} identical.

Impact of the Filter on Throughput of ASketch. ASketch update time (as well as query time) can be expressed as: $t_f + \text{filter}_{\text{selectivity}} * t_s$. Here, t_f and t_s are update times of the filter and the sketch, respectively. We define $\text{filter}_{\text{selectivity}}$ as the ratio of the count of data items that overflow the filter with respect to the total count of all data items. In the case of ASketch updates, there is an additional factor which involves *exchanging of data items* between the filter and sketch (described in our Algorithm 1). Experiments show that the number of exchanges is rather small with respect to the overall stream size and hence, we ignored it here, but analyze it in more detail in the Appendix. We evaluate the impact of this factor empirically in Section 7.

Clearly, for ASketch, we increase the processing time by t_f; however, in return, we reduce the sketch processing time by a factor of $\text{filter}_{\text{selectivity}}$. A small size of the filter (i.e., s_f) and vectorized

[2]Sketches, as well as ASketch, also allow us to model the removal of data items (see Appendix). However, for simplicity, we shall currently assume a *strict distributions* [29], that is, the stream updates are positive.

[3]For simplicity, we assume $u_t = 1$. Our analysis can easily be extended for larger values of u_t.

	Count-Min	ASketch
Freq. Estimation Time	t_s	$t_f + \left(\frac{N_2}{N}\right) t_s$
Stream Processing Throughput	$\frac{1}{t_s}$	$\frac{1}{t_f + \left(\frac{N_2}{N}\right) t_s}$
Freq. Estimation Error	$\left(\frac{e}{h}\right) N$ with prob. e^{-w}	$\left(\frac{e}{h - \frac{s_f}{w}}\right) N_2 \left(\frac{N_2}{N}\right)$ with prob. e^{-w}
Supported Queries	Frequency Estimation	Frequency Estimation, Top-k Frequent Items

Table 2: Analytic comparison between Count-Min and ASketch: w the number of hash functions, h the range of each hash function, s_f the size of the filter, t_s data-item insertion time in Count-Min, t_f data-item insertion time in the filter, N total aggregated stream size, N_1 stream size stored in the filter, $N_2 = N - N_1$, e base of natural logarithm.

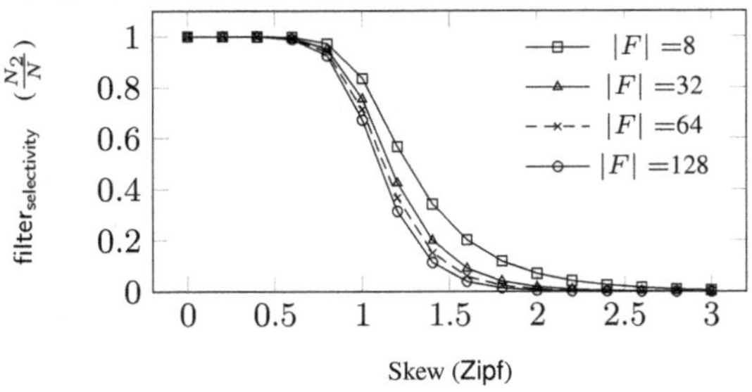

Figure 3: Filter selectivity: data stream with Zipf distribution, stream size 32M, number of distinct data items 8M. We vary the filter size $|F|$, i.e., the number of high-frequency items stored in the filter.

execution (explained in Section 6.1) keeps t_f small, in the range of a few assembly instructions. Therefore, $\text{filter}_{\text{selectivity}}$ essentially determines the overall effectiveness of ASketch.

Let us assume that out of N aggregated stream-counts, N_1 counts are processed by the filter and $(N - N_1) = N_2$ counts are processed by the sketch. Therefore, $\text{filter}_{\text{selectivity}} = \frac{N_2}{N}$. However, most real world streams exhibit skew [26]. For a Zipf distribution, we can measure the $\text{filter}_{\text{selectivity}}$ easily in the closed form by summing up the frequency counts of the top-k items [4, 32]. To demonstrate the potential effectiveness[4] of the ASketch framework, we have plotted the filter size ($|F|$) and the $\text{filter}_{\text{selectivity}}$, i.e., $\frac{N_2}{N}$ in Figure 3 on a data stream of 32M items with Zipf distribution. For a skew of 1.5, the top-32 data items account for 80% of all frequency counts, i.e., only $\frac{N_2}{N} = 20\%$ items are forwarded to the underlying sketch data structure. Therefore, we expect that the overall stream processing time of ASketch would be smaller than traditional sketches. One interesting observation from Figure 3 is that increasing the filter size beyond a certain threshold does not reduce the $\text{filter}_{\text{selectivity}}$ significantly. However, increasing the filter size, depending on the filter implementation (explained later in Section 6.1), may increase the filter processing time (t_f). Therefore, the filter in ASketch must consume a small space in order to achieve the maximum throughput gain.

Impact of the Filter on Accuracy of ASketch. ASketch improves the frequency estimation accuracy for the frequent items that are stored in the filter. In fact, if one can store the *exact* frequency counts for the items in the filter, their frequency estimation error would be zero. For the items that are stored in the sketch, we reduce their collisions with the high-frequency items, as the items stored in the filter are no longer hashed into the sketch. This reduces the possibility that a low-frequency item would appear as a high-frequency item, therefore reducing the misclassification error. However, in order to accommodate space for the filter, we now utilize a sketch structure which has a smaller size than that of the original Count-Min. This increases the frequency estimation error for low-frequency items stored in the sketch, often within a tolerable margin (see Theorem 1). Nevertheless, as mentioned earlier, it is often the frequency estimation accuracy for the high-frequency items which is more critical in actual applications (e.g., frequent pattern mining, outlier detection, load-balancing, and heavy-hitter detection) and ASketch significantly improves the frequency estimation accuracy for the high-frequency items stored in the filter. Let us assume that the frequency estimation queries are obtained by sampling the data items based on their frequencies, that is, the high-frequency items are queried more than the low-frequency items in a skewed stream. Then, the expected error in frequency estimation due to ASketch is given by: $(\frac{e}{h-\frac{s_f}{w}})N_2(\frac{N_2}{N})$, whereas the expected frequency estimation error due to Count-Min will be: $(\frac{e}{h})N$ for the same amount of storage space. Clearly, ASketch will result in a smaller expected error, since $N_2(\frac{N_2}{N}) << N$ in a skewed stream.

In the following theorem, we provide a probabilistic bound of the increase in error for the low-frequency items that reside in the underlying Count-Min sketch of ASketch, due to the reduction in Count-Min sketch size.

THEOREM 1. *The increase in error ΔE for a low-frequency item that resides in the underlying* Count-Min *sketch of* ASketch*, due to the reduction in* Count-Min *sketch size, is bounded with probability of at least $1 - e^{-w}$ as follows:*

$$\Delta E \leq (\frac{es_f}{wh(h - \frac{s_f}{w})})N \quad (1)$$

The proof can be found in the Appendix. However, one can verify that the upper bound is reasonably small even for a large size stream. In reality, the increase in error for the low-frequency items is even smaller, because the high-frequency items which constitute a significant fraction of the aggregated stream frequency, are stored in the filter, and they are not hashed into the sketch.

Summary. For a fixed ASketch size, we summarize the *trade-offs among filter size, throughput, and frequency estimation accuracy.*

- By having a larger filter, one can potentially store more high-frequency items in the filter; and this, in turn, will result in better frequency estimation accuracy for more high-frequency items. However, if we consider the expected frequency estimation error (given in Table 2), it consists of the errors due to both high-frequency and low-frequency items in the data stream. Since the high-frequency items are queried more than the low-frequency items, we find that the expected error initially decreases with the increasing filter size; but beyond a threshold filter size, it stops decreasing. This is because with increasing filter size, while we have better accuracy for more high-frequency items, we also introduce more error over the low-frequency items due to the reduced size of the underlying sketch.
- For the implementations considered, increasing the filter size increases the filter processing time t_f, without too much gain in the $\text{filter}_{\text{selectivity}}$. Therefore, beyond a threshold filter size, the throughput starts decreasing.

We empirically explore these trade-offs in Section 7.

[4]Note that the k-items in the filter are not always guranteed to be the top-k frequent items; but based on the empirical results (Table 5), we achieve high accuracy for the top-k frequent items.

5. ALGORITHM FOR ASKETCH

ASketch exchanges data items between the filter and the sketch, so that the filter stores the most frequent items of the observed input stream. Such movement of data items is a challenging problem for several reasons. First, one needs to ensure that the exchange procedure does not incur too much overhead on the normal stream processing rate. Second, it is difficult to remove the item, along with its frequency count, from the underlying sketch. This is because Count-Min only provides an over-estimation of the true frequency of an item; if we remove the over-estimated frequency count of an item from the sketch, it may violate the *one-sided accuracy guarantee* provided by the sketch. We illustrate this problem with an example:

EXAMPLE 1. *Let us assume that the data item A is currently stored in* Count-Min *and the hash cell corresponding to some hash function H_i provides the smallest frequency estimation for A. The removal of A from the sketch, along with its estimated frequency, will result in a count value of* 0 *in the hash cell corresponding to $H_i(A)$. Now, consider all items B that are also currently stored in* Count-Min*, such that $H_i(B) = H_i(A)$. After the removal of A from the sketch, the estimated frequency of all such B will become* 0*, an underestimation of their true frequencies.*

In ASketch, we want to maintain the one-sided accuracy guarantee of Count-Min, i.e., *the estimated frequency of an item reported by* ASketch *must always be an over-estimation of its true frequency*. We achieve this accuracy guarantee by introducing two different counts in the filter as described below.

Algorithm Description. ASketch consists of two data structures: *filter* (F) and *sketch* (CMS). The filter stores a few high-frequency items and two associated counts, namely new_count and old_count for each of the items that it monitors. The new_count denotes the estimated (over-estimation) frequency of an item that is currently stored in the filter. The difference between new_count and old_count represents the (exact) aggregated frequency that have been accumulated during the time a particular item resides in the filter. The sketch is implemented as the classical Count-Min, which is a two dimensional array with length (i.e., range of each hash function) h and width (number of hash functions) w, as shown in Figure 2.

The *stream processing algorithm* is shown in Algorithm 1. Every incoming tuple in the stream is represented as (k, u), where k is the key of the data item, and u is a frequency value. We first perform a lookup for the key k in the filter (lines 1-6, Algorithm 1). If k does not exist in the filter and there is an empty cell in the filter, then k is inserted in the filter with its old_count set to 0, and new_count as u (lines 4-6). Next time, whenever we find the key in the filter, we only update its new_count value without changing the old_count value (lines 2-3). If k is not found in the filter, and the filter is full (lines 7-18, Algorithm 1), then the data item is sent to the sketch. We insert the item in the sketch with the traditional sketch updating protocol, that is, k is hashed into w different rows by w different hash functions, where every hash function maps k in a range of h hash values (line 8).

Whenever we insert an item in the sketch, we get an estimate (over-estimation) of its true frequency. Now, we additionally keep track of the smallest frequency value (i.e., new_count) of any item currently stored in the filter. Thus, if the estimated frequency of the last item inserted into Count-Min is higher than the smallest frequency value in the filter, we initiate an exchange (lines 9-17, Algorithm 1). The last item that was hashed into the sketch is now moved to the filter with both its old_count and new_count set as its estimated count obtained from the sketch. However, we do not make any change in the values inside the sketch. To accommodate this item in the filter, the item with the smallest frequency in the filter is now inserted into the sketch; but we only hash its (new_count-old_count) frequency into the sketch (lines 11-12). This is because its old_count frequency can either be 0, which indicates that the item was never placed into the sketch; otherwise, its old_count frequency is already contained in the sketch since the time the item was last moved from the sketch.

Algorithm 1 Stream processing algorithm for ASketch

```
Ensure: insert tuple (k, u) into ASketch
 1: lookup k in filter
 2: if item found then
 3:     new_count[k] → new_count[k] + u
 4: else if filter not full then
 5:     new_count[k] → u
 6:     old_count[k] → 0
 7: else
 8:     update sketch with (k, u)
 9:     if (estimated freq[k] > min freq[F]) then
10:         find minimum freq item k_i in F
11:         if (new_count[k_i]-old_count[k_i])>0 then
12:             update sketch with (k_i,new_count[k_i]-old_count[k_i])
13:         end if
14:         add k to filter
15:         new_count[k] → estimated freq[k]
16:         old_count[k] → estimated freq[k]
17:     end if
18: end if
```

Algorithm 2 Query processing algorithm for ASketch

```
Ensure: estimate frequency of item k using ASketch
 1: lookup item k in filter
 2: if item found then
 3:     return new_count[k] from filter
 4: else
 5:     return estimated freq[k] from sketch
 6: end if
```

The key insight here is that we can *exactly* capture the hits for an item that is currently stored in the filter by using its (new_count-old_count) value. This has three benefits: (1) By accumulating this count in the filter, we save the cost of applying multiple hash functions in the sketch, and thus, improve the *throughput*. (2) As high-frequency items in a skewed data stream remain in the filter most of the time, we get more *accurate* frequency counts for these items. (3) The *misclassification rate* for the low-frequency items as high-frequency items also decreases, since the aggregate of the (new_count-old_count) values of the high-frequency items are not hashed into the underlying sketch .

The *query processing algorithm* is shown in Algorithm 2. For an incoming query requesting for the frequency of an item k, the algorithm first performs a lookup in the filter, and if finds the item, then returns the new_count (line 2-3); otherwise, the estimated frequency from the underlying sketch is returned (line 5).

Exchange Policy. In this section, we discuss the efficiency of the exchange policy. First, we need to keep track of the smallest frequency count in the filter. The efficiency of this step depends on the underlying data structure and the hardware implementation of the filter, which will be discussed shortly in Section 6.1. Second, we empirically found that we require a relatively small number of exchanges compared to the overall stream size in order to ensure that the high-frequency items are stored and early aggregated in the filter. As an example, even for the Uniform distribution (i.e.,

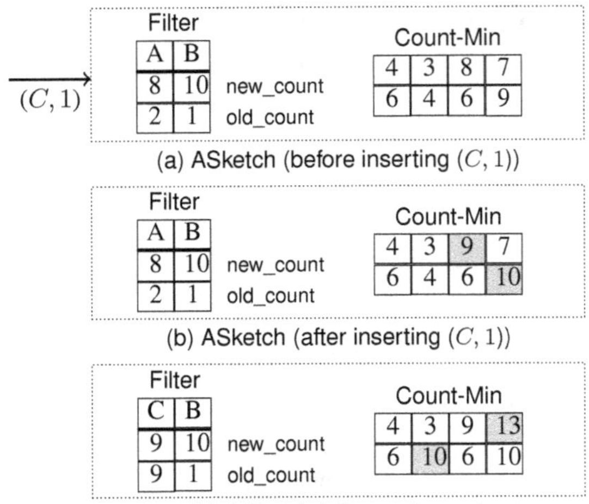

(a) ASketch (before inserting $(C, 1)$)

(b) ASketch (after inserting $(C, 1)$)

(c) ASketch (after exchange)

Figure 4: Example of stream processing by ASketch.

skew is 0), we need only about 40K exchanges for a stream of size 32M, ASketch size of 128KB, and filter size of 32 items (Figure 9). When the skew increases, the number of exchanges decreases as shown in our experimental results. Third, and perhaps more importantly, can our exchange policy trigger *multiple exchanges* between the filter and the sketch? Our exchange mechanism may indeed initiate multiple exchanges; for example, when the lowest-frequency item from the filter is moved to Count-Min, its estimated frequency (which will now be an over-estimation due to hash-based collisions) could be higher than that of the second least-frequent item in the filter. This will initiate yet another exchange. However, a careful examination reveals that multiple exchanges that happen as an after-effect of the first exchange are unnecessary and they introduce additional errors in the frequency estimation. Hence, whenever we hash an item in Count-Min because it was not found in the filter (or because the filter was full), we always restrict ourselves to *at most one exchange* between the filter and the sketch. The following lemma guarantees an upper bound on the number of times an item is inserted into the underlying sketch in the presence of our exchange policy, thereby ensuring the overall efficiency of ASketch.

LEMMA 1. *Let us assume that some data item has been appeared total t times in the stream. Then, the number of times we insert that data item in the underlying sketch by following* ASketch *algorithm is no more than t.*

Proof of the lemma follows from the fact that, in the best case, data items are early-aggregated in the filter before being inserted into the sketch. Coupled with the characteristics of our exchange policy, that is, (1) we do not perform multiple exchanges between filter and sketch for each insertion in the sketch, and (2) if the difference between the new_count and the old_count for the lowest-frequency item in the filter is zero, we do not perform any update in the sketch (line 11, Algorithm 1); we ensure that the above lemma is satisfied. While we demonstrate in our experiments (Section 7) that the number of exchanges is usually very small, we also provide theoretical bounds on the exchange policy in the Appendix.

Below, we demonstrate the key steps of our stream processing algorithm (Algorithm 1) with an example.

EXAMPLE 2. *In Figure 4, we show in three steps how a data tuple $(C, 1)$ is inserted into* ASketch. *Since the filter is full and it does not contain the data item C, the sketch is updated. We shaded the affected cells due to this update in Figure 4 (b). However, the estimated frequency of C, which is 9, is higher than the smallest frequency stored in the filter (i.e., 8 for item A). Hence, we move C into the filter with both its* old_count *and* new_count *assigned to its estimated frequency (is shown in Filter in Figure 4 (c)). We do not change anything in the sketch cells due to the movement of C. Finally, we insert A into the sketch; however, only the difference of its* (new_count-old_count) 6, *is inserted into the sketch (is shown in* Count-Min *in Figure 4 (c); affected cells are highlighted). Although, the current estimated frequency of A is 10, which is larger than the current smallest count in the filter, we do not initiate any other exchanges.*

6. ASKETCH ON MULTI-CORE

We now discuss the implementation of ASketch in modern multi-core hardware with an emphasis on (1) SIMD parallelism in the filter implementation, (2) pipeline parallelism in the ASketch framework, as well as (3) SPMD parallelism by implementing ASketch as a counting kernel in a multi-core machine.

6.1 Filter with SIMD Parallelism

Continued from the discussion in Section 4, we are aiming for a filter that is small in size. It must support the following two operations efficiently: (1) *lookup* based on the key of the data item; (2) *find* the item with the minimum new_count value. We considered several alternatives (explained below). An empirical comparison can be found in Section 7.

The Space Saving [27] algorithm also requires efficient support of the aforementioned two operations. The authors used a Stream-Summary data structure coupled with a hash table. The hash table is used for the lookup operation and the stream-summary, a linked list which keeps all the items sorted based on their count values, helps the second operation. Therefore, we used it as the first design alternative. However, this implementation has a high space overhead as it may require up to four pointers per item. Due to the large memory overhead, for the same filter size budget, it can monitor fewer items and thus performs poorly.

On modern hardware, often for small data structures, a *linear scan* performs better than a hash-based lookup, as it avoids random access and pointer chasing [32]. A linear scan is also amenable to *vectorized execution*. Therefore, we considered two array-based implementations, namely, Vector and Heap. For both implementations, we use three arrays with (id, new_count, old_count) values. The vectorized search on id to find the location of an item is shown in Algorithm 3. This is an implementation of *linear scan* with SIMD instructions[5]. The __builtin_ctz is a hardware specific high performance function implemented in assembly provided by GCC.[6] This particular function returns the count of trailing zeros in a binary representation of a number which is used to find the location of the hit. Vector also uses a linear scan for finding the element with the minimum count. We find that the Vector performs very efficiently with a skew more than 2 in a Zipf-distribution.

The Heap incurs additional overhead for maintaining the heap. However, the benefit is that the lookup of the item of minimum count becomes inexpensive. We evaluated two min-heap implementations, namely, Strict and Relaxed. For every hit in the filter, Strict-Heap rearranges the data structure so that it maintains the heap. We do not find it as efficient as the Relaxed-Heap alternative which reconstructs the heap only when there is a hit on the item with the minimum count. Based on our empirical evaluation,

[5]Details about SSE2 intrinsics can be found in https://software.intel.com/en-us/node/514275.

[6]Details can be found in https://gcc.gnu.org/onlinedocs/gcc/Other-Builtins.html.

Algorithm 3 Filtering with SSE2 SIMD intrinsics for a filter of 16 items. Implementation of linear search on the *filter_id* array.

```
/*load the input item*/
const __m128i s_item = _mm_set1_epi32(item);
/*point to the filter id array*/
__m128i *filter = (__m128i *)filter_id;
/*search 16 elements*/
__m128i f_comp = _mm_cmpeq_epi32(s_item, filter[0]);
__m128i s_comp = _mm_cmpeq_epi32(s_item, filter[1]);
__m128i t_comp = _mm_cmpeq_epi32(s_item, filter[2]);
__m128i r_comp = _mm_cmpeq_epi32(s_item, filter[3]);
/*check whether item is found*/
f_comp = _mm_packs_epi32 (f_comp, s_comp);
t_comp = _mm_packs_epi32 (t_comp, r_comp);
f_comp = _mm_packs_epi32 (f_comp, t_comp);
int found = _mm_movemask_epi8 (f_comp);
/*if found return the position*/
if (found) return __builtin_ctz(found);
else return -1;
```

the Relaxed-Heap provides the best performance among all design choices when the skew is low or even moderate (e.g., skew < 2 in a Zipf distribution).

6.2 Pipeline Parallelism: Filter and Sketch

The benefits of filtering are more pronounced when the filter and sketch are decoupled and run on separate cores. In such an implementation, shared memory access is replaced with a message passing interface between the two processors. As shown in Figure 1, the exchange of data items between the two data structures now happens through messages. Such design has been shown to be a good fit for modern hardware [32], as it avoids locking in the context of shared memory access. In ASketch, core C_0 contains the filter and consumes the input tuples. As soon as there is a miss in the filter (line 7 in Algorithm 1), it forwards the item to core C_1 that maintains the sketch. C_0 also forwards the minimum count whenever the minimum count changes. When the estimated frequency in C_1 is higher than the minimum count in C_0 (line 9 in Algorithm 1), C_1 sends the item back to C_0 and the filter is updated. The key benefit of this form of parallelism is that, as soon as C_0 forwards an item to C_1, C_0 can process new items. Therefore, we expect to see further improvements in both update and query throughput. This decoupling also allows the filter to have a small memory footprint and, hence, it may as well happen that the filter can even fit into the registers of the processor C_0 and may further improve the throughput.

6.3 SPMD Parallelism: ASketch as a Kernel

ASketch can be parallelized in an SPMD model where each processor will execute ASketch as a sequential counting kernel. Similar form of parallelism was considered by Thomas et al. [34] in the context of cell processor. We want to demonstrate the scalability of ASketch and compare its throughput with that of Count-Min when used as a kernel. We assume a multi-stream scenario where every core is consuming a different stream and applying the tuples to its own kernel. As frequency estimation is commutative in nature, when there is a query, each kernel replies its response which is later combined to produce the final result. As it is a point query, such a combination from multiple kernels is quite inexpensive. As pointed out in [34], there are also other forms of parallelism possible for sketches. For example, the sketch can be partitioned which would allow us to accommodate larger sketch sizes. However, it would also require all the sketch to process every incoming tuple both at update and query time. Therefore, we do not explore this form of parallelism in this paper.

7. EXPERIMENTAL RESULTS

We present experimental results with two real-world and one synthetic dataset. We evaluate ASketch *update efficiency*, *query processing throughput*, and *accuracy* of frequency estimation queries and compare it with that of Count-Min [11], Frequency-Aware Counting [34], Holistic UDAFs [10], and Space Saving [27]. We also provide a sensitivity analysis of ASketch by varying several parameters such as skew of the frequency distribution, filter type, and filter size.

7.1 Experimental Setup

Datasets. We summarize the datasets used below.

IP-Trace Network Stream. We used the IP-packet trace in an anonymous LAN for generating edge streams. The edge frequency is the total number of communications between two corresponding IP-addresses. Total stream size is 461 millions with 13 millions distinct edges. The maximum frequency of an edge is 17 978 588. This dataset is similar to a Zipf distribution of skew 0.9.

Kosarak Click Stream. It is an anonymized click-stream data of a hungarian on-line news portal.[7] The data set is relatively small containing 8M clicks with 40 270 distinct items. The maximum frequency of an item is 601 374. This dataset has a skew similar to a Zipf distribution of 1.0.

Synthetic Dataset. We generate a synthetic stream dataset from the skewed Zipf distribution with a stream size of 32M and the number of distinct items of 8M. We vary the skew from 0 to 3. For ease of discussion, we divide the skew range into three parts [26], and we refer to them as follows: low-skew range (0 to 1), mid-skew range or *real-world* skew range (1 to 2), and high-skew range (2 to 3).

Query and Parameters Setting. We evaluate *frequency estimation queries*: given a data item, estimate its frequency. The queries are obtained by sampling the data items based on their frequencies, that is, the high-frequency items are queried more than the low-frequency items in a skewed stream. We also perform an evaluation of the *top-k frequent items query*: determine the top-k frequent items, where k is given by the filter size of our ASketch synopsis.

We vary ASketch size from 16KB to 128KB [9, 11]. Our main focus is to operate from either the L1 or the L2 cache. Therefore, most of the experiments are done with an ASketch size of 128KB. The filter size ($|F|$) is varied from 0.1KB (8 items) to 12KB (1024 items). To keep the total synopsis size constant, we also varied the underlying sketch size. However, for a specific size of the sketch, we find that the accuracy is more sensitive towards h (i.e., range of each hash function) than towards w (i.e., the number of hash functions), especially with $w \leq 8$. Therefore, in most of our experiments, we have set $w = 8$ for all the sketch data structures, and varied h to compensate for the space of our filter. Finally, we compare the performance of four different filter implementations of ASketch as discussed in Section 6.1.

Evaluation Metrics. We measure efficiency using two metrics.

- *Stream processing throughput*, expressed in items per millisecond, measures the average number of incoming data tuples that are processed per millisecond.
- *Query processing throughput*, expressed in queries per millisecond, counts the average number of frequency estimation queries that can be answered per millisecond.

[7] Obtained from http://fimi.ua.ac.be/data/.

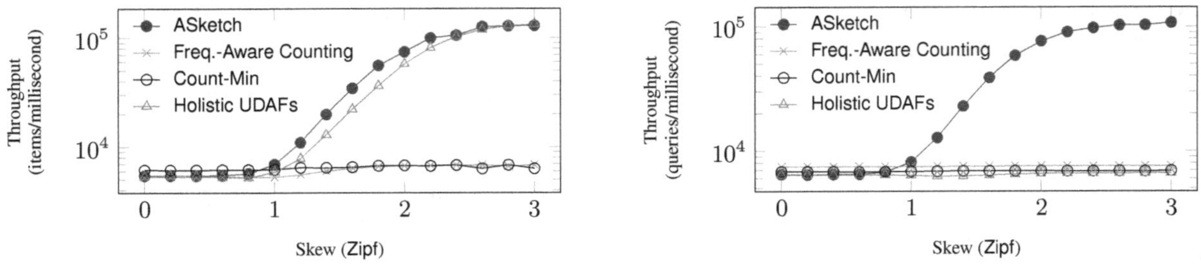

(a) Stream processing throughput with varying skew (Zipf)

(b) Query processing throughput with varying skew (Zipf)

Figure 5: Experiments on the *Synthetic* dataset; ASketch with Relaxed-Heap filter; filter size $|F|$ =32 items (~0.4KB); total synopsis size 128KB.

We evaluate the accuracy of frequency estimation queries with the two following metrics [11].

- *Observed error* is measured as the difference between the estimated frequency and the true frequency, accumulated over all the items queried. We express it as a ratio over the aggregated true frequency of all the data items queried, i.e.,

$$\text{Observed Error} = \frac{\sum_{i \in \text{Query}} |\text{estimated freq.}_i - \text{true freq.}_i|}{\sum_{i \in \text{Query}} \text{true freq.}_i}$$

- *Relative error* for one frequency estimation query is defined as the difference between the estimated frequency and the true frequency, divided by the true frequency of that data item. In our results, we report the average relative error over a pre-specified number of data items queried. Formally,

$$\text{Avg. Rel. Error} = \frac{1}{|\text{Query}|} \sum_{i \in \text{Query}} \frac{|\text{estimated freq.}_i - \text{true freq.}_i|}{\text{true freq.}_i}$$

One may note that the average relative error is biased towards the low-frequency items, due to their lower true frequency values in the denominators of the above equation.

Finally, we analyze the effectiveness of our top-k frequent items query by using *Precision-at-k*:

$$\text{Precision-at-k} = \frac{\text{true top-}k\text{ frequent items in the top-}k\text{ reported items}}{k}$$

Comparing Methods. We compare the accuracy and efficiency of ASketch with three state-of-the-art stream processing approaches[8], by assigning the same total space to all these methods.

- Count-Min (CMS) [11] applies w pairwise independent hash functions on the key k of an incoming tuple (k, u). In most of the experiments, we fixed $w = 8$ and varied h based on the total size of the synopsis.
- Frequency-Aware Counting (FCM) [34] improves the accuracy of Count-Min by using only a subset of the w hash functions for hashing each data item. Given a data item, the algorithm first applies two separate hash functions to compute an *offset* and a *gap*, which determines the subset of Count-Min hash functions to be used for hashing the data item. In addition, FCM varies the number of hash functions used for a high-frequency and a low-frequency item (e.g., $\frac{w}{2}$ hash functions for a high-frequency item and $\frac{4w}{5}$ hash functions for a low-frequency item as considered in [34]). Finally, it also uses a MG counter data structure [28] to identify the high-frequency items. For fairness, in our experiments, we have fixed the MG counter size in such a way that it stores the same number of high-frequency items as that in our filter. For lookup in the MG counter, we use the same hardware-conscious SIMD-enabled lookup code that we use for the filter lookup in ASketch.
- Holistic UDAFs (H-UDAF) [10] performs run-length aggregation in a low-level table before flushing the items into a sketch. We use a low-level table that is capable of storing the same number of data items as that in our filter, whereas the underlying sketch is implemented as Count-Min sketch. For the lookup in the low-level table, we use the same code that we use for the filter lookup.

We used publicly available source code of CMS from [11]. We implemented the codes of FCM and H-UDAF, since they are not publicly available.

Machine description. We performed all the experiments on a 2.27GHz Intel Xeon L5520 machine with 8 cores. The CPU core has 32KB L1 cache, 256KB L2 cache, and 8MB L3 cache. The operating system was Linux kernel 3.8.5. All the algorithms are implemented in C and compiled using gcc 4.7.2 with -O3 optimization. Each experimental result is averaged over 100 runs.

7.2 ASketch Performance Comparison

7.2.1 Frequency Estimation queries

We first compare ASketch with Count-Min, Frequency-Aware Counting, and Holistic UDAFs. We consider the Relaxed-Heap filter implementation for ASketch since it performs well over all skew ranges, as illustrated later in our sensitivity analysis experiments (Section 7.5)

■ **Stream Processing Throughput.** The result of the stream processing throughput comparison for all the approaches is shown in Figure 5(a). Count-Min performs almost the same over all skew ranges, since the algorithm applies the same number of hash functions irrespective of the skew. Frequency-Aware Counting throughput is lower than that of the Count-Min in low-skew range; which is caused by the overhead of MG counter and the two additional hash functions. However, for high-skew, hashing frequent items to a smaller number of hash cells compensates this overhead. Therefore, Frequency-Aware Counting throughput catches up with that of Count-Min when the skew increases. Benefits of early-aggregation is clearly visible in the throughput graph of Holistic UDAFs. In low and moderate skew ranges, the low-level aggregate table in Holistic UDAFs works as an overhead, and

[8] While Space Saving [27] can be adapted to process frequency estimation queries, usually it does not perform well in frequency estimation. We show comparision with Space Saving separately in Figure 11.

Count-Min Size	Max. # Misclassifications
16KB	27
24KB	5
32KB	8

Table 3: Misclassification statistics of Count-Min on the *Synthetic* data (Zipf skew 1.5). We report the maximum number of low-frequency items misleadingly appearing as high-frequency items over 100 runs. In our experiments with ASketch, such misclassifications did not occur.

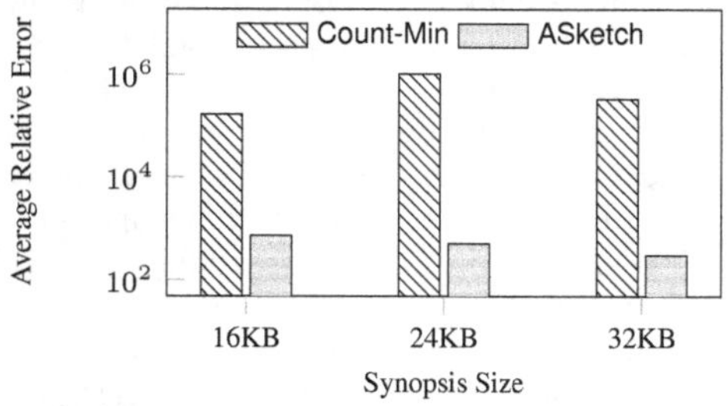

Figure 6: Average relative error over non-frequent items that appeared highly-frequent in Count-Min: *Synthetic* data with Zipf skew 1.5.

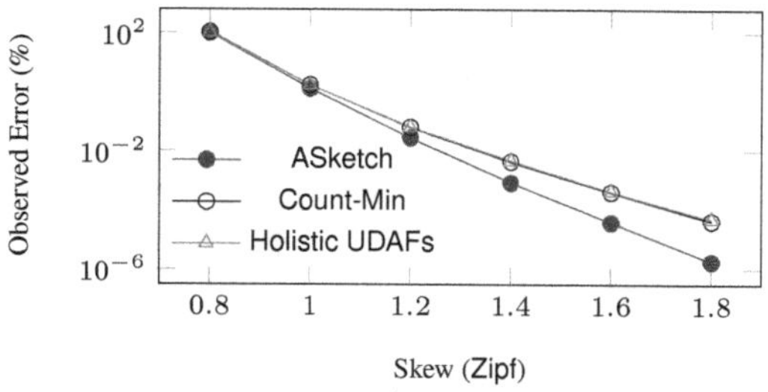

Figure 7: Observed error among ASketch, Count-Min, and Holistic UDAFs: synopsis size is 128KB.

Skew	× Improvement (Synopsis 64KB)	× Improvement (Synopsis 128KB)
0.8	1.0	1.0
1.0	1.3	1.3
1.2	2.3	2.2
1.4	5.3	5.2
1.6	11.0	10.8
1.8	28.0	23.9

Table 4: Times improvement in observed error for ASketch over Count-Min: total synopsis sizes are 64KB and 128KB.

early-aggregation does not provide any benefit. Hence, its performance drops below that of Count-Min. As the skew increases, the throughput of the algorithm also increases. At a high-skew > 2.5, a few flushings are required and thus the algorithm achieves high throughput. ASketch also behaves similarly. Even at low skew, the added overhead of filter does not deteriorate the performance significantly, compared to Count-Min. ASketch starts superseding Count-Min as soon as the skew reaches 0.8. With further increase in skew, the throughput of ASketch increases by almost an order of magnitude compared to Count-Min. In addition, we find that ASketch outperforms Holistic UDAFs in the *real-world* skew range ($1 \sim 2$), due to the overhead of flushing from the low-level aggregate table for Holistic UDAFs.

■ **Query Processing Throughput.** The query processing throughput is shown in Figure 5(b). The query items are selected uniformly from the incoming stream, that is, in a skewed data stream, the high-frequency items are queried more often compared to their low-frequency counterparts. Our results attest to the benefits of ASketch. Our filter is capable of answering most of the queries. But for Holistic UDAFs, the low-level aggregator alone is not capable of answering any query. It always requires to retrieve the frequency estimate from the underlying sketch. One may also note that Frequency-Aware Counting performs slightly better than Count-Min, since the former uses a smaller number of hash functions for answering frequency estimation queries [34]. Figure 5(b) shows that ASketch improves the query processing throughput by an order of magnitude over the existing approaches when the skew is more than 1.

■ **Avoiding Large Estimation Error.** One negative aspect of Count-Min is that if a low-frequency item always collides with the high-frequency items by applying each one of the hash functions, it then incurs a significant frequency estimation error for that low-frequency item. In such cases, the low-frequency item can be misclassified as a high-frequency item, which is often detrimental in many applications [2, 19, 30]. Although increasing the size of the sketch reduces the probability of such misclassification, we find that for relatively small-sized sketches inside the L1 cache, this situation occurs consistently when a significant number of non-frequent items get misclassified as a high-frequency item. We present the maximum number of such misclassifications over 100 runs in Table 3. The corresponding average relative error introduced by those misclassified items are shown in Figure 6. Similar situations are very unlikely to occur in ASketch as it separates the high-frequency items from the low-frequency items. This is clearly visible in Figure 6. We can see that the average relative error of Count-Min can be three order of magnitude higher than that of ASketch.

■ **Error Comparison with Count-Min and Holistic UDAFs.** We recall that any improvement by the ASketch is orthogonal to the underlying sketch. Therefore, we first compare our ASketch technique with Count-Min and Holistic UDAFs, since we have used Count-Min as the underlying sketch for both ASketch and Holistic UDAFs. The error comparison results using the percentage observed error are presented in Figure 7. We focus mainly on the skew range of 0.8 to 1.8 due to two reasons. (1) This is almost same as the *real-world* skew range. (2) For a skew higher than 1.8, the observed error by ASketch is often zero; and for a skew below 0.8, the observed errors by these three methods are very much comparable. One may observe that as we increase the skew, ASketch starts performing better than both Count-Min and Holistic UDAFs. Holistic UDAFs relies on the underlying sketch for answering the queries, therefore the performance is almost the same as that of Count-Min. For example, with skew 1.4, the observed error by both Count-Min and Holistic UDAFs is $(4 \times 10^{-3})\%$, while the observed error by ASketch is $(9 \times 10^{-4})\%$. Considering the fact that the true frequencies of the most frequent items are in the order of $10^6 \sim 10^7$, which are aggregated in the denominator to compute the observed error percentage, ASketch significantly improves the frequency estimation accuracy for the high-frequency items. In Table 4, we further show the times of improvement in observed error that ASketch achieves over Count-Min for two different synopsis sizes, i.e. 64KB and 128KB. *ASketch improves the observed error about 25 times compared to Count-Min and Holistic UDAFs, while using the same amount of storage space.*

■ **Error Comparison with Frequency-Aware Counting (FCM).** To demonstrate the *generality* of ASketch, we implement it on top of a sketch that uses the FCM principle. While running the experiments with FCM, we found that FCM performs much better in terms of the accuracy of frequency estimation queries, in comparison to the Count-Min. The main error improvement of FCM comes from the fact that it uses two additional hash functions to compute an *offset* and a *gap*, and picks a $w_1 < w$ number of sketch hash functions to apply for a particular data item. This reduces

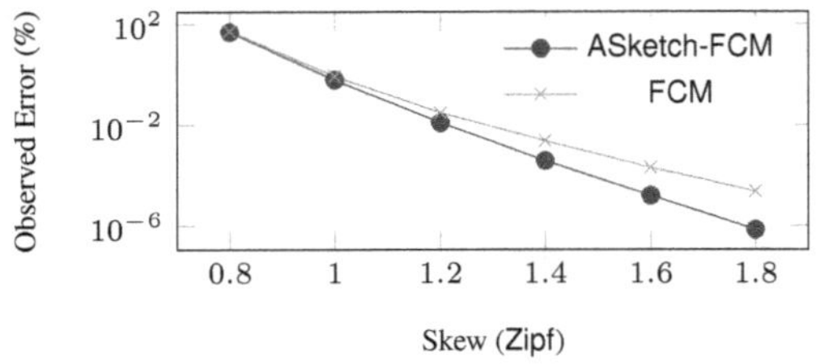

Figure 8: Observed error comparison between ASketch and FCM: Synopsis size is 128KB, ASketch-FCM is the ASketch that uses an underlying sketch based on FCM.

Skew (Zipf)	*Precision-at-k*
0.4	0.74
0.6	0.96
0.8	0.99
≥1.0	1.0

Table 5: Accuracy comparison of ASketch for top-k frequent item queries. Here, ASketch size is 128 KB, filter size is $|F| = 0.4$KB.

the number of collisions and improves the overall accuracy of the sketch. However, this approach is also compatible with ASketch. Therefore, we replace the underlying Count-Min implementation in ASketch, and incorporated an FCM-like sketch. The result of this comparison is shown in Figure 8. We find that we achieve similar levels of improvement as we have achieved before with respect to Count-Min. For example, with skew 1.6, our observed error is 13 times smaller than that of FCM. The result does emphasize the generality of ASketch as it can take advantage of any improvement in the underlying sketch.

7.2.2 Top-k Frequent Items Queries

For strict distributions [29], ASketch directly supports top-k queries where k is defined by the size of the filter. The result of *precision-at-k* for ASketch is shown in Table 5. As shown in the table, ASketch achieves high accuracy. For a skew (Zipf) of 1.0 and higher, the algorithm achieves a *precision-at-k* value of 1.0. The algorithm also exhibits high precision even at relatively small skew.

7.2.3 Number of Exchanges for ASketch.

In Figure 9, we present the statistics about the number of exchanges that happens between the filter and the sketch data structures in ASketch. As expected, the number of exchanges reduces as the skew increases. This indeed helps in improving the ASketch throughput with increasing skew in the input stream, as shown earlier in Figures 5(a) and 14. However, even with Uniform distribution (i.e., $zipf = 0$), we need only about 40K exchanges for a stream of size 32M. Our experimental evaluation indicates that the exchange of data items is not an issue.

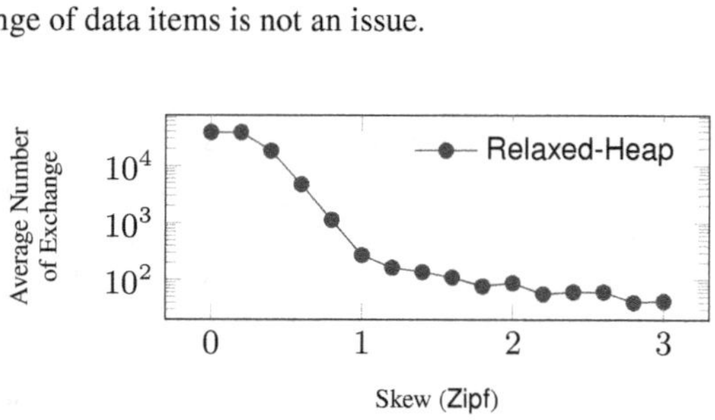

Figure 9: Average number of exchange with varying skew for ASketch: *Synthetic* dataset; Relaxed-Heap filter of size $|F|$ =32 items (~0.4KB); ASketch size is 128KB.

7.3 Experiments on Real-World Datasets

■ **Stream Processing Throughput Comparison.** The stream processing throughput on the *IP-trace* data is shown in Figure 10(a). Here, ASketch-FCM is the ASketch implementation where the underlying sketch is implemented by following the FCM principle. The throughput of ASketch is 5% higher than that of the Count-Min. Since *IP-trace* data is in the low-skew range, it is expected that ASketch will not outperform Count-Min by a significant margin. However, ASketch-FCM achieves almost 30% more throughput than that of Count-Min. It also outperforms Holistic UDAFs by almost 40%, since with low skew, the low-level aggregate table in Holistic UDAFs works as a performance bottleneck due to the excessive flushing from the table. In comparison to FCM, ASketch-FCM also achieves 40% more throughput. This is because of two reasons. (1) As explained earlier in Section 7.2.1, we consider a modified version of the FCM where we do not use the MG counter — the MG counter incurs a significant performance overhead for the original FCM technique [34]. (2) We accumulate a large number of frequency counts in the filter that are not hashed into the underlying sketch. In case of FCM, all the frequency counts are hashed into the sketch data structure.

The stream processing throughput for the Kosarak click stream is shown in Figure 10(c). The Kosarak click stream has slightly higher skew than the IP-trace stream. As a result, ASketch achieves almost 20% more throughput than Count-Min. The performance of Count-Min is skew independent, therefore, the throughput numbers are similar to that of IP-trace stream. Skew also helps Holistic UDAFs but ASketch achieves almost 10% better throughput than that of Holistic UDAFs. Similar to the IP-trace stream, FCM throughput is slightly lower than that of Count-Min due to the overhead of the MG counter. Finally, ASketch-FCM outperforms all other approaches by accumulating larger number of frequency counts in the filter. It achieves almost 70% better throughput than that of FCM.

■ **Frequency Estimation Error Comparison.** The result of frequency estimation error comparison with the *IP-trace* stream is shown in Figure 10(b). We show both implementations of ASketch — one with Count-Min as the underlying sketch; another one with FCM as the underlying sketch (abbreviated as ASketch-FCM). ASketch achieves almost 20% better observed error than both Count-Min and Holistic UDAFs. Holistic UDAFs achieves almost the same error as that of Count-Min, since it uses the underlying sketch to answer all queries. FCM achieves better accuracy than that of Count-Min as well as from ASketch. However, ASketch-FCM improves the accuracy of FCM by more than 22%.

The frequency estimation results over the Kosarak click stream are shown in Figure 10(d). ASketch outperforms both Count-Min and Holistic UDAFs by achieving almost 32% less observed error. Holistic UDAFs achieves almost the same error as that of Count-Min because it always uses the underlying sketch for answering queries. As expected, FCM achieves better accuracy than that of both ASketch and Count-Min. However, ASketch-FCM outperforms FCM by achieving almost 48% less observed error. It illustrates that the improvement of ASketch is orthogonal to the underlying sketching technique.

■ **Space Saving for Frequency Estimation.** The Space Saving [27] can be modified to answer frequency estimation queries as follows. If an item is currently monitored by the algorithm, its count can directly be used as the corresponding estimate. Otherwise, there are two approaches that can be followed. The authors in [27] suggested not to underestimate the value of the frequency and therefore, we can use the frequency of the item with

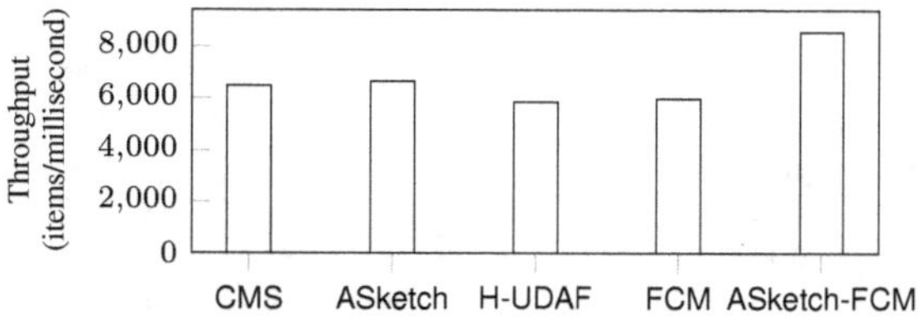

(a) Stream processing throughput on the *IP-trace* stream

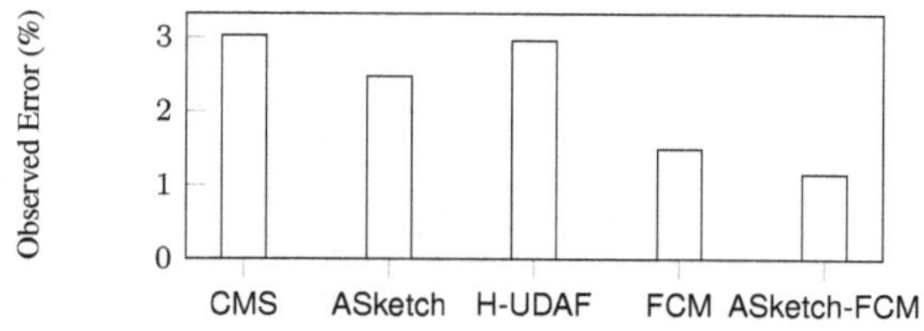

(b) Observed error comparison on the *IP-trace* stream

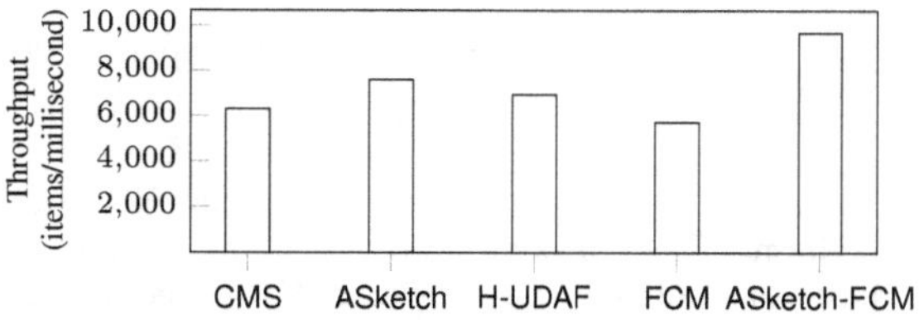

(c) Stream processing throughput on the *Kosarak* click stream

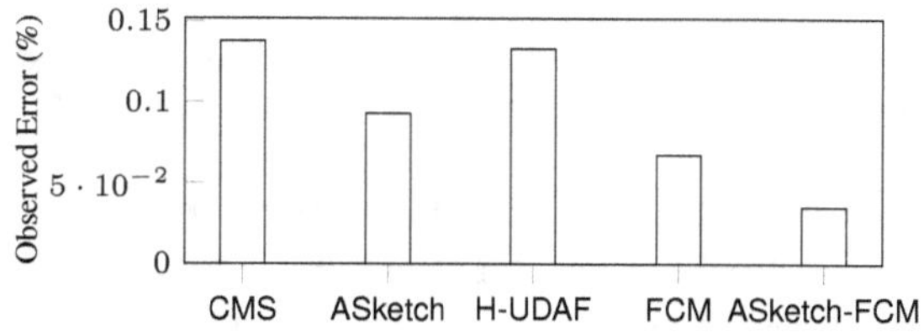

(d) Observed error comparison on the *Kosarak* click stream

Figure 10: Experiments on real-world datasets: ASketch with Relaxed-Heap filter implementation; filter size $|F|$ =32 items (~0.4KB); ASketch size is 128KB. ASketch-FCM is the ASketch that uses an underlying sketch based on FCM.

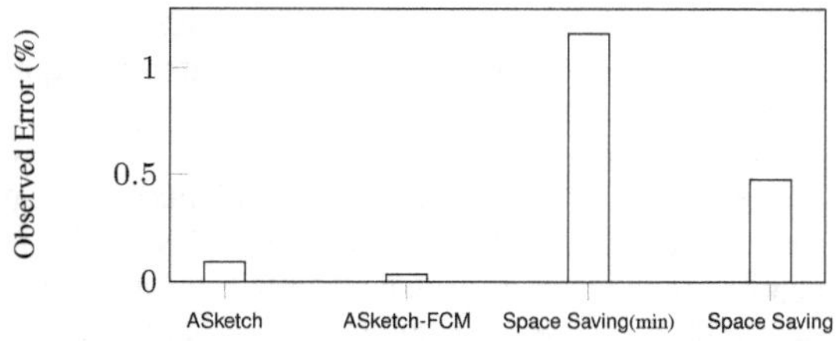

Figure 11: Observed error comparison of ASketch with Space Saving on the Kosarak click stream: ASketch with Relaxed-Heap filter; filter size $|F|$ =32 items (~0.4KB); ASketch size is 128KB. ASketch-FCM is ASketch with FCM based underlying sketch.

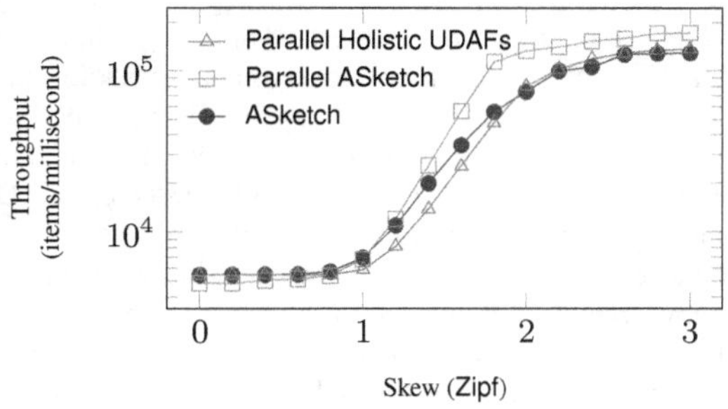

Figure 12: Stream processing throughput comparison of Parallel ASketch and Parallel Holistic UDAFs with varying skew (Zipf) on the *Synthetic* dataset; ASketch with Relaxed-Heap filter is used as a baseline; filter size $|F|$ =32 items (~0.4KB); total synopsis size is 128KB.

the minimum count as an estimate. However, the authors in [9] suggested to use 0 as the estimate of frequency for such items. In both cases, Space Saving performs poorly for frequency estimation in comparison to a same-sized sketch. To demonstrate this, we have used Space Saving to process frequency estimation queries on the Kosarak dataset, and compare this result with ASketch (presented earlier in Figure 10(d)). The result of this comparison is shown in Figure 11. Here, Space Saving(min) is the one where we use the minimum value as the estimate, and Space Saving is the one where we use 0 as the estimate. Clearly when 0 is used as estimate, Space Saving performs better. However, both implementations of ASketch achieve a much lower error in comparison.

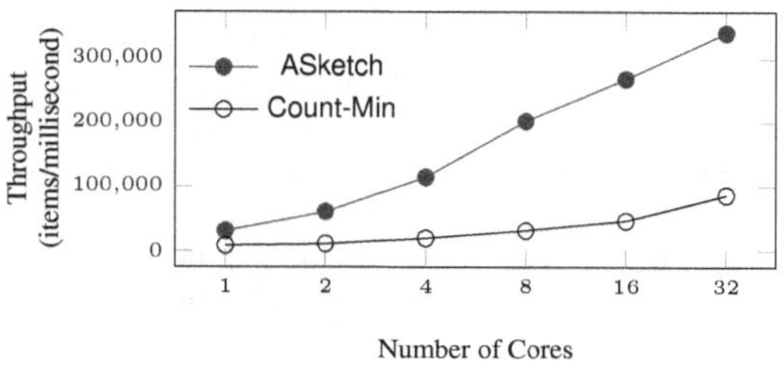

Figure 13: Throughput comparison between ASketch and Count-Min when they are used as counting kernel with varying number of cores: each synopsis size is 128KB. Here, the stream size is 1 billion tuples and the number of distinct items is 100 million, Zipf skew 1.5.

Filter Type	Observed Error (%)
Stream Summary	0.0005
Vector	0.0002
Relaxed-Heap	0.0002
Strict-Heap	0.0002

Table 6: Accuracy comparison with various filter implementations in ASketch: Vector, Stream-Summary, Strict-Heap, and Relaxed-Heap. ASketch size is 128KB, filter size $|F| = 0.4$KB, skew (Zipf)=1.5.

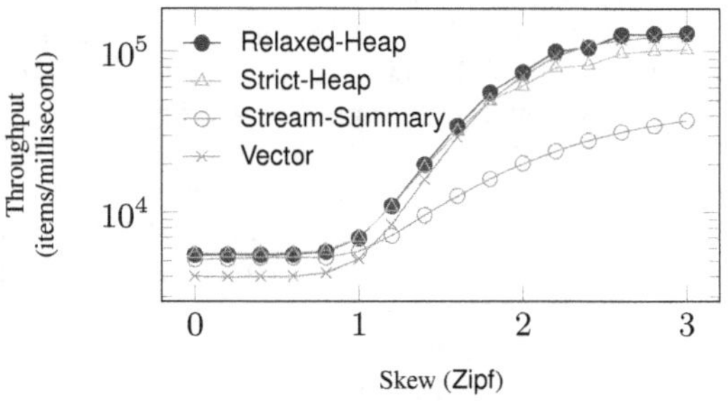

Figure 14: Stream processing throughput comparison with various filter implementations in ASketch: Vector, Stream-Summary, Strict-Heap, and Relaxed-Heap. ASketch size is 128 KB, filter size $|F| = 0.4$KB.

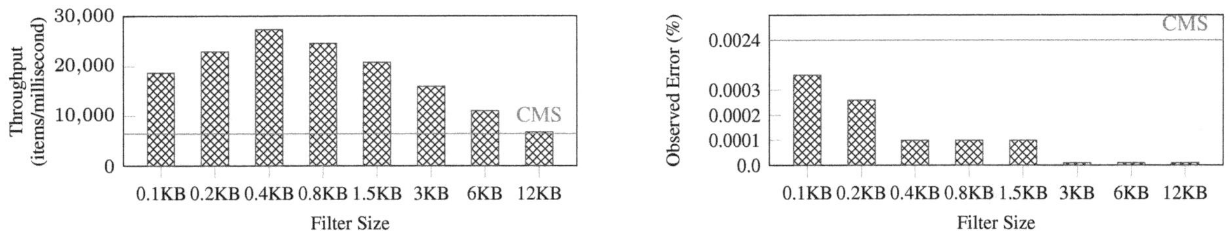

(a) Stream processing throughput

(b) Observed error comparison

Figure 15: Sensitivity analysis, w.r.t., filter sizes in ASketch: ASketch size is 128KB; *Synthetic* data; Zipf skew 1.5; Relaxed-Heap filter. Here, CMS refers to the throughput and error of Count-Min alone, shown as a point of reference for other measurements.

7.4 Experiments on Parallel ASketch

■ Throughput Benefit of Pipeline Parallelism. ASketch with pipeline parallelism (we refer to as Parallel ASketch), is the one where one core runs the filter and another core runs Count-Min algorithm. The throughput benefit of this algorithm is visible in Figure 12, especially in the skew range of 1.2 and higher. The core running the filter can start processing the next item as soon as it has forwarded the item to the core running the sketch. In fact, Parallel ASketch achieves almost twice the throughput of ASketch at a skew of 1.8. However, for a skew higher than 2.4, the throughput advantages diminish as a few items overflow. Parallel Hollistic UDAFs in Figure 12 is the implementation that is parallelized in a pipeline manner. Pipeline parallelism also benefits Parallel Hollistic UDAFs as the first core, after flushing the low-level aggregator table, can immediately start processing next items from the input stream. However, Parallel ASketch achieves almost twice the throughput of parallel Parallel Hollistic UDAFs at a skew of 1.8.

■ ASketch as a Counting Kernel. We run this experiment on an Intel Sandy-Bridge machine with 32 cores arranged in a four-socket configuration. The clock frequency is 2.40 GHz; therefore, single thread throughput is slightly higher in Figure 13 than those presented earlier in Figure 5(a). Although we do not carefully optimize the implementation for NUMA architecture, the linear scalability with increasing number of cores is clearly visible. The throughput advantage of ASketch over Count-Min is also obvious from the figure. For example, a 32 core configuration for ASketch achieves almost 4 times better throughput.

7.5 ASketch Sensitivity Analysis

Here, we analyze the performance of ASketch by varying two important parameters: the filter implementation and the filter size.

■ Impact of the Filter Implementation. We compare the trade-offs of four different filter implementations: Vector, Stream-Summary with hash table, Strict-Heap, and Relaxed-Heap. Here, we fix the total ASketch size to 128KB and fix the filter size as 0.4KB. We present the impact of varying the filter implementations on ASketch accuracy for frequency estimation queries in Table 6. Since Stream-Summary has more space overhead per item, it can accommodate only 4 items with a 0.4KB filter size; the other three filter implementations have exactly the same space overhead per item, and each of them can store 32 items within 0.4KB filter. Therefore, the Vector and both the heap-based implementations have the same accuracy; while the Stream Summary has lower accuracy.

The stream processing throughput of these four implementations are given in Figure 14. Vector performs better at a higher skew range (>2.0), since there is no overhead of maintaining the data structure, and almost all the hits go to the filter. However, it does not perform well for a skew <2.0, due to the lookup cost of the smallest count present in the filter (see line 9, Algorithm 1), which requires a linear scan on the filter.

Stream-Summary, in general, does not perform very well over all skew ranges due to its expensive data structure maintenance costs, e.g., hash evaluations, pointer chasing, collision resolutions, and also the maintenance of a doubly linked list. Nevertheless, because of the constant time access to the item with the minimum frequency count, Stream-Summary achieves better throughput at a lower skew than Vector.

Heap implementations perform better with skew <2.0, which also includes the *real-world* skew range. Particularly, Relaxed-Heap performs better than Strict-Heap, since less maintenance cost is required in the former. Both heap implementations perform better than Vector in low and medium skew ranges due to a fast access to the item with the minimum frequency count at the root of the heap. This is why we used Relaxed-Heap based ASketch while comparing with existing approaches.

■ Impact of the Filter Size. We present the impact of filter size over ASketch throughput and accuracy in Figures 15(a) and 15(b), respectively. Here, we used Relaxed-Heap. As explained earlier in Section 4, increasing the filter size beyond a threshold size (e.g., 0.4KB in our current setting) increases the filter processing time without too much gain in the filtering rate. Thus, beyond a threshold filter size, the overall ASketch throughput decreases. On the other hand, with increasing filter size, while we have better accuracy for more high-frequency items, we also introduce more error over the low-frequency items due to the reduced size of the underlying sketch data structure. Therefore, we find that the observed error stops improving after a threshold filter size, e.g., 3KB in our current setting (Figure 15(b)).

8. CONCLUSIONS

In this paper, we present ASketch — a filtering technique complementing sketches. It improves the accuracy of sketches by increasing the frequency estimation accuracy for the most frequent items and by reducing the possible misclassification of the low-frequency items. It also improves the overall throughput. ASketch outperforms the existing stream processing algorithms with an order of magnitude higher throughput and about 25 times higher accuracy, while using exactly the same amount of space. We further incorporate parallelism in ASketch to support even higher streaming rate, e.g., pipeline parallelism improves the ASketch throughput almost twice in the *real-world* skew range. ASketch also exhibits linear scalability in the case SPMD parallelism. In future work, it would be interesting to employ ASketch in a wide variety of machine learning and data mining applications where sketches are currently used.

9. REFERENCES

[1] C. Aggarwal and K. Subbian. Event Detection in Social Streams. In *SDM*, 2012.

[2] C. Aggarwal and P. S. Yu. On Classification of High-Cardinality Data Streams. In *SDM*, 2010.

[3] N. Alon, Y. Matias, and M. Szegedy. The Space Complexity of Approximating the Frequency Moments. In *STOC*, 1996.

[4] R. Berinde, P. Indyk, G. Cormode, and M. J. Strauss. Space-optimal Heavy Hitters with Strong Error Bounds. *ACM TODS*, 35(4):26, 2010.

[5] D. Bitton and D. J. DeWitt. Duplicate Record Elimination in Large Data Files. *ACM TODS*, 8(2):255–265, 1983.

[6] B. H. Bloom. Space/time Trade-offs in Hash Coding with Allowable Errors. *Comm. of ACM*, 13:422–426, 1970.

[7] M. Charikar, K. Chen, and M. Farach-Colton. Finding Frequent Items in Data Streams. In *ICALP*, 2002.

[8] G. Cormode, M. Garofalakis, P. J. Haas, and C. Jermaine. Synopses for massive data: Samples, histograms, wavelets, sketches. *Foundations and Trends in Databases*, 4(1–3):1–294, 2012.

[9] G. Cormode and M. Hadjieleftheriou. Finding Frequent Items in Data Streams. In *VLDB*, 2008.

[10] G. Cormode, T. Johnson, F. Korn, S. Muthukrishnan, O. Spatscheck, and D. Srivastava. Holistic UDAFs at Streaming Speeds. In *SIGMOD*, 2004.

[11] G. Cormode and S. Muthukrishnan. An Improved Data-Stream Summary: The Count-min Sketch and its Applications. *J. of Algorithms*, 55(1), 2005.

[12] A. Dobra, M. Garofalakis, J. Gehrke, and R. Rastogi. Processing Complex Aggregate Queries over Data Streams. In *SIGMOD*, 2002.

[13] C. Estan and G. Varghese. New Directions in Traffic Measurement and Accounting: Focusing on the Elephants, Ignoring the Mice. *ACM Trans. Comput. Syst.*, 21(3):270–313, 2003.

[14] S. Ganguly, M. Garofalakis, and R. Rastogi. Processing data-stream join aggregates using skimmed sketches. In *Advances in Database Technology-EDBT 2004*, pages 569–586. Springer, 2004.

[15] S. Ganguly, P. B. Gibbons, Y. Matias, and A. Silberschatz. Bifocal Sampling for Skew-Resistant Join Size Estimation. In *SIGMOD*, pages 271–281, 1996.

[16] M. Garofalakis and P. B. Gibbons. Wavelet Synopses with Error Guarantees. In *SIGMOD*, 2002.

[17] A. C. Gilbert, Y. Kotidis, S. Muthukrishnan, and M. Strauss. Surfing Wavelets on Streams: One-Pass Summaries for Approximate Aggregate Queries. In *VLDB*, 2001.

[18] A. C. Gilbert, Y. Kotidis, S. Muthukrishnan, and M. Strauss. How to Summarize the Universe: Dynamic Maintenance of Quantiles. In *VLDB*, 2002.

[19] A. Goyal, H. D. III, and G. Cormode. Sketch Algorithms for Estimating Point Queries in NLP. In *EMNLP-CoNLL*, 2012.

[20] S. Guha, N. Koudas, and K. Shim. Data-streams and Histograms. In *STOC*, 2001.

[21] C. Koch, S. Scherzinger, and M. Schmidt. XML Prefiltering as a String Matching Problem. In *ICDE*, pages 626–635, 2008.

[22] B. Krishnamurthy, S. Sen, Y. Zhang, and Y. Chen. Sketch-based Change Detection: Methods, Evaluation, and Applications. In *IMC*, 2003.

[23] P. Larson. Grouping and Duplicate Elimination: Benefits of Early Aggregation, 1997. Technical Report, MSR-TR-97-36.

[24] T. Liu, Y. Sun, A. X. Liu, L. Guo, and B. Fang. A Prefiltering Approach to Regular Expression Matching for Network Security Systems. In *Applied Cryptography and Network Security*, pages 363–380, 2012.

[25] Y. Lu, A. Montanari, B. Prabhakar, S. Dharmapurikar, and A. Kabbani. Counter braids: a novel counter architecture for per-flow measurement. In *SIGMETRICS*, 2008.

[26] N. Manerikar and T. Palpanas. Frequent Items in Streaming Data: An Experimental Evaluation of the State-of-the-art. *Data Knowl. Eng.*, 68(4):415–430, 2009.

[27] A. Metwally, D. Agrawal, and A. E. Abbadi. Efficient Computation of Frequent and Top-k Elements in Data Streams. In *ICDT*, 2005.

[28] J. Misra and D. Gries. Finding repeated elements. *Science of computer programming*, 2(2):143–152, 1982.

[29] S. Muthukrishnan. *Data streams: Algorithms and applications*. Now Publishers Inc, 2005.

[30] A. Pietracaprina, M. Riondato, E. Upfal, and F. Vandin. Mining top-K Frequent Itemsets Through Progressive Sampling. *Data Min. Knowl. Discov.*, 21(2):310–326, 2010.

[31] O. Rottenstreich, Y. Kanizo, and I. Keslassy. The Variable-Increment Counting Bloom Filter. *IEEE/ACM Trans. Netw.*, 22(4):1092–1105, 2014.

[32] P. Roy, J. Teubner, and G. Alonso. Efficient Frequent Item Counting in Multi-Core Hardware. In *KDD*, 2012.

[33] F. Rusu and A. Dobra. Sketches for Size of Join Estimation. *ACM TODS*, 33(3):15, 2008.

[34] D. Thomas, R. Bordawekar, C. Aggarwal, and P. S. Yu. On Efficient Query Processing of Stream Counts on the Cell Processor. In *ICDE*, 2009.

[35] W. Yan and Y. X. B. Malin. Scalable Load Balancing for MapReduce-based Record Linkage. In *IPCCC*, 2013.

[36] J. Yu, Z. Chong, H. Lu, and A. Zhou. False Positive or False Negative: Mining Frequent Itemsets from High Speed Transactional Data Streams. In *VLDB*, 2004.

[37] P. Zhao, C. C. Aggarwal, and M. Wang. gSketch: On Query Estimation in Graph Streams. In *VLDB*, 2012.

APPENDIX

A. DELETION OF ITEMS

Removal of an item from sketches is often necessary in many applications such as the conclusion of a packet flow, or the return of a previously bought item. Traditional sketches allow us to model removal of items as an update with negative counts [9]. Particularly, in the Count-Min, a negative-count-update can be performed in the same way as a positive-count-update, as long as the overall count of an item never goes negative. In the following, we shall illustrate how ASketch supports negative-count-updates.

Let us assume that the negative-count-update with the current tuple is k, that is, the item's overall frequency count needs to be reduced by an amount of k. If the item is not found in the filter, we directly apply the Count-Min technique to reduce its count by k from the sketch. On the other hand, if the item is found in the filter and its (new_count-old_count) is greater than or equal to k, then we only reduce its new_count by k. However, complexity arises if the item is found in the filter, but its (new_count-old_count) is smaller than k. Let us denote by (new_count-old_count)$= \triangle$ for that item. In such cases, we subtract k from its new_count, $(k - \triangle)$ from its old_count, and finally we also reduce its count by $(k - \triangle)$ in the underlying sketch. It is important to note that after processing a negative-count-update, we do not initiate any exchange of items between the filter and the sketch. The exchange is performed only in the successive positive-count-updates, if necessary.

B. ADDITIONAL EXPERIMENTS

B.1 Accuracy of Low-Frequency Items for ASketch

One of the key design issues of ASketch data structure is the size of the *Filter*. We have evaluated the impact of the filter size in Section 4, analytically and in Section 7.5, experimentally. We have demonstrated that increasing the filter size beyond certain threshold will decrease the stream processing throughput without any gain in accuracy of high frequency items. Therefore, we have used a small sized filter. To accommodate the filter data structure in ASketch, the same amount of space is reduced from the underlying *sketch*. As pointed out earlier, this reduction of space is very small to have any significant effect over accuracy of the low-frequency items. To demonstrate this, we have plotted the average relative error over all the low-frequency items in Figure 16. Even though the average relative error is more biased towards the low-frequency items, we do not see any differences in between Count-Min and ASketch.

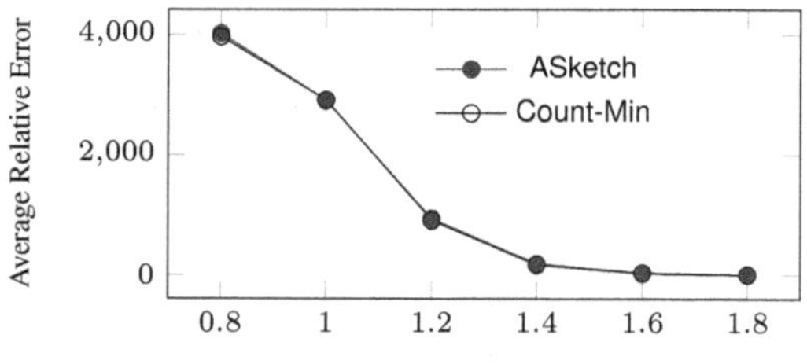

Figure 16: Average relative error comparison over all low-frequency items between ASketch and Count-Min. Stream size is 32M and alphabet size is 8M; synopsis size is 128KB.

To further emphasize that we do not introduce a high error in a few low-frequency items, we find the top-10 items with the highest accumulative error (i.e., difference between the actual count and estimated count). We show the average accumulative error over these top-10 items for both Count-Min and ASketch in Table 7. As shown in the table, there is almost no difference in the accumulative error of the top-10 error items.

Skew	Count-Min	ASketch
0.8	8013	8088
1.0	6761	6750
1.2	3541	3567
1.4	1399	1280
1.6	499	441
1.8	156	122

Table 7: Average accumulative error for top-10 error items between ASketch and Count-Min. Stream size is 32M and alphabet size is 8M; synopsis size is 128KB.

B.2 Comparison of Predicted vs. Achieved Filter Selectivity

Analytically, we have predicted the $\text{filter}_{\text{selectivity}}$ on a Zipf distribution in Section 4. To demonstrate that we achieve high $\text{filter}_{\text{selectivity}}$ with ASketch, we ran the experiment on Zipf distribution with 32M input items and tracked the number of items that are processed by the underlying sketch data structure (N_2). We compute the $\text{filter}_{\text{selectivity}}$ as the ratio of N_2 over the total number of input items (N), and plotted it in Figure 17. There are slight differences among the values which are almost not visible in the figure (e.g., for skew of 1.0, predicted is 0.75, and achieved is 0.76). For highly skewed distributions, the high-frequency items, after few updates in the sketch, gets exchanged into the filter, and then regular updates to the filter keeps them in the filter.

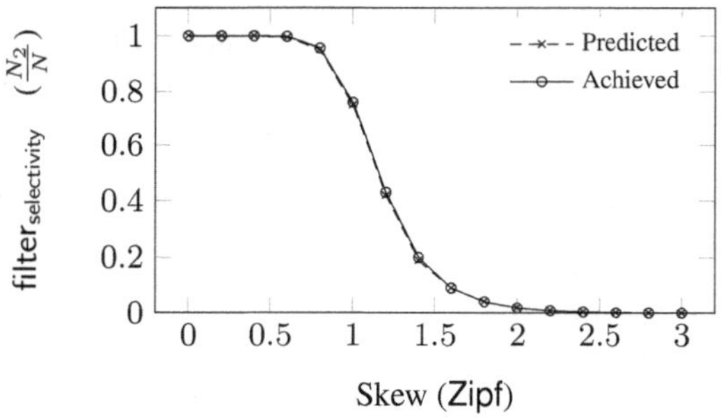

Figure 17: Filter selectivity: *Predicted* vs. *Achieved* $\text{filter}_{\text{selectivity}}$; data stream with Zipf distribution, stream size is 32M, the number of distinct data items is 8M. Here, we fixed the filter size $|F| = 32$ high frequency items.

C. ADDITIONAL ANALYSIS

C.1 Proof of Theorem 1

When the range of each hash function is h, on an average N/h items are hashed into each cell. When we allocate a size s_f to the filter, the range of each hash function reduces by s_f/w. Therefore, Ns_f/hw items get accumulated in the remaining $h - s_f/w$ cells. In other words, the expected value of the increase in the count for low-frequency items is given by $\Delta E = \frac{Ns_f}{wh(h-s_f/w)}$. Hence, by applying Markov inequality, we get:

$$P(\Delta E \geq (\frac{es_f}{wh(h - \frac{s_f}{w})})N) \leq 1/e \quad (2)$$

Since we use w pairwise independent hash functions, the overall probability that the above happens is smaller than e^{-w}. Hence, the theorem follows.

C.2 Exchange Policy

As depicted in Figure 9, if there exists skew in input data, the number of exchanges drops significantly (less than 100 exchanges for a skew of 3). In order to construct an average case scenario with uniform distribution, let us assume that no hit happens in the filter. Given that the filter monitors $|F|$ items, and the range of hash function in the sketch is h, one may require $|F|$ exchanges on an average for every h items. The intuition behind this is that once $|F|$ items are exchanged, the count of each cell in the hash function needs to be increased by 1 for the next set of $|F|$ exchanges. Therefore, with a stream size of N, the average number of exchange would be $N|F|/h$. For example, in a setup where $|F| = 32$, $h = 4084$, and $w = 1$, with 32M stream size in uniform distribution, one may require up to ~250K exchanges. However, in practice, we consider multiple hash functions in the sketch (i.e, $w > 1$), and minimum of those w values are used to estimate the frequency of an item. Also, if there are hits in the filter, the number of exchange would further decrease. Thus, the observed number of exchanges shown in Figure 9 is much lower than ~250K, more specifically ~40K for the uniform distribution.

Next, we construct a scenario with uniform distribution such that minimum number of exchanges will occur. Let us assume, $|F| = 32$, $h = 4084$, $w = 1$, stream size: $N = 32$M, and domain size: $M = 8$M. Therefore, each item occurs $\frac{N}{M} = 4$ times. Assuming these N counts get evenly distributed in each cell of the underlying sketch, the count of each cell will be $\frac{N}{h} = 7832$. The counts of each cell will come from $\frac{M}{h} = 1958$ different items. Now, we consider a scenario where these 1958 different items constitute the first 7832 counts in the stream, and they all get mapped to one particular cell in the sketch. Assuming no hits in the filter, there will be about 7832 exchanges for these items, and each item in the filter will have a count close to 7832. Now, assuming that the rest $(N - \frac{N}{h})$ counts get evenly distributed in rest of the $h-1 = 4083$ cells, there will be only few more additional exchanges due to the items with counts less than 7832 in filter. In summary, in best case, there will be in the order of $\frac{N}{h} = 7832$ exchanges. Our achieved number of exchanges are ~40K, which is much higher than the best case; however, much lower than the average case.

Below, we provide two additional lemma to derive the worst case bounds on the number of exchanges for ASketch. However, the probability of occurring such worst case scenarios are very small because the stream requires to be particularly ordered.

LEMMA 2. *Assuming no collision inside the* sketch *(i.e., the sketch is big enough to hold accurate count for all distinct keys), total number of exchanges cannot be more than $\frac{N}{2}$, where N is the total stream size.*

First, we construct an example when this happens. Let there be only two distinct items in a stream, and they are coming in the following sequence: $A\,\underline{BB}\,\underline{AA}\,\underline{BB}\,\underline{AA}\,\underline{BB}$. Assume that the filter size is 1, and the two items A and B do not collide in the sketch. This will result in $\lfloor (N-1)/2 \rfloor$ exchanges for a stream of size N. In particular, every item has an exact count in the sketch based on our assumption. We move an item from the sketch to the filter only when its count obtained from the sketch is larger than the current minimum count stored in the filter. Therefore, after an item is evicted from the filter and before it moves back again to the filter, the item will require at least 2 more hits while staying in the sketch. This is true for any item in the stream. Therefore, the maximum number of exchanges is $\frac{N}{2}$.

LEMMA 3. *Assuming there are collisions in the* sketch *(i.e., the sketch width $h << M$, the number of distinct items), total number of exchanges can be N, where N is the stream size.*

We again construct a scenario when this happens. Let there be only two distinct items in a stream, and they are coming in the following sequence: $AB\,\underline{BA}\,\underline{BA}\,\underline{BA}\,\underline{BA}\,\underline{BA}$. Assume that the filter size is 1, and each hash function in the sketch hashes both A and B to the same cell, i.e., $H_i(A) = H_i(B)$ for all $i \in (1, w)$. Hence, A and B always collide in the sketch. This results in $N-2$ exchanges for a stream of size N. We ensure that there will be no more than N exchanges, because at most one exchange can happen after one insertion in the sketch. Since the total number of insertion in the sketch is bounded by N following Lemma 1, the maximum number of exchanges cannot be more than N.

Matrix Sketching Over Sliding Windows

Zhewei Wei[1]*, Xuancheng Liu[2], Feifei Li[3], Shuo Shang[2], Xiaoyong Du[1], Ji-Rong Wen[1]†

[12]School of Information, Renmin University of China
Key Laboratory of Data Engineering and Knowledge Engineering, MOE
Beijing Key Laboratory of Big Data Management and Analysis Methods
[3]School of Computing, University of Utah
[1]{zhewei, duyong, jrwen}@ruc.edu.cn [2]{xcliu94, jedi.shang}@gmail.com [3]lifeifei@cs.utah.edu

ABSTRACT

Large-scale matrix computation becomes essential for many data data applications, and hence the problem of sketching matrix with small space and high precision has received extensive study for the past few years. This problem is often considered in the row-update streaming model, where the data set is a matrix $A \in \mathbb{R}^{n\times d}$, and the processor receives a row $(1 \times d)$ of A at each timestamp. The goal is to maintain a smaller matrix (termed approximation matrix, or simply approximation) $B \in \mathbb{R}^{\ell\times d}$ as an approximation to A, such that the covariance error $\|A^TA - B^TB\|$ is small and $\ell \ll n$.

This paper studies continuous tracking approximations to the matrix defined by a sliding window of most recent rows. We consider both sequence-based and time-based window. We show that maintaining A^TA exactly requires linear space in the sliding window model, as opposed to $O(d^2)$ space in the streaming model. With this observation, we present three general frameworks for matrix sketching on sliding windows. The sampling techniques give random samples of the rows in the window according to their squared norms. The Logarithmic Method converts a *mergeable* streaming matrix sketch into a matrix sketch on time-based sliding windows. The Dyadic Interval framework converts arbitrary streaming matrix sketch into a matrix sketch on sequence-based sliding windows. In addition to proving all algorithmic properties theoretically, we also conduct extensive empirical study with real data sets to demonstrate the efficiency of these algorithms.

*This work was partly supported by the National Key Basic Research Program (973 Program) of China (No. 2014CB340403, No. 2012CB316205), the National Natural Science Foundation of China (NSFC. 61402532, NSFC. 61502501, NSFC. 61502502, NSFC. 61502503, NSFC. 61432006). Feifei Li was supported in part by NSF grants 1251019, 1200792, and NSFC grant 61428204.

†Corresponding author.

SIGMOD'16, June 26-July 01, 2016, San Francisco, CA, USA

 ISBN 978-1-4503-3531-7/16/06...$15.00

DOI: http://dx.doi.org/10.1145/2882903.2915228

1. INTRODUCTION

Modern data sets, such as text documents, image data and social graphs, are often modeled as large matrices [23–25,30]. Such data matrices are often huge in size and generated continuously, it is essential to process them in streaming fashion and maintain an approximating summary. *Matrix sketching* is a general technique for processing these matrices to reduce the volume of data before a more refined analytic task is performed, or to directly reveal information through Principal Component Analysis (PCA), k-means clustering, or Latent Semantic Indexing (LSI) [13, 17, 21, 25, 29, 35]. Most of the matrix sketching work assume the *row-update streaming model*. In this model, the algorithm receives a row of matrix $A \in \mathbb{R}^{n\times d}$ from time to time (n increases by one after receiving a new row), and the goal is to maintain a matrix sketch structure κ that is able to produce the approximation matrix $B \in \mathbb{R}^{\ell\times d}$ with only $\ell \ll n$ rows, but guarantees that $B^TB \approx A^TA$ for the covariance matrix A^TA, i.e., B approximates A well.

In many applications, however, streams are time-sensitive: people are more interested in recent data than those in the far past. The *sliding window model* [11] is the most prominent and intuitive model to capture this essence. Inspired by this observation, we study the problem of *continuous tracking matrix sketch in the sliding window model.* We consider two types of sliding windows. A *sequence-based window* is defined by the N most recent rows. For instance, an application may restrict an analysis to the last million records received by the system. On the other hand, a *timestamp-based window* contains all rows that arrived within a fixed time interval of length Δ that covers the most recent Δ timestamps. For instance, an application may restrict an analysis to tweets that were posted within the last hour.

Motivations. A natural motivation for this problem, as argued in [4, 27, 32], is based on the observation that the sliding window model is a more appropriate model than the unbounded streaming model in many real-world applications. It is particularly the case in the areas of data analysis wherein matrix sketching techniques are widely used, since in general one is not interested in gathering information from outdated data for future predictions. For example, in a large scale text data analysis, each row in the matrix corresponds to a document (e.g. content of a tweet in twitter data) and is associated with a timestamp (e.g. time that the tweet was posted). A streaming matrix sketch is useful for analyzing text data that starts at a particular time in history. However, a far more interesting task would be analyzing tweets posted for the recent time period, say last 24 hours, or analyzing most recent tweets, say last 100,000 tweets. To meet such demands, we need a matrix sketch for a sliding window of length 24 hours or 100,000 tweets.

A more subtle motivation is due to the hardness of tracking matrix exactly on a sliding window. In the unbounded streaming model, a naive solution for the matrix sketching problem is to maintain $A^T A$ with $O(d^2)$ space and $O(d^2)$ time to process each update. This solution tracks $A^T A$ exactly with efficiency comparable to matrix sketching, as long as the data dimension d is not too large (e.g. less than 1000). In the sliding window model, however, we show that it is not possible to track $A^T A$ exactly unless we store all rows in the matrix from the most recent sliding window. This result has two impacts: 1. Sketching is essential for tracking approximation of matrices in the sliding window model, regardless of the dimension of the data; 2. Matrix sketching over sliding windows requires new techniques.

A concrete application: sliding window PCA. PCA projects high dimensional data into a lower dimensional space, and is widely used for dimensionality reduction, signal denoising, regression, visualization etc. One can use matrix sketching to perform approximate PCA, by applying PCA on the approximation B instead of the original matrix A [7].

One application of PCA is to detect changes and anomalies in multidimensional data streams [31, 33]. In this context, changes and anomalies are detected by comparing the distribution of recent data with previous data. A typical window-based solution is to extract a fixed *reference window* and to update a *test window* with newly coming data. Changes or anomalies are detected by comparing the PCA basis of data in the reference window to the test window. Results in existing literature all assume that all rows in the test window are stored in memory, and PCA is computed via svd(singular value decomposition) over all rows in the test window. This approach is inherently not scalable in applications where the window is too large to fit in memory, or the rows in the stream are too fast to apply offline PCA algorithms (or even streaming matrix sketches) on the whole window. Sliding window matrix sketching allows us to approximate PCA on sliding windows with sub-linear space, thereby giving us the ability to compute PCA for large test windows in a continuous, online fashion.

Terminologies and notations. For a vector $x \in \mathbb{R}^n$, we let $\|x\| = \sqrt{\sum_{i=1}^n x_i^2}$ denote the standard Euclidean norm of x. For a matrix $A \in \mathbb{R}^{n \times d}$, we use $\|A\| = \max_{\|x\|=1} \|Ax\|$ denote the *spectral norm* of A, and $\|A\|_F = \sqrt{\sum_{i=1}^n \|a_i\|^2}$ to denote the *Frobenius norm* of A, where a_i is the ith row of A. Intuitively, the squared spectral norm $\|A\|^2$ represents the maximum influence along any unit direction, and the squared Frobenius norm $\|A\|_F^2$ represents the total "energy" of A. The *singular value decomposition* of A, written svd(A), produces three matrices $[U, \Sigma, V]$ so that $A = U\Sigma V^T$. U is a $n \times n$ orthogonal matrix that consists of the left singular vectors $[u_1, u_2, \ldots, u_n]$, and V is a $d \times d$ matrix with columns $[v_1, v_2, ..., v_d]$ being the right singular vectors. $\Sigma = \text{diag}(\sigma_1, \ldots, \sigma_d)$ is a $n \times d$ diagonal matrix, where $\sigma_1 \geq, \ldots, \geq \sigma_r$ are the singular values of A and $r \leq d$ is the rank. From the svd, we have the spectral norm $\|A\| = \sigma_1$, and the j-th singular value $\sigma_j = \|Av_j\|$. We also let A_k be the *best rank k approximation* of matrix A, specifically $A_k = \arg\min_{X:\text{rank}(X) \leq k} \|A - X\|_F$. Note that A_k can be computed by $A = U_k \Sigma_k V_k^T$, where Σ_k is a diagonal matrix consisting of the largest k singular values, and U_k and V_k denote the matrices consisting of the first k columns of U and V, respectively.

We model a data stream as an infinite sequence $S = \{(a_i, t_i) \mid i = 1 \ldots \infty\}$, where $a_i \in \mathbb{R}^{1 \times d}$ is a row of dimension d, and $t_i \in \mathbb{R}$ denotes the timestamp of a_i. For *time-based sliding windows*, let Δ be the window size Δ and t be the current timestamp. We use the time interval $W = [t - \Delta, t]$ to denote the rows in the window when there is no confusion. We use N_W and A_W to denote the number of rows and the matrix formed by all rows in window W, respectively; or simply use A to denote A_W and N to denote N_W when there is no confusion. A *sequence-based window* W is defined by window size N, which consists of the most recent N rows. All-zero row is not allowed in a sequence-based window. For reasons will become clear later, we assume the squared norms of the rows in the window take value from $[1, R]$, that is, $1 \leq \|a\|^2 \leq R$ for all $a \in W$.

Problem definition. Given window size Δ for time-based sliding windows (or N for sequence-based sliding windows) and error parameter ε, the goal is to maintain a matrix sketch κ such that at current time t, κ can return an approximation B for $A = A_W$, where the approximation quality is measured by the *covariance error*, such that:

$$\textbf{cova-err}(A, B) = \|A^T A - B^T B\| / \|A\|_F^2 \leq \varepsilon.$$

Covariance error can also be written as $\max_{\|x\|=1}(\|Ax\|^2 - \|Bx\|^2)/\|A\|_F^2$. Intuitively, covariance error guarantees that $\|Bx\|$ preserves $\|Ax\|$, the norm (or length) of A in any direction x. For instance, when performing PCA on A, it returns the top k orthogonal directions, measured in this length. Thus by setting an error threshold ε, this bound allows one to approximately retain all important directions.

Our contributions. This work aims at understanding the sliding window matrix sketching problem and providing solutions that are both theoretically sound and practically efficient. We first present two negative results to better understand the hardness of the problem. We show that:

(1) maintaining $A^T A$ exactly on a sequence-based sliding window requires space linear to the sliding window. This result demonstrates the fundamental difference between the unbounded streaming model and the sliding window model.

(2) if the maximum norm of the rows in the window is unbounded, it is not possible to maintain a sketch κ with sub-linear space even we allow large covariance error. This lower bound suggests that we need to limit the maximum possible squared norm of all rows by a upper bound R in order to derive interesting and efficient algorithms. But this is ok in practice, since the largest squared norm for a row of data in most matrix data in real-applications is indeed bounded by some reasonable value of R [20, 21, 25].

That said, we present three techniques for the sliding window matrix sketching problem.

- The Sampling algorithms maintain random samples of rows with probabilities proportional to their squared norms in the sliding windows. Our algorithms can generate randomly sampled rows both *with and without replacement*, denoted as SWR and SWOR respectively. The sampling algorithms work for both *time-based and sequence-based sliding windows.*

sketch κ	update time	sketch size	cova-err	ℓ	window	$B \subset A$?	Need R?
Sampling (SWR)	$(d/\varepsilon^2)\log\log NR$	$(d/\varepsilon^2)\log NR$ (Expected)	$\leq \varepsilon$ w.h.p.	d/ε^2	sequence & time	✓	No
LM-FD	$d \log \varepsilon NR$	$(1/\varepsilon^2)\log \varepsilon NR$	$\leq \varepsilon$	$1/\varepsilon$	sequence & time	×	Yes
DI-FD	$(d/\varepsilon)\log R/\varepsilon$	$(R/\varepsilon)\log R/\varepsilon$	$\leq \varepsilon$	$1/\varepsilon$	sequence	×	Yes

Table 1: Comparison of various sliding-window matrix sketches. "Update cost" denotes the cost for processing a new row; "Sketch size" denotes the number of rows used by the sketch; "Cova-err" denotes the error guarantee; "ℓ" denotes the size of the final approximation B in terms of number of rows; "Window" indicates which types of sliding windows the sketch works for; "$B \subset A$" indicates if the sketch is interpretable; "Need R" indicates if the sketch needs to know the maximum squared norm R a prior.

- The *Logarithmic Method* (LM) converts a streaming matrix sketch into a sliding window matrix sketch, given that the streaming matrix sketch is *mergeable* [2]. It works for *both time-based and sequence-based sliding windows.* We combine the LM framework with Frequent Direction and obtain LM-FD.
- The *Dyadic Interval* (DI) framework converts an arbitrary streaming matrix sketch into a matrix sketch on *sequence-based sliding windows.* It has better error-space tradeoff than LM methods when the maximum squared norm in the window is small. We combine the DI framework with Frequent Direction and obtain a sliding window sketch DI-FD.

In the unbounded streaming model, it is possible to maintain B as the matrix sketch κ, e.g., the frequent direction (FD) sketch [25]. In the sliding window model, this is difficult and our algorithms maintain a sketch κ that is queryable and whenever κ is queried, it will be able to generate the approximation matrix B for the latest sliding window.

We analyze the behaviors of our algorithms with rigorous theoretical analysis in Section 5, 6 and 7.1, and present thorough experimental studies in Section 8 to verify the effectiveness of our methods in practice. All of our sketches maintain a set of *matrix rows* that are *not necessarily the rows from A.* They differ in: (1) how these rows are constructed, and (2) how these rows are stored and updated as the window moves.

To describe the strength of each method, we select three algorithms and present the theoretical results in Table 1. The *Sketch size is measured in terms of the number of rows stored by each algorithm, and update cost is measured in terms of the CPU cost.* The sampling algorithms provide sketches that are interpretable, which is a desirable property in some applications [12, 14, 17]. On the other hand, theoretical analysis and experimental studies suggest that the LM-FD algorithm provides better approximation quality and faster processing time with the same space budget. Finally, if we *only* work with sequence-based window, *and* the norms of rows in the stream are bounded (e.g. all rows are normalized and $R = 1$), the DI-FD algorithm is more efficient than LM-FD and the sampling algorithms in terms of the space usage. Note that the LM-FD and the DI-FD algorithms must know the value R a prior, while the sampling algorithms do not require the knowledge of R.

An appealing feature of our sketches is that they are in fact very easy to implement and use in practice. However, the analyses, including both error analysis and space complexity, are nontrivial and quite involved for a general audience. Thus, we only present the main results and high-level ideas of our constructions in the main text, while deferring all details of the proofs and analyses to the appendix.

2. RELATED WORK

To the best of our knowledge, this is the first work on matrix sketching in the sliding window model. There are two classes of prior work that are relevant to our study: matrix sketching algorithms in the unbounded streaming model, and streaming algorithms in the sliding window model.

Streaming matrix sketching. Streaming matrix sketching approaches can be broadly divided into three categories. The first approach is to find a small subset of matrix rows (or columns) that approximate the entire matrix. This problem is known as the *column subset selection problem* [12, 14, 17], or in our model, the *row subset section problem.* A streaming solution to the column subset selection problem is obtained by iteratively sampling rows from the input matrix with probability proportional to their squared norms. Despite this algorithm's apparent simplicity, providing tight bounds for its performance required over a decade of research [15, 17]. We will refer to this algorithm as *sampling.* The second approach is to randomly combine matrix rows via random projection. Several results exist in the literature, including random projections [34] and hashing [1,8,38]. For details of these works, we refer to the survey by Woodruff [39]. The third approach is the deterministic matrix sketching technique [25] which adapts a well-known streaming algorithm for approximating item frequencies, the MG algorithm [28], to sketching a streaming matrix through tracking *frequent directions* (FD). FD was extended to derive streaming sketching results with bounds on relative error [20], and to monitor matrix approximation in distributed setting [21]. We refer readers to recent work [19] for extensive discussion and experimental study of various streaming matrix sketching algorithms and their error bounds.

But as we explained earlier in Section 1, there are fundamental differences between streaming matrix sketching and sliding window matrix sketching (as indicated by the huge difference between the lower bounds of the exact algorithms for the two problems). Hence, all these sketching techniques cannot be directly applied to solve our problem.

Sliding window algorithms. As mentioned earlier, the bulk of existing work on the sliding-window model has focused on algorithms for maintaining simple statistics, such as count, sum, heavy hitters, and quantiles, in space and time that is significantly sublinear (typically, poly-logarithmic) in the sliding-window size. Exponential histograms [11] is a state-of-the-art deterministic technique for maintaining ε-approximate counts and sums over sliding windows. ECM-sketch [32] extends exponential histograms to distributed environment. Arasu and Manku [3] proposed an algorithm that returns ε-approximate quantiles on sliding windows. Various other queries were studied in the sliding window model, including distinct elements [22], frequency count [27], top-k [32], skyline [37] frequent pattern mining [36]. We refer interested readers to a survey by Cormode [9].

Random sampling over sliding windows is a line of work that is more related to ours. In this problem, the goal is to maintain a set of ℓ elements that is randomly drawn from the window. Babcock, Datar and Motwani [5] were the first to consider the problem, and they proposed an elegant solution by combining priority sampling with the "successors list" techniques. Since then this problem has received considerable attention [10,18]. Efraimidis and Spirakis [16] modified the priority sampling algorithm to sample weighted elements on an unbounded stream with probabilities proportional to the weights. Longbo et. al. [26] considered the weighted sampling problem over sliding windows. However, their sampling algorithm does not provide samples with probabilities proportional to the weights.

Finally, another independent related work is the sliding window sbd [6], which computes the svd over a window sliding through the rows of a matrix. However, it needs to store all rows in the sliding window, hence, is not a sketch.

3. PRELIMINARIES

This section reviews matrix sketching algorithms on an unbounded stream (i.e., streaming matrix sketching). Recall that we adapt the *row update model*, in which the algorithms receive n rows from a matrix $A \in \mathbb{R}^{n\times d}$ one after another, and the goal is to maintain a sketch κ that is able to produce the approximation matrix $B \in \mathbb{R}^{\ell\times d}$ to approximate A with only $\ell \ll n$ rows. The approximation quality is usually characterized by the covariance error $\|A^TA - B^TB\|/\|A\|_F^2$.

Row sampling. Sampling algorithms assign a probability p_i for each row a_i proportional to its squared norm, and elect ℓ rows from A into B. We have two ways for sampling rows. In the *sampling with replacement* scheme, each row a_i is sampled with probability $p_i = \|a_i\|^2/\sum_{a_k\in A}\|a_k\|^2 = \|a_i\|^2/\|A\|_F^2$. Intuitively, the squared norm of a row decides its contribution to the frequent directions for the sliding window it's in. To sample ℓ rows with replacement, we take ℓ independent copies of such random samples. Then we scale each sampled row a_i by a factor of $\sqrt{\ell}\|A\|_F/\|a_i\|$ to form the matrix B. Note that there may be duplicated rows in sampling with replacement scheme.

For *sampling without replacement*, we avoid sampling the same row by excluding sampled rows from future selection. More precisely, let S_i be the set of the first i samples. The $(i+1)$-th sample is selected from $A\setminus S_i$, and each $a_j \in A\setminus S_i$ is sampled with probability $\|a_j\|^2/\sum_{a_k\in A\setminus S_i}\|a_k\|^2$. Assuming S is the set of sampled rows, we scale each sampled row $a_i \in S$ by a factor of $\|A\|_F/\sqrt{\sum_{a_k\in S}\|a_k\|^2}$ to form the matrix B. The row sampling schemes were analyzed in [15,21], and it was shown that with $\ell = O(\frac{1}{\varepsilon^2}\log\frac{1}{\varepsilon})$ samples, both sample with and without replacement schemes achieve covariance error **cova-err** $\le \varepsilon$.

Priority sampling is a general technique for sampling rows in the streaming model. For each row a_i, we assign a random priority $\rho_i = u_i^{1/w_i}$, where u_i is a number drawn from $(0,1)$ uniformly at random. It was shown in [16] that row a_i takes the largest priority with probability $p_i = w_i/w$. To sample ℓ rows without replacement, we simply maintain a reservoir S that consists of the rows with top-ℓ priorities. Note that one can maintain top-ℓ priorities with a priority queue of size ℓ. To sample ℓ rows with replacement, we maintain ℓ independent priority samples, each consists of a single sample.

Frequent direction. In this case, the sketch κ maintains B directly, i.e., $\kappa = B$. To process each row a_i, we first check if there is an all zero row in B_{i-1}. If so, we replace the last empty row of B_i with a_i to form B_i. Otherwise, we perform $\mathsf{svd}(B_{i-1}) = U_{i-1}\Sigma_{i-1}V_{i-1}$. Let $\Sigma_{i-1} = \mathrm{diag}(\sigma_1,\ldots,\sigma_d)$, and $\lambda = \sigma_{\ell/2}^2$ where $\sigma_{\ell/2}$ is the $\ell/2$-largest singular value. We set

$$\Sigma_i = \mathrm{diag}\left(\sqrt{\sigma_1^2-\lambda},\ldots,\sqrt{\sigma_{\ell/2}^2-\lambda},0,\ldots,0\right),$$

and $B_i = \Sigma_i V_{i-1}$. Note that B_i has $\ell/2$ empty rows and can accommodate $\ell/2$ future updates. Setting $\ell = \varepsilon/2$, One can show that FD achieves **cova-err**$(A,B) \le \varepsilon$ using $O(1/\varepsilon)$ space and $O(d/\varepsilon)$ amortized update time. An extension of FD to derive streaming sketch results with bounds on relative error appeared in [20]. FD was also used to monitor matrix approximation in distributed setting [21].

4. LOWER BOUNDS

In this section, we prove two lower bounds that characterize the sliding window matrix sketching problem. We note that the lower bounds in this section will be described in the number of bits used by the algorithms, while all the upper bound results (in the rest of the paper) are presented in terms of number of rows used by the algorithms. This is because for lower bound proofs, it is not reasonable to make assumptions on how an algorithm stores its information. For simplicity, we only present the high level ideas of the proofs, and defer all details to the appendix.

A linear lower bound for exact sketching. We show that maintaining A^TA exactly on a sequence-based sliding window requires $\Omega(Nd)$ space. Note that this is the space we need to store A exactly in the sliding window. Recall that in the unbounded streaming model, we can maintain A^TA with only d^2 space, so this lower bound implies that there is a fundamental difference between streaming model and sliding window model for the matrix sketching problem.

Theorem 4.1 *An algorithm that returns A^TA for any sequence-based sliding window must use $\Omega(Nd)$ bits space.*

The proof of Theorem 4.1 relies on a reduction from the *INDEX* problem in communication complexity theory. For the details of the proof, please refer to Section B.1.

A linear lower bound for unbounded norms. The next lower bound concerns with the norm distribution in the sliding window. We show that if the maximum squared norms of rows in the matrix is unbounded, then we need linear space for the matrix sketching problem, even a constant covariance error is allowed.

Theorem 4.2 *An algorithm that returns B_W such that*

$$\mathsf{Pr}\left[\|A_W^TA_W - B_W^TB_W\| \le \frac{1}{8d}\|A_W\|_F^2\right] > \frac{1}{2}$$

for any sliding window W must use $\Omega(Nd)$ bits space.

We reduce the *d-Majority INDEX* Problem, a variation of the INDEX problem, to the matrix sketching problem. For the details of the proof, please refer to Section B.2.

Remark. By Theorem 4.2, we need to constraint the norms in the window if we aim at sub-linear space. Throughout the paper, we assume the squared norms of rows in the stream takes value from $[1, R]$, that is, $1 \le \|a_j\|^2 \le R$ for any a_j in the window. This is a mild assumption.

5. BASELINE: SAMPLING ALGORITHMS

In this section, we describe a framework for sampling matrix rows on a sliding window. Our algorithms work for both sequence-based and time-based sliding windows. Although it is a fairly common setting in many matrix sketching works to treat the sampling algorithms as the "baseline solutions", we would like to emphasize that sampling rows according to their norms over sliding windows is actually a non-trivial task. More over, analyzing the space and error bounds for such algorithms also needs novel techniques.

5.1 Algorithm Description

Row Sampling With Replacement. We first show how to sample a single row on a sliding window. Intuitively, we make slight modification to the uniform sampling algorithm on sliding windows [5] to support the row sampling schemes. For each new row a_j, we assign to it a priority $\rho_t = u_t^{1/\|a_i\|^2}$, where u_t is a random number uniformly drawn from $(0, 1)$. By the analysis of priority sampling, we need to maintain the top-1 row, that is, the row with largest priority in the window. Simply storing the top-1 row is not sufficient, since it will expire as the window moves. The idea is to maintain a list of *candidate rows*, which are defined to be the rows that could become the top-1 row in the future. More precisely, a_j is a candidate row if and only if its priority ρ_j is the largest priority between its timestamp t_j and current timestamp t_c.

Algorithm 5.1 Update algorithm of SWR at time t

Remove all (a_j, t_j, ρ_j) in Q with $t_j < t - \Delta$
if *update* $= (a_t, t)$ **then**
  Choose $u_t \in \mathsf{Unif}(0, 1)$ and set $\rho_t \leftarrow u_t^{1/\|a_t\|^2}$
  while $\rho < \rho_t$ **do**
    $(a_j, t_j, \rho_j) = Q.back$
    if $\rho < \rho_t$ **then**
      Remove (a_j, t_j, ρ_j)
  Append (a_t, t, ρ_t) to the end of Q

For the query process, we find each sampled row a_j and rescale it back by a factor of $\frac{\sqrt{\ell}\|a_j\|}{\|A\|_F}$. One technical issue is that we are not able to track the exact value of $\|A\|_F$ on a sliding window. Recall that $\|A\|_F^2 = \sum_{a \in W} \|a\|^2$, so tracking $\|A\|_F$ is equal to the problem of tracking sum on sliding windows, and is discussed thoroughly in [11]. We can maintain an exponential histogram to approximate $\|A\|_F^2$ with additive error $\varepsilon^2\|A\|_F^2$, such that we can approximate $\|A\|_F$ within $(1+\varepsilon)$ factor. As shown in [11], this requires an addition space of $O(\frac{1}{\varepsilon^2} \log NR)$. As we will show in the analysis, this will not affect the approximation quality asymptotically. We also note that in many real world applications it is possible to maintain the exact value of $\|A\|_F$ by storing the norm of each row in the window, which requires much less space than storing the original rows.

Row Sampling Without Replacement. Recall that to sample ℓ items without replacement in the streaming setting, we need to maintain top-ℓ rows, that is, the ℓ rows with highest priorities. Consider a row a_j with timestamp t_j and priority ρ_j. A simple observation is that if a_t is not a top-ℓ row in window $[t_j, t]$, it will never become a top-ℓ row from

Algorithm 5.2 Update algorithm for SWOR at time t

1: Remove all (a_j, t_j, ρ_j, k_j) in Q with $t_j < t - \Delta$
2: **if** *update* $= (a_t, t)$ **then**
3:   Choose $u_t \in \mathsf{Unif}(0, 1)$ and set $\rho_t \leftarrow u_t^{1/\|a_t\|^2}$
4:   **for** $(a_j, t_j, \rho_j, k_j) \in Q$ **do**
5:     **if** $\rho_t > \rho_j$ **then**
6:       k_j += 1
7:       **if** $k_j > l$ **then**
8:         Remove (a_j, t_j, ρ_j, k_j) from Q
9:   Append $(a_t, t, \rho_t, 1)$ to the end of Q

this time forward. Therefore, we only need to store row a_j if and only if it is a top-ℓ row in window from time t_j to current time t.

Algorithm 5.2 illustrates the pseudo code of sampling ℓ rows without replacement. We initiate a queue Q to store the candidate rows and their priorities. For each candidate row a_j with timestamp t_j, we also store its rank k_j in window between t_j and current time t. At timestamp t, we first remove all expired tuples (line 1). If there is a new row a_t coming at time t, we first assign its priority $\rho_t = u_t^{1/\|a_t\|^2}$ (line 2-3). We then scan the tuples in Q and update the rank value k_j for each tuple (a_j, t_j, ρ_j, k_j) (line 5-6). If the rank k_j is larger than ℓ, then we remove the tuple from Q (line 7). Finally, we add the tuple $(a_t, t, \rho_t, 1)$ to Q (line 8).

For the query process, we set w to the the square root of $\sum_{a_k \in S} \|a_k\|^2$, the summation of squared norms of all sampled rows. Then we find each sampled row a_j and rescale it back by a factor of $\frac{\sqrt{\ell}\|a_j\|}{\|A\|_F}$ to make up B. Here we will also use an $(1+\varepsilon)$-approximation of $\|A\|_F$ from an exponential histogram if the exact value of $\|A\|_F$ is unknown.

5.2 Analysis

Note that Algorithm 5.1 and Algorithm 5.2 follow the same framework as the uniform priority sampling algorithms in [5]. The only difference is the way we generate the priorities. However, this modification requires non-trivial analysis on the space-error tradeoffs. In the following, we will state the theorem and key lemmas, and defer all proofs in the appendix.

We first show two Lemmas on the expected number of candidate rows in Algorithm 5.1 and Algorithm 5.2 for sampling ℓ rows. We assume the maximum window size is bounded by N, and the squared norms of rows in the stream takes value from $[1, R]$.

Lemma 5.1 *The expected number of candidate rows for Algorithm 5.1 is $O(\log NR)$. Consequently, the expected number of candidate rows for sampling ℓ rows in SWR is bounded by $O(\ell \log NR)$.*

Lemma 5.2 *The expected number of candidate rows to sample ℓ rows in SWOR is bounded by $O(\ell \log NR)$.*

Recall that we need to sample $\ell = O(\frac{d}{\varepsilon^2})$ rows to achieve ε covariance error for both SWR and SWOR. Combining with Lemma 5.1 and 5.2, we have the following space-error tradeoffs for the row sampling algorithms.

Theorem 5.1 *The SWR and SWOR algorithms can return an approximation B with error* **cova-err**$(A, B) \le \varepsilon$ *using $O(\frac{d}{\varepsilon^2} \log NR)$ space in expectation. The expected update times*

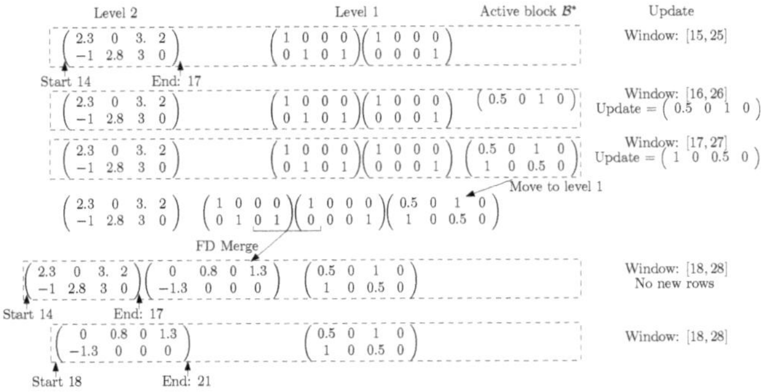

Figure 1: Running example for the LM-FD algorithm

for SWR and SWOR are $O(\frac{d}{\varepsilon^2}\log\log NR)$ *and* $O(\frac{d}{\varepsilon^2}\log NR)$, *respectively.*

6. LOGARITHMIC METHOD

In this section, we present a general framework to convert streaming matrix sketches into sliding window matrix sketches. This framework is inspired by the notion of *mergeable summaries* [2] and the logarithmic level idea of the well-known Exponential Histogram [11]. In this section, we use the Frequent Direction sketch as an example. We will show how the logarithmic method framework can cope with other mergeable sketches in the appendix.

6.1 Mergeability

Given two matrices A_1 and A_2 and their sketches $B_1 = \kappa(A_1, \varepsilon)$ and $B_2 = \kappa(A_2, \varepsilon)$, mergeability states that we can merge two sketches into a sketch for $A = [A_1; A_2]$ without increasing the size or the error. More precisely, recall that we have $\textbf{cova-err}(A_1, B_1) \le \varepsilon$ and $\textbf{cova-err}(A_2, B_2) \le \varepsilon$. More over, the space usage for both sketches are bounded by ℓ, respectively. A matrix sketch κ is *mergeable* if there is a merging algorithm such that $B = \mathsf{merge}(B_1, B_2)$ satisfies:

- The space usage for B is at most ℓ;
- The covariance error $\textbf{cova-err}(A, B)$ is at most ε.

Intuitively, if we can merge two sketches without increasing their error or size, then the sketches are mergeable. Mergeability is a very strong property, and is widely used in sensor networks and parallel computations. [2] focuses on summaries on streams of single attribute data.

Liberty [25] showed that Frequent Direction is also mergeable. Given two sketches $B_1 = \mathsf{FD}(A_1, \varepsilon)$ and $B_2 = \mathsf{FD}(A_2, \varepsilon)$, we set $C = [B_1; B_2]$ be the matrix that contains the two sketches B_1 and B_2 vertically stacked. We then run a singular decomposition on $[B_1; B_2] = U\Sigma V^T$, and let δ be the square of the ℓ-largest singular value, where $\ell = 1/\varepsilon$. We then subtract δ from all diagonal values in Σ^2, and set all negative values to be 0. Finally, we set $B = \Sigma V^T$. Liberty shows that the final sketch B can approximate $A = [A_1; A_2]$ with covariance error ε.

6.2 Algorithm Description

High Level Ideas. Figure 1 illustrates the high level idea for the LM framework. Suppose we have a streaming matrix sketch that achieves covariance error $\varepsilon/2$ with ℓ rows. For simplicity, we assume that $\ell \le R$; We will show how to remove this assumption later. We divide the window into levels of exponentially decreasing sizes. Each level is further divided into $b = \Theta(1/\varepsilon)$ blocks. The block in the leftmost level will have size roughly $\varepsilon\|A\|_F^2$, such that the expiration of some of its rows introduces a covariance error no more ε. We maintain a streaming mergeable sketch of size ℓ, for each block. For a query, we merge the sketches from each block together into an approximation B of size ℓ. By mergeability, B approximates the matrix A with covariance error $\varepsilon/2$. Finally, mergeability also ensures that we can merge two sketches in level i into a sketch in level $i+1$ without increasing the size, which is crucial for maintaining the logarithmic structure.

Data Structures. We divide the rows in the window into blocks, each covering a segment of non-overlapping consecutive rows. Each block $\mathcal{B}$ is associated with an streaming sketch of size ℓ, as well as the start time, the end time and the size of $\mathcal{B}$. We define the size of a block $\mathcal{B}$ to be the summation of the squared norms of the rows covered by $\mathcal{B}$, that is, $\mathcal{B}.size = \sum_{a\in\mathcal{B}}\|a\|^2$. We further group the blocks into levels of exponentially increasing sizes. Levels are numbered sequentially $1, \ldots, L$, with the rightmost (most recent) level to be level 1, and the leftmost (furthest) level to be level L. We maintain two invariants:

1. Each level contains $b-1$ or b blocks;
2. The size of a block in level i is between $2^{i-1}\ell$ and $2^i\ell$.

Note that since each row carries a squared norm at least 1, the second invariant ensures a block at level i covers at most $2^i\ell$ rows. We define 3 states of the block: *active*, *inactive*, *expiring*. An active block is one that receives updates ; an inactive block is one that lies completely inside the window; an expiring block is one that contains timestamp $t - \Delta$. See Figure 1. We note that there are exactly 1 active block in the sketch.

Algorithm 6.1 Update algorithm for LM (at time t)

```
1:  Remove all blocks B in L[L] with B.end < t
2:  if L[L] is empty then
3:     Remove L[L] and set L ← L − 1
4:  if update = (a_t, t) then
5:     Insert a_t to B*.sketch
6:     Set B*.end ← t and B*.size ← B*.size + ||a_t||^2
7:     if B*.size > ℓ then
8:        Append B* to L[1] and initialize an empty B* with
          B*.start = B*.end = t
9:     for i from 1 to L and L[i].length ≥ b + 1 do
10:       Find the rightmost blocks B_1 and B_2 in L[i]
11:       Construct a new block B with B.sketch =
          Merge(B_1.sketch, B_2.sketch)
12:       Set B.start ← B_1.start, B.end ← B_2.end, and
          B.size ← B_1.size + B_2.size
13:       Append B to L_{i+1} and remove B_1 and B_2 from L[i]
```

Update algorithm. Algorithm 6.1 illustrates the pseudo code of updating a LM sketch. Figure 1 use a running example to demonstrate the update process. Consider a time-based window of size 10. We set $\ell = 2$ and $d = 4$ for the LM sketch. At timestamp 25, we assume the sketch consists of 3 blocks, two from level 1 and one from level 2. We also assume the active block $\mathcal{B}^*$ is empty. Note that the rightmost block start at time 15 and end at time 18. As the window moves to $[16, 26]$, a new row $(0.5, 0, 1, 0)$ is inserted to the active block $\mathcal{B}^*$ (line 5-6 of Algorithm 6.1). Next, the window moves to $[17, 27]$. The sketch receives a new row $(1, 0, 0.5, 0)$

and insert it to $\mathcal{B}^*$. Since $\mathcal{B}^*$ is full, we move it to level 1 (line 5-6) and initialize a new active block (line 8). There are 3 blocks in level 1, so we perform the merging algorithm to the leftmost two blocks of level 1 to form a block of level 2 (line 10-14). Finally, when the window moves to $[18, 28]$, the rightmost block is expired and removed (line 2-3).

Algorithm 6.2 Query algorithm for LM (at time t)

```
Initialize B = B*
for i from 1 to L do
    for Each B in L[i] do
        B ← Merge(B, B.sketch)
```

Query algorithms. The query algorithm for LM is straightforward, and is illustrated in Algorithm 6.1. We merge all sketches in non-expiring blocks. Note that this is feasible since we require all sketches to have the same size ℓ.

Remark. Finally, we remove the assumption $\ell \leq R$. If a newly received row a_t carries a squared norm $\|a_t\|^2 \geq \ell$, we will maintain it as a single block in level 1. This row will remain untouched until its block reaches level $j = \log(\|a_t\|^2/\ell)$, which is the first level with block size larger than $\|a_t\|^2$. After level j, this row is treated as a common row and is allowed to participate merging process. As we shall see in the analysis, this will not affect the space or time bounds for the LM framework.

6.3 Analysis

We analyze the error guarantees as well as space and time complexity for the LM framework. We first prove a general Theorem that relates the complexity for LM algorithm and the streaming sketch used in each block. Then we investigate how a specific sketch can be integrate into the LM framework. In particular, assume the squared norms in the stream take value from $[1, R]$, and the maximum window size is N. We have the following Theorem for the space usage and update cost of the LM algorithm.

Theorem 6.1 *Suppose a mergeable matrix sketch κ achieves* **cova-err**$(A, B) \leq \varepsilon/8$ *with ℓ rows and update cost u in the streaming model. If we use κ as the sketch for each block in the LM algorithm and set $b = 8/\varepsilon$, we obtain a matrix sketch that works on time-based sliding window with error guarantee* **cova-err**$(A_W, B) \leq \varepsilon$ *for any given window W. The algorithm uses $O(\frac{\ell}{\varepsilon}\log \varepsilon NR)$ space and process an update in $O(u \log \varepsilon NR)$ time.*

PROOF. We first prove the error bound. Recall that the error consists of two parts: the error from the expiration of the expiring block in level L, and the error from the merged sketch for the rows in unexpired blocks. By the construction of the LM framework, there are two possibilities for the sketch in each block $\mathcal{B}$ in level i: if the size of $\mathcal{B}$ is between $2^{i-1}\ell$ and $2^i\ell$, we maintain a streaming sketch for the rows covered by $\mathcal{B}$ with size ℓ. Otherwise, we know $\mathcal{B}$ covers a single row with squared norm larger than $2^i\ell$, and we maintain that row exactly. It follows that the size of a block $\mathcal{B}$ at level i is always lower bounded by $2^{i-1}\ell$, and is upper bounded by $2^i\ell$ unless it only covers a single row. In particular, consider the level $L-1$. There are b block in this level, each with size at least $2^{L-2}\ell$. Using the simple fact that the total size in this level cannot exceeds $\|A\|_F^2$, we have $\|A\|_F^2 \geq 2^{L-2}b \cdot \ell$, and thus

$$L \leq \log \frac{\|A\|_F^2}{\ell b} + 2 \leq \log \frac{\varepsilon\|A\|_F^2}{2\ell}. \qquad (1)$$

The last inequality uses that $b \leq 8/\varepsilon$. This suggests that a block in the leftmost level L has size upper bounded by $2^L\ell = \varepsilon\|A\|_F^2/2$, unless it covers a single row. Since the expiring block is at level L, if its size is smaller than $\varepsilon\|A\|_F^2/2$, then the error contributed by it is bounded by $\varepsilon\|A\|_F^2/2$, otherwise it covers a single row and introduces no error. For the error from the merged sketch, we note that for each block $\mathcal{B}$ in level i, if the its size is between $2^{i-1}\ell$ and $2^i\ell$, the $\mathcal{B}.sketch$ uses space ℓ and approximate $\mathcal{B}$ with error bounded by $(\varepsilon/8)\cdot 2^i\ell$. Otherwise, the block covers a single row and its sketch returns no error. Therefore the total error returned by the merged sketch is bounded by

$$\sum_{i=1}^{L}(\varepsilon/8)\cdot 2^i\ell\cdot b \leq \varepsilon 2^{L+1}\ell b/8 \leq \varepsilon\cdot(\varepsilon/2)\|A\|_F^2\cdot 1/\varepsilon = \frac{\varepsilon\|A\|_F^2}{2}.$$

The last inequality is due to (1). Therefore, the error contributed by the merged sketch is also bounded by $\varepsilon\|A\|_F^2/2$, and thus the total covariance error is bounded by ε.

For the space complexity, we note that each block is maintaining a sketch with size ℓ. There are at most Lb blocks, thus the total space usage is bounded by

$$Lb\ell \leq \log\frac{\varepsilon\|A\|_F^2}{2\ell}\cdot\frac{8}{\varepsilon}\cdot\ell = O\left(\frac{\ell}{\varepsilon}\log\frac{\varepsilon NR}{s}\right) = O\left(\frac{\ell}{\varepsilon}\log\varepsilon NR\right).$$

Finally, for the update cost, note that each newly arriving row is inserted into the the sketch of the active block with $u_{1/\ell}$ update time. Moreover, we have to merge the leftmost two blocks for level i if the sum of squared norms received since last merging process exceeds $2^i\ell$, for $i = 1, \ldots, L$. To amortize this cost, we note that each row is merged at most L times, each merge process takes u time per row, so the amortized update cost is bounded by $Lu = O(u\log\frac{\varepsilon\|A\|_F^2}{\ell}) = O(u\log\varepsilon NR)$. □

Analysis for LM-FD. Recall that this algorithm uses the FD sketch for each block in the LM framework. Recall that given error parameter $\varepsilon/8$, the FD sketch uses $\ell = O(1/\varepsilon)$ rows and process an update with $u = O(d/\varepsilon)$ amortized cost. By Theorem 6.1, FM-FD achieves **cova-err** $\leq \varepsilon$ with space $O(\frac{1}{\varepsilon^2}\log\varepsilon NR)$ and amortized update cost $O(\frac{d}{\varepsilon}\log\varepsilon NR)$.

We note that the update time can be dramatically improved with a simple modification. Observe that the active block $\mathcal{B}^*$ covers at most ℓ rows. Therefore, instead of maintaining a FD sketch as $\mathcal{B}^*.sketch$, we simply store the newly receiving rows in $\mathcal{B}^*.sketch$ until its size exceeds ℓ. This will not affect the space-error tradeoffs for LM_FD, but will improve the amortized update cost to $O(d\log\varepsilon NR)$.

Corollary 6.1 *The LM-FD algorithm achieves* **cova-err** $\leq$ *ε with $O(\frac{1}{\varepsilon^2}\log\varepsilon NR)$ space and $O(d\log\varepsilon NR)$ update cost.*

7. DYADIC INTERVAL FRAMEWORK

In this section, we present another framework, termed Dyadic Interval (DI), that converts a streaming matrix sketch into a matrix sketch that works for sequence-based sliding windows. This framework is more efficient (space-wise) than the LM framework when the norms are small, and is capable of converting an arbitrary stream sketch into a sliding window matrix sketch. We use the Frequent Direction sketch to illustrate the framework in this section. We will show how the Dyadic Interval framework can cope with other streaming sketches in the appendix.

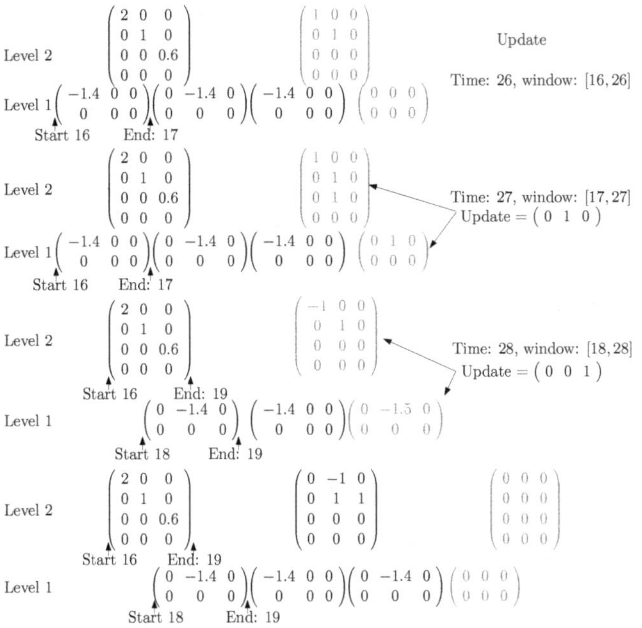

Figure 2: Illustration for Dyadic Interval method

7.1 Decomposability

DI framework is based on the *decomposability* of streaming matrix sketches. Intuitively, decomposability states that if we divide the rows of a matrix into submatrices and construct a sketch for each submatrix, we can concatenate these sketches back together to form a sketch for the original matrix. Note that decomposability is weaker than mergeability since it does not require that sketch size to remain the same after the merge, and thus is a weaker property. In fact, it is easy to show that all matrix sketches with the covariance error measure satisfy decomposability.

Lemma 7.1 (Decomposability) *Given a matrix $A_{n\times d}$, suppose we decompose A into k sub-matrices $A = [A_1; \dots; A_k]$, in which A_j is an $n_j \times d$ matrix. Suppose we compute a matrix sketch for each sub-matrix A_i, denoted B_i, such that $\|A_i^T A_i - B_i^T B_i\| \le \varepsilon_i \|A_i\|_F^2$. Then $B = [B_1; \dots; B_k]$ is an approximation for $A = [A_1; \dots; A_k]$ with error bound*

$$\|A^T A - B^T B\| \le \sum_{i=1}^{k} \varepsilon_i \|A_i\|_F^2.$$

PROOF. We observe that $A^T A = \sum_{i=1}^k A_i^T A_i$ and $B^T B = \sum_{i=1}^k B_i^T B_i$. Therefore we have

$$\|A^T A - B^T B\| \le \sum_{i=1}^{k} \|A_i^T A_i - B_i^T B_i\| \le \sum_{i=1}^{k} \varepsilon_i \|A_i\|_F^2,$$

and the Lemma follows. □

7.2 Algorithm Descriptions

High Level Ideas. The DI framework is inspired by the dyadic interval structure of the sliding window quantile structure in [3]. The high level idea is illustrated in Figure 2. We construct logarithmic number (denoted L) of levels, with each level partitions the stream into dyadic blocks. A block at the level $i+1$ contains two blocks at level i. It is easy to see that a sliding window can be decomposed into $2L$ blocks, with each level contributing at most 2 blocks. So if we maintain a streaming sketch for each block, we can concatenate the $2L$ sketches to form an approximation B for the rows in the sliding window, and the error is bounded by the decomposability property. A constraint for this dyadic structure is that it does not allow the window to shrink or expand, and thus only works for sequence-based sliding windows.

Data Structure. Suppose we have a streaming matrix sketch κ that achieves covariance error $\varepsilon/4$ with ℓ_ε rows. The notations of levels and blocks are slightly different from the ones in Section 6. We set the number of levels to be $L = \log R/\varepsilon$. For each level, we partition the stream into non-overlapping blocks, with block covers several consecutive rows in the stream. At the bottom level $\mathcal{L}[1]$, we impose a constraint such that the size of each block is between $NR/2^L$ and $NR/2^{L-1}$. We assume $2^L \le N$. Each block is associated with the following information: the start and end time and the size. We number the block in $\mathcal{L}[1]$ from old to new. For a higher level i, we make sure that each block covers exactly 2^i blocks of level 1. In particular, a block in level i covers block $j2^i$ to $(j+1)2^i - 1$ in level 1. This implies that a block in level i is of size $\Theta(NR/2^{L-i})$. Since level 1 contains at most 2^L blocks.

Following the same definitions as in Section 6, there are 3 states of the block: *active*, *inactive* and *expiring*. See Figure 2. We note that there are exactly 1 active block in each level. For the active block $\mathcal{B}^*$ at level i, we run a streaming sketch with error parameter $\varepsilon_i = 1/(2^i L)$. Once the active block $\mathcal{B}^*$ becomes full, that is, the size of $\mathcal{B}$ exceeds ℓ, the block becomes inactive. Note that this implies that an inactive block in level i stores a sketch with error parameter $\varepsilon_i = 1/(2^i L)$. To return a matrix approximation for the current window, we combine the sketches of some active and inactive blocks to determine the answer.

Algorithm 7.1 Update Algorithm for DI method

1: On receiving t-th update (a_t, t).
2: **for** $i \in [L]$ **do**
3: Remove all blocks $\mathcal{L}[i].\mathcal{B}[j]$ with $\mathcal{B}[j].end < t - N$
4: Insert a_t to $\mathcal{L}[i].\mathcal{B}^*.sketch$
5: Set $\mathcal{L}[i].\mathcal{B}^*.end \leftarrow t$
6: Set $\mathcal{L}[i].\mathcal{B}^*.size \mathrel{+}= \|a_t\|^2$
7: **if** $\mathcal{L}[1].\mathcal{B}^*.size > NR/2^L$ **then**
8: Set $v \leftarrow$ number of trailing 0's in $\mathcal{L}[i].length + 1$
9: **for** $i \in [v]$ **do**
10: Mark $\mathcal{L}[i].\mathcal{B}^*$ as inactive and append it to $\mathcal{L}[i]$
11: Initialize an empty $\mathcal{L}[i].\mathcal{B}^*$ with $\mathcal{L}[i].\mathcal{B}^*.start = \mathcal{L}[i].\mathcal{B}^*.end = t$

Update algorithms Algorithm 7.1 illustrates the pseudo code of updating a DI-based sketch. Figure 2 use a running example to demonstrate the update process. We use a sequence-based window of size 10. The sketches consists of 2 levels. For each block at level 1, we set its maximum size to be 2. Suppose at time 26, the sketch consists of 4 blocks from level 1 and 2 blocks from level 2. We use red color to mark the active blocks. Note that the active block of level 1 is empty. As the window moves to $[17, 27]$, we insert the new coming row $(0, 1, 0)$ to the active blocks in level 1 and 2 (line 4 in algorithm 7.1). Next, as the window moves to $[18, 28]$, the leftmost block of level 1 is expired and removed from the sketch (line 3). Then we insert the new coming row $(0, 0, 1)$ to the two active blocks (line 4). Since the active block of level 1 is full (the squared Frobenius norm ≥ 2), we need to mark some active blocks as inactive. To do so, note that the number of blocks in level 1 is 3, and the number of trailing 0's of (3+1=4) is 2. Thus, we set $v = 2$ (line 8) and mark the active blocks in level 1 and 2 as inactive (line 10). Finally, we initialize an new active block for each level (line 11). The final sketch at time 28 is showed in Figure 2.

Algorithm 7.2 Query process for DI method on window $(t-N, t]$

```
1: Initialize a empty matrix B
2: Initialize a = t and b = t − N
3: Find the highest level v with at least 1 active block
4: for i from v to 1 do
5:    Find the leftmost block L[i].B[j]
6:    if L[i].B[j].end ≤ a then
7:       Combine B with L[i].B[j].sketch
8:       Set a = L[i].B[j].start
9:    Find the rightmost block L[i].B[k]
10:   if k = j then
11:      Set b = L[i].B[j].end
12:   else if L[i].B[k].start ≥ b and k ≠ j then
13:      Combine B with L[i].B[k].sketch
14:      Set b ← L[i].B[k].end
```

Query algorithm. Algorithm 7.2 illustrates the pseudo code of returning a matrix sketch for window $[t-N, t]$ with a DI-based sketch. We initialize an empty matrix B (line 1) and two indicating timestamp $a = t$ and $b = t - N$. As the algorithm proceeds, the intervals $[t-N, a]$ and $[b, t]$ indicate the rows that are not covered by B. We find the highest level with at least one active block (line 3) and let v denote this level. Then we start the following process in a top-down fashion: at each level i, we find the left most block, denoted $\mathcal{L}[i].\mathcal{B}[j]$ (line 5), and check if it is in intervals $[t-N, a]$ (line 6). If so, we select it to make up the window by combining B with its sketch $\mathcal{L}[i].\mathcal{B}[j].sketch$ (line 7). Then we update a to be $L[i].\mathcal{B}[j].start$, meaning that interval $[t-N, L[i].\mathcal{B}[j].start]$ is uncovered. Then we find the rightmost block $L[i].\mathcal{B}[k]$ (line 9) and check if it is the same block as $\mathcal{L}[i].\mathcal{B}[j]$ (line 10). If so, we simply update b to be $\mathcal{L}[i].\mathcal{B}[j].end$ (line 11), meaning that interval $[\mathcal{L}[i].\mathcal{B}[j].end, t]$ is uncovered. If $\mathcal{L}[i].\mathcal{B}[k] \neq \mathcal{L}[i].\mathcal{B}[j]$, we combine B with $\mathcal{L}[i].\mathcal{B}[k].sketch$ (line 13) and update b to be $\mathcal{L}[i].\mathcal{B}[k].end$ (line 14). The query algorithm will find at most $2L$ blocks that make up the window.

7.3 Analysis

Similar to Section 6, we analyze the space and time complexity of the DI framework based on the parameters of the streaming sketch used in each block. Assume the maximum weight in the stream is R, and the window size is N. We have the following Theorem.

Theorem 7.1 *Suppose a streaming matrix sketch κ achieves* **cova-err**$(A, B) \leq \varepsilon/4$ *with ℓ_ε space and u_ε update cost. By using κ as the sketch for each block in the DI framework, we obtain a matrix sketch that works on sequence-based sliding window and gives error guarantee* **cova-err**$(A_W, B) \leq \varepsilon$ *for any given window W. The sketch uses $O(\frac{R}{\varepsilon}\sum_{i=1}^{L}(\ell_{1/(2^iL)}/2^i))$ space and process an update in $O(u_\varepsilon L)$ time, where $L = \lceil \log R/\varepsilon \rceil$.*

PROOF. We consider the error guarantee first. Recall that the error consists of two parts: the error from the expiring block in level 1, and the error from merging at most $2L$ sketches. By the fact that each row carries a squared norm at least 1 in the sequence-based sliding window, we have $\|A\|_F^2 \geq N$, and thus the size of the expiring block in level 1 is bounded by $NR/2^{L-1} \leq \varepsilon N/2 \leq \varepsilon\|A\|_F^2/2$. On the other hand, a block at level i has size at most $NR/2^{L-i}$, and maintains a sketch with error parameter $1/(2^iL)$, so a sketch at level i introduces error at most $\frac{1}{2^iL} \cdot NR/2^{L-i} = \frac{NR}{2^LL} \leq \frac{\varepsilon N}{4L}$. Summing up all $2L$ sketches follows that the error is bounded by $\varepsilon/2$. Therefore, the total covariance error is bounded by ε.

For the space usage, each block at level i maintains a sketch of size $\ell_{1/(2^iL)}$, and there are at most $2^{L-i} = \frac{8R}{2^i\varepsilon}$ blocks in level i. It follows that the space usage for level i is bounded by $8R\ell_{1/(2^iL)}/2^i$, and the total space usage is bounded by $O(\frac{R}{\varepsilon}\sum_{i=1}^{L}(\ell_{1/(2^iL)}/2^i))$.

For the update cost, we need to update L active sketches. This gives us a total update cost $u_\varepsilon L$. □

Note that if κ provides probabilistic bound, that is, κ achieves **cova-err**$(A, B) \leq \varepsilon$ with probability $1-\delta$, then DI(κ) also achieves **cova-err**$(A_W, B) \leq \varepsilon$ for any given window W with probability $1-\delta$.

DI-FD. This algorithm uses Frequent Direction sketch for each block in the DI method. Recall that given error parameter ε, the FD sketch uses $\ell_\varepsilon = O(1/\varepsilon)$ space and process an update with $u_\varepsilon = O(d/\varepsilon)$ amortized cost. By Theorem 6.1, we have the following corollary:

Corollary 7.1 *The LM-FD algorithm use $O(\frac{R}{\varepsilon}\log\frac{R}{\varepsilon})$ space and process an update with $O(\frac{d}{\varepsilon}\log\frac{R}{\varepsilon})$ amortized cost.*

8. EXPERIMENT

Algorithms. We implemented and compared the following algorithms. Note that for all sketches, our theoretical analysis only shows a loose upper bound for the sketch size in relationship to a desirable covariance error threshold ε, and the bad bases that actually meet those loose upper bounds almost never happens in real data sets. Hence, in practice, the performance of theses sketches are always much better, i.e., to meet an error threshold ε, they use much less space than what the theoretical bounds have indicated. That said, instead of setting a sketch's size based on its theoretical upper bound using an error threshold ε, we set the sketch size based on its structure and construction, as explained below, and report the *actual observed error* err in relationship to the actual size of various sketches.

(1) Baseline: Sampling algorithms. We evaluated SWR and SWOR, the row sampling with/without replacement algorithms, respectively. We also implemented a variation of SWOR, denoted as SWOR-ALL, which makes use all the candidate rows for approximating A. The intuition for SWOR-ALL is that since SWOR only returns a small portion of the candidate rows as the random samples, and it is interesting to see if the precision can be improved by using all the candidate rows in the approximation. All sampling algorithms were evaluated on both sequence-based and time-based windows. The space and error bounds were controlled by a parameter ℓ, the number of rows to be sampled. Note that the size of a sampling sketch is larger than ℓ, since it needs to generate also candidate rows in order to construct B.

(2) Logarithmic Method based algorithms. We evaluated LM-FD on both sequence-based and time-based windows.

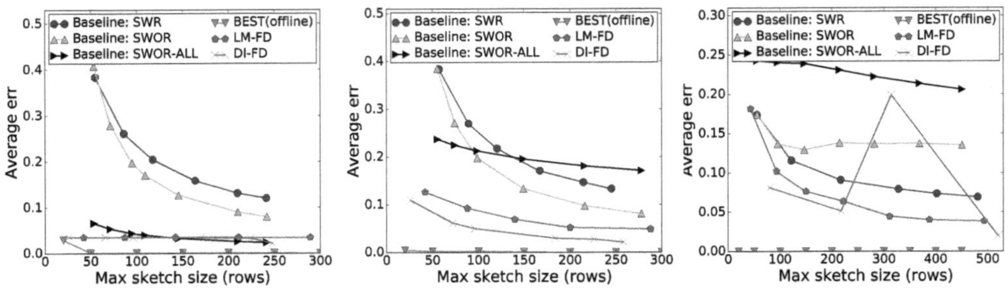

(a) SYNTHETIC (b) BIBD (c) PAMAP

Figure 3: average err vs. maximum sketch size.

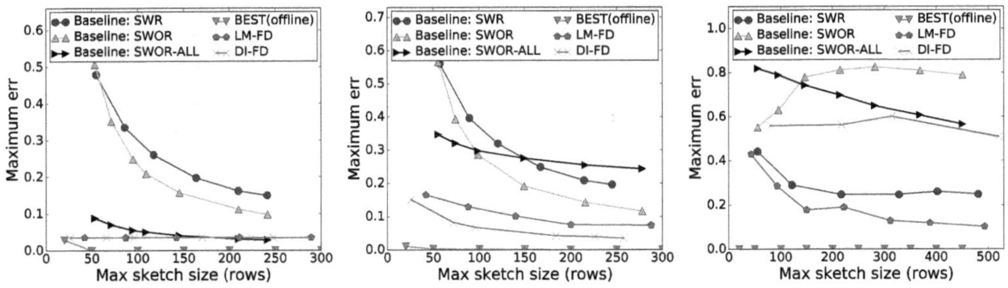

(a) SYNTHETIC (b) BIBD (c) PAMAP

Figure 4: maximum err vs. maximum sketch size.

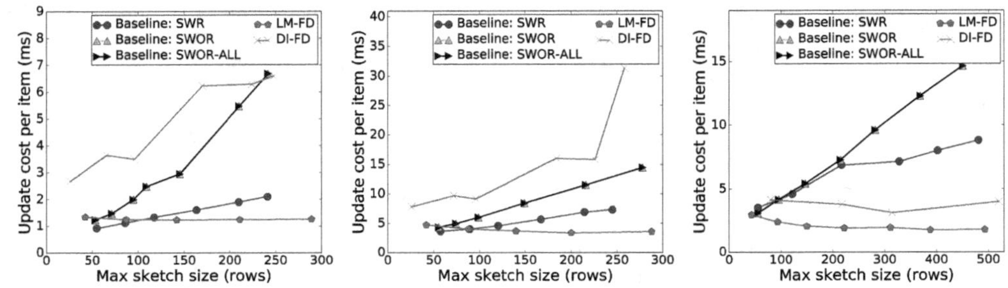

(a) SYNTHETIC (b) BIBD (c) PAMAP

Figure 5: update cost vs. maximum sketch size.

The space and error bounds were tuned by a parameter $b = \frac{1}{\varepsilon}$, the number of blocks in a level, and ℓ the size of the approximation matrix B (number of rows in B). Note that in LM-FD, each block simply stores a approximation matrix.

(3) Dyadic Interval based algorithms. We evaluated DI-FD on sequence-based sliding windows. The space and error bounds were set by the parameter $L = \log \frac{R}{\varepsilon}$, the maximum number of levels in the dyadic interval structure. Note that at the highest level, the streaming sketch has roughly $\ell/2$ rows, so that when B is constructed from all levels it has a size of roughly ℓ rows.

(4) Best rank k approximation. We evaluated BEST(offline), which is the best k-approximation for each sliding window. Note that the error provided by the best rank k approximation is theoretical optimal if the number of rows used by the sketch is bounded by k. It is not known how to compute the best rank k-approximation in the streaming model, so we compute BEST(offline) in an offline fashion.

Metrics. In the experimental study, we changed the parameters for each algorithm to show the the tradeoffs between the sketch size, actual observed error err, and running time.

- Sketch size was measured in terms of the number of rows stored for each algorithm for a sliding window. This is the dominating part of the memory usage, and is a common measurement for evaluating matrix sketching algorithms. Moreover, we measured the *maximum sketch size*, that is, the maximum number of rows stored over all appeared windows for an algorithm. For the best k approximation BEST(offline), we set k with various sizes and report its errors.
- For the approximation quality, we measured the *max error* and the *average error*, the maximum and average observed covariance error (err) over all appeared windows, using the approximation matrix B constructed by various algorithms.
- The update cost was measured by the *average processing time of one stream element (i.e., one matrix row)* for both sequenced based and time based windows. Note that we do not report the update cost of Best since it is an offline algorithm.

Setup. Since most of our sketches are randomized, we run each algorithm over each data set 20 times, and took the average for each metric to report. All algorithms were implemented in Python 2.7.6 using 32-bit addressing. The timing experiments were executed on a single idle core of an Intel Xeon E5-2620, clocked at 2.1 GHz.

Data Set	total rows n	d	N	ratio R
SYNTHETIC	10^6	300	10,000	8.35
BIBD	319,770	231	10,000	1
PAMAP	198,000	35	10,000	90089

Table 2: Data Sets for sequence-based window.

8.1 Sequence-based sliding window

We first evaluate all 6 algorithms on sequence-based sliding windows. We used two publicly available real data sets and one standard synthetic data set in the experiment.

Data Sets. SYNTHETIC is the Random Noisy matrix that has been commonly used for evaluating matrix sketching algorithms [19, 25]. Please see section D for the generating process. We generated a matrix with 300 columns and 1 million rows. All entries in SYNTHETIC are non-zeros.

BIBD[1] is the incidence matrix of a Balanced Incomplete Block Design from Mark Giesbrecht, University of Waterloo. This data set is available from the University of Florida Sparse Matrix Collection. It contains 231 columns and 319,770 rows, and 8,953,560 non-zero entries. Each entry is an 0 or 1 integer that indicates if an edge exists.

PAMAP[2] is is a physical activity monitoring data set which contains data of recorded with 8 subjects performing 14 different activities. The data set contains 45 columns, including a timestamp, an activity ID and 43 attributes of raw sensory data. In our experiments, we used a data of subject 1 with 198, 000 rows and 35 columns (removing timestamps, activity IDs and columns containing missing values). We note that the gap between two consecutive timestamps of PAMAP is fixed to 0.5 second, so this data set can be easily treated using a sequence-based sliding window.

Table 2 summarizes these data sets.

Results. We set window size to be $N = 10,000$ for all data sets. Figure 3 and 4 illustrate the the tradeoffs between the max sketch size and the average error, and between the max sketch size and the maximum error, respectively. Figure 5 shows the tradeoffs between the max sketch size and update cost. We use the same color and line style for the same algorithm across figures for better illustration. We make the following observations:

(1) The performance of SWR and SWOR varies on different data sets. A theoretical advantage of SWOR over SWR is that it does not return duplicating rows, which is more theoretically "representative". Figures 3a and 3b show that given the same space budget, SWOR provides smaller average error than SWR on SYNTHETIC and BIBD. Figures 4a and 4b indicate the same for the maximum error. However, we observe in Figures 3c and 4c that SWR provides smaller error than SWOR on PAMAP.

(2) An interesting observation from Figure 4c is that the maximum covariance error of SWOR increases with the max sketch size on PAMAP, which is counter-intuitive. To eliminate the convolution effect from the sliding window structures, we located the window where the max error was achieved (row 125,000 to row 135,000), and performed offline sampling algorithms to the rows in that window. The results is shown in Figure 6. We observe that the covariance error for SWOR indeed increases as we increase the number of rows to be sampled. One possible reason is that SWOR is not preferable when the distribution of the norms is skewed. Consider an extreme case, in which the window consists of

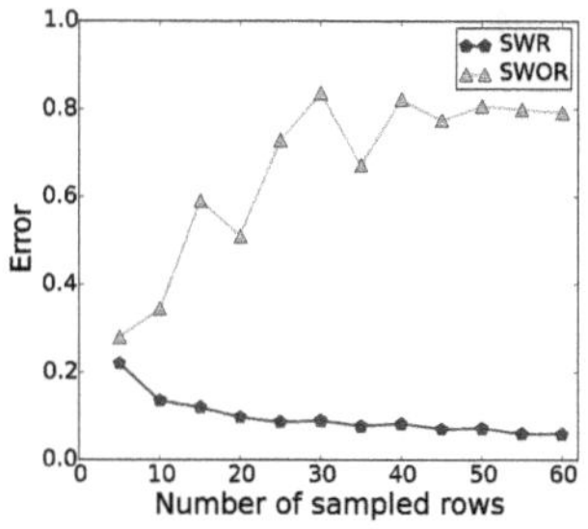

Figure 6: Covariance error vs. number of sampled rows for offline SWR and SWOR on PAMAP

$\ell - 1$ rows with very large norms, and $N - \ell + 1$ rows with very small norms. If we were to sample ℓ rows, one small row will be sampled and rescaled back according to $\|A\|_F^2$. This will over-emphasize the weight on this small row and will introduce large error.

(3) Making use of all candidate rows in the SWOR algorithm does not always give better error guarantee. While Figures 3a and 4a suggest that SWOR-ALL indeed performs better than SWR and SWOR on SYNTHETIC, the advantage becomes less obvious on BIBD (Figures 3b and 4b). Figure 3c shows that SWR or SWOR outperformed SWOR-ALL by a large margin on PAMAP in terms of average error. This can be explained by the fact that SYNTHETIC data set is a random matrix, so a candidate row acts approximately as a random sample. On the other hand, BIBD and PAMAP exhibit less randomness, so treating candidate rows as random samples may hurt the precision of estimation.

(4) The performance of DI-FD and LM-FD depends on the ratio between maximum squared norm and minimum squared norms in the data set. Figures 3b and 4b show that DI-FD achieves better error-space tradeoff than LM-FD on BIBD, while Figures 3c and 4c show the opposite results on PAMAP. Note that the ratio is 1 for BIBD, and is over 90,000 for PAMAP. This concurs with our theoretical analysis, that is, DI-FD is preferable when the ratio is small, and LM-FD is preferable when the ratio is large.

(5) Figures 3a and 4a show that for LM-FD, DI-FD and SWOR-ALL , the error does not decrease as we increase the space budget. Further investigation shows that by simply returning $B = 0$ as an approximation, one can achieve covariance error 0.0338, and any further improvement over this error may require very large space.

(6) Figure 5 shows that SWR was faster than SWOR on all three data sets. This is due to the fact that SWOR has to scan the queue Q to update the rank of each candidate row, while SWR can terminate the scan process. Figure 5 also suggests that LM-FD achieved the best performance in terms of running time. This is as expected, since the update costs for the LM-FD algorithm is bounded by $O(d \log \varepsilon NR)$, while the update costs for the DI-FD algorithm and the sampling algorithms are polynomial in d/ε. We also note that unlike the DI-FD and sampling algorithms, the running time for the LM-FD has slightly decreased as we increase the sketch size. This fits in the $O(d \log \varepsilon NR)$, since by increasing sketch size, we have effectively reduced the error threshold ε. Finally, note that it takes 20+ ms to update the DI-FD sketch on some data sets, which means it takes several hours to process 1 million rows.

8.2 Time-based sliding window

We used two real world data sets to for evaluating our algorithms on time-based sliding windows.

[1] http://www.cise.ufl.edu/research/sparse/matrices/JGD_BIBD/bibd_22_8.html

[2] http://www.pamap.org/demo.html

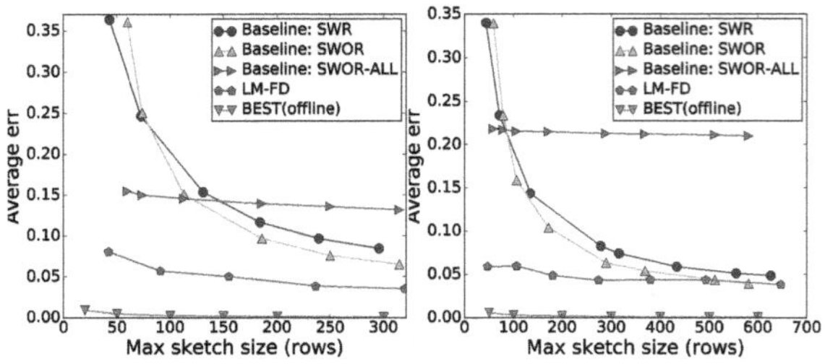

(a) RAIL (b) WIKI

Figure 7: average err vs. max sketch size.

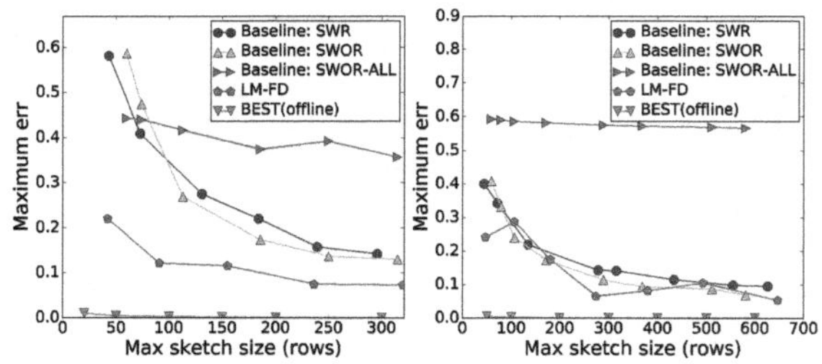

(a) RAIL (b) WIKI

Figure 8: maximum err vs. max sketch size.

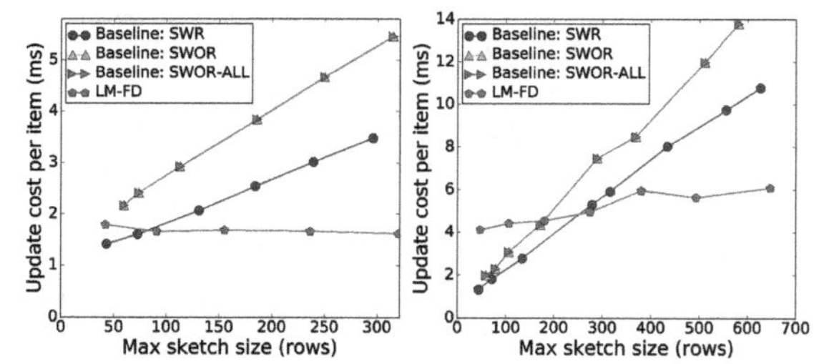

(a) RAIL (b) WIKI

Figure 9: update cost vs. sketch size.

WIKI is the text corpus built on the article dump of the Sep 2015 version of English WIKIpedia[3]. We preprocessed the data to remove the stop-words and insignificant articles. We used words occurring at least 1000 times in the entire corpus as features (columns), and selected articles with at least 500 features as rows. The entry at row i and column j is the *tf-idf weighting* of word j in article i. Each row is associated with a timestamp, which is the time that this article is published. This matrix consists of 7047 columns and 68,319 rows. The timestamps of WIKI spans over several years. We view one day as the time unit, set the window size to be 578 such that on average there are approximately 10,000 rows in a window. The maximum number of rows in a window is 62,125.

RAIL[4] is the crew scheduling matrix for the Italian railways. The entry at row i and column j is the integer cost for assigning crew i to cover trip j. This matrix contains 2586 columns and 923,269 rows, with 8,011,362 nonzero entries. We added synthetic timestamps RAIL to create a time-based stream that follows the *Poisson arrival model*, that is, the timestamps of the updates follow Poisson distribution with $\lambda = 0.5$. We set the window size to be 5,000 such that on average there are approximately 10,000 rows in a window. The maximum number of rows in a window is 10,347.

Figures 7 and 8 illustrate the the tradeoffs between the max sketch size and the average error, and between the sketch size and the maximum error, respectively. Figure 9 shows the tradeoffs between sketch size and update cost. The results suggest that the performance of the sampling and LM-FD on time-based windows is consistent with their performance on sequence-based windows. Figures 7 and 8 show that LM-FD achieved the best error-space tradeoff, followed by the two sampling algorithms.

Data Set	rows n	d	Δ	N_W	ratio R
WIKI	68,319	7047	578	$\approx 10,000$	422.81
RAIL	923,269	2586	5000	$\approx 10,000$	12

Table 3: Data Sets for time-based sliding window.

Figure 9 shows that LM-FD outperforms the sampling algorithms in terms of the update cost. This concurs with the results for sequence-based windows. However, Figure 9b suggests that the advantage of LM-FD is less obvious on the WIKI data set. This is due to the fact that in English WIKIpedia, articles are published more frequently in recent time. Thus a fixed time interval many contain very few rows at the beginning, and the queues in the sampling algorithms may be relatively small and efficient to update.

8.3 Remarks

We conclude our experimental evaluations with a few remarks. In general, the sampling algorithms performs not so well comparing to the DI-FD and the LM-FD algorithm. However, the sampling algorithms provide the desirable property that the final sketch is interpretable. Inside the family of sampling algorithms, SWR is preferred over SWOR and SWOR-ALL. We recommend LM-FD for other general analytic task, due to its overall superior efficiency in terms of both space and update cost, and to its applicability on both sequence-based and time-based windows. Finally, if the space efficiency is the main concern, the norms are strictly bounded (e.g. normalized stream), and sequenced-based window is used, DI-FD has the best performance.

We also note that the performance of our sketches is relatively stable over time, which means the overall data set size is not a critical factor in evaluating the performance of our algorithms. What really matters is the ratio R between max row norm and min row norm in a sliding window. That said, in practice, the sketch size of our design is typically much smaller than our theoretical bounds' dependence on R or $\log R$ (See the R value of PAMAP in Table 2). Finally, improving the update cost for the DI-FD algorithm is an interesting open problem.

9. CONCLUSION

This paper gives the first treatment to the sliding window sketching problem. We presented efficient algorithms for both time-based and sequence-based windows, and explored various constructions based on either sampling or embedding streaming matrix sketches (such as frequent direction) into a sliding-window data summary. We provided both formal theoretical guarantees, in terms of update cost and space–approximation error tradeoff, and extensive experimental evaluations over a large collection of real and synthetic data sets that have demonstrated the excellent performance of our algorithms in practice. Directions for future work include, but not limited to, deriving tighter theoretical bounds for some of our sketching algorithms, extending them to handle distributed data, and understanding their behaviors in different error metrics.

[3] https://en.wikipedia.org/wiki/WIKIpedia:Database_download

[4] http://www.cise.ufl.edu/research/sparse/matrices/Mittelmann/rail2586.html

10. REFERENCES

[1] D. Achlioptas. Database-friendly random projections. In *PODS*, pages 274–281. ACM, 2001.

[2] P. K. Agarwal, G. Cormode, Z. Huang, J. M. Phillips, Z. Wei, and K. Yi. Mergeable summaries. *TODS*, 38(4):26, 2013.

[3] A. Arasu and G. S. Manku. Approximate counts and quantiles over sliding windows. In *PODS*, pages 286–296. ACM, 2004.

[4] B. Babcock, S. Babu, M. Datar, R. Motwani, and J. Widom. Models and issues in data stream systems. In *PODS*, pages 1–16. ACM, 2002.

[5] B. Babcock, M. Datar, and R. Motwani. Sampling from a moving window over streaming data. In *SODA*, pages 633–634. SIAM, 2002.

[6] R. Badeau, G. Richard, and B. David. Sliding window adaptive svd algorithms. *IEEE Transactions on Signal Processing*, 52(1):1–10, 2004.

[7] C. Boutsidis, D. Garber, Z. Karnin, and E. Liberty. Online principal components analysis. In *SODA*, pages 887–901. SIAM, 2015.

[8] K. L. Clarkson and D. P. Woodruff. Low rank approximation and regression in input sparsity time. In *STOC*, pages 81–90, 2013.

[9] G. Cormode, M. Garofalakis, P. J. Haas, and C. Jermaine. Synopses for massive data: Samples, histograms, wavelets, sketches. *Foundations and Trends in Databases*, 4(1-3):1–294, 2012.

[10] G. Cormode, S. Muthukrishnan, K. Yi, and Q. Zhang. Continuous sampling from distributed streams. *JACM*, 59(2):10, 2012.

[11] M. Datar, A. Gionis, P. INDYK, and R. Motwani. Maintaining Stream Statistics over Sliding Windows. *SIAM Journal on Computing*, 31(6):1794–1813, Jan. 2002.

[12] A. Deshpande and L. Rademacher. Efficient volume sampling for row/column subset selection. In *FOCS*, pages 329–338, 2010.

[13] P. Drineas, A. Frieze, R. Kannan, S. Vempala, and V. Vinay. Clustering large graphs via the singular value decomposition. *Machine learning*, 56(1-3):9–33, 2004.

[14] P. Drineas and R. Kannan. Pass efficient algorithms for approximating large matrices. In *SODA*, pages 223–232, 2003.

[15] P. Drineas, R. Kannan, and M. W. Mahoney. Fast monte carlo algorithms for matrices i: Approximating matrix multiplication. *SIAM Journal on Computing*, 36(1):132–157, 2006.

[16] P. S. Efraimidis and P. G. Spirakis. Weighted random sampling with a reservoir. *Information Processing Letters*, 97(5):181–185, 2006.

[17] A. Frieze, R. Kannan, and S. Vempala. Fast monte-carlo algorithms for finding low-rank approximations. *JACM*, 51(6):1025–1041, 2004.

[18] R. Gemulla and W. Lehner. Sampling time-based sliding windows in bounded space. In *SIGMOD*, pages 379–392. ACM, 2008.

[19] M. Ghashami, A. Desai, and J. M. Phillips. Improved practical matrix sketching with guarantees. In *ESA*, pages 467–479. Springer, 2014.

[20] M. Ghashami and J. M. Phillips. Relative errors for deterministic low-rank matrix approximations. In *SODA*, pages 707–717. SIAM, 2014.

[21] M. Ghashami, J. M. Phillips, and F. Li. Continuous matrix approximation on distributed data. *VLDB*, 7(10):809–820, 2014.

[22] Y. Jiao. Maintaining stream statistics over multiscale sliding windows. *TODS*, 31(4):1305–1334, 2006.

[23] A. Lakhina, M. Crovella, and C. Diot. Diagnosing network-wide traffic anomalies. In *ACM SIGCOMM Computer Communication Review*, pages 219–230. ACM, 2004.

[24] A. Lakhina, K. Papagiannaki, M. Crovella, C. Diot, E. D. Kolaczyk, and N. Taft. Structural analysis of network traffic flows. In *SIGMETRICS*, 2004.

[25] E. Liberty. Simple and deterministic matrix sketching. In *SIGKDD*, pages 581–588. ACM, 2013.

[26] Z. Longbo, L. Zhanhuai, Z. Yiqiang, Y. Min, and Z. Yang. A priority random sampling algorithm for time-based sliding windows over weighted streaming data. In *SAC*, pages 453–456. ACM, 2007.

[27] G. S. Manku and R. Motwani. Approximate frequency counts over data streams. In *VLDB*, pages 346–357, 2002.

[28] J. Misra and D. Gries. Finding repeated elements. *Science of computer programming*, 2:143–152, 1982.

[29] C. Papadimitriou, P. Drineas, and M. Magdon-Ismail. Near optimal column-based matrix reconstruction. In *FOCS*, pages 305–314. IEEE, 2011.

[30] S. Papadimitriou, J. Sun, and C. Faloutsos. Streaming pattern discovery in multiple time-series. In *VLDB*, pages 697–708, 2005.

[31] S. Papadimitriou and P. Yu. Optimal multi-scale patterns in time series streams. In *SIGMOD*, pages 647–658. ACM, 2006.

[32] O. Papapetrou, M. Garofalakis, and A. Deligiannakis. Sketching distributed sliding-window data streams. *The VLDB Journal*, 24(3):345–368, 2015.

[33] A. A. Qahtan, B. Alharbi, S. Wang, and X. Zhang. A pca-based change detection framework for multidimensional data streams: Change detection in multidimensional data streams. In *SIGKDD*, pages 935–944. ACM, 2015.

[34] T. Sarlos. Improved approximation algorithms for large matrices via random projections. In *FOCS*, pages 143–152. IEEE, 2006.

[35] Q. Song, J. Cheng, and H. Lu. Incremental matrix factorization via feature space re-learning for recommender system. In *ACM Conference on Recommender Systems*, pages 277–280. ACM, 2015.

[36] S. K. Tanbeer, C. F. Ahmed, B.-S. Jeong, and Y.-K. Lee. Sliding window-based frequent pattern mining over data streams. *Information sciences*, 179(22):3843–3865, 2009.

[37] Y. Tao and D. Papadias. Maintaining sliding window skylines on data streams. *TKDE*, 18(3):377–391, 2006.

[38] K. Weinberger, A. Dasgupta, J. Langford, A. Smola, and J. Attenberg. Feature hashing for large scale multitask learning. In *ICML*, pages 1113–1120. ACM, 2009.

[39] D. P. Woodruff. Sketching as a tool for numerical linear algebra. *Theoretical Computer Science*, 10(1-2):1–157, 2014.

APPENDIX

A. OTHER LM AND FD SKETCHES

In this section, we show how the Logarithmic Method and Dyadic Interval frameworks can cope with other streaming matrix sketches. In particular, we combine the *random projection* and *Hashing* algorithms with the DI framework to obtain the DI-RP and DI-HASH algorithms, and the *Hashing* algorithms with the LM framework to obtain the LM-HASH algorithm.

Random projection. Let R be an $\ell \times n$ random projection matrix such that each cell is a random value $r_{i,j}$ selected from $\{-1/\sqrt{\ell}, 1/\sqrt{\ell}\}$ uniformly. The approximation matrix B is equivalent to the matrix RA. Note that B contains the d columns of A randomly projected from dimension n to dimension ℓ. This is easily computed in a streaming fashion with the following algorithm. On receiving the i-th row a_i, we construct a random vector $r \in R^{d\times 1}$ such that the j-th entry $r(j)$ of r is randomly selected from $\{-1/\sqrt{\ell}, 1/\sqrt{\ell}\}$. Then we set $B \leftarrow B + r \cdot a_i$. By setting $\ell = d/\varepsilon^2$, RP achieves covariance error **cova-err**$(A, B) \leq \varepsilon$ with space usage $O(d/\varepsilon^2)$ space and $O(d^2/\varepsilon^2)$ update cost. For proofs of correctness and space usage see [29,39]

Hashing. HASH is often used in practice by the machine learning community and is referred to as "feature hashing" or "hashing trick" [31] and we simply denote it as HASH. For initiation, we choose a 2-wise independent hash function $h : [n] \to [\ell]$ and a pair-wise independent hash function $g : [n] \to \{-1, +1\}$. Set $S \in R^{\ell \times n}$ to be a random sparse matrix with exactly 1 non-zero entry in each column. More precisely, S satisfies $s_{ij} = g(j)$ for $i = h(j)$, and $s_{ij} = 0$ otherwise. The approximation matrix B equals SA. HASH be be computed in a streaming fashion with the following algorithm. On receiving row a_i, we set the $h(i)$-th row of B to be $b_{h(i)} \leftarrow b_{h(i)} + g(i)a_i$. By setting $\ell = d^2/\varepsilon^2$, HASH achieves covariance error **cova-err**$(A, B) \le \varepsilon$ with space usage d^2/ε^2 space and d update cost. For proofs of correctness and space usage see [8,39].

It is easy to see that HASH is mergeable under sliding window model. Given two HASH sketches $B_1 = \mathsf{HASH}(A_1)$ and $B_2 = \mathsf{HASH}(A_2)$ with the same error parameter ε and the same hash function h and g, the merging algorithm is $\mathsf{merge}(B_1, B_2) = B_1 + B_2$. It is easy to see that $C = \mathsf{merge}(B_1, B_2)$ is a HASH sketch for $[B_1, B_2]$ with the same error parameter and space.

LM-HASH. This algorithm uses the HASH sketch for each block in the LM framework. Recall that given error parameter ε, the HASH sketch achieves **cova-err** $\le \varepsilon/8$ with high probability using $\ell = O(d^2/\varepsilon^2)$ rows and $u = O(d)$ update cost. By Theorem 6.1, we have:

Corollary A.1 *The LM-HASH algorithm achieves* **cova-err** $\le$ *ε with high probability on any given window using $O(\frac{d^2}{\varepsilon^3}\log \varepsilon NR)$ space and $O(d \log \varepsilon NR)$ amortized update cost.*

DI-RP. This algorithm uses the random projection sketch for each block in the DI framework. Recall that given error parameter ε, the PR sketch uses $\ell_\varepsilon = O(d/\varepsilon^2)$ rows and process an update with $u_\varepsilon = O(d^2/\varepsilon^2)$ amortized cost. By Theorem 7.1, we have the following corollary:

Corollary A.2 *The DI-RP algorithm use $O(\frac{Rd}{\varepsilon^2}\log\frac{R}{\varepsilon})$ space and process an update with $O(\frac{d^2}{\varepsilon^2}\log\frac{R}{\varepsilon})$ amortized cost.*

DI-HASH. This algorithm uses hash for each block in the DI framework. Recall that given error parameter ε, the HASH sketch achieves **cova-err** $\le \varepsilon/8$ with high probability using $\ell_\varepsilon = O(\frac{d^2}{\varepsilon^2})$ rows and $u = O(d)$ update cost. By Theorem 7.1, we have the following corollary:

Corollary A.3 *The DI-RP algorithm use $O(\frac{Rd^2}{\varepsilon^2}\log\frac{R}{\varepsilon})$ space and process an update with $O(d\log\frac{R}{\varepsilon})$ amortized cost.*

B. PROOFS OF TWO NEGATIVE RESULTS

B.1 Proof of Theorem 4.1

We reduce the INDEX problem to the matrix sketching problem. In an instance in the INDEX problem, a party Alice receives an n-bit string x and another party Bob receives an index $i \in [n]$. Alice sends some information to Bob, and Bob computes the i-th bit of x using these information. The *communication cost* of this problem is the number of bits sent by Alice. It is easy to see that INDEX problem can be trivially solved with $O(n)$ communication cost by sending x to Bob. A well-know lower bound in communication complexity literature is that INDEX problem also requires $\Omega(n)$ communication cost, which indicates that Alice essentially has to send all bits of x to Bob. The lower bound also holds for probabilistic protocol, that is, even if Bob is only required to compute the correct answer with probability 2/3, the communication cost is still $\Omega(n)$.

The basic idea of the reduction is to set $n = Nd$, and construct a row-update stream based on the instance in the INDEX problem. We then show that if we have a matrix sketch that uses $o(Nd)$ space and maintains A^TA exactly on any window, then we can use this sketch to solve the INDEX problem with $o(Nd)$ communication cost. This would contradict the communication lower bound of INDEX problem, which implies that we need $\Omega(Nd)$ space for the matrix sketching problem in the sliding window model.

Proof of Theorem 4.1. Suppose there is a matrix sketching algorithm κ that tracks A^TA exactly on a sliding window with $o(Nd)$ space. Given an instance of the INDEX problem with bit string x and index i, Alice will construct a stream A of size N as follow. She divides x into N chunks, such that the j-th chunk $x_{(j)}$ is a bit vector of dimension d, for $j = 1, \dots, N$. Then we let j-th row of A to be $x_{(j)}$.

Then, Alice runs the sketching algorithm κ on A, and send the memory state $\kappa(A)$ to Bob after all N rows are processed. Given the index i, Bob will first compute $k = \lceil i/N \rceil$ and $r = i - N(k-1)$. In other word, index i the entry $A_{k,r}$. To compute the value of this entry, Bob will continue running $\mathcal{A}$ with N new updates, with each update being $e_{r+1} \in \mathbb{R}^d$ is the $(r+1)$-th unit vector. Let $A(j, N+j-1)$ denote the matrix that is made up by row j to $N+j-1$. Since κ can maintain A^TA exactly, Bob can compute $\|A(j, N+j-1)x\|^2 = x^TA(j, N+j-1)^TA(j, N+j-1)x$ exactly for any vector x, at the time of the j-th update. In particular, Bob will compute $y_j = \|A(j, N+j-1)e_r\|^2$, for $j = 1, \dots, N$. Since $\|A(j, N+j-1)e_r\|^2$ is the sum of the r-th column of $A(j, N+j-1)$, and the r-th column has not been updated since Bob received it (all updates were e_{r+1}), it follows that $y_j = \sum_{m=1}^{N-j+1} A_{mr}$, where A_{mr} denotes the entry of A at row m and column r. Therefore Bob can recover x_i by $x_i = A_{k+1,r} = y_{N-k} - y_{N-k-1}$. This proves that a sliding window matrix sketch that maintains A^TA exactly with $o(Nd)$ space can be used to construct a communication protocol to solve the INDEX problem with sublinear space, which leads to a contradiction. □

Remark. It is unclear if the $\Omega(Nd)$ lower bound holds for $\varepsilon > 1/d$. In fact, for $\varepsilon > 1/\sqrt{d}$, there exists an $O(N/\varepsilon^2)$ method as follows: We compute an AMS sketch S_i of size $1/\varepsilon^2$ for each row A_i in the window. We can view S_i as a vector, such that $\left|\|S_i\|^2 - \|A_i\|^2\right| \le \varepsilon \|A_i\|^2$. This implies that we can use S_i to approximate A_i with additive error $\varepsilon\|A_i\|^2$. Hence, the total error for using $S = [S_1; \dots; S_N]$ to approximate the sliding window matrix A is bounded by $\varepsilon|A|_F^2$. (due to the fact that $\|A\|_F^2 = \sum_{i=1}^N \|A_i\|^2$). So when $\varepsilon \ge 1/\sqrt{d}$, the lower bound in Theorem 4.2 does not hold. It is unclear if the lower bound holds for $1/d < \varepsilon < 1/\sqrt{d}$. Proving an $\Omega(Nd)$ lower bound or coming up with a better upper bound for this range is an interesting open problem.

B.2 Proof of Theorem 4.2

We reduce the d-Majority INDEX problem to sliding window sketching problem with unbounded norms. Setting $n =$

Nd, the d-Majority INDEX problem is identical to the INDEX problem with only one modification: if we divide the bit vector x into N consecutive chunks, then each chunk must contain at least a half of 1 bits. In other word, for $i = 1, \ldots, N$, at least $d/2$ bits in $x_i, x_{i+1}, \ldots, x_{i+d-1}$ are 1's. We first show that the d-Majority INDEX Problem also requires $\Omega(Nd)$ communication complexity to solve.

Lemma B.1 *A one-way communication protocol that solves the d-majority index problem must use $\Omega(Nd)$ communication cost, for d sufficiently large.*

PROOF. We reduce the d-majority index problem to index problem. Assume that we have a communication protocol $\mathcal{P}$ that solves the d-majority index problem with $o(Nd)$ communication cost, we will use it to solve the index problem with sublinear communication cost. Given an instance of the index problem, we can construct an instance of the d-majority problem as follow. We set d sufficiently large and divide x into n/d chucks, each of size d. Let $x_{(j)}$ denote the bit vector corresponding to the j-th chuck. We notice that the number of 1's in $x_{(j)}$ is either larger than $d/2$ or at most $d/2$. Alice will generate a new bit vector $x'_{(j)}$ such that $x'_{(j)} = \mathbf{1} - x_{(j)}$ if the number of 1's in $x_{(j)}$ is more than $d/2$, and $x'_{(j)} = x_{(j)}$ otherwise. Alice will also generate a bit vector z such that $z_j = 1$ if $x'_{(j)} = \mathbf{1} - x_{(j)}$ and $z_j = 0$ otherwise. Finally, Alice will concatenate all $x'_{(j)}$ to generate a bit vector x', and send $\mathcal{P}(x')$ and z to Bob. Since x' is an instance of the d-Majority INDEX problem, Bob is able to figure out the i-th component x'_i of x' using $\mathcal{P}(x')$. Then Bob will return $x_i = x'_i$ if $z_{\lceil i/d \rceil} = 0$ and $x_i = 1 - x'_i$ if $z_{\lceil i/d \rceil} = 1$. This protocol correctly solves the INDEX problem using communication cost $C(\mathcal{P}) + O(n/d) = o(n/d * d) + O(n/d) = o(n)$. This contradicts with the $\Omega(n)$ communication complexity lower bound for the INDEX problem. □

PROOF OF THEOREM 4.2. Assume that κ is a sliding window matrix sketch that uses $o(Nd)$ space. Then for any window W, κ cannot produce a matrix B_W such that

$$\mathbf{Pr}\left[\|A_W^T A_W - B_W^T B_W\| \le \frac{1}{4d}\|A\|_F^2\right] > \frac{2}{3}.$$

We will show how to use κ to construct a communication protocol that solves d-Majority INDEX efficiently.

Assume that x is an instance of the d-Majority INDEX problem. Recall that x is a bit vector of size Nd divided into N chucks, such that the i-th chuck $x_{(i)}$ is a bit vector of size d, and consists of at least $d/2$ 1's. Alice will construct a matrix A with N rows, such that the i-th row $A_{(i)} = x_{(i)}/8^i$, where $x_{(i)}$ is the i-th chuck of x. Recall that $x_{(i)}$ is a bit vector of size d, with at least $d/2$ 1's. Alice will run κ on A and send the memory content $\kappa(A)$ to Bob.

Given the index i, Bob will compute $k = \lceil i/N \rceil$ and $r = i - N(k-1)$ such that $x_i = 8^k A_{k,r}$. To compute this entry, Bob will continue running κ with N new updates, with the $(N+j) - th$ update being $e_{r+1}/8^{N+j}$, for $j = 1, \ldots, N$. We let A_k denote the matrix that is made up by row k to $N+k-1$. Since κ can provide an approximation B for A_k with error guarantee

$$\mathbf{Pr}\left[\|A_k^T A_k - B^T B\| \le \frac{1}{8d}\|A_k\|_F^2\right] > \frac{2}{3},$$

it follows that for any fixed $y \in \mathcal{R}^d$,

$$\mathbf{Pr}\left[|\|A_k y\|^2 - \|By\|^2| \le \frac{1}{8d}\|A_k\|_F^2\right] > \frac{2}{3}.$$

In particular, Bob will set $y = e_r$ so that he can use $\|Be_r\|^2$ to approximate $\|A_k e_r\|^2$ with additive error at most $\frac{1}{8d}\|A_k\|_F^2$, with probability 2/3. Observe that

$$|\|A_k e_r\|^2 - A_{k,r}| = \left|\sum_{j=k}^{N} A_{j,r} - A_{k,r}\right| = \left|\sum_{j=k+1}^{N} A_{j,r}\right|.$$

Since each $|A_{j,r}|$ is bounded by 8^{-j}, we have

$$|\|A_k e_r\|^2 - A_{k,r}| \le \sum_{j=k+1}^{N} 8^{-j} \le \frac{8^{-k}}{7}.$$

This implies that $\|A_k e_r\|^2$ can approximate $A_{k,r}$ with additive error at most $8^{-k}/7$. On the other hand, $\|Be_r\|^2$ can approximate $\|A_k e_r\|^2$ with probability 2/3 and additive error

$$\frac{1}{8d}\|A_k\|_F^2 \le \frac{1}{8d}\sum_{j=k}^{\infty} d/8^j = \frac{8^{-k}}{7}.$$

It follows that with probability 2/3, $\|Be_r\|^2$ is able to approximate $A_{k,r}$ with additive error $(2/7)8^{-k}$. Since $A_{k,r} = x_i/8^k$ is either 0 or 8^{-k}, Bob is able to recover $A_{k,r}$ with probability 2/3. This contradicts to the probabilistic lower bound for d-Majority INDEX problem, and thus the Theorem follows. □

C. PROOF FOR SAMPLING ALGORITHMS

Consider a window W with row $a_1, \ldots, a_N$ in it. Let $w_1 = \|a_1\|^2, \ldots, w_N = \|a_N\|^2$ denote the squared norms in the window, with their order sorted according the receiving time. We have $1 \le w_i \le R$ for $i \in [N]$. Let $w_\ell(j)$ denote the summation of the top -$(N-j-\ell+1)$ smallest weights from $\{w_{j+1}, \ldots, w_N\}$, that is, $w_j(\ell)$ is the summation of $w_{j+1}, \ldots, w_N$, excluding the top-$(\ell-1)$ weights. We define $w(j) = w_1(j) = \sum_{k=j+1}^{N} w_k$. We first present a technical Lemma.

Lemma C.1 *Suppose $w_i \le R$ for $i = 1, \ldots, N$, then the following inequality holds*

$$\sum_{i=1}^{N-\ell+1} \frac{w_i}{w_i + w_\ell(i)} = O(\ell \log NR).$$

PROOF. We first claim that that once ℓ is fixed, $w_\ell(i)$ is strictly monotonically decreasing with i for $1 \le i \le N-\ell+1$. For a proof consider $w_\ell(i) - w_\ell(i+1)$. If w_{i+1} is not one of the top-$(\ell-1)$ weights in $w_{j+1}, \ldots, w_N$, then $w_\ell(i) - w_\ell(i+1) = w_{j+1} > 0$. Otherwise, there is a weight $w_t < w_{j+1}$ that is in top-$(\ell-1)$ for $w_{j+2}, \ldots, w_N$, and $w_\ell(i) - w_\ell(i+1) = w_t > 0$. Either way we have $w_\ell(i) - w_\ell(i+1) > 0$, and $w_\ell(i)$ is monotonically decreasing with i.

By the monotonicity of $w_\ell(i)$, we define i_k to be largest index such that $w_\ell(i_k) \ge 2^k$, and let L be the number of different k's. Since $w_\ell(0) \le NR$, we have $L \le \log NR + 1$.

Therefore

$$\sum_{i=1}^{N-\ell+1} \frac{w_i}{w_i + w_\ell(i)} \le \sum_{k=0}^{L} \sum_{i=i_k+1}^{i_{k-1}} \frac{w_i}{w_i + w_\ell(i)} \le \sum_{k=0}^{L} \sum_{i=i_k+1}^{i_{k-1}} \frac{w_i}{w_i + 2^{k-1}}.$$

The last inequality uses the fact that $w_\ell(i) \ge 2^{k-1}$ for i between $i_k + 1$ and i_{k-1}. We have

$$\sum_{i=1}^{N-\ell+1} \frac{w_i}{w_i + w_\ell(i)} \le \sum_{k=1}^{L} \frac{\sum_{i=i_k+1}^{i_{k-1}} w_i}{2^{k-1}} \le \log \ell R + \sum_{k=\log \ell R+1}^{L} \frac{\sum_{i=i_k+1}^{N} w_i}{2^{k-1}}.$$

Finally, note that $w_\ell(i) \le 2^k$ for $i \ge i_k$, and $\sum_{i=i_k+1}^{N} w_i \le w_\ell(i) + \ell R$, it follows that

$$\sum_{i=1}^{N-\ell+1} \frac{w_i}{w_i + w_\ell(i)} \le \log \ell R + \sum_{k=\log \ell R+1}^{L} \frac{2^{k+1} + \ell R}{2^k} \le \log \ell R + L + 1 = O(\log NR),$$

and the Lemma follows. □

Lemma C.2 *The probability that ρ_j is among the top-ℓ largest priorities in $\{\rho_j, \ldots, \rho_N\}$ is at most $\frac{\ell w_j}{w_j + w_j(\ell)}$*

PROOF. Consider the sampling without replacement process on $\{j, \ldots, N\}$. At each round before j is sampled, let S be the set of indices that gets sampled. Since $w_j(\ell)$ is the summation of $w_{j+1}, \ldots, w_N$ excluding the top-($\ell - 1$) weights, the probability that j gets sampled in this round is

$$\frac{w_j}{\sum_{s=j}^{N} w_s - \sum_{s \in S} w_s} \le \frac{w_j}{w_j + w_j(\ell)}.$$

Therefore, the probability that j does not get sampled is lower bounded by

$$\left(1 - \frac{w_j}{w_j + w_j(\ell)}\right)^k \ge 1 - \frac{k w_j}{w_j + w_j(\ell)},$$

which implies that the probability the j gets sampled is upper bounded by $\frac{k w_j}{w_j + w_j(\ell)}$. □

C.1 Proof of Lemma 5.1

PROOF. For sampling with replacement, we only need to prove that the expected number of rows in a sampler is $O(\log NR)$. Recall that a_i is in Q if and only if w_i is the largest weight among $w_i, \ldots, w_N$. By Lemma C.2, the probability that w_i is the largest weight among $w_i, \ldots, w_N$ is $p_i = w_i / \sum_{j=i}^{N} w_j$. Therefore the expected number of rows in the priority queue Q is

$$\sum_{i=1}^{N} p_i = \sum_{i=1}^{N} \frac{w_i}{\sum_{j=i}^{N} w_j} \le O(\log NR). \quad (2)$$

The last inequality is by setting $\ell = 1$ in Lemma C.1. □

C.2 Proof of Lemma 5.2

PROOF. By Lemma C.2, the probability that a row a_j is a candidate row is at most $\frac{\ell w_j}{w_j + w_j(\ell)}$. Thus the expected number of candidate rows is at most

$$\ell + \sum_{j=1}^{N-\ell+1} \frac{\ell w_j}{w_j + w_j(\ell)} = O(\ell \log NR).$$

The last inequality is by Lemma C.1. □

C.3 Proof of Theorem 5.1

PROOF. Assuming the algorithms know the value of $\|A\|_F^2$, the bounds of the space and update bounds directly follow from Lemma 5.1 and Lemma 5.2. Now suppose we use the approximation of $\|A\|_F^2$ from an Exponential Histogram with relative error ε. Let B be the matrix that uses $\|A\|_F^2$ for rescaling parameter, and B' be the matrix that uses the approximation of EH for rescaling parameter. It is easy to see that $B' = (1 + \alpha)B$, where $\alpha \in (-\varepsilon, \varepsilon)$. Since $\|B^T B - A^T A\| \le \varepsilon \|A\|_F^2$ and $\|B\|_F^2 = \|A\|_F^2$, it follows that

$$\|B'^T B' - A^T A\| \le \|B'^T B' - B^T B\| + \|B^T B - A^T A\| \le 3\varepsilon \|A\|_F^2,$$

and the Theorem follows. □

D. GENERATION OF SYNTHETIC

The matrix of SYNTHETIC was generated by formula $A = SDU + N/\zeta$. S is a $n \times d$ signal co-efficients matrix with each entry drawn from standard normal distribution. D is a diagonal matrix with $D_{i,i} = 1 - (i-1)/d$. U is a signal row space matrix that satisfies $UU^T = I_d$. The matrix N contributes additive Gaussian noise with $N_{i,j}$ drawn from $\mathcal{N}(0, 1)$. We set $\zeta = 10$ so that the signal SDU is recoverable.

Graph Stream Summarization

From Big Bang to Big Crunch

Nan Tang Qing Chen Prasenjit Mitra
Qatar Computing Research Institute, HBKU
{ntang, qchen, pmitra}@qf.org.qa

ABSTRACT

A graph stream, which refers to the graph with edges being updated sequentially in a form of a stream, has important applications in cyber security and social networks. Due to the sheer volume and highly dynamic nature of graph streams, the practical way of handling them is by summarization. Given a graph stream G, directed or undirected, the problem of *graph stream summarization* is to summarize G as S_G with a much smaller (*sublinear*) space, *linear* construction time and *constant* maintenance cost for each edge update, such that S_G allows many queries over G to be approximately conducted efficiently. The widely used practice of summarizing data streams is to treat each stream element independently by *e.g.,* hash- or sample-based methods, without maintaining the connections (or relationships) between elements. Hence, existing methods can only solve *ad-hoc* problems, without supporting diversified and complicated analytics over graph streams. We present **TCM**, a novel graph stream summary. Given an incoming edge, it summarizes both node and edge information in constant time. Consequently, the summary forms a graphical sketch where edges capture the connections inside elements, and nodes maintain relationships across elements. We discuss a wide range of supported queries and establish some error bounds. In addition, we experimentally show that **TCM** can effectively and efficiently support analytics over graph streams beyond the power of existing sketches, which demonstrates its potential to start a new line of research and applications in graph stream management.

CCS Concepts

•Mathematics of computing → Network flows; •Information systems → Data streams; •Theory of computation → Sketching and sampling;

Keywords

Graph streams; Data streams; Sketch; Summarization

SIGMOD '16, June 26–July 1, 2016, San Francisco, CA, USA.

DOI: http://dx.doi.org/10.1145/2882903.2915223

1. INTRODUCTION

Nowadays, massive graphs arise in many applications *e.g.,* network traffic data, social networks, and transportation networks. These graphs are highly dynamic: Network traffic data averages to about 10^9 packets per hour per router for large ISPs [23]; Twitter sees 100 million users login daily, with around 500 millions tweets per day [1].

As conventionally formulated, we consider a graph stream as a sequence of elements $(x, y; t)$[1], which indicates that the edge (x, y) is encountered at time t. A sample graph stream $\langle(a, b; t_1), (a, c; t_2), \cdots, (b, a; t_{14})\rangle$ is depicted in Fig. 1, where all timestamps are omitted for simplicity. Each edge is associated with a weight, which is 1 by default.

Practically, real-time analytics over large graph streams has wide applications, such as monitoring cyber security attacks and social network opinions. To a large extent, in the era of big data, the increasing expansion of data velocity is an open issue, and many big data is graphs inherently. Unfortunately, in a recent survey for businesses in analyzing big data streams [2], although 41% of respondents stated that the ability to analyze and act on streaming data in minutes is critical, 67% admitted that they do not have the infrastructure to support that goal. The situation is more complicated and challenging when processing graph streams. It poses unique space and time constraints on storing, summarizing and querying graph streams, due to their sheer volumes, high velocity, and the complication of analytics.

Fortunately, for the applications of data streams, fast and approximated answers are often preferred than exact answers. Not surprisingly, sketch synopses have been widely studied for data streams: approximate frequency counts [29], AMS [5], and Bottom-k [13]. Although they allow false positives, the space savings often outweigh this drawback, when the probability of an error is sufficiently low.

We illustrate by an example how approximate frequency counts [29] works. CountMin [14] improves it simply by using multiple hash functions, and gSketch [39] further improves CountMin by assuming the presence of sample data/queries that help better partition the input graph stream.

Example 1: Consider the graph stream in Fig. 1. Approximate frequency counts based methods can be used to treat each node or edge in the stream independently, by mapping them to w hash buckets. Let $w = 4$ in this example.

(1) Node sketch: It treats node labels as hash keys, *i.e.,* $\{a, b, c, d, e, f, g\}$. A hash function h is used to map these

[1]Without loss of generality, we use a directed graph for illustration. Our method can also work on undirected graphs.

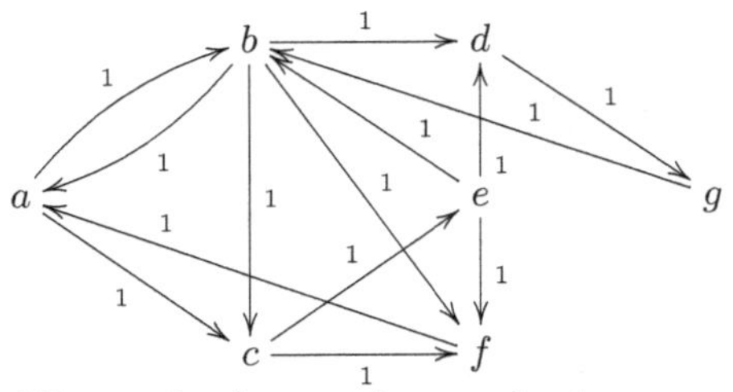

Figure 1: A sample graph stream

$h(\cdot)$	4	5	2	3
keys	a, c	b, d	e, g	f

(a) ***Node sketch***

$h'(\cdot)$	5	5	3	1
keys	ab, ac, ed, eb, ef	bc, bd, ba, bf, fa	ce, cf, gb	dg

(b) ***Edge sketch***

Figure 2: Examples of frequency counts

values to 4 buckets, *i.e.,* $h(\cdot) \rightarrow [1, 4]$, as shown in Fig. 2 (a). The first bucket sums up the in-flow weights to nodes a and c, which is 4, and similar for other buckets.

(2) Edge sketch: It treats pairs of node labels as hash keys, *e.g.,* $\{ab, ac, bc, \cdots\}$, where ab is to concatenate the two node labels for $(a, b; t_1)$. A hash function h' is used to map these values in 4 buckets, as shown in Fig. 2 (b). The value of the first bucket is the sum of weights for edges $\{ab, ac, ed, ed, ef\}$, which is 5, and similar for other buckets. □

The power of frequency counts based approaches is limited inherently by its structure: It is a vector of (hashed key, value) pairs and each hashed key is independent of each other. That is, one cannot reason for any relationships between two hashed keys. In fact, CountMin or gSketch cannot support any more queries than their frequency counts counterparts, since they are proposed to improve the accuracy. We give more details of supported queries below.

Example 2: Consider the two sketches in Example 1 that are depicted in Fig. 2. Below, we denote by ✓ the types of queries a sketch supports, and ✗ for those not supported.

(1) Node sketch (see Fig. 2 (a)).

✓ *Node queries*: It can only be used to estimate an in-flow weight of a node, *e.g.,* the estimated in-flow weight to node a is in the first bucket since $h(a) = 1$, which gives 4.

✗ *Conditional node queries*: It cannot find locally important node, *e.g.,* which is the most frequent node linking to node a, which relates to the conditional heavy hitter problem.

(2) Edge sketch (see Fig. 2 (b)). (Note: gSketch only supports the type of queries that an edge sketch supports.)

✓ *Edge queries*: What is the estimated edge weight? For instance, it is 5 for edge (a, b) from the first bucket since $h'(ab) = 1$.

✓ *Aggregate subgraph queries*: What is the aggregated weight for a graph with all edges being given explicitly? For instance, for a graph with two edges (a, c) and (c, e), the estimated weight for ac (resp. ce) is 5 (resp. 3), which sums up to be 8.

✗ *Node connectivity:* Whether two nodes are connected? It cannot answer whether there is a path from a to g. □

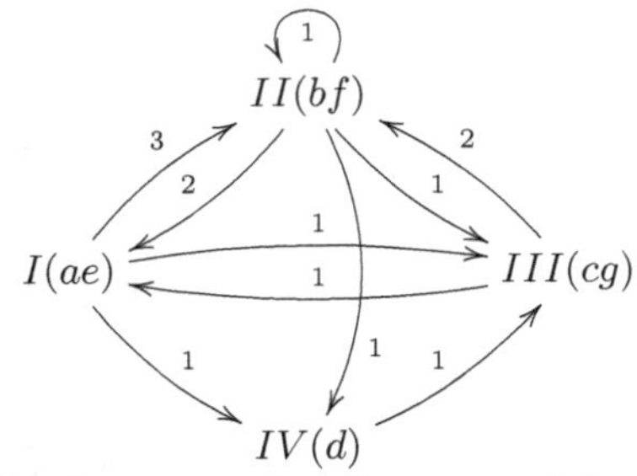

Figure 3: An example of our graphical sketch

Challenges. Designing a generalized sketch for graph streams to support all above analytics and beyond requires to satisfy the following constraints. (1) *Space constraint: sublinear* upper bound is required. (2) *Time constraint: linear* construction time is a must. Notably, this is stronger than the condition with only a constant passes over the stream. (3) *Maintenance constraint:* to maintain it for one element insertion/deletion must be in *constant* time. (4) *Graphical connectivity:* it should have a graphical model.

To solve the above challenges, we propose **TCM**, a generalized graph stream summary. Given an incoming element (*i.e.,* an edge), it summarizes both node and edge information in constant time. In contrast to previous sketches that have *one-dimensional* data structures, **TCM** is a graphical sketch with a *two-dimensional* data structure.

Example 3: Again, consider the graph stream in Fig. 1. Our proposal is shown in Fig. 3. For each edge $(x, y; t)$, **TCM** uses a hash function to map each node label to 4 node buckets *i.e.,* $h''(\cdot) \rightarrow [1, 4]$. Node I is the summary of two node labels a and e, assuming $h''(a) = 1$ and $h''(e) = 1$. The other compressed nodes are computed similarly. The edge weight denotes the aggregated weights from stream elements, *e.g.,* the number 3 from node I to II means that there are three elements as $(x, y; t)$ where the label of x (resp. y) is a or e (resp. b or f). □

From Example 3, it is easy to see that the queries supported by existing node or edge sketches are naturally supported, *e.g.,* the estimated in-flow weights to node a is 3 and the estimated weight of edge (a, b) is 3. Moreover, the other queries that are not supported by existing sketches are also supported, *e.g.,* the node that sends the most weights to node a is either b or f, and there is a path from a to d. The *essential* difference of **TCM**, compared with existing sketches, is that **TCM** keeps all structural connectivities of the original graph stream, *not only* edges, *but also* paths. For instance, the path $a \rightarrow b \rightarrow d \rightarrow g$ in Fig. 1 is captured in Fig. 3 as $I \rightarrow II \rightarrow IV \rightarrow III$. This salient property provides rich structural information to support various graph analytics (see Section 4 for a detailed discussion).

Contributions. This paper presents a novel generalized graphical sketch for summarizing graph streams, with the following contributions.

(1) We formally introduce **TCM** (Section 3). As illustrated in Fig. 3, the proposed sketch naturally preserves the graphical connections of the original graph stream, which makes it a better fit than traditional sketches in supporting analytics over graph streams.

(2) We describe algorithms to process various graph analytics on top of **TCM** (Section 4). The general purpose is, instead of proposing new algorithms, to show that **TCM**

can be easily used to support many graph queries, and *off-the-shelf* graph algorithms can be seamlessly integrated.

(3) We describe internals of **TCM** implementation (Section 5). This is important to ensure that it can be built and maintained under the hard time/space constraints for graph stream scenarios. Moreover, we propose to use non-square matrices for storage, based on which we show that CountMin is a special case of **TCM**. Furthermore, we describe its extension to support high-dimensional data streams.

(4) Using real-world and synthetic data sets, we have experimentally evaluated the power of **TCM** in supporting different analytics (Section 6), which confirms that the new sketch is indeed effective and efficient, and more general than existing sketches for graph stream applications.

In this history of graph problems over streams, unfortunately, most results showed that a large amount of space is required for *complicated* graph problems [4,30]. The present study makes an important attempt to build a generalized sketch to support various graph analytics, using only a *small* amount of space, which sheds considerable light on graph stream applications.

Organization. Section 2 discusses related work. Section 3 introduces **TCM**. Section 4 presents its supported queries. Section 5 explains implementation details and extensions. Section 6 gives experimental findings. Finally, Section 7 concludes this work, followed by our agenda for future work.

2. RELATED WORK

We categorize related work as follows.

Sketch synopses. Given a data stream, the aim of sketch synopses is to apply (linear) projections of the data into lower dimensional spaces that preserve the salient features of the data. A considerable amount of literature has been published on general data streams such as AMS [5], lossy counting [29], CountMin [14] and bottom-k [13]. The work gSketch [39] improves CountMin for graph streams, by assuming that data or query samples are given. Bloom filters have been widely used in a variety of network problems (see [10] for a survey). There are also sketches that maintain counters only for nodes, *e.g.,* using a heap for maintaining the nodes with the largest degrees for heavy hitters [15].

As remarked earlier, **TCM** is more general, since it maintains connections of all streaming edges, *without* assuming any sample data or query is given. None of existing sketches for graph streams has a graphical model.

Graph summaries. Summarizing graphs has been widely studied. The most prolific area is in web graph compression. The papers [3,35] encode Web pages with similar adjacency lists using reference encoding, so as to reduce the number of bits needed to encode a link. The work [32] groups Web pages based on a combination of their URL patterns and k-means clustering. The paper [18] compresses graphs based on specific types of queries. There are also many clustering based methods from data mining community (see *e.g.,* [24]), with the basic idea to group *similar* nodes together. Another line of work is graph sparsificaiton, which is to approximate a graph G by a sparse graph H, where H and G have the same set of vertices and H is "close" to H in some specific metric, *e.g.,* cut sparsifiers [7,8] and spectral sparsifiers [6,34].

These data structures are designed for less dynamic graphs, which are not suitable for graph streams. Another reason that graph sparsification is not used for graph streams is the metric studied for sparsifying a graph is not suitable for graph stream applications, *e.g.,* network monitoring.

Graph pattern matching over streams. There have been several work on matching graph patterns over graph streams, based on either the semantics of subgraph isomorphism [12, 20,38] or graph simulation [33]. The work [38] assumes that queries are given, and builds node-neighbor tree to filter false candidate results. The paper [20] leverages a distributed graph processing framework, Giraph, to approximately evaluate graph quereis. The work [12] uses the subgraph distributional statistics collected from the graph streams to optimize a graph query evaluation. The paper [33] uses filtering methods to find data that potentially matches for a specific type of queries, namely degree-preserving dual simulation with timing constraints.

Firstly, all the above algorithms are designed for specific types of graph queries. Secondly, most of them assume the presence of queries, so they can build indices to accelerate. In contrast, **TCM** aims at summarizing graph streams in a generalized way, so as to support various types of queries, *without* any assumption of queries.

Graph stream algorithms. There has also been work on algorithms over graph streams (see [30] for a survey). This includes the problems of connectivity [19], trees [36], spanners [16], sparsification [26], counting subgraphs *e.g.,* triangles [9,37]. However, they mainly focus on theoretical study for best approximation bound, mostly on $O(n \text{ polylog } n)$ space, with one to multiple passes over the data stream.

TCM is complementary to the above algorithms. As will be seen later (Section 4), **TCM** can treat existing algorithms as *black-boxes* to help solve existing problems.

Distributed graph systems. Many distributed graph computing systems have been proposed to conduct data processing and data analytics in massive graphs, such as Pregel [28], Giraph[2], GraphLab [27], Power-Graph [21] and GraphX [22].

They have been proved to be efficient on static graphs, but are not fully geared for analytics over big graph streams with real-time response. In practice, they are complementary to and can be used for **TCM** in distributed settings.

3. THE TCM MODEL

We first define graph streams (Section 3.1). We then formulate the studied problem (Section 3.2). Finally, we introduce our proposed graphical sketch model (Section 3.3).

3.1 Graph Streams: Big Bang

A *graph stream* is a sequence of elements $e = (x, y; t)$ where x, y are node identifiers (labels) and edge (x, y) is encountered at time-stamp t. Such a stream,

$$G = \langle e_1, e_2, \cdots, e_m \rangle$$

naturally defines a graph $G = (V, E)$ where V is a set of nodes and E is a set of edges as $\{e_1, \cdots, e_m\}$. We write $\omega(e_i)$ the weight for the edge e_i, and $\omega(x, y)$ the aggregated edge weight from node x to node y. We call m the *size* of the graph stream, denoted by $|G|$. In this work, we assume that edge weight is non-negative (*i.e.,* $\omega(e_i) \geq 0$).

Intuitively, the node label, being treated as an *identifier*, uniquely identifies a node, which could be *e.g.,* IP addresses

[2] http://giraph.apache.org

in network traffic data or user IDs in social networks. Note that, in the graph terminology, a graph stream is a *multigraph*, where each edge can occur many times, *e.g.*, one IP address can send multiple packets to another IP address. We are interested in properties of the underlying graph. This causes a main challenge with graph streams where one normally does not have enough space to record the graph that has been seen so far. Summarizing such a graph stream in one pass is important to many applications. Moreover, we do not explicitly differentiate whether the edge (x, y) is an ordered pair or not. In other words, our approach applies naturally to both directed and undirected graphs.

For instance, in network traffic data, a stream element arrives at the form: $(192.168.29.1, 192.168.29.133, 62, 105.12)$[3], where node labels 192.168.29.1 and 192.168.29.133 are IP addresses, 62 is the number of bytes sent *from* 192.168.29.1 *to* 192.168.29.133 in this captured packet (*i.e.*, the weight of the directed edge), and 105.12 is the time in seconds that this edge arrived when the server started to capture data. Please see Fig. 1 for a sample graph stream.

3.2 Graph Streams Summaries: Big Crunch

The problem of *summarizing graph streams* is, given a graph stream G, to compute another data structure S_G from G, such that:

1. $|S_G| \ll |G|$: the size of S_G is far less than G, preferably in sublinear space.
2. The time to construct S_G from G is in linear time.
3. The update cost of S_G for each edge insertion/deletion is in constant time.
4. S_G is a graph.

Intuitively, a graph stream summary has to be built and maintained in real time, so as to deal with big volume and high velocity graph stream scenarios. In fact, the CountMin [29] and its variant gSketch [39] satisfy the above conditions 1-3 (see Example 1 for more details). Unfortunately, CountMin and gSketch can support only limited types of graph analytics, since condition 4 is not satisfied.

3.3 Graphical Sketches

The graph sketch. A *graph sketch* is a graph $S_G(\mathcal{V}, \mathcal{E})$, where $\mathcal{V}$ denotes the set of vertices and $\mathcal{E}$ its edges. For a vertex $v \in \mathcal{V}$, we simply treat its label as its node identifier (the same as the graph stream model). Each edge e is associated with a weight, denoted as $\omega(e)$.

In generating the above graph sketch S_G from a graph G, we first set the number of nodes in the sketch, *i.e.*, let $|\mathcal{V}| = w$. For an edge $(x, y; t)$ in G, we use a hash function h to map the label of each node to a value in $[1, w]$, and the aggregated edge weight is calculated correspondingly.

Please refer to Fig. 3 as an example, where we set $w = 4$.

Edge weight. The edge weight for an edge e in the graph sketch is computed by an *aggregation* function of all edge weights that are mapped to e. Such an aggregation function could be min(·), max(·), count(·), average(·), sum(·) or other functions. In this paper, we use sum(·) by default to explain our method. The other aggregation functions can be similarly applied. In practice, which aggregation function to use is determined by applications. For a more general setting that requires to maintain multiple aggregated functions in a graph sketch, we may extend our model to have multiple edge weights *e.g.*, $\omega_1(e), \cdots, \omega_n(e)$, with each $\omega_i(e)$ corresponds to a distinct aggregation function.

[3]We omit port numbers and protocols for simplicity.

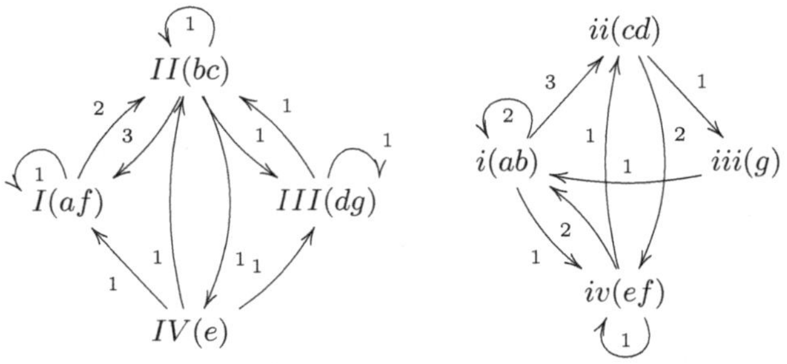

(a) Sketch S_1 (b) Sketch S_2

Figure 4: TCM with 2 hash functions

One may observe that the graph sketch model is basically the same as the graph stream model, with the main difference that the time-stamps are not maintained. This makes it very useful and applicable in many scenarios when querying a graph stream for a given time window. In other words, for a graph analytical method M that needs to run over a graph stream G, denoted as $M(G)$, one can run it directly on its sketch S_G, *i.e.*, $M(S_G)$, to get an approximate result, *without* modifying the method M.

Example 4: Consider the graph stream in Fig. 1 and its sketch in Fig. 3. Assume that query Q_1 is to estimate the aggregated edge weight from b to c. In Fig. 3, one can map b to node II, c to node III, and get the estimated weight 1 from edge (II, III), which is precise. Now consider Q_2 that is to compute the aggregated weight from g to b. One can find edge (III, II), and the estimated result is 2, which is not accurate since the real weight of (g, b) in Fig. 1 is 1. □

The above result is expected, since given the compression, no hash function can ensure that the estimation on the sketch can be done precisely. Along the same line of CountMin [14], we use multiple independent hash functions to collectively reduce the probability of hash collisions.

The TCM model. A **TCM** sketch is a set of graph sketches $\{S_1(\mathcal{V}_1, \mathcal{E}_1), \cdots, S_d(\mathcal{V}_d, \mathcal{E}_d)\}$. Here, we use d hash functions $h_1, \cdots, h_d$, where h_i $(i \in [1, d])$ is used to generate S_i. Also, $h_1, \cdots, h_d$ are pairwise independent hash functions (see Section 5.2 for more details).

Example 5: Figure 4 shows another two sketches for Fig. 1. Again, consider the query Q_2 in Example 4. Using S_1 in Fig. 4 (a), one can locate edge (III, II) for (g, b), which gives 1. Similarly, S_2 in Fig. 4 (b) will also give 1 from edge (iii, i), where g (resp. b) maps to iii (resp. i). The minimum of the above two outputs is 1, which is correct. □

Example 5 shows that using multiple hash functions can indeed improve the accuracy of estimation. In practice, using pairwise independent hash functions is a significant advance, since pairwise independent hash functions are generally easy to implement and quite efficient.

4. TCM POWERED GRAPH ANALYTICS

In this section we shall show how **TCM** can be easily used to support different graph analytics. Here, we consider the graph stream as G, and d graph sketches $\{S_1, \cdots, S_d\}$ of G, where S_i is constructed using a hash function $h_i(\cdot)$. Also, we assume that an adjacency matrix $\mathbf{M}_i$ is used for storing one graph sketch S_i. We use $\mathsf{sum}(\cdot)$ as the default aggregation function for constructing graph sketches. Whilst the exercise in this section only substantiates several types of graph queries to be addressed in this work, it is evident that the power of **TCM** is far beyond the queries listed below.

As mentioned in Section 3.3, for any graph analytics method M to run over G, *i.e.*, $M(G)$, it is possible to run M on each sketch directly, and then merge the result as: $\tilde{M}(G) = \Gamma(M(S_1), \cdots, M(S_d))$, where $\tilde{M}(G)$ denotes the estimated result over G, and $\Gamma(\cdot)$ an aggregation function (*e.g.*, min, max, conjunction) to merge results returned from d sketches. Moreover, we provide the proofs of error bounds for different queries in Appendix A.

4.1 Edge Queries

Aggregated edge weights. Given two node labels a and b, we denote by $f_e(a, b)$ the exact aggregated edge weight from node a to node b. We write $\tilde{f}_e(a, b)$ the estimated weight.

One application of such queries, taking social networks for example, is to estimate the communication frequency between two specific friends.

It is straightforward to evaluate $\tilde{f}_e(a, b)$, the weight of edge (a, b). It first gets estimated edge weight $\mathbf{M}_i[h_i(a)][h_i(b)]$ from each matrix $\mathbf{M}_i$ and then uses a corresponding function $\Gamma(\cdot)$ to merge them. The notation $\mathbf{M}_i[h_i(a)][h_i(b)]$ is the cell value relative to position $h_i(a)$ and $h_i(b)$ in matrix $\mathbf{M}_i$. It works as follows:

$$\tilde{f}_e(a, b) = \Gamma(\mathbf{M}_1[h_1(a)][h_1(b)], \cdots, \mathbf{M}_d[h_d(a)][h_d(b)])$$

In this case, the function $\Gamma(\cdot)$ is to take the minimum.

Complexity. Estimating the aggregate weight of an edge query is in $O(d)$ time, where d is a constant.

4.2 Node Queries

Aggregated node flows. For a directed graph, given a node label a, we denote by $f_v(a, \rightarrow)$ (resp. $f_v(a, \leftarrow)$) node out-flow query (resp. in-flow query), which is to tell the aggregated edge weight *from* (resp. *to*) a node with label a in the graph stream G. For an undirected graph, we write $f_v(a, -)$. Similarly, we use $\tilde{f}_v(a, \rightarrow), \tilde{f}_v(a, \leftarrow), \tilde{f}_v(a, -)$ for estimated results using sketches.

One important application of such queries is to find heavy hitters (*i.e.*, top-k nodes with highest weights of their flows) in *e.g.*, DoS (Denial-of-service) attacks for cyber security, which typically flood a target source (*i.e.*, a computer) with massive external communication requests.

Note that, CountMin has been used to solve the problem of finding heavy hitters, *i.e.*, which nodes are associated with a large number of edges or weights. Again, CountMin is a linear structure, which cannot tell any information more than a count. For a simple extended problem such as conditional heavy hitters [31], which is to find heavy hitters that are *locally* popular by considering edge connections, CountMin does not work. In contrast, the graphical structure of **TCM** provides rich information to find *conditional heavy hitters*. Please refer to Appendix-B.1 for the detailed algorithm for computing conditional heavy hitters using **TCM**.

Here, we only discuss the case $\tilde{f}_v(a, \rightarrow)$, which is to estimate the aggregate weight from node a. The other two cases, *i.e.*, $\tilde{f}_v(a, \leftarrow)$ and $\tilde{f}_v(a, -)$, can be processed analogously.

We denote by $\tilde{f}_v^i(a, \rightarrow)$ the estimated out-flow from the i-th sketch. $\tilde{f}_v^i(a, \rightarrow)$ can be computed by first locating the row in the adjacency matrix corresponding to label a (*i.e.*, $h_i(a)$), and then summing up the values in that row, *i.e.*, $\tilde{f}_v^i(a, \rightarrow) = \sum_{j=1}^{w} \mathbf{M}_i[h_i(a)][j]$. Here, w is the width of the adjacency matrix $\mathbf{M}_i$. Then,

$$\tilde{f}_v(a, \rightarrow) = \Gamma(\tilde{f}_v^1(a, \rightarrow), \cdots, \tilde{f}_v^d(a, \rightarrow))$$

The function $\Gamma(\cdot)$ is also to take the minimum.

Complexity. It is easy to see that it takes $O(d \cdot w)$ time, where both d and w are constants.

4.3 Path Queries

Reachability. Given two node a and b, a **boolean** reachability query $r(a, b)$ is to tell whether there exists a path from a to b. Also, we write $\tilde{r}(a, b)$ as the estimated reachability.

One important monitoring task, for the success of multicast deployment in the Internet, is to verify the availability of network service, which is usually referred to as *reachability monitoring*. Another application that needs to consider edge weights is IP routing, which is to determine the path of data flows in order to travel across multiple networks.

We consider the reachability query $\tilde{r}(a, b)$, which is to estimate whether b is reachable from a. For such queries, we treat any *off-the-shelf* algorithm $\mathsf{reach}(x, y)$ as a *black-box*, which returns either *true* to indicate that b is reachable from a, or *false* to represent that b is unreachable from a. It works as follows for our sketch.

P1. [Execute in parallel.] Invoke $\mathsf{reach}(h_i[a], h_i[b])$ on each sketch S_i (for $i \in [1, d]$), to decide whether the mapped node $h_i[b]$ is reachable from the mapped node $h_i[a]$ on sketch S_i.

P2. [Merge.] Merge individual results as follows:

$$\tilde{r}(a, b) = \mathsf{reach}(h_1[a], h_1[b]) \wedge \cdots \wedge \mathsf{reach}(h_d[a], h_d[b])$$

Here, the "$\wedge$" is for a boolean conjunction. Stating in another way, the estimated reachability is *true* only if the mapped nodes are reachable from all d sketches.

The complexity of the above strategy is determined by the third party solution $\mathsf{reach}()$.

4.4 Subgraph Queries

Aggregate subgraph queries. The *aggregate subgraph query* is considered in gSketch [39]. It is to compute the aggregated weight of the constituent edges of a subgraph $Q = \{(x_1, y_1), \cdots, (x_k, y_k)\}$, denoted by $f_g(Q) = \Omega(f_e(x_1, y_1), \cdots, f_e(x_k, y_k))$. Here, the function $\Omega(\cdot)$ is to sum up the weights from all $f_e(x_i, y_i)$ for $i \in [1, k]$. We write $\tilde{f}_g(Q)$ for the estimated result using sketches.

We adopt the following query semantics: if $\tilde{f}_e(x_i, y_i) = 0$ for any edge, the estimated aggregate weight should be 0, since the query graph Q does not have an exact match.

Example 6: Consider a subgraph with two edges as $\{(a, b), (a, c)\}$. The query $Q_3 : \tilde{f}_g(\{(a, b), (a, c)\})$ is to estimate the aggregate weight of the graph. The precise answer is 2, which is easy to verify from Fig. 1. □

Extensions. We consider an extension of the above aggregate subgraph query, which allows a wildcard $*$ in the node labels that are being queried. More specifically, for the subgraph

Symbols	Notations
G, S_G	a graph stream, and a graph sketch
$\omega(e)$	weight of the edge e
$f_e(a,b)$	edge weight
$f_v(a,\rightarrow)$	node out-flow weight (directed graphs)
$f_v(a,\leftarrow)$	node in-flow weight (directed graphs)
$f_v(a,-)$	node flow weight (undirected graphs)
$r(a,b)$	whether b is reachable from a
$f_g(Q)$	weight of subgraph Q

Table 1: Notations

query $Q = \{(x_1, y_1), \cdots, (x_k, y_k)\}$, each x_i or y_i is either a constant value, or a wildcard $*$ (*i.e.,* match any label). A further extension is to *bound* the wildcards to be matched to the same node, by using a subscript to a wildcard as $*_j$. That is, two wildcards with the same subscripts enforce them to be mapped to the same node.

Example 7: A subgraph query $Q_4 : \tilde{f}_g(\{(a,b),(b,c),(c,a)\})$ is to estimate the triangle, *i.e.,* a 3-clique with three vertices labeled as a, b, and c, respectively. Another subgraph query $Q_5 : \tilde{f}_g(\{(*,b),(b,c),(c,*)\})$ is to estimate paths that start at node with an edge to b, and end at any node with an edge from c, if the edge (b,c) exists in the graph. If one wants to count the common neighbors of (b,c), the following query $Q_6 : \tilde{f}_g(\{(*_1,b),(b,c),(c,*_1)\})$ can enforce such a condition, which again is a case of counting triangles. □

The extension is apparently more general, with the purpose of covering more useful queries in practice. Unfortunately, gSketch cannot support such extensions.

We next discuss the aggregate subgraph query $\tilde{f}_g(Q)$, which is to compute the aggregate weight of the constituent edges of a sub-graph Q. The process is similar to the above path queries, by using any existing algorithm subgraph(Q).

S1. [Execute in parallel.] Invoke subgraph(Q) at each sketch to find subgraph matches, and calculate the aggregate weight, denoted by $\text{weight}_i(Q)$ obtained from the i-th sketch.

S2. [Merge.] Merge individual results as follows:

$$\tilde{f}_g(Q) = \Gamma\big(\text{weight}_1(Q), \cdots, \text{weight}_d(Q)\big)$$

Here, the function $\Gamma(\cdot)$ is also to take the minimum.

Note that, running a graph algorithm on a sketch is only applicable to **TCM**. It is not applicable to gSketch since gSketch by nature is an array of frequency counts, without maintaining the graphical structure as **TCM** does. Also, in the case that $\text{weight}_i(Q)$ from some sketch says that a subgraph match does not exist, we can terminate the whole process, which provides chances for optimization that is discussed below.

Optimization. Consider a subgraph Q is defined as constituent edges as $\{(x_1, y_1), \cdots, (x_k, y_k)\}$. An alternative way of estimating the aggregate subgraph query is to first compute the minimum value among all estimated edge weights. If any $\tilde{f}_e(x_i, y_i)$ $(i \in [1,k])$ is 0, we have $\tilde{f}'_g(Q) = 0$. Otherwise, we sum them up as:

$$\tilde{f}'_g(Q) = \textstyle\sum_{i=1}^{k} \tilde{f}_e(x_i, y_i)$$

Intuitively, instead of taking the minimum weighted subgraph from all sketches, this optimization is to decompose a big problem (*e.g.,* a graph) to small pieces (*e.g.,* an edge) and locally optimize each piece. Naturally, we have

from \ to	$I(af)$	$II(bc)$	$III(dg)$	$IV(e)$
$I(af)$	1	2	0	0
$II(bc)$	3	1	1	1
$III(dg)$	0	1	1	0
$IV(e)$	1	1	1	0

Figure 5: The adjacency matrix of S_1

$\tilde{f}'_g(Q) \leq \tilde{f}_g(Q)$. Consider the two extensions of subgraph queries discussed above. For the first extension that a wildcard $*$ is used, the above optimization can be used. For instance, the edge frequency of $\tilde{f}_e(x,*)$ for a directed graph is indeed $\tilde{f}_v(x,\rightarrow)$. For the second extension that multiple wildcards $*_i$ are used to bound to the same node, this optimization cannot be applied.

Summary of notations. The notations of this paper are summarized in Table 1, which are for both directed and undirected graphs, unless being specified otherwise.

4.5 Wrap-Up

Let's conclude this section by giving some insight.

(1) One can see that we can treat existing algorithms as *black-boxes* to be applied directly on top of our sketches, *e.g.,* reach() in Section 4.3 and subgraph() in Section 4.4.

(2) One can also optimize a specific query by leveraging multiple sketches to take care of some piece of the query, *e.g.,* the edge estimation used in Section 4.4, which provides flexibility and opportunity to tune **TCM** for other specific applications.

(3) Many other graph analytics can be potentially beneficial from **TCM**, beyond what have been presented above. Please refer to Appendix B.1 about an algorithm for conditional heavy hitters, and Appendix B.2 about an algorithm for heavy triangle connections, which are important in community detection.

5. INTERNALS

Now let's shift gears and concentrate on the internals of **TCM** and its extensions (Section 5.1). We also discuss pairwise independent hash functions (Section 5.2), and a discussion of **TCM** in a distributed environment (Section 5.3).

5.1 Adjacency Matrix and Beyond

Using hash-based methods, it is evident that it only requires one-pass of the graph stream to construct/update a **TCM**. However, the linear time complexity of constructing and updating a **TCM** depends on the data structures used. For example, the adjacency list may not be a fit, since searching a specific edge on a list is not in constant time.

5.1.1 Adjacency Matrix

An adjacency matrix is a means of representing which nodes of a graph are adjacent to which other nodes.

Example 8: Consider the sketch S_1 in Fig. 4 (a) for example. Its adjacency matrix is shown in Fig. 5. □

Example 8 showcases a directed graph. In the case of an undirected graph, it will be a symmetric matrix.

Construction. Consider a graph stream $G = \langle e_1, e_2, \cdots, e_m\rangle$ where $e_i = (x_i, y_i; t_i)$. Given a number of nodes w for a graph sketch and a hash function $h(\cdot) \rightarrow [1, w]$. We use the following strategy.

from \ to	$i(abcd)$	$ii(efg)$
$I(a)$	2	0
$II(b)$	3	1
$III(c)$	0	2
$IV(d)$	0	1
$V(e)$	2	1
$VI(f)$	1	0
$VII(g)$	1	0

Figure 6: A non-square matrix

C1. [Initialization.] Construct a $w \times w$ matrix $\mathbf{M}$, with all values being initialized as 0.

C2. [Insertion of edges.] For each edge e_i ($i \in [1, m]$), compute $h(x_i)$ and $h(y_i)$, and increase the value of $\mathbf{M}[h(x_i)][h(y_i)]$ by $\omega(e_i)$, the weight of e_i.

In the above strategy, **C1** takes constant time to allocate a matrix. **C2** takes constant time for each e_i. Hence, the time complexity is $O(m)$ where m is the number of edges in G. The space complexity is $O(w^2)$.

Deletions. [Deletion of e_i.] Insertions have been discussed in the above **C2**. For the deletion of an e_i that is not of interest (*e.g.,* out of a certain time window), it suffices to decrease the value of $\mathbf{M}[h(x_i)][h(y_i)]$ by $\omega(e_i)$ in $O(1)$ time.

Alternatively, one may consider to use an adjacency *hash-list* for each node, instead of a list, to maintain its adjacent nodes using a hash table. Given an edge $e_i(x_i, y_i; t_i)$, two hash operations are needed: The first is to locate x_i, and the second is to find y_i from x_i's hash-list. Afterwards, it updates the corresponding edge weight. adjacency list is known to be suitable when graph is sparse. However, in terms of compressed graph in our case, most sketches are relatively dense, which makes the adjacency matrix the default data structure to manage our graph sketches.

5.1.2 Non-Square Matrices

In this section, we discuss the limitations of using standard adjacency matrices, followed by our proposal to relax them.

Let R be the available space for storing a graph. When using a classical adjacency matrix, we have a $n \times n$ matrix, where $n = \sqrt{R}$. Now, consider all edges from node a such as $(a, *)$. Using any hash function will inevitably hash all of these edges to the same row that is relative to node a in a matrix. For example, in Fig. 5, all edges $(a, *)$ will be hashed to the first row of the matrix.

In fact, for real-world graph data, the node degrees are skewed. It is desirable that, the nodes with higher degrees should be allocated more buckets, so as to reduce the probability of hash collisions. However, due to the lack of *a priori* knowledge of data distribution in highly dynamic graphs, it is hard to decide the right shape of a matrix. To cope with this problem, we propose to use non-square matrices.

Non-square matrices. We use a $p{*}q$ matrix with two hash functions: $h_1(\cdot) \rightarrow [1, p]$ on the *from* nodes and $h_2(\cdot) \rightarrow [1, q]$ on the *to* nodes. Let $p{*}q \approx R$ where R is the available space.

Example 9: Consider the graph stream in Fig.1. Assume that we use two hash functions: $h_1(\cdot) \rightarrow [1, 7]$ and $h_2(\cdot) \rightarrow [1, 2]$. The non-square matrix is shown in Fig. 6. □

In practice, when generating multiple sketches, we simply use matrices $n * n$, $2n * n/2$, $n/2 * 2n$, $4n * n/4$, $n/4 * 4n$, etc, without any assumption of data distribution.

5.1.3 Data Stream Sketches: A Bird's Eye View

Using non-square matrices, we can see clearly the picture of data stream summarization from a border perspective. Keep in mind that a sketch for data streams should be in *sublinear* space, *linear* construction time, and *constant* time maintenance cost per update.

One-dimensional sketch. Traditional sketches typically use a linear structure to maintain a certain type of characteristics of data streams, in real time. Taking approximate frequency counts [29] for example, they are special cases of **TCM** when setting one of our hash functions with only one bucket, *i.e.,* $h_2(\cdot) \rightarrow [1, 1]$ (see Section 5.1.2 for details).

Two-dimensional sketch. When handling two-dimensional data such as graph streams (see Section 3.1 for our formal definition) where we need to maintain the information between two items in one element, we propose to extend the sketch from a one-dimensional structure (*e.g.,* a vector) to a two-dimensional structure (*e.g.,* a matrix). The increased power with this small change is evident (see Section 4).

High-dimensional sketch. See further: When dealing with data streams that for each element $(v_1, v_2, \ldots, v_x)$, there are x intra-connected values that need to be maintained. It is natural to extend our idea to use x independent methods, $m_1, \cdots, m_x$, with each m_i working for one dimension. Here, m_i could be either a hash function, a sample-based method, or other methods such as predefined hash tags, *e.g.,* different application protocols (*e.g.,* TCP or UDP) for the Internet, or different years as a time dimension.

5.1.4 Hash Key Materialization

Obviously, there are many ways to extend **TCM**. One intuitive way is to materialize the node labels. It comes from the following observation: A hash function is a *one-way* function that is easy to compute, but hard to invert. Therefore, we hit a wall between hash keys and hash values such that it is difficult for us to do more reasonings given only hashed values. Especially when using d hash functions, we lose important connections among them since we do not keep the information of hash keys. This naturally leads to the idea of maintaining hash keys.

Extended graph sketch. Consider the graph sketch $S_G(\mathcal{V}, \mathcal{E})$ defined in Section 3.3. An *extended graph sketch* is a graph sketch $S_G(\mathcal{V}, \mathcal{E})$ that each node $v \in \mathcal{V}$ is extended with a set of node labels, denoted by $\mathsf{ext}(v)$, which records all node labels that are hashed to v.

Take Fig. 3 for example, we have $\mathsf{ext}(I) = \{a, e\}$. In fact, in Fig. 3, although we depict that with each node, the labels that it represents, *e.g.,* node I for label a and e, are not explicitly stored in the original graph sketch, but in the extended graph sketch.

Of course, this benefit comes at a cost, the extra node labels. However, this takes only $O(|V|)$ space where $|V|$ is the number of nodes in the graph stream. In terms of graph streams, the graph model is typically a multigraph with multiple edges between two nodes. Under such circumstance, the number of nodes is typically much smaller than the number of edges and maintaining them is affordable.

We will show later the usage of the extended graph sketch

in supporting the problem of heavy triangle connections (see Appendix B.2).

5.2 Pairwise Independent Hash Functions

Here, we only borrow the definition of pairwise independent hash functions.

A family of functions $\mathbf{H} = \{h|h(\cdot) \rightarrow [1, w]\}$ is called a *family of pairwise independent hash functions* if for two different hash keys x_i, x_j, and $k, l \in [1, w]$,

$$\mathsf{Pr}_{h \leftarrow \mathbf{H}}[h(x_i) = k \wedge h(x_j) = l] = 1/w^2$$

Intuitively, when using multiple hash functions to construct sketches, the hash functions used should be pairwise independent in order to reduce the probability of hash collisions. Please refer to [14] for more details.

5.3 Distributed Setup

One can see that **TCM** can be naturally deployed to a distributed environment, since the construction and maintenance of each sketch is independent of each other. Assuming we have d sketches in one computing node, when m computing nodes are available, we can use $d \times m$ sketches, which can significantly reduce the probability of hash collisions. Moreover, many analytics using **TCM** can be independently performed on multiple sketches in parallel (see Section 4), which makes a distributed environment a good fit for **TCM**.

6. EXPERIMENTS

We will start by explaining the environments where our experiments were conducted (Section 6.1). We then compare with existing approaches (Section 6.2). Finally, we summarize our experimental findings (Section 6.3).

The chief purpose of our experimental study is to prove that **TCM** should serve as the new backbone for graph stream management: **TCM** is as good as *ad-hoc* sketches for specific problems, but is much more general in supporting a wide range of analytics not supported by existing sketches.

6.1 Experimental Setup

6.1.1 Data Sets and Environment Setup

❶ ***DBLP.*** We extracted 933,530 authors as nodes and 4,918,090 author-pairs as edges from the latest DBLP archive[4]. It is an undirected graph with the weight of each streaming edge to be 1, indicating a co-authorship.

❷ ***IP flow.*** This data set contains anonymized passive traffic traces from CAIDA's equinix-chicago monitor on high-speed Internet backbone links[5]. We use one minute's traces that contain 281121 IPs and 17,721,707 traces. A trace represents a directed edge that one IP sent a packet to another IP, such as (192.168.29.1, 192.168.29.133, 62, 105.12). Here, each IP address is a node, each trace represents a directed edge, and the edge weight is the packet size, *e.g.,* 62 bytes.

❸ ***GTGraph.*** We used the well-known graph generator GTGraph[6] to generate directed graphs. We first used the R-MAT model [11] to generate a large network with power-law degree distributions. We then added weights to the edges using Zipfian distribution and the weight for each edge means the times the edge appeared in the streams. The generated network contains 10^7 vertices and $1.444 * 10^9$ edges.

❹ ***Twitter link structure.*** We used the Twitter link structure Twitter[7]. Since the released data is anonymized, we mainly used it for efficiency study. It has around 5.26 million nodes and 2 billion undirected edges, and we added random edges to simulate friendship links to make it 10 billion edges, which is 200GB on disk.

Setup. All algorithms were implemented in C++. We used the same hash functions as adopted in an open source Count-Min code[8]. All our experiments were conducted on an Intel PC with a 3.4 GHz CPU and 32GB RAM, running Ubuntu.

6.1.2 Comparison with State-of-the-Art

In sketches for data streams, there are two main types: frequency counts based (*e.g.,* CountMin and gSketch) and sample-based [29]. Take frequency counts based approaches for example, one needs to implement a node sketch by hashing nodes to support node queries, and another edge sketch by hashing edges to support edge queries (see Example 1 for more details). It is the same for sample-based solutions that different sketches are needed for *ad-hoc* problems.

We used two strategies to compare with other approaches.

(1) *Same space for an ad-hoc problem.* We used the same space for **TCM**, frequency counts-based, and sample-based approaches, for each specific problem.

(2) *Same space for a set of problems.* When giving a set of problems, *e.g.,* both edge and node queries, we only build one **TCM**, while using the same space to constructing two frequency counts-based sketches, a node sketch and an edge sketch. To better understand this comparison, please refer to Table 3 in Appendix C.1 to see the types of queries that **TCM** supports and what existing solutions support.

Note that, frequency counts-based approaches such as CountMin and **TCM** overcount the encountered elements. While sample-based approaches, on the other hand, typically undercount the elements. In fact, sample-based approaches, from the application perspective, are mainly used to estimate the *hot elements*, *i.e.,* heavy hitter problems.

6.1.3 Effectiveness Metrics

Average relative error. This measure is used for the set of queries that returns estimated frequencies, such as edge or subgraph frequencies. We used the measure defined in [39]. Given a query Q, the *relative error* is formalized as:

$$\mathsf{er}(Q) = \frac{\tilde{f}'(Q) - f(Q)}{f(Q)} = \frac{\tilde{f}'(Q)}{f(Q)} - 1$$

The *average relative error*, given a set of m queries as $\mathcal{Q} : \{Q_1, \ldots, Q_m\}$, is determined by averaging the relative errors over all queries Q_i for $i \in [1, m]$ as:

$$\mathsf{e}(\mathcal{Q}) = \frac{\sum_{i=1}^{k} \mathsf{er}(Q_i)}{m}$$

Intersection accuracy. When evaluating top-k results for heavy nodes/edges and reachability queries, we used a simple *intersection metric* [17]. Let X be the set of top-k results computed by an algorithm, and Y be the ground truth top-k

[4]http://dblp.dagstuhl.de/xml/

[5]http://www.caida.org/data/passive/passive_2015_dataset.xml

[6]http://www.cse.psu.edu/~kxm85/software/GTgraph/

[7]http://twitter.mpi-sws.org/data-icwsm2010.html.

[8]https://github.com/alabid/countminsketch/

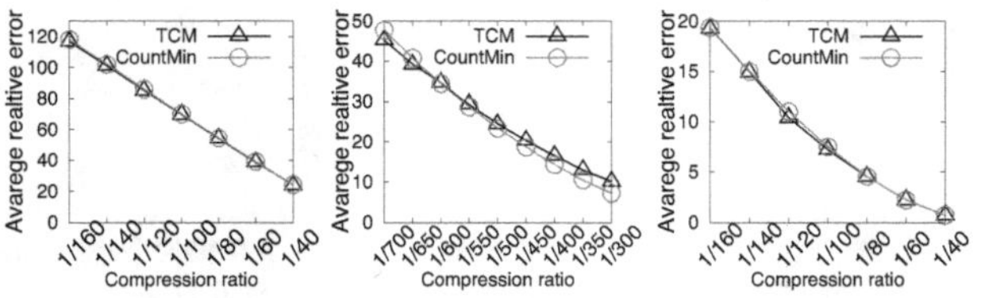

(a) DBLP (b) IP flow (c) GTGraph

Figure 7: Edge queries (varying compression ratios)

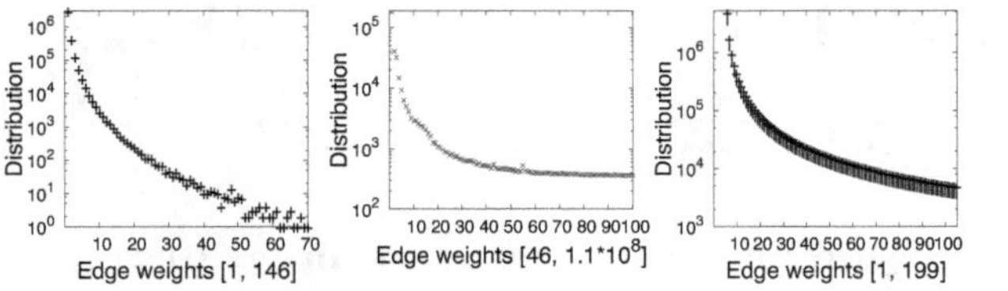

(a) DBLP (b) IP flow (c) GTGraph

Figure 8: Edge weight distribution

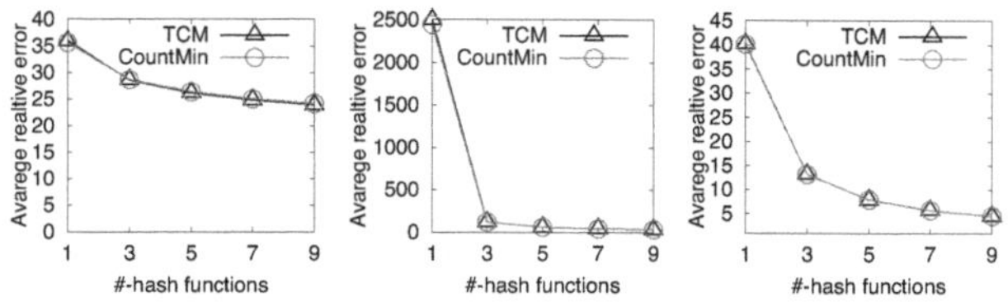

(a) DBLP (b) IP flow (c) GTGraph

Figure 9: Edge queries (fixed w, varying d)

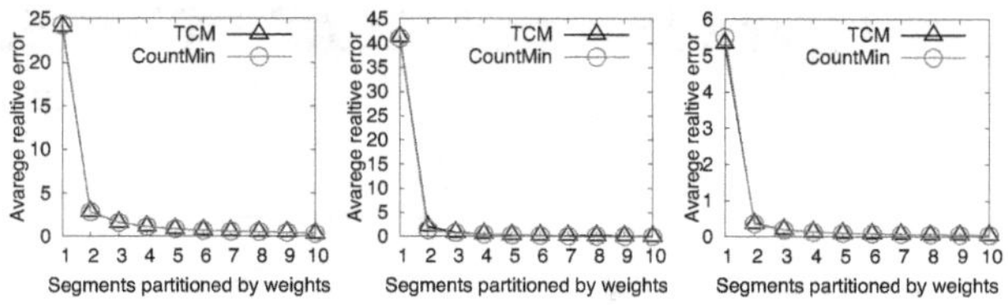

(a) DBLP (b) IP flow (c) GTGraph

Figure 10: In-depth: partition edge weights

results. The inter-accuracy is defined as $|X \cap Y|/k$, which is in $[0, 1]$, where 1 means that all real top-k results are found.

Furthermore, we used another popular measure of ranking quality for top-k results, namely normalized discounted cumulative gain (NDCG), see Appendix C.3 for more details.

6.2 Experimental Results

In this section, we show the results from five types of experiments: effectiveness for edge queries (Exp-1), effectiveness for node queries (Exp-2), effectiveness for path queries (Exp-3), effectiveness for graph queries (Exp-4), and efficiency study (Exp-5).

Exp-1: Edge queries. In the first set of experiments, we studied the performance of **TCM** in estimating edge frequencies by varying different parameters. More specifically, we varied d that is the number of hash functions, and w that is the width of the matrix.

(a) [Fixed $d = 9$, and varying w.] Here, we fixed the number of hash functions d to be 9. We varied the sizes of **TCM** by different compression ratios. Consider a graph with $|E|$ edges, the compression ratio c means that we use $|E| \times c$ space for storage. Take DBLP with 2,3425,800 edges for example, the compression ratio 1/100 indicates that the matrix used takes $2,3425,800 \times 1/100 = 234,258$ space, which is a $\sqrt{234,258} \times \sqrt{234,258}$ (*i.e.,* 484×484, or $w = 484$) matrix. For each CountMin sketch we use a vector with 234,258 cells, the same size of the matrix used by **TCM**. Figures 7(a), 7(b) and 7(c) show the results of edge frequency estimation (Section 4.1) for the data sets DBLP, IP flow, and GTGraph, respectively. The x-axis is the compression ratio and the y-axis is the average relative error of distinct edges in the graph streams.

The above results show that **TCM** and CountMin achieve comparable performance. The reason is that both approaches hashed (or compressed) all values to the same spaces having the same size $w \times w$, and the error bounds are the same (see Section A.1).

One may observe that the average relative error is relatively high for all data sets. The reason is that both **TCM** and CountMin overcount stream elements due to the compressed space. For an edge e, if its real frequency $f_e(e)$ is low, its estimated frequency $\tilde{f}(e)$ is typically much higher than $f_e(e)$ since it has chances to collide with edge e' whose real frequency is much higher than e. Figures 8(a), 8(b), and 8(c) show the edge weight distribution for DBLP, IP flow, and GTGraph, respectively. For each data set, the x-label indicates the range of edge weights. For instance, the edge weights, *i.e.,* the number of co-authorships between two authors for DBLP in Fig. 8(a), are in [1, 146]. There are 70 distinct weights, which are ranked in ascending order along the x-axis, and the y-axis indicates the number that such frequency appears. In Fig. 8(b), the edge weights have a big range $[46, 1.1 \times 10^8]$ that for the aggregated bytes transferred between two IPs. We sorted the weights in ascending order, partitioned the sorted weights in 100 equal sized bucket, and counted the number of edges in each bucket. For the value 10 in the x-axis, its y-axis value corresponds to the total number of edges appeared in the first 10 buckets. Similar for the GTGraph data in Fig. 8(c).

These figures tell us that the edge frequencies of all data sets satisfy the Zipf distribution, and edges with low frequencies dominate the results in Fig. 9. However, this will not hurt a lot in real applications. As will be shown later, the average relative error is very low for edges with high frequencies. Also, we will show that in important applications like heavy hitters, these sketches will find top-k frequent edges with high accuracy.

(b) [Fixed w, and varying d from 1 to 9.] In this set of experiments, we studied the effect of multiple pairwise independent hash functions. Figures 9(a), 9(b), and 9(c) show the results of average relative error for data sets DBLP, IP flow and GTGraph, by fixing the compression ratios to 1/40, 1/600 and 1/80, respectively. In the x-axis, we varied the number of hash functions d from 1 to 9 with a step of 2.

These results tell us that using multiple pairwise independent hash functions can indeed reduce the average relative error, since the probability of hash collisions is reduced significantly. The effect is particularly clear when the edge weights are large numbers, *e.g.,* the bytes of sent packets in IP flow data in Fig. 9(b), for both **TCM** and CountMin.

(c) [In-depth: partition edge weights.] We tested the average relative error for different ranges of edge weights, as a complementary experiment for Exp-1 (a)(b). For each data set, we first sorted all edges in ascending weight order, and partitioned the sorted edge weights in 10 groups of equal size.

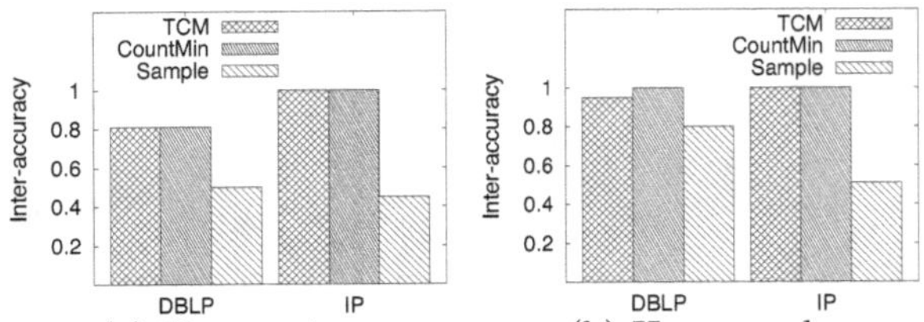

(a) Heavy edges (b) Heavy nodes

Figure 11: Heavy hitters

	$d=1$	$d=3$	$d=5$	$d=7$	$d=9$
CountMin	2434	124	62	44	36
TCM	2551	122	63	45	36
gSketch	31	13	10	9.3	8.6
TCM (edge sample)	33	13	11	9.9	9.2

Table 2: Average relative errors (IP flow)

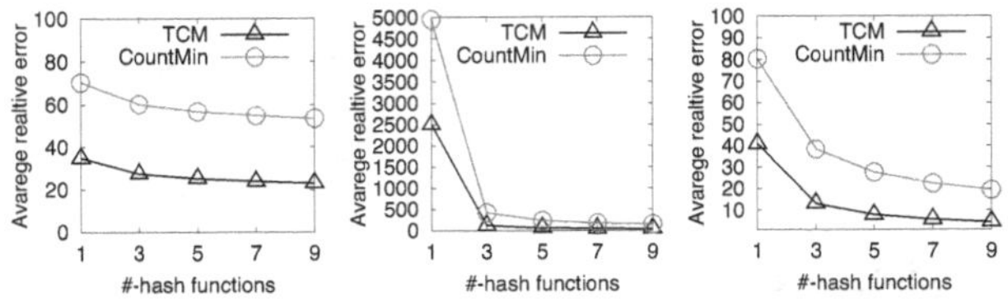

(a) DBLP (b) IP flow (c) GTGraph

Figure 12: Edge queries (sketches for > 1 function)

H. Vincent Poor	Wen Gao	Thomas S. Huang	Witold Pedrycz	Jiawei Han
Shlomo Shamai	Debin Zhao	Shuicheng Yan	Sung-Kwun Oh	Philip S. Yu
Sanjeev R. Kulkarni	Qingming Huang	Jianchao Yang	Kaoru Hirota	Deng Cai
Lalitha Sankar	Shiguang Shan	Huazhong Ning	Ho-Sung Park	Hong Cheng
Yingbin Liang	Xilin Chen	Haichao Zhang	Salvatore Sessa	Jian Pei
Mung Chiang	Tiejun Huang	Narendra Ahuja	Chang Kwak	Heng Ji

Figure 13: Conditional heavy hitters (DBLP)

Figures 10(a), 10(b) and 10(c) show the results for data sets DBLP, IP flow, and GTGraph, respectively. Here, we fixed the number of hash functions $d = 9$, and the compression ratios 1/40, 1/600 and 1/80 for the data sets DBLP, IP flow, and GTGraph, respectively.

These figures show consistent results that the average relative error is high for edges with low weights, *e.g.*, the 10% lowest weight edges *w.r.t.* x-axis value 1 in all figures. Along with the increasing edge weights, *i.e.*, the x-axis values from 2 to 10, the average relative error is significantly reduced.

(d) [Heavy edges.] We studied the performance of **TCM**, CountMin and sample-based approaches for estimating heavy edges. For each data set, we first computed top-100 edges from the original data as the ground truth. For monitoring heavy edges, we adopted a priority queue to maintain the estimated top-100 heavy edges, for each sketch. The results from the priority queue were then computed for the inter-accuracy as defined in Section 6.1.3. Also, we fixed the number of hash functions $d = 9$ and the compression ratios 1/40 and 1/600 for DBLP and IP flow, respectively. Figure 11(a) shows the results for DBLP and IP flow. GTGraph is a synthetic data, and hence its heavy edges are less of interests, which are thus not shown here. Moreover, we used the non-square matrices (Section 5.1.2) for this experiment, without assumption of the presence of any sample data. The results of using square matrices are a little bit worse than using non-square matrices, since non-square metrics can heuristically reduce the probability of hash collisions, as remarked earlier in Section 5.1.2.

The result in Fig. 11(a) tells us that **TCM** and CountMin are perfect (inter-accuracy = 1) in finding heavy edges for IP flow, for the case that the edge weights have a big range $[46, 1.1 \times 10^8]$ to represent the bytes sent between two IPs. For the edge weights that have a smaller range, *e.g.*, $[1, 146]$ for DBLP, the inter-accuracy of both **TCM** and CountMin reduced, but are still good that is 80%. For sample-based approach, we use a uniform sampling to sample a large portion (50%) of data. For both data sets, sample-based approaches perform worse than the other two.

(e) [Compare with gSketch.] We have implemented gSketch, which uses data samples to partition the graph stream by putting edges with similar weights in one partition, such that low weight edges will not collide with high weight edges when being hashed.

The result for IP flow is given in Table 2, by varying the number d of hash functions. Here, we used 10 data partitions. The result shows that the techniques proposed by gSketch can be easily integrated to **TCM**, *i.e.*, **TCM** (edge sample) in Table 2, to significantly reduce the average relative errors, when data samples are available. Moreover, the average relative errors of gSketch and improved **TCM** using edge samples are very close. The results for other data sets are given in Appendix C.2, which show similar trend.

(f) [Same space for a set of problems.] As stated in Section 6.1.2, using the same space, we built one **TCM** (with compression ratio 1/600), but two CountMin based sketches, one for edge and the other for node with equal size. The result of comparing **TCM** and edge sketches in this setting is given in Fig. 12. The result for node comparison is similar and thus omitted due to space constraints.

The result shows that **TCM** clearly outperforms CountMin in this setting. That is, by using the same space for a set of problems, **TCM** can support *ad-hoc* problems with better accuracy. Meanwhile, **TCM** can still support more analytics (see more discussion in Table 3 in Appendix C.1).

Exp-2: Node queries. In this set of experiments, we evaluated the support for heavy nodes of different sketches, as well as showing the results of using **TCM** for the conditional heavy hitter problem.

(a) [Heavy nodes.] We first studied the monitoring task of finding top-k heavy nodes. Note that, we adopted the same **TCM** sketches used in Exp-1 (d). However, for CountMin and sample-based approaches, they need to rebuild sketches for collecting node information. In other words, in order to support edge queries and point queries, both CountMin and sample-based approaches need to use extra spaces. For CountMin, we used the same space for **TCM**. For sample-based approaches, we used 50% rate for uniform sampling. For each data set, we first computed top-100 nodes from the original data as the ground truth. Similar to monitoring heavy edges, we used a priority queue to maintain the estimated top-100 heavy nodes, for each sketch. The results from the priority queue were then computed for the inter-accuracy as defined in Section 6.1.3. Figure 11(b) shows the results for DBLP and IP flow. Also, we ignored GTGraph, since it is a synthetic data, which is less of interests for heavy hitter problems.

The results show that **TCM** and CountMin perform similar with good accuracy in terms of estimating heavy nodes.

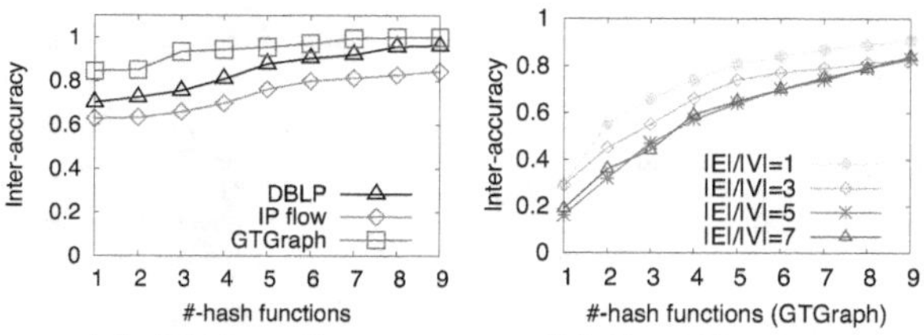

(a) All Data Sets (b) True Negatives

Figure 14: Reachability queries (varying d)

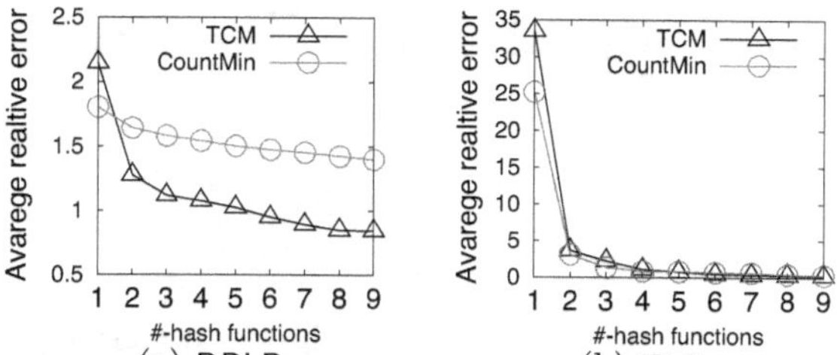

(a) DBLP (b) IP flow

Figure 15: Subgraph frequencies (varying d)

In particular, they clearly outperform sample-based approaches in both data sets, which agrees with the results from heavy edges given in Fig. 11(a).

(b) [Conditional heavy hitters.] Besides finding which nodes are most popular as heavy hitters do, conditional heavy hitters is to further find the most popular neighbors to the most popular nodes. Please find a detailed discussion and its corresponding Algorithm 1 in Appendex-B.1 for detecting conditional heavy hitters. Also, please refer to the discussion in Section 4 about why other sketches fall short of supporting the problem of conditional heavy hitters.

Since the results of DBLP are easy to understand, we only show the conditional heavy hitters detected for DBLP, as given in Fig. 13. It depicts the top-5 most productive authors such as H. Vincent Poor and Wen Gao, each of them indeed has > 700 publications. Also, it reports for each author and his top-5 most frequent collaborators. We have manually checked DBLP: 3 collaborators (Shlomo Shamai, Sanjeev R. Kulkarni, and Yingbin Liang) are indeed in H. Vincent Poor's top-5 frequent collaborators, and the other 2 are in his top-10 frequent collaborators.

Exp-3: Path queries. In this set of experiments, we evaluated the power of **TCM** in supporting reachability queries. Note that the other two types of sketches, CountMin and sample-based, cannot be used for estimating reachability queries. We fixed the compression ratios to 1/40, 1/600 and 1/80 for DBLP, IP flow, and GTGraph, respectively. We varied the number of hash functions from 1 to 9. For each data set, we randomly picked 100 pairs of nodes. The estimation is correct if either **TCM** reports that two nodes are reachable and they are indeed reachable (*i.e.*, true positives), or estimates that two nodes are not reachable and they are not connected in the original graph (*i.e.*, true negatives). The results for inter-accuracy are shown in Fig. 14(a).

The above results tell us two things. Firstly, along with the increasing number of hash functions d, the inter-accuracy of estimating reachability queries will increase, as expected. Secondly, **TCM** achieved good inter-accuracy for all data sets. For example, when $d = 9$, the inter-accuracy values for DBLP, IP flow and GTGraph are 96%, 84.5% and 100%, respectively.

<u>*In-depth: true negatives.*</u> Since **TCM** keeps all connectives of the graph stream, it only has *true positives* but no *false positives*, *i.e.*, all reachable node pairs will be detected as reachable. However, due to hash collisions, there may exist hash collisions such that **TCM** may have *false negatives*, *i.e.*, not reachable node pairs may be reported as reachable. In order to control the graph shape, we used synthetic data GTGraph by varying the ratio $|E|/|V|$ from 1 to 7, with a step of 2. Figure 14(b) shows the results for 100 not reachable pairs. It shows that when the number of hash functions is small, the inter-accuracy of *true negatives* is low. Along with increasing number of hash functions, the inter-accuracy increases significantly, with low false negatives. In fact, when $|E|/|V| > 7$, most node pairs were reachable to each other, *i.e.*, no negatives and **TCM** naturally performs well.

Exp-4: Graph analytics. In this set of experiments, we study two types of graph analytics, subgraph queries and heavy triangle connections.

(a) [Subgraph queries.] We first tested the performance of both **TCM** and CountMin in estimating subgraph queries (Section 4.4). Since subgraph queries are considered as summing up the estimated edge frequencies of all graph edges, the results are expected to be similar to the ones for edge queries. We verified the above observation by the following experiments, using only real-world data sets, *i.e.*, DBLP and IP flow. For each data set, we generated, from the original graph stream, 20 connected graphs with different shapes, such as paths, star-shaped graphs, and general graphs. Also, they have various sizes from 2 to 8 edges. We fixed the compression ratios to 1/40 and 1/600 for DBLP and IP flow, and varied the number of hash functions d from 1 to 9. Figures 15(a) and 15(b) show the results of average relative error for DBLP and IP flow, respectively. Here, the x-axis indicates the number of hash functions used, and the y-axis represents the average relative error for all tested graph queries.

The above results tell us that along with the increasing number of hash functions, the average relative error will decrease, which is expected and agrees with the results for edge queries (Exp-1 (b)). Also, the results show that the average relative error is lower than the results in Fig. 9 for edge queries. The reason is that, given a graph with several edges, if the real weight of one edge is large, it will potentially dominate the estimation of average relative error for other edges, and the overall value is thus lower. This also agrees with the results shown in Fig. 10.

(b) [Heavy triangle connections.] Intuitively, heavy triangle connections (see Appendix B.2 for a detailed discussion and its corresponding algorithm) are the set of analytics that first identify heavy edges, and then for each heavy edge (x, y), finding the nodes that communicate frequently with both x and y. We showcase DBLP here, since it is easy to understand by database researchers. We first identified top-20 heavy edges, indicating frequent collaborations, from which we selected five edges about database researchers as depicted in Fig. 16. The top-5 heavy connections with both authors are also shown. Take Charu C. Aggarwal and Philip S. Yu for example, for the 5 discovered authors that collaborate

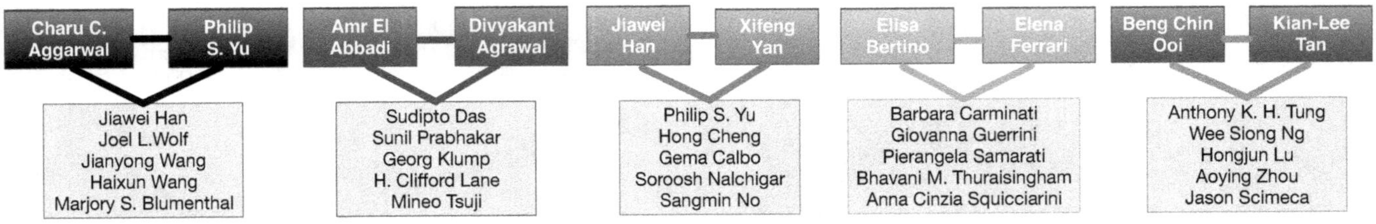

Figure 16: Heavy Triangle Connections (DBLP)

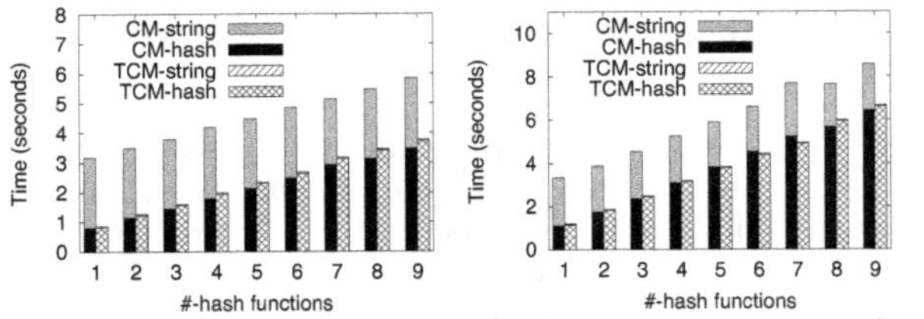

(a) DBLP ($|E| = 4.9 * 10^6$) (b) IP flow ($|E| = 1.7 * 10^7$)

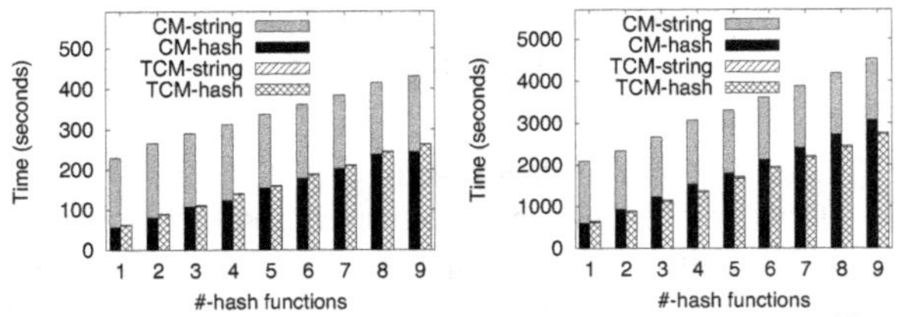

(c) GTGraph ($|E| = 1.44 * 10^9$) (d) Twitter ($|E| = 10^{10}$)

Figure 17: Efficiency

frequently with both of them, 4 are in the ground truth of top-5 results. This tells us that (i) **TCM** can discover interesting and useful results for practical applications; and (ii) the accuracy is good in practice.

Exp-5: Efficiency. In the last set of experiments, we first evaluated the efficiency of building **TCM**, as discussed in Section 5.1.1. The results of varying the number of hash functions from 1 to 9 are given in Fig. 17. In all streaming scenarios, data does not reside in disk. Hence, in our experiments, we counted the time after data is in memory.

Take DBLP in Fig. 17(a) for example. When the x-axis value is 1 that is for 1 hash function, the left (resp. right) bar represents gSketch, *i.e.*, CountMin based edge sketch, (resp. **TCM**). Each bar consists of two parts, where the upper part (-string) is for the time of string operation and the lower part (-hash) is for hashing and updating the sketch. gSketch concatenates two strings but **TCM** does not need to, that is why the upper part of CountMin takes much time but **TCM** has almost zero cost. For the cost of hashing, *i.e.*, the lower parts of both bars, the time is comparable. Moreover, when concatenating two strings a and b, sometimes the time of running the same hash function h on $h(ab)$ takes longer than on two strings $h(a)$ and $h(b)$ separately, which explains why in Fig. 17(d) the hashing time of **TCM** is even less than CountMin. Hence, the overall time of constructing gSketch is even longer than **TCM**.

The above results show that the maintenance cost of **TCM** is comparable to the state-of-the-art and also scalable, which indicates that **TCM** can be efficiently built to support real-time applications in graph streams.

Query time. After effectiveness study in Exps 1-4, we now discuss the efficiency of using **TCM** against query evaluation using the original graph stream. Note that, the **TCM** is stored as an adjacency matrix. The original graph stream, however, can only be stored using an adjacency list for two reasons: (1) one cannot know the number of nodes *a-priori*, and (2) memory limitation. Naturally, query estimation using **TCM** is orders of magnitude faster than evaluation over the graph stream. Please see Appendix C.4 for more empirical results.

6.3 Summary of Experimental Findings

We find the followings from our experimental study.

(1) **TCM** can achieve performance comparable with the state-of-the-art specialized sketches (Exp-1 (a-d), Exp-2 (a) and Exp-4 (a)). Also, the idea of gSketch can be applied to **TCM** to improve accuracy (Exp-1 (e)). Moreover, when using the same space to support different applications, **TCM** is more effective than its counterpart (Exp-1 (f)).

(2) **TCM** is much general than existing sketches, such as the conditional heavy hitters studied in Exp-2 (b), the reachability queries discussed in Exp-3, and the heavy triangle relations studied in Exp-4 (b).

(3) **TCM** is economic to maintain and efficient for query estimation (Exp-5).

These experimental results confirmed the generalization, effectiveness and efficiency of **TCM** in supporting various graph stream applications, which sheds new light on summarizing and analyzing graph streams.

7. CONCLUSION AND FUTURE WORK

We have proposed a graphical sketch **TCM** for summarizing graph streams in a sublinear space, using linear construction time, and with constant maintenance cost per update. We have demonstrated its wide applicability to many emerging applications, theoretically and experimentally. In addition, we have shown that **TCM** has comparable performance for specialized sketches for *ad-hoc* problems, and is more effective when considering a set of problems. We have also shown problems that existing sketches fail to support.

One topic for future work is to revise it in order to serve specific applications, *e.g.*, to integrate it to OpenSOC for cyber security framework. Another topic is, instead of treating it as a sketch, we plan to store extra information, use it as a filter for general (exact) query evaluation (see Section 5.1.4 for an initial discussion). Also, since evaluating queries over multiple sketches of **TCM** is naturally parallelizable, we plan to implement it on a distributed platform *e.g.*, GraphX, so as to handle big graph streams in practice, in a more scalable way. Last but not least, we plan to use it for revisiting a set of graph mining problems, *e.g.*, finding the evolution of graphs, and monitoring networks using temporal snapshots of our sketches.

8. REFERENCES

[1] Tweet statistics. *http://expandedramblings.com/index.php/march-2013-by-the-numbers-a-few-amazing-twitter-stats/10/.*

[2] Vitria. *http://www.vitria.com/solutions/streaming-big-data-analytics/benefits/.*

[3] M. Adler and M. Mitzenmacher. Towards compressing web graphs. In *Data Compression Conference*, pages 203–212, 2001.

[4] C. C. Aggarwal, editor. *Data Classification: Algorithms and Applications.* CRC Press, 2014.

[5] N. Alon, Y. Matias, and M. Szegedy. The space complexity of approximating the frequency moments. *J. Comput. Syst. Sci.*, 58(1):137–147, 1999.

[6] J. D. Batson, D. A. Spielman, and N. Srivastava. Twice-ramanujan sparsifiers. In *STOC*, pages 255–262, 2009.

[7] A. A. Benczúr and D. R. Karger. Approximating s-t minimum cuts in $\tilde{O}(n^2)$ time. In *STOC*, pages 255–262, 1996.

[8] A. A. Benczúr and D. R. Karger. Randomized approximation schemes for cuts and flows in capacitated graphs. *CoRR*, cs.DS/0207078, 2002.

[9] V. Braverman, R. Ostrovsky, and D. Vilenchik. How hard is counting triangles in the streaming model? In *ICALP*, pages 244–254, 2013.

[10] A. Z. Broder and M. Mitzenmacher. Survey: Network applications of bloom filters: A survey. *Internet Mathematics*, 1(4):485–509, 2003.

[11] D. Chakrabarti, Y. Zhan, and C. Faloutsos. R-MAT: A recursive model for graph mining. In *SDM*, pages 442–446, 2004.

[12] S. Choudhury, L. B. Holder, G. C. Jr., K. Agarwal, and J. Feo. A selectivity based approach to continuous pattern detection in streaming graphs. In *EDBT*, pages 157–168, 2015.

[13] E. Cohen and H. Kaplan. Tighter estimation using bottom k sketches. *PVLDB*, 1(1):213–224, 2008.

[14] G. Cormode and S. Muthukrishnan. An improved data stream summary: the count-min sketch and its applications. *J. Algorithms*, 55(1):58–75, 2005.

[15] G. Cormode and S. Muthukrishnan. Space efficient mining of multigraph streams. In *PODS*, pages 271–282, 2005.

[16] M. Elkin. Streaming and fully dynamic centralized algorithms for constructing and maintaining sparse spanners. *ACM Transactions on Algorithms*, 7(2):20, 2011.

[17] R. Fagin, R. Kumar, and D. Sivakumar. Comparing top k lists. In *SODA*, pages 28–36, 2003.

[18] W. Fan, J. Li, X. Wang, and Y. Wu. Query preserving graph compression. In *SIGMOD*, pages 157–168, 2012.

[19] J. Feigenbaum, S. Kannan, A. McGregor, S. Suri, and J. Zhang. On graph problems in a semi-streaming model. *Theor. Comput. Sci.*, 348(2-3), 2005.

[20] J. Gao, C. Zhou, J. Zhou, and J. X. Yu. Continuous pattern detection over billion-edge graph using distributed framework. In *ICDE*, pages 556–567, 2014.

[21] J. E. Gonzalez, Y. Low, H. Gu, D. Bickson, and C. Guestrin. Powergraph: Distributed graph-parallel computation on natural graphs. In *OSDI*, pages 17–30, 2012.

[22] J. E. Gonzalez, R. S. Xin, A. Dave, D. Crankshaw, M. J. Franklin, and I. Stoica. Graphx: Graph processing in a distributed dataflow framework. In *OSDI*, pages 599–613, 2014.

[23] S. Guha and A. McGregor. Graph synopses, sketches, and streams: A survey. *PVLDB*, 5(12):2030–2031, 2012.

[24] A. K. Jain and R. C. Dubes. *Algorithms for Clustering Data.* Prentice-Hall, 1988.

[25] K. Järvelin and J. Kekäläinen. Cumulated gain-based evaluation of IR techniques. *ACM Trans. Inf. Syst.*, 20(4), 2002.

[26] J. A. Kelner and A. Levin. Spectral sparsification in the semi-streaming setting. *Theory Comput. Syst.*, 53(2):243–262, 2013.

[27] Y. Low, J. Gonzalez, A. Kyrola, D. Bickson, C. Guestrin, and J. M. Hellerstein. Distributed graphlab: A framework for machine learning in the cloud. *PVLDB*, 5(8):716–727, 2012.

[28] G. Malewicz, M. H. Austern, A. J. C. Bik, J. C. Dehnert, I. Horn, N. Leiser, and G. Czajkowski. Pregel: a system for large-scale graph processing. In *SIGMOD*, pages 135–146, 2010.

[29] G. S. Manku and R. Motwani. Approximate frequency counts over data streams. In *VLDB*, pages 346–357, 2002.

[30] A. McGregor. Graph stream algorithms: a survey. *SIGMOD Record*, 43(1):9–20, 2014.

[31] K. Mirylenka, G. Cormode, T. Palpanas, and D. Srivastava. Conditional heavy hitters: detecting interesting correlations in data streams. *VLDB J.*, 24(3):395–414, 2015.

[32] S. Raghavan and H. Garcia-Molina. Representing web graphs. In *ICDE*, pages 405–416, 2003.

[33] C. Song, T. Ge, C. X. Chen, and J. Wang. Event pattern matching over graph streams. *PVLDB*, 8(4):413–424, 2014.

[34] D. A. Spielman and N. Srivastava. Graph sparsification by effective resistances. In *STOC*, pages 563–568, 2008.

[35] T. Suel and J. Yuan. Compressing the graph structure of the web. In *Data Compression Conference*, pages 213–222, 2001.

[36] R. E. Tarjan. Data structures and network algorithms. In *SIAM.* 1983.

[37] C. E. Tsourakakis, U. Kang, G. L. Miller, and C. Faloutsos. DOULION: counting triangles in massive graphs with a coin. In *SIGKDD*, pages 837–846, 2009.

[38] C. Wang and L. Chen. Continuous subgraph pattern search over graph streams. In *ICDE*, pages 393–404, 2009.

[39] P. Zhao, C. C. Aggarwal, and M. Wang. gSketch: On query estimation in graph streams. *PVLDB*, 5(3):193–204, 2011.

APPENDIX

A. ERROR BOUNDS

We discuss the error bounds for two basic types of queries:

edge queries and node queries. Although **TCM** is more general, we show that theoretically, it has the same error bounds as CountMin.

A.1 Edge Queries

Our proof for error bound of edge queries is an adaption of the proof used in CountMin (Section 4.1 of [14]).

Theorem 1: *The estimation $\tilde{f}_e(x,y)$ of the cumulative edge weight of the edge (x,y) has the following guarantees, $f_e(x,y) \leq \tilde{f}_e(x,y)$ with probability at least $1-\delta$, s.t., $f_e(x,y) \leq \tilde{f}_e(x,y) + \epsilon * n$, where $f_e(x,y)$ is the exact answer to the cumulative edge weight of the edge (x,y), n denotes the number of nodes, and the error in answering a query is within a factor of ϵ with probability δ*[9]. □

PROOF. Consider an edge query $f_e(x,y)$. For each stream edge $e : (x,y;t)$ and a hash function h_i, by construction, the edge weight $\omega(e)$ is added to $\mathcal{M}_i[h_i(x),h_i(y)]$, where $\mathcal{M}_i$ is the adjacency matrix corresponding to the hash function, h_i. Therefore, by construction, the answer to $f_e(x,y)$ is less than or equal to $\min_{i\in[1,d]} \mathcal{M}_i[h_i(x),h_i(y)]$, where d is the number of applied hash functions.

Consider two edges (x,y) and (z,w). We define an indicator vector $\vec{I}_{x,y,z,w}$ with d variables $[I^1_{x,y,z,w},\cdots,I^d_{x,y,z,w}]$, where $I^i_{x,y,z,w}$ corresponds to the hash function h_i. We define $I^i_{x,y,z,w}$ to be 1, if there is a collision between two disjoint edges, *i.e.*, $(x \neq z) \wedge (y \neq w) \wedge (h_i(x) = h_i(z)) \wedge (h_i(y) = h_i(w))$, and 0 otherwise. By independence assumption of hash buckets *w.r.t.* distinct hash keys, we have

$$E(I^i_{x,y,z,w}) = \mathsf{Pr}[(h_i(x) = h_i(z) \wedge h_i(y) = h_i(w)]$$
$$\leq (1/\mathsf{range}(h_i))^2 = \epsilon'^2/\mathsf{e}^2$$

where e is the base used to compute natural logarithm, and $\mathsf{range}(h_i)$ is the number of hash buckets of function h_i. Define the variable $X^i_{x,y}$ (random over choices of h_i) to count the number of collisions with the edge (x,y), which is formalized as $X^i_{x,y} = \Sigma_{z=1\ldots n,w=1\ldots n} I^i_{x,y,z,w} a_{z,w}$, where n is the number of nodes in the graph and $a_{z,w}$ is the sum of non-zero weight entries of edge (z,w). Since $a_{z,w}$ is non-negative, $X^i_{x,y}$ is non-negative. By construction, $\mathcal{M}_i[h_i(x),h_i(y)] = f_e(x,y) + X^i_{x,y}$. So clearly, $(\min_{i\in[1,d]} \mathcal{M}_i[h_i(x),h_i(y)]) \geq f_e(x,y)$. By pairwise independence of h_i, and linearity of expectation, we have

$$E(X^i_{x,y}) = E\big(\textstyle\sum_{z=1\ldots n,w=1\ldots n} I^i_{x,y,z,w} f_e(z,w)\big)$$
$$\leq \big(\textstyle\sum_{z=1\ldots n,w=1\ldots n} E(I^i_{x,y,z,w}) f_e(z,w)\big) \leq (\epsilon'/\mathsf{e})^2 * n$$

Let, $\epsilon'^2 = \epsilon$. By the Markov inequality, we get

$$\mathsf{Pr}[\tilde{f}_e(x,y) > f_e(x,y) + \epsilon * n]$$
$$= \mathsf{Pr}[\forall_i.\ \mathcal{M}_i[h_i(x),h_i(y)] > f_e(x,y) + \epsilon * n]$$
$$= \mathsf{Pr}[\forall_i.\ f_e(x,y) + X^i_{x,y} > f_e(x,y) + \epsilon * n]$$
$$= \mathsf{Pr}[\forall_i.\ X^i_{x,y} > \mathsf{e} * E(X^i_{x,y})] < \mathsf{e}^{-d} \leq \delta$$

□

Hence, **TCM** generates the same number of collisions and the same error bounds under the same probabilistic guarantees as CountMin for edge queries.

[9]The parameters ϵ and δ are usually set by the user.

A.2 Node Queries

We first discuss the query for node out-flow, *i.e.*, $f_v(a,\rightarrow)$. Consider the stream of edges $e : (a,*;t)$, *i.e.*, edges from node a to any other node indicated by a wildcard $*$. Drop the destination (*i.e.*, the wildcard) of each edge. The stream now becomes a stream of tuples $(a,\omega(t))$ where $\omega(t)$ is the sum of the weights of the outgoing edges from node a at time t. When a query is posed to find the weighted out-degree (*i.e.*, the sum of the weights of all edges whose source node is a) of node a, CountMin [14] returns the minimum of the weights in different hash buckets as the estimation of the flow out of node a. The unweighted out-degree (*i.e.*, the number of edges with source a) can be calculated similarly by setting $\omega(t)$ above to 1. Clearly, by construction, the answer obtained is an over-estimation of the true out-degree because of two reasons: (a) collisions in the hash-buckets, and (b) self-collision, *i.e.*, we do not know if an edge has been seen previously and thus count the outgoing edge again even if we have seen it.

The cases for in-flow point queries $f_v(a,\leftarrow)$ for directed graphs and flow point queries $f_v(a,-)$ for undirected graph queries can be analyzed using a similar discussion as shown above, which are thus omitted here.

Given the same number of hash buckets, the error estimates for point queries (see Sec. 4.1 of [14]) hold for these cases.

Lemma 1.2: *The estimated out-flow (in-flow) is within a factor of ϵ of the actual out-flow (in-flow) with probability δ if we use $d = \lceil ln(1/\delta)\rceil$ pair-wise independent hash functions and the number or rows $w = \lceil \mathsf{e}/\epsilon \rceil$.* □

B. ADDITIONAL ALGORITHMS

B.1 Conditional Heavy Hitters

As discussed in Section 4, different from heavy hitters, conditional heavy hitters [31] are to find heavy hitters that are *locally* popular by considering edge connections. In other words, instead of finding which nodes are most popular as heavy hitters do, it is to find the most popular neighbors to the most popular nodes.

In the following, we will present an algorithm of how **TCM** can be used to monitor a graph stream and to report conditional heavy hitters. Before we give the algorithmic details, let us define the problem first.

Conditional heavy hitters. Consider a graph stream $G = \langle e_1, e_2, \cdots, e_m\rangle$ as defined in Section 3.1. Assume *w.l.o.g.* that each edge $e_i : (x_i, y_i; t_i)$ is a directed edge from node x_i to node y_i. The problem of *conditional heavy hitters* is to find top-k heavy hitters with the most aggregate in-flow weight, and for each detected heavy hitter y, find its associated top-l nodes that send the highest weights to y.

The other two versions, the one to find nodes with top-k out-flow weights, and the other version with undirected edges, can be similarly defined. Therefore, we only present the algorithm for the problem defined above, which can be readily converted to solve other versions of conditional heavy hitter problems.

Algorithm 1. The algorithm to monitor a graph stream G to report conditional heavy hitters, is shown in Algorithm 1. Given a graph stream G, two natural numbers k and l, it outputs (estimates) top-k heavy nodes, with each one asso-

Algorithm 1: Monitoring Conditional Heavy Hitters

```
Input:  a graph stream G, a parameter k, and a parameter l.
Output: top-k heavy nodes, with each top-l heavy neighbors.
1  Initialize a TCM sketch, denote by M;
2  Initialize a global sorted list hh := ∅;
3  for each edge e_i : (x_i, y_i; t_i) in G do
4    Update the TCM sketch M using e_i;
5    Let in_weight := f̃_v(y_i, ←);
6    Let neigbor_weight := f̃_e(x_i, y_i);
7    if y_i is in hh then
8      if x_i is in y_i.hn then
9        Update the value in y_i.hn w.r.t. x_i to neigbor_weight;
10     elseif neigbor_weight > y_i.hn.min_weight then
11       if y_i.hn.size = l then
12         Delete the one in y_i.hn having the min_weight
13       Insert (neigbor_weight, x_i) to y_i.hn;
14   else                                   // y_i is not in hh
15     if in_weight > hh.min_weight and hh.size = k then
16       Delete the one in hh having the min_weight;
17     if hh.size < k then
18       Initialize a sorted list hn for y_i;
19       Insert (neigbor_weight, x_i) to y_i.hn;
20       Insert (in_weight, y_i) to hh;
21 return hh;
```

ciated with top-l heavy neighbors. It first builds a **TCM** sketch (line 1), and initializes a sorted list to maintain in order to maintain top-k heavy hitters (line 2). It then processes the incoming graph stream edges (lines 3-20). For each incoming edge, it first updates the sketch (line 4; see Section 5.1.1), and then estimates its in-flow weight (line 5; see Section 4.2) and the edge weight (line 6; see Section 4.1). If the node is already in the maintained top-k heavy hitters, it updates the associated heavy neighbors (lines 7-14). If its neighbor is already a hot neighbor (line 8), it simply updates using the new estimated edge weight (line 9). Otherwise, when either current visited node has maintained less than top-l hot neighbors, or it already has top-l hot neighbors but the new neighbor has a higher weight, it will update the hot neighbors correspondingly (lines 10-13). In the case the the currently visited node is not a heavy hitter (line 14), it first removes the maintained heavy hitter with the smallest in-flow weight, if the newly inserted node has a higher weight (lines 15-16). The heavy hitter will be updated by the new heavy hitter correspondingly (lines 17-20). Note that, if the new heavy hitter has a less weight than the minimum weight in the maintained k heavy hitters, it will not be inserted since the size of sorted heavy hitter list will not be updated (*i.e.,* lines 15-16 will not be executed). Consequently, the lines 17-20 will not be executed since the size of the maintained heavy hitter is k. Finally, it returns the top-k heavy edges, with each one associated with top-l heavy neighbors, which reflects the triangle relationships.

Complexity. It is readily to see that each step in the **for** loop (lines 3-20) will take constant time. Observe the followings. The operations for estimating the in-flow weight (line 5; see Section 4.2) and the edge weight (line 6; see Section 4.1) are in constant time. In addition, the cost of maintaining a sorted list (either the hh or a hn) is also in cost time, since the sorted list has a bounded size, k for hh and l for hn, where both k and l are constants. Hence, in total, the algorithm runs in $O(|E|)$ time, which is linear to the input.

Algorithm 2: Finding Heavy Triangle Connections

```
Input:  a graph stream G, a parameter k, and a parameter l.
Output: top-k heavy edges, with each top-l heavy connections.
1  Initialize a TCM sketch, denote by M(only one w*w matrix);
2  Find top-k heavy edges he while processing G;
3  for each edge e : (x, y) in he do
4    connections := ∅;
5    for i ∈ [1, w] do
6      if M[i][h(x)] > 0 and M[i][h(y)] > 0
7        connections := connections ∪ ext(i);
8      Rank connections by (f̃_e(z,x)×f̃_e(z,y))/(f̃_e(z,x)+f̃_e(z,y));
9      Associated top-l connections from the above ranking;
10 return heavy edges and their associated top-l connections;
```

B.2 Heavy Triangle Connections

In this section, we study a new problem for community detection.

Heavy triangle connections. Consider a graph stream $G = \langle e_1, e_2, \cdots, e_m \rangle$. The problem of *top-k triangle connections* is first to find top-k heavy edges, and then for each detected heavy edge (x, y), to find top-l nodes z ranked by the function $\big(f_e(z,x) \times f_e(z,y)\big)/\big(f_e(z,x) + f_e(z,y)\big)$.

Intuitively, the problem is to identify frequently communicated node pairs, and then identify nodes that communicate frequently with both nodes. Naturally, the detected relationships are in the shapes of triangles. In cyber security, when finding two suspicious IPs (*i.e.,* heavy edges), it is to also report other suspicious IPs. Take DBLP for another example, when identifying two authors who wrote many papers together *e.g.,* Philip S. Yu and Jiawei Han, or Divy Agrawal and Amr El Abbadi, it is to find the ones who work closely with both of them.

Note that the strategy of using **TCM** to estimate top-k heavy edges has been discussed in Section 6.2, Exp-1 (d). Given top-k heavy edges and only the **TCM**, it is not possible to identify the common neighbors since only hashed values (not the original values) are maintained. To do so, we show the power of the simple extension as discussed in Section 5.1.4, the extended graph sketch.

Algorithm 2. The algorithm to compute heavy triangle connections is shown in Algorithm 2. Given a graph stream G, two natural numbers k and l, it outputs (estimates) top-k heavy edges, with each one associated with top-l heavy connections. It first initializes a **TCM** sketch (line 1). To simplify the discussion, we consider only one hash function (*i.e.,* $d = 1$), and the case for $d > 1$ hash functions can be easily adapted. It then processes the graph stream G, maintains the sketch, and finds top-k heavy edges (line 2; see the discussion in Section 6.2, Exp-1 (d)). It then iteratively processes each heavy edge (lines 3-9). It first computes the connections for the edge being processing, using the extended graph sketch (lines 5-7). It then ranks all connections using estimated edge weights (line 8) and picks top-l of them (line 9). Finally, it returns the discovered heavy triangle connections.

Complexity. It is readily to see that for each edge, finding

	edge	node	conditional heavy nodes	path (reachability)	graph (explicit edges labels)	heavy triangle connections
TCM	✓	✓	✓	✓	✓	✓
CountMin (edge) or gSketch	✓	✗	✗	✗	✓	✗
CountMin (node)	✗	✓	✗	✗	✗	✗
sample-edge	✓	✗	✗	✗	✗	✗
sample-node	✗	✓	✗	✗	✗	✗

Table 3: Analytics supported by different sketches

	$d = 1$	$d = 3$	$d = 5$	$d = 7$	$d = 9$
CountMin	35.6	28.6	26.3	25	24
TCM	35.9	28.6	26.1	24.8	23.9
gSketch	29.8	25.2	23.5	22.5	21.8
TCM (edge sample)	29.4	24.7	23	22	21.4

Table 4: Average relative errors (DBLP)

	$d = 1$	$d = 3$	$d = 5$	$d = 7$	$d = 9$
CountMin	40.2	13.2	7.9	5.7	4.5
TCM	41	13	7.7	5.6	4.4
gSketch	5.7	3.6	3	2.63	2.4
TCM (edge sample)	5.9	3.6	3	2.6	2.3

Table 5: Average relative errors (GTGraph)

all connections will take $O(|V|)$ time. Ranking all connections will take $O(|V|log|V|)$ time. Since both k and l are constants, the total running time of Algorithm 2 is thus $O(|V|log|V|)$.

C. ADDITIONAL EXPERIMENTS

C.1 Sketch Expressiveness

The types of analytics supported by different sketches are summarized in Table 3, which tells the followings:

- For existing sketches, either frequency counts-based or sample-based, in order to support different analytics, they have to build an *ad-hoc* sketch to support a specific task, *e.g.,* edge or node.
- gSketch has been proposed to improve CountMin by considering data distribution. However, due to its inherent one-dimensional data structure, they have limited powered in supported graph analytics, which has been illustrated in Example 2.
- **TCM** is much more generalized in supporting many types of analytics in a single sketch, with the reason that **TCM** is inherent a two-dimensional structure, which keeps all graph connectivities in the original graph, as explained in Example 3. The improved power of using a two-dimensional structure vs. a one-dimensional structure is evident in supporting graph based applications.

In summary, the above analysis shows that **TCM** is much more general than *state-of-the-art* sketches.

C.2 More Comparisons with gSketch

We further show the comparisons with gSketch using DBLP and GTGraph data sets.

The result for DBLP is given in Table 4 and for GTGraph is shown in Table 5, by varying the number d of hash functions from 1 to 9 with a step of 2. Here, we used 10 data partitions.

The benefit of using data partitions for GTGraph is more significant than DBLP, in terms of the improved average relative errors. The main reasons are that (1) the range of weights for DBLP is smaller, and (2) the size of DBLP is smaller. In such case, the effect of partitioning the data to reduce the probability of hash collisions between high and low weight elements is not significant.

The above results, together with Section 6.2 Exp-1(e), show that the techniques proposed by gSketch can be easily integrated to **TCM** to reduce the average relative errors. Moreover, the average relative errors of gSketch and improved **TCM** using edge samples are very close. Again, it proves the positive result that our generalized sketch can get very close performance, when being compared with an *ad-hoc* solution.

C.3 Effectiveness with NDCG Measure

Normalized discounted cumulative gain (NDCG) [25] measures of ranking quality, which calculates the gain of a result based on its position in the result list and normalizes the score to $[0, 1]$ where 1 means perfect top-k results. Using the same setting of IP flow for heavy edges/nodes in Section 6.2, we show the NDCG results below, where he (resp. hn) is for heavy edges (resp. heavy nodes). It shows that **TCM**, as well as CountMin based method, can return top-k results with good NDCG scores. The results for other data sets are omitted for similar results and lack of space.

k	he (TCM)	he (CountMin)	hn (TCM)	hn (CountMin)
10	0.99	0.99	1	1
100	0.99	0.99	0.99	1
500	0.99	0.99	0.99	0.99

C.4 Query Time

We show the query time of edge queries for GTGraph on both the sketch and the original graph in the below table. Each row indicates the number of edge queries. For each set of edge queries, we first equally partitioned all edges in 10 buckets based on edge weights. We then picked 1/10 edges from each bucket. **TCM** is stored in an adjacency matrix and each query is in constant time, hence it is very efficient. For the original graph, it can only be stored as an adjacency list (see Section 6.2 Exp-5 for the discussion), each query needs a scan to locate the edge, which is thus very expensive. We then built a hash index on the nodes of adjacency list to favor it, such that an edge is first to use the hash index to locate the node and then scan its adjacency list to find the edge. However, as shown in the last column, it is still an order of magnitude slower than **TCM**.

#-queries	TCM (summary)	adjacency list (original graph)	hashed list (original graph)
100	0.001 secs	5.832 secs	0.013 secs
1000	0.005 secs	164.414 secs	0.072 secs
10000	0.028 secs	2022.682 secs	0.213 secs

The results for the other two data sets, DBLP and IP flow, are similar and thus omitted due to space constraints. Also, the efficiency for the other types of queries have similar conclusion, which is thus omitted.

Scalable Approximate Query Tracking over Highly Distributed Data Streams *

Nikos Giatrakos
Technical University of Crete
ngiatrakos@softnet.tuc.gr

Antonios Deligiannakis
Technical University of Crete
adeli@softnet.tuc.gr

Minos Garofalakis
Technical University of Crete
minos@softnet.tuc.gr

ABSTRACT

The recently-proposed Geometric Monitoring (GM) method has provided a general tool for the distributed monitoring of arbitrary non-linear queries over streaming data observed by a collection of remote sites, with numerous practical applications. Unfortunately, GM-based techniques can suffer from serious scalability issues with increasing numbers of remote sites. In this paper, we propose novel techniques that effectively tackle the aforementioned scalability problems by exploiting a carefully designed sample of the remote sites for efficient approximate query tracking. Our novel sampling-based scheme utilizes a sample of cardinality proportional to $\sqrt{N}$ (compared to N for the original GM), where N is the number of sites in the network, to perform the monitoring process. Our experimental evaluation over a variety of real-life data streams demonstrates that our sampling-based techniques can significantly reduce the communication cost during distributed monitoring with controllable, predefined accuracy guarantees.

1. INTRODUCTION

Efficient data stream processing algorithms have become an integral part of real-time monitoring applications, from network traffic monitoring to financial or stock data analysis and sensor data querying. Streaming tuples are rapidly produced in a number of geographically dispersed sites (routers, ATMs, sensor nodes etc) and are *continuously* processed online to provide continuous up-to-date query answers destined to support decision making procedures such as DDoS attacks, fraudulent transactions, market trend predictions, and tsunami wave detection, in a timely manner. In such distributed settings, it is imperative to design efficient algorithms that reduce the communication burden during the continuous monitoring process [4, 7], since either the available bandwidth is limited, or data transmission is a crucial factor that reduces network lifetime (e.g., for battery-powered sensor nodes [28]).

The problem of efficiently tracking the value of a function (often compared to some predefined threshold) over the union of local streams in a large-scale distributed system, lies at the core of several recent research efforts [9, 35, 7, 8, 10, 38]. Monitoring tasks may involve functions that are simple linear aggregates, such as checking whether the sum of a distributed set of variables exceeds a predetermined threshold [12, 38], thresholded counts of items [23] or frequently occurring items in a set of distributed streams [29]. More complicated function monitoring may involve holistic aggregates [9, 38], self-join as well as stream-join operations [8, 15], or general, *non-linear* function tracking [35].

The original work of Sharfman et al. [35] is the first to propose a generic, Geometric Monitoring (GM) method for monitoring *any non-linear function* f over the global average of vectors maintained at the distributed sites, with respect to some threshold T, i.e., monitoring whether $f(\cdot) \lesseqgtr T$. The GM method is a very powerful technique that has already been exploited in a wide range of applications, including: (i) outlier detection in sensor networks [1], where the monitored function is any of the L_p norms, cosine similarity, Extended Jaccard Coefficient, or correlation coefficient; (ii) tracking range, norm-aggregate and join-aggregate queries [15, 25] over distributed data streams; (iii) monitoring fragmented skyline queries [30]; (iv) detecting machines that are about to become faulty in data centers [13]; and, (v) distributed online prediction [22] by dynamically monitoring the accuracy of distributed local models. In a nutshell, the GM method can offer a general solution to any useful monitoring task (expressed over the data collected by distributed data sources), in which continuous data communication to a central site is not feasible, due to either bandwidth or energy constraints.

The basic concept utilized in [35], in order to monitor general functions, is the identification and distributed monitoring of a subset of the input domain of f where this average vector may lie (rather than the function value itself). Each site maintains a local measurements vector, produced based on the data of the site and the monitored function. The local measurements vector helps determine a monitoring zone, constructed as a proper hypersphere, of the site. Each site then checks if the function at any point of its monitoring zone exceeds/falls below the threshold T, in which case it raises an alarm that is resolved by additional communication. Geometrically, the area of the input domain that needs to be monitored is equivalent to the convex hull of the sites' local measurements vectors, which is guaranteed to contain the average vector. The union of these hyperspheres is proven to cover this convex hull, which ensures that each point of the convex hull is monitored by at least one site. Figure 1 schematically presents the above concept, details will follow in Section 3. In terms of communication efficiency, central data collection is constantly postponed until at least one site finds that input points inside its local sphere may have caused the function to cross T. In the latter case, local vectors are

*This work was supported by the European Commission under ICT-FP7-FERARI-619491 (Flexible Event pRocessing for big dAta aRchItectures).

SIGMOD'16, June 26-July 01, 2016, San Francisco, CA, USA
© 2016 ACM. ISBN 978-1-4503-3531-7/16/06...$15.00
DOI: http://dx.doi.org/10.1145/2882903.2915225

collected in a central source, an up-to-date global average is computed and f is checked to assess whether it truly crossed T or not.

In this work, we demonstrate that, despite the generic nature of the GM method as a distributed tracking scheme, it faces significant scalability issues as the number of (distributed) remote sites increases. First, we show that increasing the network scale (i.e., the number of sites, N) increases the size of the monitored area (union of balls), thus resulting in an excessive number of central data collections, even when the tracked function has not actually crossed the threshold. Such unnecessary centralization choices are referred to as False Positives (FPs). Second, the communication cost of central data collections increases proportionally to N and, thus, the total bandwidth consumption throughout the tracking process increases significantly for large values of N. Third, the above problems become even more pronounced when the monitoring query is defined over the sum (rather than the average) of the local measurements vector at the sites. This is often the case in practice, e.g., when tracking relational join aggregates over frequency distribution vectors fragmented across the sites [15].

Having identified the degree of distribution (N) as a key limitation of the GM method, we introduce an algorithmic framework that exploits a small sample (proportional to only $O(\sqrt{N})$) of the sites to perform the monitoring process, and we formally study the properties of our sampling-based geometric scheme and how it addresses the scalability issues of GM. In a nutshell, our scalable approximate monitoring algorithm exploits *Horvitz-Thompson sampling estimators* [5, 34] over a carefully built sample of the sites in order to construct low-error approximations of the average vector; furthermore, it employs multi-dimensional tail-probability bounds and thorough geometric analysis to control the effect of these approximations on the accuracy of GM. Our approach can considerably decrease the amount of false positive data centralizations and the communication burden on the network at the cost of potentially causing a few False Negatives (FNs), i.e., missing a true threshold crossing of the monitored function. Note that if such missed *threshold violations* are quickly corrected (by appropriate detection) in the immediate future, and controlled in number, then they are generally acceptable in monitoring applications where GM is employed. For example, detecting machines likely to fail in the future in large data centers (in [13]), reporting when the size of a self-join query exceeds a given threshold (in [15, 25]), or detecting when distributed online learning models have become inaccurate (in [22]) with a slight delay (e.g., over the next few data collections) has little impact on the importance and gains of distributed GM function tracking, especially when the rate of such FNs is low and can be explicitly controlled.

We provide an extensive theoretical analysis exhibiting that the amount of such false negatives is controllable, given predefined accuracy guarantees based on the desired level of communication efficiency (which is directly linked to the site-sample size). Moreover, in our experiments (Section 6.4, also see Appendix) we also demonstrate that even if FNs occur (in a controlled manner), the missed threshold crossings are detected soon afterwards, most often in the next centralization decision. We re-iterate that the communication efficiency of our techniques is essential not only in applications collecting massive amounts of data (e.g., in IP-network monitoring [11]), but also in applications characterized by power and bandwidth restrictions, as in battery-powered wireless sensor nodes, where communication is the key determinant of sensor battery life [28]. Our contributions are summarized as follows:

- We point out the limitations of the GM approach in highly distributed environments, that result in excessive false positive data centralization decisions and prohibitive communication cost.

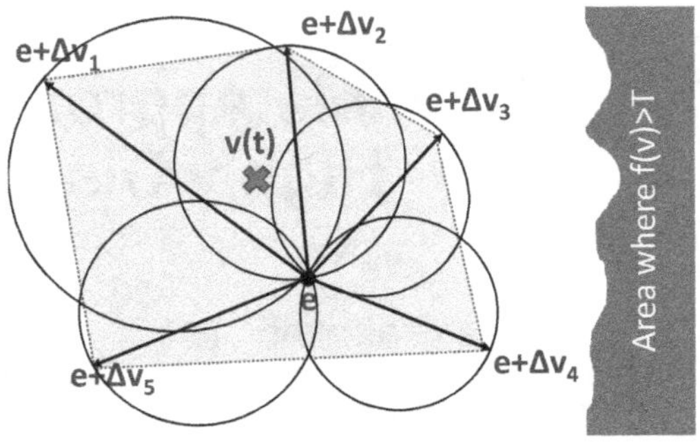

Figure 1: Illustration of GM at a given time point t. The monitored convex hull is depicted in gray, while the position of e and the current $v(t)$ are shown as well. Black spheres refer to the local constraints constructed by sites. Since none of them crosses the threshold surface, no synchronization is needed.

- Targeting the root of the above limitations, we introduce approximate algorithms for tracking any non-linear function that use only a carefully built sample of the network sites. Our techniques provide the ability to tune the sample size, and thus the anticipated communication cost according to application-defined approximation accuracy requirements. We provide an extensive theoretical analysis to formally quantify the accuracy vs. communication cost trade-off of our sampling-based techniques.
- We develop a methodology according to which a proper site sampling function is formed and parameterized. Our proposed sampling function yields a sample size proportional to only $O(\sqrt{N})$ of the total sites in the network, in contrast to $O(N)$ sites in the original GM method and its variants [16, 17].
- We conduct extensive experimentation on two real datasets, using a variety of different functions, threshold values and network sizes. Our performance comparisons are against not only the vanilla GM approach [35], but also against the balancing optimization proposed in [35] and the recently proposed prediction-based GM [16, 17]. Although these optimizations are orthogonal to our proposed framework, we show that in highly distributed environments our algorithms can ensure in most cases *one and up to two orders of magnitude less bandwidth consumption* compared to other methods, while also significantly reducing the *per site* cost (transmitted messages), even without exploiting any of these optimizations within our sampling-based scheme.

2. RELATED WORK

Abundant works have focused on efficiently performing monitoring tasks in distributed data streams. Some of them were already mentioned in Section 1, while [4] presents a recent survey on related techniques. Here, we concentrate on studies closely related to the GM framework and site sampling techniques.

Monitoring General Threshold Functions. The basic operation of the GM framework was introduced in [35]. Our work, after pointing out the shortcomings that arise in highly distributed data streams, proposes techniques to effectively confront existing scalability issues of the GM framework. [35] also proposes a balancing optimization to the basic scheme to further reduce the communication cost of their approach. However, the aforementioned balancing technique is merely a heuristic for which we experimentally (Section 6) show that is hardly adequate in highly distributed settings.

The GM framework has been enhanced in [36], where ellipsoidal instead of spherical local constraints are considered. These methods are orthogonal to the algorithms that we develop. However, [36] assumes that data follows a multivariate normal distribution; furthermore, [36] also suffers from scalability issues, since using ellipsoids instead of hyperspheres neither alters the fact that the higher N is, the higher the amount of the monitored area nor reduces the cost of a false positive central data collection.

The recently introduced prediction-based GM [16, 17] constitutes another technique that is orthogonal to the methods that we present in our work. However, [16, 17] heavily depends on accurate predictions of the local vectors maintained at each site. Nonetheless, accurately predicting several vector components over many sites becomes increasingly harder with the increase of the network scale. This is also demonstrated in our experimental evaluation.

A number of works design techniques that are geometric in nature but, contrary to our approach, focus only on specific types of functions. [32] considers functions with bounded deviation and introduces a tentative bound algorithm to monitor threshold queries in distributed databases (rather than distributed streams), while [33] focuses on vectorial top-k aggregation queries over distributed databases. Moreover, the work in [15] couples sketch summaries with the GM framework focusing on join aggregates, special cases of L_2-norms and range aggregates (e.g., quantiles, wavelets, and heavy-hitters over the streams). The work in [1] utilizes GM for outlier detection in sensor networks, reducing the problem to multiple monitoring tasks, with each task involving only the pair of nodes whose similarity is to be monitored. [24] proposes an approach, for monitoring *heterogeneous* streams by defining constraints tailored to fit the specific data distributions of sites.

Site Sampling Techniques. The sampling component that we develop as part of our tracking schemes allows the continuous monitoring on any generic function $f: \mathbb{R}^d \rightarrow \mathbb{R}$. This is the main breakthrough that distinguishes our contributions compared to individual site sampling techniques that can only handle linear functions such as counts and frequencies [39, 19, 20] or second frequency moments [27]. Besides this crucial distinction, our sampling component possesses more generic characteristics compared to existing site sampling approaches [39, 19, 20, 27]. These characteristics can be summarized as follows: (a) our analysis, from approximation quality issues to extracted estimators and expected communication savings is *multidimensional* in nature. On the contrary, [39, 19, 20, 27] define sampling schemes operating on a single dimension, (b) our techniques are destined to support *continuous monitoring* procedures while [39, 19] focus on one-shot queries, (c) Our algorithms do not incorporate any assumption about local input monotonicity or boundedness and are capable of handling *unbounded, non-monotonic local inputs* (updates). The techniques in [39, 19, 20, 27] assume bounded updates, while [39, 19, 20] are restricted to positive inputs only. (d) [39, 19, 20, 27] are focused on ensuring *accuracy relative* to the current global frequency or count which can be known only after acquiring the sample. Our algorithms abide by predetermined accuracy constraints, which is a necessary feature in our setting. Due to the above limitations, [39, 19, 20, 27] are not applicable in our setup.

3. PRELIMINARIES & MOTIVATION

In Section 3.1 we provide an overview of the Geometric Monitoring (GM) framework. Section 3.2 motivates the need for our approach, as it provides intuition on why the existing GM framework may lead to increased communication overhead when either the number of network sites increases, or when the monitored function is parameterized with the sum, rather than the global average, of local measurements vectors.

3.1 Geometric Monitoring Basics

As in previous works [9, 35, 6, 8, 36], we assume a distributed, two-tiered setting, where data arrives continuously at N geographically dispersed sites. At the top tier, a central coordinator exists that is capable of communicating with every site, while pairwise site communication is only allowed via the coordinating source. Each site S_i, $i \in [1..N]$ participating at the bottom tier periodically receives updates on its local stream and maintains a d-dimensional *local measurements vector* $v_i(t)$, capturing the current state of its local stream. The *global measurements vector (i.e., stream)* $v(t)$ at any given timestamp t, is computed as the average of $v_i(t)$ vectors, $v(t) = \frac{\sum_{i=1}^{N} v_i(t)}{N}$. The coordinator aims to continuously monitor if the value of a function $f(v(t))$, parameterized by the global average $v(t)$, lies above/below a given threshold T. We term the area of the input domain where $f(v(t)) = T$ as the *threshold surface*.

Assume that at a previous time instant t_s, the coordinator has collected the local $v_i(t_s)$ vectors. Using $e(t_s)$ to distinguish the global average $v(t_s)$ at t_s, the coordinator computes $e(t_s) = \frac{\sum_{i=1}^{N} v_i(t_s)}{N}$ at that time, subsequently broadcasting $e(t_s)$ to the sites in the bottom tier. The previous process is referred to as a *synchronization* step. Note that, until the next synchronization, the coordinator's view of the global vector stays constant at $e(t) = e(t_s)$. Following [35], upon receiving $e(t)$, sites keep up receiving updates of their local streams and accordingly maintain their $v_i(t)$ vectors. At any given timestamp, each site S_i individually computes a *deviation vector* $\Delta v_i(t) = v_i(t) - v_i(t_s)$, which depicts the change that the local vector has undergone since t_s. By attaching the deviation vector to $e(t)$, sites compute their *drift vectors* as $e(t) + \Delta v_i(t)$. Since $v(t) = \frac{\sum_{i=1}^{N} v_i(t)}{N} = e(t) + \frac{\sum_{i=1}^{N}(v_i(t) - v_i(t_s))}{N} = \frac{\sum_{i=1}^{N}(e(t) + \Delta v_i(t))}{N}$, $v(t)$ constitutes a convex combination of the drift vectors.

Consequently, $v(t)$ will always lie in the convex hull formed by the $\Delta v_i(t)$ vectors translated by $e(t)$, as depicted in Figure 1 for $d = 2$, $N = 5$: $v(t) \in Conv\ (e(t) + \Delta v_1(t), \ldots, e(t) + \Delta v_N(t))$. If the convex hull does not intersect the *inadmissible* area of the input domain (on the right of Figure 1), where the monitored inequality is reversed (from $f(v(t)) > T$ to $f(v(t)) < T$ or vice versa), it is assured that $v(t)$ cannot lie in that area either. Hence, our monitoring problem is transformed to how to decide in a distributed manner whether the convex hull intersects the threshold surface.

It has been proven [35] that if sites locally construct hyperspheres $B(e(t) + \frac{1}{2}\Delta v_i(t), \frac{1}{2}\|\Delta v_i(t)\|)$, centered at $e(t) + \frac{1}{2}\Delta v_i(t)$ with radius $\frac{1}{2}\|\Delta v_i(t)\|$, then:

$$Conv(e(t) + \Delta v_1(t), \ldots, e(t) + \Delta v_N(t)) \subset \bigcup_{i=1}^{N} B(e(t) + \tfrac{1}{2}\Delta v_i(t), \tfrac{1}{2}\|\Delta v_i(t)\|)$$

That is, the union of these hyperspheres is always guaranteed to cover the convex hull of the translated local drifts (in any dimensionality). Thus, having constructed $B(e(t) + \frac{1}{2}\Delta v_i(t), \frac{1}{2}\|\Delta v_i(t)\|)$, each site individually checks for an intersection of its local sphere with the threshold surface. In case an intersection exists in at least one S_i, a *local violation* occurs at S_i indicating that the convex hull and, thus, $v(t)$ **may** have crossed the threshold surface. Hence, a synchronization takes place where the coordinator collects the $v_i(t)$ vectors and assesses whether $f(v(t))$ truly switched sides ($\lesseqgtr$) with T. It then computes the new $e(t)$ and communicates it back to the sites. From this point forward, the tracking process can proceed as described above. If no local violation occurs (as in the example of Figure 1), then no communication is necessary.

EXAMPLE 1. *Consider a number of sensors in a server room monitoring in real-time whether uniform relative Humidity (rH) conditions exist for all the machines to operate normally. Too dry*

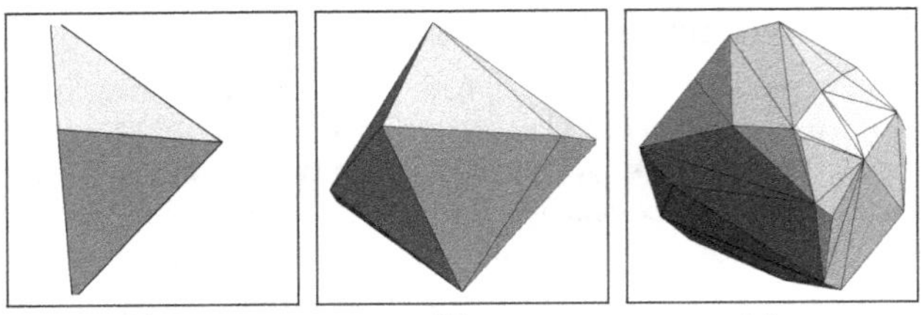

(a) $Conv(e+\Delta v_1,\ldots,e+\Delta v_5)$ (b) $Conv(e+\Delta v_1,\ldots,e+\Delta v_{10})$ (c) $Conv(e+\Delta v_1,\ldots,e+\Delta v_{100})$

Figure 2: The effect of network scale on the monitored area ($d = 3$). All Δv_i vectors are randomly chosen from the unit cube, the front view of which is the box included in each figure. As the network scale increases, more Δv_i vectors grow on the $d-$dimensional plane. Inevitably, the convex hull that needs to be monitored is enlarged favoring FP decisions.

Table 1: Frequently Used Symbols

Symbol	Description
N	The number of sites of the bottom tier
d	Dimensionality of the input domain
S_i	The i-th site, $S_i \in \{S_1,\ldots,S_N\}$
t_s	Time-point of the last synchronization
$v_i(t)$	Local measurements vector at S_i at time t
$\Delta v_i(t)$	Deviation vector at S_i at time t (equals $v_i(t)-v_i(t_s)$)
$v(t), \hat{v}(t)$	Global average & its statistic estimator at time t
$e(t)=v(t_s)$	Global average vector computed after a synchronization
$B(c,\rho)$	Hypersphere centered at c with ρ sized radius
(ε,δ)	Approximation pair denoting that $\hat{v}(t)$ should lie within ε distance from $v(t)$ with probability as least $1-\delta$
g_i	Sampling function $0 \le g_i \le 1$ for site S_i
ε_T	Minimum distance of $e(t)$ from the threshold surface

air will result in the build up of static electricity on the systems, while high humidity slowly damages equipment. To ensure uniform rH, the application continuously checks $Var(v(t)) > T$, where Var denotes the variance function [13]. Each sensor maintains a periodically updated local vector $v_i(t) = [c_i^2(t), c_i(t)]$, with $c_i(t)$ being the recent rH measurement at S_i. Variance is computed by $Var(v(t)) = \frac{1}{N}\sum_{i=1}^{N} c_i^2 + (\frac{1}{N}\sum_{i=1}^{N} c_i)^2$ and thus $v(t) = \left[\frac{1}{N}\sum_{i=1}^{N} c_i^2, \frac{1}{N}\sum_{i=1}^{N} c_i\right]$. If $v_i(t_s)$ is the last rH value S_i communicated to the coordinator, $\Delta v_i(t) = [c_i^2(t) - c_i^2(t_s),\ c_i(t) - c_i(t_s)]$. Given these, local spheres are constructed and potential threshold crossings are assessed.

Communication savings are ensured by postponing a synchronization until some site finds its local sphere intersecting the threshold surface. Also note that the convex hull or its superset, the union of local spheres, may cross the threshold surface, while the actual position of $v(t)$ may not be in the intersecting part. As a result, the framework may cause synchronizations when $f(v(t))$ has not crossed the threshold (false positives). Table 1 summarizes the main notation used in this paper.

3.2 Existing Scalability Issues

We now explain why the GM framework may result in increased communication in either highly distributed networks, or in cases where the monitored function is parameterized with the sum of the local measurements vectors.

High N values $\Rightarrow$ proneness to FP synchronizations. As already described, the area that GM needs to track is the convex hull $Conv(e+\Delta v_1(t),\ \ldots,\ e+\Delta v_N(t))$. It is not difficult to see that the more sites participate in the distributed monitoring process (and, thus, contribute their $e+\Delta v_i(t)$ in the formation of this convex hull), the larger the tracked area will be. Figure 2 schematically exhibits the effect of progressively increasing the network scale from $N=5$ sites to $N=10$ and $N=100$ in a 3-d space by randomly picking additional Δv_is from the unit cube. Larger values of N yield a convex hull that tends to cover the entire unit cube (boxed area in Fig. 2). Moreover, the hyperspheres maintained by each site in order to include the expanded convex hull will cover an even larger, compared to the expanded convex hull, area of the input domain because $Conv(e(t)+\Delta v_1(t),\ \ldots,\ e(t)+\Delta v_N(t))$ is a subset of $\bigcup_{i=1}^{N} B(e(t)+\frac{1}{2}\Delta v_i(t),\ \frac{1}{2}\|\Delta v_i(t)\|)$. This raises the potential for a larger number of FP synchronization decisions as the number of sites increases.

Note that the cost of a FP synchronization decision is equivalent to $N+1$ messages, assuming the coordinator is equipped with broadcast capabilities, or $2N$ otherwise, and that all sites are required to participate in this process. This not only increases the total communication cost per FP as the number of sites N increases, but also increases the cost per site, since a site transmits messages each time at least one site exhibits a local violation.

Problematic application on monitoring sum-parameterized functions. Consider the case where the function that needs to be monitored is parameterized with the sum rather than the global average, i.e., $f(v_{sum}(t)) \lesseqgtr T$ with $v_{sum}(t) = N \cdot v(t) = \sum_{i=1}^{N} v_i(t)$. Such functions, for instance, include L_2 norms during approximate function monitoring queries [15, 17], or statistics like the Mutual Information function in news monitoring applications [16].

Let this time $e_{sum}(t) = v_{sum}(t_s)$. The above equation shows that $v_{sum}(t)$ can be expressed as a convex combination of $(e(t)+\Delta v_i(t))$ vectors scaled by N since $N \cdot (e(t)+\Delta v_i(t)) = e_{sum}(t) + N \cdot \Delta v_i(t)$. As a consequence, $v_{sum}(t)$ lies inside the scaled convex hull $Conv(N\cdot\ (e(t)\ +\Delta v_1(t)),\ldots,N\cdot\ (e(t)\ +\Delta v_N(t)))$.

We can now perform the monitoring in a slightly modified way from the original GM scheme of Section 3.1. The difference is that the new local constraint in each site S_i is scaled by N, i.e., $B(N\cdot e(t)+\frac{N}{2}\Delta v_i(t),\ \frac{N}{2}\|\Delta v_i(t)\|)$ which is checked so as to assess whether it invades the threshold surface. Consequently, in highly distributed settings, the degree of distribution N has once again an undesirable impact on the size of the local constraints, increasing the proneness of the framework to FP synchronizations.

4. SCALABLE QUERY TRACKING

Having shown that the degree of distribution N is the factor that renders GM practically inefficient, we now design a sampling-based framework that overcomes these scalability issues. Section 4.1 first formally presents a set of requirements that any candidate sampling-based scheme for GM monitoring should adhere to, in order to both guarantee efficiency in terms of bandwidth consumption and compliance with application-defined accuracy requirements.

Then, in Section 4.2, we present our generic sampling-based GM scheme in detail. The intuition behind our approach is that, instead of monitoring the entire convex hull formed by the N sites, we choose to track a narrower convex hull composed of a carefully-crafted random sample of sites. The latter area constructs a subset of $Conv(\{e+\Delta v_i\} : \forall S_i \in \{S_1,\ldots,S_N\})$ reducing the tracked space and warding off FP synchronizations. For ease of exposition, we henceforth omit the temporal reference t where appropriate.

4.1 Efficiency and Accuracy Requirements

In addition to choosing fewer sites to reduce the monitored area, our sampling-based geometric scheme should be able to *guarantee improved communication efficiency* by ensuring that its inscribed local constraints are fully contained within the local constraints $\bigcup_{i=1}^{N} B(e+\frac{1}{2}\Delta v_i, \frac{1}{2}\|\Delta v_i\|)$ of the original GM method (Section 3.1). This guarantees that the area tracked by the sampled sites does not cross the threshold surface before the union of balls of the conventional GM does and, thus, additional FP synchronizations **cannot** be caused.

REQUIREMENT 1. **[Efficiency]** *Let Sur_{sample} denote the area monitored by a candidate sampling-based monitoring scheme. To guarantee efficiency by reducing FP synchronizations, inclusion $Sur_{sample} \subseteq \bigcup_{i=1}^{N} B(e+\frac{1}{2}\Delta v_i, \frac{1}{2}\|\Delta v_i\|)$ should hold.*

Since the monitoring process utilizes a small sample (subset) of the sites available in the network, it will be approximate in nature. At any given time t, our sampling-based geometric techniques monitor an *unbiased* (i.e., $E(\hat{v}(t)) = v(t)$) estimation $\hat{v}(t)$ of the true global average $v(t)$ originating from only a sample $K \subseteq \{S_1, \ldots S_N\}$ of sites' local vectors. We wish to keep the estimation error controllable and tunable based on *a priori* defined accuracy requirements. To control the approximation error, we employ an (ε,δ) approximation scheme. More precisely, for a priori given $0<\delta\leq 1$, $\varepsilon>0$ we shall require $v \in B(\hat{v},\varepsilon)$ with high probability, at least $1-\delta$.

REQUIREMENT 2. **[Approximation Quality]** *At any given time, the estimation $\hat{v}$ monitored by the sampled sites should not exceed $\varepsilon-$ distance from the true v, with high probability $1-\delta$; that is, for given $0<\delta\leq 1$, $\varepsilon>0$: $P(v \notin B(\hat{v},\varepsilon)) \leq \delta$.*

Due to the fact that $v(t)$ is monitored in an approximate way tuned according to (ε,δ), it is possible that a synchronization is prevented while $v(t)$ truly switched side with respect to the threshold surface. Our sampling-based scheme should enable applications to explicitly tune the probability P_{FN} of such False Negative (FN) events. This requires an additional (application-defined) input parameter apart from (ε,δ).

Nonetheless, specifying a triplet of parameters two of which refer to the input domain rather than the function value may be confusing from an application viewpoint. Application accuracy requirements should be expressed in a simple way that abstracts the actual details of the input domain of the tracking process. While it is more natural for the end user to directly specify P_{FN}, for ease of presentation we assume that the parameter specified is the δ parameter of Requirement 2. We demonstrate in Section 5 that P_{FN} is directly linked to δ. Then, our scheme can accordingly tune not only the probability of a FN, i.e., P_{FN}, but also the approximation quality in the (ε,δ) scheme. To do so, ε should be expressed as a function of δ, i.e., $\varepsilon = \varepsilon(\delta)$.

REQUIREMENT 3. **[Tunable Accuracy]** *At any given time, the proposed sampling-based monitoring algorithm should possess the ability to receive a sole tolerance value $0<\delta\leq 1$ and self-tune its Approximation Quality i.e., (ε,δ) and FN rate i.e., P_{FN}.*

Hence, we assume that the application expresses its monitoring needs in the form: $f(v(t)) \gtrless T, \delta: 0<\delta\leq 1$. We then proceed in describing the generic operation of our sampling-based framework.

4.2 Our Generic Sampling-Based Scheme

We now present our sampling-based GM algorithm and demonstrate how it satisfies Requirements 1-3. A key idea in our scheme is to independently sample each site S_i with a different probability g_i that depends on various factors. Our discussion in this section assumes that these sampling probabilities g_i have been determined, deferring the details and analysis of the g_i computation to Section 5.

Algorithmic Sketch. Consider that at a previous time, a synchronization has taken place, as described in Section 3.1, and that e has been transmitted to all $S_i \in \{S_1, \ldots, S_N\}$. At any subsequent timestamp, each S_i keeps receiving updates of its local vector v_i and computes Δv_i. In our sampling scheme, S_i constructs a local constraint in the form of a hypersphere only if it finds itself included in the sample K of sites participating in the monitoring process, i.e., $S_i \in K$. In order to determine if $S_i \in K$, each site independently flips a biased coin with success probability of g_i, where $g_i \in [0,1]$ is a sampling function independently computed by each site. Each $S_i \in K$ inscribes a sphere $B(e+\frac{1}{2}\Delta v_i, \frac{1}{2}\|\Delta v_i\|)$ which is checked for threshold crossing. In case at least one $S_i \in K$ detects a threshold crossing of its local constraint, it calls for a synchronization. During the synchronization, the coordinator initially broadcasts a message requiring only the sampled sites to contribute their Δv_i vectors. Using these vectors, it derives an unbiased estimate $\hat{v}$ (using Estimator 1 below) of v and checks (Requirement 2) whether $B(\hat{v},\varepsilon)$ crosses T. If it does not, then the coordinator deduces that this was a FP alarm with probability $1-\delta$ and the tracking continues unaffected. Otherwise, a full synchronization takes place, where also all $S_i \notin K$ contribute their Δv_is for a new e vector to be computed and communicated to the underlying sites. In the latter case, the coordinator believes that a true threshold violation may have taken place and probes the whole set of sites to compute the exact value of e. This is required to avoid an additive error in the approximation of $\hat{v}$ (see Estimator 1) as the tracking process continues.

We now provide the details of our monitoring scheme, explain our design choices (as described in the above algorithmic sketch), and discuss the accuracy guarantees of our technique. In each of these steps, we examine the satisfiability of Requirements 1-3 in conjunction with our algorithmic sketch. For ease of exposition, we start our discussion with Requirement 2.

Monitored Estimator and Approximation Quality Requirement. Consider a multivariate random variable $\Delta' v_i = \frac{\Delta v_i}{g_i}$ with probability g_i, and zero otherwise. Notice that $E[\Delta' v_i]$ is a $d-$dimensional vector and $E[\Delta' v_i] = [E[\Delta' v_{i1}], \cdots, E[\Delta' v_{id}]]$, where $\Delta' v_{ij}$ denotes the j-th component (dimension) of the vector $\Delta' v_i$. We demonstrate in Lemma 1 that, based on the drift vectors $e+\frac{\Delta v_i}{g_i}$ of the set K, an unbiased estimate $\hat{v}$ of the global average v can be derived at any given time stamp t utilizing a *Horvitz-Thompson Estimator* [5, 34]:

$$\hat{v} = e + \frac{\sum_{i=1}^{N} \Delta' v_i}{N} = e + \frac{\sum\limits_{S_i \in K} \frac{\Delta v_i}{g_i}}{N} \tag{1}$$

Note that the global average is $v = e + \Delta v$, with $\Delta v = \sum_{i=1}^{N} \Delta v_i / N$. Hence, Estimator 1 estimates Δv as $\hat{\Delta v} = \sum_{S_i \in K} \frac{\Delta v_i}{g_i} / N$. The estimator weighs each sampled site with $1/g_i$. The reason for this is fairly intuitive: If site S_i, which is sampled with probability g_i, individually appears in the sample, then, on average, we expect to have $1/g_i$ sites with similar probabilities in the full population (since $g_i \cdot 1/g_i = 1$); thus, the single occurrence of S_i in the sample is essentially a "representative" of $1/g_i$ sites in the full population [21, 34].

LEMMA 1. *For Estimator 1 the following hold:*
(a) Estimator 1 is an unbiased estimator of v when sampling $\forall S_i \in \{S_1, \ldots, S_N\}$ *with* $0 \leq g_i \leq 1$.
(b) $E[\hat{v}] \in Conv(\, e + \Delta v_1, \ldots, e + \Delta v_N)$
(c) $\hat{v} \in Conv(\{e + \frac{\Delta v_i}{g_i}\} : \forall S_i \in K)$

PROOF. See Appendix □

Since Estimator 1 is unbiased, we can utilize standard tail inequalities [14] to satisfy Requirement 2. Note that we do not assume independence of individual dimensions of either local, or global vectors that we examine. Nonetheless, according to our algorithmic sketch, S_is independently decide to include themselves in K or not, based on g_i. The Vector Bernstein's Inequality [2] (presented below) will be particularly useful in our subsequent analysis.

Vector Bernstein's Inequality [2]. Let $y_1, \ldots, y_N$ be independent random vectors with $E[y_i] = 0$. Let $B > 0$ denote an upper bound on $\|y_i\|$ (i.e., $\|y_i\| \leq B$), and let $\sigma^2 \geq \sum_{i=1}^{N} E[\|y_i\|^2]$. Then, for all $0 < \delta \leq 1$ and $0 \leq \varepsilon \leq \sigma^2/B$ such that $\varepsilon = (1 + \sqrt{\ell n(1/\delta)}) \cdot \sigma$:

$$P(\|\sum_{i=1}^{N} y_i\| \geq \varepsilon) \leq \delta \quad \square \qquad (2)$$

The inequality states that if we add N random vectors of bounded length which move around zero, their sum will produce a vector placed near (no farther than ε) to zero with probability at least $1 - \delta$. The proximity (ε) of the vector sum to zero depends on an upper bound σ on the overall standard deviation [1] and the chosen probability bound δ. Note that the above bound does not depend on the dimensionality d of the vectors. In our case, each y_i corresponds to $\frac{\Delta' v_i - \Delta v_i}{N}$. Moreover, $B \geq \{\|\frac{\Delta v_i}{N}\|, \|\frac{\Delta v_i}{g_i \cdot N} - \frac{\Delta v_i}{N}\|\}\ \forall S_i \in \{S_1, \ldots, S_N\}$ depending on whether $S_i \in K$, or not. Additionally, simple calculations show that $\sigma^2 \geq \sum_{i=1}^{N} E[\|y_i\|^2]$, as required by the Vector Bernstein's Inequality, yields $\sigma^2 \geq \sum_{i=1}^{N} \frac{\|\Delta v_i\|^2}{N^2 \cdot g_i} - \sum_{i=1}^{N} \frac{\|\Delta v_i\|^2}{N^2}$.

Using Inequality 2 we partially satisfy Requirement 2, since we have not yet discussed how B, σ and, thus, ε can be set a priori. In Section 5 we will choose a sampling function providing an ε that is upper bounded by a constant value known to each S_i before a monitoring phase begins. Based on this, we can fully satisfy Requirement 2.

Monitoring Scheme and Efficiency Requirement. Based on Lemma 1, sampled sites need to monitor $Conv(\{e + \frac{\Delta v_i}{g_i}\} : \forall S_i \in K)$ where (i) the estimation $\hat{v}$ of v lies, as Lemma 1(c) shows, and (ii) the true global average v is expected to lie since $E[\hat{v}] = v$. For ease of exposition, we assume that $\hat{v} = v$ and we will loosen this assumption later in this section. In order to track $Conv(\{e + \frac{\Delta v_i}{g_i}\} : \forall S_i \in K)$ according to the existing GM framework, each $S_i \in K$ would need to construct local hyperspheres of the form $B(e + \frac{1}{2}\frac{\Delta v_i}{g_i}, \frac{1}{2}\|\frac{\Delta v_i}{g_i}\|)$, with the union of these local hyperspheres covering the convex hull that encompasses $\hat{v}$. However, these hyperspheres are larger (by a factor of $1/g_i$) than the ones mentioned in our algorithmic sketch. Let us now examine the reason for this important difference.

Compared to the basic GM method (Section 3.1), the above scheme omits hyperspheres of sites that do not get sampled, thus reducing the monitored area. On the other hand, since $g_i \leq 1$, the hyperspheres $B(e + \frac{1}{2}\frac{\Delta v_i}{g_i}, \frac{1}{2}\|\frac{\Delta v_i}{g_i}\|)$ possess larger radii than the $B(e + \frac{1}{2}\Delta v_i, \frac{1}{2}\|\Delta v_i\|)$ used in basic GM, and the centers of the spheres are also different. As an example, Figure 3(a) depicts the area that needs to be monitored, which corresponds to the balls of sites S_2 and S_3 covering the shaded part of Figure 3(a), according to Lemma 1. Hence, the current scheme may on one hand reduce FP decisions due to the fact that it uses fewer Δv_i vectors in its convex hull, but on the other hand it may also cause more FP synchronizations because it constructs larger spherical constraints centered at different positions as shown in Figure 3(a). In other words, it may perform better than GM, but this is in no way guaranteed. Obviously, this violates Requirement 1. The following lemma builds on Lemma 1, and demonstrates how our sampling-based monitoring scheme can be validly modified to abide by Requirement 1.

[1] Note that $\sigma^2 \geq \sum_{i=1}^{N} E[\|y_i\|^2] \geq \sum_{i=1}^{N} E[\|y_i\|^2] - (E[\|y_i\|])^2 = \sum_{i=1}^{N} Var[\|y_i\|]$, therefore σ^2 bounds the sum of individual length variances.

LEMMA 2. *Provided that* $\hat{v} = v$,

$$\hat{v} \in Conv(\{e + \Delta v_i\} : \forall S_i \in K)$$

PROOF. See Appendix □

Lemma 2 shows that for the sampled sites to monitor the position of $\hat{v} = v$, they need to construct local constraints of the form $B(e + \frac{1}{2}\Delta v_i, \frac{1}{2}\|\Delta v_i\|)$ as we described in our algorithmic sketch. These balls possess the same center and radius as those in the initial GM scheme of Section 3.1 and we can choose g_i such that $|K| \ll N$. Hence, $\bigcup_{S_i \in K} B(e + \frac{1}{2}\Delta v_i, \frac{1}{2}\|\Delta v_i\|) \subseteq \bigcup_{i=1}^{N} B(e + \frac{1}{2}\Delta v_i, \frac{1}{2}\|\Delta v_i\|)$. Figure 3(b) depicts the improvement that Lemma 2 yields in the construction of local balls especially compared to the local constraints induced by Lemma 1 in Figure 3(a). Hence, the new local constraints adhere to Requirement 1 and no additional FPs can be provided by the sampling based scheme. Therefore, Lemma 2 was actually employed in our algorithmic sketch presented at the beginning of this section.

We now focus on removing the $\hat{v} = v$ assumption. Even if $\hat{v} = v$ does not hold, from Inequality 2, we know that with high probability, at least $1 - \delta$, $v \in B(\hat{v}, \varepsilon)$. When $v \in B(\hat{v}, \varepsilon)$, the worst case scenario during the monitoring process appears when $\hat{v}$ is located on the periphery of $\bigcup_{S_i \in K} B(e + \frac{1}{2}\Delta v_i, \frac{1}{2}\|\Delta v_i\|)$. Then, the fact that $\hat{v}$ lies on the edge of some GM sphere, combined with the fact that $v \in B(\hat{v}, \varepsilon)$, guarantees that the largest distance v may travel outside the union of the spheres is ε. The first option to handle this situation is to expand the radius of the balls inscribed by sites to $B(e + \frac{1}{2}\Delta v_i, \frac{1}{2}\|\Delta v_i\| + \varepsilon)$ so that with probability $1 - \delta$ they include $v \in B(\hat{v}, \varepsilon)$. However, if we do that, Requirement 1 is no longer satisfied. The second option is to allow such an error, which may, however, lead to a FN decision. We opt for the second option and focus on its effect on the FN rate.

Satisfying the Tunable Accuracy Requirement. According to our algorithmic sketch and our analysis so far, a FN decision may occur in the following mutually exclusive cases:

(a) During the distributed monitoring process, upon judging potential threshold crossings of local hyperspheres that were not expanded by an ε factor (as previously described). We consider two sub-cases: In subcase (a1), the local constraint $B(e + \frac{1}{2}\Delta v_i, \frac{1}{2}\|\Delta v_i\|)$ of every site $S_i \in K$ has a minimum distance from the threshold surface larger than ε. Subcase (a2) covers the case when the above condition does not hold for at least one $S_i \in K$.

(b) During the synchronization process, where the coordinator probes the sample and uses $B(\hat{v}, \varepsilon)$ to determine if a full synchronization is necessary.

Note however, that these types of FNs cannot occur simultaneously since case (b) can happen only when a threshold crossing is de-

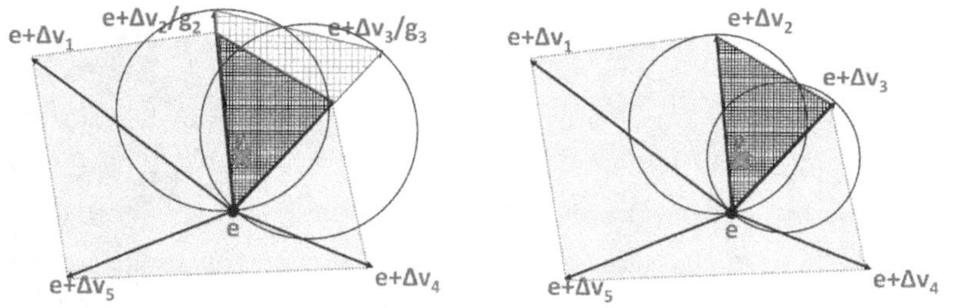

(a) Sampling-Based tracking according to Lemma 1, violating Requirement 1 ($S_2, S_3 \in K$)

(b) Requirement 1 abiding sampling-based scheme in Lemma 2 ($S_2, S_3 \in K$)

Figure 3: Sampling-based monitoring over distributed data streams. Shaded areas belong to the convex hull that needs to be monitored according to Lemma 1 and Lemma 2, respectively. The gray area corresponds to the convex hull that is formed by the whole set of sites in the network (N=5).

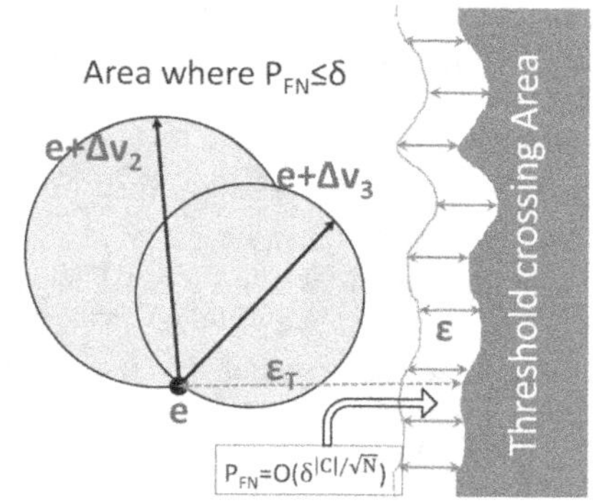

Figure 4: P_{FN} wrt the distance from the threshold surface. In the white (left) area $P_{FN} \leq \delta$ since no ball approaches the surface more than ε.

tected during the monitoring process. We set out our discussion from case (a), which is more complicated.

Case (a1). If $v \in B(\hat{v}, \varepsilon)$, whenever every S_i's $\in K$ local constraint $B(e + \frac{1}{2}\Delta v_i, \frac{1}{2}\|\Delta v_i\|)$ has a minimum distance from the threshold surface larger than ε as shown in Figure 4, our choice of not expanding these spheres to $B(e + \frac{1}{2}\Delta v_i, \frac{1}{2}\|\Delta v_i\| + \varepsilon)$ does not affect the quality of the monitoring process. This is true because even if v lies outside the monitored area, with high probability $1 - \delta$ it has not changed side with respect to T because $v \in B(\hat{v}, \varepsilon)$. Therefore, when the minimum distance of the union of balls of sampled sites from the threshold surface is larger than ε (see Fig. 4), we cannot have a FN decision unless $v \notin B(\hat{v}, \varepsilon)$. The latter has a probability of δ and $P_{FN} \leq \delta$.

Case (a2). We now examine how the P_{FN} probability is bounded when there exists at least one site $S_i \in K$ with $B(e + \frac{1}{2}\Delta v_i, \frac{1}{2}\|\Delta v_i\|)$ placed closer to the threshold surface than ε. Looking at Figure 4, this corresponds to the zone around the threshold surface marked with an ε and corresponding double arrows. If there exists $S_i \in K$ with $B(e + \frac{1}{2}\Delta v_i, \frac{1}{2}\|\Delta v_i\|)$ entering the ε-zone in Figure 4, this means that v is likely to have crossed the threshold surface despite $v \in B(\hat{v}, \varepsilon)$. Let ε_T (red, dotted line in Fig. 4) denote the minimum distance of e from the threshold surface, computed once during a full synchronization process and kept until the upcoming one. Simple calculations show that if no site S_i has a $\|\Delta v_i\| > \varepsilon_T$, the global average cannot have switched side with respect to the threshold surface and no FN decision can occur. Hence, for a FN decision to occur we need *at least one* sampled site to enter the ε-zone and there should exist a number (*at least one*) of sites in the network that have drifted more that ε_T distance from e and *are not* included in K. If at least one of the threshold crossing sites is sampled then a local violation will be detected and no FN can occur at this stage. Therefore, assuming that at a given time point $|C|$ sites cross the threshold, $P_{FN} \leq \prod_{S_i \in C} (1 - g_i)$, since a FP will occur when none of these $|C|$ sites is included in the sample. Fortunately, as we are going to show in the upcoming section, for a properly constructed g_i, even in case that for some sites their drift vectors enter the ε-zone, P_{FN} has an upper bound proportional to $\delta^{\frac{|C|}{\sqrt{N}}}$ which decreases exponentially with the number of threshold crossing sites. Moreover, as we show in Section 5, this bound on P_{FN} is pessimistic, as it is computed on the pathological case where for all $S_i \in C$, $\|\Delta v_i\| = \varepsilon_T$. What happens in practice, because v is the average of the drift vectors, is that in order for v to cross the threshold surface, the threshold surface is crossed by either several moderate in length drift vectors (in which case $|C|$ is large), or by fewer but larger drift vectors. In the latter case, we show in Section 5 that the sampling probability of such sites is larger, making it less likely that they will all be omitted from the sample.

Case (b). Please recall that in our algorithmic sketch we mentioned that during a synchronization the coordinator, in its effort to reduce the cost of a potential FP decision, first attempts to save communication by broadcasting a message and requiring only the sampled sites to contribute their Δv_i vectors in order to compute $\hat{v}$. It then checks $B(\hat{v}, \varepsilon)$ for threshold crossing before allowing a full synchronization. In this phase, an erroneous FN decision may occur only when $v \notin B(\hat{v}, \varepsilon)$ which happens with probability at most δ and thus $P_{FN} \leq \delta$.

Based on Inequality 2, we set $\varepsilon = (1 + \sqrt{\ell n(1/\delta)}) \cdot \sigma$. In the next section we provide a sampling function that upper bounds σ by a constant value and tune ε according to the application defined δ. Having bound σ, we showed in this section that P_{FN} can be also bounded by δ. Thus, Requirement 3 is satisfied as well. In the next section we further exhibit that based on the constructed g_i, δ also successfully tunes the sample cardinality $|K|$ and, thus the anticipated savings of the sampling-based scheme in terms of FP reduction and bandwidth preservation.

5. SETTING THE SAMPLING FUNCTION

In sampling-based geometric monitoring, each S_i individually decides whether to include itself in K or not, using a sampling function $0 \leq g_i \leq 1$. Our sampling-based scheme can accommodate any g_i that samples the d−dimensional local vectors of sites. However, not all functions yield desired properties for our scheme. We next present in a step-by-step fashion the elements of a suitable g_i and reason about our choices based on the properties that these elements attribute to our scheme. We eventually derive a proper g_i that simultaneously (a) ensures a sample of $O(\ell n(1/\delta)\sqrt{N})$ size, (b) upper bounds σ and, thus, ε by an a priori (before acquiring the sample) constant value controlled by δ. In that, g_i allows the sampling-based scheme to comply with Requirement 2, (c) given the previous upper bound that determines the size of the ε−zone (Fig. 4), g_i tunes the probability of false negatives (Requirement 3).

• $\|\Delta v_i\|$ **should be included in the nominator of** g_i**.** According to our algorithmic sketch in Section 4.2, upon a local violation the coordinator probes only sites $S_i \in K$ and checks $B(\hat{v}, \varepsilon)$ for threshold crossing in order to call for a full synchronization, or not. To inscribe $B(\hat{v}, \varepsilon)$, the radius ε should obtain (be bounded by) a constant value. In order to come up with a constant value for ε, according to Inequality 2, we need to bound σ. In Section 4.2, we showed that $\sigma^2 \geq \sum_{i=1}^{N} \frac{\|\Delta v_i\|^2}{N^2 \cdot g_i} - \sum_{i=1}^{N} \frac{\|\Delta v_i\|^2}{N^2}$. Apart from g_i, the only variable term included in the latter inequality is the size of the drift $\|\Delta v_i\|$. To eliminate this variable term, $\|\Delta v_i\|$ should be included in the nominator of g_i (calculations follow in the upcoming Inequality 3).

• **$\ell n(1/\delta)$ needs to be included in the nominator of g_i.** As mentioned in Requirement 3, ε should be tunable by (a function of) δ, i.e., $\varepsilon = \varepsilon(\delta)$, so as to allow the size of the $\varepsilon-$ zone to be controlled by the application. Hence, $\ell n(1/\delta)$ needs to be included in the nominator of g_i. Due to the presence of $(1 + \sqrt{\ell n(1/\delta)}) \cdot \sigma$ $(= \varepsilon)$ in Inequality 2, we will later show in Equation 4 that placing $\ell n(1/\delta)$ in the nominator of the function allows the application to express the size of the $\varepsilon-$zone as a *fraction* (< 1) of the bound of the approximation error between $\hat{v}$ and v.

• **A term N^x, $x > 0$ is needed in the denominator of g_i.** To ensure communication savings and reduced monitored area, we need $|K| \ll N$. The expected sample cardinality of our scheme is given by $\sum_{i=1}^{N} g_i$. Since this sum iterates over all the N terms, to ensure $|K| \ll N$, we need a term N^x in the denominator of g_i in order to obtain an expected communication cost of $O(N^{1-x})$. What is then required is to compute a proper value for $x > 0$.

• **A constant U such that $U > h \cdot \|\Delta v_i\|$, $h > 1$ is necessary in the denominator of g_i.** Having required that $\|\Delta v_i\|$ lies in the nominator of g_i, to achieve $O(N^{1-x})$ cardinality, the presence of a constant U such that $U > h \cdot \|\Delta v_i\|$ for some $h > 1$ in the denominator of g_i is necessary as well. For example, in a setup where sites receive ± 1 updates per dimension [39, 19, 20] over a sliding window of w size, the maximum $\|\Delta v_i\|$ that may occur is equal to $U = \sqrt{d} \cdot w$. In case of unbounded inputs, a generalization of the bound used in [19] would suffice. In particular, [19] focuses on linear functions and assumes that an estimation of the global count (in one dimension) is available beforehand. It thus sets U equal to that total count estimation. The equivalent in our multidimensional scenario is to utilize e, i.e., the last known global average estimation, and express U as a function of its norm $\|e\|$.

Summarizing, all our previous remarks are satisfied upon setting

$$g_i = \frac{\ell n(1/\delta) \cdot \|\Delta v_i\|}{U \cdot N^x}$$

The expected communication cost is a tunable (using δ) fraction of N, proportional only to $\sum_{i=1}^{N} g_i = O(\ell n(1/\delta) \cdot N^{1-x})$. We then seek for a proper value for $x > 0$. Recalling Vector Bernstein's Inequality (Inequality 2) and using the above g_i, for σ we receive:

$$\sum_{i=1}^{N} E[\|y_i\|^2] = \sum_{i=1}^{N} \frac{\|\Delta v_i\|^2}{N^2 \cdot \frac{\|\Delta v_i\| \cdot \ell n(1/\delta)}{U \cdot N^x}} - \sum_{i=1}^{N} \frac{\|\Delta v_i\|^2}{N^2} =$$

$$\sum_{i=1}^{N} \frac{\|\Delta v_i\|}{N \cdot \sqrt{N}} \frac{U \cdot N^x}{\sqrt{N} \cdot \ell n(1/\delta)} - \sum_{i=1}^{N} \frac{\|\Delta v_i\|^2}{N^2} \cdot \sum_{i=1}^{N} \left(\frac{1}{\sqrt{N}}\right)^2 \overset{Cauchy-Schwarz}{\underset{Inequality\ [3,37]}{\leq}}$$

$$2\sum_{i=1}^{N} \frac{\|\Delta v_i\|}{N \cdot \sqrt{N}} \frac{U \cdot N^x}{2 \cdot \ell n(1/\delta)\sqrt{N}} - \left(\sum_{i=1}^{N} \frac{\|\Delta v_i\|}{N \cdot \sqrt{N}}\right)^2 =$$

$$-\left(\sum_{i=1}^{N} \frac{\|\Delta v_i\|}{N \cdot \sqrt{N}}\right)^2 + 2\sum_{i=1}^{N} \frac{\|\Delta v_i\|}{N \cdot \sqrt{N}} \frac{U \cdot N^x}{2 \cdot \ell n(1/\delta)\sqrt{N}} \pm \left(\frac{U \cdot N^x}{2 \cdot \ell n(1/\delta)\sqrt{N}}\right)^2 \overset{identity}{=}$$

$$-\left(\sum_{i=1}^{N} \frac{\|\Delta v_i\|}{N \cdot \sqrt{N}} - \frac{U \cdot N^x}{2 \cdot \ell n(1/\delta)\sqrt{N}}\right)^2 + \left(\frac{U \cdot N^x}{2 \cdot \ell n(1/\delta)\sqrt{N}}\right)^2 \Leftrightarrow$$

$$\sum_{i=1}^{N} E[\|y_i\|^2] \leq \left(\frac{U \cdot N^x}{2 \cdot \ell n(1/\delta)\sqrt{N}}\right)^2 = \sigma^2 \qquad (3)$$

In our analysis we made use of the Cauchy-Schwarz Inequality [3, 37], which states that if $a_1, \ldots, a_N$ and $b_1, \ldots, b_N$ are two sequences of real numbers, then $\left(\sum_{i=1}^{N} a_i \cdot b_i\right)^2 \leq \sum_{i=1}^{N} a_i^2 \cdot \sum_{i=1}^{N} b_i^2$. The equality holds if and only if the sequences are proportional. In order to express ε as a fraction of U and as a function of δ, while at the same time avoiding an undesirable dependence on the network scale N, we pick $x = 1/2$. Then, $\varepsilon = (1 + \sqrt{\ell n(1/\delta)}) \cdot \sigma$ $= (\frac{1+\sqrt{\ell n(1/\delta)}}{2 \cdot \ell n(1/\delta)}) \cdot U$, while B can be set to $B = \frac{\|\Delta v_i\|}{N \cdot g_i} = \frac{U}{\ell n(1/\delta) \cdot \sqrt{N}}$. Notice that the choice of $\ell n(1/\delta)$ in the nominator of g_i is the lowest value that we could use in order to obtain a tunable by δ increase in the expected communication cost, while at the same time being able to express ε as a percentage of U. The latter claim is true due to the fact that $(\frac{1+\sqrt{\ell n(1/\delta)}}{2 \cdot \ell n(1/\delta)}) < 1, \forall \delta < 1/e$ (i.e., a range that contains the typical values for δ).

The Sampling Function. Pointing out the characteristics of our sampling-based *GM* scheme, for given $\delta \in (0, 1/e)$:

$$\begin{cases} g_i = \frac{\|\Delta v_i\| \ell n(1/\delta)}{U \cdot \sqrt{N}} & \text{Sampling Function} \\ \varepsilon = (\frac{1+\sqrt{\ell n(1/\delta)}}{2 \cdot \ell n(1/\delta)}) \cdot U & \hat{v} \text{ Estimation Error} \\ \sum_{i=1}^{N} g_i = O(\ell n(1/\delta)\sqrt{N}) & \text{Expected Sample Size} \end{cases} \qquad (4)$$

Notice that $g_i < 1$ and $\varepsilon \leq \sigma^2/B$ practically holds, as required by the Vector Bernstein's Inequality. In addition, ε is controllable using the δ parameter. Furthermore, note that when δ decreases, then ε also decreases, while the expected sample size increases logarithmically. This is a trade-off between bandwidth consumption and accuracy that our sampling-based scheme achieves by a single, application defined parameter δ.

Notice that the proposed g_i does not explicitly impose a lower bound on sample size. For example, if all sites have very small Δv_i vectors, then their sampling probabilities will be small. However, even if none of them gets sampled (such a case becomes less likely as the number of sites increases), our algorithm will estimate - according to Estimator 1 - that $\hat{v} = e$. That is, the current position of v coincides with the estimate vector e (the last known, due to synchronization, global average vector), leading to the conclusion that the function has not crossed the threshold. In any such case, according to our analysis using the Vector Bernstein Inequality, our estimation is accurate within ε from the true average with (controllably) high probability. On the other hand, our framework needs to ensure that it samples enough sites when the global vector v does cross the threshold surface, so as to avoid FNs. In our work (see Lemma 3 below), we bound P_{FN} based on both the number of threshold crossing sites and the distance of the spheres from the $\varepsilon-$ zone (and, thus, from the threshold surface).

EXAMPLE 2. *Recalling Example 1, we note that common relative humidity values in a server room range between 0.4 and 0.6 (i.e, 40% and 60%) rH. In such cases, the maximum $\|\Delta v_i\|$ may occur when the reading of a sensor gradually shifts from 0.4 to 0.6 (or vice versa), yielding a maximum $\|\Delta v_i\| = \sqrt{(0.6^2 - 0.4^2)^2 + (0.6 - 0.4)^2} \approx 0.28$. Thus, $U = 0.28$. The following table computes, for $N = 100$ and $N = 961$, the values of ε, the range of g_i values in this example, and $\ell n(1/\delta)\sqrt{N}$ (an upper* *bound on* $\sum_{i=1}^{N} g_i$*) for* δ *values of 0.1 and 0.05. We note that this upper bound becomes smaller compared to N as N increases. Moreover, note that smaller* δ *values result in smaller* ε *and larger* g_i *values, as smaller* δ *values point to a requirement for fewer FNs.*

δ	N	$\sqrt{N}$	Range of g_i	ε	$\ell n(1/\delta)\sqrt{N}$
0.1	100	10	[0,0.23]	0.15	24
0.1	961	31	[0,0.08]	0.15	72
0.05	100	10	[0,0.3]	0.13	30
0.05	961	31	[0,0.097]	0.13	93

Completing the puzzle for P_{FN} bounds. In Section 4.2, we mentioned that when some of the sampled sites enter the ε-zone, $P_{FN} \leq \prod_{S_i \in C}(1-g_i)$, where C the set of threshold crossing sites. Under the light of the chosen g_i we receive $P_{FN} \leq \prod_{S_i \in C}(1-\frac{\|\Delta v_i\| \ell n(1/\delta)}{U \cdot \sqrt{N}})$. However, we also noted that for a site $S_i \in C$, $\|\Delta v_i\| > \varepsilon_T$, since otherwise S_i cannot have crossed the threshold surface. Therefore, since $g_i < 1$, substituting above:

$$P_{FN} \leq (1-\frac{\ell n(1/\delta)\cdot \varepsilon_T}{U\cdot\sqrt{N}})^{|C|} \leq e^{-\frac{|C|\cdot \ell n(1/\delta)\cdot\varepsilon_T}{U\cdot\sqrt{N}}} = \delta^{\frac{|C|\cdot\varepsilon_T}{U\cdot\sqrt{N}}}$$

As mentioned in Section 4.2, this bound on P_{FN} is a worst-case bound that is derived from a pathological case, in which for all $S_i \in C$, $||\Delta v_i|| = \varepsilon_T$. However, what happens in practice, because v is the average of the drift vectors, is that in order for v to cross the threshold surface, the threshold surface is crossed (i) by either several moderate in length drift vectors, in which case $|C|$ is large and P_{FN} is small, since it decreases exponentially with the number of threshold crossing sites, or (ii) by fewer but larger drift vectors that, thus, have larger sampling probabilities. In the latter case, it is less likely that they are all omitted from the sample.

Thus, apart from ensuring $P_{FN} \leq \delta$ when no local constraint enters the ε-zone as discussed in Section 4.2, we also bounded the complementary case, and note that P_{FN} may become even lower than δ when $|C|$ is sufficiently larger than $\sqrt{N}$. We emphasize that the minimum distance of e from the threshold surface, i.e., ε_T (see Fig 4), is computed during a synchronization and is, thus, a known parameter until the next central data collection. In any case, the size of the $\varepsilon-$zone can be tuned to the desirable extend using δ as discussed above. Based on the above discussion and our analysis in Section 4.2 the following lemma comes naturally.

LEMMA 3. *The Sampling-Based GM Scheme being set according to Equation 4 yields:*

- $P_{FN} \leq \delta$ *if* $\forall S_i \in K, B(e+\frac{\Delta v_i}{2}, \frac{\|\Delta v_i\|}{2}) \cap \varepsilon-zone = \emptyset$
- $P_{FN} = O(\delta^{\frac{|C|}{\sqrt{N}}})$ *otherwise*

where C denotes the set of threshold crossing sites. Thus, one can properly tune δ *to obtain the desired FN probability.*

6. EXPERIMENTS

We develop a simulation environment in Java in order to evaluate the performance of our techniques. We compare the communication cost (number of messages) as well as the number of FP and FN synchronization decisions of our sampling-based scheme, henceforth referred to as **SGM**, against other GM related techniques that have been proposed in the literature. More precisely:

- The Geometric Monitoring framework of Section 3.1 introduced in [35], termed **GM**.
- The GM framework enhanced with the balancing optimization presented in [35], termed **BGM**. In BGM, the coordinator tries to probe a subset of Δv_is that may partially cancel out the crossing ones due to their different direction. If such a subset exists, it knows that $v(t)$ has not crossed the threshold without requiring a full synchronization. Please refer to [35] for more details.
- The Prediction-Based Geometric Monitoring Framework, and in particular the CAA technique proposed in [16, 17], henceforth referred to as **PGM**. We adopt a Velocity-Acceleration predictor and present the best performance PGM shows upon varying the window according to which predictions are formed from 3 to 10 measurements (roughly the amount of stories received hourly).

We emphasize that the BGM and the PGM approaches are orthogonal to our sampling-based GM framework. Despite this fact, to better perceive the benefits of our novel SGM approach and expose its features, in our experimentation we form a worst case scenario for SGM by not applying any orthogonal approach on top of it. Moreover, note that BGM and PGM are not orthogonal to each other, since the CAA approach [16, 17] switches among monitoring models instead of balancing their drift vectors.

Data Sets. We utilize two real world datasets. The first dataset is the Reuters Corpus (RCV1-v2) [26] data, termed *Reuters*, also used in related work [35, 36, 16]. It is composed of 804414 records of news stories which have been categorized and have been tagged with a list of terms (features). As previous works [35, 36, 16], we focus on tracking the terms *Febru, Ipo, Bosnia* and their co-occurrences with the Corporate/Industrial category. We monitor the relevance between a (term, category) pair using two different functions: the Mutual Information (MI) function and the χ^2 function (please refer to [16, 17] for more details). We use a sliding window of 200 documents for this dataset which is roughly the amount of news stories received daily [16, 17]. Since, the number of records in the data is limited, we use the Reuters data to evaluate our algorithms in mediocre distributed settings of size $N = 50$ to $N = 100$ and provide some initial comparisons with related work [35, 16, 17] where no more than 100 sites are considered.

The second dataset, termed *Jester* [18], contains 4.1 million ratings between -10 and 10 on 100 jokes from 73421 users. We use this dataset to approximately monitor the sum in buckets of equi-width histograms of the above rating range, based on L_∞ distance as well as the Jeffrey Divergence (JD) [31]. More precisely, we use these functions to measure the distance (cost) of encoding the current global histogram at each time instance, to the one communicated during the last central data collection. In addition to L_∞ and JD, the third function we experiment on (in the Appendix), is the tracking of the Self-Join (SJ) size [17, 15, 8] (essentially the L_2 Norm) of the vector hosting the expected counts in the aforementioned histogram buckets. Since users provide ratings for 100 distinct cases, we utilize a sliding window of 100 observations for this dataset. Regarding the degree of distribution, we vary N between 100 and 1000.

Metrics and Parameter Settings. Throughout our study, for each (dataset, function) pair we initially measure the number of communicated messages varying the value of the threshold, i.e., T, keeping the number of sites to a fixed value that lies in the middle ($N = 75$ for Reuters and $N = 500$ for Jester) of the aforementioned distribution ranges. This helps demonstrate the performance of the candidate schemes upon altering the placement of the threshold surface.

Then, for the middle threshold case we investigate the communication cost for increasing network scales. In the Jester dataset where larger network sizes can be tested, we also investigate the cost of messages per site (instead of just the total number of mes-

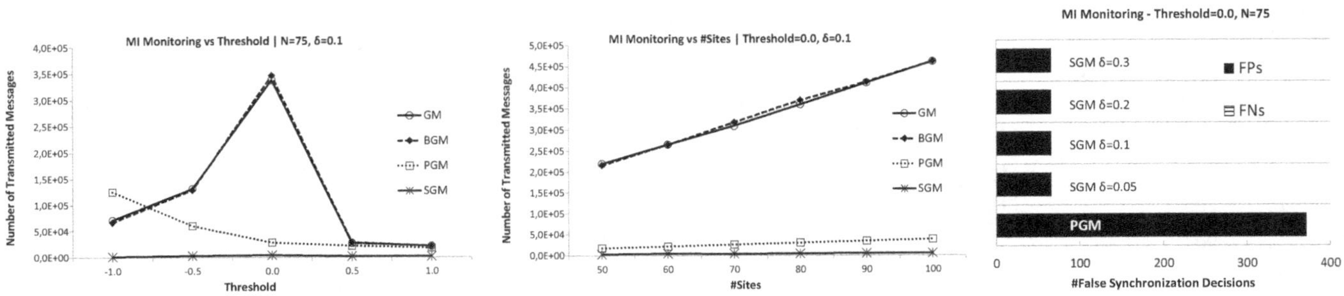

(a) MI Monitoring: Comm. Cost vs Threshold (b) MI Monitoring: Comm. Cost vs Sites (c) MI Monitoring: Sensitivity to δ

Figure 5: Reuters Data Set: Performance of our Techniques on *MI* Monitoring

sages), as this gives an indication on how the cost of each site scales when the number of sites increases. For large numbers of sites and for constrained applications such as sensor networks, where an increased number of transmitted messages results in reduced network lifetime, this per site cost should ideally remain steady (or increase at a small rate) as we scale to larger networks.

For SGM, we also vary the posed tolerance constraint i.e., the application defined probability δ, between 0.05 and 0.3 with a default value of 0.1 and perform a sensitivity analysis on the number of false (FP, FN) synchronization decisions in comparison with the FPs produced by the best (at each case) of the competitors.

Main Findings. Our experimental analysis demonstrates that our sampling-based SGM method significantly reduces the number of transmitted messages and the number of false positives, with the benefits becoming more profound when the number of sites increases. Please note that, since in GM each false positive results in communication from all sites and the coordinator, significantly reducing the number of false positives translates into a corresponding bandwidth reduction (or energy consumption reduction, in case of applications with sensor sites) on *each* site. This is validated by the scalability experiment performed on the (larger) Jester dataset, where the corresponding benefits *per site*, compared to GM, increase in larger network setups. Finally, the false negatives of SGM are in all cases lower than the specified tolerance parameter δ.

6.1 Reuters Dataset Monitoring

We first focus on the Reuters dataset. Figure 5(a) and Figure 5(b) present the communication cost of GM, BGM, PGM and SGM varying the value of the posed threshold and the scale of the distributed network for the default value of $\delta = 0.1$ when monitoring the Mutual Information function. We present results for the Febru term, as the trends are similar for the other two (Bosnia, Ipo) terms.

In both figures, the lines corresponding to GM, BGM almost coincide, showing that in this data set the balancing optimization does not reduce the communication cost. The reason is that, when many sites cross the threshold surface moving towards similar directions, an additive effect on their Δv_is naturally exists. Therefore, the coordinator probes almost all of the non-crossing sites so as to balance the added drift. On the other hand, the prediction-based mechanism of PGM reduces the communication cost by more than an order of magnitude compared to GM and BGM for different threshold values when $N = 75$. Still, our proposed sampling-based scheme SGM (star-marked line approaching the x axis in the figure) performs from 6 times (for $T = 0$) to two orders of magnitude (for $T = -1$) better than PGM across various thresholds, with at least an order of magnitude improvement for the rest of the tested threshold values. Despite its good performance, PGM performs worse than GM and BGM for $T = -1$. This is because, contrary to our sampling-based scheme, the prediction-based mechanism PGM can practically achieve (as shown in [16, 17]), but does not guarantee communication savings over the baseline solution of GM.

Moreover, in Figure 5(b) our SGM approach performs from 5 to almost an order of magnitude times better than PGM, which in turn outperforms GM and BGM for the fixed $T = 0$, across the various network scales. The benefits of SGM increase with the number of sites as, not only does it reduce the number of FPs (also depicted in Figure 5(c)), but also in each FP it requires transmission from $O(\sqrt{N})$ sites, in comparison to $O(N)$ sites for the other techniques.

Figure 5(c) presents a sensitivity analysis on the effect of δ to the number of FP, FN decisions. Recall that FPs are responsible for the unnecessary portion of communicated messages. As a result, our sensitivity analysis also exposes the trade-off among bandwidth consumption caused by FPs and accuracy in terms of FNs for SGM. The horizontal bars depict the number of FP decisions of PGM (which, as we just showed, outperforms GM and BGM) compared to the FP and FN decisions of SGM, under different δ values ranging between 0.05 and 0.3. FPs and FNs for each given δ are drawn in stacked bars as explained by the corresponding legends, while the overall length of the bars represents the total number of false decisions. As shown by the figure, the communication reduction that was observed in Figure 5(a) and Figure 5(b) for $T = 0$ is translated to a corresponding ratio (of about 6) of the FP decisions of PGM over those of SGM with $\delta = 0.1$. Moreover, we can observe that the number of FP decisions of SGM remains stable across different δ values, while the SGM framework in practice produces no FNs for this (function, dataset) pair.

Turning our interest to the χ^2 case, the main difference in Figure 6(a) and Figure 6(b) is that PGM performs only slightly (<0.2 times) better than BGM and GM. Monitoring χ^2 results in a monitoring process at a higher dimensional space (which in turns means trying to accurately predict more components of local and predicted global vectors). This affects the quality of the predictions and the size of the monitored convex hulls in PGM, therefore its limited improvements. Apart from the above remark, SGM reduces the bandwidth consumption from 3.8 times for $T = 0$, to more than an order of magnitude compared to the other candidates for the rest of threshold values (Fig. 6(a)). In addition, SGM needs more than one order of magnitude (between 13 and 16 times) fewer messages than its competitors across different network scales (Fig. 6(b)).

We now focus on Figure 6(c) and the amount of FPs, FNs depicted there. SGM ensures more than an order of magnitude reduction on the amount of false decisions (represented by the total length of the stacked bar of FP, FN counts) compared to the second best alternative of PGM. Figure 6(c) demonstrates that increasing

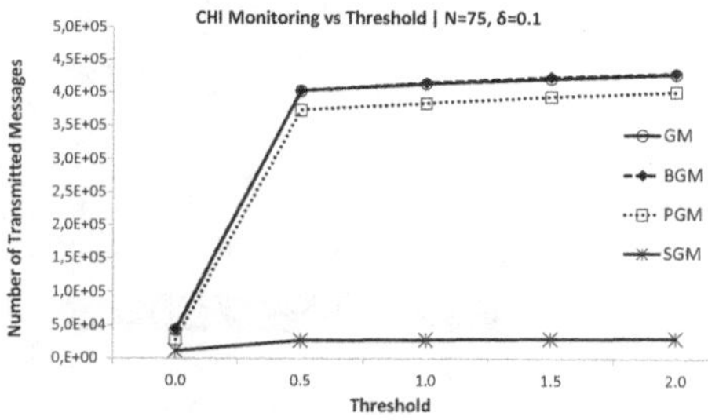

(a) χ^2 Monitoring: Comm. Cost vs Threshold

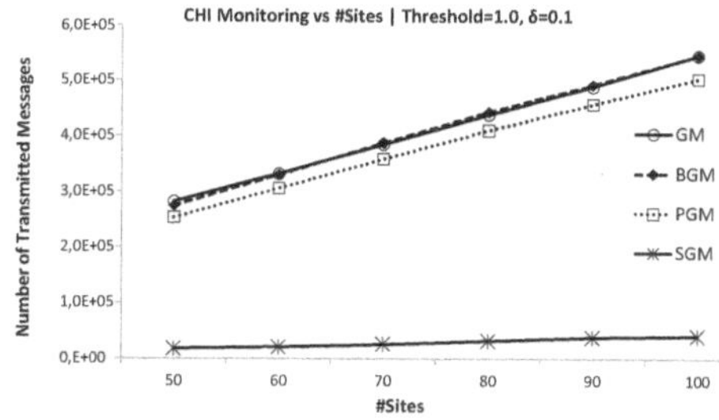

(b) χ^2 Monitoring: Comm. Cost vs Sites

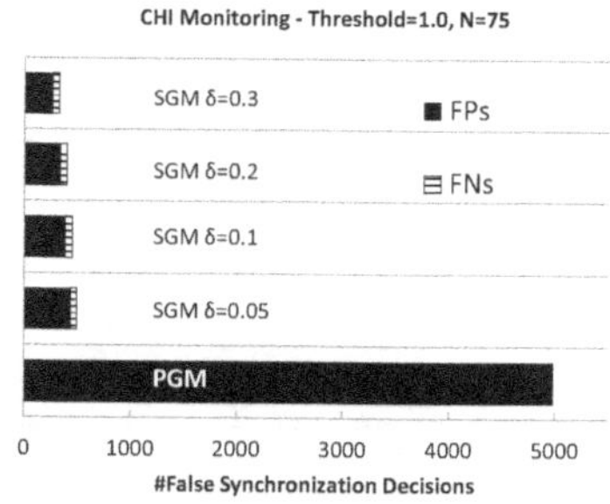

(c) χ^2 Monitoring: Sensitivity to δ

Figure 6: Reuters Data Set: Performance of our Techniques on χ^2 Monitoring

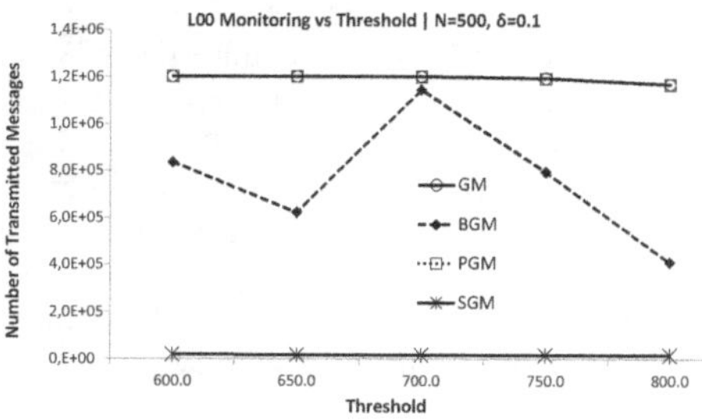

(a) L_∞ Monitoring: Comm. Cost vs Threshold

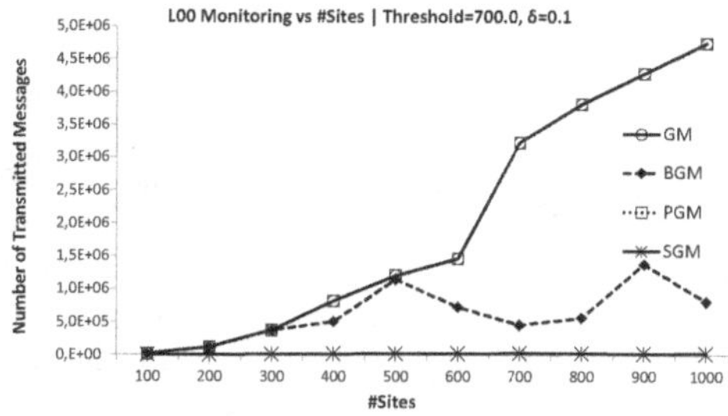

(b) L_∞ Monitoring: Comm. Cost vs Sites

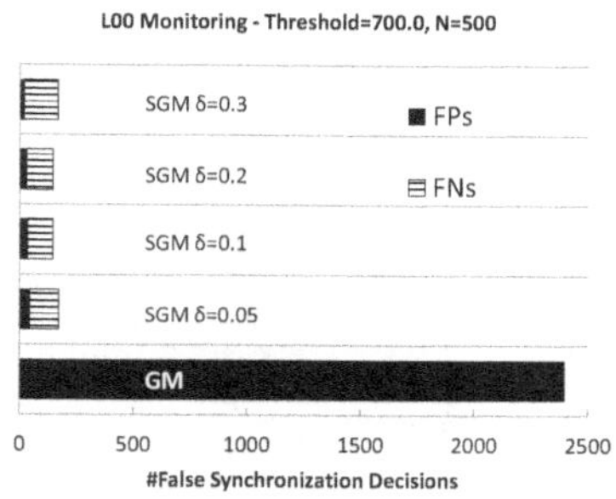

(c) L_∞ Monitoring: Sensitivity to δ

Figure 7: Jester Data Set: Performance of our Techniques on L_∞ Monitoring

δ causes FP decisions to be reduced by more than 15% in each bar of the histogram. FNs slightly increase with increased δ values, but are very rare in all cases. The reduction in FP with increased δ values is easily understood, since the expected sample size is proportional to $\ell n(1/\delta)\sqrt{N}$. Thus, increasing δ decreases the sample size and, thus, the monitored space responsible for FPs. Regarding FNs, they are rare in all cases. For instance, for SGM and $\delta = 0.05$, ~8000 updates arrive per site (see the size of the Reuters data set and $N \leq 100$) and the number of FNs is just 61, which corresponds to a ratio lower than 0.01. SGM typically provides fewer FNs (in this experiment, always by at least a factor of 5) than the posed δ according to which the tolerance to FNs is tuned.

6.2 Jester Dataset Monitoring

We now focus on the Jester dataset which, due to its larger size, allows us to also perform tests in larger topologies. The default number of sites used in this dataset is 500. Two general observations coming out of Figure 7 and Figure 8 we mention that:

- In this larger scale dataset, the performance of the PGM approach is equivalent to the baseline GM. This validates our claim in Section 2 where we noted that PGM may perform well in small to medium sized network distributions, but increasing the network scale makes the existence of inaccurate predictors in some sites more probable and, thus, PGM becomes more prone to FPs.
- Figure 7 shows that balancing may help reduce the bandwidth consumption in that particular (function, dataset) pair. Nonetheless, in Figure 8 where only the function and the threshold value (surface) is altered, BGM provides no improvements. This comes as no surprise, as BGM adopts a simple heuristic hoping to probe sites with drift vectors of opposite direction compared to the threshold crossing ones. Hence, contrary to SGM, BGM does not guarantee communication reduction. Furthermore, contrary to our proposed SGM approach, none of the BGM or PGM mechanisms provide a way to tune the expected bandwidth consumption according to posed accuracy standards.

Focusing on specific figures, in Figure 7(a) we point out that the bandwidth consumption achieved by our SGM (star-marked line approaching the x axis in the figure) approach is from 25 to 64 times lower than the best alternative (BGM). Moreover, upon varying the network scale between 100 and 1000 sites in Figure 7(b), the communication cost reduction by SGM reaches a factor of 64 for $N = 900$, while constantly being at least 20 times lower compared to BGM, for different degrees of network distribution. Comparing the cost of SGM against PGM or GM, for instance when $N = 1000$ SGM results in 206 times fewer messages, with at least 20 times fewer messages for any other network scale.

Concluding our discussion on L_∞, the sensitivity analysis in Figure 7(c) shows the trade-off among unnecessary bandwidth consumption due to FP and accuracy in terms of FN decisions for different δs. SGM is compared to the FPs in GM, as BGM causes full synchronization only progressively, thus FPs cannot be counted in a distinct manner. As this figure shows, the number of FP decisions tends to be reduced upon increasing δ, while the number of FNs tends to increase, both of which are the expected behavior. Given that about 4850 updates arrive in every site of the network using the Jester dataset, the 148 FNs for $\delta = 0.3$ correspond to a ratio of just 3% false negatives, while the corresponding ratio for the ~110-120 FNs and for the rest of the examined δ values never exceeds 2.3%. Hence, once again the amount of FNs is less than the posed δ.

In Figure 8 we focus on the Jeffrey Divergence monitoring function. In Figure 8(a) and Figure 8(b), all three competitive techniques (GM, BGM and PGM) exhibit comparable performances.

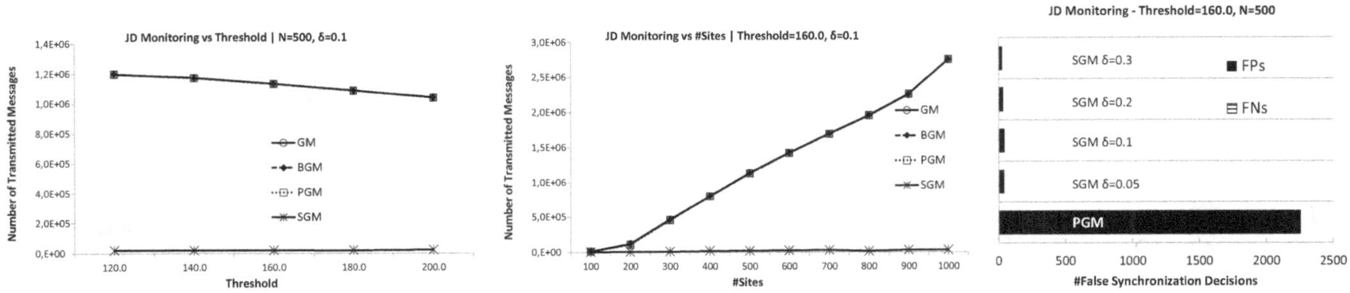

(a) JD Monitoring: Comm. Cost vs Threshold (b) JD Monitoring: Comm. Cost vs Sites (c) JD Monitoring: Sensitivity to δ

Figure 8: Jester Data Set: Performance of our Techniques on Jeffrey Divergence Monitoring

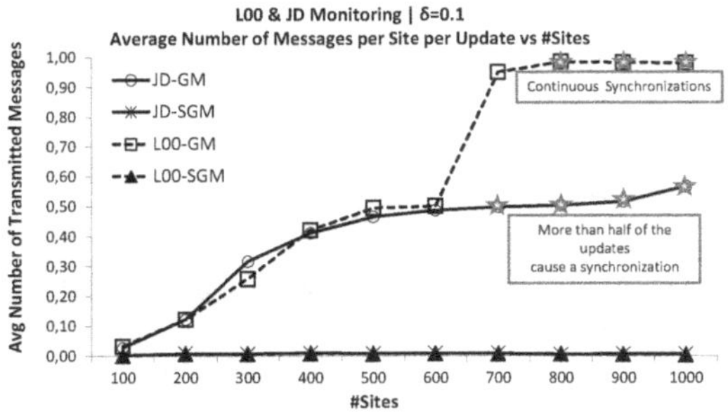

Figure 9: Average Number of Messages Transmitted by *each Site* per Data Update

Our SGM framework reduces the consumed bandwidth up to a factor of 56 across different thresholds for $N = 500$ and the communication gains progressively approach two orders of magnitude by increasing the network scale to $N = 1000$ sites (Fig. 8(b)). Regarding the number of false synchronization decisions and the sensitivity on the chosen δ, Figure 8(c) exposes the absence of FNs and the reduction of FPs by about 20% as we increase δ above 0.1.

Due to space constraints, the case of Self-Join size monitoring is summarized in Section 6.4 and then described in the Appendix.

6.3 Messages Per Site in Large Networks

In order to validate our claim regarding scalability to larger network distributions and to resource constrained environments, apart from measuring the total communication cost (number of messages) transmitted in the network, we further study the average number of messages transmitted by *each site*. That is, we measure the average number of messages a site transmitted per each update of its data. An average value close to 1 indicates that each site in the network transmitted a message after each data update, which is equivalent to a synchronization process.

Figure 9 presents the average number of transmissions per site and data update for the GM and SGM schemes in L_∞ and in Jeffrey Divergence monitoring when varying the size of the network scale. Figure 9 shows that increasing the scale in GM (and the other alternatives that have similar performance to GM in Fig. 7(b) and Fig. 8(b)) results in a continuous increase in the number of transmitted messages per site. This is more evident in L_∞ monitoring where, starting at 800 sites, GM behaves as the naive choice of continuous central data collection, since at least one site exhibits a local violation, which results in communication by all other sites as well. In Jeffrey Divergence monitoring this effect is less pronounced until $N = 500$, but still each site transmits a message in over half of its data updates for larger network sizes. On the contrary, the SGM approach is very slightly affected by the increase in network distribution, since the number of sampled sites increases with the logarithm of the network size. Thus, the benefits of SGM not only increase with larger network topologies, but it is also more appropriate for resource constrained environments, such as battery-powered sensor networks, where it is desirable to reduce the amount of communication per site in order to prolong the network lifetime.

6.4 Additional Results

In the Appendix we provide the following additional results: (a) we provide statistics on the duration of FNs, showing that even if FNs occur (in a controllable manner), the missed threshold crossings are detected soon afterwards in the future, most often in the next synchronization decision; (b) we include the analysis of Self Join size monitoring for which SGM provides more than an order of magnitude fewer transmissions compared to GM, PGM. BGM can fall short compared to our SGM up to 8 times, but typically provides between 2-3 times worse communication cost in terms of the number of transmitted messages; (c) we compare our SGM approach using the proposed g_i (Section 5) with a variant that uses the SGM framework but naively samples sites with equal probability, i.e., performs Bernoulli sampling. What we show is that SGM outperforms the Bernoulli sampling variant across different network scales with gains reaching a factor of 50.

7. CONCLUSIONS

In this work we rendered the GM framework of [35] capable to operate in highly distributed settings. We initially exhibited the culprits that cause the GM approach to become impractical due to severe scalability issues. To encounter these issues, we introduced a novel sampling-based geometric monitoring technique capable of performing the tracking process utilizing only a sample of the available sites. The sample size entailed by our methods is proportional to $\sqrt{N}$ and also dependent on application's accuracy requirements. Our experimental evaluation shows that our sampling-based techniques can significantly reduce the communication cost throughout the monitoring process with controllable accuracy guarantees, outperforming other competitors proposed in the literature.

8. REFERENCES

[1] S. Burdakis and A. Deligiannakis. Detecting outliers in sensor networks using the geometric approach. In *Proc. of ICDE Conference*, pages 1108–1119, 2012.

[2] E. J. Candès and Y. Plan. A probabilistic and ripless theory of compressed sensing. *CoRR*, abs/1011.3854, 2010.

[3] A. L. Cauchy. *Cours d'analyse de l'École royale polytechnique*. Paris, France, 1821.

[4] G. Cormode. The continuous distributed monitoring model. *SIGMOD Rec.*, 42(1):5–14, may 2013.

[5] G. Cormode and N. Duffield. Sampling for big data: A tutorial. In *Proc. of ACM SIGKDD Conference*, pages 1975–1975, 2014.

[6] G. Cormode and M. Garofalakis. Sketching streams through the net: Distributed approximate query tracking. In *Proc. of VLDB Conference*, pages 312–323, 2005.

[7] G. Cormode and M. Garofalakis. Streaming in a connected world: querying and tracking distributed data streams. In *Proc. of SIGMOD Conference*, pages 1178–1181, 2007.

[8] G. Cormode and M. Garofalakis. Approximate continuous querying over distributed streams. *ACM Transactions on Database Systems*, 33(2):9:1–9:39, 2008.

[9] G. Cormode, M. Garofalakis, S. Muthukrishnan, and R. Rastogi. Holistic aggregates in a networked world: distributed tracking of approximate quantiles. In *SIGMOD*, pages 25–36, 2005.

[10] G. Cormode, S. Muthukrishnan, and K. Yi. Algorithms for distributed functional monitoring. *ACM Trans. Algorithms*, 7(2):21:1–21:20, mar 2011.

[11] C. Cranor, T. Johnson, O. Spataschek, and V. Shkapenyuk. Gigascope: A stream database for network applications. In *ACM SIGMOD*, pages 647–651, 2003.

[12] M. Dilman and D. Raz. Efficient reactive monitoring. In *INFOCOM*, volume 2, pages 1012–1019, 2001.

[13] M. Gabel, A. Schuster, and D. Keren. Communication-efficient distributed variance monitoring and outlier detection for multivariate time series. In *IEEE IPDPS*, pages 37–47, 2014.

[14] M. Garofalakis, J. Gehrke, and R. Rastogi. Querying and mining data streams: You only get one look a tutorial. In *Proc. of SIGMOD Conference*, pages 635–635, 2002.

[15] M. Garofalakis, D. Keren, and V. Samoladas. Sketch-based geometric monitoring of distributed stream queries. *In VLDB*, 6(10):937–948, 2013.

[16] N. Giatrakos, A. Deligiannakis, M. Garofalakis, I. Sharfman, and A. Schuster. Prediction-based geometric monitoring over distributed data streams. In *SIGMOD*, pages 265–276, 2012.

[17] N. Giatrakos, A. Deligiannakis, M. Garofalakis, I. Sharfman, and A. Schuster. Distributed geometric query monitoring using prediction models. *ACM Trans. Database Syst.*, 39(2):16:1–16:42, may 2014.

[18] K. Goldberg, T. Roeder, D. Gupta, and C. Perkins. Eigentaste: A constant time collaborative filtering algorithm. *Inf. Retr.*, 4(2):133–151, 2001.

[19] Z. Huang, K. Yi, Y. Liu, and G. Chen. Optimal sampling algorithms for frequency estimation in distributed data. In *INFOCOM*, pages 1997–2005, 2011.

[20] Z. Huang, K. Yi, and Q. Zhang. Randomized algorithms for tracking distributed count, frequencies, and ranks. In *Proc. of PODS*, pages 295–306, 2012.

[21] S. R. Jeffery, M. Garofalakis, and M. J. Franklin. Adaptive cleaning for rfid data streams. In *Proceedings of the 32Nd International Conference on Very Large Data Bases*, VLDB '06, pages 163–174. VLDB Endowment, 2006.

[22] M. Kamp, M. Boley, D. Keren, A. Schuster, and I. Sharfman. Communicationefficient distributed online prediction by dynamic model synchronization. In *ECML PKDD*, pages 623–639, 2014.

[23] R. Keralapura, G. Cormode, and J. Ramamirtham. Communication-efficient distributed monitoring of thresholded counts. In *SIGMOD*, pages 289–300, 2006.

[24] D. Keren, G. Sagy, A. Abboud, D. Ben-David, A. Schuster, I. Sharfman, and A. Deligiannakis. Geometric monitoring of heterogeneous streams. *Knowledge and Data Engineering, IEEE Transactions on*, 26(8):1890–1903, 2014.

[25] A. Lazerson, I. Sharfman, D. Keren, A. Schuster, M. Garofalakis, and V. Samoladas. Monitoring distributed streams using convex decompositions. *Proc. VLDB Endow.*, 8(5):545–556, jan 2015.

[26] D. D. Lewis, Y. Yang, T. G. Rose, and F. Li. Rcv1: A new benchmark collection for text categorization research. *Journal of Machine Learning Research*, 5(Apr):361–397, 2004.

[27] Z. Liu, B. Radunović, and M. Vojnović. Continuous distributed counting for non-monotonic streams. In *Proc. of PODS*, pages 307–318, 2012.

[28] S. R. Madden, M. J. Franklin, J. M. Hellerstein, and W. Hong. Tinydb: an acquisitional query processing system for sensor networks. *ACM Trans. Database Syst.*, 30:122–173, March 2005.

[29] A. Manjhi, V. Shkapenyuk, K. Dhamdhere, and C. Olston. Finding (recently) frequent items in distributed data streams. In *ICDE*, pages 767–778, 2005.

[30] O. Papapetrou and M. N. Garofalakis. Continuous fragmented skylines over distributed streams. In *IEEE ICDE*, pages 124–135, 2014.

[31] Y. Rubner, C. Tomasi, and L. J. Guibas. The earth mover's distance as a metric for image retrieval. *Int. J. Comput. Vision*, 40(2):99–121, 2000.

[32] G. Sagy, D. Keren, I. Sharfman, and A. Schuster. Distributed threshold querying of general functions by a difference of monotonic representation. *In VLDB*, 4:46–57, 2010.

[33] G. Sagy, I. Sharfman, D. Keren, and A. Schuster. Top-k vectorial aggregation queries in a distributed environment. *J. Parallel Distrib. Comput.*, 71(2):302–315, 2011.

[34] C.-E. Särndal, B. Swensson, and J. Wretman. *"Model Assisted Survey Sampling"*. Springer-Verlag New York, Inc. (Springer Series in Statistics), 1992.

[35] I. Sharfman, A. Schuster, and D. Keren. A geometric approach to monitoring threshold functions over distributed data streams. In *SIGMOD*, pages 301–312, 2006.

[36] I. Sharfman, A. Schuster, and D. Keren. Shape sensitive geometric monitoring. In *PODS*, pages 301–310, 2008.

[37] J. M. Steele. *The Cauchy-Schwarz Master Class: An Introduction to the Art of Mathematical Inequalities, Chap.1,*. Cambridge University Press, New York, NY, USA, 2004.

[38] M. Tang, F. Li, and Y. Tao. Distributed online tracking. In *Proc. of SIGMOD Conference*, pages 2047–2061, New York, NY, USA, 2015.

[39] Q. G. Zhao, M. Ogihara, H. Wang, and J. J. Xu. Finding global icebergs over distributed data sets. In *PODS*, 2006.

APPENDIX

A. PROOFS OF LEMMA 1 AND LEMMA 2

LEMMA 1. *For Estimator 1 the following hold:*
(a) Estimator 1 is an unbiased estimator of v when sampling $\forall S_i \in \{S_1, \ldots, S_N\}$ *with* $0 \leq g_i \leq 1$.
(b) $E[\hat{v}] \in Conv(\, e+\Delta v_1, \ldots, e+\Delta v_N)$
(c) $\hat{v} \in Conv(\{e+\frac{\Delta v_i}{g_i}\} : \forall S_i \in K)$

PROOF.
(a) To prove that the estimator is unbiased we need to show that $E[\hat{v}] = v$. Recall from Equation 1 that $\sum_{S_i \in K} \frac{\Delta v_i}{g_i} = \sum_{i=1}^{N} \Delta' v_i$ and that $E[\Delta' v_i] = g_i \cdot \frac{\Delta v_i}{g_i} + (1-g_i)\cdot 0 = \Delta v_i$. By applying the properties of the expected value we get:

$$E[\hat{v}] = E[e+\frac{\sum_{i=1}^{N}\Delta' v_i}{N}] = e+\frac{\sum_{i=1}^{N}E[\Delta' v_i]}{N} = e+\frac{\sum_{i=1}^{N}\Delta v_i}{N} = v$$

(b) Obvious, since $E[\hat{v}] = v$ and $v \in Conv(\, e+\Delta v_1, \ldots, e+\Delta v_N)$.
(c) $\hat{v}$ is a convex combination of the $e+\Delta' v_i$ vectors and, therefore, lies in their convex hull. Since $\Delta' v_i = 0$ for all sites not included in the sample, the convex hulls $Conv(\{e+\frac{\Delta v_i}{g_i}\} : \forall S_i \in K)$ and $Conv(\{e+\Delta' v_i\} : \forall i \in [1,N])$ coincide. □

LEMMA 2. *Provided that* $\hat{v} = v$,

$$\hat{v} \in Conv(\{e+\Delta v_i\} : \forall S_i \in K)$$

PROOF. Lemma 1(c) we shows $\hat{v} \in Conv(\{e+\frac{\Delta v_i}{g_i}\} : \forall S_i \in K)$, and we already know that $v \in Conv(\{e+\Delta v_i\} : \forall S_i \in \{S_1, \ldots, S_N\})$. But, since $\hat{v} = v$, also $\hat{v} \in Conv(\{e+\Delta v_i\} : \forall S_i \in \{S_1, \ldots, S_N\})$ should hold. Combining the above:

$$\hat{v} \in Conv(\{e+\Delta v_i\} : \forall S_i \in \{S_1, \ldots, S_N\}) \cap Conv(\{e+\frac{\Delta v_i}{g_i}\} : \forall S_i \in K).$$

Let X_N denote the above intersection of the convex hulls when the N sites perform sampling trials. To prove the lemma it suffices to show that X_N is equivalent to $Conv(\{e+\Delta v_i\} : \forall S_i \in K)$.

Before we begin, we emphasize that in case a site gets sampled, $g_i > 0$ must hold, otherwise it cannot be included in the sample. Let $[y;w]$ denote the set of all convex combinations among $y, w \in \mathbb{R}^d$, i.e., $[y,w] = \{\forall q \in \mathbb{R}^d : q = \lambda \cdot y + (1-\lambda)\cdot w \,, 0 \leq \lambda \leq 1\}$. The proof will be derived inductively, in each of the steps abusively specifying K_N to denote a sample obtained out of N sites. Note beforehand that any intersection of convex sets is convex.

At the base case, $N = 1$ site exists, $Conv(e+\Delta v_1) = [e; e+\Delta v_1]$. If $S_1 \in K_1$, $Conv(e+\frac{\Delta v_1}{g_1}) = [e; e+\frac{\Delta v_1}{g_1}]$. Multidimensional points $e+\Delta v_1$, $e+\frac{\Delta v_1}{g_1}$ possess the same starting point e and differ only in the scale among Δv_1, $\frac{\Delta v_1}{g_1}$. Therefore, e, $e+\Delta v_1$, $e+\frac{\Delta v_1}{g_1}$ are collinear and since $g_1 \leq 1$, $[e; e+\Delta v_1] \cap [e; e+\frac{\Delta v_1}{g_1}] = [e; e+\Delta v_1]$ $\Rightarrow X_1 = [e; e+\Delta v_1] = Conv(\{e+\Delta v_i\} : \forall S_i \in K_1)$. On the other hand, if $S_1 \notin K_1$, $X_1 = e$. So, the lemma holds for $N = 1$.

We assume that the lemma holds for $N-1$ sites, i.e.,

$$X_{N-1} = Conv(\{e+\Delta v_i\} : \forall S_i \in \{S_1, \ldots, S_{N-1}\}) \cap Conv(\{e+\frac{\Delta v_i}{g_i}\} : \forall S_i \in K_{N-1}) = Conv(\{e+\Delta v_i\} : \forall S_i \in K_{N-1})$$

and examine the addition of S_N.

By adding $e+\Delta v_N$ to $Conv(\{e+\Delta v_i\} : \forall S_i \in \{S_1, \ldots, S_{N-1}\})$ we not only added the convex combinations $[e; e+\Delta v_N]$ as in the case where $N = 1$, but also all other possible convex combinations from any $y \in Conv(\{e+\Delta v_i\} : \forall S_i \in \{S_1, \ldots, S_{N-1}\})$ to the newly introduced points $[e; e+\Delta v_N]$ i.e., $[y; [e; e+\Delta v_N]]$. The same holds for $Conv(\{e+\frac{\Delta v_i}{g_i}\} : \forall S_i \in K_{N-1})$. Having said that, the candidate points for addition in X_{N-1} to form X_N are included in the intersection of the newly introduced convex combinations. That is, the set of points that X_N will add (compared to X_{N-1}) belong to the intersection of all possible convex combinations from every point included in X_{N-1} to the new $[e; e+\Delta v_N]$, $[e; e+\Delta' v_i]$: $\forall z \in X_{N-1}$ $[z; [e; e+\Delta v_N]] \cap [z; [e; e+\Delta' v_i]]$. If $S_N \notin K_N$, $[z; [e; e+\Delta v_N]] \cap [z; e] = [z; e] \Rightarrow X_{N-1} = X_N = Conv(\{e+\Delta v_i\} : \forall S_i \in K_N)$. On the other hand, when $S_N \in K_N$, taking into consideration the collinearity among e, $e+\frac{\Delta v_N}{g_N}$ and $e+\Delta v_N$, $[z; [e; e+\Delta v_N]] \cap [z; [e; e+\frac{\Delta v_N}{g_N}]] = [z; [e; e+\Delta v_N]]$. Eventually, $X_N = X_{N-1} \cup [z; [e; e+\Delta v_N]] = Conv(\{e+\Delta v_i\} : \forall S_i \in K_N)$, which completes the proof. □

B. JESTER DATASET - SJ MONITORING

In the Jester dataset we approximately monitor the sum in buckets of equi-width histograms, based on L_∞ distance as well as the Jeffrey Divergence (JD) [31]. In addition to L_∞ and JD, here we also experiment with a third function tracking the Self-Join (SJ) size [17, 15, 8] (essentially the L_2 Norm), of the vector hosting the expected counts in histogram buckets. Figure 10 presents the bandwidth consumption achieved by SGM compared to the rest of the candidates across different thresholds, network scales and values of δ. According to Figure 10(a) and Figure 10(b), SGM may require more than an order of magnitude fewer message transmissions compared to (GM, PGM) across different thresholds and network scales. SGM performs from 2 (for $T = 210$) to 8 (for $T = 180$) times better than BGM upon varying the threshold. Additionally, for network scales up to 400 sites, SGM reduces the transmitted messages up to a factor of 7 compared to BGM, while for higher amounts of distribution SGM mostly halves the number of messages BGM requires.

On the other hand, the sensitivity analysis of Figure 10(c) shows and the amount of FPs is reduced by more than an order of magnitude compared to GM for the tested tolerance δ values (recall that BGM progressively probes sites, thus FPs cannot be counted in a distinct manner). The same figure shows that increasing δ causes FP decisions to be reduced by more than 10% when switching from $\delta = 0.05$ to $\delta = 0.1$ and by almost 20% from $\delta = 0.1$ to $\delta = 0.2$. At the same time, FNs marginally increase with increased δ. Once again, the reduction in FPs with increased δ values is explained by the fact that the expected sample size is proportional to $\ell n(1/\delta)\sqrt{N}$. Thus, increasing δ decreases the sample size and the tracked area. Regarding FNs, their percentage lies below the corresponding δ value in each experiment of Figure 10(c).

Eventually, Figure 11 presents the average number of messages transmitted per site and data update for the GM and SGM schemes. It is not difficult to see that even for mediocre network scales of 100 sites, more than half of the updates caused a synchronization in GM, while this percentage exceeds 80% for topologies with 800 or more sites.

C. DURATION OF FNS

A discriminating fact among FP and FN synchronization decisions lies on the nature of their effect. FP decisions have an instant effect as the coordinator becomes aware of a FP, and the certain overhead on the consumed bandwidth it caused, by the end of a synchronization. Contrary to FPs, a FN decision has both the instant effect of saving bandwidth while it should not, as well as a persistent effect. In particular, upon a FN occurrence and for a number

	Threshold					
	0,5		1		1,5	
#Sites	Mode	Mdn	Mode	Mdn	Mode	Mdn
60	1	3	1	3	1	2
70	1	4	1	3	1	2
80	1	3	1	3	1	3
90	2	3	1	4	1	2
100	2	3	1	2	1	1

Table 2: FN Duration - χ^2 Monitoring

	Threshold					
	190		200		210	
#Sites	Mode	Mdn	Mode	Mdn	Mode	Mdn
600	2	2	1	1	1	1
700	1	1	1	1	1	1
800	1	1	1	1	2	1
900	1	1	1	1	1	1
1000	1	1	1	3	1	1

Table 3: FN Duration - *SJ* Monitoring

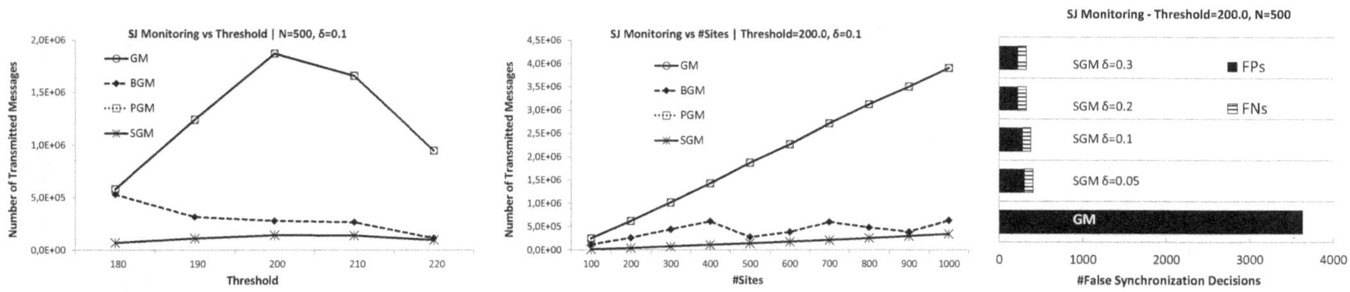

(a) *SJ* Monitoring: Comm. Cost vs Threshold (b) *SJ* Monitoring: Comm. Cost vs Sites (c) *SJ* Monitoring: Sensitivity to δ

Figure 10: Jester Data Set: Performance of our Techniques on $Self-Join$ size Monitoring

of time units, the application continuous to consider that the monitored function lies on one side of T, while $f(v(t))$ has switched side. This misconception is held by the coordinator until either a synchronization (FP or not), or $v(t)$ again switches to its initial side with respect to T. Consequently, we enhance our study by concentrating on the anticipated duration of a FN decision, indicatively providing results for χ^2 and *SJ* monitoring. In our study we report holistic aggregates and in particular the Mode and Median (denoted by Mdn) statistics for FN duration.

As both Table 2 and Table 3 demonstrate, the most frequent situation is the one where our proposed SGM approach compensates the coordinator for a FN decision immediately after its occurrence, i.e., the corresponding duration is 1 time unit. This is expressed by the Mode=1 value in the vast majority of the cases cited in the corresponding tables. On the other hand, interpreting the cited median values, we can observe that most of the times SGM needs no more than 3 time units to compensate for a FN apparition for χ^2 (Table 2), while needing 1 time unit (i.e., Mode=Mdn) for SJ (Table 3).

Overall, we can safely conclude that even when SGM does produce FN decisions (recall that JD and MI were practically FN free) it possesses the ability to immediately compensate the tracking process for them. This is due to the fact that for low δ values, the probability of missing the event of a threshold crossing in consecutive time units decreases with the number of time units.

D. COMPARISON WITH A BERNOULLI SAMPLING VARIANT

As we described in Section 2, the limitations (see points (a)-(d) in the last paragraph of Section 2) incorporated in [39, 19, 20, 27] do not allow them to become valid g_i choices for SGM. The question that naturally arises is what if we reside to a simpler g_i, instead of the one proposed in Section 5, which uses the SGM framework but naively samples sites with equal probability, i.e., performs Bernoulli sampling. For a fair comparison with our techniques, in case of this Bernoulli sampling variant each site's g_i is set to $\ell n(1/\delta)/\sqrt{N}$ yielding analogous expected sample size $(O(\ell n(1/\delta)\sqrt{N}))$ as the function that we proposed in Section 5. Please note that the Bernoulli sampling variant still utilizes optimizations that we proposed in this paper, such as the observation that sampled sites do not need to scale their Δv_i vectors by $1/g_i$.

We compare SGM incorporating the g_i of Section 5 (as in all previous evaluations), with the Bernoulli sampling variant in terms of the number of transmitted messages for different network scales. Figure 12 presents the respective comparison pairs for each monitored function (L_∞, *JD*, *SJ*) in the Jester dataset. Pairwise comparisons shown in the figure include SGM's performance marked with the respective function abbreviation (e.g. L_∞-SGM), against the respective variant (e.g., L_∞-Bernoulli).

According to Figure 12 we observe the following: (a) in SJ monitoring, SJ-Bernoulli performs 2-3 times worse than our proposed SJ-SGM across the examined network scales, (b) in Jeffrey Di-

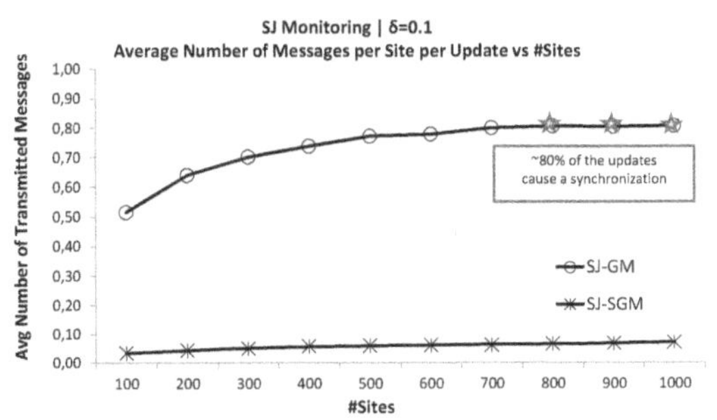

Figure 11: Average Number of Messages Transmitted by *each Site* per Data Update for SJ Monitoring

vergence monitoring, JD-Bernoulli falls short from 6 to 36 times compared to our JD-SGM and (c) L_∞−Bernoulli provides from 5 to 50 times more transmitted messages than our L_∞−SGM proposal. These ratios exhibit the ability of our proposed g_i to decrease communication burden compared to other, straightforward, sampling function choices. The differences in the performance with the Bernoulli sampling variant are mainly attributed to the fact that, contrary to the g_i we proposed in this work (Section 5), Bernoulli sampling does not take into consideration the size of the local deviation vector $\|\Delta v_i\|$. Thus, sites with small deviations that less affect the global average but lie near the threshold surface, are equally probable to be included in the sample as peers with large $\|\Delta v_i\|$ that push the global average away from it. A plausible characteristic is that such a behavior is not allowed by our proposed sampling function which incorporates $\|\Delta v_i\|$ in its calculation formula.

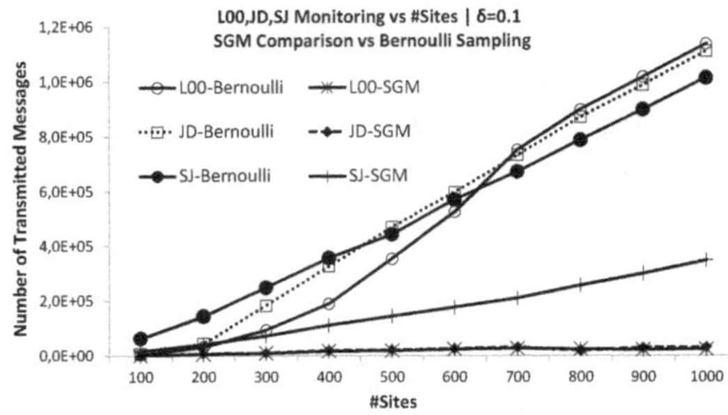

Figure 12: Comparison of SGM vs Bernoulli Sampling Variant

Author Index

www.ingramcontent.com/pod-product-compliance
Lightning Source LLC
LaVergne TN
LVHW080108011026
849160LV00013B/1054
* 9 7 8 1 4 5 0 3 4 6 0 5 4 *